THIRTY-SEVENTH EDITION

KOVELS'
ANTIQUES
& COLLECTIBLES
PRICE LIST

FOR THE 2005 MARKET
ILLUSTRATED

RANDOM HOUSE REFERENCE
NEW YORK TORONTO LONDON SYDNEY AUCKLAND

Published by Random House Reference, an imprint of the Random House
Information Group, 1745 Broadway, New York, New York 10019.
Distributed by the Random House Information Group, a division of
Random House Inc., New York, and simultaneously in Canada
by Random House of Canada Limited, Toronto.

Random House is a registered trademark of Random House, Inc.
www.randomhouse.com

Printed in the United States of America

Library of Congress Catalog Card Number: 83-643618

ISBN 0-375-72068-5

10   9   8   7   6   5   4   3   2   1

THIRTY-SEVENTH EDITION

BOOKS BY RALPH AND TERRY KOVEL

American Country Furniture, 1780–1875

A Directory of American Silver, Pewter, and Silver Plate

Kovels' Advertising Collectibles Price List

Kovels' American Antiques, 1750–1900

Kovels' American Art Pottery

Kovels' American Silver Marks, 1650 to the Present

Kovels' Antiques & Collectibles Fix-It Source Book

Kovels' Antiques & Collectibles Price List

Kovels' Bid, Buy, and Sell Online

Kovels' Book of Antique Labels

Kovels' Bottles Price List

Kovels' Collector's Guide to American Art Pottery

Kovels' Collectors' Source Book

Kovels' Depression Glass & Dinnerware Price List

Kovels' Dictionary of Marks—Pottery & Porcelain

Kovels' Guide to Selling, Buying, and Fixing
Your Antiques and Collectibles

Kovels' Illustrated Price Guide to Royal Doulton

Kovels' Know Your Antiques

Kovels' Know Your Collectibles

Kovels' New Dictionary of Marks—Pottery & Porcelain

Kovels' Price Guide for Collector Plates, Figurines,
Paperweights, and Other Limited Editions

Kovels' Quick Tips—799 Helpful Hints
on How to Care for Your Collectibles

Kovels' Yellow Pages: A Resource Guide for Collectors

The Label Made Me Buy It: From Aunt Jemima to Zonkers—
The Best-Dressed Boxes, Bottles, and Cans from the Past

INTRODUCTION

This is the 37th year *Kovels' Antiques & Collectibles Price List* has been published. And the book is still written by the original authors, Ralph and Terry Kovel. This edition has hundreds of pictures and logos, about 50,000 prices, and dozens of tips about care. It also has a special color insert, "Unique and Unusual Sales of the Year," picturing such items as a tureen shaped like a crab, cowgirl candles, a doll with seven legs, and a $604 Grape-Nuts cereal box.

READ THIS FIRST

This is a book for the collector. We check prices, visit shops, shows, and flea markets, read hundreds of publications and catalogs, check online services and the Internet, and decide what antiques and collectibles are of most interest. We concentrate on the average pieces in any category. Sometimes high-priced pieces are included so you will realize that some rarities are very valuable.

Examples of furniture, silver, Tiffany, or art pottery may sell for more than $40,000; we list a few. Highest price in this book is $48,400, for a 22-inch Tiffany nasturtium shade. Lowest price is $0.25, for a 1950s marbled yellow plastic button. Most pieces we list cost less than $10,000. We also list the weird and the wonderful. This year you can find a wooden highway sign for the town of Naromiyocknowhusunkatankshunkbrook, Connecticut, 9 by 52 inches, selling for $825. We also list a 15-inch cast-iron star-shaped bolt designed to hold a house together in an earthquake, $66; and a piece of folk art, an "alligator deterrent," with a mouth that moves when cranked, $460. The smallest item is an enameled silver button 7/16 inches in diameter, embossed with a thistle and hallmarked by Charles Horne of England for $100. Another tiny piece is an Aladdin lamp finial, $475. The biggest is a tin ceiling, 18 by 30 feet, for $800.

Prices are up in some categories. The biggest surprise is that Depression Glass has jumped in price. Rare, out-of-production Royal Doulton figurines are going up in price. A Princess Badoura figurine sold for $7,648. Furniture by George Nakashima set records, including $129,250 for a low round table. Arts and Crafts and Art Pottery continue to rise in price. A Rookwood Pottery black iris glazed vase with flying cranes and metal overlay by Kataro Shirayamadani sold for $350,750. There is continued interest in garden antiques, from old flowerpots to large fountains. Anything glass or pottery\ marked Czechoslovakia sells quickly. The flower patterns of Hull pottery are increasing in price. Vintage clothing and textiles sell quickly. Less-than-perfect antiques and collectibles are selling at prices much higher than expected—if they are rare. Many repaired pieces of rare art pottery sold this year for almost as much as perfect pieces. But Arts and Crafts furniture, especially pieces by Gustav Stickley, must have the original finish to sell at a high price. Fifties furniture is selling for high prices. Collectors were afraid the new copies sold at furniture stores would depress prices, but serious collectors still pay top prices for original examples. Chinese Export Famille Rose porcelain has gained new acceptance at museums and with collectors because recent information shows many pieces are older than first thought. A pair of urns brought a record $23,000.

Some antiques malls have closed. Others have added giftwares, flowers, and other items that interest collectors. Many offer items they also list on the Internet. Prices at large, well-advertised auctions are up. But dealers at flea markets and small shows say customers are showing less interest. Some Internet auctions are getting high prices, but Internet auction prices generally are still dropping. EBay prices are down again. And less than 45 percent of the pieces listed on eBay actually sold. The online market is international. Objects known in most of the world, such as pens, cigarette lighters, toys, and ordinary '50s furniture, are selling at the same prices as last year. Only exceptional pieces go for the extraordinary prices reported in the news media.

This year we added Bone and Patent Model as new categories. The book seems to have gotten younger over 37 years. Most items in our original book were made before 1860. Today we have pieces made as recently as the 1990s, and there is great interest in furniture, glass, and ceramics made since 1950.

The book is kept at about 900 pages so it can go with you to sales. We try to have a balanced format—not too many glass, pottery, or collectible items, furniture from the eighteenth through the twentieth centuries, not too many items that sell for over $5,000. Prices are from the American market for the American market. Few European sales are reported. We take the editorial privilege of not including prices that result from "auction fever." There is a computer-generated index. Use it often. It includes categories and much more. For example, there is a category for Celluloid. Most celluloid will be there, but a toy made of celluloid will be listed under Toy and also indexed under Celluloid. There are also cross-references in the listings and in the paragraphs. But some searching must be done. For example, Barbie dolls are in the Doll category; there is no Barbie category. And when you look at "doll, Barbie" you see a note that Barbie is under "doll, Mattel, Barbie" because most dolls are listed by maker.

All photographs and prices are new, except pictures that are pattern examples in Depression Glass and Pressed Glass. Antiques pictured are items that were offered for sale. Whenever computer-generated spaces appear, we fill them with new tips about care of collections, security, and other useful information. These tips are set in special type. Don't discard this book. Old Kovels' price books should be saved for future reference and tax and appraisal information.

The prices in this book are reports of the general antiques market. Every price in the book is new. We do not estimate or "update" prices. Prices are asking prices, although a buyer may have negotiated a price to a lower figure. No price is an estimate. We do not pay dealers and writers to estimate prices. Experience has shown us that estimated prices are usually high or low, but rarely a true report. If a price range is given, at least two identical items were offered for sale at different times. Price ranges are found only in categories like Pressed Glass, where identical items can be identified. If the price is from an auction, it includes the buyer's premium, but like all the prices, it does not include sales tax. Some prices in *Kovels' Antiques & Collectibles Price List* may seem high and some may seem low because of regional variations. But each price is one you could have paid for the object somewhere in the United States. Some Internet prices are included, but we find prices there can be misleading. Because so many people who do not collect and know little about the objects are describing and selling pieces, there are inaccuracies in the descriptions.

If you are selling your collection, do not expect to get retail value unless you are a dealer. Wholesale prices for antiques are usually 50 percent less than retail. The antiques dealer must make a profit or go out of business. Internet auction prices are less predictable. Because of the international audience and "auction fever," prices can be higher or lower than retail.

THE RECORD PRICES HYPE

The media love to report record prices, amazing auctions, and high-priced discoveries that have little to do with the antiques and collectibles market of the average collector. Great stories, but—like winning the lottery—not likely to happen to everyone. So enjoy studying auction records, but remember these are prices for the rarest and best.

RECORD-SETTING PRICES

BRONZES & SCULPTURES

Amore and Psyche carrara marble: $152,500 for a monumental carrara marble of Amore and Psyche, signed "Alba," titled and dated 1887 at base, 67 inches high x 23½ inches wide x 36-inch diameter.

CLOCKS & WATCHES

Aaron Willard tall clock: $253,000 for an Aaron Willard tall-case clock, figured mahogany with brass-fluted quarter columns and pierced fretwork, made in Roxbury, Massachusetts, between 1790 and 1810.

American clock: $803,200 for an American clock with English musical movement that plays eight tunes, Philadelphia mahogany case, dial inscribed "Paul Rimbault/London," 9 feet 3½ inches.

English clock: $1,502,967 for a Thomas Tompion No. 417 ormolu-mounted red turtle-shell grand-sonnerie table clock with pull repeat, London, c.1705, 31½ inches.

DECOYS

Canadian decoy and Thomas Chambers decoy: $187,000 for a Canadian decoy by Thomas Chambers of Toronto, Ontario; a wood duck drake with original paint with mellowed patinated surface, c.1910.

Louisiana decoy: $34,100 for a mallard hen by Marc Alcide Comardelle of Bayou Gauche, Louisiana, c.1910.

Miniature red-breasted merganser drake: $2,185 for a miniature red-breasted merganser drake on driftwood base by James Lapham of Dennisport, Massachusetts, dated February 18, 1957.

FURNITURE

20th-century chair: $970,700 for a 20th-century bronze armchair by Armand Albert Rateau, model No. 1793, with leg stamp, 36 x 24 x 20½ inches.

Chippendale bombé chest-on-chest: $1,766,600 for a Robert "King" Hooper mahogany carved Chippendale bombé chest-on-chest of Boston origin, c.1770.

George Nakashima piece: $129,250 for a George Nakashima English oak burl dining table, completely executed by Nakashima, designed in 1965 for Cuyahoga Savings, Cleveland, Ohio, 8-foot diameter.

Gustav Stickley corner cabinet: $390,000 for a Gustav Stickley early oak corner cabinet with leaded glass panes and copper hardware, c.1903.

Jacques-Emile Ruhlmann end table: $388,300 for a chocolate brown lacquer and gilt-bronze end table by Jacques-Emile Ruhlmann, with oval top and adjustable telescopic base, 1932, marked, 23½ x 34 inches.

Pierre Legrain stool: $455,500 for a stool designed by Pierre Legrain, iron and chromed metal, cube form, white-gold leaf, black lacquer at base, with ring handles, c.1922, 16 x 18¼ x 16¼ inches.

Victorian furniture piece: $189,750 for an Alexander Roux walnut server, with carved leaves, acorns, hanging grouse, flowers, and fruit, two tiers, top serving-shelf supported by two 20-inch life-size seated hunting dogs, back area carved with a 14-inch doe/deer mount, 49¼ x 48½ x 24½ inches.

GLASS

Cambridge Crown Tuscan box on nude stem: $1,524 for a Cambridge cigarette box in the Crown Tuscan color with gold-encrusted Portia etching, early 1930s, 7½ inches.

Cambridge Crown Tuscan swan bowl: $1,625 for a Cambridge Crown Tuscan swan bowl with painted Charleton decoration, label on bottom, early 1930s, 8 x 5½ x 5¾ inches.

Carved glass snuff bottle: $241,248 for a Famille Rose enameled carved glass snuff bottle, attributed to the Palace Workshops, Beijing, 1770-1799.

Enameled glass snuff bottle: $299,488 for a Famille Rose enameled glass snuff bottle, Imperial, Palace Workshops, Beijing, Qianlong (1736-1760), engraved and blue enamel-filled four-character mark.

Inside-painted snuff bottle: $226,688 for an inside-painted crystal snuff bottle, signed Ma Shaoxuan with one Shaoxuan seal, 1912.

Jumbo–Canton Pressed Glass: $9,625 for a Jumbo–Canton covered compote, with frosted elephant finial, plain hollow stem, and round stepped foot, Canton Glass Co., 1880s, 12 inches high, 7½-inch-high base.

Plated Amberina: $33,500 for a plated Amberina water pitcher, tall circular ribbed neck, protruding amber ribs, bulbous cream body with hints of green, and applied amber handle, late 1800s, 8 inches.

Wave Crest box: $17,050 for a Wave Crest box, with female portrait on lid, beading, gold trim, ormolu fittings, mark, c.1895, 6 x 5 x 5 inches.

LAMPS & LIGHTING

Jacques-Emile Ruhlmann table lamp: $421,900 for a silvered-bronze and frosted-glass table lamp by Jacques-Emile Ruhlmann, c.1925, 39½ inches.

Lighthouse burner: $2,200 for an 1860s lighthouse kerosene burner.

Tiffany Dragonfly lamp: $903,500 for a Tiffany Dragonfly leaded glass table lamp, with turtleback tile, mosaic, and bronze base, c.1906, stamped Tiffany Studios New York, 22 inches.

MISCELLANEOUS

Barrel scale: $1,100 for a "Dayton" barrel scale, Model 144, early 1900s.

Brass andirons: $88,000 for a pair of brass Chippendale andirons with ball-and-claw feet, urn-shaped finials, columnar shafts, square plinth, engraved eagles, c.1790, 28 inches.

Fraktur at auction: $366,750 for an 1801 Center County, Pennsylvania German, ink-on-paper fraktur signed by Rev. George Geistweite (c.1761-1801), decorated with figures, horses, double eagles, hens, chicks, lions, flowers, and a central panel and verse from *A Hymn to the Nightingale.*

George Washington hair: $58,139 for thousands of individual strands of President George Washington's hair, contained in a 2-inch-diameter silver snuff-type box along with his wooden ring.

Mechanical pencil sharpener: $17,050 for a 1906 abrasive-disk pencil sharpener by Chelsea Manufacturing Co.

Miniature toilet: $5,605 for a decorated miniature tradesman's-sample toilet, white glaze with colored floral design on rim interior and side, marked "The/Puritas/Washdown/Closet/Rd. No. 67021," c.1894, 8¾ inches.

NCR cash register: $3,025 for an early brass NCR register, flat scroll design, Model 33, original parts, including amount-purchased sign, clock, and customer-ordered lid plaque, all glass key checks, late 1800s.

Oak bean counter: $7,975 for a 12-foot, oak, Sherer Company bean counter, original finish, decals, labels, original drawers and hardware, late 19th century.

Railroad nameplate: $93,420 for an 84-inch-long locomotive nameplate, "Cock o' the North," restored, cast brass, A4-style lettering, early 20th century.

Urinal: $1,344 for a Rose Medallion covered urinal, with side handle, decorated with Chinese figures, late 19th century.

MUSIC

Record, single: $21,967 for the Beatles demonstration single, *Love Me Do/P.S. I Love You,* autographed by Paul McCartney, produced by Parlophone in 1962, impressed "45-R 4949," produced also with the misspelling of "Lennon – McArtney," one of only 250 printed this way.

PAPER

"I Want *You* for U.S. Army" Flagg poster: $12,650 for the James Montgomery Flagg poster, "I Want *You* . . . ," New York, 1917, Uncle Sam pointing.

St. Moritz resort/ski poster: $44,454 for the Palace Hotel, St. Moritz, resort/ski poster by Emil Cardinaux, 1920.

"Wake Up, America!" Flagg poster: $9,775 for the James Montgomery Flagg World War I poster, "Wake Up, America!"

POLITICAL

Campaign jugate pinback: $24,032 for a 1920 Cox/Roosevelt campaign jugate pinback, ⅞-inch diameter, photographic image of Cox and Roosevelt, with its original Whitehead and Hoag back paper.

POTTERY & PORCELAIN

American art pottery: $350,750 for a Rookwood black iris glazed vase decorated with flying cranes and electroplated copper and silver overlay of lotus blossoms, by Kataro Shirayamadani, 1900, 14½ inches.

Chinese Export bowl: $197,900 for a Chinese Export punch bowl, painted, one side a scene after William Hogarth's *Midnight Modern Conversation,* the other side a scene of Chinese gentlemen at supper with maidservants, c.1775, 21¼ inches.

Famille Rose urns: $23,000 for a pair of Chinese Export Famille Rose porcelain urns, with painted figural scenes, covers with figural knops, c.1840, 16½ inches.

Newcomb pottery canister: $78,400 for a Newcomb College pottery canister with cover by Henrietta Joor, decorated with tall daisy-type flowers with yellow centers, white petals, and green leaves and stems, c.1904, 8 inches high.

Royal Doulton Princess Badoura figurine: $7,648 for the Royal Doulton figurine, Princess Badoura, HN2081, introduced in 1952, dated 1994.

Virginia stoneware: $49,000 for a James River 5-gallon crock with an incised cobalt blue fighting cock, a horizontal Dutch tulip on the other side, c.1820.

PRINTS

Audubon print, American flamingo, Plate 431: $197,900 for the Audubon print, Plate 431, the American flamingo, hand-colored engraving with aqua tint and etching, 1838, 38¼ x 24¾ inches.

SILVER AND OTHER METALS

Doorstop: $16,500 for a cast-iron doorstop, football player, football tucked under arm, detailed casting and paint, 20th century, 11¼ x 6 inches.

Pewter teapot: $18,700 for a Philadelphia Queen Anne-form pewter teapot with touchmark of Cornelius Bradford, c.1752, 7 inches (replaced lid).

SPORTS

Babe Ruth rookie baseball card: $109,639 for the 1915 M101-5 Sporting News #151 Babe Ruth rookie card.

Honus Wagner white-border T-206 baseball card: $109,639 for the 1909-1911 T-206 white-border Honus Wagner baseball card, reverse advertisement for Sweet Caporal cigarettes, graded PR-FR 1 by PSA.

Individual American tackle item: $101,200 for a 19th-century "Giant" Haskell Minnow lure, made by gunsmith Riley Haskell in Painesville, Ohio; hollow copper body with scale detail, defined fins, and revolving tail, sold with slide-top wood box incised "R. Haskell," oversized, 10 inches.

Kovalovsky Big Game reel: $20,900 for a Kovalovsky-Zane Grey Big Game reel, marked on the front plate, "Arthur Kovalovsky, hand made," two-level wedding-cake construction, c.1935, 8 ½-inch diameter, 6 ½-inch-wide spool, 17 lbs.

Topps hockey five-cent wax box: $85,531 for the counter sales box of 24 five-cent packs of 1954-55 Topps hockey cards, 19 of the packs inside.

Unopened 1952 Topps baseball card set: $208,704 for an unopened 1952 Topps baseball five-cent wax box (24 packs).

TEXTILES

Bed cloth: $231,000 for a muslin bed cloth decorated in a Baltimore-album quilt style with watercolor and pigment stenciled panels depicting an ornate tree of life with birds in trees eating fruit, baskets of fruit, and vines with large clusters of grapes, 19th century, 8 x 8½ feet.

TOOLS

Center-wheel plow plane: $22,000 for a Sandusky Tool Company self-regulating, three-arm, center-wheel, rosewood plow plane, No. 141, with six ivory tips, late 19th century.

TOYS, DOLLS & GAMES

Chicago Digger arcade game: $5,500 for a "Chicago Digger" five-cent crane arcade game, c.1940, 6 feet tall, restored.

Cowboy slot machine: $22,000 for a carved five-cent Golden Nugget life-size figural cowboy slot machine, carved by Frank Polk.

Elgin bicycle: $20,900 for a 1937 Elgin drive-shaft "Robin" bicycle, with All-state ribbed white sidewall tires, speedometer, front light, and original paint.

G.I. Joe prototype: $200,000 for a handmade, hand-painted, 12-inch-tall 1963 G.I. Joe prototype, with movable limbs, wearing a stitched sergeant's uniform, with original hand-drawn box artwork for the first "Action Marine" G.I. Joe, made by Don Levine of Providence, Rhode Island.

Door of Hope "Manchu Woman" doll: $8,050 for a Door of Hope "Manchu Woman" doll, carved wood with carved headpiece and facial features, silk clothing and carved wooden arms, legs, and shoes, 11 inches. These dolls were made from 1917 to 1950 to benefit children in China.

Mills Cricket coin-drop machine: $20,900 for a five-cent Mills Cricket coin-drop machine, c.1904.

Mills Owl upright slot machine: $6,600 for a Mills Owl five-cent upright slot machine, c.1897.

Star Wars figure set: $16,261 for a 1977 complete set of 20 plastic Star Wars figures in original packaging.

A NOTE TO COLLECTORS

You already know this is a great overall price guide for antiques and collectibles. Each entry is current, every picture is new, all prices are accurate.

But things change quickly. Important sales produce new record prices. Fakes appear. Rarities are discovered. To keep up with developments, read *Kovels on Antiques and Collectibles*, a monthly newsletter with up-to-date information on collecting. It is filled with color photographs, about forty to an issue. The newsletter reports prices, trends, auction results, Internet sales, and other news for collectors *as it happens*. For a free sample of *Kovels on Antiques and Collectibles*, fill out and mail the postage-paid postcard at the back of this book. We also have a website that gives FREE pricing information, lists of publications and sources, and news. Visit www.kovels.com to learn more.

HOW TO USE THIS BOOK

There are a few rules for using this book. Each listing is arranged in the following manner: CATEGORY (such as Pressed Glass), OBJECT (such as vase), DESCRIPTION (as much information as possible about size, age, color, and pattern). Some types of glass, pottery, and silver are exceptions to this rule. These are listed CATEGORY, PATTERN, OBJECT, DESCRIPTION. All items are presumed to be in good condition and undamaged, unless otherwise noted. If a maker's name is easily recognized, like Gustav Stickley, we include it near the beginning of the entry. If the maker is obscure, the name may be at the end.

Many of the general glass entries are in special categories: Glass-Art, Glass-Blown, Glass-Bohemian, Glass-Contemporary, Glass-Midcentury, and Glass-Venetian. Major glass factories are listed under factory names. Well-known types of glass, such as cut, pressed, Depression, Carnival, etc., can be found in their own categories. You will find silver flatware in either Silver Flatware Plated or Silver Flatware Sterling. You will also find a section for Silver Plate, which includes coffeepots, trays, and other plated pieces. Solid or sterling silver is listed by country, so look for Silver-American, Silver-English, etc. Silver jewelry is listed under jewelry. Most pottery or porcelain is listed by factory name, such as Weller; or by item, such as Calendar Plate; or in sections like Dinnerware or Kitchen; or in a special section, Pottery-Art, Pottery-Contemporary, Pottery-Midcentury, etc.

Sometimes we make arbitrary decisions. Fishing has its own category, but hunting is part of the larger category called Sports. We have omitted all guns except toys. It is not legal to sell weapons without a special license, so guns are not part of the general antiques market. Airguns, BB guns, rocket guns, and others are listed in the "Toy" section. Everything is listed according to the computer alphabetizing system. This means words such as "Mt." are alphabetized as "M-T," not as "M-O-U-N-T." All numerals are before all letters; thus "2" comes before "A."

We made several editorial decisions. A butter dish is a "butter." A salt dish is called a "salt" to differentiate it from a saltshaker. It is always "sugar and creamer," never "creamer and sugar." Political collectors often refer to "pin-backs," the round celluloid or tin pins decorated with candidates' names and faces. We use the word "button" instead of "pinback." The word "button" is also used when referring to fasteners on clothing. Where one dimension is given, it is the height; or if the object is round, the dimension is the diameter. The height of a picture is listed before width. Glass is clear unless a color is indicated.

Every entry is listed alphabetically, but problems of language remain. Some antiques terms, such as "Sheffield" or "Pratt," have two meanings. Read the paragraph headings to know the meaning used. All category headings are based on the language of the average person, and we use terms like "mud figures" even if not technically correct.

This book does *not* include price listings for fine art paintings, antiquities, stamps, coins, or most types of books. *Big Little Books* and similar children's books *are* included. Comic books are *not* listed, but original comic art and cels *are* listed in their own categories.

Prices for items pictured can be found in the appropriate category. Look for the matching entry with the abbreviation "Illus."

Because of the computer, the book can be produced quickly. The last entries are added in June; the book is available in October. But human help finds prices and checks accuracy. We read everything at least three times, sometimes more. We edit more than 60,000 entries down to the 50,000 entries found here. We correct spelling, remove incorrect data, write category paragraphs, and decide on new categories. Information in the paragraphs is updated each year and this year more than fifty updates and additions were made.

Prices are reports from all parts of the United States, Canada, and Europe, converted to U.S. dollars at the rate of exchange at the time of the sale. The average rate of exchange between June 2003 and June 2004 was about $0.75 U.S. to $1 Canadian. Prices are from auctions, shops, Internet sales, and shows. Every price is checked for accuracy, but we are not responsible for errors.

We cannot answer your letters asking for price information. But please write if you have any requests for categories to be included in future editions or any corrections to the paragraphs or prices.

When you see us at shows and flea markets, stop and say hello. Don't be surprised if we ask for your suggestions. Or you can write to us at P.O. Box 22200-K, Beachwood, Ohio 44122 or visit us at our website, www.kovels.com.

RALPH & TERRY KOVEL
July 2004

ACKNOWLEDGMENTS

We give special thanks to those who helped us with pictures and deeds: Auction Team Köln; Bertoia Auctions; Charlton Hall Galleries; Christie's; Conestoga Auction Co.; Cowan's Historic Americana Auctions; Craftsman Auctions; David Rago Auctions (David Rago and John Sollo); Doyle New York; Fontaine's Auction Gallery; Garth's Auctions; Glass-Works Auctions; Green Valley Auctions; Jackson's International Auctioneers & Appraisers; James D. Julia; Lang's Sporting Collectables; MastroNet; McMasters Harris Auction House; Mid-Hudson Galleries; New Orleans Auction Galleries; Pacific Glass Auctions; Pook & Pook; Randy Inman Auctions; Robert C. Eldred Co.; Robert S. Brunk Auction Services; Samuel Cottone Auctions; Skinner; Smith and Jones; Sotheby's; Strawser Auctions; Theriault's; Treadway Gallery; Victorian Casino Antiques; Village Doll and Toy; Weschler's & Sons; William H. Bunch Auctions; William Morford Auctions; Woody's Auctions; and Wright Auctions.

To the others in the antiques trade who knowingly or unknowingly contributed to this book, we say "thank you": Aladdin Knights of the Mystic Light; Aleph-Bet Books; Alexander Autographs; Allard Auctions; American Bottle Auctions; American Cut Glass Association; Anderson Auction; Andre Ammelounx; Ark Antiques; Art & Fragrances Auctions; Arte Primitivo; Auctions Unlimited; Aumann Auctions; Baker's International Antiques & Collectibles; BBR Auctions; Be-hold (Larry Gottheim); Big Kid Collectables; Bloomington Auction Gallery; Bonhams; Candy Container Collectors of America; Canes Through the Ages Auction; Cincinnati Art Galleries; Collection Liquidations Auction; Collectors Auction Services; Collectors Choice Auction; Cook Book Collector's Club; Copake Auction; Daguerrian Society; Dallas Auction Gallery; Dargate Auction Galleries; David M. Cobb Doll Auctions; Davis Auction Service; Decoys Unlimited; DeFina Auctions; Early American Antique Tool Auctions; Early American History Auction; Early's Art Glass Auction; Faganarms; Federation of Historical Bottle Collectors; Figural Bottle Opener Collectors Club; FJN Publishers; Flashlight Collectors of America; Float About; Frank H. Boos Gallery; Franks Antiques & Auctions; Freeman's (Samuel T. Freeman & Co.); Gallery at Knotty Pine (Michael S. Pappas); Gene Harris Antique Auction Center; Gisela Antiques; Hake's Americana & Collectibles; Harvey Clar Auctioneers; Heisey Collectors of America; Henry Peirce Auctioneers; Hoosier Peddler; Hummel Collector's Club; Ivey-Selkirk Auctioneers; John Woytowicz; Joy Luke Auctioneers & Appraisers; Kevin L. Shea; L.H. Selman Ltd.; Los Angeles Modern Auctions; Lynn Geyer's Advertising Auctions; Majolica Auctions; Manion's International Auction House; Maritime Antiques Auction; Mark of Time; McCoy Lovers; McMurray Antiques & Auctions; Michael Ivankovich Antiques & Auction Co.; Mike Clum Auction Co.; Miscellaneous Man; Muddy River Trading Co. (Gary Metz); N. Bloom & Son; Naomi and Wallace Bornstein; National Association Breweriana Advertising; National Association of Milk Bottle Collectors; National Association of Paper and Advertising Collectors; National Cambridge

Collectors; National Toothpick Holder Collectors Society; Neal Auction Co.; Noel Barrett Antiques & Auctions; Norman C. Heckler & Co.; Northeast Auctions; Old Barn Auction; Old Sleepy Eye Collectors Club of America; Old World Auctions; Past Tyme Pleasures; Phillips, de Pury & Luxembourg; Phoenix Militaria Corp.; R.O. Schmitt Fine Arts; Randy's Toy Shop; Rex Stark Americana; Rich Penn Country Store and Advertising Auction; Richard Opfer Auctioneering; Ron Smith; Ruby Lane; Seeck Auctions; Serious Toyz; Shirley Dunbar; Slater's Americana; Sloans & Kenyon; Smith House Toys; Sold USA Auctions; Southern Folk Pottery Collectors Society; Stanton Auctioneers; Susanin's Auctions; Swann Galleries; Tea Leaf Club International; Team's Tiffany Treasures; Thomaston Place Auction Galleries; TIAS; Tom Harris Auctions; Tool Shop Auctions; Touch of Glass; Tradewinds Antiques; Vicki & Bruce Waasdorp; Waddington's; Watt Collectors Association; Willis Henry Auctions; Yankee Peddler Antique Toys; and Yesterday's Pastimes.

We thank all of those at Random House Reference for working through the unique way we write a price book. Our longtime editor, Dorothy Harris, guided the book through all of its stages and made sure it was better than ever and on time. David Naggar, president of the Random House Information Group; Sheryl Stebbins, vice president and publisher of Random House Reference; Beth Levy, associate managing editor; Lisa Montebello, production manager; Fabrizio LaRocca, creative director; Geraldine Sarmiento, designer; and Lindsey Glass all worked together to create the final book. Merri Ann Morrell at Precision Graphics once again solved the problems of forcing the data to create perfect printed pages and clear photographs.

The hard work of recording prices, assembling pictures and information, checking and rechecking entries for accuracy, and all the other details is done by our staff first. We thank Carmie Amata, Linda Coulter, Grace DeFrancisco, Doris Gerbitz, Marcia Goldberg, Evelyn Hayes, Katie Karrick, Kim Kovel, Liz Lillis, Heidi Makela, Tina McBean, Nancy Saada, Julie Seaman, June Smith, Cherrie Smrekar, and Katie Smrekar. The pictures seem to require new technology every year. Benjamin Margalit took many of the photographs and managed to show the details and styles that interest collectors. Karen Kneisley has conquered the problems of getting and reproducing pictures that come in all forms, from black and white glossies to digital images. But the person who keeps us all on schedule, reads and rereads the copy, keeps up-to-date information for the paragraphs, finds and solves hundreds of unexpected problems, and works around the computer glitches is Gay Hunter. This is her 24th book and her knowledge is encyclopedic. We thank all of them because we know that even though our names are on the book, we couldn't do it without their expertise.

THIRTY-SEVENTH EDITION

KOVELS'
ANTIQUES
& COLLECTIBLES

PRICE LIST

FOR THE 2005 MARKET
ILLUSTRATED

A. WALTER made pate-de-verre glass under contract at the Daum glass-works from 1908 to 1914. He started his own firm in Nancy, France, in 1919. Pieces made before 1914 are signed *Daum, Nancy* with a cross. After 1919 the signature is *A. Walter Nancy*.

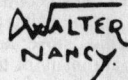

Dish, Crab, Iridescent, Yellow, Signed, c.1920, 5 3/8 In.	3585.00
Paperweight, Butterfly, 1907, 3 5/8 In.	1265.00
Paperweight, Butterfly, Wings Spread, Brown, Yellow, Green, 4 In.	3000.00
Paperweight, Crab, Brown, Green Base, c.1920, 1 7/8 In.	2390.00
Paperweight, Lobster, Mottled Shell, Yellow Base, Impressed, 3 In.	1200.00
Paperweight, Moth, Blue, Brown, Green, Yellow, 4 1/2 In.	2750.00
Vase, Nasturtium, Pink Shaded To Yellow, Matte, Signed, 6 1/2 In.	546.00

ABC plates, or children's alphabet plates, were most popular from 1780 to 1860, but are still being made. The letters on the plate were meant as teaching aids for children learning to read. The plates were made of pottery, porcelain, metal, or glass. Mugs and other items were also made with alphabet decorations.

Dispenser, Plate, Child Playing Hoops, Embossed, Tin, 19th Century, 3 In.	210.00
Plate, Brown Transfer Scene, Rugby Game, Child's, 7 In.	169.00
Plate, Dog & Palm Tree, Embossed, Glass, Ripley & Co., c.1880	85.00
Plate, Embossed Black, Green & Red, 3 Children & Dog, 6 In.	125.00
Plate, Franklin's Maxim, Save While You Can, Hand Colored Transfer, Embossed, 7 1/2 In.	325.00
Plate, Girl & Animals In Stable, Blue Transfer, Embossed, Red Border, 7 In.	150.00
Plate, Hunting Scene, Brown Transfer, Hand Colored, Embossed, 6 In.	100.00
Plate, John Gilpin Going To Edmonton, Man Riding Horse, 7 1/4 In.	67.00
Plate, Man, Horse, The Walk, Colored Transfer, Embossed, Staffordshire, c.1860, 5 In.	220.00
Plate, Marine Railway Station, Manhattan Beach Motel, Child's, 7 1/2 In.	165.00

ABINGDON POTTERY was established in 1908 by Raymond E. Bidwell as the Abingdon Sanitary Manufacturing Company. The company started making art pottery in 1934. The factory ceased production of art pottery in 1950.

Bookends, Horsehead, Black, 6 1/2 In.	145.00
Bookends, Horsehead, White, 6 1/2 In.	145.00
Console, Flower Shape, Pink, 14 In.	15.00
Cookie Jar, Clock, 9 1/2 In.	31.00
Cookie Jar, Locomotive, White, Yellow, Red, Black Trim, Marked	55.00
Vase, Art Deco, Overlapping Leaves, Yellow, 8 3/4 In.	29.00
Vase, Long Handles, Embossed Petals Around Base, Light Green, 10 In.	710.00
Vase, Ram's Head, Light Blue, Marked, 3 3/4 In.	38.00
Vase, Urn Shape, Curled Handle, Celadon Green, 6 3/4 In.	30.00

ADAMS china was made by William Adams and Sons of Staffordshire, England. The firm was founded in 1769 and became part of the Wedgwood Group in 1966. The name "Adams" appeared on various items through 1998. All types of tablewares and useful wares were made. Other pieces of Adams may be found listed under Flow Blue and Tea Leaf Ironstone.

Creamer, Adams' Rose, Rainbow, Purple, Blue, Red, Green, Spatter, 4 In.	115.00
Creamer, Adams' Rose, Rainbow, Red, Green, Purple, Blue, Spatter, 3 3/4 In.	275.00
Cup & Saucer, Adams' Rose, Blue, Red, Green, Spatter	200.00
Jug, Jasper Dip, Blue, Applied Classical Relief, Leaf Borders, c.1800, 7 1/2 In.	1060.00
Pitcher, Cream, Adams' Rose, Red, Spatter, 4 1/2 In.	105.00
Pitcher, Milk, Adams' Rose, 7 In.	165.00
Pitcher & Bowl, Adams' Rose, Leaves, Gaudy, Impressed Wood, 13 1/4 In.	1265.00
Plate, Adams' Rose, Blue, Spatter, 10 1/4 In.	715.00
Plate, Mitchell & Freeman's China & Glass Warehouse, 10 1/8 In.	865.00
Plate Set, Red Roses, Green, Cobalt Blue Leaves, 9 1/4 In., 6 Piece	315.00
Platter, Red Roses, Green & Blue, Leaves, Octagonal, 12 5/8 x 16 In.	720.00
Sugar, Cover, Mother, Child, Dog, Playing In Yard, Blue, Impressed, 6 3/4 In.	195.00
Teapot, Rose, Polychrome Flowers, 5 3/4 In.	110.00

ADVERTISING containers and products sold in the old country store are now all collectibles. These stores, with the crackers in a barrel and a potbellied stove, are a symbol of an earlier, less hectic time. Listed here are many of the advertising items. Other similar pieces may be found under the product name, such as Planters Peanuts. We have tried to list items in the logical places, so large store fixtures will be found under the Architectural category, enameled tin dishes under Graniteware, paper items in the Paper category, etc. Store fixtures, cases, and other items that have no advertising as part of the decoration are listed in the Store category.

Ad, Magazine, Alka Seltzer, Speedy, Liquid Pain Reliever, December 1959	15.00
Ad, Magazine, Green Giant, How The Green Giant Was Born, c.1946	15.00
Ad, Magazine, Kool Aid, Pitcher, Smiling, Tiny Crystals Of Concentrated Flavor, 1959	12.00
Ad, Magazine, Morton Salt, When It Rains It Pours, c.1940	15.00
Ad, Magazine, Old Crow, A Vote For Old Crow Is A Vote For Honest Pleasure	12.00
Ad, Magazine, Swan Soap, Lever Brothers, c.1940	12.00
Ashtray, Borg Cigarettes, Black, Austria, 1920s, 4 1/2 In.	120.00
Ashtray, Jaeger High Dump Mixer, Cement Truck, 8 In.	85.00
Ashtray, Jim Brown, Aluminum, 75th Birthday, 50th Anniversary, 1939	25.00
Ashtray, Wyandotte Products, Pressed Copper, Arrowhead Shape, 5 In.	35.00
Bag, Flour, Red Star Milling Co. Flour, Sample, 3 x 1 3/4 x 1 1/4 In.	75.00
Bag, Flour, Texas Pioneer Flour, Sample, 3 x 1 3/4 x 1 1/4 In.	75.00
Bag Holder, Acme Fruit Flavors, Wood, Stencil, Griffiths, Griffin & Hoxie, Utica, N.Y.	1870.00
Banner, Dee-Cee, Western Wear, Denim, Blue, Red, Yellow, 36 x 46 In.	110.00
Banner, Leg Liberty, Better Sports, Helen Wills, Tennis, Cotton, 33 1/2 x 45 1/4 In.	1955.00
Banner, Maverick Denim Jeans, Bell Bottoms, 40 x 72 In.	110.00
Banner, Purina Eggs, For Sale, Cardboard, 1954, 18 x 26 In.	28.00
Banner, Who's Your Druggist, Hang On For Pure Drugs, Ithaca, N.Y., 49 x 37 In.	489.00
Barrel, Bull Meat Brand Flour, Paper Ads, Oak, 32 1/2 x 22 1/2 In.	230.00
Barrel, Hires Root Beer, Oak, Tin, Steel Liner, Cover, 30 x 26 In.	316.00
Basket, Sno King Baking Powder, Wire, 17 1/2 x 16 x 25 In.	275.00
Belt Buckle, Borden, Elsie, Brass, 50th Anniversary, 1986	50.00
Bench, Poll-Parrot Shoes, 5 Sections, Animal Dividers, Wood, 96 In.	7370.00
Bib, Reddy Kilowatt, Little Bo Peep, Little Boy Blue, Cloth, 9 1/2 x 7 1/2 In.	65.00
Bin, A&P Coffee, Slant Front, Lift Top, Hand Painted, 25 x 13 x 13 In.	250.00
Bin, Beech-Nut Chewing Tobacco, Tin Lithograph, 8 5/8 x 10 x 8 1/4 In.	600.00
Bin, Calumet Baking Powder, Double Acting, Wood, No Lid, 25 1/2 x 17 In.	35.00
Bin, High Grade Brand Teas, Steinwender Stoffgren Coffee Co., Tin, 17 x 18 x 13 In.	330.00
Bin, Luxury Coffee, Wood, Mustard Color, 100 Lb., 32 x 21 1/2 x 16 In.	2970.00
Bin, Sure Shot Chewing Tobacco, Tin Lithograph, 6 1/2 x 15 1/4 x 10 1/4 In.	925.00 to 1045.00
Bin, Sweet Burley Tobacco, Yellow Ground, Red Letters, 10 3/4 x 8 1/4 In.	230.00
Bin & Sifter, Cream City Flour, Metal, 1893, 27 1/2 x 12 1/2 In.	770.00
Blotter, Brown's Iron Bitters, Victorian House & Family, 3 7/8 x 6 7/8 In.	49.00
Blotter, Miami Powder Co., Coil Of Fuse, Carload Of Powder, 3 7/8 x 9 1/4 In.	110.00
Books may be included in the Paper category.	
Bottles are listed in their own category.	
Bottle Carrier, Welch's Grape Juice, House & Building Forms, 1950s, 11 Piece	1470.00
Bottle Openers are listed in their own category.	
Bowl, Quaker Oats, Instant Oatmeal, It's Hot, Plastic, 1992, 6 In.	4.00
Box, see also Box category.	
Box, Ackers Dyspepsia Tablets, Girl, Fancy Hat, Cardboard, 6 x 5 1/2 In.	190.00
Box, Acme Chocolates, Paper, Cedar Rapids, Iowa, 7 1/2 x 10 1/2 In.	55.00
Box, American Youth Athletic Underwear, 10 3/4 x 9 In.	56.00
Box, Arbuckle's Coffee, Wood, Shipping, Stenciled, Impressed	110.00
Box, Arm & Hammer, Bicarbonate Of Soda, Free Sample, 2 3/8 x 1 3/4 x 1 In.	95.00
Box, Bambina Toupee Plasters, Slide Tray, Lynn, Mass., 4 1/4 x 1 5/8 In.	240.00
Box, Beech-Nut Gum, Peppermint Flavor, Green, Cardboard, 4 x 15 x 2 1/2 In.	110.00
Box, Bower & Bartlett's Favorite Boston Coffees, Black, Gold, Red, 17 x 19 x 14 In.	300.00
Box, Cigar, Brass Mounted, Stained Wood, Hinged Lid, 2 Drawers, 4 x 9 1/2 x 6 In.	195.00
Box, Cigar, Musical, Scalloped, Ebonized, Burl Walnut, c.1890, 11 1/2 x 7 1/2 In.	750.00
Box, Cigar, Pittsburg's Finest, Policeman, Wood, 10 7/8 x 7 5/8 x 7 1/2 In.	300.00
Box, Cigar, Rocky Ford, 5 x 9 In.	11.00
Box, Cigar, Santa Claus, Book Shape, Gibson-Type Woman, 6 3/4 x 8 x 6 In.	75.00

Box, Cigar, Sunset Trail, Metal & Glass Cover, 9 x 5 1/2 x 5 In. 385.00
Box, Clean-BE-Tween, Tooth Brush Refills, 3/4 x 2 1/8 x 1 1/8 In. 28.00
Box, Crane's Candy, Gessoed Wood, Parrish Rubaiyat, 1920s, 6 x 12 1/4 x 2 7/8 In. 798.00
Box, Dana's Sarsaparilla, Wood, Belfast, Maine, 11 1/4 x 10 1/4 x 9 In. 120.00
Box, Dickerman's Pen & Pencil, Oak Case, Glass Top, 2 Drawers, 6 x 15 x 11 In. 225.00
Box, Dr. Harter's Wild Cherry Bitters, Wood, 21 x 9 x 12 In. 60.00
Box, Dr. Kilmer's Headache Cure, Cardboard, Slide Tray, Contents, 2 1/2 In. 360.00
Box, Dreft Detergent, Unopened, 15 Oz., 8 1/2 x 6 x 2 1/8 In. 15.00
Box, Electric Bitters, 2 Dozen, World's Greatest Cure, Wood, 20 x 10 x 13 In. 120.00
Box, Elkay Baking Powder, Cardboard, Paper Label, Pour Spout, 5 5/8 x 3 In. 85.00
Box, Gold Dandruff Cure, Wood, Dovetailed, 9 x 8 x 10 In. 39.00
Box, Gold Dust, Twins On Front, Gold & Blue Ground, 1920s, 7 In. 685.00
Box, Heinz, Wood, Handle, Printing On 4 Sides, Pittsburgh, Pa., 22 x 10 In. 28.00
Box, Honest Weight Tobacco, Weyman & Bro., Cardboard, 1887, 9 x 12 x 5 In. 248.00
Box, Jack Sprat Tea, Consolidated Foods Corp., 4 1/4 x 3 x 2 1/4 In. 85.00
Box, Johnson's Belladonna Plaster, Cardboard, 9 x 6 In. 60.00
Box, Kibbe Bros., Molasses Candy, Wood, Springfield, Mass., 17 x 5 1/2 x 13 In. 60.00
Box, Lash's Bitters, Tonic Laxative, Dovetailed, Wood, 13 x 10 1/2 x 10 In. 85.00
Box, Lincoln Seyms & Co., Spices, Pepper, Wood, 8 1/2 x 16 In. 39.00
Box, London Cocoa, Wood, 15 1/2 x 3 1/2 x 15 In. 39.00
Box, Lydia Pinkham's Liver Pills, 12 Sealed Packages, Cardboard, 3 3/4 x 4 1/2 In. 255.00
Box, Mammoth Barkers Toilet Soap, Dovetailed, Glass Lid, 16 x 5 1/4 x 11 In. 35.00
Box, Mother Goose Child's Shoes, 7 5/8 x 4 5/8 x 3 In. 50.00
Box, None Such Mince Meat, Stenciled, Wood, 16 x 6 x 8 1/2 In. 35.00
Box, Recipe, Land-O-Lakes Butter, Tin, 5 1/2 x 3 x 3 In. 45.00
Box, Scotch Brand Oats, Cardboard, Paper Label, Quaker Oats, 9 1/2 x 5 In. 165.00
Box, Seed, D.M. Ferry & Co., Choice Flower Seeds, Oak, 11 x 7 x 4 In. 165.00
Box, Simmons Liver Regulator, 4 Individual Boxes, 2 1/8 x 7 3/4 In. 60.00
Box, Slades Pure Spices, Wood, 19 x 2 1/2 x 12 In. 50.00
Box, St. Jacob's Oil, Great German Remedy, 1 Dozen, Dovetailed, Wood, 7 x 7 x 5 In. ... 55.00
Box, St. Johnsbury Cookies, Homemade, Wood, 21 x 11 x 15 In. 165.00
Box, Sweet Clover Dairy Box, Wood, Metal On Edges, 16 x 9 x 12 In. 28.00
Box, Tennessee Biscuit Co., Glass Front, 10 1/2 x 6 In. 22.00
Box, Tiger Rolled White Oats, Snarling Tiger, Cardboard, Round, c.1930, 10 x 5 1/2 In. .. 50.00
Box, Tree Tea Orange Pekoe, Cardboard, M.J.B. Co., San Francisco, 2 5/8 x 2 In. 118.00
Box, Tru-Aspingum, Cardboard, Unopened, 5/8 x 2 3/4 x 2 1/4 In. 32.00
Box, Warner's Safe Cure, Wood, Rochester, N.Y., 10 1/2 x 10 1/2 x 14 In. 145.00
Box, Warner's Safe Yeast, Cardboard, Round, Paper Label, 5 x 2 1/4 In. 286.00
Box, Weideman Oat Flakes, Cardboard, 14 Oz., 6 1/4 x 4 1/4 In. 130.00
Broadside, Mammy With Melon, Lithograph, Paper, c.1890, 12 In. 75.00
Brochure, Stroh Brewing Co., Brewers Products, Testimonials, c.1893, 7 x 8 In. 98.00
Broom Holder, DeLaval Cream Separators, Tin Lithograph, Round, Envelope, 3 1/2 In. ... 495.00
Broom Holder, Schmidt's Blue Ribbon Bread, 2 Sides, 31 In. ....85.00 to 155.00
Butter Chip, Bordon's, Elsie The Cow, Inca Ware China, 3 In. 55.00
Buttonhook, Stetson Shoes, Metal, Marked For Men & Women, 6 In. 10.00
Cabinet, Boynton McKay Drug Store, Camden, Me., 3 Doors, Maple, 31 x 128 In. 1150.00
Cabinet, Crowley's Needles, 2 Drawers, Ruby Glass, 16 x 6 In. 358.00
Cabinet, Crowley's Needles, 2 Drawers, Ruby Glass, c.1890, 9 x 5 In. 440.00
Cabinet, DeLaval Cream Separator, World's Standard, Tin Lithograph, 17 x 23 In. 990.00
Cabinet, Diamond Dyes, Children, Balloons, Tin Lithograph, c.1890, 15 x 24 In. . .605.00 to 935.00
Cabinet, Diamond Dyes, Evolution Of Women, Tin Lithograph, c.1890, 22 x 30 In. 935.00
Cabinet, Diamond Dyes, Fairies, Wells & Richardson Co., Vt., 31 x 22 x 9 In. 3410.00
Cabinet, Diamond Dyes, Governess, Embossed, 22 1/2 x 29 x 9 In. ....825.00 to 2530.00
Cabinet, Diamond Dyes, Mansion, Oak, Tin Lithograph Door, 1910-1914, 15 x 24 In. ... 825.00
Cabinet, Diamond Dyes, Maypole, Wood, Tin Lithograph, 1906, 22 x 30 In. ...1018.00 to 2640.00
Cabinet, Diamond Dyes, Washer Woman, Blue Ground, Oak Case, 22 x 30 In. 1320.00
Cabinet, Dr. Daniels' Veterinary Medicines, Embossed, 20 x 28 1/2 x 7 In. .....3700.00 to 3850.00
Cabinet, Dr. E.S. Sloane's Medicines, Wood, Glass Paned Door, 26 x 16 x 6 In. 299.00
Cabinet, Dr. Lesure's Veterinary Medicine, Horse, Tin Lithograph, c.1910, 21 x 27 In. ... 5610.00
Cabinet, Dy-O-La, Tin Door, Packets, Booklets, Burlington, 16 x 12 x 8 In. ......230.00 to 275.00
Cabinet, German Household Dyes, Ash, Paul Oppeman Mfg., Milw., c.1890, 23 x 30 In. . 440.00
Cabinet, Goffs Braid, 2 Drawers, 17 x 8 In. 121.00
Cabinet, Humphreys' Specifics, Medicines, Cures, On Tin, Drawers, c.1900, 22 x 27 In. ... 605.00

Cabinet, Milward's Needles, 2 Drawers, Ruby Glass, c.1890, 16 x 6 In. . . . . .358.00 to 415.00
Cabinet, Munyon's Homeopathic Remedies, Wood, Tin Panel, 1905, 18 x 24 In. 660.00
Cabinet, Perfection Dyes, 2 Doors, Embossed, W. Cushing & Co., 24 x 17 In. . . . .475.00 to 530.00
Cabinet, Pratt's Veterinary Remedies, Oak, Tin Lithograph, Horses, Medicines, 17 x 30 In. 1760.00
Cabinet, Putnam Dyes, Man, On Horse, White, Metal, 28 x 11 In. 250.00
Cabinet, Putnam Dyes, Wood, Tin Lithograph, Paper Back, c.1910, 21 x 10 In. 330.00
Cabinet, Ribbon, H. Pauk & Sons, St. Louis, 37 In. 2420.00
Cabinet, Richard Hudnut Rouge, 8 Samples, 17 In. 253.00
Cabinet, Schaefer Fineline Pencils, Semicircular, 14 x 27 In. 251.00
Cabinet, Spool, Clark's O.N.T., 2 Drawers, Reverse Label, Mixed Wood Case, 22 In. 305.00
Cabinet, Spool, Clark's O.N.T., 2 Drawers, Ruby Glass, Walnut, 7 x 19 In. 205.00
Cabinet, Spool, Clark's O.N.T., 3 Drawers, Ruby Glass, Walnut, 23 x 10 In. 330.00
Cabinet, Spool, Clark's O.N.T., 4 Drawers, Decals, 19 1/4 x 14 1/4 In. 180.00
Cabinet, Spool, Clark's O.N.T., 4 Drawers, Ruby Glass Inserts, 22 x 17 In. 880.00
Cabinet, Spool, Clark's O.N.T., 5 Drawers, Embroidery, 18 1/2 x 19 x 13 1/2 In. 55.00
Cabinet, Spool, Clark's O.N.T., 6 Drawers, Ruby Glass, c.1890, 26 x 23 In. 1100.00
Cabinet, Spool, Clark's O.N.T., Roll-Top Door, Oak, Wall Mount, c.1890, 21 x 23 In. 470.00
Cabinet, Spool, Coats & Clark, 6 Drawers, Ruby Glass, c.1900, 26 x 22 In. . . . .1100.00 to 1430.00
Cabinet, Spool, Coats & Clark, 6 Drawers, Ruby Glass, Walnut, c.1890, 24 x 19 In. 935.00
Cabinet, Spool, George A. Clark, 6 Drawers, Oak, c.1900, 26 x 22 In. 1430.00
Cabinet, Spool, George A. Clark, 6 Drawers, Walnut, c.1890, 24 x 19 In. 935.00
Cabinet, Spool, J. & P. Coats', 2 Drawers, Walnut, 21 1/2 x 9 x 17 In. 215.00
Cabinet, Spool, J. & P. Coats', 6 Drawers, 24 x 20 In. 415.00
Cabinet, Spool, J. & P. Coats', 6 Drawers, Cherry, Porcelain Pulls, 22 x 26 x 20 In. 525.00
Cabinet, Spool, J. & P. Coats', Roll-Top Doors, Oak, Turntable, c.1890, 21 x 33 In. 1540.00
Cabinet, Spool, Merrick's Cotton, 6 Cord, Turns, Glass Panels, c.1890, 18 x 23 In. 1925.00
Cabinet, Spool, Merrick's Cotton, Oak, Mirror, Fold-Down Front, c.1890, 36 x 31 In. . . .   2000.00
Cabinet, Spool, Merrick's Cotton, Rack Turns, Glass Ends, Curved, 31 x 25 In. 2365.00
Cabinet, Spool, Merrick's Double, Racks Turn, Glass Ends, Curved, 31 x 25 In. 2365.00
Cabinet, Spool, Potter's Silk Thread, Oak, Glass, Turned Legs, 60 In. 2200.00
Cabinet, Spool, Potter's Silk Thread, Wood, Glass, 3 Drawers, Turns, c.1910, 18 x 33 In. . .   1870.00
Cabinet, Spool, Richardson Silks, Glass, Turns, Drawer, c.1900, 25 x 30 In. 3080.00
Cabinet, Turkish Dyes, Desert Scene, Tin Lithograph, c.1890, 23 x 33 In. 440.00
Calendars are listed in their own category.
Can, Borden, Malted Milk, 6 x 6 1/4 In. 90.00
Can, Brownie Brand Salted Peanuts, Blue, Yellow, Tin, 10 Lb., 8 1/4 x 9 In. 130.00
Can, Buffalo Brand Fancy Salted Peanuts, Tin Lithograph, E.M. Hoyt, 25 Lb., 9 In. 240.00
Can, C.F. Blanke & Co. Roasted Coffee, Our Winner, Tin, Paper Label, 13 1/2 x 20 In. 140.00
Can, Calumet Baking Powder, Tin, 5 Lb., 7 1/2 x 4 1/4 In. 75.00
Can, Campbell's Coffee, Tin, 3 Lb. 250.00
Can, Fishers's Peanuts, Tin Lithograph, 25 Lb., 20 1/2 In. 110.00
Can, Fresh Salmon, Columbia River Packers Assn., Astoria, Oregon, 4 3/8 In. . . . . . . *Illus*   10.00
Can, Hi-Plane Tobacco, 10 Cents, For Pipe & Cigarettes, Tin, Embossed, 35 x 11 In. 140.00
Can, Jumbo Blanched Salted Peanuts, Chicago, Ill., Tin, 10 Lb., 9 In. . . . . .55.00 to 66.00
Can, Sailor Boy Oysters, Gal. 75.00
Can, Southern Star Pure Lard, Cover, Tin, 115 Lb., 19 3/4 x 16 In. 200.00
Can, Venus Oil, Tin, Paper Label, 1929, 14 In. 55.00
Can Opener, Pet Irradiated Sunshine Vitamin D Milk, Wood Handle, Metal, 4 In. 55.00
Canisters, see introductory paragraph to Tins in this category.
Cards are listed in the Card category as card, advertising.
Case, Display, Adams Pepsin Tutti Frutti Gum, Oak, Mirror, c.1900, 12 x 18 In. 965.00
Case, Display, Arrows Collars, Oak, Glass, 9 x 18 In. 580.00
Case, Display, Blough Remedies, Oak, Sliding Doors, Drawers, 42 x 37 1/2 In. 800.00
Case, Display, Blue Bird Handkerchiefs, Tin Lithograph, Glass, 6 3/4 x 11 1/2 x 8 In. 495.00
Case, Display, Boston Garter, Mahogany, Glass, Lift Lid, 14 x 6 In. 215.00
Case, Display, Bower & Bartlett's Coffee, Red Shield Brand, Tin, 19 x 17 x 12 1/2 In. 420.00
Case, Display, Eveready Battery, 10 Cents Each, Tin Lithograph, Counter, 16 In. . .357.00 to 550.00
Case, Display, Eyeglass, Walnut, 7 Drawers, Porcelain Knobs, Stencil, 21 x 12 x 21 In. . . .   900.00
Case, Display, Farnam's Kalamazoo Gum, Wood, Glass, 7 1/2 x 17 x 10 In. 6160.00
Case, Display, Ingersoll Watches, Wood, Glass, 9 x 9 1/2 In. 525.00
Case, Display, J.P. Primley's California Fruit & Pepsin Gum, Oak, c.1910, 18 x 9 In. 660.00
Case, Display, Kaywoodie Pipes, 5 Pipes, Wood, Side Hinged Door, 10 x 11 In. 176.00
Case, Display, King Collar Buttons, Oak, Slant Top, Insert Card, 9 In. 330.00

Case, Display, M. Hohner's Harmonica, Wood, 9 x 11 In. 220.00
Case, Display, Marble's Outer's Knives, Bull Moose, 12 3/4 x 15 1/8 x 6 1/2 In. 600.00
Case, Display, Minters Candies, Metal, Glass, 13 x 10 x 13 1/2 In. 22.00
Case, Display, Moore's Ice Cream, Oak, Glass, 14 1/2 x 15 3/4 x 10 1/4 In. 385.00
Case, Display, Nestle Hazel Nut Milk Chocolate, 5 Cents, 4 3/4 x 10 1/8 x 7 1/5 In. 550.00
Case, Display, Tennyson, Humidor, Tin Lithograph, Countertop, 16 In. 190.00
Case, Display, Wrigley's Gum, Wrigley Man, Early 1900s, 13 x 12 In. 825.00
Case, Display, Zeno Chewing Gum, Marquee, Oak, Glass Shelves, Mirror, 18 In. ..635.00 to 825.00
Case, Verithin Colored Pencils, Wood, Glass, Interior Slots, Angled, 14 In. 95.00
Chair, Garver's Furniture & Stoves, Hagerstown, Painted, Stenciled, Child's, 18 In. 385.00
Chair, P. Nicklas's & Sons, Carpet Store, Painted, Stenciled, Wood, Child's, 18 In. 165.00
Chalkboard, Abbotts Dairy Products, Tin, Cardboard Back, Painted, 16 x 24 In. 145.00
Chalkboard, Hires, Tin, Embossed, Painted, 15 x 30 In. 55.00
Change Receiver, see also Tip Tray in this category.
Change Receiver, Swan Vestas, Smokers Match, Glass, 6 x 6 x 1 3/4 In. 145.00
Charger, Green River Whiskey, She Was Bred In Old Kentucky, 24 In. 358.00
Checkerboard, Hires Root Beer, Happy Blond Boy, Paper Lithograph, 12 x 12 In. ..110.00 to 125.00
Cigar Cutter, Aleppo Higrade Cigars, Lighter, Oil, Ruby Glass Globe, c.1880, 15 In. 1045.00
Cigar Cutter, Betsy Ross 5 Cent Cigars, Cast Iron, Lever, c.1890, 9 In. ....550.00 to 715.00
Cigar Cutter, Boston Trade, Lever, Oak Base, c.1880, 8 x 4 1/2 In. 495.00
Cigar Cutter, El Sidelo Cigars, Reverse On Glass, Frame, 21 x 15 In. 220.00
Cigar Cutter, El Tino 5 Cent Cigar, Reverse Glass, Oak, Clockwork, c.1880, 9 x 5 In. ... 578.00
Cigar Cutter, Piper Heidsieck Cigars, Cast Iron, Bottle Shape, 12 x 4 1/2 In. 750.00
Cigar Cutter, Try CCA Cigars, Lighter, 2 Wicks, Oil, Ruby Glass Globe, c.1880, 14 In. .. 1265.00
Cigar Cutter, Uwanta Cigars, 5 Cent, Indian, Horse, 9 In. 495.00
Cigar Cutter, Wm. Penn 10 Cent Cigars, King Of Havana, Rigby, 9 In. 550.00
Cigarette Pack, Lucky Strike, Contents, 1953 .... 35.00
Clicker, Red Goose Shoes, Duck Bill, Black Letters, 1 3/4 x 5/8 In. 145.00
Clicker, Red Goose Shoes, Duck Bill, Yellow & Red Letters, 1 7/8 x 5/8 In. 165.00
Clocks are listed in their own category.
Coffeepot, Sanka Instant Coffee, Minners & Co., Hall China, 4 3/4 In. 20.00
Container, Tod Co. Waxed Dental Floss, Round, Pocket Size, 1 1/4 In. 80.00
Cooler, 7-Up, c.1930, 18 x 9 x 11 1/2 In. 125.00
Cooler, Grapette Soda, Double Top, Open, Under Racks, 31 x 34 In. 625.00
Cooler, Squirt, Merry-Go-Round, Swing Handle, 14 In. 28.00
Counter Pad, Seminola 5 Cent Cigar, Indian Princess, Felt, 11 x 13 In. 885.00
Crock, Heinz, Apple Butter, Stoneware, Stone Lithograph Label, 8 x 4 In. 745.00
Crumb Scraper Set, Drake Mercantile, Kittens, Tin Lithograph, 6 1/2 x 9 1/4 In. 578.00
Decanter Set, Anheuser-Busch, Brown, Canteen Shape, 6 Cups, Box, 7 Piece 248.00
Dispenser, Alka-Seltzer, Be Wise Alkasize, Dr. Miles Laboratories, Tin, 14 1/2 In. .265.00 to 385.00
Dispenser, Alka-Seltzer, Tumbler, Chrome, Tin Lithograph, 14 5/8 x 5 In. 440.00
Dispenser, Bromo Seltzer, Cobalt Bottle, Glass, Base, c.1930, 15 In. 195.00
Dispenser, Buckeye Root Beer, Black, Cleveland Fruit Juice Co. Mfg., c.1918 .... 740.00
Dispenser, Buckeye Root Beer, Tree Stump Form, Horseshoe Ball, Pump, c.1920 .... 495.00
Dispenser, Buckeye Root Beer, White, Red Letters, Cleveland Fruit Juice Co., c.1918 ... 1430.00

Advertising, Can, Fresh
Salmon, Columbia River
Packers Assn., Astoria,
Oregon, 4 3/8 In.

Santa Claus was often pictured in a mauve or blue suit before 1930. Any Santa toy, postcard, or decoration that does not have Santa in a red suit is worth extra money.

Advertising, Display, Page &
Shaw Chocolates, Santa,
Cardboard, Lithograph, 39 In.

Dispenser, Cherry & Allen Red Tame Cherry, Frosted Glass, Marble Base, 29 x 7 In. 1760.00
Dispenser, Fowler's Cherry Mash, Ruby Glass, Nickel Plated Top & Clamp, 13 In. 305.00
Dispenser, Ginger Mint Julep, Barrel, Horseshoe Pump, Porcelain Knob, c.1920 .... 470.00
Dispenser, Green River Soda Pop, Glass Center, Metal Base, Original Jug, c.1910, 17 In. . 285.00
Dispenser, Hires Root Beer Syrup, Hourglass Shape, c.1920, 14 3/4 x 8 In. ......660.00 to 1185.00
Dispenser, Hires Root Beer, Drink Hires, It Is Pure, Painted Porcelain, 14 In. 360.00
Dispenser, Hires Root Beer, Munimaker 5500.00
Dispenser, Howel's Cherry Julep, 5 Cent, Red, Horseshoe Pump, c.1918 .... 1650.00
Dispenser, Howel's Orange Julep, 5 Cent, Horseshoe Pump, c.1918 .... 1540.00
Dispenser, Jersey Creme, Horseshoe Pump, Porcelain Knob, c.1918 .... 1650.00
Dispenser, Kenny's Iced Tea, Silver Bands, New Lid, 13 In. 65.00
Dispenser, Lash's Dixie Dew, Glass, Pedestal, Spigot, c.1900, 16 In. 745.00
Dispenser, Middleby Root Beer, Mug, Glass, Brown, Spigot, 12 In. 121.00
Dispenser, Minimax Refill, Show How To Use Minimax, Tin, Wall Mount, 14 x 4 In. 75.00
Dispenser, Mission Grapefruit, Black Base, Lid, Spigot, c.1900, 14 In. 330.00
Dispenser, Nesbitt Julep, Crock Base, Spigot, Gallon Jug, 1900-1910, 18 In. 120.00
Dispenser, Orange Crush, Black Glass Base, Frosted Globe, Metal Lid, c.1910, 17 In. ... 495.00
Dispenser, PEZ, 3 Candy Choices, Yellow, Metal, Enamel, Germany, 1950s, 30 In. 840.00
Dispenser, Safe-T-Cones, Metal, Plastic, 38 In. 50.00
Dispenser, Ver-Ba, Drink Ver-Ba 5 Cents, c.1918 .... 1210.00
Dispenser, Ward's Grape Crush, Green, Glass, c.1918 .... 885.00
Dispenser, Ward's Lemon Crush, Yellow, Green, Horseshoe Pump 1320.00
Dispenser, Ward's Orange Crush Syrup, c.1918, 14 3/4 x 8 1/2 In. 1725.00
Dispenser, Ward's Orange Crush, Orange, Green, Horseshoe Pump 770.00
Dispenser, Wrigley's Gum, Rotates, Mirrored, c.1920, 15 In. 495.00
Display, Adams Pure Chewing Gum, Jar, Glass, Acid Etched, 5 x 5 x 11 In. 85.00
Display, Aikin Lambert Co. Pens, Oak, Glass, Pens, Boxes, 41 1/2 In. 660.00
Display, Alka-Seltzer, Speedy, Vinyl, Miles Laboratory, Inc., 1963 .... 750.00
Display, Amos, From Amos 'n' Andy, Pepsodent, Die Cut, 1930, 22 In. 165.00
Display, Bayer Aspirin Pill, Felt Base, 2 x 7 In. 30.00
Display, Beech-Nut Gum, Tin Lithograph, 14 1/2 x 6 3/8 x 6 5/8 In. 2200.00
Display, Blatz Chewing Gum, Cardboard, 10 Gum Packs, 5 1/8 x 6 1/8 x 4 1/4 In. 990.00
Display, Buster Brown, In Shoe, Tige Pulling Shoe, Lithograph, Die Cut, 24 In. 9400.00
Display, Dr. Morse's Indian Root Pills, Indian, Canoe, Cardboard, 20 x 9 In. 198.00
Display, Dr. Morse's Indian Root Pills, Indians, Cardboard, 24 x 13 In. 80.00
Display, Elgin Watch, Made In America, Wood, Plastic, Light-Up, 18 x 22 In. 85.00
Display, Fairbanks Gold Dust Washing Powder, Twins Do Your Work, 60 In. 18000.00
Display, Golden Burst Popcorn, Edgewater Farms, Sterling, Ill., Metal, 17 x 16 In. 33.00
Display, Greyhound Bus Lines, Depot Timetable, 1940s ....330.00 to 690.00
Display, Johnson & Johnson, Medicated & Adhesive Plasters, Tin, 13 x 15 In. 685.00
Display, Kaiser Aluminum Shade Screen, Brett, Bart Maverick, Die Cut, 1959, 32 x 27 In. 1300.00
Display, Kodak Film, Ed Sullivan, Yellow, Blue, Red, 15 x 8 In. 22.00
Display, Mason's Challenge Blacking Shoe Polish, Wood, Box, 11 x 3 x 8 In. 55.00
Display, Mason's Challenge Blacking Shoe Polish, Wood, Box, 12 x 9 x 3 In. 110.00
Display, Maxwell House Coffee, Man, Woman, Die Cut, Cardboard, 36 x 26 In. 125.00
Display, Mays Seeds, Tin Lithograph, Wood Base, Tripod, Patent 1902, 45 In. 1430.00
Display, Mellins Food, Child, On Chair, Die Cut, 12 x 7 1/2 In. 39.00
Display, Miss Curity, First Lady Of First Aid, Plastic, c.1950, 19 In. 175.00
Display, Munsing Union Suits, Tin, 46 In. 1100.00
Display, National Biscuit, 6 Boxes, Marquee, 39 In. 165.00
Display, Nature's Remedy, Feel Like A Million, Girl, Cardboard, 13 x 17 In. 210.00
Display, Ottens Cream Nut Bread, Waterville, Me., Rope Handles, 20 1/2 x 30 In. 225.00
Display, Page & Shaw Chocolates, Santa, Cardboard, Lithograph, 39 In. ....*Illus* 60.00
Display, RCA, Eddie Cantor, Paper, c.1930, 5 3/4 In. 35.00
Display, Reddy Kilowatt, 3-D, Talking, Microphone, Speakers, Transportation Crate 2600.00
Display, Rice's Seeds, Wood, Paper Label, 23 x 35 x 9 In. 70.00
Display, Stars Of Radio & Television, Picture Cards, Bubble Gum, 1953, 24 Piece 805.00
Display, Sunbeam Bread, Holiday Dinner, 1962, 25 x 35 In. 39.00
Display, Towle's Log Cabin Syrup, Cardboard, 3-D, Woods, 16 x 28 x 10 In. 725.00
Display, Vanola Pure Mints, Winner For After Dinner, Contents, 8 1/4 x 3 In. 225.00
Display, Wheatlet Superior Oat Meal, Uncle Sam, Cardboard, 1899, 3 1/2 x 6 In. 120.00
Display, Whitman's Samplers Chocolates, Man, Cardboard, Die Cut, 40 x 24 In. 110.00
Display, Winchester Tools, 1866-1920, Easel Back, Countertop, 8 1/2 x 10 1/2 In. 468.00

Display, Winchester Tools, Best Workmanship, Cardboard, c.1920, 10 x 4 In. 275.00
Display, Wise Potato Chips, Boy & Girl, Cardboard, Easel Back, 17 x 20 In. 49.00
Display, Wolverine Action Line Boots, Shoes, Grizzly, Fiberglass, 1970s, 19 x 10 In. 28.00
Display, Wrangler Jeans, Wooden Post, 1960s, 17 x 2 3/4 In. 601.00
Display, Wrigley's Gum, Be Sure It's Wrigley's, Round, c.1900, 13 x 12 In. 825.00
Display, Wrigley's Gum, Moon-Faced Man, Tin, Die Cut, 4 Boxes, c.1920 . . . . 1430.00
Display, Yanks Chewing Gum, 20 Gum Packages, 5 Cent, 1 x 3 1/4 x 6 1/2 In. 210.00
Display, Yuengling's Pilsner Beer, Woman With Beer, Die Cut, Cardboard, 24 x 36 In. . . . 90.00
Dolls are listed in their own category.
Door Push, Canada Dry Ginger Ale, Embossed, Tin Lithograph, 9 x 3 In. 231.00
Door Push, Clicquot Club, Eskimo Boy, Embossed, Tin Lithograph, 9 x 3 In. 105.00
Door Push, Crescent Flour, Try A Sack, Embossed, Tin Lithograph, 9 5/8 x 3 3/4 In. 330.00
Door Push, Domino Cigarettes, Tin Lithograph, 14 x 4 In. 110.00
Door Push, Dr Pepper, Drink A Bite To Eat, Metal, c.1940, 4 x 8 In. 325.00
Door Push, Dr Pepper, Emergency Notification Insert, Metal, c.1940, 4 x 8 In. 365.00
Door Push, Dr. King's, Cures Consumption, Coughs & Colds, Porcelain, 7 In. . .1650.00 to 1815.00
Door Push, Edgeworth Ready Rubbed Pipe Tobacco, Tin Lithograph, 14 x 4 In. 187.00
Door Push, Ex-Lax, Get Your Box Now, Porcelain, Multicolored, 8 x 4 In. 415.00
Door Push, Kirks Flake Soap, Come In, Red, White, Porcelain, 8 1/2 x 3 1/4 In. 385.00
Door Push, Pabst Beer, Blended Splendid, Embossed, Tin Lithograph, 4 x 9 In. 65.00
Door Push, Pabst Beer, Red, White, Blue, 7 1/4 x 4 1/4 In. 125.00
Door Push, Ridgways Coffee, Yellow, Red, Metal, 3 1/4 x 9 In. 45.00
Door Push, Schmidt's Blue Ribbon Bread, Stenciled, Sheet Metal, 19 In. 175.00
Door Push, Sunbeam Blue Ribbon Bread, Stenciled, Sheet Metal, 19 In. 300.00
Door Push, Texas Punch, Hello, You'll Love It, Tin, c.1940, 9 1/2 In. 160.00
Door Push, Walgreen's, Aluminum, Embossed, 3 x 15 In. 110.00
Egg Separator, Charles Chips, Plastic, Blue, Advertising 10.00
Egg Timer, AT&T General Markets, Logo, 3 3/4 In. 20.00
Eggcup, Eat Michigan Eggs, Japan, 2 1/2 In. 35.00
Eggcup, Fanny Farmer, Chicken Shape, Yellow, 1940s, 2 1/2 x 3 1/2 In. 28.00
Fans are listed in their own category.
Figure, Air India Airlines, Composition, 1973, 12 In. 75.00
Figure, Big Boy, Elias Brothers Restaurant, Vinyl, c.1960, 8 In. 50.00
Figure, Colonel Sanders, Plastic, KFC, 1965, 12 1/2 In. 45.00
Figure, Crescent Tools, Stand-Up, Cardboard, 4 1/2 x 5 1/2 In. 28.00
Figure, Dr. Kool, Penguin, Medical Bag, Plaster, c.1950, 4 1/2 In. 165.00
Figure, Dutch Boy, Papier-Mache, 30 In. 1100.00
Figure, Eskimo Pie Kid, Plush, 1975, 15 In. 32.00
Figure, Florsheim Shoe, Painted, 3 1/2 In. 40.00
Figure, Frankenmuth Dachshund, Beer, Ale, Plaster, 1930s, 4 x 7 x 6 In. 50.00
Figure, Freddy Fast, Douglas Oil Company, Vinyl, 1976, 7 In. 110.00
Figure, Fruit Stripe Zebra, Bendable, Beech-Nut Inc., 1988, 3 In. 29.00
Figure, Gas Genie, Greater Winnipeg Canada Gas Utility Co., c.1960, 19 In. 35.00
Figure, Green River Whiskey, Black Man, Horse, Hard Rubber, 10 x 13 In. 230.00
Figure, Heinz Aristocrat Tomato, Top Hat, Ascot, Composition, 1939, 6 In. 285.00
Figure, Jaymar Occident Flour, Costs More, Worth It, Wood, c.1934, 5 1/2 In. 138.00
Figure, Keebler Elf, Ernie, Vinyl, 1974, 6 1/2 In. 25.00
Figure, King Royal, Vinyl, Nabisco, 1973, 10 In. 175.00
Figure, Miller Girl, Plastic, Gold Color, 1950s, 6 1/2 In. 65.00
Figure, Mountain Dew, Willy The Hillbilly, Vinyl, Plush, 1965, 20 In. 165.00
Figure, Nipper, Papier-Mache, Victor, 34 In. 880.00
Figure, School Crossing Guard, Hand Raised, Speed Limit Sign, Wood, 84 In. 385.00
Figure, Spuds MacKenzie, Bud Light, Plastic, Hollow, 15 x 16 In. 75.00
Figure, Spuds MacKenzie, Budweiser, Light-Up, Plastic, 15 x 10 x 18 In. 275.00
Figure, Union 76, Minute Man, Resin, Esco, c.1950, 12 In. 55.00
Flag Pole Holder, Case Tractor, Eagle On Globe, Cast Iron, c.1900, 24 x 52 In. 6325.00
Foam Scraper, Fort Pitt Beer, That's It, Red, White 45.00
Foam Scraper, Golden Glow Beer, Black, White 60.00
Golf Ball Set, Reddy Kilowatt, Titleist, Box, 1980s, 3 Piece 40.00
Jar, '76 Boot Polish, Metal Lid, Paper Label, Gadi, Memphis, 2 1/2 In. 8.00
Jar, Borden's Malted Milk, Glass Label, Embossed Lid, 9 In. . . . . .330.00 to 660.00
Jar, Chicos Peanuts, Metal Base, Lid, c.1900, 11 In. . . . . .440.00 to 495.00
Jar, John Wyeth & Bro., Compressed Tablets, Soda-Mint & Pepsin, Amber, c.1885, 2 In. . . 39.00

Jar, Kis-Me Gum, Glass, Square, Cover, Louisville, Ky., 10 1/2 x 4 5/8 In. 100.00
Jar, Tip Top Nipples, Painted Label, Whitall Tatum Company, Round, 9 x 5 1/2 In. 1265.00
Jar, Toms Toasted Peanuts, Delicious, Clear, Red Knob, 10 In. 35.00
Jug, Vat 69 Gold, White & Gold Bar, Hall China, 5 1/4 In. 25.00
Key Ring, Michelin Man, White, Plastic, c.1960, 1 1/4 In. 15.00
Kick Plate, Sir Walter Raleigh Smoking Tobacco, Ship, Porcelain, c.1930, 1 x 3 In. 1450.00
Kit, Listerine Toothbrush, Full Tube, Lithograph Toothbrush, Die Cut, Skeezix, 6 In. 175.00
Knife, Gulf Oil Co., Inlaid Enamel, Airplane, Airship, Refineries, Derricks, 3 1/4 In. 605.00
Label, Beer, Tivoli Brewing Co., Denver, 1950s, 3 x 3 1/2 In. 6.00
Label, Cigar, Sailors Hope Cigars, Woman, Standing On Dock, Frame, 10 x 6 1/2 In. 39.00
Label, Glacier National Park, See America First, Goat On Mountain, 1922, 5 In. 35.00
Label, Tobacco, Stonewall Jackson Tobacco, 1873, 12 x 12 In. 220.00
Label, Tobacco, Watson McGill, Ships, Flags, Stone Lithograph, 14 x 7 1/4 In. 99.00
Lamps are listed in the Lamp category.
Letter Opener, Welsbach Lights, 10 1/2 x 2 3/4 In. 85.00
Letter Opener, Welsbach Mantles, Spread-Wing Eagle On Shaft, Phila., 10 1/2 In. 56.00
Lunch Box, Central Union Cut Plug, U.S. Tobacco Co., Richmond, Va., 4 x 7 x 5 In. 210.00
Lunch Box, Dixie Queen Tobacco, 4 x 7 3/4 x 5 1/4 In. 65.00
Lunch Box, George Washington, Cut Plug, Tin Lithograph, Handle, 4 3/4 x 7 1/2 In. .35.00 to 44.00
Lunch Box, Just Suits Cut Plug, Tin Lithograph, Wire Handle, 8 In. 80.00
Lunch Box, Tiger Chewing Tobacco, Tin Lithograph, Red, 2 Handles, 10 In. 45.00
Lunch Boxes are also listed in their own category.
Mask, Aunt Jemima, Pancake Flour, I'se In Town Honey, Ask Your Grocer 700.00
Matchbook, Pacific Far East Line, SS Mariposa, SS Monterey 3.00

Advertising mirrors of all sizes are listed here. Advertising pocket mirrors range in size from 1 1/2 to 5 inches in diameter. Most of these mirrors were given away as advertising promotions and include the name of the company in the design.

Mirror, Angelus Marshmallows, Cherubs, 2 In. 75.00
Mirror, Beeman's Pepsin Gum, Celluloid, Round, 2 1/8 In. 275.00
Mirror, Berry Brothers Varnishes, Boy Pulling Wagon, Dog, Oval, 1 3/4 x 2 3/4 In. 220.00
Mirror, Brotherhood Overalls, H.S. Peters, Topless Woman, Round, 2 1/8 In. 435.00
Mirror, Carmen Complexion Powder, 1 3/4 In. 110.00
Mirror, Ceresota Flour, Child Cutting Bread, Brown Border, 2 1/8 In. 135.00
Mirror, Defiance Tick Mitten, World's Most Modern Canvas Glove, Celluloid 75.00
Mirror, Dockash Stoves & Ranges Are The Best, 2 In. 135.00
Mirror, Dr. Daniels Horse, Cattle & Dog Medicines, Celluloid, Round, 2 In. 120.00
Mirror, Fairbanks Gold Dust Washing Powder, 2 x 3 In. 40.00
Mirror, Fort Bedford P-Nut Butter, Largest 10 Cent Glass Sold, Celluloid, 1 3/4 In. 125.00
Mirror, Fraternal Life Insurance, Omaha, Neb., Celluloid, 2 3/4 x 1 3/4 In. 95.00
Mirror, Get A Bell Telephone, Celluloid, Oval, AT&T, 2 3/4 x 1 3/4 In. 245.00
Mirror, Goodyear's Rubber Glove Co., Celluloid, Round, Pincushion, 2 1/4 In. 65.00
Mirror, Hobo Kidney & Bladder Remedy, Celluloid, Yellow, White, Black, 2 In. 125.00
Mirror, Home Store, Millinery & Cloaks, McKeesport, 2 In. 235.00
Mirror, Horlick's Malted Milk, Woman, Cow, Stream, 2 1/8 In. 145.00
Mirror, Horlick's Original Malted Milk, Girl, Cow, Celluloid, 2 1/4 In. 40.00
Mirror, Hotel Raymond, Good For 10 Cents In Trade, Round, 2 1/4 In. 265.00
Mirror, Humphrey's, Oak Frame, 11 1/2 x 10 In. 85.00
Mirror, Hyatt, Badges & Buttons Of Every Kind, Black, White, Celluloid, 1 3/4 In. 65.00
Mirror, Kendall Friday Co., Gas Power People, Woman, Car, Celluloid, 2 1/8 In. 515.00
Mirror, Laurel Stoves, Lady Laurel, Celluloid, Oval, 2 3/4 x 1 3/4 In. 365.00
Mirror, Lucky Tiger, Cures Dandruff, Woman, Tiger, Red, Black, White, 2 1/8 In. 100.00
Mirror, Mascot Tobacco, Crushed Cut Tobacco, Dog, Celluloid, 2 1/4 In. 40.00
Mirror, Matchless Cunningham Piano, Oval, Celluloid, 1 3/4 x 2 3/4 In. 165.00
Mirror, Minneapolis School Supply Company, Weighted, Round, 3 1/2 In. 65.00
Mirror, National Ice Cream, Enjoy Eating, Bastin Bros. Co., Celluloid, 1 3/4 In. . . . .115.00 to 250.00
Mirror, Nature's Remedy Tablets, Blue Border, Celluloid, Round, 2 1/8 In. 145.00
Mirror, Norton Mercantile Co., Girl, Holding Flower, Handle, 2 x 5 1/4 In. 210.00
Mirror, Oak Motor Suit, Man In Suit, By Car, Celluloid, 2 3/4 x 1 3/4 In. 265.00
Mirror, Paperweight, New Human Interest Library, Midland Press, 3 In. 85.00
Mirror, Prisco Lanterns, Uncle Obediah, Lantern, On Crates, Celluloid, 2 1/4 In. 175.00
Mirror, Rumford Baking Powder, Wreath, Celluloid, Early 1900s, 1 3/4 In. 130.00

Mirror, San-Tox, Image Of Nurse, Celluloid, 2 3/4 x 1 3/4 In. 175.00
Mirror, Schaeffer Pianos, Tan Ground, Round, Celluloid, 2 In. 165.00
Mirror, White House Shoes, Brown Shoe Co., St. Louis, Round, 2 1/4 In. 195.00
Mixer, Malt, Hires, Porcelain, Cast Iron, Hand Crank, c.1897 . . . . 770.00
Mug, Araban H Chocolate, Restaurant Ware, Iroquois China, 1940s-1960s, 3 1/2 In. 36.00
Mug, Borden, Elsie The Cow, Flowers, Gold Trim, Child's, 3 x 4 In. 110.00
Mug, Budweiser, Holiday, Champion Clydesdales, St. Louis, Mo., 1980 . . . . 155.00
Mug, Get Me At Rockford Malt Extract Co., Stoneware 400.00
Mug, Hires Root Beer, Boy, Mug, Join Health & Cheer, Villeroy & Boch, 5 In. 125.00
Mug, North American Van Lines, State & Monroe Sts., Chicago, Blue, Gray, Miniature . . . 60.00
Mug, Try Harvester Malt Syrup, Stoneware 435.00
Pail, Armour's Veribest Peanut Butter, Chicago, 3 3/4 x 3 3/8 In. 390.00
Pail, Blue & Scarlet Plug Cut Tobacco, Tin, Handle, Booker Tobacco Co. 600.00
Pail, Bluehill Coffee, Cup That Cheers, Swing Handle, 5 Lb., 7 x 10 In. 330.00
Pail, Borden, Elsie The Cow, Tin, Wooden Handle, Ohio Art, 5 x 6 In. 65.00
Pail, Clark's Peanut Butter, Canoe, Dog Sled, Tin Lithograph, 1 Lb., 3 3/8 x 3 3/4 In. 965.00
Pail, Cream Nut Peanut Butter, Tin, Bel-Mo-Butter Co., Michigan, 3 3/8 x 3 3/4 In. 385.00
Pail, Derby's Peter Pan Peanut Butter, Free Sample, 2 1/4 x 1 5/8 In. 205.00
Pail, Gold Flake Peanut Butter, Lid, Kelly Peanut Corp., 5 Lb., 6 x 6 In. 25.00
Pail, J.O. Schimmel Preserving Co., Apple Butter, Painted, Bail Handle, 9 1/2 In. 108.00
Pail, Jackie Coogan Peanut Butter, Tin, Kelly Co., Cleveland, 12 Oz., 3 1/2 x 3 In. 375.00
Pail, John P. Squire & Co. Pure Leaf Lard, Bail Handle, 8 Lb. 10 Oz., 7 x 7 1/2 In. 26.00
Pail, Little Pig Peanut Butter, Tin, 2 7/8 x 3 1/8 In. 295.00
Pail, Monarch Peanut Butter, Tin Lithograph, 1920s, 1 Lb., 3 3/4 x 3 3/8 In. 330.00
Pail, Monarch Peanut Butter, Tin Lithograph, 1920s, 2 Lb., 4 3/4 x 4 1/4 In. 300.00
Pail, Monarch Teenie Weenie Peanut Butter, Tin, 34 x 3 3/8 In. 250.00
Pail, Nash Coffee, Milk Can Shape, Tin Wire Handle, 14 1/2 x 8 3/4 In. 45.00
Pail, O! Boy Peanut Butter, Tin Lithograph, Stone Ordean Wells, 3 3/8 x 3 3/4 In. 715.00
Pail, Peter Pan Peanut Butter, Pry Top, Tin, 2 3/4 x 3 1/2 In. 375.00
Pail, Pure Hard Candies, Tin, Lovell & Covel, Boston, 3 Oz., 2 7/8 x 2 7/8 In. 375.00
Pail, Red Luzianne, Bail Handle, 15 Cents Overprint, 7 1/2 x 6 1/8 In. 55.00
Pail, Red Luzianne, Bail Handle, New Orleans, 3 Lb., 7 1/4 x 6 1/4 In. 155.00
Pail, Sanders Satin Candy, Children, Tin Swing Handle, 2 1/2 Lb., 5 x 5 In. 100.00
Pail, Shedd's Peanut Butter, Circus, Tin, 5 Lb., 6 1/2 In. 10.00
Pail, Wishbone Combination Coffee, Bail Handle, 3 Lb., 7 1/2 x 7 1/2 In. 170.00
Pennant, Dick & Bros. Bock Beer, Goat & Barrel, 28 In. 195.00
Pin, Acme Queen Farm Machinery, 4 Jacks & A Queen, 1 1/4 In. 265.00
Pin, Atlantic City, Steel Pier, Black, White, Celluloid, c.1930, 1 1/4 In. 20.00
Pin, Austin Ammunition, 3 Dogs, Multicolored, 7/8 In. 145.00
Pin, Bond Bread, Amelia Earhart's Friendship, Multicolored, Celluloid 20.00
Pin, Buy Right In Richmond Hill, Santa, Multicolored, Celluloid, 1 1/4 In. 85.00
Pin, Champion Spark Plugs, Charlie Orbit Time, Rocket, Green, Yellow, c.1960, 3 In. 15.00
Pin, Chevrolet, Leading 6 For 46, Red, White, Blue, Celluloid, 7/8 In. 17.00
Pin, Crescent Flour Mills, Pride Of Colorado, Multicolored, Celluloid, 1 1/4 In. 49.00
Pin, Daisy Boy Air Rifle, Boy, Rifle, Celluloid, 1914, 1 1/2 In. . . . . .1500.00 to 2170.00
Pin, Deering Harvester Co., Farmer, Harvesting, Celluloid, Pinback, 1896, 1 1/4 In. 45.00
Pin, Dupont, Prosperity Follows Dynamite, Multicolored, Celluloid, 1 1/4 In. 55.00
Pin, Ford, I'm Fired Up, Flasher, Orange, Yellow, Vari-Vue, c.1960, 3 In. 30.00
Pin, Golden Sheaf Bread, Bungalow Given Away, Celluloid, 1 1/2 In. 250.00
Pin, Goodyear, Scotties Image, Listen, Wende Oil Corp., 1 1/2 In. 140.00
Pin, High Admiral Cigarettes, Yellow Kid, Me Flower, No. 11, Celluloid 45.00
Pin, High Admiral Cigarettes, Yellow Kid, Napoleon, No. 13, Celluloid 45.00
Pin, High Admiral Cigarettes, Yellow Kid, Parrot, No. 10, Celluloid 44.00
Pin, Land O' Lakes Creameries, Indian Maiden, Celluloid, 1928, 1 1/2 In. 89.00
Pin, Liquozone, Oxygen Method, Gives Life, 2 Children, Celluloid, 1 1/4 In. 90.00
Pin, Lyon's Beer, I Chirp For, Lion, Bug Shaped Clicker, Celluloid, 1 1/4 In. 149.00
Pin, Oh Boy Gum, Booster, Chew To Your Heart's Content, Celluloid, 1 1/4 In. 310.00
Pin, Orange Crush, Celluloid, Cardboard, Philadelphia Badge Co., 9 In. 165.00
Pin, Pillsbury's Best, Flour Girl, Celluloid, Somme Badge Co., 1 3/4 In. 130.00
Pin, Pure As Butterine, 2 Girls, Celluloid, 1 1/4 In. 180.00
Pin, Southwestern Iowa Firemens Assoc., Celluloid, July 4-5, 1906, 1 1/4 In. 36.00
Pin, Special Patent Flour, Ask Your Mother, Celluloid, 1 1/2 In. 200.00
Pin, Thrifty, Has Krona Chrome, Think Bug, Blue, White, c.1960, 3 1/2 In. 20.00

Pin, Tiffin Wagon Co., Green Wagon, Celluloid, Ohio, 1 1/4 In. 195.00
Pin, Yellow Kid, Ham & Eggs, Red, White, Blue, Black, Celluloid, 1 1/4 In. 50.00
Pin, Yellow Kid, Slick As De Ice, Red, White, Blue, Black, Celluloid, 1 1/4 In. 49.00
Pin, Yetter's Wallpaper, Dutch Girl, Tulip, Celluloid, Omaha, Neb., 1 1/4 In. 165.00
Plaque, Elgin Pocket Watch, My Elgin's All Right, 22 x 15 In. 290.00
Plaque, Monda Cuba Cigars, Indian, Paperboard, Frame, 10 1/2 x 12 1/2 In. 265.00
Plate, Abbottmaid Ice Cream, 6th Anniversary, Ceramic, c.1920, 6 1/2 In. 250.00
Plate, Chew Rose Leaf Fine Cut, Avalon, Pebble Ground, Applied Flowers, 8 3/4 In. 80.00
Plate, Old Barbee Whiskey, Tin Lithograph, Vienna Art, 10 In. 440.00
Punch Bowl, Trowbridge's Original Chocolate Chips, Flowers, Ironstone, 6 x 13 In. 125.00
Rack, Newspaper, Chicago Examiner, One Cent, Red Paint, 34 In. 529.00
Ring, Kellogg's, Tom Corbett Space Cadet Rocket, No. 1, Space Cadet Girl, Plastic, 1952 25.00
Ring, Kellogg's, Tom Corbett Space Cadet Rocket, No. 2, Parallo-Ray Gun, Plastic, 1952 . 25.00
Ring, Kellogg's, Tom Corbett Space Cadet Rocket, No. 8, Space Cruiser, Plastic, 1952 ... 25.00
Ring, Mr. Softee, I Like Mister Softee, Flasher, Vari-Vue 25.00
Ring, Sky King Electronic TV, Magnifier Lens, Metal Band, 1940s 125.00
Rolling Pin, Milk Glass, Nebraska Fuel Company, Pekin Coal-Best For Heating 495.00
Rolling Pin, Royal Household Flour, China, Wooden Handles, Canada, 19 1/4 x 3 In. 255.00
Safe, Meilink Safe, Stencil, Handle, Salesman's Sample, 9 1/2 x 14 In. 1320.00
Salt & Pepper Shakers are listed in their own category.
Scales are listed in their own category.
Scoreboard, Piedmont Cigarettes, Tin Lithograph, Wood Frame, c.1920, 24 x 36 In. 309.00
Scraper, Tin, American Maid Bread, Lithograph Of Loaf, Red & Blue, 1 3/4 x 3 In. 415.00
Sharpening Stone, Goodyear's Rubber Gloves, Oval, 2 3/4 x 1 3/4 In. 125.00
Shoehorn, Shinola Shoe Polish, Brush, Shoe Polish, 1 3/4 x 6 3/4 In. 120.00
Sign, 2 For 1 Orange Drink, Ace Of Fruit Drinks, Tin, Embossed, 27 x 11 In. 220.00
Sign, 3 Cent Cigars, Ask For Fame & Fortune, Cardboard, Frame, 7 1/2 x 13 1/2 In. 62.00
Sign, 7-Up, Like Lemon-Lime Flavour, White, Red, Green, Tin, 29 1/4 x 12 1/4 In. 100.00
Sign, 7-Up, The Best Stop Sign On The Road, Cardboard, Wood Frame, 13 x 22 In. 110.00
Sign, 7-Up, You Like It, Bottle Shape, Embossed Tin, 1962, 13 x 44 1/2 In. 413.00
Sign, 7-Up, Your Fresh Up, Bather On Bottle, Red, White, Green, Tin, 1947, 27 x 19 In. ... 165.00
Sign, A&P Tea Co., Woman Riding Elephant, Cardboard, Die Cut, 1884, 10 1/2 In. 60.00
Sign, A.T. Wilson & Son's Milk, Cow Head, Porcelain, 11 In. 20.00
Sign, Adams Laundry, Iron, Curved Top Bar, Hanging Sadiron, 15 x 10 In. 550.00
Sign, Alka-Seltzer, Speedy Holds Glass, Cardboard, Die Cut, Easel Back, 22 x 40 In. 130.00
Sign, All You Can Eat Seafood, Fish Shape, Wood, Carved, Painted, 14 x 47 In. 99.00
Sign, Alliance Insurance Company Of Philadelphia, Porcelain, 18 x 24 In. 45.00
Sign, Alligator Steel Belt Lacing, Tin Over Cardboard, Green, Yellow, 9 x 13 In. 110.00
Sign, Alox Shoe Laces, Good Shoe Laces For A Nickel, Paper, Frame, 14 x 26 In. 35.00
Sign, American Fire & Casualty, Shield Shape, Wood, Orlando, Florida, 16 x 15 In. 35.00
Sign, American Gentleman Shoes, John Crescenzo, Embossed, Tin, 1915, 19 x 14 In. 145.00
Sign, American Ice Cubes, Crystal Clear, Tin, 19 x 29 In. 220.00
Sign, American Stamps, We Give & Redeem, Red, Yellow, Tin, Embossed, 28 x 10 In. 165.00
Sign, Anheuser-Busch, Budweiser Girl, Victorian Lady, Red Dress, Frame, 24 x 38 In. ... 1430.00
Sign, Apco Oil Well, Edwards Field Grayburg Unit, Red, White, 10 x 26 In. 149.00
Sign, Apothecary, Stationer, Black Ground, Gold Lettering, 15 1/2 x 19 In. 575.00
Sign, Arab U-Do-It, Termite & Pest Control, Light-Up, Plastic, 15 In. 20.00
Sign, Arbuckles Coffee, Pure Wholesome, Yellow, Black, Red, 19 1/2 x 5 1/2 In. 265.00
Sign, Arden Fine Ice Cream, Delicious, Masonite, Beveled Edge, 7 1/4 x 12 In. 175.00
Sign, Arden Ice Cream, For Vital Energy, Porcelain, 28 x 32 In. 300.00
Sign, Armour's Star Brand Mince Meat, Tin Lithograph, 21 1/2 x 28 In. 560.00
Sign, Armour's Star Ham For Easter, Rabbit Shape, Die Cut, c.1920, 25 x 58 In. 600.00
Sign, Arnold L. Cochrane Electrical Contractor, Wood, Painted, 26 x 43 In. 190.00
Sign, Atkins Silver Steel Saws, Tin Lithograph, Frame, 10 x 19 In. 525.00
Sign, Aunt Jemima, String Hanger, Pancake Flour, Paper Lithograph, 2-Sided, 17 1/2 In. . 5310.00
Sign, B & R Ranch, Wm. Fish & Sons, Tin, Painted, 35 1/2 In. 85.00
Sign, B.E. Karshiner Authorized Dealer, Porcelain, White, Blue, 72 x 9 In. 45.00
Sign, Bagdad Short Cut Smoking Tobacco, Red, White, Porcelain, 7 x 18 In. 95.00
Sign, Baker's Chocolate, Enamel, 24 x 36 In. 380.00
Sign, Bakery, Pretzel, Urethane Foam, Applied Marble, c.1960, 19 x 23 In. 60.00
Sign, Bamber Funeral Home, Black, Brass, 16 1/2 x 24 In. 17.00
Sign, Bank Note Cigars, 5 Cents, 2 Men, Box Of Cigars, Frame, 22 x 30 In. 360.00
Sign, Batey's Lemonade, Porcelain, 20 x 30 In. 85.00

Sign, Beatrice Ice Cream, Ice Cream Cone, Fiberboard, Die Cut, 46 x 26 In. 35.00
Sign, Beech-Nut Tobacco, 10 Cents, Lorillard, Porcelain, 9 x 5 7/8 In. 300.00
Sign, Berkeley Gables, Dinner, Lunch, Masonite, Black Frame, 29 x 20 In. 168.00
Sign, Biberon Robert Nursing Bottles, Baby In Bird's Nest, Tin, France, 15 x 10 In. 545.00
Sign, Bickmore Easy Shave Cream, 35 Cents, Man, Cardboard, 31 x 21 In. 160.00
Sign, Bieres Excelsior, Bottle, Orange, Gold, Green Ground, c.1930, 13 In. 45.00
Sign, Big 5 Cigars Golden Veil, Frame, 16 1/2 x 21 In. 275.00
Sign, Big Boy Pale Dry, 5 Cents, In Green Bottles Only, Tin, 19 x 9 In. 330.00
Sign, Big Giant Cola, 16 Oz., Bigger, Better, Red, White, Tin, Embossed, 29 x 11 In. 250.00
Sign, Big Winston Overalls, Black, White, Red, Flange, Metal, 12 3/4 x 9 1/2 In. 880.00
Sign, Bishop & Boyden Drug Store, Gilt, Polychrome, 2-Sided, c.1915, 59 x 30 In. 1495.00
Sign, Black Cat Hosiery, Your Dollar Goes Further, Yellow, Red, Tin, 11 x 35 In. 330.00
Sign, Black Cat Silk Hosiery, Lithograph, Henry Hutt, Frame, 27 x 37 In. 3745.00
Sign, Blue Ribbon Bourbon, Farm Scene, Oil On Canvas, Frame, 29 x 39 In. 275.00
Sign, Boats For The Quarry, White, Black, Pine, Beveled Edge, 12 1/2 x 163 In. 550.00
Sign, Bond Bread, Better By Far, Red, Yellow, Black, Tin, 28 x 19 3/4 In. 80.00
Sign, Bond Bread, The Home-Like Loaf, Yellow, Black, Porcelain, 19 x 14 In. 65.00
Sign, Borax Dry Soap, For Washing Everything, Red, White, Tin, Embossed, 24 x 7 In. .. 250.00
Sign, Borden Eagle Brand, Partners Since 1857, Trolley Card, 11 x 21 In. 39.00
Sign, Borden Ice Cream, Elsie The Cow, Yellow, Red, Blue, Tin, c.1954, 28 x 54 In. 150.00
Sign, Borden, Eagle Brand Condensed Milk, Girl, Cardboard, c.1910, 10 x 14 In. 375.00
Sign, Borden, Elsie The Cow, Tin, 18 x 18 In. 330.00
Sign, Boschee's Syrup, Laboratory, Lithograph, Canvas, Frame, 27 x 35 In. 1100.00
Sign, Boston Celery Co., Kays Best, Long Wharf, Masonite, 30 1/4 x 36 In. 80.00
Sign, Boston Club Cigars & Tobacco, Boston Base Ball Club, 1889, 20 x 24 In. 4500.00
Sign, Boyle & Murphy Co. Cut Meats, Black, Gilt, Tin, Frame, 22 1/4 x 53 In. 460.00
Sign, Breyers Ice Cream, Tin Lithograph, Embossed, Oval, 51 In. 220.00
Sign, Brickmakers Arms Pub, Painted, Metal, Wood Frame, 2-Sided, 33 x 45 In. 440.00
Sign, Broadies Drug Store, Painting On Glass, Frame, c.1890, 18 x 26 In. ....900.00 to 1300.00
Sign, Bromo Seltzer, Emerson's, King & Queen, Frame, 26 x 43 In. 690.00
Sign, Brooke Bond Tea, Red, Black, Porcelain, 30 x 20 In. 110.00
Sign, Brookfield Rye, Girl Holding Bottle, Chromolithograph, 23 x 33 In. 2750.00
Sign, Brown Wagons, Plows, Cultivators, Wood, 19th Century, 23 x 33 In. 4800.00
Sign, Brown's Jumbo Bread, Elephant Shape, Die Cut, Frame, 17 x 19 In. 300.00
Sign, Brown's Jumbo Bread, Elephant, Tin Lithograph, Die Cut, c.1900, 13 In. 470.00
Sign, Browning Pistols, Renaissance Engraved, Laminated, Stand-Up, 8 x 11 In. 125.00
Sign, Brylcreem, For Smart Healthy Hair, Red Ground, Porcelain, 16 x 18 In. 250.00
Sign, BT Babbitt Soap, Child Blowing Bubbles, Frame, 21 x 34 In. 315.00
Sign, Budweiser, Custer's Last Stand, Print, Frame, 42 x 33 In. 330.00
Sign, Budweiser, On Tap, Embossed, Celluloid, Frame, 20 x 32 In. 11550.00
Sign, Buffalo Brewing Co., 4 Bottles, Tankards, Table, Tin, Frame, 22 x 28 In. ....495.00 to 525.00
Sign, Bull Durham Smoking Tobacco, Matador, Bull, Frame, 23 x 55 In. 690.00
Sign, Bull Durham Smoking Tobacco, Paper, Frame, 24 x 29 In. 990.00
Sign, Bull Durham Tobacco, Man Sitting, Cardboard, Die Cut, c.1915, 6 1/2 x 13 In. 575.00
Sign, Bulova, Give The Finest, Santa Claus, Roland Jewelers, 11 x 28 In. 11.00
Sign, Bunker Hill Breweries, Owl Musty, PB Ale, Cardboard, 1906, 14 In. 250.00
Sign, Burger Beer, Vas You Efer In Zinzinnati, Light-Up, Glass, Metal Frame, 8 x 25 In. .. 55.00
Sign, C.F. & I. Coals, Colorado Fuel & Iron Co., Porcelain, 22 x 11 In. 275.00
Sign, Camel Cigarettes, So Mild, So Good, Paper, 32 x 42 In. 28.00
Sign, Camillus Cutlery Co., Knife Opens & Closes, Electric, Animated, 14 x 24 In. 44.00
Sign, Campbell's, Tomato Soup, Porcelain, Curved, c.1920-1930, 12 x 22 1/2 In. 2300.00
Sign, Canada Dry, Green, White, Red, Yellow, Porcelain, Oval, 19 x 16 In. 90.00
Sign, Canadian Club, 5 Cent Cigars, 3 Men, Frame, 14 x 19 In. 308.00
Sign, Canoe Club Beverage, Once You Try It, Cardboard, Metal, 14 x 30 In. 248.00
Sign, Carbo Magnetic Razor, Black Triplets In Basket, They're All Alike, Tin, 13 In. 3700.00
Sign, Carnation Ice Cream, Sundae, Red, White, Green, 22 x 22 In. 385.00
Sign, Cascade Ginger Ale, A Toast In Every Glass, Cardboard, c.1920, 10 x 14 In. 340.00
Sign, Caswell Cigar Club, Fox Hunters, Hounds, Wood, 11 1/2 x 15 1/2 In. 275.00
Sign, Cedarhurst Whiskey, Bear In Mind, Brown Bear, Tin, Frame, 12 x 8 In. 650.00
Sign, Cer-Ola, A Non-Intoxicating Cereal Beverage, Bay City, Mich., 11 x 17 In. 50.00
Sign, Ceresota Flour, Boy, Carving Loaf, Tin, Embossed, Sentenne & Green, 26 x 21 In. . 960.00
Sign, Chapin's Buchu-Paiba, Great Kidney Cure, E.S. Wells, Jersey City, N.J., 7 x 5 In. .. 39.00
Sign, Chase & Sanborn, Old-Fashioned Grocery, Paper, Frame, c.1897, 23 x 25 In. .550.00 to 700.00

Sign, Cherry Blossoms Drink, In Bottles Only, Men, Cardboard, Die Cut, 7 x 16 In. 220.00
Sign, Cherry Blush, Cherries Only Rival, Tin Over Cardboard, c.1920, 6 x 9 In. ...650.00 to 850.00
Sign, Chesterfield Cigarettes, 21/20, They Satisfy, Red, White, Yellow, Tin, 18 x 24 In. 55.00
Sign, Chesterfield Cigarettes, Best For You, Black, Red, Yellow, Tin, 12 x 34 In. 39.00
Sign, Chesterfield Cigarettes, Big Clean Taste, Top Tobacco, Tin, 34 x 12 In. 55.00
Sign, Chesterfield Cigarettes, Big Clean Taste, Top Tobacco, Tin, Embossed, 19 x 29 In. ... 66.00
Sign, Chesterfield Cigarettes, Buy Chesterfield Here, Tin, 18 x 12 In. 44.00
Sign, Chesterfield Cigarettes, Tastes Great, Tin, Liggett & Myers, 19 1/2 x 24 In. 55.00
Sign, Chilean Soda, Natural, Yassuh, Uncle Natchel, Sheet Steel, 21 1/2 In. 330.00
Sign, Cigars, Vertical Letters, Hand Painted, Stepped Base, 44 In. 925.00
Sign, City Of New York Insurance, Glass, Reverse Painted, Frame, 22 x 30 In. 425.00
Sign, Clark's Mile End Cotton, Dar It Is, Man Picking Cotton, Cardboard, 22 x 17 In. 900.00
Sign, Clark's Mile End Spool Cotton, Black Man, Field, Lithograph Paper, 22 x 17 In. 1017.00
Sign, Clear Quill Flour, Tin, Cardboard Back, Self-Framed, c.1890, 14 x 20 In. ....700.00 to 900.00
Sign, Clicquot Club, Eskimo Boy, Tin Lithograph, Embossed, c.1950, 9 x 20 In. 190.00
Sign, Coach Stop, No Parking, 2-Sided, Yellow, Porcelain, Holder, 12 x 17 1/2 In. 120.00
Sign, Coles Peruvian Bark & Wild Cherry Bitters, Porcelain, c.1880, 8 x 18 In. ...700.00 to 900.00
Sign, Colonial Club, 5 Cent Cigar, 2-Sided, Metal, Flange, 18 1/2 x 9 In. 220.00
Sign, Colonial Club, 5 Cent Cigar, Woman Wearing Hat With Flowers, 27 x 32 In. .880.00 to 990.00
Sign, Columbia Insurance Company, New Jersey, Frame, 18 x 22 In. 35.00
Sign, Commercial Union Assurance, Glass, Reverse Painted, 13 1/2 x 19 1/2 In. 29.00
Sign, Consolidated Tours, Blue, White, 2-Sided, Porcelain, Die Cut, 23 x 19 In. 1275.00
Sign, Consumer's Beer, Ask Father, Embossed Tin, Hills Grove, Rhode Island, 28 x 10 In. 120.00
Sign, Converse Shoes, People, Car, Frame, c.1910, 30 x 34 In. 385.00
Sign, Cosmo Spar Varnish, Man On Horseback, Wood, Early 1900s, 21 In. 106.00
Sign, Coventry Machinists Co., Club Cycles For 1887, Frame, 15 x 21 In. 100.00
Sign, Cowboy Boot, Texas, 2-Sided, Illuminated, 96 In. 4500.00
Sign, Cracker Jack, Mother, Child, Cardboard, Lithograph, 1900, 14 1/2 x 10 3/4 In. 5500.00
Sign, Cream Of Wheat, Jack The Giant Killer, Paper, Frame, 1909, 14 x 10 In. 11.00
Sign, Cream Of Wheat, Man Holding Sign, Frame, 1913, 14 x 10 In. 11.00
Sign, Cream Of Wheat, Uncle Sam Reading Poster, Frame, 20 x 16 In. ....11.00 to 17.00
Sign, Cressmans Counsellor, 5 Cent Cigar, Linen, Lithograph, Frame, 20 x 26 In. 550.00
Sign, Cruwell Tobak, Indian Smoking Pipe, Tin, Germany, 9 3/8 x 14 1/4 In. 50.00
Sign, Cuday's Diamond C Hams, Bacon & Lard, Tin, Embossed, Frame, 25 x 32 In. 550.00
Sign, Cunard Line Agency, Berengaria Ocean Liner, Tin Lithograph, 34 x 44 In. 1430.00
Sign, Dad's Old Fashioned Root Beer, Delicious, Tin, Embossed, 1950s, 19 x 27 In. 300.00
Sign, Dakota Maid Flour, Yellow Ground, Tin Lithograph, Embossed, 9 x 19 1/2 In. 130.00
Sign, Dandy Shandy, Down Goes The Thermometer, Cardboard, Frame, 19 x 11 In. 55.00
Sign, Day's Fruit Beverage, Painted, Green Ground, Tin, 9 1/2 x 19 1/2 In. 110.00
Sign, DeLaval Cream Separators, Lady, With Separator, Tin, Frame, 41 x 29 In. 1650.00
Sign, DeLaval Cream Separators, Yellow, Black, White, Tin, Flange, 18 x 26 In. 880.00
Sign, DeLaval, Sooner Or Later You Will Buy, Kimball & Sons, 41 x 29 In. 1650.00
Sign, DeLaval, Sooner Or Later You Will Buy, Porcelain, 2-Sided, 18 x 27 In. 1980.00
Sign, Delaware Rubber Co., Washington Crossing Delaware, c.1900, 20 x 26 In. 259.00
Sign, Delmars Restaurant, Steel, Plexiglas, Reverse Painted, 2-Sided, 31 x 41 x 8 In. 58.00
Sign, Dexter Building, Applied Lettering, Egg & Dart Molding, 21 x 22 In. 58.00
Sign, Diamond Crystal Salt, The Salt That's All Salt, Red, Yellow, Black, Tin, 15 x 23 In. .. 22.00
Sign, Diamond Dyes, Busy Day In Dollville, Tin Litho, Frame, 1911, 17 x 11 1/2 In. 3850.00
Sign, Diamond Edge Tools, Frank Lominack Hardware, Tin, Embossed, 9 x 27 In. 85.00
Sign, Dilbert Bros. & Co. Cigars, Handmade, Paper Lithograph On Tin, 10 x 14 In. 495.00
Sign, Domaine Rolet Winery, Cotes Du Jura, France, c.1940, 38 x 26 In. 1035.00
Sign, Double Cola, Enjoy, Green, White, Red, Tin, 31 3/4 x 11 3/4 In. 80.00
Sign, Double Cola, Woman Holding Bottle, Frame, 27 x 22 In. 275.00
Sign, Dr Pepper, Drink A Bite To Eat, Paper Lithograph, Easel, c.1940, 9 x 11 1/2 In. 280.00
Sign, Dr Pepper, Drink Dr Pepper, Porcelain, Raised Logo, c.1940, 10 1/2 x 26 1/2 In. ... 385.00
Sign, Dr Pepper, Good For Life, Porcelain, c.1940, 10 1/2 x 26 1/2 In. ....365.00 to 390.00
Sign, Dr Pepper, Thank You, Call Again, Paper Lithograph, c.1940, 9 x 11 1/2 In. 275.00
Sign, Dr Pepper, White Letters, Red Ground, Enameled, Porcelain, 7 3/4 x 20 In. 110.00
Sign, Dr. Cox's Barbed Wire Liniment, Cardboard, Frame, 29 x 25 In. 415.00
Sign, Dr. Fenner's Remedies, U.S. Battleship Iowa, Paper, c.1898, 11 1/2 x 9 In. 240.00
Sign, Dr. Jayne's Family Medicine, Victorian Frame, 23 x 26 In. 470.00
Sign, Dr. Morse's Indian Root Pills, Cardboard, Countertop, 24 x 13 In. ....80.00 to 110.00
Sign, Dr. Murlless' Dental Purifico, To Sweeten & Cleanse, Frame, 13 x 11 1/4 In. 230.00

Sign, Dr. Odozone, Cleans Teeth Clean, It's A Fact, Cardboard, 20 x 11 In. 165.00
Sign, Dr. Prices Delicious Extract Of Vanilla, Paper, Frame, 27 1/2 x 17 1/2 In. 110.00
Sign, Dr. Russell's Pepsin Calisaya Bitters, 1880, 21 x 15 In. 8970.00
Sign, Dr. Wells Delicious Carbonated Beverage, Tin, 24 x 2 3/4 In. 145.00
Sign, Drewery's Ale & Beer, Thrill Of Lifetime, Men, Canoe, Tin Lithograph, 23 x 17 In. . . 146.00
Sign, Drink Big Boy Beverages, Drink Big Boy, Tin, Embossed, 34 x 18 In. 85.00
Sign, Du Pont Polish, Boy, Shiny Car, Die Cut, Cardboard Lithograph, Easel Back, 22 In. . . 450.00
Sign, Dubec Waterloo, Victorian Lady, Red Hat, Dress, Lithograph, Frame, 24 x 29 In. . . . 578.00
Sign, Dukes Mixture, Roll Of Fame, Porcelain, 1920-1930, 5 1/4 x 8 In. 825.00
Sign, Duraline Floor Coverings, J. Frank Darling Co., N.Y., Tin, Embossed, 5 x 28 In. 20.00
Sign, Dutch Boy Paints, Painter, Frame, 1907, 31 x 23 In. 430.00
Sign, E.D. Pinaud's Eau De Quinine, Bottle, Tin, Frame, c.1900, 17 1/2 x 23 In. 225.00
Sign, Eagle Star Insurance Co., Eagle Flying, Tin Lithograph, Over Cardboard, 9 x 12 In. . . 100.00
Sign, Eberhardt & Ober Brewing Co., Buildings, Print, Frame, 36 x 50 In. . . . . . .455.00 to 1155.00
Sign, Ed Steves & Sons Lumber, Paper Lithograph, Frame, 21 x 16 In. 100.00
Sign, Eddy Good Bread, Red, Yellow, White, Tin, 12 x 27 In. 35.00
Sign, Edgeworth Tobacco, Metal Over Cardboard, 9 1/4 x 13 1/4 In. 475.00
Sign, EFICO Equitable Fire Insurance, Charleston, Glass, Frame, 16 x 22 In. 200.00
Sign, Eggs, Write-On Board, Black, Yellow, Tin, Embossed, 24 x 7 1/4 In. 45.00
Sign, Egyptian Luxury Cigarettes, Woman, White Dress, Hat, Frame, 25 x 33 In. 330.00
Sign, Eisenlohr's Cinco 5 Cent Cigars, Same Old Quality, Frame, 33 x 47 In. 385.00
Sign, El Sidelo Cigars, Glass, Reverse Painted, Frame, 21 x 15 In. 220.00
Sign, Energos Cigars, Man, Oxen, Glass, Reverse Painted, 17 x 24 In. 578.00
Sign, Engles & Krudwig Grape Juice, Cherubs Dancing, Lithograph, 19 x 14 In. 259.00
Sign, English Fullers Beer, Independent Family Brewers, Porcelain, 21 x 25 In. 165.00
Sign, Epicerie, Galoches Et Sabots, Gold, Black Ground, 1900s, 33 1/2 x 18 In. 355.00
Sign, Erica Bicycle, Painted, Tin, Embossed, Germany, 12 x 6 1/2 In. 132.00
Sign, Escapernong Wine, Garrett & Co., Uncle Sam, Liberty, Tin, Self-Framed, 18 x 26 In. 3960.00
Sign, Evangeline Maid Bread, Stays Fresh Longer, Tin, Embossed, 24 x 48 In. 330.00
Sign, Eveready Flashlights & Batteries, Man, Batteries, Porcelain, 18 x 41 In. 715.00
Sign, Everfast Department, Molded Composite, c.1940, 10 x 28 In. 75.00
Sign, Eye Doctor, Gold Paint, Cobalt & Red Lens Glass, Cast Iron, 17 x 31 In. 2970.00
Sign, F.L. Grant Furniture-Undertaking, Salamanca, Yellow, Tin, Embossed, 28 x 5 In. . . . 39.00
Sign, Falstaff Beer, Irishman, Holding Beer, Frame, 29 x 41 In. 193.00
Sign, Fame & Fortune 3 Cent Cigars, A.K. Walch, Phila., Pa., Tin, 8 x 14 In. 275.00
Sign, Famous Beer, On Tap, Black, Red, White, Porcelain, 42 1/2 x 30 In. 550.00
Sign, Fehrs Malt Tonic, Maiden, Cherubs, Tin, Oval, Self-Framed, 28 1/4 x 22 1/2 In. 420.00
Sign, Fields Champion Whiskey, Tin, Frame, c.1890, 26 x 35 In. 1980.00
Sign, Filmer & Hardwick's Colliery Engine, Wood, Painted, 1842, 24 x 36 In. 259.00
Sign, Finks Red Bar Overalls, Wears Like A Pigs Nose, Tin, 35 1/2 x 11 In. 440.00
Sign, Firemen's Insurance Co., Newark, N.J., Aluminum, Acid Etched, Frame, 11 x 14 In. . 110.00
Sign, First National Bank, Teddy Roosevelt, Tin Lithograph, 18 x 14 In. . . . . *Illus* 300.00
Sign, Flower Shop, Faience, Multicolored Flowers In Basket, 1900s, 20 In. 632.50
Sign, Foster Hose Supports, Woman, With Hose Supports, Lithograph, 9 x 17 In. 253.00
Sign, Frog In Your Throat, 2 Girls, Cardboard, Die Cut, Frame, c.1894, 5 3/4 x 8 In. 255.00
Sign, Frog In Your Throat, Breaks Up A Cold, Frog & Scarf, Paper, Frame, 14 x 42 In. 990.00
Sign, Frostie Root Beer, Tin, 15 3/4 x 9 5/8 In. 165.00
Sign, G. Richard Cycles, G. Bataille, Stone Lithograph, France, c.1900, 51 x 37 In. 1095.00
Sign, Gardner's Corn & Bunion Remedy, Ask Druggist, Paper, Frame, 11 x 8 1/2 In. 88.00
Sign, Garland Stoves & Ranges, World's Best, Porcelain, Tin, 24 x 24 In. . . . . . .1300.00 to 1750.00
Sign, Gastobac Curing Systems, First & Best, Metal, 2-Sided, 20 x 28 In. 60.00
Sign, Gastobac Curing Systems, See Your Local Gas Company, Tin, 20 x 28 In. 45.00
Sign, Gavitt's Herb Tablets, W.W. Gavitt Medical, Paper, 12 x 7 3/8 In. 165.00
Sign, Georgia Stages, Ticket Office, Bus Station, Porcelain, Hanging, 24 x 20 In. 12000.00
Sign, Glocklers, Butcher, Bull, Meat Tools, Iron, Syracuse, Patent 1889, 33 In. 715.00
Sign, Gold Bond Stamps, We Give, Yellow, Black, Red, Metal, Flange, 28 x 17 1/2 In. 145.00
Sign, Gold Dust Washing Powder, Trolley Card, 14 1/2 x 25 In. 1200.00
Sign, Golden Fleece Knitting Yarns, Glass, Reverse Painted, Chain Hanger, 9 x 18 In. 275.00
Sign, Golden Light Coffee, Tin Over Cardboard, 15 1/2 x 8 1/4 In. 135.00
Sign, Goldenson Furniture & Carpets, Tin, Wood Frame, 29 x 10 In. 300.00
Sign, Granger Pipe Tobacco, Aviator, Smiling, Smoking Pipe, Cardboard, 11 x 15 In. 32.00
Sign, Grape Smash, You Will Like It, 5 Cents, Cardboard, 12 x 8 1/2 In. 55.00
Sign, Grape-Nuts, Girl, St. Bernard, Tin Lithograph, Self-Framed, c.1916, 20 x 31 In. 2650.00

Sign, Grapette Soda, Bottle, Die Cut, 36 In. 325.00
Sign, Grapette Soda, Neon, Porcelain, 102 In. 1100.00
Sign, Grapette Soda, Real Fruit Juice Flavor, Tin, 11 1/2 x 31 In. 175.00
Sign, Greebe & Atwater-Kent, Radios & Electrical Fixtures, Wood, 84 x 14 In. 100.00
Sign, Green River Whiskey, Black Man, Horse, Tin, Self-Framed, 41 x 31 In. 880.00
Sign, Green River Whiskey, Man Holding Horse's Bridle, Embossed, 10 x 13 In. 230.00
Sign, Groceries, Copper, Over Wood, 7 x 57 In. 550.00
Sign, Grocery, Arm Shape, Extended Finger, Green, Yellow, Glen Rock, Pa., 30 x 6 In. . . . 1125.00
Sign, H. Martindale, Boot Shape, Black, Red, Wood, 2-Sided, Iron Hook, 37 x 21 In. 2035.00
Sign, Hamilton-Brown Shoe Co., Woman, Blue Dress, Hat, Frame, 22 x 35 In. 468.00
Sign, Hanover Pure Rye, Horse, Convex Glass, Reverse Painted, c.1890, 24 In. . . . 850.00 to 1100.00
Sign, Hartford Fire Insurance, Tin Lithograph, Self-Framed, 20 x 24 In. 110.00
Sign, Harvester Cigar, Heart Of Havana, Tin Lithograph, Embossed, 9 x 13 In. 220.00
Sign, Hat Care, All Kinds Of Hats Cleaned & Blocked, Hat, Wood, c.1900, 36 x 29 In. . . . 1765.00
Sign, Hav-A-Tampa Cigar, For Good Taste, 1955, 15 x 24 In. 85.00
Sign, Headlight Union Made Overalls, Train Engine, Porcelain, 15 x 45 In. 440.00
Sign, Heath & Milligan Paints, Walter S. Edgerly, Durham, Yellow, Wood, 31 x 48 In. . . . 1180.00
Sign, Helmar Turkish Cigarettes, Porcelain, Round, 8 In. 160.00
Sign, Hershey's Ice Cream, Light-Up, Plastic Lens, Metal Frame, 15 x 29 In. 45.00
Sign, Hickman Ebbert Co. Wagons, Apple Tree, Tin, Frame, c.1906, 26 x 38 In. . 1200.00 to 1800.00
Sign, Hickok Radio & TV Instruments, Glass, Reverse Painted, 15 x 13 In. 110.00
Sign, Highland Tonic Water, Cures Brights, Diabetes, Cardboard, 11 x 14 In. 125.00
Sign, Hill Top, Black, Painted, Wood, Frame, 9 1/2 x 24 1/4 x 1 1/2 In. 200.00
Sign, Hills Bros. Coffee, Flavor Determines Value, Cardboard, c.1930, 19 x 10 In. 175.00
Sign, Hills Bros. Coffee, Flavoring Extracts, Man, Cardboard, 11 x 14 In. 65.00
Sign, Hindenburg, Zeppelin Airship, Heavy Paper, 1930s, 31 x 45 3/4 In. 4100.00
Sign, Hinkley & Garrett Country Store, Pumpkin Color Ground, 89 3/4 x 11 In. 225.00
Sign, Hires Root Beer, Bottle Shape, Tin, Die Cut, Embossed, 56 In. 330.00
Sign, Hires Root Beer, Take Home A Carton, Lady, Holding Glass, Cardboard, 9 x 11 In. . 35.00
Sign, Hires Root Beer, Triple AAA Root Beer, 5 Cents, Frame, 11 x 17 In. 17.00
Sign, Hires, Enjoy Hires, Always Pure, Girl, Hat, Tin Lithograph, Embossed, 10 x 28 In. . 525.00
Sign, Hires, Lady, Holding Glass, Hires R-J Root Beer, 1940-1950, 34 x 58 In. 250.00
Sign, Hiss Brothers Millinery, West Point, Women, Men, Paper Lithograph, 1894 . . . . 468.00
Sign, Hitch No Horses To These Sheds, Wooden, 24 x 8 In. 145.00
Sign, Hoffman Brewing Co., Paper Lithograph, Frame, 43 x 13 In. 250.00
Sign, Hoffmanettes 5 Cent Cigar, Cardboard, Wood Frame, c.1900, 16 x 22 In. . . . 350.00 to 425.00
Sign, Holsum Bakes Real Bread, Tin, 15 1/2 x 60 In. 440.00
Sign, Holsum Bread, To My Valentine, Boy, Girl, Frame, 18 x 41 In. 220.00
Sign, Home Of The Checker Smoker, Red, Gold, Reverse Painted, 33 x 14 In. 29.00
Sign, Homenta, Headaches, Coughs & Catarrh, Black Man, Articulated, 20 x 15 In. 14300.00
Sign, Homestake 5 Cent Cigar, America's Greatest, Glass, Oval, 10 x 14 In. 495.00
Sign, Honest Weight Tobacco, Weyman & Bro. Mfg., Paper, Frame, 19 1/2 x 24 In. 660.00
Sign, Honey Scotch, Ten Pieces, 5 Cents, Tin Lithograph, Embossed, 7 x 19 1/2 In. 230.00
Sign, Hood Ice Cream, Ice Cream Cone, Cow, Tin, Frame, 23 x 31 In. 330.00
Sign, Horoscope Scale, Porcelain, Die Cut, 12 x 15 In. 187.00
Sign, Horse Shoe Tobacco, Finest Quality, 10 Cents, Cardboard, 21 x 11 In. 77.00
Sign, Horseshoe Shape, Trotting Horse, Sheet Metal, 34 x 31 In. 1150.00
Sign, Horsford Baking Powder, Self Raising, Cardboard, 12 1/2 x 9 1/2 In. 165.00
Sign, Houbigant Parfums, Paper On Cardboard, Frame, 1920s, 16 1/2 x 20 1/2 In. . 250.00 to 325.00
Sign, Hubbard Bro's & Co., Wood, Painted, Black, Gold, 8 x 30 In. 45.00
Sign, Hunts Ice Cream, Celluloid, Hanger, c.1940, 9 In. 585.00
Sign, Huseman's Soda, Clear & Sparkling, Red Bud, Ill., Tin, 20 x 13 In. 55.00
Sign, Huyburs Caracas Cocoa, New York, Silver, Black, Frame, 14 1/2 x 10 1/2 In. 75.00
Sign, I.W. Harper Whiskey, Dog, Cabin, Vitrolite, Frame, 1909, 23 x 26 In. . . . . 1100.00 to 3740.00
Sign, Ide & Willson's Boots & Shoes, Lithograph, Columbus, Ohio, Frame, 23 x 18 In. . . 635.00
Sign, Imperial Tobacco Co., Indian, Celluloid, 8 x 5 1/2 In. 55.00
Sign, Indian Maid Coal, Pocahontas In Canoe, Porcelain, 24 In. 275.00
Sign, Ingersoll Watches, His First Watch, Boy, Holding Watch, Frame, 14 x 23 In. 220.00
Sign, Instruments Of Musique, Violin Form, Painted Metal, 20 x 10 In. 635.00
Sign, International Stock Food, Dan Patch, Paper, Frame, c.1910, 20 x 27 1/2 In. . 225.00 to 325.00
Sign, International System, Postal Telegraph, Blue, Porcelain, 16 x 30 In. 160.00
Sign, Invincible Motor Insurance Co., Car, Ship, Green, Yellow, Red, Tin, 9 x 20 In. 358.00
Sign, Ironbrew, We Serve Ironbrew In Bottles, Blakeslee Bros., c.1940, 9 x 12 In. 800.00

Sign, Iroquois Insurance, Metal, Die Cut, Danville, Illinois, 3 5/8 x 2 5/8 In. 85.00
Sign, J.A. Hislop & Co. Dry Goods, Wood, Tin, Frame, 41 1/2 x 19 1/2 In. 550.00
Sign, J.N. Ward & Co. Shirts, Lithograph, Cardboard, Frame, c.1880, 14 x 21 In. . .475.00 to 650.00
Sign, J.P. Alley's Hambone Cigar, Cardboard Lithograph, 2-Sided, String Hanger, 7 In. . . . 190.00
Sign, Jack Boeckmann's Musical Instrument Hospital, Iron, 25 x 47 In. 2200.00
Sign, Japps Hair Rejuvenator, Hair Color Samples, Tin, 13 1/4 x 9 1/4 In. 210.00
Sign, Jas. G. Johnson & Co., Beach, Spring, Summer 1897, Paper, Frame, 55 x 36 In. 3190.00
Sign, Jas. Johnson French Millinery, Mandolin Shape, Die Cut, 15 1/2 In. 60.00
Sign, Jay-An-Ay Ice Cream, Jessup & Antrim Ice Cream Co., 11 x 8 In. 55.00
Sign, JC Cola, It's Delightful, Glass, Reverse Painted, Dura-Products, c.1940, 9 x 12 In. . . . 845.00
Sign, Jersey Creme, Perfect Drink, 5 Cents, Tin Lithograph, 2-Sided, Flange, 6 x 6 In. . . . 798.00
Sign, Jim Hogg 5 Cent Cigars, James Stephen Hogg, Frame, 10 x 21 In. 193.00
Sign, Joe Loehndorf Painting & Decorating, Pallette, Brushes, Wood, 24 x 30 In. 440.00
Sign, John Deere Farm Implements, Red, Yellow, Black, Tin, 30 x 12 In. 468.00
Sign, Juicy Fruit Gum, Woman, Red Feather Boa, Frame, 14 x 19 In. 55.00
Sign, Julius Anderson & Sons Raw & Pasteurized Milk, Oil On Canvas, 17 x 40 In. 200.00
Sign, Kamm & Schellinger Brewing Co., Lithograph, Frame, 26 x 27 In. 578.00
Sign, KC Baking Powder, For Better Baking, Red, White, Black, 2-Sided, 26 x 11 In. 385.00
Sign, Kellogg's, Scouts Today, Leaders Tomorrow, Cardboard, 1951, 23 x 30 In. 670.00
Sign, Ken-L Ration, Feed Your Dog The Best, Yellow Dog, Tin, Die Cut, 14 x 21 In. 330.00
Sign, Kerns Bread, Take Home, Red, Yellow, Black, Tin, 54 x 14 In. 149.00
Sign, Kerns Bread, Take Home, Yellow, Red, Black, White, Tin, Flange, 14 x 18 In. 85.00
Sign, King Arthur Flour, King On Horseback, Tin, Round, Self-Framed, 26 In. 4145.00
Sign, King Quality Shoes For Men, Tin Lithograph, Die Cut, c.1920, 9 1/2 x 12 In. 35.00
Sign, Kool Cigarettes, Snow Fresh Filter, Penguin, Tin, 30 x 12 In. 28.00
Sign, Kool Cigarettes, Union Bug, 15 Cents, Cardboard, 1940s, 18 x 12 In. 200.00
Sign, Korbel Champagne, Tin Lithograph, Cardboard, Beveled, 13 x 19 In. 265.00
Sign, Korbel Champagne, Woman Holding Grapes, Bottle, Table, 1915, 13 x 19 In. 300.00
Sign, Kyra Cigar, Chicago Herald 20th Year, Cardboard, 2-Sided, Round, 5 3/8 In. 25.00
Sign, L & M Cigarettes, Filters, More Flavor, Less Nicotine, Tin, 22 x 18 In. 50.00
Sign, L & M Cigarettes, Live Modern, Smoke Modern, Tin, 17 1/2 x 12 In. 35.00
Sign, L. Hoster Brewery, Monk, Man, Sitting, Keg, Tin Lithograph, c.1890, 20 x 17 In. . . 90.00
Sign, L.O. Kelly, Ph.T., Swedish Massage, Steam Baths, Wood, c.1890, 18 x 48 In. 595.00
Sign, L.S. Benezet, Pocket Watch, Electric, 2-Sided, France, Early 1900s, 21 In. 2795.00
Sign, La Fendrich Habana Cigars, Oval, Swivels, Countertop, 10 x 10 In. 330.00
Sign, La Flor De Carvalho Havana Cigars, Tin, Frame, 1906, 15 x 21 In. 175.00
Sign, La Flor De Erb Cigar, Bearded Man, Embossed, Tin, c.1900, 6 1/8 x 13 1/2 In. 55.00
Sign, La Venga Cigars, Glass, Reverse Painted, Frame, 27 x 21 In. . . . . .550.00 to 580.00
Sign, Lakeside Club Bouquet, Milk Glass Panel, Wood Frame, 18 1/2 x 21 1/2 In. 3300.00
Sign, LaPorta Fabrics, Factory Scene, Self-Framed, 1914, 27 1/2 x 9 1/2 In. 220.00
Sign, LaPreferencia Cigar, Victorian Woman, Red Dress, Hat, Frame, 25 x 36 In. 1650.00
Sign, LaReine Rex Shoes, B. Rosenberg & Sons, Black, Yellow, Tin, 13 x 20 In. 60.00
Sign, Larkin Laundry Soap, Cat, Red Bow, Cardboard, Die Cut, Easel Back, 12 x 9 In. . . . 240.00
Sign, Le Parisien, Phili, Stone Lithograph, France, c.1934, 62 x 45 In. 805.00
Sign, Lee Jeans, Storm Rider, Lithograph, 1980s, 27 1/2 x 22 In. 30.00
Sign, Lee Overalls, Leg Kicking, Tin Lithograph, Embossed, Late 1930s, 23 In. 385.00
Sign, Levi Strauss, Neon, Plastic, 1980s, 16 In. 200.00
Sign, Liberty Beef, 49 North St., Black, Gilt, Metal, Wood Frame, 28 1/4 x 81 In. 300.00
Sign, Lime Cola, Double Size, 5 Cents, White, Red, Parker Metal Co., 3 x 20 In. 45.00
Sign, Lion Black Lead, Red, White, Porcelain, 20 x 12 In. 130.00
Sign, Lipton's Teas, Will You Have Some, Lithograph, Frame, 14 x 20 In. 2200.00
Sign, Lipton, Indian Woman, Parasol, Cardboard, Frame, 13 x 19 In. 110.00
Sign, Liquer Hanappier, Woman, With Glass, Tin, Die Cut, Embossed, 19 1/4 x 19 1/2 In. . 460.00
Sign, Lotta Cola, Serves 3, 16 Oz. Soft Drink, Tin, Embossed, 1959, 11 3/4 x 21 1/2 In. . . . 195.00
Sign, Louis B. Miele Wholesale Produce, Painted, Tin On Wood, 26 x 15 In. 135.00
Sign, Lucky Strike Cigarettes, Cardboard, Frame, 15 x 11 1/4 In. 75.00
Sign, Lucky Tiger Hair & Scalp, Blond Woman, Tiger, Cardboard, 22 x 33 1/2 In. 550.00
Sign, Lustre Cream Shampoo, Marilyn Monroe, Tin, Blue Ground, 16 x 12 In. 55.00
Sign, M. Hommel Wine, Sandusky, Ohio, Woman, Flowers, 22 x 28 In. 145.00
Sign, Ma's Root Beer, Woman, Smiling, Metal, Embossed, c.1950, 19 1/2 x 27 1/2 In. 200.00
Sign, Maffits Gold Supply Co., Wilmington, N.C., Porcelain, 30 x 21 In. 45.00
Sign, Mail Pouch Tobacco, Chew Mail Pouch, Barn Shape, Tin On Wood, 56 In. 385.00
Sign, Mail Pouch Tobacco, Girl, Straw Hat, Cardboard, Frame, 15 x 19 1/2 In. 2250.00

Sign, Makepeace Evaporated Cranberries, Wareham, Mass., Cardboard, 12 x 7 In. 35.00
Sign, Malt Nutrine, Doctor, Bag, Umbrella, Tin, Cardboard, c.1915, 7 x 12 In. . . . .250.00 to 350.00
Sign, Malt Nutrine, Stork Carries Baby, Tin, Cardboard, c.1915, 7 x 12 In. . . . . . .250.00 to 350.00
Sign, Marine Gasoline, Racing Boat, Porcelain, Octagonal, 2-Sided, 48 x 30 In. 5500.00
Sign, Mark Roger's Whiskey, 4 Men Drinking, Shadow Box, 11 1/2 x 13 1/2 In. 415.00
Sign, Masurys Marin Swedish Marine Paints, Green, White, Red, Flange, 30 x 26 In. 39.00
Sign, Matinee Cigars, Victorian Woman, In Hat, Frame, c.1880, 20 x 24 In. 418.00
Sign, Maurices Printing Ink, Eagle, Oil On Paper, 19th Century, 37 x 49 In. 470.00
Sign, Mavis, Drink, It's Real Chocolate, Tin, Embossed, Baltimore, 10 x 28 In. 198.00
Sign, Mayer Shoes, For Sale By Q.B. Stout, Tin, Embossed, 19 3/4 x 6 3/4 In. 55.00
Sign, Mayflower Great Stomach & Blood Remedy, Paper, 14 x 11 In. 45.00
Sign, Mayo's Plug Smoking Tobacco, Cock O' The Walk, Porcelain, 13 x 6 1/2 In. 550.00
Sign, Mayo's Plug Smoking Tobacco, Rooster, Lithograph On Linen, 23 x 60 In. 314.00
Sign, McCormick Deering Line, Woman In Straw Hat, Print, Frame, 12 x 18 In. . . . . : 198.00
Sign, McCormick Harvesting Machine, Chromolithograph, Frame, 25 x 32 In. 690.00
Sign, McCormick Harvesting Machine, Horse, Machine, Frame, c.1890, 33 x 43 In. 1100.00
Sign, McCormick Reapers, Back From The War, Horses, Soldier, Frame, 31 x 21 In. 220.00
Sign, McNally-Pittsburg Mfg. Corp., Designed & Built By, Porcelain, 30 x 10 In. 110.00
Sign, Meals & Lodging, Jitney Service, 2-Sided, 48 1/4 x 12 3/4 In. 759.00
Sign, Meckumfat Ground Oats, Fowl, Cardboard, c.1920, 14 1/2 x 18 1/2 In. 875.00
Sign, Mellins Food, For Infants & Invalids, Tin, Wells & Hope Co., 26 x 20 1/2 In. 349.00
Sign, Merchant Millers, Yahoo, Neb., Paper, Frame, 17 1/2 x 22 In. 715.00
Sign, Mercury Outboards, Kiekhaefer, Sales & Service, Tin, Embossed, 24 x 30 In. 495.00
Sign, Merry Prince 5 Cent Cigar, Glass, Reverse Painted, 6 x 16 In. 240.00
Sign, Merry Widow Chewing Gum, Cardboard, 8 x 6 In. 415.00
Sign, Mi-Grape Soda, The Taste Lingers, Tin, Embossed, 23 1/2 x 12 In. 110.00
Sign, Miller High Life, Easel Back, String, 14 x 10 In. 260.00
Sign, Miner's Friend Dynamite, Paper Lithograph, Frame, 9 x 14 1/4 In. 1665.00
Sign, Missing Miss Cigar, Woman, Rolled Edge, Tin, 1908, 14 1/2 x 14 1/2 In. 1020.00
Sign, Mission Of California Orange, Embossed, Tin, 24 x 24 In. 230.00
Sign, Model Smoking Tobacco, Tin, 5 3/4 x 15 In. 235.00
Sign, Moehn Brewing Company, Maltodextrine Tonic, Tin, Round, 15 In. 495.00
Sign, Mohawk Tool Works, Arrowsharp Axes, Cast Brass, 10 x 16 In. 855.00
Sign, Morea Liquid Feeds, Yellow, Black, Tin, 20 x 42 In. 60.00
Sign, Morning After Chaser Mixer, Heavy Cardboard, c.1920, 8 x 10 In. 75.00
Sign, Mortar & Pestle, Eagle Perched On Top, Gold Paint, Zinc, Molded, 32 1/4 In. 500.00
Sign, Mountain Dew, Do The Dew, Neon, 22 x 24 In. 127.00
Sign, Moxie, Die Cut, Fred Archer, Cardboard, Easel Back, 10 3/8 x 8 In. 185.00
Sign, Moxie, Drink Moxie, Red Ground, Tin Lithograph, Embossed, 6 1/4 x 19 In. 240.00
Sign, Moxie, Drink Moxie, Tin Lithograph, Embossed, 18 1/2 x 27 1/4 In. 230.00
Sign, Moxie, Drink Moxie, Tin Lithograph, Flange, 18 In. 357.00
Sign, Moxie, Yes! We Sell, Very Healthful, Convex, Tin, 19 1/2 x 27 In. 880.00
Sign, Mrs. Guntner's Wart Remedy, No More Warts, Blue, Cardboard, 13 x 7 1/4 In. 88.00
Sign, Mumm's Extra Dry Whiskey, Victorian Woman, Hat, Frame, 24 x 29 In. 578.00
Sign, Murad Turkish Cigarettes, Man On Horse, Frame, 28 x 42 In. 358.00
Sign, National Trailways System, Porcelain, 2-Sided, 18 1/4 x 22 In. 688.00
Sign, Nehi Soda, Curb Service, Tin Lithograph, Embossed, 26 3/4 x 19 3/4 In. 230.00
Sign, Nelsons Dairies, Chocolate Flavored Milk, 5 Cent, Red, White, Tin, 24 x 12 In. 300.00
Sign, Nesbitt's Orange Drink, Woman, Pool, Cardboard, Frame, 1955, 29 x 39 In. .350.00 to 450.00
Sign, New York Garment Shop, Leaded Glass, 1 Ft. 9 In. x 18 Ft. 6 In., 3 Piece 518.00
Sign, Newsboy Plug Tobacco, Paper, Frame, c.1890, 32 x 41 In. 578.00
Sign, Niagara Fire Insurance Company, Niagara Falls, Porcelain, 11 x 21 In. 1035.00
Sign, Nichol Kola, A Long Drink, America's Taste Sensation, Tin, 12 x 36 In. 110.00
Sign, Nichol Kola, America's Taste Sensation, 5 Cents, Black, Red, White, Tin, 11 x 27 In. 39.00
Sign, Nichol Kola, Toy Soldier, Bottle, Yellow, Red, White, Tin, 29 x 11 3/4 In. 70.00
Sign, Nichol Kola, Twice As Good, 5 Cent, Tin, Embossed, Parker Metal, 12 x 35 In. 138.00
Sign, Nitrolian, Leonetto Capiello, Stone Lithograph, Frame, c.1929, 62 x 47 In. 1495.00
Sign, No Smoking At Any Time, Lighted Cigars Prohibited, Porcelain, 12 x 18 In. 745.00
Sign, Norka Orange, Tastes Better, Red, White, Black, Tin, 24 x 12 1/4 In. 138.00
Sign, North American Van Lines, Oneonta Transfer & Storage, Tin, 2-Sided, 18 x 24 In. . . . 39.00
Sign, O'San Cigars, Cigar Of Smiles, Yellow, Black, Embossed, Tin, 28 x 10 In. 99.00
Sign, Ogdens St. Julien Tobacco, Cool & Fragrant, Blue, Yellow, Tin, 29 x 10 In. 22.00
Sign, Oh Boy Gum, Boy, 4 Packs Gum, Goudey, Tin Litho, Frame, c.1930, 7 x 15 In. 225.00

Sign, Oh Henry, Enjoy A 10 Cent Piece, Tin, Embossed, 1925, 27 x 13 In. 415.00
Sign, Ohio Farmers Insurance Co., Porcelain, 2-Sided, 16 x 25 In.   855.00
Sign, Ohio Sugar Co. Office, Wood, 2-Sided, 42 x 48 In. 1265.00
Sign, Old Colony Insurance Co., Boston, Glass, Reverse Painted, Frame, 18 x 24 In. 173.00
Sign, Old English Curve Cut Pipe Tobacco, Man, Pipe, Paper, Frame, 23 x 27 In. 275.00
Sign, Old Gold Cigarettes, Woman, Cigarette, Lithograph, Die Cut, Frame, 28 x 39 In. . . .   358.00
Sign, Old Hundred Cigars, W.H.I. Hayes, Cardboard, 18 1/2 x 6 In. 99.00
Sign, Old Overholt Rye, Fly Fisherman, R. Bohune, Frame, c.1913, 20 1/2 x 33 In. 495.00
Sign, Old Reliable Coffee, Always Good, Yellow, Black, Tin, c.1920, 6 1/2 x 14 In. 138.00
Sign, Old Stark Whiskey, Glass, Reverse Painted, 4 x 14 In. 190.00
Sign, Optimo Cigars, All Havana Cigars, Man, In Hat, Paper, Frame, 22 x 28 In. 140.00
Sign, Orange Crush, Feel Fresh, Crushie, Embossed, Metal, 16 3/4 x 46 1/2 In. 290.00
Sign, Orange Crush, Metal, Enamel Paint, 1968, 56 x 32 In. 295.00
Sign, Orange Julep, Couple, 2 Straws, Paper Lithograph, Frame, 7 1/2 x 12 In. 210.00
Sign, Ore-O-Dale Farms, Registered Guernseys, Cow, Porcelain, 2-Sided, 30 x 30 In. 220.00
Sign, OshKosh B'Gosh Overalls, Uncle Sam, Cardboard, c.1918, 14 x 30 In. 725.00
Sign, OshKosh B'Gosh, Union Made, Tin, Embossed, c.1930, 9 1/4 x 13 1/2 In. . . .100.00 to 150.00
Sign, OshKosh B'Gosh, World's Best Overalls, 4 Men, c.1930, 14 x 15 In. . . . . . . .175.00 to 250.00
Sign, P.H.C. Hall Dance, Pine, Red Arrow, 2-Sided, c.1930, 48 1/4 x 28 1/4 In. 805.00
Sign, Pabst Chemical Co., Okay Specific, Paper, Frame, 7 1/2 x 10 1/2 In. 240.00
Sign, Pabst Extract, Woman, Pink Dress, Gold Ground, 1916, 7 x 35 In. 315.00
Sign, Pabst Extract, Woman, Yellow Dress, 1917, 7 x 35 In. 315.00
Sign, Pabst Malt Extract, Best Tonic, Knight Riding Swan, 14 x 22 In. 375.00
Sign, Pabst, Quality Yes Suh-H, Black Waiter, Cardboard, c.1938, 24 x 34 In. . . . .300.00 to 375.00
Sign, Pabst, Smiling Man Pours Beer With Glass, Cardboard, c.1933, 20 x 26 In. 300.00
Sign, Pabst, Spanish-American War, Chromolithograph, Frame, c.1900, 33 x 27 In. 2300.00
Sign, Packard Cable, Girl In Lake, Paper, Wood Frame, c.1900, 18 1/2 x 25 1/2 In. 350.00
Sign, Park & Tilford's Chocolates, Porcelain, 15 x 48 In. 90.00
Sign, Parke, Davis & Co., Protect Your Calves, Die Cut, Cardboard, 17 1/2 x 11 In. 855.00
Sign, Parozone, Does More Than Bleach, Tin, Rolled Edge, 19 1/2 x 6 1/2 In. 70.00
Sign, Part T Pak Beverages, 10 Cent, Full Quart, Serves 6, 33 x 12 In. 110.00
Sign, Pay Car Scrap Tobacco, You'll Like, Cardboard, Trolley Car, 11 x 14 In. 100.00
Sign, Pears' Soap, Henry Ward Beecher, Actresses, Lithograph On Card, 10 x 14 In. 75.00
Sign, Pelican Cigarettes, Ch. Yzay, Lithograph, France, c.1934, 23 x 31 In. 375.00
Sign, Peninsular Furnaces, Stoves, Porcelain On Tin, c.1890, 18 x 24 In. . . . . . . .1300.00 to 1750.00
Sign, Peter Schoenhofen Brewing, Chicago, Paper, Frame, c.1890, 20 x 25 In. 415.00
Sign, Peter Schuyler Cigars, 10 Cent Cigar, Tin, Wood, Oval, Frame, 27 In. 495.00
Sign, Peter Schuyler Cigars, Get Pack Of, Blue, Yellow, White, Porcelain, 36 x 12 In. 210.00
Sign, Peter Schuyler Cigars, In Handy Packs Of 5 & 10, Frame, 15 x 25 In. 165.00
Sign, Petromax Kerosene, Famous, Sold Here, Green, Porcelain, 13 x 25 In. 220.00
Sign, Petromax Kerosene, Genuine, Sold Here, Blue, Yellow, Porcelain, 18 x 31 In. 220.00
Sign, Philip Morris Cigarettes, Bellboy, Johnny, Die Cut, Stand Up, 44 In. . . . . . . .110.00 to 660.00
Sign, Philip Morris Cigarettes, Call For, America's Finest, Tin, Embossed, 16 x 46 In. 330.00
Sign, Philips Light Bulbs, Light Bulb, Logo, Porcelain, Middle Eastern, 12 x 15 1/2 In. . . .   250.00
Sign, Phoenix Assurance Co., Wood, London, Established 1782, Frame, 18 x 22 In. 69.00
Sign, Picaninny Freeze Ice Cream, Boy, Watermelon, Cardboard, 1922, 9 x 12 In. 90.00
Sign, Picaninny Freeze, Hendler's Ice Cream, 5 Cents, Cardboard, 1922, 14 x 11 In. 575.00
Sign, Pickwick Ale & Stout, Bottle, Tin Lithograph, Embossed, 19 x 27 In. 180.00
Sign, Piedmont Cigarettes, Chalkboard, Tin Lithograph, Wood Frame, c.1920, 2 x 3 In. . . .   300.00
Sign, Piedmont Cigarettes, Cigarette Of Quality, Victorian Woman, Frame, 19 x 29 In. . . .   468.00
Sign, Piedmont Cigarettes, Washington's Return, Frame, c.1890, 24 x 30 In. 330.00
Sign, Players Cigarettes, 9 Actor & Actress Cards, Cardboard, Frame, 7 x 14 In. 75.00
Sign, Players Cigarettes, Players Please, Sailor, Porcelain, 16 x 45 In. 550.00
Sign, Pneu Velo Michelin, Michelin Man On Bike, L.T. Hingre, c.1900, 37 x 24 In. 4140.00
Sign, Poll-Parrot Shoes, Parrot In Shoes, 2-Sided, Wood, Sidewalk, 46 In. 330.00
Sign, Pompeian Beauty Products, Man, Woman, 12 x 31 In. 510.00
Sign, Pop Cola, America's Finest Cola, Mirror, Frame, c.1940, 9 x 13 In. 75.00
Sign, Popsicle, Everybody Likes, Tin Lithograph, Embossed, 9 7/8 x 27 3/4 In. 360.00
Sign, Porto Ramos-Pinto, Stone Lithograph, France, c.1932, 14 1/2 x 20 1/2 In. 430.00
Sign, Post Office, Black, Gray, 19th Century, 9 1/2 x 57 1/2 In. 690.00
Sign, Prince Albert Cigarettes, Dubec Tobacco, Victorian Woman, Frame, 24 x 29 In. 200.00
Sign, Private Closet, 5 Cents, Directions, Blue, White, Porcelain, 3 1/2 x 12 In. 300.00
Sign, Proctor's Photograph Rooms, Sewing Machines, Wood, Painted, 48 x 24 In. 4025.00

Advertising, Sign, First
National Bank, Teddy
Roosevelt, Tin
Lithograph

Advertising, Sign, Sapolio Polish, Enoch
Morgan's Sons, Cleveland, 19 1/2 x 27 1/2 In.

Sign, Profile Sign Co., Painted, Applied Cut-Out, Pine, Early 1900s, 13 x 52 In. 1530.00
Sign, Prudential Insurance, Branch Office, Porcelain, 14 x 20 In.   385.00
Sign, Purity Butter Pretzels, Boy, Pretzel, Cardboard, Diecut, Easel Back, 12 x 22 In. 120.00
Sign, Purity Ice Cream, Girl, Die Cut, Stand-Up, Wolf Adv. Co., N.Y., 12 x 12 In. 45.00
Sign, Quail Cigar, Made In Louisville, Hand Painted, Tin, Frame, 14 x 42 In. 60.00
Sign, Quaker Maid Milk, First Quality, Red Ground, Porcelain, Die Cut, 24 x 41 In. 635.00
Sign, Quill Flour, Union Mill Co., Flour, Table, Bread, Blue Ground, Tin, 1890, 14 In. . . .   800.00
Sign, Railway Express Agency, Red, White, Porcelain, 8 x 8 In.   110.00
Sign, Raleigh Cycle Co., Champion Of World, Arthur Zimmerman, 21 1/2 x 15 In. 896.00
Sign, Randolph Macon Cigars, Man, Woman, Tin Lithograph, Self-Framed, 20 x 24 In. . .   650.00
Sign, Raytheon Radio Tubes, Tube, Box, Flange, Tin, c.1934, 14 x 18 In. 270.00
Sign, RCA Victor, His Master's Voice, Dog, Phonograph, Porcelain, 24 x 18 In. . . .715.00 to 855.00
Sign, Red Cross, All May Help, Support Your 1950 Fund, Wax Board, 21 x 27 In. 22.00
Sign, Red Goose Shoes, Children Running, Celluloid, c.1910, 11 x 14 In. . . . . . .900.00 to 1300.00
Sign, Red Goose Shoes, Figural, Red, White, Porcelain, Neon, 1930s, 40 In. . . . . .875.00 to 1695.00
Sign, Red Man Tobacco, America's Best Chew, Paper, 15 x 11 In. 28.00
Sign, Red Man Tobacco, Free Baseball Cards, Enos Slaughter, Cardboard, 11 x 15 In. 600.00
Sign, Red Seal Beverages, Red, Beige, Tin, 23 1/2 x 12 In. 110.00
Sign, Reddy Kilowatt, Flameless Electric Kitchen, Star Shape, 33 x 31 In. 180.00
Sign, Redfern Rubber Heels & Shoes, Policeman, Boy, Porcelain, 20 x 48 In. 300.00
Sign, Redford's Navy Mixture, Heavy Cardboard, 1900, 8 x 12 In. 75.00
Sign, Redford's Tobaccos, Men On Plantation, Frame, 21 x 27 In. 140.00
Sign, Regina Music Boxes, 19 Different Models, Late 1800s, 17 x 22 In. 250.00
Sign, Remington U.M.C., Bear At Campsite, American Litho Co., 1919, 23 x 14 In. 748.00
Sign, Reymonds Butter Crust Bread, Quality Service, Yellow, Tin, 1939, 20 x 14 In. 35.00
Sign, Rite-Way Milker, It Milks The Right Way, Red, Black, Tin, 9 3/4 x 13 3/4 In. 40.00
Sign, Rochester Root Beer, Always Cold, Glass, Reverse Painted, Frame, 10 x 12 In. 190.00
Sign, Rolling Rock, Carry Back, Derby Winner 1961, Pressed Board, 10 1/2 x 14 In. 35.00
Sign, Rose Exterminator Co., Man Spraying, Porcelain, Die Cut, 10 3/4 In. 358.00
Sign, Rose-O-Cuba Domestic Cigar, Roses In Vase, Die Cut, 24 In. 145.00
Sign, Rough On Rats, Clears It Out, 15 Cents, Chinese Man Eating Rat, 5 x 7 In. 825.00
Sign, Rough On Rats, Woman Chases Man, Boy, Dog, Paper, 8 1/8 x 5 1/8 In. 275.00
Sign, Round Oak Stove, Doe-Wah-Jack Indian, Cardboard, Die Cut, 62 In. 3575.00
Sign, Royal Crown Cola, Bottle, Tin, Self-Framed, 16 x 36 In. 99.00
Sign, Royal Crown Cola, Diet-Rite Cola, Sugar Free, Tin, 18 x 54 In. 145.00
Sign, Royal Crown Cola, Drink RC Cola, Tin, 18 x 54 In. 300.00
Sign, Royal Crown Cola, Drink, White, Red, Blue, Tin, Embossed, 12 x 32 In. 110.00
Sign, Russells' Ales, Men Unloading Kegs, Tin, Self-Framed, 21 x 29 In. 413.00
Sign, S. & C. Paint & Hardware Co., 2-Sided, Frame, 36 x 23 In. 315.00
Sign, Safe Plate, S.C. Herring, Fire Proof Safe, Bronze, 1852, 4 1/2 x 6 1/2 In. 173.00
Sign, San-Cura Hand Ointments, Cardboard, Dunston Lith. Co., Frame, 38 x 7 In. 100.00
Sign, Sands Plumbs & Levels, Always Tell The Truth, Aluminum, c.1930, 7 x 14 In. 185.00
Sign, Sanford's Ginger, Policeman, Vegetables, Paper, Frame, c.1886, 15 x 19 In. 2860.00
Sign, Sapolio Polish, Enoch Morgan's Sons, Cleveland, 19 1/2 x 27 1/2 In. . . . . *Illus*   1500.00
Sign, Satin Skin Powder, Satin Skin Cream, Paper Lithograph, Frame, 31 x 46 In. 445.00
Sign, Scheneck's Pulmonic Syrup Sea Weed, Tin Lithograph, 27 3/4 x 22 In. 2035.00
Sign, Schlitz Famo, The Drink That Leaves No Doubt, Tin Lithograph, 8 3/4 x 19 In. 225.00
Sign, Schoenling Lager Beer, Bottle To Glass, Glass, Aluminum, 25 x 12 In. 468.00
Sign, Scotch Oil Liniment, Canvas, Roll Down, Wood Frame, c.1887, 17 x 30 1/2 In. 2420.00
Sign, Seaboard Coast Line Railroad Equipment Trust, Steel, 5 1/2 x 36 In. 190.00

Sign, Seabury Bearse Contractor Builder, Wood, 2-Sided, 17 x 41 In. 130.00
Sign, Sharples Tubular Cream Separators, World's Best, Tin, Embossed, 10 x 14 In. 175.00
Sign, Shoe Shop, Man's Shoe, Vertical Letters, Wood, 60 In. 825.00
Sign, Shoes Rebottomed Entire Length, Shoe Sole, Figural, Wood, 35 1/2 x 11 3/4 In. 865.00
Sign, Short Line, Nation Wide Bus Service, Porcelain, Flange, 20 x 30 In. 210.00
Sign, Shuttleworth, Real Estate, Red, White, Blue, Tin, c.1930, 18 1/2 x 24 x 3/4 In. 50.00
Sign, Silverwood's Deluxe Ice Cream, Metal, 2-Sided, 35 1/2 x 23 1/2 In. 140.00
Sign, Singer Sewing Machines, Lady Sewing, Red, Green, White, Porcelain, 16 x 20 In. ... 187.00
Sign, Ski Soda, Picture Of Pop Bottle Skiing, Yellow, Green, 1950s, 12 x 31 In. 410.00
Sign, Slenderize Nonfat Milk, Overeating?, Tin, 2-Sided, 24 x 40 In. 165.00
Sign, Smith's Dairy Farm, Wooden, Carved, Chain Hanger, 20 1/2 x 30 1/2 In. 45.00
Sign, Snow Boy Washing Powder, Boy On Sled, Hayes Co., 1925, 29 x 23 In. 9775.00
Sign, Solona White Port Wine, Couple Dining, Paper, Frame, c.1900, 16 x 18 In. ..175.00 to 225.00
Sign, Southern Girl Shoes, Lynchburg, Va., Tin Lithograph, Self-Framed, 16 x 19 In. 440.00
Sign, Spectacles & Eyeglasses Repaired, Glass, Reverse Painted, Frame, 15 x 22 In. 385.00
Sign, Sports Argus Magazine, First For Sport, Porcelain, 17 x 24 In. 55.00
Sign, Squeeze, Distinctive Orange Drink, Tin, Embossed, Frame, 19 x 27 In. 247.00
Sign, Squeeze, Distinctive Orange Drink, Tin, Embossed, Frame, c.1940, 18 x 26 In. 1375.00
Sign, Squires Meat, Ham-Bacon-Sausage, Pig, Human Eyes, Tin, 20 x 24 In. 495.00
Sign, Squires Meat, Pig, Seated, John P. Squire & Co., Boston, Tin, 24 x 19 In. 365.00
Sign, Squirt, Drink, Bottle, Green, Yellow, Blue, Embossed, Metal, 17 x 40 In. 245.00
Sign, Squirt, Never An After-Thirst, Tin, Embossed, 1951, 9 1/2 x 28 In. ....187.00 to 210.00
Sign, Stag Smoking Tobacco, Elk, Paper Lithograph, Frame, 28 x 42 In. 468.00
Sign, Star Steel Belt Lacing, A Better Lacing For Less Money, 8 Sizes, Tin, 14 x 19 In. .. 39.00
Sign, Star Tobacco, Best For Over 3 Generations, 10 Cents, Tin, 12 x 23 1/2 In. 165.00
Sign, Star Tobacco, Best For Over 60 Years, Cardboard, 21 x 11 In. 70.00
Sign, Sterling Beer, Super Bru, Tin Lithograph, 17 5/8 x 9 3/8 In. 495.00
Sign, Sterling Brand Seeds, Woman In Field, Ear Of Corn, Paper, 1912, 29 x 21 In. 475.00
Sign, Stewart Clipping Machine, Horses, Cardboard Lithograph, 14 x 20 In. 525.00
Sign, Strathmore Cigars, 2 Men, Sitting A Table, Tin Lithograph, 15 x 17 In. 110.00
Sign, Stud Smoking Tobacco, Bully For Makins, Cardboard, 2-Sided, 8 x 11 In. 130.00
Sign, Stutts Eas-It, For Toothache, Yellow, Black, Tin, 20 x 9 In. 415.00
Sign, Sun-Maid Raisins, Add Novelty & Zest, Cardboard, Die Cut, 21 1/2 x 34 1/2 In. ... 24.00
Sign, Sunkist Grower, Porcelain, 11 1/2 x 19 1/2 In. 305.00
Sign, Sunny South Cigarettes, Victorian Woman, Cardboard, Frame, 15 x 20 In. 300.00
Sign, Sunshine Beer, 3 Triple Crown Winners, Paper, Frame, 27 x 34 In. 275.00
Sign, Sunsweet Prunes, Trolley Card, 11 x 21 In. 22.00
Sign, Sweet Corporal Cigarettes, Majorette, Tin, Wood Frame, 61 x 19 In. 3000.00
Sign, Sweet Heart Products, Heart Shape, Red, Porcelain, c.1920, 5 x 5 In. 275.00
Sign, Sweet Orr Co. Pants, Shirts & Overalls, Tug-O-War, Tin, Frame, 23 x 29 In. 550.00
Sign, Swift's Premium Cooked Ham, Girl, Chef's Hat, Basket, Gilt Frame, 20 x 15 In. ... 315.00
Sign, Tall One Soda, Wherever You're Thirsty, Flange, c.1930, 5 x 12 In. 625.00
Sign, Taystee Bread, Best Loaf Of Bread In Town, Porcelain, 9 1/2 x 16 In. 20.00
Sign, The Brew For You, Bevel Edge, American Art Works, 1906, 17 3/4 x 14 3/4 In. 575.00
Sign, Thoroughbreds Cigarettes, Lithograph, Frame, 25 x 32 In. 220.00
Sign, Tom Keene Cigar, Curved, Porcelain, Ingram Richardson, 15 x 14 3/4 In. 635.00
Sign, Tom Moore Cigar, Lithograph, Frame, 24 x 30 In. 440.00
Sign, Toni Kola, Explorer Drinks Kola, Art Nouveau, C. Verneau, 62 x 46 In. 3450.00
Sign, Tourist Golden Rule System, Yellow, Red, Black, Porcelain, 2-Sided, 18 In. 495.00
Sign, Town Talk Flour, It Has No Equal, Cardboard, 15 x 12 In. 165.00
Sign, Triple 16 Cola, Red, White, Tin, 11 1/2 x 31 1/2 In. 275.00
Sign, Turkish Dyes, Desert Scene, Wood, Tin Lithograph, c.1890, 23 x 33 In. 440.00
Sign, Ulypto Cough Drops, Stops Coughing Instantly, Black, White, Tin, 13 x 6 In. 85.00
Sign, Uneeda Biscuit, Give The Children, Natural Biscuit Co., Trolley Card, 11 x 21 In. .. 85.00
Sign, United Brand Night Shirts, Lithograph, Frame, 19 1/2 x 27 In. 195.00
Sign, Utter Manufacturing Co., Horses, Farm Machinery, Frame, c.1880, 21 x 26 In. 415.00
Sign, Velvet Tobacco, 2 Men, Boy, Dog, Tin, Frame, 26 x 32 In. 2200.00
Sign, Velvet Tobacco, 2 Men, Sitting, Boy, Dog, Tin, 22 x 28 In. 550.00
Sign, Velvet Tobacco, Victorian Woman, Black Feathered Hat, Paper, Frame, 17 x 31 In. .. 495.00
Sign, Vigorator Hair Tonic, Head Rub, Tin Lithograph, Bellefontaine, 9 x 5 In. 130.00
Sign, Warner's Safe Yeast, Health Preserving, Indians, Canoe, Frame, 18 x 34 In. 3520.00
Sign, Washington Irving Havana Cigars, Tin Lithograph, Self-Framed, 18 x 26 In. 775.00
Sign, We Do Business Here, On Cash Basis Only, Frame, 7 x 82 In. 2645.00

Sign, Wells Fargo & Co. Express, Diamond Shape, Metal Ribbed Frame, 14 In. 1150.00
Sign, Wells, Richardson & Co. Butter Color, Boy, Cow, Paper, Frame, 21 x 42 In. 665.00
Sign, West End Brewery Co., 2 Children, On Bench, Lithograph, 17 1/2 x 13 3/4 In. 300.00
Sign, Westchester Fire Insurance, N.Y., Est. 1837, Blue, White, Porcelain, 20 x 14 In. 358.00
Sign, Wheelers Nerve Vitalizer, Epileptic Fits, Black, Yellow, Tin, 13 1/2 x 10 In. 600.00
Sign, Whistle Soda, Just Whistle, Embossed Pop, Red Ground, Blue Letters, 14 In. 475.00
Sign, Whistle Soda, Thirsty, Just Whistle, Tin Lithograph, Embossed, 7 x 10 In. 715.00
Sign, White House Shoes, Woman, Red Dress, Paper, Frame, 11 x 26 In. 330.00
Sign, Whitley Solid Steel Mower, Men, Horses, Paper, Frame, c.1890, 20 x 34 In. 660.00
Sign, Wildroot Hair Cream Oil, Fosdick, Cardboard, Die Cut, Easel Back, 30 x 30 In. 250.00
Sign, Willard's Candy Bars, Boy, Hands In Pockets, Cardboard, Die Cut, 17 x 8 3/8 In. 440.00
Sign, Willard's Candy Bars, Girl, Hands In Pockets, Cardboard, Die Cut, 17 x 8 3/8 In. ... 745.00
Sign, William Gerst Brewing Co., Nashville, Paper Lithograph, Frame, 40 x 27 In. 4300.00
Sign, Wilson Whiskey, People, Carriage, Tin Lithograph, Frame, c.1890, 38 x 50 In. 990.00
Sign, Winchester, Ranger Shot Shells, Dog, Bird In Mouth, 18 x 24 In. 198.00
Sign, Wings Cigarettes, Union Made, 10 Cents, Frame, 1934, 13 x 19 In. 68.00
Sign, Witt Cornace Company, Cincinnati, Trash Can, Porcelain, c.1930, 4 1/4 In. 650.00
Sign, Wolf Co. Flouring Mill Machinery, Pennsylvania, Paper, Frame, 13 x 21 In. 495.00
Sign, Wolverine Soap Chips, Not In Stores, Lithograph, Frame, 1900, 29 x 34 In. .750.00 to 1100.00
Sign, Woolworth, Values Our Tradition Since 1879, 30 x 18 In. 85.00
Sign, Wrigley's Delicious Flavors, Cardboard Lithograph, Easel Back, 1920s, 7 x 11 In. ... 325.00
Sign, Wrigley's Doublemint Gum, Real Peppermint Flavor, Frame, 17 x 27 In. 88.00
Sign, Wrigley's Gum, For Flavor, Yellow, Green, Red, Cardboard, 11 x 42 In. 17.00
Sign, Wrigley's Gum, Good & Good For You, Paper, Glass, Frame, 21 1/4 x 11 1/2 In. 195.00
Sign, Wrigley's Gum, Wrigley Spears, Flying, In Baskets, Frame, c.1920, 22 x 12 In. 235.00
Sign, Wrigley's P.K. Gum, Boy, Checkered Hat, Decal On Glass, 15 x 25 In. 330.00
Sign, Wrigley's P.K. Gum, In The Evening By The Moonlight, Paper, Frame, 15 x 25 In. . 290.00
Sign, Wrigley's P.K. Gum, New Handy Pack, Cardboard, Frame, c.1928, 12 x 22 In. 750.00
Sign, Wrigley's Spearmint Gum, After Every Meal, Man, Woman, Frame, 13 x 23 In. 175.00
Sign, Wrigley's Spearmint Gum, Football Stadium, Cardboard, 11 x 42 In. 22.00
Sign, Wrigley's Spearmint Gum, Wrigley Boy, Die Cut, Frame, 27 x 41 In. 523.00
Sign, Yeast Foam, Makes Delicious Buckwheat Pancakes, Girl, Paper, 9 x 14 In. 88.00
Sign, Yuengling's Beer, Glass, Reverse Painted, Round, 24 In. 2200.00
Stringholder, Post Toasties, Improved Corn Flakes, Tin Lithograph, 1916 .... 660.00
Stringholder, Postum, Health First, Tin Lithograph, Iron Frame, 11 In. 247.00
Stringholder, Walker's King Of Soap, Beehive, Cast Iron, Embossed, 4 1/2 In. 85.00
Thermometers are listed in their own category.

Advertising tin cans or canisters were first used commercially in the
United States in 1819 and were called *tins.* The English language is
sometimes confusing. Today the word *tin* is used by most collectors
to describe many types of containers, including food tins, biscuit
boxes, roly poly tobacco containers, gunpowder cans, talcum powder
sprinkle-top cans, cigarette flat-fifty tins, and more. Beer Cans are
listed in their own category. Things made of undecorated tin are listed
under Tinware.

Tin, A&P Coffee, Slant Front, Lift Top, Mounted, Light Fixture, 25 x 13 x 13 In. 250.00
Tin, Alcazar Cigar, Liberty Can Co., Lancaster, Pa., 5 1/2 x 5 In. 2200.00
Tin, Allan's Star Brand Pills, Allan-Pfeifer Chemical Co., 3 x 1 5/8 In. 44.00
Tin, Allen's Sanitary Tooth Ease, Paper Label, Contents, 4 1/8 In. 70.00
Tin, Altex Liquid Latex Condoms, Tin Lithograph, Western Rubber, 1/4 Doz., 2 x 2 In. ... 360.00
Tin, Antikamnia, Hernia & Heroin Tablets, Nov. 13, 1902, 1 1/2 x 2 1/4 In. 330.00
Tin, Arabian Scratches & Gall Cure, Long Oval, Sample, 2 1/2 In. 145.00
Tin, Aunt Jemima, Pancake, Limited Edition, Quaker Limited Edition, 1983, 6 In. 10.00
Tin, Badger Coffee, 1 Lb., 3 1/2 x 5 In. 325.00
Tin, Bagley's Wild Fruit Tobacco, 4 x 6 In. 95.00
Tin, Bailey's Supreme Coffee, Key Wind, 3 1/2 x 5 In. 110.00
Tin, Barton's Candy Almond Kisses, 9 Oz., 4 x 3 1/2 In. 25.00
Tin, Between The Acts Little Cigars, Flat Pocket, 3 3/8 x 3 x 1/4 In. 25.00
Tin, Black Boy Pure Coffee, Tin Lithograph, 1/2 Lb., 3 x 4 In. 116.00
Tin, Blue Ointment, Poison, Skull & Crossbones, Blue, Black, Round, 1 3/4 In. 15.00
Tin, Blue Plate Coffee, Blue Willow Cup & Saucer Graphic, Key, 1 Lb., 3 1/2 x 5 In. 45.00
Tin, Blue Ribbon Brand Condoms, Safety Tips, Tin Lithograph, 1 7/8 x 2 1/4 In. 1020.00

Tin, Borden's Malted Milk, Full Pry Top, 1950s, 5 1/4 x 2 3/8 In. 115.00
Tin, Bouquet Roasted Coffee, Steaming Cup, c.1900, 1 Lb., 5 1/2 x 4 1/4 In. 45.00
Tin, Briggs Pipe Mixture Tobacco, P. Lorillard Co., 1940s, 4 1/4 In. 55.00
Tin, Brights Kidney Beans For Pain In The Back, Flat, 2 1/2 x 1 1/2 In. 28.00
Tin, Brown Beauty Tobacco, Brown Ground, Woman Center, Hinged, 8 In. 140.00
Tin, Bucking Ham Cut Plug Smoking Tobacco, Trial Package, 3 x 2 1/4 In. 145.00
Tin, Bunyan Coffee, Lumberjack Holding Ax, Red & White Lettering, 1 Lb. 350.00
Tin, Cadena Fuminettes Tobacco, Black Man Holding Leaf, Lithograph, 4 1/4 In. 110.00
Tin, Cadet Baby Talc, Soldier, Cadette Products Corp., 3 Oz. 155.00
Tin, Cadette Tooth Powder, Toy Cadette, Lithograph, Gray, 7 3/8 x 2 1/4 x 1 1/4 In. 175.00
Tin, Cadette Tooth Powder, Toy Cadette, Lithograph, Red, 7 3/8 x 2 1/4 x 1 1/4 In. 700.00
Tin, Calox Tooth Powder, Oval Base, 4 3/8 x 2 1/2 x 1 3/4 In. 85.00
Tin, Camp Fire Cocoa, Pry Top, Lotus Tea Concern, 1916, 4 3/4 x 3 1/4 x 2 1/8 In. 225.00
Tin, Campfire Marshmallows, Pry Top, 12 Oz., 3 1/2 x 5 1/2 In. 210.00
Tin, CAP Drip Grind Coffee, Key Wind, Bunn Capitol Grocery, 1 Lb., 4 x 5 In. 225.00
Tin, Carbolic Toothpowder, Gold Ground, Paper Label, Round, 2 x 5/8 In. 18.00
Tin, Carmen Brand Latex Condoms, Woman, Tin Lithograph, Round, 1 5/8 x 5/8 In. 605.00
Tin, Carr's Biscuits, Double-Decker Bus Shape, Chad Valley, 1950s, 10 In. 600.00
Tin, Cascara Compound, Hinkle Pill Compound, 1 3/4 x 1 In. 48.00
Tin, Celery Pills, Stoherts LD, Atherton, Round, 3/8 x 1 1/2 In. 40.00
Tin, Chase & Sanborn High Grade Coffee, Sample, 2 5/8 x 2 1/2 In. 145.00
Tin, Checkers Tobacco, Weisert Brothers, Lithograph, 4 1/2 x 3 x 7/8 In. 580.00
Tin, Choice Family Tea, Winslow, Rand & Watson, Boston & Chicago, 4 In. 56.00
Tin, Clover Farm Ground Sage, 2 1/2 x 2 3/8 x 1 1/4 In. 68.00
Tin, Common Sense Baking Powder, 2 1/2 x 1 5/8 In. 120.00
Tin, Continental Cubes Tobacco, George Washington, Tin Lithograph, 4 3/4 x 3 In. 690.00
Tin, Continental Cubes Tobacco, George Washington, Tin Lithograph, 7 3/8 x 5 In. 4070.00
Tin, Daisy Fresh Coffee, Euclid Coffee Co., Lithograph, Key, 1 Lb., 3 5/8 x 5 In. 165.00
Tin, Dan Patch Cut Plug Tobacco, Yellow, Red, Hinged Lid, 6 x 4 In. .... *Illus* 80.00
Tin, Deep River Oysters, 5 x 2 In. 72.00
Tin, Dilworth's Golden Urn Coffee, Lithograph, Sample, 2 1/2 x 2 In. 165.00
Tin, Dixie Queen Plug Cut Tobacco, Girl In Hat, Lithograph, 6 1/4 x 4 7/8 In. ....300.00 to 660.00
Tin, Doan's Ointment, Foster Milburn Co., Buffalo, N.Y., Round, 3/4 x 1 7/8 In. 44.00
Tin, Dot Coffee, Screw Top, Sample, 2 x 2 1/2 In. 210.00
Tin, Dr. A.W. Chase Co. Herpes Ointment, Yellow, Round, 1 3/4 In. 50.00
Tin, Dr. Hess Healing Powder, 25 Cents, Contents, 4 Oz., 5 x 2 1/2 In. 30.00
Tin, Dr. Hess Healing Powder, 50 Cents, 10 Oz., 5 1/2 x 3 3/4 In. 39.00
Tin, Dr. Hess Udder Ointment, Tan Cow, Black & White Ground, Lithograph, 7 Oz. 45.00
Tin, Dr. Hobson's Carbolic Salve, Pfeiffer Chem., New York, Round, 3/4 x 2 3/4 In. 35.00
Tin, Dr. I.W. Lyons Perfect Tooth Powder, Cylindrical, Box, 3 1/2 In. 176.00
Tin, Dr. J.A. Foster's Wonder Tooth Powder, Cylindrical, 4 1/8 In. 145.00
Tin, Dr. LeGear's Lice Killer, Woman, Animals, Paper Label, Unopened, 1 1/2 x 3 In. 70.00
Tin, Dr. Rubins Vital Phosphor, Louisville Medicine Co., 2 1/2 x 1 1/2 In. 95.00
Tin, Dr. Von Breemberg's Homeopathic Bilious Powders, 4 1/4 x 1 7/8 In. 70.00
Tin, Drucker's Revelation Tooth Powder, Sample, 2 5/8 x 1 In. 35.00
Tin, Drug Pack Condoms, Nutex Co., Blue, White, Lithograph, 1 5/8 x 2 1/8 In. 190.00
Tin, Dubarry Perfume, Golden Morn, Round, Needler's Ltd., 5/8 x 1 1/4 In. 45.00
Tin, Encharma Talcum Powder, 6 x 2 1/4 x 1 1/4 In. 295.00
Tin, Epicure Coffee, John Sills & Sons, Waiter, Lithograph, 1 Lb., 6 x 4 In. 800.00
Tin, F.W. Cough Drops, Geo. Miller & Son, Philadelphia, Lithograph, 8 x 5 In. 1540.00
Tin, Fairway Brand Coffee, Children In Field, Cup Of Coffee, Key Wind, 4 x 5 In. 275.00
Tin, Farmers Pride Cloves, Hulman & Co., Lithograph, 3 1/2 x 2 1/2 x 1 1/8 In. 320.00
Tin, First Prize Coffee, Jefferson Grocery Co., Punxsutawney, Pa., Key Wind, 1 Lb. 45.00
Tin, Forest & Stream Tobacco, Man Fishing, Lithograph, 3 1/4 x 1 x 4 In. 578.00
Tin, Genuine Liquid Latex Condoms, 2 1/8 x 1 5/8 In. 175.00
Tin, Globe Tobacco, Detroit Mich., Handmade, 3 1/2 x 4 In. ....*Illus* 365.00
Tin, Glovers Imperial Liver Pills, For Dogs, Flat, 3 1/8 x 2 In. 90.00
Tin, Golden Raven Salve, Skin Disorders, Blue, Yellow, Round, 2 In. 35.00
Tin, Golliwog, Full-Figured, Orange, Plaid Outfit, Embossed, 3-Sided, 6 1/4 In. 60.00
Tin, Granger Pipe Tobacco, Rough Cut, Leaf, Blue, Red, Cream, 5 3/4 x 4 3/4 In. 20.00
Tin, Guide Pipe & Cigarette Tobacco, Larus, Lithograph, 4 1/4 x 3 In. 250.00
Tin, H-T Trout Bait, Salmon Paste, Lake With Trout, Pry Lid, 1920s, 2 x 2 In. 600.00
Tin, Half & Half Tobacco, Paper Stamps On Top, 1 Lb. 42.00

Advertising, Tin, Dan Patch
Cut Plug Tobacco, Yellow,
Red, Hinged Lid, 6 x 4 In.

Advertising, Tin,
Mennen's Borated
Talcum Toilet Powder,
Newark, N.J., 4 1/2 In.

Advertising, Tin, Globe
Tobacco, Detroit Mich.,
Handmade, 3 1/2 x 4 In.

Advertising, Tin, Possum
Cigars, Am Good &
Sweet, Red, 5 1/4 In.
Aurene, Vase, Blue, Flared,
Ruffled Edge, Signed, 6 In.

Tin, Handsome Dan, L. Studdard, 5 x 6 1/2 x 2 5/8 In.	70.00
Tin, Heekins Pure Baking Powder, Lithograph, No Lid, 27 x 15 In.	90.00
Tin, Henri Bouillon Cubes, Tin Lithograph, Cylindrical, 1 x 3 1/2 In.	45.00
Tin, Hi-Plane Smooth Cut Tobacco, Single Motor, Plane Graphic, 4 3/8 x 3 x 1 In.	.150.00 to 165.00
Tin, Hills Bros. Coffee, Regular Ground Embossed Lid, 2 Lb.	30.00
Tin, Hogg's Oysters, Round, 5 x 2 In.	275.00
Tin, Holland House Coffee, Key Wind, 1 Lb., 5 x 3 3/4 In.	65.00
Tin, Honest Labor Cut Plug Tobacco, 1 1/4 x 4 1/2 x 2 3/4 In.	55.00
Tin, Horlick's Malted Milk, Fountain Brand, Graphics On 3 Sides, 8 1/2 x 6 1/4 In.	275.00
Tin, Huntley & Palmers Biscuits, 8-Book Bundle, c.1900, 6 1/4 x 6 1/4 x 4 1/4 In.	60.00
Tin, Huntley & Palmers Biscuits, Farmhouse, c.1931, 4 1/4 x 6 1/4 x 3 3/4 In.	830.00
Tin, Huntley & Palmers Biscuits, Handbag, 7 x 6 x 2 1/4 In.	95.00
Tin, Huntley & Palmers Biscuits, Kate Greenaway, 1980, 8 In.	45.00
Tin, Huntley & Palmers Biscuits, Lantern, 9 In.	42.00
Tin, Huntley & Palmers Biscuits, Soldier Shape, 1950s	225.00
Tin, Hurley Burley Plug Cut, 5 Cents, P. Lorillard, Unopened, 4 1/8 x 2 1/2 x 7/8 In.	95.00
Tin, Index Brand Breakfast Cocoa, Montgomery Ward & Co., c.1930, 5 Lb.	40.00
Tin, International Gall Cure, Team Of Horses, Yellow, Round, 3 x 2 1/2 In.	105.00
Tin, Italina Laxative Preparation, 5 x 3 3/4 In.	75.00
Tin, Jack Sprat Tea, Square, 5 x 3 In.	175.00
Tin, Jew Davids Plaster, E. Taylor, Rochester, N.Y., Embossed, Round, 2 In.	130.00
Tin, Johnson's Baby Powder, 1940s, 5 3/4 In.	30.00
Tin, Juno Brand Ginger, Spokane, Wash., 3 1/4 x 2 3/8 x 1 3/8 In.	95.00
Tin, Juno Brand Tumeric, Spokane, Wash., 3 1/4 x 2 3/8 x 1 1/8 In.	145.00
Tin, Just Suits Tobacco, Cut Plug, Red, Gold, Black, Hinged Lid, 5 1/4 x 7 3/4 In.	90.00
Tin, Kleeko Coffee, Cup, Red, Yellow, Green, Cloverdale Co., c.1920, 1 Lb., 6 x 4 1/2 In.	45.00
Tin, Kondon's Kidney & Back Tablets, 50 Cents, 2 1/2 x 1 5/8 In.	33.00
Tin, Kuco Talc, Man Shaving, Woman Tennis Player, Sample, 2 x 1 In.	330.00
Tin, Leichner Blending Powder, 1930s, 4 In.	17.00
Tin, Liberty Coffee Additive, Cardboard, Paper Label, Sample, 1 5/8 x 1 1/8 In.	215.00
Tin, Lloyds Kidney & Rheumatism Tablets, Lloyd Preparation Co., 2 5/8 x 1 1/2 In.	60.00
Tin, Loyl Coffee, Eagle, Lithograph, Rochester Seed & Supply, 1 Lb., 6 1/4 x 4 In.	130.00
Tin, Lucky Strike, Flat Fifties, It's Toasted, Green, 4 1/2 x 5 3/4 x 1/2 In.	25.00
Tin, Lucky Strike, Genuine Roll Cut, c.1915, Vertical Pocket, 4 1/2 x 2 7/8 In.	79.00
Tin, Luden's Menthol Cough Drops, Super Deluxe, Reading, Pa., 2 1/2 x 2 1/4 In.	225.00
Tin, Luzianne Coffee & Chickory, W.B. Reilly & Co., Red, 6 In.	110.00
Tin, Luzianne Coffee, Red, 2-Color Image, Lithograph, Handle, 7 1/2 In.	90.00
Tin, Luzianne Coffee, Red, 6-Color Image, Lithograph, Handle, 7 1/2 In.	125.00
Tin, Luzianne Coffee, White, Lithograph, Handle, 3 Lb., 7 1/2 In.	85.00
Tin, Magnetic Nervine, Nerve Tonic & Restorer, 2 1/2 x 1 1/2 In.	145.00
Tin, Mammy's Favorite Brand Coffee, C.D. Kenny Co., Tin, 4 Lb., 10 3/4 x 6 In.	275.00
Tin, Mammy's Favorite Brand Coffee, Orange, Black, Louisville, Ky., 6 x 11 In.	210.00
Tin, Manru Coffee, Yellow, Red, Black, 5 Cup, c.1920, 2 1/2 x 2 In.	35.00
Tin, McKesson's Talc, 2 Nude Children, Standing By Fire, 1920s, 6 x 3 x 1 In.	55.00
Tin, Mellos Popcorn, Red, White, Blue, c.1940, 4 Lb., 6 x 4 In.	44.00

Tin, Mennen's Borated Talcum Toilet Powder, Newark, N.J., 4 1/2 In. . . . . *Illus*   150.00
Tin, Mexine Chile Powder Seasoning, Paper Label, 4 1/4 x 1 5/8 In. 50.00
Tin, Millar's Magnet Brand Coffee, Key Wind, 3 7/8 x 5 In. 85.00
Tin, Millwoods Pulvola Foot Powder, Brewer & Co. Inc., 3-Sided, 4 1/4 In. 95.00
Tin, Mohican Cinnamon, Pure Spices, 2 Oz., 2 1/4 x 1 1/4 x 3 3/4 In. 55.00
Tin, Monarch Coffee, Lion, Reid Murdoch, Chicago, 1 Lb. 35.00
Tin, Moses Cough Drops, Gold & Black Paint, Red Ground, 9 In. 138.00
Tin, Mosquito Talcum Powder, Harmony Of Boston, Embossed, 4 1/2 In. 60.00
Tin, Muratti's After Lunch Cigarettes, Man, Champagne, Hinged Lid, 3 x 3 1/2 In. 40.00
Tin, My Baby's Talcum, Sears Roebuck & Co., 6 x 2 1/8 x 1 1/4 In. 350.00
Tin, Nature's Cure, Celebrated Blood Purifier, Red, White, Flat, 3 x 2 In. 60.00
Tin, Neal's Anti Gas Tablets, Balloon Shape, 3 1/8 x 2 1/8 In. 120.00
Tin, Nerve Berries, American Medical Co., Cincinnati, O., 2 1/2 x 1 1/2 In. 687.00
Tin, Nerve Seeds, Great Nerve Restorer, Flat, 2 1/2 x 1 1/2 In. 360.00
Tin, Nigger Head Stove Polish, Lithograph, Black Man, White Can, 3 In. 240.00
Tin, Niggerhair, Big Haired Black Woman, Bones In Nose, Ears, 1878, 6 1/2 In. . . .220.00 to 260.00
Tin, Niggerhead Dates, Exaggerated Comic Black In Date Tree, 7 3/4 In. 156.00
Tin, Nottingham Menthol Cough Drops, Sold At Rexall Store, 3/4 x 3 1/4 x 2 1/4 In. 48.00
Tin, Oceanic Cut Plug Tobacco, Ocean Liner, Fish, Hinged Lid, c.1900, 4 x 6 In. 75.00
Tin, Old Dominion Oysters, 3 x 2 In. 198.00
Tin, Old Judge Nutmeg, Jesse C. Stewart, Pittsburg, Pa., 3 1/4 x 1 7/8 x 1 1/2 In. 165.00
Tin, Old Mansion Ground Cloves, Shaker Top, 3 5/8 x 2 3/8 x 1 In. 85.00
Tin, Old Squire Pipe Tobacco, Vertical Pocket, 4 x 3 x 7/8 In. 315.00
Tin, On The Square Tobacco, Embossed, Lithograph, Strat Bros., 3 1/4 x 2 x 2 In. 90.00
Tin, Orcico Cigars, 2 For 5 Cents, Indian, Lithograph, 6 x 6 x 4 In. . . . . .200.00 to 605.00
Tin, Original Pack Oysters, Chesapeake Bay's Famous Oyster Beds, Qt. 456.00
Tin, Ovaltine, Add To Your Mid-Morning Milk, c.1940, 1 3/4 In. 40.00
Tin, Parto Glory Nerve Tonic, c.1913, 5 3/8 x 2 1/2 x 2 1/2 In. 210.00
Tin, Pat Hand Globe Tobacco, Lithograph, 2 3/4 x 2 1/2 x 1 3/8 In. 145.00
Tin, Patent Superior Liquid Latex Condoms, Lithograph, Lid, 1 1/2 x 2 x 7/16 In. 468.00
Tin, Paul Bunyan Coffee, Lumberjack Holding Ax, Red Ground, 1 Lb. 350.00
Tin, Paul Jones Clean Cut Tobacco, Tin Lithograph, 4 1/2 x 3 x 7/8 In. 1925.00
Tin, Peek Frean, Makers Of Famous Biscuits, Square, 2 1/2 In.   42.00
Tin, Peek Frean, Pat-A-Cake Biscuits, Square, 3 1/2 In. 378.00
Tin, Peter Rabbit Candy, Handle, 2 3/8 x 4 1/2 x 2 3/8 In. 225.00
Tin, Pinex Laxatives, Pinex Co., Fort Wayne, Ind., 1/2 x 3 3/8 x 2 3/4 In. 18.00
Tin, Pinko-Laxin, For Constipation, St. Louis, 2 3/4 x 2 In. 85.00
Tin, Pioneer Brand Golden Flake Cavendish, Black Transfer, 1 7/8 x 7 x 4 In. 78.00
Tin, Pioneer Brand Golden Flake Cavendish, Man, Stump, Hinged Lid, c.1930, 4 x 7 In. . .   35.00
Tin, Pipe Major English Smoking Mixture, Lithograph, 4 1/2 x 3 In. 358.00
Tin, Possum Cigars, Am Good & Sweet, Red, 5 1/4 In. . . . . *Illus* 400.00
Tin, Pride Of Virginia Sliced Plug, Blue, Hinged Lid, c.1910, 2 5/8 x 4 1/2 x 5 In. 59.00
Tin, Prince Albert Chop Cut, Vertical Pocket, 1 3/4 x 3 x 7/8 In. 45.00
Tin, Princess Salted Peanuts, Lummis & Co., Philadelphia, 10 Lb., 9 1/2 In. 145.00
Tin, Princeton Mixture Fine Tobacco, Paper Lid Label, Marburg, 4 1/2 x 3 In. 440.00
Tin, Puritan Crushed Plug Mixture, Lithograph, 4 3/8 x 3 x 7/8 In. 330.00
Tin, Quaker Oats, 1896 Oatmeal Box Design, Limited Edition, 1984, 8 1/4 In. 15.00
Tin, Ramses Condoms, Julius Schmid, New York, 2 5/8 x 1 7/8 In. 180.00
Tin, Rawleigh Aspirin Tablets, Insert, Hinged Top, 3/8 x 2 3/8 x 2 In. 48.00
Tin, Rawleigh Pan-Jang Talcum Powder, Chinese Woman, Lithograph, 3 x 5 In. 120.00
Tin, Ray's Seafood Fresh Oysters, See-Through Top, 2 3/4 x 3 1/2 In. 20.00
Tin, Red Indian Cut Plug, Lithograph, 7 1/2 In. 450.00
Tin, Revivo Nerve & Sexual Disease, Royal Medicine Co., 2 1/2 x 1 1/2 In. 230.00
Tin, Rexall Briten Tooth Powder, Oval Base, 4 1/2 x 3 1/8 x 2 1/8 In. 80.00
Tin, Rexall Violet Talcum Powder, United Drug Co., Boston, Mass., 4 1/2 In. 45.00
Tin, Roly Poly, Mayo's Tobacco, Dutchman, 6 1/2 x 6 In. 460.00
Tin, Romeos Condoms, Violet Ground, Shield Emblem, Killian Co., 1 5/8 x 2 1/4 In. 415.00
Tin, Rose Chemical Co., Corn Salve, Baltimore, Md., 1/2 x 1 In. 28.00
Tin, Rowntree's Cachous Sweet, Cricket Bat Shape, c.1910, 4 1/2 In. 90.00
Tin, Royal Blue Stores Brand Pure Spices, Chicago, Ill., 4 x 2 3/8 x 1 1/4 In. 145.00
Tin, Royal Jewel Coffee, Key Wind, 2 Lb., 6 5/8 x 5 In. 110.00
Tin, Runkels Pure Cocoa, Sample, 1 5/8 x 1 1/8 x 3/4 In. . . . . .195.00 to 225.00
Tin, Sail Pipe Tobacco, Dutch, 14 Oz., 5 1/2 x 5 In. 32.00

Tin, Sailor Girl Oysters, 3 x 2 In. 22.00
Tin, Savoy Quality Certified Cocoa, Hinged Top, 6 x 3 1/4 In. 120.00
Tin, Sayman's Healing Salve, T.M. Sayman, St. Louis, 7/8 x 2 1/4 In. 48.00
Tin, Schilling Baking Powder, Paper Label, Push-On Top, 5 x 3 In. 10.00
Tin, Schilling Cayenne Pepper, Dial Top, 1940s, 3 1/2 In. 8.50
Tin, Schrafts Chocolates, Hinged Top, 1 Lb., 8 x 2 1/4 x 5 In. 32.00
Tin, Scotch Snuff, Larkin & Morrill, Byfield, Mass., 2 1/4 x 1 1/2 In. 45.00
Tin, Seal Of North Carolina Plug Cut Tobacco, Lithograph, 6 1/2 x 5 In. 415.00
Tin, Sears Roebuck Roasted Coffee, 11 x 16 In. 255.00
Tin, Silver Tex Deluxe Condoms, Askwell Corp., Akron, Ohio, 2 1/8 x 1 5/8 In. 235.00
Tin, Sozodont Powder, Cleansing The Teeth, 2 3/4 x 2 In. 175.00
Tin, Squadron Leader Tobacco, Airplane, 4 1/4 x 3 1/4 x 1 In. 122.00
Tin, Squibb's Bath Toilet Powder, 3 1/8 x 4 3/4 In. 240.00
Tin, Squirrel Peanut Butter, Tin Lithograph, Pry Lid, 3 Lb., 4 3/4 x 5 1/8 In. 467.00
Tin, Stag Tobacco, Lorillard, Jersey City, N.J., 6 1/2 In. 175.00
Tin, Stickney & Poor's, Tumeric, Shaker Top, Boston, 2 7/8 In. 38.00
Tin, Sunset Trail Cigar, White, 6 x 6 x 4 In. 325.00
Tin, Sunshine Biscuit, Flagship Of Bicentennial, Frigate Ships, 1976, 14 1/2 x 12 In. 32.00
Tin, Sykes Comfort Powder, Oval, Flat Top, Boston, 4 1/4 x 2 3/4 x 2 1/4 In. 485.00
Tin, T.A. Treakle & Son Fresh Oysters, Palmer, Virginia, Pt., 3 3/4 x 3 1/2 In. ... 32.00
Tin, Talcum Powder For Infants & Adults, Perfumed, Allen Pharm., 3 7/8 x 1 In. 245.00
Tin, Thalax Laxative, Palatable, Mild, Non-Injurious, Red, 2 1/2 x 1 1/2 In. 50.00
Tin, Three Feathers Plug Cut, Vertical Pocket, 4 1/8 x 3 1/4 x 1 1/8 In. 375.00
Tin, Three Knights Condoms, 3 Knights On Horses, Gray Ground, Goodyear Rubber 145.00
Tin, Tobacco Girl Cigar, 50 Count, Girl In Leaf, Lithograph, 5 1/2 x 6 1/4 x 4 1/4 In. 3630.00
Tin, Totem Tobacco, Totem Pole, Indian, Lithograph, 3 5/8 x 2 5/8 In. 1375.00
Tin, Towle's Log Cabin Syrup, 100 Years, Cabin Shape, 1987, 5 x 5 x 3 In. 45.00
Tin, Towle's Log Cabin Syrup, Cabin Shape, c.1950, 2 Lb., 4 1/2 x 5 x 2 3/4 In. 55.00
Tin, Towle's Log Cabin Syrup, Family, Blacksmith Shop, 4 3/4 In. ....45.00 to 179.00
Tin, Towle's Log Cabin Syrup, Frontier Inn, 5 3/4 In. 65.00
Tin, Towle's Log Cabin Syrup, Frontier Jail, Wheels 157.00
Tin, Towle's Log Cabin Syrup, Mother Cooking Hot Cakes, Bear At Door, 3 3/4 In. 168.00
Tin, Towle's Log Cabin Syrup, Mother Cooking Hot Cakes, Girl At Door, 5 7/8 In. 134.00
Tin, Town & Country Condoms, Lithograph, Nelson Products, 1 5/8 x 2 1/8 In. 1925.00
Tin, Toyland Peanut Butter, Marching Band, Elephant, Camel, Blue, Bail Handle, 1 Lb. ... 275.00
Tin, Trout Line Tobacco, Green Ground, 3 1/2 In. 770.00
Tin, Turkey Coffee, Kasper Co., Tin Lithograph, 1 Lb., 5 3/4 x 4 1/4 In. 415.00
Tin, Union Cut Plug Tobacco, Lithograph, 5 x 8 In. 72.00
Tin, Union Leader Cut Plug, Eagles, Red, Vertical Pocket, 4 x 2 In. 55.00
Tin, Union Leader Tobacco, Uncle Sam, Smoking Pipe, 4 1/2 x 3 3/8 In. 95.00
Tin, Valley Brand Malted Milk, Valley Dairy, New York, 20 Lb., 15 1/2 x 8 In. 135.00
Tin, Victory Influenza Lozenges, Insist On Having, 12 In. 143.00
Tin, Warner's Safe Asthma Remedy, Paper Label, 3 1/4 x 2 In. 255.00
Tin, Watkins Laxative & Cold Grip Tablets, Early 1900s, 3 1/2 x 2 3/4 x 1/2 In. 10.00
Tin, Watkins Sweetened Malted Milk, Pry Top, 5 3/4 x 3 3/8 In. 120.00
Tin, Weyman's Cutty Pipe, Lithograph, 13 1/2 x 10 1/4 x 9 3/8 In. 1540.00
Tin, White Manor Pipe Mixture, Southern Plantation, 3 x 3 1/2 x 1 In. 230.00
Tin, White Owl Brand Cigars, 50 Count, Lithograph, 5 3/4 x 5 1/2 In. 745.00
Tin, Wilson's Co-Re-Ga Dental Powder, Contents, Sample, 2 1/8 In. 11.00
Tin, Witch Hazel Tooth Soap, Robinson & Halstead, Flat, 3 1/8 x 2 In. 630.00
Tin, Wonder Heart Cure, Seroco Chemical Co., 3 x 1 3/4 In. 120.00
Tin, Woods Improved Lollacapop, Mosquito, Yellow, Black, 1 3/4 x 3 1/4 In. 68.00
Tin, Yankee Boy Plug Cut Tobacco, Lithograph, Pocket, 4 1/8 x 3 1/2 In. 700.00
Tin, Yellow Bonnet Coffee, Springfield, Lithograph, Key Wind, 1 Lb., 3 1/2 x 5 In. 110.00

Advertising tip trays are decorated metal trays less than 5 inches in
diameter. They were placed on the table or counter to hold either the
bill or the coins that were left as a tip. Change receivers could be made
of glass, plastic, or metal. They were kept on the counter near the cash
register and held the money passed back and forth by the cashier.
Related items may be listed in the Advertising category under Change
Receivers.

Tip Tray, Best Prepared Paint, Heath & Milligan, Chicago, 4 1/8 In. 450.00

Tip Tray, DeLaval Cream Separators, 4 1/4 In. 176.00
Tip Tray, Denby Cigars, Factory, Evansville, Ind., 6 In. 25.00
Tip Tray, Dr Pepper, Black Boy Eating Watermelon, Oval, 3 1/4 In. 425.00
Tip Tray, Fairy Soap, Girl, Sitting On Soap, Round, 4 1/4 In. 90.00
Tip Tray, Fraternal Life & Accident Insurance, 4 7/8 x 4 1/4 In. 135.00
Tip Tray, Fraternal Life Insurance, 3 White Horses, Scalloped Edge, Round, 4 1/4 In. 44.00
Tip Tray, General Arthur Cigars, Garfield's Vice President, c.1920, 4 In. 75.00
Tip Tray, Golden Dome Whiskey, Champion Of All, H. Swartz & Co., Boston, 4 In. 75.00
Tip Tray, Gottfreid Krueger Brewing Co., Round, 4 3/8 In. . . . . .125.00 to 240.00
Tip Tray, Havana Cigars, Cavalier, 4 1/4 In. 77.00
Tip Tray, Helvetia Milk Condensing Co., 3 1/2 In. 145.00
Tip Tray, Home Treasure Stoves & Ranges, Adams Furniture Co., 6 x 4 In. 138.00
Tip Tray, Indianapolis Brewing Co., Lieber's Gold Medal Beer, 9 1/4 In. 125.00
Tip Tray, Kenny's, Teas, Coffees, Drink & Enjoy, Woman, Roses, Tin Lithograph, 4 In. . . 198.00
Tip Tray, Liberty Beer, Indian Maiden, Tin Lithograph, 4 1/2 In. 256.00
Tip Tray, Mokaine Is The Best Of All Liqueurs, Rectangular, 4 5/8 x 3 In. . . . . . . .195.00 to 245.00
Tip Tray, Moxie, Woman, Glass Of Moxie, Tin Lithograph, 6 In. 55.00
Tip Tray, Muehlebagh's Pilsner Beer, Kansas City, Round, 5 1/8 In. 335.00
Tip Tray, Not Appearing At Bal Tabarin, Marilyn Monroe Nude, Crystal Bay, Nevada 150.00
Tip Tray, Olympia Beer, It's The Water, Gentleman, Holding Bottle, c.1920, 4 In. 45.00
Tip Tray, Parsley Brand Salmon, Round, 4 1/8 In. 170.00
Tip Tray, Quandt's Famous Beer & Ales, Mercury Figure Atop Globe, c.1900, 4 In. 80.00
Tip Tray, Resinol Soap & Ointment, Woman, Blue Dress, 4 1/4 In. 121.00
Tip Tray, Rockford Watches, Woman, Blue Dress, 3 1/4 x 4 3/4 In. 209.00
Tip Tray, Welsbach Mantles, Indianapolis, Indiana, 4 1/4 In. 68.00
Tip Tray, Yaka-Cola Every Hour, Take No Other, 4 1/4 In. 425.00
Tire Cover, Drink Pepsol, 1920s, 30 In. 500.00
Tobacco Pack, Bagpipe Chewing Tobacco, Unopened, 5 1/2 x 3 3/8 x 1 3/8 In. 140.00
Tobacco Pack, Brownie Smoking, E.O. Eshelby Tobacco Co., 4 Oz., 4 x 5 x 1 1/2 In. 17.00
Tobacco Pack, C & C Scrap Plain Tobacco, 4 7/8 x 3 1/4 x 1 1/2 In. 155.00
Tobacco Pack, Home Comfort Tobacco, Myers-Cox Co., Unopened, 4 1/2 x 3 x 1 In. 125.00
Tray, Tip, see Tip Trays in this category.
Tray, Anheuser-Busch, Brewery, Tin Lithograph, Oval, 15 5/8 x 18 5/8 In. 855.00
Tray, Anheuser-Busch, Malt Nutrine Woman, Vienna Art, 1905 Patent, 10 In. 100.00
Tray, Buckeye Root Beer, 5 Cents, Mug, Boy, Girl, Tin Lithograph, Square, 12 1/2 In. . . . 1300.00
Tray, C.D. Kenny Coffee & Tea, Boy & Dog, Tin Lithograph, 9 1/2 In. 385.00
Tray, C.D. Kenny Coffee & Tea, Santa Claus, Sleeping Child, Tin Lithograph, 9 1/2 In. . . 220.00
Tray, Cherry Sparkle Bottling Co., So. Milwaukee, 1930s, 13 x 10 In. 175.00
Tray, Edelweiss Beer, Girl, Short Red Hair, Tin Lithograph, Round, 1913, 13 In. 176.00
Tray, Fulgor Polish, Salvador Rull Of Barcelona, Spain, Tin, c.1920, 3 x 5 In. 35.00
Tray, Hanover Whiskey, Horse Head, Landscape, Tin Lithograph, c.1907, 28 x 38 In. 690.00
Tray, I.B. Stein & Son Distillers, Woman, Kutztown, Pa., Round, 12 In. 154.00
Tray, Iroquois Indian Head Beer & Ale, Buffalo, N.Y., 12 In. 110.00
Tray, Iroquois Indian Head Beer, Pressed Steel, International Breweries, Buffalo, 13 In. . . 30.00
Tray, Leisy Brewing, Factory, Tin Lithograph, 13 5/8 x 16 5/8 In. 850.00
Tray, Limberg's Ice Cream Co., We Do Not Make All The Ice Cream, Horse, 1912, 13 In. . 525.00
Tray, Maxwell House, Elderly Couple, Since 1892, Tin Lithograph, Oval, 17 In. 215.00
Tray, McDonald Patent Maple Syrup Spouts, Winter, Tin Lithograph, 15 1/2 x 18 In. 230.00
Tray, Nehi Soda, Woman In Wave, Soda Bottle, Tin Lithograph, Rectangular, 13 In. 275.00
Tray, NuGrape, Girl Drinking Soda, Tin Lithograph, 11 x 13 In. 180.00
Tray, NuGrape, Woman, Holding Bottle, A Flavor You Can't Forget, Tin, 12 In. 44.00
Tray, Old Dutch Premium Beer, Eagle Brewing Co., Catasauqua, Pa., 11 7/8 In. 200.00
Tray, Orange Julep, Girl, Beach, Tin Lithograph, 1920s, 13 1/4 x 10 1/4 In. 230.00
Tray, Pabst Beer, Milwaukee, Factory, Tin Lithograph, 12 1/4 x 17 1/4 In. 605.00
Tray, Perfect Brew, Bulldog, Tin Lithograph, Square, 13 In. 198.00
Tray, Polar Ginger Ale, Polar Bear, Green, Yellow, Round, 13 In. 60.00
Tray, Standard Brewing Company, Execution Of Sioux, Tin Lithograph, 12 In. 550.00
Tray, Utica Club Ale, West End Brewing Co., Round, 12 In. 50.00
Tray, Zetts Bavarian Beer, Medieval Man, Holding Beer, Staff, c.1900, 13 In. 100.00
Tray, Zipps Cherri-O, Bird, Drinking From Glass, c.1920, 12 In. . . . . .625.00 to 650.00
Tube, Darkie Tooth Paste, Contents, Box, Hawley & Hazel, 4 7/8 x 1 3/8 x 7/8 In. 85.00
Tube, Rexall Dentutex Adhesive Jelly, Box, 6 1/2 In. 48.00
Tumbler, General Electric, Greetings, R. Cooper Jr., Garland, Gold, 1940, 3 3/4 x 2 1/2 In. 22.00

Whiskey, Free's Pure Rye, Drink Our Specialty, York, Pa., 2 1/4 In. 28.00
Whiskey, William Foust Distillers, Enameled White Letters, Glen Rock, Pa., 2 In. 84.00
Whiskey, William Foust Distillers, Red Seal, Glen Rock, Pa., 2 1/4 In. 565.00
Whistle, Red Goose Shoes 54.00
Whistle, Robin Hood Shoes, Flat, 1 x 2 5/8 In. 95.00
Whistle, Twinkie Shoes For Girls & Boys, Balloon Shape, 1 1/8 x 1 1/4 In. 125.00

AGATA glass was made by Joseph Locke of the New England Glass
Company of Cambridge, Massachusetts, after 1885. A metallic stain
was applied to New England Peachblow and the mottled design char-
acteristic of agata appeared.

Finger Bowl, Underplate, Mottled, Ruffled Rim, 2 1/2 x 5 1/2 In. & 6 3/8 In. 1495.00
Tumbler, White To Pink Shading, Gold, Amethyst, c.1890, 3 3/4 In., Pair 335.00
Tumbler, Wild Rose Shaded To Mineral Stain, 3 7/8 In. 165.00
Vase, Lily, White To Pink, Amethyst, Gold, Metal Cupid Stand, c.1890, 7 1/2 In. 335.00
Vase, Lily, Wild Rose Shaded To Cream, Mineral Stain, Tapered, 7 3/4 In. 880.00
Vase, Lily, Wild Rose, Gold & Purple Stain, 6 3/4 In. 1375.00
Whiskey, Wild Rose Shaded To Mineral Stain, 2 3/4 In. 440.00

AKRO AGATE glass was made in Clarksburg, West Virginia, from 1932
to 1951. Before that time, the firm made children's glass marbles,
which are listed in this book in the Marble category. Most of the glass
is marked with a crow flying through the letter *A*.

Ashtray, Red, Marbleized, With Cigarette Jar 160.00
Cup, Green, Octagonal, 1 1/2 In. 9.00
Cup, Pink, Octagonal, 3 3/8 In. 4.00
Cup & Saucer, White, Demitasse 20.00
Desk Set, Pen, Letter Holder, Calendar Case 15.00
Drink Set, Play-Time, Box, 7 Piece 225.00
Drink Set, Play-Time, Concentric Rib, Yellow & Green, Box, 8 Piece 135.00
Fan, Electric, Oxblood, 13 In. 199.00
Flowerpot, Blue & White Marbleized, Ribbed Top, 2 1/4 In. 7.00
Flowerpot, Blue Marbleized, 3-Footed, 5 1/8 In. 90.00
Flowerpot, Cornflower Blue, Ribbed, 2 3/8 In. 6.00
Flowerpot, Orange & White Marbleized, 1 7/8 In. 7.00
Jar, Apothecary, Black, Stopper, 6 1/2 In. 43.00
Lamp, Sconce, Electric, Ivory, 7 1/8 In. 90.00
Plate, Blue, Octagonal, 4 1/4 In. 8.00
Powder Jar, Pink, 6 1/8 In. 190.00
Tea Set, Little American Maid, Cobalt, Stipple Band, Box 800.00
Teapot, Blue, Child's, 2 3/8 In. 40.00
Teapot, Raised Daisy, Opaque, Blue, 2 3/8 In. 35.00
Tumbler, Raised Daisy, Yellow, 4 Piece 159.00
Urn, Opalescent, 3 1/4 In. 8.00

ALABASTER is a very soft form of gypsum, a stone that resembles marble. It was often carved into vases or statues in Victorian times. There
are alabaster carvings being made even today.

Bust, Girl, Wearing Bonnet, Pedestal Base, 38 In. 1100.00
Bust, Pierrette, Female, Smiling Clown, Marble Base, Marked, Italy, 9 1/2 In. 260.00
Bust, Socrates, White, Black Pedestal, Plinth, c.1835, 12 1/2 x 4 1/2 In. 430.00
Figurine, Falcon, Art Deco, 17 In., Pair 770.00
Figurine, Tiger, Striding Forward, On Rocky Outcrop, Glass Inset Eyes, 24 In. 1835.00
Figurine, Woman, Wood Base, Frank Varga, c.1972, 14 In. 345.00
Group, 2 Fighting Bulls, Wood Base, Frank Varga, c.1967, 8 1/2 x 14 In. 400.00
Group, 2 Wrestlers, Rocky Base, 13 In. 1410.00
Group, 3 People Huddle Together, Wood Base, Frank Varga, 1969, 13 In. 400.00
Group, Madonna & Child, Standing, Wearing Crowns, 19th Century, 20 1/2 In. 1175.00
Group, Toilette Of Venus, Late 19th Century, 14 1/2 x 12 In. 1610.00
Group, Venus & Psyche Embracing, Kissing, Late 1800s, 20 In. 1530.00
Lamp, Kneeling Maiden, Turkish Dress, Guarding A Fire, Art Nouveau, 11 1/2 In. 2640.00
Pedestal, Classical Column, 40 In. 480.00
Pedestal, Column, Octagonal Base, 34 In. 360.00
Pedestal, Columnar, Carved, White, Italy, c.1900, 43 1/2 x 9 3/4 In., Pair 635.00

Pedestal, Spiral Reeded Column, Square Top, Victorian, 41 x 13 In., Pair 550.00
Urn, Cup Form, Grapevine Rim, Square Base, Late 1800s, 21 x 22 In. 259.00
Vase, Ribbed, Italy, c.1900, 11 In. 575.00

ALUMINUM was more expensive than gold or silver until the 1850s.
Chemists learned how to refine bauxite to get aluminum. Jewelry and
other small objects were made of the valuable metal until 1914, when
an inexpensive smelting process was invented. The aluminum collected today dates from the 1930s through the 1950s. Hand-hammered
pieces are the most popular.

Basket, Pierced Handle, Ruffled Edge, Rodney Kent, 6 3/8 In. 35.00
Candleholder, 3-Light, Semicircular Base, Art Deco, Marked, Everlast, 9 1/4 In., Pair . . . 80.00
Casserole, Cover, Beaded Trim, Scrolled Finial, Pyrex Glass Insert, 10 In. 27.00
Coaster, Ducks, Cattails, 3 3/16 In., 8 Piece 25.00
Dish, Seashell, 4 Cone Feet, Signed, Bruce Fox, 10 In. 80.00
Pitcher, Ice Lip, Hammered, Ear Handle, Everlast, 8 In. 25.00
Propeller, Kliptip-Met-L, Polished, McCauley, Dayton, Ohio, 58 In. 275.00
Salt & Pepper, Charles Sheeler, USA, 1935, 1 x 1 x 1 1/2 In. 820.00
Tidbit, 3 Tiers, Floral, Hammered, Pineapple Finial, 13 In. 40.00
Tray, 3 Sections, Hammered, Piecrust Edge, Ring Handle, Cromwell, 9 3/4 In. 25.00
Tray, Floral Band, Piecrust Edge, Buenilum, 18 In. 35.00
Tray, Paden City Plate In Center, Farberware, Scrolled Handles, 13 3/4 In. 45.00
Tray, Wheat Sheaf Center, Square, Kensington, 10 3/4 In. 23.00
Water Set, Bamboo Pattern, Everlast, Pitcher & 6 Tumblers 310.00

AMBER, see Jewelry category.

AMBER GLASS is the name of any glassware with the proper yellow-
brown shading. It was a popular color just after the Civil War and
many pressed glass pieces were made of amber glass. Depression glass
of the 1930s–1950s was also made in shades of amber glass. Other
pieces may be found in the Depression Glass, Pressed Glass, and other
glass categories. All types are being reproduced.

Candlestick, Moon & Star, L.E. Smith, 6 1/4 In. 45.00
Condiment Set, 2 Bottles, Stoppers, Metal Holder 105.00
Console, Rolled Edge, Engraved Flowers, 14 In. 175.00
Cruet, Chrome Stopper & Base, Marked, Farber Bros., Pair 35.00
Decanter, Teardrop Shape, Blown Flame Stopper, 1960s, 15 In. 70.00
Figurine, Horse, Hand Shaped, 6 In. 23.00
Figurine, Snail, Hand Shaped, Kanawha Glass Co., 3 1/2 In. 35.00
Honey Dish, Cover, Embossed Beehives, Victorian, 6 1/2 In. 60.00
Honey Dish, Cover, Embossed Bees & Hives, Hive Finial, 4-Footed, Square, 5 In. 60.00
Vase, Cover, Enameled Flowers, 15 In., Pair 880.00

AMBERETTE pieces are listed in the Pressed Glass category under the pattern name
Amberette.

AMBERINA is a two-toned glassware made from 1883 to about 1900. It
was patented by Joseph Locke of the New England Glass Company,
but was also made by other companies. The glass shades from red to
amber. Similar pieces of glass may be found in the Baccarat, Libbey,
and Plated Amberina categories. Glass shaded from blue to amber is
called *Blue Amberina* or *Bluerina*.

Basket, Applied Amber Rigaree, Applied Amber Foot, Handleless, 8 x 5 1/4 In. 115.00
Basket, Swirled Ribs, Applied Amber Rigaree & Thorn Handle, 7 In. 520.00
Bell, Inverted Thumbprint, Applied Amber Handle, 6 In. 29.00
Bowl, 3 x 4 1/2 In. 115.00
Bowl, Cover, Diamond-Quilted, Applied Amber Finial, c.1900 . . . . 560.00
Bowl, Diamond-Quilted, 1 1/2 x 4 1/4 In. 90.00
Bowl, Finger, Ruffled Rim, c.1890, 2 3/4 In. 145.00
Bowl, Ruffled, 2 1/2 x 5 1/2 In. 150.00
Bowl, Star Shape, 9 In. 110.00
Bowl, Swirled, Ribbed, Ruffled Top, Clear Pedestal, Coiled Handle, 4 x 6 1/4 In. 145.00
Celery Dish, Daisy & Button, Boat Shape, Hobbs, Brockunier & Co., 13 3/4 In. 65.00

Celery Vase, Diamond-Quilted, Scalloped Square Top, 6 1/2 In. 145.00
Celery Vase, Herringbone, Square, 6 1/2 In. 130.00
Celery Vase, Scalloped Top, Square, 6 1/2 x 3 1/2 In. 345.00
Creamer, Inverted Thumbprint, Square Mouth, Applied Handle, 4 1/4 In. 320.00
Cruet, Faceted Stopper, c.1890, 5 1/2 In. 250.00
Cuspidor, Flared Rim, 2 1/2 x 5 1/4 In. 230.00
Finger Bowl, Inverted Thumbprint, Ruffled Top, 5 1/2 x 2 3/4 In. 85.00
Finger Bowl, Rolled Scalloped Rim, 2 1/2 x 5 In. 175.00
Finger Bowl, Underplate, Ruffled Rim, c.1900, 6 In. 60.00
Goblet, Amber Stem & Foot, 6 1/4 In. 230.00
Mug, Blown Out, Swirled, Gold Enamel Leaves, Branches, Rope Handle, 5 1/2 In. 60.00
Mug, Swirled, 5 In. 80.00
Nappy, Daisy & Button, 4 1/2 In. 86.00
Pitcher, Applied Reeded Handle, 4 Pinched Sides, 7 1/2 In. 120.00
Pitcher, Daisy & Button, Applied Amber Handle, 5 In. 210.00
Pitcher, Diagonal Ribs, Applied Reeded Handle, c.1900, 8 1/2 In. 170.00
Pitcher, Inverted Thumbprint, Applied Amber Handle, c.1910, 6 1/2 In. 170.00
Pitcher, Inverted Thumbprint, Reverse Coloring, Applied Reeded Handle, 4 3/4 In. 40.00
Pitcher, Inverted Thumbprint, Ribbed Handle, Tricornered Spout, 8 1/2 In. 175.00
Pitcher, Inverted Thumbprint, Squat, Applied Reeded Handle, 7 In. 150.00
Pitcher, Inverted Thumbprint, Tricornered Top, Amber Reeded Handle, 4 3/4 In. 265.00
Pitcher, Milk, Inverted Thumbprint, Ruffled Edge, Applied Rope Handle, 6 1/4 In. 200.00
Pitcher, Milk, Inverted Thumbprint, Square Top, Applied Amber Reeded Handle, 5 In. ... 345.00
Pitcher, Ribbed, Applied Reeded Handle, 8 In. 210.00
Pitcher, Square, Ribbed Amber Handle, Red To Yellow, 9 In. 175.00
Punch Bowl, Swirled, Enameled Flowers, Peaked, Applied Handles, Oval, 11 1/4 In. 149.00
Punch Cup, Ribbed, Applied Handle, 2 1/4 In. 30.00
Sugar Shaker, Inverted Thumbprint, Geo. Hazelton Hardware, 8 1/4 In. 1438.00
Toothpick, Diamond-Quilted, Square Top, 2 3/4 In. 201.00
Toothpick, Diamond-Quilted, Tricornered, 2 1/8 In. 259.00
Toothpick, Inverted Thumbprint, Pedestal Base 250.00
Toothpick, Venetian Diamond 225.00
Tumbler, Diamond-Quilted, 3 3/4 In. 748.00
Tumbler, Inverted Thumbprint, 3 5/8 In. 58.00
Tumbler, Inverted Thumbprint, Barrel Shape, 4 In. 99.00
Tumbler, Ribbed, 4 1/4 In. 115.00
Tumbler, Whiskey, Diamond-Quilted, Ground Pontil, 2 3/4 In. 173.00
Vase, Bud, Fluted, Tapered, Cylindrical, Round Amber Disc, 12 In. 834.00
Vase, Diamond-Quilted, Egg Shape, 3 Applied Reeded Feet, 5 1/2 In. 460.00
Vase, Fold-Down Top, Tapered, Optic Ribbed Disc, 12 In. 403.00
Vase, Jack-In-The-Pulpit, Reeded, Urn Shape, 13 1/2 In. 115.00
Vase, Jack-In-The-Pulpit, Tapered Amber Stem, 10 In. 288.00
Vase, Jack-In-The-Pulpit, Tapered Amber Stem, Raised Disc Foot, 11 3/4 In. 288.00
Vase, Jack-In-The-Pulpit, Tapered Stem, Raised Disc Foot, 7 In. 288.00
Vase, Lily, Fold-Down Top, Applied Amber Foot, 6 In. 150.00
Vase, Lily, Ribbed Stem, Applied Foot, 9 In. 518.00
Vase, Ribbed, Applied Amber Handles, Applied Foot, 7 1/2 In. 86.00
Vase, Ruffled Petal Edge, 7 1/4 In. 144.00
Vase, Square, Ruffled Edge, 4 x 4 In. 230.00
Vase, Swirled Ribs, Applied Rigaree Edge, 7 In., Pair 115.00
Water Set, Inverted Thumbprint, Applied Reeded Handle, 7 Piece 420.00

AMERICAN DINNERWARE, see Dinnerware.

AMERICAN ENCAUSTIC TILING COMPANY was founded in Zanesville, Ohio, in 1875. The company planned to make a variety of tiles to compete with the English tiles that were selling in the United States for use in fireplaces and other architectural designs. The first glazed tiles were made in 1880, embossed tiles in 1881, faience tiles in the 1920s. The firm closed in 1935 and reopened in 1937 as the Shawnee Pottery.

Bookends, Cherub, Rabbit, Mark, 1926, 4 1/2 x 5 In., Pair 210.00
Tile, Cattails, Embossed, Blue Glaze, Frame, 24 x 6 In., 4 Piece 920.00
Tile, Elephant, Beige, Tan, Ivory, Marked, 4 In. 175.00
Tile, Elephant, Comical, Grass, Tan Ground, 6 In. 450.00

Tile, Female Profile, Ivory Matte, Marked, 4 In.	58.00
Tile, Geometric Design, Tan, Beige, Green, Marked, 12 In.	115.00
Tile, Girl In Bonnet, Blue, Marked, 6 In.	145.00
Tile, Jack & Jill, Marked, 6 In.	145.00
Tile, King Cole, Walter Crane Illustration, Marked, 6 In.	115.00
Tile, Little Jack Horner, Marked, 6 In.	29.00
Tile, Peacocks Complaint, Walter Crane Illustration, 6 In.	115.00
Tile, See Saw Margery Daw, Marked, 6 In.	145.00

AMETHYST GLASS is any of the many glasswares made in the dark purple color of the gemstone called amethyst. Included in this category are many pieces made in the nineteenth and twentieth centuries. Very dark pieces are called *black amethyst* and are listed under that heading.

Bowl, Egyptian Revival Holder, Winged Woman Handles, Bronze Base, 7 In.	735.00
Sugar, Blown Open, Paneled, Open Pontil, 3 1/4 In.	170.00
Wine, Freeblown Stem & Base, England, 1800s, 3 3/4 In., 4 Piece	127.00

AMPHORA pieces are listed in the Teplitz category.

ANDIRONS and related fireplace items are included in the Fireplace category.

ANIMAL TROPHIES, such as stuffed animals, rugs made of animal skins, and other similar collectibles made from animal, fish, or bird parts, are listed in this category. Collectors should be aware of the endangered species laws that make it illegal to buy and sell some of these items. Any eagle feathers, many types of pelts or rugs (such as leopard), ivory, and many forms of tortoiseshell can be confiscated by the government. Related trophies may be found in the Fishing category. Ivory items may be found in the Scrimshaw or Ivory categories.

4 American Birds, Taxidermy, Glass Dome, c.1875, 13 x 6 x 17 In.	1725.00
8 Old World Birds, Taxidermy, Glass Dome, c.1875, 10 1/4 x 13 In.	805.00
Bird, Hanging From Rope, Wooden, Germany, c.1890, 21 1/2 x 13 In.	725.00
Bobcat, Full Figure	624.00
Deer, White Tailed, 6-Point Antlers, Head Straight	88.00
Deer, White Tailed, 6-Point Antlers, Head Turned	60.00
Fish, Striped Bass, Mounted, 50 In.	220.00
Fox, Gray, Full Figure	88.00
Lamb, Persian, Black, Full Figure	22.00
Moose Antlers, 12-Point, Mounted, Circular Plaque, 48 x 40 In.	374.00
Moose Antlers, Maine, 40 In.	187.00
Mouflon, Dark Brown, 2 Curly Horns, Marked Het Loo 24, Sept. 1970	330.00
Pheasant, Male, Full Figure	22.00
Rabbit, Snowshoe, Full Figure	55.00
Rug, Bear Skin, Alaskan, White, Large	1534.00
Rug, Bear Skin, Black, 70 In.	345.00
Rug, Polar Bear Skin, Mounted Head & Claws, Lined, 7 Ft. 10 In. x 7 Ft.	700.00
Rug, Red Wolf	275.00
Rug, Zebra Skin, Black Felt Lining, 106 x 66 In.	460.00

ANIMATION ART collectibles include cels that are painted drawings on celluloid needed to make animated cartoons shown in movie theaters or on TV. Hundreds of cels were made, then photographed in sequence to make a cartoon showing moving figures. Early examples made by the Walt Disney Studios are popular with collectors today. Original sketches used by the artists are also listed here. Modern animated cartoons are made using computer-generated pictures. Some of these are being produced as cels to be sold to collectors. Other cartoon art is listed in Comic Art and Disneyana.

Cel, 3 Caballeros, Donald Duck, Jose Carioca, Panchito, Frame, 1945, 20 x 16 In.	928.00
Cel, 3 Caballeros, Rooster, Holding Donald Duck & Parrot, 1945, 10 x 6 1/2 In.	575.00
Cel, 3 Little Wolves, Big Bad Wolf, D.C. Heath, Frame, 1940, 9 x 8 1/2 In.	1200.00
Cel, Bambi, In Forest, Hand Painted, Walt Disney, 20th Century, 5 1/4 x 5 In.	1410.00
Cel, Bambi, In Snow, Hand Painted, Walt Disney, 20th Century, 6 x 5 In.	940.00
Cel, Bugs Bunny, Carnival Of The Animals, Bugs In Blue Tails, 15 1/4 x 17 1/4 In.	165.00

Cel, Flintstones, Pebbles, Bam Bam, Barney, Wilma, Signed, Frame, 12 x 8 1/2 In. 116.00
Cel, Jiminy Cricket, I'm No Fool, Mickey Mouse Club, 1950s, 12 1/2 x 12 1/4 In. .230.00 to 498.00
Cel, Lady & The Tramp, Bella Notte, 1955, 16 1/2 x 12 In. ....230.00 to 805.00
Cel, Lonesome Ghosts, Title Card Set-Up, Disney, 1937, 8 3/8 x 11 3/8 In. 2717.00
Cel, Mickey & The Seal, Pluto & Salty, Red Ball, 1948, 6 3/4 x 9 3/8 In. 335.00
Cel, Mickey Down Under, Mickey, Throwing Boomerang, Courvoisier, 1948 .... 575.00
Cel, Pink Panther, Frame, 12 x 9 In. 171.00
Cel, Pluto & Salty The Seal, Mickey & The Seal, 1948, 6 3/4 x 9 3/8 In. 335.00
Cel, Snow White & The 7 Dwarfs, Bambi, 4 Rabbits, Squirrel, 1937, 7 x 6 In. ....345.00 to 675.00
Cel, Snow White, 2 Bluebirds, In Nest, On Branch, Frame, 6 1/4 x 7 1/4 In. 525.00
Cel, Song Of The South, Br'er Rabbit, Br'er Fox, Frame, c.1950, 20 1/2 x 17 In. 498.00
Cel, Winnie The Pooh, Many Adventures Of Winnie The Pooh, 16 1/4 x 19 1/4 In. 275.00
Cel, Yogi Bear, Quick Draw McGraw, Friends, Signed, Frame, 12 x 8 In. 127.00

ANNA POTTERY was started in Anna, Illinois, in 1859 by Cornwall and
Wallace Kirkpatrick. They made many types of utilitarian wares,
bricks, drain tiles, and giftware. The most collectible pieces made by
the pottery are the pig-shaped bottles and jugs with special inscriptions, applied animals, and figures. The pottery closed in 1894.

Anna Pottery

Pitcher, Snakes, 1885 .... 3800.00

APPLE PEELERS are listed in the Kitchen category under Peeler, Apple.

ARCHITECTURAL antiques include a variety of collectibles, usually
very large, that have been removed from buildings. Hardware, back-
bars, doors, paneling, and even old bathtubs are now wanted by collectors. Pieces of the Victorian, Art Nouveau, and Art Deco styles are
in greatest demand.

Backbar, Saloon, Oak, Leaded Glass Panels, c.1900, 14 Ft. 8800.00
Bidet, Porcelain, Blue, White, Flowers, Mahogany Stand, Chinese, 26 x 25 x 15 In. 1610.00
Block, Stone, Carved, Fruit, Floral Swag, Ribbon, 25 x 8 1/2 x 6 In. 165.00
Bracket, Female Lion Shape, Marble Shelf, Composition, 31 x 48 x 20 In., Pair 165.00
Bracket, Gothic Style, Plaster, Fabric, 18 x 23 1/2 x 12 In. 880.00
Bracket, Mahogany, Carved, Gilt, Iron Base, Shell Style Finials, 1800s, 32 In., Pair 1430.00
Bracket, Wall Mount, Iron, Scrolled Feet, Planter Brackets, 78 x 59 In. 300.00
Bracket, Wall, Wood, Carved, Putto, Winged Merman, Scalloped, 20th Century, 17 In. ... 155.00
Building Bolt, Earthquake Star, Cast Iron, 15 In. 66.00
Capital, Corinthian, Pine, Carved Scrolls, Leaves, American, c.1910, 13 x 16 In., Pair ... 1725.00
Capital, Stone, Cast, Carved Leaves, Continental, Early 1900s, 17 x 21 In., Pair 3680.00
Caryatids, Female Bust, Oak, Continental, 43 In., Pair 2990.00
Ceiling, Tin, Embossed Squares, Molding, 18 x 30 Ft. 800.00
Column, Empire Style, Scagliola, Slate, Painted, 1800s, 46 In. 4995.00
Column, Gilt Bronze, Verde Antico, Rouge Royale, Marble, Caesar Head, 10 In., Pair 1095.00
Column, Half, Walnut, Carved, 42 In., Pair 210.00
Corner Guards, Horse Legs, Latticework Panels, Cast Iron, 25 In. 770.00
Cupola, Louver Slats, Swept Roof, Tin, 1800s, 114 x 42 x 42 In., Pair 2130.00
Cupola, Molded Trim, Louver Slats, Molded Tops, 108 x 42 In., Pair 2090.00
Door, Belle Epoque, Polychrome, Parcel Gilt, Beech, c.1900, 98 x 45 1/2 In., Pair 3910.00
Door, Inset Panels, Red Flame Graining, Rockingham Knob, Box Lock, 77 x 36 In. 316.00
Door, Raised Panels, Blue Sponging, York Co., Penn., 74 x 34 In. 900.00
Door, Raised Panels, Mustard Paint, Orange Decoration, Black, 78 1/2 x 34 In. 1015.00
Door, Saloon, Swinging, Walnut, Stained Glass Upper, Clear Glass, 48 In., Pair 357.00
Door Handle, Bronze, Loop Shape, Polished Brass Finish, Albert Paley, 16 In., Pair 8050.00
Door Handle, Iron, Reverse Punch, Thumb Latch, 18th Century, 16 x 3 In. 1430.00
Door Handle, Organic Design, Brown Patina, Albert Paley, 74 1/4 In., Pair 6900.00
Door Handle, Steel, Circular & Semi Circular Shapes, Albert Paley, 88 1/4 In., Pair 4600.00
Door Handle Set, Steel, Lock Plate, Walter Gropius, Berlin, 1920s, 10 In. 410.00
Doorknob, Cranberry Cut To Clear, Glass, Pair 495.00
Doorknob, Sandwich Glass, 12 Piece 230.00
Finial, Gatepost, Carved, Pineapple, Late 1800s, Pair 5500.00
Finial, Newel Post, Brass Ferule, Clambroth Hobnail Glass Top, 7 1/2 In. 220.00
Finial, Roof, Beehive Top, Copper, 1860-1880 .... 4200.00
Flower, Daisy, Bronze, Iron, 4 In. 50.00
Fountain, Wall Mount, Classical, Lion's Mask, Cast, 51 x 63 x 27 1/2 In. 1093.00

Frame, Wall Mounting Brackets, Gold Painted, Iron, 22 In., Pair 121.00
Fretwork, Stick & Ball, Center Wheel, Turned Posts, 82 1/2 In. 365.00
Frieze, Gesso, Rams' Heads, Urns, Scrolls, 18th Century, 34 In., Pair 3960.00
Gate, Iron, Circles, Scrolls, Art Deco, Early 1900s, 97 x 98 In. 3680.00
Gate, Renaissance Style, Wood, Arched Pediment, 1800s, 112 1/2 x 50 In., Pair 1610.00
Grate, Window, Iron, Flowers, Urn, Painted, Green, White, 18 x 37 In., Pair 1840.00
Hinge, Batwing, Black Paint, Lebanon Co., 7 x 2 In., 4 Piece 520.00
Hinge, Forged, Scrolled Wings, Iron, 11 In., Pair 225.00
Hinge, Incised Iron, Angel, Scroll Work, 22 In. 35.00
Hinge, Iron, Ram's Horn, 15 x 6 In., Pair 165.00
Iron Grate, Scrolled Flowers, Varity Iron Works, York, Pa., 32 1/2 x 18 In. 55.00
Jamb Hooks, Chippendale Style, Brass, Turned, Faceted Finials, 2 1/2 x 5 1/2 In., Pair . . . 56.00
Lamp Post, Fluted Columns, Floral Relief, White Cast Iron, 81 In., Pair 605.00
Letter Box, Dome Top, Flowers, Lion's Head, Cast Iron, 41 1/2 x 13 x 14 1/2 In. 546.00
Mantel, Chippendale Style, Maple Leaves, Shells, Urns, Columns, 56 x 44 In. 290.00
Mantel, Copeland Tile Inserts, England, c.1820 . . . . 1995.00
Mantel, Federal, Carved, White, Drapery Swag, New York, 63 x 88 In. 8050.00
Mantel, Federal, Fluted Pilasters, Red Paint, Breadboard Ends, 49 x 63 1/4 In. 230.00
Mantel, Iron Surround, Faux Marble Slate Top, 41 1/4 x 60 x 10 1/4 In. 275.00
Mantel, Mixed Wood, Faux Marble Painting, Pilasters, 42 x 12 x 39 1/2 In. 138.00
Mantel, Pine, Grain Paint, c.1860, 60 x 59 In. 275.00
Mantel, Pine, White Paint, Reeded Molding, 64 1/2 x 6 1/2 x 60 In. 440.00
Mantel, Softwood, Molded Opening, Mustard Paint, 55 1/2 x 42 In. 75.00
Mantel, Softwood, Scallop Edge, Classical Scene, Lady, Children, 64 x 48 x 42 In. 2250.00
Model, Bank, Wood, Painted, White, Tar Shingles, Electrified, 36 x 26 x 29 In. 290.00
Model, Horse Barn, Red Paint, White Detail, Peaked Roof, 13 x 10 x 13 In. 100.00
Molding, Anthemion, Scroll, Gilt Bronze, From Buncombe County Courthouse, 96 In. . . . 770.00
Molding, Carved, Beaded Dentil, Gadrooned Elements, Paint Traces, 85 x 7 In. 360.00
Molding, Carved, Geometric, Flowers, Vines, Hand Planed Surface, 65 x 9 In. 165.00
Mount, Iron Frame, Acanthus Leaf, Scrolling, Paint Traces, 27 x 9 x 23 In. 250.00
Newel Post, Walnut, Carved, Owl Shape, Outstretched Wings, Early 1900s, 18 In. 940.00
Ornament, Lion's Head, Carved In 1/2 Round, Painted, Late 19th Century, 8 x 7 In. 8965.00
Overdoor, Far Eastern, Wood, Painted, Carved, Structures, Deities, 37 x 83 x 4 In. 546.00
Overmantel Mirror, Aesthetic Revival, Ebonized, Carved, Corner Patera, 61 x 55 In. 705.00
Overmantel Mirror, Aesthetic Revival, Giltwood, Late 1800s, 85 x 64 x 6 1/2 In. 1495.00
Overmantel Mirror, Applied Half Turnings, Carved Corner Blocks, 22 x 53 In. 115.00
Overmantel Mirror, Carved Giltwood, Shell, Leaves, c.1865, 73 x 43 In. 2530.00
Overmantel Mirror, Continental Rococo Style, Giltwood, 3 Sections, 41 x 69 In. 1495.00
Overmantel Mirror, Gilt, 3 Part, Applied Half Turnings, 25 x 54 1/2 In. 145.00
Overmantel Mirror, Louis XVI Style, Giltwood, Mid 19th Century, 81 x 46 In. 1610.00
Overmantel Mirror, Louis XVI Style, Giltwood, Olive Leaves, c.1885, 65 x 43 In. 1265.00
Overmantel Mirror, Louis XVI Style, Mahogany, Torch, Quiver, c.1885, 92 x 53 In. 1090.00
Overmantel Mirror, Louis XVI Style, Polychrome, 40 x 30 In., Pair 375.00
Overmantel Mirror, Napoleon III, Giltwood, Carved, c.1865, 61 1/2 x 36 1/2 In. 1725.00
Overmantel Mirror, Napoleon III, Giltwood, Flowers, Cenotaph Shape, c.1865 . . . . 690.00
Overmantel Mirror, Napoleon III, Giltwood, Louis XVI Style, 67 x 32 In. 2070.00
Overmantel Mirror, Napoleon III, Giltwood, Louis XVI Style, Arch, 83 x 53 In. 2530.00
Overmantel Mirror, Neoclassical, Giltwood, American, c.1820, 31 1/2 x 60 In. 2300.00
Overmantel Mirror, Neoclassical, Giltwood, Boston, c.1825, 40 1/2 x 64 In. 8340.00
Overmantel Mirror, Neoclassical, Giltwood, Carved, Gesso, c.1810, 24 x 53 1/2 In. 1765.00
Overmantel Mirror, Regency, Oblong, 3 Sections, c.1815, 36 1/2 x 57 1/2 In. 1380.00
Overmantel Mirror, Rococo Revival, Giltwood, Mid 19th Century, 100 x 68 x 9 In. 10925.00
Overmantel Mirror, Rococo Style, Giltwood, Continental, 42 x 54 In. 1150.00
Overmantel Mirror, Rococo, Carved Wood, Gilt Gesso, 50 x 60 In. 3955.00
Overmantel Mirror, Sheraton Style, Inlaid Satinwood, Flowers, 34 3/8 x 54 In. 635.00
Overmantel Mirror, Sheraton, Gilt, Fleur-De-Lis Corners, 1800s, 35 1/2 x 65 In. 1380.00
Panel, Alabaster, Pierced, Carved, Indian, Agra, Late 1800s, 16 1/4 x 11 1/4 In. 1725.00
Panel, Oak, North Wind Decoration, Scrolled Leaf Details, 10 1/2 x 55 1/2 In. 219.00
Panel, Renaissance Style, Scrolls, Hawk Heads, Cast Iron, 38 x 24 In., Pair 195.00
Panel, Scrolled, Vertical Bars, Iron, 75 x 18 In., Pair 1320.00
Panel, Wood Carved, Flowers & Leaves, Green Paint, 27 & 37 In., 2 Piece 45.00
Pediment, Multicolored, Trompe L'Oeil Arch, Italy, 1800s, 33 x 58 In., Pair 3220.00
Post, Lead, Painted, Full Round, Hand Shape, Finger Pointing Up, 12 In., Pair 1435.00

Shutters, Green Paint, 4 Sections, Beaded Edges, 67 1/4 x 26 1/4 In., Pair 201.00
Shutters, Painted, Stationary Top Louvers, Adjustable Lowers, 18 1/2 x 61 In., Pair 412.00
Toilet, Raised Blue Heron On Front, Trenton, New Jersey, c.1870 .... 650.00
Wall Bracket, Rococo Revival, Mahogany, Carved, Openwork, 11 1/2 In., Pair 1645.00
Window, Arched, Rayed Mullions, White, Green Painted, 12 Pane, 41 x 21 1/2 In. 302.00

AREQUIPA POTTERY was produced from 1911 to 1918 by the patients
of the Arequipa Sanatorium in Marin County, north of San Francisco.
The patients were trained by Frederick Hürten Rhead, who had worked
at the Roseville Pottery.

Bowl, Pot, Beside Tree, Blue Mark, F. Rhead, 2 1/4 In. 590.00
Vase, Bulbous, Mauve Matte Glaze, Marked, 4 In. 690.00
Vase, Embossed, Branches, Fruit, Leaves, Blue Matte, Mottled Indigo, Stamped, 6 In. ... 6325.00

ARGY-ROUSSEAU, see G. Argy-Rousseau category.

ARITA is a port in Japan. Porcelain was made there from about 1616.
Many types of decorations were used, including the popular Imari
designs, which are listed under Imari in this book.

Bottle, Blue & White, Sake Tokkuri Design, Flower Sprig, Japan, 1800s, 15 In. 235.00
Bowl, Meiji, Octagonal, Footed, Japan, 11 1/4 In. 400.00
Charger, Blue & White, Dragon, Sages, Bamboo Grove, Horses, Japan, 1800s, 20 In. 940.00
Charger, Blue & White, Geometric Designs, Japan, 1800s, 20 In. 705.00
Charger, Blue & White, Shishi Design, Japan, 1800s, 23 In. 1410.00
Charger, Ships, Castles, Landscapes, Blue & White, Cheng Hua Mark, 1800s, 22 3/4 In. . 1528.00
Dish, Fan Form, Crane, Tortoise, Pine, Blue & White, c.1900, 9 1/2 In. 288.00
Garden Seat, Hourglass Shape, Shishi Mask Handles, Flowers, Japan, Late 1800s, 19 In. . 588.00
Jar, Cover, Blue & White, Egrets, Prunus, Ice Ground, Japan, Late 1800s, 23 In. 1880.00
Jar, Cover, Blue & White, Molded Crane, Leaves, Transfer Borders, Japan, c.1900, 26 In. . 353.00
Planter & Tray, Blue & White, Crane Design, Japan, Late 1800s, 9 In. 353.00
Vase, Birds, Flowers, Blue, Gray & Yellow Underglaze, Japan, 1800s, 37 In. 823.00

ART DECO, or Art Moderne, a style started at the Paris Exposition of
1925, is characterized by linear, geometric designs. All types of furniture and decorative arts, jewelry, book bindings, and even games were
designed in this style. Additional items may be found in the Furniture
category or in various glass and pottery categories, etc.

Gazelle, Hagenauer, Lying Down, Chrome Horns, Wood Carving, 8 x 14 x 4 In. 865.00
Horse, Hagenauer, Olive Wood, Wood Carving, Austria, 13 x 14 1/4 x 4 1/4 In. 1955.00
Horse, Hagenauer, Rearing, Brass Tail & Base, Wood Carving, 11 1/4 x 9 3/4 x 3 In. 2300.00

ART GLASS, see Glass-Art category.

ART POTTERY, see Pottery-Art.

ARTHUR OSBORNE plaques are found in the Ivorex category.

ARTS & CRAFTS was a design style popular in American decorative arts
from 1894 to 1923. In the 1970s collectors began to rediscover
Mission furniture, art pottery, metalwork, linens, and light fixtures
from this period. The interest has continued. Today everything from
this era is collectible, including jewelry, graphics, and silverware.
Additional items may be found in the Furniture category, various glass
categories, etc.

Card Holder, Sterling Silver, Copper Inlay, 3 1/4 x 1 3/4 In. 145.00
Vase, Green Matte Glaze, Variegated Glaze, 2 Loop Handles, 5 1/2 In. 185.00
Vase, Shouldered Shape, Thick Green Matte Glaze, 4 1/2 In. 60.00

AURENE glass was made by Frederick Carder of New York about 1904.
It is an iridescent gold, blue, green, or red glass, usually marked
Aurene or *Steuben*.

Basket, Blue, Coiled Buttons, Rolled In Rim, 8 1/2 x 7 7/8 In. 1265.00
Bottle, Scent, Blue, 7 1/2 In. 635.00
Bowl, Blue, Rolled Rim, Signed, c.1910, 4 x 7 In. 950.00
Bowl, Centerpiece, Gold Calcite Interior, Signed, 12 x 2 3/4 In. 230.00

To clean alabaster, dust with a soft brush,
then wipe with turpentine or dry-cleaning
fluid. Do not use water. Alabaster
dissolves in water.

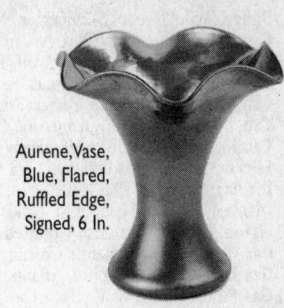

Aurene, Vase,
Blue, Flared,
Ruffled Edge,
Signed, 6 In.

Don't put an alabaster figure or vase
outside. It's more porous than marble and
will eventually fall apart if exposed to rain.

Bowl, Centerpiece, Gold, Brown Aurene Base, c.1920, 11 1/2 In.	430.00
Bowl, Gold, Applied Threading, Flared, 10 In.	1410.00
Bowl, Gold, Flower Form, Blue Base, Signed, 4 1/2 x 12 In.	1495.00
Candlestick, Blue, Saucer Base, Twisted Stem, No. 686, 8 In.	920.00
Compote, Blue, 8 x 5 In.	750.00
Finger Bowl, Gold & Blue, Ruffled Edge, 3 1/2 In., 4 Piece	700.00
Finger Bowl, Gold, Ruffled Edge, 5 1/4 In.	175.00
Goblet, Gold, Twist Stem, c.1910, 6 In.	375.00 to 730.00
Lampshade, Gold, Bulbous Form, Signed, 4 In., Pair	520.00
Salt & Pepper, Gold, Brass Tops, 6 3/4 In.	950.00
Vase, Blue, Flared, Ruffled Edge, Signed, 6 In. ....*Illus*	920.00
Vase, Blue, Ruffled Rim, Stretch Border, Disc Pedestal, Signed, 4 3/4 In.	1350.00
Vase, Blue, Silver Leaves & Vines, Gold Cuff, Zigzag Intarsia, 7 1/2 In.	25875.00
Vase, Flowerform, Tapered Stem, Circular Foot, 8 1/2 In.	1175.00
Vase, Gold, 6-Sided Rim, Pedestal Foot, No. B241, 8 In.	690.00
Vase, Gold, Bulbous, Flared Rim, 6 In.	645.00
Vase, Gold, Calcite Interior, 6 1/4 In.	490.00
Vase, Gold, Diagonal Ribs, Flared, Footed, 11 7/8 In.	2630.00
Vase, Gold, Flared, Ruffled Edge, 5 In.	635.00
Vase, Gold, Flared, Slightly Ruffled Edge, 9 1/2 In.	2160.00
Vase, Gold, Green Swirls, 4 Pinched Sides, Flared Rim, Signed, 4 1/2 In.	2013.00
Vase, Gold, Oval, Signed, 8 1/4 In.	825.00
Vase, Gold, Pulled Feather, 3 1/4 In.	1469.00
Vase, Gold, Ribbed, Flared Rim, 4 1/2 In.	430.00
Vase, Gold, Shell Form, Twisted Stem, Footed, 7 1/2 In.	3408.00
Vase, Gold, Squared Rim, Pinched, 3 1/8 In.	1610.00
Vase, Gold, Wide Mouth, Rolled Edge, 3 Handles, 5 1/8 x 9 In.	1528.00
Vase, Jack-In-The-Pulpit, Gold & Amber, 6 In.	940.00
Vase, Jack-In-The-Pulpit, Gold, Stretched Rim, 7 3/8 In.	1880.00
Vase, Stick, Blue, Ringed, Foot, 8 In.	230.00
Vase, Swirled Ribbing, Blue, 7 In.	719.00
Vase, Tree Trunk, Blue, 3 Prongs, Signed, 6 1/2 In.	1315.00 to 1800.00
Vase, Tree Trunk, Gold, 3 Prongs, Blue Foot, 6 1/4 In.	1015.00
Vase, Tree Trunk, Gold, Blue Gold Base, Signed Pontil, 8 In.	776.00
Vase, Trumpet, Blue, Applied Connector & Foot, Ruffled Edge, 8 1/2 In.	3680.00
Vase, Turquoise, Pulled Heart & Vine, Steuben, Signed, 5 1/2 In.	4830.00
Whimsey, Darner, Gold, Open Pontil, 7 In.	305.00

AUSTRIA is a collecting term that covers pieces made by a wide variety of factories. They are listed in this book in categories such as Royal Dux, or Porcelain.

AUTO parts and accessories are collectors' items today. Gas pump
globes and license plates are part of this specialty. Prices are determined by age, rarity, and condition. Signs and packaging related to
automobiles may also be found in the Advertising category. Lalique
hood ornaments will be listed in the Lalique category.

Ashtray, Pirelli, Miniature Rubber Tire, Glass Insert, 6 In.	15.00
Badge, Texaco, Name Badge, Cloisonne Enameling, 1 3/4 x 2 1/4 In.	470.00

Badge, Tydol Veedol Serviceman, Name, Inlaid Enameled Letters, 2 7/8 x 2 1/4 In. 745.00
Banner, Atlantic Motor Oil, Aviation, 100% Pennsylvania Oil, Canvas, 36 x 26 In. 90.00
Banner, Atlantic Motor Oil, Wolf, Don't Be Afraid, Big Bad Wolf, Cloth, 58 x 36 In. 230.00
Button, Esso, Merry Christmas, Santa Claus, Red, White, Blue, Celluloid, 1 1/4 In. 39.00
Can, Eveready Prestone, Perfect Anti-Freeze, Tin Lithograph, 10 In. 65.00
Can, Purity Oil Co., Transmission Grease, 5 Lb. 60.00
Catalog, Spyker Automobile, Heavy Board, Holland, England, 12 x 19 In., 10 Pages 375.00
Clicker, Sohio Oil Company, 2 3/8 x 1 1/4 In. 80.00
Display, Schrader Tire Valve Stem, Contents, Steel, Countertop, c.1925, 16 In. 525.00
Display, Tydol & Veedol Oil, Leads Its Class, Metal, Lithograph, 2-Sided, 43 In. 275.00
Figure, BP Oil Man, Arm Upraised, Arm Out, Shirt, White Hat, Vinyl, c.1950, 3 1/2 In. .. 55.00
Gas Pump Globe, Atlantic Gasoline, Reverse Painted, 2-Sided, 21 1/2 In. 470.00
Gas Pump Globe, Capitol, Atlantic Gasoline, Reverse Painted, 2-Sided, 20 In. 470.00
Gas Pump Globe, Gulf, Glass Casing & Lenses, 17 In. 415.00
Gas Pump Globe, Skelly, Fortified Gasoline, Red, White, Blue 255.00
Gas Pump Globe, Standard Oil, White, Gold, Crown, 17 In. 495.00
Lamp, Nickel Plated, 20th Century Mfg. Co., 7 In. 28.00
Lamp, Texaco, 75th Anniversary, Plastic 125.00
License Plate, Maine, 1915, Blue On White, Ing-Rich Mfg. Co. 110.00
License Plate, Massachusetts, 1910, Blue On White, Baltimore Enamel & Novelty Co. .. 65.00
License Plate, Massachusetts, 1914, Blue On White, Ing-Rich Mfg. Co., Pair 75.00
License Plate, Massachusetts, 1915, White On Blue, Ing-Rich Mfg. Co., Pair 85.00
License Plate, New Hampshire, 1914, White On Green, Balt. Enamel & Novelty Co. 170.00
License Plate, New Hampshire, 1915, Green On White, Ing-Rich Mfg. Co. ....50.00 to 130.00
License Plate, New Hampshire, 1918, White On Green, Pair 75.00
License Plate, New Jersey, 1915, Porcelain, Frame, Pair 155.00
License Plate, New York, 1917, 13 x 6 In., Pair 98.00
License Plate, Pennsylvania, 1906, White On Blue, 3 Digit, 6 1/2 x 7 In. 900.00
License Plate, Pennsylvania, 1964, Truck 12.00
Matchbook, Buick, Red Convertible, Spencer Buick, Taraval, San Francisco, 1958 ...... 12.00
Mug, Esso, Tiger Eating Ice Cream, 3 1/2 In. 8.00
Oil Can, Atlantic Oil, ODNOL, Russian Extra Heavy Mineral Oil, Gal., 10 In. 105.00
Oil Can, Boston Coach Axle Oil, Standard Oil Company, 6 In. 28.00
Oil Can, Cascade Motor Oil, Cataract Refining Co., MacDonald Mfg. Co., Toronto, Gal. . 550.00
Oil Can, Cities Service Blue Club Motor Oil, Gal. 17.00
Oil Can, Ford Motor Oil, This Can Fits Under Seat Of Ford Touring Car, British Oil Co. .. 800.00
Oil Can, Gilmore Lion Head Motor Oil, Contents, Qt. 520.00
Oil Can, Hudson Motor Oil, Oil Tanker, Tin Lithograph, Unopened, 5 1/2 x 4 In. 300.00
Oil Can, Kendall, Hypoid Lube, 90 Weight, 1 Lb., 5 1/2 In. 27.00
Oil Can, No. 6, Eagle, U.S.A., Brass 110.00
Oil Can, Polarine, Imperial Oil Co., MacDonald Mfg. Co., Gal. 675.00
Oil Can, Quaker City Bonded Motor Oil, Pennsylvania Petroleum, Qt., 5 1/2 x 4 In. 125.00
Oil Can, Red Bell Motor Oil, Sico Co., Mt. Joy, Pa., 2 Gal., 11 In. 50.00
Oil Can, Red Indian Auto Oil, McColl Bros. & Co., Gal. 2900.00
Oil Can, Sign, Boston Coach Axle Oil, Standard Oil Co., Contents, Tin, 3 x 5 1/2 x 2 In. . 35.00
Oil Can, Texaco, Motor Oil, Heavy, Pour Spout, Green, Port Arthur, Tex., 1/2 Gal., 7 In. .. 105.00
Oil Dispenser, Esso, Figural, Oil Drop Character 60.00
Pin, Valvoline, It's In The Ring, Valvoline Wins Or Else, Red, White, Blue, c.1940, 3 In. . 20.00
Pitcher, Cornfield Auto Chevrolet, Dysart, Iowa, Watt, Cherries, No. 15 .... 165.00
Plate, Mobil Oil, Pegasus, White, Scalloped Edge, Restaurant China, 10 In. 70.00
Poster, Hey Kids!, Bardahl, 5 T-Shirts, 4 Oil Filter Villains, c.1955, 11 x 22 In. 45.00
Radiator Cap, Figural, Vulcan The Smith, Leaning On Wheel, Brass 320.00
Radiator Cap, Goodyear Tires, Ned Lambert, Model T, Stenciled, Cardboard, 18 1/2 In. .. 110.00
Radiator Cap, Motor Meter, Dog Bone, Crest, Glass Eye, Nickel 129.00
Radiator Ornament, Cadillac, Flying Lady, 1931-1932 .... 120.00
Radiator Ornament, Dodge Brothers Motor Meter, Dog Bone Cap, 7 1/2 In. 120.00
Sign, AAA Approved, Red, White, Blue, Oval, Porcelain, 23 x 30 In. 165.00
Sign, Atlantic Gasoline, Porcelain, 52 In. 300.00
Sign, Atlantic Gasoline, Red, White, Black, Porcelain, 6 1/2 x 13 In. 39.00
Sign, Atlantic Motor Oil, Red, White, Blue, Porcelain, 52 In. 250.00
Sign, Atlantic White Flash Gasoline, Red, White, Black, 13 x 17 In. 275.00
Sign, Baudou Tires, Bandage Increvable, Brevele S.G.D.G., Tin Lithograph, 27 x 19 In. .. 1440.00

Sign, Cadillac Service, Black, Gold, Red, White, Round, Porcelain, c.1950, 48 In. 2310.00
Sign, Champion Spark Plugs, Dependable, Tin, Flange, c.1960, 23 3/4 x 35 1/2 In. 149.00
Sign, Chrysler Service, Black, Yellow, 2-Sided, Porcelain, 26 3/4 x 21 In. 440.00
Sign, Colonial Minuteman Regular Gasoline, Porcelain, 15 x 12 In. 770.00
Sign, Conoco Gasoline, Yellow, Red, Blue, Porcelain, 2-Sided, Round, 25 In. 2640.00
Sign, Conoco, Red, White, Tin, Metal Frame, 16 1/2 x 50 In. 165.00
Sign, De Soto, Approved Service, Red, White, Blue, Porcelain, Round, 30 In. 415.00
Sign, Dodge Trucks, Job Rated Sales & Service, Porcelain, 2-Sided, 42 In. 3400.00
Sign, Douglas Battery, Sales & Service, Red, Black, Tin, 47 x 17 1/2 In. 70.00
Sign, Du Pont Anti-Freeze Methanol, 30 Cent Qt., Cardboard, Frame, 30 x 21 In. 95.00
Sign, En-Ar-Co Motor Oil, Boy Holding Sign, Tin, 2-Sided, Round, Brackets, 40 In. 635.00
Sign, Energee True Gasoline, Pure Oil Co., Tin, Flange, Round, 17 1/2 x 20 In. 330.00
Sign, Fisk Tires, Gasoline, Auto Supplies, Porcelain, Flange, 18 x 24 1/4 In. 1020.00
Sign, Fisk Tires, Time To Re-Tire, Buy Fisk, Toddler With Tire, Porcelain, 28 x 36 In. . . . 1900.00
Sign, Ford, Neon, Porcelain, White Script Name, Oval, 72 In. 1600.00
Sign, Ford, Neon, Red Offset Letters, Decorative Molding, Oval, 72 In. 2200.00
Sign, Ford, Pickup Truck Emblem, Lightning, Cast Aluminum, 1953-1956, 21 In. 303.00
Sign, Francisco Auto Heaters, People In Car, Tin, Self-Framed, c.1920, 18 x 40 In. 1390.00
Sign, Gillette Tires, A Bear For Wear, White, Red, Black, Tin, Metal, 48 x 29 In. 90.00
Sign, Good Gulf Gasoline, White, Orange, Blue, Porcelain, Round, 10 1/2 In. 138.00
Sign, Goodrich Safety Tires, Canadian Mountie, Porcelain, 56 x 20 In. 10200.00
Sign, Goodyear Tires, Diamond Shape, Porcelain, Brackets, 2-Sided, 48 x 27 In. 385.00
Sign, Gulf Dealer, Orange, Black, 2-Sided, Round, 66 In. 210.00
Sign, Gulf Dealer, Red, White, Black, 2-Sided, Porcelain, Round, 65 In. 330.00
Sign, Highway, Naromiyocknowhusunkatankshunk Brook, Conn., Wood, 9 x 52 In. 825.00
Sign, Hudson Essex Service, Porcelain, 16 x 30 In. 385.00
Sign, Kendall Motor Oil, Red, White, Tin, 2-Sided, Round, 22 In. 55.00
Sign, Koldpruf Antifreeze, Penguin, 2-Sided, Die Cut Cardboard, 11 1/2 x 18 In. 230.00
Sign, Magnolia Petroleum Co., For Sale Here, Porcelain, 2-Sided, Round, 30 In. 525.00
Sign, Marathon Oil, Marathon Products, Green Border, 48 In. 4500.00
Sign, Miller Tires, Geared To The Road, Blue, White, Porcelain, 2-Sided, 60 x 30 In. 1100.00
Sign, Mobil Regular, Porcelain, 12 x 13 3/4 In. 95.00
Sign, Nash Authorized Service, Shield Shape, Porcelain, 2-Sided, 22 x 36 In. 2640.00
Sign, National Refining Co., Boy, Tin Lithograph, 2-Sided, c.1917, 28 x 45 In. . .2500.00 to 3500.00
Sign, OK Tires, Boy Saluting, OK On Chest, Masonite, Die Cut, 16 x 25 1/4 In. 120.00
Sign, Olixir, Unseen Power, Feel The Difference, Tin Lithograph, 20 x 22 In. 375.00
Sign, Pencoil Motor Oils, Metal, Wood Frame, 14 x 42 In. 198.00
Sign, Polarine Motor Oil, Consult Chart, White, Red, Black, Porcelain, Round, 42 In. 468.00
Sign, Red Crown Gasoline, White, Red, Porcelain, Round, 42 In. 660.00
Sign, Riley Bros. Oil, That's Oil, Yellow, Red, Black, 13 x 5 1/2 In. 90.00
Sign, Scholl's Axle Grease, Independent Oil Co., Red, Tin, 6 1/2 x 6 In. 66.00
Sign, Shell Gasoline, World Experience In Every Gallon, Stamps, Paper, 33 x 58 In. 145.00
Sign, Shell, Bulk Service, Yellow, Red, Porcelain, 18 x 24 In. 385.00
Sign, Shell-Penn Motor Oil, Scallop Shell, Yellow, Red, Porcelain, Die Cut, 30 x 29 In. . . 175.00
Sign, Sico Straight Gas, White, Blue, Porcelain, Round, 36 In. 50.00
Sign, Sinclair Dino Gasoline, Porcelain, 12 x 13 1/2 In. 149.00
Sign, Sinclair H-C Gasoline, Porcelain, 2-Sided, Round, 48 In. 45.00
Sign, Sonic Tires, The Tire Of The Future Today, 16 x 60 In. 70.00
Sign, Sonoco Gas Station, Restrooms, Porcelain, 2-Sided, Iron Bracket, 14 x 22 In. 855.00
Sign, Star Cars, Enameled, Green Background, Center Star, 2-Sided, 37 x 24 In. 450.00
Sign, Sunray D-X Petroleum Products, Octagonal, Porcelain, Orange Ground, 9 x 9 In. 1320.00
Sign, Texaco Fire Chief Gasoline, Porcelain, 1946, 12 x 18 In. . . . . .75.00 to 100.00
Sign, Texaco Fire Chief Gasoline, Porcelain, 1963, 18 x 12 In. 39.00
Sign, Texaco Kerosene, Clear Burning, Red, White, Blue, Tin, 1957, 11 3/4 x 19 3/4 In. . . . 165.00
Sign, Texaco Motor Oil, Free Crankcase Service, Porcelain, 30 x 30 In. 50.00
Sign, Texaco Sea Chief, White, Yellow, Black, Red, Tin, Embossed, 15 x 10 In. 470.00
Sign, Texaco Sky Chief Su-Preme, Petrox, Porcelain, 1962, 12 x 18 In. 110.00
Sign, Texaco Sky Chief, Green, Red, White, Porcelain, 1947, 12 x 18 In. 105.00
Sign, Texaco, Red, Green, White, Black, Leaded Glass, Round, 22 In. 770.00
Sign, Texaco, Texas Company, Petroleum Products, Metal, Round, 8 3/4 In. 110.00
Sign, Tydol Gasoline, Red, White Blue, Porcelain, Round, 42 In. 470.00
Sign, Union 76, Orange, Blue, White, 14 x 74 In. 50.00

Sign, Webaco Oil Co., Credit Cards Honored, White, Red, Black, Tin, Flange, 14 x 20 In. .   39.00
Sign, Weed Chains, For Safe Driving, Dial Price Of Gas, Tin, Wood Frame, 23 x 17 In. ...   1700.00
Sign, Whippet, Dollar For Dollar Value, Willy's Overland, 1920s, 15 x 25 In. .....125.00 to 150.00
Sign, White Star Gasoline, Staroleum, Blue, White, Porcelain, Round, 28 In. 635.00
Sign, Willy's Knight Service, Genuine Parts, Porcelain, Die Cut, 2-Sided, 30 x 40 In. 2320.00
Thermos, Esso, Happy Motoring, Metal 65.00
Tin, Goodrich Tires Repair Outfit, Best In Long Run, Instructions, 1920s, 7 x 3 x 2 In. 60.00
Tin, Hollingshead Axle Oil, Easy Pour Spout, Man & Buggy, Pt., 5 1/2 In. 30.00
Tin, Zit Automobile Dry Wash, Contents, 3 1/2 x 7 1/2 x 2 1/2 In. 35.00
Tire Pump, Brass, Cast Iron, F.E. Meyers & Bro, Patent 1894, 26 In. 95.00
Waste Bucket, Texaco, Cast Iron, Steel, 1942, 18 In. 35.00
Weather Vane, Mobil Pegasus, Cast Copper, Porcelain Die Cut Pegasus, 32 x 21 In. 4400.00

AUTUMN LEAF pattern china was made for the Jewel Tea Company
beginning in 1933. Hall China Company of East Liverpool, Ohio,
Crooksville China Company of Crooksville, Ohio, Harker Potteries of
Chester, West Virginia, and Paden City Pottery, Paden City, West
Virginia, made dishes with this design. Autumn Leaf has remained
popular and was made by Hall China Company until 1978. Some other
pieces in the Autumn Leaf pattern are still being made. For more information, see *Kovels' Depression Glass & Dinnerware Price List.*

Baker, Fort Pitt, Oval, 12 Oz. 145.00
Bean Pot, Cover, Handle, 6 1/2 In. 1000.00
Bean Pot, Handle 695.00
Berry Bowl, 5 1/2 In. ....8.00 to 12.00
Bowl, Cereal, 6 1/2 In. 15.00
Bowl, Sunshine, No. 3, 6 In. ....25.00 to 30.00
Bowl, Sunshine, No. 4, 7 1/2 In. 42.00
Bowl, Vegetable, Oval, 2 Sections, 10 1/2 In. 140.00
Bowl, Vegetable, Oval, Ruffled-D, 7 In. 40.00
Bowl Set, Nesting, 1 Qt., 2 Qt., 3 1/2 Qt., 3 Piece 70.00
Butter, Cover, 1/4 Lb. 175.00
Butter, Cover, 1 Lb. ....500.00 to 600.00
Cake Plate, 9 1/2 In. 28.00
Cake Plate, Cover, Holiday Fruit, Metal, Round 10.00
Cake Plate, Cover, Metal, Round, Cover, Paper Label 28.00
Canister, Metal, Plastic Cover 25.00
Casserole, Cover, 2 Handles, 2 Qt. ....30.00 to 35.00
Casserole, Cover, 2 Qt., 8 1/2 In. 70.00
Coffee Dispenser, Metal, Wall Bracket 325.00
Coffeepot, Jewel Best, Metal, West Bend 525.00
Coffeepot, Jordan, China, 4 Piece 350.00
Coffeepot, Percolator, Electric 400.00
Cookie Jar, Big Ear, Eva Ziesel 325.00
Cookie Jar, Tootsie 325.00
Creamer, Footed 20.00
Cup & Saucer, Tea 10.00
Custard Cup, 2 In. ....5.00 to 13.00
Jug, Rayed, 2 1/2 Pt. 7.00
Mustard Set, 3 Piece 125.00
Plate, Bread & Butter, 6 In. 12.00
Plate, Dinner, 9 In. 20.00
Salt & Pepper, Ruffled, 2 1/2 In. 18.00
Saucepan, Cover, Enameled, 2 Qt. 100.00
Saucer 6.00
Shaker, Pepper, 4 1/4 In. 20.00
Syrup, Cover 115.00
Teapot, Aladdin 110.00
Teapot, Newport, 7 1/2 In. 280.00
Tidbit, 3 Tiers 125.00
Tumbler, Frosted Glass, 5 1/2 In. 35.00
Tumbler, Libbey Glass, 6 1/2 In. 45.00
Vase, Bud, Fluted Top, 5 3/4 In. 295.00

AZALEA dinnerware was made for Larkin Company customers from 1918 to 1941. Larkin, the soap company, was in Buffalo, New York. The dishes were made by Noritake China Company of Japan. Each piece of the white china was decorated with pink azaleas.

Bowl, Vegetable, Open Handles	15.00
Bowl, Vegetable, Sections	185.00
Butter Chip, Red Wreath Mark, 3 1/4 In.	53.00
Candy Jar, Cover, 6-Sided, 5 1/8 In.	225.00 to 850.00
Eggcup	40.00
Grapefruit, Footed, 4 1/2 In.	225.00
Pitcher, 5 3/4 In.	125.00
Plate, Salad, 7 3/4 In.	10.00 to 20.00
Platter, 14 In.	20.00
Relish, 4 Sections	100.00
Salt & Pepper	23.00
Sugar & Creamer	190.00
Sugar Shaker	65.00
Teapot	75.00
Tureen, Soup, Cover	130.00
Vase, Fan, 5 3/4 In.	185.00

BACCARAT glass was made in France by La Compagnie des Cristalleries de Baccarat, located 150 miles from Paris. The factory was started in 1765. The firm went bankrupt and began operating again about 1822. Cane and millefiori paperweights were made during the 1860 to 1880 period. The firm is still working near Paris making paperweights and glasswares.

Candelabrum, 3-Light, Clear, Amber, Cranberry, 23 1/2 In.	360.00
Candelabrum, 3-Light, Molded, Frosted, Figural, 21 1/2 In., Pair	2530.00
Candlestick, Dolphin, Prisms, Signed, 13 3/4 x 6 7/8 In., Pair	840.00
Cordial, Flute Shape, 5 In., 4 Piece	90.00
Decanter, Panels, Flared Body, Stopper, Signed, 9 In.	230.00
Figurine, Dachshund, 1900s, 6 In.	100.00
Figurine, Dog, Seated, Deco Style, Signed, 7 1/8 x 3 3/4 x 1 3/4 In.	85.00
Figurine, Poodle, Standing, 5 1/4 x 4 3/4 In.	160.00
Goblet, Paneled, 6-Sided Bowl & Foot, Hexagonal Base, 6 1/4 In., 8 Piece	300.00
Knife Rest, Rectangular, Box, 12 Piece	250.00
Paperweight, Buttercup, Turquoise, White, Garland, Red & White Canes, c.1850	2185.00
Paperweight, Choufuer, Canes, Cauliflower Ground, Signed, 1848, 3 In.	11500.00
Paperweight, Garlands, Interlacing Canes, White & Red Ground, c.1850, 3 1/3 In.	1840.00
Paperweight, Macedoine, Colored Twist Canes, 2 3/8 In.	290.00
Paperweight, Multicolor Garlands, White Lace & Vaseline Ground, 1971, 3 3/8 In.	175.00
Paperweight, Mushroom, Millefiori, Blue & White Torsade Ground, 2 3/4 In.	1300.00
Paperweight, Pansy, Purple, Blue, Yellow, Honeycomb Center, c.1850, 3 1/8 In.	1840.00

Baccarat, Paperweight, Sulphide, Hunter, Dog, Ruby Ground, Faceted, 3 3/8 In.

Be careful about displaying paperweights or other heavy objects on glass shelves. It may seem safe for years, but a slight jar from a slamming door may be enough to cause the glass to crack.

Paperweight, Red Rose, Pansy, White Double Clematis, Faceted, Star Cut Base, c.1850 .. 7188.00
Paperweight, Rose, Deep Red, Star Cut Base, c.1850, 3 In. 3355.00
Paperweight, Silhouette Canes, Monkeys, Blue Carpet Ground, 3 1/8 In. 650.00
Paperweight, Silhouette Canes, Pelicans, Concentric Millefiori, 1974, 3 1/8 In. 700.00
Paperweight, Silhouette Canes, Rooster, Dog, Pheasant, Horse, Deer, Roses, 2 13/16 In. .. 1900.00
Paperweight, Silhouette Canes, Squirrel Millefiori Rings, No. 1145, Signed, 1972 . . . . . . 520.00
Paperweight, Silhouette Canes, Stork, 6 Circular Millefiori Garlands, 3 1/4 In. 550.00
Paperweight, Silhouette Canes, Zodiac, Yellow Carpet Ground, Signed, 1969 . . . . 520.00
Paperweight, Snake, Coiled, Green, Muslin Ground, Faceted, c.1850, 3 In. 3165.00
Paperweight, Snake, Coiled, Pink, Green Markings, Muslin Ground, c.1850, 3 1/8 In. . . . 7480.00
Paperweight, Strawberry, 2 Ripe Berries, 3 Leaf Clusters, c.1850, 2 1/4 In. 690.00
Paperweight, Sulphide, Hunter, Dog, Ruby Ground, Faceted, 3 3/8 In. . . . . *Illus* 5225.00
Paperweight, Sulphide, Joan Of Arc, Green Ground, Faceted, c.1850, 3 1/2 In. 1380.00
Paperweight, Sulphide, Madonna, Red Ground, Faceted, c.1850, 3 1/2 In. 805.00
Paperweight, Sulphide, Pope Pius IX, 19th Century, 8 5/8 In. 405.00
Paperweight, Triple Blue & White Bellflowers, Bud, Star Cut Base, c.1850, 2 3/4 In. 6785.00
Paperweight, Wedding Bouquet, White Star Canes, Blue, White Arrowhead, c.1850 . . . . . 10925.00
Pitcher, Rose Teinte Swirl, Round Mouth, Clear Applied Handle, 9 1/4 In. 265.00

BADGES have been used since before the Civil War. Collectors search
for examples of all types, including law enforcement and company
identification badges. Well-known prison or law enforcement badges
are most desirable. Most are made of nickel or brass. Many recent
reproductions have been made.

Air Police, Patrolman, Dover Air Force Base, USAF 150.00
Captain, Department Of Corrections, Goldtone, Pinback, New Jersey, 3 x 1 3/4 In. 52.00
Customs Special Agent, Retired, Blue Enamel, Gold Color, Bag, U.S., 1 3/4 x 2 1/2 In. . . 320.00
Deputy, U.S. Marshal, S.D.O., Shield Shape, Eagle, Nickel, Pinback, 2 x 2 3/4 In. 1725.00
Deputy Game Protectory, Nickel, Enameled Center Crest, Pennsylvania 190.00
Firefighting, Elliot Hose, 15, Crossed Trumpets & Helmet, Silver 45.00
Firefighting, Shield Shape, ST, Allentown Fire Department, 14-172, 2 1/8 In. 69.00
Firefighting, Silver, Keystone, Wagon Top Bar, C.O. Defender Reading, Pa., 1856, 2 Piece 290.00
Firefighting, ST, Fire Panoply Center, Steamer Co. No. 1, Washington, N.J., 2 1/8 In. 60.00
Firefighting, ST, Montgomery, 1-1847, Cutout Center, GT No. 1, 2 Piece 180.00
Paramedic, Ballard's Ambulance, Chula Vista, Goldtone Finish, Enamel Details, 3 1/4 In. 30.00
Police, Hartford, Shield Shape, No. 98, TM Parker, Custom Die 300.00
Police, Washington DC Metro, Silvertone, Capitol Building, 2 1/2 x 2 3/4 In. 50.00
Police Deputy Inspector, Coat Of Arms, Gold Finish, New York City, 2 1/4 x 1 3/4 In. . . . 170.00
Police Officer, Goldtone, Red Enamel, Pinback, Locking Clasp, Soviet, 2 7/8 x 2 1/2 In. . . . 50.00
Security Services, Wells Fargo, Pinback, Gold Color, Eagle At Top, Blue Enamel, 3 In. . . 30.00
Special Police, Detroit, Pierced Center Star, Number, Pinback, Silvered Finish, 2 3/4 In. .. 30.00
U.S. Capitol Police, Shield Shape, CD Reese, 122 Nassau St., N.Y. 400.00
U.S. Customs Special Agent, Retired, Enamel, Gold Color, Bag, 1 3/4 x 2 1/2 In. 250.00

BANKS of metal have been made since 1868. There are still banks,
mechanical banks, and registering banks (those that show the total
money deposited on the face of the bank). Many old iron or tin banks
have been reproduced since the 1950s in iron or plastic. Some old
reproductions marked Book of Knowledge or John Wright, or Capron
are listed. Pottery, glass, and plastic banks are also listed here. Mickey
Mouse and other Disneyana banks are listed in Disneyana. We have
added the M-numbers based on *The Penny Bank Book: Collected Still
Banks* by Andy and Susan Moore and the R numbers based on *Coin
Banks by Banthrico* by James L. Redwine.

A&P Food Stores, Glass, Vial, Dimes, 100th Anniversary, 1959, 3 3/4 In. 20.00
Acey Chicken, Artic Circle Drive-In Restaurant, Ceramic, 1964 . . . . 75.00
Alphabet, Blocks, Cast Iron, M 1064, 3 1/2 In. 1100.00
Andy Gump, Seated, Reading Newspaper, Painted, Iron, Arcade, M 217, 4 1/2 In. 935.00
Andy Gump, Thrift Bank, Save A Little, Have A Lot, Tin, M 218, 4 3/8 In. . . . . . . .240.00 to 265.00
Apple, Cast Iron, Painted, Kyser & Rex, 1882, M 1621, 5 1/2 In. 253.00
Bank, State Bank, Cast Iron, M 1633, 5 In. 176.00
Bank, State Bank, Mansard Roof, Cast Iron, Copper, Gold, 6 x 4 1/2 x 3 1/2 In. 100.00
Bank Building, Caisse, Lead, 6 1/2 In. 275.00

Bank, Bank Building, Quadrafoil,
Cast Iron, M 1003, 3 1/8 In.

**Reproduction cast-iron toys and banks
are heavier and thicker than originals.**

**To clean lithographed tin banks, try using
Sani Wax and 0000-grade steel wool, but
use with extreme caution.**

Bank Building, Columbia, Cast Iron, Kenton, c.1904, M 1077, 7 x 5 1/4 x 5 1/4 In. 188.00
Bank Building, Continental Bank, White Metal, Banthrico, R 971, 5 1/4 In. 72.00
Bank Building, Crown Bank, Japanned Cast Iron, J. & E. Stevens, M 1226, 3 1/2 In. 165.00
Bank Building, Crown Bank, On Legs, Cast Iron, M 1150, 4 5/8 In. 1045.00
Bank Building, Cupola Bank, Cast Iron, J. & E. Stevens, M 1145, 5 1/2 In. 440.00
Bank Building, Eagle Finial, Cast Iron, Painted, M 1134, 9 1/2 In. 1210.00
Bank Building, First Federal Saving Of Chicago, White Metal, Glass, Banthrico, 7 1/8 In. 110.00
Bank Building, Ford City Bank, White Metal, Banthrico, R 623, 3 3/4 In. 82.00
Bank Building, Glõbe Savings, Cast Iron, Painted, Kyser & Rex, M 1199, 7 In. . .715.00 to 1870.00
Bank Building, Home Bank, Cast Iron, H.L. Judd, M 1019, 4 In. 451.00
Bank Building, Home Savings, Dog Finial, Iron, Gold Trim, J. & E. Stevens, M 1237, 5 In. 132.00
Bank Building, Lawn Savings, White Metal, Banthrico, R 646, 3 1/8 In. 22.00
Bank Building, Minot Federal Savings, White Metal, Banthrico, R 661, 2 1/2 In. 193.00
Bank Building, Northwestern National, White Metal, Banthrico, R 737, 6 7/8 In. 17.00
Bank Building, Peoples' United States Bank, St. Louis, Pot Metal, Tin, 6 x 9 In. 605.00
Bank Building, Quadrafoil, Cast Iron, M 1003, 3 1/8 In. . . . . *Illus* 44.00
Baseball On Bat Tripod, Cast Iron, Nickel Plated, Hubley, M 1608, 5 1/4 In. 2200.00
Baseball Player, Cast Iron, Blue, Red, Flesh Tone Paint, A.C. Williams, M 19, 5 3/4 In. . . 303.00
Bear, Mother & Baby, Ceramic, 4 1/2 In. 22.00
Bear, Standing On Hind Legs, Cast Iron, Hubley, M 693, 5 1/2 In. 138.00
Bear, With Arms Folded, Seated, Lead, Continental, M 697, 3 13/16 In. 715.00
Bear Stealing Pig, Cast Iron, Painted, 5 1/2 In. 358.00
Beehive, Cast Iron, Painted, Industry Shall Be Rewarded, John Harper, M 686, 4 1/2 In. . . 440.00
Bell, Washington Silhouette, Cast Iron, Grey Iron Casting, M 784, 3 3/4 In. 11.00
Best Western, Black Top Hat, Shoes, Ceramic, Round 50.00
Big Boy, Head Slot, Soft Vinyl, 9 In. 45.00
Birdhouse On Legs, Silvered Lead, Germany, M 653, 4 1/8 In. 61.00
Boat, Battleship Indiana, Cast Iron, White, Green, Red, J. & E. Stevens, 10 In. 1820.00
Boat, Battleship Maine, Painted, Iron, Gold Trim, Grey Iron Casting, M 1440, 4 3/4 In. . . 358.00
Boat, Battleship Oregon, Cast Iron, J. & E. Stevens, M 1454, 5 In. 330.00
Boat, Steamboat, Cast Iron, Gold, Red, A.C. Williams, c.1920, M 1459, 2 1/2 x 7 1/2 In. . . 259.00
Book, Babes In The Woods, Tin, 5 5/8 In. 94.00
Book, Boulevard Bridge Bank Of Chicago, Cloth Covered Brass, Box, 6 In. 66.00
Book, Drop In Your Change For A Victrola, Steel, 4 1/8 In. 116.00
Book, Old King Cole, Humpty Dumpty, Vinyl, Brass, 4 3/4 In. 204.00
Building, 1876, Cast Iron, M 1011, 3 3/8 In. 28.00
Building, Arsenal Savings & Loan, White Metal, Banthrico, R 532, 3 1/8 In. 120.00
Building, Church, 1882, Painted Cast Iron, Kyser & Rex, M 959, 5 1/2 In. 110.00
Building, Church, Square Trap, Lithographed Tin, Chein, 1930s, 4 In. 95.00
Building, Columbia, Cast Iron, Kenton, M 1073, 8 3/4 In. 1815.00
Building, Cottage With Porch, Cast Iron, Painted, Grey Iron Casting, M 999, 4 In. 231.00
Building, Cottage, Chimney, Painted, Stenciled, Tin, George W. Brown, M 1035, 6 1/4 In. 413.00
Building, Eiffel Tower, Cast Iron, Robert Brown, Wales, M 1076, 8 1/2 In. 22.00
Building, Flat Iron Building, Cast Iron, Painted, Raised Letters, Kenton, M 1160, 6 In. . . . 413.00
Building, Hansel & Gretel House, Embossed, Tin Lithograph, Stollwerck, M 1016, 2 In. . . 28.00
Building, Independence Hall Tower, Cast Iron, Enterprise, 1876, M 1202, 9 3/4 In. 330.00

Building, Ives Palace, Trap, Key, Japanned Cast Iron, Painted, Ives, 1885, M 1116, 8 In. . . . 1265.00
Building, Litchfield Cathedral, Cast Iron, Chamberlain & Hill, M 969, 6 5/8 In. 253.00
Building, Log Cabin, Cast Iron, Kyser & Rex, M 1023, 2 1/2 In. . . . . .330.00 to 418.00
Building, Osceola County Courthouse, White Metal, R 987, 5 5/8 In. 55.00
Building, Palace, Cast Iron, Painted, Ives, 1885, M 116, 7 1/2 In. 770.00
Building, Skyscraper, 6 Gold Posts, Iron, Silver Paint, A.C. Williams, M 1241, 6 1/2 x 4 In. 303.00
Building, Tower Federal Savings, White Metal, Banthrico, R 744, 5 7/8 In. 22.00
Building, Tower, Cast Iron, Kenton, M 1173, 4 1/8 In. 308.00
Building, Tower, Japanned Cast Iron, John Harper, M 1208, 9 1/4 In. . . . . .303.00 to 341.00
Building, Villa, Japanned Cast Iron, Kyser & Rex, M 1179, 5 1/4 In. 154.00
Bullet, Preparedness, Steel, Harmo Electric, M 1408, 6 1/16 In. 33.00
Cadet, Cast Iron, Painted, Hubley, M 8, 5 3/4 In. 1760.00
Cakewalker, Black Dandy, Coin Slot In Hat, Hand Painted, 1880s, 3 1/2 In. 220.00
Calumet, Tin & Paper Lithograph, 5 1/2 In. 90.00
Camel, Cast Iron, A.C. Williams, M 767, 7 1/4 In. . . . . .125.00 to 259.00
Captain Kidd, Cast Iron, M 38, 4 1/4 In. 161.00
Car, Buick, 1953, White Metal, R 359, 8 In. 333.00
Car, Chevrolet, 1950, White Metal, Banthrico, R 366, 7 5/8 In. . . . .·. . . 198.00
Car, DeSoto, 1949, White Metal, Banthrico, R 379, 8 In. 116.00
Car, Dodge, 1951, White Metal, Banthrico, R 381, 8 In. 132.00
Car, Dodge, 1954, White Metal, Banthrico, R 383, 8 In. 143.00
Car, Ford, Model A, Touring, Arcade, 1923 . . . . 2500.00
Car, Ford, Model T, Cast Iron, M 1483, 4 In. 1430.00
Car, Pontiac, 1949, White Metal, R 406, 8 1/8 In. 116.00
Cash Register, Junior, Cast Iron, Nickeled, J. & E. Stevens, M 930, 4 1/4 In. 385.00
Cat, Head, Ceramic, M 398, 3 In. 110.00
Cat, Kitty, Painted, Cast Iron, Hubley, M 349, 4 3/4 In. 107.00
Cat, With Ball, Painted, Cast Iron, M 353, 5 1/2 In. . . . . .193.00 to 489.00
Chief Wahoo, Cleveland Indians, Stanford Pottery, Red, White, Gold Tooth, 1948, 8 In. . . . 410.00
Citizens Bank, White Metal, 4 3/4 In. 28.00
Clock, C.C. Harvey & Co. Pianos, 6 In. 132.00
Clock, Hall, Cast Iron, Tin, Painted, Paper Face, Hubley, M 1534, 5 1/4 In. 253.00
Clown, Crooked Hat, Cast Iron, Painted, M 210, 7 In. 605.00
Cow, Cast Iron, A.C. Williams, M 553, 3 3/8 In. 242.00
Curtis Candy, Plastic, Metal, 5 Cents, Marx Toy Co., 3 3/8 x 2 1/8 x 7 3/8 In. 40.00
Cylinder, Cats & Dogs, Silvered Brass, 2 1/4 In. 39.00
Daikoku, God Of Wealth, Lead, Japan, M 68, 6 In. 583.00
Desk, Roll-Top, Tin, 4 1/4 In. 66.00
Dog, Boston Bull Terrier, Cast Iron, Painted, Vindex, M 421, 5 1/2 In. 110.00
Dog, Boston Bulldog, Seated, Cast Iron, Hubley, M 413, 4 3/8 In. . . . . .193.00 to 220.00
Dog, Boxer, Cast Iron, M 357, 4 1/2 In. 110.00
Dog, Labrador Retriever, Cast Iron, Banthrico, M 412, 4 1/2 In. 748.00
Dog, Newfoundland, Cast Iron, Arcade, M 440, 5 1/4 In. . . . . .39.00 to 196.00
Dog, Reclining, With Blanket, Ceramic, 3 1/2 In. 94.00
Dog, St. Bernard, Pack, Front Paw Lifted, Iron, A.C. Williams, M 437, 5 1/2 In. . . . . .62.00 to 99.00
Donkey, Shenandoah Caverns, Virginia, White Metal, 5 1/2 In. 154.00
Donkey, White Metal, Hampton Beach, 4 In. 55.00
Duck, On Tub, Cast Iron, Painted, Hubley, M 616, 5 1/4 In. 121.00
Duck, Squawking, Lead, M 645, 4 1/4 In. 121.00
Dutch Boy, Standing, Cast Iron, M 17, 6 3/4 In. 198.00
Dutch Girl, Flowers, Cast Iron, Hubley, M 181, 5 1/4 In. . . . . .39.00 to 121.00
Edison Bank, White Metal, Banthrico, R 14, 5 3/4 In. 6.60
Elephant, Howdah, Cast Iron, A.C. Williams, M 474, 4 7/8 In. 77.00
Elephant, Howdah, Short Trunk, Cast Iron, Hubley, M 1630, 3 3/4 In. 429.00
Elephant, On Wheels, Cast Iron, A.C. Williams, M 446, 4 1/8 In. 957.00
Ever-Ready Blades, Tin, 1 3/4 x 2 x 1 In. 25.00
Fala, Cast Iron, M 430, 2 3/4 In. 253.00
Farmers & Merchants State Bank, New Ulm, Minn., House, Plastic, Metal, 4 x 3 x 3 In. . . 60.00
Fez, String Tassel, White Metal, M 1393, 3 1/8 In. 66.00
Fidelity Trust Vault, Cast Iron, J. Barton Smith, M 903, 6 1/2 In. 143.00
Fido, On Pillow, Cast Iron, Painted, Hubley, M 443, 6 In. 132.00
Fifth Northwestern National, White Metal, Banthrico, R 737, 6 7/8 In. 83.00
Fire Pumper Truck, Cast Iron, 5 1/2 In. 160.00

Fishing Creel, Ceramic, 2 1/2 In. 72.00
Football Player Holding Football Over Head, Red, Silver, Cast Iron, Hubley, M 10, 5 In.   700.00
Fort, Cast Iron, Electroplate Finish, Kenton, M 1172, 4 1/4 In. 275.00
Four Tower, Cast Iron, J. & E. Stevens, c.1895, M 1121, 5 3/4 In. 176.00
Foxy Grandpa, Cast Iron, M 320, 5 1/2 In. .... .45.00 to 154.00
Freedom 7 Space Capsule, Plastic, Silver, State Mutual Savings, Los Angeles, 1961, 5 In.   104.00
General Benjamin Butler, Iron, Painted, 1884, J. & E. Stevens, M 54, 6 1/2 In. . .935.00 to 2090.00
George Washington Bust, Prudential Insurance Co., White Metal Cast, 6 In. 143.00
George Washington Standing, Cast Iron, M 138, 6 1/2 In. 132.00
Globe, Claw & Ball Feet, Silver Color, Cast Iron, M 810, 5 In. 715.00
Globe On Wire Arc, Cast Iron, Gold Paint, Arcade, M 785, 4 5/8 In. 303.00
Golliwog, Cast Aluminum, John Harper, M 86, 6 In. 150.00
Goose, Cast Iron, Arcade, M 614, 3 3/4 In. 84.00
Gorilla, Seated, White Metal, M 744, 4 1/4 In. 99.00
Graf Zeppelin, Cast Iron, A.C. Williams, M 1428, 1 3/4 In. .... .99.00 to 143.00
Grandfather Clock, Indian Head National Bank, White Metal Cast, 7 1/2 In. 77.00
Hangar, Goodyear Zeppelin Hangar, Aluminum, Ferrosteel, M 1430, 2 5/16 In. 352.00
Hen & Chicks, Base, Silvered Brass, Stone, 3 5/8 In. 310.00
Hen On Nest, Cast Iron, Painted, M 546, 3 In. 880.00
Horse, Beauty, Prancing Horse On Oval Base, Cast Iron, M 514, 4 3/4 In. 286.00
Horse On Tub, Cast Iron, Black Paint, Orange Blanket, A.C. Williams, M 509, 5 1/2 In. . . 165.00
Ice Cream Freezer, North Pole, Iron, Grey Iron Casting, Semimechanical, M 1371, 4 In. .   475.00
Independence Hall, Cast Iron, M 1211, 6 3/8 In. 1210.00
Indian, With Tomahawk, Hand At Forehead, Cast Iron, Hubley, M 228, 6 In. . . . ...124.00 to 495.00
Indian Chief, Ancostia Federal, Bronzed Metal, Washington, D.C., Banthrico, R 27, 5 In. .   54.00
Indian Head, Headdress, Tassels, China, 4 x 2 3/4 In. 75.00
Indian In Headdress, Bust, Lead, M 221, 3 1/2 In. 231.00
Jiggs, Cigar In Mouth, Pottery, Brown, Glazed, 5 In. 220.00
Li'l Abner, Can O' Coins, Tin, 4 3/8 In. 40.00
Liberty Penny Bank, Tin Lithograph, Abraham Lincoln, Girard, 5 1/2 In. 44.00
Lion, Harris Trust & Savings Bank, White Metal, 5 x 6 In. 75.00
Lion, Tail Right, Cast Iron, Electroplated, A.C. Williams, M 755, 4 In. .... .17.00 to 39.00
Little Thrifty, Ceramic, 5 1/8 In. 77.00
Lucky Joe, Nash-Underwood Prepared Mustard, Glass, Tin, Screw-On Lid, 4 1/2 In. .56.00 to 67.00
MacArthur, Molded Composition, Save For Our Victory, 5 In. 100.00
Mailbox, U.S. Mail, On Legs, Green, Yellow, Cast Iron, Hubley, M 842, 3 3/4 In. 35.00
Main Street Trolley, Passengers, Cast Iron, Painted, A.C. Williams, 6 3/4 In. 198.00
Mammy, Ceramic, 6 1/4 In. 30.00
Mammy With Clothes Basket, Cast Metal, M 175, 5 1/4 In. 140.00
Mary & Little Lamb, Cast Iron, M 164, 4 3/8 In. 400.00

Mechanical banks were first made about 1870. Any bank with moving
parts is considered mechanical. The metal banks made before World
War I are the most desirable. Copies and new designs of mechanical
banks have been made in metal or plastic since the 1920s. The condition of the paint on the old banks is important. Worn paint can lower a
price by 90%.

Mechanical, Acrobat, Cast Iron, J. & E. Stevens, 1883 .... 1430.00
Mechanical, Artillery, Blue Coat, Cast Iron, J. & E. Stevens .... .825.00 to 1320.00
Mechanical, Artillery, Red Coat, Cast Iron, J. & E. Stevens 713.00
Mechanical, Artillery, Union Soldier, Bronze Plated Iron, J. & E. Stevens, 1892, 8 In. 1455.00
Mechanical, Bank Teller, Door Opens To Reveal Teller, Cast Iron, 4 1/2 In. 420.00
Mechanical, Boy On Trapeze, Red Shirt, Blue Pants, J. Barton, Smith, c.1891 .... 24200.00
Mechanical, Boy Robbing Bird's Nest, J. & E. Stevens, 1906 .... 9487.00
Mechanical, Boys Stealing Watermelons, Dog Chases, Iron, Kyser & Rex, 6 1/2 In. 1500.00
Mechanical, Breadwinners, Honest Labor, Painted, Cast Iron, Bailey & J. & E. Stevens .. 4400.00
Mechanical, Bulldog, Man, Japanned Cast Iron, Clockwork, Ives, 1878 .... 5170.00
Mechanical, Butting Buffalo, Lifts Head To Butt Black Boy, 1950s, 7 1/2 In. 125.00
Mechanical, Cabin, Yellow, Black Figure, Cast Iron, J. & E. Stevens ....330.00 to 805.00
Mechanical, Calumet, Paper Covered, Cardboard, Nodding Face, 5 3/4 In. 88.00
Mechanical, Chimpanzee, Cast Iron, Second Casting, Kyser & Rex 605.00
Mechanical, Clown On Globe Spins, Iron, Yellow, J. & E. Stevens, 9 In. ....2090.00 to 7425.00
Mechanical, Clown On Globe, Cast Iron, Tan Base, J. & E. Stevens ....1250.00 to 1350.00

Mechanical, Clown, Cast Aluminum, Starkie 275.00
Mechanical, Clown, Chein, Signed, Gene Bosch, 5 In. 210.00
Mechanical, Clown, Pot Belly, Eats Coins, Belly Grows, China, Box, 10 1/2 In. 17.00
Mechanical, Columbus & The Indian, 8 x 3 1/4 x 6 1/4 In. 345.00
Mechanical, Confectionery, Girl, At Counter, Cast Iron, Kyser & Rex, 1881 .... 5170.00
Mechanical, Creedmoor, Man Shooting Rifle At Target, J. & E. Stevens, 1877 .... 375.00 to 660.00
Mechanical, Darktown Battery, Baseball, Iron, Painted, J. & E. Stevens, 1888, 9 3/4 In. .. 1540.00
Mechanical, Dinah, Black Woman, Yellow Shirt, Cast Iron, John Harper .... 275.00 to 303.00
Mechanical, Dog On Turntable, Cast Iron, H.L. Judd 358.00
Mechanical, Eagle & Eaglets, Cast Iron, J. & E. Stevens, 1888, 6 3/4 In. .... 588.00 to 1265.00
Mechanical, Elephant & 3 Clowns, Cast Iron, J. & E. Stevens, 1882 .... 935.00
Mechanical, Elephant & Locked Howdah, Cast Iron, Gurney Refrigerator Co. 2750.00
Mechanical, Elephant, 3 Stars, Cast Iron, c.1884 .... 275.00
Mechanical, Elephant, Moves Trunk, Cast Iron, A.C. Williams, 4 3/4 In. .... 66.00 to 72.00
Mechanical, Football, Player Kicks Coin, Cast Iron, John Harper, 1895 .... 1210.00
Mechanical, Frog On Rock, Green, Yellow, Brown, Cast Iron, Kilgore 770.00
Mechanical, Frog On Round Lattice Base, Cast Iron, J. & E. Stevens .... 495.00 to 1500.00
Mechanical, Frogs, Small & Large Frogs, Cast Iron, 8 1/2 In. .... 468.00 to 825.00
Mechanical, Girl In Victorian Chair, Cast Iron, c.1880 .... 3465.00
Mechanical, Grenadier, Cast Iron, John Harper, c.1885 .... 303.00
Mechanical, Hall's Excelsior, Iron, Cashier, J. & E. Stevens, 6 In. .... 248.00 to 385.00
Mechanical, Hall's Excelsior, Red, White, Cast Iron, Wood, J. & E. Stevens, 6 In. 440.00
Mechanical, Hall's Liliput, Cast Iron, J. & E. Stevens 770.00
Mechanical, Hoop-La, Clown, Dog, Barrel, Yellow, White, Brown, Cast Iron, John Harper 660.00
Mechanical, Humpty Dumpty, Shepard Hardware, Shepard & Adams, 1884 Patent 440.00
Mechanical, I Always Did 'Spise A Mule, Boy, Cast Iron, J. & E. Stevens, 1879, 10 In. .. 523.00
Mechanical, Indian Shooting Bear, Cast Iron, J. & E. Stevens, 1883 .... 770.00 to 2530.00
Mechanical, Initiating, Man, Goat, Frog, Cast Iron, Mechanical Novelty Works, 1880 .... 550.00
Mechanical, Jitney, Balloon Tire Wheel Turns, Tin, TMC, c.1925, 5 In. 135.00
Mechanical, Jolly Nigger, Butterfly Tie, Cast Iron, John Harper 220.00
Mechanical, Jolly Nigger, England, 6 1/2 x 5 1/2 In. 550.00
Mechanical, Jolly Nigger, Red Shirt, Original Paint, Cast Iron, J. & E. Stevens, 4 3/4 In. ... 1763.00
Mechanical, Jolly Nigger, Top Hat, Large, Cast Iron 248.00
Mechanical, Jolly Nigger, Top Hat, Small, Cast Iron 165.00
Mechanical, Jonah & Whale, Cast Iron, Shepard Hardware, 1890 .... 1430.00 to 2000.00
Mechanical, Key, Copper Flashed Cast Iron, 5 3/4 In. 413.00
Mechanical, Kiltie, Cast Iron, John Harper, 1931 .... 605.00
Mechanical, Leap Frog, Shepard Hardware, Cast Iron, Peter Adams, 1891 .... 3300.00
Mechanical, Lion & 2 Monkeys, Cast Iron, Kyser & Rex, 1883, 9 In. .... 523.00 to 550.00
Mechanical, Little Joe, Cast Iron, John Harper, c.1924 .... 358.00
Mechanical, Magician, Coin Disappears Under Hat, Cast Iron, J. & E. Stevens, 8 In. 990.00
Mechanical, Mason, Cast Iron, Brick Layer & Carrier, Shepard Hardware, 1887 .... 4000.00
Mechanical, Memorial Money Bank, Cast Iron, Liberty Bell, Enterprise, 1875 .... 297.00
Mechanical, Monkey & Organ Grinder, Cast Iron, Hubley, 1925, 8 7/8 In. ....121.00 to 297.00
Mechanical, Monkey, With Tray, Raises Arms, Opens Mouth, Tin, Germany, 1908 ...... 450.00
Mechanical, Mule Entering Barn, Cast Iron, J. & E. Stevens, 1880 .... 900.00 to 1400.00
Mechanical, New Creedmoor, Cast Iron, J. & E. Stevens, 1877 .... 405.00 to 605.00
Mechanical, North Pole, Cast Iron, Second Casting, J. & E. Stevens 1210.00
Mechanical, Novelty Bank, Door, Teller, J. & E. Stevens, 1872, 6 3/4 x 4 1/4 In. .863.00 to 1571.00
Mechanical, Octagonal Fort, Cannon, Black, Red, Green, White, Brown, Cast Iron 825.00
Mechanical, Organ Bank, Boy & Girl, Cast Iron, Kyser & Rex, 1882 .... 1100.00
Mechanical, Organ Bank, Cat & Dog, Cast Iron, Kyser & Rex, 1882 .... 633.00 to 750.00
Mechanical, Organ Bank, Miniature, Cast Iron, Kyser & Rex, 1881 .... 468.00
Mechanical, Owl, Turns Head, Cast Iron, J. & E. Stevens, 1880, 3 7/8 In. .... 220.00 to 460.00
Mechanical, Paddy & Pig, Cast Iron, J. & E. Stevens, 1882 .... 935.00
Mechanical, Patronize The Blind, Man, Dog, Cast Iron, J. & E. Stevens, 1878 .... 2530.00
Mechanical, Peg-Leg Beggar, Cast Iron, H.L. Judd 495.00
Mechanical, Penny Pineapple, Cast Iron, July 4, 1960, Hawaii's Statehood, 8 1/2 In. 132.00
Mechanical, Pig In Highchair, Nickel Plated, Cast Iron, J. & E. Stevens 605.00
Mechanical, Pistol, Dime, Combination Lock, Elliot, Box, 1909 Patent, 6 1/2 In. 385.00
Mechanical, Postman, Puts Coin Through Letter Box, Tin, England, 1927 .... 450.00
Mechanical, Presto, Cast Iron, Building, Trick Drawer, Kyser & Rex 286.00
Mechanical, Punch & Judy, Book Of Knowledge, 7 1/4 In. 84.00

Mechanical, Punch & Judy, Iron, Large Letters, Pat. July 22, 1884, Shepard Hardware, 6 In. 5581.00
Mechanical, Rabbit, Standing, Cast Iron, Ears Move, Lockwood, Large 418.00
Mechanical, Reclining Chinaman, Cast Iron, J. & E. Stevens, 5 In. 5060.00
Mechanical, Red Riding Hood, Vending, Tin Lithograph, Stollwerck, 6 1/2 In. 165.00
Mechanical, Rooster, Lever Opens Mouth, Cast Iron, Kyser & Rex, 6 1/4 In. . . . .330.00 to 495.00
Mechanical, Santa Claus, By Chimney, Cast Iron, c.1889, Shepard Hardware 1540.00
Mechanical, Seaman, Wheel, Pot Metal, Pilot Life Insurance Co., Banthrico, R 886, 6 In. . 73.00
Mechanical, Shoot The Chute, Bronze, Boat, Figures, J. & E. Stevens, 9 1/2 In. . .770.00 to 1650.00
Mechanical, Signal Cabin, Tin Lithograph, Distler, 5 3/4 In. 193.00
Mechanical, Southern Comfort, Man Shoots Coin Into Bottle, Cast Metal, 8 1/2 In. .50.00 to 121.00
Mechanical, Speaking Dog, Cast Iron, Base, Shepard Hardware, 7 1/2 x 7 In. . . . . .550.00 to 690.00
Mechanical, Speaking Girl, Sitting Girl, Blue Dress, J. & E. Stevens 1375.00
Mechanical, Stollwerck Post Savings, Vends Chocolate, Tin Lithograph, Glass, 6 1/2 In. . . 193.00
Mechanical, Stump Speaker, Cast Iron, Shepard Hardware, Patented 1886 . . . . . .633.00 to 1265.00
Mechanical, Tabby, Cast Iron, Cat On Egg 358.00
Mechanical, Tammany, Book Of Knowledge, Cast Iron, 5 1/2 In. 62.00
Mechanical, Tammany, Gray, Black, Sliding Trap, Iron, J. & E. Stevens, 4 7/16 In. 646.00
Mechanical, Tank & Cannon, Cast Iron, Patent 122123, Brown, Green, Red, Starkie 1100.00
Mechanical, Teddy & The Bear, Cast Iron, J. & E. Stevens, 10 In. . . . . .805.00 to 3300.00
Mechanical, Toad On Stump, Black, Green, Brown, Iron, J. & E. Stevens, 4 In. . . .660.00 to 825.00
Mechanical, Trick Dog, Clown & Hoop, Barrel, 6-Part Base, Cast Iron, Hubley 3410.00
Mechanical, Trick Pony, Iron, Shepard Hardware, Pat. 1885, 8 In. . . . . .605.00 to 1540.00
Mechanical, U.S. & Spain, Cast Iron, J. & E. Stevens, 1898 . . . . 1350.00
Mechanical, Uncle Remus, White Policeman, Black Chicken Thief, 1950s, 7 1/2 In. 160.00
Mechanical, Uncle Sam, With Satchel, Cast Iron, Shepard Hardware . . . . .1045.00 to 4675.00
Mechanical, Watch Dog Safe, Combination Dial, Cast Iron, J. & E. Stevens, 1890s 330.00
Mechanical, Weeden's Plantation Darky Savings, Tin, 1890s 1250.00
Mechanical, William Tell, Cast Iron, J. & E. Stevens, 10 1/2 In. . . . . .770.00 to 1265.00
Mechanical, World's Fair, Columbus & Indian, Cast Iron, J. & E. Stevens 825.00
Mercury Project Space Capsule, Plastic, Gold, Independent Bank, c.1965, 5 In. 104.00
Middy, Boy, Cast Iron, 1887, M 36, 5 1/2 In. 240.00
Monkey, Playing Accordion, Lead, 4 3/4 In. 330.00
Monkey, Seated, With Pineapple, Ceramic, 4 1/4 In. 33.00
Mourner's Purse, Lead, M 949, 5 In. 143.00
Mulligan, Policeman, Cast Iron, A.C. Williams, M 177, 5 3/4 In. 308.00
Multiplying, Interior Mirrors, Cast Iron, J. & E. Stevens, M 1184, 6 1/2 In. 715.00
Mutt & Jeff, Cast Iron, A.C. Williams, M 157, 5 In. . . . . .77.00 to 105.00
Nash's Prepared Mustard, Joe Louis, Glass, c.1940, 8 1/2 Oz., 4 1/2 x 2 1/4 In. 30.00
New Revised Encyclopedia, 10 Cents A Day, Bookcase, Tin Lithograph, 5 In. 187.00
Nipper, RCA, Fuzzy Flocking Over Metal, Radio Corp. Coin Trap, 6 1/4 In. 255.00
Old South Church, Cast Iron, Painted, Label, M 990, 9 3/4 In. 3960.00
Olympic Federal, White Metal, Banthrico, R, 678, 3 1/2 In. 72.00
Owl, Cast Iron, Be Wise Save Money, A.C. Williams, M 598, 4 7/8 In. 220.00
Owl, Painted, Cast Iron, Vindex, M 597, 4 1/4 In. 138.00
Pail, White City No. 2, Cast Iron, Nicol, 1893, M 911, 2 5/8 In. . . . . .65.00 to 72.00
Pass A Round The Hat, Cast Iron, M 1380, 2 3/8 In. 22.00
Pig, A Christmas Roast, Embossed Side, Cast Iron, Curled Tail, M 613, 7 In. 55.00
Pig, Bank On Republic, Dressed Pig, On Base, M 330, 7 In. 113.00
Pig, Bow Tie, Jacket, Hat, Arbide Employees Federal Credit Union, Plastic, 5 In. 10.00
Pig, Cast Iron, Buy At Norco & Save, Norco Foundry, Pottstown, Pa., 6 x 3 In. 150.00
Pig, Chittenden Bank, Rubber Stopper, Porcelain, Made In USA, 3 1/2 x 6 1/4 In. 9.00
Pig, Community First, White, Plastic Stopper, 5 1/2 x 3 1/2 In. 5.50
Pig, CoreStates Bank, Blue Logo, Gold Accents, Top Slot, Ceramic 11.00
Pig, Pottery, Blue Glaze On Upper Body, Mottled Brown Base, 4 x 2 In. 124.00
Pig, Seated, Silvered Lead, M 604, 3 1/4 In. 330.00
Pig, Sewer Tile, Brown Glaze, 9 1/2 In. 440.00
Pig, Wise Pig Holding Suitcase, Thrifty, Pink, Cast Iron, Hubley, M 609, 6 5/8 In. .260.00 to 489.00
Pig, With Bow, Nickeled Cast Iron, Shimer Toy Co., 1899, M 606, 5 In. 165.00
Piggy, Scroddleware, 6 1/2 In. 46.00
Pirate, Pistols, On Chest, White Metal, M 341, 6 1/4 In. 132.00
Policeman, Cast Iron, Blue, Arcade, 1920s, M 182, 5 1/2 In. 385.00
Possum, Cast Iron, Gold Paint, Arcade, 1910, M 561, 2 3/8 x 4 3/8 In. 303.00
Prancing Horse, Pebbled Base, Iron, Painted, A.C. Williams, M 521, 6 1/2 In. . . . .28.00 to 83.00

Princess Elizabeth, Tin, 5 3/8 In. 363.00
Professor Pug Frog, Cast Iron, Painted, A.C. Williams, M 311, 3 1/2 In. 330.00
Punch & Judy, Tin Lithograph, England, M 1299, 4 1/4 In. 220.00
Purse, Cast Iron, Put Money In Thy Purse, 1886, M 1266, 3 1/2 In. 1760.00
Rabbit, Begging, Cast Iron, Painted, Gold, A.C. Williams, M 566, 5 In. 77.00
Rabbit, Lying Down, Cast Iron, M 565, 2 1/8 In. 352.00
Rabbit, On Haunches, Silvered Lead, Germany, M 571, 3 3/8 In. 242.00
Record Player, Save For Your Sunny Suds, Brass, M 824, 4 1/2 In. 116.00
Red Goose, Cast Iron, 4 1/2 In. 176.00
Refrigerator, Kelvinator, On Legs, Cast Iron, 4 1/4 In. 77.00
Register, Balfour Budget Bank, For Class Ring, Tin, Dime 99.00
Register, Be Thrifty, Save A Dime Daily, Metal, Dime Increments, 2 1/2 In. 15.00
Register, Centesimi, Tin, 4 3/4 In. . . . . *Illus* 50.00
Register, Elves Rolling Coins, Tin, Dime 50.00
Register, Pfennige, Children With Balloons, Tin, 5 In. . . . . *Illus* 35.00
Register, Pfennige, Children With Blocks, Tin, 5 In. . . . . *Illus* 85.00
Register, Popeye, Tin, Dime 39.00
Register, Uncle Sam, Dime A Day, Tin, Chein, Dime 242.00
Rex Water Heater, Tin Lithograph, 7 1/2 In. 55.00
Rhino, Cast Iron, Black, Gold Horn, Arcade, M 721, 2 5/8 x 5 In. 358.00
Rocket, Metal, First Federal Savings & Loan, Astro Mfg., c.1957, 11 In. 374.00
Rooster, Cast Iron, Hubley, M 548, 4 3/4 In. . . . . .80.00 to 113.00
Roper Stove, Cast Iron, Arcade, M 1341, 3 3/4 In. 231.00
Royal National Life Boat Institution, Tin, Decals, Lock, 14 1/2 In. 220.00
Safe, 4 Panels, Sledding, Fishing, Hoop, Bicyclist, Key, Cast Iron, 19th Century 308.00
Safe, Bank Of Commerce, Nickel Plated Cast Iron, Kenton, 6 3/4 In. 275.00
Safe, Bank Of Industry, Combination Lock, Nickel Plate, Cast Iron, Kenton, 5 x 4 In. 150.00
Safe, Bronzed Diamond, Key Locked Door, c.1900, 6 1/2 x 5 1/2 x 7 1/2 In. 184.00
Safe, Eureka Trust & Savings Bank, Cast Iron, 5 3/4 In. . . . . .190.00 to 209.00
Safe, Hexagon Door, Grill, Cast Iron, Tin, 5 3/8 In. 275.00
Safe, Ideal Security, Cast Iron, 5 1/2 In. 176.00
Safe, Radio, Combination, Cast Iron, Painted, Nickel Plated Door, Kenton, 4 3/4 In. 121.00
Safe, Roller Skaters, Cast Iron, Painted, Key, Kyser & Rex, 3 3/4 In. 138.00
Safe, Security Safe Deposit, Cast Iron, Arcade, 6 In. 220.00
Safe, Security Safe, Cast Iron, M 889, 4 1/2 In. 187.00
Safe, White City Puzzle, No. 10, Plated Cast Iron, Nicol, M 913, 4 1/4 In. 110.00
Safe, Young America, Japanned Iron, Embossed, Gold Trim, Kyser & Rex, M 881, 4 In. . . . 165.00
Sailor Boy, Lead, Continental, M 272, 4 1/8 In. 1430.00
Santa, Folded Arms, Aluminum, Reynolds, 9 3/4 In. 50.00
Santa, Holding Naughty Boy By Ear, Aluminum, Reynolds, 5 3/4 In. 60.00
Santa, Holding Small Tree, Cast Iron, Reynolds, 5 5/8 In. 50.00
Santa, In Zeppelin, Aluminum, Reynolds, 3 1/2 In. 28.00
Santa, Iron, Holding Tree, 6 In. 588.00
Santa, Sleeping In Chair, White Metal, Original Box, Banthrico, M 102, 6 1/2 In. 44.00

Bank, Register, Centesimi,
Tin, 4 3/4 In.

Bank, Register, Pfennige,
Children With Balloons, Tin, 5 In.

Bank, Register, Pfennige,
Children With Blocks, Tin, 5 In.

Santa, With Presents, Aluminum, 1958, 6 5/8 In. 22.00
Santa, With Watch, Aluminum, Reynolds, 4 7/8 In. . . . . .55.00 to 61.00
Satchel, Steel, M 1268, 3 3/8 In. 44.00
Satellite, Rocket On Top Of Globe, Gold Paint, Duro Mold & Mfg., 1950s, 10 1/2 In. . . . 322.00
Save & Smile Money Box, Black Face, Red, White Eyes, Iron, England, M 1641, 4 1/4 In. 248.00
See Your Savings Daily, Shop Peoples Drug Stores, Glass Block, 4 3/4 x 4 3/4 x 3 1/4 In. . 62.00
Sharecropper, Cast Iron, Painted, A.C. Williams, M 173, 5 1/2 In. . . . . .110.00 to 187.00
Sharecropper, Give Me A Penny, Iron, Red Shirt, Wing, 1894, M 167, 5 1/2 In. 193.00
Singer Sewing Machine, Painted, Stenciled, Tin, Decals, Key, Germany, M 1368, 5 In. . . . 165.00
Space Heater, Flowers, Lattice, Japanned Iron, Chamberlain & Hill, M 1094, 6 3/4 In. . . . 94.00
Statue Of Liberty, Cast Iron, M 1166, 9 5/8 In. 2090.00
Stove, Save Your Money & Buy A Gas Stove, Green, Silver, Cast Iron, Painted, 5 1/2 In. . 28.00
Strato Bank, Rocket & Moon, Planter's Bank, Duro Mold & Mfg., c.1950s, 7 1/4 x 3 In. . 207.00
Sunbonnet Sue, Girl In Bonnet, Parasol, Cast Iron, M 257, 7 1/2 x 4 In. . . . . .51.00 to 132.00
Tank, Where's That Blinking Kaiser?, Ceramic, England, M 297, 3 3/16 In. 61.00
Teddy, Theodore Roosevelt, Cast Iron, A.C. Williams, M 120, 5 In. 358.00
Transvaal Money Box, Man, In Top Hat, Painted Cast Iron, England, M 251, 6 In. 138.00
Turkey, Red Head, Cast Iron, Japanned Body, A.C. Williams, M 585, 4 In. 303.00
Turkey, Red Head, Cast Iron, Japanned Body, A.C. Williams, M 587, 3 3/8 In. 303.00
Typewriter, White Metal, National Products, M 1271, 1 3/4 In. 105.00
Vending, Hershey Bar Bank, Original Box, Plastic, Tin, 6 3/4 In. 39.00
Washington Monument, Cast Iron, A.C. Williams, M 1049, 7 1/2 In. 550.00
Wonderland Cottage, Tin, 5 1/2 In. 61.00

BANKO is a group of rustic Japanese wares made in the nineteenth and twentieth centuries. Some pieces are made of mosaics of colored clay; some are fanciful teapots. Redware and other materials were also used.

Dish, Leaf Shape, 3 Walnuts, 7 1/2 In. 35.00
Teapot, Egg Shape, Fish, Shellfish, Early 1900s, 5 1/2 In. 160.00
Wall Pocket, Crows, Weeping Willows, Signed, 6 3/4 In. 40.00

BARBED WIRE was first patented in 1867. Collectors want eighteen-inch samples.

Sunderland's Kirk Single Line, 1885, 18 In. 8.00
Union Pacific Railroad, Round Square, 4 Barbs, 18 In. 12.50
Waukegan, Half Round, 4 Barbs, 18 In. 7.00

BARBER collectibles range from the popular red and white striped pole that used to be found in front of every shop to the small scissors and tools of the trade. Barber chairs are wanted, especially the older models with elaborate iron trim.

Cabinet, Shaving, Oak, Glass Front, 30 In. 385.00
Chair, Child's, Horse, Red, Brown, Wood, Porcelain, Chrome, Leather, Koken, 45 In. 2970.00
Chair, Horse Head, Porcelain, Leather, Wood, Emil J. Paidar Co., Chicago, 48 In. 3520.00
Chair, Red Leather, White Porcelain, Theo. Koch Co. 350.00
Container, Steri-Tool, DeWitt, 10 x 5 In. 95.00
Mirror, Chrome Pedestal, 2 Porcelain Cups, Star Shaving Brush 155.00
Pole, Black Acorn Finials, Red & White Candy Cane Stripes, 46 In. 1610.00
Pole, Carved, Painted, Blue Sphere Finial, Red & White Striped, 24 In. 715.00
Pole, Glass, Metal, Model 405, Revolves, William Marvey Co., St. Paul, Minn., 24 In. 495.00
Pole, Koken, Red, White, Blue Stripe, Porcelain, Cast Iron, Globe, Electric, c.1920, 84 In. 1760.00
Pole, Pine, Polychrome, Red, White & Blue Paint, American, Early 1900s, 30 In. 345.00
Pole, Porcelain, Tin, Glass, Wall Mount, Cut & Shave 50 Cents, Theo. Koch, 35 In. 415.00
Pole, Red, White, Blue Stripes, Revolves, Lights, Barber Shop Globe, Porcelain, 72 In. . . 1420.00
Pole, Red, White, Blue, Electric, Wall Mounted, 27 In. 305.00
Pole, Turned Wood, Paint Layers, Ivory & Cream Over Blue & Red, 23 1/2 In. 805.00
Pole, Wood, Square, Tapered Sides, Red, White, Blue Paint, 65 In. 290.00
Razor, English Rolls, Silver Metal Case 15.00
Shaving Kit, Mahogany, Burl Wood Lid, Inlaid Corners, Fold-Up Mirror, 3 x 10 x 6 In. . . 110.00
Sign, Barber Shop, Stripes, Red, White, Blue, Curved, Porcelain, Enamel, 24 x 15 In. 225.00
Sign, Hair Cut 25 Cents, Up To 5 P.M., Glass, Reverse Painted, Shadow Box, 10 x 15 In. . 715.00
Sign, Hair Cut 50 Cents, Glass, Reverse Painted, Tin Back, 10 x 15 In. 440.00
Sign, Straight Razor, Carved, Painted, American, 19th Century, 20 In. 325.00

Sign, Straight Razor, Galvanized Metal, Wood Sheath, 42 In. 290.00
Sign, Trade, Shaving Brush, Le Figaro, Wood Base, Natural Bristles, 9 1/2 x 3 1/4 In. 580.00

BAROMETERS are used to forecast the weather. Antique barometers with elaborate wooden cases and brass trim are the most desirable. Mercury column barometers are also popular with collectors. It is difficult to find someone to repair a broken one, so be sure your barometer is in working condition.

Admiral Fitzroy, Oak, Mercury, Glass, Brass Key, England, 1881, 46 x 9 1/2 x 3 In. 690.00
Aneroid, Black Forest, Carved Walnut, Mercury Thermometer, c.1890, 22 In. 170.00
Aneroid, Emory Douglass, Brass Case, Hinged Bezel, England, c.1900, 7 1/2 In. 140.00
Aneroid, Empire Style, Giltwood, Verre Eglomise, Lyre Finial, Foiling, 34 5/8 In. 265.00
Aneroid, J. Morris Optician, Mahogany, Band Inlaid Case, Bolton, 35 In. 595.00
Aneroid, Liquid Thermometer, Carved Walnut, France, Victorian, c.1880, 26 In. 170.00
Aneroid, Taylor, Presentation, Chrome, Rochester, N.Y., 1943, 8 1/4 In. 230.00
Aneroid, V. Beaumont, Metallic, White Dial, Metal Case, New York, 1859, 5 In. 500.00
Aneroid, Wood Back, Germany, 6 1/4 In. 12.00
Banjo, A Moteni, Bubble Level, Ivory Adjustment Knob, c.1840 . . . . 805.00
Banjo, Aneroid, Thomas Armstrong & Bros., Oak, Arch Crest, Late 1800s, 40 In. 440.00
Banjo, Duncan, Mahogany, Molded Bonnet Top, Aberdeen, Scotland, 38 In. 1035.00
Banjo, Fagioli & Son, Rosewood, Scroll Decoration, Mid 19th Century, 41 In. 605.00
Banjo, J.B. Silvano, Victorian, Mahogany, Mid 19th Century, 37 1/2 In. 750.00
Banjo, J.C. Moretti/Lynn, Mahogany, Late 19th Century, 38 1/2 In. 2300.00
Banjo, Louis XVI Style, Parcel Gilt, Eagle, Italy, 37 1/2 x 14 In. 2530.00
Banjo, Mahogany, Broken Arch Top, Inlaid Shell, Flower Inlay, Early 1800s, 38 In. 1265.00
Banjo, Mercury, Flame Mahogany, Swan' Neck Pediment, c.1840, 44 In. 735.00
Banjo, Thermometer, Humidity Gauge, Mahogany, 8 x 38 1/2 In. 460.00
Brass, Carved Walnut Frame, Germany, 9 In. 66.00
Desk Top, Porcelain Dial, Germany, 5 In. 60.00
English Oak, Carved, Silvered Dials, c.1920, 35 x 10 1/4 In. 805.00
J. Robinson, Ivory Scale, Thermometer, Wood Adjustment Knob, New York 1610.00
Lighthouse, Animated, Clock, Brass, France, 17 1/2 In. 2320.00
Louis XVI Style, Giltwood, Flower Basket, Quivers Suspending Drapery, 37 3/8 In. 2350.00
Mahogany, Carved, Turned, Beveled Glass, Round, 11 In. 250.00
Mahogany, S. Lilly, Inlaid Flowers, Shell Medallions, Edinburgh, 39 In. 1090.00
Mahogany, Tn. Corti, Shell, Inlay, Engraved Face, Holb Hill, London, 38 In. 920.00
Marine, Brass, Gimbal Mounted, Plexiglass Site Tube, Engraved, 38 x 2 1/2 In. 365.00
Marine, Humphries, Stick, Rosewood, Thermometer, Ivory Scales, Hartlepool, 37 In. 2875.00
Marine, I&A Walker, Gimbal, Mahogany, Ivory Scales, Finial, Brass, Liverpool 7189.00
Marine, Negretti & Zambra, Gimbal, Scales, Thermometer, Sympiesometer, 1850 . . . . 4430.00
Nautical, Silver Dial, Leather Case Pocket 2 1/2 In. 55.00
Nautical, Thermometer, Mahogany, Pine, Porcelain Dial, 37 x 9 1/2 x 2 1/4 In. 1045.00
Oak, Carved Flowers, Scrolls, England, 27 In. 250.00
Pocket, Silver Dial, Leather Case, 2 1/2 In. 60.00
Schatz, Weather Station, Brass Case, Wall Mount, Bevel Glass, 7 x 3 1/2 In. 90.00
Shelf, Mahogany, Tambour Shelf Mount, 1922, 17 1/4 x 8 x 3 1/2 In. 50.00
Stick, Dominick Lione, Inlaid Mahogany, Glazed Door, Georgian, c.1805, 39 In. 2015.00
Stick, Duncan, Mahogany, Pewter Dial, Aberdeen, Scotland, 38 In. 1725.00
Stick, E.C. Spooner, Storm King, Silvered Tablet, Boston, American, 42 In. 565.00
Stick, George III Style, Inlaid Walnut, Mid 19th Century, 38 In. 1725.00
Stick, George III, Mahogany, Crossbanded, Engraved Steel Face, c.1800, 40 1/2 In. 2300.00
Stick, J. Kendall, Ripple Front, Mahogany, Band Inlaid Case, N.Y., 35 In. 1695.00
Stick, Mahogany, Gimbal, Silvered Dial, Brass Mounts, c.1900, 39 1/2 In. 1840.00
Stick, Oak, Ivory Tablet, Glass Tubes, Ball Type Reservoir, 36 In. 675.00
Stick, Regency, Walnut Frame, Chip Carved, Silvered Dial, N.Y., 36 1/2 In. 980.00
Table, Thermometer, Round Dial, Mahogany, England, 19th Century, 10 In. 275.00
Thermometer, Chelsea, Brass Case, Walnut Plaque, 4 1/4 x 7 1/4 In. 225.00
Thermometer, LA Smith, Mahogany, Scrolled Top, Eagle, Shield, N.Y., 37 In. 2115.00
Thermometer, Man, On High Wheel, Sign Post, Flowers, Leaves, Wood, Carved 365.00
Weather Station, Mahogany, Pine, Bull's Eye Mirror, Porcelain, 37 x 9 1/2 x 2 In. 1065.00
Wheel, Hepplewhite Style, Broken Pediment, Shell Inlay, Hexagon Frame, 34 5/8 In. 560.00
Wheel, J. Steele, George II, Inlaid Mahogany, Liverpool, 39 In. 825.00
Wood, Carved Leaf, Flowers, Bird, Germany, c.1900, 24 1/2 x 11 1/2 In. 345.00

Basalt, Teapot, Floral
Relief, c.1800, 6 In.

BASALT is a special type of ceramic invented by Josiah Wedgwood in the eighteenth century. It is a fine-grained, unglazed stoneware. The most common type is black, but many other colors were made.

Medallion, Washington, Portrait, Black, Frame, Wedgwood & Bentley, c.1779, 3 In. 2300.00
Teapot, Floral Relief, c.1800, 6 In. .... *Illus* 195.00

BASEBALL collectibles are in the Sports category, except for baseball cards, which are listed under Baseball in the Card category.

BASKETS of all types are popular with collectors. American Indian, Japanese, African, Shaker, and many other kinds of baskets can be found. Of course, baskets are still being made, so the collector must learn to tell the age and style of the basket to determine the value.

Armadillo Shell, Irregularly Shaped, Handle, 11 In.	46.00
Ash, Splint, Fixed Handle, Dome Cover, White Paint, Tapered, 10 1/2 x 11 1/2 In.	50.00
Buttocks, 14 Ribs, Splint, Overlapping Weave, Arched Handle, 6 x 5 In.	85.00
Buttocks, 20 Ribs, Splint, Bentwood Handle, 5 3/4 x 3 1/4 In.	220.00
Buttocks, 32 Ribs, Splint, Bentwood Handle, 10 1/2 In.	85.00
Buttocks, Splint, Fixed Handle, 9 1/2 In.	90.00
Buttocks, Striped Decorations, Fixed Handle, 18 In.	115.00
Carrying, Round, Splint, Bentwood Handle, Late 19th Century, 13 1/2 In.	58.00
Cat Head, Stationary Handle	7820.00
Cheese, Large	400.00
Coiled, Rounded Base, Flared Body, Wrapped Rim, 12 In.	80.00
Coiled, Rye, Round, 15 1/2 In.	17.00
Coiled, Straw, Thread Binding, Applied Bentwood Oak Handle, 11 1/2 x 14 x 11 In.	130.00
Conservatory, Plaited Wire, Circular, France, 5 1/2 x 15 1/4 In., Pair	145.00
Egg, Nesting, Split Oak, East Tennessee, Miniature, 4 x 3 In. To 1 1/2 x 1 In., 5 Piece	470.00
Egg, Split Oak, Red, Orange, Mary E. Prater, Tennessee, c.1975, 5 1/2 In.	415.00
Egg, Split Oak, Rim, Band, East Tennessee, 8 1/2 x 10 1/2 x 8 1/2 In.	415.00
Egg, Split Oak, Rim, Band, Signed Betty Tanner, 9 1/2 x 10 1/2 x 11 In.	185.00
Egg, Split Oak, Shaped Rim, Nailed Construction, 16 x 18 x 15 In.	195.00
Egg Shape, Bail Handle, Small Lid, Flared Foot, Oriental, 10 1/2 In.	220.00
Field, Ash, Splint, Notched Handle, 15 x 15 1/2 In.	85.00
Flower, Splint, Flared Rim, Looping Carry Handle, 15 In.	96.00
Gathering, 4 Handles, High Dome, 24 In.	2760.00
Gathering, Grape Harvester's, Sheet Metal, Green Paint, LT. Label, Early 1900s, 34 In. ..	325.00
Gathering, Push-Up Bottom, Double Wrap Rim, Swing Handle, 9 1/2 x 17 In.	230.00
Gathering, Splint, 2 Fixed Handles, 21 In.	70.00
Gathering, Split Oak, Compartment Basket On Side, Loop Handles, 22 x 16 In.	100.00
Hand Crocheted, Open, Rope Style Handles, Lid With Pull, 7 In.	35.00
Hanging, Wall, Half Buttocks, Splint, Bentwood Handle, 8 x 6 x 6 1/4 In.	195.00
Harvest, Ash Splint, Round, Wrapped Rim, 2 Handles, 19th Century, 10 x 17 1/2 In.	250.00
Ikebana, Egg Shape, Splint, Bamboo, 2 Color, Imbricated Design, Early 1900s, 13 In. ...	460.00
Ikebana, Round, Splint, Knotted Bamboo Handle, Early 1900s, 15 1/2 In.............	315.00
Market, Splint, Oak Handle, Light Patina, 14 In.	47.00
Market, Splint, Tapered Ribs, Round Top, 9 1/2 x 10 In.	220.00
Melon, 32 Radiating Ribs, Square Opening, Arched Handle, 7 x 6 1/2 In.	575.00
Nantucket, Arched Swing Handle, Turned Wood Base, Painted Green, 12 x 14 1/2 In. ...	980.00
Nantucket, Bentwood Handle, Dark Splint Bands, Wood Ears, 10 x 6 1/2 In.	2530.00

Nantucket, Bentwood Handle, Disc Base, Brass Ears, Boyer, 7 x 4 1/2 In. 1840.00
Nantucket, Bentwood Swing Handle, Wood Dish Base, 10 x 5 In. 520.00
Nantucket, Lightship, Swing Handle, 19th Century, 9 1/2 x 12 1/2 In. 2070.00
Nantucket, Lightship, Swing Handle, Label, 19th Century, 1/2 In. 1265.00
Nantucket, Oval, Swing Handle, Wood Base, Brass Ears, 20th Century, 6 x 11 5/8 In. 705.00
Nantucket, Oval, Swing Handle, Wood Base, Brass Ears, Late 19th Century, 4 3/8 x 8 In. 3408.00
Nantucket, Oval, Wood Swing Handle, Base, c.1900, 4 3/4 x 10 3/4 In. 645.00
Nantucket, Purse, Bentwood Handle, Discs In Lid, Bottom, 6 1/2 x 7 In. 575.00
Nantucket, Round, High Sides, Arched Handle, Brown Patina, Wood Base, 8 1/2 x 10 In. 2420.00
Nantucket, Round, Hinged Handle, Wrapped Rim, Copper Rivets, Stencil, 17 x 14 In. ... 3300.00
Nantucket, Round, Swing Handle, Base, Brass Ears, Late 18th Century, 10 5/8 x 13 In. ... 353.00
Nantucket, Round, Swing Handle, Base, Brass Ears, Late 19th Century, 8 x 11 1/2 In. ... 353.00
Nantucket, Round, Swing Handle, Base, Copper Ears, Late 19th Century, 3 x 3 3/8 In. ... 940.00
Nantucket, Round, Swing Handle, Turned Base, Late 19th Century, 7 x 5 3/8 In. 3820.00
Nantucket, Round, Swing Handle, Turned Pine Base, Hickory Staves, 11 1/2 x 15 5/8 In. 3408.00
Nantucket, Round, Swing Handle, Wood Base, Early 20th Century, 4 3/4 x 8 3/4 In. 175.00
Nantucket, Swing Handle, Ferdinand Sylvaro 1100.00
Oblong, Twin Braided Swing Handles, Cover, 10 x 16 In. 60.00
Oval, Splint, Crossing Handle Supports, Tapered Ribs, 6 x 6 In. 250.00
Oval, Splint, Tapered Ribs, 4 x 5 In. 275.00
Pack, Splint, Bulbous, Leather Straps, 19 In. 79.00
Picnic, Hinged Oak, Walnut Split, 2 Hinged Lids, Handle, 1 x 18 1/2 x 10 In. 175.00
Rye Straw, Lid, Oval, 24 x 12 In. 79.00
Shopping, River Cane, 2 Handles, Geometric, Aniline Dyes, 13 x 11 x 7 1/2 In. 85.00
Splint, Apple Green, 2 Lift Up Covers, Handle, Early 1900s, 13 x 10 x 16 In. 880.00
Splint, Ash, Cover, 3 Colors, Round To Square, 14 x 11 In. 485.00
Splint, Ash, Round, 2 Handles, Wrapped Rim, 19th Century, 10 x 17 1/2 In. 250.00
Splint, Chrome Yellow, Rectangular, Handle, 21 x 12 In. 2530.00
Splint, Painted, Gray Blue, Rectangular, 2 Carved Handles, 19th Century, 15 5/8 x 25 In. . 447.00
Splint, Round, Tapered Sides, Swing Handle, Green Paint, 16 1/2 x 10 1/2 In. 259.00
Split, Oak, Scalloped Border, Caswell County, North Carolina, 11 x 13 1/2 x 12 In. 35.00
Split Oak, Coker Creek Crafts, 12 1/2 x 13 x 10 In. 155.00
Tray, Round, Coiled, Rye Straw, 16 3/4 In. 17.00
Wishbone, Constructed Of Turkey Wishbones & Strands Of Bones, 1910, 8 In. 410.00

BATCHELDER products are made from California clay. Ernest Batchelder established a tile studio in Pasadena, California, in 1909 and expanded until 1916. Then he built a larger factory with a new partner. The Batchelder-Wilson Company made all types of architectural tiles, garden pots, and bookends. The plant closed in 1932. In 1936 Batchelder opened Batchelder Ceramics, also in Pasadena, and made bowls, vases, and earthenware pots. He retired in 1951 and died in 1957. Pieces are marked *Batchelder Pasadena* or *Batchelder Los Angeles.*

**BATCHELDER
LOS ANGELES**

Corbel, Abstract, Incised, Blue Gray Matte, Light Green Glaze, 5 3/4 x 2 3/4 In., Pair 175.00
Tile, Boy With Dragon & Knight Pull Toy, Tan, Blue, Mauve, Frame, 12 x 12 In. 770.00
Tile, Houses Along River, Sailboat, Dutch Figures, Blue, Ivory Matte Glaze, 17 x 6 In. 865.00
Tile, Hunting Scene, Marked, 4 In. 29.00
Tile, Medieval City, Behind Stone Wall, Gray, Red, Blue Engobe, Stamped, 5 3/4 In. 175.00
Tile, Peacocks, Under Grapevines, Blue Engobe, Stamped, Frame, 9 x 5 3/4 In., Pair 980.00
Vase, Dark Blue Glaze, Marked, 4 In. 490.00

BATMAN and Robin are characters from a comic strip by Bob Kane that started in 1939. In 1966, the characters became part of a popular television series. There have been radio and movie serials that featured the pair. The first full-length movie was made in 1989.

Bat Cycle, Mego, 1974, 10 1/2 In. 60.00
Bat Gloves, 1960s, Child Size, 12 In. 230.00
Bath Towel Poncho, Cape Graphic On Back, Chest On Front, 1976, 55 x 34 In. 79.00
Batman, Magnetic, Flyaway Action, Mego, Box, 1970s, 12 1/2 In. 285.00
Batmobile, Battery Operated, Tin Lithograph, Box, Taiwan, 12 In. 316.00
Batmobile, Boat & Trailer, Corgi, 1974, 11 In. 300.00
Batmobile, Bump & Go, Red, Battery Operated, Box, c.1960 ....230.00 to 730.00
Batmobile, Bump & Go, Tin, Battery Operated, Taiwan, Box, 1974, 9 3/4 In. 365.00

Batmobile, Slot Car, Aurora, 1966, 3 In. 145.00
Batmobile, Tin Lithograph, Battery Operated, Ahi, Box, Japan, 12 In. 550.00
Batmobile, Tin Lithograph, Battery Operated, Japan, 1960s, 12 In. 365.00
Batmobile, Tin, Taiwan, Box, 10 In. 310.00
Comic Book, No. 6, First Jerry Robinson Cover, 1941 .... 1035.00
Figurine, Removable Cape, Gloves & Boots, Tag, Toy & Novelty, 1966, 16 In. 85.00
Figurine, Uniform & Equipment, Captain Action, Ideal, Box, 1966 .... 975.00
Game, Board, Milton Bradley, Box, 1966, 55 Piece 115.00
Game, Playing Pieces, 3 Cardboard Batmobiles, Milton Bradley, Box, 10 x 19 In. 70.00
License Plate, Batman & Robin, City Skyline, 1966, 12 x 6 In. 69.00
Mad Magazine, Alfred As Robin, No. 105, September, 1966 .... 65.00
Model Kit, Batmobile, Assembled, Painted, Instructions, Aurora, Box, 1966, 6 1/2 In. .. 375.00
Model Kit, Batmobile, Assembled, Painted, Instructions, Japan, Box, 1960s, 6 1/2 In. 90.00
Mug, Coffee, Milk Glass, Fighting Figure 1 Side, Logo Other, 1966, 3 1/2 In. 65.00
Projector Gun, Plastic, Battery Operated, Box, Toy Biz, 10 1/2 In. 25.00
Puppets, Hand, Batman, Robin, Vinyl, National Periodical, Ideal, Box, 1966, 10 x 10 In. .. 385.00
Ring, Pewter, Hong Kong, 1960s, Child's Size 40.00
Robin, Magnetic, Flyaway Action, Mego, Box, 1970s, 12 1/4 In. 325.00
Robin, Mego, Palitoy Box, 1977, 9 1/2 In. 985.00
Soaky, Box, 1960s 140.00
Train, Boxcar, Follow Batman In DC Comics, 1977, 7 In. 55.00
Tumbler, Robin, Pepsi-Cola Super Series, 1976, 16 Oz. 20.00
Water Gun, Black Plastic, Bat Plane Shape, Chinese, 1989 .... 15.00

BATTERSEA enamels, which are enamels painted on copper, were made in the Battersea district of London from about 1750 to 1756. Many similar enamels are mistakenly called *Battersea*.

Box, Cheltenham Wells Scene, 1790, 2 1/4 x 1 3/4 In. 550.00
Box, Enameled, Heart Shape, Lid, Woman, Platter, Basket, New Mackrel, 2 3/4 x 2 1/4 In. 201.00
Box, Horseracing Scene, Blue, White, 2 1/2 x 1 1/4 In. 400.00
Box, Remember The Giver, 1790, 7/8 In. Diam. 375.00
Box, Tieback Knob, Mourning Scene, Sacred To Friendship, 1 5/8 In. Diam. 750.00

BAUER pottery is a California-made ware. J.A. Bauer bought Paducah Pottery in Paducah, Kentucky, in 1885. He moved the pottery to Los Angeles, California, in 1909. The company made art pottery after 1912 and dinnerwares marked *Bauer* in 1930. The factory went out of business in 1962. See also the Russel Wright category.

La Linda, Saltshaker 25.00
Mixing Bowl, No. 36, Speckled, Beige, 1950s, 6 In. 20.00
Monterey, Cup & Saucer 30.00
Monterey, Gravy Boat 40.00
Monterey, Sugar 20.00
Monterey, Teapot, Cover, Orange, 6 Cup 150.00
Ring, Casserole, Holder, 5 x 9 1/2 In. 75.00
Ring, Custard Cup, Yellow, 2 1/2 In. 25.00
Ring, Mixing Bowl, No. 12, Black, 9 1/2 In. 100.00
Ring, Plate, Salad, Cobalt Blue, 7 3/4 In. 25.00
Ring, Refrigerator Set, Stacking, Chartreuse, 4 Piece 300.00
Sand Jar, Vase, Yellow, No. 122, Straight Sides, 20 In. 100.00

BAVARIA is a region in Europe where many types of porcelain were made. In the nineteenth century, the mark often included the word *Bavaria*. After 1871, the words *Bavaria, Germany*, were used. Listed here are pieces that include the name *Bavaria* in some form, but major porcelain makers, such as Rosenthal, are listed in their own categories.

Berry Set, Hand Painted Roses On White, Green Border, 5 Piece 75.00
Butter, Cover, Hand Painted Fruit, 7 1/2 In. 45.00
Cake Stand, Hand Painted Roses On White, Scalloped Edge, 12 In. 160.00
Coffeepot, Hand Painted Roses, Oscar Schaller & Co., 1918-1921, 8 1/2 In. 60.00
Condensed Milk Holder, Underplate, Hand Painted Cherries, Gold Trim 135.00
Cup & Saucer, Mustache, Hand Painted Roses On White 60.00
Pitcher, Lemonade, Floral Border At Mouth, Gold Trim, 6 In. 195.00

Plate, Parcel Gilt, Flowers, Etched Geometric Bands, c.1910, 10 1/2 In., 12 Piece 590.00
Plate Set, Luncheon, Flower Center, Gold Border, Square, 8 1/2 In. 259.00
Platter, Hand Painted Roses On White, Scalloped Edge, 15 In. 70.00
Salt & Pepper, Gold Wreaths, Bulbous, 1890-1910 . . . . 55.00
Tureen, Cover, Handles, Black & Gold Trim 50.00

BEADED BAGS are included in the Purse category.

BEATLES collectors search for any items picturing the four members of
the famous music group or any of their recordings. Because these
items are so new, the condition is very important and top prices are
paid only for items in mint condition. The Beatles first appeared on
American network television in 1964. The group disbanded in 1971.
Ringo Starr and Paul McCartney are still performing. John Lennon
died in 1980. George Harrison died in 2001.

Award, Gold Record Sales, Meet The Beatles, Frame, 21 x 17 In. 115.00
Game, Flip Your Wig, Milton Bradley, NEMS Enterprises Ltd., 1964 . . . . 165.00
Lunch Box, Yellow Submarine, Metal, King Features, King Seeley Thermos, 1968 . . . . . . 880.00
Lunch Box & Thermos, Beatles Pictures, NEMS Enterprises Ltd. . . . . .255.00 to 395.00
Ornament Set, Playing Instruments, Bandstand, Hallmark, 1994 . . . . 175.00
Pencil Case, NEMS Enterprises Ltd., 1964 . . . . 100.00
Photograph, Beatles Knocked Out By Muhammad Ali, Ali Autograph, 20 x 16 In. 150.00
Pin, Guitar Shape, John Lennon Photograph, 1960s, 4 1/4 In. 57.00
Poster, Sgt. Pepper's Lonely Hearts Club Band, England, 1967, 8 x 11 1/2 In. . . . . .28.00 to 45.00
Tote Bag, TWA, Luggage Tag, Red & White Letters, Beatles To The U.S.A. August 1965 . 1150.00
Toy, 4 Pop Guitar, Plastic, Instructions 366.00
Tray, Portraits, Metal, Square, Rounded Edges, Worcester Ware, 1964, 13 x 13 In. . .85.00 to 195.00

BEEHIVE, Austria, or Beehive, Vienna, are terms used in English-
speaking countries to refer to the many types of decorated porcelain
bearing a mark that looks like a beehive. The mark is actually a shield,
viewed upside down. It was first used in 1744 by the Royal Porcelain
Manufactory of Vienna. The firm made porcelains, called *Royal
Vienna* by collectors, until it closed in 1864. Many other German,
Austrian, and Japanese factories have reproduced Royal Vienna wares,
complete with the original shield or *beehive* mark. This listing includes
the expensive, original Royal Vienna porcelains and many other types
of beehive porcelain. The Royal Vienna pieces include that name in the
description.

Coffee Set, After Dinner, Romantic Decoration, Case, Royal Vienna, c.1910, 15 Piece . . . 375.00
Cup & Saucer, Bacchanalian Revelry, Plum, Gilt, Royal Vienna, 2 5/8 In. 315.00
Cup & Saucer, Children On Parade, Instruments, Hauser, Royal Vienna, 3 3/4 In. 546.00
Cup & Saucer, Classical Scenes, Plum, Gilt, Royal Vienna, 3 1/2 In. 575.00
Cup & Saucer, Lady Rushout U. Tochter, Plum, Gilt, Footed, Royal Vienna, 2 1/2 In. 310.00
Cup & Saucer, Lavinia, Portrait, Gilt Trim, Signed, A.H., Royal Vienna, 2 1/4 In. 150.00
Cup & Saucer, Maiden With Cupid, Plum, Pink, Gilt, Bird Head Handle, Royal Vienna . . 575.00

**If you're moving, pack your plates
on their sides with pads under
and between the plates. The
weight of a stack of plates can
crack the bottom plates.**

Beehive, Plate, Classical Scene, Gold Border,
Blumen Von Forclo, Royal Vienna, 9 1/2 In.

Cup & Saucer, Maidens & Babies, Royal Vienna, 4 In. 489.00
Dessert Service, Arabesque Pattern, c.1900, Royal Vienna, 9 Piece 150.00
Figurine, Rider On Stallion, Augarten Wien, Hofbourg Wien, 9 x 8 1/2 In., Pair 770.00
Group, Woman Reading Book, Man, Wahliss, c.1910, Royal Vienna, 10 3/4 In. 264.00
Plate, 2 Maidens, Garlands, Statue, Burgundy, Jewel Border, Royal Vienna, 9 1/2 In. 748.00
Plate, 3 Women, Crying Cherub, Cobalt Blue Border, Gold Stencil, Signed, 9 1/4 In. 400.00
Plate, Classical Scene, Cobalt Blue Border, Gold Stencil Overlay, Signed, 9 1/4 In. 450.00
Plate, Classical Scene, Cobalt Blue Border, Woman, Cherubs, G. Herr, Late 1800s, 9 In. . 750.00
Plate, Classical Scene, Gold Border, Blumen Von Forclo, Royal Vienna, 9 1/2 In. . . . *Illus* 750.00
Plate, Cupid, 2 Lovers, Marked, Victoria Austria, Royal Vienna, Early 1900s, 11 1/2 In. .. 23.00
Plate, Grazien Rache, Blue, Burgundy, Pink, Jeweled Border, Royal Vienna, 9 1/2 In. 748.00
Plate, Hektors Alschied, Gilt, Blue, Jewel Border, Barschneider, Royal Vienna, 9 1/2 In. . 750.00
Plate, Hypolite U Phodrou, Blue, Burgundy, Jeweled Border, Royal Vienna, 9 1/2 In. ... 750.00
Plate, Karlder IV Prager Universitat, Center Scene, Gilt Rim, Late 1800s, 9 5/8 In. 805.00
Plate, Mars & Venus, Cobalt Blue, Gilt, Signed, Paul, Royal Vienna 140.00
Plate, Rinaldo Und Armide, Blue, Jewel Border, Barschneider, Royal Vienna, 9 1/2 In. ... 750.00
Plate, Tannhauser Scene, Act II, Royal Vienna, c.1890, 9 1/2 In. 980.00
Plate, Transfer Decoration, Classical Figures, Austria, 10 1/2 In. 29.00
Plate, Woman Reclining Near Water, White Parrot, Blue Border, Gold Stencil, 8 In. 100.00
Tray, 2 Handles, Painted, Scenic, Frolicking People, Royal Vienna, 16 1/2 In. 85.00
Tureen, Fruit, Flower Swags, Figures, Pink, Blue Ground, 15 1/4 In. 2090.00
Urn, Egg Shape, Dome Cover, Angelica Kaufmann Medallions, Brocade Ground, 23 In. ... 1035.00

BEER BOTTLES are listed in the Bottle category under Beer.

BEER CANS are a twentieth-century idea. Beer was sold in kegs or
returnable bottles until 1934. The first patent for a can was issued to
the American Can Company in September of that year; and Gotfried
Kruger Brewing Company, Newark, New Jersey, was the first to use
the can. The cone-top can was first made in 1935, the aluminum pop-
top in 1962. Collectors should look for cans in good condition, with no
dents or rust. Serious collectors prefer cans that have been opened
from the bottom.

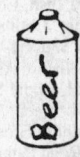

Bantam, Flat Top, Goebel Brewing Co., Detroit, Mich., 8 Oz. 75.00
Fort Pitt Beer, Cone Top, Pittsburgh, Pa. 305.00
Fox Deluxe Beer, Cone Top, Marion 565.00
Frankenmuth Premium Dry, Flat Top 45.00
Krueger Cone Top Beer Can, Cone Top, N.Y. 90.00
Lion Pilsner Crowntainer, Cone Top, Pilsner Brewing Co., N.Y. 350.00
Lubeck Royal Beer, Flat Top, 12 Oz. 2395.00
Pabst Blue Ribbon Bock Beer, Flat Top, Milwaukee, Wisconsin 230.00
Takara Lager Beer, Flat Top, Japan 365.00
Tivoli Western, Flat Top, Denver, Colo. 45.00
Velvet Glow, Flat Top, Grace Brothers, Santa Rosa, California, 16 Oz. 55.00
Wiedeman's Special Bohemian Brew, Cone Top, Newport, Kentucky 315.00

BELL collectors collect all types of bells. Favorites include glass bells,
figural bells, school bells, and cowbells. Bells have been made of
porcelain, china, or metal through the centuries.

Brass, Brass Dolphin Stand, 1900s, 12 In. 175.00
Brass, Cast Iron Yoke, R. Kern, Ligonier, Pa., 13 In. 220.00
Bronze, Fern-Like Top, Sheet Copper Pendant, Arcosanti, 38 x 10 In. 980.00
Buddhist, Acid Etched Dragons, Copper, Tokugawa Mons, Japan, c.1900, 14 In. 355.00
Church, Bronze, Mexico, 100 Lbs., Early 1800s, 13 In. Diam. 495.00
Countertop, Brass, Dome Shape, Ring Handle, Turned Oak Stand, Victorian, 10 1/2 In. .. 200.00
Countertop, Figural, Turtle, Head Is Ringer, Nickel Plated Iron, Windup, 5 1/2 In. 315.00
Cow, 2 Ladies, Golliwog, On Horse, Green, 3 1/2 x 2 x 2 3/4 In. 75.00
Hames, Conestoga Wagon, Brass, Wrought Iron Frame, 3 Piece 358.00
Hand, Cast Bronze, 8 x 14 In. 195.00
Huckster's, Brass, 12 In. 670.00
Owl, Copper Gilt, Spain, 3 1/4 In. 325.00
School, Bronze, Turned Walnut Handle, 9 In. 69.00
Sleigh, 20 Graduated Bells, Brass, Leather Strap, 82 In. 145.00

Sleigh, 29 Graduated Bells, Original Strap, 68 In. 220.00
Sleigh, Brass, Silver Finish, Leather Strap, 94 In. 45.00
Wedding, Glass, Blue, Applied Handle, Clear, 12 x 7 In. 175.00

BELLEEK china was made in Ireland, other European countries, and the
United States. The glaze is creamy yellow and appears wet. The first
Belleek was made in 1857. All pieces listed here are Irish Belleek. The
mark changed through the years. The first mark, black, dates from
1863 to 1890. The second mark, black, dates from 1891 to 1926 and
includes the words *Co. Fermanagh, Ireland*. The third mark, black,
dates from 1926 to 1946 and has the words *Deanta in Eirinn*. The
fourth mark, same as the third mark but green, dates from 1946 to
1955. The fifth mark, green, dates from 1955 to 1965 and has an R in
a circle added in the upper right. The sixth mark, green, dates after
1965 and the words *Co. Fermanagh* have been omitted. The seventh
mark, gold, was used from 1980 to 1993 and omits the words *Deanta
in Eirinn*. The eighth mark, introduced in 1993, is similar to the second mark but is printed in blue. The word *Belleek* is now used only on
the pieces made in Ireland even though earlier pieces from other countries were sometimes marked *Belleek*. These early pieces are listed by
manufacturer, such as Ceramic Art Co., Haviland, Lenox, Ott &
Brewer, and Willets.

Biscuit Jar, Cover, Basket Weave, Shamrocks, 4th Mark, 6 5/8 In. 390.00
Bowl, Shell Shape, Wave Base, 3 1/4 x 2 1/2 In. ....90.00 to 101.00
Butter, Cottage Shape, 7th Mark, 6 1/2 x 5 x 5 In. 250.00
Cheese Dish, Cover, Cottage Shape, Vine Handle, 7th Mark, 5 x 7 In. 250.00
Creamer, Undine, Girl Holding Heart, 2nd Mark, 4 In. 405.00
Cup & Saucer, New Shell, Pink, 3rd Mark 400.00
Dish, Shamrocks, Cutout Handle, Turquoise, Gold, 5th Mark 350.00
Inkwell, Apple Shape, Plate With Leaves, Purple Decoration, 1st Mark 5500.00
Jug, Aberdeen, Applied Flowers, 3rd Mark, 6 1/8 In. 270.00
Jug, White, Green Heightening, 2nd Black Mark, c.1900, 6 In. 299.00
Mug, Rope Pattern, Rope Handles, 2nd Mark, 2 3/4 x 2 3/4 In. 58.00
Pitcher, Relief Thistle, Gilt Highlights, American, 5 1/2 x 6 In. 330.00
Posy Cradle, 7th Mark, 5 1/2 x 2 3/4 x 2 In. 90.00
Teapot, Basket Weave, Shamrocks, 6th Mark 325.00
Teapot, Limpet Shape, Cob Luster Handle & Trim, 5th Mark 395.00
Teapot, Shamrocks, 6th Mark, 7 In. 195.00
Trinket Box, Cover, Acorn & Oak Leaf Finial, Trunk Shape, 1928, 2 1/2 x 3 1/2 In. 350.00
Vase, 8-Paneled Base, Shamrocks, Gold Luster, Conical Neck, Handles, 5th Mark, 8 In. .. 275.00
Vase, Shamrocks, 2 Handles, 6th Mark, 1965, 8 In. 65.00
Vase, Spill, Applied Painted Roses, Petal Rim, 6th Mark, 7 3/4 In. 195.00

BENNINGTON ware was the product of two factories working in
Bennington, Vermont. Both the Norton Company and the Lyman
Fenton Company were out of business by 1896. The wares include
brown and yellow mottled pottery, Parian, scroddled ware, stoneware,
graniteware, yellowware, and Staffordshire-type vases. The name is
also a generic term for mottled brownware of the type made in
Bennington.

Atomizer, Lid 264.00
Baking Dish, Elongated, Flint Enamel, Molded Rim, Mark A, 1849, 11 1/4 In. 1380.00
Bottle, Coachman, Barrel, Flint Enamel, 1849 Mark A, 11 In. 2070.00
Bottle, Coachman, Barrel, Mustache, Tassels, Flint Enamel, Mark A, 1849, 11 In. 1380.00
Bottle, Coachman, Impressed, Fenton, 1849, 10 1/2 In. 235.00
Bottle, Flask, Book, Bennington Battle, Flint Enamel, 2 Qt., 8 In. ....665.00 to 1150.00
Bottle, Flask, Book, Bennington Battle, Flint Enamel, 4 Qt., 11 In. 3450.00
Bottle, Flask, Book, Bennington Battle, Flint Enamel, Pt., 5 1/2 In. 975.00
Bottle, Flask, Book, Bennington Company C On Spine, 1849-1858, 7 3/4 In. 500.00
Bottle, Flask, Book, Departed Spirits, c.1849, 5 1/2 x 4 1/8 x 2 In. 595.00
Bottle, Flask, Book, Indians Lament, Flint Enamel, 6 In. 495.00
Bottle, Flask, Book, Ladies Companion, Flint Enamel, 5 1/8 In. 660.00
Bottle, Flask, Book, Ned Buntline's Bible, Flint Enamel, Signed, 1849, 6 In. 2000.00

Bottle, Flask, Book, Ned Buntline's Own, Flint Enamel, Signed, 6 In. 2310.00
Bottle, Flask, Book, Scroddled Ware, Gray, Pink, Applied Spine Star, 5 3/4 In. 1495.00
Bottle, Flask, Book, Spirits Of Bennington, Flint Enamel, 2 Qt., 8 In. 1495.00
Bottle, Flask, Book, Travelers Companion, Flint Enamel, 6 In. 605.00
Bowl, Mottled Orange & Brown, Tapered, Mark, 1849, 3 1/2 x 11 1/2 In. 81.00
Bowl, Spout, Orange & Brown, Streaks, Flint Enamel, Mark, 1849, 4 3/4 x 12 1/2 In. 403.00
Cake Mold, Mottled Orange Brown Glaze, Flint Enamel, 3 1/3 x 8 3/4 In. 230.00
Candlestick, Cylindrical, Mottled Olive Green, Brown, Flint Enamel, 6 1/2 In. 748.00
Churn, Cobalt Blue Flower, Stoneware, E. & L.P. Norton, 5 Gal. 460.00
Churn, Cobalt Leaf, Applied Handles, E. Norton & Co., 8 x 17 1/2 In. 495.00
Churn, Cover, Bird, Blue, Stoneware, E. & L.P. Norton, 3 Gal. 990.00
Churn, Light Gray, Blue Stylized Leaf, Handles, Flared Rim, No Lid, 19 In. 345.00
Creamer, Cow, Cover, Flint Enamel, 5 1/2 x 7 In. 575.00
Creamer, Cow, Cover, Graniteware, 5 1/2 x 7 In. 345.00
Crock, 3 Flowers, Jardiniere Style, Stoneware, Norton & Fenton, 2 Gal. 220.00
Crock, Cobalt Blue Feather, Applied Handles, Flared Rim, E. & L.P. Norton, 7 In. 230.00
Crock, Cobalt Blue Flower Decoration, Egg Shape, Stoneware, J. & P. Norton 195.00
Crock, Flared Rim, Flower & Dot, Dark Blue, Applied Handles, Stoneware, 11 1/2 In. . . . 360.00
Crock, Flower Leaf, Stoneware, E. & L.P. Norton, Gal. 149.00
Crock, Spray Of Flowers, Stoneware, E. & L.P. Norton, Gal. 127.00
Crock, Spray Of Flowers, Stoneware, J. & E. Norton, Gal. 290.00
Dish, Circular, Deep, Flint Enamel, Mark A, 1849, 12 3/4 In. 920.00
Dish, Soap, Ribs, Footed, Rockingham Glaze, 3 x 4 1/2 x 3 1/4 In. 81.00
Doorknob, Mottled Orange & Light Green, Round, 8-Sided Top, 2 In., Pair 86.00
Inhaler, Bulbous, Bottom Vent, 6 1/2 In. 300.00
Jar, Canning, Cobalt Blue, Flowers, Stoneware, E. & L.P. Norton, c.1880, 2 Gal., 12 In. . . 413.00
Jar, Canning, Dotted Flower Spray, Stoneware, E. & L.P. Norton, c.1880, 2 Gal., 12 In. . . 605.00
Jar, Tornado Design, Stoneware, J. & E. Norton, 2 Gal. 195.00
Jug, 3 Flowers, Stoneware, Julius Norton, 3 Gal. 165.00
Jug, Bird On Stump, Stoneware, Norton, 2 Gal. 4070.00
Jug, Blue Tulip, 2, Oval, Strap Handle, Stoneware, Norton & Son, 13 In. 430.00
Jug, Cobalt Blue Bird, Stoneware, J. & E. Norton, 11 In. 290.00
Jug, Cobalt Blue Parrot, Branch, Fanned Tail Feathers, Stoneware, E. Norton, 10 1/2 In. . . 546.00
Jug, Recumbent Deer, Fence, Stoneware, J. & E. Norton, 8 x 6 1/2 In., 3 Gal. 7150.00
Jug, Stylized Thistle, Stoneware, J. & E. Norton, Gal. 415.00
Lion, Standing, Facing Left, Coleslaw Mane, Paw On Ball, Flint Enamel, 11 x 7 1/2 In. . . 10925.00
Mixing Bowl, Sloped Sides, Spout, Flint Enamel, Mark A, 1849, 13 1/2 In. 1955.00
Paperweight, Spaniel, Lying Down, Rectangular Base, Flint Enamel, 3 x 4 1/2 In. 1035.00
Pie Plate, c.1849, 9 1/4 In. 382.00
Pipkin, Bulbous, Ribs, Flattened Knop, Flint Enamel, 6 In. . . . ; 575.00
Pipkin, Bulbous, Ribs, Flattened Knop, Flint Enamel, 7 1/2 In. 805.00
Pitcher, Alternate Rib, Flint Enamel, Mark A, 1849, 8 1/2 In. 690.00
Pitcher, Alternate Rib, Waisted, Leaf Spout, Flint Enamel, Mark A, 1849, 7 1/2 In. 690.00
Pitcher, Blue & White, Cherubs, Grapevines, Impressed, 1850, 9 In. 325.00
Pitcher, Brown Glaze, Anchor & Chain, Applied Handle, 10 1/2 x 7 1/4 x 6 1/2 In. 78.00
Pitcher, Brown, Hunting Scene, Greyhound Handle, 9 x 9 In. 115.00
Pitcher, Cupid, Psyche, Blue On White, Parian, 10 3/4 In. 259.00
Pitcher, Flint Enamel, Scalloped Ribs, Applied Handle, c.1858, 9 3/4 In. 355.00
Pitcher, Parian, Vining Roses, Branch Handle, Fenton Works, 10 1/4 In. 275.00
Pitcher, Relief Hunt Scene, Leaf Wreath, Dead Game, 9 In. 96.00
Pitcher, Rockingham, Paneled Baluster, Angular Handle, 9 In. 1265.00
Pitcher, Toby, Sitting, Grapevine Handle, Flint Enamel, Mark A, 1849, 6 5/8 In. . .460.00 to 690.00
Pitcher, Tulip & Heart, Baluster, Flint Enamel, Mark A, 1849, 9 1/4 In. . . . . . . .1265.00 to 1840.00
Pitcher & Washbowl, Alternate Rib, Flint Enamel, Mark A, 1849-1858 . . . . 2185.00
Pitcher & Washbowl, Scroddled Ware, Diamond Pattern, c.1855, 11 1/2 x 13 In. 1725.00
Snuff Jar, Toby, Cover, Flint Enamel, Mark A, 1849, 4 1/4 In. . . . . .460.00 to 748.00
Snuff Jar, Toby, Mottled Brown Glaze, Hat, Pedestal Base, Marked, 1849, 5 1/4 In. 290.00
Snuff Jar, Toby, Mottled Green Glaze, Hat, Marked, 1849, 4 1/4 In. 230.00
Sugar, Cover, Flint Enamel, 1849-1858, 10 In. 1060.00
Teapot, Cover, Ribs, Green Orange Glaze, Mark, Flint Enamel, 1849, 7 1/4 In. 865.00
Tile, Latticework Center, Olive Amber Glaze, Flint Enamel, Mark A, 1849, 7 1/4 In. 230.00
Tobacco Jar, Cover, Ribs, Yellow To Gold, Flint Enamel, 7 In. 230.00
Vase, Cottage-Type, Woman Petting Perched Bird, Glazed Leaves, Scrolls, 8 1/2 In. 105.00

Vase, Tulip, Octagonal Base, Flint Enamel, 10 In., Pair 863.00
Washbowl, Scalloped Ribs, 12-Sided, Flint Enamel, Mark A, 1849, 13 1/2 In. 1840.00

BERLIN, a German porcelain factory, was started in 1751 by Wilhelm
Kaspar Wegely. In 1763, the factory was taken over by Frederick the
Great and became the Royal Berlin Porcelain Manufactory. It is still in
operation today. Pieces have been marked in a variety of ways.

Bowl, Birds, Insects, Flowers, Handles, 4 Lobes, Scroll Feet, 6 1/4 x 14 In. 920.00
Bracket, Wall, Pink, Green, Gilt Scrollwork, Flowers, Birds, Insects, 8 3/4 In., Pair 1200.00
Figurine, Woman, Reclining, Putto, Painted, Gilt, Shaped Plinth Base, 9 1/4 In. 325.00
Plaque, 2 Boys Enjoying Humble Repast, Dog, Bread, Frame, c.1890, 13 3/4 x 11 7/8 In. .. 2705.00
Plaque, Alchemist, Late 19th Century, 11 x 8 3/4 In. 1725.00
Plaque, Children, Whispering In Stone Courtyard, Rectangular, Frame, 13 x 8 In. 9430.00
Plaque, Genre Scene, Monk, 14 x 16 In. 2800.00
Plaque, Spinster, Eating A Meal, Late 19th Century, 10 x 12 1/2 In. 3220.00
Urn, Cover, Flowers, Insects, Turquoise Ribbons, Swags, Handles, Marked, c.1860, Pair . 1000.00

BESWICK started making earthenware in Staffordshire, England, in
1936. The company is now part of Royal Doulton Tableware, Ltd.
Figurines of animals, especially dogs and horses, Beatrix Potter animals, and other wares are still being made.

Figurine, Cow, Mottled, Brown, Ivory, Arthur Gredington, 1940s, 5 x 8 1/2 In. 4950.00
Figurine, Duchess With Flowers, Beatrix Potter, 3 3/4 In. 3130.00
Figurine, Ginger Cat, No. 1883, 6 1/2 In. 515.00
Figurine, Girl On Pony, No. 1499, 1957-1965, 5 x 5 In. 525.00
Figurine, Horse, Clydesdale, Harness, 1974-1982, 10 3/4 In. 300.00
Figurine, Pheasants, No. 2078, 7 x 9 1/2 In., Pair 880.00
Figurine, Poodle & Bulldog, Near Liquor Bottle, Dubonnet, No. 264 .... 130.00
Figurine, Poodle, Standing, Dutch Clip, 6 x 5 1/4 In. 45.00
Figurine, Rooster Leghorn, 9 1/2 x 9 1/2 In. 310.00
Figurine, Stag, Golden Brown, Satin Matte, No. 2629, 1978-1980, 13 1/2 In. 295.00
Pitcher, Molded, Ivory, Flowers, Scrolls, Hand Painted, Robert Burns, Plow, Verse, 8 In. . 220.00
Vase, Marbleized, Pink, Yellow, Blue, Matte Glaze, Oval, Stamped, 11 1/2 In. 90.00

BETTY BOOP, the cartoon figure, first appeared on the screen in 1931.
Her face was modeled after the famous singer Helen Kane and her
body after Mae West. In 1935, a comic strip was started. Her dog was
named Bimbo. Although the Betty Boop cartoons ended by 1938, there
was a revival of interest in the Betty Boop image in the 1980s and new
pieces are being made.

Card Game, 1920, 3 1/4 x 6 1/4 In. 75.00
Coin Purse, Plastic, Zipper 65.00
Cookie Jar, Betty & Pudgy, Hand Painted, 7 1/2 x 4 In. 35.00
Cookie Jar, Great Stars, Betty Boop As Juliette, 14 In. 80.00
Figurine, Bow On Head, Splash Me, Marked On Back, Chalkware, 6 1/2 In. 40.00
Figurine, Celluloid, Movable Arms & Legs, Prewar, 8 In. 990.00
Hosiery, Black, Original Label, 1931, 11 In. 110.00
Light Bulb, Christmas, Milk Glass, Marked Fleishers Studios, Japan, 1931, 3 In. 42.00
Ornament, Loop & Hook, Jointed, Wood, 4 1/2 In. 70.00
Salt & Pepper, Bimbo, 1930s, 2 1/2 In. 95.00
Toy, Happy House, Celluloid, White Tower Pen Attached, Japan 950.00
Toy, Jointed, Wood, c.1930, 4 1/4 In. 175.00

BICYCLES were invented in 1839. The first manufactured bicycle was
made in 1861. Special ladies' bicycles were made after 1874. The
modern safety bicycle was not produced until 1885. Collectors search
for all types of bicycles and tricycles. Bicycle-related items are also
listed here.

Crawford, Wood Wheels, Direct Drive, Hagerstown, Md., 68 In. 605.00
High Wheel, Eagle, Roadster, Safety, Rotary Crank, c.1890, 51 In. .... *Illus* 11200.00
High Wheel, Victor, Overmann Wheel Co., 1885, 56 In. 10080.00
Huffy, Coca-Cola, Boy's, 26 x 70 In. 195.00

Iver Johnson, Wood Rims, Saddlebag, 36 In. 1375.00
Oil Lamp, Fireball, Spherical, Clear, 3 Red Jeweled Lenses, Cycle Danger Signal, 1800s . 1100.00
Pull-A-Way Cycle, Puffer Hubbard Mfg. Co., Minneapolis, 41 In. 635.00
Roadmaster, Supreme, Curved Tubes, Pedal Crank, Headlights, 1937 .... 8750.00
Roadmaster, Supreme, Dual Headlights, 1937 .... *Illus* 8792.00
Schwinn, Red Phantom, Chrome, 1940s-1950s 1000.00
Shelby, Donald Duck, Boy's, Balloon Tires, 1951, 24 In. 4200.00
Shelby, Donald Duck, Boy's, Balloon Tires, 24 In. 4200.00
Sign, Michelin Bicycle Tires, Michelin Man Riding Bicycle, Tin, 1962, 9 x 13 In. 200.00
Sign, Schwinn Bicycles, Franchised Dealer, Metal, Lithograph, 20 x 15 In. 90.00
Springfield, Roadster, Gear Driven, Mustache Handlebars, 1889, 50 In. 4800.00
Tricycle, Lever Drive, Spoke Wheels, Wicker Chair, Switzerland, c.1880 .... 9842.00
Tricycle, Steel Wheels, Cast Pedals, Wooden Handles, c.1890, 25 In. 300.00
Tricycle, Tiller, Upholstered Seat, Iron Rails, c.1880-1890 .... 250.00
Tricycle, Wood, Steel, Rubber Tires, Bell Car, 27 In. 230.00

BING & GRONDAHL is a famous Danish factory making fine porcelains from 1853 to the present. Underglaze blue decoration was started in 1886. The annual Christmas plate series was introduced in 1895. Dinnerwares, stoneware, and figurines are still being made today. The firm has used the initials B & G and a stylized castle as part of the mark since 1898.

Button, Porcelain, Denmark, Viking Ship, 1940s, 1 1/4 In. 32.00
Plate, Children's Day, Magical Tea Party, 1985 .... 30.00
Plate, Christmas, 1897, Christmas Meal Of The Sparrows 1875.00
Plate, Christmas, 1900, Church Bells Chiming In Christmas 1425.00
Plate, Christmas, 1901, Three Wise Men From The East 665.00
Plate, Christmas, 1902, Interior Of Gothic Church 545.00
Plate, Christmas, 1903, Happy Expectations Of The Children 426.00
Plate, Christmas, 1904, View Of Copenhagen 219.00
Plate, Christmas, 1905, Anxiety Of The Coming Christmas Night 219.00
Plate, Christmas, 1906, Sleighing To Church On Christmas Eve 144.00
Plate, Christmas, 1907, Little Match Girl 144.00
Plate, Christmas, 1908, St. Petri Church Of Copenhagen 111.00
Plate, Christmas, 1909, Happiness Over The Yule Tree 125.00
Plate, Christmas, 1910, Old Organist 120.00
Plate, Christmas, 1911, First It Was Sung By The Angels 105.00
Plate, Christmas, 1912, Going To Church On Christmas Eve 99.00
Plate, Christmas, 1913, Bringing Home The Yule Tree 99.00
Plate, Christmas, 1917, Arrival Of The Christmas Boat 105.00
Plate, Christmas, 1927, Skating Couple 114.00
Plate, Christmas, 1940, Delivering Christmas Letters 225.00
Plate, Christmas, 1943, Ribe Cathedral 255.00
Plate, Christmas, 1957, Christmas Candles 175.00
Plate, Christmas, 1960, Danish Village Church 205.00
Plate, Christmas, 1963, Christmas Elf 156.00
Plate, Christmas, 1975, Christmas At The Old Water Mill 30.00
Plate, Christmas, 1982, Christmas Tree 55.00
Plate, Mother's Day, 1969, Cocker Spaniel & Pups 450.00
Plate, Mother's Day, 1970, Bird & Chicks 30.00
Plate, Mother's Day, 1971, Cat & Kittens 25.00
Plate, Mother's Day, 1982, Lioness & Cubs 45.00
Plate, Mother's Day, 1989, Cow With Calf 75.00
Vase, Hydrangea, Wisteria, 17 In. 715.00

BINOCULARS of all types are wanted by collectors. Those made in the eighteenth and nineteenth centuries are favored by serious collectors. The small, attractive binoculars called *opera glasses* are listed in their own category.

Bausch & Lomb, U.S. Navy, Case, 1941, 8 In. 230.00
Brass, U.S. Signal, Lemaire, Paris 130.00
Carl Zeiss, 6 x 30, Field, Wehrmacht, Leather Covering & Strap 98.00

Carl Zeiss, Jena, 6 x 30, Black, Textured Metal Body, East Germany 69.00
Carl Zeiss, Jena, 6 x 30, Leatherette, Aluminum Body, Brass Hardware, East Germany ... 60.00
Deinstglas, 10 x 50, Field, Wehrmacht Officer's, Metal, Bakelite, Leather Strap 170.00
Dienstglas, SS, Bakelite, Leather Case 635.00
Dienstglas, WH, 6 x 30, Adjustable Eyepieces, Black Textured Surface 150.00
Dienstglas, WH, 6 x 30, Crosshair Reticule, Leather Strap, Lens Protector 130.00

BIRDCAGES are collected for use as homes for pet birds and as decorative objects of folk art. Elaborate wooden cages of the past centuries can still be found. The brass or wicker cages of the 1930s are popular with bird owners.

Bamboo, Blue & White Porcelain Feeders, Jade Perches, Iron Stand, c.1890, 21 1/2 In. ... 161.00
Bell Shape, Wire, Brass Cap, Paw Feet, Wood Perches, Old Silver Paint, 31 In. 44.00
Bird, Delft, Polychrome, Figural Design, 1700s, 18 x 7 x 10 1/2 In. 1840.00
Chip Carved, Painted, Tramp Art, Glass Water Dispenser, 16 1/4 x 12 1/2 In. 495.00
Crown-Of-Thorns Pattern, Hinged Door, Tramp Art, 1880, 13 In. 175.00
Iron, Plant Holders, Vines, Flowers, Cream Color Paint, 73 In. 176.00
Tin, Wirework, Riverboat, Painted, 4 Tiers, Paddlewheels, Sailor, Flag, 25 x 15 x 29 In. ... 2950.00
Wood, Carved, Door, Dragon Form Base, Chinese, 64 x 33 1/2 In. 316.00
Wood, Chinese, c.1900, 11 7/8 In. 201.00
Wood, Ebonized, Stand, Rectangular, Turned Finial, 63 x 22 1/2 x 17 In. 657.00
Wood, Metal Bars, Flower, Spire Details, Blue, Red, Yellow Paint, 22 In. 110.00
Wood, Reed Framework, Square Base, Octagonal Turret, Dome Top, 15 x 9 x 34 In. 220.00
Wood, Wirework, Painted, Carved Spires, 19th Century, 23 x 18 3/4 x 12 1/2 In. 2350.00

BISQUE is an unglazed baked porcelain. Finished bisque has a slightly sandy texture with a dull finish. Some of it may be decorated with various colors. Bisque gained favor during the late Victorian era when thousands of bisque figurines were made. It is still being made. Additional bisque items may be listed under the factory name.

Bust, Catherine The Great, After Jean-Dominque Rachette Model, Russia, 18 In. 8965.00
Bust, Napoleon, Round Socle, Gilt Bronze Square Plinth, France, c.1900, 11 In. 115.00
Dish, Hen On Nest, Eggs, Brown Basket Weave, Beige & White, 2 1/4 x 2 1/2 x 2 In. 75.00
Figurine, 3 Dancing Girls, Green Folklore Dresses, c.1915, 9 To 12 In., 3 Piece 660.00
Figurine, Action Babies, Naked Playful Baby, Gebruder Heubach, c.1915, 6 In., Pair 1320.00
Figurine, Ambulance Driver, Red Cross Cap, Smoking, Gebruder Heubach, c.1915, 5 In. . 550.00
Figurine, Baby In Papa's Shoe, Blond Hair, Real Lace, Gebruder Heubach, c.1912, 12 In. . 5060.00
Figurine, Bathing Boy, Standing In Tub, Gebruder Heubach, c.1910, 15 In. 3080.00
Figurine, Boy & Girl, Carrying Baskets, 8 In., Pair 100.00
Figurine, Boy In Blue Cap, Standing, Dutch Shoes, Necktie, Side Glancing Eyes, 9 In. ... 440.00
Figurine, Boy In Papa's Boots, Gebruder Heubach, c.1915, 6 In. 880.00
Figurine, Boy, Dropped Fish From Platter, Blue Coat, Striped Pants, Germany, 10 1/4 In. . 83.00
Figurine, Boy, With Hat & Flower, Girl, With Apron & Flowers, 16 In., Pair 33.00
Figurine, Bunny Child, Jointed Arms, Eggshell, Gebruder Heubach, c.1915, 6 1/2 In. 578.00
Figurine, Crawling Baby, Egg Candy Holder, 12309, Gebruder Heubach, c.1912, 6 In. ... 358.00
Figurine, Dutch Girl With Easter Eggs, Gebruder Heubach, c.1915, 6 In. 825.00
Figurine, Foxy Grandpa, Seated Pose, Hand Painted, Blue Striped Suit, Red Tie, 8 In. ... 55.00
Figurine, Girl In Blue Sunbonnet, No. 8153, Gebruder Heubach, c.1910, 8 In. 935.00
Figurine, Girl In Contemplating Pose, No. 8010, Gebruder Heubach, c.1912, 7 In. 1430.00
Figurine, Mickey McGuire, Toonerville Trolley, 2 In. 27.50
Figurine, Poodle, Seated On Back Haunches, Gebruder Heubach, c.1915, 8 In. 303.00
Figurine, Poodle, Seated, Shaggy, Gebruder Heubach, c.1912, 7 To 9 In., Pair 495.00
Figurine, Puppy, White Body, Black Ears, Face, Gebruder Heubach, c.1915, 3 In. 440.00
Figurine, Soccer Boy, Seated, Feet In Air, Blue Sweater, Gebruder Heubach, c.1910, 6 In. 385.00
Figurine, Soccer Player, S On Red Sweater, Gebruder Heubach, c.1912, 10 In. 935.00
Figurine, Woman Preparing To Dive, Blond, Blue Swimsuit, Germany, c.1910, 18 In. 1430.00
Figurine, Young Lad Contemplating, Elbows On Logs, Gebruder Heubach, c.1912, 9 In. . 1650.00
Garniture, Clock, Seated Figures, Lady, Man, Dog, Observing Lobster, 15 In., 3 Piece ... 940.00
Jardiniere, Sevres Style, Frolicking Putto Frieze, 6 1/2 In., Pair 1016.00
Mug, Happy Hooligan, Figural, Trimmed Jacket, Vest, Hand Painted, Germany, 5 1/4 In. . 55.00
Pin Tray, Woman Playing Mandolin, Art Nouveau, 5 1/2 In. 140.00
Vase, Bud, Woman Holding Ewer, Art Nouveau, 6 In. 120.00

Vase, Man & Parrot, 6 1/4 In. 22.00
Vase, Woman, 3 Children, Open Blossoms, Figural, 8 In. 25.00

BLACK memorabilia has become an important area of collecting since
the 1970s. The best material dates from past centuries, but many recent
items are also of interest. F & F is the mark used on plastic made by
Fiedler & Fiedler Mold & Die Works, Inc. in the 1930s and 1940s.
Objects that picture a black person may also be listed in this book
under Advertising, Tins; Banks; Bottle Openers; Cookie Jars; Salt &
Pepper; Sheet Music; Toys; etc.

Air Freshener, Malcolm X, 2-Sided, Any Means Necessary, 1960s, 4 1/2 In. 45.00
Ashtray, Black Boy In Tub, Ceramic, Lusterware, Prewar Japan, 4 In. 75.00
Ashtray, Holder, Golliwog Strike, Sack For Matches, Czechoslovakia, 1920s, 5 In. 225.00
Ashtray, Screaming Mammy, Terra-Cotta, Bug Eyed, Bared Teeth, Prewar Japan, 4 In. . . . 365.00
Banjo-Uke, Black Uncle Sam, Exaggerated Blackface Minstrel, Lithograph, 12 In. 45.00
Bedpan, Black & White Babies, Let's Do Business, Bisque, Austria, 1880s, 3 1/2 In. 85.00
Bell, Aunt Jemima, Cloth Dress, Holladner Novelty, Box, 5 In. 79.00
Bell, Mammy, Painted Porcelain, Hinode Stamp, Japan, 3 In. 60.00
Bike Bobber, Golliwog, Animated Eyes Blink, Wink, Spring Base, Early 1950s, 5 In. 35.00
Book, Beloved Belindy, Johnny Gruelle, Volland, Box, c.1926 . . . . 650.00
Book, Child's Story Of The Negro, Cloth, Associated Publishers, 1938, 219 Pages 350.00
Book, First Book Of Jazz, Langston Hughes, Franklin Watts, 1955, 65 Pages 250.00
Book, Ten Little Colored Boys, Die-Cut Heads, Howell Soskins, 1942 . . . . 400.00
Book, Ten Little Niggers, Uncle John's Drolleries, McLoughlin Bros., c.1876 . . . . 1500.00
Box, Display, Mason Challenge Boot Blacking, Street Scene, 1880s, 10 1/2 In. 105.00
Box, Recipe, Aunt Jemima, Embossed Face, Yellow, Prewar, 3 x 5 1/4 In. 100.00
Box, Shipping, Aunt Jemima, Cardboard Lithograph, 13 1/2 In. 180.00
Broom, Fireplace, Mammy, Carved Wood, Horsehair, Hanging Ring, 19 In. 55.00
Calendar, Baseball, Struggle On The Home Stretch, Blacksville Series, 1881, 6 1/2 In. . . . 70.00
Candle, Mammy & Uncle Mose, 6 In. 110.00
Candle, Smiling Mammy Shape, Wax, Hand Painted, 1900s, 6 In. 60.00
Candle, Uncle Remus Shape, Butler, Wax, Hand Painted, 1900s, 6 In. 70.00
Card, Playing, Coon, Circular, Black Dandy, Sutherlands, N.Y., 3 In. 190.00
Chalkboard, Black Nancy Coal, Paper On Wood, 18 In. 260.00
Cheese Container, Little Nigger, Lithograph, Cardboard, 1 1/2 In. Diam. 90.00
Cigar Box, Temptation, Lithograph, Black Boy Chased By Gator, Pyrograph, 8 In. 290.00
Cigar Holder, Black Head, Painted, Ceramic, Victoria, Carlsbad, Austria, 1880s, 4 1/2 In. . 222.00
Cigar Holder, Watermelon Girl, Ceramic, 5 In. 120.00
Cigarette & Match Holder, Black Boy, Top Hat, Lusterware, Japan, 2 3/4 In. 65.00
Cookie Jars are listed in the Cookie Jar category.
Costume, Black Tricot Face Cover, Celluloid Teeth, Lips, Straw Hat, 1890s, 6 1/2 In. 200.00
Cup & Saucer, Demitasse, Coon Chicken Inn, Incaware, Shenango Pottery, 3 In. 395.00
Display Box, Aunt Jemima, Cardboard Lithograph, 4-Sided, Stand-Up, 27 1/2 In. 310.00
Doll, Alabama Baby, Cloth, Muslin Body, Stitch-Jointed, Ella Smith, c.1910, 12 In. 880.00
Doll, Baby, Bisque Socket Head, Painted Eyes, Molded Lids, Open-Close Mouth, 11 In. . . 770.00
Doll, Beloved Belindy, Printed Fabric, Original Clothes, Tagged, Knickerbocker, 15 1/2 In. 400.00
Doll, Bisque, Socket Head, Black Woman Carries White Baby, Kuhnlenz, c.1895, 6 In. . . . 415.00
Doll, Carved Wood, Mortise & Tenon Joints, Cotton Hair, Button Pupils, 11 In. 965.00
Doll, Child, Bisque Socket Head, Ethnic Features, Sleep Eyes, Painted Lashes, 17 In. 2310.00
Doll, Cloth Head & Body, Button Eyes, Embroidered Features, String Hair, 16 In. 415.00
Doll, Cloth Head, Button Eyes, Caracul Brows, Wig, Jointed, Dress, Stockings, 25 In. . . . 360.00
Doll, Cloth, Cloth Head, Stitched Eyes, Brows, Mouth, Arms & Legs, 22 In. 635.00
Doll, Cloth, Embroidered Features, Curly Wool Wig, Kid Glove Hands, 25 In. 1210.00
Doll, Cloth, Embroidered Features, Curly Yarn Hair, 5 Stitched Fingers, 18 In. 770.00
Doll, Cloth, Embroidered Features, Wool Hair, Original Clothes, 12 In. 130.00
Doll, Cloth, Exaggerated Painted Features, Flowered Dress, 23 In. 1980.00
Doll, Cloth, Girl, Mother-Of-Pearl Button Eyes, Dress, Bonnet, Late 1800s, 20 In. 925.00
Doll, Cloth, Oil-Painted Stockinette Head, Mohair, Cloth Body, Tab-Jointed, 16 In. 495.00
Doll, Comical Figures, After 10 Lil Niggers, Original Box, 1950s, 10 In., 10 Piece 135.00
Doll, Composition, Sleep Eyes, White Dress, Baby, 13 In. 115.00
Doll, Cowboy, Posable Arms, Leather Chaps, Western Outfit, Bakelite, 7 In. 120.00
Doll, Felt Face, Shoebutton Eyes, Mohair Wig, Jointed, Oversize Feet, 19 In. 2420.00

Doll, Folk, Cotton Sateen, Pearl Button Eyes, Fleeced Hair, American, Late 1800s, 17 In. . . 495.00
Doll, Golliwog, Crocheted Wool, Red Tails, Bowtie, Prewar, England, 9 In. 55.00
Doll, Golliwog, Stuffed Corduroy, Silk, Wool Hair, Celluloid Eyes, 11 In. 100.00
Doll, Lady, Stiff Neck, Embroidered Features, Jointed, Red Velvet Shoes, 19 In. 550.00
Doll, Little Black Sambo, Stockinet Head, Painted Eyes, String Hair, Cloth Body, 22 In. . . . 2035.00
Doll, Mammy & Baby, Bisque Socket Head, Pupilless Eyes, 4 Teeth, Yarn Wig, 7 1/2 In. . . 660.00
Doll, Mammy, Oilcloth Mask Face, Cloth Body, 12 In. 30.00
Doll, Mammy, Stockinet Head, Painted Eyes, Lashes, Ethnic Features, Cloth Body, 27 In. . . 6290.00
Doll, Plush, Black Cannibal, Native Garb, Holding Spear, Felt, 8 In. 20.00
Doll, Printed Cloth, Cream Of Wheat Man, 16 1/2 In. 35.00
Doll, Stockinet Head, Sculptured Features, Shoebutton Eyes, Cloth Body, 20 In. 1130.00
Doll, Toaster Cover, Stitched Face, 7 In. 15.00
Doll, Topsey, Li'l Eva, Stuffed Cloth, Turn Upside Down, New Orleans, 9 1/2 In. 45.00
Doll, Topsy-Turvy, Composition Head & Arms, Dressed, 7 1/2 In. 70.00
Doll, Topsy-Turvy, Felt Face, Cloth Stitched Features, 17 In. 120.00
Doll, Uncle Mose, Cloth, Stuffed & Sewn, 10 1/2 In. 65.00
Doll, Ventriloquist Dummy, Papier-Mache, Wood, Checked Pants, c.1900, 38 In. 990.00
Fan, Watermelon, Waiter Serving Chicken Center, Red, Black Seeds, 13 In. 230.00
Figurine, Black Boy Eaten By Frog, Bisque, Hand Painted, Germany 130.00
Figurine, Black Minstrel, With Banjo, Bisque, Hand Painted, Austria, 1880s, 3 3/4 In. 110.00
Figurine, Boy Eating Corn, Painted Bisque, 4 1/4 In. . . . . *Illus* 135.00
Figurine, Boy Eating Watermelon, Bisque, Germany, 4 1/4 In. 100.00
Figurine, Boy Holding Pigs, Bisque, 7 1/2 In. 235.00
Figurine, Boy With Goose, Bisque, Germany, 4 1/2 In. 180.00
Figurine, Boy, Riding Alligator, Rotating Head, Cast Iron, 3 1/2 x 6 In. 250.00
Figurine, Cakewalkers, Painted Bisque, 5 1/8 In. . . . . *Illus* 225.00
Figurine, Golliwog, Eccentrically Dressed, Chalkware, Painted, Prewar Japan, 4 In. 110.00
Figurine, Mad Cannibal, Black Head, Huge Teeth, Bone In Nose, Vinyl, Box, 2 1/2 In. . . . 145.00
Figurine, Porter, Railroad, Lionel Deluxe, Valise, Golf Bag, Hand Painted, Lead, 3 1/4 In. 35.00
Figurine, Porter, Railroad, Mini Deluxe, Suitcase, Valise, Accessories, Prewar Japan, 2 In. 45.00
Figurine, Potty Baby, Boy, Holding Umbrella, Bisque, Lusterware, 1880s, 4 1/2 In. 70.00
Game, Dexterity, Voracious Nigger, Metal Balls Go Into Mouth, 3 3/4 In. 135.00
Game, Shasteen Hot Dog, Painted Fiberboard, Shasteen Studios, Toledo, Ohio, 23 In. 480.00
Hand Puppet, 5-Finger, Exaggerated Screaming Black Man's Head, 1950s, 4 1/2 In. 70.00
Hanger, String, Hamborne Cigar, Cardboard, 2-Sided, Pilot, Plane, 7 In. 170.00
Humidor, Black Boy In Barrel, Terra-Cotta, Hand Painted, c.1900, 8 In. 215.00
Humidor, Black Chauffer, Hand Painted, Austria, 1880s, 5 1/2 In. 385.00
Humidor, Dandy In Barrel, Smoking Cigar, Terra-Cotta, Hand Painted, 8 In. 545.00
Humidor, Figural, Man, Receding Hairline, Pipe, Unmarked, Conte & Bohme, 4 1/4 In. . . 135.00
Humidor, Screaming Black Man, Terra-Cotta, Hand Painted, 1880s 605.00
Jar, Cover, Black Boy, Bowtie, Straw Hat, Polychromed Plaster, 7 In. 115.00
Jug, Comic Black Hillbilly Base, Pottery, Hand Painted, Nash Welch, 9 3/4 In. 385.00
Lantern Slides, Li'l Nigger Boys, Color Lithograph On Glass, Poem, Box, 3 1/2 In. 285.00
Marionette, Speed Mitzinette, Painted Composition & Wood, Box, Ron Carr, 16 In. 250.00
Mask, 1/2 Face, Black Man, Straw Hat, Die Cut, Embossed, Lithograph, 12 In. 230.00
Mask, Papier-Mache, Exaggerated Features, Eye & Nose Holes, 1900s, 10 3/4 In. 150.00

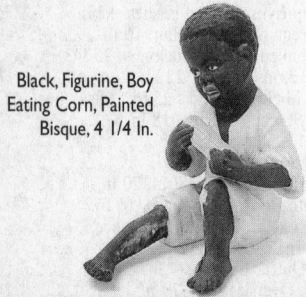

Black, Figurine, Boy
Eating Corn, Painted
Bisque, 4 1/4 In.

Black, Figurine,
Cakewalkers, Painted
Bisque, 5 1/8 In.

Match Safe, Black Man's Head, Striker, Wall Mount, Pottery, Keramic Art Works, 6 In. .. 225.00
Mug, Golliwog & Teddy, Listening To Victrola, Hand Painted, Gold Trim, Prewar Czech . 100.00
Noisemaker, Clapper, Ragtime Black Jazz Drummer, Double Die Cut Graphic, 5 3/4 In. .. 70.00
Pillow, Golliwog, Stuffed, Ruffled Edge, 10 Different Classic Poses, 36 In. 20.00
Pin Tray, Black Baby, Come Hither Pose, Bathing Outfit, Germany, c.1900, 4 3/4 In. 90.00
Pin Tray, Blackamoor Slave Holds Clamshell, Hand Painted, 17th Century, 7 3/4 In. 135.00
Pipe, Cakewalker, Hand Carved, Meerschaum Bust, Top Hat, c.1880, 4 3/4 In. 230.00
Pipe, Crying Black Man, Hand Carved, Meerschaum, France, 1870s, 2 1/4 In. 150.00
Pipe, Darkie, Full Face, Grinning, Bowtie, Screw-On Tobacco Hat, Bakelite, 5 3/4 In. ... 110.00
Pipe, Novelty, Comical Fat Black Man, Sad Faced Scowl, Terra-Cotta, 1920s, 5 1/4 In. .. 120.00
Plate, Black Man Making Pass At Chinese Girl, Octagonal, Filigree, 10 In. 95.00
Plate, Golliwog, Hand Painted, Staffordshire, England, 7 In. 170.00
Platter, Coon Chicken Inn, Incaware, Shenango Pottery, 11 1/2 In. 450.00
Postcard, Pick The Pickaninnies Puzzle 85.00
Poster, Negro Progress Exposition, Polychrome, Lincoln, Freed Slaves, 1940, 14 x 22 In. 1095.00
Pot Holder, Mammy, Cotton, Wool, Stuffed, Framed, c.1900, 13 1/2 x 8 3/8 In. 500.00
Puppet, Minstrel, Carved Wood, Painted, Cloth, Articulated, Banjo, Pelham, Box, 14 In. . 85.00
Puzzle, Golliwog, Teddy, Friends, Party, Wood, Lithograph, Prewar England, Box, 10 In. . 75.00
Puzzle, Little Black Sambo, 3 Puzzles, Hays, Akron, Saalfield, Box, 1942, 9 1/2 x 9 In. .. 650.00
Puzzle, Little Black Sambo, 4 Puzzles, Peat, Cleve., Harter, Box, 1937, 7 3/8 x 9 3/4 In. .. 850.00
Puzzle, Young Black Couple On Beach, Litho On Paper, Original Envelope, 8 In. 160.00
Rattle, Dapper Dan, Celluloid, Paper Label On Foot, 4 3/4 In. 55.00
Recipe Box, Aunt Jemima, Plastic, Green, 5 1/4 In. 190.00
Recipe Box, Aunt Jemima, Plastic, Red, 5 1/4 In. ....79.00 to 148.00
Server, Hors D'Oeuvres, Boy, Umbrella Holes For Appetizers, Silver Plate, 1890s, 6 In. .. 470.00
Sheet Music, Ashy Africa, African Native, Large Format, 1903 .... 55.00
Sheet Music, Cotton Club Parade 28th Ed, Old Plantation, Dancers, 1937 .... 40.00
Sheet Music, Entertainer, Black Entertainer, Large Format, 1902 .... 165.00
Sheet Music, Funeral Clothes, Black Man, 1926 .... 121.00
Sheet Music, Jungle Drums On Patrol, Black Americana Graphics, 1920s 125.00
Sheet Music, Mandy's Broadway Stroll, Black Woman, Parasol, Large Format, 1898 .... 415.00
Sheet Music, Old Black Joe, Black Man On Cover, Stephen Foster, 1915 .... 20.00
Sheet Music, When Our Brown Skin Soldier Boys Come Home, Large Format, 1919 .... 57.00
Smoke Set, Minstrel, Playing Accordion, Bisque, 1890s, 5 In. 235.00
Smoke Stand, Jockey, Majolica Style, Brick Wall Holds Cigars, Matches, 1880s, 6 In. ... 335.00
Soap Dish, Mammy, Open Basket, Cast Iron, 5 1/8 In. 190.00
Songbook, Little Niggers, 10 Plantation Songs, England, 1928, 24 Pages, 12 1/4 In. 55.00
Spice Set, Aunt Jemima, Painted Plastic, Box, 12 In. 735.00
Spoon, Sterling, Enameled Bowl, Boy Eating Watermelon, Getting Full, 5 1/2 In. 1600.00
Spoon, Sterling, Enameled Bowl, Boy On Fence Eating Watermelon, Tennessee, 5 1/2 In. 1100.00
Spoon, Sterling, Enameled Image, 3 Blacks In Watermelon, Tennessee, 1906, 6 In. 2300.00
Spoon, Sterling, Enameled Image, Boy Eating Watermelon, The Real Thing, Atlanta, 4 In. 1300.00
Statue, Jockey, Starters Trumpet, Stylized, Bisque, Hand Painted, Austria, 1900s, 13 In. .. 150.00
Stein, Minstrel, Dancing, Ceramic, Glaze, Base Hole For Lamp, 1961, 7 1/2 In. 95.00
Stereo Card, Black Waiter Serves White Man, Printed Joke, Comic Gems, c.1870 .... 130.00
Stereo Card, How De Debil Do Dey Make A Bike Anyway, 3 Black Boys, c.1900 .... 86.00
Stringholder, Mischievous Mammy, String Pulls From Mouth, Terra-Cotta, 1920s, 6 In. .. 169.00
Sugar & Creamer, Aunt Jemima & Butler, Plastic, F&F Mold, 4 In. ....100.00 to 285.00
Swizzle Stick Set, Zulu-Lulu, Plastic, Display Card, 6 Sticks 29.00
Table, Chicken Thief, Mission Style, Mahogany, Carved Tableaus, 1920s, 23 In. 935.00
Tickets, Anderson County Colored Fair, Coloreds Only, Cardboard, 1930s, 2 In. 25.00
Toast Rack, Golliwog, Motorcyclist, Silver Crane, England, Ceramic, 5 In. 110.00
Tobacco, Niggerhair, Chewing Tobacco, American Tobacco Co., Stamp, 1932, 6 1/2 In. .. 95.00
Toothbrush, Darkie Deluxe, Smiling Minstrel Label, Case, Original Price Tag, 6 1/2 In. .. 30.00
Towel, Pickaninny Eating Watermelon, Embroidered, Painted, 30 In. 70.00
Toy, Dancer, Man, Painted, Jointed Limbs, Wooden, Late 19th Century, 12 1/2 In. 2750.00

BLACK AMETHYST glass appears black until it is held to the light, then
a dark purple can be seen. It has been made in many factories from
1860 to the present.

Bowl, Double Shield, Square, Ruffled Edge, Handles, L.E. Smith, 10 In. 30.00
Bowl, Ribbed, Pierced Tab Handles, 5 In. 18.00

Candlestick, 1930s, 3 3/4 x 7 1/4 In., Pair 45.00
Candy Dish, Cover, 8-Sided, Knob Finial, 4 1/2 x 5 1/8 In. 20.00
Candy Dish, Flared, Footed, Art Deco, 3 1/2 x 5 1/4 In. 15.00
Flower Frog, 3 In. 20.00
Powder Jar, Chantal, Ball Shape, Domed Cover, Art Deco, 4 7/8 x 4 1/4 In. 30.00
Vase, 6-Sided, Ruffled Edge, Saucer Foot, Art Deco, 4 7/8 x 5 In. 50.00
Vase, Baluster, Ruffled Edge, 10 x 5 In. 30.00
Vase, Bud, Painted Flowers, Flattened Rolled Rim, Footed, 9 In. 45.00
Vase, Bulbous, Shoulder Rings, Flared, Handles, 6 1/2 In. 30.00

BLENKO GLASS COMPANY is the 1930s successor to several glassworks
founded by William John Blenko in Milton, West Virginia. In 1933, his
son, William H. Blenko Sr. took charge. The company made a line of
reproductions for Colonial Williamsburg. They are still in business and
are best known today for their decorative wares and stained glass.

Basket, Teal Blue, Hanging, White Cord Rope, 1960s, 8 x 6 1/2 In. 35.00
Bottle, Rialto Series, Opalescent, Sand Blasted Signature, 1960, 9 1/2 In. 405.00
Bowl, Blue Sky, Rim Fades To Green Mountains At Middle, 15 In. 175.00
Decanter, Chess Piece Shape, Amberina Orange, No. 5959, W. Husted, 1959, 15 1/2 In. ... 300.00
Decanter, Turquoise, Crackle, Bulbous Base, Long Neck, Teardrop Stopper, 18 In. 95.00
Decanter, Yellow, Embossed, Globe Stopper, Joel Myers, 1960, 10 In. 95.00
Pitcher, Tangerine, No. 976, Anderson, 1959, 19 In. 170.00
Vase, Cat Shape, Amber, Tail Handle, Applied Face, 13 3/4 In. 305.00
Vase, Emerald Green, Clear Base, Signed, 1962, 8 1/2 In. 65.00
Vase, Fish Shape, Jade Green, Wayne Husted, 1958, 8 In. 55.00
Vase, Lilac, Bulbous Midsection, Wayne Husted, 24 In. 180.00
Vase, Shamrock, Rose, 8 1/4 In. 55.00

BLOWN GLASS, see Glass-Blown category.

BLUE GLASS, see Cobalt Blue category.

BLUE ONION, see Onion category.

BLUE WILLOW, see Willow category.

BOCH FRERES factory was founded in 1841 in La Louviere in eastern
Belgium. The wares resemble the work of Villeroy & Boch. The factory is still in business.

Bowl, Low, Art Deco Flowers, Keramis, 10 1/2 In. 345.00
Lamp Base, Stylized Pattern, Turquoise, Cobalt Blue, Yellow, Crackle Ground, 13 x 6 In. .. 635.00
Vase, Abstract Flowers, Spiked Triangle Leaves, Yellow, Black, Blue, 12 In. 550.00
Vase, Art Deco, 3 Foraging Deer, Charles Catteau, 9 1/8 In. 1955.00
Vase, Bird, Egg Shape, Narrow Neck, Flared Rim, Keramis, Belgium, c.1930, 10 1/8 In. . 880.00
Vase, Blue Crackle Glaze, 8-Sided, Flared, Art Deco, 9 1/4 In. 175.00
Vase, Bulbous, Stylized Fruit, Blue, Green, Ivory Ground, 10 In. 460.00
Vase, Bulbous, Tapered, Stylized Flowers, Brown, Green, Ivory, Charles Catteau, 12 In. ... 978.00
Vase, Bulbous, Wide Mouth, Flowers, Gres Keramis, Catteau, Belgium, c.1930, 5 In. ... 499.00
Vase, Bulbous, Wide Shoulder, Short Neck, Mottled, Gres Catteau, Belgium, c.1930, 6 In. 646.00
Vase, Cylindrical, 7 Openings, Graduated Steps, Persian Blue, Belgium, c.1925, 9 3/8 In. . 382.00
Vase, Egg Shape, Drip Decoration, Gres Keramis, Catteau, Belgium, c.1930, 9 1/4 In. ... 590.00
Vase, Egg Shape, Water Lily, Mottled Blue, Gres Keramis, Belgium, c.1930, 10 In. 765.00
Vase, Egg Shape, White Glaze, Ocher Ground, Gres Keramis, Catteau, Belgium, 6 1/2 In. 705.00
Vase, Flower Baskets, Yellow, Orange, Blue, White Crackle Glaze, 8 1/2 In. 300.00
Vase, Flying Geese, Tapering Cylindrical, Gres Keramis, Belgium, c.1925, 11 1/4 In. 2115.00
Vase, Orange, Blue Flowers, White Crackle Glaze, 9 5/8 In. 518.00
Vase, Pinwheel Flowers, Blue, Yellow, Vertical Wavy Lines, Oval, 11 In. 375.00
Vase, Short Neck, Stylized Flowers & Leaves, Keramis, Belgium, c.1930, 11 In. 880.00
Vase, Spherical, Birds, Branches, Gres Keramis, Catteau, Belgium, 1930, 7 5/8 In. 825.00
Vase, Stylized Flowers, Indigo & Amber, White Crackle, Charles Catteau, 5 1/2 In. 1840.00
Vase, Swollen Cylinder, Ferns, Gres Keramis, Catteau, Belgium, c.1930, 9 1/2 In. 1528.00
Vase, Tapered, Chicken Design, Incised, Painted, Keramis, 11 In. 748.00
Vase, Tulips, Yellow, Orange, Red, Forget-Me-Nots, White Crackle Glaze, Oval, 11 In. 550.00
Vase, Vertical Panels, Half Moons, Yellow, Turquoise, Black Beads, Baluster, 11 In. 425.00

BOEHM is the collector's name for the porcelains of Edward Marshall Boehm. In 1953 the Osso China Company was reorganized as Edward Marshall Boehm, Inc. The company is still working in England and New Jersey. In the early days of the factory, dishes were made, but the elaborate and lifelike bird figurines are the best-known ware. Edward Marshall Boehm, the founder, died in 1961, but the firm has continued to design and produce porcelain. Today, the firm makes both limited and unlimited editions of figurines and plates.

Candlestick, Holly, Berries, Leaves, No. 400-62, c.1965, 10 x 3 1/2 In., Pair	316.00
Figurine, Baby Blue Jay, No. 436, Horse Head Mark, 4 1/4 In.	165.00
Figurine, Baby Bluebird, No. 442, Horse Head Mark, 4 1/2 In.	220.00
Figurine, Baby Robin, No. 437, Horse Head Mark, 3 1/2 In.	145.00 to 157.00
Figurine, Baby Wood Thrush, No. 444, Horse Head Mark, 4 1/4 In.	110.00
Figurine, Black Chickadee, No. 191, c.1976, 14 x 6 1/2 In.	920.00
Figurine, Blackbird, Cherry Blossoms, Horse Head Mark, 17 In.	1380.00
Figurine, Fledgling Magpie, No. 476, Horse Head Mark, 5 3/4 In.	165.00
Figurine, Hummingbird, Cactus, No. 440, Horse Head Mark, 8 1/2 In.	575.00
Figurine, Mallard Ducklings, Horse Head Mark, Feather, 6 In.	175.00
Figurine, Poodle, Lying Down, Show Clip, White, Pink, 3 1/2 x 6 1/2 In.	180.00
Figurine, Poodle, White, Turquoise, Lying Down, 3 1/8 x 5 1/4 In.	80.00
Group, Least Tern, No. 287, Signed, 14 1/2 In.	259.00

BOHEMIAN GLASS, see Glass-Bohemian.

BONE includes those articles made of bone not listed elsewhere in this book.

Figurine, Elephant, 1800s, 3 1/4 In.	276.00
Figurine, Woman, Standing, Chinese, 20th Century, 30 In.	316.00
Group, 7 Merchants On Bridge, Glass Pedestal, Chinese, 20th Century, 14 x 43 1/2 In.	805.00
Rouge Pot, Carved, Cover, Indian, Round, Mid 19th Century, 1 x 1 1/2 In.	460.00

BONE DISHES were considered a necessary part of a table setting for the Victorian table. The crescent-shaped dish was kept at the edge of the dinner plate so the bones removed from the fish could be stored away from the uneaten food. Some bone dishes were made in more fanciful shapes and many resemble fish.

Blue Flowers, W.H. Grindley & Co.	35.00
Butterflies, Tan Ground, Gold Trim	22.00
Floral Transfer, Brown, Edge, Malkin & Co., Burslem, England, 1891-1902	15.00
Floral Transfer, Brown, Gold Trim, Scalloped Ribs, Wheeling, 1880-1886	40.00
Gold Border, Knowles China Co.	8.00
Pink Flowers, Scalloped Edge, Henry Alcock & Co., 1880-1910	18.00
Pink Roses, Hand Painted, Mittereich, Bavaria	28.00

BOOKENDS have probably been used since books became inexpensive. Early libraries kept books in cupboards, not on open shelves. By the 1870s bookends appeared, especially homemade fret-carved wooden examples. Most bookends listed in this book date from the twentieth century. Bookends are also listed in other categories by manufacturer or material. All bookends listed here are pairs.

2 Chinese Children, 1 Seated On Stack Of Books, Cast Metal, Gold Paint, 8 3/4 x 5 In.	250.00
Arts & Crafts, Hammered Copper, 6 1/2 In.	200.00
Brass, Hartford Fire Insurance Co., 1810-1935, 5 1/2 In.	92.00
Camel, Cast Iron, 5 1/4 In.	17.00
Cat, Seated, Bronze Finish, Base, Oval, Black Enamel, Dewitt, 8 1/2 In.	80.00
Cat & Dog, Silver Plate, Art Deco Style, Marked, H. Vandaele, 6 x 3 1/2 x 3 1/4 In.	385.00
Chamberstick & Book, Wood, Applied Tooled Leather, Arts & Crafts, 5 1/2 In.	115.00
Chamois, Tree, Leaves, Tabletop Faceplate, Bark Edges, Wood, Carved, 1900, 7 x 17 In.	430.00
Copper, Craftsman, 5 x 4 1/2 In.	145.00
Copper, Roycroft, 5 x 5 In.	518.00
Dog, Boston Terrier, Bradley & Hubbard, 5 1/4 x 5 In.	165.00
Dog, Scottish Terrier, White Metal, 3 1/2 In.	90.00
Dog, Terrier, Cast Iron, Hubley, 5 x 5 In.	138.00

Elephant & Palace, Cast Iron, 5 3/4 In. 18.00
Foo Dog, Seated, Jade, Green, Early 1900s, 5 In. 400.00
Fork Halves, Die, Steel, Flatware, 9 3/4 In. 118.00
Japanese Peasant, White Metal, Patinated, c.1900, 7 In. 138.00
Maiden, Sitting On Lily Pad, Frog, Metal, Maroon Patina, Art Nouveau, 7 In. 58.00
Model 4925, Enamel, Marianne Brandt, Ruppelwerk Gotha, Germany, c.1930, 5 In. 1287.00
Mushrooms, Frog, Bronze, McClelland Barclay, 5 In. 546.00
Oak, G. Stickley, 6 x 7 x 2 1/2 In. 1035.00
Owl, Arch, Curved, Beveled, Bradley & Hubbard, 5 x 6 In. 110.00
Parrots At Fountain, Semicircular, Brass, Acid Etched, 5 x 7 In. 316.00
Peacock Design, Tooled, Cutout, Hammered Copper, Arts & Crafts, 6 In. 175.00
Sailing Ship, Cast Iron, Bronze Wash, 6 3/4 x 4 1/2 In. 75.00
Stylized Design, Hammered Copper, Jarvie, 4 1/2 In. 489.00
U.S. Constitution, Ship's Wheel, Ship's Material, Bronze, 1927, 6 x 1 1/4 x 5 3/4 In. 920.00
U.S. Frigate Constitution Keel, Wood, Brass Plaque, 1927, 6 1/2 x 7 1/2 In. 316.00
Wise Men, Sage On Base, Warrior Fighting Tiger, Soapstone, Pair, 11 1/2 In. 105.00

BOOKMARKS were originally made of parchment, cloth, or leather. Soon woven silk ribbon, thin cardboard, celluloid, wood, silver, tortoiseshell, and metals were used. Examples made before 1850 are scarce, but there are many to be found dating before 1920.

Campbell Soup, Just Add Hot Water, Multicolored, Celluloid 49.00
Comfort Soap, Paper, Child Wearing Glasses, Send 25 Wrappers For Book, 7 x 2 In. 35.00
George Washington, Woven Silk, Phoenix Silk Manufacturing Co., 8 In. 54.00
Hoyt's German Cologne, Paper, Child In Glasses, Die Cut, Lowell, Mass., 4 1/2 In. 9.00
Motto, Word Is Truth, Punchwork, Embroidered, 11 In. 15.00
Photograph, Silk Ribbon, Unique Portrait Co., Pat. Oct. 15, 1889, 8 x 2 In. 35.00
Star Spangled Banner, Woven Silk, Phoenix Silk Manufacturing Co., 8 In. 79.00

BOSSONS character wall masks, plaques, figurines, and other decorative pieces are made by W.H. Bossons, Limited of Congleton, England. The company was founded in 1946 and closed in 1996. Dates shown are the date the item was introduced.

Wall Figure, Cat Head, Black, Wall Hanging, 1958, 3 1/2 In. 75.00
Wall Figure, Cat Head, White, Hanging, 1958, 3 1/2 In. 140.00
Wall Figure, Desert Hawks, No. 63, 1961 .... 145.00
Wall Figure, Gypsy Girl 90.00
Wall Figure, Swan, Blue, 1970-1971 .... 460.00
Wall Mask, Cossack, Box 150.00
Wall Mask, Mr. Wang, Chinese Man 255.00

BOSTON & SANDWICH CO. pieces may be found in the Lutz and Sandwich Glass categories.

BOTTLE collecting has become a major American hobby. There are several general categories of bottles, such as historic flasks, bitters, household, and figural. ABM means the bottle was made by an automatic bottle machine after 1903. Pyro is the shortened form of the word *pyroglaze,* an enameled lettering used on bottles after the mid-1930s. This form of decoration is also called ACL or applied color label. For more bottle prices, see the book *Kovels' Bottles Price List* by Ralph and Terry Kovel.

Apothecary, 2 Applied Rings, Cover, Cobalt Blue Ring, 11 x 5 In. 155.00
Apothecary, 3 Blown-Out Rings, Applied Stem, Foot, Cover, 14 1/4 x 10 x 3 In. 130.00
Apothecary, Bulbous Body, Applied Collar, Pedestal, Round Footed Base, 22 3/4 In. 281.00
Apothecary, Cover, Blue, Columbia, 30 In. 2420.00
Apothecary, ESS Cloves, Globular, Carboy Type, Green, Gilt Label, 16 x 13 In. 1155.00
Apothecary, Horlick's Malted Milk, Glass Stopper, 9 1/2 In. 159.00
Armour & Co., Pottery, Cream, Butterscotch Glaze, Stopper 30.00
Barber, Armour & Co., Ceramic, Cream, Butterscotch Glaze, Stopper 30.00
Barber, Bay Rum, Milk Glass, Bird, Cattail, Pontil, Applied Mouth, 8 3/4 In. 215.00
Barber, Blue Opalescent Stripes, 8 In. 175.00
Barber, Blue, Enamel Daisies, 9 In. 275.00

Barber, Brilliantine, Purple Amethyst, Ribs, Multicolored, Flowers, Tooled Mouth, 8 In. . . . 179.00
Barber, Brilliantine, Purple Amethyst, Ribs, Multicolored, Polished Lip, 3 7/8 In. 310.00
Barber, Clear, Horizontal Gold Bands, Bulbous, 6 In. 30.00
Barber, Cobalt Blue, Gold Bands, Bulbous, 4 3/4 In. 50.00
Barber, Cobalt Blue, Mary Gregory Type, Rolled Lip, Pontil, 8 In. 336.00
Barber, Coin Spot, Multicolored Enamel Flowers, Rolled Lip, Pontil, 8 In. 310.00
Barber, Cranberry Opalescent, Coral, Pontil, Rolled Lip, 8 1/8 In. 530.00
Barber, Cranberry Opalescent, Swirled To Left, Rolled Lip, Pontil, 6 7/8 In. 125.00
Barber, Emerald Green, Yellow, Gold Trim, Rolled Lip, Pontil, Art Nouveau, 8 1/8 In. . . . 280.00
Barber, Frosted Ruby Red, Ribs, Multicolored Enamel Flowers, Pontil, 7 1/4 In. 365.00
Barber, Grape Amethyst, Yellow & Gold Enamel Flowers, Rolled Lip, Art Nouveau, 8 In. 225.00
Barber, Green, Mary Gregory Type, Rolled Lip, Pontil, 8 In. 110.00
Barber, Kennedy's Dandruff Cure Hair Restorer, Clear, Label Under Glass, 7 In. 1120.00
Barber, Light Yellow, Mary Gregory Type, White Enamel, Woman, 9 In. 50.00
Barber, Liquid Head Rest, Clear, Label Under Glass, 7 3/4 In. 305.00
Barber, Purple Amethyst, Ribs, Windmill, Toilet Water, Rolled Lip, Pontil, 7 3/4 In. 450.00
Barber, Purple Amethyst, Yellow, Flowers, Gold Trim, Rolled Lip, Pontil, 8 1/8 In. 280.00
Barber, Scalp Tonic, Clear, Horizontal Ribs, 9 In. 365.00
Barber, Shampoo, Clear, Label Under Glass, 7 5/8 In. 420.00
Barber, Teal Green, Mary Gregory Type, White Enamel, 3/4 In. 1570.00
Barber, Turquoise Opalescent, Coral, Rolled Lip, Pontil, 8 1/4 In. 840.00
Barber, Turquoise Opalescent, Swirled To Left, Rolled Lip, Pontil, 6 1/4 In. 157.00
Barber, Vegederma, Purple Amethyst, White Enamel Girl, Rolled Lip, Pontil, 8 1/8 In. . . . 390.00
Barber, Witch Hazel, Milk Glass, Multicolored Enamel, Applied Mouth, 9 In. 235.00
Barber, Yellow Green, Mary Gregory Type, White Enamel, Rolled Lip, 8 1/8 In. 224.00

Beam bottles were made to hold Kentucky Straight Bourbon, made by
the James B. Beam Distilling Company. The Beam series of ceramic
bottles began in 1953.

Beam, Antique Trader, 1968 . . . . 10.00
Beam, Blue Jay, Regal China, 1969 . . . . 20.00
Beam, Duck, Mallard, 1988 . . . . 5.00
Beam, Elks Club, 1968 . . . . 10.00
Beam, Harold's Club, Covered Wagon, Regal China, 1969 . . . . 10.00
Beam, Harry Hoffman Liquor Stores, Denver, Regal China, 1969 . . . . 10.00
Beam, Jack Rabbit, Regal China, 1971 . . . . 43.00
Beam, Koala Bear, Regal China, 1973 . . . . 24.00
Beam, Liberty, Coins, Attucks, Hamilton, Hancock, Regal China, 1970 . . . . 12.00
Beam, Mt. Rushmore, 1969 . . . . 10.00
Beam, New Hampshire, State, 1968 . . . . 15.00
Beam, Pearl Harbor, 1972 . . . . 45.00
Beam, Political, Donkey, Elephant, 1972, Pair 20.00
Beam, San Francisco Cable Car, 1968 . . . . 10.00
Beam, Sequoit Indian, Antioch Ill., 1967 . . . . 9.00
Beer, A. Werm, Honey Gold, Blob Top 59.00
Beer, Anderson & Co., Home Brewed Ale, Red Amber, Cylindrical, Sloping Collar 2016.00
Beer, Anheuser Busch Brewing, Red Amber, Embossed, 8 3/4 In. 75.00
Beer, Celery Beer, Keller Candy Company, Oakland, Ca., Amber, Tooled Top, Qt. 90.00
Beer, Elgin Eagle Brewing Co., Elgin, Ill., Aqua, Blob Top, Stopper, 9 In. 29.00
Beer, John Gompf Brewery, Ontario, Aqua, Embossed, Blob Top, 9 In. 29.00
Beer, Louis Buehler, Philadelphia, Man Pouring Beer In Glass, Aqua, Blob Top, 8 3/4 In. . 59.00
Beer, Lucky Lager, Painted Label, 1950s, 7 Oz. 15.00
Beer, M. Butterman Cronk, Citron, Squat, Blob Top 149.00
Beer, Matt Schmitt, Belle Plaine, Iowa, Embossed, c.1905-1916, 24 Oz. 500.00
Beer, New South Brewing & Ice, Middlesboro, Ky., Woman On Rock, Amber, Blob Top . 39.00
Beer, Peter Stumpf, Orange Amber, Lightning Stopper, 1893-1897, Pt., 8 3/4 In. 190.00
Beer, R.H. Inman, Huddersfield, Aqua, Cobalt Blue Lip, 8 In. 69.00
Beer, Red Top, Westheimer & Sons, Cincinnati, Ohio, St. Joseph, Mo., 4 1/4 In. 85.00
Beer, Reymann Brewing Co., Wheeling, W. Va., Aqua Blue, Blob Top, 12 In. 59.00
Beer, Saltzmann Bros., Palace Hill Brewery, Oil City, Pa., Amber, Blob Top 8.00
Beer, Schmulback Brewing Co., Wheeling, W. Va., Amber, Monogram, Tall 5.00
Beer, Shelby Street Brewery, Louisville, Ky., Orange Amber, Blob Top, 11 1/2 In. 59.00
Beer, Simon Pure, Buffalo, N.Y., Yellow Amber, Embossed, Blob Top, 9 In. 35.00

Beer, Virginia Brewing, Aqua, Baltimore Seal Type Closure, 1890-1900, 9 In. 80.00
Beer, Wm. A. Cunliffe's Botanic Beer, Orange Amber, Embossed, Blob Top, 9 1/2 In. . . . 39.00
Bininger, A.M. & Co., 19 Broad St., N.Y., Barrel, Yellow Amber, Double Collar, 9 1/2 In. 420.00
Bininger, A.M. & Co., 19 Broad St., N.Y., Cannon, Amber, Sheared Lip, 12 1/2 In. 1320.00
Bininger, A.M. & Co., 19 Broad St., N.Y., Jug, Amber, Applied Collar, 8 1/4 In. 470.00
Bininger, A.M. & Co., 19 Broad St., N.Y., Old Kentucky Bourbon, Barrel, Amber, 8 In. . . 330.00
Bininger, A.M. & Co., Barrel, Yellow Amber, Double Collar, Pontil, 8 In. 300.00
Bitters, Angostura Bark, Eagle Liquor Distiller, Amber, Bulbous Bottom, 7 In. 29.00
Bitters, Baker's Orange Grove, Yellow Amber, Square, Roped Corners, 9 1/2 In. 840.00
Bitters, Bell's Cocktail, Jas. M. Bell & Co., New York, Amber, Lady's Leg, 10 1/2 In. . . . 385.00
Bitters, Ben Franklin, Poor Richard's Tonic Barrel, Green, c.1850, 10 In. 8960.00
Bitters, Berkshire, Amann & Co., Cincinnati, O., Pig, Deep Amber, 10 1/2 In. 460.00
Bitters, Brown's Catalina, Cannon Shape, Amber, Square Lip, 11 1/4 In. 425.00
Bitters, Brown's Celebrated Indian Herb, Patented 1867, Yellow To Honey Amber, 12 In. 850.00
Bitters, Caroni, Green, Cylindrical, Tooled Square Lip, 5 1/4 In. 30.00
Bitters, Cooley's Anti-Dispeptic Or Jaundice, Aqua, Oval, Applied Mouth, 6 1/4 In. 1300.00
Bitters, Damiana, Baja, California, Lewis Hess Manufr., Blue, Aqua, Cylindrical, 11 3/4 In. 110.00
Bitters, Doyle's Hop, 1872, Amber, 4 Indented Panels, 9 1/2 In. 40.00
Bitters, Dr. Bishop's Wa-Hoo, Wa-Hooo Bitter Co., Conn., Semi-Cabin, Amber, 8 In. 900.00
Bitters, Dr. Cook's Wine Of Tar, Blue, Embossed, 9 In. 48.00
Bitters, Dr. Harter's Wild Cherry, St. Louis, Amber, 4 Indented Panels, 4 1/2 In. 40.00
Bitters, Dr. J. Boveedod's Imperial Wine, Aqua, Rectangular, Panels, 9 3/8 In. 420.00
Bitters, Dr. J. Hostetter's Stomach, Olive Yellow, Square, 1860-1870, 9 1/2 x 3 In. 520.00
Bitters, Dr. J. Hostetter's Stomach, Yellow Amber, Sloping Collar, 8 7/8 In. 50.00
Bitters, Dr. Jacob's, S.A. Spencer, New Haven, Ct., Rectangular, Aqua, 8 1/2 In. 325.00
Bitters, Dr. Langley's Root & Herb, 76 Union, Boston, Aqua, Applied Lip, 8 3/4 In. 70.00
Bitters, Dr. Langley's Root & Herb, Reverse 99, Union St., Boston, Light Green, 6 3/4 In. 340.00
Bitters, Dr. Soule's Hop Flowers & Leaf, Cabin, Amber, 9 1/2 In. 175.00
Bitters, Dr. Wheeler's Tonic Sherry Wine, Boston, Aqua, Square, Roped Edges, 9 1/2 In. . 3920.00
Bitters, Drake's Plantation, 6 Log, Cabin, Amber, 1862, 10 1/4 In. 460.00
Bitters, Drake's Plantation, 6 Log, Cabin, Deep To Medium Strawberry Puce, 10 In. 770.00
Bitters, Drake's Plantation, 6 Log, Cabin, Gold Amber, 9 3/4 In. 175.00
Bitters, Drake's Plantation, 6 Log, Cabin, Honey To Yellow Amber, 1862, 10 In. 200.00
Bitters, Drake's Plantation, 6 Log, Cabin, Patented 1862, Honey Amber, 9 3/4 In. 150.00
Bitters, Drake's Plantation, 6 Log, Strawberry Puce, 10 In. 190.00
Bitters, Flask, L.N. Kreinbrooks, Mt. Pleasant, Yellow Amber, Pa., Pt., 6 1/4 In. 1000.00
Bitters, Gold Amber, Pineapple Shape, Applied Mouth, 9 In. 360.00
Bitters, Greeley's Bourbon, Barrel, Copper Puce, Square Collar, 1860-1870, 9 1/2 In. . . . 525.00
Bitters, Greeley's Bourbon, Barrel, Strawberry Puce, 9 3/8 In. 1456.00
Bitters, Green Mountain Cider, Aqua, Round, Applied Mouth, 10 1/4 In. 45.00
Bitters, H.P. Herb Wild Cherry, Reading, Pa., Cabin, Medium Amber, Tree, 10 In. 550.00
Bitters, Hall's, E.E. Hall, New Haven, Barrel, Amber, 9 1/8 In. 90.00
Bitters, Hall's, E.E. Hall, New Haven, Barrel, Amber, Applied Square Collar, 9 In. 220.00 to 360.00
Bitters, Holtzermann's Patent Stomach, Cabin, Red Amber, 9 3/4 In. 280.00
Bitters, Home Bitters Co., St. Louis Mo., Aqua, Rectangular, Strapped Sides, 7 1/2 In. . . . 65.00
Bitters, James L. Davis' Sons, Schiedam, New York, Amber, Square, Beveled Corners, 9 In. 420.00
Bitters, Jno Moffat, Price $1, Phoenix, New York, Amber Black, Rolled Mouth, 5 1/2 In. . 2800.00
Bitters, John Moffat, Phoenix, New York, Aqua, Open Pontil, Applied Mouth, 5 1/2 In. . . 80.00
Bitters, John Moffat, Price $1, Phoenix, Aqua, Open Pontil, Rolled Lip, 7 In. 125.00
Bitters, Johnson's Calisaya Bitters, Burlington, Vt., Amber, Square, Label, 10 In. 220.00
Bitters, Kelly's Old Cabin, Patented 1863, Light To Medium Amber, 9 5/8 In, ... 3020.00
Bitters, Kelly's Old Cabin, Patented 1863, Teal Green Blue, 9 5/8 In. 29700.00
Bitters, Kelly's Old Cabin, Patented 1863, Medium Amber, 9 5/8 In. 2420.00
Bitters, Kimball's Jaundice, Troy, N.H., Olive Amber, Applied Collar, c.1845, 7 In. 1430.00
Bitters, Lacours Sarsapariphere, Light To Medium Amber, Round, Indented Panels, 9 In. . 3740.00
Bitters, Lediard's Celebrated Stomach, Blue Green, Double Roll Collar, 10 In. 2420.00
Bitters, Lediard's O.K. Plantation, 1840, Semi-Cabin, Amber, Applied Top, 10 In. 2860.00
Bitters, Lediard's, Plantation, New York, Amber, Square, Applied Top, 10 In. 1210.00
Bitters, Litthauer Stomach, Hartwig Kantorowicz, Milk Glass, Case Gin, 9 1/8 In. 45.00
Bitters, Litthauer Stomach, Josef Loewenthal, Berlin, Milk Glass, Case Gin, 9 1/2 In. . . . 150.00
Bitters, Louis Taussig & Co., San Francisco, Ca., Amber, Applied Square Lip, 8 3/4 In. . . 100.00
Bitters, Mishler's Herb, Dr. S.B. Hartman & Co., Yellow Amber, Square, 9 In. 100.00
Bitters, Napoleon Cocktail, Dingens Brothers, Yellow Amber, Lady's Leg, 10 1/2 In. 6500.00

Bitters, National, Ear Of Corn, Patent 1867, Amber, Applied Lip, 12 1/2 In. 495.00
Bitters, Old Dr. Goodhues, Root & Herb, Salem, Mass., Aqua, Rectangular, 8 7/8 In. 130.00
Bitters, Old Homestead Wild Cherry, Cabin, Amber, Applied Sloping Collar, 9 3/4 In. 440.00
Bitters, Old Sachem & Wigwam Tonic, Barrel, Amber, Applied Square Collar, 9 3/8 In. . . . 500.00
Bitters, Old Sachem & Wigwam Tonic, Barrel, Red Amber, Applied Lip, 9 1/4 In. 215.00
Bitters, Old Sachem & Wigwam Tonic, Barrel, Straw Yellow, 9 1/2 In. 9520.00
Bitters, Old Sachem & Wigwam Tonic, Barrel, Strawberry Puce, 9 3/8 In. 570.00
Bitters, Orizaba, J. Maristany Jr., Amber, Applied Mouth, 9 1/2 In. 6050.00
Bitters, Pineapple, Yellow, Olive, Diamond Diaper, Applied Mouth, Pontil, 8 7/8 In. 730.00
Bitters, Rush's, A.H. Flanders M.D., New York, Amber, Square, 8 3/4 In. 230.00
Bitters, S.B. Goff's Herb, Camden, N.J., Aqua, Beveled Edges, Double Collar, 5 3/4 In. . . 20.00
Bitters, S.O. Richardson's, South Reading, Mass., Aqua, Flared Lip, Pontil, 7 In. 100.00
Bitters, Sazerac Aromatic, Lady's Leg, Milk Glass, Applied Mouth, c.1875, 12 1/2 In. . . . 275.00
Bitters, Sazerac Aromatic, Lady's Leg, Milk Glass, Applied Ring, 12 In. 420.00
Bitters, Smyrna Stomach, Prolongs Life, Dayton, Ohio, Lady's Leg, Amber, 9 In. 190.00
Bitters, Sol Frank's Panacea, Frank Hayman & Rhine, Lighthouse, Amber, 10 1/4 In. 2450.00
Bitters, Solomon's Strengthening & Invigorating, Savannah, Ga., Cobalt Blue, 9 5/8 In. . . 1650.00
Bitters, Suffolk, Philbrook & Tucker, Boston, Pig, Amber, 10 In. 185.00
Bitters, W.C. Brobst & Rentschler, Reading, Pa., Barrel, Orange Amber, 10 5/8 In. 595.00
Bitters, Wampoo, New York, Light To Medium Amber, Applied Lip, 9 3/4 In. 209.00
Bitters, Warner's Safe, Rochester, N.Y., Amber, Double Collar, Oval, c.1860, 9 1/2 In. . . . 730.00
Bitters, Wormser Bros, San Francisco, Barrel, Amber, Applied Lip, c.1875, 9 3/4 In. 2200.00
Blown, Amethyst, Opal White Swirls, Footed, 5 7/8 In. 250.00
Blown, Chestnut, Olive Yellow, Outward Rolled Collar, 1780-1830, 6 1/2 In. 300.00
Blown, Globular, Rigaree, Bulging Neck, Tooled Lip, 2 1/8 In. 55.00
Coca-Cola bottles are listed in the Coca-Cola category.
Cordial, Wishart's Pine Tree Tar, Phila., Patent 1859, Blue Green, Square, Embossed, 8 In. 139.00
Cosmetic, Acme Hair Vigor, Label Under Glass, Embossed Wildroot Top, 9 In. 425.00
Cosmetic, Ambercrude For Hair & Scalp, Phila., U.S.A., BIMAL, Contents, Label, 8 In. . 45.00
Cosmetic, C.A.P. Mason, Hair Balm, Providence, R.I., Olive Yellow, Label, c.1870, 7 In. . 3025.00
Cosmetic, Circassian Hair Restorative, Cincinnati, Yellow Amber, 7 3/8 In. 269.00
Cosmetic, Dr. Tebbetts' Physiological Hair Regenerator, Apricot, Double Collar, 7 3/4 In. . 4480.00
Cosmetic, Dr. Tebbetts' Physiological Hair Regenerator, Deep Amethyst, 7 1/2 In. 225.00
Cosmetic, Hair Oil, Figural, Turtle, Yellow Amber, Head Stopper, 4 7/8 In. 420.00
Cosmetic, Mrs. S.A. Allen's World's Hair Balsam, N.Y., Aqua, Open Pontil, 6 3/4 In. 60.00
Cosmetic, Mrs. S.A. Allen's World's Hair Restorer, New York, Amethyst, 7 In. 110.00
Cosmetic, Pearson & Co. Circassian Hair Rejuvenator, Brooklyn, N.Y., Amber, 6 3/4 In. . 670.00
Cosmetic, Professor Motts Magic Hair Invigorator, Highgate, Vt., Aqua, 6 1/4 In. 246.00
Cosmetic, Professor Motts Magic Hair Invigorator, Highgate, Vt., Green Aqua, 7 3/4 In. . 364.00
Cosmetic, Velvetina Skin Beautifier, Milk Glass, Contents, Label, 5 1/4 In. 155.00
Cure, Ayer's Ague, Lowell, Mass., Aqua, Contents, 7 In. 35.00
Cure, Dr. C.C. Roc's Liver Rheumatic & Neuralgic, Aqua, Embossed, Contents, 8 In. 70.00
Cure, Dr. Kilmer's Swamp Root Kidney Cure, London, Sample, 3 1/8 In. 15.00
Cure, Dr. Woodruff's Wonderful Cure Co., Columbus, Ga., Gold Amber, c.1875, 8 In. . . . 155.00
Cure, Hires Cough, Phila., Pa., Aqua, Label, Contents, 1880-1900, 4 1/2 In. 210.00
Demijohn, Aqua, Bubbles, Iron Pontil, 17 1/2 In. 79.00
Demijohn, Blue Aqua, Cylindrical, Iron Pontil, c.1850-1860, 12 1/2 In. 29.00
Demijohn, Gold Amber, Sloping Collar, Pontil, 12 7/8 In. 505.00
Demijohn, Green Aqua, Applied Ribbed Collar, Open Pontil, 16 1/2 In. 44.00
Demijohn, Olive Amber, Blown, Applied Tapered Collar, Pontil, 10 5/8 In. 99.00
Demijohn, Olive Amber, Stoddard, 11 1/2 In. 85.00
Demijohn, Olive Yellow, 3-Piece Mold, Squat, Swirls, 13 1/2 In. 40.00
Figural, Dog, Dressed As Hunter, Pottery, Hat Stopper, 12 1/2 In. 725.00
Figural, Duck, In Uniform, Pottery, 13 In. 725.00
Figural, Japanese Mikado, Amber, Primicerio & Co., Japanese Polish, c.1880, 6 3/4 In. . . . 440.00
Figural, Monument, Teal Green, 4-Sided, Tooled Flared Mouth, 12 In. 1680.00
Figural, Sailor, Blue, Blown, Ground Top, c.1900, 12 In. 159.00
Flask, 16 Ribs, Swirled To Left, Blue Aqua, Sheared Mouth, 5 3/4 In. 250.00
Flask, 18 Ribs, Teardrop, Swirled To Right, Aqua, Sheared Mouth, Pontil, 1/2 Pt. 215.00
Flask, 20 Ribs, Swirled To Right, Amber, Sheared Mouth, Pontil, 6 1/8 In. 260.00
Flask, 20 Ribs, Vertical, Blue, Sheared Mouth, Iron Pontil, 1845-1860, 1/2 Pt. 200.00
Flask, Adams & Jefferson, Medium Olive Amber, Sheared Mouth, Pontil, 1/2 Pt. 476.00
Flask, Anthracite Brand, California Brandy, L. Lewith & Sons, Pa., ABM, c.1910, Qt. 39.00

Flask, Book, Departed Spirits, Enamel, c.1849, 5 1/2 x 3 3/4 In. . . . . .385.00 to 595.00
Flask, Book, Kossuth's Life & Suffering, Flint Enamel, Signed, 6 In. . . . . .440.00 to 715.00
Flask, Chestnut, Forest Green, Applied Lip, Pontil, 1780-1830, 6 5/8 In. 476.00
Flask, Chestnut, Olive Yellow, Applied Collar, 7 In. 280.00
Flask, Chestnut, Olive Yellow, Sloping Collar, Pontil, 7 In. 280.00
Flask, Chestnut, Sea Green, Sheared Lip, FB, Open Pontil, 1800-1830, Pt., 7 1/4 In. 179.00
Flask, Chestnut, Topaz, Tooled Collar, Pontil, 5 1/4 In. 336.00
Flask, Coffin, Polychrome, Deer, Flowers, 1763, 6 x 2 x 3 3/4 In. 330.00
Flask, Cornucopia & Medallion, Aqua, Sheared Mouth, Open Pontil, 1/2 Pt. 80.00
Flask, Cornucopia & Urn, Blue Green, Sheared Mouth, Pontil, 1/2 Pt. 450.00
Flask, Cornucopia & Urn, Emerald Green, Pontil, Pt. 825.00
Flask, Cornucopia & Urn, Gold Amber, Sheared Mouth, Pontil, 1/2 Pt. 95.00
Flask, Cornucopia & Urn, Light Olive, Amber, Sheared Mouth, Pontil, Pt. 269.00
Flask, Cornucopia & Urn, Olive Green, 1/2 Pt. 145.00
Flask, Cornucopia & Urn, Olive Green, Pontil, New England, 1830-1850, 1/2 Pt. 165.00
Flask, Cornucopia & Urn, Olive Green, Pt. 145.00
Flask, Cornucopia & Urn, Olive Green, Sheared Mouth, Open Pontil, 1/2 Pt. 99.00
Flask, Cornucopia & Urn, Olive Green, Tooled Lip, Pontil, Pt. 138.00
Flask, Cornucopia & Urn, Yellow Amber, Sheared Mouth, Open Pontil, Pt. 130.00
Flask, Cupid & Flowers, Renaissance Style, Silver Cup & Cap, Marked, 5 3/4 In. 275.00
Flask, Double Eagle, Blue Green, Sheared Mouth, Pontil, Pt. 365.00
Flask, Double Eagle, Dark Olive Green, Applied Ring, Pt. 390.00
Flask, Double Eagle, Emerald Green, Sheared Mouth, Pontil, Pt. 2465.00
Flask, Double Eagle, Gold Amber, Applied Collar, Pontil, Pt. 308.00
Flask, Double Eagle, Light Yellow Amber, Applied Collar, Qt. 310.00
Flask, Double Eagle, Medium Blue Green, Sheared Mouth, Pontil, Qt. 1790.00
Flask, Double Eagle, Medium Gold Amber, Sheared Mouth, Pt. 605.00
Flask, Double Eagle, Olive Green, Open Pontil, Keene, Pt. 127.00
Flask, Double Eagle, Olive Green, Sheared Mouth, Open Pontil, Stoddard, 1/2 Pt. 170.00
Flask, Double Eagle, Olive Yellow, Open Pontil, Stoddard, Qt. 330.00
Flask, Double Eagle, Olive Yellow, Sheared Mouth, Pontil, Pt. 420.00
Flask, Double Eagle, Olive Yellow, Sheared Mouth, Pontil, Qt. 4760.00
Flask, Double Eagle, Sapphire Blue, Applied, Ring, 1860-1970, Pt. 3640.00
Flask, Double Eagle, Stoddard, 1840-1860, Pt. 420.00
Flask, Double Eagle, Yellow Amber, Olive Tone, Sheared Mouth, Pontil, Stoddard, Pt. 200.00
Flask, Eagle & Banner, Gold Amber, Olive Tint, Sheared Mouth, Pontil, Pt. 3360.00
Flask, Eagle & Calabash, Green, Applied Sloping Collar, Iron Pontil, 1855-1865, Qt. 495.00
Flask, Eagle & Cornucopia, Aqua, Sheared Mouth, Pontil, 1/2 Pt. 269.00
Flask, Eagle & Cornucopia, Blue Green, Sheared Mouth, Pontil, Pt. 365.00
Flask, Eagle & Cornucopia, Gold Amber, Sheared Lip, Pontil, Pt. 99.00
Flask, Eagle & Cornucopia, Light Yellow, Olive Tone, Sheared Mouth, Pontil, Pt. 450.00
Flask, Eagle & Cornucopia, Olive To Amber, Sheared Mouth, Open Pontil, Keene, Pt. . . . 165.00
Flask, Eagle & Cornucopia, Olive Yellow, Amber Tint, Keene, c.1835, Pt. 145.00
Flask, Eagle & Cornucopia, Olive Yellow, Sheared Mouth, Pontil, Pt. 160.00
Flask, Eagle & Flag, Aqua, Sheared Mouth, Pontil, Pt. 225.00
Flask, Eagle & Indian, Shooting Bird, Aqua, Applied Ring, Qt. 190.00
Flask, Eagle & Morning Glory, Aqua, Applied Double Collar, Pt. 670.00
Flask, Eagle & Morning Glory, Mottled Brown, Tan Stoneware, Pt. 4765.00
Flask, Eagle & Westford, Yellow Amber, 1/2 Pt. 365.00
Flask, Eagle & Willington, Emerald Green, Applied Collar, Pt. 3080.00
Flask, Eagle & Willington, Forest Green, Long Neck, Double Collar, 1/2 Pt. 616.00
Flask, Eagle & Willington, Olive Green, Sheared Mouth, Pt. 310.00
Flask, Eagle & Willington, Olive Yellow, Sheared Mouth, 1860-1872, Pt. 310.00
Flask, Eagle, Liberty, Olive Yellow, Applied Double Collar, 1/2 Pt. 260.00
Flask, Embossed Map Of Australia, Basket Weave, Aqua, Applied Handle, c.1876, 8 In. . . . 90.00
Flask, Flora Temple, Apricot Puce, Applied Ring & Sloping Collar, Ring, Qt. 530.00
Flask, Flora Temple, Horse, Harness Trot, Handle, Strawberry Puce, Applied Mouth, Pt. . . . 440.00
Flask, For Pike's Peak, Prospector, Eagle, Aqua, Tooled Ring, Qt. 90.00
Flask, For Pike's Peak, Prospector, Eagle, Blue Green, Sheared Mouth, Pontil, 1/2 Pt. 300.00
Flask, Horseman & Hound, Green Aqua, Applied Double Collar, 1/2 Pt. 246.00
Flask, Hunter & Fisherman, Calabash, Copper Puce, Sloping Collar, Pontil, Qt. 420.00
Flask, Hunter & Hounds, Light Yellow Amber, Applied Collar, Qt. 1008.00
Flask, J.J. Morrison, Liquor Dealer, Lynchburg, Va., Sun-Colored Amethyst, 1890, Pt. 176.00

Flask, Jenny Lind & Glasshouse, Sapphire Blue Calabash, Open Pontil, Qt. 45.00
Flask, Kossuth & Frigate, Aqua, Applied Sloping Collar, Pontil, Pt. 365.00
Flask, Lafayette & Eagle, Aqua, Sheared Mouth, Pontil, Pt. 1065.00
Flask, Lafayette & Liberty, Olive Yellow, Sheared Mouth, Pontil, 1/2 Pt. 1905.00
Flask, Liberty, Sheaf Of Rye & Star, Gold Amber, Sheared Mouth, Open Pontil, Pt. 880.00
Flask, Lowell Railroad & Eagle, Olive Yellow, Sheared Mouth, Pontil, 1/2 Pt. 785.00
Flask, Lowell Railroad & Eagle, Yellow Green, Sheared, Mouth, Pontil, 1/2 Pt. 950.00
Flask, Masonic & Eagle, Applied Ring, Rolled Mouth, Pontil, Pt. 1570.00
Flask, Masonic & Eagle, Aqua Green, Sheared Mouth, Open Pontil, Keene, Pt. 440.00
Flask, Masonic & Eagle, Aqua Green, Tooled Lip, Open Pontil, Pt. 300.00
Flask, Masonic & Eagle, Green Aqua, Clam Broth, Sheared Mouth, Pt. 450.00
Flask, Masonic & Eagle, Green Aqua, Tooled Lip, Pontil, Pt. 670.00
Flask, Masonic & Eagle, Light Blue Green, Sheared Mouth, Pontil, Pt. 500.00
Flask, Masonic & Eagle, Light Olive Green, Open Pontil, Keene, Pt. 250.00
Flask, Masonic & Eagle, Light To Medium Blue Green, Sheared Mouth, Pontil, Pt. 560.00
Flask, Masonic & Eagle, Medium Olive Yellow, Sheared Mouth, Pontil, 1/2 Pt. 450.00
Flask, Masonic & Eagle, Olive Yellow, Sheared Mouth, Pontil, Pt. ....160.00 to 336.00
Flask, Masonic & Eagle, Yellow Amber, Inward Rolled Lip, Pontil, Pt. 3080.00
Flask, Masonic, Arch & Frigate, Aqua, Sheared Mouth, Pontil, Pt. 390.00
Flask, Masonic, Arch & Frigate, Green Aqua, Gray Tint, Sheared Mouth, Pontil, Pt. 615.00
Flask, Merry Christmas, Pumpkinseed, Plum Tree, Clear, Tooled Lip, 1885-1900, 4 5/8 In. 145.00
Flask, Old No. 12, Sheffield, Gray Green, Slab Seal, 7 3/4 In. 120.00
Flask, Pan-American Exposition, Threaded Ground Mouth, Jigger Cap, c.1900, 1/2 Pt. ... 240.00
Flask, Pitkin Type, 16 Ribs, Swirled To Right, Sea Green, Sheared Mouth, Pontil, 6 7/8 In. 670.00
Flask, Pitkin Type, 32 Ribs, Swirled To Right, Sea Green, Sheared Mouth, Pontil, 6 3/4 In. 785.00
Flask, Pitkin Type, 36 Ribs, Swirled To Right, Olive, Sheared Mouth, Pontil, 5 1/8 In. ... 615.00
Flask, Pitkin, 32 Broken Ribs, Swirled To Right, Green, Tooled Lip, c.1810, 6 7/8 In. 600.00
Flask, Pitkin, 36 Broken Ribs, Olive Yellow, Sheared Lip, Pontil, 5 3/8 In. 875.00
Flask, Pretzel Shape, Pottery, Incised 45, 6 In. 28.00
Flask, Pretzel, Foust, c.1908, 5 1/2 In. 1620.00
Flask, Puce Amber, Swirled Ribs, Sheared Mouth, Open Pontil, Midwest, 4 1/2 In. 330.00
Flask, Pumpkinseed Spider Web, Pink & White, 3 3/4 In. 35.00
Flask, Pumpkinseed, Embossed, Barrel In Wreath, Pt. 59.00
Flask, Ruby, Swirled To Right, Pontil, Early 19th Century, 8 In. 382.00
Flask, Scroll, Aqua, Sheared Mouth, Open Pontil, Pt. 66.00
Flask, Scroll, Citron, Sheared Mouth, Iron Pontil, 1845-1860, 1/2 Pt. 3640.00
Flask, Scroll, Cobalt Blue, Sheared Mouth, Iron Pontil, Qt. 6160.00
Flask, Scroll, Dark Olive Yellow, Applied Ring, Pontil, Qt. 2240.00
Flask, Scroll, Gold Amber, Sheared Mouth, Pontil, 1845-1860, 1/2 Pt. 1456.00
Flask, Scroll, Light To Medium, Topaz, Applied Ring, Pontil, Qt. 4200.00
Flask, Scroll, Lime Green, Sheared Mouth, Pontil, Pt. 1120.00
Flask, Scroll, Sapphire Blue, Sheared Mouth, Pontil, Pt. 1900.00
Flask, Scroll, Sapphire Blue, Sheared Mouth, Pontil, Qt. 3080.00
Flask, Sheaf Of Grain & Star, Gold Amber, Applied Double Collar, 1/2 Pt. 1904.00
Flask, Sheaf Of Grain & Star, Medium Olive Yellow, Applied Mouth, Ring, Double, Qt. ... 6160.00
Flask, Sheaf Of Grain & Star, Olive Yellow, Applied Double Collar, Pontil, Pt. 4200.00
Flask, Sheaf Of Grain, Westford Glass Co., Olive Amber, Double Collar, 1/2 Pt. 170.00
Flask, Sheaf Of Grain, Westford Travelers Companion, Amber, Tapered Collar, Qt. 205.00
Flask, Sheaf Of Wheat, Amber, Smooth Base, Applied Double Collar, Westford, Pt. 140.00
Flask, Sheaf Of Wheat, Amber, Smooth Base, Double Collar, Westfield Glass Co., Pt. 175.00
Flask, Shield, Stars & Stripes, Aqua, Applied Double Collar Mouth, Pt. 170.00
Flask, Sloop & Star, Aqua, Pontil, Sheared Mouth, 1/2 Pt. 120.00
Flask, Stoddard Type, Amber, Embossed Star, Metal Cap, 1/2 Pt. 27.00
Flask, Stoddard Type, Yellow Amber, Applied Sloping Collar, Pontil, 1/2 Pt. 785.00
Flask, Strap Sides, Yellow, Double Collar, 1/2 Pt., 6 In. 12.00
Flask, Success To The Railroad, Deep Olive Green, Sheared Mouth, Pontil, Pt. 365.00
Flask, Success To The Railroad, Eagle, Gold Amber, Sheared Mouth, Pontil, Pt. 179.00
Flask, Success To The Railroad, Forest Green, Sheared Mouth, Pontil, Pt. 365.00
Flask, Success To The Railroad, Olive Amber, Pt., 6 1/2 In. 247.50
Flask, Success To The Railroad, Olive Green, Pontil, Pt. 255.00
Flask, Success To The Railroad, Olive Green, Sheared Mouth, Open Pontil, Keene, Pt. ... 330.00
Flask, Success To The Railroad, Olive Yellow, Sheared Mouth, Pontil, Pt. 450.00
Flask, Sunburst, Blue Green, Inward Rolled Mouth, Pontil, 3/4 Pt. 415.00

Flask, Sunburst, Blue Green, Ribbed, Sheared Mouth, Pontil, 1/2 Pt. 365.00
Flask, Sunburst, Eagle, Dark Amber, Sheared Mouth, Pontil, Pt. 30240.00
Flask, Sunburst, Elongated, Green Aqua, Pontil, Pt. 180.00
Flask, Sunburst, Forest Green, Sheared Mouth, Pontil, Pt. 1456.00
Flask, Sunburst, Light Yellow Amber, Olive Tone, Sheared Mouth, Pontil, 1/2 Pt. 1680.00
Flask, Sunburst, Olive Yellow, Sheared Mouth, Pontil, 1/2 Pt. . . . . .308.00 to 340.00
Flask, Union, Clasped Hands & Eagle, Aqua, Applied Ring, 1/2 Pt. 215.00
Flask, Union, Clasped Hands & Eagle, Aqua, Double Collar, Iron Pontil, Pt. 70.00
Flask, Union, Clasped Hands & Eagle, Calabash, Citron, Applied Collar, Pontil, Pt. 950.00
Flask, Union, Clasped Hands & Eagle, Cornflower Blue, Applied Mouth, Ring, Qt. 6720.00
Flask, Union, Clasped Hands & Eagle, Deep Amber, 1/2 Pt. 300.00
Flask, Union, Clasped Hands & Eagle, Gold Amber, Applied Collar, 1/2 Pt. 365.00
Flask, Union, Clasped Hands & Eagle, Olive Yellow, Applied Collar, Qt. 3025.00
Flask, Warranted, Strap Side, Dark Amber, Qt. 20.00
Flask, Washington & Jackson, Amber, Sheared Mouth, Open Pontil, Pt. 94.00
Flask, Washington & Jackson, Gold Amber, Sheared Mouth, Pontil, Coventry, 1/2 Pt. 230.00
Flask, Washington & Jackson, Olive Yellow Amber, Sheared Mouth, Pontil, 1/2 Pt. 476.00
Flask, Washington & Jackson, Olive Yellow, Sheared Mouth, Pontil, Pt. 336.00
Flask, Washington & Monument, Pale Amethyst, Sheared Mouth, Pontil, Pt. 532.00
Flask, Washington & Sheaf, Aqua, Applied Double Collar, 1/2 Pt. 88.00
Flask, Washington & Taylor, Aqua, Oval, c.1848, 5 3/4 In. 780.00
Flask, Washington & Taylor, Cobalt Blue, Dyottville Glass Works, c.1850, Qt. 7840.00
Flask, Washington & Taylor, Green, c.1840, Pt. 604.00
Flask, Washington & Taylor, Medium Yellow Green, Sheared Mouth, Pontil, Pt. 392.00
Flask, Washington & Taylor, Never Surrenders, Aqua, Dyottville Glass Works, Qt. 99.00
Flask, Washington & Taylor, Never Surrenders, Aqua, Pontil, Qt. 55.00
Flask, Washington, Father Of His Country, Aqua, Dyottville, Qt. 85.00
Flask, Will You Take A Drink, Blue Green, Tooled Sloped Collar, 1/2 Pt. 785.00
Food, E.D. Pettengill Co., Portland, Horseradish, Shaker, Label, 4 3/4 In. 1035.00
Food, Liggett's Cherriade Syrup, Enamel Over Glass, 12 In. 305.00
Food, London Mustard, Aqua, Rolled Lip, Open Pontil, 6 1/4 In. 175.00
Food, Maple Sap & Boiled Cider Vinegar, East Ringe, N.H., Cobalt Blue 385.00
Food, Sherbet-Tade Syrup, Foil & Enamel Label, 12 In. 250.00
Food, Shriver's Oyster Ketchup, Baltimore, Olive Yellow, Applied Top, c.1860, 7 1/2 In. . . 1073.00
Food, Stromeyer's Grape Punch Syrup, Reverse Label On Glass, 12 1/2 In. 575.00
Fruit Jar, A. Kline, Stopple, Aqua, Marked, Patent October 27, 1862, Qt. 45.00
Fruit Jar, Crown Imperial, Blue Aqua, Screw Lid, 1/2 Gal. 39.00
Fruit Jar, Cunningham & Co., Pittsburgh, Aqua, Square Collar, 1875-1880, Qt. 130.00
Fruit Jar, Flaccus Bros., Steers Head, Milk Glass, Threaded Mouth, 1885-1900, Pt. 175.00
Fruit Jar, Globe, Yellow Amber, Glass Lid, Iron Clamp, 1885-1900, Qt. 77.00
Fruit Jar, Stephens Fruits & Jams, Gloucester, Aqua, 2 Geese, Embossed, 10 In. 17.00
Gin, A Van Hoboken & Co., Rotterdam, Sealed, Mushroom Top, Olive, Tapered, 11 1/4 In. 100.00
Gin, Case, Olive Green, Flared Lip, Open Pontil 72.00
Gin, Sapphire Blue, Neck, Teal Shoulders, Tooled Mouth, 1870-1890, 10 In. 390.00
Ginger Beer, Andrew A. Watt & Co. Ltd., Londonberry, Prancing Lion, 2-Tone, 8 In. 25.00
Ginger Beer, Arliss Robinson & Co., Sutton Surrey, Home Brewed, Blob Top, 6 3/4 In. . . . 33.00
Ginger Beer, Arnold & Co., Monks Abbey, 2-Tone, Blob Top, 7 1/4 In. 50.00
Ginger Beer, Brewster & Dodgson, Leeds, 2-Tone, Blob Top, 8 1/2 In. 17.00
Ginger Beer, Brothwell & Essam, Forncett St., Sheffield, 2-Tone, Blob Top, 7 3/4 In. 50.00
Ginger Beer, C. Robillard & Cie, Limitee, Montreal, Stoneware, Pt. 29.00
Ginger Beer, Comrie & Co., Special, Helensburgh, White, Black Transfer, Blob Top, 8 In. 92.00
Ginger Beer, D. Kelly & Co., Stone Ginger, Limited, Leith, 2-Tone, Blob Top, 8 1/4 In. . . 285.00
Ginger Beer, Firth's Darlington, Train, Blue Transfer, 2-Tone, Blob Top, 7 In. 42.00
Ginger Beer, G. Bullock & Son, Blackpool, 2-Tone, Blob Top, 8 In. 92.00
Ginger Beer, Harston & Co., Leeds, Dove, 2-Tone, Blob Top, 6 3/4 In. 50.00
Ginger Beer, J. Swenden & Co. Ltd., Darlington, Blue Transfer Print, 2-Tone, 7 3/4 In. . . 58.00
Ginger Beer, J.S. Eyre & Co., Launceston, Established 1830, 2-Tone, Blob Top, 7 In. 25.00
Ginger Beer, James Jeffery, Quencher, Jopps Lane, Aberdeen, Fireman, 8 3/4 In. 104.00
Ginger Beer, Jas Rose & Co., Oatmeal Stout, Caistor Lincoln, 2-Tone, Blob Top, 8 3/4 In. 35.00
Ginger Beer, Jas. Thatcher & Compy, West Drayton, Cottage, 2-Tone, Blob Top, 6 1/2 In. 500.00
Ginger Beer, John Fitzgerald, Darcy's, Newcastle On Tyne, Blue Transfer, 2-Tone, 7 1/2 In. 17.00
Ginger Beer, John Milne, Stonehaven, Brewed, 1846, Brown Transfer, 2-Tone, 9 In. 25.00
Ginger Beer, Marsom & Sons, Maypole, Biggleswade, Cream, Blob Top, 6 3/4 In. 25.00

To remove a cork that has fallen inside a bottle, pour some ammonia in the bottle. Let it sit for a few days. Most of the cork should dissolve and can easily be removed.

Bottle, Household, Win-Shine,
Window Cleaner, Kenmore
Co., Crown Top, 6 1/2 In.

Ginger Beer, McCall's, D. McCall & Co., Sorba Park, Oban, 2-Tone, 8 1/2 In.	84.00
Ginger Beer, Milnes & Sons, Bradford, Boy In Donkey, Blob Top, 7 In.	35.00
Ginger Beer, Murtough, Portsea, Knight On Horseback, Doulton, 2-Tone, Blob Top, 6 In. .	40.00
Ginger Beer, P. Mason, Kitt Hill, Callington, Tin Mine, White Glaze, 6 3/4 In.	159.00
Ginger Beer, Redruth Brewery Co. Ltd., Bird, Man In Basket, Moon, Tan, Blob Top, 7 In.	115.00
Ginger Beer, Rimmington & Son, Bradford, Alchemist, White Glaze, 6 3/4 In.	50.00
Ginger Beer, S.H. Ward & Co. Ltd., Renton Street, Sheffield, 2-Tone, Blob Top, 7 1/4 In. .	50.00
Ginger Beer, Skene & Company, Celebrated, Dufftown, Bagpiper, 2-Tone, 8 1/2 In.	69.00
Ginger Beer, T. Hills, 247 Beverley Road, Hull, Stone Brewed, 2-Tone, Blob Top, 8 In. . .	120.00
Ginger Beer, W & J Cruickshank, Ye Olden, Buckie, Blue Transfer, Blob Top, 8 1/2 In. . .	170.00
Ginger Beer, Wm. Hoyes, Brown Creme, Blob Top, Stoneware, Qt.	69.00
Household, Sheldon's Magic Water Proof, Boot Polish, Green, 8-Sided, 5 1/2 In.	3080.00
Household, W.E. Nye, Sperm Oil, New Bedford, Mass., Whaling, Label, Contents, 3 In. . .	345.00
Household, Win-Shine, Window Cleaner, Kenmore Co., Crown Top, 6 1/2 In. . . . . . . *Illus*	25.00
Ink, Barrel, Disc Lip, Pontil, 2 In.	280.00
Ink, Carter's, Cathedral, Cobalt Blue, 9 1/2 In.	96.00
Ink, Carter's, Emerald Green, 3-Piece Mold, Applied Lip, 10 In.	88.00
Ink, Caw's Ink, New York, Light Green, Square Lip, 2 3/8 In.	10.00
Ink, Cylindrical, Forest Green, Disc Lip, Pontil, Coventry, Conn., 1 3/4 x 2 1/4 In.	179.00
Ink, Farley's, 8-Sided, Gold Amber, Sheared Mouth, Pontil, Stoddard, N.H., 1 3/4 In. . . .	560.00
Ink, Geometric, Amber, Open Pontil, Coventry, Conn., 1 3/4 In.	61.00
Ink, Geometric, Olive Green, Open Pontil, Keene, N.H., 1 3/4 In.	33.00
Ink, Geometric, Olive Green, Pontil, Coventry, Conn., 1 1/2 In.	330.00
Ink, Harrison's Columbian, 8-Sided, Aqua, Open Pontil, Disc Lip, 3 3/4 In.	94.00
Ink, House, Amethystine, Flared Sheared Mouth, Pontil, 2 1/2 In.	952.00
Ink, John Bond's Crystal Palace, Square, Cobalt Blue, Flared Lip, Label, 1 1/2 In.	202.00
Ink, L.H. Thomas, Cone Ink, Aqua, Tooled Lip, 2 3/4 In.	39.00
Ink, M & P, New York, Umbrella, 8-Sided, Green, Inward Rolled Mouth, 2 1/2 In.	1120.00
Ink, Pitkin Type, 36 Ribs, Swirled Left, Olive Green, Cupped Lip, Pontil, 1 5/8 x 2 1/4 In.	900.00
Ink, Russia Cement, Signet, Cobalt Blue, Threaded Mouth, Metal Cap, 1905-1915, Pt. . . .	90.00
Ink, Stafford's, Teal Blue, Pt., 6 1/4 In.	70.00
Ink, Stephens, Aldersgate, London, Stoneware, Salt Glaze, Squared Lip, Contents, 6 In. . .	37.00
Ink, Stephens, Fancy Violet Writing Ink, Square, Clear, Stopper, 7 In.	20.00
Ink, Teakettle, Amethyst, Ground Lip, 2 In.	330.00
Ink, Teakettle, Domed, Yellow Green, Applied Bird, Tooled Lip, 2 5/8 In.	730.00
Ink, Turtle, Bird, Aqua, Tooled Lip, Ground Top, 2 In.	44.00
Ink, Umbrella, 8-Sided, Blue Green, Open Pontil, 2 5/8 In.	85.00
Ink, Umbrella, 8-Sided, Olive Green, Sheared Mouth, Pontil, 2 3/8 In.	340.00
Ink, Underwood's, Cobalt Blue, Master, 9 7/8 In.	90.00
Ink, W.E. Bonney, Hanover, Mass., Aqua, Square, 4 Circular Panels, Square Collar, 3 In. .	25.00
Jar, Cigar, Mercantile, Gold Amber, Stamped Tin Lid, Label, 1902-1910, 5 1/8 In.	155.00
Jar, Figural, Milk Pail, Cover, Blue, Sheared Mouth, Tin Collar, Handle, 4 1/2 In.	1230.00
Jar, Mason's Patent Nov. 30th 1858, Amber, Zinc Lid, 1870-1890, Qt.	176.00
Jar, Mason's, Patent Nov 30th 1858, Teal, Ground Lip, Zinc Lid, Qt.	275.00
Jar, Medicine, Apothecary, Cer. Plumbi Subac, Label Under Glass, Milk Glass, 6 1/2 In. . .	240.00
Jar, Newlin's Coffee, Newlin Tea Co., New York, Yellow, Tin Lid, 6 1/4 In.	1905.00

Jar, Nut House, Embossed House, Letters, 10 In. 135.00
Jar, Storage, Blue Green Glass, Pontil, Green Painted Tin Lid, 7 In. 60.00
Jar, Storage, Citron, Cylindrical, Oval Panels, Zinc Band, Ground Mouth, Pt. 215.00
Jar, Storage, Olive Amber Glass, Open Pontil, Rolled Lip, 10 1/2 In. 330.00
Jar, Storage, Olive Yellow, Cylindrical, Wide Mouth, Tooled Rim, Pontil, 8 x 4 1/4 In. 179.00
Jar, Tobacco, Belfast Cigars, United, Cut Plug, Light Yellow Amber, Tin Lid, 7 In. 70.00
Medicine, American Oil, Burkesville, Kentucky, Aqua, Pontil, c.1850, 6 3/4 In. 880.00
Medicine, Ascatco, Gnu, Wrapper, Unopened, 4 In. 30.00
Medicine, B.F. Fish's Hair Restorative, Light Blue Aqua, Applied Double Collar, 7 1/4 In.   880.00
Medicine, Barrett's Mandrake Embrocations, Ducks, Green, Rectangular, 4 3/4 In. 45.00
Medicine, Bartine's Lotion, Yellow Green, Rectangular, Beveled, Pontil, 5 5/8 In. 1460.00
Medicine, Blood Food Prepared By G. Handyside, Olive Green, Rectangular, 5 1/2 In. 55.00
Medicine, Bowman's Drug Store, Alton, Ill., Cobalt Blue, Embossed, 4 7/8 In. 365.00
Medicine, British Oil, Steelman & Archer Wholesale Druggists, Phila., ABM, 5 1/2 In. 12.00
Medicine, Bromo-Seltzer, Emerson Drug Co., Box, Cobalt Blue, 2 3/4 In. 90.00
Medicine, C. Brinkerhoff's Health Restorative, Price $1.00, Olive Yellow, 7 1/4 In. 1790.00
Medicine, C. Heimstreet & Co., Sapphire Blue, Applied Double Collar, 8-Sided, 6 7/8 In. .   390.00
Medicine, Cereal Extract Of Oats & Barley, F.R. Gross & Co., Amber, 7 1/2 In. 69.00
Medicine, Champion Liniment, 20 Different Problems, Clear, 1870-1880, 7 In. 40.00
Medicine, Constitutional Beverage, W. Olmsted & Company, Gold Amber, 10 1/8 In. 310.00
Medicine, Dr. A.C. Daniels' Disinfectant, Label, Contents, 6 In. 48.00
Medicine, Dr. Bull's, Label, Contents, Pamphlet, Box, c.1885, 5 1/4 In. 470.00
Medicine, Dr. Duncan's Expectorant Remedy, Light Green, Rectangular, Pontil, 6 1/8 In. .   3080.00
Medicine, Dr. Gordack, Pale Green, Tooled Flared Mouth, Tubular Pontil, 6 7/8 In. 476.00
Medicine, Dr. Harter's Elixir Of Wild Cherry, Aqua, Label, Contents, Box, 10 In. 1980.00
Medicine, Dr. Harter's Iron Tonic, Amber, Label, Contents, Box, 9 1/4 In. 495.00
Medicine, Dr. Harter's Liniment, St. Louis, Mo., Aqua, Label, Contents, Box, 4 3/4 In. . . .   230.00
Medicine, Dr. Harter's Lung Balm, St. Louis, Mo., Aqua, Label, Contents, Box, 5 7/8 In. .   110.00
Medicine, Dr. Harter's Lung Balm, St. Louis, Mo., Aqua, Label, Contents, Box, 7 3/4 In. .   855.00
Medicine, Dr. King's New Life Pills, Always Satisfy, 4-Sided, Stopper, 13 In. 364.00
Medicine, Dr. Miles' Cactus Compound, Aqua, Label, Contents, Box, 8 1/4 In. 165.00
Medicine, Dr. Miles' Restorative Blood Purifier, Aqua, Label, Contents, Box, 8 In. 468.00
Medicine, Dr. Miles' Tonic, Aqua, Label, Contents, Box, 8 1/4 In.   105.00
Medicine, Dr. Poland's Humor Doctor, 8 In. 30.00
Medicine, Dr. R.H. Kline's Epileptic Remedy, Aqua, Rectangular, 7 In. 48.00
Medicine, Dr. Robert's Laxative For Children, Label, Contents, Box, 6 1/2 In. 20.00
Medicine, Dr. Samuel H.P. Lee's Littenreptic, Cork, Wrapper, c.1940, 2 1/2 x 2 In. 39.00
Medicine, Dr. Shoop's Restorative, Great Nerve Tonic, Contents, Wrapper, Box, 8 In. 275.00
Medicine, Dr. Southworth's Blood & Kidney Remedy, Blue Green, Rectangular, 8 1/2 In. .   59.00
Medicine, Dr. Tebbetts' Physiological Hair Regenerator, Apricot Pink, c.1850 . . . .   4480.00
Medicine, Dr. Tebbetts' Physiological Hair Regenerator, Deep Wine Amethyst, c.1850 . . . .   365.00
Medicine, Dr. Townsend's Sarsparilla, Green, Sloping Collar, Iron Pontil, 9 1/2 In. 125.00
Medicine, E.R. Squibb, Civil War Ear Medicine, Blue Green, Wide Mouth, c.1860, 7 In. . . .   69.00
Medicine, E.R. Squibb, Teal Blue, Applied Square Color, Clear Stopper, 7 3/4 In. 468.00
Medicine, Fellows Syrup Of Hypophosphites, Aqua, Contents, Label, Canada, 5 1/4 In. . .   50.00
Medicine, Fleming's Veterinary Eye Lotion, Paper Label, Round, Contents, c.1914, 3 In. .   66.00
Medicine, Fleming's Veterinary Healing Oil, Wrap Around Label, Contents, 3 3/4 In. 99.00
Medicine, From Laboratory Of G.W. Merchant, Chemist, Lockport, N.Y., Green, 5 1/2 In.   840.00
Medicine, G.W. Merchant, Chemist, Lockport, N.Y., Blue Green, Sloping Collar, 5 1/2 In.   310.00
Medicine, Gargling Oil, Cobalt Blue, ABM, Label, Horse On Front, 5 In. 175.00
Medicine, Gargling Oil, Green, Label, Family Scene, Partial Contents, 5 1/2 In. 440.00
Medicine, Genuine Sand's Sarsaparilla, N.Y., Aqua, Embossed, Whittled, 9 3/4 In. 450.00
Medicine, Glycozone, Ch. Marchand, Contents, Label, Wrapper, 5 1/4 In. 70.00
Medicine, Gun Wa's Chinese Remedy, Golden, Applied Top, 8 In. 495.00
Medicine, H.H. Warner & Co., Tippecanoe, Rochester, N.Y., Light Amber, 9 In. 90.00
Medicine, Healy & Bigelow, Indian Sagwa, Indian, Aqua, Contents, Label, 8 1/2 In. 1375.00
Medicine, Hunt's Remedy, Aqua, Wm. E. Clarke, Pharmacist, 7 In.   15.00
Medicine, J.B. Marchisi M.D., Uterine Catholicon, Aqua, Contents, Rear Label, 8 In. 45.00
Medicine, John J. Smith, Louisville, Ky., Blue Green, Sloping Collar, Pontil, 5 3/4 In. . . .   1345.00
Medicine, Katz & Besthoff, Pharmacists, New Orleans, Cobalt Blue, 1890-1900, 7 3/4 In.   330.00
Medicine, Kickapoo Oil, Aqua, Contents, Label, Pamphlet, Box, 7 In. 90.00
Medicine, Kickapoo Sagwa, Clear, Label, Contents, C.I. Hood Co., 8 1/2 In. 155.00
Medicine, Lucien Pratte, Le Renovateur, Waterbury, Conn., Cobalt Blue, 9 1/4 In. 280.00

Medicine, Lyon's Jamaica Ginger, Embossed, Aqua, c.1855-1865, 6 1/4 In. 39.00
Medicine, Marbrie, Cobalt Blue, Opaque White Loopings, 8-Sided, 8 x 2 x 3 In. 990.00
Medicine, Medico Chirurgical Hospital, Eye Water, Cobalt Blue, Embossed, 5 In. 139.00
Medicine, Morely Bros Druggists, Gold Amber, Austin, Texas, 1880-1900, 10 1/4 In. 550.00
Medicine, Morse's Celebrated Syrup, Prov., R.I., Aqua, Oval, Collared Mouth, 9 1/4 In. . . 246.00
Medicine, Mrs. Winslow's Soothing Syrup, Curtis & Perkins, Aqua, Rolled Lip, OP, 5 In. . 39.00
Medicine, Norwood's Veratrum Viride, Clear, Label, United Society Of Shakers, 5 1/2 In. . 55.00
Medicine, Price's Candle Company Limited, Cobalt Blue, Stopper, England, 7 1/2 In. 198.00
Medicine, Professor Wood's Hair Restorative, St. Louis, Missouri, Aqua, 4-Sided, 9 In. . . 364.00
Medicine, Radium Radia, Sick Man, Cured Man, Clear, Label, Contents, 1880-1895, 5 In. 169.00
Medicine, Rawleigh's, Colic & Bloat Compound, Aqua, ABM, Label, 8 In. 105.00
Medicine, Rev. Gates Magamoose, Cathedral Panels, 8 In. 20.00
Medicine, Rheumatic Trademark Syrup, 4-Sided, Gold Amber, Wolcott, N.Y., 1882, 10 In. 179.00
Medicine, Rhodes, Antidote Malaria, Aqua, Open Pontil, Applied Mouth, 8 1/8 In. 375.00
Medicine, Sanford's Radical Cure, Sapphire, Blue, Square Collar, Paneled, 7 3/8 In. 160.00
Medicine, Shaker Cherry Pectoral Syrup, Canterbury, N.Y., Aqua, Pontil, 5 1/2 In. 130.00
Medicine, Shaker Hair Restorer, Gold Amber, Tooled Double Ring Lip, c.1880, 7 3/4 In. . . 145.00
Medicine, Shaker Syrup, Canterbury, N.H., Aqua, Embossed, Whittled, 7 1/4 . . . . 270.00
Medicine, Smelling Salts, Cobalt Blue, Bulbous Neck, 1820-1840, 2 5/8 In. 1230.00
Medicine, Sniteman's X Ray Liniment, Label, Contents, Box, Wisconsin, 12 In. 330.00
Medicine, Spark's Kidney & Liver Cure, Orange, Amber, Oval, Bust Of Man, 9 1/2 In. 229.00
Medicine, St. Antonius Liniment, Aqua, Label, Contents, 1875, 6 In. 130.00
Medicine, Sterling's Ambrosia For Hair, Blue Aqua, Neck Ring, Pontil, 6 1/2 In. 69.00
Medicine, Strickland's Wine Of Life, Amber, Cylindrical, Whiskey Shape, Label, 11 In. . . . 240.00
Medicine, U.S.A. Hosp. Dept., Blue Green Aqua, Wide Mouth, 7 1/2 In. 415.00
Medicine, U.S.A. Hosp. Dept., Emerald Green, Applied Top, 9 1/2 In. 1980.00
Medicine, U.S.A. Hosp. Dept., Light Orange Yellow, Applied Top, 9 1/4 In. 1430.00
Medicine, W. Brinker & Son Co., Druggist, New York & Brooklyn, Blob Top, 8 In. 8.00
Medicine, W.E. Hagan & Co., Light Blue, 8-Sided, Applied Top, 6 3/4 In. 385.00
Medicine, Warner's Compound Diuretic, Amber, Contents, 9 In. 145.00
Medicine, Warner's Safe Compound, Embossed, Gold Amber, 5 1/2 In. 120.00
Medicine, Warner's Safe Cure, London, Embossed, Deep Amber, 7 1/2 In. 40.00
Medicine, Warner's Safe Diabetes Cure, Yellow Amber, Contents, Box, 9 1/2 In. 770.00
Medicine, Warner's Safe Diabetes Remedy, Amber, Label, Contents, Flyers, Box, 9 1/2 In. 470.00
Medicine, Warner's Safe Nervine, Amber, Box, Fliers, 9 1/2 In. 635.00
Medicine, Warner's Safe Nervine, Embossed, Amber, 1/2 Pt. 450.00
Medicine, Warner's Safe Nervine, Embossed, Olive Green, 7 1/4 In. 40.00
Medicine, Warner's Safe Remedies, Diuretic, Amber, ABM, Label, Contents, 6 Oz., 7 In. . 90.00
Medicine, Wm. Radam's Microbe Killer, Amber, Embossed Label, 10 1/4 In. 90.00
Medicine, Wood's Liniment, Aqua, Rolled Lip, Open Pontil, 4 1/8 In. 295.00
Milk, Creamer, Mitchell's, Bridgeport, Conn., Red, 2-Sided, 3/4 Oz. 50.00
Milk, Estey's Farm Dairy, Orange ACL, Qt. 20.00
Milk, Farm Dairy, Edwardsville, Pa., Red Pyro, Qt. 25.00
Milk, Farmers Dairy, Cumberland, Md., Embossed, Pt. 16.00
Milk, Hob & Nob Farm, Crotched Mountain, Francestown, N.H. 39.00
Milk, Horlick's Malted Milk, Racine, Wis., Embossed, Screw-On Lid, 7 In. 50.00
Milk, Johnson Farms Dairy, Waterloo, Iowa, Quality You Can Taste, Qt. 30.00
Milk, Northampton Dairy, Babyface, Sample, Qt. 125.00
Milk, Perry's Creamery, Tuscaloosa, Al., Buy Defense Bonds, Qt. 45.00
Milk, Rawleigh Farms, Good Health Milk, Freeport, Ill., 1/2 Pt. 45.00
Milk, Stocker's, Easton, Pa., Have You Tried Our Other, Square, Red Pyro, Qt. 20.00
Milk, Tonne Dairy, Ft. Wayne, Ind., Cow, Qt. 125.00
Mineral Water, A.D. Rapp, New York, Cobalt Blue, Applied Sloping Collar, Pontil, 1/2 Pt. 730.00
Mineral Water, Adirondack Spring, Green, Sloping Collar, Westport, N.Y., 1865, Qt. 264.00
Mineral Water, Alburgh A Springs, Vt., Gold Amber, Stoddard, Qt. 138.00
Mineral Water, Artesian Spring Co., Emerald Green, Ballston Spa., N.Y., 1865, Pt. 112.00
Mineral Water, B & G Superior, San Francisco, Cobalt Blue, Iron Pontil, 6 5/8 In. 415.00
Mineral Water, Bangor City, Purity Guaranteed, Aqua, Codd, 8-Sided, 8 3/4 In. 69.00
Mineral Water, Beard's, Boston, Cylindrical, Blue Green, Blob Top, 1860, 7 In. 75.00
Mineral Water, Champion Spouting Spring, Saratoga, N.Y., Amber, 1865-1880, Pt 415.00
Mineral Water, Chemung Spring Water, Indian At Spring, Rocks, Amber, 1865, 1/2 Gal. . 660.00
Mineral Water, Congress & Empire Spring Co., Hotchkiss' Sons, Olive Green, Pt. 180.00
Mineral Water, Congress & Empire Spring Co., Saratoga, N.Y., Olive, Embossed, Qt. 290.00

Mineral Water, Congress Spring Co., Saratoga, N.Y., Emerald Green, Pt. . . . . .45.00 to 55.00
Mineral Water, Franklin Spring, Saratoga, N.Y., Ballston Spa, Emerald Green, 1865, Pt. . . 525.00
Mineral Water, G.H. Lyford Co., Green, Cylindrical, Collar Mouth, Iron Pontil, 1/2 Pt. . . 450.00
Mineral Water, Geo. Upp Jr., York, Pa., Cobalt Blue, Squat, 7 1/2 In. 759.00
Mineral Water, Gettysburg Katalysine, Yellow, Cylindrical, Double Collar, 9 5/8 In. 90.00
Mineral Water, Guilford Mineral Spring Water, Blue Green, Qt. 90.00
Mineral Water, Hathorn Spring, Saratoga, N.Y., Black, Applied Sloping Collar, Qt. 80.00
Mineral Water, J. Dowdall-Union Glass Works Phila., Cobalt Blue, Applied Mouth, 7 In. . 750.00
Mineral Water, M.T. Crawford, Hartford, Ct., Cobalt, Applied Sloping Collar, 1/2 Pt. . . . 420.00
Mineral Water, M.T. Crawford, Hartford, Ct., Sapphire, Blob Top, Iron Pontil, 1/2 Pt. . . . 530.00
Mineral Water, Middletown Healing Springs, Vt., Amber, Double Collar, Stoddard, Qt. . . 85.00
Mineral Water, Minnequa, Bradford Co., Pa., Blue Aqua, Applied Double Collar, Pt. 89.00
Mineral Water, Missisquoi A Springs, Light Olive, Sloping Double Collar, Qt. 80.00
Mineral Water, Patterson & Brazeau, New York, Vichy Water, Forest Green, 1/2 Pt. 220.00
Mineral Water, Saratoga Star Spring, Amber, Applied Sloping Collar, 1862-1889, Qt. 90.00
Mineral Water, Siphon Kumysgen, Cobalt, Blob Top, Contents, Label, c.1880, 9 1/4 In. . . 175.00
Mineral Water, St. Leon Spring Water, Boston, Teal Green, Wicker Cover, Qt. 670.00
Mineral Water, Star Spring Co, Saratoga, N.Y., Medium Gold Amber, 1862-1889, Pt. 120.00
Mineral Water, Star Spring Co., Saratoga, N.Y., Olive Yellow, Stoddard, Pt. 135.00
Mineral Water, Washington Spring, Saratoga, N.Y., Emerald Green, Pt. 260.00
Miniature, Delmonico Rye, L & A Scharff Distillers, St. Louis, Mo., Jug, Stoneware, 3 In. 115.00
Nailsea Type, Globular, Applied Neck, Olive Green, White Looping, Horse, 9 1/2 In. 6012.00
Pepper Sauce, Bird, Cathedral, Aqua, 1830, 11 In. 1350.00
Pepper Sauce, Cathedral, Blue Aqua, Square Base, Embossed, 10 1/4 In. 139.00
Pepper Sauce, Cathedral, Cornflower Blue, 1860-1870, 8 3/8 In. 670.00
Pepper Sauce, Cathedral, Green, 1840-1860, 8 3/4 In. 670.00
Pepper Sauce, W.J. Taylor & Co., Manchester, Aqua, Sheared Lip, 5 In. 40.00
Pepper Sauce, Wells Miller & Provst, New York, Panels, Cobalt, Applied Mouth, 8 In. . . . 775.00
Perfume bottles are listed in their own category.
Pickle, Cathedral, Aqua, 6-Sided, Rolled Lip, 1860-1875, 13 In. 110.00
Pickle, Cathedral, Aqua, Rolled Lip, 11 1/2 In. 170.00
Pickle, Cathedral, Blue Green, 4-Sided, Rolled Lip, 11 3/4 In. 785.00
Pickle, Cathedral, Green Aqua, 6-Sided, Windows, 13 1/4 In. 279.00
Pickle, Cathedral, Green, 4-Sided, Rolled Lip, 11 3/4 In. 896.00
Pickle, Cathedral, Green, 4-Sided, Tooled Collar, Pontil, 8 3/4 In. 420.00
Pickle, Richmond Pickle Co., 8-Sided, 7 In. 35.00
Pickle, Richmond Pickle Co., Richmond, Va., 8-Sided, Tapered, 8 In. 40.00
Poison, Admiralty, Cobalt Blue, Embossed, Vertical Ribs, 8 1/2 In. 468.00
Poison, Cobalt Blue, Quilted, 5 In. 45.00
Poison, Embossed Not To Be Taken, Cobalt Blue, Horizontal Ribs, 3 3/4 In. 117.00
Poison, Embossed Not To Be Taken, Cobalt Blue, Horizontal Ribs, 6 3/4 In. 260.00
Poison, Embossed Poison, Property Of Poplar Borough, Cobalt Blue, 6-Sided, 9 In. 470.00
Poison, Embossed Skull & Crossbones, Olive Green, 6-Sided, 10 3/4 In. 350.00
Poison, Embossed, S.A.R. & H. Sick Fund, Not To Be Taken, Cobalt, 6-Sided, 3 3/4 In. . . 84.00
Poison, Figural, Skull, Cobalt Blue, Tooled Flared Mouth, 1880-1900, 2 7/8 In. 3360.00
Poison, Flask, Clear, Hobnail, Open Pontil, 6 In. 50.00
Poison, H.T. Waldner, Bedbug Poison, Cobalt Blue, Cylindrical, c.1885, 8 3/4 In. 39.00
Poison, Leath & Ross Neuraline, Poison, Emerald Green, Embossed, 8-Sided, 1 1/2 In. . . 78.00
Poison, Manchester Royal Infirmary, Cobalt Blue, Embossed, 6-Sided, Ribs, 5 1/2 In. . . . 40.00
Poison, Submarine, Cobalt Blue, Tooled Flared Mouth, England, 1880-1900, 4 3/4 In. . . . 2688.00
Poison, Tinct Iodine, Cobalt Blue, 1 3/16 In. 66.00
Saki, Anchor, Blossoms, Navy, Japan, World War II, 6 In. 98.00
Saki, Anchor, Blossoms, Retirement, Navy, Japan, World War II, 6 In. 69.00
Saki, Japanese 39th Infantry Regiment, Brown, Blue, Ceramic, World War II, 6 In. 74.00
Saki, Navy, Ceramic, Battle Flag, Anchor, Blossom, World War II, 6 In. 109.00
Sarsaparilla, Dr. Ira Baker's Honduras, Aqua, Squared Collar, 1892-1906, 10 1/2 In. 120.00
Sarsaparilla, Dr. Townsend's, Albany, N.Y., Blue Aqua, Sloping Collar, Pontil, 9 1/2 In. . . 310.00
Sarsaparilla, Dr. Townsend's, Albany, N.Y., Blue Green, Iron Pontil, 9 1/2 In. 505.00
Sarsaparilla, Dr. Townsend's, Albany, N.Y., Blue Green, Iron Pontil, 9 3/4 In. 560.00
Sarsaparilla, Dr. Townsend's, Albany, N.Y., Blue Green, Sloping Collar, Iron Pontil, 9 In. 476.00
Sarsaparilla, Dr. Townsend's, Albany, N.Y., Blue Green, Sloping Collar, Square, 9 1/2 In. 100.00
Sarsaparilla, Dr. Townsend's, Albany, N.Y., Deep Olive Green, Pontil, 9 1/4 In. 530.00
Sarsaparilla, Dr. Townsend's, Albany, N.Y., Emerald Green, Iron Pontil, 10 1/8 In. 615.00

Sarsaparilla, Dr. Townsend's, Albany, N.Y., Green, Iron Pontil, 9 1/2 In. 365.00
Sarsaparilla, Dr. Townsend's, Albany, N.Y., Medium Yellow Green, Iron Pontil, 9 3/8 In. . . 530.00
Sarsaparilla, Dr. Townsend's, Albany, N.Y., Olive Yellow, Iron Pontil, 9 1/4 In. 615.00
Sarsaparilla, Dr. Townsend's, Albany, N.Y., Olive Yellow, Pontil, 9 1/2 In. . . . . . . .308.00 to 476.00
Sarsaparilla, Dr. Townsend's, Albany, N.Y., Olive Yellow, Square, Pontil, 9 3/4 In. 365.00
Sarsaparilla, Log Cabin, Rochester, N.Y., Pat. Sept 6th 1887, Amber, 9 In. 190.00
Sarsaparilla, Log Cabin, Rochester, N.Y., Pat. Sept 6th 1887, Amber, Box, Contents, 9 In. 1155.00
Sarsaparilla, Old Dr. Townsend's, N.Y., Green, Sloping Collar, c.1880, 9 3/4 In. 145.00
Sarsaparilla, Old Dr. Townsend's, N.Y., Light Blue Green, Iron Pontil, 9 1/2 In. 532.00
Scent, Glass, Millefiori, Enamel, Portraits 55.00
Scent, Sunburst, Cobalt Blue, 3 In. 880.00
Scent, Swirled Right, Black Amethyst, Pontil, 2 1/2 In. 605.00
Scent, Swirled Right, Cobalt Blue, New England, 2 3/4 In. 55.00
Scent, Swirled, Cobalt Blue, New England, 3 In. 60.00
Seal, Boar, Coronet, Olive Green, Pontil Base, Applied Double Collar, 11 1/4 In. 400.00
Seal, Lupton, Olive Green, Applied Double Collar, 11 In. 420.00
Seal, S. Young & Co., Sheffield, Olive Green, Flask, Round Shouldered, 10 In. 60.00
Seltzer, Belfast, San Francisco, Green, ACL 35.00
Seltzer, Blue, Faceted, Birds Head Spout, Pewter Tap, 12 In. 20.00
Seltzer, Havana, Pure High Class Aerated Waters, Blue, Bear, 12 1/4 In. 418.00
Seltzer, Heath Mineral Waters, Nailsea, Acid Etched, Plastic Tap, 11 3/4 In. 58.00
Seltzer, Magner's Table Waters, Bright Green, Acid Etched, Chrome Tap, 12 In. 85.00
Seltzer, San Francisco Seltzer Water, Etched 35.00
Seltzer, Scarborough & Whitby Breweries, Green, Fluted, Sloping Collar, Pewter, 7 In. . . 500.00
Smelling Salts, 20 Ribs, Swirled To Right, Emerald Green, Pontil, 2 3/4 In. 179.00
Snuff, Agate, Brown & White Bands, Oval, Flattened, Coral Stopper, 2 In. 115.00
Snuff, Agate, Figural, Kneeling Boy, Bat, Black Accents, Hair Knot Forms Stopper, 2 In. . . 1725.00
Snuff, Agate, Foo Lion In Relief, Bamboo, Honey, Spade Shape, Quartz Stopper, 2 In. . . . 115.00
Snuff, Agate, High Relief Dragon, Flask Shape, Chinese, 2 1/2 In. 259.00
Snuff, Agate, Leaves, Caramel, Double Gourd Shape, Chinese, 1800s, 2 In. 150.00
Snuff, Agate, Moss, Oval, Raised Handles, Coral Stopper, 2 1/4 In. 259.00
Snuff, Amber, Yellow, Rectangular, Beveled Corners, Flared, Pontil, 5 In. 505.00
Snuff, Amethyst, Relief Carved Leaves, Temple Jar Shape, 3 1/4 In. 185.00
Snuff, Bamboo, Amber, Oval, Jadeite Stopper, 2 In. 405.00
Snuff, Bamboo, Relief Carved Waves, Tear Drop Shape, Coral Inlaid Stopper, 3 In. 1495.00
Snuff, Cameo Agate, Bowman & Boatman In Battle, Oval, Flattened, Lapis Stopper, 3 In. 4715.00
Snuff, Cameo Agate, Carved Children & Bat, Oval, Agate Stopper, 1 7/8 In. 403.00
Snuff, Cameo Agate, Carved Sage & Attendant With Teapot, Oval, 2 1/4 In. 1150.00
Snuff, Cameo Agate, Relief Carved, Figural Landscape, Oval, Flattened, Jadeite Stopper . . 1495.00
Snuff, Cameo Agate, Tethered Horse, Bat, Red, Cream Ground, Oval, 2 1/4 In. 690.00
Snuff, Chalcedony Agate, Leaping Carp Shape, Carved Grasses, Waves, 2 1/4 In. 127.00
Snuff, Chalcedony Agate, Mandarin Duck, Dark Matrix Highlights, Oval, 2 In. 259.00
Snuff, Chloromelanite, Carved Figures By River, Pink Quartz Stopper, 2 3/4 In. 4140.00
Snuff, Cinnabar, Carved Landscape, Jade Stopper, 2 1/2 In. 173.00
Snuff, Cinnabar, Landscape, Red & Black, Oval, Jadeite Stopper, 2 1/2 In. 2415.00
Snuff, Cloisonne, Passion Flowers, Blue Ground, Oval, Jadeite Stopper, 2 In. 748.00
Snuff, Cloisonne, Passion Flowers, White Ground, Pilgrim Flask Shape, 3 In. 201.00
Snuff, E. Roome, Troy, N.Y., Light Green, Embossed, 4 In. 385.00
Snuff, Fire Opal, Melon Shape, Carved Butterfly, Vines, Coral Stopper, 2 1/4 In. 604.00
Snuff, Glass, Blown, Yellow Amber, Rectangular, Sheared Mouth, Pontil, 4 3/16 In. 476.00
Snuff, Glass, Carved Figures In Landscape, Red, Yellow Ground, 2 1/4 In. 978.00
Snuff, Glass, Clear, Blue Overlay, Bird, Flowers, Pear Shape, Jadeite Stopper 460.00
Snuff, Glass, Custard, Enameled, Grasshopper, Dragonfly, Flowers, Coral Stopper, 2 In. . . 719.00
Snuff, Glass, Flowers, Crab, 7-Color Overlay, Mock Handles, Yanchow School, 3 In. 405.00
Snuff, Glass, Green Over White, Children Playing In Garden, Chinese, 3 1/4 In. 260.00
Snuff, Glass, Olive Green, Open Pontil, New England 55.00
Snuff, Glass, Olive Yellow, Rectangular, Beveled Corners, Applied Mouth, Pontil, 6 In. . . 448.00
Snuff, Glass, Olive Yellow, Square, Beveled Corners, Tooled Mouth, Pontil, 4 5/8 In. 179.00
Snuff, Glass, Olive Yellow, Square, Sheared Mouth, Pontil, Freeblown, 6 1/4 In. 560.00
Snuff, Glass, Pink Over Blue Over White, Peony, Prunus, 2 1/2 In. 2645.00
Snuff, Glass, Red Over Clear, Leaping Carp, Plants, Chinese, 2 1/2 In. 200.00
Snuff, Glass, Red Over Opalescent, Dragon Medallions, Mask Handles, 2 1/2 In. 776.00
Snuff, Glass, Red Over Snowflake, 8 Horses, 2 1/4 In. 403.00

Snuff, Glass, Red, Green & Blue Over Snowflake, Squirrel, Grapes, 2 1/4 In. 1064.00
Snuff, Glass, Ruby, Double Gourd Shape, Faceted, 2 1/2 In. 290.00
Snuff, Glass, Taddy & Compy, Wholesale Manufacturers, Tobacco & Snuff, Square, 3 In. . 285.00
Snuff, Glass, Traveler In Landscape, Chinese, Painted Interior, 2 1/2 In. 1150.00
Snuff, Glass, Turquoise Over Clear, Deer, Crane, Mask Handles, Jade Stopper, 2 1/4 In. . . 259.00
Snuff, Glass, Yellow Over Amber Flowers, Mother-Of-Pearl Stopper, 2 1/4 In. 863.00
Snuff, Inkstone, Chinese Characters, Pear Shape, Mask Handles, Coral Stopper, 2 3/4 In. . 1150.00
Snuff, Ivory, Carved Children, Temple Jar Shape, Clenched Fist Finial, 4 1/4 In. 345.00
Snuff, Ivory, Carved Flowers, Rectangular, Chinese, 1800s, 2 3/4 In. 118.00
Snuff, Ivory, Erotic, Engraved, Polychrome Figures, Stopper, 1900s, 3 In. 150.00
Snuff, Ivory, Figural, Naked Boy Seated On Drum, 2 1/2 In. 489.00
Snuff, Ivory, Figural, Woman Riding Elephant, Head Stopper, 3 In. 115.00
Snuff, Ivory, Figures & Dragons, Spade Shape, Stopper, 2 1/2 In. 230.00
Snuff, Ivory, Mongolian Horseman, Drinking Tea, Painted, Oval, Flattened, 2 1/2 In. 316.00
Snuff, Jade, Carved Leaves & Vines, Fruit Shape, Turquoise Stopper 145.00
Snuff, Jade, Red, Brown Streaks, Pebble Shape, 2 1/4 In. 635.00
Snuff, Jade, White, Carved Man Drinking Wine Under Tree, Oval, Rose Quartz Stopper . . 719.00
Snuff, Jade, White, Double Gourd Shape, Coral Stopper, 2 In. 200.00
Snuff, Jade, White, Enameled Silver Mounts, Chinese, 1800s, 2 1/2 In. 355.00
Snuff, Jadeite, Blue, Oval, Jadeite Stopper, 2 In. 2300.00
Snuff, Jadeite, Green, Oval, Pink Tourmaline Stopper, 2 1/2 In. 805.00
Snuff, Jadeite, Green, Snow On Grasses, Spade Shape, 2 3/4 In. 1150.00
Snuff, Lac Burgaute, Sea Ear, Signed, Chinese 595.00
Snuff, Lapis Lazuli, Carved Dragon, Temple Vase Shape, 2 In. 575.00
Snuff, Lapis Lazuli, Coral & Malachite Inlay, Mongolian Style Mounts, 2 1/2 In. 460.00
Snuff, Lapis Lazuli, Gourds, Vines, Gourd Shape, Stopper, c.1910, 2 In. 80.00
Snuff, Milk Glass, Enameled Birds & Chrysanthemums, Agate Stopper, 1 3/4 In., Pair . . . 805.00
Snuff, Opal, Carved Birds & Flowers, Jadeite Stopper, 2 1/4 In. 138.00
Snuff, Porcelain, Attached Netsuke, Purse Shape, Coral Stopper, 1 3/4 In. 1610.00
Snuff, Porcelain, Aubergine & Green Glaze, Eggplant Shape, 1 1/2 In. 127.00
Snuff, Porcelain, Camel Driver & Camel By City Wall, Lapis Stopper, 1 1/2 In. 70.00
Snuff, Porcelain, Cicada On Willow Tree Branch, Oval, 3 In. 518.00
Snuff, Porcelain, Copper Red, 5-Claw Dragon, Tear Drop Shape, Wood Stopper, 3 In. 601.00
Snuff, Porcelain, Crickets, Jadeite Stopper, Oval, 1820-1850, 2 1/4 In. 635.00
Snuff, Porcelain, Dolphin's Head, Flowers, c.1720 . . . . 518.00
Snuff, Porcelain, Dragon Roundel, Bats, Purse Shape, Lapis Stopper, 2 In. 127.00
Snuff, Porcelain, Dragon, Clouds, Red, Gray Underglaze, Cylindrical, Stone Stopper, 3 In. 220.00
Snuff, Porcelain, Dragon, Red, Blue Underglaze, Cylindrical, Amethyst Stopper, 2 1/4 In. . 575.00
Snuff, Porcelain, Figural, Squirrel With Grapes, Jade Stopper, 2 3/4 In. 115.00
Snuff, Porcelain, Grasshopper Design, Pebble Shape, Coral Stopper, 2 1/4 In. 660.00
Snuff, Porcelain, Green Glaze, Double Carp Shape, Jade Stopper, 2 1/2 In. 127.00
Snuff, Porcelain, Incised Dragon, Spade Shape, Glass Stopper, 2 1/4 In. 175.00
Snuff, Porcelain, Landscape, Mountains, Teahouse, Green, 3 In. 635.00
Snuff, Porcelain, Lohan Riding Deer, Landscape, Baluster Shape, Coral Stopper, 2 3/4 In. . 750.00
Snuff, Porcelain, Pink Crackle Glaze, Meiping Shape, Jadeite Stopper, 2 3/4 In. 175.00
Snuff, Porcelain, Rose Crackle Glaze, Gourd Shape, Stone Stopper, 2 1/8 In. 127.00
Snuff, Porcelain, Yellow Glaze, Ear Of Corn Shape, Coral Stopper, 2 3/4 In. 140.00
Snuff, Rock Crystal, Figural Landscape, Painted Interior, Rose Quartz Stopper, 2 1/4 In. . . 435.00
Snuff, Shadow Agate, Agate Eye Inclusion, Flattened Oval, Jade Stopper, Chinese, 3 In. . . 520.00
Snuff, Shadow Agate, Bird On Tree Stump, Oval, Tiger's Eye Stopper, 2 1/8 In. 1495.00
Snuff, Shadow Agate, Songbirds, Flowering Tree, Flattened Oval, Stopper, 1800s, 2 In. . . 145.00
Snuff, Soapstone, Operatic Scenes, Tan, Pink & Black Marks, Chinese, 1800s, 3 1/4 In. . . 380.00
Snuff, Soochow Agate, Sages & Foo Lion In Landscape, Oval, Glass Stopper, 1 3/4 In. . . . 4255.00
Snuff, Tiger's Eye, Blue, Cameo Carved Crane, Pine Trees, Jade Stopper, 2 1/4 In. 115.00
Snuff, Turquoise, Carved Insect, Blossom, Leaves, Fruit Shape, Agate Stopper, 2 In. 520.00
Soaky, Mighty Mouse, 1960s 85.00
Soda, A. Smith, Charleston, S.C., Cobalt Blue, Cylindrical, Sloping Collar, Pontil, 1/2 Pt. . 895.00
Soda, Allegheny Bottling Co., 48 Taggart St., Pittsburgh, Pa., Aqua, Hutchinson 25.00
Soda, Arctic Soda Works, Honolulu, Aqua, Slug Plate, Tooled Lip, Cylindrical 55.00
Soda, Barrett & Elders, Aqua, Codd, Ceramic Stopper, 8 In. 200.00
Soda, Big Hit, Brunswick, Baseball Player, Embossed, Ga., 8 Oz. 85.00
Soda, Brown Stout, Teal Blue, Cylindrical, Applied Collar, Iron Pontil, 1/2 Pt. 180.00
Soda, C.B. Owen & Co., Cincinnati, Blue 200.00

Soda, C.P. Fahler, York, Pa., Green, 7 1/2 In. 225.00
Soda, Cascade Ginger Ale, 6-Pack, Box, 8 x 10 x 5 1/2 In. 17.00
Soda, Cherry Smash, Hot Soda, Metal Cap, 12 In. ....80.00 to 190.00
Soda, Cherry Smash, Reverse Glass Label, Metal Cap, 12 In. 77.00
Soda, Cyc-Kola, Extra Quality, Cliquot Club, Millis, Mass., Paper Label, 11 1/4 In. 335.00
Soda, E. Centsch, Buffalo, N.Y., Aqua, Hutchinson 25.00
Soda, F. Seitz & Bro., Easton, Pa., Sapphire Blue, Squat 130.00
Soda, F. Seitz & Bro., Premium Mineral Water, Sapphire Blue, 8-Sided 99.00
Soda, G. Hill, Aerated Water, Wombwell, Codd, Amber, 9 In. 200.00
Soda, G. Upp Jr., Green, 7 3/8 In. 200.00
Soda, G.S. Smart, Alnwick, Redfearn Bros., Emerald Green, Codd, 9 1/4 In. 69.00
Soda, Geo. R. Lamb & Co., Red Bank, N.J., Green, Squat, Crown Top, c.1880, 7 In. 45.00
Soda, Geo. Schmuck, Cleveland, O., Aqua, Hutchinson 20.00
Soda, Green Aqua, Squat, Slug Plate 99.00
Soda, Hall Ltd., Brewery, Ely, Olive Green, Codd, 7 1/2 In. 100.00
Soda, Hawaiian Soda Works, Honolulu, Hawaii, Aqua, Crown Top, 1900, 8 3/4 In. 45.00
Soda, Henry Wenzel, Covington, Ky., Sea Green, Applied Lip, c.1870, 1/2 Pt., 7 1/4 In. .. 45.00
Soda, Howell & Smith, Buffalo, N.Y., Aqua, Hutchinson 20.00
Soda, Howell & Smith, Buffalo, Yellow Green, Tapered, Cylindrical, 1845-1860 .... 1790.00
Soda, Indian Rock, Ginger Ale, Richmond, Ten Pin, 1908-1915, 7 5/8 In. 605.00
Soda, Jackson's Napa Soda, Aqua, Cap 11.00
Soda, Luke Beard, Forest Green, Ten Pin, Open Pontil 950.00
Soda, M. Felix, Harrisburg, Aqua, Squat, Slug Plate 59.00
Soda, Oakland Pioneer, Aqua, Tooled Square Lip, 13 1/2 In. 200.00
Soda, P.H. Reasbeck, Braddock, Pa., Aqua, Hutchinson 25.00
Soda, R. White, Camberwell, Aqua, Amber Lip, Codd, 7 1/4 In. 92.00
Soda, R. White, Camberwell, Rylands Barnsley, Aqua, Red Amber Lip, Codd, 9 1/4 In. .. 50.00
Soda, Richardson's Fruited Orangeade, Label Under Glass, 11 x 3 3/8 In. 1870.00
Soda, Sacramento Eagle Soda, Cobalt Blue, Blob Top, Iron Pontil, 1850, 7 1/2 In. 660.00
Soda, Smile, Contents, Box, 18 In., Gal. 550.00
Soda, Spencer Connor & Co., Manchester, Aqua, Codd, 9 In. 25.00
Soda, Wadsworth, St. Ives Hunts, Barnsley, Aqua, Cobalt Blue Lip, Codd, 8 In. 400.00
Soda, Wm. A. Kearney, Shamokin, Pa., Root Beer Amber, Hutchinson, c.1890, Qt. 415.00
Soda, Wm. H. Stall, Phoenixville, Pa., Clear, Paneled Base, Hutchinson 17.00
Soda, Wm. W. Lappeus Premium Soda, Albany, Deep Blue 900.00
Spirits, Dip Mold Cylinder, Deep Kickup, Outward Rolled Lip, c.1750, 10 1/2 In. 99.00
Stiegel Type, Enameled, Woman Carrying Pails, Pewter Collar, 1750-1850, 5 3/4 In. 230.00
Target Ball, Bogardus, Pat'd Apr 10 1877, Gold Amber, Sheared Mouth, Stopper, 2 3/4 In. 365.00
Target Ball, N.B. Glass Works, Perth, Diamond, Cobalt Blue, 3 In. 55.00
Target Ball, N.B. Glass Works, Perth, Diamond, Pale Blue 95.00
Target Ball, N.B. Glass Works, Perth, Diamond, Pale Green 100.00
Target Ball, Van Gutsema A St. Quentin, Diamond, Cobalt Blue, 3 1/4 In. 40.00
Target Ball, W.W. Greeners, St. Mary's Works, Diamond, Amethyst, 3 In. 635.00
Tonic, Dodge Brothers, Melanine, Plum Amethyst, 7 3/8 In. 1456.00
Tonic, Vernal Female Tonic For Women, Label, Contents, Pamphlet, Box, 9 In. 65.00
Whiskey, Alice In Wonderland, Amber, Painted, Chestnut Shape, Jug, 8 In., Pair 500.00
Whiskey, Apricot Puce, Dyottville Glassworks, Phila., 11 1/2 In. 39.00
Whiskey, Backbar, Horseshoe & Four Leaf Clover, Olive Yellow, Embossed, 11 In. 39.00
Whiskey, Berry's Diamond Wedding, Clear, Embossed Barrels, Qt., 12 1/4 In. 39.00
Whiskey, Brooklyn Glass Bottle Works, Gold Amber, 1865-1875, Fifth, 11 1/4 In. 300.00
Whiskey, C.A. Essman's, Shoofly, Fish Shaped Label, I Am Dry, Flask, c.1890, 5 In. 155.00
Whiskey, Chapin & Gore Sour Mash, 1861, Barrel, Amber, Stopper, 1/2 Pt. 220.00
Whiskey, Commodores Royal, O.K., Old Bourbon & Rye, Inside Screw Threads, 12 In. .. 495.00
Whiskey, Dickson & White, Kenton, O., Aqua, Applied Mouth, Flask, 1870-1880, Qt. 99.00
Whiskey, Doct. Girard's Cherry Brandy, Medium Gold Amber, Applied Band, Handle 1430.00
Whiskey, Duffy Malt Whiskey, Rochester, N.Y., Patented 1886, Amber 8.00
Whiskey, E.P. Middleton, 1825 Wheat Whiskey, Phila, Green, Double Roll Collar 303.00
Whiskey, Forest Lawn, J.V.H., Yellow Olive Amber, Onion Shape, Long Neck, 1850, 7 In. 550.00
Whiskey, Glen Garry, Very Old Scotch Whisky, Port Dundas, Stamp 29.00
Whiskey, Glenco Brand Scotch Whiskey, Thistle Transfer, Jug 129.00
Whiskey, Griffith Hyatt & Co., Baltimore, Jug, Yellow Amber, Square Collar, Pontil, 7 In. 950.00
Whiskey, Haynor's Whiskey Distillery, Troy, Ohio, Amber, 1897, Qt. 10.00
Whiskey, Henry Chapman & Co., Montreal, Flask, Red Amber, Teardrop Shape, 5 3/4 In. . 250.00

Whiskey, J.H. Cutter, Old Bourbon, A.P. Hotaling & Co., Dark Amber, Fifth 1210.00
Whiskey, Jesse Moore & Co., Louisville, Ky., Red Orange Amber, Embossed Antlers, Fifth 2420.00
Whiskey, Kelloggs Nelson County Extra Kentucky Bourbon, Dark Red Amber, Fifth 875.00
Whiskey, Laughlan Ross & Co., Aqua, Embossed Thistles & Barley, 10 1/4 In. 159.00
Whiskey, Mitchell's Old Irish Whisky, Belfast, Stoneware, Jug, 2-Tone, 7 In. 54.00
Whiskey, Monopole Rye, Black Bar, Cut Glass, Zipper Neck, Gilt, 3 3/4 x 9 1/2 In. 110.00
Whiskey, O.K. Bourbon Castle, F. Chevalier & Co., Amber, Applied Top, c.1875, 12 In. .. 1045.00
Whiskey, Old Bourbon, Honey Amber, Hog Shape, 1875-1890, 6 5/8 In. 415.00
Whiskey, Old Bourbon, Wilson Fairbank & Co, Aqua, 1870-1890, 10 In. 145.00
Whiskey, Old Prentice Whisky, Inside Fluted Panels, Ground Pontil, 3 1/2 x 11 In. 210.00
Whiskey, Reed's Old Lexington Club, Cunningham & Ihmsen, Amber, Applied Top, 11 In. 4620.00
Whiskey, Rickett's Bristol Glass Works, Olive Green, 3-Piece Mold, Sloped Top, Pontil .. 39.00
Whiskey, Schiedam Aromatic, Schnapps, Light Apple Green 55.00
Whiskey, South Carolina Dispensary, Aqua, Strap Side, c.1900, 1/2 Pt., 6 1/4 In. 176.00
Whiskey, South Carolina Dispensary, Palmetto Tree, Clear, 1900-1907, Qt., 9 1/8 In. 385.00
Whiskey, Star, New York, Yellow Amber, Cone Shape, Vertical Ribs, Handle, 8 In. 1100.00
Whiskey, Strawberry Puce, Applied Handle, Pontil, Jug, 5 7/8 In. 450.00
Whiskey, Tucker, Suspects His Master, Bulldog, Enamel Decoration, 1880-1900, 11 In. .. 660.00
Whiskey, Watson's Dundee, Stoneware, Jug, Spout, 2-Tone, 8 1/2 In. 50.00
Whiskey, Wharton's, 1850, Chestnut Grove, Gold Amber, Pocket Flask, 5 1/2 In. 229.00
Whiskey, William Jameson & Co., Dublin, Diamond, Jug 139.00
Wine, English Onion, Olive Green, Tapered, String Collar, Pontil, c.1690, 5 3/4 In. 284.00
Wine, Mallet, Olive Green, Applied String Collar, Pontil, 8 1/2 In. 70.00
Wine, Nichs Hallam 1712, Dutch Onion, Green, Applied String Collar, Pontil, 6 3/4 In. .. 5180.00
Wine, Olive Green, Cylindrical, Applied Collar, Pontil, c.1790, 8 1/4 In. 25.00
Wine, Scranton Wine & Liquor Co., Cobalt Blue, Jug, 1/2 Gal. 295.00

BOTTLE OPENERS are needed to open many bottles. As soon as the commercial bottle was invented, the opener to be used with the new types of closures became a necessity. Many types of bottle openers can be found, most dating from the twentieth century. Collectors prize advertising and comic openers.

Alligator Biting Scared Black Man, Wilton Mfg., 1920s, 4 In. 80.00
Amish Man, Cast Iron, Wall Mount, 1953, 4 1/8 x 3 5/8 In. 3800.00
Beer Drinker, Cast Iron 500.00
Boy Winking, Wall Mount, Cast Iron, 3 7/8 x 3 5/8 In. 775.00
Caddy, Cast Iron, Nickel Plated, 1932, 5 13/16 x 1 7/8 In. 550.00
Cathy Coed, Cast Iron, c.1950, 4 1/2 In. 550.00
Clown, Head, Cast Iron, 1950 .... 25.00
Cow Head, Cast Iron, Wood Handle 66.00
Cowboy, Cactus, Hollow Mold, Pot Metal, 4 5/8 x 2 3/16 In. 300.00
Dinky Dan, Cast Iron, 1948, 3 7/8 x 2 1/8 In. 290.00
Dog Head, Ebony, Brass Collar, Double Opener Blade, Evans 100.00
Duck, Mallard, Metal, Green Head Yellow Bill, Scott Products, 1970, 6 In. 80.00
Elephant, Cast Iron, 1950, 3 x 2 In. 225.00
Eskimo, Aluminum, 1956-1961 .... 300.00
Eskimo, Hollow, Pot Metal, Bronze Plated, 4 In. 700.00
Freddy Frosh, Cast Iron, c.1950, 4 x 2 In. 205.00
Knife, Remington Blade, Bottle Shape 254.00
Lucky Bop, Man On Base, Pot Metal, Brass Plated 40.00
Man, Non-Magnetic Alloy 10.00
Paddy The Pledgemaster, Cast Iron, 1948, 3 7/8 x 2 1/4 In. ....140.00 to 300.00
Parrot On Perch, Cast Iron, 4 5/8 x 3 1/4 In. 270.00
Patty Pep, Cast Iron, c.1950, 4 In. 500.00
Sailor, Aluminum 110.00
Sammy Samoa, Cast Iron, c.1950, 4 In. 180.00
Sawfish With Snout Opener, Cast Iron 225.00
Seahorse, Cast Iron, 1950, 4 1/4 x 2 1/4 In. 80.00
Skull, Drink It Here, Not Hereafter, Cast Iron, Painted White, 1930s 145.00
Stout Gentleman, Toasting With Mug Of Beer, Sprenger Brewing Co., 6 1/2 In. 169.00
Swimmer, Aluminum Alloy 950.00
Swordfish, White Metal, Painted, 1950, 1 15/16 x 5 7/8 In. 475.00

BOX 77 BOX, Candle

BOXES of all kinds are collected. They were made of thin strips of inlaid wood, metal, tortoiseshell, embroidery, or other material. Additional boxes may be listed in other sections, such as Advertising, Battersea, Ivory, Shaker, Tinware, and various Porcelain categories. Tea Caddies are listed in their own category.

Apple, Cherry, Dovetailed Construction, 9 3/4 In.	248.00
Apple, Mahogany, Nailed, 9 1/4 x 9 1/2 In.	110.00
Apple, Red Paint, Nailed Construction, 13 x 12 In.	140.00
Baleen, 3 Fingers, Oval, Incised, Trees, House, Wooden Lid, 2 3/4 x 2 In.	259.00
Baleen, Etched Decoration, House, Willow Tree, Ship, Cover, Oval, 1800s, 3 x 4 x 5 In.	345.00
Ballot, 2 Compartments, Hinged Cover, Black & White Marbles	29.00
Ballot, Walnut, Dovetailed, Hanging, Slant Lid, Arched Crest, 9 5/8 x 8 3/4 x 6 1/2 In.	259.00
Ballot, Walnut, Hinged Door, Marbles	29.00
Ballot, Wood, 2 Compartments, Sliding Cover, Marbles	45.00
Band, Wallpaper, Flowering Tree, German Newspaper Lined, 3 x 4 1/4 In.	293.00
Band, Wallpaper, Green Geometric Design, John Avery, 6 x 10 In.	350.00
Band, Wallpaper, Green, Pink Flowers, Lining, Hannah Davis, Label, 10 In.	490.00
Band, Wallpaper, Orange, Black Stylized Flowers, 19th Century, 3 1/8 x 1 3/4 x 5/8 In.	385.00
Band, Wallpaper, White, Blue Branches, 19th Century, 8 3/4 x 5 1/2 x 3 14 In.	190.00
Band, Wallpaper, White, Stripes, Blue & Green Flower, 19th Century, 8 3/4 x 5 x 4 1/4 In.	360.00
Band, Wood Finish, Marbleized Paper Interior, 2 3/4 x 7 3/4 In.	415.00
Bentwood, Bittersweet Over Putty Paint, Wrought Iron Tacks, c.1767, 8 x 6 x 3 In.	1610.00
Bentwood, Circular, Cover, Red Paint, 1800s, 6 1/2 In.	115.00
Bentwood, Oval, 1 Finger, Copper Tacks, 2 1/8 x 5 7/8 In.	375.00
Bentwood, Red, Sponge Decoration, Laced Seams, c.1835, 12 x 8 x 7 1/4 In.	345.00
Bentwood, Round, 3 Fingers, Cover, Blue Paint, 8 1/2 x 5 In.	1610.00
Bentwood, Scandinavian Decoration, Oval, Laced Fingers, Blue, Orange, 8 1/2 x 3 In.	290.00
Betel, Lacquer, Black, Cinnabar Red, Medallions, Gold, Lift-Out Lid, Burma, 7 x 7 In.	150.00
Betel, Lacquer, Gold, Black, Cinnabar Interior, Tiger On Cover, Lift-Out Tray, 6 x 4 In.	175.00
Betel, Lacquer, Gold, Cinnabar, Black, Green, Blue Stripes, Lift-Out Tray, Burma, 7 x 4 In.	115.00
Betel, Lacquer, Painted, Cinnabar, Black, Gold, Peacock Medallion, Burma, 5 x 5 In.	105.00
Bible, Baroque Carving, Pine, Ball Feet, 16 x 25 1/2 In.	345.00
Bible, Burled Walnut, Rosewood Inlay, 13 x 10 x 4 In.	255.00
Bible, Oak, Chip Carved, Dovetail Case, Medallion, Strap Hinges, 22 x 11 1/2 x 9 1/2 In.	275.00
Birchbark, Quillwork, Cover, Leaf Design, c.1900, 4 In.	115.00
Bird's-Eye Maple, Carved, Painted, 4 x 12 In.	355.00
Biscuit, Faux Tortoiseshell, Silver Plated Handles, Edwardian Style, 5 x 16 x 9 In.	1150.00
Black & Gold Lacquer, Stacked, Book Shape, Mirror, Drawer, Chinese, 4 x 7 1/4 x 10 In.	115.00
Black Base, House, Stylized Tulips, Oval, Bucher, 13 3/4 x 9 x 5 1/4 In.	1045.00
Black Base, Painted Decoration, House, Red Roof, Tulips, Bucher, 9 3/4 x 6 3/4 x 3 In.	6710.00
Black Base, Painted, Houses, Tress, Stylized Tulips, Bucher, 13 x 8 x 5 1/4 In.	1870.00
Black Base, Red, Yellow, Green, House, Flowers, Square, Bucher, 8 3/4 x 9 3/4 x 2 1/2 In.	2530.00
Blue Paint, Finger Lap Joints, Copper Nails, 19th Century, 7 x 5 x 2 In.	1540.00
Bonnet, Wallpaper Covered, Cardboard, 10 In.	345.00
Bonnet Set, Nesting, Oval, Split Beech, Oilcloth Top, 6 x 9 In., 7 x 10 In., 8 x 12 In.	670.00
Book Form, Walnut, Mahogany, Bird's-Eye Maple, Rosewood, 14 x 12 x 3 In.	405.00
Boot, Paint Decorated, Grain Painted, Yellow Ocher, Hinged Lid, 14 x 14 1/2 x 9 1/2 In.	360.00
Brass, Book Form, Hinged Lid, 1800s, 3 In.	115.00
Bride's, Hand Decorated, Polychrome On Blue, 16 In.	450.00
Bride's, Pine, Bentwood, Willow Reed, Bride, Groom, Flowers, German Verse, 7 x 18 In.	1045.00
Candle, Heart Shape Pull, Paint Decorated, Black, Red, Slide Lid, 4 5/8 x 5 3/4 x 15 1/2 In.	330.00
Candle, Ivory Decoration, Whale, Schooner, Wood, 17 x 10 1/2 x 4 1/2 In.	400.00
Candle, Maple, Dovetailed, Finger Hold, Slide Lid, 12 In.	95.00
Candle, Painted, Pierced Star Shape Carved Panel, 19th Century, 12 In.	200.00
Candle, Painted, Tulips, Leaves, Slide Lid, Pine, c.1830, 10 1/2 x 4 x 5 In. .... *Illus*	2860.00
Candle, Polychrome Tulip, Red Ground, Pine, Slide Lid, 5 x 12 1/4 In.	385.00
Candle, Rosehead Nail, Chamfered Edge, Old Red Paint, Slide Lid, 15 x 9 In.	169.00
Candle, Softwood, Dovetailed, Raised Panel, Carved Edge, Putty Paint, Slide Lid, 12 In.	310.00
Candle, Tin, Round, Hanging, Early 1800s, 10 3/4 In.	99.00
Candle, Tulip, Red Ground, Pine, Slide Lid, Anne Stauffer, 1796, 2 3/4 x 7 3/4 In.	5500.00
Candle, Wall, Birch, Dovetailed, Bowed Front, Escutcheon, Cutout Crest, 7 x 12 x 5 In.	345.00
Candle, Wall, Mahogany, Columbia, Leaf Inlays, 20 In.	540.00

Box, Candle,
Painted, Tulips,
Leaves, Slide Lid,
Pine, c.1830,
10 1/2 x 4 x 5 In.

Box, Dome
Top, Blue
Painted, Birds,
Flowers, Wire
Handle, c.1840,
11 x 7 x 7 In.

Candle, Wall, Pine, Keyhole Crest, 13 1/4 x 5 1/4 x 11 1/4 In. 300.00
Candle, Wall, Pine, Red Paint, Black Interior, Shaped Crest, Canted Front, 13 1/2 x 6 In. . 605.00
Candle, Walnut, Dovetailed, Chamfered Edges, 12 x 4 3/4 x 4 1/2 In. 250.00
Candle, Walnut, Dovetailed, Crest, 13 x 6 3/4 x 8 1/2 In. 288.00
Candy, Violin, Green, Drawer, Cardboard, Wood, 7 1/4 In. 100.00
Carved, Frisian, Time Is Money On Lid, Incised Fans, Stars, Diamonds, 9 x 6 x 7 In. 180.00
Census, Fill Out Census Blank, Drop It In Box, Mustard Paint, 18 In. 385.00
Charity, 2 Slots, 2 Doors, Brass, Molded Base, 6 1/2 In. 1645.00
Chip Carved, Trick Top, Stars, House, Flower Basket, Ezekial Holbrook Jr., c.1815 .... 2640.00
Cigarette, Drum Shape, Ebonized & Brass Drumsticks On Lid, France, 3 1/4 In. 169.00
Cigarette, Silver, Man & Seminude Woman, Running With Red Sheet, Enamel, 3 x 4 In. . 720.00
Cigarette, Silver, Nude Woman Dressing, Enamel, 4 1/2 x 3 1/2 In. 1265.00
Cloisonne, Cylinder, Dragons, Scrolled Field, 3 1/8 In. 99.00
Collection, Grain Decorated, Dovetailed Sides, Square Nails, Cutout Handle, 18 1/4 In. .. 145.00
Collection, Tin, Applied Cutout Stars, Eagle, Painted, Graduated Shape, 17 x 9 x 22 In. . 230.00
Comb, Heart Chip Carved, Painted, Yellow, Green, Scalloped Front, 10 x 4 x 10 In. 825.00
Copper, Flower Shape, Butterfly, Peonies, Ducks, Passion Flowers, 19th Century, 5 1/4 In. 115.00
Cosmetic, Teak, 3 Drawers, 2 Mirrors, Silver Plated Brass, Asia, 1800s, 8 x 10 In. 725.00
Curly Maple, Lid, Carved Bird, Worm Damage, 4 x 7 1/2 x 4 1/2 In. 110.00
Cutlery, Softwood, Rolling Pin Handle, Mortised Construction, 13 1/4 In. 140.00
Cutout Apron, Pierced Flower, Removable Lid, England, 18 1/2 x 36 1/2 x 12 In. 90.00
Decanter, Federal, Inlaid Mahogany, 11 Bottles, Boston, c.1800, 11 1/2 x 16 1/8 In. 2185.00
Decanter, Oak, 12 Bottles, Glassware, Iron Straps, 11 x 10 1/4 x 16 1/2 In. 805.00
Desk, Banded, Fruitwood, Inlaid, Cassone Shape, c.1835, 6 x 10 x 8 1/2 In. 405.00
Desk, Ebony, Scarlet Tortoiseshell, Secret Drawers, Germany, c.1885, 12 x 15 1/4 x 10 In. 2760.00
Desk, Gilt Brass Mount, Polished Moss Agate, Renaissance Style, Russia, 2 x 4 1/4 x 3 In. 460.00
Desk, Grand Tour, Peach Marble, Roman Sarcophagus Shape, 19th Century, 3 x 5 In. 575.00
Desk, Rosewood, Bone Inlay, Oblong, Anglo-Indian, c.1885, 5 x 17 1/2 x 8 1/4 In. 690.00
Desk, Rosewood, Lift-Out Interior Tray, 6 Compartments, Mid 1800s, 5 x 13 1/2 x 10 In. . 145.00
Desk, Wood, Ebonized, Inlaid, Micro Mosaic, Key, Italy, c.1865, 3 x 9 1/4 x 7 1/2 In. 460.00
Ditty, Shell Work, 10 1/2 x 7 1/2 x 3 In. 316.00
Document, Dome Top, Stamped, T. Tilden, 8 1/2 x 17 3/4 x 8 3/4 In. 4780.00
Document, English Ash, Wrought Iron Hardware, Hinged Lid, 1700s, 12 x 17 x 12 1/2 In. 200.00
Document, Grain Painted, Dovetailed, E. Morse, N.H., 1848, 14 x 11 1/4 x 5 In. 489.00
Document, Leather Bound, Handle, Brass Studs, 19th Century, 6 x 11 x 8 In. 69.00
Document, Mahogany, Maple, Diagonal Banding, Brass Bail Handle, 3 x 11 1/4 x 8 In. .. 60.00
Document, Maple, American, First Half 1800s, 12 1/2 x 24 x 11 1/2 In. 355.00
Document, Pennsylvania German Paper Decoration, c.1834, 8 x 15 In. 695.00
Document, Pine, Dovetailed, Wallpaper Lined, Iron Hasp Lock, 18 x 10 1/2 x 7 1/2 In. .. 305.00
Document, Pine, Painted Red, Brass Pull, 19th Century, 6 5/8 x 14 1/4 x 8 1/2 In. 380.00
Document, Red & Black Swirl, Pine, Dome Top, New England, 5 3/4 x 13 3/4 In. 2990.00
Document, Red, Black Primitive & Compass Designs, Pine, Lift Top, 12 x 9 8 1/2 In. ... 550.00
Document, Satinwood, Veneer, Mahogany Band, Ivory Escutcheon, 4 x 10 x 7 1/2 In. 805.00
Document, Scarlet Leather, Hetty Nutlman, Newark, American, c.1800, 6 1/2 x 13 x 8 In. 460.00
Document, Sea Lions On Ends, Yellow, Red Polka Dots, Cornucopia, Pine, 16 x 9 x 6 In. 865.00
Document, Tole, Brown Japanning, Wire Bail Handle, Flowers, Stripes, 9 x 4 3/4 x 5 In. . 250.00
Document, Wallpaper Covered, Dome Top, Tin Hasp Lock, Wire Handles, 13 x 8 x 7 In. . 375.00
Document, Walnut, Dovetailed, Molded Base, Diamond Escutcheon Inlaiy, 17 x 8 In. ... 315.00
Document, White Pine, Grain Decorated, Dovetailed, Inset Lock, 1800s, 13 x 7 1/2 x 6 In. 195.00
Dome Top, Basswood, Dovetailed, Green Paint, 22 1/2 x 12 1/4 x 9 In. 200.00

Dome Top, Blue Painted, Birds, Flowers, Wire Handle, c.1840, 11 x 7 x 7 In. ...... *Illus*   825.00
Dome Top, Flowers, 2 Birds, Ocher Painted Ground, c.1840, 16 x 10 1/2 x 9 In. 1100.00
Dome Top, Flowers, Swag, Cotter-Pin Hinges, c.1818, 12 1/2 x 8 x 8 In. 650.00
Dome Top, Green Paint, Gold & Red Decoration, 12 In. 6050.00
Dome Top, Paint Decorated, Compass Drawn Flowers, Tin Hasp, c.1815, 5 x 5 1/2 x 4 In.   7700.00
Dome Top, Painted, Stippled Panels, Flowers, Red Flame, Wire Nails, 13 1/2 x 6 3/4 In. ..   870.00
Dome Top, Painted, Yellow Ground, Bird, Flowers, 7 1/2 x 7 1/4 x 11 1/2 In. 550.00
Dome Top, Pine, Red Vinegar Decoration, Orange Ground, Hasp Lock, 18 x 9 x 9 In. 1900.00
Dome Top, Rawhide, Brass Tacks, Leather Handle, Lock, Wallpaper Lining, 14 x 9 In. ...   230.00
Dresser, 5-Point Stars, Eye Dazzler Top, Hinged Lid, Exotic Woods, 10 3/4 x 18 x 11 In. .   805.00
Dresser, Celluloid, Greek Goddess, Cherubs, 13 In. 150.00
Dresser, Dropwell, Backboard, 2 Mirrors, Tinsel Painting, Drawers, 15 x 23 x 5 1/2 In. ..   489.00
Dresser, Footed, Oval, Brass, Man, Woman Drinking Tea, Swags, Flowers, 3 x 8 1/4 x 6 In.   110.00
Dresser, General Grant & His Horse Shape, White Glaze, Gilt, Cover, 5 x 3 1/2 In. 58.00
Dresser, Marquetry Inlaid Fruitwood, Leaf Spray, Late 1800s, 10 3/4 In. 880.00
Dresser, Porcelain, Egg Shape, Cleopatra, Wagner, Germany, c.1900, 4 1/2 In. 1295.00
Dresser, Rectangular, Divided Interior, Snakeskin, Cover, 4 x 9 x 5 In. 58.00
Dresser, Rectangular, Silver, Cover, Crystal, Engraved, Russia, 7 1/2 x 1 3/4 In. 175.00
Ebonized Wood, Pietra Dura Top, Hinged Lid, White Iris, Italy, Late 1800s, 8 1/2 x 6 In. .   460.00
Enamel On Copper, Round, Dome Top, Peacock, Tail Feathers On Branch, 4 3/4 x 2 In. ...   3200.00
Enamel On Copper, Square, Luminescent, Peacock On Tree, Landscape, 4 3/4 x 1 3/4 In.   4200.00
Feed, Slant Front, Pine, Dovetail Construction, 1800s, 34 x 42 x 17 In. 290.00
Finger Jointed, Levi Beal Impression, 5 1/2 x 2 In. 115.00
Game, Chinoiserie, Lacquer, Boxes, Card Trays, Gaming Chips, c.1810, 12 x 15 x 4 In. ...   980.00
Glove, Lacewood, Inlay, Canted Corners, Hinged Lid, Feather Band, Late 1800s, 13 In. ..   355.00
Gold Lacquer, Flower, Mother-Of-Pearl Inlay, Square, 1800s, 3 In. 1725.00
Gold Lacquer, Flowers, Swirled Ground, Square, 1800s, 2 In. 150.00
Gold Lacquer, Rectangular, Paulownia, Wisteria, Nashiji Ground, 1800s, 3 1/2 In. 210.00
Grain Painted, Radiating Pattern, c.1840, 19 3/4 x 8 x 10 1/4 In. 935.00
Gum, Birch Bark, Fitted Base, Lid, Brass Bail Handle, 5 1/4 x 4 1/4 In. 110.00
Guri Lacquer, Circular, Flower Like Design, c.1800, 2 In. 375.00
Hammered Copper, Applied Lid Design, Arts & Crafts, 5 In. 85.00
Hat, Leather, Blue & White Cotton Ticking Lining, c.1850, 9 3/4 x 13 1/2 In. 75.00
Hat, Leather, Gilt Decoration, Tapering Egg Shape, 19th Century 90.00
Hat, Leather, Painted Royal Coat Of Arms, Brass Studs, England, 1800s, 13 In. 405.00
Hat, Paper On Cardboard, Hot Air Balloon Voyage 3875.00
Hat, Wallpaper Covered, Blue & Brown Flower Block Print, Green Scrolling, 8 x 4 In. ..   316.00
Hat, Wallpaper Covered, Brown, Green, Tan Block Prints, 10 3/4 x 7 In. 405.00
Hat, Wallpaper Covered, Mustard, Brown Block Print Carnation, 14 x 9 3/4 In. 489.00
Hinged Lid, Clear Glass, Etched Daisy, Metal Fittings, 2 1/2 x 6 1/2 In. 20.00
Hinged Lid, Oval, Jewels, Reticulated Silver, Beveled Glass, 3 x 7 1/2 In. 60.00
Hinged Lid, Silver Wire, Carved Cameo Medallion, Woman Feeding Bird, 2 1/2 x 4 In. ..   700.00
Hinged Lid, Tortoiseshell, Pierced Brass, Applied Mother-Of-Pearl Medallion, 6 In. 690.00
Humidor, Inlaid Walnut, Mariner's Compass, Diamond Point Edges, Tin Lined, 11 1/2 In.   45.00
Humidor, Mahogany, Porcelain Lining, 12 3/4 x 7 3/4 In. 45.00
Humidor, Marquetry Inlay, Stylized Flowers, c.1900, 10 1/2 In. 115.00
Iron, Gem, Polisher, Streeter's, Slant Back, 5 In. 248.00
Iron, Inlaid, Cylinder, Grape Leaf, Vine, Gilt Metal, Dragonfly Seal, Komei, 2 3/8 In. 575.00
Iron, Inlaid, Rounded Rectangle, Silver, Gold, Sparrow Flying, Japan, 2 7/8 x 4 x 1 1/2 In.   1540.00
Iron, Round Back, Lift Gate, England, c.1800, 6 x 2 In. 77.00
Iron, Rounded Front, Swing Gate, Heart Shape Latch, 6 1/2 In. 22.00
Ivory, Carved Oriental Scene Lid, Faux Tortoiseshell, Brass, 3 x 4 x 1 1/2 In. 220.00
Jewelry, Brass, Mother-Of-Pearl, Macassar Ebony, England, c.1885, 4 3/4 x 12 In. 575.00
Jewelry, Carved, Flowers, Hinged Lid, Deer & Tree Stump Finial, c.1910, 9 x 6 In. 513.00
Jewelry, Casket, Flowers, Foil, Enameled, Seed Pearls, Fire Gilt Bronze Frame, 7 1/2 In. .   1356.00
Jewelry, Chest, Victorian, Rosewood, Mother-Of-Pearl Inlay, Berries, Vines, 16 In. 840.00
Jewelry, Cover, English Walnut, Trays, Drawers, Elm Burl Panels, 5 x 11 1/2 x 9 1/4 In. ..   825.00
Jewelry, Edwardian, Polished Bone Mounted, Russet Tortoiseshell, c.1900, 6 x 4 In. 805.00
Jewelry, Edwardian, Yew, Polychrome, Mother Of Pearl Inlay, c.1900, 5 x 11 3/4 In. 805.00
Jewelry, Faux Tortoiseshell, Ormolu, Hinged Lid, Handle, Louis XVI Style, 9 5/8 In. 940.00
Jewelry, Gilt Metal, Dancing Cherubs, Scalloped Sides, Scroll Feet, 8 x 8 1/4 x 4 1/2 In. .   1200.00
Jewelry, Hobstar Lid, Prism Cut Body, Oval, Hinged, C.F. Monroe, 3 x 5 1/2 In. 300.00
Jewelry, Mother-Of-Pearl, Rosewood, Velvet Interior, Key, c.1850, 4 x 9 x 6 In. 230.00

Jewelry, Pinwheel Lid, Hobstar, Strawberry Diamond, Round, C.F. Monroe, 3 x 3 3/4 In. . 150.00
Jewelry, Round, Hinged, Signed Sterling Fittings, Hobstar Lid, 2 1/2 x 4 1/4 In. 225.00
Jewelry, Silver Plate, Ebony, Carved Bone, 5 Drawers, Anglo-Indian, 11 x 13 1/2 In. 920.00
Jewelry, Teakwood, Brass Inset Panels, Oriental Taste, Continental, 12 In. 345.00
Jewelry, Walnut, Marquetry, Neoclassical, Continental, 7 x 12 1/2 In. 690.00
Jewelry, Walnut, Mother-Of-Pearl Inlay, Lift Top, On Stand, 1800s, 20 x 10 In. 920.00
Jewelry, Wood, Carved, 2 Deer, Tree, On Finial, Oval, Hinged Lid, Switzerland, 7 x 8 In. . 200.00
Jewelry, Wood, Hammered Copper Panel, Arts & Crafts, England, 11 1/2 In. 430.00
Kirbitz Slide, Detailed Rosemaling, Norway, 13 In. 525.00
Knife, Chippendale Style, Mahogany, Brass Hardware, 14 1/2 x 9 x 9 In. 430.00
Knife, Curly Maple, Pine, Canted Sides, Peg Handles, 9 x 13 x 5 1/2 In. 715.00
Knife, Curly Maple, Scrubbed Surface, Arched Ends, Center Divider, 14 x 8 x 7 In. 790.00
Knife, Federal, Mahogany Inlay, Hinged Lid, Fitted Interior, c.1810, 14 In., Pair 4780.00
Knife, Federal, Mahogany Inlay, Sloped Hinged Lid, Banded Edge, c.1810, 14 In., Pair .. 15535.00
Knife, Georgian, Slant Front, Mahogany, Prince Of Whales Feathers, c.1815, 14 In., Pair . 2530.00
Knife, Hepplewhite, Mahogany Veneer, Inlay, Serpentine Front, 9 x 11 x 15 In. 750.00
Knife, Hepplewhite, Mahogany, Serpentine Front, Fitted Interior, c.1790, 14 1/4 In., Pair . 3795.00
Knife, Hepplewhite, Mahogany, Shaded Urn Inlay On Top 1155.00
Knife, Mahogany Inlay, Conch Shell, Serpentine, George III Style, 15 x 9 x 10 In., Pair ... 2990.00
Knife, Maple, Satinwood, Serpentine Front, Inlay, Ebonized, George III, 19 x 7 In. ... *Illus* 4600.00
Knife, Pine, Wall, Black Paint, 20 In. 90.00
Lacquer, Black, Gold, Lakeside Landscapes, Cover, Rectangular, 1800s, 3 x 4 In. 4140.00
Lacquer, Black, Gold, Rectangular, Deer, Flowers, c.1900, 5 1/2 x 4 1/2 In. 345.00
Lacquer, Cinnabar Red, Green, Pine Trees, Coin Designs, Cover, Japan, Late 1800s, 10 In. 180.00
Lacquer, Gold, Bamboo Fan Design, Nashiji Interior, Pewter Rim, Square, 1800s, 3 In. .. 150.00
Lacquer, Gold, Hiramakie Rose Design, Pine Tree Tray, 1800s, 5 1/4 x 7 1/4 x 3 3/4 In. ... 4140.00
Lacquer, Gold, Takarabune, Gods Of Good Fortune Relief, 1800s, 4 1/2 In. 1785.00
Lacquer, Hiramakie Scene, Ducks, Trees, Pewter Rim, Cover, 1800s, 17 x 14 1/2 x 6 In. . 2070.00
Lacquer, Mother-Of-Pearl, Polychrome, Parcel Gilt, England, c.1865, 3 x 11 3/4 x 9 In. ... 300.00
Lacquer, Rectangular, Chrysanthemum Basket, 1800s, 5 1/2 x 4 In. 275.00
Leather, Brass Mounted, Painted, Figures, Exterior Settings, Chinese, 8 x 17 x 10 1/2 In. . 165.00
Letter, English Mahogany, Slant Front, Faux Tambour Doors, c.1850, 11 x 12 x 7 In. 230.00
Letter, Grain Painted, Basswood, Hinged Lid, 5 1/2 x 16 x 12 1/4 In. 805.00
Letter, Lithographed Landscape, Rosettes, 19th Century, 21 1/2 x 13 In. 145.00
Letter, Mahogany, Burl Veneer, Slant Front Lid, Brass Lock, Drawer, 12 1/2 x 13 x 10 In. 365.00
Letter, Regency, Boulle, Asprey, Slant Lid, 6 1/2 x 8 1/2 x 4 1/2 In. 1265.00
Letter, Satinwood, Ormolu Mounts, 13 1/2 In. 259.00
Letter, Wall, Scenic Design, Ebony, 11 In. 200.00
Lift Top, Painted, Red, Black Primitive Designs, Compass Design, Pine, 12 x 9 x 8 In. ... 550.00
Lift Top, Sponge Decorated, Pine, Red, Black Paint, 12 x 23 1/2 x 11 1/2 In. 315.00
Lift Top, Sponge Decorated, Pine, Red, Black Paint, 7 1/2 x 15 x 8 In. 430.00
Liqueur, Napoleon III Style, Burlwood, Ebony, Bone Inlay, c.1885, 10 1/2 x 13 1/2 In. ... 2300.00
Lock, German Steel, Wrought Iron Bound, Scrolled Mounts, 1700s, 18 x 33 In. 2115.00
Lock, Iron, Rectangular, Dome Top, Single Hammered Strap To Top, 6 3/8 In. 380.00
Mahogany, Bird's-Eye Maple, Parquetry Lid, Mirror, c.1840, 4 x 11 x 8 In. 69.00
Mahogany, Dog, Geometric Decoration, 1800s, 6 x 15 x 10 In. 360.00
Mahogany, Dome Top, String Inlay, Geometric Patterns, Early 1800s, 20 x 34 In. 430.00
Mahogany, Stepped Lid, Late 1700s, 7 1/2 x 10 x 7 In. 200.00
Mahogany, Veneer, Inlaid, Hinged Lift Top, Brass Handles, 19th Century, 8 x 11 x 9 In. ... 1410.00
Malachite, Gilt, Octagonal, Brass Mounted, 1 1/2 x 7 x 4 1/2 In. 385.00
Marquetry, Inlaid Tulipwood, Walnut, Napoleon III, Mid 1800s, 6 x 28 x 17 1/2 In. 1175.00
Memento, Mori, Hinged Lid, Skull Cartouche, Mortality Designs, Continental, 3 1/2 In. ... 235.00
Mixed Metal, Rectangular, Wine Pot, Flowers, Butterflies, 19th Century, 4 1/2 In. 805.00
Mixed Metal, Tsuba Shape Top, Gold Inlay, Japan, 19th Century, 2 1/2 x 2 1/2 In. 880.00
Money, Hinged Cover, Brass, 4 1/4 x 9 x 4 3/4 In. 400.00
Money, Monkey Head Form, Gray, White Matte, 2 1/4 In. 50.00
Mother-Of-Pearl, Abalone, Celadon Paper Lining, Early 1900s, 2 1/4 x 6 1/2 x 3 1/4 In. ... 230.00
Necessaire, Rosewood, Fitted Tray, Sewing Implements, Brush, Comb, 8 1/2 x 3 1/2 In. .. 96.00
Nesting, Cardboard, Wallpaper Lined, Cutout Designs, Trefoils, 6 x 6 To 4 x 4 In., 3 Piece 230.00
Oak, Chip Carved, Dark Finish, Initials, IC, 1648, 50 1/2 x 25 1/2 In. 2090.00
Onyx, Enamel & Gilt Metal Mounted, 7 1/2 In. 390.00
Oval, Cover, Painted Black, Lapped Finger Construction, Levi Beal, 1800s, 1 5/8 x 4 In. . 1175.00

Box, Knife, Maple,
Satinwood, Serpentine
Front, Inlay, Ebonized,
George III, 19 x 7 In.

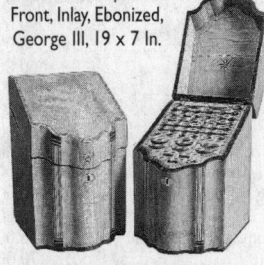

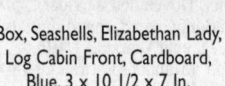

Box, Seashells, Elizabethan Lady,
Log Cabin Front, Cardboard,
Blue, 3 x 10 1/2 x 7 In.

Box, Storage, Painted, 9-Petal
Flower, Slide Lid, Pine, 18th
Century, 6 x 4 x 2 In.

Oval, Old Green Paint, 2 1/2 x 6 1/4 In.	935.00
Oval, Prussian Blue Paint, 2 x 5 1/4 In.	855.00
Pantry, Bentwood, 1 Finger, Square Nails, 2 5/8 x 9 1/4 In.	575.00
Pantry, Bentwood, Gray Paint, Inscription Inside Bottom, Bail Handle, Tacks, 11 x 7 In.	550.00
Pantry, Bentwood, Green Paint, Steel Tacks, Cover, 13 3/4 x 6 1/2 In.	230.00
Pantry, Bentwood, Lapped Seams, Iron Tacks, Green Paint, Round, 16 1/4 x 8 1/2 In.	259.00
Pantry, Bentwood, Lopped Seams, Tacks, Blue, Cover, V.D. Shattrick, 9 1/2 x 4 1/2 In.	690.00
Pantry, Bentwood, Red Paint, Wooden Bail Handle, Steel Tacks, 11 1/2 x 7 In.	520.00
Pantry, Bentwood, Round, Lapped Seams, Iron Tacks, Red Paint, Cover, 12 1/2 In.	490.00
Pantry, Bentwood, Round, Red Ground, Blue, Yellow Tulips, c.1896, 7 3/4 In.	2090.00
Pantry, Oak, Poplar, Cover, 12 1/2 x 23 1/4 x 19 3/4 In.	198.00
Pantry, Old Mustard Paint, Round, 9 1/2 In.	330.00
Pantry, Painted, Green, Ginger Stenciled Lettering, Yellow Eagle, Round, Pine, 4 x 7 In.	715.00
Pantry, Painted, Mustard, Putty, Stenciled Initials, Round, Pine, 3 3/4 x 8 In.	468.00
Pantry, Painted, Orange, Black, Pine, 4 1/2 x 8 3/4 In.	770.00
Papier-Mache, Painted, Black, Star Design, Oval, 3 1/4 x 7 x 5 In.	145.00
Patch, Enamel On Brass, Cylinder Form, Flower Decorated Cover, c.1900, 1 1/3 In.	69.00
Patch, Ivory, Plique, Rose Gold Metal Vignette, Plinth, Urn, Late 18th Century, 3 3/8 In.	295.00
Picnic, Kiriwood, 4 Drawers, Cupboard, Bamboo Handles, Late 1800s, 14 x 12 1/2 In.	145.00
Pill, Blue Agate, Metal, Early 1900s, 1 3/4 In.	105.00
Pine, Crotch Split Mahogany Veneer, 7 x 18 x 11 In.	215.00
Pine, Dovetailed, Black Over Red Painted Decoration, Iron Handles, 36 1/4 x 15 1/2 In.	305.00
Pine, Dovetailed, Square Nails, Wire Staple Hinges, Painted, 8 1/4 x 5 3/4 x 4 1/4 In.	1725.00
Pine, Green, Large Dovetails, Square Nails, Ball Feet, Hinged Lid, 18th Century, 9 In.	795.00
Pine, Hand Wrought Nails, Iron Strap Hinges, Painted Blue Fish, 6 1/2 x 13 x 7 1/2 In.	90.00
Pine, Iron Mounted, Hand Wrought Iron Strap Hinges, Early 1800s, 10 1/2 x 18 x 13 In.	140.00
Pine, Mahogany Veneer, French Polish Finish, Red Stain Interior, 7 x 18 x 11 In.	220.00
Pine, Open Bin, Shelf Top, Applied 4-Leaf Clovers, 33 x 27 x 18 1/2 In.	259.00
Pine, Painted, Angel, Red Sash, Olive Branch, Trumpet, Hinged Lid, 3 1/2 x 11 x 7 In.	7050.00
Pine, Painted, Carved Scroll Crest, Slant Lid, American, 1800s, 10 3/4 x 14 1/4 x 7 1/2 In.	1058.00
Pineapple, Black Glass, Bronze Mounted, Gilt Metal Fronds, Feather Base, 9 1/2 In.	705.00
Pipe, Mahogany, Pierced Backboard, Drawer, American, 1800s, 20 7/8 x 5 1/8 x 4 7/8 In.	1410.00
Pipe, Wall Mounted, Wood, Cut Nail Construction, Heart & Leaf Decoration, 16 1/2 In.	187.00
Pipe, Wall, Pine, 19th Century, 14 1/2 x 7 1/2 x 3 3/4 In.	140.00
Pipe, Wall, Red Paint, Tin Box In Drawer Compartment, Slide Lid, 6 x 4 x 13 In.	575.00
Pipe, White Paint, Arched, Pierced Back, Drawer, American, 1800s, 17 3/4 x 5 x 4 3/4 In.	4995.00
Polychrome Wood, Tibet, c.1830, 10 x 15 1/2 x 9 1/2 In.	295.00
Poplar, Molded Top, Dovetailed, Brass Hinges, Lock, 19th Century, 8 1/2 x 14 x 10 In.	305.00
Porcelain, Phoenix, Peony, Underglaze Blue, Red, Round, M. Kozan, 19th Century, 4 In.	4140.00
Puzzle, Pine, Carved, Applied Decoration, Black Lines, Dots, Mid 1800s, 9 1/2 x 2 x 3 In.	258.00
Quill, Ebonized Wood Trim, Panel Set Quills, Inlaid Bone, Ivory, Slide Lid, 7 x 4 x 2 In.	100.00
Razor, Carved Wood, Interior Slides Out, 2 Sections, 19th Century	185.00
Red Painted, Oval Lid, Stamped Figures, Chickens, People, Birds, Stars, 2 1/2 x 7 x 5 In.	660.00
Regency, Chinoiserie, Figures In Garden, Octagonal, c.1825, 5 x 11 1/2 x 8 1/2 In.	545.00
Renaissance Revival, Walnut, Porcelain, Ormolu Mounted, Cupid, Gilt, 11 1/4 In.	410.00
Rosemaling, Cutout Feet, Handles, Scalloped Base, Repaint, c.1895, 8 3/4 x 7 1/4 In.	230.00

Rosewood, Scrolling Flower Brass Inlay, Coffin Shape, c.1850, 13 1/4 x 7 In. 345.00
Saffron, Turned, Painted, Salmon Ground, Pomegranate, Strawberry, 4 7/8 In. 990.00
Salt, Softwood, 2 Drawers Below Bin, Cutout Crest, Hanging, 12 1/2 In. 158.00
Salt, Softwood, Dovetailed Construction, Drawer, Lemon Finials, 17 1/4 In. 90.00
Salt, Wall, Bentwood Front, Pinwheel Designs, Painted, Green, 11 x 7 1/2 In. 330.00
Salt, Wall, Dovetailed, Arched Crest, Lift Top, 10 1/2 x 6 3/4 x 8 In. 660.00
Salt, Wall, Hardwood, Copper Bands, Scrolled Cutouts, 10 1/2 x 7 x 6 3/4 In. 495.00
Scroll, Black Lacquer, Maki-e, Prunus, Bamboo, Japan, 1800s, 16 In. 150.00
Scrubbed Red, Yellow Paint, 4 1/2 x 10 1/2 In. 210.00
Seashells, Elizabethan Lady, Log Cabin Front, Cardboard, Blue, 3 x 10 1/2 x 7 In. . . *Illus* 220.00
Slide Cover, Cherry, Raised Panel, Dovetailed, Divider, 2 5/8 x 8 1/4 x 5 1/4 In. 195.00
Slide Cover, Poplar, Red Decoration, Green Ground, Initials, Swag Borders, 13 x 6 x 6 In. 460.00
Snuff, Burl Walnut, Book Shape, Soviet Union, 3 1/4 In. 90.00
Snuff, Burl Walnut, Turned Wood, Miniature Portrait Of 1800s Woman, 1900s, 4 In. 176.00
Snuff, Copper, Gilt Metal Mounts, Red Transfer Vignettes, 3 1/4 In. 170.00
Snuff, Papier-Mache, Polychrome Paint, Inlaid Stars, 3 1/2 In. 50.00
Softwood, Scrolled, Cutout Sides, Interior Compartment, 29 x 51 1/4 x 15 12 In. 1540.00
Softwood, Smoke Decorated, Green Paint, Square Nails, Unpainted Lid, 17 3/4 x 12 In. . . . 100.00
Softwood, Yellow Grained, Dovetailed Construction, 1873, 23 3/4 x 14 In. 305.00
Spirits Case, Oak, Brass Mounts, 4 Cut Glass Decanters, Stoppers, 10 1/2 x 8 3/4 x 9 In. . 220.00
Stamp, 3 British Stamps, George Heath, London, c.1890 . . . . 5570.00
Stamp, Brass, Royal Coat Of Arms, Side Door, Wharton's Rotary, 1854 . . . . 1280.00
Stamp, U.S. 2 Cent Stamp, George Heath, London, c.1890 . . . . 1835.00
Stationery, Boulle, Tortoiseshell, Brass Inlay, 2 Front Doors, 9 x 5 1/2 In. 480.00
Stationery, Rosewood, Inlaid Mother-Of-Pearl, c.1850, 12 In. 135.00
Steel, Lacquered Wood, Art Deco, 1930s, 6 x 3 1/2 x 2 In. 1055.00
Storage, Bentwood, Red Paint, Steel Tack Construction, 14 3/4 x 9 In. 520.00
Storage, Burled Walnut, Molded Base, 9 1/2 In. 135.00
Storage, Chinese Elm, Dovetailed, Trunk Shape, Hinged, c.1900, 11 x 17 1/2 x 10 1/2 In. 105.00
Storage, Chinese, Red Lacquer, 3 Round Boxes, Cover, Frame, 29 1/2 x 21 In. 405.00
Storage, Dome Top, Forged Lock, Hasp, Escutcheon, Iron Studs, Cotter Pins, 21 1/2 In. . . 525.00
Storage, Gold & Red Lacquer, Mirror, 4 Drawers, Garden, Chinese, 11 1/4 x 10 x 13 In. . 290.00
Storage, Painted, 9-Petal Flower, Slide Lid, Pine, 18th Century, 6 x 4 x 2 In. . . . . . . *Illus* 1870.00
Storage, Painted, Applied Woodcut, Man, 18th Century Clothes, Pine, 7 x 4 1/2 x 3 5/8 In. 385.00
Storage, Painted, Paper Covered, Stylized Sun, Tulip, c.1779, 15 x 5 x 8 1/2 In. 1430.00
Storage, Painted, Patinated To Black, Stylized Branches, Yellow Pine, 17 x 6 x 9 In. 825.00
Storage, Painted, Yellow Stripes, Sunburst Flowers, Pine, Mid 1800s, 10 x 5 1/2 x 4 In. . . 110.00
Storage, Pine, Vinegar Grained, Red Brown Over Yellow, 17 7/8 x 9 3/4 x 7 In. 405.00
Storage, Poplar, Green, Red, Black, Maria Halieince In Script, c.1836, 14 x 11 x 10 In. . . 750.00
Table, George VI, Rectangular, Bone Banded Burlwood, Birch Lined, 3 x 6 x 4 1/4 In. . . . 290.00
Table, Nickel, Silver Inlay, Brass Mount, Blond Tortoiseshell, Taffeta, c.1885, 4 x 3 In. . . 865.00
Tantalus, Brass Inlaid Burlwood, France, 19th Century, 10 3/4 x 13 1/2 x 10 In. 1650.00
Tantalus, Burl Walnut, 3 Cut Glass Decanters, Mirrored Back, 2 Lids, 15 1/2 x 13 5/8 In. . 1035.00
Tantalus, Ebony, Lacquered, 4 Decanters, 16 Cordials, France, c.1875, 10 x 12 x 9 In. . . . 920.00
Tantalus, Faux Tortoiseshell, 4 Cut Glass Decanters, Gilt Metal, French Style, 17 x 26 In. 1380.00
Tantalus, Napoleon II Style, Brass, Mother-Of-Pearl Inlay, c.1900, 10 3/4 x 13 x 10 In. . 825.00
Tantalus, Oak, Bronze, Lock, 3 Diamond Cut Decanters, Victorian, c.1890, 12 x 14 x 7 In. 200.00
Tea, Black Lacquer, Parcel Gilt, Wood, 2 Compartments, Chinese Export, 4 3/4 x 7 3/4 In. 1955.00
Tea, Burlwood, Banded, Geometric Inlay, England, 4 3/4 x 7 x 4 In. 110.00
Tea, Georgian, Brass Mounted, Banded Mahogany, 2 Compartments, 6 x 9 1/2 x 6 In. . . . 430.00
Tea, Mahogany, Inlaid Bone, Brass Handle, 19th Century, England, 5 1/2 x 6 1/2 x 5 In. . . 155.00
Tea, Oak, Bun Feet, Handles, 2 Compartments, Bone Escutcheon, 7 1/2 x 10 1/2 x 6 In. . . 275.00
Tea, Rosewood, String Inlay, Kite Escutcheon, Compressed Bun Feet, 6 3/4 x 12 1/4 In. . . 110.00
Tea, Tortoiseshell, 2 Compartments, Serpentine Front, England, c.1865, 3 1/2 x 5 x 3 In. . 1495.00
Tea, Walnut, Mahogany, Band Inlay, Interior Compartments, England, 5 x 7 3/4 x 5 In. . . 150.00
Tinder, Flintlock, Brass, Open Style, Pocket, 2 1/4 In. 1540.00
Tinder, Flintlock, Iron, Brass Mountings, Hinged Lid, Pocket, 1 3/4 In. 3080.00
Tinder, Tin, Flint, Metal Striker, Candle Holder Cover, 4 1/2 In. 145.00
Tobacco, Oak, Pipe & Torquay Container, 8 x 7 x 11 In. 595.00
Tobacco, Rotterdam Scene, Continents, Legends, Copper, Brass, Dutch, c.1760, 2 x 6 In. . 720.00
Tortoiseshell, William IV, Brass Ball Feet, Pewter String Lid, c.1830, 3 x 7 x 4 In. 1265.00
Traveling, Diorama, Mayan Indian, c.1930, 23 3/4 x 12 x 23 1/4 In. 300.00
Traveling, Mahogany, Lady's, Lift Out Tray, 3 Bottles, Silver Plate Lids, 5 x 10 x 7 1/2 In. 110.00

Traveling, Shoebox, Leather, Sections, Brass Hardware, 14 x 16 x 14 In. 425.00
Trinket, Lap Joints, Pin, 19th Century, 2 x 1 1/8 In. 100.00
Tulipwood & Poplar, Brown, Polychrome Flowers, Leaves, Lehn, c.1870, 6 x 14 1/2 In. . . . 4400.00
Vinegar Grained, Green, Yellow Brush Decoration, Maine, 26 In. 6900.00
Walnut, Whalebone Carving Of Sperm Whale, American, 11 1/4 x 4 1/2 x 2 3/4 In. 1150.00
Watch, Hutch, Building Shape, Brick Base, Steeple Roof, Painted, c.1850, 4 x 7 1/2 In. . . 1320.00
Whatnot, Lid, Slide Drawer, 3 Drawers, Anglo-Indian, 10 1/4 x 11 7 1/4 In. 670.00
White Cover, Enameled, Cobalt Blue, Birds, A Trifle From A Friend, 2 In. 260.00
Wood, Carved As Basket, Demon Supports, Shishi Group Finial, Japan, Late 1800s, 16 In. 590.00
Wood, Carved, 2 Mermaids, Center Medallion, 10 1/2 In. 230.00
Wood, Chamfered Top, Hinged Lid, Red Paint, Black Details, 15 In. 65.00
Wood, E.R.M. Co. 1873-75, Chamfered Slide Lid, Grain Painted, 17 In. 120.00
Wood, Egyptian Revival, Relief, Hinged Lid, Sphinxes, Pharaohs, Peasants, 12 1/2 In. . . . 235.00
Wood, Hand Carved, Country Scene, Wildflowers, Cover, Round, 7 In. 120.00
Wood, Lacquer, High Relief, Mantis Decoration, 19th Century, 2 In. 185.00
Wood, Painted Geometric Designs, Art Deco, 3 1/2 x 9 In. 145.00
Wood, Painted, Lappet Carving, Paw Feet, Italian Renaissance Revival, 9 1/2 x 13 1/2 In. 590.00
Wood, Presentation, Walnut, Eagle, Inscribed Names, 1864, 5 1/2 x 10 1/2 x 6 1/2 In. . . . 4370.00
Wood, Rosewood, Leaf Sides, Archaic Designs, Chinese, 1800s, 7 In. 120.00
Wood, Softwood, Grain Painted, Divided Lid, Dovetailed Construction, 60 In. 506.00
Wood, Turned, Painted, Salmon Ground, Pomegranate, Strawberry, 5 1/8 In. 2530.00
Wood, Walnut Veneers, Inlaid Concentric Circles, Lift Top, 1700s, 3 x 11 x 9 In. 489.00
Work, Dome Top, Brass Ring Handles, Bun Feet, England, 7 x 11 In. 450.00
Work, Pine, Oval, Lapped Joint Sewn, Geometric Decoration, 11 3/4 x 20 1/2 In. 330.00
Work, Regency, Rosewood, Brass Mount, Bone Inlay, Sarcophagus Shape, 6 x 12 1/2 In. . 405.00
Writing, Anglo-Colonial, Brass Bound, Hardwood, c.1840, 9 x 20 1/2 x 12 In. 690.00
Writing, Burl Walnut, Brass Strap Mounts, Dome Top, England, 6 5/8 x 9 1/4 In. 460.00
Writing, Lacquer, Interior Compartments, 4 x 11 x 8 In. 35.00
Writing, Mahogany, Brass Bound, 3 Secret Drawers, Brass Handles, 7 x 19 x 10 1/4 In. . . 720.00
Writing, Mahogany, Inlaid Stars, Slant Lid, 3 3/4 x 11 1/2 In. 160.00
Writing, Oak, Crystal Ink Bottles, Victorian, Late 1800s, 5 1/2 x 12 1/4 x 7 In. 115.00
Writing, Tiger Maple Inlay, Green Baize Surface, Hinged Lid, c.1840, 7 x 18 x 9 In. 225.00
Writing, Victorian, Mother-Of-Pearl, Inlaid Lacquer, c.1870, 5 1/2 x 15 1/2 x 12 In. 800.00

BOY SCOUT collectibles include any material related to scouting, including patches, manuals, and uniforms. The Boy Scout movement in the United States started in 1910. The first Jamboree was held in 1937. Girl Scout items are listed under their own heading.

Bank, In Uniform, Pack, Cast Iron, A.C. Williams, M 45, 6 In. . . . . .84.00 to 94.00
Bell, Bicycle, Scout, Embossed, Be Prepared, Handlebar Mount, 2 1/2 In. 120.00
Belt, Leather, Be Prepared Buckle, Fleur-De-Lis Style Badge, 33 In. 33.00
Cap, Air Scout, Blue, BSA Emblem, White Wing Air Scout Patch, World War II 40.00
Medal, Ribbon, Liberty Loan, U.S. Treasury Department, 1916, 1 1/4 In. 58.00
Patch, National Jamboree, Irvine Ranch, Calif., 1953, 3 In. 30.00
Patch, Scoutacular Circus, Central Indiana Council, 1958, 3 In. 29.00
Uniform, Shirt, Neckerchief, Merit Badges, Patches, 1950s 29.00
Watch, Comic Character, Ingersoll, 1920s 40.00

BRADLEY & HUBBARD is a name found on many metal objects. Walter Hubbard and his brother-in-law, Nathaniel Lyman Bradley, started making cast iron clocks, tables, frames, andirons, lamps, chandeliers, sconces, and sewing birds in 1854 in Meriden, Connecticut. The company became Bradley & Hubbard Manufacturing Company in 1875. Charles Parker Company bought the firm in 1940. Their lamps are especially prized by collectors.

Candlestick, Woman, Lying On Leaf, Bulb, Bronze, 3 1/2 x 7 In. 405.00
Desk Set, Brass, Patinated, Arts & Crafts Taste, c.1900, 8 Piece 575.00
Lamp, 4-Socket, 10-Panels, Carmel Slag Glass, Baskets, Garland, 29 In. 1380.00
Lamp, Electric, Lily Pad, Loetz Shade, 24 In. 3160.00
Lamp, Murano Panel, Glass, Overlay Base, 11 x 20 In. 1380.00
Mirror, Framed With Reticulated Flowers, 13 1/2 x 16 In. 195.00
Plant Stand, Cast Iron, Cherub, Lion's Foot, c.1870, 32 In. 750.00
Wall Sconce, Iron, Gilt, 2 Candle Cups, Mirror, Dolphins, 21 1/2 In., Pair 415.00

BRASS has been used for decorative pieces and useful tablewares since ancient times. It is an alloy of copper, zinc, and other metals. Additional brass items may be found under Bell, Candlestick, Tool, or Trivet.

Ash Can, Plaque, Cigar, Cigarette Ends, Drawer, Hairy Paw Feet, Early 1900s, 11 5/8 In. .	50.00
Ashtray, Geisha, Matchbox Holder, Freidag Metal Pattern Plate Co., Il., 6 In.	55.00
Ashtray, Standing, Floor, American Eagle, Cast Iron, Gold Color, Wood Accents	37.00
Basin, Flared Sides, Wire Reinforced Rolled Edge, Hanging Ring, 1851, 2 3/4 x 9 1/2 In. . .	70.00
Bed Warmer, Chase Decoration, Pierced Cover, Apple Wood Handle, 42 1/2 In.	405.00
Bed Warmer, Copper Hinged Cover, Stipple, Turned Handle, England, c.1900, 42 In.	69.00
Bed Warmer, Engraved, Turned Wood Handle, 45 In.	200.00
Bed Warmer, Engraved, Wood Handle, 46 1/2 In.	130.00
Bed Warmer, Flower & Scroll, Tooled, Walnut Handle	95.00
Bed Warmer, Flowers, Scrolls, Spun Pan, Cherry Handle, Engraved, 45 1/2 In.	248.00
Bed Warmer, Hinged Lid, Turned Wood Handle, Floral Punch, America, 1800s, 42 In. . . .	235.00
Bed Warmer, Hinged Lid, Wood Handle, Potted Flower, Stripes, 19th Century, 43 3/4 In. .	235.00
Bed Warmer, Iron Handle, Hinged Lid, Pierced, Punched Design, 18th Century, 44 1/4 In.	640.00
Bed Warmer, Punched Leaf Decoration, Turned Handle, 43 In.	200.00
Bed Warmer, Punched, Engraved Flowers, Turned Hardwood Handle, 11 1/2 x 43 In. . . .	230.00
Bed Warmer, Turned Handle, Peafowl Engraving, 44 In.	185.00
Bed Warmer, Turned Wood Handle, Engraved Lid, 19th Century, 45 3/4 In.	145.00
Book Holder, Indian Chief Form Ends, Expandable, 5 3/4 In.	80.00
Bowl, Petal Shape, Footed, 4 x 10 In.	90.00
Brazier, Scroll Handles, Paw Feet, England, 22 x 14 7/8 x 10 In.	259.00
Bucket, Bail Handle, Wrought Iron Swing Handle, 8 1/2 x 13 In.	98.00
Bucket, Iron Bail Handle, 1800s, 11 1/2 In.	69.00
Bucket, Wrought Iron Swing Handle, 14 1/2 x 20 In.	75.00
Canister, Oval, Footed, Geometric Engraving, 8 In.	69.00
Cauldron, Hammered, Dovetailed, Lion's Head, Paw Feet, 17 x 23 In.	125.00
Coal Scuttle, Helmet Form, Swing Handle, 1800s, 16 In.	90.00
Coal Scuttle, Removable Lid, Metal Liner, Urn Finial, Brass Feet, 17 x 15 x 14 1/2 In. . . .	165.00
Cuspidor, Albert Pick & Co., 3 3/4 x 9 1/4 In., 2 Piece	11.00
Cuspidor, Arcade, 3 1/2 x 7 1/2 In., 2 Piece	145.00
Cuspidor, Arcade, Long Neck, 10 In.	187.00
Cuspidor, Arcade, No. 401, Albert Pick & Co., 8 In. . . . . .66.00 to 143.00
Cuspidor, Arcade, No. 402, 4 x 9 In., 2 Piece	165.00
Cuspidor, Arcade, No. 403, Albert Pick & Co., 3 1/2 x 7 1/2 In., 2 Piece	22.00
Cuspidor, Burley & Co., No. 5747, 3 1/4 x 7 1/2 In., 2 Piece	45.00
Cuspidor, Burley & Co., No. 5748, 4 x 9 In., 2 Piece	65.00
Cuspidor, Cast Iron Insert, Wisconsin Governor's Office, 14 In.	440.00
Cuspidor, Polished Wrap, Cast Base, H.S.B. & Co., Chicago, Il., 4 x 10 3/4 In., 2 Piece . .	45.00
Desk Stand, 2 Inkwells, Covers, Pen Holder, Renaissance Style Border, 4 1/4 x 12 1/2 In.	140.00
Dog Collar, Cast & Hinged Construction, Engraved Initials, Dutch, c.1690	1300.00
Dog Collar, Engraved, England, Late 18th Century	1200.00
Doorknob, Turned, Molded Edge Base Plate, 3 1/4 In.	45.00
Doorknocker, S-Scroll Handle, Molded Edge Plates, 7 In.	578.00
Figurine, Bird, Exotic, Crane, Standing On Stump, Torchere, Japan, 54 x 27 x 15 In.	1320.00
Figurine, Boat, Bronze Egyptian Woman, Hagenauer, Austria, 15 x 17 1/2 In.	1150.00
Figurine, Cannon, Cast, Wooden Carriage, 10 1/2 In.	99.00
Figurine, Cannon, Wooden Carriage, 4 Wheels, 17 In.	890.00
Figurine, Hagenauer, Kneeling Figure, Profile, 10 1/4 x 8 3/4 x 2 3/4 In.	805.00
Figurine, Porte A Cigares, Napoleon III, Blackamoor, 3 Wire Baskets, c.1865, 9 In.	1265.00
Figurine, Wood, Bugle Player, Carved, Incised, Hagenauer, Austria, 6 3/4 x 10 1/4 In. . . .	865.00
Fire Rail, Tongs, 2 Tubular Levels, Brass Handles, 42 In.	115.00
Footman, Brass, Pierced, Engraved, 1800s, 13 x 11 x 10 In.	290.00
Frame, Pietra Dura, Folding, Engraved, Pieced Ferns, Black Ground, 9 x 9 3/4 In.	1035.00
Gong, Rosewood Frame, Flowers, Chinese, Late 1800s, 23 1/2 x 37 1/2 In.	325.00
Group, Oxen Pulling Plow, 2 Wheels, Marble Base, 6 12 x 14 x 4 3/4 In.	140.00
Hinge, Round Surface, 24 In., Pair	35.00
Jardiniere, Hand Hammered, Animals, Indo Persian Scenes, Dovetailed, 15 1/4 x 15 In. . .	56.00
Jardiniere, Oval, Rococo Repousse Design, Continental, Late 1800s, 18 In.	175.00
Jardiniere, Swan, Rosewood, 18 x 18 x 10 1/2 In.	201.00
Kettle Shelf, Pierced, Wrought Iron, Cabriole Legs, Penny Feet, 12 1/2 x 12 1/2 x 14 In. .	230.00

Key Rack, Bicycle, 10-Speed, Wall Mount	5.00
Ladle, Bowl, Wrought Iron Handle, Incised Arch & Dot, 19 1/2 In.	165.00
Ladle, Bowl, Wrought Iron Handle, Shaped, Flattened, Hanging Hook, 13 In.	50.00
Mold, Candle, 4 Tube, Cherry Frame, 1853, 6 1/4 In.	605.00
Monstrance, Gilt, Paste Jewel, Porcelain, Rondel Set, France, 1929, 24 1/2 In.	3680.00
Mortar & Pestle, Flowers, Handles, c.1850, 6 x 6 In.	175.00
Paper Holder, Wash Room, Nickel Plated, Woman's Head, Leaf Scrollwork, 6 x 9 x 5 In.	920.00
Pendant, Spirit Of St. Louis, Enamel On Brass, 1 1/2 In.	65.00
Perpetual Calendar, Rotating, Days Of The Month & Tides, c.1790	150.00
Picture Frame, Repousse Gilt, Green Jewels, Laurel Wreath Crest, c.1900, 7 1/2 x 1/2 In.	430.00
Pie Crimper, Ring Turned Handle, Early 19th Century, 4 1/2 In.	20.00
Pie Wheel, Tasting Spoon, 18th Century	185.00
Plaque, Poachers Shall Be Shot On 1st Sight, Questioned Afterwards, c.1868, 4 x 4 1/2 In.	45.00
Plate Pail, Brass Bound, Mahogany, Cylindrical Shape, Pierced Stick Splats, 11 x 11 In. .	12075.00
Posy Ring, Engraved, Continu Contant, Recovered From Thames River, 17th Century . . .	350.00
Pricket Stick, Iron Tips, Sheet Brass Base, 24 In., Pair	138.00
Pump, Water, Salesman's Sample, J.H. Best, Pat. 1906, 20 In.	1455.00
Rotisserie, Wheel, 5 Hanging Hooks, Winding Mechanism, Early 19th Century, 17 In. . . .	865.00
Samovar, Incised Medallions, Footed Base, Stirrup Handles, Russia, 19 x 9 In.	115.00
Samovar, Shaped Tray, 2 Handles, Russia, c.1890, 18 1/2 In.	545.00
Samovar, Tray, Turned Wood Handles, Paw Feet, Cyrillic Writing, Russia, c.1903, 25 In. .	275.00
Sconce, Candle, 3-Arm, Louis XVI Style, Gilt, Late 1900s, 19 1/2 In., Pair	175.00
Sconce, Rococo Style, Dutch, 1800s, 7 1/2 In., Pair	575.00
Sconce, Topless Women, Bouquet, Opalescent, Ruffled Shade, 24 x 12 x 8 1/2 In., Pair . .	3160.00
Seal, Glass Intaglio, Lafayette, Late 18th Century	350.00
Seal, State Of Mississippi, Southern Dist. Chancery Cohrt., Cast, 1 3/4 x 1/2 In.	44.00
Shield, Repousse, Red, White, Blue, Gilt, Initials, Republique France, 1800s, 15 x 12 In. .	385.00
Shoehorn, Curling End, Ball Terminal, 18th Century	250.00
Skimmer, Pierced Lid, Oval Nut Roaster, Early 19th Century, 21 In.	405.00
Spoon Mold, 2 Parts, For Pewter Spoon, 10 In.	145.00
Stamp Case & Damper, 3 Sections, Adolf Frankau, England, 1886	640.00
Stand, Fern, Round, 3-Footed, 31 In.	350.00
Stand, Kettle, Pierced Top, Cabriole Legs, Pad Foot, 15 x 11 3/4 In.	75.00
Sundial, Traveling, Ring, Gilding & Silvering, Marked, England, 1721	595.00
Tea Urn, George III, Early 19th Century	765.00
Teakettle, Stand, Pumpkin Shape, Stem Finial, Paw Feet, Tripod Base, 10 3/4 In.	190.00
Teapot & Stand, Hammered, WMF, 13 In.	259.00
Tobacco Jar, Cover, Late 18th Century	395.00
Tool Rest, Scrolled Top, Tapered, Twisted Legs, Spade Feet, England, 19th Century, 11 In.	55.00
Umbrella Stand, Crest, Double Eagle, Hammered, Urn Shape, Handles, 22 x 12 In.	150.00
Umbrella Stand, Tree Trunk Shape, Hunting Dog, Rifle, Bagged Hare, Pheasants, 22 In. .	295.00
Weight Set, Graduated Baluster Shape, Handles, England, 14 Lbs. To 2 Oz., 10 Piece . . .	220.00
Wreath, 26 Animal & Human Figures, Stamped	480.00
Writing Set, Traveling, 2 Inkwells, Brush, Pen, Candlestick, Brass Interior, 5 x 3 In.	650.00

BRASTOFF, see Sascha Brastoff category.

BREAD PLATE, see various silver categories, porcelain factories, and pressed glass patterns.

BRIDE'S BASKETS OR BRIDE'S BOWLS were usually one-of-a-kind novelties made in American and European glass factories. They were especially popular about 1880 when the decorated basket was often given as a wedding gift. Cut glass baskets were popular after 1890. All bride's baskets lost favor about 1905. Bride's baskets and bride's bowls may also be found in other glass sections. Check the index at the back of the book.

BRIDE'S BASKET, Blue, Faded To White, Tricorner, Silver Plated Frame, 12 x 12 In.	173.00
Blue, White & Peach Inside Ruffles, New Amsterdam Silver Co., 10 1/2 In.	255.00
Cameo, Red, Silver Plated Frame, Mt. Washington, 10 1/2 In.	600.00
Cream, Red Satin Interior, Crimped, Foldover Rim, Silver Plated Frame, 10 In.	315.00
Glass, Crimped Border, Enamel Wreath, Pairpoint Frame, 3 3/4 x 10 1/2 In.	430.00
Hobnail, White, Pink Interior, Amber Tipped, Silver Frame, 10 1/4 x 9 1/2 In.	175.00
Peachblow, 2 Cherub Medallions, Flowers, Ruffled, Frame, c.1890, 14 In.	1000.00

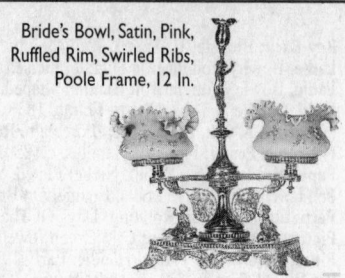

Bride's Bowl, Satin, Pink,
Ruffled Rim, Swirled Ribs,
Poole Frame, 12 In.

Bride's Bowl, Satin, Blue &
Brown, Folded, Ruffled Rim,
Timberlake Frame, 10 In.

Peachblow, Blue & Yellow Daisies, Silver Plated Frame, c.1900, 12 In.	470.00
Pink, Cased, Fan Shape, Amber Rim, Gold, Gilt Wire Handles, 16 x 14 In.	1000.00
Pink, Frosted, Ruffled, Silver Plated Frame, 8 1/2 x 10 In.	150.00
Ribbed, Deep Mahogany To Creamy White, Ruffled Rim, England, 10 3/4 In.	200.00
Yellow, Cased, Ruffled, Silver Plated Frame, 7 In.	200.00
BRIDE'S BOWL, Black, Jack-In-The-Pulpit, Bird, Branch, Enamel, Diana, Frame, 20 x 14 In.	5900.00
Blue, Enameled Flowers, Silver Plated Frame, 10 x 8 In.	200.00
Blue, Jack-In-The-Pulpit, Ruffled, Flowers, Meriden Silver Plated Frame, 13 1/2 In.	1050.00
Burmese, Melon Shape, Silver Plated Frame, 11 In.	300.00
Cranberry Opalescent, Ruffled Rim, Frame, Pairpoint, 9 In.	395.00
Hobnail, Pink & White Frosted, Webster Silver Plated Frame, 13 In.	550.00
Hobnail, White Cased To Pink, Folded, Ruffled, 4 1/4 x 11 1/2 In.	175.00
Orange, Melon Form, Ruffled, Enameled, Barbour Silver Plated Frame, 16 x 12 In.	1000.00
Orange, Yellow, Cased, Swirls, Star Crimped, Pairpoint Silver Plated Frame, 10 In.	500.00
Pink, Cased To White, Pear Branch, Southington Silver Plated Frame, 7 x 15 In.	750.00
Pink, Cased, Enameled, 12 In.	225.00
Pink, Cased, Petal Shape, Flowers, Enameled, Silver Plated Frame, 11 x 11 In.	950.00
Pink, Cased, Square, Silver Plated Frame, 10 1/2 In.	200.00
Pink, White, Cased, Ruffled, Wilcox Silver Plated Frame, 10 x 9 In.	300.00
Pink Opaque, Acid Cut, Flowers, Thistles, Wilcox, Silver Plated Frame, 14 x 9 In.	900.00
Rainbow, Cased, Enameled Scene, Meriden Silver Plated Frame, 7 1/2 x 12 1/2 In.	3400.00
Satin, Blue & Brown, Folded, Ruffled Rim, Timberlake Frame, 10 In. ....*Illus*	2800.00
Satin, Blue, Crimped, Flowers, Coralene, Aurora Silver Plated Frame, 8 x 11 In.	525.00
Satin, Blue, Ruffled, Yellow Enamel Design, Meriden Silver Plated Frame, 12 x 12 In.	350.00
Satin, Blue, Shell Form, Blossoms, White, Enameled, Silver Plated Frame, 6 x 17 In.	375.00
Satin, Green, Scalloped Rim, Enameled Leaves, Silver Plated Frame, c.1890, 11 In.	420.00
Satin, Pink, Diamond-Quilted, Blossoms, Enamel, Silver Plated Frame, 12 x 10 In.	2900.00
Satin, Pink, Herringbone, Rectangular, Aurora Silver Plated Frame, 14 x 12 In.	775.00
Satin, Pink, Ruffled Rim, Swirled Ribs, Poole Frame, 12 In. ....*Illus*	300.00
Satin, Yellow, Ruffled, Shell Edge, Meriden Silver Plated Frame, 14 x 11 In.	500.00
Tortoiseshell, Flowers, Gold, Enameled, Homan, Silver Plated Frame, 15 x 10 In.	1700.00
White, Cased Pink To Green, Melon, Ribs, Silver Plated Frame, 10 x 11 In.	550.00
White, Cased To Pink, Enameled Flowers, Meriden Frame, 17 In. ....*Illus*	8500.00
White, Cased To Pink, Enameled Flowers, Ruffled, Pairpoint Frame, 10 x 11 In.	500.00
White, Cased To Pink, Flowers, Enameled, St. Louis, Silver Plated Frame, 13 In.	350.00
White, Cased To Pink, Ruffled, Pear Branch, Silver Plated Frame, 12 1/2 In.	650.00
White, Cased To Pink, Shell Shape, Barbour, Silver Plated Frame, 12 In.	400.00
Yellow, Cased, Enameled, Simpson, Hall & Miller, Silver Plated Frame, 12 x 10 In.	1200.00

Bride's Bowl, White,
Cased To Pink, Enameled
Flowers, Meriden Frame, 17 In.

BRISTOL glass was made in Bristol, England, after the 1700s. The Bristol glass most often seen today is a Victorian, lightweight opaque glass that is often blue. Some of the glass was decorated with enamels.

Bottle, Perfume, Enameled, Parcel Gilt, White, Tussy Mussy Stopper, 11 3/4 In.	145.00
Mug, Bird On Branch, Pink Over White, Barrel Form, Applied Opal Handle, Gilt, 3 1/4 In.	40.00
Vase, House In Mountains, c.1890, 11 1/2 x 6 In., Pair	140.00
Vase, Napoleon Transfer, Baluster Form, 20th Century, 14 In.	112.00
Vase, Urn Shape, Roses, Pink, Brown, Yellow, c.1900, 13 In.	45.00

BRITANNIA, see Pewter category.

BRONZE is an alloy of copper, tin, and other metals. It is used to make figurines, lamps, and other decorative objects. Bronze lamps are listed in the Lamp category. Pieces listed here date from the eighteenth, nineteenth, and twentieth centuries.

Ashtray, Bach, Oscar, Applied Top Designs, 29 In.	45.00
Ashtray, Bach, Oscar, Ornate Tripod Base, 2 Handles, 29 In.	440.00
Basket, Dragon Handle, Japan, 16 In.	550.00
Bowl, 3-Footed, Handles, China, 5 x 7 1/4 In.	200.00
Bowl, Dragons, High Relief, Japan, Late 1800s, 9 In.	590.00
Bowl, Egg Shape, Dragon Base, Japan, Late 19th Century, 9 1/2 x 4 3/4 In.	890.00
Bowl, Gilt, Napoleon III, Neo-Grec Style, Mid 19th Century, 25 x 16 In.	1955.00
Buddha, Seated, Earth Touching Posture, Double Lotus Base, Ming Dynasty, 8 1/4 In. . . .	290.00
Bust, Bacchus, Marble Plinth, 11 In.	1243.00
Bust, Bardery, Lincoln, Carved Ivory Head, Wood Eagle Plinth, 9 1/2 In.	1075.00
Bust, Bottee, Louis-Alexandre, Girl, Headdress, Etruscan Style Pin, Tiffany, 1883, 18 In. .	1295.00
Bust, Frampton, George, Enid The Fair, Original Dark Patina, 1907, 20 1/2 x 9 In.	7475.00
Bust, Houdon, Woman Clutching Garment, Circular Pedestal, France, 24 In.	1540.00
Bust, Mercury, Bronze Plinth, 10 1/2 In.	620.00
Bust, Scott, Horton, Eagle, 20th Century, 5 In.	285.00
Bust, Stotz, Stuttgart, Hermes V. Olympia, 13 In.	495.00
Cachepot, Bronze, Relief, Row Of Horses, Cylindrical, Flared, Art Deco, 10 In., Pair	990.00
Censor, 3-Footed Base, Lion Shape Handles, Finial, Chinese, 7 1/2 In.	69.00
Censor, Taoist Dignitary, Horse, 2 Parts, Gilt, Late Qing Dynasty, 20 In.	1415.00
Column, Napoleonic, Victory, Stepped Base, Dolphins, Sphinxes, Figures, 11 1/2 In.	1840.00
Compote, Louis XVI Style, Ormolu, Glass, Putto Holding Stalk, c.1900, 14 x 11 3/4 In. . .	865.00
Crucifix, Gilt, Cold Painted Enamel, Continental, Late 19th Century, 43 In.	1265.00
Cup, Wine, Traveler's, Top Unscrews To Turn Over Stem & Base, Scotland	225.00
Desk Set, Mappin & Webb, Gilt, Neo-Grec, London, c.1900, 10 Piece	1150.00
Dish, Frog, Cast, Abalone, Art Nouveau, c.1900, 10 In.	1116.00
Dish, Shell, Cast, Seashell Feet, 7 In.	285.00
Door Knocker, Dolphin Frame, Woman's Bust, Medusa Mask, 10 x 7 1/2 In.	290.00
Door Knocker, Mercury Head, 7 1/2 In.	150.00
Door Knocker, Powder Flask Shape, Derringer Pistol, 7 In.	58.00
Door Knocker, Woman's Head Below 2 Dolphins, 19th Century, 13 In., Pair	2200.00
Ewer, Allegorical Scenes, Putti, Dolphins, Waisted Neck, Seahorse, 17 1/2 In.	598.00
Ewer, Music Trophies, Angels Playing Music, Rooster Head Handles, 15 1/2 In., Pair	3520.00
Ewer, Neoclassical Style, 21 In.	359.00
Ewer, Paillard, Victor, Louis XVI Style, Marble Socle, 26 In., Pair	3585.00
Figurine, Kwan-Ti, Buddha, Lotus Leaves, 10 In.	105.00
Flatware Service, Dirilyte, Bronze Nickel Alloy, 65 Piece	294.00
Fountain, Cherub, Clutching Dolphin, 29 1/4 In.	2530.00
Frame, Oval, Ribbon & Flower, Dutch, 1800s, 15 In.	145.00
Incense Burner, Cloud Shape Tripod Base, Dragon Finial, Japan, Late 1800s, 20 In.	470.00
Incense Burner, Crane On Lotus Leaf, Japan, 19th Century, 22 In.	230.00
Incense Burner, Flying Eagle, 3 Chains, Hanging, Japan, 19th Century, 20 x 10 1/2 In. . .	1725.00
Incense Burner, Foo Dog, Wood Base, Ming Dynasty, c.1600, 17 x 12 x 25 In.	4830.00
Jardiniere, Cast, Winged Caryatid Handles, 4 Cast Dolphin Legs, 14 1/2 x 24 In.	4520.00
Jardiniere, Champleve, c.1900, 11 x 14 In.	475.00
Jardiniere, Mythical Beast Shape, Xuande Reign Mark, 1800s, 17 In.	865.00
Jardiniere, Napoleon III, Copper Liner, Oblong, c.1865, 9 1/2 x 4 In.	980.00
Jardiniere, Openwork, Lion Masks, 9 1/2 x 9 1/2 In.	790.00
Mantel Garnitures, Cylindrical Vase, Scrolling Leaves, Late 1800s, 14 3/4 In.	460.00

Mask, Hagenauer, Stylized Woman's Face, Vienna Workshop, 10 In. 2715.00
Mask, Man, Woman, Art Deco, 11 In., Pair 1210.00
Mortar, Cast, Animal Head Handles, Scroll Bands, 19th Century, 5 3/4 In. 410.00
Mortar & Pestle, Relief Decoration, 2 Handles, 4 1/2 In. 125.00
Parrot, On Perch, Hollow Cast, Applied Black Patina, 53 1/2 In.   460.00
Parrots, On Branch, Cold Painted, 2 1/2 In. 95.00
Pen Wipe, Poodle, Show Clip, 3 x 4 In. 150.00
Pen Wipe, Poodle, Show Clip, Geschutz, 4 1/2 x 6 3/4 In. 100.00
Planter, Birds, Raised, Round, Japan, 10 In. 290.00
Plaque, Loudray, Woman & Lute, Fairy & Trumpet, 2-Sided, Late 1800s, 2 3/4 In. 45.00
Plaque, Man, Silhouette, Neck Up, Relief, 15 In. 85.00
Plaque, Palmer, Head, Winged, Hooded, c.1878, 11 x 36 In. 3300.00
Plaque, Rescue Of Captain John Smith, 19th Century, 4 1/2 x 6 1/4 In. 69.00
Plaque, Stag In Landscape, Rectangular, 10 1/4 x 8 In. 75.00
Plateau, Acanthus Frieze, Beaded Border, Scrolled Handles, 5 x 17 1/2 x 16 In. 1900.00
Safe Plate, Herring Safe Co., Factory Scene, Dolphin Mounts, c.1852, 4 1/2 x 6 1/2 In. . . .   178.00
Sconce, Candle, Flower Bouquet, Porcelain Flowers, 18 In., Pair 2260.00
Sconce, Candle, Silver Gilt Cherub, Fire Gilt Bracket, 13 In., Pair 1469.00
Sconce, Louis XVI Style, 2 Cup, Ribbon Top, Scrolled Arms, 19th Century, 19 In., Pair . .   990.00
Sculpture, 2 Tigers, Attacking Elephant, Ivory Tusks, Japan, 19th Century, 18 1/2 x 16 In.   2070.00
Sculpture, 3 Generations, Verdigris Patina, 20th Century, 13 1/2 In. 290.00
Sculpture, 3 Tigers Attack Elephant, Ivory Tusks, Japan, 19th Century, 20 x 24 1/2 In. . . .   3220.00
Sculpture, Alligator, Aggressive, Gaping Mouth, Cast, 26 x 30 x 72 In. 1265.00
Sculpture, Alliot, Lucien, Flower Girl, Marble Base, 23 x 24 1/2 In. 1440.00
Sculpture, Art Deco, Man Struggling With Winch, Green Marble Base, 25 x 27 In. 1530.00
Sculpture, Athena, Patinated, Late 19th Century, 23 x 8 1/2 In. 1380.00
Sculpture, Bacchante Family, Black Marble & Ormolu Beaded Plinth, 15 In. 1095.00
Sculpture, Bacchus & Infant, Brown Patina, Mottled Yellow Marble Base, 9 1/2 In. 1140.00
Sculpture, Barberini Venus, Standing, Nude, Dolphin, Putto, Late 19th Century, 14 3/4 In.   1035.00
Sculpture, Barger, Ray, Hope Rising From The Ashes, 1978, 6 x 4 1/2 In. 290.00
Sculpture, Barger, Ray, Seeing You, 1974, 9 3/4 x 6 1/2 In. 200.00
Sculpture, Barre, Napoleon, Holding Hat, Military Attire, Square Marble Base, 18 In. . . .   2622.00
Sculpture, Barrias, Louis-Ernest, Mozart Enfant, 1883, 45 1/2 In.   5290.00
Sculpture, Barye, Antoine-Louis, Boar, Late 1800s, 7 In. 1495.00
Sculpture, Barye, Antoine-Louis, Dog, Wolfhound, Seated, Paw Up, Marble Base, 6 In. . .   900.00
Sculpture, Barye, Bull Elephant, Running, Gilded Tusks, Marble Base, 15 x 14 x 9 In. . . .   476.00
Sculpture, Barye, Elephant, Running, Verdigris Patina, Marble Base, 15 In. 2260.00
Sculpture, Bearded Man Sitting On Rock, Holding Water Urn, 15 1/2 In. 3200.00
Sculpture, Berndorf, Boy Clutches Horse's Neck, Lost Hat, 14 x 15 1/2 In. 2375.00
Sculpture, Bird Dog, Patinated, Oval Wood Base, 12 In. 450.00
Sculpture, Bodhisattva, Burma, 12 1/2 In. 500.00
Sculpture, Bodhisattva, Tibet, 20th Century, 11 1/2 In. 385.00
Sculpture, Bodhisattva, Tibet, 20th Century, 13 In. 415.00
Sculpture, Boucher, A., Cupid, Seated, Black Marble & Wood Plinth, 12 In. 1380.00
Sculpture, Bouret, Eutrope, Au Clair De La Lune, Patinated, Late 19th Century, 18 In. . . .   920.00
Sculpture, Bouret, Eutrope, Bacchus On Column, Wine Cup, Late 1800s, 10 1/2 In. 1380.00
Sculpture, Boy, Donkey, Polychrome, Red, Blue, Gold, Silver, Austria, 3 x 3 In. 175.00
Sculpture, Buddha, Lotus Throne, 16 Arms, Multiple Heads, Late 1800s, 15 1/4 In. 345.00
Sculpture, Buddha, Standing, Tortoise, Japan, Edo Period, 3 1/2 In. 195.00
Sculpture, Buddha, Standing, Wood Lotus Base, Edo Period, 17 1/2 In. 2070.00
Sculpture, Bureau, Leon, Le Charmeur, Red Brown Patina, 14 1/4 In. 865.00
Sculpture, Camel, Hollow Cast, Wood Base, Character Signature, Oriental, 28 x 19 In. . . .   770.00
Sculpture, Caravanniez, A., Barbedienne, F., Jeanne De Arc, Brown Patina, Signed, 20 In.   600.00
Sculpture, Cherub, Stump, Bow & Quiver, Marble Base, 14 In. 905.00
Sculpture, Chiparus, St. Therese, Ivory Face & Hands, 18 In. 4600.00
Sculpture, Chipmunk, Sleeping, Tail Curled Over Head, Paul King Foundry, 4 3/8 In. . . .   590.00
Sculpture, Cobra, Polychrome, Austria, 6 x 7 In. 805.00
Sculpture, Cook, R., Horse, Stumbling, Bent On One Knee, 14 In.   120.00
Sculpture, Damosseno, Black Patina, Fonderia Sommer, Naples, Italy, Early 1900s, 24 In.   635.00
Sculpture, Davidson, Marshall Foch, Military Officer, 1918, 9 1/2 In. 1325.00
Sculpture, Delabriere, Horse By Fence, Brown Patina, 10 1/2 x 11 1/2 In. 690.00
Sculpture, Delabriere, Le Premier Gibier, Brown Patina, Marble Base, 19 x 24 In. 2300.00
Sculpture, Dionysus, Grand Tour Verte, Round Base, 1800s, 24 1/4 x 10 In. 2300.00

Sculpture, Dog, Wolfhound, Standing, Long-Haired, Marble Base, 6 x 7 1/2 In. 420.00
Sculpture, Dogs, 2 Poodles, Marble Base, 2 x 3 1/2 x 4 In. 120.00
Sculpture, Dragon, Japan, 19th Century, 30 1/2 In. 7080.00
Sculpture, Dubois, Nude, Hollow Cast, Polished, Lacquered, Signed, 13 1/2 In. 300.00
Sculpture, Elephant & Lions, Wood Base, 20 In. 1045.00
Sculpture, Elephant, Trumpeting, Ivory Tusks, Signed, 19th Century, 23 1/2 In. 920.00
Sculpture, Elephant, Wood Base, Japan, 1800s, 13 x 24 1/2 In. 1200.00
Sculpture, Erte, Emerald Vase, Marble Base, 1988, 24 x 5 1/4 In. 3105.00
Sculpture, Erte, Follies Bergere, Marble Base, 1987, 18 1/4 x 10 1/2 In. 2645.00
Sculpture, Falconer On Horseback, Brown Patina, France, c.1886, 18 x 16 In. 5750.00
Sculpture, Fayarl, Dancer, Arms Spread, Holding Skirt, Onyx Pedestal, Art Deco, 14 In. . 2415.00
Sculpture, Ferdinand, Amazone, Marble Base, Barbedienne, France, 1800s, 24 1/2 In. . . . 1380.00
Sculpture, Fraser, Teddy Roosevelt, c.1920, 12 3/4 x 10 In. 460.00
Sculpture, Fratin, Lion Marchant, Green Brown Patina, 10 1/2 x 18 In. 980.00
Sculpture, Fratin, Lionne Portant Une Gazelle, Terrain Base, c.1864, 9 3/4 x 16 In. 865.00
Sculpture, Fratin, Stallion, Standing, Naturalistic Base, Hercules, 14 x 12 1/2 In. 2705.00
Sculpture, Fremiet, Emmanuel, Le Char De Minerve, 25 x 21 x 12 1/2 In. 7190.00
Sculpture, Fremiet, La Char De Minerve, Inscription, 25 x 21 x 12 1/2 In. 7190.00
Sculpture, Fremiet, Troubadour On Horseback, 13 In. 1060.00
Sculpture, Fremiet, Two Horses & Riders, c.1800s 8355.00
Sculpture, Gardet, Dog, Great Dane, Lying Down, Brown Patina, c.1939, 15 1/2 x 27 In. . 2990.00
Sculpture, Gaudez, Gypsy Maiden, France, 34 In. 2115.00
Sculpture, Germain, Cavalier, Standing, Renaissance Style Dress, Silvered, 9 3/4 In. 235.00
Sculpture, Gillemin, Cavalier Plays Violin, Rouge Marble Base, 6 1/4 In. 345.00
Sculpture, Giraud, Joan Of Arc, Holding Pennant, Sword, Foot On Rocks, 30 1/2 In. 1760.00
Sculpture, Goddess, Nepal, 35 In. 645.00
Sculpture, Goddess, Seated On Elephant, Lotus Blossom, Pearl, Gilt, 1900s, 12 1/4 In. . . 290.00
Sculpture, Grecian Athlete, Draped, Throwing Ball, Green Brown Patina, 10 In. 875.00
Sculpture, Grecian Woman, Standing, Holding Drapery, Brown Patina, 14 In. 875.00
Sculpture, Greek Athlete, Patinated, Sienna Marble Plinth, c.1900, 9 1/4 x 7 x 7 In. 345.00
Sculpture, Guanyin, Chinese, Qing Dynasty, c.1860-1900, 18 1/2 In. 945.00
Sculpture, Hagenauer, African Woman, Stylized Hair, Austria, 14 x 10 1/4 In. 1265.00
Sculpture, Heikka, Mountain Sheep, Curled Horn, c.1928, 3 1/2 x 7 1/2 x 5 In. 490.00
Sculpture, Hen Pecking At Ground, 8 In. 300.00
Sculpture, Hercules, Holding Cornucopia, 17 1/2 In. 1540.00
Sculpture, Humphriss, Cowboy On Horse, 6 1/2 In. 805.00
Sculpture, Humphriss, Lotus Eater, Patina, 26 x 12 x 9 In. 4600.00
Sculpture, Hunter Rabbit, Vest, Rifle, Late 1800s, 5 In. 835.00
Sculpture, Hunter, On Horse, Hunting Dogs, Russia, 16 In. 7006.00
Sculpture, Hyde, Doug, Pueblo Pot, Granite Base, 1980s, 2 3/4 x 4 x 3 1/2 In. 375.00
Sculpture, Junan Sei, Stalking Tiger, Chocolate Patina, 8 x 18 In. 1120.00
Sculpture, Kaesbach, Rearing Horse, Rider, 10 1/2 In. 770.00
Sculpture, Kannon, Standing, Robes, Lotus Crown, Wood Stand, 19th Century, 19 1/2 In. 230.00
Sculpture, Kauba, Carl, Celtic Warrior On Horseback, c.1900, 12 x 14 x 5 1/2 In. 800.00
Sculpture, Kauba, Carl, Indian Children, Donkey, 13 In. 3850.00
Sculpture, Knight On Horseback, Gilt, Black Granite Plinth, 1800s, 14 3/4 x 13 x 7 In. . . . 575.00
Sculpture, Lady, Holding Glass Orbs, Art Deco, 9 3/4 In. 1090.00
Sculpture, Lautier, 3 Water Nymphs, 8-Sided Base, 12 In. 815.00
Sculpture, Liberich, Bear, Standing, c.1868, 20 1/2 In. 5750.00
Sculpture, Lion On Rock, Japan, 28 In. 805.00
Sculpture, Magna Mater, Brown Patina, Ochre Marble Base, Continental, c.1900, 26 In. . . 2300.00
Sculpture, Malfray, Woman, 24 In. 1195.00
Sculpture, Man, Riding Camel, Playing Drum, Cold Painted, 3 1/4 x 2 1/2 In. 150.00
Sculpture, Mare, Nuzzling Foal, Oval Base, Early 20th Century, 6 In. 295.00
Sculpture, Marina, Mermaid Emerging From Waves, Paris, 1923, 17 In. 2300.00
Sculpture, Mears, Helen Farnsworth, Seated Worker, Shovel, c.1900, 8 x 10 In. 1050.00
Sculpture, Men, Child, Sleigh Pulled By Horse, Oval Base, Russia, 17 In. 1800.00
Sculpture, Mene, Dog & Hare, 7 1/2 In. 1920.00
Sculpture, Mene, Dog, Whippet, Standing, Oval Marble Base, Brown Patina, 8 x 9 In. . . . 1955.00
Sculpture, Mene, Dogs, 2 Whippets & Ball, 6 1/2 In. 690.00
Sculpture, Mene, Stag Attacked By 3 Hounds, France, 12 In. 1530.00
Sculpture, Mignery, Corporate Trough, Wood Base, 1991, 11 In. 400.00
Sculpture, Military Archer, Bow, Arrow, Patinated, Chinese, Late 20th Century, 11 In. . . . 315.00

Sculpture, Moigniez, Feathers, Shoreline, Seashells, 22 In. 4520.00
Sculpture, Moigniez, Terrier & Cat, Rocky Outcrop, France, 4 1/4 x 3 In. 440.00
Sculpture, Moreau, Lovers Walking On Rocks, Green Marble Base, 23 In. 3300.00
Sculpture, Moreau, Maiden, Child, 1872, 32 In. 7150.00
Sculpture, Moreau, Nude Rising From Waves, 2 Cherubs, Signed, c.1917, 33 3/4 In. 6325.00
Sculpture, Morgan, F.J., Fox & Chicken, 4 1/4 In. 230.00
Sculpture, Muller, Horse, Groomsman, 11 In. 1100.00
Sculpture, Napoleon, Malachite Base, Gilt, Early 20th Century, 7 3/4 In. 645.00
Sculpture, Napoleon, White Marble Base, Gilt Bronze Eagle, 1800s, 11 1/2 x 3 1/4 In. ... 115.00
Sculpture, Nude Woman Standing, 1882-1954, 29 x 11 x 9 In. 4315.00
Sculpture, Oriental Dancer, Art Deco, 55 In. 715.00
Sculpture, Owl, Cold Painted, Vienna, Early 20th Century, 5 1/4 In. 175.00
Sculpture, Pautrot, Ferdinand, Finch On A Perch, Dark Brown Patina, 7 In. 230.00
Sculpture, Pedestrian Hobbyhorse, Sugino Cycle Industries Ltd., 8 1/2 x 8 1/2 In. 179.00
Sculpture, Penelope Contemplating The Portrait Of Ulysses, c.1900, 14 1/2 In. 750.00
Sculpture, Pheasant, Ring Neck, Rooster, Enameled, Bronze, Austria, 14 In., Pair 920.00
Sculpture, Picault, Harlequin With Mandolin, 19 In. 1760.00
Sculpture, Pierrot, Seated, Playing Mandolin, Ivorine Face, Incised, Art Deco, 2 3/4 In. ... 235.00
Sculpture, Powell, Surprised, Colt Discovers Saddle, c.1960s, 3 1/2 x 9 x 6 In. 196.00
Sculpture, Putto Musician, Flower Base, Brown Patina, Red Marble Plinth, 12 In. 1725.00
Sculpture, Reghier, Woman, Flowing Dress, Holding Apple, 12 In. 280.00
Sculpture, Rochard, Rhinoceros, Dark Brown Patina, Oblong Base, 15 1/2 In. 1750.00
Sculpture, Roman Soldier, Masks, 39 In. 1580.00
Sculpture, Salmson, Philosphe, France, 1800s, 10 1/4 x 4 3/4 In. 1035.00
Sculpture, Schmotz, Girl Standing, Reading Book, Marble Base, 4 1/2 In. 115.00
Sculpture, Seated Nubian Woman, Playing Lute, Cold Painted, 3 In. 290.00
Sculpture, Shattuck, Louise, Dogs, 5 Poodles, Marble Base, 8 x 13 In. 550.00
Sculpture, Shishi, Curly Hair, Menacing, 1800s, 5 1/2 In. 430.00
Sculpture, Spanish Conquistador, On Horseback, Signed, 12 In. 195.00
Sculpture, Sphinx, Gilt, Green Marble Base, Early 20th Century, 4 x 6 In., Pair 380.00
Sculpture, SS Normandie, Glass Display Case, 36 In. 1210.00
Sculpture, Stag, Standing, Cold Painted, Vienna, Late 19th Century, 4 In. 175.00
Sculpture, Title Plate, Les Harmonies, Draped Woman, Harp, Held By Man, c.1912, 41 In. 10350.00
Sculpture, Troika, Sled, Riders, 3 Horses, Brass Finish, Woerffel, Russia, 10 In. 1485.00
Sculpture, Valton, Lioness, Growling, Marble Base, France, c.1900, 17 1/4 x 12 1/2 In. ... 1045.00
Sculpture, Valton, Tiger, Wounded, Arrows, 19 In. 1100.00
Sculpture, Verdigris Patinated, La Baigneuse, Louis XVI Style, 33 x 11 In. 3910.00
Sculpture, Vestal Virgin, Flaming Urn, Bouquet, Marble Base, Late 1800s, 14 3/4 In. 920.00
Sculpture, Vienna, Arabian Merchant, Cold Painted, Early 20th Century, 4 In. 1060.00
Sculpture, Vienna, Arabian Rug Seller, Cold Painted, Early 20th Century, 7 x 8 3/4 In. 560.00
Sculpture, Vienna, Arabian Woman & Man, On Cushion & Stool, Early 1900s, 3 1/2 In. .. 529.00
Sculpture, Vienna, Exotic Dancer, Polychrome, Early 20th Century, 4 1/2 In. 345.00
Sculpture, Williams, Dancing Nude, 13 1/2 In. 460.00
Sculpture, Winged Woman, Inscribed, 36 In. 2300.00
Sculpture, Woman, Classical, Standing, Roman Clothing, Tiffany & Co., Late 1800s, 12 In. 410.00
Sculpture, Woman, Feeding Peacock, Art Nouveau, Green Marble Base, 9 x 13 x 5 In. ... 1725.00
Sculpture, Woman, Lying Down, Art Nouveau, 11 1/4 In. 330.00
Sculpture, Woman, Walking, Ascending Stair, Art Deco, 11 1/4 In. 1650.00
Seal, Figural, Silvered, Ferret, Coat Of Arms Base, 3 1/4 In. 265.00
Sphinx, Rectangular Plinth, 1800s, 5 1/2 x 7 5/8 x 2 1/2 In., Pair 520.00
Standish, Bergman, Arabian Man, Rifle, Cold Painted, Marble Base, c.1900, 14 3/8 In. .. 2468.00
Standish, Louis XVI Style, Gilt, Marble, 9 In. 210.00
Tazza, Pandora & Box, Signed, c.1860-1905, 4 In. 196.00
Teapot, Peach Shape, Branch Handle, 1800s, 6 1/2 In. 127.00
Tray, Woman, Arms Outstretched, Holding Dress, Art Nouveau, 5 1/2 In. 345.00
Urn, Classical Style, Applied Grapevines, Double Bird Handles, Leaf Pedestal, 12 1/2 In. .. 520.00
Urn, Classical Style, Janus Head, 2 Handles, Verdigris Patina, 18 1/2 In. 1410.00
Urn, Dragons, Oriental Calligraphy, 19th Century, 9 x 9 x 17 In 250.00
Urn, Female Masks, Removable Tops, 2 Snake Handles, Early 20th Century, 17 In. 670.00
Urn, Louis XVI Style, Gilt, Cherub, Cornucopia, Dome Lid, Paris, c.1850, 15 1/2 In., Pair 1610.00
Urn, Mantel, Classical Revival, Marble, Vines, Handles, Marble Plinth, 11 1/2 In., Pair ... 590.00
Urn, Neoclassical Style, Marble, Continental, Early 20th Century, 26 1/2 In., Pair 3565.00
Urn, Nude, Relief, Greek Form, Handles, Pedestal, Square Base, Elkington, 9 1/4 In., Pair 978.00

Urn, Renaissance Revival, Classical Shape, Loop Handle, Low Relief Figures, 12 3/8 In. .   120.00
Urn, Vasiform Body, Fluted, Tapered Lid, Trumpet Foot, Patinated, Mantel, 9 3/8 In., Pair   325.00
Vase, Bulbous, Grapes, 2 Handles, Presentation, Germany, 18 x 14 In. 420.00
Vase, Carp, Raised Relief, Swirling Water, 19th Century, 12 x 6 In. . . . . .385.00 to 395.00
Vase, Club Shape, Dragon Around Neck, Relief, Japan, Late 19th Century, 8 3/4 In. 290.00
Vase, Cylinder, Bamboo, Relief, Black Brown Patina, Japan, 19th Century, 12 In. 400.00
Vase, Dragon, Glass Pearl, Cast Ochre Surface, Patinated, Japan, 19th Century, 8 In. 750.00
Vase, Flowers, Animals, Relief, Patinated, Japan, c.1900, 20 In. 230.00
Vase, Hexagonal, Fan Form Cartouches, Silver Fretwork, 19th Century, 9 1/4 In. 315.00
Vase, Inlaid Pebbles, Tapered Neck, Bulbous, Leaves, Grass, 8 1/4 In. 445.00
Vase, Inverted Pear Shape, 3-Footed Wave Base, Karako Figure, 19th Century, 10 1/4 In. .   405.00
Vase, Inverted Pear Shape, Raised Drip Design, Japan, 19th Century, 22 In. 575.00
Vase, Inverted Pear, Chrysanthemum, Engraved, Patinated, c.1910, 4 1/4 In. 115.00
Vase, Mountain Scene, Waterfall, Yoshimasa, Japan, 19th Century, 1868-1912, 11 7/8 In. .   315.00
Vase, Patinated, Footed, Celestial Dragon, Japan, Late 19th Century, 21 In. 920.00
Vase, Salamander, Relief, Oval, Shouldered, Marbelized Waisted Circular Base, 8 In. 350.00
Vase, Seikoku, Baluster, Dragon, 19th Century, 10 1/2 In. 635.00
Vase, Spill, Figural, Water Nymphs Swimming, Holding Fish, Art Nouveau, Gilt, 4 1/4 In.   470.00
Vase, Urn Shape, Dragon, Clouds, Japan, Early 1900s, 37 1/2 In. 805.00
Weight, Woman's Head, Roman Period, 3 x 1 7/8 x 2 1/4 In. 5940.00

BROWNIES were first drawn in 1883 by Palmer Cox. They are characterized by large round eyes, downturned mouths, and skinny legs. Toys,
books, dinnerware, and other objects were made with the Brownies as
part of the design.

Book, Brownie Year Book, Palmer Cox, McLoughlin Bros., 1895 . . . .   450.00
Book, Brownies & The Farmer, Palmer Cox, Hubbard Publishing, 1902 . . . .   35.00
Book, Palmer Cox's Brownies & Other Stories, Hardcover, Donohue, c.1915, 62 Pages . .   10.00
Bottle, Whiskey, Small Face, 3 In. 66.00
Doll, Cloth, Uncut, 6 Dolls, Copyright Jan. 15, 1892 . . . .   180.00
Drum, Band, Embossed Wood, Paper Lithograph, Palmer Cox, 10 In. 185.00
Home Book, Palmer Cox, The Century Co., New York, 1893 . . . .   50.00
Jigsaw Puzzle, Brownie Scroll, Blindman's Bluff, The Dance, 1891, 13 x 10 In. 230.00
Puzzle, Graphic Cubes, Brownie Scenes, Paper Lithograph, Cardboard 495.00
Trade Card, Palmer Cox, Norton White Seal Flour, Color Lithograph, c.1885, 4 x 6 In. . . .   55.00

BRUSH Pottery was started in 1925. George Brush first worked in 1901
in Zanesville, Ohio. He started his own pottery in 1907, but it burned
to the ground soon after. In 1909 he became manager of the J.W.
McCoy Pottery. In 1911, Brush and J.W. McCoy formed the Brush-
McCoy Pottery Co. After a series of name changes, the company
became The Brush Pottery in 1925. It closed in 1982. Old Brush was
marked with impressed letters or a palette-shaped mark. Some new
pieces are being marked in raised letters or with a raised mark.
Collectors favor the figural cookie jars made by this company. Because
there was a company named Brush-McCoy, there is great confusion
between Brush and Nelson McCoy pieces. See McCoy category for
more information.

MARK

Beanpot, Cover, Ladle, Dark Brown Glaze, Marked, 164, 10 In. 45.00
Cookie Jar, American Eagle, 1967 . . . .   50.00
Cookie Jar, Little Red Riding Hood, 10 1/2 x 6 1/2 In. 650.00
Cookie Jar, Teddy Bear 45.00
Figurine, Cat, Tan Glaze, Miniature, c.1939 . . . .   95.00
Flowerpot, Attached Saucer, Woodgrain, Olive Green Glaze, 5 1/2 In. 25.00
Jardiniere, Arched Panels, Leafy Border, Green & Brown Majolica Glaze, 12 In. 60.00
Planter, Girl In Long Dress, Wide Brimmed Hat, Basket, 8 x 7 In. 195.00
Planter, Piggy, Aqua Glaze, 4 1/2 x 5 1/2 In. 35.00
Planter, Turtle, Green & Brown Glaze, Marked B493, USA, 7 1/2 In. 50.00
Planter, Window Sill, Embossed, Light Green Vellum Glaze, 1950s, 7 3/4 In. 13.00
Planter, Window Sill, Oblong, Ribbed, Dark Green Glaze, Marked B201-7, 7 In. 25.00
Teapot, Cloverleaf, 8 Cup, 6 1/2 In. 75.00
Vase, Fawn Vellum Glaze, Green, Squat, Handles, 5 x 6 1/2 In.   80.00
Vase, Green Matte Glaze, Handles, 12 3/4 x 7 In. 230.00

Vase, Melon Ribbed, Tan Vellum Glaze, Green Branch Handles, Footed, 12 1/2 In.	85.00
Vase, Onyx, Brown Drip Glaze At Top, Urn Shape, Handles, 8 In.	85.00
Vase, Onyx, Brown Drip Glaze, 12 In.	185.00
Vase, Onyx, Green Drip Glaze, 15 In.	110.00
Vase, Smoky Gray Glaze, Scroll Handles, Footed, Marked 594, USA, 8 1/4 In.	45.00
Wall Pocket, Dog In Doghouse, 8 x 7 In.	80.00

BRUSH MCCOY, see Brush category and related pieces in McCoy category.

BUCK ROGERS was the first American science fiction comic strip. It
started in 1929 and continued until 1967. Buck has also appeared in
comic books, movies, and, in the 1980s, a television series. Any memorabilia connected with the character Buck Rogers is collectible.

Badge, Solar Scouts, Silver Luster, Signature, Cream Of Wheat, 1936, 1 1/2 In.	215.00
Belt, Buck Logo, Tigerman, Princess Ardala, Twiki, Blue, Vinyl, 1 1/4 x 27 In.	25.00
Belt Box, Buck Rogers Over Rocket, Orange, c.1930, 2 1/4 x 7 3/4 x 1 3/4 In.	720.00
Book, Big Little Book, Buck Rogers & The Planetoid Plot, Hardcover, 1936	135.00
Book, Big Little Book, Buck Rogers & The Planetoid Plot, Whitman, No. 1197	45.00
Book, Big Little Book, Cocomalt, 1933	145.00
Book, Buck Rogers vs. The Fiend Of Space, No. 1409, 1940	56.00
Book, Pop-Up, Strange Adventures In The Spider Ship, 1935, 16 Pages	252.00
Button, 25th Century Classic Members, Buck Portrait, Cream Of Wheat Club, 1935	75.00
Catalog, Buck Rogers Space Ranger Kit, Sylvania TV, 1952, 8 1/2 x 11 In.	405.00
Colorforms, Die Cut, Vinyl, Box, Robert C. Dille, 1979, 8 x 12 1/2 In.	20.00
Figure, Draco, Box, 12 In.	125.00
Flyer, Space Ranger Kit, Sylvania, One Page, 1950s, 10 3/4 x 8 In.	125.00
Game, Battle For The 25th Century, TSR Inc., 12 1/4 x 21 3/4 In.	25.00
Game, Buck Rogers, Milton Bradley, 1979, 9 1/2 x 19 In.	45.00
Holster, Silhouette Of Buck, 5 Rivets, Brown, Leather, Daisy, 9 x 30 In.	210.00
Pistol, XZ-35, Holster, Leather, Brown, Daisy, 1935, 8 In.	920.00
Playsuit, Vest, Pants, Shirt, Helmet, Belt, Cream Of Wheat, Sackman Brothers Co., 1935 .	475.00
Popgun, 25th Century, Pressed Steel, Daisy, 10 In.	250.00
Record, Original Radio Broadcast, 33 1/3, Mark 56 Records, 12 1/4 In.	25.00
Rocket Ship, Tin Lithograph, Windup, Marx, Box, c.1927, 12 In. . . . . .1650.00 to 2500.00
Space Ranger Kit, Sylvania, 4 Pages, Newspaper Form, 1952, 12 x 16 In.	175.00
Space Ranger Kit, Sylvania, 8 Pages, 1952, 8 1/2 x 11 In.	395.00
Space Ranger Kit, Sylvania, Hardcover, Spiral Binding, 1952, 10 x 14 In.	600.00
Spaceship, Metal, Midgetoy, Packaged, 1954, 3 1/2 In.	55.00
Toy, Rocket Police Patrol, Tin Lithograph, Clockwork, Louis Marx, Box, 11 1/2 In.	2200.00
Watch, Buck & Wilma On Face, Lightning Bolt Hands, 1935, 2 In.	345.00
Watch, Pocket, Buck Rogers & Wilma, Silver Finish, Ingraham, 1935, 2 In.	310.00
Watch, Pocket, Buck Rogers In The 25th Century, Huckleberry Time Co., 2 In.	1000.00

BUFFALO POTTERY was made in Buffalo, New York, after 1902. The
company was established by the Larkin Company, famous manufacturers of soap. The wares are marked with a picture of a buffalo and
the date of manufacture. Deldare ware is the most famous pottery
made at the factory. It has either a khaki-colored or green background
with hand-painted transfer designs.

BUFFALO POTTERY, Bowl, Willow, Pink, 8 In.	50.00
Chocolate Pot, Sailing Ships, Waves, Angular Handle, Abino, C. Harris, 10 In.	750.00
Cup & Saucer, Chocolate, Windmill, Village, Boats, Abino Maritime, 1913	523.00
Cup & Saucer, George Washington, Gold Bands	200.00
Grill Plate, Willow	35.00
Medallion, Blue, Cameo Portrait, John D. Larkin, Oct. 5, 1925, 7 1/4 In.	375.00
Pitcher, Chrysanthemums, Sea Green, Gold Trim, Bulbous, Reticulated Rim, 7 In.	200.00
Pitcher, Cinderella, In Stagecoach, Glass Slipper, 1907, 6 1/2 In.	275.00
Pitcher, Holland, Girls Knitting, Mother With Bushel Of Wheat, 6 1/4 In.	325.00
Pitcher, Man On Path To Windmill, Harbor Setting, Abino Maritime, 10 x 9 In.	1320.00
Pitcher, Mason, Men Traveling In Gondolas, Transfer, Paneled, Scalloped, 8 In.	500.00
Pitcher, Roosevelt Bears, Hot Air Balloon, 1906, 4 In.	100.00
Pitcher, Sailor Portraits, Nautical Items, White, Brown Transfer, 9 In.	1500.00
Pitcher, Stags, Chased By Hunting Dogs, Mauve Poppies, 1907, 6 3/4 In.	425.00
Pitcher, White, Gilt Trim, Melon Shape, Fluted Panels, 1909, 9 In.	300.00

Plate, George Washington, Oval, Gold Bands, 9 1/2 In., Pair 150.00
Plate, Roosevelt Bears, We've Broken Something, Spattered, Scalloped Rim, 7 In. 900.00
Salt & Pepper, Pink High Glaze, Tapered, Rouge Ware, 3 In. 50.00
Sugar, Lid, Roycroft Symbol, Arts & Crafts Design, Red & Green On White, 7 In. 748.00
Tray, Roycroft Artwork, Green, Brown, Square, Rounded Corners, 10 In. 300.00
BUFFALO POTTERY DELDARE, Bowl, Nut, Squirrel, Butterflies, Emerald, 3 3/4 x 8 In. 1540.00
Bowl, Nut, Ye Lion Inn, Gentlemen, Dog, Inverted Edge, 1909, 3 3/4 x 8 In. 770.00
Candleholder, Art Nouveau Flowers, Emerald, 1911, 6 5/8 In. 1150.00
Candlestick, Gentlemen, Village Houses, 9 1/2 In., Pair 500.00
Candlestick, Shieldback, Men On Boardwalk, 7 x 6 In. 770.00
Cup & Saucer, Chocolate, Flowers, Geometrics, Butterflies, Emerald 1430.00
Humidor, Mariner, There Was An Old Sailor, Sailors, Ship Finial, 8 x 6 In. 385.00
Humidor, Ye Lion Inn, 8-Sided, Bulging Panels, Dome Shape Cover, 7 In. 715.00
Inkwell, Bands Of Butterflies, Arches, Square, Rounded Corners, 2 In. 660.00
Mug, Fallowfield Hunt, Breaking Cover, 3 3/4 In., Pair 305.00
Mug, Fallowfield Hunt, The Start, 13 1/2 In. 415.00
Mug, Ye Lion Inn, A. Wade, Ink Stamp, 1909, 4 1/4 In. 145.00
Mug, Ye Lion Inn, P. Hall, 1909, 4 1/8 In. 115.00
Pitcher, Fallowfield Hunt, The Return, 8 1/4 x 7 1/2 In. 470.00
Pitcher, To Demand My Annual Rent, Cordial Hospitality, 8 In. 360.00
Pitcher, To Spare An Old Broken Soldier, Ford, 1909, 7 In. 275.00
Plaque, Dr. Syntax Sells Grizzle, Steissel, Emerald, 1911, 13 1/12 In. 900.00
Plaque, Friday, Monks Depicting Days Of Week, Gerhardt, 12 In. 605.00
Plate, Action Between The Constitution & The Guerrier, 1911, 7 1/2 In. 2530.00
Plate, Calendar, 1910, Seasons Depicted By Elves, E. Horn, 9 1/4 In. 1300.00
Plate, Daughter Of Revolution, Woman Loading Cannon, Stuart, 9 In. 6325.00
Plate, Dr. Syntax Making A Discovery, Arched Border, Emerald, 10 In. 385.00
Plate, Dr. Syntax Misfortune At Tulip Hall, Gerhardt, Emerald, 1911, 8 In. 385.00
Plate, Fallowfield Hunt, The Start, c.1909, 9 1/4 In. 115.00
Plate, Garden Trio, Women, Music, Broel, Emerald, 1911, 9 In. 605.00
Plate, Ye Olden Times, Men On Boardwalk, 9 1/2 In. 195.00
Plate, Ye Olden Times, Men On Boardwalk, Gerhardt, 1909, 4 1/2 In. 750.00
Plate, Ye Village Gossips, c.1909, 10 In. 105.00
Platter, An Evening At Ye Lion Inn, c.1908, 13 1/2 In. 402.00
Platter, Lost Scene, c.1911, 13 1/2 In. 92.00
Punch Bowl, Fallowfield Hunt, Supper, Breaking Cover, Pedestal, 14 In. 6600.00
Punch Cup, Landscape Scene, House Inside, 2 1/4 x 4 In., Pair 413.00
Soup, Dish, Ye Village Street, 2 Men Walking, Sheehan, 9 In. 225.00
Tankard, Great Controversy, Teach The Dutchman, Ball, 12 1/4 In. 500.00
Vase, Silver Overlay Buds, Stems, Bulbous, Tapered, Flared, Emerald, 8 In. 2530.00
Vase, Vertical Bands Of Flowers, Geometrics, Baluster, Emerald, 8 1/2 In. 770.00
Vase, Ye Village Parson, Ye Village Schoolmaster, Baluster, 8 1/2 In. 440.00

BUNNYKINS, see Royal Doulton category.

BURMESE GLASS was developed by Frederick Shirley at the Mt.
Washington Glass Works in New Bedford, Massachusetts, in 1885. It is
a two-toned glass, shading from peach to yellow. Some pieces have a
pattern mold design. A few Burmese pieces were decorated with pictures or applied glass flowers of colored Burmese glass. Other factories
made similar glass also called *Burmese.* Related items may be listed in
the Fenton category, the Gunderson category and under Webb Burmese.

Biscuit Jar, Cover, Flowers, Squat, Footed, 4 x 6 In. 1265.00
Bowl, Inverted Thumbprint, Scalloped Edge, 3 x 9 In. 175.00
Bride's Basket, Tricornered, Silver Plate Holder, c.1890, 12 In. 2130.00
Condiment Jar, Ribbed Body, Silver Plated Mounts, 3 1/4 In. 60.00
Condiment Set, Gold Enameled Flowers, 3 Piece 2480.00
Creamer, Applied Handle, 3 1/2 In. .... .345.00 to 600.00
Creamer, Glossy, 3 1/2 In. 220.00
Fairy Lamp, Green Leaves, Ruffled, Clarke, 5 In. 1150.00
Finger Bowl, Ruffled Rim, 5 1/2 In. 150.00
Pitcher, Green Ivy Frame, Dickens' Verse, c.1890, 6 x 7 In. 6160.00
Plate, 5 1/4 In. 115.00
Plate, 8 In. 115.00

Plate, European Fishing Harbor Scent, Stone Fort, Mountain, 12 In. 950.00
Plate, Nesting Birds, Enameled, 10 In. 840.00
Punch Cup, Glossy, Applied Loop Handle, 2 3/4 In. 259.00
Rose Bowl, Enameled Flowers, Gold, Inverted Ruffled Edge, 6 x 7 1/2 In. 635.00
Sugar, 3 3/4 In. 375.00
Sugar, Applied Handles, 3 3/4 In. 60.00
Toothpick, Square Rim 325.00
Toothpick, Tricornered Rim 425.00
Toothpick, Tricornered Rim, Flowers 700.00
Tumbler, Glossy, 3 3/4 In. 230.00
Tumbler, Juice, 3 In. 115.00
Tumbler, Juice, Applied Handle, 3 1/2 In. 145.00
Vase, Enameled Flowers, Leaves & Stems, Ribbed, Flared, 3 1/4 In. 200.00
Vase, Enameled Flowers, Leaves, Ribbed, Ruffled Edge, 4 1/2 In. 575.00
Vase, Flared, Ruffled Edge, 6 x 6 1/2 In. 230.00
Vase, Garden Of Allah, Desert, Camels, 16 In. 7190.00
Vase, Glossy, Ruffled Edge, Footed, 4 1/2 In. 80.00
Vase, Gourd Shape, Enameled Flowers, 12 In. 2300.00
Vase, Jack-In-The-Pulpit, Glossy, 9 1/4 In. 405.00
Vase, Jack-In-The-Pulpit, Ruffled Rim, 11 In. 125.00
Vase, Lily, Raised Disc Foot, 12 In. 605.00
Vase, Lily, Ruffled Rim, 9 3/4 In. 550.00
Vase, Lily, Tapered, Raised Disc Foot, 15 In. 330.00
Vase, Ribbed, Flared Base, Scalloped Edge, 5 1/4 In. 300.00
Vase, Twist, Ruffled Edge, Tricornered, 6 1/4 In. ....150.00 to 230.00
Water Set, 7 Piece 3100.00

BUSTER BROWN, the comic strip, first appeared in color in 1902.
Buster and his dog, Tige, remained a popular comic and soon became
even more famous as the emblem for a shoe company, a textile firm,
and other companies. The strip was discontinued in 1920. Buster
Brown sponsored a radio show from 1943 to 1955 and a TV show from
1950 to 1956. The Buster Brown characters are still used by Brown
Shoe Company, Buster Brown Apparel, Inc., and Gateway Hosiery.

Bank, Buster Brown & Tige, Cast Iron, Painted, Williams, 5 1/4 In. ....165.00 to 176.00
Bank, Good Luck, Cast Iron, Painted, Arcade, 4 1/4 In. 132.00
Bank, Horse, Good Luck, Tige, Cast Iron, Arcade, 5 In. ....255.00 to 300.00
Book, Buster Brown Goes Fishing, Cloth, Akron, Saalfield, 1905 .... 300.00
Button, Buster Brown & Tige, Celluloid, 1 1/2 In. 280.00
Button, Buster Brown Bread, Tige, Multicolored, Celluloid, 1 1/4 In. 17.00
Candy Container, Tige, Composition, 6 1/4 In. ....*Illus* 1430.00
Cigar Tin, Round, 6 x 4 In. 4100.00
Clicker, Boy & Dog, Celluloid, 1 1/4 In. 275.00
Cloth, Printed, Buster Brown & Tige, Frame, c.1900, 20 x 24 In. 105.00
Dish, Cap Shape, Tige Balancing Teakettle On Nose, 4 5/8 In. 80.00
Display, Tige Pulling Buster In Shoe, Tin Lithograph, Die Cut, 24 In., 2 Piece 9400.00
Doll, Tige, Cloth, Uncut, Knickerbocker Specialty Co., 17 x 36 In. ....*Illus* 275.00
Figurine, Buster Brown, Arms Move, Embossed, Bisque, Germany, 4 In. 138.00

Buster Brown,
Candy Container,
Tige, Composition,
6 1/4 In.

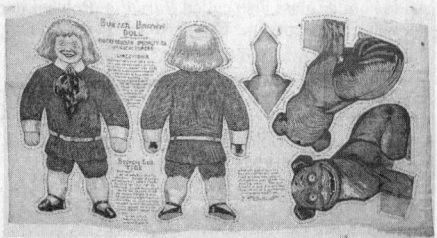

Buster Brown, Doll, Tige, Cloth, Uncut,
Knickerbocker Specialty Co., 17 x 36 In.

Keychain Fob, Blue Ribbon, Silver, Oval 28.00
Mirror, Blue Bowtie & Collar, Whitehead & Hoag, c.1905, 2 In. 176.00
Mirror, Buster & Tige, Full Length, E.G. Adams & Co., c.1900, 2 1/4 In. 240.00
Mirror, Buster, Tige, For Boys & Girls, Whitehead & Hoag, c.1910-1915, 1 3/4 In. 66.00
Plaque, Chalkware, Winking Buster, Tige, Dimensional, 17 x 18 In. 200.00
Playing Cards, U.S. Playing Card Co., c.1906, 2 1/2 In. 55.00
Pocketknife, Bilt Shoe, Ivory Grip, 3/4 x 3 3/4 In. 125.00
Pocketknife, Buster Standing Over Tige, Blue On White Pearl, 4 In. 104.00
Pocketknife, For Boys, For Girls, 1940s, 3 1/2 In. 80.00
Puzzle, Put Your Feet In Brown Bilt Shoes, Tin, Metal Ball, 2 In. 55.00
Salt & Pepper, Andy's Gang Show, Froggy The Gremlin, Japan, 6 x 3 In. 125.00
Sign, Buster Brown Bread, Golden Sheaf Bakery, Buster, Tige, Tin, 30 x 22 In. 1375.00
Toy, Dog, Tige, Mohair, Dark Brown, Tan, Steiff, c.1920, 15 In. 605.00
Tray, Shoe Advertising, Brown Grain Painting, Gold Letters, 13 3/8 In. 55.00
Waffle Iron, Cast Iron 140.00

BUTTER CHIPS, or butter pats, were small individual dishes for butter. They were the height of fashion from 1880 to 1910. Earlier as well as later examples are known.

Blue Bird, 1900s, 3 3/8 In. 27.00
Blue Danube, Scalloped Edge, Marked 29, 1890s 50.00
Keystone Pattern, 2 Red Stripes Around Edge, PRR In Center, 3 1/2 In. 25.00
Leaf, Basket Weave, 3 In. 129.00

BUTTER MOLDS are listed in the Kitchen category under Mold, Butter.

BUTTON collecting has been popular since the nineteenth century. Buttons have been known throughout the centuries, and there are millions of styles. Gold, silver, or precious stones were used for the best buttons, but most were made of natural materials, like bone or shell, or from inexpensive metals. Only a few types are listed for comparison.

Aluminum, Embossed Pinecone, Shank, 3/4 In. 2.00
Bakelite, Carved, Banana, Metal Shank, 2 3/4 In. 90.00
Bakelite, Carved, Bow, Brown, 1 1/4 In. 2.00
Bakelite, Carved, Rooster, Painted Comb & Waddle, 1 1/8 In. 75.00
Bakelite, Pharaoh's Head, Egyptian Revivial, Painted, 3 1/8 In. 25.00
Celluloid, Embossed Rooster, Gold Paint, Shank, 1 In. 115.00
Celluloid, Fan, Rhinestone Frame, Green, Shank, 1 3/4 In. 30.00
Celluloid, Gold Peacock, Painted, Shank, 2 1/2 In. 95.00
Composition, Syroco, Children Sledding, Sew Through, 2 1/8 In. 110.00
Composition, Syroco, Clock Face, Sew Through, 1 3/4 In. 90.00
Composition, Syroco, Indian Chief, Sew Through, 2 In. 105.00
Composition, Syroco, Paratrooper, Sew Through, 1 7/8 In. 110.00
Composition, Syroco, Penguin, Black Wings & Head, Sew Through, 2 In. 205.00
Glass, Amber, Rat, Sew Through, 1 1/8 In. 30.00
Glass, Jet, Embossed Teardrops, Brass Shank, c.1870, 1 1/4 In. 4.00
Glass, Lacy Pressed, Flower, Olive Green, Mercury Back, Shank, 1 In. 80.00
Glass, Pink Moonstone, Rhinestone Center, Gold Metal, Shank, 3/4 In. 1.00
Metal, Art Nouveau Design, Glass Peacock's Eye, Japanned, Openwork, Shank, 1 1/4 In. . . 305.00
Pearl, Greyhound, Metal, Shank, 1 1/8 In. 27.00
Plastic, Chunky, Marbled Yellow, Shank, 1950s, 1 1/8 In., 4 Piece 1.00
Porcelain, Woman, Satsuma, Hand Painted, Gold Beading, Shank, 1 In. 500.00
Silver, Flowers, Embossed, Enameled, Hallmark, Shank, 1 1/8 In. 305.00
Silver, Thistle, Embossed, Enameled, Shank, Hallmark, Charles Horner, 7/16 In. 100.00
Starflower, Glass, Red, Embossed, Painted, Shank, 3/4 In., 6 Piece 4.00
Steel, Cameo, Woman In Profile, Embossed, Gold Chased, Rivited Shank, 5/8 In. 5.00
Wedgwood, Flowers, Green & Gold Border, Hand Painted, Shank, 1 In. 225.00

BUTTONHOOKS have been a popular collectible in England for many years but are now gaining the attention of American collectors. The buttonhooks were made to help fasten the many buttons of the old-fashioned high-button shoes and other items of apparel.

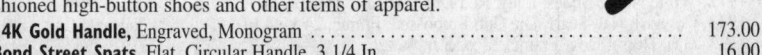

14K Gold Handle, Engraved, Monogram 173.00
Bond Street Spats, Flat, Circular Handle, 3 1/4 In. 16.00

Brown Bros. Shoes, Beloit, Wis., Flat, Circular Handle, 5 In. 16.00
J.C. Penney Co. 475 Stores, Flat, Circular Handle, 5 In. 13.00
Johnson Bros. Duds For Men, Flat Handle, Full Loop End, 3 5/8 In. 17.00
M. & K. Shoe Shop, Cincinnati, Flat, Circular Handle, 5 1/8 In. 16.00
R. E. Borst, Fine Shoes, Parish, N.Y., Flat, Circular Handle, 5 In. 11.00
Rockford E. & E. Clothing House, Daisy, Full Loop End, 1916, 3 1/8 In. 17.00
Shoehorn, Petty's Enna Jettick Shoes, Jenkins Arcade, Folding, 5 In. 28.00
Shoehorn, Petty's Shoe Repair Shop, Milady's Shoe Horn, Folding, 5 In. 28.00
Silver, Floral Embossed Handle, Leaves & Scrolls, Victorian 19.00
Sterling Silver, Floral Design, Engraved GLGVW, 6 1/2 In. 32.00
Sterling Silver, Spiral Column In Shaft, Art Nouveau Handle, Haddie D. Elkins 65.00

CALENDARS made to hang on the wall or to be displayed on a desk top
have been popular since the last quarter of the nineteenth century.
Many were printed with advertising as part of the artwork and were
given away as premiums. Calendars with guns, gunpowder, or Coca-
Cola advertising are most prized.

1891, Hood's, 3 Children Playing Instruments, Frame, 11 x 15 In. 175.00
1891, Mrs. Winslow's Soothing Syrup, Lady, Baby, Frame, 12 1/2 x 15 1/2 In. 155.00
1894, Hood's, Lady, Flowers In Hat, Frame, 9 x 12 In. 130.00
1896, Hood's, Lady, Gray Hat, Frame, 10 x 13 In. 130.00
1898, 2 Pretty Women, Pine Cones, Cardboard, Embossed 10 1/2 x 14 1/2 In. 50.00
1899, Hood's Sarsaparilla, Glass Back, Frame, 10 x 14 In. 130.00
1900, Redrick Co., Girl In Winter Coat, Chambersburg, Pa., Frame, 15 x 11 In. 80.00
1901, Baker & Osgood Hardware, Lady, Flowers, Die Cut, Frame, 13 x 24 In. 220.00
1901, Hartzler's Cash Store, Girl, Deer, Die Cut, Frame, 15 x 27 In. 190.00
1901, Singer Sewing Machines, Cardboard, Technological Advances, 11 x 15 In. 225.00
1902, Hood's Sarsaparilla, 4 Women, Frame, 8 x 21 In. 310.00
1902, Prudential Insurance, Victorian Lady, Black Hat, Frame, 15 x 17 In. 140.00
1903, Antikamnia, 11 x 8 In. 17.00
1903, C.D. Kenny, 4 Pages, Frame, 26 x 30 In. 440.00
1904, Bromo-Seltzer, Emerson Drug Co., Mechanical Trade Card, 5 x 2 1/2 In. 165.00
1905, 4 Girls With Birds, Die Cut, Lithograph, Frame, 16 x 34 In. 550.00
1905, 4 Seasons, 4 Children, Victorian Dress, Die Cut, 29 x 10 In. 230.00
1905, Girl On Swing, Die Cut, Frame, 9 x 12 In. 55.00
1905, Harrington & Richardson Arms, Lady, Gun, Lithograph, 26 x 14 In. .... *Illus* 4180.00
1905, Metropolitan Life Insurance, 4 Girls In Flowers, Frame, 7 x 24 In. 176.00
1906, Grand Union Tea Co., Girl On Swing, Die Cut, 10 x 29 In. 415.00
1906, Lafin & Rand Powder Co., Man Hiding Behind Canoe, 15 x 29 In. 2475.00
1906, Libby, McNeill & Libby, Corned Beef, Girl, In Straw Hat, Frame 190.00
1906, Mott's Department Store, Girl, Bonnet, Die Cut, Embossed, Frame, 15 x 23 In. 330.00
1907, Hood's, Sarsaparilla, Frame, 14 x 21 In. 90.00
1907, Victorian Girl With Fan, Die Cut, 11 x 5 In. 125.00
1908, 2 Girls Hugging, Frame, 12 x 20 In. 220.00
1908, Couple, In 4 Seasons, Frame, 14 x 28 In. 230.00
1908, F. Marquardsen, Cowgirl, Sitting On Rock, 11 1/4 x 21 In. 1210.00
1908, Lady Golfer, Red Skirt, White Blouse, Frame, 13 x 27 In. 265.00
1908, Lady, Black Dress, Frame, 24 x 32 In. 165.00
1908, Lady, Lavender, Die Cut, Lithograph, Frame, 17 x 24 In. 375.00
1908, Smiles & Tears, Black Girl In Dunce Cap, Raphael Tuck, Die Cut, 10 3/4 In. 275.00
1908, Tompkins Co. Fire Insurance, N.Y., L. Rhead Fishing Print, Full Pad, 6 x 3 In. 275.00
1908, Victorian Lady, Red Flowers, Die Cut, Embossed, Frame, 17 x 27 In. 360.00
1909, Osborne Harvesting Machines, Cowboy, Shooting Antelope, 14 x 20 In. 935.00
1910, Hood's, Girl, Pink Bow In Hair, Frame, 13 x 12 In. 120.00
1910, L.L. Croner, Butcher & Grocer, Boy, Girl, Die Cut, Embossed, 14 x 20 In. 250.00
1910, Peters Cartridge Co., 2 Men In Canoe, 14 x 27 In. 4400.00
1911, Hood's, Lady, Red Roses In Hair, Frame, 10 x 14 In. 155.00
1911, Pratts, Woman, Apple, Horse, 8 x 12 1/2 In. 468.00
1911, Sharples Separator Co., Lady With Separator, Frame, 12 x 19 In. 190.00
1912, Bristol Fishing Rods, Honeymoon Campers, 17 1/4 x 30 3/4 In. 415.00
1912, White House Shoes, Lady, Red Dress, Frame, 18 x 36 In. 605.00
1913, Cowgirl, Hat, Scarf, Die Cut, Embossed, Frame, 24 x 24 In. 440.00
1913, Girl, Horse, Dog, Frame, 12 x 15 In. 195.00

Calendar Paper, 1905, Harrington & Richardson Arms, Lady, Gun, Lithograph, 26 x 14 In.

Calendar Paper, 1924, Arthur L. Potter Insurance Co., Log Rollers, 10 1/4 x 3 3/4 In.

Calendar Paper, 1951, Clicquot Club Beverages, Eskimo, Girl, 22 1/2 x 14 In.

1913, O.H. Woodward-Gen. Hardware, Lady, Die Cut, Embossed, Frame, 14 x 20 In. 198.00
1913, Wm. Volkland, Kansas, Girls In Car, Frame, 14 x 20 In. 330.00
1914, Pabst Extract, Victorian Lady, Orange Dress, 10 x 37 In. 220.00
1914, Winchester, Hunter, Dogs, Corn, 15 1/4 x 30 1/4 In. 1820.00
1915, Boy, Girl Reading Book, Die Cut, Embossed, 11 x 15 In. 285.00
1915, Warren Linderman, Fishing Scene, Full Pad, Reading, Pa., 23 x 11 1/2 In. 1045.00
1916, DeLaval Cream Separators, Boy, Girl, On Counter, Frame, 16 x 28 In. 375.00
1916, Hood's Sarsaparilla, Lady, Orange Bow In Hair, Frame, 9 x 17 In. 85.00
1916, Libby, McNeil & Libby, Girl, Blue Dress, Glass Back, Frame, 12 x 18 In. 276.00
1916, P. Squillanti-Wholesale Grocer, Lady, White Dress, Linen, Frame, 22 x 27 In. 265.00
1917, Dutch Boy Painter, Armstrong & McKelvey, Frame, 20 x 44 In. . . . . .558.00 to 578.00
1917, Pabst Extract, Lady, Yellow Dress, 7 x 35 In. 315.00
1917, Pabst Extract, Lady, Yellow Dress, Black Stole, Frame, 13 x 40 In. 250.00
1918, Walker Hardware, Stagecoach Being Held Up, 20 x 16 In. 176.00
1919, Bride, Holding White Flower Bouquet, Frame, 13 x 18 In. 22.00
1921, Edison Mazda, Primitive Man, Maxfield Parrish, Frame, 23 x 12 In. 2310.00
1921, Peters Shoes, J.F. Campbell, Lady, Horse, Frame, 21 x 22 In. 305.00
1923, Trail Blazer, Cowboy On Horse, Salesman's Sample, 10 x 16 1/2 In. 198.00
1924, Arthur L. Potter Insurance Co., Log Rollers, 10 1/4 x 3 3/4 In. . . . . *Illus* 145.00
1925, Edison Mazda, Small Dream Light, Maxfield Parrish, Frame, 21 x 11 In. 470.00
1925, Remington, Let're Rain, 15 x 28 1/2 In. 358.00
1925, U.S. Cartridges Shot Shells, Duck Hunter, 34 x 16 1/4 In. 2760.00
1926, McCormick Deering Co., Lady With Basket, Frame, 18 x 30 In. 200.00
1926, V.J. Plewa, Up To Date Shoe Store, 2 Girls, Roses, Die Cut, Frame, 15 x 22 In. . . . 330.00
1928, Peters Cartridge Company, Frame, 18 x 34 In. 415.00
1928, Remington, Hunter In Cabin, Dog, Fireplace, 27 1/2 x 15 In. 405.00
1928, Western Ammunition, Snow Geese, 15 x 28 In. 525.00
1929, Sharp Bros. Milk, Lady, Red Roses, Frame, 22 x 48 In. 330.00
1929, Winchester, Game Birds, Dog, Frame, 14 3/4 x 26 In. 2080.00
1930, Dutch Boy Painter, Dutch Boy White Lead, Frame, 20 x 30 In. 550.00
1931, Dutch Boy Painter, Frame, 40 x 21 In. 440.00
1932, Dutch Boy White Lead Paint, Frame, 19 x 40 In. 250.00
1933, Thoms Murphy Co., Sunshine Pinup, Girl At Beach, 20 x 14 In. 165.00
1934, Winchester, Boy On Fence, Dog, 27 1/4 x 16 In. 2185.00
1935, Lucerne Market, Loggers, Recipe Foldout, 8 1/2 x 5 3/4 In. 165.00
1937, Corn Belt Serum Co., Baby, Chasing 2 Pigs On Bike, Frame, 17 x 23 In. 110.00
1937, Thomas Murphy Co., Sunrise, Sample, Maxfield Parrish, 13 3/4 x 7 1/2 In. 330.00
1937, Thomas Murphy Co., Sunrise, Sample, Maxfield Parrish, 18 1/2 x 10 3/4 In. 240.00
1938, Broadmoor Hotel, Celluloid, Maxfield Parrish, Pocket, 2 1/4 x 3 3/4 In. 330.00
1938, Edison Mazda, Egyptian Priestess, Parrish, 19 1/8 x 8 1/2 In. 798.00
1940, Evening Shadows, Maxfield Parrish, Brown & Bigelow, 33 3/8 x 16 In. 330.00
1940, Harley-Davidson, Tin Lithograph Back, So. Dakota Dealer, 3 x 5 3/4 In. 580.00

1943, A Perfect Day, Maxfield Parrish, 16 x 22 In. 55.00
1944, Corn Belt Laboratories, Baby With Pig, Frame, 17 x 23 In. 99.00
1947, Boy, Big Fish, Men, Small Fish, A.L. Wolf & Son, Pa., Frame, 18 x 29 In. 230.00
1947, Sacramento Rubber Co., Evening, Maxfield Parrish, Frame, 13 x 17 In. 66.00
1948, Harry's Place, Dog, Wild Turkey, 9 x 16 In. 95.00
1948, Miles City Saddlery Co., Wagon Train, 17 1/2 x 27 1/2 In. 745.00
1950, Sunlit Valley, Maxfield Parrish, Brown & Bigelow, 33 1/4 x 16 In. 210.00
1951, A.W. McGee Garage, Bayard, Iowa, Feathers, Red Felt, Cardboard, 7 x 12 In. 25.00
1951, B & B Plumbing, Girl, In Hat, Horse, Frame, 13 x 20 In. 55.00
1951, Clicquot Club Beverages, Eskimo, Girl, 22 1/2 x 14 In. .... *Illus* 72.00
1952, Gay Products Company, If It's Gay, It's Okay, Woman, 10 1/2 x 5 1/2 In. 49.00
1952, Myers Truck Lines, Knox City, Mo., Cowgirl, Horse, 12 x 20 3/4 In. 25.00
1953, Clicquot Club, Ginger Ale, Eskimo Boy, Holding Bottle, 12 x 23 In. 70.00
1954, Old Glen Mill, Maxfield Parrish, Brown & Bigelow, 33 1/2 x 16 In. 385.00
1962, Whitman's Chocolates, Yellow, Red, Tin, Paper, 13 x 19 In. 250.00
1964, Playboy Playmate, Original Sleeve 78.00
1971, Old Dutch Beer, Box 37.50
1992, Joe Camel Scenes, Camel Coupon, 2 Page Joe Camel Poster 39.00
1992, Joe Camel Year In Pictures, Joe At Piano, White Dinner Jacker 84.00
1993, Joe Camel Weekends 84.00

CALENDAR PLATES were very popular in the United States from 1906 to 1929. Since then, plates have been made every year. A calendar and the name of a store, a picture of flowers, a girl, or a scene were featured on the plate.

1909, H.C. Paulsen Jewelers, Sonora, Calif., Rose Center, Homer Laughlin 70.00
1909, V.J. Leight General Merchandise, Bird With Ribbon, House Springs, Mo. 60.00
1910, Oriental Drug Co., Children Playing, Chanute, Kansas 60.00
1911, Tinsmith Stove Roofing Co., Horse, Horseshoe, Luzerne, Penn., 7 In. 35.00
1964, Gold Tracery, Taylor, Smith & Taylor, 10 In. 17.00
1965, Blue Heaven, Blue & Black, Royal China Co. 25.00
1969, Currier & Ives, Green, Royal China Co., 10 In. 35.00
1974, God Bless Our Home, Maroon Transfer, Alfred Meakin, England, 9 In. 8.00
1976, Bicentennial, Eagle, Japan 20.00
1978, Samurai, Wedgwood, 10 1/4 In. 10.00

CAMARK POTTERY started in 1924 in Camden, Arkansas. Jack Carnes founded the firm and made many types of glazes and wares. The company was bought by Mary Daniel. Production was halted in 1983.

Figurine, Bear Lifting Fishbowl On 4 Paws, Green 160.00
Figurine, Cat Staring Into Fishbowl, Peach 175.00
Figurine, Dog, White, 12 x 8 In. 450.00
Lamp Base, Shouldered, Stylized Landscape, Blue, Gray, Ivory, Shade, 10 In. 978.00

CAMBRIDGE GLASS Company was founded in 1901 in Cambridge, Ohio. The company closed in 1954, reopened briefly, and closed again in 1958. The firm made all types of glass. Their early wares included heavy pressed glass with the mark *Near Cut*. Later wares included Crown Tuscan, etched stemware, and clear and colored glass. The firm used a C in a triangle mark after 1920. Some Cambridge patterns may be included in the Depression Glass category.

2 Kid, Flower Frog, 9 x 4 In. 330.00
2 Kid, Flower Frog, Amber, 9 1/4 In. 160.00
Apple Blossom, Compote, Willow Blue, 7 1/8 x 7 1/4 In. 275.00
Apple Blossom, Plate, Cheese & Cracker, Amber, 2 Piece 145.00
Apple Blossom, Platter, Gold Krystol, Rectangular, 3/4 x 8 1/4 In. 190.00
Apple Blossom, Relish, 3 Sections, Heatherbloom, 1 7/8 x 9 In. 250.00
Bashful Charlotte, Flower Frog, 8 1/4 x 4 1/8 In. 175.00
Bashful Charlotte, Flower Frog, Peach-Blo, 11 In. 350.00
Buzz Saw, Cruet, Marigold Carnival, 4 In. 250.00
Candlelight, Vase, Crown Tuscan, Keyhole, Gold Encrusted, 12 In. 200.00
Caprice, Bowl, Alpine, Crimped, 4-Footed, 4 x 13 In. 145.00
Caprice, Bowl, LaRosa, Crimped, 4-Footed, 12 1/2 In. 165.00

Caprice, Bowl, Moonlight Blue, 4-Footed, 13 x 3 5/8 In. 125.00
Caprice, Bowl, Moonlight Blue, Alpine, Crimped, 4-Footed, 12 In. ....185.00 to 200.00
Caprice, Bowl, Moonlight Blue, Crimped, Footed, 9 1/2 x 4 1/2 In. 140.00
Caprice, Bowl, Moonlight Blue, Footed, Flared, 12 3/4 x 3 3/4 In. 130.00
Caprice, Bowl, Moonlight Blue, Oval, Tab Handles, 4-Footed, 11 In. 165.00
Caprice, Bowl, Salad, Cupped, 4-Footed, 3 x 13 In. 195.00
Caprice, Candlestick, 2-Light, Moonlight Blue, 7 1/2 In. 800.00
Caprice, Candlestick, 2-Light, Shell Bobeches, 7 1/2 In. 265.00
Caprice, Candlestick, Moonlight Blue, Bobeche, 7 In., Pair 159.00
Caprice, Candy Dish, Cover, 3-Footed, 6 In. 120.00
Caprice, Celery Dish, 3 Sections, Moonlight Blue, 2 1/4 x 13 In. 250.00
Caprice, Compote, Moonlight Blue, 6 In. 150.00
Caprice, Cordial, Pistachio, 1 Oz. 145.00
Caprice, Cruet, Stopper, Moonlight Blue, 3 Oz. 200.00
Caprice, Ice Bucket, Alpine, 4-Footed, Chrome Handle, 5 3/4 x 6 1/2 In. 110.00
Caprice, Jug, Ball, Moonlight Blue, 80 Oz. 275.00
Caprice, Salt & Pepper, Moonlight Blue, Silver Holder 130.00
Caprice, Sherbet, Low, 6 Oz. 95.00
Caprice, Vase, Teal, Crimped Top, 4 1/2 In. 195.00
Carmen, Champagne, Clear Stem & Foot, 6 Oz. 180.00
Carmen, Console Set, Leaf, 3 Piece 900.00
Chantilly, Candlestick, Hurricane Shade, Bobeche, Keyhole Stem, 11 1/4 x 5 In. 250.00
Chantilly, Candy Dish, Cover, Sterling Silver Foot, 7 x 5 1/2 In. 200.00
Chantilly, Cordial, 1 Oz., 4 3/4 In. 125.00
Chantilly, Pitcher, Martini, Stirrer, 8 3/4 x 6 In. 300.00
Chantilly, Sherbet, Hollow Stem, 5 3/4 x 3 In. 290.00
Chantilly, Sugar & Creamer, Scrolled Handles 50.00
Cleo, Bowl, Console, Peach-Blo, 8 3/8 In. 200.00
Cleo, Candy Dish, Cover, Willow Blue 510.00
Cleo, Console, Footed, 11 In. 135.00
Crown Tuscan, Basket, 14 In. 350.00
Crown Tuscan, Bowl, Oval, Footed, 12 In. 145.00
Crown Tuscan, Bowl, Shell, 3-Toed, 10 In. 160.00
Crown Tuscan, Candlestick, Nude Stem, 8 1/2 In. 230.00
Crown Tuscan, Compote, Shell, 4 1/2 x 6 In. 60.00
Crown Tuscan, Compote, Shell, Footed, 8 In. 185.00
Crown Tuscan, Vase, Cornucopia, Footed, 9 1/2 In. 125.00
Crown Tuscan, Vase, Flowers, Gold Encrusted, Collar, Squat, 3 1/4 In. 150.00
Crown Tuscan, Vase, Gold Encrusted, 7 In. 230.00
Decagon, Sugar & Creamer, Tray, Ebony, Handles 180.00
Dolphin, Candlestick, 2-Light, Royal Blue, Pair 549.00
Draped Lady, Flower Frog, 8 1/2 In. ....165.00 to 175.00
Draped Lady, Flower Frog, Amber, 8 1/2 In. 150.00
Draped Lady, Flower Frog, Frosted, 12 1/2 In. 210.00
Draped Lady, Flower Frog, Light Emerald, 8 1/2 In. 114.00
Draped Lady, Flower Frog, Light Emerald, Oval Base, 8 1/2 In. 340.00
Draped Lady, Flower Frog, Oval Base, 12 1/2 In. 325.00
Draped Lady, Flower Frog, Peach-Blo, 8 1/2 In. 180.00
Ebony, Bookends, Scottie Dogs 100.00
Ebony, Decanter, Pinch, 6-Sided Stopper, 10 1/4 In. 110.00
Ebony, Vase, Gold Encrusted, 7 x 8 In. 80.00
Ebony, Vase, Roses, Hand Painted, 16 In. 2000.00
Elaine, Jug, Ball, Tilted, 80 Oz. 155.00
Everglade, Bowl, Buffalo Hunt, Amber, 16 In. 160.00
Everglade, Bowl, Tulip, Ebony, 15 In. 380.00
Figurine, Bridge Hound, Carmen, Hole For Pencil, 1 3/4 In. 210.00
Georgian, Tumbler, Amber 10.00
Georgian, Tumbler, Juice, 3 3/4 In. 10.00
Helio, Vase, Gold Trim, 8 In. 135.00
Heron, Flower Frog, 8 3/4 x 4 In. 130.00
Larosa, Candlestick, 3 Levels, Pair 100.00
Mandolin Lady, Flower Frog, 9 1/2 In. 240.00
Martha Washington, Vase, Milk Glass, Fan Shape, 8 1/2 In. 55.00

Mt. Vernon, Relish, Emerald Green, 5 Sections, 12 In. 85.00
No. 742, Jug, Cover, Etched, 63 Oz. 650.00
Nude, Ashtray, Carmen 255.00
Nude, Champagne, Heatherbloom Bowl, Clear Stem & Feet, 6 Oz. 435.00
Nude, Cigarette Box, Amethyst 495.00
Nude, Cigarette Box, Carmen 500.00
Nude, Cocktail, Carmen, Crackled Bowl, Clear Stem & Foot 1800.00
Nude, Cocktail, Ebony, 3 Oz., 6 1/2 In. 95.00
Nude, Cocktail, Forest Green, Frosted Stem, 3 Oz., 6 1/2 In. 110.00
Nude, Cocktail, Gold Krystol, 3 Oz., 6 1/2 In. 275.00
Nude, Cocktail, Peach-Blo, Frosted Stem, 3 Oz., 6 1/2 In. 110.00
Nude, Cocktail, Royal Blue, 3 Oz., 6 1/2 In. 205.00
Nude, Compote, 8 In. 195.00
Nude, Compote, Amber, Farberware, 7 1/4 x 5 1/2 In. 95.00
Nude, Compote, Heatherbloom, 8 In. 986.00
Nude, Cordial, Royal Blue, 1 Oz. 435.00
Nude, Ivy Ball, Carmen 395.00
Portia, Relish, 8 In. 35.00
Portia, Vase, Crown Tuscan, Gold Encrusted, 10 In. 280.00
Portia, Vase, Crown Tuscan, Keyhole, Gold Encrusted, 12 In. 400.00
Reamer, Saucer Type, Small Loop Handle, 4 1/8 In. 20.00
Rosalie, Bottle, Dressing, Green, 7 1/8 In. 270.00
Rose Point, Basket, 5 In. 330.00
Rose Point, Bowl, Crimped, 4-Footed, 12 In. 110.00
Rose Point, Bowl, Oval, Handles, 4-Footed, 12 In. 500.00
Rose Point, Butter, Cover, 1/4 Lb. 500.00
Rose Point, Butter, Cover, Round, 5 1/2 In. 175.00
Rose Point, Cake Plate, Handles, 13 1/2 In. 130.00
Rose Point, Candlestick, 3-Light, 5 1/2 x 7 1/2 In., Pair 240.00
Rose Point, Candlestick, 3-Light, 6 1/4 x 6 5/8 In., Pair 250.00
Rose Point, Candlestick, 4 In., Pair 110.00
Rose Point, Candlestick, Ram's Head, 4 1/2 x 4 3/4 In., Pair 195.00
Rose Point, Candy Box, Cover, Cut Finial, 6 In. 150.00
Rose Point, Candy Dish, Gold Encrusted, 3 1/2 x 8 In. 140.00
Rose Point, Candy Dish, Lid, 5 x 5 3/4 In. 230.00
Rose Point, Celery Dish, 11 1/2 x 5 In. 140.00
Rose Point, Claret, 4 1/2 Oz., 6 1/4 In. 130.00
Rose Point, Cocktail Shaker, 32 Oz. 175.00
Rose Point, Cocktail, 3 1/2 Oz., 6 In. 60.00
Rose Point, Compote, Handles, 8 x 9 1/4 In. 180.00
Rose Point, Cordial, 1 Oz. 85.00
Rose Point, Creamer, Footed 120.00
Rose Point, Decanter, No. 1321 .... 285.00
Rose Point, Dish, Mayonnaise, Sterling Silver Trim, 4 x 6 1/4 In. 175.00
Rose Point, Dish, Mayonnaise, Underplate, Ladle, Gold Trim 135.00
Rose Point, Goblet, 10 Oz. 40.00
Rose Point, Honey, Cover, Square, Handles ....455.00 to 510.00
Rose Point, Jam Jar, Lid, Spoon, 5 1/2 In. 230.00
Rose Point, Jug, Ball, Tilted, 80 Oz. 285.00
Rose Point, Oyster Cocktail, 4 1/2 Oz. 40.00
Rose Point, Parfait, 5 Oz., 6 1/4 In. 115.00
Rose Point, Parfait, Gold Encrusted, 5 Oz., 6 1/4 In. 230.00
Rose Point, Pitcher, Doulton, 80 Oz. 375.00
Rose Point, Pitcher, Martini, 60 Oz. 560.00
Rose Point, Plate, Dinner, 10 1/2 In. ....160.00 to 200.00
Rose Point, Relish, 3 Sections, 7 1/2 In. 70.00
Rose Point, Relish, 3 Sections, 10 In. 150.00
Rose Point, Relish, 5 Sections, 1 1/8 x 10 1/2 In. 130.00
Rose Point, Relish, Plate, Inserts, 12 In., 6 Piece 250.00
Rose Point, Salt & Pepper, Ball, 2 x 2 In. 170.00
Rose Point, Sandwich Server, Center Handle, Square, 5 1/4 x 10 3/4 In. 230.00
Rose Point, Sherbet, 7 Oz., 4 5/8 In. 135.00
Rose Point, Sherry, 2 Oz. 95.00

Rose Point, Sugar, Footed 120.00
Rose Point, Torte Plate, 14 In. 375.00
Rose Point, Tumbler, Juice, Footed, 5 Oz. 40.00
Rose Point, Tumbler, Juice, Footed, Blown, 5 Oz. 120.00
Rose Point, Vase, Bud, 10 In. 70.00
Rose Point, Vase, Cornucopia, 10 In. 200.00
Rose Point, Vase, Crown Tuscan, 6 1/8 x 2 1/4 In. 190.00
Rose Point, Vase, Flip, 8 In. 250.00
Rose Point, Vase, Globe, 6 1/2 In. 270.00
Rose Point, Vase, Keyhole Stem, Gold Encrusted, 10 1/8 In. 180.00
Rose Point, Wine, 2 1/2 Oz. 75.00
Scottie Dog, Decanter Set, Juice, Red, Enameled, 5 Piece 1000.00
Shell, Dish, Windsor Blue, Footed, 5 1/2 x 8 3/4 In. 190.00
Stackaway, Ashtray Set, Blue, Emerald, Amber, Amethyst, Clear, 5 Piece 65.00
Swan, Dish, Black, 4 In. 40.00
Swan, Dish, Dark Emerald Green, 8 1/2 In. 150.00
Swan, Dish, Ebony, Flower Block, 11 1/2 In. 275.00
Tally Ho, Hat, Amethyst, 6 3/8 x 10 1/4 In. 290.00
Tally Ho, Wine, Cobalt Blue, 2 1/2 Oz., 6 1/2 In. 90.00
Temple, Jar, Pink, 6 3/4 x 6 In. 290.00
Tulip Etch, Water Set, Light Emerald, 7 Piece 215.00
Wildflower, Candy Dish, Gold Trim, 5 1/2 x 5 3/4 In. 230.00
Wildflower, Candy Dish, Ruffled Edge, 3 1/2 x 5 1/2 In. 80.00
Windsor Etch, Vase, Castle, Ebony Foot, 12 In. 2000.00

CAMBRIDGE POTTERY was made in Cambridge, Ohio, from about 1895 until World War I. The factory made brown glazed decorated artwares with a variety of marks, including an acorn, the name *Cambridge*, the name *Oakwood*, or the name *Terrhea*.

Vase, Orange Flowers, Brown Glaze, Marked, 5 1/2 In. 115.00

CAMEO GLASS was made in much the same manner as a cameo in jewelry. Parts of the top layer of glass were cut away to reveal a different-colored glass beneath. The most famous cameo glass was made during the nineteenth century. Signed cameo glass pieces are listed under the glasswork's name, such as Daum or Galle.

Biscuit Jar, Apple Blossoms, Leaves, Silver Plated Collar & Cover, 6 1/2 x 5 In. 2875.00
Bottle, Flowers, Leaves, Lapidary Stopper, 6 1/2 In. 300.00
Bottle, Scent, Blue Over Clear, Amber Flowers, Sterling Cover, 3 3/4 In. 345.00
Bowl, Morning Glory, White Over Cranberry, Ruffled Edge, 4 x 10 In. 1150.00
Jug, Claret, Morning Glories, Leaves, Vines, Silver Handle, Rim, 8 3/4 In. 1265.00
Tumbler, Citron Flowers, Leaves, Wheel Cut Clear Base, 2 3/4 x 2 In. 60.00
Vase, Aqua Vining Foliage, Rim, Cristallerie De Pantin & TVSc, 4 1/2 In. 315.00
Vase, Arsall, Green Trees, Birds, Meadows, Orange Lake, 7 1/4 In. 690.00
Vase, Birds On Branch, Red & Black Cut To Clear, Art Nouveau, 13 In. 275.00
Vase, Brown Leaves & Berries, Yellow Ground, Weis, 1 3/4 In. 127.00
Vase, Flowers, Branches, Leaves, Maroon Over Orange, Signed, D'Argyl, 9 In. 460.00
Vase, Flowers, Stems, Butterfly, Mottled Cream & Lavender Ground, Weis, 10 In. 518.00
Vase, Maroon Iris, Dragonfly, Clear Frosted Ground, Swollen, Flattened, 14 In. 605.00
Vase, Meadow, Trees, Elk, Lake, Arsall, 14 1/4 In. 960.00
Vase, Square, Trees, Meadow, Pink, Enamel, Lamartine, 1910, 2 1/2 x 2 3/4 In. 1150.00

CAMPAIGN memorabilia is listed in the Political category.

CAMPBELL KIDS were first used as part of an advertisement for the Campbell Soup Company in 1906. The kids were created by Grace Drayton, a popular illustrator of the day. The kids were used in magazine and newspaper ads until about 1951. They were presented again in 1966; and in 1983, they were redesigned with a slimmer, more contemporary appearance.

Bank, Cast Iron, Painted, Raised Letters, Williams, 4 1/4 In. 200.00
Bank, Cast Iron, Williams, c.1910-1920 .... 345.00
Book, Campbell Kids Have A Party, Alma Lach, Rand McNally, 1954 .... 125.00
Cookie Jar, Chef Hat, Soup Bowl, M'm M'm Good, Pottery, 9 1/4 x 6 In. 11.00

Display, Tin Marquee, Metal Rack, Cooking Unit, 28 In. 330.00
Doll, Composition, Painted Features, Blue Romper, Chef's Hat, Horsman, Box, 12 In. 495.00
Doll, Composition, Painted Features, Blue Shorts, Cap, Horsman, Box, 12 In. 385.00
Doll, Paul Revere & Betsy Ross, 1976, 10 1/2 In., Pair 85.00

CANDELABRUM refers to a candleholder with more than one arm to
hold many candles; a candlestick is designed to hold one candle. The
eccentricity of the English language makes the plural of candelabrum
into candelabra.

2-Light, Art Nouveau, Figural, Flowering Iris Stems, Germany, 13 In., Pair 5875.00
2-Light, Blanc-De-Chine Porcelain, Bronze Mount, William Brownfield, 9 1/2 In. 865.00
2-Light, Brass, Iron, Prisms, Victorian, c.1860, 16 x 15 In., Pair 250.00
2-Light, Bronze, Marble, Blackamoor, Belle Epoque, c.1900, 19 In., Pair 3450.00
2-Light, Chrome, Stylized Deer, Hagenauer, Vienna, 6 1/4 x 6 1/2 In. 690.00
2-Light, Cut Glass, Bronze Mounted, Acorn Finial, Anglo Irish, 13 In. 1175.00
2-Light, Gilt Bronze, Cut Glass, Louis XVI Style, c.1900, 13 x 10 1/2 In., Pair 750.00
2-Light, Gilt Bronze, Empire Style, Tapered Ionic Columns, Scroll Feet, 22 In., Pair 2272.00
2-Light, Gilt Bronze, Louis XVI Style, 11 In., Pair 470.00
2-Light, Iron, Penny Foot Tripod Base, Adjustable, 23 In. 715.00
2-Light, Louis XV Style, Gilt Bronze, Coiled Serpents, Early 1900s, 10 In., Pair 144.00
2-Light, Louis XVI Style, Gilt Brass, Cut Glass, Electrified, 20 x 12 In., Pair 575.00
2-Light, Louis XVI Style, Sevres Biscuit, Bronze, Orry, c.1860, 12 x 8 In., Pair 2185.00
2-Light, Pewter, Celtic-Art Nouveau, Tudric, England, 10 1/2 In. 2025.00
2-Light, Polished Chrome, Chase, Walter Von Nessen, 9 1/2 x 8 3/4 In., Pair 145.00
2-Light, Silver Plate, Baluster Stem, Sheffield, c.1790, 15 3/4 x 15 In., Pair 1150.00
2-Light, Silver, Empire Style, Flame Finials, Germany, Late 1800s, 8 1/2 In., Pair 1415.00
2-Light, Wrought Iron, Samuel Yellin, 19 3/4 In. 5875.00
3-Light, .800 Sterling, Undulating Stems, Gadroon, 9 1/4 x 10 x 4 1/2 In., Pair 250.00
3-Light, Baccarat, Molded, Cut Glass, 17 1/4 In., Pair 1725.00
3-Light, Brass, Coat Of Arms, c.1880-1900, 14 1/4 x 9 x 5 In., Pair 170.00
3-Light, Bronze, Directoire Style, Colorless Glass, Early 1900s, 12 In., Pair 470.00
3-Light, Bronze, E.T. Hurley, 1918, 15 In., Pair 2070.00
3-Light, Bronze, Empire Style, Winged Figure, Bouquet, 21 1/4 In. 2390.00
3-Light, Bronze, Empire Style, Winged Maiden, Arched Garland, 16 1/4 In., Pair 1795.00
3-Light, Bronze, Scroll Arms, 8-Sided Pierced Base, Oscar Bach, 19 In. 1175.00
3-Light, Empire, Bronze, Marble, 16 1/2 In., Pair 329.00
3-Light, Figural, Classically Dressed Man, Woman, Porcelain, 19 x 7 In., Pair 560.00
3-Light, Gilt Bronze, Brass, Napoleon III, Louis XVI Style, c.1885, 12 x 8 3/4 In. 489.00
3-Light, Gilt Metal, Alabaster, Louis XVI Style, 27 In. 765.00
3-Light, Iron, Hammered, Cutout Leaf Design At Center, Arts & Crafts, 13 In. 1175.00
3-Light, Louis XV Style, Gilt Bronze, 10 In., Pair 478.00
3-Light, Molded Glass, Dolphin Standards, France, Late 1800s, 19 In. 460.00
3-Light, Patinated Bronze, Classical Style, Gilt, Maidens, Lilies, Gilt, 35 In. 2475.00
3-Light, Renaissance Revival, Gilt Bronze, Scroll Feet, Late 1800s, 18 3/4 In., Pair 520.00
3-Light, Sheffield Plate, Batwing Sconces, England, 1800s, 15 1/2 x 12 1/4 In., Pair 940.00
3-Light, Silver Plate, Sheffield, 21 1/2 x 16 In., Pair 290.00
3-Light, Silver Plate, Shell Marks, England, 20th Century, 19 1/2 In., Pair 325.00
3-Light, Silver Plate, Thistle Form Nozzle, 1900s, 19 1/4 x 18 1/2 In., Pair 635.00
3-Light, Silver, Simpson, Hall, Miller, 12 1/2 x 11 In., Pair 364.00
3-Light, Sterling Silver, 20 x 16 In. 400.00
4-Light, Argente Bronze, Napoleon III Style, Putti, Sheffield, 20 1/2 In., Pair 1495.00
4-Light, Brass, Circular Base, 11 3/4 x 12 3/4 In., Pair 1035.00
4-Light, Cherub, Gilt Bronze, Patinated, 19 In., Pair 2375.00
4-Light, Gilt, Bronze, Napoleon III, France, c.1860-1885, 22 In., Pair 1456.00
4-Light, Gilt, Eglomise Plaque, 16 x 17 In. 730.00
4-Light, Glass, Gilt Bronze, Louis XV Style, c.1900, 25 3/4 In., Pair 945.00
4-Light, Hand Painted, Flower Relief, Cherubs, Sitzendorf, c.1910, 18 x 11 In., Pair 450.00
4-Light, Louis XV Style, Gilt Bronze, Scrolling Leaves, c.1890, 17 1/4 In., Pair 1380.00
4-Light, Porcelain, Women, Putti, Flowers, Germany, Late 1800s, 16 1/2 In., Pair 460.00
5-Light, 4-Arm, Silver Plate, Beaded Edge, Central Flame, 15 1/2 x 14 1/2 In. 110.00
5-Light, Blue Opaline Glass, Ormolu, Ribbed Body, Rococo Style Base, 1800s, 27 In. 430.00
5-Light, Brass, Applied Milk Glass Flowers, Openwork Tripod Base, Gilt, 20 In., Pair . . . 195.00
5-Light, Brass, Continental, 15 1/4 In., Pair 180.00

5-Light, Brushed Metal, Incised Sunburst, Tommi Parzinger, 20 1/4 x 13 In. 1725.00
5-Light, Charles X, Gilt, Patinated Bronze, c.1825, 29 In., Pair 5465.00
5-Light, Cut Crystal, Baccarat, 10 In., Pair 708.00
5-Light, Empire Style, Porcelain, Blue, White, France, c.1900, 20 x 9 1/2 In., Pair 4200.00
5-Light, French Style, Gilt Bronze, Marble, Flower, Acanthus Leaves, c.1875, 30 In. 750.00
5-Light, Gilt & Patinated Bronze, Charles X, c.1835, 21 1/2 In., Pair 2990.00
5-Light, Gilt Bronze, Alabaster, Charles X Style, Late 1800s, 19 1/2 In., Pair 415.00
5-Light, Gilt Bronze, Champleve, Urn Form Standard, France, c.1860, 24 In., Pair 4600.00
5-Light, Gilt Bronze, Napoleon III, Cherub On Orb, c.1860, 20 In., Pair 1265.00
5-Light, Louis Philippe, Bronze, Gilded, Black, Neoclassical, c.1835, 22 1/2 In. 3910.00
5-Light, Louis XV Style, Gilt Bronze, Electrified, France, c.1810, 23 In., Pair 1150.00
5-Light, Louis XV Style, Gilt, Prism Drops, 29 In., Pair 290.00
5-Light, Louis XVI Style, Bronze, Marble, Cherub, Flower Spray, 29 In. 270.00
5-Light, Louis XVI Style, Gilt Bronze, Mounted As Lamp, 24 In. 480.00
5-Light, Louis XVI Style, Victorian, Bronze, Black Onyx, 26 1/2 In., Pair 385.00
5-Light, Porcelain, Rococo Revival, Blue, White, Figurine Base, Sitzendorf, 21 In. 2070.00
5-Light, Renaissance Revival, Ebonized, Brass, Continental, Early 1900s, 29 In. 635.00
5-Light, Renaissance Style, Brass, Continental, Early 1900s, 21 3/4 In., Pair 290.00
5-Light, Renaissance Style, Brass, Continental, Early 1900s, 24 In., Pair 290.00
5-Light, Renaissance Style, Scrolled Arms, Tripod Base, Wrought Iron, 59 In., Pair 265.00
5-Light, Scrolled, Open Work, Silver Plate, Reed & Barton, 16 In. 100.00
5-Light, Silver Plate On Copper, S-Shaped Arms, 1900s, 17 x 18 In. 920.00
5-Light, Silver Plate, Baluster Stem, Scrolling Arm Rests, Rogers, 11 1/4 In. 60.00
5-Light, Silver Plate, Gorham, 21 1/2 In., 3 Piece 235.00
5-Light, Silver Plate, Lobed Baluster Stem, Cohannet Silver Co., Mass., 20 In. 118.00
5-Light, Silver Plate, Rococo Style, Epergne, c.1900, 16 x 15 In., Pair 290.00
5-Light, Silver, Convertible, Finland, 1900s, 18 In., Pair 1725.00
5-Light, Sterling Silver, Round Base, Baluster Stem, Embossed Flowers, 15 In., Pair 7770.00
5-Light, Sterling, Convertible, 20th Century, 14 1/2 In., Pair 175.00
5-Light, Sterling, Hand Chased, Convertible, Early 20th Century, 15 5/8 In., Pair 3525.00
5-Light, Thistle Shaped Scones, Dominick & Haff, Early 1900s, 18 In., Pair 6169.00
5-Light, Wrought Iron, Cat Figure, Goberg, 13 1/2 x 11 3/4 In., Pair 230.00
6-Light, Center Socket, Candle, Bronze, Gilded, Tripod, Minerva, Cherubs, 24 1/2 In. 440.00
6-Light, Center Turn Post, 4 Columns, Beaded Edge, Silver Plate, 21 x 18 1/2 In. 250.00
6-Light, Column, Neoclassical Style, Corinthian, Pine, Painted, 54 In., Pair 1840.00
6-Light, Empire Style, Bronze, Marble, Lamp Mounted, 31 In., Pair 2150.00
6-Light, Flower Garland, Scrollwork, France, 1800s, 24 In., Pair 1840.00
6-Light, German Porcelain, Stylized Tree, Schierholz, Early 1900s, 20 In., Pair 355.00
6-Light, Gilt Brass, Black Slate, Neogrecque, Lion Masks, Napoleon III, 26 In., Pair 2070.00
6-Light, Gilt Bronze, Italy, Mid 19th Century, 26 1/2 In., Pair 1840.00
6-Light, Gilt Bronze, Marble, Louis XV Style, c.1900, 19 5/8 In., Pair 1416.00
6-Light, Louis Philippe, Tapering, Scrolled Branches, c.1840, 26 In. 2530.00
6-Light, Louis XV Style, Floriform, Bronze, 22 In., Pair 2390.00
6-Light, Louis XV Style, Gilt Bronze, Prisms, Electrified, 36 In. 956.00
6-Light, Louis XV Style, Ormolu, Putto, Verdigris Patinated Hair, c.1900, 28 In. 635.00
6-Light, Louis XVI Style, Gilt Bronze, Classical Maiden, c.1850, 27 1/2 In., Pair 1955.00
6-Light, Louis XVI Style, Gilt Bronze, Scrolled Arms, Late 1800s, 22 1/2 In., Pair 470.00
6-Light, Louis XVI Style, Neoclassical Female, Gilt Bronze, Late 1800s, Pair 1035.00
6-Light, Napoleon III, Tripodal, Gilt Bronze, 36 1/2 x 9 1/2 In., Pair 1725.00
6-Light, Paneled, Fluted, Turned Column, Scroll Arms, c.1820, 12 x 15 1/2 In. 489.00
6-Light, Putto, Seated, Grasping Torchere, Louis XVI Style, Gilt-Bronze, 26 In., Pair 6600.00
7-Light, Brass, Wrought Iron, Beveled Edge Marble Base, 19 1/4 x 26 In., Pair 460.00
7-Light, Electroplated, Mirrored Plateau, Serpentine Arms, Late 1800s, 13 5/8 In. 2470.00
7-Light, Empire Style, Columns, Gilt Bronze, 29 In., Pair 1650.00
7-Light, Gilt Bronze, Baluster, Scrolling Arms, Leaf Form, Scalloped, 27 1/2 In. 230.00
7-Light, Gilt Bronze, Neoclassical Style, Garland Leaf & Shell, c.1890, 22 In. 230.00
7-Light, Gilt Bronze, Woman, Louis XVI Style, Electrified, c.1890, 28 3/4 In., Pair 2700.00
7-Light, Gilt Metal, Marble, Napoleon III, 23 1/2 x 11 In. 560.00
7-Light, Louis XV Style, Ormolu, Bronze, Putto Clipping Wing, c.1900, 30 In. 11265.00
7-Light, Louis XVI Style, Bronze, Mounted As Lamp, 31 In., Pair 1016.00
7-Light, Napoleon III, Gilt & Patinated Bronze, Maiden, c.1850, 33 x 16 In., Pair 4600.00
7-Light, Napoleon III, Patinated Bronze, Greek Revival Style, 31 In., Pair 1840.00
7-Light, Rococo Style, Silver, Germany, c.1900, 24 In., Pair 3680.00

7-Light, Scrolled Lily, Gilt Bronze, Black Marble, France, 19th Century, 31 In., Pair 5750.00
8-Light, Louis XV Style, Flower Filled Cornucopia, Bronze, Gilt, 30 In., Pair 2475.00
9-Light, Louis XV Style, Putto, Cornucopia, Gilt, Patinated Bronze, 30 In., Pair 4400.00
10-Light, Empire Style, Bronze, Scrolled Branches, Late 19th Century, 26 In., Pair 1150.00
11-Light, Gilt Bronze, Marble, Flower Fern Arms, France, Late 1800s, 41 x 15 In. 1095.00
13-Light, Brass, Stylized Tree, Bruno Paul, Dresden, Germany, c.1901, 16 In. 1880.00
24-Light, Tin, Anniversary, Candle, Serrated Arms, New York, 16 In., Pair 130.00
Bronze, Hanging, Monkey Finial, Lion Mounts, 13 1/2 In. 259.00
Bronze, Hurley, Sea Horses, 9 x 13 In. 1150.00
Girandole, 2-Light, Mirror, Murano, Amber, Engraved Glass, 25 x 14 x 8 In., Pair 1840.00
Girandole, 3-Arm, Bronze, Lyre Form, Pair 150.00
Girandole, 3-Light, Gilt Bronze, Indians, Scout, Crystal Prisms, 17 1/2 In., Pair 480.00
Girandole, 3-Light, Gothic Revival, Gilt Brass, W.F. Shaw, Boston, c.1850, 17 5/8 In. ... 633.00
Girandole, 3-Light, Lyre Form, Gilt Metal, Prisms, Victorian, 18 1/4 x 17 In., Pair 518.00
Girandole, 5-Arm, Prisms, Cornelius, Philadelphia, c.1845, 17 x 23 In. 865.00
Girandole, Gilt Bronze, Patinated, Late Regency, c.1825, 9 In., Pair 1093.00
Porcelain, Woman By Tree, Blue & White, Germany, c.1900, 12 In. 85.00
Sconce, 2-Light, Edwardian, Silvered Nickel, Patinated Bronze, c.1900, 24 In., Pair 1840.00
Sconce, 2-Light, Silvered Nickel, Charles II Style, Eagle, c.1890, 12 x 9 In., Pair 2990.00
Sconce, Brass, Swollen Candlecup, Drip Pan, Scrolled Arm, England, 6 In., Pair 3290.00
Silver Plate, Continental, Tapered Stem, Chased Leaves, c.1880, 18 In., Pair 865.00
Silver Plate, Regency Style, 20th Century, 15 1/4 x 14 1/2 In., Pair 316.00

CANDLESTICKS were made of brass, pewter, glass, sterling silver, plated silver, and all types of pottery and porcelain. The earliest candlesticks, dating from the sixteenth century, held the candle on a pricket (sharp pointed spike). These lost favor because in times of strife the large church candlesticks with prickets became formidable weapons, so the socket was mandated. Candlesticks changed in style through the centuries, and designs range from classic to rococo to Art Nouveau to Art Deco.

Amber Glass, Pairpoint, Cut Grape Design, Hollow Stem, 10 1/2 In., Pair 400.00
Blown Glass, Sommerso, Antonio Da Ros, Italy, 1960s, 5 x 14 1/4 In., Pair 935.00
Bone, Black Details, Anglo-Indian, c.1900, 11 1/2 In., Pair 345.00
Brass, 2 Swellings On Shaft, Faceted Ridged Base, England, c.1720, 6 3/8 In. 235.00
Brass, 6-Footed, Baluster Turnings, Continental, Early 1800s, 9 1/4 In. 175.00
Brass, Acanthus Leaf Decoration, Trefoil Base, Bronze Finish, 11 In., Pair 220.00
Brass, Alpha Shape, Flat Circular Base, Arts & Crafts, Jarvie, 11 In., Pair 1175.00
Brass, Baluster Form, Georgian, Early 19th Century, 11 In., Pair 200.00
Brass, Baluster Form, Push-Up, 8 1/4 In., Pair 69.00
Brass, Baluster Form, Push-Up, 9 1/2 In., Pair 69.00
Brass, Bead & Rope Banding, Lobed Urn Sockets, Round Base, 13 In., Pair 385.00
Brass, Beehive, England, 14 In., Pair 375.00
Brass, Beta Shape, Circular Base, Arts & Crafts, Jarvie, 12 1/2 In. 1645.00
Brass, Capstan, Tooled Edge, Flared Socket, Raised Rim, 4 3/4 In. 745.00
Brass, Capstans, Lower Quarter Saucer, Dutch, 4 1/4 In., Pair 225.00
Brass, Chippendale Style, Scalloped Base, 7 3/4 In., Pair 525.00
Brass, Continental, Baluster Shaft, Bulbed Base, 1660-1670, 10 3/4 In. .... *Illus* 2115.00
Brass, Cylindrical Candlecup, Ring Turned, Baluster, Square, Paw Feet, Spain, 6 7/8 In. ... 441.00
Brass, Cylindrical Sconce, Double Knop Stem, Square Base, c.1775, 6 3/8 In., Pair 235.00
Brass, Cylindrical Sconce, Knopped Baluster Stem, Late 1700s, 7 In., Pair 440.00
Brass, Diamond Design, Push-Up, 8 In., Pair 115.00
Brass, Dome Base, Twisted Stem, Flared Socket, Hand Threaded Post, 12 1/4 In., Pair ... 360.00
Brass, Drip Pan, Handle, 4 1/4 x 6 1/4 x 7 In., Pair 230.00
Brass, Embossed Queen Of Diamonds, 11 1/2 In., Pair 250.00
Brass, Empire, Vasiform Shafts, Square Base, 8 3/4 In., Pair 25.00
Brass, Everted Top Flange, 1660-1670, 10 3/4 x 7 3/4 In. 2115.00
Brass, Extractor, Cylindrical Stem, Domed Round Foot, c.1750, 6 3/8 In., Pair 205.00
Brass, Federal, Square Base, Tapered Columns, Cast Initial H, 9 1/2 In. 110.00
Brass, Federal, Tapered Shaft, Step-Out Capitols, Square Base, 8 1/2 In., Pair 95.00
Brass, Flared Molded Base, Drip Tray, 3 1/4 In., Pair 440.00
Brass, Flared Top, Ring Turned On Flared Base, Push-Up, 6 1/4 x 3 1/4 In., Pair 110.00
Brass, Flower Blossom Punch Decoration, 17th Century, 21 3/4 x 10 3/8 In. 560.00

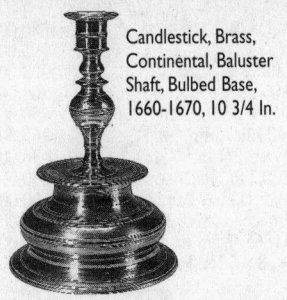

Candlestick, Brass,
Continental, Baluster
Shaft, Bulbed Base,
1660-1670, 10 3/4 In.

**Wax on your antique metal
candlesticks? Put the candlesticks
in the freezer. After a few hours,
the wax will easily flake off.**

Brass, George III, Push-Up, Columnar Standard, Circular Foot, Late 1700s, 8 In.	69.00
Brass, Good Luck Form, 1800s, 11 1/2 In., Pair	175.00
Brass, Heemskeerk, Cylindrical Sconce, Double Knop Stem, 9 1/4 In.	175.00
Brass, Hexagonal Base, Mid 17th Century, 11 1/2 In., Pair	3055.00
Brass, Hexagonal Base, Seamed Column, 6 & 5 3/4 In., Pair	259.00
Brass, Iron, Conical Green Tole Shade, Louis Philippe, c.1835, 16 In., Pair	1380.00
Brass, King Of Diamond Form, 1800s, 14 In., Pair	175.00
Brass, King Of Diamond Form, Late 1800s, 12 1/2 In., Pair	175.00
Brass, Neoclassical, Fluted Tulip Sconce, Square Foot, c.1800, 10 3/4 In., Pair	265.00
Brass, Paneled Baluster Stem, Octagonal Base, 7 1/4 In.	175.00
Brass, Patinated, Regency Style, Mounted As Table Lamps, 31 1/2 In., Pair	489.00
Brass, Queen Anne, Early 18th Century, 8 1/8 In., Pair	880.00
Brass, Queen Anne, Heavy Casting, Scalloped Base, Petal Socket, 8 3/8 In., Pair	865.00
Brass, Queen Anne, Scalloped, Center Band & Rim, Baluster Turned Stem, 7 In.	605.00
Brass, Queen Anne, Square Seamed, Scalloped Base, 6 3/4 In.	275.00
Brass, Queen Anne, Turned Shaft, Gadrooned, c.1705, 7 1/2 In.	1500.00
Brass, Ring Turned, Flared Top, Push-Up, 6 x 3 1/4 In.	112.00
Brass, Ring Turned, Rectangular Base, Push-Up, 6 x 2 1/2 x 3 In., Pair	75.00
Brass, Ring Turned, Tapered Square Base, Push-Up, 6 x 3 x 3 In., Pair	85.00
Brass, Rope Twist, Open Double Twist, Turned Base, England, c.1890, 12 In., Pair	219.00
Brass, Sand Casting, Tripod Harpy Bases, Griffins, Acanthus, 12 3/4 In.	165.00
Brass, Sconce, Fretwork, Rolled Rivet, Candleholder, 17th Century, Dutch	1400.00
Brass, Seamed Sockets, Stems, Octagonal Base, 6 1/4 In., Pair	430.00
Brass, Square Base, Push-Up, 6 1/2 In., Pair	230.00
Brass, Tapered Seams, Circular Base, Ring Turned, 19th Century, 13 1/2 In., Pair	138.00
Brass, Tapered, Oval, Circular Bases, Cupped Drip Plates, 19th Century, 16 1/8 In., Pair	195.00
Bronze, Alabaster, 3 Griffins, France, Second Empire, Late 1800s, 5 3/4 In., Pair	235.00
Bronze, Bear On Chair, Cub, Violin, Monkey, Christophe Fratin, 13 1/8 In., Pair	1175.00
Bronze, Cherub Riding Crocodile, 8 1/2 In., Pair	600.00
Bronze, Chinese, Heron Shape, Pricket, 21 1/8 In., Early 20th Century, Pair	590.00
Bronze, Gilt, Tapered, Octagonal, Leaf & Dot Borders, 19th Century, 10 1/2 In., Pair	605.00
Bronze, Louis XV Style, Holder, c.1840, 9 In., Pair	460.00
Bronze, Oval Sconce, Fluted Baluster, Foot, Ogee Base, 9 1/2 In., Pair	470.00
Bronze, Prestion, Jessie, No. 12, Anderson Foundry Mark, 8 x 13 In., Pair	4025.00
Bronze, Pricket, Gilt, Continental, 17 In., Pair	236.00
Bronze, Putto, Fruit Filled Urn, F. Barbedienne, Paris, Late 1800s, 6 In., Pair	575.00
Bronze, Rocaille Leaf Sconce, Acanthus Leaf Base, Louis XV Style, 4 In., Pair	150.00
Bronze, Wall, Mythological Figure, 1800s, 8 3/4 In., Pair	2070.00
Bronze Dore, Acorn Finial, Swan Mounted Cups, Flowers, France, 9 1/2 In., Pair	1430.00
Cast Brass, Insects, Lizards, 7 x 4 3/4 In., Pair	140.00
Chamber, Deep Dish, Loop Handle, Brass Push-Up, London, 1836, 10 1/2 x 5 1/2 In.	259.00
Chamber, Jessie Preston, Bronze Handle, 7 1/2 In.	1955.00
Chamber, Sheffield Plate, Regency, Matthew Boulton, c.1810, 4 x 5 3/4 In., Pair	635.00
Chamber, Tin, 2 Sockets, Oval Base, Crimped Edge, Finger Ring, Suffer Cap, 10 x 13 In.	201.00
Cloisonne, 2-Cup, Bird, Enamel, Bronze, Chinese, 1900s, 8 In., Pair	1800.00
Cloisonne, Deer Shape, Pricket Form, Chinese, 17 In., Pair	290.00
Copper, Hammered, Faceted, Squat, Dark Patina, Stickley Brothers, 10 In., Pair	1380.00
Copper, Hammered, Roycroft, 6 In., Pair	460.00
Copper, Hammered, Stickley, Onondaga, 9 3/4 In., Pair	1100.00

Copper Finish, Slender Stem, Jarvie, Early 1900s, 13 7/8 In. 380.00
Elephant, Lying Down, Polychrome, Porcelain, 6 x 8 In., Pair 1095.00
Fanfare, 3 Heights, Kjeel Endman, c.1960, Tallest 11 1/4 In., 3 Piece 223.00
Flared, Waisted Form, Domed Base, Flint Enamel, 8 1/2 In., Pair 805.00
Gilt Brass, Carved, Ebony Lacquered, Parcel Gilt, Napoleon III, 19 1/2 In., Pair 750.00
Gilt Brass, Louis XVI Style, Louis Philippe, Mid 19th Century, 23 In., Pair 1265.00
Gilt Bronze, Alabaster Inset, Art Nouveau, c.1900, 4 1/4 x 5 5/8 x 3 3/4 In. 30.00
Gilt Bronze, Charles X, Faceted Tiers, Octagonal Plinth, c.1825, 12 In., Pair 230.00
Gilt Bronze, Louis Philippe, Neoclassical, Ribbed Shaft, c.1830, 9 1/2 In., Pair 520.00
Gilt Bronze, Louis XVI Style, Rose Bouquet, Marble Center, France, c.1890, 16 In., Pair . 1610.00
Gilt Bronze, Urn Form Sconce, Cleopatra, Egyptian Revival, c.1865, 7 5/8 In., Pair 440.00
Gilt Metal, Egyptian Revival Style, Painted Profiles, Late 1800s, 8 x 5 In., Pair 115.00
Gilt Wood, Florentine Style, 17 1/2 In., Pair 405.00
Glass, Canary, Stepped Base, Fluted Column, Petal Socket, 9 1/2 In. 69.00
Glass, Clambroth To Pink Swirl, Hand Blown, 9 x 4 3/8 In., Pair 170.00
Glass, Dolphin, Blue & Clambroth, Dolphins On Socket, 1-Step Base, 10 1/4 In. 2935.00
Glass, Double Knop Stem, Gallery Socket, Pressed Base, Stepped, 9 3/8 In., Pair 1650.00
Glass, Florentine, Celeste Blue, Carnival Glass, 8 1/2 In. 165.00
Glass, Hand Blown, Amber, Ribbed, Twisted Hollow Stem, Saucer Foot, Flat Rim, 10 In. .. 29.00
Glass, Hand Blown, Clambroth To Pink Swirl, 9 x 4 3/8 In., Pair 150.00
Glass, Hexagonal Shape, Square Stepped Base, England, 1800s, 10 1/4 In., 4 Piece 259.00
Glass, Hexagonal, George VI, c.1900, 9 1/4 x 5 In., Pair 175.00
Glass, Ribbed Flared Socket, Pressed Base, Circular Steps, Square Foot, 11 1/2 In. 2310.00
Glass, Twisted Trefoil Form, Baccarat, 6 1/4 In., Pair 230.00
Hogscraper, Saucer Base, Bulbous Bobeche, Push-Up, Tin, 6 1/2 In., Pair 395.00
Iron, Hand Forged, Holder, 3 Legs, c.1770, 15 In. 520.00
Iron, Handwrought, Chamber, Goberg, 8 In. 145.00
Iron, Hog Scraper Style, Brass Wedding Bands, 1800s Style, 8 3/4 In., Pair 248.00
Iron, Pan, Candle Socket, Signed, 18th Century 595.00
Iron, Spiral, Wood Base, 18th Century, 8 1/4 In. 248.00
Iron, Wood Handle, Socket & Pricket Holders, Early 1800s, 11 1/2 x 3 In. 345.00
Metal, Tulip Shape Cup, Hammered, Beaded, Monogram M, 3 1/4 In., Pair 135.00
Mixed Metal, Chamber, Aesthetic Movement, Meriden, c.1890, 5 In. 265.00
Mixed Metal, Copper, Applied Bird, Frog, Chamber, Gorham, Early 1900s, 2 7/8 In. 440.00
Paktong, Column Standard, Square Stepped Base, George III, c.1790, 6 1/2 In., Pair 750.00
Paktong, Corinthian Column, Gadrooned Base, George III, c.1790, 10 5/8 In., Pair 2530.00
Paktong, Flared Leaf Cast Bobeche, George II, c.1750, 8 1/2 In., Pair 4140.00
Paktong, Lobed Bobeche, Gadroon Basea, George II, c.1750, 10 In., Pair 5750.00
Paktong, Scallop Shell Molded Leaf Base, George II, c.1750, 8 1/2 In., Pair 3450.00
Paktong, Shell Cast Bobeche, Shell & Scroll Base, George II, c.1750, 12 1/4 In., Pair ... 5750.00
Pewter, Hammered, Patina, A.M. & Co., England, Arts & Crafts, 10 In. 750.00
Porcelain, Gilt Woman Holding Calla Lily, Art Nouveau Style, Chamber, c.1900, 5 In. ... 185.00
Porcelain, Jacob Petit, Leaf Form, Flower Heads, Chamber, c.1865, 3 In. 575.00
Porcelain, Maidens Holding Torchere Candle Cups, Flowers, Germany, 45 In., Pair 345.00
Porcelain, Metal, Flowered Bough, Frog, Gilt Base, 6 3/4 In., Pair 460.00
Porcelain, Parrots On Stumps, Cherries, Gilt Brass Mounts, 1887, 14 In, Pair 3740.00
Porcelain, Rose Medallion Colors, Japan, Chamber, c.1850, 5 In. 140.00
Porcelain, Rose Medallion, Trumpet Form, Bird & Flower, 8 In., 4 Piece 1840.00
Pressed Glass, Cobalt Blue, Hexagonal, 9 1/8 In., Pair 489.00
Pressed Glass, Eiffel Tower Shape, 10 1/2 In., Pair 140.00
Pressed Glass, Hexagonal, Cobalt Blue, Boston & Sandwich Glass, 1 5/8 x 1 1/8 In. 415.00
Rock Crystal, Bronze, Dome Pedestal, 6-Sided Plinth, Electrified, 21 In., Pair 4025.00
Sheffield Plate, Columnar Stems, Reeded Nozzles, c.1900, 9 1/8 In., 4 Piece 560.00
Sheffield Plate, Egg Shape Sconces, Loop Handle, Chamber, 1800s, 4 In., 4 Piece 765.00
Sheffield Plate, Georgian, Thistle Nozzle, M. Boulton, c.1800, 12 1/4 In., Pair 1265.00
Silver, Adam Form, Corinthian Column Socles, Sheffield, c.1810, 12 1/2 In., Pair 660.00
Silver, Baroque Style, Possibly Hungary, c.1785, 13 1/2 In., Pair 1095.00
Silver, Chernigov, Russia, 1838, 9 1/2 In., Pair 2480.00
Silver, Column Form, Ponce, Continental, c.1800, 7 In., Pair 1150.00
Silver, Columnar, Beaded Stepped Base, Hawkesworth, Eyre, England, 9 In., Pair 920.00
Silver, Engraved Bands, Ball & Claw Feet, J.C. & J.C., Brazil, c.1850, 9 In., Pair 540.00
Silver, George II, Gadrooned Rim, Ionic Column, Jas. Allen, 1765, 11 1/2 In., Pair 3525.00
Silver, George III, Cylindrical Base, Snuffer, Chamber, London, 1774 .... 890.00

Silver, Knopped Stem, Octagonal Base, Anthemia, George III, England, 9 1/2 In., Pair ... 5060.00
Silver, Neoclassical, Cylindrical Sconce, Tapered Stems, Late 1700s, 9 1/4 In., Pair 1880.00
Silver Gilt, Openwork Design, Leaves, Masks, Renaissance Revival, 6 1/4 In. 265.00
Silver Plate, Adam Style, Sheffield, 12 In. 69.00
Silver Plate, Adam Style, Weighted Square Bases, Urn Sockets, 11 1/2 In., 8 Piece 2300.00
Silver Plate, Baluster, Urn Sconce, Flower Wreath, Sheffield, c.1785, 11 In., Pair 1035.00
Silver Plate, English Baroque Style, Marked, T.E. Wharton, 10 1/4 In. 190.00
Silver Plate, Federal Style, Oval, Tapered, Reeded Columns, 11 1/4 In., Pair 248.00
Silver Plate, Gadroon Decoration, England, 7 In., Pair 69.00
Silver Plate, George III Style, Flatted Oval Body, Beaded Edge, 11 1/2 In., 4 Piece 865.00
Silver Plate, Hurricane Shade, Tapered Stem, Trumpet Foot, 1800s, 20 3/4 In., Pair 529.00
Silver Plate, Leaftip Molded Nozzle, Round Foot, 5 1/2 In., 4 Piece 265.00
Silver Plate, Lyre Form, Oval, 12 1/2 x 5 x 4 1/2 In. 330.00
Silver Plate, Mounted As Lamp, Sheffield, Early 19th Century, 10 In., Pair 546.00
Silver Plate, Old Sheffield Plate, Intaglio Cut Shades, 21 In., Pair 495.00
Silver Plate, Queen Anne Style, Spink & Son, London, 6 1/2 In., 4 Piece 345.00
Silver Plate, Raised Flowers, 8 1/2 x 4 3/4 In., Pair 50.00
Silver Plate, Sheffield, Early 19th Century, 11 1/2 In., Pair 690.00
Silver Plate, Telescoping, Sheffield, 7 1/2 In., Pair 240.00
Sterling Silver, Baluster Stem, Reed & Barton, c.1900, 10 1/2 In., 4 Piece 1840.00
Sterling Silver, Baluster, Leaves, Monogram, Whiting, 19th Century, 9 In., Pair 895.00
Sterling Silver, Bell Shape Hurricane Shade, England, 20th Century, 20 5/8 In., Pair 235.00
Sterling Silver, Bell Shape, Acanthus Rim, Cylindrical Stem, England, 1800s, 11 In. 150.00
Sterling Silver, Circular, Cross-Form Pedestal Foot, Allan Adler, c.1950, 5 In., Pair 4540.00
Sterling Silver, Corinthian Column, Gorham, c.1959, 10 1/4 x 4 1/4 In., Pair 259.00
Sterling Silver, Corinthian Column, Sheffield, England, 1950, 9 In, Pair 1195.00
Sterling Silver, Danish Modern Style, Clarence Vanderbilt, c.1930, 4 x 5 In., Pair ....../. 230.00
Sterling Silver, Denmark, c.1910, 9 x 5 1/2 In., Pair 805.00
Sterling Silver, Filled, Weighted, Box, England, 9 In., Pair 440.00
Sterling Silver, George III, Masks, John Carter, c.1771, 12 1/2 In., 4 Piece 13225.00
Sterling Silver, George III, Satyr's Masks, John Carter, c.1771, 12 1/2 In., Pair ..3450.00 to 5465.00
Sterling Silver, Grape, Twist Stem, Georg Jensen, Denmark, 1920s, 5 3/4 In., Pair 4600.00
Sterling Silver, Lord Saybrook, Round Base, International, 9 1/2 x 4 1/2 In., Pair 125.00
Sterling Silver, Neoclassical Style, Weighted, Round Nozzle, Faceted Stem, 9 In. 118.00
Sterling Silver, Queen Anne Style, George V, England, 1911, 8 3/8 In., Pair 940.00
Sterling Silver, Round Base, Ribbed Edge, Tapered, Vase Shaped, France, 9 In., Pair 978.00
Sterling Silver, Round Base, Tapering, Flared Candle Holder, Continental, 8 1/2 In., Pair . 635.00
Sterling Silver, Tubular Stem, Oval Socket, Shreve, Crump & Low, c.1905, 14 In., Pair .. 5975.00
Terra-Cotta Stoneware, Enamel Band, Aesthetic Taste, c.1885, 7 In., Pair 2760.00
Wood, Carved, Irises, c.1900, 14 1/2 In., Pair 115.00
Wrought Iron, Cast, Brass, Patinated Green Finish, Arts & Crafts, 12 3/4 In., Pair 323.00
Wrought Iron, Spiral, Adjustable, Turned Wood Base, 7 1/2 In., Pair 92.00
Wrought Iron, Spiral, Scrolled Push-Up, Turned Wood Base, 8 1/4 In. 259.00
Wrought Iron, Spiral, Spike Lip Hanger, Scrolled Push-Up, Wood Base, 7 3/4 In. 413.00
Wrought Iron, Spiral, Turned Wood Base, 7 3/4 In. 220.00
Wrought Metal, Bobeche, Pierced Spear, Arts & Crafts Style, 19 1/2 In., Pair 175.00
Yellowware, Dark Green Alkaline Glaze, 6 In., Pair 855.00

CANDLEWICK items may be listed in the Imperial and Pressed Glass categories.

CANDY CONTAINERS have been popular since the late Victorian era. Collectors have long favored the glass containers, but now all types, including tin and papier-mache, are collected. Probably the earliest glass container sold commercially was the Liberty Bell made in 1876 for sale at the Centennial Exposition. Thousands of designs were made until the cost became too high in the 1960s. By the late 1970s, reproductions were being made and sold without the candy. Containers listed here are glass unless otherwise described. A Belsnickle is a nineteenth-century figure of Father Christmas. Some candy containers may be listed in Toy or in other categories.

Airplane, Liberty Motor, Biplane, Glass Body, Tin Lithograph Frame, 5 x 6 1/2 In. 1265.00
Airplane, P-38 Lightning, Coarse Glass, Vertical Tail Ribbon, c.1942, 7 1/8 In. 140.00
Airplane, T.M.A. 44, Cardboard Wings, Metal Cap, T.H. Stough, c.1939, 4 In. 165.00

Amos 'n' Andy, Open Air Taxi, Red Wheels, Victory Glass Co., 1928, 4 1/2 In. 330.00
Barney Google & Ball, Standing On Pedestal, c.1927, 3 3/4 In. 140.00
Barney Google & Bank, Ribbed Barrel, Tin Screw Cap, Coin Slot, c.1923, 3 In. 800.00
Baseball Player, Necktie, Belt, Cloth Dressed, On Base, Papier-Mache, 7 In. 1320.00
Baseball Player, Screw Metal Cap, Shaker Holes, c.1916, 5 In. 550.00
Battleship On Waves, Gold Tin Base, 5 1/4 In. 195.00
Bear In Car, Cap & Suit, Blown Glass, Metal Screw Cap, 5 In. 220.00
Bear On Circus Tub, Tin Spinner, Hose, c.1916, 4 1/4 In. 250.00
Bear Reading Book, Seated On Suitcase, Blown Glass, Metal Screw Cap, 4 1/4 In. 55.00
Bell, School, Blown Clear Glass, Metal Cap, Bead & Teardrop, 6 In. 220.00
Bell, School, Wood Handle, Blown Glass, c.1910, 7 In. 745.00
Belsnickle, Papier-Mache, Mica Base, 11 1/2 In. 1650.00
Bird On Mound, Metal Whistle Tip, c.1918, 2 3/4 In. 275.00
Boat, Cruiser, J.H. Millstein, 1945, 4 1/2 In. 11.00
Boat, Submarine F.6., Clear Glass, Tin Lithograph Tower, Tin Flag, Base, 5 3/4 In. 385.00
Bobbie Blake, Holding Rabbit, Composition, 6 In. .... *Illus* 99.00
Boot, Santa Claus's, Merry Christmas Label, 3 1/4 In. 11.00
Box, Man & Woman, Hand Painted, Paperboard, Glass Cover, Round, 3 In. .... *Illus* 175.00
Boy, On Snowball, Bisque Head, Papier-Mache, Germany, 7 In. 440.00
Bus, Electric Omnibus Company, Tin Lithograph, Meier, 3 1/4 In. 1265.00
Bus, Greyhound, Blue Paint, Paper Label, V.G. Co., 5 In. 360.00
Bus, Victory Glass Co., 3 Sections, Brown Paint, 5 3/8 In. 605.00
Bus, Victory Glass Co., 3 Sections, Green Paint, Silver Wheels, 5 3/8 In. 525.00
Bus, Victory Line Special, Blue Painted Body, 4 3/4 In. 35.00
Camera On Tripod, Red, Black, Metal Legs, Red String & Ball, 5 1/2 In. 275.00
Candy Corn, Papier-Mache, Germany, 9 1/2 In. 35.00
Cannon, Glass, 2 Wheel Mount, No. 1, Tin Carriage, c.1930, 4 1/2 In. 250.00
Cannon, Glass, 4 Wheel Mount, Tin Carriage, c.1920, 4 3/4 In. 20.00
Cannon, U.S. Defense Field Gun No. 17, Glass, Tin Barrel, Screw Cap, 4 1/4 In. 248.00
Car, Bottle Sedan, Volkswagen, Plastic Screw Back Lid, 6 In. 10.00
Car, Coupe, Glass Body, Tin Wheels, Tin Closure, 4 1/4 In. 415.00
Car, Electric Runabout, Open Top, Tin Closure, Contents, c.1914, 3 1/2 In. 35.00
Car, Flat Front, Ribbed Grill, Red Lid, 4 In. 330.00
Car, Open Top, Rubber Wheels, Cork Closure, T.H. Stough, 3 3/4 In. .... *Illus* 22.00
Car, Racing, No. 2, Clear Glass, Spoked Wheels, 3 5/8 In. 55.00
Car, Racing, No. 12, Ribbed Grill, Back Fin, Tin Closure, 5 3/8 In. 55.00
Car, Sedan, Green, Tin Wheels, Tin Closure, 5 In. 165.00
Car, Sedan, Red, Tin Wheels, Tin Closure, 5 In. 110.00
Cash Register, c.1913, 3 In. 195.00
Cat, Black Cat For Luck, Clear Glass, Seated Cat, Metal Base, 4 1/4 In. 1320.00
Cat, Winking, Stretched Neck, Black, Metal Screw Cap, 5 In. 4730.00
Chick, In Eggshell Car, U.S.A., Victory Glass Co., 4 1/4 In. 55.00
Chick, Tin Snap-On Lid, 3 5/8 In. 250.00
Chicken, On Nest, Composition, Cardboard, Rye Straw Basket, 6 In. 90.00
Chicken, Woven Basket, Scalloped Tin Closure, 1900, 2 x 2 In. 640.00
Clock, Alarm, Pressed Clear Glass, Footed, Tin Cap, c.1909, 3 1/2 In. 145.00
Clock, Mantel, Paper Clock Face, Tin Slide Lid, c.1913, 3 3/4 In. 110.00
Clock, Milk Glass, Arched Top, Painted Ocean Scene, c.1909, 3 1/4 In. 285.00

Candy Container,
Bobbie Blake,
Holding Rabbit,
Composition, 6 In.

Candy Container,
Box, Man & Woman,
Hand Painted,
Paperboard, Glass
Cover, Round, 3 In.

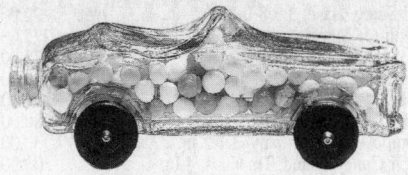 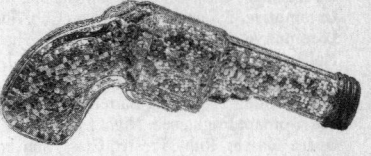

Candy Container, Car, Open Top, Rubber
Wheels, Cork Closure, T.H. Stough, 3 3/4 In.

Candy Container, Gun, Red Screw Cap,
Marked, Avor, 5 1/2 In.

Crystal Palace, 6 In.	140.00
Display Case, Showcase Full Of Candy 10 Cents, Paper Label, c.1913, 3 In.	415.00
Dog, Bulldog With Collar, Metal Screw Cap, Victory Glass Co., c.1930, 4 1/4 In.	55.00
Dog, Bulldog, Seated, Cardboard Closure, T.H. Stough, 4 In.	45.00
Dog, Spaniel, Glass Eyes, Papier-Mache, Germany, 8 In.	330.00
Dog By Barrel Bank, 1 Ear Cocked, Brown Paint, Orange Screw-On Lid, 3 1/4 In.	195.00
Doll, Basket, With Baby, Painted, Provincial Dress, Late 19th Century, 8 1/2 In.	560.00
Dolly's Bathtub, Glass Feet, Victory Glass Co., Jeannette, Pa., 4 3/4 In.	3960.00
Drum, Milk Glass, Crossed U.S. Flags, Coin Slot Metal Lid, c.1906, 1 3/4 In.	550.00
Drum Mug, Ruby Flashed, Gettysburg 50th Anniversary, c.1909, 2 1/4 In.	250.00
Duck, In Sailor Suit, Composition, 10 In.	250.00
Duck, Nesting, Round Base, Metal Screw Cap, 2 5/8 In.	275.00
Ear Of Corn, Metal Screw Cap, 6 3/4 In.	55.00
Elephant, G.O.P., 3 In.	99.00
Elephant, Gray, Papier-Mache, 8 1/2 In.	330.00
Father Christmas, Bisque Head, 9 In.	560.00
Father Christmas, Papier-Mache, Cardboard, Wood Base, 7 3/4 In.	330.00
Felix The Cat, Barrel Bank, Hand On Hip, Snap On Lid, c.1922, 3 1/2 In.	385.00
Felix The Cat, On Pedestal, Metal Screw Lid, c.1922, 3 1/4 In.	2860.00
Fire Engine, Ladder Truck, Firemen, Tin Wheels, Victory Glass, c.1936, 5 1/4 In.	155.00
Fire Engine & Boiler, Clear Glass, Tin Base, 5 1/4 In.	35.00
Fountain, Tin, Painted, Embossed, 3 1/2 In.	220.00
French Military Vehicle, Lift Up Roof, Dunlop Balloon Tires, Tin, 6 In.	110.00
Gas Pump, 23 Cents To-Day, Rubber Hose, c.1925, 4 1/4 In.	250.00
George Washington, Bisque Head, Cloth Dress, Papier-Mache Horse, 11 In.	1045.00
Globe, Metal Stand, Screw Cap, Contents, 4 1/4 In.	110.00
Gun, Cambridge Automatic, Diamond Pattern Grip, 5 In.	99.00
Gun, Kolt, Black Painted Barrel, Red Metal Screw Cap, 4 1/2 In.	55.00
Gun, Red Screw Cap, Marked, Avor, 5 1/2 In. ....*Illus*	6.00
Happifats, On Drum, Metal Screw Bottom Cap, 4 1/2 In.	195.00
Hearse, Clear Glass, Fringe Tassels, Tin Lid, 4 3/8 In.	55.00
Helicopter, Tin Propellers, Ribbed Body, Cork Closure, T.J. Stough, 4 3/8 In.	55.00
Helicopter, Tin Roof Propeller, Metal Screw Cap, Contents, 4 3/8 In.	176.00
Horn, Trumpet, Milk Glass, Gilt Handle, Boy Fishing, Renova, Pa., c.1907, 5 1/2 In.	300.00
Horn, Trumpet, Red Metal Screw Lid, 5 1/2 In.	45.00
Hot Doggie, Amber, Closure, 5 5/8 In.	880.00
House, Green Shingles, Gable Attic Window, Tin Base, Sears, c.1919, 2 3/4 In.	195.00
Independence Hall, Philadelphia Centennial Exposition, 1876, 7 1/4 In.	195.00
Iron, Rope Cord, Electric Style, Paper Closure, Pla-Toy Co., 4 1/2 In.	44.00
Jackie Coogan, The Kid, Clear, Westmoreland Specialty, 1925, 5 In. ....300.00 to 468.00	
Kiddie Kar, Horse Head, 3 Glass Wheels, Victory Glass Co., c.1923, 4 1/4 In.	165.00
Lamp, George Washington Shade, Globe Shape, Tin Base, 5 1/4 In.	605.00
Lamp, Souvenir Of Boston, Ribbed, Paper Shade, 5 1/4 In.	110.00
Lamp, Tin Shade, Ribbed, Tin Screw Cap & Shade, 5 1/4 In.	66.00
Lantern, Auto Lamp, Teal Green Glass, Square, Tin Closure, c.1911, 4 1/4 In.	55.00
Lantern, Ball Shape, Glass, Beaded, Star Design Cap, Shaker Top, c.1913, 3 1/4 In.	6.00
Lantern, Ball Shape, Glass, Flower Design, Shaker Top, 3 1/4 In.	210.00
Lantern, Japanese Paper Type Glass, Tin Top Edge, Bail Handle, c.1916, 3 In.	935.00
Lantern, Teal Green Glass, 4-Sided, Inset Medallions, Metal Base, Screw Cap, 4 In.	6.00
Lemon Head, Washer Woman, Composition, Germany, 4 In.	470.00
Liberty Bell, Blown Glass, Philadelphia Centennial Exposition, 1876, 3 3/8 In.	55.00

Liberty Bell, Glass Bracket, Bail Handle, Metal Screw Base, 3 3/8 In. 22.00
Locomotive, 2 Stacker, Ruby Glass Cab, Souvenir Of Mauston, Wis., 2 3/4 In. 275.00
Locomotive, J.J. Brainard's 1893, Red Wheels, 4 In. 175.00
Mailbox, Silver Paint, Tin Base, c.1907, 3 1/4 In. 330.00
Motorcycle, Rider, U.S.A. Indian, Jenet, Pa., 5 In. 385.00
Mule, Pulling 2-Wheeled Barrel With Driver, Victory Glass Co., 4 1/2 In. ....45.00 to 80.00
Old Woman, Frightened, Night Cap, Gown, Composition, Germany, 3 1/2 In. 330.00
Opera Glasses, Ruby, Pressed Glass, Souvenir Of Coney Island, Tin Caps, 4 In. 303.00
Pear, Face, Pull Stem, Eyes & Mouth Move, Papier-Mache, 5 In. 415.00
Pencil, Baby Jumbo, Pencil Tip Closure, c.1939, 5 1/2 In. 110.00
PEZ, Casper The Friendly Ghost, Die Cut, 1960s 130.00
PEZ, Santa, 1950s 92.00
Phonograph, Glass Horn, Tin Slide Base, c.1915, 3 1/2 In. 330.00
Phonograph, Inkwell Type, Home Sweet Home, Horn, Glass, Tin, Contents, 2 1/2 In. 415.00
Piano, Upright, Clear Glass, Gilt Finish, Tin Slide Back, Coin Slot, 2 3/4 In. 120.00
Piano, Upright, Milk Glass, Gilt Finish, Tin Slide Back, Coin Slot, 2 3/4 In. 800.00
Pig, Pink, Head Moves, Molded Papier-Mache, 11 In. 550.00
Pumpkin Head Witch, Bespectacled Orange Head, 1920s, 4 3/4 In. 600.00
Purse, Rippled Finish, Ruby Flashed Banner, Tin Slide Base, 4 In. 690.00
Rabbit, Brown, White, Glass Eyes, Papier-Mache, Germany, 3 In. 155.00
Rabbit, In Eggshell, Metal Screw Cap, 5 1/4 In. 275.00
Rabbit, Millstein, Glass, Contents, Cardboard Insert, 6 1/4 x 4 In. 79.00
Rabbit, Mother & Daughter, Green Apron, Metal Screw Cap, 5 1/8 In. 440.00
Rabbit, Papier-Mache, W. Germany, 4 In. 50.00
Rabbit, Pushing Chick In Shell Cart, 4 In. 305.00
Rabbit, Running On Log, Flat, 4 1/2 In. 140.00
Rabbit, Standing, Legs Apart, Red Head, 5 1/2 In. 165.00
Rabbit, White, Pulling Brown Rabbit In Cart, Papier-Mache, Germany, 6 In. 605.00
Rabbit, With Basket On Arm, Metal Screw Cap, 4 3/8 In. 250.00
Rabbit, With Wheelbarrow, 4 1/8 In. 55.00
Rabbit Family, Flat Dimensional, V.G. Co., Jeannette, Pa., 4 3/4 In. 635.00
Radio, Tune In, Pressed Glass, c.1925, 4 1/2 In. 55.00
Rapid Fire Gun, Enameled Metal Carriage, Tin Cannon, c.1916, 7 3/4 In. 165.00
Reindeer, Plush, Composition, Metal Antlers, 11 In. 358.00
Rocking Horse, Saddle, Harness & Mane Definition, 4 1/2 In. 110.00
Rocking Horse, With Clown Rider, c.1919, 3 5/8 In. 140.00
Rocking Settee, Pressed Glass, c.1914, 2 3/4 In. 525.00
Rolling Pin, Wood Handles, Red Screw Caps, c.1930, 7 In. 155.00
Rooster, Crowing, Metal Screw-On Cap, 5 In. 250.00
Rooster, Papier-Mache, Painted, Pair 50.00
Safe, Penny Trust, Milk Glass, Tin Lid, Coin Slot, c.1907, 3 In. 110.00
Safe, Penny Trust, Pressed Glass, Tin Lid, Coin Slot, c.1907, 3 In. 80.00
Santa Claus, Banded Coat, Metal Screw Cap, 5 1/4 In. 55.00
Santa Claus, By Chimney, Green Suit, Coin Slot Lid, 3 5/8 In. 4290.00
Santa Claus, By Chimney, Red Suit & Chimney, 3 5/8 In. 110.00
Santa Claus, Cloth Dress, Papier-Mache, Cardboard Body, 11 1/2 In. 523.00
Santa Claus, Double Cuff, Red Suit, Black Boots, c.1925, 4 3/8 In. 110.00
Santa Claus, Leaving Chimney, Screw Cap, c.1925, 5 In. 248.00
Santa Claus, Robe, Chenille, Basket, Papier-Mache, Cardboard, Japan, 9 In. 440.00
Sign, Don't Park Here, Screw Cap, c.1925, 4 1/2 In. 110.00
Snowman, Flocked Body, Spring Bobbing Head, Stovepipe Hat, 1940s, 6 In. 55.00
Soldier, By Tent, Doughboy, Flat Figure, Painted, 3 1/4 In. 2805.00
Soldier, With Sword, Double Breasted Uniform, Helmet, 5 1/8 In. 305.00
Spark Plug, Horse, Saddle Blanket, Red Tin Snap Base, c.1923, 3 In. 75.00
St. Nicholas, Papier-Mache, Mohair Wig, Feather Tree, Germany, c.1910, 15 In. 2130.00
Statue Of Liberty, Glass Pedestal, Gilded Metal Figure, 5 3/4 In. 3520.00
Suitcase, Glass, Metal Bail Handle, Tin Slide Base, c.1908, 3 1/2 In. 22.00
Suitcase, Milk Glass, Boy Fishing, Metal Bail Handle, 3 1/2 In. 415.00
Suitcase, Milk Glass, Lord & Lady In Rowboat, Metal Bail Handle, 3 1/2 In. 525.00
Suitcase, Milk Glass, Roosevelt Bears, Metal Bail Handle, 3 1/2 In. 305.00
Swan Boat, With Rabbit & Chick, 4 1/4 In. 360.00
Sweeper, Dolly Tin Snap Lid, Twisted Wire Handle, c.1914 ....140.00 to 345.00
Tank, 2 Cannons, Cardboard Closure, Khaki Paint, Victory Glass, 4 1/8 In. 22.00

Taxi, Black & White Checkered Lid, Clear Glass, Tin Wheels, c.1920, 4 1/8 In. 660.00
Taxi, Yellow, Tin Wheels, 4 1/8 In. 770.00
Telephone, Candlestick, Blue Glass, Wooden Receiver, 5 In. 66.00
Telephone, Hello Central, Glass Body, Wood Receiver, Redlich's, 6 In. 468.00
Telephone, Number Please, Blown Glass, Pewter Top, Redlich's, c.1907, 4 In. 11.00
Toonerville Trolley, Depot Line, c.1920, 3 1/2 In. 330.00
Top, Glass Spinning, Wood Launcher, Tin Bracket, Victory Glass Co., c.1920s, 4 In. 55.00
Top, Spinning, Metal Launcher, Gibbs Toy, Victory Glass Co., c.1920s, 3 3/4 In. 11.00
Train, J.J. Brainard's 1923, Tin Lithograph Scene, 5 3/4 In., 3 Piece 525.00
Train, Overland Limited, Jeannette Glass Co., 5-In. Engine, 4 Piece 470.00
Truck, Bakery, Glass Body, Tin Cab & Roof, c.1920, 4 1/4 In. 1100.00
Trunk, Milk Glass, Souvenir Of Alexandria Bay, Tin Slide Base, 2 3/4 In. 55.00
Turkey, Gobbler, Defined Feathers, Comb, Wattles, 3 1/2 In. 90.00
Uncle Sam, By Barrel, Tin Screw Cap, Coin Slot, c.1918, 3 3/4 In. 275.00
Veggie Man, Baby Face, Potato Body, Composition, Germany, 5 1/2 In. 385.00
Veggie Man & Turnip, Painted Composition, Cardboard Slide, Germany, 4 In. 880.00
Wagon, U.S. Express, Tin Wheels, Wire Handle, West Bros., 4 1/4 In. 220.00
Washstand, Dollhouse, Pressed Glass, Mirrored Top, Tin Lid, 3 3/4 In. 660.00
Watch, Glass, Leather Strap 275.00
Wheelbarrow, Clear Glass, Red Tin Wheel & Lid, c.1935, 6 In. 66.00
Windmill, 5 Windows, Ruby Glass Base & Roof, 3 7/8 In. 440.00
Windmill, Dutch, Tin Blades, Pla-Toy Co., 5 In. 35.00
Windmill, Teddy Flag, Glass, Tin Operator's Room, West Bros. Co., 6 1/4 In. 300.00
Woman, Lemon Head, Washer, Blue Scarf, On Head, Composition, Germany, 4 In. 468.00
World War I, Tank, 4 Cannons, Glass, Raised Beads, c.1919, 4 1/4 In. 44.00
Ye Olde Oaken Bucket, Milk Glass, Gilt Paint, Tin Snap Lid, Bail Handle, 2 In. 55.00

CANES and walking sticks were used by every well-dressed man in the
nineteenth century, but by World War I the style had changed. Today
canes are used by few but the infirm. Collectors prize old canes made
with special features, like hidden swords, whiskey flasks, or risqué pictures seen through peepholes. Examples with solid gold heads or made
from exotic materials are among the higher-priced canes. See also
Scrimshaw.

Antler, Hardwood, George Washington Centennial, Long Live President, 37 1/4 In. 805.00
Bakelite, Bird Inset Eyes, Amber, 1935, 39 In. 120.00
Bamboo Sword, Stag Horn Handle, 35 1/2 In. 345.00
Beadwork, Geometric, Orange, Blue, White, Yellow, Brass Ferrule, Indian, 37 In. 529.00
Captain's, Whale Ivory, Rosewood, Brass Inlay, Going Ashore, 37 In. 750.00
College, Dartmouth, Indian Head, Black Hair, Signed B.M. Scolly, c.1909, 36 1/2 In. 518.00
Dagger, Walking Stick, Stag Horn, Yew, Russia, c.1900, 33 1/2 In. 945.00
Ebony, Black Man's Head, Big Smile, Malacca Shaft, England, 36 1/4 In. 3696.00
Flute, Disassembles In Middle For Playing, Silver Mounts, Silver Valve, 6 Finger Holes .. 850.00
Glass, Aqua, Twist Handle & Stem, England, 1800s, 35 3/4 In. 90.00
Glass, Blown, Aqua, 26 1/2 In. 45.00
Glass, Blown, Aquamarine, 55 1/2 In. 55.00
Glass, Blown, Clear, Ruby Threaded Swirl, 31 1/2 In. 115.00
Glass, Blown, Clear, Swirls, 48 1/2 In. 65.00
Glass, Blown, Cobalt Blue, Brass Top, 45 1/2 In. 80.00
Glass, Blown, Green, Opal Swirl, 42 In. 85.00
Glass, Blown, Stripes, Red, White, Blue, 50 1/2 In. 220.00
Goat Antler, Hoof, Knobby Wood, Carved Location, Names, Alpine, Steel End, 39 In. 90.00
Goat Antler, Wood Shaft, Spiral Carved Writing, Metal End, Alpine, Switzerland, 39 In. . 60.00
Gun, 6-Barreled Revolver, Pepper Box, Hardwood Shaft, 5-In. Stiletto Blade, 35 In. 5875.00
Gun, Gutta-Percha, Remington Dog, 22 Caliber, c.1870, 33 In. 8960.00
Horn, Club Shape, Rosewood, Silver Collar, Glasgow, c.1904, 36 In. 235.00
Horn, Cockatiel Head, Glass Eyes, Rosewood Shaft, Chased Gilt Collar, 37 In. 560.00
Horn, Hardwood, Tapered, Civil War Battle Names, 35 3/4 In. 1265.00
Horse Measuring, Hooked End, Pullout Metal Ruler, Brass Level, 17 Hand, 37 1/2 In. ... 110.00
Hunchback, Ivory Face, Hand, Silvered, Ebonized Shaft, 33 In. 705.00
Indian, Metal Ferule, Cap, Dartmouth, Shield, Delta Delta, 1928, 36 In. 385.00
Ivory, 2 Hunting Dogs, Glass Eyes, Reed Ground, Silver Collar, Malacca Shaft, 34 1/2 In. 1120.00
Ivory, 4 Basset Hounds Under Umbrella, Malacca Shaft, England, 37 1/4 In. 1000.00

Ivory, Acorns, Gold Plated Hilt, Wood Shaft, 35 In. 115.00
Ivory, Boot, Button Front, Worn Sole, Pear Wood Shaft, France, 35 1/4 In. 2240.00
Ivory, Creole Woman's Head, Twisted Silver Collar, Malacca Shaft, 39 In. 2465.00
Ivory, Crowing Rooster, Red Glass Eyes, Amber, Malacca Shaft, France, 37 In. 2465.00
Ivory, Dog Head, Glass Eyes, Gold Color, 35 1/2 In. 460.00
Ivory, Fox, Pointed Muzzle, Bushy Tail, Malacca Shaft, 34 3/4 In. 1680.00
Ivory, Globe Knob, Compass & Sundial Inside, Braided Silver Collar, Wood Shaft, 35 In. . 2240.00
Ivory, Grim Reaper's Head, Buffalo Horn Hood, Malacca Shaft, England, 33 1/2 In. 3920.00
Ivory, Hand Holding Rodent, Buttoned Cuff, Half Bark Malacca Shaft, 37 In. 1456.00
Ivory, Lady's Leg, High Button Boots To Bloomers, Malacca Shaft, France, 36 1/2 In. . . . 3360.00
Ivory, Lion, Perched On Branch, Looking At Snake, Bronze Collar, Malacca Shaft, 33 In. . 560.00
Ivory, Monkey Head, Exaggerated Features, Red Tongue Sticks Out, Ebony Shaft, 36 In. . 2465.00
Ivory, Presentation, Whalebone, Crook Handle, U.S. Consul, Azores, c.1911 . . . . 1645.00
Ivory, Rabbit's Head, Red Glass Eyes, Chased Gilt Collar, Malacca Shaft, 36 In. 2015.00
Ivory, Rabbit, Dressed As Gentleman, Holding Hat, Flowers In Pocket, 36 3/4 In. 3810.00
Ivory, Roman Gladiator's Head, Stern Features, Helmet, Malacca Shaft, 33 In. 1905.00
Ivory, Seminude Woman, Cloth Around Waist, Ebony Shaft, France, 34 In. 2465.00
Ivory, Whalebone Shaft, William IV, Bust, 36 In. 1035.00
Ivory Handle, Clenched Fist, 3 1/4 In. 865.00
Ivory Handle, Dragon Head, Ball In Mouth, Rosewood Handle, Chinese, 34 1/2 In. 840.00
Lapis Lazuli, Swung Derby Handle, Gold Monogram, Ivory Shaft, 34 1/2 In. 5040.00
Light, Ever Ready, Fleur-De-Lis Switch, Shield Striking Plate, 1902 . . . . 1650.00
Mahogany, Silver Mounted, Early 20th Century, 34 In. 1300.00
Man's Head, Glass Eyes, Pyrographic Spots, Metal Tip, 34 In. 165.00
Maple, Bird Head, Tapered Shaft, Inscription, 36 1/2 In. 195.00
Metal, Monkey, Arms & Legs Wrapped Around, Tapered Shaft, 33 In. 110.00
Mother-Of-Pearl, Fish, Fluted, Rosewood Shaft, Italy, 36 In. 1905.00
Narwhal Tusk, Twist Carved, Turk's Head Knot Carving, 2 Baleen Rings, 33 1/4 In. 4600.00
Partridge, Single Piece, Finger Shape, Inlaid Silver Details & Fingernail, 34 3/4 In. 335.00
Patriotic Symbols, Portraits, 2 Piece Construction, Spanish American War, 32 In. 1150.00
Porcelain Knob, Painted Flowers, Meissen, Purple Collar, Purpleheart, Wood Shaft, 36 In. 1000.00
Quartz, Gold, Silver Mount, 8 Oval Panels, Lignum Vitae Shaft, 35 3/4 In. 9520.00
Rabbit Handle, Gold Washed Silver, Glass Eyes, Victorian, London, c.1898, 36 In. 590.00
Schtockschnitzler, Carved Bird, Simmons, Dogwood, 19th Century, 36 3/4 In. 770.00
Siam Horn, Exotic Bird Head, Long Beak, Glass Eyes, Rosewood Shaft, 34 3/4 In. 500.00
Silver, Art Nouveau, Flowers, Leaves, Ebony Shaft, Germany, 34 3/4 In. 390.00
Silver, Chased & Engraved Spiral Bands & Flowers, Ebony Shaft, 36 In. 335.00
Silver, Crook, Greyhound's Head, Open Mouth, Hanging Tongue, Ebony Shaft, 35 In. . . . 335.00
Silver, Dachshund, Leaves & Flowers, Opera Shape, Ebony Shaft, Germany, 34 1/4 In. . . . 1120.00
Silver, Horse Head, Braided Mane, Riding Implements, Belt Collar, Ebony Shaft, 36 In. . . 1905.00
Silver, Trumpet Handle, Hearing Aid, Cylindrical Resonance Box, Ebonized Shaft, 35 In. . 3585.00
Silver Knob, Illustrations Of Don Quixote, Malacca Shaft, 33 3/4 In. 780.00
Silver Plate, L-Shaped, Art Nouveau Flowers, Amber Tip, Malacca Shaft, Germany, 39 In. 360.00
Single Hardwood Branch, Carved Peasant's Head, Wearing Flat Hat, Folk Art, 32 1/4 In. . 500.00
Spyglass, Ebonized Shaft, 37 In. 345.00
Swagger Stick, Ivory Mounts, Hide, Horsehair, Rhinoceros Hide Covered Shaft, 36 In. . . . 176.00
Swagger Stick, Victoria Falls, Peephole, Composition, Tapered Leather Shaft, 33 In. 25.00
Sword, Chinese, Dragon Head, Copper Tube, Brass Inlays, 4 Sided Steel Spike, 15 In. . . . 140.00
Sword, Steel, Malacca, Crook Handle, Blond Horn Ferrule, France, 34 In. 450.00
Sword, Walking Stick, Bamboo, Bone Mounted, 20th Century, 35 In. 165.00
Sword, Walking Stick, Bone, 5 Gold Collars, Monkeys, Vines, Japan, c.1900 . . . . 825.00
Sword, Walking Stick, Briarwood, Victorian, c.1850, 34 5/8 In. 295.00
Tape Measure, Black Man, Smoking Cigar, Celluloid, Rosewood, 35 In. 590.00
Vertebrae, 8-Sided Wooden Knob, 35 In. 69.00
Walking Stick, Bamboo, Brass Mounts, 34 1/2 In. 175.00
Walking Stick, Bamboo, Metal Studded, Thailand, 33 In. 150.00
Walking Stick, Bone, Bamboo, Crooked Handle, Early 20th Century, 36 In. 380.00
Walking Stick, Bone, Brass, c.1845, 36 1/2 In. 420.00
Walking Stick, Briarwood, Fox, Snail, Caterpillar, Early 1900s, 36 In. 385.00
Walking Stick, Briarwood, Tiger's Eye Mounted, Blue Stone, c.1900, 33 1/2 In. 354.00
Walking Stick, Coquille, Acorn Tip, Tortoiseshell, Mother-Of-Pearl, 1800s, 36 In. 470.00
Walking Stick, Ebony, Ferrule, 14K Gold Knob, Repousse, 44 1/2 In. 360.00
Walking Stick, Ebony, Whistle Handle, Metal, Horn Ferrule, Early 20th Century, 36 In. . . 470.00

Walking Stick, Gilt Copper Mounted, Rococo Scrolls, Horn Ferrule, c.1900, 36 1/4 In. . . . 355.00
Walking Stick, Hardwood, Man's Head, Hat, Chip Carved Shaft, 29 3/4 In. 290.00
Walking Stick, Hearts, Geometric, Man, Shield, Snake Around Base, Brass Cap, 33 In. . . 115.00
Walking Stick, Horn, Whippet's Head, Yew, Early 1900s, 35 1/4 In. 770.00
Walking Stick, Ivory Topped, Engraved, Thomas Cushman, 19th Century, 45 In. 410.00
Walking Stick, Ivory, Bearded Naval Officer, Chestnut Shaft, Brass Ferrule, 36 In. 705.00
Walking Stick, Ivory, Court Jester, Carved, Ebony Shaft, 19th Century, 34 In. 2000.00
Walking Stick, Ivory, Jester's Head, Briarwood, Early 20th Century, 35 In. 590.00
Walking Stick, Ivory, Pique, Stylized Flowers, Malacca Shaft, Early 18th Century, 38 In. . 5875.00
Walking Stick, Ivory, Pique, Zigzag Incising, England, Late 17th Century, 38 In. 5170.00
Walking Stick, Ivory, Pommel, Reeded Silvered Metal Collar, c.1834, 35 In. 1295.00
Walking Stick, Ivory, Queen, Bus, Malacca, 17th Century, 37 In. 1175.00
Walking Stick, Pipe Stem Pommel, Malacca Shaft, Austria, 34 In. 355.00
Walking Stick, Poodle, Crouching, Black Forest, Sterling Silver Collar, Rosewood Shaft . 475.00
Walking Stick, Porcelain, Painted, Cherub, Cobalt, Gilt, Monogram, 6 In. 370.00
Walking Stick, Silver, Poodle Head Finial, Ebony Shaft, Birmingham 325.00
Walking Stick, Spyglass, Dolland, London, 19th Century, 36 In. 590.00
Walking Stick, Sterling, Turquoise, Rosewood, Curled End, 38 In. 50.00
Walking Stick, Tua, Derby Handle, Ivory Pique, England, 17th Century, 35 In. 6169.00
Walking Stick, Vertebrae, Turned Walnut 135.00
Walking Stick, Vine Branch, Knobbed, Kneeling Woman's Bottom, France, 35 In. 785.00
Walking Stick, Walrus Bone, Ivory, Bear Shape Finial, 21 In. 230.00
Walrus Ivory, Dragon, Long Scaled Neck, Rosewood Shaft, 34 1/2 In. 450.00
Wedding, Bone, Carved Figures, Colonial Man & Woman, Snake In Tree, 36 In. 605.00
Whale's Tooth, Sea Bird, Wood Shaft, South Seas, 36 In. 750.00
Whale's Tooth, Sperm, Whale Shaped Handle, Carved, Whalebone Shaft, 33 1/4 In. 2465.00
Whale's Tooth Ivory, Ebony, Carved Whalebone Ferrule, 35 1/2 In. 385.00
Whale's Tooth Ivory, Whalebone, 36 In. 460.00
Whalebone, 12 Abalone Diamond Inlays, Rope Carving, 33 In. 980.00
Whalebone, Clenched Fist, c.1870, 36 In. 645.00
Wood, Alligator, 35 In. 259.00
Wood, Bird Handle, Painted Yellow, 36 In. 1045.00
Wood, Bird, 28 In. 135.00
Wood, Black Panther, Open Mouth, Ebonized, 35 1/2 In. 28.00
Wood, Burled, 3 Carved Sides, E. Flint, Erie Canal Sec. 137 1855, 38 1/2 In. 115.00
Wood, Carved, Bird, Red, Green Shaft, Painted, Multicolored, 39 In. 95.00
Wood, Carved, Double Face, Human, Monkey, Knob End, 31 In. 65.00
Wood, Carved, Monkey Head, Hat, Knobby Shaft, Metal Tip, 35 In. 29.00
Wood, Carved, Snake, Swallowing Man, Black, Stripes, 36 In. 468.00
Wood, Carved, Snakes, Fish, Birds, Dog Head, Tools, Gun, Bullets, c.1800, 35 3/4 In. . . . 1100.00
Wood, Dog, On Top Of Man's Head, 36 In. 385.00
Wood, Man's Head, Twisted Shaft, Reddish Brown Stain, 31 In. 110.00
Wood, Mermaid, Diving, Fish Scale Tail, Black Hair, 38 1/4 In. 480.00
Wood, Seahorse, Scrolled 35 In. 56.00

CANTON CHINA is a blue-and-white ware made near the city of Canton, in China, from about 1785 to 1895. It is hand decorated with Chinese scenes. Canton is part of the group of porcelains known today as Chinese Export Porcelain.

Basin, 1 3/4 x 9 1/4 In. 325.00
Basket, Undertray, Reticulated, Oval, 19th Century, 4 7/8 x 8 1/2 In. 880.00
Bidet, Walnut Cover, Stand, c.1800, 23 x 15 1/2 x 5 1/2 In. 1150.00
Bowl, Cut Corners, 9 1/2 In. 355.00
Bowl, Pagoda, Trees, River, Mountains, Blue Band, Crosshatching, 9 1/2 In. 1045.00
Bowl, Scalloped Edges, Orange Peel Glaze, 3 Blue Flowers, Outside, 8 3/4 x 1 1/2 In. . . . 440.00
Bowl, Underplate, Orange Peel Glaze, Reticulated, Oval, 3 1/4 x 10 7/8 In. 546.00
Bowl, Underplate, Reticulated, 8 1/2 x 9 In. 1045.00
Bowl, Vegetable, Cover, 19th Century, 9 1/2 In. 105.00
Bowl, Vegetable, Cover, Diamond Shape, 9 3/4 x 7 1/2 In. 165.00
Bowl, Vegetable, Cover, Square, Pinecone Finial, 19th Century, 9 1/2 In. 230.00
Bowl, Vegetable, Underplate, Boar's Head Handles, Finial, Orange Peel Glaze, 3 x 7 In. . . 525.00
Creamer, Bull Nose Spout, Applied Handle, 3 1/2 In. 440.00
Creamer, c.1840, 2 3/4 In. 90.00

Dish, Entree, Cover, Entwined Handles, c.1850, 5 x 12 In. 1150.00
Dish, Late 19th Century, 10 1/2 In. 355.00
Dish, Square, 19th Century, 10 3/8 In. 470.00
Dish & Trivet Set, Oval, Pierced Border, 8 1/2 In., 8 Piece 1610.00
Eggcup Set, Landscape, 19th Century, 5 Piece 230.00
Fruit Basket, Under Liner, 9 x 7 3/4 In. 460.00
Fruit Basket, Undertray, Pierced, c.1861, 4 3/4 x 10 In. 1150.00
Garden Seat, Riveted, Barrel Shape, Openwork, Monkey Cartouches, 18 1/4 In., Pair 605.00
Ginger Jar, 6 3/4 In. 28.00
Ginger Jar, 7 3/4 x 8 1/2 In. 259.00
Gravy Boat, Oval, Cover, Twisted Handles, 12 In. 735.00
Gravy Boat, Rectangular, Cover, 12 In. 620.00
Hot Water Plate, Octagonal, 19th Century, 10 1/2 In. 200.00
Mug, Intertwined Handle, Molded Berry Ends, 4 In. 550.00
Pitcher, 7 3/4 In. 460.00
Pitcher, Cover, Oval, Double, Overlapping Strap Handles, Foo Dog Finial, 9 In. 2090.00
Pitcher, Milk, 19th Century, 6 5/8 In. 499.00
Pitcher, Molded End, Applied Handle, 7 In. 715.00
Plate, Footed, Figural Scenes, Early 1800s, 8 In., Pair 690.00
Plate Set, 8 3/4 In., 5 Piece 145.00
Plate Set, 10 In., 5 Piece 345.00
Plate Set, 10 1/4 In., 8 Piece 288.00
Plate Set, c.1830, 10 In., 7 Piece 315.00
Platter, 12 In. ....83.00 to 325.00
Platter, 16 In. 310.00
Platter, 18 In. 518.00
Platter, Cut Corner, 9 1/2 x 7 In. 259.00
Platter, Cut Corner, 11 3/4 x 9 1/4 In. 127.00
Platter, Cut Corner, 13 x 10 1/4 In. 345.00
Platter, Cut Corner, 15 1/2 x 12 1/2 In. 776.00
Platter, Cut Corner, 16 x 12 3/4 In. 200.00
Platter, Oblong, Octagonal, 19th Century, 12 1/4 x 15 3/8 In. 765.00
Platter, Octagonal, Fitzhugh Border, 14 3/4 In. 635.00
Platter, Octagonal, Pagoda, Bridge, Boat, 13 x 16 In. 375.00
Platter, On Stand, Octagonal, 18 x 20 1/2 In. 1380.00
Platter, Oval, 19th Century, 14 In. 295.00
Platter, Pagodas, Octagonal, 11 1/4 In. 140.00
Platter, Scene, Chamfered Corners, c.1770, 14 1/2 x 11 1/2 In. 545.00
Platter, Well & Tree, 11 3/8 x 14 1/4 In. 396.00
Platter, Well & Tree, Octagonal, 15 In. 405.00
Pot De Creme, Landscape Design, Cover, 19th Century, 3 In. 185.00
Punch Bowl, 5 1/2 x 13 3/8 In. 1540.00
Punch Bowl, Mid 19th Century, 14 3/4 In. 2875.00
Salad Bowl, Cut Corner, 19th Century, 4 1/2 x 10 In. 560.00
Serving Bowl, Round, 10 1/4 In. 275.00
Serving Dish, Diamond Shape, 3 3/4 x 9 1/2 x 7 In. 375.00
Serving Dish, Shrimp, 10 1/2 x 9 3/4 In. 345.00
Shrimp Dish, 10 5/8 In. 590.00
Shrimp Dish, 2 Shrimp, On Flange Handle, Acorn Shape 605.00
Sugar, Baluster, 2 Handles, Berry Form Finial, 6 In. 300.00
Sugar, Cover, Intertwined Handles, Molded Berry Ends, Finial, 6 1/4 In. 248.00
Sugar, Cover, Oval, Landscape, Mid 19th Century, 7 In. 175.00
Tea Jar, Cover, 14 In., Pair 9775.00
Tea Service, c.1850, 6-In. Teapot, 5 Piece 865.00
Tea Service, Gilt, 19th Century, 7-1/4 Teapot, 5 Piece 920.00
Teapot, Berry Finial, Handles, c.1850, 7 1/2 In. 520.00
Teapot, Cover, Cylinderical, Strap Handle, 4 3/4 In. 489.00
Teapot, Cylindrical, Fruit Finial, Entwined Lapped Handle, 19th Century, 5 3/4 In. 499.00
Teapot, Dome Cover, Pagodas, Boats, Scrolled Ear Handle, 9 3/4 In. 330.00
Teapot, Intertwined Handle, Berry Finial, 5 1/4 In. 201.00
Teapot, Intertwined Handle, Molded Berry Ends, Berry Finial, 6 In. 605.00
Tureen, Boar's Head Handles, 1800s, 14 In. 646.00
Tureen, Cover, Boar's Head Handles, Underplate, Octagonal, 1800s, 8 3/4 x 13 3/8 In. 1530.00

Tureen, Cover, Footed, Oval Base, Flared, Animal Head Handles, 13 x 9 1/2 In. 1870.00
Tureen, Cover, Underliner, Boar's Head, Oval, 8 1/2 x 12 1/2 In. 2300.00
Tureen, Sauce, Undertray, Polychrome, Figural Design, Blue Fret Border, c.1820, 8 In. . . .   690.00
Tureen, Undertray, 12 7/8 In. 165.00
Vase, Bottle Shape, Mounted As Lamp, 13 In. 1095.00
Vase, Scene, Flared, Elongated Neck, 19th Century, 18 1/4 In. 2415.00
Vase, Trumpet Form, Buddha Design, Enamel, Late 1800s, 3 1/2 In. 40.00

CAPO-DI-MONTE porcelain was first made in Naples, Italy, from 1743 to 1759. The factory moved near Madrid, Spain, reopened in 1771, and worked to 1834. Since that time, the Doccia factory of Italy acquired the molds and is using the crown and N mark. Societe Richard Ceramica is a modern-day firm often referred to as Ginori or Capo-di-Monte. This company uses the crown and N mark.

Box, Cylindrical, Figural Relief, c.1900, 3 1/2 In. 160.00
Box, Hinged Top, Oval, Venus As Vulcan's Forge, 8 In. 300.00
Group, Boy & Girl Picking Grapes, Signed, 6 In. 40.00
Inkstand, Double, Pen Trays, Goat, Satyrs, Gilt Trim, 7 1/2 x 7 1/2 In. 140.00
Plate, Napoleon, Late 19th Century, 8 In. 230.00
Plate, Relief Cherubs, Flower Spray, 10 1/2 In., 6 Piece 316.00
Plate, Relief Cherubs, Flower Spray, 10 1/2 In., Pair 144.00
Plate, Shield In Middle, People On Border, 9 In. 140.00
Stein, Figural Lid, Bacchanalian Scene, Grapevine Handle, Crowned N, 1 Liter 403.00
Stein, Figural Lid, Cherubs, Animals, 1/2 Liter 115.00
Stein, Figural Lid, Warriors, Crowned N, 1/2 Liter 280.00
Stein, Helmet, Battle Scene, Porcelain Inset Lid, Crowned N, 1/4 Liter 345.00
Stein, Lid, Bacchanalian Scene, Gilt Interior, 1/2 Liter 300.00
Stein, Lid, Battle Scene, Warrior Handle, Finial, 1 1/2 Liter, 17 In. 2010.00
Stein, Lid, Lion Finial, Battle Scene, Relief, 1/3 Liter 345.00
Stein, Lid, Lions & Warriors, Boar Finial, 1/4 Liter 230.00
Stein, Lid, Putti Around Fires In Woods, Putti Finial, Elephant Handle, 1 Liter 604.00
Urn, Feathered Rim & Base, Enamel Classical Figures, 8 1/4 In., Pair 440.00

CAPTAIN MARVEL was introduced in February 1940 in Whiz comic books. An orphan named Billy Batson met the wizard, Shazam, and whenever he said the magic word he was transformed into a superhero. A movie serial was released in 1940. The comic was discontinued in 1954. A second Captain Marvel appeared in 1966, a third in 1967. Only the original was transformed by shouting *Shazam*.

Bag, Captain Marvel Holding Jet, Travelight, Fawcett Co., 1947, 5 1/2 x 8 In. 690.00
Disk, Shazam, Cardboard, 1 1/2 In. 50.00
Drawing, Captain Marvel, Billy Batson, C.C. Beck, 1970, 9 x 10 3/4 In. 1725.00
Paint Book, Captain Marvel & Jr., 1943, 11 x 14 3/4 In., 64 Pages 202.00
Pencil Clip, Shazam, 1 1/2 In. 45.00
Pennant, Captain Marvel, Felt, Fawcett Publications, c.1946, 8 x 14 1/2 In. 160.00
Pin, Shazam Red, Blue, Cream, 7/8 In. 65.00
Toy, Magic Flute, Cardboard, Plastic, Fawcett Publications Inc., 4 3/4 In. 58.00
Toy, Tricycle, Moves In Circle, Rings Bell, Tin, Windup, Marx, Japan, 4 In. 275.00

CAPTAIN MIDNIGHT began as a radio show in September 1940. The first comic book appeared in July 1941. Captain Midnight was really the aviator Captain Albright, who was to defeat the Nazis. A movie serial was made in 1942 and a comic strip was published for a short time. The comic book Captain Midnight ended his career in 1948. The radio premiums are the prized collector memorabilia today.

Badge, Decoder, Silver Metal, 1941, 2 1/2 In. 20.00
Book, Big Little Book, Captain Midnight & Shiek Jomak Khan, 1946 . . . .   40.00
Book, Secret Squadron New Official, 1948, 6 In., 16 Pages 35.00
Decoder, Silver Dart, 1957 . . . .   185.00
Detect-O-Scope, Box, Instructions 300.00
Mug, Ovaltine, Booklet, Box 65.00
Ring, Mystic Sun God, Secret Compartment, Ovaltine Premium, 1947 . . . . .550.00 to 575.00
Ring, Siren, Whistles, Gold Metal 150.00

CARAMEL SLAG, see Imperial Glass category.

CARDS listed here include advertising cards (often called trade cards), greeting cards, baseball cards, playing cards, and others. Color pictures were rare in the nineteenth century, so companies gave away colorful cards with pictures of children, flowers, products, or related scenes that promoted the company name. These were often collected and stored in albums. Baseball cards also date from the nineteenth century when they were used by tobacco companies as giveaways. Gum cards were started in 1933, but it was not until after World War II that the bubble gum cards favored today were produced. Today over 1,000 cards are issued each year by the gum companies. Related items may be found in the Postcard and Movie categories.

Advertising, Allen's Lung Balsam, Grandmother, Child, Fireplace, Bottle Of Balsam	28.00
Advertising, Ayer's Sarsaparilla, Sunny Hours, Imprint, 5 x 2 1/2 In.	90.00
Advertising, Black, Trade, Nigger, Stone Lithograph, Album, 1882, 5 1/4 In.	198.00
Advertising, Celluloid Collars & Cuffs, Die Cut, 9 In. ....*Illus*	18.00
Advertising, Clark's O.N.T. Spool Cotton, Boy & Girl In Woods, 4 3/8 x 2 3/4 In.	23.00
Advertising, Clipper Ship Galatea, Polyphemus Crushing Acis, Greek Myth, 6 1/2 x 4 In. .	750.00
Advertising, Colgate's Ribbon Dental Cream, Mechanical, Moving Arms, 5 1/2 x 3 1/2 In. .	85.00
Advertising, Coussens & Tabler Medicine, Sick Man In Bed, Female Angel Holding Sign	308.00
Advertising, Daisy Air Rifle, Boys Duck Hunting, Description On Back, 5 1/2 x 3 1/2 In. .	415.00
Advertising, Deering & Co., Folding, Farm Settings, Farm Equipment, 14 In.	115.00
Advertising, Dr. Grove's Anodyne For Infants, Glove Shape, 6 3/8 x 2 1/8 In.	285.00
Advertising, Faricum Cough Drops, Before & After Images, 4 7/8 x 3 In.	20.00
Advertising, Hires Root Beer, Die Cut, Lithograph, 5 x 3 1/2 In.	85.00
Advertising, Hires, Woman In Black Dress, Girl Holds Root Beer Box, 3 3/4 x 5 3/4 In. ..	20.00
Advertising, Hood's Sarsaparilla, Smiling Triplets, 1889, 2 3/4 x 3 3/4 In.	20.00
Advertising, Humpty Dumpty Bank ....*Illus*	315.00
Advertising, Hunt's Remedy, Kidney & Liver, Men Discussing Remedy, 3 1/8 x 4 3/4 In. .	230.00
Advertising, IW Harper, Make A Hit, Winning Brand, Honus Wagner, 1912, 5 x 3 3/4 In. .	900.00
Advertising, J. & P. Coats' Thread, Champion, Child, Rifle, Champion Cup, 3 x 4 1/2 In. .	18.00
Advertising, Kickapoo Indian Remedies, Uncut Sheet Of 4 Cards, 4 Different Scenes	230.00
Advertising, Mail Pouch Coffee, Revolving Wheel, Ship, Train, Wagon, St. Louis	65.00
Advertising, Norton Brothers Signs, Cans, Boxes, Tin Lithograph, c.1870s, 2 3/4 x 4 In. ..	635.00
Advertising, Parker Gun, Pigeon Shoot On Front, Price List On Back, 5 3/4 x 3 1/2 In. ...	195.00
Advertising, Post Toasties Corn Flakes, 1926, 3 1/2 x 5 In.	15.00
Advertising, Snider's Catsup, Mechanical, 5 1/4 In.	86.00
Advertising, Vandergrift Washing Machine, Die Cut ....*Illus*	145.00
Advertising, White's Shoes, Louisville, Kentucky, c.1910	10.00
Baseball, Cal Ripken, Topps, No. 98T, 1982	105.00
Baseball, Hank Aaron, Rookie No. 128, Topps, 1954	4333.00
Baseball, Johnny Evers, T-206 Tobacco, Portrait, Green, Piedmont Brand, Near Mint	1428.00
Baseball, Lefty Gomez, Gum Inc., No. 72, 1942, 2 1/2 x 3 1/8 In.	50.00
Baseball, Mickey Mantle, Dan-Dee Potato Chips, 1954	4766.00
Baseball, Mickey Mantle, Stadium Sports Publishing, Hologram, Trade Show Promotion .	100.00
Baseball, Mickey Mantle, Topps, No. 50, 1966	150.00
Baseball, Pee Wee Reese, No. 54, 1942, 2 1/2 x 3 1/8 In.	75.00
Baseball, Red Stockings, Cincinnati, Peck & Snyder, 1869, 4 5/8 x 3 1/4 In.	6038.00
Baseball, Roberto Clemente, Topps No. 164, 1955	4766.00

Card, Advertising, Celluloid
Collars & Cuffs, Die Cut, 9 In.

Card, Advertising,
Humpty Dumpty
Bank

Card, Advertising,
Vandergrift Washing
Machine, Die Cut

Baseball, Ted Williams, Topps No. 250, 1954	2957.00
Baseball, Willie Mays No. 90, Topps, 1954	5245.00
Basketball, Michael Jordan, Fleer, No. 57, 1986-1987	1035.00
Basketball, Pete Maravich, Rookie, Topps, 1970-1971	2346.00
Football, Knute Rockne, Goudey, Sport Kings, No. 35, 1933	2657.00
Football, Norm Van Brocklin, Bowman, No. 1, 1952	3537.00
Greeting, Friendship, 2 Hearts, From, To, Green & Red, 1850s, 2 3/4 x 1 5/8 In.	11.00
Greeting, Friendship, Lover's Sentiments, Yellow Tulips & Poppies, 2 3/4 x 1 5/8 In.	15.00
Greeting, Tom & Jerry, Signed, MGM Animation Staff, Fred Quimby, 1951, 21 x 29 In.	575.00
Greeting, Valentine, Boy Water Bottle, Stand-Up, Color Lithography, 1920s, 5 1/2 In.	7.00
Greeting, Valentine, Coffee, Hearts, Stand-Up, White, Brown, Red, Green, 1920s, 5 1/2 In.	7.00
Hockey, Terry Sawchuk, Parkhurst, No. 61, 1951-1952	805.00
Membership, Captain Gallant, 4 x 2 1/2 In.	50.00
Playing, Edison Mazda Light Bulbs, Ecstasy, Parrish, Sealed, Box, 1930, 3 7/8 x 2 3/8 In.	358.00
Playing, Edison Mazda Light Bulbs, Waterfall, Parrish, Box, 1931, 3 7/8 x 2 3/8 In.	255.00
Playing, Hard A Port Tobacco, Scantily Clad Women, Box, c.1890, 53 Cards	1325.00
Playing, Hotpoint Automatic Home Laundry, Red Slip Finish, 1950s	18.00
Playing, Hunt & Sons, England, 1820, Deck Of 52	650.00
Playing, Stage Star Photographs, Stage No. 65, Leather Case, USPC, 1896	489.00
Target, Alf Rieckhoff Trick Shooter, Spade In Center, 6 x 4 1/8 In.	49.00
Trading, Barbie, Fashion, Nos. 141-175, Dynamic Toy Inc., c.1962, 3 1/4 x 1/2 In.	90.00

CARDER, see Aurene and Steuben categories.

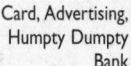

CARLSBAD is a mark found on china made by several factories in Germany, Austria, and Bavaria. Many pieces were exported to the United States. Most of the pieces available today were made after 1891.

Bowl, Flowers, Orange Ground, Rogers Silver Plated Holder, 7 x 14 In.	100.00
Oyster Plate, 6-Well, White Shells, Pink & Gilt Speckled Ground, c.1900, 9 In.	57.00
Vase, Bladder Form, Transfer Photograph, 2 Young Boys, Green, Gilt, 14 1/2 In.	127.00

CARLTON WARE was made at the Carlton Works of Stoke-on-Trent, England, beginning about 1890. The firm traded as Wiltshaw & Robinson until 1957. It was renamed Carlton Ware Ltd. in 1958. The company went bankrupt in 1995, but the name is still in use.

Biscuit Jar, Cover, Silver Plated, Peonies	305.00
Butter Tub, Cover, Cobalt, Oriental, Jeweled, Reeded Handle, Late 1950s, 5 1/4 In.	69.00
Vase, Bleu Royale, Spider Web, Jeweled, Late 1950s, 3 1/4 In.	60.00
Vase, Green Luster, Hollyhocks, 8 In.	345.00
Vase, Oriental, Blue, Jeweled, Gold Enameled, Late 1950s, 8 In.	140.00
Vase, Tropical Birds, Butterflies, Garden, 5 1/4 In., Pair	1265.00
Vase, Yen Yen Shape, Multicolored, Gold, Enamel, Oriental Landscapes, c.1900, 13 In.	294.00

CARNIVAL GLASS was an inexpensive, iridescent, pressed glass made from about 1907 to about 1925. More than 1,000 different patterns are known. Carnival glass is currently being reproduced. Additional pieces may be found in the Northwood category. Some of the high prices listed this year are from the sale of a major collection.

Acorn, Compote, Green, Ruffled Edge	3100.00

Acorn Burrs, Pitcher, Marigold, 8 3/4 In. 1050.00
Acorn Burrs, Punch Set, Green, 8 Piece 2700.00
Acorn Burrs, Water Set, Amethyst, 7 Piece 850.00
Acorn Burrs, Water Set, Green, 6 Piece 1000.00
Acorn Burrs & Bark pattern is listed here as Acorn Burrs.
Amaryllis pattern is listed here as Tiger Lily.
American Beauty Roses pattern is listed here as Wreath of Roses.
Apple Tree, Tumbler, Blue, 4 In. 45.00
Apple Tree, Tumbler, Marigold, 4 In. 10.00
April Showers, Vase, Amethyst, 12 In. 45.00
April Showers, Vase, Green, 12 In. 75.00
April Showers, Vase, Marigold, 12 In. 45.00
Asters, Rose Bowl, Marigold 160.00
Australian Swan, Sauce, Amethyst, Ruffled Edge 85.00
Australian Swan, Sauce, Marigold, Ruffled Edge 105.00
Autumn Acorn, Plate, Green, 9 In. 1100.00
Ballard-Merced, Plate, Amethyst, 6 In. 1300.00
Banded Grape & Cable, Hatpin Holder, Marigold 475.00
Banded Grape & Cable, Hatpin Holder, Purple 275.00
Basket, Amethyst . . . . .155.00 to 200.00
Basket, Aqua Opalescent 250.00
Basket, Basket, Aqua Opalescent 450.00
Basket, Green 75.00
Basket, Ice Green 155.00
Basket, Marigold 65.00
Basket, Sapphire 1600.00
Basket, Smoke 300.00
Battenburg Lace No. 1 pattern is listed here as Hearts & Flowers.
Battenburg Lace No. 2 pattern is listed here as Captive Rose.
Battenburg Lace No. 3 pattern is listed here as Fanciful.
Beaded Cable, Rose Bowl, Amethyst, Rayed Interior 80.00
Beaded Cable, Rose Bowl, Aqua Opalescent, Butterscotch, Iridescent 300.00
Beaded Cable, Rose Bowl, Blue 85.00
Beaded Cable, Rose Bowl, Green, Rayed Interior 245.00
Beaded Cable, Rose Bowl, Ice Blue 700.00
Beaded Cable, Rose Bowl, Lavender 375.00
Beaded Cable, Rose Bowl, Marigold 50.00
Beauty Bud, Vase, Marigold 35.00
Bells & Beads, Bowl, Peach Opalescent, Ruffled Edge, 7 In. 100.00
Big Fish, Bowl, Ice Cream, Green 475.00
Big Fish, Bowl, Ice Cream, Marigold . . . . .650.00 to 850.00
Bird With Grapes, Wall Pocket, Marigold 50.00
Birds & Cherries, Compote, Ruffled, Amethyst 20.00
Birds On Bough pattern is listed here as Birds & Cherries.
Birmingham Age Herald, Plate, Amethyst, 9 In. 2600.00
Blackberry & Checkerboard pattern is listed here as Blackberry Block.
Blackberry Block, Pitcher, Green, Straight Sides 1200.00
Blackberry Block, Tumbler, Blue, 4 In. 45.00
Blackberry Wreath, Bowl, Blue, Ruffled Edge, 10 In. 1200.00
Blueberry, Tumbler, Marigold 100.00
Bouquet, Pitcher, Marigold, 9 1/4 In. 125.00
Bouquet, Tumbler, Blue, 4 In. 10.00
Braziers Candies, Plate, Amethyst, Hand Grip, 6 In. . . . . .900.00 to 1100.00
Brocaded Summer Gardens, Sandwich Server, Center Handle, White 35.00
Broekers Flour, Plate, Amethyst, 6 In. 200.00
Brooklyn Bridge, Bowl, Marigold, Ruffled Edge, 10 In. 200.00
Bushel Basket pattern is listed here as Basket.
Butterflies, Bonbon, Marigold 75.00
Butterfly & Berry, Berry Set, Blue, 7 Piece 325.00
Butterfly & Berry, Tumbler, Blue, 4 1/4 In. 10.00
Butterfly & Berry, Water Set, Blue, 7 Piece 700.00
Butterfly & Cable pattern is listed here as Springtime.
Butterfly & Fern, Tumbler, Marigold 45.00

Butterfly & Fern, Water Set, Blue, 7 Piece 725.00
Butterfly & Grape pattern is listed here as Butterfly & Berry.
Butterfly & Plume pattern is listed here as Butterfly & Fern.
Butterfly & Stippled Rays pattern is listed here as Butterfly.
Butterfly & Tulip, Bowl, Square, Amethyst ....*Illus* 2600.00
Buzz Saw, Cruet, Green, Clear Stopper, 6 In. 450.00
Cambridge No. 2351, Vase, Light Marigold, Footed, 4 In. 325.00
Captive Rose, Bowl, Marigold, Ruffled Edge 50.00
Captive Rose, Compote, Amethyst, Ruffled Edge 75.00
Captive Rose, Plate, Green, 9 In. 800.00
Central Shoe Store, Plate, Amethyst, 6 In. 1300.00
Chatelaine, Tumbler, Purple 350.00
Cherry, Bowl, Amethyst, Ruffled Edge 425.00
Cherry, Bowl, Ice Cream, Marigold, Satin, 7 In. 70.00
Cherry, Compote, Amethyst 1200.00
Cherry, Pitcher, Dark Marigold 1800.00
Cherry, Pitcher, Green 1000.00
Cherry, Plate, Green, 10 In. 3700.00
Cherry, Tumbler, Marigold 230.00
Cherry Chain, Bowl, Amethyst, 10 In. 325.00
Cherry Chain, Bowl, Marigold, 6 In. 40.00
Cherry Chain, Plate, Blue, 6 In. 135.00
Cherry Wreathed pattern is listed here as Wreathed Cherry.
Christmas Cactus pattern is listed here as Thistle.
Christmas Plate pattern is listed here as Poinsettia.
Cleveland Memorial, Ashtray, Amethyst 7000.00
Cobblestone, Bowl, Amethyst, Ruffled Edge 55.00
Corn, Vase, Marigold, Plain Base 300.00
Corn, Vase, White 200.00
Courthouse, Bowl, Amethyst 1200.00
Courthouse, Bowl, Lavender, Ruffled Edge 2300.00
Dahlia, Tumbler, Amethyst 65.00
Daisy & Drape, Vase, Flared, Aqua Opalescent 625.00
Daisy & Drape, Vase, Flared, Marigold 450.00
Daisy & Drape, Vase, Flared, White 200.00
Daisy & Drape, Vase, Ice Blue, Rolled Inward Rim 2250.00
Daisy & Lattice Band pattern is listed here as Lattice & Daisy.
Daisy & Plume, Rose Bowl, Marigold 25.00
Daisy & Plume, Rose Bowl, Raspberry Interior, Amethyst, 3-Footed 175.00
Daisy & Plume, Rose Bowl, Raspberry Interior, Aqua Opal, 3-Footed ....*Illus* 7000.00
Daisy & Plume, Rose Bowl, Raspberry Interior, Marigold, 3-Footed 55.00
Daisy Band & Drape pattern is listed here as Daisy & Drape.
Dandelion, Mug, Aqua Opalescent, Pastel, Iridescent 425.00
Dandelion, Tumbler, White 95.00
Dandelion Variant pattern is listed here as Paneled Dandelion.
Davidson's Society Chocolates, Amethyst, Handgrip 1000.00
Diamond Band pattern is listed here as Diamonds.
Diamond Cut, Jardiniere, Amethyst 200.00
Diamond Points, Basket, Marigold 2100.00
Diamond Points, Vase, Blue, 10 In. 675.00
Diamonds, Tumbler, Green 100.00
Diamonds, Tumbler, Marigold 75.00
Diving Dolphins, Bowl, Marigold, Ruffled Edge, Footed, 7 In. 150.00
Diving Dolphins, Rose Bowl, Amethyst 525.00
Dogwood & Marsh Lily pattern is listed here as Two Flowers.
Dolphins, Compote, Amethyst 2500.00
Dorsey & Funkenstein, Plate, Amethyst, 6 In. 2600.00
Double Dutch, Bowl, Footed, Marigold, 9 1/2 In. 45.00
Double Scroll, Console Set, Smoke, 3 Piece 125.00
Double Star, Water Set, Green, 7 Piece 600.00
Dozen Roses, Bowl, Amethyst, Footed 900.00
Dragon & Berry, Bowl, Blue, 8 1/2 In. 250.00
Dragon & Lotus, Bowl, Blue, 9 In. ....70.00 to 90.00

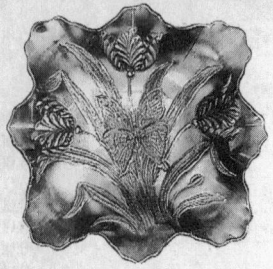

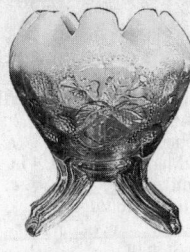

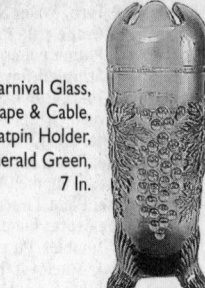

Carnival Glass,
Grape & Cable,
Hatpin Holder,
Emerald Green,
7 In.

Carnival Glass, Daisy & Plume,
Rose Bowl, Raspberry Interior,
Aqua Opal, 3-Footed

Carnival Glass, Butterfly & Tulip,
Bowl, Square, Amethyst

Dragon & Lotus, Bowl, Marigold On Moonstone, Ruffled Edge	900.00
Dragon & Lotus, Bowl, Marigold, 8 In.	60.00
Drapery, Rose Bowl, Amethyst . . . . .200.00 to 250.00	
Drapery, Rose Bowl, Aqua Opal, Butterscotch, Iridescent	250.00
Drapery, Rose Bowl, Blue	180.00
Drapery, Rose Bowl, Marigold	275.00
Drapery, Vase, Ice Blue, 8 In.	800.00
Drapery, Vase, White, 8 In.	175.00
Drapery Variant, Vase, Amethyst, 9 In.	155.00
Drapery Variant, Vase, Blue, 9 In.	165.00
Dreibus Parfait Sweets, Amethyst, Handgrip	1100.00
Eagle Furniture, Plate, Amethyst, 6 In.	1500.00
Egyptian Band pattern is listed here as Round-Up.	
Elks, Detroit, Bowl, Amethyst, Ruffled Edges, 1910	900.00
Elks, Parkersburg, Plate, Blue, 1914, 7 In.	2200.00
Emaline pattern is listed here as Zipper Loop.	
Embroidered Mums, Bowl, Amethyst, Ruffled Edge	275.00
Embroidered Mums, Bowl, Ice Green, Ruffled Edge	1400.00
Exchange Bank, Plate, Amethyst, 6 In.	1700.00
Fan & Arch pattern is listed here as Persian Garden.	
Fanciful, Bowl, Amethyst, Ruffled Edge	1300.00
Fantasy pattern is listed here as Question Marks.	
Farmyard, Bowl, Amethyst, Square	4000.00
Feather & Heart, Hair Receiver, Marigold	1600.00
Feather & Heart, Pitcher, Amethyst	300.00
Feather & Heart, Tumbler, Green	165.00
Feathered Scroll pattern is listed here as Feathered Serpent.	
Feathered Serpent, Bowl, Marigold, 5 In.	40.00
Feathers, Vase, Green, Marked, 7 In.	60.00
Fenton's Butterfly pattern is listed here as Butterfly.	
Fern Brand Chocolates, Plate, Amethyst, Handgrip	950.00
Fine Cut & Roses, Rose Bowl, Aqua Opal	950.00
Fine Cut & Roses, Rose Bowl, Dark Marigold	75.00
Fine Cut & Roses, Rose Bowl, Ice Blue	55.00
Fine Cut & Roses, Rose Bowl, Marigold	125.00
Fine Cut & Roses, Rose Bowl, Pastel Blue	175.00
Fine Cut & Roses, Rose Bowl, White	250.00
Fine Cut Flowers, Compote, Marigold, Ruffled Edge	10.00
Fine Rib, Vase, Blue, Irregular Ruffled Rim, 17 In.	175.00
Fine Rib, Vase, Marigold On Vaseline, 10 In.	50.00
Fine Rib, Vase, Red, 10 In.	350.00
Finecut & Star pattern is listed here as Star & File.	
Fish & Flowers pattern is listed here as Trout & Fly.	
Fishscales & Beads, Bowl, Amethyst, Ruffled Edge, 7 In.	145.00
Fleur-De-Lis, Bowl, Marigold	200.00
Fleur-De-Lis, Bowl, Vaseline, Square, Domed Foot	5000.00
Floral & Diamond Point pattern is listed here as Fine Cut & Roses.	
Floral & Grape, Tumbler, Amethyst, 4 In.	10.00

Floral & Grapevine pattern is listed here as Floral & Grape.

Floral & Optic, Cake Plate, Marigold, Footed 15.00
Floral & Wheat, Bonbon, White, Handles, Footed 58.00
Floral & Wheat Spray pattern is listed here as Floral & Wheat.
Florentine, Candlestick, Celeste Blue, 8 In., Pair 90.00
Florentine, Candlestick, Marigold, 10 In., Pair ....70.00 to 75.00
Florentine, Candlestick, Red, 8 In. 300.00
Flower Pot pattern is listed here as Butterfly & Tulip.
Flowers & Frames, Bowl, Amethyst, Ruffled Edge, Domed Foot 85.00
Fluffy Bird pattern is listed here as Peacock.
Fluffy Peacock, Pitcher, Blue 850.00
Fluffy Peacock, Tumbler, Marigold 20.00
Fluffy Peacock, Water Set, Amethyst, 7 Piece 800.00
Flute, Toothpick Amethyst, 2 1/2 In. 40.00
Forks, Cracker Jar, Green, No Cover 275.00
Four Flowers, Bowl, Blue, Ruffled Edge 85.00
Four Flowers, Plate, Green, 9 In. ....300.00 to 400.00
Four Pillars, Vase, Aqua Opalescent, Butterscotch Iridescent, 12 In. 235.00
Four Pillars, Vase, Marigold, 10 In. 35.00
Freefold, Vase, Amethyst, 10 In. 285.00
Frosted Block, Rose Bowl, Marigold 25.00
Fruit Salad, Punch Set, Amethyst, 6 Piece 1800.00
Garland, Rose Bowl, Amethyst 260.00
Garland, Rose Bowl, Marigold 80.00
Gay 90s, Tumbler, Amethyst 700.00
Geo. W. Getz Pianos, Plate, Amethyst, 6 In. 1300.00
Golden Harvest, Wine Set, Marigold, 7 Piece 105.00
Good Luck, Bowl, Electric Blue, 2 1/2 x 9 In. 300.00
Good Luck, Bowl, Marigold, 2 3/4 x 8 3/4 In. 50.00
Gothic Arches, Vase, Marigold, 11 x 8 In. 1200.00
Gothic Arches, Vase, Smoke, 11 x 7 1/2 In. 900.00
Grape & Cable, Banana Bowl, Swirled Smoky Blue, 6 x 12 In. 375.00
Grape & Cable, Bowl, 3-Footed, Marigold, 6 3/4 x 11 1/2 In. 150.00
Grape & Cable, Bowl, Amethyst 75.00
Grape & Cable, Bowl, Ice Cream, Basketweave Exterior, Green, 10 1/2 In. 200.00
Grape & Cable, Bowl, Marigold, Ruffled Edge, 3 1/2 x 10 In. 25.00
Grape & Cable, Bowl, Orange, Amethyst, Applied Cobalt Handle, Footed, 8 1/2 In. 2875.00
Grape & Cable, Bowl, Orange, Persian Medallion Interior, Marigold 135.00
Grape & Cable, Candle Lamp, Amethyst, 10 In. 950.00
Grape & Cable, Candlestick, Amethyst, 3/4 In., Pair 250.00
Grape & Cable, Compote, Amethyst, 8 1/2 x 10 1/4 In. 400.00
Grape & Cable, Cup & Saucer, Amethyst 170.00
Grape & Cable, Decanter, Amethyst, 9 In. 175.00
Grape & Cable, Decanter, Tumbler, Whiskey, Amethyst, 11 3/4 In., 2 Piece 1400.00
Grape & Cable, Dresser Tray, Amethyst, 11 1/4 In. 450.00
Grape & Cable, Hatpin Holder, Amethyst, 7 In. ....225.00 to 235.00
Grape & Cable, Hatpin Holder, Black Amethyst, Gold Decoration, 7 In. 145.00
Grape & Cable, Hatpin Holder, Emerald Green, 7 In. ....*Illus* 3100.00
Grape & Cable, Perfume Bottle, Amethyst ....325.00 to 700.00
Grape & Cable, Perfume Bottle, Marigold 170.00
Grape & Cable, Plate, Amethyst, 9 In. ....80.00 to 125.00
Grape & Cable, Plate, Amethyst, Stippled, Ribbed Exterior, 9 In. 1200.00
Grape & Cable, Plate, Basketweave Exterior, Amethyst, 7 3/4 In. 50.00
Grape & Cable, Plate, Basketweave Exterior, Stippled, Amethyst, 9 In. 325.00
Grape & Cable, Plate, Footed, Marigold, 9 In. 65.00
Grape & Cable, Plate, Handgrip, Basketweave Exterior, Amethyst, 8 In. 60.00
Grape & Cable, Plate, Old Rose Distilling Co., Stippled, Green, 8 3/4 In. ....300.00 to 375.00
Grape & Cable, Plate, Ribbed Exterior, Stippled, Blue, 9 In. 550.00
Grape & Cable, Plate, Stippled, Marigold, 9 In. 950.00
Grape & Cable, Powder Box, Cover, Amethyst, 3 1/2 In. 125.00
Grape & Cable, Punch Set, Amethyst, 8 Piece 750.00
Grape & Cable, Punch Set, Blue, 8 Piece 2800.00
Grape & Cable, Punch Set, Ice Blue, 13 Piece 8000.00

Grape & Cable, Sweetmeat, Amethyst, Footed, 9 In. 135.00
Grape & Cable, Sweetmeat, Cover, Amethyst, 8 1/2 In. 125.00
Grape & Cable, Table Set, Amethyst, 4 Piece 225.00
Grape & Cable, Water Set, Marigold, 7 Piece 300.00
Grape & Cable With Thumbprint, Cracker Jar, Amethyst, Handles, 7 1/2 In. 300.00
Grape & Cable With Thumbprint, Humidor, Cover, Amethyst, 7 1/2 In. 450.00
Grape & Cable With Thumbprint, Pitcher, Straight Sides, Amethyst, 9 1/2 In. 500.00
Grape & Cable With Thumbprint, Water Set, Amethyst, 2 Piece 275.00
Grape & Gothic Arches, Tumbler Set, Marigold, 4 In., 5 Piece 60.00
Grape Arbor, Tumbler, Ice Blue 130.00
Grape Arbor, Tumbler, Marigold 40.00
Grape Delight pattern is listed here as Vintage.
Grape Leaves, Bowl, Marigold, Ruffled Edge 10.00
Grape Wreath, Bowl, Marigold, 7 In. 55.00
Grape Wreath, Bowl, Variant, Green, 8 In. 115.00
Grapevine Diamonds pattern is listed here as Grapevine Lattice.
Grapevine Lattice, Plate, Marigold, 6 In. 30.00
Grapevine Lattice, Tumbler, Amethyst 20.00
Grapevine Lattice, Tumbler, White 185.00
Greek Key, Tumbler, Marigold 105.00
Greengard Furniture Co., Plate, Amethyst, Handgrip 7000.00
Harvest Flower, Tumbler, Amethyst, 4 1/4 In. 260.00
Harvest Time pattern is listed here as Golden Harvest.
Heart & Vine, Plate, Amethyst, 9 In. 250.00
Heart & Vine, Plate, Marigold, J.N. Ledford Company, Cooleemee, N.C., 9 In. 9000.00
Hearts & Flowers, Bowl, Amethyst, Ruffled Edge 475.00
Hearts & Flowers, Bowl, Aqua, Opalescent, Ruffled Edge 1000.00
Hearts & Flowers, Bowl, Green, Ruffled Edge . . . . .1300.00 to 1450.00
Hearts & Flowers, Bowl, Ice Green, Ruffled Edge 550.00
Hearts & Flowers, Bowl, Lime Green, Ruffled Edge 2100.00
Hearts & Flowers, Bowl, Marigold, Ruffled Edge 750.00
Heavy Grape, Nappy, Amethyst, Handles 40.00
Heavy Grape, Plate, Smoke, 8 In. 165.00
Heavy Iris, Tumbler, Marigold . . . . .45.00 to 85.00
Heron & Rushes pattern is listed here as Stork & Rushes.
Hobnail, Rose Bowl, Marigold 125.00
Hobnail, Swirl, Rose Bowl, Amethyst 325.00
Hobnail, Swirl, Rose Bowl, Marigold 170.00
Hobstar, Punch Cup, Marigold 50.00
Hobstar & Feather, Bowl, Diamond Shape, Marigold, 5 In. 1000.00
Hobstar & Feather, Rose Bowl, Green 1700.00
Hobstar & Torch pattern is listed here as Double Star.
Hobstar Band, Celery Vase, Marigold, Handles 55.00
Hobstar Band, Pitcher, Marigold, Footed 75.00
Hobstar Flower, Compote, Green, Ruffled Edge 80.00
Holly, Bowl, Blue Opalescent, Ruffled Edge 1050.00
Holly, Bowl, Blue, Deep, 7 1/2 In. 115.00
Holly, Bowl, Marigold Opalescent, Ruffled Edge 700.00
Holly, Plate, Marigold, 9 In. . . . . .175.00 to 300.00
Holly & Berry, Nappy, Handles, Peach Opalescent 30.00
Holly Spray pattern is listed here as Holly Sprig.
Holly Sprig, Bonbon, Green, Satin 75.00
Holly Sprig, Bonbon, Marigold 45.00
Holly Sprig, Bowl, Amethyst, Ruffled Edge, 8 In. 575.00
Holly Sprig, Bowl, Green, 7 In. 135.00
Holly Sprig, Bowl, Green, Tricornered, 6 In. 175.00
Holly Sprig, Nappy, Marigold, Handle 85.00
Holly Whirl, Bowl, Green, Ruffled Edge 145.00
Honeycomb, Rose Bowl, Peach Opalescent 95.00
Honeycomb Collar pattern is listed here as Fishscales & Beads.
Horse Medallions pattern is listed here as Horses' Heads.
Horses' Heads, Bowl, Nut, Red, Footed 1500.00
Horses' Heads, Plate, Marigold, 7 In. 225.00

Horses' Heads, Rose Bowl, Lime Green 475.00
Imperial Grape, Basket, Branch Handle, Marigold, 9 3/4 In. 115.00
Imperial Grape, Decanter, Amethyst, Stopper . . . . .250.00 to 400.00
Imperial Grape, Plate, Amethyst, 9 In. 1900.00
Imperial Grape, Plate, Green, 9 In. 35.00
Imperial Grape, Tumbler, Marigold 15.00
Imperial Grape, Wine Set, Smoke, 5 Piece 225.00
Imperial Jewels, Bowl, Square, Marigold, Marked, 7 In. 50.00
Imperial Jewels, Vase, Purple, Marked, 6 In. 65.00
Inca, Bottle, Marigold 225.00
Intaglio pattern is listed here as Hobstar & Feather.
Inverted Thistle, Bowl, Amethyst, 8 In. 200.00
Irish Lace pattern is listed here as Louisa.
Issac Benesch & Sons, Bowl, Amethyst, Ruffled Edge 425.00
Jeweled Heart, Bowl, Peach Opalescent, Ruffled Edge, 6 In. 25.00
Jockey Club, Plate, Amethyst, 6 In. 1600.00
Kittens, Cup & Saucer, Marigold 125.00
Knotted Beads, Vase, Blue, Ruffled Edge, 9 In. 35.00
Kokomo, Rose Bowl, Marigold 30.00
Kookabura, Sauce, Amethyst, Ruffled Edge 155.00
Kookabura, Sauce, Marigold, Ruffled Edge 95.00
Labelle Poppy pattern is listed here as Poppy Show.
Labelle Rose pattern is listed here as Rose Show.
Lattice & Daisy, Berry Set, Marigold, 9 Piece 300.00
Lattice & Grape, Tumbler, Blue 55.00
Lattice & Grapevine pattern is listed here as Lattice & Grape.
Leaf & Beads, Bowl, Amethyst, Rayed Interior, Domed Foot 85.00
Leaf & Beads, Bowl, Marigold, Sunflower Interior, Domed Foot . . . . .25.00 to 45.00
Leaf & Beads, Rose Bowl, Amethyst, Sunflower Interior, Domed Foot . . . . .85.00 to 95.00
Leaf & Beads, Rose Bowl, Blue, Footed 350.00
Leaf & Beads, Rose Bowl, Green, Sunflower Interior, Footed 215.00
Leaf & Beads, Rose Bowl, Ice Green, Footed 1500.00
Leaf & Beads, Rose Bowl, White, Footed 375.00
Leaf & Little Flowers, Compote, Amethyst, Miniature 325.00
Leaf & Little Flowers, Compote, Marigold, Miniature 155.00
Leaf Chain, Plate, Blue, 7 1/2 In. . . . . .70.00 to 100.00
Leaf Chain, Plate, Marigold, 7 1/2 In. 75.00
Leaf Chain, Plate, Marigold, 9 1/4 In. 575.00
Leaf Column, Vase, Green, 10 In. 190.00
Leaf Column, Vase, White, 10 In. 300.00
Leaf Medallion pattern is listed here as Leaf Chain.
Leaf Pinwheel & Star Flower pattern is listed here as Whirling Leaves.
Lined Lattice, Vase, Amethyst, 10 In. . . . . .105.00 to 195.00
Little Flowers, Chop Plate, Marigold 1400.00
Little Stars, Bowl, Green, Ruffled Edge, 7 In. 185.00
Loganberry, Vase, Amethyst 1700.00
Loganberry, Vase, Marigold 650.00
Loop & Column pattern is listed here as Pulled Loop.
Looped Petals pattern is listed here as Scales.
Lotus & Grape, Bonbon, Marigold, Handles, Folded, 7 In. 25.00
Lotus & Grape, Plate, Amethyst, 9 In. 1200.00
Lotus Land, Bonbon, Amethyst 900.00
Louisa, Rose Bowl, Green, Footed . . . . .30.00 to 55.00
Louisa, Rose Bowl, Marigold, Footed 60.00
Luster Rose, Butter, Cover, Marigold, 7 1/2 In. 40.00
Luster Rose, Fernery, Marigold 25.00
Magpie, Sauce, Marigold, Ruffled Edge 35.00
Many Fruits, Punch Set, Amethyst, 7 Piece 1050.00
Maple Leaf, Tumbler, Amethyst 20.00
Marilyn, Pitcher, Marigold 600.00
Marilyn, Tumbler, Green 190.00
Maryland pattern is listed here as Rustic.
Melinda pattern is listed here as Wishbone.

Mirrored Lotus, Rose Bowl, White 300.00
Morning Glory, Vase, Marigold, 5 In. . . . . .30.00 to 55.00
Morning Glory, Vase, Smoke, 7 In. 65.00
Multi Fruit & Flowers pattern is listed here as Many Fruits.
Mums & Greek Key pattern is listed here as Embroidered Mums.
N's Flute, Water Set, Marigold, 6 Piece 150.00
Nesting Swan, Bowl, Amethyst, 9 1/2 In. 1000.00
Nesting Swan, Bowl, Green, Deep 700.00
Night Stars, Bonbon, Amethyst 800.00
Norris N. Smith, Plate, Amethyst, 6 In. 1400.00
Nu-Art Chrysanthemum, Chop Plate, Smoke 800.00
Nu-Art Chrysanthemum, Plate, Green, 10 1/4 In. 11000.00
Nu-Art Homestead, Chop Plate, Smoke 625.00
Nu-Art Homestead, Plate, Amber, 10 1/4 In. 2000.00
Oak Leaf & Acorn pattern is listed here as Acorn.
Octagon, Vase, Marigold, 8 In. 55.00
Ogden Furniture, Plate, Amethyst, Handgrip 1100.00
Open Rose, Plate, Amethyst, 9 In. 1700.00
Open Rose, Plate, Marigold, 9 In. 55.00
Orange Tree, Hatpin Holder, Blue, 7 In. 150.00
Orange Tree, Hatpin Holder, Iridescent Chocolate 2700.00
Orange Tree, Loving Cup, Amethyst 500.00
Orange Tree, Loving Cup, Blue . . . . .200.00 to 2750.00
Orange Tree, Loving Cup, Green 1000.00
Orange Tree, Loving Cup, Marigold 175.00
Orange Tree, Mug, Marigold, 3 1/2 In. 10.00
Orange Tree, Plate, Blue, 9 1/2 In. 300.00
Orange Tree, Powder Jar, Blue, 3 1/2 In. 50.00
Orange Tree, Punch Set, Blue, 8 Piece 350.00
Orange Tree, Syrup, Blue, Whimsey 5000.00
Orange Tree, Table Set, Butter, Creamer, Spooner, Blue 225.00
Orange Tree, Tumbler, Marigold, Footed 25.00
Orange Tree & Scroll, Tumbler, Marigold . . . . .20.00 to 40.00
Oriental Poppy, Pitcher, Green 1350.00
Oriental Poppy, Pitcher, Marigold 450.00
Oriental Poppy, Tumbler, Amethyst 40.00
Oriental Poppy, Tumbler, Ice Blue, Ribbed Interior 215.00
Oriental Poppy, Tumbler, Marigold 25.00
Paneled Dandelion, Tumbler, Amethyst 55.00
Paneled Holly, Bonbon, Green 30.00
Panther, Berry Set, Marigold, 7 Piece 205.00
Panther, Bowl, Red, Ruffled Edge, 5 In. 275.00
Peach, Tumbler, Blue 100.00
Peacock, Bowl, Amethyst, 5 In. 165.00
Peacock, Bowl, Marigold, Ruffled Edge, 9 In. 350.00
Peacock, Plate, Amethyst, 6 In. 115.00
Peacock & Grape, Bowl, Blue, 9 In. 80.00
Peacock & Grape, Bowl, Peach Opalescent, Ruffled Edge 400.00
Peacock & Urn, Bowl, Ice Cream, Amethyst 350.00
Peacock & Urn, Bowl, Ice Cream, Blue, 6 In. 95.00
Peacock & Urn, Bowl, Ice Cream, Green 1000.00
Peacock & Urn, Bowl, Variant, Mystery, Green, 8 1/2 In. 400.00
Peacock & Urn, Compote, Marigold, Ruffled Edge 20.00
Peacock & Urn, Plate, Blue, 9 In. 500.00
Peacock At The Fountain, Compote, Electric Blue, 6 In. 1450.00
Peacock At The Fountain, Punch Bowl, Base, Amethyst, 10 In. 1800.00
Peacock At The Fountain, Table Set, Amethyst, 4 Piece 750.00
Peacock At The Fountain, Table Set, Marigold, 4 Piece 425.00
Peacock At The Fountain, Water Set, Amethyst, 7 Piece 1000.00
Peacock At The Fountain, Water Set, Marigold, 7 Piece 375.00
Peacock At The Urn, Bowl, Ice Cream, Cobalt Blue, Gold Iridescence, 10 In. 400.00
Peacock On Fence pattern is listed here as Peacocks.
Peacock Tail Variant, Compote, Green, Satin, Ruffled Edge 55.00

Peacocks, Bowl, Amethyst, 8 3/4 In. 310.00
Peacocks, Bowl, Aqua Opalescent, Ruffled Edge, 8 3/4 In. ....1200.00 to 1450.00
Peacocks, Bowl, Blue, Ruffled Edge, 8 3/4 In. 575.00
Peacocks, Plate, Amethyst, 9 1/4 In. 300.00
Peacocks, Plate, Blue, 9 In. 225.00
Peacocks, Plate, Blue, Stippled, 9 In. ....1000.00 to 1200.00
Peacocks, Plate, Ice Green, 9 In. 325.00
Peacocks, Plate, Marigold, 9 In. 300.00
Peacocks, Plate, Marigold, Stippled, 9 In. 650.00
Peacocks, Water Set, Electric Blue, 8 1/2 In., 7 Piece 550.00
Perfection, Pitcher, Amethyst 5500.00
Perfection, Tumbler, Amethyst 550.00
Persian Garden, Bowl, Fruit, Pedestal Base, Aqua Opalescent, 6 In. 400.00
Persian Garden, Plate, Marigold, 6 In. 50.00
Persian Medallion, Bonbon, Green 235.00
Persian Medallion, Bonbon, Marigold 65.00
Persian Medallion, Bonbon, Red 295.00
Persian Medallion, Bowl, Blue, Ruffled Edge, 10 In. 175.00
Persian Medallion, Plate, Amethyst, 6 In. 125.00
Persian Medallion, Plate, Blue, 9 In. 1000.00
Persian Medallion, Plate, Marigold, 6 In. ....150.00 to 200.00
Persian Medallion, Rose Bowl, Marigold ....35.00 to 40.00
Persian Medallion, Rose Bowl, White 110.00
Peter Rabbit, Bowl, Green, Ruffled Edge, 8 1/2 In. 2600.00
Peter Rabbit, Bowl, Marigold, Ruffled Edge, 8 1/2 In. 1200.00
Pine Cone, Plate, Marigold, 6 1/4 In. 150.00
Pine Cone Wreath pattern is listed here as Pine Cone.
Poinsettia, Pitcher, Milk, Marigold 70.00
Poinsettia, Pitcher, Milk, Smoke 255.00
Pony, Bowl, Amethyst, Ruffled Edge, 8 1/2 In. 200.00
Pony Rosette pattern is listed here as Pony.
Poppy Show, Plate, Blue, 9 In. 4900.00
Poppy Show, Plate, Ice Blue, 9 In. 2400.00
Poppy Show, Plate, Marigold, 9 In. 2500.00
Poppy Show, Vase, Marigold, 12 In. 525.00
Poppy Show, Vase, Smoke, 12 In. 4400.00
Princess Lace pattern is listed here as Octagon.
Pulled Loop, Vase, Amethyst, 9 In. 35.00
Question Marks, Cake Plate, Peach Opalescent, Ruffled Edge, Footed 175.00
Quill, Pitcher, Marigold 500.00
Quill, Tumbler, Amethyst 185.00
Raspberry, Pitcher, Milk, Marigold, 7 1/2 In. 60.00
Raspberry, Tumbler, Amethyst, 4 1/4 In. 10.00
Rays & Ribbons, Bowl, Marigold, Ruffled Edge 115.00
Rib & Panel, Vase, Marigold, 8 1/2 In. 35.00
Ripple, Vase, Blue, 11 In. 135.00
Ripple, Vase, Green, 5 In. 185.00
Ripple, Vase, Marigold, 9 1/2 In. 30.00
Robin, Water Set, Marigold, 7 Piece 275.00
Robin Red Breast pattern is listed here as Robin.
Rood's Chocolates, Plate, Amethyst, 6 In. 3600.00
Rose & Ruffles pattern is listed here as Open Rose.
Rose Show, Bowl, Amethyst, Ruffled Edge, 8 3/4 In. 300.00
Rose Show, Bowl, Aqua Opalescent, Butterscotch, Ruffled Edge, 8 3/4 In. ......650.00 to 1000.00
Rose Show, Bowl, Green, Ruffled Edge, 8 3/4 In. 1350.00
Rose Show, Bowl, Lime Green Opalescent, Ruffled Edge, 8 3/4 In. 2200.00
Rose Show, Bowl, White, 8 3/4 In. 175.00
Rose Show, Plate, Blue, 9 In. 550.00
Rose Show Variant, Plate, Marigold, 9 In. 1500.00
Roses & Fruits, Bonbon, Green 600.00
Roses & Greek Key, Plate, Smoke, Square 17000.00
Round-Up, Bowl, Amethyst, Ruffled Edge 625.00
Round-Up, Bowl, Smoke, Ruffled Edge 105.00

Rustic, Vase, Blue, 21 In. 1050.00
Rustic, Vase, Lime Green Opalescent, 17 In. 4000.00
S-Repeat, Wine Set, Blue, 11 1/2-In. Decanter, 10 1/2-In. Tray, 6 Piece 330.00
Sailboat & Windmill pattern is listed here as Sailboats.
Sailboats, Plate, Blue, 6 In. 475.00
Sailboats, Sauce, Round, Marigold 10.00
Scales, Bowl, Marigold, Ruffled Edge 30.00
Scroll Embossed, Compote, Blue, Ruffled Edge, Miniature 350.00
Scroll Embossed, Compote, File Exterior, Amethyst 375.00
Scroll Embossed, Compote, Green 40.00
Seaweed, Bowl, Ice Cream, Amethyst, 10 In. 170.00
Shell, Plate, Green, 9 In. 200.00
Shell & Wild Rose pattern is listed here as Wild Rose.
Shriners, Champagne, Louisville, 1909 . . . . 45.00
Singing Birds, Mug, Stippled, Blue 850.00
Singing Birds, Mug, Stippled, Marigold . . . . .80.00 to 85.00
Soda Gold, Tumbler, Marigold 10.00
Soldiers & Sailors, Plate, Illinois, Marigold, 7 In. 1900.00
Soldiers & Sailors, Plate, Indiana, Blue, 7 In. 15500.00
Spider Web pattern is listed here as Soda Gold.
Spiralex, Vase, Peach Opalescent, 10 In. 30.00
Spiralex, Vase, White, 12 In. 75.00
Spring Flowers pattern is listed here as Bouquet.
Springtime, Table Set, Amethyst, 4 Piece 1000.00
Stag & Holly, Bowl, Marigold, Spatula Foot, 11 In. 90.00
Stag & Holly, Plate, Marigold, 9 In. 600.00
Stag & Holly, Rose Bowl, Marigold, 3-Footed, 7 In. 150.00
Star & File, Compote, Marigold 135.00
Star & File, Rose Bowl, Marigold 50.00
Sterling Furniture Co., Plate, Amethyst, Handgrip 1800.00
Stippled Clematis pattern is listed here as Little Stars.
Stippled Diamond & Flower pattern is listed here as Little Flowers.
Stippled Leaf & Beads pattern is listed here as Leaf & Beads.
Stippled Petals, Bowl, Amethyst, Footed, Ruffled Edge 500.00
Stippled Posy & Pods pattern is listed here as Four Flowers.
Stippled Ribbons & Rays pattern is listed here as Rays & Ribbons.
Stork & Rushes, Mug, Amethyst, 4 In. 50.00
Stork & Rushes, Tumbler, Marigold 10.00
Stork & Rushes, Water Set, Blue, 7 Piece 650.00
Strawberry, Bowl, Amethyst, 8 1/2 In. 80.00
Strawberry, Plate, Green, 9 In. . . . . .100.00 to 165.00
Strawberry, Plate, Stippled, Amethyst, 9 In. . . . . .750.00 to 1100.00
Strawberry Wreath, Bowl, Amethyst, Square, 9 In. . . . . .225.00 to 350.00
Strawberry Wreath, Bowl, Vaseline, Marigold Overlay, Square 1600.00
Strawberry Wreath, Compote, Marigold, Ruffled Edge 375.00
Stream Of Hearts, Compote, Marigold, Ruffled Edge 85.00
Sunflower pattern is listed here as Dandelion.
Sunflower, Bowl, Amethyst, Footed, Ruffled Edge 700.00
Sunflower, Bowl, Blue, Footed, Ruffled Edge 1350.00
Sunflower, Bowl, Green, Footed, Ruffled Edge 1450.00
Sunflower-Wheat-Clover pattern is listed here as Harvest Flower.
Swan, Pastel, Salt, Amethyst 50.00
Swan, Pastel, Salt, Marigold 75.00
Swan, Pastel, Salt, Peach Opalescent 275.00
Thin Rib, Vase, Marigold, 16 In. 20.00
Thistle, Bowl, Amethyst 115.00
Three Fruits, Bowl, Marigold, 9 In. 105.00
Three Fruits, Plate, Amethyst, 9 In. 140.00
Three Fruits, Plate, Stippled, Aqua Opalescent, 9 In. 4500.00
Three Fruits, Plate, Stippled, Blue, 9 In. 1300.00
Three Fruits Medallion, Bowl, Aqua Opalescent, Stippled, Spatula Foot, 8 3/4 In. 350.00
Three Fruits Medallion, Bowl, Ice Green, Stippled, Spatula Foot, 9 In. 450.00
Three-In-One, Bowl, Smoke, Ruffled Edge, 9 In. 10.00

Tiger Lily, Plate, Footed, Amethyst 1600.00
Tornado, Vase, Amethyst .... .250.00 to 550.00
Tornado, Vase, Ribbed, Blue .... - 3100.00
Tree Trunk, Vase, Amethyst, 10 In. 40.00
Tree Trunk, Vase, Marigold, 12 In. 170.00
Trout & Fly, Bowl, Ice Cream, Green 750.00
Trout & Fly, Bowl, Ice Cream, Marigold 625.00
Trout & Fly, Bowl, Marigold, Square 900.00
Tulip & Cane, Wine, Marigold, 3 5/8 In. 55.00
Two Flowers, Bowl, 3-Footed, Marigold, 5 x 9 In. 40.00
Two Flowers, Rose Bowl, Lime Green Opalescent 200.00
Two Flowers, Rose Bowl, Marigold 35.00
Two Flowers, Rose Bowl, Smoky Blue 75.00
Utah Liquor Co., Plate, Amethyst, Double Handgrip 1750.00
Victorian, Bowl, Ice Cream, Amethyst, 11 In. 1200.00
Vintage, Bowl, Marigold, 7 1/2 In. 10.00
Vintage, Fernery, Blue .... .25.00 to 30.00
Vintage, Fernery, Marigold 25.00
Vintage, Nut Bowl, Amethyst, Footed, 4 1/4 In. 25.00
Vintage, Nut Bowl, Blue, Footed, 4 1/2 In. 50.00
Vintage, Rose Bowl, Amethyst 80.00
Vintage, Rose Bowl, Marigold 50.00
Whirling Leaves, Bowl, Green, Ruffled Edge 175.00
Whirling Leaves, Bowl, Green, Tricornered, Ruffled Edge 325.00
Wild Grapes pattern is listed here as Grape Leaves.
Wild Rose, Bowl, Amethyst, Open Edge, Footed 65.00
Wild Strawberry, Plate, Handgrip, Amethyst, 7 3/4 In. 80.00
Wild Strawberry, Plate, Handgrip, Green, 7 In. 125.00
Windmill, Bowl, Amethyst, Ruffled Edge 145.00
Windmill, Bowl, Marigold Milk Glass 425.00
Windmill, Pitcher, Smoke 500.00
Windmill Medallion pattern is listed here as Windmill.
Wishbone, Bowl, Amethyst, 9 In. 210.00
Wishbone, Bowl, Blue, Footed, Ruffled Edge 475.00
Wishbone, Bowl, Marigold, Footed, Ruffled Edge 95.00
Wishbone & Spades, Chop Plate, Amethyst 1000.00
Wisteria, Tumbler, Ice Blue 650.00
Wisteria & Lattice pattern is listed here as Wisteria.
Woodpecker, Wall Pocket, Marigold 70.00
Wreath Of Roses, Rose Bowl, Amethyst 30.00
Wreathed Cherry, Berry Set, Amethyst, Oval Master, 7 Piece 300.00
Zig Zag, Bowl, Ice Cream, Amethyst 325.00
Zipper Loop, Finger Lamp, Marigold .... .1050.00 to 1200.00

CAROUSEL or merry-go-round figures were first carved in the United
States in 1867 by Gustav Dentzel. Collectors discovered the charm of
the hand-carved figures in the 1970s, and they were soon classed as
folk art. Most desirable are the figures other than horses, such as pigs,
camels, lions, or dogs. A jumper is a figure that was made to move up
and down on a pole; a stander was placed in a stationary position.

Horse, Arcade, Metal, Painted Brown, White Accents, Leather Saddle, 54 x 26 In. 250.00
Horse, Carved, Painted, Leather Bridle, Iron Stirrups, Platform, 51 x 63 x 12 In. 5280.00
Horse, Jumping, Brown, Black Mane, Horsehair Tail, Green & Blue Saddle, 52 In. 1265.00
Horse, Jumping, Wood, Carved, Painted, Herschell-Spillman Co., 1903-1920, 42 x 56 In. . 3170.00
Horse, Rearing, Brown Paint, Mounted, Stepped Base, A. Saget, Canada, 1890, 51 In. ... 28000.00
Horse, Running, Cast Metal, Painted, Late 19th Century 410.00
Horse, Standing, Gustav A. Dentzel, Germantown, Pa., c.1900, 59 1/4 In. 17700.00
Horse, Steel Support, France, 1800s, 50 In. 2200.00
Horse, Wood, Carved, France, c.1900, 61 x 65 In. 840.00

CARRIAGE means several things, so this category lists baby carriages,
buggies for adults, horse-drawn sleighs, and even strollers. Doll-sized
carriages are listed in the Toy category.

Amish, Pull, Wood, Vinyl Canopy, Child's, 48 In. 440.00

Baby Buggy, Mustard Paint, Pin Striping, Rough Canopy, Victorian, 55 In.	275.00
Baby Buggy, Oak, Wicker, Parasol, 50 In.	330.00
Baby Buggy, Wicker, Natural Finish, Red & Green Accents, Heywood Wakefield, 48 In.	100.00
Baby Buggy, Wood, Cast Iron, Parasol, 48 In.	495.00
Dog Cart, Farm Wagon Style, c.1890, 93 x 23 x 20 In.	1600.00
Pram, Wood, Spoke Wheels, Canvas, Victorian, 31 1/2 x 38 x 13 In.	275.00
Pram, Woven Wicker, Spring Platform, Rubber Wheels, Corduroy, 43 x 52 x 19 In.	129.00
Sleigh, Cutter, Wood, Ribbed Seat Carving, Iron Frame, Storage Compartment, 70 In.	275.00
Stroller, Oriole Wicker, Converts To Sleeper, Withrow Mfg., 39 In.	250.00
Stroller, Wicker, Collapsible Handle, 57 In.	90.00
Stroller, Wicker, Stability Wheels, Large Spring, Rich Toy, 57 In.	130.00

CASH REGISTERS

CASH REGISTERS were invented in 1884 because an eye on the cash was a necessity in stores of the nineteenth century, too. John and James Ritty invented a large model that resembled a clock and kept a record of the dollars and cents exchanged in the store. John Patterson improved the cash register with a paper roll to record the money. By the early 1900s, elaborate brass registers were made. About World War I, the fancy case was exchanged for the more modern types.

American, Brass, Maple Base, 1909, 18 x 10 x 16 In.	1400.00
Brandt Automatic Cashier, Nickel Plated Money Changer, Griffins, 14 In.	130.00
Hough Security, Ledger Roll Top, Oak, Springfield, Mass., 17 x 10 x 19 In.	385.00
Michigan, Ornate Case, Marquee, 23 In.	176.00
National, Model 41, Brass, Walnut Base, 19 In.	220.00
National, Model 137, 25-Key, Lever & Handle, Cast Iron Case, Oak, 1901-1906	280.00
National, Model 313, 15-Key, Bronze, Nickel Plated, Oak, 11 In.	500.00 to 1130.00
National, Model 317, 15-Key, Bronze, Marble, Oak Base, 10 In.	600.00 to 1045.00
National, Model 327, 15-Key, Bronze, Marble Base, c.1908, 17 In.	745.00 to 1100.00
National, Model 332, Bronze Oak Base, Key, Marble Insert, c.1895, 17 In.	250.00
National, Model 415, 26-Key, Bronze	350.00
National, Model 441, 36-Key, Bronze, Marble, 1/4 Sawn Oak Base, 20 In.	440.00
National, Model 452, 45-Key, Bronze, Nickel Plated, Black, 24 In.	220.00
National, Model 552, 9 Drawer, Oak Base, Electrified	1100.00
National, Model 726, Wood Grain Tin, Oak, 17 In.	165.00

CASTOR JARS

CASTOR JARS for pickles are glass jars about six inches in height, held in special metal holders. They became a popular dinner table accessory about 1890. Each jar had a top that was usually silver or silver plate. The frame, also of a silver metal, had a handle that arched above the jar and a hook that held a pair of tongs. By 1900, the pickle castor was out of fashion. Many examples found today have reproduced glass jars in old holders. Additional pickle castors may be found in the various Glass categories.

Pickle, Cobalt Blue, Mary Gregory Style Boy Fishing, Silver Plated Cover, Stand	135.00
Pickle, Cranberry Glass, Enamel Pink Dogwood, Victorian	1150.00
Pickle, Cranberry, Inverted Thumbprint, Enameled	895.00
Pickle, Cranberry, Paneled Sprig, Enameled	895.00
Pickle, Green, Applied, Threading	375.00
Pickle, Melon, Ribbed, Wheel Cut Insert, Meriden Plated Holder, Tongs, 4 3/8 x 10 In.	489.00

CASTOR SETS

CASTOR SETS holding just salt and pepper castors were used in the seventeenth century. The sugar castor, mustard pot, spice dredger, bottles for vinegar and oil, and other spice holders became popular by the eighteenth century. These sets were usually made of sterling silver. The American Victorian castor set, the type most collected today, was made of silver plated Britannia metal. Colored glass bottles were introduced after the Civil War. The sets were out of fashion by World War I. Be careful when buying sets with colored bottles; many are reproductions. Other castor sets may be listed in various porcelain and glass categories in this book.

4 Bottles, Clear, Daisy & Button, Art Nouveau Silver Plated Stand, 5 1/2 In.	325.00
4 Bottles, Crosshatch Cut, Looped Handle, Sterling Silver, George III, c.1812, 6 In.	150.00

4 Bottles, Cruet, Silver Plate, Reeded Frames, Matthew Boulton, Sheffield, 6 3/4 In. 380.00
4 Bottles, Silver Plated Holder, England, 9 1/2 In. 230.00
4 Bottles, Square, 4 Ball Feet, Germany, 8 3/4 In. 260.00
5 Bottles, Clear, Engraved, Tufts Silver Plated Stand, Pedestal 65.00
5 Bottles, Cranberry, Inverted Thumbprint, Wilcox Silver Plated Stand, Dinner Bell 300.00
6 Bottles, Clear, Engraved, Meriden Brittania Style Stand 150.00

CATALOGS are listed in the Paper category.

CAULDON Limited worked in Staffordshire, Great Britain, and went
through many name changes. John Ridgway made porcelain at Cauldon
Place, Hanley, until 1855. The firm of John Ridgway, Bates and Co. of
Cauldon Place worked from 1856 to 1859. It became Bates, Brown-
Westhead, Moore and Co. from 1859 to 1862. Brown-Westhead, Moore
and Co. worked from 1862 to 1904. About 1890, this firm started using
the words *Cauldon* or *Cauldon ware* as part of the mark. Cauldon Ltd.
worked from 1905 to 1920, Cauldon Potteries from 1920 to 1962.
Related items may be found in the Indian Tree category.

Basket, Harlequin Pattern, Edith Gater, Art Deco, 10 In. 250.00
Candlestick, Roses, Hand Painted, 1920s, 7 In. 85.00
Cup & Saucer, Barberry Pattern, Demitasse 25.00
Dish, Chintz, Diamond Shape, Rounded Corners, 9 1/4 In. 150.00
Plate, Byzantine Transfer, Blue, c.1910, 6 1/2 In. 50.00
Plate, Luncheon, No. 2/2655/X, 12 Piece 530.00
Plate, Service, Flower, Gilt Leaves, Beige Border, Early 1900s, 10 3/8 In., 12 Piece 560.00
Platter, Fish, 21 1/2 In. 130.00
Tureen, Soup, Bowls, Roses, Blue Ribbon, Enamel, 13 Piece 195.00

CELADON is the name of a velvet-textured green-gray glaze used by
Chinese, Japanese, Korean, and other factories. The name refers both
to the glaze and to pieces covered with the glaze. It is still being made.

Bowl, 4-Petal Flower, 19th Century, 7 In. 29.00
Bowl, Carved Flowers, Lung Chaun, 7 1/2 In. 58.00
Bowl, Carved, Peonies, Cone Shape, 3 1/4 In. 239.00
Bowl, Inlaid, Crane, Clouds, Black & White, Peonies, Leaves, Korea, 7 3/4 In. 5520.00
Bowl, Korea, Koryo Dynasty, 4 In. 235.00
Bowl, Sawankhaloki, Ayuthya Period, 11 1/2 In., Pair 180.00
Charger, Birds, Butterflies, Flowers, Light Green Ground, Gold Edge, 14 1/2 In. 489.00
Charger, Chinese, Ming Dynasty, 14 1/4 In. 690.00
Charger, Flower Scrolling, Chinese, 1800s, 16 In. 90.00
Charger, Trigram Bands, 3 Animalistic Feet, Oval, Rolled Edge, 11 In. 345.00
Cup, Handle, Flower Shape, Dragon's Head Handle, Korea, 4 1/4 In. 2475.00
Dish, Jui Form, Figural Design, c.1840, 10 3/4 In. 635.00
Dish, Kuan Type, Brass Edge, Chinese, 1800s, 5 In. 295.00
Dish, Raised Fish Interior, Melon Ribbed Exterior, 5 1/2 In., Pair 405.00
Dish, Underglaze Blue, Iris Design, Japan, 1800s, 8 1/4 In. 69.00
Figurine, Crane, 1900s, 16 3/4 In., Pair 375.00
Fingering Piece, Frog, Early 1900s, 1 5/8 In. 29.00
Flask, Moon, Pheasants, Geese, Peonies, Chinese, 23 3/4 In. 1035.00
Jar, Oviform, Underglaze Blue & Red Fruit, 1700s, 5 In. 646.00
Jardiniere, Carved Flowers, 1900s, 20 1/2 In. 115.00
Planter, Ormolu Mounted, Flowers, Trees, Birds, Ring Handles, 12 x 15 In. 3616.00
Serving Dish, Cartouche Shape, Butterfly, Bird, 3 x 15 x 11 In. 99.00
Umbrella Stand, Enameled Birds, Flowers, Japan, c.1900, 24 In. 380.00
Vase, Blue Molded Foo Dogs & Clouds, Chinese, Late 1800s, 24 In. 410.00
Vase, Copper Red Fish, Chinese, 18th Century, 6 1/2 In. 2596.00
Vase, Hu Form, Cylindrical Handles, Late 1800s, 5 In. 46.00
Vase, Inlaid, Cranes, Willow Tree, Black, White, Mallet Shape, Fish Handles, Korea, 7 In. 8625.00
Vase, Inlaid, Flowering Tree, Pear Shape, Korea, 9 In. 5290.00
Vase, Owl, Leaves, Gold Lacquer, Crackle, Gray Green, Japan, Late 1800s, 15 1/2 In. ... 120.00
Vase, Studio, Mandarin Ducks, Japan, Early 1900s, 11 3/4 In. 345.00
Wine Pot, Inlaid, Cartouches, Willow Tree, Ducks, Palmette Band, Korea, 7 1/2 In. 2990.00
Writer's Coupe, 3-Legged Frog, Japan, 1800s, 2 1/2 In. 90.00

CELLULOID is a trademark for a plastic developed in 1868 by John W. Hyatt. Celluloid Manufacturing Company, the Celluloid Novelty Company, Celluloid Fancy Goods Company, and American Xylonite Company all used Celluloid to make jewelry, games, sewing equipment, false teeth, and piano keys. Eventually, the Hyatt Company became the American Celluloid and Chemical Manufacturing Company, the Celanese Corporation. The name *Celluloid* was often used to identify any similar plastic. Celluloid toys are listed under Toys.

Box, Collars & Cuff, Romantic Scene, Scrolling, Square, 6 1/4 In. 45.00
Box, Fan, Ivory, Blue Silk Lining, 12 x 3 3/4 In. 50.00
Box, Glove, Woman With Roses, 12 x 4 7/8 In. 40.00
Box, Ring, 4-Legged, Red, Wilkens 39.00
Dresser Set, Ivory, Brushes, Combs, Mirror, Manicure Tools, 25 Piece 70.00
Manicure Set, Leather Case, Light Blue Handles, Germany, 14 Piece 15.00
Powder Box, Cylinder, Cover, Flowers, 4 x 3 In. 25.00
Tissue Holder, Ivory, Embossed & Painted Kitten, 1950s, 3 x 4 1/2 In. 35.00
Trinket Box, Pearlescent Pink, Gold & Black Flowers, 5 x 3 In. 20.00

CELS are listed in this book in the Animation Art category.

CERAMIC ART COMPANY of Trenton, New Jersey, was established in 1889 by J. Coxon and W. Lenox and was an early producer of American Belleek porcelain. It became Lenox, Inc. in 1906. Do not confuse this ware with the pottery made by the Ceramic Arts Studio of Madison, Wisconsin.

Vase, Belleek Flower, Chrysanthemums, Slender Neck, Early 1900s, 18 3/8 In. 705.00
Vase, Indian Chief, Polychrome, Hand Painted, c.1895, 18 3/4 In. 1763.00

CERAMIC ARTS STUDIO was founded about 1940 in Madison, Wisconsin, by Lawrence Rabbett and Ruben Sand. Their most popular products were expensive molded figurines. The pottery closed in 1955. Do not confuse these products with those of the Ceramic Art Co. of Trenton, New Jersey.

Figurine, Horse Head, 3 1/2 In. 65.00
Salt & Pepper, Deer & Fawn, Betty Harrington, 4 In. 145.00
Salt & Pepper, Dog & Doghouse, 2 In. 110.00
Salt & Pepper, Polar Bear Mother & Baby, 4 1/2 In. 95.00
Salt & Pepper, Ram & Lamb, Betty Harrington, 1950s, 2 1/2 In. 79.00
Salt & Pepper, Siamese Cat & Kitten . . . . 95.00 to 115.00
Salt & Pepper, Siamese Cat, Thai & Thai-Thai, 5 In. 135.00
Salt & Pepper, Siamese Cat, Thai & Thai-Thai, Betty Harrington, 2 1/2 x 6 1/2 In. 65.00

CHALKWARE is really plaster of Paris decorated with watercolors. One type was molded from Staffordshire and other porcelain models and painted and sold as inexpensive decorations in the nineteenth century. Figures of plaster, made from about 1910 to 1940 for use as prizes at carnivals, are also known as chalkware. Kewpie dolls made of chalkware will be found in their own category.

Bank, Dog, Playing Banjo, 8 1/8 In. 11.00
Bank, Pig, Black, Gray, 16 In. 27.50
Figurine, Bird, Yellow, 19th Century, 6 1/4 In. 165.00
Figurine, Cat, Gray, Black Stripes, Green Highlights, 19th Century, 5 1/2 In. . . . . *Illus* 935.00
Figurine, Cat, Polychrome Paint, Red Ears, Brown Tail, American, c.1850, 6 3/4 In. 259.00
Figurine, Cat, Seated, 5 In. 1100.00
Figurine, Cat, Seated, Black, On White Decoration, Bow Collar, 6 3/4 In. 250.00
Figurine, Cat, Seated, Reddish Brown, Molded Collar, Tail Between Front Legs, 8 In. 338.00
Figurine, Cat, Seated, Smoking Pipe, Blue Bow Around Neck, 10 In. 225.00
Figurine, Cat, Seated, White, Red, Yellow, Black Detail, 19th Century, 10 In. . . . . . . *Illus* 3190.00
Figurine, Deer, Brown, Black, Red Paint, 10 1/2 In. 115.00
Figurine, Dog, Bulldog, Tooled Fur, White & Black Paint, 6 1/2 x 7 1/2 In. 99.00
Figurine, Dog, Poodle, White, Black Tail, Green Base, 7 In. 300.00
Figurine, Dog, Poodle, Yellow, Red Platform, Red Collar, 12 In. 10.00
Figurine, Dog, Seated, Black, On White Decoration, Polychrome Collar, 8 In., Pair 220.00

Clockwise from left: Chalkware, Figurine, Goat, White, Red Polka Dots, Yellow, Black, 19th Century, 9 In.
Chalkware, Figurine, Cat, Gray, Black Stripes, Green Highlights, 19th Century, 5 1/2 In.
Chalkware, Figurine, Peacock, Black, Green, Red, Raised Polka Dot Tail, 19th Century, 5 In.
Chalkware, Figurine, Squirrel, Eating Nut, Black Ears, Black, Yellow, Red, 19th Century, 7 In. Chalkware,
Figurine, Cat, Seated, White, Red, Yellow, Black Detail, 19th Century, 10 In.
Chalkware, Figurine, Dog, Spaniel, White, Black Ears, Black, Yellow, Red, 19th Century, 7 In.
Chalkware, Figurine, Roosters, Kissing, White, Gold Wings, Brown, Tail Feathers, 6 In.

Figurine, Dog, Spaniel, Seated, Brown, Black, 8 1/4 In. 58.00
Figurine, Dog, Spaniel, White, Black Ears, Black, Yellow, Red, 19th Century, 7 In. . . . *Illus* 990.00
Figurine, Dove, White, Yellow Feet, Cherry Branch Base, 10 1/4 In. 275.00
Figurine, Eagle, Spread Wing, On Ball, Star Band, Gilt, 18 1/2 In. 180.00
Figurine, Goat, White, Red Polka Dots, Yellow, Black, 19th Century, 9 In. .... *Illus* 5500.00
Figurine, Parrot, Detailed Feathers, Black, Brown, Yellow Green, 8 1/4 In. 495.00
Figurine, Peacock, Black, Green, Red, Raised Polka Dot Tail, 19th Century, 5 In. . . . *Illus* 1485.00
Figurine, Pigeon, 5 1/2 In. 990.00
Figurine, Rabbit, Seated, 19th Century, 5 1/2 In. 110.00
Figurine, Reindeer, Brown, Black, 10 In. 275.00
Figurine, Roosters, Kissing, White, Gold Wings, Brown, Tail Feathers, 6 In. .... *Illus* 1265.00
Figurine, Sheep, Lamb, Red Ears, Yellow Green, Orange, 6 1/4 In. 165.00
Figurine, Sheep, Ram, Ewe, Red, Black, Yellow Green Traces, 3 1/4 & 5 In., Pair 220.00
Figurine, Squirrel, Eating Nut, Black Ears, Black, Yellow, Red, 19th Century, 7 In. . . *Illus* 990.00
Figurine, Squirrel, Yellow Green, Ocher, 7 1/4 In. 300.00
Plaque, Horse Head Shape, White, Black, Red, Early 20th Century, 9 1/4 In., Pair 265.00
Plaque, Relief, Black Men Playing Pool, From N.Y. Pool Hall, 1940s, 16 In. 150.00

CHARLIE CHAPLIN, the famous comic and actor, lived from 1889 to
1977. He made his first movie in 1913. He did the movie *The Tramp*
in 1915. The character of the Tramp has remained famous, and in the
1980s appeared in a series of television commercials for computers.
Dolls, candy containers, and all sorts of memorabilia picture Charlie
Chaplin. Pieces are being made even today.

Bank, Charlie By Barrel, Glass, Tin, Borgfeldt, M 298, 3 3/4 In. 165.00
Book, Flip, Flipix, 1991, 3 x 2 In., 30 Pages 8.00
Candy Container, Barrel Bank, Tin Lid, Chaplin Along Side, Borgfeldt, 3 3/4 In. 345.00
Candy Container, Cane, Barrel Bank, L.D. Smith Co., 4 In. 495.00
Figure, Nodding, Wood, Carved, Painted, Germany, 13 In. 275.00
Film Reels, Mutoscope, German Pocket Book 1320.00
Lobby Title Card, Modern Times, Chaplin, Paulette Goddard, 1936, 11 x 14 In. 550.00
Photograph, Sepia Tone, Autograph, Inscription, Witzel Studio, Early 1920s 840.00
Postcard, Sepia, Essanay Film Studio, 1916 .... 15.00
Toy, El Vagabundo, Plastic, Windup, Spain, 7 In. 110.00
Toy, Walker, Clockwork, Composition Over Wire Body, 11 1/2 In. 360.00
Toy, Walker, Tin Lithograph, Cast Iron Shoes, Germany, 8 3/4 In. ....715.00 to 825.00

CHARLIE MCCARTHY was the ventriloquist's dummy used by Edgar Bergen from the 1930s. He was famous for his work in radio, movies, and television. The act was retired in the 1970s.

Dummy, Cardboard, Mechanical, Chase & Sanborn, 1938, 18 In.	75.00
Dummy, Gentleman, Celluloid, Japan, Box, 7 1/4 In.	965.00
Figure, Celluloid, Mouth & Chin Move, Windup, Box, C&K Japan, 1930s, 7 In.	675.00
Figure, Radio Show, Paper, Framed, 16 x 20 In.	120.00
Toy, Benzine Buggy, Tin Lithograph, Windup, Marx, American, c.1938, 8 In.	330.00
Toy, Benzine Buggy, Tin Lithograph, Windup, Marx, Box, American, c.1938, 8 In.	495.00
Toy, Car, Mortimer Snerd, Private, Tin Lithograph, Marx, Box, 1939, 17 In.	6325.00
Toy, Car, Windup, Tin Lithograph, Marx, 7 1/2 In.	275.00
Toy, Charlie Drives Car, Tin Lithograph, Windup, Marx, 8 In.	360.00
Toy, Crazy Car, Marx, 1935	495.00
Toy, Doll, Tuxedo, Hat, Lapel Pin, Effanbee, 1937, 17 In.	625.00
Toy, Gentleman Ventriloquist, Bounces, Mouth Opens, Japan, 7 1/4 In.	875.00
Toy, Krazy Car, Mortimer Snerd, Marx, 1935	495.00 to 695.00
Toy, McCarthy Strut, Tin Lithograph, Windup, Marx, Box, American, c.1940, 8 In.	385.00
Toy, Moritmer Snerd Drummer, Tin Lithograph, Louis Marx, Box, 8 1/2 In.	990.00
Toy, Mortimer Snerd Tricky Auto, Tin Lithograph, Marx, Box, 7 1/4 In.	440.00 to 660.00
Toy, Mortimer Snerd Walker, Tin Lithograph, Louis Marx, 1939, 8 3/4 In.	250.00
Toy, Mortimer Snerd's Hometown Band, Tin Lithograph, Windup, Marx, c.1940, 8 In.	580.00
Toy, Mortimer Snerd, Moves, Tin, Windup, Marx, Box, 1939, 8 1/2 In.	396.00 to 625.00
Toy, Private Car, Charlie & Mortimer Snerd, Tin Lithograph, Louis Marx, Box, 15 1/2 In.	4675.00
Toy, Walker, Tin Lithograph, Clockwork, Louis Marx, 1939, 8 3/4 In.	250.00

CHELSEA porcelain was made in the Chelsea area of London from about 1745 to 1784. Some pieces made from 1770 to 1784 may include the letter *D* for *Derby* in the mark. Ceramic designs were borrowed from the Meissen models of the day. Pieces were made of soft paste. The gold anchor was used as the mark but it has been copied by many other factories. Recent copies of Chelsea have been made from the original molds. Do not confuse Chelsea porcelain with Chelsea Grape, a white pottery with luster grape decoration.

Cup & Saucer, Flowers, Red Anchor Mark, England, c.1800	518.00
Dish, Fruiting Vines, Bouquet Of Flowers, Oval, 8 1/2 In.	745.00
Figurine, Boy On Stick Horse, Black Hat, 6 In.	198.00
Figurine, Poodle, White, On Green & Brown Mottled Base, Early 19th Century, 3 In., Pair	160.00
Lamp, Vase, Exotic Birds, Insects, 6-Sided, Flared Rim, Signed, 8 In., Pair	290.00
Plate, Flower Shape, Flower & Butterfly, Early 1800s, 9 1/2 In.	400.00

CHINESE EXPORT porcelain comprises all the many kinds of porcelain made in China for export to America and Europe in the eighteenth, nineteenth, and twentieth centuries. Other pieces may be listed in this book under Canton, Celadon, Nanking, and Rose Medallion.

Basin, Mandarin, Blue & White, Asian Life Medallion, c.1780, 4 x 11 1/8 In.	430.00
Basket, Underplate, Chestnut, Famille Rose, Scallop Rim, c.1810, 4 1/2 x 6 1/2 In.	529.00
Basket, Undertray, Lattice Sides, Cabbage Leaf, Butterfly, 1800s, 9 3/4 & 10 In.	750.00
Bottle, Gin, Cover, Blue & White, c.1700, 10 3/4 In., Pair	8963.00
Bottle, Water, Figures, Artifacts, 19th Century, 10 1/2 In.	825.00
Bottle, Water, Flowers, Roundel, Sprigs, Cobalt Blue, Gilt, Early 1800s, 10 In.	2350.00
Bough Pot, Famille Rose, Court Life Scenes, 1736-1795, 7 1/2 In.	575.00
Bough Pot, Rectangular Form, Squirrel, Grape, Rope Handles, c.1830, 7 3/4 In.	1380.00
Bourdalou, Seville Rose, Butterflies, Lid, Twisted Handle, Early 18th Century	995.00
Bowl, 5 People, Birds, 7 7/8 In.	410.00
Bowl, Armorial, Footed, 4 1/2 x 11 In.	440.00
Bowl, Armorial, Footed, Monogram Crest, Flowers, Orange Red, Sienna, 4 x 9 In.	920.00
Bowl, Bell Shape, Flowers, 18th Century, 4 3/4 In.	69.00
Bowl, Blue, White, Flowers, Landscape Border, c.1790, 11 1/4 In.	1035.00
Bowl, Cabbage Leaf Pattern, 1800s, 11 1/2 In.	865.00
Bowl, Chinese Calligraphy, Flowers, Fruit, 4 1/2 x 13 3/4 In.	170.00
Bowl, Cut Corner, Sepia, Orange, Sacred Flower, Butterfly, 1800s, 5 x 9 3/4 In.	1380.00
Bowl, Dome Lid, Armorial, Mantled Crest, Blue, Gilt, 6 x 10 3/4 In.	400.00

Bowl, Famille Jaune, Flowers, Modified Square Shape, 6 1/4 In.	69.00
Bowl, Famille Rose, 8 Panels, Center Flower, Mid 19th Century, 9 In.	60.00
Bowl, Famille Rose, Blue Interior, Scalloped, Wood Stand, c.1850, 9 x 2 3/4 In.	340.00
Bowl, Famille Rose, Flower Shape, Butterfly, Flowers, c.1840, 10 In.	690.00
Bowl, Famille Rose, Interior Figure Panels, Floral Reserves, 5 x 11 1/2 In.	1430.00
Bowl, Famille Verte, Flowering Tree, Peony, Early 1700s, 8 3/4 In.	605.00
Bowl, Fruit, Sprays, State Of New York Arms, Cobalt Blue, Gilt, c.1787, 10 1/4 In.	2350.00
Bowl, Rockefeller Pattern, Figural Design, Gold, Sepia Landscape, 1700s, 4 1/4 In.	690.00
Bowl, Rural Water Scenes, Crosshatch Border, Blue, White, 11 3/4 In.	575.00
Bowl, Silver, Melon Form, Scalloped Border, Raised Iris, 3 1/2 x 5 1/2 In.	360.00
Bowl, Silver, Raised Bamboo Trees, Moon, Sun, Stippled Field, 3 1/2 x 6 In.	360.00
Bowl, Spinach & Egg Glaze, Bell Shape, 5 3/4 In., Pair	690.00
Bowl, Tables, Vases, Jars, Boxes, Flowers, Fruit, 4 1/2 x 13 3/4 In.	165.00
Bowl, Vegetable, Rectangular, Pinecone Finial, Flowers, Cover, Late 1700s, Pair	1725.00
Brush Holder, Orange Foo Dog, 1870s, 5 In.	115.00
Candleholder, Elephant, Blue Underglaze, Red, Green, Gilt, 6 x 7 In., Pair	865.00
Candleholder, Famille Rose, Figural, Woman, Lotus Flower Holder, 17 In., Pair	1265.00
Candlestick, Dog Shape, Rose Medallion Blanket, c.1840, 5 1/4 In., Pair	5750.00
Candlestick, Elephant, Salmon Pink, Famille Rose Saddle, c.1810, 5 3/4 In.	1265.00
Candlestick, Flaring Base, Yellow, Painted Flowers, 1800s, 4 1/2 In., Pair	115.00
Card Tray, Hexagonal, Scalloped Edges, Flowers, c.1800, 5 In., Pair	375.00
Charger, Armorial, Torriano & Proli Arms, Italian Market, c.1740, 12 1/2 In.	2070.00
Charger, Blue & White, 1644-1661, 19 3/4 In.	4480.00
Charger, Blue & White, Floral Design, 15 1/2 In.	780.00
Charger, Butterfly, Flowers, Blue & White, 18 1/2 In.	200.00
Charger, Famille Rose, Ducks, Cranes, Lotus Blossoms, c.1760, 12 In.	805.00
Charger, Famille Rose, Figures In Garden, Early 20th Century, 13 1/2 In., Pair	230.00
Charger, Famille Rose, Geometric Designs, Blooming Branch, c.1750, 14 In.	2185.00
Charger, Famille Rose, Triple Border, Flowers, Center Figural Scene, 14 In.	230.00
Charger, Famille Verte, Central Bird, Chinese, Late 19th Century, 18 In.	230.00
Charger, Figural Decoration, Maiden, Sage, 1800s, 18 In.	260.00
Charger, Peony, Blue & White, c.1722, 14 In.	690.00
Coffeepot, Lighthouse Form, Blue & White, c.1790, 9 1/2 In.	1315.00
Creamer, Helmet Shape, Black Flowers, c.1800, 4 3/4 In.	105.00
Creamer, Pear Shape, Western Figures, Entwined Handle, 1700s, 5 In.	375.00
Cup, 3 Erotic Figures, Polychrome, 1900s, 3 1/4 In.	345.00
Cup, Blue Dragon, Inscribed, Underglaze, Blue & White, White Stem, 3 3/4 In.	489.00
Cup, Green, Fitzhugh, Fishbone Handles, c.1830, 3 Piece	46.00
Cup, Sang De Boeuf Glaze, Incised Dragons, Bell Shape, Stemmed, 6 1/4 In.	460.00
Cup & Saucer, Bird, Butterfly Cartouches, Lattice Ground, 1700s, Pair	259.00
Cup & Saucer, Famille Verte, Figural Design, Oversize, 1800s	315.00
Cup & Saucer, Flower & Leaf Design, 1700s	85.00
Cup & Saucer, Quaker & Cow, c.1815	1400.00
Dish, Armorial, 3 Figures, Flower Sprays, Chained Rim, c.1760, 8 1/4 In.	805.00
Dish, Armorial, Octagonal, Bruce Coat Of Arms, c.1785, 10 In.	460.00
Dish, Blue Underglaze, Island Pagodas, Figures Crossing Bridge, c.1780, 6 In.	290.00
Dish, Blue, Pagodas, Fitzhugh, Square, 10 1/4 In.	11500.00
Dish, Blue, White, Octagonal, Figural Scenes, Flowers, c.1790, 10 3/4 In., Pair	1955.00
Dish, Cabbage Leaf, Lozenge Form, Gallery Border, 1 1/2 x 15 x 11 In.	575.00
Dish, Cover, Blue Fitzhugh, Oval, Lotus Bud Finial, 4 1/2 x 11 1/2 In.	650.00
Dish, Cover, Iron Red, Gilt Highlights, Lion Knop, c.1861, 5 1/2 x 8 In., Pair	400.00
Dish, Cover, Lozenge Shape, Cobalt Blue, Rust, Flowers, Ship, 9 x 3 In., c.1800	290.00
Dish, Cover, Underliner, Famille Rose, Birds, Flowers, Butterflies, 6 x 5 In.	200.00
Dish, Cover, Undertray, Figural & Birds, Gilt Fruit Form Finial, c.1860, 5 1/2 In.	575.00
Dish, Famille Rose, Butterfly, Flowers, Gold Ground, c.1850, 15 1/4 In.	805.00
Dish, Famille Rose, Shallow Bowl, Fish & Leaves, c.1760, 8 3/4 In.	550.00
Dish, Famille Verte, Flower Basket, Butterfly Reserves, 1700s, 9 In.	265.00
Dish, Famille Verte, Oval, Aviary Reserve Cavatto, c.1840, 8 1/4 In.	290.00
Dish, Orange Fitzhugh, American Eagle, Curved Sides, Notched Corners, 8 In.	10640.00
Dish, Serpentine Rim, Flowers, Spearhead Border, 1700s, 5 1/2 In., Pair	175.00
Dish, Shrimp, Figures, Flowers, Famille Rose, c.1850, 1 3/4 x 9 1/2 x 10 1/2 In.	605.00
Dish Set, Blue & White, Landscape, Flower Medallions, Borders, 9 In., 3 Piece	145.00
Dish Set, Blue Fitzhugh, Pierced Border, c.1850, 10-In. Plate, 7 Piece	635.00

Figurine, Cockerel, Famille Rose Palette, c.1780, 9 In. 520.00
Figurine, Crane, Famille Rose, 20 1/2 In., Pair 460.00
Figurine, Ho Ho Bird, Lotus Rockwork Base, Famille Rose, c.1910, 19 In., Pair 1035.00
Figurine, Hounds, Glazed, Red Collar, Gilt Bells, 20th Century, 20 3/4 In., Pair 1265.00
Figurine, On Lotus Throne, Famille Rose, 10 In. 325.00
Figurine, Parrot, Green, Aubergine Glaze, Hardwood Stand, 1900s, 8 1/2 In., Pair 520.00
Figurine, Parrots, Lavender, Yellow, Rockwork Base, 1800s, 11 1/4 In. 1955.00
Figurine, Phoenix, Famille Rose, Early 20th Century, 16 In., Pair 560.00
Figurine, Quan Yin, Famille Rose, Seated Woman, c.1800, 8 In. 980.00
Figurine, Rooster, Polychromes, Decorated Biscuit, Terrain Base, 15 1/2 In., Pair 920.00
Fishbowl, Birds & Flowers, Famille Verte, c.1900, 18 In. 470.00
Fishbowl, Famille Rose, Children, Flowers, Aquatic Scene Inside, 18 3/4 x 21 In. 405.00
Fruit Basket, Undertray, Blue Fitzhugh, Pierced, c.1850 .... 805.00
Garden Seat, Barrel, Foo Dogs, Blue, White, 18 In. 920.00
Garden Seat, Blue Glaze, Drum Shape, 21 1/2 In. 288.00
Garden Seat, Child's, Blue, White, Floral, Raised Bosses, Pierced Cashes, 11 5/8 In. 764.00
Garden Seat, Famille Rose, Drum Shape, Openwork Sides, Gilt, 18 1/2 In. 1870.00
Ginger Jar, Blue, Rural Coastal Village Scene, Orange Peel Glaze, 16 1/2 x 6 In. 225.00
Ginger Jar, Famille Rose, Bird, Flowers, Mid 20th Century, 10 In. 115.00
Ginger Jar, Famille Verte, French Ormolu Mounts, c.1850, 16 1/2 In., Pair 3955.00
Hot Water Plate, Famille Rose, Butterfly, Flower, Monogram, c.1810, 9 3/4 In. 260.00
Hot Water Plate, Salmon, American Eagle, Monogram A.C., c.1800, 11 In. 489.00
Incense Holder, Turquoise Glaze, Famille Rose Flower Border, 1800s, 8 In. 499.00
Jar, 5-Clawed Dragon, Buddhistic Symbols, Blue & White, Melon Shape, 6 In. 1550.00
Jar, Cover, Rural Life Scene, 6-Sided, c.1900, 14 x 8 1/2 In., Pair 150.00
Jar, Famille Rose, Barrel Shape, Butterflies, Flowers, 1875-1908, 8 In., Pair 489.00
Jar, Famille Verte, Baluster, Foo Dogs, Peonies, 1800s, 12 In. 118.00
Jar, Famille Verte, Cover, Baluster, Birds, Flowers, 1800s, 16 In. 764.00
Jar, Famille Verte, Cover, Hundred Antiques, 1800s, 17 In. 588.00
Jar, Famille Verte, Ginger, Crackle Glaze, Hundred Antiques, Late 1800s, 12 In. 235.00
Jardiniere, Baluster Form, Peony, Blue, White, 12 In. 1095.00
Jardiniere, Blue & White, Foo Dog, Cloud Design, 1800s, 10 1/2 In. 200.00
Jardiniere, Famille Jaune Peach, Flowers, Early 1900s, 12 x 14 1/2 In. 259.00
Jardiniere, Famille Jaune, Landscape, Phoenixes, Peony, 13 1/2 x 15 In. 173.00
Jardiniere, Famille Verte, Cabbage Shape, 20th Century, 10 3/4 In., Pair 345.00
Jardiniere, Stand, 6-Sided, Court Life, Butterflies, Flowers, 6 3/4 In., Pair 1035.00
Lamp, Famille Rose, Male Figure, Colored Robe, On Waves, c.1900, 10 1/2 x 20 In. 90.00
Lamp Base, Oxblood Glaze, Paneled Baluster Shape, 20th Century, 15 In., Pair 705.00
Monteith, Orange Fitzhugh, American Eagle, Scalloped, Fluted, 10 3/4 In. 19550.00
Mug, Barrel Shape, Handle, Flowers, c.1800, 5 1/4 In. 520.00
Mug, Bell Shape, Figures, Flowers, Butterflies, 4 1/2 x 6 3/4 In. 375.00
Mug, Bell Shape, Flowers, Leaves, Applied Handle, Early 19th Century, 6 In. 440.00
Mug, Blue & White, Scene In Panel 700.00
Mug, Enameled Figural Decoration, Late 1700s, 5 1/4 In. 545.00
Mug, Famille Rose, Cylindrical, Braided Handle, Flowers, c.1780, 6 In. 1380.00
Mug Set, Blue Fitzhugh, Graduated, Nanking Border, Entwined Handle, 3 Piece 1495.00
Planter, Famille Rose, Bird, Flower Decoration, Late 19th Century, 7 x 10 1/2 In. 170.00
Planter, Famille Rose, Flower Panels, c.1850, 10 1/2 In., Pair 255.00
Planter, Famille Verte, Warriors, 1800s, 17 In. 1175.00
Planter, Storks In Tree, Mid To Late 19th Century, 7 x 10 1/2 In. 226,00
Plaque, Stand, Famille Rose, Porcelain, Late 19th Century, 24 x 23 In. 460.00
Plaque, Wall, Famille Rose, Flowers, Frame, 31 3/4 x 7 3/4 In., 1900s, Pair 865.00
Plate, American Eagle, E Pluribus Unum, American Embassy, Peking, 7 In. 1150.00
Plate, Armorial, Coat Of Arms, Flower Garlands, Early 19th Century, 9 1/4 In. 1840.00
Plate, Armorial, Fishscale Band, Gilt, Coat Of Arms, 9 1/4 In. 575.00
Plate, Armorial, Green Chrysanthemums, Spread Eagle, Monogram, 9 3/4 In. 1760.00
Plate, Armorial, Spearhead, Flowers, Chain Banding, c.1755, 9 In. 400.00
Plate, Famille Rose, Bamboo, Chinese Garden, Figures, c.1770, 9 In. 546.00
Plate, Famille Rose, Mythical Bird, Flowers, Wide Rim, c.1770, 9 In. 635.00
Plate, Famille Rose, Sargent Family Coat Of Arms, Motto, 9 1/2 In. ....5060.00 to 6440.00
Plate, Famille Rose, Warriors, Polychrome Enamel, Late 1800s, 9 3/4 In., Pair 145.00
Plate, Figural Landscape Center, Butterflies, Flowers, c.1800, 10 In., Pair 345.00
Plate, Flower Basket, Buddhistic Symbols, Famille Verte, 8 In. 635.00

Plate, Fruit, Flower, Butterflies, Flowers, Gold Ground, 1800s, 9 1/2 In. 69.00
Plate, Rockefeller Pattern, Gilt Border, Sepia Landscapes, 1700s, 9 3/4 In. 1840.00
Plate, Service, Green Fitzhugh, Mid 19th Century, 10 In. 200.00
Plate, Shell & Scroll Border, Flower Spray, c.1770, 8 3/4 In., Pair 865.00
Plate, Tobacco Leaf, Scrolled Flowers, Leaves, Rust, Brown, c.1765, 9 1/8 In., Pair 978.00
Plate Set, Bird, Flower, Insect, Famille Rose, 19th Century, 9 3/4 In., 4 Piece 230.00
Plate Set, Blue & White, Flowers, Diamond Hatch Rim, Chinese, c.1770, 9 In. 175.00
Plate Set, Dessert, Pseudo Tobacco Leaf, Gilt Highlights, c.1795, 8 3/4 In. 1265.00
Plate Set, Famille Rose, Bird, Butterfly, Flower, c.1850, 9 1/2 In., 12 Piece 520.00
Platter, Armorial, Stephenson Arms, Chain Bands, Oval, c.1790, 13 x 10 1/2 In. 1150.00
Platter, Blue & White, Octagonal, c.1810, 19 1/2 In. 540.00
Platter, Blue & White, Octagonal, Flowers, Trellis Border, 19th Century, 12 3/8 In. 440.00
Platter, Blue & White, Octagonal, Landscape Scene, 19th Century, 13 In. 590.00
Platter, Blue Fitzhugh, Oval, 19th Century, 20 1/8 In. 880.00
Platter, Blue Fitzhugh, Rectangular, Short Shaped Feet, c.1850, 13 1/2 In. 1150.00
Platter, Canted Corner, Figures, Garden Landscape, 14 In., Pair 1440.00
Platter, Drain Plate, Armorial, Flower, Butterfly Band, Warriors, Oval, 17 In. 3100.00
Platter, Famille Rose, Bird, Butterfly, Flowers, 19th Century 1610.00
Platter, Famille Rose, Bird, Flower, Butterfly, Ormolu Frame, c.1830, 10 1/2 In. 450.00
Platter, Famille Rose, Shaped, Scalloped, Double Spearhead Borders, 10 1/4 In. 635.00
Platter, Famille Rose, Stand, Regency, Mahogany, c.1795, 15 x 18 1/2 In., Pair 3910.00
Platter, Fitzhugh, Orange, Oval, Chinese, 1800s, 17 In. 2585.00
Platter, Flowers, Fruit, Butterflies, Sepia, Gilt, Oval, 19th Century, 18 3/4 In. 558.00
Platter, Flowers, Modified Spearhead Border, Late 1700s, 12 3/4 In. 489.00
Platter, Octagonal, Coat Of Arms, Malo Mori Quam Faedari, 11 1/2 In., Pair 1610.00
Platter, Oval, Orange Border, Orange Peel Glaze, 9 x 10 5/8 In. 1940.00
Platter, Oval, Ribbed Border, Flowers, 18 3/4 x 15 3/4 In. 145.00
Platter, Stand, Sacred Bird, Orange Red, Gilt, Mahogany Stand, 20 x 19 In. 920.00
Platter, Thousand Butterfly Pattern, Late 19th Century, 16 In. 530.00
Punch Bowl, 2 Wigged Men, Arms Of Liberty, Winged Devil, 4 1/2 x 10 1/4 In. 4715.00
Punch Bowl, American Eagle, Shield, Sepia, Gold, 11 In. 1725.00
Punch Bowl, Cabbage Leaf, 20th Century, 7 x 15 3/4 In., Pair 1095.00
Punch Bowl, Famille Rose, Blue & White Flower Border, c.1820, 5 1/2 x 14 In. 2530.00
Punch Bowl, Famille Rose, Butterflies, Bok Choy, Late 1800s, 6 3/4 x 16 In. 2300.00
Punch Bowl, Figures, Panels Of Chinese Life, Flared Rim, Famille Rose, 16 1/2 In. 520.00
Punch Bowl, People, Court Scene, Famille Rose, Cartouches, 4 x 11 1/4 In. 550.00
Salt, Trencher, Basket Form, 4 Animalistic Feet, Oval, 1700s, 3 1/2 In. 980.00
Sauceboat, Polychrome, Oval, Flower Spray, Garland, c.1780, 7 3/4 In. 315.00
Saucer, Chinese Figures, Deer, Landscape, Flower Band, c.1820, 6 1/4 In. 260.00
Screen, Figures In Palace Garden, Famille Rose, 1800s, 21 In. 765.00
Serving Dish, Famille Rose, Canton, Bird, Flower, Gilt Handle, c.1830, 10 1/2 In. 460.00
Serving Dish, Famille Rose, Octagonal, Bird, Flowers, 13 In., Pair 2130.00
Soup, Dish, Armorial, 8-Sided, Spearhead & Chain Band, 8 3/4 In. 1380.00
Soup, Dish, Armorial, Flower Sprays, Chains, Coat Of Arms, 8-Sided Rim, c.1865, 9 In. . . 865.00
Spoon Tray, Oval, Ship, American Flags, Flower Sprays, c.1790, 5 In. 4715.00
Sprinkler, Rose Water, Blue & White, 1662-1722, 10 3/4 In., Pair 13145.00
Stand, Famille Rose, Lotus Shape, 1821-1861, 9 In. 520.00
Table Screen, Famille Rose Enamel, Courtiers, Rosewood Frame, c.1890, 27 In. 705.00
Tea Box, Hinged Lid, Applied Papers, Label, Mid 1800s, 13 x 13 x 13 In. 90.00
Tea Set, Flowers, Teapot, Sugar, Cover, Creamer, Cups, Child's, 18th Century 175.00
Teabowl, Martha Washington, Border, Round Chain, 15 States Names, c.1795, 4 1/4 In. . . 9400.00
Teapot, Circular, Sepia Flower Decoration, 1800s 145.00
Teapot, Drum Shape, Cabbage Leaf Design, Entwined Handle, 1800s, 5 In. 575.00
Teapot, Egg Shape, Figural Landscape, Pink Fishscale Ground, Late 1700s, 7 In. 605.00
Teapot, Famille Rose, Circular, Marriage Design, Monogram, c.1780, 5 In. 575.00
Teapot, Famille Rose, Cylinder, Bird & Flower, c.1860, 6 In. 130.00
Teapot, Famille Rose, Landscape, Figures, Poems, c.1840, 6 1/4 In. 575.00
Teapot, Family Scenes, Spherical Body, Mandarin Cover, c.1750, 5 1/2 In. 460.00
Teapot, Flat Cover, Globular, Flowers, Scroll Handle, c.1780, 5 3/4 In. 470.00
Teapot, Globular Shape, Figural Cartouches, Lattice Ground, c.1890, 9 In. 690.00
Teapot, Globular, Women's, Scholar's Items, 4 1/2 x 6 3/4 In. 400.00
Teapot, Pear Shape, Flowering Vine, c.1760, 5 1/2 In. 1090.00
Teapot, Tobacco Leaf, Bamboo Form, Handle, Spout, c.1780, 6 1/2 In. 3220.00

Teapot, White Ground, Multicolored Flowers, Rattan Covered Handle, 5 1/2 In. 29.00
Temple Jar, Cover, Pear Shape, Figures, Bird, Flowers, 14 3/4 In. 345.00
Tray, Mandarin Design, Blue Fitzhugh Border, Late 1700s, 10 In. 520.00
Tureen, Armorial, Vegetable, Flowers, Trophies, Rectangular, c.1730, 10 1/2 x 13 In. 2875.00
Tureen, Cover, Blue & White, Peaked Loop Handles, Flower Finial, 11 In. 1380.00
Tureen, Cover, Figures, Oval, Intertwining Handles, Famille Rose, c.1870, 13 In. 748.00
Tureen, Cover, Stand, Blue & White, Early 19th Century, 10 1/2 In. 299.00
Tureen, Dome Cover, Oval, Famille Rose, Boar's Head Handles, 7 1/4 x 13 3/4 In. 520.00
Tureen, Platter, Sacred Bird, Gilt Flower Knop, Entwined Handles, c.1850 . . . . 4140.00
Tureen, Sauce, Blue & White, Monogram, Oval, Early 1800s, 8 In. 835.00
Tureen, Sauce, Thousand Butterfly Pattern, Late 1800s, 8 In., Pair 980.00
Tureen, Soup, Cabbage Leaf Design, Oval, Late 1800s, 12 1/2 In. 2070.00
Tureen, Soup, Stand, Octagonal, Chinese Landscape Scene, 14 3/4 In. 575.00
Tureen, Soup, Strap Handles, Famille Rose Flowers, Gilt, Cover, 14 In. 2185.00
Urn, Cherry Blossom, Black Field, 18th Century, 18 In. 1100.00
Urn, Cover, Flowers, Rust, Brown, Blue Rim, Gold Highlights, 17 x 9 In. 550.00
Vase, 5 Lobes, Flowers, Elongated Necks, Blue, White, 11 In., Pair 520.00
Vase, Baluster Form, Peach & Shou Design, Polychrome, c.1900, 16 1/2 In. 230.00
Vase, Baluster Form, Scalloped Ruff Neck, Celadon, Flowers, 1800s, 15 5/8 In., Pair 2470.00
Vase, Baluster, Relief Dragons, Famille Rose, 10 In., 1800s, Pair 635.00
Vase, Bamboo & Flowers, Blue & White, Pear Shape, 12 In. 1495.00
Vase, Beaker Shape, Famille Rose, Mounted As Lamp, c.1795, 13 In. 1610.00
Vase, Blue & White, Mounted As Lamp, Late 19th Century, 12 1/2 In. 520.00
Vase, Butterfly, Flowers, Turquoise Ground, Club Shape, 13 1/2 In. 640.00
Vase, Cover, Famille Rose, Enamel, Hexagonal, 21 1/2 In., Pair 17250.00
Vase, Cylinder, Blue & White, Peach Design, c.1810, 13 1/2 In. 259.00
Vase, Dragon, Phoenix, Blue & White, Club Shape, Garlic Mouth, 8 1/2 In. 920.00
Vase, Elephant, Blue & White Enamel Decoration, c.1800, 7 In. 999.00
Vase, Elephant, Saddle, Famille Rose, Double Gourd, Handles, 14 In., Pair 2530.00
Vase, Famille Rose, Bamboo Form Handles, 20th Century, 18 1/4 In. 345.00
Vase, Famille Rose, Cylindrical Neck, Flared Rim, Egg Shape Body, 12 1/4 In. 145.00
Vase, Famille Rose, Garden Panels, c.1850, 18 In. 680.00
Vase, Famille Rose, Hexagonal, Foo Dog Handles, Early 1800s, 23 In., Pair 3680.00
Vase, Famille Rose, Mythological Figures, Dragon Handles, c.1810, 24 In., Pair 4140.00
Vase, Famille Rose, Squared Baluster, Lotus, Wood Stand, c.1890, 9 In., Pair 635.00
Vase, Famille Rose, Temple, Assorted Designs, c.1850, 18 In. 1920.00
Vase, Famille Rose, Women In Palace, 1800s, 24 In. 325.00
Vase, Famille Verte, Birds, Flowers, 1800s, 24 In., Pair 2938.00
Vase, Famille Verte, Combating Warriors, 1800s, 17 In. 705.00
Vase, Famille Verte, Oviform, Flowers, K'ang Hsi Period, 5 3/4 In. 264.00
Vase, Famille Verte, Powder Blue, Fish Reserves, 1800s, 18 In. 206.00
Vase, Famille Verte, Rouleau Shape, Coral Red Ground, Early 1800s, 18 1/4 In. 489.00
Vase, Famille Verte, Rouleau Shape, Palace Scenes, 1800s, 15 In., Pair 823.00
Vase, Figures In Landscape, Blue & White, Baluster Shape, 18 In. 300.00
Vase, Fitzhugh, Orange, Reticulated Handles, Hexagon Base, 12 1/2 In. 180.00
Vase, Flattened Baluster Shape, Famille Rose, Goddesses, 1800s, 9 In., Pair 865.00
Vase, Foo Dog Design, Blue & White, Teardrop Shape, 7 1/2 In. 600.00
Vase, Green Glaze, Relief Deer, Pine Tree, Calligraphy, 10 1/4 In. 750.00
Vase, Hundred Antiques Designs, Famille Rose, Late 1800s, 15 In., Pair 410.00
Vase, Lions, Dragons, Figures, Gilt, Cartouche, Famille Rose, Baluster, 24 1/2 In. 3450.00
Vase, Nine Peaches, Famille Rose Enamel, Chinese, 19 In. 4994.00
Vase, Orange Red, Gilt Highlights, Foo Dog Handle, c.1861, 9 3/4 In., Pair 2300.00
Vase, Palmette & Flowers, Blue & White, Pear Shape, 6 In. 489.00
Vase, Peachbloom Glaze, Raised Leaves At Foot, Amphora Shape, 8 1/4 In. 865.00
Vase, Potpourri, Famille Rose, Dragon & Cloud, Cover, c.1910, 6 1/2 In. 1840.00
Vase, Stylized Lotus Pattern, Pear Shape, 12 In. 4600.00
Vase, Temple, Famille Verte, Blue & Gold Ground, c.1800, 18 In., Pair 2415.00
Vase, Turquoise Glaze, Relief Archaic Pattern, 8-Sided, 11 In. 374.00
Vase, Warriors, Flower Borders, Foo Dogs, Dragons, 1800s, 16 In. 881.00
Vase, White Glaze, Relief Tigers, Pine Trees, Calligraphy, 8 In. 690.00
Vase, Women Playing Chess, Famille Rose, 1800s, 18 In. 646.00
Wall Pocket, Famille Rose Enamel, Flowers, Yellow Ground, 7 In., Pair 382.00
Water Dropper, Famille Rose, Waterlily Pad, Bud, c.1780, 2 3/4 x 5 1/2 x 4 In. 633.00

Wine Pot, Blue, White, Mythological Figures Riding Clouds, Pear Shape, 5 In. 115.00
Wine Pot, Flowers, Blue & White, Inverted Pear Shape, 4 In. 632.00

CHINTZ is the name of a group of china patterns featuring an overall design of flowers and leaves. The design became popular with English makers about 1928. A few pieces are still being made. The best known are designs by Royal Winton, James Kent Ltd., Crown Ducal, and Shelley. Crown Ducal and Shelley are listed in their own sections.

Black Beauty, Salt & Pepper, 6-Paneled, Lord Nelson, 2 1/2 In. 125.00
Blue Pansy, Cup & Saucer, Luncheon Plate, Lawley, 3 Piece 100.00
Brama, Sauceboat, Midwinter 50.00
Briar Rose, Saucer, Lord Nelson 20.00
Chinese Rose, Bowl, Leighton Pottery, 8 In. 175.00
DuBarry, Sugar, Cover, James Kent 120.00
DuBarry, Teapot, James Kent 525.00
Elbeck, Teapot, Coffeepot, Greek Shape, Royal Winton 245.00
English Rose, Pin Tray, Royal Winton, 3 1/2 x 4 1/2 In. 80.00
Florence, Vase, 8-Paneled, Footed, Royal Winton, 6 In. 800.00
Hazel, Plate, Luncheon, Square, Canted Corners, Royal Winton, 7 In. 140.00
Hazel, Tray, Handles, Royal Winton, 11 In. 495.00
Heather, Jam Jar, Cover, Underplate, Glass Spoon, Lord Nelson 190.00
Maytime, Cake Plate, Tab Handles, Shelley, 9 3/4 In. 225.00
Old Cottage, Gem Dish, Royal Winton, 9 x 11 In. 225.00
Old Foley, Bonbon, Footed, Lord Nelson 70.00
Old Welbeck, Coffee Cann & Saucer, Royal Winton 55.00
Royal Brocade, Sugar & Creamer, Lord Nelson 175.00
Royal Tudorware, Tidbit, 2 Tiers, Brass Handle, Barket Brothers 180.00
Royalty, Breakfast Set, Royal Winton, 6 Piece 2250.00
Royalty, Sugar, Royal Winton, Ascot Shape, 2 3/4 In. 95.00
Summertime, Ashtray, Royal Winton, 4 1/4 In. 65.00
Summertime, Cup & Saucer, Luncheon Plate, Royal Winton, 3 Piece 120.00
Summertime, Tea Set, Royal Winton, 3 Piece 900.00
Sunshine, Cup & Saucer, Luncheon Plate, Royal Winton, 3 Piece 100.00

CHOCOLATE GLASS, sometimes mistakenly called caramel slag, was made by the Indiana Tumbler and Goblet Company of Greentown, Indiana, from 1900 to 1903. It was also made at other National Glass Company factories. Fenton Art Glass Co. also made chocolate glass from about 1907 to 1915. More recent pieces have been made by Imperial and others.

Cactus, Cracker Jar, Cover, Greentown, 8 In. 110.00
Cactus, Creamer, Greentown, 5 1/4 In. 65.00
Cactus, Syrup, Cover, Greentown, 6 In. 135.00
Cactus, Tumbler, Greentown, 4 In. 40.00
Indoor Drinking Scene, Mug, Greentown 100.00
Outdoor Drinking Scene, Mug, Greentown 125.00
Racing Deer & Doe, Pitcher, Greentown 400.00
Uneeda Biscuit, Tumbler 125.00

CHRISTMAS collectibles include not only Christmas trees and ornaments listed below, but also Santa Claus figures, special dishes, and even games and wrapping paper. A Belsnickle is a nineteenth-century figure of Father Christmas. A kugel is an early, heavy ornament made of thick blown glass, lined with zinc or lead, and often covered with colored wax. Christmas cards are listed in this section under Greeting Card. Christmas collectibles may also be listed in the Candy Container category. Christmas trees are listed in the section that follows.

Belsnickle, Painted Cardboard, Red, Black, White, Gold Flecks, 10 1/8 In. 144.00
Belsnickle, Painted, Red, White, Black, Gold Flecks, 7 3/4 In. 374.00
Blocks, ABC, Kris Kringle, McLoughlin Brothers, 1890s 225.00
Book, Boo-Boos & Santa Claus, Glassene, Attwell, Valentine, c.1924 .... 1200.00
Book, Life & Adventures Of Santa Claus, Bowen Merrill, 1902, 206 Pages 950.00
Button, J.N. Adam, Santa, North Pole, Polar Bear, Multicolored, Celluloid, 1 1/4 In. 201.00

Button, Quackenbush's Toyland, Out Of This World, Santa Claus, Lithograph, 1 5/8 In. ... 28.00
Button, Santa Claus Gave This To Me At Hens-Kelly, Celluloid, 1 1/4 In. 119.00
Button, Santa Claus, On My Way To Martins, Celluloid, Multicolored, 1 1/4 In. 149.00
Button, Santa Claus, Red, Yellow, Black, White, Celluloid, 1 1/4 In. 28.00
Candle, Santa, Gurley Novelty Co., 2 7/8 In. . . . . *Illus* 15.00
Card, Hubert & Muriel Humphrey, Facsimile Signatures, 4 1/2 x 6 In. 15.00
Coloring Book, Merrill, 1951 . . . . 8.00
Cookie Jar, Santa Claus, Plastic, Carolina Enterprises, 1973, 12 In. 40.00
Cracker, Red & Green, Mottoes, Set Of 12, Box, England, c.1925, 8 1/4 x 8 1/4 In. 65.00
Cubes, Jolly Santa Claus, 6 Different Santa Scenes, McLoughlin Brothers 1000.00
Doll, Santa Claus, Composition, Germany, 6 In. 65.00
Doll, Santa Claus, Pattern, Cloth, Uncut, 1800s, 24 x 18 In. 400.00
Doll, Stuffed, Edward Peck, 1880s 150.00
Doll, Stuffed, Hallmark, 1972, 5 In. 15.00
Doll, Young Girl, Period Clothing, On Rollers, Simon & Halbig, 1890 . . . . 1595.00
Figure, Santa Claus, Bisque, Germany, c.1920 . . . . 195.00
Figure, Santa Claus, Clockwork Mechanism, Walking, Ives 4950.00
Figure, Santa Claus, Composition, Red Felt Coat, Fur Whiskers, Feather Tree, 8 In. 604.00
Figure, Santa Claus, Hand Painted, Outstretched Arms, Fenton 35.00
Figure, Santa Claus, Papier-Mache, Cardboard, Chenille Robe, Basket, Japan, 8 3/4 In. . . . 440.00
Figure, Santa Claus, Papier-Mache, Wheeled Platform, Basket, Posable Head, 25 In. 4400.00
Figure, Santa Claus, Sleigh, Loofah & Straw, Cloth Dressed, Composition, 15 In. 605.00
Figure, Santa Claus, Sleigh, Wood, Cloth Dressed, Composition, 17 In. 1760.00
Figure, Santa Claus, Sleigh, Wood, Reindeer, Composition, Clockwork, 30 In. 4950.00
Figure, Santa Claus, Windup, Music, Papier-Mache, Continental, 1930s, 10 3/4 In. 275.00
Game, Card, Santa Claus, Russel, 1964 . . . . 25.00
Game, Game Of Merry Christmas, Parker Brothers, 1898 . . . . 1600.00
Game, Hi-Ho Santa Claus, Whitman, 1962 . . . . 35.00
Game, Night Before Christmas, Whitman, 1939 . . . . 150.00
Greeting Card, Decembre, Japon, Paul Jacoulet 140.00
Greeting Card, Merry Christmas & A Happy New Year, Paul Jacoulet 138.00
Greeting Card, Snowy Night, Paul Jacoulet 127.00
Kugel, Golden Amber, Embossed Brass Top, Loop Hanger, 9 1/2 In. 345.00
Lamp, Kerosene, Milk Glass, Painted, 10 In. 1540.00
Lamp, Oil, Night-Light, Santa Claus, Porcelain, Germany, 1920s 200.00
Lamp, Santa Claus, Kerosene, Milk Glass, Painted, 10 In. 1540.00
Nativity Set, Papier-Mache, Manger, Figures, Germany, c.1920, 15 Piece 430.00
Nodder, Santa Claus, Animated, Paper Lithograph, E.I.H. Co., Box, 18 In. 1760.00
Nodder, Santa, Cardboard, Wooden Box, Clockwork Mechanism, Horseman, 18 In. 1980.00
Pail, Christmas Greetings, Santa Claus, Blue Flat Tin Handle, Ohio Art, 5 In. 110.00
Paper Doll, Betty Bonnet's Christmas Party, Santa Outfit, Ladies Home Journal, 1916 . . . . 20.00
Paper Doll, Joies De Noel, Nativity Set, Tree, Animals, People, Box, 10 x 15 In. 4700.00
Pin, Eatons, Greeting From Santa Claus, Multicolored, Celluloid, 1 1/4 In. 120.00
Pin, Every Year I Am Here In Rudges Toyland, Santa, Multicolored, Celluloid, 1 1/4 In. . . 55.00
Pin, Give Something Electrical, Santa Claus, Multicolored, Celluloid, 1 1/4 In. 85.00
Pin, Glenville Banking & Trust, Santa On Phone, Multicolored, Celluloid, 1 1/4 In. 40.00
Pin, Halls, Santa Claus, Holly Wreath, Around Head, Multicolored, Celluloid, 1 1/4 In. . . 66.00
Pin, Headquarters At Hunter, Tuppens, Santa, In Chimney, Celluloid, 1 1/4 In. 100.00
Pin, Kresge Department Store, Newark, Santa Claus, Building, Celluloid, 1 1/2 In. 335.00
Pin, Sanders Candies, Santa Claus, Candle, Multicolored, Celluloid, 1 1/4 In. . . . . .100.00 to 120.00
Plates that are limited editions are listed in the Collector Plate category or in the correct
factory listing.
Postcard, Peace, Goodwill, Santa, Ringing Bell, Black & White, Signed, Nast, 6 In. 360.00
Postcard, Santa Claus, Children, Wiener Werkstatte, Number 900 . . . . 1150.00
Postcard, Santa Giving Gifts, Blue & Green Robe, Hold-To-Light 255.00
Postcard, Santa In Car, Hold-To-Light . . . . *Illus* 260.00
Postcard, Santa Loading Sleigh, Angels, Hold-To-Light, Mailick 315.00
Postcard, Santa, Children, Wiener Werkstatte, No. 900 . . . . 1150.00
Postcard, Santa, Metamorphic, Punch & Judy In Beard, Children & Cat Eyes & Ears 200.00
Postcard, Santa, Ringing Bell, Peace & Goodwill Ringing In The Air, Signed, Nast, 6 In. . . 358.00
Puzzle, Inlaid Heavy Cardboard, Santa's Workshop, Lowe, 1940s 7.00
Puzzle, Santa Claus, Scroll Puzzle, By McLoughlin, 1899 . . . . 70.00
Shoehorn, Weslows, Santa Claus, Anderson, Ind., 6 3/4 In. 40.00

Christmas, Stocking, Uncut, Muslin, Saalfield
Publishing Co., c.1907, 17 x 36 In.

Christmas,
Candle, Santa,
Gurley Novelty
Co., 2 7/8 In.

Christmas, Postcard, Santa In Car,
Hold-To-Light

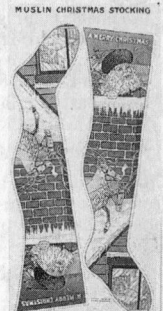

MUSLIN CHRISTMAS STOCKING

Stocking, Child, In Bed, Stockings, On Fireplace, Cloth, 29 In.	130.00
Stocking, Uncut, Muslin, Saalfield Publishing Co., c.1907, 17 x 36 In. .... *Illus*	715.00
Store Display, Santa, Plywood, Composition Figure, Electric, Germany, 23 x 21 In.	605.00
Toy, Happy Santa, Battery, Rolls Along, Head Turns, Plays Drum, Cragstan, 12 In.	105.00
Toy, Railroad Car, Santa Claus, Wood, Bisque Figures, 15 In.	275.00
Toy, Roly Poly, Santa Claus, Composition, 1910, 8 In.	550.00
Toy, Santa Claus, Fortune Telling, Battery Operated, Hong Kong, Box	20.00
Toy, Santa Claus, Nodding, Carrying Sack & Tree, Clockwork, c.1920, 27 In.	4950.00
Toy, Santa Claus, On Sled, Merry Christmas, Tin, Celluloid, Windup, Japan, Box, 7 In.	260.00
Toy, Santa Claus, On Sled, Moves, Bell Noise, Tin, Celluloid, Occupied Japan, Box, 8 In.	170.00
Toy, Santa Claus, Reindeer, Sleigh, Plastic, Canadian Cheerio, Box, 1950s	75.00
Toy, Santa Claus, Sleigh, 2 Reindeer, Cast Iron, Hubley, 16 In.	660.00
Toy, Santa Claus, Sleigh, 2 Reindeer, Tin Lithograph, Clockwork, Strauss, 11 In.	1430.00
Toy, Santa Claus, Sleigh, Loofah & Straw, Composition, 15 In.	605.00
Toy, Santa Claus, Sleigh, Nodding Reindeer, Clockwork	4950.00
Toy, Santa Claus, Sleigh, Reindeer, Composition, Wood, Bark, Clockwork, 30 In.	4950.00
Toy, Santa Claus, Sleigh, Waving, Toys, Reindeer, Tin, Celluloid, Windup, Japan, 8 In.	85.00
Toy, Santa Claus, Sleigh, Wood, Composition, Wire, 17 In.	1760.00
Toy, Santa Claus, Walking, Windup, Celluloid, Box, TN, Japan, 1930s	650.00
Toy, Santa Copter, Multiple Actions, Battery Operated, Original Box, Illsco, 1960s	145.00
Toy, Santa Skier, Tin, Vinyl Head, Windup, Japan, 1950s, 5 In.	150.00
Window Display, Santa Claus, Animated, Lithographed, Germany, 17 In.	4070.00

CHRISTMAS TREES made of feathers and Christmas tree decorations of all types are popular with collectors. The first decorated Christmas tree in America is claimed by many states, including Pennsylvania (1747), Massachusetts (1832), Illinois (1833), Ohio (1838), and Iowa (1845). The first glass ornaments were imported from Germany about 1860. Dresden ornaments were made about 100 years ago of paper and tinsel. Manufacturers in the United States were making ornaments in the early 1870s. Electric lights were first used on a Christmas tree in 1882. Character light bulbs became popular in the 1920s, bubble lights in the 1940s, twinkle bulbs in the 1950s, plastic bulbs by 1955. In this book a Christmas light is a holder for a candle used on the tree. Other forms of lighting include light bulbs. Other Christmas memorabilia is listed in the preceding section.

Candleholder, Figural Animals, Wire Holders, Box, c.1900, 23 Piece	2016.00
Feather, Brown Tape-Wrapped Trunk, Red Berries, Wood Base, 49 1/2 In.	410.00
Kugel, Emerald Green, Embossed Brass Top, Steel Hanging Loop, 7 1/2 In.	175.00
Kugel, Ruby Red, Brass Hanger, 6 In.	575.00
Lights, Bells, Plastic, Disney, Noma, Mazda Lamps, Box, 11 x 6 In.	220.00
Ornament, Angel Head, Wings, Tinsel Halo, Dresden	385.00
Ornament, Angel, 2-Sided, Cardboard, Dresden, 3 1/2 In.	550.00
Ornament, Angel, 2-Sided, Embossed, Painted, Cardboard, Dresden, 3 1/2 In.	550.00
Ornament, Blown Glass, Santa In Airplane, Wire Wings, Germany, 1950s, 5 In.	40.00

Ornament, Cap, Kugel, Green, Embossed, 4 1/2 In. 51.00
Ornament, Full-Figured Grinning Black Clown, Plays Mandolin, 1900, 4 In. 235.00
Ornament, Girl, Tennis Racket, Cotton Batting, Scrap Face, Crepe Cape, 5 1/2 In. 175.00
Ornament, Girl, With Muff, Cotton, Scrap Face, Buttons, Paper Fir Branch, 5 1/4 In. 175.00
Ornament, Santa, Stands On Swing, Crepe, Cotton, Scrap Face, Feather Trees, 5 In. 195.00
Ornament, Skis, Boots, Blue, Glass, Metal Skis, Painted, 6 1/4 In. 44.00
Stand, Musical, Clockwork, Wood Base, Lador Switzerland, 14 In. 125.00
Stand, Square, Raised Geometric, Openwork Design, c.1928, 5 x 13 In. 150.00

CHROME items in the Art Deco style became popular in the 1930s. Collectors are most interested in high-style pieces made by the Connecticut firms of Chase Brass and Copper Company, and Manning Bowman.

Bonbon, Round Sections, Basket Handle, Chase, 8 1/2 x 5 In. 35.00
Cocktail Set, Bowl Ball-Shaped Holder, Shaker, 6 Glass Tumblers, Bowler Finial 50.00
Cocktail Shaker, Beehive Ribbed, Footed, Bakelite Handle, 11 1/2 In. 55.00
Cocktail Shaker, Strainer, Cover, Black Rings At Top & Bottom, Chase, 11 1/2 In. 25.00
Ice Bucket, Cover, Black Band, Handle, Box, Kromex, 14 1/2 In. 11.00
Pitcher, Cover, Cocktail, Empire, Bakelite Finial & Stopper, Revere, 12 1/2 In. 1420.00
Pitcher, Normandie, Streamlined, P. Muller-Munk, Revere Copper & Brass, 1935, 12 In. .. 2938.00
Punch Set, Globe-Shaped Bowl, Cover, Ladle, Saturn Ring For Glass Cups, Lehman 125.00
Sculpture, Man's Head, Stylized Features & Hair, Hagenauer, 21 x 16 1/2 In. 6325.00
Sculpture, Woman's Head, Stylized Features, Hair, Choker, Hagenauer, 21 x 17 In. 6900.00
Server, Penguin Hot & Cold, Bakelite Handles, West Bend Co., 8 3/4 In. 20.00
Sugar & Creamer, Tray, Globe Shape, Revere, Art Deco 70.00
Tea Service, Ribbed Handle, Electric, Art Deco, Chase Brass & Copper Co., 8 In. .... *Illus* 315.00
Tidbit, 3 Leaf-Shaped Sections, Center Handle, 12 1/2 In. 23.00
Tumbler, Cocktail, Hemisphere, Ring Foot, Chase, 6 Piece 150.00

CIGAR STORE FIGURES of carved wood or cast iron were used as advertisements in front of the Victorian cigar store. The carved figures are now collected as folk art. They range in size from counter type, about three feet, to over eight feet high.

Indian, Hand Carved, Headdress, Cape, Ax, Wood Base, S.A. Robb, 70 In. 51750.00
Indian, Holding Box Of Cuban Cigars, Life Size, c.1900 .... 28500.00
Indian, Holding Bunch Of Cigars, Tomahawk, T In Triangle Mark, 14 In. 90.00
Indian, Pine, Multicolored, Holding Cigars, Mid 1800s, 7 x 2 1/2 x 2 In. 3850.00
Indian, Pot Metal, Plaster, Austin Prod., 20 In. 60.00
Indian, Sonoma City, California, c.1900 .... 5750.00
Young Black Man, Holding Cigar Pipe, Wood, Countertop, 25 1/2 In. 4125.00

CINNABAR is a vermilion or red lacquer. Pieces are made with tens to hundreds of thicknesses of the lacquer that is later carved. Most cinnabar was made in the Orient.

Box, 2 Conjoined Baluster Jars, 3 Stacking Sections, 2 Covers, Carved Phoenix, 11 In. ... 3145.00
Box, Carved, Figures, Landscape, Birds, Lotus, Square, Trefoil Corners, Chinese, 10 In. ... 4195.00

Chrome, Tea Service, Ribbed Handle, Electric,
Art Deco, Chase Brass & Copper Co., 8 In.

Never run an ad that says "Call after 6 p.m." It is an announcement that you are away from the house during the day. Never leave your house keys on your keychain when an attendant parks your car.

Box, Guest Being Greeted, Flower Borders, Chinese, 1800s, 5 1/2 In. 295.00
Box, Incense, Carved Flowers, Chinese, 1700s, 2 1/2 In. 325.00
Saucer, Buddhist Lions, Flowers, Brocade Ball, Chinese, Ming Period, 7 In. 1760.00
Vase, Carved, Figures, Landscape, Dragons At Foot, Bronze Elephant Heads, 18 In. 4195.00
Vase, Pear Shape, Flowering Branches, Red, Lacquer, Chinese, Qing Dynasty, 12 1/2 In. . . 885.00

CIVIL WAR mementos are important collectors' items. Most of the
pieces are military items used from 1861 to 1865. Be sure to avoid any
explosive munitions.

Badge, Confederate Veterans Reunion, Brass, Richmond, Va., 1907 . . . . 255.00
Badge, Confederate Veterans Reunion, Celluloid Scroll Shape, Memphis, May 1901 . . . . 338.00
Badge, Confederate Veterans Reunion, Enameled Flag, Shield, 2 Parts, Pewter, c.1907 . . . 255.00
Banner, Grand Reunion, Battle At Gettysburg, 1863-1889, Hand Painted, 38 x 27 In. 6050.00
Belt Buckle, Confederate, 6th Inf. NC S.T., Brass, 2 x 3 In. 6900.00
Belt Buckle, Union, Eagle, Brass 850.00
Binoculars, Brass Tubes, Adjustment Knob, French Made, 6 1/2 In. 55.00
Breastplate, Embossed Eagle, Arrows & Olive Branch, 2 1/2 In. 125.00
Broadside, $50 Reward, Run Away Slave, Maryland, 1861, 9 1/2 x 12 In. 2850.00
Broadside, Recruiting, Office Sup't, Pa., 1862, 7 3/4 x 4 3/4 In. 425.00
Broadside, War War War, Recruitment, Jefferson City, Mo., 1861, 10 1/2 x 16 1/2 In. 7750.00
Bullet Mold, .36 Caliber, Navy, Colt 805.00
Button, Naval, CSA, Gilt Brass, 2 Parts, Convex, Anchor Over Crossed Cannon, 8 In. . . . 630.00
Camp Ware, Field Flask, Tin, Pewter, Cup, Collapsing, Tin Cup, Bowl, 4 Piece 150.00
Cane, Knobby, 121 New York, Union Corps Badges, c.1862, 34 1/2 In. 1035.00
Cane, L-Shape Bone Handle, Malacca Shaft, B Co. 19 Regt. VRC, 33 3/4 In. 546.00
Cane, Pewter, Portrait Of Ulysses Grant, Eagle, Flag, Mahogany Shaft, 1892, 35 In. 250.00
Cannon Ball, Confederate, 6 Lbs., Vicksburg 90.00
Canteen, Bull's-Eye, 7 Rings, Pewter Spout, 3 Tin Sling Loops, 7 1/2 In. 422.00
Canteen, Confederate, Tin Drum, Raised Concentric Rings, Tin Spout, 6 In. 565.00
Canteen, Confederate, Wooden, Double Iron Bands, Scratched Initials, 7 x 2 1/4 In. 2415.00
Canteen, Tin Spout, 2 Tin Sling Loops, Wool Cover, 7 1/4 In. 115.00
Canteen, Union, Pewter Spout, 2 Tin Sling Loops, 7 1/2 In. 85.00
Cap Box, Infantry, Lamb's Wool & Vent Pick Inside, E. A. Crossman & Co. 340.00
Card, Southern Confederacy, US Grant Undertaker, Died April 9, 1865, 7 x 9 In. 300.00
Cartridge Box, Naval, Leather, Stamped Oval, USN, Belt Loop, 7 3/4 x 6 1/4 In. 219.00
Cartridge Box, Pistol, Officer's, Leather, U.S. Stamp On Flap, Wool Strip, 3 3/4 In. 675.00
Cartridge Pouch, Black Leather, 2-Flap Box, H. White, S.W. Young 405.00
Compass, Officer's, Brass, Glass Lens, Silver Dial, Side Freeze Lever, 1 1/4 In. 70.00
Drum, Hand Painted Band, Blue, Eagle Holding Ribbon, Red Rims, 16 x 16 In. 7475.00
Drum, Snare, Eagle, Shield, Metal Clips, Rope, Henry Eisele, New York, 12 x 16 In. 1840.00
Field Stove, Drum Shape, Tin, Painted, 4 In. 69.00
Frock Coat, Effects, West Virginia, Major Abel Houston Thayer, Surgeon's Kit 17250.00
ID Tag, Maryland, Union, Harrison E. King, c.1861 . . . . 3040.00
Letters, Burt Scott, 53rd Indiana, K.I.A., 1863-1864, 3 Piece 635.00
Medicine Chest, Field, Leather Covered Wood, Iron Handle, Velvet Lined, 12 x 7 In. 215.00
Pamphlet, Gen. Washington & Gen. Jackson On Negro Soldiers, 1863 . . . . 275.00
Pillowcase, Gettysburg 50th Anniversary, 1863-1913, 21 In. 150.00
Priming Powder Horn, Brass Fittings, Carved, Hunting & Military Scenes, 7 In. 520.00
Print, Cartoon, Jeff's Last Skedaddle, J. Davis In Dress, Knife, McLean, 14 x 20 In. 300.00
Print, Lithograph, Andersonville Prison, Henry Seibert & Bro., N.Y., Frame, 38 x 58 In. . . 920.00
Proclamation, Seeking Army Volunteers, N.H., 1863, 10 3/4 x 8 In., 4 Pages 145.00
Ribbon, Confederate Veterans Reunion, Herndon, Mosby's Men, Sept. 10, 1910 . . . . 1238.00
Ribbon, Confederate Veterans, 14th Annual Reunion, Sept. 30, 1908 . . . . 1180.00
Ribbon, Confederate Veterans, Front Royal, Mosby's Men, Aug. 18th, 1909 . . . . 730.00
Ribbon, Our Glorious Union For Ever, Silk, c.1864, 8 1/4 x 2 1/4 In. 405.00
Saber, Calvary, Confederate, Dog River, Model 1840 Type, Single Edge Blade 4315.00
Saber, Cavalry, Iron Mounted, U.S. M1840, PDL Mark 230.00
Saber, Cavalry, Millard, Model 1860, 35-In. Single Edged Blade, Carry Rings 1035.00
Scale, Recruiting Office, Padlock, Key, Fairbanks, Wood Box, 15 x 27 x 10 In. 575.00
Sewing Kit, Red & White Striped Cotton, Tie Strings, John H. Pope, OVI 160.00
Sheet Music, Little Joe The Contraband, Lucy Lovell, Mrs. Parkhurst, 1864 . . . . 85.00
Song Sheet, General Longstreet's Grand March, 1861, 14 x 10 3/4 In., 6 Pages 120.00
Song Sheet, Song Of The Privateer, Confederate, Baltimore, 1861, 8 1/4 x 3 1/4 In. 138.00

Surgeon's Kit, Saw Blades, Knives, Rosewood, Brass Bound, 12 x 4 1/2 x 3 In. 1840.00
Sword, Confederate Foot Officer's, Single Edge, Leech & Rigdon, 28-In. Blade 2875.00
Sword, Iron Scabbard, D.J. Millard, U.S., C.E.W., 1862, Double 34 7/8-In. Blade 949.00
Sword, Naval Officer's, Sharkskin Grip, Gilded Hilt, Case, Engraved, c.1860, 35 In. 430.00
Sword, Non-Regulation Officer's, Brass Hilt, 30-In. Curved Blade 565.00
Sword, Non-Regulation, Etched, Steel Scabbard, W. Clauberg-Solingen, 32-In. Blade 2935.00
Sword, Presentation, Etched Scrollwork, Eagle, Scabbard, 1860, 31 1/2-In. Blade 1475.00
Telegram, Confederate, Southern Telegraph Co., To Gen. G.T. Beauregard, 1862 .... 770.00
Telescope, 3 Draw, Brass, Officer's, Threaded Construction, 15 In. 135.00

CKAW, see Dedham category.

CLARICE CLIFF was a designer who worked in several English factories
after the 1920s, including A.J. Wilkinson Ltd., Wilkinson's Royal
Staffordshire Pottery, Newport Pottery, and Foley Pottery. She is best
known for her brightly colored Art Deco designs, including the
"Bizarre" line. She died in 1972. Reproductions have been made by
Wedgwood.

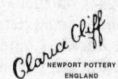

Aurea, Bizarre, Sugar & Creamer, Green, Yellow & Pink Flowers, 2 3/4 In. 195.00
Aurea, Bizarre, Sugar & Creamer, Open, Green, Yellow, Pink Flower, 2 3/4 In. 200.00
Autumn, Sugar Shaker, Conical Form, Pierced Top, Autumn Colors, 5 1/2 In. 1200.00
Bizarre, Bowl, Wide Bands, Blue, Orange, Ivory, Purple, 8 In. 650.00
Bizarre, Butter, Cover, Button Finial, Secrets, Landscape, Green, Yellow, 4 In. 550.00
Bizarre, Vase, Geometric, 6 x 5 In. 518.00
Blue Chintz, Bizarre, Cracker Jar, Cover, Blossoms, Blue, Green, Pink 1750.00
Blue Chintz, Bizarre, Plate, Stylized Flowers, Green, Blue, Pink, Marked, 9 In. 625.00
Cafe Au Lait, Pitcher, Milk, Oranges, 3 1/2 In. 295.00
Caprice, Bizarre, Bowl, Landscape, Hills, Arch, Trees, Lavender, Blue, Yellow, 8 In. 2800.00
Chintz, Bizarre, Cup, Cylindrical, D-Form Handle, Brown, Black, 1932, 4 In. 460.00
Crocus, Bizarre, Bowl, Flaring Side, 2 Bands, Crocus Blossoms, 6 1/2 In. 550.00
Crocus, Bizarre, Butter, Cover, Purple, Blue, Orange, White, 4 x 3 In. 550.00
Crocus, Bizarre, Sugar Shaker, Blue, Purple, Orange, Marked, c.1930, 5 5/8 In. 450.00
Delcia Citrus, Bizarre, Cracker Jar, Squatty, Kettle Form, Swing Bail Handle 1400.00
Delcia Citrus, Bizarre, Pitcher, Lotus Shape, Loop Handle, Orange, 12 In. 900.00
Forest Glen, Bowl, Orange, Brown Sky, Delcia Running, Orange Inside, 1936, 7 In. 280.00
Keyhole, Bowl, Upright Sides, Geometric, Yellow, Black & Green, c.1929, 8 3/8 In. 370.00
Melon, Fantasque, Pitcher, Orange & Black Bands, c.1930, 5 3/4 In. 880.00
Melon, Fantasque, Plate, Stylized Fruit, Orange Center Circle, Ink Mark, 9 In. 750.00
Melon, Jam Jar, Cover, Fruit Band, Orange, Yellow, Blue, Green, c.1930, 4 In. 700.00
My Garden, Bizarre, Vase, Relief-Molded, Orange & Yellow Flowers, 11 In. 660.00
My Garden, Candleholder, Figural, Keeling Woman, Arms Raised With Socket, 7 In. 575.00
Nemesia, Plate, Dessert, 6 In., 5 Piece 175.00
Plate, Stars, Red, Blue, Yellow Geometrics, Scalloped Edge, 5 1/2 In. 510.00
Summerhouse, Bizarre, Pitcher, Isis Shape, Yellow, Green, Purple, Red, 9 3/4 In. 3850.00
Tea For Two Set, Late 1920s, 9 Piece 3400.00
Tonquin, Bone Dish, Black 35.00
Tonquin, Bone Dish, Mulberry, Royal Staffordshire 35.00
Tonquin, Candlestick, Red, Loop Handle 35.00
Tonquin, Gravy Boat, Underplate, Black 40.00
Trees & House, Bowl, Marked, 3 1/4 x 7 3/4 In. 690.00
Trees & House, Pitcher, Hot Water, Orange, Black, Green, Pewter Lid, 1929, 7 In. 765.00
Trees & House, Plate, Dessert, 7 Piece 705.00
Wall Pocket, Lady Anne, Multicolored Flowers, No. 709, 10 1/8 In. 374.00
Woodland, Bowl, Octagonal, Landscape, Trees, Orange, Green, Black, 6 In. 550.00

CLEWELL ware was made in limited quantities by Charles Walter
Clewell of Canton, Ohio, from 1902 to 1955. Pottery was covered with
a thin coating of bronze, then treated to make the bronze turn different
colors. Pieces covered with copper, brass, or silver were also made.
Mr. Clewell's secret formula for blue patinated bronze was burned
when he died in 1965.

Bowl, Cover, Copper Clad, Bulbous, Flattened, 6 1/2 In. 1530.00
Lamp, Bronze, Incised Relief Design Repeated 4 Times, Graduated Pedestal, 14 1/2 In. .. 550.00
Pitcher, Copper Clad, Incised Flowers, 5 3/4 x 4 3/4 In. 375.00

Vase, Copper Clad Pottery, Raised Leaves, Pods, 11 In. 980.00
Vase, Copper Clad, Flower Panels, 4 x 4 1/2 In. 375.00
Vase, Copper Clad, Shouldered Shape, Marked, 8 1/2 In. 1440.00
Vase, Copper Clad, Tapered, Bulbous, 10 1/2 In. 635.00
Vase, Copper Clad, Verdigris, Bronze Patina, Bulbous, Marked, 7 x 6 In. 980.00
Vase, Footed, Orange To Blue Green Patina, No. 412-36, 8 1/2 In. 865.00

CLEWS pottery was made by George Clews & Co. of Brownhills Pottery, Tunstall, England, from 1906 to 1961. Additional pieces may be listed in the Flow Blue category.

Plate, Blue Transfer Ware, Oriental Scenes, Figures, Pagodas, 19th Century, 10 1/2 In. 66.00
Plate, Scalloped Edge, Fort Edwards, Hudson River, Mulberry, 4 1/8 In. 410.00
Plate, Toddy, America & Independence, 3-Story Building, 5 5/8 In. 345.00
Plate, Winter View Of Pittsfield, Mass., Dark Blue, 10 1/2 In. ....170.00 to 440.00
Teapot, Hunting Dogs, Dark Blue, Squat 580.00
Vase, Chameleon Ware, Blue, Brown, Orange Flowers, Yellow, Egg Shape, 8 In. 195.00
Vase, Chameleon Ware, Tree Blossom, Trumpet Shape, Blue, Yellow, No. 212/117, 9 In. ... 265.00
Vase, Chameleon Ware, Vase, Crown Pattern, Blue Ground, Egg Shape, 9 In. 195.00
Vase, Chameleon Ware, Vase, Poppy, Cylindrical, Pale Blue Ground, 11 1/2 In. 190.00

CLIFTON POTTERY was founded by William Long in Clifton, New Jersey, in 1905. He worked there until 1909 making lines including *Crystal Patina* and *Clifton Indian Ware*. Clifton Pottery made art pottery until 1911 and then concentrated on wall and floor tile. By 1914 the name had been change to Clifton Porcelain and Tile Company. Another firm, Chesapeake Pottery, sold majolica marked *Clifton Ware*.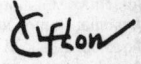

Jardiniere, Abstract Waves, Black, Beige, Terra-Cotta Ground, Incised, Tribe, 10 x 12 In. . 575.00
Vase, Bottle Form, Buff To Celadon Green, Marked, 1905, 10 1/2 In. 850.00
Vase, Brown Stylized Animals, Terra-Cotta Ground, Incised, Homolobi, 6 x 8 In. 230.00
Vase, Gourd Shape, Geometric Strips, Ivory, Red Ground, Marked, 6 1/4 x 6 1/2 In. 290.00
Vase, Gourd Shape, Petal Forms, Gray, Black, Terra-Cotta, Mississippi Tribe, 12 In. 460.00
Vase, Green Crystalline Matte Glaze, Squat, Hexagonal, Signed, 1905, 4 In. 403.00
Vase, Turquoise Matte Glaze, Handles, Marked, 1906, 6 1/2 In. 115.00
Vase, Yellow & Green Drips, Celadon Ground, 2 Handles, 1906, 4 1/2 In. 290.00

CLOCKS of all types have always been popular with collectors. The eighteenth-century tall case, or grandfather's clock, was designed to house a works with a long pendulum. In 1816, Eli Terry patented a new, smaller works for a clock, and the case became smaller. The clock could be kept on a shelf instead of on the floor. By 1840, coiled springs were used and even smaller clocks were made. Battery-powered electric clocks were made in the 1870s. A garniture set can include a clock and other objects displayed on a mantel.

Acorn, Wall, 8-Day, Thermometer, Barometer, Walnut Case, France, c.1880, 33 In. 396.00
Acorn, Wall, 8-Day, Thermometer, Barometer, Walnut Case, France, c.1880, 37 In. 425.00
Admiral Fitzroy, Barometer, Thermometer Gauge, Walnut Case, 45 In. 880.00
Advertising, 7-Up, Plastic, Flower Shape, 16 x 17 In. 66.00
Advertising, American Biscuit Mfg. Co., Regulator, 8-Day, Sessions, c.1900, 38 In. 509.00
Advertising, Beecham's Pills, Worth A Guinea A Box, Round 2695.00
Advertising, Blatz Beer, Animated, Electric, Plastic, Light-Up, 11 x 9 3/4 In. ...... *Illus* 100.00
Advertising, Cadillac, Service, Neon, c.1940 .... 990.00
Advertising, Calumet Baking Powder, Oak, 16 x 38 x 4 1/2 In. 605.00
Advertising, Calumet, Time To Buy, Oak, Reverse Glass Lettering, 39 x 18 x 5 1/2 In. 2860.00
Advertising, Capital Bread, Freshness, Flavor, Yellow, Red, Black, Plastic, Light-Up 80.00
Advertising, Dickeys Indian Blood & Liver Pills, Walnut, Waterbury Clock Co., 21 In. 660.00
Advertising, Fairacres Superior Ice Cream, Nebraska, 16 1/2 In. 200.00
Advertising, Gem Safety Razor, Wood Grain, Tin Litho, Embossed, Calendar, 28 1/2 In. ... 935.00
Advertising, Gilbert Store, Regulator, c.1910, 19 x 39 In. 325.00
Advertising, Go Greyhound & Leave The Driving To Us, Light-Up, c.1950 ......396.00 to 400.00
Advertising, Grocery & Meat Market, Round, Electric Clock Co., Chicago, 22 1/2 In. 360.00
Advertising, Irodent Tooth Paste, Electric, Square Wood Frame, 15 In. 80.00
Advertising, Iroquois Beer, Ale, Double Bubble, Light-Up, Round, 16 In. 575.00
Advertising, Josada, 10 Cent Cigars, Cast Metal, Footed, Cigar Cutter, 14 In. 990.00

Advertising, McCord Motor Gaskets, Time To Buy, 14 1/2 In. 110.00
Advertising, Mexican Cigars, Matador, Bull, Hectermann Bros., Iron, 1880, 14 x 19 In. . . 1485.00
Advertising, None Such, Pumpkin, Ribbed Cardboard, Tin Back, Round, 9 1/2 x 1 1/2 In. 1265.00
Advertising, Old Mr. Boston, Figural, Blue, White, Metal, c.1920, 22 In. 385.00
Advertising, Old Mr. Boston, Fine Liquors, Blue, Bottle Form, Metal, c.1920, 22 In. 385.00
Advertising, Penn Mutual Insurance, Banjo, Regulator, Mass., c.1860, 49 1/2 In. 3360.00
Advertising, Picadilly Ginger Ale, R.J. Holmes Carbonating Co., Mo., Brass, 15 3/4 In. . . 1375.00
Advertising, Sealtest Ice Cream, Southern Dairies, Neon, Octagonal, 18 In. 468.00
Advertising, Simmons Liver Regulator, Horseshoe Surrounds Dial, Ansonia, c.1900, 6 In. 225.00
Advertising, Tollins Dept. Store, Long Drop, Pressed Oak, c.1900, 32 In. 450.00
Advertising, Vanner & Prests Molliscorium, Baird Type, c.1890, 31 In. 550.00
Advertising, Ward's Orange Crush, Regulator, Oak Case, Ingraham Co., 32 In. 550.00
Advertising, West Point Hair Tonic, Bulova, Light-Up, 14 1/2 Diam. 120.00
Alarm, Chrome & Brass, Tifany & Co., 2 1/2 x 2 1/2 In. 150.00
Alessi, Shelf, Blond & Ebonized Wood, Pendulum, Michael Graves, 9 3/4 x 6 1/4 In. . . . 690.00
Angelus, Desk, Compendium, Weather Station, 8-Day, c.1955, 4 In. 100.00
Angelus, Globe, 8-Day, Barometer, Hygrometer, Thermometer, Swiss, c.1965, 8 In. 110.00
Animated, Black Forest, For He's A Jolly Good Fellow, c.1930, 18 In. 395.00
Animated, Bontem, Chirping Birds, Musical, c.1880, 26 In. 4400.00
Animated, Brass Cage, Singing Bird, Moves Head & Wings, 17 In. 765.00
Animated, Cat, Side-To-Side Eyes, Painted Wood Dial, Germany, 7 3/4 In. 50.00
Animated, Windmill Strut, Square, Germany, c.1930, 5 In. 50.00
Ansonia, Alhambra, Hard Rubber Dial, Open Escapement, c.1904, 18 In. 448.00
Ansonia, Banjo, No. 1, 8-Day, Windup, Sailing Ship On Glass, 17 1/2 In. 550.00
Ansonia, Black Marble, Open Escapement, c.1885, 10 1/2 In. 225.00
Ansonia, Breton, Man Carrying Clock On Shoulder, 8-Day, c.1914, 11 3/4 In. 1815.00
Ansonia, Carriage, 8-Day, Porcelain Dial, Miniature, 5 1/2 In. 198.00
Ansonia, Carriage, 30-Hour, Alarm, Miniature 225.00
Ansonia, Carriage, Vida, Gilt Spelter, c.1900, 4 In. 170.00
Ansonia, Cartel, Gold Finish Spelter Strut, Enamel Dial, Wire Stand, c.1900, 7 In. 141.00
Ansonia, Chippendale, Gilt, Faux Leather, c.1890, 18 1/2 In. 476.00
Ansonia, Columbia, Shepherd Boy, c.1905, 25 1/2 In. 3248.00
Ansonia, Cottage, Mahogany, 30-Hour Time, Strike & Alarm, Metal Dial, 11 In. 135.00
Ansonia, Crystal Regulator, Crown, 8-Day, Time & Strike, Gong, c.1914, 15 1/2 In. 565.00
Ansonia, Crystal Regulator, Crown, Porcelain Dial, Beveled Glass, 15 1/2 In. 560.00
Ansonia, Crystal Regulator, Danube, c.1920, 9 1/2 In. 198.00
Ansonia, Crystal Regulator, Elysian, 8-Day, Time & Strike, Coiled Gong, c.1914, 16 In. . . 620.00
Ansonia, Crystal Regulator, Lucia, 8-Day, Time & Strike, Beveled Glass, c.1904, 15 In. . . 1017.00
Ansonia, Crystal, Regulator, Brilliant Sash & Pendulum, c.1910, 10 In. 645.00
Ansonia, Cymric, Orchid, Art Nouveau Finish, c.1904, 24 1/2 In. 1230.00
Ansonia, Fife & Drum, 2 Figures, Gilt Copper, c.1905, 5 In. 205.00
Ansonia, Fleur-De-Lis, Orchid, Bronze Finish, c.1904, 24 1/2 In. 785.00
Ansonia, Florida, Woman On Metal Case, Flowers, Fancy Dial, 36 x 26 1/2 In. 3300.00
Ansonia, Kitchen, Oak, Gingerbread, 8-Day, Time & Strike, Alarm, 23 1/2 In. 110.00
Ansonia, Lawn Tennis, Cast Figural, c.1900, 8 In. 110.00
Ansonia, Macbeth, 8-Day, Time & Strike, Gong, c.1905, 15 In. 339.00
Ansonia, Mantel, Cygnet, Gilt Metal, Porcelain Dial, c.1905, 12 3/4 In. 335.00
Ansonia, Mantel, Music & Poetry, 2 Figures, c.1894, 20 3/4 In. 2240.00
Ansonia, Marbelite, No. 2, Porcelain Dial, Exposed Escapement, c.1885, 10 3/4 In. 280.00
Ansonia, Marbelite, No. 4, Molded Hard Rubber, Porcelain Dial, c.1885, 12 1/4 In. 250.00
Ansonia, Marbelite, No. 5, Molded Hard Rubber, Porcelain Dial, c.1885, 17 In. . . 280.00 to 390.00
Ansonia, Marbelite, No. 8, Hard Rubber Dial, Open Escapement, 15 1/2 In. 560.00
Ansonia, Novelty, Mirror, Baroque Style, Beveled Mirror, c.1890, 9 1/4 In. 728.00
Ansonia, Novelty, No. 20, Birds, c.1892, 4 1/2 In. 728.00
Ansonia, Novelty, No. 27, Masonic Themes, c.1886, 7 In. 365.00
Ansonia, Novelty, No. 254, Buenos Noches, Green, Brown, c.1914, 9 3/4 In. 896.00
Ansonia, Opera Fan, Metal Case, Paper Dial, c.1894, 8 In. 225.00
Ansonia, Parlor Ink, No. 2, Metal Dial, Silvered Chapter Ring, Gilt Center, c.1885, 8 In. . . 590.00
Ansonia, Plato, Digital, Stamped Brass Case, c.1904, 6 1/4 In. 420.00
Ansonia, Rabbit, Clock On Backpack Frame, 1-Day, c.1900, 7 1/2 In. 225.00
Ansonia, School, Regulator, 8-Day, Time Only, Oak Case, 33 In. 115.00
Ansonia, Shelf, 8-Day, Hour & 1/2, Cathedral Bell Strike, Dresden, c.1915, 12 In. 450.00
Ansonia, Shelf, Beehive, 30-Hour, Metal Dial, Decorated Lower Pane, c.1890, 19 In. 168.00

Ansonia, Shelf, Black Marble, Thoroughbred Clock Topper, French Sash Dial, 17 In. 420.00
Ansonia, Shelf, Bronze-Patinated Spelter, Pavilion Shape, c.1885, 25 1/2 x 9 1/2 In. 1610.00
Ansonia, Shelf, Criterion, Spelter, Marble, Green Onyx Inserts, c.1904, 16 3/4 In. 505.00
Ansonia, Shelf, Cygnet, Louis XVI Style, Gilt, Spelter, Rococo Sash, 8-Day, c.1906 ..... 198.00
Ansonia, Shelf, Gilt Dial Mask, Lion's Head & Feet, Black Iron, c.1900 .... 140.00
Ansonia, Shelf, Peconic, Ivory Case, Flowers, Gilt Borders, c.1900, 12 In. 620.00
Ansonia, Shelf, Porcelain H, 8-Day, Time Only, c.1895, 10 1/2 In. 196.00
Ansonia, Spelter, Key Wind, Seated Classical Figure, Putti, 19 x 11 x 9 In. 1870.00
Ansonia, Steeple, Rosewood, Masonic Tablet, 8-Day, c.1870, 20 In. 476.00
Ansonia, Swing, Fisherman, Small Diameter Arm, c.1895, 25 1/2 In. 3810.00
Ansonia, Sybil & Summer, Porcelain Dial, c.1904, 24 In. 1345.00
Art Deco, Crystal Case, Rose Face, Black Bakelite Base, Nickel, Russia, 8 1/2 In. 750.00
Art Deco, Figural, Gazelle, Marble Side Pieces, Cast Spelter, 8-Day, c.1925, 8 3/4 In. 60.00
Art Deco, Marble, 8-Day, Bell Strike, France, c.1925, 10 1/2 In. 339.00
Art Deco, Spelter Frame, Gilt Highlights, Glass Pedestals, Germany, 15 1/2 In. 195.00
Art Deco, Woman Holds Lighter, American, c.1920, 6 In. 140.00
Arts & Crafts, Wood, Green Slag Glass, Brass Numbers, 18 x 11 In. 315.00
Atkins, London, Rosewood, Half Column, Double Fusee, 30-Day, c.1865 .... 3300.00
Atkins, Shelf, Pillar, Splat, Wood, 1833 .... 99.00
Atkins Clock Co., Shelf, Tombstone, Chestnut, Walnut, Reverse Painted 17 x 11 In. 200.00
Banjo, Ansonia, No. 3, Westminster Chime, 3-Train Movement, c.1924, 40 1/2 In. 4700.00
Banjo, Ansonia, No. 3, Westminster Chimes, Crystal Glass, c.1924, 40 1/2 In. 4705.00
Banjo, Chandler, Abiel, Federal, Reverse-Painted Glass 6850.00
Banjo, Federal, Mahogany, Reverse-Painted Tablet, Battleship Scene 935.00
Banjo, G.D. Hatch, Gold Stenciled Tablets, Attleboro, Mass., c.1850, 29 In. 1905.00
Banjo, Mahogany, Black, White Dial, Gilt Side Arms, Warships, 40 In. 1725.00
Banjo, Mahogany, Presentation Dial, Eglomise Throat Glass, Ships, 28 1/2 In. 1150.00
Banjo, Mahogany, Reverse-Painted Tablet, Glass Throat, 43 In. 230.00
Banjo, New Haven, Mahogany, 8-Day, Brass Side Arms, Eagle Finial, 41 In. 365.00
Banjo, New Haven, Mahogany, Brass Side Arms, Eagle Finial, 8-Day Time, 42 1/2 In. ... 366.00
Banjo, New Haven, Mahogany, Reverse Transfer Print, Early 1900s, 41 In. 200.00
Banjo, New Haven, Mt. Vernon, Brass Eagle, Silver Dial, Mahogany Case, 42 In. 825.00
Banjo, New Haven, Westminster Chime, 8-Day, c.1930, 26 In. 198.00
Banjo, Painted Tablet, Battling Ships, Enterprise, Boxer, Eagle Finial, 30 1/2 In. 920.00
Banjo, Reverse-Painted Panel, Ships Battling, Eagle, Sweep Second Hand, 33 In. 2130.00
Banjo, Seward, Parcel Gilt, Eglomise Panel, Signed, c.1830 .... 2300.00
Banjo, Waltham, Mahogany, 8-Day, Copper-Flashed Side Arms, Eagle Finial, 41 In. 1350.00
Banjo, Waterbury, Mahogany, 8-Day Time Only, Brass Side Arms, Eagle Finial, 41 1/2 In. 620.00
Banjo, White, Black Dial, Brass Door, Side Arms, Gilt Frame, Men, Horses, 33 1/2 In. ... 4025.00
Banjo, Willard Style, Gold Stenciled Tablets, Pendulum, c.1870, 29 In. 1905.00
Banjo, Willard, Aaron, Mahogany, Eglomise, Flowers, Aurora, Chariot, 34 1/2 In. 6615.00
Banjo, Willard, Mt. Vernon, 30-Day, 42 In. 440.00
Banjo, Willard, Simon, Presentation, Eglomise, Constitution's Escape, Giltwood, 41 In. ... 9775.00
Bartholomew, E. & G., Shelf, Empire, Mahogany, Half Columns, 30-Hour, 34 3/4 In. ... 259.00
Bartholomew, E. & G., Shelf, Hollow Columns, Whaling, Paw Feet, Eagle, 38 In. 2750.00
Becker, Christoph, Vienna Regulator, Wall, Walnut, 8-Day, Germany, c.1890, 45 In. 450.00
Becker, Gustav, Regulator, Porcelain Dial, Beat Scale, 2 Weight, 48 In. 770.00
Becker, Gustav, Tambour, Mahogany, Westminster Chime, 12 x 24 1/2 In. 220.00
Becker, Gustav, Vienna Regulator, Grand Sonniere, 3 Weight, 8-Day, c.1890, 37 In. 905.00
Becker, Gustav, Vienna Regulator, Wall, 2 Weight, 8-Day, Germany, c.1890, 48 In. 1020.00
Becker, Gustav, Vienna Regulator, Wall, 2 Weight, 8-Day, Walnut Case, c.1880, 39 In. .. 905.00
Becker, Gustav, Wall, Open Well, 8-Day, Gong Strike, Germany, c.1900, 25 In. 205.00
Becker, Gustav, Wall, Walnut, Open Well, 8-Day, Gong Strike, Germany, c.1890, 36 In. .. 450.00
Biedermeier, Bracket, Rosewood, Circular Movement, Continental, c.1835, 17 In. 540.00
Bigelow & Brothers, Shelf, Bronze, Cupid, 2 Putti, Boston, 17 1/2 x 14 In. 1150.00
Bigelow & Kennard, Carriage, Grand Sonnerie, Brass, 6 1/2 x 3 1/2 x 4 1/4 In. 1955.00
Bingham, Belding, D., Regulator, Mercury Pendulum, c.1845, 95 1/2 In. 9000.00
Birge & Fuller, Steeple, Early Wagon Spring, 4 Candles, Flowers, Geometric 4400.00
Birge & Fuller, Steeple, Wagon Spring, Flowers, Geometric, 4-Candle Case, 26 In. 1770.00
Black Forest, Cuckoo, 30-Hour, Painted, Carvings, Germany, c.1868, 24 In. 960.00
Black Forest, Cuckoo, Carved, Fox Carrying Duck, Retriever Carrying Hare, 38 1/2 In. ... 2840.00
Black Forest, Cuckoo, Fox, Owl, Grapes, Leaves, Germany, c.1950, 12 x 19 In. 70.00
Black Forest, Cuckoo, Time & Strike, Roman Numerals, Relief Flowers, Animals, 25 In. . 1440.00

Clock, Advertising, Blatz Beer,
Animated, Electric, Plastic,
Light-Up, 11 x 9 3/4 In.

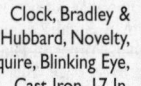

Clock, Bradley &
Hubbard, Novelty,
Squire, Blinking Eye,
Cast Iron, 17 In.

Black Forest, Wall, Convex Wood Dial, Circular, 30-Hour, c.1850, 12 In.	115.00
Black Forest, Wooden Plates Movement, Germany, c.1870, 4 1/2 In.	285.00
Boston Clock, Co., Shelf, Marble, 8-Day Time & Strike, Tandem Wind, c.1890, 9 In.	390.00
Boston Clock Co., Bronze, Tandem Wind, 8-Day, Cathedral Gong, c.1895, 8 In.	790.00
Boston Clock Co., Chelsea, Centennial Commemorative, House Strike, c.1980, 9 In.	420.00
Boston Clock Co., Rip Van Winkle, Porcelain Dial, c.1895, 14 1/2 In.	280.00
Boston Clock Co., Slate, Marble Inlay, Tandem Wind, Porcelain Dial, 9 1/4 x 12 1/2 In.	358.00
Bracket, Carved Mahogany, 3 Fusee, 8 Bells, c.1880, 42 In.	6780.00
Bracket, George III, Mahogany, Chiming, Late 18th Century, 15 x 10 x 7 3/4 In.	1840.00
Bracket, Louis XV Style, Boulle, Ormolu Mounts, c.1900, 20 x 10 x 5 In.	2015.00
Bracket, Mahogany & Oak, Carved, Dome Top, 2 Chime Dials, Germany, 22 x 14 In.	1575.00
Bracket, Pierced Mahogany, Double Fusee, 5 Pillars, England, c.1840, 17 In.	1800.00
Bracket, Teakwood, Double Fusee, Brass Plate, Dial Surround, Chinese, 13 1/4 x 9 1/4 In.	605.00
Bradley & Hubbard, Novelty, Squire, Blinking Eye, Cast Iron, 17 In. . . . . *Illus*	1500.00
Bradley & Hubbard, Topsy, Blinking Eye, Tombourine, 17 In.	5170.00
Brewster, E.C., Shelf, 30-Hour, Spring Driven, Time & Strike, c.1843, 26 In.	250.00
Brewster & Co., Shelf, 8-Day, 2 Weight, Rosewood, Mahogany, Conn., c.1855, 30 In.	290.00
Brewster Mfg. Co., Steeple, Mahogany, Metal Dial, 30-Hour, Time, Strike & Alarm, 19 In.	255.00
Bristol Brass & Clock Co., Beehive, 8-Day, Ivory Knob, c.1850, 19 In.	2296.00
British United Clock Co., Novelty, Bicycle, England, c.1900, 6 1/4 In.	950.00
Brown, J.C., Shelf, Mahogany, Double Decker, 8-Day, Brass Strap Movement, 30 1/2 In.	255.00
Brown, J.C., Steeple, 30-Hour, Time, Strike & Alarm, J.J. Beals, Boston, 19 1/2 In.	85.00
Brunfaut, Figural, Musketeer, Alabaster, Gilt Spelter, c.1890, 15 1/2 In.	200.00
Bucherer, Carriage, Gilt Metal, Enamel Face, Painted Scene, Swiss, 6 In.	295.00
California Clock Co., Electric, Pink Poodle Holds Clock Between Legs, San Juan	30.00
Camerer Kuss & Co., Trumpeter, English Oak, Carved, 8-Day, 33 x 15 x 9 In.	4615.00
Carriage, Bi-Metal Balance Platform Escapement, Round, France, c.1900, 7 1/2 In.	115.00
Carriage, Brass Case, Angle Riche, Porcelain Dial, Beveled Glass, France, c.1900, 3 In.	1900.00
Carriage, Brass Corniche, Cylinder Escapement, France, c.1910, 5 1/2 In.	254.00
Carriage, Brass, 8-Day, White Porcelain Dial, 5 1/2 x 4 3/4 x 3 3/8 In.	575.00
Carriage, Brass, Beveled Glass Panels, 8-Day, Striking Gong, Repeater, 7 x 4 x 3 In.	1000.00
Carriage, Brass, Beveled Glass Panels, White Enamel Face, Key, France, 4 1/4 In.	126.50
Carriage, Bronze, Barometer, Dual Thermometer, Compass, Leather Case, France, 5 In.	825.00
Carriage, Bronze, Engraved, Lion's Masks, Repeater, Early 20th Century, 6 1/4 In.	646.00
Carriage, Bronze, Petite Sonnerie, Repeater, Alarm, Corniche Case, France, 7 1/2 In.	1752.00
Carriage, Compendium, Barometer, Thermometer, Diamond Shape, France, c.1900, 4 In.	339.00
Carriage, English Silver, Lion, Leopard, Alarm, Leather Case, France, 4 1/4 In.	340.00
Carriage, Gilt Bronze, Porcelain, Early 20th Century, L. Malpass, 7 1/2 In.	5605.00
Carriage, Gilt Bronze, Repeating, Alarm, Monogram, France, Late 1800s, 8 1/4 In.	1410.00
Carriage, Mother-Of-Pearl, Mock Pendulum, Swiss, Miniature, 2 3/8 In.	115.00
Carriage, Patinated Bronze, Gorge Case, Asian-Style Birds, Leaves, Fitted Case, 4 In.	999.00
Carriage, Rhinestones, Gilt Mask, Enamel Dial, France, 6 In.	255.00
Cartel, Gilt Bronze, Enameled Porcelain Numbers, France, Late 19th Century, 30 In.	1356.00
Chelsea, Claremont, Brass, Bronze, Ship's Bell, Barometer, c.1973, 14 1/2 x 8 1/2 In.	785.00
Chelsea, Engine Room, U.S. Navy, Brass Dial, 8-Day, Mahogany Stand, c.1918, 12 1/2 In.	1900.00
Chelsea, Industrial, Iron Case, United Gas Improvement Co., c.1915, 6 In.	285.00
Chelsea, Marine Lever, 24-Hour Dial, Bakelite Case, Boston, c.1965, 5 1/2 In.	336.00
Chelsea, No. 1, Pendulum, Regulator, Cherry Case, c.1925, 34 In.	2090.00
Coehler, H., Cuckoo, Wooden, Birds, Leaves, Spring Wound, 1909, 20 In.	550.00

Concord Watch Co., Travel, Silver, Porcelain Dial, 8-Day, Key, Gorham, 3 x 3 In. 495.00
Dent, Regulator, Crystal, Porcelain Dial, Half-Hour Strike Movement, Brass Case, 10 In. . 96.00
Desk, Compendium, Weather Station, 4 Dials, Swivel Base, 15 Jewel, Swiss, c.1968 ..... 170.00
Desk, Dome, Battery Operated, Bar Pendulum, French Gulle, 11 In. 360.00
Desk, Pendulum, Carved Eagle, Spread Wings, Metal Ring, Shaft, 3 3/4 x 3 1/4 In. 660.00
Desk, Plato, Carriage Shape, Flip Numbers, 30 Hour, 6 In. 165.00
E. Howard & Co., Regulator, No. 10, Figure 8, Walnut, Boston, c.1874, 34 In. 8290.00
E. Howard & Co., Regulator, No. 70, Oak, Boston, c.1900, 32 In. 2130.00
E. Howard & Co., Regulator, No. 70, Walnut, Boston, c.1900, 32 In. 3135.00
E. Howard & Co., Regulator, Wall, Cherry, Boston, c.1880, 63 1/2 x 19 3/4 In. 5050.00
E. Howard & Co., Victorian, Walnut, Marble Dial, Brass Numerals, 31 1/2 In. 3680.00
E. Ingraham, School, Short Drop, Calendar, Oak Case, c.1907, 25 In. 420.00
E. Ingraham & Co., Argand, 8-Day, Time, Strike, Gesso Door, Gilt Trim, c.1880, 13 In. .. 224.00
Easel, Silvered Brass Tray, Tropical Bugs, 8-Day, Pendulette, Germany, c.1890, 11 In. ... 300.00
Eli Terry, Shelf, Scrolled Pediment, Dial, Reverse Painted Tablet, Wood Feet, 36 x 17 In. . 1840.00
Eli Terry & Sons, Pillar & Scroll, Mahogany, Reverse Painted, 31 x 16 3/4 In. 980.00
Ferguson, Inverness, Tavern, Carved Mahogany, 8-Day, Trapezoid, c.1840, 14-In. Dial ... 1980.00
Figural, Lady Sphinx, Man, Panther, Slate, Metal, Egyptian Revival, 16 1/2 x 19 In. 1920.00
Figural, Man Holding Metal Cased Clock, Upraised Arm, 20 x 16 In. 385.00
Figural, Military Officer, Sword, Marble Panels, France, 23 1/2 x 18 1/2 In. 250.00
Figural, Mystery, Swinging Ball, Woman, Wings, Gloria, 28 In. 550.00
Figural, Violinist, Jug, Tambourine, Painted Spelter, c.1900, 16 In. 285.00
Forestville, Mahogany, Ogee, 8-Day, Brass Movement, Painted Dial, 30 In. 190.00
French, Garniture Set, Flutist, Gilt Metal, Marble Base, 2 Urns, c.1920, 17 In., 3 Piece ... 255.00
French, Marble, Ormolu, Boy In Loincloth, Annular, c.1890, 11 In. 4200.00
French, Ormolu, Marble, Painted Enamel Dial, 8-Day, Bell Strike, c.1895 .... 285.00
French, Rococo, Portico, Marble, Gilt Spelter, Flower Pendulum, France, c.1900, 15 In. ... 510.00
Fuji, Diana, Swinging Arm, 8-Day, Brass Arm, Plastic Base, Japan, c.1970, 13 1/2 In. 280.00
Furtwangler, Shelf, Walnut, 8-Day, Wheel On Gong, Art Nouveau, c.1900, 17 In. 1808.00
G. Magnin, Medaille D'Argent, Figural, Le Repos, Marble Case, France, c.1890, 21 In. ... 336.00
G. Pewsey & Son, Bracket, Mahogany, Fusee, Marquetry, Chain Drive, London, 16 In. 450.00
Gale, No. 3, School, Calendar, Rosewood Case, c.1880, 30 In. 12320.00
Galt Bro. & Co., Carriage, Alarm, Oval Case, Washington, D.C., 7 In. 540.00
Garnier, Paul, Carriage, Gilt Brass, Time, Strike, Repeat, Alarm, France, c.1900, 6 1/2 In. 2240.00
Gaston Jolly, Shelf, Marble, Gilt Bronze, Paris, c.1835, 20 1/4 x 11 1/2 x 5 3/4 In. 1380.00
Gaston Jolly Fils, Shelf, Restauration, Gilt Bronze, Seated Muse, Paris, c.1815, 15 In. ... 1840.00
General Electric, Little Black Sambo, Mechanical, Poem, Box, 1940s, 8 1/4 In. 230.00
Gilbert, Occidental, Mirror Side Shelf, 8-Day, Remote Alarm, 23 In. 510.00
Gilbert, Pillar & Scroll, 8-Day, Time, Strike, Cathedral Gong, c.1925, 12 1/2 In. 310.00
Gilbert, Regulator, Wall, Pressed Oak, 8-Day, c.1900, 45 In. 960.00
Gilbert, School, Rosewood, 8-Day, Calendar, c.1910, 25 1/2 In. 226.00
Gilbert, Wm. L., Cottage, Wood Dial, S.B. Terry Alarm Movement, c.1860, 11 1/4 In. ... 785.00
Gilbert, Wm. L., Curfew, Shelf, 8-Day, Time, Strike, 18 x 17 In. 340.00
Gilbert, Wm. L., Figural, Archer, 8-Day, Time & Strike, c.1898, 32 In. 1570.00
Gilbert, Wm. L., Shelf, Army, No. 41, Pressed Oak, c.1910, 19 In. 190.00
Gilbert, Wm. L., Shelf, Mission Oak, Latch String Is Always Out, 19 1/2 In. 170.00
Griesbaum, Karl, Figural, Peddler, 30-Hour Spring, Head Turns, c.1930, 13 In. 1345.00
Hagenauer, Franz, Chrome, Sunburst Face, Outstretched Hand, Austria, 12 x 6 3/4 In. ... 4025.00
Hamburg American, Barometer, Thermometer, Half Columns, Wood Case, 30 In. 660.00
Hamburg American, Bracket, Oak, 8-Day, Time, Strike, Bell, Germany, c.1920, 20 In. ... 335.00
Hamburg American, Tambour, Mahogany, 8-Day, Sword Trademark, c.1920, 12 In. 226.00
Harris Griffin, Skeleton, Brass Chain Fusee Movement, 13 x 7 1/2 x 17 1/2 In. 1725.00
Hawkins, Bracket, Royal Exchange, Chippendale, Arched Top, Mahogany, 16 1/2 In. ... 575.00
Herman Miller, World's Fair Series, Walnut Burl, Ash, Metal, G. Rohde, 1934, 8 x 9 In. .. 2340.00
Hermet, Delmas, 2 Weight, Ding-Dong Strike, Starburst Hands, Morbier, c.1860, 56 In. . 450.00
Herschede, 9 Tube, 3 Tunes, 1/4 Chime, Bronze Numerals, c.1925, 79 1/2 In. 4030.00
Herschede, Tambour, Mahogany Case, c.1930, 8 In. 198.00
Hirschel, H., Shelf, Pillar & Scroll, 2 Columns, Brass Finials, 30 In. 250.00
Hopkins & Alfred, Shelf, Reverse Painted Lawn & Building, Claw Feet, Conn., c.1820 ... 1456.00
Howard Miller, Ball, Birch, Brass Spikes, 13 In. 865.00
Howard Miller, Ball, Black Balls, Brass Rods, G. Nelson, 1950s 575.00
Howard Miller, Ball, Multicolored Ball, Brass Spokes, G. Nelson, 14 In. 1880.00
Howard Miller, Ball, Multicolored Balls, G. Nelson, c.1948, 13 In. 3055.00

Howard Miller, Ball, White Center, Brass Spokes, G. Nelson, 13 1/2 In. 1380.00
Howard Miller, Blade, Brass, Walnut, Aluminum, Enamel, G. Nelson, c.1953, 30 In. 4095.00
Howard Miller, Meridian, Rosewood, Chrome, Arthur Umanoff, 1950, 4 x 5 1/2 In. 295.00
Howard Miller, Paddle Wheel, G. Nelson, c.1952, 11 1/4 In. 2115.00
Howard Miller, Spider Web, Enameled Steel Rods, Black Strings, G. Nelson, 18 In. 1765.00
Howard Miller, Spike, Wood, Enameled Metal, G. Nelson, 1950s, 31 x 3 1/2 In. 1404.00
Howard Miller, Starburst, Walnut Spikes, G. Nelson, 18 In. 315.00
Howard Miller, Steering Wheel, Black Enamel Ring, Brass Center, G. Nelson, 12 In. 2070.00
Howard Miller, Steering Wheel, G. Nelson, c.1952, 12 In. 525.00
Howard Miller, Walnut, Brass, Enamel, G. Nelson, 1950s, 5 1/2 x 5 x 7 In. 645.00
Howard Miller, Zoo-Timer, Fernando Fish, No. 2324, Masonite, G. Nelson, 1965 . . . .   2225.00
Howard Miller, Zoo-Timer, Samantha Swallow, Masonite, G. Nelson, 1965, 12 x 10 In. . .   1520.00
Ingeberg, Wall, Art Deco, Mahogany, 8-Day, Chime, Beveled Glass, 23 In. 225.00
Ingraham, Doric, Softwood Case, 30-Hour, Time, Strike, Alarm, Paper Dial, 16 In. 45.00
Ingraham, Kitchen, At The Well, Pressed Oak, Alarm 330.00
Ingraham, Kitchen, Gila, Pressed Oak, Calendar, 8-Day, Time & Strike, c.1915, 22 3/4 In.   198.00
Ingraham, Kitchen, Oak, Gingerbread, 8-Day Time, Strike & Alarm 115.00
Ingraham, Wall, Faux Rosewood, Grain Painted, Paper Label, c.1878, 21 1/2 In. 440.00
Ingraham, Walnut Case, Carved Crest, Calendar, 8-Day, Lewis Patent, 22 In. 675.00
Ithaca, Belgrade, Shelf, Walnut, Calendar, Time & Strike, No. 6 1/2, c.1880, 32 In. 5825.00
Ithaca, No. 10, Farmer's Model, Walnut Case, Calendar, 8-Day, Strike, Alarm, 25 In. 805.00
Ithaca, Shelf, Cottage, Walnut, Calendar, No. 7, Case, 8-Day, 2 Dials, 25 In. 575.00
Ives, Chauncey, Pillar & Scroll, Reverse Painted, c.1820 . . . .   4650.00
Jacob Petit, Paris Porcelain, Grapes, 2 Parts, c.1865, 16 1/4 x 10 1/4 In. 1840.00
Jacob Petit, Rococo, Porcelain, Flower Reserves, c.1865, 14 1/2 In. 1265.00
Japy Freres, Cartel, Ormolu Case, Porcelain Dial, 8-Day, Time & Strike, c.1890, 21 In. . .   560.00
Japy Freres, Cartel, Patinated Spelter, Sleeping Children, Angel, Bell Strike, c.1875, 13 In.   530.00
Japy Freres, Louis XV Style, Ormolu, Brass Rococo Case, 1878, 17 In. 620.00
Japy Freres, Louis XVI Style, Gilt Bronze, Marble Mounted, c.1865, 13 5/8 In. 1765.00
Japy Freres, Shelf, Figural, Seated Man At Desk, 8-Day, c.1855, 15 In. 375.00
Japy Freres, Shelf, Louis XVI Style, Putti, Birds, Marble, Bronze, 13 1/2 x 11 1/2 In. 575.00
Japy Freres, Shelf, Marble, Skeleton Movement, 8-Day, c.1890, 9 In. 448.00
Japy Freres, Wall, Bronze Nautical Design, 8-Day, Aneroid Barometer, c.1900, 20 In. 255.00
Jennings Brothers, Novelty, Owl, Head Lifts For Inkwell, c.1905 . . . .   245.00
Jennings Brothers, Silver-Colored Spelter Case, Enamel Dial, c.1910, 4 1/4 In. 140.00
Jerome, Chauncey, Shelf, Gothic, 1-Day, Rosewood Case, c.1870, 14 3/4 In. 196.00
Jerome, Chauncey, Shelf, Holloway Case, Walnut, Fusee, 30-Hour, c.1850, 15 In. 450.00
Jerome, Chauncey, Shelf, Rosewood, Gutta-Percha, 8-Day, Octagon Top, c.1870, 16 In. . .   475.00
Jerome, Chauncey, Steeple, 8-Day, Mahogany Case, New Haven, c.1850, 20 In. 196.00
Jerome, Chauncey, Wall, Octagonal, Walnut Veneer, 19th Century, 11 In. 195.00
Jerome & Co., Cottage, Rosewood, Gutta-Percha Door Inserts, 30-Hour, c.1870, 15 1/2 In.   390.00
Jerome & Co., Steeple, 8-Day, Time, Strike & Alarm, Brass Movement, 20 1/2 In. 255.00
Jerome & Co., Steeple, 30-Hour, Time, Alarm, 15 1/4 x 8 1/4 In.   170.00
Jeromes & Darrow, Shelf, Neoclassical, Mahogany, Eglomise Panel, 30 x 17 x 6 1/2 In. . .   1315.00
Johnson, William, Mahogany, Wood Dial, Ogee, 30-Hour, Patriotic Tablet, 26 1/4 In. 180.00
Joyce Whitchurch, Tavern, Flame Mahogany, 8-Day, c.1840, 52 In. 1865.00
Junghans, Ball, Copper-Patinated Metal, Wood Base, 11 1/2 In. 540.00
Junghans, Bracket, Mahogany, Westminster Chime, Alarm, Claw Feet, 14 1/4 x 12 In. 1210.00
Junghans, Cuckoo, Shelf, 8-Day, c.1890, 22 1/2 In. 425.00
Junghans, Portico, Mahogany Case, Ball Top, Pendulum, c.1915, 10 1/2 In. 226.00
Junghans, Tambour, Westminster Chime, Mahogany Case, Silvered Dial, 2 Jewel, 22 In. . .   115.00
Junghans, Wall, Mixed Wood, Calendar, 8-Day, Germany, c.1900, 27 In. 445.00
Kaiser, J., World Model, Terrestrial Globe, Halifax Moon, 400-Day, Germany, 1954, 11 In.   530.00
Kienzle, Wall, Vienna Regulator, Walnut Veneer, 8-Day, Germany, c.1890, 42 In. 255.00
Kitchen, Welch, E.N., Oak, No. 63, 8-Day, Half-Hour Strike, Tin Dial, Oak Crest, 17 In. . .   50.00
LeCoultre, Art Deco, Antique Bronze, Swiss, c.1930, 3 1/2 x 3 In. 29.00
LeCoultre, Atmos, Gilt & Glass Case, Damascene Door, Silvered Dial, 1950s, 9 In. 509.00
LeCoultre, Atmos, Gilt & Glass Case, Square Dial, Box, Papers, c.1950, 9 1/2 In. 595.00
LeCoultre, Atmos, Round, Silver Dial, c.1970, 9 x 8 In. 565.00
LeCoultre, Egyptian Revival, Obelisk, Gilt Case, c.1980, 9 1/2 In.   140.00
LeCoultre, Jaeger, 24-Hour Recital Alarm, 8-Day, Gilt Case, c.1970, 1 3/4 In. 57.00
LeCoultre, Jaeger, Mystery Timepiece, c.1950, 10 In. 565.00
LeCoultre, Musical Alarm, 8-Day, Black & Gold Dial, c.1970, 3 3/4 In. 140.00

LeCoultre, Musical Alarm, 8-Day, Lucite Dial, Butterfly, Brass Case, c.1965, 5 In. 285.00
LeCoultre, World Time, 12 Time Zones, Alarm, 8-Day, Box, Swiss, c.1964, 2 In. 224.00
Lecrosnier, Wag-On-Wall, Hour Element Cartouches, Embossed Brass Face, 57 In. 385.00
Lengsfeld, Fr., Wall, Walnut Case, Grand Sonniere, 8-Day, Germany, c.1875, 52 In. 1526.00
Lenzkirch, Shelf, Brass, Bronze, Ribbon, Acanthus, Garland, Germany, c.1900, 16 In. . . . 730.00
Lenzkirch, Wall, Balcony, Oak, 8-Day, Brass, Germany, c.1875, 36 In. 2150.00
Lenzkirch, Wall, Walnut Case, 8-Day, Germany, c.1885, 41 In. 450.00
LeRoy, Empire Style, Gilt Bronze, Cupid, Chariot, Lion, 16 x 13 In. 4185.00
Lux, Alarm, Animated, Spinning Wheel, Fireplace, c.1930, 5 In. 79.00
Lux, Black Shoeshine Boy, Woman Looking In Pocket Mirror, c.1930, 3 3/4 In. 125.00
Lux, Bulldog 1800.00
Lux, Cat, Animated, Tail Pendulum, Moving Eyes, 7 1/4 In. . . . . .135.00 to 220.00
Lyre, Mahogany Panel, Music Box, c.1825, 39 In. 4145.00
Mangiarotti, A., Secticon, Model C1, Plastic Case, Bubble Face, Swiss, 1960s, 6 In. 200.00
Mangiarotti, A., Secticon, Model T1, Plastic Case, Swiss, 1960s, 9 1/2 In. 290.00
Mangiarotti, Angelo, Secticon, Model M2, Metal Case, Swiss, 1960s, 12 In. 115.00
Marsh, George, Column & Splat, Stenciled Flowers, Pineapple, 30-Hour, Alarm, 33 In. . . 160.00
Marti, F., Bracket, Mahogany, Medallie D'Or, Gong Strike, France, c.1910, 16 In. 285.00
Marti, Regulator, Crystal, 8-Day, Coiled Gong Strike, France, c.1900, 15 1/2 In. 905.00
Marti, Shelf, Gothic Revival, Walnut, Ironwork, c.1900, 24 In. 620.00
Marti, Shelf, Napoleon III, Ormolu, Architectural, Renaissance Style, 26 1/4 In. 2070.00
Marti, Shelf, Porcelain, Floral Encrusted, Allegorical, Four Seasons, 15 3/4 In. 800.00
Mauthe, Wall, Free Swinger, 8-Day, Gong Strike, Germany, c.1920, 36 In. 509.00
Max Bill, Wall, Junghans, Glazed Ceramic, Enamel, Glass, Germany, 1954, 7 x 10 In. 2340.00
Meridian, Howard Miller, Rosewood, Aluminum, Authur Umanoff, 1950s 700.00
Montecot, Louis XVI Style, Bronze Ormolu, Marble, Enamel Dial, France, c.1850, 15 In. 620.00
Morbier, Alarm, Porcelain Dial, Brass Surround, Crest, Cornucopias, 2 Weight, 15 In. . . . 248.00
Morbier, Calendar, 30-Day, 1/4 Chime, Pinwheel, 2 Weight, Brass Musical Lyre, 26 In. . . 990.00
Morbier, Prayer, 3 Weight, Repeat Alarm, Folding Pendulum, France, 53 In. 336.00
Morbier, Wall, Prayer, 2 Weight, Repeat Alarm, Swiss Chalet Scene On Dial, 60 In. 448.00
Moreau, Mystery, Swing Arm, Woman, Cherub, c.1890, 26 1/2 In. 2875.00
Morse, Joseph, Shelf, Federal, Mahogany, Eglomise, Walpole, Mass., 32 In. 9890.00
Mougin, A.D., Atlas Carrying World, Marble, Gilt Spelter, France, c.1900, 30 In. 400.00
Mougin, A.D., Ormolu Panel, Porcelain Dial, Allegorical Case, France, c.1880, 18 1/2 In. . 452.00
Mougin, A.D., Shelf, Onyx, 8-Day, Rack Striking, France c.1890, 9 1/2 In. 198.00
Movado, Travel, Shagreen & Sterling Silver, Silvertone Dial, c.1930 . . . . 325.00
Movado, Travel, Silvertone Dial, Date, Moon Phase, Alligator Leather 825.00
Mystery, Ball On Woman's Upstretched Arm, Swinger, Spelter, France, c.1905, 39 In. . . . 4970.00
Mystery, Black Forest, 8-Day, Swinging Pendulum, Germany, c.1900, 38 In. 1130.00
Mystery, Egyptian Revival, Cleopatra Holding Candle, c.1880, 16 1/2 In. 2260.00
Mystery, Female Figure, Holding Pendulum, France, c.1885, 24 1/2 In. 3024.00
Mystery, La Science, Bronzed Spelter, August, Moreau, France, c.1890, 36 1/2 In. 4030.00
Mystery, Le Lever Du Jour, Male Statue, Bronzed Spelter, France, c.1890, 25 In. 3080.00
New Haven Clock Co., Corea, Brilliants & Emeralds, c.1900, 4 1/2 In. 360.00
New Haven Clock Co., Cut Crystal, Gilt Spelter Footed Base, c.1925, 9 In. 285.00
New Haven Clock Co., Edmond, Carriage, Repeater, Brass, Enamel Dial, c.1910, 6 In. . . . 226.00
New Haven Clock Co., Flush, Cast Metal, 17 Cards, Brilliant Bezel In Dial, c.1906, 5 In. . 335.00
New Haven Clock Co., Lucci, Porcelain Dial, Minstrel, Violin, Case, Urn Top, 21 x 19 In. 605.00
New Haven Clock Co., Minho, Mission Oak, 1-Day, Miniature Tall Case, c.1907, 12 In. . . 170.00
New Haven Clock Co., Mission, Oak, Hinged Front Door, Glass Encasement, 13 x 11 In. 193.00
New Haven Clock Co., Regulator, Crystal, Art Nouveau Gilt Spelter Case, c.1910, 16 In. 480.00
New Haven Clock Co., Regulator, Crystal, Metal Case, Gold Tone, 15 x 8 x 7 In. 375.00
New Haven Clock Co., Rosewood Case, Ogee, Etched Glass, 30-Hour, c.1880, 18 1/4 In. . 198.00
New Haven Clock Co., Shelf, Enameled Iron, 30-Hour, Porcelain Dial, 8 3/4 In. 39.00
New Haven Clock Co., Shelf, Gothic Gem, Rosewood, c.1875, 17 In. 198.00
New Haven Clock Co., Shelf, Walnut, Carved Leaves, Glazed Doors, Lines, Wheat, 22 In. 185.00
New Haven Clock Co., Steeple, 8-Day, Bell, Turner Patent Alarm, Lake Scene, 1860, 20 In. 450.00
New Haven Clock Co., Steeple, Mahogany, 8-Day, Alarm, 21 x 10 1/2 In. 425.00
New Haven Clock Co., Wall, Office, No. 1, Walnut, Weight Driven, c.1900, 41 In. 1469.00
New Haven Clock Co., Wall, Office, Oak, 30-Day, 2 Dials, 42 In. 1100.00
New Haven Clock Co., Wall, Saturn, 8-Day Spring, Paper Dial, c.1911, 35 1/2 In. 925.00
Night, Candle, Glass Dial, Boy Holding Staff, Points To Time, France, 13 In. 715.00
Night, Candle, Glass Dial, Metal Frame, Boy With Horse, 12 In. 415.00

Novelty, Goddess Of Fame, Copper Over Iron, Cherub, Eagle, Flag, 12 In. 88.00
Novelty, John Bully, Moving Eye Blinker, 30-Hour Lever, T. Kennedy, 17 In. 1130.00
Novelty, Sambo Playing Banjo, Cast Iron, Pat. May 10, 1859, 16 1/2 In. 1050.00
Orton Preston, Shelf, Pillar & Splat, 30-Hour Wood Movement, c.1810, 33 In. 345.00
Parker, Alarm, Nickel Plated, Half-Round Base, 1800s, 4 x 3 3/4 In. 690.00
Parker & Whipple, Model 200, Alarm, Embossed Base, Meriden, Conn., c.1885, 5 In. . . . 110.00
Peddler, Spelter Figure, Polychrome, Rectangular Base, 15 In. 85.00
Peddler, Whistler, Wood, Turns Head, Whistles, Sack With Clock, Germany, 13 In. 880.00
Pewter, Liberty, Copper, Enameled Face, Marked, 8 In. 4600.00
Phalibois, Automaton, Monkey Violinist, 7 Movements 4620.00
Pilling, J, S., School, Fusee, Flowers, Deer, Bird 250.00
Pratt & Frost, Shelf, Walnut, Column & Splat, 8-Day Wood Movement, 35 In. 200.00
Raingo Freres, Cartel, Louis XV Style, Gilt Bronze, Enamel Dial, Leaves, 25 In. 540.00
Raingo Freres, Shelf, Louis XVI Style, Bronze, Glass, Arrows, 18 x 10 x 5 1/2 In. 1554.00
Reading, Penelope, Shelf, Restauration, Gilt Bronze, c.1815, 13 x 12 x 6 1/2 In. 1725.00
Regulator, Baroque, Grand Sonnerie, 3 Weight, 8-Day, Germany, c.1870, 50 In. 1130.00
Regulator, Brass, 8-Day, Time & Strike, Double Vial Pendulum, 11 x 6 x 5 In. 390.00
Regulator, Crystal, 8-Day, Time & Strike, Beveled Glass, France, 8 1/2 x 5 1/2 In. 510.00
Regulator, Crystal, Brass Case, 4 Glass, 8-Day, Time & Strike, France, c.1900, 15 1/2 In. . 200.00
Regulator, Crystal, Brass, Glass Top, Germany, c.1900, 11 In. 225.00
Regulator, Crystal, Bronze, Sphere Mounted, Roman Numerals, Putti Trio, 14 In. 1035.00
Regulator, Jewelers, Oak, Lyre Pendulum, Germany, c.1900, 63 In. 3390.00
Regulator, Vienna, Wall, 2 Weight, Walnut Veneer, 8-Day, Germany, c.1885, 42 In. 678.00
Regulator, Vienna, Wall, Rosewood, 1 Weight, 8-Day, Germany, c.1875, 38 In. . . .339.00 to 424.00
Regulator, Vienna, Wall, Walnut, 1 Weight, 8-Day, Germany, c.1855, 39 1/2 In. 370.00
Regulator, Vienna, Walnut, Carved Applied Half Columns, Acorn Finials, 42 In. 370.00
Regulator, Vienna, Wood Case, 1 Weight, 8-Day, Germany, c.1870, 40 In. 450.00
Regulator, Vienna, Wood, Grand Sonnerie, 3 Weight, 8-Day, Germany, c.1880, 50 In. . . . 2260.00
Regulator, Vienna, Wood, Grand Sonniere, 3 Weight, 8-Day, Germany, c.1875, 39 In. . . . 905.00
Ruskin, Shelf, Copper, Hammered, Rivets, Spectas Fugit, England, 17 x 11 In. 3220.00
Scherraus, G.G., Art Deco, Marble, Carriage Movement, France, c.1925, 7 In. 1020.00
School, Flame Mahogany, Brass Inlay, Fusee, 8-Day, England, c.1825, 26 In. 790.00
School, Oak Box, Fruitwood Bezel, Fusee, England, c.1910, 13 x 18 In. 420.00
Seguso, Art Glass, Red Amber Glass, Folding Brass Stand, Murano, Italy, c.1965, 6 1/4 In. 295.00
Sessions, Coquette, Strut, Silver Finish, Lever Escapement, c.1940, 4 1/4 In. 115.00
Sessions, Regulator, Mission Oak, Applied Numerals, 31 1/12 In. 230.00
Sessions, Shelf, Mahogany, Lancet Case, Enamel Dial, 8-Day, Gong, c.1920, 13 In. 115.00
Sessions, Shelf, Oak, Half Columns, 8-Day, Brass Movement, Painted Dial, 15 1/2 In. 60.00
Seth Thomas, Art Deco, Walnut, Westminster Chime, No. 113, c.1928, 16 1/2 In. 565.00
Seth Thomas, Barometer, Chrome, Wood Base, 5 1/4 In. 173.00
Seth Thomas, Cast Metal, Gothic Case, Bronze, Bust Of Woman On Top, Cherubs, 15 In. 440.00
Seth Thomas, Chime, No. 64, 5-Bell Sonora, Flower Inlay, c.1915, 15 In. 1120.00
Seth Thomas, Desk, Gilt Spelter, Beveled Glass, c.1900, 3 1/2 In. 192.00
Seth Thomas, Eastlake, Wall, Office, Black Case, Time & Strike, 36 x 13 In. 865.00
Seth Thomas, Empire, No. 6, Regulator, Crystal, 8-Day, Time & Strike, c.1904, 11 1/4 In. 339.00
Seth Thomas, Empire, Oak, 8-Day, Time, Strike, 16 x 10 1/4 In. 285.00
Seth Thomas, Falsbury, Walnut, 8-Day, Time & Strike, Westminster Chime, c.1940, 9 In. . 160.00
Seth Thomas, Gingerbread, Walnut, Glass Door, Painted Ferns, 22 3/4 In. 200.00
Seth Thomas, Gothic, Bronze Case, Lancet Top, 15-Day, c.1915, 9 In. 510.00
Seth Thomas, Lodge, Metal, Log Cabin Shape, 1-Day, Time, Alarm, c.1892, 7 In. .110.00 to 140.00
Seth Thomas, Mahogany, Column & Splat, Stencil, Cornucopia, Claw Feet, 30 1/2 In. . . . 590.00
Seth Thomas, Mahogany, Tambour, Westminster, 8-Day, No. 113, c.1930, 10 1/2 In. 180.00
Seth Thomas, Oak, Gallery, 30-Day, Double Spring Movement, c.1900, 26 In. 3470.00
Seth Thomas, Office Calendar No. 5, Oak, c.1884, 50 In. 14560.00
Seth Thomas, Pillar, Alarm, 8-Day, Castle Scene, 25 1/4 In. 165.00
Seth Thomas, Regulator, Brass, Mercury Pendulum, 10 In. 230.00
Seth Thomas, Regulator, Crystal, Beveled Glass Door, Flowered Dial, 11 x 7 x 5 1/2 In. . 290.00
Seth Thomas, Regulator, Crystal, Brass Frame, Flower Urn Top, Porcelain Dial, 17 x 8 In. 525.00
Seth Thomas, Regulator, No. 1, Presentation Glass Tablet, c.1885, 34 In. 1960.00
Seth Thomas, Regulator, No. 2, Mahogany, 8-Day, Metal Dial, 32 In. 730.00
Seth Thomas, Regulator, No. 18, Long Drop, 53 1/2 x 20 x 5 3/4 In. 2970.00
Seth Thomas, Regulator, No. 70, Mahogany, Graham Escapement, c.1925, 55 1/2 In. 4145.00
Seth Thomas, Regulator, Walnut, 8-Day, Time & Strike, Brass Pendulum 750.00

Seth Thomas, Regulator, Walnut, Glass Front, Drop Pediment, 8-Day, Time & Strike 840.00
Seth Thomas, Santa Fe, Kitchen, Gilded Leaf, Alarm 770.00
Seth Thomas, Shelf, Egyptian Revival, Gilt Spelter Case, c.1880, 16 1/2 In. 170.00
Seth Thomas, Shelf, Empire, Mahogany Veneer, 17 In. 230.00
Seth Thomas, Shelf, Half Columns, 2 Weight, 1-Day, Flowers 88.00
Seth Thomas, Shelf, Iron, 18-Day, c.1885, 11 In. 140.00
Seth Thomas, Shelf, Mahogany, 30-Hour, Glass Front Door, c.1840, 25 x 15 x 4 1/2 In. ... 170.00
Seth Thomas, Shelf, Mahogany, Pillar & Scroll, 8-Day, c.1920, 17 1/2 x 5 x 32 In. 460.00
Seth Thomas, Shelf, Mahogany, Pillar & Scroll, Eglomise, 32 In. 1100.00
Seth Thomas, Shelf, Mahogany, Round Band, 8-Day, A-Frame Movement, c.1900, 16 In. . 180.00
Seth Thomas, Ship's Bell, Solid Brass, Wheel Shape, Wood Backboard 288.00
Seth Thomas, Ship's Bell, Walnut Case, Marine Lever Escapement, 7 1/2 In. 200.00
Seth Thomas, Spun Brass, Banner Lever, Double Spring Movement, c.1885, 11 In. 170.00
Seth Thomas, Wall, Oak, Gallery, 8-Day, Square, c.1940, 16 In. 170.00
Seth Thomas, Wall, Rosewood, World, 8-Day, Strike, c.1885, 32 In. 728.00
Seth Thomas, Wood, Pillar & Splat, Half Columns, Sailing Ship, 33 In. 220.00
Shelf, Annular Dial, Fire Gilt, Marble, Late 18th Century, 17 1/2 In. 9605.00
Shelf, Art Deco, Oak, Beveled Glass, Enamel Dial, 8-Day, Gong, Germany, c.1920, 15 In. 140.00
Shelf, Black Slate, Onyx, Porcelain Dial, France, c.1890, 12 1/2 In. 100.00
Shelf, Black, Starr & Frost, Louis XVI Style, Gilt Bronze, Marble, 13 x 11 In. 1435.00
Shelf, Brass, Beveled Glass, Double Mercury Pendulum, France, Early 1900s, 10 1/2 In. . 85.00
Shelf, Bronze, Gothic, Spires, Silk Thread Suspension, c.1840, 17 In. 1265.00
Shelf, Bronze, Rouge Marble, Neoclassical, Psyche & Amore, Tiffany & Co., 30 1/2 In. ... 9200.00
Shelf, Castle Scene, Moat, Brass, New England, c.1885, 12 x 10 x 5 1/2 In. 532.00
Shelf, Charles X, Ormolu Mounted, Rouge Marble, Satyr Masks, Fruit, Swags, 20 1/2 In. . 2300.00
Shelf, Cloisonne, Inlaid Brass, Glass, Miniature Ivory Portraits, France, 12 In. 920.00
Shelf, Criterion, Spelter, Marble, Red Onyx, France, c.1900, 17 In. 560.00
Shelf, Dore Bronze, Boulle, Tortoise Inlay, c.1860, 52 x 25 x 11 In. 7765.00
Shelf, Empire Style, Bronze, Marble, Drum Movement, Cupid, Psyche, 29 x 20 In. 5675.00
Shelf, Empire Style, Marble, Temple Shape, Engine-Turned Dial, Columns, 19 3/8 In. ... 560.00
Shelf, Empire Style, Parcel Gilt, Patinated Bronze, 2 Train, France, c.1910, 18 5/8 In. 650.00
Shelf, Empire, Column Supports, Inlaid Flowers & Birds, Bun Feet, 19th Century, 19 In. . 520.00
Shelf, Empire, Giltwood, Gilt Metal, Cupid Forging Arrow On Anvil, 19 x 11 1/4 In. 1150.00
Shelf, Empire, Rosewood Case, Brass Pendulum, Satinwood Inlay, Moon Hands, 18 In. ... 470.00
Shelf, Empire, Wood Face, Floral Spandrels, Ebonized, Gilt Stencil, Swag, 30 x 17 x 4 In. 715.00
Shelf, Federal, Tiger Maple, Pillar & Scroll, River Landscape, 19th Century, 31 1/2 In. 2300.00
Shelf, Figural, Female Warrior, 3 Lions, Alabaster, Gilt Spelter, c.1880, 15 In. 226.00
Shelf, Figural, Swordsmen, Spelter, 8-Day, Iron Base, 21 1/4 In. 478.00
Shelf, Incised Marble, Urn Top, Paw Feet, Hand Painted Dial, France, c.1900, 14 In. 170.00
Shelf, Louis Philippe, Sienna Marble, Patinated Bronze, Socrates, c.1835, 21 x 9 1/2 In. ... 1150.00
Shelf, Louis XV Style, Chinese Man, Parasol, Elephant, Gilt, Patinated Bronze, 18 1/2 In. 2000.00
Shelf, Louis XV Style, Gilt Brass, Chiming, Square, Flower Basket Top, c.1890, 16 In. ... 5750.00
Shelf, Louis XVI Style, 3 Cherubs, Celestial Globe, Marble Base, France, c.1875, 19 In. ... 3470.00
Shelf, Louis XVI Style, Bronze, Marble, Gilt Drum, Ebonized Figures, 20 1/2 x 27 In. ... 10755.00
Shelf, Louis XVI Style, Bronze, Marble, Sunburst Pendulum, c.1910, 16 x 8 1/2 In. 1200.00
Shelf, Louis XVI Style, Figural, Cupid, Horn & Drum, Bronze, 11 In. 750.00
Shelf, Louis XVI Style, Gilt Bronze, Marble, Putto, Grapes, Wine Cask, 14 x 16 In. 1015.00
Shelf, Louis XVI Style, Ormolu, Marble, Chiming Movement, 16 3/4 In. 295.00
Shelf, Mahogany, Domed Case, Windup, Brass Feet, Late 1800s, 12 1/2 x 9 x 5 1/2 In. ... 115.00
Shelf, Mahogany, Lancet Arch Case, 8-Day, Gong Strike, France, c.1910, 13 1/2 In. 285.00
Shelf, Marble, Enamel Dial, Open Escapement, France, c.1880, 15 In. 170.00
Shelf, Mounted Metal, Japanned, Abalone, 2 Train, Late 1800s, 13 7/8 In. 175.00
Shelf, Napoleon III, Bronze, Cloisonne, Drum Dial, Flower Urn, 18 x 9 x 5 In. 3885.00
Shelf, Ormolu Case, 2 Angels, Time & Strike, France, c.1885, 22 1/2 x 17 1/2 x 7 In. 2240.00
Shelf, Ormolu Mounted, Bronze Dore Pediment, Enameled Face, France, 24 x 8 x 8 In. . 8250.00
Shelf, Pendulum, Free Swinger, Black & Gold Case, 8-Day, Germany, 11 x 8 In. 110.00
Shelf, Pillar & Scroll, Mahogany, 30-Hour, Reverse Painted, c.1810, 17 1/2 x 32 In. 460.00
Shelf, Pillars, Marble, Porcelain, Metal Dial, Iron Finial, France, 18 x 18 3/4 In. 140.00
Shelf, Porcelain, Applied Figures, Flowers, Painted, Diana, Cherub, Father Time, 15 In. . 4255.00
Shelf, Regency Style, Gilt Bronze, Beveled Glass, France, c.1885, 18 3/4 x 10 1/2 In. 750.00
Shelf, Walnut Case, Brass Slide Shut Off, 1-Day, Alarm, Germany, c.1915, 10 In. 95.00
Shelf, Walnut Case, Full Columns, Arched Top, Metal Dials, Calendar, c.1879, 31 1/2 In. . 1069.00
Shelf, Winged Statue, Green Onyx, Gilded Spelter, Art Nouveau, France, c.1900, 29 In. ... 728.00

Sitzendorf, Porcelain, Pierced Scrolls, Flowers, Seated Figures, 20 In. 990.00
Skeleton, Brass, England, 1900s, 11 1/2 In. 560.00
Smith, Charles Alva, Wall, 8-Day, Wooden Works, Brattleboro, Vt., c.1943, 12 1/2 In. ... 1345.00
Sperry, Henry, Cottage, Grain Painted, Sponge Painted Glass, c.1855, 11 In. 550.00
Sperry & Shaw, Fenn-Type Tablet, Ogee, c.1850, 26 In. 140.00
Stickley Bros., Copper, Hammered, Square Base, Angular Body, Twisted Pillars, 9 1/2 In. 2235.00
Stoelklok, 30-Hour, Hand Painted Case, Miniature, Dutch, c.1900, 12 In. 255.00
Swiza Sheffield, Brass, Street Clock Shape, 8-Day, Alarm, Swiss, c.1965, 8 In. 90.00
Tall Case, Abel Hutchins, Federal, Cherry, 8-Day, Brass Movement, N.H., c.1810, 89 In. . 7050.00
Tall Case, Art Deco, Walnut, Continental, 75 1/2 x 22 x 11 3/4 In. 1415.00
Tall Case, Art Nouveau, Oak, Open Well, Silver & Copper Dial, Germany, c.1910, 91 In. . 2035.00
Tall Case, Arts & Crafts, Corbelled Ends, 17 x 72 x 9 In. 1610.00
Tall Case, Barraclough Haworth, Sun, Moon Dial, Birds, Flowers, Oak Inlay, 1800, 89 In. 1100.00
Tall Case, Brass Pediment & Disk Pendulum, Enameled Face, 90 x 17 x 8 In. 1450.00
Tall Case, Chelsea, No. 1, Regulator, Oak, Roman Numerals, Pendulum, c.1920, 34 In. ... 1550.00
Tall Case, Cherry, Mahogany Veneer, Painted Iron Face, Early 1800s, 98 In. .... *Illus* 5940.00
Tall Case, Cherry, Poplar, Pine, Dial Flowers, 8-Day, Pennsylvania, c.1840, 82 In. 1130.00
Tall Case, Chippendale, Figured Walnut, Pennsylvania, c.1780, 102 1/4 In. 7475.00
Tall Case, Chippendale, Walnut, Scrolled Crest, Scallop Shell, American, 91 In. 4600.00
Tall Case, Colonial Mfg., Model 1397, 3 Weight, Westminster Chime, c.1920, 77 In. 1680.00
Tall Case, Daniel Oyster, Chippendale, Cherry, 8-Day, Sun & Moon Face, Reading, Pa. ... 11500.00
Tall Case, David Blaisdell, Queen Anne, Dome Top, Amesbury, Mass., 84 In. 6040.00
Tall Case, Dutch Baroque, Walnut, Marquetry Inlay, Parcel Gilt, Figural Finials, 90 In. ... 4995.00
Tall Case, Ebonized, Hand Painted Seascape, England, 1700s, 87 3/4 x 17 x 10 3/4 In. ... 3910.00
Tall Case, Ezekiel Reed, Federal, Mahogany, 8-Day, Pierced Fret, Mass., c.1790, 92 In. ... 10000.00
Tall Case, Federal, Cherry, Inlaid, Connecticut, c.1800, 89 x 21 x 11 In. .... *Illus* 7800.00
Tall Case, Federal, Cherry, Pinwheel Inlays, Moon Phase, American, 98 In. 6900.00
Tall Case, Federal, Mahogany, Broken Arch Pediment, N.Y., c.1815, 93 x 18 x 11 3/4 In. . 2870.00
Tall Case, Flame Mahogany, 8-Day, Bell Strike, England, c.1840, 82 In. 4800.00
Tall Case, Folk Art, Paint Decorated, 1830-1870, 89 In. 15575.00
Tall Case, George Duncan, Mahogany, Inlaid, 8-Day, Enamel Dial, Banff, 83 In. 1065.00
Tall Case, George Eby, Cherry, Moon Dial, Broken Arch, Quarter-Turned Columns, 95 In. 2970.00
Tall Case, George Goodall, Musical, Walnut, Oak, Brass Works, Finials, England, 91 In. .. 4400.00
Tall Case, George III, Inlaid Mahogany, Brass Mounted, c.1765, 81 1/4 In. 3420.00
Tall Case, George III, Japanned, Arched Hood, Tombstone Door, Chinese Scenes, 93 In. ... 3819.00
Tall Case, George III, Mahogany, Oak Inlay, Early 1800s, 82 3/4 In. 1180.00
Tall Case, George IV, Inlaid Mahogany, Oak, Painted Sheet Iron Dial, c.1820, 86 1/2 In. .. 2990.00
Tall Case, Gilbert, Wm. L., Regulator, No. 12, 8-Day, Direct Drive, c.1890, 102 In. 7560.00
Tall Case, Gustav Becker, Regulator, Carved Crest, 3 Weight, 53 x 18 1/2 x 8 1/2 In. 750.00
Tall Case, Hugh Roberts, Oak, Turned Pilasters, Children On Arch, Wales, 88 1/2 In. 1760.00
Tall Case, Inglis, Mahogany, Brass Finial, Painted Face, Pendulum, 84 In. .... *Illus* 3080.00
Tall Case, J. Caillot, Burled Walnut, Inlay Flower Urns, Amsterdam, 1700s, 82 In. 5290.00
Tall Case, J.B. Garstang, Mahogany, Oak, 8-Day, Brass Dial, England, 80 In. 1015.00
Tall Case, Japanned Chinoiserie Decoration, England, c.1740, 84 In. 480.00
Tall Case, John Child, Chippendale, Mahogany, Brass Works, Philadelphia, 96 In. 9200.00
Tall Case, John Taylor, Pine, Brass Dial, 30-Hour, Petworth, England, c.1780, 76 x 16 In. . 1035.00
Tall Case, John Wainwright, George III, Oak, c.1850, 82 In. 2070.00
Tall Case, Joseph Dilger, Regency, Mahogany, Pine, Scotland, 90 In. 1725.00
Tall Case, Joshua Wilder, 8-Day, Strike, Mass., c.1815, 51 In. 18000.00
Tall Case, Junghans, Oak, Arched Top, Carved, Time & Strike, Silvered Dial, 76 In. 345.00
Tall Case, Levi Hutchins, Federal, Cherry, 8-Day, Brass Movement, N.H., 1810, 93 In. ... 10000.00
Tall Case, Louis XVI, Pine, Polychrome Flowers, c.1800, 90 1/2 x 19 In. 920.00
Tall Case, Mahogany, 5 Tube, 8-Day, Chiming, Germany, c.1925, 81 In. 2200.00
Tall Case, Mahogany, 8-Day, Bell Strike, Rolling Moon, England, c.1810, 91 In. 3110.00
Tall Case, Mahogany, Brass, Silver Face, 8-Day, England, 104 x 24 In. 7345.00
Tall Case, Mahogany, Columns, Brass & Silver Scrolled Dial, 99 In. 2300.00
Tall Case, Mahogany, Musical, Arched Pediment, 9 Tube, c.1900, 99 x 22 x 16 In. 5060.00
Tall Case, Mahogany, Painted Face, 4 Seasons Scenes, Ireland, c.1802 .... 8250.00
Tall Case, Mahogany, Painted Moon Dial, England, c.1820, 90 x 22 1/2 In. 1840.00
Tall Case, Mahogany, Swan's-Neck Pediment, England, c.1815, 88 In. 510.00
Tall Case, Mauthe, Arts & Crafts Style, Beveled Glass, Oak Case, 2 Weight, 74 1/2 In. 715.00
Tall Case, Molded Cornice, Wheat, Flowers, Enameled Face, France, 1800s, 91 1/2 In. ... 3300.00
Tall Case, Neoclassical, Polychrome, Domed Hood, 98 1/2 x 20 1/2 x 9 3/4 In. 2300.00

Clock, Tall Case, Cherry, Mahogany Veneer, Painted Iron Face, Early 1800s, 98 In.

Clock, Tall Case, Federal, Cherry, Inlaid, Connecticut, c.1800, 89 x 21 x 11 In.

Clock, Tall Case, Inglis, Mahogany, Brass Finial, Painted Face, Pendulum, 84 In.

Clock, Tall Case, Richard James, Mahogany, Cupid Heads, Painted Face, c.1775, 69 In.

Tall Case, Oak, 8-Day, Germany, Westminster Chime, c.1900, 80 1/2 In. 565.00
Tall Case, Oak, Mahogany Veneer, Bracket Feet, Decorated Face, Pilasters, 83 In. 1100.00
Tall Case, Pine, Chip Carved, Glass Enclosed Throat Door, France, Late 1800s, 84 1/2 In. . . . 865.00
Tall Case, Regency, Mahogany, Arched Hood, Crenelated Crest, Gilt Metal, 83 1/2 In. 5875.00
Tall Case, Regulator, No. 89, Oak, Roman Numerals, c.1889, 65 In. 4500.00
Tall Case, Richard James, Mahogany, Cupid Heads, Painted Face, c.1775, 69 In. . . . . *Illus* 3520.00
Tall Case, Richard Manning, Pine, Ipswich, Mass., 1748-1760, 79 1/4 In. 5875.00
Tall Case, Richard W.S. Kingerley, Mahogany, Sun & Moon Phase, R.I., 102 In. 5750.00
Tall Case, Ridgeway, Mahogany, 8-Day, Time & Strike, Moon Phase, 83 In. 345.00
Tall Case, Riley Whiting, Chippendale, Cherry, Wooden Works, Winchester, 91 3/4 In. . . . 2300.00
Tall Case, Riley Whiting, Country, Sponge & Grain Decorated, c.1820 . . . . 3740.00
Tall Case, Roberts, Oak, 8-Day, Bell Strike, Otley, England, c.1745, 28 In. 1415.00
Tall Case, Samuel Buxton, 8-Day, Bell Strike, Oak Case, England, c.1760, 78 In. 1415.00
Tall Case, Seth Thomas, Baroque Style, Mahogany, 96 In. 4125.00
Tall Case, Shaker, Poplar, Pine, Wood Works, Iron Bell, c.1840, 81 x 15 x 9 In. 3450.00
Tall Case, Stromberg, Mahogany, Electrified, e.1910, 64 1/2 x 22 x 9 In. 605.00
Tall Case, Thomas Green, Mahogany, Painted Dial, 8-Day, 94 x 23 In. 8475.00
Tall Case, Thomas Lake, Chippendale, Mahogany, Pediment Bonnet, Ball, Spire, England 6600.00
Tall Case, Tiger & Curly Maple, Separate Support Pillars, 1815-1830 . . . . 17500.00
Tall Case, W. Turnbull, Oak, Flat Bonnet Top, Brass Works, Darlington, 64 1/2 In. 1150.00
Tall Case, William McLachlan, Oak, Mahogany, New Abbey, c.1840, 91 x 21 1/2 x 10 In. 4600.00
Tall Case, William Wilson, Georgian, Mahogany, 8-Day, Pastoral Scene, c.1785, 94 In. . . . 6900.00
Terry, Samuel, Shelf, Federal, Mahogany, Pillar & Scroll, Landscape, c.1815, 31 In. 1955.00
Terryville, Glass Dome, Milk Glass Pedestal, 1852 Patent, 11 In. 1808.00
Thwaites, Wall, Rosewood, Brass Inlay, Octagonal, London, 1800s, 15 1/4 x 15 1/4 In. . . 290.00
Tiffany clocks that are part of desk sets made by Louis Comfort Tiffany are listed in the Tiffany category. Clocks sold by the store, Tiffany & Co., are listed here.
Tiffany & Co., Japy Freres Movement, Brass Case, Swags, Half Striking, 12 1/4 In. 705.00
Tiffany & Co., Shelf, Louis XV Style, Ormolu, Marti, 1900, 14 In. 1495.00
Tiffany & Co., Shelf, Patinated Copper, Slate, Marti, Late 1800s 1093.00
Travel, Walnut Finish, 15 Jewel, Box, 5 In. 150.00
Tudric, Pewter, Tooled Vines, Blue & Red Enameled Face, Archibald Knox, 5 1/2 In. 5580.00
United Clock Corp., Joe Louis, Bronzed Spelter, c.1950, 12 1/2 In. 170.00
Vincenti, Shelf, Oak, Porcelain Dial, 8-Day, Time, Strike, France, c.1910, 13 1/2 In. 450.00
Vulliamy, Benjamin, Striking Tower, Pilot Dial, Brass, c.1837, 16 x 20 In. 3136.00
Wag-On-Wall, Enameled Face, Brass, Polychrome, Continental, 54 1/2 x 13 3/4 In. 230.00
Wag-On-Wall, Wood, Painted Dial, Flowers, Brass Movement, American, 1890s, 8 3/8 In. 385.00
Waite, Bracket, William IV, Mahogany, Carved, Brass Mounts, Cheltenham, 19 In. 4150.00
Waite & Son, Fusee, Mahogany Case, Cheltenham, England, c.1860, 18 In. 595.00
Walker, Regency, Neogothic, Brass Inlaid, Ebonized, London, 16 1/4 x 9 1/8 In. 575.00
Wall, Act Of Parliament, Scene Of Junk On Waterway, Japanned, 61 1/2 x 30 1/8 In. 8225.00

Wall, Art Nouveau, Walnut, Engraved Dial & Pendulum, 8-Day, French, c.1905, 32 In. . . . 565.00
Wall, Art Nouveau, Walnut, Woman Head Pendulum, Porcelain, Calendar, Austria, 24 In. . 360.00
Wall, Baroque, Rosewood, 8-Day, Gong Strike, Victorian, Germany, c.1870, 37 In. 790.00
Wall, Brass, Striking, Lyre Pendulum, Cast Iron Weights, 1800s, 52 1/2 x 10 3/4 In. 860.00
Wall, Chevalier, Brass, Lyre Pendulum, France, 1800s, 54 3/4 x 13 x 7 1/2 In. 805.00
Wall, Ebonized Frame, Mother-Of-Pearl Inlay Dial, 8-Day, 24 x 19 1/2 In. 115.00
Wall, Gallery, 8-Day, Gong Strike, Ebonized Case, Round, France, c.1890, 16 In. 226.00
Wall, Mahogany, Tunbridge Marquetry, Steel Key, England, c.1865, 38 x 16 x 5 1/4 In. . . 520.00
Wall, Musical, Harbor Town, Reverse Painted, Frame, Austria, 1900s, 23 x 28 In. 315.00
Wall, Ormolu, Cartel, 8-Day, Enamel Cartouche, France, c.1870, 20 In. 226.00
Wall, Prayer, Oval, Oak, Bull's-Eye, Carved Leaves, Flowers, Fruit, 29 In. 660.00
Wall, Walnut, Carved, Thermometer, Barometer, Winged Griffins, Fruit, 38 x 20 In. 1155.00
Wall, Walnut, Open Balcony, Free Swinger, 8-Day, c.1900, 37 In. 540.00
Waltham, Desk, Partner's, Art Deco, 2 Dials, Chrome, Glass, 8-Day, c.1920, 4 In. 165.00
Waltham Watch Co., Travel, Sterling Silver Case, W.B. Kerr, c.1900, 4 x 3 3/4 In. 320.00
Waterbury, Augusta, Wall, Oak, Dragons, 2 Brass Weights, Pendulum, 48 In. 2750.00
Waterbury, Cottage, Peak Top, Gold Gilt, Blue, Gold Glass, 8-Day, Time & Strike, 13 In. 225.00
Waterbury, Dijon, Regulator, Crystal, Brass, Beveled Glass, 8-Day, c.1909, 13 In. 620.00
Waterbury, Dresden, Regulator, Walnut Case, Enamel Dial, 30-Day, c.1900, 49 In. 1075.00
Waterbury, Figural, Golden Retriever, Bronzed Cast Iron, c.1895, 5 1/2 In. 150.00
Waterbury, Library, Free Swinging Pendulum, Porcelain Dial, 2 Weight, 45 In. 2860.00
Waterbury, Porcelain, White, Roses, 30-Hour, 9 In. 225.00
Waterbury, Regulator, Crystal, 8-Day, Gong Strike, c.1900, 11 In. 370.00
Waterbury, Regulator, Crystal, 8-Day, Time & Strike, Coiled Gong, c.1900, 10 In. 254.00
Waterbury, Regulator, No. 60, Oak, c.1900, 72 1/2 In. 5880.00
Waterbury, Sage, Carriage, Repeating, Brass Case, Beveled Glass, c.1910, 5 3/4 In. 200.00
Waterbury, School, Long Drop, Oak, 8-Day, c.1910, 32 In. 225.00
Waterbury, School, Painted Metal Dial, Calendar, Mahogany Case, 28 In. 115.00
Waterbury, School, Rosewood, 8-Day, Time Only, Paper Dial, Calendar, 22 In. 56.00
Waterbury, Seine, Louis IV Style, Pendulum, Cast Spelter, c.1910, 13 In. 198.00
Waterbury, Shelf, Cast Spelter, Angels On Porcelain, c.1915, 12 In. 225.00
Waterbury, Shelf, Half Columns, Lion's Heads, Metal Trim, Black 99.00
Waterbury, Shelf, Mahogany Veneer, Pine, 30-Hour, 10 1/4 x 4 1/2 x 13 3/4 In. 69.00
Waterbury, Shelf, Onyx, Gilt Metal Portico Case, c.1900, 17 In. 510.00
Waterbury, Ship's Wheel, 8-Day, Brass, Jeweled, Turn Helm To Wind, 6 1/4 In. 375.00
Waterbury, Tampa, Oak, Calendar, 8-Day Time & Strike, Stork Tablet, 22 In. 225.00
Waterbury, Wall, Oak, Carved, Lady's Head, 2 Weight, 30 In. 850.00
Welch, E.N., 1-Day, Time & Strike, Amber Glass, Jewel Paperweight, c.1885, 4 In. 280.00
Welch, E.N., Beehive, Rosewood, 8-Day, Gong Strike, Alarm, c.1880, 19 In. 220.00
Welch, E.N., Briggs Rotary, 30-Hour, Steel Ball Pendulum, Dome, Wood Base, 1878, 8 In. 728.00
Welch, E.N., Gale Drop, Calendar, No. 3, Rosewood Case, Paper Dial, c.1880, 30 In. . . . 12320.00
Welch, E.N., Gentry Calendar, Wall, Pressed Oak, 8-Day, c.1900, 26 In. 450.00
Welch, E.N., Kitchen, 8-Day, Time, Strike, Pendulum, 20 1/2 In. 396.00
Welch, E.N., Kitchen, Calendar, Thermometer, Barometer, Oak, Swans, Grapes 259.00
Welch, E.N., Kitchen, Fedora, Walnut 248.00
Welch, E.N., Kitchen, Perpetual Calendar, Ben Franklin 745.00
Welch, E.N., School, Round Corners, 8-Day, Mahogany Veneer, 25 In. 250.00
Welch, E.N., Shelf, Rosewood, 8-Day, Time & Strike, 12 x 5 3/4 x 20 1/2 In. 1095.00
Welch, E.N., Shelf, Walnut, Glass Door, Painted Scene, Ships, 26 1/2 In. 259.00
Welch, E.N., Wall, Gale Drop, Walnut, Carved, Calendar, 2 Dials, 42 In. 3300.00
Welch Spring, Kitchen, Walnut, Sandwich Glass, 8-Day, Gong, c.1875, 23 In. 311.00
Welch Spring, Shelf, Parippa, Rosewood, 8-Day, c.1875, 22 In. . . . . .110.00 to 680.00
Werner, C., Wall, Burl Walnut, Pendulum, 8-Day, c.1880, 31 In. 226.00
Westclox, Bronze, Scrolled Case, Cherub Panel, 11 In. 50.00
Windmill Shape, Barometer, Silvered, Gilt Metal, Continental, 18 In. 1793.00
Winterhalder & Hoffmeier, Mahogany, Round Dial, 8-Day, Germany, c.1900, 13 In. 250.00
Woody Woodpecker, Alarm, Metal, Instructions, Walter Lantz, Box, 1959, 5 In. 385.00

CLOISONNE enamel was developed during the tenth century. A glass
enamel was applied between small ribbons of metal on a metal base.
Most cloisonne is Chinese or Japanese. Pieces marked *China* are
twentieth-century examples.

Bonbon, Celadon, Nickel Mounted, Japan, Showa Export, 7 x 6 In. 145.00

Bowl, Bulb, 5-Claw Dragon, White Ground, Oval, 9 In. 218.00
Bowl, Peonies, Black Ground, Chinese, 1800s, 13 In. 410.00
Bowl, Phoenix, Flower, Late 19th Century, 4 3/4 In. 1725.00
Box, Blue Ground, Round, 17th Century, 5 1/8 In. 2390.00
Box, Butterfly, Peony, Leaf, Pink, Blue, Japan, Late 19th Century, 2 1/2 x 5 x 4 In. 200.00
Box, Duck, Black Bill, Yellow, Blue, Green Feathers, Blue Interior, c.1850, 7 In., Pair ... 540.00
Box, Inaba, Phoenix, Wisteria, Round, Late 19th Century, 3 1/2 In. 230.00
Candlestick, Figural, Deer, Pricket, 17 In. 320.00
Censer, Passion Flowers, Blue Ground, Oval, Cylindrical Legs, Loop Handles, 9 In. 1955.00
Charger, Dragon, Bird, Flowers, Late 19th Century, 17 1/2 In. 604.00
Charger, Fan Design, Golden Yellow Ground, Late 19th Century, 12 In. 196.00
Charger, Flower Cart, 6 Lobes, Bird, Butterfly, Metal Legs, c.1890, 16 In. 690.00
Charger, Hawk, Peony, Blue Ground, Late 19th Century, 24 In. 690.00
Ewer, Ram Shape, Cup Stopper, Blue Ground, Chinese, Late 1800s, 6 In. 175.00
Figure, Deer, Blue Ground, Multicolored, Copper, 14 1/2 x 16 In. 115.00
Jar, Cover, Black Ground, 18th Century, 7 1/8 In., Pair 3346.00
Jar, Cover, Peacocks, Butterfly, Bronze Foo Dog Finial, Footed, 6 1/2 x 4 1/2 In. 60.00
Jar, Dome Cover, Egg Shape, Butterfly, Flower, Flower Finial, 19th Century, 3 3/4 In. ... 160.00
Jar, Egg Shape, Wisteria Design, Japan, Late 19th Century, 3 3/4 In. 85.00
Jardiniere, Cylinder, Butterflies, Japan, Late 19th Century, 6 In. 90.00
Jardiniere, Napoleon III Style, Gilt Bronze Mounted, 15 3/4 x 19 In. 2390.00
Moon-Flask, Chinese, Qing Dynasty, 4 3/4 In. 945.00
Pin, Oval, Flower Design, Black Ground, 1 1/2 In. 29.00
Pitcher, Water, 5-Toed Dragons, c.1900, 10 x 9 In. 730.00
Planter, Brass, Oriental Jade Tree, Orange Flowers, 15 1/2 In. 450.00
Planter, White Flowers, Tree, Leaves, Foil Under Enameling, 10 1/2 In. 1639.00
Plate, Butterfly, Chrysanthemum, Dragons, Black Ground, Late 19th Century, 12 In. 374.00
Plate, Flower Shape, Phoenix, Late 19th Century, 9 3/4 In. 259.00
Plate, Ho Bird, Brocade Design, Late 1800s, 7 In. 80.00
Plate, Prunus, Transparent Green Ground, 1900s, 5 In. 30.00
Teapot, Egg Shape, Insect, Flower, 1800s, 5 1/2 In. 210.00
Teapot, Pear Shape, Gods Of Fortune Symbols, Scrolled, Late 19th Century, 5 In. 718.00
Teapot, Totai, Grisaille Landscape, Polychrome Flowers, Japan, Late 1800s, 5 In. 230.00
Tray, Cast Brass Rim, Handles, Flowers, Arabesque Designs, 8 1/4 x 14 1/2 In. 175.00
Urn, Egg Shape, Loop Handles, Butterflies, Flowers, Late 19th Century, 8 1/2 In. 259.00
Vase, Baluster Shape, 5-Claw Dragon, Red Ground, Early 1900s, 9 In. 58.00
Vase, Bird, Tree, Shaded Blue Ground, Late 19th Century, 9 1/2 In. 400.00
Vase, Blue Ground, Dragons, Clouds, Flowers, Butterflies, Wood Stand, 25 In., Pair 575.00
Vase, Bud, Carved Wood, Flower, Butterfly, Late 19th Century, 7 1/2 In. 424.00
Vase, Burgundy, Eagles Perched On Blossoming Branches, Blue Interior, 24 In., Pair 770.00
Vase, Butterfly & Flower Panels, Multicolored, 7 In., Pair 90.00
Vase, Champleve, Enamel, Animal Head Handles, Oriental, 12 1/2 In. 250.00
Vase, Chrysanthemum, Transparent Foil Ground, Japan, Late 19th Century, 4 3/4 In. 175.00
Vase, Club Form, Phoenix, Aventurine Ground, Japan, Late 19th Century, 11 1/4 In. 460.00
Vase, Club Shape, Butterfly, Flower, Aventurine, Late 19th Century, 7 In. 210.00
Vase, Dragon, Transparent Ground, Late 19th Century, 3 1/2 In. 288.00
Vase, Egg Shape, Flowers, Green Ground, 1900s, 10 1/2 In. 430.00
Vase, Egg Shape, Snow Crane, Red Ground, Late 19th Century, 5 In. 405.00
Vase, Flowering Plants, Dark Blue Ground, Japan, c.1900, 29 In. 645.00
Vase, Foil Fish, Red & Gray, 7 1/2 In. 158.00
Vase, Gold, Silver Wirework, Butterflies, Flowers, Phoenix, Late 19th Century, 6 In. 1955.00
Vase, Hexagonal, Dragon Design, Green Ground, Late 19th Century, 4 3/4 In. 290.00
Vase, Hexagonal, Dragon, Phoenix, Black Ground, Late 19th Century, 5 3/4 In., Pair 489.00
Vase, Inverted Pear Shape, Bird, Butterfly, Flower, Brown Ground, 19th Century, 9 In. ... 300.00
Vase, Inverted Pear Shape, Chrysanthemum, Fuji Mark, Late 19th Century, 9 1/2 In. 315.00
Vase, Inverted Pear Shape, Figure & Brocade Design, Late 19th Century, 9 3/4 In. 290.00
Vase, Inverted Pear Shape, Grapevine, Pink Ground, Late 19th Century, 5 1/8 In. 259.00
Vase, Inverted Pear Shape, Prunus Design, Japan, Late 19th Century, 5 In. 259.00
Vase, Iris, Waisted, 5 3/4 In. 250.00
Vase, Landscape, Flowers, Hayashi Kodenji, Japan, 19th Century, 12 In. 28200.00
Vase, Midnight Blue Ground, Hardwood Stand, Japan, c.1926, 14 3/4 In., Pair 635.00
Vase, Monster Masks, Flared Handles, Pierced, Dome Cover, 3 Cabriole Legs, 8 In. 413.00
Vase, Multicolored Flowers, Gold Colored Inner Neck, 7 In. 30.00

Vase, Mums, Red, Yellow, Green, White, Vines, On Blue Ground, 19th Century, 18 In. 259.00
Vase, Oval, Flared Rim, Peonies, Chrysanthemums, Lily, Copper Mounts, 5 In. 1100.00
Vase, Oval, Flared Rims, Weeping Cherry Trees, Flowers, Birds, 7 x 1 x 1/2 In., Pair 1650.00
Vase, Oval, Flattened, Cranes, Goldstone Ground, Japan, Late 19th Century, 6 In., Pair . . . 825.00
Vase, Oval, Short Necks, Everted Rims, Irises, Navy Blue Ground, Stand, 5 In., Pair 1210.00
Vase, Pink & White Prunus Design, Japan, Early 1900s, 7 1/2 In. 98.00
Vase, Polychrome Grapevines, Blue Ground, Geometric Bands, 18 In. 200.00
Vase, Polychrome Roses, Pink & Black, Red Ground, Floral Scrolls On Neck, 12 In. 85.00
Vase, Powder Blue Ground, Hardwood Stand, c.1926, 2 3/4 In., Pair 1265.00
Vase, Tapered Cylinder, Bird, Chrysanthemum, Ando, Late 19th Century, 11 1/2 In. 175.00
Vase, Teardrop Shape, Dragon, Mandarin Duck, Late 19th Century, 9 1/4 In. 290.00
Vase, Transparent, Seed Form, Chrysanthemum Design, Late 19th Century, 3 1/2 In. 150.00
Vase, Well Bucket Shape, Flower, Butterfly, Aventurine, Late 19th Century, 6 In. 345.00
Wine Pot, Butterfly, Flower, Aventurine Ground, Late 19th Century, 4 3/4 In. 315.00

CLOTHING of all types is listed in this category. Dresses, hats, shoes, underwear, and more are found here. Other textiles are to be found in the Coverlet, Movie, Quilt, Textile, and World War I and II categories.

Apron, Cotton, Gingham Poodles On Base & Pocket 5.00
Blouse, Striped, Oatmeal Linen, No. 185, Hemmingway & Sons, c.1914, 15 x 7 In. 260.00
Corset, Linen, 1786, 2 Piece 2800.00
Cowgirl Outfit, Black Suede, Fringe, Jacket, Skirt, Medium, 2 Piece 45.00
Denim Jeans, Tuf Nut Westerns, Original Tags, 1950s, 30 x 34 In. 185.00
Dress, Andy Warhol Souper, Campbell's Soup, 80% Cellulose, 20% Cotton, 1960 . . . . 1175.00
Dress Coat, Helmet & Belt, Artillery 1885 . . . . 2750.00
Dress Coat, Service Stripes, Cavalry 1885 . . . . 2200.00
Hat, Black Velvet, Matte Satin, 9 In. 10.00
Hat, Jack-Tar, British Navy, Black Beaver, c.1810 . . . . 3740.00
Hat, Organ Grinder's Monkey, Leather, Silk Liner, Bronze Button, Hatbox, Early 1900s . . 440.00
Helmet, Police, Wool Cover, Metal Badge, Crown Rosette, British Gibraltar, Small 69.00
Jacket, Denim, Indigo, Big E, Lot 70505, 2 Chest Pockets, Levi's, Size 36-38 . . . . 60.00
Jacket, Denim, Indigo, Lot 71205, Rivet Buttons, Levi's, 1970, Size 42 . . . . 40.00
Jacket, Leather, Biker, 3 Zipper Slot Pockets, Waist Belt, Excelled, U.S.A., Size 16 . . . . . 40.00
Jacket, U.S. Army, Duck Hunter Camouflage, 5 Pockets, Early Vietnam 40.00
Jeans, Big E, Levi's, Polyester, Cotton, Sta-Prest, Flare, 1970s, Size 31 x 32 . . . . 40.00
Jeans, Denim, Indigo, Big E, Akamimi, 501, Levi's, 26 x 25 In. 100.00
Jeans, Denim, Indigo, Talon 42 Zipper Fly, Copperhead, 27 x 36 In. 90.00
Jeans, Denim, Indigo, Talon 42 Zipper Fly, Straight Legs, Lee Riders, 1970s, 28 x 36 In. . . 79.00
Jeans, Levi's, Saddleman Boot, Zipper Fly, 1970s, 27 x 32 In. 35.00
Kimono, Silk & Metallic Thread, Wisteria, Fans, c.1900 . . . . 720.00
Kimono, Silk Crepe, Flowers, Early 1900s 160.00
Mittens, Wool, Pink, Dog Applique, Flannel Lined, Mounted, Amish, 6 1/4 x 4 In. 250.00
Overcoat, Crochet & Taped Lace, White Linen, Ankle Length, 1800s, Woman's 550.00
Priest's Robe, Gold Brocade, Orange Ground, Pomegranates, Japan, 1800s, 74 x 24 In. . . 355.00
Priest's Robe, White Brocade, Purple, Blue, Tan Flowers, Japan, 1800s, 48 x 42 In. 355.00
Robe, Brocade, Pleated, Red Silk, Chinese, Early 1900s, Woman's 235.00
Robe, Embroidered, Chain Stitch, Midnight Blue Ground, Flowers, Chinese, 1800s 175.00
Robe, Embroidered, Gold Dragons, Blue Ground, Chinese, 1800s 825.00
Robe, Embroidered, Silk, Iron Red, Early 20th Century 470.00
Robe, Official, Silk, K'o-Ssu Work, 5-Clawed Dragon, Imperial Family, Chinese, c.1800 . 6170.00
Robe, Priest's, Gold Brocade Kesa, Blue Ground, Japan, 1800s, 80 x 38 In. 825.00
Robe, Tapestry Weave, Empress Dowager, Flowers, Shou Characters, Chinese, c.1900 . . . 2350.00
Robe, Yellow, Silk Brocade, Embroidered Blue Flowers, Chinese, Early 1900s, Woman's . 265.00
Scarf, Silk, Les Oiseaux Du Roy, Hooded Falcons, Handler, Blue, Red, Hermes 235.00
Shako, West Point Cadet, Black, Brass Colored Trim, Plume, Front Crest, c.1923, 7 In. . . . 259.00
Shawl, Kashmir, Boteh Design, White Ground, c.1900, 124 x 62 In. 175.00
Shawl, Paisley, Black Center, Fringe, 129 x 63 In. 275.00
Shawl, Paisley, Boteh Design Variation, Fringe, 136 x 63 In. 300.00
Shirt, Work, Gray, Cotton, Rayon, Long Sleeves, 2 Pockets, Lee, 1960, Size 14 . . . . 50.00
Shoes, Laces, High Top & Heels, Very Pointed Toes, Beige Leather, c.1910, Size 8 1/2 . . . 90.00
Shoes, Wedding, Leather, Pearl Buttons, Scalloped High Top, White, c.1900 . . . . 70.00
Shoes, Wood, Repousse Silver Mounted, Spanish Colonial, c.1900, 8 1/2 In., Pair 230.00
Surcoat, Silk, Gold Thread, Dragon, Peony, Frame, Chinese, 1800s, 46 1/2 x 33 1/2 In. . . 1840.00

Sweatshirt, Cotton, Long Sleeve, White, Unopened, Fruit Of The Loom, Size 34-36 ....   50.00
Tie, Peek-A-Boo, Silk, Jacquard Style, Nude Woman Inside, Nat Nast, Box, 1950s 50.00
Uniform, Cadet, Hat, Jacket, Trousers, USAF Academy, 1970s 29.00
Uniform, Royal Canadian Mounted Police, Tunic, Trousers, Size 38, 33 x 32 In. 176.00
Uniform, U.S. Military Academy, Blue Wool, Ivory, Silver Buttons, 1880s, Medium 75.00
Work Shirt, Olive Drab, Tags, Dickies, c.1950s 45.00

CLUTHRA glass is a two-layered glass with small air pockets that form
white spots. The Steuben Glass Works of Corning, New York, made it
in 1920. Kimball Glass Company of Vineland, New Jersey, made
Cluthra from about 1925. Victor Durand signed some pieces with his
name. Related items are listed in the Steuben category.

Vase, Amethyst, White, 8 1/4 In. 920.00
Vase, Sky Blue, Applied Crystal Foot, Kimble, 8 1/2 In. 345.00
Vase, Tapered, Oval, Flared Rim, Red, Yellow, Gray, Signed, 8 1/2 In. 719.00
Vase, White, Frothy, Translucent, Ground Pontil, Signed, 8 1/2 In. 345.00
Vase, Yellow Amber, Bulbous, Flared Rim, 10 1/4 x 9 In. 1955.00

COALBROOKDALE was made by the Coalport porcelain factory of
England during the Victorian period. Pieces are decorated with floral
encrustations.

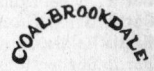

Bowl, Handles, Cover, Encrusted & Painted Flowers, 1840, 5 In. 95.00
Vase, Handles, Encrusted Flowers, 12 In. 225.00

COALPORT ware has been made by the Coalport Porcelain Works of
England from 1795 to the present time. Early pieces were unmarked.
About 1810–1825 the pieces were marked with the name *Coalport* in
various forms. Later pieces also had the name *John Rose* in the mark.
The crown mark has been used with variations since 1881. The date
1750 is printed in some marks, but it is not the date the factory started.
Some pieces are listed in Indian Tree.

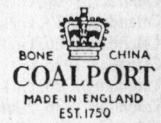

Basket, Relief Flowers, Rectangular, Entwined Handle, Early 1800s, 10 1/4 In. 545.00
Box, Cover, Gilt Design, Blue Enamel Beading, 5 In. 1020.00
Cup & Saucer, Demitasse, Bluebird, Gilt, c.1890, 1 3/4 In. 240.00
Cup & Saucer, Demitasse, Gilt, Burgundy, Jeweled, Early 20th Century, 1 3/4 In. 175.00
Cup & Saucer, Demitasse, Shell Pattern, Pink Interior, Gilt, No. 6294, 1 3/4 In. 105.00
Cup & Saucer, Demitasse, Turquoise, Gilt, Jeweled, Early 20th Century, 3 In. 300.00
Cup & Saucer, London Shape Cup, Imari Taste, c.1815, 2 1/2 In. 105.00
Cup & Saucer, Scene, Jeweled, Gilt, Late 19th Century, 1 5/8 In. 400.00
Lamp Base, Birds, Parcel Gilt, Urn Shape, England, c.1861-1875, 16 1/2 In. 3175.00
Letter Holder, Flowers, Birds, Gilt, Blue Ground, Waisted, Crest, 7 In., Pair 2645.00
Platter, Oriental Flowers & Leaves, Scalloped Border, 14 In. 175.00
Sugar, Scrolling Handles, Landscapes, Pedestal Base, c.1885, 3 1/2 x 5 In. 690.00
Vase, Cover, Woman's Portrait, Ivory & Pink Ground, 8 1/2 In. 1980.00

COBALT BLUE glass was made using oxide of cobalt. The characteris-
tic bright dark blue identifies it for the collector. Most cobalt glass
found today was made after the Civil War. There was renewed interest
in the dark blue glass in the late 1930s and dinnerwares were made.

Condiment & Spoon, Roly Poly, Metal Cover, Black Wooden Knob 25.00
Dish, Maple Leaf Shape, 1930s, 7 In. 30.00
Tumbler, Art Deco Decoration, 3 3/4 In., 6 Piece 75.00
Vase, Bud, Cone Shape, Flared Rim, Clear Foot, 11 1/2 In. 50.00
Vase, Bud, Enameled Flowers, Clear Stem & Foot, 10 In. 60.00
Vase, Egg Shape, Red Threading At Neck, Flared Rim, 6 1/2 In. 375.00

COCA-COLA was first served in 1886 in Atlanta, Georgia. It was adver-
tised through signs, newspaper ads, coupons, bottles, trays, calendars,
and even lamps and clocks. Collectors want anything with the word
Coca-Cola, including a few rare products, like gum wrappers and cigar
bands. The famous trademark was patented in 1893, the *Coke* mark in
1945. Many modern items and reproductions are being made.

Ad, Magazine, Ozzie & Harriet Ice Skating, Full Color, 1961, 10 x 13 In. 20.00

Ad, Magazine, Patrons In Soda Shop, Massengale Magazine, c.1905, 10 3/4 x 15 In. 60.00
Ad, Magazine, Raquel Welch, 1970, 14 x 10 1/2 In. 25.00
Ad, Sunday Newspaper Magazine, Santa, 1952 . . . .   20.00
Art, Original, Drink Coca-Cola, Happy Woman, Striped Shirt, Oil On Canvas, 21 x 46 In.   305.00
Ashtray, Coke Bottle, Under Green Lampshade, Match Pull, Bakelite, c.1930, 7 1/2 In. . .   850.00
Ashtray, Cup Holders, During The Game Enjoy Coca-Cola, Metal, 8 1/2 x 8 1/2 In. 149.00
Bank, Musical, Die Cast Metal, 2 Songs, Certificate, Instructions, 6 x 6 In. 50.00
Bank, Santa Claus, At Fireplace, Plastic, Mechanical 10.00
Bank, Santa Claus, With Train, Plastic, Mechanical 15.00
Booklet, Bottler, 1959 . . . .   35.00
Booklet, Bottler, January 1960 . . . .   39.00
Booklet, Bottler, Mar.-Sept. 1946 . . . .   28.00
Bottle, Blue Ridge Bottling Works, Staunton, Va., c.1910, 7 3/4 In. 65.00
Bottle, Embossed, Enameled Script, Metal Cap, c.1910, 12 In. 360.00
Bottle, Grand Opening Of World Of Coca-Cola, Atlanta, 1990 . . . .   65.00
Bottle, In Lucite, 75th Anniversary 75.00
Bottle, Jelly Belly, 75th Anniversary, Clear, Full Of Jelly Bellies, 1978, 10 Oz. 95.00
Bottle, Syrup, Drink Coca-Cola, Foil Label, 1920s, 12 In. 523.00
Bottle, Syrup, Green, Lid, 1940s, Gal. 25.00
Bottle Holder, Shopping Cart, Wire, Red Plaque, Enjoy Coke While You Shop 65.00
Bottle Opener, Brass, Patent 2335000, Starr X, 4 x 1 1/2 In. . . . . .48.00 to 50.00
Bottle Opener & Ice Pick, Wood, Red Drink Coca-Cola Bottles, 10 In. 55.00
Button, Bottle, Red Ground, Tin, 1949, 2 In. . . . . .800.00 to 845.00
Calendar, 1896, Lady With Birds, 10 1/2 x 6 1/2 In. 7150.00
Calendar, 1907, Girl With Green Dress, Holding Glass, 14 x 7 In. 11000.00
Calendar, 1919, Girl With Knitting Bag, 21 x 40 In. 1540.00
Calendar, 1920, Golfer Girl, 12 x 27 1/2 In. 3400.00
Calendar, 1926, Girl With Tennis Racket, 18 1/2 x 10 In. . . . . .900.00 to 1013.00
Calendar, 1926, Girl With Tennis Racket, Frame, 23 x 15 In. 330.00
Calendar, 1936, 50th Anniversary, N.C. Wyeth, Frame, 24 1/4 x 11 3/4 In. 647.00
Calendar, 1936, Girl, Boat, Fisherman Holding Bottle, Frame, 10 x 18 1/2 In. 625.00
Calendar, 1938, Girl At Shade, Yellow Hat . . . . .210.00 to 400.00
Calendar, 1952, Square Dance, 22 x 12 1/2 In. 165.00
Calendar, 1958, Santa Claus, Starts December 1957, 22 x 12 In.   225.00
Calendar, 1980, Olympics, 17 1/2 x 11 In. 160.00
Carrier, 6-Pack, Aluminum, 6 For 25 Cents, 8 1/2 In. 65.00
Carrier, 6-Pack, Bentwood, Handle 230.00
Carrier, 6-Pack, Different Bottlers, Metal, 1950s 150.00
Carrier, 12-Pack, Aluminum, Capacity, Reynolds Aluminum, 16 1/2 x 5 1/4 x 9 In. 150.00
Carrier, Grocery Cart, 2-Bottle Holder, Enjoy Coca-Cola While You Shop, 1950s 58.00
Case Holder, Wire, Drink Coca-Cola, Fishtail Sign, Hooks 225.00
Catalog, Merchandising, Vol. 1, 4-1-58 . . . .   176.00
Cigarette Case, Frosted Glass, Embossed, 1936, 2 Piece . . . . .425.00 to 450.00
Clock, Cola Clan Convention Award, 17 x 41 In. 83.00
Clock, Drink Coca-Cola, Square, Pam, 1950s 120.00
Clock, Drink Coke In Bottles, Plastic Face, Wire Frame, Lighted, 1950s, 64 In. 137.00
Clock, Ice Cold Coca-Cola, Silhouette Girl, Light-Up, Pam, Round 220.00
Clock, Most Refreshing Drink In The World, Battery Operated, Frame, 25 x 13 In. 299.00
Clock, Octagonal, Mahogany, Drink Coca-Cola, Key, Paperwork, 20 x 12 In. 385.00
Clock, Regulator, Delicious, Refreshing, 5 Cents, Oak Case, Ingraham, 40 In. 577.00
Clock, Silhouette Girl, Neon Motion, c.1941, 18 In. 2090.00
Clock, Telechron, 1950s, 18 In. 220.00
Clock, Wood Frame, Selected Devices, c.1940, 16 x 16 x 3 3/4 In. 330.00
Coin Changer, Have A Coke, Get Your Nickels Here, Metal, Vendo, 1950s, 16 In. 935.00
Coin-Operated Machine, 10 Cent, Cavalier, Restored, 57 In. 1265.00
Coin-Operated Machine, 10 Cent, Model No. 23, 38 x 24 In. 1430.00
Coin-Operated Machine, Cavalier Model C-51 . . . .   635.00
Coin-Operated Machine, Cooler, Beverageair, No. 8416291, 34 x 25 x 24 1/2 In. 1200.00
Coin-Operated Machine, Vendo, No. 23, 38 x 24 In. 1430.00
Coin-Operated Machine, Vendo, No. 39, 60 x 27 In. 2310.00
Coin-Operated Machine, Vendolator, No. 33, 10 Cent 660.00
Coin-Operated Machine, Vendolator, No. 39, Red Metal, 1950s, 27 1/2 x 58 x 16 In. 6500.00
Cooler, Airline, Red, 17 x 12 x 6 1/2 In. . . . . .250.00 to 420.00

Cooler, Bottle Opener, Drain, Handle, 1950s, 17 x 17 x 11 In. 285.00
Cooler, Bottle Opener, Original Tray, Drain Spigot, 18 In. 220.00
Cooler, Chest Type, Salesman Sample, Ads In Doors, 1939, 10 x 12 In. 1980.00
Cooler, Drink Coca-Cola, Metal Handle, 16 x 11 x 9 1/4 In. 325.00
Cooler, Handle, Embossed, Drink Coca-Cola In Bottles, Red, 18 In. 210.00
Cooler, Model 240T, Westinghouse, 91 In. 110.00
Cooler, Picnic, Bottle Opener, Drain, Plug, Actong Mfg., 17 1/2 x 12 x 16 1/2 In. 185.00
Cooler, Tray, Bottle Opener, Red, Vinyl, 17 x 14 x 11 1/2 In. 250.00
Cooler, Westinghouse, Embossed Metal, Restored, 34 In. 525.00
Couch, Coca-Cola Cooler Loveseat, Red, White, Embossed Lettering 495.00
Cutouts, Circus, Frame, 1927, 12 1/2 x 15 1/2 In. 100.00
Decal Sheet, Sprite Boy, Bottles Of Coke, 26 x 20 In. 175.00
Dish, Pretzel, 3 Bottles, Around Bowl 248.00
Dish, World, Fluted, Coke In Different Languages, 7 1/2 In. 100.00
Dispenser, Barrel, Oak, 7-Up, Root Beer, Countertop, 26 In. 275.00
Dispenser, Syrup, Barrel, Wood, 2 Tin Signs, Multiplex Faucet Co., 29 In. 250.00
Dispenser, Syrup, Frosted Glass Body, Porcelain Base, c.1930, 17 In. 6500.00
Display, Bottle, Patent D, Cap, 20 In. 425.00
Display, Old Man North Holding Bottle, Easel Back, Cardboard, 1953, 16 x 21 In. 445.00
Doll, Santa, Dakin, Rich's Atlanta, 1988, 16 In. 89.00
Doll, Santa, Ruskin, Electric, Mechanical, 39 In. 145.00
Door Push, Delicious & Refreshing, 5 Cents, Aluminum, c.1905, 3 x 8 In. 955.00
Door Push, Drink Coca-Cola, Blue, White, Aluminum, c.1905, 3 x 8 In. 1015.00
Doorknob, Porcelain, Drink Coca-Cola, Metal Stem 525.00
Festoon, Icicles, c.1930, 5 Piece 2000.00
Figure, Policeman, Iron Base, Slow School Zone, Sheet Steel, 1950s, 63 In. . . . . .907.00 to 1375.00
Fountain Dispenser, Painted Metal, Embossed Letters, Countertop Type, 20 In. 242.00
Frame, Coke Bottle Crest, Wood, Gilt, Applied Metal Plaque, 49 x 28 1/2 In. 113.00
Glass, Diamond, Coke Trademark, 1960s, 12 Fl. Oz. 85.00
Glass, Flared, Syrup Line, c.1910, 3 3/4 In. 375.00
Glass Holder, Logo, Silver, c.1900, 2 1/2 In. . . . . .1400.00 to 1463.00
Globe, Frosted, Green, Pinstripe, Milk Glass, c.1930, 12 In. 800.00
Globe, Hanging, Frosted, Metal Tassel, Chain, c.1930 . . . . 3600.00
Golf Bag, Vinyl, 36 In. 17.00
Jug, Stoneware, Brown & White, Paper Label, Wm. Smith & Co., York, Pa., 11 In. 96.00
Kick Plate, Drink Coca-Cola, Embossed Tin, 1933, 11 x 34 In. 647.00
Kick Plate, Drink Coca-Cola, Fountain Service, Porcelain, c.1950, 12 x 28 In. 550.00
Kick Plate, Fountain Service, Porcelain, c.1950s, 12 x 28 In. 565.00
Lunch Box, Coke Bottle Handle, 10 x 7 x 5 In. 50.00
Lunch Box, Silver, Bottle Shape Handle, Thermos Holder, 8 1/2 x 10 x 4 1/2 In. 48.00
Machine, Glasscock Jr., 4 Tin Embossed Signs 1750.00
Match Striker, Drink Coca-Cola, Porcelain, Yellow, White, Canada, 1939 . . . . 425.00
Match Striker, Drink Coca-Cola, Strike Matches Here, 4 1/2 x 4 1/2 In. 800.00
Menu Board, Diamond Coke Can 425.00
Menu Board, Drink Coca-Cola, Wood, Masonite, 1939, 26 In. 415.00
Mirror, Bastian Bros. Co., Rochester, N.Y., 1908, Pocket 1140.00
Mirror, Cardboard, Glass, White Cat, Drink Coca-Cola In Bottles, Germany, 1925, 2 In. . . . 440.00
Payroll Check, Coca-Cola Bottling Works, Lebanon, Tennessee, 1957 . . . . 25.00
Pencil Box, 3 Pencils, Pen, Ruler, Eraser, 2 Blotters, 1930s 60.00
Plaque, Dalton CC Bottling Co., 1946 & 1956, 18 x 7 1/2 In. 220.00
Plate, Bottle, Glass Of Coke, Knowles China, 1931, 7 1/4 In. 500.00
Plate, Drink Coca-Cola, Bottle, Cup, Knowles, 1931, 7 1/4 In. 535.00
Plate, Topless Woman, Vienna Art 1610.00
Playing Cards, Airplane Spotter, Blue Ground, 54 Cards, Box, 1943 . . . . 125.00
Postcard, Soda Fountain, Welch's Grape Juice Bottles, 3 1/2 x 5 1/2 In. 275.00
Poster, Home Hospitality, 3 People Singing, 1951, 30 x 50 In. 700.00
Radio, Bottle Shape, AM, Plastic, 1970s 45.00
Radio, Cassette Player, Box 55.00
Radio, Figural, Bottle, Bakelite, 1933, 23 1/2 In. 5750.00
Scooter, Brakes, 47 In. 35.00
Sewing Kit, Woman, Large Brim Hat, 1981, 2 3/4 x 1 3/4 In. 20.00
Sheet Music, Rum & Coca-Cola, Amsterdam, Sullavan, Baron, L. Feist, 1944, 2 Pages . . . 7.00
Shirt, Cream, Short Sleeves, Poly-Cotton, Medium To Large, 33 x 42 x 50 In. 38.00

Shirt, Tan, Short Sleeves, Poly-Cotton, Medium To Large, 33 x 42 x 50 In. 35.00
Sign, 2-Sided, Die Cut, Tin, Triangle, Iron Bracket, 1936, 28 x 36 . . . . 1365.00
Sign, 2-Sided, Light-Up, Plastic, Red Ground, White Letters, Round, 16 In. 495.00
Sign, 2-Sided, Light-Up, Rotates, Plastic, Metal, c.1950 . . . . 1600.00
Sign, 2-Sided, Light-Up, Rotating Halo, Metal, Plastic, Neon Products, c.1950s 1800.00
Sign, 6-Pack, Big King Size, 1961, 20 x 28 In. 2815.00
Sign, 50th Anniversary, Tin, Embossed, Round, 1936 . . . . 1650.00
Sign, Accepted Home Refreshment, Fireplace, Lithograph Cardboard, 1942, 27 x 56 In. . . . 130.00
Sign, Be Refreshed, Cardboard, Frame, 1952, 34 In. 99.00
Sign, Bottle Shape, Sheet Steel Lithograph, 108 In. 220.00
Sign, Bottle, Die Cut, Porcelain, 1940-1950, 16 1/2 x 5 In. 365.00
Sign, Bottle, Ice Cold, 2-Sided, Die Cut, Tin, Flange, 1951, 18 x 22 In. 620.00
Sign, Cap, Coca-Cola, Red, Aluminum, 12 In. 138.00
Sign, Cap, Drink Coca-Cola, Ice Cold, Blue, Porcelain, 14 In. 523.00
Sign, Cap, Drink Coca-Cola, Red, White, Porcelain, 36 In. 330.00
Sign, Coca-Cola, Please Pay When Served, Plastic, Wood, Price Bros., 17 1/2 In. 880.00
Sign, Coca-Cola, Red, White, Porcelain, 16 x 44 In. 230.00
Sign, Coke Adds Life To Everything Nice, Metal, 18 x 36 In. 110.00
Sign, Coke Time, Join The Friendly Circle, Cardboard, Frame, c.1954, 36 x 20 In. 470.00
Sign, Coke, Bottle, Brown, Green, White, Porcelain, Die Cut, 1940-1950, 16 1/2 x 5 In. . . . 330.00
Sign, Cool Contrast To A Summer Sun, Frame, 1941, 64 x 34 In. 495.00
Sign, Counter, Light-Up, Pause That Refreshes, 1940-1950 . . . . 2700.00
Sign, Delicious & Refreshing, Man, Woman, Tin, 20 x 28 In. 220.00
Sign, Delicious & Refreshing, Porcelain, 2-Sided, 1932, 36 x 60 In. . . . . *Illus* 600.00
Sign, Die Cut, 2-Sided, Tin, Triangle, Iron Bracket, 1936, 28 x 36 In. 1412.00
Sign, Disc Shape, Bottle In Center, Tin Lithograph, 24 In. 125.00
Sign, Distributor, Drink Coca-Cola, Porcelain, Tennessee Enamel Co., 72 x 96 In. 1155.00
Sign, Dole Deluxe Fountain Dispenser, 2-Sided, Porcelain, c.1950, 28 x 28 In. 2145.00
Sign, Drink Coca-Cola In Bottles, 5 Cents, Tin, Embossed, 1908, 11 3/4 x 35 1/2 In. 550.00
Sign, Drink Coca-Cola, A.A. Ardinger, Painted Tin, Frame, 27 x 69 In. 440.00
Sign, Drink Coca-Cola, Bottle, Tin Lithograph, Embossed, c.1931, 12 1/4 x 4 1/2 In. 690.00
Sign, Drink Coca-Cola, Cowboy Holding Hat & Bottle, Cardboard, 1941 . . . . 1595.00
Sign, Drink Coca-Cola, Fountain Service, Porcelain, c.1930 . . . . 2225.00
Sign, Drink Coca-Cola, Good With Food, White, Red, Aqua, c.1960, 1 1/2 x 8 In. 300.00
Sign, Drink Coca-Cola, Ice Cold, Flange, Tin, 22 In. . . . . .275.00 to 440.00
Sign, Drink Coca-Cola, Porcelain, 1927, 10 x 30 In. 350.00
Sign, Drink Coca-Cola, Porcelain, Die Cut, 60 x 38 In. 300.00
Sign, Drink Coca-Cola, Refreshing New Feeling, Fishtail, Horizontal, 1960s, 53 In. 305.00
Sign, Drink Coca-Cola, Sign Of Good Taste, Fishtail, Vertical, 1963, 53 In. 360.00
Sign, Drink Coca-Cola, Tin, Embossed Letters, 1940s, 19 x 54 In. 85.00
Sign, Drink Coca-Cola, Waitress, Car, White, Red, Black, Porcelain, 36 x 54 In. 2420.00
Sign, Drink Coca-Cola, Wood, Metal Filigree, Kay Display, 1930s, 11 3/8 x 9 In. 850.00
Sign, Enjoy Coca-Cola, 24 x 10 In. 55.00
Sign, Enjoy That Refreshing New Feeling, 2-Sided, Flange, October, 1961, 15 x 18 In. 420.00
Sign, Fountain Service, 2 Taps, Porcelain, c.1930s 2275.00
Sign, Fountain Service, 2-Sided, Die Cut, 1930s, 22 x 26 In. 385.00
Sign, Fountain Service, Delicious & Refreshing, 2-Sided, Porcelain, 1934, 60 x 42 In. 910.00
Sign, Fountain Service, Drink Coca-Cola, Enamel, Tin, 1933, 25 1/2 x 23 In. 1725.00
Sign, Fountain Service, Dual Taps, Porcelain, c.1930 . . . . 2295.00
Sign, French Canadian, Buvez, Self-Framed, Tin, c.1930, 17 1/4 x 53 In. 165.00
Sign, Gas Today, Drink Coca-Cola While You Wait, Embossed Tin, 1930s, 20 x 28 In. 910.00
Sign, Girl Holding Glass, Red Background, Oval, 1926, 7 1/2 x 11 In. 2660.00
Sign, Girl In Swimsuit, Frame, 1941, 64 x 34 In. 495.00
Sign, Good With Food, c.1960s, 1 1/2 x 8 In. 310.00
Sign, Have A Coke Now, Cardboard, 2-Sided, 1951, 16 x 27 In. 375.00
Sign, Ice Cold Coca-Cola Sold Here, Embossed Tin, 1933, 19 1/2 In. 650.00
Sign, Ice Cold, Coke Bottle, 2-Sided, Die Cut, Flange, 1951, 18 x 22 In. 600.00
Sign, Lady, Groceries, Cardboard, 1946, 16 x 27 In. 1465.00
Sign, Lunch & Soda, Porcelain, c.1950, 18 x 30 In. 1126.00
Sign, Pick Up 6, Pilaster Form, c.1950, 54 In. 2800.00
Sign, Please Pay When Served, Light-Up, Plastic, Metal, 1948, 20 In. 1485.00
Sign, Please Pay When Served, Plastic, Glass, Wood, Countertop, c.1948 . . . . 540.00
Sign, Police Crossing Guard, Cast Iron Base, c.1950 . . . . 3400.00

Coca-Cola, Sign, Delicious & Refreshing,
Porcelain, 2-Sided,
1932, 36 x 60 In.

Coca-Cola,
Tray, 1922,
Summer Girl,
Holding Glass,
13 1/4 x 10
1/2 In.

Sign, Red Button, Steel, 1950s, 36 In. 255.00
Sign, Red Syrup Dispenser, 2-Sided, Porcelain, 1939 . . . .   1430.00
Sign, Refresh Yourself, Tin, Wood Frame, St. Thomas Metal Signs, 56 x 20 In. 1450.00
Sign, Refreshing New Feeling, 2-Sided, Tin, Flange, October 1961, 15 x 18 In. 425.00
Sign, Refreshing New Feeling, Woman In Water, Cardboard, 1960s, 26 x 56 In. 55.00
Sign, Refreshment Center, Metal, 46 x 10 In. 125.00
Sign, Rotating Halo, Light-Up, 2-Sided, Metal, Plastic, c.1950 . . . .   1800.00
Sign, Sidewalk, Take Home A Carton, Big King Size, Frame, 1961, 20 x 28 In. 2815.00
Sign, Sign Of Good Taste, 2-Sided, Tin, Flange, February, 1959, 15 x 18 In. . . . . . .   .400.00 to 420.00
Sign, Take A Case Home Today, Tin, 1950s, 19 x 28 In. 357.00
Sign, Take Home A Carton, Big King Size, Frame, 1961, 20 x 28 In. 2700.00
Suit, Wool, Polyester, French Writing, Riverside, Ireland, Size 38 Jacket, Size 33 Pants   . .   100.00
Syrup Jug, Case, Atlanta, Gal., 12 In., 4 Piece 30.00
Telephone, Disc, Neon Lights, Musical Finger, Box 20.00
Thermometer, Bottle Shape, 17 In. . . . . .80.00 to 150.00
Thermometer, Bottle Shape, Christmas, 16 3/4 x 4 7/8 In. 245.00
Thermometer, Dial Type, Glass Front, Metal Sides, 1950s, 12 x 2 In. 198.00
Thermometer, Die Cut Bottle, 16 1/4 In. 68.00
Thermometer, Drink Coca-Cola, Sign Of Good Taste, Red, White, c.1950, 8 x 30 In. 575.00
Thermometer, Embossed Tin, Red Ground, 16 In. 60.00
Thermometer, Gold Bottle, Metal, 1923 . . . .   110.00
Thermometer, Sign Of Good Taste, Red, White, Tin, c.1950, 8 x 30 In. 590.00
Thermometer, Tin Lithograph, Bottle, 1958, 30 In. 105.00
Tin, Polar Bears Playing Winter Sports, 1994, 6 x 5 In. 10.00
Tip Tray, 1907, Relieves Fatigue Woman, Oval, 6 In. 525.00
Tip Tray, 1913, Hamilton King Girl, Oval, 6 In. 132.00
Tip Tray, 1916, Girl With Basket Of Flowers, 6 1/8 x 4 1/4 In. . . . . .275.00 to 303.00
Tip Tray, 1920, Golfer Girl, Oval, 6 1/4 x 4 1/2 In. . . . . .303.00 to 431.00
Token, Drink Coca-Cola, Bottle, USC Football Schedule, Aluminum, 1957 . . . .   65.00
Toy, Car, 1957 Chevrolet, No. H862, Ertl 25.00
Toy, Car, Refresh With Zest, Red, White, 10 1/2 In. 95.00
Toy, Cars, Corgi Turbo Racing Team, Die Cast, Box, 3 1/2 In., 3 Piece 75.00
Toy, Drink Dispenser, Plastic, 4 Coke Glasses, Box, Insert 145.00
Toy, Fire Engine, Holiday, Die Cast Metal, Certificate, Box, Matchbox, 9 In. 85.00
Toy, Prop Rod, Thimble Drome Racer, Plastic, Aluminum, 12 In. 149.00
Toy, Truck, 6 Soda Cases, Hand Truck, Marx, c.1955, 12 1/2 x 13 In. 475.00
Toy, Truck, 10 Glass Bottles, In Racks, Every Bottle Sterilized, Metalcraft, 11 In. 365.00
Toy, Truck, 10 Glass Bottles, Lights, Pressed Steel, Metalcraft, Box, c.1930, 12 In. 800.00
Toy, Truck, Brute Super Steel, Box, Buddy L, No. 4959, 1970 . . . .   85.00
Toy, Truck, Buddy L, Pressed Steel, Bottles, Cases, Dollies, Box, 1960s, 16 In. 825.00
Toy, Truck, Coke Bottles, Goodrich Tires, 1934 . . . .   595.00
Toy, Truck, Coke Soda Pop Stop, Steel, No. 4990, Buddy L 75.00
Toy, Truck, Decals, Bottles, Metalcraft 1200.00
Toy, Truck, Delivery, 2 Tiers, Divided Bay, Case, Pressed Steel, Buddy L, c.1960, 14 In. . . .   39.00
Toy, Truck, Delivery, No. 4942, Steel, Buddy L, Box, 1970, 5 In. 60.00
Toy, Truck, Delivery, Woody, Wyandotte, 11 In. 195.00
Toy, Truck, Die Cast, Box, England, 1967 . . . .   60.00

Toy, Truck, Die Cast, Corgi Jr., Box Van, 3 1/2 In. 120.00
Toy, Truck, Die Cast, Keg Delivery, Box, 1967, 4 In. 12.00
Toy, Truck, Enjoy Coca-Cola, Hand Truck, Cases Of Bottles, Buddy L 65.00
Toy, Truck, Mack Trailer, No. 5262, Buddy L, Box, 14 In. 95.00
Toy, Truck, No. 37, Lesney Karrier Bantam, England, 2 14 x 1 In. 100.00
Toy, Truck, Pressed Steel, Canadian Lincoln, Box, c.1950, 16 In. 295.00
Toy, Truck, Route, Battery Operated, Tin, Japan, Box, 1957 .... 495.00
Toy, Truck, Stake, Sprite Boy Logo, Pressed Steel, Marx, 20 In. 180.00
Toy, Truck, Yellow, White, Battery Operated, Sanyo, Box, c.1950, 12 1/2 In. ...... .450.00 to 478.00
Train, Pewter, Limited Edition, Engine, Coke Bottle, Bear, Caboose, 2 In., 4 Piece 275.00
Tray, 1900, Hilda Clark, At Table, Coke Glass, 9 1/4 In. 7000.00
Tray, 1908, Topless Woman, High Balls, Gin Rickies, Restored, Round, 12 In. ...2475.00 to 3850.00
Tray, 1914, Betty, Oval, 15 1/2 x 12 3/8 In. .... .275.00 to 575.00
Tray, 1916, Girl With Basket Of Flowers, Yellow Dress, 19 x 8 1/2 In. 220.00
Tray, 1922, Summer Girl, Holding Glass, 13 1/4 x 10 1/2 In. .... *Illus* 286.00
Tray, 1923, Flapper Girl, 13 1/4 x 10 1/2 In. 248.00
Tray, 1925, Party Girl, 13 x 10 1/2 In. .... .358.00 to 385.00
Tray, 1928, Soda Jerk, 13 x 10 1/2 In. 220.00
Tray, 1929, Girl In Yellow Bathing Suit, 13 x 10 1/2 In. .... .286.00 to 525.00
Tray, 1930, Bather Girl, 13 1/2 x 10 1/2 In. 220.00
Tray, 1930, Telephone Girl, 13 1/4 x 10 1/2 In. .... .198.00 to 315.00
Tray, 1933, Francis Dee, 13 1/4 x 10 1/2 In. 140.00
Tray, 1934, Weismuller & O'Sullivan, 13 1/4 x 10 1/2 In. 225.00
Tray, 1935, Madge Evans, American Art Works, 13 1/4 x 10 In. 215.00
Tray, 1936, Hostess, 13 1/4 x 10 1/2 In. .... .220.00 to 250.00
Tray, 1937, Running Girl, 13 1/4 x 10 1/2 In. .... .130.00 to 316.00
Tray, 1938, Girl At Shade, 13 1/4 x 10 In. .... .143.00 to 210.00
Tray, 1939, Springboard Girl, 13 1/2 x 10 1/2 In. .... .165.00 to 253.00
Tray, 1940, Sailor Girl, 13 1/4 x 10 1/2 In. .... .155.00 to 343.00
Tray, 1941, Skater Girl, 13 1/4 x 10 1/2 In. .... .240.00 to 295.00
Tray, 1942, 2 Girls At Car, 13 1/4 x 10 1/2 In. .... .165.00 to 209.00
Tray, 1950, Girl With Wind In Her Hair, 13 1/4 x 10 1/2 In. 95.00
Tray, 1953, Menu Girl, Sports Theme Border, 13 1/4 x 10 1/2 In. .... .51.00 to 95.00
Tray, 1980, Georgia Bulldogs Commemorative, Dawgs Undefeated Season, 18 x 13 In. ... 50.00
Tray, 1982, Sprite Boy, Bottle, 8th Annual Coke Clan Convention, 13 1/4 x 10 1/2 In. 85.00
Tray, 1985, Coca-Cola International Collectors Club, Anaheim, Ca., 13 1/4 x 10 1/2 In. .. 60.00
Tray, Romance Of Coca-Cola, 30th Anniversary, Tin, England, 16 1/2 x 12 3/4 In. 250.00
Tumbler Set, Olympic, Gold, Clear, 4 Languages, Box, 12 Oz., 4 Pieces 50.00
Wagon, Horse Drawn, 8 Coke Cases, Umbrella, Cast Iron, 15 x 5 1/2 In. 48.00

COFFEE MILLS are also called coffee grinders, although there is a difference in the way each grinds the coffee. Large floor-standing or
counter-model coffee mills were used in the nineteenth-century country store. Small home mills were first made about 1894. They lost
favor by the 1930s. The renewed interest in fresh-ground coffee has
produced many modern electric mills and hand mills and grinders.
Reproductions of the old styles are being made.

AC Williams, No. 867, Pine, Cast Metal, Ravenna, Ohio, c.1905, 2 1/2 x 4 In. 86.00
American Duplex, Electric, 32 In. 66.00
Arcade, Bell, Wall Mount, 16 In. 853.00
Arcade, Crystal, No. 1, Wall Mount, 14 In. 120.00
Arcade, Crystal, No. 3, Nickel Plated, Wall Mount, 18 3/4 In. 385.00
Arcade, Crystal, No. 3, Wall Mount, 18 3/4 In. .... .176.00 to 253.00
Arcade, Crystal, No. 4, Wall Mount, 15 1/2 In. .... .145.00 to 195.00
Arcade, Electric, Store Display, Windmill, 25 In. 605.00
Arcade, No. 25, Atwood, Metal Bracket, Glass Top, No Catch Cup, 11 1/2 In. 150.00
Arcade, No. 77, Royal, Side Mount, 8 In. 39.00
Arcade, No. 77, Royal, Wall Mount, Embossed Steel Hopper, 14 In. 77.00
Arcade, No. 9010, Aromatic, Wall Mount, 16 In. 187.00
Arcade, Telephone, Bronze Finish, 13 1/2 In. 550.00
Arcade, Telephone, Nickel Plated, 13 1/2 In. 798.00
C.S. Bell, No. 1 1/2, Cast Iron, Hillsboro, Ohio 220.00
Cha's Parker, No. 502, Cast Iron, 13 1/2 In. 468.00

Coffee Mill, Enterprise,
No. 6, Cast Iron,
Nickel, Plated Hopper,
12-In. Wheels, 24 In.

Coffee Mill, Enterprise,
No. 16, Cast Iron
Hopper, Lid, 31 In.
Wheels, 65 In.

Coffee Mill,
Ever-Ready, Tin,
Cast Iron, Wood,
Wall Mount, 12 In.

Cha's Parker, No. 606, Copper Hopper, 17 In. 665.00
Cha's Parker, No. 3000, Cast Hopper, 11-In. Wheels, 15 In. 1210.00
Cha's Parker, No. 4000, Nickel Plated Hopper, 11-In. Wheels, 23 In. 4070.00
Cha's Parker, Red Paint, Stenciled, Meriden, Conn., c.1830 .... 1815.00
Elgin National, No. 40, Cast Iron, Countertop, 19 1/2-In. Wheels, 30 In. 690.00
Elma, Table Model, c.1930, 7 3/4-In. Wheel, 12 In. ....165.00 to 198.00
Enterprise, No. 1, Iron Hopper, Lid, 12 1/2 In. 440.00
Enterprise, No. 2, Cast Iron, Old Paint, c.1880, 9-In. Wheels, 13 In. 385.00
Enterprise, No. 2, Cast Iron, Red, Blue, Gilt, 9-In. Flywheels, 12 In. 823.00
Enterprise, No. 2, Iron Hopper, Lid, 8 3/4-In. Wheels, 10 1/2 In. ....605.00 to 935.00
Enterprise, No. 2, Nickel Hopper, 8 3/4-In. Wheels, 16 In. 1100.00
Enterprise, No. 2 1/2, Nickel Plated Hopper, 8 3/4-In. Wheels, 15 In. 5500.00
Enterprise, No. 3, Iron Hopper, Lid, 10-In. Wheels, 15 In. 770.00
Enterprise, No. 5, Iron Hopper, Lid, 12-In. Wheels, 17 In. 1540.00
Enterprise, No. 6, Cast Iron, Nickel, Plated Hopper, 12-In. Wheels, 24 In. .... *Illus* 1320.00
Enterprise, No. 7, Cast Hopper, Lid, c.1904, 17-In. Wheels, 24 In. 7150.00
Enterprise, No. 7, Iron Hopper, Lid, 17-In. Wheels, 22 In. 1100.00
Enterprise, No. 8, Eagle Finial, 15-In. Wheels, 21 In. 7150.00
Enterprise, No. 16, Cast Iron Hopper, Lid, 31-In. Wheels, 65 In. .... *Illus* 3410.00
Enterprise, No. 91, Electric, 29 In. 95.00
Enterprise, No. 100, Wall Mount, 14 1/2 In. 310.00
Enterprise, No. 350, Wall Mount, Swinging Catch Cup, 16 5/8 In. 580.00
Ever-Ready, Tin, Cast Iron, Wood, Wall Mount, 12 In. .... *Illus* 193.00
Freidag, Diamond Cut, Wall Mount, 16 In. 130.00
George Pritz, Tiger Maple, Pewter Bowl, Hanover, York Co., Pa., c.1834, 8 In. 620.00
Golden Rule, Wall Mount, Citizens Wholesale Supply, 17 In. 413.00
Grand Union, Cast Iron, Red Paint, 11 1/2 In. 403.00
Grand Union, Tin Lithograph Canister, Wall Mount, c.1907, 15 In. 55.00
Griswold Mfg., Lift Front Door, 10 1/2 In. 715.00
Hollands, No. 1, Tabletop, 9 In. 578.00
Husqvarna, No. 5, Bench Mount, Sweden, 12 In. 22.00
Jabez Burns & Sons, Electric, Mounted On Base, 12 x 16 In. 88.00
John Chatillon, No. 11, Table, 12 1/2 In. 440.00
John Wright, Cast Hopper, Lid, 1958-1968, 6 3/4-In. Wheels, 11 In. ....165.00 to 220.00
Landers, Frary & Clark, No. 0014, Table Mount, 1917-1926, 11 1/4 In. 44.00
Landers, Frary & Clark, No. 01, Table Mount, 13 In. 39.00
Landers, Frary & Clark, No. 01, Table Mount, Maroon Enamel, Decals, 13 In. 22.00
Landers, Frary & Clark, No. 11, Cast Hopper, Lid, Maroon Enamel, 12 1/2 In. ....230.00 to 743.00
Landers, Frary & Clark, No. 20, Cast Hopper, Lid, 8 3/4-In. Wheels, 12 1/2 In. ..633.00 to 1430.00
Lane Brothers, Swift Mill, No. 12 1/2, Iron Hopper, Lid, 9-In. Wheels, 15 In. 880.00
Logan & Strobridge, No. 250, Side Mount, On Board, 6 x 8 In. 28.00
Logan & Strobridge, Queen, Wall Mount, 14 In. 310.00
National Specialty Mill, Cast Hopper, Lid, 8 3/4-In. Wheels, 12 In. 2970.00
National Specialty Mill, Cast Hopper, Lid, 9-In. Wheels, 13 1/2 In. 1595.00
National Specialty Mill, Cast Hopper, Lid, 10 3/4-In. Wheels, 17 In. 853.00
National Specialty Mill, Cast Hopper, Lid, 13 1/2 In. 880.00
National Specialty Mill, Nickel Hopper, 10 3/4-In. Wheels, 21 1/2 In. 1045.00
National Specialty Mill, No. 9, Cast Hopper, Lid, 20-In. Wheels, 24 In. 770.00

New Union, Second New Model, Freeport, Ill., 6 In. 275.00
Norton Bros., Tin Lithograph, Tabletop, 12 In. 523.00
S.H. Co. Koffee Krusher, No. KK/13, 10 3/4-In. Wheels, 15 In. . . . . .689.00 to 2200.00
Star, No. 8, Nickel Plated Hopper, 20-In. Wheels, 28 In. 523.00
Star, No. 10, Nickel Plated Hopper, 23-In. Wheels, 33 In. 578.00
Swift, No. 13, Iron Hopper, 12-In. Wheels, 18 In. 523.00
Woodruff & Edwards, No. 50, Little National, 9 3/4-In. Wheels, 12 1/2 In. 660.00

COIN SPOT is a glass pattern that was named by the collectors for the
spots resembling coins, which are part of the glass. Colored, clear, and
opalescent glass was made with the spots. Many companies used the
design in the 1870–1890 period. It is so popular that reproductions are
still being made.

Sugar Shaker, Blue, Brass Cover 110.00
Sugar Shaker, Clear, Tin Cover, 5 In. 80.00
Sugar Shaker, Cranberry, Tin Cover 75.00
Wine, Vaseline, Flared Foot, 7 1/4 In., 8 Piece 500.00

COIN-OPERATED MACHINES of all types are collected. The vending
machine is an ancient invention dating back to 200 B.C., when holy
water was dispensed in a coin-operated vase. Smokers in seventeenth-
century England could buy tobacco from a coin-operated box. It was
not until after the Civil War that the technology made modern coin-
operated games and vending machines plentiful. Slot machines, arcade
games, and dispensers are all collected.

Basketball Game, Paperboard Backdrop, 11 x 22 In. 660.00
Booz Barometer, Sobriety Test, 5 Cent, Metal, Wood, c.1930 . . . .   950.00
Candy, Gum, Chocolate, Essex, 1 Cent, L-Shaped 1320.00
Candy, Gum, Chocolate, Stollwerck, L-Shaped 1100.00
Cigar, Uwanta, Cigar Cutter, Indian, 5 Cent, 9 In. 495.00
Cigarette, Chat Noir 9 . . . .   588.00
Cigarette, Jennings, 5 Cents, 6 Brands, Art Deco, Floor Model 3300.00
Cigarette, Mirror, Viewing Window, Wall-Mount, c.1930, 35 x 13 In. 330.00
Cigarette, Rowe, Matches, 15 Cent Cigarettes 250.00
Cigarette, Stewart & McGuire, Painted Metal, 35 In. 250.00
Crane Digger, Novelty Merchantman, Exhibit Supply Co., Oak, 1933 . . . .   4180.00
Electric Shock, Electricity Is Life, Cured Illness, Iron, c.1910, 12 x 19 In. 2860.00
Fortune Teller, Arcade, Confucius Says, 25 Cent 2860.00
Fortune Teller, Fortune Told By Astrology, Oak Case, 1 Cent, 70 x 47 In. 3300.00
Fortune Teller, Swami, Penny For Fortune, Napkin, Chrome, 1950s 110.00
Gum, Adams, Pepsin, Tutti-Frutti, Wood, Porcelain, c.1898, 29 x 11 In. 6038.00
Gum, Baseball Card, Penny, Metal, Key, 4 Cards, Countertop, 1950s 2715.00
Gum, Blue Bird, Super Mint, Chrome 315.00
Gum, Chocolate, Selecto-Vend, 1 Cent, Revolves, c.1945, 18 In. 55.00
Gum, Dentyne, L-Shaped, Porcelain Sign, 21 x 9 In. 550.00
Gum, Dr. King's Peppermint Fruitlets Pepsin Gum, Porcelain, 1 Cent 2500.00
Gum, Freeport Novelty, Chew Goo Goo Gum, 18 In. 4950.00
Gum, H.C. Evans, Saratoga Sweepstakes, Glass, c.1933, 19 x 20 In. 1760.00
Gum, Mansfield, Pepsin, 5 Cent, Glass, Metal, 1912, 17 In. . . . . .855.00 to 1540.00
Gum, Moderne, Spearmint, 1 Cent, 18 In. 220.00
Gum, Pulver, 1 Cent, Porcelain, Green, Cop, Clockwork, 9 x 20 In. 1265.00
Gum, Pulver, 1 Cent, Porcelain, White, Woodpecker, Clockwork, 9 x 20 In. 1320.00
Gum, Pulver, Clown, Red, Yellow, 1 Cent, 21 In. 770.00
Gum, Pulver, Porcelain, Red, Cop, Clockwork, 9 x 20 In. 880.00
Gum, Pulver, Yellow Kid, Porcelain, Red, Clockwork, 9 x 20 In. 1045.00
Gum, Rock-Ola, Official Sweepstakes, 1 Cent, c.1933, 12 x 15 In. 2200.00
Gum, Zeno, 1 Cent, Oak Case, Clockwork, c.1900, 16 In. . . . . .855.00 to 1210.00
Gum, Zeno, 1 Cent, Porcelain Case, Clockwork, c.1908, 17 In. 470.00
Gumball, 1 Cent, Cast Iron Base, Red, Round Globe, c.1900, 16 In. 320.00
Gumball, Ad-Lee, E-Z, 1908 Patent 605.00
Gumball, Baker Boy, 1 Cent, Clockwork Mechanism 3565.00
Gumball, Columbus, 1 Cent, Cast Iron, c.1914, 15 In. . . . . .275.00 to 358.00
Gumball, Columbus, Bi-More, 2 Glass Globes, 1930s 1870.00

Gumball, Columbus, Model 14, Profit Sharing, Decal, c.1924, 14 1/2 In. 1210.00
Gumball, Columbus, Model 38, Tri-More, 3 Globes, Metal Floor Stand, 1939 . . . . 1430.00
Gumball, Ford, 1 Cent, Brass Label 77.00
Gumball, Glass Dome, Aluminum Base, 11 In. 55.00
Gumball, National, Double Nugget, Silver Lid, Base, Case, c.1937, 17 In. 485.00
Gumball, National, Hunter, Duck Shooting Gallery, 19 In. 360.00
Gumball, Norris, Master, 1 Cent, Nickel, Red, Black Base, c.1930, 16 In. 495.00
Gumball, Norris, Master, No. 2, Gooseneck, 1920-1930, 16 In. 580.00
Matches, 1 Cent, Metal, 15 In. 165.00
Matches, Diamond, 1 Cent, Metal, Round, 14 In. . . . . .413.00 to 465.00
Matches, Madison, Rushour, 1 Cent, Decal, Countertop, c.1927, 16 1/2 In. 130.00
Music Box, Lochmann, 12 Bells, 24 1/2-In. Discs, 9 Discs, c.1900, 60 x 32 x 17 In. 9775.00
Music Box, Regina, Model 14, Oak Case, May 18, 1897, 15 1/2-In. Disc 3600.00
Music Box, Regina, Oak, Etched Glass, Couple On Beach, 27-In. Disc 8625.00
Nut, Climax, 10 Cent, Early 1900s, 20 In. 1650.00
Peanut, Barbequed Cocktail Almonds, 10 Cent, 9 In. 70.00
Peanut, Columbus, 1 Cent, Green Painted Metal, Glass, 14 In. 220.00
Peanut, Columbus, Cast Iron, 6-Sided Globe, c.1920 . . . . 285.00
Peanut, Columbus, Model 21, Porcelain, c.1934, 13 In. 385.00
Peanut, Columbus, Model A, Cast Iron, c.1910 . . . . .275.00 to 330.00
Peanut, Ideal, 1 Cent 2645.00
Peanut, Regal, c.1940, 12 In. 66.00
Peanut, Silver King, 5 Cent, 1950s 66.00
Peanut, Silver King, 5 Cent, Hot Nut, c.1947, 15 1/2 In. 90.00
Peanut, Smilin' Sam From Alabam, 1 Cent, Red, c.1931, 14 In. . . . . .2970.00 to 3740.00
Peanut, Smilin' Sam From Alabam, c.1970s, 14 In. 468.00
Perfume, Continental Novelty, Bull's Head, 1 Cent, Iron, c.1908, 14 In. 7370.00
Pinball, College Football, Wood, Countertop, 1934, 38 x 20 x 11 In. 745.00
Poker, Bally, Reel Deal, 25 Cent, c.1960s 990.00
Poker, Mills, 1 Cent, Marquee, Poker Cards On Wheels, c.1890, 10 x 15 In. 935.00
Polyphon, Upright, Electrified, 11 Disks 2750.00
Skill, Bryans Elevenses, 5 Cent, 34 In. 385.00
Skill, Lindy Striker, 1 Cent, Win Gumball, c.1930 . . . . 1815.00
Slot, Bally, Model 873, 25 Cent, c.1971 . . . . 660.00
Slot, Buckley, 5 Cent, Enameled Iron, Oak, 26 1/4 x 15 1/2 x 16 In. 1400.00
Slot, Caille, Superior, Naked Lady, 25 Cent, c.1926 . . . . 1450.00
Slot, Extrabell, Revamping Kit, 25 Cent, c.1950 . . . . 1980.00
Slot, Jennings, 5 Line Pioneer Club, 5 Cent, c.1975 . . . . 550.00
Slot, Jennings, Duchess, 5 Cent, Mint Vendor, c.1932 .1210.00 to 1430.00
Slot, Jennings, El Dorado, 25 Cent, c.1956 . . . . 1925.00
Slot, Jennings, Golf Ball, 25 Cent, c.1932 . . . . 7150.00
Slot, Jennings, Little Duke, 1 Cent, Cast Front, Oak, 23 In. 1595.00
Slot, Jennings, Poinsettia, c.1925 . . . . 1925.00
Slot, Jennings, Silver Chief, 5 Cent, c.1937 . . . . 1430.00
Slot, Jennings, Victoria, 5 Cent, Aluminum, Peacocks, c.1930, 23 In. 2000.00
Slot, Jokers Wild, 10 Cents, Yellow, Red, Black, 31 x 16 x 17 In. 440.00
Slot, Las Vegas, 10 Cent, Red, Black 660.00
Slot, Liberty Bell, Gum, Fruit, 5 Cent, Cast Iron, Marquee, 20 1/2 x 13 In. 8050.00
Slot, Mills, Bell-O-Matic, 5 Cent, 1940s 1210.00
Slot, Mills, Cherry Bell, Hightop, 10 Cent . . . . .1375.00 to 1980.00
Slot, Mills, Golden Falls, 50 Cent, c.1948 . . . . 2310.00
Slot, Mills, Gooseneck, Fancy Front, 5 Cent, c.1933 . . . . 1155.00
Slot, Mills, Operator Bell, 5 Cent, c.1918 . . . . 1650.00
Slot, Mills, Operator Bell, 25 Cent, Aluminum, Oak Stand, 1921, 59 x 18 In. 1668.00
Slot, Mills, Owl, Upright, Floor Model, 5 Cents, c.1910 . . . . 6930.00
Slot, Mills, Pirate, Parrot, 25 Cents, 70 In. 3320.00
Slot, Pace, Comet, 10 Cent, Aluminum Case, Aeronautic Design, 1940 . . . . 2500.00
Slot, Pace, Comet, 5 Cent, c.1946 . . . . 1210.00
Slot, Pace, Comet, Art Deco Aluminum Case, 1936 . . . . 1700.00
Slot, Pace, Floor Model, Console, 1940s . . . . .950.00 to 1300.00
Slot, Rock-Ola, Super Triple, 5 Cents, Oak Case, 26 In. 1760.00
Slot, Roosevelt, Wheel, Upright, Wood, Metal, 5 Cents 8800.00
Slot, Watling, Baby Lincoln, 5 Cent, c.1933 . . . . 1100.00

Slot, Watling, Rol-A-Top, 5 Cent, c.1935 ....3630.00 to 3740.00
Slot, Watling, Rol-A-Top, 25 Cent, c.1936 .... 3960.00
Slot, White, Chicago Ridge, 5 Cent, c.1900 .... 13500.00
Stamp, Dillon, American Postmaster, 25 Cent, 10 In. 80.00
Stamp, Drop 2 Pennies, Stamp Delivery, Top Glass, 10 In. 1870.00
Strength Tester, Great Lakes System, Mercury, Metal Case, Mich., 16 In. 385.00
Strength Tester, Mills, Squeeze Grip, Cast Iron, c.1920, 26 In. 1210.00
Trade Stimulator, 20th Century Novelty Co., Oak, c.1903, 10 x 17 In. 1045.00
Trade Stimulator, Buckley, Cent-A-Pack, Cigarette Packs, c.1935, 12 In. 523.00
Trade Stimulator, Cigar, Bicycle Wheel, Oak Case, c.1895, 14 x 20 In. 3850.00
Trade Stimulator, Cigar, Fairest Wheel, Oak Case, c.1880, 24 In. .... 715.00 to 1100.00
Trade Stimulator, Cigarette, Ginger, Line-Up, 15 Cent, Key 440.00
Trade Stimulator, Daval, Chicago Club House, Poker, 1933 .... 550.00
Trade Stimulator, Griswold, Cigar, 5 Cent, Marquee, Oak Case, 19 In. .... 605.00 to 880.00
Trade Stimulator, Gumball, Push-O-Reel, Poker Game, Pull Lever, 1930s 660.00
Trade Stimulator, Mills, Puritan Bell, Fruit Reels, c.1926 .... 1155.00
Trade Stimulator, Pace, Whiz-Ball, Aluminum, Glass, c.1931 .... 440.00
Trade Stimulator, Rex, Gum, Line-Up, Key 385.00
Vending, 7-Up, Vendo 81, 10 Cent, c.1957 .... 2250.00
Vending, Collar Button, Zeno, 10 Cent, Glass 770.00
Vending, Combination Vendor, 4 Items, Wood, 1910-1920, 25 x 14 In. 1210.00
Vending, Handkerchief, Hav-A-Hank, 25-Cent, Wall Mount, 1960s, 24 In. 85.00
Vending, Hershey Chocolate, Steel, Glass, 18 In. 440.00
Vending, Kleenex, 5 Cent, Metal, 7 x 37 In. 220.00
Vending, Moderne Vendor, Hershey's Chocolate Bars, Chrome, 12 x 4 In. 120.00
Vending, Peerless, Surete Condoms, Skyscraper, 20 x 6 1/2 x 5 1/2 In. 825.00
Vending, Pencil, Victor, Vendorama, Long Boy Sticks, c.1960 .... 70.00
Vending, Stollwerck, 1 Cent, L-Shaped, Porcelain Marquee, 1900, 32 In. 990.00
Vending, Supreme Bulk, 1 Cent, c.1930 .... 470.00
Vendor, National Hunter Ball Gum, Duck Shooting Gallery, 19 In. 357.00
Viewing, Art Show, 5 Cent, Key 385.00
Viewing, Sculptoscope, Painted Metal, Key, Patent 1922, 14 In. 690.00
Viewing Mutoscope, Beauty Galore 770.00

COLLECTOR PLATES are modern plates produced in limited editions.
Some may be found listed under the factory name, such as Bing &
Grondahl, Royal Copenhagen, Royal Doulton, and Wedgwood.

    Arabia, Finns Watching The Whales, Marked, No. 8, A Alariesto, Finland, 4 1/2 In. 15.00
    Christopherson, Little House On The Prairie, 1986, 9 1/2 In. 30.00
    Franklin Mint, Mother's Little Helpers, Bears, Ed Bierly 10.00
    Glenrice, Gunfighter, John Wayne, Clint Eastwood, 1987, 10 1/4 In. 95.00
    Gorham, Pride Of Parenthood, 4 Seasons, Norman, Rockwell, 1958, 10 1/2 In. 41.00
    Hamilton, Hanging Out, Puppy Playtime Series, 1987 .... 18.00
    James Kent Ltd., Crinoline, Marked, No. 2519, Fenton, 7 3/4 In. 12.00
    Knowles, Jack & The Beanstalk, Classic Fairy Tales Series, 1987 .... 10.00
    Knowles, Puss In Boots, Classic Fairy Tales Series, 1992 .... 35.00
    Knowles, Scarlett, Gone With The Wind, Raymond Kursar, 1978, 8 1/2 In. 45.00
    Knowles, Three Little Pigs, Classic Fairy Tales Series, 1992 .... 25.00
    Knowles, Toymaker, Norman Rockwell, Heritage Collection 40.00
    Knowles, Wonderful Wizard Of Oz, 1979, 8 1/2 In. 36.00
    Porsgrund, Christmas Plate, Box, 1968 .... 56.00
    Syracuse, Legend Of Dogwood, 10 1/2 In. 15.00

COMIC ART, or cartoon art, is a relatively new field of collecting.
Original comic strips, magazine covers, and even printed strips are collected. The first daily comic strip was printed in 1907. The paintings
on celluloid used for movie cartoons are listed in this book under
Animation Art.

    Drawing, Cover, Action Comics, No. 499, Ross Andru, Dick Giodano, Pencil, Ink, 1979 .. 1500.00
    Drawing, Cover, Batman, No. 388, Tom Mandrake, Pencil & Ink, DC Comics, 1983 ..... 750.00
    Drawing, Cover, Captain America, No. 182, Wilson & Giacoia, Pencil, Ink, Marvel, 1975 . 1500.00
    Drawing, Cover, Flash, No. 11, Steve Lightle, Pencil & Ink, 1988 .... 550.00

Drawing, Cover, Green Lantern, No. 104, Mike Grell, Pencil & Ink, DC Comics, 1978 ... 4500.00
Drawing, Cover, Iron Man, No. 26, D. Heck, F. Giacoia, Pencil & Ink, 1970 .... 1800.00
Drawing, Cover, Spiderman, No. 135, Pencil & Ink, Marvel Comics, 1988 .... 900.00
Drawing, Cover, Spiderman, No. 240, Pencil & Ink, Marvel Comics, 1990 .... 750.00
Drawing, Cover, Superman, No. 12, Page 1, John Byrne, DC Comics, 1981 .... 1000.00
Drawing, Page, Captain America, No. 109, Kirby & Shores, Pencil, Ink, Marvel, 1968 ... 1400.00
Page, Comic Book, Annie Oakley & Tagg, Ziegler, 1951, 16 x 12 In. 22.00
Page, Fat Freddy Underground, 13 1/2 x 15 In., c.1970 .... 950.00
Page, Sunday, Captain & The Kids, Rudolph Dirks, Feb. 18, 1940, 13 1/2 x 20 1/2 In. ... 205.00
Page, Sunday, Clarence The Cop, Charles W. Kahles, c.1900, 10 x 19 1/2 In. 365.00
Panel, Superman, Boring, Kaye, Matted & Shrink Wrapped, c.1940, 6 1/2 x 6 1/2 In. 88.00
Strip, Amazing Spiderman, John Romita, Sr., 8/31/77, 5 x 17 In. 1800.00
Strip, Animal Crackers, Roger Bollen, June 17, 1970, 6 x 20 In. 50.00
Strip, Bugs Bunny, Ralph Heimdahl, March 21, 1966, 6 x 20 In. 88.00
Strip, Drawing, Schulz, Peanuts, Snoopy, May 17, 1962, Pencil, Ink, 7 1/2 x 28 1/2 In. ... 9500.00
Strip, Family Circus, Bil Beane, February 10, 1967, 8 x 8 In. 127.00
Strip, Little Lulu, Marge, January 10, 1967, 6 x 20 In. 85.00
Strip, Mary Worth, Ken Ernst, Allen Saunders, June 5, 1960, 6 x 18 1/2 In. 74.00
Strip, Scamp, Walt Disney Studio, January 24, 1966, 5 1/2 x 19 1/2 In. 99.00
Strip, The Flibbertys, Ray Helle, January 1, 1967, 4 1/2 x 14 In. 39.00
Strip, The Saint, Leslie Charteris, John Spranger, July 15, 1955, 6 x 21 In. 28.00

COMMEMORATIVE items have been made to honor members of royalty and those of great national fame. World's fairs and important historical events are also remembered with commemorative pieces. Related collectibles are listed in the Coronation and World's Fair categories.

Ax, SS Aberytwyth Castle, Launched By Mrs. Evans, Gilpin, c.1875, 15 1/2 In. 178.00
Bandanna, Lafayette's Visit To America, 1824, 7 1/2 x 11 In. 415.00
Bracelet, Bangle, Queen Victoria's Jubilee, Sterling Silver, England, 1887 .... 920.00
Creamer, Dewey, Olympia, Flags, Eagle Spout, Cook Pottery, Trenton, 4 In. 150.00
Cup & Saucer, U.S. Centennial, Aqua Glaze, Glasgow Pottery Co., Trenton 405.00
Drums, Regimental, Metal, Vellum, Leather, Twine, London, 3 1/2 In., Pair 118.00
Kerchief, Queen Victoria Jubilee, Tartan Border, 1887, 17 In. 150.00
Kerchief, Uncle Sam's Souvenir In Honor Of Adm. George Dewey, Silk 100.00
Mug, Boxing, Humphrys & Mendoza Fight, Odiham, Hampshire, c.1788 .... 7240.00
Mug, Edward VIII, Stylized Profile, Porcelain, 4 In. 35.00
Mug, George IV, Queen Caroline On Scales Of Justice, c.1820s 1465.00
Mug, Queen Victoria, End Of Transvaal War, Thomas Goode Commission 1449.00
Plate, Washington, His Country's Father, Liverpool Style, 1800s, 6 x 5 1/2 In. 210.00

COMPACTS hold face powder. A woman did not powder her face in public until after World War I. By 1920, the beauty parlor, permanent waves, and cosmetics had become acceptable. A few companies sold cake face powder in a box with a mirror and a pad or puff. Soon the compact was designed by jewelers and made of gold, silver, and precious materials. Cosmetic companies began to sell powder in attractive compacts of less valuable metal or plastic. Collectors today search for Art Deco designs, commemorative compacts from world's fairs or political events, and unusual examples. Many were made with companion lipsticks and other fittings.

Celluloid, Blue, Carved, Flowers, Rope Handle, Edwardian, 12 1/2 In. 125.00
Celluloid, Butterflies & Flowers, Clear Cover, 1 1/2 In. 11.00
Celluloid, Pearlescent Ivory, Roses, Square, 2 1/2 In. 15.00
Gucci, 18K Gold, Applied Leaf Accent, Mirrored Interior 645.00
Kigu, Brass, Globe, c.1940, 2 In. 545.00
Komei Damascene, Cranes, Iris, Dragon, Fuji, Early 1900s, 3 1/2 In. 200.00
Mirage, Gold, Black, Flat, Oval, Geometric, c.1928, 1 3/4 x 2 1/2 In. 545.00
Princess Pat, Metal Lacquered, Geometric Art Deco, Molded, c.1930, 1 1/2 In. 1345.00
Richard Hudnut, Cigarette Case, Silver, Lacquered, 2 Sections, c.1925, 4 1/4 x 3 In. 1515.00
Roger & Gallet, Lucite, Flat, Square, Gilded, Stylized Face, Sunburst, 1946 .... 420.00
Sterling Silver, Box & Tied Ribbon, Channel Set Ruby, Leather Case, Signed, 14K 440.00
Van Cleef & Arpels, 18K Gold, Mesh, Mirror 880.00

CONSOLIDATED LAMP AND GLASS COMPANY of Coraopolis, Pennsylvania, was founded in 1894. The company made lamps, tablewares, and art glass. Collectors are particularly interested in the wares made after 1925, including black satin glass, Cosmos (listed in its own category in this book), Martele (which resembled Lalique), Ruba Rombic (1928–1932 Art Deco line), and colored glasswares. Some Consolidated pieces are very similar to those made by the Phoenix Glass Company. The colors are sometimes different. Consolidated made Martele glass in blue, crystal, green, pink, white, or custard glass with added fired-on color or a satin finish. The company closed for the final time in 1967.

Plate, Dancing Nymph, Satin, 8 3/8 In.	68.00
Shade, Diving Girl, Ivory, 16 In.	690.00
Sugar, Cover, Bulging Loops, Blue, Opal Lining, 5 1/4 In.	300.00
Tumbler, Dancing Nymph, 3 1/2 In.	90.00
Vase, Catalonian, Chartreuse, 6 5/8 In.	70.00
Vase, Dogwood, Coral & Blue On Ivory, 10 1/2 In.	140.00
Vase, Foxglove, Green & Blue On Ivory, 10 1/4 In.	100.00
Vase, Hummingbird, White, Pastel Stain, 5 1/2 In.	90.00
Vase, Peony, White, Stained Flowers, 9 1/2 In.	105.00
Vase, Pine Cone, Green & Brown On Ivory, 7 In.	130.00

CONTEMPORARY GLASS, see Glass-Contemporary.

COOKBOOKS are collected for various reasons. Some are wanted for the recipes, some for investment, and some as examples of advertising. Cookbooks and recipe pamphlets are included in this category.

Baker's Best Chocolate Recipes, Softcover, Saddle-Stapled, 1932, 60 Pages	15.00
Better Homes Recipe Book, 1933, 448 Pages	15.00
Better Meals For Less, Softcover, 1930, 128 Pages	15.00
Crisco, New Recipes For Good Eating, Procter & Gamble, 1948	8.00
Dainty Desserts, Carrie Dudley & Ida Bailey Allen, c.1930, 58 Pages	32.00
Easy Triumphs With The New Minute Tapioca, Softcover, 1934, 45 Pages	10.00
Gem Chopper, B. Prugh & Sons, Linen Cover, 1902	18.00
Household Searchlight Recipe Book, Black Cloth Hardboards, 1945	38.00
How To Cook With Budweiser Beer, 1950s, 42 Pages	50.00
Illuminating Company New Cooks, 1953, 53 Pages	7.00
Jell-O, Genesee Pure Food Company, Rockwell Paintings On Covers, 1923	20.00
Junior Auxiliary Of Louisville, Mississippi, 1968, 259 Pages	8.00
Meta Given's Modern Encyclopedia Of Cooking, Vol. 1, Hardcover, 1959	45.00
Pillsbury, 2nd Grand National 100 Prize Winning Recipes, 1951, 100 Pages	30.00
Pillsbury, 3rd Grand National 100 Prize Winning Recipes, 1952, 96 Pages	20.00
Pillsbury, 4th Grand National 100 Prize Winning Recipes, 1953, 96 Pages	15.00
Pillsbury, 6th Grand National 100 Prize Winning Recipes, 1955, 96 Pages	15.00
River Road Recipes, Junior League Of Baton Rouge, 1979, 262 Pages	4.00
Taylor Home Set, Taylor Instrument Companies, 1928, 88 Pages	30.00
The Western Junior League, 1979, 542 Pages	6.00
Working Wives (Salaried Or Otherwise) Cookbook, Crown Pub., N.Y., 1963	38.00

COOKIE JARS with brightly painted designs or amusing figural shapes became popular in the mid-1930s. Many companies made them and collectors search for cookie jars either by design or by maker's name. Listed here are examples by the less common makers. Major factories are listed under their own names in other categories of the book, such as Abingdon, Brush, Hull, McCoy, Red Wing, and Shawnee. See also the Disneyana category.

Aunt Jemima, Painted Plastic, 10 In.	235.00
Aunt Jemima, Plastic, Black Face, F & F, 11 1/4 In.	315.00 to 365.00
Dreyers Grand Ice Cream, Treasure Craft, 10 x 8 1/2 In.	150.00
Ernie The Keebler Elf, Red Hat, F & F Mold & Dye Works, 12 In.	79.00
Famous Amos, Clear Glass, Decal, Box, Anchor Hocking, 13 1/4 x 8 1/2 In.	55.00
Fifi Poodle, Standing On Haunches, Ball, Head Is Lid, No. 1163, Miller, 11 1/2 In.	450.00
Kellogg, Tony The Tiger, Ceramic, 1977, 10 1/2 In.	220.00
M&M Bag, Ceramic, Box, 9 1/2 x 6 x 6 3/4 In.	40.00
Mammy, Ceramic McCoy Style, Signed Mann, Japan, 10 In.	339.00

Mammy, Yellow, Mosaic Tile Co., 12 1/2 In.	255.00
Mountain Dew, Can Shape, Limited Edition, Ceramic, Box, 11 In.	55.00
Oreo Truck, Nabisco, Box, 6 1/4 In.	55.00
Pepperidge Farm, Milano, No. 1 In Series, 400P	75.00
Poodle, At Cookie Counter, Twin Winton, California, U.S.A., 13 1/2 In.	70.00
Poodle, Brown, Pink Ribbon & Nails, Deforrest, California, 1960, 12 In.	40.00
Poodle, Brown, Upright, Pink Bow, Sierra Vista Ceramics, California, 1956, 12 3/4 In.	50.00
Poodle, Gray, Upright, Pink Bow, Sierra Vista Ceramics, California, 1956, 12 3/4 In.	70.00
Quaker Oats, Regal China, 9 1/2 x 5 1/2 In.	125.00
Raggedy Andy, 1940-1950, 4 3/4 In.	45.00
Raggedy Ann, Red Heart, Blue Scarf, Cuffs, Pastel Paint, 11 In.	144.00
Volkswagen, Lady Bug, 10 1/2 In.	38.00
Watermelon Choir Girl, Ceramic, Pearl China, 11 In.	790.00

COORS ware was made by a pottery in Golden, Colorado, a company founded with the help of the Coors Brewing Company. Its founder, John Herold, started the Herold China and Pottery Company in 1910. The company name was changed in 1920, when Herold left. Dishes and decorative wares were produced from the turn of the century until the pottery was destroyed by fire in the 1930s. The name *Coors* is marked on the back. The company is still in business making industrial porcelain. For more information, see *Kovels' Depression Glass & Dinnerware Price List*.

COORS
U.S.A.

Baker, Ribbed, Thermo Porcelain, Brown & Ivory Glaze, 6 In.	14.00
Cake Plate, Rosebud, Maroon, Yellow Flowers, 11 In.	110.00
Custard Cup, Rosebud, Blue, 4 In.	27.00
Custard Cup, Rosebud, Pink, 4 In.	27.00
Mixing Bowl, Orange, 6 In.	40.00
Mortar & Pestle, Ivory, 5 1/2-In. Mortar, 7 3/4-In. Pestle	85.00
Mortar & Pestle, Ivory, 7-In. Mortar, 6 3/4-In. Pestle	95.00
Pie Plate, Rosebud, Orange, Tab Handles, 10 In.	75.00
Pitcher, Tilt Ball, Green, Ice Lip, 8 In.	95.00
Plate, Thermo Porcelain, Open Window, 11 1/4 In.	30.00
Soup, Dish, Rosebud, Blue, 8 In.	5.00
Tray, Green, Square, 5 In.	12.00
Vase, Golden, Yellow, Matte White Interior, 2 Handles, Art Deco, 5 1/2 x 6 1/2 In.	145.00

COPELAND pieces listed here are those that have a mark including the word Copeland used between 1847 and 1976. Marks include Copeland Spode and Copeland & Garrett. See also Copeland Spode and Royal Worcester.

Bust, Alexandra, Mary Thornycroft, Art Union, Parian, England, c.1868, 15 In.	470.00
Bust, Apollo, C. Delpech, Art Union Of London, Parian, England, 1861, 10 1/4 In.	500.00
Bust, Lord Byron, Circular Socle Mount, Parian, England, c.1870, 24 In.	1765.00
Bust, Prince Of Wales, Parian, c.1863	719.00
Butter Chip, Pansy, Burgundy, Yellow, Cobalt Blue	275.00
Figurine, Beatrice, Gilt & Enamel Trimmed Dress, Parian, England, c.1860, 21 1/2 In.	880.00

Coverlets made before the 1830s were done on a loom that was no more than 40 inches wide. Old coverlets are made of two panels joined at the center seam.

Copeland, Teapot, Blue Jasper, White Design,
Early 20th Century, 5 1/2 In.

Figurine, Go To Sleep, Girl With Lap Dog, Brass Base, Parian, c.1862, 17 In. 355.00
Figurine, Maidenhood, Edgar Papworth Jun Sc., Parian, England, c.1873, 22 In. 880.00
Figurine, Woman Feeding Birds, Parian, 19th Century, 15 x 5 1/2 x 6 In. 250.00
Pitcher, Dragonfly & Fan, 8 1/2 In. 880.00
Pitcher, Egyptian Lotus, 8 1/2 In. 3025.00
Pitcher, Squat Baluster Body, Grapevine Band, Putti, Enamel, Vine Handle, 8 In. 150.00
Plate, Hand Painted, Hilly Landscape, Black Cock In Flight, 1800s, 9 1/2 In. 90.00
Platter, Oriental Transfer, Flowers, Baby Bird, Blue & White, Crown Mark, 21 In. 290.00
Teapot, Blue Jasper, White Design, Early 20th Century, 5 1/2 In. .... *Illus* 138.00
Tile, St. Bernard, 1888 .... 1035.00
Tureen, Turquoise Decoration, Orange Highlights, Geometric Borders, 10 1/2 x 14 In. ... 275.00
Urn, Cover, Floral, Pink Ribbon Finial, Cobalt Blue, 12 1/2 In. 335.00

COPELAND SPODE appears on some pieces of nineteenth-century English porcelain. Josiah Spode established a pottery at Stoke-on-Trent, England, in 1770. In 1833, the firm was purchased by William Copeland and Thomas Garrett and the mark was changed. In 1847, Copeland became the sole owner and the mark changed again. W.T. Copeland & Sons continued until a 1976 merger when it became Royal Worcester Spode. Pieces are listed in this book under the name that appears in the mark. Copeland Spode, Copeland, and Royal Worcester have separate listings.

Dinner Service, Transfer Printed, Earthenware, Gone Away, c.1900, 48 Piece 690.00
Pitcher, Chicago Events, People, Blue Ground, 8 1/2 In. 489.00
Plate, Green Borders, Gilt Designs, 9 1/4 In., 12 Piece 300.00
Plate Set, Olive & Gilt Borders, 12 Piece 110.00
Platter, Tower, 14 3/4 x 11 3/4 In. 145.00
Platter Set, Tower, Graduated, 14 3/4 x 11 3/4 In. 546.00
Serving Dish, Tower, 10 1/2 x 8 x 1 3/4 In., Pair 375.00
Tea Set, Relief Hunt Scenes, Blue Ground, 3 5/8 In., 3 Piece 248.00
Tea Set, Tower, Teapot, Cover, Sugar, Creamer, Blue, White, 3 Piece 230.00
Tower, Platter, Red Transfer, Gadroon Border, 1 3/4 x 23 x 18 1/4 In. 448.00
Tray, Tower, Round, 14 1/2 In. 115.00
Tureen, Tray, Cover, Tower, Ladle Slot, Blue, White, 3 Piece 920.00

COPPER has been used to make utilitarian items, such as teakettles and cooking pans, since the days of the early American colonists. Copper became a popular metal with the Arts & Crafts makers of the early 1900s, and decorative pieces, like desk sets, were made. Other pieces of copper may be found in the Arts & Crafts, Bradley & Hubbard, Kitchen, and Roycroft categories.

Backpack Vase, Lions Flanking Shield, Leather Straps, Cylindrical, 1773, 35 In. 881.00
Bas Relief, Wolf's Head, Inverted Ankh Symbol, Gilt, Mid 1800s, 12 1/2 x 11 1/2 In. 95.00
Bed Warmer, Brass, Cherry Handle, Late 19th Century, 50 In. 140.00
Bed Warmer, Engraved Flowers On Lid, Turned Wood Handle, 42 In. 145.00
Bed Warmer, Hinged Cover, Turned Handle, England, c.1900, 47 In. 69.00
Bedpan, Pierced, Grape Motif, Turned Wood Handle, 19th Century, 37 x 10 x 2 In. 575.00
Beverage Set, Tray, 6 Square Coasters, P. Blanchard, c.1955, 12 x 18 & 6 x 6 In. 800.00
Bowl, Arts & Crafts, Hammered, Cutout Grape Designs, 7 In. 520.00
Bowl, Brass Mounts & Feet, Arts & Crafts, 11 In. 175.00
Bowl, Flared Rim, 7 Lobed Sides, Arts & Crafts, Joel F. Hewes, 1980, 2 1/2 x 10 1/8 In. ... 410.00
Bowl, Footed, Deep, Hammered, Gebelein, Boston, Early 1900s, 4 1/2 x 6 3/8 In. 235.00
Bowl, Hammered, Applied Silver M, Medium Patina, Stamped, Kalo, 7 In. 430.00
Bowl, Hammered, Bulbous, Arts & Crafts, Jarvie, 8 In. 765.00
Bowl, Hammered, Embossed Acanthus Leaves, Arches, Incised, Wehde, 3 In. 259.00
Bowl, Hammered, Flower Form, Verdigris Rutile Interior, John J. Brennan, 10 In. 345.00
Bowl, Hammered, Harry Dixon, 8 In. 633.00
Bowl, Hammered, Jauchens, 3 x 10 In. 400.00
Bowl, Hammered, S Monogram, F. Novick, Chicago, Early 1900s, 3 1/8 x 7 3/8 In. 235.00
Box, Cover, Hammered, Grapes, Leaves, Enameled, Rivets, Boston School, 2 x 4 In. 2645.00
Box, Cover, Hammered, Turned-In Rim, Salmon Color Enamel, Sailing Ship, 3 x 5 In. ... 750.00
Box, Hammered, Landscape, House, Windmill, John Pearson, 12 x 4 In. 865.00
Brush Holder & Ink Case, Relief Gilt Lion, Vajra Design, 19th Century 200.00

Bucket, Coal, Brass Mounted Wood Handle, Scoop, Dutch, 22 x 19 x 13 In. 575.00
Bucket, Coal, Brass, Dutch, 10 1/2 x 13 1/2 In. 345.00
Bust, Military Figure, Plaster, Patinated, France, 20th Century, 23 1/2 In. 660.00
Canister, Trophy, Antler Feet, Hammered, Indian Harbor Yacht Club, 1906, 8 In. 1175.00
Chamber Pot, Dovetail, 18th Century 295.00
Chamberstick, Hammered, Hand, Wax Tray, G. Stickley, 9 In. 635.00
Charger, Fish, Flowers, Hammered, Guild Of Handicraft, 29 In. 1380.00
Charger, Hammered, Dodo Bird, John Pearson, 13 In. 460.00
Charger, Hammered, Incised, Flowers, Rebaje, 23 3/4 In. 259.00
Coal Bucket, Hand Wrought, Coiled Overlay, Albert Paley, 14 1/2 In. 3105.00
Coffee Urn, Hammered, Scroll Handles, Warranted Best London Manufacture, 17 In. 259.00
Coffeepot, Bottom Made To Set In Wood Cookstove, 11 In. 70.00
Coffeepot, Cylindrical, Brass Spout, Wood Grip, F. Hagenauer, Austria, 8 3/4 x 8 1/2 In. . . 430.00
Creamer, August Maag, Baltimore, Md., 4 1/2 In. . . . . *Illus* 120.00
Creamer, Cover, Conical Shape, Loop Handle, Riveted Spot, 5 In. 110.00
Cup, Spirit, Hudson Bay Company, Stamped HBC, c.1800 . . . . 165.00
Desk Set, Gustav Stickley, Workshop, Hammered, Impressed Mark 2935.00
Dish, Fern, Hammered, Applied Feet, Benedict, 11 x 6 In. 690.00
Dish, Fern, Hammered, Iron Feet, G. Stickley, 11 1/2 In. 2300.00
Dish, Hammered To Form, Patina, 18th Century, 14 1/2 In. 195.00
Etui, Gilt Copper, Continental, Early 19th Century, 4 x 4 1/4 x 2 1/4 In. 1535.00
Figure, Lobster, Gilded, Full-Bodied, 72 x 50 In. 6325.00
Ice Bucket, Applied Brass Trim, Riveted Handles, Hagenauer, 14 1/4 x 8 1/2 In. 1840.00
Jardiniere, Hammered, Fluted, Verdigris Patina, Stamped, Jauchens, 9 3/4 x 11 1/2 In. . . . 805.00
Jardiniere, Repousse Leaves, Lion's Mask Ring Handles, Oval, Compressed, Italy, 9 In. . . . 875.00
Kettle, Acorn Finial, Dovetail Construction, 19th Century, 11 1/4 In. 138.00
Kettle, Acorn Finial, Dovetail Construction, 19th Century, 12 1/4 In. 115.00
Kettle, Apple Butter, Stamped, John W. Schlosser, York Pa., 1785-1860 . . . . 175.00
Kettle, Candy, Riveted Iron Handles, 25 1/2 x 13 1/2 In. 290.00
Kettle, Dovetail Construction, Acorn Finial, 1800s, 12 1/4 In. 50.00
Kettle, Hot Water, Brass, Acorn Finial, 10 1/4 In. 69.00
Kettle, Hot Water, Brass, Dovetail Construction, Acorn Finial, 12 1/2 In. 65.00
Kettle, Hot Water, Dovetail Construction, Acorn Lid Finial, England, 1800s, 13 In. 127.00
Kettle, Hot Water, Dovetail Construction, Scrolled Finial, 19th Century, 9 1/2 In. 58.00
Kettle, Wrought Iron Handle, 35 In. 715.00
Lantern, Pierced, c.1790 . . . . 1600.00
Lavabo, Basin, Brass Mounted, 2 Sections, Mid 19th Century, 21 x 9 In. 290.00
Mirror, Arts & Crafts, Applied Sheet Copper, Ship, 30 x 38 In. 1295.00
Mirror, Cosmetic, Illuminated, Marked, Acme Specialty Mfg. Co., 10 x 8 In. 165.00
Molds are listed in the Kitchen category.
Mug, Hammered, Tapered, Tooled Lip, Looped & Riveted Handle, Stickley, 5 3/4 In. 165.00
Mug, Straight-Sided, Applied Loop Handle, Rolled Rim, Stamped, 4 1/4 In. 110.00
Mug, Strap Handle, Dovetailed, Tapered Body, Rolled Lip, Signed, W. Apple, 5 1/2 In. . . . 1320.00
Pail, Wrought Iron Swing Handle, Brass Brackets, H.W. Hayden, 6 1/2 x 9 1/2 In. 358.00
Pan, Candy, Folded Rim, Brass Turned Handles, 19th Century, 7 x 20 In. 2300.00
Pan, Frying, Iron Handle, Late 19th Century, Marked, L.F.D. & H. N.Y., 2 x 7 1/2 In. 315.00
Pan, Tin Lining, Dovetail, Spade Mount & Pierced Handle, 5 1/8 x 9 3/4 x 10 3/4 In. 58.00

Copper, Creamer, August
Maag, Baltimore, Md.,
4 1/2 In.

Copper, Pitcher, Rolled
Spout, Strap Handle, Signed,
B. Budde, N.Y., 8 1/4 In.

Copper, Teakettle, Gooseneck Spout,
Signed, Thos. M. Hammett, Philad.,
10 3/4 In.

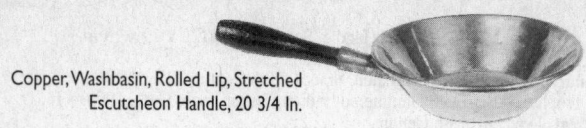

Copper, Washbasin, Rolled Lip, Stretched
Escutcheon Handle, 20 3/4 In.

Panel, Monkey, Dolce Far Niente, Maria Longworth Nichols Storer, 1906, 6 x 5 In.	920.00
Pie Pan, Hook, Hanging, 19th Century, 10 In.	207.00
Pitcher, Cream, Flared Base, Applied Spout, Handle, Signed August Maag, 4 1/2 In.	120.00
Pitcher, Milk, Manning Quality, Meriden, Conn., 12 In.	55.00
Pitcher, Rolled Spout, Strap Handle, Signed, B. Budde, N.Y., 8 1/4 In. . . . . *Illus*	110.00
Planter, Art Nouveau, Embossed, Brass Handles, WMF, 8 1/2 In.	226.00
Pot, Drum Shape, Applied Handles, Early 19th Century	525.00
Pot, Lid, Dovetailed Construction, Stamped Signature, 24 1/4 x 9 In.	165.00
Saucepan, Hammered, Iron, Rattail Handle, Mid 19th Century, 5 x 11 1/2 In.	748.00
Sieve, Patent Papers, C.V. Porter, 6 1/4 In.	35.00
Spoon, Hammered, Impressed Mark, Novick, 9 In.	58.00
Stockpot, Cover, Brass Spigot, 20th Century, 17 In.	145.00
Stockpot, Riveted Wrought Iron Handles, Brass Spout, Signed, 20 In.	145.00
Tankard, Hammered, Flared Base, Tooled Lip, Angular Handle, Stickley, 7 1/2 In.	195.00
Tankard, Loop Handle, Brass Collar, Base, Shield Medallion, W.O. Hickok, Pt., 4 1/2 In. .	3575.00
Tea Service, Brass Parts, Wood Handle, Oval Tray, K. Hagenauer, Austria, 4 Piece	690.00
Teakettle, Cover, Gooseneck, Swing Handle, Dovetailed	35.00
Teakettle, Gooseneck Spout, Brass Knob, Early 19th Century, 10 Liter, Marked, 11 1/2 In.	1150.00
Teakettle, Gooseneck Spout, Crown Handle, Brass Finial, Signed, John Getz, 16 In.	9350.00
Teakettle, Gooseneck Spout, Low Arc Dome Lid, Brass Mushroom Finial, 12 1/2 In.	1430.00
Teakettle, Gooseneck Spout, Low Arc Lid, Brass Mushroom Finial, 10 1/2 In.	635.00
Teakettle, Gooseneck Spout, Low Arc Lid, Mushroom Finial, Heis & Justice, 9 3/4 In. . .	715.00
Teakettle, Gooseneck Spout, Low Arc Lid, Scrolled Finial, Flare Handle Tabs, 11 1/4 In. .	660.00
Teakettle, Gooseneck Spout, Signed, Thos. M. Hammett, Philad., 10 3/4 In. . . . . *Illus*	2970.00
Teapot, Dovetailed, Shaped Handle, Hinged, Early 19th Century, 8 x 13 x 8 1/2 In.	248.00
Teapot, Gooseneck Spout, Dovetailed Body, Brass Finial, Signed, W. Cummings, 6 3/4 In.	5500.00
Teapot, Gooseneck Spout, Dovetailed Seams, Brass Handle, Acorn Finial, 10 3/4 In.	200.00
Teapot, Handle, Mark, AP.H, 19th Century, 27 In.	69.00
Tinderbox, Pocket, Striker, Flint, 18th Century	195.00
Tray, G. Stickley, Hammered, Oval, Riveted Copper Handle, Als Ik Kan, 21 x 11 In.	805.00
Tray, Hammered Geometric Shape, Tooled Edge Design, Fred Bossi, Round, 12 1/2 In. . .	173.00
Tray, Hammered, 4-Sided, Pierced Handles, Repousse, New Patina, G. Stickley, 19 In. . . .	1725.00
Tray, Hammered, Cutout Design, Arts & Crafts, 11 1/2 In.	86.00
Tray, Hammered, Old Mission Kopperkraft, 6 1/2 In.	58.00
Tray, Leaf Shape, Rebaje, 22 3/4 x 13 3/4 In.	200.00
Tray, Old Mission, Hammered, Tooled Design, 6 1/4 In.	115.00
Urn, Brass Finial, Spout, Acanthus Handles, c.1800-1820, 18 1/2 x 9 3/4 In.	1995.00
Urn, Underplate, Hot Water, Orb Finial, Late 19th Century, 20 In.	632.00
Vase, Arts & Crafts, Hammered, 2 Handles, Patina, 11 In.	200.00
Vase, Hammered, Flared, Arts & Crafts, 7 1/2 In.	115.00
Vase, Hammered, Flared, Flower Form, Stamped, Marie Zimmerman, 7 x 11 1/2 In.	1265.00
Vase, Hammered, Silver Plate Interior, Gebelin, Boston, 10 1/2 In.	58.00
Vase, Hammered, Tapered, Petal Shaped Mouth, Large Looped Handles, Stickley, 14 In. . .	415.00
Vase, Handle, Hammered, Stickley Brothers, 10 1/2 In.	288.00
Wall Sconce, Arts & Crafts, Hammered, Patina, 12 In.	290.00
Warming Pan, Brass Lid, Turned Wooden Handle, Repousse Designs, 1800s, 35 x 11 In. . .	85.00
Washbasin, Oblong, Handle, Rolled Edge, 19 In.	70.00
Washbasin, Rolled Lip, Stretched Escutcheon Handle, 20 3/4 In. . . . . *Illus*	297.00
Washbowl, Flared Rim, 19th Century, 6 x 18 In.	345.00

COPPER LUSTER items are listed in the Luster category.

CORALENE glass was made by firing many small colored beads on the
outside of glassware. It was made in many patterns in the United States
and Europe in the 1880s. Reproductions are made today. Coralene-
decorated Japanese pottery is listed in the Japanese Coralene category.

Bowl, Pink, Leaf Shape, Allover Seaweed, Satin, 11 In.	45.00
Vase, Amber Iridescent, Lion Head Cabochon, Pedestal, 6 In.	225.00

Vase, Gourd, Rainbow Mother-Of-Pearl, Diamond-Quilted, England, 5 In. 748.00
Vase, Mother-Of-Pearl, White, Apricot, Diamond-Quilted, Satin, 4 5/8 In. 230.00
Vase, Orange, Allover, Coral, Ruffled Edge, Satin, 3 3/4 In. 60.00

CORKSCREWS have been needed since the first bottle was sealed with a cork, probably in the seventeenth century. Today collectors search for the early, unusual patented examples or the figural corkscrews of recent years.

Cork Puller, Bar Screw, Arcade, Champion, Deco Style, 10 In. . . . . .145.00 to 175.00
Cork Puller, Bar Screw, Arcade, Daisy, Bench Mount, 7 In. 495.00
Cork Puller, Bar Screw, Invincible, Bench Mount, 9 In. . . . . .33.00 to 77.00
Heart Handle, England, 18th Century 225.00

CORONATION souvenirs have been made since the 1800s. Pottery, glass, tin, silver, and paper objects with a picture of the monarchs and date have been sold at many coronations. The pieces that mention King Edward VIII, the king who was never crowned, are not rare; collectors should be sure to check values before buying. Related pieces are found in the Commemorative category.

Mug, Queen Elizabeth II, Wade, 1953, 4 In. 25.00
Plate, King George IV & Queen Elizabeth, Granite Coronation, Moffats Ltd., 9 1/4 In. . . .   145.00
Plate, King George V & Queen Mary, 1911, 7 3/4 In. . . . . *Illus*   58.00
Plate, King George VI, Scalloped, Square, Sepia, Royal Crest, May, 1937, 6 1/4 In. 25.00
Ribbon, Queen Elizabeth II, June 2, 1953, 1 1/4 x 4 In. 30.00
Spoon, Queen Elizabeth II, Sterling Silver, Box, England, 1952, 10 In. 86.00
Tin, Candy, Queen Elizabeth II, England, 1953 . . . .   10.00
Tin, King Edward VII & Queen Alexandra, June 26th, 1902, 2 x 5 In. . . . . *Illus*   15.00

COSMOS is a pressed milk glass pattern with colored flowers made from 1894 to 1915 by the Consolidated Lamp and Glass Company. Tablewares and lamps were made in this pattern. A few pieces were also made of clear glass with painted decorations. Other glass patterns are listed under Consolidated Lamp and also in various glass categories. In later years, Cosmos was also made by the Westmoreland Glass Company.

Condiment Set, Salt & Pepper, Mustard, Tray 355.00
Creamer, 4 3/4 In. 76.00
Spooner, 4 In. 55.00
Sugar, Cover, 5 3/4 In. 80.00

COVERLETS were made of linen or wool during the nineteenth century. Most of the coverlets date from 1800 to the 1880s. There was a revival of hand weaving in the 1920s and new coverlets, especially geometric patterns, were made. The earliest coverlets were made on narrow looms, so two woven strips were joined together and a seam can be found. The weave structures of coverlets can include summer and winter, double weave, overshot, and others. Jacquard coverlets have elaborate pictorial patterns that are made on a special loom or with the use of a special attachment. Quilts are listed in this book in their own category.

Agriculture & Manufacturers, Eagles, Masonic, Independence Hall, N.Y., 80 x 104 In. . . .   1320.00

Coronation, Plate, King George V & Queen Mary, 1911, 7 3/4 In.

Coronation, Tin, King Edward VII & Queen Alexandra, June 26th, 1902, 2 x 5 In.

Broadcloth, Red, Blue, Green, Center Flowers & Geometrics, 84 x 104 In. 252.00
Broadcloth, Red, White, Blue, Flowers, 2 Panel, 76 x 86 In. 310.00
Candlewick, Woven, 8-Pointed Stars, Multiple Borders, c.1810, 62 x 84 In. 290.00
Crib, Single Weave, Red, White, Red Floral Borders, Stylized Pineapple, 33 x 41 In. 230.00
Double Weave, Blue & White, Floral Wreaths, Ithaca, 2 Panel, c.1833, 79 x 84 In. 715.00
Double Weave, Blue & White, Peter Grimm, 1859, 70 1/2 x 83 1/2 In. 355.00
Double Weave, Ivory Ground, Salmon, Navy, Fruit, Flower Urns, 2 Panel, 76 x 81 In. ... 475.00
Double Weave, Red, Blue, Wool, Natural Cotton, Brown, Fringe, 86 x 71 In. 250.00
Double Weave, Snowball, Blue & White, Tree Border, Fringe, 99 x 74 In. 495.00
Double Weave, Snowballs & Roses, Tree Border, Fringe, 2 Panel, 1800s, 87 x 75 In. 165.00
Double Weave, Snowflakes, Optical Pattern Border, 2 Panel, 68 x 90 In. 190.00
Double Weave, Squares & Tables, Blue, Top Hem, 2 Panel, 87 x 75 In. 220.00
Double Weave, Wool, Ivory Ground, Pink, Navy, Flowers, Scrolls, c.1839, 74 x 80 In. .. 365.00
Eagle, Diamond Border, Red, Navy, John Long, Holmes County, Ohio, 1851, 68 x 80 In. . 489.00
Jacquard, 3 Color, Interlocking Blue Rings, Tree Border, 2 Panel, 90 x 60 In. 415.00
Jacquard, Biederwand, Blue, Natural, Medallions, Flower Urn Border, 68 x 80 In. 1035.00
Jacquard, Biederwand, Floral Medallions, Pear Trees, Samuel Meily, 1850, 72 x 77 In. .. 633.00
Jacquard, Biederwand, Rose Medallions, 2-Headed Eagle Border, 1841, 78 x 85 In. 1320.00
Jacquard, Biederwand, Roses, Hearts, Eagle, Tree Border, Bellville, Ohio, 1850, 74 In. .. 145.00
Jacquard, Black & White, Js. Craig, Andersonville, Fl. Co. IA, 1851, 78 x 90 In. 863.00
Jacquard, Blue, Red, White Ground, Flowers, Bird, Flower Border, 75 x 82 1/2 In. 230.00
Jacquard, Blue, White, Eagles, Tree Borders, c.1857, 67 x 78 In. 173.00
Jacquard, Floral Medallions, Diamonds, Double Border, Birds, Towers, 76 x 84 In. 635.00
Jacquard, Linen & Wool, Red. Blue, Green, White Ground, Flowers, 78 x 78 In. 235.00
Jacquard, Linen, Red & White, Flowers, Flower Border, 68 x 80 In. 230.00
Jacquard, Red, White, Blue, Brown, Daniel Goodman, 1842, 76 x 93 In. 315.00
Jacquard, Rose Medallions, Circles, Fruit & Basket Border, Blue, Natural, 78 x 83 In. ... 230.00
Jacquard, Rose Medallions, Floral Rectangles, Blue, Red, Green, Natural, 74 x 82 In. ... 258.00
Jacquard, Rose, Sun Medallions, Navy, Blue, Red, Olive, 2 Panel, 76 x 86 In. 770.00
Jacquard, Star & Flower Center, House Border, Animals, J. Schnell, 102 x 92 In. 1915.00
Jacquard, Star Center, Scroll Border, Eagle Corners, Multicolored Borders, 74 x 82 In. 920.00
Overshot, 3 Colors, Squares, Rectangles, Wool, Linen, 2 Panel, 90 x 67 In. 65.00
Overshot, 4 Colors, Chariot Wheels, Cotton Ground, Mid 1900s, 85 1/2 x 62 In. 110.00
Overshot, Blue & White, Linen, Wool, L. Post Benton N.Y., 1833, 75 x 87 In. 765.00
Overshot, Blue & White, Linen, Wool, Signed, A.H. Church Ill., 1840, 78 x 85 In. 1645.00
Overshot, Blue, Red, White, Grid Pattern, Tied Fringe, 70 x 82 In. 345.00
Overshot, Diamond & Triangle Pattern, Red, Navy & Olive, 77 x 91 In. 230.00
Overshot, Geometric Repeat, Red & Brown, 2 Panel, 89 x 78 In. 155.00
Overshot, Plaid Pattern, Woven Wool, Early 19th Century, 88 x 94 In. 205.00
Overshot, Red, White, Blue, Green, Alternating Geometric Rows, 74 x 100 In. 395.00
Round Flower Panels, H&A Seifert, Mechanicsburg, Pa., 1848, 90 x 66 In. 395.00
Summer, Winter, Flowers, Geometrics, 84 x 104 In. 250.00
Summer, Winter, Fruit, Urns, Birds, Borders, Houses, Trees, 76 x 81 In. 468.00
Wool, Off-White Ground, Flower, Scrolls, 1839, 74 x 80 In. 360.00

COWAN POTTERY made art pottery and wares for florists. Guy Cowan
made pottery in Rocky River, Ohio, a suburb of Cleveland, from 1913
to 1931. A stylized mark with the word *Cowan* was used on most
pieces. A commercial, mass-produced line was marked *Lakeware*.
Collectors today search for the Art Deco pieces by Guy Cowan, Viktor
Schreckengost, Waylande Gregory, or Thelma Frazier Winter.

Bowl, Black Matte Glaze, Green Interior, 10 In. 30.00
Bowl, Console, Flared, Green, High Glaze, Marked, 13 In. 85.00
Candelabra, Pavlova, Ivory Glaze, 6 3/4 In. 290.00
Charger, Polo Players, Horses, Sun, Relief, Rust, Impressed Mark, 11 In. 635.00
Charger, Stylized Flowers, Molded, Orange Matte Glaze, Impressed Mark, 13 In. 489.00
Decanter, Ribbed, Purple To Maroon High Glaze, Marked, 10 1/2 In. 201.00
Figurine, Dove, Black Matte Glaze, 8 In. 118.00
Figurine, Flamingo, Ivory, High Glaze, 11 In. 230.00
Figurine, Flamingo, Mottled Orange Matte Glaze, 11 In. 405.00
Figurine, Horse, Ivory, Brown, Impressed Mark, 8 In. 489.00
Figurine, Huntsman, Ivory, Impressed Mark, 8 In. 460.00
Figurine, Introspection, Black Glaze, A. Drexler Jacobson, 8 1/4 In. 865.00

Figurine, Woodland Nymph, Ivory, Impressed Mark, 13 In. 2645.00
Flower Frog, Ivory, High Glaze, Impressed Mark, 12 In. 805.00
Flower Frog, Mushrooms, Ivory, High Glaze, Marked, 4 In. 145.00
Lamp Base, 3 Female Angels, Pink & Ivory Mottled Glaze, 9 In. 200.00
Pin Tray, Clown, Kneeling, Ivory Glaze, 3 In. 29.00
Trivet, Molded Flowers, Tan High Glaze, Marked, 5 1/2 In. 29.00
Vase, 3 Women, Wooded Landscape, Mottled Brown, Purple, Green, High Glaze, 8 In. 1095.00
Vase, Copper Glaze, 7 3/8 In. 90.00
Vase, Glazed, Printed Ink Mark, Stylized R, 9 1/4 In. 82.00
Vase, Inverted Pear Shape, Lavender Blue Glaze, 1900s, 5 In. 29.00
Vase, Mottled Yellow & Mauve High Glaze, Impressed Mark, 12 In. 259.00
Vase, Peach Crackle Glaze, Dark Gray Lid & Base, 14 x 6 1/2 In. 805.00
Vase, Pomegranates, Molded, Mottled Orange Matte Glaze, Impressed Mark, 12 In. 635.00
Vase, Sea Horse, 7 In. 125.00
Wall Plaque, The Hunt, Viktor Schreckengost, Polychrome Glazes, 11 1/4 In. 1495.00

CRACKER JACK, the molasses-flavored popcorn mixture, was first made in 1896 in Chicago, Illinois. A prize was added to each box in 1912. Collectors search for the old boxes, toys, and advertising materials. Many of the toys are unmarked.

Book, Riddles, 2 3/4 x 5 In., 40 Pages 35.00
Charm, Trumpet, Metal, 1950s, 1 1/4 In. 18.00
Pin, Truck, Angelus Marshmallows, c.1930, 1 5/8 In. 60.00
Toy, Spinner, Always On Top, White, Blue 95.00
Toy, Spinner, World's Famous Confections, Red, Blue 95.00
Toy, Train, Locomotive, 2 Cars, Tin Lithograph, 2 1/4 In. 145.00
Toy, Truck, Delivery, 1 1/2 x 7/8 In. 78.00
Toy, Whistle, Flat, 1 x 2 5/8 In. 110.00
Toy, Whistle, Large Mouthed Man, Tin, Gold Color, 2 1/4 In. 35.00
Watch, Pocket, Tin, c.1930s, 1 1/2 x 1/4 In. 40.00

CRACKLE GLASS was originally made by the Venetians, but most of the ware found today dates from the 1800s. The glass was heated, cooled, and refired so that many small lines appeared inside the glass. It was made in many factories in the United States and Europe.

Basket, Sapphire Blue, Applied Clear Handle, 5 1/2 In. 45.00
Bottle, Figural, Fish, Amber, Applied Mouth, Eyes & Fins, Cork Stopper, 15 x 8 In. 125.00
Bowl, Handkerchief, Amethyst, 6 x 7 1/2 In. 150.00
Cigarette Set, Cobalt Blue, Gold Metal Rims, Holder & Ashtray, 1950s, 2 Piece 95.00
Cruet, Amber, Bulbous, Clear Reeded Handle, Amber Ball Stopper, 6 1/2 In., Pair 130.00
Cruet, Amberina, Triple Ball Stopper, 6 3/4 In. 90.00
Cruet, Green, Clear Handle, Clear Round Flattened Stopper, 7 In., Pair 125.00
Decanter, Amberina, Elongated Neck, Ruffled Rim, Flame-Shaped Stopper, 13 In. 85.00
Figurine, Apple, Cranberry, Green Leaf & Stem, 4 1/2 In. 75.00
Figurine, Pear, Cobalt Blue, Green Leaf & Stem, 6 1/2 In. 85.00
Figurine, Pear, Ruby, Clear Stem, 7 1/2 In. 125.00
Lemonade Set, Clear, Elongated Shape, 12-In. Pitcher, 7 Piece 275.00
Lemonade Set, Topaz, Cone-Shaped Footed Glasses, 8 1/4-In. Pitcher, 7 Piece 295.00
Pitcher, Amberina, Elongated Spout, Applied Handle, Kanawha, 14 1/2 In. 75.00
Pitcher, Orange, Pinched Sides, Applied Handle, 10 In. 95.00
Pitcher, Pink Overshot, Swirled, Clear Reeded Handle, 7 1/2 In. 350.00
Pitcher, Ruby, Flared Rim, Applied Clear Handle, 6 3/4 In. 110.00
Pitcher, Ruby, Pinched Waist, Applied Amber Handle, 7 In. 95.00
Pitcher, Sapphire Blue, Bulbous, Applied Handle, 5 1/2 x 5 In. 190.00
Punch Set, Gilt Trim, Covered Bowl, Ladle, 6 Cups 170.00
Vase, Ruby, Flared Ruffled Rim, 7 x 8 In. 125.00
Vase, Turquoise, Tapered, Pinched Sides, 9 In. 121.00

CRANBERRY GLASS is an almost transparent yellow-red glass. It resembles the color of cranberry juice. The glass has been made in Europe and America since the Civil War. It is still being made, and reproductions can fool the unwary. Related glass items may be listed in other categories, such as Northwood, Rubena Verde, etc.

Basket, Opalescent Lattice, Ruffled Edge, 3 1/2 x 10 In. 175.00

Basket, Opalescent Ribs, Square, Ruffled Edge, Applied Twisted Handle, 8 In.	120.00
Bottle, Scent, Double, Cut Design, Brass Covers At Each End, 5 In.	115.00
Bowl, Embossed Cherubs & Scrolls, Silver Frame, 4 1/2 In.	60.00
Bowl, Enameled Insects, 4 Applied Green Feet, Rolled Edge, 11 In.	385.00
Bowl, Hobnail, Frosted, 4 x 9 In.	50.00
Celery Vase, Inverted Thumbprint, Enameled Flowers, 6 In.	135.00
Compote, Satin, Clear Dolphin Stem	200.00
Epergne, Ruffled Edge Vases, Wavy Rim Bowl, c.1870, 22 x 16 In.	315.00
Epergne, Ruffled Edge, Cranberry Trumpets & Basket, c.1900, 20 In.	980.00
Goblet, Cut, Gold Enameled, c.1900, 6 1/2 In., 7 Piece	750.00
Pitcher, Shaded To Vaseline, Hobnail, 5 3/4 In.	150.00
Pitcher, Water, Inverted Thumbprint, Ruffled Edge, Applied Handle, 9 In.	190.00
Powder Box, Cove, White & Gold Enameled, 6 1/2 In.	325.00
Salt, Inverted, Enameled Flowers, 1800s, 3 3/4 In.	80.00
Sugar Shaker, Faceted, Silver Plated Cover, c.1900, 5 1/2 In.	65.00
Vase, Diamond-Quilted, Satin, Ruffled Edge, Egg Shape, 6 1/2 In.	115.00
Water Set, Bulging Loop, Enameled Flowers, 4 Tumblers, 8 1/2 In.	175.00
Wine, Cut To Clear, Bouquet, Drapery, 1910, 7 1/2 In.	370.00

CREAMWARE, or queensware, was developed by Josiah Wedgwood about 1765. It is a cream-colored earthenware that has been copied by many factories. Similar wares may be listed under Pearlware and Wedgwood.

Bowl, Cover, Cauliflower, Scallop Rim, Leaf Molding, c.1775, 4 3/8 In.	2820.00
Bowl, Cover, Marbleized Rust & White Glaze, Handles, Geoffroy Et Cie, Gien, 6 In. *Illus*	200.00
Canister, Tea, Cauliflower, Green Leaves, Florets, c.1775, 4 In.	705.00
Canister, Tea, Lead Glazed, Tortoiseshell, 18th Century, 3 3/8 In.	499.00
Chamber Pot, Presentation, Black Transfer, Liverpool Style, c.1810, 9 x 5 3/4 In.	470.00
Charger, Lead Glazed, Octagonal, Reeded Rim, Tortoiseshell, 13 3/4 In.	470.00
Charger, Lead Glazed, Paneled Border, Mottled Ground, 12 3/8 In.	1410.00
Dish, Lead Glazed, Octagonal Shape, Leafy Cartouches, 10 3/8 In.	590.00
Figurine, Dog Seated Holding Bone In Mouth, 6 3/4 In.	230.00
Jug, Lead Glazed, Pear Shape, 3 Mask & Paw Feet, c.1770, 4 7/8 In.	380.00
Pie Plate, Cover, Bird Finial, 4 In.	50.00
Plate, Soup, Lead Glazed, Tortoiseshell Glaze, Octagonal, 8 1/2 In.	205.00
Plate, Vine Border, Central Flower Spray, 9 In., Pair	375.00
Soup, Dish, Ship Transfer, Herculaneum, Flower Vine Border, 10 1/4 In.	230.00
Teapot, Cover, Lead Glazed, Globe Shape, Relief Vines, 3 3/4 In.	1645.00
Teapot, Cover, Lead Glazed, Pot Shape, Crabstock Handle, 5 1/2 In.	1060.00
Teapot, Lead Glazed, Side Handle, Mottled Brown, c.1770, 3 5/8 In.	410.00
Teapot, Prince & Princess Of Orange, Portrait, Ribs, Intertwined Handle, 3 1/2 In.	275.00
Teapot, Transfer, Corey & Vilbourne, 19th Century	290.00
Toilette Basin, Spode, Polychrome, Chinese Flowers, c.1885, 5 x 16 1/4 In.	145.00
Vase, Greatbatch, Hand Painted, Blue, Chinoiserie, c.1770, 9 1/2 In.	675.00

CREDIT CARDS, credit tokens, metal charge plates, phone cards, and other similar collectibles that replace money are now part of the numismatic collecting hobby.

Bloomingdale's, Metal, 1980	14.00

Don't put a message on your answering machine indicating when you will return.

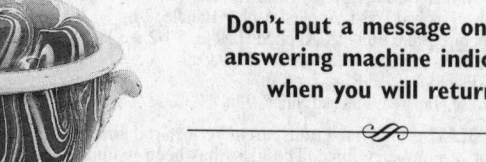

Creamware, Bowl, Cover, Marbleized
Rust & White Glaze, Handles,
Geoffroy Et Cie, Gien, 6 In.

Crown Derby,
Teapot, Imari Style,
Oval, c.1850, 7 In.

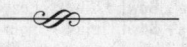

**The longer the cylinder
on an old music box,
the higher the price.**

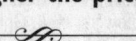

Standard Oil, Sohio, National, Expired December 1960	20.00
Telephone, AT&T, Rock & Roll Hall Of Fame, Cleveland, Ohio	15.00
Telephone, Cable & Wireless, Colonel, Kentucky Fried Chicken	7.00
Telephone, GTE, Aloha Fest, Girl, Riding Horse, 1993	28.00
Telephone, MCI, Statue Of Liberty, U.S. Flag	8.00
Telephone, Sprint, World Trade Center, Vista Hotel	14.00

CROWN DERBY is the name given to porcelain made in Derby, England, from the 1770s to 1935. Pieces are marked with a crown and the letter *D* or the word *Derby*. The earliest pieces were made by the original Derby factory, while later pieces were made by the King Street Partnerships (1848–1935) or the Derby Crown Porcelain Co. (1876–1890). Derby Crown Porcelain Co. became Royal Crown Derby Co. Ltd. in 1890. It is now part of Royal Doulton Tableware Ltd.

Basket, Flowers, Blue, Gilt, Pierced Border, Trefoil Shape, Footed, 1800s, 8 In.	310.00
Dish, Blue, Orange Decorations, Cover, Gilt, 12 In.	540.00
Dish, Rectangular, Chamfered Corners, Imari Style, c.1850, 10 x 8 1/2 In., Pair	259.00
Plate, Blue Tree, Orange Flowers, 10 In., 12 Piece	1020.00
Plate, Poppy, Tulip, Cobalt Blue Border, Gilt Decoration, 8 3/4 In., Pair	850.00
Platter, Flowers, Flowering Tree, Imari Style, Late 19th Century, 20 1/2 In.	650.00
Soup, Dish, Blue Tree, Orange Flowers, 10 1/2 In., 12 Piece	900.00
Soup, Dish, Imari Style, c.1880, 9 3/4 In., Pair	200.00
Teapot, Imari Style, Oval, c.1850, 7 In. *Illus*	276.00
Vase, Central Flower Vase, Panel, Gilt Decoration, Cobalt Blue, 11 In.	5650.00
Vase, Ginger Jar Shape, Yellow, Oriental Decoration, Late 1800s, 8 3/4 In., Pair	275.00
Vase, Imari Style, Handles, Early 20th Century, 5 In.	160.00

CROWN DUCAL is the name used on some pieces of porcelain made by A. G. Richardson and Co., Ltd., of Tunstall and Cobridge, England. The name has been used since 1916.

Bowl, Vegetable, Cover, Blink Bonnie Thistle, 10 1/2 In.	45.00
Candlestick, Tulip Freesia, Hand Painted, Pair	150.00
Gravy Boat, Underplate, Blink Bonnie Thistle	45.00
Pitcher, Ankara, Floral Body, Blue Top & Base, Charlotte Rhead, 8 1/4 In.	255.00
Pitcher, Stitch, Geometric Body, Rust Top & Base, Charlotte Rhead, 6 In.	145.00
Plate, Dinner, Florentine, 10 1/2 In.	125.00
Teapot Trivet, Ivory Chintz, 6 1/2 In.	225.00
Vase, Patch, Geometric Body, Rust Top & Base, Charlotte Rhead, 7 In.	140.00

CROWN MILANO glass was made by Frederick Shirley at the Mt. Washington Glass Works about 1890. It had a plain biscuit color with a satin finish. It was decorated with flowers and often had large gold scrolls.

Biscuit Jar, Acorn & Leaf Tracery, Opal Body, 8 In.	315.00
Biscuit Jar, Cover, Flowers, Gold, Black, Peach Shaded To Tan, Handle, 9 In.	315.00
Biscuit Jar, Cover, Leaves, Acorns, Yellow Shaded To Rose, c.1880, 8 In.	450.00
Biscuit Jar, Enameled Daisies, Peach Shaded To Yellow, Cylindrical, 5 3/4 In.	260.00
Biscuit Jar, Flowers, Gold, Green, Aqua Shaded To Cream, Melon Ribbed, 7 In.	575.00
Biscuit Jar, Gold Lotus Flower, Bulbous, Hobnail, Signed, 6 1/2 x 7 In.	520.00
Biscuit Jar, Melon Ribbed, Flower Panels & Gold Netting, Signed, 5 3/4 In.	575.00

Biscuit Jar, Poppies, Gold Flowers, Turquoise, Ribbed, 6 1/4 x 7 1/2 In. 345.00
Bride's Bowl, Flowers, Leaves, Gold, Ruffled, Bird, Silver Plated Holder, 12 1/2 In. 2015.00
Bride's Bowl, Yellow, Silver Plated Holder, Bird Handles, 9 x 11 In. 575.00
Ewer, Light Green, Lotus Flowers, Gold, Bulbous, Serpent Handle, Signed, 8 In. 1925.00
Ewer, Lily-Of-The-Valley, 9 3/4 In. 750.00
Jar, Cover, Flowers, Enameled, Opal Body, Repousse Lid, Turtle, 4 3/4 In. 600.00
Jar, Cover, Flowers, Gilt, Opal Body, 4 1/4 In. 1125.00
Pitcher, Enameled Flowers, Gold Scrolls, Handle, Signed, 7 In. 950.00
Pitcher, Flowers, Pink, Gold, Beaded, Applied Handle, 10 1/2 In. 360.00
Rose Bowl, Pink Flowers, 3 1/2 In. 335.00
Vase, Gold Dragons, Melon Ribbed, Applied Ribbed Handles, 12 In. 2590.00
Vase, Persian, Scrolls, Gold, Pink, Blue, Brown Beading, Bulbous, 11 1/4 In. 1610.00
Vase, Snow Geese Flying, Sunset, Gold Scrolls, Pedestal, Signed, c.1880, 14 3/4 In. 2575.00
Vase, Swirled Bulbous, Ruffled Edge, Gold Floral Enamel, 7 1/4 In. 600.00
Vase, Tulips, Scrolls, Leaves, Melon Ribbed, Tricornered, Signed, 13 1/2 In. 4600.00

CROWN TUSCAN pattern is included in the Cambridge glass category.

CRUETS of glass or porcelain were made to hold vinegar, oil, and other
condiments. They were especially popular during Victorian times and
have been made in a variety of styles since the eighteenth century.
Additional cruets may be found in the Castor Set category and also in
various glass categories.

Apple Green Glass, Bulbous Base, Stopper, 1920s-1930s, 6 1/2 In. 55.00
Blue Glass, Reflecting Fans Pattern, Pointed Stopper, Belmont Glass Co., 6 1/4 In. ...*Illus* 180.00
Clear Glass, Gold & Multicolored, Man & Woman Scene, Oval, 19th Century 545.00
Cobalt Blue Glass, Mary Gregory Style, Stopper, 6 1/2 In. 70.00
Cranberry Glass, Inverted Thumbprint, Gold Enameled Flowers, 7 In. ....*Illus* 100.00
Craquelle Glass, Cranberry, Clear Stopper, Hobbs Brockunier, 6 1/2 In. 100.00
Emerald Green Glass, S-Repeat Pattern, Gold Trim, Stopper 7 3/4 In. 125.00
Vaseline Glass, Daisy & Button Pattern, Faceted Stopper, 7 1/4 In. ....*Illus* 130.00

CUP PLATES are small glass or china plates that held the cup while a
diner of the mid-nineteenth century drank coffee or tea from the
saucer. The most famous cup plates were made of glass at the Boston
and Sandwich factory located in Sandwich, Massachusetts. There have
been many new glass cup plates made in recent years for sale to gift
shops or limited edition collectors. These are similar to the old plates
but can be recognized as new. Glass cup plates are here. Pottery or
porcelain cup plates may be listed in other categories.

4 Hearts & Leaves, Rosettes, 24 Bull's-Eye Scallops & Points Rim, 3 7/16 In. 45.00
4 Leaves, Star Ground, Oak Leaves, Scrolls, 19 Scallops & Points Rim, 3 9/16 In. 35.00
5-Point Star With Rays, Plain Border, 50 Scallops Rim, Amethyst, 3 1/16 In. 110.00
6-Point Star, Acorns, 18 Wheat Sheaf Scallops Rim, 3 9/16 In. 3850.00
7-Petal Rosette, 3 Sawtooth Arcs, Stippled, 58 Scallops Rim, Peacock Blue, 3 3/8 In. . . . 550.00
8-Point Bull's-Eye Tipped Star, Rosette Border, 39 Scallops Rim, 3 5/16 In. 65.00
Anchor, Stippled, Stars, 24 Large Beads & Reels, 3 1/4 In. 55.00
Center Rivet, Rosette & Diamond Dart, 61 Scallops Rim, Emerald Green, 3 1/2 In. 2310.00

Cruet, Blue Glass, Reflecting
Fans Pattern, Pointed Stopper,
Belmont Glass Co., 6 1/4 In.

Cruet, Cranberry
Glass, Inverted
Thumbprint, Gold
Enameled Flowers,
7 In.

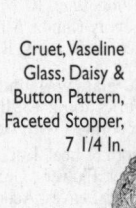

Cruet, Vaseline
Glass, Daisy &
Button Pattern,
Faceted Stopper,
7 1/4 In.

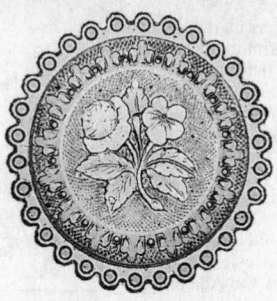

Cup Plate, Rose & Pansy, Stippled,
30 Bull's-Eye Scallops Rim, Soft Blue, 3 In.

Cup Plate, Star, Fleur-De-Lis, 10 Scallops
& Rope Rim, Light Green, 3 7/16 In.

Diamond Weave Center & Border, 60 Scallops Rim, Fort Pitt Glass Works, 3 5/8 In. 250.00
Eagle, 1832 In Border, Olive Branches, 79 Scallops Rim, Violet Blue, 3 1/2 In. 3575.00
Eagle, Plain Border, 24 Bull's-Eye Scallops & Points Rim, 3 1/2 In. 100.00
Eagle & Shield, 13 Stars, Plain Border, Octagonal, Scalloped Rim, Blue, 2 7/8 In. 990.00
Eagle & Shield, Egg & Palmette Border, Octagonal, Palmette Corners, 3 1/2 In. 715.00
Eagle & Shield, Laurel Wreath & Rope Borders, Acorns, Oak Leaves, Plain Rim, 3 In. ... 330.00
Flower, Floral & Leaf Border, 72 Scallops Rim, Deep Green, 3 3/8 In. 7150.00
Fort Pitt, 20 Large & Small Scallops Rim, Cobalt Blue, 3 11/16 In. 3575.00
Geometric, 3-Piece Mold, Folded Scalloped Rim, Amber, 3 3/4 In. 330.00
George Washington, Rayed, Laurel Border, Octagonal, Scalloped Rim, 3 1/2 In. 935.00
Heart & Bull's-Eye, 24 Beads & Reels Rim, Midwestern, 3 3/16 In. 120.00
Henry Clay, Pomegranate Border, 51 Scallops Rim, Blue, 3 9/16 In. 65.00
Liberty Torch, Scrolls, Stippled, 34 Bull's-Eye Scallops Rim, 3 9/16 In. 65.00
Log Cabin, Plain Border, 48 Scallops, 3 1/2 In. 100.00
Lyre, Stippled Border, 30 Even Scallops Rim, Midwestern, 3 1/4 In. 525.00
Maltese Cross, Rayed Darts, Uneven Serrated Border, Plain Rim, White, 3 5/16 In. 55.00
Napoleon Cameo Bust, Facing Right, 15 Palmette Scallops Rim, 3 3/8 In. 440.00
Opalescent Opaque, Shading To Clear Plain Outer Rim, 3 5/8 In. 154.00
Overlapping Hearts, 9 Scallops & Hearts Rim, Amethyst, 3 3/8 In. 3300.00
Overlapping Hearts, 9 Scallops & Hearts Rim, Opalescent, 3 3/8 In. 100.00
Porthole, Roman Rosette Borders, 34 Bull's-Eye Scallops Rim, Amethyst, 3 9/16 In. 1540.00
Porthole, Stippled, 6 C-Scrolls, Leaves, 34 Bull's-Eye Scallops Rim, 3 9/16 In. 100.00
Queen Victoria Bust, Plumes, Uneven Scalloped Border, Blue, 3 5/8 In. 155.00
Repeal Erin Go Bragh, Irish Harp, Heart & Clover Border, 38 Scallops Rim, 3 1/2 In. ... 605.00
Roman Rosette, Fleur-De-Lis, Quatrefoils, 66 Scallops Rim, Dark Blue, 3 5/16 In. 100.00
Rose & Pansy, Stippled, 30 Bull's-Eye Scallops Rim, Soft Blue, 3 In. .... *Illus* 1210.00
Rosette, Waffle Ground, 20 Bull's-Eye Scallops & Points Rim, 3 1/8 In. 45.00
Rosette & Diamond Dart, 38 Even Scallops, Clear, Black Inclusions, 3 5/8 In. 130.00
Rosette & Diamond Dart, Hearts Border, 56 Scallops Rim, Electric Blue, 3 7/16 In. 65.00
Ship, Plain & Stippled Ropes, 24 Bull's-Eye Scallops & Points Rim, 3 1/2 In. 1870.00
Star, Fleur-De-Lis, 10 Scallops & Rope Rim, Light Green, 3 7/16 In. .... *Illus* 3300.00
Steam Ship, Benjamin Franklin, Stars, Anchors, 48 Scallops Rim, Alabaster, 3 1/2 In. ... 1320.00
Steamboat, Shields & Scrolls, 25 Bull's-Eye Scallops & Points Rim, 3 7/16 In. 470.00
Stippled, Stippled Palm Border, 10 Scallops & Rope Rim, 3 5/8 In. 65.00
Sunburst, Concentric Bands, 60 Scallops Rim, Fort Pitt Glass Works, 3 5/8 In. 65.00
Sunburst, Target Center, Plain Border, 66 Scallops Rim, Red Amber, 3 5/16 In. 65.00
Sunburst With Dot, Plain Border, 22 Scallops & Point Rim, Blue, 3 In. 65.00
Swirled, 15 Scallops & Points Rim, 3 3/4 In. 130.00
Tiny Star, Floral Border, Plain Rim, Opaque Light Blue, 3 3/8 In. 330.00
Valentine, Flowers & Leaves, Stippled, Uneven Scalloped Rim, 3 1/2 In. 300.00
Waffle, Scrolls, Bull's-Eyes, 33 Bull's-Eye Scallops Rim, 3 1/16 In. 525.00

Keep art, paintings, prints, and textiles away from sunny windows.

CURRIER & IVES made the famous American lithographs marked with their name from 1857 to 1907. The mark used on the print included the street address in New York City, and it is possible to date the year of the original issue from this information. Earlier prints were made by N. Currier and use that name from 1835 to 1847. Many reprints of the Currier or Currier & Ives prints have been made. Some collectors buy the insurance calendars that were based on the old prints. The words *large*, *small*, or *medium folio* refer to size. The original print sizes were very small (up to about 7 x 9 in.), small (8.8 x 12.8 in.), medium (9 x 14 in. to 14 x 20 in.), large (larger than 14 x 20 in.). Other sizes are probably later copies. Other prints by Currier & Ives may be listed in the Card category under Advertising and in the Sheet Music category. Currier & Ives dinnerware patterns may be found in the Adams or Dinnerware categories.

American Fireman, Pulling Wagon, Signed, L. Maurer, Frame, 28 1/2 x 23 In.	660.00
American Prize Fruit, Colored, 14 x 17 1/4 In.	175.00
American Prize Fruit, Frame, 21 x 27 5/8 In.	2420.00
Bower Of Roses, Frame, 19th Century	375.00
Burning Of The Steamship, Golden Gate, Hand Colored Lithograph, 10 x 14 In.	525.00
Camping Out, Some Of The Right Sort, Walnut Frame, 21 x 28 In.	2185.00
Celebrated Stallions, George Wilkes & Commodore Vanderbilt, Frame, 23 x 32 In.	1650.00
Central Park In Winter, 9 7/8 x 13 7/8 In.	2468.00
Clipper Ship Nightingale, N. Currier, Frame, 1854, 22 5/8 x 22 1/2 In.	2938.00
Darktown Fire Brigade, Saved, Frame, 1884	200.00
Darktown Fire Brigade, Taking A Rest, Frame, Joseph Koehler	220.00 to 315.00
Darktown Trolley, Color Lithograph, Frame, 1896, 11 1/4 x 13 1/2 In.	550.00
Destruction Of Tea At Boston Harbor, c.1846, 10 x 14 In.	635.00
Explosion Of The Peacemaker, Frigate Princeton, N. Currier, 1844, 9 x 14 In.	195.00
Express Train, Hand Colored Lithograph, 1870, 10 5/8 x 14 3/4 In.	655.00
Fiend Of The Road, Farm Wagon, In Front Of 3 Racing Sleighs, Frame, 22 x 32 In.	990.00
General George Washington, The Father Of His Country, 19 x 15 1/2 In.	315.00
George Washington, First In War, N. Currier, Frame, 13 1/2 x 9 1/2 In.	374.00
Grand Drive, Central Park, N.Y., Frame, 1869, 21 x 31 In.	4700.00
Great Fire At Boston, Wood Frame, Gold Liner, 14 1/2 x 18 1/2 In.	420.00
Great Navel Victory In Mobile Bay, Frame, 19th Century, 8 x 12 In.	69.00
Haunted Castle, Frame, 10 x 14 In.	100.00
Home To Thanksgiving, Frame, 1867, 19 3/8 x 21 1/8 In.	14100.00
Landscape, Fruit & Flowers, Frame, 1862, 22 1/4 x 29 7/8 In.	2820.00
Last War Whoop, Frontiersman, Indian, Horses, N. Currier, Frame, 24 x 30 In.	1540.00
Lieutenant General Ulysses S. Grant, Frame, c.1860, 13 1/4 x 9 1/2 In.	240.00
Life Of A Fireman, The Metropolitan System, Frame, 23 7/8 x 32 3/8 In.	3115.00
Life On The Prairie, Buffalo Hunt, Frame, 21 1/4 x 29 1/2 In.	5300.00
Little Harry, Painted Softwood Frame, 9 1/2 x 13 1/2 In.	70.00
Major General Franz Sigel, Color Lithograph, Fame, 13 5/8 x 9 1/2 In.	315.00
Major General Henry W. Halleck	125.00
Major General Joseph Hooker, Color Lithograph, Frame, 12 x 8 1/2 In.	345.00
Minute-Men Of The Revolution, 12 x 15 In.	460.00
My Favorite Pony, Boy Feeding Pony, Frame, 13 1/2 x 9 1/2 In.	75.00
Old Norman Castle, N. Currier, Lithograph, Colored, Mat, 19th Century	160.00
Preparing For Market, Lithograph, N. Currier, Frame, 21 3/4 x 29 1/2 In.	3055.00
Presidents Of United States, N. Currier, Frame, 1842, 13 1/4 x 9 1/2 In.	345.00
Sale Of Pet Lamb, N. Currier, 16 1/4 x 20 3/8 In.	259.00
Saratoga Springs, N.Y., Street, Hotels, Mahogany Frame, c.1875, 18 x 14 In.	336.00
Spring, Hand Colored, Lemon Gold Molded Frame, 12 x 16 In.	140.00
St. Cecelia, Lithograph, 19th Century, 11 x 15 In.	50.00
Staten Island, Hand Colored Lithograph, 1861, 18 x 23 1/4 In.	1675.00
Steamship Bothnia Of The Cunard Line, 13 1/2 x 17 3/4 In.	275.00
Summer Morning, Children, Playing Under Trees, Frame, 13 1/2 x 17 1/2 In.	175.00
Summer Ramble, Couple Walking, Children, Oak Frame, 21 1/2 x 17 1/4 In.	550.00
Surrender Of Lord Cornwallis At Yorktown, N. Currier, Frame, 21 3/8 x 28 1/2 In.	5300.00
View Of New York From Brooklyn Heights, N. Currier, 1849, 15 x 19 3/8 In.	1765.00
Winter Evening, N. Currier, Frame, 11 1/2 x 15 1/2 In.	1295.00
Winter In The Country, Cold Morning, 19 x 26 In.	12925.00

Winter Morning, Lithograph, Frame, 12 5/8 x 17 3/8 In. 2235.00

CUSTARD GLASS is a slightly yellow opaque glass. It was first made in England in the 1880s and was first made in the United States in the 1890s. It has been reproduced. Additional pieces may be found in the Cambridge, Fenton, Heisey, and Northwood categories. Custard glass is called Ivorina Verde by Heisey and other companies.

Argonaut Shell, Sugar & Creamer, Green & Gold Trim	125.00
Chrysanthemum Sprig, Sugar & Creamer, Gold Trim, Blue Stain	385.00
Chrysanthemum Sprig, Water Set, 7 Piece	1200.00
Diamond Maple Leaf, Berry Bowl, Gold Trim, 10 1/2 In.	190.00
Geneva, Butter, Cover, Stained Trim, Flowers, 6 1/2 In.	165.00
Geneva, Tumbler, Custard, Enameled Trim, 3 3/4 In.	30.00
Maize is its own category in this book.	
Punty Band, Creamer, Souvenir, Child	35.00
Punty Band, Mug, Souvenir, 6 Oz.	50.00
Ring Band, Creamer, Gold Trim, Flowers, 4 In.	90.00
Ring Band, Toothpick, Souvenir	45.00
Winged Scroll, Celery Vase, Gold Trim, 5 In.	405.00
Winged Scroll, Toothpick, Gold Trim	215.00

CUT GLASS has been made since ancient times, but the large majority of the pieces now for sale date from the brilliant period of glass design, 1880 to 1905. These pieces have elaborate geometric designs with a deep miter cut. Modern cut glass with a similar appearance is being made in England, Ireland, and the Czech and Slovak republics. Chips and scratches are often difficult to notice but lower the value dramatically. A signature on the glass adds significantly to the value. Other cut glass pieces are listed under factory names.

Banana Bowl, Hobstar Clusters, Strawberry-Diamond & Hobstar, 4 x 11 In.	125.00
Basket, Fern, American Glass Co., 16 x 12 In.	1100.00
Basket, Geometric, Intaglio, 16 1/4 x 12 x 7 1/4 In.	1365.00
Basket, Hobstar & Pinwheel, Footed, 8 x 8 1/2 In.	1025.00
Basket, Pinwheel, Hobstar, Crosscut Diamond, Double Thumbprint Handle, 14 In. . . .	900.00
Bonbon, Hobstar & Vesica, Engraved Daisy, Serrated Edge, Handle, 5 1/4 In. . . . . . . *Illus*	80.00
Bonbon, Hobstar, Strawberry-Diamond & Fan, 3 Corner, 6 In.	75.00
Bottle, Ketchup, Hobstars, Pedestal Shape, 7 1/2 x 3 1/2 In.	345.00
Bottle, Wide Step Cut, 24-Point Hobstars, Teardrop, Stopper, 9 1/2 In., Pair	695.00
Bowl, Alternating Ovals, Star Of David Interior, Hobstar Center, 9 1/2 In.	500.00
Bowl, Cane Vesicas, Hobstar, Strawberry-Diamond & Fan, 2 Handles, 9 In.	600.00
Bowl, Centerpiece, Engraved Chrysanthemums, Feathering, American, 17 In.	1035.00
Bowl, Cover, Diamond, Anglo-Irish, Early 19th Century, 7 1/2 x 7 In.	460.00
Bowl, Diamond Point, England, 9 In.	70.00
Bowl, Eggnog, Hobstars, Nailhead Diamonds, Cut Foot, 7 3/4 x 10 3/4 In.	1180.00
Bowl, Engraved Chrysanthemum, 6 In.	75.00
Bowl, Etched, Grape Leaves, Clusters, Footed, Anglo-Irish, Late 1800s, 9 3/4 In.	400.00
Bowl, Flashed Hobstar, Crosscut Diamond, Strawberry-Diamond & Fan, J. Hoare, 8 In. . .	30.00
Bowl, Flashed Hobstar, Vesica, Hobstar & Fan, 8 In.	90.00
Bowl, Flashed Hobstar, Vesica, Strawberry-Diamond & Fan, Pitkin 7 Brooks, 8 In.	175.00
Bowl, Fruit, Hobstar Design, 4 3/4 x 8 x 5 1/2 In.	385.00
Bowl, Fruit, Russian Pattern, American, c.1890, 5 x 10 In.	520.00
Bowl, Gothic Style Arches, Feather & Vesica Center, 4 Hobstars Border, 9 In.	100.00

A signature adds 25 percent to the value of cut glass.

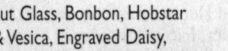

Cut Glass, Bonbon, Hobstar
& Vesica, Engraved Daisy,
Serrated Edge, Handle, 5 1/4 In.

Bowl, Hobstar & Fan, 3 3/4 x 8 In. 45.00
Bowl, Hobstar & Fan, 6 x 12 In. 100.00
Bowl, Hobstar & Tusk, Oval, 4 x 11 1/4 x 7 3/4 In. 485.00
Bowl, Hobstar Clusters, Strawberry-Diamond, Sterling Rim, 4 1/4 x 8 1/2 In. 225.00
Bowl, Hobstar Corners, Vesica Center, Cane & Russian, Square, 8 In. 200.00
Bowl, Hobstar, 3-Footed, 4 1/2 x 9 In. 380.00
Bowl, Hobstar, Split Vesica, 8 In. 75.00
Bowl, Hobstar, Strawberry-Diamond & Vesica, 10 In. 200.00
Bowl, Hobstar, Strawberry-Diamond, Cane & Fan, Crimped, 9 1/2 In. 90.00
Bowl, Hobstar, Strawberry-Diamond, Low, 7 In. 80.00
Bowl, Hobstar, Vesica, Prism & Fan, Oblong, Square, Signed, J. Hoare, 9 1/2 In. 300.00
Bowl, Hobstar, Vesica, Strawberry-Diamond & Step, 8 In. 125.00
Bowl, Hobstars, Crossed Bars, Square, Signed, Egginton, 8 1/2 In. 1150.00
Bowl, Hobstars, Fans, Scalloped Edge, Fan Bottom, 8 1/2 x 3 1/2 In. 425.00
Bowl, Intaglio Flowers, Openwork Sterling Rim, 3 x 9 1/2 In. 165.00
Bowl, Jubilee Pattern, 4 1/2 x 9 3/4 In. 495.00
Bowl, Lattice, Rosette Style Center, Flower Border, Square, 9 In. 250.00
Bowl, Parisian Pattern, Dorflinger, 4 x 9 In. 345.00
Bowl, Pears & Grapes, Signed, Sinclaire 1150.00
Bowl, Pinwheel, Bar, Diamond, 8 In. 150.00
Bowl, Roxbury Pattern, Hobstar, Clark, 9 In. 100.00
Bowl, Royal Pattern, Hunt's, 8 In. 100.00
Bowl, Russian Pattern, 8 In. 150.00
Bowl, Russian-Cut Rim, Hobstar, Cane, Crosshatch Leaf Shaped Cuts, Low, 9 In. ...130.00 to 145.00
Bowl, Spokane Pattern, 8 x 2 In. 300.00
Bowl, Starburst Center, Banded, 9 3/4 In. 150.00
Bowl, Strawberry-Diamond, Footed, 8 In. 200.00
Bowl, Sunburst & Crown, Scalloped Sawtooth Rim, 9 In. 190.00
Bowl, Sunburst, Scalloped Sawtooth Rim, 8 In. ....85.00 to 100.00
Bowl, Sunburst, Square, Brilliant Period, 6 1/2 In. 130.00
Bread Tray, Flashed Hobstar, Cane & Fan, 13 3/4 x 6 1/2 In. 375.00
Butter Chip, 2 Hobstars, Strawberry-Diamond & Fan, Round, 6 Piece 140.00
Candlestick, Notched Teardrop Stem, Faceted Knops, 8 1/4 In., Pair 325.00
Carafe, Hobstar, Crosshatch, 8 x 6 In. 195.00
Carafe, Hobstar, Nailhead Diamond, Strawberry-Diamond, Block & Fan, 8 1/4 In. 90.00
Carafe, Russian Pattern, 7 1/2 In. 130.00
Celery Dish, Etched, Engraved Bowl, Roses, Ferns, Pittsburgh, 3 1/2 x 9 1/4 In. 75.00
Celery Dish, Harvard Pattern, Canoe Shape, 11 1/2 In. 120.00
Celery Dish, Hobstar, 11 3/4 In. 30.00
Celery Dish, Hobstar, Strawberry-Diamond & Split Vesica, 11 1/4 In. 75.00
Chalice, Russian Pattern, Hollow Stem, Rayed Foot, 4 1/2 x 9 In. 225.00
Cheese & Cracker Dish, Hobstar 450.00
Cheese Dish, Underplate, Hobstar, File, Zipper, Fan, 7 x 10 In. 675.00
Claret Jug, Figural Strapwork Panels, Renaissance Revival, 14 3/4 In. 1765.00
Claret Jug, French Silver Top & Handle, Etched Crystal Body, c.1885, 5 1/2 In., Pair 2500.00
Claret Jug, Strawberry, Diamond, Fan, Stopper, 10 1/2 In. 490.00
Cocktail Mixer, Intaglio Cut Body, Gamecock, Silver Trim, Hawkes, c.1925, 9 1/2 In. ... 635.00
Compote, Amber, Diamond-Cut Bands, Footed, Edwardian Style, c.1900, 5 x 7 In., Pair . 345.00
Compote, Doughnut Bowl, Convex, Daisy Flower Cutting, 9 x 2 1/2 In. 115.00
Compote, Elmira Pattern, Teardrop Stem 325.00
Compote, Fairview Pattern, Hobstar On Base, Quaker City, 7 x 4 1/2 In. 250.00
Compote, Hobstar, Vesica, Hobnail & Fan, Teardrop Stem, Rayed Foot, 8 x 6 In. 90.00
Compote, Hobstars, Caning, Teardrop Stem, 12 In. 750.00
Compote, Parisian Pattern, Neck Ring, Hollow Stem, Hobstar, Dorflinger, 8 x 6 In. 695.00
Compote, Pinwheel, Strawberry-Diamond, Pitkin & Brooks, 6 1/2 x 4 1/4 In. 80.00
Compote, Snowflake & Fan, Sawtooth Rim, 8 In. 110.00
Compote, Swirl Strawberry-Diamond, Notched Petticoat Base, 7 x 8 In. 100.00
Compote, Zipper Cut Stem, Flared Bowl, 8 3/4 x 7 1/2 In. 430.00
Cordial Set, Strawberry-Diamond, Rayed Base, Pittsburgh, 4 3/8 In., 7 Piece 490.00
Creamer, Flower, Brilliant Period, 4 3/4 In. 70.00
Cruet, Flutes & Hobstars, 20-Point Hobstar Base, Stopper, 7 1/4 x 3 3/4 In. 195.00
Cruet, Greek Key, Engraved Daisies, Faceted Stopper, 7 In. 200.00
Cruet, Hobstar & Sheaf Of Wheat, Stopper, 6 1/2 In. 150.00

Cruet, Hobstar & Strawberry-Diamond, Double Goose Neck, Stopper, 7 1/4 In. 150.00
Decanter, Diamond Point, Mushroom Stopper, c.1825, 10 In. 70.00
Decanter, Drape, Double Goose Neck, Faceted Stopper, Straus, 12 In. 150.00
Decanter, Etched, Tapered Body, Ribbed Spout, H & H, Silver Plate, c.1900, 10 1/2 In. . . .   115.00
Decanter, Flashed Hobstar, Meriden, 10 In. 50.00
Decanter, Hobstar & Fan, Notched Prisms, Faceted Neck Ring & Stopper, 10 x 4 In. 445.00
Decanter, Pinwheel, 16 In. 60.00
Decanter, Ship's, Prism & Feather, Hobstar, Nailhead, Strawberry-Diamond & Fan, 12 In.   600.00
Decanter, Square, Caned Lower Half, 9 1/4 In. 60.00
Decanter, Stars & Diamond Drapes, Ring-Cut Neck, Stopper, 9 In. 110.00
Decanter, Thistle Shape, Acorn Stopper, Birmingham, Sterling Silver, 1912, 10 1/2 In. . . .   288.00
Decanter, Turquoise To Clear, Hobstar, Diamond, Double Goose Neck, 12 In. 10000.00
Decanter Set, Strawberry-Diamond, Applied Neck Rings, 8 3/8 In., 7 Piece 260.00
Decanter Set, Wine, Green, 19th Century, 10 Piece, 10 In. 800.00
Dish, Hobstar, Button & Strawberry-Diamond, Oval, J. Hoare, 7 1/4 In. 90.00
Dish, Russian Pattern, Leaf Shape, 9 1/2 In. 575.00
Dish, Sweet Meat, Engraved, Flower Basket, Cornucopia, 13 1/2 In. 790.00
Ewer, Geometric Swirl, Silver Mounts, Grape, Tiffany & Co., 12 1/2 In. 4255.00
Finger Bowl, Interlaced Hobstar & Fan, c.1915, 2 1/2 x 4 3/8 In., 8 Piece 800.00
Goblet, Cane, Strawberry-Diamond, Split Vesica & Fan, 6 In., 2 Piece 60.00
Goblet, Hobstar, Strawberry-Diamond & Fan, 6 In., 6 Piece 70.00
Ice Bucket, Hobstar Vase, Strawberry-Diamond, Flashed Fan, Tab Handles, 5 1/2 x 7 In. .   125.00
Ice Bucket, Hobstar, Star, Strawberry-Diamond & Fan, Tab Handles, 4 1/2 x 5 In. 150.00
Ice Bucket, Hobstars, Fans, Step Cut, 2 Handles, 5 1/2 x 8 In. 700.00
Jam Jar, Russian Pattern, Silver Plate Lid & Bail, 6 In. 250.00
Jar, Cover, Chestnut Shape, Diamond Point, Mushroom Finial, Ireland, c.1820, 15 In., Pair   3220.00
Jug, Arch, Fan, Roundel, Diamond, Bulbous Shape, Applied Handle, 7 x 4 1/4 In. 240.00
Jug, Whiskey, Hobstars, Prisms, Notched, Crosshatch, Rayed Star Base, 12 In. 1350.00
Jug, Whiskey, Marilyn Pattern, William C. Anderson, 8 x 4 3/4 In. 525.00
Knife Rest, Paneled, 4 1/4 In. 30.00
Knife Rest, Rayed Star, 4 1/2 In. 55.00
Loving Cup, Hobstar, 3 Handles, Sterling Silver Collar, Monogram, Dated 1899, 6 In. 690.00
Nappy, Cane, Star-Cut Buttons, Handle, 6 In. 60.00
Nappy, Hobstar & Fan, 6 In. 40.00
Nappy, Hobstar & Strawberry-Diamond, Leaf Shape, 7 In. 50.00
Nappy, Hobstar, Fan, Applied Handles, 11 3/4 In. 127.00
Nappy, Maltese Cross, Russian & Diamond, Hobstars, 6 In. 75.00
Nappy, Royal Pattern, Leaf Shape, Handle, Hunt, 9 In. 375.00
Pitcher, 16-Point Stars, Notched Faceted Base, Brilliant Period, American 650.00
Pitcher, Champagne, Carnation, Sunburst, American, c.1900, 12 3/4 In. 115.00
Pitcher, Hobstar & Sheaf, Sunburst-Cut Loop Handle, American, c.1900, 7 3/4 In. 115.00
Pitcher, Hobstar, Alternating Intaglio Flowers, 11 1/2 x 5 In. 1050.00
Pitcher, Hobstar, Cane, Crosshatch, 13 3/8 In. 1100.00
Pitcher, Hobstar, Crosshatch, 11 1/4 x 5 In. 375.00
Pitcher, Hobstars, Spouted Rim, Silver Collar, Gorham, 1915, 10 5/8 In. 895.00
Pitcher, Hobstars, Triple Notched Handle, 24-Point Rayed Base, 8 In. 330.00
Pitcher, Milk, Hobstars, Vesicas, Triple Cut Handle, Meriden, 8 1/2 x 5 In. 395.00
Pitcher, Prism Body, Hobstar, Cane & Strawberry-Diamond, 2-Notch Handle, 4 1/2 In. . .   200.00
Pitcher, Sawtooth Pattern, Applied Strap Handle, 19th Century, 8 3/4 In. 230.00
Pitcher, Strawberry Harvard, Scalloped Rim, Applied Cut Handle, 14 In. 230.00
Plate, Hobstar & Strawberry-Diamond Border, Hobstar Wafer Base, Roden Bros, 7 In. 150.00
Plate, Hobstar Center, Crosscut Diamond, Strawberry-Diamond & Star, 7 In. 25.00
Plate, Hobstar, 7 In. 90.00
Plate, Hobstar, Cane & Fan, 7 In. 75.00
Plate, Hobstar, File, Star & Fan, 9 In. 175.00
Plate, Ivy & Berry Border, Rayed Center, Wafer Base, 7 In. 25.00
Plate, Magnet, 8 Fans, Crosshatch, Scalloped Border, 11 In. 375.00
Plate, Seneca Pattern, Empire, 7 In. 325.00
Plate, Strawberry-Diamond, Crosshatch, Fans, 7 In. 135.00
Plate, Sunburst, Brilliant Period, 6 3/4 In. 90.00
Platter, Stars & Diamonds, Round, Brilliant Period, American, 13 1/2 In. 3500.00
Punch Bowl, Base, Chrysanthemum & Fan, American, Early 1900s, 7 3/4 x 10 In. 635.00
Punch Bowl, Base, Hobstar, 9 1/2 x 10 In. 500.00

Punch Bowl, Base, Hobstar, Crossed File, Small Hobstar Chain, 12 x 12 In. 475.00
Punch Bowl, Starburst & Torch, Scalloped Sawtooth Rim, 14 In. 500.00
Relish, Scalloped Rim, 14 1/4 In. 115.00
Relish Tray, Intaglio, 8 x 4 x 2 In. 300.00
Rose Bowl, Vaseline To Clear, Crosscut Diamond, Strawberry-Diamond, Star, Fan, 5 In. ... 450.00
Salt, Hobstar, Prism, Signed, Maple City, 6 Piece 125.00
Sandwich Server, Hobstar, Center Handle, 6 1/2 x 10 1/2 In. 575.00
Shade, Globe Shape, Cranberry & Amber Cut To Clear, Strawberry-Diamond, 6 x 4 In. ... 280.00
Sherry, Prism & Fan, 4 1/2 In., 4 Piece 25.00
Sugar, Greek Key 525.00
Sugar & Creamer, Handles, Triple Notched, 6 x 5 In., 4 x 2 1/2 In. 400.00
Sugar & Creamer, Starflower, Hobstar Base, 2 Thumbprint Handles, Pedestal, 4 1/2 In. ... 125.00
Sweetmeat Dish, Cover, Waffle Pattern, 19th Century, 9 1/4 In. 60.00
Syrup, Pinwheel, Vesica, Silver Plated Top, 5 1/2 In. 200.00
Tankard, Champagne, Blank & Cutting, Dorflinger, No. 50 .... 900.00
Tray, Hobstar, Crossed Bars & Fan, 10 In. 70.00
Tray, Ice Cream, Buffalo Pattern, Niagara, 18 x 10 In. 1450.00
Tray, Ice Cream, Hobstar, Hobnail, Pinwheel & Fan, 14 1/4 x 7 1/2 In. 125.00
Tray, Ice Cream, Interlaced Miter-Cut Rings, Lobed, c.1915, 12 1/4 In. 1035.00
Tray, Ice Cream, Pinwheel & Cane, 13 3/4 In. 400.00
Tray, Ice Cream, Seneca Pattern, Fishtail Shape, Empire, 10 x 18 In. 1850.00
Tumbler, Hobstar & Star, c.1915, 4 1/4 In., 6 Piece 175.00
Tumbler, Iced Tea, Solano, 3 1/8 x 2 1/4 In. 385.00
Tumbler, Monarch Pattern, J. Hoare, 4 In. 40.00
Vase, Cane Vesica, Stars, 32-Point Hobstar Scalloped, Pedestal, 12 1/4 x 7 In. 650.00
Vase, Comet Pattern, Bowling Pin Shape, J. Hoare, 14 In. 3600.00
Vase, Fans & Diamonds, Hobstars, Crosshatch, Bulbous Base, Flared Neck, 10 x 5 In. 450.00
Vase, Grapes, Vines, Flared, Gilt, Sterling Silver Collar, c.1903, 13 3/4 x 6 1/4 In. 1155.00
Vase, Hobstar & St. Louis Diamond Columns, Corset Shape, Hobstar Base, 13 1/2 In. ... 850.00
Vase, Hobstar, Cane, Fan, 11 1/2 In. 69.00
Vase, Hobstar, Cane, Strawberry-Diamond, Fan, Teardrop Shape, 3 Handles, 11 In. 2600.00
Vase, Hobstar, Fan, Crosshatch, Scalloped, Notched Edge, Hobstar Base, 12 In. 425.00
Vase, Hobstars, Fan Shape, Flared, Heavy Hobstar Footed Base, 7 1/2 In. 625.00
Vase, Marquise Pattern, J. Hoare, 12 In. 1250.00
Vase, Ruby Cut To Clear, Fan, Fine Cut, Handles, 10 In. 80.00
Vase, Sheldon Pattern, Chalice Shape, 12 1/2 x 5 1/4 In. 780.00
Vase, Trumpet, 2 Cane Bands, 2 Flower Panels, 16 In. 175.00
Vase, Trumpet, Pinwheel, Crosscut Diamond, Strawberry-Diamond, Prism, 13 3/4 In. 125.00
Water Set, Flower, Hoare, 7 Piece 375.00
Wine, Russian Pattern, Elongated Teardrop Stem, 5 In., 4 Piece 275.00

CZECHOSLOVAKIA is a popular term with collectors. The name, first
used as a mark after the country was formed in 1918, appears on glass
and porcelain and other decorative items. Although Czechoslovakia
split into Slovakia and the Czech Republic on January 1, 1993, the
name continues to be used in some trademarks.

CZECHOSLOVAKIA GLASS, Basket, Spattered, Yellow, Pink, Orange, Clear Twisted Handle .. 150.00
Candy Jar, Cover, Mottled Orange, Red, Green, Yellow, Urn Shape, 9 In. 175.00
Condiment Set, 2 Cruets, Tray, Pressed Waffle Blocks, Cut Stoppers 65.00
Epergne, Single Lily, Cobalt Blue, Enameled Flowers, 17 x 14 In. 290.00
Jar, Cover, Cobalt Blue, Gold Trim, Free-Blown, Art Deco, 6 1/2 In. 55.00
Perfume Bottle, Malachite, Frolicking Nudes Stopper, Art Deco, 8 In. 144.00
Vase, Aqua, Art Deco Cutting, Flared, 6 3/4 In. 225.00
Vase, Black Enameled Sweet Peas, Lines, Baluster Shape, Art Deco, 10 In. 440.00
Vase, Gold Iridescence, Helmet Shape, 7 1/2 x 5 1/4 In. 300.00
Vase, Opalescent, Crystal, Pulled, Ribbed, Swirls, Ornaments, 7 3/4 In. 2185.00
Vase, Orange Ground, Blue, White, Black Inclusions, Footed, 8 In. 85.00
Vase, Orange, Dark Blue Lily Pad Base, 4 1/2 In. 135.00
Vase, Orange, Mottled Blue & Orange Foot, Fan Shape, Art Deco, 8 In. 275.00
Vase, Pink, Iridescent Blue Oil Spots, Dark Amethyst Ground, 8 1/4 In. 960.00
Vase, Red, Swirled Black, Black Ribs, Red Tripod Foot, 5 1/2 In. 80.00
CZECHOSLOVAKIA POTTERY, Flower Frog, Ball Shape, Orange, Blue, Yellow Band, 3 1/4 In. 95.00
Pitcher, Fruits, Red & Yellow Ground, Hand Painted, 6 In. 40.00

Vase, Green Ground, Pink & Yellow Flowers, Hand Painted, 5 1/2 In. 85.00
Vase, Pink & Yellow Flower Transfer, Brown Ground, Handles, 7 In. 45.00
Wall Pocket, Bird & Birdhouse On Branch, 6 In. 45.00

D'ARGENTAL is a mark used in France by the Compagnie des Cristalleries de St. Louis. The firm made multilayered, acid-cut cameo glass in the late nineteenth and twentieth centuries. D'Argental is the French name for the city of Munzthal, home of the glassworks. Later they made enameled etched glass.

Vase, 2 Lakeside Deer, Amber, Blue Forest, Mountains, Cameo, Signed, c.1900, 12 In. 3360.00
Vase, Blossoms, Leaves, Stems, Blue On Yellow, Cameo, Signed, 6 In. 690.00
Vase, Flowers, Leaves, Rust On Amber, Cameo, Signed, 14 In. 2300.00
Vase, Green Leaves, Rose Ground, Cameo, 8 In. 635.00
Vase, Lavender Bleeding Hearts, Blue Ground, Cameo, 5 In. 300.00
Vase, Leaves, Flowers, Vine, Slender Neck, Flared, Cameo, 10 1/2 In. 1495.00
Vase, Orchids, Frosted, Tapered, Cameo, Signed, 13 1/2 In. 2760.00

DAUM, a glassworks in Nancy, France, was started by Jean Daum in 1875. The company, now called *Cristalleries de Nancy*, is still working. The *Daum Nancy* mark has been used in many variations. The name of the city and the artist are usually both included.

Bookends, 3-Sided, 5 x 4 In. 115.00
Bowl, 4 Flowers, Pink, Purple, Red, Yellow, Green Leaves, Round, Cameo, 6 In. 1980.00
Bowl, Brown Leaves, Frosted Ground, Insects, Shallow, Square, Cameo, Signed, 5 1/2 In. 1725.00
Bowl, Columbines, Blue, Leaves, Hammered Tortoise Shell Ground, Flared, Signed, 8 In. . 1380.00
Bowl, Holly Leaves, Berries, Chipped Ice Ground, Cameo, Signed, 3 1/4 x 5 In. 420.00
Bowl, Lake Scene, Green, Mottled Orange & Red Ground, Oval, Cameo, Signed, 2 3/4 In. 880.00
Bowl, Mistletoe, Berries, Clear To Green Ground, Cameo, 5 1/2 In. 690.00
Bowl, Nude Man & Woman, Intertwined, Morphing Into Tree, Pate-De-Verre, 14 3/4 In. .. 600.00
Bowl, Peach Branches, Flowering, Mottled Orange & White, Squat, Cameo, Signed, 5 In. . 1320.00
Bowl, Red Clover, Leaves, Opalescent, Enameled, Gold Highlights, Cameo, 2 3/4 In. 1500.00
Bowl, Trees & Mountains, Mottled, Cameo, 10 x 5 1/2 In. 2070.00
Bowl, Tricornered, Yellow, 3 Patches Of Pink, Cabochon Insets, 3-Footed, 6 In. 747.00
Bowl, Winter Scene, Buildings, Windmills, Pond, Trees, Enameled, Cameo, 4 x 6 x 3 In. . 1725.00
Box, Cover, Thistles, Vines, Enameled, Cameo, Signed, 3 1/4 In. 990.00
Candelabrum, 2-Light, Tree Shape, Snail, Turquoise, Brown, Pate-De-Verre, 8 In. 440.00
Chandelier, Bronze, Glass, Mottled Orange, Yellow, 4 Domed Shades, 28 x 24 In. 1795.00
Creamer, Cameo Purple Ground, Flowers, Stems & Leaves, Gilt Foot, 2 1/2 In. 480.00
Cruet, Yellow & Orange, Red Poppies, Green Stems, 1900, 6 1/2 In. 4600.00
Dish, Leaf Shape, Applied Salamander, Yellow, Green, Violet, Pate-De-Verre, 5 In. 275.00
Fernery, Strand Of Trees, Summer Foliage, Orange Sky, Hexagonal Base, 17 In. 13800.00
Figurine, Elephant, 12 In. 175.00
Figurine, Goose, In Flight, Signed, 11 x 8 In. 145.00
Figurine, Horse, Le Ba Dang, 9 1/2 x 6 In. 1020.00
Figurine, Mouse, Translucent Blue, Green, Rust, Pate-De-Verre, Signed, 4 3/4 In. 250.00
Figurine, Owl, Clear & Green, Pate-De-Verre, 7 1/4 In. 220.00
Figurine, Polar Bear, Pate-De-Verre, Opaque White, Signed, 6 1/4 x 4 In. 315.00
Figurine, Snail, 9 3/4 In. 175.00
Lamp, Stylized Flowers & Leaves, Mushroom Shape, Cameo, 14 In. 11615.00
Lamp, Tree Trunk Stem, Climbing Ivy, Leaves, Birds, Cameo Shade, Metal Base, 64 In. .. 9200.00
Lamp Base, Forest Lake Scene, Crimson, Amber Body, Cameo, c.1900, 32 In. 1570.00
Lamp Base, Orange Cut To Clear, Art Deco, Bronze Tone Metal Foot, 23 In. 1440.00
Mug, Flowers, Gold Enameled, Signed, 2 1/4 In. 430.00
Night-Light, Leaves & Flowers, Green, Brown, Metal Base, Tumbler Body, 7 In. 1725.00
Pitcher, Flowers, Leaves, Branches, Frosted, Gold Enameled, Cameo, Signed, 9 1/2 In. ... 1100.00
Pitcher, Flowers, Ruby, Gold Enameled, Cameo, Silver Mounted, 4 1/2 In. 880.00
Pitcher, Flowers, Vines, Applied Handle, Enameled, Cameo, Signed, 5 3/4 In. 1380.00
Pitcher, Green, Bands Of Flowers, Gold Enameled, Cameo, Signed, 9 3/4 In. 420.00
Rose Bowl, Tulips, Mottled Pink & Green Ground, Enameled, Cameo, Signed, 2 1/2 In. .. 880.00
Salt, Intaglio Flowers, Oval, Gold Enameled, Sterling Filigree Holder, 3 1/4 In. 525.00
Salt, Snowy Woodland, Gold Ground, Cameo, Marked, 2 1/8 In. 1045.00
Sculpture, Bird, Pate-De-Verre, Signed, 16 In. 550.00
Toothpick Holder, Pink, Lily Of The Valley, Gold Enameled, Cameo, 2 In. 690.00

Tumbler, Amethyst & Frosted, Fuchsia Blossoms In Purple, Barrel Shape, 1900, 4 3/4 In. 1265.00
Tumbler, Orange Ground, Leafless Trees, Snowy Ground, Cameo, Signed, 2 In. 1150.00
Vase, Autumn Leaves, Burnt Orange, Green, Cameo, Bulbous, Flared, Signed, 20 In. 4020.00
Vase, Berries, Leaves, Enameled, Mottled, Frosted Ground, Shouldered, Wide Mouth, 7 In. 5975.00
Vase, Birch Trees, Autumn Colors, Foggy Lake, Cylindrical, Rolled Rim, Cameo, 6 1/4 In. 4025.00
Vase, Blossom, Leaf, Stem, Vine, Green, Brown, Frosted, Cameo, Signed, 10 In. 12075.00
Vase, Blown, Applied Glass Discs, 5 1/2 x 5 In. 245.00
Vase, Blue Flowers, Green Frosted & Blue Mottled Ground, Bulbous, Footed, 4 1/2 In. .. 2350.00
Vase, Blue, Irregular Vertical Lines, Oval, Waisted, Cameo, 7 In. 990.00
Vase, Boats At Sea, Flying Birds, Yellow, Rose Mottled Ground, Flared, Cameo, 19 1/2 In. 4900.00
Vase, Boats, Trees, Brown, Orange, Yellow, Pillow Shape, Square Rim, Cameo, 7 In. 1080.00
Vase, Branch, Berries, Enameled, Maroon, Peach Ground, Club Shape, Cameo, 6 1/2 In. . 990.00
Vase, Branches, Chestnuts, Green On Orange Mottled Ground, Gourd, Marked, 7 1/2 In. . 1380.00
Vase, Brown Leaves, Thorn Stems, Clusters Of Brown & Black Flowers, Yellow, 6 1/2 In. 575.00
Vase, Brown Shaded To Yellow, Red, Green Columbine, Cameo, Signed, 15 In. 3680.00
Vase, Cameo, Purple Leaves & Berries, Mottled Blue & Green Ground, 12 In. ..... *Illus* 3220.00
Vase, Chinese Boats, Sunset, Mottled Yellow, Swollen, Cameo, 7 1/4 In. 2200.00
Vase, Dutch Winter Scene, Blue Ground, Snow, Windmills, Pillow, 3 1/4 In. 2242.00
Vase, Earthtone, Brown Leaves, Vines, Orange & Yellow Ground, Cameo, 11 1/4 In. 1020.00
Vase, Enameled Flowers, Bulbous, Ruffled Top, Vitrified, Cameo, Signed, 3 1/2 In. 1430.00
Vase, Flowers, Banner, Green, Gold Enameled, Cameo, Signed, 4 3/4 In. 600.00
Vase, Flowers, French Verse, Textured, Bulbous, Flared Rim, Cameo, Signed, 3 1/4 In. ... 230.00
Vase, Flowers, Leaves, Butterfly, Textured Ground, Enameled, Cameo, 4 In. 520.00
Vase, Flowers, Leaves, Gold Enameled Highlights, Opalescent Ground, Cameo, 3 1/4 In. . 200.00
Vase, Forest Lake Scene, Amber, Orange & Green, Cameo, 1910, 13 In. 1840.00
Vase, Fuchsia Flowers, Enamel, White Mottled & Frosted Ground, Rolled Base, 6 In., Pair 6575.00
Vase, Fuchsia, Mottled Purple & White Ground, Block Shape, Cameo, Signed, 4 3/4 In. .. 1980.00
Vase, Girl With Pigtails, Enameled, Geese, Blue Ground, Cameo, 3 1/2 In. 1540.00
Vase, Green Ground, Green Rings & Buttons, Cameo, 5 1/4 In. 990.00
Vase, Green, Clematis Blossoms, Gray Ground, Flared Rim, Cameo, 1910, 14 In. 1610.00
Vase, Green, Holly Design, Pewter Overlay, Signed, M. Maurice, 7 1/2 In. 260.00
Vase, Iris, Green & Yellow, Gray Textured Ground, Cameo, 9 In. 2530.00
Vase, Lake Scene, Amber, Crimson, Flat Sided, Footed, Cameo, c.1900, 6 x 8 In. 1790.00
Vase, Lake Scene, Gray & Blue, Yellow & Crimson Trees, Shore, Cameo, 1900, 6 In. 3565.00
Vase, Landscape, Trees, Grass, Water, Mountains, Blue Ground, Cameo, 4 1/2 In. 2127.00
Vase, Leaves, Flowers, Vines, Red Orange, Yellow Ground, Tumbler Shape, Cameo, 5 In. 1320.00
Vase, Leaves, Pods, Opalescent Green, Amber, Flared, Cameo, Signed, 5 3/4 In. 430.00
Vase, Leaves, Yellow, Green, Blue Pods, Mottled Green, Amethyst Ground, Cameo, 17 In. 2480.00
Vase, Lilies Of The Valley, Gold Opalescent, Frosted, Square, Cameo, Signed, 4 3/4 In. .. 750.00
Vase, Lilies, Enameled, Mottled Yellow, Purple, Baluster Shape, Cameo, 15 1/2 In. 8960.00
Vase, Mauve, Art Deco Design, Cameo, c.1925, 8 1/2 x 9 In. 420.00
Vase, Morning Glories, Purple & Green, Gray Ground, Bulbous, Cylindrical, Cameo, 4 In. 2090.00
Vase, Pink & Orange Flowers, Green Leaves, Frosted Ground, Baluster, 10 1/2 In. 4540.00
Vase, Pod & Stem, Yellow, Green, Squat, Signed, 5 In. 415.00
Vase, Purple & Red Fuchsia Blossoms, Gray, Enameled, Rectangular, 1910, 13 In. 1840.00
Vase, Raspberries, Canes, Leaves, Frosted To Umber, Flared, Conical, Cameo, 12 In., Pair 575.00
Vase, Red Berries, Green Leaves, Enameled, Cameo, Signed, 13 3/4 In. 8050.00

**If there are raised applied
decorations on your art glass, be
careful when cleaning it. Gold or
silver accents, painted enamel
decoration, and beads must be
kept in fine condition to
maintain the value of the glass.**

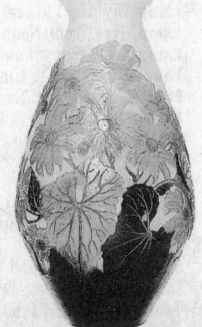

Daum, Vase, Cameo,
Purple Leaves &
Berries, Mottled Blue &
Green Ground, 12 In.

Vase, Red Flowers, Green Leaves, Opalescent Textured Ground, Cameo, Signed, 2 1/2 In. 520.00
Vase, Red Flowers, Leaves, Mottled Yellow & Red Ground, Cameo, 9 In. 1955.00
Vase, Red Foxgloves, Gold Enameled Leaves, Etched, Bottle Shape, Signed, 13 1/2 In. . . 1840.00
Vase, Red Landscape, Red, Yellow Ground, Cameo, 26 1/2 In. 4025.00
Vase, Red Poppies, Enameled, Yellow Ground, Gold Trim, Baluster, Footed, 8 5/8 In. 2870.00
Vase, Snow Scene, Crows, Flying, Perched In Trees, Cameo, Signed, 2 In. 2200.00
Vase, Spider Web, Green Iris, Leaves, Chipped Ice Ground, Gold, Cameo, Signed, 9 In. . . 5465.00
Vase, Spring Flowers, Mottled Green & Pink, Enameled, Cameo, 5 In. 3050.00
Vase, Stems & Leaves, Tangerine, White Snowberries, Gold Enameled, Cameo, 5 In. 520.00
Vase, Stick, White Flowers, Long Stems, Mottled Blue Ground, Etched Foot, Cameo, 17 In. 9560.00
Vase, Stick, Winter Scene On Bulbous Bottom, Enameled, Frosted Ground, 6 1/2 In. 3585.00
Vase, Summer Scene, Green Trees, Foliage, Orange & Yellow Ground, Cameo, 4 3/4 In. . 690.00
Vase, Sweet Pea Vines, Maroon, Light Blue, Fire Polished, Cameo, Signed, 11 In. 3850.00
Vase, Swirled Leaves & Spider Web, Purple Bottom, Yellow Top, Cameo, 6 x 5 In. 4600.00
Vase, Thistles, Enameled, Gold Highlights, Cameo, 4 3/4 In. 230.00
Vase, Thistles, Green To Yellow To Pink Ground, Cameo, 1914, 4 1/4 In. 1555.00
Vase, Thistles, Iridescent Ground, Enameled, Cameo, 4 1/2 In. 460.00
Vase, Trees In Winter, Black Birds, Enameled, Blue, Frosted, Wide Mouth, Cameo, 4 In. . 5020.00
Vase, Trees, Grasses, Yellow, Mottled Orange, Cameo, Signed, 6 1/8 In. 660.00
Vase, Trees, Lake, Mocha Cut To Green, Mottled Orange Ground, Flared, Cameo, 9 In. . . 5040.00
Vase, Trees, River, Brown, Amber, Tapered, Cupped Rim, Cameo, Signed, 24 x 8 1/2 In. . 4025.00
Vase, Violets, Leaves, Gold Enameled, Pillow, Cameo, 1 5/8 In. . . . . : . 1495.00
Vase, Violets, Mottled, Frosted Clear To Amber, Baluster, Cameo, Signed, 8 In. 2080.00
Vase, White Branches, Martele Flowers, Pinched Neck, Square Body, Footed, 9 1/2 In. . . 8965.00
Vase, White, Red & Black, Amethyst, Applied Square Handle, Ribbed, 3 1/2 In. 1100.00
Vase, Wildflowers & Leaves, Yellow & Purple Ground, Tumbler Shape, Cameo, 4 In. 1200.00
Vase, Windmill, Boats, Enameled, Cameo, Signed, 2 In. 460.00
Vase, Winter Landscape, Enameled, Goblet Shape, Cameo, Signed, 5 1/2 In. 3575.00
Vase, Winter Landscape, Light Blue, Enameled, Cameo, 5 In. 3450.00
Vase, Winter Village, Gray, Blue & Amber, 1910, 8 In. 1325.00
Vase, Yellow Martele Ground, Pink Flowers & Leaves, Cameo, 18 3/4 In. 4600.00
Vase, Yellow, Orange Flowers, Green Leaves, Mottled, Cameo, 10 In. 2070.00

DAVENPORT pottery and porcelain were made at the Davenport factory in Longport, Staffordshire, England, from 1793 to 1887. Earthenwares, creamwares, porcelains, ironstone, and other ceramics were made. Most of the pieces are marked with a form of the word *Davenport*.

DAVENPORT
LONGPORT
STAFFORDSHRE

Bowl, Amoy, Open, Flow Blue, 8 In. 595.00
Plate, Imari Style, Iron Red, Green, 1870-1886, 9 1/2 In., 6 Piece 900.00
Plate, Oriental Scene, Building, People, Palm Trees, Blue & White, 9 3/4 In. 80.00
Platter, Chinese Birds, Transfer, 19 In. 255.00
Platter, Ching, Flow Blue, 15 1/2 In. 440.00
Tray, Japan Pattern, Iron Red Factory Mark, c.1850, 19 In. 690.00

DAVY CROCKETT, the American frontiersman, was born in 1786 and died in 1836. The historical character gained new fame in 1954 when the Walt Disney television show ran a series of episodes featuring Fess Parker as Davy Crockett. Coonskin caps and buckskins became popular and hundreds of different Davy Crockett items were made.

Bank, Register, Frontier, Tin, Dime 429.00
Bowl, Cereal, Milk Glass, Hero Of Alamo, 1950s, 5 In. 45.00
Lunch Box, Davey & Indian Fighting, With Knives, Metal, Thermos, 6 x 8 x 4 In. 256.00
Memo Pad, Pen, Davy Holding Rifle, Black, Plastic, Fosta, c.1950s, 2 x 3 1/2 In. 25.00
Pail, Red Ground, White Interior, Flat Blue Handle, Tin, Ohio Art, c.1955, 7 3/4 In. 83.00
Pocketknife, Double Blades, Celluloid Grip, Rawhide, Colonial U.S.A., c.1955, 3 3/8 In. . . 40.00
Toy, Indian Fight Fur Hat, Fess Parker On Box, 1950s 995.00
Toy, Indian Target Set, Keystone Wood Toys, No. 827, c.1950s, 19 x 22 1/2 In. 200.00
Wristwatch, Powder Horn, Rawhide String, Price Tag, WDP, 1954, 7 1/2-In. Box 340.00

DE VEZ was a signature used on cameo glass after 1910. E. S. Monot founded the glass company near Paris in 1851. The company changed names many times. Mt. Joye, another glass by this factory, is listed in its own category.

Vase, Blue Trees, Lake, Mountain, Cream Ground, 6 In. 520.00

Vase, Cherries, Leaves, Mountains, Cream Ground, Signed, 6 1/4 In. 315.00
Vase, House, Barn, Man, Child, Trees, Shaded Red To Amber, Baluster, Signed, 6 In. 495.00
Vase, Landscape, Mountains, Island, Buildings, Black, Salmon, Pearl Ground, 8 In. 515.00
Vase, Leaves, Trees, Mountains, Gardens, Maiden, White Ground, 10 1/4 In. 780.00
Vase, Leaves, Vines, Flowers, Buds, Frosted Ground, 8 In. 460.00
Vase, Man, On Gondola, Trees, City, Blue, Cranberry, On Amber, Signed, 7 1/2 In. 800.00
Vase, Meadow, Trees, Castle, Grape Leaf, Vines, Green, Pink, 10 In. 575.00
Vase, Palm Trees, Mountains, Blue, Cranberry, On Amber, Signed, 7 1/2 In. 800.00
Vase, Sailboats On Water, Frosted Yellow, Spherical, Knopped Neck, Signed, 9 3/4 In. 990.00
Vase, Scenic View, Wooded Lake, Mountains, Pink Details, 6 1/4 In. 460.00
Vase, Tree Island, Building, Mountains, Amethyst, Russet, Cameo, Signed, 12 3/4 In. ... 1073.00
Vase, Trees, Water, Islands, Blue, On Green Ground, Signed, 3 1/2 In. 480.00
Vase, Trumpet, Castle, Boats, Canopy Of Branches, Frosted Pink, Signed, 8 In. 1210.00

DECORATED TUMBLERS have been made by Anchor Hocking, Federal, Hazel Atlas, Libbey, and other companies since the 1930s, when the pyroglaze process of printing was introduced. The barware and other glasses feature drinking jokes, characters, or decorative geometric patterns. Swankyswigs are listed in their own category. Decorated tumblers may also be listed in Advertising, Coca-Cola, Pepsi-Cola, and many other categories.

Tumbler, 2 Seated Black Poodles, Flower, Frosted, 4 3/4 In., 6 Piece 50.00
Tumbler, Casper The Friendly Ghost, Nightmare The Horse, Arby's, 1976, 5 In., Pair 20.00
Tumbler, David Copperfield, Frosted, Federal, 5 1/2 In. 10.00
Tumbler, Flowers, Carriage, House, Magic Milk Shake, Intact Label, Hocking, 5 1/8 In. ... 30.00
Tumbler, Iced Tea, Poodle, Black & White, Red Swirl Pattern, 7 In., 6 Piece 20.00
Tumbler, Li'l Abner Pappy Yokum, Shmoo, Green, 1949, 5 In. 26.00
Tumbler, Li'l Abner, Shmoo, Red, 1949, 5 In. 26.00
Tumbler, Michigan, Mackinac Bridge, Frosted, Hazel Atlas, 7 In. 8.00
Tumbler, Michigan, Water Wonderland, Frosted, Hazel Atlas, 6 3/4 In. 8.00
Tumbler, New Years, Clock At Midnight, Federal, 4 3/4 In. 8.00
Tumbler, Polka Dots, White Ground, Federal, 5 In., 6 Piece 30.00
Tumbler, Poodle, Black & White, Red Swirl Pattern, 5 In., 6 Piece 30.00
Tumbler, Thanksgiving, Campfire, Brown, Yellow, Green, Federal, 4 3/4 In. 9.00
Tumbler, Thanksgiving, Hat & Turkey, Brown, Yellow, Green, Federal, 4 3/4 In. 8.00
Tumbler, Tiny Tim, Frosted, Federal, 5 1/2 In. 10.00

DECOYS are carved or turned wooden copies of birds, fish, or animals. The decoy was placed in the water or propped on the shore to lure flying birds to the pond for hunters. Some decoys are handmade; some are commercial products. Today there is a group of artists making modern decoys for display, not for use in a pond.

American Widgeon, Scenic Painted Base, Signed, Joe Revello, 15 In. 146.00
Black Duck, Canvas, Back Bay, 1930s-1950s, 6 1/2 x 16 In. 149.00
Black Duck, Carved Cork 115.00
Black Duck, Cork, Pine, Corbin Reed, Virginia 70.00
Black Duck, Inlet Head, Carved Eyes, Molded Wing, Augustus Aaron Wilson 800.00
Black Duck, Madison Mitchell, Maryland, c.1970 .... 160.00
Black Duck, Molded Wing, Glass Eyes, Joseph Lincoln, Massachusetts 725.00
Black Duck, Sectional Body, Tail Open, Alfred Gardner 75.00
Black Duck, Signed, Joe Revello, 16 In. 180.00
Black Duck, Solid Body, Glass Eye, Inlet Head, Christie Bros., Michigan, c.1913 .... 550.00
Black Duck, Standard Grade, Mason Factory, Michigan, 1896-1924 .... 90.00
Black Duck, Turned Head, Glass Eye, A.E. Crowell, Massachusetts, c.1915, Oversize 4200.00
Black Duck, White, Yellow Bill, Tack Eyes, Stamped Leoh, 13 1/2 In. 109.00
Black-Bellied Plover, Bull Head, Carved Wing Outlines, c.1890 .... 1700.00
Black-Bellied Plover, Glass Bead Eyes, Split & Hollowed, Reynolds 2750.00
Black-Bellied Plover, Glass Eyes, Carved Wings, Bill, Lou Reineri, Va., 11 1/2 x 11 In. .. 90.00
Blue Heron, Carved, Painted, 1920s, 43 In. 5600.00
Blue-Winged Teal Drake, Cypress Root, c.1920 .... 2100.00
Bluebill, Scenic Base Design, Signed, Joe Revello, 10 1/2 In. 158.00
Bluebill Drake, Madison Mitchell, Maryland 145.00
Bluebill Drake, Outer Banks, North Carolina, 1930s-1950s 140.00

Bluebill Drake, Painted Eyes, Madison Mitchell, Maryland	80.00
Bluebill Drake, Solid Body, Glass Eye, Hays Factory	325.00
Bluebill Drake, Wood, Painted Eyes, Carved Feathered Back, 14 In.	59.00
Bluebill Hen, Carved, Signed, Bill Rose, Mich., 12 1/2 In.	169.00
Bluebill Hen, Chauncey Wheeler, Alexandria Bay, N.Y.	1610.00
Bluebill Hen, Solid Body, Glass Eye, Hays Factory	375.00
Bluebill Hen, Solid Body, Turned Head, Painted Eye, Comb Painted, Paddle Tail	150.00
Brant, Canvas Over Slat Wood, Wood Base, Martin Collins	200.00
Brant, Harve De Grace Style, Madison Mitchell, Maryland	69.00
Brant, Solid Body, Staple Tie Eye, 1930s-1950s	305.00
Bufflehead, Hand Carved, 1930s-1950s, 5 x 10 In.	195.00
Bufflehead, Log Base, Steve Oneshuk, 11 In.	140.00
Bufflehead, North Carolina, 1930s-1950s, 10 1/2 x 5 1/2 In.	110.00
Bufflehead, Scenic Decoration On Bottom, Signed, Joe Revello, 13 1/2 In.	115.00
Bufflehead, Tack Eyes, Flat Lead Weight, 1930s-1950s	165.00
Canada Goose, Canvas Over Slat Wood, Wood Base, Martin Collins, Massachusetts	225.00
Canada Goose, Canvas Over Wire, Wood Head, Painted, 23 1/2 In.	170.00
Canada Goose, Challenge, Solid Body, Glass Eye, Mason Factory, Michigan, 1896-1924 .	1100.00
Canada Goose, Flying, Tack Eyes, Scalloped Wings, Iron Mount, Mass., 20 x 24 In.	3565.00
Canada Goose, Hollow Body, Painted, 24 In.	255.00
Canada Goose, Log Base, Signed, John Kouchinsky, c.1976, 9 In.	135.00
Canada Goose, Miniature, Signed, Dan Brown, Maryland, c.1975, 9 1/2 In.	169.00
Canada Goose, Oakracoke Island, North Carolina, 1930s-1950s	190.00
Canada Goose, Pine, Painted, Laminated, Lead Weight, 19 x 11 3/4 In.	465.00
Canvasback, Bark Base, Signed, George Becker, c.1974, 14 1/4 In.	140.00
Canvasback, Stone Base, Signed, Benes, Miniature, 1978, 5 In.	68.00
Canvasback Drake, Glass Eyes, Solid Body, Mason Factory, Michigan, 1896-1924	290.00
Canvasback Drake, Madison Mitchell, Maryland, 1946	220.00
Canvasback Drake, Painted Eyes, Carved Bill, Eastern Shore	205.00
Canvasback Hen, Tie Eye, Madison Mitchell, Maryland, 1958	182.00
Coot, Canvas Covered, Carved Head, 1930s-1950s	290.00
Coot, Fresh Water, Solid Body, Glass Eye, Gus Nelow, Wisconsin, c.1940	275.00
Coot, Original Weight & Tie Eye, North Carolina, 10 x 7 1/2 In.	320.00
Coot, Ward Foundation World Championship Ribbon, Jacob Alexander, 1975, 11 In. ...	79.00
Curlew, Hollow, Glass Eye, Carved Wings, Raised Wing Tips, Dropped Tail, 16 1/2 In ...	300.00
Curlew, Preening, Glass Eyes, Carved Bill & Wing Feathers, Lou Reineri, Virginia	215.00
Curlew, Signed, Herb Daisy Jr., Chincoteague, Va.	130.00
Dove, Glass Eyes, Drift Wood Base, Lou Reineri, Virginia, 10 1/2 x 11 In.	165.00
Duck, Mallard Hen, Wood, Metal Eyes, Illinois, 16 In.	230.00
Duck, Wood, Glass Eyes, William Pratt, Joliet, Ill., 16 1/2 In.	120.00
Duck, Wood, Mississippi River, 1940-1950s, 11 In.	80.00
Fish, Aluminum Fins, Original Package, Bear Creek, 9 1/2 In.	90.00
Fish, Brook Trout, Ernie Peterson, McMillan, Michigan, 8 In.	11.00
Fish, Brown Trout, Glass Eyes, Ernie Peterson, McMillan, Michigan, 9 In.	55.00
Fish, Carved, Painted, Metal Fins, Curved Tale, Red, Brown, Yellow, 7 In.	275.00
Fish, Musky, Perch Scales, Split Metal Tail, Glass Eyes, Heddon, 6 In.	250.00
Fish, Perch Scales, Split Metal Tail, Glass Eyes, Heddon, 5 1/4 In.	1375.00
Fish, Perch, Ross Allen Sr., Wisconsin, c.1970s, 7 1/2 In.	550.00
Fish, Perch, Russ Hurlburt, Newberry, Michigan, 1960s, 8 In.	250.00
Fish, Perch, Vernon Baggs Sr., Kalkaska, Michigan, 10 In.	45.00
Fish, Pike, Wood, Type I, Bear Creak Bait Co., Kaleva, Michigan, c.1947	175.00
Fish, Rainbow Trout, John Eddy, Cheboygan, Michigan, 7 1/2 In.	33.00
Fish, Salmon, Glass Eyes, Metal Fins, Carl Christiansen, Dafter, Mich., 20 In.	120.00
Fish, Sturgeon, Glass Eyes, Wire, Metal, Carl Christiansen, Dafter, Mich., 25 In.	415.00
Frog, Green, Yellow, Brown, Leather Feet, No. 2, Ralph Hocker, 9 1/2 In.	95.00
Frog, Jointed Legs, John Fairfield, 4 3/4 In.	140.00
Goldeneye Drake, Cork Body, Pine Head & Keel, Irving Torrey	40.00
Goldeneye Drake, Solid Body, Painted Eye, John Smith, Nova Scotia	225.00
Goldeneye Drake, Tack Eyes, Standard Grade, Mason Factory, Michigan.	290.00
Goose, Carved, Painted, Applied Nails As Feet, 12 1/2 x 33 1/2 In.	90.00
Goose, Laminated Pine, Painted, Glass Eyes, Incised Tail Feathers, 17 1/2 x 12 In.	110.00
Greater Golden Plover, Carved Bill, Nostrils, Glass Eyes, Lou Reineri, Va., 7 1/2 x 4 In. .	55.00
Greater Golden Plover, Carved, Breeding Plumage, Painted Eyes, c.1890	1000.00

Greater Golden Plover, Split Tail, Breeding Plumage, Joseph Lincoln, Mass., c.1890	3500.00
Green Heron, Carved, Shaped Wood Base, Driftwood Perch, Signed, Pete Miciche, 7 In. .	115.00
Green-Winged Teal, George Frederick	3600.00
Green-Winged Teal, Shaped Board, Signed, John Sawyer, 1974	225.00
Green-Winged Teal Hen, Turned Head, Molded Wings, Split Tail, Painted Eyes, c.1910 . .	1000.00
Indigo Bunting, Turned Head, Glass Eye, Painted Base	425.00
Laughing Gull, Glass Eyes, Carved Wooden Base, 1/4 Size	375.00
Lesser Yellowlegs, Glass Eyes, Lou Reineri, Virginia, 9 x 8 In.	41.00
Long-Billed Curlew, Tack Eyes, 2 Knots, Herbert Randall	75.00
Long-Billed Curlew, Turned Head, Tack Eyes, Carved Wing, Herbert Randall	400.00
Loon, U.S. National Decoy Show Ribbon, Signed, Bob Biddle, c.1975, 28 In.	730.00
Mallard, Signed, Miles Hancock, Chincoteague, Va., Miniature, 6 1/4 In.	115.00
Mallard, Tack Eye, Detroit Grade, Mason Factory, Michigan, 1896-1924	350.00
Mallard Drake, Cypress Root Wood, Michael Aguzin, c.1935	325.00
Mallard Drake, Dodge Factory, Detroit, Mich., 1884-1894, 15 In.	120.00
Mallard Drake, Glass Eye, Carved Wing Outline, Omar Perez, c.1900	500.00
Mallard Drake, Glass Eyes, Mississippi River, 16 In.	35.00
Mallard Drake, Painted Eyes, Mason Factory, Michigan, 1896-1924	430.00
Mallard Drake, Signed, Walter Watson, c.1974, 17 1/2 In.	236.00
Mallard Drake, Tucked Head, Glass Eyes, Carved Wing, J. McLoughlin	400.00
Mallard Drake, Wood, Carved, Green Head, Bill, Blue, White Striped Wings, 17 1/2 In. . .	90.00
Mallard Drake & Hen, Sleeping, Canvas Over Cork, Herter Co., Pair	250.00
Mallard Drake & Hen, Wood Base, Gravel, Greg Daisy, Miniature, 4 1/4 In., Pair	190.00
Mallard Hen, Tack Eye, Antonaise St. Germain, c.1920	2000.00
Mallard Hen, Turned Head, Glass Eye, Heart Shape Wing, Feather Paint, J.C. Young, 1940	1950.00
Mallard Hen, Wood, Glass Eyes, Herter Body & Weight, 18 In.	39.00
Merganser, Alrin Meeken, Harper Island	880.00
Merganser, Hurley Conklin, New Jersey, 18 In.	590.00
Merganser, Painted, Carved, Applied Glass Eyes, Shaped Bill, 9 x 20 In.	110.00
Merganser, Silhouette Style, Rig, Centerville, Mass.	69.00
Merganser Drake, Carved Wing, Tail, Crest, Oversize	100.00
Oldsquaw Drake, Painted, Nova Scotia	200.00
Pheasant, Lady Amherst, Driftwood Base, Harold N. Gibbs	600.00
Pintail Drake, Byron Bruffee, Middleboro, Mass.	300.00
Pintail Drake, Cypress Wood, William Howard, c.1910	1000.00
Pintail Drake, Glass Eyes, Leopold Koehler, Illinois, c.1920	150.00
Pintail Drake, Signed, Ronald C. Laber, Pasadena, Md., 1972	110.00
Pintail Hen, Carved Body & Bill, Glass Eyes, Flat Applied Bottom	182.00
Prairie Chicken Hen, Carved Wood, Brown & Mustard Paint, 20 In.	353.00
Ptarmigan, Resting, Eclipse Plumage, Harold N. Gibbs	600.00
Red-Breasted Merganser Hen, Benjamin D. Smith, Massachusetts	3000.00
Redhead, Carved Bill, Tack Eyes, Elizbeth City Cast Steel Weight, 1930s-1950s	248.00
Redhead, Sink Box Type, No Weights, Early 1900s	212.00
Redhead Drake, Hollow, Carved, Harry Shourds, New Jersey, c.1910	300.00
Redhead Drake, Hollow, Glass Eyes, Comb, Chris Smith, Michigan	650.00
Redhead Drake, Molded Wings, Painted Eyes, James Look, c.1900	1200.00
Redhead Drake, Painted, C.W. Stevens Company, Weedsport, N.Y.	345.00
Redhead Drake, Signed, Don Briddell, Dallastown, Penn., 1976, 13 In.	236.00
Redhead Drake, Sleeper, Solid Body, Dogbone Weight, Fulcher, N.C., 1930-1950	220.00
Ruddy Duck, Sanding, Turned Head, Homer Lawrence, Connecticut, c.1930-1940	2750.00
Ruddy Duck, Ward Foundation, World Championship Ribbon, Joe Revello, c.1976, 11 In.	169.00
Sandhill Crane, Driftwood Base, Miniature, Harold N. Gibbs	500.00
Surf Scoter, Hollow Carved, Glass Eye, Carved Wing & Tail, Marty Hanson, Minn.	625.00
Swan, Signed, Paul Shaubach, 1976, 1/4 Size	83.00
White-Winged Scoter, Breast Preening, Carved Eyes, Molded Wings, A.A. Wilson, 1900 .	7500.00
White-Winged Scoter, Glass Eyes, Cork Body, Wood, America, 6 x 7 3/4 x 17 1/2 In. . . .	881.00
Widgeon Hen, Orange Glass Eyes, Brown, Tan, New Jersey, c.1890, 15 In.	495.00
Willet, Aluminum Billed, Tack Eyes, E.B. Smith	1500.00
Wood Duck, Signed Don Briddell, Dallastown, Pa., c.1974, 13 In.	366.00
Wood Duck Drake, Standing, Carved, A.E. Crowell, Massachusetts	425.00
Woodcock, Resting, Harold N. Gibbs	800.00
Yellowlegs, Glass Eyes, Carved Bill, Lou Reineri, Virginia, 13 1/2 x 10 1/2 In.	72.00
Yellowlegs, Hollow, Painted Eyes, c.1890-1910	2250.00

DEDHAM Pottery was started in 1895. Chelsea Keramic Art Works was established in 1872 in Chelsea, Massachusetts, by members of the Robertson family. The factory closed in 1889 and was reorganized as the Chelsea Pottery U.S. in 1891. The firm used the marks *CKAW* and *CPUS*. It became the Dedham Pottery of Dedham, Massachusetts. The factory closed in 1943. It was famous for its crackleware dishes, which picture blue outlines of animals, flowers, and other natural motifs.

Birds In Potted Orange Tree, Plate, 10 In.	385.00
Birds In Potted Orange Tree, Plate, Blue Stamp, 6 In.	375.00
Birds In Potted Orange Tree, Plate, Relief, Impressed Rabbit, 6 In.	415.00
Boot, Figural, Toothpick, Blue Laces, 2 1/2 x 2 In.	468.00
Butter Pat, Star Shape, Reticulated Edges, Embossed Blue Rim, 1931, 3 1/4 In.	1100.00
Butterfly, Cup & Saucer	300.00
Butterfly, Plate, Dots, Stripes, 6 1/4 In.	410.00
Clover, Plate, 10 In.	1100.00
Crab, Plate, 8 In.	661.00
Day Lily, Plate, Cobalt Blue Center Ground, 6 In.	935.00
Dolphin, Plate, CPUS, 8 1/2 In.	605.00
Double Turtle, Plate, 6 In.	550.00
Duck, Creamer, Looped Handle, 3 In.	385.00
Duck, Cup & Saucer	275.00
Duck, Plate, 5-Sided, Early 1900s, 7 1/8 In.	205.00
Duck, Tufted, Plate, 8 1/2 In.	275.00
Elephant, Bowl, No. 5, 4 1/4 In.	660.00
Elephant, Creamer, 2 1/4 x 5 1/2 In.	770.00
Elephant, Cup & Saucer	660.00
Elephant, Mustard Jar, Flat Cover, 3 In.	1760.00
Elephant, Plate, Deep Blue Ground, Impressed Rabbit, 6 1/4 In.	825.00
Grape, Plate, Blue Stamp, Signed, 8 1/4 In.	345.00
Grape, Plate, Grape Clusters Extend Into Center, M. Davenport, 10 In.	220.00
Horse Chestnut, Plate, 6 In.	60.00
Horse Chestnut, Plate, 10 In.	250.00
Horse Chestnut, Plate, Raised Design, 6 In.	165.00
Horse Chestnut, Tazza, H. Robertson, Impressed Rabbits, 7 In.	1540.00
Iris, Coaster, 4 In.	360.00
Magnolia, Plate, 2 Impressed Rabbits, 7 1/2 In.	165.00
Magnolia, Plate, 10 In.	220.00
Moth, Plate, Alternating Moths & Moons, Impressed Rabbit, 8 3/4 In.	715.00
Mushroom, Plate, Maude Davenport, 6 In.	880.00
Mushroom, Plate, Spotted & Striped Mushrooms, Impressed Rabbit, 8 1/4 In.	525.00
Pineapple, Plate, Flowers, CPUS, 10 1/4 In.	330.00
Polar Bear, Plate, Snow Covered Mountains, 9 3/4 In.	495.00
Pond Lily, Plate, 8 1/2 In.	195.00
Pond Lily, Plate, Blue, Ivory, 10 In.	200.00
Pond Lily, Plate, Blue, White, Impressed Mark, 10 In.	145.00
Pond Lily, Plate, Railed Leaves, Pools Of Water, Impressed Rabbit, 10 In.	248.00
Poppy, Dish, 5-Sided, 7 1/2 In.	935.00
Poppy, Plate, Center Poppy, Jagged Leaf, Blue Ground, Buds Along Border, 8 1/2 In.	195.00
Rabbit, Bowl, 4 1/2 In.	220.00
Rabbit, Bowl, 4 3/4 In.	127.00
Rabbit, Bowl, 5 1/2 In.	196.00
Rabbit, Bowl, Cover, Blue, Gray Crackle Glaze, Wide Flattened Rim, Stamped, 9 In.	440.00
Rabbit, Candleholder, Pair	325.00
Rabbit, Coffeepot, Bell Shape Cover, Square Handle, 8 3/4 In.	1100.00
Rabbit, Creamer, 3 1/2 In.	240.00
Rabbit, Cup & Saucer	175.00 to 185.00
Rabbit, Humidor, Bulbous, Rolled Mouth, Dome Cover, Knob Finial, 6 1/2 In.	1210.00
Rabbit, Knife Rest, Elongated Ears, Cobalt Blue Lines, 2 3/4 x 3 3/4 In.	525.00
Rabbit, Marmalade Jar, Cover, Globe Shape, 5 In.	605.00
Rabbit, Paperweight, 3 In.	1045.00
Rabbit, Pitcher, Bulbous Base, 5 1/4 x 4 1/2 In.	385.00
Rabbit, Pitcher, Floral Border, Flared Neck, Impressed Rabbit, 8 1/2 In.	1100.00
Rabbit, Pitcher, Milk, 4 1/2 In.	130.00

Rabbit, Plate & Bowl, 10 In., 5 x 2 1/2 In., 2 Piece 290.00
Rabbit, Plate, 6 In. 90.00
Rabbit, Plate, 7 1/2 In. 175.00
Rabbit, Plate, 8 1/2 In. ....127.00 to 175.00
Rabbit, Plate, 9 1/2 In. 165.00
Rabbit, Plate, Signed, Maude Davenport, 8 1/2 In. 290.00
Rabbit, Plate, Square Mark, 8 1/2 In., 4 Piece 375.00
Rabbit, Plate, Stamped, 10 In. 295.00
Rabbit, Platter, Oval, 12 1/4 In. 825.00
Rabbit, Relish, 8 In. 440.00
Rabbit, Stein, Signed Maude Davenport, Impressed Rabbit, 4 In. 495.00
Rabbit, Sugar, Cover, 4 1/2 In. 300.00
Seafaring, Plate, Lobster, Crab, Seaweed, Waves, 8 1/2 In., Pair 1430.00
Snowtree, Plate, 2 Impressed Rabbits, 8 1/4 In. 250.00
Swan, Cup & Saucer 430.00
Swan, Marmalade Jar, Cover, Globe Shape, 5 x 4 1/4 In. 715.00
Swan, Plate, Impressed Rabbit, 8 1/2 In. 385.00
Tapestry Lion, Plate, Raised Lions, Moon Lit Sky, Impressed Rabbit, 8 1/2 In. 1210.00
Turkey, Plate, Early 1900s, 9 5/8 In. 175.00
Turkey, Plate, Impressed Rabbit, 10 In. 275.00
Vase, Applied Rose Branch, Blue-Gray Glaze, J. Day, Chelsea Keramic, 6 3/4 In. 805.00
Vase, Freehand Design, Japanesque Manner, 6 3/4 In. 2200.00
Vase, Iridescent Red High Glaze, Streaks, H. Robertson, 6 1/2 In. 1650.00
Vase, Mottled Green Glaze, Marked, H.C. Robertson, 8 1/2 In. 920.00
Vase, Volcanic, Frothy Chocolate, Indigo, Green, Glaze, Bulbous, Incised, 7 x 3 3/4 In. .. 920.00
Wild Rose, Plate, Rose Spray, Leaves, Buds, H. Robertson, 9 3/4 In. 2970.00

DEGUE is a signature acid-etched on pieces of French glass made in the early 1900s. Cameo, mold blown, and smooth glass with contrasting colored rims are the types most often found.

Chandelier, Bronze, Frosted Glass, 3-Part Clamshell, Pendant Shades, 22 x 17 In. 1315.00
Vase, Cobalt Leaves, On Mottled Pink Ground, Chalice Shape, Signed, 11 1/4 x 4 1/4 In. .. 1035.00
Vase, Geometric Cut Design, Green, Brown, Yellow Ground, Art Deco, 18 1/4 In. 1495.00
Vase, Purple & Red Stylized Flowers, Beige Ground, Shouldered, Cameo, 9 3/4 In. 660.00
Vase, Water Buffalo, Frosted Amber Ground, Cobalt Ruffled Edge, Signed, 8 3/4 In. 880.00

DELATTE glass is a French cameo glass made by Andre Delatte. It was first made in Nancy, France, in 1921. Lighting fixtures and opaque glassware in imitation of Bohemian opaline were made. There were many French cameo glass makers, so be sure to look in other appropriate categories.

Vase, Flowers, Burgundy, Frosted Pink, Cylindrical, Signed, 8 In. 440.00
Vase, Grape Vine, Lavender, Yellow Ground, 5 In. 550.00
Vase, Intaglio Roses, Yellow, Handles, Flat Sided, c.1920, 6 3/4 In. 560.00
Vase, Pink Roses, Purple Leaves, Frosted, Cream, Pink, Yellow, Ground, Signed, 7 1/2 In. 605.00
Vase, Purple Honeysuckle Vines, Yellow Ground, Egg Shape, Signed, 7 1/2 In. 468.00
Vase, Tall Trees, Perched Owl, Hillside Village, Royal Blue, Cameo, 9 In. 1232.00

DELDARE, see Buffalo Pottery Deldare.

DELFT is a tin-glazed pottery that has been made since the seventeenth century. Delft was made in England in the eighteenth century. It is decorated with blue on white or with colored decorations. Most of the pieces sold today were made after 1891, and the name *Holland* usually appears with the Delft factory marks. The word *delft* also appears on twentieth-century pottery from Asia and Germany.

Barber's Bowl, Blue & White, 18th Century 595.00
Bowl, Children, Skating, Sledding, Building, Light & Dark Plum, Footed, 5 x 10 In. 1035.00
Bowl, Insects, Baskets Of Flowers, Diaper Ground, Blue Underglaze, 3 In. 253.00
Chamber Pot, White, Dutch, 17th Century 395.00
Chandelier, Blue On White, Flowers, Drip Pans, Peter Fitting, 26 x 26 1/2 In. 165.00
Charger, Fruit Vase, Bird, Fruit Border, Blue, White, Tin Glaze, Earthenware, 1700s, 13 In. 978.00
Charger, Oriental Design, 10 1/2 In. 660.00

Charger, Oriental Pot Center, Blue Flowers, Alternating Bands, Gold, Yellow, 14 In. 489.00
Charger, Polychrome, Chinoiserie Fishing Scene, c.1765, 12 In. 1750.00
Charger, War Bonnet, 12 In. 440.00
Charger, War Bonnet, 18th Century, 13 3/4 In. 660.00
Figurine, Cow, Flowers, Painted, 7 In., Pair 1130.00
Figurine, Cow, Gilt Traces, Hand Painted, Red, Green, Blue, Gilt Horns, 5 1/4 In. 220.00
Figurine, Cow, Reclining, Blue & White, Flowers On Back, Circlet On Neck, 1900s, 9 In. 235.00
Plaque, Genre Scene, 3 Figures, Dutch Interior, N. Artz, 1900s, 14 1/8 x 8 7/8 In. 150.00
Plaque, Quatrefoil Shape, Earthenware, Landscape, c.1850, 15 1/2 x 13 In. 150.00
Plate, Blue Dash, Blue & White, Pear Center, Holland, c.1640 . . . . 695.00
Plate, Blue Oriental Design, House Center, Floral Border, Hand Painted, 9 In. 315.00
Plate, Fenced Garden, Rocks, Flowers, Trees, England, 9 In., Pair 690.00
Plate, Flower Basket, Flower & Leaf Spray, K, 8 5/8 In., Pair 635.00
Plate, Oriental Figure, Seated On Wall, Tin Glaze, Yellow Rim, 8 7/8 In. 69.00
Plate, Polychrome, Chinese Man, England, c.1760, 10 1/2 In. 975.00
Plate, Queen Mary Of England, March 15, 1695 . . . . 3200.00
Plate, Stylized Butterflies, Central Feather, Urn, Polychrome Enamels, Marked, 9 1/8 In. . 200.00
Serving Dish, Tin Glaze, Scrollwork, Satyr Mask, Lion Head Handles, 10 x 15 x 3 In. . . . 165.00
Tankard, Pear Form, Pewter Lid, 8 In. 550.00
Tankard, White, Tin Glaze, Blue, Green, Purple, Yellow Flower Basket, Pewter Lid, 9 In. 360.00
Tile, 2 Flying Ducks, Crystalline Matte Glaze, 8 3/4 x 4 3/4 In. 345.00
Tile, 2 Owls, Brown, White, Ruins Ground, De Porceleyne Fles, Stamped, TL, 4 3/4 x 9 In. 546.00
Tile, 2 Owls, On Stone Wall, Arch, De Porceleyne Fles, 4 3/4 x 9 In. 690.00
Tile, 2 Sailboats, Sepia Painted, Marked, Utrecht, Holland, Arts & Crafts Frame, 5 3/4 In. 290.00
Tile, Bakery Zeeland, 50th Anniversary, Bakery Scene, 1950, 11 3/8 x 7 7/8 In. 316.00
Tile, Biblical Figural Scene, Fruitwood Frame, c.1790, 21 Piece 2185.00
Tile, Biblical Scenes, Blue & White, Square, c.1750, 4 1/2 In., Pair 290.00
Tile, Casting Joseph Into Pit, Bible Verse, Blue & White, England, c.1725, 5 In. 115.00
Tile, Cat, Brown, Book, White Wall, Raised Outline, De Porceleyne Fles, 8 3/4 x 4 3/4 In. 1285.00
Tile, Dutch Man, Dock, Marken, Crystalline Glaze, 5 7/8 x 4 In. 105.00
Tile, Dutch Woman, Sea, Zeeland, Crystalline Matte Glaze, 5 3/4 x 3 7/8 In. 105.00
Tile, Flying Duck, Boat, Windmill, Crystalline Matte Glaze, 8 3/4 x 4 3/4 In. 345.00
Tile, Goose, Marsh, Multicolored Raised Outline, De Porceleyne Fles, 4 1/4 x 12 1/2 In. . . 520.00
Tile, Ibis, Oasis, Pyramids, Green Glaze Border, De Porceleyne Fles, 13 1/2 x 5 In., Pair . 690.00
Tile, Man, Woman, Pastoral Landscape, Blue, White, Pewter Mounts, Square, 1700s, 5 In. 69.00
Tile, Parrot, Facing Left, Crystalline Matte Glaze, 12 7/8 x 4 5/8 In. 375.00
Tile, Parrot, Facing Right, Crystalline Matte Glaze, 12 3/4 x 4 5/8 In. 635.00
Tile, Peacock, Brick Wall Ground, De Porceleyne Fles, Stamped Bottle, TL, 13 x 4 3/4 In. 430.00
Tile, Peacock, Carved, Colorful, Arts & Crafts Oak Frame, Impressed Mark, 17 x 5 In. . . . 865.00
Tile, Peacock, Facing Left, Crystalline Matte Glaze, 12 7/8 x 4 3/4 In. 345.00
Tile, Peacock, Multicolored, White Crystalline Ground, De Porceleyne Fles, 4 3/4 x 17 In. 2415.00
Tile, Pelican, Feeding Young, Outline, Blue Ground, De Porceleyne Fles, 13 1/2 x 5 In. . . 1725.00
Tile, Rabbit, Brown, Hopping, Trees, Raised Outline, De Porceleyne Fles, 4 1/4 x 8 1/4 In. 1095.00
Tile, Rooster, White, Crystalline Matte Glaze, 9 x 4 7/8 In. 489.00
Tile, Rooster, White, Indigo Ground, Raised Outline, De Porceleyne Fles, 8 1/4 x 4 1/4 In. 430.00
Tile, Tiger, Leaping, Outline, Multicolored, Border, De Porceleyne Fles, 5 1/4 x 13 1/2 In. 1285.00
Tile, Tulips, Windmill, Crystalline Matte Glaze, 8 3/4 x 4 In. 210.00
Tile, Viking Ship, Seahorse Prow, Outline, Square, De Porceleyne Fles, Frame, 8 In. 520.00
Tile, Wading Bird, Pyramids, Crystalline Matte Glaze, 12 1/4 x 4 1/8 In. 345.00
Tile, Windmill, Sailboat, House, Crystalline Matte Glaze, 8 3/4 x 4 3/4 In. 290.00
Vase, Double Gourd, Flowers, Blue, White, Paneled Neck, Foot, England, c.1735, 11 In. . 1095.00
Vase, Figures, Waterside Windmill, Satyr Handles, Dolphins Base, Mark, c.1890, 20 In. . . 980.00
Vase, Man Playing Bagpipes, Blue, 9 1/4 In. 220.00

DENTAL cabinets, chairs, equipment, and other related items are listed here. Other objects may be found in the Medical category.

Cabinet, Burled Walnut, Roll Top, Mirror, 69 x 29 x 16 1/2 In. 5750.00
Cabinet, Wood, Beveled Glass Mirror, Roll Top, Upper Door, c.1890, 28 x 69 In. 2145.00
Cabinet, Wood, Tools, 45 In. 593.00
Chisel, Ivory Handle, 1700s, 2 3/4 In. 258.00
Compressor, For Dental Tools, Ritter Dental Mfg., Co., N.Y. 200.00
Medical Box, Hardwood, Ivory Handle, Contents, c.1870s, 11 3/4 x 6 1/4 x 7 In. 1006.00

DEPRESSION GLASS was an inexpensive glass manufactured in large quantities during the 1920s and early 1930s. It was made in many colors and patterns by dozens of factories in the United States. Most patterns were also made in clear glass, which the factories called *crystal*. If no color is listed here, it is clear. The name *Depression glass* is a modern one. For more descriptions, history, pictures, and prices of Depression glass, see the book *Kovels' Depression Glass & Dinnerware Price List*.

Adam, Ashtray, Pink, 4 1/2 In.	35.00
Adam, Bowl, Cover, Pink, 9 In.	55.00
Adam, Bowl, Green, Oval, 10 In.	52.00
Adam, Butter, Cover, Pink, Square, 6 In.	130.00
Adam, Candlestick, Pink, 4 In., Pair	125.00
Adam, Creamer, Pink	30.00
Adam, Grill Plate, Green, 9 In.	30.00
Adam, Plate, Salad, Pink, 7 3/4 In.	25.00
Adam, Platter, Pink, 11 3/4 In.	45.00
Adam, Relish, Sections, Pink, 8 In.	28.00
Adam, Saltshaker, Pink, Footed, 4 In.	55.00
Adam, Saucer, Green, Square, 6 In.	6.00
Adam, Sherbet, Green, 3 In.	37.50
Adam, Tumbler, Iced Tea, Green, Footed, 5 1/2 In.	50.00
American Pioneer, Bowl, Pink, Handles, 9 In.	60.00
American Pioneer, Cup & Saucer, Green	15.00
American Pioneer, Cup & Saucer, Pink	29.00
American Pioneer, Plate, Green, 8 In.	15.00
American Sweetheart, Creamer, Monax	12.00
American Sweetheart, Cup & Saucer, Monax	15.00
American Sweetheart, Plate, Dinner, Monax, 10 1/4 In.	30.00
American Sweetheart, Plate, Salad, Monax, 8 In.	11.00
American Sweetheart, Tumbler, Pink, 10 Oz., 4 3/4 In.	220.00
Anniversary, Plate, Dinner, 10 In.	6.00
Anniversary, Plate, Dinner, Pink, 10 In.	6.00
Anniversary, Soup, Dish, Pink, 7 3/8 In.	6.00
Anniversary, Vase, Pink, 6 1/2 In.	43.00
Anniversary, Wine, Pink, 2 1/2 Oz., 4 1/8 In.	26.00
Apple Blossom pattern is listed here as Dogwood.	
Aunt Polly, Bowl, Iridescent, Handle, 5 1/2 In.	14.00
Aunt Polly, Pitcher, Blue, 48 Oz., 8 In.	235.00
Aurora, Bowl, Cereal, Cobalt Blue, 5 3/8 In.	17.00 to 19.00
Aurora, Bowl, Cereal, Pink, 5 3/8 In.	17.00
Aurora, Cup, Cobalt Blue	18.00
Aurora, Cup, Pink	15.00
Aurora, Plate, Cobalt Blue, 6 1/2 In.	12.50 to 16.00
Aurora, Sherbet, Cobalt Blue	30.00
Aurora, Tumbler, Cobalt, 10 Oz., 4 3/4 In.	15.00
Avocado, Bowl, Green, Footed, 6 In.	35.00
Avocado, Bowl, Green, Oval, Handle, 7 In.	35.00
Avocado, Bowl, Salad, 7 1/2 In.	15.00 to 25.00
Ballerina pattern is listed here as Cameo.	
Banded Rib pattern is listed here as Coronation.	
Banded Rings pattern is listed here as Ring.	
Basket pattern is listed here as No. 615.	
Block pattern is listed here as Block Optic.	
Block Optic, Cup, Green	8.00
Bouquet & Lattice pattern is listed here as Normandie.	
Bowknot, Tumbler, Green, Flared, 10 Oz., 5 In.	27.00
Bubble, Berry Bowl, Footed, 8 3/8 In.	10.00
Bubble, Berry Bowl, Forest Green, 8 3/8 In.	10.00
Bubble, Candleholder, 3 x 4 3/4 In.	11.00
Bubble, Candleholder, Pair	11.00
Bubble, Creamer, Milk White	15.00
Bubble, Sherbet, 3 1/2 In.	10.00

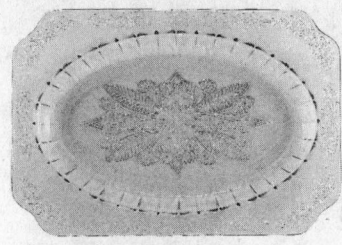

Depression
Glass, Adam

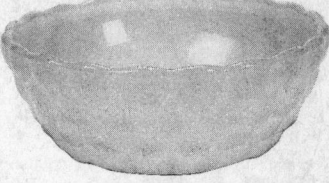

Depression Glass, Bubble

Bubble, Sugar, Milk White 15.00
Bubble, Tumbler, Iced Tea, Royal Ruby, 12 Oz., 4 1/2 In. 15.00
Bullseye pattern is listed here as Bubble.
Buttons & Bows pattern is listed here as Holiday.
Cabbage Rose pattern is listed here as Sharon.
Cameo, Console, 3-Footed, Pink, 11 In. 95.00
Cameo, Creamer, Yellow 25.00
Cameo, Cup, Green 22.00
Cameo, Plate, Dinner, Yellow, 9 1/2 In. ....15.00 to 18.00
Cameo, Platter, Green, Handles, 10 1/2 In. 35.00
Cameo, Tumbler, Green, Footed, 9 Oz., 5 In. 30.00
Cameo, Vase, Green, 8 In. 65.00
Candlewick pattern is listed in the Imperial Glass category.
Capri, Ashtray, Blue, 3 Sides, 6 7/8 In. 10.00
Capri Blue, Ashtray, 3 Sides, 6 7/8 In. 10.00
Capri Blue, Bowl, Colony Square, Oval, 7 3/4 In. 10.00
Capri Blue, Plate, Dinner, 9 7/8 In. 8.00
Capri Blue, Snack Set, Seashell, Box, 8 Piece 40.00
Caprice pattern is included in the Cambridge Glass category.
Charm, Plate, Luncheon, Forest Green, Square, 8 1/2 In. 10.00
Charm, Plate, Luncheon, Royal Ruby, 8 3/8 In. 15.00
Cherry Blossom, Berry Bowl, Pink, 8 1/2 In. ....45.00 to 56.00
Cherry Blossom, Bowl, Cereal, Green, 6 In. 39.00
Cherry Blossom, Bowl, Fruit, Pink, 3-Footed, 10 1/2 In. ....100.00 to 115.00
Cherry Blossom, Butter, Cover, Pink 105.00
Cherry Blossom, Cake Plate, Pink, 3-Footed, 10 1/4 In. 45.00
Cherry Blossom, Child's Set, Pink, 14 Piece 310.00
Cherry Blossom, Coaster, Green 15.00
Cherry Blossom, Creamer, Child's, 3 1/4 In. 40.00
Cherry Blossom, Cup & Saucer, Delphite, Child's 60.00
Cherry Blossom, Cup & Saucer, Pink 30.00
Cherry Blossom, Cup, Green 25.00
Cherry Blossom, Plate, Delphite, Child's, 6 In. 15.00
Cherry Blossom, Plate, Dinner, 9 In. 30.00
Cherry Blossom, Platter, Green, Oval, 11 In. 10.00
Cherry Blossom, Platter, Oval, 11 In. 50.00
Cherry Blossom, Saucer, Green 5.00
Cherry Blossom, Saucer, Pink 7.00
Cherry Blossom, Sugar, Cover, Green 48.00
Chevron, Creamer, Cobalt Blue, 3 In. 15.00
Cloverleaf, Cup & Saucer 15.00
Cloverleaf, Cup & Saucer, Green 11.00
Cloverleaf, Plate, Luncheon, Black, 8 In. 15.00
Cloverleaf, Salt & Pepper, Black 125.00
Cloverleaf, Saltshaker, Black 60.00
Cloverleaf, Saltshaker, Green 11.00
Cloverleaf, Sherbet, Green, 3 In. 6.00
Cloverleaf, Sugar, Green 10.00
Colonial Block, Bowl, Green, 4 In. 11.00
Colonial Block, Butter, Cover ....29.00 to 48.00
Colonial Block, Butter, Cover Only, Green 35.00

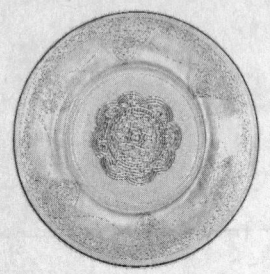

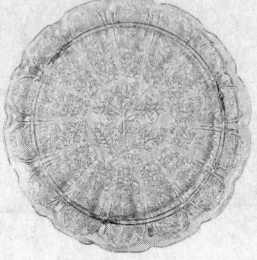

Depression Glass,
Cameo

Depression Glass,
Cherry Blossom

Depression Glass,
Chevron

Colonial Block, Candy Jar, Cover Only, Green 28.00
Colonial Block, Goblet, Green, 5 3/4 In. 13.00
Colonial Block, Goblet, Pink, 5 3/4 In. 15.50
Colonial Block, Sugar, Cover Only 17.00
Colonial Block, Sugar, Cover, Pink 29.00
Colonial Fluted, Cup, Green 10.00
Columbia, Bowl, Cereal, 5 In. 17.00
Columbia, Bowl, Ruffled Edge, 10 1/2 In. 11.00
Columbia, Butter, Cover 10.00
Columbia, Cup & Saucer 10.00
Columbia, Platter, 11 In. 9.00
Columbia, Snack Set, 2 Piece 10.00
Columbia, Soup, Dish, 8 In. 20.00
Constellation, Bowl, Salad, 10 1/2 In. 21.00
Coronation, Berry Bowl, Royal Ruby, Handles, 4 1/4 In. 8.25
Criss Cross, Butter, Cover Only, Cobalt, 1 Lb. 30.00
Criss Cross, Butter, Cover Only, Green, Rectangular, 1/4 Lb. ....27.00 to 45.00
Criss Cross, Refrigerator Dish, Cover, Green, 4 x 8 In. 45.00
Cube pattern is listed here as Cubist.
Cubist, Bowl, Gold Trim, 4 1/2 In. 6.00
Cubist, Candy Dish, Cover, Green, 6 1/4 In. 55.00
Cubist, Pitcher, Pink, 45 Oz., 8 3/4 In. ....275.00 to 350.00
Cubist, Powder Jar, Cover, Pink, Footed, 5 In. ....38.00 to 40.00
Cubist, Saucer, Green 4.00
Cubist, Sugar & Creamer, 2 3/8 In. 6.00
Cubist, Sugar & Creamer, White, 2 3/8 In. 6.00
Cubist, Tumbler, Pink, 9 Oz., 4 In. 85.00
Daisy pattern is listed here as No. 620.
Dancing Girl pattern is listed here as Cameo.
Dewdrop, Cup 4.00
Diamond pattern is listed here as Miss America.
Diamond Point, Candy Dish, Footed, 4 1/2 In. 20.00
Diamond Point, Candy Jar, Cover, 15 1/2 In. ....15.00 to 25.00
Diamond Point, Candy Jar, Cover, Amber, 15 1/2 In. 30.00
Diamond Point, Compote, 7 1/4 In. 15.00
Diamond Point, Vase, Footed, 8 In. 12.00
Diana, Bowl, Cereal, Pink, 5 In. 10.00
Diana, Bowl, Fruit, Amber, 11 In. ....18.00 to 28.00
Diana, Bowl, Scalloped Edge, 12 In. 16.00
Diana, Cup & Saucer, After Dinner 13.00
Diana, Cup & Saucer, Amber 9.00
Diana, Cup, After Dinner 8.00
Diana, Plate, Pink, 9 1/2 In. 20.00
Diana, Platter, Amber, 12 In. 15.00
Diana, Sandwich Server, Amber, 11 3/4 In. 8.00
Dogwood, Berry Bowl, Pink, 8 1/2 In. 75.00
Dogwood, Cup & Saucer, Pink, Thin 35.00

Dogwood, Plate, Green, 8 In. 12.00
Dogwood, Salver, Monax, 12 In. 30.00
Dogwood, Sugar & Creamer, Pink, Thick 38.00
Doric, Bowl, Pink, Oval, 9 In. . . . . 42.00 to 47.00
Doric, Candy Jar, Cover, Pink 48.00
Doric, Plate, Sherbet, Green, 6 In. . . . . 16.00 to 17.00
Doric, Saltshaker, Green 60.00
Doric, Saucer, Pink, 5 5/8 In. 4.00
Doric & Pansy, Cup & Saucer, Ultramarine 35.00
Doric & Pansy, Cup, Ultramarine 22.00
Doric & Pansy, Plate, Sherbet, Pink, 6 In. 8.00
Doric & Pansy, Saucer 3.00
Doric & Pansy, Sugar & Creamer 250.00
Doric & Pansy, Sugar, Pink, Child's 38.00
Early American Prescut, Ashtray, 7 3/4 In. 15.00
Early American Prescut, Candy Dish, Cover, 5 1/2 In. 11.00
Early American Prescut, Candy Dish, Cover, 7 1/2 In. 12.00
Early American Prescut, Plate, 11 In. 12.00
Early American Prescut, Platter, 13 1/2 In. 15.00
Early American Prescut, Syrup, 6 In. 15.00
Early American Prescut, Vase, Forest Green, Flared, 8 3/8 In. 15.00
Early American Rock Crystal pattern is listed here as Rock Crystal.
Fine Rib pattern is listed here as Homespun.
Fire-King, Ashtray, Swedish Modern, Iridescent Pink, 5 3/4 x 5 In. 15.00
Fire-King, Mixing Bowl Set, Ivory, Graduated, 3 Piece 15.00
Floragold, Bowl, Dessert, Square, 4 1/2 In. 5.00
Floragold, Bowl, Salad, Deep, 9 1/2 In. 43.00
Floragold, Candy Dish, 4-Footed, 5 1/4 In. 8.00
Floragold, Cup 6.00
Floragold, Pitcher, Ice Lip, 64 Oz. 53.00
Floral, Berry Bowl, Cover, Pink, 4 In. 25.00
Floral, Bowl, Cover, Vegetable, Green, 8 In. 49.00
Floral, Bowl, Vegetable, Oval, 9 In. 55.00
Floral, Butter, Cover, Green 180.00
Floral, Butter, Cover, Pink 125.00
Floral, Candy Jar, Cover, Green 48.00
Floral, Candy Jar, Cover, Pink 50.00
Floral, Coaster, Green, 3 1/4 In. 15.00
Floral, Cup, Pink 15.00
Floral, Lamp, Green, 4 1/4 In. 290.00
Floral, Plate, Sherbet, Pink, 6 In. . . . . 8.00 to 9.00
Floral, Salt & Pepper, 6 In. 55.00
Floral, Shaker, Salt & Pepper, Footed, Pink, 4 In. 50.00
Floral, Sugar, Cover, Green 45.00
Floral, Tumbler, Green, Footed, 7 Oz., 4 3/4 In. 35.00
Floral, Vase, Cone, 8 In. 50.00
Floral, Vase, Custard, Ruffled Edge, 6 7/8 In. 15.00
Florentine No. 1, Butter, Cover Only, Green 75.00
Florentine No. 1, Creamer, Green 11.00
Florentine No. 1, Grill Plate, Pink, 10 In. 11.00

Depression Glass,
Cubist

Depression Glass,
Dogwood

Florentine No. 1, Pitcher, Green, Footed, 36 Oz., 6 1/2 In. 45.00
Florentine No. 1, Plate, Dinner, 10 In. 12.50
Florentine No. 1, Plate, Sherbet, Pink, 6 In. 12.00
Florentine No. 1, Sherbet, 3 Oz. 11.50
Florentine No. 1, Sherbet, Green, 3 Oz. 12.00
Florentine No. 1, Sugar & Creamer, Pink 40.00
Florentine No. 1, Tumbler, Juice, Green, Footed, 5 Oz., 3 3/4 In. 17.00
Florentine No. 1, Tumbler, Juice, Yellow, Footed, 5 Oz., 3 3/4 In. 25.00
Florentine No. 2, Berry Bowl, Yellow, 4 1/2 In. 24.00
Florentine No. 2, Berry Bowl, Yellow, 8 In. 32.00
Florentine No. 2, Candlestick, Yellow, 2 3/4 In. ....33.00 to 38.00
Florentine No. 2, Cup & Saucer 18.00
Florentine No. 2, Cup, Yellow 10.50
Florentine No. 2, Pitcher, 48 Oz., 7 1/2 In. 28.00
Florentine No. 2, Pitcher, Footed, Yellow, 28 Oz., 7 1/2 In. 50.00
Florentine No. 2, Plate, Dinner, 10 In. 13.00
Florentine No. 2, Plate, Dinner, Yellow, 10 In. ....16.00 to 20.00
Florentine No. 2, Plate, Yellow, Sherbet, 6 In. 6.00
Florentine No. 2, Platter, Yellow, Oval, 11 In. 25.00
Florentine No. 2, Saucer, Yellow 8.00
Florentine No. 2, Sherbet, Green 10.50
Florentine No. 2, Sherbet, Yellow 12.00
Florentine No. 2, Soup, Cream, Green, 4 3/4 In. 18.00
Florentine No. 2, Soup, Cream, Pink, 4 3/4 In. 17.00
Florentine No. 2, Sugar, Yellow 12.00
Florentine No. 2, Tumbler, Footed, Green, 9 Oz., 5 In. 32.00
Florentine No. 2, Tumbler, Footed, Juice, 5 Oz., 3 3/8 In. 18.00
Florentine No. 2, Tumbler, Green, 9 Oz., 4 In. 20.00
Florentine No. 2, Tumbler, Pink, 9 Oz., 4 In. 16.00
Flower & Leaf Band pattern is listed here as Indiana Custard.
Forest Green, Bowl, 4 x 5 5/8 In. 15.00
Forest Green, Mixing Bowl, Splashproof, 5 5/8 In. 15.00
Forest Green, Tumbler, Iced Tea, 16 Oz. 12.00
Georgian, Berry Bowl, Green, 4 1/2 In. 9.00
Georgian, Butter, Cover Only, Green 38.00
Georgian, Butter, Cover, Green 110.00
Georgian, Sugar, Green 37.00
Golden Glory, Cup & Saucer 7.00
Golden Glory, Plate, Dinner, 9 In. 8.00
Golden Glory, Soup, Dish, 8 In. 8.00
Golden Glory, Sugar, Cover 7.00
Hairpin pattern is listed here as Newport.
Harvest Grape, Pitcher, Milk Glass, Indiana Glass, 10 1/2 In. 19.00
Harvest Grape, Sugar & Creamer, Underplate, Milk Glass 18.00
Harvest Grape, Vase, Green, Footed, 9 3/4 In. 18.00
Harvest Grape, Vase, Milk Glass, Footed, 9 3/4 In. 15.00
Hawaiian Leaf, Snack Set, Leaf-Shaped Plates, Box, 8 Piece 18.00
Heritage, Berry Bowl, 5 In. 16.00
Heritage, Bowl, Fruit, Gold Trim, 10 1/2 In. 8.00
Heritage, Plate, Dinner, 9 1/4 In. 10.00
Heritage, Plate, Luncheon, 8 In. 18.00
Hex Optic pattern is listed here as Hexagon Optic.
Hexagon Optic, Pitcher, Footed, 48 Oz., 9 In. 55.00
Hexagon Optic, Pitcher, Green, 70 Oz., 8 In. 295.00
Hexagon Optic, Plate, Luncheon, Green, 8 In. 6.00
Hexagon Optic, Saltshaker, Green 25.00
Hexagon Optic, Sherbet, Pink 4.00
Hexagon Optic, Sugar, Green 7.00
Hexagon Optic, Sugar, Pink 9.00
Hexagon Optic, Tumbler, Pink, 9 Oz., 3 3/4 In. 7.00
Hobnail pattern is listed in the Hobnail category.
Hobnail Anchor Hocking, Plate, Sherbet, Pink, 3 1/4 In. 15.00
Hobnail Anchor Hocking, Tumbler Set, Chrome Holder, 16 Oz., 8 Piece 25.00

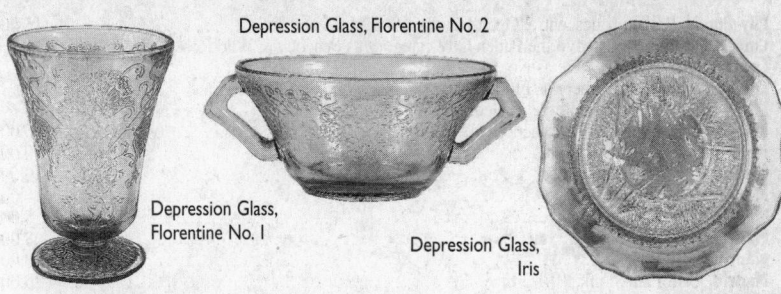

Depression Glass, Florentine No. 2

Depression Glass,
Florentine No. I

Depression Glass,
Iris

Hobnail Anchor Hocking, Tumbler, Footed, 5 1/2 In.	11.00
Hobnail Anchor Hocking, Tumbler, Milk Glass, Footed, 5 1/2 In.	15.00
Hobnail Anchor Hocking, Vase, Milk Glass, Ruffled Edge, 9 1/2 In.	10.00 to 15.00
Holiday, Pitcher, Pink, 52 Oz., 6 3/4 In.	45.00
Homespun, Coaster	2.00
Homespun, Creamer, Pink	7.00
Homespun Lookalike, Tumbler, Iced Tea, Cobalt Blue, 4 In.	30.00
Honeycomb pattern is listed here as Hexagon Optic.	
Horizontal Ribbed pattern is listed here as Manhattan.	
Horseshoe pattern is listed here as No. 612.	
Indiana Custard, Berry Bowl, 5 1/2 In.	11.25
Indiana Custard, Berry Bowl, 9 In.	35.00 to 50.00
Indiana Custard, Creamer, Footed	15.00
Indiana Custard, Sugar, Cover Only	24.00
Indiana Custard, Sugar, Footed	15.00
Iris, Bowl, Cereal, 5 In.	140.00
Iris, Bowl, Fruit, Frosted, 11 1/2 In.	45.00
Iris, Butter, Cover	48.00
Iris, Candlestick, 2-Light, 5 1/4 In., Pair	38.00
Iris, Candlestick, 2-Light, Iridescent, 5 1/2 In.	23.00
Iris, Candy Jar, Cover	230.00
Iris, Coaster	140.00
Iris, Cup	5.00
Iris, Cup & Saucer, 3 In.	45.00
Iris, Nut Set, 11 3/4 In.	130.00
Iris, Pitcher, Footed, 9 1/2 In.	40.00
Iris, Pitcher, Footed, Iridescent, 9 1/2 In.	55.00
Iris, Plate, Dinner, 9 In.	50.00
Iris, Plate, Dinner, Iridescent, 9 1/2 In.	45.00
Iris, Plate, Luncheon, 8 In.	105.00
Iris, Plate, Luncheon, Frosted, 8 In.	125.00
Iris, Sandwich Server, Iridescent, 11 3/4 In.	45.00
Iris, Saucer	8.00
Iris, Soup, Dish, 7 1/2 In.	50.00
Iris, Sugar, Cover	15.00
Iris, Tumbler, 4 In.	160.00
Iris, Wine, 3 Oz., 4 1/2 In.	12.00
Iris & Herringbone pattern is listed here as Iris.	
Jadite, Bowl, Vertical Rib, 8 In.	48.00
Jadite, Canister, Child's	45.00
Jeannette, Saucer, Ultramarine, 6 In.	4.00
Jubilee, Creamer, Yellow	20.00
Jubilee, Cup & Saucer, Yellow	22.00
Jubilee, Plate, Salad, Yellow, 7 In.	14.00
Jubilee, Saucer, Yellow	8.00
Jubilee, Sugar, Yellow	20.00
Laurel, Berry Bowl, French Ivory, 9 In.	10.00
Laurel, Platter, French Ivory, Oval, 10 3/4 In.	25.00
Lily Ponds, Bowl, Marigold, 8 3/4 In.	25.00

Lily Ponds, Relish, Iridescent, 2 Open Handles, 9 1/2 In. 15.00
Line 300 pattern is listed in the Paden City category as Peacock & Wild Rose.
Lorain pattern is listed here as No. 615.
Louisa pattern is listed here as Floragold.
Lovebirds pattern is listed here as Georgian.
Madrid, Bowl, Vegetable, Amber, Oval, 10 In. 30.00
Madrid, Coaster, 5 In. 30.00
Madrid, Console, 11 In. 10.00
Madrid, Creamer, Footed 10.00
Madrid, Cup & Saucer 8.00
Madrid, Cup, Amber 8.00
Madrid, Cup, Pink 8.00
Madrid, Grill Plate, Pink, 10 1/2 In. 20.00
Madrid, Jell-O Mold, Amber 9.00
Madrid, Pitcher, Amber, Square, 60 Oz., 8 In. 40.00
Madrid, Plate, Dinner, Green, 10 1/2 In. 70.00
Madrid, Plate, Dinner, Pink, 10 1/2 In. 18.00
Madrid, Plate, Luncheon, Amber, 8 7/8 In. . . . . .8.00 to 9.00
Madrid, Platter, Oval, 11 1/2 In. 16.00
Madrid, Sherbet, Green 9.00
Madrid, Soup, Dish, 7 In. 20.00
Madrid, Soup, Dish, Amber, 7 In. 10.00
Madrid, Sugar & Creamer 13.00
Madrid, Sugar, Cover 30.00
Madrid, Sugar, Cover, Green 73.00
Madrid, Tumbler, Amber, 12 Oz., 5 1/2 In. . . . . .19.00 to 24.00
Madrid, Tumbler, Amber, Footed, 10 Oz., 5 1/2 In. 33.00
Madrid, Tumbler, Pink, 9 Oz., 4 1/2 In. 20.00
Manhattan, Berry Bowl, Handles, 7 1/2 In. 25.00
Manhattan, Bowl, Handles, 4 1/2 In. 12.00
Manhattan, Candlestick, Square, 4 1/2 In. 11.00
Manhattan, Candy Dish, Pink, 3-Footed, 6 1/2 In. 15.00
Manhattan, Cup & Saucer 32.00
Manhattan, Pitcher, 24 Oz. 35.00
Manhattan, Pitcher, Tilt, 80 Oz. 40.00
Manhattan, Sandwich Server, 14 In. 30.00
Manhattan, Sherbet 12.00
Martha Washington pattern is included in the Cambridge Glass category.
Mayfair Federal, Cup & Saucer 18.00
Mayfair Federal, Cup, Amber 10.00
Mayfair Federal, Grill Plate, 9 1/2 In. 9.00
Mayfair Federal, Plate, Dinner, 9 1/2 In. 18.00
Mayfair Federal, Tumbler, Amber, 9 Oz., 4 1/2 In. . . . . .30.00 to 35.00
Mayfair Open Rose, Creamer, Footed, Pink. 35.00
Mayfair Open Rose, Plate, Luncheon, Pink, 8 1/2 In. 35.00
Mayfair Open Rose, Sandwich Server, Green, Center Handle 38.00
Mayfair Open Rose, Vase, Sweet Pea, Blue 145.00
Milano, Pitcher, Honey Gold, 9 In. 33.00
Miss America, Relish, 4 Sections, Divided, 9 In. 35.00
Miss America, Relish, 4 Sections, Pink, 8 3/4 In. 25.00
Moderntone, Berry Bowl, Cobalt Blue, 5 In. 24.00
Moderntone, Creamer, Footed 10.00
Moderntone, Cup & Saucer, Cobalt Blue 13.00
Moderntone, Cup, Cobalt Blue 12.00
Moderntone, Plate, Dinner, Amethyst, 8 7/8 In. 6.00
Moderntone, Plate, Dinner, Cobalt Blue, 8 7/8 In. 13.00
Moderntone, Plate, Luncheon, Cobalt Blue, 7 3/4 In. 11.00
Moderntone, Plate, Salad, Cobalt Blue, 6 3/4 In. . . . . .11.00 to 15.00
Moderntone, Plate, Sherbet, Cobalt Blue, 5 7/8 In. 7.00
Moderntone, Platter, Cobalt Blue, Oval, 11 In. 55.00
Moderntone, Sandwich Server, Cobalt Blue, 10 3/4 In. 59.00
Moderntone, Sugar, Cobalt Blue, Footed 13.00
Moderntone, Sugar, Footed 10.00

Moderntone, Tumbler, Cobalt Blue, 9 Oz., 4 1/4 In. 47.00
Moderntone Little Hostess, Saucer, Bright Pink 10.00
Moderntone Little Hostess Party, Cup, Black 13.00
Moderntone Little Hostess Party, Cup, Gold 12.00
Moderntone Little Hostess Party, Cup, Gray 10.00
Moderntone Little Hostess Party, Cup, Green 12.00
Moderntone Little Hostess Party, Cup, Lemon 16.00
Moderntone Little Hostess Party, Cup, Rust 12.00
Moderntone Little Hostess Party, Cup, Turquoise 12.00
Moderntone Little Hostess Party, Plate, Turquoise, 5 1/4 In. 12.00
Moderntone Little Hostess Party, Saucer, Bright Pink 10.00
Moderntone Little Hostess Party, Saucer, White 12.00
Moderntone Little Hostess Party, Sugar, Pink 16.00
Moderntone Little Hostess Party, Teapot, Burgundy 46.00
Moderntone Platonite, Bowl, Pink, 8 In. 30.00
Moderntone Platonite, Creamer, Yellow, Footed 10.00
Moderntone Platonite, Cup, Gray ....10.00 to 12.00
Moderntone Platonite, Plate, Dinner, Pink, 8 7/8 In. 12.00
Moderntone Platonite, Plate, Sherbet, Green, 6 3/4 In. 7.00
Moderntone Platonite, Platter, Yellow, Oval, 12 In. 25.00
Moderntone Platonite, Saltshaker, White, 4 1/4 In. 10.00
Moderntone Platonite, Saucer, Pink 7.00
Moderntone Platonite, Sherbet, Blue 10.00
Moderntone Platonite, Sherbet, Green 8.00
Moderntone Platonite, Sherbet, Pink ....8.00 to 10.00
Moderntone Platonite, Sherbet, White 10.00
Moderntone Platonite, Sherbet, Yellow 10.00
Moderntone Platonite, Soup, Cream, Gray, 4 3/4 In. 11.00
Moderntone Platonite, Soup, Cream, Pink, 4 3/4 In. 17.00
Moderntone Platonite, Sugar, Burgundy, Footed 13.00
Moderntone Platonite, Sugar, White, Red Stripes, Footed 10.00
Moderntone Platonite, Tumbler, Turquoise, 9 Oz., 4 1/4 In. 17.50
Moondrops pattern is listed in the New Martinsville category.
Moonstone, Candy Dish, Handles, Cover, 6 In. 40.00
Moonstone, Relish, Sections, 7 3/4 In. 38.00
Moroccan Amethyst, Bowl, Salad, 6 In. 10.00
Moroccan Amethyst, Celery Dish, 9 1/2 In. 16.00
Moroccan Amethyst, Cocktail Shaker, Aluminum Top ....29.00 to 50.00
Moroccan Amethyst, Snack Plate, Fan Shape, 10 In. 8.00
Mt. Vernon pattern is included in the Cambridge Glass category.
New Century, Cocktail, 3 1/2 Oz., 4 In. 29.00
New Century, Creamer, Green, Footed 20.00
New Century, Plate, Dinner, 10 In. 17.00
New Century, Platter, Oval, 11 In. 24.00
New Century, Salt & Pepper, Red Tops, Red Trim 47.00
New Century, Sugar, Footed 11.00
New Century, Tumbler, Amethyst, 5 Oz., 3 1/2 In. 15.00
New Century, Wine, Green, 2 1/2 Oz. 33.00
New Century Platonite, Butter, No Cover, Green 40.00
Newport, Berry Bowl, Amethyst, 4 3/4 In. 17.00
Newport, Berry Bowl, Amethyst, 8 1/4 In. 40.00
Newport, Berry Bowl, Platonite, Fired-On Blue, 4 3/4 In. 8.00
Newport, Berry Bowl, Platonite, Fired-On Pink, 4 3/4 In. 10.00
Newport, Berry Bowl, Platonite, Fired-On Red, 4 3/4 In. 8.00
Newport, Berry Bowl, Platonite, Fired-On Yellow, 4 3/4 In. 8.00
Newport, Plate, Dinner, Cobalt Blue, 8 3/4 In. 27.00
Newport, Plate, Luncheon, Amethyst, 8 1/2 In. 11.00
Newport, Plate, Luncheon, Platonite, 8 1/2 In. 11.00
Newport, Plate, Sherbet, Cobalt Blue, 5 7/8 In. ....7.50 to 12.00
Newport, Sandwich Server, Platonite, Fired-On Yellow, 11 In. 18.00
Newport, Soup, Cream, Platonite, 4 3/4 In. 11.00
Newport, Soup, Cream, Platonite, Gold Rim, 4 3/4 In. 11.00
Newport, Sugar & Creamer, Cobalt Blue, Footed 40.00

Newport, Sugar, Cobalt Blue, Footed 16.00
Newport, Tumbler, Platonite, Fired-On Blue, 9 Oz., 4 1/2 In. 30.00
Newport, Tumbler, Platonite, Fired-On Green, 9 Oz., 4 1/2 In. .... 24.00 to 30.00
Newport, Tumbler, Platonite, Fired-On Pink, 9 Oz., 4 1/2 In. 24.00
Newport, Tumbler, Platonite, Fired-On Yellow, 9 Oz., 4 1/2 In.. .... 30.00
No. 601 pattern is listed here as Avocado.
No. 612, Cup, Green 15.00
No. 612, Cup, Yellow 17.00
No. 612, Plate, Salad, Green, 8 3/8 In. 12.00
No. 612, Sandwich Server, Green, 11 1/2 In. 25.00
No. 612, Sherbet, Yellow 18.00
No. 612, Sugar, Green, Footed 18.00
No. 612, Sugar, Yellow, Footed 20.00
No. 612, Tumbler, Green, 9 Oz., 4 1/4 In. 15.00
No. 615, Creamer, Yellow 30.00
No. 615, Cup & Saucer, Green 18.00
No. 615, Plate, Luncheon, Green, 8 In. 15.00
No. 615, Plate, Salad, 7 3/4 In. ....13.00 to 15.00
No. 615, Platter, Green, 11 1/2 In. 25.00
No. 615, Relish, 4 Sections, 8 In. 12.00
No. 615, Sugar, Green 13.00
No. 615, Tumbler, Footed, Green, 9 Oz., 4 3/4 In. 19.00
No. 615, Tumbler, Footed, Yellow, 9 Oz., 4 3/4 In. 30.00
No. 616, Sugar, Footed 18.00
No. 616, Sugar, Yellow, Footed 30.00
No. 616, Tumbler, 5 In. 16.00
No. 618, Compote, Diamond Shape, 4 1/8 x 6 1/2 x 3 In. 18.00
No. 618, Plate, Dinner, 9 1/4 In. 24.00
No. 618, Relish, Sections, 11 1/2 In. 12.00
No. 618, Sandwich Server, 11 1/4 In. 20.00
No. 620, Berry Bowl, 9 1/4 In. 33.00
No. 620, Berry Bowl, Green, 7 1/2 In. 13.00
No. 620, Bowl, Vegetable, Amber, Oval, 10 In. ....20.00 to 23.00
No. 620, Cup & Saucer 12.00
No. 620, Cup & Saucer, Amber 14.00
No. 620, Grill Plate, 10 1/8 In. 15.00
No. 620, Grill Plate, Green, 10 1/8 In. 14.00
No. 620, Platter, Amber, Oval, 10 3/4 x 8 In. 16.00
No. 620, Relish, Amber, 3 Sections, 8 3/8 In. 24.00
No. 620, Sandwich Server, Amber, 11 1/2 In. ....12.00 to 15.00
No. 620, Soup, Cream, Amber, 4 1/2 In. 12.00
No. 622 pattern is listed here as Pretzel.
Normandie, Berry Bowl, Amber, 5 In. 10.00
Normandie, Bowl, Cereal, Iridescent, 6 1/2 In. 10.00
Normandie, Bowl, Vegetable, Amber, Oval, 10 In. 20.00
Normandie, Cup, Amber 8.00
Normandie, Plate, Dinner, Amber, 11 In. 33.00
Normandie, Salt & Pepper, Amber 50.00
Normandie, Sherbet, Pink 10.00
Normandie, Sugar & Creamer, Amber 7.00
Normandie, Sugar, Amber 8.00
Normandie, Sugar, Cover Only, Amber 95.00
Old Cafe, Vase, 7 1/4 In. 15.00
Old Colony, Bowl, Vegetable, Pink, 9 1/2 In. 35.00
Old English, Tumbler, Amber, Footed, 4 1/2 In. 25.00
Old Florentine pattern is listed here as Florentine No. 1.
Open Rose pattern is listed here as Mayfair Open Rose.
Optic Design pattern is listed here as Raindrops.
Ovide, Bowl, Cereal, Aqua, 5 1/2 In. 12.00
Ovide, Bowl, Cereal, Burgundy, 5 1/2 In. 8.00
Ovide, Bowl, Cereal, Gray, 5 1/2 In. 12.00
Ovide, Bowl, Cereal, Green, 5 1/2 In. ....8.00 to 12.00
Ovide, Creamer, Pink & Black Trim 12.00

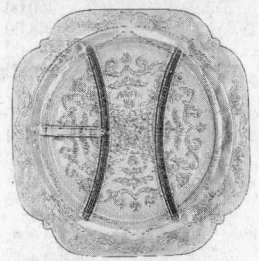

Depression Glass, Madrid   Depression Glass, No. 615   Depression Glass, Princess

Ovide, Creamer, Rust 11.00
Ovide, Cup, Aqua 8.00
Ovide, Cup, Flying Geese, Orange Trim 10.00
Ovide, Cup, Rust 8.00
Ovide, Plate, Dinner, Burgundy, 9 In. 8.00
Ovide, Plate, Dinner, Dark Green, 9 In. 8.00
Ovide, Plate, Dinner, Gray, 9 In. 8.00
Ovide, Plate, Dinner, Yellow, 9 In. 8.00
Ovide, Plate, Luncheon, Aqua, 8 In. 10.00
Ovide, Plate, Luncheon, Platonite, Flying Geese, 8 In. 10.00
Ovide, Salt & Pepper, Black 28.00
Ovide, Salt & Pepper, Green 26.00
Ovide, Sherbet, Black 11.00
Ovide, Sherbet, Black Flower, Red & Yellow Trim 18.00
Ovide, Sugar & Creamer, Red Edge Trim 32.00
Ovide, Sugar & Creamer, Yellow 12.00
Ovide, Tumbler, Aqua 10.00
Ovide, Tumbler, Black, 9 Oz., 4 3/4 In. 29.00
Ovide, Tumbler, Green, 9 Oz., 4 3/4 In. 29.00
Oyster & Pearl, Relish, Sections, 10 1/2 In. 11.00
Parrot pattern is listed here as Sylvan.
Patrician, Berry Bowl, Golden Glo, 8 1/2 In. 44.00
Patrician, Bowl, Cereal, Golden Glo, 6 In. 28.00
Patrician, Bowl, Vegetable, Green, Oval, 10 In. 40.00
Patrician, Butter, Cover 95.00
Patrician, Butter, Cover Only, Golden Glo 35.00
Patrician, Butter, Cover, Golden Glo 90.00
Patrician, Butter, Cover, Green .... 140.00 to 170.00
Patrician, Butter, No Cover, Green 70.00
Patrician, Cookie Jar, Cover 64.00
Patrician, Cookie Jar, Cover, Golden Glo .... 69.00 to 95.00
Patrician, Cup, Golden Glo 10.00
Patrician, Cup, Green 16.00
Patrician, Grill Plate, Iridescent, Experimental, 11 In. 130.00
Patrician, Jam Dish, Golden Glo, 6 3/4 In. 29.00
Patrician, Jam Dish, Green, 6 3/4 In. 35.00
Patrician, Pitcher, Golden Glo, 75 Oz., 8 In. 95.00
Patrician, Plate, Dinner, Golden Glo, 10 1/2 In. .... 7.00 to 8.00
Patrician, Plate, Sherbet, Golden Glo, 6 In. .... 9.00 to 10.00
Patrician, Platter, Golden Glo, Oval, 11 1/2 In. 32.00
Patrician, Platter, Green, Oval, 11 1/2 In. 29.00
Patrician, Platter, Oval, 11 1/2 In. 34.00
Patrician, Platter, Pink, Oval, 11 1/2 In. 18.00
Patrician, Salt & Pepper, Golden Glo .... 59.00 to 65.00
Patrician, Saltshaker 9.00
Patrician, Saucer, Pink 9.50
Patrician, Sherbet, Golden Glo .... 9.00 to 10.00
Patrician, Soup, Cream, 4 3/4 In. 17.00

Patrician, Sugar, Golden Glo, Madrid Style Cover, Round Knob 250.00
Patrician, Tumbler, 14 Oz., 5 1/2 In. 48.00
Patrician, Tumbler, 9 Oz., 4 1/4 In. 19.00
Patrician, Tumbler, Golden Glo, 4 1/4 In. 36.00
Patrician, Tumbler, Golden Glo, 9 Oz., 4 1/4 In. 30.00
Patrician, Tumbler, Golden Glo, Footed, 8 Oz., 5 1/4 In. 16.00
Peach Lustre, Vase, Ribbed, 7 1/4 In. 10.00
Peacock & Wild Rose pattern is listed in the Paden City category.
Pear Optic, Cup & Saucer, Green 10.00
Pear Optic, Plate, Sherbet, Green, 6 In. 10.00
Pineapple & Floral pattern is listed here as No. 618.
Pinwheel pattern is listed here as Sierra.
Pioneer, Plate, 12 In. ....16.00 to 18.00
Pioneer, Plate, Fruit Center, 12 In. 20.00
Pioneer, Plate, Salad, 8 In. 8.00
Poinsettia pattern is listed here as Floral.
Poppy No. 1 pattern is listed here as Florentine No. 1.
Poppy No. 2 pattern is listed here as Florentine No. 2.
Pretty Polly Party Dishes, see also the related pattern Doric & Pansy.
Pretzel, Celery Dish, 10 1/4 In. 12.00
Pretzel, Sandwich Server, 11 1/2 In. 20.00
Pretzel, Soup, Dish, 7 1/2 In. ....12.00 to 18.00
Pretzel, Sugar & Creamer 18.00
Princess, Candy Dish, Cover, Blue, 6 In. 18.00
Princess, Cup, Green 14.00
Princess, Salt & Pepper, Green 60.00
Prismatic Line pattern is listed here as Queen Mary.
Provincial pattern is listed here as Bubble.
Queen Mary, Creamer, Oval, 5 In. 10.00
Queen Mary, Sandwich Server, 12 1/2 In. 28.00
Queen Mary, Sugar & Creamer 15.00
Raindrops, Berry Bowl, 7 1/2 In. 62.00
Raindrops, Cup & Saucer, Green 12.00
Raindrops, Sugar, Cover Only, Green 45.00
Raindrops, Tumbler, Whiskey, 2 Oz., 2 1/8 In. 10.00
Raindrops, Tumbler, Whiskey, Green, 2 Oz., 2 1/8 In. 7.00
Ribbon, Berry Bowl, Green, Flared, 9 In. 35.00
Ribbon, Bowl, Fruit, Green, 4 1/2 In. 10.00
Ribbon, Candy Dish, Cover, Green, 6 1/2 In. 55.00
Ribbon, Sugar & Creamer, Green 30.00
Ring, Pitcher, 80 Oz., 8 1/2 In. 30.00
Ring, Vase, Green, 8 In. 35.00
Ripple, Bowl, Cereal, Fired-On Blue, 5 5/8 In. 8.00
Ripple, Bowl, Cereal, Fired-On Pink, 5 5/8 In. 8.00
Ripple, Plate, Luncheon, Pink Trim, 8 7/8 In. 8.00
Rock Crystal, Candlestick, 2-Light 25.00
Rock Crystal, Relish, 5 Sections, 12 1/2 In. 30.00
Rope pattern is listed here as Colonial Fluted.
Rose Cameo, Berry Bowl, Green, 4 1/2 In. 18.00
Rose Cameo, Plate, Salad, Green, 7 In. 17.00
Roxana, Tumbler, Juice, Yellow, 9 Oz., 4 1/4 In. 24.00
Royal Lace, Berry Bowl, Pink, 10 In. 33.00
Royal Lace, Bowl, Ruffled Edge, 3-Footed, 10 In. 58.00
Royal Lace, Candlestick, Cobalt Blue, Straight Edge 59.00
Royal Lace, Cookie Jar, Cover 50.00
Royal Lace, Creamer, Green, Footed. 45.00
Royal Lace, Cup 11.00
Royal Lace, Cup & Saucer, Cobalt Blue 55.00
Royal Lace, Cup & Saucer, Green 45.00
Royal Lace, Cup & Saucer, Pink 32.00
Royal Lace, Cup, Pink 24.00
Royal Lace, Grill Plate, 9 7/8 In. 10.00
Royal Lace, Pitcher, Cobalt Blue, 48 Oz., 8 In. 235.00

Royal Lace, Plate, Dinner, Cobalt Blue, 9 7/8 In. . . . . .50.00 to 55.00
Royal Lace, Plate, Luncheon, Cobalt Blue, 8 1/2 In. 60.00
Royal Lace, Plate, Sherbet, Cobalt Blue, 6 In. 16.00
Royal Lace, Saucer, Pink 7.00
Royal Lace, Soup, Cream, Cobalt Blue, 4 3/4 In. . . . . .50.00 to 55.00
Royal Lace, Sugar, Green 27.00
Royal Lace, Tumbler, 5 Oz., 3 1/2 In. 25.00
Royal Lace, Tumbler, 9 Oz., 4 1/8 In. 17.00
Royal Ruby, Ashtray, Square, 6 In. 30.00
Royal Ruby, Plate, Dinner, 9 1/8 In. 15.00
Royal Ruby, Tumbler, 9 1/2 Oz., 4 In. 10.00
Sail Boat pattern is listed here as Sportsman Series.
Sandwich Anchor Hocking, Bowl, 8 1/2 In. 15.00
Sandwich Anchor Hocking, Cup & Saucer 10.00
Sandwich Indiana, Candlestick, Amber, 3 1/2 In., Pair 20.00
Saxon pattern is listed here as Coronation.
Sharon, Berry Bowl, Golden Glo, 5 In. 9.00
Sharon, Berry Bowl, Green, 5 In. 18.00
Sharon, Bowl, Cereal, Pink, 6 In. 9.00
Sharon, Bowl, Fruit, 10 1/2 In. 23.00
Sharon, Bowl, Fruit, Pink, 10 1/2 In. 45.00
Sharon, Bowl, Oval, Pink, 9 1/2 In. 36.00
Sharon, Bowl, Vegetable, Oval, Golden Glo, 9 1/2 In. 16.00
Sharon, Cake Plate, Footed, 11 1/2 In. 10.00
Sharon, Candy Jar, Cover, Pink, 8 In. 40.00
Sharon, Creamer, Green 20.00
Sharon, Creamer, Pink 20.00
Sharon, Cup & Saucer, Golden Glo . . . . .10.00 to 16.00
Sharon, Cup & Saucer, Pink . . . . .29.00 to 30.00
Sharon, Cup, Pink . . . . .16.00 to 19.00
Sharon, Jam Dish, Pink, 7 1/2 In. 290.00
Sharon, Pitcher, Ice Lip, Pink, 80 Oz. 100.00
Sharon, Plate, Bread & Butter, Pink, 6 In. 10.00
Sharon, Plate, Dinner, Golden Glo, 9 1/2 In. 13.00
Sharon, Plate, Dinner, Pink, 9 In. 20.00
Sharon, Salt & Pepper, Golden Glo 70.00
Sharon, Salt & Pepper, Pink 75.00
Sharon, Saucer, Pink 10.00
Sharon, Sherbet, Pink 18.00
Sharon, Soup, Cream, Pink, 5 In. 49.00
Sharon, Soup, Dish, Pink, 7 3/4 In. 60.00
Sharon, Sugar & Creamer, Cover, Pink 60.00
Sharon, Sugar & Creamer, Golden Glo 45.00
Sharon, Sugar & Creamer, Pink 35.00
Sharon, Tumbler, Golden Glo, 9 Oz., 4 1/8 In. 50.00
Sharon, Tumbler, Pink, 9 Oz., 4 1/8 In. 50.00
Sierra, Bowl, Cereal, Green, 5 1/2 In. 25.00
Sierra, Saltshaker, Green 32.00
Skol, Bowl, Fruit, Capri Blue, 4 7/8 In. 16.00
Skol, Sherbet, Capri Blue, 3 3/4 In. 16.00
Skol, Tumbler, 5 In. 10.00
Skol, Tumbler, Capri Blue, 4 Oz., 3 1/8 In. 15.00
Skol, Tumbler, Capri Blue, 8 Oz., 4 In. . . . . .15.00 to 17.00
Skol, Tumbler, Capri Blue, 9 Oz., 5 1/4 In. 18.00
Skol, Tumbler, Juice, Capri Blue, 5 Oz., 3 5/8 In. 16.00
Soreno, Vase, Avocado, 7 1/4 In. 12.00
Spoke pattern is listed here as Patrician.
Sportsman Series, Cocktail Mixer, Cobalt Blue, White Ship, 4 1/2 x 4 1/4 In. 45.00
Sportsman Series, Cocktail Mixer, Cobalt Blue, Windmill, 4 3/4 x 4 1/4 In. 50.00
Sportsman Series, Roly Poly, Windmill, Cobalt Blue, Hazel Atlas, 6 Oz. 10.00
Star, Bowl, Dessert, 5 1/4 In. 10.00
Star, Pitcher, Ice Lip, 85 Oz., 9 1/4 In. 18.00
Star, Pitcher, Juice, 36 Oz., 5 3/4 In. 9.00

Star, Plate, Salad, Yellow, 6 1/2 In. 10.00
Star, Tumbler, Whiskey, 1 1/4 Oz., 2 1/4 In. 8.00
Starlight, Creamer 10.00
Starlight, Cup, White 7.00
Starlight, Plate, Luncheon, 8 1/2 In. 8.00
Starlight, Salt & Pepper 35.00
Sunburst, Berry Bowl, 4 3/4 In. 7.50
Sunburst, Saucer 6.00
Swirl Fire-King, Bowl, Vegetable, Ivory, 7 1/4 In. 17.00
Swirl Jeanette, Saucer, Delphite, 5 3/4 In. 5.00
Swirl Jeannette, Candlestick, 2-Light, Ultramarine, Pair 55.00
Swirl Jeannette, Candy Dish, Cover, 6 In. 170.00
Swirl Jeannette, Cup, Pink, 3 In. 8.00
Sylvan, Bowl, Vegetable, Green, Oval, 10 In. 80.00
Sylvan, Butter, No Cover, Green 55.00
Sylvan, Creamer, Green 68.00
Sylvan, Cup, Green 29.00
Sylvan, Grill Plate, Round, Green, 10 1/2 In. ....33.00 to 40.00
Sylvan, Plate, Dinner, Green, 9 In. ....58.00 to 69.00
Sylvan, Platter, Oval, Green, 11 1/4 In. 64.00
Sylvan, Saltshaker, Green, Footed 150.00
Sylvan, Saucer, Green 20.00
Sylvan, Sherbet, Amber, Cone, 2 7/8 In. 56.00
Sylvan, Soup, Dish, Green, 7 In. ....55.00 to 59.00
Sylvan, Sugar, Cover, Green 200.00
Sylvan, Tumbler, Green, 10 Oz., 4 1/2 In. 175.00
Tea Room, Candlestick, Green 55.00
Tea Room, Candlestick, Pink, Pair 110.00
Tea Room, Creamer, Footed, Pink, 4 1/2 In. 30.00
Teardrop, Cake Plate, Amber, 11 In. 24.00
Teardrop, Compote, Amber, 7 1/2 In. 24.00
Teardrop, Compote, Avocado Green, 7 1/2 In. 18.00
Teardrop, Compote, Milk Glass, 7 1/2 In. 15.00
Teardrop, Compote, Satin Green, 7 1/2 In. 15.00
Thistle, Bowl, Cereal, Pink, 5 1/2 In. 35.00
Threading pattern is listed here as Old English.
Thumbprint pattern is listed here as Pear Optic.
Vernon pattern is listed here as No. 616.
Vertical Ribbed pattern is listed here as Queen Mary.
Waffle pattern is listed here as Waterford.
Waterford, Plate, Dinner, 9 5/8 In. 11.00
Waterford, Tumbler, Footed, 10 Oz., 4 7/8 In. 15.00
Wexford, Bowl, Fruit, Footed, 10 In. 15.00
Wexford, Cake Stand, 12 In. 35.00
Wexford, Candleholder, 3 x 5 In. 35.00
Wexford, Candy Dish, Cover, 6 3/4 In. 10.00
Wexford, Ice Bucket, 10 1/2 In. 27.00
Wexford, Lamp, Oil 35.00

Depression Glass, Sharon

Depression Glass, Windsor

Wexford, Lazy Susan, 6 Inserts, 13 1/2 In. 35.00
Wexford, Salt & Pepper, 4 1/4 In. 15.00
Whirly-Twirly, Tumbler, Juice, 3 In. 25.00
White Ship pattern is listed here as Sportsman Series.
Wild Rose pattern is listed here as Dogwood.
Wild Rose With Leaves & Berries, Tray, 2 Handles, Indiana Glass 15.00
Windmill pattern is listed here as Sportsman Series.
Windsor, Ashtray, Pink, 5 3/4 In. 43.00
Windsor, Bowl, Boat Shape, Pink, 11 3/4 x 7 In. 50.00
Windsor, Bowl, Pink, 3-Footed, 7 1/8 In. 45.00
Windsor, Bowl, Salad, 10 1/2 In. 22.00
Windsor, Candy Dish, Heart Shape, 5 1/2 In. 38.00
Windsor, Creamer, Footed 7.00
Windsor, Cup 3.00
Windsor, Cup, Pink 12.00
Windsor, Plate, Sherbet, 6 In. 8.00
Windsor, Sandwich Server, 10 1/4 In. 6.00
Windsor, Saucer 2.00
Windsor, Saucer, Green 6.00
Windsor, Sherbet, Pink 12.00
Windsor Diamond pattern is listed here as Windsor.
Yorktown, Berry Bowl, Master, 9 1/2 In. 10.00
Yorktown, Bowl, Footed, Amber, 10 In. 18.00
Yorktown, Punch Cup 18.00

DERBY has been marked on porcelain made in the city of Derby, England, since about 1748. The original Derby factory closed in 1848, but others opened there and continued to produce quality porcelain. The Crown Derby mark began appearing on Derby wares in the 1770s.

Bowl, Flowers, Gold Rim, 9 3/4 In. 565.00
Coffee Cann & Saucer, Imari Pattern, Early 19th Century, 3 x 5 3/4 In. 58.00
Dish, Scalloped, Flowers, Blue Vine Design, Gold Trim, 9 1/2 In., Pair 1017.00
Garniture Set, Bowl, 2 Vases, Flowers, Green Ground, Gold Beading, 9 1/2 In., 3 Piece .. 1695.00
Urn, Imari Pattern, 19th Century, 3 In. 105.00
Vase, Arabesque, Bottle Shape, Octagonal Base, Beaded, Raised, 1887, 13 In. 3520.00
Vase, Baluster, Flowers, c.1810, 3 1/4 In. 259.00
Waste Bowl, Underplate, Pink Band, Pearl, Diamond Border, Gold, Cream, Black, 7 3/4 In. 160.00

DICK TRACY, the comic strip, started in 1931. Tracy was also the hero of movies from 1937 to 1947 and again in 1990, and starred in a radio series in the 1940s and a television series in the 1950s. Memorabilia from all these activities are collected.

Book, Celebrated Cases Of Dick Tracy, 1931-1951, Bonanza Books, c.1970, 291 Pages .. 65.00
Doll, Bonny Braids, Original Clothes, Box, Marx, 1951, 11 1/4 In. 500.00
Police Station, Car, In Garage, Shoots Out, Tin, Plastic, Marx FAS, 9 In. 580.00
Poster, Dick Tracy vs. Crime Inc., Fatal Hour, Ralph Byrd, 1941, 27 x 41 In. 450.00
Squad Car, Tin Lithograph, Battery Operated, Siren, Windup, Marx, Box, 1949, 11 1/2 In. 220.00
Squad Car, Tin Lithograph, Friction, Marx, 8 In. 198.00
Squad Car, Tin Lithograph, Windup, Battery Operated Light, Marx, 11 In. .... 415.00 to 490.00
Toy, B.O. Plenty, Tin Lithograph, Windup, Marx, Box, c.1939, 6 In. 360.00
Toy, B.O. Plenty, Waddles, Holds Baby Sparkles, Tin, Windup, Marx, Box, 9 In. 495.00

DICKENS WARE pieces are listed in the Royal Doulton and Weller categories.

DINNERWARE used in the United States from the 1930s through the 1950s is listed here. Most was made in potteries in southern Ohio, West Virginia, and California. A few patterns were made in Japan, England, and other countries. Dishes were sold in gift shops and department stores, or were given away as premiums. Many of these patterns are listed in this book in their own categories, such as Autumn Leaf, Azalea, Coors, Fiesta, Franciscan, Hall, Harker, Harlequin, Red Wing, Riviera, Russel Wright, Vernon Kilns, Watt, and Willow. For more information, see *Kovels' Depression Glass & Dinnerware Price List.*

American Rose, Platter, Oval, Paden City Pottery, 13 3/4 In. 30.00

Apple, Berry Bowl, Skyline Shape, Master, 8 3/4 In. 33.00
Apple, Gravy Boat, Skyline Shape, Blue Ridge 30.00
Apple, Plate, Dinner, Skyline Shape, Blue Ridge, 10 1/2 In. 23.00
Autumn Harvest, Cup, Taylor, Smith & Taylor 10.00
Autumn Harvest, Plate, Dinner, Taylor, Smith & Taylor, 10 In. 7.00
Autumn Leaves, Berry Bowl, Taylor, Smith & Taylor, 5 1/2 In. 7.00
Bak-Serv, Casserole, Cover, Pink & Yellow Flowers 45.00
Bak-Serv, Teapot, Paden City 95.00
Ballerina, Bowl, Fruit, Forest Green, Universal, 5 In. 5.00
Ballerina, Bowl, Fruit, Poppies, Universal, 5 1/2 In. 5.00
Ballerina, Bowl, Vegetable, Tab Handles, Moss Rose, Universal 25.00
Ballerina, Bowl, Vegetable, Universal, 9 In. 18.00
Ballerina, Chop Plate, Chartreuse, Universal, 11 3/4 In. 25.00
Ballerina, Cup & Saucer, Forest Green, Universal 15.00
Ballerina, Plate, Bread & Butter, Jonquil Yellow, Universal, 6 In. 6.00
Ballerina, Plate, Bread & Butter, Poppies, Universal, 6 In. 5.00
Ballerina, Plate, Dinner, Dove Gray, Universal, 9 1/4 In. 6.00
Ballerina, Plate, Dinner, Jade Green, Universal, 9 1/4 In. 8.00
Ballerina, Plate, Dinner, Moss Rose, Universal, 10 In. 15.00
Ballerina, Plate, Luncheon, Moss Rose, Universal, 9 In. 7.00
Ballerina, Platter, Tab Handles, Pink, Universal, 11 1/2 In. 15.00
Ballerina, Salt & Pepper, Moss Rose, Universal 23.00
Baltic, Berry Bowl, Adams, 5 1/4 In. 8.00
Baltic, Bowl, Cereal, Adams, 6 In. 8.00
Baltic, Plate, Dinner, Adams, 10 In. 12.00
Baltic, Plate, Salad, Adams, 7 1/2 In. 9.00
Baltic, Soup, Dish, Adams 10.00
Baltic Ivy, Plate, Dinner, Blue Ridge, 10 1/4 In. 17.00
Biscayne, Cup & Saucer, Salem China 10.00
Biscayne, Plate, Dinner, Salem China, 10 In. 8.00
Biscayne, Salver, Salem China, 12 In. 25.00
Bittersweet, Cup & Saucer, Universal 35.00
Bittersweet, Plate, Dinner, Universal, 9 1/4 In. 35.00
Bittersweet, Plate, Luncheon, Universal, 7 1/4 In. 35.00
Blue Moon, Plate, Dinner, Blue Ridge, 10 1/8 In. 48.00
Boutonniere, Bowl, Cereal, Taylor, Smith & Taylor, 4 3/4 In. 6.00
Boutonniere, Plate, Dinner, Taylor, Smith & Taylor, 10 In. 10.00
Boutonniere, Plate, Luncheon, Taylor, Smith & Taylor, 8 In. 7.00
Briar Rose, Cup & Saucer, Salem China 6.00
Briar Rose, Plate, Bread & Butter, Salem China, 6 In. 6.00
Briar Rose, Plate, Dinner, Salem China, 9 In. 10.00
Briar Rose, Platter, Oval, Tab Handles, Salem China, 11 1/2 In. 25.00
Briar Rose, Sugar, Salem China 10.00
Brocatelle, Platter, Oval, Taylor, Smith & Taylor, 13 1/2 In. 30.00
Bucks County, Casserole, Cover, Yellow, Royal China 120.00
Bucks County, Platter, Round, Royal China, 13 In. 45.00
Bucks County, Teapot, Yellow, Droop Spout, Royal China 120.00
Calico Fruit, Bowl, Salad, Universal, 9 3/4 In. 45.00
Cathay, Plate, Dinner, Taylor, Smith & Taylor, 10 1/2 In. 10.00
Cattail, Cup & Saucer, Universal 11.00
Cattail, Pie Dish, Universal, 10 In. 20.00
Cattail, Plate, Bread & Butter, Universal, 6 1/4 In. 5.50
Cattail, Plate, Dinner, Universal, 9 1/4 In. ....15.00 to 35.00
Cattail, Platter, Oval, Universal, 11 1/2 x 10 In. 25.00
Cattail, Sugar, Cover, Universal 15.00
Chicory, Plate, Luncheon, Blue Ridge, 9 1/2 In. 12.00
Cock O' The Walk, Platter, Oval, Blue Ridge, 12 In. 55.00
Colonial Homestead, Salt & Pepper, Royal China 40.00
Colonial Homestead, Teapot, Droop Spout, Royal China ....90.00 to 110.00
Colonial Homestead, Tidbit, 2 Tiers, Royal China 60.00
Conversation, Bowl, Vegetable, Oval, Taylor, Smith & Taylor, 9 3/4 In. 20.00
Conversation, Plate, Dinner, Taylor, Smith & Taylor, 10 In. 16.00
Conversation, Platter, Oval, Taylor, Smith & Taylor, 13 In. 22.00

Country Home, Casserole, Cover, Crooksville, 8 1/2 In. 65.00
County Fair, Plate, Salad, Candlewick Shape, Blue Ridge, 8 1/2 In. 20.00
Currier & Ives, Bowl, Cereal, Pink, Schoolhouse In Winter, Royal China, 6 3/8 In. 25.00
Currier & Ives, Cake Plate, Blue, Footed, Royal China, 10 In. 150.00
Currier & Ives, Casserole, Cover, Blue, Tab Handles, Royal China 175.00
Currier & Ives, Casserole, Cover, Pink, Fashionable Turnouts, Royal China 100.00
Currier & Ives, Chop Plate, Blue, Royal China, 11 In. 240.00
Currier & Ives, Chop Plate, Pink, Getting Ice, Royal China, 12 1/4 In. 68.00
Currier & Ives, Chop Plate, Pink, Royal China, 11 In. 300.00
Currier & Ives, Creamer, Tall, Pink, Express Train, Royal China 100.00
Currier & Ives, Egg Plate, Blue, Royal China, 10 1/4 In. 150.00
Currier & Ives, Gravy Boat, Pink, Dad Is Home, Royal China 45.00
Currier & Ives, Mug, Blue, Express Train, Royal China, 3 1/4 In. 75.00
Currier & Ives, Platter, Pink, Old Inn In Winter, Royal China, 13 In. 55.00
Currier & Ives, Platter, Round, Blue, Snowy Morning, Royal China, 13 In. 125.00
Currier & Ives, Platter, Round, Pink, Snowy Morning, Royal China, 13 In. 175.00
Currier & Ives, Salt & Pepper, Pink, Royal China 60.00
Currier & Ives, Sugar, Cover, Blue, On The Mississippi, Royal China 75.00
Currier & Ives, Teapot, Blue, Clipper Ship, Royal China ....135.00 to 150.00
Day Lily, Plate, Dinner, Taylor, Smith & Taylor, 10 In. 10.00
Derwood, Plate, Dinner, W.S. George, 10 In. 10.00
Duchess, Platter, Oval, Paden City Pottery, 13 3/4 In. 28.00
Early American, Bowl, Cereal, W.S. George, 5 1/2 In. 5.25
Early American, Cup, W.S. George 7.50
Early American, Saucer, W.S. George 2.50
English Abbey, Cup & Saucer, Taylor, Smith & Taylor 30.00
English Abbey, Gravy Boat, Underplate, Taylor, Smith & Taylor 75.00
English Village, Cup & Saucer, Salem China 22.00
English Village, Plate, Dinner, Salem China, 9 3/4 In. 28.00
Fair Oaks, Bowl, Vegetable, Royal China, 10 In. 25.00
Fair Oaks, Butter, Cover, Royal China 40.00
Fair Oaks, Plate, Salad, Royal China, 10 In. 25.00
Fair Oaks, Platter, Oval, Royal China, 11 x 9 In. 40.00
Fair Oaks, Salt & Pepper, Royal China 40.00
Fairlane, Butter, Cover, Steubenville 15.00
Fairlane, Plate, Dinner, Steubenville, 10 1/2 In. 10.00
Fairlane, Salt & Pepper, Steubenville 10.00
Fairmont, Bowl, Vegetable, Divided, Blue Ridge, 8 1/2 In. 25.00
First Love, Creamer, Blue Ridge 13.00
Floral Wreath, Bowl, Vegetable, Steubenville, 8 1/2 In. 13.00
Floral Wreath, Casserole, Cover, Steubenville 85.00
Floral Wreath, Plate, Dinner, Steubenville, 9 3/4 In. 12.00
Floral Wreath, Platter, Steubenville, 15 In. 50.00
Foxfire, Plate, Dinner, Blue Ridge, 91/2 In. 28.00
French Peasant, Chocolate Pot, Cover, Blue Ridge, 9 In. 550.00
Godey Prints, Platter, Blue Trim, 11 In. 10.00
Gray-Lure, Plate, Dinner, Hibiscus Decal, Crooksville, 10 In. 8.00
Gray-Lure, Plate, Salad, Hibiscus Decal, Crooksville, 7 In. 10.00
Green Wheat, Cup, Leigh 12.00
Green Wheat, Plate, Salad, Leigh, 7 In. 8.25
Green Wheat, Saucer, Leigh 5.00
Iva-Lure, Berry Bowl, Wildflowers Decal, Crooksville, 5 1/2 In. 9.00
Iva-Lure, Creamer, Wildflowers, Crooksville 12.00
Iva-Lure, Plate, Dinner, Wildflowers Decal, Crooksville, 10 In. ....12.00 to 15.00
Iva-Lure, Plate, Salad, Wildflowers Decal, Crooksville, 8 In. 12.00
Iva-Lure, Platter, Oval, Tab Handles, Wildflowers Decal, Crooksville, 11 1/2 In. 15.00
Iva-Lure, Platter, Oval, Tab Handles, Wildflowers Decal, Crooksville, 15 In. 22.00
Jonquil, Bowl, Vegetable, Paden City Pottery, 9 1/4 In. 22.00
Jonquil, Plate, Bread & Butter, Paden City Pottery, 6 1/2 In. 7.00
Jonquil, Plate, Dinner, Paden City Pottery, 10 In. 14.00
Jonquil, Plate, Luncheon, Paden City Pottery, 9 In. 10.00
Jonquil, Platter, Oval, Paden City Pottery, 14 x 11 In. 35.00
Jonquil, Soup, Dish, Paden City Pottery, 8 In. 15.00

Lazy Daisy, Platter, Oval, Taylor, Smith & Taylor, 13 1/2 In. 20.00
Liberty Blue, Cup & Saucer, Enoch Wedgwood 12.00
Lido, Bowl, Fruit, W.S. George, 5 1/2 In. 12.00
Lido, Plate, Bread & Butter, W.S. George, 6 1/2 In. 12.00
Lu-Ray, Eggcup, Double, Windsor Blue, Taylor Smith & Taylor 45.00
Memory Lane, Butter, Cover, Royal China 45.00
Memory Lane, Casserole, Cover, Royal China 90.00
Memory Lane, Teapot, Royal China 90.00
Minion, Platter, Square, Maroon, Paden City Pottery, 13 1/2 In. 20.00
Monticello, Berry Bowl, Salem China, 5 1/2 In. 10.00
Monticello, Bowl, Vegetable, Salem China, 9 In. 20.00
Monticello, Creamer, Salem China 20.00
Monticello, Platter, Oval, Salem China, 13 3/4 In. 15.00
Monticello, Sugar, Cover, Salem China 20.00
Morning Glory, Plate, Luncheon, Paden City Pottery, 9 1/4 In. 15.00
Old Curiosity Shop, Bowl, Cereal, Tab Handles, Royal China, 6 3/8 In. 40.00
Old Curiosity Shop, Casserole, Cover, Royal China 90.00
Old Curiosity Shop, Mug, Royal China 50.00
Old Curiosity Shop, Plate, Luncheon, Royal China, 9 In. 24.00
Old Curiosity Shop, Platter, Round, Royal China, 13 In. 80.00
Old Curiosity Shop, Sugar & Creamer, Royal China 40.00
Old Curiosity Shop, Teapot, Royal China 90.00
Opulence, Pitcher, Bulbous, Blue Ridge, 6 1/4 x 8 1/2 In. 290.00
Peach Blossom, Plate, Dinner, W.S. George, 9 1/4 In. 9.00
Pebbleford, Cup & Saucer, Mint Green, Taylor, Smith & Taylor 9.00
Pebbleford, Plate, Bread & Butter, Mint Green, Taylor, Smith & Taylor, 6 In. 6.00
Pebbleford, Plate, Bread & Butter, Pink, Taylor, Smith & Taylor, 6 1/2 In. 6.00
Pebbleford, Plate, Dinner, Mint Green, Taylor, Smith & Taylor, 10 In. 6.00
Pebbleford, Plate, Salad, Pink, Taylor, Smith & Taylor, 8 In. 6.00
Pebbleford, Platter, Sand, Taylor, Smith & Taylor, 13 In. 20.00
Petal Lane, Plate, Salad, Taylor, Smith & Taylor, 7 In. 7.50
Petit Point Basket, Casserole, Cover, Salem China, 9 In. 78.00
Petit Point Basket, Cup, Salem China 8.00
Petit Point Basket, Plate, Dinner, Salem China, 9 1/2 In. 14.00
Petit Point Basket, Platter, Oval, Salem China, 11 1/4 In. 19.00
Petit Point House, Chop Plate, Crooksville, 12 In. 38.00
Petit Point House, Plate, Dinner, Crooksville, 10 In. 33.00
Petit Point House, Platter, Oval, Crooksville, 11 1/4 In. 29.00
Petit Point House, Platter, Oval, Crooksville, 13 1/4 In. 40.00
Petit Point Leaf, Gravy Boat, Underplate, Crooksville 22.00
Poinsettia, Eggcup, Double, Blue Ridge 55.00
Quaker Apple, Plate, Luncheon, Blue Ridge, 9 1/2 In. 18.00
Quban Royal, Bowl, Vegetable, Royal China, 9 In. 30.00
Quban Royal, Chop Plate, Royal China, 12 In. 30.00
Quban Royal, Salt & Pepper, Royal China, 9 In. 30.00
Radisson, Bowl, Fruit, W.S. George, 5 In. 8.00
Radisson, Platter, Oval, W.S. George, 13 1/2 In. 10.00
Rooster, Bowl, Vegetable, Oval, Blue Ridge, 9 1/2 In. 50.00
Rose Marie, Creamer, Blue Ridge 63.00
Rose Marie, Sugar, Blue Ridge 33.00
Sculptured Fruit, Jug, Blue Ridge, 32 Oz., 6 3/4 In. 85.00
Sea Shell, Creamer, Taylor, Smith & Taylor, 8 In. 12.00
Sea Shell, Plate, Dinner, Taylor, Smith & Taylor, 10 1/4 In. 11.00
Sea Shell, Soup, Dish, Taylor, Smith & Taylor, 8 In. 13.00
Sheffield, Bowl, Vegetable, Salem China 25.00
Sheffield, Cup & Saucer, Salem China 12.00
Sheffield, Plate, Dinner, Salem China, 9 5/8 In. 14.00
Sheffield, Platter, Oval, Salem China, 11 3/4 In. 25.00
Sheffield, Soup, Dish, Salem China, 8 1/2 In. 13.00
Sheffield, Sugar, Cover, Salem China 25.00
Silver Elegance, Plate, Bread & Butter, Salem China, 6 In. 6.00
Silver Elegance, Plate, Salad, Salem China, 7 In. 7.00
Song Bird, Plate, Salad, Blue Ridge, 8 1/2 In. 140.00

Star Glow, Bowl, Vegetable, Royal China, 9 3/4 In.	26.00
Star Glow, Butter, Cover, Royal China	30.00
Star Glow, Coffeepot, Royal China	75.00
Star Glow, Salt & Pepper, Royal China	30.00
Star Glow, Teapot, Royal China	60.00
Strawberry, Plate, Dinner, Blue Ridge, 10 1/2 In.	19.00
Twyla, Bowl, Vegetable, Oval, W.S. George, 9 3/8 In.	24.00
Twyla, Platter, Oval, W.S. George, 11 1/2 In.	25.00
Violet Spray, Butter, Cover, Blue Ridge	60.00
Whimsey, Bowl, Cereal, Salem China, 6 In.	9.00
Woodfield, Snack Set, Jungle Green, Leaf Shape Plate, 9-In. Plate, 2 Piece	18.00
Woodfield, Snack Set, Salmon Pink, Leaf Shape Plate, 9-In. Plate, 2 Piece	18.00
Woodfield, Snack Set, Salmon Pink, Steubenville, 8 1/2 In., 2 Piece	25.00
Woodland, Chop Plate, Blue Ridge, 12 In.	14.00
Zinnia, Chop Plate, Blue Ridge, 12 In.	14.00

DIONNE QUINTUPLETS were born in Canada on May 28, 1934. The publicity about their birth and their special status as wards of the Canadian government made them famous throughout the world. Visitors could watch the girls play; reporters interviewed the girls and the staff. Thousands of special dolls and souvenirs were made picturing the quints at different ages. Emilie died in 1954, Marie in 1970, and Yvonne in 2001. Annette and Cecile still live in Canada.

Advertisement, Karo Syrup, Look At The Quintuplets, 1937, 12 x 8 1/2 In.	13.00
Book, Wonderful Dionne Quintuplets, Whitman, 1934-1935	45.00
Bowl, Cereal, Embossed Faces, Inscribed Names, Aluminum, 5 In.	35.00
Calendar, 1938, Mother Goose, Torrington Creamery	38.00
Doll, Madame Alexander, Composition, Human Hair, 11 In., 5 Piece	2310.00
Doll, Madame Alexander, Composition, Toddler, 7 1/2 In., 5 Piece	965.00 to 1650.00
Magazine, Click, Quintuplets Cover Story, June 1940, 52 Pages	8.00
Paper Doll, Punch-Out Cover, Mailer, Colgate, 1937, 9 1/4 x 9 3/4 In.	40.00
Paper Doll Set, Shackman, New York, 10 x 14 1/2 In.	15.00
Photograph, Quintuplets In Basket, 1936, 8 x 10 In.	35.00

DIRK VAN ERP was born in 1860 and died in 1933. He opened his own studio in 1908 in Oakland, California. He moved his studio to San Francisco in 1909 and the studio remained under the direction of his son until 1977. Van Erp made hammered copper accessories, including vases, desk sets, bookends, candlesticks, jardinieres, and trays, but he is best known for his lamps. The hammered copper lamps often had shades with mica panels.

Basket, Flower, Copper, Hammered, 8 x 11 In.	2012.00
Bookends, Copper, Hammered, Cutout Stylized Tulip, 4 1/2 x 6 In.	400.00
Bookends, Copper, Hammered, Overlay Oak Trees & Hills, 4 1/2 x 5 3/4 In.	1495.00
Bookends, Copper, Hammered, Shield Form, Pine Needle, Medium Patina, 6 x 5 In.	345.00
Bowl, Copper, Hammered, Darcy Gaw, 2 3/4 x 12 In.	1495.00
Bowl, Copper, Hammered, Medium Patina, Stamped, 9 1/2 In.	805.00
Bowl, Copper, Hammered, Open Box Mark, 2 1/8 x 4 1/2 In.	750.00
Bowl, Copper, Hammered, Organic Shape, Signed Harry Dixon, 12 In.	550.00
Bowl, Flared, Copper, 3 1/2 x 18 1/2 In.	920.00
Box, Copper, Hammered, Hinged Lid, Monogram, Original Patina, 3 1/2 In.	765.00
Coal Bucket, Copper, Hammered, Riveted Brass Bands, Dark Patina, 17 x 10 In.	4600.00
Crumber Set, Copper, Hammered, 9 In., 2 Piece	345.00
Lamp, Hammered Copper, Bulbous Base, 4-Panel Mica, Copper Shade, 11 x 11 In.	8625.00
Letter Opener, Copper, Hammered, Open Box Mark, 11 1/2 In.	230.00 to 575.00
Vase, Copper, Hammered, 2 7/8 In.	1090.00
Vase, Copper, Hammered, 4 1/2 x 6 In.	2185.00
Vase, Copper, Hammered, 5 1/4 In.	980.00
Vase, Copper, Hammered, Bulbous, Medium Patina, 3 x 4 In.	575.00
Vase, Copper, Hammered, Medium Patina, Shouldered, Wide Mouth, 8 1/2 In.	1765.00
Vase, Copper, Hammered, Open Box Mark, 5 1/2 In.	1725.00
Vase, Copper, Hammered, Round, Impressed Open Box Mark, 4 1/2 In.	1410.00
Vase, Copper, Hammered, Signed, 2 In.	690.00

Vase, Copper, Hammered, Signed, Closed Box Mark, Darcy Gaw, 4 In. 1725.00
Vase, Copper, Hammered, Spherical, Original Patina, 5 1/4 x 7 In. 3100.00
Vase, Copper, Hammered, Tapered, Closed Rim, Dark Patina, 8 x 5 1/2 In. 2875.00
Vase, Tapered, Closed Box Mark, 8 1/2 In. 2415.00
Vase, Warty, Open Box Mark, 7 In. 2415.00

DISNEYANA is a collector's term. Walt Disney and his company introduced many comic characters to the world. Collectors search for examples of the work of the Disney Studios and the many commercial
products modeled after his characters, including Mickey Mouse and
Donald Duck, and recent films, like *Beauty and the Beast* and *The
Little Mermaid.*

Bank, Donald Duck, Composition, Walt Disney Enterprise, 1938, 6 In. . . . . .165.00 to 187.00
Bank, Mickey Mouse, Book, Embossed, Key, Zell, c.1933, 3 x 4 1/2 In. 385.00
Bank, Mickey Mouse, Composition, Walt Disney Crown Toy, 6 In. 165.00
Bank, Mickey Mouse, Delaware Water Gap, Yellow Shorts, Metal, 3 1/2 In. 1555.00
Book, 3 Caballeros, Random House, 1944 . . . .   1200.00
Book, 3 Orphan Kittens, Whitman, 1935, 47 Pages 750.00
Book, Donald Duck, Grosset & Dunlap, 1936 . . . .   600.00
Book, Life Of Donald Duck, Random House, 1941, 72 Pages 475.00
Book, Mickey Mouse Mother Goose, Whitman, 1937 . . . .   750.00
Book, Mickey Mouse Presents Nursery Stories, Whitman, 1937 . . . .   450.00
Book, Mickey Mouse Silly Symphonies, Pop-Up, Dust Wrapper, 1933 . . . .   1500.00
Book, Robber Kitten, Whitman, 1935 . . . .   350.00
Bottle Stopper, Pinocchio, Long Nose, Silver Plated, 1940s, 4 1/2 In. 95.00
Box, Mickey & Minnie Mouse, Yellow, Red, Tin Lithograph, Germany, c.1935, 10 x 8 In.   390.00
Box, Mickey Mouse, Cookies, Nabisco, c.1948 . . . .   70.00
Box, Paint Set, Donald Duck, Mickey Mouse, Watercolor, 5 3/4 x 4 1/2 In. 50.00
Box, Pinocchio Chewing Gum, Cardboard, Dietz Gum Co., 1940 . . . .   325.00
Box, Tin, Mickey Mouse, Pie-Eyed, 1933, 10 x 8 x 7 In. 675.00
Button, Mickey Mouse, Hits Wolf With Toothbrush, Good Teeth, Dental Association 165.00
Cel, see Animation Art category.
Clock, Alarm, Donald Duck, Plastic, Germany, 7 In. 10.00
Clock, Alarm, Mickey Mouse, Bayard Mickey, Rocking Head, France, c.1977, 6 In. 160.00
Clock, Pluto, Electric, Plastic, Allied, 1950s, 9 In. 105.00
Condiment Set, Mickey Mouse, Salt, Pepper, Sugar, Cover, Ladle, Tray, Germany, c.1930   460.00
Costume, Zorro, Mask, Skirt, Cape, Pants, Ben Cooper, Box 195.00
Dish, Mickey Mouse, Baby Food, 6 1/2 In. 65.00
Doll, Donald Duck, Celluloid, Jointed, c.1940, 3 In. 85.00
Doll, Donald Duck, Cloth, Knickerbocker, 17 In. 495.00
Doll, Donald Duck, Composition Head, Marionette, Madame Alexander, c.1940, 9 In. . . .   405.00
Doll, Donald Duck, Composition, Movable Head, Knickerbocker, c.1936, 5 1/2 In. 470.00
Doll, Donald Duck, Felt, 13 In. 205.00
Doll, Dopey, Ventriloquist, Composition, Cloth, Stuffed, Ideal, 20 In. 165.00
Doll, Jiminy Cricket, Wood Jointed, Socket Neck, Ideal, 1940, 9 In. 410.00
Doll, Jiminy Cricket, Wood, Flexible, Top Hat, Umbrella, Ideal, c.1935, 9 In. 840.00
Doll, Mickey Mouse, Bandmaster, Cloth, Composition, c.1935, 19 In. 1320.00
Doll, Mickey Mouse, Button, Chest, Ear Tag, Open Mouth, Steiff, 12 In. 4400.00
Doll, Mickey Mouse, Celluloid, Jointed, c.1940, 6 In. 140.00
Doll, Mickey Mouse, Cowboy, Cloth, Composition, Leather, Gun, Knickerbocker, 10 In. . .   935.00
Doll, Mickey Mouse, Cowboy, Guns, Lasso, Hat, Knickerbocker, 1936, 13 In. 2640.00
Doll, Mickey Mouse, Lollipop Hands, Wood Jointed, Leather Ears, 6 1/2 In. 605.00
Doll, Mickey Mouse, Lollipop Hands, Wood, Disney, c.1930, 9 In. 650.00
Doll, Mickey Mouse, Mohair, Steiff, Box, 14 In. 120.00
Doll, Mickey Mouse, Open Mouth, Pie Eyes, Whiskers, Buttons, Steiff, 8 3/4 In. 1240.00
Doll, Mickey Mouse, Stuffed, Corduroy, Velveteen, c.1930, 21 In. 165.00
Doll, Mickey Mouse, Stuffed, Velveteen, Cloth, France, c.1930, 10 In. 195.00
Doll, Mickey Mouse, Wood, Jointed, 9 1/2 In. 1155.00
Doll, Mickey Mouse, Wood, Jointed, Decal, 5 In. 220.00
Doll, Pinocchio, Composition Head, Wood, Painted, Ideal, 7 In. 140.00
Doll, Pinocchio, Composition, Wood Jointed, Ideal Novelty & Toy Co., c.1940, 12 In. . . .   275.00
Doll, Pinocchio, Composition, Wood, Jointed, Painted, Ideal, 7 1/2 In. 110.00
Figurine, Donald Duck, Ceramic, Japan, 3 In. 50.00

Figurine, Donald Duck, Plays Violin, Bisque, 1930s, 4 1/2 In. 475.00
Figurine, Florida Orange Bird, Vinyl, Disney, 1973, 5 In. 45.00
Figurine, Mickey & Minnie Mouse, Hand Painted, Continental, c.1930, 5 In. 210.00
Figurine, Mickey Mouse, Carousel, Wood, H. Oevos, France, 1930s, 36 x 28 In. 1100.00
Figurine, Mickey Mouse, Ceramic, Marked, Walt E. Disney, 3 In. 20.00
Figurine, Mickey Mouse, With Sword, Bisque, Prewar Japan, 4 In. 210.00
Figurine, Minnie Mouse, Carousel, Wood, H. Oevos, France, 1930s, 36 x 28 In. 495.00
Figurine, Minnie Mouse, With Umbrella, Bisque, Prewar Japan, 4 In. 210.00
Figurine, Minnie Mouse, Wood, c.1930, 5 In. 175.00
Figurine, Snow White & 7 Dwarfs, Knickerbocker Toy, c.1940, 9 & 15 In., 8 Piece 3960.00
Figurine Set, Winnie The Pooh, Walt Disney, Beswick, 1971-1990, 8 Piece 689.00
Game, Mickey Mouse, Dominoes, Cardboard Box, Halsam, 1 x 8 5/8 x 2 In. 245.00
Game, Monorail, Parker Brothers, 1960 . . . . 25.00
Game, Silly Symphony, Donald, Mickey, Minnie, Horace, Card, 4 x 3 In. 135.00
Game, Winnie The Pooh, Parker Brothers, 1933 . . . . .230.00 to 340.00
Game, Zorro, Box, 1966 . . . . 115.00
Game, Zorro, Parker Brothers, 1966 . . . . 600.00
Globe, Mickey Mouse, Rand McNally, Tin Base, Early 1960s, 6 In., 6 1/2-In. Base 65.00
Lighter, Donald Duck, Slim, Zippo, 1976 . . . . 46.00
Lunch Box, Disney On Parade, Metal, Aladdin, 1970 . . . . 20.00
Lunch Box, Mickey Mouse, Lunch Kit, Hinged Handles, Tin Lithograph, 1935, 5 x 8 In. . . 660.00
Lunch Box, Peter Pan, Metal, Thermos, Aladdin, 1960s 69.00
Lunch Box, School Bus, Aladdin, c.1960 . . . . 40.00
Lunch Pail, Mickey Mouse, Tin Lithograph, 7 1/2 In. 130.00
Lunch Tin, Snow White, Scenes, Tin, Handles, Walt Disney, Belgium, c.1939, 8 In. 385.00
Movie Projector, Mickey Mouse, 4 Film Rolls, 11 In. 140.00
Movie Projector, Mickey Mouse, Movie Jecktor, Tin, 6 Films, Boxes 169.00
Napkin Ring, Mickey Mouse, Celluloid, Hand Painted, England, 1930s 265.00
Nodder, Donald Duck, Celluloid, Prewar Japan, 6 In. 525.00
Nodder, Mickey Mouse, Celluloid, Japan, c.1930, 7 In. 1100.00
Pail, Donald Duck, Mickey, Pig, Tin, Happynak, England, c.1930, 4 1/2 In. 245.00
Pail, Donald Duck, Tug Of War, Blue, Tin, Bail Handle, Ohio Art, 1949, 4 1/4 In. 250.00
Pail, Mickey & Minnie Mouse, At Beach, Yellow Handle, Green, Tin, U.S.A., 8 In. 800.00
Pail, Mickey Mouse, Emergency Road Repair, Yellow, Tin, Bail Handle, Ohio Art, 8 In. . . 935.00
Pail, Mickey Mouse, Mickey's Ice Cold Drinks, Blue, Tin, Bail Handle, Ohio Art, 3 In. . . 250.00
Pail, Snow White & 7 Dwarfs, Tin Lithograph, Ohio Art Co., 1938, 6 x 5 3/4 In. 580.00
Pail, Snow White & 7 Dwarfs, Yellow, Tin, Bail Handle, Ohio Art, 1939, 5 3/4 In. 330.00
Pail, Tin, Lithograph, Willow Australia, c.1939, 6 In. 415.00
Pencil Box, Peter Pan, Snap Front, Sliding Drawer Inside, 1950s, 8 3/4 x 5 In. 25.00
Pencil Sharpener, Mickey Mouse, Celluloid, Prewar Japan, 3 In. 100.00
Pennant, Disneyland, Park That Walt Built, Early 1960s 35.00
Pin, Uncle Remus, Brer Rabbit, c.1930, 1 1/4 In. 25.00
Pitcher, Mickey Mouse, Ceramic, Prewar Japan, 7 In. 170.00
Pitcher, Mickey Mouse, Porcelain, 4 In. 145.00
Plaque, Fantasia, Pewter Rim, Vernon Kilns, 14 1/2 In. 730.00
Poster, Snow White & 7 Dwarfs, 1943 Re-release, 27 x 41 In. 605.00
Projector, Mickey Mouse, Mickey Mouse Club Newsreel, Strip, Box, 1950s 305.00
Puppet, Dopey, Composition Head, Cloth Body, Hat, Painted Features, 10 In. 11.00
Puppet, Mickey Mouse, Hand, Whiskers, Button In Ear, Steiff, 9 1/2 In. 1210.00
Salt & Pepper, Alice In Wonderland, White Rabbit, Stacking, Japan, 4 In. 85.00
Salt & Pepper, Doc & Bashful, Marked, Foreign, 1930s, 2 7/8 In. 85.00
Salt & Pepper, Donald Duck, 3 1/4 In. 70.00
Salt & Pepper, Donald Duck, Dan Brechner, 1961, 4 7/8 In. 95.00
Salt & Pepper, Dumbo, Leeds, 1940s, 4 3/8 In. 95.00
Salt & Pepper, Goofy & Pluto, Anthropomorphic Car, Japan, 1930s, 4 1/4 x 4 In. 295.00
Salt & Pepper, Mickey & Minnie Mouse, Ceramic, 3 In. 6.00
Salt & Pepper, Mickey & Minnie Mouse, Ceramic, Leeds, c.1935, 3 1/4 In. 95.00
Salt & Pepper, Pinocchio, Porcelain, Bisque, Japan, 5 In. 125.00
Sign, Donald Duck, Bread, Oven Fresh Flavor, Cardboard, 1950s, 25 x 11 In. 55.00
Sign, Donald Duck, Sunoco Winter Oil, Grease, Walt Disney Ent., 1938, 58 x 36 In. 330.00
Soaky, Pinocchio, Colgate-Palmolive, 1965, 10 In. 60.00
Tin, 25th Anniversary Of Walt Disney World, Nestle Toll House, 1996, 6 1/2 In. 12.00
Tin, Donald Duck Chocolate Syrup, Walt Disney Productions, 4 1/2 x 2 5/8 In. 190.00

Tin, Donald Duck Tomato Juice, Unopened, Empty, NAAS, Indiana, 3 3/4 x 2 1/8 In. 95.00
Toothbrush Holder, 3 Little Pigs, Ceramic, Japan, 4 In. 100.00
Toothbrush Holder, Donald Duck, Bisque 350.00
Toothbrush Holder, Mickey & Minnie Mouse, Ceramic, Japan, 4 1/2 In. 1545.00
Toothbrush Holder, Mickey Mouse, Ceramic, 5 In. 185.00
Toothbrush Holder, Mickey Mouse, Wiping Pluto's Nose, Bisque 350.00
Toothbrush Holder, Mickey Mouse, Yawning, Porcelain, 1960s, 4 3/4 In. 135.00
Toothbrush Holder, Snow White, Doc, Porcelain, c.1950, 4 1/4 In. . . . . : 175.00
Toy, 3 Little Pigs, Instruments, Cloth Over Tin, Clockwork, Schuco, c.1930, 4 1/2 In. 660.00
Toy, Buzz Buzz The Bee, Whirligig, Box, c.1960 . . . . 350.00
Toy, Car, Parade, Plastic Figures, Tin Lithograph, Windup, Marx, 11 In. 450.00
Toy, Disney Express, Engine, 3 Cars, Tin Lithograph, Linemar, Box, c.1950s, 12 In. 275.00
Toy, Disneyland Ferris Wheel, Tin, Windup, J. Chein, 1955, 17 In. 550.00
Toy, Disneyland Ferris Wheel, Windup, Chein, Box, American, c.1940s, 16 In. 715.00
Toy, Disneyland Roller Coaster, Tin, Windup, J. Chein, 1955, 20 x 9 1/2 In. 700.00
Toy, Donald Duck & Goofy, Dancing, Tin Lithograph, Windup, Marx, 1946, 10 1/2 In. 520.00
Toy, Donald Duck & Huey, Tin, Linemar, Box, 5 1/2 In. 1045.00
Toy, Donald Duck & Pluto, Car, Roadster, Sun Rubber, 6 1/2 In. . . . . : . 115.00
Toy, Donald Duck & Pluto, Handcar, Windup, Tin, Composition, Box, Lionel, 10 1/2 In. . . 1380.00
Toy, Donald Duck & Pluto, Rail Car, Composition, Lionel, Box 825.00
Toy, Donald Duck, Bubble Duck, Blows Bubbles, Box, c.1940 . . . . 225.00
Toy, Donald Duck, Car, Dipsy, Tin, Plastic, Windup, Marx WDP, Box, 6 In. . . . . . .525.00 to 550.00
Toy, Donald Duck, Car, Drives, Convertible, Tin, Friction, Linemar, c.1950, 6 In. 145.00
Toy, Donald Duck, Car, Flivver, Tin, Friction, Linemar, Box, 5 1/2 In. 635.00
Toy, Donald Duck, Carousel, Windup, Celluloid, 8 In. 2640.00
Toy, Donald Duck, Carousel, Windup, Prewar Japan, Borgfeldt Walt Disney, Box, 8 In. . . . 2900.00
Toy, Donald Duck, Cart, Pulled By Pluto, Celluloid, Windup, Prewar Japan, 9 In. 2200.00
Toy, Donald Duck, Donald Drums, Goofy Dances, Tin, Marx, Box, 1946, 10 In. . . .785.00 to 910.00
Toy, Donald Duck, Drummer, Tin, Windup, WDP, Box, 6 1/2 In. 456.00
Toy, Donald Duck, Duet, Windup, Tin, Marx, 1949 . . . . 695.00
Toy, Donald Duck, Fireman, Ladder, Tin, Linemar, Box, 1950s, 6 x 14 In. . . . . . . .360.00 to 688.00
Toy, Donald Duck, Gymnast, Celluloid, Wire Apparatus, Windup, 1930s 350.00
Toy, Donald Duck, Nodder, Celluloid, Metal, 6 In. 305.00
Toy, Donald Duck, Nodder, Windup, Celluloid, Metal Base, 6 In. 550.00
Toy, Donald Duck, Skiing, Tin Lithograph, Windup, Linemar, Japan, c.1950s, 6 In. 825.00
Toy, Donald Duck, Straight Shooter, Tin, Plastic, Windup, Box, 1950s, 6 In. 275.00
Toy, Donald Duck, Tin, Plastic, Windup, Schuco, Box, 1950s, 6 1/2 In. 450.00
Toy, Donald Duck, Tractor, Dipsy, Windup, Tin, Plastic, Marx, 1950 . . . . 550.00
Toy, Donald Duck, Tractor, Plastic, Friction, 4 In. . . . . .78.00 to 115.00
Toy, Donald Duck, Tricycle, Windup, Tin Litho, Celluloid, Linemar, Box, 4 In. . . . .300.00 to 400.00
Toy, Donald Duck, Truck, Gasoline, Tin, Friction, Linemar, 13 In. 495.00
Toy, Donald Duck, Walker, Celluloid, Windup, Borgfeldt, 3 1/4 In. 675.00
Toy, Donald Duck, Walker, Celluloid, Windup, Borgfeldt, Box, 3 1/4 In. 875.00
Toy, Donald Duck, Walker, Celluloid, Windup, Box, Geo Borgfeldt, 5 1/2 In. 2100.00
Toy, Donald Duck, Walker, Composition, Windup, Borgfeldt, Lewis, Scott, 1930s, 11 In. . . 550.00
Toy, Donald Duck, Whirling Tail, Bounces, Plastic, Windup, Marx, Box, 6 1/2 In. 140.00
Toy, Donald Duck, Xylophone, Pull, Wood, Fisher Price, 1946, 13 x 11 In. 195.00
Toy, Dopey, Walker, Windup, Tin Lithograph, Marx, Box, 8 In. . . . . .410.00 to 750.00
Toy, Dumbo, Acrobat, Tin, Windup, Marx, Box, 1941, 4 In. 385.00
Toy, Dumbo, Acrobat, Windup, Walt Disney, Box 825.00
Toy, Dumbo, Carousel, 3 Dumbos, Tin, Windup, Marx, Japan, WDP, 5 1/2 In. 990.00
Toy, Ferdinand The Bull & Matador, Flat, Windup, Marx, Box, American, c.1930, 7 In. 935.00
Toy, Ferdinand The Bull, Rubber, Seiberling, 1930s, 6 In. 125.00
Toy, Ferdinand The Bull, Tin Lithograph, Windup, Linemar, c.1940s, 5 1/2 In. . . . .210.00 to 305.00
Toy, Ferris Wheel, Tin, Windup, Lithograph, Marx WDP, 17 In. 470.00
Toy, Figaro, Roll Over, Tin, Windup, Box 450.00
Toy, Goofy, Gardener, Walks, Legs Move, Clockwork, Marx, Box 780.00
Toy, Goofy, Lawn Mower, Bump-N-Go, Battery Operated, Walt Disney, Box 50.00
Toy, Jiminy Cricket, Hops, Squeeze Handle, Tin, Linemar, WDP, 7 In. 330.00
Toy, Ludwig Von Drake, Tin, Windup, Linemar, 1950s 425.00
Toy, Mickey & Minnie Mouse, Acrobats, Celluloid, George Borgfeldt, Box, 13 In. 605.00
Toy, Mickey & Minnie Mouse, Fishing Kit, Tin Lithograph, 1920s, 4 1/2 x 7 1/2 In. 550.00
Toy, Mickey & Minnie Mouse, Playland, Celluloid, Clockwork, Box, Japan, c.1930 . . . . . 1725.00

Toy, Mickey & Minnie Mouse, Watering Can, Tin 100.00
Toy, Mickey Mouse & Betty Boop, Umbrella, Celluloid, 7 In. 2970.00
Toy, Mickey Mouse & Minnie Mouse, Organ Grinder, Windup, Tin Lithograph, 7 1/2 In. . 4950.00
Toy, Mickey Mouse, Acrobat, Pie-Eyed, Prewar Japan, Geo Borgfeldt 1995.00
Toy, Mickey Mouse, Bendy, Rubber, England, 11 In. 6.00
Toy, Mickey Mouse, Car, Dipsy, Windup, Linemar, Box ....775.00 to 875.00
Toy, Mickey Mouse, Car, Dipsy, Windup, Tin Lithograph, Linemar, 6 In. 415.00
Toy, Mickey Mouse, Car, Krazy, Battery Operated, Louis Marx & Co., Box 85.00
Toy, Mickey Mouse, Car, Oldtimer, Tin, Plastic, Lever Action, Box, Japan, 4 1/2 In. 17.00
Toy, Mickey Mouse, Crib, Composition, Jointed, 7 In. 250.00
Toy, Mickey Mouse, Cyclist, Moves In Circle, Bell Rings, Linemar, Box, c.1950, 6 1/2 In. 3376.00
Toy, Mickey Mouse, Doctor's Kit, 1978 .... 15.00
Toy, Mickey Mouse, Drum, Drumsticks, Disney Ent., 1930s, 6 1/2 In. 195.00
Toy, Mickey Mouse, Drummer, Battery Operated, Tin Lithograph, Linemar, Box, 11 In. ... 1795.00
Toy, Mickey Mouse, Drummer, Yellow Green Drum, Mechanical, c.1930, 7 In. 1320.00
Toy, Mickey Mouse, Handcar, Composition Figures, Clockwork, Lionel, Box 55.00
Toy, Mickey Mouse, Handcar, Composition, Track, Wells, Box, England, 7 1/2 In. 2065.00
Toy, Mickey Mouse, Horse, Windup, Celluloid, Japan, 7 1/2 In. 2185.00
Toy, Mickey Mouse, Library Of Games, 1946, 6 In. 20.00
Toy, Mickey Mouse, Magic Lantern, 8 Slides, The Castaway, 1930-1950 .... 205.00
Toy, Mickey Mouse, Magician, Chick, Tin, Battery Operated, Linemar, Box, 10 In. 1930.00
Toy, Mickey Mouse, Magician, Tin Lithograph, Linemar, Japan, c.1950s, 6 In. 1350.00
Toy, Mickey Mouse, Magician, Waves Wand, Drops Hat, Tin, Linemar, Box, c.1950, 10 In. 1650.00
Toy, Mickey Mouse, Mickey's Delivery, Tin, Friction, Linemar, Japan, 1950s, 5 1/2 In. 305.00
Toy, Mickey Mouse, Movers Truck, Tin, Friction, Linemar, WDP, 13 In. 250.00
Toy, Mickey Mouse, Musician, Marx, Box, 1950s, 11 In. ....550.00 to 650.00
Toy, Mickey Mouse, Plays Mandolin, Bisque, c.1930, 3 1/2 In. 250.00
Toy, Mickey Mouse, Rambler, Waddles, Celluloid, Windup, Prewar Japan, 8 In. .1760.00 to 2875.00
Toy, Mickey Mouse, Riding Pluto, Celluloid, Windup, Occupied Japan, 6 1/2 In. 2090.00
Toy, Mickey Mouse, Rubber, Seiberling, 1930s, 3 1/2 In. 95.00
Toy, Mickey Mouse, Rubber, Seiberling, 1930s, 6 In. 145.00
Toy, Mickey Mouse, Sax Player, Flat, Tin, Squeeze, c.1932, 6 In. 690.00
Toy, Mickey Mouse, Scooter, Moves Leg, Plastic, Windup, Mavco, Box, 6 1/2 In. 220.00
Toy, Mickey Mouse, Scooter, Peddles, Tin, Windup, Linemar WDP, 4 1/2 In. .....400.00 to 495.00
Toy, Mickey Mouse, Stockings, Paper Bands, Tags, Box, 7 x 11 In. 605.00
Toy, Mickey Mouse, Tambourine, Tin, Paper Lithograph, 7 In. 285.00
Toy, Mickey Mouse, Telephone, Steel, Wood, Paper Lithograph, 7 In. 150.00
Toy, Mickey Mouse, Train, Circus, Metal, Tin, Engine, Tender, 3 Cars, Lionel, c.1930 .... 1870.00
Toy, Mickey Mouse, Train, Circus, Spins, Tin, Windup, Wells England, Box, 1930, 18 In. . 965.00
Toy, Mickey Mouse, Train, Circus, Tin Lithograph, Composition Mickey, Lionel, 28 In. ... 1320.00
Toy, Mickey Mouse, Train, Express, Tin Lithograph, Marx, c.1930s, 9 In. 550.00
Toy, Mickey Mouse, Trapeze, Somersaults On Metal Rod, Celluloid, Windup, 1930s 375.00
Toy, Mickey Mouse, Unicycle, Tin Lithograph, Windup, Linemar, c.1950s, 5 In. 415.00
Toy, Mickey Mouse, Whirligig, Borgfeldt, Japan, Box, c.1934, 10 In. 4620.00
Toy, Mickey Mouse, Whirligig, Celluloid, Windup, Tin Platform, Box, Borgfeldt, 8 In. ... 2200.00
Toy, Mickey Mouse, Xylophone Player, Tin, Windup, Linemar WDP, 6 1/2 In. 385.00
Toy, Mickey Mouse, Xylophone, Tin Lithograph, Linemar, Japan, c.1950s, 6 In. 440.00
Toy, Mickey Mouse, Xylophone, Tin, Windup, Linemar, Box, 7 In. 360.00
Toy, Minnie Mouse, In Rocker, Knits, Tin, Windup, Linemar, Box, 7 In. ....450.00 to 850.00
Toy, Minnie Mouse, Marionette, England, Box, c.1950 .... 75.00
Toy, Minnie Mouse, Shopping Cart, Plastic, Battery Operated, Walt Disney, Box 30.00
Toy, Minnie Mouse, Washing Machine, Revell Plastics, Box, 1950s, 8 1/2 In. 210.00
Toy, Nodder, Mickey Mouse, Banjo, Celluloid, Windup, Copt. 1928, 7 In. 805.00
Toy, Peter Pan, Television Studio Kit, Admiral Television, Unopened, Box, 1953 .... 250.00
Toy, Pinocchio, Acrobat, Tin Lithograph, Clockwork, Marx, 1939, 16 1/2 In. 275.00
Toy, Pinocchio, Battery Operated, Rosko, Box, 10 In. 155.00
Toy, Pinocchio, Paper Doll, 1939 .... 295.00
Toy, Pinocchio, Walker, Tin Lithograph, Clockwork, Linemar, 6 In. 250.00
Toy, Pinocchio, Walker, Tin Lithograph, Clockwork, Walt Disney Ent., 1939, 8 1/2 In. ... 385.00
Toy, Pinocchio, Walker, Tin, Linemar, Box, 6 In. 550.00
Toy, Pinocchio, Windup Walker, Tin Lithograph, Marx, Box, 8 1/2 In. 415.00
Toy, Pinocchio, Xylophone, Tin, Rubber, Battery Operated, Video Craft, Japan, Box, 1962 160.00
Toy, Pluto & Goofy, Vibrates, Tails Spin, Tin, Windup, Linemar, Box, 5 1/2 In. 1320.00

Toy, Pluto, Bee On Nose, Plush, Battery Operated, Box, 10 In. 65.00
Toy, Pluto, Cast Lead, Painted, Allied Toys, 2 1/4 In. 11.00
Toy, Pluto, Delivery Wagon, Celluloid, Tin, Linemar, Box, 5 1/2 In. 495.00
Toy, Pluto, Friction, Tin Lithograph, Marx, c.1939, 9 In. 79.00
Toy, Pluto, Moves, Megaphone Sounds, Tin, Windup, Linemar, Box, 6 1/2 In. 310.00
Toy, Pluto, Rollover, Tin, Windup, Box, 1930s 475.00
Toy, Pluto, Running Rubber Ears & Tail, Linemar, Box, 7 In. 600.00
Toy, Pluto, Sniffing Ground, Tin Lithograph, Clockwork, Louis Marx, Box, c.1939, 8 In. .. 468.00
Toy, Pluto, Tin Lithograph, Friction, Linemar, 4 1/2 In. 90.00
Toy, Pluto, Tin Lithograph, Friction, Linemar, 6 1/2 In. 210.00
Toy, Professor Von Drake, Walker, Tin, Linemar, Box, 6 In. 635.00
Toy, Roller Coaster, Tin, Windup, Chein, Box, 19 In. 506.00
Toy, Roo Kangaroo, Plush, Straw Filled, Shoe Button Eyes, 19 In. 55.00
Toy, Snow White & 7 Dwarfs, Vinyl, Box, c.1950, 22-In. Snow White 385.00
Toy, Snow White & 7 Dwarfs, Washing Machine, Windup, Revell, Box 66.00
Toy, Snow White, Washing Machine, Pink, Revell Plastics, Box, 1950s, 9 In. 265.00
Toy, Stroller, Oswald The Rabbit, Tin, 6 In. 250.00
Toy, Target Set, Tin Lithograph, Plastic, Figures, Target, Gun, 9 x 14 In. 45.00
Toy, Tea Set, Cinderella, Original Box, 18 Piece 295.00
Toy, Train Set, Mechanical, Platform, Windup, Marx, Box, c.1950, 22 x 13 In. 850.00
Toy, Train, Disneyland Express, Casey Jr., Windup 375.00
Toy, Train, Disneyland, 5 Cars, Tin Lithograph, Windup, Marx, Japan, 15 In. 220.00
Toy, Winnie The Pooh, Ferris Wheel, Music, Plastic, Tin, Chein, Box, 1964, 12 In. 220.00
Toy, Woodburning Set, 6 Tiles, Watercolors, Brush, Tray, Electric Pen, Box, c.1950 ...... 145.00
Toy Chest, Mickey Mouse, Carousel, Corrugated Board, Odora Co., 1933, 15 x 27 In. ... 230.00
Tumbler Set, Disney Collectors Series, Burger King, Plastic, Box 90.00
Watch, Pocket, Mickey Mouse On Face, 3 Mickey's On Smaller Dial, Ingersoll, 1934 ... 910.00
Watch, Pocket, Mickey Mouse, Ingersoll, Original Strap, Fob, c.1934 .... 495.00
Watch, Pocket, Mickey Mouse, Ingersoll, Tag, Inserts, Box, c.1934 .... 990.00
Watch, Pocket, Mickey Mouse, Long Nose, Ingersoll, England, c.1933 .... 359.00
Watch Fob, Mickey Mouse, Ingersoll, Silver Over Brass, c.1930s, 1 1/8 In. 250.00
Wristwatch, Alice In Wonderland, Blue Band, Walt Disney, Timex, Box 220.00
Wristwatch, Mickey Mouse, Bradley, WDP, Swiss, Box 99.00
Wristwatch, Mickey Mouse, Mickey Images On Metal Link Band, Ingersoll, c.1933 .... 495.00
Wristwatch, Mickey Mouse, Red Band, Walt Disney Timex, Box 220.00

DOCTOR, see Dental; Medical

DOLL entries are listed by marks printed or incised on the doll, if possible. If there are no marks, the doll is listed by the name of the subject or country or maker. Notice that Barbie is listed under Mattel. G.I.
Joe figures are listed in the Toy section. Eskimo dolls are listed in the
Eskimo section and Indian dolls are listed in the Indian section. Doll
clothes and accessories are listed at the end of this section. The twentieth-century clothes listed here are in mint condition.

A.M., 200, Bisque Socket Head, Sleep Eyes, Tongue Tip, Wig, 5-Piece Composition, 9 In. 1595.00
A.M., 241, Bisque Socket Head, Googly Eyes, Mohair Wig, 5-Piece Body, Toddler, 11 In. . 3000.00
A.M., 251, Bisque Socket Head, Sleep Eyes, Stroke Brow, Open-Close Mouth, 12 1/2 In. . 305.00
A.M., 253, Bisque Socket Head, Sleep Eyes, Googly, Mohair, 5-Piece Composition, 7 In. . 770.00
A.M., 323, Bisque Socket Head, Googly Eyes, Alsatian Costume, c.1925, 10 In. 1540.00
A.M., 323, Bisque Socket Head, Sleep Eyes, Googly, Wig, Composition Body, 7 In. 660.00
A.M., 341, Bisque Socket Head, Domed, Sleep Eyes, Composition, Vintage Dress, 8 In. . 115.00
A.M., 351, Black Bisque Socket Head, Set Eyes, 2 Teeth, Composition Body, Baby, 17 In. 415.00
A.M., 370, Bisque Head, Sleep Eyes, Open Mouth, 4 Teeth, Wig, Kid Body, Dress, 20 In. . 115.00
A.M., 371, Bisque Socket Head, Blue Sleep Eyes, Bent-Limb Baby Body, 8 In. 150.00
A.M., 390, Bisque Head, Blue Eyes, 3 Teeth, Wig, Composition, Ball-Jointed, 11 1/2 In. .. 75.00
A.M., 390, Bisque Head, Open Mouth, 3 Teeth, Unattached Wig, 18 In. 115.00
A.M., 390, Bisque Head, Sleep Eyes, Brown Wig, Composition, Ball-Jointed, 18 In. 127.00
A.M., 390, Bisque Head, Sleep Eyes, Open Mouth, 4 Teeth, Composition, Ball-Joint, 23 In. 175.00
A.M., 390, Bisque Socket Head, Mohair Wig, Composition, Ball-Jointed, 16 In. 145.00
A.M., 390, Bisque Socket Head, Sleep Eyes, Mohair Wig, Composition, Ball-Joint, 21 In. . 155.00
A.M., 390, Bisque Socket Head, Sleep Eyes, Mohair, Composition, Ball-Jointed, 26 In. ... 275.00
A.M., 390, Black Bisque Head, Sleep Eyes, Open Mouth, 4 Teeth, Wig, Composition, 28 In. 690.00
A.M., 390n, Bisque Socket Head, Glass Sleep Eyes, Mohair, Composition, Child, 12 In. .. 200.00

A.M., 590, Bisque Socket Head, Set Eyes, Mohair Wig, Composition, Wood, Jointed, 18 In.   990.00
A.M., 760, Bisque Shoulder Head, Sleep Eyes, Teeth, Mohair, Baby, 13 In. 250.00
A.M., 971A, Bisque Socket Head, Sleep Eyes, Composition, Crier, 16 1/2 In. 50.00
A.M., 975, Bisque Socket Head, Sleep Eyes, Mohair Wig, Starfish Hands, 9 1/2 In. 290.00
A.M., 1894, Bisque Head, Open Mouth, 4 Teeth, Wig, Composition, Ball-Jointed, 13 In. ..   115.00
A.M., 1894, Bisque Head, Open Mouth, Teeth, Wig, Composition Body, 10 In. 160.00
A.M., 1894, Bisque Socket Head, Mohair Wig, Composition Body, Ball-Jointed, 20 In. 250.00
A.M., Bisque Head, Little Red Riding Hood, Kid Body, 15 In. 35.00
A.M., Darling, Bisque Shoulder Head, Cloth Body, Composition Limbs, 20 In. 130.00
A.M., Darling, Bisque Shoulder Head, Sleep Eyes, Mohair, Kid Body, Gusset Joints, 9 In. .   95.00
A.M., Fanny, Bisque, Pouty, Blue Eyes, Molded Hair, Houndstooth Outfit, 17 1/2 In. 920.00
A.M., Florodora, Bisque Shoulder Head, Mohair, Kid Body, Rivet & Gusset Joints, 17 In. .   105.00
A.M., Florodora, Bisque Socket Head, Brown Sleep Eyes, Composition, Ball-Joint, 25 In. .   275.00
A.M., Florodora, Bisque, Sleep Eyes, Open Mouth, Wig, Composition, Ball-Jointed, 12 In.   130.00
A.M., Indian, Bisque Socket Head, 5-Piece Composition Body, 8 1/2 In. 95.00
A.M., Just Me, Bisque Socket Head, 5-Piece Composition Body, c.1925, 9 In. 1155.00
A.M., Just Me, Bisque Socket Head, Blue Sleep Eyes, Rosebud Mouth, 9 In. 1540.00
A.M., Just Me, Bisque, Blue Sleep Eyes, Blond Mohair Wig, Sundress, Hat, 8 In. 1140.00
A.M., Just Me, Bisque, Side Sleep Eyes, 5-Piece Composition Body, c.1928, 11 In. 2420.00
A.M., Mabel, Bisque Shoulder Head, Mohair, Kidolene Body, Rivet, Gusset Joints, 11 In. .   49.00
A.M., Mabel, Bisque Shoulder Head, Mohair Wig, Kid Body, Rivet, Gusset Joints, 19 In. .   110.00
A.M., Queen Louise, Bisque Socket Head, Sleep Eyes, Open Mouth, Teeth, Hair, 23 In. .   250.00
A.M., Queen Louise, Bisque Socket Head, Sleep Eyes, Painted Lashes, 4 Teeth, 23 In. 415.00
A.M., Queen Louise, Open Mouth, 4 Teeth, Wig, Composition, Ball-Jointed, 24 In. 290.00
Adelina Patti, Shoulder Head, Painted Eyes, Hair, Cloth Body, China Limbs, 11 1/2 In. ..   690.00
Advertising, Betsy Ross, Blue Bonnet Margarine, Mail-In Premium, Box, 1969, 8 In. 50.00
Advertising, Big Boy, Vinyl, Plush, Nanco, 1980, 10 In. 65.00
Advertising, Buddy Lee, Grapette Soda 200.00
Advertising, Clown, Kellogg's Sugar Smacks, Premium, Paul Jung, 1953 ....   50.00
Advertising, Cookie Crisp Crook, Plush, Premium, Box, 12 In. 30.00
Advertising, Cream Of Wheat Man, Stuffed, 16 x 7 In. 46.00
Advertising, Daddy Bear, Kellogg's, Cloth, Early 1900s 80.00
Advertising, Goldilocks & 3 Bears, Kellogg's, Printed Cloth, 12 In., 4 Piece 240.00
Advertising, Kellogg's Puppets, Snap, Crackle, Pop, Dancing, 1984, 4 1/2 In., 3 Piece ...   100.00
Advertising, McDonald's Hamburglar, Plush, Cape, Label, 1970s, 16 In. 25.00
Advertising, Pillsbury Finger Puppet, Flapjack, Popper, Poppin Fresh, Box, 1974, 3 Piece   150.00
Advertising, Willie Wirehand, Rural Electric, Bobbin' Head, Hand Painted, Box, 8 In. ...   30.00
Alabama Baby, Stockinette Head, Painted Features, Hair, Cloth Body, Pants, Shirt, 22 In. .   1430.00
Alexander dolls are listed in this category under Madame Alexander.
Alt Beck & Gottschalck, 639, Bisque Head, Closed Mouth, Kid Body, Silk Dress, 16 In. .   405.00
Alt Beck & Gottschalck, 880, Bisque Shoulder Head, Painted Features, 20 In. 440.00
Alt Beck & Gottschalck, 1000, Kid Body, Bisque Arms, Rivet & Gusset Joints, 14 In. 171.00
Alt Beck & Gottschalck, 1046, Porcelain Shoulder Head, Cloth Body, c.1885, 22 In. 770.00
Alt Beck & Gottschalck, 1123, Bisque Shoulder Head, Human Hair, Kid Body, 24 In. 385.00
Alt Beck & Gottschalck, 1367, Bisque Socket Head, Sleep Eyes, Composition, 15 In. 95.00
Alt Beck & Gottschalck, Baby Bo-Kaye, Bisque Head, Flanged Neck, Sleep Eyes, 16 In. .   2000.00
Alt Beck & Gottschalck, Baby Bo-Kaye, Bisque, Sleep Eyes, c.1923, 5 In. 935.00
Armand Marseille dolls are listed in this category under A.M.
Automaton, Bebe Bouquetiere, Bisque Head, Mohair Wig, Lambert, c.1890, 20 In. 7150.00
Automaton, Bebe Cage, Bisque Head, Paperweight Eyes, Lambert, c.1890, 20 In. 12650.00
Automaton, Bebe Russe, Bisque Head, Pours Tea, Blond, Lambert, c.1890, 20 In. 6600.00
Automaton, Bird In Cage, Floral Garland Perch, Beaded Base, France, c.1900, 11 3/4 In. .   805.00
Automaton, Bisque Head, Glass Eyes, Mohair Wig, Painted Face, Windup, France, 22 In.   5500.00
Automaton, Bowling, 3 Bisque-Head Dolls, Steel Ball, Otto Eichenburger, c.1907 ......   17600.00
Automaton, Cabbage Head, White Fur, Popping Glass Eyes, Musical, 7 x 3 In. 3808.00
Automaton, Clown On Music Box, Bisque Head, Open Mouth, 3 Teeth, 9 In. 430.00
Automaton, Happy Patissier, Bisque Head, Auburn Mohair Wig, Lambert, c.1892, 20 In. ..   12100.00
Automaton, Lady With Harp, Bisque Head, Mohair Wig, Velvet-Covered Base, 23 In. 7425.00
Automaton, Magician, Lambert, c.1890, 38 In. 12650.00
Automaton, Man Riding Donkey, Bisque Head, Simon & Halbig, France, c.1890, 12 In. .   4180.00
Automaton, Patissier A La Brioche, Bisque, Roullet Et Decamps, France, c.1895, 11 In. ...   4400.00
Automaton, Smoking Moor, Cross Legged, Velvet Jacket, Lambert, c.1890 ....   8800.00
Automaton, Woman Knitting, Bisque, Windup, Seated, Tete Jumeau, 17 x 10 In. 3630.00

Automaton, Young Count Playing Violin, Velvet-Covered Stool, c.1865, 13 In. 6820.00
Averill, Bonnie Babe, Bisque Flange Head, Sleep Eyes, Open Mouth, Cloth Body, 22 In. . . 310.00
Averill, Bonnie Babe, Bisque Flange Head, Sleep Eyes, Painted Hair, Cloth Body, 17 In. . . 469.00
Averill, Bonnie Babe, Domed Bisque Head, Painted, 2 Teeth, Cloth Body, c.1925, 15 In. . . 2090.00
Averill, Nancy, Comic Strip Character, Cloth, Tag, Box, c.1945, 14 In. 990.00
Bahr & Proschild, 204, Bisque, Glass Inset Eyes, 2 Teeth, Mohair Wig, c.1890, 11 In. . . . 1045.00
Bahr & Proschild, 300, Bisque Socket Head, Set Eyes, Lashes, Teeth, Jointed, 19 In. 1018.00
Bahr & Proschild, 585, Bisque, Sleep Eyes, 2 Teeth, Mohair, Composition Body, 10 In. . . 385.00
Bahr & Proschild, 604, Bisque Socket Head, Sleep Eyes, Synthetic Wig, Baby, 12 In. . . . 220.00
Bahr & Proschild, 620, Bisque Socket Head, Sleep Eyes, Teeth, Mohair, Toddler, 14 In. . . 330.00
Bahr & Proschild, 624, Bisque Socket Head, Sleep Eyes, Mohair, Composition, 17 In. . . . 330.00
Bahr & Proschild, Bisque Socket Head, Open Mouth, Composition, Jointed, 19 In. 365.00
Barbie dolls are listed in this category under Mattel.
Barrois, Fashion, Bisque Swivel Head, Kid Body, Gusset Joints, c.1878, 15 In. . . . . : 4180.00
Becassine, Composition Head, Composition Body, France, 15 In. 635.00
Beecher, Stockinette Head & Body, Painted Features, Yarn Hair, Lace Dress, Baby, 21 In. 990.00
Belton-Type, 137, Bisque Socket Head, Paperweight Eyes, Mohair, Jointed Body, 26 In. . . 2200.00
Belton-Type, 183, Bisque Socket Head, Paperweight Eyes, Composition, Jointed, 23 In. . . 1650.00
Belton-Type, 183, Bisque Socket Head, Paperweight Eyes, Human Hair Wig, 13 1/2 In. . . 1650.00
Belton-Type, TR809, Bisque Socket Head, Paperweight Eyes, Composition, Wood, 17 In. 660.00
Bergmann dolls are also in this category under S & H and Simon & Halbig.
Bergmann, Bisque Socket Head, Sleep Eyes, Hair, Cardboard Pate, Composition, 29 In. . . 495.00
Bergmann, Bisque Socket Head, Sleep Eyes, Teeth, Composition, Wood, Jointed, 26 In. . . 470.00
Berwick, Famlee, 5 Heads, Baby, Nurse, Sailor, Crying Baby, Clown, c.1921, 26 In. 259.00
Bisque, Blue Eyes, Wig, Composition Body, 9 In. 90.00
Bisque, Blue Set Eyes, Wig, Composition Body, Lavender Dress, Marked, 12 In. 75.00
Bisque, Closed Mouth, Painted Features, Human Hair Wig, Jointed Limbs, 4 In. 39.00
Bisque, Closed Mouth, Painted Features, Jointed Limbs, Painted Shoes, 4 In. 60.00
Bisque, Molded Hair, Blue Eyes, Molded Shoes, Boy, 7 In. 160.00
Bisque, Set Brown Eyes, Mohair Wig, Jointed Shoulders, Hips, Girl, 9 In. 250.00
Bisque, Shoulder Head, Painted Eyes, Molded Curls, Cloth, Bisque Limbs, Child, 15 In. . . 715.00
Bisque, Shoulder Head, Sculpted Bonnet, Kid Body, Mitten Hands, Stitch-Jointed, 10 In. . 580.00
Bisque, Socket Head, Closed Mouth, Mohair Wig, Jointed Limbs, 5 In. 55.00
Bisque, Socket Head, Sleep Eyes, Mohair, Composition, Toddler, 14 In. 1000.00
Bisque, Swivel Head, Bisque Shoulder Plate, Enamel Eyes, Mohair Wig, 16 In. 3080.00
Black dolls are included in the Black category.
Borgfeldt, 255, Bisque Socket Head, Intaglio Eyes, Googly, Watermelon Smile, 8 In. 920.00
Boudoir, Painted, Pink & Green Dress, 28 In. 127.00
Bru Jne, 3, Bisque Swivel Head, Inset Eyes, Closed Mouth, Kid Body, c.1885, 14 In. 11000.00
Bru Jne, 7, Bisque Swivel Head, Paperweight Eyes, Kid Body, c.1888, 17 In. 13570.00
Bru Jne, 8, Bisque Swivel Head, Human Hair, Kid Body, Gusset Joints, 18 In. 250.00
Bru Jne, Bisque Socket Head, Paperweight Eyes, Mohair, Composition, Wood, 22 In. 4000.00
Bru Jne, Bisque Socket Head, Wig, Walker, Kiss Throwing, Composition, Wood, 22 In. . . 660.00
Bru Jne, Bisque Swivel Head, Bosom, Enamel Eyes, Lamb's-Wool Wig, Bebe, 12 In. 8000.00
Bru Jne, Bisque Swivel Head, Kid-Edge Shoulder Plate, Glass Eyes, Wig, Bebe, 11 In. . . 8800.00
Bru Jne, Bisque Swivel Head, Paperweight Eyes, O-Shaped Mouth, Mohair, Bebe, 24 In. . 8500.00
Bru Jne, Bisque Swivel Head, Shoulder Plate, Glass Eyes, Wooden Body, Jointed, 13 In. . 6165.00
Bru Jne, Fashion, Bisque Socket Head, Shoulder Plate, Paperweight Eyes, Gussets, 16 In. 2970.00
Bruckner, Lady, Printed Cloth Face, Horsehair Wig, Jointed Cloth Body, 12 In. 275.00
Bruckner, Topsy-Turvy, Cloth, 2 Heads, Black, White, 2 Sets Of Arms, 12 In. 440.00
Buddy Lee, Plastic, Painted Side Eyes, Lashes, Smiling, 1-Piece Jointed Body, 13 In. 220.00
Bye-Lo, Bisque Flange Head, Sleep Eyes, Cloth Body, Celluloid Hands, 9 1/2 In. 275.00
Bye-Lo, Bisque Flange Head, Sleep Eyes, Cloth Body, Celluloid Hands, 19 In. . . . .358.00 to 495.00
Bye-Lo, Bisque Head, Flanged Neck, Sleep Eyes, Muslin Body, Celluloid, 12 In. 3190.00
Bye-Lo, Bisque, Blue Sleep Eyes, Christening Gown, Diaper, Laced Booties, 9 In. 545.00
Bye-Lo, Bisque, Domed Socket Head, Sleep Eyes, Celluloid Hands, 18 1/2 In. 358.00
Bye-Lo, Composition Body, White Dress, Wicker Doll Carriage, Baby, 11 & 22 In. 145.00
Bye-Lo, Composition Body, Wicker Doll Carriage, Baby, 16 & 33 In. 175.00
Cameo Doll Co., Scooties, Composition, Swivel Head, Molded Hair, Jointed, 13 In. 160.00
Cameo Doll Co., Scooties, Swivel Head, Closed Mouth, Painted, Jointed Limbs, 10 In. . . . 205.00
Celluloid, Blue Glass Eyes, Kid Body, Green & White Dress, Girl, 12 In. 65.00
Chad Valley, Girl, Cloth Mask Face, Mohair Wig, Jointed Cloth Body, 14 In. 149.00
Chad Valley, Royal Guard, Felt Swivel Head, Glass Eyes, 5-Piece Body, c.1937, 17 In. . . . 605.00

Chase, Painted Features, Leather Shoes, Child, 19 In. 345.00
Chase, Painted Stockinette Head, Limbs, Jointed, Stitched Fingers, Toes, 12 In. 300.00
Chase, Painted Stockinette Head, Painted Eyes, Lashes, Textured Hair, 12 1/2 In. 358.00
Chase, Painted Stockinette Head, Sateen Body, Jointed, 16 In. 468.00
China Shoulder Head, Blue Eyes, Molded Black Hair, Center Part, Cloth Body, 22 In. . . . 248.00
China Shoulder Head, Painted Blue Eyes, Molded Curly Hair, Cloth Body, 15 In. 385.00
China Shoulder Head, Painted Eyes, Curls, Cloth Body, Kid Hands, Fingers, 26 In. 2970.00
China Shoulder Head, Painted Eyes, Curls, Kid Body, Gusset Joints, 20 1/2 In. 770.00
China Shoulder Head, Painted Eyes, Hair, Closed Mouth, Gusset Joints, 21 In. 385.00
China Shoulder Head, Painted Eyes, Hair, Cloth Body, Leather Arms, 24 In. 550.00
China Shoulder Head, Painted Eyes, Hair, Cloth Body, Leather Arms, Jointed, 22 In. 440.00
China Shoulder Head, Painted Eyes, Hair, Mustache, Sideburns, Cloth Body, 5 1/2 In. . . . 250.00
China Shoulder Head, Painted Eyes, Hair, Wooden Body, China Limbs, Joints, 5 In. 1815.00
China Shoulder Head & Arms, Painted Features, Cloth Body, Bonnet, 18 In. 1210.00
Christopher Robin, Felt Swivel Head, Body, Painted Features, Mohair, Jointed, 18 In. . . . 935.00
Cloth, Brown, Defined Nose, Yarn Hair, Stuffed With Sawdust, Blue Dress, 19 In. 525.00
Cloth, Composition Mask, Swivel Head, Googly, Mohair, Felt, Jointed, 10 1/2 In. 495.00
Cloth, Composition Mask, Swivel Head, Googly, Mohair, Felt, Jointed, 14 In. 605.00
Cloth, Imprinted Face, Seated, Bent Knees, Waterproof, 11 1/2 In. 495.00
Cloth, Ink-Drawn Face, No Wig, Cotton Twill Body, 20 In. 3960.00
Cloth, Ink-Drawn Features, String Hair, Unjointed Arms & Legs, 16 In. 1980.00
Cloth, Lollipop Head, Pencil Face, Sewn Hands & Fingers, Red Calico Dress, 17 1/2 In. . . 575.00
Cloth, Muslin, Painted Features, Mohair Wig, Stitch-Jointed, 14 In. 100.00
Cloth, Muslin, Painted Features, Stitched-Jointed, Dress, Bonnet, Pinafore, c.1920, 17 In. . 1760.00
Cloth, Oil-Painted Eyes, Nostrils, Shaded Lips, Stitched Fingers, 31 In. 2365.00
Cloth, Oil-Painted Face, Glass Eyes, Painted Brows, Stuffed, No Joints, 19 In. 825.00
Cloth, Oil-Painted, Flat Dimensional, Muslin Body, Stitch-Jointed, Late 1800s, 15 In. 1210.00
Cloth, Oil-Painted, Muslin Body, Stitch-Jointed, American, c.1890, 32 In. 880.00
Cloth, Painted Face, Eyes, Jointed Knees, 35 In. 3740.00
Cloth, Painted Face, Hands, Legs, Socks, Boots, 27 In. 1210.00
Cloth, Painted Features & Hair, Shoulder-Jointed, Heavy, 21 In. 415.00
Cloth, Painted Features, Mohair Braid, Stitched Fingers, Leather Boots, 13 1/2 In. 360.00
Cloth, Painted Features, Stitch-Jointed, Velvet Cape, 25 In. 1320.00
Cloth, Stiff Neck, Painted Features, Stitched Fingers, Toes, 17 1/2 In. 1540.00
Cloth, White, Layered Faces, Lobster-Claw Hands, Pink Checked Dress, 21 In. 875.00
Cloth, Yellow Kid, Stuffed, Kidisms On Nightshirt, 1899, 8 In. 975.00
Columbian, Cloth, Oil Painted, Head, Rosebud Mouth, 19 1/2 In. 9900.00
Columbian, Cloth, Painted Features, Jointed Body, Dress, Underclothing, 30 In. 3960.00
Columbian, Cloth, Painted, Shoulder & Hip Joints, Stitched Fingers & Toes, 19 In. 4070.00
Composition, 6 Interchangeable Heads, Swivel Head & Limbs, Cloth Body, 16 In. 259.00
Cosmopolitan, Ginger, Hard Plastic, Sleep Eyes, 5-Piece Body, Walker, 7 1/2 In. 175.00
Deluxe Reading Co., Candy, Fashion, 4 Outfits, 3 Dress Forms, Box, DeLuxe Reading Co. . 70.00
Door Of Hope, Bride, Carved Pear-Wood Head, Painted Black Eyes, 11 In. 1155.00
Door Of Hope, Child, Carved Wood Head, Arms, Cloth Body, Painted Features, 6 1/2 In. . . 1100.00
Door Of Hope, Children, Carved Wood, Silk Outfits, Headpieces, 6 In., Pair . . . . *Illus* 5175.00
Door Of Hope, Chinese Bride, Silk Outfit, Flowers, Headdress, 11 1/2 In. . . . . *Illus* 1438.00
Door Of Hope, Farmer, Carved Pear-Wood Head, Black Eyes, Rake, Clothes, 12 In. 990.00

Doll, Door Of Hope,
Children, Carved Wood, Silk
Outfits, Headpieces, 6 In., Pair

Doll, Door Of Hope, Chinese
Bride, Silk Outfit, Flowers,
Headdress, 11 1/2 In.

Door Of Hope, Old Man, Carved Wood Head, Wrinkles, Painted Eyes, Cloth Body, 11 In.   770.00
Door Of Hope, Old Woman, Carved Wood Head, Mouth, Wrinkles, Painted Eyes, 11 In. . .   770.00
Dressel, 1349, Bisque Socket Head, Sleep Eyes, Teeth, Real Lashes, 15 In. 495.00
Dressel, Farmer, Bisque Socket Head, Mohair, Composition, Wood, 1900s, 11 In. 1430.00
Dressel, Jutta, Bisque Socket Head, Sleep Eyes, Open Mouth, Composition, 14 In. 145.00
Dressel, Jutta, Bisque, Blue Sleep Eyes, Real Lashes, Open Mouth, Wobble Tongue, 15 In.   550.00
E.D., Black Bisque Socket Head, Paperweight Eyes, Teeth, Hair, Jointed, French, 20 In. . . .   825.00
Effanbee, Anne Shirley, Composition, Sleep Eyes, Closed Mouth, Hair, c.1930, 15 In. 71.00
Effanbee, Baby Bubbles, Composition, 17 In. 90.00
Effanbee, Baby Tinyette, Composition Swivel Head, Molded Hair, Jointed, 7 1/2 In. 45.00
Effanbee, Bridesmaid, Composition Head, Flirty Eyes, Hair, 5-Piece Body, 21 In. . .150.00 to 175.00
Effanbee, Composition Socket Head, Painted Eyes, Human Hair, 5-Piece Body, 14 In. . . .   350.00
Effanbee, Girl Scout, Vinyl, Sleep Eyes, Closed Mouth, Wig, 1960, 14 1/2 In. 90.00
Effanbee, Honey, Plastic, Sleep Eyes, Floss Hair, Closed Mouth, Schiaparelli Dress, 18 In.   495.00
Effanbee, Little Lady, Composition Head, Sleep Eyes, Human Hair, 5-Piece Body, 21 In. .   250.00
Effanbee, Majorette, Composition Socket Head, Sleep Eyes, Mohair, 5-Piece Body, 14 In.   350.00
Effanbee, Nun, Composition, Blond Molded Hair, Blue Eyes, Open Mouth, 22 In. 29.00
Effanbee, Patricia, Composition, Sleep Eyes, Closed Mouth, Wig, 14 In. 125.00
Effanbee, Patsy Ann, Composition, Sleep Eyes, Closed Mouth, Wig, 19 In. 85.00
Effanbee, Patsy Joan, Composition, Sleep Eyes, Red Polka-Dot Dress, 16 In. 385.00
Effanbee, Patsy, Composition, Brown Eyes, Pursed Mouth, Molded Hair, c.1930, 14 In. . .   140.00
Effanbee, Patsyette, Red Riding Hood, Composition, Painted, 5-Piece Body, Box, 9 In. . . .   500.00
Effanbee, Sweetie Pie, Composition Flange Head, Flirty Eyes, Wig, 19 In. 115.00
Fashion, Bisque Shoulder Head, Enamel Eyes, Mohair, Kid Body, Gusset, c.1865, 13 In. . 3075.00
Fashion, Bisque Socket Head, Paperweight Eyes, Painted Lashes, France, 11 1/2 In. 1100.00
Fashion, Bisque Socket Head, Shoulder Plate, Human Hair, Cloth Body, 21 In. 600.00
Fashion, Bisque Socket Head, Shoulder Plate, Mohair Wig, Kid Body, France, 12 In. 2750.00
Fashion, Bisque Swivel Head, Bulbous Neck, Wood, Fully Jointed, c.1905, 18 In. 9900.00
Fashion, Bisque Swivel Head, Enamel Eyes, Mohair Wig, Gusset Joints, France, 17 In. . 2900.00
Fashion, Bisque Swivel Head, Enamel Eyes, Mohair, Wooden, Dowel Joints, 12 In. 6100.00
Fashion, Bisque Swivel Head, Kid Edge, Human Hair, Wood, Jointed, 17 In. 6325.00
Fashion, Bisque Swivel Head, Shoulder Plate, Enamel Eyes, Wig, c.1870, 17 In. 8140.00
Franz Schmidt, Bisque Socket Head, Sleep Eyes, Mohair, Composition, Jointed, 22 In. . . . 1045.00
French, Bisque Head, Rattling, Blue Eyes, Wooden Limbs, Clown Dress, 16 In. 145.00
French, Bisque Head, Wig, Closed Mouth, Pierced Ears, Composition Body, 17 In. 489.00
French, Bisque Shoulder Head, Enamel Eyes, Hair, Gusset Joints, Accessories, 30 In. 7250.00
French, Bisque Shoulder Head, Glass Inset Eyes, Kid Body, Gusset Joints, c.1861, 18 In. . 4675.00
French, Bisque Socket Head, Glass Eyes, Composition, Jointed, c.1900, 20 In. 9350.00
French, Bisque Socket Head, Glass Eyes, Mohair Wig, Composition Body, Bebe, 9 In. . . .   500.00
French, Bisque Socket Head, Paperweight Eyes, Hair, Composition, Wood, Bebe, 28 In. . . . 3200.00
French, Bisque Socket Head, Paperweight Eyes, Wig, Composition, Ball-Jointed, 12 In. . . . 3100.00
French, Bisque Swivel Head, Enamel Inset Eyes, Wig, Peg-Jointed, c.1875, 5 In. 3190.00
French, Bisque Swivel Head, Glass Eyes, Human Hair, Kid Body, Gusset Joints, 16 In. . . . 2700.00
French, Bisque Swivel Head, Glass Eyes, Mohair Wig, Kid Body, Gusset Joints, 10 In. 2530.00
French, Bisque Swivel Head, Glass Eyes, Mohair Wig, Kid Body, Gusset Joints, 18 In. 4510.00
French, Bisque Swivel Head, Shoulder Plate, Enamel Eyes, Kid Body, Gussets, 17 In. . . . 2420.00
French, Bisque Swivel Head, Shoulder Plate, Enamel Eyes, Mohair, Muslin Body, 11 In. . .   800.00
French, Bisque Swivel Head, Shoulder Plate, Enamel Eyes, Muslin Body, c.1868, 11 In. . . 2860.00
French, Bisque Swivel Head, Shoulder Plate, Enamel Eyes, Wig, Wooden Arms, c.1870 . . 5940.00
French, Bisque Swivel Head, Shoulder Plate, Enamel Eyes, Wood Body, c.1867, 18 In. . . 7700.00
French, Bisque Swivel Head, Shoulder Plate, Enamel Eyes, Wood Body, c.1870, 15 In. . . 4730.00
French, Bisque Swivel Head, Shoulder Plate, Enamel Eyes, Wood Body, c.1870, 20 In. . . 9350.00
French, Bisque Swivel Head, Shoulder Plate, Glass Eyes, Leather Body, Gussets, 17 In. . . 8500.00
French, Bisque Swivel Head, Shoulder Plate, Inset Eyes, Kid Body, Gusset Joints, 17 In. . . 4180.00
French, Bisque Swivel Head, Shoulder Plate, Inset Eyes, Mohair Wig, Wood Body, 15 In. 5720.00
French, Bisque Swivel Head, Shoulder Plate, Inset Eyes, Wig, Kid Body, c.1865, 17 In. . . 9075.00
French, Bisque Swivel Head, Shoulder Plate, Kid Body, Gusset Joints, c.1865, 5 In. 4400.00
French, Bisque Swivel Head, Shoulder Plate, Spiral Eyes, Hair, Kid Over Wood, c.1870 . . 4180.00
French, Bisque, Kid Edge, Inset Eyes, Mohair Wig, Painted Face, Peg-Jointed, 5 1/2 In. . . 1540.00
French, Brown Bisque Socket Head, Sleep Eyes, Wig, Composition, Wood, Bebe, 16 In. . 2500.00
French, Composition, Shoulder Head, Human Hair, Wire Arms, Soldier Uniform, 17 In. . . .   770.00
French, Papier-Mache Shoulder Head, Inset Eyes, Accented Features, Kid Body, 23 In. . . . 7975.00
French, Porcelain Shoulder Head, Glass Eyes, Kid Body, Jointed, 14 In. 1980.00

French, Pressed Leather, Painted Features, Bent-Limb Body, c.1920, 4 1/2 In. 1430.00
Frozen Charlotte, China, Painted Hair, Brown Eyes, Boy, 16 In. 490.00
G.I. Joe figures are listed in the Toy category.
Gaultier, Bisque Shoulder Head, Painted Eyes, Mohair Wig, Kid Body, c.1880, 16 In. . . . 1980.00
Gaultier, Bisque Socket Head, Glass Inset Eyes, Human Hair, c.1882, 9 1/2 In. 3520.00
Gaultier, Bisque Socket Head, Human Hair, Composition, Wood, Jointed, 15 1/2 In. 2200.00
Gaultier, Bisque Socket Head, Paperweight Eyes, Wig, Composition, Wood, Bebe, 20 In. . 2320.00
Gaultier, Bisque Socket Head, Spiral-Threaded Eyes, Blond Mohair, Bebe, c.1878, 15 In. . 4510.00
Gaultier, Bisque Swivel Head, Shoulder Plate, Enamel Eyes, Kid Body, c.1878, 16 In. . . . 3630.00
Gaultier, Bisque Swivel Head, Shoulder Plate, Enamel Eyes, Metal Armature, 19 In. 4400.00
Gaultier, Fashion, Bisque Head & Hands, Swivel Head, Gesland Body, c.1875, 24 In. 4840.00
Gaultier, Fashion, Bisque Swivel Head, Blue Eyes, Pierced Ears, Wig, Kid Body, 11 In. . . . 980.00
Gaultier, Fashion, Bisque Swivel Head, Pierced Ears, Closed Mouth, Kid Body, 13 In. . . . 750.00
Gebruder Heubach dolls are also in this category under Heubach.
Gebruder Heubach, 1233, Dancing Girl, Bisque, Blue Intaglio Eyes, Unjointed, 11 In. . . . 165.00
Gebruder Heubach, 6970, Bisque Socket Head, Pouty, Ball-Jointed, c.1912, 20 In. 2530.00
Gebruder Heubach, 6971, Bisque Socket Head, Laughing, Ball-Jointed, c.1912, 17 In. 1650.00
Gebruder Heubach, 7307, Bisque Socket Head, Glass Eyes, Ball-Jointed, c.1915, 16 In. . . 3740.00
Gebruder Heubach, 7407, Bisque Socket Head, Composition, Ball-Jointed, c.1912, 16 In. . 3190.00
Gebruder Heubach, 7602, Bisque Socket Head, Pouty, Composition, Wood, c.1912, 15 In. . 1210.00
Gebruder Heubach, 7622, Bisque Socket Head, Wood Body, Ball-Jointed, c.1912, 19 In. . . 2530.00
Gebruder Heubach, 7628, Bisque Socket Head, Composition, Ball-Jointed, c.1912, 18 In. . 1650.00
Gebruder Heubach, 7671, Brown Bisque Socket Head, Composition Body, c.1915, 11 In. . . 1210.00
Gebruder Heubach, 7744, Bisque Socket Head, Wood Body, Ball-Jointed, c.1912, 17 In. . . 7260.00
Gebruder Heubach, 7759, Domed Bisque Socket Head, Sculpted Hair, c.1912, 16 In. 3190.00
Gebruder Heubach, 7760, Bisque Socket Head, Bent-Limb Baby Body, c.1912, 14 In. 4950.00
Gebruder Heubach, 7764, Bisque Socket Head, Composition, Ball-Jointed, c.1912, 14 In. . 6160.00
Gebruder Heubach, 7788, Coquette, Bisque Socket Head, Wooden Joints, c.1912, 17 In. . 2530.00
Gebruder Heubach, 7865, Bisque Socket Head, Composition, Wood Joints, c.1912, 13 In. . 7700.00
Gebruder Heubach, 7865, Bisque Socket Head, Pensive, Ball-Jointed, c.1912, 12 In. 4180.00
Gebruder Heubach, 7911, Happy Boy, Bisque Socket Head, Ball-Jointed, c.1912, 16 In. . 2310.00
Gebruder Heubach, 7975, Baby Stuart, Bisque Socket Head, Glass Eyes, c.1915, 11 In. . . 1760.00
Gebruder Heubach, 7977, Baby Stuart, Bisque Socket Head, c.1915, 16 In. 1375.00
Gebruder Heubach, 8244, Bisque Socket Head, Sleep Eyes, Ball-Jointed, c.1915, 13 In. . 2420.00
Gebruder Heubach, 8413, Bisque Socket Head, Composition, Ball-Jointed, c.1915, 24 In. . 7700.00
Gebruder Heubach, 8774, Whistling Boy, Bisque Head, Intaglio Eyes To Side, 13 In. . . . 635.00
Gebruder Heubach, 9573, Bisque Socket Head, Googly, Russian Costume, c.1915, 7 In. . 3080.00
Gebruder Heubach, 9573, Bisque Socket Head, Googly, Watermelon Smile, 7 In. 900.00
Gebruder Heubach, Bisque Head, Composition Body, Windup, Walker, c.1912, 7 In. 580.00
Gebruder Heubach, Bisque Socket Head, Ball-Jointed, Boy, c.1915, 19 In. 1210.00
Gebruder Heubach, Bisque Socket Head, Intaglio Eyes, Open-Close Mouth, 9 1/2 In. . . . 300.00
Gebruder Heubach, Bisque Socket Head, Sleep Eyes, Ball-Jointed, c.1915, 15 In. 3740.00
Gebruder Heubach, Bisque, Loop-Jointed Arms, Legs, Brown Shoes, c.1915, 8 In. 825.00
Gebruder Heubach, Bisque, Musical, Squeak, Late 1800s, 9 In. 1430.00
Gebruder Kuhnlenz, 165, Bisque Socket Head, Wig, Composition, Ball-Jointed, 34 In. . . 550.00
Gebruder Kuhnlenz, Bisque Shoulder Head, Paperweight Eyes, Hair, Kid Body, 13 In. . . 550.00
Gebruder Kuhnlenz, Bisque Socket Head, Papier-Mache Body, Asian Child, c.1895, 9 In. 330.00
German, Bisque Head, Wig, Blue Eyes, Composition Body, Lace Dress, 5 In. 90.00
German, Bisque Head, Wig, Blue Eyes, Open Mouth, Composition Body, 7 1/2 In. 90.00
German, Bisque Head, Wig, Brown Eyes, Kid Body, White Dress, 24 In. 255.00
German, Bisque Head, Wig, Painted Eyes, Composition Body, Dress, Stamped, 6 1/2 In. . 80.00
German, Bisque Shoulder Head & Limbs, Enamel Eyes, Muslin Body, 15 In. 4400.00
German, Bisque Shoulder Head & Limbs, Sculpted Hair, Muslin Body, 17 In. 3200.00
German, Bisque Shoulder Head, Glass Eyes, Muslin, Stitch-Jointed, c.1870, 17 In. 1595.00
German, Bisque Shoulder Head, Glass Eyes, Painted Hair, Cloth Body, 25 In. 495.00
German, Bisque Shoulder Head, Inset Eyes, Muslin Body, Bisque Limbs, c.1875, 15 In. . . . 1380.00
German, Bisque Shoulder Head, Open Mouth, Teeth, Kid Body, Rivet Joints, 18 In. 149.00
German, Bisque Shoulder Head, Painted, Cardboard Body, Kid Arms, Brass Feet, 10 In. . 1760.00
German, Bisque Shoulder Head, Sculpted Braids, Painted, Muslin, Stitch-Jointed, 24 In. . 1265.00
German, Bisque Shoulder Head, Sculpted Hair, Painted Eyes, Muslin Body, c.1870, 16 In. 1100.00
German, Bisque Shoulder Head, Sculpted Hair, Painted Face, Muslin Body, c.1880, 3 In. . 485.00
German, Bisque Shoulder Head, Set Eyes, Painted Lashes, Mohair, Kid Body, 11 1/2 In. . 275.00
German, Bisque Shoulder Head, Waved Hair, Muslin Body, Bisque Limbs, 9 In. 650.00

German, Bisque Socket Head, Painted Features, Composition, Wood, Jointed, 23 In. 935.00
German, Bisque Socket Head, Set Eyes, Teeth, Human Hair, Composition, Jointed, 17 In. 385.00
German, Bisque Socket Head, Shoulder Plate, Hair, Kid Body, Gussets, Child, 14 1/2 In. . 440.00
German, Bisque Socket Head, Sleep Eyes, Human Hair, Composition, Wood, 18 In. 385.00
German, Bisque Socket Head, Sleep Eyes, Mohair Wig, Composition, Wood, 24 1/2 In. .. 385.00
German, Bisque Socket Head, Sleep Eyes, Plaster Pate, Teeth, Mohair Wig, Jointed, 20 In. 880.00
German, Bisque Swivel Head, Sculpted Hair, Muslin Body, Pierced Ears, c.1870, 17 In. ... 1650.00
German, Bisque Swivel Head, Sleep Eyes, Wig, Bisque Arms, Legs, Peg-Jointed, 4 In. 500.00
German, Bisque, Blond Wig, Blue Eyes, Open Mouth, Teeth, Composition Body, 6 In. 240.00
German, Bisque, Blond Wig, Sleep Eyes, Closed Mouth, Jointed, Molded Boots, 7 3/4 In. 375.00
German, Bisque, Blond Wig, Sleep Eyes, Open Mouth, 4 Teeth, Kid Body, Dress, 20 In. . 58.00
German, Bisque, Glass Eyes, Muslin Stitch-Jointed Body, Leather Hands, c.1875, 22 In. . 880.00
German, Bisque, Googly, Blue Socks, Brown Shoes, Marked, 5 In. 460.00
German, Bisque, Molded Hair, Blue Eyes, Painted Stockings, Brown Shoes, 4 In. 69.00
German, Bisque, Sculpted Hair, Painted Face, Muslin Arms, Legs, Underwear, 8 In. 2310.00
German, Bisque, Wig, Set Eyes, Open Mouth, 4 Teeth, Composition, Italian Peasant, 9 In. 65.00
German, Bisque, Wig, Sleep Eyes, Open Mouth, Teeth, Composition, Ball-Jointed, 16 In. . 405.00
German, Black Porcelain Shoulder Head, Upper-Glancing Eyes, Cloth, c.1890, 12 In. ... 1155.00
German, China Head, Molded Hair, China Limbs, Painted Shoes, 18 In. 115.00
German, China Head, Molded Hair, Kid Body, China Limbs, Marked Bertha, 24 In. 130.00
German, China Head, Molded Hair, Kid Body, Leather Hands, 20 In. 230.00
German, China, High Brow, Alphabet Cloth Body, 11 In. 85.00
German, Coquette, Bisque, Intaglio Eyes, Closed Mouth, Molded Hair, Jointed, 9 In. 635.00
German, Coquette, Bisque, Sculpted Hair, Painted Face, Loop-Jointed, c.1920, 8 In. 715.00
German, Countess Dagmar, Bisque Shoulder Head, Painted Eyes, Hair, Kid Limbs, 25 In. 495.00
German, Ebony Bisque Socket Head, Enamel Eyes, 5-Piece Papier-Mache Body, 6 In. ... 525.00
German, Empress Eugenie, China Shoulder Head, Painted Eyes, Molded Hair, 22 In. 385.00
German, Fortune Teller, Porcelain Head, Sculpted Hair, Painted, Kid Body, 17 In. 3800.00
German, HeBee, Bisque, Painted Features, Molded Clothes, Bib, 4 In. 605.00
German, Indian, Bisque Socket Head, 5-Piece Composition Body, 8 In. 49.00
German, Jester, Porcelain Shoulder Head, Mustache, Goatee, Cloth Body, c.1890, 14 In. . 825.00
German, Jester, Porcelain Shoulder Head, Mustache, Goatee, Cloth Body, c.1890, 18 In. . 825.00
German, Porcelain Head, Muslin Body, Stitch-Jointed, Porcelain Limbs, c.1880, 23 In. ... 990.00
German, Porcelain Head, Painted Features, Papier-Mache Body, Muslin Limbs, 9 In. 5060.00
German, Porcelain Head, Sculpted Hair, Muslin Body, Stitch-Jointed, c.1870, 22 In. 1650.00
German, Porcelain Head, Sculpted Hair, Muslin Body, Stitch-Jointed, c.1875, 20 In. 3190.00
German, Porcelain Head, Snood, Sculpted Hair, Muslin, Stitch-Jointed, c.1870, 16 In. 3410.00
German, Porcelain Shoulder Head & Limbs, Painted Hair, Blue Eyes, Muslin Body, 18 In. 1500.00
German, Porcelain Shoulder Head, Glass Eyes, Sculpted Hair, Cloth Body, c.1865, 17 In. . 2310.00
German, Porcelain Shoulder Head, Human Hair, Folklore Costume, c.1870, 17 In. 1430.00
German, Porcelain Shoulder Head, Painted Eyes, Muslin Body, Leather Arms, Boy, 14 In. 750.00
German, Porcelain Shoulder Head, Painted Face, Muslin Body, Stitch-Jointed, 4 1/2 In. .. 1430.00
German, Porcelain Shoulder Head, Painted Face, Wood Body, Dowel, Boy, 3 1/2 In. 990.00
German, Porcelain Shoulder Head, Painted Features, Articulated Wood Body, c.1845, 6 In. 1210.00
German, Porcelain Shoulder Head, Sculpted Hair, Ears, Muslin Body, c.1870, 22 In. 5060.00
German, Porcelain Shoulder Head, Sculpted Hair, Eyelids, Kid Body, c.1870, 14 In. 4070.00
German, Porcelain Shoulder Head, Sculpted Hair, Finger Curls, Cloth, c.1865, 18 In. 2750.00
German, Porcelain Shoulder Head, Sculpted Hair, Muslin, Leather Limbs, c.1865, 25 In. .. 1870.00
German, Porcelain Shoulder Head, Sculpted Hair, Muslin, Leather Limbs, c.1870, 23 In. . 5060.00
German, Porcelain Shoulder Head, Sculpted Hair, Muslin, Stitch-Jointed, c.1880, 15 In. .. 1760.00
German, Porcelain Shoulder Head, Sculpted Hair, Muslin, Stitch-Jointed, c.1880, 21 In. .. 1540.00
German, Porcelain Shoulder Head, Sculpted Hair, Painted Eyes, Stitched Body, 16 In. ... 1900.00
German, Porcelain Shoulder Head, Sculpted Hair, Painted, Cloth Body, c.1865, 19 In. ... 2750.00
German, Porcelain, Painted Features, Closed Mouth, Baby Boy, c.1875, 8 In. 900.00
German, Porcelain, Painted Pate, Eyes, Human Hair, Stitch-Jointed, 21 In. 650.00
German, Porcelain, Steiner-Style Body, Sculpted Hair, Painted Eyes, c.1885, 20 In. 1870.00
German, Tauflinge, Porcelain Swivel Head, Sculpted Hair, Crier, Baby, c.1860, 12 In. ... 6490.00
German, Wax & Papier-Mache Shoulder Head, Mohair, Muslin, Stitch-Jointed, 15 In. ... 750.00
German, Wooden, Carved Shoulder Plate, Cleavage, Dowel Joints, c.1830, 12 In. 2750.00
German, Wooden, Painted Hair, Face, Turquoise Eyes, Dowel Joints, c.1850, 5 In. 825.00
Globe, Bisque Socket Head, Sleep Eyes, Mohair Wig, 5-Piece Composition, Baby, 8 In. ... 250.00
Grace Corry Rockwell, Bisque Head, Cloth Body, Composition Limbs, c.1935, 18 In. ... 7260.00
Greiner, Papier-Mache Shoulder Head, Muslin Body, American, c.1875, 27 In. 550.00

Greiner, Papier-Mache Shoulder Head, Painted Face, Muslin Body, c.1865, 23 In. 1430.00
Grodner Tal, Wooden Head & Body, Painted Hair, Dowel Joints, c.1840, 8 In. 660.00
Grodner Tal, Wooden Head & Body, Sculpted Hair, Painted Features, c.1830, 15 In 2640.00
Gunther Heine, Papier-Mache Socket Head, Painted, Muslin, Composition, 17 In. 1000.00
Half Dolls are listed in the Pinchushion category.
Handwerck, 31, Bisque Socket Head, Human Hair, Composition, Ball-Jointed, 26 In. 195.00
Handwerck, 79, Bisque Socket Head, Sleep Eyes, Composition, Wood, Jointed, 42 In. ... 1210.00
Handwerck, 79, Bisque Socket Head, Sleep Eyes, Mohair, Composition, Jointed, 22 In. . 580.00
Handwerck, 89, Bisque Socket Head, Sleep Eyes, Composition, Wood, 8 In. 1700.00
Handwerck, 89, Bisque Socket Head, Sleep Eyes, Mohair, Composition Body, 16 In. 580.00
Handwerck, 99, Bisque Socket Head, Sleep Eyes, Mohair, Wardrobe, 21 1/2 In. 2310.00
Handwerck, 109, Bisque Socket Head, Hair, Composition Body, Ball-Jointed 30 In. 660.00
Handwerck, 109, Bisque, Blue Glass Sleep Eyes, 4 Teeth, Mohair Wig, c.1910, 18 In. ... 715.00
Handwerck, 109, Bisque, Wig, Sleep Eyes, 5 Teeth, Composition, Ball-Jointed, 24 In. ... 315.00
Handwerck, 119, Bisque Head, Wig, Sleep Eyes, Teeth, Composition, Ball-Jointed, 23 In. 230.00
Handwerck, 119, Bisque Socket Head, Sleep Eyes, Painted Lashes, Teeth, Hair, 27 In. ... 440.00
Handwerck, Bisque Head, Wig, Sleep Eyes, Composition, Ball-Jointed, Blue Dress, 10 In. 1965.00
Handwerck, Bisque Socket Head, Composition, Ball-Jointed, c.1900, 32 In. 1650.00
Handwerck, Bisque Socket Head, Glass Eyes, Wig, Composition, Ball-Jointed, 38 In. 2000.00
Handwerck, Bisque Socket Head, Sleep Eyes, Composition, Ball-Jointed, Child, 18 In. ... 275.00
Handwerck, Bisque Socket Head, Sleep Eyes, Teeth, Hair, Composition, Jointed, 30 In. .. 470.00
Handwerck, Bisque Socket Head, Sleep Eyes, Teeth, Mohair Wig, Wood, Jointed, 31 In. . 660.00
Handwerck, Bisque Socket Head, Sleep Eyes, Teeth, Mohair, Composition, Jointed, 27 In. 525.00
Handwerck, Bisque, Blue Glass Sleep Eyes, 4 Teeth, Mohair Wig, Child, c.1910, 28 In. ... 1210.00
Handwerck, Soldier, Bisque Socket Head, Googly, Painted Lashes, 12 In. 1155.00
Handwerck, Uncle Sam, Bisque Socket Head, Googly, Painted Lashes, 13 In. 2000.00
Heine & Schneider, Cloth, Oil-Painted Head, Eyes, Hair, Composition Arms, 18 In. 2860.00
Hermann Steiner, 0, Bisque Socket Head, Composition, Ball-Jointed, 14 In. 95.00
Hertel Schwab, 136, Bisque Socket Head, Mohair Wig, Composition, Ball-Jointed, 27 In. 165.00
Hertel Schwab, 142, Bisque Socket Head, Glass Eyes, Composition, 10 1/2 In. 135.00
Hertel Schwab, 142, Bisque, Domed Socket Head, Bent-Limb Baby Body, c.1915, 10 In. . 715.00
Hertel Schwab, 152, Bisque Socket Head, 5-Piece Composition Body, Baby, 33 In. 1100.00
Hertel Schwab, 152, Bisque Socket Head, Sleep Eyes, Composition, Baby, 23 In. 200.00
Hertel Schwab, 163, Bisque, Googly, Sculpted Hair, c.1915, 16 In. 6050.00
Hertel Schwab, 165, Bisque Socket Head, Blue Sleep Eyes, Jointed, Toddler, 15 In. 6600.00
Hertel Schwab, 165, Bisque Socket Head, Googly, Composition, Wood, Jointed, 11 In. ... 4840.00
Hertel Schwab, 173, Bisque Socket Head, Googly, Wig, Jointed, Toddler, 15 In. 6050.00
Hertel Schwab, Bisque Socket Head, Googly, Sculpted Hair, Smiling, 10 In. 3600.00
Heubach dolls are also in this category under Gebruder Heubach.
Heubach, 262, Bisque Socket Head, Googly, Upper Teeth, 7 In. 520.00
Heubach, 275, Bisque Head, Wig, Sleep Eyes, 4 Teeth, Kid Body, Green Dress, 17 In. ... 140.00
Heubach, 302, Bisque Socket Head, Composition, Ball-Jointed, 26 In. 330.00
Heubach, 320, Bisque Head, Open Mouth, Pierced Nostrils, Composition Body, 9 In. 440.00
Heubach, 5636, Bisque Socket Head, Sleep Eyes, 2 Lower Teeth, Human Hair, 13 1/2 In. . 770.00
Heubach, 7109, Bisque Socket Head, Intaglio Eyes, Closed Mouth, Molded Hair, 15 In. .. 690.00
Heubach, 7246, Bisque Socket Head, Sleep Eyes, Composition, Ball-Jointed, 12 In. 2200.00
Heubach, 7602, Bisque Socket Head, Painted Features, Composition, Ball-Jointed, 10 In. . 330.00
Heubach, 7620, Bisque Socket Head, Intaglio Eyes, Teeth, Composition, Wood, 20 In. ... 650.00
Heubach, 7671, Black Bisque Socket Head, Composition, Wood, Jointed, c.1915, 8 In. 1430.00
Heubach, 8191, Bisque Socket Head, Googly Eyes, Molded Hair, 8 In. 300.00
Heubach, 8192, Bisque Socket Head, Sleep Eyes, Mohair, Composition, Jointed, 14 In. .. 600.00
Heubach, 8733, Bisque Socket Head, Molded Eyelids, Hair, Composition, 7 1/2 In. 360.00
Heubach, 9573, Bisque Socket Head, Googly Eyes, Wig, Composition, c.1915, 7 In. 2090.00
Heubach, Bisque Shoulder Head, Intaglio Eyes, Cloth Body, 10 In. 635.00
Heubach, Bisque Shoulder Head, Sculpted, Mohair, American Indian, c.1910, 13 In. 3740.00
Heubach, Bisque Socket Head, Googly, 5-Piece Composition Body, c.1920, 7 In. 605.00
Heubach, Bisque Socket Head, Googly, Composition, c.1920, 11 In. 1540.00
Heubach, Bisque Socket Head, Sleep Eyes, Lashes, Teeth, Mohair, Composition, 13 In. .. 360.00
Heubach, Bisque, Googly Eyes, Pug Nose, Mohair Wig, Kidolene Body, 12 In. 3850.00
Heubach, Bisque, Socket Head, Intaglio Eyes, Molded Hair, 5-Piece Body, 7 In. 715.00
Honey West, Karate Outfit, Lipstick Whistle, Handcuff Bracelet, Accessories 115.00
Horsman, Babyland Rag, Cloth Head, Hand Painted Eyes, Teeth, Human Hair, 14 In. 495.00
Horsman, Babyland Rag, Cloth Head, Painted Face, Eyes, Nostrils, Cloth Body, 19 1/2 In. 415.00

Horsman, Babyland Rag, Cloth Head, Painted Features, Jointed, Dress, Socks, 15 In. 275.00
Huret, Bisque Head, Paperweight Eyes, Mohair Wig, Wood Body, Bebe, c.1880, 18 In. . . 27025.00
Huret, Bisque Socket Head, Wood Body, Man, c.1910, 18 In. 6050.00
Huret, Porcelain Head, Painted Eyes, Wig, Articulated Body, c.1860, 17 In. 9900.00
Ideal, Baby Snooks & Mortimer Snerd, Composition Heads, Painted Eyes & Hair, 12 In. .   690.00
Ideal, Betsy McCall, Vinyl Head, Brown Sleep Eyes, Hair, 5-Piece Plastic Body, 14 In. . . .   220.00
Ideal, Betsy McCall, Vinyl Head, Sleep Eyes, Brunette Wig, Plastic Body, 14 In. 230.00
Ideal, Betsy Wetsy, Blows Nose, Sheds Tears, Sleeps, Drinks & Wets, Vinyl Body, 15 In. .   450.00
Ideal, Dorothy Hamill, Ice Skating Rink, Gold Medal, Box, 1970s, 11 In. 90.00
Ideal, Joan Palooka, Rubber, 14 In. 121.00
Ideal, Saucy Walker, Plastic, Green Dress, c.1955, 22 In. 29.00
Ideal, Toni, Plastic, Blue Sleep Eyes, Brunette Hair, Box, c.1955, 14 In. 190.00
Ideal, Toni, Plastic, Sleep Eyes, Nylon Wig, Play Wave, Accessories, Box, 16 In. 880.00
Indian dolls are listed in the Indian category.
Izannah Walker, Cloth Head, Painted Eyes, Hair, Closed Mouth, Cloth Body, 29 In. 8250.00
Izannah Walker, Cloth, Molded, Painted Features, Central Falls, R.I., 27 1/2 In. 8815.00
Izannah Walker, Cloth, Painted Head, Eyes, Hair, Arms, Legs, Shoes, 16 1/2 In. 4400.00
J.D.K. dolls also may be listed in this category under Kestner.
Jacob Petit, Porcelain Shoulder Head, Painted Eyes, Stuffed Muslin, c.1850, 22 In. 3300.00
Japanese, Bisque, Closed Mouth, Painted Features, Jointed Arms, Nippon, 4 In. . . . . .30.00 to 39.00
Julius Hering, Bisque Socket Head, Mohair Wig, Composition Body, Baby, 12 In. 165.00
Jumeau, 1, Bisque Socket Head, Composition, Wood, Ball-Jointed, c.1880, 11 In. 7425.00
Jumeau, 2, Bisque Socket Head, Paperweight Eyes, Human Hair, Bebe, c.1888, 11 In. . . .   3410.00
Jumeau, 3, Bisque Socket Head, Paperweight Eyes, Composition, Wood, Jointed, 12 In. . .   4400.00
Jumeau, 4, Bisque Socket Head, Almond-Shaped Glass Enamel Eyes, c.1878, 22 In. 23100.00
Jumeau, 5, Bisque Socket Head, Paperweight Eyes, Mohair Wig, Bebe, 13 In. 6380.00
Jumeau, 7, Bisque Socket Head, Paperweight Eyes, c.1885, 17 In. 6600.00
Jumeau, 8, Bisque Socket Head, Spiral-Threaded Eyes, Blond Lamb's-Wool Wig, 18 In. . .   7700.00
Jumeau, 11, Bisque Socket Head, Paperweight Eyes, Hair, Composition, c.1884, 23 In. . . 14850.00
Jumeau, 12, Bisque Socket Head, Paperweight Eyes, Blond Mohair, Bebe, c.1885, 25 In. . 10450.00
Jumeau, Bisque Head, Wig, Pierced Ears, 6 Teeth, Composition, Ball-Jointed, 17 1/2 In. .   1200.00
Jumeau, Bisque Socket Head, Almond Shaped Glass Enamel Eyes, c.1878, 15 In. 14850.00
Jumeau, Bisque Socket Head, Blue Sleep Eyes, Wig, Composition, Wood, Jointed, 22 In. .   1650.00
Jumeau, Bisque Socket Head, Composition, Wood, Ball-Jointed, Bebe, c.1880, 19 In. 7700.00
Jumeau, Bisque Socket Head, Composition, Wood, Jointed, c.1890, 20 In. 3960.00
Jumeau, Bisque Socket Head, Glass Eyes, Composition, Wood, Jointed, c.1885, 22 In. . . .   1485.00
Jumeau, Bisque Socket Head, Key-Wind Phonograph, Bebe, c.1893, 24 In. 6050.00
Jumeau, Bisque Socket Head, Paperweight Eyes, Composition, Wood, Jointed, 19 In. 6160.00
Jumeau, Bisque Socket Head, Paperweight Eyes, Composition, Wood, Jointed, 24 In. 4620.00
Jumeau, Bisque Socket Head, Paperweight Eyes, Jointed Body, Bebe, c.1885, 17 In. 7700.00
Jumeau, Bisque Socket Head, Paperweight Eyes, Mohair, Composition, Bebe, 17 In. 2310.00
Jumeau, Bisque Socket Head, Paperweight Eyes, Mohair, Composition, Jointed, 20 In. . .   3800.00
Jumeau, Bisque Socket Head, Paperweight Eyes, Mohair, Composition, Wood, 14 In. 3200.00
Jumeau, Bisque Socket Head, Paperweight Eyes, Mohair, Wood, Jointed, Bebe, 10 1/2 In.   1870.00
Jumeau, Bisque Socket Head, Paperweight Eyes, Spiral Threading, Mohair, c.1886, 13 In.   3740.00
Jumeau, Bisque Socket Head, Set Eyes, Teeth, Hair, Composition, Wood, Jointed, 35 In. .   1320.00
Jumeau, Bisque Socket Head, Shoulder Plate, Paperweight Eyes, Pierced Ears, 19 In. . . .   2090.00
Jumeau, Bisque Socket Head, Shoulder Plate, Threaded Eyes, Hair, Kid Body, 23 In. 2475.00
Jumeau, Bisque Socket Head, Sleep Eyes, Composition, Wood, Jointed, c.1887, 18 In. . . .   4290.00
Jumeau, Bisque Socket Head, Sleep Eyes, Porcelain Teeth, Hair, Composition, 26 In. . . .   2100.00
Jumeau, Bisque Swivel Head, Glass Eyes, Composition, Wood, Bebe, 1885, 15 In. 8000.00
Jumeau, Bisque Swivel Head, Shoulder Plate, Enamel Eyes, Kid Body, c.1870, 19 In. . . .   4620.00
Jumeau, Bisque Swivel Head, Shoulder Plate, Enamel Eyes, Mohair, Kid Body, 13 In. . . .   3000.00
Jumeau, Bisque Swivel Head, Shoulder Plate, Enamel Eyes, Wooden Body, c.1875, 14 In.   5940.00
Jumeau, Brown Bisque Socket Head, Paperweight Eyes, Composition, Jointed, 10 In. . . .   1700.00
Jumeau, Paperweight Eyes, Ball-Jointed, Tete, Silk Dress, 26 In. 3450.00
K * R, 39, Bisque Socket Head, Flirty Sleep Eyes, Tin Lids, Feathered Lashes, 14 1/2 In. .   880.00
K * R, 100, Bisque Socket Head, Painted Blue Eyes, Molded Hair, Baby, 15 In. 431.00
K * R, 100, Bisque Socket Head, Painted Eyes, Hair, Composition, 14 1/2 In. 255.00
K * R, 100, Bisque Socket Head, Painted Eyes, Hair, Composition, Baby, 13 In. 214.00
K * R, 100, Bisque Socket Head, Painted Eyes, Molded Hair, Composition, Baby, 14 In. . .   470.00
K * R, 100, Bisque Socket Head, Painted Eyes, Open-Close Mouth, Composition, 15 In. .   248.00
K * R, 100, Black Bisque Socket Head, Bent-Limb Body, Baby, 18 In., c.1910 . . . .   1705.00

K * R, 101, Bisque Socket Head, Painted Eyes, Pouty, 16 In. 1980.00
K * R, 101, Bisque Socket Head, Painted Eyes, Pouty, Mohair Wig, Layette, 9 In. 2420.00
K * R, 101, Bisque Socket Head, Pouty, Mohair Wig, Composition Body, Jointed, 8 In. . .   1320.00
K * R, 101, Marie, Bisque Socket Head, Composition, Wood, Ball-Jointed, c.1910, 15 In. .   4400.00
K * R, 101, Marie, Bisque Socket Head, Composition, Wood, Jointed, c.1910, 18 In. 4180.00
K * R, 101, Marie, Bisque Socket Head, Composition, Wood, Jointed, c.1915, 10 In. 1430.00
K * R, 101, Marie, Bisque Socket Head, Painted Eyes, Mohair Wig, 19 1/2 In. 5500.00
K * R, 101, Peter, Bisque Socket Head, Painted Eyes, Wig, Wood, Composition, 10 1/2 In.   935.00
K * R, 109, Bisque Socket Head, Composition, Wood, Ball-Jointed, c.1910, 17 In. 6325.00
K * R, 114, Bisque Socket Head, Sleep Eyes, Pouty, Mohair, Composition, Jointed, 17 In.   5000.00
K * R, 114, Gretchen, Bisque Socket Head, Painted Features, c.1910, 22 1/2 In. 6375.00
K * R, 114, Gretchen, Bisque Socket Head, Painted Features, Pouty, c.1910, 18 In. 3960.00
K * R, 114, Hans, Bisque Socket Head, Composition, Wood, Jointed, c.1910, 16 1/2 In. . .   3960.00
K * R, 115, Phillip, Bisque Domed Socket Head, Sleep Eyes, Ball-Jointed, c.1912, 15 In. .   3410.00
K * R, 115A, Phillip, Bisque Socket Head, Sleep Eyes, Composition, Wood, c.1915, 15 In.   3300.00
K * R, 115A, Phillip, Bisque Socket Head, Sleep Eyes, Mohair Wig, c.1912, 19 In. 2860.00
K * R, 116, Bisque Socket Head, Painted Hair, Composition, Wood, c.1912, 20 In. 2530.00
K * R, 116A, Bisque Socket Head, Sleep Eyes, Dimples, Wig, Composition, Baby, 25 In. .   2475.00
K * R, 117, Mein Liebling, Bisque Socket Head, Composition, Wood, c.1912, 23 In. 4950.00
K * R, 117, Mein Liebling, Bisque Socket Head, Brown Glass Sleep Eyes, c.1912, 16 In. .   5225.00
K * R, 117A, Mein Liebling, Bisque Socket Head, Blue Glass Sleep Eyes, c.1912, 8 In. . . .   3960.00
K * R, 117A, Mein Liebling, Bisque Socket Head, Sleep Eyes, Composition, 1915, 27 In.   6050.00
K * R, 117n, Bisque Socket Head, Flirty Eyes, Human Hair, Composition, Jointed, 30 In. .   770.00
K * R, 117n, Bisque Socket Head, Sleep Eyes, Tin Lids, 4 Teeth, Mohair, 20 1/2 In. 715.00
K * R, 121, Bisque Socket Head, Sleep Eyes, Teeth, Wig, Jointed, Toddler, 16 In. 1210.00
K * R, 121, Bisque Socket Head, Sleep Eyes, Wig, Jointed, Composition, Wood, 16 In. . .   1210.00
K * R, 122, Bisque Socket Head, Gray Blue Eyes, Wobble Tongue, Hair, Baby, 24 In. . . .   605.00
K * R, 126, Bisque Socket Head, Composition, 5-Piece Body, Toddler, c.1920, 8 In. 770.00
K * R, 126, Bisque Socket Head, Flirty Sleep Eyes, Teeth, Spring Tongue, Baby, 22 In. . .   330.00
K * R, 126, Bisque Socket Head, Glass Eyes, Painted, Wig, 5-Piece Body, Toddler, 8 In. .   825.00
K * R, 126, Bisque Socket Head, Sleep Eyes, 2 Teeth, Starfish Hands, Toddler, 7 1/2 In. . .   550.00
K * R, 126, Bisque Socket Head, Sleep Eyes, Painted Face, Composition, Toddler, 9 1/2 In.   1045.00
K * R, 126, Bisque Socket Head, Sleep Eyes, Painted Lashes, 2 Teeth, Baby, 19 1/2 In. . .   385.00
K * R, 127, Bisque Socket Head, Molded Hair, Blue Glass Sleep Eyes, c.1915, 21 In. 1870.00
K * R, 131, Bisque Socket Head, Googly, Mohair, Ball-Jointed, Toddler, 15 In. 5000.00
K * R, 131, Bisque, Googly Eyes, Watermelon Slice Smile, Mohair Wig, c.1915, 15 In. . . . 14300.00
K * R, 135, Bisque Socket Head, Sleep Eyes, Teeth, Composition, Wood, Toddler, 16 In. . .   1540.00
K * R, 136, Bisque Socket Head, Sleep Eyes, Bent-Limb Body, Baby, c.1912, 23 In. 2530.00
K * R, 146, Bisque Socket Head, Brown Blue Sleep Eyes, Teeth, Human Hair, 16 1/2 In. .   360.00
K * R, 170, Bisque Head, Sleep Eyes, Muslin, Composition Hands, Baby, c.1925, 13 In. .   1980.00
K * R, 192, Bisque Socket Head, Sleep Eyes, Lashes, Wig, Composition, Jointed, 21 In. . .   360.00
K * R, 192, Bisque Socket Head, Sleep Eyes, Open Mouth, Hair, Composition, 18 In. 440.00
K * R, 192, Bisque Socket Head, Sleep Eyes, Teeth, Mohair, Composition, Jointed, 16 In.   360.00
K * R, 403, Bisque Socket Head, Blue Glass Sleep Eyes, Blond Mohair, c.1915, 20 In. . . .   935.00
K * R, 403, Bisque Socket Head, Cardboard Pate, Sleep Eyes, Wig, Walker, 25 In. 330.00
K * R, 403, Bisque Socket Head, Glass Sleep Eyes, Blond Mohair Wig, 4 Teeth, 18 In. 715.00
K * R, 403, Bisque Socket Head, Sleep Eyes, Teeth, Wig, Composition, Wood, 22 In. 330.00
K * R, Bisque Socket Head, Flirty Eyes, Mohair Wig, Composition, Ball-Jointed, 16 In. . .   4750.00
K * R, Bisque Socket Head, Sleep Eyes, Human Hair, Composition, Wood, 26 In. 1050.00
K * R, Bisque Socket Head, Sleep Eyes, Pouty Lips, Mohair, Composition, Wood, 13 In. .   3600.00
K * R, Bisque Socket Head, Sleep Eyes, Teeth, Hair, Composition, Wood, Child, 31 In. . .   440.00
K * R, Cloth, Stockinette Head, Wire-Frame Body, Felt Suit, c.1926, 13 In. 580.00
K * R, Marie, Bisque Socket Head, Painted, Wig, Composition, Wood, Jointed, 10 In. . . .   1760.00
K * R, Scottish Boy, Sleep Eyes, Open Mouth, Teeth, Blond Mohair, 5-Piece Body, 9 In. .   315.00
K.P.M., Porcelain Shoulder Head, Sideburns, Cloth Body, c.1850, 18 In. 5060.00
Kamkins, Cloth Swivel Head, Oil Painted Eyes, Mohair Wig, Stitched Joints, 19 In. 3190.00
Kamkins, Cloth Swivel Head, Painted Eyes, Human Hair, Cloth Body, 18 In. 2420.00
Kamkins, Cloth Swivel Head, Painted Features, Jointed Body, Cherry Outfit, 19 In. 2310.00
Kathe Kruse, Cloth, Oil-Painted, Stitch-Jointed, Series I, c.1925, 17 In. 2530.00
Kathe Kruse, Cloth, Oil-Painted, Stitch-Jointed, Type X, c.1930, 14 In. 1650.00
Kathe Kruse, Cloth, Painted Face, Hair, Muslin Body, Jointed, Boy, c.1915, 17 In. 3190.00
Kathe Kruse, Cloth, Painted Features, Hair, Muslin Body, Stitch-Jointed, 1940, 13 In. . . .   935.00
Kathe Kruse, Cloth, Painted Features, Hair, Muslin Body, Stitch-Jointed, 1940, 20 In. . . .   1650.00

Kathe Kruse, Cloth, Painted Features, Muslin Body, Stitch-Jointed, c.1940, 20 In. 2640.00
Kathe Kruse, Plastic Socket Head, Closed Mouth, Human Hair, Cloth Body, 14 In. 385.00
Kathy Kruse, Cloth, Brown Eyes, Hair, Dress, Hat, 17 In. 1610.00
Kenner, Shaun Cassidy, Guitar, Hardy Boy Box, 1970s 95.00
Kestner dolls are also in this category under J.D.K.
Kestner, 16, Bisque Socket Head, Sleep Eyes, Composition, Wood, c.1890, 27 In. 12650.00
Kestner, 16, Bisque Socket Head, Sleep Eyes, Porcelain Teeth, Composition, 28 In. 1210.00
Kestner, 130, Bisque, Sleep Eyes, Painted Lashes, Mohair Wig, c.1910, 8 In. 825.00
Kestner, 143, Bisque Socket Head, Brown Sleep Eyes, Painted Lashes, 2 Teeth, 12 In. 660.00
Kestner, 143, Bisque Socket Head, Plaster Pate, Sleep Eyes, Jointed, 14 In., Twins 1430.00
Kestner, 143, Bisque Socket Head, Sleep Eyes, Composition, Ball-Jointed, c.1910, 9 In. ... 578.00
Kestner, 143, Bisque Socket Head, Sleep Eyes, Open Mouth, Wig, Dress, 17 In. 990.00
Kestner, 148, Bisque Shoulder Head, Arms, Mohair Wig, Kid Body, Gusset Joints, 20 In. . . 305.00
Kestner, 150, Bisque, Sleep Eyes, 4 Upper Teeth, Mohair Wig, Flowered Dress, 8 1/2 In. . 415.00
Kestner, 150, Bisque, Sleep Eyes, Painted Lashes, Mohair Wig, c.1910, 6 In. 330.00
Kestner, 153, Bisque, Swivel Head, Brown Glass Sleep Eyes, 4 Teeth, c.1890, 8 In. 2420.00
Kestner, 154, Bisque Shoulder Head, Rivet Jointed Kid Body, Mohair Wig, 18 In. 140.00
Kestner, 155, Bisque Socket Head, Glass Sleep Eyes, Mohair, Composition, Wood, 9 In . . 600.00
Kestner, 161, Bisque Socket Head, Sleep Eyes, Red Mohair Wig, Crier, 14 1/2 In. 600.00
Kestner, 162, Bisque Socket Head, Sleep Eyes, Human Hair, Jointed, Lady, 17 1/2 In. 990.00
Kestner, 164, Bisque Head, Brown Sleep Eyes, Open Mouth, Teeth, Blond Mohair, 25 In. . 660.00
Kestner, 164, Bisque Socket Head, Sleep Eyes, Composition, Wood, c.1900, 25 In. 1045.00
Kestner, 167, Bisque Socket Head, Set Eyes, Painted Lashes, Human Hair, 4 Teeth, 15 In. . 300.00
Kestner, 167, Bisque Socket Head, Sleep Eyes, Teeth, Wig, Wood, Composition, 9 In. ... 690.00
Kestner, 167, Bisque Socket Head, Sleep Eyes, Wood, Composition, Jointed, 23 In. 580.00
Kestner, 169, Bisque Socket Head, Sleep Eyes, Hair, Wood, Composition, Jointed, 29 In. . 660.00
Kestner, 169, Bisque Socket Head, Sleep Eyes, Open-Close Mouth, Composition, 13 In. . 1000.00
Kestner, 171, Bisque Socket Head, Porcelain Teeth, Human Hair, Composition, 32 In. ... 1000.00
Kestner, 171, Bisque Socket Head, Sleep Eyes, Open Mouth, Composition, 19 In. 180.00
Kestner, 171, Bisque Socket Head, Sleep Eyes, Painted Lashes, 3 Teeth, Jointed, 26 In. .. 525.00
Kestner, 171, Bisque Socket Head, Sleep Eyes, Teeth, Synthetic Wig, Jointed, 28 1/2 In. . 495.00
Kestner, 171, Daisy, Bisque Socket Head, Plaster Pate, Teeth, Mohair, Jointed, 18 In. 1100.00
Kestner, 171, Daisy, Bisque Socket Head, Sleep Eyes, Blond Mohair Wig, 18 In. 1045.00
Kestner, 171, Daisy, Bisque Socket Head, Sleep Eyes, Lashes, Open Mouth, 18 In. 1760.00
Kestner, 172, Gibson Girl, Bisque Shoulder Head, Kid Body, Wool Suit, c.1910, 20 In. ... 3190.00
Kestner, 172, Gibson Girl, Bisque Shoulder Head, Sleep Eyes, Kid Body, 15 In. 525.00
Kestner, 195, Bisque Shoulder Head, Sleep Eyes, Fur Brows, Kid Body, Jointed, 20 In. ... 470.00
Kestner, 208, Bisque, Brown Wig, Open-Close Mouth, Clothes, Shoes, 7 In. 290.00
Kestner, 211, Bisque Socket Head, Composition Body, Bent Limbs, c.1912, 11 In. 990.00
Kestner, 211, Bisque Socket Head, Hair, Composition Body, Bent Limbs, c.1912, 17 In. ... 1045.00
Kestner, 211, Bisque Socket Head, Sleep Eyes, Mohair Wig, Composition, Baby, 11 In. .. 385.00
Kestner, 211, Bisque Socket Head, Sleep Eyes, Wig, Composition Body, 1915, 16 In. 825.00
Kestner, 214, Bisque Socket Head, Open Mouth, Teeth, Composition, Ball-Jointed, 19 In. . 345.00
Kestner, 215, Bisque Socket Head, Sleep Eyes, Real Lashes, Fur Eyebrows, 23 1/2 In. 470.00
Kestner, 221, Bisque Socket Head, Googly Eyes To Left, Blond Mohair, c.1912, 15 In. .. 7150.00
Kestner, 221, Bisque Socket Head, Googly Eyes To Right, Blond Mohair, c.1912, 11 In. . .5500.00
Kestner, 221, Bisque Socket Head, Googly Eyes, Mohair, Composition, Wood, 13 In. 6250.00
Kestner, 221, Bisque Socket Head, Googly Eyes, Wig, Composition, Toddler, 11 In. 770.00
Kestner, 226, Bisque Socket Head, Sleep Eyes, Composition Body, Baby, 15 1/2 In. 550.00
Kestner, 243, Bisque Socket Head, Sleep Eyes, Composition, Chinese Baby, 1915, 15 In. . . 3410.00
Kestner, 247, Bisque Socket Head, Sleep Eyes, Mohair Wig, 2 Teeth, c.1912, 11 In. 1155.00
Kestner, 247, Bisque Socket Head, Sleep Eyes, Teeth, Wig, Composition, Baby, 16 In. 935.00
Kestner, 247, Bisque Socket Head, Sleep Eyes, Teeth, Wig, Jointed, Toddler, 16 In. 990.00
Kestner, 257, Bisque Socket Head, Brown Sleep Eyes, Blond Mohair, 2 Teeth, 9 1/2 In. .. 690.00
Kestner, 257, Bisque Socket Head, Sleep Eyes, Tin Lids, Wig, Composition, Baby, 18 In. . . 305.00
Kestner, 260, Bisque Socket Head, Set Eyes, Teeth, Composition, Jointed, 35 In. 1870.00
Kestner, 260, Bisque Socket Head, Sleep Eyes, Composition, 5-Piece Body, c.1915, 6 In. . . 635.00
Kestner, 267, Bisque Socket Head, Inset Eyes, Composition, Wood, 28 In. 3000.00
Kestner, Bisque Shoulder Head, Set Eyes, Human Hair, Kid Body, Gussets, 19 1/2 In. . . . 230.00
Kestner, Bisque Shoulder Head, Set Eyes, Painted Lashes, Closed Mouth, 17 1/2 In. 470.00
Kestner, Bisque Shoulder Head, Sleep Eyes, Kid Body, Gusset Joints, c.1885, 15 In. 1100.00
Kestner, Bisque Shoulder Head, Turned, Sleep Eyes, Teeth, Wig, Kid Body, 15 In. 265.00
Kestner, Bisque Socket Head, Blond, Composition, Wood, Ball-Jointed, c.1900, 32 In. . 1980.00

Kestner, Bisque Socket Head, Blue Sleep Eyes, Composition Body, Ball-Jointed, 15 In. . . . 440.00
Kestner, Bisque Socket Head, Closed Mouth, Ball-Jointed, Child, c.1885, 14 In. 3080.00
Kestner, Bisque Socket Head, Composition, Ball-Jointed, Child, c.1895, 13 In. 3080.00
Kestner, Bisque Socket Head, Domed, Sleep Eyes, Teeth, Composition, Baby, 20 In. 605.00
Kestner, Bisque Socket Head, Set Eyes, Painted Lashes, Pouty Mouth, Jointed, 15 In. . . . 990.00
Kestner, Bisque Socket Head, Sleep Eyes, Composition Body, Ball-Jointed, 24 In. 550.00
Kestner, Bisque Socket Head, Sleep Eyes, Painted Lashes, Open Mouth, 2 Teeth, 24 In. . . 935.00
Kestner, Bisque Socket Head, Sleep Eyes, Teeth, Hair, Jointed, Composition, 28 In. 635.00
Kestner, Bisque Socket Head, Sleep Eyes, Teeth, Mohair Wig, Ball-Jointed, 16 In. 550.00
Kestner, Bisque Socket Head, Sleep Eyes, Teeth, Mohair, Composition, Wood, 13 In. 770.00
Kestner, Bisque Swivel Head, Glass Eyes, 3 Teeth, Mohair Wig, Peg-Jointed, 9 1/2 In. . . . 5170.00
Kestner, Bisque Swivel Head, Glass Inset Eyes, Loop-Jointed, c.1885, 6 1/2 In. 3190.00
Kestner, Bisque Swivel Head, Sleep Eyes, Dimples, Blond Wig, c.1885, 10 In. 2860.00
Kestner, Bisque Swivel Head, Yellow Boots, Loop-Jointed, c.1885, 9 In. 3960.00
Kestner, Bisque, Wig, Set Eyes, Pierced Ears, Open Mouth, 3 Teeth, 8 In. 518.00
Kestner, Hilda, Bisque Socket Head, Domed, Painted Hair, Sleep Eyes, 17 In. 3750.00
Kestner, Hilda, Bisque Socket Head, Painted Features, Sleep Eyes, c.1915, 16 In. 2860.00
Kestner, Hilda, Bisque Socket Head, Sleep Eyes, Bent Limbs, Baby, c.1915, 10 In. 2860.00
Kestner, Hilda, Bisque Socket Head, Sleep Eyes, Bent Limbs, Baby, c.1915, 25 In. 6270.00
Kestner, Hilda, Brown Sleep Eyes, 5-Piece Papier-Mache Body, Baby, 1912, 22 In. 2640.00
Kewpie dolls are listed in the Kewpie category.
Kley & Hahn, 157, Bisque Socket Head, Sleep Eyes, Mohair, Composition, Baby, 11 In. . . 275.00
Kley & Hahn, 169, Bisque Socket Head, Sleep Eyes, Human Hair, Composition, 19 In. . . . 1600.00
Kley & Hahn, 525, Bisque, Glass Sleep Eyes, Mohair Wig, Toddler, c.1912, 18 In. 1870.00
Kley & Hahn, 526, Bisque Socket Head, Mohair Wig, Composition, Jointed, 20 In. 3850.00
Kley & Hahn, 526, Bisque, Painted Features, Closed Mouth, Blond Wig, c.1910, 15 In. . . . 3630.00
Kley & Hahn, 531, Bisque Socket Head, Intaglio Eyes, Composition, Wood, 17 In. 525.00
Kley & Hahn, Bisque Socket Head, Composition, Wood, Ball-Jointed, 1912, 14 In. 2530.00
Kley & Hahn, Bisque Socket Head, Domed, Blond, Sleep Eyes, Ball-Jointed, 15 In. 1600.00
Kley & Hahn, Dollar Princess, Bisque Socket Head, Sleep Eyes, Painted Lashes, 23 In. . . 330.00
Kling, 123, Bisque Shoulder Head, Blue Set Eyes, Mohair Wig, Cloth Body, 11 In. 495.00
Kling, 189, Porcelain Shoulder Head, Blond Sculpted Hair, Cloth Body, c.1885, 20 In. . . . 800.00
Kling, Bisque Socket Head, Painted Eyes, Painted Socks, Boots, 5-Piece Body, 3 1/2 In. . . 140.00
Konig & Wernicke, Bisque Socket Head, Blue Sleep Eyes, 2 Teeth, Hair, Toddler, 11 In. . . 863.00
Lenci, Cloth, Blue Googly Eyes Eyes To Left, Blue Dress, Box, 20 In. 265.00
Lenci, Felt Swivel Head, Googly, Auburn Curly Wig, 1939, 21 In. 3850.00
Lenci, Felt Swivel Head, Painted Googly Eyes, 8 1/2 In. 220.00
Lenci, Girl, Felt Swivel Head, Mohair Wig, 5-Piece Body, Cage Of Lovebirds, 20 In. 3000.00
Lenci, Girl, Felt Swivel Head, Painted Features, Mohair Wig, Muslin Body, 14 In. 475.00
Madame Alexander, Alice In Wonderland, Composition, Sleep Eyes, Human Hair, 13 In. . . 275.00
Madame Alexander, American Girl, Plastic, Sleep Eyes, Walker, 8 In. 275.00
Madame Alexander, Amy, Plastic, Sleep Eyes, Synthetic Wig, Curlers, Box, 15 In. 415.00
Madame Alexander, Annabelle, Plastic, Sleep Eyes, 5-Piece Body, 1952, 18 In. 880.00
Madame Alexander, Binnie Walker, Plastic, Sleep Eyes, Synthetic Wig, Jointed, 18 In. . . . 660.00
Madame Alexander, Blue Boy, Plastic, Vinyl, Box, 11 In. 22.00
Madame Alexander, Bride, Composition Brown Sleep Eyes, c.1940, 14 In. 880.00
Madame Alexander, Bridesmaid, Composition Head, 5-Piece Body, c.1940, 18 In. 550.00
Madame Alexander, Cherie, Me & My Shadow, Plastic Socket Head, Pink Coat, 18 In. . . . 3630.00
Madame Alexander, Cissette, Plastic, Sleep Eyes, Wig, Jointed, Red, White Dress, 10 In. . . 385.00
Madame Alexander, Cissette, Queen, Hard Plastic, Sleep Eyes, Tiara, 10 In. 330.00
Madame Alexander, Cissy, My Fair Lady, Hard Plastic, 7-Piece Vinyl Body, 20 In. 1430.00
Madame Alexander, Easter Girl, Plastic Head, Sleep Eyes, Prototype, c.1968, 8 In. 495.00
Madame Alexander, Edith, Vinyl, Sleep Eyes, Rooted Hair, Swivel Waist, Jointed, 20 In. . . 275.00
Madame Alexander, Elise, Vinyl Socket Head, Pink Gown, Hat, c.1975, 17 In. 85.00
Madame Alexander, Fairy Princess, Composition, Sleep Eyes, Red Gown, c.1938, 15 In. . . 660.00
Madame Alexander, Gold Rush, Hard Plastic, Sleep Eyes, Blond Wig, Box, 10 In. 330.00
Madame Alexander, Groom, Sleep Eyes, Closed Mouth, Wig, String Tag, 17 In. 380.00
Madame Alexander, Iceland, Plastic, Blue Sleep Eyes, Wig, Jointed, Taffeta Dress, 10 In. . 220.00
Madame Alexander, Jane Withers, Yellow Dress, Bonnet, c.1937, 13 In. 770.00
Madame Alexander, Jenny Lind, Plastic, Sleep Eyes, Wig, Jointed, High Heels, 10 In. 195.00
Madame Alexander, Jo, Little Women, Plastic, Synthetic Wig, Hat Box, Box, 15 In. 605.00
Madame Alexander, Kate Greenaway, Composition, Brown Sleep Eyes, c.1940, 13 In. 467.00
Madame Alexander, Laurie, Little Men, Box, 8 In. 55.00

Madame Alexander, Lissy, Bride, Hard Plastic, Blue Eyes, 7-Piece Body, 12 In. 415.00
Madame Alexander, Little Shaver, Cloth, Mitten Hands, Blouse, Skirt, 20 In. 825.00
Madame Alexander, Little Shaver, Cloth, Mitten Hands, Blue Blouse, Peach Skirt, 20 In. . 495.00
Madame Alexander, Little Women, Plastic, 5-Piece Body, Dress, 1954, 14 In., 5-Piece . . . 880.00
Madame Alexander, Madelaine, Composition, Sleep Eyes, Human Hair, 14 In. 1150.00
Madame Alexander, Maggie Mix-Up, Plastic, Vinyl Arms, Sleep Eyes, Jointed, 15 In. . . 470.00
Madame Alexander, Maggie, Plastic, Sleep Eyes, 5-Piece Body, Walker, Dress, 18 In. . . . 2200.00
Madame Alexander, Margot, Plastic, Blue Sleep Eyes, Synthetic Hair, Jointed, Box, 10 In. 415.00
Madame Alexander, Marie, Composition, Sleep Eyes, Closed Mouth, Metal Tag, 20 In. . . 255.00
Madame Alexander, Marlo Thomas, That Girl, Vinyl, Sleep Eyes, Jointed, 1967, 17 In. . . 220.00
Madame Alexander, Marmie, Little Women, Plastic, Synthetic Wig, Box, 15 In. 1020.00
Madame Alexander, McGuffey Ana, Composition Socket Head, Sleep Eyes, Hair, 15 In. . 425.00
Madame Alexander, McGuffey Ana, Composition, Sleep Eyes, Human Hair, 12 In. 700.00
Madame Alexander, Meg, Little Women, Plastic, Synthetic Wig, Tag, Box, 15 In. 360.00
Madame Alexander, Poodle, Velvet, Yarn, Black, c.1950, 16 In. 295.00
Madame Alexander, Posey Pet, Cat, Brown Plush, Striped Dress, c.1940, 17 In. 220.00
Madame Alexander, Posey Pet, Rabbit, White Plush, Organdy Dress, c.1940, 17 In. 310.00
Madame Alexander, Princess Elizabeth, Composition Head, Sleep Eyes, Hair, 13 In. 400.00
Madame Alexander, Princess Elizabeth, Composition Head, Sleep Eyes, Hair, 15 In. 275.00
Madame Alexander, Princess Elizabeth, Composition Head, Sleep Eyes, Mohair, 19 In. . . 415.00
Madame Alexander, Princess Elizabeth, Lavender Gown, Tiara, c.1937, 13 In. 220.00
Madame Alexander, Princess Elizabeth, Magenta Gown, Box, c.1937, 17 In. 440.00
Madame Alexander, Princess Margaret Rose, Hard Plastic, 5-Piece Body, Walker, 18 In. . . 3740.00
Madame Alexander, Queen Elizabeth, Hard Plastic, 5-Piece Body, Walker, 18 In. 1980.00
Madame Alexander, Renoir, Plastic, Sleep Eyes, Closed Mouth, Synthetic Wig, 10 In. . . . 220.00
Madame Alexander, Rosamund Bridesmaid, Plastic, 5-Piece, Walker, Yellow Gown, 18 In. 415.00
Madame Alexander, Rosamund Bridesmaid, Plastic, Blue Sleep Eyes, Wig, 15 In. 305.00
Madame Alexander, Scarlett O'Hara, Composition, Sleep Eyes, 5-Piece Body, 14 In. 550.00
Madame Alexander, Scarlett O'Hara, Composition, Sleep Eyes, Closed Mouth, 21 In. . . . 140.00
Madame Alexander, Scarlett O'Hara, Plastic Socket Head, White Gown, c.1958, 20 In. . . 1100.00
Madame Alexander, Shari Lewis, Hard Plastic, 5-Piece Body, Red Dress, c.1959, 14 In. . . 440.00
Madame Alexander, Sonja Henie, Composition, Ivory Skating Costume, c.1940, 13 In. . . . 1660.00
Madame Alexander, Sonja Henie, Composition, Pink Skating Costume, c.1940, 20 In. . . . 1250.00
Madame Alexander, Sonja Henie, Composition, Ski Costume, Red Shirt, c.1942, 15 In. . . 770.00
Madame Alexander, Sonja Henie, Composition, Yellow Skating Costume, c.1940, 15 In. . 575.00
Madame Alexander, Southern Belle, Plastic, Sleep Eyes, Wig, Jointed, 1963, 8 In. 165.00
Madame Alexander, Stuffy, Little Men, Plastic, Sleep Eyes, Synthetic Wig, 15 In. 660.00
Madame Alexander, Susie Q & Bobbie Q, Cloth, Mitten Hands, Blue Eyes, 13 In., Pair . . 1870.00
Madame Alexander, Tiny Betty, Composition, Painted Eyes, Blond Mohair, c.1935, 7 In. . 150.00
Madame Alexander, W.A.A.C., Composition, World War II Uniform, c.1943, 15 In. 1100.00
Madame Alexander, W.A.V.E., Composition, World War II Uniform, c.1943, 15 In. 580.00
Madame Alexander, Wendy Ann, Composition, Glassine Sleep Eyes, Jointed, 13 In. 70.00
Madame Alexander, Wendy Ann, Hard Plastic, 5-Piece Body, Party Dress, c.1949, 21 In. . 1760.00
Marilyn Neuhart, Wool, Silk, Red, Yarn Hair, Wings, Heart On Belly, 1961, 6 In. 935.00
Marion, China Shoulder Head, Black Hair, Kidolene Body, Rivet Joints, 12 In. 55.00
Martha Thompson, Fashion, Bisque, Muslin Body, Bonnet, c.1953, 15 In. 798.00
Mary Hoyer, Plastic, Sleep Eyes, Caracul Wig, 5-Piece Body, 14 In. 523.00
Mattel, Allan, Painted Red Hair, Bendable Legs, Red Jacket, Blue Swim Trunks, Box . . . 145.00
Mattel, Allan, Painted Red Hair, Blue Swim Trunks, Sandals, Stand, 1968, Box 65.00
Mattel, Allan, Red Brown Hair, Blue Swim Trunks, Striped Jacket, Box 85.00
Mattel, Barbie & Ken, Gift Set, Ken, Blond, Barbie, Bubble Cut, Accessories, Box 575.00
Mattel, Barbie, American Girl, Ash Blond, Striped Swimsuit . . . . .225.00 to 325.00
Mattel, Barbie, American Girl, Ash Blond, Striped Turquoise Swimsuit, Stand, Box 400.00
Mattel, Barbie, American Girl, Tan Lips, 1-Piece Swimsuit, Turquoise Shoes, Box 500.00
Mattel, Barbie, Bubble Cut, Blond, Red Swimsuit, Pearl Earrings, Stand, Box 150.00
Mattel, Barbie, Bubble Cut, Platinum Blond, Red Swimsuit, Stand, Box 175.00
Mattel, Barbie, Bubble Cut, Titian Hair, Blue Eyes, Beige Lips, Red Swimsuit 85.00
Mattel, Barbie, Bubble Cut, Titian Hair, Pearl Earrings, Red Swimsuit, Box 140.00
Mattel, Barbie, Career Girl, Black & White Suit, Accessories, No. 954 . . . . 80.00
Mattel, Barbie, Color Magic, Blond, Diamond Print Suit, Turquoise Belt, Shoes 400.00
Mattel, Barbie, Eskimo, International Series, Box, 1981 . . . . 85.00
Mattel, Barbie, Fashion Queen, Painted Hair, Gold & White Swimsuit, 3 Wigs 165.00
Mattel, Barbie, Golden Anniversary, Mattel 50th Anniversary, Limited Edition, Box 105.00

Mattel, Barbie, Guinevere, Bubble Cut, Titian Hair, Blue Velvet Gown, Booklet, Box	250.00
Mattel, Barbie, Let's Dance, Blue Dress, Floral Print, Accessories, No. 978	55.00
Mattel, Barbie, Miss Barbie, Bendable Legs, Wigs, Lawn Swing, Accessories, Box	275.00
Mattel, Barbie, No. 1, Blond, Ponytail, Black & White Swimsuit, Accessories, Box	3300.00
Mattel, Barbie, No. 1, Blond, Ponytail, Black & White Swimsuit, Box	2200.00
Mattel, Barbie, No. 2, Blond, Ponytail, Black & White Striped Swimsuit, Stand, Box	2500.00
Mattel, Barbie, No. 3, Brunette, Ponytail, Striped Swimsuit, Shoes, Glasses	525.00
Mattel, Barbie, No. 4, Blond, Ponytail, Black & White Striped Swimsuit, Accessories . . .	225.00
Mattel, Barbie, No. 4, Blond, Ponytail, Black & White Striped Swimsuit, Stand, Box	350.00
Mattel, Barbie, No. 4, Brunette, Ponytail, Accessories	225.00
Mattel, Barbie, No. 5, Brunette, Blue Eyes, Black & White Striped Swimsuit, Stand	175.00
Mattel, Barbie, No. 5, Brunette, Ponytail, Striped Swimsuit, Accessories, Stand, Box	275.00
Mattel, Barbie, No. 5, Titian Hair, Black & White Striped Swimsuit, Stand, Box	400.00
Mattel, Barbie, No. 5, Titian Hair, Blue Eyes, Black & White Striped Swimsuit	300.00
Mattel, Barbie, Orange Blossom, Yellow Dress, Accessories, No. 987	50.00
Mattel, Barbie, Ponytail, Brunette, Black & White Striped Swimsuit, Montgomery Ward .	200.00
Mattel, Barbie, Ponytail, Brunette, Blue Eyes, Nostril Paint, Khaki Coat, Open Road	190.00
Mattel, Barbie, Ponytail, No. 1, Pedestal Stand, Black Plastic, 2 Metal Prongs	1300.00
Mattel, Barbie, Ponytail, Swirl, Blond, Blue Eyes, White Lips, Red Swimsuit	225.00
Mattel, Barbie, Ponytail, Swirl, Blue & White Swimsuit, Stand, Shoes, Jewelry, Box	281.00
Mattel, Barbie, Ponytail, Swirl, Brunette, Blue Eyes, Red Swimsuit, Booklet, Box	600.00
Mattel, Barbie, Ponytail, Swirl, Brunette, Red Swimsuit, Stand, Box	425.00
Mattel, Barbie, Ponytail, Swirl, Platinum Blond, Red Swimsuit, Accessories, Box	550.00
Mattel, Barbie, Theatre Date, Green Skirt, Bolero Jacket, Hat, Blouse, Shoes	60.00
Mattel, Barbie, Twist 'n Turn, Blond, Bendable Legs, Diamond Checked Swimsuit, Box .	300.00
Mattel, Barbie, Twist 'n Turn, Blond, Quick Curl, Pink & White Gingham Dress	95.00
Mattel, Barbie, Twist 'n Turn, Brunette, Orange Swimsuit, Net Cover-Up	215.00
Mattel, Barbie, Twist 'n Turn, Brunette, Orange Vinyl Swimsuit, Cover-Up, Stand, Box . .	325.00
Mattel, Barbie, Twist 'n Turn, Brunette, Pink & White Swimsuit, Stand, Box	375.00
Mattel, Cheryl Ladd, Box, 1970s, 11 In.	75.00
Mattel, Chris, Blond, Bendable Arms, Accessories, Box	155.00
Mattel, Christie, Black Hair, Print Top, Orange Shorts, Talking, Box	200.00
Mattel, Christie, Twist 'n Turn, Red Brown Hair, Pink & Yellow Swimsuit, Stand, Box . .	275.00
Mattel, Color Magic, Midnight, Ruby Hair, Bendable Legs, Accessories, Box	1600.00
Mattel, Francie, Ash Blond, Green & Pink Swimsuit, Bendable Legs	95.00
Mattel, Francie, Blond, 2-Piece Red & White Swimsuit, Accessories, Stand, Box	175.00
Mattel, Francie, Blond, Growing Pretty Hair, Pink Lame & Satin Dress, Box	175.00
Mattel, Francie, Brunette, String Holding Hair In Place, 2-Piece Swimsuit, Stand, Box . .	260.00
Mattel, Francie, Twist 'n Turn, Brown Hair, Bendable Legs, 2-Piece Swimsuit, Box	1900.00
Mattel, Francie, Twist 'n Turn, Brown Hair, Brown Eyes, Real Eyelashes, Nude	275.00
Mattel, Francie, Twist 'n Turn, Brunette, Accessories, Stand, Box	300.00
Mattel, Jamie, Furry Friends Set, Blond, Brown Eyes, Gray Poodle, Accessories, Box	575.00
Mattel, Julia, Brown Hair, Nurse Uniform, Accessories, Box . . . . · . . .	200.00
Mattel, Ken, 30th Anniversary, Limited Edition, No. 1110, Box	60.00
Mattel, Ken, Blond Flocked Hair, Red Swim Trunks, Accessories, Stand, Box	65.00
Mattel, Ken, Blond Flocked Hair, Straight Legs, Red Swim Trunks, Booklet, Box	95.00
Mattel, Ken, Blond Painted Hair, Red & White Jacket, Red Swim Trunks, Stand, Box . . .	120.00
Mattel, Ken, Brown Flocked Hair, Red Swim Trunks, Sandals, Stand, Box	70.00
Mattel, Ken, Brown Painted Hair, Bendable Legs, Accessories, Stand, Box	125.00
Mattel, Ken, Brown Painted Hair, Red & White Striped Jacket, Red Swim Trunks	50.00
Mattel, Kiddle Kolognes, Rosebud, Honeysuckle, Apple Blossom, Box, 3 Piece	285.00
Mattel, Kiddle Kolognes, Violet, Sweet Pea, Lily Of The Valley, Box, 3 Piece	205.00
Mattel, Liddle Kiddle, Brunette, Blue Dress, Kitchen, Plastic, Box	200.00
Mattel, Liddle Kiddle, Skediddle, Sheila, Red Hair, Yellow Dress, Orange Walker, Box . .	55.00
Mattel, Liddle Kiddle, Windy Fliddle, Blond, Blue Eyes, Airplane, On Card	230.00
Mattel, Lori & Rori, Blond, Blue Eyes, Striped Dress, Teddy Bear, Pretty Pairs	150.00
Mattel, Midge, Brunette Flip, 2-Piece Swimsuit, Stand, Box	165.00
Mattel, Midge, Brunette, Blue Ribbon Hair Band, Striped Knit Swimsuit	185.00
Mattel, Midge, Brunette, Painted & Molded Hair, 2-Piece Chartreuse, Orange Swimsuit . .	850.00
Mattel, Midge, Brunette, Striped Swimsuit, Stand, Box	230.00
Mattel, Midge, Titian Hair, 2-Piece, Yellow & Orange Swimsuit, Stand, Box	150.00
Mattel, Midge, Titian Hair, Striped Shirt, Black Pants, Plaid Bag, White Coat	85.00
Mattel, Ricky, Red Painted Hair, Striped Jacket, Blue Swim Trunks, Sandals	40.00

Mattel, Ricky, Red Painted Hair, Striped Jacket, Blue Swim Trunks, Stand, Box	70.00
Mattel, Skipper, Blond, Red & White Swimsuit, Accessories, Stand, Box	95.00
Mattel, Skipper, Brunette, Red & White Swimsuit, Stand, Box	150.00
Mattel, Skipper, Dramatic New Living, Blond, Bendable, Box	65.00
Mattel, Skipper, No. 1, Plastic Carrying Case, 1964, 9 In.	35.00
Mattel, Skipper, Titian Hair, Red & White Striped Swimsuit, Accessories, Stand, Box . . .	105.00
Mattel, Skooter, Blond, 2-Piece Swimsuit, Accessories, Stand, Box	125.00
Mattel, Stacey, Blond, Blue & Silver Lame Swimsuit, Talking, Box	325.00
Mattel, Storybook Kiddle, Liddle Middle Muffet, Red Hair, Accessories, On Card	300.00
Mattel, Storybook Kiddle, Robin Hood, Maid Marion, Necklace, On Card	110.00
Mattel, Truly Scrumptious, Blond, Pink Dress, Box	325.00
Mattel, Tutti, Blond, Blue Eyes, Flowered Dress, Accessories, Box	100.00
Mattel, Tutti, Walkin' My Dolly, Blond, Red & White Gingham Dress, Buggy, Box	145.00
Mego, Cher, Gypsy Box, 1976, 12 In.	196.00
Mego, Cowardly Lion, Wizard Of Oz, Box, 1974, 8 In.	40.00
Mego, Dorothy & Toto, Wizard Of Oz, Box, 1974, 8 In.	40.00
Mego, Dr. Zaius, Planet Of The Apes, On Card, 1967, 5 In.	26.00
Mego, Glinda The Good Witch, Wizard Of Oz, Box, 1974, 8 In.	90.00
Mego, Scarecrow, Wizard Of Oz, Box, 1974, 8 In.	40.00
Mego, Tin Woodsman, Wizard Of Oz, Box, 1974, 8 In.	40.00
Mego, Toni Tenille, Box, 1977, 12 In.	85.00
Mego, Wicked Witch, Wizard Of Oz, Box, 1974, 8 In.	65.00
Mego, Wizard, Throne, Magic Spinning Crystal Ball, Wizard Of Oz, Box, 1974, 8 In.	40.00
Morimura, Bisque Socket Head, Mohair Wig, Composition, Baby, 8 In.	49.00
Nancy Ann Storybook, Bisque, Western Miss, Painted Features, Jointed, 5 In.	900.00
Norah Wellings, Boy, Flat Swivel Head, Painted Features, Mohair Wig, Owl, 14 In.	330.00
Norah Wellings, Chinese Man, Cloth, 7 1/2 In.	35.00
Norah Wellings, Old Man & Woman, Felt Face, Muslin Body, c.1930, 24 In., Pair	1760.00
Norah Wellings, Policeman, Cloth, Painted Features, Tag, 8 In.	116.00
Norah Wellings, Sailor, Celluloid Face, Cotton Body, 11 In.	29.00
Norah Wellings, Sailor, Felt Head, Hands, Feet, Velveteen Body, Jointed, Tag, 8 In.	39.00
Ohlhaver, Bisque Shoulder Head, Sleep Eyes, Painted Lashes, 4 Teeth, Hair, 25 In.	440.00
Ohlhaver, Bisque Socket Head, Painted, Composition, Ball-Jointed, Coquette, 12 In.	550.00
Paper dolls are listed in their own category.	
Papier-Mache, Bisque Socket Head, Glass Eyes, Mohair, Wire Arms, Pull, Germany, 7 In.	850.00
Papier-Mache, Black, Painted Features, Fleecy Wig, Wooden Limbs, c.1865, 8 1/2 In. . . .	605.00
Papier-Mache, Domed Head, Inset Eyes, Painted, Muslin, Wooden Limbs, Germany, 21 In.	3000.00
Papier-Mache, Domed Head, Painted, Enamel Eyes, Kid Arms, Mechanical, 9 In.	3100.00
Papier-Mache, French Sailor, Socket Head, Mustache, 5-Piece Composition Body, 15 In. .	165.00
Papier-Mache, Shoulder Head, Enamel Eyes, Human Hair, Gusset Joints, 16 In.	2200.00
Papier-Mache, Shoulder Head, Flirty Eyes, Muslin Body, Wooden Limbs, c.1840, 22 In. .	3960.00
Papier-Mache, Shoulder Head, Painted Face, Mohair Wig, Wood Body, Man, 23 In.	4400.00
Papier-Mache, Shoulder Head, Painted Features, Hair Braids, Kid Body, Gussets, 20 In. . .	1980.00
Papier-Mache, Shoulder Head, Painted Features, Kid Body, Wooden Limbs, 14 In.	1375.00
Papier-Mache, Shoulder Head, Painted Features, Kid Body, Wooden Limbs, c.1850, 9 In. .	2640.00
Papier-Mache, Shoulder Head, Pupilless Glass Eyes, Painted Lashes, Hair, Jointed, 30 In.	900.00
Papier-Mache, Shoulder Head, Pupilless Glass Eyes, Painted Lashes, Teeth, 32 In.	550.00
Papier-Mache, Shoulder Head, Ringlet Curls, Muslin Body, Germany, c.1860, 21 In.	1100.00
Papier-Mache, Shoulder Head, Solid Dome, Painted Eyes, Wig, Kid Body, c.1850, 20 In. .	1100.00
Papier-Mache, Shoulder Head, Teeth, Painted Hair, Kid Body, 21 In.	770.00
Papier-Mache, Shoulder Head, Wax-Dipped Shell Body, France, c.1840, 9 In.	330.00
Papier-Mache, Shoulder Head, Wood, Milliner Model, Germany, c.1830, 18 In.	470.00
Papier-Mache, Smiling Aged Woman, Long Nose, Muslin Body, Germany, c.1890, 14 In. .	1210.00
Papier-Mache, Wax Shoulder Plate, Wood Upper Body, Germany, c.1885, 14 In.	440.00
Parian, Molded Hair, Blue Eyes, Parian Arms, Kid Body, Dress, 19 In.	90.00
Parian, Shoulder Head, Blond Curly Hair, Kid Body, Rivet & Gusset Joints, 17 In.	165.00
Parian, Shoulder Head, Pierced Ears, Braided Hair, Cloth Body, 20 In.	3025.00
Pierotti, Wax Shoulder Head, Stuffed Muslin Body, Velvet Dress, England, c.1870, 17 In.	880.00
Pincushion dolls are listed in their own category.	
Porcelain, Hand Pressed, Sculpted Eyes, Muslin Body, Stitch-Jointed, c.1850, 25 In.	9350.00
Porcelain, Hand Pressed, Solid Dome, Hair, Painted Eyes, Muslin Body, 1850, 13 In.	2750.00
Porcelain, Shoulder Head, Limbs, Muslin Body, Cinch Waist, Germany, c.1865, 8 In.	470.00
Poulbot, Bisque Socket Head, Mohair Wig, Composition Body, Jointed, c.1915, 14 In.	7700.00

Puppet, Monkey, Mohair, Felt, Brown, Inset Celluloid Eyes, Feathered Hat, 8 In. 118.00
Puppet, Panda Bear, 1930s, 7 In. 29.00
Puppet, Poodle, Mustache, Rose Ribbon Around Neck, Steiff, No. 317, Germany 20.00
Puppet, Punch, Cloth, Painted Features, 15 In. 45.00
Radiquet & Cordonnier, Fashion, Bisque Swivel Head, Stuffed Kid Body, c.1880, 17 In. . 9350.00
Raggedy Andy, Cloth, I Love You Heart, Button Eyes, Yarn Hair, Averill, 19 In. 465.00
Raggedy Ann, Cloth, Shoebutton Eyes, Dash Brows, Triangle Nose, Yarn Hair, 16 In. 1100.00
Raggedy Ann, Cloth, Shoebutton Eyes, Painted Features, Yarn Hair, Volland, 15 In. 385.00
Raggedy Ann, Striped Stockings, Volland Co., 1915, 16 In. 1600.00
Raggedy Ann & Andy, Cloth, Button Eyes, Embroidered, Yarn Hair, 18 & 19 In. 275.00
Raggedy Ann & Andy, Cloth, Button Eyes, Painted Lashes, Yarn Hair, 19 In. 1045.00
Raggedy Ann & Andy, Muslin, Averill, American, c.1950, 20 In., Pair 2420.00
Recknagel, Bisque Socket Head, Mohair Wig, 5-Piece Composition Body, 1914, 12 In. 130.00
Reliable, Barbara Ann Scott, Skater, Composition, Mohair Wig, Jointed, Box, 15 In. 80.00
Rohmer, Bisque, Swivel Head, Neck Socket, Shoulder Plate, Enamel Eyes, c.1867, 19 In. 9350.00
Rohmer, Porcelain Swivel Head, Glass Eyes, Kid Body, Jointed, c.1858, 15 In. 4840.00
Rohmer, Porcelain Swivel Head, Shoulder Plate, Wig, Ball-Jointed, 14 In. 3630.00
Rollinson, Cloth, Painted Head, Unjointed Neck, Lashes, Human Hair, 22 In. 600.00
Rollinson, Oil-Painted Stockinette Head, Painted Eyes, Lashes, Hair, 19 In. 880.00
Roullet & Decamps, Composition Socket Head, Grinning, Hair, Mechanical, Girl, 13 In. . 3100.00
Royal Copenhagen, Porcelain Shoulder Head, Oval Face, Leather Body, c.1950, 16 In. ... 4950.00
S & H dolls are also listed here as Bergmann and Simon & Halbig.
S.F.B.J., 60, Bisque Socket Head, Sleep Eyes, Composition Body, Ball-Jointed, 21 In. .. 275.00
S.F.B.J., 225, Bisque Socket Head, Enamel Eyes, Composition, Wood, Jointed, 22 In. 3700.00
S.F.B.J., 233, Bisque Socket Head, Composition Body, Jointed, c.1912, 18 In. 2640.00
S.F.B.J., 236, Bisque Socket Head, Blue Sleep Eyes, 2 Teeth, Bent-Limb Body, 12 In. 360.00
S.F.B.J., 236, Bisque Socket Head, Sleep Eyes, Hair, Composition Body, Baby, 19 In. ... 660.00
S.F.B.J., 236, Bisque Socket Head, Sleep Eyes, Mohair, Composition, Toddler, 19 In. 3100.00
S.F.B.J., 236, Bisque Socket Head, Sleep Eyes, Teeth, Hair, Composition, Baby, 19 In. ... 660.00
S.F.B.J., 237, Bisque Socket Head, Jewel Eyes, Composition, Wood, Jointed, 16 In. 3520.00
S.F.B.J., 245, Bisque Socket Head, Googly Eyes To Right, Dimples, c.1915, 8 In. 2820.00
S.F.B.J., 247, Bisque Socket Head, Sleep Eyes, Hair, Composition, Wood, Toddler, 12 In. . 1800.00
S.F.B.J., 252, Bisque Socket Head, Inset Eyes, Composition, Wood, Jointed, 11 In. 5720.00
S.F.B.J., 252, Bisque, Pouty, Composition Body, Jointed, c.1912, 9 In. 2640.00
S.F.B.J., 301, Bisque Socket Head, Cardboard Pate, Sleep Eyes, Hair, Tete Jumeau, 18 In. . 413.00
S.F.B.J., 301, Bisque Socket Head, Sleep Eyes, Hair, Composition, Wood, Jointed, 8 In. ... 450.00
S.F.B.J., 301, Bisque Socket Head, Sleep Eyes, Painted Lashes, Teeth, Human Hair, 20 In. . 440.00
S.F.B.J., 301, Bisque Socket Head, Sleep Eyes, Teeth, Hair, Composition, Wood, 18 In. 495.00
S.F.B.J., 301, Bisque Socket Head, Sleep Eyes, Teeth, Mohair, Composition, Lady, 19 In. . 385.00
S.F.B.J., 301, Bisque Socket Head, Sleep Eyes, Teeth, Wig, Composition, Jointed, 10 In. ... 600.00
S.F.B.J., Bisque Socket Head, Flirty Eyes, 4 Teeth, Human Hair, Walker, 10 1/2 In. 770.00
S.F.B.J., Bisque Socket Head, Set Blue Eyes, Teeth, Wig, Walker, Bebe, 22 In. 415.00
Schlaggenwald, Porcelain, Solid Dome, Human Hair, Muslin, c.1850, 18 In. 2310.00
Schmidt, 2023, Bisque Socket Head, Painted Eyes, Composition, Wood, Jointed, 16 In. ... 990.00
Schmitt & Fils, Bisque Socket Head, Enamel Eyes, Mohair, Composition, Wood, 11 In. ... 8500.00
Schmitt & Fils, Bisque Socket Head, Inset Eyes, Mohair, Composition, Wood, 17 In. 9500.00
Schoenau & Hoffmeister, 109, Bisque Head, 4 Teeth, Composition, Ball-Jointed, 23 In. ... 200.00
Schoenau & Hoffmeister, 5800, Bisque Socket Head, Composition, Ball-Jointed, 24 In. ... 300.00
Schoenau & Hoffmeister, Bisque Head, Sleep Eyes, Fly-Away Brows, Hair, Baby, 19 In. .. 540.00
Schoenau & Hoffmeister, Bisque Socket Head, Sleep Eyes, Composition, Baby, 20 In. ... 715.00
Schoenau & Hoffmeister, Bisque Socket Head, Sleep Eyes, Jointed, Toddler, 14 In. 550.00
Schoenhut, 102, Wood, Socket Head, Intaglio Eyes, Jointed Body, c.1915, 19 In. 3190.00
Schoenhut, 300, Wood, Socket Head, Carved, Wig, Spring-Jointed Body, c.1915, 16 In. ... 1045.00
Schoenhut, 308, Wood, Socket Head, Carved, Spring-Jointed, Child, c.1911, 19 In. 2420.00
Schoenhut, Rolly Dolly, Dutch Girl, Papier-Mache, Painted, Red, Green, White, 9 In. 140.00
Schoenhut, Wood, Socket Head, Carved, Brown Eyes, Spring-Jointed, c.1912, 14 In. 1870.00
Schoenhut, Wood, Socket Head, Carved, Painted Features, Blond Mohair, c.1920, 22 In. . 1210.00
Schoenhut, Wood, Socket Head, Decal Eyes, Wig, Spring-Jointed, Boy, 1911, 16 In. 330.00
Schoenhut, Wood, Socket Head, Intaglio Eyes, Pouty Mouth, Spring-Jointed, 16 In. 790.00
Schoenhut, Wood, Socket Head, Painted Eyes, Mohair, Spring-Jointed, Toddler, 11 In. ... 440.00
Schoenhut, Wood, Socket Head, Pouty, Brunette Mohair, Spring-Jointed, c.1912, 15 In. ... 2310.00
Schoenhut, Wood, Wig, Painted Eyes, Open Mouth, 16 In. 175.00
Shirley Temple dolls are included in the Shirley Temple category.

Simon & Halbig dolls are also listed here under Bergmann and S & H.
Simon & Halbig, 151, Bisque Socket Head, Painted, Teeth, Dimples, Human Hair, 14 In. . . 3630.00
Simon & Halbig, 540, Bisque Socket Head, Sleep Eyes, Painted Lashes, 4 Teeth, 21 In. . . . 440.00
Simon & Halbig, 739, Brown Bisque Socket Head, Set Eyes, Mohair, Jointed, 14 In. 1870.00
Simon & Halbig, 886, Bisque, Swivel Head, Sleep Eyes, Mohair Wig, 1890, 8 In. 2310.00
Simon & Halbig, 908, Bisque Socket Head, Kid Body, Gusset Joints, c.1880, 16 In. 1100.00
Simon & Halbig, 939, Bisque Head, Pierced Ears, Composition, Ball-Jointed, 8 In. 160.00
Simon & Halbig, 939, Bisque Socket Head, Sleep Eyes, Teeth, Hair, Jointed, 34 In. 2310.00
Simon & Halbig, 949, Bisque Socket Head, Blue Glass Inset Eyes, Child, c.1885, 25 In. . . . 3520.00
Simon & Halbig, 949, Bisque Socket Head, Wood Body, Jointed, c.1885, 15 In. 1980.00
Simon & Halbig, 949, Brown Bisque Socket Head, Sleep Eyes, Mohair, 17 In. 1500.00
Simon & Halbig, 1009, Bisque Head, 4 Teeth, Wig, Composition, Ball-Jointed, 25 In. 145.00
Simon & Halbig, 1009, Brown Bisque Socket Head, Paperweight Eyes, Black Wig, 22 In. . . 1680.00
Simon & Halbig, 1039, Bisque Socket Head, Flirty Eyes, Key Wind, Walker, 17 In. 770.00
Simon & Halbig, 1039, Bisque Socket Head, Flirty Eyes, Painted Lashes, 4 Teeth, 16 In. . . 495.00
Simon & Halbig, 1039, Bisque Socket Head, Flirty Eyes, Walker, Throws Kisses, 22 In. . . . 495.00
Simon & Halbig, 1040, Bisque Shoulder Head, Sleep Eyes, Military Uniform, 26 In. 660.00
Simon & Halbig, 1078, Bisque Head, Teeth, Composition, Ball-Jointed, 36 In. 230.00
Simon & Halbig, 1078, Bisque Socket Head, Sleep Eyes, 4 Teeth, Hair, Jointed, 19 In. . . . 374.00
Simon & Halbig, 1078, Bisque Socket Head, Sleep Eyes, 4 Teeth, Lashes, Hair, 42 In. . . . 3740.00
Simon & Halbig, 1079, Bisque Socket Head, Blue Sleep Eyes, Teeth, Mohair Wig, 28 In. . . 360.00
Simon & Halbig, 1079, Bisque Socket Head, Sleep Eyes, Mohair, Composition, 20 In. 850.00
Simon & Halbig, 1079, Bisque Socket Head, Sleep Eyes, Wig, Composition, 29 In. 495.00
Simon & Halbig, 1079, Brown Bisque Socket Head, Eyes, Mohair, Composition, 20 In. . . . 550.00
Simon & Halbig, 1159, Bisque Socket Head, Sleep Eyes, Teeth, Wig, Jointed, 17 1/2 In. . . 880.00
Simon & Halbig, 1159, Fashion, Bisque, 4 Teeth, Ball-Jointed, c.1900, 23 In. 2640.00
Simon & Halbig, 1199, Bisque, Side-Slanted Sleep Eyes, Asian Child, c.1895, 12 In. 2090.00
Simon & Halbig, 1249, Bisque Socket Head, Sleep Eyes, Mohair Wig, c.1895, 31 In. 1650.00
Simon & Halbig, 1249, Bisque Socket Head, Sleep Eyes, Mohair, Child, 35 In. 2860.00
Simon & Halbig, 1249, Bisque Socket Head, Sleep Eyes, Porcelain Teeth, Wig, 27 In. 1600.00
Simon & Halbig, 1249, Santa, Bisque Socket Head, Sleep Eyes, Composition, 25 In. 605.00
Simon & Halbig, 1279, Bisque Socket Head, Sleep Eyes, Mohair, Jointed, 25 In. 3850.00
Simon & Halbig, 1279, Bisque Socket Head, Sleep Eyes, Painted, Jointed, 22 1/2 In. 715.00
Simon & Halbig, 1294, Bisque Socket Head, Sleep Eyes, Teeth, Mohair, Toddler, 8 In. . . . 825.00
Simon & Halbig, 1294, Bisque Socket Head, Sleep Eyes, Teeth, Toddler, 19 1/2 In. 990.00
Simon & Halbig, 1329, Bisque Head, 4 Teeth, Human Hair, Composition, Asian, 15 In. . . 3850.00
Simon & Halbig, 1358, Brown Bisque Socket Head, Glass Eyes, Teeth, c.1910, 12 In. . . . 3520.00
Simon & Halbig, 1358, Brown Bisque Socket Head, Sleep Eyes, Caracul Wig, 17 In. 4950.00
Simon & Halbig, 1368, Brown Bisque Socket Head, Glass Eyes, Teeth, c.1910, 14 In. . . . 3850.00
Simon & Halbig, 1428, Bisque Socket Head, Sleep Eyes, Composition, Baby, 13 In. 1100.00
Simon & Halbig, 1448, Bisque Socket Head, Sleep Eyes, Mohair, Composition, 11 In. . . . 4750.00
Simon & Halbig, 1469, Bisque Swivel Head, Glass Eyes, Mohair Wig, 1910, 14 In. 7480.00
Simon & Halbig, Bisque Head, Glass Eyes, Muslin Body, Bisque Limbs, c.1875, 9 In. . . . 1980.00
Simon & Halbig, Bisque Socket Head, Mohair, Composition, Wood, Toddler, 18 In. 1000.00
Simon & Halbig, Bisque Socket Head, Paperweight Eyes, Mohair, Composition, 25 In. . . . 2300.00
Simon & Halbig, Bisque Swivel Head, Enamel Inset Eyes, c.1890, 7 1/2 In. 3960.00
Simon & Halbig, Bisque Swivel Head, Glass Eyes, Peg-Jointed, c.1875, 7 In. 6600.00
Simon & Halbig, Bisque Swivel Head, Glass Eyes, Wig, Peg-Jointed, 1885, 7 In. 4620.00
Simon & Halbig, Bisque Swivel Head, Shoulder Plate, Sculpted Hair, Inset Eyes, 17 In. . . . 2100.00
Simon & Halbig, Farmer, Bisque Head, Jointed Wood Body, Beard, Straw Hat, 13 In. 470.00
Sonneberg, Taufling, Papier-Mache, Swivel Head, Set Eyes, Painted Features, 6 In. 440.00
Steiff, Felt, Swivel Head, Shoebutton Eyes, Applied Ears, Mohair Wig, 10 1/2 In. 910.00
Steiff, Mama Katzenjammer, Felt, Jointed Arms, Blouse, Skirt, Button In Ear, 16 In. 440.00
Steiner, Bisque Socket Head, Blue Paperweight Eyes, Wig, Composition, Jointed, 21 In. . 2200.00
Steiner, Bisque Socket Head, Cardboard Pate, Paperweight Eyes, Wig, Jointed, 27 In. . . . 2750.00
Steiner, Bisque Socket Head, Paperweight Eyes, Human Hair, Composition, 20 In. 4250.00
Steiner, Bisque Socket Head, Paperweight Eyes, Human Hair, Jointed, Bebe, 33 In. 9350.00
Steiner, Bisque Socket Head, Paperweight Eyes, Mohair Wig, Composition, 24 In. 10000.00
Steiner, Bisque Socket Head, Paperweight Eyes, Mohair Wig, Composition, Bebe, 8 In. . . 4200.00
Steiner, Bisque Socket Head, Paperweight Eyes, Painted Lashes, Closed Mouth, 20 In. . . . 2860.00
Steiner, Bisque Socket Head, Paperweight Eyes, Painted Lashes, Human Hair, 21 In. 3410.00
Steiner, Bisque Socket Head, Paperweight Eyes, Painted, Mohair Wig, Walker, 18 In. 1650.00
Steiner, Bisque Socket Head, Sleep Eyes, Closed Mouth, Mohair, Bebe, c.1885, 15 In. . . . 5170.00

Steiner, Bisque Socket Head, Sleep Eyes, Composition Body, Bebe, c.1885, 16 In. 6600.00
Steiner, Le Parisien, Bisque Socket Head, Papier-Mache, Sleep Eyes, Teeth, 12 In. 990.00
Swaine & Co., DIP, Bisque Socket Head, Mohair, 5-Piece Composition Body, 11 In. 605.00
Terri Lee, 1379, Hard Plastic, Painted Features, Wig, Jointed, 16 In. 440.00
Terri Lee, 2860, Jerri Lee, Hard Plastic, Painted Features, Caracul Wig, Jointed, 16 In. 605.00
Terri Lee, Plastic Head, Painted Features, Gingham Shirt, Bib Overalls, 16 In. 385.00
Terri Lee, Plastic Head, Painted Features, School Dress, 16 In. 220.00
Terri Lee, Vinyl, Brown Painted Eyes, Blond Hair, Box, 1951, 16 In. 410.00
Vichy, Bisque Head, Glass Eyes, Carton Body, On 3-Wheel Base, Windup, c.1875, 10 In. .. 4840.00
Vogue, Brikette, Sleep Eyes, Hair, Red Fingernails, Cowgirl, Box, c.1950, 22 In. 140.00
Vogue, Ginny, Bo Peep, Mohair, Painted Features, Pink & White Dress, Lamb, 8 In. 540.00
Vogue, Ginny, Plastic, Blond Wig, Painted Lashes, Blue Eyes, Ski Outfit, 7 In. 550.00
Vogue, Ginny, Plastic, Sleep Eyes, Wig, 5-Piece Body, Walker, Suitcase, Box, 7 1/2 In. 495.00
Vogue, Toddles, Wee Willie Winkie, Blue Googly Eyes, Composition, Box, 8 In. 330.00
W.P.A., Cloth, Painted Stockinette Head, Painted Eyes, String Wig, Jointed, 23 In. 1100.00
Walkure, Bisque Socket Head, Set Eyes, Synthetic Wig, Composition, Wood, 39 In. 660.00
Wax, Blond Wig, Blue Sleep Eyes, Green Dress, 21 In. 145.00
Wax, Over Composition, Shoulder Head, Sleep Eyes, Closed Mouth, Pierced Ears, 15 In. .. 248.00
Wax, Over Papier-Mache, Boy, Shoulder Head, Cloth Body, Composition Limbs, 12 In. ... 60.00
Wax, Over Papier-Mache, Domed, Socket Head, Sleep Eyes, Composition, Wood, 11 In. .. 880.00
Wax, Over Papier-Mache, Glass Eyes, Human Hair, Cloth Body, 12 1/2 In. 358.00
Wax, Over Papier-Mache, Glass Sleep Eyes, Mohair, Normandy Costume, c.1885, 13 In. .. 550.00
Wax, Shoulder Head, Muslin Body, Stitch-Jointed, England, Peddler, c.1840, 13 In. 2420.00
Wooden, Carved Head, Painted Eyes, Hair, Smiling Mouth, 23 In. 600.00
Wooden, Carved, Cameo-Shaped Face, Shaped Bosom, Dowel Joints, c.1840, 5 In. 660.00
Wooden, Carved, Carved Hat, Dowel Joints, Germany, c.1840, 7 In. 550.00
Wooden, Carved, Mohair Wig, Tattoos, Asian Man, 19th Century, 12 In. 210.00
Wooden, Carved, Painted Features, Dowel Joints, Muslin Arms, 19th Century, 18 In. 1760.00
Wooden, Carved, Painted Features, Hair, Comb, Wooden Body, Ball-Jointed, 18 In. 4125.00
Wooden, Carved, Painted Features, Sculpted Hair, Dowel Joints, 19th Century, 28 In. 5830.00
Wooden, Carved, Painted, Loose Jointed Limbs, Harlequin, Attached Strings, 13 In. 1210.00
Wooden, Carved, Shaped Bosom, Dowel Joints, 19th Century, 14 In. 4180.00
Wooden, Carved, Swivel Head, Painted, Dowel Joints, Metal Hands, Feet, 1875, 12 In. .. 770.00
Wooden, Carved, Swivel Head, Painted, Human Hair, Dowel Joints, c.1870, 13 In. 1430.00
Wooden, Carved, Swivel Neck, Carved Necklace, Dowel Joints, c.1820, 16 In. 5720.00
DOLL CLOTHES, Barbie, American Airlines Stewardess, Blue Outfit, Accessories, No. 984 .. 90.00
Barbie, Apron & Accessories, Red Apron, Metal Utensils, Rolling Pin, On Card 60.00
Barbie, Arabian Nights, Pink Satin, Chiffon Skirt, Blouse, Sari, Accessories, No. 874 .... 115.00
Barbie, Barbie Learns To Cook, Flower Print Dress, Accessories, No. 1634 .... 85.00
Barbie, Benefit Performance, Red Tunic, White Skirt, No. 1667 .... 145.00
Barbie, Bride's Dream, Wedding Gown, Accessories, Box, No. 947 .... 265.00
Barbie, Candy Striper Volunteer, Accessories, No. 889 .... 130.00
Barbie, Cinderella, Poor Dress, Gown, Accessories, No. 872 .... 100.00
Barbie, Color Kick, Multicolored Bodysuit, Plush Skirt, Box, No. 3422 .... 155.00
Barbie, Crisp 'n Cool, Red Skirt, White Blouse, Accessories, Box, No. 1604 .... 165.00
Barbie, Enchanted Evening, Pink Gown, Fur Stole, 1959, Box, No. 983 .... 200.00
Barbie, Evening Splendor, Gold & White Brocade Dress, Coat, Accessories, No. 961 .... 105.00
Barbie, Fraternity Dance, Fuchsia Chiffon Gown, Accessories, No. 1638 .... 110.00
Barbie, Friday Night Date, Blue Jumper, White Dress, Accessories, No. 979 .... 55.00
Barbie, Gay Parisienne, Navy Pindot Bubble Dress, Accessories, 1959, No. 964 .... 525.00
Barbie, Gold 'n Glamour, Golden Tweed Outfit, Accessories, No. 1647 .... 405.00
Barbie, Happy Go Pink, Pink & White Organza Dress, Accessories, Box, No. 1868 ..... 135.00
Barbie, Junior Prom, Red Gown, Accessories, No. 1614 .... 165.00
Barbie, Midnight Blue, Blue Silk Gown, Cape, Accessories, No. 1617 .... 210.00
Barbie, Open Road, Striped Pants, Khaki Coat, Accessories, No. 985 .... 95.00
Barbie, Peachy Fleece Coat, Accessories, No. 915 .... 45.00
Barbie, Picnic Set, Blue Jeans, Red & White Shirt, Accessories, No. 967 .... 135.00
Barbie, Plantation Belle, Dotted Dress, Petticoat, Accessories, No. 966 .... 145.00
Barbie, Red Velvet Coat, Accessories, Box, No. 0939 .... 140.00
Barbie, Resort Set, Red Jacket, White Shorts, Striped Shirt, Accessories, No. 963 .... 30.00
Barbie, Ruffles & Swirls, Turquoise & Pink Swirled Dress, Box, No. 1783 .... 75.00
Barbie, Senior Prom, Blue & Green Satin Tulle Gown, Accessories, No. 951 .... 85.00
Barbie, Sheath Sensation, Red Dress, Straw Hat, Accessories, No. 986 .... 40.00

Barbie, Singing In The Shower, Yellow Robe, Accessories, No. 988 .... 40.00
Barbie, Sophisticated Lady, Rose Velvet & Pink Satin Gown, Accessories, No. 993 ...... 50.00
Barbie, Stormy Weather, Yellow Trench Coat, Hat, Boots, Umbrella, No. 949 .... 25.00
Barbie, Suburban Shopper, Blue & White Striped Sundress, Accessories, No. 969 .... 110.00
Barbie, Sweet Dreams, Yellow Baby Doll, Accessories, No. 973 .... 25.00
Barbie, Tropicana, Dress, Flower, Accessories, Box, No. 1460 .... 125.00
Boots, Ankle, Canvas, Leather, Hand-Stitched Lacing Holes, Cord Laces, 3 In. 220.00
Boots, Leather, Brown, Lacing, Brass-Edged Grommets, Wooden Heels, 3 In. 525.00
Chemisette, Linen, V-Shaped Collar, Faux Pockets, Buttons, Snood, c.1860, 14 In. 440.00
Chemist Outfit, Chemcraft, No. 2, Porter Co., Unopened, 14 In. 195.00
Coat, Cashmere, Velvet, Taupe, Brown, Scalloped Shaped Collar, 18 In. 300.00
Coat, Mohair, Wool Trim, Cream, Aqua, Double Breasted, Bebe Jumeau, Size 8 .... 385.00
Coat, Mohair, Wool Trim, Cream, Round Collar, Soutache Trim, 18 In. 330.00
Coat, Textured Velvet, Maroon, Box Pleated, 3/4 Sleeves, Shaped Collar, 24 In. 360.00
Dress, Bengaline Skirt, Batiste Blouse, Silk Ribbons, Lace, c.1868, 13 In. 330.00
Dress, Blue, Cream, Shadowpane, Checkered, Fitted Bodice, Trumpet Sleeves, 17 In. 220.00
Dress, Brown Calico, Gigot Sleeves, Dropped Shoulders, Fitted Bodice, 12 In. 110.00
Dress, Cotton, Brown, Dropped Shoulders, Full Skirt, Pleated, 15 In. 275.00
Dress, Cotton, Cream, Printed, Shirred Waist, Trumpet Sleeves, 16 In. 220.00
Dress, Pique, White, Black Soutache, Ribbed, Pleated, Sash, 14 In. 880.00
Dress, Pique, White, Soutache, Scalloped Collar, Pagoda Sleeves, 16 In. 1485.00
Dress, Voile, White, Cream, Shirred Waist, Juliette Sleeves, 30 In. 330.00
Francie, Curly Fur Coat, Aqua Skirt, Accessories, Box, No. 1234 .... 125.00
Francie, Long On Looks, White Blouse, Pink Skirt, Accessories, Box, No. 1227 .... 115.00
Francie, Tennis Tunic, Accessories, Box, No. 1221 .... 95.00
Francie, Waltz In Velvet, Evening Gown, Muff, Accessories, Box, No. 1768 .... 235.00
Francie, White Organdy Gown, Accessories, No. 1260 .... 100.00
Francie & Casey, Satin Happenin', Pink Jumpsuit, Accessories, Box, No. 1237 .... 105.00
Gown, Black Taffeta, Silk Edging, Parasol, Bone Handle, France, 15 In. 605.00
Gown, Cashmere, Purple, Cream, Embroidery, Rickrack, Box Pleats, 12 In. 385.00
Gown, Cotton Pique, Waffle Weave, White, Fitted Bodice, Bretelles, 14 In. 440.00
Gown, Dotted Swiss, White, Ruffle Collar, Trumpet Sleeves, Full Bodice, 13 In. 300.00
Gown, Muslin, Peach, Puffed Sleeves, Lace Trim, Bonnet, c.1867, 13 In. 715.00
Gown, Silk Taffeta, Bronze, Fitted Jacket, Full Skirt, Pleated, Bonnet, 16 In. 690.00
Gown, Silk Taffeta, Brown, Gored Skirt, Shaped Sleeves, Train, Bonnet, 17 In. 715.00
Gown, Silk, Blue Print, Velvet Trim, Caplet Sleeves, Box Pleated, 16 In. 1870.00
Gown, Silk, Mauve, Ecru, Striped, Black Lace Trim, Long Sleeves, 16 In. 770.00
Gown, Voile, White, Lavender Polka Dots, Full Bodice, Pleated, 17 In. 330.00
Gown, Woven Cotton, Cream, Flat Front, Lace, Pleats, Tucked, Bustle, 15 In. 2145.00
Jacket, Middy, Wool, Navy Blue, Front Opening, Brass Buttons, 12 In. 250.00
Jacket, Velvet, Burgundy, Double Breasted, Pearl Buttons, Beret, 28 In. 470.00
Jacket, Wool, Red, Flat Front, Wide Collar, Full Sleeves, Silk Cuffs, Tam, 24 In. 415.00
Ken, Arabian Nights, Red Velvet Coat, Turban, Box, No. 0774 .... 125.00
Ken, Army & Air Force, Box, No. 797 .... 155.00
Ken, Big Business, Black & White Houndstooth Suit, Accessories, Box, No. 1434 ...... 75.00
Ken, Blue & White Striped Uniform, Red Trim, Accessories, No. 792 .... 60.00
Ken, College Student, Plaid Jacket, Brown Pants, Accessories, Box, No. 1416 .... 295.00
Ken, Country Clubbin', Black & White Houndstooth Jacket, Pants, Box, No. 1400 ...... 125.00
Ken, Drum Major, White Jacket, Red Pants, Accessories, Box, No. 0775 .... 155.00
Ken, Goin' Huntin', Plaid Shirt, Blue Jeans, Accessories, Box, No. 1409 .... 115.00
Ken, Graduation, Black Robe, Accessories, Box, No. 795 .... 35.00
Ken, Holiday, White Shirt, Blue Pants, Accessories, Box, No. 1414 .... 185.00
Ken, In Holland, Box, No. 0777 .... 125.00
Ken, In Mexico, Bolero Jacket, Sombrero, Accessories, Box, No. 0778 .... 155.00
Ken, In Switzerland, Gray Lederhosen, Accessories, Box, No. 0776 .... 155.00
Ken, Mr. Astronaut, Silver Jumpsuit, Accessories, Box, No. 1641 .... 285.00
Ken, Party Fun, Princess Phone, Ukulele, Clock, TV, Invitations, Microphone, Box 65.00
Ken, Prince Outfit, Green Brocade Jacket, Accessories, Box, No. 0772 .... 215.00
Ken, Rovin' Reporter, Red Jacket, Blue Pants, Accessories, Box, No. 1417 .... 270.00
Ken, Special Date, Blue Jacket, Pants, Shirt, Tie, Accessories, Box, No. 1401 .... 120.00
Ken, Terry Togs, Robe, Briefs, Accessories, Box, No. 784 .... 80.00
Ken, The Night Scene, Burgundy Tuxedo, Accessories, Box, No. 1496 .... 85.00
Ken, Time For Tennis, Sweater, Shirt, Shorts, Accessories, Box, No. 790 .... 115.00

Ken, Victory Dance, White Pants, Red Vest, Blue Blazer, Accessories, Box, No. 1411 .... 125.00
Penny Brite, Singing In The Rain, Black & White Checkered Raincoat, Box 30.00
Sailor Hat, Leather, Tan, Brown Grosgrain Ribbon, Mignon Label, 4 1/2 In. 385.00
Sailor Hat, Wool, Navy Blue, Grosgrain Ribbon, Gilt Aviation Stamp, 4 In. 330.00
Sailor Hat, Wool, Navy Blue, Wire Frame, Grosgrain Band, Streamers, 4 1/2 In. 385.00
Sailor Suit, Dress, Cotton, Blue, Blouson Bodice, Middy Collar, 23 In. 550.00
Sailor Suit, Pique, Sateen, White, Blue, Jacket, Short Pants, Bebe Jumeau, 11 In. 800.00
Sailor Suit, Wool, Navy Blue, Middy Collar, Blue Over-Collar, 35 In. 635.00
Skipper, Land & Sea, Denim Outfit, Accessories, Box, No. 1917 .... 125.00
Skipper, Long 'n Short Of It, Red Mini Dress, Coat, Scarf, Accessories, Box, No. 3478 .. 75.00
Skipper, Sunny Pastels, Striped Dress, Accessories, Box, No. 1910 .... 110.00
Skipper, Town Togs, Green Coat, Jumper, Stockings, Box, No. 1922 .... 125.00
Suit, Black Wool Jacket, Pants, Vest, Wool, Wooden Shoes, 17 In. 1210.00
Suit, Jacket, Round Collar, Pleats, Button-Front Pants, Baggy, 30 In 250.00
Suit, Wool, Fitted Jacket, Flat-Front Skirt, Silk Parasol, 17 In. 580.00
Tutti, Skippin' Rope, Red Floral Dress, Blue Tights, Accessories, Box, No. 3604 .... 50.00

DONALD DUCK items are included in the Disneyana category.

DOORSTOPS have been made in all types of designs. The vast majority of the doorstops sold today are cast iron and were made from about 1890 to 1930. Most of them are shaped like people, animals, flowers, or ships. Reproductions and newly designed examples are sold in gift shops.

2 Footmen, Red, Black, Gold Epaulets, Cast Iron, Signed Fish, Hubley, 9 In. 633.00
Alligator, Cast Iron, c.1910, 16 In. 288.00
Aunt Jemima, Cast Iron, 12 In. 209.00
Aunt Jemima, Hand Painted, Cast Iron, Hubley, 1930s, 8 1/2 x 5 1/2 In. 975.00
Badger, Cast Iron, 6 x 10 1/2 In. 350.00
Basket Of Flowers, Cast Iron, 9 In. ....39.00 to 55.00
Bathing Lady, Seated, Cast Iron, 7 In. 161.00
Bear, Cast Iron, 5 1/2 In. 55.00
Bell Shape, Brass, Rope Twist Handle, England, 1800s, 17 1/2 In. 45.00
Bird Of Prey, Cast Iron, England 450.00
Black Man, On Cotton Bale, Cast Iron, 9 In. 2200.00
Bobby Blake, Teddy Bear, Blue Shirt, Black Pants, Grace Drayton, Hubley 950.00
Boy, With Teddy Bear, Cast Iron, Hubley, 9 1/2 In. 145.00
Boy & Girl, Dutch, Kissing, No. 332, Hubley, 1930s 250.00
Brass, Napoleonic Military Figure, Sword, 1800s, 15 x 9 1/4 In. 490.00
Cape Cod, Hubley, 5 1/2 x 7 3/4 In. 305.00
Cat, Black & White, Seated, Cast Iron, Marked, 15, 11 1/2 x 6 1/2 In. 220.00
Cat, Original Paint, Cast Iron, Hubley, 8 1/2 In. 40.00
Cat, Persian, Painted, Cast Iron, 8 1/2 In. 145.00
Cat, Seated, Ribbon, Cast Iron, 8 In. 40.00
Cat, Sleeping, Cast Iron, Late 19th Century, Life Size 1450.00
Cat, Walking, Raised Tail, Cast Iron 175.00
Cat, White Paint, Cast Iron, Early 20th Century, 10 1/2 In. 195.00
Cat, White, Seated, Blue Bow, Glass Eyes, Cast Iron, England, 14 1/2 x 8 1/4 In. 155.00
Chinese Man, Cast Iron, 7 In. 80.00
Christmas Carolers, Painted, Cast Iron, John Wright Toys 425.00
Clipper Ship, Cast Iron, 1925, 9 3/4 In. 150.00
Clipper Ship, Hand Painted, 1930 .... 375.00
Cockatoo, On Perch, White, Brown, Cast Iron, 19th Century, 12 1/4 x 7 1/2 x 3 1/4 In. 150.00
Cottage, Hand Painted, Cast Iron, 1920s 525.00
Cottage, Paint, Cast Iron, 8 1/2 In. 175.00
Dancers, Cast Iron, Hubley, Anne Fish, 9 In. 550.00
Deco Lady, Arms Extend At Sides Holding Up Green Dress, Judd Mfg. Co. 950.00
Dog, 2 Scotties, Bradley & Hubbard, 9 In. 155.00
Dog, Boston Terrier, Black & White, Seated, Facing Right, Cast Iron, 8 x 6 1/4 In. 176.00
Dog, Boston Terrier, Black & White, Standing, Facing Right, Cast Iron, 10 1/4 x 10 In. 88.00
Dog, Boston Terrier, Cast Iron, 9 1/2 In. 260.00
Dog, Boston Terrier, Cast Iron, 9 1/4 x 9 In. 50.00
Dog, Boston Terrier, Chain Collar, Cast Iron, 5 1/4 x 5 1/2 In. 155.00

Dog, Boston Terrier, Facing Forward, Painted, Cast Iron, 9 1/2 In. 395.00
Dog, Boston Terrier, Facing Left, Painted, Cast Iron, 9 1/2 In. ....225.00 to 535.00
Dog, Boston Terrier, Facing Right, Painted, Cast Iron, 9 In. 90.00
Dog, Boston Terrier, Facing Right, Painted, Cast Iron, 10 In. 115.00
Dog, Boston Terrier, Seated, Iron, Painted, England, 8 x 7 1/2 In. 345.00
Dog, Boxer, Hubley, 8 1/2 x 9 In. 525.00
Dog, Bulldog, Black & White, 2 Leather Collars, 8 1/2 x 8 1/2 x 3 1/4 In. 250.00
Dog, Bulldog, Standing, Polychrome, Iron, 6 In. 375.00
Dog, Cocker Spaniel, Blond, Standing, Cast Iron 340.00
Dog, Cocker Spaniel, Hubley, 6 3/4 x 11 In. 385.00
Dog, Dachshund, Full Figure, Black, Tan Paint, Red Collar, Cast Iron, 9 1/2 x 6 In. 525.00
Dog, Doberman Pinscher, Cast Iron, 6 1/4 x 7 In. 39.00
Dog, Doberman Pinscher, Hubley, 8 x 8 1/2 In. .... , 825.00
Dog, French Bulldog, Painted, Cast Iron, 8 In. ....,.... 85.00
Dog, German Shepherd, Painted, Cast Iron, Hubley, 9 1/2 In. 50.00
Dog, Greyhound, Standing, White, Cast Iron, 10 x 15 In. 250.00
Dog, Pug, Cast Iron, 8 1/4 In. 310.00
Dog, Scottie, Black, Original Paint, Cast Iron, 11 In. 115.00
Dog, Scottie, Painted, Cast Iron, 10 In. 140.00
Dog, Scottie, Seated, Black, Iron, 16 1/2 In. 310.00
Dog, Scottie, Seated, Cast Iron, Wilton Products Inc., 7 3/4 In. 50.00
Dog, Seated, Cast Iron, 6 In. 1105.00
Dog, Setter, Bronze Wash, Wood Base Mount, Cast Iron, 15 In. 115.00
Dog, Spaniel, King Charles, Black & White, 9 1/4 x 4 3/4 2 1/4 In. 550.00
Dog, Spaniel, Painted, Cast Iron 146.00
Dog, Spaniel, Potter, Gray, Black Features, 8 In. 150.00
Dog, Terrier, Cast Iron, Vindex, 9 In. 220.00
Dog, Terrier, Cast Iron, Vindex, 10 In. 250.00
Dog, Terrier, Painted, Cast Iron, 8 1/2 In. 250.00
Dog, Terrier, Red Polychrome, Cast Iron, c.1900, 8 1/2 In. 130.00
Dog, Terrier, Spelter, 11 In. 105.00
Dog, Terrier, White, Brown, Iron, Standing, 8 1/2 x 8 In. 240.00
Dolphin, Gilt Bronze, Breakfront Bowed Plinth Base, 8 In. 1495.00
Drum Major, Cast Iron, 13 In. 45.00
Duck, Black, Cast Iron, Richard F.H. Clancy, Needham, Mass., 14 1/2 In. 105.00
Dutch Girl, Carrying Buckets, Littco Prod., 1920s-1930s 950.00
Dwarf, Cast Iron, Painted, 10 In. 55.00
Eagle, FOE, Marked, Aerle 782, 1880s 950.00
Elephant, Gray, Green, Brown, 14 In. 530.00
Elephant, Mounted On Wood Base, Gold Paint, Cast Iron, 9 1/2 In. 11.00
Fawn, Taylor Cook, 1930 .... 475.00
Fisherman, Cast Iron, 8 In. 80.00
Fisherman, Cast Iron, 11 In. 275.00
Flower Basket, Colorful Flowers, Woven Basket, Marked W.S., 1926 .... 450.00
Flower Basket, Painted, Cast Iron, Hubley, Cast Iron, 10 In. 150.00
Flower Basket, Tulips, Star Flowers, Hubley, 9 3/4 x 5 1/2 In. 140.00
Flower Basket, White, Green Leaves, Hubley, 1920s-1930s 425.00
Flower Vase, Bradley & Hubbard, 11 3/4 x 6 In. 495.00
Flowerpot, Tulips, Red, Pink, Yellow, Cast Iron, 8 1/4 In. 140.00
Frog, Cast Iron, 5 1/2 In. ....44.00 to 62.00
Frog, Cast Iron, 6 In. 18.00
Frog, Cast Iron, 7 In. 50.00
Frog, Cast Iron, 8 In. 35.00
Fruit Basket, Albany Foundry, 10 1/8 x 7 1/2 In. 195.00
Fruit Bowl, Fruit, Daisies, Green Leaves, Yellow Bowl, Hubley, 1930s 395.00
Fruit Cornucopia, Cast Iron, 7 1/2 In. 56.00
Geese, Fred Everett, Hubley, 8 x 8 In. 935.00
Gentleman, Top Hat, Monocle, 8 In. 275.00
Gnome, Original Paint, Cast Iron, 13 1/2 In. 169.00
Goat, Cast Brass, 9 1/2 In., Pair 198.00
Golfer, Cast Iron, 8 1/2 In. 360.00
Golfer, Putting, Painted, Cast Iron, Stamped No. 34, 8 1/2 x 7 In. 300.00
Horse, Brass, England, 12 1/2 In. 285.00

Horse, Painted, Cast Iron, 10 1/2 In. . . . . .140.00 to 155.00
House, Edgar Allen Poe, Bradley & Hubbard 1980.00
House, John Humphrey, Green Base, 5 1/8 x 7 1/4 In. 605.00
House, On Platform, Original Paint, Cast Iron, A A Richardson Quincy, 1927, 5 x 8 x 3 In. 150.00
Humpty Dumpty, Green Bowtie, Red Suit, 1920s-1930s 750.00
Humpty Dumpty Gentleman, Cast Iron 855.00
Irises, Purple, White, Green, Cast Iron, Marked, 469, 11 x 6 1/2 In. 240.00
Jockey & Horse, Jumping Over Fence, Original Paint, Sculptured Metal Studios 1200.00
Kitten, Black, Cast Iron, Hubley, 8 1/4 In. 115.00
Kittens, Cast Iron 468.00
Lady, Cast Iron, 7 In. 66.00
Lady, Cast Iron, 16 In. 375.00
Lady, Holding Up Dress, Cast Iron, 9 In. 127.00
Lilies Of The Valley, No. 189, Hubley, 1930s 395.00
Lion, Cast Iron 285.00
Little Red Riding Hood & Wolf, National Foundry, 7 1/4 x 5 3/8 In. 525.00
Lizard, Cast Iron, 7 In. 35.00
Lizard, Cast Iron, Sherwin Williams Paint, 8 In. 80.00
Loon, Cast Iron, Signed Estelle Knapp, c.1989, 20 In., Pair 85.00
Major Domo, Blue Coat, Judd Co., 8 3/8 In. 195.00
Mammy, 2 Piece Casting, Hubley, 10 x 5 In. 300.00
Mammy, Black, Red Paint, Cast Iron, 10 In. 290.00
Mammy, Cast Iron, 9 In. 220.00
Mammy, Cast Iron, Hubley, 12 In. 150.00
Mammy, Hand Painted, Cast Iron, Hubley, Early 1900s, 10 x 5 In. 975.00
Man, Holding Flashlight, Magnifying Glass, Cast Iron, The Snooper, 13 1/4 x 4 1/4 In. . . . 408.00
Man, Holding Tire, Cast Iron, 10 In. 75.00
Man, With Sword, Colonial, Cast Iron, 11 3/4 In. 80.00
Monkey, Cast Iron, Hand Painted, 1930s, 7 x 5 1/2 In. 750.00
Monkey, Seated, Painted, Cast Iron, 9 In. 633.00
Old Salt, Yellow Slicker, Black Hat, Hands In Pockets, Cast Iron, 8 In. 125.00
Old Salt, Yellow Slicker, Black Hat, White Pants, Cast Iron, 11 1/4 In. 175.00
Old Salt, Yellow Slicker, Hat, Black Boots, Hands In Pocket, Cast Iron, 14 1/2 In. 500.00
Owl, No. 1237 CJO, Judd, 10 x 6 In. 825.00
Owl, Painted, Cast Iron, 7 3/4 In. 85.00
Pansy Bowl, Hubley, 7 x 6 1/2 In. 275.00
Parrot, Cast Iron, 7 1/2 In. 187.00
Parrot, Cast Iron, 8 In. 198.00
Parrot, In Ring, Bradley & Hubbard 250.00
Penguin, Cast Iron, 10 1/2 In. 440.00
Pheasant, Original Paint, Cast Iron, Signed, Fred Everett, 8 1/4 In. . . . . .135.00 to 195.00
Pirate, Sitting On Treasure Chest, Painted, Cast Iron, 6 3/4 In. 169.00
Punch, With Dog, Hollow Back, Painted, Cast Iron, 12 x 9 x 3 1/2 In. 450.00
Quail, Signed, Everett, 7 1/4 In. 420.00
Rabbit, Begging, Cast Iron, Bradley & Hubbard, 15 In. 855.00
Rabbit, Bradley & Hubbard, 15 1/4 In. 3080.00
Rabbit, Gentleman, Eating Carrot, Cast Iron 990.00
Rabbit, Gentleman, Hunting Pinks, Top Hat, Cast Iron 770.00
Rabbit, Old White Paint, Cast Iron, 6 1/2 In. 25.00
Ram, Iron, 9 x 7 In. 85.00
Scot, In Kilt, Cast Iron, Mid 19th Century, 14 x 13 In. 365.00
Ship, 2 Masts, Full Sail, Painted, Cast Iron, 9 1/2 x 6 x 3 In. 115.00
Ship, 3 Masts, 9 In. 175.00
Ship, Constitution Clipper, A.M Greenblatt Studios, 1924 . . . . 495.00
Ship, Constitution, Full Sail, Painted, Cast Iron, 194, 11 3/4 x 8 1/2 x 3 In. 300.00
Spanish Girl, Hand Painted, Hubley, 1920s 450.00
Sperm Whale, Cast Iron, 13 In. 259.00
Squirrel, Eating Nut, On Log, Bushy Tail, Cast Iron, 11 1/4 x 9 3/4 In. 415.00
Squirrel, On Tree Stump, Painted, Cast Iron, 1930s 495.00
Squirrel, Seated, On Log, Eating Nuts, Cast Iron, Nitney 660.00
Totem Pole, Hand Painted, Cast Iron, 8 1/2 In. 220.00
Tree & Fence, Cast Iron, Bradley & Hubbard, Early 1900s, 10 In. 450.00
Tulip Pot, 1930s 495.00

Turtle, Cast Iron, 8 1/2 In.	28.00
Victorian Woman, Garden Setting, Gloved Hand On Hip, Rose Brimmed Hat, 11 1/2 In.	6875.00
Wolf's Head, Tail, Upright, Bronze, Cast Iron, c.1880	475.00
Woman, Arms Outstretched, Holding Dress Edges, Bronze, Art Nouveau, 9 x 8 In.	518.00
Woman, Art Deco, Cast Iron, 7 1/4 In.	35.00
Woman, Holding Basket, Umbrella, Cast Iron, B & H, 11 In.	110.00
Woman, Holding Flower Basket, Cast Iron, 7 In.	165.00
Woman, Holding Flowers & Hat, Cast Iron, 11 1/2 In.	250.00
Woman In Long Dress, Carrying Shawl, Flowers, Cast Iron, Painted, 8 x 4 1/2 x 1 3/4 In.	84.00
Zinnias & Daisies, Cast Iron	200.00

DORCHESTER POTTERY was founded by George Henderson in 1895 in Dorchester, Massachusetts. At first, the firm made utilitarian stoneware, but collectors are most interested in the line of decorated blue and white pottery that Dorchester made from 1940 until it went out of business in 1979.

**DORCHESTER
POTTERY WORKS
BOSTON, MASS.**

Foot Warmer, Henderson, Stamped, 11 1/2 In.	130.00
Pitcher, Cover, Vertical Blue Stripes, Stylized Leaves, Signed, C.A.H., 5 3/4 In.	75.00
Plate, Fisherman, Signed, Knesseth Denisons, 7 1/2 In.	130.00
Plate, Painted Fruit, Knesseth Denisons, 7 1/2 In.	75.00

DOULTON pottery and porcelain were made by Doulton and Co. of Burslem, England, after 1882. The name *Royal Doulton* appeared on their wares after 1902. Other pottery by Doulton is listed under Royal Doulton.

Bowl, Gloire De Dijon, Roses, Butterflies, Gilt Decorated, Blue, White, Burslem, 16 In.	835.00
Bowl, Incised & Beaded Lines, White Enamel Flower Bands, Lambeth, 9 x 6 1/2 In.	115.00
Bowl, Persian Spray, Blue & White, c.1890	2100.00
Bowl Set, Burslem, David Dewsberry, 3 Piece	958.00
Centerpiece, Chang	2300.00
Clock, Mantle, Blue & White, Burslem	1185.00
Cup, Commemorative, Nelson, Lambeth	1050.00
Ewer, Multicolored Flowers, Cream Ground, Pedestal, Burslem, 11 1/2 In.	140.00
Figurine, Comerant, Lambeth	2300.00
Figurine, Elephant, Chinese Jade, C.J. Noke	1400.00
Ink Pot, Votes For Women, Lambeth	1055.00
Jardiniere, Brown, White Slip, Leaf Border, Lambeth, Late 1800s, 9 3/4 In.	470.00
Jug, Diamond Jubilee, Lambeth	190.00
Jug, Queen Victoria, Salt Glazed	1055.00
Lamp, Oil, Stoneware, Lambeth, 1882	4140.00
Loving Cup, Coronation, 1937, Twin Handle	805.00
Match Holder, Sterling Lid, Applied Leaves, Rosettes, No. 8570, 3 3/4 In.	115.00
Oil Lamp, Mark Marshall	2875.00
Paperweight, Fox Inviting Stork To Dinner, Salt Glazed, Stoneware, Lambeth, c.1882	5175.00
Pitcher, Brown On Brown, Lambeth, England, 7 In.	35.00
Pitcher, Deer Hunt, Men At Tables, 2-Tone Brown Glaze, Impressed, Lambeth, 6 1/2 In.	87.00
Pitcher, Incised Flower Medallions, Indigo, Amber, Dots, White, Blue, Lambeth, 8 1/2 In.	115.00
Pitcher, Swirls Of Wheat, Carved, Mottled Amber Ground, Bulbous, Lambeth, 7 In.	375.00
Plate, Egerton, Flow Blue, 8 1/2 In.	65.00
Plate, Egerton, Flow Blue, 9 1/2 In.	90.00
Plate, Egerton, Flow Blue, 10 1/2 In.	100.00
Platter, Egerton, Flow Blue, 12 In.	165.00
Platter, Egerton, Flow Blue, 16 In.	400.00
Platter, Egerton, Flow Blue, 18 In.	500.00
Platter, Madras, Flow Blue, 17 1/2 In.	190.00
Tankard, Hinged Pewter Lid, Tooled Leaves, Brown, Beige, Mark, Lambeth, 10 1/2 In.	175.00
Teapot, Flowers, Tan, Yellow, Gilt, Burslem, c.1890, 7 In. ....*Illus*	275.00
Toby Jug, Double XX, Barrel, Harry Simeon, Lambeth	3065.00
Umbrella Stand, Blue, White, Gilt Flowers, Burslem, 24 1/2 In.	1064.00
Vase, Applied Flowers, Garlands, Salt Glaze, Gannett, No. 590, 5 3/8 In.	58.00
Vase, Blue Iris, Gilt, Tapered, Marked, No. X53, 14 In.	250.00
Vase, Bulbous, Flowers, Initials, R.A. 2088 Luscian Wear, c.1895, 5 1/4 In.	259.00
Vase, Lambeth Silicon, Applied Garlands, Rosettes, 5 1/4 In.	115.00

Doulton, Teapot,
Flowers, Tan, Yellow,
Gilt, Burslem, c.1890, 7 In.

Dresden, Figurine, Pug Dog,
5 In., Pair

Vase, Lizard, Stoneware, Baluster Shape, Lambeth, Early 20th Century, 6 3/4 In.	205.00
Vase, Sgraffito Decoration, Egg Shape, Scrolled Flowers & Leaves, 7 3/8 In.	205.00
Vase, Sung, Charles Noke, Fred Moore, 6 1/8 In.	1150.00

DRAGONWARE is a form of moriage pottery made since the late 19th century. Moriage is a type of decoration on Japanese pottery. Raised white designs are applied to the ware. White dragons are the major raised decorations on the moriage called *dragonware*. The background can be one of many different colors. It is still being made.

Cup & Saucer, Demitasse, Gray, Blue, Green, Rose, Red Mark, Japan	25.00
Plate, Moriage Dragon, Black & Brown, Reticulated Edge, 6 1/4 In.	55.00
Salt & Pepper, Ball Jug Shape, Gray, 2 3/4 In.	45.00
Sugar & Creamer, Blue, 3 1/4 In.	40.00
Tea Set, Gray, Blue, Pink, Kutani, 24 Piece	325.00
Teapot, Raised Dragon, Black Matte, Gold Trim, Early 1960s, 5 In.	95.00

DRESDEN china is any china made in the town of Dresden, Germany. The most famous factory in Dresden is the Meissen factory. Figurines of eighteenth-century ladies and gentlemen, animal groups, or cherubs and other mythological subjects were popular. One special type of figurine was made with skirts of porcelain-dipped lace. Do not make the mistake of thinking that all pieces marked *Dresden* are from the Meissen factory. The Meissen pieces usually have crossed swords marks, and are listed under Meissen. Some recent porcelain from Ireland, called *Irish Dresden*, is not included in this book.

Basket, Flowers, Hand Painted, Pierced Rim, Late 20th Century, 10 In.	138.00
Bowl, Courting Scene, Flowers, 19th Century, 8 In.	110.00
Bowl, Flowers, Applied, Hand Painted, Marked, Late 20th Century, 16 In.	105.00
Box, Cover, Metal, Jewels, 3 x 5 In.	215.00
Bust, Boy, White, 14 In.	185.00
Candelabrum, 3-Light, Figural, Flowers, Vine Leaves, Marked, c.1910, 21 x 10 In., Pair .	840.00
Candlestick, Flowers, Embossed, Gilt, 7 1/2 x 4 1/4 In., Pair	100.00
Candy Box, Tambourine, Bells, Red, White, Blue, Gold, Cardboard, 2 1/2 In.	780.00
Candy Box, Tambourine, Red, Blue, Gold, Bells, Cardboard, 2 1/4 In.	80.00
Chocolate Pot, Flowers, 19th Century, 7 In.	335.00
Chocolate Set, Classical Scenes, Red, Green, Gold Highlights, 10 x 14 1/2 In.	476.00
Compote, Applied Flowers, Cherubs, Reticulated Base, Marked, c.1910, 14 1/2 x 11 In. . . .	390.00
Cup & Saucer, Man, Gilt, Jeweled, Marked, Josephine, E.M., 2 1/2 In.	1035.00
Cup & Saucer, Portrait, Dutch Maid, Flowers, Bird Head Handle, 3 1/2 In.	405.00
Dinner Service, Flowers, White Ground, Blue & Gold Mark, 95 Piece	1380.00
Dresser Box, Flowers, Gilt, Round, 5 1/2 In.	150.00
Dresser Box, Hinged Lid, Courting Scene, Border, Flowers, Marked, 5 1/2 x 2 1/2 In. . . .	200.00
Figurine, 3 Figures At Musical Recital, c.1950, 11 x 7 x 10 In.	230.00
Figurine, Exotic Bird, Polychrome, 14 x 9 In.	1500.00
Figurine, Foo Dog, Meissen Style, Curly Fur, 20th Century, 9 1/4 In.	410.00
Figurine, Fox, Full Figure, Glass Eyes, 19th Century	675.00
Figurine, Girl Standing Near Post, Flower Basket, Signed, 4 3/4 In.	200.00
Figurine, Male Flutist, Woman, c.1950, 11 1/2 x 6 1/2 x 9 In.	115.00

Figurine, Man, Woman By Piano, Flower Base, Gilt, Late 19th Century, 10 x 13 1/2 In. ...   364.00
Figurine, Monkey, Seated, With Apple, Early 20th Century, 15 3/4 In. 920.00
Figurine, Pug Dog, 5 In., Pair ....*Illus*   515.00
Figurine, Royal Carriage, Escorts, Horsemen, Scrollwork Base, 1900s, 6 x 5 x 20 In. 115.00
Figurine, Woman, Children, c.1950, 9 1/2 x 6 1/2 x 7 In. 175.00
Group, 2 Ladies, Sitting On Sofa, Table, Oval, Gilt, Marked, c.1930, 7 x 10 x 5 1/2 In. 195.00
Mirror, Flower Relief, Hand Painted, c.1900, 18 x 13 In. 840.00
Plaque, Vestalin, Classical Figure, Oil Lamp, Frame, c.1900, 5 1/2 x 3 1/2 In. 2585.00
Plate, Cabinet, Preciosa, Gypsy, Green Luster Rim, Art Nouveau, c.1900, 9 1/8 In. 705.00
Plate, Portrait Of Girl, 9 1/2 In. 495.00
Sconce, Cartouche Shaped Mirror, 3 Candle Arms, 34 x 20 In. 3285.00
Stein, Battle Scene, Porcelain Lid, Helmet Finial, 1 Liter 605.00
Teapot, Courting Scene, Gilt, Rococo Style, 20th Century, 5 1/2 In. 375.00
Teapot, Fishermen, Boats, Cobalt Blue, Gold, 5 In. 430.00
Urn, Flowers, Gilt, Blossom Finial, 20th Century, 16 1/4 In. 110.00
Vase, Hunting Scene, Puce Ground, Oval, Flared Foot, Neck, 14 In., Pair 750.00
Vase, Maiden, Long Hair, Cobalt Blue Ground, Jewels, Gilt, Cylindrical, Handles, 11 1/2 In.
2620.00
Vase, Portrait, Flowers, Filigree, Woman, Gold Frame, 6 1/2 In. 540.00

DUNCAN & MILLER is a term used by collectors when referring to glass
made by the George A. Duncan and Sons Company or the Duncan and
Miller Glass Company. These companies worked from 1893 to 1955,
when the use of the name *Duncan* was discontinued and the firm
became part of the United States Glass Company. Early patterns may
be listed under Pressed Glass.

American Way, Vase, Handkerchief, 8 x 7 5/8 In. 150.00
Ashtray, Duck, 4 In. 10.00
Canterbury, Bowl, Cape Cod Blue, Crimped, 10 In. 100.00
Canterbury, Bowl, Dressing, Sections, 5 1/4 In. 11.00
Canterbury, Candlestick, 2-Light, Chartreuse, Pair 105.00
Canterbury, Candy Dish, Cover, Ruby, Footed, 9 x 6 1/4 In. 175.00
Canterbury, Celery Dish, 2 Sections, Oblong, 10 1/2 x 6 In. 35.00
Canterbury, Condiment Tray, 4 Sections, Handles, 8 1/4 In. 30.00
Canterbury, Dish, Marmalade, Underplate, 5 x 3 In. 28.00
Canterbury, Goblet, 9 Oz., 6 In. 15.00
Canterbury, Goblet, Chartreuse, 9 Oz., 5 1/4 In. 18.00
Canterbury, Pitcher, Martini, 32 Oz. 85.00
Canterbury, Relish, 3 Sections, 10 1/2 x 6 In. ....25.00 to 30.00
Canterbury, Rose Bowl, 5 1/4 x 3 1/4 In. 25.00
Canterbury, Salt & Pepper, 3 1/2 In. 13.00
Canterbury, Sugar & Creamer 16.00
Canterbury, Vase, Cornucopia, Chartreuse 85.00
Caribbean, Bowl, Blue, Handle, 3 1/2 x 5 In. 100.00
Caribbean, Bowl, Floral, Blue, Oval, Handles, 10 3/4 In. 95.00
Caribbean, Vase, Blue, Squat, Flared, Rolled Rim, 2 1/2 x 7 In. 85.00
Cloverleaf, Vase, Cape Cod Blue, 5 In. 50.00
Dover, Champagne, Ruby, 6 Oz., 4 1/2 In. 25.00
Dover, Cocktail, Ruby, Crystal Stem & Base, 3 1/2 Oz., 4 In. 20.00
Dover, Wine, Ruby, Crystal Stem & Base, 3 Oz., 4 3/4 In. 20.00
Ellrose, Berry Set, 7 Piece 125.00
Figurine, Fat Goose, 7 1/4 x 5 In. 175.00
First Love, Cigarette Box, Cover, 3 x 4 3/4 x 3 3/4 In. 130.00
First Love, Sugar, Handles, 3 x 4 In. 24.00
First Love, Vase, 4 7/8 In. 80.00
Hobnail, Basket, Cape Cod Blue, 10 x 4 3/4 In. 113.00
Hobnail, Champagne, 5 Oz., 4 1/2 In. 16.00
Hobnail, Cocktail, 3 Oz., 4 1/8 In. 12.00
Hobnail, Ivy Ball, Cape Cod Blue, Ruffled Edge, Footed, 7 1/2 In. ....70.00 to 95.00
Hobnail, Ivy Bowl, 7 1/2 In. 35.00
Hobnail, Vase, Cape Cod Blue, Flip, 8 x 6 In. 130.00
Hobnail, Vase, Footed, 4 In. 40.00
Hobnail, Vase, Hat, 3 1/2 x 5 1/4 In. 25.00

Indian Tree, Champagne, 5 Oz. 30.00
Mardi Gras, Sugar & Creamer 50.00
Mardi Gras, Vase, Chartreuse, 8 In. 75.00
Pall Mall, Candlestick, Swan, Emerald Green, 6 In. 75.00
Pall Mall, Swan, 3 In. 20.00
Pall Mall, Swan, 5 In. 40.00
Pall Mall, Swan, 12 In. 75.00
Pall Mall, Swan, Blue, 6 In. 200.00
Pall Mall, Swan, Chartreuse, 5 In. 175.00
Pall Mall, Swan, Emerald Green, 12 In. 250.00
Pall Mall, Swan, Green Opalescent, 13 In. 250.00
Pall Mall, Swan, Green, 10 In. ....65.00 to 75.00
Sandwich, Basket, 11 1/2 x 4 In. 235.00
Sandwich, Bowl, Ruffled Edge, 4 x 11 In. 75.00
Sandwich, Bowl, Salad, 12 In. 75.00
Sandwich, Candlestick, 4 In. 18.00
Sandwich, Candlestick, Prisms, Bobeche, 10 In. 125.00
Sandwich, Candy Dish, Cover, Footed, 8 1/2 In. 100.00
Sandwich, Champagne, 5 Oz., 5 1/4 In. 18.00
Sandwich, Cheese & Cracker Set, 2 Piece 75.00
Sandwich, Cigarette Box, Cover, 4 In. 60.00
Sandwich, Coaster, 5 In. 18.00
Sandwich, Cocktail, 3 Oz., 4 1/4 In. ....20.00 to 30.00
Sandwich, Creamer, 3 In. 18.00
Sandwich, Creamer, Footed, 4 In. 18.00
Sandwich, Cup 12.00
Sandwich, Cup & Saucer, Chartreuse 20.00
Sandwich, Dish, Mayonnaise, Plate, Ladle 40.00
Sandwich, Dish, Mint, Handle, 7 In. 25.00
Sandwich, Finger Bowl, 4 In. 18.00
Sandwich, Goblet, 9 Oz., 6 In. 19.00
Sandwich, Ice Cream, Footed, 5 Oz., 4 1/4 In. 15.00
Sandwich, Ice Cream, Footed, Green, 5 Oz., 4 1/4 In. 18.00
Sandwich, Nappy, Heart Shape, 2 3/4 x 6 1/4 In. 50.00
Sandwich, Nappy, Ring Handle, 5 In. ....20.00 to 25.00
Sandwich, Nut Dish, 2 1/2 In. 18.00
Sandwich, Pitcher, Ice Lip, 64 Oz., 8 In. 170.00
Sandwich, Plate, 13 In. 55.00
Sandwich, Plate, Green, 6 In. 10.00
Sandwich, Plate, Scalloped Rim, 8 In. 4.00
Sandwich, Relish, 3 Sections, 12 In. 16.00
Sandwich, Saucer 5.00
Sandwich, Sugar, 2 3/4 In. 18.00
Sandwich, Tray, Oval, Handles, 8 In. 20.00
Sandwich, Tumbler, Iced Tea, Footed, 9 Oz., 4 3/4 In. 20.00
Sandwich, Tumbler, Iced Tea, Footed, 13 Oz., 5 1/2 In. 35.00
Sandwich, Tumbler, Iced Tea, Footed, Yellow, 13 Oz., 5 1/2 In. 40.00
Sandwich, Tumbler, Juice, Footed, 5 Oz., 3 3/4 In. 15.00
Spiral Flutes, Cup, Amber 9.00
Sylvan, Candy Dish, Cover, Leaf Shape, Crystal, 8 In. 125.00
Sylvan, Dish, Leaf Shape, 7 x 6 1/2 In. 10.00
Sylvan, Vase, Milk Glass, 5 3/4 x 8 1/2 In. 125.00
Tear Drop, Ashtray, Pair 15.00
Tear Drop, Bowl, Olive, Sections, Handles, 6 1/2 In. ....12.00 to 15.00
Tear Drop, Cup & Saucer ....17.00 to 20.00
Tear Drop, Nut Dish, 2 Sections, 6 In. ....12.00 to 15.00
Tear Drop, Plate, 7 1/2 In. 5.00
Tear Drop, Plate, 8 1/2 In. 6.00
Tear Drop, Plate, Sweetmeat, Center Handle, 6 1/2 In. 55.00
Tear Drop, Relish, 5 Sections, 12 In. 30.00
Tear Drop, Relish, Heart Shape, 2 Sections, 7 1/2 In. 20.00
Tear Drop, Salt & Pepper, 3 1/2 In. 30.00
Tear Drop, Sherbet, 5 Oz., 3 1/2 In. ....6.00 to 8.00

Tear Drop, Sugar & Creamer	25.00
Tear Drop, Tumbler, Hi-Ball, 12 Oz., 5 1/2 In.	15.00
Tear Drop, Tumbler, Whiskey, 2 Oz., 2 1/4 In.	20.00
Terrace, Relish, 3 Sections, 14 In.	29.00
Venetian, Vase, Ruby, 10 1/2 In.	150.00

DURAND art glass was made from 1924 to 1931. The Vineland Flint Glass Works was established by Victor Durand and Victor Durand, Jr., in 1897. In 1924 Martin Bach, Jr., and other artisans from the Quezal glassworks joined them at the Vineland, New Jersey, plant to make Durand art glass.

Compote, Blue, Amber, Threading, Flared, 5 In.	635.00
Compote, Gold Iridescent, Signed, 16 1/4 In.	800.00
Lamp Base, Lady Gay Rose, Cherry Red, Ginger Jar, 11 1/4 In.	4485.00
Luminaire, Mosaic, Brass Base, Dolphin Feet, 4 x 6 1/8 In.	545.00
Plate, Green, White Pulled Feathers, Roses & Leaves, Border, 8 In.	980.00
Shade, Gold Threading, Gold Ground, Baluster, 12 x 7 In.	690.00
Torchiere, King Tut, Green, Gold Iridescent, c.1925, 15 1/2 In.	1230.00
Vase, Beehive, Blue Iridescent, Signed, 12 3/8 In. ....1200.00 to	1380.00
Vase, Blue & Gold Iridescent, Coils, Alabaster Stem & Foot, c.1925, 10 In.	1570.00
Vase, Blue Gray Pulled Leaves, Vines, Orange Iridescent, 8 1/2 In.	865.00
Vase, Blue Iridescent, Golden Foot, Stout, Signed, 8 1/4 In.	920.00
Vase, Blue Iridescent, Green Highlights, White Lotus Leaves, Trailing Vines, 7 3/4 In.	980.00
Vase, Blue Iridescent, Heart & Vine, Flared Rim, 6 3/4 In.	1150.00
Vase, Blue Iridescent, Opal Leaf & Vine, Spherical, Trumpet Neck, Signed, 6 3/4 In. ..	935.00
Vase, Blue Iridescent, Opal Pulled Heart & Vine, Flared Ruffled Edge, Tapered, 5 In.	940.00
Vase, Blue Iridescent, Shoulder, Allover White Pulled Vine, Signed, 7 In.	1035.00
Vase, Blue Iridescent, Threading, Signed, 9 1/4 In.	575.00
Vase, Blue Pulled Feather, Opal, Gold Threading, c.1920, 9 3/4 In.	1065.00
Vase, Blue Tipped Pulled Feather, Gold Threading & Body, c.1925, 8 1/4 In.	500.00
Vase, Blue, Pulled Heart & Trailing Vine, Gold Ground, Signed	1200.00
Vase, Blue, Pulled Heart & Trailing Vine, Peach Ground, 10 1/2 In.	1495.00
Vase, Cobalt Blue, White & Blue Pulled Feathers, 8 3/4 In.	1035.00
Vase, Cypriot, Blue & Lavender Iridescent, Pinched Side, Rolled In Ruffled Rim, 4 1/2 In.	230.00
Vase, Gold Iridescent, Allover Pulled Vines, 10 In.	1550.00
Vase, Gold Iridescent, Bulbous Body, Flared Neck, c.1925, 9 1/2 In.	230.00
Vase, Gold, Iridescent Orange Interior, Tapered, Oval, Flared, 6 3/4 In.	250.00
Vase, Green, Gold Iridescent, Pulled Feathers, Threading, Shoulder, Signed, 7 1/4 In.	635.00
Vase, Green, Gold, Pulled Hearts, White Ground, Gold Threading, 6 In.	920.00
Vase, King Tut, Apple Green, Trumpet, Signed, 12 In.	2300.00
Vase, King Tut, Blue Iridescent, White, Yellow, Signed, 8 1/2 In. ....*Illus*	2300.00
Vase, King Tut, Blue, White Ground, 10 1/2 In.	1955.00
Vase, King Tut, Gold Iridescent, Tapered, Waisted Neck, Flared, Signed, 12in.	1430.00
Vase, King Tut, Gold Iridescent, White, Bulbous, Signed, c.1925, 16 In.	1792.00
Vase, King Tut, Gold Iridescent, White, Signed, 10 In.	1610.00
Vase, King Tut, Green, Silver Iridescent, Signed, 8 1/2 In.	2300.00
Vase, Lady Gay Rose, 5 Cut Rosettes, Leaves, 8 In.	400.00
Vase, Opalescent, Random Heart & Vine Design, Trumpet, 10 In.	550.00

Durand, Vase, King Tut,
Blue Iridescent, White,
Yellow, Signed, 8 1/2 In.

Do not light a cabinet filled with glass with light bulbs over 25 watts. Stronger bulbs generate too much heat. Some new types of bulbs are brighter and give off less heat.

Vase, Ruby Cut To Clear, Faceted Optical Windows, 8 3/8 In. 1380.00
Vase, Ruby Cut To Clear, Stylized Design, Tapered, Oval, 8 1/2 In. 1035.00
Vase, Ruby, Opal Feather Pulls, 8 1/8 In. 920.00
Vase, Trumpet, Blue Iridescent, Gold, Signed, 12 In. 715.00
Vase, Trumpet, Green & Gold Leaves, Threading, Gold Iridescent Interior, Signed, 12 In. . 660.00
Vase, White, Pulled Blue Design, Shouldered, Flared, 9 1/2 In. 1150.00
Vase, Yellow Iridescent, Trumpet, Footed, Signed, 9 3/4 In. 495.00
Vase, Yellow, Engraved Leaves & Flowers, Saucer Foot, Flared, 6 In. 230.00
Wine, Red, Opal & Red Pulled Feather, Clear Stem, Light Green Base, 5 1/2 In. 330.00

ELVIS PRESLEY, the well-known singer, lived from 1935 to 1977. He
became famous by 1956. Elvis appeared on television, starred in
twenty-seven movies, and performed in Las Vegas. Memorabilia from
any of the Presley shows, his records, and even memorials made after
his death are collected.

Candy Box, Heart Shape, Love Me Tender, Russel Stover, Cardboard, Army Uniform 45.00
Game, Elvis Welcomes You To His World, Duff Sisters, 1978 . . . .   46.00
Guitar, Gibson Dove, Custom, Used In Concert From 1973 To 1975 . . . . 29375.00
NOW Magazine, Fringed Outfit, Microphone, Inscription, Autograph, 1971 . . . . 635.00
Photograph, White Jump Suit, Inscription, Autograph, Frame, 12 x 15 In. 368.00
Poster, Love Me Tender, 20th Century Fox, 1956, 30 x 20 In. 330.00

ENAMELS listed here are made of glass particles and other materials
heated and fused to metal. In the eighteenth and nineteenth centuries,
workmen from Russia, France, England, and other countries made
small boxes and table pieces of enamel on metal. One form of English
enamel is called *Battersea* and is listed under that name. There was a
revival of interest in enameling in the 1930s and a new style evolved.
There is now renewed interest in the artistic enameled plaques, vases,
ashtrays, and jewelry. Enamels made since the 1930s are usually on
copper or steel, although silver was often used for jewelry.
Graniteware is a separate category, and enameled metal kitchen pieces
may be included in the Kitchen category.

Ashtray, Leaf Border, Jean Samuel, 1965, 6 3/4 In. . . . . *Illus*   5.00
Bottle, Scent, Woman In Garden, Hinged Lid, Glass Stopper, 2 1/2 In. 1323.00
Bowl, Abstract Burst Design, Edwards Steel Original, For Gumps, 9 3/4 In. . . . . *Illus*   65.00
Bowl, Brass, Fantoni, Raymore, Italy, c.1955, 1 1/2 x 13 x 3 1/2 In. 823.00
Bowl, Lid, Pedestal, Marianne Brandt, Ruppelwerk Gotha, Germany, c.1930, 8 x 5 In. . . . 2106.00
Bowl, Silver, Maidens, Cupids, Winged Maiden, Ball Feet, 3 1/2 x 2 1/4 x 2 1/4 In. 840.00
Box, Motto, May We Live In Plenty, Peace & Love, Oval, Hinged Cover, Battersea 550.00
Box, Oval Scene, Woman, 3 Boys, Field, Woods, Sterling Silver, 3 3/8 x 2 1/2 In. 575.00
Box, Silver, Man Tying Ribbon In Woman's Hair, France, 2 1/2 x 2 x 1 In. 900.00
Censer, Duck Shape, Champleve, Late 1800s, 6 3/4 In. 130.00
Cigarette Case, Silver, Cottage Scene, Austria, 4 1/4 x 3 1/4 In. 720.00
Eggcup, Gilt, Roundels With Floral Sprays, Shaped Rim, Trumpet Foot, 2 1/4 In. 2350.00
Jar, Inverted Pear Shape, Bird, Flower, Tree Bark, Cover, Late 19th Century, 6 3/4 In. . . . 130.00

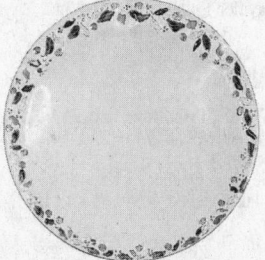

Enamel, Ashtray, Leaf Border,
Jean Samuel, 1965, 6 3/4 In.

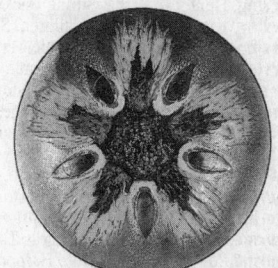

Enamel, Bowl, Abstract Burst Design,
Edwards Steel Original, For Gumps, 9 3/4 In.

Jewel Casket, Man Serenading Woman, Key, Gamet, France, 8 3/4 x 6 3/4 x 4 1/4 In.	1380.00
Plaque, Courting Couple, 18th Century Dress, Easel Back Frame, Early 1900s, 8 3/8 In. . .	1528.00
Spoon, Dessert, Silver Gilt, Rock Crystal Bowls, Renaissance Style, c.1875, 6 Piece	1150.00
Tea Set, Courting Couples, Cupids, Nymphs, Garden, Austrian, Miniature, 7 Piece	2128.00
Tray, Aluminum, Marianne Brandt, Ruppelwerk Gotha, Germany, c.1930, 9 3/4 In.	1170.00
Urn, Cover, Gilt Decorated, Cobalt Blue Ground, Hardwood Stand, Chinese, 1800s, 17 In.	259.00
Vase, Gu-Form, Floor, Champleve, Bronze, Cast Relief, Cranes, Pine Tree, 24 In.	575.00
Vase, Paolo De Poli, Copper, Green, Italy, 1960, 3 x 3 x 10 In.	1287.00
Vase, Viennese, Baluster Shape, Birds Perched On Branches, Early 1900s, 14 1/2 In.	295.00

ERPHILA is a mark found on Czechoslovakian and other pottery and porcelain made after 1920. The mark was used on items imported by Ebeling & Reuss, Philadelphia, a giftware firm that is still operating in Pennsylvania. The mark is a combination of the letters *E* and *R* (Ebeling & Reuss) and the first letters of the city, Phila(delphia). Many whimsical figural pitchers and creamers, figurines, platters, and other giftwares carry this mark.

Bowl, Floral Transfer, Spaghetti Lattice Border, Square, Stamped, 8 In.	80.00
Creamer, Deep Pink, Black & White Cat Climbing Side, Stamped, 5 3/4 In.	80.00
Figurine, Scottie Dog Mother & Pups, Black & White, Stamped, 4 Piece	135.00
Pitcher, Bird, Red & Black, Stamped, 9 In.	275.00
Pitcher, Green Plaid, Airbrushed, Stamped, 5 In.	30.00
Plaque, Embossed Flower Basket, Blue Border, Round, Stamped, 7 3/4 In.	40.00
Teapot, Cat, Figural, Black & White, Red Bow Collar, Stamped, 8 In.	170.00
Teapot, Dachshund, Figural, Brown & Black, Stamped, 8 In.	175.00
Teapot, Poodle, Figural, Gray & Black, Stamped, 8 1/4 In.	175.00

ES GERMANY porcelain was made at the factory of Erdmann Schlegelmilch from 1861 to 1937 in Suhl, Germany. The porcelain, marked *ES Germany* or *ES Suhl*, was sold decorated or undecorated. Other pieces were made at a factory in Saxony, Prussia, and are marked *ES Prussia*. Reinhold Schlegelmilch made the famous wares marked *RS Germany*.

Bowl, Bird, 4-Sided, Handles, Prov. Saxe E.S. Mark, 5 3/4 In.	35.00
Nappy, Stage Coach Scene, Prov. Saxe E.S. Mark, Early 20th Century, 8 In.	69.00
Nappy, Stagecoach Scene, Marked, 20th Century, 8 In.	70.00
Vase, Purple Violets, ES Prussia Mark, Early 20th Century, 4 1/2 In., Pair	81.00
Vase, Purple Violets, Marked, Early 20th Century, 4 1/2 In.	80.00

ESKIMO artifacts of all types are collected. Carvings of whale or walrus teeth are listed under Scrimshaw. Baskets are in the Basket category. All other types of Eskimo art are listed here. In Canada and some other areas, the term *Inuit* is used instead of Eskimo.

Basket, 2-Color Checkered Accents, Lid, Hooper Bay, c.1910, 10 x 9 In.	315.00
Basket, Carved Ivory, Polar Bear Finial, Painted Eyes, Nose, With Book, 3 1/4 x 3 1/4 In.	1760.00
Basket, Inuit, Bowl, Coil, Checkered Design, Globe Shape, Cover, 8 1/2 In.	176.00
Carving, Bear Attacks Seal, Soapstone, Inuit, Joanassie, Quebec, c.1987, 15 x 12 In.	1790.00
Carving, Hawk & Chicks, Soapstone, Inuit, Echaluk Nutalak, 1988, 12 1/2 x 8 1/2 In. . . .	1568.00
Carving, Hunter In Parka, Sitting Backwards On Walrus, Soapstone, 12 1/2 In.	560.00
Carving, Kneeling Woman, Children, Soapstone, Inuit, Davidee Enkok, 10 x 7 1/2 In.	2015.00
Carving, Madonna & Child, Whale Vertebra, Inuit, 13 In.	650.00
Carving, Male Torso, Soapstone, Inuit, 5 In.	85.00
Carving, Polar Bear, Standing, Soapstone, Inuit, 6 1/2 x 3 In.	145.00
Carving, Seal, Outstretched, Soapstone, Inuit, 8 In.	85.00
Cribbage Board, Inuit, Ivory, Engraved, Hunter, Kayak, Walrus, Fish, Bone End, 25 In. . .	705.00
Cribbage Board, Ivory, Dog Sled, Cityscape, Nome, Alaska, c.1900, 8 3/4 In.	575.00
Doll, Sealskin Outfit, Hide Face, 1900, 18 x 7 In.	635.00
Figurine, Bear Attacking Seal, Soapstone, Black, Joanassie Jack, Quebec, 7 1/2 x 8 In.	800.00
Figurine, Bear On Hind Legs, Soapstone, Thomassie Turalak, Quebec, 1990, 14 x 13 In. .	325.00
Figurine, Man Fishing, Dog, Walrus Tusk	248.00
Figurine, Man Paddling Kayak, Harpoons, Pack, Ivory, 6 In.	340.00
Figurine, Polar Bear & Seal, Carved, 5 1/4 In.	175.00
Figurine, Sea Gull & Chick, Gray, Soapstone, J.S. Sivaurapik, Quebec, 1989, 10 1/2 x 9 In.	500.00
Hook, Halibut, Northwest Coast, Wooden, Abstract Fish Shape, Metal Point, 10 In.	295.00

Knife, Scrimshaw Moose, Inuit, 9 In. 145.00
Mask, Cedar, Hand Carved, Stained, Painted, c.1950, 10 x 6 x 1 1/2 In. 375.00
Moccasins, Athabascan, Beaded, Moose Hide, Flowers, Tall Cuff, 10 In. 67.00
Mukluks, Fur, Woman's, 1920s, 9 1/2 x 8 1/2 In. 35.00
Quiver, Kutchin, Elk Hide, Painted, Beaded Trim, 8 Arrow Shafts, 26 In. 940.00
Sculpture, Polar Bear, Fish In Mouth, Ivory, High Polish, c.1950, 2 1/2 x 1 1/2 x 3 In. . . . 259.00
Trade Beads, Alaska, Cobalt, Russian Faceted, Hudson Bay Beaver Token, c.1820, 42 In. 259.00
Walrus Tusk, Engraved, Whale Hunting Scenes, 19th Century, 12 In. 529.00

FAIENCE refers to tin-glazed earthenware, especially the wares made in
France, Germany, and Scandinavia. It is also correct to say that faience
is the same as majolica or Delft, although usually the term refers only
to the tin-glazed pottery of the three regions mentioned.

Bowl, Scalloped Rim, Bandwork Border, Portrait Of A Man, French Text, 3 x 10 In. 575.00
Castor, Figural, Chinese Man Seated Cross-Legged, Green Robe, Continental, 6 1/4 In. . . 230.00
Centerpiece, Lambrequin Designs, Central Well, France, 4 3/4 x 11 1/2 x 18 In. 290.00
Compote, Polychrome Flowers, Prophet, 3-Sided Bowl, Ringed Standard, Italy, 6 x 12 In. 400.00
Inkstand, Boat Shape, Acanthus Leaf Feet, 2 Lidded Inks, Painted, 6 1/2 x 4 3/4 In. 290.00
Jar, Cover, Rouen, Delft Style Polychrome Decoration, c.1900, 14 1/2 In. 150.00
Jar, Dome Cover, Blue & White, Koi, Waves Around Base, Cherubs, Butterfly, 19 1/4 In. . 115.00
Plate, Birds, Yellow Sprigs, Leaves, Scalloped Rim, 8 3/4 In. 170.00
Shaving Bowl, Cow, Landscape, Reeded, Oval, Marked, J Pain, 2 1/4 x 14 x 10 In. 2070.00
Tile, Purple On White, Chinoiserie, Moses On The Mount, Nativity, Italy, 5 x 5 In., Pair . . 160.00
Vase, Eagle, Instruments, Weapons, Remembering The War Years, c.1916, 9 In. 110.00
Vase, Rouen, Delft Style Polychrome Decoration, c.1900, 10 1/2 In. 150.00
Vase, Rouen, Gourd Shape, Delft Style Polychrome Decoration, Ribbed, c.1900, 15 In. . . . 185.00
Wall Pocket, Violin Form, Desvres Area, 13 In. 185.00

FAIRINGS are small souvenir china boxes and figurines that were sold
at country fairs during the nineteenth century. Most were made in
Germany. Reproductions of fairings are being made, especially of the
famous *twelve months of marriage* series.

Trinket Box, 1/2 Circles, Paper Covered, Incised, Elongated Oval, 6 1/2 x 3 x 2 1/2 In. . . 800.00
Trinket Box, 1/2 Circles, Polka Dots, Painted, Elongated Oval, 4 1/2 x 2 1/2 x 6 In. 635.00
Trinket Box, Circles, Flowers, Paper Covered, Red, Black Paint, Late 1700s, 10 x 16 In. . 495.00
Trinket Box, Pietra Dura, Gilt Metal, Hinged Lid, Lining, Oblong, Italy, 1900s, 4 In. 650.00
Trinket Box, Polka Dots, Vines, Painted, Paper Covered, Oval, 8 1/2 x 4 1/2 In. 385.00
Trinket Box, Porcelain, Peasant Woman, Distaff, Cat, Germany, Late 19th Century, 12 In. 382.00
Trinket Box, Porcelain, Woman, With Cigar, Germany, c.1860, 10 1/2 In. 110.00
Trinket Box, Ribbed, Cover, Rectangular, Bunches Of Grapes, Leaves, 4 In. 40.00
Trinket Box, Silver Gilt, Amethyst, Pearl, Engraved, Openwork, Early 20th Century, 5 In. 940.00
Trinket Box, Silver Gilt, Hardstone, Pearl, Rococo Revival, Early 20th Century, 3 1/2 In. . 825.00
Trinket Box, Starburst, Flowers, Yellow, Pink, Black, Red, 3 3/4 x 2 1/2 x 1 3/4 In. 690.00
Trinket Box, Tunbridgeware, Inlaid, Geometric, Manor House, Metal Mounted, 8 7/8 In. . 4465.00
Trinket Box, Woman, 3-Tiered Dress, Yellow Bonnet, Germany, c.1850s, 7 1/2 In. 90.00
Trinket Box, Woman, Seated, 2 Fruit Baskets, Germany, 5 In. 295.00
Trinket Box, Woman, Seated, Blue Outfit, Musket, Drum, Late 19th Century, 10 1/2 In. . . 118.00

FAIRYLAND LUSTER pieces are included in the Wedgwood category.

FAMILLE ROSE, see Chinese Export category.

FANS have been used for cooling since the days of the ancients. By the
eighteenth century, the fan was an accessory for the lady of fashion,
and very elaborate and expensive fans were made. Sticks were made
of ivory or wood, set with jewels or carved. The fans were made of
painted silk or paper. Inexpensive paper fans printed with advertising
were giveaways in the late nineteenth and early twentieth centuries.
Electric fans were introduced in 1882.

Advertising, Armour Pork & Beans, 19 Characters, Paper, Fold-Out, 12 In. 45.00
Advertising, Kis-Me Chewing Gum, Paper, 9 1/2 x 15 In. 65.00
Advertising, Lamb's Music House, Pottstown, Pa., Bathing Beauty, 1920s, 10 1/2 x 10 In. 22.00
Advertising, Moxie Soft Drink, Girl Wearing Moxie-Man Necklace, 1923 . . . . 85.00
Advertising, Moxie, Blond Woman Looks In Mirror, Man On Reverse, 1925 . . . . 60.00

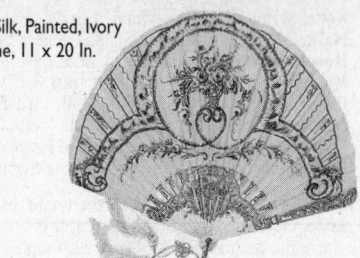

Fan, Silk, Painted, Ivory Frame, 11 x 20 In.

Fan, Celluloid, Ivory, Feathers, Silk Cord, 10 x 18 In.

Advertising, Singer, 51st Season, 2 Parakeets, 3 Sewing Machines 30.00
Advertising, Sorin Cognac, Green Cloaked Figure In White, Holding Glass, 7 1/2 In. 25.00
Brise, Ivory, Animals In Landscape, c.1800, 7 3/4 In............................ 805.00
Celluloid, Ivory, Feathers, Silk Cord, 10 x 18 In. ....*Illus* 200.00
Electric, Bersted, Eskimo, Black Base & Cage, Tin Blades, 10 In......... 50.00
Electric, Ceiling, General Electric, No. 822193, Cast Iron, Wooden Blades, 13 In. 250.00
Electric, Chicago Electric, Handybreeze, No. 8-879-E, Aqua Painted Blades & Base, 12 In. 60.00
Electric, Detroit Mfgs. Supply Co., Whirlwind, Chrome & Aluminum, 20 In. 50.00
Electric, Diehl, No. J16912, Black Painted Cage & Blades, 1950s, 21 In. 125.00
Electric, Eck, Tigre Cyclone, Oscillating, Brass Blades & Cage, Black Base, c.1910, 18 In. 660.00
Electric, General Electric, Whiz, No. 257599, Brass Blades, Painted, 9 In. 120.00
Electric, Gilbert, Polar Cub, No. P1849, Brass Base & Cage, 10 In.................... 75.00
Electric, Oscillating, Brass Blades & Cage, Robbins & Meyers 3000.00
Evening, Lady's, Lace, Silk, Ivory Sticks, Shadowbox, Mid 1800s, 14 1/2 x 18 1/2 In. ... 201.00
Fly, Spring-Driven Clock Mechanism, Cast Iron Base, Black Muslin Paddles, 29 x 5 In. .. 1150.00
Ivory, Indian Court Scene, Watercolor, Silver, c.1830, 10 1/2 x 20 In. 750.00
Ivory, Watercolor, Barucci, Cipriani, Bartolini, Tarenghi, Italy, Frame, 1800s, 8 x 2 In. ... 1150.00
Ivory Sticks, Lithograph, Courtship Scene, Mirror, Silk Tassel, Victorian, 10 1/2 In. 58.00
Ivory Sticks, Openwork, Painted, Courting Scene, Classical Figures, 1700s, 11 x 19 In. .. 415.00
Mother-Of-Pearl, Printed, Painted, Pierce Carved Sticks, Rosewood Box, 11 5/8 In. 120.00
Mother-Of-Pearl Sticks, Continental Lace, Demilune Mahogany Shadowbox, 20 1/2 In. .. 70.00
Ogi, Dance Fan, Snow Scene, White Egrets, Ivory Guards, Ladybugs, Japan, c.1920 ..... 426.00
Paper, Figural Landscape, Shibayama Guard Sticks, 1800s, 11 1/2 In. 800.00
Rococo Style, Beechwood, Carved, Parcel Gilt, France, Late 19th Century, 16 In., Pair ... 58.00
Silk, Ivory, Painted, Continental, Gilt Wood Frame, 16 x 23 In. 720.00
Silk, Painted, Ivory Frame, 11 x 20 In. ....*Illus*
Tortoiseshell, Faux, Applied Metal, On Lace, 8 1/2 In: 29.00

FAST FOOD COLLECTIBLES may be included in several categories, such as Advertising, Coca-Cola, Toy, etc.

FEDERZEICHNUNG, see Loetz category.

FENTON Art Glass Company, founded in Martins Ferry, Ohio, by Frank L. Fenton, is now located in Williamstown, West Virginia. It is noted for early carnival glass produced between 1907 and 1920. Some of these pieces are listed in the Carnival Glass category. Many other types of glass were also made. Spanish Lace in this section refers to the pattern made by Fenton.

Aqua Crest, Vase, Trumpet, c.1948, 6 1/2 In. 55.00
Black Rose, Bowl, Ruffled Edge, 1953-1954 .... 225.00
Blue Ridge, Basket, 9 In. 200.00
Cactus, Compote, Milk Glass, 1967 .... 30.00
Coin Dot, Basket, Cranberry Opalescent, 8 In. 65.00
Coin Dot, Jug, Blue Opalescent, Crimped Handle, Clear 165.00
Coin Dot, Vase, Blue Opalescent, 10 In. 200.00
Coin Dot, Vase, Cranberry Opalescent, 8 1/2 In. 65.00
Coin Dot, Vase, Cranberry, Snow Crest Edging, 11 In. 415.00
Coin Dot, Vase, French Opalescent, 11 In. 45.00
Daisy & Button, Basket, Colonial Amber, 6 In. 25.00

Daisy & Fern, Pitcher, Cranberry Opalescent, Ruffled Rim, Clear Handle, 9 1/4 In. 145.00
Daisy & Fern, Vase, Cranberry, Ruffled Rim, Egg Shape Body, 11 In. 230.00
Daisy & Fern, Water Set, Cranberry Opalescent, 8 Piece 290.00
Diamond Optic, Tumbler, Amberina, 3 Molded Base Rings, 4 In. 22.00
Diamond Optic, Vase, Ruby Overlay, 5 1/2 In. 40.00
Dolphin, Bonbon, Aquamarine Blue, Wheel Cut, c.1928, 6 1/2 In. 35.00
Emerald Crest, Bowl, 11 In. 55.00
Figurine, Bird, Blue Satin, Pair 60.00
Figurine, Butterfly On Twig, Custard 25.00
Florentine Green, Guest Set, 2 Piece 185.00
Gold Crest, Jug, 8 In. 90.00
Gold Crest, Vase, 6 In. 35.00
Grecian Gold, Guest Set, Blue Handle, 2 Piece 150.00
Hanging Hearts, Vase, Bittersweet, 7 7/8 In. 80.00
Hobnail, Basket, Blue Opalescent, 10 In. 200.00
Hobnail, Basket, Blue Opalescent, Low Foot, 5 1/2 In. 75.00
Hobnail, Basket, Cranberry Opalescent, 7 In. 95.00
Hobnail, Basket, French Opalescent, 4 1/2 In. 45.00
Hobnail, Basket, Milk Glass, 12 In. 50.00
Hobnail, Basket, Topaz Opalescent, 4 1/2 In. 150.00
Hobnail, Basket, Topaz Opalescent, 7 In. 150.00
Hobnail, Bell, Ruby, Christmas, 1981, 5 In. 20.00
Hobnail, Bowl, Colonial Ruby, 3-Footed, 7 In. 30.00
Hobnail, Bowl, Emerald Opalescent, 9 In. 125.00
Hobnail, Butter, Cover, Milk Glass 150.00
Hobnail, Candlestick, Milk Glass, Pair 75.00
Hobnail, Candy Box, Cover, Milk Glass 150.00
Hobnail, Candy Jar, Cover, Colonial Green, Footed 30.00
Hobnail, Candy Jar, Cover, Topaz Opalescent 200.00
Hobnail, Epergne, 3 Lilies, Milk Glass, c.1960, 3 1/2 x 7 1/2 In. 75.00
Hobnail, Fairy Light, Milk Glass 110.00
Hobnail, Ivy Ball, Topaz Opalescent, Footed 100.00
Hobnail, Jug, Apple Green Overlay, 12 Oz. 45.00
Hobnail, Jug, Blue Opalescent, 5 1/4 In. 125.00
Hobnail, Jug, Cranberry Opalescent, 4 1/2 In. 95.00
Hobnail, Jug, Milk Glass, 80 Oz. 125.00
Hobnail, Lamp, Oil, Milk Glass 125.00
Hobnail, Rose Bowl, Colonial Blue, Footed, c.1962 .... 22.00
Hobnail, Tray, Fan, French Opalescent 35.00
Hobnail, Vase, Blue Opalescent, 4 In. 25.00
Hobnail, Vase, Bud, Amber, 10 1/2 In. 15.00
Hobnail, Vase, Bud, Emerald Green Opalescent, 9 In. 55.00
Hobnail, Vase, Cranberry Opalescent, 6 In. 95.00
Hobnail, Vase, Cranberry Opalescent, 8 In. 145.00
Hobnail, Vase, Honey Amber Overlay, 11 In. 110.00
Hobnail, Vase, Milk Glass, 3-Footed, 12 In. 200.00
Ivory Crest, Hat, 7 In. 65.00
Peach Crest, Hat, 4 In. 45.00
Peach Crest, Hat, 10 In. 200.00
Peach Crest, Powder Jar, Cover 35.00
Peach Crest, Vase, 6 In. 70.00
Persian Medallion, Bonbon, Lime Green, Marigold Iridescence 120.00
Persian Medallion, Candy Box, Violets In The Snow On Cover 85.00
Persian Medallion, Plate, Lime Green, 6 In. 115.00
Pinwheel, Compote, Lime Sherbet 50.00
Poppy, Lamp, Wisteria 105.00
Rib Optic, Lemonade Set, Green Opalescent, Cobalt Blue Handles, c.1924, 6 Piece 430.00
Rose Crest, Vase, Hat, 4 In. 45.00
Silver Crest, Banana Boat, Low Foot 55.00
Silver Crest, Basket, 7 In. 50.00
Silver Crest, Basket, Hat Shape, White Handle, 5 In. 45.00
Silver Crest, Bonbon, Footed, c.1948 .... 40.00
Silver Crest, Candlestick, 6 In., Pair 75.00

Silver Crest, Candy Dish, Cover, Footed 50.00
Silver Crest, Jug, 8 In. 90.00
Silver Crest, Vase, 12 In. 95.00
Silver Crest, Vase, Fan, Hand Painted Flowers, c.1948 .... 50.00
Spiral Optic, Basket, Topaz Opalescent, 7 In. 150.00
Valencia, Candy Dish, Cover, Orange 50.00
Vasa Murrhina, Basket, Autumn Orange, 7 In. 85.00
Vasa Murrhina, Vase, Rose, Aventurine Green, 4 In. 75.00
Water Lily, Basket, Lime Sherbet, 7 In. 55.00
Water Lily, Bowl, Rosalene, 3-Footed 50.00
Water Lily, Candlestick, Rosalene, Pair 70.00
Water Lily, Candy Box, Cover, Rosalene, Footed 85.00
Willow Green, Perfume Bottle, 7 1/2 In. 40.00
Wisteria, Candlestick, No. 649, 1920s, 10 In., Pair 450.00

FIESTA, the colorful dinnerware, was introduced in 1936 by the Homer
Laughlin China Co., redesigned in 1969, and withdrawn in 1973. It
was reissued again in 1986 in different colors and is still being made.
The simple design was characterized by a band of concentric circles,
beginning at the rim. Cups had full-circle handles until 1969, when
partial-circle handles were made. Harlequin and Riviera were related
wares. For more information about Fiesta, its colors and prices, see the
book *Kovels' Depression Glass & Dinnerware Price List*.

Chartreuse, Chop Plate, 13 In. 60.00
Chartreuse, Mug 27.00
Chartreuse, Plate, 7 In. 45.00
Cobalt Blue, Ashtray 45.00
Cobalt Blue, Creamer, Stick 27.00
Cobalt Blue, Plate, 6 In. 6.00
Cobalt Blue, Spoon, Kitchen Kraft 60.00
Cobalt Blue, Stacking Unit, Kitchen Kraft .... 25.00 to 32.00
Cobalt Blue, Sugar 32.00
Cobalt Blue, Tumbler, Juice 35.00
Cobalt Blue, Tumbler, Water 52.00
Forest Green, Bowl, Fruit, 4 3/4 In. 18.00
Forest Green, Mug 27.00
Gray, Mug 22.00
Ivory, Ashtray 40.00
Ivory, Bowl, Fruit, 5 1/2 In. 32.00
Ivory, Candleholder, Bulb, Pair 150.00
Ivory, Candleholder, Tripod, Pair 400.00
Ivory, Chop Plate, 13 In. 27.00
Ivory, Creamer, Stick 25.00
Ivory, Plate, 6 In. 4.00
Ivory, Soup, Cream 60.00
Ivory, Tumbler, Water .... 40.00 to 50.00
Light Green, Bowl, Fruit, 5 1/2 In. .... 20.00 to 58.00
Light Green, Carafe 138.00
Light Green, Chop Plate, 13 In. 50.00
Light Green, Cup, Tea 25.00
Light Green, Jar, Cover, Kitchen Kraft, Large 165.00
Light Green, Jar, Cover, Kitchen Kraft, Medium .... 140.00 to 150.00
Light Green, Jar, Cover, Kitchen Kraft, Small 140.00
Light Green, Plate, 6 In. 10.00
Light Green, Salad, Footed 275.00
Light Green, Soup, Cream 42.00
Light Green, Stacking Unit, Kitchen Kraft .... 33.00 to 55.00
Light Green, Tumbler, Juice 40.00
Medium Green, Dessert, 6 In. 375.00
Medium Green, Mug 60.00
Medium Green, Plate, 6 In. 46.00
Medium Green, Plate, 9 In. .... 50.00 to 60.00
Red, Ashtray 45.00

Red, Candleholder, Bulb, Pair ....150.00 to 170.00
Red, Candleholder, Tripod, Pair 400.00
Red, Chop Plate, 13 In. 35.00
Red, Creamer, Stick 25.00
Red, Cup, After Dinner 60.00
Red, Jar, Cover, Kitchen Kraft, Large 80.00
Red, Plate, 6 In. 24.00
Red, Plate, 7 In. 30.00
Red, Plate, 9 In. 22.00
Red, Soup, Cream 60.00
Red, Stacking Unit, Kitchen Kraft 275.00
Red, Sugar & Creamer 70.00
Red, Tumbler, Water 30.00
Rose, Bowl, Fruit, 4 3/4 In. 18.00
Rose, Chop Plate, 13 In. 40.00
Rose, Plate, 6 In. 32.00
Rose, Plate, 7 In. 18.00
Turquoise, Bowl, 5 1/2 In. 25.00
Turquoise, Candleholder, Tripod 450.00
Turquoise, Casserole, Cover, 7 3/4 In. 75.00
Turquoise, Chop Plate, 13 In. ....25.00 to 50.00
Turquoise, Creamer, Stick 37.00
Turquoise, Mug 32.00
Turquoise, Mug, Tom & Jerry 25.00
Turquoise, Plate, 10 In. 25.00
Turquoise, Soup, Cream 42.00
Turquoise, Tumbler, Water 75.00
Yellow, Ashtray 45.00
Yellow, Bowl, Fruit, 5 1/2 In. 25.00
Yellow, Bowl, Salad 85.00
Yellow, Cake Plate, 11 In. 45.00
Yellow, Creamer, Individual 100.00
Yellow, Cup, After Dinner ....50.00 to 60.00
Yellow, Cup, Tea 25.00
Yellow, Jar, Cover, Kitchen Kraft, Medium 170.00
Yellow, Mug 15.00
Yellow, Nappy, 8 1/2 In. 40.00
Yellow, Plate, 6 In. ....4.00 to 8.00
Yellow, Plate, 9 In. 12.00
Yellow, Plate, 10 In. 25.00
Yellow, Salad, Individual 40.00
Yellow, Soup, Cream 42.00
Yellow, Stacking Unit, Kitchen Kraft ....22.00 to 55.00
Yellow, Tumbler, Juice 24.00
Yellow, Tumbler, Water ....27.00 to 40.00

FINCH, see Kay Finch category.

FINDLAY ONYX AND FLORADINE are two similar types of glass made
by Dalzell, Gilmore and Leighton Co. of Findlay, Ohio, about 1889.
Onyx is a patented yellowish white opaque glass with raised silver
daisy decorations. A few rare pieces were made of rose, amber, orange,
or purple glass. Floradine is made of cranberry-colored glass with an
opalescent white raised floral pattern and a satin finish. The same
molds were used for both types of glass.

Creamer, Silver Flowers, Leaves, Opal Handle, 4 1/2 In. 248.00
Pitcher, Floradine, 4 3/4 In. 2130.00
Spooner, 4 1/2 In. 180.00
Sugar Shaker 1290.00
Toothpick, Opal, Silver Flowers, Leaves, 2 1/2 In. 430.00
Tumbler, Silver Flowers, Barrel Shape, 3 3/4 In. ....330.00 to 405.00
Vase, Silver Flowers, 9 In. 805.00
Water Set, Opalescent, Silver Flowers, 7 Piece 2300.00

FIREFIGHTING equipment of all types is wanted, from fire marks to uniforms to toy fire trucks. It is said that every little boy wanted to be a fireman or a train engineer 75 years ago and the collectors today reflect this interest.

Alarm, Cast Iron, Fire Alarm Telegraph Station, Gamewell, No. 173	145.00 to 300.00
Alarm, Cast Iron, Fire Department Of New York, Motor, Bell, Wood Base, 23 In.	764.00
Alarm Box, Gamewell	138.00
Alarm Station, Cast Iron, Samewell Co., Newton, Mass., 68 In.	1295.00
Alarm Transmitter, 60 Brass Code Wheels, Oak Case, Gamewell	4025.00
Ax, Cast Iron, Advertising, Comp. Weldon Fire Co., 9 1/2 In.	104.00
Ax, Chromed Blade, Wooden Handle, Applied Eagle & Swastika, 15 1/4 In.	518.00
Ax, Fire Police, Steel Head, Oak Handle, Leather Belt Carrier, Germany, 15 1/2 In.	62.00
Ax, Hand, Nickel Plated Head, Oak Handle, Germany, 1940s, 15 In.	166.00
Ax, Viking Style, Parade, Aluminum, Maltese Cross, Wood Handle, 28 1/2 In.	86.00
Ax Head, Curved Blade, Diamond Points, 1800s, 8 1/4 x 12 1/2 In.	90.00
Ax Head, Curved Blade, Diamond Points, 1800s, 8 x 13 1/2 In.	120.00
Baton, Presentation, Chris A. Robertson Esq., Saint John, N.B., c.1883	500.00
Bell, Brass, Engraved 12WH, 6 In.	184.00
Bell, Brass, Oak Mount, Coils On Brass Ball Hammer, 8 In.	28.00
Bell, Fire Engine, Chrome, 8 1/2 In.	345.00
Bell, Gamewell, 6 In.	1017.00
Bell, Muffin, Brass, Wood Handle, 3 1/2 x 8 1/2 In.	345.00
Bell, Muffin, Brass, Wood Handle, 5 In.	345.00
Bell, Muffin, Brass, Wood Handle, 5 1/2 x 12 In.	316.00
Bell, Muffin, Brass, Wood Handle, Whalebone Separator, 3 1/2 x 8 1/2 In.	230.00
Belt, Ax Carrier, Black Leather, Steel, Germany, Word War II Era, Size 38 1/2	45.00
Belt, Delta City, Leather, Sliding Bead, Nickel Plated Brass Buckle, 46 1/4 In.	300.00
Belt, Leather, Stitched, Raised Lettering, Huttig Hose Co., 19th Century, 37 In.	115.00
Bridle & Bit, Leather, Red, Maltese Cross In Center	345.00
Broadside, Watchman's Calendar, Framed, Philadelphia, 1841, 19 x 15 In.	115.00
Bucket, Leather Shot, Embossed, Coat Of Arms Decal, White Canvas Lining, 22 In.	86.00
Bucket, Leather, 12 In.	350.00
Bucket, Leather, Black Paint, Red Letters, City Of Lynn, No. 19, 1868, 12 In.	575.00
Bucket, Leather, Cairns	90.00
Bucket, Leather, Copper Rivets, 16 In.	248.00
Bucket, Leather, Gold 2, Handle	130.00
Bucket, Leather, Green Paint, Mustard Lettering, GT. Falls, B&M, Handle	1035.00
Bucket, Leather, Green, E.S. Towle, American, 13 1/4 In.	660.00
Bucket, Leather, Green, T. Cole, Watertown, No. 2	1840.00
Bucket, Leather, Joseph Loring 1811	358.00
Bucket, Leather, Painted, Green, W Currier No. 1, White Lettering, 13 1/2 x 7 3/4 In.	625.00
Bucket, Leather, Painted, State House 27, 13 In.	2750.00
Bucket, Leather, Painted, United Fire Society No. 4, 1837, 12 1/4 In.	565.00
Bucket, Leather, Painted, Varrell, No. 1 & No. 2, 1812, 13 In., Pair	4675.00
Bucket, Leather, Powder Blue Paint, M. Shop 21, Early 19th Century, 17 3/4 In.	1116.00
Bucket, Lexington, Mass	2530.00
Bucket, Painted, State House	2750.00
Bucket, Rubber Over Canvas, Black, Gold 14	430.00
Bucket, Varrell No. 1 & No. 2, Handle, 1812, 13 In., Pair *Illus*	4675.00
Button, Wisconsin Firemen's Tournament, Celluloid, 1905, 1 1/2 In.	60.00
Cap, Parade, Painted, Duck Bill	1100.00
Certificate, Fairmount Fire Engine Co. No. 32, Philadelphia, 1864, 21 x 24 In.	950.00
Dish, Montgomery Hose & S.F.E., No. 1, Liberty Of Reading, Nov. 26, 1908, 6 1/2 In.	35.00
Engine Plate, James Boyd & Bro. Inc., Philadelphia	130.00
Extinguisher, Ceiling Mount, Glass, Shur Spray, Chemical Sprinkler	50.00
Extinguisher, Ceiling Mount, Shur Spray	45.00
Extinguisher, Copper, Brass, Badger's Pony Fire Extinguisher, UL Plaque	80.00
Extinguisher, Dry Chemical, Sphinx Image, Ramses	40.00
Extinguisher, Mounting Bracket, Paper Labels, Boyce, 12 In.	210.00
Extinguisher, Presto, Bucket	46.00
Extinguisher, Rex, Soda Acid Type, 2 1/2 Gal.	35.00
Extinguisher, Tin Tube, Dry Chemical, Contents, Phoenix	25.00
Extinguisher, Tin Tube, Dry Powder Type, Phoenix	50.00

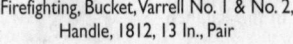

Firefighting, Bucket, Varrell No. 1 & No. 2,
Handle, 1812, 13 In., Pair

Firefighting, Helmet,
Chief, F.F.D., White
Cairns, Aluminum

Fire Alarm, Pillar Box, Peaked Roof, Iron, Cincinnati, 68 In.	1265.00
Fire Mark, Alliance Assurance Co., Copper, London, 9 x 9 In.	50.00
Fire Mark, Cast Iron, Embossed 1794, Clasped Hands, Gold, Black, 10 x 10 In.	385.00
Fire Mark, Cast Iron, FA Fire Mark, Fire Association, 11 1/4 x 7 1/4 In.	90.00
Fire Mark, London Assurance, Incorporated 1720, Felt, Frame, 20 x 16 In.	50.00
Gong, Brass, Plaque, Gamewell Moses Crane Style, 10 x 24 In.	3105.00
Gong, Turtle, Brass, 10 In.	125.00
Grenade, Blue, Quilted, Footed Base, Harden's, Contents, Label	105.00
Grenade, Harden's Hand, Cobalt Blue, Ribs, Sealed, Contents, 6 1/2 In.	90.00
Grenade, Harden's Hand, Star, Aqua, Ribs, Contents, 6 1/2 In.	150.00
Grenade, Harden's Hand, Star, Fire Extinguisher, Turquoise Blue, 6 5/8 In.	50.00
Grenade, Harden's, Star Hand Fire Extinguisher, Blue, Contents, Paper Label	85.00
Grenade, Harden, Footed, Threaded Top	430.00
Grenade, Hardens, Improved, 2 Piece, Patent Oct. 7, 1884	1325.00
Grenade, Hayward, Gray Green, Contents, Patent Aug. 8, 1871	575.00
Grenade, Hayward, Light Green, Medium Size, Contents	315.00
Grenade, Hayward, Pleated Design, Clear, Contents	230.00
Grenade, Kalamazoo, Automatic & Hand Fire Extinguisher, Cobalt Blue	1035.00
Grenade, Yellow, Contents, Systeme Labbe, France	435.00
Helmet, Aluminum, Liner, Leather Front Piece, CRFD, Red, Cairns	127.00
Helmet, Black, Leather, High Eagle, Liner, Cairns & Bro. NY 32, Poughkeepsie, 1886	605.00
Helmet, Black, Leather, High Eagle, Liner, John Olson Co. NY 64, Altoona, 1895	719.00
Helmet, Black, Leather, Liner, Cairns, EFD-1-227	290.00
Helmet, Black, Plastic, Leather Front Piece, Roving Captain NFD	69.00
Helmet, Chief, F.F.D., White Cairns, Aluminum *Illus*	116.00
Helmet, Leather, Embossed Eagle, Cairns & Bro.	110.00
Helmet, Leather, High Eagle, John Olson Company, Riverton Fire Co 1, Felt Liner	405.00
Helmet, Leather, High Eagle, Liner, Yellow, Brass Eagle, Marion 10 Reading, Cairns	1495.00
Helmet, Tin, Brass Front Plate Holder, Cairns & Brothers, Initials BVFD	39.00
Helmet, White Leather, Liner, 64 Comb, High Eagle, Hoboken F.D., 8 In.	545.00
Horn, Silver, Presentation, 1853	6900.00
Kerchief Slide, Cairns, ST, Shield Shape 7, 2 In.	185.00
Key, Fire Alarm, Brass, Wooden Block	290.00
Lamp, Engine, Side Mount, Brass, Ruby Glass, Pair	1100.00
Mug, Doylestown Fire Co., Old Home Week; 1912	20.00
Nozzle, Brass, Copper, AJ Morse Flow Control, Boston, Mass., 1917	127.00
Nozzle, Brass, Flow Control, 8 1/2 In.	50.00
Nozzle, Brass, H.N. Stone, Boston, 39 In.	39.00
Nozzle, Brass, Self Propelling Nozzle Co., New York, Patent 1916	115.00
Photograph, AJ Kennedy, President Int. Assn. Fire Engineers, NJ Car Spring	40.00
Rattle, Alarm, Single Reed, Wooden, Turned Wood Handle	69.00
Rattle, Watchman's, Brass Ends, No. 6 S.G.	115.00
Shield Holder, Beaver Front	1760.00
Sign, Ladder Truck, Lithograph, Cowing & Gleason, Seneca Falls, N.Y., 12 x 19 In.	600.00
Siren, Hand Operated, Sterling	635.00
Torch, Nickel, Brass, For Horse Drawn Fire Apparatus	145.00
Torch, Parade, Nickel, Brass, 3 In.	12.00
Trumpet, Brass, Presentation, 1851	1825.00

Trumpet, Marked, Charlestown 1760.00
Trumpet, Nickel, Brass, Foreman's, Brass Button, No. 2, 20 1/2 In. 430.00
Trumpet, Presentation, Red Cord Tassel, Engraved, Hackensack, N.J., 18 In. 719.00
Trumpet, Silver Metal, Speaking, Presentation, American Eagle, c.1853, 21 In. 6900.00
Trumpet, Silver Plate, Engraved, Fire Pumper, Trumpet, Ax, Monogram, 23 In. 1725.00
Trumpet, Silver, Speaking, Presentation, Tassel, John R. Platt, Melmora, 1862, 17 In. 949.00
Trumpet, Sterling Silver, Presentation, Engraved, 1855, 14 In. 5720.00
Trumpet, Sterling, Protector Engine Co. No. 2, Dorchester, Mass., 1855, 14 1/2 In. 5720.00

FIREPLACES were used to cook food and to heat the American home in
past centuries. Many types of tools and equipment were used.
Andirons held the logs in place, firebacks reflected the heat into the
room, and tongs were used to move either fuel or food. Many types of
spits and roasting jacks were made and may be listed in the Kitchen
category.

Andirons, Aluminum, Iron Arms, Elongated Petal, Scrolled Base, Art Deco, 22 In. 550.00
Andirons, Arts & Crafts, 3 Rooks, Nesting On Tree Stump, Iron, 30 In. 2750.00
Andirons, Arts & Crafts, Hammered Cube, Over 4-Sided Shaft, 18 1/2 x 11 3/4 In. 546.00
Andirons, Arts & Crafts, Rectilinear, Faux Rivets, Log Holder, Stamped 133, 18 x 11 In. . 115.00
Andirons, Arts & Crafts, Rectilinear, Faux Rivets, Stamped 1900, 18 x 11 In. 144.00
Andirons, Bell Metal, Lemon Top, 17 In. 690.00
Andirons, Brass, 4 Domed Feet, Scrolled Legs, Ring Turned Tops, Log Rests, 14 1/2 In. ... 115.00
Andirons, Brass, Ball Feet, Cabriole Legs, Seamed Column, Urn Top, 20 In. 635.00
Andirons, Brass, Ball Finials, Baluster Plinths, American, Early 1800s, 13 x 15 1/2 In. ... 200.00
Andirons, Brass, Ball Top, Log Guards, 15 x 24 In. ....300.00 to 460.00
Andirons, Brass, Ball, Spire Ball & Claw Feet, 26 1/2 x 22 1/4 In. 690.00
Andirons, Brass, Baluster Turned Shafts, Spurred Legs, Ball Feet, 16 1/2 In. 340.00
Andirons, Brass, Baluster, Lion Head Base, Feet, Flame Finial, 23 1/2 In. 115.00
Andirons, Brass, Blade, Iron Base, Donald Deskey, 1960s, 19 1/4 x 8 1/2 x 18 3/4 In. 920.00
Andirons, Brass, Cabriole Legs, Shaped Columns, Lobed Base, Urn Tops, 1900s, 26 In. .. 220.00
Andirons, Brass, Chippendale Style, Engraved, Urn Finial, Plinth Base, 29 In. 400.00
Andirons, Brass, Chippendale Style, Steeple Top, c.1900, 26 1/2 In. 259.00
Andirons, Brass, Chippendale Style, Urn Top Finials, Cabriole Legs, Spurred Knees, 21 In. 280.00
Andirons, Brass, Chippendale, Wrought Iron, Ball Finial, Feet, Late 1700s, 13 1/2 x 16 In. 185.00
Andirons, Brass, Dogs, Wrought Iron, 15 x 21 In. 175.00
Andirons, Brass, Double Lemon Top, John Bailey, c.1815, 23 1/4 x 12 1/4 x 22 1/4 In. ... 120.00
Andirons, Brass, Empire, Beehive Finials, Baluster Shafts, Spurred Legs, 13 1/2 In. 338.00
Andirons, Brass, Federal Style, 8-Sided Plinths, Baluster Turned Post, 24 In. 140.00
Andirons, Brass, Federal Style, Lemon Top, 22 In. 345.00
Andirons, Brass, Federal Style, Octagonal Plinth, Spur Arch, Ball Feet, 21 In. 305.00
Andirons, Brass, Federal, Acorn Finial, Ring-Turned Plinth, c.1820, 22 In. 3345.00
Andirons, Brass, Federal, Arched Supports, Ball Feet, 19 1/2 x 9 3/4 x 14 1/2 In. 230.00
Andirons, Brass, Federal, Iron, Ball Top, Feet, Column Plinths, c.1800, 18 1/2 In. 529.00
Andirons, Brass, Federal, Iron, Urn Top, Faceted Columns, Early 19th Century, 24 5/8 In. 1410.00
Andirons, Brass, Federal, Lemon Top, Log Stops, Arching Ball & Claw Feet, 22 In. 520.00
Andirons, Brass, Federal, Steeple Top, John Bailey, N.Y., c.1800, 19 In. 900.00
Andirons, Brass, Georgian Style, Flame Finials, Scroll Feet, 22 1/2 x 8 x 11 In., Pair 1380.00
Andirons, Brass, Ionic Columns, Wreaths, Cornucopia, Paw Feet, Acanthus Finials, 13 In. 165.00
Andirons, Brass, Iron, Acorn Top, Columns, Engraved Eagle, Late 18th Century, 20 In. .. 940.00
Andirons, Brass, Iron, Ball Top, Square Plinth, Cabriole Legs, Boston, c.1800, 23 In. 881.00
Andirons, Brass, Iron, Federal, Urn, Punchwork Swag, Beaded, Vines, Chevron, 31 In. ... 4112.00
Andirons, Brass, Iron, Federal, Urn-On-Urn Top, Swag, Tassel, Cabriole Leg, 26 x 11 In. . 940.00
Andirons, Brass, Iron, Lemon Top, Early 19th Century, 15 1/2 x 8 3/8 x 16 In. 600.00
Andirons, Brass, Iron, Lemon Top, Tapered Column, Square Plinth, 18th Century, 23 In. . 4406.00
Andirons, Brass, Iron, Urn Top, Knife Blade, Shield, Penny Feet, 18th Century, 23 In. ... 999.00
Andirons, Brass, Lacquered, Cabriole Legs, Tapered Columns, Urn Tops, 1900s, 24 In. ... 182.00
Andirons, Brass, Lemon Top, Turned Shafts, Cabriole Legs, Ball Feet, 19 1/2 In. 253.00
Andirons, Brass, Polished, Boston Ball Top, Log Stops, 16 1/2 x 19 x 11 In., Pair 305.00
Andirons, Brass, Queen Anne Style, Ball Finial, Feet, Scroll Legs, Williamsburg, 18 In. ... 315.00
Andirons, Brass, Queen Anne, Steeple & Urn Tops, 20 x 20 In. 290.00
Andirons, Brass, Turned Standards, American, 19 In., Pair 115.00
Andirons, Brass, Urn Finial, Cabriole Legs, Ball & Claw Feet, Phila., 1700s, 25 In. 2250.00
Andirons, Bronze, George Washington, Figural, American, 1800s, 20 1/4 x 19 In. 1410.00

Andirons, Bronze, Louis XV Style, Gilt, 19th Century, 14 1/2 In. 470.00
Andirons, Bronze, Louis XVI Style, Gilt, Blue Paint, 17 In. 1650.00
Andirons, Bronze, Peacock, Verdigris, 8-Sided Base, Ball Perch, Iron, 32 x 35 In. 5600.00
Andirons, Cast Iron, Arched Base, Reeded Pedestal, 18th Century, 15 1/2 In. 1375.00
Andirons, Cast Iron, Ball Top, 22 In. 52.00
Andirons, Cast Iron, Black Cat, Seated, Glass Eyes, Scroll Base, Early 1900s, 17 In. 355.00
Andirons, Cast Iron, Black Man, Hands On Knees, 18 1/2 In. 705.00
Andirons, Cast Iron, Boston Bull Terrier, Howes, American, c.1900, 17 x 7 x 17 In. 355.00
Andirons, Cast Iron, Brass, Donald Deskey, Bennett, 7 1/2 x 18 x 15 1/2 In. 2415.00
Andirons, Cast Iron, Cat, Seated, Glass Eyes, Scrolled, Footed Base, 17 1/2 In. 220.00
Andirons, Cast Iron, Christmas Tree, Brass Finials, 10 In. 90.00
Andirons, Cast Iron, Dogs, St. Bernards, c.1880, 12 x 13 In. 495.00
Andirons, Cast Iron, Fleur-De-Lis Top, No. 3539, Bradley & Hubbard, 28 In. 90.00
Andirons, Cast Iron, Hessian Soldier, 19th Century, 19 3/4 In. 1910.00
Andirons, Cast Iron, Hessian, Striding Position, Red Coat, Helmet, Saber, 19 3/4 In. 750.00
Andirons, Cast Iron, Indian Braves, Figural, Late 19th Century, 20 x 19 In. 4255.00
Andirons, Cast Iron, Owl Form, Glass Eyes, Stand, Tongs, 14 In. 150.00
Andirons, Cast Iron, Owl Glass Inset Eyes, 15 In. 359.00
Andirons, Cast Iron, Ringed Tops, Reeded Columns, Arched Feet, 12 x 12 In. 375.00
Andirons, Cast Iron, Sailing Ship, Double Fluted Anchor, 19 x 19 x 10 1/2 In. 400.00
Andirons, Federal, Brass, Wrought Iron, Knife Blade, Early 19th Century, 23 In. 1495.00
Andirons, Federal, Engraved, Urn Shape Finials, Classical Column, c.1810 .... 21510.00
Andirons, Federal, Knife Blade, Turned Brass Finial, Penny Feet, 19 1/2 In. 169.00
Andirons, Figural, Mythical Birds, Boy Carrying Bowl Of Flames, Bronze, 21 In. 85.00
Andirons, Figural, Winged, 2 Griffin Base, Bronze, Baluster, 19th Century, 37 In., Pair ... 1150.00
Andirons, Fire Tools, Screen, Chippendale, Brass, Ring & Urn Turned, c.1825, 24 In. 10160.00
Andirons, Georgian Style, Urn Form Finial, Ionic Column, Early 1900s, 23 1/2 In. 750.00
Andirons, Iron, Arts & Crafts, Forged, American, Early 1900s, 22 In. 225.00
Andirons, Iron, Brass Finial, Knife Blade, Penny Feet, Arching Legs, 21 In. 660.00
Andirons, Iron, Brass, Lemon Finials, Hand Forged Joint, Arched Feet, 21 1/2 In. 110.00
Andirons, Iron, Brass, Orb Finials, Adjustable Spit Hooks, c.1800, 18 1/2 x 27 In. 575.00
Andirons, Iron, Hammered, Arts & Crafts, Cannonball, Arched Feet, 9 x 22 x 13 In. 490.00
Andirons, Iron, Hammered, Raised Diamond, Bradley & Hubbard, 11 x 21 x 23 In. 690.00
Andirons, Iron, Hammered, Strap & Rivet Details, Arts & Crafts, 10 x 17 x 18 In. 315.00
Andirons, Iron, Horseshoe Form, Iron Crop, 23 x 21 x 21 In. 330.00
Andirons, Iron, Keyhole, Leaf Work On Stems, 11 1/2 In. 60.00
Andirons, Iron, Nickel Plated, Owl, Glass Eyes, 1870-1880, 13 x 17 x 8 In. ......275.00 to 308.00
Andirons, Iron, Outlaw Cowboy, Bowlegged, Ready To Draw Guns, 19 1/4 In. 1495.00
Andirons, Iron, Posset Potholders, Scrolled, Spit Hook Holders, Penny Style Feet, 24 In. . . 115.00
Andirons, Iron, Renaissance Style, Seated Lion Finial, 49 In. 4780.00
Andirons, Iron, Woman, 19th Century, 12 x 10 1/2 In. 415.00
Andirons, Metal, Chippendale, Steeple Top, Bell, 18th Century, 24 x 19 In. 430.00
Andirons, Old Boston Style, Brass Ball Top, Octagonal Stems, 1800s, 19 In. 230.00
Andirons, Poker, Shovel, Tongs, Fluted Shaft, Chippendale, Daniel King, c.1770, 26 In. ... 3345.00
Andirons, Sheet & Cast Iron, Renaissance Revival Style, Late 1800s, 29 x 9 x 27 In. 345.00
Andirons, Wrought Iron, Arched Bases, Shoe Feet, Flat Columns, Knob Finials, 19 1/2 In. 345.00
Andirons, Wrought Iron, Arts & Crafts, Riveted, 30 x 39 In. 705.00
Andirons, Wrought Iron, Brass, Shaped Urn Front, Brass Plate, Finials, 18 3/4 In. 660.00
Andirons, Wrought Iron, Brass, Urn Form Finial, Spit Hooks, Arched Feet, 31 In. 520.00
Andirons, Wrought Iron, Forge Welded Legs, Rosehead Rivets, 14 x 18 1/2 x 11 In. 250.00
Andirons, Wrought Iron, Lacquered Finish, Penny Feet, Arts & Crafts, 21 In. 110.00
Andirons, Wrought Iron, Medieval Revival, Cast, Tapered, Ball Finial, c.1920, 48 In. 460.00
Andirons, Wrought Iron, Paneled Brass, Baronial Style, Edwardian, c.1900, 26 In. 175.00
Andirons, Wrought Iron, Welded Legs, Riveted Log Holders, 14 x 18 x 11 In. 250.00
Andirons, Wrought Metal, Spade Shape, Gilt Figure, Palmetto Tree, 16 In. 145.00
Bellows, 2 Face, Leather, Wrought Iron, 68 x 36 x 24 In. 110.00
Bellows, Brass, Mahogany, Mechanical, England, 28 In. 460.00
Bellows, Chinoiserie Design, Green Paint, 18 1/2 In. 315.00
Bellows, Flowers, Stenciled, Painted, Gilt, Faux Rosewood, 17 In. 86.00
Bellows, Fruit, Green, Black, Red Leaves, Yellow Ground, Brass Spout, 17 In. 145.00
Bellows, Leaves, Fruits, Mustard Paint, 19 1/4 In. 345.00
Bellows, Stenciled, Green Ground, 18 In. 200.00
Bellows, Turtle Back, Basket Of Fruit, Leaves, Brass Nozzle, Mustard Paint, 18 1/4 In. 200.00

Bellows, Turtle Back, Cornucopia, Stenciled Fruit, Leaves, Painted, Brass, 19 In. 525.00
Bellows, Turtle Back, Flowers, Leather, Gold & Black, 18 In. 230.00
Bellows, Turtle Back, Red Paint, Gold Fruit, Leaves, Turned Brass Spout, 17 1/2 In. 175.00
Bellows, Turtle Back, Red, Green Paint, Chrome Yellow Details, 1800s, 18 1/4 In., Pair . .   80.00
Bellows, Wooden, Painted Yellow, Stenciled Harvest, Ruth Black, 11 1/4 In. 138.00
Chenet, Andirons, Bronze, Winged Griffins, 16 In. 145.00
Chenet, Andirons, Cherub, Bronze, 12 In., Pair 1469.00
Chenet, Andirons, Gilt Bronze, Louis XVI Style, Putto On Balustrade, 13 1/4 In. 1016.00
Chenet, Andirons, Merman, Bronze, 16 x 18 In. 3955.00
Coal Bin, Art Nouveau, Marquetry Inlaid, 34 In. 1760.00
Coal Hod, Brass, Copper, Metal Liner, Slant Top, Handles, Paw Feet, 22 1/2 In. 110.00
Coal Hod, Brass, Footed, Curved Body, Repousse Flowers, Shovel, 17 x 19 x 13 In. 100.00
Coal Scuttle, Cast Iron, Footed, Enameled Lid, Green, 10 1/2 x 13 1/2 x 20 In. 55.00
Coal Scuttle, Mahogany, Inlaid Wood, Brass Handles, Trim, Scoop, 18 x 13 x 12 1/2 In. .   225.00
Coal Scuttle, Oak, Metal Inner Liner, Early 20th Century, 15 x 15 In. 195.00
Coal Scuttle, Scoop, Iron, Late 19th Century, 19 x 14 x 7 In. 55.00
Fender, Brass & Steel, Serpentine, Scrolled Wire Design, 15 x 54 In. 430.00
Fender, Brass & Wire, 10 1/4 x 45 1/2 In. 605.00
Fender, Brass & Wire, 21 x 34 x 14 In. 978.00
Fender, Brass & Wire, 3 Turned Finials, 15 1/2 x 45 x 16 In. 978.00
Fender, Brass & Wire, Ball Finials, 1800s, 56 In. 1000.00
Fender, Brass & Wire, D-Form, Swag Design, 10 x 45 1/2 In. 805.00
Fender, Brass & Wire, Late 19th Century, 9 x 41 1/2 x 12 In. 145.00
Fender, Brass & Wire, Rail, Scroll Design, 12 1/2 x 90 1/2 In. 999.00
Fender, Brass & Wire, Scrolled Design, Early 1800s, 10 1/2 x 48 3/4 x 18 3/4 In. 489.00
Fender, Brass & Wire, Serpentine, Scroll Design, 1790-1840, 16 1/4 x 54 7/8 In. 3175.00
Fender, Brass Footed, Pierced, 13 x 41 x 12 In. 230.00
Fender, Brass, 3 Parts, Adjustable Center Railing, Urn Ends, Lion Heads, 56 x 34 x 15 In.   460.00
Fender, Brass, Acorn Finials, Wire Front, Curved Front, c.1900, 25 1/2 x 42 In. 1380.00
Fender, Brass, D-Form, Reticulated Leaves & Flowers, Georgian Style, c.1900, 48 1/2 In.   288.00
Fender, Brass, Geometric Piercings, Rosettes, Lion's-Head Feet, 54 x 14 x 11 In. 259.00
Fender, Brass, Iron, 19th Century, 14 x 39 In. 300.00
Fender, Brass, Pierced, 19th Century, 9 1/2 x 47 1/4 x 8 In. 978.00
Fender, Brass, Pierced, 9 1/2 x 42 x 9 In. 865.00
Fender, Brass, Pierced, Bun Feet, 44 In. 575.00
Fender, Brass, Pierced, Garland Design, Turned Posts, Hepplewhite Style, 53 In. 520.00
Fender, Brass, Pierced, Tool Stand, 20 1/2 x 36 3/4 x 15 In. 1064.00
Fender, Brass, Reticulated, Cast Applied Paw Feet, 8 3/4 x 60 In. 195.00
Fender, Brass, Reticulated, Lion's Mask Corners, 11 1/4 x 37 1/4 x 13 In. 345.00
Fender, Brass, Ribbed Moldings, Blocked Feet, Mid 19th Century, 7 x 41 x 8 1/4 In. 520.00
Fender, Brass, Serpentine Rail, Turned Knopped Supports, 20 x 54 In. 805.00
Fender, Brass, Serpentine, Pierced, Medallions, Iron Base, 20th Century, 49 x 17 In. 230.00
Fender, Brass, Sheet Iron, Belle Epoque, c.1900, 10 x 42 x 9 1/4 In. 520.00
Fender, Brass, Swags, Pierced, Cartouche On Corners, Louis XV Style, 7 5/8 x 51 1/2 In.   978.00
Fender, Brass, Tassel Feet, 10 x 56 x 13 1/2 In. 1725.00
Fender, Brass, Urn Finials, 9 x 49 1/2 x 12 3/8 In. 1208.00
Fender, Brass, Wirework, Serpentine, Georgian Style, c.1890, 13 x 36 x 12 In. 345.00
Fender, Bronze, Patinated, Neoclassical, Parcel Gilt, Pierced, c.1820, 8 x 41 In. 635.00
Fender, Copper Frame, Cushions, Leather Lift Top Tools, England, 15 x 16 In. 690.00
Fender, Cut, Cast Brass, D-Form, 3 Stylized Paw Feet, 8 1/2 x 51 x 13 In. 460.00
Fender, English Oak, Spiraled Rail, Turned Posts, 19th Century, 8 x 54 x 15 In. 248.00
Fender, Gilt Brass, Steel, Restauration, Cut, 19th Century, 6 3/4 x 34 3/4 x 2 1/4 In. 978.00
Fender, Iron, Hammered, Bronze Wash, 3 Horizontal Bars, 6 Columns, 43 x 12 x 10 In. . .   315.00
Fender, Jamb Tool Holder, Tools, Pierced Brass, D-Shape, Paw Feet, 48 x 13 1/2 In. 660.00
Fender, Steel, Brass, Lattice & Rope, 38 In. 29.00
Fender & Tool Set, Brass, Regency Style, 42 x 12 1/2 x 9 In., 5 Piece 489.00
Fire Cone, Cast Iron, Fleur-De-Lis, 16 x 19 x 12 1/2 In. 375.00
Fire Starter, Tin, Tansey's Fire Kindler, 6 x 10 In. 130.00
Fireback, Cast Iron, Cavalier On Horseback, Relief, 43 1/2 x 28 In. 275.00
Fireback, Cast Iron, Eagles, Serpents, 24 x 22 1/2 In., Pair 805.00
Fireback, Cast Iron, Urn, Flowers, Vines, Handles, 28 x 24 In. 805.00
Fireboard, Oil, On Panel, Green Louvers, Cream Surround, 1830-1850, 39 1/2 x 53 In. . . .   765.00
Goffer, Forged, Footed Cast Tripod Base, S-Standard, 10 x 7 In.   120.00

Grate, Wrought Iron, Iron Brush, Early 1900s, 17 x 16 1/2 In. 310.00
Griddle, Cast Iron, Revolving Hanger, 3-Footed, 13 x 12 In. 90.00
Gridiron, Circular, Revolving, Tripod, Handle, 3 1/4 x 22 1/2 In. 415.00
Guard, Bronze, Patinated, Gilt, Charles X, 10 x 38 x 2 1/2 In. 1035.00
Hearth Set, Brass, Fire Dogs, Pierced Fire Fender, 3 Tools, Early 20th Century, 6 Piece . .   405.00
Insert, Iron, Brass, Split Column, Empire Style Finials, Ash Pan, 23 1/2 x 32 x 14 In. 305.00
Insert, Softwood, Frame Molded Case, Cornice, Gray, Maroon, 36 1/2 x 38 1/2 In. 2925.00
Log Holder, Bronze, 8 Uprights, 2 Crescents, Albert Paley, 36 1/2 x 72 x 25 In. 6900.00
Log Holder, Cast Iron, Fire Basket, No. H606, G. Nelson, Howard Miller, 21 x 9 In. 690.00
Log Holder, Cast Iron, Turned Brass Finials, 16 1/2 x 27 x 12 1/2 In. 200.00
Log Holder, Stickley Brothers, No. 152, 5 Vertical Slats, Copper Trim, 18 x 19 x 20 In. . .   865.00
Mantel is listed in the Architectural category.
Plate Warmer, Cast Iron, 18th Century 2250.00
Screen, Arts & Crafts, 3 Panels, Floral Carving, Inscriptions, 36 x 27 In. 1150.00
Screen, Black Forest, Tapestry, German Word Friede, 19th Century 990.00
Screen, Brass, Peacock Fan, Griffin Fronted Frame, France, 26 1/2 In. 145.00
Screen, Brass, Wire Mesh, Folding, Swag & Scroll Design, 30 1/4 x 42 In. 2300.00
Screen, Burled Walnut, Renaissance Revival, Gilt, Mid 19th Century, 47 x 30 x 16 In. . . .   805.00
Screen, Cast Iron, Rococo Openwork, Vining, Scrolls, 3 Panels, 39 x 27 In. 140.00
Screen, Chenet, Rococo, Cast Brass, Wire Mesh, 31 x 29 In., 3 Piece 2150.00
Screen, Fan Shape, Retractable, 20th Century, 29 x 39 In. 340.00
Screen, Faux Bamboo, R.J. Honer, c.1890, 50 1/2 x 35 In. 1207.00
Screen, Indian, Headdress, Mixed Wood, Polychrome, Gary Birch, 24 x 27 1/2 In. 1150.00
Screen, Iron, Hand Forged, Wire Mesh, Scroll, Flowers, Birds, 43 x 39 x 16 In. 2465.00
Screen, Iron, Peacock Fan, Scroll, Strap Feet, Twisted Handle, 27 x 24 x 5 1/2 In. 275.00
Screen, Louis XVI Style, Carved Walnut, Needlework Panel, 41 x 27 In. 896.00
Screen, Louis XVI Style, Gilt Wood, Petit & Gros Point Panel, 45 1/2 x 29 1/2 In. 896.00
Screen, Mahogany, Chinese Silk Needlework, Queen Anne Style, c.1900, 55 x 14 In. 865.00
Screen, Mahogany, Needlepoint Insert, Scroll Feet, Carved, 39 1/2 x 27 In. 495.00
Screen, Mahogany, Sliding Side Extensions, Brass, Regency, 49 1/4 x 28 In. 345.00
Screen, Mahogany, Stick & Ball, Canvas Panel, Classical Figures, 51 x 26 x 12 In. 140.00
Screen, Mahogany, Tapestry, Louis Philippe, Scrolling Crest, c.1850, 42 1/2 x 25 In. 1035.00
Screen, Needlework Emblem, Renaissance Style, Continental, c.1860, 43 x 28 x 14 In. . . .   86.00
Screen, Pierced Flower, Engraved, Fleur-De-Lis Mounts, 1800s, 26 x 22 In. 400.00
Screen, Pole, George III Style, Mahogany, Flemish Tapestry Panel, Tripod, 59 x 18 In. . . .   805.00
Screen, Pole, Mahogany, Adjustable Drop Leaf, c.1850, 58 In. 410.00
Screen, Pole, Queen Anne Style, Needlework Flower, Mahogany Frame, 51 In. 460.00
Screen, Pole, Walnut, Needlepoint Panel, Scotsman, Tripod, Snake Feet, 59 In. 115.00
Screen, Rosewood, Fabric Panel, William IV, c.1830, 41 1/2 x 22 x 16 In. 575.00
Screen, Rosewood, Figural Carved, Scenic Needlepoint, 58 1/2 In, Pair 1265.00
Screen, Rosewood, Needlework, Beadwork, Barley Twist Base, c.1865, 64 In. 1035.00
Screen, Wirework, Mesh, 3 Panels, 23 x 31 x 1/2 In. 489.00
Screen, Wrought Iron, Copper Center Shield, Arts & Crafts, 25 1/2 x 21 1/4 In. 140.00
Stand, Hearth, Wrought Iron, 11 Meat Hooks, 32 3/4 x 59 In. 660.00
Stand, Kettle, Brass, Iron, Pierced Scalloped Apron, Penny Feet, 15 x 13 1/4 In. 56.00
Surround, Cast Iron, Victorian, Mantle, Early 1900s, 42 x 46 x 6 In. 260.00
Surround, Marble, Green, Blue, Flower Molding, Carved Heads, 50 x 65 x 10 1/2 In. 9460.00
Surround, Marble, Louis XVI Style, 52 x 49 In. 956.00
Surround, Marble, Rouge Royale, Canted Legs, Louis XV Style, 48 x 59 x 18 In. 3450.00
Surround, Painted Crowns, Doves, Mortised, Pegged, Scandinavia, c.1830, 82 x 52 In. 1410.00
Surround, Renaissance Revival, Burled Walnut, c.1865, 52 1/2 x 61 In. 750.00
Surround, Wood, Mortise & Tenon, Arched Top Lintel, c.1820, 47 x 60 In. 440.00
Surround & Shelf, Blue Gray Paint, 1800s, 61 x 50 1/2 In. 230.00
Surround & Shelf, Red Paint, Rectangular Shelf, Molded Pilasters, 51 3/4 x 68 In. 345.00
Tinder Lighter, Brass, Wood, Pistol Form, Engraved Flowers, Burgess, 4 x 5 In. 518.00
Tongs, Iron, Boot & Leg Shape, 12 1/2 In. 220.00
Tool Set, Andirons, Lemon Top, Brass Finial, Shovel, Poker, Chippendale Style 280.00
Tool Set, Andirons, Tools, Fender, Turned Brass, Wire, Serpentine, 20 & 58 In. 1840.00
Tool Set, Bronze, Polished Brass Finish, Albert Paley, 36 1/4 x 21 x 10 1/4 In. 4313.00
Tool Set, Fender, Andirons, Chrome, Copperplated Brass, Art Deco, 1940, 6 Piece 1840.00
Tool Set, Raised Diamond, Stand, Bradley & Hubbard, 12 x 8 x 31 In., 5 Piece 920.00
Tool Set, Renaissance Style, Gilt Bronze, 3 Tools, 36 In. 538.00
Tool Set, Stand, Brush, Shovel, Poker, Log Tongs, Albert Paley, 67 x 20 In., 5 Piece 9200.00

Tool Set, Steel, Travertine, Rosewood, England, Alessandro Albrizzi, c.1968, 10 x 35 In. . 1755.00
Tool Set, Wood Box, Brass Clad, Lion Mask Handles, 20 x 16 x 7 In., 5 Piece 175.00
Trammel, Wrought Iron, Sawtooth, 22 In. 195.00
Trivet, Heart, Wrought Iron, 36 x 9 5/8 In. 280.00
Wood Box, Scalloped Ends, Lift Lid, Strap Hinges, Dovetailed Drawers, Mustard Paint . . 900.00

FISCHER porcelain was made in Herend, Hungary, by Moritz Fischer.
The factory was founded in 1839 and continued working into the twentieth century. The wares are sometimes referred to as *Herend* porcelain.

MF

Candelabrum, 5-Light, 2 Putti, Reticulated Base, Puce, Gilt, White, Marked, 16 1/2 In. . . . 431.00
Dinner Service, Chinese Bouquet Green, 44 Piece 2530.00
Ewer, Moorish Style, Reticulated, Hungary, c.1910, 18 3/4 In. 705.00
Figurine, Bisque, Boy & Dog, 6 3/4 In. 62.00
Figurine, Hand Painted, Depicting Woman & Harvest Basket, 9 x 3 In. 110.00
Figurine, Parrot, Blue Mark, Incised, 9 3/4 In., Pair 920.00
Figurine, Rothschild Bird, 71 Piece 3680.00
Figurine, Woman, Harvest Basket On Back, Hand Painted, 9 x 3 In. 100.00
Plate, Salad, Rothschild Bird, Herend, 8 1/4 In., 10 Piece 575.00
Teapot, Birds, Flowers, Butterflies, Bugs, Herend, 20th Century, 4 In. 207.00
Tureen, Mandarin, Lemon Finial, Applied Flowers, Chinese Red, Cover, c.1950, 13 x 8 In. 460.00
Vase, Cylindrical Neck, Egg Shape, Hungary, Late 1800s, 12 1/2 In. 355.00

FISHING reels of brass or nickel were made in the United States by
1810. Bamboo fly rods were sold by 1860, often marked with the
maker's name. Lures made of metal, or metal and wood, were made in
the nineteenth century. Plastic lures were made by the 1930s. All fishing material is collected today and even equipment of the past thirty
years is of interest if in good condition with original box.

Bucket, Minnow, Shakespeare, Honor Built, No. 7780, Metal Handles, 17 x 16 In. 85.00
Cabinet, Lure Display, 3 Drawers, Magazine Rack Top, 3 Painted Names, 17 x 25 x 48 In. 28.00
Canoe Seat, Rattan, Folding, Leather Covered Legs, Under Seat Storage 39.00
Catalog, Creek Chub Bait Co., Color, Dingbat, Champ, Wee-Dee, 1937, 31 Pages 220.00
Catalog, Heddon, Lures, Rods, Baits, 1939, 44 Pages 248.00
Creel, Camp Or Canoe, Woven Reed, Belt Buckle Lid Latch, 13 x 18 x 13 In. 70.00
Creel, Cedar, Curved Back, Leather Strap, Handmade, Maine 330.00
Creel, George Lawrence Co., Split Willow, Tooled Leather, Pouch, Portland, Oregon 1650.00
Creel, George Lawrence Co., Whole Willow, Leather, Portland, Oregon 1320.00
Creel, Masonite Corp., Birchbark, Basket Weave, Leather Hinges, 8 1/2 x 11 1/2 In. 90.00
Creel, Splint, Green Paint, 6 1/2 In. 2185.00
Creel, Tight Rattan Weave, High Turtle, Bulbous, 5 1/2 x 13 x 6 1/2 In. 303.00
Creel, Whitney Sporting Goods, Harness, Colorado 1200.00
Creel, Wicker, Decorative Front Weaving, Lift-Out Tray, Sliding Peg Latch 660.00
Creel, Wicker, Woven, Leather, Shoulder Strap, Canvas Pouch, Hooks, 9 x 19 x 7 1/2 In. . 196.00
Creel, Wood, Demilune Shape, Leather Loops, Metal Rings, 1800s, 14 1/2 x 7 1/2 In. 1210.00
Fish Scaler, Rock-It, Automatic, Tow Behind Boat, 10 x 21 In. 90.00
Float, Pequa, Red, White & Blue, Strasburg, Pa., 13 In. 440.00
Fly, Richard Talleur, Mickey Finn Streamer, Cherry Frame, Mat 95.00
Fly, Salmon, Jerome Francis Molloy, Full Dressed, Container, St. John, New Brunswick . . 55.00
Fly Case, Hardy Brothers, Neroda, Tortoiseshell, England, 1930s 400.00
Fly Tying Chest, 6 Aluminum Drawers, Bottle Rack, Contents, 12 x 17 x 18 In. 55.00
Fly Tying Kit, Leather Wallet, Folding, Tools, Thread, Hook Containers, Italy 85.00
Fly Tying Vise, Bill Hunter, Stainless Steel, Limited Edition, HMH, Mahogany Box, 1970s 525.00
Gaff, Hardy, Brass, Telescopic, Lignum Handle 165.00
Gaff, Iron Hook, Wood Handle, Handmade, c.1850, 14 In. 198.00
Gaff, Marble's, Arms, Clinching, Trout Nippers, Handheld, Gladstone, Mich., c.1915 . . . . 440.00
Gaff, Shakespeare, Aluminum, Hand 94.00
Ice Saw, Spud, Metal, Heart Shaped Spud Holder, 16 In. 165.00
Knife, Abercrombie & Fitch, Priest, Scaler, Wood Handle Scale 140.00
Knife, E.V. Hofe, Russell Green River Works, Scaler, Wood Handle, Sheath, 4-In. Blade . . 85.00
Knife, H.L. Leonard Rod Co., Priest, Brass, Wood Handle, 6 1/2 In. 110.00
Knife, Puma, Priest, Scaler, Kilo Marked Scale 70.00
Knife, Schrade, Uncle Henry, Leather Sheath, Original Papers & Box 77.00
Knife, Stainless Steel, Serrated Blade, Disgorger, Metal Rule, Luna, Italy 10.00

License, 1929, Pennsylvania Non-Resident, Pinback Button, Green, Blue, White 170.00
License, 1943, Pennsylvania Non-Resident, Pinback Button, 3-Day, Blue & White 100.00
Line Dryer, Brass, Collapsible, Mahogany Base, Revolving Plate Reel, 11 In. Frame 210.00
Line Dryer, E.V. Hofe, Brass, Collapsible, C-Clamp 195.00
Lure, Abbey & Imbrie, Glowbody Minnow, Glass Tube, c.1920 . . . . 60.00
Lure, Arbogast, Tin Liz, Perch Finish, Glass Eyes, Paper, Box, 2 1/4 In. 165.00
Lure, Archer, Wakeman, Trolling Hook, Devon Style, Mounted, Oak Case, Patent 1879 . . 525.00
Lure, Bite-Em-Bate Co., Bite-Em Water Mole, Type 2, Metal Spoon On Underside, 3 In. . 50.00
Lure, Byler, Muskie-Duc, Wood Duck Shape, Metal Wings, Yellow Body, Paper, Box 550.00
Lure, Calkin, Minnow, Split Tail, Raised Eyes, Feathered Tail Hook, 4 1/2 In. 1155.00
Lure, Chapman & Son, Pike Spinner, Copper Finish, Oval, Size 3, Rochester, N.Y. 28.00
Lure, Charmer Minnow, Gold, Red Stripe, Glass Eyes, German Silver Props, c.1910 . . . . . 300.00
Lure, Cod Or Halibut, Fish Shape, Lead, Gill & Fin Details, Treble Hook, 9 In. 22.00
Lure, Creek Chub, Beetle, Black, Red & Yellow Wing Finish, Bead Eyes, 2 Pearl Spinners 85.00
Lure, Creek Chub, Dinger, Glass Eyes, Red Side, Brass Head Plate & Hook Hanger, Box . 165.00
Lure, Creek Chub, Giant Jointed Pikie, Tack Eyes, Blue Flash Finish, Box 70.00
Lure, Creek Chub, Husky Ding-Bat, No. 5300, Pikie Scale Finish, Glass Eyes 155.00
Lure, Donaly, Jersey Wow, Hand Painted, White, Black, Red, Bloomfield, N.J., 3 In. 220.00
Lure, Donaly, Red Fin Floater, Oversized Front Prop, Hand Painted, c.1916, 2 3/4 In. 110.00
Lure, Donaly, Red Fin Minnow, Glass Eyes, Metal Flappers, Hand Painted, c.1911 . . . . . . 1540.00
Lure, F.C. Woods, Expert Minnow, 3 Hooks, Round Body, c.1904, 3 In. 195.00
Lure, F.C. Woods, Expert Minnow, 5 Hooks, Green Back, Red Sides, Gold Belly, 3 3/4 In. 220.00
Lure, Florida Casting Bait Co., Pemberton Busy Bait, Fat Body, 2 1/2 In. 60.00
Lure, Frederick Flood, Florida Spinner, Green, Gold, Metal Fins, Screw Eyes, Box, 6 In. . 1760.00
Lure, G.M. Skinner, Turkey Wing Spinner, No. 15, Feathered Treble, 2 1/8 In. 330.00
Lure, Haas, Liv-Minno, 3-Section Body, c.1939, 4 1/4 In. 160.00
Lure, Heddon, Crab Wiggler, No. 1800, Flyer, Instructions, Leaping Bass Box, 3 7/8 In. . . 250.00
Lure, Heddon, Dowagiac Minnow, No. 0, Glass Eyes, 5 Sides 149.00
Lure, Heddon, Dowagiac Minnow, No. 100, Slim Body, White, Wood Box, c.1910 . . . . . . 1210.00
Lure, Heddon, Dowagiac Minnow, No. 150, Painted Eyes, Flyer, Box 90.00
Lure, Heddon, Musky Vamp, Glass Eyes, White Body, Green & Red Dots 825.00
Lure, Heddon, Musky Vamp, No. 7600, Glass Eyes, Green Scale Finish, 1925-1930 . . . . . 825.00
Lure, Heddon, Musky Vamp, No. 7600, Red Head, White, Glitter, Box 770.00
Lure, Heddon, Punkinseed, No. 730, Bluegill Finish, Box 160.00
Lure, Heddon, Punkinseed, No. 740, 2 Piece Hardware, Crappie Finish 90.00
Lure, Heddon, S.O.S. Wounded Minnow, Glass Eyes, 2 Piece Hardware, Flyer, Box 190.00
Lure, Heddon, Spin Diver, No. 3000, Glass Eyes, L-Rig Hardware, Leaping Bass Box . . . 2750.00
Lure, Heddon, Vampire, No. 7300, Glass Eyes, Jointed, Perch Finish, L-Rig Hardware . . . 70.00
Lure, Heddon, Vampire, No. 7500, Glass Eyes, L-Rig Hardware, Green Scale Finish, Box 165.00
Lure, Heddon, Vampire, No. 7500, Glass Eyes, L-Rig Hardware, Pike Scale Finish, Box . . 250.00
Lure, Heddon, Weedless Widow, No. 220, 2 Piece Hardware, Box, 2 3/4 In. 330.00
Lure, Hendryx, Snake Wood Minnow, Green, Red Spiral Metal Fin, Treble Hook, 3 In. . . . 415.00
Lure, James Harvey, Mouse, Molded Plastic, Red Herringbone Fin, Weighted, 2 3/4 In. . . 39.00
Lure, Jim Pfeffer, Orlando Shiner, Hand Carved, Green, Silver, Yellow, 2 Props, 4 In. 116.00
Lure, Joe E. Pepper, Fish Spinner, Wood, Aluminum Belly, 1900s, 4 In. 1100.00
Lure, Joe E. Pepper, Revolving Minnow, Adjustable Fins, Yellow, Red, c.1911, 3 1/4 In. . . 385.00
Lure, Joe E. Pepper, Roman Spider, White, Red Head, Yellow Eyes, Thread Legs, 3 In. . . 300.00
Lure, Johnson, Automatic Striker, Green Scales, Swing-Away Hook, Red Hair, 2 1/4 In. . . 165.00
Lure, K&K Animated Minnow, Metal Tail, Glass Eyes, 1907 Patent, Flyer, Box 6710.00
Lure, Lane, Automatic Minnow, Brown & White, Wire, Shipping Box, c.1913, 3 1/4 In. . . 4290.00
Lure, Lowell Calkin, Frog, Hollow Body, Molded Wire Line Ties, 3 3/4 In. 1210.00
Lure, Lowell Calkin, Minnow, Hollow Body, Molded Details & Line Ties, 6 1/4 In. 1155.00
Lure, McCagg, Barney Bait Frog, Long Front Prop, Celluloid-Top Box, 2 1/4 In. 70.00
Lure, Musky Sucker Bait Co., Flexie Bait, Rubber, Glass Eyes, Instructions, Box, 10 In. . . 80.00
Lure, Oliver & Gruber, Glowworm, Red & White, Jointed, Metal Diving Lip, 4 1/2 In. 195.00
Lure, Outing, Getum, Hollow Metal, Detachable Hooks, Green, White, Box 275.00
Lure, Pflueger, All In One, Glass Eyes, Bulldog Marked Lip, 1911 . . . . 358.00
Lure, Pflueger, Catalina, Second Style Round Body, Glass Eyes, Canoe Box, 4 1/4 In. . . . 195.00
Lure, Pflueger, Kent Frog, Double Belly Hook, Glass Eyes, Card, Box, c.1924 . . . . 1485.00
Lure, Pflueger, Kingfisher Wood Minnow, 3 Hooks, Glass Eyes, Box 468.00
Lure, Pflueger, Muskellunge Minnow, Rubber, Wire Rigging, Metal Fins, c.1895, 6 1/2 In. 880.00
Lure, Pflueger, Neverfail Minnow, Glass Eyes, 5 Single Hooks 220.00
Lure, Pflueger, Neverfail Minnow, Glass Eyes, Green Crackleback 165.00

Lure, Shakespeare, Hydroplane, White, Red Head, Screw Eye, Washer Hangers, 4 In. 110.00
Lure, Shakespeare, McCormic's Mermaid, Yellow, Picture Box, c.1917, 3 3/4 In. 330.00
Lure, Shakespeare, Musky Minnow, 3 Hooks, Green Crackle Back, Glass Eyes, 5 1/4 In. . .   880.00
Lure, Shakespeare, Punkinseed, White, Green Back, Feathered Rear Treble, 3 1/2 In. 140.00
Lure, Shakespeare, Rhodes Mechanical Swimming Frog, No. 3, Wood Box, c.1906 . . . . .   3850.00
Lure, Shakespeare, Slim Jim, White, Red Head, Glass Eyes, 2 Trebles, 3 5/8 In. 85.00
Lure, Shakespeare, Strike-It, Jointed, Black, Red, Yellow Belly, Glass Eyes, 1930, 3 In. . .   165.00
Lure, Shakespeare, Underwater Minnow, No. 44, Green, Pink, White, 5 Trebles, 3 3/4 In. .   140.00
Lure, South Bend, Vacuum Bait, Tack Eyes, White Body, Red Decoration, Box 220.00
Lure, South Bend, Whirl-Oreno, Revolving Head, Red, White 130.00
Lure, T.H. Bates, Serpentine Spinner, Hollow Metal, Spiral Fin, 1855 Patent, 2 1/2 In. . . .   1155.00
Lure, Transparent Fishing Tackle Co., Crawfish Or Frog Container, No. 3, 3 Hooks, Box .   660.00
Lure, Utica Tackle Co., Success Spinner, Hollow Metal, Revolving Head, 3 Hooks, Box . .   525.00
Lure, Wakeman Skeleton, Trout, 1886 Patent, Size 0, 2 1/2 In. 220.00
Lure, Weed King, Weedless Plug, White, Red Head, Metal Lever, Picture Box, 3 3/4 In. . . .   275.00
Lure, Winchester, Fluted Spinner, No. 9642, Nickel Plated Blade, 1 1/4 In. 66.00
Lure, Winchester, Minnow, Treble Hook 578.00
Lure, Winchester, Wobbler, No. 9203, Scale Finish, Gold Color 440.00
Minnow Tube, Detroit Glass, Trout Size, 3 1/4 In. 825.00
Minnow Tube, Glass, Tin Cap & Straps, 13 1/2 x 7 In. 80.00
Minnow Tube, Lowell B. Calkin, Glass, Wire Hook Hangers, Cork Stoppers, 2 1/8 In. . . .   2200.00
Net, Atherton & Son, Triangular Folding, Wood, Cane Handle, Brass, Sheffield, 43 In. . . .   55.00
Net, Landing, Turned Maple & Tiger Maple Handle, Metal Frame, Adjustable, 82 In. 58.00
Net, Trout, Brass Fixtures, Collapsible, Bent Wood Rim, Mottle Cane Handle, 20 In. 99.00
Net, W.H. Reisner, Minnow, King, Folding Umbrella, Hagerstown, Md., Bag, Tag 28.00
Reel, A. Coates, Trout, Side Mount, Variable Use, Pat. Mar. 20th 88, 2 In. 1100.00
Reel, ABU Ambassadeur, Deluxe No. 5000 C, Walnut Presentation Box 385.00
Reel, ABU Ambassadeur, No. 9000, Light Salt Walter, Red, Line 110.00
Reel, Ari Hart, Large, Leather Case, 4 1/8 x 1 1/8 In. 385.00
Reel, B.F. Meek & Sons, Blue Grass, No. 3, Leather Case, 2 x 1 5/8 In. 330.00
Reel, Billy Pate, Bluefin Model, Anti Reverse, 5 1/2 x 1 1/8 In. 358.00
Reel, Billy Pate, Fly, Salmon, Saltwater, Black, Box, Papers, Case, 3 3/4 x 1 In. 220.00
Reel, Bogdan, Salmon, Gold Anondized Frame, Engraved Name, 3 1/4 x 1 3/8 In. 935.00
Reel, C.F. Orvis, Bass, Wide Spool, 1874, 2 7/8 x 1 In. 1045.00
Reel, Charles Farlow, Mahogany, Ebonite, Ventilated, England, c.1910 . . . .   425.00
Reel, Clark & Co., Plated, Ball Handle, 3 In. 300.00
Reel, Clark Horrocks, Nickel-Plated Brass, Birdcage Side Mount, Folding Handle, 3 In. . .   2310.00
Reel, E.C. Koenig, Trout Fly, German Silver, c.1880, 2 1/4 In. 1430.00
Reel, E.V. Hofe, Model 360, No. 3 Size, Pat. Jan. 23, 83, 2 1/2 In. 7150.00
Reel, E.V. Hofe, Model 621, Size 6/0 . . . .   360.00
Reel, E.V. Hofe, Salmon, 423 6/0, Nameplate, Leather Case, 4 1/4 x 1 3/4 In. 1870.00
Reel, E.V. Hofe, Salmon, C-1926 Model 484, German Silver, 3 1/8 In. 4950.00
Reel, E.V. Hofe, Trout, Marked Perfection, Model Size 1 Hand, German Silver, 3 In. 3850.00
Reel, E.V. Hofe, Trout, Perfection, Model 360, Leather Case, 1/0 Size 5500.00
Reel, Farlow, Fly, Trout, c.1930 . . . .   145.00
Reel, Fin-Nor, Fly, No. 1, Anti Reverse, Spare Spool, Box, Bag, 2 7/8 x 7/8 In. 330.00
Reel, Fin-Nor, Saltwater Salmon, Wedding Cake, Model 3, 4 x 1 In. 935.00
Reel, Fin-Nor, Trout, Wedding Cake, Size 1, Spare Spool, Case, 3 x 3/4 In. 1870.00
Reel, H.I. Leonard, Trout, Click, Model 44a, Crank Handle, Raised Puller, No. 191813 . . .   3190.00
Reel, Hardy, Bougle, Alnwick, Left Hand Wind, Leather Case, 3 1/4 x 7/8 In. 3850.00
Reel, Hardy, Featherweight, Trout, 1 Screw Line Guide, 2 7/8 In.   165.00
Reel, Hardy, Perfect, 4 Cusp, Left Hand Wind, Red Agate, Leather Case, c.1905, 3/4 In. . .   2750.00
Reel, Hardy, Perfect, Brass Foot, A&F Leather Case, c.1912, 2 7/8 x 5/8 In. 525.00
Reel, Hardy, Perfect, Brass Foot, Bag, c.1915, 3 1/8 x 5/8 In. 300.00
Reel, Hardy, Princess, Trout, Reversible Line Guide, Pouch, Box, 3 1/2 In. 160.00
Reel, Hardy, St. George, Junior Trout, Wide Spool, Grooved Aluminum Foot, 2 9/16 In. . .   1155.00
Reel, Hardy, St. George, Trout, Pink Agate Line Guide, 3 Screw Design, 3 In. 605.00
Reel, Hardy, St. John, Salmon, 3 Screw Model, 3 7/8 x 7/8 In. 110.00
Reel, Hardy, St. John, Salmon, Spare Spool, Pouch, Box, 3 7/8 x 7/8 In. . . . . .149.00 to 195.00
Reel, Hardy, Uniqua, Trout, Box, 3 1/8 x 3/4 In. 195.00
Reel, Heddon, Bait Casting, No. 45, Non Level Wind, German Silver, c.1905 . . . .   470.00
Reel, Heddon, Pal P-41, Bait Casting, Paper, Bag, Box 95.00
Reel, J.A. Coxe, Model 25-2, Bait Casting, Free Spool, Leather Case, 2 1/8 x 1 3/4 In. . . .   80.00

Reel, J.A. Coxe, Model 25-3, Bait Casting, German Silver, Leather Case, Box 70.00
Reel, J.V. Hofe, Salmon, Multiplying, Hard Rubber, Nickel Silver, T. Conroy, 4 In. 275.00
Reel, J.V. Hofe, Trout, Click Reel, Square Corner, German Silver, Size 3, c.1880 .... 1650.00
Reel, J.V. Hofe, Trout, Hard Rubber, Strong Click, Size 4, 2 1/8 In. 440.00
Reel, J.V. Hofe, Trout, Size 3, 2 1/2 x 1 In. 330.00
Reel, J.W. Young Landex, Fly, Free Spool, Drag Regulator, Box, Bag, 3 3/8 x 7/8 In. 110.00
Reel, Marryatt, Salmon, Model 9A, Spare Spool, Suede Pouch, 3 1/2 x 3/4 In. 140.00
Reel, Marryatt, Trout, Model 7/5Asuede Pouch, 2 7/8 x 3/4 In. 220.00
Reel, Meek & Milam, No. 2, Brass, Casting, Spool Bait, Handmade, Ky., 1 7/8 x 1 3/4 In. 3850.00
Reel, Nottingham, Star Back Brace, Slater Latch, Walnut, Brass, 4 1/2 In. 195.00
Reel, Nottingham, Walnut, Brass, Star Back Brace, Horn Handle, Shallow Spool, 3 In. ... 140.00
Reel, Orvis, CFO III, Trout, Line, England, 3 x 5/8 In. 220.00
Reel, Orvis, CFO, Model 26L, Suede Pouch, Papers, 3 x 3/4 In. ....·..... 95.00
Reel, Orvis, Fly, Bass, Plated, Strong Clicker, Model 1874, Walnut Box 1870.00
Reel, Orvis, Fly, Lord 1, Multiplying, Spare Spool, Pouch, 3 1/2 x 3/4 In. 198.00
Reel, Orvis, Model 1874, 1st Model, 2 7/8 x 1/2 In. 715.00
Reel, Orvis, Saltwater Fly, Anti Reverse, 4 x 1 In. ....110.00 to 120.00
Reel, Orvis, Trout, SSS 6-7 D-Drive, Disc Drag, 3 1/4 x 7/8 In. 85.00
Reel, Otto Zwarg, Salmon, Model 300, Size 1/0, Florida, Box, 3 1/8 x 1 1/4 In. 4620.00
Reel, Peerless, Salmon, Model 5A, Pouch, 3 1/4 x 1 In. 330.00
Reel, Penn, International 20, Big Game, Gold, Slide Free Spool, Torpedo Handle ..165.00 to 195.00
Reel, Penn, Senator, No. 116A, 10/0, Yellow Torpedo Handle, Box 155.00
Reel, Pezon Et Michel, Trout, Super Parabolic, No. 76, 3 In. 410.00
Reel, Pflueger, Hawkeye, 80 Yard, 2 1/2 x 1 1/8 In. 415.00
Reel, Pflueger, Hawkeye, Trout, 60 Yard, 2 1/2 x 7/8 In. 525.00
Reel, Pflueger, Model 1392, Sculptured Pillars, Celluloid Handle, 2 7/8 x 7/8 In. 215.00
Reel, Pflueger, Salmon, 577, Anti Reverse, Adjustable Drag, Pouch, 3 5/8 x 3/4 In. ..88.00 to 165.00
Reel, Pflueger, Summit, No. 1993, Level Wind, Jeweled Side Plates 22.00
Reel, Redifor, Bait Casting, Wood Box, Warren, Ohio, Flyer, Bag, 2 x 2 1/2 In. 1210.00
Reel, Robert Haskell, Trout, Line Guide, Click Switch, Handmade, Case, 1980 .... 220.00
Reel, Ronson, Mercury, Level Wind, Bakelite Double Handle, Chrome Side 17.00
Reel, Salmon, Loop, Model 3, Pouch, 4 1/4 x 7/8 In. 220.00
Reel, Saracione Deluxe, Trout, Delrin Side Plates, Leather Case, 2 3/4 x 1 1/4 In. 1210.00
Reel, Seamaster, Mark II, Salmon, Saltwater, Anti Reverse, Handmade, 3 3/8 x 1 1/4 In. ... 990.00
Reel, Seamaster, Tarpon, Anti Reverse, Bag, Box, 3 7/8 x 1 1/16 In. 880.00
Reel, Thomas & Thomas, Kosmic, Trout, Silver Raised Pillar, 2 1/4 In. 1540.00
Reel, Thomas & Thomas, Salmon, Tournament, Spare Spool, Pouch, Box, 3 5/8 x 7/8 In. . 110.00
Reel, Trout, Brass, Sliding Stop, Extended Handle, 1800s, 1 5/8 x 1 1/4 In. 330.00
Reel, Walker, Trout, TR1, Leatherette Pouch, 2 1/2 x 7/8 In. 2310.00
Reel, William Mills & Son, Trout, Wide Spool, N.Y., 2 1/16 In. 2090.00
Reel, William Mills, Fairy, Long Foot, Side Plate, Rubber Handle, 2 In. 1540.00
Reel, Winchester, Casting, Model 4250 Takapart, 80 Yard 110.00
Reel, Winchester, Casting, Model 4328, Non Level Wind, 2 1/8 x 1 5/8 In. 175.00
Reel, Winchester, Model 4256, Click Switch, 1921 Patent, Box, 2 x 1 5/8 In. 360.00
Reel, Wm. H. Talbot, Casting, Meteor, German Silver, Ivory Grasp, 2 x 2 5/8 In. ..·.... 300.00
Reel, Zenith, Trout, Wide Spool, 3 3/8 In. 165.00
Rod, Abbey & Imbrie, Fly, Pritchard's Patent, 2 Tips, Wood Case, 10 1/2 Ft., 3 Piece 660.00
Rod, Abercrombie & Fitch, Trolling, Yellowstone, 2 Tips, 9 Ft., 3 Piece 60.00
Rod, Bob Gorman, Green River, Impregnated, 2 Tips, 3 Weights, Bag, Tube, 6 Ft., 2 Piece 660.00
Rod, Chubb, Fly, Lancewood, German Silver Reel, 2 Tips, Wood Case, 10 1/2 Ft., 3 Piece 1018.00
Rod, Chubb, Salmon, Lancewood, Nickel Silver Guides, 2 Tips, Bag, 12 Ft., 3 Piece 275.00
Rod, Dickerson, Trout, Model 7012-E, 7 Ft., 2 Piece 3300.00
Rod, E.V. Hofe, Trout, 1 Tip, 9 1/2 Ft., 3 Piece 55.00
Rod, F.E. Thomas, Special Streamer, 2 Tips, Bag, Tube, 9 Ft., 3 Piece 880.00
Rod, F.E. Thomas, Special Trolling, 2 Tips, Bag, Tag, Tube, 8 Ft. 6 In., 3 Piece 85.00
Rod, F.E. Thomas, Trolling, Dame Staddard Hub, 2 Tips, Wooden Case, 8 Ft., 2 Piece ... 165.00
Rod, H.L. Leonard, Bait Casting, Detachable Handle, Canvas Sack, Tag, 5 Ft. 6 In. 220.00
Rod, H.L. Leonard, Catskill, Model 36, 2 Tips, Red Wrap, Bag, Tube, 7 Ft. 6 In., 3 Piece . 3300.00
Rod, H.L. Leonard, Duracane, Appalachian Trail, 1 Tip, Bag, Tube, 7 Ft., 4 Piece 1100.00
Rod, H.L. Leonard, Fairy Catskill, 2 Tips, Bag, Tube, 7 Ft., 2 Piece 3080.00
Rod, H.L. Leonard, Prefire, Catskill Trout, 7 Ft., 3 Piece 2750.00
Rod, Hardy, St. Leonard, No. 1, Wood, Heavy Wire 60.00
Rod, Heddon, Bait Casting, Staggered Rings, 5 Ft., 2 Piece 99.00

Rod, Heddon, Deluxe, Peerless, Model 35, 2 Tips, Bag, Tube, Size 2 Ferrule, 8 Ft., 3 Piece	330.00
Rod, Heddon, Model 14, 2 Tips, 9 Ft., 3 Piece	195.00
Rod, Heddon, Trout, 2 Tips, Plastic Reel Seat, Made For Macy's, 8 Ft., 3 Piece	115.00
Rod, Hoagy Carmichael, Model 204, 2 Tips, Bag, Tube, 7 Ft. 3 In., 2 Piece	4290.00
Rod, Hurd, Super Caster, Steel, Walnut Handle	115.00
Rod, Jim Payne, Trout, Model 201, Made For Abercrombie & Fitch, 8 Ft.	6325.00
Rod, Mark Aroner, Fly, Hunt Pattern, 2 Tips, 3-Weight Line, Bag, Tube, 6 Ft., 3 Piece	2310.00
Rod, Mark Spittler, Fly, Quadrate, Dark Flamed Cane, Bag, Tube, 8 Ft., 2 Piece	1650.00
Rod, Milward Flymaster, Cotton Case, Labels, 9 Ft.	56.00
Rod, Milward Flymaster, Hexacane Rod, Cotton Case, England, 9 Ft.	50.00
Rod, Montague, Fishkill, 2 Tips, Bag, 7 Ft. 6 In., 3 Piece	275.00
Rod, Montague, Trolling, Split Bamboo, Wood Handle, Nickel, Brass, Sleeve, 1951	220.00
Rod, Nat Uslan, 2 Tips, 5 Sides, Bag, Tube, 9 Ft., 2 Piece	140.00
Rod, Orvis, Battenkill, 2 Tips, Bag, Tube, 7 Ft. 6 In., 2 Piece	440.00
Rod, Orvis, Battenkill, Impregnated, Bag, Tube, 8 Ft.	415.00
Rod, Orvis, Battenkill, Trout, 2 Tips, Light Line, Original Bag & Tube, 7 Ft. 9 In., 3 Piece	715.00
Rod, Orvis, Far & Fine, MCL, 2 Tips, 5-Weight Line, Bag, Tube, 7 Ft. 6 In.	715.00
Rod, Orvis, Fly, Battenkill, Impregnated, Japanned Guides, Aluminum Tube, 7 1/2 Ft.	720.00
Rod, Orvis, Fly, Impregnated, Bag, Tube, 6 Ft. 6 In., 2 Piece	495.00
Rod, Orvis, HLS Graphite, 1 Tip, For 12-Weight Line, Bag, Tube, 9 Ft., 2 Piece	70.00
Rod, Orvis, Model 99, Impregnated Rod, Bag, Tube, 7 Ft. 6 In., 2 Piece	300.00
Rod, Orvis, Salmon, Light, 2 Tips, Butt Extension, Bag, Tube, 8 1/2 Ft., 2 Piece	495.00
Rod, Orvis, Trolling, Tips, Calcutta Cane, Cord-Wrapped Handle, Bag, Case, 9 Ft., 3 Piece	140.00
Rod, Orvis, Wes Jordan Series, 2 Tips, Right Handed, Bag, Tube, 7 1/2 Ft., 2 Piece	1100.00
Rod, Payne, Model 101, 2 Tips, Bag, Tube, 7 Ft. 6 In., 2 Piece	4730.00
Rod, Payne, Model 101, Made For Abercrombie & Fitch, 7 Ft.	3300.00
Rod, Payne, Spinning, 1 Tip For Light Lures, Bag, Tube, 7 Ft., 2 Piece	435.00
Rod, Payne, Trout, Parabolic, 2 Tips, Original Bag & Tube, 7 Ft. 1 In., 2 Piece	3300.00
Rod, Per Brandin, Quad, 2 Tips, 3-Weight Line, Bag, Tube, 7 Ft., 2 Piece	3080.00
Rod, Phillipson, Trout, Peerless, Impregnated, Model 5, Bag & Tube, 8 Ft., 3 Piece	580.00
Rod, Ron Kusse, 2 Tips, Tiger Maple Grip, Bag, Tube, 7 Ft. 6 In., 2 Piece	2585.00
Rod, Sam Carlson, Quad, 2 Tips, Bag, Tube, 7 Ft. 6 In., 2 Piece	5060.00
Rod, Thomas & Thomas, 20th Anniversary Commemorative, 1989, 8 Ft., 3 Piece	4265.00
Rod, Thomas & Thomas, Classic Dryfly, Tips, Impregnated, Bag, Tube, 7 Ft. 6 In., 2 Piece	990.00
Rod, Thomas & Thomas, Fountainhead, Commemorative, No. 8 Of 20, 7 Ft. 6 In., 3 Piece	3410.00
Rod, Thomas & Thomas, Montana, 2 Tips, 7-Weight Line, 8 Ft. 6 In., 3 Piece	1210.00
Rod, Thomas & Thomas, Sans Pareil, 2 Tips, Bag, Tube, 7 Ft. 6 In., 2 Piece	1540.00
Rod, Tom Maxwell, 2 Tips, 4-Weight Line, Bag, Tube, 7 Ft., 2 Piece	2970.00
Rod, Tom Maxwell, 2 Tips, For 5-Weight Line, Bag, Tube, 7 1/2 Ft., 2 Piece	1870.00
Rod, Tony Maslan, Hollow Built Powell, Tips, 5/6-Weight Line, Bag, Tube, 9 Ft., 2 Piece	1210.00
Rod, Walton Powell, 2 Tips, Bag, Tube, 9 Ft., 3 Piece	690.00
Rod, Wright & McGill, Favorite, 2 Tips, Unused, 8 1/2 Ft., 3 Piece	495.00
Rod, Wright & McGill, Trout, Granger Victory, German Silver Reel Seat, 8 Ft., 2 Piece	275.00
Rod Bag, Orvis, 4 Rod Capacity	60.00
Salmon Tailer, Alloy Construction, Cork Grip, 30 In.	20.00
Salmon Tailer, Brass Fixtures, Metal, Rubber Grip, Wrist Thong, Scotland, 30 In.	35.00
Sign, C.F. Orvis, Tackle, Mill, Angler & Sweetheart, Frame, 14 1/2 x 21 In.	3080.00
Spear, Hand Forged, 2 Branched Head, 10 Tines, Michigan, 7 3/4 x 15 In.	330.00
Spear, W.F. Hoppe, Forged, 9 Tines, 6 3/4-In. Head	165.00
Tackle Box, Creek Chub Bait Co., Famous Pikie Minnow, Catches More Fish, No. 2718	110.00
Tackle Box, Creek Chub Bait Co., No. 2600	120.00
Tackle Box, Creek Chub Bait Co., Pikie Minnow, No. 2701, Sticker, 12 Lure Capacity	240.00
Tackle Box, Fye, For Flies, Aluminum, 2 Fold-Down Trays, Hollidaysburg, Pa., 5 x 6 In.	110.00
Tackle Box, Green Paint, Hand Painted Pike, 26 x 8 x 8 In.	1725.00
Tackle Box, Ice Fishing, Sled, Metal Bottom, Hinged Lid, Jigging Rods, 15 x 26 x 13 In.	55.00
Tackle Box, Kingfisher Decal, Tin, Crescent Shape, 2 Bands, Stars, Spring-Loaded Wires	385.00
Tackle Box, Satchel Shape, Metal Swing Handle, Perforated Lid, Ring Grasp	110.00
Tackle Box, Wood, Fish Egg Shipper, Pyrographics, L.F. Grammes, Pa., 10 x 12 x 7 In.	130.00
Trophy, Pike, Mounted	125.00
Trophy, Sea Turtle, Polished Blond Carapace, Taxidermy Figure, 14 1/4 In.	1380.00
Trophy, Swordfish Bill, Carved Decoration, 32 1/2 In.	81.00
Trophy, Walleye, Mounted	95.00

FLAGS are included in the Textile category.

FLASH GORDON appeared in the Sunday comics in 1934. The daily strip started in 1940. The hero was also in comic books from 1930 to 1970, in books from 1936, in movies from 1938, on the radio in the 1930s and 1940s, and on television from 1953 to 1954. All sorts of memorabilia are collected, but the ray guns and rocket ships are the most popular.

Figure, Ming The Merciless, On Card, Mego, 1976, 9 In.	50.00
Necktie	68.00
Toy, Gun, Click Ray Pistol, Tin, Marx KFS, Box, 10 In.	660.00
Toy, Ray Gun, Battery Operated, Marx, Box, 10 In.	950.00
Toy, Rocket Fighter, Tin Lithograph, Windup, Marx, 12 In.	330.00 to 715.00
Toy, Wagon, Space Design, Tin, Strato, Wyandotte Toys, 1940s	210.00
Toy, Water Pistol, Holster, NASTA, Hong Kong, 1975, 8 In.	75.00
Toy, Water Pistol, NASTA, Hong Kong, 1975, 8 In.	50.00
Toy, Water Pistol, Whistle End, Marx, 1940s, 7 1/2 In.	225.00

FLOW BLUE was made in England and other countries about 1830 to 1900. The dishes were printed with designs using a cobalt blue coloring. The color flowed from the design to the white body so that the finished piece has a smeared blue design. The dishes were usually made of ironstone china. More Flow Blue may be found under the name of the manufacturer.

Bone Dish, Blue Danube, Gilt Highlights, Johnson Brothers, 6 Piece	110.00
Bowl, Aldine, Covered, Footed, 12 In.	300.00
Bowl, Cover, Flowers, Scrolled Leaves, Octagonal, 8-Footed, Handles, 5 x 11 x 9 In.	130.00
Bowl, Delph, Blue Flower Border, Central Basket Of Flowers, 2 3/4 x 10 1/4 In.	40.00
Bowl, Footed, Scinde, Alcock, 6 3/4 x 11 1/2 x 8 1/4 In.	220.00
Compote, Gaudy Strawberry, Brushstroke, 8 1/2 x 11 In.	1430.00
Cup & Saucer, Leaf & Vine, Green, Morning Glories, Blue	75.00
Dish, Celtic, Oval, 6 x 4 1/2 In., 6 Piece	370.00
Pitcher, Kyber, 7 1/2 In.	255.00
Pitcher, Scinde, 8 Panels, Bulbous, Alcock, 6 In.	470.00
Pitcher, Scinde, Alcock, 12 In.	825.00
Plate, F. & Sons, Ltd., Devon, 10 1/2 In.	79.00
Plate, Manilla Pattern, 9 1/2 In., 4 Piece	305.00
Plate, Mongolia, Johnson Brothers, 10 1/2 In., Pair	127.00
Plate, Watteau, Courting Couple, Festooned Border, c.1895, 9 3/4 In., 6 Piece	400.00
Platter, Byzantine, Blue Flower, Rim, 16 1/4 x 12 1/4 In.	120.00
Platter, Canton, 15 1/2 In.	170.00
Platter, Hong Kong, Meigh, 13 3/4 In.	360.00
Platter, Oregon, Cut Corner, Blue Design, 12 1/2 x 9 1/2 In.	230.00
Platter, Scinde, Mark, Oriental Stone, Alcock, 16 x 13 In.	635.00
Platter, Temple, Podmore Walker, 15 3/4 In.	275.00
Sugar, Pagoda, Applied Handles, 7 In.	180.00
Teapot, Pelew, Lantern Shape, 9 In.	580.00
Teapot, Shell, Lantern Shape, 9 In.	715.00
Toilet Bowl, Florentine Pattern, T. Wyford Pottery, c.1890, 15 x 19 x 16 1/2 In.	575.00

FLYING PHOENIX, see Phoenix Bird category.

FOLK ART is also listed in many categories of this book under the actual name of the object. See categories such as Box, Cigar Store Figure, Paper, Weather Vane, Wooden, etc.

African American Boy, Fish On Line, Pine, Signed Sherman Hensal, 35 1/2 In.	575.00
Alligator, Alligator Deterrent, Mouth Moves When Cranked, Mounted, 53 In.	460.00
Angel, With Trumpet, Painted Metal, Full-Bodied, 19th Century, 19 x 16 3/4 In.	2090.00
Ax, Wood, Elks, Minstrels, Woodman Spare That Tree, 1912, 39 3/4 x 10 1/2 In.	520.00
Banjo, Celluloid Inlaid Finger Board, 30-Bracket Pot, 5 Strings, 34 x 11 x 3 In.	*Illus* 605.00
Bank, Tupelo Gumwood, Round, Black Voodoo Faces, Polychrome, 4 x 3 1/4 In.	1100.00
Barn, Packing Crates, Doors, Pierced Sunburst Ends, Green, Red Roof, 17 3/4 In.	35.00
Biplane, Wood, Carved Propeller, c.1925, 48 x 22 In.	345.00
Biplane, Yellow, Red Propeller, Blue, Red, White Tail Stripes, Wood, Tin Wings, 15 In.	468.00
Bird In A Cage, White, Black Wings, Tail, Glass Eyes, Red & White Cage, 12 x 6 x 8 In.	495.00

Folk Art, Banjo,
Celluloid Inlaid
Finger Board,
30-Bracket Pot,
5 Strings,
34 x 11 x 3 In.

Never plug more than 1500 watts into any one circuit. You probably have several plugs on one circuit. This is an easy mistake to make when decorating for the holidays. Don't encourage fires.

Bird Tree, 9 Birds, Carved, Painted, Natural Wood Base, 27 1/2 In.	230.00
Bird Tree, 10 Painted Birds, Glass Eyes, 27 In.	10175.00
Bird Tree, Carved, 5 Birds, Nails, Wire Legs, Wisc., Early 20th Century, 8 3/4 x 6 1/4 In.	2475.00
Birdhouse, Chalet Style, 4 Tiers, Asphalt Shingle Roof, Painted, 31 x 21 x 11 3/4 In.	250.00
Birdhouse, Martin, 2 Story, Peaked Roof, Red, Scalloped Gable Ends, Blue, 35 In.	395.00
Birdhouse, Peaked Entry, Painted Windows, Applied Shutters, Blue, Yellow, 11 In.	56.00
Birdhouse, Polychrome, Wood, Church, Picket Fence, Display Stand, 23 x 13 x 22 In.	1125.00
Box, Dome Lid, Poplar, Bracket Feet, Painted, Blue Ground, 5 3/4 x 4 1/8 x 8 In.	24750.00
Box, Painted, Yellow Ground, Flowers, Lancaster, c.1855, 2 1/4 x 2 1/4 x 4 1/4 In.	4950.00
Box, Plywood, Pine, Applied Carvings, Stylized Leaves, Alligator Finish, 13 x 9 x 6 In.	115.00
Box, Wall, Red, Green, Mustard, Black, Carving, Flowers, 14 x 24 In.	90.00
Building, Bell Tower, Pine, Painted, 32 Stenciled Windows, Red Roof, 7 x 4 x 5 1/2 In.	39.00
Bus, Double Decker, Northeast Coast Exhibition, Express Bus, New Castle, 45 x 23 In.	910.00
Bust, Wood, Carved, Man, Woman, 19th Century Clothing, Painted, 11 1/2 In., Pair	705.00
Carving, Lovebirds, Basswood, Polychrome, Wire Feet, Forked Branch, 1920, 10 x 5 In.	750.00
Carving, Shepherd, Staff, Dog, Sheep, Applied Wool, Wilhelm Schimmel, 10 x 7 x 15 In.	690.00
Cat, Seated, Bank, Carved, White Paint, 12 In.	1725.00
Cat, Walnut, Carved, Applied Glass Eyes, Popeye Reed, 12 1/4 In.	375.00
Chest, Mechanic's, Birch, Walnut, Brass Bound, Diamonds, 13 x 24 In.	690.00
Chest, Trinket, Compass Decorated, Dome Top, Blue, Flowers, 5 3/8 x 5 x 7 In.	7150.00
Chipmunk, Wood, Carved, Silvio Peter Zoratti, c.1979, 12 1/2 In., Pair	230.00
Coat Rack, Cat On Top, 4 Dogs Around Base, 1930-1940s, 51 In.	106.00
Cowboy, On Horse, Holding Hat, Gun, Wood, 20th Century, 28 1/2 x 25 x 9 1/2 In.	2310.00
Cup, Eagle, Arrows, Shield, Justice & Liberty Banner, Silver Rim, Cow Horn, 1818	5500.00
Cutout, Tulips, Men, Women, Animals, Fish, Birds, Cross Corner Frame, 11 x 15 In.	520.00
Dancing Man, Jointed, Sheet Tin, White Face, Green & Blue Body, Mid 1800s, 12 1/2 In.	360.00
Deer, Wooden, Full-Bodied, Painted Brown, White & Black Highlights, 33 x 34 In.	700.00
Diorama, Work Projects Administration, Carved Wood, c.1935, 13 x 9 x 5 7/8 In.	500.00
Dog, Pine, Carved, Painted, Wilhelm Schimmel, c.1890, 2 3/4 x 4 1/2 In.	23100.00
Dog, Pine, Carved, White, Black Spots, Wilhelm Schimmel, 2 1/2 x 4 1/8 In.	12100.00
Doll, Sailor, Suede Head, Canvas Body, 19th Century, 20 In.	115.00
Drum Box, Wood, German Band, Cheese Box	22.00
Eagle, Base, Wooden, Paint Over Gesso, 70 In.	1100.00
Fire Engine, Horse Drawn, Firemen, Fire Buckets, Red, Black, Gold, 12 x 4 1/2 In.	2310.00
Fish, Wood, Carved, Painted, Yellow, White, Blue, Black, 24 x 10 In.	290.00
Frame, Layers, Cutout Hearts, Diamonds, Scalloped Opening, 17 x 17 In.	345.00
Group, 3 Dogs, Treed Raccoon, Carved, Painted, 14 x 16 x 8 In.	130.00
Head, Carved, Weathered, Whitewash Finish, Gary Birch, 5 x 4 3/4 x 10 1/2 In.	1060.00
Head, Clown, Wood, Red Hat, Black Buttons, Hand Painted, 12 1/2 In.	330.00
Head, Pine Boards, Carved, Man's Head, Sideburns, 11 3/8 In.	230.00
Horse, Stuffed With Unbleached Cotton, Wood Frame, Mexico, 25 In.	300.00
Horse, Wood, Carved, Pegged Legs, Painted, Chestnut, Flaxen Mane, Tail, 9 5/8 In., Pair	175.00
Mask, Hispanic, Wood, Carved, Hair, Flower Details, Gesso, Black Paint, 9 3/4 In.	345.00
Men On A Stand, Pine, Carved, Painted, Late 19th Century, 11 x 10 In.	715.00
Millinery Head, Wallpaper Dress, 1840s	2400.00
Niddy Noddy, Oak, Maple, Carved, Pierced Hearts, Chip Carved Circles, 18 x 13 x 13 In.	336.00
Otter, Papier-Mache, Smiling, Dancing, Holding Cane, 44 In.	2240.00

Owl, Wood, Carved, Painted, 14 1/2 In. 1380.00
Oxen, 4 Men, Pulling Stumps, Basswood, A. Dule, 11 1/2 x 35 x 9 1/2 In. 748.00
Panel, Carved Relief, Leaping Dog, Hunter Shooting Duck, 39 x 26 In. 505.00
Pipe, Wood, Black Boy On Log, Alligator, Late 19th Century, 9 In. 690.00
Pipe Bowl, Burlwood, Carved, Head, American, 1800s, 2 7/8 In. 470.00
Planter, Round, Raised Band At Base, Relief Faces On Sides, Popeye Reed, 13 3/4 x 9 In.   635.00
Planter, Wood Slats, Birds, In Trees, Penn., Early 20th Century, 26 x 8 3/4 x 16 In. 4125.00
Plaque, Crow, Wood, Carved, Painted, Black, Popeye Reed, 16 3/4 x 10 3/4 In., Pair 546.00
Plaque, Wood, Silhouette Shape, Painted, Excursion Boat, Welcome Crest, c.1900 . . . . . .   3360.00
Retablo, Painted, Virgin Mary, Queen Of Heaven, 13 x 10 In. 115.00
Rooster, Polychrome Paint, Over Gesso, 19th Century, 6 In. 365.00
Rooster, Wood, Carved, Painted, Red, Green, Signed, Keith Collis, 15 x 15 3/4 In. 175.00
Sailing Ship, Matchstick, c.1940s, 64 In. 330.00
Screen, Scroll, Flowers, Birds, Mesh Panel, Sheet Metal, 43 x 39 x 16 In. 2420.00
Shelf, Victorian Cathedral, Band Saw Cut, Inset Clock, 61 x 35 In. 1955.00
Ship In Bottle, Village Scene, 12 In. 66.00
Sign, Oil Paint, USS Maine, Eagle On American Flag, Union Forever, 15 x 15 In. . . .   530.00
Snake, Rattler, Carved Root, Decorated, c.1940, 32 In. 770.00
Spire, Architectural, Blue, Gold, Red, White, Green, 47 In. 650.00
Squirrel, Seated, Eating Nut, Polychrome, Wood Carving, 3 1/2 In. 295.00
Stand, Black Man, Holding Tray, Wood, White Shirt, Yellow Pants, 33 3/4 In. 358.00
Stand, Cherry, Painted, Animal Heads Carved On Feet, Songbirds, Popeye Reed, 17 In. . .   405.00
Stand, Smoking, Wood, House Shape, 28 1/2 x 13 1/2 x 14 In. 50.00
Stand, Twig, Chestnut Top, Pop Bottle Lid Border, Chip Carved Base, 25 x 20 x 24 In. . .   165.00
Stand, Waiter, Carved, Painted, Standing, Black Man, White Coat, Holding Tray, 36 In. . .   765.00
Stool, Sheet Iron, Cube Shape, Pierced Flowers & Figures, 15 x 15 In., Pair 290.00
Top Hat, Cast Iron, 7 x 7 1/2 In. 176.00
Whimsy, Bottle, Gold Painted, Wooden Cross, Posts, American Flags, 10 1/2 In. 175.00
Whirligig, 2 Figures, Push Pull Handle, 8 Blades, Red, White, Blue, Iron Base, 70 x 48 In.   225.00
Whirligig, 2 Men Sawing Wood, Red, Blue, White, Black, c.1950, 32 1/2 x 40 In. 230.00
Whirligig, Eagle, Art Deco Style, Metal Stand, Rotating Wings, 1930s, 29 x 20 1/2 In. . . .   525.00
Whirligig, Goose, Painted, 22 x 5 3/4 x 5 1/8 In. 118.00
Whirligig, Horse, 6 Blades, Black, White, Red, c.1950, 36 1/2 x 35 In. 115.00
Whirligig, Indian In Canoe, Paddle Arms, Glass Bead Eyes, Wooden, c.1920, 16 1/2 In. . .   1610.00
Whirligig, Indian, Red Graining, Green Outfit, Feather, 20th Century, 10 5/8 In. 550.00
Whirligig, Man Chopping Wood, Wood, Metal, Painted, c.1978, 29 x 38 x 23 In. 250.00
Whirligig, Man On Horse, Cut Tin, Movable Legs, Wind Blades, Arrow Tail, 21 In. 550.00
Whirligig, Man Sawing Log, Windmill Base, Painted, 65 1/4 In. 175.00
Whirligig, Man, Wearing Top Hat, Carved, Painted, 14 In. 935.00
Whirligig, Red Baron, Airplane, 15 In. 198.00
Whirligig, Soldier, Civil War, Standing, Pine, Paint Traces, Late 1800s, 17 In. 880.00
Whirligig, Welder, Tanks, Black, White, Silver Paint, 20 1/2 x 17 In. 410.00
Windmill, Wood, Polychrome, Tin Roof, 18 In. 95.00

FOOT WARMERS solved the problem of cold feet in past generations.
Some warmers held charcoal, others held hot water. Pottery, tin, and
soapstone were the favored materials to conduct the heat. The warmer
was kept under the feet, then the legs and feet were tucked into a blanket, providing welcome warmth in a cold carriage or church.

    Brass, Punched Holes, Bail Handle, Dutch, c.1700 . . . .   550.00
    Pierced Tin, Wood Frame 110.00
    Tin, Iron, Pierced Stars & Scrollwork, Handle, Footed 55.00

FOOTBALL collectibles may be found in the Card and the Sports categories.

FOSTORIA glass was made in Fostoria, Ohio, from 1887 to 1891. The
factory was moved to Moundsville, West Virginia, and most of the
glass seen in shops today is a twentieth-century product. The company
was sold in 1983; new items will be easily identifiable, according to
the new owner, Lancaster Colony Corporation. Additional Fostoria
items may be listed in the Milk Glass category.

American, Ashtray, Hat, 2 1/8 In. 16.00
American, Bonbon, Blue, 3-Footed, 7 In. 250.00
American, Bonbon, Footed, 7 In. 15.00

American, Bonbon, Yellow, 3-Footed, 7 In. 290.00
American, Bottle, Bitters, Square, 5 3/8 In. 130.00
American, Bowl, 6 3/4 In. 30.00
American, Bowl, Trophy, Handles, 8 In. ....75.00 to 95.00
American, Bowl, Vegetable, 2 Sections, Oval, 10 x 7 In. 25.00
American, Box, Cover, Handkerchief, Blue, 5 1/2 x 4 In. 830.00
American, Cake Stand, Square, 7 x 10 In. 220.00
American, Candlestick, 2-Light, 4 1/4 x 8 1/4 In., Pair ....115.00 to 150.00
American, Candlestick, Short Stem, 3 1/4 In. 16.00
American, Candy Jar, Cover, Footed, 9 In. 55.00
American, Celery Dish, Oval, 10 In. 29.00
American, Chamberstick, 2 x 4 1/2 In. 75.00
American, Cheese & Cracker Set, 12 In. 40.00
American, Cracker Jar, Cover, 8 7/8 In. ....250.00 to 325.00
American, Decanter, Square, Stopper, 24 Oz., 9 x 3 1/2 In. 125.00
American, Dish, Jelly, 4 1/4 In. 25.00
American, Dish, Lemon, 5 3/8 In. 40.00
American, Dish, Mayonnaise, Underplate, Spoon 55.00
American, Dish, Pickle, 8 In. 25.00
American, Hat, 2 1/2 x 3 3/4 In. 18.00
American, Ice Bucket, Handle, 4 1/2 x 7 In. 115.00
American, Jam Jar, Cover, Silver Spoon, 4 1/4 In. 150.00
American, Jug, 3 Pt., 6 1/2 In. 75.00
American, Nappy, Cover, 5 1/4 In. 30.00
American, Oyster Cocktail, 4 1/2 Oz., 3 1/2 In. 20.00
American, Pitcher, 48 Oz., 8 In. 95.00
American, Pitcher, Ice Lip, 1/2 Gal., 8 1/4 In. 120.00
American, Pitcher, Pt., 5 1/2 In. 27.00
American, Plate, Bread & Butter, 6 In. 9.00
American, Plate, Luncheon, 9 1/2 In. 24.00
American, Plate, Salad, 8 1/2 In. ....16.00 to 25.00
American, Platter, Oval, 10 1/2 In. 35.00
American, Puff Box, Cover, 2 3/4 x 3 In. 200.00
American, Punch Bowl, Stand, 12 1/2 x 18 1/2 In. 650.00
American, Relish, 2 Sections, Handles, 12 x 5 1/2 In. 55.00
American, Relish, 4 Sections, Square, 10 3/4 In. 125.00
American, Relish, Boat Shape, 12 x 5 1/2 In. ....18.00 to 35.00
American, Relish, Oval, Handles, 12 In. 25.00
American, Rose Bowl, 5 1/2 In. 25.00
American, Saucer, 5 5/8 In. 20.00
American, Sherbet, Flared, 6 Oz., 4 1/4 In. ....18.00 to 22.00
American, Soup, Cream, Footed, Handles, 4 3/4 In. 95.00
American, Sugar & Creamer, Tray ....40.00 to 50.00
American, Syrup, Bakelite Handle, 5 1/4 In. 225.00
American, Tidbit, 3-Toed, 7 In. 28.00
American, Tray, Muffin, Handles, 4 x 8 In. 30.00
American, Tumbler, Iced Tea, Footed, 12 Oz., 5 1/2 x 3 3/8 In. 25.00
American, Tumbler, Old Fashioned, 6 Oz., 3 3/8 In. 15.00
American, Vase, 3 3/4 In. 28.00
American, Vase, Bud, Cupped Rim, 6 1/4 In. 18.00
American, Vase, Bud, Flared, Footed, 8 1/4 x 3 1/8 In. 25.00
American, Vase, Flared, 6 In. 30.00
American, Vase, Flared, 10 x 8 1/4 In. 260.00
American, Vase, Flared, Squat, 5 1/2 In. 30.00
American, Vase, Footed, 8 In. 25.00
American Lady, Claret, 3 Oz., 4 x 2 3/4 In. 20.00
Arbor, Candy Dish, Cover, Amber, 3 Sections, 5 x 7 In. 75.00
Arcady, Candlestick, 5 1/2 x 4 1/4 In., Pair 55.00
Argus, Sherbet, Cobalt Blue, 8 Oz., 5 In. 50.00
Argus, Sherbet, Olive Green, 8 Oz., 5 In. 50.00
Argus, Tumbler, Old Fashioned, Ruby, 10 Oz., 3 7/8 In. 25.00
Arlington, Saltshaker & Pepper Mill, Milk Glass, 5 In. 75.00
Art Glass, Lamp, Electric, Gold Threading, Leaves, Vines, Gold Luster, 16 In. 3700.00

Baroque, Bowl, Topaz, 11 In. 75.00
Baroque, Candlestick, 2-Light, 4 1/4 x 7 1/2 In. 29.00
Baroque, Console, 3-Footed, 12 In. 20.00
Baroque, Creamer, Silver Overlay Blossom, Footed, 3 1/2 In. 30.00
Baroque, Cruet, Topaz, Clear Stopper, 5 1/2 x 3 In. 270.00
Baroque, Dish, Pickle, Shirley Etch, Oval, 1 1/4 x 8 In. 27.00
Baroque, Pitcher, Ice Lip, 7 In. 130.00
Baroque, Plate, Salad, 7 In. 15.00
Baroque, Sugar, Silver Overlay Blossom, Footed, Handles, 3 1/2 In. 30.00
Baroque, Sugar, Topaz, Handles, 3 1/2 In. ....17.00 to 23.00
Baroque, Tidbit, Azure, 3-Footed 40.00
Baroque, Torte Plate, 14 In. 35.00
Baroque, Vase, Yellow, 7 In. 135.00
Betsy Ross, Sugar & Creamer, Milk Glass, Handles 40.00
Beverly, Plate, Bread & Butter, Amber, 6 In. 4.00
Bookends, Eagle, 7 1/2 x 5 In. 270.00
Bookends, Lyre, 7 3/8 x 5 1/2 In. 190.00
Bookends, Polar Bear, 4 5/8 x 4 In. 190.00
Brocade, Bowl, Pink, Scroll Handles, 10 In. 350.00
Buttercup, Sherbet, 6 Oz., 4 3/4 In. 18.00
Celestial, Bowl, 6 In. 5.00
Celestial, Bowl, Green, 11 In. 25.00
Celestial, Plate, Smoke, 11 In. 28.00
Celestial, Vase, Green, 8 In. 22.00
Century, Bowl, Oval, Handles, 10 In. 28.00
Century, Candlestick, 4 1/2 x 4 In. 20.00
Century, Goblet, 10 Oz., 5 3/4 In. 23.00
Century, Pitcher, 48 Oz., 7 1/8 In. ....90.00 to 130.00
Century, Plate, Salad, Crescent, 7 1/2 In. 40.00
Century, Relish, 3 Sections, 11 x 9 In. 25.00
Century, Sherbet, 5 1/2 Oz., 4 In. 16.00
Century, Tidbit, 3-Footed, 8 1/8 In. 18.00
Chateau, Champagne, 5 1/2 Oz., 5 3/8 In. 18.00
Chateau, Goblet, 10 Oz., 6 5/8 In. 25.00
Chateau, Wine, 4 Oz., 5 In. 18.00
Chintz, Bowl, 3-Toed, 7 In. 30.00
Chintz, Bowl, Flared Rim, 12 In. 95.00
Chintz, Champagne, 6 Oz., 5 1/2 In. 20.00
Chintz, Cocktail, 4 Oz., 5 In. 24.00
Chintz, Compote, 4 5/8 x 3 3/4 In. 30.00
Chintz, Goblet, 9 Oz., 7 5/8 In. 28.00
Chintz, Plate, Salad, 7 1/2 In. ....18.00 to 20.00
Chintz, Relish, 2 Sections, 10 x 7 3/4 In. 72.00
Chintz, Sauceboat, Oblong, 6 1/2 x 5 1/4 In. 135.00
Chintz, Tidbit, 3-Footed, 8 1/4 In. 50.00
Coin, Bowl, Ruby, 7 1/2 In. 85.00
Coin, Bowl, Ruby, Oblong, 9 In. 50.00
Coin, Candlestick, Amber, 4 3/4 x 3 1/4 In. 29.00
Coin, Candlestick, Olive Green, 8 In., Pair 95.00
Coin, Candy Dish, Cover, 4 1/4 x 6 3/8 In. 40.00
Coin, Compote, Amber, 8 1/2 In. 100.00
Coin, Cruet, Stopper, Handle, 6 1/4 In. 38.00
Coin, Dish, Jelly, Olive Green, Footed, 3 3/4 In. 15.00
Coin, Nappy, Empire Green, Handle, 5 3/8 In. 22.00
Coin, Nappy, Olive Green, Handle, 5 3/8 In. 18.00
Coin, Pitcher, Amber, Qt., 6 1/2 In. 55.00
Coin, Pitcher, Blue, Qt., 6 1/2 In. 220.00
Coin, Plate, 8 In. 17.00
Coin, Sugar & Creamer, Olive Green 55.00
Coin, Toothpick, 3 1/2 In. 20.00
Coin, Toothpick, Blue, 3 1/2 In. 70.00
Coin, Tumbler, Old Fashioned, 9 Oz., 3 5/8 In. 25.00
Coin, Urn, Cover, Ruby, 13 x 5 In. 125.00

Coin, Vase, Amber, Footed, 8 x 3 In. 22.00
Colony, Bowl, Gold Trim, Scalloped Rim, 5 1/2 x 10 1/2 In. 26.00
Colony, Bowl, Oblong, 8 In. 30.00
Colony, Bowl, Oval, Footed, 4 1/2 x 10 3/4 In. 125.00
Colony, Candlestick, 2-Light, 8 1/2 In., Pair 70.00
Colony, Candlestick, 7 In., Pair 100.00
Colony, Candy Dish, Cover, 4 x 6 1/2 In. 25.00
Colony, Compote, 5 In. 18.00
Colony, Cup 7.00
Colony, Goblet, 9 Oz., 5 1/2 In. .... 17.00 to 25.00
Colony, Plate, Salad, 7 In. 7.00
Colony, Sherbet, 5 Oz., 3 5/8 In. 18.00
Colony, Sugar & Creamer, Red, Maypole 90.00
Colony, Tidbit, 2 7/8 x 7 In. 75.00
Colony, Tumbler, Footed, 12 Oz., 5 3/4 In. 22.00
Colony, Wine, 3 1/4 Oz., 4 1/4 In. 30.00
Contour, Goblet, 10 1/2 Oz., 5 7/8 In. 15.00
Coronet, Bowl, Whipped Cream, Handles, 5 In. 22.00
Coronet, Creamer 25.00
Coronet, Dish, Mayonnaise, Footed, 3 1/2 x 5 In. 26.00
Corsage, Candlestick, 5 1/2 In. 30.00
Corsage, Cocktail, 3 1/2 Oz., 5 In. 20.00
Corsage, Relish, 3 Sections, Handles, 2 1/8 x 12 1/4 In. 50.00
Corsage, Sherbet, 5 1/2 Oz., 4 1/2 In. 16.00
Corsage, Tumbler, Footed, Plum Bowl, Clear Stem & Foot, 9 Oz., 5 1/2 In. 20.00
Cynthia, Bowl, 2 x 4 1/2 In. 20.00
Cynthia, Cocktail, 3 Oz., 5 In. 15.00
Cynthia, Cordial, 3/4 Oz., 3 7/8 In. 25.00
Cynthia, Goblet, 9 Oz., 7 1/2 In. 20.00
Cynthia, Juice, 5 Oz., 4 3/4 In. 15.00
Daisies, Puff Box, Cover, 3 3/8 x 5 1/2 In. 55.00
Fairfax, Bowl, Sugar, Topaz, 3 1/2 In. 10.00
Fairfax, Chop Plate, 13 In. 50.00
Fairfax, Compote, Green, 7 In. 40.00
Fairfax, Cup & Saucer, After Dinner, Topaz, 2 5/8 x 2 3/8 In. 18.00
Fairfax, Plate, Bread & Butter, Green, 6 In. 15.00
Fairfax, Plate, Bread & Butter, Topaz, 6 In. 3.00
Fairfax, Plate, Salad, Amber, 7 1/2 In. 8.00
Fairfax, Plate, Salad, Green, 7 1/2 In. 4.00
Fairfax, Plate, Salad, Topaz, 7 1/2 In. .... 8.00 to 15.00
Fairfax, Relish, 3 Sections, 10 In. 20.00
Fairfax, Sherbet, Topaz, 6 Oz., 6 In. 18.00
Fairfax, Sugar & Creamer, Ebony 125.00
Fairfax, Sugar, Handles, Amber, Footed 20.00
Fairfax, Tumbler, Juice, Footed, Azure, 5 Oz., 4 1/2 In. 15.00
Figurine, Lute & Lotus, Ebony, Gold Trim, 12 1/2 In., Pair 660.00
Figurine, Madonna, Satin Mist, 10 In. 70.00
Flame, Plate, Blue, Center Handle, 4 1/4 x 11 1/2 In. 79.00
Heather, Cake Stand, 12 1/8 In. 90.00
Heather, Goblet, 9 Oz., 6 3/8 x 3 3/4 In. 30.00
Heather, Sherbet, 7 Oz., 4 3/4 In. 22.00
Heather, Tumbler, Juice, 4 Oz., 4 7/8 In., 8 Piece 260.00
Heirloom, Bowl, Blue Opalescent, 9 In. 95.00
Heirloom, Bowl, White Opalescent, 7 In. 50.00
Heirloom, Candlestick, Blue Opalescent, 2 3/4 In., Pair 55.00
Heirloom, Candlestick, Ruby, 3 1/2 In. 85.00
Heirloom, Vase, White Opalescent, 7 3/4 In. 55.00
Holly, Bowl, 5 3/8 In. 18.00
Holly, Champagne, 6 Oz., 5 5/8 In. 20.00
Holly, Cocktail, 3 1/2 Oz., 5 1/4 In. 15.00
Holly, Wine, 3 1/2 Oz., 6 In. 20.00
Jamestown, Goblet, Blue, 9 1/2 Oz., 5 3/4 In. 24.00
Jamestown, Plate, Ruby, 8 In. 25.00

Jamestown, Sherbet, Pink, 6 1/2 Oz., 4 1/4 In. 15.00
Jamestown, Tumbler, Green, 9 Oz., 4 1/4 In. 15.00
Jamestown, Tumbler, Iced Tea, Green, Footed, 11 Oz., 6 In. . . . . .18.00 to 20.00
Jamestown, Tumbler, Iced Tea, Pink, Footed, 11 Oz., 6 In. 24.00
Jamestown, Tumbler, Juice, Footed, Ruby, 5 Oz., 4 3/4 In. 26.00
Jamestown, Wine, Blue, 4 Oz., 4 1/2 In. 24.00
June, Candlestick, Rose, 5 In., Pair 170.00
June, Centerpiece, Flared Rim, 3-Footed, 12 In. 95.00
June, Plate, Salad, 7 1/2 In. 20.00
Kent, Plate, 12 In. 38.00
Lafayette, Creamer, Gold Tint 26.00
Lafayette, Cup & Saucer, After Dinner 20.00
Lafayette, Relish, Dark Amethyst, Divided, Handles, 7 1/2 In. 50.00
Lafayette, Sugar, Handles 26.00
Laurel, Sherbet, 6 Oz., 5 1/2 In. 15.00
Lido, Bowl, Handles, 4-Footed, 10 1/2 In. 40.00
Lido, Candy Dish, 3 Sections, 6 1/4 In. 100.00
Lido, Plate, Salad, 7 1/2 In. 8.00
Lido, Tumbler, Footed, 9 Oz., 5 1/2 In. 15.00
Lido, Vase, 9 5/8 In. 265.00
Lyre, Candlestick, 6 1/2 In., Pair 85.00
Manor, Ice Bowl, 5 In. 38.00
Manor, Plate, Bread & Butter, 5 1/4 In. 17.00
Manor, Saucer, Square, 5 In. 4.00
Mayfair, Plate, Ebony, Square, 8 1/4 In. 15.00
Mayfair, Saucer, Amber, 5 In. 6.00
Mayfair, Soup, Cream, Amber, Handles, 4 1/2 In. 20.00
Mayfair, Sugar, Handles, Topaz, Tea 25.00
Mayfair, Syrup, Cover, Green, 5 1/2 In. 125.00
Mayflower, Champagne, Saucer, 6 Oz., 5 1/2 In. 18.00
Mayflower, Cup, Footed, After Dinner 17.00
Mayflower, Goblet, Water, 9 Oz., 7 1/4 In. . . . . .25.00 to 28.00
Mayflower, Plate, Salad, 7 In. 25.00
Mayflower, Salt & Pepper, Sterling Silver Tops, 3 1/2 In. 85.00
Mayflower, Wine, 3 1/2 Oz., 5 3/8 In. 30.00
Meadow Rose, Bowl, 11 3/4 In. 70.00
Meadow Rose, Champagne, 6 Oz., 5 5/8 In. 22.00
Meadow Rose, Cheese Dish, Footed, 3 x 5 1/4 In. 40.00
Meadow Rose, Plate, Luncheon, Center Handle, 11 1/2 In. 42.00
Meadow Rose, Plate, Salad, 7 1/2 In. 18.00
Meadow Rose, Sherbet, 6 Oz., 4 3/8 In. 26.00
Mesa, Goblet, Olive Green, 5 In. 15.00
Mesa, Plate, Smokey Brown, 8 In. 16.00
Mesa, Tumbler, Ruby, 5 1/2 In. 16.00
Midnight Rose, Vase, Footed, 7 1/2 x 5 In. 125.00
Moon Ring, Wine, 4 1/4 Oz., 4 3/8 In. 16.00
Moonstone, Sherbet, Apple Green, 7 Oz., 5 1/2 In. 15.00
Moonstone, Sherbet, Blue, 7 Oz., 5 1/2 In. 15.00
Moonstone, Sherbet, Yellow, 7 Oz., 5 1/2 In. 15.00
Navarre, Bell, 6 1/4 In. 85.00
Navarre, Bowl, Handles, 10 1/2 In. 55.00
Navarre, Cake Plate, Handles, 12 1/2 In. 55.00
Navarre, Candlestick, 2-Light, 4 1/2 In. 45.00
Navarre, Cocktail, 3 1/2 Oz., 5 1/4 In. 25.00
Navarre, Creamer, Tea 18.00
Navarre, Torte Plate, 14 In. 90.00
Navarre, Tumbler, Juice, Footed, 5 Oz., 4 5/8 In. 25.00
Pioneer, Plate, Amber, 8 In. 8.00
Plymouth, Goblet, 10 Oz., 5 1/2 In., 8 Piece 195.00
Queen Anne, Compote, Crystal, Green Stem, Base, 8 1/2 x 10 1/2 In. 150.00
Raleigh, Cup & Saucer 15.00
Rambler, Bowl, Salad, Ruby, 3 7/8 x 10 1/2 In. 125.00
Rogene, Tumbler, 4 1/8 In. 35.00

Romance, Candlestick, 3-Light, Pair	150.00
Romance, Creamer, 3 1/4 In.	18.00
Romance, Cup & Saucer, Footed	25.00
Romance, Soup, Dish, Flat Rim, 7 3/4 In.	100.00
Romance, Tumbler, 12 Oz., 6 In.	28.00
Romance, Vase, 9 1/2 In.	130.00
Royal, Blue, 5 1/4 In.	26.00
Royal, Soup, Dish, Flat, Rimmed, 7 3/4 In.	30.00
Santa Claus, Lamp, Oil, Milk Glass, 9 1/2 In.	4400.00
Shirley, Sugar, Handles, 3 3/4 In.	29.00
Spiral Optic, Plate, Salad, 7 1/4 In.	5.00
Starflower, Plate, 9 1/2 In.	50.00
Sun Ray, Candy Jar, Cover, 7 x 4 1/16 In.	50.00
Sun Ray, Goblet, 9 Oz., 5 3/4 In.	16.00
Sun Ray, Relish, 2 Sections, Handles, 11 5/8 x 4 1/2 In.	18.00
Sun Ray, Relish, 2 Sections, Handles, Ruby, 11 5/8 x 4 1/2 In.	40.00
Trojan, Chop Plate, 13 In.	80.00
Trojan, Ice Bucket, Rose, Tongs, 6 x 5 In.	175.00
Trojan, Tumbler, Iced Tea, Topaz, 12 Oz., 6 In.	30.00
Vernon, Candlestick, Orchid, 4 3/4 In.	30.00
Versailles, Champagne, Topaz, 6 Oz., 6 In.	30.00
Versailles, Cruet, Topaz, Footed, Sterling Stopper, 7 x 3 In.	800.00
Versailles, Cup & Saucer, Azure	43.00
Versailles, Finger Bowl, Underplate, 4 5/8 In.	100.00
Versailles, Plate, Rose, 9 1/2 In.	20.00
Versailles, Tumbler, Whiskey, Footed, Topaz, 2 1/2 Oz.	53.00
Virginia, Goblet, 10 Oz., 7 1/4 In.	20.00
Virginia, Tumbler, Iced Tea, Footed, Dark Blue, 13 Oz., 6 7/8 In.	15.00
Willowmere, Vase, Handles, 6 In.	100.00
Winburn, Nappy, Heart Shape, Milk Glass, 6 x 5 In.	10.00
Woodland, Compote, Green, Footed, 5 1/2 x 4 1/2 In.	15.00

FOVAL, see Fry category.

FRAMES are included in the Furniture category under Frame.

FRANCISCAN is a trademark that appears on pottery. Gladding, McBean and Company started in 1875. The company grew and acquired other potteries. They made sewer pipes, floor tiles, dinnerwares, and art pottery with a variety of trademarks. In 1934, dinnerware and art pottery were sold under the name Franciscan Ware. They made china and cream-colored, decorated earthenware. Desert Rose, Apple, El Patio, and Coronado were best-sellers. The company became Interpace Corporation and in 1979 was purchased by Josiah Wedgwood & Sons. The plant was closed in 1984 but a few of the patterns are still being made. For more information, see *Kovels' Depression Glass & Dinnerware Price List.*

Amapola, Plate, Dinner, 10 1/2 In.	12.00
Amapola, Sugar & Creamer	35.00
Apple, Bowl, Vegetable, 8 1/2 In.	90.00
Apple, Butter, Cover	51.00
Apple, Chop Plate, 14 In.	126.00 to 195.00
Apple, Cup & Saucer	20.00
Apple, Pitcher, Milk, 6 1/2 In.	100.00
Apple, Relish, 3 Sections, Handles, 11 3/4 In.	97.00
Apple, Tidbit, 3 Tiers, Center Handle	130.00
Apple, Tureen, Cover, 13 In.	385.00
Coronado, Ashtray, Shell Shape, 4 1/2 In.	30.00
Coronado, Bowl, Vegetable, Oval, 10 1/2 In.	35.00
Coronado, Gravy Boat, Underplate, Satin Yellow	55.00
Coronado, Salt & Pepper, Coral	30.00
Coronado, Soup, Dish	24.00
Coronado, Teapot, Turquoise	30.00
Daisy, Sugar, Cover	42.00
Desert Rose, Baking Dish, 13 1/2 x 8 1/2 In.	200.00
Desert Rose, Cigarette Box, 4 1/2 In.	150.00

Desert Rose, Compote, 3 3/4 x 8 In.	90.00
Desert Rose, Cookie Jar, 10 1/2 x 6 1/2 In.	300.00
Desert Rose, Eggcup	35.00
Desert Rose, Ginger Jar, Cover, Insert, 4 3/4 x 3 1/4 In.	430.00
Desert Rose, Salt & Pepper, 6 1/4 In.	75.00
Desert Rose, Saltshaker, Rose Bud	25.00
Desert Rose, Snack Plate, 10 1/4 In.	153.00
Desert Rose, Teapot	125.00
Desert Rose, Tureen, Cover, 12 x 7 3/4 In.	625.00
El Patio, Bowl, Vegetable, Turquoise, 9 In.	30.00
El Patio, Chop Plate, Turquoise, 11 In.	47.00
El Patio, Sugar & Creamer, Pink Matte	35.00
El Patio, Sugar & Creamer, Yellow	65.00
Forget-Me-Not, Bowl, Cereal, 7 In.	23.00
Forget-Me-Not, Creamer	33.00
Forget-Me-Not, Cup & Saucer	27.00
Fremont, Cup & Saucer	38.00
Fremont, Gravy Boat, Underplate	120.00
Fremont, Platter, Oval, 16 In.	130.00
Hacienda Gold, Creamer	14.00
Hacienda Gold, Plate, Dinner, 10 3/4 In.	15.00
Hacienda Gold, Sugar, Cover	12.00
Hacienda Green, Bowl, Vegetable, 7 1/2 In.	14.00
Hacienda Green, Cup & Saucer	16.00
Ivy, Bowl, Vegetable, Divided, 12 In.	95.00
Ivy, Chop Plate, 11 3/4 In.	95.00
Ivy, Cup & Saucer	95.00
Ivy, Soup, Dish	30.00
Ivy, Sugar, Cover	35.00
Ivy, Teapot, 6 1/4 In.	290.00
Mariposa, Salt & Pepper	98.00
Moondance, Berry Bowl	15.00
Moondance, Plate, Dinner, 10 1/2 In.	19.00
Moondance, Plate, Salad, 8 1/2 In.	14.00
October, Cup & Saucer	14.00
October, Pitcher, 7 1/2 In.	130.00
October, Platter, Oval, 14 x 11 In.	45.00
October, Salt & Pepper	20.00
October, Snack Plate, Square, 8 1/4 In.	90.00
Picnic, Coffeepot, 10 In.	80.00
Poppy, Plate, Dinner, 10 1/2 In.	40.00
Renaissance Gold, Bowl, Vegetable, Oval, 9 x 6 1/2 In.	250.00
Renaissance Gold, Plate, Dinner, 10 1/2 In.	55.00 to 74.00
Renaissance Gold, Platter, Oval, 15 1/2 x 12 In.	280.00
Spice, Butter, Cover	12.00
Spring Song, Coffeepot, 9 1/2 In.	55.00
Starburst, Bowl, Salad, 11 7/8 In.	95.00
Starburst, Bowl, Vegetable, Divided, Cover	60.00
Starburst, Butter, Cover	35.00
Starburst, Relish, 3-Sided, 3 Sections, 7 In.	95.00
Strawberry, Berry Bowl, Master, 8 1/2 In.	60.00
Strawberry, Platter, Oval, 14 1/2 In.	80.00
Tuliptime, Bowl, Cereal, 6 In.	12.00
Tuliptime, Plate, Dinner, 10 1/2 In.	18.00
Tuliptime, Sugar & Creamer	43.00
Woodside, Cup & Saucer	38.00
Woodside, Gravy Boat	137.00

FRANKART, Inc., New York, New York, mass-produced nude *dancing lady* lamps, ashtrays, and other decorative Art Deco items in the 1920s and 1930s. They were made of white lead composition and spray-painted. *Frankart Inc.* and the patent number and year were stamped on the base.

Candleholder, Nudes, Sitting, Arms Folded, Marked, 1928, 4 3/4 In.	600.00

FRANKOMA POTTERY was originally known as The Frank Potteries when John F. Frank opened shop in 1933. The factory is now working in Sapulpa, Oklahoma. Early wares were made from a light cream-colored clay from Ada, Oklahoma, but in 1956 the company switched to a red burning clay from Sapulpa. The firm makes dinnerwares, utilitarian and decorative kitchenwares, figurines, flowerpots, and limited edition and commemorative pieces. John Frank died in 1973 and his daughter, Joniece, inherited the business. Frankoma went bankrupt in 1990. It was bought by Richard Bernstein in 1991 and is still in business.

Ashtray, Arrowhead, Desert Gold, Brick Red Clay	17.00
Ashtray, Clover, Desert Gold, Brick Red Clay	7.50
Ashtray, Freeform, Prairie Green, Ada Clay	15.00
Baker, Open Handles, Plainsman, Prairie Green, Brick Red Clay	15.00
Batter Set, Pitcher, Creamer, Sugar, Syrup, Prairie Green, Ada Clay	130.00
Bookends, Irish Setter, Desert Gold, Ada Clay	200.00
Bowl, Knobby Cactus, Ada Clay, 4 In.	50.00
Bowl, Prairie Green, Red Clay, 15 In.	12.00
Bowl, Vegetable, Plainsman, Terra-Cotta Rose	10.00
Bowl, Willie Wirehand, Raised Image, Indian Electric Co-Op, 7 1/2 In.	80.00
Creamer, Plainsman, Prairie Green, Brick Red Clay	10.00
Creamer, Westwind, Autumn Yellow	10.00
Cup, Plainsman, Prairie Green, Brick Red Clay	4.50
Figurine, Charging Tiger, Iridescent Black, Ada Clay, 13 In.	3000.00
Figurine, Gardener Boy, Prairie Green	125.00
Figurine, Nude, Brown & Green Crystalline Glaze, 8 In.	290.00 to 375.00
Figurine, Star Boot, Prairie Green, Ada Clay, Miniature	35.00
Gravy Boat, Plainsman, Prairie Green, Brick Red Clay	9.00
Gravy Boat, Plainsman, Woodland Moss	15.00
Mug, Barrel, Desert Gold, Brick Red Clay	10.00
Mug, Political, Donkey, 1978	8.00
Pitcher, Plainsman, Desert Gold, Brick Red Clay	20.00
Planter, Dutch Shoe, Woodland Moss	25.00
Planter, Log, Desert Gold, Ada Clay	20.00
Plate, Dinner, Plainsman, Brown Satin, Brick Red Clay	6.00
Plate, Dinner, Plainsman, Prairie Green, Brick Red Clay	6.00
Plate, Dinner, Plainsman, Terra-Cotta Rose	6.00
Plate, Dinner, Westwind, Autumn Yellow	6.50
Plate, Salad, Plainsman, Terra-Cotta Rose	4.50
Salt & Pepper, Plainsman, Brown Satin, Brick Red Clay	10.00
Salt & Pepper, Teepee, Desert Gold, Ada Clay	15.00
Salt & Pepper, Wheat Stock, Desert Gold, Ada Clay	20.00
Teapot, Brown Satin, Brick Red Clay	12.00
Teapot, Prairie Green, Brick Red Clay	30.00
Trivet, Liberty Bell, Flame, 1976	10.00
Trivet, Prairie Green	8.00
Vase, Bud, Modern, Woodland Moss	8.00
Vase, Bud, Snail, Red Bud, Ada Clay	60.00
Vase, Fan Shell, Clay Blue, Ada Clay	25.00
Vase, Flying Goose, Desert Gold	40.00
Vase, Pillow, Prairie Green, Ada Clay, 5 In.	40.00

FRATERNAL objects that are related to the many different fraternal organizations in the United States are listed in this category. The Elks, Masons, Odd Fellows, and others are included. Also included are service organizations, like the American Legion, Kiwanis, and Lions Club. Furniture is listed in the Furniture category. Shaving mugs decorated with fraternal crests are included in the Shaving Mug category.

G.A.R., Mug, Weapons, Cannon, Multicolored, c.1900, 4 In.	75.00
G.A.R., Program, Official, Nation, 39th, Denver, 1905	50.00
Knights Of Columbus, Hat, Black Body, Gold Bullion Cross, Ostrich Feather, Size 7 1/2	95.00
Knights Of Columbus, Kepi Cap, Officer, 1895 Style, Lacquered Visor, Small	109.00
Knights Of Columbus, Sword, Lodge, Wood Grip, Bust Pommel, 28 1/4 In.	565.00
Knights Of Columbus, Sword, Steel Blade, Aluminum Guard, Steel Scabbard, 27 In.	75.00

Knights Of Columbus, Watch Fob, Bronze, Satin Ribbon, World War I Veteran 40.00
Knights Of Pythias, Sword, Lodge, Wood Grip, Armored Knight Pommel, 23 In. 39.00
Knights Of Pythias, Sword, Lodge, Wood Grip, Armored Knight Pommel, 28 1/4 In. 56.00
Masonic, Apron, Pillars, Compass, Square, Eye, No. 9, Leather, Silk, Frame, 19 x 20 In. . .   200.00
Masonic, Arch, Wood, Carved, Painted, Columns, Symbols, 99 x 64 x 12 In. 1320.00
Masonic, Bible Box, Folk Art, Cherry, Birch Inlaid Compass, Late 1800s, 3 x 9 x 12 In. . . .   230.00
Masonic, Cane, Carved, 19 Symbols, 32nd Degree Eagle, Trowel, 36 1/4 In. 690.00
Masonic, Clock, Silvered Brass, Calipers & Square, American, c.1900, 6 1/4 In. 125.00
Masonic, Lodge Apron, White Leather, Gray Ribbon Trim, Red Triangles, 13 x 14 In. 40.00
Masonic, Medallion, Rose Gold, Ashlor Lodge No. 105, Case, c.1900, 4 1/2 x 2 In. 195.00
Masonic, Pin, Insignia, In Hoc Signo Vinces, Tiger Claw, 14K Gold, Diamond 560.00
Masonic, Soup Spoon, Masonic Hall In Script On Handle, Reed & Barton 10.00
Masonic, Sword, Wood Handle, Steel Scabbard, Bent & Bush, Boston, 28-In. Blade 115.00
Masonic, Watch Fob, 32nd Degree, 2-Headed Eagle, Gold, Enamel, 1 x 1 In. . . . . .195.00 to 218.00
Odd Fellows, Badge, 10K Gold, Rhinestones, 2 5/8 x 1 1/2 In. 44.00
Odd Fellows, Pipe Bowl, Carved Wood, Oak Leaves, Eagle, J.C. Lare, 1867, 2 7/8 In. 1410.00
Shriner, Jacket, Police, Ararat Provost Marshall, Chain Stitched Back Star, Size 46R 48.00

FRY GLASS was made by the H. C. Fry Glass Company of Rochester,
Pennsylvania. The company, founded in 1901, first made cut glass and
other types of fine glasswares. In 1922, they patented a heat-resistant
glass called *Pearl Ovenglass*. For two years, 1926–1927, the company
made Fry Foval, an opal ware decorated with colored trim.
Reproductions of this glass have been made. Depression glass patterns
made by Fry may be listed in the Depression Glass category. Some
pieces of cut glass may also be included in the Cut Glass category.

FRY, Bowl, Cut, Hobstar, Flashed Star, Round, Flared, Signed, 10 1/2 In. 175.00
Cheese & Cracker Server, Strawberry-Diamond Cutting, Vesicas & Daisy, 10 In. 175.00
Compote, Blue Teardrop Stem, Raised Foot, Flared, 7 In. 230.00
Compote, Strawberry-Diamond Cutting, Star & Fan, Signed, 3 3/4 x 6 In. 25.00
Pitcher, Undertray, Blue, Threaded Band, Air-Trap Body, Raised Pedestal, 9 1/2 x 9 In. . . .   288.00
Vase, Bud, Cut Jade Body, Opalescent Foot, 7 1/4 In. 21.00
Vase, Double Gourd, Flared, Blue Rim, Ball Feet, 5 3/8 In. 115.00
Vase, Petaled Flower, Blue Rim, Tapered, Opalescent Stem, Raised Foot, 10 1/4 In. 345.00
FRY FOVAL, Coffeepot Set, Percolator, Cups, Saucers, 9 Piece 370.00
Creamer, Opal, Delft Blue Foot & Handle 100.00
Lemonade Set, Pitcher, Cover, White Opalescent, Jade Handle, 9 1/2-In. Pitcher, 7 Piece .   720.00
Tumbler, Lemonade, Rockwell Silver Rim, Delft Blue Handle & Foot, 5 In. 51.00
Vase, Jack-In-The-Pulpit, Opalescent, Translucent, Jade Rim, 10 In. 165.00

FULPER Pottery Company was incorporated in 1899 in Flemington,
New Jersey. They made art pottery from 1910 to 1929. The firm had
been making bottles, jugs, and housewares from 1805. Doll heads were
made about 1928. The firm became Stangl Pottery in 1929. Fulper art
pottery is admired for its attractive glazes and simple shapes.

Bowl, 3 Bun Feet, Chinese Blue Flambe Exterior, Oatmeal Interior, 4 7/8 x 11 1/4 In. 374.00
Bowl, Cafe Au Lait Glaze, Geometric Band, Buttressed Handles, Marked, 3 x 6 In. 374.00
Bowl, Flemington Green, 2 x 6 In. 92.00
Bowl, Frothy Blue & White Glaze Dripping, Famille Rose, Footed, Flared, 4 x 10 In. 144.00
Bowl, Green, Blue Matte Crystalline Glaze, Lavender Matte Ground, Marked, 3 x 6 In. . . .   345.00
Bowl, Lobed, Green & Blue Mottled Glaze, Caramel Interior, Stamped, 13 In. 290.00
Bowl, Low, Embossed Sides, Blue & Green Flambe, 2 7/8 x 10 1/2 In. 290.00
Bowl, Low, Ivory, Crystalline Amber Flambe, Mustard, Closed-In Rim, Marked, 10 In. . . .   259.00
Bowl, Moss To Rose Flambe Glaze, Flared, Footed, Stamped, 3 1/2 x 7 1/2 In. 1064.00
Bowl, Moss To Rose Flambe Glaze, Frothy Blue & White 259.00
Bowl, Oriental Flambe, Embossed Repeated Design, 3 x 10 1/4 In. 495.00
Bowl, Scalloped Edges, Multitone Green, Brown, Ivory Flambe Glaze, Stamped, 15 In. . . .   375.00
Bowl, Shell, Frog Rim, Green, Ivory, 3 3/4 x 11 1/2 In. 140.00
Bowl, Turquoise, Olive, Blue, Runny Glaze, Footed, Impressed, 4 x 11 1/2 In. 400.00
Candleholder, Matte Brown, New Bedford Hotel, Racetrack Mark, 2 1/4 In. 115.00
Candlestick, Blue Crystalline Glaze, 3 Handles, Marked, 1 1/4 x 6 In. 175.00
Candlestick, Chinese Blue Flambe Glaze, Twisted, Marked, 8 In.   90.00
Cider Set, Mottled Leopard Skin Crystalline Glaze, Embossed S, 6 Piece 980.00

Crock, Bird, Blue, Flemington, N.J., 3 Gal. 250.00
Figurine, Cat, Leopard Skin Crystalline Glaze, Vertical Stamp, 7 x 8 3/4 In. 750.00
Flowerpot, Flared, Brown, Gray, Yellow Crystalline Flambe Glaze, 13 x 16 In. 635.00
Powder Box, Art Deco, Young Woman, Wide Skirt, 6 1/4 In. 230.00
Urn, Colonial Revival, 2 Handles, Cobalt Blue, Rust Flambe Glaze, 17 5/8 In. 575.00
Urn, Leopard Skin Crystalline Glaze, Squat, Ridged, Marked, 7 1/2 In. 290.00
Vase, 2 Handles, Green, Brown Crystalline Glaze, 10 In. 690.00
Vase, 2 Handles, Mottled Green, Brown Crystalline Glaze, 8 In. 805.00
Vase, Basket Shape, Ruffled Rim, Twisted Handle, Turquoise Glaze, Vertical Mark, 9 In. . 115.00
Vase, Black Mirror Glaze Over Butterscotch, 3 Angular Buttressed Handles, 6 1/2 In. 415.00
Vase, Blue & Copper Dust Flambe Glaze, Baluster, Marked, 15 1/2 x 7 3/4 In. 750.00
Vase, Blue & Tan Flambe Glaze, 12 1/2 In. 520.00
Vase, Blue Crystalline Glaze, Multitoned Green Drip, Shouldered Shape, 5 1/2 In. 690.00
Vase, Blue Flambe, Bulbous, 2 Squared Handles, 6 1/4 In. 850.00
Vase, Blue, Purple & Green Drip Glaze, Bulbous, 11 In. 1410.00
Vase, Blue, Red Drip Glaze, 5 3/4 In. 230.00
Vase, Blue, Tan & Brown Flambe Glaze, 2 Handles, 10 In. 400.00
Vase, Blue, Tan Flambe Glaze, 12 1/2 In. 920.00
Vase, Blue, Yellow, Brown Crystalline Glaze, Bulbous Shape, Flared Rim, Mark, 7 3/4 In. 290.00
Vase, Bottle Shape, Brown, Green, Blue Gray Glaze, Vertical Mark, 8 In. 290.00
Vase, Bottle Shape, Flemington Green Crystalline Flambe Glaze, Prang Mark, 5 3/4 In. .. 460.00
Vase, Brown & Green Flambe Glaze, Tapered Shape, 7 In. 175.00
Vase, Brown Crystalline Glaze, Bulbous, Rolled Rim, 5 1/2 In. 325.00
Vase, Brown Drip Over Gold High Glaze, Handles, Impressed Mark, 4 1/2 In. 345.00
Vase, Bud, Frothy Gray, Brown & Beige Glaze, Over Mustard, Bullet Shape, 5 3/4 In. .. 175.00
Vase, Cat's-Eye Flambe Glaze, Bullet Shape, 3 Buttressed Handles, Marked, 6 1/2 In. ... 430.00
Vase, Cat's-Eye Flambe Glaze, Flared Mouth, Black Mirror Glaze, 7 1/2 In. 330.00
Vase, Cucumber Matte Glaze, Impressed Mark, 5 In. 259.00
Vase, Deep Brown Matte Glaze, Handles, 6 1/2 In. 405.00
Vase, Elephant's Breath, High Gloss, Leopard Skin Flambe, Barrel Shape, 7 x 5 1/2 In. .. 2300.00
Vase, Embossed Collar, Semiglossy, Green Flambe & Mottled, No. 524, 9 7/8 In. 518.00
Vase, Famille Rose Glaze, Squat, Marked, 5 3/4 x 9 In. 345.00
Vase, Famille Rose Matte Glaze, Round, Closed Rim, Marked, 6 In. 546.00
Vase, Flambe Glaze, Blue, Beige, Purple Matte, Baluster, Marked, 11 In. 430.00
Vase, Frothy Blue Over Famille Rose Glaze, Squat, 4 Buttresses, Marked, 13 x 10 In. 4025.00
Vase, Frothy Flemington Green Glaze, 4 Buttresses, Tapered, Marked, 8 1/4 In. 635.00
Vase, Frothy Gunmetal, Ivory Flambe Matte Glaze, Over Mustard Matte, 12 In. 1840.00
Vase, Frothy Indigo Matte Glaze, Tapered, 2 Handles, Horizontal Mark, 7 x 7 1/2 In. ... 200.00
Vase, Frothy Matte Amber Glaze, Corseted, Buttressed Handles, Marked, 8 x 6 1/4 In. ... 200.00
Vase, Frothy Mottled Chinese Blue Glaze, Flat Shoulder, Collared Rim, 4 1/2 x 6 1/2 In. . 260.00
Vase, Glossy Amber & Turquoise Glaze, Tapered, 4 Buttresses, Marked, 8 1/2 In. 175.00
Vase, Glossy Amber Glaze, Dripping Over Mirror Brown Base, Baluster, 13 x 6 1/2 In. .. 2300.00
Vase, Green & Black Crystalline Glaze, 3 Handles, Impressed Mark, 7 In. 400.00
Vase, Green & Brown Flambe, Blue Crystalline, Shouldered, Squared Handles, 10 In. ... 1528.00
Vase, Green Cucumber Crystalline Glaze, Slender, 2 Handles, 11 In. 865.00
Vase, Green Mirrored Glaze, Bulbous, Cylindrical Neck, Marked, 8 x 5 1/4 In. 430.00
Vase, Green, Cobalt, Turquoise Matte Glossy Glaze, Ultramarine Ground, Handles, 7 In. . 920.00
Vase, Leopard Skin Crystalline Glaze, Charcoaling, Melon Shape, 5 1/2 x 7 In. 550.00
Vase, Leopard Skin Crystalline Glaze, Faceted, Flat Embossed Shoulder, 4 x 3 3/4 In. 460.00
Vase, Leopard Skin Crystalline Glaze, Handles, Corseted, Marked, 4 1/2 x 6 In. 405.00
Vase, Leopard Skin Crystalline Glaze, Spherical, Closed In Rim, Marked, 5 1/2 In. 290.00
Vase, Leopard Skin Crystalline Glaze, Squat, Angular Chinese Handles, Marked, 4 3/4 In. 316.00
Vase, Maroon & Tan Matte Glaze, 3 Handles, Impressed Mark, 6 1/2 In. 290.00
Vase, Mirror Black Glaze, Tapered, 13 x 8 In. 2185.00
Vase, Mirror Blue & Green Frothy Glaze, Bulbous, 7 1/4 x 5 3/4 In. 315.00
Vase, Moss To Rose Flambe Glaze, 3 Handles, Horizontal Stamp, 6 1/2 x 7 1/2 In. 230.00
Vase, Mottled Blue Matte Glaze, Tapered Shape, 7 In. 405.00
Vase, Mottled Brown Glaze, Green Drip, Bulbous, 5 Buttresses At Top, 5 In. 176.00
Vase, Mottled Brown Matte Glaze, Blue Flambe Drip, Bulbous, 9 1/2 In. 290.00
Vase, Purple & Amber Flambe Glaze, Fan, 2 Handles, Marked, 8 In. 430.00
Vase, Purple Glaze, Slender Curvilinear Shape, Stamped Vertical Mark, 9 In. 345.00
Vase, Purple Microcrystalline Glaze, 3 Handles, Marked, 4 1/4 In. 230.00
Vase, Rose Drip Glaze Over Blue & Green, Famille Rose, Angular Handles, 11 1/4 In. 495.00

Vase, Turquoise Crackled Glaze, Beehive Form, Marked, 3 1/2 In. 145.00
Vase, Turquoise Matte Glaze, Tapered, Pedestal, Impressed Mark, 9 In. 115,00
Vase, Yellow Flambe, Chinese Blue & Chocolate Brown High Glaze, Baluster, 9 1/4 In. ... 275.00

FURNITURE of all types is listed in this category. Examples dating from the seventeenth century to the 1970s are included. Prices for furniture vary in different parts of the country. Oak furniture is most expensive in the West; large pieces over eight feet high are sold for the most money in the South, where high ceilings are found in the old homes. Condition is very important when determining prices. These are NOT average prices but rather reports of unique sales. If the description includes the word *style*, the piece resembles the old furniture style but was made at a later time. It is not a period piece. Garden furniture is listed in the Garden Furnishings category. Related items may be found in the Architectural, Brass, and Store categories.

Armchairs are listed under Chair in this category.
Armoire, Cherry, Cabriole Legs, Drawers, La., Mid 19th Century, 87 In. .... *Illus* 12075.00
Armoire, Continental Style, Oak, Arched Molded Cornice, Bun Feet, 83 x 72 x 22 In. 545.00
Armoire, Continental, Mixed Wood, 85 3/4 x 51 1/2 x 19 1/4 In. 290.00
Armoire, Edwardian, Mahogany, Crossbanded, Paneled Doors, Drawer, 84 x 21 x 51 In. ... 570.00
Armoire, Edwardian, Painted Satinwood, Mirror, c.1900, 83 x 63 1/2 x 23 In. 3105.00
Armoire, Empire Style, Mahogany, Gilt, 96 x 56 x 27 In. 1560.00
Armoire, French Provincial, Kingwood, Walnut, Late 1800s, 102 x 59 x 20 In. 2185.00
Armoire, French Provincial, Mahogany, 2 Doors, 2 Drawers, c.1890, 85 1/2 x 52 In. 1380.00
Armoire, French Provincial, Oak, 2 Doors, 3 Drawers, Early 1800s, 95 x 63 x 22 In. 3680.00
Armoire, George III, Inlaid Mahogany, 2 Doors, c.1800, 81 x 52 1/2 x 24 In. 1725.00
Armoire, George III, Mahogany, Channel Islands, c.1865, 82 x 52 x 33 1/2 In. 1725.00
Armoire, George IV, Mahogany, 2 Doors, Drawer, c.1835, 91 x 62 In. 1840.00
Armoire, Gothic Revival, Walnut, Arched Pediment, American, c.1855, 97 x 62 x 26 In. .. 4140.00
Armoire, Henri IV Style, Oak, Carved, France, Late 1800s, 95 x 69 x 26 1/2 In. 1265.00
Armoire, Jacobean Style, Oak, Carved Frieze, 2 Doors, Early 1900s, 71 x 42 x 21 In. 765.00
Armoire, Louis XIII, Wild Cherry, Diamond Pattern, France, 1600s, 62 x 31 x 17 In. 5000.00
Armoire, Louis XV Style, 2-Paneled Doors, c.1850, 91 1/2 x 54 1/2 x 23 In. 2760.00
Armoire, Louis XV Style, Fruitwood, 2 Doors, Molded Cornice, c.1890, 85 x 56 In. 2185.00
Armoire, Louis XV Style, Mahogany, Walnut, Early 1900s, 99 x 81 1/2 x 25 In. 575.00
Armoire, Louis XV Style, Oak, Molded Cornice, Leaf Carved Doors, 82 x 69 x 27 In. ... 880.00
Armoire, Louis XV Style, Oak, Painted, 89 x 68 x 27 In. 1530.00
Armoire, Louis XV, Oak, c.1750, 79 x 58 1/2 x 23 In. 2715.00
Armoire, Louis XV, Walnut, 2-Paneled Doors, Molded Cornice, c.1800 .... 2350.00
Armoire, Mahogany, 2 Doors, England, c.1865, 85 x 54 x 24 In. 1095.00
Armoire, Mahogany, Crossbanded, Swan Neck Pediment, 3 Drawers, 91 x 50 x 26 In. ... 1265.00
Armoire, Mahogany, Shelves, Drawers, New York, c.1825, 91 x 64 x 27 1/2 In. 13800.00
Armoire, Napoleon III, Rosewood, Burled Ash Bands, Mirror, c.1860, 93 x 42 x 19 In. ... 4890.00
Armoire, Neoclassical, Mahogany, Flared & Molded Cornice, American, Early 1800s 9200.00
Armoire, Oak, Scalloped Raised Panel Doors, Italy, 1700s, 75 x 51 1/2 x 24 1/2 In. 1610.00
Armoire, Painted, Gray, 2 Doors, 5 Raised Panels, Bracket Base, 99 x 70 x 27 In. 865.00
Armoire, Rococo Revival, Oak, 2-Paneled Doors, Crest, 90 x 62 x 26 In. 355.00
Armoire, Rococo Revival, Rosewood, Bonnet Top, Mid 1800s, 114 x 57 x 24 1/2 In. 19550.00
Armoire, Rococo, Rosewood, Scrolled Pediment, New York, c.1855, 110 x 64 In. 4600.00
Armoire, Rosewood, Mirrored Doors, 2 Drawers, c.1860, 97 x 67 In. 2760.00
Armoire, Stained Cypress, 3-Paneled Doors, Early 1900s, 108 x 85 x 29 In. 3160.00
Armoire, Walnut, Panel Doors, Creole, Late 18th Century, 89 1/2 x 56 x 24 In. 25300.00
Baker's Rack, French Provincial, Fruitwood, Slat Supports, Cup Hooks, 39 x 51 In. 325.00
Bar, Art Deco, Wood Veneer, Composite Surface, c.1935, 42 x 35 x 17 In. 380.00
Bar, Phil Powell, Walnut, Brass, Free Edge, 3 Drawers, 39 x 106 3/4 x 27 1/2 In. 9200.00
Bar Cart, Edwardian, Mahogany, Brass Inlay, Early 1800s, 39 1/2 x 31 x 19 In. 1725.00
Bar Cart, J. Adnet, Wood, Metal, c.1950, 30 1/2 x 21 1/2 x 32 1/2 In. 6465.00
Barstool, Plycraft, Walnut Plywood, Naugahyde, 17 1/4 x 37 In., Pair 1955.00
Barstool, Warren McArthur, White Leather Upholstery, 1937, 30 In., Pair ...... 1410.00 to 1750.00
Bed, Adam Style, Portrait Headboards, Pineapple Footboard, c.1900, Single, Pair 1325.00
Bed, Black Walnut, 4 Cylindrical Rails, Mattress, Rope Lacing, New England, c.1810 ... 495.00
Bed, Black, Wood, Gilt Decorated, Undulating Headboard, Mid 1800s, 57 x 66 x 78 In. .. 1380.00
Bed, Brass, Tubular, Turned Decoration, Post Caps, c.1890, 59 1/2 x 56 x 78 In. 375.00

Bed, Cannonball, Cypress, Red Stain, Louisiana, Early 1800s 3450.00
Bed, Cannonball, Maple, Scrolled Head & Footboard, 51 x 50 x 71 In. 980.00
Bed, Cannonball, Walnut, Pine, Rope, 19th Century 975.00
Bed, Cherry, Pine, Low Posts, c.1840, Pair 2500.00
Bed, Empire Style, Mahogany, Side Columns, c.1850, 43 x 48 1/2 x 80 In. 865.00
Bed, Empire, Cherry, Bell & Ball Posts, Queen, 54 1/4 In......................... 60.00
Bed, Empire, Cherry, Birch, Ball Posts, Carved Acanthus Columns, 45 1/2 In. 400.00
Bed, Empire, Cherry, Pine, Low Posts, American, c.1840, 43 1/2 x 81 x 44 In., Pair 2125.00
Bed, Empire, Pine, Mahogany, Pineapple Carved Posts, Single, 46 1/4 In., Pair 575.00
Bed, Federal, Maple, Canopy, Turned & Reeded Foot Posts 1195.00
Bed, Federal, Tiger Maple, c.1810, 68 x 54 1/4 x 78 3/4 In. 2070.00
Bed, Four-Poster, Arts & Crafts, 13 Vertical Slats, Tapered, 84 x 58 x 53 In. 2645.00
Bed, Four-Poster, Cherry, Rope, Gooseneck Headboard, Ohio, 53 x 80 In............ 1380.00
Bed, Four-Poster, Empire, Tiger Maple, American, c.1840, Double, 76 x 76 3/4 x 53 In. ... 700.00
Bed, Four-Poster, Federal, Birch, Arched Headboard, Early 1800s, 56 x 76 In. 3525.00
Bed, Four-Poster, Federal, Mahogany, Early 1800s, Double, 86 x 79 1/2 x 59 1/2 In. 1300.00
Bed, Four-Poster, Federal, Maple, Arched Headboard, c.1820, 84 x 47 x 72 In. 2820.00
Bed, Four-Poster, Federal, Maple, Pine, Urn Finials, 60 x 55 In. 805.00
Bed, Four-Poster, Jacobean Style, Oak, Carved Panels, 88 x 85 x 57 In. 10000.00
Bed, Four-Poster, Mahogany, Inlaid, Carved, Canopy, Mid 1900s, 86 x 57 3/4 x 81 In. ... 489.00
Bed, Four-Poster, Mahogany, Ogee Molded, Mississippi Valley, c.1840, 97 x 67 x 86 In. .. 6325.00
Bed, Four-Poster, Maple, Cone & Ring Finials, Rolling-Pin Crests, Rope, 45 x 48 In. 460.00
Bed, Four-Poster, Maple, Turned Urn Finials, Rope, 84 x 84 x 55 In. 770.00
Bed, Four-Poster, Neoclassical, Mahogany, Carved Fruit, Leaves, 96 x 52 x 79 In. 3680.00
Bed, Four-Poster, Neoclassical, Mahogany, Paneled Headboard, 90 x 76 In. 2585.00
Bed, Four-Poster, Neoclassical, Walnut, Mahogany, American, c.1835, 110 x 72 x 91 In. ... 3680.00
Bed, Four-Poster, P. Evans, Canopy, Chrome Patchwork, Directional, 80 x 90 In. 575.00
Bed, Four-Poster, Poplar, Mushroom Finials, Trundle, 60-In. Rails, 43 3/4 In. Wide 230.00
Bed, Four-Poster, Renaissance Style, Mahogany, Portugal, c.1850, 117 x 58 x 85 In. 8625.00
Bed, Four-Poster, Sheraton Style, Carved Pineapple, 63 x 38 x 77 In., Pair 1095.00
Bed, Four-Poster, Sheraton, Mahogany, Flat Headboard, 87 x 52 x 72 In. 1575.00
Bed, Four-Poster, Sheraton, Mahogany, Leaf Carving, Shaped Headboard, c.1820 .... 1265.00
Bed, Four-Poster, Sheraton, Softwood, Flat Head & Footboard, 81 x 62 x 83 In. 280.00
Bed, Four-Poster, Tiger Maple, 8-Sided Legs, Cannonball Feet, c.1850, 54 x 60 In. 360.00
Bed, Four-Poster, Walnut, Paneled Headboard, c.1835, Queen 4370.00
Bed, G. Nakashima, Walnut, Platform, Pegged Construction, Double, 10 x 54 x 76 In. ... 3740.00
Bed, G. Nelson, Walnut, Cane, Metal, Thin Edge, Herman Miller, 38 x 34 x 84 In., Pair .. 10530.00
Bed, G. Stickley, 2 Horizontal Rails, Cloud Lift, 3/4 Size, 79 x 46 x 38 In. 2300.00
Bed, G. Stickley, Reverse Tapered Posts, Slats, Side Rails, 48 x 59 x 79 In. 5175.00
Bed, Hepplewhite, Birch, Pencil Posts, Red Paint, New England, 85 x 52 1/2 In. 6325.00
Bed, Indonesian, Scroll & Leaf, Shell Pediment, 1900s, King, 60 x 82 x 89 In. 1320.00
Bed, Iron, Painted, Scroll, X-Decorated Head, Footboard, Canopy, 95 x 52 x 48 In. 330.00
Bed, Louis Philippe, Mahogany, Mid 19th Century, 39 x 40 1/2 x 74 In. 805.00
Bed, Louis XV Style, Polychrome, c.1900, 36 1/2 x 40 x 81 In. 1380.00
Bed, Louis XVI Style, Upholstered, 55 x 47 x 78 In., Pair 850.00
Bed, Maple, Low Posts, American, c.1835, Double, 42 1/4 x 77 x 53 In. 710.00
Bed, Maple, Pine Headboard, Blanket Roll Footboard, 46 x 42 In., Pair 115.00
Bed, Napoleon III, Fruitwood, Polychrome, c.1865, 47 1/2 x 53 x 71 1/2 In. 4830.00
Bed, Napoleon III, Rosewood, Burled Ash Bands, c.1860, 56 x 51 x 80 In. 805.00
Bed, Neoclassical, Mahogany, Gothic Spire Uprights, American, c.1840, 42 x 58 x 83 In. .. 1380.00
Bed, Neoclassical, Mahogany, Posts, Shells, Scrolling Leaves, c.1830, 91 x 64 x 82 In. ... 5060.00
Bed, Neoclassical, Mahogany, Tester, American, c.1890, 104 x 72 x 90 In. 3450.00
Bed, Neogrecque, Walnut, Pediment Headboard, American, c.1865, 86 x 67 x 89 In. 1840.00
Bed, Nutting, Mahogany, Branded Signature, Twin, 44 1/2 In., Pair 2300.00
Bed, Oak, Paneled Headboard, Applied Scroll & Bead Carving, 72 In. 340.00
Bed, Pine, Poplar, Vinegar Grain, Rope, Pennsylvania, 51 1/4 x 36 1/2 In. 575.00
Bed, Pine, Scrolled Headboard, Vase-Form Legs, American, c.1850, 63 x 53 x 71 In. 400.00
Bed, Renaissance Revival, Oak, Parcel Gilt, Low Posts, Spain, c.1910, 62 x 60 x 76 In. .. 1060.00
Bed, Renaissance Revival, Walnut, Half-Tester, Anthemion, c.1865, 129 x 72 x 88 In. 8625.00
Bed, Rococo Style, Mahogany, Carved Backrest, Footboard, Asian Export, 63 1/2 In. 205.00
Bed, Rohde, Paldao Wood, Curved Footboard, Herman Miller, 58 1/2 x 31 x 34 In....... 145.00
Bed, Rosewood, Latticework Canopy & Gallery, Chinese, 94 x 87 x 59 In. 3450.00
Bed, Rosewood, Whalebone-Tipped Posts, Mass., 1800s, 10 x 10 x 7 In. 1265.00

Bed, Roycroft, Headboard, Baseboard, Vertical Slats, Mackmurdo Feet, 49 x 55 x 80 In. . . . 6900.00
Bed, Russel Wright, Maple, American Modern, Conant & Ball, 58 x 34 In. 235.00
Bed, Shaker, Cherry, 3-Board Headboard, 2-Board Footboard, c.1860, 67 x 31 In. 3960.00
Bed, Shaker, Four-Poster, Pine, Straight Rails, Turned, Dark Stain, 34 x 70 In. 880.00
Bed, Shaker, Head & Footboards, Mortise & Tenon Posts, Ky., c.1830, 26 x 77 x 46 In. . . . 360.00
Bed, Shaker, Pine, Maple, Wheels, New Lebanon, c.1840, 34 x 78 3/4 x 41 1/2 In. 1150.00
Bed, Sheraton, Birch, Acorn Finials, New England, 48 x 56 1/2 x 81 In. 460.00
Bed, Sheraton, Maple, Cannonball, Turned, Blocked Legs, Single, Pair 1265.00
Bed, Sheraton, Maple, Knopped Foot & Head Posts, New England, 35 x 51 1/2 In. 575.00
Bed, Sheraton, Mushroom Finials, Painted, New England, 48 x 51 1/2 In. 1150.00
Bed, Sleigh, Crotch Split Mahogany Veneer, Contoured Rails, 40 x 58 x 76 In. 1100.00
Bed, Sleigh, Neoclassical, Mahogany, S-Scrolled Ends, American, c.1850, 55 In. 470.00
Bed, Sleigh, Split Mahogany Veneer, Dated Dec 10-56, 40 x 58 x 76 In. 1120.00
Bed, V. Kagan, Walnut, Sculpted Cane Headboard, King, 36 3/4 x 83 3/4 x 80 In. 1840.00
Bed, Victorian, Walnut, Carved Crest, Curved Footboard, Full, c.1855, 81 x 63 In. 5750.00
Bed, Victorian, Walnut, Framed Medallion, Carved Bonnet Finial, 82 x 72 x 62 In. 430.00
Bed, Victorian, Walnut, Racetrack Molding, Carved Crest, Footboard, 59 1/2 x 58 In. 280.00
Bed, Walnut, Poplar, Turned Legs, Mushroom Top, Rope, 17 x 28 In. 550.00
Bed Steps, Regency, Mahogany, Leather, Commode, England, 28 x 20 x 33 In. 1380.00
Bed Steps, William IV, Mahogany, 3 Tiers, Tooled Leather, c.1835, 26 x 18 x 26 In. 2530.00
Bedroom Set, Cottage, Blue Ground, Bird, Scroll, High-Back Bed, 7 Piece 2365.00
Bedroom Set, Davis Cabinet Co., Cherry, Mirrored Dresser, Nashville, 1940s, 5 Piece . . . 2310.00
Bedroom Set, Donald Deskey, Ivory & Green Enamel, Valentine-Seaver Co., 4 Piece 1150.00
Bedroom Set, Eastlake, Carved Flowers, Late 19th Century, 3 Piece 750.00
Bedroom Set, Eastlake, Half-Tester, Carved, Burl, 4 Piece 4370.00
Bedroom Set, Empire Style, Mahogany, Polychrome Decoration, 5 Piece 4140.00
Bedroom Set, Faux Bamboo, 3-Drawer Chest, Bed, American, c.1890, 2 Piece 5465.00
Bedroom Set, Federal Style, Mahogany, White Furniture Co., 5 Piece 1180.00
Bedroom Set, French Bombay, Painted, Dovetailed, Birds, Flowers, Gold Trim, 9 Piece . . 8050.00
Bedroom Set, Heywood-Wakefield, Blond Wood, Sable Finish, 6 Piece 460.00
Bedroom Set, Mahogany, Sleigh Bed, Dresser, Mirror, Scrolling, Bed 54 x 59 x 75 In. . . . 460.00
Bedroom Set, Oak, Marble Top, Dresser, 2 Nightstands, Bed, Armoire, 84 x 55 x 22 In. . . . 1265.00
Bedroom Set, Renaissance Revival, Burled Walnut, Marble Top, c.1870, 2 Piece 3795.00
Bedroom Set, Renaissance Revival, Pediment Bed, Marble Top Dresser, Commode 6000.00
Bedroom Set, Renaissance Style, Burled Elm, Walnut, c.1900, 6 Piece 4830.00
Bench, Arts & Crafts, Oak, Lift Seat, Flat Flared Arms, 3 Back Slats, 41 x 40 x 16 In. 635.00
Bench, Arts & Crafts, Rectangular Top, Horizontal Stretcher, 40 x 15 x 20 In. 1150.00
Bench, Baroque Style, Turned Oak, Tapestry, Franco-Flemish, 11 x 57 x 13 In. 690.00
Bench, Bucket, Pine, 2 Open Shelves, Frame & Panel Doors, 55 x 58 x 13 1/2 In. 990.00
Bench, Bucket, Pine, Grain Painted, Brown Over Ocher, 19th Century, 25 x 30 x 9 In. . . . 470.00
Bench, Bucket, Pine, Gray Paint, Dropped Sides, 49 In. 45.00
Bench, Bucket, Pine, Mustard Paint, Scrubbed Top, Apron Sides, 65 In. 165.00
Bench, Bucket, Pine, Old Red Paint, Cutouts, 3 Shelves, 43 x 13 x 41 1/2 In. 2760.00
Bench, Bucket, Poplar, 2 Shelves, Canted Ends, Cutouts, Square Nails, 47 x 43 x 12 In. . . 1095.00
Bench, Bucket, Poplar, Pine, 4 Shelves, Canted Top, 20th Century, 40 x 10 x 50 In. 175.00
Bench, Bucket, Scalloped Legs, Buttressed Corners, Blue Paint, 49 In. 69.00
Bench, Bucket, Softwood, 2 Shelves, Dovetailed, Mortised, Tapered, 51 x 42 x 20 In. 1155.00
Bench, Bucket, Softwood, 2 Tiers, Shaped Crest, Half-Moon Cutout Ends, 38 x 25 In. 425.00
Bench, Bucket, Softwood, Deep Well, Open Shelf, Scalloped Sides, 51 x 29 x 24 In. 535.00
Bench, Bucket, Weathered, Old Paint, Purple, Gray, Bootjack Legs, 60 x 11 x 20 In. 115.00
Bench, Cast Iron, Monkey Legs, Stepped Cross Stretcher, Artichoke Finial, 20 x 14 In. 415.00
Bench, Cast Iron, Pierced, Leafy Branches, American, c.1850, 36 x 40 x 31 In. 1265.00
Bench, Cast Iron, Scrolled Arms, Demilune Backs, England, 1800s, 33 x 52 In., Pair 5940.00
Bench, Cast Iron, Scrolled Supports, Winged Griffins, c.1920, 25 In. 69.00
Bench, Chippendale Style, Mahogany, 6 Legs, Silk Slip Seat, Arms, c.1900, 47 x 36 In. . . . 1320.00
Bench, Church, Frank Lloyd Wright, Hinged Back, Unitarian Church, 1947, 21 x 28 In. . . . 1955.00
Bench, Church, Pine, Bookracks, Yellow Paint, 37 x 62 In. 110.00
Bench, Deacon's, Birch, Pine, 8 Legs, Spindle Back, 31 x 7 1/2 x 17 In. 550.00
Bench, Deacon's, Flame Birch, Pine, 8 Legs, Spindle Back, Arms, 31 x 7 1/2 x 17 In. 560.00
Bench, Deacon's, Maple, Spindle Back, Curved Arms, 1-Board Seat, 79 In. 415.00
Bench, Deacon's, Painted Flowers, Black Ground, 8 Legs, 19th Century, 24 1/2 x 34 In. . . 470.00
Bench, Deacon's, Sheraton, Curly Maple, Cane Seat, 32 x 73 In. 3105.00
Bench, Deacon's, Yellow Paint, Wm. O. Haskell & Son, Boston, 72 In. 489.00

Furniture, Armoire,
Cherry, Cabriole Legs,
Drawers, La.,
Mid 19th Century, 87 In.

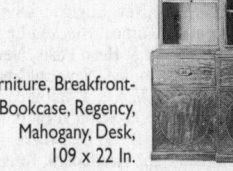

Furniture, Breakfront-
Bookcase, Regency,
Mahogany, Desk,
109 x 22 In.

Bench, Depot, Mahogany, Spindle Back, 5 Seats, 91 In. 220.00
Bench, Ebonized Oak, Chromium, Slat, Knoll, 15 1/2 x 54 x 18 In. 645.00
Bench, Empire Style, Giltwood, Ivory, Upholstered, 20 x 94 x 17 In. 960.00
Bench, Fin Juhl, Teak, Brass, Bovirke, Denmark, c.1952, 88 x 18 x 17 1/2 In. 3510.00
Bench, Florence Knoll, Enameled Steel, Walnut, Upholstered, 1950s, 61 x 18 x 15 In. ... 1120.00
Bench, G. Nelson, Birch Top, Slat, Ebonized Wood Legs, Herman Miller, 72 x 18 3/4 In. .. 1725.00
Bench, G. Nelson, Birch, Steel, Slat, Herman Miller, 1955, 48 x 18 1/2 x 14 1/2 In. 2800.00
Bench, G. Nelson, Blond Wood, Slatted, Ebonized Legs, 14 x 48 x 18 1/2 In. 690.00
Bench, G. Nelson, Ebonized Birch, Slat, Herman Miller, 1950s, 56 1/2 x 19 x 14 In. 805.00
Bench, G. Nelson, Ebonized Legs, Primavera Finish, Slat, Herman Miller, 48 x 18 In. ... 655.00
Bench, G. Nelson, Ebonized Supports, Slat, Herman Miller, 14 x 102 x 18 In. 980.00
Bench, G. Nelson, Ebonized Top & Legs, Slat, Herman Miller, 1950s, 48 x 18 3/4 In. 865.00
Bench, G. Nelson, Ebonized Top & Legs, Slat, Herman Miller, 48 x 14 In. 690.00
Bench, G. Nelson, Maple Slats, Platform, Herman Miller, c.1947, 14 x 68 1/4 In. 690.00
Bench, G. Nelson, Slat, Birch, Herman Miller, c.1948, 48 x 19 x 14 In. 1400.00
Bench, G. Nelson, Slat, Birch, Herman Miller, c.1948, 68 x 18 1/2 x 14 In. 935.00
Bench, G. Stickley, No. 224, Paneled Back, Lift Seat Compartment, 48 x 23 x 42 In. 4600.00
Bench, H. Bertoia, Walnut, Slat, Tubular Y-Shaped Legs, 15 1/2 x 72 x 18 1/2 In. 1495.00
Bench, Hall, Limbert, Left Seat, 47 1/2 x 46 1/2 x 19 1/2 In. 1670.00
Bench, Hall, Victorian, Oak, Mirror, Arms, Storage, 75 x 27 In. 520.00
Bench, Jean Prouve, Metal, Oak, Blue Enamel, c.1950 .... 14040.00
Bench, Karl Springer, Snakeskin, Steel Base, 18 1/2 x 36 x 15 1/4 In. 3740.00
Bench, Klismos, Iron, Brass, U Brackets, Scrolled Ends, Brass Handles, 28 x 21 1/4 In. .. 170.00
Bench, Louis XVI Style, Giltwood, Padded Seat, Arms, c.1900, 27 x 40 x 16 1/4 In. 865.00
Bench, Louis XVI Style, Pickled Beechwood, Curule Shape, 28 x 46 x 18 In. 290.00
Bench, Maple, Base Drawers, Cutout Ends, 20 3/4 x 14 2/4 In. 169.00
Bench, Mission, Arched Center, Open Carved Back, 3 Parts, 73 x 20 x 25 In. 1725.00
Bench, Molave Wood, Low Back, Cane Seat, Scroll Arms, Chinese, 35 x 61 x 29 In. 170.00
Bench, Neoclassical, Mahogany, Lyre Shape, Needlepoint Seat, c.1840, 22 x 41 In. 980.00
Bench, Oak, Cane Seat, Stretcher Base, Carved Frieze, 20 x 39 x 16 1/2 In. 495.00
Bench, Piano, Needlework Top, 19 x 36 x 15 In. 185.00
Bench, Pine, Iron Mounted, Hand Wrought Iron Stretchers, 20 x 91 x 14 In., Pair 415.00
Bench, Pine, Scrolled Sides, 34 In. 70.00
Bench, Prayer, Grain Painted, Late 1800s, 78 In. 45.00
Bench, Roycroft, Rectangular Seat, Slab Sides, Numbers A203, 47 x 17 x 25 In. 1840.00
Bench, Shaker, Hardwood, Pine, Bootjack Sides, Shirley, Mass., c.1850, 19 x 37 In. 13800.00
Bench, Shaker, Meetinghouse, Walnut, 22 Back Supports, Union Village, 89 In. 9200.00
Bench, Shaker, Pine, Red & Green Paint, Union Village, 72 1/2 x 14 x 31 1/2 In. 546.00
Bench, Shaker, Prayer, Pine, Poplar, Arched Leg Cutouts, Hancock, 36 x 6 1/2 x 6 3/8 In. .. 575.00
Bench, Shaker, Red Stain, Raked Cylindrical Legs, 18 3/4 x 13 1/2 x 30 In. 635.00
Bench, Shoe Foot, Oak, 14 x 60 x 12 In., Pair 460.00
Bench, Softwood, 2-Board Top, Cutout Ends, Drawer, 34 x 64 In. 505.00
Bench, Thonet, Aluminum Base, Turquoise Vinyl, 1960s, 39 x 22 x 29 In. 145.00
Bench, Victorian Style, Cast Iron, Wood, Bear Figure Cartouche, 20 x 16 x 13 In. 105.00
Bench, Victorian, Cast, Wrought Iron, Upholstered, 17 x 48 x 12 In. 140.00
Bench, Walnut, Chinese, c.1880, 19 1/2 x 44 1/2 x 10 1/4 In., Pair 385.00
Bench, Walnut, Cut Nail Construction, Painted, Ohio, c.1840, 16 x 157 x 12 1/2 In. 300.00
Bench, Wendell Castle, Walnut, Rosewood, Lift Top, c.1976, 17 1/2 x 70 x 21 In. 2530.00

Bench, William IV, Mahogany, Leather, Paw Feet, 15 1/2 x 54 x 33 In. 2990.00
Bench, Window, Chippendale Style, Cherry, Silk, 43 x 18 x 31 In. 275.00
Bench, Window, Limbert, Geometric Cutouts, Cushion, 24 x 24 1/2 x 18 In. 8625.00
Bench, Window, Victorian Style, Mahogany, Silk, Leaf Carved Apron, 40 In. 440.00
Bench, Windsor, Arrow Back, Plank Seat, Salmon Paint, 8 Legs, 32 1/2 x 77 1/2 In. 1150.00
Bench, Work, Ju Mu Wood, Chinese, 19th Century, 18 x 10 x 15 1/2 In. 230.00
Bench, Wormley, Square, Cushion Top, Wood Legs, Dunbar, c.1948, 22 1/2 x 16 In. 1295.00
Bench, Wormley, Walnut, Bentwood Hairpin Legs, Dunbar, 84 x 19 x 11 In. 1380.00
Bin, Pine, Lift Top, 3 Compartments, Caster, Gray Green Paint, 34 In. 132.00
Bookcase, 2 Doors, Copper Pulls, Hinges, Backsplash Galley, 52 x 40 x 14 In. 2185.00
Bookcase, 2 Glass Doors, Brass Pulls, Arched Stretchers, 56 x 57 1/4 x 13 1/2 In. 2070.00
Bookcase, Arts & Crafts, 2 Doors, Vertical Mullions, 6 Shelves, 47 x 13 x 58 In. 520.00
Bookcase, Barrister, Mahogany, 6 Sections, Globe-Wernicke, c.1910, 34 x 61 1/2 In. 520.00
Bookcase, Barrister, Oak, 3 Sections, 3 Doors, Globe-Wernicke, c.1900, 49 x 34 In. 400.00
Bookcase, Barrister, Oak, Stacking, Cornice, Glazed Doors, Early 1900s, 103 x 34 In. . . . 1840.00
Bookcase, Biedermeier, Fruitwood, Tympanum Drawers, 1800s, 76 x 48 x 21 In. 1530.00
Bookcase, Biedermeier, Mahogany, 2 Glass Paneled Doors, c.1825, 80 x 46 x 13 In. 1610.00
Bookcase, Biedermeier, Walnut, Ebonized, 2 Glazed Paneled Doors, 66 1/2 x 45 In. 3910.00
Bookcase, Charles Limbert, Glazed Oak, 2 Doors, 4 Glass Panel, 1906, 48 In. 2340.00
Bookcase, Charles X, Mahogany, Arched Grillwork, Doors, c.1835, 94 x 59 x 20 In. 6900.00
Bookcase, Corner, Mission, Oak, Geometric Glazed Doors, 52 x 36 1/2 x 27 In. 430.00
Bookcase, Empire Style, Mahogany, Brass, Grill Inset Doors, 78 x 63 x 9 In. 1880.00
Bookcase, Empire, Mahogany, Mullioned Double Doors, Paw Feet, 64 x 50 In. 450.00
Bookcase, Flower Decoration, Molded Base, 2 Doors, Shelves, 43 x 12 1/2 x 38 In. 250.00
Bookcase, French Empire, Black Lacquer, Gilt Bronze, Inlaid, 19th Century, 44 x 43 In. . . 690.00
Bookcase, G. Nakashima, Walnut, 2 Adjustable Shelves, c.1977, 36 x 40 x 12 In. 2760.00
Bookcase, G. Nakashima, Walnut, 2 Adjustable Shelves, c.1977, 48 x 48 x 9 3/4 In. 2760.00
Bookcase, G. Stickley, 2 Doors, 24 Glass Panes, Through Tenon, 56 1/2 x 60 x 13 In. 7200.00
Bookcase, G. Stickley, 2 Doors, Key Tenon, 16 Glass Panes, c.1904, 46 x 56 In. 8625.00
Bookcase, G. Stickley, No. 716, 2 Doors, Glass, Iron Hardware, 43 x 12 x 56 In. 5750.00
Bookcase, G. Stickley, No. 717, 2 Doors, Glass Panes, Through Tenon, 47 x 13 x 56 In. . . 4900.00
Bookcase, George III Style, Mahogany, 2 Astragal Glazed Doors, 88 x 44 x 13 In. 3910.00
Bookcase, George III Style, Mahogany, 2 Astragal Glazed Doors, 90 x 70 1/2 In. 920.00
Bookcase, George III Style, Mahogany, 2 Astragal Glazed Doors, 94 x 88 x 17 In. 1380.00
Bookcase, George III Style, Mahogany, 4 Glazed Doors, 80 x 43 x 17 1/2 In. 1530.00
Bookcase, George III Style, Mahogany, Broken Pediment, 86 1/2 x 52 1/4 In. 1035.00
Bookcase, George III Style, Mahogany, Glazed Doors, c.1900, 34 x 35 In. 1150.00
Bookcase, George III, Mahogany, 2 Doors, 4 Drawers, c.1785, 92 x 40 x 22 1/2 In. 8915.00
Bookcase, George III, Mahogany, 2 Glazed Doors, 2 Cupboard Doors, 76 x 41 In. 1095.00
Bookcase, George III, Sheraton Style, Mahogany, 4 Doors, 2 Glazed, 87 x 45 1/2 In. 3220.00
Bookcase, Gothic Revival, Walnut, 2 Glass Doors, c.1850, 71 3/4 x 84 x 19 In. 7170.00
Bookcase, Gothic Revival, Walnut, 3 Glass Doors, c.1850, 71 3/4 x 107 x 19 In. 11355.00
Bookcase, Irish Regency, Mahogany, Adjustable Shelves, 97 x 78 x 16 In. 4600.00
Bookcase, L. & J.G. Stickley, No. 326 1/2, Door, 12 Panes, Key Tenon, 33 x 56 In. 12650.00
Bookcase, L. & J.G. Stickley, No. 637, 2 Doors, Arched Apron, 55 x 36 x 13 3/4 In. 3335.00
Bookcase, L. & J.G. Stickley, No. 641, Door, Cooper Pull, 16 Panes, 55 x 30 x 12 In. 5175.00
Bookcase, L. & J.G. Stickley, No. 643, 2 Doors, Glass Panes, 56 x 40 In. 5300.00
Bookcase, L. & J.G. Stickley, No. 645, 2 Doors, 12 Panels, 52 x 12 x 56 In. 7475.00
Bookcase, Lifetime, 1 Panel Glass Door, Mullion Overlay, 53 1/2 x 27 x 13 In. 1440.00
Bookcase, Lifetime, No. 7218, Door, 10 Top Squares, Copper Hardware, 28 x 56 In. 3105.00
Bookcase, Limbert, 3 Doors, 57 x 66 1/2 x 14 In. . . . . 3680.00 to 6900.00
Bookcase, Mahogany, Carved Base, Winged Griffin Supports, c.1880, 92 x 108 In. 9775.00
Bookcase, Mahogany, Wood Screws, 2 Drawers, England, c.1850, 58 x 26 x 15 In. 1265.00
Bookcase, McCobb, Birch, 2 Open Shelves, Black Metal Stand, 33 x 36 x 12 In. 520.00
Bookcase, McCobb, Directional, Saffron Finish, 2 Shelves, 32 x 14 1/4 In. 70.00
Bookcase, Michigan Chair Co., 2 Doors, Glass Panes, Through Tenon, 36 x 12 x 45 In. . . 2990.00
Bookcase, Mission, Limbert, Heart Cutouts, 58 x 39 3/4 x 13 In. 1265.00
Bookcase, Neoclassical, Mahogany, Open, North Italy, c.1835, 39 x 39 In., Pair 7200.00
Bookcase, Oak, Double Doors, Brass Floral Basket Hinges, American, 65 x 56 In. 450.00
Bookcase, Oak, Quartersawn, 2 Doors, Fixed Shelves, 63 x 54 1/2 x 17 1/2 In. 600.00
Bookcase, Oak, Quartersawn, Sliding Glass Doors, Lock, 52 x 35 1/2 x 14 In. 590.00
Bookcase, Queen Anne Style, Sliding Doors, c.1920 . . . . 500.00
Bookcase, Queen Anne Style, Walnut, Waterfall, 2 Drawers, 44 1/2 x 23 In., Pair 980.00

Bookcase, Regency Style, Mahogany, 2 Glazed Doors, c.1850, 85 x 36 x 24 In. 980.00
Bookcase, Regency, Mahogany, 2 Split Pane Doors, Beaded, c.1835, 36 1/2 x 31 In. 1495.00
Bookcase, Regency, Mahogany, 4 Open Shelves, c.1815, 41 x 37 In., Pair 6325.00
Bookcase, Regency, Mahogany, Open, Early 19th Century, 33 x 28 1/2 x 14 In. 1150.00
Bookcase, Regency, Rosewood, Brass Inlay, Grill Inset Doors, 75 x 39 x 21 1/2 In. 825.00
Bookcase, Renaissance Revival, Walnut, 3 Doors, Ebonized, Burled, c.1875, 78 In. 2590.00
Bookcase, Renaissance Revival, Walnut, Arched Glass Door, 99 In. 8250.00
Bookcase, Revolving, Barrister, Mahogany, 4 Tiers, Molded Slats, 59 x 24 In. 700.00
Bookcase, Revolving, Edwardian, Mahogany, Crossbanded, Quatrefoil Base, 32 x 19 In. . 370.00
Bookcase, Revolving, George III Style, Inlaid Satinwood, Circular, 39 x 17 1/4 In. 1770.00
Bookcase, Revolving, Regency Style, Inlaid Yew, Circular Top, 31 x 20 1/2 In. 575.00
Bookcase, Revolving, Victorian, Mahogany, Satinwood Strung, c.1890, 32 x 21 In. 1610.00
Bookcase, Roycroft, 1 Door, 16 Glass Panes, Iron Handle, 40 x 15 x 55 In. 8225.00
Bookcase, Roycroft, Mahogany, Open, 3 Shelves, c.1910, 38 x 15 1/2 x 53 In. 2600.00
Bookcase, Stacking, Mission, 3 Sections Over Drawer, 48 x 34 1/2 x 23 In. 920.00
Bookcase, Stickley Bros., 2 Doors, Copper Hardware, Handle Cutouts, 29 x 54 x 31 In. . 2185.00
Bookcase, Walnut, 2 Doors, Columns, Burled Crest, c.1880, 84 1/2 x 47 x 20 In. 3740.00
Bookcase, Walnut, 3 Sections, Glass Doors, Half Spiral Columns, 63 x 128 x 19 In. 1150.00
Bookcase, Walnut, 3 Vertical Compartments, 3 Drawers, Victorian 2200.00
Bookcase, Walnut, Carved Crest, Burled Drawer Base, c.1880, 91 x 43 x 17 In. 2760.00
Bookcase, Wormley, K 89-4, Pyramid, Mahogany, Drexel, 1956, 55 x 19 x 24 In. 1520.00
Bookcase-Cabinet, Cherry, 2 Sections, American, Late 1800s, 97 x 72 x 18 In. 1555.00
Bookcase-Cabinet, George III Style, Mahogany, Glazed Doors, 83 x 47 1/2 In. 1265.00
Bookcase-Cabinet, George III, Mahogany, 4 Doors, c.1780, 89 x 47 x 17 In. 8225.00
Bookcase-Cabinet, Regency Style, Rosewood, Marble Top, Gilt Mount, 38 x 60 x 14 In. . 2235.00
Bookrack, Brass, Camels, Painted, Adjustable, c.1895, 5 1/2 x 22 In. Open 175.00
Bookrack, G. Stickley, No. 74, Oak, V-Top, D-Shape Handles, 31 x 30 x 10 In. 1295.00
Bookrack, G. Stickley, Peaked Crest Rail, Arched Stretchers, 45 1/2 x 19 x 12 In. 1440.00
Bookrack, Mathsson, Maple, Teak, Sweden, c.1959, 20 x 11 In. 820.00
Bookstand, George III Style, Mahogany, 46 x 19 1/4 x 15 1/4 In. 920.00
Bookstand, Sheraton Style, Mahogany, Adjustable, Slant Front, 1900s, 28 x 24 In. 375.00
Bookstand, Victorian, Mahogany, Tilt Top, Tripod, c.1860, 31 x 19 x 13 1/2 In. 355.00
Bookstand, Wormley, Mahogany, Brown Leather, Swivel Base, 29 x 35 1/2 In. 2300.00
Bootjack, Victorian, Walnut, Grape, Leaf Carvings, c.1870, 31 1/2 x 12 x 16 In. 515.00
Box, G. Stickley, No. 95, Shirtwaist, Cedar Lined, Lock, Hardware, 16 x 32 x 17 In. 4025.00
Breakfront, Chippendale Style, Mahogany, Chinoiserie Panels, c.1910, 60 1/2 x 81 In. ... 5750.00
Breakfront, George III Style, Mahogany, 92 1/2 x 144 x 17 In. 1725.00
Breakfront, George III Style, Mahogany, Banded, 2 Parts, 94 x 104 In. 5500.00
Breakfront, George III, Mahogany, 6 Drawers, Glazed Doors, 91 1/2 x 53 1/2 In. 1955.00
Breakfront, Mahogany, Serpentine Arched Top, 8-Pane Doors, c.1920s, 99 x 107 In. 4615.00
Breakfront, McCobb, Irwin Collection, 1953, 71 1/4 x 19 1/4 x 83 3/4 In. 2230.00
Breakfront, Parzinger, Etched Glass Doors, 2 Parts, 75 x 60 1/2 x 15 1/2 In. 5175.00
Breakfront, Wormley, 4 Doors, 3 Drawers, Sliding Doors, Pullout Trays, 72 x 81 In. 2070.00
Breakfront-Bookcase, George III Style, Mahogany, Mid 1900s, 92 x 77 x 18 In. 3680.00
Breakfront-Bookcase, George III, Mahogany, c.1800, 96 x 89 In. 6615.00
Breakfront-Bookcase, George III, Mahogany, Inlaid, 3 Doors, 100 x 78 In. 4675.00
Breakfront-Bookcase, Georgian Style, Mahogany, 8 Doors, c.1890, 98 x 65 x 19 In. 4830.00
Breakfront-Bookcase, Regency Style, Mahogany, 6 Doors, 6 Drawers, 92 x 83 1/2 In. ... 4140.00
Breakfront-Bookcase, Regency, Mahogany, Desk, 109 x 22 In. .... *Illus* 27600.00
Breakfront-Bookcase, Rococo Revival, Mahogany, Mid 1800s, 96 x 85 x 16 1/2 In. 6040.00
Breakfront-Bookcase, William IV, Mahogany, 4 Doors, Glazed Panels, 88 x 90 In. 2185.00
Breakfront-Bookcase, William IV, Mahogany, 91 x 96 x 23 In. 11160.00
Buffet, Blond Wood, 3 Drawers, Leather Door Front, 2 Trays, 32 x 66 x 20 1/2 In. 115.00
Buffet, Brown-Saltman, Oak Veneer, 4 Drawers, 2 Doors, 31 3/4 x 66 x 19 In. 575.00
Buffet, Charles X, Ash, 3 Doors, 3 Frieze Drawers, Late 1800s, 37 1/2 x 70 1/2 In. 2185.00
Buffet, G. Nelson, Walnut, Thin Edge, Herman Miller, c.1954, 80 x 20 x 33 1/2 In. 3510.00
Buffet, Heywood-Wakefield, Champagne Finish, 3 Drawers & Doors, 33 x 60 In. 345.00
Buffet, James Mont, 2 Drawers, 2 Cabinets, 37 1/2 x 84 x 18 1/2 In. 2760.00
Buffet, John Stuart, 4 Drawers, 4 Doors, Asian Style Drop Pulls, 32 x 80 x 21 In. 230.00
Buffet, Louis Philippe Style, Fruitwood, Early 1900s, 39 1/2 x 87 x 22 In. 6040.00
Buffet, Louis Philippe, Cherry, 38 1/2 x 79 3/4 x 23 1/4 In. 3220.00
Buffet, Louis Philippe, Fruitwood, 2 Parts, 4 Doors, 2 Drawers, c.1850, 113 x 66 In. 3910.00
Buffet, Louis XV Style, Oak, 6 Doors, 6 Drawers, c.1890, 106 x 79 In. 4600.00

Buffet, Louis XV Style, Oak, 88 1/2 x 56 1/4 x 21 1/2 In. 700.00
Buffet, Louis XV Style, Walnut, 2 Drawers, Doors, Carved Panels, 38 x 52 x 24 In. 2235.00
Buffet, Oak, Claw Feet, Mirror & Lamp Shelves 5000.00
Buffet, Parzinger, Ivory Lacquer, 5 Doors, Drawers, Shelves, 1950s 8000.00
Buffet, Pine, 2 Doors, Scroll, Carved Flowers, 2 Parts, France, 88 x 51 x 18 In. 415.00
Buffet, Renaissance Revival, Oak, Flowers, Leaves, Pierced Crest, 88 x 69 x 24 In. 4255.00
Buffet, Rohde, Paldao, Herman Miller, c.1940, 72 x 20 x 34 1/2 In. 3820.00
Buffet, Walnut, Carved Pediment, Glass Panes, Doors, Drawers, France, 108 x 59 In. 3080.00
Buffet, Wormley, Ebonized, 3 Drawers, 3 Sliding Doors, 32 x 61 1/2 x 18 1/4 In. 4025.00
Buffet, Wormley, Rosewood, Ebonized Oak, 9 Drawers, Brass Pulls, 30 x 69 x 18 In. 1840.00
Bureau, Biedermeier, Ebonized Fruitwood, Sliding Writing Surface, 43 x 38 x 21 In. 1880.00
Bureau, Camphorwood, Drawer, Molded Top, Wooden Pulls, 35 x 38 x 18 1/2 In. 1955.00
Bureau, Chippendale, Applewood, 4 Drawers, Cock-Beaded, Late 1700s, 35 x 34 In. 7050.00
Bureau, Chippendale, Cherry, Banded Veneer, 6 Drawers, Scrolled, 41 x 37 x 18 In. 2990.00
Bureau, Chippendale, Mahogany, Serpentine, 4 Drawers, R.I., Late 1700s, 33 x 35 In. . . . 15275.00
Bureau, Dutch Rococo Style, Mahogany, Marquetry, Slant Front, 43 x 43 1/2 x 25 In. . . . 2070.00
Bureau, Empire, Mahogany, 4 Drawers, Ogee Bracket Base, 41 1/2 x 37 1/2 x 19 In. 400.00
Bureau, Empire, Mahogany, Mirror, Brass Ornaments, Child's, 54 x 29 1/2 x 16 1/2 In. . . 1090.00
Bureau, Empire, Mahogany, Scrolled Splashguard, 4 Drawers, American, 41 x 44 In. 720.00
Bureau, Federal, Cherry, Inlaid, Mass., 1810-1815, 39 x 39 x 20 In. 3820.00
Bureau, Federal, Mahogany, Inlaid, Bowfront, Mass., c.1800, 31 1/2 x 38 1/2 x 21 In. . . . 4400.00
Bureau, Federal, Tiger Maple, 4 Graduated Drawers, 1810-1820, 42 x 39 x 19 In. 2470.00
Bureau, George III Style, Walnut, Slant Front, 19th Century, 42 x 37 3/4 x 20 In. 800.00
Bureau, George III, Mahogany, Slant Front, c.1780, 43 x 42 1/4 x 21 1/2 In. 2530.00
Bureau, George III, Mahogany, Slant Front, Late 18th Century, 42 x 40 x 20 1/4 In. 1955.00
Bureau, George III, Oak, Slant Front, 4 Drawers, c.1785, 40 x 36 x 20 In. 865.00
Bureau, Hepplewhite, Cherry, 4 Drawers, Drawers, French Feet, 38 x 43 x 21 In. 1495.00
Bureau, Hepplewhite, Mahogany, Bowfront, 4 Drawers, 32 x 40 1/2 x 21 3/4 In. 865.00
Bureau, Hepplewhite, Mahogany, Bowfront, Drawers, c.1890, 39 x 42 1/2 x 21 1/2 In. . . . 4255.00
Bureau, Hepplewhite, Mahogany, Bowfront, Drawers, French Feet, 36 x 40 1/2 x 21 In. . . 5290.00
Bureau, Hepplewhite, Ribbon & Diamond Inlay, 5 Drawers, c.1810, 12 x 14 In. 1955.00
Bureau, Hepplewhite, Tiger Maple, 4 Drawers, American, 37 x 41 1/2 In. 2645.00
Bureau, Louis XV Style, Kingwood, Leather Inset Top, 30 x 50 In. 1000.00
Bureau, Mahogany, Bowfront, Inlaid Apron, 4 Drawers, c.1760, 36 x 42 In. 2300.00
Bureau, Mahogany, Veneers, 4 Drawers, French Feet, c.1800, 36 x 38 1/2 x 19 1/2 In. . . . 1150.00
Bureau, Maple, Curly Maple, 4 Drawers, Turned Feet, 35 3/4 x 41 x 20 1/2 In. 1150.00
Bureau, Modernmate, Birch, 9 Drawers, Conant & Ball, 30 1/4 x 58 x 18 In. 470.00
Bureau, Neoclassical, Mahogany, Veneer, Carved, Stenciled, c.1829, 62 x 36 x 20 In. . . . 3525.00
Bureau, Pine, Walnut Top, Bamboo Turnings, 3 Drawers, Late 1800s, 8 1/4 x 10 1/4 In. . . 345.00
Bureau, Pine, Wood Pulls, Wax Finish, 7 Drawers, England, 1800s, 48 x 48 In. 1035.00
Bureau, Polychromed, Carved, Parcel Gilt, Brass Mounted, Germany, 78 x 3 x 20 In. 3680.00
Bureau, Queen Anne Style, Walnut, Mahogany, Slant Front, c.1900, 37 x 33 In. 520.00
Bureau, Sheraton, Cherry, Mahogany, Veneer, Turned Legs, 42 1/2 x 43 x 19 In. 980.00
Bureau, Sheraton, Empire, Mahogany, Veneer, 2 Over 4 Drawers, 51 x 43 x 21 In. 865.00
Bureau, Sheraton, Mahogany, 3 Over 4 Drawers, Rope Turned Pilasters, 47 1/2 x 47 In. . . 520.00
Bureau, Sheraton, Mahogany, Molded Cornice, Drawers, 49 x 39 x 18 In. 1095.00
Bureau, Sheraton, Mahogany, Veneer, 4 Drawers, Bowfront, American, 39 x 40 In. 1150.00
Bureau, Walnut, 4 Drawers, Marble Top, Victorian, 32 x 44 In. 115.00
Bureau, Walnut, Burl Inlay, 3 Drawers, Italy, Late 1700s, 30 1/2 x 44 x 21 In. 2645.00
Bureau, Walnut, Inlaid, Slant Front, 3 Drawers, Italy, Late 1700s, 43 x 43 x 23 In. 4140.00
Bureau-Bookcase, Burl Walnut, Slant Front, Pigeonholes Over 3 Drawers, 40 x 47 In. . . . 1750.00
Bureau-Bookcase, Eastlake, Walnut, 2 Glazed Doors, c.1880, 88 1/2 x 38 x 24 In. 700.00
Bureau-Bookcase, Empire, Mahogany, Glazed Doors, 10 Panes, 77 x 44 x 23 In. 440.00
Bureau-Bookcase, George III Style, Gilt, Scarlet Japanned, Slant Front, 93 x 39 x 20 In. . 4600.00
Bureau-Bookcase, George III Style, Mahogany, Swan's Neck Crest, 88 x 36 x 17 In. 1295.00
Bureau-Bookcase, George III, Mahogany, Inlaid, Slant Front, c.1790, 86 x 49 x 22 In. . . . 5175.00
Bureau-Bookcase, George III, Mahogany, Leather, Glazed Doors, c.1815, 36 x 81 In. 7475.00
Bureau-Bookcase, George III, Mahogany, Slant Front, 4 Drawers, c.1785, 82 x 41 In. 4115.00
Bureau-Bookcase, Queen Anne Style, Walnut, Double Dome Top, 82 x 38 x 19 In. 2470.00
Bureau-Bookcase, Walnut, Slant Front, 4 Drawers, Domed Top, Glazed Door, 76 x 22 In. 2100.00
Cabinet, Aalto, Birch Plywood, Artek, Finland, 1950s, 43 x 20 x 29 1/2 In., Pair 2225.00
Cabinet, Aesthetic Revival, Ebonized Walnut, c.1880, 44 x 50 1/2 x 20 1/2 In. 1265.00
Cabinet, Aesthetic Revival, Walnut, Marble, Marquetry, England, c.1885, 37 x 80 In. 1840.00

Cabinet, Altar, Rosewood, Dragons, Clouds, Chinese, Early 1900s, 73 x 35 x 18 1/2 In. . . . 470.00
Cabinet, Andre Arbus, Parchment Over Wood, Brass, 2 Drawers, 36 1/2 x 15 x 32 In. 7020.00
Cabinet, Art Deco, Exotic Wood Veneers, 4 Doors, 38 1/4 x 84 1/2 x 23 1/2 In. 1150.00
Cabinet, Art Nouveau, Steel, Bronze, 74 x 38 x 23 In. 8050.00
Cabinet, Arthur Klepper, Mahogany, Lacquer, Wor-De-Klee, 1940s, 57 x 18 x 62 In. 935.00
Cabinet, Baroque Style, Japanned, Brass Mounted, 2 Doors, 40 x 36 x 22 In. 940.00
Cabinet, Baroque Style, Walnut, Carved, 2 Doors, 68 x 46 x 24 In. 1100.00
Cabinet, Biedermeier, Ebonized Wood, Cherry Inlay, Mid 1800s, 64 x 34 x 15 In. 1840.00
Cabinet, Biedermeier, Ebony, Fruitwood, Demilune, Continental, 30 x 33 x 17 In. 2070.00
Cabinet, Black Lacquer, 2 Doors, Interior Shelves, Chinese, Early 1900s, 69 x 54 In. 575.00
Cabinet, Black Lacquer, Gilt, Interior Rod, Early 20th Century, 71 x 60 x 22 In. 1150.00
Cabinet, Black On Yellow, Smoke Decoration, Black & Red Doors, 13 x 12 x 15 In. 489.00
Cabinet, China, 2 Doors, Slag Glass Inserts, 59 1/2 x 37 x 15 1/2 In. 520.00
Cabinet, China, Arts & Crafts, 2 Doors, Top Plate Rail, 3 Shelves, 42 x 15 x 62 In. 635.00
Cabinet, China, Corner, Claw Feet, Bellflower, Drawer, 4 Shelves, 74 x 36 x 24 In. 2470.00
Cabinet, China, Flared Legs, Backsplash, 3 Shelves, Brass Pull, 59 x 45 1/2 x 14 In. 980.00
Cabinet, China, G. Nelson, Walnut, 2 Doors, Herman Miller, 34 x 18 1/2 x 58 In. 750.00
Cabinet, China, G. Stickley, No. 803, Door, 3 Adjustable Shelves, 36 x 15 x 60 In. 4600.00
Cabinet, China, G. Stickley, No. 815, 2 Glass Doors, 42 x 15 x 64 In. 9200.00
Cabinet, China, G. Stickley, No. 820, 12-Pane Door, Copper Pulls, 62 x 36 x 16 In. 6325.00
Cabinet, China, Glass Door, Scalloped Trim, Bellflowers, c.1900, 74 x 48 x 13 In. 840.00
Cabinet, China, John Widdicomb, Walnut Veneer, 3 Drawers, 77 x 56 x 20 In. 460.00
Cabinet, China, Mahogany, 2 Doors, Mirror Back, 3 Shelves, 63 x 50 x 18 In. 1485.00
Cabinet, China, Mahogany, String Inlay, 2 Parts, American, Early 1900s, 79 x 41 In. 460.00
Cabinet, China, Oak, Curved Glass, 4 Shelves, Mirror, c.1900, 37 x 60 x 14 In. 550.00
Cabinet, China, Oak, Curved Glass, Carved Feet, 3 Shelves, Mirror, c.1900, 38 x 59 In. . . . 600.00
Cabinet, China, Oak, Maiden Heads, Crest, Cupid & Flowers, 78 x 51 x 18 In. 4600.00
Cabinet, China, Oak, Oval Mirror Over 3 Curved Panels, Paw Feet, 66 x 36 In. 489.00
Cabinet, China, Oak, Quartersawn, Bowed Glass Door, American, c.1885, 84 x 49 In. 6900.00
Cabinet, China, Oak, Quartersawn, Winged Griffins, Bowed Glass, c.1885, 72 x 50 In. . . . 3450.00
Cabinet, China, Oak, Serpentine Front, Bowed Sides, Applied Scroll Carving, Claw Feet . 620.00
Cabinet, China, Rohde, Burl, Mahogany Veneer, Mirrored Top, 60 x 36 x 16 In. 1955.00
Cabinet, China, Rohde, Maidou, Mahogany, 2 Doors, Herman Miller, 36 x 57 1/2 In. 4025.00
Cabinet, China, Rohde, Paldao, Herman Miller, c.1940, 69 1/2 x 16 x 33 In. 2000.00
Cabinet, China, Shop Of The Crafters, Glass Doors, Side Cabinets, 43 x 16 x 64 In. 2300.00
Cabinet, Chippendale Style, Cherry Veneer, Beveled Glass, Drawer, 2 Doors, 2 Piece 330.00
Cabinet, Chippendale Style, Mahogany, Pedestal, c.1860, 47 x 20 1/2 In., Pair 1725.00
Cabinet, Chippendale Style, Teak, 2 Drawers, 14 1/2 x 14 1/2 In. 750.00
Cabinet, Chippendale, Pine, Stained, 2 Sections, 2 Drawers, c.1800, 86 x 60 x 20 In. 4185.00
Cabinet, Corner, 3 Barley Twist Legs, Carved, Brass Hinges, 1800s, 62 In. 975.00
Cabinet, Corner, Cherry, 4 Doors, 3 Shelves, American, Early 1800s, 75 1/2 x 48 In. 2645.00
Cabinet, Corner, French Provincial, Pine, 19th Century, 94 x 37 x 25 In. 4830.00
Cabinet, Corner, George III Style, Mahogany, 2 Doors, c.1800, 30 x 77 1/2 In. 3450.00
Cabinet, Corner, George III, Mahogany, 3 Open Shelves, 4 Bowfront Drawers, 67 In. 700.00
Cabinet, Corner, Georgian Style, Mahogany, 1900s, 81 1/2 x 27 1/2 x 15 In. 1035.00
Cabinet, Corner, Georgian, Walnut, Broken Arch Pediment, Paneled Doors, 84 x 45 In. . . . 1049.00
Cabinet, Corner, Golden Oak, Carving, 5 Shelves, 1900s, 71 x 33 x 19 1/2 In. 785.00
Cabinet, Corner, Hanging, Pine, Double Frame & Panel Doors, 35 x 37 x 19 In. 470.00
Cabinet, Corner, Hanging, Regency, Oak, Parcel Gilt, Chinoiserie, c.1835, 37 x 24 In. . . . 1380.00
Cabinet, Corner, Hepplewhite, Mahogany, Sunburst, England, Early 1800s, 73 1/2 In. 3220.00
Cabinet, Corner, Hepplewhite, Walnut, Inlaid, American, 78 1/4 x 44 x 29 In. 5900.00
Cabinet, Corner, Mahogany, Convex, 4 Doors, 2 Mirrored, Russia, c.1825, 75 x 25 In. . . . 5290.00
Cabinet, Corner, Maple, 3 Doors, Drawer, Shelves, 1800s, 87 x 46 x 24 In. 1910.00
Cabinet, Corner, Mother-Of-Pearl Inlay, Carved, Late 1800s, 87 1/2 x 33 x 18 In. 1150.00
Cabinet, Corner, Oak, Pine, 2 Doors, Polychrome Garden Scene, c.1750, 36 x 23 In. 3220.00
Cabinet, Corner, Pine, Painted, Late 19th Century, 73 x 28 1/2 x 29 In. 175.00
Cabinet, Corner, Rococo, Walnut, 2 Parts, Bowed, Mirror, c.1865, 76 x 35 In. 2530.00
Cabinet, Corner, Victorian, Walnut, 3 Tiers, Central Doors, Late 1800s, 75 1/2 In. 1175.00
Cabinet, Corner, Walnut, Marquetry, 4 Doors, Continental, 87 1/2 x 52 In. 3450.00
Cabinet, Cypress, Copper, 2 Sections, Japan, Early 1900s, 44 x 37 x 17 In. 650.00
Cabinet, Display, A. Szoeke, Mahogany, Inlaid Couple, House, 1950s, 48 x 54 In. 1755.00
Cabinet, Display, Aesthetic Revival, Mahogany, 2 Drawers, Doors, c.1890, 72 x 61 In. . . . 2820.00
Cabinet, Display, Baroque, Walnut, Barley Twist Columns, Italy, 1700s, 29 1/2 In. 1530.00

Cabinet, Display, Bombe Form, Ormolu Mount, France, c.1925, 74 1/2 x 34 1/4 In. 2240.00
Cabinet, Display, Bonnet Top, Curved Glass, Mirror Back, Lighted, c.1910, 69 x 34 In. . . 560.00
Cabinet, Display, Bonnet Top, Serpentine Glass, c.1885, 69 x 34 x 16 In. 1725.00
Cabinet, Display, Bowed Front, 3 Glass Shelves, 1900s, 61 1/2 x 26 x 12 1/2 In. 560.00
Cabinet, Display, Carved Flowers, Paw Feet, Chinese, Late 1800s, 35 x 46 1/2 x 16 In. . . 700.00
Cabinet, Display, Chinese Red Lacquer, Moon, Round, 2 Drawers, 71 x 35 x 10 In. 230.00
Cabinet, Display, Edwardian Style, Mahogany Inlay, Paneled Doors, 69 x 43 x 14 In. 1610.00
Cabinet, Display, Edwardian, Mahogany, Bowfront Glazed Doors, c.1900, 83 x 60 In. . . . 2300.00
Cabinet, Display, Georgian, Mahogany, 4 Doors, Broken Arch., c.1830, 42 1/2 x 101 In. . . 5290.00
Cabinet, Display, Glass Front, Sides, Ormolu, France, 20th Century, 63 x 29 In. . . . . *Illus* 620.00
Cabinet, Display, Glass, 4 Panels, 2 Shelves, Ormolu, France, c.1925, 57 x 23 In. . . . . *Illus* 840.00
Cabinet, Display, Glass, Lighted, Adjustable Shelves, 70 x 36 In., Pair 1345.00
Cabinet, Display, Gold, Black Lacquer, Japan, 19th Century, 22 x 20 x 10 In. . . . . . . *Illus* 8225.00
Cabinet, Display, Hanging, Continental, Arched Top, 26 1/2 x 27 x 5 1/2 In. 150.00
Cabinet, Display, Hanging, Empire Style, Brass, Glass, Mirrored Back, 1900s, 36 x 26 In. 650.00
Cabinet, Display, Hanging, George III Style, Mahogany, 1800s, 38 1/2 x 26 1/2 In. 920.00
Cabinet, Display, Hardwood, 4 Drawers, 2 Doors, Chinese, c.1920, 64 x 46 x 16 In. 460.00
Cabinet, Display, Hardwood, Carved Scrolling Flowers, 2 Doors, c.1890, 39 x 82 In. 2760.00
Cabinet, Display, Hardwood, Carved, Pierced Fretwork, Chinese, 69 1/2 x 44 x 23 In. . . . 175.00
Cabinet, Display, M. Bellini, Walnut, Glass, Mirror, 32 1/2 x 60 x 18 In. 130.00
Cabinet, Display, Mahogany, Arched Beveled Glass Doors, c.1880, 73 x 53 x 14 In. 2590.00
Cabinet, Display, Mahogany, Bowfront, Glass Doors, Mirror Back, 56 x 30 x 16 In. 865.00
Cabinet, Display, Mahogany, Curved Glass Front, American, c.1925, 62 x 39 In. 308.00
Cabinet, Display, Mahogany, Door, Beveled Glass Doors, 2 Shelves, 65 x 34 x 13 In. 460.00
Cabinet, Display, Mahogany, Mirror Back, 4 Curved Legs, 62 1/2 x 27 1/2 x 13 1/2 In. . . 400.00
Cabinet, Display, Mahogany, Shallow Drawers, 1800, 10 1/2 x 10 1/4 x 14 In. 500.00
Cabinet, Display, Oak, 4 Glass Shelves, American, Early 1900s, 71 x 54 1/2 x 18 In. 2575.00
Cabinet, Display, Oak, Cane, Bowed Glass, Wood Divider, Mirror, 35 x 46 In. 1125.00
Cabinet, Display, Oak, Glass Sides, Top, Hinged Doors, Latch, 30 x 22 1/2 x 22 1/2 In. . . 200.00
Cabinet, Display, Oak, Oval, Cabriole Legs, Gallery Top, c.1895, 56 x 25 x 40 In. 2875.00
Cabinet, Display, Rosewood, Carved Panels, Chinese, 1800s, 101 x 46 x 34 In. 7200.00
Cabinet, Display, Vernis Martin Style, Glass, Lighted, c.1910, 65 1/2 x 27 x 17 In. 1000.00
Cabinet, Dutch Neoclassical, Inlaid Mahogany, 32 1/2 x 32 1/2 x 16 In. 1195.00
Cabinet, Eastlake, Walnut, Marble Top, American, c.1890, 36 1/2 x 54 x 22 1/2 In. 1415.00
Cabinet, Edwardian, Mahogany, Carved, Door, Demilune, c.1900, 36 x 40 x 20 In. 2530.00
Cabinet, Edwardian, Mahogany, Checkerband Inlay, Glazed Doors, 4 Drawers, 45 In. 570.00
Cabinet, Edwardian, Rosewood, Marquetry, Glazed Doors, Open Shelf, 93 x 60 In. 2450.00
Cabinet, Elm, Black Lacquer, Chinese, c.1860, 73 x 45 1/2 x 20 In. 295.00
Cabinet, Elm, Red Lacquer, c.1850, 62 x 39 x 17 1/4 In. 325.00
Cabinet, Empire Style, Mahogany, Bronze Mounted, Pedestal, 42 x 25 x 19 In. 2690.00
Cabinet, Empire, Fruitwood, Mid 19th Century, 35 x 51 x 21 In. 1955.00
Cabinet, Faux Bird's-Eye Maple Graining, 2 Doors, 2 Shelves, 31 1/2 x 37 1/2 In. 460.00
Cabinet, Federal, Cherry, Flared Cornice, 2 Glass Paned Doors, 41 x 43 x 12 1/2 In. 777.00

Furniture, Cabinet, Display, Glass
Front, Sides, Ormolu, France,
20th Century, 63 x 29 In.

Furniture, Cabinet, Display, Glass,
4 Panels, 2 Shelves, Ormolu,
France, c.1925, 57 x 23 In.

Furniture, Cabinet, Display, Gold,
Black Lacquer, Japan, 19th Century,
22 x 20 x 10 In.

Cabinet, Federal, Mahogany, Inlaid, 2 Doors, 2 Drawers, c.1820, 18 1/2 x 18 In. 4700.00
Cabinet, Federal, Walnut, Doors Open To Shelves, Early 1800s, 84 x 49 x 18 In. 1840.00
Cabinet, Fornasetti, Painted, 2 Doors, Tapered Brass Legs, 1950 .... 4885.00
Cabinet, French Provincial, Fruitwood, Mahogany, Early 1800s, 13 1/2 x 8 1/2 In. 750.00
Cabinet, French Provincial, Pine, 2 Doors, Shaped Panels, 73 x 60 x 23 1/2 In. 999.00
Cabinet, Fruitwood, Stumpwork Panels, Embroidery, Mirror, 17th Century, 17 x 18 In. 10000.00
Cabinet, G. Nakashima, Black Walnut, Maple, Grass Cloth, 2 Sliding Doors, 1958, 80 In. 10500.00
Cabinet, G. Nakashima, Laurel, 4 Drawers, Brass Trim, Widdicomb, c.1958, 36 x 32 In. . 1035.00
Cabinet, G. Nakashima, Laurel, Walnut, 12 Drawers, Widdicomb, c.1958, 89 x 32 In. 2990.00
Cabinet, G. Nakashima, Walnut, 3 Sliding Doors, 1963, 96 x 20 x 32 In............... 10500.00
Cabinet, G. Nakashima, Walnut, Free Edge, Slab Top, 2 Doors, 71 1/4 x 21 x 32 1/2 In. ... 10350.00
Cabinet, G. Nakashima, Walnut, Raised Case, Grass Cloth, 2 Doors, 48 x 50 In. 6900.00
Cabinet, G. Nelson, Basic Series, 5 Drawers, Herman Miller, 40 x 18 x 34 In. 575.00
Cabinet, G. Nelson, Primavera, 3 Drawers, Door, Herman Miller, 34 x 18 1/2 x 30 In. ... 1265.00
Cabinet, G. Nelson, Primavera, 5 Drawers, Herman Miller, c.1948, 24 x 20 x 40 In. 2000.00
Cabinet, G. Nelson, Primavera, Glass Shelves, Doors, Herman Miller, 34 x 30 In. 1035.00
Cabinet, G. Nelson, Rosewood Case, Lift Top, 3 Doors, Herman Miller, 56 x 40 In. 4315.00
Cabinet, G. Nelson, Steel Frame, Metal, Wood, Herman Miller, 1950s, 34 x 30 In. 1520.00
Cabinet, G. Nelson, Thin Edge, 2 Doors, 4 Drawers, Herman Miller, 67 x 18 x 32 In. 4315.00
Cabinet, G. Nelson, Thin Edge, 3 Doors, 4 Drawers, Herman Miller, 80 x 18 x 33 In. 4025.00
Cabinet, G. Nelson, Thin Edge, Oak, Steel, Herman Miller, c.1953, 40 x 19 x 36 In. 3275.00
Cabinet, G. Nelson, Thin Edge, Rosewood, 7 Drawers, Herman Miller, 1955, 68 x 23 In. . 10530.00
Cabinet, G. Nelson, Thin Edge, Rosewood, 10 Drawers, Herman Miller, 67 x 32 In. 4600.00
Cabinet, G. Nelson, Thin Edge, Rosewood, Aluminum, Herman Miller, 1955, 34 x 31 In. . 2100.00
Cabinet, G. Nelson, Thin Edge, Teak, 5 Drawers, Door, Herman Miller, 56 x 41 In. 4900.00
Cabinet, G. Nelson, Thin Edge, Walnut, Aluminum, Herman Miller, 56 x 19 x 41 In. 4025.00
Cabinet, G. Nelson, Walnut Veneer, Brushed Chrome, Drawers, Shelves, 30 x 56 x 20 In. . 1150.00
Cabinet, G. Nelson, Walnut, Door, Open Shelf, Herman Miller, 56 x 18 1/2 x 29 In. 800.00
Cabinet, G. Stickley, Harvey Ellis, Arched Doors, V-Board Back, 36 x 15 x 60 In. 4315.00
Cabinet, George III Style, Mahogany, 2 Glazed 2-Paneled Doors, 79 x 45 In. 1265.00
Cabinet, George III Style, Mahogany, 4 Doors, c.1900, 90 x 39 x 13 1/2 In. ....2990.00 to 4600.00
Cabinet, George III Style, Satinwood, Mahogany, Kensington Co., 1900s, 35 x 60 In. 460.00
Cabinet, German Baroque Style, Walnut, Carved, 2 Sections, 2 Doors, Drawer, 86 x 45 In. 5750.00
Cabinet, Gilt, Red Lacquer, Chinese, c.1830, 55 3/4 x 37 3/4 x 17 1/2 In. 470.00
Cabinet, Gilt, Red Lacquer, Chinese, c.1860, 68 x 44 x 18 In. 945.00
Cabinet, Gilt, Red Lacquer, Shanxi, Chinese, c.1830, 45 x 37 x 19 In. 590.00
Cabinet, Gilt, Red Lacquer, Shanxi, Chinese, c.1830, 57 x 36 1/2 x 18 In. 470.00
Cabinet, Glass Door Top, 2 Door Bottom, Continental, 1800s, 87 x 48 In. 4995.00
Cabinet, Gun, Arts & Crafts, 3 Doors, Center Glass, Drawers, Open Shelves, 71 x 42 In. .. 865.00
Cabinet, Hanging, Adams Style, Flowers, Griffins, 1900s, 33 x 18 x 12 1/2 In. 660.00
Cabinet, Hanging, Florence Knoll, Drop Front Doors, 2 Compartments, 18 x 72 x 16 In. . 1380.00
Cabinet, Hanging, Mahogany, Victorian, Medieval Knights, 32 1/2 x 23 1/2 In. 460.00
Cabinet, Hardware, Revolving, Octagonal Top, 80 Drawers, Porcelain Knobs, 35 In. 1240.00
Cabinet, Hardwood, 2 Drawers, Square Legs, Chinese, 20th Century, 39 3/4 x 34 In. 315.00
Cabinet, Hardwood, Carved, Burma, 19th Century, 51 1/2 x 48 1/2 x 15 In. 1610.00
Cabinet, Hepplewhite Style, Inlay, 2 Panels, c.1820, 51 1/2 x 25 x 11 In. 1035.00
Cabinet, Italian Rosewood, Ebony, Ivory, Mid 19th Century, 110 x 52 x 21 In. 16675.00
Cabinet, James Mont, 4 Drawers, Rubbed Silver Finish, Pedestal Vase, 26 x 28 x 17 In. ... 1265.00
Cabinet, James Mont, Wood Veneer, Lacquered, 2 Doors, Shelves, 40 x 39 3/4 x 17 In. ... 2760.00
Cabinet, Jewelry, Lacquer, Shishi, Peony, Waterfall, Japan, 1800s, 19 x 18 1/2 In........ 529.00
Cabinet, Jewelry, Oak, 20 Drawers, 26 In. 635.00
Cabinet, Kiri Wood, 2 Sections, Shiga, Japan, Late 1800s, 34 x 48 3/4 In. 530.00
Cabinet, Knoll, Burl Veneer, 2 Doors, Pink, Black Marble, Shelves, 23 x 36 x 20 In. 460.00
Cabinet, Knoll, Walnut, 4 Drawers, Chrome Legs, Pulls, c.1960, 26 x 36 x 20 In. 90.00
Cabinet, Lacquer, 2 Doors, Chinese, 19th Century, 36 x 28 1/2 x 17 In................ 295.00
Cabinet, Louis Philippe, Brass Inlay, Ebony, Marble Top, 40 x 44 x 19 In. 705.00
Cabinet, Louis XIV Style, Mahogany, 2 Doors, 34 x 48 x 20 In. 440.00
Cabinet, Louis XV Style, Parquetry, Marble Top, 2 Doors, 29 x 29 x 14 In., Pair 850.00
Cabinet, Louis XVI Transitional Style, Tulipwood, Marquetry, 33 x 22 x 13 In. 3290.00
Cabinet, Mahogany, Circular Top, Pedestal, Continental, 1800s, 33 x 15 In. 630.00
Cabinet, Mahogany, Egg & Dart Molding, Doors, 49 1/2 x 40 5/8 x 13 3/4 In. 635.00
Cabinet, Mahogany, Marble Top, Composition Inlay, Signed Susini, 39 x 43 x 21 In. 8800.00
Cabinet, Mahogany, Tambour Front, Tray Top, England, c.1805, 32 x 21 x 16 3/4 In. 900.00

Cabinet, McCobb, Planner Group, Maple, 3 Drawers, Brass Legs, 36 x 31 1/2 In. 230.00
Cabinet, McCobb, Planner Group, Maple, Winchendon, 60 x 18 1/2 x 32 1/2 In. 175.00
Cabinet, Music, G. Stickley, No. 70, Paneled Doors, Through Tenon, 20 x 16 x 47 In. 9200.00
Cabinet, Music, Lifetime, Paneled Doors, 5 Shelves, Slab, Through Tenon, 34 x 26 In. 1115.00
Cabinet, Music, Louis XV Style, Painted, 48 x 25 x 16 In. 495.00
Cabinet, Music, Victorian, Cherry, American, c.1890, 63 x 38 x 14 1/2 In. 1120.00
Cabinet, Napoleon III, Ebonized, Ormolu Mounted, 54 x 43 x 14 In. 1380.00
Cabinet, Napoleon III, Marble Top, Brass Inlay, Tortoiseshell, Ebony, 41 x 33 x 15 In. .. 705.00
Cabinet, Napoleon III, Marble Top, Bronze, Pewter, France, c.1850, 53 x 48 x 18 In. 7500.00
Cabinet, Neoclassical, Inlaid Mahogany, Dutch, c.1800, 35 x 40 In. 4465.00
Cabinet, Neoclassical, Mahogany, Glass Doors, Brass, Russia, c.1825, 42 x 27 In. 2760.00
Cabinet, Neoclassical, Mahogany, Glazed Panel Doors, American, c.1890, 72 x 48 In. ... 1840.00
Cabinet, Neoclassical, Painted, Classical Figures, 78 x 41 x 13 In. 3450.00
Cabinet, Neoclassical, Walnut, 2 Doors, Drawer, Columns, Baltic, c.1840, 33 x 40 In. ... 4600.00
Cabinet, Oak, 1 Door, Strapwork Handle, England, 1900s, 77 3/4 x 33 x 15 1/2 In. 325.00
Cabinet, Oak, 3 Sections, Step Back, Leaded Glass Panels, Bun Feet, 91 x 56 x 22 In. ... 920.00
Cabinet, Oak, 36 Thin & 4 Large Drawers, Paneled Ends, 36 x 58 1/2 x 15 1/2 In. 675.00
Cabinet, Oak, Bentwood, 2 Glazed Paneled Doors, 2 Shelves, 30 1/4 x 18 x 7 1/2 In. 400.00
Cabinet, Painted, Mustard Over Bittersweet 2 Sections, 4 Open Shelves, Lower Door 2950.00
Cabinet, Pierced, Carved, Door, Drawer, Chinese, 1800s, 62 x 35 1/2 In. 1035.00
Cabinet, Pine, 4 Dovetailed Drawers, Bun Feet, Old Green Paint, 27 x 17 x 12 In. 90.00
Cabinet, Pine, 24 Flatwork Drawers Over 24 Drawers, Cast Iron Pulls, 59 x 33 In. 490.00
Cabinet, Pine, Bamboo & Burl Veneer, Copper Mounts, Japan, c.1925, 25 x 28 x 13 In. .. 175.00
Cabinet, Pine, Dovetailed, Painted Panel Door, 19th Century, 26 x 19 x 13 1/2 In. 110.00
Cabinet, Pine, Grain Painted, 2 Doors, 4 Shelves, 72 1/2 x 55 1/2 x 21 1/2 In. 1320.00
Cabinet, Pine, Painted, Sweden, c.1790, 38 1/2 x 22 1/2 x 12 3/4 In. 1415.00
Cabinet, Polychrome Wood, Tibet, c.1810, 40 x 49 1/2 x 16 3/4 In. 649.00
Cabinet, Polychrome Wood, Tibet, c.1850, 39 x 52 1/2 x 16 1/4 In. 590.00
Cabinet, Queen Anne Style, Walnut, Overhang Top, 2 Drawers, 54 x 29 x 32 In. 1015.00
Cabinet, Red & Black Lacquer, Leaves, Butterflies, Chinese, Late 1800s, 35 x 52 In. 1150.00
Cabinet, Red Lacquer, c.1850, 36 1/2 x 43 1/4 x 17 3/4 In. 470.00
Cabinet, Red Lacquer, Carved, Gilt, Green, Interior Shelves, Chinese, 77 1/2 x 38 x 9 In. . 315.00
Cabinet, Red Lacquer, Gilt, 2 Shelves, 3 Drawers, Early 1900s, 63 x 47 x 24 In. 750.00
Cabinet, Red Lacquer, Gilt, Shelf, Drawers, Early 1900s, 71 x 50 x 20 In. 1265.00
Cabinet, Red Lacquer, Gold, Maroon Butterflies, Vines, Chinese, 1900s, 69 x 33 x 18 In. . 345.00
Cabinet, Regency Style, Satinwood, Crossbanded, 3 Drawers, 20 x 25 x 12 In. 1645.00
Cabinet, Regency, Ebonized Wood, Inlaid Mahogany, Glass Shelves, 78 x 29 x 13 In. 6900.00
Cabinet, Renaissance Revival, Rosewood, Gilt Bronze Mounted, c.1875, 62 x 63 In. 6570.00
Cabinet, Renaissance Revival, Walnut, Brocatel Marble Insets, c.1870, 56 x 56 In. 3220.00
Cabinet, Renaissance Revival, Walnut, Carved, 4 Columns, Eagle, Ball Feet, 61 x 51 In. . 2300.00
Cabinet, Robsjohn-Gibbings, Walnut Veneer, 2 Doors, 31 x 34 x 20 1/2 In. 345.00
Cabinet, Rohde, 2 Sliding Glass Doors, Herman Miller, 25 x 36 x 13 In. 575.00
Cabinet, Rohde, Blond Wood Inlay, Handles, Herman Miller, c.1930, 44 x 34 x 19 In. ... 480.00
Cabinet, Rohde, Mahogany, Sliding Glass Doors, Herman Miller, 36 x 16 x 65 In. 690.00
Cabinet, Rohde, Paldao, 2 Doors, Herman Miller, 42 x 40 x 17 In. 1150.00
Cabinet, Rosewood, Brass, Mirrored Back, 3 Shelves, 64 x 54 x 16 In. 1915.00
Cabinet, Rosewood, Inlaid, Peacocks, 2 Doors, 2 Drawers, Anglo-Indian, 72 x 42 In. 1410.00
Cabinet, Rosewood, Ormolu Mounted, Continental, Late 19th Century, 29 x 62 In. 2875.00
Cabinet, Sheraton, Fruitwood, Thumbnail Molded Top, Drawers, 41 3/4 x 20 x 36 In. 2080.00
Cabinet, Smoking, English Oak, Quartersawn, Tobacco Finish, 2 Doors, 14 x 14 x 7 In. .. 390.00
Cabinet, Smoking, L. & J.G. Stickley, Divided Sections, 20 x 29 x 15 In. 4025.00
Cabinet, Smoking, Oak, Brass Hardware, Royal Ciphers, 3 Drawers, Cutter, 1900, 11 In. . 375.00
Cabinet, Smoking, Oak, Quartersawn, 2 Doors, Tabletop, England, 14 1/2 x 14 x 7 1/2 In. 350.00
Cabinet, Softwood, Russet Lacquer, Japan, Late 1800s, 24 1/2 x 34 1/2 x 15 In. 5230.00
Cabinet, Spice, Hanging, Oak, 8 Rows, Stenciled Spice Names, 17 x 10 3/4 In. 340.00
Cabinet, Spice, Hanging, Pine, 11 Drawers, Porcelain Pulls 275.00
Cabinet, Spice, Mahogany, On Stand, 3 Compartments, 23 x 16 x 12 In. 495.00
Cabinet, Spice, Pine, 8 Graduated Drawers, Wooden Pulls, 14 x 6 x 12 3/4 In. 1035.00
Cabinet, Spice, Pine, 10 Drawers, Hand Wrought Nail Construction, 22 x 27 x 10 In. 250.00
Cabinet, Spice, Poplar, 8 Dovetailed Drawers, Wooden Pegs, 24 x 19 x 9 In. 195.00
Cabinet, Spice, Softwood, 8 Drawers, Porcelain Knobs, Bun Feet, 18 x 14 x 6 In. 450.00
Cabinet, Stereo, G. Nelson, Thin Edge, Walnut, Herman Miller, c.1956, 80 x 35 In. 2340.00
Cabinet, Stereo, G. Nelson, Walnut, Aluminum, Herman Miller, c.1950, 56 x 39 In. 410.00

Cabinet, Stuart McDougal, Walnut, Lacquered, American, c.1958, 21 x 19 x 51 In. 1870.00
Cabinet, Sugi Wood, Iron Mounts, 2 Sections, Japan, Early 1900s, 34 1/2 x 43 x 16 In. ... 175.00
Cabinet, Tea, Sugi & Kiri Woods, 2 Parts, Copper Mounts, Japan, 1800s, 32 x 53 In. 355.00
Cabinet, Television, Trunk, Rivets, Leather Cover, Motorized Platform, 34 x 37 In. 670.00
Cabinet, Tommi Parzinger, Cube, Drop Front, Enamel, 17 1/4 x 20 x 16 In. 4315.00
Cabinet, Victorian, Burl Walnut, Lock End, Late 19th Century, 15 In., Pair 120.00
Cabinet, Victorian, Mahogany, 2 Beveled Glass Doors, 2 Drawers, 55 x 68 x 21 In. 1970.00
Cabinet, Victorian, Oak, Curved Glass End Panels, Scalloped Mirror Top, 72 x 57 In. 2070.00
Cabinet, Victorian, Rosewood, Mirrored Backsplash, c.1880, 51 x 21 1/2 x 15 In. 200.00
Cabinet, Violin Maker's, Pine, 24 Labeled Drawers, c.1900, 35 x 8 x 14 In. 1610.00
Cabinet, Walnut, 2 Grill Front, Pandanus Cloth, 36 In. 10000.00
Cabinet, Walnut, Pine, Plank Door, Shelves, Bracket Feet, Late 1700s, 27 x 18 x 11 In. .. 2530.00
Cabinet, Walnut, Polychromed, Bone Inlay, Door, 6 Drawers, Spain, c.1800, 22 x 35 In. ... 3450.00
Cabinet, Walnut, Slant Front, Lift Top, Door, Shelf, 37 1/2 x 32 x 20 1/2 In. 330.00
Cabinet, Wegner, Teak, Laminate Top, 4 Shelves, 4 Drawers, 22 1/2 x 30 x 17 1/2 In. 1840.00
Cabinet, Wendell Castle, Rosewood Doors, Carved Log Sides, c.1976, 40 x 26 In. 1150.00
Cabinet, Wine, Carved, Spread Wing Eagles, Griffiths, 67 3/4 x 74 1/2 x 21 In. 1010.00
Cabinet, Wood, Red, Black Lacquer, 2 Doors, Chinese, 1800s, 33 1/2 x 29 In. 545.00
Cabinet, Wormley, Mahogany, 2 Doors, Drawers, Dunbar, 41 1/2 x 18 x 38 1/2 In. 4900.00
Cabinet, Wormley, Mahogany, 2 Drawers, Woven Slat Sliding Doors, 32 x 41 x 18 In. ... 635.00
Cabinet, Zelkova & Sugi Wood, Red Lacquer, Japan, 32 1/2 x 35 In. 590.00
Cabinet-On-Cabinet, Fruitwood, Marquetry, Parquetry, 80 x 46 1/2 x 25 In. 2350.00
Cabinet-On-Chest, George III, Oak, c.1770, 68 3/4 x 50 x 20 In. 1495.00
Cabinet-On-Chest, Rosewood, 4 Drawers, Glazed Door, Baudouine, c.1855, 90 x 48 In. ... 4900.00
Cabinet-On-Stand, Chippendale Style, Gilt, Japanned, 2 Doors, Shelves, 63 x 46 x 18 In. . 1880.00
Cabinet-On-Stand, Chippendale Style, Lacquer, Chinese Decoration, 62 x 38 x 19 In. ... 1610.00
Cabinet-On-Stand, Marriage, Red Lacquer, 3 Shelves, 2 Drawers, 1800s, 70 x 42 In. *Illus* 635.00
Cabinet-On-Stand, Red Lacquer, 2 Doors, Chinese, c.1890, 61 x 80 In. 750.00
Cabinet-On-Stand, Red Lacquer, Mid 19th Century, 69 x 38 1/2 x 17 1/2 In. 1495.00
Candlestand, Ash, Hickory, Cherry Top, Round, Stick Legs, Turned Column, 17 x 22 In. .. 575.00
Candlestand, Birch, Tripod, New England, c.1800 .... 520.00
Candlestand, Black Lacquer, Bouquet, Gold Leaf Scroll, Tilt Top, c.1860, 27 In., Pair ... 2200.00
Candlestand, Checkerboard Surface, Tilt Top, 3 Cabriole Legs, England, 7 1/2 In. 60.00
Candlestand, Cherry, Lozenge Top, Spider Foot, 28 1/2 x 23 x 19 In. 470.00
Candlestand, Cherry, Oval Top, Tilt Top, Birdcage Support, Snake Feet, 21 x 16 x 29 In. .. 1690.00
Candlestand, Cherry, Round Top, Painted, Grapes, Grape Leaves, 25 x 19 1/2 In. 115.00
Candlestand, Cherry, Round Top, Vase-Turned Shaft, New England, 15 1/2 x 24 In. 790.00
Candlestand, Cherry, Round, Dish Top, Turned Support, Tripod, Late 1700s, 27 x 16 In. . 1000.00
Candlestand, Cherry, Serpentine, New England, Late 1700s, 27 1/2 x 16 In. ....*Illus* 2940.00
Candlestand, Cherry, Square, Beaded, Drawer, Tripod, Conn., Late 1700s, 28 x 18 In. ... 1645.00
Candlestand, Cherry, Turned Post, Cabriole Legs, 28 In. 160.00
Candlestand, Cherry, Vase-Form Pedestal, 3 Snake Feet, American, 26 1/2 x 17 In. 560.00
Candlestand, Chippendale Style, Mahogany, Tripod Base, 1800s, 28 1/2 x 17 1/2 In. 440.00
Candlestand, Chippendale, Black Over Salmon Paint, Cabriole Legs, 16 x 26 In. 440.00
Candlestand, Chippendale, Cherry, Cabriole Legs, Snake Feet, 27 x 17 x 26 1/2 In. 750.00
Candlestand, Chippendale, Cherry, Dish Top, Cabriole Legs, Urn Column, 28 x 18 In. ... 690.00

Furniture, Cabinet-
On-Stand, Marriage,
Red Lacquer,
3 Shelves, 2 Drawers,
1800s, 70 x 42 In.

Valuable old wicker should never be painted. It should be misted once a month. Vacuum and dust it regularly. Once a year wash it with Murphy's Oil soap. If wicker furniture becomes mildewed, wash it with a disinfectant cleaner.

Candlestand, Chippendale, Cherry, Ring & Vase Column, Tripod Base, 25 1/2 In. 865.00
Candlestand, Chippendale, Cherry, Square, Turned, Tripod, New England, 25 x 15 In. ... 1295.00
Candlestand, Chippendale, Cherry, Turned, Tapered, Column, Cabriole Legs, 25 x 13 In. .. 345.00
Candlestand, Chippendale, Curly Maple, Cabriole Legs, Pad Feet, 14 x 25 In. 825.00
Candlestand, Chippendale, Mahogany, Round, Turned Post, Tripod, c.1780, 27 x 19 In. ... 1000.00
Candlestand, Chippendale, Mahogany, Square, Carved, Tilt Top, Late 1700s, 27 x 17 In. . 1645.00
Candlestand, Chippendale, Tiger Maple, Dish Top, Snake Feet, Phila., 28 x 19 x 19 In. ... 2360.00
Candlestand, Chippendale, Walnut, Cabriole Legs, Snake Feet, 13 x 14 x 27 In. 290.00
Candlestand, Eastlake, Pietra Dura Top, Ebonized Base, c.1880, 29 x 17 In. 1265.00
Candlestand, Federal Style, Walnut, Tilt Top, Tripod Saber Legs, 1900s, 28 x 25 In. 415.00
Candlestand, Federal, Cherry, Inlay, Octagonal Top, c.1810, 26 1/2 x 19 x 13 1/2 In. 650.00
Candlestand, Federal, Cherry, Inlay, Square Top, Urn Support, c.1810, 26 x 13 x 13 In. ... 4780.00
Candlestand, Federal, Cherry, Mahogany, Carved, Tilt Top, c.1815, 27 x 18 In. ...... *Illus* 2700.00
Candlestand, Federal, Cherry, Spider Legs, Turned Post, Cutout Corner Top, 27 x 22 In. .. 150.00
Candlestand, Federal, Cherry, Tilt Top, Oval, Tripod, Spade Feet, c.1810, 28 x 16 In. 880.00
Candlestand, Federal, Cherry, Tripod, New England, c.1800, 26 x 17 1/2 In. 375.00
Candlestand, Federal, Cherry, Turned Post, Tripod, c.1790, 27 x 17 1/2 x 17 In. 1880.00
Candlestand, Federal, Mahogany, Inlay, Tilt Top, Tripod Spider Legs, 29 1/4 x 26 In. 2300.00
Candlestand, Federal, Mahogany, Oval Top, Mass., 1800s, 29 1/2 x 12 1/2 x 17 In. 1015.00
Candlestand, Federal, Mahogany, Tilt Top, Cabriole Legs, c.1810, 28 x 23 x 16 In. 3100.00
Candlestand, Federal, Mahogany, Tilt Top, Round, Birdcage, Tripod, c.1790, 28 x 9 In. ... 2470.00
Candlestand, Federal, Maple, Tripod, New England, c.1820, 28 x 15 x 19 In. .....520.00 to 920.00
Candlestand, Federal, Rosewood, Satinwood, Mahogany, Tripod, 1800, 30 x 21 x 15 In. .. 2990.00
Candlestand, George III, Dish Top, Tripod Pedestal, England, 1700s, 21 In. 1035.00
Candlestand, Hepplewhite, Birch, Red Wash, Spider Base, 21 x 16 x 29 In. 230.00
Candlestand, Hepplewhite, Birch, Tilt Top, Saber Legs, Stacked Ring Turnings, 29 In. ... 230.00
Candlestand, Hepplewhite, Cherry, Tilt Top, Turned Column, Tripod, 20 x 28 x 24 In. 690.00
Candlestand, Hepplewhite, Cherry, Tip Top, Arch Legs, c.1800, 32 1/2 x 21 3/4 In. 635.00
Candlestand, Hepplewhite, Cherry, Urn Column, Notched, Spider Base, 26 x 17 In. 520.00
Candlestand, Hepplewhite, Mahogany, Turned Pedestal, Tripod Base, 27 x 16 In. 550.00
Candlestand, Hepplewhite, Maple Stain, Ring & Urn Pedestal, 29 x 16 x 15 In. 310.00
Candlestand, Hepplewhite, Maple, Ring, Urn, Turned Post, Tripod, 29 x 16 x 15 In. 300.00
Candlestand, Iron, Seahorse Heads, 3-Footed, 38 In. 1208.00
Candlestand, Mahogany, Boxwood Inlay, 3 Snake Legs, 1700s, 28 1/2 x 17 3/4 In. 1150.00
Candlestand, Mahogany, Checkered Inlay Top, Tilt Top, Tripod Base, 27 x 14 x 20 In. 320.00
Candlestand, Mahogany, Dish Top, Birdcage, Turned Shaft, Pad Feet, 21 x 30 In. 13500.00
Candlestand, Mahogany, Gallery, Pull Slide, Tapered Legs, 1900s, 26 x 10 1/2 In. 280.00
Candlestand, Mahogany, Piecrust Carved Top, Birdcage Support, Claw & Ball Feet 365.00
Candlestand, Mahogany, Reeded Column, 3 Legs, Pad Feet, 64 x 12 1/2 In., Pair 2875.00
Candlestand, Mahogany, Round Top, Molded Edge, 3 Arched Legs, 28 x 19 In. 1265.00
Candlestand, Mahogany, Round Top, Spider Legs, c.1800, 28 x 18 In. 1065.00
Candlestand, Mahogany, Tilt Top, Acanthus Carved Pedestal, Legs, 28 x 27 x 16 In. 575.00
Candlestand, Mahogany, Tilt Top, Turned Column, Cabriole Legs, 18 x 17 x 26 In. 260.00
Candlestand, Maple, Octagonal Top, Spider Legs, c.1800, 29 x 14 x 16 In. 265.00

Furniture, Candlestand, Cherry,
Serpentine, New England, Late
1700s, 27 1/2 x 16 In.

Furniture, Candlestand, Federal,
Cherry, Mahogany, Carved, Tilt
Top, c.1815, 27 x 18 In.

Furniture, Candlestand, Queen
Anne, Walnut, Tilt Dish Top,
Birdcage, Late 1700s, 29 In.

Candlestand, Maple, Shaped Top, Turned Pedestal, Tripod, Spider Legs, c.1810	345.00
Candlestand, Maple, Spider Base, 27 1/2 x 13 1/2 x 14 In.	175.00
Candlestand, Nutting, No. 17, Windsor, Tiger Maple, 3 Legs, Signed	1125.00
Candlestand, Poplar, Walnut, Red Wash, c.1830, 14 x 17 x 25 3/4 In.	635.00
Candlestand, Queen Anne, Black Paint, Turned Pedestal, Tripod Base, 27 x 19 In.	290.00
Candlestand, Queen Anne, Cherry, Carved Corner Top, Tripod, 26 x 18 x 17 1/2 In.	920.00
Candlestand, Queen Anne, Cherry, Dish Top, Turned Post, Tripod, c.1780, 25 x 20 In. . . .	1175.00
Candlestand, Queen Anne, Cherry, Molded Serpentine Top, 28 x 14 x 14 1/2 In.	460.00
Candlestand, Queen Anne, Cherry, Serpentine Top, Cabriole Legs, 28 x 17 x 18 In.	635.00
Candlestand, Queen Anne, Curly Maple, 3 Snake Legs, c.1775, 26 1/2 x 17 In.	980.00
Candlestand, Queen Anne, Mahogany, Oval, Tilt Top, Vase Turned Column	4600.00
Candlestand, Queen Anne, Mahogany, Round, Tilt Top, 3 Snake Legs, 29 x 23 In.	800.00
Candlestand, Queen Anne, Mahogany, Tilt Top, Serpentine Edge, Mass., 27 x 18 In.	2875.00
Candlestand, Queen Anne, Round, Turned Shaft, 3 Cabriole Legs, 26 x 15 x 15 1/2 In. . .	200.00
Candlestand, Queen Anne, Satinwood Inlay, Oval Top, 28 1/2 x 23 x 15 1/2 In.	230.00
Candlestand, Queen Anne, Walnut, Tilt Dish Top, Birdcage, Late 1700s, 29 In. . . . . . *Illus*	5288.00
Candlestand, Shaker, Birch, Round, 3 Snake Legs, Enfield, N.H., c.1825, 23 1/2 x 14 In. .	3450.00
Candlestand, Shaker, Butternut, Red Stain, Snake Leg, c.1840, 26 1/4 x 17 In.	4025.00
Candlestand, Shaker, Cherry, Maple, Round, Tripod Legs, 26 1/2 x 15 1/2 In.	520.00
Candlestand, Shaker, Cherry, Round Top, Snake Legs, 25 x 16 3/4 In.	4315.00
Candlestand, Shaker, Cherry, Round Top, Spider Legs, Hancock, c.1840, 24 3/4 In.	6900.00
Candlestand, Shaker, Cherry, Snake Legs, Hancock, c.1825, 26 1/4 x 15 3/4 In.	2875.00
Candlestand, Shaker, Pine, Butternut, Snake Legs, Watervliet, c.1840, 27 x 22 In.	920.00
Candlestand, Sheraton, Cherry, Turned Pedestal, Spider Base, 27 x 17 x 19 In.	320.00
Candlestand, Tilt Top, Canted Corners, Turned, Spider Foot, 1832, 28 x 21 x 18 In.	1760.00
Candlestand, Victorian, Papier-Mache, Japanned, Mother-Of-Pearl Inlay, 26 x 20 In.	225.00
Candlestand, Walnut, Bulbous Turned Shaft, Snake Feet, 27 x 18 1/2 In.	400.00
Candlestand, Walnut, Dish Top, Birdcage Support, Vase Turned Shaft, 19 x 29 In.	1240.00
Candlestand, Walnut, Maple, Turned Shaft, Cabriole Legs, Pad Feet, 14 1/2 In.	420.00
Candlestand, Walnut, Round Top, Turned Center Spindle, 3 Curved Legs, 30 In.	110.00
Candlestand, Yew, Walnut, Ring-Turned Column, Domed Base, 18th Century, 44 In.	1150.00
Cane Holder, Arts & Crafts, Walnut, Visible Joinery, 20th Century, 36 1/4 In.	175.00
Cane Holder, Round, Curved Glass, Lift Top, Sailing Ship, 22 x 42 In.	2890.00
Canterbury, George III Style, Mahogany, 4 Sections, 2 Drawers, 22 x 19 In. . . . . *Illus*	518.00
Canterbury, Georgian, Mahogany, Divided Top, Drawer, Turned Legs, 12 x 18 In.	1490.00
Canterbury, Gothic Revival, 3 Sections, Arches, Drawer, c.1860, 22 x 19 x 14 In.	1265.00
Canterbury, Regency Style, Mahogany, 4 Compartments, Drawer, 23 1/2 x 18 1/2 In.	460.00
Canterbury, Rosewood, Drawer, 3 Spindled Compartments, c.1850, 18 x 22 x 16 In.	1150.00
Canterbury, Sheraton Style, Mahogany, 21 x 18 x 13 In.	300.00
Canterbury, Sheraton, Rosewood, Drawer, Turned Post, 3 Compartments, 22 x 21 In.	900.00
Canterbury, Victorian, Rosewood, Lyre Ends, Drawer, 17 x 19 1/2 x 13 1/2 In.	1435.00
Canterbury, Walnut, Lyre Dividers, American, c.1860, 22 x 15 In.	460.00
Cart, Bar, Aero, Removable Tray, Aluminum & Lucite, 1935, 33 1/2 In.	1400.00
Cart, Bar, Tony Paul, Plywood, Black Metal, 1954, 33 In.	610.00
Cassone, Walnut, Carved, Italy, Late 17th Century, 25 1/4 x 54 3/4 x 22 In.	2000.00
Cassone, Walnut, Rectangular, Hinged Lid, Italy, Late 1800s, 22 1/2 x 68 x 22 In.	1380.00
Cellarette, Brass Mounted, Russet Leather, 19 x 27 x 20 In.	1380.00
Cellarette, Chippendale Style, Mahogany, Tin Interior, Early 1900s, 17 x 13 In.	375.00
Cellarette, G. Stickley, No. 87, Copper Tray, Drawer, Door, 22 x 16 x 40 In.	2415.00
Cellarette, George III, Mahogany, Brass Bound, 28 1/2 x 16 3/4 In.	1265.00
Cellarette, Georgian, Boxwood, Inlaid Mahogany, Square Tapered Legs, 24 x 14 x 14 In. .	940.00
Cellarette, Georgian, Mahogany, Molded Lift Top, Zinc Lined Interior, 26 x 65 In.	675.00
Cellarette, Georgian, Mahogany, Sarcophagus Shape, c.1850, 23 x 19 1/2 In.	1495.00
Cellarette, Mahogany Veneer, Lift Top, Drawer, Recessed Panel Door, 33 x 17 x 20 In. . .	785.00
Cellarette, Mahogany, Crotch Split, Recessed Panel Doors, Lift Top, 34 x 18 x 20 In.	770.00
Cellarette, Mahogany, Doe Feet, Inlay, 27 In.	2350.00
Cellarette, Mahogany, Inlay, Dome Top, Stand, England, 30 1/2 x 21 1/2 In.	1840.00
Cellarette, Mahogany, Inlay, Slant Front, Serpentine Front, 45 x 26 x 17 In.	4115.00
Cellarette, Rococo Style, Mahogany, Carved Skirt, Arched Panels, 33 1/2 x 68 x 28 In. . .	3450.00
Chair, Rocker, is listed under Rocker in this category.	
Chair, Aalto, Lounge, Birch, Artek, Finland, 1931, 23 3/4 x 29 x 23 1/2 In.	3510.00
Chair, Aalto, No. 44, Maple Plywood Frame, Upholstered, Arms, 24 x 25 In.	1840.00
Chair, Aalto, No. 44, Upholstered, Continuous Birch Legs, Artek, c.1931	750.00

Chair, Adam Style, Cane Back, Faux Bamboo Turned Legs, 33 x 21 x 21 In., Pair 489.00
Chair, Adam Style, Pierced Splats, Padded Seat, Arms, c.1900s, 38 In. 1150.00
Chair, Adam Style, Shieldback, Paint Decorated, Cane Seat, Late 1800s, Pair 6050.00
Chair, Adirondack, Twig, Black & Silver Paint, Child's, 26 In. 22.00
Chair, Arne Jacobsen, Egg, Upholstered, Swivel Metal Base, 1960, 42 In. 1410.00
Chair, Arne Jacobsen, Oxford, Leather, Aluminum, Steel, 50 x 19 x 24 In. 529.00
Chair, Arne Jacobsen, Swan, Aluminum, Upholstered, Fritz Hansen, 1958, 29 x 27 In. ... 1170.00
Chair, Arne Norell, Lounge, Black Channeled Leather, Steel Base, 34 x 26 x 30 In. 575.00
Chair, Arne Vodder, Teak Frame, Leather Seat, Cane Back, Swivel Base, 20 x 34 In., Pair . 115.00
Chair, Art Deco, Bamboo, Bent, 2 Cushions, 30 In. 145.00
Chair, Artifort, No. 560, Tubular Steel, Foam, Ottoman, P. Paulin, Dutch, 25 & 14 In. 260.00
Chair, Artifort, No. 577, Tubular Steel, Rubber, Blue Fabric, P. Paulin, 24 x 33 x 34 In. .. 600.00
Chair, Arts & Crafts, 3 Thin Slats, Vine, Leaves, Triple Stretcher, 48 1/2 x 18 1/4 In. 300.00
Chair, Arts & Crafts, 5 Back Slats, Shoefoot Base, Arms, 24 x 19 x 46 In. 290.00
Chair, Arts & Crafts, Barrel Shape, Vertical Slats To Floor, Ball Feet, 42 x 24 x 19 In. ... 700.00
Chair, Arts & Crafts, Curved Rail, Spindle Back, Arms, England, Early 1900s, 37 In. 90.00
Chair, Arts & Crafts, Mahogany, Leather Upholstered Arms, Back, 30 x 28 x 38 In. 345.00
Chair, Arts & Crafts, Oak, Trapezoid Seat, Flared Legs, Cross Stretcher, Cutout Crest 45.00
Chair, B. Tobacoff, Lucite, Steel, Vinyl, Mobilier Modulaire, 1971, 29 x 25 In., Pair 2225.00
Chair, Bamboo, Bentwood, Pretzel, Upholstered, Arms, c.1955, 31 x 26 In. 185.00
Chair, Bamboo, Pretzel, Curved Arm & Leg Supports, c.1955, 31 x 26 In. 185.00
Chair, Banister Back, Heart Cutout, Rush Seat, Arms, 46 1/2 In. 4315.00
Chair, Banister Back, New England, c.1700, Pair 750.00
Chair, Banister Back, Rush Seat, Arm 490.00
Chair, Banister Back, S-Scroll Crest, 6 Vertical Slats, Leather Slip Seat, Arms, Pair 115.00
Chair, Banister Back, Splint Seat, Arms, Converted To Rocker, 18th Century 220.00
Chair, Baroque Style, Walnut, Carved, Spain, 19th Century 175.00
Chair, Barrel Back, Gray Paint, Late 19th Century, 17 1/2 In. 1380.00
Chair, Beechwood Arms, Carved, Damask Upholstery, 43 In., Pair 3520.00
Chair, Belter, Carved, Fountain Elms Pattern, Arms, 43 In. 10925.00
Chair, Belter, Rosewood, Laminated, Henry Clay Pattern, Arms, 39 1/2 x 24 1/2 x 32 In. . 1150.00
Chair, Belter, Rosewood, Laminated, Pierced, Arms, 46 x 25 1/2 x 35 In. 9200.00
Chair, Bergere, Beech, Serpentine Seat, Closed Arms, c.1785 .... 470.00
Chair, Bergere, Empire Style, Mahogany, Gilt Bronze, Closed Arms, c.1920, 37 In., Pair .. 1840.00
Chair, Bergere, Louis XV Style, Beech, Floral Chintz, Closed Arms, 1900s 325.00
Chair, Bergere, Louis XV Style, Carved, Giltwood, Closed Serpentine Arms, 40 In. 230.00
Chair, Bergere, Louis XV Style, Fruitwood, Closed Arms, 35 In. 3680.00
Chair, Bergere, Louis XV Style, Giltwood, Cane Back, Closed Arms, c.1885, 43 1/4 In. ... 1495.00
Chair, Bergere, Louis XV Style, Giltwood, Cane Back, Closed Arms, Late 1800s, 42 In. ... 1095.00
Chair, Bergere, Louis XV Style, Giltwood, Closed Arms, Late 19th Century, 44 In., Pair .. 2990.00
Chair, Bergere, Louis XV Style, Padded, Closed Arms, c.1910, 39 In., Pair 2185.00
Chair, Bergere, Louis XV Style, Walnut, Closed Arms, c.1875, 38 x 29 x 20 In. 980.00
Chair, Bergere, Louis XV Style, Walnut, Flower Crest, Scrolling Closed Arms, 37 In. 750.00
Chair, Bergere, Louis XV Style, Walnut, Padded, Closed Arms, c.1865, 39 In., Pair 3450.00
Chair, Bergere, Louis XV, Beechwood, Upholstered, Cabriole Legs, Closed Arms, 1900s . 1000.00
Chair, Bergere, Louis XV, Cane, Beech, Closed Arms, 1700s 880.00
Chair, Bergere, Louis XVI Style, Beechwood, Cushion, Closed Arms, 33 In., Pair 2760.00
Chair, Bergere, Louis XVI Style, Giltwood, Upholstered, Closed Arms 390.00

Furniture,
Canterbury,
George III Style,
Mahogany,
4 Sections,
2 Drawers,
22 x 19 In.

Furniture, Chair, Hunzinger,
Folding, Ecclesiastical
Needlework, 37 In.

Chair, Bergere, Louis XVI Style, Mahogany, Upholstered, Closed Arms, c.1890, 39 In. 2185.00
Chair, Bergere, Louis XVI Style, Polychrome, Closed Arms, Late 1800s, 46 In. 2990.00
Chair, Bergere, Louis XVI Style, Upholstered, Tapered Legs, Closed Arms, 36 In., Pair . . 1650.00
Chair, Bergere, Louis XVI Style, Walnut, Arched, Closed Arms, 40 1/2 x 23 x 20 In. 230.00
Chair, Bergere, Napoleon III, Walnut, Carved, Parcel Gilt, Closed Arms, c.1860, Pair 2600.00
Chair, Bergere, Padded Back, Cushion, Closed Arms, Early 1900s, 45 In., Pair 4370.00
Chair, Biedermeier, Cherry, Arms, Early 19th Century, 37 In. 1380.00
Chair, Biedermeier, Flame Mahogany, Curved Back, Downswept Arms, Saber Legs, Pair . 480.00
Chair, Biedermeier, Satinwood Flame Veneer, Pierced Slat, Sweden, 33 1/4 In. 330.00
Chair, Bone Veneer, Velvet, Anglo-Indian, 34 In., Pair 2070.00
Chair, Booster, Colonial Revival, Maple, Rush Seat, 20th Century, 37 1/2 In. 165.00
Chair, Bradington Young, Leather, Rolled Armrests, Swivel Base, Casters 520.00
Chair, C. Hansen, Wood, Rush, Green Painted, H. Wegner, c.1950, 31 In., Pair 120.00
Chair, C. Jacobs, Plywood, Beech, Kandya, c.1970, 28 In., Pair 835.00
Chair, C. Pollock, Corduroy Upholstery, Swivel Base, Knoll, 32 x 26 x 20 In. 60.00
Chair, Campaign, Mahogany, Leather, Scrolling Back, c.1900, 40 In. 2760.00
Chair, Carved Seat, Miniature, Green Over Salmon, 13 x 8 1/4 In. 275.00
Chair, Carved, Dragon Arms, Cabriole Legs, Chinese, Early 1900s, 33 In. 330.00
Chair, Carved, Dragon, Phoenix, Scrolls, Flowers, Open Arms, Chinese, Pair 1495.00
Chair, Charles II Style, Oak, Needlepoint Tapestry, c.1885 . . . . 259.00
Chair, Chinese Chippendale, Shaped Top Rail, Pierced Splat, Pair 200.00
Chair, Chinese Elm, Round Crest Rail, Back Support, Plank Seat, c.1900, Pair 230.00
Chair, Chinese Official's, Black, Incised Border, Arched Crest, Flared Ears, 47 In., Pair . . 290.00
Chair, Chippendale Style, Corner, Walnut, Upholstered, Pierced Splat 100.00
Chair, Chippendale Style, Mahogany, Arms, Early 19th Century, 38 In., Pair 1380.00
Chair, Chippendale Style, Mahogany, Needlework Seat, Pierced Splat, 37 In. 90.00
Chair, Chippendale Style, Mahogany, Pierced Back, Slip Seat, c.1780, 38 1/2 In., Pair . . . 4370.00
Chair, Chippendale Style, Mahogany, Stretcher Base, Slip Seat, 35 x 19 x 35 In. 1610.00
Chair, Chippendale Style, Oak, Mortise & Peg Construction, Velvet, Arms, 1800s, 42 In. . 360.00
Chair, Chippendale, Birch, Maple, Black Paint, Rush Seat, Pierced Splat, 39 In. 300.00
Chair, Chippendale, Birch, Slip Seat, Pinned Construction, Red Paint, New England 145.00
Chair, Chippendale, Cherry, Beaded Edges, Stretcher Base, Crewelwork Seat, 16 In. 990.00
Chair, Chippendale, Cherry, Pierced Ladder Back, Shaped Crest 400.00
Chair, Chippendale, Cherry, Serpentine Crest, Pierced Splat, c.1790, 39 In., Pair 940.00
Chair, Chippendale, Fruitwood, Slip Seat, Rush Cover, England, 17 1/2 x 32 In. 385.00
Chair, Chippendale, Mahogany, Bird's Head Arms, Needlepoint Seat, Ireland, Pair 2530.00
Chair, Chippendale, Mahogany, Carved, Serpentine Crest, 1760-1780, 39 In. 530.00
Chair, Chippendale, Mahogany, Gothic Arched Pierced Splat, Philadelphia, c.1775 . . . . . . 600.00
Chair, Chippendale, Mahogany, Ladder Back, Philadelphia, c.1770, Pair 2070.00
Chair, Chippendale, Mahogany, Open Slat Back, Slip Seat, Dovetailed Stretcher 55.00
Chair, Chippendale, Mahogany, Padded Seat, c.1785 . . . . 690.00
Chair, Chippendale, Mahogany, Serpentine Crest Rail, Upholstered Seat, New England . . . 2875.00
Chair, Chippendale, Mahogany, Upholstered, Carved Wing, c.1900, 47 1/4 x 16 In. 635.00
Chair, Chippendale, Maple, Cupid's-Bow Crest, Pierced Splat, Reed Seat, New England . . 310.00
Chair, Chippendale, Maple, Pierced Heart Splat, Padded Seat, Pair 4950.00
Chair, Chippendale, Maple, Upholstered Seat, c.1800 . . . . 375.00
Chair, Chippendale, Pierced Heart Splat, Rush Seat, New England 115.00
Chair, Chippendale, Tiger Maple, Pierced Splat, Rush Seat, 40 x 19 x 14 1/2 In. 715.00
Chair, Chippendale, Walnut, Serpentine Fan, Scroll, Upholstered, Mass., c.1780, 36 In. . . . 1110.00
Chair, Chippendale, Walnut, Upholstered, Slip Seat, Maryland, Late 1700s 550.00
Chair, Chrome Wire, Angled Sides, Tubular Base, Foam Seat, Back, Wool, 32 x 21 In. . . . 430.00
Chair, Club, Art Deco, Leather, France, 33 x 30 x 37 In., Pair 1725.00
Chair, Club, Art Deco, Mahogany, Leather, Square Russet Cushion, 1930, 30 In., Pair 1955.00
Chair, Club, Wood, Leather, 36 x 33 x 36 In., Pair 1765.00
Chair, Colonial Revival, Beech, Barrel Form, Serpentine Front, Arms, Early 1900s 400.00
Chair, Columbo, Elda, Plastic Swivel Base, Leather Cushions, Stendig, 1960s, 37 In. 1765.00
Chair, Commode, Federal, Walnut, Arms, Maryland, c.1800 . . . . 400.00
Chair, Corner, Baroque Style, Mahogany, Upholstered 660.00
Chair, Corner, Chippendale, Mahogany, England, c.1785, 31 1/2 x 29 In. 750.00
Chair, Corner, Chippendale, Mahogany, R.I., c.1790, 31 1/4 x 17 3/4 In. 8815.00
Chair, Corner, Eastlake, Walnut, Upholstered Crest Rail, Casters, c.1875 . . . . 175.00
Chair, Corner, George III Style, Mahogany, Lyre Splats, c.1900, 31 In. 575.00
Chair, Corner, George III, Mahogany, U-Shaped Crest, Balloon Splats, Late 1700s 560.00

Chair, Corner, Ladder Back, Rush Seat, Curved Back Rail, Arms, New England 575.00
Chair, Corner, Mahogany, Brass Fitting, Woven Cane Seat, Scroll Arm, 28 x 26 x 24 In. ... 560.00
Chair, Corner, Maple, Birch, Rush Seat, Curving Arms, 18th Century, 31 x 16 In. 1295.00
Chair, Corner, Maple, Rush Seat, Pad Feet, c.1730 .... 1250.00
Chair, Corner, Mixed Hardwoods, Bentwood Back, Oak Split Seat, 25 x 26 In. 275.00
Chair, Corner, Pine, Yew, Pencil Post Legs, 8 Spindles, Denmark, 29 In. 290.00
Chair, Corner, Queen Anne Style, Cabriole Legs, Pierced Splat, Duck Feet, 1700s 660.00
Chair, Curly Maple, Rush Seat, Saber Legs, 33 In., Pair 375.00
Chair, Desk, Aluminum, Steel, Plywood, Coated Canvas, General Fireproofing Co. 165.00
Chair, Desk, Arne Jacobsen, No. 3107, Plywood, Steel, F. Hansen, 32 x 18 x 22 In. 865.00
Chair, Desk, G. Stickley, 4 Vertical Slats, Cushion, Rope Foundation, 19 x 19 x 39 In. ... 690.00
Chair, Directoire Style, Mahogany, Bowed Seat, Arms, 37 1/2 In., Pair 2875.00
Chair, Don Petitt, Walnut, Bentwood, Upholstery, Knoll, 22 x 24 x 32 In., Pair 230.00
Chair, Dunbar, Leather, Stainless Steel Frame, 1972, 35 1/2 x 30 x 26 In., Pair 2070.00
Chair, Duncan Phyfe Style, Balloon Seat, Mahogany, Carved Crest, Pair 316.00
Chair, Dux, Birch Frame, Webbed Seat, Removable Cushions, 27 x 30 x 28 In. 115.00
Chair, Dux, Walnut, Curved Back & Arms, Spindles, Sweden, 30 x 30 x 24 In., Pair 230.00
Chair, Eagle Slats, Rush Seat, Gold Paint, Black Stenciling, 18 x 35 In. 230.00
Chair, Eames, Aluminum Group, Red Sling Seat, Herman Miller, 20 1/2 x 33 1/2 In. 175.00
Chair, Eames, Black Wire Frame, Vinyl Pad, Dowel Legs, Herman Miller, 32 x 19 In. ... 750.00
Chair, Eames, DAR-1, Fiberglass, Vinyl, Eiffel Tower Base, Herman Miller, 25 x 31 In. .. 290.00
Chair, Eames, DAX, Fiberglass Shell, Zinc Rod Base, Herman Miller, 25 x 24 x 31 In. ... 175.00
Chair, Eames, DCM, Birch, Plywood, Herman Miller, 19 1/2 x 21 1/2 x 29 1/2 In. 259.00
Chair, Eames, DCM, Ebonized Finish, P. Evans, 29 1/2 x 19 1/4 x 19 1/2 In. 290.00
Chair, Eames, DCW, Ash Plywood, Herman Miller, c.1950, 19 x 19 x 29 In., Pair 1110.00
Chair, Eames, DCW, Red Aniline Dyed Finish, Herman Miller, 28 1/2 x 19 1/2 x 18 In. .. 980.00
Chair, Eames, DKR, Wire, White Vinyl, Eiffel Tower, Herman Miller, 32 In., Pair 430.00
Chair, Eames, LAR, Fiberglass, Upholstered, Steel, Herman Miller, 1950s, 25 x 24 In. ... 645.00
Chair, Eames, LAX, Fiberglass, Herman Miller, 25 x 26 In. 290.00
Chair, Eames, LCW, Birch, Molded Plywood, Herman Miller, 22 x 25 x 27 In. 920.00
Chair, Eames, LCW, Walnut, Plywood, Herman Miller, 1950s, 22 x 25 1/2 x 27 1/2 In. ... 545.00
Chair, Eames, MKX-1, Black Wire, Vinyl Seat, Herman Miller, 19 x 22 x 28 1/2 In. 85.00
Chair, Eames, PAW, Birch, Fiberglass, Swivel, Arms, Herman Miller, 1952, 25 x 31 In. .. 1055.00
Chair, Eames, PKW, Wire Seat, Leather Cushion, Herman Miller, 19 x 21 x 31 1/2 In. ... 805.00
Chair, Eames, Soft Pad, Aluminum, Leather, Arms, Herman Miller, 23 x 24 x 32 In. 403.00
Chair, Eames, Zenith, Fiberglass, Shell, Rope Edge, X Base, 29 1/2 x 25 In. 410.00
Chair, Edwardian, Cock-Fighting, Leather, Splayed Legs, c.1900, 32 In., Pair 3450.00
Chair, Edwardian, Ebonized, Polychrome, Woven Seat, c.1900, 36 In., Pair 170.00
Chair, Edwardian, Mahogany, Leather Seat & Back, Ram's Horn Legs & Arms 565.00
Chair, Edwardian, Rosewood, Mother-Of-Pearl, Brass Inlay, c.1905 .... 235.00
Chair, Eero Aarnio, Mushroom, Woven Rattan, 28 1/4 x 33 1/2 x 32 In. 575.00
Chair, Eero Aarnio, Pastille, Fiberglass, Polyester, Asko, Finland, 1967, 36 x 21 In. 470.00
Chair, Eero Aarnio, Pastille, Molded Plastic, Yellow, Asko, Finland, 36 x 22 In. 978.00
Chair, Eero Saarinen, Grasshopper, Birch Frame, Upholstered, Knoll, 34 x 27 x 30 In. ... 1840.00
Chair, Eero Saarinen, Womb, Foam, Fabric-Covered Shell, Steel Legs, Knoll, 36 x 39 In. . 999.00
Chair, Eero Saarinen, Womb, Naugahyde, Steel Shell, 39 x 35 1/2 x 35 1/2 In. 1610.00
Chair, Egmont Arens, Plastic, Enameled Metal, c.1951, 17 1/2 x 20 x 30 1/2 In. 470.00
Chair, Ekstrom, Lounge, Teak, Oak, Lamb's Wool, 39 1/2 x 39 x 28 In. 1265.00
Chair, Ekstrom, Oak, Teak, Brown Leather, 40 x 27 1/4 x 25 In. 1495.00
Chair, Elias Svedberg, Birch Legs, Upholstered, Knoll, 28 x 36 In. 375.00
Chair, Empire Style, Mahogany, Leaf & Berry Carved Crest, Upholstered, Arms, 38 In. ... 1150.00
Chair, Empire, Acanthus Carved Crest Rail, Splat, Hairy Ankle, Paw Feet, 34 1/2 In. 1650.00
Chair, Empire, Mahogany, Bowed Seat, Turned Legs, Downswept Arms, Boston 230.00
Chair, Empire, Mahogany, Upholstered, Arched Back, Scroll Support Armrests, Pair 4370.00
Chair, Empire, Painted, Gold Decoration, Carved Arms, France, Pair 1725.00
Chair, Erberto Carboni, Delfino, Brass, Wool, Arflex, Italy, 1954, 28 x 34 In., Pair 4680.00
Chair, Ettore Sottsass, Mandarin, Bentwood Arms, Knoll, 26 x 24 x 32 1/2 In., Pair 115.00
Chair, F. Albini, Birch Frame, Upholstered, Squared Arms, Knoll, 22 x 24 x 30 In. 490.00
Chair, F. Albini, Upholstered, Arms, Poggi, 1950s, 29 1/2 In. 2390.00
Chair, Fabricius & Kastholm, Bird, Steel, Leather, Germany, 1960s, 28 x 27 x 41 In., Pair 2925.00
Chair, Federal, Mahogany, Flame Birch, Gothic Details, Boston 1725.00
Chair, Federal, Mahogany, Shaped Crest, Scrolled Arms, c.1815, 46 3/4 x 17 1/2 In. 3175.00
Chair, Federal, Mahogany, Swing-Out Tablet, Underseat Drawer, c.1820 .... 690.00

Chair, Federal, Mahogany, Upholstered, Serpentine Crest, c.1810, 41 In. 4185.00
Chair, Federal, Satinwood, Mahogany, Shieldback, c.1800, Pair 1610.00
Chair, Fin Juhl, Bwana, Teak, Vinyl, Dowel Legs, Arms, 36 x 34 3/4 x 30 In. 1495.00
Chair, Fin Juhl, Chieftain, Leather Upholstery, Dowel Leg Frame, 36 1/2 x 40 x 35 In. 7475.00
Chair, Fin Juhl, Lounge, Teak, Wool, Bovirke, Denmark, 1953, 29 x 30 x 26 In., Pair 3159.00
Chair, Flemish Style, Carved, Upholstered Seat, Open Arms, 60 x 30 x 22 In. 480.00
Chair, Flemish Style, Mahogany, Velvet, Scrolled Feet, Arm Supports, c.1910, 51 In. 415.00
Chair, Flemish, Walnut, Arched Back, Scrolled Arms, Late 18th Century, 42 In. 2070.00
Chair, Florence Knoll, Lounge, Parallel Bar, Steel, Leather, 1950s, 24 1/2 x 30 In., Pair . . 4095.00
Chair, Folding, Beechwood, Converts To Ladder, 34 In. 90.00
Chair, Folding, Painted, Black, Red, Gold, Butterfly, Child's, 29 In. 30.00
Chair, Folding, Red & Gold Lacquer, Oxbow Back, Brass Mounts, 1800s 260.00
Chair, Fornasetti, Lyre, c.1950, 16 x 20 x 36 1/2 In. 2940.00
Chair, Frank Gehry, Cross Check, Laminated Bentwood, Arms, 1992, 34 x 27 x 27 In. . . . 1265.00
Chair, Frankl, Art Deco, Pretzel, Bamboo, 5 Layers, Loose Cushions, 30 In. 145.00
Chair, French Colonial, Oak, Woven Cane, Early 19th Century, 42 x 20 x 25 In. 1725.00
Chair, French Provincial, Ash, Walnut, Ladder Back, Rush Seat, Early 19th Century 105.00
Chair, French Provincial, Fruitwood, Faux Bamboo, Spindles, Cane Seat, c.1900, 33 In. . . . 70.00
Chair, French Provincial, Fruitwood, Rush Seat, Open Arms 230.00
Chair, French Provincial, Walnut, Ladder Back, Rush Seat, Arms, Pair 60.00
Chair, Friedeberg, Wood, Hand Carved, Lacquer & Gold Leaf, 1960s, 36 x 21 x 19 In. . . . 3055.00
Chair, Fruitwood, Carved, Stylized Fan Backrest, Slip Seat, Baltic, c.1820, Pair 530.00
Chair, G. Nakashima, Lounge, Walnut, Hickory, Saddle Seat, Writing Arm, 33 x 31 In. . . . 3450.00
Chair, G. Nakashima, Lounge, Walnut, Upholstered, Widdicomb, 1958, 32 x 41 1/2 In. . . . 1870.00
Chair, G. Nakashima, Mira, Walnut, Sea Grass Seat, Arms, c.1959, 26 1/2 In., Pair 2750.00
Chair, G. Nakashima, Sundra, Cushion, Writing Arm, Widdicomb, 34 In. 1840.00
Chair, G. Nakashima, Walnut, Sculptural, Dowels, Arms, 24 1/2 x 28 1/2 In. 920.00
Chair, G. Nakashima, Walnut, Upholstered, Shaped Armrests, Widdicomb, 38 In. 1115.00
Chair, G. Nelson, Coconut, Gray Velour, Steel, Foam, 32 x 40 In. 3175.00
Chair, G. Nelson, DAF, Fiberglass, Arms, Herman Miller, 1956, 29 x 25 x 28 In. 2575.00
Chair, G. Nelson, Kangaroo, Plywood, Upholstered, Steel, Herman Miller, 1956, 39 In. . . 2690.00
Chair, G. Nelson, MAA, Fiberglass, Swag Leg, Herman Miller, c.1959, 28 x 33 1/2 In. 2530.00
Chair, G. Nelson, MAF, Fiberglass, Steel, Rubber, Herman Miller, 1958, 28 x 24 x 33 In. . 2800.00
Chair, G. Nelson, No. 4671, Aluminum, Upholstered, Herman Miller, 20 x 21 x 33 In. . . . 235.00
Chair, G. Nelson, No. 4674, Birch, Upholstered, Herman Miller, c.1950, 34 x 29 x 31 In. . 935.00
Chair, G. Nelson, Pretzel, Plywood, Vinyl, Herman Miller, 1957 . . . . 1528.00
Chair, G. Nelson, Square, Steel Legs, Low Arms, Herman Miller, 31 x 32 x 27 In. 575.00
Chair, G. Stickley, 3 Back Slats, Pegged, Plank Seat, 35 x 17 x 15 In., Pair 550.00
Chair, G. Stickley, 5 Back Slats, Corbels, Spring Seat, Arms, 29 x 30 x 28 In. 1150.00
Chair, G. Stickley, Chestnut, U-Back, Notched Top Rail, Rush Seat, 38 x 19 x 18 In. 825.00
Chair, G. Stickley, Morris, 4 Pegged Corbels, Paddle Arms, 33 x 31 1/2 x 34 In. 1380.00
Chair, G. Stickley, Morris, No. 367, 5-Slat Arms, 33 x 38 x 39 In. 6900.00
Chair, G. Stickley, Morris, Rewoven Seat, Bow Arms, Red Decal, 29 x 31 x 37 In. 8625.00
Chair, G. Stickley, No. 306, 3 Horizontal Slats, Rush Seat, 16 x 16 x 34 1/2 In., Pair 1610.00
Chair, G. Stickley, No. 308, H-Back, Leather Seat, 17 x 16 x 40 In., Pair 980.00
Chair, G. Stickley, No. 318, 5 Vertical Slats, Leatherette Cushion, Arms, 27 x 23 x 38 In. . 1265.00
Chair, G. Stickley, No. 349 1/2, Ladder Back, Leather Seat, Arms, 27 x 23 x 38 In. 2070.00
Chair, G. Stickley, No. 363, Leather Seat, Back, Revolving Base, 26 x 23 x 37 In. 3740.00
Chair, George II Style, Hardwood, Ebonized, Painted 299.00
Chair, George II Style, Mahogany, Shaped Crest, Padded Seat, Cabriole Legs, 41 In. 345.00
Chair, George II Style, Mahogany, Shell Carved Crest, Shaped Splat, 41 In., Pair 1035.00
Chair, George II, Walnut, Looped Arm Ends, Claw & Ball Feet, England 10280.00
Chair, George III Style, Mahogany, Architectural Splat, Arms, c.1850, 35 1/2 In., Pair 575.00
Chair, George III Style, Mahogany, Open Arms, 39 x 23 In. 200.00
Chair, George III Style, Mahogany, Pierced Ribbon Splat, c.1900, 40 In. 290.00
Chair, George III Style, Mahogany, Pierced Wheel Splat, Late 1800s, 38 In., Pair 1955.00
Chair, George III Style, Mahogany, Polychrome, Shieldback, 42 In., Pair 400.00
Chair, George III Style, Mahogany, Serpentine Crest Rail, Carved, 38 x 22 x 17 1/2 In. . . . 230.00
Chair, George III Style, Mahogany, Serpentine Top, Cushion, Scrolled Arms, 39 In. 750.00
Chair, George III Style, Mahogany, Shaped Top Rail, Pierced Splat, Slip Seat, Arms 145.00
Chair, George III Style, Walnut, Needlepoint Flower Tapestry, Arms, c.1915 . . . . 860.00
Chair, George III Style, Walnut, Parcel Gilt, Leather Upholstery, 46 In., Pair 3740.00
Chair, George III, Beech, Molded Backrest, Arms, Upholstered, c.1810 . . . . 375.00

Chair, George III, Gothic Revival, Mahogany, Scroll Ears, Drop Seat, c.1775, Pair 1175.00
Chair, George III, Mahogany, Pierced Splat, Upholstered Seat, Arms, c.1770 .... 980.00
Chair, George III, Mahogany, Pierced Vase-Form Splat, Drop Seat, Late 1700s, Pair 700.00
Chair, George III, Mahogany, Pierced Vase-Form Splat, Slip Seat, Arms, c.1785 .... 500.00
Chair, George III, Mahogany, Ribbonback, Arms, c.1770 .... 1645.00
Chair, George III, Mahogany, Shell Carved Crest, Ireland, c.1775, 42 1/2 In., Pair 6325.00
Chair, George III, Windsor, Elm, Maple, H-Stretcher, Arms, c.1800, 42 In. 1725.00
Chair, George Mann Niedecken, Full Slat Back, Solid Seat, 17 x 20 x 33 In. 1840.00
Chair, Georgian Style, Mahogany, Hairy Paw Feet, Open Arms, 39 x 24 In. 1360.00
Chair, Georgian Style, Mahogany, Red Velvet Upholstery, Padded Back, Arms, 47 In. 765.00
Chair, Georgian, Mahogany, Carved, Pierced Gothic Splat, Arms, c.1775 .... 529.00
Chair, Georgian, Mahogany, Carved, Pierced Splat, Upholstered Seat, c.1785, Pair 1175.00
Chair, Georgian, Mahogany, Pierced Splat, Overupholstered Seat, 18th Century, Pair 470.00
Chair, Georgian, Mahogany, Shaped Crest, Pierced Splat, Slip Seat, Cabriole Legs 1700.00
Chair, Georgian, Pierced, Overupholstered Seat, Claw & Ball Feet, Pair 590.00
Chair, Georgian, Scrolling Crest Rail, Tapestry Slip Seats, c.1820, 37 1/2 In., Pair 980.00
Chair, Giltwood, Lyre Back, Upholstered Seat, c.1885, 33 1/2 x 16 x 15 1/2 In. 489.00
Chair, Giltwood, Marquetry, Padded Seat, c.1885, 32 x 19 x 23 In. 545.00
Chair, Gio Ponti, Bonacina, Rattan, Upholstered, Italy, 39 3/4 In. 1135.00
Chair, Gio Ponti, Superlegerra, Cassina, c.1957, 13 x 17 x 33 In., Pair 1060.00
Chair, Gothic Revival, Domed Back, Plank Seat, Open Arms, Stretchers, Pair 575.00
Chair, Gothic Revival, Mahogany, Arched, Trefoil Carved, 46 In., Pair 1035.00
Chair, Gothic Revival, Mahogany, Gothic Arched Back, Saber Legs, c.1850, 35 In., Pair .. 980.00
Chair, Gothic Revival, Oak, Rectangular Backrest, Linenfold Panels, Arms, 1800s 470.00
Chair, Grain Painted, Rush Seat, Stencil, Writing Arm, 19th Century 175.00
Chair, Grete Jalk, Teak, Bentwood Seat, Cushions, Sled Base, 34 3/4 x 24 x 27 1/2 In. 1495.00
Chair, H. Bertoia, Bird, Chrome Wire Frame, Wool Cover, 38 x 38 x 36 In. 1035.00
Chair, H. Bertoia, Black Wire, Vinyl Seat, Knoll, Child's, 13 x 13 1/2 x 20 In., Pair 520.00
Chair, H. Bertoia, Diamond, Wire, Steel Finish, Knoll, 27 1/4 x 44 1/4 x 31 In., Pair 85.00
Chair, H. Probber, Wood Feet, Upholstered, c.1960, 24 3/4 In. 1790.00
Chair, Hardwood, Carved Splat, Arms, Chinese, Late 1800s, 39 1/4 In. 550.00
Chair, Hardwood, Padded Seat, Mother-Of-Pearl Inlay, Persia, Late 1800s, 41 In. 800.00
Chair, Hardwood, Shaped Crest, Inlaid Back, Arms, North Africa, c.1900, 45 In., Pair 1380.00
Chair, Hepplewhite Style, Mahogany, c.1900, 38 1/2 In., Pair 1380.00
Chair, Hepplewhite Style, Mahogany, Shieldback, Padded Seat, Arms, 39 In. 200.00
Chair, Hepplewhite Style, Mahogany, Upholstered Seat, Oval Back, c.1820, 37 1/2 In. ... 310.00
Chair, Hepplewhite Style, Satinwood, Pierced Shield, Painted Flower Urn, Arms, Pair ... 920.00
Chair, Hepplewhite Style, Shieldback, Vertical Splats, Pair 315.00
Chair, Hepplewhite, Mahogany, Arched Back, Arms, Upholstered, 1790 .... 510.00
Chair, Hepplewhite, Mahogany, Tapered Legs, Stretcher, Upholstered, Arms, 45 x 15 In. . 635.00
Chair, Hepplewhite, Mahogany, Upholstered, S-Curve Arms, c.1795, 18 In. 489.00
Chair, Herbert Von Thaden, Plywood, Bent, Metal Fasteners, 1947, 36 1/4 In. 9500.00
Chair, Hitchcock Style, Stenciled Gold Cornucopia, Rush Seats, 32 1/2 In., Pair 375.00
Chair, Hitchcock, Cane Seat, 19th Century, Child's 185.00
Chair, Hitchcock, Fruit Basket Stencil, Cane Seat, 34 3/4 In., Pair 175.00
Chair, Horn, Upholstered, Arms, Boston 880.00
Chair, Horseshoe Back, Carved Foo Dog Panel, Arms, Chinese, Pair 230.00
Chair, Howell, Chrome, Arms, Leatherette Upholstery, Karl Springer, 1935, 31 In., Pair .. 115.00
Chair, Hunzinger, Ebonized, Gilt, Upholstered Seat, Back, Late 19th Century 520.00
Chair, Hunzinger, Folding, Ecclesiastical Needlework, 37 In. .... *Illus* 1035.00
Chair, Hunzinger, Folding, Walnut, c.1875, 29 1/2 x 23 x 20 In. 1150.00
Chair, Hunzinger, Walnut, c.1875, 34 x 19 1/4 x 26 In. 690.00
Chair, Hunzinger, Walnut, Faux Bamboo, Arms, c.1875, 32 1/2 x 20 x 22 In. 860.00
Chair, Hunzinger, Walnut, Maiden Head Arms & Crest, c.1875, 39 1/2 x 24 x 28 In. 2875.00
Chair, Hvidt & Molgaard-Nielsen, Teak, Beech, Cushions, France & Son, 1950s, Pair 920.00
Chair, Iberian Style, Beech, Rush Seat, Spindle Balusters, Child's, 27 In., Pair 345.00
Chair, Ico Parisi, Lounge, Rosewood, Leather, Metal, MIM, Italy, 1950s, 32 x 29 In., Pair 4975.00
Chair, Irish Chippendale, Mahogany, Carved, Pierced Splat, Arms, c.1890, 40 In. 2070.00
Chair, Italian Baroque Style, Giltwood, Upholstered Backrest, Putti Arms, 1800s 3055.00
Chair, Italian Provincial, Fruitwood, Cane Seat, Back, 30 x 18 1/2 In., Pair 255.00
Chair, Italian Rococo, Parcel Giltwood, Arms, 39 In., Pair 4025.00
Chair, Italian Rococo, Polychrome Paint, Needlework Slip Seat, c.1750, Arms 2000.00
Chair, J. Hansen, No. 503, Teak, Leather, H. Wegner, c.1976, 30 3/8 In. 1015.00

Chair, J.M. Young, Morris, Slat Sides, 28 x 31 1/2 x 36 1/2 In. 1750.00
Chair, Jacobean Style, Leatherette, Animal Carved Crest 29.00
Chair, Jacobean Style, Oak, Rope Twist Columns, Animal Heads, Arms, c.1890, Pair 920.00
Chair, Jacobean, Oak, Wainscot, Leaf Carved Backrest, Plank Seat, Arms, 1600s 1060.00
Chair, James Mont, Barrel Back, Upholstered, Silver Rubbed Finish, 25 x 22 In., Pair . 3450.00
Chair, James Mont, Lounge, Wood Frame, Velvet Upholstery, 29 1/2 x 33 In., Pair 2645.00
Chair, James Mont, Upholstered, Enameled Wood Legs, 28 1/2 x 29 1/2 In. 633.00
Chair, Jean Royere, Scotch Club, Stained Oak, c.1946, 33 7/8 In., Pair 9560.00
Chair, Jeanneret, Scissor, Maple, Brass Struts, Webbed, Cushions, 28 1/2 x 23 x 27 In. 920.00
Chair, Joe, Baseball Glove, Cotton Upholstery, 29 x 68 x 48 In. 1765.00
Chair, Jorgen Hovelskov, Harp, Ebonized Frame, Denmark, 1968, 36 x 52 In. 2575.00
Chair, Josef Hoffman, Bentwood, Black Lacquer, Arms, J. & J. Kohn, Pair 1795.00
Chair, Jules Leleu, Lounge, Oak, Leather Upholstery, 1940s, 32 x 34 x 34 In., Pair 2925.00
Chair, K. Christensen, Steel, Leather, Arms, Poul Kjaerholm, c.1960, 27 3/4 In. 1910.00
Chair, K. Kukkapuro, Fiberglass, Vinyl, Haimi-Oy, c.1965, 35 3/8 In. 775.00
Chair, K. Savvaerk, Teak, Leather, Ditzel, c.1958, 25 1/4 In. 4780.00
Chair, Kaare Klint, Safari, c.1933, 31 1/2 x 22 1/2 x 22 1/2 In. 1058.00
Chair, Katavolos Littell & Kelley, Lounge, Leather, Tubular Steel Legs, 28 1/2 In. 805.00
Chair, Kem Weber, Lounge, Chromium Plated Steel, Leather, Wood, 1934, 29 x 39 In. ... 3800.00
Chair, Klismos, Ebonized Wood Frame, Silk Moire, 1930s, 36 x 20 x 33 3/4 In. 1380.00
Chair, L. & J.G. Stickley, 3 Vertical Back Slats, Solid Seat, 48 x 28 x 30 In. 800.00
Chair, L. & J.G. Stickley, 8 Back Slats, 6 Arm Slats, 25 x 25 x 32 In. 7480.00
Chair, L. & J.G. Stickley, Morris, 5-Slat Sides, 43 x 32 x 36 In. 4900.00
Chair, L. & J.G. Stickley, Morris, Arched Apron, Corbels, 39 x 31 1/2 x 36 In. 3050.00
Chair, L. & J.G. Stickley, No. 360, Ladder Back, 3 Slats, 17 x 16 x 35 In., Pair 400.00
Chair, L. & J.G. Stickley, Peaked Crest Rail, Arched Stretchers, Pair, 8 x 18 1/4 x 17 In. ... 920.00
Chair, L. & J.G. Stickley, Slat Sides, Leather Seat, Arms, 38 x 28 1/2 x 25 1/4 In. 860.00
Chair, Ladder Back, 3 Serpentine Arched Ladders, Reeded Seat, Arms, France 225.00
Chair, Ladder Back, 3 Slats, Woven Splint Seat, Blue Paint, 1700s, 23 x 15 x 12 In. 420.00
Chair, Ladder Back, 3 Slats, Woven Splint Seat, Child's, Blue Paint, 23 x 15 x 12 In. 415.00
Chair, Ladder Back, 4 Arched Ladders, Painted, Ball Feet 340.00
Chair, Ladder Back, 4 Slats, Mule Ear Posts, Orange Paint, Ohio, 37 In. 880.00
Chair, Ladder Back, 5 Slats, Serpentine Slats, Rush Seat, Front Stretcher, Ball Finials 169.00
Chair, Ladder Back, Front & Rear Posts, Mule Ear Top, Turned Arms, 36 1/2 In. 165.00
Chair, Ladder Back, Maple, Ash, Mushroom Finials, Oak Split Seat, Late 1700s, 38 In. ... 55.00
Chair, Ladder Back, Maple, Bulbous Stretcher, Rush Seat, Ball Feet, 16 x 41 In. 345.00
Chair, Ladder Back, Maple, Oak, Rush Seat, Pair 140.00
Chair, Ladder Back, Maple, Oak, Splint Seat, Turned Finials, 23 1/2 x 14 1/2 x 11 In. 170.00
Chair, Ladder Back, Maple, Oak, Woven Splint Seat, 23 1/2 x 14 1/2 x 11 In. 175.00
Chair, Ladder Back, Maple, Rush Seat, 3 Slats, Double Box Stretcher, 33 In., Pair 60.00
Chair, Ladder Back, Maple, Woven Splint Seat, 3 Slats, Raised Rings, 15 x 32 1/2 In. 85.00
Chair, Ladder Back, Oak, 5 Slats, 20th Century, 42 In., Pair 255.00
Chair, Ladder Back, Old Black Paint, 3 Slats, Arched Crest, 43 In. 230.00
Chair, Ladder Back, Shaker, Black Paint, 2, Woven Splint Seat, Arched Slat, 33 1/2 In. 345.00
Chair, Larsen & Madsen, Rosewood, Leather, Pontoppidan, Denmark, 26 x 32 1/2 In. 1035.00
Chair, Le Corbusier, Basculent, Chrome, Leather, Arms, 25 x 23 1/4 x 25 1/4 In., Pair ... 2530.00
Chair, Legislator's, Leather, Wood Base, Swivel, Maine, 34 x 18 In. 290.00
Chair, Lifetime, 3/4 Drop, Oversize, Arms, 32 1/2 x 28 x 29 In. 1840.00
Chair, Lifetime, Morris, Pegged, Arched Stretcher, Leather, Arms, 40 x 29 1/2 x 36 In. ... 1265.00
Chair, Limbert, 3 Back Slats, Slat Seat, Arms, 37 1/2 x 27 1/2 x 22 In. 345.00
Chair, Limbert, Leather, Block Legs, Paddle Arms, 32 1/2 x 32 x 32 In. 2875.00
Chair, Limbert, Leather, Brass Studs, Pair 150.00
Chair, Lolling, Chippendale Style, Mahogany, Stretcher Base, Upholstered, Arms, 42 In. . 315.00
Chair, Lolling, Federal, Mahogany, Concave Back, Bowfront, Beaded, c.1805, 42 x 15 In. 2470.00
Chair, Lolling, Federal, Mahogany, Inlaid, Serpentine, New England, c.1790, 46 1/2 In. .. 7640.00
Chair, Lolling, Federal, Mahogany, Serpentine Crest, Upholstered Arms, 37 x 16 In. 1530.00
Chair, Lolling, Hepplewhite, Mahogany, Upholstered, Box Stretcher, Curved Arms 1265.00
Chair, Lolling, Mahogany, Linenfold, Molded Arms, Tapered Legs, Box Stretcher 3680.00
Chair, Lolling, Martha Washington, Mahogany, Reeded Legs, 38 x 24 x 27 In., Pair 365.00
Chair, Lolling, Sheraton Style, Mahogany, Curved Arm Supports, Silk, 45 In. 1090.00
Chair, Lolling, Sheraton Style, Mahogany, Curved Arm Supports, Silk, 48 In. 1200.00
Chair, Louis Durot, La Spirale, Fiberglass, 1 Piece, 33 x 27 In. 750.00
Chair, Louis Philippe, Rosewood, Upholstered, Arms, 40 1/2 In., Pair 2300.00

Chair, Louis Sognot, Chrome, Cushion, Arms, c.1930, 28 1/2 x 20 1/4 x 22 In. 1725.00
Chair, Louis XIII Style, Walnut, Padded Seat & Back, Arms, 47 x 26 In., Pair 2990.00
Chair, Louis XIV Style, Fruitwood, Needlework, Flat Back, Arms, 41 x 26 x 32 In. 1840.00
Chair, Louis XIV Style, Mahogany, Needlework Upholstery, Arms 840.00
Chair, Louis XIV Style, Walnut, Chintz Upholstery, Arms 230.00
Chair, Louis XIV Style, Walnut, Upholstered, Arms 175.00
Chair, Louis XV Style, Beech, Cartouche Shaped Backrest, Arms, 1900s, Pair 355.00
Chair, Louis XV Style, Beech, Upholstered, Curved Back, Arms, Pair 1530.00
Chair, Louis XV Style, Beech, Upholstered, Flat Back, Arms, Late 1800s, 44 In., Pair 2185.00
Chair, Louis XV Style, Carved Back, Upholstered, Arms, France, c.1900, 37 In., Pair 8050.00
Chair, Louis XV Style, Flower Carved Crests, Flat Back, Upholstered, Arms, Pair 2010.00
Chair, Louis XV Style, Fruitwood, c.1900, 38 1/2 x 27 x 22 In., Pair 1840.00
Chair, Louis XV Style, Fruitwood, Upholstered, Arms, Pair . . . . .420.00 to 1550.00
Chair, Louis XV Style, Gilt, Carved, Upholstered, Curved Back, Arms, 41 1/2 In., Pair . . . 405.00
Chair, Louis XV Style, Giltwood, Aubusson Tapestry, Arms, Pair 5680.00
Chair, Louis XV Style, Giltwood, Padded, Medallion Back, Arms, c.1900, 42 In., Pair . . . 750.00
Chair, Louis XV Style, Giltwood, Upholstered, Arms, Late 1800s, 43 x 28 x 22 In. 1265.00
Chair, Louis XV Style, Giltwood, Upholstered, Curved Back, Arms, France, 36 In., Pair . . 400.00
Chair, Louis XV Style, Gros & Petit Point Upholstery, Curved Back, Arms 470.00
Chair, Louis XV Style, Mahogany, Parcel Gilt, Upholstered, Arms, 41 In., Pair 2875.00
Chair, Louis XV Style, Polychrome, Arched Back, Cushion, Arms, 35 x 29 In., Pair 2760.00
Chair, Louis XV Style, Walnut, Cane, Fan Back, 35 3/4 In. 690.00
Chair, Louis XV Style, Walnut, Padded, Needlework Seat, Arms, c.1900, 35 In. 259.00
Chair, Louis XV, Beech, Cane, Serpentine Seat, Cabriole Legs, c.1750 . . . . 210.00
Chair, Louis XV, Beech, Flat Back, Serpentine Seat, Upholstered, Arms, c.1760 . . . . 1410.00
Chair, Louis XV, Beech, Gilt, Cane Backrest, Mid 1700s, Pair 175.00
Chair, Louis XV, Beech, Upholstered, Curved Back, Leaf Carved Frame, Feet, Arms 295.00
Chair, Louis XV, Cane Back, Padded Leather Seat, Flower Carvings, c.1765, 40 In. 750.00
Chair, Louis XV, Fruitwood, Upholstered, Flat Back, Arms, c.1750, 32 In. 1610.00
Chair, Louis XV, Walnut, Upholstered, Flat Back, Arms, Mid 18th Century 800.00
Chair, Louis XVI Style, Beech, Grisaille, Gray Paint, Oval Back, Arms, 37 1/2 In. 145.00
Chair, Louis XVI Style, Beech, Grisaille, Gray Paint, Scrolled Arms, c.1900, 38 In. 460.00
Chair, Louis XVI Style, Beech, Silk, Arms, 20th Century, Pair 520.00
Chair, Louis XVI Style, Flat Back, Upholstered, Arms, Late 1800s, Pair 2070.00
Chair, Louis XVI Style, Fruitwood, Grisaille, Gray Paint, Arms, Early 1900s, 36 In., Pair . 980.00
Chair, Louis XVI Style, Fruitwood, Padded Seat & Back, Arms, c.1850, 34 In. 1840.00
Chair, Louis XVI Style, Fruitwood, Upholstered, Arms, 36 In., Pair 750.00
Chair, Louis XVI Style, Gilt, Wreath Crest, Padded Back & Seat, 36 In., Pair 1380.00
Chair, Louis XVI Style, Giltwood, Ormolu Mounted, Bonheur De Jour, c.1890, 33 In. 1410.00
Chair, Louis XVI Style, Giltwood, Pair 480.00
Chair, Louis XVI Style, Giltwood, Upholstered, Arms, Pair 1910.00
Chair, Louis XVI Style, Limed Wood, Pair 300.00
Chair, Louis XVI Style, Mahogany, Upholstered, Arms, Pair 1795.00
Chair, Louis XVI Style, Oval Backrest, Voluted Supports, Upholstered, Arms, Pair 235.00
Chair, Louis XVI Style, Padded Seat, Oval Backrest, Tapered, Fluted Legs, Arms 750.00
Chair, Louis XVI Style, Polychrome, Early 19th Century, 46 1/4 x 27 x 28 In. 4830.00
Chair, Louis XVI Style, Polychrome, Mid 19th Century, 34 1/2 x 23 x 16 In. 1150.00
Chair, Louis XVI, Carved Crest, Padded Seat, Back, Tapered Legs, c.1800, 37 In., Pair . . . 1150.00
Chair, Lounge, Art Deco, Molded Birch, Curved Arms, Upholstered, 28 x 33 x 30 In. 460.00
Chair, Lounge, Eero Aarnio Style, Rattan, Metal, 1960s, 34 x 27 x 30 In. 145.00
Chair, Lounge, Suede, Wood, Leather, 1950s, 31 x 29 x 34 In., Pair 1175.00
Chair, M. Bellini, No. 412, Leather, Embossed Plastic, Cassina, c.1976, 32 In. 6570.00
Chair, Mahogany, Carved, Dragon Heads, Crest Rail, Paw Feet, 42 In. 260.00
Chair, Mahogany, Flower Carved Crest, Slip Seat, Gondola Style, c.1835, Pair 345.00
Chair, Mahogany, Griffin Arms, Flared Front Feet, Velvet Upholstery, 18 x 36 In., Pair . . . 990.00
Chair, Mahogany, Lyre Splat, Mid 19th Century, Child's, 21 In. 1840.00
Chair, Mahogany, Marquetry, Domed Crest, Dutch, Early 1800s, 44 In., Pair 3105.00
Chair, Mahogany, Marquetry, Padded, Barrel Crest, Arms, Dutch, c.1850, 34 In. 1095.00
Chair, Mahogany, Openwork Splat, Shaped Crest Rail, Stretcher, Early 1800s, 36 1/2 In. . . 250.00
Chair, Mahogany, Padded, Tufted Back, Scrolling Arms, c.1865, 45 1/2 In. 2185.00
Chair, Mahogany, Scrolled, Carved Back, Splat, Needlepoint Seat, 38 x 17 x 17 In. 69.00
Chair, Mahogany, Shaped Crest, Gothic Pierced Splat, Slip Seat, Philadelphia 1915.00
Chair, Mahogany, Wheel Back, Feather Rosette, 1900s, 37 x 23 In. 565.00

Furniture, Chair, Napoleon III, Giltwood, Shaped
Back, Upholstered, Scrolled Crest, 44 In.

Furniture, Chair, Paint Decorated, Flowers,
Bootjack, Pa., 34 In., Pair

Chair, Maple, Ash, Banister Back, Turned, New England, 1700s, 42 1/8 x 17 In.	295.00
Chair, Maple, Banister Back, Rush Seat, 19th Century	80.00
Chair, Maple, Banister Back, Turned, New England, 1700s, 42 x 16 1/8 In.	295.00
Chair, Maple, Carved Crest Rail, Rush Seat, Turned Legs, 18th Century, 40 x 19 In., Pair .	2530.00
Chair, Maple, Red Wash, Bamboo Turned Stretchers, Woven Seat, Arms, 37 In., Pair	940.00
Chair, Maple, Vase-Form Slats, Cane Seat, c.1840, 32 In., Pair	750.00
Chair, Maple, Yellow Poplar, Carved Crest, Leather Seat, Arms, c.1725, 51 In.	6575.00
Chair, Marcel Breuer, B3, Chrome, Leather, Stendig, Italy, Pair	1175.00
Chair, Marcel Breuer, Wassily, Leather, Steel Frame, Stendig, 30 1/2 x 29 1/2 In., Pair . . .	460.00
Chair, Marco Zanuso, Lady, Ribbed Upholstery, Brass Legs, 36 x 27 x 30 In., Pair	2185.00
Chair, Marco Zanuso, Lady, Wood, Upholstered, Arflex, Italy, 1951, 31 x 33 In., Pair	7605.00
Chair, Marco Zanuso, Lambda, Enameled Steel, Ollpa, Italy, 1962, 19 x 19 x 31 In.	1400.00
Chair, Marco Zanuso, Senior, Plywood, Upholstered, Arflex, Italy, 1951, 33 x 37 In., Pair .	3800.00
Chair, Mario Bellini, Cab, Gray Leather, Arms	260.00
Chair, Massimo Iosa Ghini, Numero 1, Leather, Tubular Frame, Arms, 30 x 24 x 33 In. . .	1725.00
Chair, Mies Van Der Rohe, Barcelona, Leather, c.1929, Pair	2875.00
Chair, Mies Van Der Rohe, Lounge, MR, Steel, Suede, Arms, Knoll, 25 1/2 x 34 In., Pair .	2300.00
Chair, Mies Van Der Rohe, Tubular Chromed Steel, Leather Seat, Knoll, 19 x 18 In.	460.00
Chair, Ming Style, Elm, Chinese, c.1850, Pair	770.00
Chair, Mollino, Brass, Velvet, Turin, 1951, 33 1/4 In.	4540.00
Chair, Morris, American Modern, Arms, Conant & Ball, 36 1/4 x 26 1/2 x 33 1/2 In.	520.00
Chair, Morris, Bow, Arched Apron, 32 x 17 x 37 In.	2015.00
Chair, Morris, Mahogany, Lion Heads, Claw Feet, 39 x 29 x 35 In.	2070.00
Chair, Morris, Oak, Slat Sides, Pegged, Through Tenon Legs, 41 x 32 x 36 In.	1495.00
Chair, Morris, Walnut, Upholstered, Writing Arm, Hardy Patent, 1800s	290.00
Chair, Nanna Ditzel, Mahogany, Wicker, c.1950, 32 x 29 x 29 In.	470.00
Chair, Napoleon III, Giltwood, Shaped Back, Upholstered, Scrolled Crest, 44 In. . . . . *Illus*	5750.00
Chair, Neoclassical, Beech, Carved, Concave Backrest, Outscrolled Padded Arms	705.00
Chair, Neoclassical, Burl, Rosewood, Mahogany, Arms, Russia, 36 1/2 In.	1725.00
Chair, Neoclassical, Cane Back, Chinoiserie, Tub Form, Open Arms, 34 In., Pair	1840.00
Chair, Neoclassical, Cherry, White Leather, Barrel Back, Arms, Continental, 1800s, Pair . .	1150.00
Chair, Neoclassical, Mahogany, Padded Seat, 1900s, 37 x 16 1/2 x 16 In., Pair	1380.00
Chair, Norman Cherner, Molded Plywood, Plycraft, Arms, 31 x 25 1/4 x 18 In.	690.00
Chair, Norman Cherner, Walnut Plywood, Plycraft, Arms, 19 x 26 x 31 In., Pair	1520.00
Chair, Nutting, 8 Spindles, Vase Turnings, Stamped Under Seat	900.00
Chair, Oak, Carved, Scrolling, Upholstered Seat, Back, Early 1900s, 46 x 28 x 28 In.	225.00
Chair, Oak, Mortised, Plank Seat, Stretcher Base, Arms, England, 32 1/2 In.	200.00
Chair, Oak, Pierced Carved Back, Claw Feet, c.1885, 48 1/2 x 25 1/2 x 25 In., Pair	690.00
Chair, Oak, Pierced Gothic Arch Back, Reeded Legs, c.1885, 46 In., Pair	2070.00
Chair, Oak, Spindle Back, Rush Seat, 1800s, Child's, 30 In.	1495.00
Chair, Oak, Upholstered, France, 1940s, 22 x 28 x 30 In.	760.00
Chair, Oak, Vase-Form Splat, Turned Stretchers, c.1720	650.00
Chair, Onondaga, Cedar, Pegged Construction, Rope Weave Seat, 44 x 29 1/2 x 25 In.	520.00
Chair, Oriental, Rosewood, Round Emblem Back, Arms, 35 1/4 x 24 1/2 x 18 1/2 In.	230.00
Chair, Oriental, Teak, Carved, Cabriole Legs, Scrolled Feet, Dragon Arms, 44 1/2 In.	575.00
Chair, Oriental, Teak, Carved, Dragon Arms, Iris, Flowers, Bats, 17 x 44 In.	550.00

Chair, Osvaldo Borsani, Lounge, P 40, Tecno, Italy, 27 1/2 x 59 x 33 1/2 In. 865.00
Chair, Overstuffed, Cut Velvet Upholstery, Arms, Early 20th Century 175.00
Chair, P. Evans, Cube, Patchwork Burl Veneer, Velvet Upholstery, Swivel Base, 34 In. ... 460.00
Chair, P. Goldman, Walnut-Faced Plywood, Plycraft, c.1950, 31 1/2 In. 2630.00
Chair, Paint Decorated, Flowers, Bootjack, Pa., 34 In., Pair .... *Illus* 715.00
Chair, Paulin, Foam-Covered Steel, Green Stretch Fabric, 1970s, 24 x 36 In., Pair 940.00
Chair, Paulin, Molded Seat, Back, Wool, Pedestal Base, Artifort, 28 x 30 In., Pair 1380.00
Chair, Paulin, Ribbon, Canvas, Steel, France, 1950s, 32 x 26 x 26 1/2 In., Pair 1405.00
Chair, Pesce, UP3, C&B Italia, c.1969, 38 x 27 In. 1530.00
Chair, Plank Bottom, Mid 19th Century, 15 1/2 x 7 1/2 x 7 3/4 In. 1155.00
Chair, Plank Bottom, Red Paint, Yellow Pinstripes, Child's, 17 3/4 In. 50.00
Chair, Plank Bottom, Shaped Splat, Crest, Salmon, Yellow Pinstripes, Child's, 17 In. 1350.00
Chair, Potthast Bros., Federal Style, Mahogany, Arms, Baltimore, c.1925 .... 1035.00
Chair, Potty, Ladder Back, 5 Slats, Cherry Arms, Jennersville, Pa. 900.00
Chair, Queen Anne Style, Fruitwood, Cane, Pair 230.00
Chair, Queen Anne Style, Hardwood, Rush Seat, Mortise & Peg, 40 1/2 In. 110.00
Chair, Queen Anne Style, Mahogany, Spoon Back, American, c.1735, 40 1/2 In. 865.00
Chair, Queen Anne Style, Mahogany, Upholstered Seats, Scalloped Crest, 41 In., Pair ... 175.00
Chair, Queen Anne Style, Mahogany, Upholstered, Cabriole Legs, 1800s, 40 In., Pair 2200.00
Chair, Queen Anne Style, Mahogany, Upholstered, Cabriole Legs, Arms, 37 In., Pair 230.00
Chair, Queen Anne Style, Upholstered, Shell Carved Cabriole Legs, Arms, 46 In. 305.00
Chair, Queen Anne Style, Walnut, Open Arms, c.1800, Child's, 26 1/2 In., Pair 12500.00
Chair, Queen Anne Style, Walnut, Upholstered, Arched Back, Arms, c.1900, 39 1/4 In. 920.00
Chair, Queen Anne, Balloon Seat, Dark Finish, Yoked Crest, New England 1495.00
Chair, Queen Anne, Ballooned Slip Seat, Scrolled Splat, 1700s, 39 1/2 x 17 In. 1150.00
Chair, Queen Anne, Birch, Hickory, Rush Seat, Vase Splat, Arch Crest, 38 In. 175.00
Chair, Queen Anne, Black Paint, Ribbon Seat, Urn Shaped Splat, Arms, 38 In. 175.00
Chair, Queen Anne, Cherry, Blocked, Turned Stretchers, Pad Feet 4900.00
Chair, Queen Anne, Cherry, Rush Seat 315.00
Chair, Queen Anne, Mahogany, Relief Carved Acanthus Leaves, Scrolls, 40 1/4 In. 575.00
Chair, Queen Anne, Mahogany, Spoon Back, Cupid's-Bow Crest, Club Feet 565.00
Chair, Queen Anne, Maple, Rush Seat, Ash Stretchers, c.1780 .... 230.00
Chair, Queen Anne, Oak, Tuned Supports, Ball Stretcher, Arms 28.00
Chair, Queen Anne, Rush Seat, Spanish Feet, c.1715, 42 x 18 x 20 1/2 In. 2500.00
Chair, Queen Anne, Shaped Crest, Slip Seat, Late 18th Century, Pair 705.00
Chair, Queen Anne, Urn Splat, Upholstered Seat, 42 1/2 In. 490.00
Chair, Queen Anne, Walnut, Blocked, Turned Stretchers, Pad Feet 3450.00
Chair, Queen Anne, Walnut, Crest Rail, Cabriole Legs, Bellflower Knees, 1740 .... 2115.00
Chair, Queen Anne, Walnut, Inlaid, Rear Stretcher, c.1780 .... 575.00
Chair, Queen Anne, Walnut, Trapezoid Slip Seat, Cabriole Legs, England 575.00
Chair, Queen Anne, Walnut, Vase Splat, Cabriole Legs, H-Stretcher, Pad Feet, c.1800 .... 460.00
Chair, Queen Anne, Walnut, Yoked Crest, Mass., c.1760, 39 3/4 x 16 1/2 In. 1530.00
Chair, Queen Anne, Yoked Crest, Curved Shoulders, Slip Seat, Bermuda 6900.00
Chair, R. Neutra, Wood, Nylon Webbing, c.1950, 28 1/2 In., Pair.................... 2150.00
Chair, Red Lacquered Wood, Chinese, c.1860, Child's, Pair 295.00
Chair, Regency Style, Giltwood, Upholstered, Flat Back, Arms, c.1850, 46 x 24 In. 1840.00
Chair, Regency Style, Mahogany, Padded Seat, Paneled Crest, c.1910, 34 In., Pair 200.00
Chair, Regency Style, Mahogany, Red Leather Back, Seat, Reeded Scroll Arms, Pair 489.00
Chair, Regency Style, Openwork Crest Rails, Oriental Decoration, 35 1/2 In., Pair 275.00
Chair, Regency Style, Walnut, Needlepoint Upholstery, Pair 3000.00
Chair, Regency, Black Lacquer, Polychrome, Upholstered, Arms, 1800s, 31 x 21 x 20 In. . 2530.00
Chair, Regency, Mahogany, Lyre Carved Slats, Scroll Open Arms, c.1810, Pair 650.00
Chair, Regency, Mahogany, Rectangular Back, Lyre Splat, Padded Seat, Saber Legs, Pair . 335.00
Chair, Regency, Painted, Gilt, Cane Seat & Back, Arms, c.1815, 33 1/2 In., Pair 4140.00
Chair, Regency, Parcel Gilt, White Paint, c.1800 .... 1150.00
Chair, Renaissance Revival, Ebonized Walnut, Gilt Incised, Arms, Child's, 26 1/2 In. ... 635.00
Chair, Renaissance Revival, Hunzinger, Folding, Walnut, Arms, Mid 19th Century, 37 In. . 1035.00
Chair, Renaissance Revival, Oak, Lion's Mask, Arms, Late 1800s, 55 In. 690.00
Chair, Renaissance Revival, Palazzo, Carved Walnut, Italy, Early 1900s, Pair 3420.00
Chair, Renaissance Revival, Rosewood, Bronze Inlay, Arms, c.1870, 36 x 34 x 32 In. 1610.00
Chair, Renaissance Revival, Rosewood, Fruit, C-Scrolls, Cane Seat, Arms, Pair 450.00
Chair, Renaissance Revival, Rosewood, Gilt Incised, c.1865, 37 In., Pair 980.00
Chair, Renaissance Revival, Walnut, Damask Upholstery, Child's, 30 In. 545.00

Chair, Renaissance Revival, Walnut, Floral Chintz Upholstery, Turned Legs, c.1880 . . . . . 50.00
Chair, Renaissance Style, Curule, Walnut, Tapestry Upholstery, Arms, c.1900 . . . . 375.00
Chair, Renaissance Style, Mahogany, Curule, Padded, Saddle Seat, Italy, 35 In., Pair 3165.00
Chair, Renaissance Style, Oak, Carved, Grotesque Heads, Paw Feet, 56 In., Pair 360.00
Chair, Restauration Style, Fruitwood, Upholstered, Arms, 35 1/2 In. 575.00
Chair, Restauration, Mahogany, Leaf Scroll Ends, Open Arms, 40 1/4 In., Pair 2300.00
Chair, Risom, 654L, Birch, Canvas, Knoll, 1950s, 20 x 28 x 30 In. 380.00
Chair, Risom, Blond Wood, Black Canvas Webbing, 29 1/2 x 24 x 26 In. 345.00
Chair, Risom, Teak Base, Silk, Down Cushions, Arms, 36 x 36 x 28 In. 2415.00
Chair, Risom, Upholstered, Continuous, Birch Legs, Knoll, 29 1/2 x 20 1/2 x 24 1/4 In. . . . 490.00
Chair, Robert Propst, Leather, Aluminum, Herman Miller, 41 x 29 In. 403.00
Chair, Robsjohn-Gibbings, Mahogany, Green, Arms, Widdicomb, 21 1/2 x 24 In., Pair . . . 1095.00
Chair, Robsjohn-Gibbings, Walnut, Leather Straps, Arms, c.1940, 33 1/2 In., Pair 1315.00
Chair, Rocker is listed under Rocker in this category.
Chair, Rococo Revival, Fruit Carved Crest, American, 1800s 85.00
Chair, Rococo Revival, Laminated Rosewood, Arms, Mid 1800s, 43 x 24 x 24 In. 2530.00
Chair, Rococo Revival, Laminated Rosewood, Hourglass Back, c.1850, 41 1/2 In. 3680.00
Chair, Rococo Revival, Rosewood, Pierced Back, Upholstered Seat, c.1855, Child's 1015.00
Chair, Rococo Revival, Walnut, Woman's Portrait, Black, Continental 120.00
Chair, Rococo, Rosalie Without Grapes, Laminated Rosewood, Arms, c.1850, 40 In. 2070.00
Chair, Rohde, Vinyl, Wood Base, Continuous Seat, 32 x 16 x 18 In. 105.00
Chair, Roman Style, Brass, Iron Frame, Cross Hatch, Arm Supports, 35 x 27 x 21 In. 1100.00
Chair, Rope, High Back, Solid Arms, Cross Design 275.00
Chair, Rosewood, Burl Inset Panels, Cushions, Carved Legs, 41 3/4 x 21 3/4 x 18 In. 300.00
Chair, Rosewood, Scaly Dragons, Horned Heads, Chinese, c.1900, 36 In. 860.00
Chair, Roycroft, 4 Back Slats, Mackmurdo Feet, Leather Seat, 38 x 18 x 17 In. 1495.00
Chair, Ruhlmann, Mahogany, Leather, c.1930, 32 3/4 In. 4065.00
Chair, S. Karpen Bros., Oak, Barrel Sides, 32 x 35 1/4 x 26 In. 1380.00
Chair, Savonarola, Walnut, Carved, Italy, Late 19th Century 410.00
Chair, Scrolled Crest Rail, Vine, Flower Frieze, Arms, 17th Century, 43 x 25 x 25 In. 3730.00
Chair, Sedan, George III, Wooden, Gesso, Leather, Flower Bouquet, 64 x 31 x 39 In. 770.00
Chair, Shaker, 3 Slats, Tape Seat, Arms, Mt. Lebanon, c.1930, 18 1/4 x 41 1/2 In. 1840.00
Chair, Shaker, 3 Slats, Tapered Posts, Egg Shape Finials, Woven Tape Seat, 40 1/2 In. . . . 165.00
Chair, Shaker, Birch, 2-Rail Back, Rush Seat, Mt. Lebanon, c.1900, 17 1/2 x 28 In. 460.00
Chair, Shaker, Birch, 3 Arched Slats, Cane Seat, Enfield, N.H., c.1830, 41 In. 1530.00
Chair, Shaker, Birch, 3 Slats, Tape Seat, Tilters, New Lebanon, c.1860 . . . . 805.00
Chair, Shaker, Birch, Maple, Cane Seat, Tilters, Enfield, N.H., c.1840, 13 x 30 3/4 In. 1265.00
Chair, Shaker, Birch, Tape Seat, Tilters, Enfield, N.H., c.1840, 17 x 41 In. 3450.00
Chair, Shaker, Birch, Tilters, Brown, 3 Arched Slats, Rush Seat, N.H., 18 x 41 In. 2070.00
Chair, Shaker, Curved Back Rail, 4 Spider Legs, Swirl, Mt. Lebanon, 25 1/2 In. 5750.00
Chair, Shaker, Dining, Nipple Finials, Rush Seat, 28 In. 440.00
Chair, Shaker, Ladder Back, 3 Slats, Cane Seat, Painted, Enfield, Conn. 495.00
Chair, Shaker, Ladder Back, 3 Slats, Cane Seat, Wooden Pegs, Paint Trace, Pair 1760.00
Chair, Shaker, Ladder Back, 3 Slats, Stepped Finials, Tape Seat, Painted, Enfield, Conn. . . 330.00
Chair, Shaker, Ladder Back, 3 Slats, Woven Splint Seat, Child's, 37 1/4 In. 175.00
Chair, Shaker, Ladder Back, 4 Slats, Turned Arms, Mule Ear Corners, Cane Seat, 44 In. . . 715.00
Chair, Shaker, Ladder Back, Maple Posts, Painted, Oak Split Seat, 36 x 18 x 14 In. 250.00
Chair, Shaker, Ladder Back, Maple, Stepped Finials, 38 In. 385.00
Chair, Shaker, Ladder Back, Oval Finials, Wood Peg Construction 4180.00
Chair, Shaker, Ladder Back, Pegged Maple, Painted, Inscription, 36 x 19 x 14 In. 220.00
Chair, Shaker, Ladder Back, Splint Seat, Double Box Stretchers, Red Paint, Arms 375.00
Chair, Shaker, Low Back, Plank Seat, 6 Spindles, Canterbury, 25 1/2 In. 1840.00
Chair, Shaker, Maple, 2 Arched Slats, Tape Seat, Tilters, 2 Box Stretchers 1380.00
Chair, Shaker, Maple, 3 Slats, Perforated Seat, Mt. Lebanon, c.1876, 15 1/2 x 34 In. 635.00
Chair, Shaker, Maple, 3 Slats, Splint Seat, New Lebanon, c.1830, 16 x 41 1/2 In. 805.00
Chair, Shaker, Maple, 3 Slats, Tape Seat, Mt. Lebanon, c.1920, 40 1/2 In. 690.00
Chair, Shaker, Maple, 3 Slats, Tape Seat, Tilters, Mt. Lebanon, c.1870, 34 1/2 In. 1265.00
Chair, Shaker, Maple, 3 Slats, Tilters, Tape Seat, New Lebanon, c.1830, 17 x 42 In. 805.00
Chair, Shaker, Maple, Cane Seat, 2 Slats, Enfield, N.H., c.1840, 12 1/3 x 29 1/2 In. 1840.00
Chair, Shaker, Maple, Low Back, Tilters, Tape Seat, New Lebanon, 26 In., Pair 1380.00
Chair, Shaker, No. 1, Maple, Tape Back, Seat, Mt. Lebanon, c.1880, Child's, 28 1/2 In. . . 1495.00
Chair, Shaker, No. 2, Ladder Back, 3 Arched Slats, Taped Seat, Mt. Lebanon, 34 In. 1095.00
Chair, Shaker, No. 3, 3 Shaped Slats, Acorn Pommels, Tape Seat, Mt. Lebanon, 34 In. . . . 380.00

Chair, Shaker, No. 3, Dark Finish, Rush Seat, Arms, Mt. Lebanon 518.00
Chair, Shaker, No. 3, Maple, 3 Slats, Tape Seat, Mt. Lebanon, 15 x 33 1/2 In., Pair 1035.00
Chair, Shaker, No. 5, 3 Slats, Rush Seat, Mt. Lebanon, 16 x 37 1/2 In. 1380.00
Chair, Shaker, No. 5, 3 Slats, Tape Seat, Arms, Mt. Lebanon 520.00
Chair, Shaker, No. 5, Dark Finish, 3 Slats, Blue Tape Seat, Arms, Mt. Lebanon 635.00
Chair, Shaker, No. 6, Birch, Cane Seat, Tilters, Enfield, N.H., c.1835, 17 1/4 In. 4025.00
Chair, Shaker, No. 6, Dark Stain, Slat Back, Shawl Bar, Arms, Mt. Lebanon 750.00
Chair, Shaker, No. 7, 4 Slats, Paper Rush Seat, Mt. Lebanon 460.00
Chair, Shaker, No. 7, Maple, Tape Seat, Shawl Bar, Arms, Mt. Lebanon, c.1870, 39 In. 2015.00
Chair, Shaker, No. 7, Tape Seat & Back, Single Slats, Arms, Mt. Lebanon, 41 In. . . .805.00 to 920.00
Chair, Shaker, No. 7, Tape Seat, 2 Slats, Shawl Bar, Mt. Lebanon, 41 1/2 In. 4255.00
Chair, Shaker, No. 9, 3 Graduated Arched Slats, Legs Rise Over Seat, Enfield 2185.00
Chair, Shaker, Plank Seat, 3 Slats, Acorn Finials, Swivel, New Lebanon, 36 1/2 In. 2300.00
Chair, Shaker, Shaped Splats, Concave Edge Curve, Finials, Kentucky, Child's, 32 In. . . . 1100.00
Chair, Shaker, Slat Back, 3 Graduated Arched Slats, Rush Seat, Double Stretchers 430.00
Chair, Shaker, Slat Back, 4 Arched Slats, Rush Seat, Elongated Finials 115.00
Chair, Shaker, Tiger Maple, Arched Slat Back, Tilters, Rush Seat, Cylindrical Legs 4140.00
Chair, Sheraton Style, Painted, Cane, Reeded Stiles, Arms, c.1900, Pair 1150.00
Chair, Sheraton, Arrow Back, Yellow, 19th Century, Child's 265.00
Chair, Sheraton, Black Paint, Gold Stenciled Eagle On Crest, Rush Seat, 35 In. 170.00
Chair, Sheraton, Curly Maple, Bowed Stretcher Front, Turned Crest Rail, 34 In. 259.00
Chair, Sheraton, Mahogany, Reeded X-Shape Back, Carved Crest, 33 1/2 In. 165.00
Chair, Sheraton, Rush Seat, Stencil, Scrolling Armrests, New England, c.1815, Pair 1150.00
Chair, Sheraton, Shieldback, Serpentine Seat, Upholstered, 1800s, Pair 690.00
Chair, Sheraton, Thumb Back, Sausage Turned Arms, Mushroom Caps, American, 1800s . 200.00
Chair, Shoeshine, Steel, Wire, Pullout Footstool, 53 In. 305.00
Chair, Shop Of The Crafters, Peaked Top, Cutout Slats, Arms, 26 x 23 x 42 In. 489.00
Chair, Slipper, Rococo Revival, Laminated Rosewood, c.1850, 37 1/4 In., Pair 3450.00
Chair, Slipper, Rococo Revival, Walnut Turned Stiles, Mid 19th Century, 41 In., Pair 920.00
Chair, Slipper, Steer Horn Frame, Cushion Seat, Victorian 920.00
Chair, Softwood, Fretwork Apron, Garden Scene, Chinese, Late 1800s, 40 3/4 In., Pair . . . 175.00
Chair, Stickley Bros., 3 Vertical Slats, Plank Seat, 38 1/4 x 16 1/4 x 15 In. 315.00
Chair, Stickley Bros., Morris, 3 Slats, Through Post Construction, 31 x 36 x 36 In. 920.00
Chair, Thaden-Jordan Furniture Co., Bent Plywood, Birch Face, Metal, 1947, Pair 8815.00
Chair, Tito Agnoli, Korium, Leather, Plastic Casters, Arms, 34 3/4 x 24 1/2 x 17 1/2 In. . . 1380.00
Chair, Tobia Scarpa, Bastiano, Oak, Black Wool Upholstery, Knoll, 36 x 30 x 28 In., Pair . 865.00
Chair, Tub, Biedermeier, Birch, Ebony Inlay, Padded Back, Arms, c.1910, 38 In. 750.00
Chair, Tub, Louis Phillipe Style, Fruitwood, Curved Back, Arms, c.1910, 30 In. 1035.00
Chair, Tub, Papier-Mache, Black Lacquer, Padded Seat, c.1850, 37 x 23 x 18 In. 2185.00
Chair, Tub, Reeded Crest Rail, Cabriole Legs, England, Early 20th Century, Pair 980.00
Chair, Tub, Walnut, Mahogany, Pierced Splat, Downswept Arms, Italy, c.1910, 30 In. 575.00
Chair, Turkish Style, Carpet Upholstery, Arms, Victorian, Child's, Pair 540.00
Chair, Turkish Style, Velvet Upholstery, Arms, Victorian, Pair 1910.00
Chair, V. Kagan, Cosmos, Plexiglas, Upholstered, Wood, 1970, 28 x 60 x 35 1/2 In. 4095.00
Chair, V. Kagan, Cubist Style, Cherry Frame, Cushions, Arms, 1967, 32 x 23 x 25 1/2 In. . 920.00
Chair, V. Panton, Cone, Black Vinyl, Steel Base, 1960s, 23 x 23 In. 700.00
Chair, V. Panton, Cone, Wire Form, Blue Wool Cushion, Plus-Ligne, 25 x 29 In. 920.00
Chair, V. Panton, Green Plastic, Herman Miller, 1973, 19 x 24 x 32 1/2 In. 200.00
Chair, V. Panton, Heart, Wool, 4-Point Base, Plus-Linje, c.1960, 40 x 25 x 36 In. 3450.00
Chair, V. Panton, Stacking, Molded Plastic, Black, 1970 . . . . 325.00
Chair, Victorian, Black Lacquered, Domed Crest, Mid 1800s, 33 In., Pair 750.00
Chair, Victorian, Black Walnut, Balloon Back, Upholstered, Casters, 44 x 26 x 32 In. 280.00
Chair, Victorian, Carved Roses, Pink Floral Silk Upholstery, Mid 1900s, 45 x 26 In. 345.00
Chair, Victorian, Carved, Upholstered Seat, Open Arms, 36 1/2 In., Pair 210.00
Chair, Victorian, Mahogany, Carved, Upholstered Seat, Back, Arms, 43 1/2 In., Pair 450.00
Chair, Victorian, Mahogany, Leather Upholstery, Arms, Casters, 39 x 24 x 21 In. 365.00
Chair, Victorian, Oak, Barley Twist, Padded, Arms, c.1865, 53 1/2 In. 1265.00
Chair, Victorian, Walnut Frame, Classical Crest Figure, Upholstered, 1800s 259.00
Chair, Victorian, Walnut, Carved Crest, Lion Mask Arms, c.1865, 47 1/2 In. 490.00
Chair, Victorian, Walnut, Carved Oval Back, Carved Pediment, Early 1900s, Pair 290.00
Chair, Victorian, Walnut, Flower Upholstery, Open Arms, 39 x 29 In. 230.00
Chair, Victorian, Walnut, Needlework Seat, Finger Carved, Open Arms, 40 x 16 In. 230.00
Chair, Victorian, Walnut, Open Back, Carved Crest, Needlework Seat, 32 1/2 In., Pair . . . 120.00

Chair, W. Platner, High Back, Wire Base, Wool, Knoll, 1970s, 41 x 35 x 39 In. 800.00
Chair, W. Platner, Lounge, Nickel Rod Wire Base, White Wool Upholstery, 40 x 41 In. . . . 2235.00
Chair, W. Platner, Lounge, Wool, Bronze Wire Base, Knoll, 1970s, 36 x 24 x 30 In. 200.00
Chair, W. Platner, Wire, Nickel Finish, Wool, Knoll, 1972, 27 x 21 x 27 In., Pair 690.00
Chair, W.D. Teague, Lounge, Brushed Metal, New Cushion, 29 1/2 x 70 1/4 x 39 In. 489.00
Chair, Walnut, Balloon Back, Curved Seat, Cabriole Legs, Arms, c.1850, 42 In. 170.00
Chair, Walnut, Bargello Upholstery, Arms, 17th Century 575.00
Chair, Walnut, Carved Feet, Philadelphia, c.1760 . . . . 4315.00
Chair, Walnut, Carved Leaves, Gadroon, Needlepoint Seat, c.1890, 38 x 16 In. 140.00
Chair, Walnut, Carved Tablet Back, Arched Crest, Lift Seat, c.1850, 46 1/2 In., Pair 1035.00
Chair, Walnut, Carved, Mermaids, Putti, Pierced Scrolls, Flowers, c.1890, 53 x 22 In. 200.00
Chair, Walnut, Carved, Molded Back Crest, Padded Arms, Philadelphia, c.1850, 44 In. . . . 690.00
Chair, Walnut, Cupid's Bow Crest, Slip Seat, Cabriole Legs, Philadelphia 1915.00
Chair, Walnut, Ladder Back, 3 Splats, 35 In., Pair 330.00
Chair, Walnut, Oval Molded Back, Flower Pediment, Continental, c.1925, Pair 315.00
Chair, Walnut, Pierced Crest, Padded, Arms, Flemish, c.1850, 55 In., Pair 2070.00
Chair, Walnut, Pierced Open Splats, Rush Seat, Continental, Pair 69.00
Chair, Walnut, Spoon Back, Vase Splat, Upholstered, Continental, c.1720, 42 In. 375.00
Chair, Walnut, Turned Columns, Carved Crest, Needlepoint Seat, 38 3/4 x 17 x 16 In. 250.00
Chair, Walnut, Upholstered, Padded Back, Seat, Arms, Carved Paws, Continental, Pair . . . 1265.00
Chair, Walnut, Upholstered, Scrolled Feet & Arms, c.1900, 51 x 28 x 24 In. 670.00
Chair, Walter Lamb, Bronze Frame, Rush Seat, Back, Brown Jordan, 20 1/2 x 33 In. 1150.00
Chair, Wanscher, Mahogany, Curved Crest Rail, Leather Seat, 32 x 19 x 18 In. 520.00
Chair, Warren McArthur, Lounge, Aluminum Frame, Canvas, 32 x 26 1/2 x 35 1/2 In. 4315.00
Chair, Warren McArthur, Lounge, Aluminum, Upholstered, 1930s, 28 x 36 x 33 In. 7020.00
Chair, Warren McArthur, Tubular Aluminum, Rubber, Sling Seat, c.1935, 32 In. 1675.00
Chair, Wegner, Contoured Frame, Exposed Arms, 33 x 27 1/2 x 20 In., Pair 920.00
Chair, Wegner, Executive, c.1955, 29 x 23 x 29 1/2 In. 4995.00
Chair, Wegner, Folding, Teak, Cane Seat, Johannes Hansen, 30 x 24 1/2 x 30 In. 1955.00 to 2185.00
Chair, Wegner, Folding, Woven Reed, 30 1/2 x 24 x 27 In. 1380.00
Chair, Wegner, Kastrup, Leather, Chrome Plated Steel, 29 1/2 x 23 1/4 x 22 In. 575.00
Chair, Wegner, Lounge, Papa Bear, Teak, Upholstered, Ottoman, Denmark, 1950s, 39 In. . . 3820.00
Chair, Wegner, Teak Armrests & Legs, Upholstered, Denmark, 1950s, 33 In. 825.00
Chair, Wegner, Teak Frame, Leather Seat, J. Hansen, 24 1/2 x 20 1/2 x 29 3/4 In. 575.00
Chair, Wegner, Teak, Cane, J. Hansen, Denmark, 30 In. 470.00
Chair, Wegner, Valet, Teak, Flip-Up Back, Denmark, 1958, 37 In. 4350.00
Chair, Wendell Castle, Laminated Walnut, Barrel Back, Writing Arm, c.1978, 29 x 31 In. . . 2760.00
Chair, Wendell Castle, Oak, Barrel Back, Writing Arm, c.1976, 28 x 31 x 23 In. 1840.00
Chair, William & Mary Style, Oak, Upholstered Seat & Back, Arms, 40 In. 220.00
Chair, William & Mary, Hardwood, Rush Seat, American, Early 1700s, 42 In. 520.00
Chair, William IV, Mahogany, Mid 19th Century, 35 In., Pair 2990.00
Chair, William IV, Mahogany, Shell & Scroll Carved Back, c.1835, 32 In., Pair 2530.00
Chair, William IV, Rosewood, Upholstered, Brass Cup Casters, Scrolled Arms, c.1830 . . . 865.00
Chair, Windsor, 4 Spindles, Serpentine Crest, Writing Arm, Late 1700s, 37 x 17 In. 3525.00
Chair, Windsor, Bamboo Turnings, Green Paint, Pair 430.00
Chair, Windsor, Birdcage, 7 Bamboo Turnings, Red Grained Paint 450.00
Chair, Windsor, Birdcage, 7 Spindles, Shaped Seat, 32 1/2 x 16 x 18 In., Pair 660.00
Chair, Windsor, Birdcage, Bamboo Turnings, Black Paint, c.1800, Pair 460.00
Chair, Windsor, Birdcage, Bamboo, Black Paint, 1820, Set Of 7 . . . . 2070.00
Chair, Windsor, Black Paint, Bamboo Turnings, Arms 115.00
Chair, Windsor, Bow Back, 7 Spindles, Green, Arms, Lancaster County, Pa. 1915.00
Chair, Windsor, Bow Back, Bamboo Turnings, c.1800, 37 x 16 1/2 In. 1035.00
Chair, Windsor, Bow Back, Black Over Green Paint, Bulbous Turned Legs, Late 1700s . . 110.00
Chair, Windsor, Bow Back, Paint Decorated, Red Ground, Black, Yellow, 16 1/2 x 9 In. . . 1100.00
Chair, Windsor, Bow Back, Rush Seat, Pierced Splat 160.00
Chair, Windsor, Brace Back, 7 Spindles, Rhode Island, 38 1/2 x 17 1/4 In. 3165.00
Chair, Windsor, Brace Back, Painted, Continuous Arm, 36 x 18 In. 3900.00
Chair, Windsor, Butterfly Birdcage, 7 Spindles, 13 1/2 x 34 1/4 In., Pair 770.00
Chair, Windsor, Butterfly, 7 Bamboo Turnings 25.00
Chair, Windsor, Carved Saddle Seat, Painted, Splayed Legs, Arms, 37 1/2 x 17 In. 1035.00
Chair, Windsor, Comb Back, 5 Spindles, Drawer, Early 1800s, 48 In. 2420.00
Chair, Windsor, Comb Back, 7 Spindles, Crest Rail, Arms, 1780, 40 In. 2700.00
Chair, Windsor, Comb Back, 7 Spindles, Serpentine Crest, Late 1700s, 37 x 17 In. 1765.00

Chair, Windsor, Comb Back, Bamboo Turnings, Drawer, Writing Arm, New England 4315.00
Chair, Windsor, Concave Crest Rail, Arrow Spindle Back, Stretcher, Late 1800s 45.00
Chair, Windsor, Elm, Curved Stretchers, England, 1800s, Pair 1035.00
Chair, Windsor, Elm, Yew, Yoke Crest, Vase Splat, 19th Century 1880.00
Chair, Windsor, Fanback, 7 Spindles, Saddle Seat, Splayed Legs, 37 x 17 In., Pair 1380.00
Chair, Windsor, Fanback, 7 Spindles, Shaped Seat, New England, 18 In. 225.00
Chair, Windsor, Fanback, 8 Spindles, 36 x 17 1/2 In. 375.00
Chair, Windsor, Fanback, 9 Spindles, Arms, Pennsylvania, 1700s, 44 1/2 x 16 3/4 In. 8050.00
Chair, Windsor, Fanback, 9 Spindles, Shaped Crest, Saddle Seat, c.1790, 36 In., Pair 1475.00
Chair, Windsor, Fanback, Carved Ears, Arms, Turned Base 140.00
Chair, Windsor, Fanback, Connecticut, 1700s, 35 3/4 x 17 1/2 In., Pair 2415.00
Chair, Windsor, Fanback, Eared Crest Rail, H-Stretcher, American, c.1800, 38 1/2 In. 1265.00
Chair, Windsor, Fanback, Nutting, No. 310 .... 750.00
Chair, Windsor, Fanback, Serpentine Crest, H-Stretcher, New England, Pair 1150.00
Chair, Windsor, Fanback, Turned Legs, Scrolled Ears, Arms 1150.00
Chair, Windsor, Green Paint, Stenciled, Arms 69.00
Chair, Windsor, Hickory, Pine, Hoop Back, American, Early 1900s 415.00
Chair, Windsor, Hoop Back, 9 Spindles, Turned Legs, Stretchers, Flat Arm, Green 3095.00
Chair, Windsor, Mahogany, Hickory, 15 Spindles, Continuous Arm, 17 1/2 x 34 In. 200.00
Chair, Windsor, Maple, Pine, Bamboo Turnings, Step-Down, 19th Century, Pair ...230.00 to 316.00
Chair, Windsor, Nutting, Brace Back, 7 Spindles, Turned Base, 37 1/2 In. 345.00
Chair, Windsor, Nutting, Comb Back, Arms, 44 In. 1955.00
Chair, Windsor, Nutting, Comb Back, Plank Seat, Arms, 42 In. 1150.00
Chair, Windsor, Nutting, No. 211, Comb Back, Arms, Child's ....2700.00 to 2970.00
Chair, Windsor, Nutting, No. 301, Brace Back ....550.00 to 680.00
Chair, Windsor, Nutting, No. 401, Continuous Arm 605.00
Chair, Windsor, Nutting, No. 415, Comb Back, Arms 700.00
Chair, Windsor, Painted, 7 Spindles, Flat Bow Crest, Arms, Bamboo, Legs 845.00
Chair, Windsor, Pine, Plank Seats, 6 Spindles, Bamboo Turnings, 35 In., Pair 275.00
Chair, Windsor, Plank Seat, 4 Spindles, Turned Legs, Stretcher, 15 x 15 In. 60.00
Chair, Windsor, Plank Seat, Bamboo Turnings, Rectangular Crest, Downsloped Arms 85.00
Chair, Windsor, Poplar, Sack Back, Shaped Seat, Arms, 37 1/2 In. 190.00
Chair, Windsor, Sack Back, 7 Spindles, Bamboo Turnings, Oval Seat, Arms 4400.00
Chair, Windsor, Sack Back, 7 Spindles, Painted, Bowed Crest, c.1800, 29 x 18 In. 1995.00
Chair, Windsor, Sack Back, Black Paint, Saddle Seat, Arched Crest, Knuckle Arms 690.00
Chair, Windsor, Sack Back, Carved Knuckles, Splayed Legs, H-Stretcher, 35 1/2 In. 3850.00
Chair, Windsor, Sack Back, Shaped Seat, Stretcher Base, 37 1/2 In. 385.00
Chair, Windsor, Saddle Seat, 7 Spindles, Bamboo Turned Legs, 19th Century 259.00
Chair, Windsor, Saddle Seat, Black, Arms, 20th Century, Pair 2800.00
Chair, Windsor, Salmon Paint, Pine Seat, Step-Down, 36 1/2 x 17 3/4 In. 575.00
Chair, Windsor, Thumb Back, Mustard Paint, Black, Bamboo Turned Legs, 33 In., Pair .. 259.00
Chair, Windsor, Thumb Back, Plank Seat, 4 Spindles, Stretcher, 32 1/2 x 15 x 15 In. 60.00
Chair, Windsor, Writing Arm, Green Paint 990.00
Chair, Wing, Chippendale Style, Mahogany, Claw & Ball Feet, 17 1/2 x 46 1/2 In. .440.00 to 545.00
Chair, Wing, Chippendale Style, Mahogany, Stretcher Base, Upholstered, 46 In. 550.00
Chair, Wing, Chippendale Style, Mahogany, Upholstered, 44 In. 545.00
Chair, Wing, Chippendale, Mahogany, American, c.1780 .... 4425.00
Chair, Wing, Edwardian, Leather Upholstery, Padded, Tufted, c.1900, 47 In., Pair 4830.00
Chair, Wing, George III Style, Mahogany, Padded Back, Scrolled Arms, 43 1/2 In. 345.00
Chair, Wing, George III Style, Mahogany, Red Velvet Upholstery, Late 19th Century 1175.00
Chair, Wing, Georgian Style, Black Leather Upholstery, Brass Studs, Mid 20th Century .. 750.00
Chair, Wing, Georgian Style, Leather, Brass Tacks, Cabriole Legs, Pad Feet, 44 In. 385.00
Chair, Wing, Georgian Style, Shaped Back, Upholstered, Scroll Arms, 1900s, 40 In. 69.00
Chair, Wing, Hepplewhite Style, Mahogany, Upholstered, 18 1/2 x 46 In. 190.00
Chair, Wing, Hepplewhite, Centennial, Brocade Upholstery 520.00
Chair, Wing, Hepplewhite, Upholstered, Stretchers, 47 In., Pair 230.00
Chair, Wing, Jacobean Style, Walnut, Stretchers, Upholstered, 49 1/4 In. 2420.00
Chair, Wing, James Mont, Upholstered, Wood Feet, 32 x 36 1/2 x 28 In., Pair 2150.00
Chair, Wing, Louis XVI Style, Giltwood, Carved Leaves, Tabouret 765.00
Chair, Wing, Mahogany, Carved Leg, Scroll Arms, Upholstery, 1930s, 43 x 31 x 30 In. 390.00
Chair, Wing, Pine, Woven Seat & Back, Child's, 31 In. 175.00
Chair, Wing, Queen Anne Style, Mahogany, Mohair Upholstery, Arms, 47 In. 575.00
Chair, Wing, Queen Anne Style, Serpentine Crest, Outscrolled Arms 290.00

Chair, Wing, Queen Anne Style, Shell & Scroll Carved Legs, Upholstered 260.00
Chair, Wing, Queen Anne Style, Striped Upholstery, Pad Feet, 43 x 31 In. 395.00
Chair, Wing, Queen Anne, Mahogany, Dome Top, Mid 18th Century, 50 In. 2070.00
Chair, Wing, Queen Anne, Walnut, Carved, Arms, 18th Century, 45 1/2 x 21 x 33 In. 5175.00
Chair, Wing, Queen Anne, Walnut, Upholstered, Massachusetts 5175.00
Chair, Wood, Floral Splat, Dragon Carved Arms, Japan, Late 19th Century 345.00
Chair, Wood, Nylon Webbing, Continuous, Arms, 36 3/4 x 26 3/4 x 28 In. 400.00
Chair, Wood, Urn-Shaped Arms, Turned Legs, 1900s, 37 In., Pair 2090.00
Chair, Wormley, Alexandria, Mahogany, Oval Seat, Dunbar, 1960s, 33 In., Pair 3055.00
Chair, Wormley, Cube, Brown Mohair, 36 x 34 x 24 In., Pair 1610.00
Chair, Wormley, Light Mahogany, Upholstered, Dunbar, 26 x 30 x 29 In., Pair 805.00
Chair, Wormley, Lounge, Janus, Walnut, Leather, Dunbar, c.1960, 27 x 30 In., Pair 1755.00
Chair, Wormley, Lounge, Mahogany, Upholstered, Dunbar, 25 x 31 In., Pair 2070.00
Chair, Wormley, Lounge, Square, Brown Leather, Dunbar, 25 x 38 In., Pair 1880.00
Chair, Wormley, Lounge, U-Shape, Mahogany, Wool, Dunbar, 34 x 26 1/2 In., Pair 2645.00
Chair, Wormley, U-Shape, Swivel Base, Arms, Dunbar, 30 1/2 x 27 1/2 In., Pair 1840.00
Chair & Ottoman, Archizoom, Mies Style, Steel, Rubber, Calf, Italy, 1969, 52 x 30 In. . . .   2340.00
Chair & Ottoman, Arne Jacobsen, Egg, Fritz Hansen, c.1958, 32 x 29 x 40 In. 7640.00
Chair & Ottoman, B. Mathsson, Pernilla, Beech Frame, Hemp Webbing, Sweden 1150.00
Chair & Ottoman, Eames, 670, Rosewood, Aluminum, Steel, Leather, 33 x 33 In. 3525.00
Chair & Ottoman, Eames, Aluminum Group, Herman Miller, c.1958, 26 x 27 x 39 In. 940.00
Chair & Ottoman, Eames, Aluminum Group, Swivel Base, 39 1/2 x 26 x 27 In. 1150.00
Chair & Ottoman, Eames, No. 670, Black Leather, Herman Miller, 32 In. 1175.00
Chair & Ottoman, Eames, No. 670/671, Rosewood, Leather, Aluminum, c.1970 . . . .   3500.00
Chair & Ottoman, Eames, Rosewood Plywood, Leather, Herman Miller, 32 In. 2115.00
Chair & Ottoman, Eames, Rosewood, Leather, Herman Miller, 1960s, 33 x 32 x 33 In. . . .   1380.00
Chair & Ottoman, Eames, Soft Pad, 4 Point Aluminum, Leather, Herman Miller 1380.00
Chair & Ottoman, Frank Gehry, Easy Edges, 1972 . . . .   4400.00
Chair & Ottoman, Frank Gehry, Power Play, Bentwood, Enamel, Arms, Knoll 1840.00
Chair & Ottoman, G. Nakashima, Black Walnut, Maple, Slat Back, Arms, 1950s 3800.00
Chair & Ottoman, G. Nelson, Coconut, Steel, Upholstered, Herman Miller, 1956 . . . . 43900.00
Chair & Ottoman, George Mulhauser, Walnut, Vinyl, Laminated, c.1970, 34 In. 300.00
Chair & Ottoman, H. Bertoia, Bird, Chrome Wire Frame, Wool, 38 x 38 x 36 In. 1495.00
Chair & Ottoman, L. & J.G. Stickley, Morris, Arms, Leatherette, 40 x 33 In. 2600.00
Chair & Ottoman, Mies Style, Poltronova, c.1969, 51 1/2 x 29 x 30 In. 3525.00
Chair & Ottoman, Pace, Chrome, Lucite, Rust Suede, 1975 . . . .   510.00
Chair & Ottoman, Paulin, Artifort, c.1960, 37 x 38 1/2 x 36 In. 1760.00
Chair & Ottoman, Risom, Blond Wood, Arms, Black Canvas Webbing, Knoll 575.00
Chair & Ottoman, W. Platner, Corduroy, Wire Frame, Arms, Knoll 1725.00
Chair & Ottoman, W. Platner, Steel Rod Base, Tweed Upholstery, Knoll 2070.00
Chair Rococo, Revival, Laminated Rosewood, American, c.1850, 41 1/2 In., Pair 4370.00
Chair Rococo, Revival, Laminated Rosewood, Arms, American, c.1850, 47 In. 8625.00
Chair Rococo, Revival, Laminated Rosewood, Arms, American, c.1850, 48 In. 6900.00
Chair Set, Aesthetic Revival, Mahogany, Overupholstered, 1 Armchair, c.1890, 10 . . . . . .   4110.00
Chair Set, Andre Frechet, Walnut, c.1925, 37 In., 6 . . . .   7170.00
Chair Set, Arne Vodder, Teak, Cane, Leather, Denmark, 1960s, 20 x 20 x 33 In., 8 . . . . . .   1755.00
Chair Set, Arts & Crafts, 4 Slats, Crocker Chair Co., 22 x 21 x 37 In., 12 . . . .   1840.00
Chair Set, Arts & Crafts, Mahogany, 3 Vertical Splats, England, 1900s, 40 1/2 In., 4 . . . . .   530.00
Chair Set, Arts & Crafts, Oak, Horizontal Splat, Upholstered Seat, c.1916, 37 In., 6 . . . . .   1645.00
Chair Set, Arts & Crafts, Oak, Slat Back, Leather Seat, Square Legs, 40 In., 4 . . . .   290.00
Chair Set, Beech, Gilt, Painted, Slat Back, Bowed Seat, Early 1800s, 33 3/4 In., 6 . . . . . .   3680.00
Chair Set, Beech, Ladder Back, 2 Armchairs, Lancashire, 43 In., 10 . . . .   2530.00
Chair Set, Biedermeier, Fruitwood, Bowed Crest, Upholstered Seat, c.1840, 4 . . . .   645.00
Chair Set, Biedermeier, Maple, C-Shape Crest, Overupholstered Seat, c.1820, 6 . . . .   1645.00
Chair Set, Carlo Di Carli, Walnut, Upholstered, Singer & Sons, c.1952, 19 x 33 In., 4 . . . .   1170.00
Chair Set, Chippendale Style, Mahogany, Mid 1900s, 36 1/2 In., 8 . . . .   805.00
Chair Set, Chippendale Style, Mahogany, Overupholstered, 2 Armchairs, 4 . . . .   1295.00
Chair Set, Chippendale Style, Mahogany, Padded Seat, 35 In., 12 . . . .   5750.00
Chair Set, Chippendale Style, Mahogany, Pierced Splat, 2 Armchairs, 40 In., 8 . . . .   1150.00
Chair Set, Chippendale Style, Mahogany, Pierced Splat, Slip Seat, 1 Armchair, 8 . . . .   4830.00
Chair Set, Chippendale Style, Mahogany, Pierced, 1 Armchair, 40 x 19 1/2 In., 10 . . . . . .   5750.00
Chair Set, Chippendale Style, Mahogany, Scroll Crest, 2 Armchairs, c.1950, 12 . . . .   3450.00
Chair Set, Chippendale Style, Mahogany, Upholstered, Claw & Ball Feet, 39 In., 6 . . . .   230.00

Chair Set, Chippendale Style, Pierced Splat, Claw & Ball Feet, 8 .... 1725.00
Chair Set, Chippendale, Mahogany, Carved Crest, Splat Back, 1 Armchair, 8 .... 4830.00
Chair Set, Chippendale, Mahogany, Carved, Pierced Splat, Claw & Ball Feet, 8 .... 5775.00
Chair Set, Chippendale, Slat Backs, Claw & Ball Feet, 41 x 22 x 18 In., 6 .... 3105.00
Chair Set, Dan Johnson, Gazelle, Cast Aluminum, 1956, 18 x 17 x 31 In., 4 .... 3510.00
Chair Set, David Rowland, Stacking, Orange, Yellow, Wire, Soflex, 22 1/2 x 30 In., 6 ... 865.00
Chair Set, Directoire, Mahogany, Slip Seat, Shaped Backrest, 2 Armchairs, c.1810, 8 .... 1765.00
Chair Set, Don Chadwick, Modular, Foam, Herman Miller, 1970s, 27 In., 4 .... 230.00
Chair Set, Dunbar, Brass Handrail, Vinyl, 31 1/4 x 18 1/4 x 19 In., 4 .... 4900.00
Chair Set, Eames, DCM, Teak Plywood, Steel, Herman Miller, c.1965, 19 x 29 In., 6 .... 1870.00
Chair Set, Eames, DCW, Molded Plywood, Calico Ash Veneer, 29 1/2 x 19 1/2 In., 6 .... 2760.00
Chair Set, Eames, LAX, Seafoam Green Fiberglass, Herman Miller, 25 x 28 In., 4 ...... 978.00
Chair Set, Eames, LKR, Fiberglass, Vinyl, Steel, Herman Miller, 1950s, 19 x 28 In., 6 ... 500.00
Chair Set, Eames, Molded Plastic, Black Rod Legs, Herman Miller, 1950s, 6 .... 200.00
Chair Set, Eero Saarinen, Tulip, Fiberglass, Knoll, 32 x 20 x 22 In., 8 .... 350.00
Chair Set, Elizabethan Style, Walnut, Spindle Back, Stretcher Base, 34 1/2 In., 6 ...... 165.00
Chair Set, Elm, Ladder Back, Rush Seat, Shaped Splat, Turned Legs, Continental, 10 .... 2530.00
Chair Set, Empire Style, Shaped & Carved Crest Rails, 2 Armchairs, 35 1/2 In., 8 ...... 660.00
Chair Set, Empire, Cane Seat, Reeded & Tapered Legs, 2 Armchairs, 35 In., 8 .... 990.00
Chair Set, Faux Bamboo, Flat Back, Gold Velvet Seat, Cane Legs, 6 .... 920.00
Chair Set, Faux Bamboo, Rush Bottom, Painted, Balloon Seat, Early 1900s, 6 .... 1265.00
Chair Set, Federal Style, Mahogany, Shieldback, 2 Armchairs, Early 1900s, 8 .... 3585.00
Chair Set, Federal Style, Mahogany, Shieldback, Carved Leaves, 8 .... 3220.00
Chair Set, Federal Style, Maple, Rolled Crest, Front Stretcher, Cane Seat, 34 In., 4 ...... 375.00
Chair Set, Federal, Mahogany, Carved, Serpentine Crest Rail, c.1810, 38 1/2 In., 4 ...... 4780.00
Chair Set, Fournier, Fantasy, Carved, Elephant Ear Crest, Hoof Feet, 42 In., 4 .... 3220.00
Chair Set, French Provincial, Cherry, Wheat Pattern, Spindle Backrest, Rush Seat, 6 ..... 825.00
Chair Set, French Provincial, Elm, Leaf Carved Crest, Rush Seat, Peg Feet, 43 1/2 In., 6 . 750.00
Chair Set, French Provincial, Elm, Rush Seat, 33 1/2 In., 10 .... 2185.00
Chair Set, French Provincial, Fruitwood, Horizontal Splat, Rush Seat, 35 In., 5 .... 200.00
Chair Set, Fruitwood, Walnut, Ivory Inlay, 4 High Side, 2 Slipper, 2 Armchairs, 8 .... 700.00
Chair Set, G. Nakashima, Black Walnut, Grass Seats, 1956, 23 x 26 In., 4 .... 3395.00
Chair Set, G. Nakashima, Walnut, Grass Cord, 27 x 18 x 18 In., 6 .... 4700.00
Chair Set, G. Nelson, Birch, Vinyl, Arms, Herman Miller, c.1949, 23 x 24 x 30 In., 6 .... 1400.00
Chair Set, G. Stickley, Inverted Arched Crest Rail, Leather Seat, 1 Armchair, 4 .... 1955.00
Chair Set, G. Stickley, Ladder Back, 3 Horizontal Back Slats, Leather Seat, 5 .... 4900.00
Chair Set, G. Stickley, Ladder Back, 3 Horizontal Slats, Leather Seat, 36 In., 6 .... 3220.00
Chair Set, G. Stickley, No. 349 1/2, Ladder Back, Leather Seat, 1 Armchair, 37 In., 6 .... 12650.00
Chair Set, G. Stickley, No. 380, 4 Vertical Slats, Leather Seat, 40 In., 6 .... 7050.00
Chair Set, George II Style, Walnut, Leaf Crest, Leather, c.1850, 40 In., 4 .... 980.00
Chair Set, George II, Faux Burl Walnut, Shaped Crest, Leather Seat, 2 Armchairs, 12 .... 4370.00
Chair Set, George II, Walnut, Vase-Form Splat, Padded Seat, 2 Armchairs, 39 In., 12 .... 5060.00
Chair Set, George III Style, Elm, Turned, Rush Seat, 19th Century, 4 .... 375.00
Chair Set, George III Style, Elm, Yew, Windsor, Braced, Wheel Back, 4 .... 690.00
Chair Set, George III Style, Mahogany, Cane, Arms, c.1900, 34 In., 4 .... 1265.00
Chair Set, George III Style, Mahogany, Carved, Shieldback, Swags, 37 In., 10 .... 2875.00
Chair Set, George III Style, Mahogany, Inlaid, Shieldback, Upholstered, 6 .... 1470.00
Chair Set, George III Style, Mahogany, Ladder Back, 3 Armchairs, 7 .... 1495.00
Chair Set, George III Style, Mahogany, Mid 19th Century, 36 In., 6 .... 5750.00
Chair Set, George III Style, Mahogany, Pierced Fretwork, Early 1900s, 10 .... 5520.00
Chair Set, George III Style, Mahogany, Pierced Splat, 2 Armchairs, 38 In., 12 .... 8970.00
Chair Set, George III Style, Mahogany, Upholstered Seat, 2 Armchairs, 39 In., 12 .... 5000.00
Chair Set, George III Style, Mahogany, Vase-Form Splat, 2 Armchairs, 39 In., 8 .... 4300.00
Chair Set, George III Style, Oak, Shaped Crest, Padded Seat, c.1900, 39 1/2 In., 4 ...... 1150.00
Chair Set, George III, Mahogany, Carved Top Rail, Leather Slip Seat, c.1890, 4 .... 800.00
Chair Set, George III, Mahogany, Shaped Crest, Vase-Form Splat, Slip Seat, 5 .... 2415.00
Chair Set, Georgian Style, Mahogany, Cane Seat, Arms, 8 .... 3165.00
Chair Set, Georgian Style, Mahogany, Serpentine, Upholstered, 2 Armchairs, 10 .... 6325.00
Chair Set, Gio Ponti, Walnut, Leather, Singer, Italy, 18 x 24 x 33 1/2 In., 4 .... 865.00
Chair Set, H. Bertoia, Black Wire, Knoll, 21 x 24 x 29 1/2 In., 4 .... 345.00
Chair Set, H. Bertoia, Chromed Steel Rod, Knoll, Child's, 16 x 15 1/2 x 24 In., 4 .... 375.00
Chair Set, H. Bertoia, Plastic-Coated Metal, Knoll, 1950, 21 x 22 x 29 1/2 In., 4 .... 760.00
Chair Set, H. Probber, Walnut Frames, Tapered Legs, 23 x 23 x 28 In., 4 .... 115.00

Chair Set, H. Wegner, Oak, Teak, 3 Legs, Stacking, 28 1/2 x 20 1/2 x 18 1/2 In., 8 ...... 1840.00
Chair Set, Hans Olsen, Teak, Naugahyde, 3 Legs, Frem Rojle, Denmark, 20 x 29 In., 6 .. 545.00
Chair Set, Hepplewhite Style, Mahogany, Domed Crest, Pierced Splat, 1 Armchair, 6 .... 750.00
Chair Set, Hepplewhite Style, Mahogany, Padded Seat, 2 Armchairs, 37 1/2 In., 12 ...... 3220.00
Chair Set, Hepplewhite Style, Mahogany, Shieldback, Upholstered Seat, 6 .... 880.00
Chair Set, Hepplewhite, Mahogany, Leaf Carved Panel, Slip Seat, Square Legs, 6 ..... 4310.00
Chair Set, Hepplewhite, Mahogany, Upholstered Seat, 2 Armchairs, England, 8 .... 1495.00
Chair Set, Hitchcock Alford, Sheraton, Cane Seats, 19th Century, 6 .... 600.00
Chair Set, Hitchcock, Pillow Back, 6 .... 1440.00
Chair Set, Hitchcock, Pillow Back, Leaf Stencils, Rush Seat, Cylinder Legs, 6 .... 750.00
Chair Set, Hitchcock, Rush Seat, Black Painted, Stenciled, 4 .... 400.00
Chair Set, J. Hoffman, Bentwood, Velour, c.1910, 29 5/98 In., 4 .... 7400.00
Chair Set, J. Hoffman, Cafe, 31 x 19 x 17 In., 4 .... 4600.00
Chair Set, James Mont, Silver Gilt Finish, Porthole Cutout Back, Upholstered, 4 .... 2875.00
Chair Set, Johnson Furniture, Enameled Wood, Leather, 34 x 21 x 18 In., 10 .... 1035.00
Chair Set, Katavalos Littell & Kelley, T-Chair, Steel, Leather, 1952, 22 x 33 In., 6 ...... 7020.00
Chair Set, L. & J.G. Stickley, Pegged, Arched Stretchers, 42 x 32 x 30 In., 3 .... 2300.00
Chair Set, Lancaster, Mixed Wood, Rush Seat, 2 Armchairs, 43 In., 8 .... 2530.00
Chair Set, Louis XIV Style, Limed Fruitwood, Upholstered, 2 Armchairs, 6 .... 900.00
Chair Set, Louis XV Style, Cane Back, Upholstered Seat, 6 .... 400.00
Chair Set, Louis XV Style, Fruitwood, Late 19th Century, 34 In., 6 .... 1725.00
Chair Set, Louis XV Style, Giltwood, Aubusson Tapestry Upholstery, 6 .... 7170.00
Chair Set, Louis XV Style, High Cane Backrest, 2 Armchairs, 1900s, 5 .... 500.00
Chair Set, Louis XV, Beech, Cartouche Back, 2 Armchairs, 6 .... 1650.00
Chair Set, Louis XVI Style, Upholstered, Arms, Oval Back, Fluted Tapered Legs, 8 ..... 1955.00
Chair Set, Mahogany Veneer, White Upholstered Seat, Scroll Feet, 37 1/2 In., 8 .... 900.00
Chair Set, Mahogany, Bentwood, Openwork Decoration, Leather Fringe, 34 In., 4 ...... 110.00
Chair Set, Mahogany, Lyre Back, Upholstered, 2 Armchairs, c.1925, 32 1/2 x 19 In., 6 ... 2185.00
Chair Set, Mahogany, Lyre Splat, 2 Armchairs, Italy, Early 1900s, 35 In., 6 .... 1495.00
Chair Set, Maple, Hickory, Ladder Back, Split Oak Seat, 35 x 17 In., 6 .... 440.00
Chair Set, McCobb, Corseted Back Rail, Upholstered Seat, Calvin, 35 x 22 x 20 In., 4 ... 230.00
Chair Set, Mies Van Der Rohe, MR10, Chrome, Black Leather, Knoll, 6 .... 2820.00
Chair Set, Mies Van Der Rohe, Steel, Upholstered, Brno, 1960s, 22 x 23 1/2 x 31 In., 4 .. 2000.00
Chair Set, Milano, Wicker, Mahogany, Tub Shape, Cabriole Legs, 4 .... 460.00
Chair Set, Mixed Wood, Bamboo Turned Stile, 5 Spindles, Plank Seat, 35 1/2 In., 6 ..... 440.00
Chair Set, Neoclassical, Cherry, Upholstered Seats, Continental, c.1800, 4 .... 1150.00
Chair Set, Neoclassical, Mahogany, Brass Inlay, Sloping Backrest, c.1810, 4 .... 1175.00
Chair Set, Neoclassical, Mahogany, Carved, Rosette Splat, c.1840, 32 In., 8 .... 3825.00
Chair Set, Neoclassical, Mahogany, Gondola Form, Vase-Form Splat, Late 1800s, 6 ..... 1380.00
Chair Set, Neoclassical, Mahogany, Needlework Seat, Saber Legs, 6 .... 460.00
Chair Set, Neoclassical, Walnut, Brass Mounted, Continental, 6 .... 1610.00
Chair Set, Oak, Carved Lion's Head, 1 Armchair, 27 x 41 x 19 In., 5 .... 575.00
Chair Set, Oak, Carved, Rush Seat, Shaped Crest Rail, Continental, 10 .... 2645.00
Chair Set, Paine Furniture Co., Mahogany, Leather, Boston, 39 x 18 x 18 In., 6 .... 250.00
Chair Set, Painted Wings On Crest, Plank Seat, Half Spindle Back, 33 In., 6 .... 1100.00
Chair Set, Painted, Gilt, Thumb Back, Stenciled Fruit, Balloon Seat, 1800s, 6 .... 920.00
Chair Set, Piedmont, Woven Seat, 37 1/2 In., 4 .... 120.00
Chair Set, Pillow Back, Yellow Stencil, W. Smith Stencils, New England, 4 .... 140.00
Chair Set, Pine, Spindle Back, Plank Seat, 32 In., 6 .... 200.00
Chair Set, Plank Seat, Green Paint, Pennsylvania, 6 .... 975.00
Chair Set, Queen Anne Style, Solid Vase-Form Splat, Drop Seat, 6 .... 1645.00
Chair Set, Queen Anne Style, Walnut, Drop-In Cushions, 2 Armchairs, 38 In., 6 ...... 1265.00
Chair Set, Queen Anne, Mahogany, Slip Seat, Spoon Back, Early 1700s, 4 .... 1840.00
Chair Set, Queen Anne, Mahogany, Splat Back, Upholstered, c.1740, 6 .... 4140.00
Chair Set, Queen Anne, Rush Seat, Vase Back, New England, 42 In., 6 .... 575.00
Chair Set, Regency Style, Mahogany, Leather Seat, Scrolling Apron, 35 In., 12 .... 5520.00
Chair Set, Regency Style, Mahogany, Reeded Splat, 2 Armchairs, 34 1/2 In., 12 .... 2530.00
Chair Set, Regency, Mahogany, Curved Backrest, 2 Armchairs, c.1810, 8 .... 7050.00
Chair Set, Regency, Mahogany, Inlaid, 2 Armchairs, c.1815, 32 1/2 In., 4 .... 2070.00
Chair Set, Regency, Mahogany, Inlaid, Rectangular Crest, 2 Armchairs, 8 .... 8915.00
Chair Set, Restauration, Fruitwood, Padded Seat, Hoof Feet, c.1865, 33 In., 4 .... 920.00
Chair Set, Richard Schultz, Wool, Plastic Shell, Knoll, 1960s, 20 x 22 1/2 x 32 1/2 In., 6 . 750.00
Chair Set, Risom, Wood, Nylon Webbing, Knoll, 30 1/2 x 22 1/2 x 17 3/4 In., 4 .... 800.00

Chair Set, Robert Bliss, Kiss Me Kate, Wood, Bliss & Campbell, 14 1/4 x 39 1/2 In., 3 .. 460.00
Chair Set, Robsjohn-Gibbings, Beech, Upholstered, Widdicomb, 2 Armchairs, 34 In., 6 .. 980.00
Chair Set, Robsjohn-Gibbings, Mahogany, Velour, 33 x 19 x 23 In., 6 . . . . 1175.00
Chair Set, Rococo Revival, Rosewood, 2 Armchairs, c.1855, 4 . . . . *Illus* 11950.00
Chair Set, Rococo, Oak, Pierced Crest, Upholstered, 2 Armchairs, American, c.1850, 10 . 3105.00
Chair Set, Rococo, Polychrome, Shaped Crest, Vase Splat, Padded Seat, Italy, 1700s, 6 .. 4140.00
Chair Set, Rohde, Birch, Upholstered Seat & Back, Herman Miller, 32 x 24 In., 6 . . . . . . 2350.00
Chair Set, Rosewood, Arms, Chinese, c.1900s, 4 . . . . 1760.00
Chair Set, Shaker, Ladder Back, 3 Slats, Cane Seat, Painted, South Union, Ky., 37 In., 4 . 470.00
Chair Set, Sheraton Style, Mahogany, Carved, 2 Armchairs, 1900s, 8 . . . . 860.00
Chair Set, Sheraton, Curly Maple, Pillow Back, Rush Seat, 4 . . . . 690.00
Chair Set, Sheraton, Curly Maple, Pillow Back, Rush Seat, American, 6 . . . . 1725.00
Chair Set, Sheraton, Mahogany, Inlaid, X-Shape Splat, Upholstered Seat, 8 . . . . 2360.00
Chair Set, Sheraton, Rush Seat, Stenciled, 6 . . . . 690.00
Chair Set, Sheraton, Tiger Maple, Carved, Pierced Back, Rush Seat, 8 . . . . 6900.00
Chair Set, Tapiovaara, Birch, Domus, Finland, 1946, 22 x 20 x 31 In., 4 . . . . 1050.00
Chair Set, Thayer Coggin, Steel, Upholstered, American, 1960s, 19 x 26 x 30 In., 8 . . . . . 3800.00
Chair Set, V. Panton, Cone, Leather, Steel, Rubber, Plus-Linje, c.1960, 33 1/8 In., 6 . . . . . 3585.00
Chair Set, V. Panton, VP, Plastic, Herman Miller, 1974, 19 x 20 1/2 x 33 In., 8 . . . . 1755.00
Chair Set, Victorian, Mahogany, Pierced Splat, Early 1900s, 4 . . . . 430.00
Chair Set, Walnut, Cane Seat, Spindle Back, Turned Legs, 37 In., 5 . . . . 275.00
Chair Set, Walnut, Carved, Continental, c.1900, 6 . . . . 345.00
Chair Set, Walnut, Leaf Carved Crest, American, 2 Armchairs, Late 1800s, 38 In., 8 . . . . . 920.00
Chair Set, Walnut, Pierced Scroll Carved Crest, Saber Legs, 6 . . . . 300.00
Chair Set, Wegner, No. 501, Teak, Leather, J. Hansen, Denmark, 24 3/4 x 30 In., 4 . . . . . . 4025.00
Chair Set, Wegner, Teak, Leather, Johannes Hansen, Denmark, 1960s, 30 In., 6 . . . . 4095.00
Chair Set, Wegner, Teak, Paper Cord Seat, Carl Hansen & Son, 20 1/2 x 30 In., 4 . . . . . . 320.00
Chair Set, Wicker, Tie-On Cushions, Early 20th Century, 4 . . . . 230.00
Chair Set, William & Mary, Upholstered, Trumpet Legs, Stretchers, 34 In., 6 . . . . 2990.00
Chair Set, William IV Style, Mahogany, Silk Padded Seat, 35 In., 12 . . . . 3700.00
Chair Set, William IV, Mahogany, Carved & Pierced Splat, Gadroon Legs, 6 . . . . 3000.00
Chair Set, William IV, Mahogany, Shaped Splat, Slip Seat, c.1835, 8 . . . . 1530.00
Chair Set, Windsor Style, Oak, Raked Hoop Back, Saddle Seat, Arms, 1800s, 6 . . . . 1495.00
Chair Set, Windsor, Arrow Back, Thumb Back, Green Paint, Red & Gold Design, 6 . . . . . 3600.00
Chair Set, Windsor, Fanback, 7 Spindles, Turned Legs, Stretchers, Early 1800s, 4 . . . . . . 3565.00
Chair Set, Windsor, Low Back, 8 . . . . 1750.00
Chair Set, Windsor, Painted, Red, Yellow, Black, Green, Miniature, 4 . . . . 450.00
Chair Set, Windsor, Rod Back, Plank Seat, Bamboo Turning, 33 In., 4 . . . . 230.00
Chair Set, Windsor, Step-Down, Bentwood Back, Boston, c.1800, 6 . . . . 10350.00
Chair Set, Wormley, Ebonized Frame, Upholstered Seat, 33 x 20 x 21 1/2 In., 6 . . . . 4025.00
Chair Set, Wormley, Mahogany Legs, Upholstered, Tufted Back, Dunbar, 24 In., 6 . . . . . . 1495.00
Chair Set, Wormley, Mahogany, Cane Back, Leather Seat, Dunbar, 32 1/2 In., 4 . . . . 575.00
Chair Set, Wormley, Orange Wool, Mahogany Legs, Dunbar, 2 Armchairs, 36 In., 6 . . . . . 1380.00
Chair Set, Yellow Paint, Black Lines, Thumb Back, Plank Seat, 6 . . . . 660.00
Chair Set, Yellow Paint, Thumb Back, 4 . . . . 1320.00
Chair-Table, Hand-Wrought Hardware, Cutout Heart, Round Top, 54 x 29 In. 285.00
Chair-Table, Pine, Oxblood Paint, Round Top, 48 In. 265.00
Chair-Table, Softwood, 2-Board Top, Stretcher Base, Round, New England, 37 x 29 In. .. 845.00

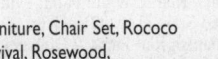

Permanent marker stains can be removed from most wood or textiles by wiping with a cloth soaked in rubbing alcohol.

Furniture, Chair Set, Rococo
Revival, Rosewood,
2 Armchairs, c.1855, 4

Chaise Longue, Adirondack Style, Rattan, Early 1900s, 43 1/2 x 23 x 60 In. 805.00
Chaise Longue, Art Deco, Rattan, White Paint, Cushions, Wheels, 35 x 49 x 66 In. 728.00
Chaise Longue, Biedermeier, Fruitwood, Turned Crest, Canted Seat, 80 x 31 In. 3175.00
Chaise Longue, Down Filled, Damask Upholstery, Tufted Back, Early 1900s, 62 In. 115.00
Chaise Longue, Enameled Iron, Scroll Arms, Wire Mesh, Adjustable, 38 x 25 x 59 In. . . . 520.00
Chaise Longue, Fiberglass, O. Mourque, Arconas, c.1970, 24 1/4 x 24 1/2 x 55 In. 1910.00
Chaise Longue, Louis XV Style, Rosewood, Parcel Gilt, Upholstered, Late 1800s, 33 In. . . 230.00
Chaise Longue, Louis XV, Beechwood, Tapestry Upholstery, Mid 1700s, 35 x 64 In. 2530.00
Chaise Longue, Louis XVI Style, Polychrome, Cane, c.1900, 35 x 37 x 26 In. 1265.00
Chaise Longue, Marcel Breuer, 6 Wheels, Chrome Steel, Wicker, Tecta, 24 x 69 x 25 In. . 1755.00
Chaise Longue, Rattan, White Paint, Cushions, Reed Mfg., Fla., 35 x 49 x 66 In. 650.00
Chaise Longue, V. Kagan, 1 Armrest, Steel Base, Suede, 33 3/4 x 27 1/2 x 52 1/2 In. 4315.00
Chaise Longue, Wegner, 2-Piece, Cushions, Adjustable Back, 32 x 30 x 73 In. 2530.00
Chaise Longue & Ottoman, Warren McArthur, Tubular Aluminum Frame, Canvas 4600.00
Cheese Rack, Provincial, Oak, Lattice Work, France, 19th Century, 9 x 28 x 20 In. 1410.00
Chest, 5 Drawers, Inlaid Leaves, Flowers, Ormolu Pulls, Beading, France, 40 x 27 In. . . . 375.00
Chest, Aesthetic Revival, Walnut, Marble Top, c.1875, 30 1/2 x 58 In. 1880.00
Chest, Arts & Crafts, Oak, Carved, 3 Drawers, Early 1900s, 37 x 33 x 17 1/2 In. 140.00
Chest, Arts & Crafts, Walnut Finish, 10 Drawers, Sliding Door Top, 50 x 15 x 26 In. 440.00
Chest, Ash, Oyster Veneered Walnut, 5 Drawers, c.1875, 40 x 38 x 21 In. 1955.00
Chest, Bachelor's, Veneer, Marble Top, Rassnick & Co., 49 x 25 x 54 In. 1150.00
Chest, Baroque Style, Oak, Iron Strap Mounted, Dome Top, 31 x 46 x 24 In. 635.00
Chest, Batchelder, Incised Daffodils On Front Panel, 13 3/4 x 27 1/2 x 14 1/2 In. 8050.00
Chest, Birch, Cherry, 6 Graduated Lipped Drawers, New England, 37 x 52 x 18 In. 1125.00
Chest, Birch, Eastern Pine, 4 Drawers, Bracket Feet, Overhang Top, New Hampshire 6800.00
Chest, Bird's-Eye Maple, Birch, 6 Drawers, Maine, 54 x 39 1/2 x 18 1/4 In. 4600.00
Chest, Black Walnut, Burl Drawers, 5 Drawers, Molded Front, 43 1/2 x 33 1/2 x 21 In. . . . 500.00
Chest, Blanket, 2 Drawers, New England, 18th Century 7500.00
Chest, Blanket, Blue Paint, Gold Flecks, Lift Top, Dovetailed Corner, 32 x 28 In. 330.00
Chest, Blanket, Blue Paint, Turned Legs, 19th Century, 26 x 46 x 20 1/2 In. 1495.00
Chest, Blanket, Cedar, Lift Top, Carved Molding, 25 x 44 x 24 In. 115.00
Chest, Blanket, Cherry, Paneled Sides, Turned Feet, 22 x 38 In. 345.00
Chest, Blanket, Chippendale Style, Pine, Bracket Base, Dovetailed, 16 x 9 x 10 In. 165.00
Chest, Blanket, Chippendale, Pine, Blue Paint, Bracket Feet, Dovetailed, 49 x 26 In. 1150.00
Chest, Blanket, Chippendale, Pine, Paneled, Bracket Feet, 36 x 52 In. 14340.00
Chest, Blanket, Chippendale, Tiger Maple, 2 Drawers, c.1800, 28 x 51 x 21 1/2 In. 1610.00
Chest, Blanket, Chippendale, Walnut, 3 Drawers, 48 1/2 x 24 x 28 3/4 In. 800.00
Chest, Blanket, Chippendale, Walnut, 3 Drawers, Strap Hinges, Ogee Feet, Pa. 3375.00
Chest, Blanket, Chippendale, Walnut, Burl, Applied Molding, 12 x 5 1/2 x 7 In. 2415.00
Chest, Blanket, Chippendale, Walnut, Pennsylvania, 24 1/2 x 53 1/2 x 23 In. 1095.00
Chest, Blanket, Dovetailed, Red Paint, Till, Turned Tall Feet, 12 3/4 x 5 3/4 In. 650.00
Chest, Blanket, Grain & Geometric Painted, Bucks County, Pa., 16 x 13 In. . . . . *Illus* 5775.00
Chest, Blanket, Grain Painted, Block Feet, c.1840, 21 x 42 x 19 In. 785.00
Chest, Blanket, Grain Painted, Dovetailed, Strap Hinges, 17 1/2 x 36 1/2 x 17 1/2 In. 195.00
Chest, Blanket, Grain Painted, Ebonized, Drawer, Shaped Supports, 47 In. 1368.00
Chest, Blanket, Grain Painted, Green, Yellow, Ocher, c.1840, 16 1/2 x 10 x 11 In. 1925.00
Chest, Blanket, Grain Painted, Hinged Top, Bracket Feet, c.1840, 27 x 51 x 21 In. 5975.00
Chest, Blanket, Grain Painted, Paneled Sides, Till, 1800s, 24 x 38 x 19 In. 480.00
Chest, Blanket, Grain Painted, Yellow, Till, Dovetailed, Ball Feet, 40 In. 535.00
Chest, Blanket, Green Paint, Hand Wrought Iron Lock, 10 1/2 x 21 x 15 In. 80.00
Chest, Blanket, Hardwoods, Cut Nail Construction, Chamfered Lid, 18 x 36 x 17 In. 110.00
Chest, Blanket, Hinged Lid, Bracket Feet, c.1800, 24 x 50 x 24 1/2 In. 259.00
Chest, Blanket, Jacobean, Carved Oak, Leaf Bands, 1600s, 30 x 48 x 21 In. 645.00
Chest, Blanket, Jacobean, Oak, Lift Top, Geometric, Flower Panels, 57 x 19 x 28 In. 405.00
Chest, Blanket, Joseph Lehn, Flower Decals, Red, Gold, c.1860, 13 1/2 x 7 x 7 1/2 In. 3025.00
Chest, Blanket, Lift Top, Blue Over Red Paint, Batwing Brasses, 4 Drawers 7500.00
Chest, Blanket, Lift Top, Frame & Panel Construction, Carved Frieze, 28 x 53 x 22 In. . . . 440.00
Chest, Blanket, Lift Top, Molded Edge, Scroll Bracket Base, 27 x 44 x 20 In. 2590.00
Chest, Blanket, Lift Top, Painted, Flowers, Birds, 18th Century, 25 1/2 x 49 x 21 In. 316.00
Chest, Blanket, Lift Top, Pine, Red & White Paint, 19th Century, 9 x 16 x 6 In. 240.00
Chest, Blanket, Lift Top, Red Stain, 23 x 47 x 17 In. 230.00
Chest, Blanket, Lift Top, Spanish Red Paint, 2 Drawers, 3 False Drawers, 37 3/4 x 44 In. . . 3250.00
Chest, Blanket, Maple, Red Brown Paint, c.1870, 16 x 7 x 6 1/2 In. 595.00

Chest, Blanket, Mixed Hardwoods, 28 x 73 x 24 In. 360.00
Chest, Blanket, Oak, Carved, Iron Strap Hinges, 22 1/2 x 39 1/2 x 21 1/2 In. 193.00
Chest, Blanket, Oak, Cathedral Arches, Greek Key, Flowerettes, c.1831 .... 619.00
Chest, Blanket, Paint Decorated, Bucks Co., Pa., c.1830, 20 x 16 1/4 x 13 In. 5775.00
Chest, Blanket, Paint, Paneled Front, Flower Bouquets, 21 x 47 x 24 In. 1076.00
Chest, Blanket, Pine, 3-Panel Front, Dovetailed, Iron Hardware, 19 x 48 x 23 In. 748.00
Chest, Blanket, Pine, 6-Board, Child's, 13 3/4 x 18 3/4 x 10 3/4 In. 265.00
Chest, Blanket, Pine, 6-Board, Scalloped Cutouts, Paint Traces, 43 x 21 x 29 In. 715.00
Chest, Blanket, Pine, 6-Board, Till, Blue, c.1810, 39 x 20 1/2 x 13 1/2 In. 1450.00
Chest, Blanket, Pine, Angled Stripes, Red Wash, Turned Feet, Dovetailed, 40 x 24 In. 259.00
Chest, Blanket, Pine, Ash, 6-Board, Turned Acorn Feet, 9 1/2 x 14 3/4 x 8 In. 145.00
Chest, Blanket, Pine, Blue Paint, Dovetailed Case, New England, 16 x 44 x 18 In. 403.00
Chest, Blanket, Pine, Blue Paint, Scalloped Ends, 48 x 17 x 24 In. 1495.00
Chest, Blanket, Pine, Bootjack Ends, Drawer, 19th Century, 36 x 44 x 19 In. 575.00
Chest, Blanket, Pine, Flame Grained, Bootjack Ends, Covered Till, Drawer, 44 x 24 In. .. 400.00
Chest, Blanket, Pine, Flowers, Geometric Stencils, c.1850, 39 1/4 x 22 1/4 In. 420.00
Chest, Blanket, Pine, Grain Painted, 4 Drawers, New England, c.1840, 37 x 41 x 20 In. .. 1380.00
Chest, Blanket, Pine, Grain Painted, American, c.1850, 27 x 45 x 21 1/2 In. 1020.00
Chest, Blanket, Pine, Lift Top, 2 Drawers, Cutout Skirt, Sides, 37 x 43 x 19 1/2 In. 400.00
Chest, Blanket, Pine, Lift Top, 2 Faux Over 3 Real Drawers, 47 x 39 x 19 In. 1150.00
Chest, Blanket, Pine, Lift Top, 3 Drawers, c.1820, 114 x 17 x 42 In. 3300.00
Chest, Blanket, Pine, Lift Top, Bootjack Ends, Ditty Box Interior, 26 x 43 x 18 In. 345.00
Chest, Blanket, Pine, Lift Top, Drawer, 18th Century, 36 1/2 x 42 x 20 In. 259.00
Chest, Blanket, Pine, Lift Top, Drawer, Applied Molded Lid, Hinges, 40 x 37 x 19 In. 715.00
Chest, Blanket, Pine, Lift Top, Drawer, Scrolled Apron, Bracket Base, 33 x 38 x 19 In. ... 720.00
Chest, Blanket, Pine, Lift Top, Painted, Drawer, Bootjack Ends, 40 x 37 x 19 In. 730.00
Chest, Blanket, Pine, Maple Lid, Sponge Decoration, Drawer, 30 1/2 x 39 1/2 In. 9490.00
Chest, Blanket, Pine, Poplar, Grain Painted, c.1820, 24 x 45 1/2 x 20 1/2 In. 575.00
Chest, Blanket, Pine, Poplar, Red Over Yellow Graining, 44 x 21 x 26 In. 805.00
Chest, Blanket, Pine, Red Brown Finish, Bootjack Ends, 3 Drawers, 21 x 9 x 12 In. 750.00
Chest, Blanket, Pine, Red Flame Graining, Yellow Ground, 37 x 18 1/2 x 19 1/2 In. 690.00
Chest, Blanket, Pine, Red Paint, Square Nails, 48 x 34 In. 250.00
Chest, Blanket, Pine, Red Paint, Tang Hinges, Hand Wrought Nails, 11 x 18 x 12 In. 165.00
Chest, Blanket, Pine, Red Paint, Till, Hinged Lid, New England, 23 x 17 x 48 1/2 In. 290.00
Chest, Blanket, Pine, Red, Hinged Lid, New England, 23 1/2 x 36 1/2 x 17 1/2 In. 520.00
Chest, Blanket, Pine, Salmon Paint, Black Squiggles, Till, c.1850, 9 1/2 x 18 x 10 In. 750.00
Chest, Blanket, Pineapple Design On Lid, Hand Wrought Hardware, Scandinavia, 1806 .. 470.00
Chest, Blanket, Pinwheel, York County, Pa., Early 1800s, 45 x 21 x 25 In. ....*Illus* 4675.00
Chest, Blanket, Poplar, Dovetailed, Grain Painted, Molded Top, Till, 20 x 38 x 19 In. 195.00
Chest, Blanket, Poplar, Dovetailed, Turned Feet, Covered Till, Lid, 38 x 22 In. 460.00
Chest, Blanket, Poplar, Grain Painted, Lidded Till, Pa., c.1850, 6 1/2 x 12 3/4 x 6 In. 230.00
Chest, Blanket, Poplar, Red Brown Paint, Covered Till, 50 x 22 1/2 x 29 1/4 In. 690.00
Chest, Blanket, Poplar, Red Paint, Black Graining, Pennsylvania, 24 x 39 In. 3165.00
Chest, Blanket, Poplar, Red Stain, 4 Drawers, New England, c.1830, 40 x 43 x 18 In. 1090.00
Chest, Blanket, Poplar, Red, Black, Stenciled, 1920 .... 550.00
Chest, Blanket, Shaker, 6-Board, Blue Paint, Alfred, Maine, 24 x 50 x 18 In. 5875.00
Chest, Blanket, Shaker, Cherry, Poplar, Drawer, Watervliet, N.Y., c.1850, 35 x 43 In. 4900.00
Chest, Blanket, Shaker, Pine, 2 Dovetailed Drawers, Watervliet, N.Y., c.1840, 42 x 37 In. .. 9200.00

Furniture, Chest, Blanket, Grain
& Geometric Painted, Bucks
County, Pa., 16 x 13 In.

Furniture, Chest, Blanket, Pinwheel, York
County, Pa., Early 1800s, 45 x 21 x 25 In.

Chest, Blanket, Shaker, Pine, Poplar, 6-Boards, Watervliet, N.Y., c.1830, 23 x 50 In. 5460.00
Chest, Blanket, Shaker, Pine, Red Paint, Hinged Top, Watervliet, N.Y., 23 x 51 x 19 In. . . 1410.00
Chest, Blanket, Shaker, Poplar, Red Paint, Drawer, Hinged Lid, 35 x 19 1/2 x 43 In. 2300.00
Chest, Blanket, Sheraton, Cherry, Kentucky, c.1820, 18 x 26 x 20 1/2 In. 1090.00
Chest, Blanket, Smoke Decoration, Till, Hinged Lid, New England, 24 x 17 x 46 In. 460.00
Chest, Blanket, Softwood, 3 Arched Molded Panels, Flowers, Red, Yellow, 1837 . . . . 420.00
Chest, Blanket, Softwood, Blue Paint, Dovetailed, Tapered Feet, 22 x 11 1/2 x 13 In. 340.00
Chest, Blanket, Softwood, Brown Combed, Turned Feet, Dovetailed, 16 x 9 x 11 In. 1520.00
Chest, Blanket, Softwood, Brown Grain Paint, Dovetailed, 46 In. 135.00
Chest, Blanket, Softwood, Dovetailed, Scalloped, Pierced Feet, 26 1/2 x 50 x 21 In. 4070.00
Chest, Blanket, Softwood, Grain, Bracket Feet, Dovetailed, c.1873, 11 x 6 x 8 In. 956.00
Chest, Blanket, Softwood, Mustard Paint, Dovetailed, Till, Iron Strap Hinges, 17 x 9 In. . . 280.00
Chest, Blanket, Softwood, Red Sponge Decoration, Till, Dovetailed, 41 1/4 In. 619.00
Chest, Blanket, Softwood, Tulip Painted Panels, Dovetailed, Turned Feet 310.00
Chest, Blanket, Tiger Maple, Faux & Real Drawers, Cabriole Legs, 49 x 38 x 18 In. 1955.00
Chest, Blanket, Walnut, 2 Drawers, Dovetailed Construction, 13 3/4 x 8 3/4 In. 225.00
Chest, Blanket, Walnut, Dovetailed, Hinges, Bracket Feet, 25 x 50 x 18 3/4 In. 1430.00
Chest, Blanket, Walnut, Dovetailed, Lidded Till, Iron Strap Hinges, 20 x 41 x 19 In. 330.00
Chest, Blanket, Walnut, Dovetailed, Molded Lid, Bracket Feet, 16 x 9 In. 2250.00
Chest, Blanket, Walnut, Pennsylvania, 19th Century, 20 1/4 x 32 1/4 x 16 In. 630.00
Chest, Blanket, Walnut, Wrought Iron Hinges, Early 1700s, 36 1/2 x 48 1/4 In. 345.00
Chest, Blanket, Walnut, Yellow Pine, Inlay, 42 1/2 x 19 1/4 x 24 1/2 In. 1495.00
Chest, Blanket, Yellow Pine, Dovetailed Drawer, Mid 1800s, 36 x 39 x 19 1/2 In. 520.00
Chest, Blanket, Yellow Pine, Tang Hinges, Late 1700s, 20 1/2 x 41 1/2 x 19 1/2 In. 250.00
Chest, Blanket, Yellow Pine, Wrought Iron Strap Hinges, 43 1/2 x 18 x 20 1/2 In. 330.00
Chest, Bone Inlay, India, Early 20th Century, 20 x 34 x 14 1/2 In. 60.00
Chest, Bowfront, 4 Drawers, Ogee Bracket Feet, New England, 1700s, 32 x 35 In. 2530.00
Chest, Bowfront, Tiger Maple, 4 Drawers, Ohio, 39 x 40 In. 2200.00
Chest, Butler's, Biedermeier, Satinwood, Drop Front, 80 x 43 x 20 3/4 In. 7700.00
Chest, Butler's, Chippendale Style, Mahogany, 4 Drawers, 46 x 48 x 21 In. 4370.00
Chest, Butler's, Hepplewhite, Mahogany, Veneers, 6 Drawers, American, 42 x 43 In. 2875.00
Chest, Campaign, British Colonial, Camphorwood, Brass Mounts, 42 x 42 x 22 In. 1645.00
Chest, Campaign, Georgian, Mahogany, 2 Parts, 1800s, 42 x 30 x 18 1/2 In. 3335.00
Chest, Campaign, Mahogany, 2 Parts, 4 Over 2 Drawers, England, 1800s, 45 x 40 In. 2990.00
Chest, Campaign, Teak, 6 Drawers, Anglo-Indian, Late 1800s, 24 1/2 x 36 In. 750.00
Chest, Camphorwood, Brass Binding, Chinese, 19th Century, 17 x 37 x 17 1/2 In. 375.00
Chest, Camphorwood, Brass Bound, Leather, Inscribed, Chinese, 1860, 20 x 41 In. 1410.00
Chest, Camphorwood, Hinged Lid, 3 Inlaid Stars, 18 1/2 x 37 x 17 1/4 In. 800.00
Chest, Camphorwood, Lift Top, Inlaid, 18 1/2 x 35 x 18 1/2 In. 2300.00
Chest, Cherry, 2 Over 3 Drawers, Split Scrolled Columns, 41 1/2 x 44 1/2 x 20 In. 495.00
Chest, Cherry, 3 Over 4 Drawers, Fluted Pilasters, 1800s, 54 x 45 x 21 In. 2530.00
Chest, Cherry, 4 Drawers, Eastern Kentucky, c.1835, 47 x 21 x 43 In. 1700.00
Chest, Cherry, 8 Drawers, Scalloped Backsplash, Lewis Spohn, Ohio, 1903, 41 x 49 In. . . 1725.00
Chest, Cherry, Bird's-Eye Maple, 4 Drawers, c.1835, 40 1/2 x 39 x 20 3/8 In. 1380.00
Chest, Cherry, Bowfront, 4 Graduated Drawers, Reeded Edge, 40 x 30 x 17 1/2 In. 1350.00
Chest, Cherry, Bowfront, Brass, French Feet, 4 Drawers, 36 In. 4400.00
Chest, Cherry, Butternut, Drawer, 26 1/2 x 40 1/2 In. 7475.00
Chest, Cherry, Mahogany, 4 Drawers, D-Form Top, Bowfront, 41 x 22 1/4 In. 1150.00
Chest, Cherry, Poplar, Walnut, 3 Drawers, Bracket Base, Relief Base, 24 x 9 x 25 In. 980.00
Chest, Chippendale Style, Cherry, 4 Drawers, American, 1800s, 41 x 42 x 22 In. 2350.00
Chest, Chippendale Style, Mahogany, 20th Century, 35 x 36 x 17 In. 145.00
Chest, Chippendale Style, Mahogany, 5 Drawers, 19 x 15 1/4 x 8 3/4 In. 1265.00
Chest, Chippendale Style, Mahogany, Block Front, 4 Drawers, 1900s, 31 x 27 x 19 In. 590.00
Chest, Chippendale, 4 Drawers, Molded Base, 38 x 40 1/2 x 20 In. 2700.00
Chest, Chippendale, 4 Drawers, Ogee Bracket Feet, Connecticut, 37 x 38 1/2 x 22 In. 5465.00
Chest, Chippendale, Birch, 5 Drawers, Dovetailed, Batwing Brass, 41 x 20 x 43 In. 4950.00
Chest, Chippendale, Birch, Cock-Beaded, Late 18th Century, 37 x 40 x 19 In. . . . . *Illus* 2115.00
Chest, Chippendale, Birch, Ogee Bracket Base, 4 Drawers, 32 x 38 x 17 1/2 In. 670.00
Chest, Chippendale, Birch, Thumb-Molded Edge, Late 1700s, 37 x 40 1/2 x 19 In. 2115.00
Chest, Chippendale, Cherry, 4 Drawers, Beaded Edges, Pine Inlay, 32 x 42 x 18 In. 1925.00
Chest, Chippendale, Cherry, 4 Drawers, Conn., Late 1700s, 37 x 45 3/4 x 20 1/4 In. 5975.00
Chest, Chippendale, Cherry, 4 Drawers, Molded Top, Conn., 42 x 19 x 34 In. 2025.00
Chest, Chippendale, Cherry, 4 Drawers, Pennsylvania, c.1800, 39 3/4 x 37 1/2 In. 1380.00

Furniture, Chest,
Chippendale, Birch,
Cock-Beaded, Late 18th
Century, 37 x 40 x 19 In.

Furniture, Chest, Federal,
Cherry, Mahogany,
Bird's-Eye Maple, Inlaid,
39 x 39 x 20 In.

Chest, Chippendale, Cherry, 4 Drawers, Serpentine Front, New England, 33 3/4 x 39 In. . . . 4315.00
Chest, Chippendale, Cherry, 4 Graduated Drawers, Molded Top, 41 x 40 x 21 In. 1015.00
Chest, Chippendale, Cherry, 5 Drawers, New England, Late 1700s, 50 x 35 x 15 In. 3055.00
Chest, Chippendale, Cherry, 6 Drawers, New England, 58 1/2 x 17 1/2 In. 3450.00
Chest, Chippendale, Cherry, 9 Drawers, Dovetailed, Bracket Feet, 64 x 43 x 21 In. 3740.00
Chest, Chippendale, Curly Maple, Pine, 6 Drawers, c.1790, 40 x 18 3/4 x 53 1/2 In. 7475.00
Chest, Chippendale, Figured Maple, 5 Drawers, New England, 47 x 36 In. 3165.00
Chest, Chippendale, Mahogany, 2 Over 3 Drawers, Chamfered Corners, 42 x 42 In. 1008.00
Chest, Chippendale, Mahogany, 2 Over 3 Drawers, Ogee Feet, 36 x 37 x 20 In. 2475.00
Chest, Chippendale, Mahogany, 4 Drawers, Maryland, c.1770, 35 x 41 x 21 1/2 In. 2760.00
Chest, Chippendale, Mahogany, 4 Drawers, Ogee Bracket Feet, c.1790, 34 x 41 x 21 In. . . 4540.00
Chest, Chippendale, Mahogany, 4 Drawers, Serpentine Apron, 36 1/4 x 41 1/8 In. 1150.00
Chest, Chippendale, Mahogany, Pediment, Tall Finials, 94 x 43 x 23 In. 10755.00
Chest, Chippendale, Mahogany, Reverse Serpentine, c.1780, 23 x 42 In. 27485.00
Chest, Chippendale, Maple, 3 Over 4 Drawers, Bracket Feet, 1760, 50 x 40 x 19 In. 7500.00
Chest, Chippendale, Maple, 5 Drawers, Thumbmolded, 43 x 35 x 19 In. 2700.00
Chest, Chippendale, Maple, 6 Graduated Drawers, Cock-Beaded, 56 1/2 x 36 x 18 In. . . . 2760.00
Chest, Chippendale, Maple, 7 Drawers, New England, Late 1700s, 48 x 39 In. 1645.00
Chest, Chippendale, Maple, Birch, 4 Drawers, Dovetailed, Ogee Feet, 35 1/2 x 41 In. 1090.00
Chest, Chippendale, Pine, Birch, 4 Drawers, Applied Ogee Bracket, 32 x 38 x 18 In. 660.00
Chest, Chippendale, Walnut, 2 Over 4 Drawers, American, 60 x 41 3/4 x 23 In. 1000.00
Chest, Chippendale, Walnut, 2 Over 5 Drawers, Late 1700s, 61 x 42 x 21 In. 1435.00
Chest, Chippendale, Walnut, 3 Over 5 Drawers, Dovetailed Top, 60 1/4 x 39 In. 6900.00
Chest, Chippendale, Walnut, 4 Drawers, Ogee Feet, American, 19 x 36 x 41 In. 3160.00
Chest, Chippendale, Walnut, 4 Drawers, Pa., Late 1700s, 38 1/2 x 40 x 22 In. 3000.00
Chest, Chippendale, Walnut, 8 Drawers, Scalloped Bracket Feet, 41 x 23 x 55 In. 3025.00
Chest, Chippendale, Walnut, Pine, 9 Drawers, Ball Feet, 40 x 23 x 59 1/2 In. 3300.00
Chest, Chippendale, Walnut, Yellow Pine, 5 Drawers, 35 1/2 x 39 3/4 In. 5060.00
Chest, Crackle Finish, 2 Over 4 Drawers, Brass Pulls 1195.00
Chest, Curly Maple, Poplar, 4 Drawers, 2-Board Top, 45 x 21 x 44 In. 1430.00
Chest, Curved Front, Lobed Corners, 4 Drawers, Scotland, c.1830, 41 x 48 In. 2185.00
Chest, Deal, Elm, 5 Drawers, Turned Drawer Pulls, 1800s, 12 3/4 x 11 In. 400.00
Chest, Dower, 2 Drawers, Polychrome Flowers, Painted, Dovetailed, 27 x 50 In. 7700.00
Chest, Dower, Blue, Salmon, Medallions, Blue & White, Bracket Feet, Pa., c.1788 . . . . . . 6300.00
Chest, Dower, Unicorn, Lion, Tulips, Birds, c.1787, 23 x 50 x 22 3/4 In. 7700.00
Chest, Dunbar, 2 Doors, Brass Hinges, 2 Interior Shelves, 34 1/4 x 38 x 20 1/2 In. 1495.00
Chest, Eastlake, Lingerie, Walnut, Side Lock, Swivel Mirror, 79 1/2 x 28 x 14 In. 1555.00
Chest, Elm, Red Lacquer, Chinese, c.1850, 9 1/4 x 40 1/4 x 6 3/4 In. 210.00
Chest, Empire Style, Cherry, Mahogany Veneer, 4 Drawers, 15 1/2 x 10 x 17 In. 715.00
Chest, Empire Style, Fruitwood, 2 Columns, Painted Capitals, 4 Drawers, 14 3/4 In. 1060.00
Chest, Empire Style, Mahogany, Partially Painted, Drawers, 59 x 41 x 21 In. 1135.00
Chest, Empire, Cherry, 3 Drawers, 32 x 36 x 19 In. 1645.00
Chest, Empire, Flamed Cherry, 2 Over 3 Drawers, Well Top, Scrolled Feet, 25 x 20 In. . . . 395.00
Chest, Empire, Pine, Chestnut Back, Grain Painted, 4 Drawers, c.1840, 13 x 9 x 18 In. . . . 690.00
Chest, Empire, Pine, Poplar, Flame Grain Mahogany Veneer, 7 Drawers, 49 x 22 In. 990.00
Chest, Empire, Walnut, Poplar, Red Flame Graining, Stripes, Polka Dots, 42 x 20 x 45 In. . 460.00
Chest, Federal, Birch, 4 Drawers, New England, c.1815, 38 1/4 x 38 1/4 x 18 In. 1535.00
Chest, Federal, Bird's-Eye Maple, 6 Drawers, Paw Feet, Carved Splashback 980.00
Chest, Federal, Cherry, 3 Over 5 Drawers, Flared Feet, Pennsylvania, c.1800, 65 In. 6500.00
Chest, Federal, Cherry, 4 Drawers, Delaware Valley, c.1820, 42 x 45 x 21 In. 750.00

Chest, Federal, Cherry, 4 Drawers, Pennsylvania, c.1800, 40 x 43 x 20 1/4 In. 1150.00
Chest, Federal, Cherry, 4 Drawers, Reeded Pilasters, New England, 41 x 18 x 41 1/2 In. . . .   920.00
Chest, Federal, Cherry, 4 Drawers, Shaped Apron, Early 1800s, 36 x 39 x 19 In. 1060.00
Chest, Federal, Cherry, 4 Graduated Drawers, c.1810, 36 x 42 x 20 In. 4185.00
Chest, Federal, Cherry, Bowed Top, c.1810, 35 x 39 x 21 In. 3585.00
Chest, Federal, Cherry, Bowfront, 4 Drawers, New England, c.1800, 36 x 42 x 21 In. 3285.00
Chest, Federal, Cherry, Chestnut, 4 Drawers, Curved Front, Early 1800s, 39 x 42 x 25 In. . .   3080.00
Chest, Federal, Cherry, Figured Maple, 4 Drawers, c.1825, 22 x 43 x 21 In. 3350.00
Chest, Federal, Cherry, Inlaid, 4 Graduated Drawers, c.1810, 37 x 43 x 20 In. 4540.00
Chest, Federal, Cherry, Mahogany, Bird's-Eye Maple, Inlaid, 39 x 39 x 20 In. . . . . . *Illus*   3819.00
Chest, Federal, Cherry, Maple, Inlaid, Mass., c.1815, 42 x 44 x 22 In. 8225.00
Chest, Federal, Cherry, Maple, Inlaid, Panels, Mahogany, c.1815, 42 x 44 x 21 3/4 In. . . .   5580.00
Chest, Federal, Cherry, Veneer, Bowfront, c.1810, 36 1/2 x 41 x 23 3/4 In. 3820.00
Chest, Federal, Mahogany Inlay, Bonnet, 3 Long Drawers, c.1810, 44 x 45 x 22 In. 2390.00
Chest, Federal, Mahogany Veneer, 4 Drawers, c.1820, 45 1/2 x 45 x 20 In. 2700.00
Chest, Federal, Mahogany Veneer, 7 Drawers, Jewelry Box, Columns, 49 x 47 x 23 In. . . .   550.00
Chest, Federal, Mahogany Veneer, Cherry Inlay, 4 Drawers, c.1810, 40 x 42 x 19 In. 3055.00
Chest, Federal, Mahogany Veneer, Ogee Backsplash, 3 Over 4 Drawers, 48 x 47 x 23 In. . .   560.00
Chest, Federal, Mahogany, 4 Drawers, 1 2-Part Drawer, c.1800, 43 x 47 1/4 x 21 In. 2760.00
Chest, Federal, Mahogany, 4 Drawers, 39 1/2 x 40 1/2 x 19 1/2 In. 1435.00
Chest, Federal, Mahogany, 4 Drawers, Bowfront, French Feet, 41 x 17 1/2 x 35 1/2 In. . . .   560.00
Chest, Federal, Mahogany, 4 Drawers, Cock-Beaded, c.1810, 42 x 42 x 21 1/4 In. 1035.00
Chest, Federal, Mahogany, Bird's-Eye Maple, 6 Drawers, Spiraled Acanthus Columns . . .   865.00
Chest, Federal, Mahogany, Bird's-Eye Maple, Satinwood, 4 Drawers, c.1810 . . . .   2875.00
Chest, Federal, Mahogany, Bowfront, 4 Drawers, D-Top, Mass., 38 1/4 x 39 1/4 In. 5750.00
Chest, Federal, Mahogany, Bowfront, Cookie Corners, Brass Pulls, c.1810 . . . .   2070.00
Chest, Federal, Mahogany, Cherry, c.1810, 35 1/4 x 42 1/2 x 18 1/2 In. 1090.00
Chest, Federal, Mahogany, Figured Maple, Early 19th Century, 43 1/4 x 42 x 19 1/2 In. . . .   805.00
Chest, Federal, Mahogany, Inlaid, 4 Drawers, Bracket Feet, 35 1/4 x 39 3/4 In. 4370.00
Chest, Federal, Mahogany, Inlaid, 4 Drawers, c.1805, 31 1/2 x 31 1/2 x 18 1/4 In. 2530.00
Chest, Federal, Mahogany, Inlaid, 4 Drawers, Early 1800s, 37 1/2 x 42 x 19 In. 1555.00
Chest, Federal, Mahogany, Inlaid, New England, c.1800, 50 1/2 x 46 3/4 x 21 1/2 In. 1435.00
Chest, Federal, Mahogany, Inlaid, Reeded Columns, Drawers, 37 x 42 x 21 In. 2640.00
Chest, Federal, Mahogany, Serpentine Front, 4 Drawers, Early 1800s, 41 x 48 x 23 In. . . .   9560.00
Chest, Federal, Mahogany, Step-Down, 3 Over 4 Drawers, Columns, 45 x 42 x 19 In. 460.00
Chest, Federal, Mahogany, Veneer, Swell Front, 4 Drawers, c.1800, 37 x 19 x 22 In. 1645.00
Chest, Federal, Mahogany, Wood Pulls, 3 Drawers, c.1820, 31 1/2 x 33 x 20 In. 1035.00
Chest, Federal, Paneled, 4 Drawers, Turned Legs, New York, c.1810, 40 x 43 x 23 In. 1270.00
Chest, Federal, Red Paint, 4 Drawers, New England, 42 1/3 x 41 x 17 12 In. 575.00
Chest, Federal, Satinwood, Cherry Inlay, 4 Drawers, c.1810, 41 x 39 x 20 In. 1150.00
Chest, Federal, Tiger Maple, 4 Drawers, Applied Columns, 46 1/2 x 49 1/2 x 19 In. 7700.00
Chest, Federal, Walnut, 5 Over 4 Drawers, Pennsylvania, c.1800, 61 x 41 x 21 In. 3585.00
Chest, Federal, Walnut, Bowfront, 4 Drawers, Wood Pulls, 38 x 41 1/4 x 22 In. 825.00
Chest, Frank Lloyd Wright, 6 Drawers, 2 Doors, Heritage Henredon, 36 x 20 x 53 In. 1725.00
Chest, French Provincial, Mahogany, Inlaid, 1700s, 32 x 39 x 16 In. 3175.00
Chest, Fruitwood, Marquetry, Ogee Frieze, 3 Long Drawers, 1800s, 37 x 49 x 22 In. 1410.00
Chest, G. Nakashima, 11 Drawers, Cabinet Door, 49 1/4 x 47 x 21 1/2 In. 2760.00
Chest, G. Nakashima, Walnut, 4 Drawers, Trestle Base, 31 1/2 x 36 x 21 1/4 In. 5465.00
Chest, G. Nelson, Primavera, Oak, Silver Plated Brass, Herman Miller, 40 x 40 x 20 In. . . .   470.00
Chest, G. Nelson, Rosewood, 8 Drawers, c.1956, 46 3/4 x 18 1/2 x 30 3/4 In. 6465.00
Chest, G. Nelson, Thin Edge, 4 Drawers, Chrome Pulls, Tapered Legs, 33 x 34 x 19 In. . . .   4600.00
Chest, G. Nelson, Walnut Veneer, 5 Drawers, Chrome Pulls, 39 1/2 x 40 x 19 In. 805.00
Chest, G. Stickley, 2 Over 4 Drawers, 32 x 19 x 46 In. 980.00
Chest, G. Stickley, 2 Over 4 Drawers, 42 x 37 x 19 In. 2875.00
Chest, G. Stickley, 5 Drawers, V-Shaped Backsplash, c.1904, 52 5/8 x 40 x 22 In. 11750.00
Chest, G. Stickley, 9 Drawers, Arched Apron, Mushroom Pulls, 50 1/2 x 36 x 20 In. 8050.00
Chest, G. Stickley, No. 621, 5 Drawers, Paneled Sides, Iron Pulls, 42 x 36 x 20 In. 6900.00
Chest, G. Stickley, No. 626, 5 Drawers, Through Tenon, 36 x 20 x 43 In. 10925.00
Chest, G. Stickley, No. 913, 9 Drawers, Oak Knobs, Hammered Pulls, 50 x 36 x 2 In. 8625.00
Chest, George II Style, Burl Walnut, 5 Drawers, c.1860, 41 1/2 x 47 In. 1840.00
Chest, George II Style, Burl Walnut, Inlaid, 2 Over 3 Drawers, c.1850, 38 x 41 In. 3680.00
Chest, George III Style, Mahogany, 3 Drawers, Bracket Feet, 1800s, 24 x 21 x 17 In. 590.00
Chest, George III Style, Mahogany, Bowfront, 5 Drawers, c.1840, 43 x 42 x 20 In. 1955.00

Chest, George III Style, Mahogany, Bowfront, 2 Over 3 Drawers, 42 x 43 x 21 In. 1150.00
Chest, George III Style, Mahogany, Bowfront, 3 Drawers, Mid 1800s, 34 x 35 x 18 In. . . . 1955.00
Chest, George III Style, Oyster Walnut, Brass Mount, 4 Drawers, 35 x 40 In. 1380.00
Chest, George III Style, Satinwood, Inlay, Ebonized, 5 Drawers, 44 x 43 x 20 In. 920.00
Chest, George III Style, Walnut, 4 Drawers, Bracket Feet, 20 1/2 x 20 1/2 x 11 In. 618.00
Chest, George III Style, Walnut, Rosewood, 5 Drawers, c.1890, 40 x 38 1/4 In. 3105.00
Chest, George III, Mahogany, 4 Drawers, Late 1700s, 32 x 31 In. 2990.00
Chest, George III, Mahogany, 6 Drawers, Banded Top, c.1900, 43 x 48 1/2 In. 1955.00
Chest, George III, Mahogany, Bowfront, 2 Over 3 Drawers, c.1785, 40 1/2 x 41 In. 1380.00
Chest, George III, Mahogany, Bowfront, 3 Drawers, c.1800, 33 x 26 x 22 1/2 In. 1530.00
Chest, George III, Mahogany, Bowfront, 3 Drawers, Pullout Side, 40 x 42 x 20 In. 1150.00
Chest, George III, Mahogany, Bowfront, 4 Drawers, Late 1700s, 36 x 4 1/2 x 22 In. 1495.00
Chest, George III, Mahogany, Bowfront, 5 Drawers, c.1800, 37 x 42 x 20 1/2 In. 2185.00
Chest, George III, Mahogany, Bowfront, Banded, 2 Drawers, c.1800, 42 x 43 x 23 In. . . . 2300.00
Chest, George III, Mahogany, Bowfront, c.1800, 41 x 39 1/2 x 19 1/2 In. 1725.00
Chest, George III, Mahogany, Inlaid, Bowfront, 5 Drawers, c.1800, 39 x 40 x 19 In. 1295.00
Chest, George III, Mahogany, Inlaid, Serpentine, 4 Drawers, 39 1/4 x 47 In. 3450.00
Chest, George III, Mahogany, Serpentine Front, 4 Drawers, c.1775, 35 x 42 x 22 In. 2235.00
Chest, George III, Mahogany, Serpentine Front, 5 Drawers, c.1780, 31 x 27 x 20 In. 5580.00
Chest, George III, Oak, Inlaid, 2 Short Over 3 Long Drawers, c.1790, 48 x 40 x 19 In. 546.00
Chest, George III, Walnut, Oyster Veneer, 4 Drawers, 31 1/2 x 43 x 20 1/2 In. 1610.00
Chest, George IV, Mahogany, Inlaid, Bowfront, 5 Drawers, c.1850, 42 x 40 1/2 In. 1495.00
Chest, George IV, Mahogany, Linenfold Inlay, 5 Drawers, c.1830, 41 x 40 In. 2415.00
Chest, Georgian Style, Bowfront, 5 Drawers, Inlaid Top, c.1840, 39 x 47 In. 1150.00
Chest, Georgian Style, Burl Walnut, Brass Mounted, 4 Drawers, 30 x 36 In. 575.00
Chest, Georgian Style, Mahogany, 2 Short Over 3 Long Drawers, 1800s, 15 x 20 In. 440.00
Chest, Georgian Style, Mahogany, Bowfront, 5 Drawers, c.1840, 43 x 47 In. 1955.00
Chest, Georgian, 5 Drawers, Serpentine Top, Late 1800s, 34 1/2 x 36 1/2 x 19 1/2 In. . . . 2070.00
Chest, Georgian, Mahogany, 3 Over 3 Drawers, c.1850, 38 3/4 x 44 1/2 x 22 1/4 In. 2350.00
Chest, Georgian, Mahogany, Bow Top, 4 Drawers, 42 1/2 x 45 1/2 x 23 1/2 In. 1955.00
Chest, Georgian, Mahogany, Bowfront, 2 Over 3 Drawers, c.1800, 46 x 42 x 20 In. 999.00
Chest, Georgian, Mahogany, Brass Mounted, 5 Drawers, c.1815, 37 x 39 In. 865.00
Chest, Georgian, Mahogany, Inlaid, Shell, Beaded Edge, c.1850, 39 1/2 x 53 x 21 In. 1095.00
Chest, Georgian, Walnut, Banded, Brass Mounted, 4 Drawers, c.1715, 29 x 33 1/2 In. 3450.00
Chest, Gothic Revival, Oak, 69 x 29 x 23 In. 1195.00
Chest, Grain Painted, 6 Drawers, 62 x 32 1/2 In. 155.00
Chest, H. Probber, Rosewood & Oak Veneer, Jewelry, 8 Drawers, 36 x 14 x 14 In. 3740.00
Chest, Hardwood, Dome Top, Iron Bound, Continental, 1802, 26 x 50 x 23 In. 330.00
Chest, Hardwood, Painted, Iron Bound, Continental, 1812, 28 x 46 x 23 In. 540.00
Chest, Hepplewhite Style, Mahogany, Bowfront, 4 Drawers, 40 x 36 x 21 1/2 In. 800.00
Chest, Hepplewhite, Bowfront, 4 Drawers, James Dinsmore, c.1810, 41 In. 4025.00
Chest, Hepplewhite, Bowfront, Mahogany, Flame Veneer, England, 35 x 19 x 35 In. 1610.00
Chest, Hepplewhite, Cherry, Inlaid, 4 Drawers, Beaded Edge, Conn., 42 1/4 x 42 In. 1725.00
Chest, Hepplewhite, Cherry, Inlay, 4 Dovetailed Drawers, Brasses, 42 x 20 x 41 In. 1840.00
Chest, Hepplewhite, Cherry, Inlay, 5 Drawers, Dovetailed, Scalloped Apron, 40 x 20 In. . . 1870.00
Chest, Hepplewhite, Mahogany Inlay, Bowfront, 4 Drawers, 36 x 39 1/2 In. 2590.00
Chest, Hepplewhite, Mahogany Veneer, 4 Drawers, Shaped Apron, 38 x 39 x 18 In. 660.00
Chest, Hepplewhite, Mahogany Veneer, Flame Grain, Bowfront, 5 Drawers, 42 1/2 In. . . . 2530.00
Chest, Hepplewhite, Mahogany Veneer, Pine, 4 Drawers, 37 1/2 x 39 x 17 1/2 In. 670.00
Chest, Hepplewhite, Mahogany, 4 Drawers, Bone Shield Escutcheon, 35 1/2 x 36 In. 920.00
Chest, Hepplewhite, Mahogany, 5 Drawers, Pennsylvania, c.1835, 44 x 22 In. 1610.00
Chest, Hepplewhite, Mahogany, Bowfront, 4 Cock-Beaded Drawers, 41 x 18 x 40 In. 2025.00
Chest, Hepplewhite, Mahogany, Bowfront, 4 Drawers, Dovetailed, 35 3/4 x 37 x 21 In. . . 920.00
Chest, Hepplewhite, Mahogany, Bowfront, 4 Drawers, New England, 35 x 39 In. 1610.00
Chest, Hepplewhite, Mahogany, Inlaid, Bowfront, 4 Drawers, 36 1/4 x 41 In. 5465.00
Chest, Hepplewhite, Mahogany, Pine, Bowfront, 38 3/4 x 21 1/4 x 33 In. 1380.00
Chest, Jacobean Style, Oak, 4 Drawers, Fluted Skirt, Early 1900s, 39 x 30 x 17 In. 495.00
Chest, Jacobean, 5 Drawers, Elaborate Front, Bun Feet, England, 36 3/4 x 37 In. 8050.00
Chest, Lacquer, Figures, Landscapes, Wood, Chinese, 1800s, 21 x 36 x 19 1/2 In. 635.00
Chest, Lingerie, Victorian, Burled Walnut Panels, Spindled Gallery, 79 x 38 x 20 In. 1380.00
Chest, Louis XVI Style, Walnut, 2 Drawers, Leaf Carved, c.1850, 33 x 49 x 23 In. 4370.00
Chest, Mahogany, 2 Drawers, Marble Top, Octagonal Mirror, 62 x 43 x 21 In. 2070.00
Chest, Mahogany, 2 Drawers, Molded Top, Fluted Pilasters, c.1900, 10 x 16 In. 520.00

Chest, Mahogany, 2 Over 3 Drawers, Bracket Feet, 19th Century, 40 x 42 x 21 In. 715.00
Chest, Mahogany, 3 Drawers, Concave Corner Stiles, Bracket Feet, 12 x 8 x 13 1/2 In. 290.00
Chest, Mahogany, 4 Drawers, Molded Top, 19th Century, England, 41 x 47 x 23 In. 715.00
Chest, Mahogany, 4 Drawers, Turned Feet, Early 19th Century, 43 x 44 x 19 1/2 In. 1380.00
Chest, Mahogany, 4 Long Graduated Drawers, Bracket Feet, c.1800, 33 x 33 x 17 In. 805.00
Chest, Mahogany, 5 Drawers, Bracket Feet, Brass, c.1835, 30 x 43 x 22 In. 1530.00
Chest, Mahogany, 5 Drawers, Ebony Pulls, Molded Top, c.1800, 10 1/2 x 11 1/2 In. 750.00
Chest, Mahogany, Black Marble Top, New York, c.1825, 40 x 42 1/2 In. 1495.00
Chest, Mahogany, Bowfront, 2 Over 3 Drawers, Cock-Beaded, 41 1/2 x 41 x 20 1/2 In. .. 1210.00
Chest, Mahogany, Bowfront, 4 Drawers, Brass Bail Handles, Beaded Edge, 34 x 40 In. .. 1095.00
Chest, Mahogany, Bowfront, Ribbon Inlay, Reeded Legs, c.1810, 40 1/2 x 45 x 21 In. ... 3680.00
Chest, Mahogany, Bowfront, String Inlay, 6 Graduated Drawers, 48 x 43 x 25 In. 880.00
Chest, Mahogany, Cock-Beaded Drawers, Bracket Feet, 41 1/2 x 38 x 19 1/2 In. 715.00
Chest, Mahogany, Contrasting Veneers, 4 Drawers, c.1800, 40 3/4 x 39 x 21 1/2 In. 2240.00
Chest, Mahogany, Dovetailed, Carved, Animals, Leaves, Paw Feet, 24 x 44 x 22 1/2 In. .. 575.00
Chest, Mahogany, Flat Top, Brass Corners, 19th Century, 41 x 19 x 20 1/2 In. 675.00
Chest, Mahogany, Inlaid, 4 Drawers, Brass Pulls, Scalloped Skirt, 1800s, 36 x 37 In. 1540.00
Chest, Mahogany, Inlaid, 5 Drawers, England, c.1850, 45 3/4 x 51 x 21 3/4 In. 2070.00
Chest, Mahogany, Mahogany Veneers, Bowfront, 4 Drawers, 12 x 10 1/2 x 9 1/2 In. 315.00
Chest, Mahogany, Poplar, Ogee Bracket Feet, Mid-Atlantic States, c.1780, 38 x 41 In. ... 4715.00
Chest, Mahogany, Serpentine, Drexel, 52 1/2 x 38 x 21 1/2 In. 345.00
Chest, Mahogany, Yellow Pine, 3 Drawers, 38 1/2 x 43 x 23 1/2 In. 2860.00
Chest, Maple, 2 Over 3 Dovetailed Drawers, 19th Century, 48 x 35 1/2 x 18 In. 715.00
Chest, Maple, 6 Drawers, Dovetailed, American, Late 1700s, 62 x 38 x 18 1/2 In. 2750.00
Chest, Maple, Pine, Queen Anne, Batwing Brasses, 35 x 29 In. 15400.00
Chest, Maple, Softwood, Slant Front, Beadboard, Turned Feet, Blue Paint, 62 x 37 In. ... 620.00
Chest, Maple, Tiger Maple, Pine, 6 Drawers, Scrolled Bracket Base, 56 x 39 x 19 In. 2760.00
Chest, Marble Top, Mirror, Serpentine Front, 3 Drawers, Top Crest, 87 x 55 x 24 In. 540.00
Chest, McCobb, 8 Drawers, Calvin, c.1958, 66 x 18 x 34 In. 1060.00
Chest, McCobb, Birch, 7 Drawers, Rosewood Pull, 1950s, 41 x 38 x 18 In. 520.00
Chest, McCobb, Planner Group, 3 Black Drawers, Blond Bench, 39 1/4 x 48 x 18 In. 635.00
Chest, McCobb, Planner Group, Birch, Brass, Modular Base, Pair 590.00
Chest, McCobb, Planner Group, Walnut Finish, 4 Drawers, 42 1/4 x 36 x 18 In. 235.00
Chest, Mennonite, 5 Drawers, 11 Tiered Upper Drawers, Lancaster County. 12500.00
Chest, Molded Top, 5 Drawers, Turned Pulls & Feet, 1800s, 10 1/2 x 9 1/2 In. 1035.00
Chest, Mule, Chippendale, Mahogany, 8 Drawers, Ogee Feet, c.1785, 46 x 68 In. 4370.00
Chest, Mule, Chippendale, Pine, Dovetailed, 2 Drawers, 2 False Fronts, 42 x 41 In. 1610.00
Chest, Mule, Curly Maple, 2 Drawers, Scalloped Base, 37 3/4 x 14 3/4 x 38 In. 865.00
Chest, Mule, Curly Maple, Pine, Scallop Cutouts, 2 Drawers, Brass, 41 x 18 x 39 In. 4400.00
Chest, Mule, George III, Oak, c.1790, 28 x 50 x 20 In. 1035.00
Chest, Mule, Grain Painted, 2 Drawers, 37 x 17 1/4 x 36 In. 1380.00
Chest, Mule, Grain Painted, 2 Drawers, Lift Top, American, c.1825, 19 x 38 x 38 In. 2300.00
Chest, Mule, Pine, 2 Dovetailed Drawers, Bracket Feet, Scalloped Returns, 37 x 39 In. ... 1320.00
Chest, Mule, Pine, 2 Drawers, Dovetailed, Covered Till, Interior Drawer, 37 x 38 In. 2415.00
Chest, Mule, Pine, 2 Drawers, Dovetailed, Wooden Pulls, Molded, 38 x 38 x 17 In. 1035.00
Chest, Mule, Pine, Grain Decorated, 2 Drawers, Bracket Feet, 38 1/2 x 17 1/2 x 37 In. ... 1955.00
Chest, Mule, Pine, Lift Top, 2 Drawers, Early 1800s, 43 x 46 1/2 x 18 In. 750.00
Chest, Mule, Pine, Oxblood, Lift Top, Drawer, 34 x 32 In. 715.00
Chest, Mule, Pine, Poplar, Flame Decorated, Scalloped Base, 37 x 18 x 31 In. 1265.00

**Pembroke tables with square legs sell
for higher prices than Pembroke tables
with turned or reeded legs.**

Furniture, Chest, Mule, Poplar,
Painted, Lift Top, Wooden Knobs,
Cutouts, 37 x 38 x 18 In.

Chest, Mule, Poplar, Painted, Lift Top, Wooden Knobs, Cutouts, 37 x 38 x 18 In. . . . *Illus* 2300.00
Chest, Neoclassical, Fruitwood, 2 Drawers, Square Legs, c.1810, 31 x 32 1/2 x 17 In. . . . 1880.00
Chest, Neoclassical, Grain Painted, Splash Board, 2 Over 3 Drawers, 49 x 42 x 20 In. . . . 940.00
Chest, Neoclassical, Mahogany, 4 Drawers, Column Pilasters, c.1830, 46 x 47 x 24 In. . . . 575.00
Chest, Neoclassical, Mahogany, 4 Drawers, Mid 1800s, 35 1/2 x 38 1/2 x 21 In. 2530.00
Chest, Neoclassical, Mahogany, 5 Drawers, American, c.1835, 46 1/2 x 44 1/2 In. 805.00
Chest, Neoclassical, Mahogany, 6 Drawers, American, c.1835, 44 1/2 x 42 In. 1035.00
Chest, Neoclassical, Tiger Maple, 4 Drawers, New England, c.1850, 46 x 43 x 23 In. 600.00
Chest, Nutting, Chippendale Style, Mahogany, 4 Drawers, 36 1/2 x 38 x 19 In. 4715.00
Chest, Oak, 2 Over 2 Drawers, Reeded Molding, Brass Pulls, 30 1/2 x 37 x 17 1/2 In. . . . 900.00
Chest, Oak, 2 Over 3 Drawers, Bracket Feet, 19th Century, England, 38 x 37 x 19 In. 935.00
Chest, Oak, 2 Over 3 Drawers, Molded Front, Bracket Feet, England, 36 x 41 x 23 In. 1380.00
Chest, Oak, Blind Panels, Split Columns, Mid 18th Century, 31 1/2 x 40 x 25 In. 1150.00
Chest, Oak, Star & Urn Inlay, Early 18th Century, 30 1/2 x 56 x 28 1/2 In. 1610.00
Chest, Ormolu Mounted, Inlaid, Satin Lined, Cabriole Legs, Continental, 32 x 27 In. 200.00
Chest, Paint Decorated, Brown Graining, Black Molding, Ball Feet, 11 x 9 x 16 In. 825.00
Chest, Paint Decorated, Gilt, 3 Over 4 Drawers, Soap Hollow, c.1870, 53 x 39 x 21 In. . . . 28600.00
Chest, Parquetry, 3 Drawers, Canted Corners, Continental, c.1800, 11 x 7 x 6 In. 3000.00
Chest, Pine, 3 Drawers, Porcelain Knobs, 30 x 32 In. 145.00
Chest, Pine, 3 Drawers, Rounded Front Corners, Bracket Feet, c.1840, 40 x 43 x 19 In. . . 635.00
Chest, Pine, 4 Drawers, Board & Batten Backing, Early 1900s, 32 x 34 x 18 1/2 In. 330.00
Chest, Pine, 4 Drawers, Bun Feet, Painted, Continental, c.1850, 49 x 39 1/2 In. 750.00
Chest, Pine, 4 Drawers, Turned Pulls, 1800s, 12 x 12 1/2 In. 259.00
Chest, Pine, 6-Board, Blue Paint, Early 19th Century, 23 x 41 x 18 In. 1175.00
Chest, Pine, 6-Board, Hinged Top, Chamfered Edge, Early 1800s, 11 x 35 x 16 In. 560.00
Chest, Pine, 6-Board, Red & Green Paint, Flat Iron Hinges, 15 x 39 x 16 In. 280.00
Chest, Pine, Flowers, Drawers, Teardrop Pulls, 54 x 24 x 18 In. 550.00
Chest, Pine, Grain Paint, 3 Drawers, Ceramic Pulls, 1800s, 13 3/4 x 14 In. 315.00
Chest, Pine, Green Sponging, Tombstone Panels, Dovetailed, 19th Century, 19 x 9 In. . . . 575.00
Chest, Pine, Painted, Late 18th Century, 36 3/4 x 44 3/4 x 18 In. 3055.00
Chest, Pine, Polychrome, Mirror, Backsplash, Miniature, 16 x 10 x 6 In. 2750.00
Chest, Pine, Poplar, 9 Drawers, Cut Nail, Dovetailed, c.1850, 21 x 12 x 8 In. 1320.00
Chest, Pine, Red Paint, 4 Drawers, Carved Feet, 11 x 7 x 14 1/2 In. 200.00
Chest, Pine, Red, Ocher Grain Painted, 5 Drawers, Ball Feet, 41 x 39 x 18 1/2 In. 1210.00
Chest, Polychrome, 3 Drawers, Bun Feet, Italy, Late 1700s, 36 x 53 x 24 1/2 In. 4830.00
Chest, Polychrome, 3 Drawers, Landscape Drawer Fronts, 33 x 41 1/2 x 26 1/2 In. 3680.00
Chest, Polychrome, Serpentine Top, 3 Drawers, Bun Feet, Italy, 33 x 48 x 26 1/2 In. 2185.00
Chest, Poplar, Lift Top, Paneled Front, Yellow Wash, Tapered Legs, 27 1/2 x 43 In. 1550.00
Chest, Queen Anne Style, Walnut, 2 Over 3 Drawers, 35 1/2 x 43 1/2 x 22 1/2 In. 1495.00
Chest, Queen Anne Style, Walnut, 3 Drawers, Oyster Panels, 34 1/2 x 41 1/2 In. 920.00
Chest, Queen Anne Style, Walnut, 3 Over 3 Drawers, 35 x 39 1/2 x 21 1/2 In. 1265.00
Chest, Queen Anne Style, Walnut, 5 Drawers, Stringing, 37 1/2 x 42 1/2 x 21 In. 1495.00
Chest, Queen Anne Style, Walnut, Satinwood, 2 Over 2 Drawers, 29 x 42 In. 1380.00
Chest, Queen Anne Style, Walnut, Starburst Inlay, 5 Drawers, 39 x 40 x 23 In. 980.00
Chest, Queen Anne Style, Walnut, Starburst Inlay, 5 Drawers, 45 1/2 x 40 1/2 In. 2070.00
Chest, Queen Anne Style, Walnut, String Inlay, Oyster Veneers, 32 x 33 x 21 In. 1380.00
Chest, Queen Anne, Cherry, Carved, 11 Drawers, Mass., c.1760, 69 1/2 x 38 3/4 In. 8800.00
Chest, Queen Anne, Curly Maple, 5 Drawers, c.1760, 50 1/4 x 37 3/4 x 18 1/2 In. 3680.00
Chest, Queen Anne, Walnut, Mid 18th Century, 35 x 37 1/2 x 19 1/2 In. 1150.00
Chest, Red Lacquer, Gilt, Qing Dynasty, Chinese, c.1860, 15 x 27 x 18 In. 415.00
Chest, Red Paint, 3 Drawers, 2 False Drawers, Molded Front, 36 In. Wide 8500.00
Chest, Red Paint, Original Knobs, Connecticut River Valley, c.1790 . . . . 4800.00
Chest, Regency Style, Mahogany, 2 Drawers, Scrolling Patterns, 34 1/2 x 47 In. 1840.00
Chest, Regency, Mahogany, Bowfront, 2 Over 2 Drawers, c.1815, 34 x 42 x 21 In. 1095.00
Chest, Regency, Mahogany, Bowfront, 2 Over 3 Drawers, 39 x 40 1/2 x 21 In. 2070.00
Chest, Regency, Mahogany, Bowfront, 2 Over 3 Drawers, c.1815, 40 x 41 In. 1380.00
Chest, Regency, Mahogany, Bowfront, 2 Over 3 Drawers, c.1815, 42 x 40 x 21 In. 1725.00
Chest, Regency, Mahogany, Bowfront, 3 Drawers, c.1815, 35 x 40 x 21 1/2 In. 1610.00
Chest, Regency, Mahogany, Bowfront, 5 Drawers, c.1815, 41 x 41 1/2 x 20 In. 1150.00
Chest, Regency, Mahogany, Bowfront, 5 Drawers, c.1815, 43 x 39 x 22 In. 1150.00
Chest, Regency, Mahogany, Bowfront, Early 19th Century, 40 1/2 x 40 x 20 In. 1840.00
Chest, Renaissance Revival, Oak, Parcel Gilt, 8 Drawers, Spain, c.1910, 48 x 41 x 22 In. . . 1060.00
Chest, Restauration, Mahogany, Bird's-Eye Maple, Feet, 7 x 13 x 10 In. 520.00

Chest, Rohde, 5 Drawers, Inlaid Bands, Bakelite Pulls, 46 x 33 x 19 1/2 In. 5465.00
Chest, Rosewood Grain Decoration, 6 Drawers, Early 1800s, 41 1/2 x 20 x 41 In. 1140.00
Chest, Rosewood, 3 Parts, 4 Doors, 5 Drawers, Stepped, Korea, Late 1800s, 65 x 47 In. ... 1150.00
Chest, Shaker, 6 Drawers, Dovetailed Top, Alfred, Maine, 61 x 40 x 20 In. 8625.00
Chest, Shaker, Cherry, Pine, 4 Drawers, Ohio, c.1835, 42 x 42 x 18 In. 4025.00
Chest, Shaker, Cherry, Pine, 4 Drawers, Whitewater, Ohio, c.1840, 40 x 40 In. 3450.00
Chest, Shaker, Pine, 4 Graduated Drawers, Angled Feet, Mt. Lebanon, N.Y., 37 x 30 In. ... 1115.00
Chest, Shaker, Pine, 10 Drawers, Sabbathday Lake, Me., c.1850, 56 1/2 x 33 1/2 In. ... 5750.00
Chest, Shaker, Pine, Red, Till, Bootjack Ends, Harvard, Mass., c.1820, 21 x 33 x 16 In. ... 1495.00
Chest, Sheraton Style, Mahogany, Glass Knobs, 1800s, Miniature, 11 x 13 x 5 In. 605.00
Chest, Sheraton, 2 Over 3 Drawers, Reeded Stiles, Scalloped Skirt, 40 1/2 x 18 x 43 In. ... 450.00
Chest, Sheraton, Cherry, 4 Drawers, Dovetailed, Turned Feet, Backsplash, 43 x 21 In. ... 660.00
Chest, Sheraton, Cherry, 4 Graduated Drawers, Molded Lip, Panels, 17 1/2 x 16 In. 3040.00
Chest, Sheraton, Cherry, Bowfront, 4 Graduated Beaded Drawers, Scalloped Skirt, 41 In. . 675.00
Chest, Sheraton, Cherry, Bowfront, D-Form Top, 4 Drawers, Conn., 40 1/2 x 40 In. 2875.00
Chest, Sheraton, Cherry, Mahogany, Bowfront, 4 Drawers, Tall Turned Legs 1690.00
Chest, Sheraton, Cherry, Maple, Bird's-Eye Maple, 6 Drawers, Backsplash, c.1835 ..... 980.00
Chest, Sheraton, Cherry, Poplar, Variegated Line Inlay, 42 1/2 x 21 1/2 x 41 1/2 In. 3105.00
Chest, Sheraton, Mahogany, 6 Drawers, Reeded Stiles, Turned Feet, 24 x 24 x 13 In. ... 2700.00
Chest, Sheraton, Mahogany, Bowfront, 4 Cock-Beaded Drawers, 40 1/2 x 19 x 40 In. ... 1070.00
Chest, Sheraton, Mahogany, Corinthian Capitals, 43 x 42 In. 790.00
Chest, Sheraton, Maple, 4 Drawers, Porringer Top, c.1815, 36 1/2 x 39 x 19 In. 1610.00
Chest, Softwood, 4 Drawers, Cock-Beaded, Yellow, Red Ground, New England 3375.00
Chest, Spanish Baroque, Drawers, Door, Columns, Bun Feet, 1600, 21 x 34 x 13 In. 5750.00
Chest, Spanish Colonial, Dower, Pine, Painted, 1800s, 16 x 32 3/4 x 16 1/2 In. 770.00
Chest, Spice, Shaker, Poplar, Butternut, 5 Drawers, N.Y., c.1850, 27 x 27 x 12 3/4 In. 3450.00
Chest, Spice, Softwood, 6 Over 1 Wide Drawer, Arched Crest, 9 1/2 x 18 In. 310.00
Chest, Storage, Black Lacquer, Birds, Mythical Animals, Chinese, 1800s, 12 1/2 x 27 In. .. 520.00
Chest, Storage, Black Lacquer, Garden, Pavilion, Chinese, 1800s, 12 x 25 1/2 x 17 In. .. 260.00
Chest, Sugar, Cherry, Dovetailed, Till, Lock, Va., 1830-1860, 34 x 41 x 19 1/2 In. 6800.00
Chest, Sugar, Cherry, Ivory Escutcheon, c.1820, 29 x 36 x 20 In. 3740.00
Chest, Sugar, Federal, Walnut, Lift Top, Drawer, American, Late 1700s, 38 x 27 In. 6325.00
Chest, Sugar, Walnut, Dovetailed Case, Drawer, 1800s, 37 x 31 x 20 In. 3520.00
Chest, Sugar, Walnut, Lift Top, Dovetailed Case, Drawer, 31 x 29 x 30 In. 2925.00
Chest, Teak, Iron Bound, Lift Top, Continental, 23 x 49 In. 210.00
Chest, Tiger Maple, 3 Drawers, Peaked Backsplash, Paneled Ends, 40 x 36 1/2 In. 395.00
Chest, Tommi Parzinger, 4 Drawers, Green Marbled Leather Front, 34 x 44 x 19 In. 3220.00
Chest, Victorian, Mahogany, 2 Over 3 Drawers, Mid 19th Century, 42 x 42 x 22 In. 1150.00
Chest, Victorian, Mahogany, 4 Drawers, Bracket Feet, c.1840, 40 x 42 x 18 1/2 In. 235.00
Chest, Victorian, Mahogany, Marble Top, 4 Drawers, c.1870, 35 x 41 x 18 In. 235.00
Chest, Victorian, Oak, Marble Top, 4 Graduated Drawers, Carved Pulls, 33 x 41 x 20 In. .. 59.00
Chest, Victorian, Walnut, Burl Walnut, Mirror, 5 Drawers, 65 x 43 x 21 In. 650.00
Chest, Victorian, Walnut, Paneled, 6 Drawers, c.1890, 43 x 42 In. 260.00
Chest, Victorian, Walnut, Raised Panels, 4 Drawers, c.1890, 38 x 40 In. 115.00
Chest, Walnut, 2 Drawers, Early 1800s, 10 1/4 x 9 1/2 In. 489.00
Chest, Walnut, 2 Over 3 Graduated Drawers, Turned Feet, 11 1/2 x 12 In. 1180.00
Chest, Walnut, 3 Drawers, Porcelain Knobs, Carved Pilasters, 1800s, 11 3/4 x 10 1/2 In. .. 430.00
Chest, Walnut, 3 Drawers, Porcelain Pulls, c.1850, 11 3/4 x 10 1/2 In. 315.00
Chest, Walnut, 4 Drawers, Pennsylvania, 1780, 37 x 42 x 23 In. 2700.00
Chest, Walnut, 8 Drawers, Dovetailed Case, Quarter Columns, 48 x 47 x 23 In. 1760.00
Chest, Walnut, Banded Inlay, 2 Over 2 Drawers, England, 36 1/2 x 37 1/2 x 18 In. 660.00
Chest, Walnut, Burled Panels, Drop Down, Side Lock, 34 x 37 1/4 x 19 1/4 In. 920.00
Chest, Walnut, Cherry, Bonnet Over 3 Drawers, 19th Century, 47 x 42 x 20 1/2 In. 825.00
Chest, Walnut, Inlaid & Burl, 5 Drawers, 29 3/8 x 26 1/4 x 15 1/2 In., Pair 2070.00
Chest, Walnut, Inlaid Compass, Star, Hearts, Lines, Scalloped Skirts, 31 x 17 x 12 In. ... 115.00
Chest, Walnut, Inlaid, Bellflowers, Splayed Feet, c.1830, 40 x 40 x 19 1/2 In. 1150.00
Chest, Walnut, Pine, Red Flame Painting, 4 Drawers, 44 x 20 x 35 In. 1035.00
Chest, Walnut, Rosewood, Carved Heads, Fruits, 38 1/2 x 46 1/2 x 22 1/2 In. 3450.00
Chest, Walnut, String & Bellflower Inlay, 4 Dovetailed Drawers, 38 x 34 x 18 In. 2200.00
Chest, William & Mary Style, 4 Drawers, Bun Feet, 25 1/2 x 13 x 21 In. 460.00
Chest, William & Mary Style, Burl Walnut, 5 Drawers, c.1850, 36 1/4 x 40 1/2 In. 2875.00
Chest, William & Mary Style, Burl Walnut, Inlaid, 5 Drawers, c.1890, 40 x 39 In. 2300.00
Chest, William & Mary Style, Olive Wood, Oyster Veneer, 5 Drawers, 37 1/2 x 39 In. ... 3680.00

Chest, William & Mary Style, Walnut, Sunburst Inlay, 5 Drawers, 37 x 38 x 21 In. 2185.00
Chest, William & Mary, Oak, c.1700, 39 1/2 x 44 1/2 x 22 In. 1610.00
Chest, William & Mary, Walnut, 5 Drawers, Bun Feet, 1700s, 39 x 34 1/2 In. 2875.00
Chest, William IV Style, Mahogany, Canted Top, Turned Legs, 22 x 20 x 13 1/2 In. 1060.00
Chest, William IV, Satinwood, 3 Drawers, Molded Top, c.1835, 10 1/2 x 12 x 9 In. 1265.00
Chest, William IV, Walnut, 4 Drawers, Columns, Plinth Base, c.1840, 38 x 51 x 25 In. ... 980.00
Chest, Wormley, Drawer, 2 Doors, Brass Ring Pulls, 25 x 32 x 15 In. 1985.00
Chest, Wormley, Mahogany, 2 Over 3 Drawers, Recessed Pulls, 32 x 41 1/2 x 18 In. 920.00
Chest, Wormley, Mahogany, 7 Drawers, Recessed Pulls, Dunbar, 34 x 20 x 53 In. 1380.00
Chest, Wormley, Mahogany, Leather-Wrapped Plinth Base, 32 x 41 x 18 In. 1150.00
Chest-On-Chest, Chippendale Style, Mahogany, American, c.1850, 60 x 42 1/2 In. 1000.00
Chest-On-Chest, Chippendale, Tiger Maple, 9 Drawers, Bracket Feet, 75 x 38 x 19 In. ... 24675.00
Chest-On-Chest, George II Style, 9 Drawers, Pullout Slide, c.1900, 69 x 33 In. 3680.00
Chest-On-Chest, George II Style, Walnut, 9 Drawers, 74 1/2 x 44 1/2 x 22 1/2 In. 2645.00
Chest-On-Chest, George III, Mahogany, 2 Short Over 6 Long Drawers, 76 x 44 In. 4370.00
Chest-On-Chest, George III, Mahogany, 8 Drawers, c.1765, 72 x 41 x 21 In. 2350.00
Chest-On-Chest, George III, Mahogany, Pine, 8 Drawers, 69 x 43 In. 7015.00
Chest-On-Chest, Nutting, Chippendale Style, Mahogany, 7 Drawers, 63 x 38 In. 7590.00
Chest-On-Chest, Shaker, Cherry, Tiger Maple, 2 Over 4 Drawers, 52 x 38 In. 5580.00
Chest-On-Frame, G. Nelson, Walnut, Birch, Ebonized Legs, Herman Miller, c.1950 ..... 805.00
Chest-On-Frame, George III, Mahogany, 71 x 42 x 21 In. 2990.00
Chest-On-Frame, Georgian, 8 Drawers, Cabriole Legs, 18th Century, 51 x 40 x 18 In. 2235.00
Chest-On-Frame, Hepplewhite, Mahogany, Veneer, Inlay, Pine, Oak, 43 x 20 x 76 In. 4140.00
Chest-On-Frame, Teak, Brass Mounted, Zanzibar, 1800s, 25 1/2 x 46 x 19 1/2 In. 415.00
Chest-On-Stand, Federal, Walnut, Inlaid, Late 18th Century, 46 x 43 x 21 In. 690.00
Chiffonnier, Eastlake, Walnut, Marble Top, American, c.1880, 81 3/4 x 43 x 18 In. 650.00
Chiffonnier, Italian Neoclassical, Fruitwood, Inlaid, c.1810, 27 x 17 x 13 In. 440.00
Chiffonnier, Lifetime, No. 4000, Single-Panel Door, Drawer, Brass Pull, 60 x 24 In. 3175.00
Chiffonnier, Regency Style, Rosewood, Brass, Fabric Door Panels, c.1890, 47 x 41 In. 2300.00
Clothespress, Mahogany, England, c.1890, 76 x 77 1/2 x 24 In. 1265.00
Clothespress, Neoclassical, Mahogany, Carved, Cornice, c.1820, 92 x 52 x 23 In. 11950.00
Clothespress, Red Lacquer, Gold Decoration, Chinese, 52 x 24 x 69 In. 1375.00
Coat Rack, Bruce Tippet, Renna, White Paint, Gavina, Italy, 1970s 4200.00
Coat Rack, Carved, Ram, Leaves, Ibex, Glass Eyes, 3 Hooks, Swiss, c.1910, 10 x 19 In. . 605.00
Coat Rack, Hat, Walnut, Horn & Brass Hooks, 1934, 11 x 51 In. 1495.00
Coat Rack, Mahogany, Turned Column Post, 4 Legs, Brass Hooks, 67 x 22 In. 150.00
Coffer, Charles I, Cedar, Paneled Sides, Columns, Lift Top, 31 x 64 x 22 In. 2800.00
Coffer, Mahogany, Early 19th Century, 21 x 21 x 13 1/2 In. 690.00
Coffer, Mahogany, Leaf Carvings, Paw Feet, Flemish, c.1850, 25 1/2 x 60 In. 1840.00
Coffer, Oak, Arched Lid, Iron Strapwork, England, Late 18th Century, 28 x 51 x 24 In. 1725.00
Coffer, Oak, Star & Geometric Inlay, Iron Handles, England, 1800s, 28 x 61 x 26 In. 1955.00
Coffer, Victorian, Mahogany, Rectangular, Leather Lining, Pen Tray, 1845, 13 In. 630.00
Coffer, William IV Style, Leather Upholstered, Lift Top, c.1900, 19 x 52 x 22 In. 3910.00
Commode, Biedermeier, Birch, 3 Drawers, Corner Columns, c.1815, 31 1/2 x 38 In. 2300.00
Commode, Biedermeier, Blond Wood, 3 Drawers, 32 x 40 x 20 In. 4140.00
Commode, Biedermeier, Flame Mahogany, 3 Graduated Drawers, 37 x 25 x 54 In. 4020.00
Commode, Biedermeier, Maple, Marble Top, 4 Drawers, c.1910, 34 x 51 In. 1610.00
Commode, Biedermeier, Satinwood, Walnut, Marquetry, c.1840, 37 x 49 x 25 In. 1610.00
Commode, Bombe, Louis XV Style, King & Tulipwood, P. Bernard, c.1750, 36 x 42 In. ... 9200.00
Commode, Burl Walnut, Kettle Form, 3 Drawers, Continental, c.1840, 33 x 33 x 22 In. ... 4830.00
Commode, Charles X, Mahogany, Marble Top, 4 Drawers, c.1835, 38 x 51 x 22 1/2 In. ... 1265.00
Commode, Charles X, Walnut, Marble Top, 4 Drawers, c.1850, 38 1/2 x 50 1/2 In. 1725.00
Commode, Edwardian, Satinwood, Painted, Red Marble Top, Demilune, 36 In. 1430.00
Commode, French Empire, 4 Drawers, Marble Top, Ormolu, 36 x 48 1/2 In. 3280.00
Commode, French Provincial, Painted, Bracket Feet, 33 x 42 x 19 In. 200.00
Commode, French Provincial, Walnut, 3 Drawers, Late 1700s, 37 x 52 x 26 In. 7475.00
Commode, Fruitwood, Inlaid Mulberry, Serpentine Front, Panels, 45 In. 4370.00
Commode, Fruitwood, Mahogany, 3 Drawers, Italy, Late 1700s, 36 x 49 x 24 In. 5060.00
Commode, George III Style, Mahogany, Drop Front, Late 1800s, 27 x 12 x 22 In. 920.00
Commode, George III Style, Mahogany, Lift Top, 32 1/2 x 19 1/2 x 17 1/2 In. 520.00
Commode, George III Style, Satinwood, Mahogany, Demilune, c.1920, 33 x 45 In. 2875.00
Commode, George III, Mahogany, Lift Top, Bracket Feet, 29 x 24 x 15 1/4 In. 690.00
Commode, George III, Oak, Hinged Lid, c.1790, 17 3/4 x 21 1/2 x 17 1/2 In. 259.00

Commode, Italian Neoclassical, Painted, Scarlet Ground, c.1800, 39 x 54 x 24 In. 4600.00
Commode, Italian, Walnut, 2 Drawers, Candle Drawer, Carved, 43 x 62 x 22 In. 5290.00
Commode, Louis Philippe Style, Burl Walnut, Late 1800s, 31 x 30 1/2 x 18 In. 1150.00
Commode, Louis Philippe, Burl Walnut, Marble Top, Mid 1800s, 37 x 42 x 22 In. 1610.00
Commode, Louis Philippe, Kingwood, Mahogany, 3 Drawers, c.1835, 28 x 19 x 14 In. 1840.00
Commode, Louis Philippe, Mahogany, Marble Top, 5 Drawers, 38 x 48 x 21 1/2 In. 1610.00
Commode, Louis Philippe, Walnut, 2 Drawers, Bracket Feet, c.1840, 39 x 45 x 21 In. 630.00
Commode, Louis Philippe, Walnut, Marble Top, 4 Drawers, 39 x 51 x 24 In. 2760.00
Commode, Louis Philippe, Walnut, Marble Top, 5 Drawers, c.1850, 42 x 49 In. 1265.00
Commode, Louis XV Style, 2 Drawers, Serpentine Front, Austria, 1700s, 28 x 23 In. 1495.00
Commode, Louis XV Style, Bombe, Black Lacquer, Marble Top, c.1890, 34 x 45 In. 4600.00
Commode, Louis XV Style, Bombe, Parquetry, Marble Top, 34 x 46 In., Pair 3000.00
Commode, Louis XV Style, Bow Top, 2 Drawers, Late 1800s, 12 x 17 x 9 In. 1840.00
Commode, Louis XV Style, Chinoiserie, Ebonized, 4 Drawers, 34 x 45 x 20 In. 1380.00
Commode, Louis XV Style, Mahogany, Marquetry, Marble Top, 32 x 32 1/2 In. 540.00
Commode, Louis XV Style, Mahogany, Parquetry, Marble Top, 3 Drawers, 33 x 51 In. 2300.00
Commode, Louis XV Style, Parquetry, 1800s, 32 x 21 In., Pair 1725.00
Commode, Louis XV, Elm, Serpentine Bombe, 38 x 5 1/2 x 31 In. 9775.00
Commode, Louis XV, Kingwood, Tulipwood, Marble Top, 4 Drawers, 36 x 44 x 33 In. .. 1765.00
Commode, Louis XV, Oak, 4 Drawers, Bowed, c.1750, 33 1/2 x 46 x 24 In. 5060.00
Commode, Louis XV, Walnut, 4 Drawers, Scalloped Apron, 31 x 49 1/2 In. 3165.00
Commode, Louis XVI Style, Cupid, Gilt Metal Mount, 30 x 16 x 13 1/2 In., Pair 1035.00
Commode, Louis XVI Style, Mahogany, D-Shape Top, 4 Drawers 2185.00
Commode, Louis XVI Style, Mahogany, Early 1900s, 43 1/2 x 36 x 20 In. 805.00
Commode, Louis XVI Style, Mahogany, Marble Top, 3 Drawers, 34 1/2 x 19 1/2 In. ... 4250.00
Commode, Louis XVI Style, Tulipwood, Gilt Bronze, Marble Top, 36 x 51 x 21 In. 4700.00
Commode, Louis XVI Style, Walnut, Marble Top, 2 Doors, 41 1/2 x 52 x 21 In. 2300.00
Commode, Louis XVI, Plum Pudding Mahogany, Marble Top, 33 x 49 x 22 In. 1265.00
Commode, Louis XVI, Walnut, 3 Drawers, Early 1800s, 32 x 43 1/2 In. 3175.00
Commode, Mahogany, Mirror In Top, Stencil Decoration, 2 Doors, 33 x 36 x 22 In. 1725.00
Commode, Neoclassical, Birch, Kingwood, 3 Drawers, Sweden, c.1825, 34 x 42 x 19 In. .. 4830.00
Commode, Neoclassical, Burled Walnut, Mahogany Inlay, 3 Drawers, c.1840 .... 5900.00
Commode, Neoclassical, Fruitwood, 3 Drawers, c.1835, 36 x 25 x 17 1/2 In. 1725.00
Commode, Neoclassical, Fruitwood, Inlaid Walnut, 2 Drawer, c.1800, 32 x 46 x 22 In. .. 7050.00
Commode, Neoclassical, Mahogany, Gilt, 4 Drawers, Russia, c.1825, 41 x 41 x 19 In. ... 5520.00
Commode, Neoclassical, Tambour Doors, Dutch, Early 1900s, 32 x 31 In. 750.00
Commode, Neoclassical, Walnut, 3 Drawers, c.1800, Italy, 32 x 52 x 23 In. 1955.00
Commode, Neoclassical, Walnut, Polychrome, 4 Drawers, 2 Doors, Italy, 41 x 82 In. 3165.00
Commode, Pine, Carved, 2 Drawers, Canada, 1700s, 27 1/2 x 38 x 22 In. 5500.00
Commode, Pine, Red Paint, Lift Top, 2-Door Base, 32 x 28 x 17 1/2 In. 200.00
Commode, Regency Style, Mahogany, Marble, 3 Drawers, Late 1800s, 36 x 45 x 23 In. .. 920.00
Commode, Regency, Tulipwood, Amaranth Parquetry, Marble Top, 33 x 47 x 24 In. 2950.00
Commode, Renaissance Revival, Walnut, Marble Top, Drawer, c.1865, 27 1/2 x 19 In. ... 750.00
Commode, Renaissance Revival, Walnut, Marble Top, Drawer, c.1870, 33 x 22 In. 920.00
Commode, Renaissance Style, French Oak, Late 18th Century, 70 x 38 x 19 In. 1265.00
Commode, Restauration, Pine, 4 Drawers, Block Feet, c.1850, 38 x 49 x 21 1/4 In. 1265.00
Commode, Restauration, Walnut, Marble Top, 4 Drawers, c.1850, 38 x 50 1/2 In. 2530.00
Commode, Rococo, Rosewood, Marble, Drawer, American, c.1850, 32 x 20 In., Pair 7200.00
Commode, Rococo, Serpentine Front, 4 Inlaid Drawers, Italy, 43 x 60 x 24 In. 7765.00
Commode, Rococo, Walnut, Serpentine Front, Continental, Late 1700s, 38 1/2 x 54 In. 3220.00
Commode, Venetian Style, Bombe, Polychromed, Marble, 2 Drawers, 34 1/2 x 58 In. 980.00
Commode, Venetian, Painted, Serpentine Top, Drawers, 1800s, 30 x 27 x 14 In. 2760.00
Commode, Victorian, Walnut, Carved, Marble, Mirror, 2 Drawers, 2 Doors, 36 x 74 In. .. 800.00
Commode, Walnut, Geometric Inlay, 3 Drawers, Germany, Late 1700s, 16 x 20 In. 1610.00
Commode, Walnut, Marble Top, 3 Drawers, Continental, Late 1700s, 32 x 20 x 14 In. ... 6325.00
Commode, Walnut, Scrolled, Carved, Drawers, Cabriole Legs, France, 34 x 39 x 21 In. .. 7700.00
Cradle, Blue Gray, Red Paint, 18 1/2 x 31 In. 205.00
Cradle, Cherry, Poplar, Black Paint, Hooded, Dovetailed, Handles, 23 x 42 In. 290.00
Cradle, French Provincial, Fruitwood, Arched Headboard, c.1850, 16 x 34 In. 460.00
Cradle, Hand Painted, Strap Holes, Norway, 28 In. 45.00
Cradle, Hooded, Grain Painted Frame, Sunken Rosewood Grained Panels 169.00
Cradle, Hooded, Grain Painted, Blue, Black & Red Exterior, 25 x 37 x 23 In. 150.00
Cradle, Pine, France, c.1900, 42 In. 275.00

Cradle, Pine, Hooded, Dovetailed, Hand-Cut Nails, 19th Century, 29 1/2 x 40 x 23 In. 140.00
Cradle, Pine, Hooded, Gray Paint, Pa., Early 19th Century, 28 x 37 1/2 In. 300.00
Cradle, Renaissance Revival, Walnut, Burl, Carved, c.1875, 41 x 42 x 27 In. 1035.00
Cradle, Victorian, Wrought Iron, Basket Shape, Twist Supports, 1800s, 36 x 39 x 24 In. .. 1150.00
Credenza, Aesthetic Revival, Cherry, Lacquer, Gold Trim, Drawer, 2 Doors, 38 In. 800.00
Credenza, Arne Vodder, Rosewood, Enameled, Denmark, 1960s, 72 x 30 In. 3510.00
Credenza, Burl Walnut, Inlaid, Glass Doors, 44 x 72 x 15 In. 2420.00
Credenza, Central Door, Inlaid Star, Drawers, Continental, 1700s, 33 x 30 x 13 In. 4620.00
Credenza, Dyrlund, Teak, 4 Drawers, 2 Doors, Denmark, c.1960, 35 x 83 x 18 In. 940.00
Credenza, Florence Knoll, Rosewood, Bronze Base, 4 Drawers, 2 Doors, 75 In. 2585.00
Credenza, French Empire, Black Lacquer, Gilt Bronze Inlay, Marble, c.1850, 55 x 45 In. .. 2300.00
Credenza, G. Nelson, EOG, Walnut, Steel, Herman Miller, 1971, 74 x 19 x 26 In. 820.00
Credenza, G. Nelson, Thin Edge, Walnut Veneer, 2 Doors, Aluminum Legs, 33 x 67 In. ... 4315.00
Credenza, G. Nelson, Walnut, 5 Drawers, Locking Doors, Herman Miller, 80 x 30 In. 2300.00
Credenza, Mahogany Veneer, Chrome Frame, Marble Top, 2 Cabinets, 26 x 76 x 21 In. .. 1380.00
Credenza, McCobb, Planner Group, 2 Doors, 4 Drawers, 33 x 6 x 18 1/4 In. 690.00
Credenza, Victorian, Mahogany, Satinwood Inlay, Marble Top, 35 x 59 x 17 1/2 In. 1675.00
Credenza, W. Sklaroff, Rosewood, Fiberglass, c.1972, 29 x 73 x 20 In. 1840.00
Credenza, Walnut, Inlaid, Demilune Top, 2 Curved Glazed Doors, Plinth Base, 60 In. 3146.00
Crib, Flame Birch, Turned Legs, Casters, New England, c.1820 .... 1100.00
Crib, Pine, Rockers In Long Direction, Heart Cutouts, Dovetailed, 20 x 33 x 15 In. 850.00
Cricket, Wooden, Red Paint, 19th Century, 6 1/2 x 12 x 7 1/2 In. 69.00
Cupboard, Ash, 4 Doors, Glass In Upper Doors, 42 x 80 In. 365.00
Cupboard, Bamboo, Leather, Glazed Door, Anglo-Indian, c.1885, 36 x 21 x 14 1/2 In. ... 635.00
Cupboard, Biedermeier, Walnut, Marble Top, Pedestal, Fluted Sides, 30 x 16 In. 1530.00
Cupboard, Bittersweet Paint, 2-Compartment Bin, 2 Doors, c.1880, 35 x 67 In. 1650.00
Cupboard, Blue Over Red Paint, Step Back, Open, New England, c.1780 .... 4200.00
Cupboard, Bucket, Pine, Red Paint, 38 x 61 In. 440.00
Cupboard, Burl, Cornice, Scalloped Crest, 18th Century, 86 x 51 x 20 1/2 In. 2530.00
Cupboard, Cherry, 3 Shelves, Door, Flatware Notches, c.1850, 77 1/4 x 36 1/2 In. 840.00
Cupboard, Cherry, 6-Pane Doors, Lancaster Co., Pa., 85 x 55 x 21 In. 6865.00
Cupboard, Cherry, Poplar, Door, 3 Shelves, Mortise, Tenon, c.1840, 58 1/2 x 28 In. 5465.00
Cupboard, Cherry, Walnut, Red Over Orange Vinegar Graining, 35 x 11 1/2 x 51 In. 8050.00
Cupboard, Chip Carved, Door, 2 Drawers, 2 Shelves, England, c.1800, 13 1/2 x 11 In. 575.00
Cupboard, Chippendale, Cherry, Step Back, 2 Sections, c.1780, 86 x 59 x 20 In. 5740.00
Cupboard, Corner, Amish, Red, Green Paint, Blind Front, 4 Doors, Cornice Trim, 72 In. . 4900.00
Cupboard, Corner, Biedermeier, Fruitwood, Glass Door, c.1820, 80 x 35 x 19 In. 2470.00
Cupboard, Corner, Blue Paint, Dentil Molding, Maryland 22000.00
Cupboard, Corner, Butternut, Inlay, Inset Panels, Western Pa., 1815-1820 ....11500.00
Cupboard, Corner, Butternut, Pine, Green Paint, 4 Doors, 1830, 48 1/2 In. 2990.00
Cupboard, Corner, Butternut, Pine, Spruce, 2 Over 2 Doors, c.1845, 48 1/2 x 20 x 72 In. . 2990.00
Cupboard, Corner, Cherry Glaze, Double Doors, 16 Panels, c.1850, 54 x 86 1/2 In. 2070.00
Cupboard, Corner, Cherry, 4-Pane Doors, 3 Drawers, Scalloped Skirt, 84 x 57 x 22 In. ... 2310.00
Cupboard, Corner, Chestnut, Black Paint, 4 Doors, Rhode Island, 76 x 39 In. 575.00
Cupboard, Corner, Chippendale, Walnut, 3 Doors, Pennsylvania, 85 x 41 In. 4025.00
Cupboard, Corner, Federal, Pine, 2 Upper Windowed Doors, Shelves, 100 x 65 x 31 In. .. 9200.00
Cupboard, Corner, Federal, Tiger Maple, 2-Part Blank Door, 96 x 53 x 27 In. 13200.00
Cupboard, Corner, Flame Mahogany, Pine, Grain Painted, 80 1/2 x 45 1/2 x 22 1/2 In. ... 1725.00
Cupboard, Corner, Grain Painted, 12 Panes, 2 Parts, American, 90 x 41 x 25 In. 4600.00
Cupboard, Corner, Grain Painted, Drop Front Desk, 4 Panes, 51 x 94 In. 1155.00
Cupboard, Corner, Hepplewhite, Walnut, Glass Panes, American, 78 1/4 x 44 In. 6960.00
Cupboard, Corner, Mahogany, Broken Arch, Leaf Carved, Claw & Ball Feet, 82 x 31 In. . 2938.00
Cupboard, Corner, Mahogany, Fluted Frieze, Frame, Panel Doors, 88 x 27 x 20 In. 6160.00
Cupboard, Corner, Pine, Molded Cornice, American, 75 1/2 x 38 In. 520.00
Cupboard, Corner, Pine, Paneled Lower Door, 9-Pane Upper Door, 82 In. 690.00
Cupboard, Corner, Pine, Poplar, Arched Door, c.1800, 47 x 23 x 92 1/2 In. 7800.00
Cupboard, Corner, Pine, Poplar, Red Wash, 4 Doors, c.1850, 43 3/4 x 21 x 85 1/2 In. 2875.00
Cupboard, Corner, Pine, Poplar, Red Wash, Double Blind Doors, 1840, 85 In. 2875.00
Cupboard, Corner, Pine, Porcelain Pulls, Norway, Late 1800s, 35 x 22 x 13 In. 1760.00
Cupboard, Corner, Pine, Red Wash, 3 Doors, Drawer, Pennsylvania, 81 In. 1725.00
Cupboard, Corner, Pine, Scalloped Sections, 2-Paneled Doors, 75 x 43 x 23 In. 520.00
Cupboard, Corner, Pine, Stained, 2 Sections, Mid 19th Century, 82 1/4 x 45 x 26 In. 2530.00
Cupboard, Corner, Red Paint, 2 Glass Doors Over 4 Drawers Over 2 Doors, 84 In. 3625.00

Cupboard, Corner, Softwood, 2 Sections, 6-Pane Doors, Feathered Grain, 85 In. 4050.00
Cupboard, Corner, Softwood, 2 Sections, 12-Pane Door, Columns, Ogee Feet, 81 In. 2700.00
Cupboard, Corner, Softwood, Feather Grain Painted Decoration, 80 x 50 x 25 1/2 In. 6050.00
Cupboard, Corner, Softwood, Green, Door, Interior Shelves, Tabletop, 30 x 25 In. 450.00
Cupboard, Corner, Walnut, 3 Sections, Scalloped Cornice, 2 6-Pane Doors, 83 In. 1575.00
Cupboard, Corner, Walnut, Dental Cornice, 2 Doors, 6 Panes, 2 Sections, 88 1/2 In. 15200.00
Cupboard, Corner, Walnut, Paint Decoration, Scandinavia, c.1825, 72 x 101 In. 1645.00
Cupboard, Corner, Walnut, Poplar, 2-Paneled Doors, Bracket Feet, 55 x 21 x 82 In. 3520.00
Cupboard, Corner, Walnut, Poplar, 4-Paneled Doors, 48 x 18 1/2 x 82 1/2 In. 2185.00
Cupboard, Cypress, Painted, Paneled Doors, 66 x 37 1/2 x 20 1/2 In. 1150.00
Cupboard, Dunbar, Wood Veneer, Steel Pulls, Shelves, 20 x 80 x 18 In. 1495.00
Cupboard, Edwardian, Mahogany, Inlaid, Glazed Door, c.1900, 36 x 30 x 11 In. 375.00
Cupboard, Elizabethan Style, Oak, Carved, Inlaid, England, c.1890, 71 x 76 x 20 In. 2530.00
Cupboard, Elm, 5 Doors, 3 Drawers, England, c.1850, 92 x 67 x 21 1/2 In. 2645.00
Cupboard, George III, Mahogany, 4 Doors, c.1885, 95 1/2 x 49 1/2 x 24 1/2 In. 1150.00
Cupboard, Green Paint, 2 Doors, Backsplash, Ohio, 1876, 45 x 31 1/2 x 19 In. 3700.00
Cupboard, Hanging, Corner, 2-Paneled Door, 36 x 25 In. 795.00
Cupboard, Hanging, Corner, Cherry, Poplar, Carved, Iron Latch, 26 1/2 x 30 3/4 x 18 In. . .   1380.00
Cupboard, Hanging, Corner, Chippendale Style, Walnut, Paneled Door, Shelves, 31 In. . .   170.00
Cupboard, Hanging, Corner, George III, Japanned, Bowfront, Painted, 49 x 26 x 18 In. . . .   1495.00
Cupboard, Hanging, Corner, Mahogany, Oak, Bowfront, 25 x 18 x 41 1/2 In. 345.00
Cupboard, Hanging, Corner, Softwood, Blind Door, Painted, 1800s, 28 x 27 x 15 In. 468.00
Cupboard, Hanging, Grain Painted, 3 Shelves, 2 Doors, 33 x 28 In. 220.00
Cupboard, Hanging, Oak, Green Paint, Paneled Door, 2 Interior Shelves, 40 x 25 In. 290.00
Cupboard, Hanging, Pine, Blue Paint, 2 Arched Doors, Switzerland, 44 In. 3800.00
Cupboard, Hanging, Pine, Mortised Construction, 21 x 26 In. 115.00
Cupboard, Hanging, Pine, Poplar, Door, 4 Glass Panes, 2 Shelves, 32 x 11 x 36 In. 750.00
Cupboard, Hanging, Pine, Poplar, Dovetailed, 3 Shelves, 16 x 22 In. 520.00
Cupboard, Hanging, Queen Anne, Walnut, Stepped Cornice, Shelf, Door, 30 x 37 x 9 In. . .   5625.00
Cupboard, Hanging, Walnut, Raised Panel Door, 2 Shelves, 14 1/2 x 9 1/2 x 23 In. 1265.00
Cupboard, Hooded, 3 Open Shelves, Vermont, 1780-1800 . . . .   13500.00
Cupboard, Jelly, 2-Paneled Door, Scalloped Base, 3 Interior Shelves, 45 x 48 In. 800.00
Cupboard, Jelly, Alligatored Red Paint, 2 Drawers Over 2 Doors 975.00
Cupboard, Jelly, Pine, Drawer, 2 Doors, American, 55 x 45 x 16 1/2 In. 520.00
Cupboard, Jelly, Pine, Green Paint, Beaded Boards, 4 Interior Shelves, 53 x 42 In. 520.00
Cupboard, Jelly, Softwood, 2 Drawers, 2 Sunken-Panel Doors, Stippling 900.00
Cupboard, Jelly, Softwood, Backsplash, 2 Drawers, Sunken-Panel Doors, Shaped Feet . . .   310.00
Cupboard, Jelly, Softwood, Shaped Backsplash, 2 Drawers Over 2 Sunken-Panel Doors . .   340.00
Cupboard, Jelly, Walnut, Pine, Arched Cutouts, Door, Brass, 43 x 16 x 49 1/2 In. 990.00
Cupboard, Jelly, Yellow Pine, Scalloped Gallery, 4 Drawers, c.1840 . . . .   3495.00
Cupboard, Louis Philippe Style, Elm, 35 x 28 1/2 x 19 1/2 In., Pair 1265.00
Cupboard, Louis XV Style, Fruitwood, c.1900, 106 x 62 1/2 x 23 1/2 In. 2760.00
Cupboard, Milk, Bittersweet Paint, Screened Paneled Door, 72 In. 550.00
Cupboard, Milk, Softwood, Door, Shelves, Cutout Half-Moon Ends, 38 x 54 x 19 In. 255.00
Cupboard, Milk, Softwood, Painted, 2 Doors, Sunken Panels, Ball Feet, 42 x 56 x 20 In. .   620.00
Cupboard, Mixed Wood, 2-Part Blind Door, Step Back, Bracket Feet, 75 x 40 x 27 In. . . .   3850.00
Cupboard, Mustard Paint, Feather Grained, 2 Doors, American, 78 x 53 In. 1495.00
Cupboard, Mustard Paint, Step Back, Cubbyholes, Boone, Mo., c.1870, 48 x 92 In. 1100.00
Cupboard, Oak, Ash, 3 Tiers, Open Plate Rack, Sled Runner Feet, 56 x 26 x 12 In. 110.00
Cupboard, Oak, Carved, 2 Doors, Drinking Scenes, Green Man Frieze, 61 x 52 x 24 In. . .   440.00
Cupboard, Painted, Leaves & Scrolls, Bracket Feet, Italy, 1700s, 41 x 84 In. . . . . *Illus*   8915.00
Cupboard, Paneled Doors, Figures & Flowers, Chinese, 18th Century, 64 x 24 x 63 In. . . .   8500.00
Cupboard, Pine, 2 Shelves, Hudson Valley, 60 1/4 x 47 1/2 x 18 1/4 In. 375.00
Cupboard, Pine, 2-Paneled Doors, Drawer, Molded Cornice, 81 x 55 x 20 In. 890.00
Cupboard, Pine, 4 Glazed Doors Over 4 Drawers, Bracket Feet, 76 In. 230.00
Cupboard, Pine, Bittersweet Paint, Step Back, Open Top, Door, Child's, 19 x 43 In. 290.00
Cupboard, Pine, Blue Paint, Step Back, Open Front, Square Nails, 46 x 80 In. 325.00
Cupboard, Pine, Brown Paint, Door, Dovetailed Corners, 38 x 28 In. 110.00
Cupboard, Pine, Closed Face, 4 Beveled Doors, 91 x 55 1/2 x 21 1/2 In. 315.00
Cupboard, Pine, Cornice, 2 Shelves, Plate Rim, Openwork, 74 x 61 x 18 In. 605.00
Cupboard, Pine, Drawer, 29 1/2 x 15 1/2 x 75 In. 1695.00
Cupboard, Pine, Flour & Spice Boxes, 1880s, 32 x 61 In. 715.00
Cupboard, Pine, Grain Painted, Step Back, 2 Parts, c.1890, 50 x 18 x 75 In. 2850.00

Cupboard, Pine, Maple, Poplar, Painted, Preserve Rack, Open Shelves, Rails, 63 x 37 In. . . 3600.00
Cupboard, Pine, Mustard Paint, Flaring Cornice, 3 Shelves, 1830, 77 In. 4700.00
Cupboard, Pine, Open Top, 2 Door Base, Shaped Bottom Apron, 72 x 31 x 15 In. 1980.00
Cupboard, Pine, Open Top, Pegged Door Base, 2 Panels, 66 x 48 x 19 In. 1925.00
Cupboard, Pine, Oxblood, Open Top, 2 Doors, 70 x 42 In. 990.00
Cupboard, Pine, Painted, Step Back, 78 In. . . . . *Illus* 6900.00
Cupboard, Pine, Painted, Step Back, Panel & Diamond Doors, 65 x 32 x 22 In. 315.00
Cupboard, Pine, Paneled, Recessed Doors, 2 Shelves Top, 1 Shelf Down, 1830, 77 In. 4700.00
Cupboard, Pine, Plank Door, Drawer, Continental, c.1875, 68 1/2 x 48 x 21 In. 550.00
Cupboard, Pine, Poplar, Step Back, Arched Pie Shelf, 2 Parts, 61 x 21 x 83 In. 2300.00
Cupboard, Pine, Raised Panels, Forged Hardware, Scandinavia, 66 x 48 x 19 In. 1960.00
Cupboard, Pine, Stained, 3 Shelves, American, Miniature, 17 1/2 x 11 In. 175.00
Cupboard, Pine, Step Back, 2 Doors Over Door, Pie Shelf, Scalloped, 81 x 28 In. 1925.00
Cupboard, Pine, Step Back, 2 Parts, 19th Century, 82 x 35 x 18 1/2 In. 375.00
Cupboard, Pine, Step Back, 2 Parts, Plate Bar, Spoon Notches, 82 x 81 x 17 In. 7635.00
Cupboard, Pine, Step Back, Hand-Wrought Hinges, Square Nails, 77 x 36 In. 550.00
Cupboard, Pine, Step Back, Open Top, 2 Doors, Shaped Apron, 72 x 31 x 15 In. 2015.00
Cupboard, Pine, Step Back, Plank Doors, 3 Shelves, 81 x 45 x 23 In. 2090.00
Cupboard, Pine, Straight Front, 3 Doors Over 3 Drawers, 6 Panes, 61 x 86 In. 940.00
Cupboard, Pine, White Over Green Over Blue Over Red Wash, Step Back, 44 x 19 In. . . . 6900.00
Cupboard, Poplar, Red Paint, 2 Sections, Bracket Feet, 49 x 20 1/2 x 83 In. 10065.00
Cupboard, Red Paint, 2 Glass Doors, 2 Inner Shelves, Dovetailed, 36 1/2 x 38 x 12 In. . . . 750.00
Cupboard, Red Paint, Mustard, Step Back, Wainscoted Back, c.1880, 53 x 88 In. 4400.00
Cupboard, Red Paint, Scalloped Cant Back Sides, Open Top, 18th Century 14500.00
Cupboard, Regency, Mahogany, Circular, Marble Top, c.1815, 27 1/2 x 15 In. 400.00
Cupboard, Regency, Mahogany, Leather Top, c.1810, 44 x 22 In., Pair 1955.00
Cupboard, Shaker, Cherry, Hanging, 2 Doors, 3 Shelves, Enfield, 24 x 9 x 31 1/2 In. 1280.00
Cupboard, Shaker, Hanging, Pine, Butternut, Watervliet, N.Y., c.1870, 30 x 16 In. 3740.00
Cupboard, Shaker, Hanging, Pine, Dovetailed, Steel Hangers, c.1850, 41 x 26 x 7 In. 4600.00
Cupboard, Shaker, Hanging, Pine, Raised Panel Door, c.1850, 26 3/4 x 22 In. 1495.00
Cupboard, Shaker, Pine, 2 Doors, 5 Drawers, New Lebanon, c.1840, 75 In. 5750.00
Cupboard, Shaker, Pine, 2 Doors, Cherry Knobs, 75 x 24 3/4 x 13 1/2 In. 4600.00
Cupboard, Shaker, Pine, Red Paint, 2 Parts, 3 Drawers, Harvard, Mass., 78 x 39 x 19 In. . 1035.00
Cupboard, Shaker, Pine, Red Wash, Panel Door, 4 Shelves, Harvard, Mass., 68 x 21 In. . . 5075.00
Cupboard, Shaker, Trustee's, Dovetailed, 16 Compartments, c.1850, 25 x 18 1/4 In. 2760.00
Cupboard, Softwood, 6-Pane Doors, 3 Drawers, Pennsylvania Dutch, 89 x 20 x 63 In. . . . 4950.00
Cupboard, Softwood, Blue Paint, 7 Drawers, Raised Panel Door, 58 x 35 In. 340.00
Cupboard, Softwood, Molded Cornice, Door, Raised Panels, Yellow, 70 x 34 x 13 In. 1575.00
Cupboard, Softwood, Open Top, 3 Shelves, Plate Rails, 39 x 66 In. 1915.00
Cupboard, Softwood, Painted, Paneled Doors, Cutout Feet, 23 x 39 1/4 x 13 1/2 In. 1760.00
Cupboard, Softwood, Shaped Gallery, Double Raised-Panel Doors, 51 x 24 In. 169.00
Cupboard, Softwood, Step Back, Stepped Cornice, Shelves, Panel Door, 75 x 35 x 18 In. . 2625.00
Cupboard, Step Back, 2 Drawers, 4 Doors, Glass Panes, c.1850, 77 1/4 x 43 3/4 In. 2760.00
Cupboard, Step Back, 2 Drawers, 4 Doors, Glass Panes, Pa., c.1850, 86 x 56 1/4 In. 1840.00
Cupboard, Step Back, 4 Raised-Panel Doors, Scrolled Skirt, 52 x 83 In. 1485.00
Cupboard, Sugar Pine, 12 Panes, 1820s 2150.00
Cupboard, Tiger Maple, Walnut, Step Back, 2 Parts, c.1830, 82 x 55 x 19 In. 10340.00
Cupboard, Victorian, Mahogany, Paneled Door, Shelves, Mid 1800s, 32 x 22 x 22 In. 1495.00

Furniture, Cupboard, Painted, Leaves & Scrolls, Bracket
Feet, Italy, 1700s, 41 x 84 In.

Furniture, Cupboard,
Pine, Painted, Step
Back, 78 In.

Cupboard, Walnut, 4 Doors, 2 Drawers, 2 Parts, Continental, 55 x 87 3/4 In. 600.00
Cupboard, Walnut, 4-Paneled Doors, 2 Drawers, 2 Parts, 56 x 17 1/2 x 84 1/2 In. 2475.00
Cupboard, Walnut, Burled Panels, 12 Panes, 2 Parts, Bracket Feet, 80 In. 4840.00
Cupboard, Walnut, Paneled Doors, Lap-Jointed Backsplash, c.1870, 25 x 56 x 16 In. 250.00
Cupboard, Walnut, Pennsylvania Dutch, Lancaster Co., 87 x 62 x 21 In. 14060.00
Cupboard, Walnut, Pine, Painted, Scrubbed Top, 2 Parts, 3 Drawers, 82 1/2 x 63 In. 2700.00
Cupboard, Walnut, Pinwheel, Star Tins, Bracket Feet, 2 Panel Doors, 51 x 18 x 82 In. 3850.00
Cupboard, Walnut, Step Back, 6-Paneled Doors, 2 Half Drawers, 86 x 43 x 18 In. 635.00
Cupboard, William IV, Mahogany, Mid 1800s, 31 x 19 1/2 x 23 1/2 In., Pair 1610.00
Cupboard, William IV, Mahogany, Mid 1800s, 35 x 19 x 22 1/2 In., Pair 2185.00
Cupboard, Yellow Pine, Poplar, Step Back, 2 Shelves, Plate Rack, 72 x 34 x 17 In. 1210.00
Cupboard, Yellow Pine, Step Back, 3 Shelves, Lower Plank Doors, 80 x 40 x 21 In. 770.00
Cupboard, Yew, Red Lacquer, Gold, Black Paint, Butterflies, 2 Doors, 51 x 34 In. 345.00
Cupboard, Zelkova, Sugi & Kiri Woods, Japan, Late 1800s, 37 x 67 1/2 In. 1175.00
Daybed, Brown Leather, Round Bolster, Tubular Steel Legs, Stendig, 17 x 78 x 36 In. 4110.00
Daybed, Charles X Style, Mahogany, Upholstered, c.1890, 35 x 41 x 86 In. 920.00
Daybed, Empire, Bird's-Eye Maple, American, c.1815, 26 1/2 x 77 1/2 x 36 In. 825.00
Daybed, Empire, Fruitwood, Gilt Bronze Mounted, Early 1800s, 42 x 42 x 76 In. 2070.00
Daybed, Florence Knoll, Charles Niedringhaus, Steel Frame, 29 x 82 x 41 In. 1725.00
Daybed, G. Nakashima, Walnut, Plank Support, Oval Legs, 10 1/2 x 30 x 74 1/4 In. 2875.00
Daybed, G. Nelson, Birch, Dowel Legs, Upholstered, Herman Miller, 75 x 33 x 25 In. 1150.00
Daybed, Louis Philippe, Mahogany, Scrolled Headboard, 33 x 61 In., c.1835 . . . .   1150.00
Daybed, Louis XV Style, Fruitwood, Upholstered, c.1900, 36 x 78 x 32 1/2 In. 1495.00
Daybed, Louis XVI Style, Beech, Padded, Reeded Frame, Late 1800s, 38 x 78 x 39 In. 1610.00
Daybed, Louis XVI Style, Cane, Polychrome, Early 1900s, 34 x 34 x 80 In. 920.00
Daybed, Mahogany, Scrolling Crest Rail Ends, France, c.1850, 45 x 43 In. 1610.00
Daybed, Mies Van Der Rohe, Rosewood, Leather, Steel, Knoll, 1960s, 77 x 39 x 24 In. . . .   5850.00
Daybed, Neoclassical Style, Mahogany, Cane, Padded Backrest, Late 1800s, 65 In. 235.00
Daybed, Victorian, Chestnut, Blanket Storage, 70 x 37 x 23 1/2 In. 850.00
Daybed, Walnut, Curved Crest Rails, Upholstered, France, c.1900, 37 x 77 In. 1150.00
Daybed, Wormley, Mahogany, Upholstered, 1957-1965, 85 x 30 x 28 In. 5560.00
Desk, Aalto, Birch, Double Pedestal, Artek, Finland, 1940s, 59 x 28 x 29 In. 2106.00
Desk, Adam Style, Mahogany, Inlaid, c.1900, 40 1/2 x 48 x 26 In.   1265.00
Desk, Art Deco, Maple, Black Top, 2 Sliding Glass Doors, 42 x 20 In. 169.00
Desk, Arts & Crafts, Drawer, Copper Hardware, Slatted Shelves, 42 x 28 x 29 In. 230.00
Desk, Arts & Crafts, Drawer, Early 1900s, 29 1/2 x 27 1/4 x 48 In. 410.00
Desk, Arts & Crafts, Drop Front, Oak, Early 1900s, 60 1/2 x 25 5/8 x 10 1/8 In. 410.00
Desk, Arts & Crafts, Oak, Central Drawer, Lift Top, Inkwell, 30 x 45 1/2 x 27 In. 250.00
Desk, Baroque, Mahogany, Ornate Carving, 31 x 54 x 30 In. 540.00
Desk, Baroque, Slant Front, Fruitwood, Flowers, Marquetry, Walnut, 43 x 40 x 21 In. 6756.00
Desk, Biedermeier, Walnut, Lift Top, Drawer, c.1850, 33 x 30 x 21 In. 1650.00
Desk, Blond Wood, Leather Cover, Frosted Glass, Herman Miller, 27 x 48 x 20 In. 460.00
Desk, Butler's, Federal, Mahogany, Figured Maple, c.1815, 50 1/2 x 45 1/2 x 23 In. 9775.00
Desk, Butler's, Federal, Satinwood, Rosewood, Mahogany, c.1805 x 41 x 41 x 20 In. 3220.00
Desk, Butler's, George III, Mahogany, c.1810, 40 x 43 x 20 In. 2000.00
Desk, Butler's, Hepplewhite, 2 Fold-Down Drawers, 41 x 21 x 42 In. 2815.00
Desk, Butler's, Mahogany, Cherry Top, Brass Pulls, c.1875, 47 1/2 x 63 x 23 In. 5200.00
Desk, Butler's, Mahogany, Fold-Out, c.1830, 38 x 36 1/2 x 18 In. 3680.00
Desk, Butler's, Mahogany, Inlaid, 4 Drawers, 43 1/2 x 46 x 20 1/2 In. 575.00
Desk, Butler's, Sheraton, Drop Front, Mahogany, 3 Drawers, 41 1/2 x 42 x 44 In. 635.00
Desk, Butler's, Sheraton, Drop Front, Mahogany, Philadelphia, 45 x 46 In. 3165.00
Desk, Butler's, Slant Front, Pullout Stays, 5 Drawers, Ohio, c.1830, 52 x 43 x 21 In. 2420.00
Desk, Butler's, Victorian, Mahogany, Siding Secretary Drawer, 43 x 45 x 22 In. 120.00
Desk, Campaign, Camphorwood, 2 Parts, 4 Drawers, Chinese, 45 x 43 x 19 In. 4025.00
Desk, Cherry, Poplar, Red Paint, Hinged Top, Drawer, c.1790 . . . .   1200.00
Desk, Chippendale Style, Slant Front, Burl Maple, New England, 1800s, 23 x 23 In. 8050.00
Desk, Chippendale, Block Slant Front, Mahogany, 4 Drawers, 42 x 40 x 21 In. 31070.00
Desk, Chippendale, Cherry, 3 Drawers, Ogee Bracket, 46 x 39 x 20 1/2 In. 430.00
Desk, Chippendale, Curly Maple, 4 Graduated Drawers 2070.00
Desk, Chippendale, Drop Front, Maple, Red Stain, Tiger Maple Interior, c.1780 . . . .   2645.00
Desk, Chippendale, Mahogany, Block Front, Hinged Lid, c.1800, 44 1/2 x 39 In. 3165.00
Desk, Chippendale, Mahogany, Oxbow, Mass., c.1780, 46 x 32 x 21 In. 5580.00
Desk, Chippendale, Slant Front, 4 Drawers, Claw & Ball Feet, Late 1700s, 39 1/2 In. 4994.00

Furniture, Desk, Chippendale,
Slant Front, Maple,
Dovetailed, Carved,
41 1/2 x 39 x 19 In.

Furniture, Desk, Davenport,
Victorian, Satinwood, Inlaid Burl
Walnut, 35 x 21 In.

Desk, Chippendale, Slant Front, Birch, 4 Graduated Drawers, 43 x 39 3/4 x 18 1/2 In. . . . 3165.00
Desk, Chippendale, Slant Front, Cherry, 4 Drawers, 38 1/2 x 36 x 18 1/2 In. 5980.00
Desk, Chippendale, Slant Front, Cherry, American, c.1800, 38 1/2 x 36 1/4 x 18 In. 1180.00
Desk, Chippendale, Slant Front, Cherry, Dovetailed, 4 Drawers, Conn., 42 x 44 x 20 In. . . 3450.00
Desk, Chippendale, Slant Front, Mahogany, 4 Drawers, 40 x 40 x 19 1/2 In. 1090.00
Desk, Chippendale, Slant Front, Mahogany, 4 Drawers, c.1870, 41 x 39 1/2 x 19 1/2 In. . . 2940.00
Desk, Chippendale, Slant Front, Mahogany, 4 Drawers, Dovetailed, 43 1/4 x 41 x 24 In. . . 3450.00
Desk, Chippendale, Slant Front, Mahogany, 10 Drawers, Pigeonholes, Mass., 43 x 41 In. . . 3525.00
Desk, Chippendale, Slant Front, Mahogany, Inlaid Heart, 8 Drawers, c.1780, 40 x 35 In. . . 2000.00
Desk, Chippendale, Slant Front, Mahogany, Oxbow, Massachusetts, 43 1/2 x 41 In. 10925.00
Desk, Chippendale, Slant Front, Mahogany, Oxbow, Mid 1700s, 44 x 42 x 23 In. 15525.00
Desk, Chippendale, Slant Front, Maple, 4 Drawers, New England, 42 1/4 x 39 In. 3740.00
Desk, Chippendale, Slant Front, Maple, 4 Graduated Drawers, Bracket Feet, 30 x 36 In. . . 2475.00
Desk, Chippendale, Slant Front, Maple, Dovetailed, Carved, 41 1/2 x 39 x 19 In. . . . *Illus* 3740.00
Desk, Chippendale, Slant Front, Pine, 2 Drawers, New England, 38 1/2 x 36 x 17 In. 575.00
Desk, Chippendale, Slant Front, Pine, 4 Drawers, c.1770, 21 1/2 x 18 x 11 In. 9560.00
Desk, Chippendale, Slant Front, Walnut, 4 Graduated Drawers, 33 x 38 In. 1350.00
Desk, Chippendale, Slant Front, Walnut, American, Child's, 25 1/4 x 23 3/4 In. 4600.00
Desk, Chippendale, Slant Front, Walnut, Maple, 4 Drawers, Dovetailed, 43 x 37 x 20 In. . 1840.00
Desk, Chippendale, Slant Front, Walnut, Prospect Door, Drawers, 1770, 43 x 40 x 22 In. . 2300.00
Desk, Chippendale, Walnut, Sliding Compartment, Dovetailed, Bracket Feet, 43 x 49 In. . 7910.00
Desk, Count Sakhnoffsky, 7 Drawers, 6 Angled, Double Pedestal, 30 x 49 1/2 x 24 In. 460.00
Desk, Curly Maple, 4 Drawers, Glass Pulls, Dovetailed, 42 x 21 x 58 In. 11000.00
Desk, Davenport, Burl Walnut, Hinged Writing Surface, c.1850, 37 x 22 In. 1175.00
Desk, Davenport, Rosewood, Bird's-Eye Maple, Marquetry, 21 x 21 x 35 In. 890.00
Desk, Davenport, Victorian, Satinwood, Inlaid Burl Walnut, 35 x 21 In. . . . . *Illus* 745.00
Desk, Directoire Style, Roll Top, Retractable Lid, Mahogany, Late 1800s, 49 x 54 In. 2300.00
Desk, Drop Front, Ash, Pigeonholes, c.1910, 26 x 40 In. 145.00
Desk, Drop Front, Carved Panels, c.1880, 60 1/2 x 33 x 11 3/4 In. 805.00
Desk, Drop Front, Softwood, Red Paint, Slotted Interior, 2 Drawers, 16 3/4 x 16 3/4 In. . . 1465.00
Desk, Edwardian, Mahogany, Crossbanded, 4 Drawers, Square Tapered Legs, 30 x 47 In. . 395.00
Desk, Edwardian, Satinwood, Inlaid Mahogany, Carlton House, 42 x 45 x 24 In. 1380.00
Desk, Egyptian Revival, Drop Front, Walnut, 3 Sections, 4 Drawers, 64 x 38 x 16 In. 460.00
Desk, Eliel Saarinen, 4 Drawers, Pedestal, Johnson Furniture, 30 x 48 x 27 3/4 In. 690.00
Desk, Elizabethan Revival, Mahogany, 2 Over 2 Drawers, Trestle Base 800.00
Desk, Elm, Chinese, c.1890, 34 3/4 x 39 3/4 x 24 1/2 In. 355.00
Desk, Empire Style, Mahogany, Pedestal, 31 x 62 1/2 In. 1500.00
Desk, Empire, Mahogany, 4-Drawer Back, Leather Top, 2 Drawers, c.1820, 35 x 37 In. . . 1840.00
Desk, Federal, Cherry, Mahogany Veneer, Joseph Morrill, Vermont, c.1826 . . . . 5580.00
Desk, Federal, Slant Front, Birch, Inlaid Walnut, New England, c.1810, 46 x 40 x 20 In. . . 2760.00
Desk, Federal, Slant Front, Mahogany, Pigeonholes, c.1775, 43 x 41 x 22 In. 3450.00
Desk, Federal, Slant Front, Maple, 6 Drawers, Document Slots, c.1810, 44 x 42 x 19 In. . . 1150.00
Desk, Federal, Slant Front, Tiger Maple, Fan Carved 8800.00
Desk, Florence Knoll, Rectangular Top, Chrome Plated Steel Pedestal, 30 x 72 x 36 In. . . 860.00
Desk, G. Nakashima, Free Edge, Walnut Top, 2 Bookcases, 46 1/4 x 144 x 21 1/4 In. 4315.00
Desk, G. Nakashima, Walnut, Slab Sides, Sapwood Streak, 2 Drawers, 38 x 28 3/4 In. . . . 11500.00
Desk, G. Nelson, Action Office, Roll Top, 2 Drawers, Trestle, 34 x 54 x 30 In. 805.00
Desk, G. Nelson, Action Office, Roll Top, Walnut, Herman Miller, 64 x 40 In. 2760.00

Desk, G. Nelson, Drop Front, 3 Drawers, Herman Miller, 40 x 25 x 29 1/2 In. 1175.00
Desk, G. Nelson, Leather Surface, 2 Sliding Doors, c.1948, 40 1/2 x 54 x 28 In. 4995.00
Desk, G. Nelson, Primavera, Steel Frame, Laminate, Herman Miller, 1956, 36 x 30 In. . . . 1120.00
Desk, G. Nelson, Roll Top, Rosewood, Pedestal, Herman Miller, 1955, 42 x 35 In. 5265.00
Desk, G. Nelson, Walnut, Laminate, Steel, Plastic, 39 x 28 1/2 x 33 1/2 In. 4115.00
Desk, G. Stickley, Drawer, Kneehole Compartment, Copper Hardware, 42 x 24 x 29 In. . . . 1150.00
Desk, G. Stickley, Drop Front, Mahogany, Paneled, Drawer, 46 1/2 x 32 x 12 In. 1840.00
Desk, G. Stickley, No. 459, Iron Pulls, Paneled Sides, Back 2875.00
Desk, G. Stickley, No. 505, Chalet, Drop Front, c.1902, 46 x 22 In. 2990.00
Desk, G. Stickley, No. 713, Roll Top, 60 x 32 x 46 In. 9200.00
Desk, G. Stickley, No. 732, Drop Front, 2 Over 2 Drawers, Slab Sides, 44 x 32 In. 2115.00
Desk, G. Stickley, Oak, Leather Top, Paneled Sides, Through Tenon, 30 x 54 In. 3450.00
Desk, George III Style, Pedestal, Mahogany, Leather Top, Kittinger, 31 x 72 x 36 In. 1495.00
Desk, George III Style, Polychromed, Satinwood, Carlton House, c.1875, 37 x 42 In. 8050.00
Desk, George III Style, Slant Front, Mahogany, Bracket Feet, 39 1/2 x 34 1/2 x 18 In. . . . 750.00
Desk, George III, Lacquered, Japanned, Bowfront, 3 Graduated Drawers, 48 In. 3495.00
Desk, George III, Mahogany, Kneehole, c.1800, 33 x 42 In. 3450.00
Desk, George III, Slant Front, Mahogany, 4 Drawers, Pigeonholes, 39 3/4 x 41 3/4 In. . . . 5465.00
Desk, George III, Slant Front, Mahogany, Inlaid, 4 Drawers, Fitted Interior, 36 In. 875.00
Desk, Georgian Style, Black Lacquer, Chinoiserie Decoration, 34 1/2 x 44 x 32 In. 1435.00
Desk, Georgian Style, Mahogany, Leather, Drawer, c.1900, 30 1/2 x 42 1/2 x 45 In. 460.00
Desk, Georgian Style, Slant Front, Mahogany, Inlaid, 6 Sections, 41 x 36 x 20 1/2 In. 990.00
Desk, Georgian, Chinoiserie, Block Front, 2 Drawers, Cabriole Legs, 60 x 31 In. 1725.00
Desk, Georgian, Slant Front, 4 Drawers, Bracket Base, 18th Century 1440.00
Desk, Hepplewhite Style, Mahogany, Kneehole, 29 1/2 x 48 x 24 1/2 In. 935.00
Desk, Hepplewhite, Slant Front, Mahogany, Pine, 4 Drawers, Nested Interior, Brass 1290.00
Desk, Hongmu, Wood, 8 Drawers, Brass Pulls, Chinese, c.1875, 55 x 23 x 33 In. 2800.00
Desk, L. & J.G. Stickley, Copper Pulls, Through Tenon, 29 x 36 x 24 In. 2590.00
Desk, L. & J.G. Stickley, Drop Front, 5 Drawers, Open Ends, 40 x 45 x 21 In. 1955.00
Desk, L. & J.G. Stickley, No. 414, 5 Drawers, Kneehole, 40 x 22 x 35 In. 1380.00
Desk, L. & J.G. Stickley, No. 501, 5 Drawers, Through Tenon, 48 x 30 x 29 In. 3450.00
Desk, L. & J.G. Stickley, No. 505, Overhanging Top, Blind Drawer, 48 x 30 In. 1410.00
Desk, Lifetime, Drop Front, 4 Drawers, 33 1/2 x 16 x 63 In. 1840.00
Desk, Lifetime, No. 8568, Slant Front, 2 Drawers, Shelf, Copper Hardware, 43 x 34 In. . . 1290.00
Desk, Limbert, 2 Drawers, Slat Sides, Arched Crest Rail, 43 1/2 x 32 x 15 1/2 In. 980.00
Desk, Louis Philippe, Mahogany, Kneehole, Brass Mounted, c.1865, 28 1/2 x 38 In. 635.00
Desk, Louis Phillipe Style, Slant Front, Mahogany, Marquetry, 45 x 26 x 18 In. 1400.00
Desk, Louis XV Style, Kingwood, Slide Top, Kidney Shape, Late 1800s, 29 1/2 x 36 In. . . 1725.00
Desk, Louis XV Style, Kneehole, Leather Inset Top, Bronze Mounted, 30 x 36 x 22 In. . . 1600.00
Desk, Louis XV Style, Mahogany, Parquetry, Bowfront, Marble Top, France 1345.00
Desk, Louis XV Style, Rosewood, Kingwood, Marquetry, 39 x 28 x 19 In. 710.00
Desk, Louis XV, Mahogany, Inset Leather Top, 3 Drawers, c.1780, 29 x 39 x 22 In. 2530.00
Desk, Louis XVI Style, Black Lacquer, Ormolu Trim, 51 x 27 1/2 x 30 In. 1095.00
Desk, Louis XVI Style, Mahogany, Bronze Mounted, Cylinder, 62 x 35 x 21 In. 1675.00
Desk, Mahogany, 2 Columns Of 3 Drawers, Inset Leather, Turned Feet, 29 x 23 x 40 In. . . 1049.00
Desk, Mahogany, 8 Drawers, Molded Leather Top, 29 1/4 x 54 x 27 In. 325.00
Desk, Mahogany, 9 Drawers, Leather Top, 2 Pedestals, c.1850, 33 1/2 x 60 x 41 1/2 In. . . 2185.00
Desk, Mahogany, 9 Drawers, Leather Top, Pedestal, 1800s, 31 x 47 x 27 In. 880.00
Desk, Mahogany, Inlaid, Oval Panel, Pullout Writing Surface, 38 x 30 x 17 1/2 In. 1650.00
Desk, Mahogany, Kidney Shape, Floral Marquetry, 43 In. 540.00
Desk, Mahogany, Winged Griffin Supports, Carved Apron, c.1885, 29 x 55 x 36 In. 5175.00
Desk, Majorelle, Carved Corners, Stencils, 29 x 54 x 31 In. 2300.00
Desk, Melodeon, Mahogany, Half Lift Top, Writing Surface, 34 1/2 x 42 x 21 In. 180.00
Desk, Neoclassical Style, Slant Front, Fruitwood, Marquetry, 49 1/2 x 46 x 21 In. 1295.00
Desk, Oak, Brass, Leather, Mastercraft, 31 x 56 x 28 In. 1880.00
Desk, Oak, Figural Carved, 2 Drawers, c.1885, 30 x 60 x 36 In. 7190.00
Desk, Oriental, Slant Front, Mother-Of-Pearl Inlay, 4 Drawers, 1900s, 36 x 17 x 42 In. . . . 385.00
Desk, Partners, Chippendale Style, Mahogany, Flat Top, 30 x 72 x 45 In. 2530.00
Desk, Partners, Florence Knoll, Rosewood, Steel, 1960s, 72 x 38 x 28 1/2 In. 4095.00
Desk, Partners, George II Style, Walnut, Serpentine, Leather Surface, 66 x 31 In. 2990.00
Desk, Partners, George III Style, Mahogany, Leather, 2 Pedestals, 30 x 71 x 48 In. 5750.00
Desk, Partners, George III Style, Walnut, Leather Top, c.1900, 31 x 60 x 39 In. 3565.00
Desk, Partners, George III, Mahogany, Leather Top, 9 Drawers, c.1900 . . . . 6615.00

Furniture, Desk,
Queen Anne, Slant Front,
Tiger Maple, Dovetailed,
43 1/2 x 36 x 20 1/2 In.

Furniture, Desk,
Sheraton, Slant
Front, Mahogany,
Maple, Birch, Carved,
78 x 40 x 20 In.

Desk, Partners, Georgian Style, Burl Walnut, Leather Top, 31 x 68 1/4 x 44 1/4 In. 2300.00
Desk, Partners, Georgian Style, Mahogany, Leather Top, c.1890, 32 x 66 x 54 In. 2530.00
Desk, Partners, Louis XVI Style, Mahogany, Ormolu Mounted, 31 x 71 x 42 In. 1725.00
Desk, Partners, Mahogany, Felt Top, Brass Pulls, 18 Drawers, 30 3/4 x 49 In. 1200.00
Desk, Partners, Mahogany, Lion Mask Pilasters, England, 32 x 79 x 50 1/2 In. 4600.00
Desk, Partners, Mahogany, Raised Panel, Green Felt Top, 30 3/4 x 49 In. 1345.00
Desk, Partners, Mahogany, Ribbon Inlay, 30 x 58 x 38 In. 3160.00
Desk, Partners, Tommi Parzinger, Ebonized, Charak Modern, 28 1/2 x 48 x 28 In. 2990.00
Desk, Pickled Pine, 2 Pedestal, Late 19th Century, 31 x 45 1/2 x 22 1/4 In. 1035.00
Desk, Pine, Kneehole, England, 29 1/2 x 49 1/4 x 24 In. 920.00
Desk, Pine, Lift Top, 6 Compartments, Turned Legs, 18 In. 415.00
Desk, Pine, Lift Top, Red Wash, Mortised Side Aprons, 34 1/2 x 28 x 38 In. 325.00
Desk, Plantation, Cherry, 2 Sections, c.1850, 51 1/2 x 37 x 21 In. 865.00
Desk, Plantation, Sheraton, Slant Front, Maple, Birch, 3 Shelves, 81 x 37 x 23 In. 4600.00
Desk, Plantation, Walnut, Scrolled Sides, Sloped Lid, 37 x 60 1/2 x 33 In. 28750.00
Desk, Poplar, Painted, 3 Drawers, c.1860, 30 1/4 x 10 1/4 x 33 1/4 In. 345.00
Desk, Queen Anne Style, Slant Front, Oak, 3 Drawers, Claw & Ball Feet, 39 x 30 x 17 In. 355.00
Desk, Queen Anne Style, Walnut, Kneehole, Leather Surface, 7 Drawers, Door, 32 x 29 In. 865.00
Desk, Queen Anne, Slant Front, Maple, Curly Maple, 3 Graduated Drawers, 41 1/2 In. . . . 1955.00
Desk, Queen Anne, Slant Front, Tiger Maple, Dovetailed, 43 1/2 x 36 x 20 1/2 In. . . *Illus* 33350.00
Desk, Queen Anne, Slant Front, Walnut, Maple, 42 x 36 x 18 In. 8800.00
Desk, Red Lacquer, Qing Dynasty, Chinese, c.1890, 32 x 45 1/4 x 20 1/4 In. 649.00
Desk, Renaissance Revival, Slant Front, Burled Walnut, c.1865, 61 x 38 x 20 In. 2300.00
Desk, Renaissance Revival, Walnut, 2 Pedestals, Late 1800s, 30 1/4 x 72 1/2 x 38 In. 1840.00
Desk, Renaissance Revival, Walnut, 5 Drawers, Pedestal, c.1875, 29 x 62 x 33 1/2 In. 4900.00
Desk, Rococo Revival, Walnut, Drop Front, American, c.1865, 50 x 26 x 16 In. 1955.00
Desk, Rococo Style, Walnut, Carved Crest, Leather Top, 47 x 38 1/2 x 23 1/2 In. 1380.00
Desk, Roger Sprunger, Rosewood, Chromium Sheet Steel, Dunbar, c.1970, 84 x 30 In. . . . 4095.00
Desk, Roll Top, 3 Drawers, Pullout Writing Surface, Scandinavian, 38 x 36 In. 460.00
Desk, Roll Top, Mahogany, Fitted Interior, Brass Handle, Plate, 15 x 18 x 14 1/2 In. 635.00
Desk, Roll Top, Mahogany, Marquetry, 38 x 30 x 17 1/2 In. 1680.00
Desk, Roll Top, Oak, 7 Drawers, Paneled 2-Pedestal Base, c.1910, 50 In. 805.00
Desk, Roll Top, Oak, Double Bank, 6 Drawers, 41 1/2 x 48 x 31 1/2 In. 700.00
Desk, Rosewood, Flowering Plum Branches, Birds, c.1900, 46 1/2 x 38 1/2 In. 1150.00
Desk, Schoolmaster's, Hepplewhite Style, Lift Top, Mid 19th Century, 31 x 26 x 38 In. . . 259.00
Desk, Schoolmaster's, Slant Front, Oak, Pine, Drawer, Pigeonholes, 28 1/2 x 22 x 35 In. . 605.00
Desk, Schoolmaster's, Softwood, Slide Writing Surface, 3 Drawers, Tapered Legs 255.00
Desk, Shaker, Drop Front, Pine, Hinged Lid, Watervliet, c.1845, 61 x 36 1/2 In. 3740.00
Desk, Shaker, Trustee's, Butternut, Poplar, 2 Parts, c.1840, 86 x 36 In. 5175.00
Desk, Shaker, Trustee's, Cherry, Poplar, 2 Parts, Glass, c.1835, 84 x 41 1/2 In. 6900.00
Desk, Shaker, Trustee's, Drop Front, Cherry, Poplar, Canterbury, N.H., c.1830, 56 x 27 In. 8340.00
Desk, Sheraton, Lift Top, 2 Drawers, 6 Pigeonholes, American, 36 x 42 In. 210.00
Desk, Sheraton, Slant Front, Mahogany, Maple, Birch, Carved, 78 x 40 x 20 In. . . . . *Illus* 10350.00
Desk, Sheraton, Slant Front, Tiger Maple, Pullout Writing Surface, 4 Drawers 2800.00
Desk, Sheraton, Slant Front, Walnut, American, 42 x 40 x 19 1/2 In. 1200.00
Desk, Slant Front, Birch, William Cole, Maine, 1812, 43 1/4 x 36 x 17 1/4 In. 3740.00
Desk, Slant Front, Cherry, 10 Interior Drawers, 4 Outside Drawers, 42 1/2 x 36 x 18 In. . . 2415.00
Desk, Slant Front, Cherry, Carved & Pierced Gallery, 2 Drawers, 44 1/4 x 28 x 16 In. 259.00

Desk, Slant Front, Mahogany, 4 Graduated Drawers, New England, 33 x 45 1/2 x 22 In. . . . 1915.00
Desk, Slant Front, Mahogany, 9 Interior Drawers, Mass., 41 1/2 x 22 x 32 In. 2025.00
Desk, Slant Front, Mahogany, Oxbow Front, Rhode Island, 48 x 40 x 24 In. 4025.00
Desk, Slant Front, Oak, 4 Drawers, Ball Feet, England, 1700s, 37 1/2 x 38 1/2 In. 1725.00
Desk, Slant Front, Pine, Lift Top, Paneled Doors, Porcelain Knobs, 1890s, Child's, 58 In. . . 415.00
Desk, Slant Front, Pine, Poplar, Tapered Legs, Sections, 19th Century, 36 x 31 x 23 In. . . . 990.00
Desk, Slant Front, Poplar, Grain Painted, Center Drawer, c.1840, 39 x 36 3/4 x 23 3/4 In. . . 590.00
Desk, Slant Front, Rosewood, Maple, Interior Compartments, 4 Drawers, 40 x 39 In. 1265.00
Desk, Slant Front, Southern Pine, Arched Pediment, Frieze Drawer, 69 x 33 1/2 x 30 In. . . 920.00
Desk, Slant Front, Walnut, Serpentine, Scalloped Skirt, 19 x 23 In. 2035.00
Desk, Star Inlaid Top, 2 Drawers, Continental, Early 1800s, 40 x 24 x 31 In. 575.00
Desk, Stickley Bros., Bookshelves, Drawer, Slats, 29 x 40 x 26 In. 1095.00
Desk, Stickley Bros., Slant Front, Oak, 3 Drawers, Compartments, 46 x 17 In. 1575.00
Desk, Tiger Maple, Tambour, Lift Top, 9 Pigeonholes, 2 Sections, 46 x 31 x 19 In. 575.00
Desk, V. Kagan, Exotic Wood Veneer, 4 Drawers, 29 1/4 x 62 1/2 x 29 1/2 In. 2415.00
Desk, V. Kagan, Oval Roll Top, Walnut, Plexiglas Legs, 35 x 44 1/2 x 24 In. 1840.00
Desk, Victorian, Chestnut, Spindle Mounts, Drawer, 30 1/2 x 40 x 27 In. 220.00
Desk, Victorian, Mahogany, Brass Mounted, Leather Writing Surface, 7 x 21 x 11 In. 345.00
Desk, Victorian, Slant Front, Mahogany, Pedestals, 4 Drawers, 47 x 58 x 32 In. 940.00
Desk, Victorian, Walnut, Ebonized Finish, 47 1/4 x 18 1/4 x 12 3/4 In. 400.00
Desk, W. Platner, Walnut Veneer, Polished Chrome, Leather Top, 30 x 96 x 40 In. 8050.00
Desk, W. Sklaroff, Uniplane, Rosewood, Fiberglass, Early 1970s, 29 x 71 1/2 x 36 In. 1610.00
Desk, Walnut Top, Aluminum, Black Enameled Drawers, 30 1/2 x 78 x 40 1/4 In. 690.00
Desk, Walnut, Lift Top, Door, Drawers, 1800s, 39 x 27 1/2 x 25 1/2 In. 3960.00
Desk, Walnut, Lift Top, Drawer, Turned Legs, 35 x 30 1/2 x 21 In. 300.00
Desk, Walnut, Serpentine, Brass Gallery, Marquetry, Continental, c.1900, 34 x 45 In. 4140.00
Desk, Walnut, Slant Lift Top, 2 Drawers, Pigeonholes, 63 x 50 In. 750.00
Desk, Wendell Castle, Laminated Walnut, V-Shape, Drawer, 18 1/2 x 52 x 28 1/4 In. 2760.00
Desk, William IV, Mahogany, Drawers, Pedestal, c.1835, 30 1/2 x 49 1/2 In. 1060.00
Desk, Wooton, No. 10, Walnut, Double Pier Standard, Cylinder Top, 1880, 56 x 70 In. 3575.00
Desk, Wormley, Roll Top, Rosewood, Ebonized Frame, 3 Drawers, 35 x 75 x 28 In. 5465.00
Desk, Wormley, Rosewood, Mahogany, Dunbar, 1960s, 74 1/2 x 28 x 35 In. 4680.00
Desk Box, Shaker, Pine, Slanted Lift Lid, Brass Hinges, c.1845, 4 1/2 x 21 1/2 x 12 In. . . 920.00
Dining Set, Adjustable Table Height, 2-Slide Out Leaves, Denmark, c.1960, 9 Piece 940.00
Dining Set, Arts & Crafts, Oak, 8 Leaves, 7 Chairs, 30 1/2-In. Table, 8 Piece 1265.00
Dining Set, Dyrlund, Rectangular Top, Woven Seats, c.1950, 28 3/4-In. Table, 6 Piece . . . 470.00
Dining Set, Eero Saarinen, Marble Top, 6 Pedestal Chairs, Knoll, 54 x 29 In., 7 Piece 2935.00
Dining Set, H. Wegner, Teak Veneer, Beech Legs, Round, 6 Chairs, F. Hansen 3055.00
Dining Set, Hans Olsen, Teak, 3-Leg Chairs, Frem Rojle, Denmark, 5 Piece . . . .1150.00 to 3220.00
Dining Set, John Stuart, Extension Table, 2 Armchairs, Johnson Furniture, 7 Piece 750.00
Dining Set, Mahogany, Bernhardt Furniture Co., 10 Piece 1400.00
Dining Set, Mahogany, Prince Of Wales Feathers, Carved, 37 1/2 In., 8 Piece 4140.00
Dining Set, McCobb, Planner Group, Maple, Black Metal, 60 x 38 In., 7 Piece 1495.00
Dining Set, Oak, Inlaid, China Cabinet, Sideboard, Table, 6 Chairs, 9 Piece 2875.00
Dining Set, Rohde, Paldao, Herman Miller, c.1940, 9 Piece 4400.00
Dining Set, Teak, Table, 6 Chairs, Woven Cord, Denmark, 28 1/2 x 48 x 45 In., 7 Piece . . . 1295.00
Dining Set, Victorian, Cast Iron, Round Table, 4 3-Leg Chairs, Balloon Back, 5 Piece . . . 785.00
Dining Set, W. Platner, Rosewood Top, Bronze Wire Base, Wool, 4 Chairs, 5 Piece 2990.00
Dining Set, Wormley, 2 Leaves, 6 Chairs, Dunbar, c.1958, 29 x 54-In. Table Closed 3760.00
Dresser, American Aesthetic, Mahogany, Mixed Metals, Late 1800s, 81 x 53 In. 1150.00
Dresser, Cherry, 4 Tiger Maple Drawers, Gebhard Harland, Station, Ind., 42 In. 385.00
Dresser, Cherry, Mahogany Veneer, Mirror, Eastern Kentucky, 66 x 19 x 39 In. 725.00
Dresser, Cottage Pine, Mirror, 5 Drawers, Backsplash, Carved Knobs, 51 x 30 x 20 In. . . . 310.00
Dresser, Cottage, Softwood, 3 Drawers, Carved Pulls, Glove Boxes, Candle Shelves 280.00
Dresser, Dunbar, 2 Sliding Doors, 12 Over 6 Inside Drawers, 5 Legs, 34 x 60 x 18 In. 290.00
Dresser, Empire, Mahogany Veneer, 4 Drawers, 3 Glove Drawers, 64 x 36 1/2 x 22 In. . . . 1000.00
Dresser, Empire, Mahogany, 4 Drawers, Glove Box, Mirror, 64 x 36 1/2 x 22 In. 990.00
Dresser, Florence Knoll, Wood Grain, Drawers, Metal Legs, 27 x 36 x 18 In. 1380.00
Dresser, Frankl, 10 Drawers, Brass Pulls, Johnson Furniture, 72 1/2 x 32 1/2 In. 400.00
Dresser, G. Nelson, Steel Frame, 4 Drawers, Herman Miller, 33 1/2 x 17 x 37 In. . .575.00 to 750.00
Dresser, G. Nelson, Thin Edge, 4 Drawers, Herman Miller, 27 1/2 x 34 x 20 In. 2185.00
Dresser, G. Nelson, Walnut Veneer, 3 Drawers, Plank Leg Base, 29 3/4 x 24 x 20 In. 520.00
Dresser, H. Probber, Mahogany, 6 Drawers, 6 Legs, 76 x 20 x 31 1/2 In. 978.00

Dresser, Jacobean Style, Oak, 2 Drawers, Ball Feet, 34 x 52 1/2 x 21 In. 1150.00
Dresser, Louis XV Style, Bombe, Flowers, Gilt Trim, Widdicomb, 48 x 23 x 33 1/2 In. . . . 748.00
Dresser, Mahogany, 2 Over 3 Drawers, Bracket Feet, 38 x 45 x 22 In. 2015.00
Dresser, Mahogany, 6 Drawers, Oval Mirror, Wishbone Frame, 78 x 56 x 25 1/2 In. 375.00
Dresser, Mahogany, 7 Drawers, Oval Beveled Mirror, c.1920, 73 x 40 x 23 In. 325.00
Dresser, Mahogany, Bowfront, 4 Drawers, Oval Beveled Mirror, 71 x 45 x 23 In. 200.00
Dresser, Mahogany, Mirror, 5 Drawers, 2 Scrolled Stiles, Paw Feet, 43 1/2 In. 140.00
Dresser, McCobb, Planner Group, Maple, 8 Drawers, 60 x 18 x 33 In. 345.00
Dresser, Neoclassical, Mahogany, 5 Drawers, Mirror, c.1841, 34 x 29 1/4 x 10 In. 230.00
Dresser, Neoclassical, Mahogany, Oval Mirror, American, c.1830, 67 x 42 x 20 In. 2185.00
Dresser, Oak, 2 Over 2 Drawers, Corbelled Mirror, 73 x 43 x 21 In. 1210.00
Dresser, Oak, 4 Over 4 Drawers, Through Tenon Stretcher, Legs, 53 x 40 x 22 In. 5465.00
Dresser, Oak, Pine, 4 Doors, Dovetailed Drawers, 2 Parts, Wales, 1800s, 47 1/4 x 77 In. . . 990.00
Dresser, Pine, 5 Drawers, Mirror, Posts, Backsplash, Carved Knobs, 51 x 30 x 20 In. 305.00
Dresser, Pine, Poplar, American, 19th Century, 71 3/4 x 43 3/4 x 21 1/2 In. 649.00
Dresser, Pine, Poplar, Green Paint Interior, 1800s 765.00
Dresser, Renaissance Revival, Marble Top, Carved, Victorian, 84 x 59 x 21 1/2 In. 2530.00
Dresser, Renaissance Revival, Walnut, Crest, Mirror, 3 Drawers, c.1880, 41 x 95 In. 750.00
Dresser, Renaissance Revival, Walnut, Marble, Mirror, c.1870, 92 x 54 x 25 In. 1725.00
Dresser, Robsjohn-Gibbings, Bleached Mahogany, 4 Drawers, 32 x 35 In. 1120.00
Dresser, Rococo, Mahogany, Marble Top, Mirror, American, c.1850, 92 x 43 x 20 In. 1035.00
Dresser, Rohde, Paldao, 4 Drawers, Brass Pulls, Herman Miller, 48 x 18 x 32 1/4 In. 1725.00
Dresser, Rosewood, Marble Top, 3 Drawers, Mirror, New York, c.1850, 84 x 50 In. 4900.00
Dresser, Rosewood, Marble Top, Scrolled, Winged Angel, c.1860, 91 x 50 x 24 In. 9200.00
Dresser, Roycroft, 4 Drawers, Mirror, Mackmurdo Feet, 61 x 43 In. 10350.00
Dresser, V. Kagan, Cherry, 3 Drawers, Sculpted Base, 31 3/4 x 40 x 19 In. 2875.00
Dresser, Victorian, Black Walnut, Burl, Marble Top, Candle Shelf, 80 x 43 x 20 1/2 In. . . 615.00
Dresser, Victorian, Oak, 4 Serpentine Drawers, Wishbone Mirror, c.1900, 44 x 74 In. 259.00
Dresser, Victorian, Walnut, Burl, Wishbone Mirror, 5 Drawers, 72 x 41 In. 500.00
Dresser, Victorian, Walnut, Marble Top, Applied Racetrack Molding, 32 x 44 x 19 In. 390.00
Dresser, Victorian, Walnut, Marble, Mirror, Writing Slide, c.1895, 78 x 47 x 21 In. 175.00
Dresser, Walnut, Marble Top, Swing Mirror, Bowed Drawers, Scroll Feet 500.00
Dresser, Welsh, Oak, 3 Shelves, Drawer, 2 Doors, England, c.1900, 90 x 62 x 17 In. 825.00
Dressing Stand, Empire, Mahogany, Swing Mirror, 6 Drawers, 35 1/2 x 60 x 18 1/2 In. . . 2025.00
Dressing Stand, Empire, Walnut, Swing Mirror, 5 Drawers, 78 x 38 x 25 In. 450.00
Dry Sink, Grain Painted, Hinged Lid, 2 Doors, Pa., Late 1800s, 37 x 19 x 31 In. 1045.00
Dry Sink, Green Paint, 3 Drawers Flanked By 2 Plank Doors, 63 In. 3450.00
Dry Sink, Hardwood, Lift Top, Dovetailed Well, 2 Drawers, 2 Doors, 13 x 13 1/2 In. 2025.00
Dry Sink, Mahogany, Maple, Cupboard Base, Continental, 30 x 59 x 24 In. 1555.00
Dry Sink, Mixed Woods, Hutch Top, 2 Doors, Drawer, 48 1/4 x 81 1/2 In. 730.00
Dry Sink, Oak, Hutch Top, 4 Doors, 3 Drawers, Shaped Cutout Ends, 36 x 72 In. 395.00
Dry Sink, Paint Decorated, Interior Shelf, Drawer, 19th Century, 16 x 10 x 21 In. 2200.00
Dry Sink, Pine, 2 Parts, Pennsylvania, c.1850, 88 x 50 x 21 In. 8800.00
Dry Sink, Pine, Paint, 2 Cabinet Doors, 3 Drawers, 65 x 36 x 18 In. 359.00
Dry Sink, Pine, Poplar, Red Wash, Recessed Panel Doors, Shelf, 54 x 19 x 38 In. 3740.00
Dry Sink, Pine, Poplar, Yellow, Thos. Underwood, Ohio, c.1881, 42 x 18 x 41 In. 4025.00
Dry Sink, Pine, Red Paint, 2 Doors, Square Nails, 59 x 36 In. 385.00
Dry Sink, Pine, Robin's-Egg Blue Paint, Lift Top, 35 x 37 In. 360.00
Dry Sink, Poplar, 2 Doors, Mortise, Pegged, Square Nail, 34 3/4 x 63 1/2 In. 935.00
Dry Sink, Red, Beige Paint, Tray Top, 2-Paneled Doors, 1800s, 32 x 39 x 18 1/2 In. 690.00
Dry Sink, Softwood, Shelf Back, Scalloped Support, Drawer, 2 Doors, 54 1/4 In. 900.00
Dry Sink, Softwood, Single Drawer, 2 Sunken-Panel Doors, 27 x 16 In. 450.00
Dry Sink, Softwood, Yellow Grain Paint Over Green, Door, 26 1/2 x 28 x 20 In. 620.00
Dry Sink, Walnut, Red Wash, Pegged Gallery, Panel Doors, c.1840 . . . . 2295.00
Dry Sink, Yellow Paint, Paneled Ends, 2 Doors, 46 1/2 x 34 In. 450.00
Dumbwaiter, Chippendale, 3 Graduated Tiers, Tripod Base, Snake Feet, England, 45 In. . 1610.00
Dumbwaiter, Chippendale, Mahogany, 3 Tiers, Snake Legs, Tripod, England, 42 In. 920.00
Dumbwaiter, Edwardian, Mahogany, 2 Tiers, c.1900, 33 x 24 In. 520.00
Dumbwaiter, George III Style, Mahogany, 3 Round Tiers, 46 x 22 In. 775.00
Dumbwaiter, George III, Mahogany, 3 Tiers, Baluster Supports, Tripod Base, 44 In. 1575.00
Dumbwaiter, George III, Mahogany, 3 Tiers, Piecrust Edge, c.1810, 28 x 44 In. 1495.00
Dumbwaiter, George III, Mahogany, Pivot Cleats, c.1800, 43 x 23 In. 1725.00
Dumbwaiter, Georgian Style, Mahogany, 3 Round Tiers, Pad Feet, Miniature, 12 In., Pair 380.00

Dumbwaiter, William IV, Mahogany, Revolving, Tabletop, c.1830, 4 1/2 x 21 1/2 In. 575.00
Easel, Aesthetic Revival, Palette & Brushes Top Carving, Black Finish, 28 x 78 In. 2300.00
Easel, Eastlake, Walnut, Carved Flowers, 3-Leg Base, 30 x 74 In. 805.00
Easel, Hardwood, Carved, Anglo-Indian, Mid 19th Century, 62 x 35 x 18 In. 1840.00
Easel, Oak, Iron Adjusting Mechanism, 72 x 32 x 31 In. 715.00
Easel, Renaissance Revival, Ebonized Walnut, Gilt Incised, 72 1/2 x 28 1/2 In. 2530.00
Etagere, Beveled Mirror, c.1890, 72 1/2 x 39 x 16 In. 1380.00
Etagere, Chinese Chippendale, Mahogany, Early 1900s, 70 x 51 x 13 In. 5465.00
Etagere, Corner, Victorian, Bird's-Eye Maple, Glass, 62 x 32 x 24 In. 805.00
Etagere, Dunbar, Cream Lacquer, Square, Geometric Cutouts, 3 Glass Shelves, 79 In. . . . 2585.00
Etagere, Federal, Drawer, Red Wash, Bamboo Supports, 3 Tiers, 52 1/2 x 18 In. 1035.00
Etagere, Gothic Revival, Mahogany, 6 Side Shelves, Center Mirror, Marble Base 2970.00
Etagere, Hunzinger Style, Beveled Mirrors, Claw Feet, c.1885, 75 x 41 x 10 In. 1495.00
Etagere, Louis XVI Style, Mahogany, Bronze Mounted, 2 Tiers, 46 x 13 In. 325.00
Etagere, Mahogany, 4 Shelves, 2 Drawers, American, c.1830, 62 x 23 x 18 In. 1725.00
Etagere, Mahogany, Pierced Brass Gallery, France, c.1885, 32 x 18 x 10 In., Pair 12650.00
Etagere, McCobb, Birch, Metal, 2 Beech Shelves, 48 x 47 x 13 In. 690.00
Etagere, Napoleon III, Brass Mounted, 4 Tiers, 43 x 17 In., Pair 540.00
Etagere, Oak, Cartouche, 3 Carved Panels, Reeded Columns, Bun Feet, 93 In. 460.00
Etagere, Regency Style, Mahogany, 3 Shelves, Ball Feet, 37 1/2 x 40 x 16 In. 460.00
Etagere, Renaissance Revival, Rosewood, Cabinet Base, 2 Parts, c.1865, 108 x 56 In. 6040.00
Etagere, Rococo Revival, Rosewood, Carved, Mirror, c.1850, 64 x 40 1/2 In. . . . . . . *Illus* 3884.00
Etagere, Rococo Revival, Rosewood, Carved, Mirror, Marble, c.1855, 94 x 48 In. . . *Illus* 7770.00
Etagere, Rococo, Rosewood Grained, Mirror Top, Mid 19th Century, 92 x 52 In. 3450.00
Etagere, Rosewood, Carved, Open Shelves, Paw Feet, East Asia, 70 1/2 x 39 x 17 In. 1150.00
Etagere, Sheraton Style, Mahogany, American, Early 1800s, 43 x 34 1/2 In. 1035.00
Etagere, Victorian, Bamboo, Lacquered, Ivory, 4 Tiers, 56 x 33 x 20 1/2 In. 540.00
Etagere, Victorian, Oak, Bamboo, c.1890, 46 x 19 1/2 x 9 In. 175.00
Etagere, Victorian, Rosewood, Pierced, Carved, 6 Tiers, Drawer, 67 1/2 x 43 In. 1785.00
Footstool, Black Leather, Brass Tacks, Cabriole Legs, 16 1/2 x 12 x 13 In. 220.00
Footstool, G. Stickley, No. 300, Arched Seat Rail, Through Tenon, 20 x 16 x 15 In. 2185.00
Footstool, G. Stickley, No. 302, Leather Cover, Flared Feet, 12 x 12 x 5 In. 635.00
Footstool, L. & J.G. Stickley, Leather Tacked Upholstery, Arched Apron, 18 x 15 In. 545.00
Footstool, Lakeside Craftshop, Slatted, Through Tenon Construction, 18 x 18 x 15 In. . . . 575.00
Footstool, Limbert, Cricket, Rectangular Top, Central Cutout, 18 x 10 x 6 In. 145.00
Footstool, Louis XVI Style, Painted, Ivory, Oval, 8 1/2 x 14 1/2 x 11 1/2 In., Pair 840.00
Footstool, Napoleon III, Ebonized, Parcel Gilt, 17 x 16 1/2 In., Pair 520.00
Footstool, Neoclassical, Rosewood, Upholstered, American, c.1840, 12 x 19 x 16 In. 345.00
Footstool, Oak, Heart Cutout, Splayed & Scalloped Ends, Relief Carving, c.1818 . . . . 300.00
Footstool, Pine, Black Over Red Graining, Bronze Stenciling, 6 3/4 x 13 x 5 7/8 In. 320.00
Footstool, Pine, Needlework Upholstery, 19th Century, 6 1/2 x 16 In. 235.00
Footstool, Poplar, Red Brown Wash, Scalloped Legs, Beaded Aprons, 15 x 9 x 8 In. 190.00
Footstool, Regency, Mahogany, Tapered Padded Top, c.1900, 9 x 12 In., Pair 2185.00
Footstool, Shaker, Dark Stain, Mt. Lebanon, Early 1900s, 6 1/8 x 11 3/4 x 11 In. 355.00
Footstool, Shaker, Plank Top, Fabric Cover, Turned Legs, Mt. Lebanon, 7 x 12 1/2 In. . . . 230.00
Footstool, Shaker, Splint Woven Seat, Natural Finish, Tapered Legs, 11 1/4 x 12 1/2 In. . . 175.00
Footstool, Victorian, Floral Beadwork, Brass Ball Feet, 10 7/8 x 5 1/2 In., Pair 225.00

Furniture, Etagere,
Rococo Revival,
Rosewood, Carved,
Mirror, c.1850,
64 x 40 1/2 In.

Furniture, Etagere,
Rococo Revival,
Rosewood, Carved,
Mirror, Marble, c.1855,
94 x 48 In.

Furniture, Frame, Italian Baroque,
Gilt, Carved Wood,
17th Century, 72 x 53 In.

Furniture, Frame, Italian Baroque,
Gilt, Carved Wood, Lilies,
17th Century, 80 1/2 x 63 In.

Furniture, Frame, Louis XIII
Style, Gilt, Carved Wood,
19th Century, 85 x 51 1/2 In.

Footstool, Victorian, Mahogany, Carved, Pierced, Turned Stretcher, 16 x 20 x 14 In. 195.00
Footstool, Victorian, Petit & Gros Needlework, 1900s, 7 1/2 x 13 1/2 In. 90.00
Footstool, Victorian, Rosewood, Upholstered, 13 x 13 In. 165.00
Footstool, Victorian, Walnut, Upholstered 175.00
Footstool, Walnut, Cane, 19th Century, 15 1/2 x 10 x 13 1/2 In.   28.00
Footstool, Walnut, Drawers, Upholstered, Ball Feet, 39 1/2 x 13 1/2 In. 180.00
Footstool, Walnut, Mahogany Veneer, Stumpwork Cat, Red Ground, 13 x 10 x 9 In. 520.00
Footstool, Walnut, Molded Base, Needlepoint Cover, Stepped Feet, 12 x 18 In. 145.00
Footstool, Windsor, Oval, Turned & Canted Legs, 18 1/4 x 12 1/4 In. 280.00
Frame, Alligator Hide, 6 3/8 x 5 3/8 x 1 1/4 In. 460.00
Frame, Baroque Style, Composition, Gilt, Scroll & Leaf, 19th Century, 26 x 22 In. 165.00
Frame, Baroque, Gilt, Pebbled, Rope Edge, Victorian, 30 1/2 x 25 1/2 In. 785.00
Frame, Caned Border, Arts & Crafts, 7 x 9 In. 90.00
Frame, Corner Block, Inlaid, Mid 19th Century, New England, 17 x 15 In. 305.00
Frame, Gilt, Cove Molded, 19th Century, 31 3/4 x 27 3/4 In. 22.00
Frame, Gilt, Gesso, Leaves, Scrolls, American, c.1850, 45 x 55 1/4 In. 630.00
Frame, Gilt, Mid 19th Century, 5 3/4 x 8 In., Pair 220.00
Frame, Italian Baroque, Gilt, Carved Wood, 17th Century, 72 x 53 In. . . . . *Illus*   5060.00
Frame, Italian Baroque, Gilt, Carved Wood, Lilies, 17th Century, 80 1/2 x 63 In. . . . *Illus*   2970.00
Frame, Jade, Gilt Center, Medallion, 20th Century, 7 x 5 x 1/2 In. 560.00
Frame, Louis XIII Style, Gilt, Carved Wood, 19th Century, 85 x 51 1/2 In. . . . . *Illus*   3190.00
Frame, Napoleon III, Gilt, Plaster, Carved, 19th Century, 18 1/2 x 16 1/2 In. 175.00
Frame, Oak, Carved, Ivy Leaves, Vines, Berries, 9 x 11 In. 300.00
Frame, Paint Decorated, Gold Lines, Late 1800s, 8 1/2 x 6 1/8 In. 55.00
Frame, Paint Decorated, Striped Design, Pa., Mid 19th Century, 17 x 13 In. 220.00
Frame, Painted, Corn Block, Applied Half-Round Turnings, 20th Century, 18 x 16 In. 300.00
Frame, Pewter, Hammered, Organic Design, Aquamarines, Arts & Crafts, Round, 8 In. 500.00
Frame, Pinwheel, Corner Block, Paint Decorated, Pa., Mid 1800s, 19 x 15 1/2 In. 935.00
Frame, Redwood, Carved, Scroll Shape, Arts & Crafts, 35 x 13 1/2 In. 470.00
Frame, Shadow Box, Walnut, Gilt, Botanical Prints, c.1900, 15 x 13 1/2 In., Pair 145.00
Frame, Stenciled, Gold, Red Brown Ground, Flowers, Leaves, Mid 1800s, 10 x 7 In. 99.00
Frame, Tan Suede Leather, Arts & Crafts, 8 x 10 In. 59.00
Frame, Tiger Maple, 14 x 18 In. 110.00
Frame, Tiger Maple, Applied Molding, Label, E. Goss, Salem, Mass., 1800s, 16 x 20 In. . .   560.00
Frame, Wood, Inlaid Mother-Of-Pearl, Ivory, Bronze, Easel, Arts & Crafts, 11 x 16 1/2 In.   410.00
Frame, Wood, Turned Columns, Old Glass, 19th Century, 16 5/8 x 14 5/8 In. 85.00
Hall Stand, Aesthetic Revival, Walnut, Carved, Vine Borders, Hooks, Mirror, 52 x 41 In. .   940.00
Hall Stand, Mirror, Marble-Top Glove Box, 2 Umbrella Holders 715.00
Hall Stand, Oak, Keyhole-Shaped Mirror, Carved Crest, Rolled Arms 1700.00
Hall Stand, Oak, Mirror, Brass Double Hooks, Arms, Seat, c.1910, 75 x 25 x 15 In. 335.00
Hall Stand, Polished Steel, Foliate Crest, Oval Mirror, 1859, 88 x 38 x 12 In. 8050.00
Hall Stand, Renaissance Revival, Oak, Broken Arch, Urn Finial, c.1880 . . . .   805.00
Hall Stand, Renaissance Revival, Walnut, Mirror, Drawer, c.1865, 89 1/2 x 51 x 17 In. 2760.00

Hall Stand, Victorian Style, Oak, Mirror, Applied Decoration, Marble Top, 75 In. 315.00
Hall Stand, Walnut, Mirror, Marble, Umbrella Rests, c.1875, 91 x 36 In. 920.00
Hall Tree, Aesthetic Revival, Embossed, Leather, Mirror, Late 1800s, 35 In. 235.00
Hall Tree, Arts & Crafts, Oak, Bowed Slat Sides, Mortised Geometric Stretcher 340.00
Hall Tree, Bentwood, 8 Curved Arms At Top, Shaft Lower Ring, 4 Arched Legs, 81 In. . . . 530.00
Hall Tree, Gothic, Carved Gallery, Spire Finials, c.1880,'93 x 40 x 12 In. 2475.00
Hall Tree, Renaissance Style, Grapevine, 7 Hooks, Lion's Head, Iron, 78 x 32 x 12 In. . . . 3960.00
Hall Tree, Tiger Bamboo, Wood, Rattan Strapping, 1800s, 55 1/2 x 51 In. 520.00
Hall Tree, Victorian, Walnut, Marble Top, Mirror, Drawer, 2 Umbrella Holders, 81 In. 460.00
Hall Tree, Victorian, Walnut, X-Crossed Arms, White Tack-Button Arms, 88 In. 225.00
Hat Rack, American Empire, Bamboo-Carved Post, 10 Pegs, Tripod Base, 79 In. 1495.00
Hat Rack, Art Deco, Mirror, Curled Hooks, Flowers, Shelf, France, 24 x 9 x 16 In. 750.00
Hat Rack, Walnut, Mirror, 15 Cattle Horns, Wall Mounted, c.1892, 76 x 26 1/2 In. 805.00
Hat Rack, Wood, Mountain Goat Horn, 13 1/2 x 28 In. 80.00
Headboard, Frank Lloyd Wright, Taliesin Border, Heritage Henredon, 54 x 39 In. 345.00
Headboard, G. Nakashima, Laurel Veneer, Bowed, Widdicomb, c.1958, 127 x 38 1/2 In. . 980.00
Headboard, G. Nakashima, Pagoda Shape, Widdicomb, 37 3/4 x 55 1/2 In. 2070.00
Headboard, G. Nelson, Thin Edge, Rosewood, Herman Miller, 116 x 12 x 40 In., Pair . . . 3450.00
Headboard, H. Probber, Light & Dark Mahogany, King Size, 80 x 39 In. 260.00
Headboard, Mahogany, Arch Crest, Carved Leaves, Tufted Upholstery, 55 x 84 In. 460.00
Headboard, Wormley, Ebonized Oak, Drop-Down Armrests, Wool, 38 x 81 In. 1840.00
High Chair, Arrow Back, Plank Bottom, Green, Red Paint Traces, 19th Century, 34 In. . . . 130.00
High Chair, Banister Back, Rush Seat, c.1700, 37 x 19 x 15 In. 2500.00
High Chair, Bentwood, Plank Seat, Yellow Paint, Footrest, 26 1/2 In. 140.00
High Chair, Bentwood, Spindle Turned Supports, Black Paint, Late 1800s, 32 In. 220.00
High Chair, Georgian, Separates From Table Base, Cane Seat, Back, England, 40 In. 895.00
High Chair, Maple, Hickory, Ladder Back, 2 Slats, Cornhusk Seat, Ky., 35 1/2 In. 185.00
High Chair, Mixed Wood, Ladder Back, 3 Arched Slats, Ball Finials, Nipple Feet 255.00
High Chair, Oak, Curved Back, Cane Seat, 38 In. 55.00
High Chair, Plank Seat, Shaped Crest, Painted, Fruit, Leaves, House, Barn 365.00
High Chair, Rush Seat, Ladder Back, Arms, Black Ground, Red, 37 In. 470.00
High Chair, Windsor, Bow Back, 5 Spindles, Shaped Seat, Scrolled Arms 960.00
High Chair, Windsor, Comb Back, Turned Stretcher, Red Over Green Paint, 20 In. 580.00
High Chair, Windsor, Red & Black Grain Painted, Stencil, Arrow Spindles, 36 1/2 In. 290.00
Highboy, Cherry, Flat Top, String Inlay, New Hampshire, c.1780 . . . . 13500.00
Highboy, Chippendale Style, Mahogany, Potthast Bros., c.1925, 80 1/2 x 38 In. 5060.00
Highboy, Chippendale Style, Mahogany, Rolled Broken Arch, Shells, 87 x 43 In. 3615.00
Highboy, Chippendale, Bonnet Top, Claw & Ball Feet, 40 x 20 x 86 In. 2300.00
Highboy, Chippendale, Mahogany, Scroll Top, Philadelphia, 81 x 38 x 22 In. . . .2360.00 to 2785.00
Highboy, George II Style, Mahogany, Bowfront, 51 1/2 x 36 1/2 x 22 1/2 In. 1840.00
Highboy, Japanned, Raised, Gilt, Red Ground, England, c.1890 . . . . 8800.00
Highboy, Oak, 5 Serpentine Drawers, Hat Box Door, c.1900, 36 x 48 In. 315.00
Highboy, Queen Anne Style, Mahogany Veneer, 8 Drawers, Child's, 30 x 56 In. 1870.00
Highboy, Queen Anne, Carved Maple, 8 Drawers, New England, 66 x 37 In. 6615.00
Highboy, Queen Anne, Cherry, Drawers, Cabriole Legs, 18th Century, 89 x 38 x 20 In. . . . 6440.00
Highboy, Queen Anne, Curly Maple, 8 Drawers, Drop Pendants, 73 x 39 In. 9200.00
Highboy, Queen Anne, Maple, 10 Drawers, New England, 65 x 36 In. 3680.00
Highboy, Queen Anne, Maple, 2 Long Drawers, Pinwheel, c.1760, 36 x 39 x 19 In. 2585.00
Highboy, Queen Anne, Walnut, 8 Drawers, Long Island, 66 1/2 x 41 In. 5465.00
Highboy, Queen Anne, Walnut, Bonnet Top, 10 Drawers, 88 1/4 x 40 3/4 x 22 In. 14375.00
Highboy, Queen Anne, Walnut, Stepped Cornice, 7 Drawers, Phila., 89 x 38 x 21 In. 12375.00
Highboy, Rohde, Paldao, 5 Drawers, Brass Pulls, Herman Miller, 33 x 18 x 42 In. 1370.00
Highboy, William & Mary Style, Cherry, 8 Drawers, 59 1/2 x 34 1/2 In. 2300.00
Highboy, William & Mary Style, Trumpet-Turned Legs, American, 60 1/4 x 39 3/4 In. . . . 3450.00
Huntboard, Chippendale, Figured Maple, 43 x 61 x 18 1/2 In. 2990.00
Huntboard, Flaming Birch, White Pine, Writing Surface, Drawer, Pigeonholes, c.1800 . . . 8250.00
Huntboard, Georgian, Crescent Top, Reeded Edges, Fluted Tapered Legs, 60 In. 1485.00
Huntboard, Georgian, Mahogany, Satinwood Inlay, Serpentine, Square Legs, 1800s 4140.00
Huntboard, Hepplewhite Style, Mahogany, Oak, 2 Drawers, Kittinger, 48 x 21 x 35 In. . . . 1265.00
Huntboard, Hepplewhite, 2 Drawers, Vermont, 33 1/2 x 38 1/2 x 15 3/4 In. 1725.00
Huntboard, Walnut, Pine, Tapered Legs, c.1850 . . . . 8000.00
Hutch, H. Probber, Mahogany, Glass, 70 1/2 x 18 x 79 1/2 In. 460.00
Hutch, Heywood-Wakefield, Glass Doors, 2 Piece, 72 x 54 x 19 In. 1610.00

Hutch, John Stuart, Walnut, Brass, 2 Pieces, Johnson Furniture, 75 x 61 x 20 1/4 In. 1265.00
Hutch, Peter Hunt, Hearts & Flowers, Shelves, Drawers, Doors, 53 x 30 x 17 In. 490.00
Hutch, Pine, 2 Doors, 2 Drawers, Shelves, Continental, 1800s, 81 x 52 In. 1955.00
Hutch, Robsjohn-Gibbings, Walnut Veneer, 2 Pieces, 2 Glass Doors, 60 x 35 x 21 In. 345.00
Hutch, Shaker, Walnut, Mid 1800s, 89 x 53 1/4 x 21 3/4 In. 1770.00
Hutch, Windsor, Maple, Woven Splint Seat, New England, c.1850 .... 2800.00
Kas, Blue Paint, Rosehead Nail Construction, Hudson River 10400.00
Kas, Cherry, Walnut, Oak, Raised Panel Door, 3 Drawers, 79 1/2 x 60 x 24 1/2 In. 3740.00
Kas, William & Mary, Walnut, 2 Parts, 2 Doors, Drawer, Ball Feet, New York, 81 x 70 In. . 2875.00
Kneeler, Prie Dieu, Baroque, Oak, Splayed Ring-Turned Legs, Continental, 27 x 22 In. .. 205.00
Kneeler, Prie Dieu, Directoire Style, Fruitwood, Padded, 33 In. 115.00
Kneeler, Prie Dieu, Mahogany, Parquetry, Continental 955.00
Kneeler, Prie Dieu, Renaissance Style, Oak, Carved, Angel Masks, 72 x 26 x 22 In. 2530.00
Lap Desk, Anglo-Indian, Ebony, Quill, Ivory Roundel, Marquetry, 17 x 10 In. 999.00
Lap Desk, Burl Veneer, Geometric Inlay, Mother-Of-Pearl, Leather, 6 x 12 x 9 In. 410.00
Lap Desk, Burl, Brass, 3 Hidden Drawers, Velvet, Stand, c.1830, 25 1/2 x 20 In. 920.00
Lap Desk, Crocodile, Brass Inlay, 2 Ink Bottles, c.1885, 5 1/4 x 12 1/2 x 10 In. 1725.00
Lap Desk, Inlaid, Geometric Bands, Pen Tray, 2 Pens, 5 1/2 x 11 3/4 x 8 1/2 In. 385.00
Lap Desk, Mahogany, Brass Bound, Fitted Interior, England, Early 1800s, 11 3/4 In. 200.00
Lap Desk, Mahogany, Inlaid Brass, England, 7 x 20 x 10 1/2 In. 230.00
Lap Desk, Maple, Mahogany, Side Drawer, Brass Handles, 7 x 21 x 10 1/2 In. 230.00
Lap Desk, Rosewood Veneer, Brass Bound, Velvet Writing Surface, 5 x 15 x 10 In. 195.00
Lap Desk, Rosewood Veneer, Brass, Velvet Writing Surface, Leather Inkwell, 15 x 10 In. . 190.00
Lap Desk, Rosewood, Brass Bound, Ink Bottles, Felt Surface, c.1850, 4 x 14 x 10 In. 140.00
Lap Desk, Rosewood, Brass Mounts, Folding Brass Pull Drawer, 7 x 18 x 10 In. 300.00
Lap Desk, Rosewood, Tortoiseshell, Brass Inlay, 4 3/4 x 14 x 11 In. 495.00
Lap Desk, Rosewood, Tortoiseshell, Brass Inlay, Tooled Leather, 5 x 14 x 11 In. 500.00
Lap Desk, Slant Front, Walnut, Dovetailed, 2 Drawers, Compartments, 19 x 16 In. 225.00
Lap Desk, Tunbridge, Elm, Burl, Baize Surface, c.1865, 6 x 11 3/4 x 8 1/2 In. 259.00
Lap Desk, Tunbridge, Elm, Mahogany, Key, Oblong, England, 7 x 19 1/2 In. 630.00
Lap Desk, Walnut, Brass Bound, Hidden Drawers, Fitted Stand, 1800s, 24 x 20 In. 920.00
Lap Desk, Walnut, Brass Mounted, Tooled Leather, Late 1800s, 6 x 16 x 9 In. 290.00
Lectern, Champleve, Enamel, Bronze, Continental, c.1900, 6 5/8 x 12 3/8 x 15 In. 710.00
Library Steps, Chair, Arts & Crafts, Oak, Pierced Back Rails, c.1900 .... 375.00
Library Steps, Regency Style, Mahogany, Gilt, Tooled Leather, 6 Steps, c.1900, 88 In. 2300.00
Library Steps, Regency Style, Mahogany, Tooled Gold Leather, 63 x 19 x 18 In. 175.00
Library Steps, Regency Style, Rosewood, 4 Fan-Shape Steps, 71 In. 575.00
Library Steps-Chair, Divided Seat, 4 Steps, England, c.1890, 35 In. 290.00
Library Steps-Chair, Regency Style, Mahogany, Carved, 34 1/2 In. 460.00
Library Steps-Chair, Regency, Mahogany, Slung Seat & Back, c.1815, 35 x 24 x 29 In. .. 2070.00
Linen Press, Chippendale, Mahogany, 2 Doors, 5 Drawers, c.1791, 81 x 49 x 21 In. 9560.00
Linen Press, G. Nakashima, Cherry, Fabric-Backed Sliding Doors, 80 x 57 In. 11750.00
Linen Press, George III Style, Oak, Japanned, Parcel Gilt, c.1900, 58 x 34 x 17 1/2 In. 520.00
Linen Press, George III, Burl Walnut, 4 Drawers, c.1815, 82 x 51 In. 6900.00
Linen Press, George III, Mahogany, 2 Drawers, 2 Faux Drawers, c.1785, 83 x 50 In. 1840.00
Linen Press, George III, Mahogany, Brass Mounted, Beaded, c.1800, 88 x 48 In. 1725.00
Linen Press, George III, Mahogany, Late 18th Century, 73 1/2 x 47 1/2 x 23 1/2 In. 2530.00
Linen Press, George III, Mahogany, Scrolled Pediment, Late 1700s, 87 In. 6325.00
Linen Press, Mahogany, 2 Sunken-Panel Doors, 4 Over 2 Drawers, 22 1/2 x 8 x 11 In. 2200.00
Linen Press, Oak, Stepped Cornice, Arched Paneled Doors, 6 Drawers, 85 x 51 In. 1925.00
Linen Press, Parquetry, Broken Arch Pediment, 2 Doors, 3 Drawers, Dutch, 92 x 65 In. .. 4185.00
Linen Press, Pine, Green Paint, 2 Drawers, 2-Paneled Doors, 3 Inside Shelves, 61 In. 1440.00
Linen Press, Queen Anne Style, Walnut, 2 Doors, 4 Drawers, 90 x 43 x 24 In. 2990.00
Linen Press, Regency, Mahogany, Inlaid, 3 Part, 2 Doors, 4 Drawers, 86 3/4 x 50 In. 4025.00
Love Seat, Biggs, No. 2408, Hepplewhite Style, Mahogany, 1900s, 36 x 54 In. 460.00
Love Seat, Florence Knoll, No. 1206, Velvet, Steel Base, 1970s, 62 x 31 1/2 x 30 In. 800.00
Love Seat, Louis XV Style, Wood, Trapunto, Meyer Gunther & Martini, 54 In. 315.00
Love Seat, Majorelle, Ombelles Pattern, 62 In. 2530.00
Love Seat, Renaissance Revival, Walnut, c.1870, 66 In. 230.00
Love Seat, Thayer Coggin, Black Enamel Base, Naugahyde, 55 x 31 x 28 In., Pair 460.00
Love Seat, V. Kagan, No. 100B, Green Chenille, Walnut Legs, 35 1/2 x 58 x 22 In. 6900.00
Love Seat, Victorian, Walnut, Carved, Tufted Velour Upholstery, 37 x 60 x 17 In. 400.00
Love Seat, Victorian, Walnut, Rose Carving, Tufted Pink Upholstery, 54 In. 60.00

Lowboy, Chippendale Style, Walnut, Block Front, 1900s, 28 1/2 x 19 1/4 x 32 In. 545.00
Lowboy, George III, Walnut, Oak, Drawers, Cabriole Legs, Duck Feet, 1700s, 29 x 29 In. . . 4140.00
Lowboy, Oak, 3 Drawers, Fretwork Corner Braces, Chamfered Legs, England, 28 x 34 In. 565.00
Lowboy, Queen Anne Style, Gilt, Japanned Decoration, 30 1/2 x 33 3/4 x 20 1/4 In. 185.00
Lowboy, Queen Anne Style, Walnut, 3 Drawers, Cabriole Legs, c.1910, 30 x 27 In. 470.00
Lowboy, Queen Anne, Fruitwood, 3 Drawers, Pad Feet, Mid 1700s, 27 1/2 x 34 x 21 In. . . 2530.00
Lowboy, Queen Anne, Herringbone, Crossband Walnut Veneer, c.1760, 33 x 44 x 22 In. . . 1380.00
Lowboy, Queen Anne, Mahogany, Molded Top, Leaf & Scroll Carving, 28 x 27 x 18 In. . . 900.00
Lowboy, Queen Anne, Maple, Birch, 4 Drawers, Fan Carving, c.1750, 30 x 32 In. 10925.00
Lowboy, Queen Anne, Maple, Pine, 1 Long Over 3 Short Drawers, 31 x 31 x 16 In. 1265.00
Lowboy, Queen Anne, Oak, 3 Drawers, Cabriole Legs, Shaped Apron, 28 x 33 x 20 In. . . . 1150.00
Lowboy, Queen Anne, Walnut, 3 Drawers, Cabriole Legs, Pa., 28 1/2 x 19 x 36 In. 5750.00
Lowboy, Queen Anne, Walnut, Cabriole Legs, 3 Dovetailed Drawers, 34 x 27 3/4 In. 3335.00
Mirror, 3 Parts, Basket Of Wheat, Ogee, 19th Century, 37 x 22 In. 145.00
Mirror, Adam Style, Giltwood, Oval, Carved, Eagle Crest, 1800s, 51 In. 1035.00
Mirror, Art Nouveau, Disc Shape, Above Kneeling Female Figure, Bronze, 28 In. 2200.00
Mirror, Art Nouveau, Giltwood, Painted, Carved, Flowers, Scrolling, 70 x 49 In. 345.00
Mirror, Arts & Crafts, Hammered Brass, England, 1909, 15 x 19 In., Pair 1495.00
Mirror, Arts & Crafts, Hammered Copper, Fish, Newlyn, England, 19 In. 3450.00
Mirror, Arts & Crafts, Hammered Pewter, 22 1/2 x 33 1/2 In. 635.00
Mirror, Arts & Crafts, Leather, Brass Studded 2200.00
Mirror, Baroque Style, Carved Giltwood, Florence, Italy, Late 1800s, 53 x 38 In. 1495.00
Mirror, Baroque Style, Giltwood, Highly Carved, Florence, Italy, 50 x 36 In. 1725.00
Mirror, Baroque Style, Giltwood, Mercury's Head, Plumes, Italy, c.1885, 43 x 24 In. 1610.00
Mirror, Baroque Style, Wood, Painted, Gilt Gesso, Continental, 24 1/2 x 23 In. 575.00
Mirror, Beaux Arts Style, Giltwood, Carved, Reeded Rails, 42 1/2 x 32 In. 980.00
Mirror, Black Forest, Carved, Pierced, Scrolled, Rope Border, c.1875, 60 x 42 1/4 In. 505.00
Mirror, Black Forest, Pine, Carved, Climbing Bear, Late 1800s 7500.00
Mirror, Black, Urn & Flowers, 2 Brass Hooks, 25 x 16 1/4 In. 125.00
Mirror, Brass, Carved Ebony, Dutch, 53 x 32 In. 2875.00
Mirror, Brass, Silvered Rim, Flower Feet, Plateau, 14 In. 55.00
Mirror, Bugatti, Semicircular Panel, Pewter Inlay, 3 Shelves, 49 x 30 In. 12650.00
Mirror, Bull's-Eye, Gilt, Winged Phoenix, Early 1800s 4675.00
Mirror, Bull's-Eye, Regency Style, Giltwood, Convex, Eagle, c.1865, 40 x 25 In., Pair . . . 2990.00
Mirror, Bull's-Eye, Regency Style, Giltwood, Leaf & Shell Pendant, Late 1800s, 34 In. . . 1530.00
Mirror, Bull's-Eye, Regency Style, Giltwood, Parcel Ebonized, Convex, 35 3/4 In. 1955.00
Mirror, Burl Elm, Birch, Ebonized, Ormolu Mounted, c.1835, 55 x 29 In. 1495.00
Mirror, Carved Frame, Scrolls, Winged Heads At Top, Bottom, 16 1/2 x 13 In. 195.00
Mirror, Carved, Insects, Flowers & Bat Inlay, Chinese, Early 1900s, 48 1/2 x 21 In. 120.00
Mirror, Chariot Of Apollo Lithograph, Oblong, Italy, c.1885, 22 1/2 x 13 3/4 In. 690.00
Mirror, Cheval, Cherry, Scrolled Posts, Carved Paw Feet, 72 1/2 x 33 In. 775.00
Mirror, Cheval, Edwardian, Mahogany, Splayed Legs, c.1900, 69 x 36 1/2 In. 2300.00
Mirror, Cheval, Faux Bamboo, 80 x 29 In. 2240.00
Mirror, Cheval, Mahogany, Beveled Glass, Urn-Form Finial, 82 x 34 1/4 In. 345.00
Mirror, Cheval, Mahogany, Beveled, Octagonal Columns, 1900s, 33 x 71 1/2 In. 575.00
Mirror, Cheval, Mahogany, Molded Saber Legs, England, 57 x 26 In. 2130.00
Mirror, Cheval, Rococo Style, Mahogany, Yoke Crest, c.1850, 71 x 32 x 29 In. 290.00
Mirror, Cheval, Rosewood, Carved Flowers, Chinese, 1800s, 36 x 86 x 27 1/2 In. 940.00
Mirror, Chippendale Style, Broken Arch Top, Flower Rosettes, 63 x 32 In. 620.00
Mirror, Chippendale Style, Gilt Gesso, Broken Arch, Flower Urn, 54 1/2 x 23 In. 960.00
Mirror, Chippendale Style, Giltwood, 48 x 31 In. 1120.00
Mirror, Chippendale Style, Giltwood, Carved, Scrolling Leaves, c.1910, 53 x 26 1/2 In. . . 865.00
Mirror, Chippendale Style, Giltwood, Rococo Scrolling Leaf, 53 1/2 x 35 1/2 In. 375.00
Mirror, Chippendale Style, Mahogany, 20th Century, 51 x 32 In. 115.00
Mirror, Chippendale Style, Mahogany, Figured Veneer, Scroll, Early 1900s, 25 x 15 In. . . 290.00
Mirror, Chippendale Style, Mahogany, Flame Figured, 38 1/2 x 19 In. 200.00
Mirror, Chippendale Style, Mahogany, Parcel Gilt, Late 19th Century, 39 x 20 In. 405.00
Mirror, Chippendale Style, Mahogany, Pine, Scroll, Pierced Crest, 1800s, 30 x 18 In. 230.00
Mirror, Chippendale, Cherry, Parcel Gilt Border, Scrollwork, Bird, c.1800, 26 x 15 In. . . . 920.00
Mirror, Chippendale, Gilt Eagle, Late 1800s, 27 1/2 In. 750.00
Mirror, Chippendale, Gilt, Scrolled Ears, Openwork, 41 In. 1840.00
Mirror, Chippendale, Mahogany Veneer, Pine, 20 1/2 x 13 In. 300.00
Mirror, Chippendale, Mahogany Veneer, Pine, Scalloped, 38 x 20 3/4 In. 400.00

Mirror, Chippendale, Mahogany Veneer, Pine, String Inlay, 20 1/2 x 13 In. 310.00
Mirror, Chippendale, Mahogany, Applied Phoenix Crest, 24 1/2 x 14 In. 550.00
Mirror, Chippendale, Mahogany, Eagle Crest, Scroll, Gilt, 31 x 17 In. 385.00
Mirror, Chippendale, Mahogany, Gilt Eagle Pediment, 27 x 14 In. 160.00
Mirror, Chippendale, Mahogany, Gilt Gesso, Late 18th Century, 44 x 19 1/2 In. 3055.00
Mirror, Chippendale, Mahogany, Gilt Gesso, Scrolled Frame, c.1750, 41 x 20 In. 1880.00
Mirror, Chippendale, Mahogany, Gilt Gesso, Scrolled Frame, Flowers, 37 x 20 In. 1060.00
Mirror, Chippendale, Mahogany, Giltwood, 2 Parts, 35 x 20 In. 5750.00
Mirror, Chippendale, Mahogany, Giltwood, Phoenix, 32 x 17 1/4 In. 575.00
Mirror, Chippendale, Mahogany, Giltwood, Phoenix, 36 x 19 1/2 In. 460.00
Mirror, Chippendale, Mahogany, Giltwood, Scrolled Crest, 41 1/2 x 22 In. 4600.00
Mirror, Chippendale, Mahogany, Line Inlay, Scroll Cut, Applied Floral Brass, 20 In. 290.00
Mirror, Chippendale, Mahogany, Parcel Gilt, Oval, Beveled, Carved Leaves, 34 x 22 In. . . . 285.00
Mirror, Chippendale, Mahogany, Scrolled Cutouts, 25 3/4 In. 140.00
Mirror, Chippendale, Mahogany, Scrolled Ears, Arched Crest, 31 x 15 1/2 In. 565.00
Mirror, Chippendale, Mahogany, Scrolled, Molded Liner, 1790, 38 x 20 In. 585.00
Mirror, Chippendale, Mahogany, Scrolled, Gilt, Eagle, Molded, c.1810, 23 x 12 In. 530.00
Mirror, Chippendale, Mahogany, Scrolled, Molded Liner, 35 x 18 In. 940.00
Mirror, Chippendale, Mahogany, Scrolling Crest, Base, Late 1700s, 20 1/2 x 12 1/4 In. . . . 575.00
Mirror, Chippendale, Mahogany, Scrollwork, 2 Birds, 19 1/2 In. 540.00
Mirror, Chippendale, Mahogany, Scrollwork, 39 x 19 In. 345.00
Mirror, Chippendale, Mahogany, Top Crest, Concave Gilt Carving, 29 x 17 3/4 In. 315.00
Mirror, Chippendale, Walnut, Parcel Gilt, Pierced Gilt Crest Shell, 44 3/4 x 24 In. 3450.00
Mirror, Chippendale, Walnut, Parcel Gilt, Scrolled Crest, Gilded Eagle, 32 x 18 In. 920.00
Mirror, Convex, Gilt Carved, Eagle Girandole, Applied Leaf Carving, 46 In. 4315.00
Mirror, Directoire Style, Gilt Metal, Starburst, Twisted Inner Border, 41 In. 290.00
Mirror, Directoire Style, Giltwood, Sunburst, c.1935, 35 In. 805.00
Mirror, Directoire Style, Leaves, Sunburst, Wrought Iron, Continental, 18 In., Pair 1095.00
Mirror, Directoire Style, Wrought Iron, Gilt, Sunburst, Round, Spain, 21 In. 635.00
Mirror, Dressing, Art Nouveau, Silver Plated, 22 x 15 In. 5380.00
Mirror, Dressing, Beveled, Brass, 3 Parts, Scroll, 10 1/4 In. 85.00
Mirror, Dressing, Hagenauer, Brass, Stylized Head, Austria, 24 1/2 x 17 x 3 1/2 In. 4890.00
Mirror, Dressing, Mahogany, 2 Drawers, Brass Knob, Ball Feet, 18 3/4 x 21 x 7 1/2 In. . . 120.00
Mirror, Dressing, Mahogany, 3 Drawers, Bracket Feet, 29 1/2 x 28 x 10 In. 175.00
Mirror, Dressing, Mahogany, Drawer, Boston, c.1830, 20 x 22 x 8 1/2 In. 750.00
Mirror, Dressing, Mahogany, Marquetry, Frieze Drawers, Anglo-Dutch, 27 x 21 x 12 In. . . 635.00
Mirror, Dressing, Ormolu, Fan Form, Lacy Edging, Tassel Base, Easel Back, 18 1/2 In. . . 295.00
Mirror, Dressing, Silver, Cherub, Dolphin, Leaves, Oval, Easel Back, 17 x 13 1/4 In. 1150.00
Mirror, Dressing, Victorian, Mahogany, 2 Compartments, c.1840, 24 x 22 x 9 1/2 In. 200.00
Mirror, Eastlake, Carved, Molded, Gilt, 24 x 54 In. 115.00
Mirror, Eastlake, Walnut, Carved Scrolls, Panels, 24 x 57 In. 70.00
Mirror, Edwardian, Convex, Giltwood, Parcel Ebonized, c.1900, 30 x 23 In. 1610.00
Mirror, Embossed, Cut Brass Mount, Ebonized, Dutch, 30 1/2 x 27 In. 545.00
Mirror, Empire, Gilt Gesso, Applied Half Turnings, Acanthus Leaves, 23 3/4 x 41 In. 600.00
Mirror, Empire, Reverse Painted, Woman With Child, 37 1/2 x 22 1/2 In. 400.00
Mirror, Empire, Split Spindle Columns, Stepped Plinth, Frieze, Reverse Painted, 25 In. . . 275.00
Mirror, Empire, Split Spindle, Reverse Painted, Dancing Woman, 35 x 18 1/2 In. 770.00
Mirror, Federal Style, Gilt, Folky Flower Watercolor Upper Panel, 1800s 230.00
Mirror, Federal, 2 Panels, Reverse Painted, Victorian Lady, 29 x 13 1/2 x 2 1/2 In. 55.00
Mirror, Federal, 2 Panels, Sailing Ship, Split Column, Gold Frame, 34 x 18 3/4 x 2 In. . . . 580.00
Mirror, Federal, Convex, Giltwood, Dolphin Pediment, Leaf Drop, 42 x 14 1/2 In. 8050.00
Mirror, Federal, Convex, Giltwood, Eagle, 2 Candle Arms, Frame, 39 x 24 In. 3885.00
Mirror, Federal, Gilded, 2 Parts, Columns, Corner Blocks, Rosettes, 43 x 23 x 2 5/8 In. . . 275.00
Mirror, Federal, Gilded, Rosettes, Tuned Half Columns, Corner Blocks, 43 x 23 x 3 In. . . 280.00
Mirror, Federal, Gilt Gesso, Painted, Split Baluster, c.1825, 24 x 13 In. 560.00
Mirror, Federal, Gilt Gesso, Reverse Painted, Naval Scene, c.1820, 38 x 18 In. 4700.00
Mirror, Federal, Gilt, Silver Decoration, Reverse Painted, House, Tree, Lake, 52 In. 565.00
Mirror, Federal, Giltwood, Reverse Painted, House, Landscape, Mass., 32 x 19 In. 1495.00
Mirror, Federal, Giltwood, Reverse Painted, Landscape, Boston, 35 3/4 x 21 3/4 In. 2415.00
Mirror, Federal, Gold Leaf, Sand Textured, Split Column, 32 x 16 x 2 In. 195.00
Mirror, Federal, Gold Leaf, Split Column, 32 x 16 x 2 In. 195.00
Mirror, Federal, Mahogany Veneer, Bone Drawer Pulls, 19 x 17 1/2 In. 200.00
Mirror, Federal, Mahogany Veneer, Reverse Painted, Cottage, Landscape, 17 x 10 In. 495.00

Mirror, Federal, Mahogany, 2 Sections, Reverse Painted, 31 1/2 x 15 3/4 In. 230.00
Mirror, Federal, Mahogany, Inlaid Shell, Scrolled Crest, c.1810, 44 x 24 In. 1075.00
Mirror, Federal, Mahogany, Inlaid, Parcel Gilt, Early 1800s, 52 x 23 In. 5975.00
Mirror, Federal, Reverse Painted, Eagle, Swags, Cove Molded Frame, 38 x 22 In. 520.00
Mirror, Federal, Reverse Painted, Sailing Ship, Split Columns, 34 x 19 x 2 In. 590.00
Mirror, Federal, Softwood, Grain Painted, 18 3/4 x 12 In. 690.00
Mirror, Flowers, Leaves, Chinese, 1800s, 60 x 55 In. 880.00
Mirror, Fornasetti, Reverse Painted, Italy, c.1952, 12 x 13 1/2 In. 2340.00
Mirror, Fruitwood, Inlaid, Molded Frame, Arching Crown, 46 x 26 In. 2090.00
Mirror, G. Nakashima, Walnut, Widdicomb, c.1958, 52 x 4 x 43 In. 2300.00
Mirror, G. Stickley, No. 916, Peaked Top Rail, Label, Red Decal, 35 x 23 In. 1035.00
Mirror, George I, Mahogany, Wave Edge Mold, Early 1700s, 43 x 12 1/4 In. 259.00
Mirror, George III Style, Giltwood, Oval, Garlands, Festoons, Swags, Birds, 48 x 25 In. ... 1315.00
Mirror, George III Style, Mahogany, Parcel Gilt, Broken Arch Pediment, Eagle 655.00
Mirror, George III Style, Parcel Gilt, Carved, 61 1/2 x 32 In. 1770.00
Mirror, George III Style, Walnut, Parcel Gilt Gesso, 1900s, 55 x 28 3/4 In. 800.00
Mirror, George III, Mahogany, c.1800, 26 x 13 3/4 In. 230.00
Mirror, George III, Walnut, Parcel Giltwood, 27 In. 11750.00
Mirror, George V, Giltwood, Parcel Ebonized, Convex, c.1900, 17 3/4 In. 290.00
Mirror, George V, Japanned, Blue & Gold, Round, c.1900, 21 In. 345.00
Mirror, Georgian Style, Glass Spherules On Frame, Oval, Ireland, 1800s, 20 1/2 In. 120.00
Mirror, Gilt & Silvered Wood, Fruit Basket, Italy, Early 1800s, 45 x 34 In., Pair 1725.00
Mirror, Gilt Bronze, Lion, Laurel Wreath, 3-Arm Candle Sockets, 19th Century, 20 In. ... 175.00
Mirror, Gilt Bronze, Reticulated Scrolls, 19th Century, 20 In. 115.00
Mirror, Gilt Frame, Arched Carved Crest, Corners, 20th Century, 54 x 57 In. 280.00
Mirror, Gilt Gesso, Shell Crest, Scrolled Corners, 43 x 35 3/4 In. 315.00
Mirror, Gilt, Gesso, Scrolling, Shells, Stepped Inner Liner, 31 x 36 In. 405.00
Mirror, Gilt, Polychrome, Armorial Crest, Oval, 72 x 50 In. 4830.00
Mirror, Gilt, Rounded Corner Top, Beaded Edge Decoration, France, 25 x 20 1/2 In. 230.00
Mirror, Gilt, Wrought Iron, Sunflower, Curled Tips, Italy, 26 In. 545.00
Mirror, Giltwood, 2 Parts, Scrolled Acanthus Leaf Design, Shepherds, Goats, 62 x 20 In. . 400.00
Mirror, Giltwood, Beveled Glass Panels, Early 1900s, 57 x 43 In., Pair 2530.00
Mirror, Giltwood, Cartouche Form, Phoenixes, Italy, Early 1900s, 32 x 21 In. 345.00
Mirror, Giltwood, Carved, Half Columns, Spearhead Corners, c.1890, 27 x 47 In. 230.00
Mirror, Giltwood, Carved, Late 1800s, 91 x 65 In. 2530.00
Mirror, Giltwood, Carved, Shells, Scroll, Wave, 49 x 34 1/2 In. 375.00
Mirror, Giltwood, Eagle, Shield, Laurel Boughs, American, c.1850, 74 x 54 3/4 In. 7820.00
Mirror, Giltwood, Gothic Arch, c.1890, 42 3/4 x 30 In. 345.00
Mirror, Giltwood, Leaf Scrolls, Italy, c.1885, 49 x 30 In. 3680.00
Mirror, Giltwood, Reeded Sunburst, Gesso, Pentagonal, Continental, 14 In. 200.00
Mirror, Giltwood, Reeded, Lotus Pilasters, N.Y., c.1815, 45 x 23 1/2 In. 1035.00
Mirror, Giltwood, Shepherds, Goats, 2 Parts, Scroll Acanthus Leaf, 62 x 19 3/4 In. 450.00
Mirror, Giltwood, Sunburst, Oval, Italy, 34 x 25 In. 1265.00
Mirror, Giltwood, Wrapped Leaf & Berry Border, Oval, 34 x 39 In. 575.00
Mirror, Gio Ponti Style, Art Deco, Chrome, Steel, Italy, 63 x 35 In. 500.00
Mirror, Girandole, Gilt, 2 Fish, Flame, 2 3-Light Candelabra, c.1800, 37 x 28 In. 3910.00
Mirror, Girandole, Renaissance Revival, 3-Light, Brass, Early 1900s, 23 x 10 In., Pair ... 405.00
Mirror, Girandole, Rococo, 2 Iron Candlearms, Italy, 1700s, 19 x 11 In., Pair 230.00
Mirror, Gold Gesso, Scrolling, Rectangular, 27 x 31 In. 85.00
Mirror, Gold Leaf, Carved Corners, Ivory Crackle Glaze, c.1920, 31 x 43 In. 125.00
Mirror, Gothic Revival, Mahogany, Carved Pediment, Continental, c.1840, 77 x 31 In. ... 1840.00
Mirror, H. Probber, Light & Dark Mahogany, 30 x 47 3/4 In. 635.00
Mirror, Heavy Brass, Iron Scrolled Rim, Flower-Form Feet, Plateau, 14 In. 35.00
Mirror, Italian Rococo, Giltwood, Gray Paint, 19th Century, 29 1/2 x 19 In. 1725.00
Mirror, J. Adnet, Leather Over Steel, Brass, France, 1950s, 14 1/2 x 19 In. 2340.00
Mirror, L. & J.G. Stickley, No. 65, Arched Top, Copper Hooks, 40 x 27 In. 1495.00
Mirror, Louis XIV Style, Beech, Giltwood, Plaster, Carved, 64 x 41 In. 800.00
Mirror, Louis XV Style, Black, Gilt, Cartouche Shape, Leaves, Scrolls, 50 x 44 In. 2870.00
Mirror, Louis XV Style, Carved Wood, Gilt, Acanthus Leaf & Flower, 43 x 49 In. 605.00
Mirror, Louis XV Style, Giltwood, Plaster, c.1885, 66 1/2 x 52 1/2 x 6 In. 1380.00
Mirror, Louis XVI Style, Gilt & Silvered Wood, Fruits, Flowers, Oval, 60 x 47 In. 1555.00
Mirror, Louis XVI Style, Gilt Bronze, Pierced, Beveled Glass, 36 x 20 In. 1265.00
Mirror, Louis XVI Style, Giltwood, Beaded, Molded, c.1900, 56 x 29 In. 1090.00

Mirror, Louis XVI Style, Giltwood, Carved Birds, Garlands, 60 x 41 x 4 In. 2530.00
Mirror, Louis XVI Style, Giltwood, Carved Vines, France, Late 1800s, 41 x 24 In. 3220.00
Mirror, Louis XVI Style, Giltwood, Convex, Molded Frame, Notched Rays, Italy, 24 In. . . 400.00
Mirror, Louis XVI Style, Giltwood, Flowers, Leaves, 46 x 36 In. 8365.00
Mirror, Louis XVI Style, Giltwood, Openwork Crest, Flower Basket, Garlands, 43 In. . . . 2115.00
Mirror, Louis XVI Style, Giltwood, Rocaille Corner Leaves, 27 In., Pair 440.00
Mirror, Louis XVI Style, Giltwood, Turquoise Paint, 59 x 35 In. 1195.00
Mirror, Louis XVI, Giltwood, Pierced Carved Crest, Rectangular, 45 x 67 In. 1660.00
Mirror, Mahogany, 2 Parts, Peter Grinnell & Son, Rhode Island, 42 x 23 In. 1035.00
Mirror, Mahogany, Line & Band Inlay, Beveled Glass, Brass Urn Finials, 31 In., Pair 850.00
Mirror, Mahogany, Ogee, Applied Gilt Gesso Scrolled Corners, 19th Century, 23 x 43 In. . 140.00
Mirror, Mahogany, Painted Oak Leaf, Flowers, Oval, 25 x 35 x 1 In. 560.00
Mirror, Napoleon III, Giltwood, Oval, c.1865, 41 x 32 In. 1265.00
Mirror, Neoclassical, Gesso, Giltwood, Ebonized, Convex, American, 27 x 19 In. 200.00
Mirror, Neoclassical, Gilt, Painted, Brass Rosettes, c.1825, 36 3/4 x 17 In. 2115.00
Mirror, Neoclassical, Giltwood, Carved, c.1840, 62 x 32 1/2 In. 2990.00
Mirror, Neoclassical, Giltwood, Molded Frame, American, c.1830, 40 x 25 1/2 In. 345.00
Mirror, Neoclassical, Giltwood, Polychrome, Italy, 60 x 41 In. 4025.00
Mirror, Neoclassical, Giltwood, Rectangular, Italy, 18th Century, 37 x 22 In. 1035.00
Mirror, Neoclassical, Giltwood, Stepped Molded Cornice, 50 x 27 1/2 In., Pair 14340.00
Mirror, Neoclassical, Mahogany, Molded, American, c.1830, 39 x 27 In. 145.00
Mirror, Neoclassical, Walnut, Eglomise Panel, 40 x 23 In. 230.00
Mirror, Nutting, Colonial Style, Phoenix Crest, Scrolled Pediment, 42 x 23 1/2 In. 2300.00
Mirror, Oak, Eagle Pediment, Fruit, 19th Century, 23 x 15 In. 880.00
Mirror, Oak, Gilt Gesso, Beveled Glass, Double, 48 x 26 In. 190.00
Mirror, Openwork Pediment, Stylized Flowers, Gilt Liner, 33 x 18 1/2 In. 880.00
Mirror, Oriental Style, Carved, Scroll & Leaf Decoration, 54 x 35 1/2 In. 440.00
Mirror, Painted Flowers, Early 1900s, 29 x 18 In. 29.00
Mirror, Parcel Gilt, Polychrome, Rectangular, Italy, 20 x 16 In. 290.00
Mirror, Pier, Aesthetic Revival, Giltwood, American, c.1885, 108 x 52 In. 2185.00
Mirror, Pier, Eastlake, Carved Crest, Gold Highlights, 59 x 28 1/2 In. 240.00
Mirror, Pier, Empire Style, Giltwood, 61 x 37 In. 660.00
Mirror, Pier, Federal, Giltwood, Greek Key Frieze, Beveled Glass, 61 In. 8340.00
Mirror, Pier, George III Style, Giltwood, Pilasters, 55 x 43 x 6 In. 630.00
Mirror, Pier, Gilt, Broken Arch Pediment, Egg & Dart Border, Putti, 84 x 46 In. 1650.00
Mirror, Pier, Giltwood, Arched, Marble Shelf, c.1850, 122 1/2 x 50 In. 6900.00
Mirror, Pier, Louis XV Style, Hardwood, Ivory Paint, 61 x 37 In. 359.00
Mirror, Pier, Napoleon III, Giltwood, Finger-Molded Frame, c.1860, 44 x 32 In., Pair 2070.00
Mirror, Pier, Neoclassical, Giltwood, c.1830, 72 x 42 1/2 In. 1840.00
Mirror, Pier, Neoclassical, Giltwood, Oak Leaves, Sweden, c.1810, 65 1/2 x 39 1/4 In. . . . 1840.00
Mirror, Pier, Neoclassical, Giltwood, Spiral Turned Columns, c.1825, 37 x 25 In. 920.00
Mirror, Pier, Neoclassical, Giltwood, Tympanum Form, c.1815, 81 x 38 In. 1840.00
Mirror, Pier, Regency, Reverse Painted Glass, Cove Molded, 95 x 43 In. . . . . *Illus* 10350.00
Mirror, Pier, Renaissance Revival, Burl, Gilt Incised, Ebony, 113 x 37 In. 1265.00
Mirror, Pier, Renaissance Revival, Marble, Hat Hooks, 108 x 54 In. 3850.00
Mirror, Pier, Rococo, Giltwood, Arched, Molded Frame, c.1855, 84 x 56 x 6 In. 6900.00
Mirror, Pine, Black Paint, Corner Blocks, Rosettes, c.1984, 19 x 15 In. 259.00

**Don't use window cleaner to wipe
off mirror frames or picture frames.
It may remove the gilding.**

**Early (18th-century) glass is thinner
than later glass. Early mirrors reflect a
darker image than new mirrors.**

Furniture, Mirror,
Pier, Regency,
Reverse Painted
Glass, Cove
Molded, 95 x 43 In.

Mirror, Pine, Cutout, Red Paint, Yellow Trim, 14 1/2 x 9 In. 1325.00
Mirror, Pine, Molded Frame, Flemish, c.1885, 22 1/2 x 29 1/2 In., Pair 1840.00
Mirror, Pine, Painted, Half Turnings, Raised Corner Blocks, 12 5/8 x 10 3/4 In., Pair 440.00
Mirror, Pine, Red On Black Grain Painting, Tombstone Shape, Gilt, 34 x 18 In. 345.00
Mirror, Pine, Reeded Frame, Reverse Painted, Covered Bridge, 16 1/2 x 9 3/4 In. 460.00
Mirror, Queen Anne Style, Black Paint, Chinoiserie, c.1910, 34 In. 825.00
Mirror, Queen Anne Style, Japanned, Shaped Bird Crest, Leaves, 21 1/4 In. 530.00
Mirror, Queen Anne Style, Mahogany Veneer, Pine, Carved Urn, 1800s, 40 x 21 1/2 In. . . 690.00
Mirror, Queen Anne, Mahogany, 2 Panels, 48 x 18 1/2 x 7/8 In. 250.00
Mirror, Queen Anne, Mahogany, Burl, Pierced, Scrolled Crest, c.1720, 51 x 21 In. 2300.00
Mirror, Queen Anne, Mahogany, Scrolled Crest, Gilded Phoenix, 32 In. 790.00
Mirror, Queen Anne, Pine, Painted, New England, c.1780, 21 1/4 In. 430.00
Mirror, Queen Anne, Walnut, Cushion Molded, 2 Parts, Beveled Glass, 50 x 19 1/2 In. . . . 2530.00
Mirror, Queen Anne, Walnut, Giltwood, Open Crest, Bird, Leaves, Baltic, 38 In. 805.00
Mirror, Queen Anne, Walnut, Molded Edge, 33 1/2 x 14 3/4 In. 1095.00
Mirror, Queen Anne, Walnut, Parcel Gilt, 2 Sections, Fretted Crest, 48 3/8 In. 590.00
Mirror, Queen Anne, Walnut, Parcel Gilt, Scrolled Crest, Beaded Edge, 31 In. 470.00
Mirror, Queen Anne, Walnut, Scrolled Crest, 18th Century, 43 1/2 x 15 In. 1765.00
Mirror, Regency Style, Gilt, Convex, 52 x 44 In. 2015.00
Mirror, Regency Style, Giltwood, 3 Palm Fronds, France, c.1865, 46 x 24 In. 1725.00
Mirror, Regency Style, Giltwood, Parcel Ebonized, England, 40 1/2 x 26 3/4 In. 1150.00
Mirror, Regency, Giltwood, Black Lacquer, Convex, England, c.1815, 43 x 24 3/4 In. 3450.00
Mirror, Regency, Giltwood, Carved, Parcel Ebonized, Convex, 26 In. 1095.00
Mirror, Regency, Giltwood, Convex, Molded Frame, Eagle, Early 1800s, 43 x 26 In. 3450.00
Mirror, Renaissance Revival, Ebonized Gessoed Wood, Parcel Gilt, c.1900, 37 x 50 In. . . 460.00
Mirror, Renaissance Revival, Mahogany, Leaves, Heads, Victorian, 62 x 10 1/2 In. 1195.00
Mirror, Renaissance Revival, Mahogany, Ribbon & Bead, Late 1800s, 27 x 27 In. 115.00
Mirror, Renaissance Revival, Pressed Tin, Faux Tortoiseshell, 46 x 25 In. 1435.00
Mirror, Rococo Taste, Giltwood, Cartouche, Italy, 60 x 34 In. 920.00
Mirror, Rococo, Brass Frame, 37 x 46 In. 230.00
Mirror, Rococo, Carved Wood, 11 Dancing Cherubs, 59 x 74 In. 3575.00
Mirror, Rococo, Gilt, Rosebuds, Leaves, Cherub, 20 x 29 In. 1050.00
Mirror, Rococo, Giltwood, Cartouche, Leaves, Vines, Italy, 47 x 31 In. 690.00
Mirror, Rococo, Giltwood, Cherubs, Leaves, Gesso, Oval, 49 x 27 In. 1915.00
Mirror, Rococo, Giltwood, Gesso, Cartouche, Italy, c.1835, 65 x 28 1/2 In. 1610.00
Mirror, Rococo, Giltwood, Ivory Enamel Band, Oval, Italy, 59 x 35 In., Pair 2530.00
Mirror, Satinwood, Inlaid, Flowers, Crossbanded, Continental, 50 x 36 1/4 In., Pair 980.00
Mirror, Shaker, Pine, Mitered, Pierced Backboard, Enfield, N.H., 14 7/8 x 8 3/4 In. 920.00
Mirror, Shaving, Bronze, Scrolled & Leaf Surrounds, Oblong, Late 1800s, 20 In. 750.00
Mirror, Shaving, Drawer, Bun Feet, String Inlay, 18 x 13 1/4 x 6 1/2 In. 290.00
Mirror, Shaving, George III, Mahogany, c.1790, 20 x 15 x 7 3/4 In. 470.00
Mirror, Shaving, Mahogany, Dovetailed Drawers, Acorn Finials, Turned Feet, 23 x 9 In. . . 175.00
Mirror, Shaving, Mahogany, Raised Lip, Pedestal, Tripod, 62 x 16 In. 635.00
Mirror, Shaving, Queen Anne, Mahogany, Dovetailed, 3 Drawers, 18 x 8 x 26 In. 750.00
Mirror, Shaving, Sheraton Style, Satinwood Veneer, 3 Drawers, 22 x 8 x 25 In. 145.00
Mirror, Shell Art, Plaster Frame, 22 1/2 x 29 In. 135.00
Mirror, Sheraton, Gilt, 2 Parts, Reverse Painted, Sailboat, 245 1/2 x 13 1/2 In. 260.00
Mirror, Sheraton, Reverse Painted, 2 Parts, 26 x 14 1/2 In. 315.00
Mirror, Sheraton, Reverse Painted, Battleship, 1800s, 32 x 15 1/2 In. 290.00
Mirror, Sterling, Heart Shape, William Comyns, London, 1898, 16 1/2 x 14 1/2 In. 1225.00
Mirror, Tabernacle, Federal, Gilt Gesso, Molded Cornice, c.1815, 29 1/2 x 15 In. 1530.00
Mirror, Tabernacle, Federal, Giltwood, Reverse Painted, Allegorical Liberty, 39 x 25 In. . . 1150.00
Mirror, Tabernacle, Neoclassical, Reverse Painted, Early 1900s, 43 x 24 In. 345.00
Mirror, Tabernacle, Sheraton, Mahogany, Rope-Turned Columns, American, 41 x 19 In. . . 800.00
Mirror, Tabernacle, Sheraton, Rope-Turned Pilasters, 19th Century, 32 x 17 1/2 In. 145.00
Mirror, Trumeau, Beechwood, Parcel Gilt, c.1900, 76 x 46 In. 3680.00
Mirror, Trumeau, Louis XV Style, Giltwood, Cream Paint, 63 x 47 1/2 x 2 In. 1725.00
Mirror, Venetian, Crested Top, Beveled, Etched, Octagonal, 49 x 31 In. 1150.00
Mirror, Venetian, Etched Glass, Shaped Crest, Starburst, Early 20th Century, 60 In. 3055.00
Mirror, Venetian, Reverse Engraved, Leaves, Fleurettes, Late 1800s, 58 x 29 In. 6040.00
Mirror, Venetian, Reverse Engraved, Oblong, 55 1/2 x 28 x 1 In. 520.00
Mirror, Venetian, Rococo Style, Cartouche Form, Italy, c.1900, 35 x 23 In. 635.00
Mirror, Victorian, Carved, Gilded, Oval, Deer Figure On Top, 59 x 29 1/2 In. 895.00

Mirror, Walnut, Black Forest, Carved, Eagle Top, 40 x 22 In. 3000.00
Mirror, Walnut, Mahogany Veneer Liner, 22 1/2 x 17 In. 77.00
Mirror, Walnut, Molded, Arch, Gilt Liner, c.1880, 3 x 20 In. 260.00
Mirror, Walnut, Shadow Box, Victorian, Oval, 22 In. 150.00
Mirror, William & Mary, Early 1700s, 16 3/4 x 10 1/2 In. 1210.00
Mirror, William IV Style, Giltwood, Gesso, c.1835, 44 1/2 x 26 1/2 In. 1265.00
Mirror, Wood, Gilt Gesso, Flowers, Acanthus Leaves, 36 x 30 In. 60.00
Mirror, Wrought Iron, Cut Brass, 2 Laurel Leaf Sprays, Oval, Italy, 37 x 25 In. 980.00
Ottoman, Aesthetic Revival, Cherry, Lacquer, Upholstered, c.1875, 16 x 15 In., Pair 900.00
Ottoman, Arts & Crafts, Box Stretcher, Square, Tobey Furniture Co., 16 x 22 In. 690.00
Ottoman, Frank Gehry, Easy Edges, Laminated Corrugated Cardboard, 16 x 17 In. 1495.00
Ottoman, G. Nakashima, Walnut, Cushion, Cross Base, c.1977, 13 3/4 x 21 In. 3105.00
Ottoman, G. Nakashima, Walnut, Maple, 1960s, 20 x 20 x 11 In. 1520.00
Ottoman, H. Bertoia, No. 242, Vinyl, Steel, Knoll, c.1950, 15 x 24 x 17 In., 4 Piece 2629.00
Ottoman, Oak, Zebra Skin, Padded, 2 Compartments, c.1885, 18 x 42 x 25 In. 4370.00
Ottoman, Victorian, Leather, Tufted Top, Compartment, c.1890, 20 1/2 x 55 x 22 In. 1725.00
Ottoman, Victorian, Mahogany, Leather, Plinth Base, 18 x 42 1/2 x 25 In. 2300.00
Ottoman, W. Plattner, Nickel Plated Wire Base, Mohair Upholstery, Round, 16 x 25 In. ... 820.00
Overmantel, see Architectural category.
Parlor Set, Adam Style, Satinwood, Flowers, Armchair, Settee, Side Chair, 3 Piece 920.00
Parlor Set, Arts & Crafts, Barrel Shape, Woven Diamond Design, 3 Piece 2415.00
Parlor Set, Haywood-Wakefield, Wicker, Cushions, Sofa, Chair, Rocker, 3 Piece 2185.00
Parlor Set, Wicker, Black Paint, Flowers, Macaw On Settee, c.1925, 6 Piece 1900.00
Parlor Set, Wicker, Black, Flowers, Macaw On Settee, c.1925, 6 Piece 1700.00
Parlor Set, Wicker, Rolled Arms, Back, Whitney, Ashburnham, Mass., 4 Piece 600.00
Pedestal, Alabaster, Italy, Early 20th Century, 39 1/4 In., Pair 800.00
Pedestal, Brass Mount, Reeded Column, Octagonal Base, 44 1/2 In., Pair 880.00
Pedestal, Bronze, Marble, Corinthian Capitals, Square Top, 46 x 11 3/4 In., Pair 518.00
Pedestal, Empire Revival, Cast Iron, Black, Crossed Arrows, c.1910, 47 3/4 In., Pair 1410.00
Pedestal, Empire Style, Gilt Bronze Mounts, Green Marble, 45 In. 3585.00
Pedestal, Empire Style, Rosewood, Ebonized Mahogany, Bronze, 46 x 22 1/4 x 14 In. ... 540.00
Pedestal, Gothic Revival, Pine, Columns, Egg & Dart Molding, 35 x 17 x 16 In. 330.00
Pedestal, Gothic Revival, Pine, Waxed, Mid 19th Century, 70 x 26 x 25 In. 430.00
Pedestal, Green Onyx, Column, 30 In., Pair 700.00
Pedestal, Hardwood, Carved, Marble Dish Top, Carved Base, Early 1900s, 39 x 16 In. ... 290.00
Pedestal, Hardwood, Inlaid, Hexagonal, Block Feet, North Africa, c.1900, 25 x 14 In. ... 750.00
Pedestal, Hardwood, Mother-Of-Pearl, Octagonal, North Africa, 24 x 17 1/2 In. 690.00
Pedestal, L. & J.G. Stickley, No. 27, Square Top, Corbels, Flared Base, 36 x 19 In. 3290.00
Pedestal, L. & J.G. Stickley, Oak, 42 x 13 x 13 In. 2990.00
Pedestal, Limbert, No. 246, Round Top, 2 Lower Shelves, Arched Sides, 42 x 14 In. 4400.00
Pedestal, Louis XVI Style, Onyx, Octagonal Top, Late 1800s, 42 1/2 x 20 x 10 In. 1840.00
Pedestal, Louis XVI Style, Parcel Giltwood, Square, Tapered, Bows, Swags, 44 In., Pair . 575.00
Pedestal, Louis XVI Style, Walnut, Marble Top, Ormolu Mounted, 45 x 21 In. 2070.00
Pedestal, Mahogany, Pierced Brass Gallery, X-Brace Stretchers, 40 1/2 x 12 In. 145.00
Pedestal, Marble Top, Gilt Painted Base, Wrapped Columns, Paw Feet, 41 x 14 x 14 In. ... 300.00
Pedestal, Marble, Cream & Gray, Continental, c.1900, 48 1/4 x 14 x 13 3/4 In. 860.00
Pedestal, Marble, Swirled Body, Octagonal Base, Canted Corners, 35 1/2 In. 250.00
Pedestal, Marble, Verde Antico, c.1885, 42 x 19 1/2 x 19 1/2 In. 1095.00
Pedestal, Marble, White, Black, Variegated, Spiral, Late 1800s, 42 x 10 In. 460.00
Pedestal, Napoleon III, Mahogany, Marble Top, Tapered, c.1890, 46 x 18 In., Pair 2530.00
Pedestal, Napoleon III, Walnut, Scroll Brackets, Urns, Leaves, c.1865, 47 x 17 In. 1150.00
Pedestal, Neoclassical, Black Variegated Marble, Block Feet, 44 In., Pair 2070.00
Pedestal, Neoclassical, Gilt Bronze Mount, 39 In. 1315.00
Pedestal, Neoclassical, Gilt Decoration, Italy, 49 x 20 In., Pair 5750.00
Pedestal, Neoclassical, Green Marble, Column, 41 In. 660.00
Pedestal, Neoclassical, Mahogany, Marble Top, Brass Mounted, c.1910, 48 1/4 In. 575.00
Pedestal, Neoclassical, Marble, Column, Square Top, c.1900, 35 x 10 In. 315.00
Pedestal, Neoclassical, Marble, Flower Swags, Continental, 35 x 18 In. 2030.00
Pedestal, Neoclassical, Marble, Square Top, Column, 34 x 14 In., Pair 1035.00
Pedestal, Neoclassical, Onyx, Bronze Mounted, Continental, 37 1/2 In., Pair 3680.00
Pedestal, Neoclassical, Parcel Giltwood, Verte Peinte, 32 x 22 1/2 In., Pair 1265.00
Pedestal, Neoclassical, Wood, Painted, 3 Columns, 28 3/4 x 15 3/4 x 17 1/4 In., Pair ... 240.00
Pedestal, Oak, Carved Panels, Tapered, Egg & Leaf Molding, 52 x 13 x 11 In. 1650.00

Pedestal, Onyx, White, 7 Sections, Lobed Urn Center, Octagonal Base, 44 x 11 In. 400.00
Pedestal, Onyx, Yellow, 42 In. 1725.00
Pedestal, Openwork Top, Scrolling, Tripod Base, Cast Iron, 30 x 19 In. 99.00
Pedestal, Regency Style, Ebonized Wood, Ormolu Mounted, 1880s, 56 x 20 x 12 In. 1610.00
Pedestal, Regency Style, Polychrome, Circular Top, Early 1900s, 38 1/2 In., Pair 1265.00
Pedestal, Renaissance Revival, Mahogany, Ebonized, Gilt Decorated, 40 In., Pair 1430.00
Pedestal, Renaissance Revival, Marble, 3 Columns, Tripod, 35 1/4 In., Pair 1840.00
Pedestal, Rosewood, Tapered, Circular Top, Tripod Scrolled Feet, 29 1/2 x 18 1/2 In. 990.00
Pedestal, Satinwood, Parquetry, Ormolu, 2 Jasperware Oval Medallions, 46 x 12 In. 2825.00
Pedestal, Victorian Style, Cast Iron, Marble, Scrolling Flowers, 29 x 36 x 13 In., Pair . . . 550.00
Pedestal, Victorian, Marble, Verde Antico, Revolving Top, c.1900, 38 In. 980.00
Pie Safe, Amish, 16 Punched Tin Panels, Drawer, Ky., 68 x 42 In. 6000.00
Pie Safe, Cherry, 2 Drawers, 12 Pierced Tin Panels, 2 Doors, Va., c.1850, 51 x 39 In. 1395.00
Pie Safe, Cherry, 2 Drawers, 2 Doors, 4 Pierced Tin Raised Panels, 54 x 44 x 21 In. 2310.00
Pie Safe, Cherry, 2 Drawers, Pierced Tin Doors, Raised Panels, 54 x 44 x 20 1/2 In. 2350.00
Pie Safe, Green Paint, 2 Doors, 12 Tin Panels 420.00
Pie Safe, Green Paint, Flour, Sugar & Pie, c.1880s, 40 x 67 In. 1100.00
Pie Safe, Hanging, Painted, Pinwheel, Flowers, Stars In Circle, 30 x 32 In. 115.00
Pie Safe, Mustard Paint, Screen, Round, 60 In. 580.00
Pie Safe, Painted, Leaf Design, Pierced Tin, Early 19th Century, 36 x 39 In. 405.00
Pie Safe, Pine, 2 Dovetailed Drawers, Punched Tin Doors, 51 x 41 x 19 In. 385.00
Pie Safe, Pine, Brown Paint, 8 Punched Tin Panels, 2 Doors, Bracket Feet, 50 x 42 In. . . . 750.00
Pie Safe, Pine, Door, Iron & Brass Latch, Screen Panels, 2 Shelves, 27 x 16 1/2 In. 415.00
Pie Safe, Pine, Paneled, 2 Drawers Over 2 Doors, 42 x 47 In. 195.00
Pie Safe, Pine, Red Paint, Punched Tin, 2 Doors, Drawer, 70 In. 300.00
Pie Safe, Poplar, Pine, Scalloped Gallery, 2 Drawers Over 2 Doors, c.1880 . . . . 3650.00
Pie Safe, Shaker, Yellow Paint, 2 Doors, Punched Tin Panels, 5 Shelves, 77 In. 3820.00
Pie Safe, Softwood, 2 Doors, 3 Star Punched Tin Panels, Dovetailed Drawer 1400.00
Pie Safe, Softwood, Dovetailed Top, Double Sunken Panels, Brown Paint 845.00
Pie Safe, Tin Door, Punched Hearts, Stars, American, c.1875, 48 3/4 x 43 x 22 1/4 In. . . . 1120.00
Pie Safe, Walnut, 1 Over 2 Drawers, Pierced Star, Tin Doors, Side Panels, 50 x 41 In. 1100.00
Pie Safe, Walnut, 2 Doors, Punched Tin Panels, 2 Drawers, Turned Legs, 42 x 54 In. 575.00
Pie Safe, Walnut, 2 Drawers, 2 Doors, 3 Pinwheel Pierced Tin Sides, 51 x 40 x 18 In. 990.00
Pie Safe, Walnut, 2 Drawers, Panel Doors, Pinwheel Pierced Tin, 51 x 39 x 18 In. 1000.00
Pie Safe, Walnut, 12 Panels, Vertically Split Turnings, 54 x 41 1/2 x 17 In. 1495.00
Pie Safe, Walnut, 12 Punched Tin Pinwheel Panels, 2 Drawers, 52 1/2 x 40 x 18 In. 2310.00
Pie Safe, Walnut, Pine, Drawer, Tin Doors, Pierced Star, 49 1/2 x 41 x 16 1/2 In. 1120.00
Planter, Teak Case, Frame, Zinc Insert, Scandinavian, 19 3/4 x 14 x 16 1/2 In. 460.00
Planter, V. Panton, Enameled Metal, X Design, Denmark, 1970s, 16 x 16 In., Pair 935.00
Plate Rack, Wrought Iron, Tripod Shape, 5 Graduated Shelves, 40 1/2 x 11 In. 115.00
Podium, Wendell Castle, Walnut Laminate, Stack Slanted, Drawer, 51 x 64 x 32 In. 3450.00
Rack, Baker's, Iron, 3 Tiers, Brass, Rays Ironworks, Los Angeles, 83 x 96 x 19 In. 600.00
Rack, Baker's, Iron, Brass, 3 Shelves, Scrolled Center Supports, Crest, 76 x 47 1/2 In. . . . 980.00
Rack, Baker's, Victorian, Iron, Brass Bound, 3 Open Shelves, 70 x 35 x 18 In. 865.00
Rack, Baker's, Victorian, Iron, Brass Bound, 3 Shelves, 79 x 28 1/2 x 9 In. 405.00
Rack, Bread, Louis XV, Walnut, Kneeling Woman, 33 1/2 x 29 3/4 x 16 In. 805.00
Rack, Drying, Herb, Folding, Green Paint, 2 Sections, Leather Hinges, 48 x 46 1/2 In. . . . 145.00
Rack, Drying, Shaker, Cherry, 2 Bars, Mortised, Arched Foot, 33 x 30 In. 920.00
Rack, Magazine, G. Stickley, Paneled Sides, Leather Straps, 35 x 15 x 145 In. 6900.00
Rack, Magazine, Hanging, Eagle & Flag, White Porcelain Tack Accents, 34 In. 60.00
Rack, Magazine, J. Adnet, Bamboo, Brass, Rattan, France, 1950s, 16 x 9 x 21 1/2 In. 1755.00
Rack, Magazine, J. Adnet, Leather, Steel, Brass, France, 1950s, 12 x 7 x 16 In. 2000.00
Rack, Magazine, Slatted Sides, Cutout Handle, Arts & Crafts, 20 x 16 x 22 In. 325.00
Rack, Magazine, Wire, Dog Form, c.1950 . . . . 127.00
Rack, Magazine, Wormley, No. 4765, Tree, Walnut, Birch, Dunbar, c.1952, 28 x 25 In. . . . 4680.00
Rack, Plate, Hanging, Wrought Iron, Domed, Fleur-De-Lis, 13 3/4 In. 175.00
Rack, Plate, Painted, Black, Cup Hooks, 3 Drawers, c.1890, 46 In. 440.00
Rack, Plate, Pine, Mortised Joints, 36 x 28 In. 120.00
Rack, Plate, William & Mary Style, Oak, England, Early 1900s, 24 1/4 x 18 In. 175.00
Rack, Quilt, Folding, 2 Sections, Pine, Medallion Top, Shoe Feet, 65 x 46 1/2 In. 200.00
Rack, Quilt, Folding, 2 Sections, Pine, Painted, Gray, Beaded Edges, 74 x 72 In. 230.00
Rack, Quilt, Walnut, Tongue In Groove Construction, Early 19th Century, 20 In. 220.00
Recamier, Biedermeier, Maple, Scrolled Ends, Stepped Backrest, c.1820, 64 In. 1175.00

Recamier, Empire Style, Mahogany, 26 x 80 x 30 In. 1300.00
Recamier, Federal Style, Mahogany, Saber Legs, Ormolu, Brocade, Baker, 81 x 34 In. . . . 2970.00
Recamier, Mahogany, Ram's Head, Leaves, Rolled Arm, Velvet Upholstery, 31 x 33 In. . . 650.00
Recamier, Neoclassical, Cane Seat, Scrolling Head & Footboard, Legs, 33 x 74 In. 9430.00
Recamier, Neoclassical, Mahogany, Carved, Curved Back, Feet, c.1830, 31 x 72 x 22 In. . 4185.00
Rocker, Arts & Crafts, 3 Horizontal Slats, Through Tenon Construction, 27 x 29 x 33 In. . 115.00
Rocker, Arts & Crafts, 6 Narrow Vertical Slats, Saddle Seat, 17 x 28 x 29 In. 400.00
Rocker, Bentwood, Austrian, c.1890, 36 In. 230.00
Rocker, Black Paint, 6 Slats, Ring Turned Legs, Baluster Turned Supports, 17 x 48 In. . . . 345.00
Rocker, Boston, Cane Seat, Fruit Stencil, Brown Black Ground, 41 In. 100.00
Rocker, Boston, Shell & Leaf, Grain Painted Ground, 19th Century 115.00
Rocker, Cane Seat, 5 Slats, Turned Front Posts, Arms, Ohio, 43 1/2 In. 600.00
Rocker, Carousel Carriage Form, Horse, Adams, Marlboro, N.H., Child's, 42 In. 800.00
Rocker, Curly Maple, Ladder Back, Armless, Front Comma Cutouts, 41 In. 660.00
Rocker, Eames, Birch, Strut Frame, Banner Metals, Wire Seat, Leather, c.1950, 28 In. 960.00
Rocker, Eames, Fiberglass, Parchment, Birch Sleighs, Herman Miller, c.1950, 27 In. 1435.00
Rocker, Eames, Orange Fiberglass, Metal Rod Base, Wooden Rockers, 1958, 26 1/2 In. . . . 645.00
Rocker, Eames, RAR, Birch, Fiberglass, Zinc, Herman Miller, c.1950, 25 x 27 x 27 In. . . . 935.00
Rocker, Eames, Zenith, Yellow Fiberglass, Herman Miller, 25 x 27 In. 1265.00
Rocker, G. Nakashima, Walnut, Hickory Spindles, 1976, 32 1/2 x 18 1/2 x 29 In. 4315.00
Rocker, G. Stickley, 4 Slats, Curved Top Rail & Arms, 37 x 25 x 28 In. 590.00
Rocker, G. Stickley, Arched Stretchers, 36 x 24 1/2 x 21 In. 690.00
Rocker, G. Stickley, Leather Cushion, 1901, 36 x 25 x 24 In. 2015.00
Rocker, G. Stickley, Mahogany, Web Seat, 35 x 28 1/2 x 23 In. 460.00
Rocker, G. Stickley, No. 393, 5 Vertical Slats, Curved Arms, 27 x 30 x 44 In. 4315.00
Rocker, Green Paint, Flower Decal, Plank Bottom, Child's, 20 1/2 In. 96.00
Rocker, Green Paint, Woven Splint Seat, Shaped Splat, Child's, 22 In. 565.00
Rocker, Green Paint, Yellow, Brown, Black Flowers, Wheat Tops, 18 In. 115.00
Rocker, Heywood-Wakefield, Wicker, Leatherette Seat, Scrolled Arms, Child's 55.00
Rocker, Hickory, 4 Split Log Slats, Curved Slatted Seat, 36 In. 570.00
Rocker, Hitchcock, Black Paint, Pillow Back, 1800s 160.00
Rocker, J.M. Young, Leather Seat, 39 1/2 x 26 x 31 In. 520.00
Rocker, L. & J.G. Stickley, Back Slats, Arched Side, Stretchers, 39 x 32 x 30 In. 1495.00
Rocker, L. & J.G. Stickley, Morris, Leather Cushions, Even Arms, 38 x 31 x 35 In. 2128.00
Rocker, L. & J.G. Stickley, Morris, Slat Sides, Leather Upholstery, 36 1/2 x 35 x 32 In. . . . 2415.00
Rocker, L. & J.G. Stickley, No. 460, Slat Sides, 31 x 18 x 29 In. 2215.00
Rocker, L. & J.G. Stickley, Slat Sides, 38 x 28 1/2 x 25 1/2 In. 1440.00
Rocker, L. & J.G. Stickley, Vertical Slats, Arms, Arched Apron, 35 x 28 x 29 In. 690.00
Rocker, L. & J.G. Stickley, Vertical Slats, Drop-In Seat, 35 x 27 x 30 In. 1150.00
Rocker, Ladder Back, 2 Slats, Red Paint, Tape Seat, Child's, 20 1/2 In. 85.00
Rocker, Ladder Back, 3 Slats, Splint Seat, Blue Paint 230.00
Rocker, Ladder Back, 4 Graduated Slats, Mortise & Tenon Construction, 42 In. 360.00
Rocker, Ladder Back, 4 Slats, Woven Rush Seat, Arms, 40 x 25 x 20 In. 550.00
Rocker, Ladder Back, Acorn Finials, Turned Arms, Red Paint Traces, Fiber Seat, 23 In. . . . 130.00
Rocker, Ladder Back, Birch, Hickory, Woven Seat, 7 x 21 1/2 In. 250.00
Rocker, Ladder Back, Maple, Hickory, Paper Rush Seat, 3 Arched Slats, Child's, 23 In. . . . 125.00
Rocker, Ladder Back, Maple, Turned Front Posts, Woven Fiber Seat, 41 1/2 In. 770.00
Rocker, Ladder Back, Mixed Wood, Arched Slats, Red Stain Trace, c.1825, 44 x 21 In. . . . 145.00
Rocker, Ladder Back, Red Paint, 3 Arched Slats, Splint Seat, Child's, 24 In. 630.00
Rocker, Ladder Back, Rope Seat, Turned Finials, Double Stretcher Base, Early 1800s 127.00
Rocker, Ladder Back, Shaped Finials, Paint Traces, Hickory Bark Seat, 39 In. 220.00
Rocker, Lime Green Paint, Black Highlights, Crest Rail, Plank Bottom, 29 1/2 In. 120.00
Rocker, Lincoln Style, Cane Seat, Back, c.1890, 27 In. 127.00
Rocker, Lincoln Style, Maple, Cane Seat, Back, c.1890, 40 In. 80.00
Rocker, Lincoln Style, Walnut, Carved Crest, Upholstered, 37 1/2 x 24 1/2 x 27 In. 140.00
Rocker, Lincoln Style, Walnut, Serpentine Back, Upholstered, Padded Arms, 39 In., Pair . 300.00
Rocker, Molded Fiberglass, Steel Rod Base, Birch Runners, Herman Miller, 26 In. 500.00
Rocker, Oak, Cane, Painted, R.L. Bryan Co., 1920s, Child's, 29 In. 80.00
Rocker, Oak, Metal Frame, Upholstered, 32 x 23 1/2 x 28 In. 345.00
Rocker, Painted, Stencils, Cane Seat, c.1860, Child's 315.00
Rocker, Pennsylvania Dutch, Red, High Back, 42 x 25 x 19 1/2 In. 840.00
Rocker, Red Paint, Shaped Crest, Rolled Arms, Seat, Plank Bottom, Child's, 24 In. 169.00
Rocker, Red, Yellow, Black, 5 Shaped Slats, Woven Splint Seat, Walnut Paddle Arms 365.00

Rocker, Roycroft, Chestnut, Leather Seat, Carved Orb, 36 x 25 1/4 x 22 In. 2300.00
Rocker, Roycroft, No. 039, Flared Back, Leather Seat, 25 x 31 x 36 In. 1955.00
Rocker, Shaker, Birch, 4 Slats, Scroll Arms, Alfred, Me., c.1830, Child's, 13 1/2 x 41 In. . . 4025.00
Rocker, Shaker, Birch, Maple, 4 Slats, Tape Seat, Arms, 15 x 44 In. 690.00
Rocker, Shaker, Brown Paint, Red & Blue, 3 Slats, Woven, Tape Seat, 14 1/2 x 35 In. 360.00
Rocker, Shaker, Ladder Back, 4 Shaped Slats, Acorn Finials, Low Rush Seat, 42 1/2 In. . . 715.00
Rocker, Shaker, Ladder Back, Bird's-Eye & Curly Maple, Rounded Arms, 45 In. 1320.00
Rocker, Shaker, Ladder Back, Straight Back Posts, Turned Arms, Early 1800s, 45 In. 220.00
Rocker, Shaker, Maple, 3 Slats, Rush Seat, New Lebanon, c.1825, 13 1/2 x 31 1/4 In. 1150.00
Rocker, Shaker, Maple, 4 Slats, Rush Seat, Scroll Arms, New Lebanon, c.1835, 46 In. . . . 5175.00
Rocker, Shaker, Maple, 4 Slats, Tape Seat, Arms, Harvard, Mass., c.1840, 16 1/2 x 46 In. . 2015.00
Rocker, Shaker, Maple, Splint Seat, Mushroom Caps, Enfield, Conn., c.1820, 47 In. 5290.00
Rocker, Shaker, Maple, Tape Back, Seat, Arms, Mt. Lebanon, c.1880, 12 x 28 3/4 In. 3450.00
Rocker, Shaker, Maple, Tiger Maple, 3 Arched Splats, Arms, Watervliet, c.1820, 34 In. . . . 3450.00
Rocker, Shaker, No. 0, Maple, Ladder Back, Mt. Lebanon, c.1880, 9 x 24 In. . . .3450.00 to 3680.00
Rocker, Shaker, No. 1, Black Paint, 3 Slats, Mt. Lebanon, N.Y., 29 In. 480.00
Rocker, Shaker, No. 1, Maple, Tape Back, Seat, Mt. Lebanon, 13 x 29 1/2 In. 2070.00
Rocker, Shaker, No. 3, 3 Arched Slats, Rush Seat, Mt. Lebanon, 35 In. 430.00
Rocker, Shaker, No. 3, Acorn Finials, Cane Seat, Ky. 990.00
Rocker, Shaker, No. 3, Maple, 3 Slats, Tape Seat, Mt. Lebanon, 15 1/2 x 35 In. 800.00
Rocker, Shaker, No. 3, Maple, Tape Seat, Shawl Bar, Arms, Mt. Lebanon, c.1870, 34 In. . 1035.00
Rocker, Shaker, No. 3, Padded, 3 Slats, Decal, Arms, Mt. Lebanon 460.00
Rocker, Shaker, No. 4, Ladder Back, Mt. Lebanon 345.00
Rocker, Shaker, No. 4, Maple, 3 Slats, Rush Seat, Mt. Lebanon, 15 1/2 x 35 1/2 In. 690.00
Rocker, Shaker, No. 6, Maple, Ebony, Arms, Mt. Lebanon, c.1875, 15 1/2 x 42 In. 1035.00
Rocker, Shaker, No. 6, Tiger Maple, Shawl Bar, Rush Seat, Curved Arms, Mt. Lebanon . . 345.00
Rocker, Shaker, No. 7, 4 Slats, Rush Seat, Armless, Mt. Lebanon, N.Y., 45 In. 380.00
Rocker, Shaker, No. 7, Capped Arms, Black & Burgundy Tape Seat, Shawl Bar, 40 In. . . . 935.00
Rocker, Shaker, No. 7, Ladder Back, 4 Slats, Woven Rush Seat, Arms, 40 x 25 x 20 In. . . . 560.00
Rocker, Shaker, No. 7, Maple, 4 Slats, Arms, Cane Seat, Mt. Lebanon, c.1880, 16 x 42 In. . 3795.00
Rocker, Shaker, No. 7, Maple, Ladder Back, Mt. Lebanon, c.1880, 15 x 41 1/2 In. 1150.00
Rocker, Shaker, No. 7, Maple, Shawl Bar, Arms, Mt. Lebanon, 17 1/2 x 39 1/2 In. 2645.00
Rocker, Shaker, No. 7, Maple, Shawl Bar, Arms, Mt. Lebanon, c.1880, 16 x 41 In. 2415.00
Rocker, Shaker, No. 7, Maple, Tape Back, Seat, Mt. Lebanon, 17 x 42 In., Pair 4600.00
Rocker, Shaker, No. 7, Maple, Tape Seat, Arms, Mt. Lebanon, 17 x 41 In. 3165.00
Rocker, Shaker, Painted, 3 Arched Slats, Splint Seat, Scrolled Arms, 43 1/2 x 14 In. 765.00
Rocker, Shaker, Ring Base, Graduated Splats, Shaped Arms, Oval Finials, Ky., 45 In. 275.00
Rocker, Shaker, Shaped Arms, Acorn Finials, Broad Cane Seat, Late 1800s, 34 1/2 In. . . . 220.00
Rocker, Shaker, Tiger Maple, 4 Arched Slats, Rush Seat, Arms, Enfield, 45 In. 3565.00
Rocker, Sheraton, Painted, Brown, Gold Stencil, Rush Seat, 28 In. 80.00
Rocker, Spindle Back, Cane Seat, Arms, Painted, Stenciled, 21 x 14 x 19 In. 56.00
Rocker, Spindle Back, Cane Seat, Bentwood Arms, 21 x 14 x 19 In. 55.00
Rocker, Spinning Wheel Back, Red & Gilt Paint, c.1900 . . . . 1200.00
Rocker, Spinning Wheel, Gold Highlights, Spindle Turnings, Pennsylvania 895.00
Rocker, Stickley Bros., Oak, Glazed Canvas, Brass Tag, 28 x 20 1/2 x 23 In. 295.00
Rocker, Thonet, Bentwood, Spirals, Adjustable Cane Back, 38 x 21 x 66 In. 499.00
Rocker, Victorian, Walnut, Cane Seat, Back, Carved Hip Rests, 33 1/2 In. 120.00
Rocker, Victorian, Walnut, Carved, Flowers, Acanthus Crest, 35 In. 175.00
Rocker, Walter Lamb, Brown Jordan, c.1950, 20 x 32 x 32 In. 4700.00
Rocker, Windsor, 3 Arrow Back Slats, 5-Rod Comb, Green Paint, Stencil, 41 x 16 In. 605.00
Rocker, Windsor, Arrow Back, Painted, 31 In. 40.00
Rocker, Windsor, Arrow Back, Plank Seat, Double Crest Rail, Black, 40 x 19 x 24 In. . . . 225.00
Rocker, Windsor, Sack Back, Plank Seat, England, 36 x 24 x 28 In. 99.00
Rocker, Windsor, Yellow, Gold, Black Line Edging, Fruit, Bamboo Turnings, 46 1/2 In. . . 1265.00
Screen, 2-Panel, Dragon & Cloud Design, Wood Frame, 19th Century, 54 x 48 In. 405.00
Screen, 2-Panel, Enamel, Baluster Gallery, Scenic, Slender Legs, 9 In. 2940.00
Screen, 2-Panel, Ivory, Mother-Of-Pearl Inlay, Birds, Flowers, Wood Frame, 65 1/2 In. . . . 405.00
Screen, 2-Panel, Mahogany Frame, Mortise & Tenon, Fabric, 45 x 19 In. 670.00
Screen, 2-Panel, Tiger On Cliff In Rain, Folding, c.1800, 68 x 74 In. 4025.00
Screen, 2-Panel, Wood, Lacquer, Carved Ivory, Horn Accents, Plants, 73 x 68 In. 605.00
Screen, 3-Panel, Arts & Crafts, Walnut, Leather, Red, Green Flowers, 54 x 71-In. Panels . 489.00
Screen, 3-Panel, Chinoiserie, Painted Canvas, Asian Garden, Red Ground, 68 x 18 In. 175.00
Screen, 3-Panel, Inlaid Ivory, Wooden, 30 In. 110.00

Screen, 3-Panel, Louis XV Style, Beech, Carved, Gilt, Upholstered, 80 x 81 In., Pair 1725.00
Screen, 3-Panel, Louis XV Style, Giltwood, Putto, 83 In. 7770.00
Screen, 3-Panel, Painted Copper, Fish, Shells, Carved Wood Top, 1885, 65 x 75 In. 3740.00
Screen, 3-Panel, Painted Fabric, 20th Century, 60 x 54 1/4 In. 310.00
Screen, 3-Panel, Rococo Revival, Canvas, Painted, Late 19th Century, 67 x 20 In. 410.00
Screen, 3-Panel, Rococo, Canvas, Painted, Continental, 59 1/2 x 75 In., Pair 2300.00
Screen, 3-Panel, Satinwood, Spider Web Mount, Fabric, c.1900, 67 x 49 1/2 In. 805.00
Screen, 3-Panel, Shaker, Infirmary, Pine, Louvered, c.1850, 80 1/2 x 24 In. Each 3165.00
Screen, 3-Panel, Stickley Bros., 3 Vertical Slats Over Leather Insert, 20 x 66 In. 1840.00
Screen, 4-Panel, Aesthetic Revival, Ebonized, American, c.1875, 70 1/2 In. 2350.00
Screen, 4-Panel, Black Lacquer, Applique, Chinese, 71 1/2 x 72 In. 1150.00
Screen, 4-Panel, Canvas, Napoleonic War Scenes, Brass Nails, c.1900, 51 x 52 In. 1495.00
Screen, 4-Panel, Children, Birds, Medallion, Royalty, Cutout, 1874, 78 x 116 In. 1900.00
Screen, 4-Panel, Dragons, Greek Key Carved Frames, Embroidered, 100 In. 80.00
Screen, 4-Panel, Ebonized, Pierced, Carved, Fabric Panels, c.1880, 62 x 22 In. 390.00
Screen, 4-Panel, Edwardian, Mahogany, 36 Glazed Panes, Silk Upholstery, 70 x 72 In. . . . 1265.00
Screen, 4-Panel, Edwardian, Polychrome, Chinoiserie, c.1900, 72 x 22 1/2 In. 805.00
Screen, 4-Panel, Elm, Red Lacquer, c.1800, 82 1/2 x 21 In. Each 385.00
Screen, 4-Panel, Lacquered Wood, Intaglio Scenes, Polychrome, Gilt, 72 x 64 In. 127.00
Screen, 4-Panel, Lacquered Wood, Painted Canvas, Mother-Of-Pearl Trim, 69 x 96 In. . . . 175.00
Screen, 4-Panel, Louis XVI Style, Giltwood, Fabric Panels, 60 x 54 In. 440.00
Screen, 4-Panel, Oak, Fabric Panels, Glass Inserts, c.1905, 68 x 20 In. 660.00
Screen, 4-Panel, Paper, Irises, Leaves, Frame, Japan, c.1925, 36 1/2 x 71 3/4 In. 345.00
Screen, 4-Panel, Restauration, Polychrome Paper, Chinoiserie, 51 3/4 x 22 1/2 In. 1840.00
Screen, 4-Panel, Silk, Landscape, Japan, Early 1900s, 23 x 80 In. 60.00
Screen, 4-Panel, Swimming Ducks, Marsh Grass, Japan, 40 x 56 In. 230.00
Screen, 4-Panel, Wormley, Cedar, Geometric Design, Paper Backing, Dunbar, 84 In. 2940.00
Screen, 5-Panel, Flower Drape, Shells, Canvas, Peach, Gray, 103 x 21 In. 200.00
Screen, 6-Panel, Birds, Flowers, Landscape, c.1790, 67 x 138 In. 800.00
Screen, 6-Panel, Coromandel, Lacquer, Landscape, Birds, Chinese, Early 1800s, 77 In. . . . 1840.00
Screen, 6-Panel, Eames, FSW-6, Birch Plywood, Canvas Webbing, 60 x 68 In. 4200.00
Screen, 6-Panel, Eames, FSW-6, Ebonized Ash Plywood, Herman Miller, 60 x 68 In. 2590.00
Screen, 7-Panel, Coromandel, Figures, Pavilions, Chinese, 71 x 90 In. 2590.00
Screen, 8-Panel, Eames, FSW-8, Ash, Canvas, Herman Miller, c.1950, 80 x 68 In. 6325.00
Screen, 12-Panel, Black Coromandel Lacquer, Chinese, 19 1/2 x 108 In. Each 3660.00
Screen, Elm, Lacquer, Marble Dreamstone Inset, Chinese, 1800s, 9 x 10 In. 90.00
Screen, Famille Rose Enamel Plaque, Rosewood Stand, Chinese, c.1910, 23 In. 470.00
Screen, Fornasetti, Milan Cathedral Transfer, Italy, c.1960s, 52 x 54 In. 4095.00
Screen, Jade, Wood, Fruit Carved Panel, Pierced Wood Stand, 1700s, 10 x 8 In. 775.00
Screen, Napoleon III, Needlework, Velvet, Carved Crest, Ebonized, 43 1/2 In. . . . . . . *Illus* 520.00
Screen, Regency, Needlework, Rosewood Frame, Pedestal Base, England, 56 In. 290.00
Screen, Rococo Style, Giltwood, 134 x 156 In. 8965.00
Screen, Rosewood Frame, Longevity Figures, Chinese, c.1900, 29 In. 175.00
Screen, Rosewood, Variegated Marble, Chinese, 97 x 50 In. 885.00
Secretary, American Empire, Rosewood, 2 Parts, Early 1800s 2785.00
Secretary, Baroque Style, Mahogany, 96 x 50 x 25 In. 3885.00
Secretary, Black Walnut, Cylinder Roll, Pullout Surface, 79 1/2 In. 850.00

Furniture, Screen,
Napoleon III, Needlework,
Velvet, Carved Crest,
Ebonized, 43 1/2 In.

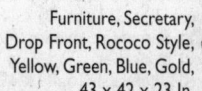

Furniture, Secretary,
Drop Front, Rococo Style,
Yellow, Green, Blue, Gold,
43 x 42 x 23 In.

Secretary, Butler's, Empire, Mahogany, Bracket Base, c.1850, 89 x 46 1/2 x 20 1/2 In. . . . 2010.00
Secretary, Chippendale Style, Mahogany, American, c.1850, 80 x 40 In. 1770.00
Secretary, Chippendale Style, Slant Front, Walnut, c.1900, 36 x 80 In. 3220.00
Secretary, Chippendale Style, Slant Front, Walnut, c.1900, 82 x 30 1/4 In. 2760.00
Secretary, Chippendale, Slant Front, 2 Doors, 4 Drawers, 4 Sections, 86 x 42 x 23 In. . . . 2420.00
Secretary, Chippendale, Slant Front, Cherry, Conn., c.1800, 90 x 37 x 18 In. 4480.00
Secretary, Chippendale, Walnut, 2-Paneled Doors, 84 x 38 In. 8815.00
Secretary, Colonial Revival, Governor Winthrop, Serpentine Front, 1900s 660.00
Secretary, Drop Front, Cherry, Walnut, 2 Parts, 85 x 41 x 22 In. 7190.00
Secretary, Drop Front, Felt Surface, Continental, c.1835, 37 3/4 x 59 3/4 In. 1265.00
Secretary, Drop Front, Flame Mahogany, Marble Top, c.1850, 55 1/2 x 38 3/4 In. 3680.00
Secretary, Drop Front, Parquetry, Marble Top, 2 Doors, 54 1/2 x 35 x 15 1/2 In. 1175.00
Secretary, Drop Front, Ripple Molding, Gallery Top, c.1850, 64 x 35 x 19 In. 690.00
Secretary, Drop Front, Rococo Style, Yellow, Green, Blue, Gold, 43 x 42 x 23 In. . . . *Illus* 2185.00
Secretary, Drop Front, Walnut, Spindles, 2 Slide-Out Compartments 2420.00
Secretary, Drop Front, Walnut, Tapered Legs, American, 2 Parts, 59 x 39 x 24 In. 4315.00
Secretary, Edwardian, Mahogany Inlay, c.1900, 79 x 35 x 17 1/2 In. 230.00
Secretary, Edwardian, Roll Top, Stainwood, 4 Doors, 92 x 36 In. 7170.00
Secretary, Edwardian, Satinwood, Mahogany, Cylinder, 2 Parts, 88 x 53 In. 4185.00
Secretary, Empire Style, Drop Front, Mahogany, Gilt Brass, Italy, c.1815, 56 x 35 In. 3220.00
Secretary, Empire, Drop Front, Mahogany Veneer, 2 Parts, 75 1/2 x 39 In. 1840.00
Secretary, Empire, Drop Front, Mahogany, 3 Sections, Glazed Doors, 96 x 43 x 21 In. . . . 1265.00
Secretary, Empire, Flame Mahogany, Gothic Arched, Glass Front Doors 4400.00
Secretary, Empire, Mahogany, 2 Parts, American, c.1840, 75 3/4 x 47 x 21 1/4 In. 1000.00
Secretary, Empire, Rosewood, American, c.1835, 86 x 43 3/4 In., 2 Piece 2360.00
Secretary, Federal Style, Mahogany Inlaid, 3 Doors, Drawers, 75 x 37 x 19 In. 1590.00
Secretary, Federal, 6-Pane, Windowed Doors, 77 x 42 x 18 1/2 In. 1650.00
Secretary, Federal, Mahogany, Cornice, Doors, Early 1800s, 57 x 35 x 17 1/2 In. 2760.00
Secretary, Federal, Mahogany, Doors, Brass, c.1815, 57 x 39 x 23 In. 8365.00
Secretary, Federal, Mahogany, Glazed, c.1800, 77 3/4 x 39 x 19 In. 4400.00
Secretary, Federal, Windowed Doors, 76 1/2 x 42 x 18 1/2 In. 1680.00
Secretary, G. Nelson, Drop Front, 3 Drawers, 2 Shelves, U-Pulls, 46 x 56 x 19 In. 1265.00
Secretary, George III, Fiddle, Mahogany, 90 1/2 x 47 x 22 In. 3220.00
Secretary, George III, Mahogany, 2 Glazed Doors, c.1785, 83 x 38 In. 1840.00
Secretary, George III, Mahogany, 2 Glazed Doors, c.1785, 93 x 40 In. 2530.00
Secretary, George III, Mahogany, 98 x 42 x 22 1/2 In. 2760.00
Secretary, George III, Mahogany, Cornice, 2 Doors, 96 x 46 x 22 1/2 In. 2760.00
Secretary, George III, Mahogany, Inlaid, 19th Century, 48 x 94 1/2 In. 4025.00
Secretary, George III, Mahogany, Late 1700s, 90 1/2 x 44 x 22 In. 4600.00
Secretary, George III, Mahogany, Late 18th Century, 88 1/2 x 42 x 22 In. 5290.00
Secretary, George III, Slant Front, Mahogany, 4 Drawers, 1700s, 97 x 47 In. 6900.00
Secretary, Georgian Style, Japanned, Double Pediment, Early 1900s, 84 x 43 x 22 In. . . . 2200.00
Secretary, Georgian, Mahogany, Broken Arch, 5 Drawers, 88 x 44 x 22 1/2 In. 5650.00
Secretary, Gothic Revival, Mahogany, Baltimore, c.1830, 100 x 47 In. 4140.00
Secretary, Hepplewhite, Drop Front, Pine, 2 Parts, 78 1/2 x 47 1/4 In. 690.00
Secretary, Hepplewhite, Slant Front, Cherry, 2 Parts, 2 Upper Doors, c.1795, 86 x 41 In. . 5750.00
Secretary, Louis Phillipe Style, Kingwood, Serpentine, 48 x 26 1/2 In. 460.00
Secretary, Louis XV Style, Walnut, Mid 20th Century, 32 x 17 x 72 In. 375.00
Secretary, Louis XVI Style, Slant Front, Rosewood, American, c.1865, 53 x 31 In. 2760.00
Secretary, Louis XVI, Drop Front, Mahogany, Early 1800s, 54 x 30 x 15 In. 350.00
Secretary, Louis XVI, Drop Front, Mahogany, Late 1700s, 57 x 37 x 15 1/2 In. 920.00
Secretary, Mahogany, 3 Drawers, Block Front Base, 77 In. 630.00
Secretary, Mahogany, Cathedral Cutout Top Doors, 3 Drawers, 2 Parts, 56 x 39 In. 690.00
Secretary, Mahogany, Fold-Out, American, c.1840, 72 x 39 x 18 3/4 In. 920.00
Secretary, Mahogany, Tambour Slides, 2 Parts, 3 Bottom Drawers, 50 1/4 x 41 3/4 In. . . . 2400.00
Secretary, Neoclassical, Mahogany, 5 Drawers, American, c.1840, 78 x 45 In. 1495.00
Secretary, Oak, 2 Doors, 5 Pigeonholes, Shelves, Germany, 18th Century 2500.00
Secretary, Pine, Raised Panel Doors, Sweden, 1800s, 83 x 56 1/2 x 22 In. 990.00
Secretary, Pine, Slanted Lift Top, 2 Doors, Turned Legs, 80 x 44 In. 520.00
Secretary, Plantation, Walnut, Dentil Top, Serpentine Interior, 59 x 39 In. 8495.00
Secretary, Queen Anne Style, Drop Front, 2 Drawers, 72 x 33 x 17 In. 1035.00
Secretary, Regency, Mahogany, 2 Glazed Doors, c.1815, 89 x 42 1/2 In. 5290.00
Secretary, Regency, Mahogany, Inlaid, Ebonized, Satinwood, 84 x 40 x 21 In. 3910.00

Secretary, Renaissance Revival, Walnut, 2 Parts, Doors, c.1865, 112 x 60 In. 5750.00
Secretary, Renaissance Revival, Walnut, Bird's-Eye Maple Interior, 2 Arched Doors 4840.00
Secretary, Roll Top, Lacquered, Draw Front, 77 x 42 x 22 1/2 In. 1840.00
Secretary, Sheraton, Bird's-Eye Maple, 2-Door Bookcase, c.1830, 60 x 42 x 19 In. 1440.00
Secretary, Sheraton, Cherry, Curly Maple, 2 Parts, Star Inlay, 105 x 42 In. 7190.00
Secretary, Sheraton, Cherry, Maple Inlay, 3 Drawers, 8 Doors, N.H., c.1800, 87 x 43 In. . . 8625.00
Secretary, Sheraton, Mahogany, 2 Parts, 4 Drawers, 4 Doors, Mass., 87 x 43 In. 7190.00
Secretary, Sheraton, Mahogany, Blind Front, 5 Drawers, 2 Doors, American, 68 x 38 In. . .   920.00
Secretary, Sheraton, Mahogany, Bonnet Top, Glazed Doors, Drawers, 67 x 38 x 20 In. 1150.00
Secretary, Sheraton, Mahogany, Figured Birch, New England, 78 x 40 x 20 1/2 In. 10350.00
Secretary, Slant Front, Burled Walnut, Carved Crest, 82 1/2 x 39 1/2 x 18 In. 1440.00
Secretary, Slant Front, Pine, Painted, Panel Doors, 72 x 36 x 17 In. 145.00
Secretary, Victorian, Black Walnut, Burl, 2 Sections, Cylinder Roll, 79 x 34 x 20 In. 950.00
Secretary, Victorian, Roll Top, 83 x 33 x 20 In. 1555.00
Secretary, Walnut, 2 Glass Doors, 2 Bird's-Eye Maple Drawers, 79 x 30 In. 900.00
Secretary, Walnut, Carved Crest, Slotted Interior, 82 In. 450.00
Secretary, William IV, Drop Front, Mahogany, Mid 19th Century, 54 x 33 x 17 In. 2990.00
Semainier, Empire Style, Mahogany, 7 Drawers, Gilt Bronze Mounts, 61 x 34 In. 805.00
Semainier, Mahogany, 7 Drawers, Marble Top, France, Late 1800s, 65 x 32 x 16 In. 2645.00
Server, Aesthetic Revival, Mahogany, 2 Drawers, American, Late 1800s, 38 x 52 In. 1060.00
Server, Bamboo Style, Geometric Inlay, 52 3/4 x 59 x 21 In. 1840.00
Server, Baroque Style, Carved Panel Doors, Early 1900s, 47 1/2 x 19 x 35 In. 175.00
Server, Empire, Mahogany, Crotch Veneer, 19th Century, 43 1/2 x 47 1/2 x 22 In. 520.00
Server, Empire, Mahogany, Salmon, Ivory Marble Top, Ball Feet, 36 x 46 x 22 In. 2860.00
Server, G. Stickley, 2 Drawers, Slat Back Rail 8625.00
Server, G. Stickley, Arched Apron, Red Decal, 42 x 36 x 18 In. 4600.00
Server, G. Stickley, No. 819, 4 Drawers, Iron Hardware, 48 x 20 x 39 In. 6325.00
Server, G. Stickley, Plate Rail, 3 Drawers, Oval Pull, 44 x 48 x 21 In. 3740.00
Server, George III Style, Mahogany, Inlaid, Bowed, Crossband Top, 36 x 48 x 27 In. 1265.00
Server, L. & J.G. Stickley, Blind Drawers, 32 x 18 x 32 In. 805.00
Server, Limbert, No. 403, Copper Hardware, 2 Drawers, 2 Shelves, 40 x 18 x 44 In. 1095.00
Server, Louis XVI Style, Fruitwood Marquetry, Ormolu Mount, c.1880, 35 x 30 In. 4115.00
Server, Mahogany, 2 Tiers, Scrolling Elements, c.1875, 45 x 54 x 24 In. 825.00
Server, Mahogany, Drawer, Turned Legs, c.1810, 29 1/2 x 40 x 22 In. 115.00
Server, Marble Top, 2 Drawers, 2 Panel Doors, 1800s, 48 x 20 x 38 In. 290.00
Server, Neoclassical, 2 Doors, Columns, Ormolu, Paw Feet, American, 50 x 22 x 34 In. . .   805.00
Server, Neoclassical, Mahogany, 3 Drawers, American, c.1835, 35 1/2 x 36 In. 865.00
Server, Oak, Carved Lion Heads Columns, 42 x 48 x 22 In. 690.00
Server, Paul Evans, Metal, Wood, Composition, Slate, Sculptured, 32 x 48 x 20 1/2 In. 410.00
Server, Queen Anne Style, Walnut, Mid 20th Century, 34 1/2 x 40 1/2 x 18 1/4 In. 178.00
Server, Rococo, Rosewood, Marble Top, Cabriole Legs, 71 x 41 x 16 1/2 In. 1495.00
Server, Sheraton, 4 Drawers, Red Flame Graining, 34 1/2 x 20 x 35 1/2 In. 1375.00
Server, Walnut, 2 Parts, Frieze Drawers, Cupboard, c.1885, 38 x 37 1/2 x 24 In. 805.00
Server, Walnut, Mahogany, Marble, 2 Drawers, Brass Pulls, 32 x 35 x 18 In. . . .1925.00 to 1960.00
Server, Walnut, Marble Top, 2 Drawers, 2 Panel Doors, American, c.1875, 39 x 48 x 20 In. 170.00
Server, Walnut, Relief Carving, Marble Top, 3 Sections, Mirror, 59 x 21 x 79 1/2 In. 1265.00
Server, William IV, Mahogany, Marble Top, Mid 1800s, 35 x 49 1/2 x 21 3/4 In. 3910.00
Server, Wormley, No. 5433, Walnut, Drop Leaf, Dunbar, 21 x 28 x 31 1/2 In. 5465.00
Settee, Baroque Style, Beech, Floral Carved Frame, Bowfront, 20th Century 880.00
Settee, Blue Paint, Double Shaped Crest, Scroll Arms, c.1870, 25 x 9 x 17 In. 13200.00
Settee, Chippendale Style, Padded, Outscrolled Arms, c.1890, 40 x 97 x 35 In. 4370.00
Settee, Dunbar, Wood, Cane Back & Sides, Cushions, 26 1/2 x 60 x 23 1/2 In. 2070.00
Settee, Empire Style, Mahogany, Gilt Bronze Mount, c.1900, 35 x 51 In. 920.00
Settee, Empire, Mahogany, Serpentine, Bracket Legs, Upholstered, 33 x 43 x 22 In. 405.00
Settee, Federal Style, Mahogany, Chair Back, 59 In. 1195.00
Settee, G. Nakashima, Maple, Black Walnut, Slat Back, 1955, 47 1/2 x 35 x 31 In. 2460.00
Settee, G. Stickley, No. 165, Tapered Pyramid Posts, Arched Slats, 40 x 59 In. 6325.00
Settee, George III Style, Triple Chairback, Woven Splat, Cushion, 37 x 54 x 24 In. 690.00
Settee, George IV, Mahogany, Triple Chairback, c.1815, 36 1/2 x 56 x 17 1/2 In. 2300.00
Settee, Giltwood, Cabriole Legs, Scrolled Arms & Feet, France, 39 x 50 x 27 In. 250.00
Settee, Green, Yellow Paint, John Sweeny, Pennsylvania, 19th Century, 17 x 26 In. 12100.00
Settee, L. & J.G. Stickley, 22 Back Slats, Cushion, 60 x 21 x 33 In. 6325.00
Settee, Lloyd, Tubular Chrome, Bakelite Armrests, Oilcloth, 48 x 32 x 34 In. . . . . . . *Illus*   259.00

Furniture, Settee, Lloyd,
Tubular Chrome, Bakelite
Armrests, Oilcloth,
48 x 32 x 34 In.

Furniture, Settee,
Rococo Revival,
Rosewood, Carved,
Upholstered, c.1855,
64 3/4 In.

Settee, Louis XIV Style, Giltwood, Upholstered, 69 1/2 In. 840.00
Settee, Louis XVI Style, Carved Flowers, Tapered & Fluted Column Legs, 52 In. 315.00
Settee, Louis XVI Style, Giltwood, Needlepoint Back, Oval, 60 In. 550.00
Settee, Mahogany, Carved Frame, Ribbon Crest, Open Gadroon Border, 37 x 52 x 26 In. . .   550.00
Settee, Mahogany, Carved, Reeded Apron, Upholstered, Paw Feet, 53 x 21 x 33 In. 190.00
Settee, Mahogany, Ruffled Ribbon Crest, Upholstered, France, 37 x 52 x 26 In. 560.00
Settee, Meridienne, Belter, Rococo Revival, Rosalie Without Grapes, c.1850, 36 1/2 In. . .   3910.00
Settee, Neoclassical Style, Mahogany, American, 62 In. 840.00
Settee, Neoclassical, Birch, Maple, Scroll Arms, Klismos Legs, 33 1/2 x 14 x 62 1/2 In. .   2940.00
Settee, Neoclassical, Mahogany, Outscrolled Arms, Boston, c.1825, 78 In. 2150.00
Settee, Pine, Blue Gray Paint, Bootjack Ends, Curved Arms, 31 x 42 In. 1725.00
Settee, Pine, Pennsylvania, Mid 19th Century, 71 1/2 In. 290.00
Settee, Red, Plank Seat, Square Arms, Chamfered Tapered Legs, 28 x 64 x 23 In. 660.00
Settee, Renaissance Revival, Mahogany, Pierced Crest, Leaves, 74 In. 1435.00
Settee, Rococo Revival, Rosewood Laminate, American, c.1850, 49 x 66 x 27 In. 5520.00
Settee, Rococo Revival, Rosewood Laminate, Hawkins Pattern, 50 x 65 x 40 In. 10925.00
Settee, Rococo Revival, Rosewood, American, Mid 19th Century, 35 x 61 x 27 In., Pair . .   920.00
Settee, Rococo Revival, Rosewood, Carved, Upholstered, c.1855, 64 3/4 In. . . . . *Illus*   7768.00
Settee, Rococo Revival, Rosewood, Pierced Crest, Ivy, Flowers, N.Y., c.1855, 79 In. 9560.00
Settee, Rococo Revival, Rosewood, Shaped Crest, Flowers, c.1855, 64 3/4 In. 7170.00
Settee, Rosewood Grain Painted, Strawberry, Flowers, 16 3/4 x 10 1/4 In. 2420.00
Settee, Shaker, Tape Seat & Back, Curved Armrests, Mt. Lebanon, 40 1/2 In. . . .6325.00 to 8340.00
Settee, Stickley Bros., Cherry, Tripleback, Spindles, c.1910 . . . .   230.00
Settee, Teak, Wool Upholstered Seat & Back, 26 1/2 x 49 1/4 x 22 In. 2185.00
Settee, Turkish Style, Velvet Upholstery, 60 In. 1015.00
Settee, Victorian, Burl Walnut, Upholstered, 63 In. 290.00
Settee, Victorian, Walnut, Carved, Upholstered, 35 1/2 x 63 1/2 x 32 In. 450.00
Settee, Vinyl, Laminate Top Side Table, Steel Frame, J.G. Furniture, 30 x 66 In. 510.00
Settee, Walnut, Finger Carved, Upholstered, 35 1/2 x 63 1/2 x 32 In. 400.00
Settee, Warren McArthur, Aluminum, Upholstered, Rubber, 1930s, 47 x 34 x 33 In. 3160.00
Settee, Wendell Castle, Molar, Molded Fiberglass, Red, High Gloss, 48 x 33 x 26 In. 460.00
Settee, Windsor, Birdcage Back, Bamboo Turnings, Plank Seat, 1820s, 77 In. 3900.00
Settee, Windsor, Double Back, 2 Horizontal Slats, 12 Spindles, 1840 . . . .   1535.00
Settee, Windsor, Painted, Bamboo Turnings, Early 19th Century, 36 x 18 In. 4350.00
Settle, Drop Arm, Slat Back, 36 x 85 1/2 x 33 In. 1725.00
Settle, G. Stickley, Mahogany, Drop Arms, 17 Slats, Leather Cushion, 72 x 28 x 38 In. . . .   2415.00
Settle, G. Stickley, V Back, Leather Seat, 36 x 47 x 24 In. 4025.00
Settle, L. & J.G. Stickley, No. 232, 2 Horizontal Rails, Cushion, 72 x 24 x 33 In. 2500.00
Settle, L. & J.G. Stickley, Slat Sides, Leather Cushion, 34 x 76 x 31 In. 6900.00
Settle, L. & J.G. Stickley, Slats, Pegged, Leather Upholstery, c.1910, 28 x 72 x 27 In. 2990.00
Settle, Oak, Panels, Shaped Arms, Scrolled, 17th Century, England, 40 x 72 x 26 In. 2750.00
Settle, Oak, Solid Back, Padded Seat, Arms, England, Early 1800s, 40 x 55 x 28 In. 1265.00
Settle, Old Hickory Style, Turned Legs, Rungs, Woven Bark Seat, Back, 34 1/2 x 36 In. . .   195.00
Settle, Pine, Shaped Top, Arched Feet, England, c.1820, 58 x 49 x 16 In. 495.00
Settle, Queen Anne, Oak, 3 Raised Panels, Loose Cushion, England, 54 In. 345.00
Settle, Shop Of The Crafters, 8 Flared Slats, Peaked Top Rail, Cutout, 77 x 30 x 37 In. . .   2415.00
Settle, Stickley & Brandt Co., Spindles, Spring Seat, Leatherette, 31 x 52 x 26 In. 2015.00
Settle, Stickley Bros., Trapezoid Slats, Beveled Knobs, 72 x 32 x 35 In. 3170.00
Settle, Windsor, Bow Back, 2 Drawers, 54 x 40 In. 1325.00
Sewing Cabinet, Shaker, 2 Stacks Of 12 Chamfered Drawers, 34 3/4 x 16 3/4 x 7 1/2 In. . .   6440.00
Shelf, 3 Tiers, Heart-Shape Mirror, Arrow-Topped Spindles, 21 x 6 1/2 x 2 1/2 In. 1430.00

Shelf, Baroque Style, Giltwood, Bracket, Italy, c.1900, 25 x 5 In., Pair 3220.00
Shelf, Cherry, Whale Side, 34 1/2 x 26 1/2 In. 635.00
Shelf, Corner, Chinoiserie, Lacquer, Black, Gold, Landscape, France, 1700s, 31 In., Pair . . 5290.00
Shelf, Corner, Hanging, Louis XVI Style, Giltwood, France, 18 1/2 x 13 1/2 In. 980.00
Shelf, Corner, Victorian, Ebonized, Pierce Carved, 18 x 21 x 9 3/4 In. 290.00
Shelf, Corner, Walnut, 5 Shelves, Cutout Back, Supports, 60 x 17 x 24 In. 90.00
Shelf, Corner, Walnut, Cutout Backs, Finials, 5 Shelves, 60 x 14 To 24 In. 105.00
Shelf, Display, Pine, Painted, Hat & Coat Rack, Contemporary, 14 x 41 In. 22.00
Shelf, Dunbar, 4 Tiers, White Enameled Wood, 4 Glass Shelves, 79 x 20 In., Pair 4900.00
Shelf, Eames, ESU-200, 3 Sliding Doors, 2 Pullout Shelves, 32 1/4 x 47 x 16 1/2 In. 3105.00
Shelf, Eames, ESU-400, Iron Frame, 3 Drawers, Black Laminate, 55 x 47 x 17 In. 5465.00
Shelf, Folding, Parcel Gilt, Lacquer, Chinoiserie, England, c.1835, 14 x 10 In., Pair 690.00
Shelf, G. Nakashima, Walnut, Iron Mounting Brackets, 116 x 21 In. 8815.00
Shelf, Giltwood, Demilune, Stylized Cruciform Back, Italy, c.1900, 24 x 15 x 7 In. 1095.00
Shelf, Giltwood, Scrolled Acanthus Shape, Bracket, 14 1/4 x 12 x 7 In. 200.00
Shelf, Hanging, Burl Veneers, Ormolu Mounts, Continental, 1800s, 32 x 28 x 11 In. 1035.00
Shelf, Hanging, Egyptian Revival, Wood, Gesso, Painted, 1900s, 13 1/4 In., Pair 1410.00
Shelf, Hanging, Gilt Lacquered Brass, Patinated Metal, 12 1/2 x 15 3/4 In., Pair 1150.00
Shelf, Hanging, Louis XIV Style, Giltwood, 40 x 12 x 11 In. 390.00
Shelf, Hanging, Louis XVI Style, Kingwood, Inlaid, Serpentine Shelves, 30 x 19 x 6 In. . . 90.00
Shelf, Hanging, Mahogany, Satinwood, Demilune, Pendant Drop, 14 x 22 In., Pair 1265.00
Shelf, Hanging, Pine, Basswood, Ogee Frame, 3 Shelves, Painted, 26 x 32 1/4 In. 1725.00
Shelf, Hanging, Pine, Black & Red, Whale End, 4 Shelves, 33 x 8 x 39 In. 1840.00
Shelf, Hanging, Pine, White & Blue Paint, 41 1/2 x 20 1/2 x 7 1/2 In. 300.00
Shelf, Hanging, Regency Style, Giltwood, Carved, Serpentine, c.1875, 13 x 11 In., Pair . . 1265.00
Shelf, Hanging, Renaissance Revival, Walnut, Female Bust, c.1865, 13 x 9 1/2 x 9 In. . . . 2760.00
Shelf, Hanging, Rococo Revival, Giltwood, Early 1900s, 9 1/2 In., Pair 200.00
Shelf, Hanging, Rococo, Walnut, Pierced Scrolled Sides, American, c.1850, 34 x 32 In. . . 230.00
Shelf, Hanging, Rosewood, Grain Painted, 3 Tiers, 23 x 19 3/4 x 5 In. 365.00
Shelf, Hanging, Shaker, Pine, Arched Sides, Dovetailed Base, c.1850, 20 1/2 x 7 In. 1035.00
Shelf, Hanging, Walnut, 4 Shelves, Ring-Turned Supports, Finials, 23 3/4 x 6 3/8 In. 190.00
Shelf, Hanging, Walnut, 4 Shelves, Scalloped Sides, Patina, 21 x 12 In. 340.00
Shelf, Hanging, Walnut, Whale Side, 2 Drawers, 37 3/4 x 24 3/4 x 8 1/4 In. 2015.00
Shelf, Hanging, Walnut, Whale Side, 8 Shelves, 74 x 21 In. 2875.00
Shelf, Hanging, Whale Form, 4 Tiers, Rippled Edge, 19th Century, 33 x 27 1/2 In. 230.00
Shelf, Knoll, Ivory Enamel, Semicircular, 3 Shelves, Crescent Top Shelf, 38 x 15 In. 489.00
Shelf, Mahogany, Whale Side, 19th Century, 32 x 22 In. 690.00
Shelf, Olaf Von Bohr, Modular, Orange, ABS Plastic, Kartell, 74 x 63 1/2 x 11 In. 980.00
Shelf, Pine, Bucket, 4 Shelves, Dry Mustard Paint, 48 x 52 In. 1155.00
Shelf, Red Paint, Whale Back, 4 Shelves, c.1800, 31 x 25 1/2 In. 2160.00
Shelf, Shaker, Pegboard, Red, Oblong, 2 Hanging Rods, 32 x 24 x 6 In. 1035.00
Shelf, Shaker, Pine, 5 Graduated Open Shelves, Arched Feet, 76 x 52 In. 590.00
Shelf, Walnut, Carved, Spread-Wing Eagle On Perch, Nut & Leaf Carving, 14 x 17 In. . . . 675.00
Shelf, Walnut, Flat Back, 6 Shelves, Graduated, 69 x 14 To 34 In. 145.00
Shelf, Wooden, Deer Head, Germany, c.1920, 13 x 13 In. 145.00
Shelves, Hanging, Eastlake, Walnut, Pierced Sides, c.1880, 30 1/2 x 24 x 10 In. 540.00
Shelves, Oak, Carved Corner Posts, Vining, Open Twist, 3 Shelves, 68 x 24 x 70 In. 1725.00
Sideboard, Aesthetic Revival, Mahogany, 3 Drawers, 2 Doors, c.1890, 40 x 58 In. 705.00
Sideboard, Art Deco, Calamander, Inset Marble, Early 1900s, 43 x 65 1/2 x 21 In. 6325.00
Sideboard, Arts & Crafts, Oak, 4 Drawers, 2 Doors, 57 x 39 x 21 In. 750.00
Sideboard, Dominique, Rosewood, Parchment, Bronze, France, 1930s, 78 x 22 x 40 In. . . 4680.00
Sideboard, Eastlake Style, Walnut, 2 Parts, American, c.1880, 80 x 54 x 23 1/2 In. 3335.00
Sideboard, Edwardian, Mahogany, Satinwood Inlay, 38 x 72 x 24 In. 4480.00
Sideboard, Empire, Mahogany, 1 Short & 2 Long Drawers, 3 Doors, 66 x 23 x 43 In. 730.00
Sideboard, Empire, Mahogany, 4 Doors, 4 Drawers, Marble Top, 67 x 59 In. 3160.00
Sideboard, Federal Style, Cherry, Satinwood Inlay, c.1875, 42 x 60 x 20 In. 2530.00
Sideboard, Federal Style, Mahogany, Inlaid, Satinwood, Serpentine Front, 39 x 72 In. . . . 1900.00
Sideboard, Federal Style, Satinwood, Mahogany, Serpentine, 1900s, 71 x 39 1/2 In. 1840.00
Sideboard, Federal, Mahogany, 3 Drawers, New England, c.1810, 40 x 61 x 23 In. 3000.00
Sideboard, Federal, Mahogany, Bowfront Drawers, 40 1/2 x 71 1/2 x 21 1/2 In. 3585.00
Sideboard, Federal, Mahogany, Convex & Concave Doors, Fluted Legs, 36 x 90 In. 7865.00
Sideboard, Federal, Mahogany, Drawer, 4 Doors, Early 1900s, 70 x 27 1/2 x 40 In. 1440.00
Sideboard, Federal, Mahogany, Inlaid, Canted Panels, c.1790, 42 x 63 x 27 In. 9990.00

Sideboard, Federal, Mahogany, Inlaid, Early 1800s, 40 x 72 x 25 1/2 In. 3885.00
Sideboard, Federal, Mahogany, Inlaid, Satinwood, Serpentine, 40 x 63 1/4 x 24 In. 12650.00
Sideboard, Federal, Mahogany, Serpentine Front, Bowed Drawers, 72 x 40 x 28 In. 6415.00
Sideboard, Fin Juhl, Walnut, 2 Doors, 5 Drawers, Dowel Legs, 30 1/4 x 66 x 19 In. 1495.00
Sideboard, G. Stickley, 3 Over 2 Drawers, Doors, Copper Hinges, 44 x 48 x 18 In. 3450.00
Sideboard, G. Stickley, Plate Rail, 4 Drawers, 2 Cupboards, 48 x 19 x 45 In. 4315.00
Sideboard, George III Style, Mahogany, Inlaid, Bowfront, 2 Drawers, 36 x 61 x 24 In. . . . 1955.00
Sideboard, George III Style, Mahogany, Serpentine, Early 1900s, 41 x 60 x 26 In. 1035.00
Sideboard, George III, Mahogany, Bowfront, Late 1700s, 38 x 66 x 27 In. 3680.00
Sideboard, George III, Mahogany, Drawer, 2 Doors, c.1800, 36 x 74 1/4 x 29 In. 4200.00
Sideboard, George III, Mahogany, Inlaid Shell Medallions, Brass Gallery, 82 In. 6470.00
Sideboard, George III, Mahogany, Inlaid, Bowfront, c.1790, 37 x 23 x 51 In. 8525.00
Sideboard, George III, Mahogany, Marquetry, Early 1800s, 37 x 67 x 25 In. 12650.00
Sideboard, George IV Style, Mahogany, Early 1900s, 44 1/2 x 84 x 24 1/2 In. 1265.00
Sideboard, Georgian Style, Mahogany, Serpentine Top, Drawer, 2 Doors, 37 x 58 In. 1095.00
Sideboard, Georgian, Mahogany, Bowfront, Brass Mount, c.1800, 36 x 72 In. 3910.00
Sideboard, Georgian, Mahogany, Inlaid, Serpentine, Late 1800s, 36 x 54 x 23 In. 1955.00
Sideboard, Grain Painted, 2 Doors, 2 Drawers, American, c.1875, 62 1/2 x 41 In. 840.00
Sideboard, Green, Cream, 3 Over 2 Doors, c.1890 . . . . 1850.00
Sideboard, Hepplewhite Style, Mahogany, 2 Doors, Drawer, 38 x 78 x 26 In. 1495.00
Sideboard, Hepplewhite Style, Mahogany, 7 Drawers, Bowfront, 37 x 63 1/2 x 31 In. 1495.00
Sideboard, Hepplewhite Style, Mahogany, Line, Shell, Bellflower Inlay, 36 x 61 In. 2760.00
Sideboard, Hepplewhite, Mahogany, 3 Drawers, New England, 42 3/4 x 71 1/2 In. 7200.00
Sideboard, Hepplewhite, Mahogany, Bowfront, 3 Drawers, 4 Doors, 41 x 60 In. 1380.00
Sideboard, Hepplewhite, Mahogany, Bowfront, 3 Drawers, England, c.1780, 36 x 67 In. . . 4140.00
Sideboard, Hepplewhite, Mahogany, Bowfront, Inlaid, Wine Drawers, 37 x 76 x 22 In. . . . 3800.00
Sideboard, Hepplewhite, Mahogany, D-Shape Front, 4 Drawers, 67 x 29 x 40 In. 9900.00
Sideboard, Hepplewhite, Mahogany, Inlaid, 3 Drawers, 36 3/4 x 51 1/2 In. 4600.00
Sideboard, Hepplewhite, Mahogany, Inlaid, 5 Drawers, 2 Doors, N.Y., 42 x 66 In. 5175.00
Sideboard, Hepplewhite, Walnut, Bowfront, Drawer, Doors, 70 x 40 x 24 1/2 In. 2300.00
Sideboard, L. & J.G. Stickley, No. 731, 5 Drawers, 2 Doors, 72 x 50 In. 4700.00
Sideboard, Lifetime, Beveled Mirror Backsplash, Plate Rack, 52 1/2 x 54 x 22 In. 1050.00
Sideboard, Mahogany, 3 Silver Drawers Over Linen Drawers, 3 Doors, 48 x 66 x 25 In. . . 670.00
Sideboard, Mahogany, 4 Drawers, 2 Pedestals, c.1835, 49 x 75 In. 4370.00
Sideboard, Mahogany, D-Shape, Backsplash, 2 Drawers, 1900s, 39 x 71 x 23 In. 1150.00
Sideboard, Mahogany, Drawer, 2 Cupboards, c.1865, 36 x 60 x 21 In. 1150.00
Sideboard, Mahogany, Ormolu, 3 Drawers, Pedestal Base, Boston, 46 x 69 In. 5465.00
Sideboard, Marble Top, Carved Birds, Candle Holders, Drawers, Doors, 86 x 51 x 21 In. . 5125.00
Sideboard, McCobb, Mahogany, 2 Trifold Doors, Calvin, 71 x 19 x 34 1/2 In. 1095.00
Sideboard, McCobb, Walnut, 8 Drawers, 2 Doors, Travertine Top, 71 x 19 x 32 In. 1725.00
Sideboard, McCobb, Walnut, Brass, Travertine Top, Calvin 1175.00
Sideboard, Milo Baughman, Marble, Brushed Chrome, Thayer Coggin, 30 x 64 x 21 In. . . 460.00
Sideboard, Neoclassical, Curly & Bird's-Eye Maple, c.1820, 47 1/2 x 65 1/2 x 23 In. 2990.00
Sideboard, Neoclassical, Mahogany, c.1830, 50 1/2 x 73 1/4 x 27 In. 1090.00
Sideboard, Neoclassical, Paneled Doors, 3 Drawers, c.1890, 79 x 24 x 61 In. 115.00
Sideboard, Oak, Carved, Eagles, 67 x 62 In. 9900.00
Sideboard, Oak, Carved, Scenic Top Crest, Fan-Shape Spindles, 65 x 51 x 19 1/2 In. 575.00
Sideboard, Oak, Mirror Back, 2 Piece, 3 Drawers, Panel Doors, 72 3/4 x 60 In. 920.00
Sideboard, Oak, Pollard Oak, 2 Drawers, 2 Doors, c.1870, 81 x 73 x 21 In. 1410.00
Sideboard, Parzinger, 4 Doors, Leather, Brass, 32 3/4 x 64 1/2 x 17 In. 5750.00
Sideboard, Pine, Waxed Finish, 7 Drawers, Cupboard, England, 1800s, 34 x 70 x 21 In. . . 1380.00
Sideboard, Poplar, 6 Legs, 3 Dovetailed Over 3 Large Drawers, 38 x 54 x 21 In. 1760.00
Sideboard, Queen Anne Style, Walnut, Mid 20th Century, 37 x 72 x 23 In. 200.00
Sideboard, Queen Anne, Cherry, 3 Drawers, Fan Carving, 30 1/2 x 42 x 22 In. 575.00
Sideboard, Queen Anne, Mahogany, 4 Drawers, Shell Carving, Newport, 1700s 5175.00
Sideboard, Regency Style, Mahogany, 2 Pedestal Cabinets, c.1890, 43 x 83 In. 2645.00
Sideboard, Regency Style, Mahogany, 3 Doors, Drawers, Early 1900s, 36 x 60 x 21 In. . . . 990.00
Sideboard, Regency Style, Mahogany, Serpentine Front, 5 Drawers, 33 x 46 x 24 In. 770.00
Sideboard, Renaissance Revival, Burled Walnut, 2 Parts, Mirror, c.1865, 86 x 73 In. 3910.00
Sideboard, Renaissance Revival, Walnut, Marble Top, Oval-Panel Burl Doors 1815.00
Sideboard, Renaissance Revival, Walnut, Marble Top, 90 x 55 x 24 In. 1900.00
Sideboard, Rococo Revival, Oak, Marble Top, Carved Stag's Head, c.1865 . . . . 4600.00
Sideboard, Rohde, Maidou, Mahogany, Rosewood, 4 Doors, Herman Miller, 72 x 21 In. . . 2300.00

Sideboard, Rosewood Veneer, 5 Doors, Denmark, 35 1/2 x 97 1/2 x 18 In. 920.00
Sideboard, Rosewood, Grain Painted, Marble, 2 Shelves, 37 1/2 x 59 x 22 In. 415.00
Sideboard, Sheraton Style, Cherry, 3 Drawers, 4 Doors, 74 x 47 x 24 In. 1210.00
Sideboard, Sheraton, Mahogany, Cellarette, Candle Drawers, Philadelphia, c.1800 . . . . . . 4400.00
Sideboard, Sheraton, Mahogany, D-Shape, 3 Drawers, 4 Doors, 60 x 23 x 42 In. 565.00
Sideboard, Stickley & Brandt Co., Plate Rack, Gallery, 53 x 56 x 27 In. 1670.00
Sideboard, Stickley Bros., Mirror, 3 Drawers, 2 Doors, 51 x 60 x 23 In. 1725.00
Sideboard, Victorian, Walnut, Marble Top, Oval Panels, c.1865, 53 x 20 x 104 In. 2875.00
Sideboard, Walnut, 4 Posts, 2 Cup Holder Back Bars, Drawers, c.1830, 47 x 55 x 23 In. . . . 2640.00
Sideboard, Walnut, Marble Top, 2 Drawers Over 2 Sunken-Panel Doors, 46 x 21 In. 375.00
Sideboard, Walnut, Marble Top, Molded Doors, American, c.1870, 73 x 70 1/2 In. 3220.00
Sideboard, Walnut, Marble Top, Panels, Columns, c.1880, 84 1/2 x 47 x 20 In. 2940.00
Sideboard, William IV, Mahogany, 3 Drawers, 2 Pedestals, c.1850, 36 x 71 x 26 In. 1840.00
Sideboard, William IV, Mahogany, 3 Drawers, Pedestal, c.1850, 37 x 73 x 25 In. 1035.00
Sideboard, William IV, Mahogany, Paneled, Carved, Mid 1800s, 45 x 80 x 28 1/2 In. 4370.00
Sideboard, Wormley, No. 6421, 3 Drawers, 4 Doors, Dunbar, 33 x 80 x 19 In. 3105.00
Silver Chest, George III Style, Mahogany, Inset Top, Gadrooned Edge, 21 1/4 x 23 In. . . . 405.00
Silver Chest, George III Style, Mahogany, Pierced Gallery, 28 x 34 x 19 In. 865.00
Silver Chest, Neoclassical, Mahogany, 3 Drawers, Turned Legs, c.1820, 36 x 29 x 20 In. . . 3585.00
Silver Chest, Oak, 4 Drawers, 2 Doors, Hertz, c.1875, 41 1/2 x 21 x 16 1/2 In. 2300.00
Silver Chest, Oak, Quartersawn, Inlaid Brass Shield, 5 Drawers, 16 x 23 x 18 In. 390.00
Snack Tray, Mahogany, Turned, 3 Sections, Prestini, 18 In. 2070.00
Sofa, Biedermeier, Burled Walnut, Highback, Upholstered, 64 x 29 In. 520.00
Sofa, Biedermeier, Rectangular Backrest, Paneled Seat Rail, c.1885, 71 1/2 In. . . 1645.00
Sofa, Cappellini, White, Upholstered, Wood Feet, M. Bellini, 24 1/2 x 88 x 42 In. 540.00
Sofa, Chesterfield, Edwardian, Leather Upholstery, Tufted, 29 x 104 x 38 In. 3680.00
Sofa, Chesterfield, Overstuffed, Brown Tufted Leather, Brass Tacking, 72 In. 2350.00
Sofa, Chippendale Style, Mahogany Base, Upholstered, 1900s, 68 1/2 x 36 1/2 In. 660.00
Sofa, Chippendale Style, Mahogany, Camelback, Upholstered, 84 x 32 x 42 In. 575.00
Sofa, Chippendale Style, Mahogany, Upholstered, Chinese, 1900s, 74 x 34 1/2 In. 660.00
Sofa, Chippendale Style, Shaped Crest, Tapered Legs, Upholstered, 76 In. 310.00
Sofa, Chippendale, Mahogany, Camelback, Scroll Arms, Upholstered, 38 x 78 x 30 In. . . . 3300.00
Sofa, Chippendale, Mahogany, Camelback, Tapestry Upholstery, 38 x 78 x 30 In. 3360.00
Sofa, Chippendale, Mahogany, Serpentine Back, Upholstered, c.1790, 34 x 80 x 29 In. . . . 4230.00
Sofa, Eames, Girard Upholstery, Steel Frame, Herman Miller, 36 x 72 x 29 In. 1265.00
Sofa, Eames, No. 3473, Aluminum, Naugahyde, Herman Miller, 1964, 72 x 33 In. 2925.00
Sofa, Eames, Steel Frame, Striped Wool Fabric, 1950s, 72 x 30 x 34 In. 1150.00
Sofa, Federal, Mahogany, Carved Flowers & Greek Key, Splayed Legs, 88 In. 400.00
Sofa, Federal, Mahogany, Carved Frame, Pineapple Finial, Cornucopia, 34 x 77 x 25 In. . . 990.00
Sofa, Federal, Mahogany, Carved, Scrolled Arms, Upholstered, 34 x 77 x 25 In. 1000.00
Sofa, Fin Juhl, Leather, Bronze, Teak, Bovirke, Denmark, c.1953, 75 1/2 x 30 x 30 In. . . . 6435.00
Sofa, Florence Knoll, No. 26, Upholstery, Conical Wood Legs, 90 In. 460.00
Sofa, Florence Knoll, No. 1207, Velvet, Steel Base, Knoll, 90 x 31 1/2 x 30 In. 1840.00
Sofa, Florence Knoll, Tubular Aluminum, Upholstered, 72 x 27 x 29 In. . . . . *Illus* 1265.00
Sofa, Florence Knoll, Wool Upholstery, Steel Base, Knoll, 29 1/2 x 62 x 32 In. 2645.00
Sofa, French Provincial, Walnut, Silk Upholstery, Shaped Top Rail, c.1950, 84 In. 1725.00
Sofa, G. Nakashima, Walnut, Upholstered, 2-Piece, 1961, 102 x 32 x 31 In. 5265.00
Sofa, G. Nelson, Folding, Birch, Metal, Canvas, Cushions, Herman Miller, 96 x 28 In. . . . 1495.00
Sofa, G. Nelson, Sleeper, Hinged Back, Herman Miller, 1960s, 82 x 36 x 28 In. 3220.00

Furniture, Sofa, Florence Knoll, Tubular
Aluminum, Upholstered, 72 x 27 x 29 In.

**If heavy furniture legs have left
dents in your carpet, put an ice
cube on the spot and wait for the
carpet to spring back.**

Sofa, G. Nelson, Sling, Chromed Steel, Leather, Herman Miller, 87 1/2 x 32 x 29 In. 2990.00
Sofa, G. Nelson, Upholstered, Steel, Herman Miller, 1956, 105 In., 4 Piece 1110.00
Sofa, G. Nelson, Vinyl, Wool, 6 Cushions, Steel Legs, Herman Miller, 80 x 30 x 30 In. ... 575.00
Sofa, George III Style, Mahogany, Camelback, Early 1900s, 39 x 72 In. 2530.00
Sofa, George III, Upholstered, Mahogany, Rolled Arms, 1700s, 50 In. 2875.00
Sofa, Georgian Style, Upholstered, Crewel Upholstery, Skirt, 74 In. 260.00
Sofa, Gilt Gesso Frame, Flower Carving, Upholstered, Continental, 82 In. 489.00
Sofa, Gilt Gesso, Acanthus Leaf, Scroll Arms Supports, 41 x 57 x 26 In. 1320.00
Sofa, Henredon, 3 Cushions, Linen Upholstery, Floral Print, 105 In. 670.00
Sofa, Herman Miller, No. 4678, Birch, Upholstered, G. Nelson, c.1950, 80 x 31 x 31 In. ... 1870.00
Sofa, J. Hoffman, Kubus, Leather, Wood Frame, Ebonized, Silver Feet, 82 x 29 In. 4025.00
Sofa, Jydsk Mobelvaerk, Teak, Wool Upholstery, Steel Legs, Denmark, 88 x 30 x 24 In. ... 690.00
Sofa, K. Christensen, Steel, Leather, 2 Seats, Poul Kjaerholm, c.1960, 28 x 54 x 27 In. 3465.00
Sofa, K. Christensen, Steel, Upholstered, Poul Kjaerholm, 1958, 28 x 79 x 25 In. 5975.00
Sofa, Kittinger, Chippendale Style, Rolled Arms, Camelback, Mahogany, 39 x 94 In. 1540.00
Sofa, Le Corbusier, LC2, Chrome, Leather, Nylon, Cassina 4700.00
Sofa, Leather, 3 Fixed High Cushion Seats, Roll Arms, 40 x 76 x 38 In. 489.00
Sofa, Louis XV Style, Beech, C-Shaped Backrest, Gray Paint, 1800s, 48 In. 1880.00
Sofa, Louis XV Style, Beech, Painted, Leaf Carved Crest, Late 1800s, 51 In. 765.00
Sofa, Louis XV Style, Carved Wood Crest Rail, Upholstered, 85 In. 460.00
Sofa, Louis XV Style, Giltwood, Aubusson Tapestry Upholstery, 61 In. 8965.00
Sofa, Louis XV Style, Giltwood, Aubusson Tapestry Upholstery, 80 In. 7770.00
Sofa, Louis XV Style, Upholstered, 3 Sections, Cabriole Legs, Early 1800s, 68 In. 4370.00
Sofa, Louis XV Style, Walnut, Leaf Carved Serpentine Frame, Red Velvet, 71 In. 470.00
Sofa, Louis XV Style, Walnut, Upholstered Back, Cushions, Late 1800s, 43 x 91 In. 690.00
Sofa, Louis XVI Style, Mahogany, Silk Upholstery, Scrolled Arms, 72 In. 590.00
Sofa, Mahogany, Camelback, Serpentine, Scrolled Backrest, Arms, c.1850, 77 In. 3055.00
Sofa, Mahogany, Carved, Acanthus, Rolled Crest, Upholstered, 33 x 78 In. 1645.00
Sofa, Mahogany, Flame Veneer, Carved, Velvet Upholstery, Paw Feet, 95 x 23 x 36 In. ... 1955.00
Sofa, Mahogany, Scrolled Arms, Velvet, Saber Legs, Brass Casters, 1800s, 77 1/2 In. 4600.00
Sofa, Milo Baughman, Wool, Chromed Steel, Thayer-Coggin, 68 x 32 x 25 In. 865.00
Sofa, Modular, Blue Vinyl, Molded Plastic Base, Herman Miller, 1970s, 11 Piece 2470.00
Sofa, Modular, Don Chadwick, Molded Foam, Plastic Base, Herman Miller, 7 Piece 1380.00
Sofa, Modular, Jan Ekselius, Steel, Foam, Stendig, 27 x 26 1/2 x 33 In., 4 Piece 690.00
Sofa, Neoclassical Revival, Carved Mahogany, c.1890, 35 1/2 x 85 3/4 In. 865.00
Sofa, Neoclassical Style, Mahogany, Scrolled Rail, Arms, Paw Feet, c.1890, 60 x 25 In. .. 1495.00
Sofa, Neoclassical, Mahogany, Carved Armrests, Upholstered, 38 x 90 x 29 In. 2200.00
Sofa, Neoclassical, Mahogany, Maple Veneer, c.1820, 32 x 92 In. 805.00
Sofa, Neoclassical, Mahogany, Molded Crest, Outscrolled Arms, Boston, c.1830, 82 In. .. 660.00
Sofa, Neoclassical, Mahogany, Scroll Arms, American, c.1835, 36 x 75 x 23 In. 860.00
Sofa, Neoclassical, Mahogany, Upholstered Back & Arms, Continental, c.1870, 77 In. 3450.00
Sofa, Neoclassical, Rosewood, Mahogany, Scroll Arm, American, c.1890, 33 x 91 In. 1150.00
Sofa, Neoclassical, Walnut, 3 Pierced Splats, Italy, Early 1800s, 33 1/2 x 65 In. 1150.00
Sofa, Regency Style, Mahogany, Dome, Padded Back, Early 1900s, 31 x 76 x 29 In. 1495.00
Sofa, Renaissance Revival, Ebonized Walnut, Gilt, 19th Century, 45 1/2 x 69 x 2 In. 5750.00
Sofa, Rococo Revival, En Cabriolet, Giltwood, Italy, 19th Century, 77 In. 210.00
Sofa, Rococo, Mahogany, Carved, American, Mid 19th Century, 45 x 87 x 32 In. 3680.00
Sofa, Rococo, Mahogany, Flower Crest, Mid 19th Century, 33 x 75 1/2 x 26 1/2 In. 810.00
Sofa, Rococo, Rosewood Laminate, Carved Rose Crest, c.1860, 65 1/2 x 47 In. 5500.00
Sofa, Rococo, Rosewood Laminate, Closed Arms, c.1850, 76 x 52 In. 7765.00
Sofa, Rococo, Rosewood Laminate, Rosalie Without Grapes, c.1850, 40 x 75 In. 3220.00
Sofa, Rococo, Rosewood, Carved, Floral Crests, Upholstered, c.1865, 88 In. 1765.00
Sofa, Rococo, Rosewood, Carved, Top Rail, Mid 1800s, 45 x 76 x 32 In. 1265.00
Sofa, Rosewood, Carved, Marble Inlaid Back, Chinese, 1900s, 75 x 24 x 46 In. 235.00
Sofa, Rosewood, Low Relief-Carved Aprons, Low Back, Chinese, c.1900, 75 In. 825.00
Sofa, Sheraton, Cannon Barrel, Maple, Red Homespun Seat Cushion, 27 x 72 In. 260.00
Sofa, Stendig, Non-Stop, Black Leather, Modular, c.1978, 204 In. 10575.00
Sofa, Stipple-Punched Ground, Velvet Upholstery, Scroll Arms, 33 x 28 x 85 In. 575.00
Sofa, Studio 65, Marilyn, Upholstered Foam, Red Lips, Gufram, Italy, 82 x 29 x 33 In. ... 5290.00
Sofa, Ueli Berger, DS-600, Tan Leather, 22 Sections, De Sede 10575.00
Sofa, V. Kagan, 150BC, Cloud, Biomorphic, Leather, Chrome Base, 32 x 112 x 46 In. 4025.00
Sofa, V. Kagan, R7076, Omnibus, L-Shaped Back, Upholstered, 30 x 80 x 33 1/2 In. 3105.00
Sofa, V. Kagan, Unicorn, Leather, Steel Base, 31 x 102 x 32 In. 8050.00

Sofa, V. Kagan, Walnut, Upholstered, Black Wool, 27 3/4 x 107 x 27 1/4 In. 3740.00
Sofa, V. Panton, Steelstyle, Wire Frame, Upholstered, F. Hansen, 4 Piece 2700.00
Sofa, Victorian, Burl Arm Supports, Frieze, Upholstered, Turned Legs, 29 x 74 x 32 In. . . 140.00
Sofa, Victorian, Mahogany, Carved Top Rail, Serpentine Front Rail, c.1850, 86 In. 175.00
Sofa, Victorian, Triple Arch, Upholstered, Rolled Arms, c.1885, 41 x 82 x 26 1/2 In. 896.00
Sofa, Victorian, Walnut, Split Cushion Back, Double, 40 x 79 1/2 x 33 1/2 In. 800.00
Sofa, W.D. Teague, Brushed Metal, Vinyl Cushions, Arms, 29 1/2 x 70 1/4 x 39 In. 690.00
Sofa, Walnut, 3-Section Back, Flower Crest, Upholstered, Victorian, 83 1/2 In. 100.00
Sofa, Walnut, Serpentine Seat, Shaped Wings, Leaf Carved Legs, c.1850, 60 In. 590.00
Sofa, Wedge Back, Wool Upholstery, 3 Geometric Pillows, 90 x 30 x 28 In. 1380.00
Sofa, Wegner, Wicker, Upholstery, Teak, Getama, Denmark, 1960s, 78 x 26 3/4 In. 5558.00
Sofa, William & Mary Style, Mahogany, Flame Stitched Upholstery, 47 In. 3055.00
Sofa, Wormley, Chrome Base, Square, Brown Leather, Dunbar, 67 In. 1000.00
Sofa, Wormley, Mahogany Base, Even Arm, Silk, Dunbar, 88 x 31 x 30 In. 1725.00
Sofa, Wormley, Mahogany, Wool Upholstery, Dunbar, 73 x 33 x 26 In. 1380.00
Spice Cabinet, Walnut, 50 Drawers, Porcelain Pulls, 17 In. 165.00
Spice Chest, 3 Drawers, Cut Nail Pulls, Mustard Paint, 9 In. 99.00
Spice Chest, 8 Drawers, Black Paint, c.1875, 12 In. 175.00
Spice Chest, Tole, Mustard Decoration, 10 Drawers, 21 1/2 x 39 1/2 In. 460.00
Stand, Adirondack, Painted, White 1850.00
Stand, Art Nouveau, Patinated Metal, Oriental Animal-Form Top, Square, 14 In. 259.00
Stand, Arts & Crafts, Adjustable Top Shelf, Lower Shelf, 32 x 13 x 30 In. 290.00
Stand, Arts & Crafts, Square Top, Raised Cutout Handles, 26 x 14 x 14 In. 529.00
Stand, Bamboo, Door, Rattan Top, 2 Interior Shelves, 36 x 22 1/2 x 15 1/2 In. 250.00
Stand, Baroque, Walnut Inlay, Basket Shape, Anglo-Dutch, 16 x 14 1/2 In. 460.00
Stand, Biedermeier, Fruitwood Veneer, 8 Sections, Ebonized Molding, 30 x 24 x 18 In. . . 550.00
Stand, Birch, Basswood, Drawer, Tapered Legs, Maine, 27 1/2 x 16 3/4 x 17 1/2 In. 4140.00
Stand, Blackamoor, Venetian Baroque, Gilt, Polychrome, Lacquer, 34 x 19 x 13 In. 3220.00
Stand, Buddha, Gold Lacquer, Lotus Base, Mandala Back, 1800s, 22 1/2 In. 400.00
Stand, Cast Iron, Tripod, Round Top, Openwork, Relief, Scrolled Legs, White, 28 In. 220.00
Stand, Cast Iron, Verdigris Brass, Tripod, Indo-Persian, c.1910, 22 1/2 x 19 3/4 In. 200.00
Stand, Cherry, Bird's-Eye Maple, Banded Mahogany Inlay, 2 Drawers, 28 x 21 x 18 In. . . 660.00
Stand, Cherry, Drawer, Oval Corners, Tall Turned Legs, New England 730.00
Stand, Cherry, Drawer, Rectangular Top, Rounded Corners, 27 1/2 x 18 1/2 x 24 In. 1295.00
Stand, Cherry, Splayed, Turned Legs, Lancaster Co., Pennsylvania 480.00
Stand, Chinese Altar, Plank Top, 3 Drawers, Stretcher Base, 34 x 84 1/2 x 20 In. 330.00
Stand, Corner, Arts & Crafts, 3 Tiers, Inset Tiles, 28 In. 80.00
Stand, Eames, Plywood, Masonite, 3 Drawers, Shelf, Steel, Herman Miller 11700.00
Stand, Elm, Lacquered, Chinese, c.1830, 33 1/2 x 17 In., Pair 470.00
Stand, Empire Style, Mahogany, Banded Top, Oval Corners, Pedestal Shaft, Pair 900.00
Stand, Empire Style, Marble Top, Winged Female Figure Mounts, 24 x 35 x 24 In. 360.00
Stand, Federal Style, Hardwood, Biscuit Corner Top, 2 Drawers, 28 x 22 1/2 x 16 In. 605.00
Stand, Federal, Birch, Cherry, Drawer, Straight Skirt, c.1810, 28 1/2 x 21 x 16 1/2 In. . . . 1175.00
Stand, Federal, Cherry, Bird's-Eye Maple, Early 1800s, 27 1/2 x 19 x 16 1/2 In. 750.00
Stand, Federal, Cherry, Inlaid, Drawer, 1/4 Fans, Serrated Banding, c.1790, 27 x 17 In. . . 16450.00
Stand, Federal, Cherry, Inlaid, Drawer, Rectangular Top, 1800s, 27 x 18 x 17 1/4 In. 900.00
Stand, Federal, Cherry, Inlaid, Tray Top, New England, 27 1/4 x 13 1/2 x 13 3/4 In. 4315.00
Stand, Federal, Cherry, Tripod, Circular Top, Snake Feet, 27 x 17 3/4 In. 390.00
Stand, Federal, Mahogany, Cherry, New England, c.1825, 39 x 22 x 18 1/2 In. 1410.00
Stand, Federal, Mahogany, Drawer, Brass Pull, c.1800, 29 1/4 x 18 x 16 In. 1410.00
Stand, Federal, Mahogany, Inlaid, Drawer, Cock-Beaded, c.1812, 28 x 20 x 17 In. 4400.00
Stand, Federal, Mahogany, Inlaid, Drawer, Square, Turned, Reeded Legs, 28 x 17 In. 1410.00
Stand, Federal, Tiger Maple, Drawer, Overhanging Top, Peg Feet, 1820, 28 In. 2000.00
Stand, Fern, Mahogany, Barley Twist Supports, Brass Dragon Heads, 29 x 21 In. 169.00
Stand, French Provincial, Fruitwood, Drawer, Stretcher Shelf, 23 x 18 In. 430.00
Stand, G. Nakashima, Drawer, Brass Pulls, Widdicomb, 21 x 22 x 21 In., Pair 1955.00
Stand, G. Nelson, Rosewood, Aluminum, Herman Miller, 1950s, 18 x 24 In., Pair 4680.00
Stand, G. Nelson, Steel Frame, Drawer, Herman Miller, 17 x 17 x 25 In. 175.00
Stand, G. Nelson, Thin Edge, Rosewood, Drawer, Herman Miller, 18 x 18 1/2 x 22 In. . . . 980.00
Stand, G. Stickley, No. 641, 2 Drawers, Wood Knobs, 20 x 18 x 30 In. 1840.00
Stand, G. Stickley, Round, Cutout Legs, Signed, 29 x 30 In. 1200.00
Stand, George III, Mahogany, c.1800, 30 x 23 x 17 In. 320.00
Stand, Gilt Decorated, Black Lacquered, Birdcage, Tripod, Chinese, 30 x 33 In. 1095.00

Stand, Grain Painted, Stencil, 28 1/2 x 20 x 18 In. 290.00
Stand, Hepplewhite Style, Mahogany, Hekman Furniture Co., 27 x 16 x 23 In., Pair 375.00
Stand, Hepplewhite, 3 Drawers, Mirror, c.1820, 20 1/2 x 19 1/2 x 9 In. 250.00
Stand, Hepplewhite, Birch, Red Wash, Drawer, Tapered Legs, 28 1/2 x 20 1/4 x 16 In. ... 400.00
Stand, Hepplewhite, Cherry, Bird's-Eye Maple Inlay, 2 Tiers, 29 1/2 x 15 1/2 x 17 In. 3680.00
Stand, Hepplewhite, Cherry, Drawer, Banded Inlay, American, 30 x 16 In. 400.00
Stand, Hepplewhite, Cherry, Tray Top, Drawer, 29 x 19 1/2 In. 800.00
Stand, Hepplewhite, Cherry, Tray Top, Drawer, American, 28 x 17 1/2 x 17 In. 980.00
Stand, Hepplewhite, Curly Maple, Cherry, 2 Drawers, Glass Pulls, 22 x 21 x 30 In. 575.00
Stand, Hepplewhite, Curly Maple, Tapered Legs, 17 1/2 x 18 7/8 x 27 7/8 In. 690.00
Stand, Hepplewhite, Mahogany, C-Scroll Brackets, 27 1/2 x 12 x 12 In., Pair 690.00
Stand, Hepplewhite, Mahogany, Satinwood Inlay, 2 Drawers, 27 1/2 x 15 x 20 1/2 In. ... 4830.00
Stand, Hepplewhite, Pine, Drawer, 28 1/2 x 17 1/2 x 17 1/2 In. 230.00
Stand, Hepplewhite, Pine, Drawer, Tapered Legs, 29 x 17 1/2 x 17 In. 300.00
Stand, Hepplewhite, Walnut, 3 Cock-Beaded Drawers, 29 x 16 x 18 In. 700.00
Stand, Hepplewhite, Walnut, Beaded Drawer Front, Brass Pull, 25 x 16 x 19 1/2 In. 225.00
Stand, Hepplewhite, Walnut, Drawer, Tapered Legs, 24 x 21 In. 175.00
Stand, Hepplewhite, Walnut, Tapered Legs, Beaded Drawer, Brass Pulls, 25 x 16 In. 220.00
Stand, Iron, Ceramic Tile Top, Scrolled Feet, 24 x 18 x 13 1/2 In. 220.00
Stand, Iron, Marble Top, Tripod Legs, Angels In Relief, 30 x 24 In. 1430.00
Stand, Iron, Tripod, Hoof Feet, Acanthus Leaf, Scroll, Round Top, 30 x 16 In. 550.00
Stand, Iron, Tripod, Latticework, Women Heads, Hoof Feet, 28 x 24 In. 550.00
Stand, Limbert, Oak, Square Top, Arched Apron, Cane Panels, Flared Legs, 34 x 14 In. .. 2940.00
Stand, Lion, Ivory, Rosewood, Column Standard, Turned Base, 9 In. 315.00
Stand, Louis Philippe, Walnut, Marble Top, 3 Drawers, c.1850, 27 x 17 x 12 In. 300.00
Stand, Louis XV Style, Marble Top, 2 Drawers, Oval, Late 1800s, 29 x 23 In. 375.00
Stand, Louis XVI Style, Marble Top, Cartouche Shape Top, 28 x 20 x 16 In. 825.00
Stand, Louis XVI, Fruitwood, Marble Top, Tambour Door, 28 x 17 1/2 x 12 In. 880.00
Stand, Luggage, J. Adnet, Leather Over Iron, Brass, France, 1950s, 24 x 21 x 21 In. 1755.00
Stand, Macassar Ebony, Lacquer, Aluminum, France, 1930s, 19 x 20 In., Pair 820.00
Stand, Magazine, Eastlake, Ebonized, Parcel Gilt, Adjustable Racks, c.1880, 45 x 19 In. .. 825.00
Stand, Magazine, G. Stickley, 5 Shelves, Wide-Slat Side, 30 x 12 x 47 In. 2300.00
Stand, Magazine, G. Stickley, No. 79, 4 Shelves, Arched Toe Board, 14 x 9 x 40 In. 3740.00
Stand, Magazine, G. Stickley, No. 514, Tongue & Grooved Panels, 35 x 14 In. 8050.00
Stand, Magazine, G. Stickley, Square Top, 4 Shelves, Paneled Sides, 16 x 16 x 44 In. ... 2300.00
Stand, Magazine, G. Stickley, Tapered Sides, Tree Of Life, 4 Shelves, Leather, 43 In. 4900.00
Stand, Magazine, L. & J.G. Stickley, No. 46, 4 Shelves, Slats, 42 1/4 x 20 x 12 In. 3450.00
Stand, Magazine, Lakeside Craft Shops, Mahogany, 32 1/2 x 18 1/2 x 13 1/2 In. 575.00
Stand, Magazine, Limbert, 4 Shelves, 42 x 16 x 12 In. 1265.00
Stand, Magazine, Roycroft, Mahogany, 3 Shelves, Canted Sides, Arched, 37 x 18 In. 2990.00
Stand, Magazine, Stickley Bros., 31 x 26 x 13 In. 1100.00
Stand, Magazine, Stickley Bros., No. 4706, 4 Shelves, Side Spindles, 39 x 27 In. 1295.00
Stand, Mahogany, 3 Tiers, Nathan Margolis, Hartford, Conn., 41 3/4 x 19 In. 345.00
Stand, Mahogany, Carved Leaf Skirt, 8-Sided Marble Top, c.1900, 30 x 28 In. 300.00
Stand, Mahogany, Cherry, Inlaid, Serpentine Front, 2 Drawers, c.1830, 31 x 21 In. 2150.00
Stand, Mahogany, Leather, Tambour Doors, 28 1/2 x 22 3/8 x 18 In., Pair 1150.00
Stand, Mahogany, Reticulated Carved Leaf Skirt, Marble Top, c.1900, 30 x 28 In. 340.00
Stand, Maple, Cut Corner Top, Vase Turned Pedestal, Spider Legs, 28 1/4 x 22 x 15 In. .. 489.00
Stand, Maple, Walnut Lift Top, Swing-Out Supports, 4 Drawers, Turned Legs, 29 x 25 In. 1265.00
Stand, Marble Top, Cast Iron Base, Arched Stretcher, 29 1/2 x 31 1/2 x 20 In., Pair 275.00
Stand, Marble Top, Drawer, Gold Painted Bases, 1900s, 24 1/2 x 17 1/2 x 15 In., Pair ... 300.00
Stand, McCobb, Leather Top, Drawer, 2 Doors, 24 x 22 x 21 In., Pair 630.00
Stand, McCobb, Walnut, White Glass, Steel, c.1956, 22 x 21 x 24 In., Pair 1640.00
Stand, Mixed Wood, Parquetry, Drawer, 29 1/2 x 18 x 14 In. 200.00
Stand, Music, G. Stickley, Mahogany, 4 Shelves, 19 x 39 x 15 In. 1610.00
Stand, Music, Papier-Mache, Mid 19th Century, 43 x 18 x 18 In. 2300.00
Stand, Music, Renaissance Revival, Ebonized, Gilt Bronze Mounted, c.1870, 32 x 28 In. .. 800.00
Stand, Music, Renaissance Revival, Walnut, 2 Fold-Out Shelves, c.1865, 45 x 15 In. 230.00
Stand, Neoclassical, Blond Wood, Egg Shape, 26 x 23 x 18 In., Pair 1725.00
Stand, Neoclassical, Cherry, Drawer, Conn., c.1825, 27 3/4 x 18 1/2 x 18 In. 2235.00
Stand, Nutting, No. 653, Round, Turned Splayed Legs, Label 500.00
Stand, Oak, Tambour Doors, Drawer, Continental, 19th Century, 27 x 18 x 12 In. 410.00
Stand, Oriental, Teak, Carved Legs, Pierced Leaves On Apron, 15 1/2 x 13 In. 290.00

Stand, Painted Wood, Urn Shape, Gilt Highlights, Drawer, 30 x 17 1/2 In. 495.00
Stand, Painted, Tole Tray, Serpentine Side, Mid 1800s, 21 x 21 In. 175.00
Stand, Parquetry, 3 Drawers, Serpentine Front, Continental, 29 3/4 x 18 x 14 In. 405.00
Stand, Pine, 2 Drawers, Dovetailed, Flared Legs, 30 x 19 x 15 1/2 In. 140.00
Stand, Pine, Drawer, Turned Legs, Gray Blue Paint, 30 x 32 1/2 x 21 In. 275.00
Stand, Pine, Hardwood, Frieze Drawers, Square Legs, American, c.1810, 30 1/2 x 16 In. .. 300.00
Stand, Pine, Red Finish, Square Tapered Legs, 19th Century, 29 x 19 x 19 In. 175.00
Stand, Plant, Aesthetic Revival, Maple, Faux Bamboo, Folding Tripod, 1900, 38 In. 635.00
Stand, Plant, Arts & Crafts, Walnut, Square, Arched Stretcher, 15 x 15 x 31 In. 320.00
Stand, Plant, Empire Style, Ebonized Wood, Inverted Pear Shape, Enameled, 31 1/2 In. ... 355.00
Stand, Plant, G. Stickley, Splay Legs, 18 x 18 x 20 In. 4715.00
Stand, Plant, George III Style, Giltwood, Acanthus & Scroll, Tripodal, 43 In., Pair 1150.00
Stand, Plant, Graduated 3 Tier, Demilune, Pine, 34 x 47 1/2 x 22 In. 250.00
Stand, Plant, Green Paint, 2 Tiers, 13 Arms, 19th Century, 55 In. 1925.00
Stand, Plant, Hardwood, Carved, Flowers, Masks, Marble Top, Chinese, c.1890, 33 In. .. 520.00
Stand, Plant, Hunzinger, Walnut, 9 Circular Platforms, Turned Spindles, 1860, 55 In. 1195.00
Stand, Plant, Louis XVI Style, Giltwood, 3 Tapered Legs, Circular Top, 53 1/2 x 14 In. ... 320.00
Stand, Plant, Marble, Brass, Scroll Feet, Onyx & Brass Finials, 18 x 18 x 34 1/2 In. 220.00
Stand, Plant, Painted, 5 Shelves, Tripod Base, Early 20th Century, 51 x 20 In. 940.00
Stand, Plant, Pine, 3 Graduated Tiers, Demilune, 34 x 47 1/2 x 22 In. 250.00
Stand, Plant, Pine, Pinwheel Design, 4 Turned Uprights, 19th Century, 55 In. 1925.00
Stand, Plant, Robert Adam Style, Polychromed, c.1900, 41 1/2 x 18 In. 430.00
Stand, Plant, Softwood, 5 Half Tiers, Brown Paint, 51 In. 420.00
Stand, Plant, Stickley Bros., Mahogany, Square Top, Tapered Base, 13 x 13 x 34 In. 1035.00
Stand, Plant, Stickley Bros., Square Top, Tapered Base, 13 x 13 x 34 In. 520.00
Stand, Plant, Victorian, Cast Iron, Stepped, Tripod, Hoof Feet, 19 x 66 1/2 x 14 1/2 In. .. 1035.00
Stand, Plant, Victorian, Wirework, 3 Tiers, Center Mounted Basket, 51 x 30 x 26 In. 420.00
Stand, Plant, Wire, Oval Shelf, Gallery, Center Holder, 45 x 35 1/2 x 11 In. 185.00
Stand, Plant, Wire, Stepped Shelves, Gallery, Top Holder, 49 x 30 x 24 In. 145.00
Stand, Poplar, 1-Board Top, Frieze, Turned Legs, Paint Traces, 28 x 20 x 17 In. 360.00
Stand, Portfolio, Gothic Revival, Burl Walnut, American, 19th Century, 46 x 27 In. 5400.00
Stand, Queen Anne Style, Mahogany, c.1800, 31 1/2 x 12 1/2 In., Pair 2530.00
Stand, Queen Anne, Ash, Pine, Drawer, Pad Feet, Painted, 28 1/2 x 28 x 21 1/2 In. 1100.00
Stand, Red Paint, Square Top, Tripod Splayed Legs, Connecticut, 27 x 12 In. 1840.00
Stand, Regency Style, Fruitwood, Tapered, 3-Part Base, c.1900, 25 x 14 In. 800.00
Stand, Regency Style, Mahogany, Circular Tops, Molded Frieze, Paw Feet, 42 In., Pair .. 600.00
Stand, Rohde, Paldao Wood, Door, Brass Pulls, Herman Miller, 17 x 25 In., Pair 1380.00
Stand, Rosewood, Carved, Chinese, 36 x 10 1/2 In. 150.00
Stand, Rosewood, Famille Rose Porcelain Inset, Chinese, Early 1900s 470.00
Stand, Rosewood, Inlaid Marble Top, Chinese, Late 1800s, 16 1/2 x 12 1/2 x 32 In., Pair . 530.00
Stand, Roycroft, Little Journey's, 2 Shelves, Through Tenon, 26 x 14 x 26 In. 980.00
Stand, Roycroft, Little Journeys, With Memorial Edition Books, 26 x 14 x 26 In. 520.00
Stand, Shaker, Cherry, Drawer, Rounded Corners, Mt. Lebanon, 28 3/4 x 19 x 34 In. 1495.00
Stand, Shaker, Cherry, Poplar, Dovetailed Drawer, Turned Legs, 1800s, 27 x 21 x 10 In. . 770.00
Stand, Shaker, Tiger Maple, Drop Leaf, 2 Drawers, 2 Leaves, Tapered Legs 7875.00
Stand, Shaker, Walnut, Drawer, 2 Board Top, Ohio, 28 1/2 x 32 1/2 x 21 In. 605.00
Stand, Shaving, George III, Mahogany, 3 Drawers, Mirror, 21 1/2 x 17 1/2 x 10 In. 660.00
Stand, Shaving, Mahogany, Mirror, Cabinet, Shelf, Late 1800s, 61 x 13 In. 259.00
Stand, Shaving, Mahogany, Spiral Column, Cabriole Legs, c.1890, 73 x 17 x 17 In. 1670.00
Stand, Sheraton Style, Cherry, Turned Legs, Drawer, 25 x 17 x 14 In. 400.00
Stand, Sheraton Style, Mahogany, 4 Tiers, 25 1/2 x 19 x 14 In. 50.00
Stand, Sheraton Style, Mahogany, Flame Grain, Drawer, Late 1800s, 18 x 15 In. 920.00
Stand, Sheraton, Cherry, Burl Veneer, 2 Drawers, Dovetailed, 18 1/2 x 18 1/2 x 31 In. ... 550.00
Stand, Sheraton, Cherry, Drawer, Dovetailed, Reeded Legs, 25 3/4 x 18 x 17 1/2 In. 635.00
Stand, Sheraton, Cherry, Drawer, Dovetailed, Turned Legs, Ball Feet, 20 3/4 x 19 1/2 In. . 415.00
Stand, Sheraton, Cherry, Drawer, Turned & Tapered Legs, 19 x 20 x 29 In. 259.00
Stand, Sheraton, Cherry, Drop Leaf, Drawer, American, 28 x 15 x 17 In. 575.00
Stand, Sheraton, Cherry, Pine, Ogee Drawer Front, 19 1/4 x 29 In. 250.00
Stand, Sheraton, Cherry, Poplar, Drawer, 20 1/4 x 21 x 29 1/2 In. 250.00
Stand, Sheraton, Cherry, Turned Legs, Ball Feet, 28 1/2 x 19 1/2 x 19 In. 315.00
Stand, Sheraton, Curly Maple, Poplar, Drawer, 22 x 21 1/2 x 29 1/2 In. 1610.00
Stand, Sheraton, Drawer, Spiral, Ring Carved Legs, 28 1/2 x 19 1/2 x 17 In. 575.00
Stand, Sheraton, Mahogany, 2 Drawers, Carved Legs, 29 x 19 1/4 x 15 3/4 In. 1150.00

Stand, Sheraton, Mahogany, 2 Drawers, Rope Twist Legs, New England, 28 1/2 x 21 In. . . 1495.00
Stand, Sheraton, Mahogany, Bird's-Eye Maple, Brass, Drawer, 29 x 17 x 16 In. 335.00
Stand, Sheraton, Mahogany, Bird's-Eye Maple, Drawer, Brass Knob, 30 x 17 x 16 In. . . . 330.00
Stand, Sheraton, Maple, Pine, Drop Leaf, 2 Drawers, Brass Pulls, 28 1/2 x 17 x 18 In. . . . 280.00
Stand, Sheraton, Pine, Brown Paint, Drawer, Turned Legs, 28 1/2 x 16 x 18 In. 520.00
Stand, Sheraton, Pine, Maple, Drawers, Turned Legs, Dovetailed Drawers, 20 x 19 3/4 In. 545.00
Stand, Sheraton, Pine, Mixed Wood, Drawer, American, 29 x 16 1/2 x 22 1/2 In. 345.00
Stand, Sheraton, Poplar, Pine, Red Wash, Dovetailed Drawers, c.1840, 20 1/2 x 29 3/4 In. 545.00
Stand, Sheraton, Tiger Maple Top, Bird's-Eye Maple Drawer Front, 29 x 22 x 19 In. 375.00
Stand, Sheraton, Walnut, Poplar, Pine, 2 Dovetailed Drawers, 21 1/4 x 29 1/2 In. 430.00
Stand, Sheraton, Walnut, Tapered Legs, 19th Century, 27 1/4 x 24 x 17 1/2 In. 575.00
Stand, Smoking, Black Butler, Cast Iron, c.1925, 33 In. 750.00
Stand, Smoking, Folk Art House, Wooden, 28 1/2 x 13 1/2 x 14 In. 55.00
Stand, Smoking, L. & J.G. Stickley, No. 515, Octagonal Top, Shoefoot, 21 x 21 x 24 In. . . 4025.00
Stand, Tea Urn, George III Style, Mahogany, Early 20th Century, 25 x 13 x 13 In. 1035.00
Stand, Teak, Carved, Soapstone Top Inset, 18 1/4 x 19 In. 345.00
Stand, Telephone, Elliot Noyes, Laminate Top, Tripod Base, Knoll, 22 x 22 x 19 In. 545.00
Stand, Telephone, Limbert, Oak, Shelf, Chair, 1906, 30 In. 765.00
Stand, Telephone, Mahogany, Lift Top, Leather Writing Surface, 26 x 14 x 18 In. 300.00
Stand, Telephone, Square, Arched Apron, Lower Shelf, Tapered Legs, 18 x 18 x 29 In. . . . 489.00
Stand, Tiger Maple, Dish Top, Spider Legs, Turned Post, 28 1/2 x 17 x 17 In. 550.00
Stand, Tilt Top, Cherry, Tiger Maple, Turned Shaft, Cabriole Legs, 29 x 22 3/4 In. 960.00
Stand, Tilt Top, Federal Style, Mahogany, Inlaid, Spider Legs, 29 x 14 3/4 x 22 3/4 In. . . . 1495.00
Stand, Tilt Top, Mahogany, Molded Edge, Turned Pedestal, 30 x 23 1/2 In. 140.00
Stand, Tilt Top, Mahogany, Pedestal, Snake Foot, 3-Footed, 25 x 26 In. 495.00
Stand, Twig, Crossed Tripod Base, Square Top, Scalloped Apron, 11 1/2 x 26 In. 315.00
Stand, Victorian, Walnut, Oval, Marble Top, Cutout Legs, 28 x 22 x 17 In. 230.00
Stand, Walnut, 1-Board Top, Tapered Legs, Skirt Border, 1800s, 26 x 22 x 19 1/2 In. 360.00
Stand, Walnut, Drawer, Tapered Splay Legs, 27 1/2 x 23 1/2 x 31 In. 1350.00
Stand, Walnut, Inlaid, 2-Board Top, Diamonds, Flowers, 30 1/2 x 37 x 29 In. 1045.00
Stand, Walnut, Marble Top, Beale & Hooper, 32 x 18 x 16 1/4 In. 489.00
Stand, Walnut, Mortise & Tenon Joints, 2 Drawers, 19th Century, 28 x 19 x 17 In. 195.00
Stand, Walnut, Pegged Legs, Penny Feet, 27 1/2 In. 145.00
Stand, Walnut, Pietra Dura Mounted Top, 32 1/2 x 17 1/2 In. 750.00
Stand, Walnut, Square Top, Drawer, Platform Stretcher, 27 5/8 x 14 x 14 In. 69.00
Stand, Walnut, Tilt Top, Wood Latch, Turned Pedestal, 3 Saber Legs, 28 x 20 x 21 In. . . . 470.00
Stand, Walnut, Veneer Over Pine, 2 Drawers, Tapered Legs, 31 x 18 x 18 In. 195.00
Stand, Wendell Castle, Walnut, Rosewood, Door, 21 x 16 x 23 1/2 In., Pair 865.00
Stand, Widdicomb, Black Lacquer, 2 Drawers, 23 1/4 x 18 In., Pair 2415.00
Stand, Widdicomb, Louis XV Style, Bombe, Flowers, Gilt Trim, 30 x 28 In., Pair 400.00
Stand, William IV, Mahogany, 3 Rectangular Tiers, Trestle Base, 45 x 19 x 46 In. 2970.00
Stand, Wood, Carved, Marble Top, Chinese, 1800s, 32 x 17 1/2 In. 460.00
Stand, Wood, Marble Top, 2 Tiers, Chinese, 1800s, 32 x 12 x 16 1/2 In. 316.00
Stool, Achille Castiglioni, Sella, Leather Bike Seat, 1957 . . . . 2460.00
Stool, Arts & Crafts, Thebes, Concave Cutout Top, Turned Legs, 16 x 16 x 14 In. 345.00
Stool, Arts & Crafts, Thebes, Concave, Slatted Seat, 3 Spindles, 16 x 16 x 15 In. 575.00
Stool, Beech, Polychrome, Square Upholstered Seat, France, c.1865, 19 x 13 In. 520.00
Stool, Biedermeier, Cherry, Mortise & Tenon, 11 1/2 x 23 1/2 x 11 In. 90.00
Stool, Biedermeier, Fruitwood, Ebonized, Parcel Gilt, Tufted Cushion, c.1825, 19 In. 2940.00
Stool, Chippendale Style, Mahogany, Carved Legs, Ball Feet, 1800s, 18 x 27 x 19 In. 1870.00
Stool, Chippendale Style, Mahogany, Needlepoint Upholstery, 1900s, 19 x 20 In. 750.00
Stool, Chippendale Style, Mahogany, Serpentine, 19 1/2 x 23 1/2 x 18 In. 115.00
Stool, Cricket, Red Paint 1210.00
Stool, Duncan Phyfe, Mahogany, Bowed Seat, 15 x 21 x 16 In., Pair 10158.00
Stool, Eero Saarinen, Enameled Metal, Terrycloth Upholstery, Knoll, 17 1/4 In. 95.00
Stool, Eero Saarinen, Wool, Swivel, Aluminum Pedestal Base, 16 x 15 In., Pair 470.00
Stool, Elm, Through Tenon, 3 Legs, 24 In. 55.00
Stool, Empire Style, Upholstered, Paw Feet, Rolled Arms, 1900s, 27 x 31 x 16 In., Pair . . 440.00
Stool, F. Gehry, Wiggle, Cardboard, Masonite, Easy Edges, 1972, 14 x 17 x 16 In. 2340.00
Stool, G. Nakashima, Triangular Top, 3 Legs, 1 Free Edge, 12 1/2 x 19 x 17 In. 1035.00
Stool, G. Nelson, Ebonized Wood, Wool, Herman Miller, 21 x 15 1/2 x 18 1/2 In. 145.00
Stool, George II Style, Mahogany, Oblong, Upholstered, 18 x 26 x 18 In., Pair 750.00
Stool, George II Style, Walnut, Padded, Late 1800s, 19 x 24 1/2 x 20 1/2 In., Pair 920.00

Stool, George III Style, Mahogany, 1900s, 18 x 17 1/2 In. 460.00
Stool, George III Style, Mahogany, Carved, Curule Form, Upholstered, 20 x 20 In. 865.00
Stool, George III Style, Mahogany, Oval, 17 x 22 In. 600.00
Stool, George III Style, Mahogany, Padded, Rectangular, c.1890, 19 x 21 x 17 In. 805.00
Stool, George III, Mahogany, c.1800 .... 920.00
Stool, Georgian, Mahogany, Slip Seat, 20 x 15 1/2 x 19 In. 170.00
Stool, Gerrit Rietveld, Military, Wood, Black, White, 1950s, 17 x 16 x 16 In. 7170.00
Stool, Giltwood, Carved, Italy, 18 1/2 x 23 x 18 In. 489.00
Stool, Giltwood, Pillow Top, Baluster Legs, Italy, 25 x 17 In., Pair 1840.00
Stool, Gothic Revival, Mahogany, Square, Upholstered Seat, c.1850, 17 x 20 x 20 In. 2630.00
Stool, Gothic Revival, Oak, Quatrefoil Carved Knees, c.1850, 18 x 18 x 13 1/2 In., Pair .. 805.00
Stool, Irish Georgian Style, Mahogany, Leaf Carved Apron, 21 x 24 x 17 In., Pair 750.00
Stool, Jacobean, Fruitwood, Vase Turnings, Rush Seat, 14 x 26 In. 635.00
Stool, Joe Colombo, Birillo, Chromed Steel, Leather, Plastic, Italy, 1970, 18 1/2 x 42 In. . 1640.00
Stool, L. & J.G. Stickley, Mahogany, 7 Vertical Spindles, Leather Top, 18 x 13 In. 765.00
Stool, Larsen & Madsen, Teak, Leather, Denmark, 23 x 15 1/2 x 16 In. 430.00
Stool, Louis XV Style, Giltwood, Padded Seat, Cabriole Legs, c.1885, 19 x 35 x 20 In. .. 575.00
Stool, Louis XV Style, Giltwood, Upholstered, 16 x 16 In. 300.00
Stool, Louis XVI Revival, Gilt Bronze Mounted, Ebonized, 19 x 22 x 17 In. 1910.00
Stool, Louis XVI Style, Beech, Upholstered, France, 18 x 26 x 19 In., Pair 2760.00
Stool, Louis XVI Style, Giltwood, Padded, Rectangular, c.1890, 19 x 39 1/4 x 20 In. 489.00
Stool, McCobb, Directional, Brass, Upholstered, 1954, 20 x 20 x 15 In., Pair 2340.00
Stool, Milking, Windsor, Splayed Leg, Ring-Turned Mortised Legs, Early 1800s, 14 In. .. 660.00
Stool, Napoleon III, Adjustable, Ebonized, Column Supports, c.1865, 19 1/2 x 13 In. 400.00
Stool, Napoleon III, Giltwood, Padded Top, Gilt Rope-Form Base, 15 x 23 In. 1955.00
Stool, Napoleon III, Giltwood, Paneled Frieze, Round Seat, c.1860, 17 x 26 In. 860.00
Stool, Nutting, No. 171, Jacobean, Upholstered, Signed 725.00
Stool, P. Evans, Riveted Patchwork, Velvet Cushion, 20 x 20 x 13 In., Pair 2990.00
Stool, Perriand, Ebonized Wood, France, 1960s, 13 x 16 In. 1755.00
Stool, Peter Hunt Style, Bootjack, 8 x 16 x 8 In. 80.00
Stool, Piano, Empire, Mahogany, Rosewood, Octagonal Top, 18 1/2 x 14 In. 460.00
Stool, Piano, Federal, Mahogany, Round, c.1820, 20 1/2 In. 3585.00
Stool, Piano, George IV, Mahogany, Circular Seat, Early 1800s, 20 x 12 In. 140.00
Stool, Piano, Louis Philippe, Mahogany, Adjustable, 3 Legs, c.1835, 19 1/2 x 13 In. 230.00
Stool, Piano, Victorian, Cast Iron, Cushioned Top, Tripod Base, Openwork Legs, 18 In. .. 29.00
Stool, Pine, Splayed Legs, Pennsylvania, 8 x 14 1/2 x 8 In. 69.00
Stool, Pine, Square Leather Top, Flat Stretchers, 28 In. 105.00
Stool, Queen Anne Style, Mahogany, Padded, Cabriole Legs, 19 1/2 x 19 In. 518.00
Stool, Regency Style, Giltwood, Padded Seat, Scrolled Arms, c.1880, 27 x 38 In., Pair ... 2990.00
Stool, Regency Style, Mahogany, Padded Top, Faux Bamboo Base, 20 x 51 x 17 In. 1380.00
Stool, Regency Style, Mahogany, Padded, Brass Nail Heads, 14 x 48 x 22 In. 1495.00
Stool, Rosewood, Basketwork, Carved, Burl Inlay, Chinese, c.1890, 19 In., Pair 410.00
Stool, Rosewood, Carved Frieze, Cabriole Legs, Scroll Feet, 17 x 24 x 16 In. 1210.00
Stool, Russell Woodard, Extruded Aluminum, Leather, U.S.A., 1960s, 21 x 17 In., Pair .. 2225.00
Stool, Scrub Top, Sponge Decoration, Maine, 7 1/2 x 18 3/4 x 8 1/2 In. 748.00
Stool, Shaker, Green Paint, Bootjack Ends, Rectangular, Enfield, Conn., 10 x 9 x 19 In. .. 646.00
Stool, Shaker, Maple, Wool Tape Seat, Mt. Lebanon, c.1885, 16 x 13 1/2 In. 2415.00
Stool, Shaker, Oak, Hickory, Gray Paint, Scrubbed Seat, 12 1/4 x 25 1/4 In. 863.00
Stool, Shaker, Painted, Turned Legs, River Cane Seat, c.1860, 9 1/2 x 12 x 11 1/2 In. 715.00
Stool, Shaker, Pine, 3 Steps, Arched Feet, Enfield, Conn., c.1840s, 26 x 4 1/2 x 13 In. ... 1440.00
Stool, Shaker, Pine, Dark Stain, Enfield, Conn., c.1840, 30 x 18 1/2 x 22 In. 3819.00
Stool, Shaker, Pine, Red Paint, Arched Sides, Hinged Top, 17 x 20 x 17 In. 325.00
Stool, Shaker, Revolving, Maple, Pine, Round Seat, 4 Arched Feet, 20 x 14 3/4 In. 3165.00
Stool, Shaker, Taped Top, Double Box Stretcher, Mt. Lebanon, 16 1/2 x 14 1/4 In. 1265.00
Stool, Shaker, Walnut, Button Turned Tops, Oak Split Seat, 10 x 13 In. 220.00
Stool, Sheraton, Cherry, Needlework Seat, Late 1800s, 13 x 16 x 16 In. 175.00
Stool, Softwood, Cutout Apron, Shaped, 14 x 8 In. 68.00
Stool, Upholstered, 8 Buffalo Horn Feet, 22 x 20 1/2 x 11 In. 635.00
Stool, V. Kagan, Lucite, Vinyl, Tufted Cushion, 16 x 20 In. 489.00
Stool, V. Panton, No. 250S, Metal, Upholstered, X-Design, 1971, 32 In., Pair 3805.00
Stool, Vanity, Colonial Revival, Ebonized Walnut, Slip Seat, Cabriole Legs, 20 x 22 In. .. 380.00
Stool, Victorian, Burgundy, Tack Head Trim, Serpentine Sides, c.1870, 14 x 19 x 19 In. .. 530.00
Stool, Victorian, Lift Top, Upholstered, Pinched Waist, c.1900, 18 1/2 x 19 In. 545.00

Stool, Victorian, Mahogany, Carved, Pierced, Stretcher, Pine Frame, 16 x 20 x 14 In. 110.00
Stool, Victorian, Mahogany, Needlework Upholstery, c.1880, 16 1/2 x 31 In. 230.00
Stool, Walnut, Padded Top, Needlework, Cabriole Legs, 27 x 19 In. 1310.00
Stool, Walnut, Rectangular Shaped Top, Continental, 1800s, 20 x 21 x 13 1/2 In. 200.00
Stool, Walnut, Upholstered, Cabriole Legs, Spanish Feet, 17 1/2 x 18 1/2 x 14 1/2 In. 175.00
Stool, Warren McArthur, Tubular Aluminum Base, Vinyl Seat, 30 x 14 3/4 In. 1955.00
Stool, William & Mary Style, Ash, Turned Stretcher, Early 1900s, 19 x 18 x 15 In. 275.00
Stool, William & Mary, Upholstered Top, Spanish Feet, 17 x 15 1/2 x 18 1/2 In. 690.00
Stool, William IV, Mahogany, Leather Upholstery, Scroll Shape, 20 x 35 x 20 1/2 In. 750.00
Stool, Wood Frame, Tongue & Groove, Peg Feet, Woven Cane Top, 13 x 10 In. 120.00
Stool, Woodard & Sons, Wire, Steel, Painted, 14 x 20 x 20 In., Pair 705.00
Stool, Yew, Walnut, Oval Seat, Thick Splayed Legs, England, 13 1/4 x 17 1/2 In. 195.00
Stool Set, Aalto, 3 Laminated Bent Birch Legs, Round Seat, c.1950, 3 .... 635.00
Stool Set, Bar, Richard Neutra, Chromed Metal, Upholstered, 33 In., 4 .... 1790.00
Stool Set, G. Nakashima, High Mira, Walnut, Poplar, 1961, 20 x 19 x 33 In., 4 .... 4975.00
Table, 2 Drawers, Pierced Apron, Chinese, 33 x 62 x 24 In. 1265.00
Table, Aalto, Blond Wood, Bentwood, Shelf, Artek, 22 x 23 x 17 In. 520.00
Table, Aalto, Molded Birch Frame, Glass Top, Artek, 27 1/2 In. 144.00
Table, Aesthetic Revival, Pietra Dura, Tripod, American, Late 1800s, 30 1/2 x 18 In. 1180.00
Table, Aldo Tura, Mahogany, Lacquered Goatskin, Brass, Italy, 1950s, 26 x 17 In. 1755.00
Table, Alfonse Bach, Black Lacquered Wood, 2 Tiers, Stepped, Chromed Tubular, Pair ... 1380.00
Table, Altar, Black Lacquer, Chinese, c.1800, 35 1/2 x 63 3/4 x 14 In. 470.00
Table, Altar, Distressed Wood, Carved Floral Supports, Chinese, 1800s, 32 x 96 In. 1265.00
Table, Altar, Elm, Chinese, c.1800, 34 x 61 x 11 In. 410.00
Table, Altar, Hardwood, Incised Dragon & Key Border, Oriental, 32 x 72 x 18 In. 630.00
Table, Altar, Scroll Top, Flowers, Latticework, Chinese, 1800s, 47 x 32 1/2 In. 940.00
Table, Altar, Softwood, 2 Drawers, Southern Chinese, Late 1800s, 33 x 51 In. 520.00
Table, Altar, Upturned Corners, Carved Aprons, Chinese, Early 1900s, 64 x 33 In. 325.00
Table, Art Deco, Bamboo, Bent, Demilune, 21 In., Pair 430.00
Table, Art Deco, Bamboo, Bent, Walnut Top, 16 1/2 x 36 In. 145.00
Table, Art Deco, Birch, Inlaid Top, Curved Floor Stretcher, 30 x 20 x 25 In. 430.00
Table, Art Deco, Blond Mahogany, Round, Chinoiserie, Early 1900s, 17 1/2 x 35 In. 290.00
Table, Art Deco, Carved Swan Supports, Beveled Glass, 60 x 13 x 30 In. 230.00
Table, Arts & Crafts, 4 Decorated Tiles, Wrought Iron Base, 13 x 13 x 20 In. 345.00
Table, Arts & Crafts, 4 Flower Tiles, Wrought Iron Base, 3 Legs, 16 x 21 In. 375.00
Table, Arts & Crafts, 4 Tiers, Cast Brass Feet, 17 x 17 x 30 In. 1380.00
Table, Arts & Crafts, Inset Earthtone Tiles, Wrought Iron Base, 19 x 13 x 19 In. 520.00
Table, Arts & Crafts, Quartered Top, Macmurdo Feet, 30 x 28 In. 1095.00
Table, Arts & Crafts, Square Top, Lower Shelf, Stretchers, 24 x 24 x 29 In. 750.00
Table, Bamboo, Hardwood Top, Drawer, Straight Legs, Openwork Skirt, 37 1/2 x 32 In. .. 520.00
Table, Bamboo, Lacquered, Anglo-Indian, c.1900, 28 x 18 In. 315.00
Table, Bamboo, Sea Grass, Octagonal, Anglo-Indian, c.1900, 28 1/2 x 22 In. 175.00
Table, Baroque, Walnut, Carved, Octagonal Top, Sham Drawers, Italy, 29 x 41 1/2 In. 1410.00
Table, Baroque, Walnut, Oak, 2 Drawers, Continental, 1600s, 32 x 72 x 27 In. 4995.00
Table, Batchelder, Enameled Iron Base, Rectangular Tile Top, 19 x 18 x 12 In. 1035.00
Table, Beech, Octagonal, Pierced Carving, Continental, c.1900, 30 x 29 x 26 In. 315.00
Table, Belle Epoque, Alabaster, Gilt Bronze Mounted, Tiers, Round, 34 x 17 In. 920.00
Table, Biedermeier, Burl Walnut, Faceted Stem, Tripod Base, 29 x 17 1/2 In., Pair 2235.00
Table, Biedermeier, Burl Walnut, Round Top, Trefoil Pedestal, 30 x 65 1/2 In. 2875.00
Table, Biedermeier, Cherry, Square, Figured Top, Inlay, 30 x 30 1/2 x 29 In. 1495.00
Table, Biedermeier, Fruitwood Inlay, Gilt, Ebonized, c.1825, 30 x 20 In. 2820.00
Table, Biedermeier, Fruitwood, Ebonized, Felt Playing Surface, c.1810, 30 x 36 x 18 In. ... 1530.00
Table, Biedermeier, Walnut, Frieze Drawers, c.1830, 30 1/2 x 41 1/2 x 35 In. 705.00
Table, Birch, Chrome, Draw Leaf Extensions, c.1930, 25 x 40 x 30 In. 85.00
Table, Black Enamel, Marble Top, Ormolu Trim, Bun Feet, 20 x 29 x 25 In. 110.00
Table, Bone Inlay, Octagonal, Pierced Pedestal, Anglo-Indian, 30 x 42 1/2 x 45 In. 115.00
Table, Burl Walnut, Mahogany, Serpentine, Cabriole Legs, England, 29 1/2 x 16 3/4 In. ... 115.00
Table, Burl Walnut, Organic Shape, 4 Saber Legs, Vermont, 16 x 36 1/2 x 17 In. 1150.00
Table, Burl Walnut, Satinwood Inlay, Parcel Ebonized Wood, c.1880, 27 x 46 x 34 In. 1610.00
Table, Butterfly, Faux-Grained, Norway, c.1870s, 42 x 80 In. Open 2640.00
Table, Byrdcliffe, 2 Drawers, Shelf, Splayed Side Panels, 63 x 28 x 30 In. 10350.00
Table, Card, Adam Style, Satinwood, Painted Details, 30 3/4 x 35 3/4 x 18 In. 1555.00
Table, Card, Chippendale Style, Mahogany, Flip Top, 1800s, 28 x 32 x 19 1/2 In. 730.00

Table, Card, Chippendale, Mahogany, Drawer, Cabriole Legs, 28 1/2 x 32 1/2 In. 7765.00
Table, Card, Chippendale, Mahogany, Fold Top, Marlborough Legs, c.1780, 29 x 32 In. . . 2235.00
Table, Card, Edwardian, Mahogany, Fold Top, X-Shape Trestle, 30 x 30 In. 999.00
Table, Card, Empire, Mahogany, Pine, Veneer, Platform Base, 34 1/2 x 18 x 29 In. 345.00
Table, Card, Empire, Walnut, Foldover, American, c.1840, 30 x 41 1/4 x 18 In. 445.00
Table, Card, Federal Style, Mahogany, Demilune, Fold Top, c.1900, 29 x 34 1/2 In. 405.00
Table, Card, Federal, Mahogany Inlay, Bird's-Eye Maple Panels, 30 x 36 x 18 In. 6575.00
Table, Card, Federal, Mahogany, D-Shape Top, Reeded Edge, c.1815, 29 x 36 x 18 In. . . . 3110.00
Table, Card, Federal, Mahogany, D-Shape, Rhode Island, Early 1800s, 29 x 35 x 17 In. . . 2390.00
Table, Card, Federal, Mahogany, Drawer, Breadboard Ends, c.1800, 28 x 36 In. 1380.00
Table, Card, Federal, Mahogany, Foldover, Mass., Early 1800s, 29 x 36 x 17 1/2 In. 840.00
Table, Card, Federal, Mahogany, Foldover, Rhode Island, Early 1800s, 28 x 36 x 18 In. . . 3345.00
Table, Card, Federal, Mahogany, Foldover, Serpentine Front, 29 3/4 x 36 x 18 In. 2990.00
Table, Card, Federal, Mahogany, Inlaid, Birch Oval, Signed I & S, 29 x 35 1/2 In. 17250.00
Table, Card, Federal, Mahogany, Inlaid, c.1790, 28 1/2 x 36 x 17 3/4 In. 3400.00
Table, Card, Federal, Mahogany, Inlaid, Fold Top, c.1800, 30 x 36 x 16 1/2 In. 7640.00
Table, Card, Federal, Mahogany, Inlaid, Fold Top, c.1820, 31 x 32 3/4 x 17 In. 2820.00
Table, Card, Federal, Mahogany, Inlaid, Fold Top, Oval Corners, c.1790, 29 x 35 In. 2000.00
Table, Card, Federal, Mahogany, Inlaid, Fold Top, Oval Corners, c.1800, 29 x 36 In. 2585.00
Table, Card, Federal, Mahogany, Inlaid, Hinged Top, 5 Legs, Boston, 29 1/4 x 35 1/2 In. . 4830.00
Table, Card, Federal, Mahogany, Inlaid, Serpentine Front, 36 In. 5465.00
Table, Card, Federal, Mahogany, Maple, Seymour School, Boston, 30 x 42 x 20 1/2 In. . . 5750.00
Table, Card, Federal, Mahogany, Veneer, Reeded Legs, Foldover, 36 x 18 x 29 In. 2000.00
Table, Card, Flame Mahogany, Demilune, 4 Tapered Legs, 1930s, 31 x 36 x 18 In. 475.00
Table, Card, Flame Mahogany, Inlay, Demilune, Column Legs, 1930s, 31 x 36 x 18 In. . . . 530.00
Table, Card, George III, Demilune, D-Shaped Top, c.1790, 28 x 36 In. 705.00
Table, Card, Georgian, Mahogany, Accordion Back Legs, Green Felt, 33 x 16 x 29 In. . . . 2250.00
Table, Card, Hepplewhite, Flame Birch, Square Legs, New England, 29 x 36 x 17 In. 630.00
Table, Card, Hepplewhite, Mahogany, Demilune, Swing Leg, 29 1/2 x 36 x 18 In. 920.00
Table, Card, Hepplewhite, Mahogany, Serpentine Front, 29 x 36 x 17 1/2 In. 790.00
Table, Card, Hepplewhite, Mahogany, Straight Front, Shaped Ends, 29 x 36 x 17 1/2 In. . . 1015.00
Table, Card, Hepplewhite, Mahogany, Tapered Legs, c.1800, 28 3/4 x 36 x 17 1/4 In. 1265.00
Table, Card, Hepplewhite, Mahogany, Urn, Inlaid Drapery Top, Felt Surface, 29 x 36 In. . 1920.00
Table, Card, Hepplewhite, Walnut, Inlaid, D-Form, Hinged, 28 x 35 1/4 x 17 In. 920.00
Table, Card, Lucite, 26 1/4 x 30 x 30 In. 130.00
Table, Card, Mahogany, Serpentine Front, c.1876, 29 3/4 x 36 In. 920.00
Table, Card, Mahogany, Serpentine Front, Hinged Top, New England, 29 1/4 In. 14950.00
Table, Card, Mahogany, Shaped Front, Cabriole Legs, Claw & Ball Feet 340.00
Table, Card, Neoclassical, Mahogany, Carved Flowers, Acanthus, 29 x 35 x 18 In. 420.00
Table, Card, Neoclassical, Mahogany, Foldover, Phila., c.1825, 31 x 35 x 18 In. 1795.00
Table, Card, Queen Anne, Walnut, Crossbanded, Accordian, 20 3/4 x 33 1/2 In. 2235.00
Table, Card, Sheraton, Mahogany, Bird's-Eye Maple, Rosewood, Mass., 29 x 34 In. 2875.00
Table, Card, Sheraton, Mahogany, D-Shaped Fold Top, 29 1/4 x 35 1/4 In. Open 1035.00
Table, Card, Sheraton, Mahogany, Flame Birch, Israel Sack, 29 1/2 x 36 x 17 1/4 In. 7130.00
Table, Card, Sheraton, Mahogany, Inlaid, Serpentine Front, 29 1/2 x 33 3/4 x 18 In. 6325.00
Table, Card, Sheraton, Mahogany, Reeded Edge, Legs, 29 x 36 In. 730.00
Table, Card, Sheraton, Mahogany, Serpentine Top, McIntyre School, Mass., 30 x 37 In. . . 4025.00
Table, Cast Iron Base, Scrolled, Openwork Decoration, 29 x 40 x 22 In. 770.00
Table, Cast Iron, White Paint, Mahogany Top, Cabriole Legs, Shelf, 26 x 29 In. 260.00
Table, Center, Aesthetic Revival, Ebonized, Parcel Gilt, Octagonal, England, 29 x 41 In. . . 1610.00
Table, Center, Biedermeier, Cherry, Frieze Fitted, Drawer, Cabriole Legs, 30 In. 1495.00
Table, Center, Biedermeier, Elm, Drawer, Concave Stretcher, c.1825, 29 x 49 x 35 In. 4140.00
Table, Center, Biedermeier, Mahogany, Stretcher Shelf, 3 Legs, c.1820, 29 x 46 In. 4370.00
Table, Center, Cast Iron, Lattice, Zodiac, 28 x 32 In. 1200.00
Table, Center, Charles X, Mahogany, Marble Top, Pedestal, 3 Legs, c.1835, 25 x 38 In. . . 2760.00
Table, Center, Empire Style, Rosewood, Bronze Mount, Octagonal, Pedestal, 28 x 34 In. . 660.00
Table, Center, Italian Renaissance, Walnut, Drop Leaf, Triangular, D-Leaves, 21 x 44 In. . 1880.00
Table, Center, Louis XV Style, Marble Top, 2 Tiers, Oval, France, 1900s, 38 1/2 x 28 In. . 230.00
Table, Center, Louis XVI Style, Giltwood, Marble, c.1885, 30 1/2 x 41 x 24 1/4 In. 1955.00
Table, Center, Mahogany, Marble Top, Continental, c.1850, 30 x 57 x 40 In. 1035.00
Table, Center, Mahogany, Serpentine Marble Top, 30 3/8 x 30 x 37 In. 2990.00
Table, Center, Marble Top, Wrought Iron, Scroll Legs, X-Stretcher, Italy, 29 x 42 In. 2530.00
Table, Center, Napoleon III, Fruitwood, Gilt Brass Mounted, c.1865, 31 x 50 In. 4370.00

Table, Center, Napoleon III, Kingwood, Marquetry, c.1865, 29 x 55 In. 7200.00
Table, Center, Neoclassical, Giltwood, Marble Top, Pedestal, Paw Feet, France, 30 In. . . . 2070.00
Table, Center, Neoclassical, Mahogany, American, c.1840, 30 x 35 1/2 x 35 1/2 In. 400.00
Table, Center, Neoclassical, Mahogany, Octagonal Top, c.1850, 29 3/4 x 33 In. 1000.00
Table, Center, Regency, Mahogany, Tilt Top, 3-Part Base, 29 1/2 x 52 1/2 In. 2530.00
Table, Center, Regency, Mahogany, Tilt Top, Rectangular, c.1815, 28 1/2 x 38 1/2 In. 1150.00
Table, Center, Regency, Tilt Top, Rosewood, 3-Part Base, c.1835, 30 x 54 In. 4600.00
Table, Center, Renaissance Revival, Ebonized Cherry, Marquetry, c.1870, 29 x 30 In. 4025.00
Table, Center, Rococo Revival, Rosewood, Marble Top, c.1855, 31 x 44 x 25 1/2 In. 6575.00
Table, Center, Rococo, Turtle Marble Top, Carved Knees, c.1850, 37 x 23 x 29 1/2 In. . . . 2300.00
Table, Center, Stickley Bros., Round, Cross Stretcher, Lower Shelf, 30 x 40 In. 575.00
Table, Center, Victorian, Turned Pedestal, Oval, Flat Carved Legs, 30 x 30 x 22 In. 260.00
Table, Center, Victorian, Walnut Burl Top, 1880s, 41 x 25 x 28 In. 1800.00
Table, Center, Victorian, Walnut, Carved, Turned Decoration, Marble Top, 32 x 29 In. . . . 520.00
Table, Center, William IV, Mahogany, Mid 19th Century, 27 1/2 x 41 In. 2530.00
Table, Center, William IV, Mahogany, Specimen Mineral Top, Carved Paw Feet 11500.00
Table, Center, William IV, Mahogany, Sunburst Inlay, c.1850, 27 1/2 x 47 In. 1610.00
Table, Charles X Style, Mahogany, Brass Mounted, 27 1/2 x 30 1/4 In. 1020.00
Table, Charles X Style, Mahogany, Ebonized, Bronze Mounted, 29 x 31 x 26 1/2 In. 1555.00
Table, Cherry, Drawer, Square, Tapered Legs, c.1830, 27 x 29 x 18 1/2 In. 865.00
Table, Cherry, Tiger Maple Side Panels, End Drawers, 40 x 27 In. 145.00
Table, Chinese Style, Softwood, Carving, 21 x 33 x 19 1/2 In. 165.00
Table, Chippendale Style, Gallery Top, Pedestal, c.1900, 28 x 21 1/2 In. 460.00
Table, Chippendale Style, Mahogany, Drawer, Ireland, c.1900, 35 1/2 x 42 1/2 In. 2760.00
Table, Chippendale Style, Mahogany, Fretwork, Mirrored Tray, Chinese, 30 x 19 x 19 In. . 1200.00
Table, Chippendale Style, Mahogany, Shaped Square Top, Drawer, 28 x 18 In. 620.00
Table, Chippendale Style, Mahogany, Trumpet Shape, Cabriole Legs, 27 x 30 In. 175.00
Table, Chippendale, Mahogany, Serpentine Top, 2 Leaves, 27 1/2 x 34 1/2 x 17 1/2 In. . . . 865.00
Table, Chrome, Metal, Travertine, 15 3/4 x 20 x 20 In. 740.00
Table, Coffee, American Modern, Freeform, c.1954 . . . . 2645.00
Table, Coffee, Amoeba, Ash, Birch, Bleached, Inset Glass, c.1950, 52 x 30 In. 520.00
Table, Coffee, Andre Bus, Acclaim, Oak, Walnut, 2 Parts, Swivel, Lane, 15 x 53 x 20 In. . 290.00
Table, Coffee, Arne Jacobsen, Rosewood Veneer, Aluminum Pedestal, 20 x 35 In. 460.00
Table, Coffee, Black Lacquer, Hardstone, Flowers, Chinese, 16 x 30 x 30 In. 400.00
Table, Coffee, Black Walnut, Free-Edge Top, Plank Legs, 18 x 57 x 19 In. 175.00
Table, Coffee, Bronze, Cruciform Base, Rectangular, Glass Top, 17 x 46 x 29 In. 1380.00
Table, Coffee, Cini Boeri, Lunario, Glass, Metal, Knoll, c.1972, 58 x 43 x 17 In. 3510.00
Table, Coffee, Eames, Ash Plywood, Black Paint, Herman Miller, c.1950, 15 x 34 In. 1910.00
Table, Coffee, Eero Saarinen, Laminate Top, Cast Iron Base, Knoll, 42 x 15 1/4 In. 400.00
Table, Coffee, Florence Knoll, Rosewood Top, Chrome Frame, 17 x 45 x 23 In. 320.00
Table, Coffee, Frankl, Amoeba, Cork Top, Mahogany Legs, 14 1/2 x 47 1/2 x 35 1/2 In. . . 1955.00
Table, Coffee, Frankl, Biomorphic, Laminated Cork Veneer Top, 14 1/2 x 72 x 36 In. 3220.00
Table, Coffee, G. Nakashima, Black Walnut, Sapwood Edges, 58 x 29 x 18 In. 6900.00
Table, Coffee, G. Nakashima, Walnut, Slab Top, Free Edge, Rosewood Butterfly Joint 10925.00
Table, Coffee, G. Nelson, Primavera, Birch, Herman Miller, c.1950, 48 x 22 x 15 In. 995.00
Table, Coffee, G. Nelson, Walnut Top, Ebonized Legs, Herman Miller, 32 x 15 In. 430.00
Table, Coffee, G. Nelson, Walnut Veneer, Laminate Top, Steel Base, 14 3/4 x 48 x 27 In. . 1725.00
Table, Coffee, G. Nelson, Walnut Veneer, Square Top, Herman Miller, 15 1/4 x 32 In. 260.00
Table, Coffee, Glass Top, Inlaid, Brass Frame, Crossbanded, Ormolu, c.1950, 18 x 29 In. . . 140.00
Table, Coffee, H. Probber, Nuclear, Bleached Mahogany, c.1952, 24 x 78 x 15 In. 4680.00
Table, Coffee, I. Noguchi, Walnut, Glass Top, Herman Miller, 1985, 50 x 36 x 15 3/4 In. . . 800.00
Table, Coffee, Iron Frame, Rope Twist & Scroll, Flower Tile Top, 30 1/2 In. 100.00
Table, Coffee, John Keil, Birch, Brown Saltman, U.S.A., 1950s, 29 1/2 x 64 x 14 1/2 In. . 585.00
Table, Coffee, Julio Katinsky, Rosewood, Glass, Brazil, 1960s, 51 x 18 x 16 In. 1755.00
Table, Coffee, Karl Springer Style, Wood, Lacquer Finish, 1940s, 48 x 22 x 18 In. 865.00
Table, Coffee, Kingwood, Inlaid, Bronze Mounted, Continental, 20 x 32 x 22 In. 100.00
Table, Coffee, Kraft Associates, c.1958, 19 1/2 In. 500.00
Table, Coffee, Louis Sognot, Walnut, Steel, Glass, 1950s, 35 1/2 x 25 3/4 x 17 1/2 In. . . . 1170.00
Table, Coffee, Louis XV Style, Onyx Cover, Gilt Metal Base, c.1930, 17 x 39 x 20 In. . . . 90.00
Table, Coffee, Louis XVI Style, Gilt Bronze, Glass Top, 18 x 48 x 30 In. 1100.00
Table, Coffee, Marble Top, Aluminum, Round, 15 x 42 In. 430.00
Table, Coffee, McCobb, Beech, Metal, Bamboo, 2 Drawers, 16 x 59 In. 750.00
Table, Coffee, McCobb, Planner Group, Maple, Drawer, Winchendon, 54 x 20 x 16 In. 145.00

Table, Coffee, McCobb, Woodgrain Formica Top, Drawer, Shelf, Calvin, 17 x 54 x 32 In. .   259.00
Table, Coffee, Michael Coffey, Walnut, Wave Shaped, 17 x 47 1/2 x 23 1/2 In. 5175.00
Table, Coffee, Mies Van Der Rohe, Barcelona, Chrome-Plated Brass, 17 x 40 In. 155.00
Table, Coffee, Neoclassical, Gilt Marble Top, 20 1/2 x 40 x 17 1/2 In. 315.00
Table, Coffee, Oak, Granite Tile Top, Sallingboe, Jelling, Denmark, 17 x 52 x 27 1/2 In. . . .   175.00
Table, Coffee, P. Evans, Molded Mahogany Plywood, 1940s, 41 1/2 x 30 x 15 In. 995.00
Table, Coffee, P. Evans, Sculpted Bronze Base, Glass Top, 1970, 16 1/4 x 72 x 36 In. 865.00
Table, Coffee, P. Evans, Walnut Plywood, c.1947, 15 1/2 x 34 1/2 In. 895.00
Table, Coffee, Paul Evans, Directional, Patchwork Metal, Slate Top, 30 x 30 x 24 In. 690.00
Table, Coffee, Philip & Kelvin Laverne, Bronze, Chinese Scenes, 17 x 35 1/2 In. 1150.00
Table, Coffee, Philip & Kelvin Laverne, Tree Of Life, 6 Pullout Leaves, 18 x 54 In. 9200.00
Table, Coffee, Pietra Dura Inlay, Urn, Lamp, Flower, Early 1900s, 20 x 22 x 34 In. 3795.00
Table, Coffee, Pine, Painted, Birds, Hieroglyphics, 18 x 96 x 37 In. 260.00
Table, Coffee, Plate Glass Top, Iron Base, Black, Scrolled Designs, 40 x 31 x 18 1/2 In. . .   250.00
Table, Coffee, Poul Kjaerholm, Glass Top, Chrome Plated Base, 1955, 13 1/2 x 31 In. . . .   3740.00
Table, Coffee, Red Lacquered Wood, Cutout, Steel Legs, 54 x 30 x 15 1/2 In. 290.00
Table, Coffee, Robsjohn-Gibbings, Amoeba, Walnut, Brass Legs, 17 x 54 x 30 In. 920.00
Table, Coffee, Rohde, Acacia Burl Top, Kidney Shape, 15 1/4 x 41 x 26 In. 3220.00
Table, Coffee, Rosewood, Teak, Steel, Denmark, 17 1/3 x 28 1/3 x 28 1/3 In. 190.00
Table, Coffee, Tapio Wirkkala, Asko, Finland, c.1955, 49 x 24 1/2 x 15 3/4 In. 3525.00
Table, Coffee, Travertine, No. 3399-1, Walnut, Widdicomb, c.1958, 16 x 20 x 22 In. 2340.00
Table, Coffee, W. Haines, Mahogany Veneer, Brass Legs, c.1950, 17 x 72 x 24 In. 2630.00
Table, Coffee, W. Platner, Steel Rod, Glass Top, Knoll, 33 1/2 x 15 1/4 In. 1150.00
Table, Coffee, Walnut, Serpentine, 20 1/2 x 59 x 36 In. 145.00
Table, Coffee, Walnut, Slab Top, Splayed Tapered Legs, 31 x 31 x 18 In. 2185.00
Table, Coffee, Wendell Castle, Walnut, Rosewood, Round, c.1976, 14 1/2 x 43 1/2 In. 1150.00
Table, Coffee, Wormley, No. 5424, Brass, Glass Top, Dunbar, c.1950, 16 x 45 x 17 In. . . .   1555.00
Table, Coffee, Wormley, Walnut, Steel, Laminate, Dunbar, c.1960, 72 x 17 x 15 1/4 In. . . .   2810.00
Table, Coffee, Wrought Iron, 21 Polychrome Tiles, Fiorano, Italy, 18 x 42 x 18 In. 635.00
Table, Communion, Mixed Wood, Open Shelf, Pegged, Snow Hill, 29 x 48 x 20 In. 440.00
Table, Conference, Florence Knoll, Rosewood Veneer, Steel Pedestal, 29 x 96 x 54 In. . . .   2070.00
Table, Conference, George III Style, Mahogany, 2 Pedestals, 31 x 90 x 132 In. 2070.00
Table, Conservatory, Iron, Marble Top, Inlaid Pattern, Brass, 23 1/2 x 32 1/2 In. 635.00
Table, Conservatory, Scagliola Marble, Star Inlay, Griffin Supports, 30 x 74 1/2 In. 2530.00
Table, Conservatory, Victorian, Cast Iron, Specimen Marble Top, 34 x 46 x 35 In. 2185.00
Table, Console, Adam Style, Painted, Gilt, Flowers, 1800s, 32 1/2 x 40 In. 1785.00
Table, Console, Art Deco, Walnut, Birch, Early 20th Century, 26 1/2 x 39 x 22 In. 69.00
Table, Console, Art Deco, Wrought Iron, Marble, Bracketed Support, 36 x 43 1/2 In. 978.00
Table, Console, Art Deco, Wrought Iron, Rouge Marble Top, 36 x 60 x 18 In. 1100.00
Table, Console, Biedermeier, Walnut, Cherry, 3 Drawers, 32 x 43 x 20 1/2 In. 4830.00
Table, Console, Blackamoor Figure, Polychrome Wood, Gesso, Italy, 35 x 35 x 12 In. 950.00
Table, Console, Carved & Gilt Decoration, Marble Top, Mirror, 36 x 53 x 15 1/2 In. 575.00
Table, Console, Chinese Chippendale Style, Blind Fret Carving, England, c.1750, 32 In. . . .   3910.00
Table, Console, Elm, Marble Top, Shelf, Continental, c.1865, 39 1/2 x 53 x 26 1/2 In. . . .   3680.00
Table, Console, Empire Style, Burl, Marble, Gilt Bronze, 34 1/2 x 41 x 16 1/2 In., Pair . . .   1725.00
Table, Console, Empire Style, Terra-Cotta, Dolphin Shape, Entwined Fish, 1900s, 29 In. . . .   150.00
Table, Console, Empire, Gilt Bronze Mounted, Marble Top, c.1810, 35 x 45 1/2 In. 1115.00
Table, Console, Federal Style, Mahogany, Demilune, 28 3/4 x 46 3/4 x 23 In. 710.00
Table, Console, George III Style, Mahogany, Demilune, Carved, 35 x 42 x 21 In. 2590.00
Table, Console, George III Style, Satinwood, Demilune Top, 29 x 36 x 15 In., Pair 2300.00
Table, Console, George III Style, Yew, Demilune Top, Sunburst, 33 x 44 In., Pair 3680.00
Table, Console, George III, Mahogany, Late 18th Century, 28 x 48 1/2 x 23 In., Pair 2070.00
Table, Console, George III, Mahogany, Marble Top, Ireland, c.1785, 31 1/2 x 54 x 32 In. .   3220.00
Table, Console, Gesso & Painted, Faux Marble Top, Italy, 31 x 52 In. . . . . *Illus*   3680.00
Table, Console, Giltwood, Carved, Fabric-Covered Inset, Continental, 38 x 48 x 21 In. . . .   635.00
Table, Console, Hardwood, Flowers, Masks, Chinese, Late 1800s, 33 x 56 x 22 In. 980.00
Table, Console, Ico Parisi, Italian Walnut, Brass, Singer & Sons, 77 x 20 x 30 In. 11115.00
Table, Console, Iron, Marble, Scrolled Base, Brass Acanthus, 26 x 12 x 31 In., Pair 935.00
Table, Console, Louis Philippe, Mahogany, Marble Top, Drawer, c.1850, 34 x 31 x 15 In. . .   1610.00
Table, Console, Louis XIV Style, Mahogany, 28 x 31 x 22 In., Pair 777.00
Table, Console, Louis XV Style, Black, Gilt, Marble Top, Scrolls, 1900s, 30 x 44 In. 777.00
Table, Console, Louis XV Style, Giltwood, Green Marble Top, 41 x 54 In. 2475.00
Table, Console, Louis XV Style, Giltwood, Marble Top, C-Scroll Legs, c.1890, 33 x 35 In.   2185.00

Furniture, Table, Console, Gesso & Painted,
Faux Marble Top, Italy, 31 x 52 In.

Furniture, Table, Drop Leaf,
Sheraton, Tiger Maple,
Cherry, c.1840, 28 x 39 In.

Table, Console, Louis XV Style, Giltwood, Marble Top, Flowers, c.1865, 36 x 32 1/2 In. . .	3450.00
Table, Console, Louis XV Style, Ivory Paint, Marble Top, 29 1/2 x 49 1/2 x 22 In.	540.00
Table, Console, Louis XV Style, Marble Top, Cabriole Legs, 1800s, 36 x 63 x 25 In.	5280.00
Table, Console, Louis XV Style, Openwork Leaf Frieze, Marble Top, 1900s, 33 x 47 In. . . .	355.00
Table, Console, Louis XV Style, Wrought Iron, Serpentine, Marble Top, 33 x 55 In., Pair .	2300.00
Table, Console, Louis XV, Walnut, Serpentine, Mid 18th Century, 25 x 36 24 1/2 In.	750.00
Table, Console, Louis XVI Style, Black Marble Top, Bowed Stretchers, 36 x 19 x 30 In. .	410.00
Table, Console, Louis XVI Style, Giltwood, Marble Top, 32 3/4 x 24 In., Pair	1955.00
Table, Console, Louis XVI Style, Giltwood, Marble Top, c.1850, 34 x 23 x 12 In.	2185.00
Table, Console, Louis XVI Style, Giltwood, Marble Top, Late 1800s, 34 x 18 x 11 In.	1035.00
Table, Console, Louis XVI Style, Giltwood, Marble Top, Late 1800s, 36 x 40 x 18 In.	2070.00
Table, Console, Louis XVI Style, Oak, Marble Top, Reeded Frieze, 35 1/2 x 36 x 18 In. . . .	2200.00
Table, Console, Louis XVI Style, Painted, Gilt, Demilune, Mirror, 102 x 27 In.	650.00
Table, Console, Louis XVI, Giltwood, Marble Top, Pierced Frieze, 33 x 29 x 14 In.	2350.00
Table, Console, Mahogany, Applied Molding, Stepped Out, England, 36 x 59 x 17 In.	635.00
Table, Console, Mahogany, Line Inlay, Demilune, 28 x 47 x 22 In.	175.00
Table, Console, Marble Top, Silver & Gilt, Continental, 33 x 67 x 24 In.	1095.00
Table, Console, Mirrored, Tier Edge, Late 1800s, 34 x 59 1/2 x 20 3/4 In.	730.00
Table, Console, Napoleon III, Carved Giltwood, c.1865, 30 x 31 1/2 In.	4140.00
Table, Console, Neoclassical, Gilt, Ebonized Wood, Marble Top, 37 x 49 1/2 In., Pair	7770.00
Table, Console, Neoclassical, Mahogany, American, c.1840, 28 x 35 1/2 x 20 In.	400.00
Table, Console, Neoclassical, Mahogany, Marble Top, Italy, c.1850, 37 x 43 x 20 In.	3910.00
Table, Console, Neoclassical, Marble Top, Iron, 37 1/2 x 63 In.	3220.00
Table, Console, Neoclassical, Marble Top, Parcel Gilt, Italy, c.1800, 37 1/2 x 38 In.	1610.00
Table, Console, Neoclassical, Marble, Continental, 35 x 55 In.	1910.00
Table, Console, Neoclassical, Oak, Pine, Polychrome, 33 1/2 x 40 x 19 In.	920.00
Table, Console, Oak, Rattan, Openwork Apron, Late 20th Century, 32 x 31 x 22 In.	345.00
Table, Console, Painted Flowers, 3 Drawers, Continental, c.1900, 30 x 45 x 23 In.	1095.00
Table, Console, Queen Anne Style, Burl Walnut, Scalloped Frame, 35 1/2 x 54 1/2 In. . . .	920.00
Table, Console, Regency Style, Mahogany, Leaf & Shell Carving, 36 x 60 x 20 In.	1150.00
Table, Console, Robsjohn-Gibbings, Mahogany, 2 Tiers, Widdicomb, 48 x 18 x 28 3/4 In. .	405.00
Table, Console, Rococo Revival, Painted, Ivory, Verdigris, Marble Top, 33 x 62 x 30 In. . .	6575.00
Table, Console, Rococo Style, Giltwood, Marble Top, Continental, 31 x 37 In.	605.00
Table, Console, Rococo, Marble Top, Shell Carved Apron, 48 x 24 x 20 In.	1725.00
Table, Console, Rococo, Rosewood, Serpentine Top, American, c.1850, 36 x 44 x 20 In. . .	2300.00
Table, Console, Rosewood, Drawer, Heavily Carved Apron, Legs, 26 1/2 x 51 In., Pair . . .	750.00
Table, Console, Stickley Bros., 6 Barley-Twist Legs, Cross Stretcher, 31 x 72 x 32 In. . . .	1380.00
Table, Console, Victorian, Mahogany, Scalloped Top, c.1900, 31 x 54 x 18 In.	1150.00
Table, Console, Wood, Carved, Serpentine, Faux Painted, Continental, 36 x 51 x 23 In. . .	550.00
Table, Corner, L. & J.G. Stickley, 2 Tiers, Pegged, Stretchers, 29 x 24 x 24 In.	1095.00
Table, Corner, L. & J.G., Stickley, No. 580, 29 x 36 x 36 In.	1898.00
Table, Cube, Marble Top, Chrome Base, 42 3/4 x 42 1/2 In.	440.00
Table, Dinette, Eero Saarinen, Laminate Top, Cast Iron Base, Knoll, 42 x 28 1/2 In.	460.00
Table, Dining, Aesthetic Revival, Mahogany, 5 Leaves, Late 1800s, 29 1/2 x 60 In.	1998.00
Table, Dining, Andreas Tuck, Teak, Round Top, Steel, Extension, Wegner, 28 x 53 In. . . .	750.00
Table, Dining, Art Deco, Exotic Wood Veneers, Oval Band, 30 3/4 x 80 x 45 In.	865.00
Table, Dining, B. Mathsson, Teak, Sweden, 1960s, 36 x 110 1/2 x 26 3/4 In.	1120.00
Table, Dining, Bertha Schafer, Walnut, Round, 4 Leaves, Singer, 38 x 29 1/4 In.	690.00
Table, Dining, Borge Mogensen, Teak, 4 Leaves, F. Stolefabrik, 1960s, 67 x 51 x 29 In. . .	2460.00

Table, Dining, Drop Leaf, Cherry, Extension, American, Late 1800s, 30 1/2 x 66 x 46 In. . 825.00
Table, Dining, Drop Leaf, Chippendale Style, Late 1800s, 28 x 48 x 19 1/2 In. 1610.00
Table, Dining, Drop Leaf, Chippendale, Mahogany, Double Swing Leg, 28 1/4 In. 560.00
Table, Dining, Drop Leaf, Federal, Mahogany, Inlaid, Overhang, 4 Square Legs, 1800 . . . 700.00
Table, Dining, Drop Leaf, Federal, Mahogany, Inlaid, Rectangular, 28 x 48 x 49 In. 645.00
Table, Dining, Drop Leaf, French Provincial, Cherry, Leaves, 29 1/2 x 46 1/2 In. 2820.00
Table, Dining, Drop Leaf, George III, Mahogany, 28 x 48 In. 2070.00
Table, Dining, Drop Leaf, George III, Mahogany, Demilune, Late 1700s, 29 x 61 In. 690.00
Table, Dining, Drop Leaf, George III, Oval Top, c.1875, 29 x 46 1/2 In. 865.00
Table, Dining, Drop Leaf, Hepplewhite, Black, Maine, c.1800, 28 3/4 x 48 x 16 In. 1265.00
Table, Dining, Drop Leaf, Hepplewhite, Pine, Maple Base, 28 x 25 x 44 1/2 In. 500.00
Table, Dining, Drop Leaf, Louis Philippe, Mahogany, 29 1/2 x 46 In. 1725.00
Table, Dining, Drop Leaf, Mahogany, Marquetry, Dutch, c.1865, 29 1/2 x 30 x 63 In. 2760.00
Table, Dining, Drop Leaf, Neoclassical, Mahogany, N.Y., c.1825, 31 x 22 3/4 x 48 In. . . . 720.00
Table, Dining, Drop Leaf, Queen Anne, Mahogany, Round, c.1760, 28 x 48 In. 5875.00
Table, Dining, Drop Leaf, Queen Anne, Maple, Round, New England, 1700s, 28 x 48 In. . 1765.00
Table, Dining, Drop Leaf, Sheraton, Mahogany, Spiral Carved Legs, 29 x 48 x 17 In. 300.00
Table, Dining, Edwardian, Walnut, Burl, Oval, Cabriole Legs, c.1900, 29 x 41 1/2 In. 630.00
Table, Dining, Eero Saarinen, Laminate Top, Pedestal Base, 29 x 96 x 54 In. 4315.00
Table, Dining, Eero Saarinen, Tulip, Laminate Top, Pedestal, Knoll, 28 1/2 x 54 In. 1840.00
Table, Dining, Eero Saarinen, Tulip, Walnut Top, Pedestal Base, Oval, 29 x 77 x 48 In. . . . 3740.00
Table, Dining, Eero Saarinen, Walnut Top, Pedestal, Elliptical, Knoll, 78 x 48 x 29 In. . . . 2300.00
Table, Dining, Federal, Inlaid, 3 Sections, 2 Demilune, c.1810, 30 x 44 x 109 1/2 In. . . 14340.00
Table, Dining, Federal, Mahogany, 2 Parts, American, 30 1/2 x 45 x 92 In. 1495.00
Table, Dining, Federal, Mahogany, Demilune, 2 Sections, Inlaid Apron, 28 3/4 x 72 In. . . . 2590.00
Table, Dining, G. Nakashima, Cherry, Rosewood, Trestle, Leaves, 1955, 28 x 72 x 40 In. . 6465.00
Table, Dining, G. Nakashima, Walnut, Trestle, Free Edge Top, 1978, 35 x 59 x 42 In. 6900.00
Table, Dining, G. Nelson, Chromed Steel, Laminate, Herman Miller, 1950s, 42 x 27 In. . . 645.00
Table, Dining, G. Nelson, Walnut, Metal, Pedestal, Herman Miller, c.1956, 72 x 29 In. . . . 935.00
Table, Dining, George III Style, Mahogany, 1 Leaf, c.1890, 28 1/2 x 49 1/2 x 88 In. 2530.00
Table, Dining, George III Style, Mahogany, 3 Pedestals, 2 Leaves, 29 x 48 x 108 In. 3450.00
Table, Dining, George III Style, Mahogany, Inlaid, Oval, 29 x 70 1/2 x 51 1/2 In. 1380.00
Table, Dining, George III, Mahogany, 3 Sections, c.1800, 28 1/2 x 115 x 47 1/2 In. 1610.00
Table, Dining, George III, Mahogany, 3 Sections, Late 18th Century, 38 x 115 1/2 In. 5175.00
Table, Dining, Georgian Style, Mahogany, Inlaid, Oval, 29 1/2 x 45 3/4 x 96 In. 315.00
Table, Dining, Georgian Style, Satinwood, Inlaid, 2 Pedestals, 29 3/4 x 48 In. 2415.00
Table, Dining, Georgian, Mahogany, 3 Pedestals, Leaf, c.1830, 28 x 90 In. 3900.00
Table, Dining, Gio Ponti, Walnut, Brass, Singer & Sons, Italy, 1950s, 65 x 19 x 30 In. . . . 4400.00
Table, Dining, Hepplewhite, Maple, Tapered Legs, c.1800, 28 1/2 x 36 1/2 x 27 In. 575.00
Table, Dining, Heywood-Wakefield, Champagne Finish, Extension, 29 x 60 x 42 In. 690.00
Table, Dining, I. Noguchi, Laminate Top, Chrome Plated Column, Round, 29 x 48 In. 1495.00
Table, Dining, Kristian Vedel, Rosewood, Soren Willadsens, 26 x 70 3/4 x 47 In. 750.00
Table, Dining, L. & J.G., Stickley, Exposed Through-Tenon Legs, 2 Leaves, 30 x 48 In. . . 2645.00
Table, Dining, Limbert, Square Top, 5 Leaves, Tapered Pedestal Base, 41 x 35 x 29 In. . . . 3220.00
Table, Dining, Louis XV Style, Walnut, Shaped Frieze, 2 Leaves, 29 1/2 x 43 In. 1530.00
Table, Dining, Louis XVI Style, Mahogany, Ormolu Mounted, 2 Leaves, 29 x 42 In. 635.00
Table, Dining, Mahogany, Block Pedestal, 4 Scroll Feet, 5 Leaves, 30 x 54 In. 2050.00
Table, Dining, Mahogany, Extending, c.1925, 30 x 66 x 46 1/2 In. 9560.00
Table, Dining, Mahogany, Pedestal Base, 7 Leaves, 54 x 29 1/2 In. 1345.00
Table, Dining, Mahogany, Round, Square Block Pedestal, 5 Leaves, 30 x 54 In. 2296.00
Table, Dining, McCobb, Walnut, Oval Top, Chrome Frame, Extension, 29 x 62 x 40 In. . . 1150.00
Table, Dining, Neoclassical, Mahogany, 2 Parts, New York, c.1825, 31 x 42 x 51 In. 3000.00
Table, Dining, Neoclassical, Mahogany, Parquetry, Round, Leaf, 46 In. 605.00
Table, Dining, Neoclassical, Round Extension, Mahogany, 1800s, 29 x 54 In. 1150.00
Table, Dining, Oak, Checkerboard Inlay, Draw Leaf, 30 x 36 x 56 In. 150.00
Table, Dining, Oak, Quartersawn, 5 Legs, 5 Leaves, c.1910, 30 x 44 x 43 1/2 In. 350.00
Table, Dining, Oak, Square, Cutout Stretchers, 5 Leaves, 48 x 28 1/2 x 48 In. 1955.00
Table, Dining, Oak, Winged Griffins, Center Support Column, 29 x 54 In. 2300.00
Table, Dining, P. Evans, Bronze Panel Base, Glass Top, 1971, 29 x 48 x 96 In. 2415.00
Table, Dining, P. Evans, Chrome Patchwork, 29 x 84 x 40 In. 2300.00
Table, Dining, Parzinger, Inlaid Diamond-Pattern Top, 29 3/4 x 68 x 38 In. 5175.00
Table, Dining, Queen Anne Style, Mahogany, 2 Leaves, 30 1/2 x 42 x 93 In. 230.00
Table, Dining, Regency Style, Mahogany, 2 Pedestals, 2 Leaves, 29 x 86 x 40 1/2 In. 1295.00

Table, Dining, Regency Style, Mahogany, 2 Pedestals, 2 Leaves, 30 x 122 x 46 In. 3740.00
Table, Dining, Regency Style, Mahogany, 2 Pedestals, c.1900, 29 1/4 x 40 1/4 x 91 In. 1150.00
Table, Dining, Regency Style, Mahogany, 3 Pedestals, 2 Leaves, 29 x 53 x 150 In. 5750.00
Table, Dining, Regency Style, Mahogany, 10 Leaves, Early 1900s, 29 x 47 x 196 In. 1000.00
Table, Dining, Regency Style, Mahogany, Horseshoe Shape, 30 x 62 In. 2070.00
Table, Dining, Renaissance Revival, Mahogany, Frieze, Early 1900s, 29 x 44 x 44 In. 110.00
Table, Dining, Rohde, Flip Top, 2 Leaves, 29 x 1/4 x 36 x 20 In. 865.00
Table, Dining, Rohde, Mahogany, X-Stretcher, Herman Miller, 68 x 40 x 29 In. 1150.00
Table, Dining, Shaker, Tiger Maple, Walnut, Trestle Base, 24 1/2 x 32 3/4 x 59 1/2 In. 2760.00
Table, Dining, Sheraton Style, Mahogany, Oak, Pine, 6 Legs, 48 x 24 x 20 1/2 In. 315.00
Table, Dining, Sheraton, Cherry, Mahogany, 2 Parts, Rope Twist Legs, 47 x 30 x 20 In. ... 1015.00
Table, Dining, Sheraton, Drop Leaf, Cherry, D-Shaped Leaves, 29 x 42 1/4 x 19 1/4 In. .. 230.00
Table, Dining, Sheraton, Mahogany, 2 Drawers, Turned Legs, Caster Feet, 29 x 56 In. 520.00
Table, Dining, Sheraton, Mahogany, 3 Pedestals, D-Shaped Ends, 29 x 48 x 127 In. 4600.00
Table, Dining, Sheraton, Mahogany, Heavy Turned Legs, Extension, 29 x 39 1/2 x 42 In. . 225.00
Table, Dining, Sheraton, Mahogany, Molded Skirt, Casters, Extension, 29 x 40 x 42 In. ... 220.00
Table, Dining, Sheraton, Pine, Maple, Green Paint, 28 1/2 x 38 1/2 x 39 In. 420.00
Table, Dining, Stickley Bros., Oak, Round Top, Rope Twist Legs, Bin Feet, 48 In. 290.00
Table, Dining, Victorian, Mahogany, Oval Top, 2 Leaves, c.1870, 29 1/2 x 48 x 64 In. 1955.00
Table, Dining, Victorian, Oak, Pedestal, Carved Legs, 3 Leaves, 1880s, 84 In. 1800.00
Table, Dining, Walnut, 3-Board Top, Drawer, Turned Legs, 28 1/2 x 79 x 38 1/2 In. 300.00
Table, Dining, Walnut, Carved Cabriole Legs, Bun Feet, Leaves, France, 29 x 49 x 99 In. . 770.00
Table, Dining, Walnut, Parquetry, 2 Leaves, 30 x 123 In. 518.00
Table, Dining, Walnut, Turned Legs, 6 Leaves, c.1870, 120 In. 2375.00
Table, Dining, Wormley, 3 Leaves, Dunbar, c.1957-1965, 72 x 42 x 29 1/2 In. 9360.00
Table, Dining, Wormley, Blond Wood, Extension, Drexel, 29 x 64 x 40 In. 345.00
Table, Dining, Wormley, Ebonized Trestle Base, Extension, Dunbar, 29 x 66 x 42 In. 4025.00
Table, Dining, Wormley, Round Top, Pedestal, Dunbar, c.1948, 39 1/2 x 27 In. 1880.00
Table, Dining, Wormley, Walnut Veneer, Ebonized Finish, 29 1/2 x 66 x 44 In. 3450.00
Table, Directoire Style, Fruitwood, 27 x 18 x 12 1/2 In. 500.00
Table, Directoire, Walnut, Gris De St. Anne Marble Top, c.1830 .... 1725.00
Table, Drafting, Gray Laminate Top, 5 Drawers, Tubular Metal Base, 30 x 78 x 38 In. ... 690.00
Table, Drafting, Lift Top, Ratchet Mechanism, Trestle Cross Stretcher, 37 x 42 x 29 In. .. 250.00
Table, Dressing, Beau Brummel, George III Style, Mahogany, Satinwood, 31 x 27 In. 1150.00
Table, Dressing, Beau Brummel, Georgian, Mahogany, Double Hinge Top, 31 x 29 In. 999.00
Table, Dressing, Belter, Rosewood, Stretcher, 21 x 16 x 31 In. 865.00
Table, Dressing, Belter, Rosewood, Walnut, 21 x 16 x 32 In. 1150.00
Table, Dressing, Chippendale, Walnut, 4 Drawers, Trifid Feet, c.1770, 29 x 30 x 19 In. ... 11355.00
Table, Dressing, Federal, Mahogany, Satinwood, Mirror, Potthast Bros., c.1925 .... 1150.00
Table, Dressing, French Provincial, Cherry, Brass, Lift Top, c.1835, 29 x 32 x 18 In. 1150.00
Table, Dressing, G. Stickley, No 914, 2 Drawers, Mirror, 33 x 18 x 55 In. 3740.00
Table, Dressing, George II, Walnut, c.1750, 28 3/4 x 31 x 18 1/4 In. 1610.00
Table, Dressing, George III Style, Mahogany, Inlaid, 2 Parts, c.1890, 30 1/2 x 45 In. 1115.00
Table, Dressing, George III, Mahogany, 27 1/2 x 31 x 17 3/4 In. 1610.00
Table, Dressing, George III, Mahogany, Ebony Inlay, Bowfront, Ivory Feet, 22 In. 1580.00
Table, Dressing, Hepplewhite, Mustard Paint, Fruit Stencil, Drawer, Maine, 34 x 33 In. .. 805.00
Table, Dressing, Hepplewhite, Pine, Graining, Tapered Legs, 2 Drawers, 36 x 33 In. 1150.00
Table, Dressing, Louis XV Style, Mahogany, Marquetry, 28 1/2 x 32 1/2 In. 840.00
Table, Dressing, Louis XV, Mahogany, Satinwood, Doors, Cane Inset, 61 x 49 In. 1045.00
Table, Dressing, Mahogany, 4 Drawers, Mirror, c.1840, 71 x 39 x 21 In. 2530.00
Table, Dressing, Mahogany, Mirror, c.1940s, 67 x 44 x 18 1/2 In. 175.00
Table, Dressing, Mahogany, Serpentine, Accordion Mirror, Chair, 1890-1900 .... 1595.00
Table, Dressing, Mahogany, Veneer, 4 Drawers, Rope Turned Legs, 36 1/2 x 36 x 17 In. .. 660.00
Table, Dressing, Neoclassical, Burl Walnut, Inlaid Fruitwood, 33 1/2 x 30 x 19 In. 235.00
Table, Dressing, Neoclassical, Fruitwood, False Frieze Drawers, Italy, 31 x 38 x 19 In. ... 235.00
Table, Dressing, Neoclassical, Mahogany, Boston, c.1825, 76 1/2 In. 1610.00
Table, Dressing, Pine, 3 Drawers, Button Feet, New England, 36 x 32 1/2 x 15 1/2 In. ... 175.00
Table, Dressing, Pine, Black & Red Graining, Drawer, Wooden Pull, 36 x 18 x 28 1/2 In. . 430.00
Table, Dressing, Pine, Splashguard, 29 1/2 x 23 x 11 In. 400.00
Table, Dressing, Queen Anne Style, Walnut, 5 Drawers, 31 1/2 x 42 x 24 In. 235.00
Table, Dressing, Queen Anne, Mahogany, Top Drawers, X-Stretcher, Spanish Foot 845.00
Table, Dressing, Queen Anne, Walnut, 4 Drawers, Early 1700s, 28 x 30 x 19 In. 1880.00
Table, Dressing, Rococo Revival, Walnut, Mirror, Pierced Crest, c.1865, 75 x 48 1/2 In. ... 4830.00

Table, Dressing, Rococo Style, Mahogany, Pewter Inlay, 63 x 53 x 26 In. 1195.00
Table, Dressing, Rococo Style, Marquetry, Ebonized Burl, 29 x 44 x 18 In. 1150.00
Table, Dressing, Rococo Style, Painted, Mirror, 60 x 41 x 24 In. 650.00
Table, Dressing, Rococo, Duchesse, Mahogany, Mirror, New Orleans, c.1850, 78 x 39 In. . 4315.00
Table, Dressing, Roycroft, Drawer, Mirror, Mackmurdo Feet, 56 x 39 x 17 1/2 In. 7475.00
Table, Dressing, Sheraton Style, Mahogany, Concave, Ribbed Legs, 30 x 38 x 28 In. 1325.00
Table, Dressing, Sheraton, Curly Maple, Drawer, 34 1/2 x 17 x 34 3/4 In. 1495.00
Table, Dressing, Walnut, Pine, Drawer, Spool Turned Legs, 30 x 37 x 18 In. 195.00
Table, Dressing, Yellow Paint, Scrolled Backboard, 2 Glove Drawers, 1825, 38 In. 1170.00
Table, Drop Leaf, Arts & Crafts, Circular, Shoefoot Base, 30 x 31 x 17 In. 230.00
Table, Drop Leaf, Arts & Crafts, Kendal Oak, Rotating Top, England 530.00
Table, Drop Leaf, B. Mathsson, Teak, Birch Legs, K. Mathsson, Sweden, 40 x 29 In. 1725.00
Table, Drop Leaf, Biedermeier, Pine, Figured Veneer, Paw Feet, 33 x 28 x 30 In. 980.00
Table, Drop Leaf, Black Forest, Walnut, 20th Century, 28 1/2 x 29 1/4 In. 805.00
Table, Drop Leaf, Bleached Maple, Barley Twist Legs, c.1850, 29 1/2 x 45 In. 260.00
Table, Drop Leaf, Cherry, Gateleg, 2 Leaves, 29 x 46 1/2 x 16 In. 175.00
Table, Drop Leaf, Cherry, Ring-Turned Legs, New York, c.1855, 84 x 44 In. 2375.00
Table, Drop Leaf, Cherry, Spiraled Legs, Iron Hinges, 19th Century, 29 x 19 x 46 In. 275.00
Table, Drop Leaf, Chippendale Style, Gadrooned Border, Cabriole Legs, 29 x 19 x 32 In. . 80.00
Table, Drop Leaf, Chippendale, Birch, 1-Board Top, 46 1/2 x 14 1/2 x 14 In. 460.00
Table, Drop Leaf, Chippendale, Mahogany, Oak, England, 27 1/2 x 46 In. 470.00
Table, Drop Leaf, Cypress, Poplar, Drawer, Early 19th Century, 29 x 42 x 20 In. 1035.00
Table, Drop Leaf, Diamond & Rectangular Whalebone Inlay, 28 x 25 x 21 In. 550.00
Table, Drop Leaf, English Oak, Gateleg, Elliptical Top, c.1910, 28 3/4 x 21 x 41 1/2 In. . . 175.00
Table, Drop Leaf, Federal, Cherry, New England, c.1820, 26 1/2 x 19 1/2 x 46 In. 315.00
Table, Drop Leaf, Federal, Cherry, New England, c.1820, 29 x 18 1/2 x 21 In. 430.00
Table, Drop Leaf, Federal, Mahoganized Birch, Round Corners, 29 1/2 x 38 In. 29.00
Table, Drop Leaf, Federal, Mahogany, Acanthus Carved Legs, 29 1/2 x 39 1/2 x 25 In. . . . 2300.00
Table, Drop Leaf, Federal, Mahogany, Brass Mounts, c.1815, 28 3/4 x 24 1/2 x 51 In. 1725.00
Table, Drop Leaf, Federal, Mahogany, Carved, Turned Legs, New York, 29 x 24 x 40 In. . . 460.00
Table, Drop Leaf, Federal, Mahogany, New England, c.1815, 29 x 21 1/4 x 52 1/2 In. 800.00
Table, Drop Leaf, Federal, Mahogany, Pedestal, Baltimore, c.1820 . . . . 1495.00
Table, Drop Leaf, Federal, Swing Leg, Drawer, Early 19th Century, 48 x 25 1/2 x 30 In. . . 575.00
Table, Drop Leaf, G. Stickley, No. 666, Gateleg, Drawer, 9 x 22 x 26 In. Open 1610.00
Table, Drop Leaf, G. Stickley, No. 673, Oval, Shoefoot Base, 44 x 14 x 29 In. 2645.00
Table, Drop Leaf, George III Style, Mahogany, Turned Pedestal, Saber Legs, 29 x 29 In. . 230.00
Table, Drop Leaf, George III, Mahogany, c.1770, 27 x 12 x 36 In. . . . . .800.00 to 1265.00
Table, Drop Leaf, George III, Mahogany, Oval, c.1785, 28 x 30 In. 805.00
Table, Drop Leaf, George III, Oak, Gateleg, Mid 18th Century, 28 x 22 x 49 3/4 In. 1380.00
Table, Drop Leaf, George III, Satinwood Inlay, Drawers, 1800s, 29 x 59 x 27 In. 3525.00
Table, Drop Leaf, Georgian, Mahogany, Oval, Molded, Claw & Ball Feet, 40 x 18 In. 1125.00
Table, Drop Leaf, H. Wegner, Teak & Oak, X-Leg Base, 28 x 93 1/2 x 33 3/4 In. 2070.00
Table, Drop Leaf, Hepplewhite, Birch, American, 11-In. Leaves, 29 x 42 x 20 In. 415.00
Table, Drop Leaf, Hepplewhite, Mahogany, 3 Sections, 23 x 47 In. 2875.00
Table, Drop Leaf, Hepplewhite, Mahogany, Double Swing Leg, 28 x 46 x 17 1/2 In. 335.00
Table, Drop Leaf, Hepplewhite, Mahogany, Tapered Legs, 27 3/4 x 46 1/4 x 17 1/2 In. . . . 330.00
Table, Drop Leaf, Hepplewhite, Maple, Square Legs, 13 1/2 In. Leaves, 28 1/2 x 43 In. . . . 175.00
Table, Drop Leaf, Hepplewhite, Pine Top, Maple Base, Tapered Legs, 28 x 25 x 45 In. . . . 495.00
Table, Drop Leaf, Hepplewhite, Square Tapered Legs, Leaves, 19th Century, 42 x 15 In. . . 375.00
Table, Drop Leaf, Hepplewhite, Tiger Maple, Cherry Base, Swing Leg, 28 x 42 x 15 In. . . . 2090.00
Table, Drop Leaf, Jacobean Style, Oak, Gateleg, c.1900, 27 x 11 x 23 3/4 In. 545.00
Table, Drop Leaf, Mahogany, 2 Drawers, Turned Legs, New England, c.1825, 28 x 20 In. . 1150.00
Table, Drop Leaf, Mahogany, 2 Frieze Drawers, 6 Tapered Legs, 30 1/2 x 40 x 63 In. 175.00
Table, Drop Leaf, Mahogany, Blanket Roll Top, 2 Leaves, Claw & Ball Feet 420.00
Table, Drop Leaf, Mahogany, Cock-Beaded, Rope Turned Legs, 29 x 17 x 18 In. 575.00
Table, Drop Leaf, Mahogany, Oval Top, Pedestal Base, 29 1/4 x 18 1/2 x 42 In. 1035.00
Table, Drop Leaf, Mahogany, Rope Turned Legs, Tripod Base, 2 Leaves, 36 x 17 3/4 In. . . 375.00
Table, Drop Leaf, Maple, Gateleg, Bowed Ends, Drawer, American, 27 x 32 In. 2300.00
Table, Drop Leaf, Neoclassical, Frieze Drawers, American, c.1835, 29 1/2 x 52 x 41 In. . . . 920.00
Table, Drop Leaf, Neoclassical, Mahogany, American c.1825, 30 1/2 x 26 x 38 1/2 In. . . . 690.00
Table, Drop Leaf, Neoclassical, Mahogany, American, c.1825, 28 1/2 x 22 x 38 In. 520.00
Table, Drop Leaf, Neoclassical, Mahogany, Pedestal, 4 Legs, Drawer, 31 1/2 In. 2585.00
Table, Drop Leaf, Neoclassical, Pedestal, American 29 x 42 In. 115.00

Table, Drop Leaf, Oak, 2 Swing Legs, Hinges, England, 18th Century, 26 1/2 x 24 In. . . . 3960.00
Table, Drop Leaf, Pine, Gateleg, 30 x 47 x 46 In. 175.00
Table, Drop Leaf, Queen Anne Style, Pegged, Dovetailed, c.1810, 29 1/4 x 42 x 16 In. 2240.00
Table, Drop Leaf, Queen Anne Style, Satinwood, Banded Mahogany, 28 x 36 x 50 In. . . . 940.00
Table, Drop Leaf, Queen Anne, Cutout Apron, Late 1700s, 27 1/2 x 35 1/2 x 47 In. 999.00
Table, Drop Leaf, Queen Anne, Mahogany, Cabriole Legs, 28 x 36 x 11 1/2 In. 2760.00
Table, Drop Leaf, Queen Anne, Mahogany, Club Feet, 44 x 13 1/2 x 13 1/2 In. 1295.00
Table, Drop Leaf, Queen Anne, Mahogany, Oval Top, England, 33 x 14 In. 690.00
Table, Drop Leaf, Queen Anne, Maple, Cusped Corners, New England, 28 x 44 1/2 In. . . . 1725.00
Table, Drop Leaf, Queen Anne, Tiger Maple, 27 x 43 x 12 In. 400.00
Table, Drop Leaf, Queen Anne, Tiger Maple, Bowed Ends, Oval Leaves, 28 x 42 In. 3160.00
Table, Drop Leaf, Queen Anne, Walnut, Cabriole Legs, Pad Feet, 1700s, 26 x 39 x 13 In. . 1610.00
Table, Drop Leaf, Queen Anne, Walnut, Oval, Hinged, England, 26 1/2 x 36 In. 1150.00
Table, Drop Leaf, Regency, Mahogany, c.1835, 29 x 20 x 39 In. 1035.00
Table, Drop Leaf, Regency, Mahogany, Inlaid, c.1835, 57 3/4 x 26 3/4 In. 2530.00
Table, Drop Leaf, Renaissance Revival, Ebonized, Gilt Bronze Mounts, 29 x 30 In. 960.00
Table, Drop Leaf, Rosewood, Scandinavian, 34 1/2 x 8 1/2 x 29 In. 635.00
Table, Drop Leaf, Shaker, Cherry, Whitewater, Ohio, c.1840, 29 x 38 1/2 x 44 In. 1265.00
Table, Drop Leaf, Sheraton, Apple Wood, Turned Legs, 10-In. Leaves, 1800s, 29 x 36 In. . 185.00
Table, Drop Leaf, Sheraton, Cherry, Dovetailed Drawers, Turned Legs, 36 x 19 x 29 In. . . . 420.00
Table, Drop Leaf, Sheraton, Cherry, Scalloped Leaves, 28 3/4 x 37 In. 440.00
Table, Drop Leaf, Sheraton, Cherry, Turned Legs, 13-In. Leaves, 29 x 48 x 19 1/2 In. 175.00
Table, Drop Leaf, Sheraton, Cherry, Turned Legs, Drawer, 27 3/4 x 38 3/4 x 21 In. 260.00
Table, Drop Leaf, Sheraton, Mahogany, 2 Drawers, 28 1/2 x 16 1/4 x 17 In. 260.00
Table, Drop Leaf, Sheraton, Mahogany, 2 Drawers, 29 x 15 1/2 x 17 In. 315.00
Table, Drop Leaf, Sheraton, Mahogany, Fluted Legs, 28 1/4 x 38 In. 345.00
Table, Drop Leaf, Sheraton, Mahogany, New England, 29 x 18 1/2 x 17 3/4 In. 1035.00
Table, Drop Leaf, Sheraton, Mahogany, Ribbed Legs, Casters, 29 x 36 x 18 In. 1725.00
Table, Drop Leaf, Sheraton, Mahogany, Turned Legs, 28 x 35 3/4 x 17 1/2 In. 315.00
Table, Drop Leaf, Sheraton, Mahogany, Turned Legs, 28 x 48 x 18 1/2 In. 460.00
Table, Drop Leaf, Sheraton, Pine Top, Maple Base, Swing Leg, 28 x 43 x 16 In. 560.00
Table, Drop Leaf, Sheraton, Pine Top, Maple, Swing Leg, 28 1/2 x 43 x 16 1/2 In. 550.00
Table, Drop Leaf, Sheraton, Pine, Red Paint, 2-Board Top, 41 x 17 x 11 In. 1035.00
Table, Drop Leaf, Sheraton, Tiger Maple, Cherry, c.1840, 28 x 39 In. . . . . *Illus* 165.00
Table, Drop Leaf, Sheraton, Tiger Maple, Turned Legs, 39 1/2 x 18 x 30 In. 1465.00
Table, Drop Leaf, Victorian, Mahogany, H-Shape Trestle, Mid 1800s, 28 x 30 In. 700.00
Table, Drop Leaf, Victorian, Walnut, Round, Urn Shaped Shaft, 30 x 18 x 36 In. 300.00
Table, Drop Leaf, Victorian, Walnut, Turned Legs, 30 x 40 In. 80.00
Table, Drop Leaf, Walnut, Turned, Swing Legs, 59 In. 395.00
Table, Drop Leaf, William & Mary Style, Oak, Leaves, Box Stretcher, 29 x 54 x 23 In. 2705.00
Table, Drop Leaf, William & Mary, 2 Drawers, Molded Square Legs, c.1730, 48 In. 12500.00
Table, Drop Leaf, William & Mary, Maple, Gateleg, Oval Top, Massachusetts, 26 x 44 In. . 6040.00
Table, Drop Leaf, William & Mary, Oak, Oblong Top, Rounded Leaves, Shaped Skirt 1675.00
Table, Drop Leaf, William IV, Satinwood, Mahogany, c.1830, 29 x 45 x 26 In. 2300.00
Table, Drum, George III Style, Satinwood, Inlay, Leather Inset Top, 30 x 36 In. 3220.00
Table, Eames, Aluminum, Walnut Veneer, Round, Herman Miller, 29 3/4 x 25 1/2 In. 60.00
Table, Eames, DTM, Laminated Plywood, Steel Legs, Herman Miller, 34 x 28 1/2 In. 690.00
Table, Eames, DTM-20, Walnut Plywood, Chrome, Herman Miller, 1952, 34 x 29 In. 995.00
Table, Eames, IT-1, Birch Top, Steel Folding Legs, Herman Miller, 21 1/2 x 17 In. 1035.00
Table, Eames, LTR, Birch Top, Zinc Wire Base, Herman Miller, 15 x 13 x 10 In. . .200.00 to 345.00
Table, Eames, Plywood, Enameled Metal, Herman Miller c.1952, 10 x 16 x 13 In. 2030.00
Table, Eames, Plywood, Steel, Herman Miller, c.1950, 17 x 21 1/2 x 18 In. 960.00
Table, Eames, Surfboard, Plywood, Wire, Herman Miller, c.1950s, 89 x 29 x 10 In. 4025.00
Table, Eames, Universal Base, Oak Top, 4-Point Aluminum Base, Round, 42 x 28 3/4 In. . 115.00
Table, Edwardian Style, Mahogany, Banded Oval Top, 28 x 22 1/2 x 17 1/2 In., Pair 1380.00
Table, Edwardian Style, Oak, Leather, 8 Sides, 27 1/2 x 18 In. 1840.00
Table, Edwardian, Inlaid Mahogany, Leather Writing Surface, c.1900, 30 x 42 x 19 In. . . . 350.00
Table, Edwardian, Walnut, Satinwood, c.1900, 28 x 24 x 15 1/2 In. 980.00
Table, Eero Saarinen, Italian Marble Top, Pedestal, Cast Iron Base, Knoll, 36 x 28 1/2 In. . 1380.00
Table, Eero Saarinen, Walnut Top, Pedestal, Cast Iron Base, Knoll, 20 x 20 1/2 In. 550.00
Table, Eero Saarinen, White Laminate, Round, Pedestal, Metal Base, Knoll, 20 x 20 In. . . 320.00
Table, Eero Saarinen, White Marble Top, Pedestal, Enameled Base, Knoll, 16 x 20 In. . . . 345.00
Table, Elizabethan Style, Oak, Open Shelf, Frieze Drawers, Vine, 45 x 42 x 15 In. 295.00

Table, Elm, Chinese, c.1810, 11 1/4 x 28 1/2 x 17 In. 265.00
Table, Elm, Chinese, c.1810, 33 x 67 x 23 1/2 In. 210.00
Table, Elm, Chinese, c.1850, 13 x 27 In., Pair 175.00
Table, Elm, Lute, Chinese, c.1830, 33 1/2 x 42 x 17 3/4 In. 945.00
Table, Empire Style, Fruitwood, Ormolu Mounted, 3 Frieze Drawers, 31 x 68 x 30 In. 1295.00
Table, Empire Style, Mahogany, Applied Frieze, Round Top, c.1900, 29 1/2 x 33 In. 1610.00
Table, Empire Style, Mahogany, Gilt, 3 Drawers, Inset Leather, 30 x 55 In. .... *Illus* 1380.00
Table, Empire Style, Mahogany, Leather Surface, 3 Drawers, 29 1/2 x 57 x 27 In. 2990.00
Table, Empire Style, Mahogany, Lyre Pedestal, c.1850, 29 x 34 In. 260.00
Table, Empire Style, Mahogany, Marble Top, c.1900, 24 1/2 x 19 In. 1610.00
Table, Empire Style, Mahogany, Marble Top, Late 19th Century, 23 x 15 3/4 In. 690.00
Table, Empire Style, Mahogany, Pedestal, c.1890, 29 1/2 x 52 In. 345.00
Table, Empire Style, Marble Noir, Brass, Tripod, 26 1/2 x 17 In. 1035.00
Table, Empire Style, Marble Top, Brass, Tripod, 26 1/4 x 17 In., Pair 1150.00
Table, Empire Style, Marble Top, Mahogany, Early 20th Century, 23 x 16 In. 800.00
Table, Empire Style, Marble Top, Serpentine Legs, Tops, 36 x 42 x 23 In. 220.00
Table, Empire Style, Rosewood, Gilt Bronze, France, c.1900, 32 1/2 x 47 In. 5750.00
Table, Empire, Mahogany, Foldover, Pedestal, American, 29 1/2 x 36 x 17 3/4 In. 710.00
Table, Empire, Mahogany, Marble Top, Flower & Scroll Border, 30 x 31 x 46 In. 2300.00
Table, Empire, Mahogany, Marble Top, Pedestal, c.1815, 32 x 13 1/2 In., Pair 2530.00
Table, Empire, Mahogany, Octagonal, France, c.1865, 30 x 35 In. 345.00
Table, Empire, Mahogany, Trestle Base, Saber Legs, Paw Feet, 1820, 29 x 24 In. 4620.00
Table, English Export, Regimental Drum, WWI Insignia, 1st Irish Guard, 20 x 15 In. 295.00
Table, F. Gehry, Easy Edge, Cardboard, Masonite, 1972, 20 1/2 In. 935.00
Table, Faux Tortoiseshell, Boulle Work, Drawer, Square Pedestal, 18 1/4 x 30 3/4 In. 920.00
Table, Federal Style, Mahogany, Inlaid, 3 Parts, 30 1/2 x 113 1/2 x 46 In. 1770.00
Table, Federal Style, Walnut, Drawer, Bamboo Turned Legs, 30 x 18 x 18 In. 240.00
Table, Federal, Cherry, 2 Drawers, Early 1800s, 30 1/2 x 37 x 18 In. 780.00
Table, Federal, Mahogany Inlay, Oval Top, Squared Frame, Drawer, c.1790, 23 1/2 In. ... 23900.00
Table, Federal, Mahogany, 2 Drawers, N.Y., c.1820, 36 x 36 x 18 1/2 In. 1795.00
Table, Federal, Mahogany, Drawers, Boston, 1810-1825, 27 x 39 1/2 In. 3410.00
Table, Federal, Mahogany, Hairy Paw Platform Base, Brass Casters, 28 1/2 x 36 x 21 In. .. 600.00
Table, Federal, Mahogany, New England, c.1815, 29 1/2 x 41 3/4 x 20 3/4 In. 865.00
Table, Federal, Mahogany, Veneer, 2 Parts, New York, c.1825, 29 1/2 x 53 1/2 In. 3055.00
Table, Federal, Walnut, 19th Century, 27 1/2 x 14 1/2 In. 460.00
Table, Figures In Garden, Chinese, Early 1900s, 14 1/2 x 47 1/4 x 23 3/4 In. 980.00
Table, Florence Knoll, Marble Top, Chrome Base, 16 3/4 x 27 In. 460.00
Table, Florence Knoll, Tubular Steel Base, Chrome, Cremo Marble, 27 x 27 x 17 In. 230.00
Table, Folding, Herman Miller, c.1970, 59 x 23 1/2 x 15 In. 355.00
Table, Folding, Wormley, Glass Tile Top, Dunbar, c.1957, 25 x 22 1/2 x 21 1/2 In. 1645.00
Table, Frank Lloyd Wright, Hexagonal Top, 3 Slab Base, Henredon, 25 x 29 x 26 In. 980.00
Table, Frank Lloyd Wright, Square Top, Cube Base, Taliesin Edge, Henredon, 26 x 13 In. 2115.00
Table, Frank Lloyd Wright, Taliesin Design, Heritage Henredon, 60 x 20 x 14 In. 1530.00
Table, Frank Lloyd Wright, Taliesin Edge, Drawer, Shelf, Henredon, 26 x 27 x 23 In. 800.00
Table, Frankl, Cork Veneer, Triangular Top, Mahogany Veneered Shelf, 24 x 25 x 27 In. .. 750.00
Table, French Provincial, Fruitwood, Draw End, Early 19th Century, 30 x 51 x 32 In. 1955.00
Table, French Provincial, Maple, Walnut, c.1810, 30 x 14 1/2 x 12 1/2 In. 189.00
Table, French Provincial, Oak, Rectangular Top, Square Legs, Stretchers, 29 x 71 x 21 In. 650.00
Table, French Provincial, Pine, 2 Frieze Drawers, 29 1/2 x 63 x 30 1/2 In. 1035.00

Furniture, Table, Empire Style,
Mahogany, Gilt, 3 Drawers, Inset
Leather, 30 x 55 In.

Furniture, Table, Game, Federal, Mahogany,
Carved, Gilt, c.1815, 30 x 36 x 18 1/2 In.

Table, French Walnut, Demilune, Early 19th Century, 28 x 20 x 12 In. 865.00
Table, Fruitwood, Carved, Marble Top, 18 1/2 x 24 x 17 1/2 In., Pair 115.00
Table, Fruitwood, Checkered Marble Top, 2 Tiers, c.1900, 31 1/2 x 17 x 17 In. 520.00
Table, Fruitwood, Molded Drawers, Carved Apron, Breadboard Ends, 11 x 7 1/2 x 8 In. .. 450.00
Table, Fruitwood, Pine, Oak, Gateleg, Turned Feet, Stretchers, 36 x 16 1/2 x 16 In. 770.00
Table, Fruitwood, Planked Top, Shaped Legs, 18 x 52 1/2 x 22 In. 635.00
Table, G. Nakashima, Cherry, Free Edge, Triangular, 3 Dowel Legs, 41 x 21 1/2 In. 1725.00
Table, G. Nakashima, Minguren, Walnut, Free Edge, Rectangular, 21 x 28 x 20 In. 5750.00
Table, G. Nakashima, Square Top, 1 Free Edge, Drawer, 21 x 28 x 28 1/4 In. 3740.00
Table, G. Nakashima, Walnut, Free Edge, 4 Dowel Legs, 27 x 25 x 17 In. 1725.00
Table, G. Nelson, Lazy Susan, Laminate, Metal Base, Herman Miller, 47 1/2 x 29 In. 865.00
Table, G. Nelson, No. 4656, Primavera, Birch, Gateleg, Herman Miller, 1948, 65 x 30 In. . 700.00
Table, G. Nelson, Primavera, Birch, Herman Miller, c.1950, 23 x 16 x 21 In. 500.00
Table, G. Nelson, Rosewood Top, Ebonized Legs, Herman Miller, 72 x 40 x 29 In. 1955.00
Table, G. Nelson, Walnut Tray Top, Chrome, Enameled Base, Herman Miller, 18 x 17 In. . 800.00
Table, G. Nelson, Walnut Veneer, 2 Tiers, Blind Drawers, 18 x 30 1/2 x 18 In., Pair 3450.00
Table, G. Nelson, Walnut Veneer, Drawer, Cubby Hole, Plank Legs, 24 x 18 x 20 In. 575.00
Table, G. Nelson, Walnut Veneer, Glass Top, Drawer, Herman Miller, 22 x 18 x 35 In. ... 635.00
Table, G. Nelson, Walnut, Steel, Enamel, Herman Miller, 1950s, 18 x 17 In. 700.00
Table, G. Nelson, Walnut, Steel, Herman Miller, 24 x 17 x 18 1/2 In., Pair 1755.00
Table, G. Stickley, Cut Corner Top, Shelf, Arched Cross Stretchers, 24 x 24 x 29 In. 2875.00
Table, G. Stickley, Mahogany, Round Top, Arched Cross Stretcher Base, 36 x 29 In. 2070.00
Table, G. Stickley, No. 436, Circular, Cross Stretcher, Mortised, 28 x 23 1/2 In. 9200.00
Table, G. Stickley, No. 441, Cross Stretcher, Through Tenon, c.1902, 36 x 29 In. 10925.00
Table, G. Stickley, No. 612, Cut Corner Top, Shelf, Through Tenon, 30 x 30 x 29 In. 4900.00
Table, G. Stickley, No. 634, 2 Leaves, Arched Cross Stretcher, 54 x 29 In. 13800.00
Table, G. Stickley, No. 637, Trestle, Shelf, Shoefoot Base, 48 x 30 x 29 In. 1150.00
Table, G. Stickley, Trestle, Shelf, Through Tenon Stretchers, 48 x 30 In. 2820.00
Table, Galle, Fruitwood, Marquetry, c.1920, 26 x 16 1/2 x 14 1/2 In. 720.00
Table, Game, Arts & Crafts, Oak, Cloth, Flip Top, Padded 235.00
Table, Game, Biedermeier, Fruitwood, Gateleg, Demilune, 29 x 39 x 20 In. 700.00
Table, Game, Biedermeier, Fruitwood, Inlaid, Felt Lined Interior, 31 x 16 1/2 x 33 In. ... 470.00
Table, Game, Biedermeier, Fruitwood, Plain Frieze, c.1815, 30 1/2 x 33 1/2 In. 920.00
Table, Game, Burl, Flip & Swivel Top, Brass Cuffs, 30 x 35 x 17 In. 715.00
Table, Game, Chippendale, Mahogany, Carved, Apron, N.Y., Late 1700s, 27 x 31 In. 12925.00
Table, Game, Directoire, Mahogany, Baize Lined Top, Early 1800s, 29 x 31 x 32 In. 690.00
Table, Game, Directoire, Mahogany, Flip Top, Frieze Drawers, 29 1/2 x 34 x 16 1/2 In. .. 650.00
Table, Game, Empire, Mahogany, Apron, Ogee Molding, Vase Shape Shaft 450.00
Table, Game, Empire, Mahogany, Lyre Support, Flared Pedestal, 36 x 29 In. 260.00
Table, Game, Federal, Flip Top, Bowfront, Drawer, Early 1900s, 36 x 18 x 31 In. 315.00
Table, Game, Federal, Mahogany, Carved, Gilt, c.1815, 30 x 36 x 18 1/2 In. .... *Illus* 32400.00
Table, Game, Federal, Mahogany, Flip Top, American, c.1900, 30 x 36 In. 920.00
Table, Game, Federal, Mahogany, Massachusetts, Early 1800s, 29 1/2 x 36 x 18 In. 2300.00
Table, Game, Federal, Mahogany, Satinwood Inlay, 32 1/2 x 16 1/8 x 26 1/8 In. 2185.00
Table, Game, Flip Top, Mahogany, Satinwood, Marquetry, Italy, c.1815, 29 x 36 In. 4370.00
Table, Game, George III Style, Mahogany, Flip Top, Leather Inset, Cabriole Legs, 33 In. . 990.00
Table, Game, George III, Mahogany, Flip Top, c.1810, 30 x 35 1/8 x 17 In. 1035.00
Table, Game, George III, Mahogany, Inlaid, D-Shape Top, 29 x 36 x 35 In. Open 2300.00
Table, Game, George III, Mahogany, Inlaid, Felt Surface, c.1800, 29 x 37 x 18 In., Pair .. 2700.00
Table, Game, George III, Mahogany, Satinwood Threading, c.1800, 30 x 36 In. 1495.00
Table, Game, George III, Mahogany, Satinwood, Demilune, Flip Top, 28 x 35 x 18 In. 2990.00
Table, Game, George III, Mahogany, String Inlaid, Flip Top, 30 x 17 x 35 1/2 In. 520.00
Table, Game, Georgian, Mahogany, Shell, Bellflower Knees, Carved, 28 1/2 x 33 In. 1920.00
Table, Game, Georgian, Mahogany, Swivel Top, Flared Platform, Scroll Feet, 36 In. 570.00
Table, Game, Hepplewhite, Cherry, Swing Leg, Drawers, 29 1/2 x 38 x 50 1/2 In. 1150.00
Table, Game, Hepplewhite, Mahogany, Bellflower Inlay, 30 1/2 x 36 x 18 In. 1725.00
Table, Game, Hepplewhite, Mahogany, Eagle Panel, Flip Top, 1900s, 35 x 17 In. 520.00
Table, Game, Hunzinger, Oak, Flip Top, Round, Felt, Paw Feet, Aug. 5-90, 33 In. 1790.00
Table, Game, Mahogany, Acanthus Carved Pedestal, Paw Feet, Brass, 28 x 36 In. 1380.00
Table, Game, Mahogany, Handkerchief, Duck Feet, 3-Part Top, 1700s, 37 In. 635.00
Table, Game, Mahogany, Marquetry, Bronze Ormolu, X-Stretcher, 1900s, 30 x 27 In. 400.00
Table, Game, Mahogany, Parquetry, Flowers, France, c.1890, 30 x 39 x 20 In. 635.00
Table, Game, Mahogany, Urn Shaped Pedestal, American, c.1840, 29 x 36 x 18 1/4 In. 405.00

Table, Game, Mixed Wood, Black Paint Pedestal, c.1900, 14 x 14 x 22 In. 259.00
Table, Game, Napoleon III, Kingwood, Brass Inlay Top, c.1860, 30 x 33 1/2 x 18 In. 315.00
Table, Game, Napoleon III, Mahogany, Inlaid, Handkerchief, 29 x 22 x 22 In. 495.00
Table, Game, Neoclassical, Mahogany, American, c.1840, 28 1/2 x 36 x 18 In. 290.00
Table, Game, Queen Anne Style, Cherry, Leather Top, c.1810, 30 1/2 x 36 x 35 In. 920.00
Table, Game, Queen Anne Style, Red Lacquer, Mid 1800s, 30 1/2 x 31 1/2 x 13 1/2 In. . . 3680.00
Table, Game, Queen Anne, Mahogany, Triple Flip Top, 29 3/4 x 33 1/2 In. 7475.00
Table, Game, Regency, Mahogany, Flip Top, D-Shape, Saber Legs, 29 1/2 x 41 x 18 In. . . 2310.00
Table, Game, Regency, Mahogany, Inlaid, Ebonized Wood, Flip Top, 29 x 36 x 17 In. 575.00
Table, Game, Rococo Revival, Rosewood, Late 1800s, 30 x 36 x 18 In. 2185.00
Table, Game, Victorian, Papier-Mache, Tilt Top, 27 x 22 In. 1080.00
Table, Game, Victorian, Walnut, Bulbous Turned Legs, c.1895, 35 x 98 x 53 In. 5750.00
Table, Game, Walnut, Gateleg, Demilune, Raised Fluted Legs, 29 x 18 In. 660.00
Table, Game, Walnut, Handkerchief, Drawer, Continental, c.1910, 30 1/2 x 28 In. 1150.00
Table, Game, William IV, Leather Inset, Round Corners, Quatrefoil Base, 29 x 36 In. 1140.00
Table, Game, William IV, Mahogany, 3-Drawer Chest, c.1835, 30 x 26 In. 1150.00
Table, Game, Wormley, Wood Frame, Leather Top, Dunbar, 28 x 36 In. 750.00
Table, George I, Mahogany, Porringer Corners, England, Early 1700s, 33 In. 7820.00
Table, George II Style, Walnut, Double Pedestal, 2 Leaves, 30 x 48 x 145 In. 2760.00
Table, George III Style, Mahogany, 2 Pedestals, 5 Leaves, c.1950, 29 1/2 x 72 In. 920.00
Table, George III Style, Mahogany, 3 Pedestals, c.1925, 28 1/2 x 48 x 106 In. 1265.00
Table, George III Style, Mahogany, Cabriole Legs, Pad Feet, 28 1/2 x 48 x 68 In. 1725.00
Table, George III Style, Mahogany, Demilune Drop Leaves, 29 1/2 x 84 In. 575.00
Table, George III Style, Mahogany, Inlaid, 2 Columns, Kittinger, 29 x 113 1/2 x 48 In. . . . 2360.00
Table, George III Style, Mahogany, Quarter Veneer, 28 3/4 x 27 In. 405.00
Table, George III Style, Mahogany, Rosewood, Demilune, 33 x 44 x 19 In., Pair 3450.00
Table, George III Style, Satinwood, Ebonized, Inlaid Mahogany, 29 x 34 x 18 In. 635.00
Table, George III Style, Satinwood, Mahogany Inlay, Harewood Crossband, 34 x 49 In. . . 10925.00
Table, George III, Mahogany, 3 Drawers, c.1760, 28 x 30 In. 1265.00
Table, George III, Mahogany, Carved, 3 Pedestals, 1800s 8625.00
Table, George III, Mahogany, Inlaid, c.1800, 27 1/4 x 17 x 16 3/4 In. 805.00
Table, George III, Mahogany, Inlaid, Leather Inset, c.1800, 28 x 24 x 16 In. 3910.00
Table, George III, Mahogany, Sunburst, Demilune, c.1785, 30 x 57 1/2 x 25 In. 1725.00
Table, Georgian Style, Mahogany, Early 20th Century, 30 x 18 x 66 In. 230.00
Table, Georgian Style, Mahogany, Inlaid, 3 Leaves, 13 In., 31 x 40 x 21 In. 690.00
Table, Georgian Style, Mahogany, Inlaid, Serpentine Gallery, 31 x 16 x 16 In. 1060.00
Table, Georgian Style, Mahogany, Reeded Edge, 3 Pedestals, 2 Leaves, 156 x 29 In. 3100.00
Table, Georgian Style, Walnut, Black Marble, Lattice Apron, 28 x 18 x 20 In. 175.00
Table, Georgian, Mahogany, 4 Saber Legs, Oval, c.1835 . . . . 4140.00
Table, Georgian, Mahogany, Satinwood Inlay, Serpentine Front 1600.00
Table, Gilt, Marble Top, Wood Trumpet Legs, Oval, Italy, 34 x 33 1/2 x 27 In. 3565.00
Table, Giltwood, Oval, Tripod, Italy, c.1865, 31 x 19 x 15 In. 1265.00
Table, Gio Ponti, Italian Walnut, Brass, 3 Leaves, Singer & Sons, 1950s, 40 x 29 In. 4400.00
Table, Gothic Revival, Cast Iron, Openwork, Stretcher Base, N.C., 29 x 39 x 25 In. 275.00
Table, Green Lacquer, Demilune, Women, Garden, Chinese, 1800s, 34 x 17 x 32 1/2 In. . . 529.00
Table, Green Marble Inset, Bronze Angle Iron Frame, 24 x 26 In., Pair 690.00
Table, Gueridon, Cast Iron, Arrow Shape, Round Glass, Tripod Base, 35 1/2 x 13 In. 125.00
Table, Gueridon, Charles X Style, Mahogany, Marble Top, Parcel Gilt, 27 1/2 x 20 In. . . . 445.00
Table, Gueridon, Empire Style, Mahogany, Bronze Mounted, Malachite Top, 32 x 24 In. . 1380.00
Table, Gueridon, Empire Style, Mahogany, Specimen Marble, Round Top, 29 x 36 In. . . . 4600.00
Table, Gueridon, Empire Style, Marble Top, Ormolu, 29 x 27 1/2 In., Pair 3680.00
Table, Gueridon, Fruitwood, Circular Top, Inlaid Star, Continental, c.1850, 36 x 15 In. . . . 200.00
Table, Gueridon, George III Style, Bronze Mounted, Marble, 32 x 16 In. 2760.00
Table, Gueridon, Louis XV Style, Giltwood, Round Marble Top, Frieze, 29 In., Pair 400.00
Table, Gueridon, Louis XVI Style, Mahogany, Gilt Bronze, Marble Top, c.1910, 32 In. . . . 1380.00
Table, Gueridon, Napoleon III, Mahogany, Marble Top, c.1865, 29 1/2 x 26 1/2 In. 1380.00
Table, Gueridon, Restauration Style, Burled Elm, Marble Top, 31 x 32 In. 1610.00
Table, Gueridon, Restauration, Mahogany, Marble Top, c.1815, 31 x 38 In. 3680.00
Table, Harvest, Cherry, Drop Leaf, Turned Legs, Stretcher Base, 72 x 26 x 30 In. 900.00
Table, Harvest, Cherry, Turned Leg, Molded Edge, 30 1/2 x 30 1/2 x 73 In. 980.00
Table, Harvest, French Provincial, Fruitwood, Mid 19th Century, 29 x 65 x 27 In. 1840.00
Table, Harvest, Fruitwood, Cut Corners, Pegged, c.1850, 31 x 117 x 32 In. 550.00
Table, Harvest, Pine, 4-Board, Rough Hewn, Stretcher Base, 29 x 72 x 26 In. 336.00

Table, Harvest, Pine, Drop Leaf, 19th Century, 30 1/2 x 22 x 90 In. 1095.00
Table, Harvest, Pine, Poplar, 4 Vase & Ring Turned Legs, c.1830, 29 x 67 x 26 In. 1410.00
Table, Harvest, Pine, Scrubbed Top, Blue Base, 106 In. 190.00
Table, Harvest, Softwood, Green Paint, Drop Leaf, Drawer, Turnip Feet, 28 x 53 1/2 In. . . 2025.00
Table, Hepplewhite Style, Birch, Yellow Inlay, Drawer, Brass Pull, 29 x 19 x 17 In. 850.00
Table, Hepplewhite Style, Mahogany, Double Pedestal, 10 Leaves, 29 x 70 In. 6040.00
Table, Hepplewhite Style, Mahogany, String Inlaid, Demilune, 29 x 45 x 20 In., Pair 750.00
Table, Hepplewhite, Birch, Pine, Pegged Joints, Tapered Legs, 27 1/2 x 38 3/4 x 29 In. . . . 520.00
Table, Hepplewhite, Pine, Drawer, Dovetailed, Tapered Legs, 30 1/4 x 45 1/2 x 29 In. . . . 1095.00
Table, Hepplewhite, Poplar, 2-Board Pine Top, Old Red Wash, c.1830, 29 x 31 x 21 In. . . 489.00
Table, Hepplewhite, Walnut, Eagle Inlay, 3 Drawers, American, 28 3/4 x 16 x 33 In. 1725.00
Table, Howell, Wood, Chrome, 2 Semicircular Shelves, 22 x 25 x 13 In. 635.00
Table, Hugh Acton, Travertine, Brass, U.S.A., 1950s, 30 x 20 x 15 1/2 In. 1755.00
Table, I. Noguchi, Black Enamel, Cast Iron Base, Knoll, 23 1/2 x 19 3/4 In. 1265.00
Table, I. Noguchi, Cyclone, White Laminate Top, Chrome Wire Shaft, Knoll, 29 x 36 In. . . 1495.00
Table, I. Noguchi, Laminate Top, Cast Iron Base, Steel Wire, Knoll, 34 x 29 In. 920.00
Table, Ice Cream Parlor, Attached Stools, Lift Top, Cast Iron Legs, c.1900 . . . . 1375.00
Table, Ice Cream Parlor, Oak, Twisted Wire, 2 Chairs, 24-In. Table 440.00
Table, Ice Cream Parlor, Simulated Milk Glass Top, Swivel Iron & Wood Seats, 30 In. . . . 330.00
Table, Irish Chippendale Style, Walnut, Carved, 34 1/2 x 54 1/2 x 20 1/2 In. 1610.00
Table, Iron, Glass Top, Painted Base, 4 Ivy-Wrapped Legs, 20 x 30 In. 220.00
Table, Iron, Scrolled Frame, Leaf Mounts, Glass Top, France, c.1850, 21 x 36 x 18 In. . . . 345.00
Table, J. Adnet, Leather Over Steel, Brass, France, 1950s, 10 x 16 1/2 In. 1400.00
Table, Jacobean Style, Oak, Carved Scroll Border, Baluster Legs, 31 x 51 x 32 In. 1320.00
Table, Jean-Michel Frank, Parchment, c.1940, 19 3/4 x 24 3/4 x 15 In., Pair 4780.00
Table, Karl Springer, Glass Top, Angled Brass Pedestal, c.1980 . . . . 825.00
Table, Kingwood, Gilt Bronze Mounts, 3 Drawers, France, c.1890, 29 x 55 x 31 In. 4140.00
Table, L. & J.G. Stickley, No. 536, Round Top & Apron, Stretcher Base, 29 x 24 In. 1295.00
Table, L. & J.G. Stickley, No. 542, Round Top, Lower Open Shelf, 36 x 29 In. 1880.00
Table, L. & J.G. Stickley, No. 559, Octagonal, Through Post, 18 x 18 x 20 In. 2185.00
Table, L. & J.G. Stickley, No. 573, Round, Arched Cross Stretchers, 29 x 18 In. 880.00
Table, L. & J.G. Stickley, No. 574, Cut Corner, Shelf, 18 x 18 x 29 In. 460.00
Table, L. & J.G. Stickley, No. 599, Mouse Hole, Slab Legs, Through Tenon, 60 x 32 In. . . . 8050.00
Table, L. & J.G. Stickley, No. 716, Circular Top, Pedestal Base, 3 Leaves, 45 x 29 In. . . . 1035.00
Table, L. & J.G. Stickley, No. 717, Pedestal Base, 6 Leaves, 54 x 30 In. 3450.00
Table, Lacquered Bamboo, Wood, Red, Chinese, Early 1900s, 34 x 67 x 29 In. 800.00
Table, Lacquered, High Relief Dragons, Japan, Late 1800s, 37 x 31 x 24 1/4 In. 1060.00
Table, Lacquered, Parcel Gilt, Papier-Mache, Mother-Of-Pearl, c.1850, 30 x 20 1/2 In. . . . 1610.00
Table, Late Regency, Rosewood, Coin Molded Frieze, c.1825, 24 1/2 x 18 x 13 In. 6900.00
Table, Library, 2 Drawers, Carved Skirt, Reeded, 29 1/2 x 78 x 2 In. 2875.00
Table, Library, G. Stickley, 2 Drawers, Corbels, Cross Stretcher, 30 x 48 x 29 1/2 In. 1150.00
Table, Library, G. Stickley, Arched Skirt Board, 30 x 50 x 30 In. 2590.00
Table, Library, G. Stickley, No. 614, 2 Drawers, Iron Pulls, Corbelled Legs, 42 x 30 In. . . 2235.00
Table, Library, G. Stickley, No. 616, Oak, 2 Drawers, c.1915, 30 1/2 x 54 x 32 In. 1265.00
Table, Library, George III Style, Mahogany, Carved, 19th Century, 30 x 54 x 30 In. 4315.00
Table, Library, L. & J.G. Stickley, 2 Drawers, Brass Pulls, Through Tenon 2015.00
Table, Library, L. & J.G. Stickley, 2 Tiers, Apron, Arched Stretchers, Round, 29 x 36 In. . . 1200.00
Table, Library, L. & J.G. Stickley, Drawers, Copper Hinge Plates, Pulls, 56 x 36 x 14 In. . . 2300.00
Table, Library, L. & J.G. Stickley, No. 520, Drawer, Copper Pulls, 36 x 24 x 29 In. 1035.00
Table, Library, L. & J.G., Stickley, Through Tenon, Drawer, Pulls, 29 x 42 x 28 In. 1725.00
Table, Library, Lifetime, Copper Pulls, Through Tenon, Stretcher, 29 3/4 x 54 x 32 In. . . . 1335.00
Table, Library, Lifetime, No. 914, 2 Drawers, Iron Pulls, 60 x 36 In. 2120.00
Table, Library, Limbert, Blind Drawers, Lower Shelf, Shaped Side Slats, 42 x 28 x 30 In. . . 635.00
Table, Library, Limbert, No. 1129, Oak, Drawer, Arched Apron, 48 x 28 x 29 In. 1060.00
Table, Library, Mahogany, Barley Twist Turned Legs, 28 3/4 x 40 x 29 1/4 In. 230.00
Table, Library, Mahogany, Blind Drawers, Lower Shelf, 42 x 28 x 30 In. 1380.00
Table, Library, Mahogany, Gallery, 2 Drawers, Stretcher, 1800s, 35 x 48 x 24 In. 550.00
Table, Library, Neoclassical, Mahogany, Carved, Drop Leaf, c.1825, 29 x 52 x 36 In. 5975.00
Table, Library, Onondaga Shops, 2 Drawers, Side Slats, Arched Apron, 29 x 42 x 28 In. . . 2590.00
Table, Library, Regency Style, Mahogany, 2 Leaves, c.1890, 29 1/2 x 42 x 76 In. 1610.00
Table, Library, Renaissance Revival, Mahogany, c.1870, 28 x 53 1/2 x 34 In. 3885.00
Table, Library, Renaissance Revival, Oak, Guilloche Borders, Twist Legs, 29 x 48 x 28 In. 880.00
Table, Library, Rosewood, 3 Drawers, Spain, Early 1800s, 29 x 53 x 26 In. 2185.00

Table, Library, Rosewood, Drop Leaf, Drawer, England, Late 1700s, 29 x 37 x 23 In. 2300.00
Table, Library, Stickley Bros., No. 2561, Drawer, 2-Slat Stretcher, 44 x 28 x 31 In. 690.00
Table, Library, Stickley Bros., Through Tenon Stretcher, Splined Top, 30 x 46 x 27 In. . . . 1035.00
Table, Library, Victorian, Mahogany, Felt Top, 2 Drawers, 30 x 72 x 36 In. 1700.00
Table, Library, Walnut, Marble Top, White, 30 x 30 In. 275.00
Table, Limbert, No. 148, Circular Top, Splayed Legs, Wide Cross Stretchers, 30 x 29 In. . 5750.00
Table, Limbert, Oak, Oval, Splined Top, Splay Ends, 29 x 45 x 30 In. 3220.00
Table, Limbert, Trestle, Shelf, Slab Sides, Through Tenon, 50 x 28 x 29 In. 2990.00
Table, Limbert, Vertical Lower Stretcher, Rectangular Cutouts, Round Top, 30 x 29 In. . . . 3335.00
Table, Limed Oak, Patinated Bronze, G. Y. Gastou, c.1952, 25 1/2 x 23 1/2 In. 4480.00
Table, Louis Philippe, Mahogany, Tripod, Haunched Paw Feet, c.1835, 31 x 39 1/2 In. . . . 2185.00
Table, Louis XV Style, Gilt Bronze Mounted, Marble Top, 28 x 23 x 14 1/2 In. 530.00
Table, Louis XV Style, Kingwood, 3 Frieze Drawers, 30 x 46 x 24 1/2 In. 840.00
Table, Louis XV Style, Kingwood, Drawers, Gilt Bronze Mounted, 29 x 48 x 34 In. 1645.00
Table, Louis XV Style, Kingwood, Gilt Bronze, Paw Feet, c.1920, 29 x 18 x 18 In. 260.00
Table, Louis XV Style, Mahogany, Bronze Mounted, Leather, Drawers, 30 x 45 x 25 In. . . 775.00
Table, Louis XV Style, Mahogany, Gilt Bronze Mounted, 31 x 69 x 38 In. 4780.00
Table, Louis XV Style, Marble Top, Kidney Shape, 3 Drawers, 29 x 24 x 14 In. 720.00
Table, Louis XV Style, Oak, Cabriole Legs, 20th Century, 27 x 22 x 9 In., Pair 765.00
Table, Louis XV Style, Parquetry, Oak, 2 Draw Leaves, 1900s, 29 1/2 x 43 x 57 In. 1410.00
Table, Louis XV Style, Serpentine, Drawer, Cabriole Legs, Stencil, 15 x 27 In., Pair 635.00
Table, Louis XV Style, Tulipwood, Bronze Mounting, 30 1/2 x 14 x 14 In., Pair 489.00
Table, Louis XV Style, Tulipwood, Gilt Bronze, Porcelain Mounted, 28 x 23 x 17 In. 645.00
Table, Louis XV Style, Tulipwood, Marble Top, Gilt Bronze, 20 x 24 x 19 In. 705.00
Table, Louis XV/XVI Style, Tulipwood, Marble Top, Kidney Shape, 26 x 25 x 12 In. 410.00
Table, Louis XVI Style, Giltwood, 27 1/2 x 24 In. 2300.00
Table, Louis XVI Style, Giltwood, Marble Top, Carved Frieze, 38 x 56 x 28 In. 980.00
Table, Louis XVI Style, Giltwood, Marble Top, Mid 19th Century, 31 x 31 x 19 In. 1495.00
Table, Louis XVI Style, Giltwood, Marble Top, Oval, c.1910, 30 x 30 1/2 x 22 In. 520.00
Table, Louis XVI Style, Mahogany, Brass Banded, c.1900, 30 x 21 x 20 3/4 In. 2070.00
Table, Louis XVI Style, Mahogany, Marble Top, Brass Gallery, c.1910, 30 x 20 In. 690.00
Table, Louis XVI Style, Mahogany, Marble Top, Early 1800s, 31 1/2 x 40 x 22 In. 2070.00
Table, Louis XVI Style, Mahogany, Ormolu, Octagonal, 29 x 21 x 16 1/2 In., Pair 1150.00
Table, Louis XVI Style, Mahogany, Red Marble Top, Bronze Mounted, 28 x 29 In. 1600.00
Table, Louis XVI Style, Mahogany, Round, Early 1900s, 28 1/2 x 24 1/2 In., Pair 1495.00
Table, Louis XVI Style, Tulipwood, Marquetry, Leather Surface, Drawer, 42 x 32 In. 460.00
Table, Louis XVI Style, Tulipwood, Parquetry, Gilt Bronze Mounted, 31 x 43 x 26 In. . . . 3820.00
Table, Magazine, Risom, Walnut, c.1949, 17 1/2 x 25 x 18 In. 2460.00
Table, Magazine, Wormley, Dunbar, c.1948, 25 x 22 In. 1765.00
Table, Mahogany, Basket-Weave Top, 24 x 25 x 26 In. 175.00
Table, Mahogany, Bowfront Frieze, Drawer, Oval Top, Trestle Base, 27 x 30 In. 440.00
Table, Mahogany, Bowfront, Drexel, 28 1/2 x 22 x 16 In. 69.00
Table, Mahogany, Demilune, Tapered Feet, c.1810, 29 x 20 x 41 In. 895.00
Table, Mahogany, Drawer, Frame Molded Top, Drawer Pulls, 27 x 22 x 16 In. 330.00
Table, Mahogany, Drawer, Mushroom Drawer Pulls, Turned Legs, 27 x 22 x 16 In. 335.00
Table, Mahogany, Federal, Hairy Paw, Platform Base, 28 1/2 x 36 x 21 In. 615.00
Table, Mahogany, Hinged, Swing Top, 2 Drawers, Serpentine Front, 29 x 22 x 15 In. 230.00
Table, Mahogany, Lift Top, Cock-Beaded Drawers, Brass Mounts, 28 1/2 x 18 x 14 In. . . . 825.00
Table, Mahogany, Maple, New England, c.1820, 33 3/4 x 32 x 20 In. 885.00
Table, Mahogany, Marble Top, 3 Leopards' Heads Pedestal, 38 1/2 x 22 1/2 In., Pair 345.00
Table, Mahogany, Marble Top, Brass Banding, France, 28 1/4 x 34 x 18 In., Pair 1495.00
Table, Mahogany, Medallion, Line Inlay, Oval Top, 4 Cuffed Legs, X-Stretcher, Finial . . . 225.00
Table, Mahogany, Pietra Dura Marble Top, American, c.1880, 31 x 25 In. 3290.00
Table, Mahogany, Round Piecrust Top, Carved Pedestal, 28 x 30 1/2 In. 345.00
Table, Mahogany, Scalloped Top, Tripod, Cabriole Legs, 28 x 18 x 22 In. 290.00
Table, Mahogany, Shell Border, Carved Urn Pedestal, 1900s, 27 x 24 In. 565.00
Table, Mahogany, Split Pedestal Base, 6 Leaves, c.1885, 29 x 59 x 60 In. 3910.00
Table, Mahogany, Top Gallery, Platform Stretcher, 1900s, 26 1/2 x 15 x 20 In., Pair 175.00
Table, Mahogany, Turned Pedestal, Tripod Base, Snake Feet, 27 1/2 x 28 In. 1090.00
Table, Majorelle, Marquetry Top, Flowers, Shelf, Triangular, 3 Legs, 28 x 30 In. 3450.00
Table, Maple, Pine, Overhang Top, Early 1700s, 25 1/2 x 24 1/2 x 19 3/4 In. 10000.00
Table, Marble Top, Serpentine Marble Top, 30 x 51 x 35 In. 385.00
Table, Marble Turtle Top, Finger Carved Apron, Shaped Scrolled Legs, X-Stretcher 365.00

Table, McCobb, No. 7014, Wedge, Mahogany, Calvin, 24 x 20 In. 200.00
Table, Mies Van Der Rohe, Barcelona, Square Glass Top, Steel Frame, Knoll, 17 x 40 In. . 880.00
Table, Mirror, Wood, Carved, Marble Top, 2 Sections, 82 x 45 1/2 x 13 In. 405.00
Table, Mixed Wood, Inlaid, Octagonal, 1910-1930 . . . . 2800.00
Table, Napoleon III, Beechwood, Cream Paint, Parcel Gilt, c.1860, 30 x 51 x 27 In., Pair . 3910.00
Table, Napoleon III, Mahogany, Circular, Gilt Bronze Mounts, c.1865, 30 x 37 In. 1495.00
Table, Napoleon III, Mahogany, Kingwood, Marble Top, 2 Drawers, c.1865, 30 x 22 In. . . 980.00
Table, Napoleon III, Marble Top, Pierced Gallery, Fluted Legs, Early 1900s, 32 x 10 In. . . 230.00
Table, Napoleon III, Red Lacquer, Mid 19th Century, 27 x 17 x 11 In. 1495.00
Table, Neoclassical, Alabaster, Cartouche Shape, Shelf Stretcher, 29 In. 360.00
Table, Neoclassical, Burl Walnut, Drawer, Continental, c.1800, 28 1/2 x 25 1/2 In. 2300.00
Table, Neoclassical, Drop Leaf, Mahogany, Drawers, American, c.1825, 29 x 23 x 44 In. . 1495.00
Table, Neoclassical, Fruitwood, Gilt Bronze Mount, Inset Marble, 37 x 29 x 21 In., Pair . 2350.00
Table, Neoclassical, Mahogany, 2 Drawers, American, c.1830, 29 x 21 1/2 x 16 1/2 In. . . . 1035.00
Table, Neoclassical, Mahogany, Frieze Drawers, Oval, Dutch, Early 1800s, 30 x 43 In. . . . 1495.00
Table, Neoclassical, Mahogany, Inlaid, Verde Eglomise Mounted, 31 x 24 x 15 In. 700.00
Table, Neoclassical, Mahogany, Marble Top, Drawer, c.1835, 37 x 30 x 18 In. 4600.00
Table, Neoclassical, Mahogany, Rosewood Banding, Mid 1800s, 30 x 19 x 13 In. 1265.00
Table, Neoclassical, Mahogany, Round, 4-Sided Base, c.1845, 29 x 26 In. 175.00
Table, Neoclassical, Pietra Dura Marble, Bronze, Gallery, 31 1/2 x 30 In. 1175.00
Table, Nesting, George III Style, Mahogany, Inlaid, 1900s, 26 x 20 1/2 In., 3 Piece 235.00
Table, Nesting, Majorelle, Flowers & Leaves Inlay, 30 To 16 In., 4 Piece 2590.00
Table, Nesting, Murano Glass, Wrought Iron Base, 12 1/2 x 12 1/2 x 16 In., 3 Piece 690.00
Table, Nesting, Oak, Cube, 16 3/4 x 15 3/4 x 15 3/4 In., 3 Piece 60.00
Table, Nesting, Robsjohn-Gibbings, Mahogany, Widdicomb, 24 x 26 In., 3 Piece 880.00
Table, Nesting, Rosewood, Chinese, 28 x 19 x 13 3/4 In., Pair 130.00
Table, Nesting, Rosewood, Chinese, Early 20th Century, 2 Piece . . . . *Illus* 700.00
Table, Nesting, Teak, Square, Tapered Dowel Legs, Denmark, 16 x 18 In., 4 Piece 230.00
Table, Oak Parquetry, Bulbous Pedestals, France, 29 x 39 x 110 In. 1095.00
Table, Oak, Cylindrical, Toby, 29 x 40 In. 1095.00
Table, Oak, Gateleg, Folding, 3 Turned Legs, England, c.1710, 27 x 30 In. 805.00
Table, Oak, Octagonal, 28 x 20 x 20 In. 1035.00
Table, Oak, Parquetry, Draw Leaf, Continental, c.1865, 29 1/2 x 39 x 78 In. 1495.00
Table, Oak, Rectangular Top, Frieze, Box Stretcher, 28 x 32 x 19 1/2 In. 865.00
Table, Oak, Round, 3 Leaves, Octagonal Pedestal Supports, 30 x 50 In. 430.00
Table, Oriental, Carved, Red Marble Insert, Vines, Flowers, Claw Feet, 32 x 21 In. 430.00
Table, Oriental, Mahogany, Glass Top, Round, Carved Battle Scene, 29 x 18 1/2 In. 340.00
Table, Oriental, Teak, Hexagonal Top, Greek Key Edge, 6 Legs, 27 x 32 x 28 In. 400.00
Table, P. Frankl, Mahogany, 2 Ebonized Wood Shelves, Brown Saltman, 21 x 27 In. 1530.00
Table, Painted, Decorated, Scrub Top, Blue Green Legs, 19th Century, 29 x 34 x 22 In. . . . 300.00
Table, Papier-Mache, Mother-Of-Pearl Inlay, Cast Iron Feet, 27 x 26 x 21 In. 410.00
Table, Paul Laszlo, Step, Mahogany, Brown Saltman, California, 21 x 28 x 24 1/4 In. 460.00
Table, Pembroke, Federal, Cherry, c.1815, 25 3/4 x 20 1/2 x 23 3/4 In. 315.00
Table, Pembroke, Federal, Cherry, Drawer, Early 1800s, 28 1/2 x 20 1/2 x 30 1/2 In. 720.00
Table, Pembroke, Federal, Cherry, Drawer, New England, c.1800, 28 1/2 x 33 1/2 In. 880.00
Table, Pembroke, Federal, Cherry, Drawer, Square Legs, Early 1800s, 28 x 20 x 30 In. . . . 359.00
Table, Pembroke, Federal, Mahogany, c.1810, 27 x 41 x 26 In. 6575.00
Table, Pembroke, Federal, Mahogany, Demilune Leaves, Drawer, c.1795, 27 x 20 In. 16730.00
Table, Pembroke, Federal, Mahogany, Inlaid, Drawer, c.1790, 27 1/2 x 29 In. 2940.00
Table, Pembroke, Federal, Maple, Figured, c.1820, 28 x 26 x 41 In. 3825.00
Table, Pembroke, Federal, Satinwood, Inlaid Walnut, c.1800, 29 x 21 x 32 1/4 In. 345.00
Table, Pembroke, George III Style, Mahogany, Inlaid, c.1835, 27 x 18 x 32 In. 635.00
Table, Pembroke, George III, Harewood, Satinwood Inlay, c.1790, 28 x 17 x 22 In. 3450.00
Table, Pembroke, George III, Mahogany, Drawer, Square Legs, c.1800, 28 x 34 1/2 In. . . . 1380.00
Table, Pembroke, George III, Mahogany, Inlaid Satinwood, 28 x 30 1/2 x 19 In. 6900.00
Table, Pembroke, George III, Satinwood, Crossbanded, c.1790, 28 x 32 x 38 In. 3175.00
Table, Pembroke, George III, Satinwood, Hardwood, Inlay, c.1790, 27 x 20 x 30 In. 6900.00
Table, Pembroke, George III, Satinwood, Inlaid Mahogany, c.1800, 27 x 20 1/2 In. 635.00
Table, Pembroke, George IV, Mahogany, Drawer, c.1840, 25 x 20 1/2 x 36 In. 865.00
Table, Pembroke, Hepplewhite, Checkerboard Inlay, American, 28 1/2 x 33 x 44 In. 5175.00
Table, Pembroke, Hepplewhite, Cherry, 10-In. Leaves, 29 1/2 x 34 1/2 x 18 In. 635.00
Table, Pembroke, Hepplewhite, Cherry, Beaded Drawers, American, 29 x 31 1/4 In. 9200.00
Table, Pembroke, Hepplewhite, Mahogany, Barber Pole Inlay, 28 3/4 x 34 In. 2185.00

Furniture, Table, Nesting, Rosewood, Chinese,
Early 20th Century, 2 Piece

Furniture, Table, Rococo Revival, Rosewood,
Marble Top, Pierced, c.1855, 30 x 44 In.

Table, Pembroke, Hepplewhite, Mahogany, Bird's-Eye Maple, 28 x 33 x 20 In.	3795.00
Table, Pembroke, Hepplewhite, Mahogany, Inlaid, Bow Ends, 32 x 39 In.	9315.00
Table, Pembroke, Hepplewhite, Mahogany, X-Stretcher, 28 x 36 x 19 In.	750.00
Table, Pembroke, Hepplewhite, Maple, Drawer, American, c.1790, 27 x 36 In.	865.00
Table, Pembroke, Hepplewhite, Walnut, Drawer, Boxwood Beaded Edge, 30 1/2 In.	620.00
Table, Pembroke, Mahogany, Bowed Ends, 28 3/4 x 30 x 19 In.	1295.00
Table, Pembroke, Mahogany, Drawer, American, 12-In. Leaves, c.1810, 27 x 46 1/2 In. . .	1440.00
Table, Pembroke, Mahogany, Drawer, England, c.1800, 28 1/2 x 19 1/2 x 33 In.	560.00
Table, Pembroke, Mahogany, Drawer, Ring-Turned Legs, c.1825, 29 x 36 x 23 In.	2185.00
Table, Pembroke, Mahogany, Drawer, Tapered Legs, Brass, Late 1700s, 28 x 30 In.	1265.00
Table, Pembroke, Mahogany, Geometric Band Inlay, Drawer, 28 1/2 x 19 x 35 1/2 In.	415.00
Table, Pembroke, Neoclassical, Mahogany, Drawer, 29 x 38 x 19 1/2 In.	805.00
Table, Pembroke, Regency, Mahogany, 2 End Drawers, c.1815, 28 1/2 x 36 In.	1840.00
Table, Pembroke, Serpentine Top, Drawer, Tapered Legs, 28 x 36 x 16 In.	800.00
Table, Pembroke, Sheraton Style, Mahogany, Satinwood Inlay, 28 x 34 x 21 1/4 In.	400.00
Table, Pembroke, Sheraton, Mahogany, Drawer, 12-In. Leaves, American, 28 x 39 In.	920.00
Table, Pembroke, Sheraton, Mahogany, Drawer, 29 1/2 x 38 x 24 In.	805.00
Table, Pembroke, Sheraton, Mahogany, Drawer, Sham Drawers, N.Y., 26 3/4 x 34 In.	1725.00
Table, Pembroke, Sheraton, Mahogany, Drawers, c.1820, 28 x 22 1/4 x 36 In.	4600.00
Table, Pembroke, Sheraton, Mahogany, Drawers, Scalloped Leaves, 32 x 20 In.	1380.00
Table, Pembroke, Sheraton, Mahogany, Inlaid, Square Leaves, Mass., 28 1/2 x 36 In.	5750.00
Table, Pembroke, Tapered Legs, Drawer, Cross Stretcher, 27 1/2 x 36 1/2 x 32 In.	900.00
Table, Pembroke, Walnut, 2 Drawers, American, c.1845, 39 1/2 x 20 1/2 In.	405.00
Table, Pembroke, Walnut, Inlaid Skirt, X-Stretcher, c.1820, 29 1/2 x 36 1/2 x 17 1/2 In. . .	310.00
Table, Pembroke, Yew, Crossbanded, Short Drawers, Chamfered Legs, 37 In.	3670.00
Table, Pennsylvania Dutch, Red Stain, Hex Symbol, c.1860, 30 x 40 x 34 In.	1345.00
Table, Philippe Starck, Driade, Cast Aluminum, Glass, c.1989, 22 x 27 In.	820.00
Table, Phillip LaVerne, Bronze, Pewter, Sculpted, Chinoiserie Design, 41 x 31 In.	2990.00
Table, Pier, Louis XVI Style, Parcel Gilt, Painted, White Marble, 32 x 51 x 25 In.	1725.00
Table, Pier, Neoclassical, Mahogany, Marble Top, American, c.1890, 37 x 38 In.	1955.00
Table, Pier, Neoclassical, Mahogany, Marble Top, c.1830, 35 x 42 x 17 In., Pair	35850.00
Table, Pier, Neoclassical, Mahogany, Ormolu Mount, Early 1800s, 36 x 40 x 17 In.	2070.00
Table, Pierced Supports, Shaped, Iron Stretchers, Spain, 31 x 82 x 38 In.	1150.00
Table, Pine Slab, Poplar Top, Birch Legs, 29 x 30 x 30 In.	165.00
Table, Pine Top, Walnut, Overhanging, Cabriole Legs, 3 Drawers, 29 x 60 x 32 In.	1265.00
Table, Pine, 2-Board Top, Tapered Legs, 28 x 29 x 19 In.	45.00
Table, Pine, 4-Board Top, Log Legs, Stretcher, 29 x 72 x 26 In.	330.00
Table, Pine, Oak Legs, Round, Tongue & Groove Top, 28 1/2 x 39 In.	100.00
Table, Pine, Painted, Short Drawers, Stretchers, Early 1900s, 27 x 38 x 24 In.	105.00
Table, Pine, Red Brown Wash, Arched Cutouts, 3-Board Top, 48 x 35 x 28 In.	2200.00
Table, Pine, Red Paint, Turned Legs, 29 x 42 x 41 In.	110.00
Table, Pine, Stripped, 5 Drawers, 2 Tiers, Continental, 29 x 35 x 25 1/2 In.	260.00
Table, Plate Glass Top, Round, Pink Hand Base, 30 x 40 In.	1035.00
Table, Poplar Top, Pine Slab Skirt, Birch Legs, 29 x 30 x 30 In.	170.00
Table, Poplar, Grain Painted, Overhanging Top, Swelled Legs, 1830, 30 1/2 In.	1530.00
Table, Poplar, Green Paint, Arched Base Cutouts, 40 x 31 x 28 3/4 In.	1150.00

Table, Prestini, Turned Wood, Steel, c.1946, 15 1/2 x 20 1/2 In. 5875.00
Table, Queen Anne, Mahogany, Gateleg, Beaded Apron, Reeded Edges, 29 1/2 x 40 In. . . 865.00
Table, Queen Anne, Walnut, Frieze Drawers, Round Legs, Pad Feet, 27 x 28 x 14 In. 440.00
Table, Queen Anne, Walnut, Turned Feet, Stretcher Base, 48 x 29 1/2 x 27 In. 165.00
Table, Rectangular, Chinese, c.1890, 29 1/2 x 82 1/2 x 31 In. 400.00
Table, Red, White Paint, 2-Board Top, Dovetailed Skirt, 27 1/2 x 42 x 29 In. 400.00
Table, Reeded Cloud Apron, Chinese, 1800s, 33 x 85 x 25 In. 1035.00
Table, Refectory, Baroque, Oak, Draw Leaf, Bulbous Legs, Continental, 29 1/2 x 47 In. . . 1840.00
Table, Refectory, Elizabethan Style, Oak, Late 1800s, 70 x 20 1/2 x 29 In. 590.00
Table, Refectory, Oak, Oblong Plank Top, Continental, c.1885, 28 1/2 x 84 In. 1150.00
Table, Refectory, Tudor Style, Oak, Arched Supports, Stepped Feet, 84 x 30 In. 230.00
Table, Refectory, Walnut, Bulbous Turned Legs, France, c.1750, 31 x 66 In. 7190.00
Table, Refectory, Walnut, Polychromed Wood, Italy, c.1900, 31 x 84 x 36 In. 3910.00
Table, Regency Style, Mahogany, 2 Pedestals, 30 x 114 x 51 1/2 In. 3100.00
Table, Regency Style, Mahogany, 3 Pedestals, D-Ends, England, 29 1/2 x 47 In. 6040.00
Table, Regency Style, Mahogany, 4 Tiers, Lazy Susan, Drawers, 54 x 36 In. 5520.00
Table, Regency Style, Mahogany, Horseshoe, 5 Extension Leaves, 30 x 62 1/2 In. 1955.00
Table, Regency Style, Mahogany, Inlaid, Round, 28 x 21 In., Pair 520.00
Table, Regency Style, Mahogany, Late 19th Century, 27 1/2 x 23 In. 635.00
Table, Regency Style, Mahogany, Parcel Gilt, 2 Pedestals, 1900s, 28 3/4 x 75 1/2 In. 4405.00
Table, Regency Style, Mahogany, Round, 31 1/2 x 36 In. 1535.00
Table, Regency, Faux Rosewood, Marble Top, Paw Feet, Mid 1800s, 30 x 17 In. 2760.00
Table, Regency, Mahogany Inlay, Splayed Legs, c.1820, 28 1/2 x 19 1/2 x 12 In. 940.00
Table, Regency, Mahogany, 4 Scrolling Supports, Early 1800s, 37 1/2 x 78 x 27 In. 4140.00
Table, Regency, Mahogany, Hidden Drawers, c.1900, 26 1/4 x 19 x 13 In., Pair 201.00
Table, Regency, Mahogany, Panel Standard, Paw Feet, 19th Century, 29 1/2 x 71 In. 11500.00
Table, Regency, Rosewood, Mahogany, Pedestal, 3 Lion Feet, c.1815, 28 3/4 x 52 In. 3220.00
Table, Renaissance Revival, Burl Panels, Marble Top, Turned Legs, 31 x 42 x 26 In. 1870.00
Table, Renaissance Revival, Burl Walnut, Marble Top, c.1865, 28 1/2 x 38 1/2 In. 1265.00
Table, Renaissance Revival, Walnut, Inset Marble Top, c.1870, 29 1/2 x 39 x 23 In. 750.00
Table, Renaissance Revival, Walnut, Marble Top, American, c.1875, 28 1/2 x 30 x 21 In. . 290.00
Table, Renaissance, Oak, Lion Masks, Dolphin Feet, Late 1800s, 30 x 48 x 40 In. 1725.00
Table, Renaissance, Oak, Round, Carved, Mid 1800s, 28 1/2 x 42 In. 1035.00
Table, Restauration Style, Mahogany, Marble Top, c.1900, 17 1/2 x 26 x 17 3/4 In. 1265.00
Table, Restauration, Mahogany, Marble Top, Plinth Shelf, Tripodal, c.1865, 29 x 26 In. . . 1955.00
Table, Restauration, Mahogany, Marble Top, Reeded Vase Standard, 29 x 38 In. 2530.00
Table, Restauration, Mahogany, Marble Top, Round, Frieze, 3 Legs, 29 1/2 x 35 1/2 In. . . 2070.00
Table, Richard Schultz, Petal, White Enameled, Octagonal, Pedestal, 19 x 16 In. 4600.00
Table, Risom, Walnut, Rectangular, Tapered Ends, 96 x 42 x 30 In. 635.00
Table, Robsjohn-Gibbings, Mahogany, 2 Tiers, Widdicomb, 30 x 18 x 20 In. 345.00
Table, Robsjohn-Gibbings, No. 1764, Mahogany, Widdicomb, 1952, 48 x 29 In. 3740.00
Table, Rococo Revival, Rosewood, Marble Top, Pierced, c.1855, 30 x 44 In. . . . . *Illus* 6575.00
Table, Rococo, Mahogany, Square Top, Shaped Frieze, 23 x 23 1/2 In. 120.00
Table, Rococo, Rosewood, Marble Turtle Top, c.1855, 29 1/2 x 51 1/2 x 26 In. 3450.00
Table, Rohde, Cloud, Biomorphic Glass, Wood Legs, Herman Miller, 27 x 21 x 26 In. 1495.00
Table, Rohde, Maidou, Mahogany Patchwork Top, 2 Leaves, Herman Miller, 72 x 30 In. . 6900.00
Table, Rohde, Paldao, Biomorphic, 3 Legs, Herman Miller, 27 x 27 x 21 1/2 In. 1495.00
Table, Rosewood, Archaic Designs, Rectangular, Chinese, c.1900, 36 x 14 1/2 x 60 In. . . . 590.00
Table, Rosewood, Gilt Mounted, Turned Pedestal, Round, Tripod Base, 25 x 14 In. 745.00
Table, Rosewood, Marble Top, Rectangular, Chinese, 19 1/4 x 16 x 12 In., Pair 500.00
Table, Rosewood, Marble Turtle Top, 19th Century, 52 x 26 x 29 In. 2415.00
Table, Rosewood, Removable Tray Top, Royal Copenhagen Tiles, 19 x 20 x 15 In. 320.00
Table, Roycroft, Oak, Flared Legs, Seahorse Keys, Octagonal, c.1920, 28 x 42 In. 1035.00
Table, Sawbuck, Pin, Nail Construction, Cross Stretcher, Dovetailed, 41 x 24 In. 1725.00
Table, Scrubbed Lift Top, Compartment, Yellow Grained, 52 1/2 x 36 In. 790.00
Table, Sewing, 2-Board Top, 2 Doors, Beaded Legs, Chinese, 79 3/4 x 28 In. 495.00
Table, Sewing, Biedermeier, Fruitwood, Hinged Top, c.1825, 32 x 22 x 18 In. 1840.00
Table, Sewing, Bird's-Eye Maple, Drop Leaf, 2 Drawers, c.1820, 31 x 20 x 16 In. 410.00
Table, Sewing, Chinoiserie, Lacquer, Checkerboard Lift Top, 28 x 20 x 24 In. 750.00
Table, Sewing, Empire, Mahogany, Lift Top, Drawer, American, c.1845, 15 x 22 x 31 In. . 635.00
Table, Sewing, Federal, Mahogany, 2 Drawers, Pedestal, c.1820, 28 1/2 x 20 x 18 In. 590.00
Table, Sewing, Federal, Mahogany, 2 Drawers, Turned Legs, c.1827, 30 x 23 x 18 In. 5020.00
Table, Sewing, Federal, Mahogany, Veneer, Salem, c.1820, 30 x 20 x 16 1/2 In. 3525.00

Table, Sewing, Fruitwood, Marquetry, c.1845, 30 x 19 1/2 x 18 1/2 In. 560.00
Table, Sewing, George IV, Rosewood, Drop Leaf, 2 Drawers, c.1825, 30 1/2 x 19 In. 2070.00
Table, Sewing, George IV, Rosewood, Drop Leaf, c.1825, 30 1/2 x 15 1/2 x 19 In. 2070.00
Table, Sewing, Hepplewhite Style, Maple, Drawer, 25 x 17 x 14 In. 460.00
Table, Sewing, Inlaid Pattern, Lift Top, Cabriole Legs, 1880, 16 x 26 In. 315.00
Table, Sewing, Japanned, New England, c.1835, 29 x 24 x 20 In. 2875.00
Table, Sewing, Neoclassical, Mahogany, 2 Drawers, American, c.1835, 32 x 22 x 17 In. . . 260.00
Table, Sewing, Neoclassical, Mahogany, 2 Frieze Drawers, c.1835, 31 x 24 x 20 In. 690.00
Table, Sewing, Neoclassical, Mahogany, Carved, Drop Leaf, c.1825, 29 x 21 x 18 In. 2030.00
Table, Sewing, Neoclassical, Mahogany, Cherry, Mid 19th Century, 32 x 21 x 17 In. 575.00
Table, Sewing, Neoclassical, Mahogany, Drop Leaf, 2 Drawers, 29 3/4 x 20 In. 1150.00
Table, Sewing, Neoclassical, Mahogany, Inlaid, Red, White, Blue, 30 x 19 x 17 In. 2390.00
Table, Sewing, Neoclassical, Mahogany, Lift Top, American, c.1835, 33 x 25 In. 920.00
Table, Sewing, Neoclassical, Mahogany, Paw Feet, c.1900, 28 1/2 x 19 x 18 In. 460.00
Table, Sewing, Neoclassical, Maple, Mahogany, 3 Drawers, 29 x 20 x 16 In. 540.00
Table, Sewing, Regency, Mahogany, Drop Leaf, c.1835, 28 1/2 x 20 x 20 In. 9780.00
Table, Sewing, Regency, Mahogany, Octagonal, 29 x 17 In. 540.00
Table, Sewing, Shaker, Birch, Cherry, Pine, Drawer, New Lebanon, N.Y., c.1855, 28 In. . . 920.00
Table, Sewing, Shaker, Butternut, Pine, Dovetailed Drawers, 41 1/2 x 31 1/2 x 24 In. . . . 18400.00
Table, Sewing, Shaker, Cherry, 2-Board, Birch Legs, Wheels, 30 1/2 x 66 x 28 In. 6900.00
Table, Sewing, Shaker, Cherry, Butternut Drawer Front, Pittsfield, Mass., 29 x 20 In. 1955.00
Table, Sewing, Shaker, Cherry, Poplar, Pine, Drawer, c.1840, 29 x 28 x 21 1/2 In. 1495.00
Table, Sewing, Shaker, Maple, Birch, Drawer, Enfield, N.H., c.1830, 27 x 36 In. 6900.00
Table, Sewing, Shaker, Maple, Opposing Drawers, 27 1/4 x 17 x 23 1/4 In. 3450.00
Table, Sewing, Shaker, Maple, Walnut, Lift Top, Oval, Harvard, c.1860, 22 1/2 x 42 In. . . 4025.00
Table, Sewing, Shaker, Painted, Enfield, New Hampshire, c.1835 . . . . 12500.00
Table, Sewing, Shaker, Pine, Cherry, Birch, Pegged, c.1835, 26 x 42 In. 4600.00
Table, Sewing, Shaker, Pine, Maple, 2-Board Top, Drawer, N.H., c.1800, 29 x 45 In. 2875.00
Table, Sewing, Shaker, Red Painted Base, Scrubbed Top, Drawer, 30 x 37 3/4 x 22 In. . . . 2300.00
Table, Sewing, Sheraton, Bleached Mahogany, Drawer, American, 28 1/2 x 18 x 19 In. . . . 375.00
Table, Sewing, Sheraton, Cherry, Drawer, American, 28 1/2 x 18 1/2 x 20 1/2 In. 545.00
Table, Sewing, Sheraton, Cherry, Drop Leaf, 2 Drawers, American, 29 x 15 x 22 In. 520.00
Table, Sewing, Sheraton, Cherry, Maple, Drawers, Turned Legs, 28 x 18 1/2 x 18 1/2 In. . . 400.00
Table, Sewing, Sheraton, Mahogany, 2 Drawers, Turned Legs, 29 x 16 1/2 In. 750.00
Table, Sewing, Sheraton, Mahogany, Drop Leaf, 2 Drawers, American, 29 x 16 In. 460.00
Table, Sewing, Sheraton, Mahogany, Lift Top, Dividers, 28 1/2 x 15 1/2 x 22 1/2 In. 1240.00
Table, Sewing, Sheraton, Mahogany, Turned Legs, 2 Drawers, 29 x 17 1/2 x 17 In. 400.00
Table, Sewing, Sheraton, Pine, Drop Leaf, 2 Drawers, Pumpkin Pine Finish, 29 x 18 In. . . 210.00
Table, Sewing, Softwood, Red Paint, 1-Board Top, Turned Legs, 29 x 31 1/2 x 20 In. 470.00
Table, Sewing, Tiger Maple, Glass Drawer Pulls, 30 x 18 1/2 x 20 In. 750.00
Table, Sewing, Victorian, Rosewood, Drop Leaf, Drawer, c.1850, 27 x 22 1/2 x 22 In. . . . 345.00
Table, Sewing, Walnut, 2 Drawers, Brass Pulls, Basket Slide, 30 1/2 x 18 x 16 In. 290.00
Table, Sewing, Walnut, Long, Wood Bag Drawers, Victorian, 30 1/2 x 24 In. 575.00
Table, Sewing, Walnut, Molded Legs, Cross Brace, Marble Top, 30 x 31 x 18 In. 275.00
Table, Sewing, Wood, Whalebone & Ivory Fittings, Tambour Sides, 9 x 11 1/2 In. 460.00
Table, Shaker, Bittersweet Red Paint, 3-Board Top, 2 Drawers, 27 x 128 x 28 In. 3450.00
Table, Shaker, Butternut, Birch, Drop Leaf, N.H., 28 1/4 x 36 x 15 1/2 In. 1040.00
Table, Shaker, Pine, Square Top, Drawer, Squared Tapered Legs, c.1830, 26 x 17 In. 1410.00
Table, Shaker, Trestle, Cherry, 2-Board Top, Arched Feet, Harvard, Mass., 72 x 30 In. 4400.00
Table, Shaker, Walnut, Maple, Oak, Tilt Top, Tripod Base, Harvard, Mass., 25 x 36 In. . . . 5580.00
Table, Sheraton Style, Cherry, Mahogany, Banded Inlay, Reeded Legs, 30 x 33 In. 460.00
Table, Sheraton Style, Mahogany, 3 Pedestals, 2 Leaves, 1900s, 40 x 138 In. 1100.00
Table, Sheraton Style, Mahogany, Leather, Drawers, Late 1800s, 29 x 40 x 25 In. 690.00
Table, Sheraton, 2 Parts, D-Shaped Ends, Massachusetts, 29 1/2 x 84 In. 4600.00
Table, Sheraton, Mahogany, 2 Parts, Casters, 28 3/4 x 52 1/2 x 84 In. 2300.00
Table, Sheraton, Maple, Curly Maple, Drawer, Turned Legs, 32 x 21 x 29 In. 690.00
Table, Sheraton, Pine, Maple, Round Corners, Turned Legs, 28 1/2 x 38 1/2 x 38 In. 415.00
Table, Sheraton, Tiger Stripe & Bird's-Eye Maple, 2 Pine Drawers, Turned Legs, 28 In. . . 575.00
Table, Sheraton, Walnut, Drawer, c.1800, 32 x 29 x 20 In. 460.00
Table, Shop Of The Crafters, Cut Corner Top, Lower Shelf, Cutouts, 52 x 35 x 30 In. 1265.00
Table, Side, A. Girard, Marble, Aluminum, Herman Miller, 1967, 20 x 20 x 20 In. 1755.00
Table, Side, Baroque Style, Mahogany, Marquetry, X-Stretcher, 30 1/2 x 31 In. 1320.00
Table, Side, Cherry, 2 Drawers, Ball Feet, American, c.1825, 29 x 20 x 17 In. 520.00

Table, Side, Chippendale, 3 Drawers, Shaped Top, 35 x 48 In., Pair 1955.00
Table, Side, Cloud Apron, Demilune, Chinese, 1800s, 33 1/4 x 36 x 17 1/2 In. 750.00
Table, Side, Directoire Style, Mahogany, 29 x 16 1/2 x 9 In., Pair 840.00
Table, Side, Directoire, Mahogany, Marble Top, Cupboard, c.1800, 32 x 12 x 12 In. 635.00
Table, Side, Edwardian, Harewood, Fruitwood, Mahogany, c.1900, 28 1/2 x 16 x 12 In. ... 1295.00
Table, Side, Edwardian, Lacewood, Crossbanded, Drawer, c.1900, 26 x 20 x 14 In., Pair .. 2235.00
Table, Side, Empire Style, Gilt Bronze, Marble Top, 15 x 19 3/4 x 21 1/2 In., Pair 5675.00
Table, Side, Federal, Satinwood, Cherry Inlay, c.1800, 26 1/4 x 18 3/4 x 14 1/4 In. 1610.00
Table, Side, French Provincial, Open Cupboard, Fruitwood, Drawer, 1800s, 29 x 15 In. ... 345.00
Table, Side, George III, Mahogany, Demilune, c.1815, 28 x 46 x 22 1/2 In., Pair 1840.00
Table, Side, George III, Mahogany, Drawers, Late 1700s, 33 1/2 x 72 x 29 1/2 In. 4600.00
Table, Side, George III, Mahogany, Oblong, Dish Top, c.1800, 30 x 36 1/4 x 25 In. 3450.00
Table, Side, Georgian, Satinwood, Banded, Drawer, c.1815, 29 x 36 x 24 In. 1495.00
Table, Side, J. Adnet, Brass, Steel, France, 1950s, 21 x 10 1/2 x 22 In. 1170.00
Table, Side, J. Adnet, Glass, Leather Over Steel, Brass, France, 1950s, 17 1/2 x 20 In. .. 1520.00
Table, Side, J. Adnet, Leather, Steel, Brass, Parchment, France, 1950s, 21 x 18 In., Pair . 4390.00
Table, Side, Jacobean, Oak, 1600s, 27 1/2 x 35 1/2 x 20 In. 1175.00
Table, Side, Louis XV Style, Mahogany, Oval Top, Cane Sides, 25 1/2 x 23 1/2 In., Pair .. 239.00
Table, Side, Mahogany, Leather Inset, Art Deco, 26 1/2 x 26 In. 359.00
Table, Side, Mahogany, Marble Turtle Top, Shelf, 29 x 35 In. 759.00
Table, Side, Napoleon III, Mahogany, Bronze Mounted, 16 x 16 x 16 In. 149.00
Table, Side, Neoclassical, Beech, Parcel Gilt, Italy, Late 1700s, 37 x 31 In., Pair 6615.00
Table, Side, Neoclassical, Satinwood, Inlaid Mahogany, 30 x 30 x 18 In. 605.00
Table, Side, Neoclassical, Walnut, Mahogany, Star Inlay, Baltic, c.1835, 30 x 29 In. 2300.00
Table, Side, Oak, Bellflower, Acanthine Carving, 2 Drawers, Italy, c.1900, 36 x 60 In. ... 1725.00
Table, Side, Philip LaVerne, Bronze, Pewter, Chinoiserie, 1950s, 16 x 18 In., Pair 1840.00
Table, Side, Pine, Maple, Oval, Hinged Top, New England, 24 x 28 1/2 x 30 In. 5750.00
Table, Side, Queen Anne Style, Mahogany, Demilune Top, 29 x 42 In., Pair 1495.00
Table, Side, Regency Style, Mahogany, Fold-Out, c.1900, 31 x 62 1/2 x 19 1/2 In. 3220.00
Table, Side, Robsjohn-Gibbings, Bleached Mahogany, Rattan, Widdicomb, 24 In., Pair ... 2585.00
Table, Side, Rohde, Semicircular, Glass Shelf, 21 1/4 x 14 1/2 In. 2760.00
Table, Side, Saarinen, Tulip, White Laminate Top, Pedestal Base, Knoll, 20 1/2 x 20 In. .. 520.00
Table, Side, Tiger Birch, Drawer, Splayed Legs, 27 1/2 In. 145.00
Table, Side, V. Kagan, Triangular Glass Top, Walnut Base, 19 x 29 3/4 x 24 In. 865.00
Table, Side, V. Kagan, Walnut, Triangular Top, Tripod Pedestal Base, 21 x 24 In. 865.00
Table, Side, Walnut, Exotic Bird Inlay, Drawer, c.1870, 27 x 24 x 18 In. 10160.00
Table, Side, Walnut, Oak, Serpentine Shaped Leaves, Drawer, c.1760, 29 1/2 In. 1670.00
Table, Side, William & Mary Style, Oak, Frieze Drawers, 22 x 25 x 22 In. 295.00
Table, Side, Wormley, Round Glass Top, Steel Base, 27 1/2 x 40 In. 1150.00
Table, Side, Yellow Pine, Demilune, American, 27 x 34 x 17 1/2 In. 260.00
Table, Single Board Top, Pegged Construction, 18th Century, 48 x 29 In. 4900.00
Table, Slate Top, Deep Carved Apron, Shell Supports, Claw & Ball Feet, Ireland, 55 In. ... 3059.00
Table, Split Bamboo, Red Lacquer, Flowers, Chinese, 1800s, 22 x 63 x 23 In. 750.00
Table, Stickley Bros., 5 Exposed Through Tenon Legs, 4 Leaves, 30 x 54 In. 1900.00
Table, Stickley Bros., Splined Top, Exposed Through Tenon, 30 x 40 In. ....920.00 to 1210.00
Table, Sutherland, Mahogany, Marquetry, Leaves, 6 1/2 x 22 x 22 3/4 In. 695.00
Table, Tavern, 1-Board Oval Top, 4 Turned Legs, 24 x 31 x 23 In. 4715.00
Table, Tavern, 3-Board Top, Center Stretcher, Square Leg, 26 x 39 x 37 In. 315.00
Table, Tavern, Breadboard Ends, Scrub Top, Drawer, 27 3/4 x 45 1/2 x 30 1/2 In. 920.00
Table, Tavern, Chippendale, Maple, New England, 1760-1780, 25 x 24 1/2 x 29 1/2 In. ... 805.00
Table, Tavern, Elm, Box Stretcher, England, 1700s, 25 x 30 x 18 In. 940.00
Table, Tavern, Hepplewhite, Maple, Butternut, 2-Board Top, Drawer, 44 x 28 x 29 In. ... 2415.00
Table, Tavern, Indian Brown Paint, Drawer, Breadboard Ends, American, 26 1/2 x 37 In. . 1955.00
Table, Tavern, Maple, 2-Board Pine Top, Dovetailed Drawers, Stretcher Base, 47 x 30 In. . 750.00
Table, Tavern, Maple, Oval, Box Stretcher, 25 1/2 x 25 x 33 1/2 In. 920.00
Table, Tavern, Maple, Pine, 2-Board Top, 29 x 41 3/4 x 26 1/4 In. 550.00
Table, Tavern, Maple, Pine, Breadboard Top, Block, Vase & Ring-Turned Legs, 27 In. 2940.00
Table, Tavern, Maple, Pine, Drawer, Stretcher Base, Turned Legs, 1700, 25 In. 4880.00
Table, Tavern, Maple, Pine, Stretcher Base, Splay Legs, New England 2700.00
Table, Tavern, Pine, 2-Board Top, Breadboard, Stretcher, c.1800, 58 x 36 x 27 In. 1275.00
Table, Tavern, Pine, Other Woods, Breadboard Ends, Drawer, Button Feet 1265.00
Table, Tavern, Pine, Pegged Construction, Late 1700s, 29 1/2 x 19 1/2 x 26 In. 1350.00
Table, Tavern, Queen Anne, Birch, Pine, Drawer, Tapered Legs, 53 x 30 1/2 In. 1760.00

Table, Tavern, Queen Anne, Cherry, Walnut, Turned, Frieze Drawers, 29 x 53 x 36 In. . . . 1840.00
Table, Tavern, Queen Anne, Maple, Brown Over Red Paint, 27 3/4 x 17 1/2 x 26 In. 21850.00
Table, Tavern, Queen Anne, Maple, Painted, Oval, 25 3/4 x 32 x 25 In. 5175.00
Table, Tavern, Sheraton, Maple, Pine, 2-Board Top, Red Paint, 29 x 42 x 26 In. 560.00
Table, Tavern, Sheraton, Maple, Pine, 2-Board Top, Turned Leg, 29 x 41 3/4 x 26 In. 550.00
Table, Tavern, Tiger Maple, Drawer, Pegged Construction, c.1850, 28 x 29 1/2 x 23 In. . . 2130.00
Table, Tavern, Walnut, 3-Board Top, 3 Drawers, 60 x 38 x 28 In. 2250.00
Table, Tavern, Walnut, Drawer, Breadboard Ends, H-Stretcher, 27 3/4 x 28 1/2 In. 345.00
Table, Tavern, Walnut, Other Woods, Square Legs, 18th Century, 29 x 36 x 25 In. 750.00
Table, Tavern, Walnut, Pine, Stretcher, Drawer, 39 1/2 x 23 1/4 x 32 In. 770.00
Table, Tea, Black Over Red Wash, Tray Top, Slipper Feet, 31 1/2 x 21 1/2 In. 7700.00
Table, Tea, Chippendale Style Mahogany, Carved, X-Stretcher, 28 x 34 x 19 In. 805.00
Table, Tea, Chippendale Style, Mahogany, c.1940, 30 x 29 1/2 In. 400.00
Table, Tea, Chippendale Style, Mahogany, Piecrust Top, Birdcage, Colonial Mfg. 420.00
Table, Tea, Chippendale, Cherry, Tripod, 29 x 34 1/2 In. 480.00
Table, Tea, Chippendale, Mahogany, Carved, Piecrust, Spiral Post, Tripod Base, 29 In. . . . 2820.00
Table, Tea, Chippendale, Mahogany, Urn Pedestal, Pad Feet, 28 1/2 x 35 1/2 x 36 In. 415.00
Table, Tea, Federal, Cherry, Foldover, c.1810, 29 x 35 3/4 x 17 3/4 In. 2360.00
Table, Tea, Federal, Mahogany, Inlaid, Foldover, Serpentine, c.1800, 28 x 36 x 18 In. 2480.00
Table, Tea, French Provincial, Fruitwood, Drawer, 26 1/2 x 24 x 16 1/2 In. 690.00
Table, Tea, George III Style, Mahogany, Tripod Pedestal, Paw Feet, 30 x 30 In. 430.00
Table, Tea, George III, Mahogany, Fold Top, c.1750, 28 x 27 x 13 In. 1495.00
Table, Tea, George III, Mahogany, Inlaid, Foldover, c.1800, 29 1/2 x 36 x 17 1/2 In. 2125.00
Table, Tea, George III, Mahogany, Serpentine, Fold Top, c.1790, 28 1/2 x 36 x 18 In. 575.00
Table, Tea, George IV, Burl Elm, 4 Hinged Caddies, c.1820, 29 x 19 x 13 In. 635.00
Table, Tea, Georgian, Tilt Top, Mahogany, Carved, Piecrust Top, 29 x 22 1/2 In. 1645.00
Table, Tea, Hardwood, Octagonal Top, Tripod Base, Anglo-Indian, 29 x 29 In. 410.00
Table, Tea, Hepplewhite Style, Mahogany, Round Top, Kittinger, 24 3/4 x 16 1/4 In. 315.00
Table, Tea, L. & J.G. Stickley, No. 508, Round, Shelf, 24 1/2 x 24 In. 1725.00
Table, Tea, Queen Anne Style, Mahogany, Candle Slides, 28 x 18 x 25 1/2 In. 330.00
Table, Tea, Queen Anne Style, Mahogany, Flip Top, Hidden Drawers, c.1910, 16 x 30 In. . . 460.00
Table, Tea, Queen Anne Style, Mahogany, Gallery, Cup Rests, 1800s, 28 x 31 x 21 In. . . . 1645.00
Table, Tea, Queen Anne Style, Tiger Maple, Eldred Wheeler, 25 1/2 x 17 1/2 x 26 In. 520.00
Table, Tea, Queen Anne, Cedar, Tripod Base, Slipper Feet, 28 1/2 x 32 In. 635.00
Table, Tea, Queen Anne, Dish Top, Mahogany, Padded Slipper Feet, 24 1/2 x 28 3/4 In. . . 345.00
Table, Tea, Queen Anne, Maple, Red Paint, Drop Leaf, Cabriole Legs, Mass., 26 x 30 In. . 7050.00
Table, Tea, Queen Anne, Walnut, Rectangular Top, Drawer, 28 x 26 x 18 In. 480.00
Table, Tea, Regency, Mahogany, Pedestal Base, England, c.1810, 31 x 18 1/2 x 12 In. 980.00
Table, Tea, Regency, Rosewood, Tapered, 4 Canisters, 2 Wells, c.1825, 30 1/2 x 16 In. . . . 1115.00
Table, Tea, Scalloped Top, Cabriole Legs, Continental, c.1800, 29 1/2 x 40 1/2 In. 2875.00
Table, Tea, Tilt Top, Cherry, Dish Top, Birdcage, Tripod, American, c.1790, 29 x 36 In. . . . 1955.00
Table, Tea, Tilt Top, Chippendale, Mahogany, Round, New England, c.1780, 28 x 31 In. . . . 2235.00
Table, Tea, Tilt Top, Chippendale, Mahogany, Serpentine, Turned, Tripod, 29 x 31 In. 2705.00
Table, Tea, Tilt Top, Chippendale, Walnut, Tripod Cabriole Legs, Boston, 28 x 32 In. 10350.00
Table, Tea, Tilt Top, George III, Mahogany, Birdcage Mechanism, 29 x 27 In. 2070.00
Table, Tea, Tilt Top, Mahogany, 3-Footed Base, Snake Feet, 25 x 26 In. 500.00
Table, Tea, Tilt Top, Mahogany, Brass Latch, Late 1700s, 28 x 27 x 28 In. 935.00
Table, Tea, Tilt Top, Mahogany, Molded Top, Carved Corners, 28 1/2 x 35 1/2 x 36 In. . . . 1725.00
Table, Tea, Tilt Top, Queen Anne, Cherry, 29 x 30 1/2 In. 550.00
Table, Tea, Tilt Top, Queen Anne, Cherry, Cabriole Legs, Dutch Feet, 28 3/4 x 35 In. 748.00
Table, Tile Top, Enameled Iron Pedestal Base, 2 Ring Drink Holders, 24 x 15 In. 805.00
Table, Tilt Top, Cherry, Cut Corner Top, Turned Pedestal, Snake Feet, 26 1/2 x 33 1/2 In. . 600.00
Table, Tilt Top, Chippendale Style, Cherry, Tripod, American, 27 x 20 In. 240.00
Table, Tilt Top, Chippendale Style, Mahogany, Claw Feet, 29 x 32 In. 960.00
Table, Tilt Top, Chippendale Style, Mahogany, Inlaid, Tripod Base, 30 1/2 x 36 In. 470.00
Table, Tilt Top, Chippendale Style, Mahogany, Tripod Base, 27 x 20 x 27 In. 200.00
Table, Tilt Top, Chippendale, Mahogany, Birdcage Base, Snake Feet, 34 1/2 In. 1610.00
Table, Tilt Top, Chippendale, Mahogany, Tripod, Birdcage Support, 28 1/2 x 36 In. 825.00
Table, Tilt Top, Chippendale, Maple, Inlaid, Tripod, American, c.1810, 24 1/2 x 16 In. 770.00
Table, Tilt Top, Edwardian, Mahogany, Circular Top, Tripod, c.1850, 28 x 31 3/4 In. 920.00
Table, Tilt Top, Federal, Mahogany, Clover-Leaf Top, 3 Saber Legs, 28 3/4 x 25 In. 690.00
Table, Tilt Top, Federal, Mahogany, Inlaid, Serpentine, Tripod, c.1800, 28 x 20 In. 3940.00
Table, Tilt Top, Federal, Mahogany, Tripod, Early 1800s, 28 x 18 1/4 x 18 3/4 In. 1195.00

Table, Tilt Top, George II, Mahogany, Ebonized & Brass Bands, Paw Feet, 44 x 63 In. 5245.00
Table, Tilt Top, George III Style, Mahogany, Tripod, Late 1800s, 30 x 33 In. 1610.00
Table, Tilt Top, George III, Mahogany, Dish Top, Birdcage Support, Tripod, 28 x 23 In. .. 235.00
Table, Tilt Top, George III, Mahogany, Oval, Beehive Stem, Downswept Legs, 28 1/2 In. . 1645.00
Table, Tilt Top, George III, Mahogany, Oval, c.1800, 29 x 53 x 43 In. 520.00
Table, Tilt Top, George III, Mahogany, Round, Tripod Base, 30 In. 830.00
Table, Tilt Top, George III, Mahogany, Square, Tripod Base, 33 x 33 In. 2270.00
Table, Tilt Top, George III, Mahogany, Tripod, Late 18th Century, 28 1/2 x 33 1/2 In. ... 1035.00
Table, Tilt Top, George III, Oak, Tripod, Baluster Splat, Cabriole Legs, 29 x 27 x 26 In. ... 920.00
Table, Tilt Top, Georgian Style, Mahogany, Tripod Base, 27 1/2 x 32 1/2 In. 470.00
Table, Tilt Top, Mahogany, Dish Top, Tripod Base, England, 27 x 27 1/2 In. 1495.00
Table, Tilt Top, Mahogany, Inlaid Portraits Of Washington & Lafayette, 26 x 28 In. 4500.00
Table, Tilt Top, Mahogany, Marquetry, Continental, c.1850, 27 x 18 1/4 In. 1610.00
Table, Tilt Top, Mahogany, Pedestal, Spider Legs, Slipper Feet, 1700s, 28 x 24 In. 775.00
Table, Tilt Top, Mahogany, Turned Pedestal, Oval, England, 54 x 42 In. 230.00
Table, Tilt Top, Maple, Tiger Maple, Turned Pedestal, Tripod, 29 1/2 x 32 x 33 1/2 In. .. 2300.00
Table, Tilt Top, Marble, Maiden Heads, Claw Feet, 31 In. 8625.00
Table, Tilt Top, Neoclassical, Rosewood, Giltwood, Ormolu, 28 1/4 x 23 In. 4315.00
Table, Tilt Top, Papier-Mache, Black Lacquer, Round, c.1850, 27 1/2 x 24 1/2 In. 3740.00
Table, Tilt Top, Papier-Mache, Oval, Scalloped Edge, Painted Flowers, Pedestal, 27 In. .. 525.00
Table, Tilt Top, Pine, Blue & Bittersweet Paint, Fancy Raised Edge, Tripod, c.1800s 330.00
Table, Tilt Top, Queen Anne, Gateleg, Oblong, Drawer, c.1715, 32 x 80 x 50 In. 1150.00
Table, Tilt Top, Regency, Mahogany, 4 Reeded Splayed Legs, c.1815, 30 1/2 x 48 In. 3450.00
Table, Tilt Top, Regency, Mahogany, Banded, England, c.1815, 27 x 42 In. 2300.00
Table, Tilt Top, Regency, Mahogany, Paw Feet, Casters, Early 1800s, 29 1/2 x 40 1/2 In. . 920.00
Table, Tilt Top, Regency, Mahogany, Round, 3 Feet, c.1815, 29 x 45 3/4 In. 3220.00
Table, Tilt Top, Regency, Mahogany, Round, Pedestal, c.1815, 28 1/2 x 47 In. 1725.00
Table, Tilt Top, Sheraton, Mahogany, Saber Legs, Paw Feet, 52 x 39 x 38 In. 2860.00
Table, Tilt Top, Victorian, Mahogany, Scalloped Edge, Pedestal Base, 28 x 32 x 26 In. ... 615.00
Table, Tilt Top, William IV, Mahogany, c.1835, 28 1/2 x 57 x 44 In. 2300.00
Table, Tray, George III Style, Mahogany, Arched Frieze, 28 1/2 x 22 x 16 In. 400.00
Table, Tray, George III, Mahogany, Folding, c.1800, 30 1/2 x 21 In. 520.00
Table, Tray, George III, Mahogany, Stand, c.1800, 17 x 35 x 26 In. 805.00
Table, Tray, Papier-Mache, Black Lacquer, Folding, Early 1900s, 31 x 24 In. 865.00
Table, Tray, Queen Anne Style, Mahogany, Painted Top, c.1900, 20 x 23 x 16 In. 320.00
Table, Tray, Victorian, Mahogany, 19th Century, 19 x 38 x 44 In. 1175.00
Table, Tray, Victorian, Mahogany, Carrying Handles, 17 x 30 x 21 In. 470.00
Table, Trestle, G. Stickley, No. 424, Overhang Top, Cross Stretcher, 29 1/2 x 40 x 28 In. . 3165.00
Table, Trestle, Pine, Mortised, Scalloped, 3-Board Top, Essex, Mass., 64 x 34 In. 575.00
Table, Trestle, Walnut, Spindled Gallery, Runner Feet, Italy, c.1710, 31 x 43 In. 2990.00
Table, V. Kagan, Walnut, Frosted Glass Top, Kidney Shape, 15 x 49 x 32 In. 1495.00
Table, V. Panton, Cone, Black Laminate Top, 3-Point Base, Plus-Linje, 32 x 16 In. 750.00
Table, V. Panton, Wire, Lacquered Wood, X-Design, Denmark, 1970s, 36 x 18 In. 940.00
Table, Victorian, Black Lacquer, Figural Landscape, Mid 19th Century, 28 x 19 1/2 In. 805.00
Table, Victorian, Black Walnut, Marble Top, Urn Center Finial, 30 1/2 x 30 x 21 1/2 In. .. 365.00
Table, Victorian, Cast Iron, Round Marble Top, Brass Bound, Late 1800s, 28 x 20 In. 290.00
Table, Victorian, Eastlake, Rectangular, 4 Flat Carved Legs, 28 x 28 x 19 In. 90.00
Table, Victorian, Lacquered, Stylized Flower, Shelf, Bamboo Turnings, 29 x 20 In. 115.00
Table, Victorian, Mahogany, c.1850, 29 x 31 x 17 1/2 In. 920.00
Table, Victorian, Mahogany, Demilune, Carved Lion Heads & Feet, 24 x 28 In. 259.00
Table, Victorian, Mahogany, Serpentine Sides, Fruit, Leaf Border, 28 x 55 x 39 In. 1530.00
Table, Victorian, Marble Top, Oval, Carved Knees, Apron, c.1860, 28 1/2 x 38 x 26 In. .. 1725.00
Table, Victorian, Walnut, Marble Top, 4 Flat Cut Legs, 29 x 21 x 28 In. 290.00
Table, Victorian, Walnut, Marble Top, c.1880, 28 x 19 x 14 In. 105.00
Table, Victorian, Walnut, Marble Top, Dolphin Legs, 30 x 36 In. 525.00
Table, Victorian, Walnut, Marble Top, Early 20th Century, 28 1/2 x 15 1/2 In. 230.00
Table, Victorian, Walnut, Marble Top, Oval, Pedestal, 27 x 27 x 20 In. 170.00
Table, Victorian, Walnut, Pink & Ivory Marble Top, Stretcher Base, 29 1/2 x 35 x 22 In. .. 495.00
Table, Victorian, Walnut, Rotary, Sliding Top, Clowes & Gates, 1877 Patent, 31 x 32 In. .. 420.00
Table, W. Platner, Walnut, Bronze, Knoll, 16 x 18 In. 1110.00
Table, Walnut Top, Beveled Edge, Nickel Wire Base, Round, 36 x 28 In. 1530.00
Table, Walnut, 2-Board Top, Drawer, Tapered Legs, 18th Century, 28 x 37 1/2 x 26 In. .. 3960.00
Table, Walnut, 4-Board Top, Tapered Legs, 31 x 92 x 36 In. 660.00

Table, Walnut, Beveled Top, Drawer, Turned Legs, 19th Century, 29 x 36 x 20 In. 200.00
Table, Walnut, Chamfered Legs, Turned Stretchers, 24 x 15 x 18 1/2 In. 345.00
Table, Walnut, Dovetailed, 2 Drawers, Turned, Tapered Legs, Mortise, 30 x 33 x 60 In. .. 1725.00
Table, Walnut, Frieze Drawers, Turned Legs, Italy, Early 18th Century, 32 x 46 x 23 In. .. 1955.00
Table, Walnut, Mahogany, Piecrust Edge, England, 17 x 21 In. 175.00
Table, Walnut, Marble Top, Molded Frieze, American, c.1875, 30 x 17 In. 115.00
Table, Walnut, Marble Top, Oval, Eagle Heads, c.1870, 30 x 26 x 35 In. 2875.00
Table, Walnut, Marble Turtle Top, Carved Base, c.1870, 30 x 3 x 27 In. 2300.00
Table, Walnut, Olive Wood, Kidney Shaped Top, Italy, c.1885, 26 x 20 x 15 In., Pair 750.00
Table, Walnut, Oval Top, Urn Stem, American, c.1875, 28 1/2 x 21 1/2 In. 85.00
Table, Walnut, Pine, Green Over Red Paint, Turned Legs, 2 Drawers, 53 x 30 x 28 In. ... 440.00
Table, Walnut, Serpentine Top, Cabriole Legs, France, 27 x 16 x 13 In. 460.00
Table, Walnut, Tiger Maple Inlay, Dovetailed Drawers, Spool Legs, 29 x 12 In. 290.00
Table, Walnut, Victorian, Pedestal Base, Claw Feet, c.1880, 29 1/2 x 60 In. 3450.00
Table, Warren McArthur, Aluminum, Laminate, Rubber, 1930s, 24 x 24 x 29 In. 2460.00
Table, Wendell Castle, Walnut Laminate, Triangular, c.1976, 22 x 31 In. 2875.00
Table, William & Mary, Cherry, Gateleg, Drawer, Leaves, 18th Century, 26 x 42 x 13 In. .. 1150.00
Table, William & Mary, Walnut, Gateleg, Early 1700s, 28 1/2 x 18 x 46 1/2 In. 5975.00
Table, William IV, Burl Walnut, Gilt Bronze Mounted, c.1835, 28 1/2 x 42 In. 8225.00
Table, William IV, Mahogany, 3 Tiers, Square, c.1830, 26 x 17 1/2 In. 1495.00
Table, William IV, Mahogany, Brass Casters, 2 Leaves, c.1820, 30 x 55 x 52 In. 805.00
Table, William IV, Mahogany, Hinged Top, c.1830, 30 x 37 x 26 In. 1035.00
Table, William IV, Rosewood, Ebony Band, Bone Inlay, c.1835, 29 x 52 In. 1265.00
Table, William IV, Rosewood, Marble Top, Baluster Standard, c.1835, 28 1/2 x 26 In. 1495.00
Table, Wood, Ebonized, 3 Tiers, c.1850, 31 1/2 x 14 1/2 x 11 1/2 In. 690.00
Table, Wood, Malachite Center, Turned Legs, Gilt Decoration, 29 1/2 x 20 In., Pair 690.00
Table, Wood, Polychrome, Mongolia, c.1810, 9 3/4 x 25 1/4 x 12 1/2 In. 325.00
Table, Wood, Polychrome, Tibet, c.1800, 11 x 24 1/2 x 11 1/2 In. 325.00
Table, Wormley, Mahogany, Glass, Dunbar, c.1950, 20 x 24 3/4 x 22 In. 1790.00
Table, Wormley, No. 3349, Bleached Mahogany, 2 Tiers, 25 x 24 x 19 In. 440.00
Table, Wormley, No. 3349, Mahogany, 2 Tiers, Dunbar, 18 1/2 x 24 x 25 In., Pair 1265.00
Table, Wormley, No. 4475, Mitered, Dunbar, 31 1/2 x 27 1/4 In. 230.00
Table, Wormley, No. 5313, Walnut, Mahogany, Triangular, Dunbar, c.1952, 25 x 22 In. 1755.00
Table, Wormley, No. 5426, Tile, Murano Glass, Brass, c.1960, 25 1/2 x 24 x 16 In. 1400.00
Table, Wormley, Walnut Veneer, Rosewood, Chinese Style, 22 x 27 1/2 x 27 In., Pair 690.00
Table, Writing, Arts & Crafts, Oak, Quartered, Wolverine, American, c.1910, 29 x 43 In. . 385.00
Table, Writing, Biedermeier, Cherry, Parcel Ebonized, c.1825, 35 1/2 x 38 x 23 In. 1610.00
Table, Writing, Bonheur Du Jour, Napoleon III, c.1865, 71 x 38 1/2 x 20 In. 1495.00
Table, Writing, Bonheur Du Jour, Napoleon III, Mahogany, Bronze Mounted, 40 x 30 In. .. 540.00
Table, Writing, Bonheur Du Jour, Vernis Martin Style, Giltwood, Bronze Mount, 34 In. ... 1910.00
Table, Writing, Eastlake, Drawer, Burl Front, 30 x 36 x 24 In. ....*Illus* 315.00
Table, Writing, George III, Mahogany, 2 Drawers, Late 1700s, 29 1/2 x 39 x 24 In. 1035.00
Table, Writing, George III, Mahogany, Leather Panel, Late 1700s, 30 x 59 x 36 In. 14660.00
Table, Writing, Louis XVI Style, Kingwood, Marquetry, 30 x 26 x 16 1/4 In. 470.00
Table, Writing, Regency Style, Mahogany, Kidney Shape, 3 Drawers, 30 x 41 x 20 In. 1265.00
Table, Writing, Regency Style, Mahogany, Leather Top, c.1815, 30 x 58 x 38 1/2 In. 2300.00
Table, Writing, Regency Style, Satinwood, Leather Top, 2 Drawers, 32 5/8 x 60 1/4 In. 1495.00
Table, Writing, Victorian, Elm, Gilt, Tooled Leather, c.1850, 31 x 50 x 38 In. 2530.00
Table, Writing, Victorian, Mahogany, Drawer, c.1865, 29 1/4 x 36 x 19 1/2 In. 635.00
Table, Writing, Victorian, Molded Skirt, Long Drawers, Fluted Legs, 1890, 30 x 50 In. ... 690.00
Table, Writing, William IV, Mahogany, Leather Surface, c.1840, 29 x 54 x 41 In. 3680.00
Table, Wrought Iron Base, 2-Tile Top, Horse-Drawn Carriage, California, 19 x 16 In. 290.00
Table, Wrought Iron Base, 2-Tile Top, Peacocks, Medallion, Midwestern, 22 x 11 In. 115.00
Table, Wrought Iron Base, Tile Top, White Paint, Persian Carpet Pattern, 20 x 18 In. 200.00
Table Set, Hickory, 2 Chairs, Table, 30 x 23 1/2 x 23 1/2 In., 3 Piece 1495.00
Table Set, John Risley, Wrought Iron, Glass Top, 2 Chairs, 1960s, 36 x 30-In. Table 1725.00
Tabouret, Arts & Crafts, 3 Sides, Cut Corner Top, Splayed Legs, 15 x 17 x 20 In. 230.00
Tabouret, G. Stickley, No. 52, Tapered Posts, 4 Iron Hooks, 23 x 23 x 72 In. 489.00
Tabouret, G. Stickley, No. 53, 2 Tapered Posts, Iron Hooks, 72 x 14 x 23 In. ...2760.00 to 3525.00
Tabouret, G. Stickley, Round Top, Notched Lower Stretcher, 14 x 16 In. 345.00
Tabouret, L. & J.G. Stickley, No. 558, Octagonal Top, Cross Stretchers, 17 x 15 In. 865.00
Tabouret, L. & J.G. Stickley, No. 559, Octagonal Top, Cross Stretchers, 20 1/4 x 18 In. .. 1380.00
Tabouret, L. & J.G. Stickley, Octagonal Top, Arched Cross Stretchers, 18 x 18 x 20 In. .. 980.00

Furniture, Table, Writing, Eastlake,
Drawer, Burl Front, 30 x 36 x 24 In.

Furniture, Umbrella Stand,
Little Red Riding Hood,
Germany, Late 1800s

Tabouret, Louis XVI Style, Giltwood, Late 19th Century, 14 1/2 In. 945.00
Tabouret, Oriental, Mahogany, Octagonal Top, Claw & Ball Feet, 37 x 13 In. 900.00
Tabouret, Oriental, Rosewood, Octagonal Top, Marble Insert, Openwork, 24 x 12 In. 255.00
Tabouret, Oriental, Rosewood, Round Top, Marble Insert, Openwork, 24 x 11 In. 680.00
Tabouret, Rosewood, Carved, Marble Inlaid Top, Chinese, Late 1800s, Pair 825.00
Tabouret, Rosewood, Marble Inlaid Top, Chinese, Late 1800s . . . . .120.00 to 470.00
Tabouret, Roycroft, No. 050, Square Top, Flared, Tapered Legs, Incised Orb, 12 x 12 In. . . 1410.00
Tabouret, Stickley Bros., Square, 2 Level Stretchers, 16 1/4 x 13 In. 635.00
Tea Cart, Arthur Klepper, Mahogany, Wor-De-Klee, 1951, 35 x 18 x 28 In. 585.00
Tea Cart, Edwardian, Mahogany, 2 Tiers, Floral Marquetry, 27 1/2 In. 440.00
Tea Cart, Frankel, Bamboo, 1950s, 31 x 37 1/2 x 20 In. 400.00
Tray On Stand, Card, Blackamoor Holding Oval Lacquered Tray, 17 1/2 In. 715.00
Tray On Stand, Card, Walnut, Black Forest, Cub Holding Tray, Barley Twist, 32 x 18 In. . . 1380.00
Tray On Stand, George III Style, Mahogany, c.1900, 22 x 26 x 19 In. 315.00
Tray On Stand, George III Style, Mahogany, Curved Sides, 29 1/2 x 38 x 28 In. 865.00
Tray On Stand, Victorian, Papier-Mache, Oval, 19 x 30 x 24 In. 1195.00
Trolley, Cheese, William IV, Mahogany, c.1835, 7 1/4 x 18 x 9 In. 520.00
Trolley, Mahogany, 3 Tiers, Graduated Shelves, Trestle Base, 63 x 60 x 27 In. 1725.00
Umbrella Stand, Arts & Crafts, Green Matte Glaze, Raised Decoration, 10 x 21 In. 635.00
Umbrella Stand, Cast Iron, Nautical Design, Sailor, Anchor, Paddle, 27 In. 1900.00
Umbrella Stand, Flower Shaft, Openwork, Scrolled Arms, Lion Head Terminals, 27 In. . . 62.00
Umbrella Stand, Fornasetti, Brass, Hat Stand Transfer, Italy, c.1954, 10 x 22 In. 1990.00
Umbrella Stand, G. Stickley, No. 54, 4 Tapered Posts, Copper Pan, 12 x 12 x 33 In. 1495.00
Umbrella Stand, G. Stickley, No. 100, Tapered Slats, 24 x 11 1/2 In. 1380.00
Umbrella Stand, G. Stickley, No. 273, Hammered Copper, 12 x 28 In. 2070.00
Umbrella Stand, G. Stickley, Slatted, Flaring, 24 In. 1725.00
Umbrella Stand, Little Red Riding Hood, Germany, Late 1800s . . . .*Illus* 4950.00
Umbrella Stand, Stylized Peacocks, Copper Insert, 28 1/2 x 11 In. Square 2760.00
Vanity, G. Nelson, Thin Edge, Rosewood, 2 Cabinets, Herman Miller, 88 x 27 1/4 In. 4600.00
Vanity, G. Stickley, No. 907, Mirror, 5 Drawers, Wrought Iron Pulls, 55 x 48 x 22 In. 4315.00
Vanity, G. Stickley, No. 914, 2 Drawers, Arched Apron, Mirror, 54 x 36 x 18 1/2 In. 2415.00
Vanity, Gothic Revival, Marble Sill, 2 Swing Mirrors, Scrolled Supports, 66 x 22 In. 575.00
Vanity, Mahogany Inlay, Serpentine Front, Kneehole, 70 1/2 x 46 x 19 In. 390.00
Vanity, Pine, Grain Painted, Stenciled, Turned Legs, 1800s, 29 x 33 x 15 In. 345.00
Vanity, Relief Carved, Dragon, Flower, Bird, Scrolls, Oval Mirror, Chinese, 70 In. 1150.00
Vanity, Rohde, Mirror, Drum Shaped Side Pedestals, 3 Drawers, 66 x 52 x 16 In. 9200.00
Vanity, Wood Veneer, Mirror Top, 2 Drawers, Serpentine Front, 76 x 49 x 16 1/2 In. 230.00
Vitrine, Biedermeier, Birch, Door, X-Form Mullions, Pilasters, c.1825, 67 x 40 x 25 In. . . 2070.00
Vitrine, Biedermeier, Walnut, Early 19th Century, 68 1/4 x 48 1/2 x 15 1/2 In. 2990.00
Vitrine, Chippendale Style, Tiger Maple, 20 x 30 x 20 In. 1380.00
Vitrine, Corner, Edwardian, Mahogany, Inlaid, 2 Bowfront Glass Doors, 51 x 22 In. 765.00
Vitrine, Curved Glass, Mirrored Back, Countryside Scenes, Shelves, 56 x 29 x 17 In. 715.00
Vitrine, Edwardian, Mahogany, 2 Doors, 70 x 41 1/2 In. 600.00
Vitrine, Edwardian, Mahogany, Inlaid, Hinged Glass Top, c.1910, 29 x 24 In. 410.00
Vitrine, Edwardian, Mahogany, Serpentine, 2 Shelves, c.1900, 28 x 24 In. 920.00
Vitrine, Fruitwood, Sunburst, 2 Glass Doors, Germany, Early 1900s, 73 x 44 x 15 In. 2115.00
Vitrine, George III Style, Mahogany, 3 Astragal-Glazed Doors, 79 1/2 x 76 In. 1610.00
Vitrine, George III Style, Mahogany, 84 x 56 x 16 In. 2629.00

Vitrine, Gesso Molded, Side Glass, 55 1/2 x 29 x 17 In. 605.00
Vitrine, Hanging, Victorian, Bentwood, 33 x 21 x 9 In. 480.00
Vitrine, Hepplewhite Style, Fruitwood, Glass Panes, Tapered Legs, Italy, 25 x 19 In. 145.00
Vitrine, Hepplewhite Style, Mahogany, Veneers, Tapered Legs, 29 x 30 x 18 1/2 In. 400.00
Vitrine, Louis XV Style, Bronze Mounted, 29 3/4 x 28 x 16 In. 1795.00
Vitrine, Louis XV Style, Giltwood, 65 1/2 x 28 x 15 In. 1195.00
Vitrine, Louis XV Style, Kingwood, Gilt Bronze Cartouches, Landscapes, 27 x 63 In. . . . 920.00
Vitrine, Louis XV Style, Kingwood, Serpentine, Late 1800s, 64 x 33 x 16 In. 750.00
Vitrine, Louis XV Style, Mahogany, Bronze Mounted, 72 x 52 x 17 In. 6000.00
Vitrine, Louis XV Style, Mahogany, Gilt Metal, Vernis Martin, Painted, 26 x 14 In. 940.00
Vitrine, Louis XV Style, Ormolu Mounted, Glass, Vernis Martin, c.1910, 55 In. 1175.00
Vitrine, Louis XV Style, Ormolu, Parcel Ebonized Parquetry, 66 x 31 x 17 In. 1150.00
Vitrine, Louis XV Style, Serpentine Front, Vernis Martin, Early 1900s, 57 x 27 x 15 In. . . 560.00
Vitrine, Louis XV, Mahogany, Serpentine, Door, 59 x 26 x 18 In. 1000.00
Vitrine, Louis XVI Style, Giltwood, 58 x 27 x 17 In. 1135.00
Vitrine, Louis XVI Style, Giltwood, High Relief Leaves, Arrows, 1800s, 72 x 40 In. 4350.00
Vitrine, Louis XVI Style, Giltwood, Red Velvet Interior, 67 x 30 x 16 In., Pair 2200.00
Vitrine, Louis XVI Style, Ivory Painted, 70 x 36 x 15 In. 540.00
Vitrine, Louis XVI Style, Mahogany, Bronze Mounted, Demilune, 62 x 33 x 16 In. 660.00
Vitrine, Louis XVI Style, Mahogany, Oval, 31 x 27 x 19 1/2 In. 1795.00
Vitrine, Louis XVI, Giltwood, Glass Front, Sides, Mirror Back, 62 x 31 x 18 In. 3055.00
Vitrine, Mahogany, Giltwood, Vernis Martin Style, 68 x 29 x 21 In. 65.00
Vitrine, Mahogany, Glass Top, 6 Reeded Legs, 42 x 45 1/2 x 18 1/2 In. 980.00
Vitrine, Mahogany, String Inlay, Glazed Doors, Straight Legs, 54 x 24 In. 430.00
Vitrine, Napoleon III Style, Kingwood, Ormolu Mounted, c.1875, 78 x 41 x 17 In. 4140.00
Vitrine, Napoleon III, Ebony, Bronze, 2 Parts, 85 x 47 x 15 1/2 In. 2150.00
Vitrine, Napoleon III, Mahogany, Oval Painted Plaque, Late 1800s, 67 x 29 1/2 In. 1840.00
Vitrine, Napoleon III, Marble Top, c.1865, 51 x 30 In. 2185.00
Vitrine, Neoclassical, Marble Top, Gilt Metal Mounts, 64 x 31 3/4 x 16 1/2 In. 1150.00
Vitrine, Neoclassical, Painted, Giltwood, Italy, 42 x 24 In. 1195.00
Vitrine, Regency Style, Mahogany, Glass Inserts, 29 1/2 x 20 In., Pair 805.00
Vitrine, Regency, Mahogany, Early 19th Century, 72 x 23 1/2 x 15 1/2 In., Pair 2760.00
Vitrine, Rococo Revival, Mahogany, 52 x 21 x 8 In. 960.00
Vitrine, Rococo Revival, Oak, Serpentine Crest, Mullioned Drawers, Dutch, 28 x 24 In. . . 560.00
Vitrine, Satinwood, Inlaid, Musical Instruments, Continental, 72 x 26 1/8 x 17 In. 1035.00
Vitrine, Tabletop, Walnut, Carved Pine Madonna, Child, Mid 1800s, 22 x 13 x 11 In. 920.00
Vitrine, Victorian, Glass Panels, Serpentine Side, American, 44 1/2 x 16 In. 650.00
Wall Unit, Anna Castelli, Roundup, 4 Sections, Slide Doors, Plastic, 12 x 30 In. 259.00
Wall Unit, Joe Columbo, Molded Plastic, Orange, 66 x 12 x 40 1/2 In. 1095.00
Wall Unit, McCobb, Walnut, 2 Doors, 2 Drawers, Winchedon, 3 Piece 460.00
Wall Unit, McCobb, Walnut, 2 Pieces, Shelves, Drawers, 81 3/4 x 72 x 18 In. 1840.00
Wall Unit, Swedish Modern, Ladder Shelf, Wood, Metal, c.1951 . . . . 1410.00
Wardrobe, Galle, Art Nouveau, Pine, Bird's-Eye Maple, 83 x 43 1/2 x 18 In. 6000.00
Wardrobe, H. Probber, Mahogany, 8 Drawers, Glass Shelves, 38 x 20 x 54 In. 1495.00
Wardrobe, Napoleon III, Mahogany, 4 Doors, 2 Glazed, c.1900, 79 x 90 x 24 3/4 In. 1955.00
Wardrobe, Neoclassical, Mahogany, Ogee Cornice, c.1830, 70 x 27 1/2 In. 3738.00
Wardrobe, Oak, 2 Doors, 2 Drawers, Angled Crown Molding, Knockdown, 48 x 86 In. . . . 300.00
Wardrobe, Pine, Dovetailed Top & Bottom, Amana, Iowa, 1870s, 48 x 77 In. 715.00
Wardrobe, Pine, Mustard Paint, 4-Paneled Door, Beveled Corners, 51 x 81 In. 499.00
Wardrobe, Pine, Painted Urns, Copper Hinges & Decorations, 1920s, 76 In. 220.00
Wardrobe, Pine, Robin's-Egg Blue & Black, Door, 7 Chamfered Panels, 38 x 75 In. 470.00
Wardrobe, Regency, Mahogany, 5 Drawers, 2 Cupboards, c.1815, 65 3/4 x 84 In. 1150.00
Wardrobe, Regency, Mahogany, Bowfront, 2 Doors, Drawer, 81 1/2 x 50 x 24 In. 2585.00
Wardrobe, Rosewood, Iron Mounts, 3 Sections, Japan, Early 1900s, 47 x 61 x 16 In. 825.00
Wardrobe, Teak, Oak, Laminate, 54 x 42 x 18 1/2 In. 700.00
Wardrobe, Victorian, Bird's-Eye Maple, Drawer, 2 Doors, 89 x 60 x 23 In. 635.00
Wardrobe, Victorian, Burl Walnut, 2 Drawers, Ornate Top, Knockdown 2400.00
Wardrobe, Victorian, Mahogany, 5 Drawers, 4 Doors, c.1850, 81 1/2 x 84 x 20 In. 2185.00
Wardrobe, Victorian, Mahogany, Ebonized, Mirrored Doors, Drawer, 101 x 18 x 52 In. . . 790.00
Wardrobe, Walnut, 2 Gothic Arched Panel Doors, Drawer, 81 x 52 In. 290.00
Wardrobe, William IV, Mahogany, 2-Paneled Doors, c.1835, 88 x 62 x 24 1/2 In. 1725.00
Washstand, Bamboo, Pine Drawer Front, Walnut Top, 1800s, 9 1/2 x 6 In. 315.00
Washstand, Biedermeier, Serpentine Front, Mid 1800s, 34 x 32 x 21 In. 550.00

Washstand, Cherry, Carved Backsplash, Drawer, Lower Shelf, 34 x 20 In.	340.00
Washstand, Corner, George III Style, Mahogany, 2 Shelves, c.1885, 32 x 24 In.	375.00
Washstand, Corner, Hepplewhite, Mahogany, Drawer, 1900s, 41 3/4 x 17 1/2 In.	750.00
Washstand, Corner, Hepplewhite, Mahogany, Inlaid, Shelf, 40 3/4 x 25 In.	1265.00
Washstand, Federal, Mahogany, Flame Veneer, Pine, 18 3/4 x 16 x 37 1/2 In.	315.00
Washstand, Hepplewhite Style, Tiger Maple, Swing-Out Drawers, 32 x 32 x 13 In.	1720.00
Washstand, Louis Philippe Style, Burl Walnut, Hinged Top, 4 Drawers, 39 x 37 x 19 In.	2990.00
Washstand, Mahogany, Cutout Drawers, Galleried Top, 37 1/2 x 21 x 17 In.	865.00
Washstand, Mahogany, Inlaid, Marble Top, Tiled Splat, c.1900, 43 x 42 x 20 In.	115.00
Washstand, Mahogany, Marble Top, Scrolling Support, c.1865, 36 x 36 x 18 In.	200.00
Washstand, Mahogany, Molded Top, Drawer, 2 Sunken-Panel Doors, 28 3/4 In.	225.00
Washstand, Mahogany, Veneer Inlay, Drawer, 31 In.	490.00
Washstand, Mustard Paint, Green Decoration, 39 In.	315.00
Washstand, Pine, Grain Painted, Turned Legs, Dovetailed Drawers, 17 x 14 x 37 In.	440.00
Washstand, Pine, Poplar, Splash Panel, 38 x 28 x 18 In.	770.00
Washstand, Shaker, Poplar, Drawer, Shelf, Whitewater, Ohio, c.1850, 34 1/2 x 20 In.	1265.00
Washstand, Shaker, Red Paint, Drawer, Scrolled Gallery, 36 x 17 x 16 In.	345.00
Washstand, Sheraton, Black, Stencil, Drawer, Backsplash, 38 x 17 x 14 In.	365.00
Washstand, Sheraton, Cherry, Pine, Brass Pull, 15 x 15 1/4 x 33 In.	290.00
Washstand, Sheraton, Drawer, High Backsplash, Cutout Top, 38 x 17 x 14 In.	360.00
Washstand, Sheraton, Mahogany, Splashboard, Convex, 30 1/2 x 22 x 15 1/2 In.	400.00
Washstand, Victorian, Corner, Mahogany Inlay, Splashboard, Shelf, 49 x 31 In.	295.00
Washstand, Victorian, Mahogany, Marquetry, Backsplash, Paw Feet, 40 x 32 x 19 In.	865.00
Washstand, Walnut, 3 Drawers, 36 x 30 In.	260.00
Washstand, Walnut, 3 Drawers, Carved Pulls, Towel Spindle, 33 x 34 In.	210.00
Wastebasket, Arts & Crafts, Notched Sides, Arched Lower Support, 13 x 13 x 20 In.	490.00
Wastebasket, G. Stickley, No. 94, Slatted, Tapered, Iron Hoops, 12 x 14 In.	2185.00
Wastebasket, Mathieu Mategot, Steel, Perforated, Enameled, France, 1950s, 10 x 15 In.	1755.00
Wastebasket, Slatted Sides, Wood Through Tenon Handles, 12 x 15 x 16 In.	750.00
Wastebasket, Stickley Bros., Metal Tag, 17 1/2 x 14 1/4 In.	690.00
Whatnot Shelf, George III Style, Mahogany, 3 Tiers, Drawer, 19 1/4 x 42 In.	690.00
Whatnot Shelf, Hanging, Mahogany, 3 Parts, Pagoda Tops, Scalloped Front, 37 x 25 In.	200.00
Whatnot Shelf, Hanging, Walnut, Scalloped Sides, 4 Shelves, 29 x 30 In.	85.00
Whatnot Shelf, Mahogany, 5 Demilune Shelves, American, 1800s, 62 x 27 x 19 In.	115.00
Whatnot Shelf, Mahogany, 6 Tiers, c.1900, 65 x 30 x 16 In.	145.00
Whatnot Shelf, Regency, Mahogany, 3 Tiers, Drawer, 19th Century, 45 In.	1410.00
Whatnot Shelf, Regency, Mahogany, 3 Tiers, Early 1800s, 45 1/2 x 18 1/2 x 18 In.	2185.00
Whatnot Shelf, Regency, Mahogany, 4 Shelves, c.1815, 55 x 24 x 18 In.	2070.00
Whatnot Shelf, Victorian, Mahogany, Drawer, 55 In.	7050.00
Whatnot Shelf, William IV, Mahogany, Mid 19th Century, 70 x 23 1/2 x 16 1/4 In.	1955.00
Window Seat, Louis XV Style, Giltwood, Cane Seat, Late 1800s, 26 x 30 1/2 In.	800.00
Window Seat, Mahogany, Scrolling Ends, Upholstered, 6 Legs, 45 x 22 1/2 In.	460.00
Window Seat, Neoclassical, Fruitwood, Continental, c.1815, 31 x 45 x 17 In., Pair	4370.00
Window Seat, Regency Style, Mahogany, Padded Seat, Lyre Arms, 33 x 47 x 18 In.	1095.00
Window Seat, Upholstered, Cabriole Legs, Carved, 27 x 38 x 17 1/2 In.	140.00
Wine Cooler, Elm, Round, Incised Lines, Handled Liner, 5 x 19 In.	575.00
Wine Cooler, George III, Inlaid Mahogany, Octagonal, c.1800, 29 x 18 In.	1530.00
Wine Cooler, Hinged Top, 3 Copper Bands, 17 x 24 1/2 x 19 In.	805.00
Wine Cooler, Regency Style, Mahogany, Brass Bound, c.1890, 24 1/2 x 30 1/2 In.	1035.00
Wine Cooler, William IV, Mahogany, Sarcophagus, 17 x 25 1/2 x 17 1/2 In.	1295.00

FURSTENBERG Porcelain Works was started in Furstenberg, Germany, in 1747. It is still working. Many of the modern products are made in the old molds.

Bowl, Many Flowers, Octagonal, 7 1/2 In.	75.00
Coffee Set, Lottine, 8 Piece	70.00
Figurine, Swans, Natural Coloration, Late 1700s, 5 1/2 In., Pair	430.00
Pin Dish, Hummingbird, Gold Trim, Marked, Late 1800s, 4 In.	20.00
Pin Dish, Parrot, Gold Trim, Late 1800s, 4 In.	20.00
Platter, Many Flowers, Octagonal, Marked, 12 In.	80.00
Sugar, Cover, Many Flowers, Octagonal, Marked	50.00
Vase, Pink Roses, Urn Shape, 1980s, 8 1/4 In.	35.00

G. ARGY-ROUSSEAU is the impressed mark used on a variety of objects in the Art Deco style. Gabriel Argy-Rousseau, born in 1885, was a French glass artist. In 1921, he formed a partnership that made pate-de-verre and other glass. He worked until 1952 and died in 1953.

G-ARGY-
ROUSSEAU

Bowl, Black-Eyed Susans, Pate-De-Verre, 3 1/2 In.	990.00
Bowl, Frosted, Geometric Band, Amethyst, Oval, Cameo, Pate-De-Verre, 2 In.	1640.00
Bowl, Leaf, Vine, Pate-De-Verre, Signed, c.1900, 3 1/2 x 1 1/2 In.	1230.00
Figurine, Buddha, Jade Green, Pate-De-Verre, Signed, 3 In.	1100.00
Pendant, Scarab, Orange, Red, Black, Oval, Pate-De-Verre, Signed, 2 1/2 In.	1650.00
Pendant, Turquoise Petals, Purple Center & Edge, Pate-De-Verre, 2 1/2 In.	1800.00
Vase, Anemones, Pate-De-Verre, c.1920, 3 In.	5975.00
Vase, Chameleons, Green, Amethyst, Cream, Urn, Rolled Rim, Pate-De-Verre	4315.00
Vase, Chardon, Pate-De-Verre, c.1915, 3 7/8 In.	5020.00
Vase, Purple, Red, Brown & Peach, Triangle Shapes, Pate-De-Verre, 6 In.	6035.00
Vase, Red Thistles, Green Leaves, Pate-De-Verre, Signed, 6 x 3 1/2 In.	4900.00
Vase, Spider & Web, Black, Maroon, Green Vine, Globular, Pate-De-Verre, 5 In.	4450.00
Vase, Wolves, Black, Purple & Green Ground, White Snow, Signed, 10 In.	4875.00
Vase, Woman Picking Apples, Pate-De-Verre, 9 1/2 In.	9500.00

GALLE was a designer who made glass, pottery, furniture, and other Art Nouveau items. Émile Galle founded his factory in France in 1874. After Galle's death in 1904, the firm continued to make glass and furniture until 1931. The name *Galle* was used as a mark, but it was often hidden in the design of the object. Galle glass is listed here. Pottery is in the next section. His furniture is listed in the Furniture category.

Galle

Bottle, Scent, Green, Daises, Cameo, Signed, 5 1/2 In.	1670.50
Bottle, Scent, Green, Leaves & Stems, Lilac Flowers, Frosted Stopper, Cameo, 6 1/2 In.	840.00
Bottle, Scent, Leaves, Vines & Berries, Pink & Cream, Frosted Stopper, Cameo, 4 In.	980.00
Bottle, Scent, Pillow, Green Cut To Clear, Ferns & Leaves, Signed, Frosted Stopper, 4 In.	780.00
Bottle, Scent, Transparent Brown, Blue, Yellow, Purple Flowers, Flying Insects, 6 In.	805.00
Bowl, Centerpiece, Amethyst Flowers, Leaves, Stems, Frosted, Cameo, Signed, 12 In.	1100.00
Bowl, Clover Leaf Shape, Pansies, Leaves, Pink, Blue, Green, Cameo, 2 5/8 x 6 3/4 In.	520.00
Bowl, Cover, Purple Flowers, Cameo, Signed, 6 In.	770.00
Bowl, Enameled Chrysanthemums, Smoky Ground, 10 1/2 In.	480.00
Bowl, Glossy Tangerine Flowers, Frosted Ground, Cameo, 4 1/2 In.	400.00
Bowl, Orange Poppies, Footed, Cameo, Signed, 4 3/4 In.	990.00
Bowl, Red Flowers & Leaves, White Frosted Ground, Ruffled Edge, Cameo, 9 x 3 1/2 In.	7170.00
Box, Cover, Enameled, Thistle, Amber Ground, Round, Signed, 6 In.	990.00
Box, Glossy Flowers, Red, Leaves, Amber Ground, Round, Cameo, Signed, 3 x 5 In.	660.00
Champagne, Gold Enamel, Faceted Jewels, Applied Foot, Signed, 4 1/2 In.	1840.00
Cordial, Cherries, Pale Brown, Gold, Signed, 2 1/2 In.	750.00
Cruet, Enameled, Praying Mantis, Clover, Amber Ground, Signed, 8 In.	2475.00
Cup & Saucer, Enameled Blue Flowers, Blue & White Dragonflies, Clear Ground	800.00
Dresser Set, Amber, Flowers, White, Turquoise, Green, Gold Enamel, Signed, 4 Piece	880.00
Ewer, Enameled, Man Playing Bagpipe, Pheasants, Round Handle, Signed, 8 x 6 In.	900.00
Ewer, Silver Overlay, Flowers & Leaves, Chipped Ice Ground, Cameo, Signed, 10 In.	1670.00
Lamp, Purple Flowers, Yellow Ground, Cameo, 19 x 12 In.	7350.00
Lamp, Yellow Ground, Red Flowers, Cameo Base & Shade, 11 In.	16950.00
Lamp Base, Crimson Flowers, Citron Ground, Cameo, Signed, c.1900, 10 1/2 In.	450.00
Perfume Lamp, Trees, Amber Ground, Cameo, Metal Burner, Lampe Berger, 6 In.	1440.00
Pitcher, Burgundy Leaves, Etched, Fire Polished, Applied Fluted Shaped Handle, 7 In.	2150.00
Pitcher, Handles, Leaves, Flowers, Vines, Green, Lavender, White, Peach, Cameo, 5 In.	750.00
Tray, Clear, Enameled Flowers, Leaves, Dragonfly, Rolled Gold Rim, Signed, 10 x 8 In.	1130.00
Tumbler, Water Lily, Amber, Light Blue Frosted Ground, Cameo, 4 In.	750.00
Urn, Green Thistles, Mottled Pale Pink, Frosty Ground, Cameo, 3 In.	375.00
Vase, Amber Poppies, On Light Gray Ground, Cameo, Signed, 7 1/4 In.	1955.00
Vase, Amethyst Flowers, Flared, Conical, Cameo, Signed, 8 1/2 In.	1700.00
Vase, Amethyst Flowers, Peach Frosted Ground, Double Gourd, Cameo, 4 1/4 In.	360.00
Vase, Amethyst Trees, Blue Mountains, Frosted, Lozenge Shape, Cameo, Signed, 5 1/2 In.	1035.00
Vase, Amethyst, White, Red & Black Fleur-De-Lis, Square Handles, Ribbed, 10 In.	460.00
Vase, Banjo, Flowers, Amethyst, Citron Shaded To Apricot, Frosted, Signed, 5 5/8 In.	465.00
Vase, Banjo, Purple Flowers, Amber Round, Cameo, Signed, 6 3/4 In.	630.00

Vase, Banjo, Woodland & Lake Scene, Birds In Flight, Frosted, Cameo, Signed, 7 In. 800.00
Vase, Bee, Honeycomb, Branches, Flowers, On Translucent Brown, Ribbed, Signed, 4 In. 1955.00
Vase, Berries, Leaves, Red, On Yellow Ground, Cameo, Signed, 6 1/2 In. 1380.00
Vase, Bleeding Heart, Amethyst, Frosted, Bell Shape, Cameo, 4 3/4 In. 345.00
Vase, Blossoms, Leaves, Green, Yellow, Frosted Ground, Bulbous, Handles, Cameo, 5 In. 1400.00
Vase, Blue Flowers, Blue To Mottled White Ground, Cameo, 10 1/2 In. 960.00
Vase, Blue Flowers, Citron, Footed, Cameo, Signed, c.1890 .... 1460.00
Vase, Brown & Green Cameo Trees, Apricot Ground, Signed, 5 In. 630.00
Vase, Brown & Green Leaves, Stems & Flowers, Green, Pink & Cream, Cameo, 16 In. 2300.00
Vase, Brown & Green Trees, Pink Ground, Cameo, 6 1/2 In. 520.00
Vase, Brown Leaves & Flowers, Frosted Cream, Pink & Yellow Ground, Cameo, 6 In. ... 920.00
Vase, Brown Leaves & Flowers, Salmon Ground, Cameo, 4 In. 175.00
Vase, Brown Leaves & Flowers, Seafoam Green Ground, Cameo, Signed, 7 1/2 In. 3450.00
Vase, Brown Leaves, Vines & Flowers, Green Ground, Cameo, 10 In. 540.00
Vase, Bud, Hanging Flowers, Pods, Clear To Amethyst, Frosted, Cameo, Signed, 6 1/8 In. 375.00
Vase, Bud, Maroon Cut To Copper, Flowers, Cameo, Signed, c.1900, 4 x 2 3/4 In. 335.00
Vase, Bud, Russet, Amber Poppies, Frosted Salmon Ground, Flared Base, Cameo, 7 In. .. 460.00
Vase, Burgundy Orchids, Olive Green Ground, Egg Shape, Cameo, 4 3/4 In. 990.00
Vase, Carved Brown & Green Irises, Frosted, Mottled Pink Ground, Cameo, 16 In. 2300.00
Vase, Chrysanthemums, Incised, Orange, Pink & Brown Ground, Cameo, 14 In. 2000.00
Vase, Citron Flowers, Leaves, Flat Sides, Flared, Cameo, c.1900, 5 1/2 In. 2130.00
Vase, Clematis, Leaves, Light Pink, Amethyst, Frosted, Tapered, Cameo, Signed, 6 1/2 In. 3650.00
Vase, Clover Flower, Leaves, Peach Ground, Cameo, c.1900, 4 3/4 In. 750.00
Vase, Crocus, Blown-Out, Yellow Ground, Cameo, Tapered Neck, 8 1/2 In. 4400.00
Vase, Egg Shape, Leaves & Flowers, Green, Yellow, Signed, Cameo, 3 In. 2015.00
Vase, Enameled Poppies, Ice Green Ground, Cameo, Signed, 7 1/4 In. 1250.00
Vase, Entwined Fish Shape, Iridescent Amber, Violet, Cabochon Eyes, Signed, 5 3/4 In. .. 1322.00
Vase, Ferns, Dark Green, Green Frosted Ground, Cameo, Signed, 3 1/4 In. 200.00
Vase, Ferns, Green Ground, Cameo, Signed, 16 In. 3410.00
Vase, Figure On A Bridge, Brown & Green, Elongated Teardrop Shape, Cameo, 10 1/2 In. 1540.00
Vase, Flowers & Vines, Red, Clear Ground, Cameo, Signed, 8 1/2 In. 2415.00
Vase, Flowers, Amethyst, Yellow Frosted, Double Gourd, Cameo, Signed, 4 3/4 In. 345.00
Vase, Flowers, Apricot, Burgundy, Frosted, Tapered, Waisted Neck, Signed, 6 1/2 In. ... 440.00
Vase, Flowers, Blue & Green, White Frosted Ground, Tapered Neck, Cameo, 10 In. 4780.00
Vase, Flowers, Brown & Orange, Mottled Yellow Ground, Tapered, Cameo, Signed, 10 In. 3825.00
Vase, Flowers, Leaves, Amethyst, Blue Ground, Tapered, Oval, Cameo, 6 In. 690.00
Vase, Flowers, Leaves, Apricot, Frosted Ground, Bottle Shape, Cameo, Signed, 9 1/2 In. . 460.00
Vase, Flowers, Leaves, Brown, Yellow Shaded To Cream, Cameo, Signed, 7 1/4 In. 1035.00
Vase, Flowers, Pods, Leaves, Red, Umber, Frosted, Cameo, Tapered, 5 3/4 In. 385.00
Vase, Grape Vines, Umber, Amber, Tapered, Cameo, Signed, 8 In. 490.00
Vase, Green & Brown Landscape, Pink & Frosted Ground, Cameo, 9 In. 2875.00
Vase, Green Berries, Leaves, Branches, Amber Ground, Cameo, Signed, 14 1/4 In. 2240.00
Vase, Green Leaves & Flowers, Pink Ground, Cameo, 2 1/4 x 2 3/4 In. 210.00
Vase, Green Leaves & Vines, Flower, Green To Blue, Peach Ground, Cameo, 3 In. 290.00
Vase, Green Thistles, Peach Ground, Flattened Club Shape, Cameo, Signed, 8 1/2 In. ... 825.00
Vase, Green, Peach & Brown Flowers, Peach Ground, Egg Shape, Cameo, 7 In. 635.00
Vase, Iris, Ferns, Amethyst, Green, Mottled Blue & Yellow, Signed, Cameo, 15 In. 4430.00
Vase, Iris, Leaves, Amethyst, Frosted, Baluster, Cameo, Signed, 7 1/2 In. 400.00
Vase, Iris, Pink, Green Ground, Wheel Carved, Cameo, Signed, 15 In. 25300.00
Vase, Iris, Purple, Frosted & Purple Ground, Cameo, 7 1/2 In. 1175.00
Vase, Lady's Slipper, Green, Frosted Pink Ground, Cameo, 8 1/2 In. 2875.00
Vase, Lake Como, Peacock, Amethyst, Blue, Amber Ground, Cameo, Signed, 14 In. 28750.00
Vase, Landscape, Purple, Green, Frosted Green, Brown Ground, Cameo, 18 In. 5750.00
Vase, Landscape, Trees, Lake, Yellow Ground, Bulbous, Tapered Neck, Cameo, 9 In. 5735.00
Vase, Landscape, Trees, Water, Boulders, Mountain Range, Purple, 18 1/2 In. 4025.00
Vase, Lavender & Blue Flowers, Cream To Yellow Ground, Cameo, 9 3/4 In. 1840.00
Vase, Lavender & Blue Flowers, Leaves, Frosty Pale Citron Ground, Cameo, 6 1/8 In. ... 1725.00
Vase, Lavender Fuchsias, Light Brown Leaves, Citron Ground, Tapered, 4 3/4 In. 345.00
Vase, Lavender Leaves, Vines, Flowers, Yellow To Clear Ground, Cameo, 9 3/4 In. 900.00
Vase, Leaf & Berry, Blown-Out, Green & Brown, Frosted Ground, 9 In. .... *Illus* 5175.00
Vase, Leaves, Flowers, Amber Ground, Clear Frosted Strip, Bell Shape, Cameo, 4 1/4 In. .. 300.00
Vase, Leaves, Seedpods, Green, Frosted Ground, Peach Shaded To Cream, Cameo, 10 In. .. 980.00
Vase, Leaves, Vines, Seedpods, Dark Green, White Ground, Signed, Cameo, 9 In. 780.00

Vase, Maroon Berries, Vines, Glossy, Brown Ground, Club Shape, Cameo, 9 3/4 In. 2150.00
Vase, Maroon Leaves, Stems & Flowers, Frosted Ground, Cameo, 7 1/2 In. 865.00
Vase, Maroon Snapdragons, Pink Ground, Elongated Teardrop Shape, Cameo, 7 In. 715.00
Vase, Morning Glories, Leaves, Frosted Yellow Ground, Oval, Cameo, Signed, 12 1/2 In. . 5000.00
Vase, Nasturtiums, Orange Cut To Clear, Cylindrical, Cameo, Signed, 13 In. 1980.00
Vase, Olive Green Eucalyptus Branch, Pearl Gray Ground, Tapered, Signed, 25 1/2 In. . . . 3100.00
Vase, Orange Spider Mums, Pearl Gray Ground, Flared, Cupped Rim, Signed, 15 x 5 In. . 1610.00
Vase, Orchids, Green & Maroon Mottled Ground, Cylindrical, Signed, 13 1/2 In. 2200.00
Vase, Pastel Blue, Green Flowers, Leaves, Stems, Mottled White Ground, 7 1/2 In. 345.00
Vase, Peonies, Green, Red Brown Ground, Baluster, Cameo, Signed, 4 3/4 In. 1540.00
Vase, Pilgrim, Panoramic View Of Lake, Trees, Green, Orange, Frosted Ground, 5 In. 1265.00
Vase, Pillow, Lavender & Olive Hydrangea On Buff, Handles, Cameo, Signed, 11 1/2 In. . 230.00
Vase, Poppy Pods, Ferns, Green, Pink, Yellow, Flattened, Flared Top, Cameo, 10 x 12 In. . 4025.00
Vase, Purple & Green Flowers, Leaves, Cylindrical Top, Bulbous Base, Cameo, 18 In. . . . 1380.00
Vase, Purple Bell Flowers, Leaves, Frosted Amber Ground, Footed, 6 1/2 In. 920.00
Vase, Purple Sweet Pea Branches, Chartreuse, Yellow Ground, Bullet Shape, 14 In. 1495.00
Vase, Purple Trees, Blue To White Frosted Ground, Tapered, Cameo, Signed, 8 In. 2630.00
Vase, Red Flowers, Frosted, Yellow Ground, Cameo, 9 1/2 In. 3335.00
Vase, Red Leaves, Cherry Blossom In Windowpane, Cameo, 14 1/2 In. 4315.00
Vase, Red Orchids, Frosted, Yellow Ground, Slender, Footed, Cameo, 9 1/2 In. 2185.00
Vase, Red, Leaves, Blue & Green, Grasshopper, Wheel Carved, Signed, 3 In. 6325.00
Vase, Scarlet Berries, Leaves, Citron, Frosty, Cameo, 2 3/8 In. 375.00
Vase, Stick, Brown & Green Stems, Leaves, Flared Rim, Cameo, 12 In. 900.00
Vase, Stick, Brown Berries, Leaves, Vines, Frosted Ground, Cameo, 8 1/4 In. 635.00
Vase, Stick, Cranberry Flowers, Leaves, Frosted Ground, Ruffled Edge, Foot, Cameo, 9 In. 800.00
Vase, Stick, Flowers, Yellow, Leaves, White Frosted Ground, Bulbous Base, 17 In. 2630.00
Vase, Stick, Frosty Pink, Green, Thistles, Cameo, Signed, 3 3/4 In. 345.00
Vase, Sweet Pea Vines, Green, Pink Ground, Globular Base, Cameo, 11 In. 1045.00
Vase, Tan Flowers, Leaves, Frosted Ground, Bottle Shape, Cameo, Signed, 11 In. 3450.00
Vase, Thistle, Green, Cream, Pink Ground, Signed, Cameo, 5 3/4 In. 150.00
Vase, Thistle, Olive Green, Amber Ground, Cylindrical Top, Square Base, Cameo, 24 In. . 3080.00
Vase, Thistles, Brown, Pink, Amber Ground, Ruffled Foot, Crimped Rim, Signed, 7 In. . . 1100.00
Vase, Thistles, Frosted Pink, Cream Ground, Cameo, 9 3/4 In. 980.00
Vase, Trees, Amber, Green Lake, Flattened, Flared, Cameo, Signed, 13 In. 7200.00
Vase, Trees, Amber, Lake, Mottled Yellow, Frosted Neck, Flattened Oval, Cameo, 13 In. . 1480.00
Vase, Trees, Summer Foliage, Water, Frosted, Apricot Tint, Cameo, Signed, 9 1/2 In. 1925.00
Vase, Trumpet, Flowers, Leaves, Amethyst, Blue, Frosted Green Ground, Signed, 14 In. . . 4600.00
Vase, Veronica Blossoms, Lavender, Green, Cylindrical, Cameo, Signed, 19 In. 2750.00
Vase, Vines, Brown, Gray, Purple Ground, Cameo, 8 1/2 In. 865.00
Vase, Violet, Flower Cut To White, Cream & Red Ground, Cameo, Signed, 5 In. 575.00
Vase, Water Lilies, Blue, Purple, Frosted Yellow Ground, Cameo, 12 In. 1265.00

GALLE POTTERY was made by Emile Galle, the famous French designer, after 1874. The pieces were marked with the initials *E. G.*
impressed, *Em. Galle Faiencerie de Nancy*, or a version of his signature. Galle is best known for his glass, listed above.

Basket, Tree Trunk, Enameled, Cherry Tree, Earthenware, Late 1800s, 14 In. 175.00
Ewer, Pansies, Mottled Ground, Yellow, Blue, White, Cobalt Blue, Brown, 9 In. 990.00
Figurine, Pug Dog, Yellow On White, Blue Spots, Glass Eyes, Faience, c.1880, 12 In. . . . 5020.00
Pitcher, Dragonflies, Pinched Neck, Ruffled Edge, 5 1/2 In. 1540.00
Pitcher, Man's Portrait, Wide Brimmed Hat, Bulbous, Pinched Neck, 8 1/2 In. 1210.00
Vase, Jack-In-The-Pulpit, Mountains, Trees, Building, Ribbed, Faience, 11 In. 400.00
Vase, Raised Flowers, Butterflies, Twig, Multicolored, 8 1/4 In. 3000.00
Vase, Sunflowers Forming Pocket, Footed, Faience, Signed, 7 x 7 x 5 In. 525.00

GAME collectors like all types of games. Of special interest are any
board games or card games. Transogram and other company names are
included in the description when known. Other games may be found
listed under Card, Toy, or the name of the character or celebrity fea-
tured in the game.

5 Jolly Darkies, Crank, Wood, Paper Lithograph, Reed, 8 3/4 In. 825.00
Arithmetic, Tin Lithograph, Spring Motor, Buffalo Toys, 6 In. 35.00
Backgammon, Mahogany, Satinwood, Sycamore, Dice Tumbler, Box, c.1890, 16 x 11 In. . 288.00

Galle, Vase, Leaf &
Berry, Blown-Out,
Green & Brown,
Frosted Ground,
9 In.

Printed game boards from the
1940s–1960s fade very
quickly. Older printing seems
to be damaged less by
exposure to ultraviolet light.

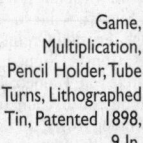

Game,
Multiplication,
Pencil Holder, Tube
Turns, Lithographed
Tin, Patented 1898,
9 In.

Bagatelle, Folding Mahogany Board, 9 Numbered Pockets, Balls, Cue, 23 x 37 x 20 In. . .	415.00
Baseball, Pinball Style, Hand Held, 4 1/2 In.	55.00
Baseball Card, 94 Cards, Instruction Booklets, Geo. Norris Co., 1903 Patent	310.00
Beany & Cecil Ring Toss, Box	60.00
Board, Burgundy, Green, Yellow, Gallery Rim, 13 x 13 1/4 In.	690.00
Board, Checkers & Backgammon, Inlaid Parquetry, Applied Edge, 18 x 18 In.	260.00
Board, Checkers & Parcheesi, Black Border, Gold Striping, Green, 22 1/2 In.	495.00
Board, Checkers & Parcheesi, Edge Molding, Multicolor, 35 x 21 1/2 In.	3850.00
Board, Checkers & Parcheesi, Gallery Rim, 20 1/4 x 20 1/4 In.	14375.00
Board, Checkers & Parcheesi, Painted, Red, Black, Yellow, Green, Orange, 18 x 18 In. . . .	1795.00
Board, Checkers, Black, White Squares, Argyle Border, American, 1800s, 18 x 18 In.	16450.00
Board, Checkers, Breadboard Ends, Red & Black Squares, Yellow Striping, 14 x 16 In. . .	695.00
Board, Checkers, Carved Borders, Dividers, Black & Red Brown, 15 1/4 x 15 1/8 In. . . .	575.00
Board, Checkers, Engraved Glass, 4 Inscribed Names, Pennsylvania, 1869, 19 3/8 In.	999.00
Board, Checkers, Figured Tiger Maple Border & Squares, Alternate With Walnut, 18 In. . .	750.00
Board, Checkers, Incised Layout, Rimmed Border, 11 3/4 x 11 3/4 In.	175.00
Board, Checkers, Inlaid, Light & Dark Wood, Rayed Corners, Ebony Pegged Frame	265.00
Board, Checkers, Pine Board, Red Stain, Black & White, 3/4 x 15 x 8 1/2 In.	110.00
Board, Checkers, Pine, Black Paint, Natural Finish, 12 x 12 In.	190.00
Board, Checkers, Pine, Black, White, Pink, Man, Woman, Barns, 1800s, 26 x 18 In.	4185.00
Board, Checkers, Pine, Breadboard Ends, Painted, Gold, Red, Salmon, 20 x 17 1/2 In. . . .	345.00
Board, Checkers, Pine, Red Stain, Black & White, 3/4 x 15 x 8 1/2 In.	110.00
Board, Checkers, Plywood, Black, Red, Hand Painted, 19 x 16 In.	69.00
Board, Checkers, Red & Black Blocks, Single Wide Board, 24 1/2 x 18 1/2 In.	880.00
Board, Checkers, Wood, Robin's-Egg Green Paint, 11 x 17 In.	60.00
Board, Chess, Carved Walnut, Glass Inserts, JP Monogram, 19 x 29 In.	290.00
Board, Grand Jeu Du Bebe Jumeau, Paris Exposition, Eiffel Tower, 1889, 18 x 27 In.	410.00
Board, Groucho T.V. Quiz, 1954, 18 1/4 x 13 1/2 In.	235.00
Board, Mustard & Green Squares, Applied Molded Edge, 25 x 12 1/2 In.	400.00
Board, Painted, Red, Black, Yellow, Mickey Mouse Head At Top, 25 x 3 1/4 In.	55.00
Board, Parcheesi, Groups Of Birds, Different Seasons, Hand Painted, 1933, 28 In.	1850.00
Board, Parcheesi, Painted, Green, Tan, Mustard, Gold, Walnut Trim, 20 1/4 x 20 3/4 In. . .	5460.00
Board, Parcheesi, Painted, R.W. Turner, 2-Sided, Christmas 1900	300.00
Board, Parcheesi, Red, White, Blue, Eagle Corner Blocks, Folk Art, 22 x 16 3/4 In.	2475.00
Board, Pine, Grid Drilled Holes, Whittled Pegs, c.1922, 1 1/2 x 12 1/2 x 11 1/2 In.	56.00
Board, Pine, Red Paint, Black Checker Squares, Backgammon On Reverse, 15 x 15 In. . .	720.00
Bowling, Kingpin Jr., Tin Lithograph, Pins, Baldwin	45.00
Buffalo Bill Jr. Cattle Round-Up, Dick Jones On Cover, 1950s	85.00
Capt. Quantum vs. The Ugly Druggies, Play To Win Inc., Board, 1990	85.00
Car Race, Automatic, 3 Cars, Tin Lithograph, Haji, Japan, Box, 1950s, 6 x 6 In.	209.00
Carpet Ball, Various Colors, Circles, Plaids, Children's, 2 3/4 In., 5 Piece	1393.00
Chess Set, Alabaster Board & Pieces, 6 1/4 In.	130.00
Chess Set, Brass, American Revolution Bicentennial, Dovetailed Box, E.H. Cloutier	1800.00
Chess Set, Ebony, Ivory, Classical Form, No Board, c.1900, 3 1/2-In. Kings	259.00
Chess Set, Ivory, Carved, 32 Figures	173.00
Chess Set, Ivory, Mixed Wood Board, Case, Haryuki, Japan, 1900s, 15 1/2 x 15 3/4 In. . .	545.00

Chess Set, Ivory, Stained, Red & White, Chinese Characters, 1920, 4 In. 390.00
Christmas Stocking, McLoughlin, Board, 1899, 6 x 4 1/2 In. 715.00
Combat, Ideal, Board, Box, 1963 . . . .   85.00
Cowboys & Indians, Ed-U-Cards, Card, Box, 1949 . . . .   30.00
Croquet Set, Child's, Little Folks, Case 69.00
Day At The Circus, McLoughlin Bros., Board, 1898 . . . .   900.00
Dice Machine, Automatic, Nickel, Clawson, Shakes, Tosses, 1890, 9 x 26 In. 3680.00
Dice Shaker Set, Boxwood, Turned, Pair Of Bone Dice, 18th Century 185.00
District Messenger Boy, McLoughlin, Board, 17 x 9 In. 330.00
Dominoes, Bone & Ebony, Dovetailed Wood Box, Slide Lid, 28 Dominos, 19th Century .   150.00
Dominoes, Express Dominoes, Train Art, Box 85.00
Dominoes, Mail Pouch, Box, Instructions, 6 1/2 x 2 In. 1000.00
Donkey Shooting, Donkey Kicks, Cork Rifle, Tin Lithographed Strauss, 1920s, 15 In. . . .   1960.00
Double Gameboard, Football, Baseball & Checkers, Parker Brothers, 1940s 45.00
Elsie & Her Family, Selchow & Righter, N.Y., Board, 1941, 12 1/2 x 14 In. 65.00
Erector Set, No. 8 1/2, All Electric, How To Make 'Em Book, 1938 . . . .   80.00
Fish Pond Game, New & Improved, Lithograph Paper, 4 Poles, McLoughlin Bros., c.1890   10.00
Football, Cast Iron, Wood, Rubber Footballs, Woolsey Mfg. Co., Minneapolis, 7 x 20 In. .   770.00
Game Of Cats & Mice, McLoughlin Bros., Board, Box, 13 1/2 x 7 In. 25.00
Gee-Wiz Horse Race, Pressed Steel Flywheel, Wolverine, 1920s, 15 1/2 In. 110.00
Gesichterspiel, Faces, Interchangeable Pieces, Lithograph, Box, Germany, 19th Century . .   705.00
Grandma's Arithmetical, Milton Bradley, Card, Box, Early 20th Century, 6 1/4 x 8 1/4 In.   20.00
Have Gun Will Travel, Parker Brothers, Board, 1959 . . . .   1300.00
Horse Race, Mechanical, 7 Horses, Cardboard Case, France, c.1920 . . . .   310.00
Infallible Indicator, Hercules Powder, Heavy Stock, 1923, 5 3/8 x 3 1/2 In. 195.00
Jigsaw Puzzle, As You Like It, Paper, On Wood, Ives, Box, 10 x 7 3/4 In. 1100.00
Jigsaw Puzzle, Fall River Line, Boat Under Brooklyn Bridge, McLoughlin, 12 x 9 In. . . .   525.00
Jigsaw Puzzle, Locomotive, McLoughlin, Box, 13 x 10 1/2 In. 250.00
Jigsaw Puzzle, Pastime Puzzle, Jigsaw, Lithographed Wood, Parker Brothers, 1917 . . . . . .   22.00
Jigsaw Puzzle, Si Cowlick & Pepper Prank 50.00
Jigsaw Puzzle, U.S. Sailor, Nurse & Soldier, Guild, Whitman Pub., Box, 1940s 40.00
Jigsaw Puzzle, Wild West, Stagecoach, McLoughlin, 12 x 8 1/2 In. 550.00
Jigsaw Puzzle, Wood, Fred Robinson, England 39.00
Jolly Darkie Target, Man, Open Mouth & Holes, Paper Lithograph, McLoughlin Bros. . . .   770.00
Knockout, Electronic Boxing, Northeastern Products, Box, 1950s 45.00
Lincoln Highway & Checkers, Lithograph Paper, Parker Brothers, Box, 1920s 50.00
Little Rascals Our Gang Clubhouse Bingo, 1958 . . . .   68.00
Magnetic Circus, Red, Yellow, Metal Board, Metal Figures, Smethport Co., 1920s 110.00
Magnetic Fish Pond, McLoughlin, 1891, 15 x 15 In. 248.00
Mah Jongg Set, Leather Case, Pong-Chow 105.00
Mansion Of Happiness, 1894, Parker Brothers, Board, 21 x 14 In. 220.00
Marbelator, No. 3, Metal, Toy Creation Station, c.1930, 21 In. 200.00
Merry Milkman, Pieces, Instructions, Hasbro, Board, c.1950, 12 x 18 In. 180.00
Messenger Boy & Checkers, Milton Bradley Co., Board, 17 x 8 3/4 In. 140.00
Mini Golf, Molded Plastic, Technofix, West Germany, 1960s, 22 x 19 In. 160.00
Multiplication, Pencil Holder, Tube Turns, Lithographed Tin, Patented 1898, 9 In. . . *Illus*   85.00
Nancy Drew Mystery Game, Parker Brothers, Board, 1957 . . . . .230.00 to 340.00
Old Maid & Old Bachelor, Board, 1894, 13 1/2 In. 605.00
Outer Limits, Milton Bradley, Board, 1964 . . . . .230.00 to 340.00
Phil Silvers' You'll Never Get Rich, Sgt. Bilko, Gardner Games, Board, 1955 . . . .   55.00
Pickwick Ten Pins, Wood, Paper Lithograph, Horsman, 7 1/2 In.   2420.00
Pinball, 5 In 1, Wood, Glass, Northwestern Products, c.1940, 13 x 23 In. 58.00
Ping-Pong Ball Dispenser, 19 In. 50.00
Puzzle, Blocks, 6 Animals, Cardboard, Paper Lithograph, 35 Cubes, Box, 18 x 13 In. 385.00
Puzzle, Blocks, Animals, Paper Lithograph, On Wood, Box, Germany 88.00
Puzzle, Blocks, Child, Dolls, Lithograph On Wood, Box, Germany, c.1900 . . . .   72.00
Puzzle, Blocks, Children Playing, Airplanes, Box, Germany 95.00
Puzzle, Blocks, Children, Turn-Of-The-Century, Paper Lithograph, On Wood, Box 39.00
Puzzle, Blocks, Goats, Lithograph Paper, Wood, Germany 8.00
Puzzle, Blocks, Little Dame Grump, Aunt Louisa's, Guide, McLoughlin, Box, 11x 12 In. .   165.00
Puzzle, Blocks, Little Red Riding Hood, Paper Lithograph, On Wood, Germany 66.00
Puzzle, Blocks, Noah's Ark, Box, Germany 66.00
Puzzle, Cube, Santa Claus, Lithograph, Wood, 3 Pictures, McLoughlin Bros., c.1890 . . . .   880.00

Puzzle, Darktown Fire Brigade, Cardboard, Parker Brothers, 1890s, 7 3/4 x 9 1/2 In. 468.00
Puzzle, Foiled By Essolube, Dr. Seuss, 150 Pieces, Envelope, c.1930s, 17 x 11 1/2 In. ... 750.00
Puzzle, Fuzzy Wuzzy Series, Pandora Picture Puzzles, Selcher & Righter Co., 7 x 9 In. .. 25.00
Puzzle, Gilbert Puzzle Parties, Booklet, Box 45.00
Puzzle, Hood Farm Puzzle Box, Cow, Chickens, Pig, Box, 1905 .... 35.00
Puzzle, Hood's Sarsaparilla, 4 In 1, Box, 32-Page Booklet, c.1896, 18 1/4 x 11 1/4 In. ... 90.00
Puzzle, Jaynes Expectorant, Bottle Shape, Attached Malady, Remedy Paddles, 5 1/2 In. .. 45.00
Puzzle, Locomotive, McLoughlin Bros., Box, c.1887 .... 225.00
Puzzle, Make Your Own Funnies, Wood, Instructions, Jaymar, Box, c.1930 .... 1450.00
Puzzle, Riverboat, City Of Worcester, Litho, McLoughlin Bros., Box, 1889, 38 x 14 In. .. 690.00
Puzzle, United States Map, Lithographed Wood, Parker Brothers, Box 50.00
Puzzle, Wild West, Assembled, Frame, Box, 11 x 19 In. 275.00
Puzzle, Zoo, Animals, 6 Sections, Paper On Wood, Lithograph, Germany, 10 x 14 In. 98.00
Quick Draw McGraw, Private Eye, Milton Bradley, Board, 1960, 16 x 18 In. 15.00
Reading, Rip Van Winkle, Milton Bradley, Box, 1909, 5 1/2 x 6 3/4 In. 20.00
Red Riding Hood, Parker Brothers, Board, 21 x 10 1/2 In. 660.00
Risk, Wood Pieces, Parker Bros., Board, 1960s 29.00
Rival Doctors, Board, 1893, 10 1/2 x 11 In. 880.00
Rudolph The Red-Nosed Reindeer, Parker Brothers, Board, 1948 .... 275.00
Sand Chessmen, Whalebone, Toothpick Ends, Figural Tops, 4 1/4 To 5 1/2 In. 175.00
Scratch, Spinner, Teaches Math, Tin Plate, Bird Mfg., U.S.A., Box, 10 In. 45.00
Shooting Gallery, Space Shooting Range, Tin, Windup, Automatic Toy Co., Box, 19 In. ... 355.00
Shooting Target, Pig, Astride Wall, Tin, Sheet Metal, Early 20th Century, 15 x 17 In. 965.00
Spider-Man, Web Spinning Action, Figures Of Spidey & Villains, Ideal, 18 x 16 In. 75.00
Squad Leader, Game Of Infantry Combat In WWII, Avalon Hill, Baltimore, 1977 .... 35.00
Squadron Scramble Card Game No. I, No. 3937, Whitman Publishing, U.S.A., 1942 ... 25.00
Stanley In Africa, Lithograph Paper, Board, Bliss, Box, 1891, 15 x 13 1/2 In. 1760.00
Steeple Chase, McLoughlin, Board, 1890s, 10 1/2 x 20 In. 55.00
Steeple Chase, McLoughlin, Board, 1890s, 21 x 31 In. 220.00
Target, Chuck, Black Man, In Watermelon Patch, Ottman, 17 1/2 x 8 In. 770.00
Target, Knight, Armor, Hit Shield, Raises Sword, Tin, Battery Operated, MT, Box, 12 In. . 550.00
Target, Mighty Kong, Battery Operated, Box, 9 In. 545.00
Target, Mother Goose, Ball Hits Button, Characters Pop Up, Wood, Paper Litho, 18 In. .. 550.00
Target, Quick Draw McGraw, Shooting, 1960s 60.00
Target, Shoot 'Em Ups, Hit Target & Cowbay Falls, Battery Operated, Vanity Fair, Box .. 30.00
Target, Shooting Gallery, Battleship, Cast Iron, 10 x 5 In. 56.00
Telegraph Boy, McLoughlin, Board, 1888, 17 1/4 x 9 1/2 In. .... 165.00 to 195.00
Throw, Cat, Sitting, Black, Plywood, Painted, Revere Beach, 39 1/2 x 24 In. 230.00
Toy Town Post Office, Milton Bradley 110.00
Twilight Zone, Unopened Contents, Ideal, Board, 1964 .... 190.00
Uncle Sam's Spelling Board, Wood, Cardboard, Metal, Durable Toy & Novelty, 10 x 15 In. 105.00
United States Air Mail, Parker Brothers, Box, 1930s 30.00
Visit Of Santa Claus, Lithographed, Milton Bradley, Board, Box 345.00
Washington Crossing The Delaware, Singer, Box 30.00
Wheel, Chance, Wood Stand, Nickel & Brass Hardware, c.1880s, 53 x 32 1/2 In. 3089.00
Wheel, Gambling, Reverse Painted, Famous Race Horses, Wood, Iron, H.C. Evans, 88 In. . 4950.00
Wheel, Roulette, Accessories, Mahogany Box, England, c.1925, 6 x 22 x 14 1/2 In. 690.00
Wheel, Roulette, Horse Race, Painted Wood, 44 In. 2420.00
Wheel, Roulette, Mahogany, Table Top, Copper, Brass, Pewter, 14 In. 280.00
Wheel, Roulette, Wheel Crate, Legs, Stretcher, Albert Pick, c.1910, 23 In. 660.00
Wheel, Roulette, Wood Rimmed Bicycle Wheel, Early 20th Century 345.00
White Elephant Question, Paper Lithograph, Elephant Trunk Points, France, 10 x 11 In. . 220.00
Wild Bill Hickok, Cavalry & Indians, Guy Madison On Lid, Built Rite, 1950s 85.00
Yacht Race, McLoughlin, Board, 1887, 16 1/2 x 8 1/2 In. 1045.00
Zoom Game Of Skill, Cast Aluminum Front, Airplane Graphics, Box, 1940s, 14 x 24 In. . 825.00
Zorro, Whitman, Board, 1965 .... 25.00

GARDEN FURNISHINGS have been popular for centuries. The stone or
metal statues, wire, iron, or rustic furniture, urns and fountains, sundi-
als, and small figurines are included in this category. Many of the
metal pieces have been made continuously for years.

    Armillary Sphere, Bronze, Pedestal, Georgian, Carved Putti, Limestone, c.1780, 68 In. 2300.00
    Armillary Sphere, Carved Limestone, Iron, 72 1/2 x 20 x 19 In. .... *Illus* 3520.00

Basket, Wirework, Applied Flowers, Leaves, Painted, Tin, 1800s, 17 x 11 x 9 1/2 In. 252.00
Bench, Aesthetic Style, Flower Medallions, Hunting Dog, Cast Iron, 1900s, 31 x 51 In. .. 345.00
Bench, Branches, Green Paint, Cast Iron, Oak Slats, 48 In. 483.00
Bench, Fan Shape Back, Strapwork Arms, Cast Iron, Victorian, 46 In. .... *Illus* 980.00
Bench, Gauche Pattern, Floral Crest, Cast Iron, 34 1/4 x 43 x 16 In. .... *Illus* 1265.00
Bench, Gothic Arches, Shaped Feet, Iron, 1800s, England, 41 1/2 x 66 x 18 In. 2200.00
Bench, Gothic, Pierced Scrollwork, Cast Iron, Late Victorian, 44 x 17 1/2 x 36 In. 1495.00
Bench, Oak Leaves, Dog Heads, Cast Iron, Wood, Victorian, 37 1/2 x 59 In. 750.00
Bench, Openwork Seat, Back, Cabriole Legs, Cast Iron, 35 x 47 x 20 In. 990.00
Bench, Openwork Seat, Scrolled Panel, White, Washington Iron Works, Cast Iron, 45 In. .. 230.00
Bench, Openwork, Scrolls & Swags, Curved Legs, White Paint, Cast Iron, 36 x 30 In. 115.00
Bench, Pierced Fan, Trefoil, Arched Back Rest, Scrolled Arms, Cast Iron, 47 In., Pair 3220.00
Bench, Tudor Rose, Green Paint, Oak Slats, Cast Iron, 48 In. 440.00
Bench, Windsor, Fern, White, Cast Iron, 32 x 94 x 15 In. 2875.00
Bench, Winged Griffin, Branching Flowers, Cast Iron, Late Victorian, 39 x 24 x 29 In. ... 1150.00
Birdbath, Scallop Form, 2 Ducks, White Paint, Cast Iron, 13 In. 185.00
Birdhouse, Gothic Style, Gray, White, Red Roof, Iron, 10 1/2 x 14 1/2 x 11 In. 2013.00
Boot Scraper, Horseshoe Shape, Mounted, Rimmed Base, Iron, 9 x 11 In. 2530.00
Boot Scraper, Quatrefoil Base, Iron, 5 1/2 x 10 1/2 x 11 In. 633.00
Chair, W. Guhl, Concrete, Eternit, c.1954, 21 5/8 In. 2270.00
Chair, Wagon Wheel Spring Seat, White Enamel Paint, Wrought Iron, 31 x 16 x 22 In. ... 170.00
Chair Set, Openwork, Coat Of Arms, Victorian, Cast Iron, England, 3 Piece 1955.00
Chair Set, Sunburst Crest, Scrolled Lyre Backs, Cast Iron, Victorian, 3 Piece 715.00
Cherub, Playing Drums, Cymbals, Cast Iron, Wood Bases, c.1900, 14 1/2 In., Pair 115.00
Figure, 4 Seasons Set, Putto On Sphere, Rococo Style, Cast Iron, 40 In. 2760.00
Figure, Alligator, Cast Iron, 29 In. 345.00
Figure, Buddha, Seated, Green Patina, Concrete, 11 1/2 In. 175.00
Figure, Bulldog, Cast Iron, 16 x 29 In. 920.00
Figure, Crane, Japanese Style, One Head Up, Other Preening, 53 In., Pair 575.00
Figure, Dog, Bulldog, Sitting, Polychrome, Patina, Iron, 7 In. 385.00
Figure, Dog, Great Dane, Seated, Rectangular Plinth, 43 x 19 x 22 In., Pair 1150.00
Figure, Eagle, Spread Wing, Gilt, Black Painted Plinth, Iron, 19th Century, 15 1/4 x 8 In. . 825.00
Figure, Foo Dog, Seated, Weathered Surface, 15 1/2 x 21 1/2 & 15 x 20 In., Pair 220.00
Figure, Foo Dogs On Medallions, Flowers, Stone, 27 x 9 x 37 In. 440.00
Figure, Frog, Red Marble Eyes, Cement, 11 In. 158.00
Figure, Gnome, Holding Basket, Wood, Swiss, c.1920, 5 1/4 In. 240.00
Figure, Jockey, Outstretched Arm, Red, Black, White Paint, Cast Iron, 24 In. 190.00
Figure, Lion, Lying Down, Rectangular Plinth, Iron, Victorian, 14 1/2 In., Pair 805.00
Figure, Lion, Seated, Resting Paw On Shield, Cast Stone, 33 x 14 x 18 1/2 In., Pair 430.00
Figure, Male Torso, Cast Iron, Marble Base, 20 x 39 & 14 x 20 In. 1875.00
Figure, Monk, Seated On Rough Cut Block, Stone, Gray Patina, 24 In. 220.00
Figure, Puppy, Reclining, Cast Iron, 19 In. 335.00
Figure, Rabbit, Cast Iron, White Paint, 11 x 9 1/2 In. 290.00
Figure, Rabbit, White Paint, 2-Piece Casting, Iron, 11 5/8 In. 200.00
Figure, Rooster, White Paint, Iron, 14 In. 150.00
Figure, Victorian Style, 8-Point Buck, Cast Iron, 71 x 18 x 40 In. 2300.00
Figure, Victorian Style, Doe, Head Raised, 60 x 15 x 48 In. 1495.00

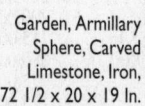

Garden, Armillary
Sphere, Carved
Limestone, Iron,
72 1/2 x 20 x 19 In.

Garden, Bench, Fan-
Shaped Back, Strapwork
Arms, Cast Iron,
Victorian, 46 In.

Garden, Bench, Gauche
Pattern, Floral Crest, Cast
Iron, 34 1/4 x 43 x 16 In.

Garden, Fountain, Figural,
Genevieve, Bronze,
Patina, Marked, E. Berge
1917, 33 x 20 In.

Garden, Urn, Relief Frieze, Neoclassical
Figures, Carved, Marble, 29 x 24 In., Pair

Fountain, 3 Tiers, Tazza Shape Bowls, Swan Pedestal, Cast Iron, Victorian, 97 x 46 In.	1035.00
Fountain, Basin Shape, Square Stepped Pedestal, Footed, Cast Iron, c.1865, 46 x 40 In.	1610.00
Fountain, Conservatory, Patinated Bronze, Classical Maiden, France, 56 1/2 In. . .920.00 to	1200.00
Fountain, Figural, Child Riding Fish, Cast Lead, 13 1/2 In.	440.00
Fountain, Figural, Genevieve, Bronze, Patina, Marked, E. Berge 1917, 33 x 20 In. . . *Illus*	1980.00
Fountain, La Source, Terra-Cotta Stain, Cast Stone, 60 x 39 In.	2530.00
Fountain, Renaissance Style, Boy With Dolphin, Verdigris, Patinated Bronze, 48 1/2 In.	2530.00
Fountain, Victorian Style, Putto, Lobed Bowl, 3 Dolphin Pedestal, Cast Iron, 47 x 26 In.	865.00
Fountain Head, Carved, Classical Figures, Stone Slab Mount, c.1804, 14 1/2 x 10 In.	230.00
Gate, Rose Design, Iron, 48 In., Pair	1100.00
Group, Deer Family, Tan Paint, Cast Iron, Buck 49 In., Doe 47 In., Fawn 30 In.	4950.00
Hitching Post, Column, Roof Style Top, Green, Gold, Cast Iron, 69 1/2 In.	230.00
Hitching Post, Finial, Elephant, Cast Iron, 8 1/2 In.	825.00
Hitching Post, Horse Head, Animated, Octagonal Base, Side Ring, Black, Iron, 13 1/4 In.	410.00
Hitching Post, Horse Head, Cast Iron, 12 1/4 In., Pair	98.00
Hitching Post, Horse Head, Cast Iron, Mid 19th Century, 68 In.	1265.00
Hitching Post, Horse Head, Fluted Column, Cast Iron, Painted Black, 47 5/8 x 24 In.	705.00
Hitching Post, Horse Head, Marten & Anderson Yankton, Black, Iron, 31 1/2 In.	825.00
Hitching Post, Horse Head, Mouth Loop, Entrance Bell, Cast Iron, 10 x 8 x 11 1/2 In.	35.00
Hitching Post, Indian, Cast Iron, Top Hair Knot, Feathers, Turned Post, 55 In.	14950.00
Hitching Post, Jockey, Black & Light Blue Diamond Shirt, Cast Iron, 48 In.	588.00
Hitching Post, Jockey, Iron Base, McKittrick Foundry, Union Beach, New York, 47 In.	1100.00
Hitching Post, Tree Trunk Shape, Cut Off Branches, Cast Iron, 52 1/2 In.	345.00
Jardiniere, Blue & White Enamel, Flaring, Mask Handles, Cast Iron, c.1840, 16 In.	1955.00
Kneeling Stool, Pine, Nailed, Cutout Bootjack Ends, 7 x 29 1/5 x 7 In.	28.00
Lantern, Iron, Japan, Early 1900s, 60 In.	2470.00
Lawn Mower, 2 Handles, Sickle Bar, 1900	248.00
Lawn Sprinkler, Mallard Duck, Molded Metal, 15 In.	275.00
Ornament, Fruit Basket, Concrete, Green Paint, 22 In.	230.00
Ornament, Pineapple, Faience, Yellow Glaze, Black Diamond Points, 22 In., Pair	1380.00
Pagoda, Concrete, 22 In.	160.00
Pedestal, Square, Corinthian, Cast Iron Capitals, Marble Top, 30 In.	5980.00
Plant Stand, 2 Tiers, Wirework, Hour Glass Shape, Casters, Victorian, 43 x 20 In.	470.00
Plant Stand, 3 Tiers, Wirework, Pedestal, Basket, Victorian, 51 x 30 1/4 x 26 In.	415.00
Plant Stand, Flower Top, Scrolling Brackets, Dolphin Feet, Cast Iron, 28 x 14 In., Pair	403.00
Plant Stand, Wire Work, 2 Tiers, Round, Hour Glass Shape Base, Victorian, 43 x 20 In.	476.00
Plant Stand, Wire Work, 3 Tiers, Arbor Top, Hanging Basket, Victorian, 78 x 46 x 29 In.	505.00
Planter, Bowl, Copper, Iron Swags, Iron Rope Twist Tripod Legs, 35 1/2 In., Pair	170.00
Planter, Octagonal, Swag, Terra-Cotta, 14 x 17 x 17 In., Pair	770.00
Planter, Tree Trunk Shape, Composition, 41 x 20 In., 2 Piece	220.00
Planter, Wall, Pierce-Work Backplate, Cast Iron, 25 x 14 1/4 x 5 1/4 In.	200.00
Porch Swing, Wicker, Painted Cream, Arched Back, Suspended By Chains, 22 x 55 In.	115.00
Seat, Blue & White, Drum Shape, Flowers Scrolling, Ceramic, Chinese, 1800s, 19 In.	880.00
Seat, Blue Design, White Glaze, Round, Ceramic, Chinese, c.1835, 18 In.	1975.00
Seat, Brown Lacquer, Passion Flowers, 1900s, 17 1/2 In., Pair	175.00
Seat, Chinese Style Decoration, Lion Masks, Blue Ground, 18 1/4 In.	764.00
Seat, Courtier Design, Mask Handles, Japan, c.1900, 19 In.	176.00
Seat, Drum Shape, Blue, White Birds, Flowers, Porcelain, Chinese, Late 1800s, 18 In.	1528.00

Seat, Elephant Shape, Multicolored Glaze, Porcelain, Chinese, 22 x 10 1/2 x 21 In., Pair	196.00
Seat, Famille Noire, Exotic Bird, Peonies, Porcelain, 19 1/2 In.	115.00
Seat, Famille Rose, Flowers, Drum Shape, Coin Piercings, Chinese, 1800s, 19 In.	440.00
Seat, Rose Medallion, Drum Shape, Porcelain, Chinese, 1800s, 19 In.	2470.00
Set, Renaissance Revival Style, Green Paint, Cast Iron, Atlanta Stove Works, 6 Piece	2530.00
Settle, Stone, Carved, Circular Top, Tapered Base, 25 1/2 x 20 x 20 In., Pair	2200.00
Sprinkler, Mallard Duck, Brace Spinner, Cast Iron, Victorian, 13 In.	1540.00
Sprinkler, Merganser Duck, Large Feet, Cast Iron	660.00
Sundial, Anno Dom MXCXI, 3 Stanchions, Bronze Hand, 18th Century, 8 In.	300.00
Sundial, Bronze, Terra-Cotta, 8-Sided, Urn Form Pedestal, 19th Century, 39 1/2 x 20 In.	770.00
Sundial, Engraved Numerals, Skull, Sickle, Life's But A Shade, Bronze, c.1675, 8 In.	460.00
Sundial, Hemispherical, Vines, Grape Cluster, Bird, Bronze, 1800s, 15 3/8 x 34 x 17 In.	940.00
Sundial, Sun Face, Roman Numerals, Brass, 8 In.	298.00
Sundial, Wooden, Folding, Pocket, Embossed, 4 x 2 x 1/4 In.	55.00
Table, Rococo Scrolled Base, Latticework, Round Top, Painted, Cast Iron, 38 x 27 In.	110.00
Table, Victorian Style, Round Top, Pierced Flowers, Cast Iron, 27 1/2 x 22 1/2 In., Pair	175.00
Topiary, 3 Graduated Holly Spherules, Leaves, Berries, Painted, Metal, 32 In., Pair	470.00
Urn, Campana Shape, White Paint, Cast Iron, 11 1/2 In., Pair	150.00
Urn, Classical, Plinth Base, Cast Iron, 23 x 17 1/2 In.	595.00
Urn, Gothic Style, Footed, Terra-Cotta, Cast Stone, 20 In., Pair	520.00
Urn, Medici Style, Carved Outswept Rim, Fluted Body, Marble, England, 28 In., Pair	1150.00
Urn, Neoclassical, 2 Mask Handles, Fluted Pedestal, Iron, 23 x 32 1/2 In., Pair	545.00
Urn, Neoclassical, Flared Rim, Flowers, Ram's Head Handles, Bronze, 27 x 20 In., Pair	1035.00
Urn, Neoclassical, Tazza Form, Egg & Dart Molding, Cast Iron, 39 x 37 In., Pair	1265.00
Urn, Pegasus, Twisted Handles, Reeded Foot Base, Cast Lead, 18th Century, 20 x 12 In.	495.00
Urn, Relief Frieze, Neoclassical Figures, Carved, Marble, 29 x 24 In., Pair *Illus*	1700.00
Urn, Ruffled Top, Lion Heads, Swing Handles, Square Base, Cast Iron, 14 1/2 x 21 1/2 In.	865.00
Vase, Campana Shape, Square Pedestal, Terra-Cotta, Cast Stone, France, 49 In., Pair	865.00
Wardian Case, Rococo Revival Frame, Iron, Glass, c.1855, 18 1/2 x 29 x 15 1/4 In.	1207.00

GAUDY DUTCH pottery was made in England for America from about 1810 to 1820. It is a white earthenware with Imari-style decorations of red, blue, green, yellow, and black. Only sixteen patterns of Gaudy Dutch were made: Butterfly, Carnation, Dahlia, Double Rose, Dove, Grape, Leaf, Oyster, Primrose, Single Rose, Strawflower, Sunflower, Urn, War Bonnet, Zinnia, and No Name. Other similar wares are called *Gaudy Ironstone* and *Gaudy Welsh*.

Bowl, War Bonnet, 9 1/2 In.	260.00
Coffeepot, Dome Top, Carnation, 10 1/4 In.	1100.00
Coffeepot, Dome Top, Single Rose, 10 1/2 In.	3300.00
Creamer, Single Rose, 4 1/2 In.	1150.00
Cup & Saucer, Single Rose	375.00
Cup & Saucer, Sunflower	635.00
Cup & Saucer, War Bonnet	635.00
Cup Plate, Butterfly, 3 7/8 In.	4830.00
Cup Plate, Dahlia, Green, Gold, Blue, Brown, Scalloped, Fish Scale, 4 1/4 In.	1210.00
Cup Plate, Double Rose, 3 5/8 In.	1320.00
Cup Plate, Grape, 3 1/2 In.	990.00
Cup Plate, Single Rose, 4 In.	990.00
Cup Plate, Urn, 3 3/4 In.	2200.00
Cup Plate, War Bonnet, 3 1/2 In.	1375.00
Pitcher, War Bonnet, 5 1/2 In.	2300.00
Plate, Butterfly, 8 3/8 In.	1540.00
Plate, Carnation, 9 3/4 In.	1840.00
Plate, Double Rose, 7 1/8 In.	345.00
Plate, Double Rose, 8 1/4 In.	690.00
Plate, Dove, 10 In.	1925.00
Plate, Grape, 5 7/8 In.	290.00
Plate, Grape, 7 In.	385.00 to 460.00
Plate, Grape, 8 In.	575.00
Plate, Grape, 9 3/4 In.	1095.00
Plate, Grape, Blue, Yellow, Green, Orange, 7 1/8 In.	440.00
Plate, Primrose, Impressed, Riley, 8 3/8 In.	4140.00

Plate, Single Rose, 8 In. ....290.00 to 415.00
Plate, Urn, 6 1/4 In. 690.00
Plate, War Bonnet, 8 In. 690.00
Teapot, Oyster, 6 3/4 In. 715.00
Teapot, Urn, Gooseneck Spout, Scroll Handle, 6 5/8 In. 845.00
Teapot, War Bonnet, 6 1/2 In. 3910.00
Toddy, Grape, 4 1/2 In. 920.00
Waste Bowl, Dove, Orange, Cobalt Blue, Yellow, 6 1/4 x 3 In. 358.00

GAUDY IRONSTONE is the collector's name for the ironstone wares
with the bright patterns similar to Gaudy Dutch. It was made in
England for the American market after 1850. There may be other
examples found in the listing for Ironstone or under the name of the
ceramic factory.

Charger, Center Yellow Flower, Red & Green, Black Lion Mark, 13 1/2 In. 172.00
Child's Set, Wagon Wheel, Sugar, Lid, Creamer, 5-In. Teapot & Lid, 6 Plates 400.00
Chop Plate, Flowers, Pagoda, Bridge, Ashworth Bros., England, 12 1/2 In............. 110.00
Creamer, Grape Octagon Form, Overglaze Green Sprigs, 6 In. 350.00
Plate, Half-Ripe Strawberries, Paneled, 9 1/2 In. 275.00
Plate, Soup, Grape, 10 3/4 In. 300.00
Platter, Cobalt Blue, Red, Purple Flowers, Davenport, 13 1/2 x 16 3/4 In. 250.00
Platter, Flow Blue Design, Stylized Roses, Scrolls, Swags, 14 x 17 1/2 In. 600.00
Platter, Grape, Canted Corners, Orange & Green Shoots, Leaves, 11 x 14 1/2 In. 450.00
Platter, Relief Border Panels, 11 x 15 1/2 In. 300.00
Platter, Strawberry, Canted Corners, 10 1/4 x 13 1/2 In. 850.00
Punch Bowl, 10 In. 330.00
Sugar, Lid, Pinwheel, Finial 250.00
Teapot, Adams Rose, Green Leaves, Yellow & Cobalt Blue Details, 4 1/4 In. 60.00
Teapot, Morning Glory, Paneled, Pedestal Foot, Cockcomb Handle, 10 In. 425.00
Teapot, Pinwheel, Red-Orange Luster, Leaves, Finial Lid, 9 In. 300.00
Wash Pitcher, Morning Glory, 12 1/4 In. 750.00
Wash Pitcher, Strawberry, Freehand Flow Blue Design, 12 1/2 In. 850.00
Waste Bowl, Strawberry, Paneled, 3 3/4 x 6 In. 550.00

GAUDY WELSH is an Imari-decorated earthenware with red, blue,
green, and gold decorations. Most Gaudy Welsh was made in England
for the American market. It was made from 1820 to about 1860.

Jug, Oyster, Copper Luster, 20th Century, 2 1/4 x 1 3/8 In. 99.00
Mug, Gate, Cobalt Blue, Green, Orange, Luster, 4 1/4 In. 165.00
Mug, Urn, Paneled, Molded Leaves On Handle, 3 3/8 In. 405.00
Mustard Pot, Spoon, 19th Century, 4 x 2 1/4 x 2 1/4 In. 165.00
Pitcher, Cream, Oyster, Iron Red, Copper Luster, Mid 19th Century, 4 3/8 x 4 In. 143.00
Pitcher, Flower, Stripes, 7 1/2 In. 305.00
Pitcher, Petunias, Pink & Copper Luster, Panels, Scrolled Handle, 7 1/4 In. 259.00
Pitcher, Roses, Red, Blue, Green Leaves, Molded Rim, Base, 7 3/4 In. 145.00
Pitcher, Sunflowers, Panels, Pink & Copper Luster, 7 1/4 In. 115.00
Plate, Oyster, Iron Red, Blue, Copper Luster, 19th Century, 6 3/4 In. 145.00
Platter, Blackberry Design, Cobalt Blue, Yellow, Orange, Gilt, 9 1/4 x 11 3/4 In. 316.00
Platter, Flowers, Jagged Leaves, Wavy Stems, Copper Luster, Octagonal, 12 x 15 In. 460.00
Soup, Dish, Dahlia, 19th Century, 1 1/4 x 7 1/2 In. 55.00
Teapot, Blackberry Design, Cobalt Blue, Yellow, Orange, Gilt, Fruit Finial, 9 1/2 In. 489.00
Toothpick Holder, Oyster, Allerton, 19th Century, 1 5/8 x 1 3/4 In. 99.00
Washbowl & Pitcher, Chinoiserie Figural Design, Early 1800s, 3 In. 145.00

GENE AUTRY was born in 1907. He began his career as the *Singing
Cowboy* in 1928. His first movie appearance was in 1934, his last in
1958. His likeness and that of the Wonder Horse, Champion, were used
on toys, books, lunch boxes, and advertisements.

Button, Cowboy Star, Multicolored, Celluloid, 1 3/4 In. 22.00
Cap Gun, Cast Iron, Single Shot & Action, Plastic Grip, Kenton, 8 In. 55.00
Cap Gun, Short Barrel, Pearlized Grips, Cast Iron, Kenton, c.1940, 6 1/4 In. 125.00
Cap Gun, Short Barrel, Pearlized Grips, Cast Iron, Kenton, c.1940, 8 In. 125.00
Cap Gun Set, 2 Holsters, Belt, Guns, 6 1/2 In. 155.00

Holster, Black Leather Belt, Plastic Jewels, Brown Pockets, c.1940, 10 1/4 In. 80.00
Horse, Champion, Vinyl, Inflatable, Bouncing, 1950s, 23 In. 80.00

GIBSON GIRL black-and-blue decorated plates were made in the early 1900s. Twenty-four different 10 1/2-inch plates were made by the Royal Doulton pottery at Lambeth, England. These pictured scenes from the book *A Widow and Her Friends* by Charles Dana Gibson. Another set of twelve 9-inch plates featuring pictures of the heads of Gibson Girls had all-blue decoration. Many other items also pictured the famous Gibson Girl.

Box, Cover, Cameo Of Girl, Pyrography, 15 x 12 x 5 In. 50.00
Plate, Miss Babbles Brings Morning Paper, Royal Doulton, Signed, 10 1/2 In. 100.00
Plate, Royal Doulton, c.1900, 10 1/2 In., 6 Piece 575.00
Postcard, The New Gibson Girl, Photo, 1919 . . . .   5.00

GILLINDER pressed glass was first made by William T. Gillinder of Philadelphia in 1863. The company had a working factory on the grounds at the Centennial and made small, marked pieces of glass for sale as souvenirs. They made a variety of decorative glass pieces and tablewares.

GILLINDER

Bread Tray, Washington Centennial, 1876 . . . .   120.00
Bust, Admiral Dewey, Milk Glass, Frosted, 5 1/2 In. 300.00
Bust, Lincoln, 1876, 6 In. 424.00
Figurine, Buddha, Seated, Cobalt Blue, 5 1/2 In. 85.00
Salt & Pepper, Melon Ribbed, Opal, Enameled Flowers, 3 In. 90.00

GIRL SCOUT collectors search for anything pertaining to the Girl Scouts, including uniforms, publications, and old cookie boxes. The Girl Scout movement started in 1912, two years after the Boy Scouts. It began under Juliette Gordon Low of Savannah, Georgia. The first Girl Scout cookies were sold in 1928.

Lunch Box, Candy, 3 x 6 x 3 3/4 In. 365.00
Pencil Case, Girl Playing Bugle, Wallace Pencil Co., Tin Lithograph, 7 3/4 x 3 1/2 In. 125.00
Poster, Build For American Girlhood, Cardboard, Lester Raidh, c.1920s, 11 x 16 In. 65.00

GLASS-ART. Art glass means any of the many forms of glassware made during the late nineteenth or early twentieth century. These wares were expensive and production was limited. Art glass is not the typical commercial glass that was made in large quantities, and most of the art glass was produced by hand methods. Later twentieth-century glass is listed under Glass-Contemporary, Glass-Midcentury, or Glass-Venetian. Even more art glass may be found in categories such as Burmese, Cameo Glass, Tiffany, and other factory names.

Basket, Amber, Ribs, Pink Twist Handle, 6 1/2 In. 60.00
Basket, Blue Opalescent, Thorn Handle, Enameled Acorn Design, 6 1/4 In. 50.00
Basket, Cased Pink, Flowers, Applied Clear Handle, 7 In. 70.00
Basket, Cased Yellow Over Tomato, Swirled Ribs, Ruffled Rim, Thorn Handle, 6 x 7 In. . .   115.00
Basket, Cranberry Opalescent Stripes, Pink Twist Handle, 5 In. 80.00
Basket, Lavender Opalescent Swirl, Vaseline Twist Handle, Yellow Blossoms, 6 1/2 In. . . .   100.00
Basket, Lavender, Handle, Yellow Opalescent, Plumes, 5 1/2 In. 200.00
Basket, Opaque Blue, Applied Clear Handle, Footed, 6 1/2 In. 60.00
Basket, Pink, Silver Mica Highlights, Cased, Clear Twist Thorn Handle, 7 In. 60.00
Basket, Yellow, Gold Mica Highlights, Cased, Clear Twist Handle, 7 1/2 In. 90.00
Biscuit Jar, Opaque Green, Enameled Flowers, Silver Plated Lid, Bail Handle, 6 1/2 In. . .   225.00
Bowl, Acid Etched, Female Figure, Bird, Ann Warff, Sweden, c.1980, 5 7/8 In. 90.00
Bowl, Chinese Overlay, Green On White, Carved Landscape, Rosewood Stand, 6 In., Pair   575.00
Bowl, Hand Blown Glass, Vertical Ribbing, Silver Mica Flecks, 5 3/4 x 3 1/2 In. 290.00
Box, Hinged Cover, Egg Shape, Clear, Violets, Enamel, 4 In. 50.00
Compote, Cherub Shape Handles, Cast Metal Stand, 13 In. 115.00
Creamer, Pink, Yellow, Blue, White Swirl, Enameled, Pink Interior, Handleless, 3 3/4 In. . .   460.00
Decanter, Enameled Poppies, Green Pedestal, 14 In. 100.00
Epergne, Pedestal Bowl, Opaque Pink, Lily, 10 1/2 In. 130.00
Epergne, Scrolled Canes, Hanging Bouquet Holders, Ruffled Edge, c.1870, 19 In. 690.00

Pitcher, Cranberry, Vaseline, Hobnail, 7 3/4 In. 375.00
Pitcher, Enameled Ferns & Bees, Ribbed Handle, Bulbous, Continental, 8 In. 705.00
Pitcher, Opaque Pink, Enameled Chrysanthemum, Flat, 9 3/4 In. 250.00
Salt & Pepper, Opaque Blue, Gold Trim, 3 1/4 In., Pair 70.00
Shade, Blue Iridescent Trailing, Gold Ground, White Interior, 4 3/4 In., 4 Piece 3335.00
Sugar Shaker, Beaded Grape, Pink Satin, 5 1/2 In. 140.00
Sugar Shaker, Blue Opaque, Ribs, Lattice, 5 In. 180.00
Sugar Shaker, Embossed Flowers, Lime Green, 4 In. 100.00
Sugar Shaker, Pink, End Of Day, 5 In. 90.00
Sugar Shaker, Quilted Pine Cone, Pink, Cased, 5 1/4 In. 140.00
Tumbler, Diamond-Quilted, Pink Opalescent To Clear, Barrel Shape, 3 1/2 In. 50.00
Tumbler, Inverted Baby Thumbprint, Bluerina, Hobbs, Brockunier, 3 3/4 In. 155.00
Tumbler, Inverted Baby Thumbprint, Bluerina, Rosette & Thumbprint Base, 4 In. 165.00
Tumbler, Pink Shaded To Deep Blue, Ribbed Optic, 3 3/4 In. 130.00
Tumbler Set, Polka Dot, Various Colors, Hobbs, No. 290, Box, 3 3/4 In., 12 Piece 3740.00
Vase, Aventurine, Cased, Blue Interior, Berries, Petal Base, 4 1/2 x 6 3/4 In. 115.00
Vase, Bottle Shape, Mottled Yellow & White, Kimball, 4 In. 50.00
Vase, Campana, Enameled Flowers, Horned Animals, Handles, 1900s, 8 3/8 In. 205.00
Vase, Clear Body, Red & Amber Splashes, 2 Red Handles, St. Louis, 4 x 5 In. 175.00
Vase, Dimpled Sides, Iridescent Threaded Design, Yellow Ground, Austria, 6 3/4 In. 120.00
Vase, Embossed Elephants, Frosted, D'Avesn France, 8 1/2 x 7 1/2 In. 175.00
Vase, Etched, Egg Shape, Geometric Patterns, Blue, Catteau, Belgium, c.1915, 8 In. 382.00
Vase, Flashed Yellow Ground, Green, Iridescent Frosted Scrolls, Honesdale, 3 1/4 In. 85.00
Vase, Floral Overlay, Iridescent Glass, Pinched Rim, 5 1/4 In. 460.00
Vase, Forest Relief, Tapered Cylinder, Wide Mouth, Continental, 10 1/8 In. 235.00
Vase, Iridescent Amethyst, 4 Folded Handles, Austria, 8 In. 315.00
Vase, Iridescent Fuchsia Red, Applied Threading, Textured Oil Spot, Dimpled, 13 In. 345.00
Vase, Iridescent Gold Zipper, Pink Rope, Frosted, Rolled Rim, Correia, 4 3/4 In. 45.00
Vase, Iridescent, Gold Green, Threaded Body, Applied Cherries, Early 1900s, 5 In. 705.00
Vase, Mold Blown, Pinched Sides, Blue Iridescent, Green Glass Body, Austria, 4 3/4 In. ... 230.00
Vase, Opaque Pink, Ribs, Clear Beveled Foot, Mirror Base, 3 1/4 In. 175.00
Vase, Pulled Feather, Gold Trim, Iridescent Rim, Trevais, 3 x 3 1/2 In. 230.00
Vase, Red Ground, Smoky Gray Design, Bulbous, Austria, 9 In. 115.00
Water Set, 6-Sided Pitcher, Tree Trunk, Goblets, Victorian, 5 Piece 300.00

GLASS-BLOWN was formed by forcing air through a rod into molten
glass. Early glass and some forms of art glass were hand blown. Other
types of glass were molded or pressed.

Apothecary Jar, Steeple Stopper, England, c.1900, 30 1/2 In. 375.00
Basket, Beaded Loop Pattern, Everted Rim, Snap Pontil, Applied Handle, 4 x 4 In. 58.00
Bottle, Dress, Silver Overlay Flowers, 3 1/2 In. 46.00
Cake Dome, Folded Rim, Dome Top, Applied Handle, Wafer, 12 x 9 1/2 In. 200.00
Canister, Cover, Cobalt Blue Rings, Tall Finial, Pittsburgh, 12 3/4 In. 600.00
Compote, Cut, Scallop Edge, Air Trap Stem, Pittsburgh, 9 x 8 1/2 In. 173.00
Cordial Set, Flint, Wafer Stem, 4 To 4 1/4 In., 5 Piece 200.00
Creamer, Cobalt Blue, Applied Handle, 4 In. 550.00
Crystal Ball, Hardwood Stand, Chinese, c.1900, 6 In. 575.00
Cuspidor, Pillar Mold, Tulip Form, Ruffled Rim, Pontil, 6 1/2 In. 220.00
Decanter, 3-Piece Mold, 19th Century, 11 1/4 In. 290.00
Decanter, Bulbous, Round Foot, Folded Rim, Ball Stopper, 4 x 3 1/2 x 2 In. 210.00
Decanter, Canary, Reeded, Paneled, Swirled Stoppers, 10 1/2 In., Pair 470.00
Decanter, Cobalt Blue, Flared Rim, Stopper, 9 1/2 In., Pair 520.00
Decanter, Molded, Stopper, Waffle & Diamond Bull's-Eye Pattern, 10 1/2 In., Pair 805.00
Decanter, Pillar Molded, Flint, 8 Ribs, Blown Stopper, Ground Pontil, 13 In. 150.00
Goblet, Double White, Air-Twist Stem 330.00
Hat, Black Amethyst, Polished Pontil, 7 x 12 In. 200.00
Hat, Cobalt Blue, Open Pontil, 2 1/2 In. 65.00
Hat, Emerald Green, Snap Pontil, 4 x 6 1/2 In. 144.00
Hat, Light Amethyst, Pinched, Pontil, 3 7/8 In. 220.00
Hat, Olive Green, Pinched, Rolled Rim, Pontil, 3 1/8 In. 195.00
Hat, Sunburst, Cobalt Blue, Iridescent, 3-Piece Mold, Rolled Rim, Pontil, 2 1/8 In. 635.00
Jar, Cover, Cobalt Blue, Spool Shaped Knops, 1800s, 11 7/8 x 12 1/2 In., Pair 1410.00
Mug, Enameled, Flared Rim, Applied Handle, Penn., Early 1800s, 3 1/2 In. 60.00

Mug, Fiery Opalescent, Remember Me, Blue, Red Flowers, Applied Handle, 4 1/2 In. 60.00
Pan, Olive Amber, Folded Rim, Pontil, 13 x 3 1/2 In. 1495.00
Pickle Jar, Aqua, Molded, Gothic Arches, Iron Pontil, 8 3/4 In.   115.00
Pitcher, Green, Footed, Applied Handle, South Jersey, 4 3/4 In.   20.00
Pitcher, Milk, Stiegel Type, Cobalt Blue, Fluted, Footed, Applied Handle, 5 In. 330.00
Pitcher, Pillar Mold, Applied Curved Handle, 8 3/4 In. 375.00
Salt, Short Knop Stem, Applied Round Foot, Flint, 2 1/2 x 2 3/8 In. 330.00
Salt, Stiegel Type, Amethyst, Footed, 2 1/4 In. 1045.00
Salver, Low Foot, Pulled Rim, Applied Folded Foot, 3 1/2 x 16 1/2 In. 715.00
String Holder, Applied Cobalt Blue Rings, Engraved Flowers, 5 x 4 1/2 In. 230.00
Sugar, Dome Cover, Cobalt Blue, Applied Foot, 6 1/2 In. 200.00
Tumbler, Cobalt Blue, Pontil, 3 5/8 x 2 7/8 In. 65.00
Tumbler, Flip, 3-Piece Mold, Pontil, 5 In. 260.00
Tumbler, Flip, Engraved Flower Basket, American, Early 1800s, 4 x 5 In. 230.00
Tumbler, Yellow Tint, Top Band, 3 3/8 x 2 3/8 In. 130.00
Vase, Clear, Tapered, Rings, 19th Century, 13 In. 275.00
Vase, Green, Threaded, Frosted, Ruffled Edge, c.1900, 8 1/2 x 12 In. 1035.00
Vase, Hyacinth, Violet Blue, Pontil, 7 In. 160.00
Whimsy, Woman Spinning Yarn, Polychrome, Wooden Base, 5 3/8 In. 440.00
Wine, Amethyst, U-Shape Bowl, Applied Stem, Foot, Flint, 4 3/4 x 2 3/8 In. 65.00
Wine, Hollow Stem Containing 1846 Quarter, 5 In. 260.00
Witch's Ball, Ruby, Rough Open Pontil, 7 3/4 In. 1045.00

GLASS-BOHEMIAN Bohemian glass is an ornate overlay or flashed
glass made during the Victorian era. It has been reproduced in
Bohemia, which is now a part of the Czech Republic. Glass made from
1875 to 1900 is preferred by collectors.

Ale, Amber, Engraved, Deer In Forest, 1890s, 7 1/2 In. 115.00
Beaker, Ruby Cut To Clear, Flowerhead Medallions, Sulphide Bust, 5 In. 745.00
Decanter, Amber Cut To Clear, Vintage Pattern, Stopper, 11 1/2 In., Pair 60.00
Decanter, Cranberry Cut To Clear, Canes, Lighthouse Shape, c.1900, 14 3/4 In. 315.00
Decanter, Engraved Stag, Tree, Ferns, Grass, 9 3/4 In. 110.00
Goblet, Cover, Amber, Engraved, Animals, Hunters, Medallions, 1890s, 9 In. 255.00
Goblet, Gold Enameled Scroll Leaves, 7 In., 4 Piece 115.00
Jar, Cover, Ruby Cut To Clear, Landscape, Animals, 13 In., Pair 290.00
Pokal, Cover, Ruby Cut To Clear, Waffle, 6-Sided Stem, 11 In., Pair 230.00
Powder Jar, Cover, Scrolls, Flowers, Parcel Gilt, Enameled, Cut, 4 1/2 In. 260.00
Salver, White Cut To Clear, Gold Enamel, Late 1800s, 14 3/8 In. 235.00
Urn, Enameled Flower Sprays, White Ground, 1800s, 6 1/2 In., Pair 175.00
Vase, Amber, Engraved Forest Landscape, Baluster, Late 19th Century, 12 In. 175.00
Vase, Cranberry Cut To Clear Panels, 6 Sides, c.1900, 12 In., Pair 2070.00
Vase, Fan, Iridescent, Green Oil Spot, Burgundy Rim, Rindskopf, 11 In. 560.00
Vase, Gold Iridescent, Ruffled Edge, Footed, Late 1800s, 10 In.   265.00
Vase, Green, Silver Enameled Birds, 1800s, 4 In. 210.00
Vase, Lattimo, Green, Gold, Lancet Arches, France, c.1865, 18 In. 1035.00
Vase, Ruby Cut To Clear Circles, Peacock, 7 1/2 In. 145.00
Vase, Ruby Cut To Clear, Flowers, c.1900, 9 1/2 In. 105.00
Vase, Ruby Cut To Clear, Oculus & Hobstar, c.1900, 8 x 8 1/2 In. 290.00
Vase, Sapphire Blue, White Enameled Portrait, Wreath, c.1900, 10 1/2 In. 45.00
Water Set, Gold Enameled Band, 11 1/4 In. 60.00
Wine Set, Ruby Cut To Clear, Elk, Trees, 5 Piece 115.00

GLASS-CONTEMPORARY includes pieces by glass artists working after
1975. Many of these pieces are free-form, one-of-a-kind sculptures.
Paperweights by contemporary artists are listed in the Paperweight category. Earlier studio glass may be found in Glass-Venetian.

Sculpture, Breakthrough, Clear, Pink, Blue, Labino, 1978, 7 In. 4250.00
Sculpture, Emergence, Clear, Pink Interior Veils, Labino, 1978, 7 In. 4200.00
Vase, Blue Iridescent, Rust, Gold, Lotton, c.1985, 7 3/4 In. 440.00
Vase, Bulbous, Iridescent, Stylized Circle & Line, Orient & Flume, 6 In. 205.00
Vase, Cased Butterscotch, Combed Feathers, Blue Tips, Lundberg Studios, 4 In. 115.00
Vase, Cobalt Vines, Leaves, Lundberg Studios, 1976, 2 7/8 In. 185.00
Vase, Egg Shape, Tall Flowers, Grass, Mark Peisner, 1978, 5 7/8 In. 355.00

Vase, Glass, Clear Over Pink, Gold Iridescent, Pinched Interior, Labino, 4 In. 165.00
Vase, Glossy Burgundy, Brick Shoulder, Signed, Sweet, 1979, 4 1/2 In. 35.00
Vase, Iridescent Blue, 2 Pulled Festoons, Lundberg Studios, 1975, 4 In. 290.00
Vase, Iridescent, Cylindrical, Flared Rim, Pulled Feather, Eickholt, c.1990, 8 In. 265.00
Vase, Jack-In-Pulpit, Iridized Blue Pan, Stretched Border, Altoman, 15 x 9 In. 545.00
Vase, Melon Shape, 16 Ribs, Blue Iridescent, Orient & Flume, 4 5/8 In. 120.00
Vase, Pulled Zipper, Green & Brown, Orient & Flume, No. 73032, 5 1/2 In. 90.00
Vase, Silhouette, Skyline, Keys To The City, Blue, Green, White, McCobb, 16 In. 1210.00
Vase, Snail, Blown, 15 3/4 In. 105.00
Vase, Spring Plum Series, Lampwork Flowers, Heilman-Roessler, 1982, 6 In. 175.00
Vase, Stick, Iridescent Glass, Copper, Lundberg, 11 In. 120.00
Vase, Threaded, Squared, Whitefriars, England, S11, 1969, 5 3/4 In. 259.00

GLASS-CUT, see Cut Glass category.

GLASS-DEPRESSION, see Depression Glass category.

GLASS-MIDCENTURY refers to art glass made from the 1950s to the
1980s. Some glass factories, such as Baccarat or Orrefors, are listed
under their own categories. Earlier glass may be listed in the Glass-Art
and Glass-Contemporary categories. Italian glass may be found in
Glass-Venetian.

Bowl, Platter, Siamese, Purple, Blue, Green, Higgins, 12 1/2-In. Platter 345.00
Carafe Set, Romantica, Tapio Wirkkala, Littala, 1960, 9 Piece 590.00
Charger, Fused, Abstract Design, Michael & Francis Higgins, USA, 1960s, 15 In. 2000.00
Dish, Aalto Flower, Alvar Aalto, Karhula, Finland, 1939, 12 x 12 x 3 In. 1755.00
Fish Platter, Fish Shape, Enamel, Maurice Heaton, USA, 1950s, 15 x 7 In. 820.00
Plate, Riviera Pattern, Blues, Greens, Higgins, 10 1/2 x 10 1/2 In. 145.00
Platter, Tapio Wirkkala, Littala, c.1950, 2 x 17 x 5 In. 2350.00
Tray, Rectangular, Blue & Gold Branch Like Designs, Higgins, 10 In. 115.00
Vase, Bamboo Style, Tapio Wirkkala, Littala 54, 9 1/4 x 4 1/4 In. 2820.00
Vase, Kaj Franckc, For Nuutajarvi, Engraved Mark, 10 In. 155.00
Vase, Per Lutkin, Holmegaard, 1952, 16 1/2 In. 235.00
Vase, Tuone Virta, Tapio Wirkkala, Littala, c.1948, 15 In. 2940.00

GLASS-VENETIAN. Venetian glass has been made near Venice, Italy,
since the thirteenth century. Thin, colored glass with applied decoration is favored, although many other types have been made. Collectors
have recently become interested in the Art Deco and 1950s designs.
Glass was made on the Venetian island of Murano from 1291. The out-
put dwindled in the late seventeenth century but began to flourish
again in the 1850s. Some of the old techniques of glassmaking were
revived, and firms today make traditional designs and original modern
glass. Since 1981, the name *Murano* may only be used on glass made
on Murano Island. Other pieces of Italian glass may be found in the
Glass-Contemporary and Glass-Midcentury categories of this book.

Bottle, Dresser, Gold Aventurine, Lavender, Swan Finials, c.1900, 14 In., Pair 460.00
Bowl, Black & Red Swirl, Flared, Footed, Venini, 11 In. 265.00
Bowl, Centerpiece, Free Form, Orange Interior, Milk White Exterior, Murano, 20 In. 60.00
Bowl, Shell Form, Iridescent, Barovier & Toso, Murano, 1940s, 9 In., Pair 690.00
Compote, Amethyst, Dolphin Base, 9 In. 60.00
Compote, Applied Grape & Leaf, Ribbon Twist Stem, 7 x 11 In.   70.00
Compote, Pink, Applied Threading, Gold Inclusions, 5 7/8 x 7 In. 85.00
Ewer, Enamel & Gold Grapes, Waisted, Bulbous Base, 16 1/8 In. 175.00
Figurine, Anthony, Cleopatra, 20th Century, 25 1/2 In., Pair 1535.00
Figurine, Bird, Oval Base, Trapped Air Bubble, Green Amber, Murano, 12 In., Pair 80.00
Figurine, Fish, Black Band, Clear Cased, G. Cenedese, Murano, 14 1/2 In. 235.00
Figurine, Fish, Gray, Green, Pinched Fins, Eyes, Mouth, Murano, 20th Century, 17 In. . . .   380.00
Figurine, Poodle, Green, Blue, Gold, Red Features, Murano, 6 In. 40.00
Pitcher, Cover, Millefiori, Tapered, Pulled Handle, 9 1/4 In. 480.00
Plate, Enameled Flowers, Gold Enameled Scrolled Border, Green, 8 1/2 In., 12 Piece 575.00
Tumbler, Apple Green, Enameled Flowers, Ribbed, 5 3/8 In., 12 Piece 805.00
Vase, Ambrato, Tear Shape, Swirling Color, Ercole Barovier, c.1955, 9 1/2 x 5 1/2 In. 2185.00
Vase, Bottle, A Canne, Green, Red, c.1968, 11 In. 345.00

Vase, Fazzeletto, Handkerchief, White Opaque, Clear Cased, Venini, 1950s, 9 In. 235.00
Vase, Gold Inclusions, Trapped Bubbles, Heavy Cased, c.1940s, 9 In. 865.00
Vase, Green & Opaque White Vertical Stripes, Murano, 6 3/4 In. 60.00
Vase, Iridescent, Carlo Scarpa, No. 11011, Venini, Italy, c.1933, 6 3/4 x 10 In. 3045.00
Vase, Pezzato, Red, Blue & Clear Patches, Venini, 10 In. 50.00
Vase, Pillow, Swirled Bluish Purple, Archimede Seguso, 7 1/4 x 5 3/4 In. 230.00
Vase, Smoky Gray, Striated Organic Shapes, Gold Inclusions, 10 1/2 In. 690.00
Vase, Swan, Green Jade, Alabaster, Archimede Seguso, Murano, 6 1/2 In. 69.00

GLASSES for the eyes, or spectacles, were mentioned in a manuscript in 1289 and have been used ever since. The first eyeglasses with rigid side pieces were made in London in 1727. Bifocals were invented by Benjamin Franklin in 1785. Lorgnettes were popular in late Victorian times. Opera Glasses are listed in their own category.

Lorgnette, Reeded Case, 14K Gold, Initials, Art Deco, Lugeni, c.1930, 2 1/2 x 3/4 In. . . . 460.00
Lorgnette, Sterling, Art Nouveau 250.00
Magnifying Glass, Bentwood Frame, Thick Bubbled Lens, c.1700 . . . . 250.00
Pince-Nez, Gilt Metal Wire Frames, Oval Lenses, Hard Case, Velvet Lining, 1900s 29.00
Spectacles, Martin's Margin's, Iron Frame, Horn Insets, England, c.1750 . . . . 395.00
Spectacles, Octagonal Lens, Case, Embossed Lid, c.1860 . . . . 113.00
Sun, Cartier, 188 Collet-Set Diamonds, Black Acetate Inset, Cartier, France 6325.00
Sun, Yellow Glass Lenses, Flexible Earpiece, Leather Case, Ray Ban, Bausch & Lomb . . . 30.00

GLIDDEN Pottery worked in Alfred, New York, from 1940 to 1957. The pottery made stoneware, dinnerware, and art objects.

Bowl, Seated Black Poodles, Square, No. 17, 4 1/4 x 8 In. 10.00
Casserole, Cover, Seated Black Poodle, Handles, No. 167, 5 x 6 In. . . . . .10.00 to 25.00
Condiment Tray, 3 Sections, Seated Black Poodles, No. 300, 9 x 12 In., Pair 45.00
Condiment Tray, 5 Sections, Seated Black Poodles, No. 280, 11 1/2 x 15 In. 40.00
Plate, Seated Black Poodle, Square, No. 19, 4 In., Pair 10.00
Plate, Seated Black Poodle, Square, No. 31, 9 3/4 In., Pair . . . . .45.00 to 70.00
Tray, Seated Black Poodle, Handle, Square, No. 025, 7 3/4 x 8 In. 40.00
Tumbler, Poodle, Black, Seated, White Ground, No. 1127, 5 3/4 In. . . . . *Illus* 30.00
Vase, Pillow, Draped Pattern, Blue, Turquoise, Black, 16 3/4 x 14 3/4 In. 920.00

GOEBEL is the mark used by W. Goebel Porzellanfabrik of Oeslau, Germany, now Rodental, Germany. Many types of figurines and dishes have been made. The firm is still working. The pieces marked *Goebel Hummel* are listed under Hummel in this book.

Figurine, Poodle, Black, Seated, Extended Paw, No. 3004030, 12 1/4 In. 70.00
Group, Bearded Man, Young Woman, 16th Century Costume, L. Ispanky, 11 1/2 In. 230.00
Pincushion, Lady, Placing Red Flower In Hair, 1926, 5 1/2 In. 80.00
Salt & Pepper, Black Children With Banjo, 3 3/8 In. 195.00
Salt & Pepper, Black Children, Hugger, 3 In. 195.00
Salt & Pepper, Boy & Girl, Platinum Trim, 3 In. 59.00
Salt & Pepper, Bride & Groom, Kissing, 1940-1955, 3 3/8 In. 59.00
Salt & Pepper, Cardinal Tuck, Holding Books, 3 1/4 In. 195.00
Salt & Pepper, Cat & Dog, 1926, 2 3/8 & 1 3/8 In. 75.00
Salt & Pepper, Golfer, Golf Club Tray, 3 3/4 x 5 In., 3 Piece 145.00

GOLDSCHEIDER has made porcelains in three places. The family left Vienna in 1938 and started factories in England and in Trenton, New Jersey. The New Jersey factory started in 1940 as Goldscheider-U.S.A. In 1941 it became Goldscheider-Everlast Corporation. From 1947 to 1953 it was Goldcrest Ceramics Corporation. In 1950 the Vienna plant was returned to Mr. Goldscheider, and the company continues in business. The Trenton, New Jersey, business, now called *Goldscheider of Vienna*, imports all of the pieces.

Figurine, Deer, Standing, 6 1/2 In. 60.00
Figurine, Equestrienne Jumping Horse Over Fence, Austria, 14 x 16 1/2 x 6 In. 575.00
Figurine, Girl, Butterfly Wing Dress, Bass Drum, Austria, 12 x 9 x 4 1/2 In. 750.00
Figurine, Nude Woman, Butterfly Wings, Multicolored, Austria, 11 x 12 1/2 In. 1380.00

Figurine, Nude, Black Cape, Feathered Headdress, Thumasch, Austria, 18 x 8 In. 1840.00
Figurine, Woman, Green Dress, Blue Flowers, Austria, 16 x 16 x 5 In. 750.00
Figurine, Woman, Standing, With Umbrella, 11 1/4 In. 69.00
Figurine, Young Boy, Blue Flower Bouquet, Austria, 5 5/8 In. 345.00
Wall Mask, Woman In Repose, Pink, Blue, Brown, Austria, 12 3/4 x 8 1/4 In. 115.00

GOLF, see Sports category.

GOSS china has been made since 1858. English potter William Henry
Goss first made it at the Falcon Pottery in Stoke-on-Trent. The factory
name was changed to Goss China Company in 1934 when it was taken
over by Cauldon Potteries. Production ceased in 1940. Goss China
resembles Irish Belleek in both body and glaze. The company also
made popular souvenir china, usually marked with local crests and
names.

W.H.COSS

Cheese Dish, Cover, 3 Tiger Heads, Scrolled Floreat Salopian, 3 x 2 In. 85.00
China Jug, Shows Crest Of The Cat & Fiddle, Buxton 50.00
Figurine, Parian, The Devil Looking Over Lincoln, Gothic Script At Base, 5 1/2 In. 135.00
Jug, Water, Hand Painted Red & Blue Flowers, W.H. Goss Stamp On Base, 6 In. 140.00
Teapot, White, Red & Blue Flowers, Marked W.H. Goss, 4 1/2 In. 410.00

GOUDA, Holland, has been a pottery center since the seventeenth century. Two firms, the Zenith pottery, established in the eighteenth century, and the Zuid-Hollandsche pottery made the brightly colored art
pottery marked *Gouda* from 1898 to about 1964. Other factories followed. Many pieces featured Art Nouveau or Art Deco designs.
Pattern names in Dutch, listed here, seem strange to English speaking
collectors.

Bowl, Anjer, Blue Flowers, Orange & Rust Field, Swirl & Dot Border, 1922, 4 x 9 In. . . . 125.00
Bowl, Blue, Yellow, Magenta Flower, 5-Sided, Footed, 2 3/4 x 10 In. 80.00
Bowl, Fella, Yellow Sun Rays, Aqua Leaves, Blue Trim, Yellow Ground, 1929, 14 In. 225.00
Bowl, Herman, Burgundy, Orange Abstract Design, Scalloped, Striped Pedestal, 4 x 5 In. . 80.00
Bowl, Ivora, Bird, Blue Chest, Green Feathers, Flowers, Triangle & Dot Border, 12 In. . . . 500.00
Bowl, Orient, Stylized Flowers, Arches, Dots, Teal, Orange, Blue, 4-Footed, 6 x 7 In. 150.00
Bowl, Yellow, No. 4238, Squat Form, Glossy, Plazuid, 8 1/4 x 2 1/2 In. 115.00
Candlestick, Brown Ground, Cobalt Grapes, Orange, Lavender, Teal, 9 1/4 In. 55.00
Candlestick, Yellow Sunrays, Leaves, Tapered, Double Bud Neck, Crimped, 12 In., Pair . 225.00
Dish, Lydia, Brown Matte Glaze, Flowers, Scalloped Edge, Handle, 7 1/4 In. 70.00
Ewer, Art Nouveau Tulips, Purple, Tan, Yellow Stars, High Glaze, Stopper, 9 3/4 In. 500.00
Ewer, Red Flowers, Running Blue & Green Ground, Marked, 11 3/4 In. 375.00
Ewer, Rhodian PZH, Holland, c.1915, 11 x 6 In. 325.00
Jardiniere, Stylized Daisies, Blue & Ocher Trim, Aqua Leaves, Brown Ground, 8 x 10 In. . 150.00
Jardiniere, Tan Flowers, Brown Matte Glaze, Bulbous, Triple Banded Neck, 8 1/2 In. 200.00
Jardiniere, Triangles, Pansies, Geometric Border, Green, Lavender, Yellow, 1926, 5 x 6 In. 100.00
Lamp, Oil, Cobalt Blue, Mottled Orange, Green Ground, Hangs On Wall, 7 x 5 In. 175.00
Match & Candle Holder, Mauve & Violet Pansies, Aqua Accents, Tray Body, 4 x 9 In. . . . 200.00
Pitcher, Brown & Pumpkin Abstract Design, Green Neck, Bulbous, 7 1/2 In. 175.00
Pitcher, Candia, Rust, Yellow Dots In Blue Waves, Green Ground, Tankard Shape, 7 In. . . 150.00
Pitcher, Chartreuse, Tan, Green Stylized Flowers, Bulbous Midsection, 8 In. 125.00
Pitcher, Plata, Stylized Berries, Rust Abstract Design, Green Matte Glaze, 10 1/2 In. 500.00
Planter, Hanging, Orange & Mahogany Flowers, White Field, Brown Ground, 8 1/2 In. . . 125.00
Plaque, Dolores, Flowers, Orange, Green, Blue, Fluted Panels Along Rim, 18 In. 200.00
Plaque, Madeleine, Flower, Yellow Sunray Petals, Lavender, Green, 1930, 9 In. 200.00
Plaque, Mero, Art Nouveau Design, Orange, Yellow Blue Ovals & Bands, 1923, 9 In. . . . 200.00
Plaque, Seafaring, White Birds, Clouds, Waves, Gray, Purple, Cobalt Blue, Black, 10 In. . 375.00
Tazza, Rhodian, Green, Abstract, Blue, Rust, Green, Yellow Trim, 2 Handles, 10 In. 150.00
Tile, Sailboats, Windmill, Church, Painted, Frame, Signed, Zuid-Holland VW, 6 In. 115.00
Tray, Yellow Flowers, Cobalt Medallions, Scalloped, Stamped, Fanny Gouda, 10 x 13 In. . 175.00
Tray, Yselstroom, Stylized Flowers, Orange, Teal, Ivory, Blue, Diamond Shape, 18 In. . . . 200.00
Vase, Ada, Stylized Flowers, Purple, Rust, Yellow & Blue Dots, Buttressed Handles, 8 In. . 150.00
Vase, Amphora, Pastel Flowers, Ovoid, Ocher Pedestal Base, 7 1/2 In. 175.00
Vase, Art Nouveau Leaves, Purple, Teal, Orange, Brown, High Glaze, 1918, 6 x 4 In. 150.00
Vase, Astra, Yellow & Orange Stars, Multicolored Geometrics, Baluster Shape, 18 In. 650.00
Vase, Averil, Orange Flowers, Oak Leaves, Turquoise & Black Bands, 10 3/4 In. 300.00

Vase, Butterfly, Pansies, Leaves, High Glaze, Double Gourd Shape, 5 x 3 1/2 In. 400.00
Vase, Candia, Sage Green Glaze, Rust Designs, Blue & White Accents, Flared, 12 In. 200.00
Vase, Corel, 2 Handles, Schoon Hovendahl, Holland, 1925, 10 1/2 x 6 1/4 In. 325.00
Vase, Deco Butterfly, Blue, Gold, Caterpillar Bands, Violet, Green Ground, Baluster, 12 In. 550.00
Vase, Distel, Black Stylized Lion, Swirls, White Ground, Green Band, 10 1/4 In. 300.00
Vase, Distel, Boy & Girl Skating, Art Nouveau Design On Rim, 2 Angular Handles, 11 In. 750.00
Vase, Distel, Girl Skipping Rope, Tan, Brown, Mauve, Green Ground, Tapered, 5 1/4 In. . 225.00
Vase, Distel, Rust Lions & Swirls, Green Trim, White Ground, 9 x 7 In. 325.00
Vase, Dutch Girl, Burgundy, Green, Blue, Bulb Shaped Neck, 2 Handles, 6 x 5 In. 100.00
Vase, Gambir, Burgundy, Black Stylized Poppies, Yellow Tendrils, High Glaze, 11 In. 500.00
Vase, Gelria, Pansies, Leaves, Purple, Green, Orange, Brown Ground, Tapered, 8 In. 375.00
Vase, Herman, Burgundy & Orange Abstract Design, Gray Ground, 2 Handles, 5 1/4 In. .. 100.00
Vase, Massa, Ovals Within Ovals, Dotted Waves, Green, Ivory, Bulbous, 5 x 5 1/2 In. 125.00
Vase, Orange & Lavender Relief Hearts, Cobalt Blue Ground, 7 x 4 1/2 In. 100.00
Vase, Purple Pansies, Painted, Art Nouveau Style, Marked, 14 1/2 In. 300.00
Vase, Quatrefoil Flowers, Blue, Yellow, Orange, Red, Ivory Ground, 5 3/4 In. 55.00
Vase, Regina, Double Gourd Shape, Marked & X'ed, 8 1/2 In. 175.00
Vase, Regina, Flowers, 2 Sweeping Handles, Art Nouveau, 11 In. 500.00
Vase, Regina, Gourd Shape, Black Flowers, Amber & Black Ground, Marked, 8 In. 374.00
Vase, Roda, Stylized, Red, Yellow, White Ground, Gold Trim, Twisted Handle, 8 In. 150.00
Vase, Yellow Petals Spiral Around Body, Brown Ground, Flared Rim, 1924, 8 In. 125.00

GRANITEWARE is an enameled tinware that has been used in the kitchen
from the late nineteenth century to the present. Earlier graniteware was
green or turquoise blue, with white spatters. The later ware was gray
with white spatters. Reproductions are being made in all colors.

Ant Trap, Gray, 1 1/8 x 4 3/4 In. 300.00
Ashtray, Light Blue & White, 4 5/8 In. 17.00
Basin, Cobalt Blue & White, 4 3/8 In. 120.00
Basin, Cream, Green, Paper Label Crest, 11 3/4 In. 35.00
Basin, European Gray, Salesman's Sample, 4 7/8 In. 20.00
Basin, Gray, Stamped, Columbian, 4 In. 30.00
Basin, Handles, Green & White Swirl, 22 In. 28.00
Batter Bucket, White, Blue Trim, Paper Label, 9 In. 35.00
Berry Bucket, Cover, Brown & White, 5 1/2 In. 413.00
Berry Bucket, Cover, Dark Green & White, 6 In. 330.00
Berry Bucket, Cover, Tin, American Gray, 4 In. 85.00
Berry Bucket, Cover, Tin, Gray, 4 1/4 In. 60.00
Berry Bucket, Cover, Tin, Gray, Bail Handle, 4 3/4 In. 99.00
Berry Bucket, Green & White, 5 1/4 In. 305.00
Biscuit Cutter, Gray 415.00
Bread Box, White, Oblong 70.00
Bundt Pan, Gray, 10 In. 28.00
Cake Pan, American Gray, 16 x 11 In. 20.00
Canister, Cover, European Gray, 3 3/4 In. 28.00
Cider Server, Blue & White, 15 In. 495.00
Coaster, Bluebelle Ware, 4 In. 30.00
Coaster, Green & White, 4 1/8 In. 60.00
Coffee Boiler, Brown, 14 In. 5.50
Coffeepot, Blue & White Swirl, 10 In. 35.00

Graniteware, Kettle, Blue &
White Marble, Wooden Bail
Handle, 7 3/4 x 8 1/2 In.

Glidden, Tumbler,
Poodle, Black,
Seated, White
Ground, No. 1127,
5 3/4 In.

Coffeepot, Blue & White, 12 In. 45.00
Coffeepot, Brown & White, 8 In. 300.00
Coffeepot, Cover, Tin, Gray, Marked, L. & G. Mfg. Co., 6 3/4 In. 165.00
Coffeepot, Dark Blue, 11 In. 47.00
Coffeepot, Green & White, Blue Handle, Trim, 11 In. 495.00
Coffeepot, Robin's-Egg Blue, White Interior, 6 1/2 In. 45.00
Coffeepot, Thistle, 9 1/2 In. 50.00
Colander, Blue, White Swirl, 10 In. 40.00
Colander, Gray, 1 3/4 x 3 3/4 In. 470.00
Colander, Green & White, 5 1/8 x 10 In. 165.00
Cream Pail, Blue & White, Bail Handle, 7 1/2 In. 360.00
Cup, American Gray, 2 3/4 In. 120.00
Cup, Coffee, Blue & White, 1 1/4 In. 195.00
Cup, Green & White, 2 1/4 x 4 1/4 In. 275.00
Cuspidor, American Gray, 6 3/4 In. 45.00
Dish, Feeding, Mary Alice, Blue, White, 8 In. 40.00
Double Boiler, Blue & White, 8 1/2 In. 35.00
Double Boiler, Blue & White, 10 In. 25.00
Double Boiler, Brown & White Swirl 150.00
Flask, Cover, Tin, Gray, 4 1/2 In. 415.00
Funnel, American Gray, 5 In. 15.00
Funnel, American Gray, Applied Handle, 7 1/4 In. 15.00
Funnel, Blue & White, Squat, Black Handle, Trim, 3 1/4 In. 105.00
Invalid Feeder, White, Navy Trim 20.00
Kettle, Blue & White Marble, Wooden Bail Handle, 7 3/4 x 8 1/2 In. . . . . Illus   300.00
Kettle, Green & White, Berlin Style, 5 1/4 In. 248.00
Kettle, Preserve, Chrysolite Swirl, 6 In. Diameter 95.00
Kettle, Preserve, Cover, Blue, White Swirl, 10 1/2 In. 30.00
Ladle, Oyster, American Gray 40.00
Ladle, Thistle Ware, 12 In. 60.00
Measure, Liquid, American Gray, 1/2 Qt. 190.00
Milk Can, Cover, Tin, Green & White, 10 1/4 In. 250.00
Milk Can, Emerald Ware, 10 1/2 x 5 1/4 In. 300.00
Milk Carrier, Cover, Cobalt Blue & White Swirl, 9 In. 1000.00
Milk Carrier, Tin Lid, American Gray, 8 1/2 In. 35.00
Milk Pail, Cover, Tin, Gray, Bail Handle, 9 In. 85.00
Milk Pail, Green & White, Bail Handle, 10 1/4 In. 935.00
Mixing Bowl, Blue, 10 1/4 In. 14.00
Mixing Bowl, Blue, 11 1/2 In. 35.00
Mold, Ear Of Corn, Oval, Fluted, American Gray, 6 In. 65.00
Mold, Shell, Blue, 3 In. 25.00
Muffin Pan, Cobalt Blue & White Swirl, 8 Cups 200.00
Muffin Pan, Individual, Cream & Green, 3 1/2 In. 30.00
Mug, Blue, White Swirl, 5 In. Diameter 25.00
Mug, Chrysolite, 3 1/2 In. 30.00
Pan, Pudding, Blue & White, 1 x 3 3/8 In. 138.00
Pan, Pudding, Green & White, 3 x 8 1/2 In. 120.00
Pan, Pudding, Navy Blue, White Swirl, 7 3/4 In. 15.00
Pan, Pudding, Shamrock, 12 In. 20.00
Pan, Pudding, Thistle Ware, 13 1/4 In. 40.00
Pan, Roaster, Brown, White Swirl, 19 In. 75.00
Pan, Turk's Head, Gray, 1 1/4 x 3 3/8 In. 60.00
Pie Pan, Brown & White, 9 In. 17.00
Pie Pan, Green & White, 10 In. 85.00
Pie Plate, Blue Ribbon, 9 3/4 In. 25.00
Pie Plate, Blue Swirl, 10 In. 80.00
Pie Plate, Brown, White Swirl, 8 In. 22.00
Pie Plate, Cobalt Blue, White Swirl, 9 7/8 In. 45.00
Pie Plate, Emerald Swirl, 9 In. 20.00
Pie Plate, Green, White Swirl, 10 1/8 In. 40.00
Pitcher, Measurer, Blue & White, 3 In. 690.00
Pitcher, Measurer, Brown & White, 6 1/2 In. 90.00
Pitcher, Molasses, Cover, Gray, 5 3/4 In. 60.00

Pitcher, Water, Blue & White Swirl, 8 1/4 In. 40.00
Pitcher, Water, Brown & White, 9 1/4 In. 165.00
Plate, Soup, Blue, White Swirl, 9 1/4 In. ....50.00 to 85.00
Pot, 2 Handles, Blue & White, 12 1/2 In. 8.00
Pot, Cover, Green & White Swirl, Bail Handle 28.00
Pot, Cover, Tin, Dark Green & White, Berlin Style, 4 x 6 1/4 In. 132.00
Pot, Green & White Swirl, Cover, Cobalt Blue Handle, 8 x 16 In. 66.00
Roaster, Bluebelle, 19 In., 2 Piece 30.00
Roaster, Shamrock, Insert, 17 1/2 In. 65.00
Salt, Hanging, Green, 7 1/2 In. 70.00
Saucepan, Bluebelle Ware, 10 In. 10.00
Saucepan, Cover, Bluebelle Ware, 10 In. 18.00
Scoop, Candy, Robin's-Egg Blue, 4 1/4 In. 55.00
Scoop, Sugar, American Gray, Riveted, 5 1/2 In. 65.00
Scoop, Thumb, American Gray, 6 1/2 In. 75.00
Scoop, Thumb, Cobalt Blue, White Swirl, 7 In. 375.00
Soap Dish, Blue, Marbling, Wall Mount 165.00
Soap Dish, Hanging, Green, White Soap Saver, 7 In. 65.00
Spoon Rest, Horse Head, Brown, Over Cast Iron 45.00
Strainer, Blue, White, Inside Handle 25.00
Strainer, Wire, American Gray, 7 1/2 In. 50.00
Sugar & Creamer, Green & White, 4 1/4 In. 120.00
Tea Set, American Gray, Pewter Trim, Tray, Square, 12 In., 4 Piece 725.00
Tea Steeper, Granite Lid, American Gray, 6 In. 50.00
Tea Steeper, Green & White, 5 In. 330.00
Tea Strainer, Blue, White Swirl 55.00
Teakettle, American Gray, 7 In. 45.00
Teakettle, Blue, White Shaded, 8 In. 100.00
Teapot, Bonnie Blue, 7 1/2 In. 45.00
Teapot, Chrome Lid, Cream, 9 1/2 In. 20.00
Teapot, Cream & Green, 8 1/2 In. 40.00
Teapot, Gray, Squat, Pewter Trim, 8 1/4 In. 195.00
Teapot, Hinged Cover, Cobalt Blue & White, Wood Finial, 7 1/4 In. 140.00
Teapot, Tin Lid, Brown Relish, Wood Knob, Handle, 9 1/2 In. 55.00
Teapot, Tin Lid, Gray, Iron Handle, 8 1/2 In. 30.00
Trivet, White, Blue Bird 55.00
Utility Rack, European Gray, Zeep, Zand, Soda 75.00
Wash Basin, Emerald Swirl, 12 In. 40.00

GREENTOWN glass was made by the Indiana Tumbler and Goblet Company of Greentown, Indiana, from 1894 to 1903. In 1899, the factory became part of National Glass Company. A variety of pressed glass was made. Additional pieces may be found in other categories, such as Chocolate Glass, Holly Amber, Milk Glass, and Pressed Glass.

Austrian, Creamer, Canary, Child's 90.00
Austrian, Punch Cup, Amber 130.00
Austrian, Punch Cup, Emerald Green 130.00
Dewey, Creamer, Amber 175.00
Dewey, Cruet, Amber, Stopper 110.00
Dewey, Cruet, Nile Green, Stopper 210.00
Dustpan, Amber 150.00
Hen On Nest Cover, Dish, Blue 325.00
Herringbone Buttress, Bowl, Clear Gold Trim 75.00
Herringbone Buttress, Vase, Green 150.00
Teardrop & Tassel, Butter, Cover 260.00

GRUEBY Faience Company of Boston, Massachusetts, was incorporated in 1897 by William H. Grueby. Garden statuary, art pottery, and architectural tiles were made until 1920. The company developed a matte green glaze that was so popular it was copied by many other factories making a less expensive type of pottery. This eventually led to the financial problems of the pottery.

Bowl, Green Matte Glaze, Swirled Interior, Marked, 9 In. 805.00

Bowl, Leathery Green Matte Glaze, Marked, 7 3/4 In. 374.00
Humidor, Green Matte Ground, Blossoms, Ivory, Yellow, Wilhemina Post, 7 1/2 In. 4600.00
Inkwell, Hand-Hammered Sterling Fittings, Squat, Bigelow, Kennard & Co., 4 3/4 In. ... 1495.00
Paperweight, Scarab, Green Glaze, 1 1/2 x 4 x 2 3/4 In. 525.00
Paperweight, Scarab, Green Matte Glaze, 1 1/4 x 3 7/8 In. 1150.00
Paperweight, Scarab, Green Matte Glaze, Marked, 3 3/4 x 2 3/4 In. 1380.00
Paperweight, Scarab, Olive Green, Dark Green Charcoaling, 4 In. 605.00
Tile, 2 Geese, Stylized Trees, Green, Blue, Mauve, Amber, Raised Outline, 4 In. 1150.00
Tile, 2 Pine Trees, Hills, Raised Outline, Green, Blue, Brown, Signed, MD, 6 In. 6325.00
Tile, Arts & Crafts Geometric Design, Green, Brown Matte Glaze, Oak Frame, 8 In. 1495.00
Tile, Cherubic Boy, Winged, Tan, Gold Ground, Arts & Crafts Frame, 6 In. 1150.00
Tile, Dog, White, Yellow Blossoms, Green Leaves, Blue Ground, 6 In. 3105.00
Tile, Frieze Of White Horses, Blue Sky, Green Ground, Signed, KY, Frame, 6 In. 4600.00
Tile, Geese, Intertwined, Under, Arc Of Green Trees, Raised Outline, Blue Ground, 4 In. . 3740.00
Tile, Geometric, Floral, Dark Clay, Green Matte Glaze, Stamped, 8 1/4 In. 980.00
Tile, Grape Cluster, Blue, Green Leaves, Beige Ground, Frame, 6 In. 635.00
Tile, Pines, Landscape, Green, Blue, Brown, Square, Signed, 6 In. 6325.00
Tile, Rabbit, Crouching, Ivory, Blue, Green Raised Outline, 4 In. 635.00
Tile, Rabbit, Crouching, Ivory, Lettuce Field, Green Ground, Raised Outline, 6 In. 3740.00
Tile, Sailing Ship, Curdled Glaze, Blue, Green, Brown, Raised Outline, Square, 8 In. ... 4315.00
Tile, Saint Louis, On Horse, Mosaic, Multicolored Matte Glaze, Frame, 48 x 42 1/2 In. ...21850.00
Tile, Ship, Curly Waves, Brown, Orange Boat, Green Ground, Raised Outline, 6 In. 2875.00
Tile, Ship, Waves, Raised Outline, Unglazed Outline, Matte Glaze, 8 In. 7475.00
Tile, St. George & Dragon, Curdled Matte Glaze, 8 In. 24150.00
Tile, Stylized Cherub, Brown Clay, Yellow Matte Ground, Arts & Crafts Oak Frame, 6 In. 650.00
Tile, Stylized Landscape, Trees, Green, Blue, Ivory Matte Glaze, Frame, 4 In. 1955.00
Tile, Stylized Rose, Brown Matte Glaze, Stamped, 4 In. 175.00
Tile, Stylized Tan Flower, Black Glaze Background, Frame, 13 In. 920.00
Tile, Tall Ship, On Seas, Ivory, Brown, Blue-Gray, Raised Outline, Square, 6 In. 1380.00
Tile, Tulip, Purple, Green Leaves, Raised Outline, Green Ground, Signed RE, Frame, 6 In. 4900.00
Tile, Tulip, Yellow, Leaves, Bronze Frame, Tiffany Mount, 4 Petal Feet, 1 3/8 x 6 x 6 In. . 5060.00
Tile, Turtle, Brown, Beige, Ivory, Green Leaves, Dark Brown Ground, Frame, 6 In. 4900.00
Tile, White Rabbit, Blue Ground, Oatmeal Glaze, Square, 4 In. 920.00
Tile, White Water Lilies, Green Leaves, Raised Outline, Paper Label, 6 In. 3105.00
Tile, Winged Bird, Green On Blue, Arts & Crafts Frame, 7 1/2 In. 1380.00
Vase, Applied Broad Leaves, Blossoms, Green Matte Glaze, Wilhemina Post, 4 1/2 In. .. 8625.00
Vase, Applied Jonquils, Feathered Green Matte Glaze, Ivory, Yellow, Burgundy, 11 In. ...12650.00
Vase, Applied Leaves & Buds, Green Matte Glaze, 7 1/2 In. 2425.00
Vase, Applied Leaves, Green Matte Glaze, Yellow Buds, 6-Sided Top, Stamped, 7 3/4 In. . 8050.00
Vase, Applied Overlapping Leaves, Green Matte Glaze, Tapered, 7 1/2 In. 3290.00
Vase, Brown Matte Glaze, Shouldered, 9 1/2 In. 2235.00
Vase, Carved & Applied Leaves, Yellow Buds, Green Matte Glaze, Swollen, 10 In. 8225.00
Vase, Carved Leaves, Textured Green Matte Glaze, Tapered, Flared Rim, 6 1/2 In. 1175.00
Vase, Curdled Deep Mauve Glaze, Applied Stacked Leaves, Marie Seaman, 8 1/2 x 5 In. . 4600.00
Vase, Feathered Green Matte Glaze, Round Leaves, Buds, Squat Base, 7 1/2 x 5 In. 2875.00
Vase, Flaring, Bulbous Bottom, Carved Leaves, Dark Green Matte Glaze, 7 1/2 In. 1725.00
Vase, Frothy Sand Matte Glaze, Tooled Leaves, Bulbous, Gertrude Priest, 5 x 4 In. 1955.00
Vase, Green Matte Glaze, Broad Leaves, Bulbous, 5 1/4 x 4 In. 2185.00
Vase, Green Matte Glaze, Broad Leaves, Oval, Stamped, E.R.F., 10 x 6 In. 6900.00
Vase, Green Matte Glaze, Carved, Rounded Leaves, Bulbous, Stamped, 7 1/4 x 4 1/4 In. . 1725.00
Vase, Green Matte Glaze, Embossed Flowers & Buds, Bulbous, 13 1/2 In. 15150.00
Vase, Green Matte Glaze, Flower Form, 7 Handles, Stamped, 12 1/2 x 10 1/2 In. 49000.00
Vase, Green Matte Glaze, Pulled, Feathered, Yellow Buds, Leaves, 23 x 8 In. 1495.00
Vase, Hexagonal Rim, Cylindrical, Leaf & Bud Design, Green Glaze, Marked, 1904, 7 In. 4110.00
Vase, Indigo Matte Glaze, Curdled, Ridges, Cylindrical, Stamped, 9 x 3 3/4 In. 2530.00
Vase, Indigo Matte Glaze, Oatmeal, Flat Shoulder, Stamped, 3 3/4 x 3 In. 1035.00
Vase, Leathery Green Matte Glaze, Applied Jonquils, Ivory, Yellow, Burgundy, 11 In. 12650.00
Vase, Leathery Green Matte Glaze, Broad Leaves, Round, Marked, ERF, 4 x 4 3/4 In..... 5750.00
Vase, Low, Textured Green Matte Glaze, 7 1/2 In. 405.00
Vase, Mottled Blue Gray Ground, Applied Leaves, White Crocus Buds, Bulbous, 5 In. ... 4310.00
Vase, Oatmeal Glaze, Veined, Spherical Base, Raised Bands, Flared Mouth, 3 x 5 In. 990.00
Vase, Shouldered Shape, 3 Carved Daffodils, Green Matte Glaze, 3 1/2 In. 1725.00
Vase, Tapered, Incised Lines, Green Matte Glaze, 7 In. 2760.00

Vase, Textured Brown Matte Glaze, 8 In. 690.00
Vase, Trumpet, Green Glaze, 7 x 5 1/4 In. 1430.00
Water Lilies, White, Lily Pads, Green, Dark Green Ground, 6 x 18 1/4 In., 3 Piece 6325.00

GUNDERSEN glass was made at the Gundersen-Pairpoint Glass Works of New Bedford, Massachusetts, from 1952 to 1957. Gundersen Peachblow is especially famous.

Decanter, Peachblow, Bulbous Stopper, 11 3/4 In. 405.00
Vase, Jack-In-The-Pulpit, Peachblow, Flower, Opal Border, Tapered, Raised Disc, 9 In. 173.00
Vase, Peachblow, Lily, Disc Foot, 9 In. 230.00

GUNS that may be classed as toys, such as BB guns, air rifles, and cap guns, are listed in the Toy category.

GUSTAVSBERG ceramics factory was founded in 1827 near Stockholm, Sweden. It is best known to collectors for its twentieth-century art- **Gustafsberg** wares, especially a green stoneware with silver inlay called *Argenta*.

Bowl, Concentric Rings, Green, Applied Silver, Argenta, Wilhelm Kage, 3 3/8 In. 104.00
Butter Chip, Flowers, Argenta, 3 1/2 In. 20.00
Vase, Brown, Glazed Porcelain, Stig Lindberg, Sweden, 1950s, 4 x 3 1/2 x 8 1/4 In. 585.00
Vase, Flowers, Turquoise Matte Glaze, Flared, Footed, Signed, 7 1/2 In. 175.00
Vase, Glazed Stoneware, Wilhelm Kage, Sweden, 1950s, 7 x 7 In. 585.00
Vase, Pungo, Glazed, Stig Lindberg, Sweden, 1950s, 5 1/2 x 4 1/2 x 9 1/2 In. 1170.00
Vase, Soaring Birds, Turquoise Matte Glaze, Cylindrical, Footed, Signed, 8 In. 175.00
Vase, Surrea, Wilhelm Kage, c.1940, 13 In. 1880.00
Vase, Veckla, Glazed Porcelain, Stig Lindberg, Sweden, 7 1/2 In. 58.00
Vase, Winged Creature, Turquoise Matte Glaze, Flared, Signed, 6 In. 115.00

GUTTA-PERCHA was one of the first plastic materials. It was made from a mixture of resins from Malaysian trees. It was molded and used for daguerreotype cases, toilet articles, and picture frames in the nine- teenth century.

Chain, Pocket Watch, Circular Links, Brass Connectors, 12 1/2 In. 15.00
Mirror, Hand, Embossed Flowers, Diatite Pat 1868, March 19 1872, 8 3/4 In. 100.00
Pipe, Figural, The Smoking Gun, Italy, 5 In. 355.00
Revolver Case, Smith & Wesson First Model Tip Up, Eagle, Leaves, 8 x 4 x 2 In. 4313.00
Tieback, Embossed Grapes & Vines, Gilt Center, Patented 1868, 3 1/2 In. 10.00
Union Case, Woman Holding Wreath, Ship, Train, Littlefield, Parsons, 1857, 4 In. 50.00

HAEGER Potteries, Inc., Dundee, Illinois, started making commercial artwares in 1914. Early pieces were marked with the name *Haeger* written over an *H*. About 1938, the mark *Royal Haeger* was used in honor of Royal Hickman, a designer at the factory. The firm is still making florist wares and lamp bases. See also the Royal Hickman category.

Ashtray, Boomerang Form, 6 Rests, Agate Glass, 12 1/2 In. 35.00
Ashtray, Hyde Park, Mottled Green, Brass Initial D, 8 1/4 In. .... *Illus* 25.00
Ashtray, No. 2001, Red Matte Glaze, 5 Holder, Geometric, Rectangular, 9 In. 18.00
Ashtray, No. 2069, Earth Wrap, 3 Holder, Brown & Orange On Olive, 1970s, 8 In. 23.00
Ashtray, No. SP-12, 7 Holders, Briar Agate, 3-Footed, 13 In. 44.00
Box, No. R-1166, Chartreuse Agate, 3 x 10 x 6 In. 38.00

Haeger, Ashtray, Hyde Park, Mottled Green, Brass Initial D, 8 1/4 In.

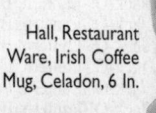

Hall, Restaurant Ware, Irish Coffee Mug, Celadon, 6 In.

Console, Green Agate, 13 x 6 In.	20.00
Figurine, Cat, Black, Egyptian, 20 1/2 In.	125.00
Figurine, Giraffe, Mother & Baby, Glossy Brown Glaze, Wood Base, 13 In.	175.00
Figurine, Woman, Holding Bowl, Glossy Green, Yellow, Brown Glaze, 10 x 10 1/2 In.	58.00
Lamp, Gazelle Heads, Green Glaze, 30 In., Pair	55.00
Pitcher, Pink, 6 x 6 3/4 In.	50.00
Vase, Bands, Gold, Brown, Over Speckled Ivory Glaze, Marked, 16 x 9 1/2 In.	58.00
Vase, No. 4030, Black, Peacock Glaze, 12 In.	92.00
Vase, No. 4162X, Orange Peel, Cylindrical, 1976, 7 In.	120.00

HALF-DOLL, see Pincushion Doll category.

HALL CHINA Company started in East Liverpool, Ohio, in 1903. The firm made many types of wares. Collectors search for the Hall teapots made from the 1920s to the 1950s. The dinnerwares of the same period, especially Autumn Leaf pattern, are also popular. The Hall China Company is still working. For more information, see *Kovels' Depression Glass & Dinnerware Price List.* Autumn Leaf pattern dishes are listed in their own category in this book.

HALL'S
SUPERIOR
QUALITY
KITCHENWARE

Aristocrat, Leftover, Ivory, 7 x 4 In.	100.00
Blue Blossom, Jug, Donut, 7 1/2 In.	390.00
Cactus, Bowl, Salad, 9 In.	18.00
Chinese Red, Mixing Bowl, 8 1/2 In.	40.00
G.E., Water Server, Addison Gray, 8 1/4 In.	100.00
Hotpoint, Leftover, Sandust, Rectangular, 3 1/2 In.	100.00
Montgomery Ward, Bowl, Delphinium, 7 In.	30.00
Montgomery Ward, Water Server, Delphinium, 1940s	100.00
Orange Poppy, Coffeepot, Bellevue, 2 Cup	2900.00
Poppy & Wheat, Teapot, 6 Cup	390.00
Refrigerator Ware, Water Server, Plaza, Red, 6 5/8 In.	390.00
Restaurant Ware, Irish Coffee Mug, Celadon, 6 In. .... *Illus*	15.00
Royal Rose, Jug, Ball, Platinum Trim, 2 Qt.	100.00
Taverne, Baker, French, Fluted, 8 x 2 3/4 In.	25.00
Taverne, Bowl, Salad, 9 In.	20.00
Taverne, Coaster, 3 1/2 In.	20.00
Taverne, Coffeepot, Banded, 9 In.	112.00
Taverne, Jar, Drip, Cover, 4 1/4 In.	79.00
Taverne, Teapot, New York, 6 Cup	195.00
Taverne, Tray, Rectangular, Metal	8.00
Teapot, Boston, Black Apple, Gold Trim, 6 1/4 In.	479.00
Teapot, Boston, Lipton Tea, Light Yellow, 5 1/2 In.	20.00
Teapot, Los Angeles, Chinese Red, 7 1/4 In.	500.00
Teapot, Rhythm, Cobalt Blue, 6 In.	370.00
Teapot, Rutherford, Chinese Red, Ribbed, 6 3/8 In.	390.00
Wildfire, Teapot, Sani-Grid, 6 Cup	370.00

HALLOWEEN is an ancient holiday that has changed in the last 200 years. The jack-o'-lantern, witches on broomsticks, and orange decorations seem to be twentieth-century creations. Collectors started to become serious about collecting Halloween-related items in the late 1970s. The papier-mache decorations, now replaced by plastic, and old costumes are in demand.

Book, Owen's Halloween Tales, 2nd Edition, Ethel Owens, Dust Jacket, 1931, 6 x 8 In.	95.00
Candy Container, Baker, Pumpkin Head, Plaid Pants, Composition, 3 1/2 In.	305.00
Candy Container, Black Cat Policeman, Papier-Mache, Germany, 5 1/2 In.	605.00
Candy Container, Black Cat, Crouching, Painted Plaster, Original Ribbon, 6 In.	990.00
Candy Container, Ghost, Nodder, Composition, Cardboard, Crepe, 5 1/2 In.	250.00
Candy Container, Jack-O'-Lantern, Bell Shape, Screw Base, 3 3/4 In.	935.00
Candy Container, Jack-O'-Lantern, Brownie Policeman, 4 3/4 In.	1430.00
Candy Container, Jack-O'-Lantern, Bulging Eyes, Teeth, Wire Bail Handle, 4 In.	330.00
Candy Container, Jack-O'-Lantern, Clown, Gold Tin Screw Base, 4 3/4 In.	250.00
Candy Container, Jack-O'-Lantern, Papier-Mache, Pull Slide, Huylers-New York, 4 In.	415.00
Candy Container, Jack-O'-Lantern, Pop Eyed, Metal Screw Lid, Coin Slot, 2 1/2 In.	525.00

Halloween,
Candy
Container,
Veggie Man
& Turnip,
Composition,
Painted,
Germany, 4 In.

Halloween, Jack-O'-Lantern, Paper
Pulp, Glazed, Orange, Green
Highlights, American, 8 In.

Halloween, Toy,
Witch, Squeak,
Cloth, Cardboard,
Composition,
Germany, 6 1/2 In.

Candy Container, Policeman Jr., Metal Screw Cap, Wire Bail Handle, 4 1/2 In.	798.00
Candy Container, Pumpkin Head Man, Devil Shape Hat	1760.00
Candy Container, Pumpkin Head Man, Witch Shape Hat, 6 1/2 In.	1430.00
Candy Container, Veggie Man & Turnip, Composition, Painted, Germany, 4 In. ..... *Illus*	880.00
Candy Container, Witch, Black Cat, Painted, Composition, Germany, 4 In.	525.00
Candy Container, Witch, Broom, Painted Composition, Crepe Paper Hair, Germany, 6 In.	385.00
Candy Container, Witch, Riding Broom, Composition, 3 1/2 In.	305.00
Costume, Clown, Orange & Black, Bells, Hat, Yankiboy, 1920s, Box	185.00
Costume, Frankenstein, 1970s	15.00
Costume, Miss Kitty, Gunsmoke, Mask, Blouse, Pants, Halco, Box	85.00
Costume, Spiderman, Ben Cooper, Box, 1965, Medium	110.00
Fan, Cat, Wood, Tissue Fur Body, Cardboard Face & Tail, Printed, Germany, 12 In.	155.00
Figure, Witch, Red Dress, Broom, Papier-Mache, Cardboard, Germany, 6 In.	275.00
Horn, Jack-O'-Lantern, Black Cat, Orange Crepe Paper, 8 1/2 x 11 1/2 In.	58.00
Jack-In-The-Box, Jack-O'-Lantern, Papier-Mache, Wood, 8 1/2 x 3 1/2 In.	1635.00
Jack-O'-Lantern, Battery Operated, Box, 5 In.	127.00
Jack-O'-Lantern, Glass, Painted, Metal Rim, Handle, 4 1/2 In.	360.00
Jack-O'-Lantern, Lipstick Mouth, Pressed Cardboard, Germany, 4 3/4 In.	110.00
Jack-O'-Lantern, On Cat Body, Tail In Back, Paper Pulp, 7 3/4 In.	360.00
Jack-O'-Lantern, Orange, Pressed Cardboard, Ribbon, Wire, 6 1/2 x 9 In.	330.00
Jack-O'-Lantern, Paper Pulp, Glazed, Orange, Green Highlights, American, 8 In. .... *Illus*	160.00
Jack-O'-Lantern, Papier-Mache, Open Eyes, Mouth, Paper Insert, Bail Handle, 4 1/2 In. ...	230.00
Jack-O'-Lantern, Papier-Mache, Original Paint, Wire Bail Handle, 7 3/4 In.	200.00
Jack-O'-Lantern, Papier-Mache, Paper Insert, 4 3/4 x 4 In.	58.00
Jack-O'-Lantern, Papier-Mache, Paper Inserts, Wire Bail Handles, 4 1/4 x 4 3/4 In.	144.00
Jack-O'-Lantern, Pressed Cardboard, Ribbon, Wire, 6 1/2 x 9 In.	330.00
Jack-O'-Lantern, Singing, Paper Pulp, Battery Operated, Pulpco, 4 1/2 In.	190.00
Jack-O'-Lantern, Tin, Hand Painted, Pole Mount, 9 In.	740.00
Lantern, Black Cat, Honeycomb, Cardboard, Crepe, 11 In.	120.00
Lantern, Black Cat, On Fence, Glazed Paper Pulp, 7 1/2 In.	220.00
Lantern, Black Cat, Pressed Cardboard, Dimensional Ears, Germany, 3 1/2 In.	660.00
Lantern, Hexagonal, Die Cut Cardboard, Tissue Paper Transparencies, Germany, 9 In.	195.00
Mask, Chief Sitting Bug, Paper, Child's, 1930s-1940s	12.00
Nodder, Black Cat, Orange Collar, Papier-Mache, Germany, 2 3/4 In.	240.00
Nodder, Black Cat, Papier-Mache, Cardboard, 5 In.	300.00
Nodder, Black Cat, Spring Head, Papier-Mache, Cardboard, 5 In.	300.00
Nodder, Jack-O'-Lantern, Screamer, Composition, Cardboard, 5 In.	330.00
Nodder, Witch, Painted Composition, Wood Base, 7 In.	690.00
Noisemaker, Devil Ratchet, Bobbing, Painted Composition, Wood, Crepe, 8 1/2 In.	300.00
Noisemaker, Frying Pan Clanger, Tin Lithograph, Wood, Pat. June 1906, 10 3/4 In. ...	50.00
Postcard, 6 Children, Green Hair, Red Ear Of Corn, Whitney Samuel Schmucker	46.00
Postcard, A High, Old Time This Hallowe'en, Witch Flying On Broom, Cat, 4 Bats	46.00
Postcard, All Halloween, Verse, Witch On Broom, Winsch Schmucker, 1911 .....145.00 to	195.00
Postcard, Greetings At Hallowe'en, Woman, Black Gown, John Winsch Schmucker	127.00
Postcard, Hallowe'en Greetings, Pumpkin, 2 Green Imps, 2 Leaves, Checkered Border ..	46.00
Postcard, My Best Wishes For Halloween, Child, Pumpkin	25.00
Postcard, On Hallowe'en We'll Steal The Gate, 4 Pumpkin Headed Children	25.00
Ratchet, Pumpkin Head Man, Crepe Collar, Composition, Wood Body, 10 In.	15.00

Rattle, Jack-O'-Lantern, 2 Faces, Lithograph, Pressed Cardboard, Germany, 3 1/2 In. 88.00
Rattle, Jack-O'-Lantern, Printed Paper, Cardboard, Crepe Trim, C.A. Reed Co., 8 1/4 In. .   80.00
Skeleton, Couple, Painted Composition, Springy Arms & Legs, 4 In. 38.00
Tin, Tindecco Candy, Young Witch, Broom, Jack-O-Lantern, 1 5/8 x 6 1/8 In. 265.00
Toy, Jack-In-The-Box, Jack-O'-Lantern, Papier-Mache, Wood Box, 8 1/2 x 3 1/2 In. 635.00
Toy, Jack-O'-Lantern, Pressed Cardboard, Wood, Squeak 855.00
Toy, Pumpkin Head Man, Ratchet, Composition, Crepe Collar, Wood, 10 In. 14.00
Toy, Tambourine, Black Cat, Orange, Tin Lithograph, Chein, 7 In. 77.00
Toy, Witch, On Rocket, Pull Toy, Hard Plastic, 4 1/2 In. 130.00
Toy, Witch, On Rocking Chair, Wood, Cloth, Papier-Mache, Mechanical, 7 1/2 x 7 In. 415.00
Toy, Witch, Red Dress, Broom, Papier-Mache, Cardboard, Germany, 6 In. 275.00
Toy, Witch, Riding Motorcycle, Hard Plastic, 7 In. 200.00
Toy, Witch, Squeak, Composition, Cloth, Cardboard, Germany, 6 1/2 In. . . . . *Illus*   1265.00
Walker, Man, Jack-O'-Lantern Head, Composition, Wood, Clockwork Mechanism 3080.00

HAMPSHIRE pottery was made in Keene, New Hampshire, between 1871 and 1923. Hampshire developed a line of colored glazed wares as early as 1883, including a Royal Worcester-type pink, olive green, blue, and mahogany. Pieces are marked with the printed mark or the impressed name *Hampshire Pottery* or *J.S.T. & Co., Keene, N.H.* Many pieces were marked with city names and sold as souvenirs.

Bowl, Cerulean Blue Glaze, Spherical, 3 x 6 In. 358.00
Bowl, Embossed Geometric Pattern, Green Matte Glaze, Squat, 2 1/2 x 5 1/2 In. 345.00
Chamberstick, Green Matte Glaze, Marked, 4 x 7 In. 345.00
Chamberstick, Pinched Base, Loop Handle, Green, No. 31, Early 1900s, 3 x 7 1/8 In. . . .   175.00
Cup, Green Matte Glaze, 3 Handles 300.00
Lamp, Floral Bud, Green Matte Glaze, Bulb Shaped Upper Body, Circular Base, 11 In. . . .   935.00
Lamp, Twisted Pond Lily, Green Matte Glaze, Circular Pedestal, 15 1/2 In. 1320.00
Lamp Base, Green Matte Glaze, Embossed Leaves, Bud, Trumpet Shape, 14 1/2 x 8 In. . .   978.00
Lamp Base, Green Matte Glaze, Embossed Tulips, Squat, Stamped, 6 x 11 1/2 In. 1150.00
Lamp Base, Green Matte Glaze, Water Lily, Flared, No. 0013, 11 1/4 x 7 1/2 In. . .400.00 to 450.00
Pitcher, Blue Green Feathered Glaze, Squat, Stamped, 3 1/4 x 7 In. 230.00
Pitcher, Green Matte Glaze, Footed, Marked, 14 1/2 In. 145.00
Pitcher, Green Matte Glaze, Melon Shape, 4 x 5 In. 220.00
Pitcher, Green Matte Glaze, Tapered, Embossed Handle, 11 1/2 In. 358.00
Stein, Green Matte Glaze, 7 In. 149.00
Stein, Green Matte Glaze, Incised Art Nouveau Design, Bands, Tankard Handle, 9 In. . . .   195.00
Tumbler, Cerulean Blue Glaze, Mottled, Green Accents, 5 1/4 x 3 In. 250.00
Umbrella Stand, Green Matte Glaze, Embossed Ivy, Bamboo Ground, 17 1/2 x 8 In. 1955.00
Urn, Green Matte Glaze, Leathery, Stamped, 14 1/2 In. 1495.00
Vase, Alternating Leaves, Buds, Blue Feathered Matte Glaze, Stamped, 6 1/2 x 4 In. 1255.00
Vase, Alternating Leaves, Buds, Green Matte Glaze, Stamped, 7 x 4 In. 800.00
Vase, Bag, Embossed, Green Matte Glaze, Ribbon At Neck, Crimped Mouth, 11 In. 880.00
Vase, Bleeding Heart Flowers, Fernlike Leaves, Green Matte Glaze, 4 1/2 x 5 In. 660.00
Vase, Blue Gray Mottled Matte Glaze, Cylindrical, Early 1900s, 11 1/4 In. 645.00
Vase, Blue Matte Glaze, Cylindrical, 7 In. 350.00
Vase, Blue Mottled Glaze, Paneled, Egg Shape, Rolled Mouth, 6 3/4 In. 415.00
Vase, Buds, Embossed, Blue & Green Feathered Matte Glaze, Bulbous, 7 3/4 x 7 In. 1265.00
Vase, Cerulean Blue, Mottled, Veined, Oval, 6 1/4 x 4 In. 550.00
Vase, Cerulean Blue, Raised Mottled Shoulder, Black Veining, Egg Shape, 8 3/4 In. 605.00
Vase, Cerulean Blue, Stylized Waves, Mottled, Cylindrical, 7 1/2 x 4 In. 660.00
Vase, Cucumber Green Glaze, 3 Pinched Sections, Reticulated Mouth, 3 x 3 In. 330.00
Vase, Flowers, Embossed, Stems To Base, Blue, Mottled Green, Egg Shape, 7 In. 1760.00
Vase, Full Height Leaves, Embossed, Blue Green Matte Feathered Glaze, Marked, 7 In. . .   1095.00
Vase, Genie Bottle, Cerulean Blue Glaze, Green Accents, 2 Angular Handles, 7 In. 715.00
Vase, Green Matte Glaze, Bulbous, Wide Mouth, Linear Decoration, Early 1900s, 4 In. . .   355.00
Vase, Green Matte Glaze, Melon Shape, 2 3/4 In. 525.00
Vase, Khaki Green, Brown Streaks, Egg Shape, 5 In. 358.00
Vase, Lavender, Mint Green Mottled Glaze, Paneled Lower Half, Rolled Rim, 3 1/2 In. . .   248.00
Vase, Leaves & Buds, Embossed, Green & Brown Frothy Matte Glaze, 6 3/4 In. 748.00
Vase, Leaves, Buds, Green & Blue Feathered Glaze, Stamped, 6 3/4 x 4 In. 865.00
Vase, Leaves, Full Height, Cafe Au Lait Veined Glaze, On Dark Brown Ground, 7 In. 316.00
Vase, Lily Pad, Mottled Green Glaze, Raised Collar, Apple Shape, No. 92, 9 1/4 In. 2300.00

Vase, Lotus Leaves, Buds, Green Matte Glaze, Bulbous, Marked, 7 In. 1095.00
Vase, Mocha Brown Glaze, Paneled, Ovoid, Rolled Mouth, 4 1/2 In. 605.00
Vase, Molded Panels, Cream, Rose Matte Glaze, 4 1/2 In. 518.00
Vase, Overlapping Leaves, Multitoned Blue, Gray Matte Glaze, 7 1/2 In. 1380.00
Vase, Raised Swirl, Reptilian Turquoise, Olive & Brown Glaze, Squat, 3 1/4 x 4 In. 750.00
Vase, Trees, Embossed, Under Veined Green Matte Glaze, Squat, Marked, 5 1/2 In. 230.00
Vase, Tulips, Embossed, Green Matte Glaze, Bulbous, Marked, 8 1/2 In. 635.00
Vase, Water Lily, Green Matte Glaze, Embossed Closed Buds, Egg Shape, 7 x 5 In. 1430.00

HANDEL glass was made by Philip Handel working in Meriden, Connecticut, from 1885 and in New York City from 1893 to 1933. The firm made art glass and other types of lamps. Handel shades were made not only of leaded glass in a style reminiscent of Tiffany but also of reverse painted glass. Handel also made vases and other glass objects.

Ash Receiver, Dog, 4-Footed, Removable Base, 3 x 4 In. 345.00
Ash Receiver, Monk Reading Newspaper, Removable Base, Mounted Collar, 3 x 3 1/2 In. 345.00
Ashtray, Golfing Scene, Bronze Mounts, 5 In. . . . . *Illus* 1550.00
Ashtray, Hinged Screen, Brass Collar, Cigarette Rests, Deer, Signed, 7 1/2 x 4 1/2 In. 690.00
Ashtray, White, Purple Flowers, Heart Shape, Breaded Rim, Signed, 1897, 4 1/2 In. 115.00
Ashtray, Woman At Waterfront, Bronze Collar, Cigarette Rests, Stamped, 5 In. 1150.00
Bowl, Pink Rose, Gold Enameled, Pedestal Foot, 6 In. 285.00
Bowl, Yellow, Frosted, Art Deco, Cameo, 7 In. 2300.00
Candlestick, Glass, Windmills, Frosted, Stamped, 8 1/2 In. 1090.00
Celery Dish, Flowers, Shamrock, Green Enameled Mosserine, Oval, 11 x 5 In. 1150.00
Cigar Jar, Hinged Cover, Hunter & Companion, Signed, 6 1/2 x 3 In. 1150.00
Cigarette Jar, Embossed Scrolls, Dog Head, Handles, 3 1/2 In. 230.00
Cigarette Jar, Horse, Bronze Handles, 3 x 3 In. 460.00
Hatpin Holder, Blue, Pink Flowers, Stamped, 6 In. 460.00
Humidor, Cover, Green, Pine Needle, 5 1/2 In. 2590.00
Humidor, Hinged Cover, 2 Dogs, Brown, Green, Signed, 5 In. 575.00
Humidor, Hinged Cover, 2 Indians, Hexagon, 8 x 6 In. 3450.00
Humidor, Hinged Cover, 3 Dogs, Red, Green, Signed, Bauer, 7 x 5 In. 920.00
Humidor, Hinged Cover, 3 Dogs, Red, Green, Signed, Bauer, 7 x 7 1/2 In. 575.00
Humidor, Hinged Cover, Dogs Running, Signed Bauer, 7 x 6 In. 920.00
Humidor, Hinged Cover, Indian Chief, Headdress, Signed, 6 x 3 In. . . . . *Illus* 2300.00
Humidor, Hinged Cover, Indian On Horseback Spearing Buffalo, 6 x 4 In. 3740.00
Humidor, Horse Head, Cigars On Lid, Raised Scroll Design, Marked, 6 x 3 In. 430.00
Jar, Cover, Yellow, Frosted, Cameo, 7 1/2 In. 400.00
Lamp, 6 Panels, Metal Overlay, Iris, Slag Glass, Bronze Base, 15 x 22 In. 2530.00
Lamp, 7 Panels, Metal Overlay, Daffodils, White, Hampshire Pottery Base, 21 In. 6325.00
Lamp, 12 Panels, Metal Overlay, Flowers, Green, Yellow Slag, Gilt Base, 21 1/2 In. 2110.00
Lamp, Adjustable, Shade, Maple Leaves, 66 In. 1955.00
Lamp, Art Deco, Enameled, Roses, Aqua Ground, 8 x 15 In. 1840.00
Lamp, Bell Shade, Fir Trees, Forest Scene, Bronze Base, 14 1/2 In. 4025.00
Lamp, Chipped Ice Shade, Flowers, Mauve, Blue, Purple, Yellow Ground, 13 3/4 In. 2860.00
Lamp, Chipped Ice Shade, Landscape, Early 1900s, 14 1/4 In. 1150.00

Handel, Ashtray, Golfing Scene,
Bronze Mounts, 5 In.

Handel, Humidor,
Hinged Cover, Indian
Chief, Headdress,
Signed, 6 x 3 In.

Lamp, Daffodils, Baluster Base, 18 In. 11500.00
Lamp, Desk, Metal Overlay, Diamond, Yellow & Green Slag Glass, Adjustable, 10 In. 1765.00
Lamp, Desk, Metal Overlay, Palm Tree, Multicolored Glass, Bronze Base, 11 x 14 In. 2300.00
Lamp, Desk, Moonlit River Scene, Patinated Metal Base, 13 1/4 In. 1000.00
Lamp, Domed Shade, Birds & Flowers, Green Ground, 7 1/2 x 14 1/2 In. 4420.00
Lamp, Domed Shade, Birds In Flight, 7 x 15 In. 4310.00
Lamp, Domed Shade, Butterflies, Flowers, Ferns, Bronze Base, 4 Flared Feet, 28 In. 1410.00
Lamp, Domed Shape, Flowers, Yellow Ground, Recessed Forest Scene, Signed, 7 x 14 In. 5750.00
Lamp, Flowers, Ribbed Base, No. 6422, Signed, 16 x 22 In. 3450.00
Lamp, Hanging, 6 Panels, Metal Overlay, Mottled Glass, 20 In. 3100.00
Lamp, Hanging, Jungle Bird, Signed, 10 In. 4600.00
Lamp, Hanging, Metal Overlay, Mushroom Shape, Palm Trees, Bronze, 7 x 11 In. 4715.00
Lamp, Hanging, Metal Overlay, Trellis, Red Wreaths, Green, Caramel Slag, 10 In., Pair .. 2645.00
Lamp, Hanging, Slag, Yellow, Swirl Leaf, Signed, 18 In. 1380.00
Lamp, Hanging, Tropical Island, Swirls Over Green Panels, 28 In. 6040.00
Lamp, Harp, Art Deco, Hexagonal Shade, Frosted, 7 x 18 In. 1320.00
Lamp, Harp, Yellow, Black, Flowers, 6 x 11 In. 1725.00
Lamp, Jungle Bird, Hexagonal, 7 x 14 In. 8050.00
Lamp, Landscape, Hexagonal, Ribbed, Signed, 7 1/2 x 13 1/2 In. 2300.00
Lamp, Landscape, Water, Birds, Orange Ground, Signed, 23 1/2 In. 5060.00
Lamp, Maple Leaf Shade, 23 In. 2750.00
Lamp, Metal Overlay, Chipped Ice Glass, 4-Socket, Double Shaft, 27 1/2 x 20 In. 6325.00
Lamp, Metal Overlay, Tropical Landscape, Multicolored Slag Glass, 3-Socket, 25 x 20 In. 6325.00
Lamp, Metal Overlay, Tulips, Caramel & White Slag Glass, Bronzed Metal Base, 15 In. ... 980.00
Lamp, Parrots, Flowers, Hexagonal, Signed, 7 1/2 x 14 In. 1840.00
Lamp, Red Roses, Oval Shade, Signed, 10 x 5 x 15 In. 2645.00
Lamp, River, Trees, Pink & Yellow Sky, Bronze Base, 15 x 21 1/2 In. 3680.00
Lamp, Trees, Meadows, Cloudy Skies, 3-Socket Base, Acorn Pulls, 18 In. 6040.00
Lamp, Trees, Textured Metalwork, Signed, 17 3/4 x 23 In. 2300.00
Lamp, Tropical Scene, Reverse Painted, Bronze Base, 14 1/2 x 8 In. 1380.00
Lamp, Tulip, Leaded Petals, Green, White, Bronze Lily Pad Base, c.1910, 14 In. 1035.00 to 1880.00
Lamp Base, 3-Light, Flowers, Bronzed Metal, 24 In. 440.00
Match Safe, Indian Chief, Metal Collar, 3 x 3 In. ....515.00 to 800.00
Mug, Animals, Birds, Monk, Inscriptions, 2 In., 10 Piece 1440.00
Pitcher, Cover, Green Enameled Mosserine, 3 Leaf Clover, Etched Flowers, 9 In. 290.00
Pitcher, Pink Roses, 10 3/4 In. 1035.00
Punch Bowl Set, Grape, Gold Rim & Handles, 11 Piece 5175.00
Shade, Globe Shape, White, Pink, Flowers, 9 In. 230.00
Shade, Teroma, Pale Yellow Ground, 5 1/4 In., Pair 545.00
Smoking Set, Buffalo, Indian, Horses, Ash Receiver, Match Holder, Humidor, 4 Piece ... 1670.00
Stylized Flowers, Green, Red, Yellow Ground, Bronze Base, 22 In. 4115.00
Tea Set, Flowers, Gold Trim, Porcelain, 21 Piece 1725.00
Tobacco Jar, Hinged Cover, 3 Dogs, Rectangular, Signed, Kelsey, 5 x 6 In. 1150.00
Tobacco Jar, Metal Overlay, Removable Pipe, Setter At Point, Signed, 5 x 5 1/2 In. 920.00
Vase, Tazza, Pink, White Flowers, Leaves, Porcelain, 8 1/2 x 5 In. 805.00
Vase, Tazza, Roses, Thorned Stem, Porcelain, 9 1/2 x 5 In. 3160.00
Vase, Teroma, Alpine Scene, Signed, 9 1/2 In. 1150.00
Vase, Teroma, Birch & Fir Trees, Signed, 8 In. 920.00
Vase, Teroma, Green, Brown, Flowers, 7 In. 520.00
Vase, Teroma, Pine Needles, 8 1/2 In. 460.00
Vase, Woman, Porcelain, Mounted Brass Collar, Signed, 12 In. 690.00

HARDWARE, see Architectural category.

HARKER Pottery Company was incorporated in 1890 in East Liverpool, Ohio. The Harker family had been making pottery in the area since 1840. The company made many types of pottery but by the Civil War was making quantities of yellowware from native clays. They also made Rockingham-type brown-glazed pottery and whiteware. The plant was moved to Chester, West Virginia, in 1931. Dinnerwares were made and sold nationally. In 1971 the company was sold to Jeannette Glass Company and all operations ceased in 1972. For more information, see *Kovels' Depression Glass & Dinnerware Price List.*

Alpine, Plate, Dinner, Intaglio, Cameoware, 10 In. 10.00

Alpine, Salt & Pepper, Intaglio, Cameoware 18.00
Alpine, Sugar & Creamer, Intaglio, Cameoware 16.00
Amy, Pie Server, 9 1/4 In. 35.00
Blue Basket, Creamer 16.00
Chesterton, Casserole, Cover, Gray, Tab Handles, 9 1/2 x 10 In. 25.00
Chesterton, Oval, Platter, Gray, 13 1/2 In. 20.00
Emmy, Salt & Pepper, Skyscraper Shape, Poppies, 4 1/2 In. 40.00
Emmy, Syrup, Cover, 5 1/2 In. 35.00
Ivy Vine, Gravy Boat 19.00
Ivy Vine, Platter, Oval, 16 In. 46.00
Mallow, Bowl, 10 In. 45.00
Mallow, Cake Plate, 11 x 12 1/2 In. 35.00
Mallow, Casserole, Cover, Qt., 6 1/2 x 4 1/2 In. 56.00
Mallow, Salt & Pepper, Skyscraper Shape, 4 1/2 In. 43.00
Modern Tulip, Casserole, Cover, 8 5/8 In. 45.00
Modern Tulip, Water Jug, Cover, 8 In. 28.00
Oriental Poppy, Jug, Gargoyle, Qt., 6 1/4 In. 30.00
Petit Point, Canister, Cover, Paneled Sides, 6 In. 125.00
Petit Point, Coffee Server, 4 Cups, 7 1/2 In. 48.00
Petit Point, Creamer 28.00
Petit Point, Sugar, Cover 28.00
Petit Point Rose, Casserole, Cover, 8 1/2 In. 50.00
Petit Point Rose, Platter, Oval, 14 In. 35.00
Pine Cone, Bowl, Cereal, 6 1/4 In. 7.00
Pine Cone, Soup, Dish 8.00
Red Apple, Bowl, Swirled Sides, 9 In. 38.00
Red Apple, Cake Plate, 11 3/8 In. 30.00
Silhouette, Bowl, 9 1/4 In. 39.00
Silhouette, Pie Dish, 10 1/4 In. 30.00
Silhouette, Rolling Pin, Fireplace Woman, Stopper, 15 In. 189.00
Tulip, Rolling Pin, Stopper, 15 In. 145.00
White Rose, Pie Baker, Blue, Carv-Kraft, 10 In. 29.00
White Rose, Plate, Dinner, Cameoware, 10 In. 23.00
White Rose, Platter, Blue, Cameoware, Carv-Kraft, 11 x 12 In. 40.00
White Rose, Teapot, Blue, Cameoware, 4 1/2 In. 70.00
Wild Rose, Cake Plate, 11 x 12 1/2 In. 35.00

HARLEQUIN dinnerware was produced by the Homer Laughlin
Company from 1938 to 1964, and sold without trademark by the F. W.
Woolworth Co. It has a concentric ring design like Fiesta, but the rings
are separated from the rim by a plain margin. Cup handles are triangular in shape. Seven different novelty animal figurines were introduced
in 1939. For more information on Harlequin dinnerware, see *Kovels'
Depression Glass & Dinnerware Price List*.

Chartreuse, Creamer 11.00
Chartreuse, Cup & Saucer 12.00
Chartreuse, Platter, 11 In. ....10.00 to 18.00
Chartreuse, Soup, Cream 25.00
Forest Green, Plate, 10 In. 6.00
Forest Green, Salt & Pepper ....27.50 to 30.00
Gray, Shaker 8.00
Gray, Sugar 12.50
Light Green, Creamer 5.00
Maroon, Bowl, Baker, Oval 30.00
Mauve Blue, Bowl, Baker, Oval 30.00
Mauve Blue, Bowl, Nut 12.00
Mauve Blue, Cup & Saucer 20.00
Mauve Blue, Cup, After Dinner 36.00
Mauve Blue, Sugar 5.00
Medium Green, Plate, 9 In. ....9.00 to 19.00
Medium Green, Plate, 10 In. 80.00
Medium Green, Salad, Individual 15.00
Red, Soup, Cream 42.00

Red, Tumbler, Water	18.00
Rose, Platter, 13 In.	9.00
Turquoise, Bowl, Nappy, 9 In.	22.00
Turquoise, Platter, 11 In.	6.00
Turquoise, Salad, Individual	6.00
Turquoise, Salt & Pepper	11.00
Turquoise, Sugar & Creamer	5.00 to 26.00
Turquoise, Teapot	50.00
Turquoise, Tumbler, Water	11.00
Yellow, Bowl, Nappy, 9 In.	22.00
Yellow, Creamer, High Lipped	200.00
Yellow, Cup, After Dinner	65.00
Yellow, Marmalade	150.00
Yellow, Salad, Individual	16.00
Yellow, Sugar & Creamer	18.00

HATPIN collectors search for pins popular from 1860 to 1920. The long pin, often over four inches, was used to hold the hat in place on the hair. The tops of the pins were made of all materials, from solid gold and real gemstones to ceramics and glass. Be careful to buy original hatpins and not recent pieces made by altering old buttons.

Micro Mosaic, Millefiori Tesserae Stars Surrounding Center Garden, 2 3/4 In.	80.00
Rhinestone, Crystal & Red, Brass Setting, Gold Plated, North Bohemia, c.1900, 11 In.	85.00
Rhinestone, Shamrock, Purple, Green, 6 In.	8.00
Satsuma Cap, Bezel Set, Hand Painted, Imari Colored Flowers, Leaves, 1-In. Round, 8 In.	140.00

HATPIN HOLDERS were needed when hatpins were fashionable from 1860 to 1920. The large, heavy hat required special long-shanked pins to hold it in place. The hatpin holder resembles a large saltshaker, but it often has no opening at the bottom as a shaker does. Hatpin holders were made of all types of ceramics and metal. Look for other pieces under the names of specific manufacturers.

Ebony, Sterling Silver, Inlaid Word Hatpins, England, 1918, 5 1/2 In.	280.00
Glass, Engraved Notches, Silver Plated Top, England, 9 In.	35.00
Hand Painted Flowers, Pink, Blue Yellow, Cobalt Blue & Gold Trim, 4 In.	65.00
Limoges, Boot Shape, Pink & Yellow Flowers, 6 In.	40.00
Nippon, Souvenir, Washington, D.C., Moriage Trim, 5 In.	80.00
Noritake, Butterfly & Blossoms, Pink Ground, Hand Painted, 5 In.	65.00
Royal Bayreuth, Dachshund, Figural	500.00
Royal Vienna, Pink Roses & Buds, Scalloped Panels & Feet, 5 In.	225.00
RS Prussia, Pink Roses, Green Ground, 7 In.	180.00
RS Prussia, Yellow Calla Lily, 4 1/4 In.	175.00
Schafer & Vater, Jasperware, Green, White Classical Woman, 5 1/4 In.	630.00

HAVILAND china has been made in Limoges, France, since 1842. The factory was started by the Haviland Brothers of New York City. Pieces are marked *H & Co.*, *Haviland & Co.*, or *Theodore Haviland*. It is possible to match existing sets of dishes through dealers who specialize in Haviland china. Other factories worked in the town of Limoges making a similar chinaware. These porcelains are listed in this book under Limoges.

HAVILAND & CO.

Boullion, Pemberton Pattern, Pink & Blue Flowers, Handles, Theodore Haviland	35.00
Bowl, Vegetable, Cover, Blue & Pink Asters, Gold Trim, Theodore Haviland, 11 In.	110.00
Bowl, Vegetable, Cover, Embossed Cartouches, Pale Blue Flowers, 1894-1931, 11 In.	230.00
Bowl, Vegetable, Cover, Juliet Pattern, Pink Floral Sprays, Theodore Haviland, 8 In.	200.00
Bowl, Vegetable, Cover, Wedding Ring Pattern, 1876-1886, 8 In.	125.00
Butter, Cover, Hand Painted Pink Flowers, Bow Finial, Strainer, 7 3/4 In.	230.00
Cake Plate, Pink Rose, Green Foliage, Handles, 12 In.	80.00
Cup, Juliet Pattern, Pink Flowers, Theodore Haviland	15.00
Cup, Wild Irises, Lavender, Gold Trim, Scrolled Handle, 1890s	35.00
Dish, Leaf Shape, Pink Roses, Green Foliage, Gold Trim	30.00
Gravy Boat, Attached Underplate, Lancaster Pattern, Theodore Haviland, 7 1/2 In.	130.00
Oyster Plate, 5 Wells, Turkey, Seafoam Green Ground, 8 3/4 In.	360.00
Oyster Plate, 6 Wells, Flowers, Gold, 9 In.	140.00

Haviland, Pitcher, Gold
Plums, Deep Pink
Ground, Marked CF,
20th Century, 8 In.

**Never use hot or cold water on
glass. Use dishwashing liquid, a
soft toothbrush, and warm
water. Rinse, then dry with a
terrycloth towel.**

Oyster Plate, 6 Wells, Yellow Ground, Gold Flowers, Pink Wells, Octagonal	220.00
Pitcher, Gold Plums, Deep Pink Ground, Marked CF, 20th Century, 8 In. .... *Illus*	207.00
Plate, Bread & Butter, French Garden Pattern, Pink Roses, Green Swags	25.00
Plate, Dinner, Forever Spring, 10 1/8 In.	12.00
Plate, Dinner, Old Blackberry Pattern, 1876-1889, 9 1/2 In.	25.00
Plate, Dinner, Pink Floral Swags, Gold Trim, 1894-1931, 8 3/4 In.	30.00
Plate, Longfellow, C. Piton, France, Late 1800s, 8 3/8 In., 12 Piece	999.00
Platter, Canvasback Duck, Chesapeake, White House, Theo. Davis, Limoges, 18 1/2 In. .	5650.00
Platter, Pink Chrysanthemums, Gold Trim, Oval, 13 1/2 In.	80.00
Soup, Dish, Sylvia Pattern, Pink Roses, Green Foliage, Theodore Haviland, 7 In.	22.00
Sugar & Creamer, Helene Pattern, Pink Flowers, Theodore Haviland	115.00
Tea Set, Blue Flowers, C-Scroll Handles, Johann Haviland, Bavaria, 3 Piece	145.00

HAWKES cut glass was made by T. G. Hawkes & Company of Corning,
New York, founded in 1880. The firm cut glass blanks made at other
glassworks until 1962. Many pieces are marked with the trademark, a
trefoil ring enclosing a fleur-de-lis and two hawks. Cut glass by other
manufacturers is listed under either the factory name or in the general
Cut Glass category.

Berry Bowl, Queens Cutting, Signed, 5 1/2 In.	125.00
Bowl, 4 Large Hobstar Fields, Square, 8 1/2 In.	450.00
Bowl, Center Star, Flower Vases, Fruit Bowl, Engraved, 1910-1930, 12 In.	510.00
Bowl, Centerpiece, Chrysanthemum Cutting, 12 In.	900.00
Bowl, Diamonds, Stars, Fans, Arches, Signed, 9 In.	259.00
Bowl, Hobstar, 8 x 3 1/4 In.	200.00
Bowl, Iris, Ray Center, Signed, 8 In.	90.00
Bowl, Whipped Cream, Hobstar, Crosscut Diamond, Signed, 6 In.	125.00
Butter, Cover, Venetian Cutting, Octagonal, Straus, 6 1/2 x 9 In.	700.00
Candlestick, Hollow Stem, Pyramidal Star Base, Signed, 9 In.	725.00
Candy Dish, Cover, Intaglio, Flower Bouquets, Lattice, Sterling Silver Finial, 5 x 9 In.	250.00
Carafe, Water, Chrysanthemum Cutting, 8 In.	600.00
Cocktail Shaker, Engraved Leaves, Silver Mounts, 9 1/4 x 11 In.	129.00
Cocktail Shaker, Engraved Rooster, Silver Rim & Spout, 1901, 9 In. ....110.00 to	125.00
Cologne, Brazilian Cutting, 5 In.	290.00
Decanter, Rouen Cutting, Faceted Stopper, Signed, 10 1/2 In., Pair	1250.00
Goblet, Queens Cutting, Signed, 6 In.	200.00
Jug, Florence Cutting, Squat, 2 Pt., 6 In.	175.00
Plate, 6 Hobstars, Engraved Bands, Rayed Center, Signed, 9 3/4 In.	100.00
Plate, 12 Heavy Flutes, 20-Point Hobstar Center, Signed, 6 In.	25.00
Plate, Brazilian Variation, Crosscut Diamond, 7 In.	50.00
Plate, Chrysanthemum Cutting, 7 In.	350.00
Sugar & Creamer, Brunswick Cutting, Signed	450.00
Toothpick, Carnation, Gravic, Signed	250.00
Toothpick, Gladys Cutting, Barrel Shape, 2 1/2 In.	75.00
Tray, Klondike Cutting, Signed, 10 In.	4000.00
Tray, North Star Cutting, Round, Scalloped Edge, 15 In.	2645.00
Trivet, Gravic Flower Design, Signed, 8 1/2 In.	200.00
Vase, Diamonds, Ribbed Panels, 9 3/4 In.	260.00
Vase, Fluted, Stars On Frosted Panels, Stamped, 11 1/2 In.	260.00
Vase, Horizontal Bars, Stars, Signed, 12 In.	195.00

Vase, Lorraine Cutting, 16 In. 3950.00
Water Set, Star Garland, Intaglio Flowers, Signed, 6 1/2 In., 3 Piece 175.00

HEAD VASES, generally showing a woman from the shoulders up, were used by florists primarily in the 1950s and 1960s. Made in a variety of sizes and often decorated with imitation jewelry and other lifelike accessories, the vases were manufactured in Japan and the U.S.A. Less elaborate examples were made as early as the 1930s. Religious themes, babies, and animals are also common subjects. Other head vases are listed under manufacturers' names and can be located through the index at the back of this book.

Mitzie Gaynor, Wearing White Flower In Upswept Hair, Hand On Chin, 6 3/4 In. 655.00
Teen, Blond, Pink Bow, Blue Eyes, Pouty Coral Lips, Purple Blouse, Enesco, 7 In. 455.00
Teen, Blond, Red Heart Pendant, Original Foil Napco Label, Marked, 7 In. 1080.00
Woman In Hat, Rhinestones, Napcoware, 6 In. 375.00

HEDI SCHOOP Art Creations, North Hollywood, California, started about 1945 and was working until 1954. Schoop made ceramic figurines, lamps, planters, and tablewares.

Figurine, Dutch Girl, Holding Apron, 11 In. 90.00
Figurine, Flower Girl, Head, Leaning To Side, 9 1/2 In. 80.00
Figurine, Poodles Admire Each Other, Carved Black Fur, Pair, 12 In. 100.00
Figurine, Woman & Poodle, Black Dress, 10 1/2 In. .... 15.00 to 30.00
Figurine, Woman, Holding Book, 9 In. 95.00
Vase, Figural, Young Woman, Gray Dress, Kerchief, Signed, 12 3/4 In. 145.00

HEINTZ ART Metal Shop used the letters *HAMS* in a diamond as a mark. Otto Heintz took over the Arts & Crafts Company in Buffalo, New York, in 1903. By 1906 it had become the Heintz Art Metal Shop. It remained in business until 1930. The company made ashtrays, bookends, boxes, bowls, desk sets, vases, trophies, and smoking sets. The best-known pieces are made of patinated bronze with silver overlay. Similar pieces were made by Smith Metal Arts and were marked *Silver Crest*. Some pieces by both companies are unmarked.

Ashtray, Matchbox Holder, Golfer, Silver On Bronze, Patina, Stamped, 4 x 7 In. 145.00
Box, Cover, Hunting Scene, Silver On Bronze, Dark Green Patina, 2 1/4 x 4 3/4 In. 470.00
Humidor, Cylindrical, Overlay, Silver On Bronze, Monogram, Diamond Mark, 5 x 4 In. ... 115.00
Jar, Cover, Bronze, Applied Sterling Silver Design On Top, 7 In. 175.00
Lamp, Bulbous, Bronze, Sterling Silver Bird Design, Bird Cutout Shade, 8 x 11 1/2 In. 1265.00
Lamp, Geometric Band, Silver On Bronze, Original Patina, 10 1/2 x 8 In. 635.00
Lamp, Goldenrod, Silver On Bronze, Verdigris Patina, 11 x 8 In. 805.00
Lamp, Helmet Shade, Amethyst Jewels, Silver On Bronze, Cleaned Patina, 14 x 9 1/2 In. .. 920.00
Lamp, Helmet Shade, Pussywillows, Silver On Bronze, Patina, 11 x 8 In. 375.00
Lamp, Helmet Shade, Silver Leaf Overlay, 10 1/2 In. 920.00
Vase, Goldenrod Overlay, Oval, Silver On Bronze, Medium Patina, 12 x 6 In. 460.00
Vase, Wild Rose, Flared Mouth, Silver On Bronze, Dark Green Patina, Silvercrest, 9 In. ... 140.00

HEISEY glass was made from 1896 to 1957 in Newark, Ohio, by A. H. Heisey and Co., Inc. The Imperial Glass Company of Bellaire, Ohio, bought some of the molds and the rights to the trademark. Some Heisey patterns have been made by Imperial since 1960. After 1968, they stopped using the *H* trademark. Heisey used romantic names for colors, such as *Sahara*. Do not confuse color and pattern names. The Custard Glass and Ruby Glass categories may also include some Heisey pieces.

Angel Fish, Bookends 180.00
Animal, Airedale 1800.00
Animal, Asiatic Pheasant .... 225.00 to 325.00
Animal, Baby Chick 45.00
Animal, Bull 3500.00
Animal, Bunny, Head Down, Pair 375.00
Animal, Bunny, Head Up, Pair 350.00
Animal, Clydesdale 595.00

Animal, Colt, Kicking	325.00
Animal, Colt, Rearing	325.00
Animal, Colt, Standing	60.00 to 75.00
Animal, Donkey	250.00 to 285.00
Animal, Duckling, Floating, Pair	375.00
Animal, Duckling, Standing	165.00
Animal, Elephant, Large	295.00
Animal, Elephant, Medium	295.00 to 350.00
Animal, Elephant, Small	260.00
Animal, Fighting Rooster	195.00
Animal, Flying Mare	5000.00
Animal, Gazelle	3000.00
Animal, Giraffe	130.00 to 200.00
Animal, Goose, Wings Down	475.00
Animal, Goose, Wings Half	75.00
Animal, Goose, Wings Up	65.00 to 95.00
Animal, Hen	1200.00
Animal, Mallard, Wings Down	315.00
Animal, Mallard, Wings Half	160.00
Animal, Mallard, Wings Up	125.00 to 160.00
Animal, Pig, Mama	975.00
Animal, Piglet	40.00 to 50.00
Animal, Plug Horse, Sparky	125.00
Animal, Pouter Pigeon	1300.00
Animal, Rabbit, Mother	3500.00
Animal, Ring-Necked Pheasant	160.00
Animal, Rooster, Vase	100.00
Animal, Scottie Dog	95.00 to 110.00
Animal, Show Horse	1500.00
Animal, Sparrow	65.00 to 100.00
Animal, Swan	1100.00
Arch, Tumbler, Amber	160.00
Aristocrat, Candlestick, 7 In., Pair	160.00
Aristocrat, Candy Jar, Cover, Cobalt Blue, Footed, 1/2 Lb.	1750.00
Athena, Bowl, Hexagonal, 11 In.	25.00
Athena, Candlestick, 2-Light	35.00
Ball, Vase, 6 In.	45.00
Banded Flute, Jar, Horseradish, Cover	85.00
Banded Flute, Tray, 13 In.	125.00
Beaded Panel & Sunburst, Toothpick, 2 1/2 In.	120.00
Beaded Panel & Sunburst, Toothpick, Clear	165.00
Beaded Swag, Mug, Souvenir, Ruby Stain, 6 Oz.	35.00
Beaded Swag, Toothpick, 2 1/4 In.	30.00
Beaded Swag, Toothpick, Ruby Stain, 2 1/4 In.	12.00
Cathedral, Vase, Antarctic Etch, Flared, 8 In.	195.00
Cathedral, Vase, Sahara, Flared, 8 In.	125.00
Colonial, Basket, Round, Handle, 8 In.	160.00
Colonial, Goblet	20.00
Colonial, Jug, Molasses, Hinged Cover, 8 Oz.	85.00
Colonial, Salt & Pepper	35.00
Colonial, Spice Tray, 10 In.	30.00
Colonial, Spice Tray, Colonial Carving, 10 In.	35.00
Colonial, Sugar & Creamer	30.00 to 55.00
Colonial, Sugar & Creamer, Sterling Base	75.00
Colonial, Tumbler, Gold Trim	20.00
Crystolite, Bottle, Bitters	175.00
Crystolite, Candleblock, Rosette, Pair	25.00
Crystolite, Candleblock, Square, Pair	40.00
Crystolite, Candleblock, Swirl, Pair	55.00
Crystolite, Cheese Plate, Oval, Handles, 8 In.	40.00
Crystolite, Cigarette Set, Box, Cover, Ashtrays, 5 Piece	55.00
Crystolite, Compote, Blown	285.00
Crystolite, Dish, Mayonnaise, Oval, Handles, 6 In.	40.00

Crystolite, Dish, Pickle, Handle, 9 In. 35.00
Crystolite, Lamp, Electric, Cloth Shade, 13 In. 65.00
Crystolite, Pitcher, 1/2 Gal. 100.00
Crystolite, Plate, 10 In. 45.00
Crystolite, Puff Box, Cover 40.00
Crystolite, Punch Cup 10.00
Crystolite, Relish, 5 Sections, Round 35.00
Crystolite, Relish, Cloverleaf 20.00
Crystolite, Salt & Pepper, Nickel Tops 40.00
Crystolite, Sugar & Creamer, Tray 60.00
Daisy & Leaves, Basket, 8 In. 250.00
Daisy & Leaves, Basket, Fruit, 8 In. 150.00
Empress, Bowl, Nasturtium, Moongleam, Dolphin Footed 210.00
Empress, Bowl, Sahara, 8 In. 50.00
Empress, Bowl, Sahara, Rolled Edge, 8 In. 40.00
Empress, Candy Box, Cover, Flamingo, 6 In. 55.00
Empress, Candy Box, Cover, Sahara, Dolphin Footed 195.00
Empress, Celery Dish, Sahara 45.00
Empress, Dish, Mayonnaise, Sahara, Dolphin Footed 55.00
Empress, Dish, Pickle & Olive, Moongleam, 12 In. 45.00
Empress, Ice Tub, Moongleam, Antarctic Etch, Silver Plated Handle 170.00
Empress, Mustard, Cover, Sahara 110.00
Empress, Plate, 9 In. 50.00
Empress, Plate, Alexandrite, 8 In. . . . . .60.00 to 100.00
Empress, Plate, Tangerine, 8 In. 150.00
Empress, Platter, Sahara, Oval, 14 In. 60.00
Empress, Relish, Triplex, 3 Sections, Flamingo, 7 In. 65.00
Empress, Sugar & Creamer, Flamingo 75.00
Essex, Candlestick, 9 In., Pair 290.00
Fancy Loop, Punch Cup . . . . .15.00 to 25.00
Fancy Loop, Relish 30.00
Fancy Loop, Sugar & Creamer, Emerald Green, Gold Trim 100.00
Fancy Loop, Toothpick, 2 1/4 In. . . . . .40.00 to 75.00
Fancy Loop, Toothpick, Emerald Green, Gold Trim, 2 1/4 In. 65.00
Fancy Loop, Tumbler, Emerald Green, Gold Trim, 3 3/4 In. 55.00
Fancy Loop, Water Set, Emerald Green, Gold Trim, 7 Piece 310.00
Fancy Loop, Wine, 3 Oz. 40.00
Fandango, Bowl, 3 Sides, 8 In. 45.00
Fandango, Bowl, 8 In. 30.00
Fandango, Bowl, Flared, 9 In. 40.00
Fandango, Butter, Cover 120.00
Fandango, Cake Salver, Footed 65.00
Fandango, Cruet 25.00
Fandango, Sugar & Creamer 45.00
Fandango, Toothpick 90.00
Fern, Dish, Mayonnaise, Handles 45.00
Flat Panel, Cruet 35.00
Flat Panel, Jar, Cover, Crushed Fruit 275.00
Flat Panel, Sugar & Creamer, Butter Chip, Stacked Set 80.00
Flat Panel, Toothpick . . . . .65.00 to 75.00
Flower Frog, Flamingo 30.00
Flower Frog, Moongleam 40.00
Gascony, Tumbler, Juice, Sahara, Wide Optic, 5 Oz. 45.00
Georgian, Candlestick, 9 In., Pair 145.00
Glory, Wine, 2 Oz. 12.00
Greek Key, Celery Dish, 9 In. 35.00
Greek Key, Pitcher, 3 Pt. 225.00
Greek Key, Pitcher, Straight Sides, 1/2 Gal. 410.00
Greek Key, Tray, French Roll, 12 1/2 In. 150.00
Half Circle, Sugar & Creamer 185.00
Half Circle, Sugar & Creamer, Flamingo 120.00
Half Circle, Sugar & Creamer, Sahara 95.00
Horse Head, Bookends 195.00

Jamestown, Goblet, Barcelona Cutting, 10 Oz. 30.00
Kohinoor, Cocktail, Zircon Bowl, Clear Stem & Foot 85.00
Lariat, Basket, 8 1/2 In. 160.00
Lariat, Candlestick, 3-Light, Pair 95.00
Lariat, Cologne, Stopper, 4 Oz. 110.00
Lariat, Creamer 15.00
Lariat, Relish, 3 Sections, 12 In. 30.00
Lariat, Sugar & Creamer 30.00
Legionnaire, Goblet, 10 Oz. 25.00
Locket On Chain, Butter, Cover 200.00
Locket On Chain, Wine 75.00
Mayflower, Champagne, Moongleam Stem & Foot, 5 1/2 In. 55.00
McGrady, Syrup, Flamingo, 5 Oz. 90.00
Military Cap, Ashtray ....25.00 to 35.00
Minuet, Tumbler, Iced Tea, Footed, 12 Oz. 60.00
Narrow Flute, Condiment Set, 5 Piece 200.00
Narrow Flute, Creamer, Enameled Flower 30.00
Narrow Flute, Dish, Lemon, 6 1/2 In. ....25.00 to 30.00
Narrow Flute, Marmalade, Cover 115.00
Narrow Flute, Mustard, Cover 90.00
Narrow Flute, Nappy, Flared, 8 In. 30.00
Narrow Flute, Relish, 3 Sections, Moongleam 65.00
Narrow Flute, Sugar & Creamer 35.00
Narrow Flute, Sugar & Creamer, Cover 40.00
Narrow Flute, Sugar & Creamer, Individual 35.00
New Era, Goblet, 10 Oz. 25.00
Octagon, Basket, Flamingo, 5 In. 325.00
Octagon, Bowl, Floral, Moongleam, 12 In. 60.00
Octagon, Dish, Dessert, Pink 20.00
Octagon, Dish, Mayonnaise, Diamond Optic, Moongleam, Footed, Handles 35.00
Old Colony, Candy Dish, Yeoman, Green, Handles 75.00
Old Sandwich, Cruet, Stopper ....70.00 to 95.00
Old Sandwich, Dish, Sundae, Moongleam 40.00
Old Sandwich, Sugar & Creamer 75.00
Old Sandwich, Tumbler, Soda, Footed, 12 Oz. 20.00
Old Williamsburg, Candelabrum, 3-Light, Sahara, 15 1/2 In., Pair 1300.00
Old Williamsburg, Candlestick, 9 In., Pair 120.00
Old Williamsburg, Eggcup 12.00
Old Williamsburg, Goblet 25.00
Old Williamsburg, Sugar, Cover 10.00
Omega, Goblet, Star Cutting 25.00
Orchid Etch, Bowl, Floral, Waverly, 12 In. 75.00
Orchid Etch, Candlestick, 3-Light, Cascade, Pair 280.00
Orchid Etch, Compote, Knee & Step, 5 1/2 In. 45.00
Orchid Etch, Pitcher, Donna, 1/2 Gal. 285.00
Orchid Etch, Salt & Pepper, Waverly 120.00
Orchid Etch, Sugar & Creamer, Waverly ....60.00 to 65.00
Orchid Etch, Vase, Fan, Lariat, 7 In. 140.00
Oxford, Goblet 25.00
Parallel Quarter, Bowl, Floral, Etched, 11 In. 40.00
Parallel Quarter, Candlestick, 3 In., Pair 50.00
Peerless, Cup 8.00
Peerless, Decanter, Stopper, Pt. 50.00
Peerless, Plate, 6 In. 10.00
Peerless, Sugar 15.00
Peerless, Sugar & Creamer, Individual 30.00
Peerless, Toothpick 70.00
Peerless, Tumbler 30.00
Peerless, Wine 10.00
Petal, Sugar & Creamer, Crystal 85.00
Petal, Sugar & Creamer, Flamingo 70.00
Petal, Sugar & Creamer, Moongleam 75.00
Picket, Basket, Daisy Cutting, 10 In. 230.00

Pillows, Butter, Cover 90.00
Pillows, Compote, 5 1/2 In. 85.00
Pillows, Rose Bowl, 6 1/2 In. 150.00
Pillows, Rose Bowl, Footed, 4 In. 325.00
Pillows, Spooner 160.00
Pillows, Vase, Ball, 4 1/2 In. 75.00
Pineapple & Fan, Cup, Ruby, Clear, 3 1/4 In. 60.00
Pineapple & Fan, Jug, Molasses, Hinged Cover, 10 Oz. 135.00
Pineapple & Fan, Mug, Gold Trim, 6 Oz. 40.00
Pineapple & Fan, Nappy, 8 In. 40.00
Pineapple & Fan, Rose Bowl, 3 In. 115.00
Pineapple & Fan, Toothpick 130.00
Pineapple & Fan, Toothpick, 2 1/4 In. 50.00
Pineapple & Fan, Toothpick, Clear, Gold Trim 115.00
Pineapple & Fan, Toothpick, Green, Gold Trim, 2 1/4 In. 80.00
Pineapple & Fan, Tumbler, Ruby Stain, Mother 40.00
Pineapple & Fan, Water Set, Emerald Green, Gold Trim, 7 Piece 265.00
Pinwheel & Fan, Basket, Variant 310.00
Pinwheel & Fan, Bowl, 8 In. 40.00
Pinwheel & Fan, Pitcher, 3 Pt. 180.00
Pinwheel & Fan, Punch Cup 10.00
Pinwheel & Fan, Punch Cup, Moongleam 55.00
Plantation, Candlestick, 2-Light, Pair 120.00
Plantation, Candlestick, 5 In., Pair 250.00
Plantation, Coaster, Pair 20.00
Plantation, Compote, Footed 35.00
Plantation, Relish, 4 Sections, 8 In. 100.00
Plantation, Salt & Pepper 50.00
Plantation, Sugar & Creamer ....45.00 to 60.00
Plantation, Tray, Condiment, 8 1/2 In. 135.00
Plantation, Tray, Ivy Etch, Flared Edge, 14 In. 140.00
Pleat & Panel, Compote, Covered, Footed 40.00
Pluto, Candlestick, Moongleam, Pair 80.00
Prince Of Wales, Pitcher, 1/2 Gal. 290.00
Prince Of Wales, Toothpick, Gold Trim 195.00
Priscilla, Mustard, Cover 40.00
Priscilla, Toothpick, Etched Flowers 60.00
Provincial, Sherbet 7.00
Punty Band, Toothpick, Ruby Stain, Souvenir 45.00
Puritan, Cake Plate, 4 x 12 In. 240.00
Puritan, Candy Jar, Cover 225.00
Puritan, Compote, Silver Overlay, 6 x 10 In. 130.00
Puritan, Jelly, Footed, 5 In. 25.00
Puritan, Pitcher, Cover, Straight Sides, Qt. 165.00
Puritan, Salt & Pepper 25.00
Queen Ann, Celery Dish, Moongleam, 8 In. 40.00
Queen Ann, Marmalade, Cover 45.00
Queen Ann, Nappy, 8 In. 130.00
Recessed Panel, Candy Jar, Cover, Enameled Trim, 10 In. 60.00
Revere, Dish, Lemon, 5 In. 30.00
Rib & Panel, Basket, Moongleam 275.00
Ridgeleigh, Bowl, Floral, Sahara, Oval, 12 In. 125.00
Ridgeleigh, Cake Plate, Fin Handles, 12 In. 300.00
Ridgeleigh, Cigarette Box, Cover, Round 90.00
Ridgeleigh, Cigarette Set, Box, Cover, Ashtrays, 5 Piece 65.00
Ridgeleigh, Coaster Set, Box, 8 Piece 75.00
Ridgeleigh, Coaster Set, Carrier, Handle, 6 Piece 65.00
Ridgeleigh, Cup & Saucer 15.00
Ridgeleigh, Dish, Dessert, Handles 75.00
Ridgeleigh, Dish, Lemon, Cover 40.00
Ridgeleigh, Goblet, 8 Oz. 25.00
Ridgeleigh, Plate, 8 In. 15.00
Ridgeleigh, Punch Cup 10.00

Ridgeleigh, Relish, Star, 5 Sections, 10 In. 40.00
Ridgeleigh, Vase, 9 In. 80.00
Ridgeleigh, Vase, Candle Insert, Sahara, 6 In., Pair 150.00
Ridgeleigh, Vase, Sahara, Footed, Flared, 5 In. 140.00
Rococo, Bonbon, 5 1/2 In. 35.00
Rose, Torte Plate, 14 In. 100.00
Rose Etch, Basket, 8 In. 180.00
Rose Etch, Candlestick, 3-Light, Cascade, Pair ....165.00 to 175.00
Rose Etch, Celery Dish, Waverly, 13 In. 52.00
Rose Etch, Ice Tub, Waverly, Handles ....350.00 to 450.00
Rose Etch, Plate, Waverly, 8 In. 15.00
Rose Etch, Sherbet, Waverly 35.00
Rose Etch, Sugar & Creamer, Tray, Waverly 125.00
Rose Etch, Sugar & Creamer, Waverly 65.00
Rose Etch, Vase, 8 In. 200.00
Sahara, Mayonnaise Ladle 50.00
Saturn, Cruet, Dawn, Stopper 220.00
Saturn, Dish, Mayonnaise, 5 In. 40.00
Saturn, Mustard, Cover 45.00
Saturn, Vase, Ball, Cut, 5 In. 150.00
Sawtooth Band, Saltshaker, Ruby Stain, Souvenir 30.00
Stanhope, Champagne, Zircon Foot & Bowl 75.00
Stanhope, Punch Cup 15.00
Sunburst, Celery Dish, 12 In. 40.00
Sunburst, Compote, 8 3/4 In. 70.00
Sunburst, Jug, Molasses, Hinged Cover, 16 Oz. 225.00
Sunburst, Nappy, 7 In. 80.00
Sunflower, Sugar & Creamer 65.00
Tally Ho, Tumbler, Whiskey, 2 1/4 In. 75.00
Thumbprint & Panel, Vase, Flared 80.00
Town & Country, Tumbler, Dawn, Flared, 8 Oz. 40.00
Trident, Candlestick, Sahara, Pair 180.00
Tudor, Jelly, Moongleam, Footed, 5 In. 30.00
Tudor, Mug 100.00
Tudor, Sherbet, 5 Oz. 15.00
Twist, Bowl, Footed, 8 In. 50.00
Twist, Bowl, Marigold, Floral Carving, Low Foot 45.00
Twist, Celery Dish, Moongleam, 13 In. 40.00
Twist, Plate, Marigold, 7 In. 40.00
Twist, Salt & Pepper 35.00
Urn, Jug, Molasses, 14 Oz. 135.00
Victorian, Bowl, 8 In. 25.00
Victorian, Celery Dish, 12 In. 25.00
Victorian, Compote, 2-Ball Stem ....20.00 to 30.00
Victorian, Goblet 25.00
Victorian, Punch Cup 10.00
Victorian, Sherbet, 5 Oz. 15.00
Victorian, Vase, 4 In. 50.00
Victorian, Vase, Flared, 8 1/2 In. 160.00
Warwick, Toothpick, Cobalt Blue 125.00
Warwick, Vase, 2 1/2 In., Pair 45.00
Warwick, Vase, 5 In., Pair 65.00
Warwick, Vase, 7 In., Pair 85.00
Warwick, Vase, 9 In., Pair 95.00
Waverly, Goblet, 10 Oz. 35.00
Waverly, Salt & Pepper ....15.00 to 40.00
Waverly, Sandwich Server, Center Handle, 14 In. 45.00
Waverly, Sugar & Creamer 40.00
Whirlpool, Sugar & Creamer, Tray 85.00
Whirlpool, Vase, Violet, 5 In. 150.00
Yeoman, Celery Dish, Moongleam, 9 In. 35.00
Yeoman, Compote, Sahara, Diamond Optic 60.00
Yeoman, Sugar & Creamer 15.00

Yeoman, Sugar & Creamer, Carved 35.00
Yeoman, Sugar & Creamer, Oval, Floral Carved, Hotel 40.00
Yeoman, Vase, Candle Insert 95.00

HEREND, see Fischer category.

HEUBACH is the collector's name for Gebruder Heubach, a firm working in Lichten, Germany, from 1840 to 1925. It is best known for bisque dolls and doll heads, their principal products. They also manufactured bisque figurines, including piano babies, beginning in the 1880s, and glazed figurines in the 1900s. Piano Babies are listed in their own category. Dolls are included in the Doll category under *Gebruder Heubach* and *Heubach*. Another factory, Ernst Heubach, working in Koppelsdorf, Germany, also made porcelain and dolls. These will also be found in the Doll category under Heubach Koppelsdorf.

Figurine, Baroque Man & Woman, Bisque, 18 In., Pair 150.00
Figurine, Dog, Pointer, Gray, White, Green Base, 7 x 14 In. 460.00
Figurine, Dutch Girl, Orange Skirt, Green Scarf, 3 1/2 In. 320.00
Figurine, Elegantly Dressed Man & Woman, Green Tones, c.1900, 15 In., Pair ..... *Illus* 290.00
Figurine, Snowy Owl, Porcelain, 1909-1945, 11 1/2 In. 240.00
Piano Baby, Baby Sucking On Toe, Bisque, 18 In. 650.00
Piano Baby, Boy Eating Chocolate Bar, Bisque, 11 In. 1650.00
Vase, Blue Ground, Figural Mermaid, Bisque, 9 In. 950.00
Vase, Pink Ground, Art Nouveau Woman, Handles, Pate-Sur-Pate, 1884, 7 In. 500.00

HISTORIC BLUE, see factory names, such as Adams, Clews, Ridgway, and Staffordshire.

HOBNAIL glass is a style of glass with bumps all over. Dozens of hobnail patterns and variants have been made. Clear, colored, and opalescent hobnail have been made and are being reproduced. Other pieces of hobnail may also be listed in the Duncan & Miller, Fenton, and Francisware categories.

Bowl, Shell Footed, No. 323, Ruby Hobnail, Dew Drop, Hobbs, Brockunier, 8 1/2 x 6 In. .. 168.00
Bowl, White Over Pink, Cased, Ruffled Edge, 1870s, 10 In. 350.00
Bowl, White Over Raspberry, Ruffled Edge, Hobbs, Brockunier, 8 x 2 1/8 In. 193.00
Decanter, Stopper, 11 In. 35.00
Egg Plate, 15 Wells, 11 In. 20.00
Lamp, Oil, Milk Glass, 6 1/4 In. 35.00
Pitcher, Amber, Blown, c.1900, 7 In. 150.00
Pitcher, Milk, 1/2 Gal. 35.00
Pitcher, Opalescent, Dew Drop, No. 323, Hobbs, Brockunier, 4 1/2 In. 132.00
Vase, White, Blue Interior, Ruffled Edge, Kanawha Glass Co. 25.00

HOCHST, or Hoechst, porcelain was made in Germany from 1746 to 1796. It was marked with a six-spoke wheel. Be careful when buying Hochst; many other firms have used a very similar wheel-shaped mark.

Figurine, Boy, Holding Spaniel, 6 1/4 In. 220.00
Figurine, Boy, With Basket, Signed, E. Werner, 6 1/8 In. 330.00
Figurine, Colonial Woman, Curtseying, Wheel Mark, 7 1/4 In. 325.00

HOLLY AMBER, or golden agate, glass was made by the Indiana Tumbler and Goblet Company of Greentown, Indiana, from January 1, 1903, to June 13, 1903. It is a pressed glass pattern featuring holly leaves in the amber-shaded glass. The glass was made with shadings that range from creamy opalescent to brown-amber.

Berry Set, 5 Piece 950.00
Bowl, 4 1/2 In. 290.00
Bowl, 7 1/2 x 4 1/2 In. 335.00
Bowl, 8 1/2 In. 665.00
Bowl, Oval, 7 1/4 In. .... .655.00 to 690.00
Butter, Cover, 7 1/2 In. .... .1450.00 to 1725.00
Compote, 4 1/2 x 4 In. 1000.00
Compote, 7 1/4 x 8 1/4 In. 730.00

Heubach, Figurine,
Elegantly Dressed Man
& Woman, Green Tones,
c.1900, 15 In., Pair

Horn, Wine Cup, Rhinoceros,
Dragon Handles, Wood Plum
Branch Stand, Chinese, 7 3/4 In.

Compote, Cover, 9 x 6 1/4 In.	950.00
Dish, Pickle, 8 3/4 In.	460.00
Plate, 7 1/2 In.	300.00
Syrup, Silver, Cover	1100.00
Vase, 6 1/4 In.	670.00

HOLT-HOWARD was an importer who started working in 1949 in Stamford, Connecticut. The company sold many types of table accessories, such as condiment jars, decanters, spoon holders, and saltshakers. The figures shown on some of his pieces had a cartoon-like quality. The company was bought out by General Housewares Corporation in 1969. Holt-Howard pieces are often marked with the name and the year or *HH* and the year stamped in black. The HH mark was used until 1974. There was also a black and silver label. Production of Holt-Howard ceased in 1990. Similar pieces by the same Holt-Howard designer are being made today and are marked GHA.

Ashtray, Cozy Kitten, 4 3/4 In.	95.00
Bank, Cozy Kitten, Bobbing Head, 5 1/2 In.	290.00
Chocolate Set, Holly Berry, 1959, 7 Piece	60.00
Dish, Mayonnaise, Cover, Ladle, Pixie Ware, c.1958	325.00
Honey Pot, Pixie Ware, c.1958	235.00
Hors D'Oeuvre Holder, Pixie Ware, c.1958	275.00
Memo Holder, Cozy Kitten, Adhesive Label, 6 7/8 In.	190.00
Mug, Rooster, Coq Rouge	15.00
Olive Jar, Pixie Ware, c.1958	155.00
Pitcher, Cloud Santa, 1967, 7 1/4 In.	35.00
Pitcher, Coq Rouge, Yellow Rooster, Tail Handle, 9 1/2 In.	130.00
Salt & Pepper, Holly Girls, 4 In.	30.00
Shaker, Powdered Cleanser, Cozy Kitten, 6 3/4 In.	230.00
Spoon Rest, Coq Rouge, Sitting Rooster, 3 3/4 In.	50.00
Stringholder, Cozy Kitten, 4 1/2 In.	135.00
Sugar & Creamer, Pixie Ware, c.1958	290.00
Tray, Christmas Tree, 3 Sections, Adhesive Lable, 14 x 8 1/2 In.	30.00

HOPALONG CASSIDY was a character in a series of twenty-eight books written by Clarence E. Milford, first published in 1907. Movies and television shows were made based on the character. The best-known actor playing Hopalong Cassidy was William Lawrence Boyd. His first movie appearance was in 1919, but the first Hopalong Cassidy film was not until 1934. Sixty-six films were made. In 1948, William Boyd purchased the television rights to the movies, then later made fifty-two new programs. In the 1950s, Hopalong Cassidy and his horse, named *Topper*, were seen in comics, records, toys, and other products. Boyd died in 1972.

Bowl & Plate, Marked, W.S. George	30.00
Button, Country Club Dairy, Black, Yellow, Lithographed	16.00
Button, Hoppy's Favorite, Polk Dairy	30.00

Cap Gun Set, 2 Holsters, Belt, Guns 605.00
Chair, Director's, Vinyl, Wood, Fringe, c.1950, 23 In. . . . . .230.00 to 604.00
Costume, Cowboy, Gun, Holster, Box 220.00
Ear Muffs, Plastic, Tin Strap, Bailey, Box, c.1950 . . . . 180.00
Game, Milton Bradley, Box, 1950 . . . . 85.00
Lamp, Aladdin, Bullet, Shade 190.00
Lamp, Aladdin, Gun In Holster, Wall 200.00
Mask, Latex, Box, 1950 . . . . .230.00 to 450.00
Pencil Case, Paper Insert With 3 Hoppy Scenes, 1950s, 8 1/4 x 4 1/2 In. 130.00
Radio, Red, Metal, Foil Front, Model 441T, Arvin, 8 1/4 In. 365.00
Toy, Shooting Gallery, Tin, Automatic Toy, Box, 20 In. 260.00
Toy, Twirls Lasso On Horse, Windup, 1940s 375.00
Tumbler, 4 7/8 In. 50.00
Tumbler, Breakfast Milk, 1950s, 5 In. 55.00
Watch, Leather Band, Metal Buckle, White Face, Hopalong's Picture 60.00

HORN was used to make many types of boxes, furniture inlays, jewelry,
and whimsies.

Hide Scraper, Elk, Elbow Form, Decoration, Tinting, c.1850, 13 1/2 x 1 3/4 In. 690.00
Libation Cup, Brown, Carved Berries, Leaves, Rootstock Handle, Stand, Chinese, 1800s . 6325.00
Mirror & Comb, Traveling, Mahogany, c.1800 . . . . 150.00
Snuff Mull, Silver Mounted, Engraved, Pig Tail End, Scotland, Georgian, c.1835, 3 1/2 In. 375.00
Spoon, Variegated Beadwork On Handle, c.1890, 7 1/4 x 2 1/2 In. 230.00
Whistle, Stag, Scallop Shell Shape, 1800s, 1 1/2 In. 12.00
Wine Cup, Rhinoceros, Dragon Handles, Plum Branch Stand, Chinese, 7 3/4 In. . . . . *Illus* 2000.00

HOWARD PIERCE began working in Southern California in 1936. In
1945, he opened a pottery in Claremont. He moved to Joshua Tree in
1968 and continued making pottery until 1991. His contemporary-
looking figurines are popular with collectors. Though most pieces are
marked with his name, smaller items from his sets often were not
marked.

Howard Pierce

Bowl, Fluted, Flared, Blue, Black Accents, Marked, 1983, 4 1/4 x 7 1/4 In. 150.00
Figurine, Bear, Brown, 7 In. 85.00
Figurine, Circus Horse, Leaping, Head Down, Tail Straight, Blue, 6 1/2 x 7 1/2 In. 245.00
Figurine, Man, Holding Bird, Extended Arm, Textured Glaze, Stamped, 11 In. 195.00
Figurine, Mouse, Pink, Ivory, Stamped, 2 x 3 1/4 In. 380.00
Figurine, Native Woman, Long Body, Arms Behind Back, Mottled Glaze, 16 1/2 In. 245.00
Figurine, Owl, Gray, 5 In. 50.00
Figurine, Panther, Pacing, Brown Glaze, 2 3/4 x 11 1/2 In. 400.00
Figurine, Rabbit, Pale Green, White Cement, 10 1/2 x 5 1/2 In. 380.00
Group, 2 Owls, Tree, On Branch, Small Flowers, Marked, 13 In. 240.00
Group, 3 Monkeys, Stacked, Black, 15 In. 360.00
Magnet, Dinosaur, Gray Glossy Glaze, 1 1/2 x 3 In. 110.00
Pencil Holder, Women, Nude, Relief, Tan & Brown Glaze, 1980, 4 1/2 x 3 1/2 In. 170.00
Vase, Viking Boat, Brown, Rectangular, 5 x 9 In. 25.00
Wall Plaque, Birds In Relief, Pale Green Ground, Rectangular, 6 1/4 19 In. 445.00
Whistle, Bird, Gray, White, Textured Glaze, 3 1/2 In. 100.00
Whistle, Snake, Crawling, M Shape, Brown, White Glaze, 2 3/4 x 3 1/4 In. 155.00

HOWDY DOODY and Buffalo Bob were the main characters in a children's series televised from 1947 to 1960. Howdy was a redheaded
puppet. The series became popular with college students in the late
1970s when Buffalo Bob began to lecture on campuses.

Bag, Apple, Little Chief Washington State Apples, Sanson & Sons, c.1955 . . . . 15.00
Bank, Riding Pig, Marked Bob Smith U.S.A., Shawnee, 6 3/4 In. 550.00
Clock-A-Doodle, Howdy On Swing, Clarabell On Dial, Key Wind 2800.00
Clock-A-Doodle, Tin, Kagran Corp., Bandai, Japan, Box, 1950s, 9 1/2 In. 4180.00
Cookie Jar, 9 3/4 In. 900.00
Doll, Wood Jointed, 12 1/2 In. 395.00
Marionette, Princess Summerfall-Winterspring, Peter Puppet Playthings, 13 In. 220.00
Puppet, Clarabell, Composition Head, Painted Features, Hinged Jaw, Box, 15 In. 400.00
Puppet, Composition Head, Hands, Feet, 16 In. 50.00

Puppet, Composition Head, Painted Features, Hinged Jaw, Controlled, Box, 16 In. 265.00
Puppet, Dilly-Dally, Composition Head, Plastic Glasses, Hinged Jaw, Box, 14 In. 440.00
Puppet, Flub-A-Dub, Composition Head, Sleep Eyes, Lashes, Hinged Jaw, 11 1/2 In. 363.00
Puppet, Kagran Wonder Bread Premium, Cardboard, Jointed, c.1950 .... 105.00
Puppet, Mr. Bluster, Composition Head, Painted Features, Hinged Jaw, Box, 14 In. 485.00
Puppet Show Set, Hard Plastic Figures, 1950s, 4 In., 5 Piece 137.00
Ring, Flashlight, Premium 245.00
Sign, Polaroid Television Filter, c.1950, 18 1/2 x 25 In. 865.00
Toy, Band, Buffalo Bill Plays Piano, Tin, Unique Art, Box, 8 In. ....1485.00 to 2310.00
Toy, Clarabell The Clown, Jumps With Cable Squeeze, Linemar, c.1950 .... 275.00
Toy, Clock-A-Doodle, Tin, Windup, Bandai, 1950s, 9 1/2 In. 3800.00
Toy, Howdy & Bob, Piano, Clockwork, Tin Lithograph, Unique Art, 7 x 8 1/2 In. 825.00
Toy, Howdy Doody Band, Tin Lithograph, Windup, Unique Art, c.1950s, 6 1/2 In. 800.00
Tumbler, Flub-A-Dub On Train, Blue, Circus Series 10.00

HULL pottery was made in Crooksville, Ohio, from 1905. Addis E. Hull bought the Acme Pottery Company and started making ceramic wares. In 1917, A. E. Hull Pottery began making art pottery as well as the commercial wares. For a short time, 1921 to 1929, the firm also sold pottery imported from Europe. The dinnerwares of the 1940s, including the Little Red Riding Hood line, the high gloss artwares of the 1950s, and the matte wares of the 1940s, are all popular with collectors. The firm officially closed in March 1986.

Hull
U.S.A.

Bow Knot, Tea Set, Pink, Blue, 3 Piece 450.00
House & Garden, Mixing Bowl, 7 In. 13.00
Little Red Riding Hood, Salt & Pepper, Gold Trim, 3 1/2 In. 95.00
Parchment & Pine, Basket, 16 In. 150.00

HUMMEL figurines, based on the drawings of the nun M.I. Hummel (Berta Hummel), are made by the W. Goebel Porzellanfabrik of Oeslau, Germany, now Rodenthal, Germany. They were first made in 1935. The *Crown* mark was used from 1935 to 1949. The company added the *bee* marks in 1950. The *full bee* with variations, was used from 1950 to 1959; *stylized bee,* 1957 to 1972; *three line mark,* 1964 to 1972; *last bee,* sometimes called *vee over gee,* 1972 to 1979. In 1979 the V bee symbol was removed from the mark. *U.S. Zone* was part of the mark from 1946 to 1948; *W. Germany,* was part of the mark from 1960 to 1990; The *Goebel, W. Germany* mark, called the *missing bee* mark, was used from 1979 to 1990; *Goebel, Germany* with the crown and WG, originally called the *new mark,* was used from 1991 through part of 1999. The newest version of the bee mark with the word *Goebel,* the *current mark* or *Goebel with full bee,* was adopted in 2000. A special *Year 2000* backstamp was also introduced. Porcelain figures inspired by Berta Hummel's drawings were introduced in 1997. These are marked BH followed by a number. They are made in the Far East, not Germany. Other decorative items and plates that feature Hummel drawings have been made by Schmid Brothers, Inc., since 1971.

Figurine, No. 5, Strolling Along, Stylized Bee 280.00
Figurine, No. 11/0, Merry Wanderer, Last Bee 135.00
Figurine, No. 11/2/0, Merry Wanderer, Full Bee 196.00
Figurine, No. 13/0, Meditation, Three Line Mark 175.00
Figurine, No. 15/2/0, Hear Ye, Hear Ye, Missing Bee 145.00
Figurine, No. 16/1, Little Hiker, Missing Bee 260.00
Figurine, No. 42/0, Good Shepherd, Full Bee 128.00
Figurine, No. 43, March Winds, Last Bee 46.00
Figurine, No. 47/0, Goose Girl, Last Bee 125.00
Figurine, No. 52/0, Going To Grandma's, Missing Bee 320.00
Figurine, No. 57, Chick Girl, Vee Over Gee 75.00
Figurine, No. 57/0, Chick Girl, Missing Bee 35.00
Figurine, No. 58/0, Playmates, Vee Over Gee 46.00
Figurine, No. 59, Skier, New Mark 113.00
Figurine, No. 66, Farm Boy, Three Line Mark 300.00

Figurine, No. 67, Doll Mother, Stylized Bee 104.00
Figurine, No. 70, Holy Child, New Mark 94.00
Figurine, No. 74, Little Gardener, Missing Bee 58.00
Figurine, No. 85/0, Serenade, Full Bee 145.00
Figurine, No. 98, Sister, Stylized Bee 240.00
Figurine, No. 99, Eventide, Missing Bee ....115.00 to 195.00
Figurine, No. 111/1, Wayside Harmony, Missing Bee 225.00
Figurine, No. 112/3/0, Just Resting, Stylized Bee 225.00
Figurine, No. 141X, Apple Tree Girl, Vee Over Gee, 32 In. 5390.00
Figurine, No. 142/3/0, Apple Tree Boy, Vee Over Gee 175.00
Figurine, No. 142X, Apple Tree Boy, Stylized Bee, 30 In. 6250.00
Figurine, No. 153/1, Auf Wiedersehen, New Mark 102.00
Figurine, No. 176/0, Happy Birthday, New Mark 160.00
Figurine, No. 182, Good Friends, Crown Mark 403.00
Figurine, No. 186, Sweet Music, Stylized Bee 240.00
Figurine, No. 214/D, Angel Serenade, Missing Bee 35.00
Figurine, No. 255, Stitch In Time, Last Bee 94.00
Figurine, No. 304, Artist, Vee Over Gee 350.00
Figurine, No. 311, Kiss Me, Stylized Bee 302.00
Figurine, No. 317, Not For You, Last Bee 295.00
Figurine, No. 333, Blessed Event, Last Bee 69.00
Figurine, No. 344, Feathered Friends, Missing Bee 90.00
Figurine, No. 346, Smart Little Sister, Missing Bee 88.00
Figurine, No. 374, Lost Stocking, Three Line Mark 480.00
Figurine, No. 378, Easter Greetings, Missing Bee 35.00
Figurine, No. 380, Daisies Don't Tell, Missing Bee 275.00
Figurine, No. 382, Visiting An Invalid, Three Line Mark 145.00
Figurine, No. 399, Valentine Joy, Missing Bee 250.00
Figurine, No. 421, It's Cold, Missing Bee 350.00
Figurine, No. 422, What Now, Vee Over Gee 350.00
Figurine, No. 431, Surprise, Missing Bee 300.00
Plaque, No. 310, Searching Angel, Missing Bee 150.00
Plaque, No. 323, Merry Christmas, Missing Bee 150.00
Plaque, No. 690, Smiling Through, Vee Over Gee. 75.00
Plate, Annual, 1971, Heavenly Angel 750.00
Plate, Annual, 1972, Hear Ye, Hear Ye 130.00
Wall Vase, No. 360/C, Girl, Vee Over Gee 210.00

HUTSCHENREUTHER Porcelain Company of Selb, Germany, was established in 1814 and is still working. The company makes fine quality porcelain dinnerwares and figurines. The mark has changed through the years, but the name and the lion insignia appear in most versions.

LORENZ
HUTSCHEN REUTER

GERMANY

Bowl, Plumes, Purple, Green Luster, Flowers, Signed, E. Dennie, 12 In. 145.00
Figurine, Dog, Dachshund, Stand, 1940s, 5 x 3 1/4 In. 225.00
Figurine, Dog, Fox Terrier, Sitting, White & Tan, Black Spots, Red Collar, 5 1/2 In. 245.00
Figurine, Dog, Poodle, White, Seated, 6 1/2 In. 80.00
Figurine, Dog, Poodle, White, Seated, No. 2477/3f, 145/1011, 6 1/2 In. 80.00
Figurine, Dog, Poodle, White, Standing, No. 2478/31, 6 1/4 x 7 In. 80.00
Figurine, Girl Feeding Fawn, Oval Base, Marked C. Werner, 12 1/2 In. 150.00
Figurine, Ladies Dancing, Gilt Border Dresses, 11 In., Pair 195.00
Figurine, Man, Running With Pig, 5 In. 46.00
Group, 2 Horses, Running, White Glaze, 16 In. 290.00
Plaque, Seminude Woman, Erbluht, After A. Asti, Frame, 5 In. 940.00
Plaque, Tess Of Yarborough, After Gainsborough, 5 In. 440.00
Vase, Sevres Style, Multicolor Portrait, Blue, Handles, Cover, c.1880, 7 In., Pair 575.00

ICONS, special, revered pictures of Jesus, Mary, or a saint, are usually Russian or Byzantine. The small icons collected today are made of wood and tin or precious metals. Many modern copies have been made in the old style and are being sold to tourists in Russia and Europe and at shops in the United States. Rare, old icons have sold for over $50,000.

    Assembly Of Archangel Michael, Holding Sword, Throngs Of Angels, Russia, 21 x 17 In.   1725.00

Baptism Of Christ, St. John, Angels, Wood, Painted, Gilt Metal, Faux Pearls, 4 1/4 In. 1058.00
Christ The Pantocrator, Painted, On Board, Russia, 19th Century, 10 1/2 x 8 1/2 In. 235.00
Guardian Angel, Pendant, Silver Mounted, Mother-Of-Pearl, Russia, c.1917, 3 1/2 In. 588.00
Jesus, Embossed, Engraved, Russia, Late 19th Century, 10 1/2 x 8 3/4 x 1 In. 86.00
Jesus, Holding Bible, Chromolithograph, Embossed Sheet, On Wood, Case, 14 x 12 In. . . 220.00
Life Of Christ, Wood Panel, Gesso, Gilt, Painted Scenes, Geometric Border, 14 x 12 In. . . 230.00
Madonna & Child, Carved Wood, Anri, c.1960, 16 In. 259.00
Madonna & Child, White Glaze, Ceramic, Marked AVF, 24 In. 1018.00
Mary, Baby Jesus, 7 Saints, Brass Riza, Polished & Matte Finish, Russia, 7 3/8 x 6 In. . . . 415.50
Mary, Baby Jesus, Brass Riza, Repousse, Engraved, Gilt Frame, Wood Case, 9 x 8 3/8 In. 220.00
Mary, Jesus, Silver, Engraved Border, Enamel, Silver Riza, Repousse, 7 x 6 In. 330.00
Mother Of God, Theodore, Saints Around Border, Russia, 14 x 12 In. 230.00
Mother Of God, Vladimir, Russia, 19th Century, 17 x 15 In. 635.00
St. John The Forerunner, Gold Highlights, Russia, c.1800, 15 x 19 In. 978.00
St. Seraphim Of Sarov, Seraphim Holding Chotki, Delivering Blessing, Russia, 9 x 7 In. . 230.00
Triptych, Carved Bone, Crucifixion Mourners, Hinged Doors, Giltwood Frame, 11 1/4 In. 1880.00
Triptych, Christ's Crucifixion, Apostles, Giltwood Frame, Early 20th Century, 11 In. 705.00
Virgin, Oil & Gilt On Panel, Greco-Russian School, Early 20th Century, 10 1/2 x 8 1/4 In. 345.00
Virgin & Child, Wood, Gilt, Multicolored, South Germany, Signed F., c.1960, 21 In. 489.00
Virgin Of Tenderness, Riza, Beadwork, Muslin Ground, Russia, 12 In. 88.00

IMARI porcelain was made in Japan and China beginning in the 17th century. In the 18th century and later, it was copied by porcelain factories in Germany, France, England, and the United States. It was especially popular in the 19th century and is still being made. Imari is characteristically decorated with stylized bamboo, floral, and geometric designs in orange, red, green, and blue. The name comes from the Japanese port of Imari, which exported the ware made nearby in a factory at Arita. *Imari* is now a general term for any pattern of this type.

Bowl, 10 Petals, Japan, Late 19th Century, 9 1/2 In. 315.00
Bowl, Alternating Swirls Of Underglaze Blue & Red, Gilt, Japan, 1800s, 9 3/4 In. 440.00
Bowl, Bamboo, Pine, Prunus, 3 Friends, Leaf Edges, Cover, 1800s, 9 1/2 In., Pair 825.00
Bowl, Blue, White Design, Scalloped Rim, 3 1/2 x 8 1/2 In. 40.00
Bowl, Calligraphy Outer Panels, 4 Inner Panel Scenes, c.1815, 9 1/2 In. 735.00
Bowl, Central Flower Rondel, Dragons, Phoenixes, 1800s, 12 In. 440.00
Bowl, Central Medallion, Blue Flowers, Gilt, 3 x 15 1/4 In. 605.00
Bowl, Chrysanthemum Shape, Flower Brocade Design, 1800s, 4 3/4 In. 150.00
Bowl, Chrysanthemums, Japan, 1800s, 14 In. 1880.00
Bowl, Flowering Vine, Cover, Japan, 19th Century, 4 3/4 In. 50.00
Bowl, Flowers, Chinese, c.1740, 7 3/4 In. 236.00
Bowl, Flowers, Pinwheel Border, Late 1800s, 13 3/4 In. 489.00
Bowl, Foo Dog, Brocade Ball Center, 3 Friends, Brocade Border, 1800s, 8 1/2 In. 145.00
Bowl, Fukagawa, Center Carp, Japan, Late 19th Century, 7 1/2 x 14 In. 2373.00
Bowl, Low, Fukagawa, Dragon Design, Late 19th Century, 10 1/2 In. 565.00
Bowl, Nut, Flower Center, Brocade Border, Multicolored Enamels, Japan, c.1900, 6 In. . . . 35.00
Bowl, Orange, Blue, Scalloped Rim, 11 In. 675.00
Bowl, Paneled Egg Shape, Flower Garden, Shishi, 1800s, 10 In. 690.00
Bowl Set, Flower Shape, 6 Poets, Pine Landscape, Japan, 19th Century, 6 In., 12 Piece . . . 288.00
Bowl Set, Nesting, Peony Center, Flower Brocade Border, Japan, 19th Century, 3 Piece . . 1200.00
Bowl Set, Nesting, Phoenix Center, Cranes, Prunus, 1800s, 7 1/2 & 8 In. 259.00
Bowl Set, Nesting, Stylized Bird, 1800s, 7 1/4, 8 1/2 & 9 3/4 In. 315.00
Bowl Set, Shoe Design, Crane, Flowers, Late 1800s, 4 3/4 In., 4 Piece 90.00
Box, Scholars & Scroll, Egg Shape, Flower Borders, Koransha, Japan, c.1810, 3 3/4 In. . . 150.00
Cachepot, Courtesans In Garden, Japan, 1800s, 10 1/2 x 13 1/2 In. 865.00
Changer, Iron Red, Blue, Green, Central Medallion, Flower Vase, 12 In. 140.00
Charger, 3 Phoenix Bird Panels, First Half 19th Century, 21 1/2 In. 1800.00
Charger, Blue, Red, Green, Gilt Highlights, 14 3/4 In. 250.00
Charger, Blue, White, Peonies, Scalloped Rim, 18 In. 375.00
Charger, Carp, Flowers, 21 In. 3390.00
Charger, Chrysanthemum, Multicolored, 20th Century, 17 1/2 In. 405.00
Charger, Court Scene, Gilt Ground, Brocade Borders, Japan, 1800s, 22 In. 1175.00
Charger, Curtain Center, Shishi, Peonies, Prunus, Bamboo, 1800s, 24 1/4 In. 460.00
Charger, Dragon Center, Sparrow & Flower Cartouches, c.1850, 22 In. 1150.00

Bone china is a special type of porcelain that has bone ash added to the clay. This makes a stronger, whiter porcelain.

Imari, Charger, Vase Of Flowers,
Geometric Decorations,
Scalloped Border, 18 1/4 In.

Charger, Figural & Lion Fan Form Cartouche, 1800s, 18 In. 375.00
Charger, Floral Reserve Panels, Underglaze Blue & Multicolored Enamels, 1800s, 16 In. . 518.00
Charger, Flower Center, Birds, Cranes, 1800s, 15 In. 460.00
Charger, Flower Form, Bamboo & Peacock Design, Late 1800s, 11 In. 130.00
Charger, Flower Form, Flower Basket Center, Peonies, Blue Flowers, 1800s, 14 1/2 In. ... 518.00
Charger, Flower Form, Phoenix, Blue Flowers, Mandarin Duck, 1800s, 16 In. 430.00
Charger, Flower Vase, Veranda, Brocade, 6 Spurs & Flowers On Base, 1700s, 13 In. 705.00
Charger, Flowering Branch, Floral Medallions, Rust, Gold Scrolls, Exterior Horses, 19 In. 720.00
Charger, Flowers, 6 Panels, 19th Century, 16 In. 185.00
Charger, Flowers, Central Medallion, Brocade, Japan, 19th Century, 22 In., Pair 885.00
Charger, Landscape Screens, Brocade Ground, Late 1800s, 12 In., Pair 520.00
Charger, Landscape, 19th Century, 18 1/4 In. 315.00
Charger, Multicolored Enamel, Bamboo Medallion, Garden, Japan, c.1910, 12 1/4 In. 105.00
Charger, Paneled, Multicolored, Blue, Rust, Green, 19th Century, 11 3/4 In. 80.00
Charger, Phoenix, Blue Flowers, Cranes, Pavilions, 1800s, 12 1/2 In., Pair 550.00
Charger, Phoenix, Peony Garden, Octagonal Form, 1800s, 13 In. 315.00
Charger, Scalloped Edge, Flower Basket, Fan Shape Border, Japan, 1800s, 18 In., Pair ... 1410.00
Charger, Scalloped Rim, Cranes & Tortoises Border, Japan, c.1860, 12 3/4 In. 290.00
Charger, Shishi & Peony, c.1850, 18 In. 520.00
Charger, Upswept Rim, Phoenix, Trees, Flowers, Japan, Late 1800s, 12 In. 175.00
Charger, Vase Of Flowers, Geometric Decorations, Scalloped Border, 18 1/4 In. ..... *Illus* 880.00
Charger, Wisteria, Figures, Dragon Screen, Flower, 1800s, 14 1/2 In. 891.00
Cup & Saucer, Chrysanthemum Form, Floral Brocade Design, 1800s, 3 In. 80.00
Cup Set, Sake, Poets, Pine Tree Landscape, Blue Ground, 19th Century, 12 Piece 160.00
Dish, Abalone Shell Shape, Aquatic Scene, Japan, Early 1900s, 9 In. 259.00
Dish, Deep, Oval, Scalloped Rim, Japan, 12 x 9 3/8 In. 201.00
Dish, Fan Form, Flowers, 1800s, 10 In. 150.00
Dish, Rabbit, Chrysanthemum, Fuku Mark, Square, 1800s, 5 1/2 In., 6 Piece 345.00
Garden Seat, Multicolored, Pierced, Riveted Barrel Shape, 20th Century, 19 3/4 In., Pair . 2530.00
Jar, Dome Cover, Inverted Pear Shape, Melon Ribbing, Bird, Flower, 1800s, 16 In. 1035.00
Jardiniere, Ribbed Form, Flower Molded Edge, 1800s, 8 x 12 In. 940.00
Plate, Basket Of Flowers Center, Flowerhead Shape, Japan, 19th Century, 12 In. 315.00
Plate, Bird, Flower Garden, Dragons, Phoenix, 1868-1912, 12 In. 220.00
Plate, Center Blue Dragon, 4 Alternating Designs, Fukagawa, Late 19th Century, 8 1/2 In. 170.00
Plate, Flower Basket Center, 9 1/2 In. 40.00
Plate, Flower Centers, Fish, Sea Grasses, c.1850, 4 1/2 In., Pair 105.00
Plate, Flower Shape, 3 Friends, Urns, Dragons, 1800s, 8 1/2 In., Pair 140.00
Plate, Flower Shape, 6 Poets, Bamboo Grove, 19th Century, 8 1/2 In., 12 Piece 460.00
Plate, Flower Shape, Pinwheel Design, 19th Century, 8 1/2 In. 65.00
Plate, Flower Shape, Shou Center, Books, Scrolls, 1800s, 8 1/2 In., Pair 140.00
Plate, Flower Vase Center, Flower Brocade Border, Chinese, 1700s, 9 1/4 In. 345.00
Plate, Flowers, Red & Orange Enamels, Gilt, Japan, 1700s, 9 In., 10 Piece 1175.00
Plate, Fukagawa, Scalloped Edges, Ribbed, Signed, c.1820 .... 395.00
Plate, Pomegranate Center, Stylized Flowers, 1800s, 10 In., Pair 175.00
Platter, Flowers, Oval, White Ground, c.1840, 18 In. 375.00
Punch Bowl, Crane & Tortoise Inside, Peonies & Brocadework Out, 1800s, 14 1/2 In. ... 1095.00
Punch Bowl, Flower Scrolling, Brocade Patterns, Japan, 1800s, 12 1/2 In. 620.00
Punch Bowl, Peacock & Flowers Interior, Phoenix & Flower Exterior, Japan, 1800s 1765.00

Punch Bowl, Samurai Panels, Scalloped Rim, c.1890, 15 x 6 1/2 In. 1790.00
Serving Dish, Boat Shape, Fan Form Cartouches, Flowers, Fish, 19th Century, 11 In., Pair 1495.00
Soup, Dish, Poets, Pine Tree Landscape, 19th Century, 4 1/2 In., 12 Piece 200.00
Tazza, Footed, 8-Point Star Shape, Circular Foot, Brocade Design, 1800s, 8 1/2 In. 315.00
Tea Caddy, Blue & Red Flowers, Gilded Rims, Cover, Round, c.1720, 3 3/4 x 5 In. 635.00
Umbrella Stand, Multicolored, Ribbed, Cylindrical, 20th Century, 22 1/4 In. 315.00
Vase, Cylindrical, 2 Figural Reserves, Flower Ground, 1868-1912, c.1885, 12 In., Pair ... 978.00
Vase, Palace, Trumpet Form, Carp Design, 1800s, 36 1/2 In. 2300.00
Vase, Pencil Neck, Orange Flowers, Blue Leaves, 19th Century, 5 1/2 In. 170.00
Vase, Phoenixes, Dragons, Japan, 1800s, 18 In. 1058.00
Vase, Ribbed, Pavilions In Gardens, Peony Trees, Japan, 1800s, 18 1/2 In. 865.00
Vase, Women, Children, Phoenixes, Dragons, Flowers, Japan, 1800s, 15 In. 1058.00

IMPERIAL GLASS Corporation was founded in Bellaire, Ohio, in 1901.
It became a subsidiary of Lenox, Inc., in 1973 and was sold to Arthur
R. Lorch in 1981. It was sold again in 1982, and went bankrupt in
1984. In 1985, the molds and some assets were sold. The Imperial
glass preferred by the collector is freehand art glass, carnival glass,
slag glass, stretch glass, and other top-quality tablewares. Tablewares
and animals are listed here. The others may be found in the appropriate sections.

Animal, Donkey, Caramel Slag, 6 1/2 In. 50.00
Animal, Scottie Dog, Caramel Slag, Marked, 3 1/2 x 4 1/2 In. 315.00
Animal, Tiger, Caramel Slag, Paperweight, 2 3/4 x 8 In. 130.00
Art Glass, Vase, Blue Pulled Heart & Vine, Orange Iridescent, c.1920 .... 310.00
Art Glass, Vase, Cobalt Blue, Iridescent Orange, Pulled Heart & Vine, Flared, 7 1/4 In. .. 980.00
Art Glass, Vase, Cobalt Blue, Orange Iridescent Interior, Flared Rim, 6 3/4 In. 175.00
Art Glass, Vase, Jewel, Ruby, Iridescent, Stretched Rim, Ground Pontil, 8 3/4 In. 200.00
Art Glass, Vase, Navy Blue, Orange Iridescent Interior, Long Flaring Neck, 10 In. 300.00
Art Glass, Vase, Orange Iridescent, 10 In. 60.00
Art Glass, Vase, Orange Iridescent, Pulled Design, Bulbous, Flared Neck, 7 1/4 In. 315.00
Art Glass, Vase, Purple, Red, Green & Gold Iridescent, Pinched, Flared Rim, 7 In. 560.00
Art Glass, Vase, Red Iridescent, Slender, Flared, 10 In. 460.00
Art Glass, Vase, Yellow, Opal Festoons, Orange Iridescent Neck, 8 5/8 In. 315.00
Beaded Block, Celery Dish, Marigold, 8 1/2 In. 90.00
Beaded Block, Plate, Square, 7 1/4 In. 50.00
Beaded Block, Plate, Square, Green, 7 1/4 In. 50.00
Beaded Block, Plate, Square, Pink, 7 1/4 In. 50.00
Candlewick, Basket, Beaded Handle, 5 In. 350.00
Candlewick, Bonbon, Handles, Black, 10 1/8 In. 200.00
Candlewick, Bottle, Oil, Footed, 9 In. 170.00
Candlewick, Bottle, Vinegar, Apple Etch, 8 1/8 In. 150.00
Candlewick, Bowl, Black, Gold Flowers, 4-Toed, Square, Fluted Rim, 9 x 7 In. 425.00
Candlewick, Bowl, Centerpiece, Oval, 13 1/2 In. 250.00
Candlewick, Bowl, Heart Shape, Handled, 9 In. ....175.00 to 200.00
Candlewick, Bowl, Salad, With Fork & Spoon, 3 1/2 x 10 In. 110.00
Candlewick, Bowl, Vegetable, Cover, 8 In. 300.00
Candlewick, Cake Plate, Birthday, 72 Candleholders, 13 In. 325.00
Candlewick, Candlestick, 3-Light, Cupped, 5 1/2 In. 250.00
Candlewick, Candy Box, Cover, 2-Bead Finial, 6 1/2 In. 450.00
Candlewick, Candy Dish, Cover, 3 Sections, 7 In. ....150.00 to 290.00
Candlewick, Chip & Dip Plate, 14 In. 650.00
Candlewick, Claret, Ruby, 4 Oz., 4 3/4 In. 135.00
Candlewick, Cocktail, Shrimp, 4 5/8 In. 260.00
Candlewick, Cordial, 1 Oz., 4 In. 210.00
Candlewick, Dish, Baked Apple, Blue, 6 1/2 In. 139.00
Candlewick, Gravy Boat, Underplate 150.00
Candlewick, Ice Bucket, 7 3/4 In. 190.00
Candlewick, Nappy, 3-Toed, 2 3/4 x 4 1/2 In. 65.00
Candlewick, Pitcher, 80 Oz. 165.00
Candlewick, Pitcher, Lilliputian, 16 Oz., 6 1/2 In. 285.00
Candlewick, Pitcher, Manhattan, 40 Oz., 9 1/2 In. 275.00
Candlewick, Plate, Dinner, 10 In. 50.00

Candlewick, Platter, Oval, 17 In. 185.00
Candlewick, Platter, Steak, Oval, 12 3/4 In. 65.00
Candlewick, Relish & Dressing Set 150.00
Candlewick, Relish, 4 Sections 15.00
Candlewick, Relish, 5 Sections, 11 In. 80.00
Candlewick, Salad Set, Mallard Etch, 4 Piece 250.00
Candlewick, Sherbet, 5 Oz. 15.00
Candlewick, Sugar & Creamer, Beaded, Handles, Footed 70.00
Candlewick, Tray, Fruit, 7 1/2 In. 250.00
Candlewick, Tray, Handle, Black, 8 1/2 In. 290.00
Candlewick, Tray, Lemon, Handle, 5 1/2 In. 75.00
Candlewick, Tumbler, 10 Oz. 18.00
Candlewick, Tumbler, 12 Oz. 500.00
Candlewick, Vase, 7 In. 375.00
Candlewick, Wine, 4 Oz., 3 In. 35.00
Cape Cod, Bowl, Centerpiece, Oval, 13 In. 150.00
Cape Cod, Bowl, Salad, 11 In. 45.00
Cape Cod, Cake Plate, 4-Footed, 10 In. 165.00
Cape Cod, Cake Stand, 10 1/2 In. 50.00
Cape Cod, Candlestick, 5 1/4 In., Pair 50.00
Cape Cod, Candy Jar, Cover, 10 x 3 1/2 In. 130.00
Cape Cod, Cigarette Box, Cover, 5 1/2 In. 50.00
Cape Cod, Cigarette Lighter, Black, 4 5/8 In. 70.00
Cape Cod, Cocktail, 3 1/2 Oz. 8.00
Cape Cod, Compote, Cover, 10 1/4 x 6 1/4 In. 90.00
Cape Cod, Cup, Coffee 15.00
Cape Cod, Finger Bowl, 4 1/4 In. 25.00
Cape Cod, Goblet, 9 Oz. 12.00
Cape Cod, Goblet, 10 Oz. 10.00
Cape Cod, Parfait, 6 Oz. 12.00
Cape Cod, Pitcher, Ice Lip, 2 Qt. 150.00
Cape Cod, Plate, Bread & Butter, 6 1/2 In. 10.00
Cape Cod, Relish, 5 Sections, 11 1/2 In. 50.00
Cape Cod, Sherbet, 6 Oz., 4 In. 30.00
Cape Cod, Sherbet, 6 Oz., 5 In. 30.00
Cape Cod, Tumbler, Juice, 5 1/2 In. 30.00
Cape Cod, Vase, 11 In. 50.00
Cape Cod, Wine, 3 Oz. 8.00
Caramel Slag, Box, Dog, Cover, 6 1/2 In. 100.00
Caramel Slag, Compote, 7 In. 190.00
Caramel Slag, Compote, Oval, 6 1/4 In. 85.00
Caramel Slag, Cruet, Stopper, 6 7/8 In. 70.00
Caramel Slag, Dish, Rooster, Cover, 8 x 7 3/8 In. 175.00
Caramel Slag, Pitcher, Handled, 36 Oz., 8 In. 85.00
Caramel Slag, Pitcher, Mini, 3 1/8 In. 45.00
Caramel Slag, Salt & Pepper, 3 1/2 In. 50.00
Caramel Slag, Sugar & Creamer 65.00
Caramel Slag, Tumbler, 5 1/4 In. 70.00
Cathay, Bowl, Centerpiece, Cranberry, 3 3/4 x 10 1/2 In. 75.00
Corinthian, Candlestick, 4 1/2 In. 45.00
Loganberry, Vase, Milk Glass, 6 In. 45.00
Pansy, Nappy, Handled, Iridescent Amber, Handles 25.00
Ruby Slag, Vase, Dancing Ladies, Dog Watching, 8 3/8 In. 125.00
Stretch-Glass, Vase, Iridescent Blue, 6 1/2 In. 70.00
Waterlily, Bowl, Footed, Marigold, 9 In. 45.00
Windmill, Bowl, Caramel Slag, 9 In. 50.00
Windmill, Pitcher, Caramel Slag, 6 1/2 In. 80.00

INDIAN art from North America has attracted the collector for many years. Each tribe has its own distinctive designs and techniques. Baskets, jewelry, pottery, and leatherwork are of greatest collector interest. Eskimo art is listed in another category in this book.

Adze, Plains, Bone, Leather Wrapped, 11 In. 2150.00

Indian, Basket, Cherokee, Double
Woven, River Cane, Geometric
Lid, 10 1/2 x 7 1/4 In.

Indian, Basket, Cherokee, Shopping,
Maple Split, Curled Design,
Handles, 13 In.

Indian, Basket, Choctaw,
Laundry, River Cane, Red, Blue
Aniline Dye, Lid, 22 x 19 In.

Amulet, Plains, Lizard, Beaded, Hide, Green Design, 7 In. 1230.00
Awl & Case, Kiowa, Blue Seed Beads, German Silver Cones, c.1890, 7 1/4 x 15 In. 3680.00
Awl & Case, Sioux, Cylindrical Beading, Cone & Feather Drop, c.1890, 15 In. 316.00
Awl & Knife Case, Sioux, Sinew Sewn, Seed Beads, Silver Bead Accents, c.1910, 4 In. . . 145.00
Awl Case, Plains, Rawhide Wrapped, Beaded, Buckskin Flap, c.1900, 15 In. 430.00
Ax, Plains, Pipe, Tomahawk, Forged Brass, Hardwood Stem, c.1890, 21 x 6 1/2 In. 2590.00
Bag, Apache, Drawstring, Fringe, 1930s, 11 In. 165.00
Bag, Cheyenne, Tobacco, Beaded Strips, Flagged Bards, Leather Fringe, c.1890, 29 In. . . . 1265.00
Bag, Nez Perce, Corn Husk Back, Vegetable Dye, c.1900, 13 1/2 x 20 In. 2875.00
Bag, Nez Perce, Twined Corn Husk, Geometric Designs, c.1900, 13 1/2 x 16 In. 1095.00
Bag, Plains, Hide, 27 Beadwork Rows, Rawhide Pulls & Handle, 12 1/2 x 8 In. 3585.00
Bag, Plateau, Buckskin, Fully Beaded Front, Flowers, Leaves, Blue, c.1910, 15 x 13 In. . . 978.00
Bag, Plateau, Buckskin, Tanned, Beaded, Flowers, Fringe, c.1920, 9 1/2 x 11 In. 90.00
Bag, Plateau, Corn Husk, Stacked Rows Of Stepped Diamonds, Rectangular, 11 In. 265.00
Bag, Plateau, Fully Beaded, Flowers, c.1930, 12 x 9 1/2 In. 360.00
Bag, Sioux, Quill, Beaded, Ribbon Trim, Beaded Border, Fringe, c.1890, 9 1/4 In. 980.00
Bag, Sioux, Tobacco, Beaded, Bars, Feathers, Fringe, c.1890, 27 In. 2875.00
Bag, Sioux, Tobacco, Hide, Beaded, Diamond, Square, 3 Crosses, 34 In. 4780.00
Bag, Woodland, Flowers, Drawstring, Fringe, c.1890, 7 In. 575.00
Bag, Yakima, Eagle, Old Glory, Fully Beaded, Flat, c.1930, 12 x 14 In. 865.00
Bandolier, Chippewa, Beaded Flowers, Velvet, Muslin Lined, c.1910, 42 x 13 In. 2588.00
Bandolier, Chippewa, Beaded, Velvet, Trade Bead, Wool Tassels, c.1900, 12 x 46 In. 1380.00
Bandolier, Chippewa, Hand Beaded, Flowers, Leaves, c.1880, 46 x 19 x 13 3/4 In. 1725.00
Bandolier, Chippewa, Loom Beaded, Flowers, Leaves, c.1880, 37 x 19 x 11 1/4 In. 2415.00
Bandolier, Great Lakes, Red Wool Trade Cloth, Beaded, Geometric, 41 x 11 In. 2300.00
Bandolier, Winnebago, Flowers, Leaves, Oak Shadowbox Frame, 1890s, 16 x 41 In. 4290.00
Basket, Aleut, Twined, Braided Rim, Multicolored Yarn Design On Top, 8 x 11 In. 353.00
Basket, Algonquin, Orange, Brown Wicker, Ribbon Sides, Lid, c.1940, 6 1/2 x 9 In. 138.00
Basket, Apache, Bowl, Coil, 3-Petal Radiating Design, Triangles, c.1900, 13 1/2 In. 705.00
Basket, Apache, Bowl, Multicolored, People, Dogs, Crosses, c.1900, 4 x 13 1/2 In. 3163.00
Basket, Apache, Bowl, Radiating Steps, Geometrics, c.1900, 2 x 8 In. 431.00
Basket, Apache, Multicolored, Star, Checkered Band, c.1910, 4 x 13 1/2 In. 2588.00
Basket, Apache, Tray, Squash Blossom Center, Willow, Devil's Claw, 1 1/2 x 9 1/2 In. . . . 375.00
Basket, Chehalis, Banded Designs, Gold Butterfly Accents, c.1940, 4 x 7 1/2 In. 375.00
Basket, Cherokee, 2 Handles, Maple Split, Curled Maple Decoration, 13 In. 185.00
Basket, Cherokee, Banded Geometric Designs, Jar Shape, Square Bottom, 15 In. 470.00
Basket, Cherokee, Double Woven, Geometrics Lid, 10 1/2 x 7 x 7 In. 1430.00
Basket, Cherokee, Double Woven, River Cane, Butternut Dye Geometrics, 8 x 8 x 7 In. . . 140.00
Basket, Cherokee, Double Woven, River Cane, Geometric Lid, 10 1/2 x 7 1/4 In. . . . *Illus* 1300.00
Basket, Cherokee, Double Woven, River Cane, Geometrics Lid, 13 3/4 x 8 x 8 In. 2090.00
Basket, Cherokee, Gathering, River Cane, Wrapped Rim, Oak Handles, 10 x 21 x 16 In. . 1210.00
Basket, Cherokee, Honeysuckle, Wrapped Oak Split Rim, 11 1/2 In. 165.00
Basket, Cherokee, Multicolored, Geometrics, Wood Handle, c.1920, 7 x 9 1/2 x 11 In. . . . 520.00
Basket, Cherokee, River Cane, Double Woven, Butternut & Bloodroot Dye, Lid, 9 1/2 In. 935.00

Basket, Cherokee, River Cane, Geometric Bands, Walnut Dye, 13 1/2 x 10 1/2 x 7 In. 250.00
Basket, Cherokee, River Cane, Square-To-Round Design, Oak Rim, 13 x 16 x 16 In. 1100.00
Basket, Cherokee, River Cane, Square-To-Round, Bloodroot & Walnut Dyes, 14 1/2 In. .. 605.00
Basket, Cherokee, River Cane, Walnut & Yellowroot Dyes, Oak Handle, 15 x 14 x 12 In. . 715.00
Basket, Cherokee, Shopping, Maple Split, Curled Design, Handles, 13 In. .... *Illus* 170.00
Basket, Chitimacha, Bowl, Twilled Design, Red & Black, Natural Ground, 3 x 5 In. 295.00
Basket, Chitimacha, River Cane, Double Woven, Diagonal Bands, Brown, Red, 2 x 6 In. . 220.00
Basket, Choctaw, Laundry, River Cane, Red, Blue Aniline Dye, Lid, 22 x 19 In. ..... *Illus* 1100.00
Basket, Choctaw, River Cane, Aniline Dye, Wrapped Handle, 11 1/2 x 10 x 10 In. 99.00
Basket, Choctaw, River Cane, Wrapped Handle, c.1930, Mississippi, 12 x 9 1/2 In. 88.00
Basket, Choctaw, River Cane, Wrapped Handle, Mellow Patina, 7 1/4 x 7 In. 110.00
Basket, Choctaw, Trinket, 2 Neck, Plaited, Woven Handle, c.1920, 9 x 12 x 4 In. 315.00
Basket, Coiled, California, Flat Bottom, Zigzags, Flared Sides, 11 x 17 In. 1765.00
Basket, Hopi, Multicolored, Coil, Squash Blossom Design, c.1950, 2 1/4 x 13 In. 230.00
Basket, Hupa, Bowl, Twined, Diagonal Chevrons & Triangles, Sawtooth Edge, 12 x 8 In. . 1410.00
Basket, Hupa, Hat, Twined, Brown Parallelograms, 7 In. 500.00
Basket, Hupa, Open Weave, Banded Geometric Designs, c.1940, 3 x 4 In. 230.00
Basket, Karok, Burden, Stacked Vertical Steps, 13 x 13 1/2 In. 1530.00
Basket, Karok, Woven, Geometric Designs, c.1930, 3 1/2 x 5 In. 288.00
Basket, Klamath, Bowl, 3 Bands, Track-Like Pattern, Cone Shaped Bottom, 4 1/2 x 16 In. 235.00
Basket, Klamath, Burden, Twined, Zigzag Bands, Flared, Flat Bottom, 13 In. 3645.00
Basket, Klamath, Cooking, Twined, Staggered Stepped Triangles, 9 1/2 In. 235.00
Basket, Klamath, Flat Bottom, Checkered, Rhomboid, Fine Weave, c.1930, 4 x 7 In. 260.00
Basket, Klamath, Round Bowl, Multicolored Stepped Rectangles, c.1930, 4 1/2 x 8 In. ... 546.00
Basket, Klamath, Straight Sides, Geometrics, Yellow Accents, c.1920, 5 x 7 In. 230.00
Basket, Lillooet, Fine Weave, Pedestal, Diamond, Multicolored, Flat Lid, 1930, 5 x 8 In. . 520.00
Basket, Maidu, Bowl, Coil, Spiral Stepped Design, Flared Sides, Flat Bottom, 11 x 21 In. 940.00
Basket, Makah, Bowl, Red & Orange Rim & Bottom Bands, c.1940, 3 1/2 x 7 In. 144.00
Basket, Makah, Trinket, Floating Arrow, Z Designs, Starburst Lid, c.1930, 2 x 4 In. 60.00
Basket, Mission, Bowl, Coil, Interlocking Diamonds, Globe Shape, Flat Bottom, 8 In. ... 355.00
Basket, Mission, Bowl, Coil, Polychrome, Geometric Designs, Oval, 14 x 12 In. 176.00
Basket, Mohegan, Splint, Square Bottom, Round Top, Pointed Lid, Painted, 17 In. 470.00
Basket, Navajo, Wedding, Multicolored, Braided Rim, c.1900, 3 3/4 x 14 1/2 In. 230.00
Basket, Northwest, Imbricated, Stepped Diamonds, 2 Buckskin Straps, 13 In. 499.00
Basket, Panamint, Jar, Coiled, Frets, Crosses, c.1925, 5 1/8 x 6 1/2 In. 1090.00
Basket, Papago, Concentric Frets, Triangles, 4 1/2 x 10 In. 86.00
Basket, Papago, Flared, Coiled, Geometric Decoration, Light Field, 8 1/2 In. 415.00
Basket, Papago, Jar, Coiled, Split Stitch, Whirling Log, c.1925, 7 1/4 x 9 1/2 In. 460.00
Basket, Papago, Lid, Large, c.1930 .... 4500.00
Basket, Papago, Tohono O'odham, Stepped Design, Devil's Claw, Yucca Root, 6 x 4 In. ... 110.00
Basket, Papago, Tohono O'odham, Whirling Log, Devil's Claw, 8 1/4 x 5 In. 220.00
Basket, Pima, Bowl, Coiled, Double Stepped Terrace, c.1970, 1 3/4 x 2 In. 375.00
Basket, Pima, Bowl, Coiled, Repeated Frets, c.1925, 3 1/2 x 13 1/8 In. 775.00
Basket, Pima, Bowl, Coiled, Stylized Hourglass, Crosses, c.1925, 5 3/4 x 17 In. 1150.00
Basket, Pima, Coiled, Stepped Terrace, Diamonds, c.1925, 7 1/4 x 15 1/2 In. 605.00
Basket, Pima, Flat Bowl, Black Geometrics, c.1940, 3 x 13 In. 546.00
Basket, Pima, Flat, Dark Center, Squash Blossom Variation, c.1920, 3 x 11 In. 748.00
Basket, Pima, Plaque, Coil, Man-In-Maze Design, 14 In. 1765.00
Basket, Pima, Radiating Stepped Terrace, c.1900, 5 x 20 In. 690.00
Basket, Pima, Stepped Terrace Diamond Willow, Devil's Claw, 4 x 5 3/4 In. 175.00
Basket, Pima, Stitched Coil, Running S, c.1940, 2 1/2 x 3 3/4 In. 145.00
Basket, Pima, Tray, Concentric Frets, Willow, Devil's Claw, 2 1/2 x 14 In. 4140.00
Basket, Pit River, Burden, Conical, Top Knot Design, Woven, c.1910, 19 x 20 In. 2185.00
Basket, Pomo, Bowl, Coiled, Diagonal Lightning Bands, Flattened Shape, 7 In. 265.00
Basket, Pomo, Coil, Wide Bands, Seed Bead Trim, Flat Globe Shape, 5 1/2 In. 355.00
Basket, Salish, Trunk, Lid, 3 Color, Butterfly, Flower, c.1930, 10 x 15 x 9 In. 431.00
Basket, Salish, Trunk, Trees, Stepped Terrace, Cylinder, Lid, c.1930, 18 x 21 In. 1150.00
Basket, San Carlos Apache, Bowl, Coiled, Saguaro, Cross Design, c.1925, 3 x 15 In. 3680.00
Basket, San Carlos Apache, Tray, Coiled, Fret, Center Starburst, c.1940, 1 3/4 x 8 3/4 In. . 720.00
Basket, Shasta, Globe Shape, Geometric Top Knot Design, c.1910, 8 x 13 In. 978.00
Basket, Tlingit, Bold Crosses, Rattle-Top Cover, Pinwheel Design On Knob, 8 1/2 In. 1765.00
Basket, Tlingit, Twined, 3 Bands Of Fret & Zigzags, Cylindrical, Lid, c.1900, 10 In. 1175.00
Basket, Tubatulabal, Bowl, Coil, 3 Bands Of Hourglass Designs, Flared, 13 3/4 In. 1998.00

Basket, Winnebago, Woven Split Ash, Handle, Vegetal Dye, c.1920, 8 x 12 In. 80.00
Basket, Winnebago, Woven Split Ash, Lid, Vegetal Dye, c.1920, 6 x 12 1/2 In. 115.00
Basket, Yokuts, Bowl, Geometric, Polychrome, Coiled, 10 1/2 In. 3000.00
Basket, Yurok, Triangle Designs, c.1900, 5 x 9 In. 1610.00
Belt, Fabric, Beaded, Faces, Birds, Reptiles, Shell Borders, Multicolored, 51 In. 110.00
Belt, Navajo, Concha, Silver, Turquoise, 44 In. 1050.00
Belt, Nez Perce, Beaded, Flowers, Butterflies, 1920s, 4 x 32 In. 120.00
Belt, Yakima, Beaded, Geometric, White Field, Orange, Blue, Green, 1920, 4 x 38 1/2 In. . 220.00
Belt Bag, Nez Perce, Cornhusk, Beaded Flower Flap, c.1910, 5 x 6 In. 489.00
Blanket, Chimayo, Blue Ground, Stepped Terrace, Gray, Red, Hand Woven, 57 x 64 In. ... 110.00
Blanket, Hudson Bay, 4 Point, Trade, Tag, c.1930, 86 x 70 In. 150.00
Blanket, Kiowa, Ceremonial, Ribbonwork, c.1920, 70 x 56 1/2 In. 230.00
Blanket, Navajo, Beige Ground, White, Dark Brown, 65 x 37 In. 575.00
Blanket, Navajo, Double Saddle, Gray Center, Serrated Red Border, 24 x 50 In. 2070.00
Blanket, Navajo, Eye Dazzler, Geometric, Black, Gray, Off-White, Field, 84 x 48 In. 230.00
Blanket, Navajo, Eye Dazzler, Red, Black, Gray, Off-White Field, 38 x 60 In. 315.00
Blanket, Navajo, Red Field, Off-White & Black, Double Diamond Pattern, 36 x 64 In. ... 460.00
Blanket, Navajo, Saddle, Stripes, Yellow, Red, Brown, Geometric End, 28 x 59 In. 90.00
Blanket, Navajo, Wool, Eye Dazzler, c.1910, 52 x 34 In. 1095.00
Blanket, Osage, Hand Designs, Navy Trade Cloth, Silk, c.1900, 51 x 54 In. 1380.00
Blanket, Plains, Beaded Strip, Silk Border, Olivella Shell Drops, 72 x 59 In. 2185.00
Blanket, Plains, Trade, 3 Groups Of Flowers At Each Edge, c.1925, 57 x 74 In. 1090.00
Blanket, Plains, Trade, 3 Rows Of Silk Ribbon, Hand Stitched, 60 x 67 In. 460.00
Blanket, Plains, Trade, 6 Bands, Flowers, Crystal Beads, c.1950, 66 x 57 In. 575.00
Blanket Strip, Sioux, Patriotic Design, Red & White Stripes, 4 Medallions, 56 1/2 In. ... 750.00
Bow, Mojave, Painted, Hand Carved, Black, Red Geometric, c.1900, 57 x 1 3/4 In. 431.00
Bow, Osage, Rosewood, Rawhide, Tribal, Mid 19th Century, 51 In. 56.00
Bow Case & Quiver, Cheyenne, Beaded Panel, Red Tradecloth Rim, c.1900, 38 x 6 In. .. 1150.00
Bowl, Blackware, San Ildefonso, Maria Martinez, 1943-1956 .... 3450.00
Bowl, Haida, Wood, Carved, Dogfish Shaped Ends, Abalone Inlay, 15 1/2 In. 235.00
Bowl, Maricopa, Eye In The Wave Design, Red, E.M., c.1925, 3 x 5 1/4 In. 173.00
Bowl, Pima, Basket, Coiled, Flared Sides, Sawtooth Bands, Early 1900s, 5 1/4 x 12 In. ... 489.00
Bowl, San Ildefonso, Pottery, Matte Geometrics, Black Ground, Globe Shape, 9 In. 588.00
Bowl, Santa Clara, Blackware, Polished Surface, Applied Black Matte Design, 3 x 5 In. .. 195.00
Bowl, Woodlands, Burl, Oval, Flat Bottom, 19th Century, 13 3/4 In. 999.00
Bowl, Zuni, Earthenware, Slip Decoration, Male & Female Figures, 4 x 9 x 9 1/4 In. 66.00
Bowl, Zuni, Pottery, Polychrome, Turreted Rim, Painted Frog, Tadpoles, Serpent, 10 In. .. 2689.00
Box, Cover, Micmac, Bark, Oval, Quill Wrapped Slats, Polychrome Geometrics, 12 In. ... 881.00
Bracelet, Navajo, 3 Turquoise Stones, Silver, Leaf Designs, c.1950, 8 1/4 x 1 1/4 In. 207.00
Bracelet, Navajo, 5 Spider Web Turquoise Cabochons, Stampwork, c.1974, 3 In. 150.00
Bracelet, Navajo, Silver, Watch, 40 Natural Morenci Turquoises Stones, c.1950, 2 1/2 In. . 115.00
Bracelet, Navajo, Sterling Silver, 7 Green Turquoise Stones, c.1960, 8 1/4 x 1/2 In. 140.00
Bracelet, Navajo, Sterling Silver, Bisbee Turquoise Stone, c.1970, 7 x 3 3/4 In. 196.00
Bracelet, Zuni, 3 Clusters, Turquoise, c.1974, 2 3/4 In. 196.00
Breastplate, Hair Pipe, Leather Bands, Blue, White Beads, 20 x 11 In. 55.00
Breech Cloth, Blackfoot, Velvet, Sequins, Basket Beads, c.1920, 51 x 15 1/2 In. 105.00
Bridle, Plains, Beaded, Quilled, Pinwheel Design, Red, White, 47 In. 2465.00
Bridle, Plains, Geometric Beading, Lazy Stitch, Cones, Tassels, c.1900, 19 x 8 In. 1840.00
Calling Horn, Chippewa, Birch Bark, Moose, Flying Geese, Incised, c.1920 .... 460.00
Candlestick, Zuni, Pottery, Birds, Geometric Designs, Jaguar Handles, 6 In., Pair 1295.00
Candlestick, Zuni, Pottery, Painted, Knifewing Man, Rectangular, Handle, 7 In., Pair 600.00
Canoe, Birch Bark, Abenaki, Late 1800s, 15 Ft. 8 In. 6200.00
Canoe, Chippewa, Toy, Birch Bark, Incised Interior, Carved Spreaders, c.1920, 48 In. 690.00
Canoe, Northwest Coast, Carved, Painted, Wolf Heads, White, Black, Red, 24 In. 600.00
Canteen, Cochiti, Pottery, Geometric Designs, Globe Shape, Spout, Lug Handles, 6 In. .. 825.00
Canteen, Hopi, 2 Handles, Polychrome, Painted Designs, c.1890, 5 x 7 In. 3450.00
Canteen, Zuni, Pottery, Red & Black Spiral, Globe Shape, 2 Knobs, 7 In. 650.00
Cap, Sioux, Boy's, Beaded Geometric Designs, c.1900, 2 1/2 x 6 1/2 x 5 1/2 In. 1725.00
Choker, Plains, Glass Tube Beads, Leather Spacers, c.1930, 15 In. 85.00
Cigar Box, Maliseet, Birch Bark, Moose Hair Embroidery, Figures, Animals, Leaves, 6 In. 1880.00
Club, Cheyenne, Stone, Beadwork, Hide Trimmed Shaft, Horsehair Tassel, 31 In. 956.00
Club, Cheyenne, Stone, Beadwork, Hide, Horsehair Tassel, Feather Trim, 26 In. 775.00
Club, Crow, Spiral Carved Stone Head, Rawhide Wrapped, Beaded Handle, c.1890, 24 In. . 375.00

Club, Plains, Slapper Type, Rawhide Wrapped, Horsehair Drop, c.1860s, 17 In. 276.00
Coat, Cheyenne, Infant's, Frock, Buckskin, Fringed Cape Collar, Seed Bead Trim, 21 In. . .   4700.00
Coat, Chippewa, Man's, Beaded, Fringe, 42 x 29 In. 360.50
Coat, Plains, Hide, Beaded Geometric Strips, Standup Collar, Fringe, 19th Century, 46 In.   4995.00
Coat, Sioux, Boy's, Horse, Deer, Buffalo, Bird, Pipe Beaded, Fringe, c.1890, 41 In. 13225.00
Cradle, Buffalo Hide, Canvas, Beaded, Stepped Triangles, Diamonds, 26 1/2 In. 8815.00
Cradle, Hupa, Basketry, Polychrome, Geometrics, Conical Sun Shade, c.1920, 10 x 21 In.   980.00
Cradle, Lakota Sioux, Toy, Quilled, Beaded, Hawkbell Trim, c.1940, 3 1/2 x 18 x 4 1/2 In.   920.00
Cradle, Northeast, Splint, Ash, Porcupine Stitch, Braided Trim, Wooden Rocker, 18 In. . . .   323.00
Cradle, Shoshone, Wood, Muslin Cover, Beaded Trim, Doll Inside, 17 1/2 In. 940.00
Cradle, Umatilla, Denim Body, Buckskin Trim, Rawhide, Shade, c.1950, 37 x 12 x 10 In. .   104.00
Cradle, Ute, Toy, Hide Doll, Geometric Beadwork, c.1880, 2 1/2 x 12 x 5 1/2 In. 1265.00
Cradle Hood Cover, Sioux, Quilled Hide, Beadwork Trim, Wool, 26 1/2 x 12 In. 1912.00
Cradleboard, Apache, Bentwood Frame, Handle Top, Applied Fabric, 37 x 13 1/2 x 13 In.   110.00
Cradleboard, Mohawk, Iroquois, Chip Carved Flowers, Polychrome, c.1845 . . . .   12600.00
Cradleboard, Navajo, Cedar, Entwood Handle, Applied Leather Straps, 30 In. 80.00
Cuffs, Sioux, Buffalo Hide, Beadwork American Flags, Geometrics, c.1890, 7 x 5 In. 230.00
Cushion, Iroquois, Beaded Trim, Bird, Lavender Velvet, 8 x 8 In.   220.00
Dance Apron, Plains, Glass Beaded Flowers & Leaves, c.1915, 20 x 17 1/2 In., Pair 316.00
Dance Ball, Arapaho, Fully Beaded, Grass, c.1920, 3 In. 489.00
Dance Wand, Plains, Buffalo Horn, Beaded, Fringe, c.1890, 18 x 12 1/2 x 2 1/4 In. 545.00
Dance Wand, Plains, Rawhide Wrapped Handle, 13 1/2 x 7 1/2 In. 200.00
Doll, Mesquaki, Hide, Cloth, Beaded, Bear Claw Necklace, Yarn Sash & Turban, 6 In. . . .   1175.00
Doll, Northeast, Blue Cloth Shirt & Leggings, Hide Moccasins, Beaded, Yarn Sash, 11 In.   529.00
Doll, Plains, Beaded Vest & Moccasins, Cloth Shirt, Fringed Leggings, Horsehair, 11 In. .   2235.00
Doll, Plains, Male, Hide, Stuffed, Beaded Eyes, Mouth, Silver Cross Pendant, 15 In. 6575.00
Doll, Plains, Woman, Hide, Stuffed, Beaded Eyes & Mouth, Fringed Dress, 14 In. 4185.00
Doll, Sioux, Buckskin Body, Brown Braids, Beaded Yoke, Belt, Moccasins, 1900, 8 In. . .   420.00
Doll, Sioux, Cloth, Painted Face, Beaded Buckskin Moccasins, 1950, 15 x 5 1/2 In. 45.00
Doll, Skookum, Beaded Leather Moccasins, Necklace, Papoose, 11 1/2 In. 140.00
Doll, Skookum, Brave, Composition, Woven Blanket, Headdress, 19 In. 325.00
Doll, Skookum, Chief, Celluloid Face, 8 In. 35.00
Doll, Skookum, Chief, Store Display, Headdress, Blanket, 36 In. 2070.00
Doll, Skookum, Man, Blanket, Side Glancing Eyes, Human Hair, Beads, c.1920, 21 In. . . .   550.00
Doll, Skookum, Traditional Outfit, Beaded Necklace, Composition Face, 13 1/2 In. 125.00
Doll, Skookum, Traditional Outfit, Composition Face, 15 In. 140.00
Doll, Skookum, Traditional Outfit, Composition Face, Label Under Foot, 14 In. 135.00
Doll, Skookum, Woman, With Baby, Braided Hair, Flannel Blanket, Bead Earrings, 19 In.   590.00
Doll, Ute, Woman, Beaded Cloth, Stuffed Calico, Beaded Leggings, c.1900, 11 In. 259.00
Doll, Ute, Woman, Beaded Hide, Wool Leggings, Beaded Moccasins, c.1900, 21 In. 545.00
Drum, Great Lakes, Rawhide Face, Wooden Hoops & Pegs, 19th Century, 13 1/2 In. 150.00
Drum, Pueblo, Cottonwood, Rawhide Beads, Pigment Painted, c.1900, 7 1/2 x 6 x 7 In. . .   489.00
Drum, Southwest, Wood, Hide, Painted, Elongated Triangles, Rawhide Lacing, 21 1/2 In. .   1000.00
Drum Stick, Great Lakes, Wood, Curved, Faceted, Horse Head Beater, Hide Wrap, 11 In. .   440.00
Effigy, Plains, Umbilical Turtle, Beaded, c.1890, 5 3/4 In. 635.00
Fetish, Kiowa, Hide, Beaded, Triangular, Wrapped Leather Dowel, Hide Fringe, 25 1/2 In.   4481.00
Figure, Zuni, Owl, Pottery, 3 Small Owl Head Projections, Painted, Red & Black, 11 In. . .   2705.00
Gloves, Plateau, Gauntlets, Brave On Horse, Fringed Cuffs, c.1900, 15 1/4 In. 1840.00
Gloves, Plateau, Gauntlets, Leaves, Flowers, Buckskin, Fringed Cuffs, c.1920, 13 In. 145.00
Gloves, Umatilla, Child's, Beaded Flowers, Tanned Buckskin, Parade, c.1950, 9 x 3 In. . . .   58.00
Hair Ornament, Sioux, Brass Pendant, 5 Quill Strands, Leather Mount, 16 1/2 In. 305.00
Hat, Nez Perce, Cornhusk Fez, Hemp Base, Wool Yarn, Trade Bead, Shell, c.1900 . . . . . .   635.00
Horse Blanket, Southern Plains, Beaded Stroud, Cotton, c.1900, 62 x 21 1/2 In. 1265.00
Jacket, Blackfoot, Beaded, Buckskin, 1941 . . . .   650.00
Jacket, Plains, Beaded Flowers On Pockets, Fringe, c.1925, 53 In. 259.00
Jar, Acoma, Multicolored, Concave Base, Geometric, Abstract Birds, 5 3/4 x 7 1/2 In. . . .   375.00
Jar, Acoma, Multicolored, Cross, Whirling Logs, c.1925, 4 x 4 1/2 In. 259.00
Jar, Acoma, Multicolored, Swirl, Red Band Interior, c.1925, 6 1/2 x 8 1/4 In. 635.00
Jar, Hopi, Parrot, Birds, Pendant Form Rim, Hopi VI, c.1925, 5 1/2 x 3 3/4 In. 230.00
Jar, Mojave, Figures, 2-Sided Human Head Handle, Incised Features, 4 Spouts, 6 x 5 In. .   470.00
Jar, Santa Clara, Blackware, Flower Band, Lightning Bolt, Birdell, 4 1/2 In. 400.00
Jar, Santa Clara, Carved Blackware, Feather Design, Reycita Naranjo, c.1925, 5 x 8 In. . .   315.00
Jar, Yokuts, Coiled, Bottleneck, Multicolored Pictorial, 7 1/2 In.   7200.00

Jar, Zia, Pottery, Red & Black Geometrics, High Shoulder, Flared Neck, 8 1/2 In. 245.00
Jar, Zuni, Multicolored, Geometric Designs, c.1923, 9 x 12 1/2 In. 3680.00
Kachina, Hopi, Bird, 1 Piece, c.1940, 13 x 4 1/2 x 4 In. 345.00
Kachina, Hopi, Cottonwood, Flared Kilt, Sash, 16 1/12 In. 646.00
Kachina, Hopi, Cottonwood, Wearing Manta & Skirt, Turquoise Inlaid Earrings, 19 In. . . . 382.00
Kachina, Hopi, Pop Eyes, Feather Ears, Marked Holi-Wah, 8 In. 192.50
Kachina, Wood Carved, Painted Wood, c.1930, 9 1/2 x 2 x 2 In. 52.00
Knife, Plains, Beaver Tail, Metal, Wooden Handle, 6 Copper Rivets, 14 1/2 In. 8225.00
Knife & Sheath, Sioux, Bone Handle, Beaded, Sinew Sewn 770.00
Knife & Sheath, Sioux, Red, Orange, Blue Beads, Lazy Stitch, c.1910, 8 In. 144.00
Knife Sheath, Cheyenne, Beaded, 2 Twisted Fringe Drops, Tin Cone Danglers, 7 In. 999.00
Knife Sheath, Cheyenne, Beaded, Sinew Sewn, Late 1800s, 8 1/2 x 2 3/4 In. 990.00
Knife Sheath, Cheyenne, Buffalo Hide, Sinew Sewn, c.1880, 3 x 10 In. 1150.00
Knife Sheath, Lakota Sioux, Cowhide, Beaded, Quill, Late 1800s, 6 1/2 In. 900.00
Knife Sheath, Lakota, Hide, Beaded, Triangles, Chevrons, Stripes, Fringe, 10 In. 1765.00
Knife Sheath, Ojibwa, Hide, Beaded Seam, Top, Danglers, c.1900, 9 1/2 In. 600.00
Knife Sheath, Plains, Beaded, Lazy Stitch, c.1900, 12 In. 259.00
Knife Sheath, Plateau, Beaded, Flowers, 8 1/2 In. 440.00
Knife Sheath, Sioux, Hide, Beadwork, Fringe, Tin Cones, 10 In. 1555.00
Knife Sheath, Sioux, Parfleche, Lazy Stitch, Bar Design, Cones, Feathers, c.1890, 9 In. . . . 863.00
Ladle, Northwest Coast, Ceremonial, Wood, Shaman Handle, c.1960s, 4 1/2 x 13 In. 259.00
Ladle, Woodlands, Wood, Oval Scoop, Carved Effigy, Stylized Otter, 6 3/4 In. 3410.00
Ladle, Woodlands, Wood, Round Scoop, Carved Handle, Bird's Head Under Wing, 11 In. . . 650.00
Leggings, Cheyenne, Child's, Beaded, Green Bar Elements, Crosses, c.1890, 11 1/2 In. 805.00
Leggings, Kiowa, Hide, Beadwork Fringe, 28 In., Pair 7170.00
Leggings, Nez Perce, Beaded, Cloth, 13 x 11 1/2 In. 860.50
Leggings, Plains, Buffalo Hide Strips, Beaded Stepped Triangles, Fringed Flaps, 31 In. . . . 3290.00
Leggings, Plains, Hide, Beaded, Cloth, Multicolored Geometric Designs, 11 x 4 In. 1230.00
Leggings, Santee, Openwork, Beaded, Flags, Flowers, Symbols, c.1925, 15 In. 978.00
Leggings, Sioux, Beaded, Painted, Geometric Design, 22 1/2 In., Pair 1675.00
Leggings, Sioux, Buffalo Hide, Wool Stroud Cloth, Sinew Sewn, c.1880, 12 1/2 x 30 In. . . 865.00
Leggings, Sioux, Hide, Beaded, Beadwork Cuff, 18 1/2 In. 2689.00
Leggings, Sioux, Red Trade Cloth, Geometric Strips, Early 1900s, 29 x 13 In., Pair 375.00
Leggings, Southern Plains, Hide, Flared, Beaded, Painted, Crosses, Circles, Lizards, 32 In. 7770.00
Log Carrier, Penobscot, Wood, Birch Bark, Warrior, Moose, Elk, Geometrics, 19 In. 1175.00
Moccasins, Apache, High Top, Beaded, Rawhide Soles, 1880s 3630.00
Moccasins, Apache, High Top, Beadwork, Yellow Ocher, c.1900, 15 1/2 x 11 1/2 In. 1150.00
Moccasins, Arapaho, Beaded, Buckskin, Buffalo Sole, Ocher, c.1930, 10 In. 230.00
Moccasins, Arapaho, Child's, Beaded Boxes & Borders, Buffalo Hide, 10 In. 705.00
Moccasins, Arapaho, Fully Beaded, Buffalo Hide, Sinew Sewn, 1800s, 10 1/2 In. 1955.00
Moccasins, Arapaho, Leaves, Floating Crosses, Beaded Sole Border, c.1905, 8 In. 403.00
Moccasins, Arapaho, Millefiori Beads, c.1890, 10 1/4 In. 604.00
Moccasins, Blackfoot, Ceremonial, Black, Beaded Vamp, Lazy Stitch, c.1890, 10 1/2 In. . . 1380.00
Moccasins, Blackfoot, Child's, Beaded, Fringed, 5 3/4 In. 137.00
Moccasins, Central Plains, Geometric Beading, Quilled Vamps & Slats, Hide, 10 1/2 In. . . 3290.00
Moccasins, Cheyenne, Arapaho, Beaded, Hide, Brown, White, Orange, Blue, 6 In., Pair . . 201.00
Moccasins, Cheyenne, Beaded, Brain Tanned Uppers, Rawhide Soles, 1870s 495.00
Moccasins, Cheyenne, Beaded, Multicolored, High Tops, Brown Leather Bottoms, 4 In. . . 138.00
Moccasins, Cheyenne, Beaded, Orange, Black, Silver, 4 In. 150.00
Moccasins, Cheyenne, Child's, Beaded, Stepped Terrace, Pink, Green, c.1890, 5 1/4 In. . . 1955.00
Moccasins, Cheyenne, Green, Cross, Stepped Terrace Sole Design, c.1920, 11 1/4 In. 748.00
Moccasins, Cheyenne, Women's, Beaded Buckskin, Hard Soles, c.1900, 15 In. 805.00
Moccasins, Cree, Beaded Crosses, Red, Blue, White, Buffalo Hide, Muslin Cuffs, 9 1/2 In. 1116.00
Moccasins, Crow, Beaded, Circular Geometrics, c.1940, 4 x 11 x 4 In. 460.00
Moccasins, Crow, Flat Beaded, High Top, Elk Hide, c.1960, 8 x 4 x 9 1/2 In. 127.00
Moccasins, Crow, Toe Beadwork, Rawhide Soles, Buckskin, c.1880, 3 x 10 x 4 In. 316.00
Moccasins, Eastern Woodlands, Beaded, White, Rose, Red, Blue, Brown, Hide, 10 In. . . . 253.00
Moccasins, Eastern Woodlands, Beadwork, Multicolored, Cloth Uppers, 5 In. 290.00
Moccasins, Flathead, Woman's, Seed & Cut Beads, Stylized Leaves, c.1890, 9 1/4 In. 7590.00
Moccasins, Geometric Beading, Red, Blue, Green, White, 10 1/4 In. 880.00
Moccasins, Great Lakes, Child's, Porcupine Quill Decoration, 1890-1920, 7 1/2 In. 180.50
Moccasins, Great Lakes, Men's, Beaded, 1890-1910, 9 3/4 In., Pair 280.50
Moccasins, Lakota, Hide, Beaded Uppers, Triangles, Purple, Brown Buffalo Tracks, 10 In. 1058.00

Moccasins, Ojibwa, Beaded Flowers, Cloth Vamps & Cuffs, Hide, Yarn Ties, 9 In. 206.00
Moccasins, Plains, Beaded, Hide, Ceremonial, 10 In. 3942.00
Moccasins, Plains, Quilled, Red, Green Triangles, Bead Border, c.1880, 10 1/2 In. 2415.00
Moccasins, Shoshone, Beaded Vamps, Multicolored Diamonds, Buffalo Hide, Child's 823.00
Moccasins, Sioux, Beaded Hide, Dragonfly Soles, Child's 3000.00
Moccasins, Sioux, Beaded, Star, Lazy Stitch, Hard Sole, c.1900, 10 In. 1035.00
Moccasins, Sioux, Beaded, Stepped Terrace, Parfleche Soles, c.1890, 10 1/4 In. 978.00
Moccasins, Sioux, Beaded, White, Blue, Diamond, Parfleche Soles, c.1890, 10 1/2 In. 1200.00
Moccasins, Sioux, Beadwork, Lazy Stitch, Buffalo Hide, c.1890, 4 x 11 x 4 In. 863.00
Moccasins, Sioux, Child's, Ceremonial, Beaded Sole, Crimped Cuffs, c.1900, 6 1/2 In. 805.00
Moccasins, Sioux, Fully Beaded, Multicolored, Parfleche Soles, c.1910, 10 1/2 In. 575.00
Moccasins, Tlingit, Beaded, Buckskin, c.1900, 10 In. 431.00
Moccasins, Ute, Beaded, Elk Hide, Sinew Sewn, Buffalo Soles, c.1885, 10 1/2 In. 3450.00
Moccasins & Leggings, Chippewa, Child's, 1900-1920s, 12 In. 220.00
Necklace, Blackfoot, Bear Claws, Trade Beads, c.1890, 24 In. 1095.00
Necklace, Great Lakes, Multicolored Beaded Thunderbirds, Hide Ties, 2 x 5 In. 1528.00
Necklace, Navajo, 3 Rows Sterling Beads, Squash Type, 14 Turquoise Stones, c.1970 .... 345.00
Necklace, Navajo, Squash Blossom, 10 Turquoise Blossoms, Naja, 32 In. 403.00
Necklace, Navajo, Sterling, Turquoise, Coral Squash Blossom, c.1970, 31 In. 288.00
Necklace, Plains, Badger Claw, 30 Claws, Chief Beads, Leather Thong, 1860s-1870s 4125.00
Necklace, Pueblo, 7 Strand, Coral, Silver, Turquoise, Bone, c.1974, 26 In. 405.00
Necklace, Trade Bead, Deep Blue, Crystal Dutch Glass, 1800s, 24 In. 115.00
Necklace, Trade Bead, Faceted Blue Russian Beads, 7 Cut Sides, 1800s, 30 In. 138.00
Necklace, Trade Bead, Pottery, Hand Worked Beads, Carvings, 1800s, 26 In. 58.00
Olla, Acoma, Black & Orange Geometrics & Flowers, Tapered, Concave Base, 11 In. 4995.00
Olla, Acoma, Black Hatched Geometric Designs, Tapered Neck, Concave Base, 10 In. ... 765.00
Olla, Acoma, Orange & Black Geometric, High Shoulders, Concave Base, 12 In. 1765.00
Olla, Tesuque, Black Geometric, Red Band, Globe Shape, Flared Neck, 10 x 8 1/2 In. 765.00
Parfleche, Crow, Painted, Geometric Designs, c.1900, 4 x 15 x 28 In. 805.00
Parfleche, Plains, Green, Yellow, Blue & Red Designs, c.1890, 25 x 14 3/4 In. 1725.00
Parfleche, Plains, Painted Hide, Geometric & Tepee Design, 14 x 52 In. 7170.00
Pin, Navajo, Sterling, 3-1/2 Rosettes, 42 Turquoise Stones, c.1960, 3 1/2 x 1 1/2 In. 90.00
Pin, Zuni, Silver, Stone, Inlaid, Rainbow Man, 2 1/2 In. 150.00
Pipe, Blackfoot, Catlinite, Pewter, Inlaid Black Slate, Mid 1900s, 6 3/4 In. 315.00
Pipe, Blackfoot, Ceremonial, Black Stone, Unused, c.1900, 3 x 6 x 1 1/4 In. 195.00
Pipe, Lakota, Sioux, Ash Stem, Portrait, Warrior, Tomahawk, Red Pipestone Bowl, 22 In. .. 4405.00
Pipe, Plains, Ash Stem, Carved Turtle & Elk Head Effigies, Tomahawk Bowl, 18 In. 3175.00
Pipe, Plains, Ash Stem, File Branding, Brass Tacks, Red Pipestone Bowl, 21 1/2 In. 1530.00
Pipe Bag, Arapaho, Beaded Borders, Panels, Symbols, Quilled Slats, Fringe, 30 In. 1295.00
Pipe Bag, Beaded, Buckskin, Geometric, 3 Tassels, Red, Green, Blue, Yellow, 36 In. 1430.00
Pipe Bag, Blackfoot, Antelope Hide, Beaded, Ocher, Fringe, c.1880, 7 x 30 In. 1265.00
Pipe Bag, Blackfoot, Geometrics, Beaded, Brain Tanned Leather, 1880s, 32 In. 1815.00
Pipe Bag, Cheyenne, Beaded Border, Arrow, Diamonds, Leather Fringe, c.1890, 39 In. ... 1265.00
Pipe Bag, Cheyenne, Beaded, Buckskin, 8-Point Star, Quilled, Fringe, c.1900, 25 x 7 In. .. 3165.00
Pipe Bag, Cheyenne, Beaded, Buckskin, Geometric, Quilled, Fringe, c.1920, 25 x 7 In. .. 2185.00
Pipe Bag, Lakota, Beaded, Hide, Hourglass, Quilled, Fringe, Horsehair Danglers, 35 In. .. 2470.00
Pipe Bag, Plains, Beaded, Hide, Quilled, Metal Tassels, Horsehair, 35 x 8 In. 2710.00
Pipe Bag, Plains, Beaded, Quilled, American Flags, Geometric Designs, 29 x 7 In. 3940.00
Pipe Bag, Plains, Flowers, Beaded, Quilled, Hide, 29 x 7 In. 1848.00
Pipe Bag, Plains, Flowers, Beaded, Quilled, Hide, 29 x 8 In. 2340.00
Pipe Bag, Plains, Geometric, Beaded, Quilled, Hide, 29 x 8 In. 3200.00
Pipe Bag, Sioux, Beaded, Quilled, 1880s, 26 In. 1650.00
Pipe Bag, Sioux, Fully Beaded, Quilled Slats, Hide, Sinew, Tin Cones, c.1890, 8 x 28 In. .. 2185.00
Pipe Bowl, Ojibwa, Black Pipestone, Flared Bowl, Lead Inlay, Stripes, Checks, 7 In. 1175.00
Pipe Bowl, Pawnee, Red Pipestone, Elbow Shape, Pierced, Notched Bowl, Incised, 5 In. .. 1528.00
Pipe Bowl, Plains, Red Pipestone, Keg Shaped Bowl, 19th Century, 3 3/4 In. 940.00
Pot, Acoma, Bird Effigy, Handle, 1940s 105.00
Pot, Acoma, Parrot Design, Handle, 2 Spouts, 1940s, 7 x 10 In. 195.00
Pottery, Acoma, Owl, 20th Century, 8 x 10 In. 290.00
Pottery, Zuni, Owl, 3 Babies, 7 x 7 In. 210.00
Pouch, Apache, Buckskin, Beaded, Flowers, Fringe, E.H. Rhodes, c.1880, 9 1/2 In. 1116.00
Pouch, Buckskin, Beaded, Horse, Cross, Star, Crescent, Tassels, 9 1/2 In. 495.00
Pouch, Crow, Beaded Cloth, Hide, Cross & Hourglass, Blue Ground, Drawstring, 7 1/2 In. 940.00

Pouch, Crow, Ration, Beaded, 5 3/4 In. 190.00
Pouch, Dakota, Beaded, Flowers, Hide, Roll Beaded Fringe, c.1900, 11 In. 118.00
Pouch, Kiowa, Strike-A-Lite, Trade Beads, German Silver Decorations, c.1890, 4 1/4 In. . 3335.00
Pouch, Micmac, No. 16 Beaded, 19th Century, 4 1/2 x 6 In. 115.00
Pouch, Plains, Beaded, Flowers, Blue Ground, Leather Drawstringc.1900, 6 1/4 In. 145.00
Pouch, Plains, Beaded, Hide, U.S. Flags, Fringe, 7 In. 1135.00
Pouch, Plains, Strike-A-Lite, Geometric, Bars, Blue Ground, c.1890, 4 In. 1035.00
Pouch, Plains, Strike-A-Lite, Hourglass Shape, Beaded, Tin Cone Danglers, 5 In. 2350.00
Pouch, Santiee Sioux, Beaded, 4 Sides, Fringe, Drawstring, 7 In. 165.00
Pouch, Sioux, Beaded, Oval, Checkerboard, Cut Fringe, c.1880, 5 In. 345.00
Pouch, Southern Plains, Geometrics, Bead Lace Border, c.1900, 4 3/4 In. 430.00
Pouch, Southern Plains, Geometrics, Metal Bead Trim, Drawstring, c.1890, 6 In. 315.00
Pouch, Southern Plains, Whirling Log, Polychrome Bead Border, Fringe, c.1910, 5 In. .. 145.00
Pouch, Ute, Leather, Beaded Flap, Geometrics, Tin Cone Danglers, Trapezoidal, 5 1/2 In. . 825.00
Purse, Naliseet, Beadwork, Cluster Flower, Black Velvet, c.1880, 6 1/4 In. 690.00
Purse, Northeast, Beadwork, Cluster Flower, Black Velvet, Double Flap, c.1880, 6 In. ... 144.00
Purse, Sioux, Beaded, Brass Hardware, Geometric Designs, c.1880, 9 1/2 x 12 In. 1150.00
Quirt, Plains, Wood Handle, Rawhide Lash, Fringed & Beaded Strap, 14 In. 588.00
Quiver, Algonquin, Plaited, Woven Birch Bark, Feathers, Moosehide, c.1920, 27 x 4 In. .. 520.00
Quiver & Arrows, Hand Tooled Leather, 12 Metal Tip Arrows, Feathers, 1920, 28 x 2 In. . 30.00
Rattle, Hopi, Ceremonial, Rawhide, Yellow Ocher, Painted, c.1930, 8 1/2 x 4 x 2 1/2 In. . 290.00
Rattle, Pueblo, Gourd, Painted Head, Cotton Wrapped Handle, c.1900, 10 1/2 x 4 1/4 In. . 315.00
Rosette, Shoshone, Beaded, 4-Point Design, Hide, Red Cloth Back, Fringed, 10 In. 1410.00
Rug, Chimayo, Red, Waterbug & Line Designs, Runner, c.1950, 62 x 18 1/2 In. 150.00
Rug, Diamond Lozenge Medallion, White, Red, Black & Brown Border, 60 x 32 In.. .... 370.00
Rug, Navajo Yei, Figures, Center Corn Plant, Brown, Natural, Orange, 25 x 37 In. 110.00
Rug, Navajo, 2 Serrated Diamond Lozenges, Ivory, Gray, Black, Tan, 60 x 41 In. 525.00
Rug, Navajo, 3 Diamonds, Black & Red, Charcoal Field, 60 x 30 In. 330.00
Rug, Navajo, 3 Medallions, Black, Beige, Turquoise, Yellow Field, 65 x 28 In. 210.00
Rug, Navajo, 3 Squash Flower Medallions, Black, Ivory, Red, Green Field, 59 x 24 In. ... 219.00
Rug, Navajo, Central X Design, Red, Beige, Gray Field, Geometric Borders, 28 x 45 In. .. 195.00
Rug, Navajo, Chinle Area, Geometric Designs, Beige, Brown, White, c.1920, 45 x 80 In. . 1725.00
Rug, Navajo, Concentric Bands, Multicolored, 57 x 33 In. 2200.00
Rug, Navajo, Concentric Serrated Diamonds, Ivory, Brown, Red, Charcoal, 36 x 55 In. ... 220.00
Rug, Navajo, Cornstalk Yei, Figures, Handspun Wool, c.1940, 29 x 33 In. 259.00
Rug, Navajo, Crystal Area, Central Lozenge Pattern, c.1940, 88 x 66 In. 1840.00
Rug, Navajo, Crystal Area, Central Lozenge, Runner, c.1935, 66 x 31 In. 545.00
Rug, Navajo, Crystal Style, Storm Variant, Eye In The Diamond, c.1940, 36 x 48 In. 2415.00
Rug, Navajo, Crystal Variation, Double S Lozenge, Terrace Edge, c.1930, 77 x 43 In. 1035.00
Rug, Navajo, Crystal Variation, Fishhooks, Crosses, Swastika, c.1935, 54 x 40 In. 345.00
Rug, Navajo, Crystal Variation, Squash Blossom In Lozenge, c.1930, 86 x 44 1/2 In. 1495.00
Rug, Navajo, Crystal Variation, Triple Stepped Terrace, c.1940, 73 1/2 x 40 1/2 In. 750.00
Rug, Navajo, Diagonal Serrated Stripes, Red & Brown, Ivory Ground, Wool, 79 x 50 In. . 575.00
Rug, Navajo, Diamonds, Red Field, Multiple Serrated Borders, 79 x 53 In. 5500.00
Rug, Navajo, Diamonds, Tan, Brown, Red Cross Centers, Brown Border, 36 x 72 In. 200.00
Rug, Navajo, Eye Dazzler, Center Cross, Handspun, Aniline Dyes, c.1890, 81 x 57 In. ... 4370.00
Rug, Navajo, Ganado Trading Post, Linked Diamonds, Gray Ground, Red, 48 x 71 In. ... 330.00
Rug, Navajo, Ganado Variation, Crystal Chain, Double Lozenge, c.1930, 81 x 54 1/2 In. .. 2990.00
Rug, Navajo, Ganado, Lozenge, Serrated, T Border, Handspun, c.1940, 87 1/2 x 57 1/2 In. 3565.00
Rug, Navajo, Geometric, Red, Brown, Ivory Ground, 41 x 69 In. 430.00
Rug, Navajo, Geometric, Stepped, Brown, Ivory, Gold, 61 x 33 In. 360.00
Rug, Navajo, Geometric, Stripes, Red, Green, Black, Yellow, Ivory Ground, 28 x 40 In. .. 375.00
Rug, Navajo, Natural Wool, Fishhook Designs, c.1950, Runner, 98 x 39 In. 1380.00
Rug, Navajo, Red Mesa, Border, 55 x 76 In. 4370.00
Rug, Navajo, Serrated Diamond Rows, Red Field, 56 x 80 In. 415.00
Rug, Navajo, Serrated Diamonds, Brown, Ivory, Charcoal, 34 x 55 In. 110.00
Rug, Navajo, Serrated Diamonds, White, Red, Brown, Gray Runner, 167 x 82 In. 5290.00
Rug, Navajo, Star, Simple Border, Vegetal & Aniline Dyes, 41 1/2 x 54 3/4 In. 545.00
Rug, Navajo, Stepped Diamond & Cross, Brown, Red, Orange, Wool, 74 x 46 In. 750.00
Rug, Navajo, Stepped Triangles, Muted Colors, c.1930, 69 x 46 In. 635.00
Rug, Navajo, Storm Variation, Bows, Arrows, Whirling Logs, Bugs, c.1930, 82 x 48 In. ... 1725.00
Rug, Navajo, Triangle & Diamond, Serrated Diamond Border, Red, Brown, 38 x 57 In. .. 440.00
Rug, Navajo, Two Grey Hills Variation, Celtic Cross, Fish Hooks, c.1970, 45 x 62 In. 2185.00

Rug, Navajo, Two Grey Hills Variation, Double Lozenge, c.1950, 45 x 81 In. 3220.00
Rug, Navajo, Two Grey Hills Variation, Spider Woman Cross, c.1935, 71 1/2 x 54 1/2 In. . 2070.00
Rug, Navajo, Vertical Lines, Mustard, Blue, Black, Ivory Field, 60 x 32 In. 245.00
Rug, Navajo, Wool, Corner Designs, c.1910, 56 x 33 In. 1095.00
Rug, Navajo, Yei, 4 Figures, Handspun, Vegetal & Analine Dyes, 41 x 59 In. 660.00
Rug, Navajo, Yei, 6 Figures, Handspun, Vegetal & Aniline Dyes, c.1950, 23 x 36 In. 460.00
Rug, Navajo, Yei, 7 Corn Dancers, Off-White Field, Multicolored, 37 x 39 In. 385.00
Rug, Navajo, Yei, Feathers, Figures, Handspun, Analine Dyes, c.1930, 33 x 52 In. 1035.00
Saddle, Cree, Stirrups, Tanned Hide, Beaded Teardrops, c.1885, 22 x 29 1/2 In. 3565.00
Saddle, Plains, Leather, Antler Frame, Leather Harnessing 2270.00
Saddle Blanket, Central Plains, Hide, Canvas, Beaded Geometrics, Long Fringe, 38 In. . . 1645.00
Saddle Blanket, Navajo, Center Cross, Geometric Corner Squares, 53 x 34 In. 999.00
Saddle Blanket, Navajo, Image Of Cow's Head, Word Cow, 30 x 30 In. 1290.00
Saddle Blanket, Navajo, Wool, Red, Stripes, Checkered Corners, 33 x 29 In. 470.00
Saddlebag, Lakota Sioux, Double, Buffalo Hide, Pockets, Beaded, Teepees, Fringe, 35 In. 9400.00
Saddlebag, Plains, Hide, 6 Geometric Beaded & Hide Fringe, 72 In. 13145.00
Sally Bag, Wasco, Buckskin Top, Drawstring, Twined Basketry Bottom, 7 In. 355.00
Sash, Choctaw, Red Cloth, Green Geometric Appliques, Blue Border, White Beads, 45 In. 7638.00
Sash, Great Lakes, Beaded, Geometrics, White Ground, Red Braided Wool Ties, 30 In. . . . 470.00
Sash, Great Lakes, Wool, Beaded, Stripes, Zigzags, Diamonds, Fringe, 72 In. 9400.00
Seed Jar, Hopi, Multicolored, Squat Shape, Bands, Early 1900s, 2 1/2 x 7 In. 175.00
Shirt, Blackfoot, Beaded, Tanned Hide, Fringe, Red Cloth Cuffs, Antler Buttons, 22 In. . . 410.00
Shirt, Blackfoot, War, Beaded Neck, Wrist Cuffs, Fringe, Sinew Sewn, 1870s-1880s 1760.00
Skullcap, Sioux, Stepped Terrace, Cross, Cotton Lining, c.1890, 6 1/4 In. 1210.00
Sleeves, Plains, Beaded, Geometrics, Painted Hide, 18 1/2 In., Pair 1910.00
Sleeves, Sioux, Beadwork, Geometrics, Fabric, Hide, 14 1/4 In., Pair 1135.00
Spoon, Northwest Coast, Mountain Goat Horn, Carved Handle, c.1900, 10 1/4 In. 1095.00
Spoon, Tlingit, Totemic, Mountain Sheep Horn, c.1850, 13 In. 1840.00
Tepee Bag, Plains, Horsehair & Metal Fringe, Beaded Ends, 18 1/2 x 24 In. 2030.00
Tile, Acoma, 2-Headed Waterbird, c.1920s, 6 x 6 In. 430.00
Totem Pole, Figures, Carved, Painted Bear, Whale, Eagle, 16 In. 250.00
Totem Pole, Haida, Cedar, Bird Atop Other Figures, c.1925, 24 x 3 3/4 x 4 1/2 In. 1265.00
Totem Pole, Northwest Coast, Wood, Painted, 5 Animals, Abalone Eyes, 39 In. 4481.00
Toy, Ute, Cradleboard, Doll, Beadwork, c.1902, 6 1/4 x 3 1/4 In. 1000.00
Tray, Apache, Coil, Radiating Stacked Triangles, 11 1/4 In. 825.00
Tray, Apache, Coiled, 5 Sided Center Stars, Geometrics, 15 x 3 1/2 In. 3520.00
Tray, Cahuilla, Coil, 3 Bands Of Connected Triangles, 16 3/4 In. 529.00
Tray, Hupa, Winnowing, Brown, Stepped Spirals, 21 In. 1645.00
Tray, Huron, Moose Hair Embroidery, Flowers, 5 Sections, Birch Bark, 5 1/4 In. 470.00
Tray, Karok, Flour, Twined, Interlocking Diamonds, Brown, 25 In. 590.00
Tray, Pima, Coil, 5-Point Center, Band Of Stepped Triangles, 7 1/2 In. 380.00
Tray, Thompson River Basin, Flat, Handles, Black & Red Designs, 1940, 2 x 14 x 13 In. . 290.00
Tray, Wedding, Navajo, Coil, Red Band, Black Stepped Triangles, 15 1/2 In. 765.00
Trousers, Santiee Sioux, Beaded, 1880 . . . . 3850.00
Vase, Hopi, Black, Feathers, Orange Ground, Cylindrical, Tapered, c.1940, 9 In. 325.00
Vase, Pueblo, Tewa, Wedding, 2 Necks, Black On Black, c.1930, 11 x 8 x 8 In. 230.00
Vest, Beaded, Arrowhead, Feathers, Diamonds Under Pockets, Pinwheel On Back, 23 In. . 310.00
Vest, Beaded, Hide, Stylized Flowers, Borders, Crimped Edge, Early 20th Century, 20 In. 170.00
Vest, Beaded, Horse, Blue, Black, Geometric Bands, Flower, Turquoise Leaves, 22 In. . . . 620.00
Vest, Buffalo Hide, Flowers, Pockets, Buttons, c.1890, 21 x 17 In. 635.00
Vest, Plains, Beaded, Flowers, Birds, Blue Trade Cloth, Velvet Trim, c.1890, 20 x 18 In. . 1090.00
Vest, Plains, Hide, Quilled, Flower Front, Starburst Back, 20 x 18 In. 4680.00
Vest, Sioux, Beaded, Deer, Blue Ground, Lazy Stitch, c.1880, 20 x 17 1/2 In. 3680.00
Vest, Sioux, Child's, Beaded, Geometric, Leaves, Sinew Sewn, c.1900, 15 x 16 In. 1725.00
Wall Pouch, Tlingit, Beadwork, Flowers, Moosehide, Fringe, Early 1900s, 17 1/2 x 6 In. . 690.00
War Club, Catlinite, Hide Covering, Double Sided Blunt End, Beveled, 22 x 4 1/2 x 2 In. . 345.00
War Club, Plains, Stone Head, Rawhide, Wrapped, Beaded, c.1890, 18 x 2 1/2 x 2 In. . . . 290.00
War Club, Plains, Stone, Beaded, Rawhide Handle, c.1880, 15 1/2 x 2 3/4 x 2 In. 520.00
War Club, Sioux, Steatite Rock Head, Beaded, Wood Handle, Hide Covering, 17 x 6 In. . . 405.00
War Club, Sioux, Stone, Ghost Dancer, Hide Covered Handle, 21 In. 220.00
Water Basket, Apache, Parfleche, 10 In. 83.00
Weaving, Navajo, Concentric Diamonds, Banded Zigzags, 74 x 55 In. 600.00
Weaving, Navajo, Cow's Head, Cow, Stripes On Ends, 30 x 30 In. 1295.00

Weaving, Navajo, Eagle Center, Handspun, c.1940, 51 x 32 In. 315.00
Weaving, Navajo, Eye Dazzler, Red Ground, 27 x 32 In. 590.00
Weaving, Navajo, Shiprock Area, Tree Of Life, Horses, Birds, c.1980, 27 x 30 In. 345.00
Weaving, Navajo, Storm Pattern Sampler, c.1970, 16 x 20 In. 35.00
Weaving, Navajo, Wool, Chief's Pattern, Crosses, Red & Brown Stripes, 75 x 59 In. 6465.00
Weaving, Navajo, Wool, Diagonal Sawtooth, Bright Colors, 93 x 54 In. 705.00
Weaving, Navajo, Wool, Third Phase Chief's Pattern, Red, Blue, Brown, 76 x 55 In. 4406.00
Whistle, Metal, Engraved, Capt. J.S. Loud Dec 29-30, 1890, Wounded Knee, 3 In. 1880.00

INKSTANDS were made to be placed on a desk. They held some type of container for ink, and possibly a sander, a pen tray, a pen, a holder for pounce, and even a candle to melt the sealing wax. Inkstands date to the eighteenth century and have been made of silver, copper, ceramics, and glass. Additional inkstands may be found in these and other related categories.

6 Division Stamp Box, Pen Case, Wood Lined, Betheman & Sons, London 1650.00
Brass, Pharoah Head, 2 Glass Wells, Egyptian Revival, 9 1/2 x 8 In. 690.00
Bronze, Hinged Top, Stylized Leaves, Berried Branches, Art Nouveau, Late 1800s, 9 In. . 235.00
Bronze, Marble Base, Mountain Lion, 2 Inkwells, T.F. Cartier Model, 1900s, 17 In. 1300.00
Copper, Bird & Vine, Milk Glass Inkwells, Sponge Holder, Pen Rest, 1 5/8 x 5 x 3 In. . . . 110.00
Gilt Bronze, Cornucopia, Cherub Lid, Faux Tortoiseshell, 7 1/2 x 8 3/4 In., Pair 550.00
Iron, 2 Revolving Glass Fonts, Ground Lips, 4 1/4 In. 110.00
Iron, Branch, Rooster, Hen, Cabbage, Porcelain Inkwell, Hinged Lid, 1 3/4 x 5 1/4 In. . . . 308.00
Rosewood, Tiger-Eye Stones, Brass, George Dowler, Victorian, c.1857, 5 x 12 In. 145.00
Silver, Horseshoe, Austria, 2 1/4 x 3 3/4 x 2 In. 135.00
Silver, Scroll & Shell Handle, Gadroon Rim, 4 Panel Feet, London, 1755, 6 In. 920.00
Silver Plate, 2 Glass Inkwells, Pierced & Shaped Lids, Ball Final & Feet, 8 x 2 3/4 In. . . . 224.00

INKWELLS, of course, held ink. Ready-made ink was first made about 1836 and was sold in bottles. The desk inkwell had a narrow hole so the pen would not slip inside. Inkwells were made of many materials, such as pottery, glass, pewter, and silver. Look in these categories for more listings of inkwells.

Brass, Building, Samuel Thompson & Sons, Midland Maltings, 6 1/4 x 10 3/4 In. 420.00
Brass, Circular Pot, Reticulated Tray, Art Nouveau, c.1895, 8 In. 45.00
Brass, Double, Standish, Late 1800s, 11 1/2 In. 90.00
Brass, Gilded, Double Chain, Engraved Fleur-De-Lis, Hinged, Malachite, 2 1/2 x 3 In. . . . 420.00
Brass, Snail, Revolving, Butterflies, Cast Brass Support, 4 In. 198.00
Bronze, Barefoot Sailor On Bow Of Dory, c.1900, 9 x 18 1/4 x 5 1/2 In. 880.00
Bronze, Child & Dog, Doghouse, Tree Stump Penholder, c.1900, 6 In. 500.00
Bronze, Gnomes, Toadstool, Hinged Cover, Enameled, Austria, 1800s, 4 1/2 In. 518.00
Bronze, Marble, 2 Wells, Center Relief Plaque, Ormolu Trim, Signed, H. Chapu, 16 In. . . 1650.00
Bronze, Urn Bowl, 3 Half Figures, Hinged Lid, Paw Feet, Copper Liner, 7 1/2 In. 140.00
Brownware, 3 Coin Medallions, Round, 4 1/2 In. 65.00
Cast Iron, Crab, 7 In. 90.00
Cast Iron, Double Pressed Glass Wells, Pen Rest, Calendar Dials, Victorian, 5 x 9 x 6 In. . 280.00
Ceramic, Dolphin, Cream Luster Glaze, Perry & Co., 4 1/2 In. 25.00
Ceramic, Dumfries, A. Loneburne, Angel, Holding Staff, Beveled Corners, Porcelle, 2 In. . 17.00
Ceramic, Rugby Ball, Light Brown, Metal Cap, 2 1/2 In. 135.00
Cloisonne Enamel, Bronze, Egg Shape Well, Butterfly Lid Finial, Late 1800s, 9 In. 118.00
Copper, Silver, Art Nouveau, 6 1/2 x 3 In. 470.00
Cut Glass, Blue, Faceted Top, Brass Collar, Anchor, Flowers, 3 x 2 1/2 x 2 1/2 In. 350.00
Frosted Blue Glass, Art Deco, Plastic Pen, Eversharp, France, 4 3/4 x 4 1/4 In. 115.00
Glass, Black Amethyst, Sengbusch, 4 3/4 x 3 1/4 In. 185.00
Glass, Blown, Amber, Olive, Pontil Base, Tooled Rim, Mouth, Continental, 1 5/8 In. 125.00
Glass, Blown, Blue Green, Pontil Base, Applied Disc Mouth, 1 7/8 x 1 1/2 In. 45.00
Glass, Blown, Cobalt Blue, Pontil, Tooled Rim, Mouth, Continental, 2 In. 168.00
Glass, Blown, Olive Green, 3-Piece Mold, 1 1/2 x 2 1/2 In. 145.00
Glass, Blown, Sapphire Blue, Gallery Rim, Iron Pontil, 2 1/2 x 2 In. 230.00
Glass, Cobalt Blue, Cylindrical, Unspillable, Tapered, Pontil Scar, 2 1/4 In. 60.00
Glass, Cobalt Blue, Tooled Funnel Type, 1 3/4 In. 90.00
Glass, Crosscut Diamond, Silver Plated Lid & Base, Reed & Barton, 3 In. 325.00
Glass, Cylindrical, Hyde, London, Cobalt Blue, Pouring Lip, Embossed, 6 In. 17.00

Glass, Olive Green, Diamond Diaper, 1 7/8 x 2 1/4 In.	66.00
Glass, Sterling Silver Cover, Rectangular, Monogram, 3 In.	80.00
Glass, Teakettle, Cobalt Blue, Straight Spout, Gold Top, Cap, Box, 2 In.	420.00
Leather, Brass Poodle, Brass Encased Glass Inkwell, Traveling, 2 1/4 x 2 1/2 In.	60.00
Metal, Patinated, Owl, Wood Base, 7 1/4 x 2 5/8 In.	345.00
Metal, Putto, Hinged Cover, Gilt, 7 3/8 In.	546.00
Milk Glass, Beveled Block Cherub, 3 3/4 x 4 In.	65.00
Pewter, Brown Glass Insert, 3 x 3 1/2 In.	184.00
Pewter, Raised, Incised Rings, 8 3/4 x 3 3/4 In.	110.00
Pewter, Round Base, Hinged Lid, Gray Ceramic Insert, 7 3/4 x 2 1/2 In.	105.00
Porcelain, 2 Seated Poodles, Square On Rectangular Base, Penholder, 3 x 4 1/2 In.	325.00
Porcelain, Bird On Nest, Snake Stealing Eggs, Staffordshire, Late 1800s, 2 1/2 x 2 3/4 In.	60.00
Porcelain, Cherub, Bird, Nest, Eggs, 3 Pen Holes, Staffordshire, 8 1/2 x 2 1/2 x 4 In.	75.00
Porcelain, Dog, Reclining Red Whippets, Blue Base, Gilt Trim, Staffordshire, 6 3/4 In., Pair	200.00
Porcelain, Dog, Whippet, Staffordshire, 7 In.	95.00
Porcelain, Dog, White, Black Spots, Cobalt Blue Base, Staffordshire, 4 In., Pair	550.00
Porcelain, Man, Leaning On Barrel, Holding Jug, Staffordshire, 4 1/4 x 2 3/4 x 3 1/4 In.	88.00
Porcelain, Man, Leaning On Beer Keg, Pitcher, Staffordshire, 4 1/4 x 2 3/4 x 3 1/4 In.	145.00
Porcelain, Man, Sleeping Holding Jug, Mug, 2 Holes, Staffordshire, 3 x 2 1/4 x 2 3/4 In.	65.00
Porcelain, Pink Shoe, Man, Tricornered Hat, Staffordshire, 1800s, 4 1/2 x 7 In., 2 Piece	635.00
Porcelain, Whippet, Staffordshire, 8 In., Pair	400.00
Pottery, Graniteware, Lion's Head, Figural, 2 Quill Holes, Filler Hole, 2 3/8 In.	56.00
Pottery, Tan, Molded Pour Spout, 4 1/4 x 2 1/4 In.	90.00
Rosewood, Barrel Shape, Glass Insert, c.1860, 2 1/4 x 1 1/2 In.	300.00
Soapstone, Carved, Rectangular, 2 1/8 In.	45.00
Spelter, Camel, Lying Down, Multicolored, Glass Well, 8 1/2 In.	200.00
Sterling Silver, George V, Turned Cover, 4 Pen Receptacles, Inscription, c.1924, 6 In.	350.00
Stoneware, Blue, Splotching, Sloped Rim, Blue Band At Base, 3 3/4 x 2 In.	2250.00
Stoneware, Dark Brown, Albany Glaze, 4 Quill Holes, 1 7/8 x 4 1/8 In.	670.00
Stoneware, Frogskin Albany Slip Glaze, Signed, c.1960, 3 In., Pair	120.00
Stoneware, Manganese Glaze, Arched Panels, 1 7/8 In.	28.00
Wood, Bear, Black Forest, Carved, Glass Eyes, Open Mouth, Crooked Front Paw, 6 In.	535.00
Wood, Bear, Walking Along Tree Stump, Glass Insert, Switzerland, 5 1/2 x 8 In.	470.00
Wood, Black Forest Carved, Poodle Head, Glass Eyes, Brass Inkwell, 5 1/4 x 4 1/4 In.	60.00
Wood, Footed, Porcelain Containers, Gilt, Late 19th Century, 9 1/2 x 5 1/2 In.	250.00
Wood, Nest, Flowers, Leaves, Bird Cover, Pen Rest, Glass Insert, 4 x 11 In.	460.00

INSULATORS of glass or pottery have been made for use on telegraph or telephone poles since 1844. Thousands of different styles of insulators have been made. Most common are those of clear or aqua glass; most desirable are the threadless types made from 1850 to 1870.

A.A., Side Wire Groove, Double Petticoat, Threaded, Milky Fizzy Aqua	330.00
American, Side Wire Groove, Double Petticoat, Threaded, Yellow Green	250.00
Brookfield, No. 20, Side Wire Groove, Single Petticoat, Threaded, Amber, Green Aqua	3.00
Brookfield, No. 20, Side Wire Groove, Single Petticoat, Threaded, Aqua	1.00
Brookfield, No. 20, Side Wire Groove, Single Petticoat, Threaded, Dark Aqua	1.00
Cable, Cable Top, Threaded, 2 Ears, Emerald Green	1017.00
California, No. A007, Side Wire Groove, Single Petticoat, Threaded, Light Purple	15.00
Columbia, No. 2, Cable Top, Saddle Wire Groove, 2 Ears, Threaded, Teal Green	400.00
Cutter, Coffin Bottom, Aqua	500.00
Diamond, Side Wire Groove, Single Petticoat, Threaded, Teal Blue	330.00
Dominion, No. 10, Straw, Side Wire Groove, Single Petticoat, Threaded, Flat Top	12.00
Gayner, No. 48-400, Aqua, Black Swirls, Side Wire Groove, Double Petticoat, Threaded	410.00
H.G. Co., No. 7, Milky Aqua, Side Wire Groove, Single Petticoat, Threaded	165.00
H.G. Co., Oxblood, Side Wire Groove, Double Petticoat, Threaded	1870.00
Hemingray, No. 10, Aqua, 2 Piece, Side Wire Groove, Single Petticoat, Threaded, Flat Top	95.00
Hemingray, No. 10, Clear, Side Wire Groove, Single Petticoat, Threaded, Flat Top	2.00
Hemingray, No. 20, Dark Yellow Amber, Side Wire Groove, Theaded	30.00
Hemingray, No. 100HV, Clear, Side Wire Groove, Triple Petticoat, Theaded	1.00
Hemingray, No. 110, Dead End Spool, 2 Wire, Blue	5.00
Jumbo, Side Wire Groove, Single Petticoat, Threaded, Aqua	155.00
Knowles, No. 2, Cable, Cable Top, Threaded, Multitone, Blue, Green, Amber	130.00
Locke, No. 16, Saddle Groove, Triple Petticoat, Threaded, Yellow, Green, Amber	130.00

Manhattan, Cable Top, Threaded, Green, Amber 465.00
Maydwell, No. 20, Side Wire Groove, Double Petticoat, Threaded, Milk Glass 30.00
Maydwell, No. 20, Side Wire Groove, Double Petticoat, Threaded, Milk Glass, Swirls 250.00
McLaughlin, No. 9, Side Wire Groove, Single Petticoat, Threaded, Light Blue 5.00
McLaughlin, No. 14, Side Wire Groove, Double Petticoat, Threaded, Blue Aqua 10.00
McLaughlin, No. 14, Side Wire Groove, Double Petticoat, Threaded, Olive Green, Black .   10.00
McLaughlin, No. 16, Side Wire Groove, Single Petticoat, Threaded, Light Green 15.00
McLaughlin, No. 19, Side Wire Groove, Double Petticoat, Threaded, Bubbly Lime Green .   60.00
McLaughlin, No. 19, Side Wire Groove, Double Petticoat, Threaded, Dark Emerald Green   40.00
McLaughlin, No. 20, Side Wire Groove, Double Petticoat, Threaded, Smoke Straw 20.00
McLaughlin, No. 20, Swirled Citrine, Side Wire Groove, Double Petticoat, Threaded 650.00
McLaughlin, No. 40, Side Wire Groove, Double Petticoat, Threaded, Aqua 250.00
McLaughlin, No. 40, Side Wire Groove, Double Petticoat, Threaded, Aqua, Bubbly 10.00
McLaughlin, No. 40, Side Wire Groove, Double Petticoat, Threaded, Blue Aqua 7.00
McLaughlin, No. 42, Side Wire Groove, Double Petticoat, Threaded, Blue, Emerald Green   125.00
McLaughlin, No. 42, Side Wire Groove, Double Petticoat, Threaded, Sage Green 8.00
N.E.G.M., Cable Top, Threaded, 2-Tone, Amber, Aqua 90.00
National, No. 110.6, Blue Aqua 1700.00
Oakman, No. 14, Side Wire Groove, Double Petticoat, Threaded, Ice Blue Aqua 825.00
Whitall, Tatum, No. 010, Saddle Groove, Double Petticoat, Threaded, Green 35.00
Whitall, Tatum, No. 010, Saddle Groove, Double Petticoat, Threaded, Root Beer Amber . .   10.00

IRISH BELLEEK, see Belleek category.

IRON is a metal that has been used by man since prehistoric times. It is
a popular metal for tools and decorative items like doorstops that need
as much weight as possible. Items are listed here or under other appropriate headings, such as Bookends, Doorstop, Kitchen, Match Holder,
or Tool. The tool that is used for ironing clothes, an iron, is listed in the
Kitchen category under Iron and Sadiron.

Ashtray, Cowboy Hat, Texas Centennial, Arcade, 1936, 4 In. 1045.00
Bootjack, Folding, Brass Hinges, Early 1800s, 10 1/4 x 2 In. 120.00
Bull's Head, Red Gold Painted Finish, France, 19th Century, 25 In. 1955.00
Bullet, Mold, 38 Caliber, Wood Handles, Stamped, 9 In. 20.00
Bung Puller, Corkscrew Shape, England, 17th Century 160.00
Cigar Cutter, High Toned, That Good 5 Cent Cigar, Lever, 1880, 8 x 5 In. 415.00
Cuspidor, Tortoise Shape, Push Head To Open, Bradley & Hubbard, 4 1/2 x 13 x 11 In. . . .   300.00
Dutch Bonnet Roller, c.1840, 3 3/4 x 3 1/4 In. 220.00
Eagle, Spread Wings, U.S. Shield, Multicolored, America, 1800s, 8 5/8 x 15 1/8 In. 1645.00
Figure, Dog, Boston Terrier, Seated, Cast, Painted, England, 8 x 7 1/2 In. 345.00
Figure, Pheasant, Marble Plinth, 6 x 17 3/4 x 4 In. 95.00
Figure, Pontiac Indian Head, Cast, 13 In. 250.00
Figure, Rabbit, Painted White, Seated On Hind Haunches, Perked Ears, Cast, 15 In. 145.00
Gas Jet, Acme, c.1888, 4 1/2 In. 110.00
Gas Jet, Hollow Body, Ox Tongue Shape, Front Vents, Bakelite Handle, Ostarica, 8 In. 11.00
Hook, Crown, Wrought, 8 Hooks, Swan Decoration, 20th Century, 15 1/2 x 15 In. 165.00
Hook, Scroll Ends, Applied Leaf, 8 In. 28.00
Hook, Wrought, Birds, Scroll, Pair 305.00
Horse, On Platform, 63 x 50 x 23 In. 7700.00
Jardiniere, Oval Basin, Bud Finials, Pinch Waist, Scrolled Feet, Continental, 44 x 35 In. . . .   2530.00
Lamp Base, Urn Shape, Faux Marble Paint, 14 In., Pair 22.00
Mold, Minnie Ball, 3 3/4 In. 10.00
Ox Bow Pin, Hand Forged, 4 1/2 In., Pair 170.00
Paperweight, Lighthouse, Painted, 5 3/4 In. 55.00
Planter, 4 Graduated Tiers, Victorian, 26 x 7 1/2 x 66 In. 345.00
Plaque, George Washington Profile, Multicolored Paint, Laurel Leaves, 39 In. 4945.00
Plaque, Theodore Roosevelt, Cast, James Earle Fraser, c.1920, 10 x 13 In. 130.00
Shackles, Leg, Revolutionary War 250.00
Stove Plate, Anchor, Tulip & Heart Medallion, Colebrookdale Furnace, 24 x 26 In. 195.00
Stove Plate, Arches, Tulips, Inscriptions, Amos Geret, c.1752, 27 x 28 1/2 In. 660.00
Stove Plate, Flowers, Scrolls, H.R. Stiegel, c.1769, 19 1/2 x 24 In. 990.00
Urn, 2 Handles, Art Deco Design, France, 21 1/2 In., Pair 1150.00
Urn, Classical, Scroll, Leaf Applied Handles, Rolled Edge, Pedestal, 28 x 21 In. 440.00
Urn, Victorian, Scrolled Lip, Fluted Base, 17 x 20 In., Pair 440.00

Vase, Teardrop, Iris, Goose, Crane, Grapevine, Dragonfly Mark, Komei, c.1910, 4 In. 805.00
Windmill Weight, Rooster, Silver & Red Paint, Hummer, Elgin Wind Power, 8 1/2 In. . . .   935.00

IRONSTONE china was first made in 1813. It gained its greatest popularity during the mid-nineteenth century. The heavy, durable, off-white pottery was made in white or was decorated with any of hundreds of patterns. Much flow blue pottery was made of ironstone. Some of the decorations were raised. Many pieces of ironstone are unmarked, but some English and American factories included the word *Ironstone* in their marks. Additional pieces may be listed in other categories, such as Chelsea Grape, Chelsea Sprig, Flow Blue, Gaudy Ironstone, Mason's Ironstone, Moss Rose, Staffordshire, and Tea Leaf Ironstone.

Bowl, Blue Willow, Pearl, Marked, Oval, Mid 19th Century, 2 1/2 x 12 1/4 In. 140.00
Bowl, Leaves, Teal, Green, Red Drape Design, 3 1/2 x 7 In. 110.00
Bowl, Men, Women, On Boneshaker, Velocipede, Transfer, c.1870, 6 3/4 In. 896.00
Bowl, Octagonal, Sepia Print, J. Clementson, Staffordshire, c.1850, 13 3/8 In. 165.00
Chamber Pot, Willow Transfer, Bishop & Stonier, c.1936, 6 x 9 1/2 In. 115.00
Chamber Set, Carnation Pattern, Green Transfer, 7 Piece . . . . .300.00 to 336.00
Coffeepot, Blue Transfer, Snowflake Dome Top, 9 1/4 In.   385.00
Coffeepot, Old English Simpsons, Ivy, Marlborough, 8 3/4 In. 45.00
Cup & Saucer, English Chippendale, Johnson Bros., Oversize, 9 1/2 & 11 1/2 In. 85.00
Cup & Saucer, Handleless, Snowflake Pattern, Blue Transfer 138.00
Cup Plate, Wheat & Clover, Turner & Tomkinson, 4 7/8 In. 35.00
Dinnerware Set, Paris White, Burleigh Ware, England, 198 Piece 230.00
Jug, Puzzle, Elsmore & Forster, 1867 . . . .   480.00
Jug, Puzzle, Harlequins, Fighting Cocks, Elsmore & Forster, 1867, 8 1/2 In. 460.00
Jug, Puzzle, Harlequins, Marbleized Green, Black Transfer, Elsmore & Forster 330.00
Pitcher, Dragon Handle, Flowers, Imari, c.1840, 5 In. 210.00
Pitcher, Hudson Democratic Society, Gold, New Jersey Seal, 1893, 9 In. . . . . *Illus*   575.00
Pitcher, Sheaf Of Wheat, 8 1/2 In. 135.00
Pitcher, Syrup, Imari, Hinged Pewter Lid, 19th Century, 7 1/4 In. 140.00
Plate, American Eagle & Shield, Flower & Geometric Border, Blue Transfer, 9 1/4 In. 855.00
Plate, Dinner, Multicolored Oriental Decoration, 10 1/2 In., 8 Piece 185.00
Platter, Blue Sponge, 13 1/2 In. 155.00
Platter, Blue Sponge, Rectangular, 13 1/2 x 10 In. 125.00
Platter, Exotic Birds, Blue Transfer, Hicks, Meigh & Johnson, 1822-1835 . . . .   805.00
Platter, Imari, Flower Filled Urn, Leaf & Scroll Border, Gilt, 1800s, 19 In. 470.00
Platter, Oriental Decoration, Ashworth, c.1875, 21 x 16 5/8 In. 546.00
Platter, Trees, Flowers, Imari, Scalloped Edge, England, c.1850, 17 In. 415.00
Platter, Well & Tree, Cunard Steamship, Crystal, John & George Alcock, 1839-1846 . . .   1495.00
Punch Bowl, Blue Transfer, Flowers, Scrolls, Gold Rim, Footed, c.1860, 9 1/2 In. 225.00
Tea Set, Mulberry, Sugar, Creamer, Waste Bowl, Teapot, 4 Piece 550.00
Teapot, Molded Ribs, Copper Luster Stripes, Flow Blue Leaves, Fruit Finial, 9 1/4 In. 115.00
Tobacco Jar, Cover, Flowers, Gold Lettering, Pipe Finial, 6 x 5 x 3 In., 2 Piece 80.00
Tray, Serving, Brown, White, 11 x 8 3/4 In. 290.00
Tureen, Ladle, Aesthetic, Songbirds, Japanese Fans, Brown Transfer, c.1879, 10 1/4 In. . .   288.00
Tureen, Ladle, White, Marked, Red Cliff 34.00
Tureen, Sauce, Cover, Dragon Handles, Imari Flowers, Octagonal, c.1850, 9 1/4 In. 635.00

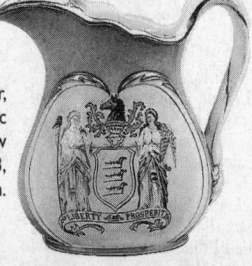

Ironstone, Pitcher,
Hudson Democratic
Society, Gold, New
Jersey Seal, 1893,
9 In.

Jasperware,
Cachepot, Greek
Scene, Teal Blue,
Impressed, Dudson,
England, 7 1/2 In.

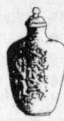

IVORY from the tusk of an elephant is thought by many to be the only true ivory. To most collectors, the term *ivory* also includes such natural materials as walrus, hippopotamus, or whale teeth or tusks, and some of the vegetable materials that are of similar texture and density. Other ivory items may be found in the Scrimshaw and Netsuke categories. Collectors should be aware of the recent laws limiting the buying and selling of elephant ivory and scrimshaw.

Baton, Conductor's, Gold Star Of David On Knob, 19th Century, 7 1/2 In..	670.00
Bottle, Snuff, Gourd, Insect, Carved, Chinese, 3 In.	185.00
Box, Cylinder, Chrysanthemum Design, Kazuyuki, 1868-1912, 2 1/2 In.	17.00
Box, Cylinder, Turtle Design, 1868-1912, 3 3/4 In.	575.00
Box, Dragons, Clouds, Japan, 1800s, 3 1/2 In.	940.00
Box, Dressing Table, Carved, Flower Bouquet, Round, Mid 19th Century, 1 x 2 3/4 In. . . .	1035.00
Box, Incense, Leaf Edge, 2 Phoenixes, Japan, 1800s, 2 3/4 In.	940.00
Box, Military Victory Commemoration, Continental, 8 1/2 In.	4480.00
Box, Oval Outline, Relief Figures, Elephants, Macaques, Japan, 19th Century, 3 x 4 In. . .	175.00
Bracelet, Asian Warrior Carving, Gold Tone Filigree Links, Wirework, Beads, 7 In.	206.00
Brushpot, Carved, African Male Lions, Signed, Japan, Early 20th Century, 3 x 2 1/2 In. . .	265.00
Brushpot, Warriors, Chinese, 1800s, 7 1/4 In.	1295.00
Card Case, Figural Cartouche, Flowers, Landscape, Early 1800s, 4 1/2 In.	575.00
Corkscrew, Whale Tooth Handle, Silver, PHV & C, England, 4 3/4 x 4 In.	259.00
Cross, High Relief, Roses, Lilies, Leaved Branches, Italy, 1800s, 3 1/2 In.	2300.00
Demi-Paure, Pin, Earrings, Grape Clusters, Leaves, Morning Glories, 1800s, 3 Piece	2070.00
Figurine, Bird, On Tree Stump, Vines, Carved, Wood Base, Ebonized, 9 1/4 In., Pair	405.00
Figurine, Buddha, Seated On Lotus Throne, Contemplative Pose, 4 3/4 In.	190.00
Figurine, Cherub, 5 1/4 In., Pair	2868.00
Figurine, Chinese Woman, Lying Down, Chinese, 1800s, 7 1/2 In.	315.00
Figurine, Cormorant Fisherman, 2 Cormorants, c.1900, 13 In.	1210.00
Figurine, Corpus Christi, Ebony Cross Molded Frame, Continental, 19th Century, 20 In. . .	2530.00
Figurine, Craftsman, Seated, Tools, Boxes, Signed, 1868-1912, 2 1/4 In.	520.00
Figurine, Dog, Long Fur, Inlaid Eyes, Early 1900s, 4 In.	230.00
Figurine, Elephant, 7 In.	45.00
Figurine, Emperor, Empress, Chinese, 8 3/4 In., Pair	885.00
Figurine, Emperor, Empress, Standing, 15 1/2 In., Pair	1535.00
Figurine, Farmer Gathering Cucumbers, Mitsuyuki, 1868-1912, 6 In.	805.00
Figurine, Farmer, Holding Rake, Sickle, 1868-1912, 9 In.	259.00
Figurine, Fate, Book, Flax Spindle, Renaissance Style, Germany, c.1885, 5 In.	260.00
Figurine, Female Nude, Holding Flower, Art Nouveau Style, 1900s, 8 In.	290.00
Figurine, Fisherman, Net, Pole, Basket, 1868-1912, 6 1/2 In.	400.00
Figurine, Fisherman, Running Through Waves, Carrying Basket, 8 In.	630.00
Figurine, Fisherman, Straw Hat, Grass Apron, Carrying Net, Conch Shell, 7 1/2 In.	550.00
Figurine, Foo Dog, On Pedestal, Loose Pearl In Mouth, Incised Signature, 4 In., Pair	400.00
Figurine, Gnome, Pedestal, Classical Enamel, Painted Band Of Children, 4 In.	367.00
Figurine, Horse, Chinese, 8 In.	500.00
Figurine, Kwan Yin, Elongated Features, Flowing Robe, Flower Basket, 9 1/2 In.	385.00
Figurine, Madonna & Child, Christ Child Holds Dove, Germany, 6 3/4 In.	480.00
Figurine, Man, Drinking Sake, Eating Fish, Masakazu, 1868-1912, 3 1/2 In.	375.00
Figurine, Man, Oriental, Dragon Robe, Sword, Elephant Headdress, Wood Base, 14 In. . .	525.00
Figurine, Man, Woman, Holding Broom, Signed, 4 1/8 x 4 1/4 In., Pair	259.00
Figurine, Mansai Dancer, Japan, Late 1800s, 5 1/4 In.	765.00
Figurine, Meiren Head, Chinese, 20th Century, 5 In.	470.00
Figurine, Meiren, Immortal, Chinese, 12 In., Pair	825.00
Figurine, Moses, Triptych, Hinged Robe, Discovery Of Baby Moses Inside, c.1910, 11 In.	865.00
Figurine, Mountain Climber, RAJ Initials, Continental, Early 20th Century, 4 1/2 In.	316.00
Figurine, Nio Holding Boxwood Mohyoku, Falling Demons, Japan, 1800s, 11 1/2 In.	3055.00
Figurine, Official, Woman, Hardwood Stand, Early 1900s, 12 In., Pair	748.00
Figurine, Oni, Basket Of Crabs, Gyokuzan, 1868-1912, 5 3/4 In.	375.00
Figurine, Penguin, Scrimshaw Eyes, 3 5/8 x 1 x 1 1/4 In.	300.00
Figurine, Puppeteer, Engraved Kimono, Kneeling, Holding Samurai Puppet, Japan, 6 In. .	805.00
Figurine, Seated Sage, Tatami Mat, Basket, Multicolored, Kyokusen, 1900s, 9 In.	690.00
Figurine, Sheep, Black Inked Eyes, Long Tails, 4 1/4 In., Pair	138.00
Figurine, Shoki Battles 2 Oni, Japan, 1868-1912, 6 1/4 In.	489.00

Figurine, Shou-Lao, Seated, Reading, Tiger, Clouds, Wood Stand, Japan, 1800s, 11 In. 1150.00
Figurine, Standing Maiden, Gilt Bronze, 13 In. 2868.00
Figurine, Swan, Wings Meeting Over Back, Amber Eyes, Silver Metal Beak, Feet, 2 In. ... 316.00
Figurine, Traveler By Signpost, Packages, Signed, c.1900, 8 1/2 In. 430.00
Figurine, Woman Holding Birdcage, Cockatoo, Removable Cover, 1868-1912, 9 1/2 In. ... 1670.00
Figurine, Woman Pulled In Rickshaw, Japan, 1800s, 6 1/2 In. 520.00
Figurine, Woman, Elderly, Brown Vest, Detailed Hair, Wood Base, Early 1900s, 10 1/2 In. 1095.00
Figurine, Woman, Oriental, Feeds Stork, Bird In Hair, 12 In. 240.00
Figurine, Woman, Oriental, Holding Vase, 4 1/2 In. 120.00
Figurine, Woman, Oriental, Holds Fan, 13 In. 205.00
Figurine, Woman, Oriental, Holds Sword, 12 In. 150.00
Figurine, Young Woman, 4 1/2 In. 310.00
Figurine, Young Woman, Fire Gilt, Sterling Base, Hase, 1920-1930s Style, 5 In. 255.00
Group, 2 Immortals, Hardwood Stand, Chinese, 19th Century, 23 1/2 In. 2875.00
Group, Foo Dog & Puppies, Wood Base, Chinese, c.1950, 7 1/2 In. 400.00
Group, Mask Seller, Oni, Japan, 1868-1912, 3 In. 185.00
Group, Washington Crossing The Delaware, Leather Case, Late 1800s, 7 1/2 x 9 3/4 In. ... 5020.00
Group, Woman In Rickshaw, Signed, 1868-1912, 6 3/4 In. 1380.00
Group, Young Woman Laborer, Water Buffalo, Wood Base, Chinese, c.1950, 9 1/2 In. ... 460.00
Incense Burner, Chinese, 8 In. 470.00
Magnifying Glass, Ivory Handle, Turtles On Tree Stump, 1868-1912, 10 1/2 In. 115.00
Match Holder, Initials, Silver Decoration, 2 x 1 In. 150.00
Miniature, Portrait, Child, Bonnet, Apple, Brass Frame, Liner, Smart, 5 1/2 x 4 1/2 In. ... 523.00
Miniature, Portrait, Gentleman, Blue Eyes, Sideburns, Cape, Frame, 8 3/4 x 7 1/2 In. 430.00
Miniature, Portrait, George Washington, Flowers, Copper, Gainsborough, 5 1/2 x 5 In. ... 303.00
Miniature, Portrait, George Washington, Frame, Sarah Goodridge, 6 7/8 x 5 7/8 In. 1840.00
Miniature, Portrait, Girl In White Dress, Glazed Gold Locket, c.1790, 2 1/4 x 2 1/4 In. ... 590.00
Miniature, Portrait, Girl, Dress, Dog, Romney, Frame, Oval, Ribbon Crest, 4 3/4 x 3 In. .. 374.00
Miniature, Portrait, John Barry, Black Frame, H. Frost, c.1830, 5 3/4 x 4 3/4 In. 1150.00
Miniature, Portrait, Lady Blessington, Initialed TH, 1832, 4 x 3 3/4 In. 345.00
Miniature, Portrait, Louis XVI, Lady Of Fashion, Frame, Weber, Riaolet, c.1885, 3 3/4 In. 201.00
Miniature, Portrait, Louis XVI, Landscape Setting, Frame, 5 3/4 x 4 3/4 In. 259.00
Miniature, Portrait, Man, Seated By Window, Red Curtain, Brass Frame, 3 1/2 x 2 1/2 In. 230.00
Miniature, Portrait, Man, Wearing Glasses, Signed, M. Hart, c.1885, 3 1/4 In. 476.00
Miniature, Portrait, Mary, Queen Of Scots, Frame, Brass Acorn, c.1820, 5 3/4 x 5 In. 230.00
Miniature, Portrait, Medieval Woman, Pearl Earrings, Castle, Rene, Frame, 4 5/8 x 4 In. . 230.00
Miniature, Portrait, Military Officer, Blue Jacket, Gold Epaulettes, Brass Frame, 4 x 3 In. 86.00
Miniature, Portrait, Patrick Henry, Signed, J. Smart, Frame, 8 1/4 x 7 1/4 In. 805.00
Miniature, Portrait, Persian Sultan, Ebony Easel Frame, 5 x 3 1/4 In. 83.00
Miniature, Portrait, Queen, Gold Crown, Pearls, Ermine Wrap, Derval, Frame, 4 x 3 In. .. 805.00
Miniature, Portrait, Thomas Sumter, Ebonized Frame, Sarah Goodridge, 6 3/8 x 5 1/4 In. . 1955.00
Miniature, Portrait, Woman, Blue Dress, Frame, c.1810, 4 x 4 1/2 In. 365.00
Miniature, Portrait, Woman, Pearls, Flowers In Hair, Frame, R. Carriera, 4 1/4 x 3 1/2 In. . 403.00
Miniature, Portrait, Woman, Wig, Brass Frame, R. Cosway, 1778, 3 x 2 3/8 In. 330.00
Miniature, Portrait, Young Man, Curly Hair, Gray Eyes, Brass Rope Frame, 3 1/4 In. 290.00
Okimono, Ashinaga Holds Basket, Fish, Signed, Late 1800s, 9 In. 891.00
Okimono, Cat, Lotus, Carp, 1868-1912, 4 In. 575.00
Okimono, Farmer, Peasant, Landscape, Pine Trees, 1868-1912, 5 1/4 In. 230.00
Okimono, Fisherman Standing On One Foot, Fish, Basket, Pole, 8 1/2 In. 472.00
Okimono, Hawk On Tree Stump, Signed, 1868-1912, 2 1/2 In. 259.00
Okimono, Inkwell, 2 Dragons, Round, 4 In. 354.00
Okimono, Man Cutting Large Radish, 1868-1912, 2 1/2 In. 316.00
Okimono, Man, Woman, Large Clamshell, 1800s, 3 3/4 In. 431.00
Okimono, Man, Woman, Tying Treasure Sack, Tomochika, Late 1800s, 3 In. 690.00
Okimono, Noh Mask Carver Holding Basket & Doll, 6 In. 767.00
Okimono, Short Man, Long Beard, Holds Stick, Japan, 1926-1989, 3 In. 153.00
Okimono, Takarabune, Gods Of Good Fortune, Early 1900s, 3 3/4 In. 259.00
Okimono, Woman Carrying Child On Back, Comb Shopping, 1800s, 2 3/4 In. 230.00
Pagoda, 5 Tiers, Japan, Late 1800s, 19 In. 195.00
Pie Crimper, Pierced Carved Hearts, Scrolling, 2 1/4 In. Wheel, 7 1/4 In. 1380.00
Pillbox, Figural Landscape, High Relief, Chinese Export, c.1830, 1 1/2 In. 40.00
Plaque, Ancestral, Rectangular, Man With Masonic Medal, 1770-1848, 5 1/2 x 4 1/2 In. ... 715.00
Pokal, Battle Scene, Pedestal Base, c.1850, 10 3/4 In. 1708.00

THE UNIQUE AND UNUSUAL SALES OF THE YEAR

Innumerable antiques and collectibles are sold every year. Collectors buy for many reasons—nostalgia, usefulness, artistic value, historic importance, humor factor, or emotional appeal. This is a picture gallery of pieces we would have liked to own. Some we bid on and lost; some we passed at flea markets. But we learned long ago that "you only regret what you don't buy." Here are this year's regrets.

Several companies made unusual Art Nouveau-inspired pottery in the Teplitz-Turn area of Bohemia. This elaborate 21-inch vase by the Amphora Porcelain Works is a nineteenth-century example. Scrambling up the side through the blackberries are lifelike children. This piece would be noticed in any room. It sold for $ 2,300.

No question: This is an Egyptian Revival piece that might have looked great with our Egyptian Revival chair. But the 6-foot-wide screen was too large and cost $10,600, so it now belongs to another collector.

Photo credit: New Orleans Auction Galleries, New Orleans, Louisiana

We had never before seen a Bakelite candlestick phone decorated in an Arts and Crafts hammered copper casing. This 1910 American Bell Telephone Company phone was embellished by the famous Roycrofters, which explains the $8,000 price.

Photo credit: David Rago Auctions, Lambertville, New Jersey

Modern reproduction flasks are easy to find for under $10, but a true collector wants the real thing, even if it costs $56,100. That was the price of this very rare eagle-eaglet yellow-olive-colored flask with a green mouth, made in Pittsburgh between 1825 and 1835.

Flag-decorated antiques are always popular. This unique American mahogany writing table, made in about 1900, has a military theme. The legs and tabletop corners look like cannon barrels and cannon balls. The crosspieces between the legs are shaped like muskets. The trim looks like pyramids of cannon balls. But the wooden red, white, and blue flag top is the ultimate expression of the designer-carver's patriotism. This table, estimated at $6,000 to $8,000, sold for $42,000.

This pensive crab is actually a tureen, probably for a fish stew or crab bisque. The eighteenth-century Chinese Export tureen, only 8 ⁵⁄₈ inches long, created a stir when it sold at auction for $276,300.

Colored glass became fashionable just after the Civil War, with many new types available on the market. This pink shaded glass with a mother-of-pearl herringbone pattern has enameled floral designs on the outside and yellow glass on the inside. The silver-plated base is marked Meriden. It was included in a large sale of Victorian art glass and auctioned for $1,840.

Tiffany Studios made famous lamps with leaded glass shades and smaller decorative pieces like glass vases or bronze desk sets. About twenty desk set patterns were made. A basic desk set had six pieces: a letter rack, blotter ends, inkstand, box, pen tray, and letter opener. You could also get a matching calendar, stamp box, pen holder, ashtray, picture frame, thermometer, or bookends. This bronze and colored enamel set in the Bookmark pattern sold for $22,705 to a collector who must have a neater desk than ours.

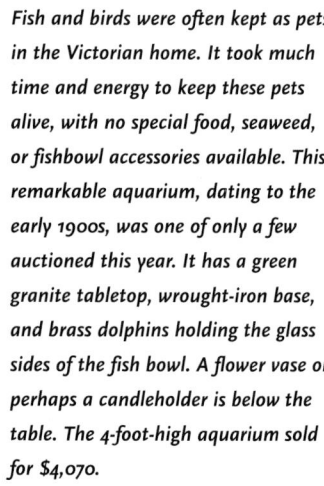

Fish and birds were often kept as pets in the Victorian home. It took much time and energy to keep these pets alive, with no special food, seaweed, or fishbowl accessories available. This remarkable aquarium, dating to the early 1900s, was one of only a few auctioned this year. It has a green granite tabletop, wrought-iron base, and brass dolphins holding the glass sides of the fish bowl. A flower vase or perhaps a candleholder is below the table. The 4-foot-high aquarium sold for $4,070.

Birdcages from the nineteenth century were often fanciful creations. This painted tin and wirework riverboat birdcage has four tiers, tin paddlewheels, floors, smokestacks, a sailor, and even an American flag. Not much room for the bird, because it is only 25 1/4 inches wide by 29 inches long. Still, it brought $2,940 at auction.

Victorian dining room sideboards and servers were often made with three-dimensional carvings of edible mammals, like pigs and deer, and edible fish, birds, and plants. We wonder why this walnut server by Alexander Roux of New York featured a pair of life-size dogs. Perhaps they are hunting dogs. The other carvings include oak leaves and acorns, grapes, grouse, a frog, flowers, and leaves. The 49 1/2-inch-high server sold at auction for a record $189,750.

This silvered bronze head of a mean-looking bull-mastiff is hiding an inkwell. The hinged head opens to reveal a brass and glass well. The brass tag on the collar opens into a locket for pictures, or perhaps the hair of a loved one. It may have been made by Franz Xavier Bergman, a nineteenth-century Austrian. Although only 6 inches high, it sold for $4,600.

Fenton glass does not have to be old or expensive to be collectible. The company, founded in Martins Ferry, Ohio, operates today in Williamstown, West Virginia. This light blue satin glass candy dish, 6 $1/2$ inches high, was made between 1973 and 1984. The Persian medallion mold for the piece was originally used for carnival glass. This year the dish is worth $30.

Bessie must have had fun with this painted wood and iron sled. The top of the sled has a scenic picture of sailboats on a mountain lake, an odd decoration for a toy that was used in the snow. The iron strapwork and runners are typical of the work found on sleds of the late nineteenth century. It sold as a piece of folk art for $764.

Beauties of 100 years ago were not as thin as those admired today. This early twentieth-century figure shows a voluptuous woman bathing. It is signed on the bottom with the pink triangle mark of the Royal Dux porcelain factory of Dux, Bohemia (now Duchov, Czech Republic). It attracted a buyer at $865.

In the 1980s, iridescent glass was identified as Tiffany or Steuben or probably just considered "unknown." Now collectors seek the iridescent glass of Loetz, Durand, and others, and experts can identify each type from the design and color of the glass. Glass made years ago by Loetz, an Austrian company, is now a favorite of collectors and is getting more expensive. This 9 ½-inch textured glass vase has a blue oilspot finish and applied seashells. It auctioned for $3,910. But pieces of Loetz are rarely marked and can be found at bargain prices at house sales and rummage sales.

Pressed glass made in the 1800s is back in favor. This amber-colored deer and pine tree mug sold for $45 a few years ago. Today it costs $70. Watch out for reproductions made in the 1930s and 1950s, and even more recently.

"American Satsuma" seems like a strange name, since Satsuma is a Japanese pottery. During World War I (1914–1918), American women who decorated china could not buy pieces made in Germany. Instead they used Satsuma. The pieces, like this potpourri jar, were painted with western-style designs. This piece is even signed by the decorator, "Luman." It is worth $200, but this type of Satsuma is not well-known. We have collected it for years.

Dresser sets were different during the Edwardian era. This set has a tray, a hair receiver, a hatpin holder, and a dish for soap or pins. The birds were hand-painted on this yellow tray, made by John Tams Ltd. of England. The signature dates the piece to after 1912. It sold for only $50, the value of the hatpin holder or the tray.

Unusual kitchen stuff is fun and often useful. This 3 $^3/_8$-inch-high figure of a chimney sweep holds an egg timer. This type of egg timer was popular starting in the 1920s and is still made today. They were made in Germany, Japan, and England as inexpensive trinkets, but today the chimney sweep sells for $65.

In the 1960s, these cowgirl candles were used on a birthday cake. They were just one of many figural candle sets made by the Gurley Novelty Company of Buffalo, New York. The colored candles have faded, and the blue eyes and colorful dresses are just a memory. The package of six candles sold for 25 cents when new. Today candle collectors will pay $15.

Folk art is a term that includes many different types of carvings, paintings, and ceramics made by untrained artists. This painted wooden eagle from a Hudson River steamboat, carved in about 1850, sells as folk art today. It is 41 inches long and sold for $19,360 at auction.

One of these figurines is missing its head and hands, but both were saved because they belonged to George Washington. The 6-inch figurines are made of English soft-paste porcelain. A 1759 invoice recording the purchase by Col. George Washington sold with the figurines. That's why they were auctioned for $45,410. Without the invoice, they would have sold for less than $7,000.

Drop-leaf tables were made to take up a small space near a wall and open up to be a large table for playing cards or dining. This cherry Queen Anne table, made in Massachusetts in about 1760, is as useful today as it was in the past and looks great in a dining room. At $7,200, it's a good investment.

A lesson in "good, better, best" in Sandwich glass—all sold at the same auction. The hexagonal candlestick in canary glass sold for $55, the Dolphin canary candlestick was $187, and the blue and clambroth Acanthus Leaf candlestick was $660.

The Door of Hope Mission in China made and sold dolls from 1917 to 1950. This pair of 6-inch child dolls, made of carved wood and wearing silk outfits, auctioned for $5,175.

Everyone wants to own a "museum piece." Museums "edit" collections by selling some pieces at public sales. The Metropolitan Museum deaccessioned this 79-inch-long Rococo Revival settee made in New York in 1855. Why? Because the museum owns a similar sofa that was displayed in its 1976 "19th Century America" exhibit. It sold for $9,560.

We wanted to bid on this Faience Manufacturing Company potpourri keeper, but we knew the $500 to $700 estimate was too low. It was. The spectacular piece, 19 inches high and made in about 1885 in Greenpoint, New York, sold to a museum for $9,000.

There is still much confusion about the age of Rose Medallion and related porcelain from China. The Rose Medallion pattern has a bird or peony in its medallions and the surrounding panels show people. This ware was out of fashion with collectors in the United States from 1900 until the mid-1990s. Rose Medallion porcelain has been made since the eighteenth century; this vase probably dates from the late nineteenth century. Prices have been rising, so the 17 1/2-inch-high vase sold for $750.

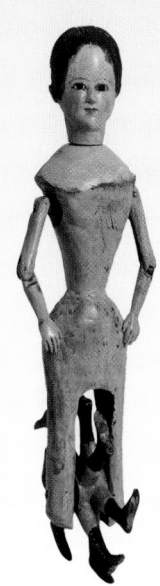

Some antiques are just plain fun! This early nineteenth-century wooden doll has seven legs so it can "walk." The legs act like spokes on a revolving wheel and when a dress covers all but the doll's feet, it looks as if she has two walking legs. The doll is made of carved wood, with head, arms, and, of course, legs that move. It is rare, valuable, and entertaining, so a determined bidder paid $6,390 to own her.

Hot air balloons were oddities and wonders as early as the eighteenth century. This mechanical tin Ferris wheel, only 4 inches high, was a penny toy when new. This year it sold for $4,070.

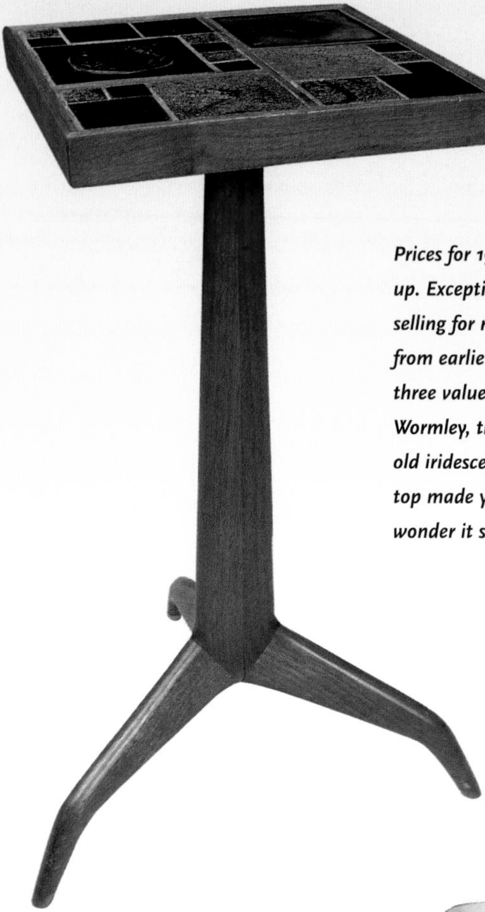

Photo credit: Jackson's Auctioneers & Appraisers, Cedar Falls, Iowa

Prices for 1950s furniture are moving up. Exceptional designer pieces are selling for more than good furniture from earlier centuries. This table has three value pluses: the designer Edward Wormley, the maker Dunbar, and the old iridescent Favrile glass tiles on the top made years before by Tiffany. No wonder it sold for $8,280.

Photo credit: Jackson's Auctioneers & Appraisers, Cedar Falls, Iowa

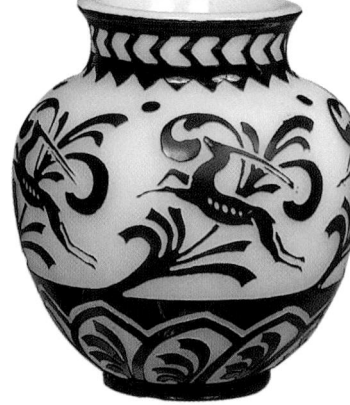

Sometimes an antique or collectible triggers an emotional reaction. We remember Mother's Steuben acid-etched lamp in black over alabaster, so this vase seemed like it belonged with us. But we did not bid, even though the Art Deco leaping gazelle pattern was appealing. Estimated at under $2,500, it sold for $5,060.

These tin candy container buildings have been selling regularly for over thirty years. A dealer in advertising collectibles found hundreds of the flat pieces of tin, and he and his friends bent them into shape. They sold them without the glass containers that they would have covered. This lot probably was not part of that great find, because each tin building has its original glass liner impressed "West Bros. Co., Grapeville, Pa., Net Wt. 1 ¼ oz., Serial No. 2862." The set was shown in a 1914 wholesale catalog. No wonder the bid for all 14 was $2,860—about $200 each.

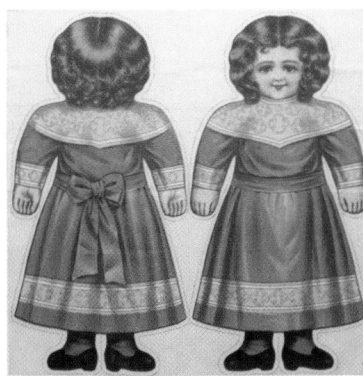

Cloth dolls have been made from printed fabric since the end of the nineteenth century. This doll, marked "Art Rag Doll, Thompson's Mail Order" was offered for sale in about 1900. Cut out the front and back, sew them together, stuff them, and you have a 14-inch doll. The uncut fabric is worth $105.

Who would ever save empty cereal boxes? If the box pictures a figure from sports, television, radio, or the comics, there are lots of collectors willing to pay for it. This empty 1936 Post Grape-Nuts cereal box picturing Dizzy Dean, the great baseball pitcher, auctioned for $604. We understand why someone would buy it today. What amazes us is that the empty box has been carefully preserved for 70 years. It may be the only surviving complete box.

Sometimes collectors long for a huge item but settle for a small one because of space or money. There are 4-foot-high Mr. Peanut iron scales that have sold for over $8,000, and a larger-than-life-sized Mr. Peanut costume was offered at a flea market a few years ago for $700. But one collector delighted in this 9-inch-high plastic Mr. Peanut wind-up walker toy that sold for only $230.

The upper class in Victorian England liked to use a special dish for each type of food. This stand with six removable eggcups helped make breakfast look like a feast. George Jones & Sons made the colorful majolica stand that attracted a buyer at $1,792.

Puzzle Ball, 7 Balls, Figural Handle, Ivory Chain, Wood Case, 1800s, 7 1/2 In. 863.00
Puzzle Ball, Ball In Dragon, 3 Elephant Form Supports, Stand, 1800s, 5 3/4 In. 230.00
Puzzle Ball, Stand, Brocade, Dragon Pattern, 1800s, 3 1/2 x 14 1/4 In. 2185.00
Seal, Elephant Shape, Chinese, 1800s, 2 3/4 In. 230.00
Serving Set, Fork, Spoon, Shovel Form Handles, 10 In. 259.00
Shoehorn, Horse Hoof Handle, Brass, Wood, Leather Loop, Hermes, 1930s, 21 In. 175.00
Snooker Ball, Globe, Engraved, 1900s, 2 1/4 In. 115.00
Snuffbox, Carved, Chinese, 7/8 x 1 In. 81.00
Spoon, Snuff, Stand, 1 1/4 In. 92.00
Table Screen, Figures Smoking Pipes, Monkeys, Japan, 1868-1912, 8 1/2 x 7 In. 5635.00
Tusk, 14 Elephants, Graduated Row, Carved Wood Base, 23 x 4 1/2 In. 300.00
Tusk, Figures, Flower Landscape, Wood Stand, Chinese, Late 20th Century, 19 In. 345.00
Tusk, Pavilions, Gardens, Chinese, 8 In. 235.00
Urn, Classical Style, Wood Base, 8 In. 225.00
Vase, Dragons After Flaming Pearl, Pierced, Hardwood Stand, 19th Century, 10 In. 290.00
Wand, Hand, 19 In. 230.00

JACK-IN-THE-PULPIT vases, oddly shaped like trumpets, resemble the
wild plant called jack-in-the-pulpit. The design originated in the late
Victorian years. Vases in the jack-in-the-pulpit shape were made of
ceramic or glass, and the complete list of page references can be found
in the index.

Vase, Gold Iridescent, Threaded, Glass, 8 In. 357.00
Vase, Iridescent Amber, Clear Stem, Black Disc, Signed, Rick Strini, 10 In. 155.00
Vase, Iridescent Green, Gold Pulled Feathers, Button Pontil, Signed, 13 1/2 In. 630.00
Vase, Opalescent, Ribbed, Silver Plated Foot Holder, 8 1/4 In., Pair 259.00
Vase, Pastel Green, Satin, Vertical Ribs, 5 1/2 In. 140.00
Vase, Pink Flower, Yellow Ribs, Cased Stem, Raised Disc, 14 1/4 In., Pair 518.00
Vase, Pink Shaded To White, Ruffled Edge, Applied Foot, Italy, 12 In. 109.00
Vase, Shaded Blue Satin To Pearl Gray, Bulbous, 6 In. 165.00
Vase, Vertical Latticinio, Ribbon Canes, Italy, 7 In. 120.00

JADE is the name for two different minerals, nephrite and jadeite.
Nephrite is the mineral used for most early Oriental carvings. Jade is a
very tough stone that is found in many colors from dark green to pale
lavender. Jade carvings are still being made in the old styles, so collectors must be careful not to be fooled by recent pieces. Jade jewelry
is found in this book under Jewelry.

Archer's Thumb Ring, Convex Cylindrical Sides, Dark Green, Chinese, 18th Century 130.00
Bi-Disk, Serpentine, Chinese, 3 3/4 In. 35.00
Bowl, Carved, Nephrite, Dragon, Wooden Stand, Mid 20th Century, 9 1/2 x 8 1/2 x 3 In. . .   1008.00
Bowl, Celadon Stone, Bat Carved Handle, Tao Tieh Masks, Chinese, 1700s, 6 In. 380.00
Bowl, Cover, Green, Carved His Hsuang Characters, Bats, Flowers, c.1800, 5 1/2 In. 1880.00
Brush Rest, Gray, Crane & Deer In Pine Grove, 6 3/4 In. 175.00
Carving, Buddha's Hand, Fruit, Celadon, Wooden Stand, 1700s, 6 1/2 In. 5175.00
Carving, Goddess Of Mercy, Green, Chinese, Late 1800s, 8 3/4 In. 1410.00
Carving, Goddess Quan Yin, Pale Green, Chinese, 1900s, 5 1/2 In. 355.00
Carving, Green Yellow, 2 Puppies, Ling Chih Boughs In Mouth, Chinese, 1800s, 3 In. 410.00
Censer, Yellowish Celadon, Chinese, 5 1/2 In. 295.00
Cup, Bell Shape, Early 1900s, 2 1/4 In. 29.00
Dish, Smokey, Foo Dog Cover, 2 Pierced Handles, 3 Legs, 4 x 3 In. 58.00
Figurine, Camel, Lying Down, Head Resting Between 2 Humps, Sage Green, 5 In. 345.00
Figurine, Horse, Celadon, Chinese, Late 1800s, 5 1/2 In. 175.00
Figurine, Man, Riding On Mountain, Carved Wooden Base, Mid 20th Century, 11 x 10 In.   1456.00
Figurine, Mandarin Duck, Lying Down, Pale Gray Celadon, Chinese, c.1900, 8 In. 635.00
Figurine, Pi, Pierced Floral Design, White Jade, Wooden Stand, 1800s, 4 3/4 In. 196.00
Figurine, Sage, Branch Of Peaches, White, c.1900, 2 1/4 In. 35.00
Fingering Piece, 3 Cats, Late 1800s, 1 1/2 In. 90.00
Fingering Piece, Liu Hai, String Of Cash, 3-Legged Frog, White, 1800s, 2 In. 160.00
Fingering Piece, White, Monkey & Young, 1800s, 1 3/8 In. 29.00
Fingernail Guard, Bat, Shou, Coin, White, 1800s, 2 3/8 In. 29.00
Foo Dog, Green, Chinese, 1800s, 5 1/2 In. 470.00
Group, 2 Boys, Russet Light Celadon, Chinese, 1900s, 5 In. 460.00

Group, Lino, Brocade Ball, Pup, 1800s, 2 1/2 In. 949.00
Hairpin, White, Bow Shape, 1800s, 3 1/2 In. 40.00
Libation Cup, Green, Pale Blue, Clouds, Dragons, 1800s, 4 3/4 In. 575.00
Paperweight, Yellow White, Pair Of Peaches, Leaves, Bird, Chinese, 1800s, 4 In. 176.00
Scepter, Ju-I Carved, Ling Chih, Pale Green White, Chinese, 1800s, 17 In. 880.00
Scroll Weight, White, Rectangular, Monkeys Gathering Peaches, 1700s, 8 In., Pair 2875.00
Sculpture, Carved, Grapevine, Branches, Chinese, 11 1/2 x 9 In. 805.00
Seal, Double, Huan Form, Mythical Animal, White, Brown Marks, Chinese, 1700s, 2 In. . . 118.00
Spoon, Branch Form, Relief Carved Leaves & Flowers, 1800s, 4 1/2 In. 69.00
Toggle, Amber, Boy & Foo Dog, Chinese, 1800s, 2 In. 264.00
Vase, 3 Friends, Flowering Prunus, Bamboo, Pine, Black, White, Chinese, 1800s, 5 In. . . . 1295.00
Vase, 3-Section Jade Tree, Multicolored Jade Leaves, Flowers, 20 x 20 In. 345.00
Vase, Cover, Mogul Style, Relief Carved Flowers, c.1800, 6 In. 4600.00
Vase, White, Jug Form, Late 1700s, 7 1/2 In. 7360.00

JAPANESE WOODBLOCK PRINTS are listed in this book in the Print category under
Japanese.

JASPERWARE can be made in different ways. Some pieces are made
from a solid colored clay with applied raised designs of a contrasting
colored clay. Other pieces are made entirely of one color clay with
raised decorations that are glazed with a contrasting color. Additional
pieces of jasperware may also be listed in the Wedgwood category or
under various art potteries.

Biscuit Jar, Dark Blue, White, Hunt Scene, Silver Plated Fittings, Adams, 7 In. 275.00
Cachepot, Greek Scene, Teal Blue, Impressed, Dudson, England, 7 1/2 In. . . . . *Illus* 185.00
Pitcher, Blue & White, Classical Figures, Adams, Early 1900s, 6 In. 80.00
Pitcher, Blue & White, Grapes, Grapevine, Early 1900s, 6 1/2 In. 65.00
Plaque, Indian Chasing Buffalo, Green, White, Oval, 5 3/4 x 5 In. 135.00
Tankard, White Classical Figures, Blue, Sheffield Silver Rim, England, c.1790, 6 In. 560.00

JEWELRY, whether made from gold and precious gems or plastic and
colored glass, is popular with collectors. Values are determined by the
intrinsic value of the stones and metal and by the skill of the craftsmen
and designers. Victorian and older jewelry have been collected since
the 1950s. More recent interests are Art Deco and Edwardian styles,
Mexican and Danish silver jewelry, and beads of all kinds. Copies of
almost all styles are being made. American Indian jewelry is listed in
the Indian category. Tiffany jewelry is listed here.

Arm Cuff, Snake, Mesh, Braided, 18K Gold 700.00
Belt, Link, Silver, Niello, Imperial Russian, 1 1/2 x 30 In. 290.00
Belt, Mesh, Silver, Vermeil, Crystal Buckle, Adjustable, 31 x 1 1/4 In. 259.00
Belt, Silver, Flowers, Butterflies, Pierced, Rectangular, c.1900, 33 In. 259.00
Belt Buckle, Sterling Silver, Tortoiseshell Plaque, Silver Rivets, Pineda, Mexico, 1950 . . . 380.00
Bracelet, 12 Mine Cut Diamonds, 14K White Gold, Art Deco, c.1920, 6 1/2 In. 1955.00
Bracelet, 15 Diamonds, 15 Sapphires, 14K Yellow Gold, Tiffany & Co. 2000.00
Bracelet, Agate, Cairngorms, Bloodstone, Gold Mounted, Scotland, c.1850, 7 In. 3200.00
Bracelet, Bangle, 10 Diamonds, 18K Gold, Hinged, Tiffany & Co. 1410.00
Bracelet, Bangle, 15K Yellow Gold, England, c.1865, 1 1/2 In. Wide 900.00
Bracelet, Bangle, 4-Leaf Clover, Seed Pearl, Green Stones, 14K Gold, Hinged, Edwardian 265.00
Bracelet, Bangle, Bakelite, Flower Band, Green, Hinged 200.00
Bracelet, Bangle, Bakelite, Leaf Band, Ivory, Pierced & Carved 230.00
Bracelet, Bangle, Bakelite, Sunflower, Ivory, Carved 215.00
Bracelet, Bangle, Bakelite, Zigzag, Green, Yellow 240.00
Bracelet, Bangle, Coral, Scrolling Leaf, 14K Gold, Riker Brothers, 1907 . . . . 880.00
Bracelet, Bangle, Filigree, Iridescent Pink Beads, Miriam Haskell 79.00
Bracelet, Bangle, Flower, Leaf Scrolls, Tooled Ground, 14K Gold, Oval, Victorian 375.00
Bracelet, Bangle, Hinged, 10 Diamonds, Platinum, 18K Gold, Tiffany & Co., 5 1/2 In. . . . 1495.00
Bracelet, Bangle, Hinged, Buckle, 14K Gold, Engraved, c.1900 . . . . 780.00
Bracelet, Bangle, Hinged, Cameo, Classical Profiles, Roberge, 18K Gold, 7 In. 1495.00
Bracelet, Bangle, Hinged, Cultured Pearl, Diamond, 14K Gold, Edwardian 1000.00
Bracelet, Bangle, Hinged, Rose Cut Diamond, Seed Pearls, Bead, Wirework, 15K Gold . . 645.00
Bracelet, Bangle, Hinged, Stirrup, Sterling Silver, Gucci 380.00
Bracelet, Bangle, Hinged, Wirework, Twisted, Stylized Lion Heads, 18K Gold 801.00

Bracelet, Bangle, Lapis, Beaded Wirework, 18K Gold, Etruscan Revival 3408.00
Bracelet, Bangle, Love, 18K Gold, Screwdriver, Cartier, Box ....1610.00 to 1765.00
Bracelet, Bangle, Pearl, Diamond, Openwork, Black, Starr & Frost, Edwardian 1530.00
Bracelet, Bangle, Ribbed Design, 18K Yellow Gold, Cartier, Box 880.00
Bracelet, Bangle, Serpent Shape, Garnet Eyes, 14K Gold, c.1885 .... 920.00
Bracelet, Bangle, Sterling Silver, Aquamarine, 14K Gold, D. Yurman 765.00
Bracelet, Bangle, Turquoise, Cultured Pearl, 14K Yellow Gold, c.1960 .... 300.00
Bracelet, Bangle, Twisted, 18K Gold, Italy 1035.00
Bracelet, Blue Enamel, Mother-Of-Pearl, Paste Diamond, Gold, Victorian .... *Illus* 600.00
Bracelet, Book, Rose Cut Diamond Binding, Flowers, Enamel, 7 In................. 2000.00
Bracelet, Cameo, Diamond Border, 15K Yellow Gold, c.1880 .... 1680.00
Bracelet, Cameo, Pearl Border, Openwork Band, 14K Gold, Box 1020.00
Bracelet, Cameo, Shell, Profile, Classical Woman, 15K Gold, England, c.1880, 5 In. 600.00
Bracelet, Carnelian, Agate, Silver, Engraved, Scotland, c.1900 .... 345.00
Bracelet, Chain D'Ancre, Sterling Silver, Toggle Clasp, Signed, Hermes, 8 In. 940.00
Bracelet, Chain, Maple Leaves, Carved Red Celluloid, 7 1/2 In. 65.00
Bracelet, Charm, 30 Assorted Charms, Silvertone & Sterling Silver, Monet 42.00
Bracelet, Charm, Fleur-De-Lis, Faux Turquoise, Goldtone Metal, 7 In.............. 42.00
Bracelet, Charm, Hawaiian, Pink & Yellow Enamel, Rhinestones, 1950s 80.00
Bracelet, Charm, Scottie Dog, Dangling In Dog House, Goldtone Metal, Monet 20.00
Bracelet, Charm, Scottie Dogs, Pearl Discs, Monogram, Bird In Cage, 14K Yellow Gold . 415.00
Bracelet, Coiled Wire, Peridot, Tourmaline, Sapphire Beads, Gold, Feldbaum, 7 1/2 In. .. 765.00
Bracelet, Coin, Love Token, Engraved Reverse, 1875-1883, 7 1/2 In. .... *Illus* 85.00
Bracelet, Coin, Pesos, Mexican, 18K Gold, 1945 .... 705.00
Bracelet, Cuff, Abstract, Rolled Edge, Sterling Silver, Elsa Peretti, Tiffany & Co. 316.00
Bracelet, Cuff, Black Leather, Gold Pyramid Accents, Hermes, 7 1/2 In............ 500.00
Bracelet, Cuff, Brass, Applied Sterling Silver Wire, Art Smith 10000.00
Bracelet, Cuff, Burgundy Leather, Gold Pyramid Accents, Hermes, 7 1/2 In. 410.00
Bracelet, Cuff, Clear Rhinestones, Blanket Set, Monet, 1 1/2 In. Wide 32.00
Bracelet, Cuff, Etruscan Style, 15K Gold, Engraved, Gretchen Danz, c.1890 .... 660.00
Bracelet, Cuff, Hinged, Rope Twist, Silver, Ball Terminals, 14K Gold, Yurman 355.00
Bracelet, Cuff, Hinged, Tapered, Engraved Flowers, Brushed, 18K Gold 410.00
Bracelet, Cuff, Sterling Silver, Georg Jensen, c.1940 .... 865.00
Bracelet, Cultured Pearl, 14K Gold Mount, Mikimoto, 7 1/4 In. 1295.00
Bracelet, Cultured Pearl, 18K Gold, Silver Clasp, Buccellati, 7 In. 825.00
Bracelet, Curb Link, Flattened, Diamond, 18K Gold, Tiffany, 6 7/8 In. 1530.00
Bracelet, Daisies, Vines, Leaves, Diamond, 18K Bicolor Gold, Paul Morelli, 7 In. 940.00
Bracelet, Diamond Melee, Bezel Set, Mesh, 18K Gold, Boucheron, Paris, 6 3/4 In. 5580.00
Bracelet, Diamond, 14K White Gold, c.1960, 6 3/4 In. 865.00
Bracelet, Diamond, Art Deco, Platinum, c.1930, 7 1/4 In......................... 4830.00
Bracelet, Diamond, Brickwork Mesh, 14K Gold, Van Cleef & Arpels, Silk Pouch, 7 In. .. 3760.00
Bracelet, Diamond, Leaves, 18K Gold, Angela Cummings, 1986 .... 1175.00
Bracelet, Dome Shape, Blue Enamel, Rose Cut Diamonds, 15K Gold, England, c.1840 .. 780.00
Bracelet, Double Link, Rope Twist, Diamond, Platinum, Art Deco, 6 3/4 In. 360.00
Bracelet, Dragonfly, Pierce Wings, Sterling Silver, Art Nouveau, 2 3/8 In. 345.00
Bracelet, Flexible, Square Box Illusion, Platinum, Diamond, Art Deco, c.1920, 7 In. 2530.00
Bracelet, Garter, Ribbon, Mesh, Ogee Slide, 18K Gold, Victorian 635.00
Bracelet, Green Chrysoprase, 18K Gold Hand Clasp, G. Kiss, 7 1/2 In. 880.00
Bracelet, Hinged, Bear, Diamond In Teeth, 14K Gold, Art Nouveau, Alling & Co. 2235.00
Bracelet, Hinged, Serpent Shape, Ruby Eyes, 14K Yellow & Pink Gold, Victorian, 6 In. ... 405.00
Bracelet, Jadeite, Carved Flowers, Pierced Plaques, Gilt Silver Mount, 6 1/2 In. 411.00
Bracelet, Lapis, Turquoise, 10 Strands, 18K Gold Clasp, Verdura, 8 In................ 3290.00
Bracelet, Link, 15K Yellow Gold, England, c.1890 .... 510.00
Bracelet, Link, Amethyst, Scrolls, Art Nouveau, 14K Gold, 7 1/2 In.................. 5175.00
Bracelet, Link, Amethyst, Seed Pearls, Filigree, 6 1/4 x 1/2 In. 520.00
Bracelet, Link, Diamond, White Gold, Art Deco, 7 In............................ 1380.00
Bracelet, Link, Hammered Sterling Silver, Organic Design, Arts & Crafts, 7 In. 145.00
Bracelet, Link, Quatrefoil, Repousse, 14K Gold, Guard, 1887, 6 1/4 In. 430.00
Bracelet, Link, Rectangular, Stamped Flowers, Georg Jensen, Denmark 410.00
Bracelet, Link, Snake, Turquoise, 15K Yellow Gold, England, c.1840, 7 1/4 In. 900.00
Bracelet, Mask, Comedy & Tragedy, Coral, Fox Head, Ruby Eyes, 14K Gold 440.00
Bracelet, Moonstone, Ruby, Round, Banded Links, 14K Gold, R.C. Yard, 7 In. 1880.00
Bracelet, Moonstone, Silver, Curved Links, Antonio Pineda, Mexico, 7 In. 1530.00

Jewelry, Bracelet,
Coin, Love Token,
Engraved Reverse,
1875-1883, 7 1/2 In.

Jewelry, Bracelet, Blue Enamel,
Mother-Of-Pearl, Paste Diamond,
Gold, Victorian

Jewelry, Earrings, Coral, Cherub
Heads, Bows, Dangling Greek
Vases, 1 3/8 In.

Bracelet, Opal, Buttercup Design, 14K Yellow Gold 1095.00
Bracelet, Peridot, Citrine, Sapphire, Amethyst, Aquamarine, P. Papi, 7 In. 530.00
Bracelet, Pink Cameo, Reverse Carved, Apple Juice Links, Elastic 700.00
Bracelet, Pink Sapphire, Oval, 18K Gold, Robin Rotenier, 6 3/4 In. 2115.00
Bracelet, Platinum, 3 Diamond Shape Links, Diamond, Art Deco, 1830 .... 4830.00
Bracelet, Platinum, 36 Old Mine Diamonds, Art Deco, c.1930, 7 1/4 In. 5750.00
Bracelet, Platinum, Sapphire, Diamond, Art Deco, Tiffany, 7 In. 4406.00
Bracelet, Rope Twist, Lily Pad Ends, 22K Yellow Gold, Bright Engraving 635.00
Bracelet, Sapphire, Diamond, Tapered Links, Herringbone Edge, 18K Gold, Cartier, 7 In. 1175.00
Bracelet, Seed Pearls, Crystal, 14K Gold, Art Deco, c.1925, 7 1/4 x 1 1/4 In. 460.00
Bracelet, Silver, Hammered, Quatrefoil, Wood Grain, Orb Mark 300.00
Bracelet, Slide, Mesh, Cameo, Woman's Profile, 18K Gold, American, c.1900, 7 x 1 In. ... 1140.00
Bracelet, Slide, Mesh, Flexible, 14K Gold, American, c.1890 .... 840.00
Bracelet, Slide, Mesh, Gold Filled, Carved Tiger Eye, Fringed Ends, Pair 115.00
Bracelet, Slide, Pearl, Tracery, 14K Gold, American, c.1900 .... 600.00
Bracelet, Snake, Mouth Grasping Tail, Diamond Eyes, 14K Gold, 7 1/4 In. 705.00
Bracelet, Star Of David, Gold Braided Wire, Medallion Clasp, Middle Ages, 6 1/2 In. ... 1380.00
Bracelet, Sterling Silver, Alternating Oakleaf Links & Balls, Georg Jensen, c.1952, 7 In. . 750.00
Bracelet, Sterling Silver, Curb Links, Buckle Clasp, Hermes 880.00
Bracelet, Sterling Silver, Curved Links, Cabochon Moonstones, Pineda, Mexico, 7 In. ... 1530.00
Bracelet, Sterling Silver, Curved Plaques, Stylized Blossom, Laurence Foss, 7 5/8 In. 245.00
Bracelet, Sterling Silver, Flower-Shaped Links, Georg Jensen, 7 In. 500.00
Bracelet, Sterling Silver, Flowers, Lapis, Georg Jensen 1560.00
Bracelet, Sterling Silver, X-Shaped Links, Beaded Edge, Aquilar, Mexico, 7 1/2 In. 1115.00
Bracelet, Woman With Flowing Hair, Onyx, Full Cut Diamond, Ruby, 14K Gold, c.1950 . 650.00
Bracelet & Earrings, Bakelite, Brown, Yellow Random Dots 845.00
Bracelet & Earrings, Bangle, Rope Twist, Silver, Gems, Clip-On, David Yurman 1060.00
Buckle, Snake, Curved, Green Stone Eyes, 14K Gold 529.00
Buckle, Stylized Leaves, Sterling Silver, Hammered, Oval, F.G. Hale, 1 1/4 x 1 5/8 In. 1500.00
Chain, Vest, Rope, Quarter Eagle, 14K Rose & White Gold, 1905, 16 In. 405.00
Chain, Watch, 2, Slides, Gold, 1863, 26 In. 405.00
Chain, Watch, Rope, Twist, 14K Gold, 19th Century, 50 In. 259.00
Charm, Snowman, Pave Diamonds, Emerald, Ruby & Onyx 745.00
Choker, Bracelet & Earrings Set, Snake Design, 18 K Gold, Elsa Peretti, Tiffany 1725.00
Cigarette Case, 14K Gold, Leaf Engraved Edges, American, c.1930 .... 1410.00
Cigarette Case, 14K Yellow Gold, Monogram, Men's, 4 1/8 x 3 1/2 x 1/4 In. 405.00
Cigarette Case, Herringbone Engraving, 14K Gold, Tiffany 1060.00
Cigarette Case, Nude Woman, Man Holding Towel, Silver, France, 1800s, 3 1/2 In. 1495.00
Cigarette Case, Reeded Design, Initialed Spring Bar, 14K Gold, Cartier, c.1930, 5 1/2 In. . 1150.00
Cigarette Case, Reeded Edge, Platinum, Bicolor 18K Gold Marquetry, Art Deco 1400.00
Cigarette Case, Sterling Silver, Art Nouveau, Flowers, Vines, Link Chain 440.00
Clasp, Cape, Cameo, Gold, Tortoise Shell, Pearls, Flower, Links, 6 1/4 In. 400.00
Clasp, Woman's Left Eye, 8 Amethysts, Braided Hair, 1840, 3/8 In. 1816.00
Clip, 3-Petal Flower, Embossed Cabochons, Red, Blue, Green, Rhinestones, Trifari, 2 In. . 185.00
Clip, Cat's Eye, Chrysoberyl, Platinum, 50 Diamonds, Art Deco, 1 x 3/4 In. 5750.00
Clip, Doorknocker, Blue Rhinestones, Turquoise Cabochon, Coro, 3 In. 225.00
Clip, Dress, Amethyst, Frosted Rock Crystal, Oval, 18K Gold 5300.00
Clip, Grapes Cluster, Leaves, Moonstone Rhinestones, Silvertone Metal, 3 In. 43.00
Clip, Green Glass Rhinestones & Cabochons, Art Deco, 2 1/2 In. 100.00
Clip, Nosegay, Opaque Pink & Turquoise Rhinestones, Enameled, Trifari, 2 1/2 In. 260.00

Compact, Flower, Scroll, Rouge Pots, Mirror, Lipstick Case, 14K Gold, Mesmer, 3 In. . . .	635.00
Compact, Oval, Gold Tone, Blue Enamel Top, Turquoise Poodle, Dorset Fifth Avenue . . .	30.00
Compact, Sterling Silver, Applied Enameled Gold Lady Bug, 2 1/2 x 2 1/2 In.	575.00
Compact, Sterling Silver, Gold, Stone Set, Art Deco, American, c.1920-1930, 3 1/2 In. . . .	176.00
Cuff Links, 14K Gold, Diamond, Double Oval Links, Crosshatch Design, Tiffany	380.00
Cuff Links, 2 Knots Joined By Bar, 18K Gold, Schlumberger, Tiffany	880.00
Cuff Links, Baseball & Bat, 14K Gold, Engraved, c.1920	765.00
Cuff Links, Diamond, 18K Yellow Gold, Textured, Alluvial, Rectangular	690.00
Cuff Links, Double Link, Basket Weave, 18K Gold, R.C. Yard	600.00
Cuff Links, Double Link, Incised Squares, Sapphire, 14K Gold, Tiffany & Co.	825.00
Cuff Links, Double Oval Link, Beaded Edge, 14K Gold, Art Nouveau, Tiffany & Co.	600.00
Cuff Links, Geometric Shape, Sterling Silver, Ronald Pearson, 1950s, 3/4 In.	440.00
Cuff Links, Gorilla Head & Hands, Sapphire Eyes, Link Chain	7640.00
Cuff Links, Lion Head, Diamond, Ruby, 14K Gold	460.00
Cuff Links, Love, D-Shape, 18K Gold, Cartier	1116.00
Cuff Links, Oval, Sterling Silver, Blue Chalcedony, Georg Jensen, 1945	460.00
Cuff Links, Platinum, Star Sapphire, Baguette Diamond, 3 Studs, 1930	3295.00
Cuff Links, Ruby, 6-Star Set Diamonds, Platinum, 18K Gold, Edwardian	3055.00
Cuff Links, Sapphire, 18K Gold, Cartier, France, c.1930, 1 In.	1610.00
Cuff Links, Wheel Of Life, Jade, Diamond, 14K Gold, Tiffany & Co.	575.00
Earrings, 3 Interlocking Circles, 18K Gold, Paloma Picasso, Tiffany, Box	440.00
Earrings, 3 Sapphire Drops, Diamond, Platinum, 14K Gold, c.1930	2990.00
Earrings, 7 Flowers, Emeralds, Crescent Shape, 18K Gold, Cartier	3055.00
Earrings, Alhambra, Coral Quatrefoil, 18K Gold, Van Cleef & Arpels	1645.00
Earrings, Amethyst, Circular Cut, 14K Gold, Cartier	470.00
Earrings, Angels, Sterling Silver, 18K Yellow Gold, Marked SG, 1 1/8 x 1 1/8 In.	300.00
Earrings, Blue Star Sapphire, Screwback, 14K Gold, c.1950	290.00
Earrings, Blue Topaz, Pyramid Shaped Cabochon, 18K Bicolor Gold, Clip-On, Bulgari . .	2235.00
Earrings, Butterfly, Onyx, Opal, 18K Gold, Angela Cummings, Tiffany	765.00
Earrings, Citrine, Ribbed Half Hoop, 18K Gold, Boucheron	1175.00
Earrings, Coral, Cherub Heads, Bows, Dangling Greek Vases, 1 3/8 In. . *. . . . . *Illus*	350.00
Earrings, Cowboy Boot, Lasso, Red Rhinestones, Yellow Enamel, Screwback, 1 In.	65.00
Earrings, Diamond, Brickwork, Half Hoop, 18K Gold, Cartier	3760.00
Earrings, Diamond, Half Hoop, 18K Gold, Hammered	1410.00
Earrings, Diamond, Interlocking Hearts, 18K Gold	2585.00
Earrings, Diamond, Leaf Cluster, 18K Gold, Buccellati	2000.00
Earrings, Diamond, Onyx, Oval, 18K Yellow Gold, Denise Roberge, 1 1/4 In.	865.00
Earrings, Diamond, Pink Sapphires, Pave Set, Silver Mount	1765.00
Earrings, Diamond, Sapphire Bee, Blue Topaz Head, 18K White Gold	235.00
Earrings, Dome Shape, Hammered, 18K Gold Enamel, Clip-On, David Webb	1410.00
Earrings, Drop, 15K Yellow Gold, Egyptian Revival Style, Victorian, c.1875	1265.00
Earrings, Drop, Chalcedony, 14K Yellow Gold	300.00
Earrings, Green Onyx, Quatrefoil Mount, 22K Gold, Maya Neimans	410.00
Earrings, Half Hoop, Pink Sapphires, Full Cut Diamonds, Brickwork, 18K Gold	2235.00
Earrings, Half Sphere Shape, Faceted, 18K Rose Gold, c.1940	1175.00
Earrings, Hoop, Diamonds, Ruby, Gypsy Set, 14K Gold	2585.00
Earrings, Hoop, Rope Twist, Diamonds, Flowers, 18K Gold, Vourakis	880.00
Earrings, Intaglio, Pearls, Bezel Set, Elizabeth Locke, 18K Gold	865.00
Earrings, Mabe, Pearl, 18K Gold Frame, Radiating Lines, Clip-On, Tiffany	1000.00
Earrings, Openwork, Curved, 14K Gold, Clip-On, Tiffany	500.00
Earrings, Pearl, Diamond Border, Platinum-Plated, 18K Gold, Edwardian	1765.00
Earrings, Pearl, Intaglio, Man & Woman, 18K Gold, Clip-On, Elizabeth Locke	2235.00
Earrings, Pearl, Paste, Engraved Flowers, 9K Gold, England, Victorian, c.1880	1380.00
Earrings, Pearl, South Sea, 18K Gold Mounts, Studs	825.00
Earrings, Pendant, Citrine, Scrolls, Wirework, Beaded Accents, 14K Gold	1115.00
Earrings, Pendant, Flowers, Insect, Amethysts, Diamonds, Seed Pearls, Enamel, 14K Gold	470.00
Earrings, Ruby, Diamond Border, Diamond Set Bow, 14K White Gold, 1 1/2 In.	1150.00
Earrings, Stylized Blossom, Sterling Silver, Bead, Screwback, C.P. Petersen, 1 1/4 In. . . .	195.00
Earrings, Sunburst, 18K Gold, 3 Prong Set Diamonds, DeScenza	530.00
Earrings, Tourmaline, Multicolored, 14K Gold, Clip-On, France, 1 In.	905.00
Earrings, Turbo Shell, Coral Cabochons, 18K Gold, Clip-On, Seaman Schepps	940.00
Earrings, Turbo Shell, Emerald, 14K Gold, Clip-On, Seaman Schepps	825.00
Earrings, Wire Cage, Sterling Silver, Tumbled Turquoise Beads, Ed Wiener	765.00

Earrings, Wire Twist, Cabochon, 14K Gold, Screwback, Tiffany, 3/4 In. 200.00
Earrings, Wooden Scroll, Sterling Silver Mount, William Spratling, Mexico 325.00
Earrings, Yellow Beryl, Lemon Slice, Bezel Set Diamond, 18K Gold 500.00
Hatpins are listed in this book in the Hatpin category.
Lavaliere, Black Opal, Diamonds, Platinum, Art Deco, c.1920, 17-In. Chain 489.00
Lavaliere, Diamond, Red Spinel, 14K White Gold, c.1930, 14 1/2 In. 1265.00
Lavaliere, Link, Filigree, Crystal, Diamond Panels, Art Deco, Chain, White Gold, 15 In. . . . 750.00
Lavaliere, Pendant, Flower, Platinum, Seed Pearls, Diamonds, Box, Edwardian, 15 1/2 In. 3055.00
Lavaliere, Pharaoh's Bust, Turquoise, Pearls, Art Nouveau, 2 Chains, 14K Gold, 9 1/2 In. . 635.00
Lavaliere, Rose, Stem, Pearls, Enamel Overlay, Krementz, 14K Gold, Art Nouveau 300.00
Lipstick Case, Woven Design, 18K Gold, Van Cleef & Arpels 430.00
Locket, Flowers, Enamel, 14K Gold, c.1920 . . . . 660.00
Locket, Sterling, Walnut Shape, Perfume Compartments, Photo, Mirror, 1 3/4 x 1 1/2 In. . 360.00
Locket, Woman's Head, Flowing Hair, Garlands, 18K Gold, Art Nouveau, 1 1/4 In. 385.00
Locket, Woman's Left Eye, Heart Shape, Gold, Turquoise, Seed Pearls, 1/2 In. 1725.00
Money Clip, Oversized Paperclip, 14K Gold, Tiffany, Box 235.00
Necessaire, Diamond, Sapphire, Mirror, Writing Surface, Edwardian, Box 1765.00
Necessaire, Engraved, Blue Cabochon Clasp, Chain, c.1900, 3 1/2 x 2 1/2 In. 315.00
Necklace, 67 Onyx Beads, 18K Gold, Angela Cummings, Tiffany, 33 3/4 In. 470.00
Necklace, Amethyst, 18K Gold, Hinged Bail, Kohn, c.1900, 17 1/2 In. 825.00
Necklace, Angel Skin Coral Beads, Single Strand, c.1915, 25 In. 200.00
Necklace, Bakelite, Red Apples, Chain, Green Leaves, 16 In. 510.00
Necklace, Bezel Set, Labradorite, Sterling Silver, Georg Jensen 3175.00
Necklace, Brass, Patina, Art Smith, USA, c.1950 . . . . 1170.00
Necklace, Cameo, Shell, Gentleman, Etruscan Style Frame, Chain, Fiorentini, c.1860 . . . . 2400.00
Necklace, Carnelian, Enamel, Art Deco, 16 1/2 In. 4700.00
Necklace, Choker, 14K Gold, Silver Peridot, Hobe, 16 1/2 In. 1725.00
Necklace, Choker, Platinum, Diamonds, Seed Pearls, Edwardian, c.1910, 13 1/2 In. 4025.00
Necklace, Collar, Sodalite, Round, Tapered Panels, 18K Yellow Gold, Lalaounis, 17 In. . . 2875.00
Necklace, Coral Bead, Angelskin, 3 Strands, Carved Rose, 17 In. 410.00
Necklace, Daisies, Vines, Leaves, Diamond, 18K Gold, Morelli, 15 1/4 In. 3055.00
Necklace, Dragon Design, Silver, Turquoise Bead, 1900s, 31 In. 75.00
Necklace, Earrings, Bracelet, Amethyst Rhinestones, Silvertone Metal, Sarah Coventry . . . 50.00
Necklace, Earrings, Bracelet, Contessa, Faux Opal Cabochons, Sarah Coventry 53.00
Necklace, Faux Sapphires, Pearls, Leaf, Neoclassical Style, Krementz, 14K Gold, 15 In. . . . 750.00
Necklace, Flowers & Leaves, Coral, Bezel Set, Georg Jensen, 15 In. 1765.00
Necklace, Flowers, White Jade Panels, Mogul Style, Gold Chain, c.1900, 16 In. 600.00
Necklace, Garnets, 10K Gold, Victorian, Late 1800s, 17 In. 1380.00
Necklace, Glass, Green, Cabochons, Jugendstil, Marked DLH Depose, 18 x 3 In. 145.00
Necklace, Glass, Jadeite, Moss In Snow, Seed Pearls, Silver Gilt Mount, 16 1/2 In. 765.00
Necklace, Guilloche Enamel, Blue & White, Platinum, Diamond, Edwardian, 19 In. 1645.00
Necklace, Jade, Beaded Fringe, Art Deco, Czechoslovakia, 24 In. 375.00
Necklace, Jadeite Bead, 14K Gold Barrel Clasp, Buccellati, 22 In. 2350.00
Necklace, Jadeite, Carved Flowers, Pierced, Links, c.1930, 15 In. 4700.00
Necklace, Jadeite, Graduated Beads, 27 1/2 In. 500.00
Necklace, Lapis Lazuli, 41 Beads, Gold Filled Clasp, 18 In. 69.00
Necklace, Lariat, Foxtail Mesh, 18K Gold, 16 In. 1175.00
Necklace, Leaf Chain, Clear Rhinestones, Silvertone Metal, Sarah Coventry 26.00
Necklace, Link, 2 Rows, Oval, Flattened, 14K Gold, Tongue Clasp, c.1940 . . . . 489.00
Necklace, Link, Block Shape, Incised Lines, 14K Gold, Tiffany, 17 In. 825.00
Necklace, Link, Navette Shape, 5 Rows, Brickwork, 18K Gold, Cartier, 16 1/2 In. 2585.00
Necklace, Locket, Guilloche Enamel, Sapphire, 14K Gold, 1910 . . . . 3720.00
Necklace, Medallion, Crescent Shape, 18K White Gold, Diamonds, c.1930, 21 1/2 In. . . . 1035.00
Necklace, Moonstone Beads, Graduated, 18K Gold Clasp, Buccellati 1530.00
Necklace, Pastel Lucite Beads, Clustered, Monet, 35 In. 30.00
Necklace, Pendant Cross, Sapphires, Link Chain, 14K Gold Mount, Tiffany & Co., 32 In. . 3820.00
Necklace, Pendant, 25 Pearls, Old Mine & Rose Cut Diamonds, 14K Gold, c.1870 . . . . . . 520.00
Necklace, Pendant, Amethyst, Link Chain, Victorian, 15 In. 1880.00
Necklace, Pendant, Berry & Leaf, Flower Links, Sterling Silver, Georg Jensen 15 1/2 In. . 1645.00
Necklace, Pendant, Citrine Squares, Links, Retro, Signed Tiffany & Co., 14K Gold 8815.00
Necklace, Pendant, Coral, 14K Gold, Racaille Design Links, Krementz, c.1930, 17 1/4 In. 499.00
Necklace, Pendant, Heart Shape, Baton Links, Georg Jensen, 33 In. 499.00
Necklace, Pendant, Heart, Diamond, Trace Link Chain, 18K Gold, Tiffany, 16 1/2 In. 1880.00

Necklace, Pendant, Imitation Opal, 14K Gold, Art Nouveau, 16 1/2 In. 500.00
Necklace, Pendant, Silver, Hammered, Inset Coral, Arts & Crafts, Holland, 1 1/2 In. 345.00
Necklace, Pendant, Silver, Rose Design, Inset Mother-Of-Pearl, Arts & Crafts, 1 1/2 In. . . 115.00
Necklace, Pendant, Strawberry, Steuben Glass, 14K Gold Chain, Box, 24 In. 405.00
Necklace, Pendant, Turquoise Cabochons, Mine Cut Diamond, Domed, Oval, Cain, 17 In. 325.00
Necklace, Pendant, Turquoise, Silver, Hector Aguilar, Taxco, Mexico, c.1945, 17 1/4 In. . . 2530.00
Necklace, Peridot, Tourmaline, Sapphire, Pearls, 14K Gold, N. Feldbaum, 15 1/2 In. 2235.00
Necklace, Plastic Disc, Silver Ball, Cross, Leather Cord, Arnoldo Pomodoro 645.00
Necklace, Platinum, Diamond, Cultured Pearl, Black Onyx, Silk, Art Deco, c.1920, 36 In. 1840.00
Necklace, Rope Twist, Cylindrical Beads, Foxtail Chain, Signed Lalaounis, 15 In. 765.00
Necklace, Rose Diamond Swallows, 18K Gold, 19th Century 6675.00
Necklace, Silver & White Pearls, Citrine Beads, Fringe, 18K Gold, Marina B., 18 In. 1765.00
Necklace, Silver, Curved Links, Moonstone, Antonio Pineda, Taxco, Mexico, 16 1/2 In. . . 2000.00
Necklace, Silver, Hammered, 2 Inset Amethysts, Murle Bennett, 10 In. 690.00
Necklace, Silver, Pierced, Turquoise, Enamel, 3 Baroque Pearls, Liberty & Co. 470.00
Necklace, Snake, Coiled, Rope Twist Body, Molded Head, Tail, Gold Filled, 17 3/4 In. . . . 120.00
Necklace, Squash Blossom, Horseshoe-Shaped Pendant, Silver, 28 In. 220.00
Necklace, Sterling Silver, Curved Links, Cabochon Moonstones, Pineda, Mexico, 17 In. . . 2000.00
Necklace, Sterling Silver, Dangling & Inset Lapis, Kalo, 17 In. 3820.00
Necklace, Sterling Silver, Ebony, Betty Cooke, USA, c.1950 . . . . 1755.00
Necklace, Sterling Silver, Flowers Links, Georg Jensen, 16 1/2 In. 765.00
Necklace, Sterling Silver, Leaf & Bud Links, Georg Jensen, 1967, 17 1/4 In. 880.00
Necklace, Tahitian Pearl, 18K Gold, Fireworks Collection, Tiffany, 15 In. 865.00
Necklace, Tubogas, 18K Gold, Chain, Tiffany, 16 In. 2585.00
Necklace, Turquoise, Seahorse, Fish, Eel, Scallops, Chain, 14K Gold, 2 1/4 x 1 1/2 In. . . . 2185.00
Necklace & Bracelet, Connections, 18K Gold, Paloma Picasso, Tiffany, 16 1/2 & 7 1/2 In. 2235.00
Necklace & Earrings, Leaf Strands, Jade Lucite, Goldtone Metal, Trifari 60.00
Pendant, 2 Cherubs, Enamel, 18K Gold, France, c.1870 . . . . 1680.00
Pendant, Amethyst Cabochon, Swirling, Sterling Silver, Chain, 1 3/4 In. 350.00
Pendant, Butterfly Wing, Sterling Silver, Stylized Leaves, Bead, Teardrop Shape, 2 In. . . . 375.00
Pendant, Coin, Queen Victoria, St. George, 14K Gold, 1887 . . . . 295.00
Pendant, Cross Frame, Bezel-Set Emerald, 18K Gold, Signed, Parenti, 2 1/2 In. 590.00
Pendant, Cross, Emerald, 18K Gold, Parenti Sisters 590.00
Pendant, Double Acorn, Steuben, 18K Yellow Gold 460.00
Pendant, Faience Scarab, Carnelian Batton Carved, 18K Yellow Gold, 3 1/2 x 2 In. 1725.00
Pendant, Flowering Gourds, Lapis, 14K White Gold, Art Deco 265.00
Pendant, Gem Set, Enamel, Beadwork Accents, 18K Gold, Edwin Streeter, Box 2235.00
Pendant, Grape Cluster, Platinum, Diamond, Pearl, Edwardian Style 9295.00
Pendant, Jade, White, Bell Shape, Scroll Carving, Early 1900s, 2 1/4 In. 29.00
Pendant, Jadeite, Carved Relief Dragon, Double Gourd Shape, c.1900, 1 1/2 In. 115.00
Pendant, Lavender, Jade, Carved, Double Gourd Shape, Jade Top, 14K Gold, 1900 . . . . . . 4056.00
Pendant, Locket, Emerald, 4 Diamonds, Beads, 14K Gold Mount, Victorian 765.00
Pendant, Onyx, Snake, 14K Gold, Diamond Eyes, c.1920 . . . . 1080.00
Pendant, Rose Quartz, Fruit Carving, Oval, Early 1900s, 2 In. 29.00
Pendant, Scarab, 15K Gold, Egyptian Revival, 1880 . . . . 2110.00
Pendant, Sterling Silver, Peridots, Pearl, Citrine, Leaves, Beads, Scrolls, Chain, 1 In. 975.00
Pendant, Sterling Silver, Stylized Flowers, Amethyst Cabochon, Chain, 2 In. 235.00
Pendant, White Jade, Baby Lock, Musical Stone Carving, Jui, c.1900, 2 1/2 In. 260.00
Pill Box, Poodle Shape, 14K Gold, Sapphire & Ruby Collar, Twist Head, 2 In. 895.00
Pin, 2 Acorns, Leaf, Sterling Silver, Oval, Georg Jensen, 2 1/4 In. 240.00
Pin, 2 Birds, Wheat Sheaf, Sterling Silver, Square, Georg Jensen, Denmark, 1 1/2 In. 265.00
Pin, 2 Circle, 3 Diamonds, 14K Gold, Cartier, 1 1/4 x 1 1/2 In. 690.00
Pin, 3 Flowers, Enamel, Diamond, 14K Gold, c.1885, 1 x 1 1/2 In. 750.00
Pin, 3 Swirling Leaves, Sterling Silver, Frame, Hammered, No. 101, Georg Jensen 325.00
Pin, 10 Diamonds, 11 Seed Pearls, 14K Gold, Crescent Shape, c.1910, 3 In. 635.00
Pin, 11 Diamonds, Gold & Black Enamel, 14 Pearls, Victorian 2300.00
Pin, Abstract Shape, Sterling Silver, Art Smith, USA, 1950s, 3 1/4 In. 1287.00
Pin, Abstract Shape, Sterling Silver, Harry Bertoia, USA, c.1943, 2 1/2 In. 4970.00
Pin, Abstract, Black Bead, Sterling Silver, No. 328, Georg Jensen, Denmark 355.00
Pin, Amethyst, Pearls, Grapevine, Leaf, 14K Gold, Pre-Raphaelite, 43 Ct. 1380.00
Pin, Bakelite, Bulldog, Carved, Orange Dye, Celluloid Teeth & Eyes, 3 In. 500.00
Pin, Bakelite, Diamond, Emeralds, 14K Gold Mount 705.00
Pin, Bakelite, Fishbowl, Root Beer, Reverse Carved Fish, Paint, 2 3/4 In. 260.00

Pin, Bakelite, Green Helmet, Yellow Uniform, Soldier, Rotating Arm, 3 In. 1300.00
Pin, Bakelite, Hand, Black, Wearing Goldtone Metal Chain Bracelet, 4 In. 290.00
Pin, Bakelite, Moon & Palm Tree, Butterscotch, Painted, 2 1/2 In. 1400.00
Pin, Bakelite, Scottie Dog, Red, Black Paint, 3 In. 210.00
Pin, Ballerina, Light Blue & Clear Rhinestones, Silvertone Metal, 2 1/2 In. 45.00
Pin, Bar, Chrysoprase, 18K Yellow Gold, Elsa Peretti, 3 In. 315.00
Pin, Bar, Crown, Opal, Seed Pearls, 15K Gold, c.1885, 2 1/4 In. 1035.00
Pin, Bar, Diamond, 14K Gold, 20th Century, 2 x 12 In. 345.00
Pin, Bar, Diamond, Platinum, Filigree, Art Deco, c.1935 . . . . 1380.00
Pin, Bar, Diamond, Sapphire, Art Deco, Cartier, Box 7640.00
Pin, Bar, Filigree, 14K White Gold, Diamond, Sapphires, Edwardian, c.1910 . . . . 259.00
Pin, Bar, Mythological God, 15K Gold, Edwardian, 1900 . . . . 670.00
Pin, Bar, Oval, Leaves, Vines, Opal Cabochon, 3/8 x 2 1/2 In. 495.00
Pin, Bar, Platinum, 17 Diamonds, 14K Gold Stem, J.E. Caldwell & Co., Art Deco 1175.00
Pin, Bar, Ribbon, Platinum, Diamonds, Art Deco, c.1925, 2 1/4 In. 1955.00
Pin, Bar, Sapphire, Seed Pearls, 14 K Gold, Art Deco, c.1930 . . . . 400.00
Pin, Bar, Sterling Silver, Stylized Tree, Inset Jewel, Arts & Crafts, 2 In. 120.00
Pin, Bar, Sterling Silver, Turquoise Matrix, Cabochon Center, M. Turner, 1/2 x 1 7/8 In. . . 335.00
Pin, Bar, Turquoise, 14K Yellow Gold, Etruscan Revival Frame, Victorian, c.1880 . . . . . . 315.00
Pin, Bar, White & Yellow Gold, Mine Cut Diamonds, Late 1800s, 2 1/2 In. 720.00
Pin, Basket, Emerald, Sapphire & Ruby Flowers, Diamond, 18K Gold, Tiffany & Co. 2470.00
Pin, Bean Shape, Open, Veined Leaf, Bead, Scroll, Gilbert Oakes, 1 1/4 x 1 5/8 In. 2700.00
Pin, Bee, Emerald Eyes, 18K Gold, Chaumet, Pair 999.00
Pin, Bellflower, Green Stone Pendants, Georg Jensen, Denmark 2235.00
Pin, Bird Among Leaves, Sterling Silver, No. 123, Georg Jensen . . . . .235.00 to 295.00
Pin, Bird In Wreath, Sterling Silver, No. 165, Georg Jensen 205.00
Pin, Bird, Spread Wings, Ruby, 18K Gold, Tiffany, 1 x 1 In. 524.00
Pin, Black Opal Slab, Oval, Diamond Border, Platinum Mount, Birks, 1 1/4 In. 8050.00
Pin, Blackamoor, Diamond, Rubies, Turquoise Cabochon, 18K Gold 1060.00
Pin, Blackamoor, Turban, Bead Set, Diamonds, Emeralds, 18K Gold, G. Nardi 7050.00
Pin, Bloodhound, Enamel, Ruby & Diamond Eyes, 1970s 2705.00
Pin, Blossom, Vines, Sterling Silver, Amber, Chalcedony, Georg Jensen 3055.00
Pin, Bow, Diamond & Sapphire, Platinum Mount, Art Deco 6465.00
Pin, Bow, Diamond, Platinum, 1950s 3915.00
Pin, Bow, Floppy, Diamond, Platinum, 1950s 4985.00
Pin, Bowknot, Diamond, Palladium, c.1900, 1 3/4 x 1 In. 2530.00
Pin, Bumblebee, Emerald, Diamond, Ruby, Opal, 14K Rose Gold, 1900s 2300.00
Pin, Butterfly, Coral Cabochons, White Enamel, Trifari, 1960s, 2 In. 100.00
Pin, Butterfly, Diamond, Sapphire, Ruby, Pearl, England, c.1890, 1 1/4 x 1 In. 1020.00
Pin, Butterfly, Faceted Jet, Wire Frame, C-Clasp, 1920s, 2 In. 65.00
Pin, Butterfly, Rhinestone Body, Goldtone Metal, Coro, 2 In. 40.00
Pin, Butterfly, Rubies, Sapphires, Rose Cut Diamonds, Pearls, c.1880, 1 3/4 x 1 1/4 In. . . . 1440.00
Pin, Calla Lily, 2 Leaves, Sterling Silver, Hand Wrought, Peer Smed, 2 1/2 In. 200.00
Pin, Cameo, 2 Women, Cherub, Owl, Moon, Oval, 2 1/4 In. 500.00
Pin, Cameo, 18K Gold Frame, England, c.1865 . . . . 840.00
Pin, Cameo, Agate, Pearl Frame, England, c.1880 . . . . 1080.00
Pin, Cameo, Bar, Sardonyx, Woman, 14K Gold 295.00
Pin, Cameo, Carnelian Agate, Lady In Profile, Seed Pearl, Diamond Frame 980.00
Pin, Cameo, Diana The Huntress, Round, 2 1/2 In. 1050.00
Pin, Cameo, Lava, Cherub & Dog, 2 1/2 In. 850.00
Pin, Cameo, Locket, Pendant, 14K Yellow Gold, c.1860 . . . . 980.00
Pin, Cameo, Madonna & Child, Gold, 2 1/2 In. 650.00
Pin, Cameo, Malachite, Artemis, 18K Gold Frame, c.1890 . . . . 2040.00
Pin, Cameo, Man & Woman Riding Horse, Clouds, Oval, 2 1/2 In. 1200.00
Pin, Cameo, Onyx, Woman With Rose In Hair, Seed Pearl Frame, 14K Gold Mount 765.00
Pin, Cameo, Portrait Of Man, Ebony Frame, Oval, 1 1/4 In. 300.00
Pin, Cameo, Rose Cut Diamonds, Silver & 15K Gold Frame, England, c.1890, 1 1/4 In. . . 900.00
Pin, Cameo, Sardonyx, Half Pearls, Diamonds, 14K Gold, Victorian, 1 3/4 In. . . . . . . *Illus* 1035.00
Pin, Cameo, Shell, Athena & Owl, 18K Gold Frame, c.1900, 2 x 1 1/2 In. 960.00
Pin, Cameo, Shell, Madonna & Child, Pedestal, Victorian, 2 1/2 x 2 1/4 In. 115.00
Pin, Cameo, Shell, Woman, Carved Rocaille Frame, Victorian 200.00
Pin, Cameo, Shell, Woman, Flowing Hair, Diamond Earring, 14K White Gold, Art Deco . 175.00
Pin, Cameo, Venus Riding Shell, Drawn By Dolphins, R. Rosi 1000.00

Pin, Cameo, Village Scene, Rectangular, Wooden Frame, 1 1/2 In. 175.00
Pin, Cameo, Woman At Wall, With Basket, Oval, 2 1/4 In. 150.00
Pin, Cameo, Woman Feeding Eagle, Oval, 2 In. 900.00
Pin, Cameo, Woman Smelling Rose, Oval, 2 1/4 In. 600.00
Pin, Cameo, Woman's Profile, Carved Flowers, Diamond Pendant, c.1910, 2 1/2 In. 375.00
Pin, Cameo, Young Woman, Curly Hair, Oval, 1 1/2 In. 125.00
Pin, Cartoon Hound, Enamel, Black, Red & White, 1970 . . . .   1480.00
Pin, Cherries, Leaves, Silver, Hammered, Kalo, 2 In. 470.00
Pin, Chick On Branch, Turquoise, Rubies, Diamond, 18K Gold, Van Cleef & Arpels 1880.00
Pin, Chrysanthemum, 6 Mine Cut Diamond, 14K Gold, Germany 690.00
Pin, Circle, Diamond, Onyx, European & French Cut, Art Deco 1175.00
Pin, Circle, Open, Platinum, Diamond, c.1920, 1 1/2 In. 1610.00
Pin, Circle, Sterling Silver, Pierced, Chased Cardinal On Branch, Emily A. Day, 2 1/8 In. .   85.00
Pin, Cloissone, Pharaoh Profile, Vulture Wings 590.00
Pin, Cockatoos, Green, Yellow Tourmaline, Diamond, 18K Gold, Gage 4700.00
Pin, Cocker Spaniel, Emerald Eyes, Ruby Mouth, Diamond Collar, D. Frere 200.00
Pin, Coin, Egyptian, Pharaoh In Chariot, 14K Gold 470.00
Pin, Copper, Hammered, Amber Inset, Arts & Crafts, Dutch, 3 1/2 In. 58.00
Pin, Coral, Carved Rose, Bee, Gold, Signed, Constantine, 1986, 2 1/2 In. 430.00
Pin, Coral, Pearls, Rose Cut Diamond, Victorian 690.00
Pin, Crane, Bird, Round, Sterling, Georg Jensen, c.1917 . . . .   315.00
Pin, Crown, Jewels Of India Line, Green, Red, Clear Cabochons, Goldtone, 3 1/2 In. 760.00
Pin, Cut Glass Stones, Eisenberg, 2 1/2 x 1 5/8 In. 110.00
Pin, Cut Glass Stones, Floral Bouquet Mount, Eisenberg, 1930s, 3 3/4 x 2 1/4 In. 330.00
Pin, Diamond, 14K Gold, Silver, Flowers, Oval, c.1840, 1 1/2 In. 1035.00
Pin, Diamond, Bezel & Bead Set, Platinum Mount, Art Deco 2470.00
Pin, Diamond, Blue Sapphire, Emerald, 14K Gold, c.1900 . . . .   1150.00
Pin, Diamond, Pearls, Sapphire, 14K Yellow & White Gold, c.1950 . . . .   405.00
Pin, Diamond, Platinum, Art Deco, Bead-Set, Cartier 8225.00
Pin, Diamond, Stag With Arrow, Sapphire Eye, 9K Rose Gold Mount 1765.00
Pin, Diamonds, Oval, Key Fret Design, 14K White & Yellow Gold, Art Deco, c.1925 . . . .   805.00
Pin, Dog Head, Rubies, Diamonds, 15K Gold, England, c.1890 . . . .   1080.00
Pin, Dog, Pug, Diamond Eye, 18K Gold 2110.00
Pin, Dog, Pug, Silver & Gold, Diamond Eyes, 1890 . . . .   835.00
Pin, Doggy, Emerald Eyes, 1970s 2110.00
Pin, Dragonfly, Diamonds, 14K White Gold, England, c.1900 . . . .   2040.00
Pin, Dragonfly, Diamonds, Rubies, 15K Gold, England, c.1890 . . . .   1140.00
Pin, Emerald, 39 Diamonds, 14K Gold, c.1900, 2 1/4 x 1 1/4 In. 1150.00
Pin, Enamel, Bird, Bezel Set Full Cut Diamond Eye, 18K Gold 320.00
Pin, Enamel, Grapevine, Carnelians, Art Nouveau Style, Chinese, 2 1/2 x 3 1/2 In. 320.00
Pin, Enamel, Seed Pearls, Diamond, 14K Gold, c.1880, 1 1/2 x 1 1/4 In. 520.00
Pin, Filigree Cluster, Citrine Rhinestones, Oval, Hollycraft, 1 In. 75.00
Pin, Fish, Silver, Gold Washed, Pearl Body, Diamonds, c.1890, 2 In. 2040.00
Pin, Flapper Walking Greyhound, Goldtone Metal, Engraved, 1920s, 2 1/2 In. 70.00
Pin, Flower Basket, Emerald Glass Flowers, Rhinestone Centers, Goldtone, Trifari, 2 In. . .   130.00
Pin, Flower Shape, 20 Round Diamonds, 18K Yellow Gold 345.00
Pin, Flower Spray, Diamonds, Platinum Plated, Edwardian 1295.00
Pin, Flower Spray, Diamonds, Platinum, Meister, 1 3/4 In. 2530.00
Pin, Flower Spray, Seed Pearls, Diamonds, Leaves, 18K Gold, Anna Bachelli 7640.00
Pin, Flower, 5 Petals, Diamond, 18K White Gold Mount, Tiffany 9400.00
Pin, Flower, Chrysophase, Cabochon, Sterling Silver, Oval, Georg Jensen, Denmark 410.00
Pin, Flower, Clustered Petals, Seed Pearls, Burnished Goldtone, Haskell, 1 3/4 In. 95.00
Pin, Flower, Diamonds, 8K Yellow & White Gold, Satsky, 1 3/4 x 2 3/4 In. 920.00
Pin, Flower, Enamel, Diamonds, 18K Gold, Tiffany 1840.00
Pin, Flower, Pearls, Swirled Wirework Petals, 14K Gold, Nikki Feldbaum 999.00
Pin, Flower, Ruby Center, Full Cut Diamond, 14K Gold Mount, Signed Cartier 2470.00
Pin, Flower, Spade Shape Leaves, Ruby, Emerald, Amethyst, 14K Gold, Tiffany, 2 1/2 In.   489.00
Pin, Flowerpot, Onyx, Diamond, Scroll Frame, 15K Gold, Portugal 235.00
Pin, Flowers, Jadeite, Ruby, Vines, 14K Gold, Art Deco, Tiffany, c.1930, 1 x 2 In. 1035.00
Pin, Flowers, Leaves, Stems, 160 Diamonds, Platinum, 14K Gold, c.1900, 3 1/2 x 2 In. . .   3680.00
Pin, Flowers, Pendants, Foxtail Chain, Emerald, 14K Gold, Victorian 825.00
Pin, Flowers, Sterling Silver, Wirework, Lapis Lazuli, Oval, Georg Jensen 1060.00
Pin, Fly, Diamond Body & Wings, Rose Cut Ruby Eyes 560.00

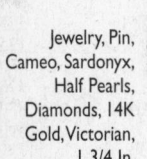

Jewelry, Pin,
Cameo, Sardonyx,
Half Pearls,
Diamonds, 14K
Gold, Victorian,
1 3/4 In.

Jewelry, Pin,
Mourning, In
Memory Of, Black
Enamel, Locks

Pin, Fox, Diamond, 18K Gold, Victorian, 1885 . . . . 3295.00
Pin, Frog, Jelly Belly, Green Rhinestone Eyes, Sterling Silver, Trifari, 3 In. 310.00
Pin, Geometric Shape, Sterling Silver, Oval Blister Pearl, 3/4 x 2 5/8 In. 295.00
Pin, Girandole, Crystals, Scrolled Frame, 14K Gold, Georgian 230.00
Pin, Griffin, Pierced, Chased, Nickel-Plated Silver, Cabochon, Forest Craft Guild, 2 In. . . 275.00
Pin, Horned Beetle, 4 Marquis Rubies, Diamond & Ruby Eyes, 1 1/4 In. 225.00
Pin, Horseshoe & Hammer, Diamond, Ruby, 18K 1510.00
Pin, Horseshoe, Mine Cut Diamonds, 18K Gold Mount 1175.00
Pin, Hound, Seated, Enameled Face, 18K Gold, 1970s 2280.00
Pin, Insect, Mine Cut Diamond, Mother Of Pearl, Sapphire, Ruby, 14K Gold Mount 3290.00
Pin, Irish Harp, Clover, Applied Rope Twist Wire, 15K Gold, Box 700.00
Pin, Jade, Leaves, Seed Pearls, 14K Gold, Potter & Mellen, Inc., 5/8 x 2 5/8 In. 2400.00
Pin, Jadeite, Pagoda Shape, Enameled, 14K Gold Mount, Art Deco, Sloan & Co. 3055.00
Pin, King Of Hearts, Diamond, Enamel, 18K Gold, Cartier, Paris, Box, c.1950 . . . . 8400.00
Pin, Knot Shape, 8 Sapphires, 18K Gold, Tiffany, 2 x 1 3/4 In. 750.00
Pin, Krazy Kat, Black Enamel, Brass, Cat Playing Banjo, Red Rhinestone Eyes, 1 3/8 In. . 125.00
Pin, Ladybug, 18K White Gold, Diamond, Enamel, Art Deco, Cartier, c.1930, 1 In. 6900.00
Pin, Lapel, Bicycle, Diamond, Platinum, Revolving Wheels, 15K Gold, 1900 . . . . 3295.00
Pin, Leaf & Berry Design, Sterling Silver, Arts & Crafts, 1 In. 86.00
Pin, Leafy Swirl, Sterling Silver, Round, Moonstone, Georg Jensen 765.00
Pin, Leaves, Sterling Silver, Curved, Oval Frame, Georg Jensen 380.00
Pin, Leaves, Vines, Berries, Topaz, Tear Drop Shape, 14K Green Gold, 1 1/4 In. 2800.00
Pin, Leopard, Rhinestones, Black Enamel, Moving Tail, Florenza, 2 In. 90.00
Pin, Lion, Emerald Eyes, 1970s 2110.00
Pin, Lizard, Yellow Gold, Green Garnet, Diamond, c.1890 . . . . 3600.00
Pin, Love Birds, Pearl Bodies, French, 1940 . . . . 1675.00
Pin, Lover's Eye, Carved Coral, Gold Pinback, c.1810, 1 1/8 x 1 In. 2640.00
Pin, Man & Woman, Red Stone Accent, 18K Gold & Mixed Metal, M.S. Owens 175.00
Pin, Matrix Mask, Scrolling Headdress, 3 Arrowheads, Sterling Silver, Turquoise 295.00
Pin, Mexican Guitarist, Painted, Bakelite, 3 In. 200.00
Pin, Mosaic, Peacock, Set In Dyed Chalcedony, Yellow Gold Frame, 1 3/8 x 3/4 In. 1200.00
Pin, Mourning, In Memory Of, Black Enamel, Locks Of Hair, 2 1/4 In. . . . . *Illus* 85.00
Pin, Mourning, Oval, Sword, Oak Tree Branch, Shield & Ribbon, Silver, Scotland, c.1860 85.00
Pin, Navette Shape, Sterling Silver, Applied Blossom, Leaves, Oval Pearl, 7/8 x 2 3/8 In. . 325.00
Pin, Nest Of Baby Birds, Gilt Mount, Lalique, c.1920 . . . . 205.00
Pin, Palm Leaves, Ruby Cabochons, 18K Gold, Tiffany, 2 x 1 In. 690.00
Pin, Pearl Leaf, Translucent Enamel, Art Nouveau, 14K Gold, 1890 . . . . 2110.00
Pin, Pearl, Amethyst, Split Pearls, 9K Yellow Gold Frame, Edwardian 145.00
Pin, Pendant, Bouquet, Bakelite, Butterscotch, Carved Leaves, Glass Flowers, 4 1/4 In. . . 1135.00
Pin, Pietra Dura, 2 Butterflies, Lapis, Malachite, Jasper, Agate, 18K Gold, c.1851 . . . . 705.00
Pin, Platinum, Diamond, Blue Sapphire, Art Deco, c.1920, 1 1/4 x 1 In. 2530.00
Pin, Platinum, Diamond, Seed Pearls, Kunzite, C.F. Carlman, Box, c.1940, 3/5 x 1/2 In. . . 4230.00
Pin, Plique-A-Jour, Dragonfly, Diamonds, Emeralds, Sapphire, Enamel, 18K Gold, 2 In. . . 1035.00
Pin, Plique-A-Jour, Lotus Leaves, Pearls, Blue Stone, Sterling Silver, Art Nouveau 1150.00
Pin, Plique-A-Jour, Winged Figure, Diamonds, Emerald, Pearl, 14K Gold, Art Nouveau . . 1920.00
Pin, Poodle, Black & White Polka Dots, Goldtone Metal, 1950s, 2 In. 42.00
Pin, Poodle, Seated, 14K Gold, Tiffany & Co. 90.00
Pin, Poodle, Standing, Show Clip, Rhinestone, Bauer 60.00
Pin, Putti, Amethysts, Diamonds, 18K Gold, Renaissance Revival, Tiffany & Co., c.1900 . 5175.00
Pin, Queen Of Hearts, 18K Gold, Enamel, Diamond, Cartier, Paris, Box, c.1950 . . . . 8400.00
Pin, Rabbit, Ruby, 18K Gold, Tiffany, 1 1/2 x 1 In. 630.00

Pin, Rabbit, Ruby, Orange Coral, 18K Gold, Tiffany, 1 1/4 x 3/4 In. 1095.00
Pin, Racehorse, Enameled Jockey, Diamond, Platinum 4480.00
Pin, Red Cross, Laurel Wreath Border, Enamel, Gold, c.1910 .... 170.00
Pin, Ribbons, 5-Petal Flower Shape, Clear Rhinestones, Hattie Carnegie, 2 In. 125.00
Pin, Ringlet Of Budding Leafy Branches, Sterling Silver, No. 159, Georg Jensen 350.00
Pin, Rose, Full Cut Diamond Dewdrop, 20K Gold, Tiffany 1880.00
Pin, Saint Andrew's Cross, Engraved Sterling Silver, Agate, c.1870 .... 145.00
Pin, Saint Simon's Anchor, Silver, Agate, Scotland, c.1870 .... 160.00
Pin, Salamander, Demantoid Garnets, Silver, 15K Gold, England, c.1850 .... 1320.00
Pin, Santa Claus, Red, Pink, Blue, Clear Rhinestones, Dangling Beard, 3 In. 80.00
Pin, Sapphire, Diamond, Platinum Mount, Black Starr & Frost, Art Deco, 6 7/8 In. 4700.00
Pin, Scottie Dog, Carved White Celluloid, Painted, 1 1/2 In. 43.00
Pin, Scroll, Diamond, Austrian, 14K Gold, 1890 .... 1300.00
Pin, Scrolled Ribbons, Leaves, Prong Set & Baguette Diamonds, Platinum, Art Deco 8050.00
Pin, Sea Gull In Flight, Sterling Silver, Round, Pierced, Chased, Panis Gallery, 1 3/4 In. .. 165.00
Pin, Serpent, Enamel, Emerald, Swag, Tassel, 2 1/2 x 2 1/2 In. 400.00
Pin, Serpent, Enamel, Rose Cut Diamonds, Pearls, Reversible, c.1860, 14K Gold 2530.00
Pin, Shamrock, Seed Pearls, Diamond, Enamel, 14K Gold, c.1900 .... 1380.00
Pin, Shield Shape, Embossed, Enameled Domed, 14K Gold, Victorian, 2 1/4 x 1 In. 330.00
Pin, Silver, Amethysts, Garnets, Topaz, Citrines, Retro, c.1940, 1 3/4 x 1 1/2 In. 230.00
Pin, Silver, Hammered, Cherries, Leaves, Kalo, 2 In. 489.00
Pin, Silver, Hammered, Coral Inset, Stuber & Kay, Hamburg, 1 1/2 In. 58.00
Pin, Snake, Diamond, Emerald, 15K Gold, England, c.1880 .... 840.00
Pin, Spider, Opal, Diamond, Demantoid Garnets, Gold, c.1910 .... 3120.00
Pin, Star Shape, Silver, Green Enamel, Circular, Applied Wire, 1 1/8 In. 95.00
Pin, Star, Silver, 15K Gold Washed, Diamond Center, England, c.1910 .... 1080.00
Pin, Starburst, Diamonds, 18K Gold, Webb 1645.00
Pin, Starfish, Rhinestones, Goldtone Metal, Castlecliff, 2 1/4 In. 55.00
Pin, Sterling Silver, Gold Washed, Jade, Agate, Quartz, Chinese, c.1900 .... 165.00
Pin, Sterling Silver, Green Chalcedony, Bezel Set, Georg Jensen 440.00
Pin, Sterling Silver, Hammered, Applied Snake, Inset Painted Stone, Arts & Crafts, 2 In. . 175.00
Pin, Sterling Silver, Hammered, Inset Amethyst, Stylized Design, Arts & Crafts, 2 In. 300.00
Pin, Sterling Silver, Inset Turquoise, Dangling Pearls, Arts & Crafts, 1 3/4 In. 560.00
Pin, Stork & Bird, Sterling Silver, Georg Jensen 355.00
Pin, Strawberry, Engraved Leaves, 18K Yellow Gold, Tiffany, 1 3/4 x 2 1/8 In. 1870.00
Pin, Stylized Horse, Sterling Silver, Paul Lobel 500.00
Pin, Stylized Horse, Sterling Silver, Signed Paul Lobel, c.1945 .... 500.00
Pin, Thistle, Gilt Metal, Round, Engraved, c.1890 .... 46.00
Pin, Tree, 11 Rubies, 18K Gold, Tiffany, 1 1/4 x 1 1/2 In. 635.00
Pin, Tree, Emerald Leaves, Banded Agate Pot, 18K Gold Mount, Buccellati 2705.00
Pin, Tulip, Ruby, Enamel, 14K Gold, Cartier, 1 1/2 In. 1840.00
Pin, Victory, Snail Form Tank, English & American Flags, Gold, 1945 .... 4478.00
Pin, Winged Deer, Oval, Georg Jensen, c.1924, 2 x 2 1/4 In. 489.00
Pin, Woman Chinese Dress, Flowers, Vines, Opal, Diamond, 18K Bicolor Gold 1175.00
Pin, Woman's Head, Red Clay, Art Deco, 2 1/2 In. 60.00
Pin, Woman, Diadem, Headdress, Sterling Silver, Diamond Ear Pendants, 14K Gold, Erte 529.00
Pin, Woman, Profile, Wearing Turban, 4 Diamonds, 14 K Gold, Art Nouveau 250.00
Pin, Wreath & Bird, Sterling Silver, Denmark 265.00
Pin, Wreath, Laurel Branch, Gold Mesh, Jade Jonquil Rhinestones, Hobe, 2 In. 85.00
Pin, Wreath, Platinum, 17 Old Mine Cut Diamonds, Art Deco, c.1920, 1 In. 1380.00
Pin, Zebra, Carved Wood, Yellow Stripes, Glass Eyes, 1940s, 2 1/2 In. 42.00
Pin & Earrings, Aspen Leaf, Openwork, Goldtone Metal, Sarah Coventry 40.00
Pin & Earrings, Bird Of Paradise, Turquoise & Red Paste Gems, Pot Metal, 1930s 100.00
Pin & Earrings, Cameo, Sardonyx, Brown & White, 14K Yellow Gold, c.1890 .... 805.00
Pin & Earrings, Jelly Belly, Penguin, Pave Diamonds, Sterling Silver, Trifari 200.00
Pin & Earrings, Leaf Shape, Sterling Silver, Green Stone, Georg Jensen 265.00
Pin & Earrings, Tulip Design, Sterling Silver, Georg Jensen 375.00
Ring, 2 Scarabs, Sapphire, 14K Gold, Egyptian Style, Art Nouveau, Size 6 .... 430.00
Ring, 2 Synthetic Sapphires, Diamonds, 14K White Gold, Art Deco, c.1920, Size 5 3/4 ... 375.00
Ring, 3 Diamonds, Box Mounted, F & F Felger, c.1925, Size 6 1/2 .... 805.00
Ring, 3 Diamonds, Sapphire, Gypsy Mount, 14K Yellow Gold, c.1930, Size 10 1/2 ...... 4600.00
Ring, 18K Gold, Bisected Circle, Georg Jensen, Size 7 3/4 .... 440.00
Ring, Amethyst, 2 Diamonds, Bezel Set, Leaves, Gilbert Oakes, Size 8 1/2 .... 3900.00

Ring, Aquamarine, Oval, Blossoms, Leaves, Vine Frame, 14K Gold, Arts & Crafts 470.00
Ring, Band, 3 Bars Bezel Set Coral, 18K Gold, Alesaro, Size 2 1/2 .... 120.00
Ring, Band, Sapphire, Diamond, Platinum, Art Deco, c.1930, Size 7 1/4 .... 1380.00
Ring, Band, Tapered, Ribbed, Crossed Diamond Ribbons, 18K Gold, Tiffany, Size 6 1/4 .. 470.00
Ring, Belle Epoque Diamond, Platinum Front, 14K Gold, 1910 .... 4060.00
Ring, Brass, England, Engraved Date 1681 .... 150.00
Ring, Brilliant Cut Diamond, 14K White Gold, c.1920 .... 600.00
Ring, Cameo, Agate, Diamond Border, 18th Century 2960.00
Ring, Cameo, Classical Maiden, 6 Seed Pearls, 10K Gold Mount, Victorian, Size 7 1/2 .. 175.00
Ring, Cameo, Intaglio Carnelian, George Washington, Yellow Gold, England, c.1840 .... 780.00
Ring, Cameo, Satyr, Goat, Diamond, Silver, Georgian, Size 8 .... 980.00
Ring, Cocktail, Platinum, Diamond, Sapphires, Art Deco, Size 7 1/2 .... 635.00
Ring, Cornucopia, Diamond, Enamel, 18K Gold, 1900 .... 4140.00
Ring, Diamond & Emerald, Baguettes, Tiffany & Co., Size 6 1/4 .... 2470.00
Ring, Diamond, 14K Yellow & White Gold, Art Deco, Size 6 .... 865.00
Ring, Diamond, 14K Yellow & White Gold, c.1900, Size 7 .... 1610.00
Ring, Diamond, Champagne Color, Bezel Set, Art Deco, Size 6 1/2 .... 1765.00
Ring, Diamond, Pink, Flower Mount, Enamel Beading, Art Deco, Size 3 3/4 .... 4700.00
Ring, Diamond, Platinum, 14K Gold, c.1960, Size 5 3/4 .... 2470.00
Ring, Diamond, Platinum, Tiffany & Co., Size 3 1/2 .... 2875.00
Ring, Diamond, Red Spinel, Platinum, Art Deco, c.1930, Size 6 3/4 .... 1955.00
Ring, Diamond, Solitaire, Platinum, Art Deco, c.1920 In., Size 5 3/4 .... 3220.00
Ring, Diamonds, Enamel, Intertwined Tendrils, Art Nouveau, 14K Gold 1150.00
Ring, Dinner, 14K Gold, Sapphire, 12 Diamonds, c.1900, Size 6 1/4 .... 4140.00
Ring, Dinner, Aquamarine, Emerald Cut, 14K White Gold, c.1940, Size 6 1/2 .... 865.00
Ring, Dinner, Caramel Sapphire, 14K Gold, Art Deco, c.1930, Size 6 1/2 .... 920.00
Ring, Dinner, Diamond, Sapphire, 14K White Gold, c.1930, Size 5 1/2 .... 575.00
Ring, Dinner, Diamond, Surrounded By 24 Diamonds, 12 Emeralds, Platinum, Art Deco .. 2600.00
Ring, Dinner, Platinum, Diamond, Art Deco, c.1920, Size 5 .... 1955.00
Ring, Dinner, Sapphire, Diamond, Art Deco, c.1930, Size 5 1/4 .... 920.00
Ring, Emerald & Diamond, Blue Enamel, Applied Bird, 14K Gold, 1800s 565.00
Ring, Emerald, 2 Diamonds, Platinum & 18K Gold Mount, Tiffany 3290.00
Ring, Emerald, 17 Old Rose Cut Diamonds, 18K Gold 1430.00
Ring, Emerald, 34 Single Cut Diamonds, 18K Bicolor Gold, Art Deco, c.1930 .... 2990.00
Ring, Eternity Band, Diamond, Platinum, Art Deco, c.1930, Size 7 3/4 .... .635.00 to 1035.00
Ring, Eternity Band, Platinum, 24 Old European Cut Diamonds, Art Deco, c.1930, Size 7 . 920.00
Ring, Eternity Band, Ruby, Platinum, Art Deco, c.1920 .... 430.00
Ring, Filigree, Platinum, Diamond 1430.00
Ring, Filigree, Platinum, Diamonds, c.1920, Size 6 3/4 .... 4025.00
Ring, Gargoyle, Emerald Eyes, 18K Gold, Hand Wrought, 1920 .... 720.00
Ring, Garnet, 13 Round Cut Stones, 10K Yellow Gold, Mid 1900s, Size 9 1/2 .... 90.00
Ring, Girl's Head, Enamel, Limoges, Art Nouveau, 18K Gold, 1890 .... 1510.00
Ring, Half Pearl, Translucent Red Enamel, 1810 .... 2280.00
Ring, Heart Shape, Diamond, Platinum, 14K White Gold, Art Deco, c.1930, Size 3 1/4 ... 750.00
Ring, Human Hair Band, Rolled 14K Gold Center, Blue Enamel, Early 19th Century 90.00
Ring, Jade, Marquise Shape, 9K Gold, 1910 .... 1440.00
Ring, Knot, Textured, Ring Guard, 18K Gold, Tiffany, Size 3 1/2 .... 440.00
Ring, Opal, Surrounded By 14 Diamonds, 14K Yellow Gold, c.1890, Size 8 1/4 ...... 1610.00
Ring, Pearl, 8 Old Mine Cut Diamonds, Edwardian, Size 5 1/2 .... 825.00
Ring, Pearl, Black Onyx, Flower Border, 14K Gold, c.1915, Size 4 3/4 .... 4000.00
Ring, Platinum, 14 Diamonds, Heart Shape, Art Deco, c.1930, Size 3 1/4 .... 1265.00
Ring, Platinum, Alexandrite, 12 Diamonds, Art Deco, c.1930, Size 6 .... 2070.00
Ring, Platinum, Gold Wash, Old Mine Cut Diamond, Art Deco, c.1920, Size 2 1/2 In. ... 805.00
Ring, Platinum, Serpentine Links, Leaves, Old Mine Cut Diamonds, c.1925 .... 5060.00
Ring, Red Coral, Cabochon, Bezel Set, Engraved Snakes, 14K Gold, Size 8 .... 295.00
Ring, Reeded I Design, 18K Gold, Tiffany, Box, Size 5 1/4 .... 470.00
Ring, Rubies, Sapphires, Diamonds, Red, White & Blue, 14K Gold, J.E. Caldwell & Co. . 290.00
Ring, Ruby, Diamond, 18K Gold & Platinum, Oscar Heyman 2820.00
Ring, Ruby, Diamond, Mine Cut, Bicolor 18K, 14K Gold, Size 6 .... 2350.00
Ring, Sapphire, 2 Mine Cut Diamonds, Gypsy Mount, 14K Rose Gold 865.00
Ring, Sapphire, Diamond, Cushion Shape, Art Deco, Size 5 1/2 ....10575.00
Ring, Sculptured Band, Diamonds, 18K Bicolor Gold, Henry Dunay, Size 6 .... 865.00
Ring, Signature, 15 Diamonds, 18K Yellow Gold, Tiffany & Co., 6 1/2 In. 635.00

Ring, Silver, Gold Washed, 30 Mine Cut Diamonds, c.1900 .... 660.00
Ring, Snake, Diamonds, Cushion & Cut, 18K Gold, Victorian, c.1890 .... 540.00
Ring, Sphere, 18K Gold, Tapered Shank, Dinh Van, Size 6 1/2 .... 560.00
Ring, Stag, Signet, Bloodstone, Rectangular, Pink Gold, Victorian, Size 4 3/4 ...... 200.00
Ring, Star Sapphire, Lavender, 6 Diamonds, Pear Shape, Platinum, Art Deco, Size 4 1/2 .. 4025.00
Ring, Sterling Silver, 2 Flower Buds Flanked By Leaves, Henry Pilstrup 206.00
Ring, Sterling Silver, 3 Women, Flowing Hair, Flowers, Art Nouveau, Size 7 1/2 In. 380.00
Ring, Sterling Silver, Labradorite, Leafy Shoulders, Georg Jensen, Size 6 3/4 .... 206.00
Ring, Sterling Silver, Lapis Lazuli, Leaf & Bud Frame, Georg Jensen, Size 6 .... 235.00
Ring, Stylized Bull's Head, Ruby, Wirework, Bezel Set, 18K Gold, Lalounis, Size 4 ..... 440.00
Ring, Tanzanite, Diamond, 14K Gold, Peter & Dawn Fisher, Size 7 1/4 .... 235.00
Ring, Tourmaline, Abstract Design, 18K Yellow Gold, Man's 69.00
Ring, Tourmaline, Green, Faceted, 3 Pearls, 14K Gold, Gilbert Oakes, Size 8 .... 3100.00
Ring, Tourmaline, Openwork, Basket Weave, 18K Gold, Mauboussin, Size 6 .... 705.00
Ring, Turquoise Cabochon, 18 Mine Cut Diamonds, 14K Gold Mount, Size 4 .... 880.00
Ring, Vines & Flowers, 18K Gold, Anna Bachelli 765.00
Stickpin, Agate, Shield Shape, Engraved, c.1880 .... 80.00
Stickpin, Baby's Face, Carved Moonstone, Diamond Bonnet, Box, Edwardian 1645.00
Stickpin, Circle, 2-Sided, Platinum, Diamond, 18K Gold Mount, Art Deco, Cartier, Box .. 3290.00
Stickpin, Gold, Moonstone, Tiffany 315.00
Stickpin, Hummingbird, Bead Set Diamond Body, 14K Gold 150.00
Stickpin, Interlocking Scroll Design, Impressed Mark, Liberty, 1 3/4 In. 150.00
Stickpin, Owl On Log, Diamonds, Emeralds, Platinum & 14K Gold 825.00
Tiara, Flowers, Diamond, Seed Pearls, Hand-Sewn Wire Frame, 14K Gold, c.1870 ...... 2300.00
Tie Bar, Mesh, 18K Gold, Tiffany & Co., 3 In. 500.00
Watches are listed in their own category.
Wristwatches are listed in their own category.

JOHN ROGERS statues were made from 1859 to 1892. The originals were bronze, but the thousands of copies made by the Rogers factory were of painted plaster. Eighty different figures were created. Similar painted plaster figures were produced by some other factories. Rights to the figures were sold in 1893 and they were manufactured for several more years by the Rogers Statuette Co. Never repaint a Rogers figure because this lowers the value to collectors.

Group, Photographer, 1878, 18 1/2 In. 3750.00
Group, The Council Of War, President Lincoln, General Grant, 1868, 24 In. 1500.00

JOSEF ORIGINALS ceramics were designed by Muriel Joseph George. The first pieces were made in California from 1945 to 1962. They were then manufactured in Japan. The company was sold to George Good in 1982 and he continued to make Josef Originals until 1985. The company was then sold to Southland Corporation. The name is now owned by Applause, and the Birthday Girl series is still being made.

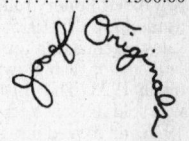

Figurine, Colonial Days Series, Caroline, Girl In Pink Dress & Bonnet, 9 1/2 In. 190.00
Figurine, Doberman Pinscher, 3 3/4 x 6 In. 65.00
Figurine, Girl With Parasol, White Dress With Flowers, 8 3/4 In. 180.00
Figurine, Little International Series, America, Indian Girl, 3 1/2 In. 80.00
Figurine, Mama Ostrich, Sitting On Egg, 5 1/4 In. 70.00
Music Box, Lara's Theme, Russian Boy & Girl On Top, 6 x 4 1/2 In. 125.00
Music Box, Mary Had A Little Lamb, Mary & Lamb, 5 3/8 x 4 1/2 In. 90.00

JUDAICA is any memorabilia that refers to the Jews or the Jewish religion. Interests range from newspaper clippings that mention eighteenth- and nineteenth-century Jewish Americans to religious objects, such as menorahs or spice boxes. Age, condition, and the intrinsic value of the material, as well as the historic and artistic importance, determine the value.

Bag, Matzoh, Silk, Embroidered, Lion, Crown, Leaves, Ivory Ground, 15 In. 176.00
Box, Etrog, Silver, Fruit Shape, Hebrew Text, Ball Feet, Germany, 20th Century, 4 1/2 In . 590.00
Box, Etrog, Silver, Fruit, Branch Finial, Loop Handle, St. Petersburg, Russia, 1900s, 5 In. . 5875.00
Box, Etrog, Silver, Squirrel Finial, Twist Lobed Cover, Scrolled Stem, Russia, 10 3/4 In. .. 150.00
Breastplate, Torah, Sterling Silver, Cartouche, Crown, Scrolls, Cast Leaves, 1936, 13 In. . 705.00

Candelabrum, 7-Light, Branch Arms, Octagonal Stepped Base, Bronze, 15 In., Pair	118.00
Candlestick, Sabbath, Cast Bronze, Fox Hunt, Menorah & Star Of David On Base, 11 In. .	235.00
Candlestick, Sabbath, Silver Plate, Neoclassical Designs, Scroll Feet, Poland, 13 In., Pair .	646.00
Candlestick, Silver, Repousse, Tulip Shaped Holders, A. Reiner, Warsaw, 12 In., Pair	1293.00
Carafe, Wine, Shabbat, Pottery, Painted Lions, Grapes, Vines, Hebrew Text, Dutch, 11 In.	441.00
Carpet, Wool, Rachel's Tomb, Menorahs, Zion, Bezalel, Marvadia, Jerusalem, 20 x 43 In.	3819.00
Container, Charity, Barrel Shape, Ribbed, Slot Top, Handle, Copper, 19th Century, 7 1/2 In.	176.00
Container, Charity, Synagogue Shape, Damascene, Hebrew Text & Symbols, 10 In.	705.00
Cup, Kiddush, Flared Rim, Circumcision Inscription, Silver, Dutch, 1927, 3 1/2 In.	765.00
Cup, Kiddush, Silver, Etched Palm Trees, Hebrew Text, Tapered, Flared Foot, Bezalel, 4 In.	940.00
Cup, Kiddush, Silver, Filigree, Medallions, Early 20th Century, Bezalel, Jerusalem, 5 In. .	881.00
Cup, Kiddush, Silver, Flared Rim, Planters, Trees, Hebrew Inscription, Poland, 2 1/2 In. .	940.00
Cup, Kiddush, Silver, Flared, Slender Stem, Square Foot, Germany, 19th Century, 5 1/2 In.	590.00
Cup, Kiddush, Silver, Leaf Band, Scroll, Hebrew Inscription, Poland, 19th Century, 2 In.	323.00
Curtain, Torah, Velvet, Embroidered, Lion, Leaves, Hebrew Lettering, Gold Thread	1763.00
Knife, Shabbat, Metal, Mother-Of-Pearl, Hebrew Inscription, Czechoslovakia, 5 1/2 In. . .	176.00
Lamp, Hanukah, Brass, Copper, Shaped Backplate, Applied Hearts, Stars, Paw Feet, 12 In.	588.00
Lamp, Hanukah, Brass, Openwork Backplate, Lions, Crown, Heart, Candleholders, 10 In.	588.00
Lamp, Hanukah, Bronze, Shaped Backplate, Star, Lion, Oil Wells, Poland, 9 1/2 In.	1058.00
Lamp, Hanukah, Servant, Brass, Lions, Menorah, Hebrew Words, Bezalel, 6 In.	705.00
Lamp, Hanukah, Servant, Oil Fonts, Bronze, Arched, Figure Of Judith, Scrolls, Italy, 8 In.	1763.00
Lamp, Hanukah, Wood, Carved, Incised Designs, Folk Art, Central America, 1970s, 15 In.	118.00
Megillah, Brass Case, Serpentine Thumb Piece, Parchment Scroll, Purim Story, 13 In.	2700.00
Megillah, Silver Repousse Case, Flattened Onion Top, Sephardic Script Scroll, 10 In.	2700.00
Mezuzah, Silver, Ivory, Carved, Crown, Lions, Scrolled Backplate, Coral Cabochon, 7 In.	323.00
Noisemaker, Purim, Silver, Filigree, Applied Turquoise, Carnelian, Hebrew Text, 12 In. . .	1528.00
Plaque, Bronze, Mother & Child Putting Money In Tzdaka Box, B. Schatz, 6 3/8 In.	823.00
Plate, Seder, Rose, Yellow & Brown Transfers, Aqua Border, Flowers, Shaped Rim, 9 In. .	588.00
Pointer, Torah, Bone, Turned Shaft & Knops, Pointed Hand, Compartment In Finial, 12 In.	705.00
Spice Box, Cover, Silver, Rectangular, Fruit Finial, 3 Sections, Ball Feet, Germany, 2 1/2 In.	1175.00
Spice Box, Tower, Silver, Tapered Spire, Filigree Compartment, Footed, Germany, 7 In. . .	1645.00
Spice Container, Silver, Fish Shape, Removable Head, Red Stone Eyes, 5 1/2 In.	118.00
Spice Tower, Silver, Filigree, Flag, Birds, Bells, Circular Base, Leaf & Berry, Russia	2000.00
Spice Tower, Silver, Filigree, Late 19th Century, Germany, 12 In.	58.00
Tapestry, Wool, Aviva Margalit, Ein Hod Artists Village, Israel, 1950s, 66 x 46 In.	646.00
Torah Pointer, Silver, Knop, Bells, Cuffed Hands, Hebrew Inscription, Poland, 9 In.	823.00

JUGTOWN Pottery refers to pottery made in North Carolina as far back as the 1750s. In 1915, Juliana and Jacques Busbee set up a training and sales organization for what they named *Jugtown Pottery*. In 1921, they built a shop at Jugtown, North Carolina, and hired Ben Owen as a potter in 1923. The Busbees moved the village store where the pottery was sold to New York City. Juliana Busbee sold the New York store in 1926 and moved into a log cabin near the Jugtown Pottery. The pottery closed in 1959. It reopened in 1960 and is still working near Seagrove, North Carolina.

Bowl, Applied Handles, Brown, Orange Glaze, 3 1/4 x 10 In.	195.00
Bowl, Blue Glaze, Marked, 4 1/2 In.	145.00
Jar, Cracker, Orange, Red Lead Glaze, Groove Top Handles, 1930s, 7 1/2 In.	413.00
Vase, Baluster, Red, Mottled Glaze, Impressed, 9 x 6 1/2 In.	1265.00
Vase, Bud, Beaker Form, Blue Glaze, Marked, 3 1/2 x 3 1/2 In.	145.00
Vase, Oval, Lug Handles, Frogskin, Olive, Yellow, Amber Glaze, 7 1/2 In.	400.00
Vase, Pear Shape, Blue Glaze, Red Flashes, Stamped, 6 x 5 In.	1150.00
Vase, Round, Shaped Shoulder, Blue Glaze, 5 3/4 x 4 1/2 In.	385.00
Vase, Round, Stepped, Flared Rim, Blue Glaze, Frogskin Interior, 9 x 6 In.	305.00
Vase, Squat, Blue, Mottled Glaze, Impressed, 5 1/2 x 6 In.	2070.00

JUKEBOXES play records. The first coin-operated phonograph was demonstrated in 1889. In 1906 the *Automatic Entertainer* appeared, the first coin-operated phonograph to offer several different selections of music. The first electrically powered jukebox was introduced in 1927. Collectors search for jukeboxes of all ages, especially those with flashing lights and unusual design and graphics.

Rock-Ola, Model 1422, 20 Selections, 78 RPM, 1946	4180.00

Seeburg, Model 146M, Symphonola, Trashcan, 20 Selections, 78 RPM, 1946 . . . .   750.00
Seeburg, Model 148SL, Trash Can, Aluminum, 20 Selections, 78 RPM, 1948 . . . .   3355.00
Wurlitzer, Model 24, Light Up, 24 Selections, 78 RPM, 1938 . . . .   2875.00
Wurlitzer, Model 700, Coin-Operated, 24 Selections, 78 RPM, 1940 . . . .   4000.00
Wurlitzer, Model 1015, 24 Selections, 78 RPM, 1946-1947, 59 In. . . . . .6500.00 to 6900.00

KATE GREENAWAY, who was a famous illustrator of children's books, drew pictures of children in high-waisted Empire dresses. She lived from 1846 to 1901. Her designs appear on china, glass, and other pieces.

Bonbon, Cherubs Carrying Cornucopia Of Flowers, Shell Shape, 4 3/4 In. 8.00
Book, Almanack For 1889, Routledge 175.00
Book, Children's Birthday, F.E. Weatherly, With Other Illustrators, W. Mack, 1880 . . . . . .   250.00
Book, Marigold Garden, Woodblock Designs On Cover 25.00
Book, Pink & Blue Affair, Ruth Campbell, 1923 . . . .   60.00
Calling Card Tray, Figural, Sisters & Their Dog, Derby, 7 1/4 In. 550.00
Card, Advertising, Boy In Coat, Streeter, Brimmer & Olean, Watertown, N.Y., 4 In. 15.00
Napkin Ring, Figural, Boy, Openwork Ring, Tufts 995.00
Napkin Ring, Figural, Boy, With Bat & Ball 1100.00
Napkin Ring, Figural, Girl, Seated On Branches 1250.00
Salt & Pepper, Boy & Girl, In Victorian Dress, 4 3/4 In. 95.00
Salt & Pepper, Boy & Girl, Pottery, Continental, 4 3/8 In. 95.00
Salt & Pepper, Boy & Girl, Ribbed Base, Purple Flower, 2 3/4 In. 95.00

KAY FINCH Ceramics were made in Corona Del Mar, California, from 1935 to 1963. The hand-decorated pieces often depicted whimsical animals and people. Pastel colors were used.

Kay Finch
CALIFORNIA

Figurine, Cat, Whimsical, Pink, Purple, Green, Blue, Signed, 7 In. 104.00
Figurine, Godey Man, 8 In. 75.00
Figurine, Pig 150.00
Figurine, Poodle, No. 5203, Pearlized Gray & Gold, 10 In. . . . . *Illus*   400.00
Figurine, Poodle, No. 5304, Playful 400.00

KAYSERZINN, see Pewter category.

KELVA glassware was made by the C. F. Monroe Company of Meriden, Connecticut, about 1904. It is a pale, pastel-painted glass decorated with flowers, designs, or scenes. Kelva resembles Nakara and Wave Crest, two other glasswares made by the same company.

KELVA

Box, Green Mottled Ground, Pink Flowers, Gilt Metal Base, Hinged Cover, 2 1/2 x 3 In. . .   1050.00
Box, Mottled Green, Pink Flowers, Beading, Hinged Cover, Signed, 2 3/4 x 4 1/2 In. 375.00
Box, Mottled Red, Blue Flowers, Hinged Cover, New Lining, Signed, 2 3/4 x 4 1/2 In. . . .   325.00
Box, Pink Flowers, Green Mottled Ground, Hinged Cover, Signed, 3 1/2 x 8 In. .1000.00 to 1150.00
Jewelry Box, Mottled Pink, Blue Flowers, Lining, Hinged Cover, Signed, 2 1/2 x 3 3/4 In. .   175.00
Jewelry Box, Mottled Red, Flowers, Linging, Hinged Cover, Signed, 2 1/2 x 3 1/2 In. 250.00
Vase, Gray Mottled Ground, Pink Flowers, Gilt Metal Handles, Base, 9 1/2 In. 650.00
Vase, Stick, Mottled Green Ground, Pink Flowers, Gilt Metal Feet, 9 In. 425.00

Kay Finch, Figurine,
Poodle, No. 5203,
Pearlized Gray & Gold,
10 In.

Kew Blas, Vase, Green,
Gold, Iridescent, Hooked
Feathers, Gold Interior,
Signed, 9 In.

KENTON HILLS Pottery in Erlanger, Kentucky, made artwares, including vases and figurines that resembled Rookwood, probably because
so many of the original artists and workmen had worked at the
Rookwood plant. Kenton Hills opened in 1939 and closed during
World War II.

Ashtray, Fish Shape, Green Majolica Glaze, Marked, 8 3/4 In.	230.00
Figurine, Dove, Green, David Seyler, 4 3/8 x 7 In.	375.00
Vase, Sung Plum Glaze, 5 1/4 In.	115.00
Vase, Tapered, Light Blue High Glaze, Black Highlights, Marked, 5 In.	400.00

KEW BLAS is the name used by the Union Glass Company of Somer-
ville, Massachusetts. The name refers to an iridescent golden glass
made from the 1890s to 1924. The iridescent glass was reminiscent of
the Tiffany glass of the period.

Bowl, Green Iridescent, Rectangular Mouth, Signed, 2 x 4 1/2 In.	385.00
Chalice, Reddish Blue Iridescent, Flared, Raised Disc Foot, Signed, 5 x 6 In.	415.00
Compote, Green, Pink, Gold Iridescent, Ruffled Edge, Knopped Stem, Signed, 6 1/2 In.	440.00
Compote, Green, Purple, Gold Iridescent, Optic Ribs, Raised Disc Foot, Signed, 5 3/4 In.	360.00
Finger Bowl, Underplate, Gold Iridescent, Ruffled Edge, Ribs, Signed, 2 1/2 In.	360.00
Pitcher, Pulled Feathers, Gold Iridescent Interior, Early 1900s, 4 3/8 In.	765.00
Saucer, Gold Iridescent, Scalloped Edge, 6 3/4 In.	145.00
Vase, Gold Iridescent, Green Pulled Feathers, White Ground, Ruffled Edge, 6 1/2 In.	2185.00
Vase, Green & Gold Pulled Feathers, Opal Ground, Bulbous, Signed, 4 1/4 In.	785.00
Vase, Green & Gold Pulled Feathers, White Ground, Gold Interior, Signed, 8 1/4 In.	1120.00
Vase, Green Pulled Feathers, Gold Iridescent, Ruffled Edge, Signed, 8 1/2 In.	1430.00
Vase, Green, Gold, Iridescent, Hooked Feathers, Gold Interior, Signed, 9 In. .... *Illus*	920.00
Vase, Linear Pattern, Gold Iridescent Interior, Flared Rim, Bulbous, Early 1900s, 3 In.	530.00
Vase, Pulled Feathers, Gold Iridescent, Scalloped Rim, c.1920, 8 In.	530.00

KEWPIES, designed by Rose O'Neill, were first pictured in the *Ladies'
Home Journal.* The figures, which are similar to pixies, were a success,
and Kewpie dolls and figurines started appearing in 1911. Kewpie pictures and other items soon followed. Collectors search for all items that
picture the little winged people.

Bisque, Bride & Groom, Germany, 4 1/2 In., Pair	115.00
Bisque, Jointed, Painted Side-Glancing Eyes, Smiling, Wings, Crossed Arms, 4 In.	300.00
Bisque, Standing, Jointed Shoulders, 5 In.	100.00
Bisque, Thinker, Sitting, Elbows On Knees, Chin In Hand, Painted Eyes, Smiling, 7 In.	205.00
Bisque, Wide Brim, Brown Hat, Jointed Arms, O'Neill On Feet, Germany, c.1915, 6 In.	4620.00
Candy Container, Barrel Bank, Side-Glancing Eyes, Metal Snap Lid, 3 In.	90.00
Celluloid, Groom, Japan, 3 In.	50.00
Composition, Painted Features, 5-Piece Body, Sunsuit, Socks, Shoes, Cameo, 12 In.	440.00
Composition, Painted Features, Molded & Painted Hair, Jointed Arms, Wings, 11 In.	65.00
Doll, Cloth, Mask Face, Rosy Cheeks, Painted Features, Wings, Soft Stuffed, 18 In.	690.00
Plate, 5 Kewpies At Play, Porcelain, Rose O'Neill, 7 In.	115.00
Salt & Pepper, Porcelain, Seated, Bunny, Chick, Germany, c.1920, 3 In., Pair	825.00

KIMBALL, see Cluthra category.

KING'S ROSE, see Soft Paste category.

KITCHEN utensils of all types, from eggbeaters to bowls, are collected
today. Handmade wooden and metal items, like ladles and apple peelers, were made in the early nineteenth century. Mass-produced pieces,
like iron apple peelers and graniteware, were made in the nineteenth
century. Also included in this category are utensils used for other
household chores, such as laundry and cleaning. Other kitchen wares
are listed under manufacturers' names or under Advertising, Iron, Tool,
or Wooden.

Applesauce Pot, Brass, Copper Handles, Dutch, 11 1/2 x 18 In.	375.00
Batter Bowl, Burl, Tapered Sides, Carved Handle, Wrought Iron Handle, 11 x 6 In.	891.00
Batter Bowl, Glass, Ovenware, White, Handle, Federal, 7 3/4 In.	50.00
Board, Cheese, Mahogany, Silver Plate Mounts, 8 x 8 x 4 1/2 In.	250.00
Board, Dough, Heart Cutout, Rectangular, Rounded Corners, Pennsylvania, 22 x 16 In.	650.00

Bowl, Chopping, Burl, Maple, American, c.1800, 18 In. 3795.00
Bowl, Chopping, Pine, Rectangular, 6 1/2 x 26 x 17 In. 195.00
Bowl, Dough, Cherry, Cover, Stand, Late 19th Century, 30 x 26 x 29 In. 115.00
Bowl, Dough, Hewn, Painted, Blue Green, Winter Scene, 22 x 15 1/2 x 6 In. 260.00
Bowl, Dough, Rolling Pin, Maple, Hand Carved, 19 x 13 x 4 1/2 & 19 x 2 1/2 In. 145.00
Bowl, Salad, Green Paint, American, 1800s, 20 x 12 1/2 In. 259.00
Box, Lift Top, Drawer, Yellow Painted, 11 x 10 1/2 x 8 In. 240.00
Butcher Tool Set, Dippers, Bow, Forks, Spatula, Dipper, Skimmer, Forged Iron, 8 Piece . . 145.00
Butter Bowl, Wooden, Interior Painted, Indians, Canoes, White Water, 15 In. 300.00
Butter Bowl, Wooden, Interior Winter Scene, Painted, Church, Stream, 13 1/2 In. 300.00
Butter Mold, look under Mold, Butter in this category.
Butter Paddle, Bird's-Eye Maple, Hook Handle, 10 In. 165.00
Butter Paddle, Wooden, Carved, 9 1/4 In. 39.00
Butter Stamp, 2 Birds, In Shield, Holding Pinecones, Wooden, Carved, 4 3/4 x 4 1/2 In. . 83.00
Butter Stamp, 2-Sided, Eagle, Vining, X Design Reverse, Wooden Handle, 4 1/2 In. 358.00
Butter Stamp, 3 Tulips, Hatched Border, Oval, 3 3/4 x 5 1/2 In. 1155.00
Butter Stamp, 6-Lobed Star, Hatching, Round, 4 1/2 In. 60.00
Butter Stamp, 6-Point Star, Round, 3 1/2 x 3 1/2 In. 250.00
Butter Stamp, 6-Point Star, Round, Chip Carved Border, 1 x 4 In. 140.00
Butter Stamp, Acorn & Fern Leaf, Arch & Block Border, 4 In. 105.00
Butter Stamp, American Eagle, Double, Facing Each Other, Shields, Arrows, 3 1/2 In. . . 590.00
Butter Stamp, Carved Initials, Detachable Handle, Round, 4 x 6 In. 165.00
Butter Stamp, Cow & Fence, Rope Border, 2 Parts, 3 1/2 In. 220.00
Butter Stamp, Cow, Doll, Handle, 3 1/8 In. 259.00
Butter Stamp, Cow, Leaves, Gouged Border, 3 x 3 1/2 In. 145.00
Butter Stamp, Cow, Nell, Leaf, Stem, Rope Border, 3 3/8 In. 525.00
Butter Stamp, Crosshatched Heart, Feathered, 3 3/8 In. 288.00
Butter Stamp, Double Acorn, Leaf, 2 Parts, 3 7/8 In. 70.00
Butter Stamp, Double Thistle, Leaf, 2 Parts, 4 In. 200.00
Butter Stamp, Eagle, 8-Point Star, 3 3/4 In. 220.00
Butter Stamp, Eagle, Flower, Notched Border, 3 3/4 In. 365.00
Butter Stamp, Eagle, Leaves, Treen, 2 1/2 x 4 3/4 In. 154.00
Butter Stamp, Eagle, On Branch, 8-Point Star, Concentric Ring Border, 4 1/2 In. 220.00
Butter Stamp, Eagle, On Branch, Handle, 2 7/8 In. 575.00
Butter Stamp, Fish, Swimming, Water Plants, Handle, 3 In. 690.00
Butter Stamp, Flower Basket, Scrubbed Surface, 3 1/2 In. 144.00
Butter Stamp, Flower, Thistle, Leaf, 2 Parts, 4 In. 85.00
Butter Stamp, Flowers, Applied Handle, Round, 5 x 4 3/8 In. 250.00
Butter Stamp, Flowers, Letters, 7 1/2 x 3 3/4 In. 130.00
Butter Stamp, Fox, Running, Handle, 3 1/2 In. 85.00
Butter Stamp, Game Bird, Long Legs, Short Beak, Threaded Handle, 3 3/4 In. 259.00
Butter Stamp, Half Moon, Star & Leaf Border, 3 1/4 x 4 1/8 In. 155.00
Butter Stamp, Heart, Flower, Zigzag Border, Oval, Pine, 3 1/2 x 5 1/2 In. 2090.00
Butter Stamp, Heart, Tulip, 8-Point Star, Geometric & Zigzag Border, 3 3/8 In. 910.00
Butter Stamp, Hen, Threaded Handle, 4 In. 575.00
Butter Stamp, Initial M, Cut Leaf, Round Handle, 4 In. 330.00
Butter Stamp, Leaf, Rake, Pitchfork, Wales, 1768 . . . . 350.00
Butter Stamp, Lollipop, Chip Carved, Elongated, Center Flower, 12 1/8 In. 80.00
Butter Stamp, Lollipop, Double, Maple 2070.00
Butter Stamp, Lollipop, Star Center, Carved Border, Metal Handle, 9 In. 275.00
Butter Stamp, Lollipop, Stylized Eagle, Curly Maple, 4 x 9 In. 385.00
Butter Stamp, Lollipop, Sunburst, Starflower Center, 9 In. 145.00
Butter Stamp, Lollipop, Tulip, Carved Handle, 4 1/4 x 7 1/2 In. 2090.00
Butter Stamp, Pennsylvania German Heart, Tulip, Compass Star, Pine, 6 1/2 x 4 In. 4620.00
Butter Stamp, Pheasant, Inset Handle, 4 3/8 In. 288.00
Butter Stamp, Pineapple, Flower, Leaf, 4 1/4 In. 110.00
Butter Stamp, Pinwheel, Rosette, 3 3/4 In. 105.00
Butter Stamp, Pinwheel, Triangle Handle, Round, 4 1/4 In. 110.00
Butter Stamp, Ram, Curled Horns, Double Scalloped Border, 3 1/2 In. 345.00
Butter Stamp, Sheaf Of Wheat, Fern Leaf, Notched Border, Oblong, 5 7/8 In. 825.00
Butter Stamp, Sheaf Of Wheat, Gouged Border, 3 x 4 1/2 In. 72.00
Butter Stamp, Sheaf Of Wheat, Threaded Handle, 4 1/8 In. 86.00
Butter Stamp, Songbird, 3 Leaves, Handle, 3 3/4 In. 175.00

Butter Stamp, Songbird, Flower, Handle, 3 1/2 In. 115.00
Butter Stamp, Star, Flowers, Bull's-Eye, Star, Coggled Rim, 2 Parts, 4 3/4 In. 195.00
Butter Stamp, Star, Round, Pine, 3 1/2 In. 105.00
Butter Stamp, Strawberry, Leaf, 2 Parts, 4 1/4 In. 220.00
Butter Stamp, Sunflower, Leaf, 4 1/4 In. 200.00
Butter Stamp, Swan, In Lake, 2 Parts, 4 In. 190.00
Butter Stamp, Thistle, Leaf, 4 In. 85.00
Butter Stamp, Tulip, 2 Stars, 3 1/4 x 4 3/4 In. 525.00
Butter Stamp, Tulip, Leaf, Coggled Rim, 3 3/4 In. 220.00
Butter Stamp, Tulip, Leaf, Star, 4 3/4 In. 220.00
Butter Stamp, Tulip, Star Center, Chip Carved Border, 3 x 4 1/2 In. 770.00
Butter Stamp, Tulip, Stars, 1-Piece Handle, 4 7/8 In. 288.00
Butter Stamp, Woman, Churning Butter, Leaves, Fluted & Ring Border, 4 In. 800.00
Butter Stamp, Woman, Polka Dot Dress, Maple, Shenandoah Valley, Va., 3 x 1 3/4 In. 1265.00
Cabbage Cutter, Board, Chestnut, Single Blade, Heart Cutout, Arched Top, 15 In. 176.00
Cabbage Cutter, Hand Crank, Horizontal Blade, 1890 .... 275.00
Cake Board, Geometric, Figures, Conger Style, Round, Chip Carved, c.1880, 11 x 11 In. .. 1880.00
Cake Board, Jenny Lind, Chip Carved, c.1860, 8 1/2 x 5 x 1 In. 375.00
Cake Board, Jenny Lind, Opera Singer, Ferns, American, c.1855, 8 1/2 x 5 x 1 In. 375.00
Cake Board, Walnut, 2-Sided, Man Riding Pig Backward, Pony, c.1840, 5 1/2 x 8 In. 1430.00
Canister, Banded Decoration, Bun Feet, Lignum Vitae, Mid 1800s, 9 In. 145.00
Canister Set, Blown Glass, Tin Lid, 4 1/2 x 6 In. & 4 3/4 x 11 1/2 In., 2 Piece 315.00
Casserole, Cover, White, Black & Gold Diamonds, Federal Glass, 2 1/2 Qt. 16.00
Cauldron, Cast Iron, Chinese Bronze Style, Double Loop Handle, 3-Footed, 14 x 22 In. .. 80.00
Charcoal, Cast Iron, High Sheen Polished, Japan, 6 1/4 In. 220.00
Charcoal, Iron, Upright Chimney, Portugal, 7 3/4 In. 286.00
Cheese Strainer, Wood, Rack, Round, 25 In. 220.00
Chestnut Roaster, Brass Pan, Turned Wood Handle, Pierced, Hinged Lid, 22 x 6 3/4 In. . 145.00
Chestnut Roaster, Copper, Brass Handle, England, c.1845, 5 x 21 In. 145.00
Churn, 5 Overlapping Bands, Rosehead Nails, Lollipop Handle, Painted, 45 1/2 In. 575.00
Churn, Ballard, Cobalt Blue, Flower Branch, Double Crescent Handles, 18 3/4 In. 290.00
Churn, Black Over Red Graining, White Scrolling, c.1868, 17 x 34 In. 275.00
Churn, Blue Tin, Iron Frame, Handle 90.00
Churn, Countertop, Wood, Hand Crank, Yellow Paint, 14 In. 385.00
Churn, Cylinder Shape, Wood Dasher, Lid, 16 In. 135.00
Churn, Dazey, Glass, Metal, 2 Qt. 220.00
Churn, Flower, Glass Jar Bottom, Dazey, Qt. 1760.00
Churn, Funk's Champion, Wood, Stenciling, 1865 Patent, 33 In. 190.00
Churn, Glass, Metal, Dazey, 2 Qt. 220.00
Churn, Glass, Raised Cow, Electric, Gem Dandy, Alabama Mfg., Birmingham, 25 In. 77.00
Churn, Glass, Round Paper Label, Dazey, Qt. 1320.00
Churn, Glass, Wood Dasher, Iron Top, 14 1/4 In. 20.00
Churn, Glass, Wood Handle, Iron Crank, Fulton Glass, 14 In. 79.00
Churn, Glass, Wood Handle, Iron Crank, Tin Lid, Germany, 13 1/4 In. 45.00
Churn, Iron Bands, Wooden, 29 x 18 In. 595.00
Churn, Maple, Hickory, Stave Construction, 4 Iron Bands, c.1800, 36 1/2 In. 460.00
Churn, Metal, Hand Crank, Wood Cover, 20th Century, 14 In. 160.00
Churn, Rosewood, Grain Painted, E.H. Funks Champion, 1868 Patent, 40 1/4 In. 900.00
Churn, Square, Iron Crank Handle, Red Paint, 1870 Patent, 32 x 18 x 19 In. 115.00
Churn, Stave Construction, Iron Bands, Varnished, American, 39 In. 259.00
Churn, Stave Construction, Lid, Loop Handle, Red Paint, American, 48 In. 115.00
Churn, Staved Construction, Barrel Shape, Knopped Handle, American, 44 1/2 In. 259.00
Cleaver, Angel Shape, Polished Steel, Tiger Maple Handle, Brass, 12 3/4 In. 1630.00
Coffee Grinders are listed in the Coffee Mill category.
Coffee Maker, Naperian, Copper Beaker, Flask, Tap, Burner, Britain, 19th Century, 12 In. .. 206.00
Coffee Mills are listed in their own category
Cookie Board, 2-Sided, Cat 1 Side, Dog Other Side, Fruitwood, 14 In. 530.00
Cookie Board, 4 Incised Figures, Men On Horseback, Carved, 3 1/2 x 16 In. 165.00
Cookie Board, Compass Stars, Geometric Corner Designs, Wood, 6 3/4 x 12 3/4 In. 468.00
Cookie Board, King In Robe & Crown, Wood, Scandinavia, 33 In. 47.00
Cookie Board, Man 1 Side, Man & Woman Other Side, 39 1/2 x 9 1/2 In. 403.00
Cookie Board, Rooster, Horse & Rider, Man On Barrel, Ship, 3 3/4 x 24 In. 110.00
Cookie Board, Rooster, In Heart, Vine Heart, Red Stain, 7 1/8 In. 190.00

Cookie Board, Snail, On Leaf, Ash, 4 3/8 x 3 1/8 In.	580.00
Cookie Cutter, 4 Hearts, Tin, 1 7/8 x 3 1/2 In.	17.00
Cookie Cutter, Acorn, Handle, Fluted, Shaped Back Plate, Tin, 3 1/2 x 3 1/4 In.	195.00
Cookie Cutter, Belsnickle, Santa, Long Beard, c.1900, 6 In.	209.00
Cookie Cutter, Bird, Long Tail, Tin, 5 x 3 In.	358.00
Cookie Cutter, Birds, Animals, Boot, Top Hat, Tin, 13 Piece	403.00
Cookie Cutter, Church, Tin, 4 1/4 x 3 3/4 In.	11.00
Cookie Cutter, Civil War Soldier, 3/4 Profile, 19th Century, 8 1/2 In. .... *Illus*	2090.00
Cookie Cutter, Eagle, Spread Wing, Tin, 4 3/4 x 5 1/2 In.	633.00
Cookie Cutter, Flower, Leaf, Tin, 5 x 2 3/4 In.	28.00
Cookie Cutter, Goose, Tin, 5 3/4 x 5 1/8 In.	84.00
Cookie Cutter, Horse, Galloping, Tin, 2 3/4 x 3 3/4 In.	18.00
Cookie Cutter, Horse, Trotting, Tin, Folded Rim, 6 x 8 5/8 In.	195.00
Cookie Cutter, Man, On Horse, Tin, 4 1/4 x 5 1/2 In.	140.00
Cookie Cutter, Rooster, Looking Backward, Handle, Tin, 6 x 5 In.	110.00
Cookie Cutter, Rooster, Tin, 4 1/8 x 4 In.	50.00
Cookie Cutter, Rooster, Tin, 6 x 4 3/4 In.	85.00
Cookie Cutter, Rooster, Tin, Copper, Applied Handle, 6 x 5 3/4 In.	110.00
Cookie Cutter, Spingerle, Christmas Tree, 18th Century	750.00
Cookie Cutter, Sprinperle, Easter, Tin, 7 1/2 x 11 In.	95.00
Cookie Cutter, Violin, Tin, 7 1/4 x 3 1/2 In.	220.00
Cookie Cutter, Whale, Applied Handle, Tin, 1 3/4 x 3 3/4 In.	35.00
Cookie Cutter, Woman, Head Turned To Side, Applied Handle, 19th Century, 8 1/4 In.	990.00
Cookie Mold, Springerle, 4 Rows Of 4 Carved Blocks, c.1830, 5 x 7 & 2 x 5 In., Pair	575.00
Cookie Mold, Springerle, 8 Carved Blocks, Maple, Late 1700s, 3 3/4 x 7 1/4 x 9 In.	750.00
Cookie Pan, Brass, Wire Reinforced Rolled Rim, Wrought Iron Handle, 13 x 13 1/2 In.	72.00
Cork Extractor, Champion, Cast Iron, Embossed, Wooden Handle, c.1898, 9 In.	316.00
Cream Spoon, Stainless, Imperial, USA, 4 1/2 In.	18.00
Cutlery Tray, Bird's Eye Maple, American, 19th Century, 5 x 15 x 9 1/2 In.	290.00
Cutlery Tray, Scalloped Sides, Open Center Handle, 3 1/2 In.	195.00
Cutting Board, Maple, Heart Shape Cutout, Natural Finish, 21 3/4 In.	250.00
Cutting Board, Oak, Heart Shape Cutout, Scrolled Top, 20 x 7 1/2 In.	176.00
Cutting Board, Pine, 16 x 10 In.	5.50
Cutting Board, Poplar, Heart-Shaped Cut Out, 8 x 21 1/2 In.	195.00
Cutting Board, Poplar, Rounded Bottom Corner, 15 x 10 3/4 In.	22.00
Cutting Board, Single, Oak, 3-Footed, 18th Century, 10 In.	350.00
Cutting Board, Tiger Maple, 44 1/2 x 11 In.	200.00
Cutting Board, Tiger Maple, Round, 9 1/2 In.	495.00
Dish, Baking, Slipware, 18th Century, 11 In.	1400.00
Dish, Wooden, Cherry, Footed, 18th Century, 12 In.	850.00
Dispenser, Coffee Bean, Nickel, Brass, Cylindrical, 25 In.	165.00
Dough Box, Beveled, Lid, Mortis & Tenon Construction, Scalloped Skirt, 27 x 42 x 22 In.	440.00
Dough Box, Floor, Stand, 1-Board Top, Turned Legs, Scroll Handles, 28 x 36 x 17 In.	175.00
Dough Box, Grain Painted, Lift Top, 2 Drawers, Legs, Amish, 45 In.	470.00
Dough Box, Green Paint, c.1880s, 45 In.	230.00
Dough Box, Painted, Red Wash, Black Stripes, Splay Legs, 1800s, 40 x 18 x 28 In.	990.00
Dough Box, Pine, Hinged Lid, Tapered Base, 30 x 38 1/2 x 20 1/2 In.	110.00

Kitchen, Cookie
Cutter, Civil War
Soldier, 3/4 Profile,
19th Century,
8 1/2 In.

Kitchen, Food
Chopper, Glass,
Measuring,
Lithographed Tin
Cover, Hazel
Atlas, 7 1/2 In.

**If your old cast-iron pan
without a wooden handle
is dirty, clean it in a
self-cleaning oven.**

Dough Box, Pine, Lift Top, Dovetailed, Drawer, Tray, Iron Hinges, 40 x 31 1/2 x 23 In. . . . 495.00
Dough Box, Provincial, Carved, Trapezoidal, Flowers, Louis XVI, 1800s, 28 x 46 In. 940.00
Dough Box, Splayed Legs, Skirt, Stand, Slide Top, Pumpkin Pine Finish, 27 x 34 x 18 In. 259.00
Dough Box, White Pine, Dovetailed, Removable Lid, Painted, Blue, 9 x 31 x 6 In. 795.00
Dough Scraper, Brass, Iron, Peter Derr, 1840 . . . . 1495.00
Dough Scraper, Wrought Iron, Heart Cutout Blade, Tapered Handle, 4 1/2 In. 195.00
Dough Tray, Oak, Dovetailed, Tapered Splay Legs, Breadboard Ends, 66 x 26 x 30 In. . . . 960.00
Drying Rack, Plate, Painted Blue, 2 Levels, 36 x 24 In. 395.00
Drying Rack, Wire Mesh, Wood, U.S. Cook Stove, E.G. Farney, Waynesboro, Pa., 25 In. . 198.00
Dutch Oven, Griswold, No. 8, Lid 225.00
Dutch Oven, Martin Stove, No. 8 . . . . 25.00
Eggcup, Wooden, Painted, Salmon Ground, Strawberry 935.00
Eggcup, Wooden, Painted, Tan Ground, Blue, Red, Green, Applied Decal, 3 1/2 In. 825.00
Flatiron, Central, Model M, Cast Iron Heat Shield 20.00
Fluter, Brass, Cast Iron, Built In Slug, Geneva, c.1870, 6 In. 330.00
Food Chopper, Fox Shape, Curved Blade, Brass Handle, 1800s, 13 1/2 In. 1069.00
Food Chopper, Glass, Measuring, Lithographed Tin Cover, Hazel Atlas, 7 1/2 In. . . . *Illus* 12.00
Food Cutter, Cast Iron, Tin, Enterprise, Philadelphia, Pa., 17 In. 275.00
Fork, Sweetmeat, Folding, Pearl Panels, 18th Century 165.00
Funnel, Tapered, Spout, 2 Wooden Staves, Green Paint, 9 x 7 1/2 In. 330.00
Game Hook, 3 Swivel 4-Prong Hooks, Swivel Ring Hanger, Iron, 7 3/4 x 9 In. 165.00
Game Rack, Gothic Window Shape, Top Arches, Iron, 17 1/2 x 13 1/4 In. 330.00
Game Rack, Stepped Crest, Twisted & Scrolled Designs, 5 Hooks, Black, Iron, 17 1/4 In. . 175.00
Grater, Brass, Tabletop, Footed, 18th Century 395.00
Grater, Nutmeg, Japanned Tin, Paper Label, 6 In. 250.00
Grater, Nutmeg, Ribbed Melon Shape, Monogram, Hinged Grill, Silver, 2 In. 520.00
Grater, Nutmeg, Silver Mounted, Demilune Steel Body, George III, London, 1816, 4 In. . 1410.00
Grater, Nutmeg, Turned Wood Handle, Spring Action Loader, 6 1/4 In. 85.00
Grater, Nutmeg, Wood, Tin, Cast Iron, Edgar Mfg. Co., c.1891, 7 In. 95.00
Grater Box, Tin, Punched, Handles, Clark, Sawyer & Co., 11 1/2 x 7 In. 295.00
Griddle, Stove & Range, Martin, No. 8 . . . . 45.00
Griddle, Wagner, No. 14, Bail Handle 85.00
Griddle, Wrought Iron, Hand Forged, Long Handle, 3 x 18 3/4 x 10 In. 58.00
Grinder, Bench Mount, Schofield, 10 In. 28.00
Grinder, Corn Sheller, Bench Mount, Brady Mfg., 12 In. 470.00
Grinder, Octagonal, Tabletop, Embossed, A & K Sons, 7 1/2 In. 550.00
Ice Box, Oak, 3 Doors, Brass Nameplate, The Odorless, Chattanooga, Tenn. 330.00
Ice Cream Freezer, Glass, Whip, Eggbeater, Butter Churn, Dazey, 11 In. 950.00
Ice Cream Freezer, Peerless, Green Paint, Paper Label 310.00
Ice Cream Maker, Cedar Bucket, Brass Bands, White Mountain Junior, 7 1/2 x 5 1/2 In. . . 195.00
Iron, Case, Dovetail Box, Instructions, Enterprise, Philadelphia, 18 1/2 In. 440.00
Iron, Electric, Streamline, Cordlessmatic, Red, Aluminum, Plastic . . . . *Illus* 72.00
Iron, Feather Bed Smoother, KMD Monogram, Norwegian, 1820, 22 In. 355.00
Iron, Flat, Rooster Latch, Double Dolphin Handle, Sphinx 60.00
Iron, Fluter, Cast Iron, Brass, Slug, Geneva, c.1870, 5 3/4 In. *Illus* 105.00
Iron, Fluter, Eureka, Octagon Base, 4 3/4 In. 275.00

Kitchen, Iron, Electric,
Streamline, Cordlessmatic, Red,
Aluminum, Plastic

Kitchen, Iron, Fluter, Cast
Iron, Brass, Slug, Geneva,
c.1870, 5 3/4 In.

Kitchen, Iron, Sadiron, Cast
White Metal, Relief Roses,
5 3/4 In.

Iron, Fluter, Machine, Motor Or Hand Driven, 8-In. Rollers, Banner Electric 105.00
Iron, Fluter, Rocker, Gold Luck, Cast Horseshoe, Marked ....'....................... 39.00
Iron, Fluter, Rocker, Star, 3 x 5 In. 50.00
Iron, Fluter, Roller, Shaper, White Metal, Cast Iron, Pat. Dec. 17 1878, 4 1/4 x 6 3/4 In. ... 35.00
Iron, Fluter, Tong Scissor, Decorative Handles, Flowers, 5 Tongs, 13 In. 8.00
Iron, Gas, Otto, Side Mount, Double Pointed, Heat Shield, Trivet 105.00
Iron, Gas, Rose, Woman Ironing, Stylized R, Rosenburg Mfg. Co., N.Y. 165.00
Iron, Goffering, Rat Tail, Curlicue, Double Barrels, Tripod Base, c.1800, 10 In. 2090.00
Iron, Goffering, Tripod Base, Revolving Barrel, Brass, 10 1/2 In. 95.00
Iron, Polishing, Boat Shape, Round Bottom, M.A.B. Cook, Pat'd Dec. 5 1848, 5 1/4 In. ... 28.00
Iron, Porcelain, Metal Sole, Electric, 110V 72.00
Iron, Sadiron, Cast White Metal, Relief Roses, 5 3/4 In. ....*Illus* 14.00
Iron, Sadiron, Kenrick, Double Pointed, 5 1/4 In. 11.00
Iron, Sleeve, Myers, Mini, Detachable Handle, Center Mount, 4 1/4 In............... 440.00
Iron, Smoothing, Revolving Rotary, Gasoline, Jeremiah W. Brown, c.1854 .... 85.00
Iron, Tailor's, Liquid Fuel Tank, 11 1/2 In. 220.00
Iron, Tailor's, Side Mounted Gas Tank, American Gas Machine Co., 17 Lbs., 11 In. 149.00
Iron, Travel, Electric, 100-220 Volts, Red Box, Germany, 1930s 55.00
Jar, Lid, Wooden, Footed, Pease, Bail Handle, 11 x 8 1/4 In. 1035.00
Jar, Milk Glass, Drippings On Cover, 3 x 4 In. 50.00
Jug, Batter, Snowflake Stencil, Accent Brushstroke, Tin Lid, Bail Handle, 9 In. 1690.00
Juicer, Cast Aluminum, Ebaloy, 12 In. 11.00
Juicer, Daisy, Bench Mount, Arcade, 12 In. 248.00
Juicer, Meat & Juice Press, Cast Iron, Osborne Newark, N.J., c.1884 .... 50.00
Juicer, Rapid, Bench Mount, Albert Pick & Co., Chicago, 16 In. 155.00
Juicer, Wall Mount, Matt Redlinger, Freeport, Il., 9 In. 145.00
Kettle, Apple Butter, Brass, Handle, 13 1/2 In. 58.00
Kettle, Apple Butter, Brass, Handle, Waterbury, Conn., 13 In. 69.00
Kettle, Apple Butter, Copper, Dovetailed, Iron Handle, 25 x 29 1/4 In. 330.00
Kettle, Apple Butter, Copper, Dovetailed, Iron Swing Handle, Tripod Stand, Iron Ladle .. 535.00
Kettle, Brass, Iron Handle, Hoop, 19th Century, 12 1/4 x 18 In. 575.00
Kettle, Butchering, Ears Of Corn On Door, Kenwood, No. 131, Wehrle Co., Ohio, 36 In. . 165.00
Kettle, Cover, Copper, 2 Handles, Spout, New York, c.1830, 22 In. 750.00
Kettle, Griswold, Aluminum, Wood Handle, Flat Bottom, Cover, 1/2 Qt. 200.00
Kettle, Griswold, No. A41 1/2C, Flat Bottom, Cover, Aluminum, Wood Handle, 1 1/2 Qt. 200.00
Kettle, Stand, Iron, Scrolled Top, Rope Twist Supports, Penny Feet, Forged Iron, 12 In. .. 295.00
Kettle Stand, Brass, 2 Levels, Ringed Feet, England, Early 19th Century, 14 x 15 In. 200.00
Knife Sharpener, Cast Iron, Dazey Sharpit, Dazey Churn & Mfg. Co., St. Louis, 5 1/2 In. 25.00
Kraut Cutter, Dovetailed Hopper, Pierced Handle, Curly Maple, 12 x 42 In. 715.00
Ladle, Burl, 15 1/2 In. 65.00
Ladle, Coconut Shell, Ivory & Silver Mounts, Wood Handle, 1800s, 15 1/2 In. 1265.00
Ladle, Coconut Shell, Whalebone Handle, Pewter Mounts, 1800s, 14 In. 230.00
Ladle, Hanging, Engraved, Birds, Branches, Flowers, Iron 248.00
Ladle, Pewter, Brass, Richard Lee, Springfield Vermont, c.1816, 11 1/8 In. 1410.00
Ladle, Wooden, Carved, Swan Neck Handle, 19 In. 190.00
Ladle, Wrought Iron, Rolling Pin Profile Handle, 18 In. 415.00
Laundry Boiler, Hescock, Agitator, Hubbard, Ohio, c.1877, 8 In. 55.00
Mangle Board, Round Carved Decoration, Initials L.M.T., c.1858, 33 x 6 1/2 x 4 In. 176.00
Marshmallow Toaster, Angelus-Campfire Bar-B-Q, 3 1/4 In. ....*Illus* 55.00
Masher, Wood, Maple, Carved, Turned, Etched Fraktur Type Birds, Bonhoff Banner, 9 In. 358.00
Match Holders can be found in their own category.
Match Safes can be found in their own category.
Meat Rack, Daisy, Butcher Shop, S. Birkenwald Co., Iron, 70 In. 1100.00
Meat Tenderizer, Embossed, Wooden Handle, 1877, 10 In. 110.00
Meat Tenderizer, Tiger Maple Handle & Head, Steel Teeth, 13 1/4 In. .... *Illus* 125.00
Mixer, Malt, Hamilton Beach 165.00
Mixer, Milkshake, Hamilton Beach, No. 10, White Porcelain, 18 In. 70.00
Mixer, Milkshake, Multi-Mixer, Porcelain, Chrome, 18 In. 330.00
Mixer, Stainless Steel, Bicor Battery Power, Japan, 9 In. 15.00
Mixing Bowl, Cattail, Universal, 10 1/2 In... 30.00
Mixing Bowl, Platonite, Black Flower, Rim Rings, Hazel Atlas, 9 x 4 1/2 In. 45.00
Mixing Bowl, White, Black Flower, Rim Rings, Hazel Atlas, 3 1/2 x 7 In. 30.00
Mixing Bowl Set, Snowflakes, Milk Glass, Federal Glass, 2 1/2 Qt. & 1 1/2 Qt., 2 Piece .. 19.00

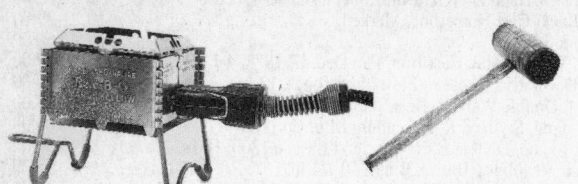

Kitchen, Marshmallow Toaster,
Angelus-Campfire Bar-B-Q, 3 1/4 In.

Kitchen, Meat Tenderizer,
Tiger Maple Handle &
Head, Steel Teeth, 13 1/4 In.

Kitchen, Mold, Blanc Mange,
Copper, 6 1/2 x 5 1/2 In.

Mold, Ice Cream, see also Pewter category.
Molds may also be found in the Pewter and Tinware categories.
Mold, 6-Point Star, Scalloped Rim, Copper, Tin Lined, Brass Ring, 2 1/2 x 11 In. 195.00
Mold, Blanc Mange, Copper, 6 1/2 x 5 1/2 In. .... *Illus* 259.00
Mold, Butter, Heart Shape, Wood, Carved WC & Heart, 10 In. 105.00
Mold, Butter, Heart Shape, Wood, Tin Surround, Carved Cross, 4 In. 275.00
Mold, Butter, Heart Shape, Wood, Tin Surround, Carved M.J. Initials, 8 In. 150.00
Mold, Butter, Heart Shape, Wood, Tin Surround, Carved Script Writing, 7 In. 70.00
Mold, Butter, Pineapple, 4 3/4 In. 50.00
Mold, Butter, Swan, Wood, 3 1/2 In. 58.00
Mold, Butter, Swan, Wood, 4 3/4 In. 70.00
Mold, Cake, Lamb, Griswold, No. 866, Cast Iron, 13 In. .... .85.00 to 99.00
Mold, Cake, Rabbit, Griswold, Cast Iron, 12 In. 176.00
Mold, Cake, Reverse Lamb, Griswold, Plated 115.00
Mold, Cake, Santa, Black, Griswold, Cast Iron 475.00
Mold, Cake, Santa, Griswold, Cast Iron 465.00
Mold, Candle, see Tinware category.
Mold, Chocolate, Harley-Davidson, With Rider, Dresden, Germany, Early 1920s 3300.00
Mold, Cookie, 2-Sided, Man, Woman, Carved Wood, Pennsylvania, 17 1/2 x 7 In. 127.00
Mold, Food, Eléphant, Scalloped Edges, Ironstone, 6 x 8 x 3 1/2 In. 330.00
Mold, Food, Swirl Pattern, Glazed, Redware, 2 1/4 x 4 In. 165.00
Mold, Food, Turk's Head, Fluted Rim, Copper, Late 1800s, 3 1/4 x 8 1/2 In. 575.00
Mold, Food, Turk's Head, Fluted, Copper, Tin Lined, 4 1/2 x 11 In. 275.00
Mold, Food, Turk's Head, Manganese Splotching, Redware, 7 3/4 In. 39.00
Mold, Food, Turk's Head, Red & Brown Alkaline Glaze, 1850, 3 x 9 1/2 In. 45.00
Mold, Food, Turk's Head, Redware, Mottled Glaze, Fluted, Henne, 2 3/4 x 5 1/2 In. 1650.00
Mold, Food, Turk's Head, Redware, Peppered Alkaline Glaze, 1840, 10 1/2 x 3 3/4 In. ... 45.00
Mold, Food, Turk's Head, Salt Glaze, 2-Tone Stoneware, 1 3/4 x 3 3/4 In. 99.00
Mold, Food, Yellow Slip, Leaves Around Fluted Rim, Bottom Swirl, Redware, 7 In. 280.00
Mold, Ice Cream, Slanting Sides, Byrnes & Kleifer Co., Pittsburgh, 3 7/8 x 2 3/4 x 4 In. .. 28.00
Mold, Lobster, Graniteware, Blue, White, 7 In. 28.00
Mold, Popsicle, Copper Exterior, 18 In. 963.00
Mold, Pudding, Lobed, Star Center, Copper, 19th Century, 5 1/2 x 10 In. 605.00
Mold, Springerle, Paddle Shape, Leaf Designs, Wooden, 2 1/2 x 15 1/2 In. 28.00
Mold, Wood, Walnut, 2-Sided, Carved, Flowers, Wheel, Beehive, Feather, 8 x 6 In. 55.00
Mop, Rag, Cherrywood, Threaded Spindle, Original Red Wash, 18th Century 285.00
Mortar & Pestle, Burlwood, Ash, Turned, 6 & 9 1/4 In. 360.00
Mortar & Pestle, Wood, Robin's-Egg Blue, c.1840 .... 500.00
Muffin Pan, Griswold, No. 14 .... 290.00
Muffin Pan, Wagner, Marked Q, Open Frame 35.00
Mug, Yellow Polka Dots, Platonite, Glass, Hazel Atlas, 1950s 40.00
Noggin, Wooden, Straight Sides, Slightly Flared Spout, Cutout Handle, 6 3/4 In. 85.00
Pan, Bread, Erie, No. 24 .... 660.00
Pan, Corn Stick, Griswold, No. 273, Pattern 930 .... 35.00
Pan, French Bread, Wagner Ware, No. 1162, 12 x 4 In. 100.00
Pan, Frying, Brass, Handle, Wood, Iron, Mid 19th Century, 1 1/2 x 11 In. 633.00
Pan, Gem, No. 50, Heart & Star 1600.00
Pan, Popover, Griswold, No. 10, Pattern 948 .... 60.00
Pan, Popover, Wagner Ware, No. 1323 .... 30.00

Pan, Wagner Ware, Little Gem, 9 Cups	125.00
Pastry Board, Woman, Tree With Flags, Jumping Jack, Drum, 11 1/4 x 10 1/2 In.	380.00
Pastry Wheel, Round Blade, Pierced Heart Cutout, Heart Scroll End, Iron, 16 1/2 In.	960.00
Patty Bowl, Griswold, No. 72	60.00
Pie Board, Teardrop Shape, Slate, 24 x 20 In.	250.00
Pie Crimper, Brass, 4 1/2 In. ....*Illus*	95.00
Pitcher, Milk, White Glass, 2 Cup, 1920s-1930s, 5 3/8 In.	24.00
Poached Egg Cutter, Made In Germany, Hoffritz, New York, 5 1/4 In.	45.00
Portable Kitchen, 6 Canisters, Tin, Porcelain Knobs, 33 x 14 In.	140.00
Pot, Bread, Enamel, Blue, 24 In.	50.00
Pot Rack, Iron, 9 Tiers, Penny Feet, Green Paint, 72 In.	99.00
Pot Rack, Iron, Penny Feet, Cobalt Blue Paint, 72 In.	115.00
Potato Cooker, Top-O-Stove, Pewter, Steel, Single Potato, 1930s	556.00
Press, Fruit & Jelly, Cast Iron, Wood Handle, 1873, 6 In.	120.00
Press, Fruit, Maple Frame, Tin Cylinder, Spout, Iron Handle, 13 In.	75.00
Rack, Hanging, 3 Chains, Round, Hooks, Iron, France, 19th Century, 32 In.	295.00
Rack, Utensil, 5 Hooks, Scrolled Decoration, Wrought Iron, 7 1/2 x 21 1/2 In.	192.50
Reamers are listed in their own category.	
Roaster, Adjustable Rack, 4 Prongs, 3-Footed, Wrought Iron, 25 In.	200.00
Roaster, Chestnut, Heart Top, Engraved Tulip, Brass, Wrought Iron, Wood Handle, 35 In.	120.00
Roaster, Coffee Bean, Burner, Early 1900s, 18 In.	132.00
Roaster, Griswold, No. 5, Trivet A485T, Oval	50.00
Roaster, Tin Cover, Cast Iron, Oval, 19th Century, 8 x 15 1/2 In.	175.00
Roaster, Wagner Ware, No. 8, Aluminum, Oval, Raised Letter Lid, Trivet	95.00
Roaster, Wagner, No. 4265, Magnalite, Trivet	85.00
Roaster, Wagner, No. 4269, Magnalite, Trivet, Oval	165.00
Roaster, Wild Game, Tin, Spit, Hearth, 19 x 18 In.	230.00
Roasterette, Wagner, No. 4263, Magnalite, Trivet	75.00
Roasting Rack, Iron, Hinged, Notched Clasp, Stretcher, 18 1/2 x 12 1/2 x 7 3/4 In.	1320.00
Roasting Stand, Scroll Top, Adjustable Fork & Pan, Iron, 23 1/2 x 9 1/2 x 11 In.	1430.00
Rolling Pin, Bird's-Eye Maple, Sheet Metal Wall Mounted Holder, 19 1/2 In.	440.00
Rolling Pin, Curly Maple, Ridges, 19 In.	275.00
Rolling Pin, Glass, 2-Masted Brig, Mary Goodal Whitby, c.1853, 14 1/2 In.	200.00
Rolling Pin, Glass, Blue, Nautical Scenes, 29 In.	175.00
Rolling Pin, Glass, Dark Green, White Pulled Stripes, 14 In.	140.00
Rolling Pin, Glass, Onyx, Etched, Village Scene, Isabell Davie, c.1860, 14 In.	470.00
Rolling Pin, Glass, Pink, White Pulled Swags, 10 1/2 In.	260.00
Rolling Pin, Glass, Rose & White Looping, 15 1/2 In.	160.00
Rolling Pin, Glass, Ship Scene, Cobalt Blue, 14 1/2 In.	105.00
Rolling Pin, Glass, Tapered, Fitted Wooden Mounting Bracket, 16 In.	110.00
Rolling Pin, Glass, White, Light Blue Pulled Stripes, 15 In.	130.00
Rolling Pin, Stoneware, Wilson's Variety Store, Trade With Us & Save Dough, 7 In.	600.00
Rolling Pin, Walnut, Pennsylvania, 18th Century	150.00
Rug Beater, Wooden, Decorative Edges, Compass Pinwheel Designs	70.00
Salt, Burl, Wood Carved, Inscribed, Initials, 1806	525.00
Salt, Master, Wooden, Painted, Blue Base, Strawberry, Yellow Interior, Treen, 2 3/4 In.	715.00
Salt & Pepper Shakers are listed in their own category.	
Scoop, Grain, Tiger Maple, 10 In.	250.00
Scoop, Ice Cream, Cone Dispenser, Wood Handle, 5 1/4 x 9 In.	2200.00
Scoop, Ice Cream, Square, Prince Castle, c.1940	400.00
Skewer Hanger, Scroll Designs, Handwrought Iron, 1800s, 11 1/4 x 5 1/2 In.	1100.00
Skillet, Center Star, Surrounding Hearts Design, Handle, Cast Iron, 15 In.	55.00
Skillet, Favorite Piqua Ware, No. 3	20.00
Skillet, Griddle, Griswold, No. 7	120.00
Skillet, Griddle, Wagner Ware, No. 7	35.00
Skillet, Griswold, No. 3, 709 L, Smooth Bottom	15.00
Skillet, Griswold, No. 4, 702A, Smooth Bottom	60.00
Skillet, Griswold, No. 5, Hinge, Smooth Bottom	55.00
Skillet, Griswold, No. 6, Smooth Bottom	45.00
Skillet, Griswold, No. 7, Smooth Bottom	45.00
Skillet, Griswold, No. 8, Cover, Pattern 77A	120.00
Skillet, Griswold, No. 8, Square	75.00
Skillet, Griswold, No. 9, 1710, Heat Ring	65.00

Skillet, Legs, Long Handle, Iron, 12 In. 176.00
Skillet, Wagner Ware, No. 2 .... 120.00
Skillet, Wagner Ware, No. 10, Sidney 45.00
Skillet, Wagner Ware, No. 12 .... 65.00
Skillet Lid, Griswold, No. 9 .... 40.00
Smoothing Board, Chestnut, Rope Twist Edges, Vining Tulips, Paint Traces, 30 In. 300.00
Smoothing Board, Horse Handle, Molded Edge, J.R., M.H.D., 1816, 26 In. 1375.00
Smoothing Board, Paint Decorated, Carved Horse Handle, Green, Red, 21 1/2 x 5 x 5 In. 290.00
Smoothing Board, Wood, Inset Handle, Carved, Horse, Heart, Painted, 26 1/2 In. 460.00
Sock Dryer, 2-Sided, Children's, Pine, Signed S.E. Keesey, 13 1/2 In. 330.00
Sock Dryer, Pine, 9 3/8 In., Pair 110.00
Spatula, Iron, Punched Dot Design, Date, Pennsylvania, 1820, 16 In. 295.00
Spatula, Wrought Iron, Long Handle, Cast Stamp End, Reverse Double Rs, 11 1/4 In. 110.00
Spatula, Wrought Iron, Shaped Blade, Flattened Handle, Incised Line, Circle, 14 In. 30.00
Spatula, Wrought Iron, Shaped Blade, Flattened Handle, Scrolled Hook, 19 1/4 In. 55.00
Spice Box, Slide Lid, Dovetailed Joints, Compartment Interior, Red Paint, 11 x 5 1/2 In. ... 330.00
Spice Box, Treen, Red Paint, New England, 18th Century 225.00
Spice Box, Walnut, Dovetailed Case, Chamfered Slide Lid, Sectioned Interior 450.00
Spice Box, Walnut, Wall, Dovetailed, Flared Back, Brass Pulls, 17 x 10 3/4 x 8 1/4 In. ... 2200.00
Spoon, Wooden, Carved Handle, Hearts, Cross, Will Reese, Cardiff, Wales, Aged 15, 1845 495.00
Strainer, Tin, Punched, Pinwheel Design, Scalloped Ends, 19th Century, 22 x 11 x 3 In. ... 440.00
Straw Hat Press, Hinge Top, Movable Plates, T-Handle, Gas Heated, 18 x 14 x 9 In. 280.00
Stringholder, 6-Point Star, Flowers, Ribbed Sphere, Iron, 19th Century, 7 3/4 In. 265.00
Stringholder, Ball Of Yarn Shape, Cast Iron, 5 In. 85.00
Sugar, Cover, Burl, Inscribed Anne Tomas, 1852 .... 1200.00
Sugar, Cover, Maple, Oval, 8 1/2 x 4 1/2 In. 895.00
Sugar Nippers, Flame Engraving 250.00
Sweater Dryer, Folding, Hinges, Pine, 11 1/2 x 22 In. 415.00
Table, Dough, French Provincial, Walnut, Mid 19th Century, 37 x 50 1/2 x 22 1/2 In. 3450.00
Teakettle, Copper, Swing Handle, Gooseneck Spout, Signed D. Stoehr, 12 In. 450.00
Teakettle, Griswold, No. 7, Erie 70.00
Toast Rack, Brass, Crossed Rifles, Laurel Wreath Handle, Ball Feet, 6 x 4 In. ...... *Illus* 765.00
Toaster, Flip Over, Drop Handles, Nickel Body, Flowers, Universal, c.1929, 9 In. 350.00
Toaster, Forged Iron, Ram's Horn, Long Handle, Lollipop End, 36 In. 280.00
Toaster, Iron, Hinged, Wooden Handle, 6 x 21 In. 250.00
Toaster, Long Swing Handle, 26 1/2 x 13 In. 60.00
Toaster, Wrought Iron, Fleur-De-Lis Scrollwork, 18 In. 290.00
Tray, Heart & Pony, Peter Hunt, 17 3/4 In. 80.00
Trivet, see Trivet category.
Utensil Set, Spatula, Ladle, Taster, Brass, Rivets, F.B.S. Canton, O., c.1886, 3 Piece 145.00
Waffle Iron, Iron, B. & S. Co., Chatham, New England, Early 19th Century 295.00
Wash Basin, Duplex, Collapsible, Stenciled Information, Round, 10 In. 39.00
Wash Boiler, Tin, Patent Model, Raleigh, N.C., c.1874, 10 x 5 x 9 In. 360.00
Washboard, Mechanical, Wonder Labor Saver, Tin, Wood Frame, Hand Crank, 26 x 12 In. 70.00
Washboard, Stoneware, Wood Frame, Bennington Pottery, 23 x 13 In. 95.00
Washboard, Stoneware, Wooden Frame, Nut Brown, Yellow, 21 1/2 x 13 In. 358.00
Washing Machine, Rocker Style, Red Paint, Salesman Sample, Wood, 17 x 19 x 10 In. 105.00
Washing Machine, Wood, Cast Iron Flywheel, Ribbed Rocker, 40 In. 395.00
Whisk, Tin, Tubular Handle, Hanging Ring, 19th Century, 10 1/4 In. 360.00
Whiskbroom, Silver Banded, Pearl Handle, Victorian 85.00
Wringer, Bench, Anchor Brand, 48 In. 130.00

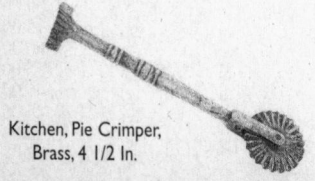

Kitchen, Pie Crimper,
Brass, 4 1/2 In.

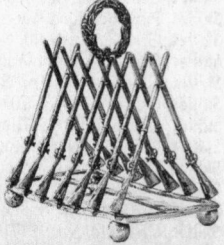

Kitchen, Toast Rack,
Brass, Crossed Rifles,
Laurel Wreath Handle,
Ball Feet, 6 x 4 In.

KNIFE collectors usually specialize in a single type. In the 1960s, the United States government passed a law that required knife manufacturers to mark their knives with the country of origin. This seemed to encourage the collectors, and knife collecting became an interest of a large group of people. All types of knives are collected, from top quality twentieth-century examples to old bone- or pearl-handled knives in excellent condition.

Bolo, Wood Handle, Leather Sheath, Philippines, c.1918, 15 1/2-In. Blade	85.00
Bowie, 2-Piece Scale Grips, J Nowill, Sheffield, England, 5 3/4-In. Blade	425.00
Bowie, Leather Scabbard, Rogers & Sons, Sheffield, England, 6 7/8-In. Blade	400.00
Bowie, No. 13, Ground Clip Point Blade, Black Horn Handle, Sheath, Collins, 9 1/4 In.	290.00
Bowie, Survival, Steel Blade, Brass, Collins Legitimus, 9 1/2-In. Blade	730.00
Cattle, Cracked Ice Celluloid Handles, 3 Blades, Germany, c.1950, 3 5/8 In.	65.00
Cheese, Case Bros., Little Valley, N.Y., 1900-1912, 16 In.	70.00
Combat, Oval Steel Guard, Wood Handle, Steel Scabbard, Italy, 13 In.	120.00
Curved Blade, Rosewood Handle, Leather Sheath, Brass Throat, Middle Eastern, 15 In.	75.00
Dagger, Africa, Silver Trim Handle, Alligator Skin Scabbard, 10 1/4 In.	155.00
Dagger, Aikuchi Type, Carved Bone Grip, Copper, Wood Scabbard, Japan, 13 3/4 In.	175.00
Dagger, Bone Grip, Brass Guard, England, 17th Century	375.00
Dagger, Bone Grips, Brass Sheath, Wood Scabbard, Bosnia, c.1800, 6 3/4-In. Blade	175.00
Dagger, Carved Wood, Mask, Serpent, 3 Faces, Tibet, c.1880, 10 1/2 In.	70.00
Dagger, Cinqueda, Round Pommel, Wire Wrapped Grip, Heavy, Broad Blade, 37 5/8 In.	880.00
Dagger, Eickhorn, German Shooting Association Dress, Leather Scabbard, 21 In.	1150.00
Dagger, Hand Forged Blade, Steel, Wood Handle, Leather Sheath, Danakil, Africa, 12 In.	60.00
Dagger, Japan, Ivory Mounts, Cranes & Clouds Carvings, Late 1800s	1410.00
Dagger, Japan, Metal, Flower Inlay, Hand Forged Blade, Rhino Horn Scabbard, 8 x 5/8 In.	440.00
Dagger, Leaf Shaped Blade, Leather Scabbard, Mediterranean, c.1850, 5 3/4-In. Blade	165.00
Dagger, Luftwaffe, Officer, White Grip, Scabbard	605.00
Dagger, Luftwaffe, Swastikas, Chain Hanger, Leather Grip, Scabbard, 18 1/4 In.	460.00
Dagger, Main Gauche, Sail Form Guard, Left Hand, Spain, c.1660, 20 1/4-In. Blade	8750.00
Dagger, Marine Officer, Scabbard, Chain, RZM 7/66, NSKK, 1940, 13 3/4 In.	3240.00
Dagger, Nazi, Eagle, Wood Handle, Motto, Scabbard, 14 3/4 In.	290.00
Dagger, Nazi, Luftwaffe Officer, 1st Pattern, Leather Scabbard, Weyersberg, 17 3/4 In.	575.00
Dagger, Nazi, SA Roundel, Scabbard, Wood Grip, Carl Jul Krebs, Solingen, 13 3/4 In.	345.00
Dagger, Nazi, SA, Motto, Nickel Guard, Scabbard, Ernst Erich Witte, World War II, 13 In.	440.00
Dagger, Nazi, SS Roundel, Eagle, Wood Grip, Anodized Scabbard, 13 3/4 In.	1030.00
Dagger, Nazi, Wehrmacht Officer, Orange Spiral Grip, Scabbard, P.D. Luneschloss, 15 In.	345.00
Dagger, Officer's Dress, Romania, King Michael I, Steel Scabbard, 5 3/8-In. Blade	230.00
Dagger, Officer's, Eagle, Swastika, Composition Handle, Scabbard, Army, 10-In. Blade	1205.00
Dagger, Repousse Silver Mounts, Thailand, 1800s, 14 In.	150.00
Dagger, Silver Inlay, Flower Design, Cloth Covered Scabbard, India, c.1910, 15 1/4 In.	150.00
Dagger, SS Officer, RZM, 120/34, Scabbard, Nickel Guard, Wood Grip, 13 3/4 In.	795.00
Dagger, Tibet, Ceremonial, Bronze, Dragon, 3-Headed Demon, 1800s, 17 1/2 In.	920.00
Dagger, Wood Grip, Nickel Guard, Scabbard, SA, Chirstianswerk, 13 1/2 In.	375.00
Dirk, Case, Double Edge Fuller Blade, Iron Guard & Pommel, 1800s, 16-In. Blade	460.00
Dirk, Ivory Handle, Hexagonal Blade, German Silver Scabbard, 5-In. Blade	290.00
Dirk, Silver Mounted, Pressed Horn Handle, Leather Scabbard, American, 9 3/4 In.	2645.00
Fighting, Wood Handle, Steel Guard, Steel Scabbard, Web Belt Loop, Austria, 13 1/2 In.	100.00
Folding, Etched Blade, Hunting Scene, Horn Handles, V.D. Kerkhove, France, 19 In.	575.00
Folding, Nickel Silver, Horn, Eagle, Shield, Liberty Cap, Stars, Edward Barnes, 6 x 10 In.	745.00
Gaucho, Silver Handle, Heart, Flowers, Leather Sheath, Argentina, 13 In.	800.00
Gravity, Paratrooper, Plastic Handle, Eickhorn, Folding Spike, West Germany, 4-In. Blade	75.00
Hewer, Red Cross EM, Sawtooth Back, Plastic Grip, Scabbard, Ges. Geschutzt	489.00
Hunting, 175th Anniversary, Walnut Display, Remington, Box, 1991, 4 1/2-In. Blade	90.00
Hunting, No. 57, German Stag Handles, Marbles, Gladstone, Mich., 1907, 5-In. Blade	1650.00
In-Out, Green Camouflage, Top Automatic, FES Rostfrei Blade, 8 In.	60.00
Jack, Moby Dick, Limited Edition, Bone Inserts, Whale, Ship, Case, U.S.A., 5 1/4 In.	120.00
Kabar, No. 1152, Pocket, 4 Blade, Screwdriver, Can, Bottle Opener, Stag Handles, 3 5/8 In.	30.00
Kris, Serpentine Blade, Bone Handle, Wood Scabbard, 9 In.	139.00
Kris, Wavy Blade, Wood Handle & Scabbard, Java, 13 1/4 In.	145.00
Leatherworkers', Half Moon, Sheath, Sorby	45.00
Marble Woodcraft, Leather Handle, Aluminum Pommel, 4 1/2-In. Blade	30.00
Marbles Ideal, Stag Handle, Aluminum Pommel, 6 7/8-In. Blade	220.00

NATO Military, Autoknife, Black Cast Handle, 3 3/8-In. Stainless Blade 49.00
Nazi, HJ, Black Checker Grip, Motto, Scabbard, Leather Loop, Waffen Wyersberg, 10 In. . 275.00
Nazi, HJ, Diamond Inset, Checkered Grip, Scabbard, Leather Belt Loop, 9 1/2 In. 170.00
Paratrooper, Gravity, Take Down Style, Plastic Grip, Bund, West Germany, 9 7/8 In. 79.00
Paratrooper Take Down, Plastic Handle, Eickhorn, West Germany, 4-In. Blade 65.00
Paring & Grapefruit, Sunoco, Wood Handles, Box 10.00
Quill, Bone Handle, Lion Lying Down, England, c.1800 .... 185.00
Schrade, Old Timer, No. 165, Brown Plastic Grip, Brass Guard, Leather Sheath, 9 1/2 In. . 40.00
Springfield, U.S. Army Issue, 1880s 1250.00
Switchblade, Aluminum Handle, Pocket Handle, US Military, Smith & Wesson, 8 1/2 In. . 90.00
Tanto, 440 Stainless Steel, Leather Sheath, Box, Bear Brand, 1970s, 11 1/4 In. 30.00
Tanto, Slightly Curved Blade, Copper Seppa, Wooden Kozuka & Saya, Japan, 10 3/4 In. . 145.00
Van Montagu, Steel Blades, Silver Mounted Ivory Handles, Set, 24 Piece 315.00
Whaler's, Scrimshaw, Walrus Tusk Handle & Sheath, Ship & Anchor On Blade, 10 1/2 In. 920.00

KNOWLES, TAYLOR & KNOWLES items may be found in the KTK and Lotus Ware
categories.

KOREAN WARE, see Sumida.

KOSTA, the oldest Swedish glass factory, was founded in 1742. During
the 1920s through the 1950s, many pieces of original design were
made at the factory. In 1971, Kosta became part of the Afors Group. In
1976, the name *Kosta Boda* was adopted. The company merged with
Orrefors in 1990 and is still working.

KOSTA

Bowl, Boat Shape, Opaque Medium Blue, Clear Cased, Signed, 6 1/2 In............... 55.00
Bowl, Centerpiece, Smoky Purple, Clear Cased, 3 3/4 x 18 In. 175.00
Decanter, Scala, Patches, Coral Ground, C. Von Sydow, Late 1980s, 7 3/4 x 6 1/4 In. 460.00
Paperweight, Crystal, Ballerina, Triangular, Signed, Sweden, 1900s, 3 7/8 In. 295.00
Vase, Amber, Cased Clear, Applied Foot, Signed, 5 1/2 In. 55.00
Vase, Amethyst, Cased In Clear, Air Bubbles, Signed, 8 1/2 In. 65.00
Vase, Black Trees, Multicolored Leaves, Clear Cased, Signed, 6 In. 1295.00
Vase, Magenta, Blue, Etched, Oval Window, Clear Cased, Signed, c.1985, 7 In. 265.00
Vase, Melon Shape, Ribbed, Vaseline, No. 49481, A. Whelstrom, Boda, 1900s, 13 In. 59.00
Vase, Pillow, Black, Clear Cased, Controlled Air Bubbles, Signed, 3 1/4 In. 55.00
Vase, Trees In Fog, Vicke Lindstrand, c.1950, 9 1/2 In. 2350.00
Vase, Twisted Ribbed Front, Smooth Back, No. 49241, Boda, c.1985, 9 3/4 In. 176.00

KPM refers to Berlin porcelain, but the same initials were used alone
and in combination with other symbols by several German porcelain
makers. They include the Konigliche Porzellan Manufaktur of Berlin,
initials used in mark, 1823–1847; Meissen, 1723–1724 only; Krister
Porzellan Manufaktur in Waldenburg, after 1831; Kranichfelder
Porzellan Manufaktur in Kranichfeld, after 1903; and the Kister
Porzellan Manufaktur in Scheibe, after 1838.

K.P.M

Basket, Transfer, Painted, Open Work Basket Dish, 9 In. 400.00
Bottle, Tea, Egg Shape, Gilt Enamel, Rocaille Vines, Dome Lid, c.1890, 4 1/4 In. 120.00
Bowl, Birds, Gilt Edge, Modified Oval, 13 1/2 In. 200.00

KPM, Lithophane, Women
& Children, Ruby Over
Clear Glass Border,
Etched, 16 In.

KPM, Vase, Neoclassical
Figures, Raised Gold
Trim, 1800s, 9 In.

Bowl, Brown Tortoise Interior, Gilt Border, 19th Century, 12 In.	130.00
Bowl, Center Crest, Bird, Scepter, Crown, Swirl, Basket, Gilt Decoration, Square, 9 In.	339.00
Bowl, Flower Bouquet, Reticulated Rim, Blue Scepter Mark, 7 1/2 In.	105.00
Cup, Chocolate, Portrait, Brunette Beauty, Porcelain, Egg Shape, c.1875, 5 1/8 In.	470.00
Cup & Saucer, Lungerfest Scene, Scroll Handles, Signed, J. Neumann, 4 1/2 In.	980.00
Figurine, Cherub, Holding Hammer, Dog, 7 1/2 In.	345.00
Figurine, Cupid, Holding Flower, Bow & Arrow, Oval Plinth, Marked, c.1900, 15 x 7 In.	1230.00
Figurine, Lady, Holding Pouch, 19th Century, 7 In.	375.00
Figurine, Lady, Smelling Flower, 6 1/2 In.	345.00
Figurine, Man, Being Bitten By Serpent, 19th Century, 7 In.	400.00 to 490.00
Lamp Shade, Lithophane, 5 Paneled Scenes, 6 1/2 In.	750.00
Lithophane, Women & Children, Ruby Over Clear Glass Border, Etched, 16 In. .... *Illus*	950.00
Plaque, Enameled, Woman In Velvet Chair, Frame, 6 x 8 In.	4255.00
Plaque, Girl, Lying Down, Reading, Blue Blanket, 13 x 16 In.	7770.00
Plaque, Lovers On A Swing, Mark, Late 1800s, 15 3/8 x 9 5/8 In.	16450.00
Plaque, Madonna, Painted Porcelain, Oval, Frame, c.1900, 10 1/4 x 21 x 19 1/4 In.	1410.00
Plaque, Maiden, Wearing Ivy Crown, Long Hair, Frame, Signed, Wagner, 17 x 19 In.	4700.00
Plaque, Melon Eaters, 11 x 8 3/4 In.	4125.00
Plaque, Peasant Girl, White Headdress, Mahogany Frame, Oval, c.1900, 10 5/8 In.	3055.00
Plaque, Portrait, Old Man, Painted, Rectangular, Wagner, Scepter Mark, Frame, 11 x 9 In.	4370.00
Plaque, Ruth, 11 x 18 1/2 In.	5320.00
Plaque, Smiling Woman, Carl Meinelts, 15 x 12 In.	12075.00
Plaque, Tavern Girl Resisting Cavalier, Mark, Late 1800s, 9 3/4 x 7 3/8 In.	4405.00
Plaque, Woman Bathing, Man Spying, Mark, Early 20th Century, 12 1/2 x 10 In.	9400.00
Plaque, Young Woman, Blond Hair, Pink Ribbon, White Flowers, Austria, 9 3/4 x 7 In.	3680.00
Plaque, Young Woman, Brown Hair, Profile, Gold & Pearl Necklace, 9 x 6 3/4 In.	2530.00
Plaque, Young Woman, Frame, Fabric Back, Late 19th Century, 6 x 4 In.	1610.00
Plate, Mythological Design, Enameled, Jeweled, c.1860, 9 1/2 In., Pair	10640.00
Plate, Portrait, Girl, Dress, Blue Scarf, Cobalt Enamel, Zuleika, Grace Bishop, Dresden	2185.00
Platter, Fish, Embossed Swirl, Basket Weave Border, 24 1/2 In.	254.00
Punch Bowl, Cover, Men, Women, Children, Flowers, Cherub Finial, 13 x 10 1/2 In.	1600.00
Stand, Condiment, Florals, Marked, 7 1/4 In.	145.00
Stein, Parian Band Of Composers Bust, Porcelain, Pewter, Inscribed, 1884, 3 Liter	240.00
Stein, Sunburst Design, Porcelain, Pewter Lid, 2 Liter	195.00
Teapot, Flowers, 19th Century, 4 In.	175.00
Tureen, Bird & Berry, Cover, Caduceus Mark, 12 1/4 In.	207.00
Tureen, Cover, Bacchanalian Figural Finial, 11 In.	550.00
Urn, Cover, Scene Of Cherub Medallions, Green, White, Gold Ribbon Handles, 11 In.	225.00
Vase, Flower Bouquet, White Ground, Gold Rim, Blue Scepter Mark, 9 1/2 In.	90.00
Vase, Flowers, Female Portraits, 19th Century, 23 In.	635.00
Vase, Neoclassical Figures, Raised Gold Trim, 1800s, 9 In. .... *Illus*	290.00

KTK are the initials of the Knowles, Taylor & Knowles Company of East Liverpool, Ohio, founded by Isaac W. Knowles in 1853. The company made many types of utilitarian wares, hotel china, and dinnerwares. They made the fine bone china known as Lotus Ware from 1891 to 1896. The company merged with American Ceramic Corporation in 1928. It closed in 1934. Lotus Ware is listed in its own category in this book.

K.T.&K.
CHINA

Bowl, Turquoise, Irregular Shape, Applied Ribbon Trim, 13 1/2 x 7 1/2 In.	39.00
Bowl, Vegetable, Oval, Rust Center Medallion, Floral Border, 9 3/4 x 7 1/2 In.	65.00
Celery Dish, Pink & White Daisies, Green Leaves, Gold Trim, Irregular Shape, 13 In.	35.00
Chamber Pot, Blue Flowers, Gold Trim	100.00
Pitcher, Milk, White, Ironstone, Scroll Handle, 7 In.	250.00
Plate, Old Glory & Her Allies, Flags, World War I, 9 1/2 In.	35.00
Platter, Oval, Liverpool Flower Border, 15 1/2 x 11 1/2 In.	38.00
Serving Dish, Cover, Flowers, 11 x 7 1/2 In.	98.00
Vase, White, Ironstone, Embossed Leaves, Flared Neck, Scalloped Foot & Rim, 4 1/2 In.	39.00

KU KLUX KLAN items are now collected because of their historic importance. Literature, robes, and memorabilia are available. The Klan was outlawed in 1869 and reemerged in 1915. It is still in existence, so new material is found.

Belt Buckle, Klansman Holds Flag, Cast Metal, Brass Finish, Embossed, 3 3/4 In.	85.00

Belt Buckle, Knight Rider, Flag, Fiery Cross, Attack Church Roman Dragon, Brass, 3 In. .   65.00
Broadside, Flyer, Klorero, Knight Rider, Flaming Cross, Rearing Horse, 1926, 10 In. 75.00
Brochure, Stop Negro-White Marriages, Fold-Out, Racist Quotations, 12 In. 30.00
Card, Christmas, Rider, Flaming Cross, I'm Dreaming Of A White Christmas, 7 1/2 In. 25.00
Cuspidor, Embossed, Brass, 11 In. 138.00
Figure, Red Blood Drop Cross Patch, Rope Lynching Noose, Carved, 1920s, 12 In. 368.00
Flag, Parade, By This Sign Conquer, Washington Labor Day March, Linen, 18 In. 180.00
Jackknife, 2 Blades, Engraved Hood, Cross, Bone, Celluloid, Metal, c.1917, 6 3/4 In. 149.00
Magazine, Kluxer, Flag Cover, Vol. 1, No. 32, Mar. 1924, 11 In., 35 Pages 45.00
Membership Card, Official Knights Of The Ku Klux Klan, 2-Sided, c.1916, 4 In. 40.00
Patch, Texas, Embroidered Cotton, Comic Image, Invisible Empire, 3 3/4 In. 42.00
Photograph, Klansmen, On Horses, Sepia, Black & White, c.1923, 5 1/2 In. 45.00
Photograph, Parade, Klansmen Marching, Float, Hooded Children, 1920s, 4 1/2 In. 20.00
Pin, 100% American, The Flag I Love, Hidden Message, 1 1/4 In. 75.00
Plate, God Give Us Men, Over Cross, 100% American, 24K Gold, c.1919, 6 1/4 In. 105.00
Plate, Latin Inscription, Not For Self, But For Others, Flaming Cross, 1920, 6 1/2 In. 127.00
Sheet Music, KKK Hooded Knight On Horseback 45.00

KUTANI porcelain was made in Japan after the mid-seventeenth century. Most of the pieces found today are nineteenth-century. Collectors often use the term *Kutani* to refer to just the later, colorful pieces decorated with red, gold, and black pictures of warriors, animals, and birds.

Bowl, Figural Landscape, Pilgrim, Holy Man, 12 In. 230.00
Bowl, Mythological Figural Landscape, 13 In. 230.00
Bowl, Pierced Border, Bronze Mounted, Elephant Form Feet, c.1890, 14 1/2 x 6 In. 1380.00
Bowl, Pine, Prunus Decoration, Fuku Mark, 1800s, 13 1/2 In. 590.00
Brush Holder, Flowers, Butterfly, Late 19th Century, 4 1/2 In. 170.00
Chalice, Red, Cranes On Exterior, Landscape Reserves Inside, 1800s, 7 In., Pair 175.00
Charger, Children & Brocade, 1800s, 15 In. 400.00
Dish, Fan Shape Medallions, Figure, Birds, Flowers, 1800s, Pair 235.00
Dish, Square, Mandarin Duck Design, Blue Green, 8 In. 60.00
Ewer, 3 Round Scenes, People, Flowers, Rust, Gold, Signed, 10 1/2 In. 200.00
Figurine, Woman Seated On Elephant, Japan, 1800s, 9 1/2 In. 499.00
Group, Noh Actors, Blue Green, Early 1900s, 11 In. 375.00
Incense Burner, Birds, Flowers, Wiseman Finial, 3 Chinese Boy Supports, 1800s, 9 In. ...   176.00
Jar, Cover, Ginger, Flowers, Footed, Signed, 6 In. 280.00
Jar, Cover, Ginger, Scribed, Signed, 5 3/4 In. 127.00
Jar, Cover, Hundred Wisemen, Pear Shape, 1800s, 13 In. 235.00
Jardiniere, Green, Landscapes, Brocade Patterns, Gilt, 1800s, 14 In. 470.00
Plate, 4 Different Asian Mountain Scenes, Late 19th Century, 8 1/2 In., 4 Piece 85.00
Plate, Dragon, Phoenix, Bird, Signed, 19th Century, 7 1/2 In. 40.00
Plate, Figural Landscape, Blue Green, c.1900, 9 1/4 In., Pair 115.00
Plate, Figures, Flowers, 20th Century, 10 In., 8 Piece 325.00
Plate, Samurai On Horseback, 10 3/4 In. 80.00
Punch Bowl, 1800s, 14 x 5 In. 400.00
Teapot, Baluster, Dragon Handle, Spout, Signed, 19th Century, 11 In. 345.00
Teapot, Barrel Shape, Rattan Handle, 7 1/2 In. 45.00
Teapot, Oval, Signed, 19th Century, 5 In. 69.00
Teapot, Pear Shape, Signed, 19th Century, 6 1/4 In. 80.00
Tile, Samurai Warrior, 2 Maids, Teakwood Frame, Round, 1800s, 15 In. 345.00
Vase, Bird Of Paradise, Stylized Dragon Handles, Signed, 19th Century, 14 In. 400.00
Vase, Elongated Bottle Shape, Figures, Garden Scene, Red, Gilt, 1800s, 12 In. 230.00
Vase, Geisha, Bird, Signed, 19th Century, 9 1/2 In. 210.00
Vase, Molded Aquatic Life, Painted Flowers, Japan, 1800s, 8 In. 80.00
Vase, Orange, Gilt Decoration, Landscape, Flower Cartouche, c.1870, 10 In., Pair 575.00
Vase, Pencil Neck, Insect, Butterfly, Late 19th Century, 7 1/2 In. 150.00

LACQUER is a type of varnish. Collectors are most interested in the Chinese and Japanese lacquer wares made from the Japanese varnish tree. Lacquer wares are made from wood with many coats of lacquer. Sometimes the piece is carved or decorated with ivory or metal inlay.

Basket, Cover, Handle, Red, 1800s, 12 1/2 In. 50.00

Bowl, Mother-Of-Pearl Inlay, Flowers, Leaves, Ogata Korin, 1700s, 15 1/2 In. 1150.00
Box, 2 Tiers, Footed Tray, Gold, Silver, Minogami, River Bank, Landscape, 10 x 8 x 8 In. 4400.00
Box, 5 Tiers, Red, Yellow, Black, Trays, Inverted Fan Shaped Opening, 8 x 5 x 6 In. 330.00
Box, Cosmetic, Mon & Vine, 4 Drawers, Black, Gold, 1800s, 14 x 12 1/4 In. 115.00
Box, Cover, Mother-Of-Pearl Inlay, Phoenix, Flower, Black Ground, Korea, 14 x 11 In. .. 520.00
Box, Cylindrical, Landscape Design, 8-Sided Base, Black, Gold, Early 1900s, 16 x 21 In. . 230.00
Box, Desk, Chinese Export, Black, Gold, Mandarins Decor, c.1835, 4 x 12 1/4 x 8 In. 980.00
Box, Egg Shape, Loop Handle, Red, c.1900, 18 In. 90.00
Box, Fans, Silver Peonies, Nashiji Ground, Japan, Early 1900s, 7 x 3 1/4 In. 235.00
Box, Games, 6 Compartments, Lift-Off Lid, Chinese Export, Late 1800s, 15 In. 960.00
Box, Incense, Boats, Torii Gate, Prayer Flags, 2 5/8 x 6 1/4 x 2 In. 250.00
Box, Letter, Black, Gold, Mon & Vine Design, Contents, Late 1800s, 15 In. 430.00
Box, Longevity Tortoise, Round, Japan, 1800s, 5 In. 120.00
Box, Ribbed Cylinder, Butterfly, Tripod Base, Brass Bound, c.1910, 16 1/2 x 14 1/2 In. .. 115.00
Box, Rooster, Maple Tree, Red, Gold, Japan, Early 1900s, 11 In. 29.00
Butsudan, Home Altar, Black, Buddha, Lotus Throne, Metalwork Mandala, 1800s, 7 In. . 210.00
Compact, Black, Gold, Exotic Birds, Weeping Cherry Tree, Early 1900s, 3 1/2 In. 290.00
Decanter Case, Red, Gilt, Stags In Wooded Landscape, 8 1/2 x 8 1/2 x 9 1/2 In. 99.00
Dish, Black, Gold, Rectangular, Herdsman Riding Water Buffalo, Early 1800s, 6 x 7 In. .. 145.00
Dish, Saucer Form, Red, Riverside Landscape Design, 1800s, 5 1/2 In. 29.00
Dish, Saucer, Wood, Cicada Design, Late 19th Century, 5 In. 29.00
Easter Egg, Red, Enamel, Scenic, Christ Rising From Tomb, Gilt, Late 1800s, 6 1/2 In. .. 1175.00
Figurine, Buddha, Wood, 2-Tier Lotus Base, Cobra Form Mandala, Early 1800s, 13 1/2 In. 405.00
Figurine, Dancer, Han Style, Black, Red Lacquer, 15 1/2 In. 175.00
Kogo, Incense Container, Clamshell Shape, Dragon King Palace, 1800s, 4 In. 3450.00
Kogo, Incense Container, Hanging Kimono, Low Relief Pine Tree, 1800s, 3 3/4 In. 750.00
Kogo, Incense Container, Koto Shape, Hiramakie Strings, Wood Graining, 1800s, 6 In. 2300.00
Kogo, Incense Container, Wood, Mask Form, Bulging Eyes, Late 19th Century, 3 In. 90.00
Letter Box, Gold, 3-Leaf Mon Design, Nashihi Ground, Japan, Late 19th Century, 12 In. . 175.00
Mask, Wood, Heroic, Red Tengu King, Gold Eyes, Japan, 1900s, 18 In. 345.00
Noh Mask, Ghost, Wood, 1800s, 8 In. 1150.00
Parasol Handle, Bamboo, Flowering Vine, Wasp, Late 1800s, 14 1/2 In. 360.00
Plate, 5 Dragons, Leaf Rim, Metal Rim & Foot, Wood Stand, 1800s, 13 In., Pair 2300.00
Sake Bottle, 3-Petal Tokugawa, Mashiji Ground, 1800s, 8 1/2 In., Pair 175.00
Serving, Dish, Fish Shape, Red, Early 1900s, 15 In. 29.00
Stand, Cloisonne Enamel Inset, Gilt, Polychrome, 1900s, 22 1/2 x 16 In. 230.00
Tea Caddy, Cylindrical, Waves, Nets, Pewter, Mother-Of-Pearl Inlay, 1800s, 2 3/4 In. 1955.00
Tray, Black, Gold, Moonlit Landscape, Square, Japan, Meiji Period, 10 In. 230.00
Tray, Gold, Footed, Flowers, Nashji Ground, Square, 1800s, 10 3/4 In. 255.00
Tray, Gold, Lotus Leaf Shape, Seed Pods, Peony Basket, 1800s, 24 In. 865.00
Tray, Gold, Round, Hiramakie Butterfly Design, Nashiji Ground, Early 1800s, 10 1/4 In. . 130.00
Tray, Round, Maki-e Design, Pelican, Yoshihara, Japan, Early 1900s 940.00
Tray, Victorian, Black, Shaped, Gilt Border, Mapplebeck & Lowe, 22 x 31 1/2 x 24 In. 1610.00

LADY HEAD VASE, see Head Vase.

LALIQUE glass was made by Rene Lalique in Paris, France, between the 1890s and his death in 1945. The glass was molded, pressed, and engraved in Art Nouveau and Art Deco styles. Pieces were marked with the signature *R. Lalique*. Lalique glass is still being made. Pieces made after 1945 bear the mark *Lalique*. Jewelry made by Rene Lalique is listed in the Jewelry category.

R.LALIQUE

Ashtray, Alaska, Opalescent, Stenciled R. Lalique, c.1931, 4 In. 920.00
Ashtray, Archers, Amber, Frosted, 4 1/2 In. 1434.00
Ashtray, Caravelle, Ship Form Handle, 4 In. 80.00
Ashtray, Chien, Dog, Yellow, Engraved R. Lalique, c.1926, 4 In. 690.00
Ashtray, Clos St. Odile, Clear, Frosted, Sepia Patina, R. Lalique, c.1922, 5 1/2 In. 460.00
Ashtray, Dindon, Turkey, Mint Green Opalescent, Engraved R. Lalique, c.1925, 4 In. 750.00
Ashtray, Fauvettes, Warblers, Clear, Frosted, Sepia Patina, R. Lalique, c.1924, 7 In. 290.00
Ashtray, Feuilles, Leaves, Clear, Frosted, Blue Patina, R. Lalique, c.1924, 7 In. 230.00
Ashtray, Lapin, Rabbit, Opalescent, Engraved R. Lalique, c.1925, 4 In. 690.00
Ashtray, Moineau, Sparrow, Clear, Frosted, Engraved R. Lalique, c.1925, 4 1/2 In. 400.00
Atomizer, Calendal, Molinard, Dancers, Clear, Frosted, Sepia, Lalique, c.1927, 5 1/2 In. ... 980.00

Atomizer, Epines, Thorns, Intaglio Frosted Design, Metal Collar, 3 3/4 In. 345.00
Atomizer, Figurines No. 1, Marcas Et Bardel, Frosted, Blue, R. Lalique, c.1924, 5 In. 750.00
Atomizer, Figurines No. 1, Marcas Et Bardel, Frosted, Green, R. Lalique, c.1924, 3 3/4 In. . . 750.00
Atomizer, Figurines No. 2, Marcas Et Bardel, Frosted, Green, R. Lalique, c.1926, 5 In. . . . 490.00
Atomizer, Le Parisien, Molinard, Clear, Frosted, Sepia Patina, R. Lalique, c.1923, 5 In. . . 980.00
Blotter, Rocker, Feuilles D'Artichaut, Leaves, Frosted, Sepia, R. Lalique, c.1920, 6 1/2 In. 1095.00
Bookends, Hirondelle, Swallow, Frosted, Stenciled R. Lalique, c.1942, 6 1/2 In., Pair 1150.00
Bowl, Actinia, Swirls, Opalescent, Stenciled R. Lalique, c.1933, 10 In. 375.00
Bowl, Algues, Seaweed, Open Coupe, Opalescent, Stenciled R. Lalique, c.1933, 14 1/2 In. 690.00
Bowl, Anges, Angels, Opalescent, Sepia Patina, Stenciled R. Lalique, c.1930, 15 In. 3740.00
Bowl, Asters, Open Coupe, Stenciled R. Lalique, c.1935, 10 In. 400.00
Bowl, Bulbes No. 2, Opalescent, Stenciled R. Lalique, c.1935, 8 1/4 In. 375.00
Bowl, Bulbes No. 2, Open Coupe, Opalescent, R. Lalique, c.1935, 10 In. 490.00
Bowl, Bulbes, Opalescent, Clear, 3 1/2 x 7 7/8 In. . . : 290.00
Bowl, Bulbes, Open Coupe, Opalescent, Clear, 1 7/8 x 9 7/8 In. 259.00
Bowl, Calypso, Mermaids, Coupe, Opalescent, Stenciled R. Lalique, c.1931, 12 In. 2760.00
Bowl, Chene, Oak Leaves, Stems, Molded, Frosted, c.1950, 18 In. 805.00
Bowl, Chiens, Dogs, Clear, Frosted, Sepia Patina, Molded, R. Lalique, c.1921, 9 1/4 In. . . 550.00
Bowl, Coquilles, Shells, Opalescent, R. Lalique, c.1924, 9 1/2 In. 575.00
Bowl, Coquilles, Shells, Opalescent, Signed, c.1930, 12 In. 616.00
Bowl, Fleur, Flower, Clear, Frosted, Green Patina, Black Enamel, Lalique, c.1912, 4 1/2 In. 980.00
Bowl, Fleurons No. 2, Stenciled R. Lalique, c.1935, 8 1/4 In. 375.00
Bowl, Graines D'Asperges No. 2, Asparagus Seeds, Opalescent, Molded, c.1921, 8 1/4 In. 345.00
Bowl, Gui, Mistletoe, Green Stain, 9 1/4 In. 495.00
Bowl, Lys, Lilies, Molded Flowers, Frosted, Blue Patina, R. Lalique, c.1924, 9 1/2 In. . . . 980.00
Bowl, Marguerites, Daisies, Frosted, Stenciled R. Lalique, c.1933, 11 In. 259.00
Bowl, Martigues, Fish, Opalescent, Molded R. Lalique, c.1920, 14 1/2 In. 3450.00
Bowl, Mont-Dore, Opalescent, Molded R. Lalique, c.1928, 8 1/2 In. 290.00
Bowl, Nemours, Flowers, Black Enamel Centers, 10 In. 230.00
Bowl, Ondines, Water Nymphs, Opalescent, Stenciled R. Lalique, c.1921, 8 1/4 In. 920.00
Bowl, Ormeaux No. 2, Elm Leaves, Frosted, Blue Patina, R. Lalique, c.1931, 13 In. 520.00
Bowl, Oursins, Graduated Bubbles, Clear Opalescent, 3 3/8 x 8 In. 345.00
Bowl, Paons, Peacocks, Opalescent, Engraved R. Lalique, c.1932, 12 1/4 In. 690.00
Bowl, Paquerettes, Daisies, Frosted, Sepia Patina, Stenciled R. Lalique, c.1931, 10 In. . . . 490.00
Bowl, Perruches, Parakeets, Opalescent, Blue Green Patina, R. Lalique, c.1931, 9 1/2 In. . 4600.00
Bowl, Poissons No. 1, Fish, Opalescent, Stenciled R. Lalique, c.1931, 9 In. 690.00
Bowl, Poissons No. 2, Fish, Opalescent, Stenciled R. Lalique, c.1921, 9 1/2 In. 345.00
Bowl, Saint James, Open Coupe, Etched Rim, Jagged Oval Links, 1935-1947, 14 In. 295.00
Bowl, Tournon, Flowers, Opalescent, Relief Decoration, 1928, 11 7/8 In. 1295.00
Bowl, Trepied Sirene, Mermaid, Opalescent, Molded R. Lalique, c.1920, 14 In. 8625.00
Bowl, Volubulis, 3 Morning Glories, Flower Veins Make Feet, Amber, 8 1/2 In. 345.00
Bowl, Volubulis, 3 Morning Glories, Opalescent, R. Lalique, c.1921, 8 1/4 In. 400.00
Bowl, Volubulis, 3 Morning Glories, Yellow, R. Lalique, c.1921, 8 1/2 In. . . . . .520.00 to 920.00
Bowl, Volutes, Spiraling Bubbles, Opalescent, Stenciled R. Lalique, c.1934, 10 In. 520.00
Box, Cleones, Raised Beetles, Ferns, Amber, 6 3/4 In. 1095.00
Box, Cover, Amour Assis, Boy, Clear, Frosted, Blue Patina, R. Lalique, c.1919, 6 In. 3740.00
Box, Cover, Cigales, Cicadas, Opalescent, Molded R. Lalique, c.1921, 10 In. 2070.00
Box, Cover, Cyprins, Cover, Opalescent Fish, 10 x 2 In. 3165.00
Box, Cover, Deux Sirenes, 2 Mermaids, Opalescent, Molded R. Lalique, c.1931, 10 In. . . . 4315.00
Box, Cover, Eglantine, Wild Rose, Clear, Frosted, 4 1/8 x 5 3/8 In. 210.00
Box, Cover, Libellules, Dragonflies, Opalescent, Molded R. Lalique, c.1921, 7 In. 1725.00
Box, Cover, Muguets, Lilies Of The Valley, Green Opalescent, R. Lalique, c.1921, 10 In. . 1650.00
Box, Cover, Quatre Flacons, Houbigant, Opalescent, Molded R. Lalique, c.1928, 5 1/2 In. 375.00
Box, Cover, Quatre Scarabees, 4 Beetles, Black, White, R. Lalique, c.1911, 3 1/2 In. 2070.00
Box, Cover, Six Dahlias, Opalescent, Molded R. Lalique, c.1922, 8 1/2 In. 800.00
Candlestick, Mesanges, Birds, Frosted, Gray, Bobeches, R. Lalique, c.1943, 7 In., Pair . . . 1150.00
Chandelier, Chamres, Leaves, Clear, Frosted, Original Cords, R. Lalique, c.1924, 14 In. . . 3740.00
Clock, Deux Colombes, 2 Doves, Opalescent, Blue Patina, Molded, R. Lalique, 9 In. 4600.00
Clock, Deux Figuerines, Frosted, Molded Glass 9400.00
Clock, Inseperables, Birds, Branch, Opalescent, Alabaster, Molded R. Lalique, c.1926, 4 In. 2415.00
Clock, Moineaux, 4 Sparrows, Clear, Frosted, Sepia, Molded R. Lalique, c.1924, 6 1/4 In. 3740.00
Clock, Quatre Moineaux Du Japon, 4 Sparrows, Frosted, R. Lalique, c.1931, 7 1/2 In. 6400.00
Crucifix, Christ, Clear, Frosted, Chromed Metal, Stenciled R. Lalique, c.1930, 16 In. 1610.00

Decanter, Marguerites, Daisies, Clear, Frosted, Engraved R. Lalique, c.1920, 14 1/4 In. ... 1035.00
Figurine, Danseuse Bras Baisse, Dancer, Arms Down, Engraved Lalique, c.1975, 9 1/2 In. 690.00
Figurine, Danseuse Bras Leves, Dancer, Arms Up, Engraved Lalique, c.1975, 9 1/2 In. 690.00
Figurine, Floreal, Nude Woman, Engraved Lalique, No. 11904, c.1975, 3 1/2 In. 200.00
Figurine, Grande Nue, Socle Lierre, Nude, Clear, Frosted, c.1919, 16 1/2 In. 17250.00
Figurine, Isis, Nude, Engraved Lalique, c.1975, 13 1/2 In. 1265.00
Figurine, Panther, Spotted, Black, 14 1/2 In. 1495.00
Figurine, Vierge Mains Jointes, Praying Madonna, Frosted, 10 In. 230.00
Hood Ornament, Archer, Clear, Frosted, Molded, 4 3/4 In. 2115.00
Hood Ornament, Libellule Grande, Dragonfly, Clear, Frosted, Molded R. Lalique, 8 In. ... 8625.00
Hood Ornament, Longchamp, Horse Head, Clear, Frosted, c.1929, 5 1/4 In. 2645.00
Hood Ornament, St. Christophe, Clear, Frosted, Chrome, Celluloid Stand, R. Lalique, 8 In. 2070.00
Hood Ornament, Tete D'aigle, Eagle Head, Clear, Frosted, R. Lalique, c.1928, 4 1/4 In. . 1840.00
Hood Ornament, Tete De Coq, Rooster, Clear, Frosted, Black Base, Lalique, c.1928, 7 In. 1035.00
Ice Bucket, Clos St. Odile, Clear, Frosted, Sepia Patina, R. Lalique, c.1922, 9 1/2 In. 3740.00
Ice Pail, Fougeres, Leaves, Blue Stain, Tapered, Cylinder, R. Lalique, c.1924, 8 3/4 In. .. 1380.00
Inkwell, Trois Papillons, 3 Butterflies, Frosted, Sepia, Engraved Lalique, c.1912, 4 In. 2645.00
Mirror, Anemones, Clear, Frosted, Metal, Pink Foil, c.1913, 15 1/2 x 15 1/2 In. 6900.00
Paperweight, Barbillon, Fish, Clear, Frosted, Stenciled R. Lalique, c.1931, 3 1/4 In. 520.00
Paperweight, Bison, Clear, Frosted, Stenciled R. Lalique, c.1931, 5 In. 635.00
Paperweight, Bison, Etched Glass, 3 3/4 x 4 7/8 In. ....150.00 to 518.00
Paperweight, Chouette, Owl, Engraved Lalique, c.1980, 3 In. 145.00
Paperweight, Chrysis, Clear, Frosted, Stamped, 5 1/4 In. 188.00
Paperweight, Coq Nain, Cockerel, Frosted, 8 1/8 In. 400.00
Paperweight, Daim, Deer, Clear, Frosted, Stenciled R. Lalique, c.1926, 3 1/4 In. 460.00
Paperweight, Deux Aigles, 2 Eagles, Topaz Glass, Molded Lalique, c.1914, 4 In. 2185.00
Paperweight, Deux Tourterelles, 2 Turtledoves, Clear, Frosted, R. Lalique, c.1925, 5 In. .. 980.00
Paperweight, Double Marguerites, Daisies, Clear, Frosted, Yellow, Lalique, c.1919, 4 In. . 1150.00
Paperweight, Masque Noir, Black Satyr Mask, Palm Fronds, 4 1/2 x 3 3/4 x 2 1/4 In..... 225.00
Paperweight, Moineau Timide, Sparrow, Clear, Frosted, Sepia, R. Lalique, c.1929, 5 In. . 290.00
Paperweight, Tete D'Aigle, Eagle Head, Frosted, 4 1/4 In. ....345.00 to 355.00
Paperweight, Tete De Coq, Rooster Head, Frosted, 7 In. 375.00
Paperweight, Toby, Elephant, Engraved R. Lalique, c.1929, 3 1/2 In. 1955.00
Perfume Bottle, Danae, Magasin Du Louvre, Clear, Frosted, Sepia, Lalique, c.1930, 3 In. 1840.00
Perfume Bottle, Dans La Nuit, Worth, Clear, Frosted, Stopper, R. Lalique, 1925, 9 1/2 In. 2695.00
Perfume Bottle, Dans La Nuit, Worth, Frosted, Stars, Moon, R. Lalique, Box, 1924, 6 In. 1346.00
Perfume Bottle, Deux Figurines, Bouchon, Clear, Frosted, Sepia, R. Lalique, c.1912, 5 In. 8050.00
Perfume Bottle, Fille D'Eve, Nina Ricci, Apple, Clear, Frosted, Lalique, c.1965, 4 In. 315.00
Perfume Bottle, Fougeres, Lady Portrait, Frosted, Green, Gold Foil, c.1912, 3 3/4 In. ... 11500.00
Perfume Bottle, Je Reviens, Worth, Blue, Cylindrical, Stopper, Box, 1928, 5 1/4 In. 2860.00
Perfume Bottle, L'Air Du Temps, Nina Ricci, Dove, Frosted, Lalique, c.1960, 12 1/2 In. . 1380.00
Perfume Bottle, L'Air Du Temps, Nina Ricci, Screw Cap, M. Lalique, Box, 1948, 1 In. .. 168.00
Perfume Bottle, L'Air Du Temps, Nina Ricci, Swirls, M. Lalique, Box, 1951, 2 1/2 In. .. 715.00
Perfume Bottle, La Phalene, D'Heraud, Butterfly, Amber, R. Lalique, c.1923, 3 1/2 In. . 5750.00
Perfume Bottle, Le Baiser Du Faune Molinard, Clear, Frosted, R. Lalique, c.1928, 6 In. . 11500.00
Perfume Bottle, Leurs Ames, D'Orsay, Women, Tree, Clear, Frosted, Sepia, Lalique, 5 In. 8050.00
Perfume Bottle, Myosotis, No. 3, Nude Stopper, Frosted, Green, R. Lalique, c.1928, 9 In. 4715.00
Perfume Bottle, Pomme, Apple, Frosted, M. Lalique, 5 1/4 In. 290.00
Perfume Bottle, Rosace Figurines, Clear, Frosted, Sepia, R. Lalique, c.1912, 4 1/2 In. ... 2300.00
Perfume Bottle, Roses, D'Orsay, Woman Stopper, Frosted, Sepia, Lalique, c.1912, 4 In. . 3000.00
Perfume Bottle, Salamandres, Clear, Frosted, Blue Patina, R. Lalique, c.1914, 3 1/2 In. .. 1725.00
Perfume Bottle, Sans Adieu, Worth, Green, Circular, Stopper, R. Lalique, 1929, 3 In. 1515.00
Perfume Bottle, Volnay, Violette, Clear, Stopper, R. Lalique, c.1919, 5 In. 5725.00
Perfume Burner, Sirenes, Mermaids, Frosted, Blue, Molded R. Lalique, c.1920, 7 In. ... 2530.00
Plaque, Les Parfums De Coty, Brass, Leather Back, R. Lalique, c.1911, 10 x 4 1/4 In. ... 3335.00
Plaque, Masque De Femme, Woman's Face, Fish, Chrome Stand, Lalique, c.1975, 13 In. . 3740.00
Plate, Algues, Seaweed, Opalescent, Stenciled R. Lalique, c.1933, 15 1/4 In. 750.00
Plate, Asters No. 2, Opalescent, c.1935, 11 In. 400.00
Plate, Chasse Chiens, Dogs, Clear, Frosted, Blue, Engraved R. Lalique, c.1914, 8 1/2 In. . 575.00
Plate, Coquilles, Shells, Opalescent, Molded R. Lalique, c.1924, 11 1/2 In. 750.00
Plate, Dauphins, Fish In Waves, Opalescent, Stenciled R. Lalique, c.1931, 12 In. 750.00
Plate, Marienthal, Grape Clusters, Frosted Glass, Molded R. Lalique, c.1932, 7 In. 145.00
Plate, Ondines, Water Nymphs, Opalescent, R. Lalique, c.1921, 11 In. 2300.00

Keep your collection of glassware away from the speakers of your sound system. Heavy bass and high-pitched sounds can crack the glass.

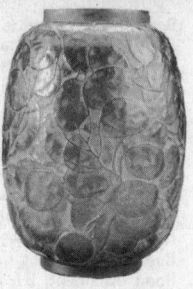

Lalique, Vase, Monnaie
Du Pape, Deep Red
Amber, R. Lalique,
1914, 9 1/2 In.

Plate, Oursins, Graduated Bubbles, Clear, Opalescent, 10 7/8 In.	345.00
Seal, Figurine Mains Jointes, Woman, Clear, Frosted, Sepia, R. Lalique, c.1920, 3 1/2 In.	2070.00
Seal, Sauterelle, Grasshopper, Electric Blue, Molded Lalique, c.1912, 1 3/4 In.	690.00
Swizzle Stick, Barr, Masks, Clear, Frosted, Box, c.1931, 5 In., 12 Piece	6900.00
Vase, Acanthes, Egg Shape, Thistles In Frosted Glass, 1921, 11 In.	2465.00
Vase, Aras, Birds Perched On Foliage, Spherical, R. Lalique, 1924, 10 In.	2200.00
Vase, Archer, 10 Archers & Birds, Frosted Amber, Opalescent Liner, 10 1/2 In.	11500.00
Vase, Archers, Amber, Engraved R. Lalique, c.1921, 10 1/4 In.	8050.00
Vase, Archers, Yellow, Molded R. Lalique, c.1921, 10 1/4 In.	8625.00
Vase, Avallon, Birds & Berries, 5 1/4 In., Pair	780.00
Vase, Bacchantes, Dancers, Frosted Glass, 9 1/2 In.	1795.00
Vase, Bagatelle, Fledglings, Leaves, Frosted, 6 5/8 In.	80.00
Vase, Camaret, Fish, Engraved R. Lalique, c.1928, 5 1/2 In.	1095.00
Vase, Camaret, Fish, Frosted, 5 In.	1320.00
Vase, Ceylan, Opalescent, Signed, 9 3/8 In.	4185.00
Vase, Ceylan, Parakeets, Frosted, Blue Stain, 9 1/4 In.	4125.00
Vase, Chardons, Thistles, Clear, Frosted, Sepia Patina, c.1922, 7 1/2 In.	865.00
Vase, Coqs Et Plumes, Roosters & Feathers, Frosted, 6 In., Pair	2030.00
Vase, Coqs Et Plumes, Roosters & Feathers, Frosted, Stenciled R. Lalique, c.1928, 6 In.	1150.00
Vase, Coquilles, Shells, Blue Stain, Frosted Foot & Neck, 7 1/2 In.	1495.00
Vase, Coquilles, Shells, Clear, Frosted, Blue Patina, Molded R. Lalique, c.1920, 7 1/2 In.	1380.00
Vase, Danaides, Nude Maidens, Water Pouring From Urns, Frosted, 7 1/8 In.	1955.00 to 2200.00
Vase, Deux Anneaux, Pigeons, Handles, Opalescent, Engraved Lalique, c.1919, 13 In.	9900.00
Vase, Domremy, Thistles, Frosted, 8 1/4 In.	1035.00
Vase, Espalion, Ferns, Bulbous, Blue, 7 In.	2875.00
Vase, Espalion, Ferns, Opalescent, Green Patina, Engraved R. Lalique, c.1927, 7 In.	1095.00
Vase, Espalion, Ferns, Opalescent, Mauve Patina, Engraved R. Lalique, c.1927, 7 In.	980.00
Vase, Esterel, Oleander, Opalescent, Blue Patina, Engraved R. Lalique, c.1923, 6 In.	1095.00
Vase, Esterel, Oleander, Yellow, Sepia Patina, Molded R. Lalique, c.1923, 6 In.	2530.00
Vase, Eucalyptus, Leaves, Opalescent, c.1931, 6 1/2 In.	1840.00
Vase, Formose, Fish, Opalescent, Blue Patina, Engraved R. Lalique, c.1924, 6 1/2 In.	2300.00
Vase, Formose, Fish, Red, White Patina, Molded R. Lalique, c.1924, 6 1/2 In.	9200.00
Vase, Formose, Fish, Topaz, Sepia Patina, Molded R. Lalique, c.1924, 6 1/2 In.	3105.00
Vase, Grignon, Clear, Frosted, Stenciled R. Lalique, c.1932, 7 1/4 In.	575.00
Vase, Gui, Mistletoe, Opalescent, Blue Patina, Molded R. Lalique, c.1920, 7 In.	1265.00
Vase, Gui, Mistletoe, Opalescent, Green Patina, Molded R. Lalique, c.1920, 7 In.	1380.00
Vase, Gui, Mistletoe, Teal Green, c.1920, 7 In.	4600.00
Vase, Helder, Frosted, Blue Patina, Carafe Form, Stenciled R. Lalique, c.1929, 9 In., Pair	1150.00
Vase, Honfleaur, Clear, Frosted, Sepia Patina, Wing Handles, c.1927, 5 1/2 In.	865.00
Vase, Languedoc, Leaves, Opalescent, Stenciled R. Lalique, c.1931, 11 In. Diam.	6900.00
Vase, Lierre, Ivy, Clear, Frosted, Sepia Patina, c.1930, 6 1/2 In.	690.00
Vase, Lotus, Lotus Blossom, Molded, Frosted Ground, Ribbed, R. Lalique, 5 3/4 In.	700.00
Vase, Monnaie Du Pape, Deep Red Amber, R. Lalique, 1914, 9 1/2 In. *Illus*	4600.00
Vase, Oleron, Fish, Opalescent, Engraved R. Lalique, c.1927, 4 In.	980.00
Vase, Ormeaux, Elm Leaves, Clear, Frosted, Engraved R. Lalique, c.1926, 6 In.	920.00
Vase, Ormeaux, Elm Leaves, Glossy Veins, Frosted, Round, 6 1/2 x 6 In.	850.00
Vase, Palmes, Palm Leaves, Frosted, Green Patina, Molded R. Lalique, c.1923, 4 1/2 In.	980.00
Vase, Penthievre, Fish, Topaz, White Patina, Engraved R. Lalique, c.1928, 10 1/4 In.	6900.00
Vase, Piriac, Medial Band Of Fish & Waves, Blue, Stenciled R. Lalique, c.1930, 7 In.	5750.00

Vase, Rampillon, Cabochons, Flowers, Opalescent, Blue Gray Patina, c.1927, 5 In. 1150.00
Vase, Renoncules, Ranuculus Flowers, Clear, Frosted, c.1930, 6 In. 635.00
Vase, Ronces, Thorny Vines, Amber, c.1921, 9 1/2 In. 4025.00
Vase, Ronces, Thorny Vines, Blue Patina, Molded R. Lalique, c.1921, 9 1/2 In. 1265.00
Vase, Ronces, Thorny Vines, Emerald Green, R. Lalique, c.1921, 9 1/2 In. 5750.00
Vase, Ronces, Thorny Vines, Yellow Opalescent, Engraved R. Lalique, c.1921, 9 In. 4315.00
Vase, Tourbillons, Scrolls, Frosted, Bronze Base, Stenciled R. Lalique, c.1926, 8 1/2 In. ... 13800.00
Vase, Tournai, Band Of Leaves, Opalescent, c.1930, Signed, 5 1/2 x 3 1/4 In. 615.00
Vase, Tournai, Leaf Panels, Topaz, White Patina, Molded R. Lalique, c.1924, 5 In. 1150.00
Vase, Tournesols, Sunflowers, Electric Blue, Engraved R. Lalique, 4 1/2 In. 2875.00
Vase, Vase, Koudour, Frosted, Black Enamel, Zigzags, Molded R. Lalique, c.1926, 7 In. ... 4900.00
Vase, Vichy, Flower Garlands, Clear, Frosted, Sepia Patina, c.1937, 6 3/4 In. 750.00

LAMPS of every type, from the early oil-burning Betty and Phoebe lamps to the recent electric lamps with glass or beaded shades, interest collectors. Fuels used in lamps changed through the years; whale oil (1800–1840), camphene (1828), Argand (1830), lard (1833–1863), turpentine and alcohol (1840s), gas (1850–1879), kerosene (1860), and electricity (1879) are the most common. Other lamps are listed by manufacturer or type of material.

Advertising, Elsie The Cow, Daisy Necklace, c.1960, 9 x 8 In. 395.00
Advertising, Insure With Glens Falls Before The Fire, Burning Building, 17 1/2 x 24 In. ... 635.00
Advertising, Moxie, Drink Moxie, Hanging, 10 In. 550.00
Aladdin, B-26, Simplicity, Decalcomania 225.00
Aladdin, B-30, Simplicity, White 125.00
Aladdin, B-41, Washington Drape, Amber, Round Base 150.00
Aladdin, B-55, Washington Drape, Amber, Plain Stem 120.00
Aladdin, B-55, Washington Drape, Green, Plain Stem 150.00
Aladdin, B-60, Short Lincoln Drape, Alacite 625.00
Aladdin, B-75, Tall Lincoln Drape, Alacite 90.00
Aladdin, B-75, Tall Lincoln Drape, Alacite, Burner 110.00
Aladdin, B-77, Tall Lincoln Drape, Ruby 600.00
Aladdin, B-81, Beehive, Green 160.00
Aladdin, B-82, Beehive, Light Amber 190.00
Aladdin, B-83, Beehive, Ruby ....400.00 to 500.00
Aladdin, B-85, Diamond Quilt, White Moonstone 330.00
Aladdin, B-86, Diamond Quilt, Green Moonstone 225.00
Aladdin, B-88, Vertique, Yellow Moonstone 675.00
Aladdin, B-90, Quilt, White Moonstone Font, Black Crystal Foot 300.00
Aladdin, B-91, Quilt, White Moonstone Font, Rose Moonstone Foot 250.00
Aladdin, B-100, Corinthian, Clear 80.00
Aladdin, B-104, Corinthian, Clear, Black 120.00
Aladdin, B-122, Vertique, Pink Moonstone 350.00
Aladdin, B-134, Orientale, Bronze 70.00
Aladdin, B-136, Treasure, Ducks Shade, 14 In. 150.00
Aladdin, G-15, Floral Base, Crystal 200.00
Aladdin, G-16, Figurine, Shade 575.00
Aladdin, G-16, Table 40.00
Aladdin, G-43, Boudoir, Pair 25.00
Aladdin, G-44, Deco, Crystal, Figural 200.00
Aladdin, G-142, Etched Crystal 170.00
Aladdin, G-156, Moonstone 50.00
Aladdin, G-202, Alacite, Buckle Finial, Desk 70.00
Aladdin, G-211, Candelabra, Alacite 200.00
Aladdin, G-212, Fluted Shade, Alacite, Illuminated Base 90.00
Aladdin, G-237, Alacite Font, Metal Foot 110.00
Aladdin, G-258, Oak Leaf, Illuminated Base, Moonsheaf Final, Pair 110.00
Aladdin, G-282, Turnkey, Whip-O-Lite Shade ....50.00 to 175.00
Aladdin, G-322, Stanley Lamp, Lime Green, Illuminated Base, Pair 10.00
Aladdin, G-375, Dancing Ladies Urn ....700.00 to 1350.00
Aladdin, Model B, No. 104, Colonial, Clear 110.00
Aladdin, Model B, No. 105, Colonial, Green 200.00
Aladdin, Model B, No. 106, Colonial, Amber 110.00

Argand, 2-Light, Gilt Bronze, Square Standard & Base, Scroll Feet, 17 1/2 In. 600.00
Argand, Brass, Urn Form, Greek Key, Tapered Column, Circular Base, 24 In., Pair 4840.00
Argand, Bronze Base, Air Holes, 1783 .... 5000.00
Argand, Empire Style, Gilt Metal, 14 In., Pair 1195.00
Art Deco, Bronze, Sea Horse, Cylindrical Standard, Oscar Bach, c.1930, 65 3/4 In. 1295.00
Astral, Brass Standard, 2-Step Marble Base, Cut & Etched Shade, c.1840, 25 In. 1265.00
Astral, Brass, Etched Glass Shade, Glass Pendants, Victorian, 28 1/2 In., Pair 1555.00
Astral, Brass, Glass, Marble, Late 19th Century, 20 1/2 In. 440.00
Astral, Brass, Reeded Standard, 2-Step Marble Base, Etched Shade, Prisms, 30 In. 1090.00
Astral, Cornelius, Brass, Cut & Etched Shade, c.1840, 24 In. 1495.00
Astral, Embossed Base, Cut & Etched Shade, 3-Footed, 24 In. 1495.00
Astral, Neoclassical, Ormolu, Marble, Cut Glass, 29 1/2 In. 1380.00
Betty, Brass & Iron, Original Hanger & Pick, Chain, Peter Derr, Signed P.D., 1843 ..... 2310.00
Betty, Cast Iron, Hook, 5 1/2 In. 90.00
Betty, Double, Iron, Back Bar Ratchet, Hanging Hook, 7 In. 248.00
Betty, Double, Wrought Iron, Twisted Rattail Hanging Pick, c.1800, 4 1/2 x 12 1/2 In. ... 85.00
Betty, Forged Iron, Split Tail Finial, Rope Twist Hanger, 6 1/2 In. 135.00
Betty, Iron, Hanging Hook, Hinged Lid, Shaped Finial, 5 In. 66.00
Betty, Iron, Heart Finial, 5 In. 95.00
Betty, Iron, Hinged Lid, Y-Shape Finial, Iron Hanger, Rope Twist, 4 In. 310.00
Bouillotte, 2-Light, Louis XVI Style, Brass, Black Tole, Parcel Gilded, Adjustable, 24 In. 345.00
Bouillotte, 2-Light, Neoclassical, Silver Plate, Red Tole Shade, Electric, 19 x 11 1/2 In. ... 575.00
Bouillotte, 3-Light, Louis XVI Style, Gilt Brass, Crimson, Tole, 26 In. 1095.00
Bouillotte, Louis XV Style, Argente Bronze, Scrolled Feet, 24 1/2 In. 865.00
Bouillotte, Louis XVI Style, Gilt Bronze, 20 In. 1435.00
Bouillotte, Louis XVI Style, Gilt Bronze, 27 In. 1195.00
Bradley & Hubbard lamps are included in the Bradley & Hubbard category.
Chandelier, 1-Light, Gilt Metal, Glass Beads, Smoky Glass Prisms, 15 In. 440.00
Chandelier, 2-Light, Louis XVI Style, Bronze, Putto In Wreath, Holding Torches, 12 In. ... 2640.00
Chandelier, 3-Light, Empire Style, Gilt Bronze, Angel Atop Orb, Holding Wreath, 20 In. . 2090.00
Chandelier, 3-Light, Louis XV Style, Gilt Bronze, Glass, 15 In. 560.00
Chandelier, 3-Light, Louis XV Style, Gilt Bronze, Putto Holding Lamp, 34 In. 1675.00
Chandelier, 3-Light, Restauration Style, Gilt Brass, Green Tole, Chain, c.1850, 18 x 19 In. 635.00
Chandelier, 4-Arm, Gas, Openwork, Nickel-Plated Iron Teardrop, Electrific, 27 In. 1230.00
Chandelier, 4-Light, Art Nouveau, Gilt Bronze, Flower Shaped Shades, 40 In. 2090.00
Chandelier, 4-Tier, Belle Epoque, Graduated, 21 x 10 1/4 In. 460.00
Chandelier, 5-Arm, Tin, Double-Cone Central Section, 23 x 21 In. 375.00
Chandelier, 5-Light, Arts & Crafts, Hammered Copper, Heart Cutouts, 18 x 18 x 36 In. .. 2645.00
Chandelier, 5-Light, Louis XV Style, Cut Glass, Ormolu, 1900s, 28 x 30 In. 865.00
Chandelier, 5-Light, Painted Tin, Scrolled Candle Arms, Cone Standard, Electrific, 27 In. . 956.00
Chandelier, 5-Light, Venetian Rococo Style, Murano Glass, Blue, Clear, 29 x 23 In. ... 575.00
Chandelier, 6-Arm, Rococo Gilded Brass, Round Bracket, Cut Prisms, 51 x 28 In. 3300.00
Chandelier, 6-Light, Belle Epoque, Louis XVI Style, Brass, c.1900, 28 x 17 1/2 In. 980.00
Chandelier, 6-Light, Double Antler, Brass Mounted, Continental, Early 1900s, 36 x 33 In. 345.00
Chandelier, 6-Light, Dutch Rococo, Brass, Brass Snuffer, Early 18th Century, 18 x 23 In. . 2760.00
Chandelier, 6-Light, Empire Revival, Balloon Shape, Glass, Metal, Electric, 29 In. 3820.00
Chandelier, 6-Light, Empire Style, Gilt Metal, Glass, 26 In. 470.00
Chandelier, 6-Light, George III Style, Cut Glass, 1900s, 42 x 36 In. 1150.00
Chandelier, 6-Light, Gothic Style, Giltwood, Gesso, 20 x 30 In. 149.00
Chandelier, 6-Light, Louis XIV Style, Giltwood, Electrific, France, c.1900, 30 x 25 In. ... 750.00
Chandelier, 6-Light, Louis XV Style, Cage Form, Gilt Brass, France, 19 1/2 x 13 1/2 In. . 1150.00
Chandelier, 6-Light, Louis XV Style, Gilt, Patinated Bronze, Elephant Standard, 30 In. .. 5975.00
Chandelier, 6-Light, Louis XV Style, Ormolu, Glass, 20th Century, 36 x 22 In. 1955.00
Chandelier, 6-Light, Louis XVI, Cage Form, Gilt Brass, Cut Glass, France, 27 1/2 In. 690.00
Chandelier, 6-Light, Multicolored, Carved Wood, Swan, Leaves, Italy, c.1925, 35 x 33 In. 1035.00
Chandelier, 6-Light, Neoclassical, Cut Glass, Inverted Balusters, Electrific, 19 In. 825.00
Chandelier, 6-Light, Regency Style, Antiqued Brass, Cut Glass, 28 x 22 In. 575.00
Chandelier, 6-Light, Restauration Style, Gilt Brass, Electric, c.1900, 30 x 14 1/2 In. 3680.00
Chandelier, 6-Light, Rococo Style, Brass, Electric, Dutch, 1900s, 26 1/4 x 26 1/2 In. 865.00
Chandelier, 6-Light, Rococo Style, Paktong Type, Electric, Early 1900s, 25 x 27 1/2 In. ... 3220.00
Chandelier, 6-Light, Swan, Gilt Brass, Tole, Electric, c.1900, 30 x 24 1/2 In. 805.00
Chandelier, 6-Light, Venetian Glass, Light Blue Shaded To Clear, 33 In. 1725.00
Chandelier, 7-Light, Arts & Crafts, Brass, Paneled Body, Early 1900s, 59 x 27 In. 315.00

Chandelier, 7-Light, Empire Style, Gilt Bronze, Patinated, Brass Chain, 32 x 23 In. 1840.00
Chandelier, 8-Arm, Brass, Cupids, Scrolled Mounts, Artichoke Drop Finial, 30 x 30 In. .. 1430.00
Chandelier, 8-Light, Brass, Cut Glass, Electric, Continental, c.1885, 30 x 22 1/2 In. 1840.00
Chandelier, 8-Light, Catherine II Style, Brass, Giltwood, Electric, Russia, c.1900, 37 In. . 4600.00
Chandelier, 8-Light, Frosted Glass, Brass, Black Enamel, Germany, 26 1/2 x 43 1/2 In. .. 690.00
Chandelier, 8-Light, George III Style, Brass, Glass, 1900s, 36 x 32 In. ....460.00 to 575.00
Chandelier, 8-Light, George III Style, Cut, Faceted Glass 5465.00
Chandelier, 8-Light, Louis XV Style, Brass, Prisms, Cage Form, Electric, France, 32 In. .. 865.00
Chandelier, 8-Light, Louis XVI Style, Cut Glass, Gilt Brass, Electric, France, 38 x 22 In. . 805.00
Chandelier, 8-Light, Louis XVI Style, Flower-Form Sockets, Iron, France, 42 x 32 1/2 In. 1150.00
Chandelier, 8-Light, Louis XVI Style, Gilt Brass, Cut Glass, France, 41 x 23 In. 750.00
Chandelier, 8-Light, Louis XVI Style, Gilt Bronze, Glass, Electric, France, 35 x 24 In. ... 2070.00
Chandelier, 8-Light, Louis XVI Style, Gilt Bronze, Prisms, 24 x 22 In. 1015.00
Chandelier, 8-Light, Louis XVI Style, Gilt Bronze, Prisms, 34 In. 5225.00
Chandelier, 8-Light, Louis XVI Style, Gilt Metal, Glass, Early 20th Century, 48 x 29 In. . 2760.00
Chandelier, 8-Light, Louis XVI Style, Gilt, Iron, Cage Form, Cut Glass, 37 x 29 In. 865.00
Chandelier, 8-Light, Louis XVI Style, Wrought Iron, Tin, Continental, 40 1/2 x 36 In. ... 345.00
Chandelier, 8-Light, Regency Style, Gilt Brass, Pendalogues, England, c.1935, 33 x 27 In. 1265.00
Chandelier, 8-Light, Seguso, Venetian Glass, 28 x 30 In. 3000.00
Chandelier, 8-Light, Waterfall Form, Gilt Brass, Electric, Italy, 40 x 31 In. 2760.00
Chandelier, 8-Light, Wrought Iron, 20th Century, 18 x 36 In., Pair 175.00
Chandelier, 9-Light, Belle Epoque, Gilt Bronze, Electric, c.1900, 32 1/2 x 20 1/2 In. 920.00
Chandelier, 9-Light, Contempo, Wrought Iron, Glass, c.1952, 22 In. 380.00
Chandelier, 9-Light, Louis XVI Style, Bronze, Prisms, 38 In. 4675.00
Chandelier, 9-Light, Louis XVI Style, Glass, Brass, Electric, France, c.1900, 40 x 24 In. . 3220.00
Chandelier, 9-Light, Regency Style, Gilt Brass, Electric, England, c.1865, 46 x 21 In. 2760.00
Chandelier, 10-Arm, 31-Light, Brass, Prisms, Mid 20th Century, 34 x 42 In. 825.00
Chandelier, 10-Light, Louis XV Style, Brass, Cut Glass, 20th Century, 24 x 25 In. 1610.00
Chandelier, 10-Light, Louis XVI Style, Gilt Brass, Cut Glass, 31 x 24 In. 978.00
Chandelier, 11-Light, Belle Epoque, Cut Glass, Gilt Brass, Bead Chains, 38 x 21 In. 1955.00
Chandelier, 12-Arm, Brass, Chain Mount, 43 x 48 In. 330.00
Chandelier, 12-Light, Emerald Glass, Hurricane Shades, Electrific, c.1910, 42 x 33 In. ... 2990.00
Chandelier, 12-Light, George III Style, Waterford Glass, 1900s, 39 x 36 In. 1650.00
Chandelier, 12-Light, George V, Brass, 2 Tiers, S-Scroll Arms, c.1915, 32 x 32 In. 1610.00
Chandelier, 12-Light, Iron, Crystal, Prism Drops, 26 x 27 In. 920.00
Chandelier, 12-Light, Louis XVI Style, Gilt Brass, France, 38 x 31 In. 2990.00
Chandelier, 12-Light, Neoclassical Revival, Glass, Electric, c.1910, 16 In. 265.00
Chandelier, 12-Light, Swirl, Teardrop Shades, Electric, 60 In. 5750.00
Chandelier, 12-Light, Tin, 3 Tiers, Candle Sockets, Tulip Petals, Wood, 1900s, 30 In. 330.00
Chandelier, 14-Light, Gilt Brass, Crystal, Cage Form, Bulbous Stem, 32 x 35 In. 865.00
Chandelier, 15-Light, Rococo, Gilt, Baluster Shape, Free Flowing Arms, 40 In. 5245.00
Chandelier, 18-Light, Louis XV Style, Wrought Iron, Cage Form, France, 54 x 44 In. 4830.00
Chandelier, 24-Light, Louis XV Style, Bronze, Cut Glass, Cage, Electric, France, 38 In. ... 2990.00
Chandelier, Art Deco, Aluminum, Curved Clear Glass Rods, Etching, 1940s, 17 x 20 In. . 115.00
Chandelier, Art Nouveau, Wrought Iron, White Opaline Glass, 11 x 13 In. 1380.00
Chandelier, Belle Epoque, Louis XVI Style, Brass, Cut Glass, c.1900, 25 x 10 1/2 In. 1380.00
Chandelier, Brass, Round, Dome Shade, Glass Beads, Silk Fringe, 21 x 21 In. 470.00
Chandelier, Convex Sunburst, Wheat Spears, Wrought Iron, Gilded, France, 6 3/4 x 28 In. 920.00
Chandelier, Louis XVI Style, Brass, Cut Glass, 30 x 16 In. 1035.00
Chandelier, Paavo Tynell, Brass, Pierced Dome, Pleated Silk Shade, 35 1/2 In. 4315.00
Chandelier, Wood, Carved, Painted, White, Gold Detail, Acanthus Leaves, 38 x 39 1/2 In. 1265.00
Electric, 1-Arm, Brass, Urn Font, John B. Jones, Boston, 19 3/4 In., Pair 1375.00
Electric, 2-Light, Arts & Crafts, Leaded Glass, Floral Shade, Oak, 35 x 19 3/4 x 19 3/4 In. 1090.00
Electric, 2-Light, Boudoir, Venetian Glass, 18 1/2 In., Pair 1195.00
Electric, 2-Light, Bronze, Cloisonne, Flowers, Blue Ground, Round Base, Oriental, 70 In. 690.00
Electric, 2-Light, Maria Pergay, Brushed Chrome, Wedge Shape, Brass, 20 x 8 In. 3220.00
Electric, Aalto, Spot, 2 Cylinders, Black Enameled Exterior, Poulsen, 13 1/4 x 5 In., Pair . 69.00
Electric, Achille & Pier Giacomo Castiglioni, Marble, Aluminum, Arco, Italy, 1962, 96 In. 4400.00
Electric, Achille & Pier Giacomo Castiglioni, Plastic, Wire, Wood, Gatto Flos, 12 In., Pair 920.00
Electric, Alabaster, Blossoming Flower, Square Base, 12 1/2 In. 165.00
Electric, Alabaster, Carved, Girl Seated On Stone Wall, Under Lantern, Pedestal, 66 In. .. 1923.00
Electric, Alabaster, Carved, Romeo, Juliet, Continental, 30 In. 777.00
Electric, Aluminum, Brass, 14-Tiered Metal Shade, 8 x 37 In. 4390.00

Electric, Angle, Chimney, Upper Pair, Translucent White, Crimped Rims, 8 1/4 In. . . . . . .　210.00
Electric, Arredoluce, Aluminum, Magnet, Enameled Metal, Italy, 1960s, 2 3/4 x 14 In. . . .　1520.00
Electric, Arredoluce, Chromed Steel, Marble, Nanda Vigo, Italy, 1960s, 9 x 19 x 71 In. . .　1755.00
Electric, Arredoluce, Chromed Steel, Metal, Marble, Adjustable, Italy, 1960s, 65 In., Pair .　2690.00
Electric, Art Deco, Ludwig Fuchs, Chubby Youth Holding Lamp Socket Aloft, 28 In. . . . .　1035.00
Electric, Art Nouveau, Blue Mottled Glass Panel, Geometric Shade, 21 x 19 In. . . . .　60.00
Electric, Art Nouveau, Bronze, Leaded Glass Shade, Scalloped Rim, Nude Figures, 33 In.　316.00
Electric, Art Nouveau, Bronze, Shell Molded Feet, 63 In. . . . .　115.00
Electric, Art Nouveau, Figural, Neoclassical Woman & Child, Metal, 29 In. . . . .　175.00
Electric, Art Nouveau, Woman Holds 2 Lights, Hammered Brass Shades, 6 x 20 In. . . . . .　920.00
Electric, Arteluce, Enameled Metal, Steel, Marble, Adjustable, Italy, 1950s, Floor . . . .　2575.00
Electric, Arts & Crafts, 6 Panels, Hammered Copper, Metalwork, 26 In. . . . .　460.00
Electric, Arts & Crafts, Bronzed Metal Base, Brown, Ivory Leaded Glass, 18 x 23 In. . . . .　635.00
Electric, Arts & Crafts, Bronzed Metal, Slag Glass Inserts, 19 1/2 In. . . . .　490.00
Electric, Arts & Crafts, Green Mottled Glass, Oak Base, Hexagonal, 15 x 22 In. . . . .　430.00
Electric, Arts & Crafts, Hammered Copper, Mica Shade, 18 x 16 In. . . . .　5175.00
Electric, Arts & Crafts, Iron Base, Chain, Green Glass Shade, 15 x 15 x 19 In. . . . .　230.00
Electric, Audoux-Minet, Woven & Braided Sisal, Iron, Parchment, France, 1940s, Floor . .　150.00
Electric, Baltensweiler, No. 60, Steel, Enameled Metal, Germany, 1951, 14 x 63 In. . . . . .　2100.00
Electric, Baroque Style, Gilt Bronze, Pottery, Alabaster Shade, 76 In. . . . .　2030.00
Electric, Bear Holding Lamppost, Wood, Carved, Swiss, c.1910, 14 In. . . . .　1270.00
Electric, Blanc De Chine, Urn, Pedestal Shape, Gilt Bronze Base, Early 1900s, 11 In., Pair　575.00
Electric, Bottle-Shaped, Flowers, Men, Board Game, Enamel, Chinese, c.1910, 19 In., Pair　880.00
Electric, Brass, Inlaid Pewter, Rectangular, Mythological Figures, 1900s, 16 In., Pair . . . .　230.00
Electric, Brass, Shoeshine, Foot Supports Mounted To Base, 16 3/4 In., Pair . . . .　29.00
Electric, Bridge, Hand Kneeling Hammered Iron, Adjustable, Tripod Base, 65 In. . . . .　130.00
Electric, Bronze, Kneeling Figure At Mosque, Cold Painted, Austria, 30 In. . . . .　5225.00
Electric, Bronze, Marble, Obelisk Stem, Gothic Arch, Leaves, 20th Century, 19 1/2 In. . . .　230.00
Electric, Bronze, Woman Dancing, Tree, Glass Dome, Yellow, Green Leaves, 12 x 8 In. . . .　2875.00
Electric, Bronze, Woman, Holding Torches, Iridescent, Art Nouveau, E. Villanis, 20 In. . . .　440.00
Electric, Buggy, Cast Drapery Detail, Eagle Finials, 4 Panes, 30 In., Pair . . . .　470.00
Electric, C. Hartman, Chrome, Signed, 43 1/2 In., Pair . . . .　1675.00
Electric, Cameo Glass, Flowers, Orange, Yellow, 11 In. . . . .　850.00
Electric, Caramel Slag Glass, Classical Metal Overlay, 6 Panels, c.1930, 15 1/2 x 22 In. . .　265.00
Electric, Cast Iron, Frog Base, Hotel Desk Bell, 12 In. . . . .　2970.00
Electric, Cedric Hartman, Bronze, American, 1960s, 11 x 13 x 37 In., Pair . . . .　2575.00
Electric, Ceiling, 3-Light, George III Style, Brass, Glass, 20 1/2 x 8 1/2 In., Pair . . . .　520.00
Electric, Ceiling, Alabaster, Tassels, 12 In. . . . .　8365.00
Electric, Ceiling, Brass, Cased Green Glass Shade, c.1910 . . . .　350.00
Electric, Ceiling, Panton, Flowerpot, 4 Dome Shades, Louis Poulsen, 25 x 15 1/4 In. . . . .　635.00
Electric, Ceiling, Panton, Fun 1 DM, Shell Disks, Chromed Metal Frame, J. Luber, 24 In.　1150.00
Electric, Chase, Flat, Circular Mica Shade, 2 Painted Parrots, 13 1/2 In. . . . .　259.00
Electric, Christian Dell, Enamel, Chrome, Bakelite, Model 6580, Kaiser, Germany, 1933 .　1755.00
Electric, Classique, Reverse Painted Shade, Flowers, Bronze Base, 22 In. . . . . *Illus*　1840.00
Electric, Crystal, Brass, Urn Form, Glass Flowers, Basket, Brass Leaves, 17 x 7 In., Pair　920.00
Electric, Cut Glass, Egg Shape Base, Shade, Daisy Heads, Starbursts, Early 1900s, 26 In. .　590.00
Electric, Design Line, Ball Top, Black Base, c.1968, 16 1/2 In. . . . .　235.00
Electric, Design Line, Stemlite, Egg Shape, Enameled Metal Base, 19 1/4 x 9 In. . . . .　259.00
Electric, Design Line, Stemlite, Mushroom Shade, White Enamel Base . . . .　175.00
Electric, Desk, Arts & Crafts, Brass, Glass, Openwork, Adjustable, Brass Shade, 11 In. . . .　250.00
Electric, Desk, Emerald Light, Adjustable Brass Base, 13 1/2 In. . . . .　345.00
Electric, Desk, Fase, Brushed Chrome, Arc, Clock, Spain, 14 1/4 x 25 In. . . . .　978.00
Electric, Desk, Jorge Pensi, Aluminum, Double-Rod Shaft, 22 1/2 x 10 In. . . . .　865.00
Electric, Desk, Pulled Feather Glass Shade, Bronze, Round Base, Tiffany Style, 8 In. . . . . .　1200.00
Electric, Duffner & Kimberly, Leaded Glass, Flowers, Bronze, 21 x 16 In. . . . .　8050.00
Electric, Elio Martinelli, 1-Piece Molded Plastic, Italy, 18 x 18 In. . . . .　259.00
Electric, Empire Style, Green Onyx, Mahogany, Gilt Metal, 60 In. . . . .　329.00
Electric, Enameled Metal, Black Spherical Fixture, Italy, 1950s, 14 1/2 x 8 1/4 In. . . . . . .　175.00
Electric, Faience, Green, Brown Glazed Yellowware, Wooden Mounts, 1800s, 16 In. . . . .　355.00
Electric, Faience, Jar, Oval, Handles, Yellow Bands, Angel, Dragon, Double Socket, 21 In.　275.00
Electric, Fontana Arte, Glass, Chromed Steel, Italy, 1960s, 12 x 56 In. . . . .　2106.00
Electric, Frederick Weinberg, Horse Head, Rattan, Metal, Parchment Shade, 34 x 21 In. . .　690.00
Electric, G. Nakashima, Cherry Plank Base, Parchment Shade, 32 1/4 x 15 3/4 In. . . . . . .　10925.00

Lamp, Electric, Classique,
Reverse Painted Shade, Flowers,
Bronze Base, 22 In.

Lamp, Electric, Jefferson,
Reverse Painted, Scenic,
Gilt Bronze Base, 23 In.

Lamp, Electric, Phoenix,
Reverse Painted, River Scene,
Bronze Base, 24 In.

Electric, G. Nakashima, Cherry, Rosewood, Parchment Shade, 1970, 29 3/4 x 12 3/4 In. . . . 9775.00
Electric, G. Nakashima, Free-Form Walnut Base, Parchment Shade, 31 1/2 x 13 1/2 In. . . . 3220.00
Electric, G. Nakashima, Oak Burl Base, Parchment Shade, 19 x 9 3/4 In. 4600.00
Electric, G. Nakashima, Walnut Base, Holly Rings, Cylindrical Shade, 58 1/2 x 16 1/2 In. . 9200.00
Electric, G. Nakashima, Walnut, 2 Shafts, Holly Rings, Parchment Shade, 19 x 9 3/4 In. . . 3450.00
Electric, G. Nelson, Bubble, Fiberglass, Enamel, Howard Miller, 1950s, 28 x 22 In. 1870.00
Electric, G. Stickley, Grooved Shaft, Hammered Iron Accents, Inverted Base, 57 x 11 In. . 2700.00
Electric, G. Stickley, Mahogany, Silk Lined, Wicker Shade, Buttressed Base, 58 In. 2990.00
Electric, G. Stickley, No. 295, Copper, Cylindrical, Handles, Wicker Shade, 14 x 18 In. . . 4315.00
Electric, George Kovacs, Brass Base, Cantile-Covered Lucite, Shades, 13 x 24 In., Pair . . 865.00
Electric, Gilbert Watrous, Brass, Enameled Metal, Heifetz, 1951, 9 x 30 In. 1520.00
Electric, Giltwood, Multicolored, Spiral Reeded, Acanthine Accents, Italy, c.1900, 73 In. . 635.00
Electric, Giltwood, Turned Standard, Fluted, Round Base, Italy, 63 In. 635.00
Electric, Gorham, Geometric Shade, Leaded, Caramel, Spider Web, 16 x 22 In. 2875.00
Electric, Gothic Style, Basalt, Candlestick, Octagonal, England, 26 In., Pair 316.00
Electric, Green Slag Glass, Rectangular, 19 In. 175.00
Electric, Greta Grossman, Enameled Metal, Ralph O. Smith, c.1950, 15 x 19 x 48 In. 1055.00
Electric, H.G. Cleveland, Arts & Crafts, Copper, Flower Shape, Boston, 10 In. 750.00
Electric, Hanging, 5-Light, Bronze, Shade, 5 1/2 x 28 In. 1495.00
Electric, Hanging, 5-Light, Bronze, White Globes, 30 In. 2300.00
Electric, Hanging, Achille Castiglioni, Frisbi F79, Ateler International, c.1978 . . . . 235.00
Electric, Hanging, Arne Jacobsen, Royal Mini, Louis Poulsen, Denmark, 14 3/4 x 7 In. . . 259.00
Electric, Hanging, Art Deco, Brass Frame, Milk Glass Panel, Hexagonal, 14 1/2 In., Pair . 85.00
Electric, Hanging, Art Deco, Star Shape, Frosted Slag Glass Panels, 17 In. 380.00
Electric, Hanging, Arts & Crafts, Cast Iron, Slag Glass 275.00
Electric, Hanging, AV Mazzega, Steel, 12 Murano Glass Cubes, Italy, c.1970, 27 x 34 In. . 1380.00
Electric, Hanging, Brass, Basket Weave, Petal Decoration, Pink Glass Shades, 32 x 15 In. 415.00
Electric, Hanging, G. Nelson, Bubble Cluster, Model B-3-740, c.1958, 12 x 32 In. 3510.00
Electric, Hanging, G. Nelson, Bubble, Howard Miller, c.1950, 23 x 12 In. 2070.00
Electric, Hanging, G. Stickley, Lantern, Amber Shade, Pierced Hearts, 12 x 6 In. 1495.00
Electric, Hanging, G. Stickley, Lantern, Hammered Amber Glass, Pierced Sides, 14 x 9 In. 3335.00
Electric, Hanging, Glass Globe, Smoke Bell, Brass Mounts, 18 In. 165.00
Electric, Hanging, Gorham, Leaded Shade, Flowers, Leaves, Caramel Ground, 20 x 25 In. 7200.00
Electric, Hanging, Henningsen, PH-3, Enameled Aluminum, Poulsen, Denmark, 19 x 10 In. 410.00
Electric, Hanging, Iron, Rooster Finial, U-Shaped Hanger, Twisted Hook, 8 1/2 x 5 In. . . . 275.00
Electric, Hanging, Leaded, Poinsettias, 18 x 23 In. 345.00
Electric, Hanging, Panton, Flowerpot, Yellow, Poulsen, c.1970, 20 x 16 In. 865.00
Electric, Hanging, Panton, Fun, Shells, AG Luber, Swiss, 1964, 12 x 17 In. 1725.00
Electric, Hanging, Sputnik, Brass Rods, Brass Ball Center, 1950s, 25 x 18 In. 748.00
Electric, Hula Girl, Skirt Moves, Dodge Mfg., c.1940, 18 In. 578.00
Electric, Isamu Noguchi, Parchment, Knoll, c.1950, 16 In. 1880.00
Electric, J. Adnet, 2-Light, Burgundy Leather, c.1950, 26 1/2 In. 5975.00
Electric, J. Adnet, Bamboo, Brass, Leather, France, 1950s, 58 1/2 In. 7020.00
Electric, J. Adnet, Black Leather, Paper Shade, c.1950, 18 1/4 In. 5975.00

Electric, J. Adnet, Leather Over Iron, Brass, Adjustable, 1950s, 16 x 32 x 68 1/2 In. 6435.00
Electric, J. Adnet, Leather Over Iron, Brass, Cone Base, France, 1950s, 67 1/2 In. 1755.00
Electric, J. Adnet, Leather Over Iron, Brass, Enameled Metal, France, 1950s, 76 In. 1870.00
Electric, J.T. Kalmar, Leather, Iron, Brass, Parchment, Austria, c.1950, 18 x 28 x 64 In. . . 2225.00
Electric, James Mont, Carved Leaf Base, Gilt Finish, 27 x 18 1/4 In., Pair 2185.00
Electric, James Mont, Distressed Wood Base, Drum Shade, Brushed Bronze, 44 x 22 In. . . 489.00
Electric, James Mont, Urn Base, Silver Leaf, Silver Leaf Drum Shade, 36 x 17 In., Pair . . 1725.00
Electric, Jean Royere, Iron, France, c.1947, 61 1/2 In. 4095.00
Electric, Jefferson, Reverse Painted, Scenic, Gilt Bronze Base, 23 In. . . . . *Illus* 1955.00
Electric, Joe Colombo, O-Luce, Acrylic, Lucite, Enameled Metal, Italy, 1962, 9 1/2 In. . . . 7020.00
Electric, Kaiser & Idell, Adjustable Shade, Enameled Metal, Swiss, 8 x 18 In. 115.00
Electric, Koch & Lowy, Half Nelson, Chrome Metal, G. Nelson, c.1960, 16 x 20 In. 935.00
Electric, Kurt Versen, Copper, Glass, Nickel Plated, c.1934, 10 x 14 In. 4975.00
Electric, Laurel, Brushed Chrome, Wood Shaft, Mushroom Shade, 56 1/4 x 11 3/4 In. . . . 690.00
Electric, Laurel, Cylindrical Covered Shade, Glass Shelf, Chrome Wire Base, 57 x 20 In. . . 690.00
Electric, Laurel, Egg Shape, Frosted Glass Shade, Brass-Finished Chrome, 13 x 9 1/2 In. . . 175.00
Electric, Laurel, Mushroom, Opaque Frosted Glass Shade, Black Enameled Base, 56 In. . . 410.00
Electric, Lightolier, 3 Adjustable Plastic Shades, Tapered Column, 60 In., Pair 460.00
Electric, Lightolier, Metal Column, Plastic Shade, Perforated Metal Diffuser, 18 x 52 In. . . 29.00
Electric, Luigi Caccia Dominioni, LP 11, Metal, Glass, Italy, 1958, 13 x 45 In., Pair 1755.00
Electric, Mahogany, Bobbin Turned, Faux Candle Inserts, Fabric Clip Shades, 13 In., Pair . 118.00
Electric, Mario Botta, Shogun, Artemide, c.1985, 23 x 13 In. 1410.00
Electric, Martine Bedin, Super, Plastic, Rubber, Memphis, Box, 1981, 24 x 7 x 14 In. 635.00
Electric, Metal, Figural, Boy & Girl, 18th Century Dress, Reading Book, 1910s, 23 In., Pair 175.00
Electric, Miller, Caramel Slag Glass, 6 Panels, Flower Design Base, Early 1900s 520.00
Electric, Miller, Green Slag, Spelter, 8 Panels, Bronze & Iron Base, 23 In. 345.00
Electric, Moe Bridges, Reverse Painted, Red, Purple & Yellow Dahlias, 18 In. 9900.00
Electric, Mosaic, Leaded Shade, Flowers, Leaves, Caramel Swirl, 24 x 31 In. 4600.00
Electric, Murano Glass, Mushroom Shape, Swirling White Canes, 11 1/2 x 9 1/2 In. 575.00
Electric, Nessen, Chrome-Plated Steel, Adjustable Arm, Metal Diffuser Shade, 4 x 16 In. . . 60.00
Electric, Oak, Turned Base, Spiral Reeding, Fluted Column, 67 1/4 In. 165.00
Electric, Onyx Base, White Marble Top, Octagonal Granite Base, 29 x 9 1/2 In. 85.00
Electric, Opalescent Art Glass, Snail, Footed Pillow Shape, Ormolu, 1900s, 17 1/2 In. 1060.00
Electric, Oscar Bach, Leaded Mica Shade, Painted, Bronzed Base, Dragon, 13 x 61 In. . . . 2185.00
Electric, Oscar Bach, Pewter, Brass Base, Bleached Leather Shade, 19 In. 2300.00
Electric, Panton, Flowerpot, 3 Shades, Louis Poulsen, c.1969 . . . . 265.00
Electric, Panton, Fun 2 TA, Shells, AG Luber, Swiss, 1964, 11 x 17 In. . . . . .1035.00 to 1095.00
Electric, Perko, Solid Brass, Clear Ribbed Lens, 17 In. 90.00
Electric, Pewter, Dolphin Shape, 19 3/4 In., Pair 299.00
Electric, Phoenix, Reverse Painted, River Scene, Bronze Base, 24 In. . . . . *Illus* 2185.00
Electric, Piano, Onyx Inset, Reticulated Metal Base, Late 1800s, 58 In. 259.00
Electric, Pierre Guariche, Brass, Fabric, Disderot, France, 1950s, 48 x 62 In. 5265.00
Electric, Pierre Guariche, Extending Arm, Brass, Enameled Metal, Fabric, Diserot, 1950s . 1170.00
Electric, Pierre Paulin, Enameled Metal, Elysee Series, 1971, 12 x 53 In. 1112.00
Electric, Pine Slab Base, Birch Center Post, Birch Twig Shade, 23 x 18 x 17 1/2 In. 140.00
Electric, Pittsburgh, Reverse Painted, Flowers, Handel Base, 24 In. . . . . *Illus* 1265.00
Electric, Polished Chrome, 5 Fixtures, Graduated Height, 32 1/4 In. 345.00
Electric, Porcelain, Blue & White, Scrolls, Symbols, Chinese, Late 1800s, 23 In. 175.00
Electric, Porcelain, Phoenix, On Black Ground, Gilt, Baluster, Chinese, 16 In. 325.00
Electric, Porcelain, Red Sang De Boeuf Glaze, Wood Base, Brass Top, 2 Sockets, 26 In. . . 110.00
Electric, Porcelain, Square, Narrow Mouth, Blossoms, Blue & White, Chinese, 24 1/2 In. . . 175.00
Electric, Red Enameled Metal Shade, Brass Arm, Adjustable, Swiss, 1950s, 20 x 17 In. . . 430.00
Electric, Reggiani, 4 Brass Stems, Opaque White Glass Ball Shades, 1950s, 66 In. 645.00
Electric, Reverse Painted, Riverscape, Dome Shade, c.1918, 17 1/4 x 9 3/4 In. 325.00
Electric, Reverse Painted, Winter Landscape, 2 Sockets, c.1910, 16 x 24 5/8 In. 1410.00
Electric, Reverse Painted, Wooded Landscape, Gilt Iron Base, 22 x 16 In. 460.00
Electric, Robert Sonneman, Chrome, Arched Shaft, Adjustable Arm, 62 1/2 x 50 In. 375.00
Electric, Rodolfo Bonetto, Plastic, Mirrored Surface, Italy, 1972, 7 1/2 x 10 1/2 In. 460.00
Electric, Rougier, Egg Shape, Molded Plastic Cylinders, Brass Base, 30 1/2 x 12 3/4 In. . . 1035.00
Electric, Roycroft, Hammered Copper, Helmet Shade, 13 1/2 In. 2070.00
Electric, Roycroft, Hammered Copper, Square Base, Mica Inserts In Shade, 13 x 7 In. 3450.00
Electric, Rustic, Pine Base, Birch Post, Twig Shade Frame, Wire, 23 x 18 x 17 In. 140.00
Electric, Sale Brothers, Slag Glass, 15 In. 290.00

Electric, Salterini, Bronze, Cone-Shaped Mica Shade, 3-Sided Base, Etched, 62 In. 1410.00
Electric, Sergio Asti, Chrome, Tubular Pole, Adjustable Ball Shade, Knoll, 60 In. 1410.00
Electric, Slag Glass, Metal Overlay, Octagonal Shade, Cherries, 1900s, 25 x 18 3/4 In. . . . 1998.00
Electric, Spelter, Caramel Slag Glass, Dome Shade, 19 In. 450.00
Electric, Stair Post, Paint Decorated, Black, Red, Black Base, White Shade, 32 In., Pair . . 50.00
Electric, Stemlite, Mushroom, Opaque Frosted Glass, Black Enameled Base, 42 In., Pair . 560.00
Electric, Stickley Brothers, Hammered Copper, Flower Cutouts, 16 x 22 In. 4600.00
Electric, Stickley, Wooden Pedestal Base, Beaded, Rattan Shade, Green Linen, 24 In. 1430.00
Electric, Stiffel, Rocket Ship, Brass, Adjustable Base & Shade, 1950s, 22 In. 650.00
Electric, Stilnovo, Enameled Metal, Brass, 6 Adjustable Shades, Italy, 1950s, 28 x 81 In. . 2450.00
Electric, Student, Brass, Double, Cased Green Shade, 25 In. 545.00
Electric, Teaque Polaroid, Dome Resin Shade, Walter Doren, Mass., c.1940, 13 x 12 In. . . 1295.00
Electric, Tin, Tripod Base, Twig & Vine Design, White Paint, Twig Finial, 64 In. 275.00
Electric, Tommi Parzinger, Wood Base, 2 Sockets, Silk Shade, Shelf, 63 x 18 In. 2990.00
Electric, Tommi Parzinger, Wrought Iron, Enamel, 4 Candlestick Fixtures, 74 1/2 In. 1610.00
Electric, Triennale, Gino Sarfatti, 3 Chrome Arms, Marble Base, Cone Shades, 56 x 43 In. 4315.00
Electric, Turned Wood, Parcel Gilt, Crimson, Chinoiserie, Tole, 29 In., Pair 1095.00
Electric, Unique Art, Leaded, Cone Shade, Flowers, Leaves, Branches, 19 x 30 In. 9200.00
Electric, Vase, Orange & White, Flowers, Birds, Oriental, 22 In., Pair 145.00
Electric, Victorian, Shell Globe, 59 x 12 In. 2010.00
Electric, Wagon Wheel, Iron Bands, 30 1/2 In. 99.00
Electric, Walter Dorwin Teague, Bakelite Base, Aluminum, Polaroid, 12 3/4 x 11 1/4 In. . 1150.00
Electric, Walter Von Nessen, Aluminum, Cloth, Adjustable, American, 1950s, 14 x 17 In. . 470.00
Electric, Walter Von Nessen, Brushed Steel, Shade, Diffuser, Hang Tag, 37 1/2 In. 175.00
Electric, Walter Von Nessen, Glass, Chromed Steel, Fabric Shade, c.1950 . . . . 645.00
Electric, Walter Von Nessen, Plastic Dome, Chrome Column, Walnut Base, 15 1/2 x 28 In. 115.00
Electric, Walter Von Nessen, Swing Arm, Satin Chrome, Shade, c.1970, 31 x 50 In., Pair . 1265.00
Electric, Walter Von Nessen, White Plastic Dome, Satin Chrome Base, 15 1/2 x 51 In. . . . 115.00
Electric, Wilkinson, Leaded Glass Shade, Bronzed Metal Base, 22 In. . . . . *Illus* 630.00
Electric, Wilkinson, Water Lily, Beaded, Pink, Purple, Red, White, 30 x 18 In. 4600.00
Electric, Wood, Metal Arm, Rope Twist Column, Cone Shade, c.1950, 60 In. 705.00
Eletric, Green Slag, Metal Overlay, Hexagonal, R.O. Co., Chicago, 1940, 14 x 25 In. 705.00
Fairy, Cased Pink, White, Frosted Stripe Shade, Pressed Base, Candle Cup, 4 3/4 In. 198.00
Fairy, Figural, Satin Glass 2-Faced Baby, S. Clarke Fairy Pyramid Mark, 4 In. 236.00
Fluid, Amethyst Font, Twinkle, 7 1/4 In. 20.00
Fluid, Blown Glass, Peg, Wood Base, 8 1/2 In. 275.00
Fluid, Blown Glass, Pewter Collar, Cut, Bladed Wafer, Pressed Base, 10 3/4 In. 220.00
Fluid, Blue Foot & Stem, Applied Clear Font, Twin Tube Burner, 7 1/2 In. 518.00
Fluid, Blue Opaline Glass, Red, Gilt Leaves 105.00
Fluid, Clambroth Glass, Tulip Pattern Font, Columnar Standard, Square, 11 In. 310.00
Fluid, Cut Glass Overlay, Opaque Cut To Clear, Brass, 1860-1870, 13 In. 880.00
Fluid, Cut Glass, Heart Pattern, Hexagonal Base, Early 19th Century, 8 1/2 In., Pair 259.00
Fluid, Cut Glass, Opaque Blue To White, Star, Oval, Late 1800s, 14 1/2 In. 1058.00
Fluid, Cut Glass, Opaque To Clear, Green Font, Flower, Leaf, Late 1800s, 13 3/4 In. 1998.00
Fluid, Cut Glass, Opaque To Clear, Ruby Font, Oval, Punty, Slash, Late 1800s, 13 In. 499.00
Fluid, Dalzell, Gilmore & Leighton, Sweetheart, Green Font, Base, Miniature 250.00
Fluid, Flint Glass, Bull's-Eye, Fleur-De-Lis, Brass Plinth, Marble Base, 1800s, 9 1/4 In. . . 200.00

Lamp, Electric,
Pittsburgh, Reverse
Painted, Flowers,
Handel Base, 24 In.

Lamp, Electric,
Wilkinson, Leaded
Glass Shade, Bronzed
Metal Base, 22 In.

Fluid, Molded Font, Green, Gilded, Brass Collar, Beehive Stem, Marble Base, 10 1/4 In. . . 385.00
Fluid, Peg, Brass Candlestick, Twist Column, Frosted Cut To Yellow, 17 1/2 In., Pair 630.00
Fluid, Peg, Paneled, Pewter Candlestick, Brass Collar, Fluid Burner, 7 In., Pair 495.00
Fluid, Pewter, Candlestick Form, Spring Loaded, Signed, 10 1/2 In. 330.00
Fluid, Pewter, Finger, 2-Tube Burner, Caps, Partial Chain, Footed, 5 1/2 In. 385.00
Fluid, Pressed Glass, Inverted Diamond, Thumbprint, Brass Collar, Marble Base, 10 In. . . 110.00
Fluid, Pressed Glass, Paneled Waffle, Pewter Collar, Wafer, Hexagonal Base, 11 1/2 In. . . 145.00
Fluid, Skater's, Brass, Green Globe, Swing Carry Handle 309.00
Fluid, Thuro 3-99A, Swan, Pressed Glass, Glass Font, Brass Collar, 9 1/2 In. 1725.00
Fluid, Tin, Half Circle Tank, Red Paint, Finger, 6 3/4 In. 124.00
Fluid, Tin, Oval Tank, Round Shaft, Saucer Base, Loop Handle, 7 1/2 In. 110.00
Gas, Ansonia, Man Holding Jug, Woman Wih Pitcher, New Globes, c.1895, 38 In., Pair . . 1790.00
Gas, Gasolier, 4-Light, Crystal, Prisms, Baluster Stem, Anglo-Irish, 1800s, 52 1/2 x 33 In. 1725.00
Gas, Gasolier, 6-Arm, Rococo Revival, Brass, Bronze, Brass, Electric, 37 x 38 In. 10350.00
Gas, Gasolier, 6-Light, Neoclassical, Gilt Brass, Beads, 5 Tiers, Electric, c.1860, 46 In. . . . 4140.00
Gas, Gasolier, 10-Light, Louis XVI Style, Dore, Brass, Molded Faces, Shade, 26 x 30 In. . 2300.00
Gas, Tin Vent, Shade, Wood Finial, Asbury Park Boardwalk, 32 In. 110.00
Grease, Copper, Handmade, 11 1/2 In. 230.00
Grease, Double, Wrought Iron, Reflecting Disks, Early 19th Century, 7 3/4 In. 75.00
Grease, Tin, Hanging, Hollow Stem, Semicircular Lid, Scrolled Finial, Cone Base, 7 In. . . 275.00
Handel lamps are included in the Handel category.
Kerosene, Adams & Company, Bradford, Brass Collar, Stand, 11 In. 55.00
Kerosene, Amber Base, Stand, No. 2 Slip Burner, Chimney, Tin Connector, 9 1/2 In. 90.00
Kerosene, Amber Font, Stand, Opaque White Base, Brass Collar, No. 2 Slip Burner, 9 In. . 65.00
Kerosene, Amber Stained, Engraved Panels, Finger, Footed, No. 0 Slip Burner, 5 In. 440.00
Kerosene, Angle, Globe, Translucent White Chimney, Embossed, 12 3/4 In. 80.00
Kerosene, Aquarius, Finger, Footed, Blue, Brass Collar, No. 1 Slip Burner, Chimney, 5 In. 99.00
Kerosene, Aquarius, Stand, Blue, Brass Collar, No. 2 Slip Burner, Crimp Top, 10 In. 210.00
Kerosene, Banquet, Bohemian Glass, Globular Shade, 24 In. 345.00
Kerosene, Banquet, Pink Cased Hobnail 1980.00
Kerosene, Banquet, Silver Plate, Milk Glass Shade, Pink Flowers, 19 x 6 1/2 In., Pair 400.00
Kerosene, Barn, Brass, Double Burner, Glass Chimney, Wire Frame, 29 In. 65.00
Kerosene, Basket Weave, Medallions, Stand, Amber, No. 1 Slip Burner, Chimney, 9 In. . . 165.00
Kerosene, Belmont, Canary Base, Brass Collar, No. 1 Slip Burner, Chimney, 9 In. 303.00
Kerosene, Bethesda, Opaque Base, No. 1 P&A Lip Burner, Pearl-Top Chimney, 10 In. . . . 330.00
Kerosene, Blown Font, Blue Baroque Base, No. 2 Slip Burner, Ball Shade, 12 3/4 In. 605.00
Kerosene, Blown Font, Opaque, Square Base, No. 2 Novelty Burner, Oregon Shade, 12 In. 330.00
Kerosene, Blown Font, Translucent Red, Stepped, Brass, Starch Blue Base, 9 3/8 In. 110.00
Kerosene, Blown, Cut & Frosted, Ledge Font, Quatrefoil & Punty Cut, 10 1/2 In. 165.00
Kerosene, Blown-Out Grapes, Vine, Brass Collar, Burner, Chimney, Umbrella Shade, 5 In. 55.00
Kerosene, Boiler, Patented Wm. F. Rossman, 1868, 9 In. 250.00
Kerosene, Brass Collar, String Burner, Applied Handle, Rayed Base, Finger, 3 In. 33.00
Kerosene, Brass, Clockwork Mechanism, c.1874, 19 1/2 In. 169.00
Kerosene, Brass, Stepped Base, Flower Medallions, Etched Satin Glass Shade, 23 In. 110.00
Kerosene, Brown, Red, Pink, White Spatter, Glass Leaf Handle, Brass, Finger, 4 1/2 In. . . 39.00
Kerosene, Buggy, Brass, Tail, H & B Lamp No. 1109, Beveled Lens, Fixed Handle, 10 In. 115.00
Kerosene, Buggy, Brass, Tin, Beveled Lens, Arrow Shape Mounting Bracket, 10 In., Pair . 85.00
Kerosene, Buggy, Napoleon III, Brass, Glass, Copper Mounted, c.1865, 12 x 3 1/4 In., Pair 200.00
Kerosene, Butter Cup, Amber, Brass Collar, Burner, Chimney, Applied Handle, 2 3/4 In. . 80.00
Kerosene, Butter Cup, Green, Brass Collar, Burner, Chimney, Applied Handle, 2 3/4 In. . . 155.00
Kerosene, Carlisle, Stand, Blue, Brass Collar, Burner, Chimney, 6 In. 80.00
Kerosene, Cobalt Blue Glass, Mary Gregory Design, Children In Snow, No. 2 . . . . 800.00
Kerosene, Composite, Brass, Wide Plate Collar, Acid Etched, Enameled Glass, 13 3/4 In. . 145.00
Kerosene, Cut Glass Globe, Drop Prisms, American Brilliant Period 1000.00
Kerosene, Cut Glass, Mushroom Shade, Prisms, American Brilliant, 1900s, 25 x 12 3/8 In. 590.00
Kerosene, Cut Overlay, Cranberry Cut To Clear, Pear Shape Font, Oregon Shade, 11 In. . 440.00
Kerosene, Cut Overlay, Green Cut To Clear, Washington, Brass Stem, Marble, 15 In. 110.00
Kerosene, Cut Overlay, Opalescent Cut To Clear, Pear-Shape Font, Ball Shade, 12 1/2 In. . 715.00
Kerosene, Cut Overlay, White Cut To Cranberry, Brass Stem, Marble Base, 11 1/2 In. . . . 360.00
Kerosene, Dodge Type, Molded Font, Cobalt Blue To Clear Cut Overlay Stem, 13 5/8 In. . 385.00
Kerosene, Double Arm, Brass, Iron Hanger, Glass Lamps, Overpainted Red, 31 In. 195.00
Kerosene, Dresden Type, Multicolored, Enameled Fleur-De-Lis, Egg-Shape Shade, 8 In. . 155.00
Kerosene, Eason, Stand, Opalescent Font, Black Base, Brass No. 2 Collar, 9 In. 265.00

Kerosene, Engraved, Swag & Tassel, Opaque Gem Base, Gilding, No. 2 Slip Burner, 12 In.   230.00
Kerosene, Erin Fan, Stand, Green, Brass Collar, No. 1 Slip Burner, Chimney, 8 1/2 In. 99.00
Kerosene, Female Bust, Spelter, Brass Plated, Iron Base, 11 1/4 In. 66.00
Kerosene, Finger, Brass Collar, Burner, Chimney, c.1868, 3 In. 660.00
Kerosene, Finger, Footed, Amber, Paneled, Embossed Design, Brass Collar, Burner, 3 In. .   130.00
Kerosene, Finger, Lomax Globe, Brass Collar, Molded Handle, Oil Guard, c.1870, 4 In. . . .   70.00
Kerosene, Finger, Nutmeg, Opaque White, Brass Collar, Burner, Chimney, 2 1/2 In. 35.00
Kerosene, Gone With The Wind, Egyptian Scene, Blown-Out Lion's Head, 22 In. 400.00
Kerosene, Gone With The Wind, Green, White Flowers, 22 In. 315.00
Kerosene, Hanging, Country Store, Brass, Iron, Milk Glass Shade, Smoke Bell, 32 In. 110.00
Kerosene, Hanging, Cranberry Shade, Floral Design, 14 In. 1500.00
Kerosene, Hanging, Iron, Birdcage Shape, Glass Globe, Flowers, Painted, 18 x 17 In. 100.00
Kerosene, Hanging, Opaque White Shade, Snow Scene, Brass Smoke Bell, 37 In. 360.00
Kerosene, Hanging, Stained Glass, 10 Bent Panels, Green, Red Trim, Victorian, 25 In. 300.00
Kerosene, Laurel, Frosted Glass, Mushroom Shape, Black Enamel Base, 56 x 12 3/4 In. . .   460.00
Kerosene, Little Harry's, Cobalt Font, Milk Glass Shade, Miniature 470.00
Kerosene, Milk Glass, Multicolored Flower Base, Pierced Metal Shade, c.1880, 7 3/4 In. . .   40.00
Kerosene, Milkmaid, Ruby Stained, Reverse Painted Flowers, 9 3/4 In. 415.00
Kerosene, Miller, Copper, Brass, Caramel & White Slag Glass Shade, 18 In. 290.00
Kerosene, Nickel Chrome, Reflector, Iron Base, c.1885, 20 1/2 x 5 In. 125.00
Kerosene, Opalescent Font, Stepped Rib, Enameled Flowers, Gilding, Brass, 13 3/8 In. . .   70.00
Kerosene, Opaque Blue, Stand, White Enamel Leaves, Brass Collar, Burner, Chimney, 6 In.   50.00
Kerosene, Opaque White, Enamel Flowers, Brass Collar, Burner, Chimney, Shade, 4 In. . .   80.00
Kerosene, Owl, Applied Eyes, Multicolored, Brass Collar, Burner, Chimney, 6 1/2 In. 198.00
Kerosene, Parlor, Bronze, Brass, Tripod, Paneled Column, Scroll Feet, 30 In. 575.00
Kerosene, Parlor, Painted Brown, Dome Shade, Enameled Flowers, Brass Collar, 8 1/2 In.   99.00
Kerosene, Periwinkle, Brass Collar, No. 0 Slip Burner, Petal-Top Chimney, 9 In. 165.00
Kerosene, Pressed Glass, Atterbury, Prism With Loops, Milk Glass, No. 2 Collar, 12 In. . .   70.00
Kerosene, Pressed Glass, Atterbury, Starburst, Brass No. 1 Collar, c.1868, 4 In. 330.00
Kerosene, Pressed Glass, Bull's-Eye & Fleur-De-Lis, Wafer, Pressed Base, Brass, 9 In. . . .   120.00
Kerosene, Pressed Glass, Bull's-Eye, Brass Collar, No. 2 Slip Burner, Chimney, 10 In. . . .   110.00
Kerosene, Pressed Glass, Cable & Dart, Opalescent, Lip Burner, Marble Base, 8 3/4 In. . .   195.00
Kerosene, Pressed Glass, Cathedral, Amber, Blue Base, No. 2 Slip Burner, Chimney, 12 In.   550.00
Kerosene, Pressed Glass, Coolidge Drape, Cobalt Blue, No. 1 Slip Burner, Chimney, 8 In.   275.00
Kerosene, Pressed Glass, Corn In Shield, Brass Collar, No. 1 Slip Burner, Chimney, 8 In. .   99.00
Kerosene, Pressed Glass, Cosmos, Daisy, Cased Pink, Brass Collar, Burner, Chimney, 4 In.   39.00
Kerosene, Pressed Glass, Cosmos, Paneled, Milk Glass, Flowers, Ball Shade, 4 1/4 In. . . .   35.00
Kerosene, Pressed Glass, Daisy, Finger, Footed, Brass Collar, Burner, Chimney, 3 3/4 In. .   45.00
Kerosene, Pressed Glass, Diamond & Fan, Finger, Footed, No. 0 Slip Burner, 5 1/2 In. . . .   155.00
Kerosene, Pressed Glass, Empress, Green, No. 1 Slip Burner, Riverside Glass Works, 8 In.   99.00
Kerosene, Pressed Glass, Feather Duster, No. 0 Slip Burner, Piecrust Chimney, 3 1/2 In. . .   155.00
Kerosene, Pressed Glass, Fishscale, Finger, Footed, No. 1 Slip Burner, Handle, 6 1/2 In. . .   120.00
Kerosene, Pressed Glass, Fleur-De-Lis, Gold Painted, Eagle Glass & Mfg., 3 1/4 In. 55.00
Kerosene, Pressed Glass, Greek Key Band, Enameled Font, Miller Lip Burner, 11 In. 165.00
Kerosene, Pressed Glass, Greek Key, Brass Collar, Burner, Matching Chimney, 5 In. 90.00
Kerosene, Pressed Glass, Hobbs' Coin Dot, Finger, Blue Opalescent, No. 0 Burner, 3 In. .   145.00
Kerosene, Pressed Glass, Hobbs' Double Diamond Cluster, Miller Lip Burner, 11 In. 145.00
Kerosene, Pressed Glass, Hobnail, Stand, Brass Collar, Burner, Chimney, 4 1/2 In. 80.00
Kerosene, Pressed Glass, Inverted Thumbprint & Fan, No. 2 Slip Burner, 9 3/4 In. 110.00
Kerosene, Pressed Glass, Inverted Thumbprint, Finger, Footed, Canary Opalescent, 5 In. .   495.00
Kerosene, Pressed Glass, Inverted Thumbprint, Opalescent, No. 1 Burner, 7 1/4 In. 360.00
Kerosene, Pressed Glass, King's Heart, Finger, Footed, No. 1 Slip Burner, 6 1/2 In. 175.00
Kerosene, Pressed Glass, Marsh Fern, Finger, Footed, Brass Collar, No. 1 Slip Burner, 5 In.   285.00
Kerosene, Pressed Glass, Naomi, Finger, Footed, Brass Collar, Applied Handle, 5 1/2 In. . .   145.00
Kerosene, Pressed Glass, Onion Base, Mottled Opaque Blue, Blown Font, 13 1/4 In. 2530.00
Kerosene, Pressed Glass, Paneled Bull's-Eye, Brass Connector, Starch Blue, 8 3/8 In. 300.00
Kerosene, Pressed Glass, Peacock Feathers, No. 2 Slip Burner, Piecrust Chimney, 10 In. . .   165.00
Kerosene, Pressed Glass, Peanut, Brass Collar, No. 2 Slip Burner, Chimney, 9 1/2 In. 275.00
Kerosene, Pressed Glass, Primrose, Opalescent, No. 0 Burner, Piecrust Chimney, 3 In. . . .   660.00
Kerosene, Pressed Glass, Prince Edward, Finger, Footed, No. 1 Slip Burner, 5 1/2 In. 275.00
Kerosene, Pressed Glass, Princess Feather, No. 2 Slip Burner, Piecrust Chimney, 9 1/2 In.   220.00
Kerosene, Pressed Glass, Princess, Satin Finish Font, Brass Collar, Scroll Foot, 11 In. . . .   165.00
Kerosene, Pressed Glass, Prism & Diamond Point, Baroque Base, Brass, 12 3/4 In. 99.00

Kerosene, Pressed Glass, Ripley, Hollow Stem, Stand, Brass Collar, No. 1 Slip Burner, 9 In. 80.00
Kerosene, Pressed Glass, Ripley, Sconce, Cast-Iron Hook Handle, Brass Collar, 2 7/8 In. . 275.00
Kerosene, Pressed Glass, Seaweed, Cranberry Opalescent, Cranberry Chimney, 4 1/2 In. . 660.00
Kerosene, Pressed Glass, Sheldon Swirl, Pink, Opalescent Font, No. 1 Slip Burner, 9 In. . 275.00
Kerosene, Pressed Glass, Sheldon Swirl, Yellow Opalescent, No. 1 Slip Burner, 8 3/4 In. . 250.00
Kerosene, Pressed Glass, Snowflake, Blue Opalescent, Brass No. 2 Collar, 9 In. 1265.00
Kerosene, Pressed Glass, Snowflake, Cranberry Opalescent, Brass No. 2 Collar, 9 In. 715.00
Kerosene, Pressed Glass, Snowflake, Opalescent, No. 0 Burner, Piecrust Chimney, 3 In. . . . 1210.00
Kerosene, Pressed Glass, Swirl, Amber, No. 1 Slip Burner, Piecrust Chimney, 7 3/4 In. . 155.00
Kerosene, Pressed Glass, Thousand Eye, Diamond & Dot Font, No. 2 Slip Burner, 12 In. . . 230.00
Kerosene, Pressed Glass, Turkey Track, Finger, Footed, No. 1 Slip Burner, Chimney, 6 In. 155.00
Kerosene, Pressed Glass, Venice, Yellow Opalescent Font, No. 1 Slip Burner, 8 1/2 In. 185.00
Kerosene, Pressed Glass, Whirlpool, Blue, Brass Collar, No. 2 Slip Burner, Chimney, 9 In. 310.00
Kerosene, Pressed Glass, Zipper Loop, Marigold, 6 1/2 x 4 In. 750.00
Kerosene, Pressed Glass, Zipper Loop, Marigold, 7 1/2 x 5 1/2 In. 525.00
Kerosene, Pressed Glass, Zipper Loop, Marigold, 7 x 4 1/4 In 325.00
Kerosene, Scalloped Foot Base, Brass Collar, No. 0 Slip Burner, Piecrust Chimney, 9 In. . 55.00
Kerosene, Sconce, Swirled Ribbed Tank, Tall Match Cylinders, 12 1/2 In. 39.00
Kerosene, Ships, Brass, Gimbal Mounted, Mask Arm Terminals, Ribbed Shade, 14 In. . . . 115.00
Kerosene, Spanish Lace, Cranberry Opalescent, Burner, Chimney, 3 3/4 In. 440.00
Kerosene, Student, Brass, Milk Glass Shade, Husk Finial, Trumpet Base, 26 In. 175.00
Kerosene, Student, Brass, Shade Ring, Milk Glass & Amber Shades, 23 In., Pair 410.00
Kerosene, Student, Brass, Spiral Ribbing, Milk Glass Shade, Pat May 27, 1922 . . . . 330.00
Kerosene, Student, Leader, Nickel Plated, Opaque White Shade, No. 1 Burner, 18 In. 220.00
Kerosene, Vase, Spelter, Nickel-Plated Draft Burner, Reflector, Soapstone Foot, 5 1/2 In. . 120.00
Kerosene, Wright & Butler, Putty Color, Multicolored Enamel Flowers, Finger, 3 1/2 In. . 300.00
Lard, Tin, Flat Wick, Saucer Base, 1851, 6 1/2 In. 99.00
Lard, Tole, Blue Paint, Signed Leitersburg Lamp Tinware, 6 1/2 In. 1980.00
Lard, Ufford, Tin, Iron Base, Boston, 10 1/2 In. 275.00
Lard, Ufford, Tin, Iron Base, Kennear Patent, 1851, 8 1/2 In. 195.00
Oil, 2-Cup, Hand Wrought, Tripod Penny Feet, Adjustable, 58 In., Pair 1320.00
Oil, Amber Globe, Enamel Hummingbird, 4-Sided Green Glass Base, Victorian, 21 In. . . . 230.00
Oil, Brass, Repousse, Cased Glass Shade, Electric, Juno Lamp Co., 16 1/2 In. 90.00
Oil, Brass, Ships, Candlestick, Gimbal-Mounted Bowl, 9 1/4 In. 255.00
Oil, Camphor, Louis Philippe, Gilt Bronze, Bulbous Frosted Shade, 11 In., Pair 1725.00
Oil, Capen & Molineaux, Pewter, Cast Foliate Burner, 12 In. 460.00
Oil, Cut Glass, Silver Plate, Columnar, Electrified, England, 19 1/2 In. 345.00
Oil, Cut Overlay, Cranberry Cut To White, Stepped Marble Base, 14 1/4 In., Pair 520.00
Oil, Egg Shape, Brass & Steel Base, Double Burner, Vasa Murrhina, 15 1/2 In. 360.00
Oil, Loom, Hanging, Heart Finial, Single Socket, Iron, 17 3/4 In. 195.00
Oil, Marble Column, Ornate Cast Metal Mounts, Scrolls, Shells, 1893 Patent, 20 1/2 In. . . . 220.00
Oil, Miner's Safety, Aluminum, American Co., Scranton Pa., 10 1/2 In. 345.00
Oil, Miner's Safety, Brass, Engraved, Hammer & Pick On Heart Shield, 7 1/4 In. 110.00
Oil, Miner's Safety, Brass, Hughes Bros., Scranton, Pa., 8 1/2 In. 300.00
Oil, Miner's Safety, Brass, Tin, Signed J. Anton & Son, c.1904, 4 1/4 In. 100.00
Oil, Miner's Safety, Brass, Watson, New Castle, Pa., 9 1/2 In. 175.00
Oil, Miner's Safety, Cylindrical, Bail Handle, Mesh, Key, Brass, Potter & Hoffman, 9 In. . 290.00
Oil, Miner's Safety, Eagle & Shield Trademark, Geo. Anton, Monongahela City, Pa., 3 In. 70.00
Oil, Miner's Safety, Iron & Brass, Wolf Co., 8 1/2 In. 28.00
Oil, Miner's Safety, Tin, W.G. Dowd, Patent Model, 1869, 3 In. 415.00
Oil, Neoclassical, Egg Shape, Bronze Plinth Base, Late 1800s, 14 3/4 In., Pair 410.00
Oil, Onion Globe, Brass Top, Wire Guards, Bail Handle, 10 x 12 In. 300.00
Oil, Onion Globe, Hand Blown, Clear Stem, Rayo Queen Anne Burner, 10 1/2 In. 29.00
Oil, Pattern Molded, Emerald Green, Applied Solid Handle, 3 1/2 In., Pair 690.00
Oil, Pattern Molded, Raised Oval Designs, Gilt Detail, Stepped Marble Base, 15 In. 145.00
Oil, Petaled, Amethyst Font, Milk Glass Base 385.00
Oil, Pewter, Brass Burner, Bulbous Tank, Finger, R. Gleason, c.1830, 5 1/2 In. 900.00
Oil, Pewter, Brass Burner, Ribbed Base Border, 8 1/2 In. 200.00
Oil, Pewter, Saucer Base, Tall Shaft, Shaped Handle, Elongated Arm, 9 1/2 In. 180.00
Oil, Pewter, Saucer Base, Tall Shaft, Shaped Handle, Elongated Arm, 11 In. 100.00
Oil, Porcelain, Flower Decoration, 19th Century, 17 In. 46.00
Oil, Pressed Glass, Bellflower, Bracket, Original Brass Collars, 5 3/4 x 5 1/2 In. 290.00

Oil, Pressed Glass, Harp, Flowers, Red, Yellow, Blue, Green 195.00
Oil, Pressed Glass, Purple Slag Glass Base, 13 In. 400.00
Oil, Pressed Glass, Riverside Clinch, Flowers, Wafer, 2 Piece, 6 1/2 x 5 1/4 In., Pair 195.00
Oil, Sinumbra, Brass, Bronze, Column Standard, Square Base, American, 29 In. 6038.00
Oil, Sinumbra, Brass, Bronze, H.N. Hooper, Boston, c.1855, 26 1/4 In. 7765.00
Oil, Tin, Saucer Base, Finger Handle, 7 1/2 In. 200.00
Pairpoint lamps are in the Pairpoint category.
Perfume, Painted Glass Shade, 7 1/2 In. 245.00
Regency, Gilt Bronze, Etched Glass Shade, Argand, Early 1800s, 17 In. 520.00
Rush, Beechwood, White Painted, Polychromed, Parcel Gilt, Carved, Early 1800s, 57 In. .. 1093.00
Rush, Forged Iron Clamp, Single Arm, Mounted To Wood Base, 8 1/2 In. 450.00
Rush, Forged Iron, Twisted Shaft, Tripod Base, Penny Feet, 8 1/4 In. 225.00
Rush, Iron, Holder, Round Platform, 3 Legs, 12 1/2 In. 275.00
Rush, Iron, Wood Block Base, Twisted Post, Knob Holder, 11 1/2 In. 430.00
Rush, Wrought Iron, Holder, Tripod Base, Brass Disk, Snake Feet, 8 3/4 In. 290.00
Sconce, 1-Light, George III Style, Brass, Glass, Shield Support, 1900s, 14 1/4 In., 6 Piece 575.00
Sconce, 1-Light, Louis XVI Style, Gilt Bronze, Opalescent Shade, 16 1/2 In., Pair 2390.00
Sconce, 1-Light, Tin, Shield Shaped Plaques, Angel, Gilt Drape, 1800s, 10 x 7 In., Pair .. 1840.00
Sconce, 2-Light, Brass, Crest, Dolphins, Openwork, Beveled Mirror, Prism, 18 In. 160.00
Sconce, 2-Light, Bronze, Ribbon & Flower, Early 1900s, 12 1/2 In., Pair 185.00
Sconce, 2-Light, Candleholder, Wall, Ornate Brass, Beveled Glass, 24 x 10 1/2 In. 375.00
Sconce, 2-Light, Directoire Style, Faux Candles, Nickel, France, 17 1/2 x 8 1/2 In., Pair .. 460.00
Sconce, 2-Light, Georgian Style, Giltwood, Mirror Back, 48 x 22 In., Pair 2750.00
Sconce, 2-Light, Gilt Bronze, Cut Glass, Electric, France, 14 x 14 x 6 1/4 In. 460.00
Sconce, 2-Light, Louis XV, Giltwood, Ribbon, Bowl, Tassels, Eagle, 43 1/2 In., Pair 2940.00
Sconce, 2-Light, Louis XVI Style, Gilt Brass, Jewel Cut Glass Beads, 13 x 11 In., Pair ... 546.00
Sconce, 2-Light, Louis XVI Style, Gilt Bronze, 36 In. 2875.00
Sconce, 2-Light, Neoclassical, Bronze, Glass, Rock Crystal, 1800s, 15 In., Pair 1840.00
Sconce, 2-Light, Neoclassical, Cut Glass, Backplate, Electric, Early 1900s, 12 In., Pair .. 500.00
Sconce, 2-Light, Rococo Revival, Bird, Silvered Wood, Metal, Glass, 2 In., Pair 1015.00
Sconce, 3-Light, George III Style, Demilune, Brass, Glass, 1900s, 14 x 31 x 15 In., Pair .. 345.00
Sconce, 3-Light, Gilt Brass, Tulip-Shape Holders, Winding Vine, Leaf Arms, 16 In., Pair . 500.00
Sconce, 3-Light, Gilt Iron, Glass, Rock Crystal, Leaf Design, Early 1800s, 15 In. 975.00
Sconce, 3-Light, Italian Rococo, Giltwood, 35 1/2 In., Pair 210.00
Sconce, 3-Light, Louis XIV Style, 17 1/2 In., Pair 236.00
Sconce, 3-Light, Louis XV Style, Gilt Brass, White Faux Candle, Mid 1900s, 26 x 16 In. .. 1150.00
Sconce, 3-Light, Louis XVI Style, Bronze, 22 In., Pair 1200.00
Sconce, 3-Light, Louis XVI Style, Gilt Metal, 36 In., Pair 1195.00
Sconce, 3-Light, Louis XVI Style, Gilt Metal, Wood, c.1910, 18 3/8 In., Pair 560.00
Sconce, 3-Light, Louis XVI Style, Giltwood, Metal, Flower Crest, 39 In., Pair 1200.00
Sconce, 3-Light, Neoclassical, Gilt Metal, Cut Glass, 1900s, 32 x 20 x 18 In., 4 Piece 1725.00
Sconce, 3-Light, Neoclassical, Gilt Metal, Cut Glass, 32 x 20 x 18 In., 4 Piece 2300.00
Sconce, 4-Light, Rose Spray, Electric, Continental, c.1900, 24 1/2 x 28 In., Pair .1380.00 to 1840.00
Sconce, 5-Light, Cast Iron, Electric, Anglo-American, c.1865, 27 1/2 x 16 1/2 In., Pair ... 2185.00
Sconce, 5-Light, George III Style, Cut Glass, 25 In., Pair 900.00
Sconce, 5-Light, Louis XVI Style, Gilt Bronze, Scrolled Arms, Urn, Swag, 20 1/2 In., Pair 770.00
Sconce, 5-Light, Louis XVI Style, Ormolu, Cut Glass, 12 In., Pair 800.00
Sconce, 5-Light, Louis XVI Style, Ormolu, Cut Glass, 20th Century, 24 x 18 x 12 In., Pair 920.00
Sconce, 6-Light, Gilt Bronze, Cut Glass, Electric, Continental, 15 1/2 x 16 1/2 In., Pair .. 1150.00
Sconce, 6-Light, Louis XV Style, Ormolu, Leaves, Scrolling Arms, 1890s, 18 In. 1150.00
Sconce, 6-Light, Louis XVI Style, Gilt Bronze, Barbedienne, Paris, c.1885, 21 In., Pair .. 6900.00
Sconce, 6-Light, Napoleon III, Candle, Gilt Bronze, Lily, c.1865, 22 x 19 x 12 In., Pair .. 1725.00
Sconce, Arne Jacobsen, Visor, Enameled, Louis Poulsen, Denmark, 6 1/2 x 14 In., Pair ... 575.00
Sconce, Brass, Openwork, Bow & Bird's Heads, Vine & Berry, 19 In., Pair 160.00
Sconce, Cylinder, Crimped Drip Pan, Finger Hole, 12 x 9 1/2 In. 1095.00
Sconce, Disderot, Brass, Enamel, Saucer Shape, 14 1/2 x 13 In. 1035.00
Sconce, George Nelson, Bubble, Howard Miller, c.1952 .... 1645.00
Sconce, Heifetz, Wood, Brass, Male, Female Profiles, Shades, 15 1/2 x 6 1/2 x 50 In., Pair 635.00
Sconce, James Mont, Pickled Oak, Cantilevered Arm, 36 x 22 In. 690.00
Sconce, Neoclassical, Cast Iron, Winged Putto, c.1900, 21 x 11 x 14 In., Pair 690.00
Sconce, Paavo Tynell, Brass, Taito, Finland, c.1948, Pair 2800.00
Sconce, Tin, Candleholder, Saucer Base, Crimped Rim, Sunflower, 12 1/2 In. 845.00

Sconce, Tin, Mirror Back, Crimped Drip Pan, Red Paint, 15 1/4 In. 169.00
Sconce, Tin, Oval Reflectors, Crimped, Flared Rim, Drip Pan, 13 In., Pair 115.00
Sconce, Wood, White Glass Shade, Denmark, c.1960, 28 In. 235.00
Skater's, Amethyst Shade 1130.00
Skater's, Brass, Embossed Dietz Boy On Shade, Bail Handle, 6 1/2 In. 170.00
Skater's, Cobalt Blue Shade 605.00
Skater's, Red Globe, Metal Framework 1760.00
Skater's, Ruby Shade 3630.00
Tiffany lamps are listed in the Tiffany category.
Torchere, 5-Light, Frosted Glass Shades, Scrolled Feet, c.1900, 76 In., Pair 3055.00
Torchere, 9-Light, Scrolled Base, Wrought Iron, 72 In., Pair 1495.00
Torchere, 13-Light, Pricket Top, Iron, 66 In. 1438.00
Torchere, Art Nouveau, Nymph Among Reeds, Electric, Early 1900s, 55 x 44 In. 1610.00
Torchere, Baroque Style, Silvered Metal, 30 In., Pair 239.00
Torchere, Egyptian Revival, Alabaster, Jar-Shape Globes, c.1930, 68 In. 2530.00
Torchere, George III Style, Mahogany, Piecrust Top, 52 x 15 In. 290.00
Torchere, Hammered, Shelf, Milk Glass Globe, Late 1800s, 62 1/4 x 71 In. 1880.00
Torchere, Louis XVI Style, Giltwood, 78 In., Pair 3000.00
Torchere, Scroll, Shell, Guilloche Carving, 3-Part Base, Italy, c.1850, 78 In. 1610.00
Torchere, Tripod, Multicolored, Baluster Form, Continental, 60 1/2 x 16 In. 550.00
Vianne, Electric, Marble Base, Glass Shade, c.1960s, 12 In. 85.00
Whale Oil, 3-Printie Block, Amethyst, Hexagonal Base, Pewter Collar, 8 1/4 In. 715.00
Whale Oil, Bigler, Tapered Font, Wafer, Square Base, Brass Collar, 9 5/8 In. 55.00
Whale Oil, Blown Glass, Blue Base, Clear Font, American, 7 In. 8050.00
Whale Oil, Blown Glass, Bulbous, Wafer, Pressed Glass Base, Brass Collar, 10 5/8 In. . . 35.00
Whale Oil, Blown Glass, Bulbous, Wafer, Pressed Glass Base, Pewter Collar, 5 1/8 In. . . . 275.00
Whale Oil, Blown Glass, Cone Font, Wafer, Pressed Glass Base, 6 3/4 In. 65.00
Whale Oil, Blown Glass, Finger, Applied Handle, Flared Foot, 3 1/4 In. 110.00
Whale Oil, Blown Glass, Lion's Head, Basket Of Flowers Base, Opaque White, 7 3/4 In. . 715.00
Whale Oil, Brass, Round Base, Baluster-Turned Column, Inverted-Bell Font, 8 1/2 In. . . . 165.00
Whale Oil, Brass, Saucer Base, Dolphin Finger Handle, Double Burner, 7 In., Pair 460.00
Whale Oil, Brass, Urn Shape, Octagonal Base, Chain Hangers, Late 1800s, 2 In. 55.00
Whale Oil, Bronze, Snake Terminal, Ratchet, Scrolled Lid, Pharaoh's Head, 7 In. 420.00
Whale Oil, Bulbous Font, Globe Wafer, Pressed Glass Base, Pewter Collar, 10 1/2 In. 65.00
Whale Oil, Gimbal-Mounted Pewter, Saucer Base, Finger Hold, 2 Burners, 5 1/4 In. 135.00
Whale Oil, Glass, Candlestick Form, Baluster Shaft, Polished Pontil, 9 3/4 In., Pair 1380.00
Whale Oil, Homan, Pewter, Gimbal, Finger Ring, Wall Mount Ring, Cincinnati, 5 In. 518.00
Whale Oil, Onion Shape, Beehive Font, 19th Century, 5 1/2 In. 58.00
Whale Oil, Pressed Glass, Bull's-Eye & Fleur-De-Lis, Flint, 1800s, 10 In. 316.00
Whale Oil, Pressed Glass, Bull's-Eye & Rosette, Hexagonal Base, Brass, 9 1/2 In., Pair . . 220.00
Whale Oil, Pressed Glass, Bull's-Eye, Inverted Sawtooth, 19th Century, 9 1/2 In. 127.00
Whale Oil, Pressed Glass, Cable & Fan, Flint, 8 3/4 In. 150.00
Whale Oil, Pressed Glass, Circle & Ellipse, Brass, Stem Reeded, Marble Base, 9 1/2 In. . . 55.00
Whale Oil, Pressed Glass, Cut Font, Opaque Globe, 17 In. 140.00
Whale Oil, Pressed Glass, Excelsior With Maltese Cross, Pewter, 5 3/4 In. 22.00
Whale Oil, Pressed Glass, Flattened Sawtooth, Brass Stem, Marble Base, 12 In. 22.00
Whale Oil, Pressed Glass, Heart, Sawtooth & Thumbprints, Hexagonal Base, 8 3/4 In. . . . 45.00
Whale Oil, Pressed Glass, Lyre, 6-Panel Font, Twin-Tube Brass Burner, 11 1/4 In. 98.00
Whale Oil, Pressed Glass, Sandwich Star, Hexagonal Base, Brass Collar, 10 1/2 In., Pair . 55.00
Whale Oil, Pressed Glass, Star & Punty, Wafer, Hexagonal Base, 9 3/4 In., Pair 75.00
Whale Oil, Pressed Glass, Sweetheart, 19th Century, 10 1/4 In., Pair 259.00
Whale Oil, Pressed Glass, Tulip, Hexagonal Base, 1845-1870, 9 3/4 In., Pair 499.00
Whale Oil, Pressed Glass, Waffle & Thumbprint, Applied Handle, Brass Collar, 4 1/2 In. . . 33.00
Whale Oil, Pressed Glass, Waffle, 11 1/2 In. 115.00
Whale Oil, Pressed Glass, Waisted Loop, Gilded Stem, Marble Base, Brass Collar, 11 In. . 22.00
Whale Oil, Tin, Rectangular Saucer Base, Loop Carry Ring, 6 1/4 In. 28.00
Whale Oil, Tin, Saucer Base, 7 In. 33.00
Whale Oil, Tin, Wood, Long Handle, Double Burner, Parade Type, 18 x 5 1/2 In. 60.00
LAMP SHADE, Glass, Iridescent, Austria, 9 x 4 3/4 In. 107.00
Glass, Jefferson, Reverse Painted, Art Deco Chevron Designs, 6 Panels, 14 x 9 In. 865.00
Glass, Quilted, Cranberry Opalescent, Crimped Rim, 5 In. 165.00
Glass, Red Threaded Rim, Acid-Etched Flower Design, Goffered Rim, 4 In. 140.00

Pressed Glass, Inverted Thumbprint, Amber, Goffered Rim, 4 In. Fitter, 6 In., Pair 17.00

LANTERNS are a special type of lighting device. They have a light
source, usually a candle, totally hidden inside the walls of the lantern.
Light is seen through holes or glass sections.

Arts & Crafts, Hanging, Bronzed Metal, Mica Inserts, Ceiling Cap, 14 In. 690.00
Arts & Crafts, Hanging, Bull's-Eye Glass, Iron, 11 1/4 In. 529.00
Arts & Crafts, Hanging, Slag Glass Panels, 13 In. 200.00
Arts & Crafts, Leaded Glass, Ivory, Green, Purple, 10 In. 633.00
Brass, Blown Glass Globe, E.J. Hale, Mid 19th Century, 15 1/2 In. 550.00
Brass, British Coal Mining Co., Serial No. 58767, Wales, U.K., 8 1/2 In. 56.00
Brass, Clear Globe, Property Of Pullman Silver Palace Car Co., 20 1/2 In. 195.00
Brass, Hand Inspection, 360 Degree, Ribbed Lens, Oil Burner, Handle, 17 In. 345.00
Brass, Hexagonal, Glass Panes, Candle, Smoke Shield, Embossed, 18 In., Pair 55.00
Brass, Pierced Bottom & Top, Candle, Cover, Swing Handle, Accordion Shape, 7 In. 39.00
Bulbous Globe, Slide Door, Base Collar, Swing Handle, 11 1/4 In. 235.00
Bulbous Globe, Star, Diamond-Shape Holes, Round Handle, 17 1/2 In. 200.00
Chinese, Canvas On Wooden Ribs, Hand Painted, Warrior Figures 65.00
Copper, Glass, Oil Lamp, 20 x 11 x 9 In. 776.00
Copper, Pierced, Turkish Style, 2 Tiers, 27 x 22 In. 840.00
Dietz, Blizzard, No. 2, Green Globe, 20 In. 66.00
Dietz, King Fire Dept., American LaFrance Fire Engine, Elmira, New York 575.00
Dietz, King Fire Dept., Red Paint, Red Globe, Brass, Copper, Tin 140.00
Dietz, King Fire Dept., Seagrave, Nickel, Brass, Columbus, Ohio, Aug. 27, '07 . . . .   805.00
Dietz, Little Giant, 17 In. 22.00
Dietz, Vista, Red Globe, 17 In. 17.00
Dietz, Wizard, Red Globe, 16 In. 11.00
Driving, Beveled Glass, Tin, Red Lens, Brass, Mounts, 21 x 5 1/2 x 5 1/2 In., Pair 112.00
Floor, Black Lacquer, Gilt Decoration, Chinese, c.1900, 76 1/2 In., Pair 1610.00
Floor, Giltwood, Multicolored, Putto Heads, Winged Dragon, Italy, c.1900, 93 In. 1495.00
G. Stickley, Hanging, Copper, Hammered, Amber Glass, 16 x 5 x 5 In. 1880.00
Garden, Bronze, Dragons, Clouds, Japan, Late 1800s, 19 In., Pair 120.00
Garden, Toro, Composite, Calligraphy, Patinated, Japan, 53 In. 345.00
Gas, Vieux Carre, Copper, Glass Panes, Iron Scrolls, 38 x 16 1/2 x 16 1/2 In. 750.00
Hall, Blown Glass, Engraved, Frosted, Brass Mounted, Continental, c.1810, 18 x 10 In. . .   750.00
Hall, Blown Glass, Leaf Engraved, Brass Mounted, Early 19th Century, 31 1/2 x 9 1/2 In.   345.00
Hall, Gilt Brass, Etched Glass, Flowers, 19th Century Style, England, 37 x 16 In., Pair . . .   805.00
Hall, Louis XVI Style, 3-Light, Convex Glass, Gilt Brass, Suspension Chain, 32 x 7 In. . .   920.00
Hanging, Tin, Wire, Clear Glass Shade, 12 In. 248.00
Heart Cutouts, Iron, G. Stickley, 13 x 6 In. 1150.00
Kerosene, Bell System Etched In Globe, Red Globe, Embury Manufacturing 70.00
Pole, Tin, Blue Paint, Cylindrical Case, Corbel Decoration, Italy, 1800s, 78 In., Pair 880.00
Porcelain, Famille Rose Enamels, Courting Scenes, Chinese, Early 1900s, 12 In., Pair 646.00
Portico, Amethyst Glaze, Hexagonal, Wrought Iron, Brass, Continental, 46 x 31 In. 635.00
Portico, Baronial Style, Iron, Stained Glass, Tapered Square, England, c.1900, 27 x 12 In.   405.00
Portico, Gothic Revival, Wrought Steel, Hexagonal, 3 Lights, England, 32 x 15 In., Pair .   4140.00
Portico, Louis XVI Style, Brass, Patinated, Hexagonal, France, 33 x 20 In. 2300.00
Tin, 2 Green & 2 Clear Glass Panels, Loop Carry Handle, 15 In. 110.00
Tin, Glass Panels, Swing Handle, Wood, Footed, Late 1800s, 2 1/2 x 1 1/2 x 4 3/4 In. 1045.00
Tin, Half Round, Punched Cone Shaped Top, Ring Handle, Hinge Door, Candle, 15 In. . . .   460.00
Tin, Pierced, Barn, Early 1800s, 13 In. 60.00
Tin, Pierced, Hinged Door, Glass Lens, Black, Red, Ocher, 17 x 8 In. 125.00
Tin, Punched, Cylindrical, Cone Top, Hanging Ring, Hinged Door, Handle, Candle, 16 In.   330.00
Tin, Punched, Patinated, Green, Blue & Clear Pressed Glass Panels, Middle East, 29 In. . .   575.00
Tin, Punched, Paul Revere Style, 13 In. 90.00
Tin, Punched, Paul Revere Style, Starburst, Ring Hanger, 15 In. 275.00
Tin, Punched, Rosettes & Fan Panels, Glass Panes, Cone Top, Ring Carrier, 13 In. 230.00
Tin, Round Lenses, Round Frame, Pierced Vent Cap, Fixed Handle, 14 1/2 In. 310.00
Tin, Sliding Glass Panels, Peaked Top, Ring Handle, Wire Guards, Candle, 14 1/2 In. 138.00
Wood, Green Paint, Yellow Glass, Candle, 18 In. 255.00
Wrought Iron, Black Frame, Glass Panes, Iron Bracket, 18 In. 110.00

Le Verre Francais, Vase,
Stylized Plant, Orange,
Brown, Green, On Clear
Ground, 20 In.

Rubber cement solvent, available at art
and office supply stores, has many uses.
Put a few drops on a paper towel and
rub off ink smudges, adhesive tape glue,
or label glue from glass or porcelain.

LE VERRE FRANCAIS is one of the many types of cameo glass made in
France. The glass was made by the C. Schneider factory in Epinay-sur-
Seine from 1918 to 1933. It is a mottled glass, usually decorated with
floral designs, and bears the incised signature *Le Verre Francais*.

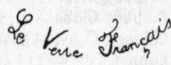

Atomizer, Cameo Leaves, Yellow Ground, Brass Top, 5 1/2 In.		360.00
Bowl, Art Deco, Thorny Branches, Flowers, Mottled Orange, Oblong, 4 x 7 3/4 In.		690.00
Compote, Mottled Purple Stem & Foot, Yellow Bowl, 10 x 8 In.		1380.00
Compote, Pine Branches, Burgundy, Amber Ground, 5 1/2 x 11 In.		980.00
Lamp Base, Purple Cameo Glass, Bulbous, Sunflowers, Early 1900s, 12 3/4 In.		940.00
Lampshade, Orange, Brown, Green Design, Mottled Ground, 5 1/2 In.		430.00
Vase, 3 Dahlias, Purple, Pink Ground, 6 In.		978.00
Vase, Art Deco, Frosted White, Pink, Mottled Ground, Charder, 11 1/4 In.		1785.00
Vase, Berries, Mottled Brown, Orange, Red, On Yellow Ground, 4 In.		460.00
Vase, Blue, Green Mottled Leaves, Orange Stylized Flowers, 11 In.		2415.00
Vase, Blue, Medallions Cut, Flowers, 3 3/4 In.		300.00
Vase, Flowers, Mottled Yellow, Orange Ground, Footed, c.1920, 12 In.		1905.00
Vase, Footed Cylinder, Mottled, Green, Orange, Cameo, Leaves, c.1920, 16 In.		1120.00
Vase, Geese, In Flight, Amethyst, Blue, On Mottled Chartreuse, 14 In.		4315.00
Vase, Mottled Brown Rim, Cameo Leaves, Stems, Flowers, Charder, 6 1/2 In.		1380.00
Vase, Orange Foxglove, On Pink Mottled Ground, 19 x 6 In.		1840.00
Vase, Red Cameo Over Yellow, Orange Ground, Cherries, Footed, 10 3/4 In.		1553.00
Vase, Red Roses, Thorny Stems, Yellow Ground, Green Mottled Base, 10 In.		1150.00
Vase, Slender, Cut Design, Brown, Orange, Yellow Ground, 7 1/2 In.		200.00
Vase, Stylized Flowers, Amethyst, Mottled Rose, Urn Shape, 12 1/8 In.		825.00
Vase, Stylized Flowers, On Mottled Orange, Yellow, 9 In.		550.00
Vase, Stylized Plant, Orange, Brown, Green, On Clear Ground, 20 In.	*Illus*	3335.00
Vase, Swans, Mirrored, Aubergine, Orange & Yellow Ground, 10 1/4 In.		3160.00

LEATHER is tanned animal hide and it has been used to make decorative and useful objects for centuries. Leather objects must be carefully
preserved with proper humidity and oiling or the leather will deterio-
rate and crack. This damage cannot be repaired.

Belt, Studded, 1822, 36 In.		55.00
Book Cover, Hand Tooled, Arts & Crafts Trees, Frame, 9 1/2 x 5 3/4 In.		520.00
Bridle, Hitched Headstall Horsehair Rosettes, Tasseled Reins, American Flags, 19 In.		4400.00
Gun Case, Paper Labels, Mahogany Stand, 24 In.		275.00
Holster, Browning High Power, Black, Hardshell, Magazine Pouch, Larsen Trademark		65.00
Saddle, Steel Mounted, Wood Frame, Batting, Rosette Bolts, Medieval Style, 21 1/2 In.		235.00
Shotgun Case, Fitted, Brass Mounted, Stenciled Lettering, c.1943, 14 x 32 x 4 In.		360.00
Strap, 3 Polished Brass Sleigh Bells, 13 1/2 In.		90.00
Strap, Nickel Plating, 46 Brass Bells, 93 In.		415.00
Tobacco Pouch, Basketry Design, Brass Kanemono, Water Buffalo, Herd Boy, 1800s		115.00

LEEDS pottery was made at Leeds, Yorkshire, England, from 1774 to
1878. Most Leeds ware was not marked. Early Leeds pieces had distinctive twisted handles with a greenish glaze on part of the creamy
ware. Later ware often had blue borders on the creamy pottery. A

LEEDS POTTERY.

Chicago company named Leeds made many Disney-inspired figurines.
They are listed in the Disneyana category.

Charger, Blue Feather, Multicolored Flowers, 13 1/4 In.	385.00
Coffeepot, Blue & Green Floral Sprays, Swags, Bulbous, Dome Lid, 10 3/8 In.	287.00
Cup & Saucer, Handleless, Blue, Green, Brown Flowers, Leaves	165.00
Cup Plate, Eagle, Brown, Shield, Gold, Branch, Green, Scalloped, Blue Edge, 4 3/8 In. ..	1980.00
Cup Plate, Peafowl, Orange, Gold, Blue, Tree Branch, Green, Brown Feather Edge, 4 In. .	990.00
Platter, Blue, Octagonal, Lobed Rim, 19 x 14 1/2 In.	185.00
Teapot, Flowers, Pear Shape, Multicolored, Pearlware Body, Dome Lid, c.1815, 11 In.	518.00

LEFTON is a mark found on pottery, porcelain, glass, and other wares
imported by the Geo. Zoltan Lefton Company. The company began in
1941 and is still in business. It was restructured in 2002 and is now
called the Lefton Company. The company mark has changed through
the years; but because marks have been used for long periods of time,
they are of little help in dating an object.

Ashtray, Blue Paisley, Crown Insignia, No. NE2344, 5 1/2 In.	18.00
Bank, Lion, Stopper, No. H13384, 7 3/4 x 4 In.	25.00
Bank, Piggy, Black, White, Stopper, No. 07176, 6 x 5 x 5 1/2 In.	145.00
Bank, Retirement, Rocking Grandma	24.00
Bell, Dinner, Flowers, No. 01990, 3 1/4 x 2 3/4 In.	18.00
Bookends, Owl, Label, No. H483	18.00
Bowl, Cover, 3-Footed, Green, Cream, No. 4387, 4 x 3 In.	65.00
Bowl, Footed, Roses, Leaves, 8 x 4 1/2 x 3 In.	280.00
Candy Dish, Pastel Green, Fluted Gold Edge, Cherub, Pearlized, No. 837, 7 In.	240.00
Canister Set, Lids, Corks, 4 Piece	115.00
Coffee Set, Pot, Sugar, Creamer, Green Heritage, No. 3065 & 3066	160.00
Coffeepot, Green Heritage, Rose, Gold Handle, Spout, No. 3065, 9 x 8 1/2 In.	140.00
Coffeepot, Heirloom Heritage, 3-Footed, No. 1075, 8 In.	85.00
Coffeepot, Lid, Brown Heritage, Crown Logo, Sticker, No. 1866, 8 1/2 In.	105.00
Coffeepot, Lid, Green Heritage, Handle, Sticker, Crown, No. 3065	105.00
Coffeepot, Lid, Rose Chintz, Sticker, No. 560R, 9 In.	105.00
Coffeepot, Violet Chintz, Gold Handle, No. 660V	145.00
Compote, Yellow Daisy, No. 5005, 5 3/4 In.	25.00
Cookie Jar, Country Charm Rooster, 6 In.	55.00
Decanter, Stopper, Monk, Sticker, No. 166, 8 1/2 In.	85.00
Dish, Leaf, Shabby Chic, 2-Sided, Flowers, Leaves, No. 4674, 6 1/2 x 4 3/4 In.	20.00
Dresser Box, Swan, Applied Flowers, Bisque, No. 08156, 2 1/2 x 2 1/2 In.	18.00
Eggcup, Blue Paisley, No. NE2131, 3 1/8 x 2 3/8 In.	28.00
Figurine, Angel January, No. 3322, 4 1/8 In.	25.00
Figurine, Artist Painting Landscape, Bisque, No. 7800, 6 1/2 In.	55.00
Figurine, Cat, No. H4032, 5 x 2 1/2 In.	20.00
Figurine, Child Of Prague, Boy, 5 x 3 5/8 In.	75.00
Figurine, Child Of Prague, Girl, 5 x 3 7/8 In.	75.00
Figurine, Girl In Bonnet, No. 06025, 2 1/2 In.	15.00
Figurine, Girl, Flowers, No. 1448, 4 1/2 In.	24.00
Figurine, Hobo, No. 3217, 5 In.	15.00
Figurine, Panda Bear Eating Bamboo, No. 1697	15.00
Figurine, Pink Poodle With Hat, Flowers	85.00
Figurine, Poodle, Spaghetti Trim, 3 1/2 In.	65.00
Figurine, Swan, Flowers, Leaves, 6 1/2 x 3 1/2 x 5 1/2 In.	45.00
Figurine, Unicorn, Gold Horn, Shamrock Necklace, No. 4938, 4 1/2 In.	15.00
Group, Vet Gives Poodle A Shot, No. 7270, 5 3/4 In.	30.00
Hankie Holder, Violet Chintz, 3-Footed, No. E4986	28.00
Head Vase, Horse, 6 1/2 x 7 x 4 7/8 In.	49.00
Honey Pot, Fruit Of Italy, No. 623	22.00
Honey Pot, Pineapple, Wooden Spoon, Sticker, No. 2539	25.00
Jam Jar, No. H5070, 5 1/2 In.	20.00
Jewelry Box, Flowers, Bisque, Sticker, Round, No. 12152, 4 3/4 In.	30.00
Nappy, Flowers, No. E3310, 7 In.	32.00
Nappy, Green Heritage, Flowers, Leaf Shape, No. 1860, 6 1/2 x 5 In.	20.00
Pitcher, Poinsettia, Logo, No. 4389, 6 1/2 In.	75.00
Pitcher, Tree Trunk, Mushrooms, Leaves, No. 6466, 7 x 3 1/2 In.	40.00

Pitcher, Vase, White, Blue Grapes, No. 2188, 4 1/2 In. 49.00
Pitcher, Water, Green Heritage, Rose, Gold Handle, Crown, Logo, Sticker, No. NE796 ... 115.00
Planter, Donkey & Cart, 5 x 6 x 3 1/2 In. 15.00
Planter, Fishing Hat, Pole, No. H6591, 7 1/8 x 4 3/4 x 3 7/8 In. 18.00
Plate, Chintz, No. NE2338, 7 In. 22.00
Plate, Dinner, Roses, Gilt, Swirled Rim, No. 3168 .... 20.00
Plate, Guardian Angel, No. 01357, 9 In. 50.00
Plate, Salad, Poinsettia, Green, Cream, No. 4395, 6 3/4 In. 25.00
Plate, Serving, Green Holly, Sticker, No. 2048, 9 In. 18.00
Plate, Violet, No. 212, 9 In. 68.00
Salt & Pepper, Flowers, Orange, Green, No. 5400, 7 In. 15.00
Salt & Pepper, Miss Priss, No. 1511, 3 1/2 & 2 3/4 In. 35.00
Shoe, Pink, Logo, No. 1204, 4 1/2 In. 25.00
Snack Set, Christmas Holly, Plates, Cups, Mug, 8 Piece 25.00
Snack Set, Sugar & Creamer, 4 Trays, 4 Cups, Rose Chintz 300.00
Snack Set, Tea Rose, No. 2759 .... 18.00
Sugar & Creamer, Green Holly, No. 1355, 3 1/2 x 4 In. 35.00
Sugar & Creamer, Miss Priss, No. 1508 .... 75.00
Teapot, Dutch Girl, Removable Lid, Stamped Numbers On Bottom 75.00
Teapot, Embossed Rose, Crown Logo, No. 952, 9 x 6 In. 165.00
Teapot, Green Heritage, Rose, 8 1/2 In. 95.00
Teapot, Lid, Green Heritage, Sticker, Crown, No. 5857, 6 In. 105.00
Teapot, Rose Chintz, 6 1/2 x 8 1/4 In. 75.00
Teapot, Sugar & Creamer, Stackable, Rose, No. 885 .... 72.00
Tidbit, 2 Tiers, Della Robbia Fruit, Metal Handle, No. 2090 .... 55.00
Tidbit, 2 Tiers, Poinsettia, Green, Cream, No. 4391, 6 3/4 & 8 3/4 In. 65.00
Tidbit, Rose Chintz, Gold Tone Handle, 6 1/4 In. 25.00
Toothbrush Holder, Flowers, No. 270, 3 3/4 In. 15.00
Tray, Serving, Embossed Grape, Leaves, Fruit, No. 1160A, Square 12 In. 65.00
Trinket Box, Clown, 3 1/2 In. 18.00
Tumble-Up, Green Heritage, Crown Logo, Sticker, No. 1266, 7 In. 115.00
Vase, Egg, Cracked, Rose, No. H183, 5 In. 45.00
Vase, Green Heritage Rose, No. 748, 5 1/2 In. 18.00
Vase, Pedestal, Shabby Chic, Flowers, No. 1190, 4 x 4 1/2 x 2 3/4 In. 23.00
Vase, White, Matte, No. 2488W, 4 1/2 x 4 In. 15.00
Wall Plaque, Man With Pipe, Bisque, Matte, No. 471, 5 In. 25.00
Wall Plaque, Railway Man With Pipe, Bisque, Matte, No. 4713, 5 In. 25.00

LEGRAS was founded in 1864 by Auguste Legras at St. Denis, France.
It is best known for cameo glass and enamel-decorated glass with Art
Nouveau designs. Legras merged with Pantin in 1920 and became the
Verreries et Cristalleries de St. Denis et de Pantin Reunies.

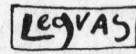

Bowl, Strawberries & Leaves, Rectangular Top, Round Base, Cameo, 4 x 2 1/4 x 2 In. ... 520.00
Powder Jar, Cover, Brown, Black Trees, Painted Ground, Russet To Gold, 4 3/4 x 3 In. .. 345.00
Rose Bowl, Snowy Landscape, Birds Flying, Enameled, Crimped Edge, Signed, 4 1/4 In. .. 345.00
Tray, Winter Landscape, Walnut Frame, Signed, 9 x 5 In. 575.00
Vase, Apple Blossom, Pastel, Bowling Pin Shape, Signed, 7 In. 900.00
Vase, Cherries, Leaves, Textured Green Ground, Cameo, Signed, 8 In. 260.00
Vase, Enameled Flowers, Leaves, Flared Base, 13 1/2 In. 880.00
Vase, Flowers, Blue, Cascading, Signed, c.1920, 9 1/2 In. 420.00
Vase, Flowers, Leaves, Berries, Textured Ground, Cameo, 8 1/4 In. 420.00
Vase, Green Aventurine, Raised Gilt Mistletoe, Opalescent Berries, Handles, 12 In., Pair .. 1575.00
Vase, Landscape, Blue, Green, Yellow, Tricornered Rim, c.1918, 4 In. 355.00
Vase, Leafy Branches, Holly Blossoms, Tricornered Rim, Cameo, Signed, 4 1/2 x 3 1/4 In. . 520.00
Vase, Leaves, Amber, Frosted Ground, Cameo, Signed, 5 1/4 In. 260.00
Vase, Leaves, Berries, Pink Ground, Cameo, 11 1/4 In. 520.00
Vase, Maroon Leaves, Vines, Peach Ground, Cameo, 6 In. 115.00
Vase, Pink, Green, Violets, Cameo, Signed, 4 In. 350.00
Vase, Purple Flower Clusters, Leaves, Textured, Mauve Shoulder, Signed, c.1900, 16 In. . 1230.00
Vase, Rayed Celestial Cameo Band, Teal, Rust, White Ground, Art Deco, 8 1/4 In. 690.00
Vase, Snow Scene, Enameled Trees Rising On Sunlit Sky, Square, Signed, 8 1/4 In. 385.00
Vase, Stylized Ribbon, Chipped Ice Ground, Enamel, Cameo, 12 1/2 In. 315.00
Vase, Trees, Meadows, Mountains, Orange & Yellow Ground, Cameo, Enamel, 6 1/2 In. .. 800.00

Vase, Trees, Pond, Forested Ground, Enamel, Cameo, 6 In. 215.00
Vase, Trees, Sailboats, Green Leaves, Frosted, Cameo, Signed, 8 1/4 In. 800.00
Vase, Trees, Spanish Moss, Red, Twilight Blue, Cameo, Signed, 9 1/4 In. 690.00
Vase, Underwater Scene, Apricot Ground, Brown, Yellow, Enamel, Cameo, Signed, 22 In. 1035.00
Vase, Violets, Leaves, Enamel, Frosty Texture, Cameo, Art Deco, 9 1/2 In. 400.00
Vase, Winter Woodland Scene, Snow, Trees, Village, Cameo, Signed, 5 1/4 x 4 In. 1150.00

LENOX is the name of a porcelain maker. Walter Scott Lenox and
Jonathan Coxon, Sr., founded the Ceramic Art Company in Trenton,
New Jersey, in 1889. In 1906, Lenox left and started his own company
called *Lenox.* The company makes a porcelain that is similar to Irish
Belleek. The marks used by the firm have changed through the years
and collectors prefer the earlier examples. Related pieces may also be
listed in the Ceramic Art Co. category.

Dinner Set, Essex, 12 Place Settings 2950.00
Dinner Set, Jewel, Plates, Serving Pieces, 56 Piece 405.00
Fish Set, Hand Painted, Gray, Green, Gilt Rim, Tiffany & Co., W.H. Marley, 9 In. 1295.00
Plate, Birds, Boehm Decoration, Annual Plates, 1970-1981, 10 3/4 In. 690.00
Plate, Place, Blue Ground, Green Marks, 11 1/4 In., 12 Piece 1535.00
Stein, Men Playing Cards, Porcelain, Copper & Silver Lid, 1/2 Liter 805.00
Stein, Men Playing Cards, Porcelain, Copper & Silver Lid, 1 Liter 1035.00
Urn, 2 Nude Women, Bathing, Signed, May Pepperdine, Belleek, 1897-1898, 18 1/2 In. .. 2185.00
Vase, Roses, Pink, White, Bulbous, George Morley, 14 3/4 x 9 In. 1495.00

LETTER OPENERS have been used since the eighteenth century. Ivory
and silver were favored by the well-to-do. In the late nineteenth century, the letter opener was popular as an advertising giveaway and
many were made of metal or celluloid. Brass openers with figural handles were also popular.

Bronze, Nymph, Water Reed Blade, Clio Baker Model, Art Nouveau, 14 3/4 In. 470.00
Dagger, Scrolled Handled & Hilt, Mother-Of-Pearl Inlay, Brass, Sheath, 10 In. 30.00
Dwarf Miner, Ivory Type Material, c.1910, 8 1/2 In. 133.00
Empire Varnish Company, Gold Metal, Cleveland, Oh., 8 In. 3.00
Fuller, Salesman On Handle, Brown Plastic, 7 In. 5.00
Fuller, Salesman On Handle, Pink Plastic, 7 In. 20.00
Horse Head, Sterling Silver, Read & Barton, 10 In. 95.00
Indian Motif, Turquoise Plastic, 8 In. 8.00
Mother-Of-Pearl, Carved Handle, 7 1/2 In. 95.00
Neighborhood News, Silver Metal, Nordman Printing Co., 9 3/4 In. 10.00
Poodle, Running, Sterling Silver, 1 1/2 x 8 In. 125.00

LIBBEY Glass Company has made many types of glass since 1888,
including the cut glass and tablewares that are collected today. The
stemwares of the 1930s and 1940s are once again in style. The Toledo,
Ohio, firm was purchased by Owens-Illinois in 1935 and is still working under the name *Libbey Incorporated.* Maize is listed in its own
category.

Bowl, 6 Engraved Flower Panels, Notched Prism Borders, 4 1/4 In. 140.00
Bowl, Amberina, Ruffled Edge, 7 In. 575.00
Bowl, Amberina, Ruffled Edge, Signed, 1 3/4 x 7 In. 345.00
Bowl, File & Fan, Alternating, Hobstar Border, Signed, 9 In. 175.00
Bowl, Glorietta Cutting, Signed, 2 x 8 In. 370.00
Bowl, Greek Key, Shallow, 9 In. 650.00
Champagne, Clear Bowl, Stem, Cranberry Egg-Shaped Knop, Nash, 1931-1941, 5 1/2 In. . 170.00
Champagne Set, Patrician Cutting, 6 In., 8 Piece 115.00
Cheese Dish, Cover, Strawberry & Diamond, Signed, 1896-1906, 9 x 6 In. 650.00
Compote, Engraved Flowers & Chain, Swirl Stem, Signed, 8 x 6 1/4 In. 60.00
Compote, Flower Form, Amberina, Knopped Teardrop Stem, Signed, c.1917, 10 In. 3105.00
Compote, Flower Form, Amberina, Signed 3025.00
Decanter, Empress Cutting, Bowling Pin Shape, Stopper, 1896-1906, 12 1/2 In. 595.00
Goblet, Clear Bowl, Cranberry Egg-Shaped Knop, Nash, 1931-1941, 5 1/2 In. 185.00
Goblet, Embassy Pattern, Walter Dorwin Teague, 1939, 4 x 6 In., 4 Piece 935.00
Nappy, Gem Cutting, Round, Signed, 6 In. 40.00

Nappy, Glenda Cutting, Signed, 6 In. 125.00
Nappy, Stratford Cutting Variation, Tricornered, 6 In. 75.00
Plate, Ellsmere Cutting, Signed, 7 In. 775.00
Plate, Gloria Cutting, 10 In. 225.00
Plate, Harvard Cutting, 7 In. 140.00
Plate, Hobstar, Strawberry Diamond & Fan, Pedestal, Signed, 3 1/2 x 9 In. 250.00
Relish, Glenda Cutting, Sections, Signed 195.00
Salt, Stratford Cutting, Pedestal, Scalloped Hobstar Base, Signed, 3 In. 350.00
Sugar & Creamer, Star & Feather, Signed 250.00
Tazza, Ozella Cutting, Signed, 5 1/4 x 8 In. 460.00
Toothpick Holder, Crosshatch, Bull's-Eye, Pinched Waist, 2 1/4 In. 40.00
Tumbler, New Brilliant Pattern, 3 3/4 In. 45.00
Tumbler Set, Berry Festival Pattern, Safedge No. 185, 6 Piece 55.00
Vase, Amberina, Optic Ribbed, Double Wafers, Fuchsia Disc Foot, Signed, 10 3/4 In. 3050.00
Vase, Amberina, Oval, Waisted Neck, Flared, Optic Ribbed, Signed, 9 In. 2990.00
Vase, Amberina, Ribbed Baluster, Flared, Optic Ribbed Disc Foot, Signed, 8 In. 1035.00
Vase, Amberina, Ribbed, Flared, Bubble Ball Connector, 8 In. 518.00
Vase, Amberina, Ribbed, Oval, Cylindrical Neck, Ruffled Edge, Signed, 13 3/4 In. 2365.00
Vase, Amberina, Ruffled Edge, Optic Ribbed Disc Foot, Signed, Pontil, 10 3/4 In. 575.00
Vase, Engraved Flowers, Everted Lip, Footed, c.1900, 12 In. 200.00
Vase, Jack-In-The-Pulpit, Amberina, Bulbous, Optic Ribbed, Signed, 5 In. 695.00
Vase, Jack-In-The-Pulpit, Amberina, Bulbous, Optic Ribbed, Signed, 17 In. 1840.00
Vase, Opalescent, Blue Applied Rim, Applied Clear & Opalescent Foot, 6 1/2 In. 60.00
Vase, Sweet Pea, Intaglio Flower, Signed.4 1/4 x 6 In. 225.00
Vase, Trumpet, Bull's-Eye & Flowers, Pedestal, Signed, 9 3/4 In. 325.00
Vase, Trumpet, Green Cut To Clear, Harvard, 12 1/4 In. 1400.00
Water Set, Hobstar, Notched Fan Prisms, Signed, 8 1/2 In., 7 Piece 350.00

LIGHTERS for cigarettes and cigars are collectible. Cigarettes became popular in the late nineteenth century, and with the cigarette came matches and cigarette lighters. All types of lighters are collected, from solid gold to the first of the recent disposable lighters. Most examples found were made after 1940. Some lighters may be found in the Jewelry category in this book.

Bronica, World Clock, Gas, Battery Ignition, Box, c.1969, 8 In. 22.00
Cigar, Aleppo Higrade Cigars, Nickel Pot, Oil, Ruby Globe, Cigar Cutter, c.1880, 15 In. ... 1045.00
Cigar, Angel, Carrying Torch, Ruby Globe, Gas, c.1900, 18 In. 660.00
Cigar, CCA Cigars, 2 Wicks, Oil, Ruby Globe, Cigar Cutter, c.1880, 14 In. 1265.00
Cigar, Cupid, Cobalt Glass Globe, Cast Metal Base, Gas, c.1900, 17 In. 770.00
Cigar, Elephant, Gray, Yellow, White Globe, Cast Iron, Gas, c.1900, 12 In. 605.00
Cigar, Green Swirl Globe, Tank, Oil, c.1880, 10 In. 415.00
Cigar, Horse, Cinco Globe, 3 Wicks, Metal, Oil, c.1900, 17 In. 385.00
Cigar, Indian, Feathers, Yellow Glass Globe, Metal, Gas, c.1900, 20 In. 660.00
Cigar, John Anderson & Co., Paperboy, Streetlight, Cigar Cutter, 1890, 23 In. 2640.00
Cigar, Knight, Yellow Glass Globe, Metal, Gas, c.1900, 20 In. 715.00
Cigar, Man, Drinking Next To Streetlight, Marble Base, 10 In. 248.00
Cigar, McNeil & Higgins, Guarantee, Ruby Globe, Cutter, 2 Wicks, Oil, 13 In. 935.00
Cigar, Piedmont, Glass Front, Cigar Cutter 935.00
Cigar, Read Tobacco Flotilla Superior Quality, White Globe, Cutter, Iron, Oil, 1880, 12 In. ... 1045.00
Cigar, Ruby Swirl Glass Globe, Enameled Glass, Square Base, 2 Wicks, Oil, c.1880, 11 In. 440.00
Cigar, Uncle Remus, 5 Cent Cigar, Ruby Globe, 2 Wicks, Cutter, Oil, 14 In. 1045.00
Cigar, White Glass Globe, Enameled Glass, Square Base, 2 Wicks, Oil, c.1880, 11 In. 330.00
Cigar, Woman, Art Nouveau, Marble Base, 2 Wicks, Amber Swirl Glass, 1880, 12 In. 935.00
Cigar, Woman, Art Nouveau, Metal, Gas, c.1900, 20 In. 825.00
Demley, French 75 mm Howitzer, Black, Green Enamel Paint, 4 1/4 x 9 1/2 x 4 In. 50.00
Dunhill, Lift Arm, Silver Plate, 4 1/4 In. 35.00
Dunhill, Sterling, Trench Style, Instructions, Box 66.00
Dunhill, Watch, Unique Sports, Sterling, 15 Jewel Movement 1295.00
Flintlock Tinder, Iron, Wood, Military Engravings, England, c.1770, 5 In. 690.00
Midland Jump Spark, Oak Case ....195.00 to 275.00
Park Brand, First Place Safety Award, Great Lakes Steel Corporation, Box, 1955 .... 30.00
Poodle, Standing, Bronze Finish, 4 x 5 In. 45.00
Ronson, Pist-O-Lighter, Pistol, Nickeled Cast Iron, 1910 Patent 470.00

Thorens, Cowboy Boot, Copper Plated, White Metal, Switzerland, 5 1/4 In. 50.00
Zippo, Allied Chemical, Monogram, Versel, 5-Barrel Hinge, 2 x 1 In. 29.00
Zippo, D-Day Commemoration, Black Crinkle Finish, Bronze Shield, Tin Box, 1994 . . . .   50.00
Zippo, Korean War, 98th Bomb Group, Bowling Trophy, Instructions, Box, 1951 . . . .   110.00
Zippo, U.S. Army, Armored Division, Polished Silvertone, Insignia, 1977, 1 1/4 x 2 1/4 In.   58.00
Zippo, U.S. Army, Caribbean, Brushed Silvertone, Etched Insignia, 1957, 1 3/4 x 2 1/4 In.   75.00
Zippo, U.S. Army, Signal Corps, Polished Silvertone, Vietnam War, 1 1/2 x 2 1/4 In. 98.00
Zippo, Vietnam 33 Beer Bottle Cap, Brushed Silvertone, 1962, 1 1/2 x 2 1/4 In. 110.00

LIGHTNING ROD and lightning rod balls are collected. The glass balls
were at the center of the rod that was attached to the roof of a house or
barn to avoid lightning damage.

Glass Ball Center, Tripod Base 135.00
Horse, Blue Globe, 56 In. 595.00
Scroll Finials, Iron, 60 1/4 In., Pair 55.00

LIMOGES porcelain has been made in Limoges, France, since the mid-
nineteenth century. Fine porcelains were made by many factories,
including Haviland, Ahrenfeldt, Guerin, Pouyat, Elite, and others.
Modern porcelains are being made at Limoges and the word *Limoges*
as part of the mark is not an indication of age. Haviland, one of the
Limoges factories, is listed as a separate category in this book.

Biscuit Jar, Cover, Flowers, Yellow, Gold Enamel, T & V France, 8 x 5 In. 150.00
Bowl, Center, Hand Painted, Gilt, Grape Decoration, Early 1900s, 13 1/4 x 5 7/8 In. 200.00
Box, Black Poodle, Standing, FB, 2 1/2 x 2 3/4 In. 120.00
Box, Cover, Egg Shape, Light Blue, Cherub Feeding Chicks, Medallion, 4 x 6 In. 80.00
Box, Hat Shape, White, Gilt, Pink Ribbon, Round, 1 3/4 In. 50.00
Box, Hinged Cover, Blue Flowers, Embossed, White Ground, Round, 2 In. 50.00
Box, Hinged Cover, Clam Shape, Iridescent Purple Spot, 2 In. 40.00
Box, Hinged Cover, Mill Scene, Book Shape, Blue, 1 3/4 In. 50.00
Box, Poodle, Gray, Standing On Teal Base, Poodle Head Clasp, Signed, 2 x 2 In. . . . *Illus*   40.00
Charger, 2 Women In Dress, Near Street Corner, Signed, 13 In. 300.00
Charger, American Indian Chief, Hand Painted, Early 1900s, 11 5/8 In. 470.00
Charger, Roses Near Stream, Signed, 13 In. 350.00
Chocolate Pot, Art Nouveau, Hand Painted, White Art Co., 11 x 8 1/2 In. 518.00
Crepe Server, Cover, Flowers, Gilt Trim, Marked, T & V France, c.1900, 9 In. 160.00
Cup & Saucer, Demitasse, Transfer Flower, Gold Banding, 2 1/4 In., 12 Piece 339.00
Cup & Saucer, Yellow, Floral, Marked, T & V, 20th Century . . . . *Illus*   92.00
Dessert Service, 5 Cups & Saucers, 6 Plates, Early 20th Century, 7 7/8 In. 60.00
Dinner Service, Chrysanthemum, c.1900, 77 Piece 1495.00
Dish, Leaf Shape, Man, Woman, Child, Cobalt Blue Ground, 7 1/2 In. 50.00
Ewer, Fern & Grass, Salmon Ground, Gilt, Early 1890s, 9 1/2 In. 350.00
Fish Set, 12 Plates, Platter, Fish Scenes, Scalloped Gilt Rim, c.1890, 9 1/2 In., 13 Piece . .   2300.00
Fish Set, 12 Plates, Sauceboat, 24-In. Platter, Pitkin & Brooks Mark 1500.00
Jardiniere, Egg Shape, Courting Couple, Cavalier, Hand Painted, Early 1900s, 10 In. 235.00
Oyster Plate, 5 Wells, Marine Designs, c.1896, 7 3/4 In. 310.00
Pitcher, Cider, Roses, Marked, J & C, c.1910, 7 In. 160.00
Pitcher, Pear, Gilt, Hand Painted, Pickard, 13 3/4 In. 950.00
Plaque, Cavaliers In An Interior, Enamel, Gilt Monogram, Ormolu Frame, 11 x 9 In. 2530.00
Plaque, Cavaliers Playing Chess, Enamel, Giltwood Frame, 20th Century, 8 1/2 x 12 In. . . .   1725.00

Limoges, Box,
Poodle, Gray,
Standing On
Teal Base,
Poodle Head
Clasp, Signed,
2 x 2 In.

Limoges, Cup & Saucer,
Yellow, Floral, Marked,
T & V, 20th Century

Don't sticky-tape a top on a
teapot. The decoration may
come off with the tape.
Secure a top with dental wax
or earthquake wax.

Limoges, Teapot, Pink
Flowers, Blue, Gilt Trim,
c.1900, 6 1/4 In.

Plaque, Enamel, 2 Men & Woman In Tavern, Gilt Metal Frame, Late 1800s, 2 3/4 x 4 In.	720.00
Plaque, Enamel, Cavalier, Wood & Metal Frame, Late 1800s, 8 x 4 1/2 In.	1210.00
Plaque, Nude Woman, Books, Skull, Angel, Oval, Mat, Frame, c.1900, 5 7/8 In.	380.00
Plaque, Pate-Sur-Pate, Classical Woman, Harp, CP, Early 1900s, 10 5/8 In.	295.00
Plate, 2 Rabbits, Signed, Pradet, 10 In.	100.00
Plate, 4 Shorebird Scene, Blue, Gilt Border, Hand Painted, 9 In., 4 Piece	90.00
Plate, Dinner, Louis XVI Style, Gilded, C. Ahrenfeldt, c.1885, 10 3/4 In., 12 Piece	2300.00
Plate, Fish, Hand Painted, Late 19th Century, 9 In., 8 Piece	520.00
Plate, Game Birds, 9 In., 10 Piece	1035.00
Plate, Game, 2 Birds Among Flowers, Signed, 10 3/4 In.	70.00
Plate, Game, 2 Pheasants, Signed, Coudert, 10 3/4 In.	50.00
Plate, Game, 2 Quail, Signed, Coudert, 10 3/4 In.	80.00
Plate, Game, Bird Scene, Dark Blue, Gold Trim, 10 1/2 In.	100.00
Plate, Game, Birds In Flight, Signed L. Labania, Gilt Scrolled Rim, 9 5/8 In., 12 Piece	705.00
Plate, Game, Chinese Pheasant, Green Border, Signed, Hucks, 12 In.	100.00
Plate, Monk Sipping Coffee, Green Ground, Signed LE Pie, 10 In.	60.00
Plate, President Harrison Service, Scallop Rim, Gilt Border, France, c.1892, 8 5/8 In.	499.00
Plate, Quail Scene, Signed, Edmund, 10 1/4 In.	90.00
Plate, Seafood, Fish, Seaweed, 9 1/4 In.	110.00
Plate, Soup, Florence Pattern, c.1900, 9 In., 12 Piece	710.00
Plate, Violets, Hand Painted, 9 1/2 In.	100.00
Serving Dish, Parcel Gilt, Putti, Gilt Enamel, Rococo Revival, Early 1900s, 4 Piece	295.00
Teapot, Pink Flowers, Blue, Gilt Trim, c.1900, 6 1/4 In. *Illus*	150.00
Vase, Enameled Multicolored Flowers, Metallic Ground, 4 1/2 In.	1035.00
Vase, Hand Painted Flowers, Signed, Gretchen Blesey, 16 In.	420.00
Vase, Hand Painted Irises, 21 In.	1430.00
Vase, Poppies, Hand Painted, Gilt Rim, Signed, 1910, 10 1/8 In.	395.00
Vase, Tapered, High Rounded Shoulder, Blue Irises, 11 1/2 In.	415.00
Wall Pocket, Bagpipe, Transfer, People, Dancing Around Bonfire, Ribbon, c.1880, 13 In.	375.00

LINDBERGH was a national hero. In 1927, Charles Lindbergh, the aviator, became the first man to make a nonstop solo flight across the
Atlantic Ocean. In 1932, his son was kidnapped and murdered, and
Lindbergh was again the center of public interest. He died in 1974. All
types of Lindbergh memorabilia are collected.

Bookends, Engine, Propeller, Bust, Cast Iron, Copper Plate, 4 3/4 x 6 3/4 In.	230.00
Button, Captain Charles A. Lindbergh, Celluloid Over Metal, Pinback, 1 1/4 In.	95.00
Button, Lindbergh, With Mom, Black, White, Celluloid, Buffalo, N.Y., July 29, 1927	99.00
Button, Lucky Lindy Welcome, Blue, Brown, White, Celluloid	75.00
Button, Plucky Lindy, Horseshoe, Celluloid Over Metal, Pinback, 1 1/4 In.	95.00
Button, Plucky Lindy, Horseshoe, Wishbone, Celluloid Over Metal, Pinback, 1 1/4 In.	85.00
Button, Plucky Lindy, Portrait, Horseshoe, Multicolored	45.00
Button, Universal Lindbergh Day, May 21, Red, Black, White, Celluloid, 1 1/4 In.	128.00
Button, Welcome Lindy, Blue Center, Red Rim, White Letters & Plane	250.00
Candy Container, Spirit Of St. Louis, Glass Wings, 2 Stars, Red Propeller, 5 In.	110.00
Candy Container, Spirit Of St. Louis, Tin Wings, Green Glass, 1927, 4 1/2 In.	300.00
Letter Opener, Brass, 7 1/4 In.	65.00
Notebook, Lindy, Spirit Of St. Louis, 6 3/4 x 8 1/2 In.	50.00
Pencil, Lindy Bread, Bullet, Celluloid, Red, White, Blue, Spirit Of St. Louis Picture	125.00
Pennant, Spirit Of St. Louis, Welcome Home, Blue, White, Felt, 1927, 29 In.	230.00

Photo Card, Lindy & Mother, Car, Blank Back 25.00
Pin, Photograph, Sepia, Celluloid, Silver Frame, 1 1/4 In. 215.00
Pin, Pride Of U.S.A, Picture, Black, White, Celluloid, Ribbon, Metal Plane 150.00
Pin, Spirit Of St. Louis, Brass, 1 1/4 In. 65.00
Pin, Spirit Of St. Louis, Rhinestones 40.00
Pin, Spirit Of St. Louis, Side View, Rhinestones, Original Card 75.00
Pin, Welcome Home Lindy, Picture, Black, White, Celluloid, Ribbon, Metal Plane 70.00
Pin, Welcome Home, Capt. Chas. Lindbergh, Red, White, Blue, Celluloid, 7/8 In. 100.00
Plate, May 1927, 8 1/2 In. 85.00
Plate, Statue Of Liberty, White, Yellow, 1927, 8 In. 95.00
Pocket Watch, Nickel Plated Case, Spirit Of St. Louis Over Ocean 175.00
Poster, Welcome Home Our Lindy, Brown On Tan, Brooklyn Daily Times, 21 x 16 In. ... 990.00
Quilt, Spirit Of St. Louis, Brown Planes, White Ground, Hand Sewn, c.1927, 70 x 84 In. . 865.00
Ribbon, Welcome, Our Hero, Red, Black, White 140.00
Sheet Music, Spirit Of St. Louis March, 1927 .... 35.00
Sheet Music, When Lindy Comes Home, 1927 .... 45.00
Token, Historic Flight, Lucky Lindy, Copper 15.00
Toy, Airplane, Spirit Of St. Louis, Metalcraft, 1930s .... 145.00 to 500.00

LITHOPHANES are porcelain pictures made by casting clay in layers of various thicknesses. When a piece is held to the light, a picture of light and shadow is seen through it. Most lithophanes date from the 1825–1875 period. A few are still being made. Many lithophanes sold today were originally panels for lampshades.

Lamp, Woman Knitting, Child At Knee, Brass Base, KPM, Victorian, 18 In. 2900.00
Lampshade, Bell Shape, Figural & Animal Design, 1800s, 7 In. 490.00
Panel, Girl, Writing Lesson, KPM, 1800s, 3 x 3 5/8 In. 230.00
Panel, Lighthouse, Coast, France, c.1870, 4 x 4 1/4 In. 185.00
Panel, Woman Lying Down, Reading, Landscape, Brass Stand, Frame, 7 x 10 In. 920.00
Panel, Women By Fireplace, Cast-Iron Frame, 4 x 4 In. 300.00

LIVERPOOL, England, was the site of several pottery and porcelain factories from 1716 to 1785. Some earthenware was made with transfer decorations. Sadler and Green made print-decorated wares from 1756. Many of the pieces were made for the American market and feature patriotic emblems, such as eagles, flags, and other special-interest motifs. Liverpool pitchers are always called Liverpool jugs by collectors.

Bowl, Ben Franklin, George Washington, Ship, Black Transfer, 9 x 4 In. 1265.00
Bowl, George Washington, On Horseback, c.1780, 4 x 9 3/4 In. 5830.00
Creamer, Custom Is Second Nature, Scene, 5 1/4 In. 575.00
Jug, 3-Masted Ship, Woman Resting Against Anchor, HG & E, 1801, 9 1/2 In. 805.00
Jug, By Virtue & Valor We Have Freed Our Country, Transfer Printed 5800.00
Jug, Come Ever Smiling Liberty, Black Transfer Scenes, Applied Handle, 6 In. 335.00
Jug, George Washington Portrait, c.1790s 7680.00
Jug, God Speed The Plough, Black Transfer Scenes, Applied Handle, 8 In. 390.00
Jug, Masonic Verse In Wreath, Black On White Transfer, J.D.P., 10 In. 630.00
Jug, Masonic, Pillars, All-Seeing Eye, Veritas Est Intus, c.1800, 7 3/4 x 4 1/4 In. 840.00
Jug, Sailing Ship, Coat Of Arms, Behold Our Support, Black Transfer, 6 3/4 In. 230.00
Jug, Ship, Brig Adventure Of Salem, Washington On Reverse, 9 1/4 In. 4675.00
Jug, Union Of The 2 Great Republics, Black Transfer, England, Early 1800s, 6 5/8 In. ... 2235.00

LLADRO is a Spanish porcelain. Juan, Jose, and Vicente Lladro opened a ceramics workshop in Almacera in 1951. They soon began making figurines in a distinctive, elongated style. In 1958 the factory moved to Tabernes Blanques, Spain. The company makes stoneware and porcelain figurines and vases in limited and unlimited editions. Dates given are first and last years of production.

LLADRÓ°

Figurine, All Aboard, Boy With Train, No. 7619, 1992 .... 150.00
Figurine, Cadet Captain, No. 5404, 12 1/2 In. 165.00
Figurine, First Kiss, Girl & Boy On Bench, No. 7635, 1985-1995 .... 210.00
Figurine, Girl, With Umbrella, No. 7036 .... 315.00
Figurine, High Society, No. 1430, 14 1/4 In. 220.00
Figurine, Idyll, No. 1017, 14 1/4 In. 198.00

Figurine, Maiden Picking Flowers, 8 In. 69.00
Figurine, Morning Delivery, Basset Hound, No. 6398, 6 3/4 In. 175.00
Figurine, Picture Perfect, Girl, With Umbrella, Dog In Lap, No. 7612 . . . .   290.00
Figurine, Playful Dogs, 2 Poodles, Spilled Fruit Basket, No. 1367, c.1980 . . . .   475.00
Figurine, Poodle, No. 39, Standing, 5 3/4 x 6 3/4 In. 225.00
Figurine, Poodle, No. 6557, Standing On Hind Legs, Holding Ball, 9 1/2 x 13 1/2 In. 400.00
Figurine, Tennis Player Boy, No. 4894, 10 1/2 In. 130.00
Figurine, Woman, With Flowers, No. E-2M, 7 1/4 In. 127.00

LOETZ glass was made in many varieties. Johann Loetz bought a glassworks in Austria in 1840. He died in 1848 and his widow ran the company; then in 1879, his grandson took over. Most collectors recognize
the iridescent gold glass similar to Tiffany, but many other types were
made. The firm closed during World War II.

Loetz Austria

Biscuit Jar, Green, Crackled Finish, Silver Plated Rim & Lid, 7 In. 115.00
Bottle, Blue Iridescent, Flanged Rim, Pinched Body, 6 1/2 In. 260.00
Bowl, Gold Iridescent, Papillion, c.1900, 9 1/2 x 4 In. 250.00
Bowl, Green & Gold Iridescent, 6 Applied Handles, 9 1/2 In. 545.00
Bowl, Oil Spot, Gold Iridescent, Blue, 3 1/2 x 10 In. 200.00
Bowl, Yellow Iridescent, Applied Random Threading, Ruffled Edge, 5 x 2 3/4 In. 300.00
Candlestick, Figural, Flower, Blue Iridescent Stems, Opaline Blossom, c.1910, 6 1/4 In. . . . 1065.00
Candlestick, Gold Iridescent, Applied, Rings, Drip Pan, Domed Foot, 15 1/4 In. 1495.00
Compote, Oil Spot, Red Iridescent, Silver Plated, Pedestal, c.1900, 11 x 7 1/2 In. 420.00
Coupe, Chartreuse Iridescent, Dark Brown Flowers, Signed, c.1925, 7 1/4 In. 785.00
Ewer, Oil Spot, Gold Iridescent, Art Nouveau, 4-Footed Northwind Frame, 11 In. 1800.00
Rose Water Sprinkler, Iridescent, Pinched, Bulbous, Flared, Shaped Mouth, 9 1/2 In. 690.00
Vase, Amber Iridescent, Trefoil Rim, Iridescent Blue Overlay, Signed, 5 1/4 In. 1400.00
Vase, Amber Iridescent, Wide Swirling Silver Blue Iridescent Lines, Signed, 7 1/4 In. . . . 2530.00
Vase, Blue Iridescent Pulled Feathers, Green Ground, 10 1/2 In.   920.00
Vase, Blue Iridescent Swirls, Amber, Signed, 6 In. 550.00
Vase, Blue Iridescent Swirls, Dots, Gold Iridescent, Purple, Ruffled Edge, 7 In. 2875.00
Vase, Blue Iridescent, Gold Waves, Dark Amber, Signed Pontil, 7 1/2 In. 2015.00
Vase, Blue Iridescent, Purple Swirls, Flared Rim, Double Conical Stem, Footed, 6 1/2 In. . 1210.00
Vase, Blue Iridescent, White Marbled Design, Waisted, Tapered, Ruffled Edge, 9 In. 220.00
Vase, Candia Silberiris Astartig, Iridescent Amber, 3 Hooked Spouts, 6 In. 1116.00
Vase, Candia Silberiris Decoration, Flared, Ruffled Edge, 14 In. 2940.00
Vase, Candia Silberiris, Gold Iridescent Gold, Rolled Rim, 3 3/8 In. 345.00
Vase, Candia Silberiris, Gold Iridescent, c.1900, 2 In. 225.00
Vase, Candia Silberiris, Gold Iridescent, Magenta, Rolled Rim, 4 1/8 In. 345.00
Vase, Coppelia, Frosty Yellow, Tricornered Rim, Applied Fleur-De-Lis, 3 3/8 In. 160.00
Vase, Craquelle, Emerald Green Iridescent, 4 1/2 In. 115.00
Vase, Crimson Red Iridescent, Ruffled Edge, Stretched Rim, 10 In. 430.00
Vase, Faceted, Green Swirls, Ruffled Edge, Gold Oil Spot Base, 9 1/2 x 7 1/2 In. 460.00
Vase, Federzeichnung, Air Trapped Octopus, Gold Tracery, Signed, 13 In. 2576.00
Vase, Federzeichnung, Round, Brown, Mother-Of-Pearl, Gold Squiggles, 5 1/4 In. 1725.00
Vase, Flower Form, Green Oil Spot, Light Green Stem, Foot, 9 1/2 In. 920.00
Vase, Frog, Green Iridescent, Ribbed, Applied Feet, 7 1/4 In. 2415.00
Vase, Gold Iridescent Over Purple, Cameo, Bulbous, c.1899, 8 1/2 In. 1520.00
Vase, Gold Iridescent, Applied Silver & Gold Iridescent Prunts, 4 3/4 In. 2070.00
Vase, Gold Iridescent, Flat, Craquelle, Wide Neck, Rolled Rim, 5 3/4 x 6 1/2 In. 285.00
Vase, Gold, Purple Iridescent, Pulled Feathers, Egg Shape, Signed, 8 1/2 In. 1315.00
Vase, Green & White, Drips Of Red, Red Streaking On Bottom, Ruffled Edge, 6 3/4 In. . . .   250.00
Vase, Green Iridescent, Applied Lattice Work, Bulbous, Pinched, Flared Rim, 5 In. 880.00
Vase, Green Iridescent, Dimples, Ground Pontil, 5 1/2 In. 144.00
Vase, Green Iridescent, Enameled, Flowering Clover, Spiral Ribs, Egg Shape, 10 In. 500.00
Vase, Green Iridescent, Squat, 4 Applied Handles, Wide Mouth, 3 In. 235.00
Vase, Green Iridescent, Twisted Handle, Footed, 8 In. 575.00
Vase, Green Mottled Glass, White Pulled Decoration, Bulbous, 5 In. 460.00
Vase, Green, Pulled Blue & Purple Drape, Fluted Top, 10 In. 575.00
Vase, Iridescent, Blue Pulled Design, 3-Footed Copper Stand, 7 3/4 In. 920.00
Vase, Jack-In-The-Pulpit, Gold Iridescent, Green Swirl, 13 1/4 In. 470.00
Vase, Light Blue Iridescent, Silver Flower & Ribbon Overlay, Art Nouveau, 8 In. 2280.00
Vase, Marmorierte, Agate, Painted Collar, Oval, c.1900, 4 1/2 In. . . . . *Illus*   460.00

Loetz, Vase,
Marmorierte, Agate,
Painted Collar, Oval,
c.1900, 4 1/2 In.

Loetz, Vase, Papillon,
Seashell, Green, Iridescent
Blue, c.1900, 7 In.

Vase, Marmorierte, Malachite, Flower Garlands, Gold & White Enamel, 5 3/4 In. 230.00
Vase, Moon Crater, Gold Iridescent, 6 In. 325.00
Vase, Neptune, Silver Green, Tricornered Rim, Pinched Body, Thorn Branches, 4 In. 345.00
Vase, Octopus, Swirls, Scrolls, Enameled, Leaves, Vines, Brown Over White, 10 1/4 In. . . .   2070.00
Vase, Oil Spot, Amber To Rose, Blue, Tricornered Rim, c.1900, 7 1/2 In. 1065.00
Vase, Oil Spot, Gold & Carmel, Bulbous Base, Ruffled Edge, 11 1/2 In. 460.00
Vase, Oil Spot, Gold Iridescent, Pinched Top, 6 1/2 In. 460.00
Vase, Oil Spot, Green, Blue Iridescent, Blue Ground, 4 Waist Indentations, 5 In. 1035.00
Vase, Oil Spot, Melon Ribbed, Peacock Blue Trails, 3 1/2 In. 95.00
Vase, Oil Spot, Purple & Blue Iridescent, Ruffled Rim, 11 In. 230.00
Vase, Oil Spot, Silvery Blue Iridescent, Amber, Bulbous, Irregular Fluted Rim, 5 In. 275.00
Vase, Opal Amber Iridescent, Dimpled Shoulders, Trefoil Rim, Iridized, Pulled Coils, 8 In.   460.00
Vase, Opalescent, Green, Gold, Swirls, Waisted, Tapered Neck, Rolled Rim, Signed, 5 In. .   415.00
Vase, Papillon, Amber Shaded To Blue, Oil Spot, c.1900, 8 1/2 x 9 In. 950.00
Vase, Papillon, Blue Iridescent, 3 In. 345.00
Vase, Papillon, Green, Dimpled Sides, 3 Applied Handles, 5 1/4 In. 315.00
Vase, Papillon, Green, Quatrefoil Rim, Pinched Body, 6 1/4 In. 345.00
Vase, Papillon, Green, Rainbow Highlights, Irregular Tricornered Rim, 5 3/4 In. 315.00
Vase, Papillon, Seashell, Green, Iridescent Blue, c.1900, 7 In. . . . . *Illus*   3335.00
Vase, Papillon, Yellow Iridescent, Cobalt, Flared Rim, 6 x 8 In. 400.00
Vase, Phanomen, Applied Silver Threading & Flowers, 4 In. 4115.00
Vase, Phanomen, Green Iridescent, Squat, 3 1/2 x 5 In. 1610.00
Vase, Platinum, Purple Highlights, Green, Shouldered, Textured Surface, 6 1/2 In. 400.00
Vase, Purple Iridescent, Green Highlights, Slender Neck, Bulbous, 12 1/2 In. 460.00
Vase, Purple Iridescent, Green, Blue, Gold Loopings & Trailings, Flared, Signed, 14 In. . . .   715.00
Vase, Purple, Pulled Blue, Green, Gold, Shouldered, Flared Rim, 9 1/4 In. 2000.00
Vase, Rusticana, Thumbprint Pontil, 4 In. 175.00
Vase, Seashell, Gold Iridescent, Seaweed, Rigaree Foot, c.1900, 14 In. 1900.00
Vase, Seashell, Spiral, Gold Iridescent, Coral Base, 9 In. 990.00
Vase, Silver Blue Iridescent Threading, Amethyst Ground, 6 1/4 In. 260.00
Vase, Tango, Tangerine, Amethyst Design, Oval, Flattened Rim, Signed, 8 1/2 In. 275.00
Vase, Yellow Pulled Green Iridescent Tendrils, Slender, Shouldered, 8 1/4 In. 635.00
Vase, Yellow, Blue, Metallic Inclusions, Woven Design, Flared, Clear Handles, 11 In. 620.00

LONE RANGER, a fictional character, was introduced on the radio in
1932. Over three thousand shows were produced before the series
ended in 1954. In 1938, the first Lone Ranger movie was made.
Television shows were started in 1949 and are still seen on some sta-
tions. The Lone Ranger appears on many products and was even the
name of a restaurant chain for several years.

Badge, 2 Shades Brass Luster, Starburst Design, Round Up Products, c.1950, 1 1/2 In. . . .   3065.00
Badge, Die-Cut Star, Brass Luster, Supplee, c.1938, 1 3/8 In. 145.00
Badge, Lone Ranger's Face, Tin, Lithograph, Crescent Toy Co., c.1966, 2 In. 100.00
Badge, Safety Scout, Indian Shooting Bow, Silvercup Bread, c.1934, 3 5/8 x 5 3/8 In. 45.00
Badge Set, Tin, Mask, Sheriff Badge, Gun, Japan, 1960s 10.00
Bank, Book, Leather, Brass, Embossed, Knights Life Insurance Co., 1 x 3 x 3 1/2 In. 150.00
Book, Hi-Yo Silver, Lone Ranger To The Rescue, c.1937, 8 1/2 x 11 3/8 In., 48 Pages . . .   175.00
Book, Lone Ranger Rides, Hardcover, Putnam Sons, NY, c.1941, 5 1/4 x 7 1/4 In. 150.00
Cap Gun, Cast Iron, Replaced Wood Grips, Kilgore, 8 1/2 In. 55.00

Card, Chief Scout, 2nd Degree, Premium, Silvercup Bread, c.1934, 3 3/4 x 7 1/2 In. 135.00
Card, Flasher, Lone Ranger, Tonto, Firing Guns, 2 x 2 1/2 In. 45.00
Card, Safety Club Pledge, 2-Sided, Butter Nut Bakery, c.1938, 3 1/4 x 5 In. 230.00
Costume, Cowboy, Vest, Chaps, Holster, TLR Inc., Box, c.1930, 12 1/2 x 13 In. 375.00
Cup, Lone Ranger & Tonto Riding Horses, Milk Glass, White, Handle, 2 1/2 x 3 1/2 In. ... 45.00
Figurine, Lone Ranger, White Hat, Pink Neckerchief, Flat Back, Plaster, 14 1/4 In. 75.00
Flashlight, Signal Siren, Lithograph, Battery Operated, Usalite, Box, c.1955 ......115.00 to 407.00
Game, Board, Hi-Yo Silver, Box 175.00
Game, Board, Milton Bradley, 1966 .... 70.00
Game, Parker Brothers, 1950s 125.00
Game, Target, Marx, 27 In. 66.00
Game, Target, Metal Gun, Darts, Box, Marx, 1946 .... 550.00
Gum Wrapper, Lone Ranger, Hi-Yo Silver, Bowman Gum, 4 1/2 x 6 In. 330.00
Holster, Belt, Lone Ranger, Leather, White, Plastic Jewels, Fringe, c.1950s, 3 1/2 x 29 In. 87.00
Lucky Piece, Silvers Lucky Horseshoe, Brass Luster, 1938, 1 1/4 In. 35.00
Mask, Paper, Die Cut, Merita Bread, TLR Inc., c.1940, 8 1/2 In. 199.00
Movie Viewer Set, Lone Ranger Rides Again, Viewer, 3 Films, Acme Plastic Toys, Box .. 100.00
Neckerchief, Steer Slide, Lone Ranger, Silver, Silk, c.1950s, 17 1/2 In. 65.00
Newspaper, Lone Ranger Roundup, Safety Club, Vol. 1, Bond Bread, 8 x 10 3/4 In. 150.00
Newspaper, Lone Ranger Roundup, Safety Club, Vol. 2, Bond Bread, 7 1/2 x 10 In. 100.00
Pencil, Floating, Mechanical, Red Barrel, Progressive Products, Late 1940s, 5 3/8 In. 150.00
Pencil Case, Lone Ranger Firing Gun, Outlaws, Blue, Textured, 5 x 8 1/2 In. 75.00
Photograph, Lone Ranger, On Silver, TV Star For Nestles Quik, Glossy, 8 x 9 3/4 In. ... 110.00
Picture, Lone Ranger, On Silver, Twirling Lasso, Signed, To Oscar, 7-Up, 8 x 10 In. 95.00
Picture, Lone Ranger, Tonto, On Horse, Look Into Sun, Horlicks Malted Milk, 8 x 10 In. . 65.00
Pin, Lone Ranger On Silver, Brass Luster, TLR, 1939, 1 1/4 In. 35.00
Pin, Lone Ranger Radio Station, Charleston's Pioneer, WCFC 1390, c.1938, 1 1/2 In. 100.00
Pin, Lone Ranger Wafers, Smiths Food Group, Wrather Corp., 1966, 1 1/4 In. 95.00
Pin, Silver's Lucky Horseshoe, TLR, 1939, 1 1/2 In. 65.00
Postcard, Lone Ranger Twirling Lasso, Butter Nut Bread Premium, 3 3/8 x 5 5/8 In. 235.00
Poster, Lone Ranger & Lost City Of Gold, Clayton Moore, 1958, 27 x 41 In. 575.00
Poster, Lone Ranger, Tonto, Horses, Signed, Clayton Moore, Jay Silverheels, 24 x 30 In. .. 616.00
Program, Arena Thrill Winter Circus, Cleveland Arena, 1940, 8 1/2 x 11 In., 8 Pages 1405.00
Program, Rodeo, Madison Square Garden, 1951, 8 1/2 x 11 In., 48 Pages 115.00
Radio, Lone Ranger, Silver, Dial, Bakelite, Handle, c.1938, 6 3/4 x 14 1/2 x 9 In. 2500.00
Ring, Army Air Corps, Silver Luster, Kix Premium, 1942 .... 229.00
Ring, Atomic Bomb, Lightning Bolt, Atoms, Kix Premium, 1948 .... 475.00
Ring, Flashlight, Kix Premium, General Mills, 1948, 1 3/4 In. ....115.00 to 145.00
Sign, Merita Bread, Tin, 24 x 36 In. 495.00
Snow Globe, Red Shirt, Black Pants, Yellow Base, Plastic, c.1950, 2 1/2 In. 25.00
Toy, Bullet, 45 Caliber, Secret Compartment, Aluminum, Kix Premium, 1947, 1 3/4 In. 40.00
Toy, Gun, First Click, Lone Ranger, Smiling, Black, Tin Lithograph, Marx, 1938, 7 1/4 In. 95.00
Toy, Hi-Yo Silver, Lone Ranger, On Silver, Lasso, Tin, Windup, Marx, Box, 1938, 8 In. .. 963.00
Toy, Pistol, Flashlight, Instruction Sheet, Mailer, Box, Cheerios, c.1949, 5 1/2 In. 225.00
Toy, Range Rider, Tin Lithograph, Rocker Base, Windup, Marx, Box, 1938, 11 In. .273.00 to 588.00
Vanity Set, Brush, Comb, Hi-Yo Silver, No. 2807, Box 125.00
Wallet, Bullet, Spur, Mask, Gun, Leather, Brown, Embossed, Zipper, 3 1/2 x 4 1/2 In. ... 75.00

LONGWY Workshop of Longwy, France, first made ceramic wares in 1798. The workshop is still in business. Most of the ceramic pieces found today are glazed with many colors to resemble cloisonne or other enameled metal. Many pieces were made with stylized figures and Art Deco designs. The factory used a variety of marks.

Box, Birds Under Crowns, Silver Plated Cover, Bail, 4 3/8 In. 375.00
Box, Flowers, Bowtie Shape, Cover, 2 1/8 x 5 In. 259.00
Box, Flowers, Round, Cover, 2 x 3 5/8 In. 230.00
Charger, 2 Flying Ducks, Sunset, Art Deco Design, 15 In. 1150.00
Charger, Birds Perched Over Water, 14 1/2 In. 330.00
Charger, Persian Mosaic, Signed, c.1880, 17 In. 500.00
Planter, Flowers, Brass Mounts, 8 3/4 x 11 1/4 In. 2070.00
Plate, Copper Luster Flowers, Ivory Cartouche, Cobalt Border, 8 1/4 In. 140.00
Plate, Fish, Green, Gray, Geometric Blue Field, 8 3/4 In. 250.00
Plate, Flower Cartouche, Ivory Ground, Flower Borders, Scroll & Snowflakes, 9 In. 165.00

Plate, Flowers, Japanese Style, 9 5/8 In.	220.00
Plate, Sloped Square Shape, Round Foot Ring, 10 x 10 In.	110.00
Platter, Serving, Flowers, Scalloped Rim, Blue Field, 11 x 9 1/2 In.	220.00
Trivet, Bird, Flowering Branches, Wood Base, 11 In.	315.00
Trivet, Woman, Tree, Large Flower, Blue, Red, Amber, Stamped, 8 In.	230.00
Vase, Black Design, Blue Field, Bottle Shape, Wood Stand, 11 3/4 In.	715.00
Vase, Flowers, Multicolored, Turquoise Crackle Glaze, Gargoyle Handles, 13 In.	1095.00
Vase, Geometric, Multicolored, 6 1/2 In.	978.00
Vase, Primavara, Black Art Deco Design, Blue Ground, 12 1/2 In.	860.00

LONHUDA Pottery Company of Steubenville, Ohio, was organized in 1892 by William Long, W. H. Hunter, and Alfred Day. Brown underglaze slip-decorated pottery was made. The firm closed in 1896. The company used many marks; the earliest included the letters *LPCO*.

LONHUDA

Vase, Hooked Fish, On Shoulder, Bulbous, Marked, 8 1/4 x 5 3/4 In.	575.00
Vase, Yellow Flowers, Standard Glaze, Applied Handles, Marked, 6 In.	290.00

LOTUS WARE was made by the Knowles, Taylor & Knowles Company of East Liverpool, Ohio, from 1890 to 1900. Lotus Ware, a thin porcelain which resembles Belleek, was sometimes decorated outside the factory. Other types of ceramics that were made by the Knowles, Taylor & Knowles Company are listed under KTK.

Biscuit Jar, Cover, Fishnet, Flower Panels, Stamped, 6 3/4 In.	316.00
Biscuit Jar, Cover, Pink Flowers, Green Vines, Raised Net, KTK Co., 7 x 4 In.	400.00
Bowl, Flowers, Gold, Ruffled, Beaded Rim, Stamped, 4 1/4 In.	315.00
Bowl, Pink & Yellow Roses, Gilt, Applied Medallions, Beaded, Ruffled Rim, 4 1/2 In.	400.00
Bowl, Raised Flowers, Reticulated Medallions, Beaded Gilt Rim, Stamped, 4 In.	259.00
Bowl, Rose, Gold Highlights, Gilt Beaded, Ruffled Rim, Stamped, 4 1/4 In.	170.00
Bowl, Roses, Green Leaves, Thorny Stems, Bulbous, Beaded Gilt Ring, Stamped, 4 1/4 In.	200.00
Ewer, Pink, Yellow Flowers, Leaves, Mottled Olive Ground, Applied Handle, 10 In.	200.00
Ewer, Vines, Leaves, Flowers, Pale Green, White, Etruscan, Bulbous, Stamped, 9 1/2 In.	259.00
Jug, Daisy Band, White Shaded To Apricot, Gilt, Applied Twig Stem, Stamped, 5 1/4 In.	115.00
Jug, Fishnet, Applied Twig Handle, Valenciennes, Stamped, 3 3/4 In.	175.00
Jug, Green Fishnet, Alternating Flowers, Gilt, Applied Twig Handle, Stamped, 4 1/4 In.	460.00
Jug, Roses, Red, Yellow, Pink, Leaves, Thorns, Applied Twig Handle, Stamped, 3 3/4 In.	115.00
Jug, White, Gold Fishnet, Bulbous, Applied Twig Handle, Gilt, Stamped, 3 3/4 In.	144.00
Tray, Shell, Hand Painted Flowers, Ruffled Rim, Gilt, Stylized Branch Base, 8 1/2 In.	210.00
Tray, Shell, Wild Flower, Over Pink Blush, Ruffled Edge, Gilt Footed, DF, 8 1/2 In.	295.00
Vase, Baluster, Fluted, Applied Scroll Handles, Cremonian, Stamped, 6 In.	144.00
Vase, Blue, Over Fuji Mum, Thebian, Double Gourd, Gilt, Stamped, 8 1/4 In.	345.00
Vase, Enameled Flowers, Curved Arms, Round Neck, Geometric, Gilt, Stamped, 7 3/4 In.	290.00
Vase, Flared, Mold Decorated Neck, Applied Handles, Bulbous, Parmian, Stamped, 10 In.	144.00
Vase, Leaves, Berries, Applied Gilt Scrolled Handles, Bulbous, Flared, Stamped, 8 1/4 In.	400.00
Vase, Pale Green, White Flowers, Vines, Leaves, Bulbous, Umbrian, Stamped, 8 1/4 In.	750.00
Vase, Violets, Green Leaves, Bulbous, Handles, Venetian, Stamped, 8 In.	200.00

LOW art tiles were made by the J. and J. G. Low Art Tile Works of Chelsea, Massachusetts, from 1877 to 1902. A variety of art and other tiles were made. Some of the tiles were made by a process called *natural*, some were hand modeled, and some were made mechanically.

J.&J.G.LOW

Tile, First Love, Older Couple, Brown Glaze, Signed, Arthur Osborne, 6 In.	289.00
Tile, Maiden's Head, Profile, Brown Glossy Glaze, Brass Frame, Round, 4 1/2 In.	115.00
Tile, Medieval Violin Player, Embossed, Ivy Wreath, Green Glaze, Stamped, 6 In. Diam.	200.00
Tile, Old Man, Nunovam Satis, Cobalt Blue Glaze, Arthur Osborne, Stamped, 6 In.	144.00
Tile, Tree Branches, Brown, Embossed, Aesthetic Movement Design, Stamped, 6 In.	145.00
Tile, Woman, Bearded Man, Embossed, Amber Glossy Glaze, Frame, 6 In., Pair	115.00

LOWESTOFT was a factory in Suffolk, England, which from 1757 to 1802 made many commemorative gift pieces and small, dated, inscribed pieces of soft paste porcelain. Related items may be found in the Chinese Export category.

Mug, Central Crest, Crown, Roses, Blue & White, Dragon Handle, 4 3/4 In.	920.00

LOY-NEL-ART, see McCoy category.

LUNCH BOXES and lunch pails have been used to carry lunches to school or work since the nineteenth century. Today, most collectors want either early tobacco advertising boxes or children's lunch boxes made since the 1930s. These boxes are made of metal or plastic. Boxes listed here include the original Thermos bottle inside the box unless otherwise indicated. Movie, television, and cartoon characters may be found in their own categories. Tobacco tin pails and lunch boxes are listed in the Advertising category.

LUNCH BOX, A-Team, Orange, Plastic, Canadian Thermos Products, 1983, 8 x 10 x 5 In. . . .	25.00
Astronauts, On Moon, Spaceships, Metal, Dome, c.1963	220.00
Barbie, Lunch Bag, Pink, Flowers, Vinyl, White Handle	65.00
Barbie, Ponytail, Black Vinyl, 2 Compartments, 1962	150.00
Barbie & Francie, Black Vinyl, Black Handle, Metal Closure, 1965	95.00
Barbie & Midge, Brunch Bag, Black Vinyl, Metal Zipper, 1963	105.00
Casey Jones, Metal, Dome, Universal, c.1960	290.00
Central Station, Fire Safety Rules, American Thermos Products, 1959, 7 x 9 x 4 1/4 In. . . .	360.00
Children Playing, Tin Lithograph, Square, Double Swing Handles, 7 In.	85.00
Fall Guy, Metal, Aladdin, 1981	45.00
Girl & Poodle, School House, Blue, Vinyl, Ardee, c.1960, 6 1/2 x 8 1/4 x 3 1/2 In. . . .	75.00
Hanna-Barbera, Funtastic World, Metal, King Seeley Thermos, 1977, 6 3/4 x 8 In.	45.00
Hogan's Heroes, Metal, Dome, Aladdin, 1966	375.00
Incredible Hulk, Metal, Aladdin, 1978	39.00
Jetsons, Metal, Dome, Aladdin, 1963	825.00
Julia, Metal, King Seeley Thermos, 1969	25.00
Lance Link, Metal, King Seeley Thermos, 1971	50.00
Lost In Space, Metal, Dome, King Seeley Thermos, 1967, 7 x 9 x 4 1/4 In.	650.00
Man From U.N.C.L.E., Metal, King Seeley Thermos, 1966	250.00
Miss America, Metal, Aladdin, 1972	415.00
Munsters, Metal, King Seeley Thermos, 1965 . . . . .172.00 to	225.00
Pete's Picture Party, 2 Kids, Balloons, Vinyl, Flasher, c.1960, 7 x 9 x 3 1/2 In.	150.00
Porky's Lunch Wagon, Metal, Dome, American Thermos, 1959, 6 1/2 x 9 In.	60.00
Red Barn, Metal, Dome, American Thermos, c.1957, 7 x 9 x 4 1/2 In.	40.00
Rough Rider, Metal, Aladdin, 1973, 7 x 8 x 4 In.	45.00
Tom Corbett, Space Cadet, Metal, Aladdin, 1954, 7 x 8 x 4 In.	350.00
U.S. Space Shuttle Challenger, Vinyl, Nappe-Babcock, 1986, 8 x 10 x 4 In.	50.00
Voyage To The Bottom Of The Sea, Metal, Aladdin, 1967	220.00
Wagon Train, Metal, King Seeley Thermos, 1964	175.00
Washington Redskins, Helmet, Metal, Okay Industries, c.1970, 7 x 9 x 3 1/2 In.	95.00
Wild Wild West, Metal, Aladdin, 1969	225.00
Zorro, Scenes, Tooled Leather Design, Metal, Aladdin, c.1958, 7 x 8 x 4 In.	173.00
LUNCH BOX THERMOS, Little Miss Dutch, Girl Rolling Hoop, Universal, c.1959, 7 3/4 In. . .	40.00
Munsters, Metal, Tan Cup, King Seeley Thermos, c.1965, 6 1/2 In.	67.00
Pebbles & Bamm-Bamm, Teenagers, Aladdin, 1971, 6 5/8 In.	30.00
Rifleman, On Horseback, Aladdin, 1961, 6 1/2 In.	95.00
Treasure Chest, Metal, Aladdin, 1961, 6 1/2 In.	145.00

LUSTER glaze was meant to resemble copper, silver, or gold. The term *luster* includes any piece with some luster trim. It has been used since the sixteenth century. Some of the luster found today was made during the nineteenth century. The metallic glazes are applied on pottery. The finished color depends on the combination of the clay color and the glaze. Blue, orange, gold, and pearlized luster decorations were used by Japanese and German firms in the early 1900s. Tea Leaf pieces have their own category.

Copper, Pitcher, Canary Band, White Reserves, Pink Transfer Scenes, 6 1/4 In.	115.00
Copper, Pitcher, General Jackson, Hero Of New Orleans, 5 1/2 In.	4750.00
Copper, Pitcher, Kiddle & Bryan Longton Clock, Yellow Band, 5 1/2 In.	85.00
Copper, Pitcher, Lafayette, 4 In.	440.00
Copper, Pitcher, Lafayette, Cornwallis, Black Transfer, Yellow Band, c.1871, 6 1/2 x 5 In.	250.00
Copper, Pitcher, Women Playing Badminton, 3 Cavettos, Chartreuse Band, England, 9 In.	545.00
Fairyland luster is included in the Wedgwood category.	
Pink, Figurine, Poodle, Show Clip, England, 2 1/2 x 3 1/2 In.	90.00
Pink, Plate, Central Butterfly Decoration, 19th Century, 4 In.	115.00

Pink, Teapot, Figures, Landscape, 7 1/2 In. 150.00
Silver, Mug, Blue Transfer, Hunter, 2 Hounds, Village Landscape, England, 3 3/8 In. 295.00
Silver, Mug, Flower Banner, Porter, Pearlware, Applied Angle Handle, c.1820, 3 1/4 In. . . .   210.00
Silver, Tea Set, Goose Neck Coffeepot, Teapot, Water Pot, 6 Piece 280.00
Sunderland luster pieces are listed in the Sunderland category.
Tea Leaf luster pieces are listed in the Tea Leaf Ironstone category.

LUSTRE ART GLASS Company was founded in Long Island, New York, in 1920 by Conrad Vahlsing and Paul Frank. The company made lampshades and globes that are almost indistinguishable from those made by Quezal. Most of the shades made by the company were unmarked.

Shade, Trumpet, Internal Ivory & Green Swirl, Signed, 5 1/8 In. 230.00

LUSTRES are mantel decorations or pedestal vases with many hanging glass prisms. The name really refers to the prisms, and it is proper to refer to a single glass prism as a lustre. Either spelling, luster or lustre, is correct.

Amber Cut To Clear, Etched Flowers, 8 Pendants, Bohemia, 12 1/2 In., Pair 400.00
Blue Opaline, Crystal Drops, Fleur-De-Lis, Pinched Waist, c.1890, 11 In., Pair 420.00
Clear, Flowers, Gilt, Hanging Crystals, Late 19th Century, 14 x 7 In. 420.00
Clear, Trumpet Shape, Serrated Rim, Prisms, 7 1/2 In., Pair 500.00
Cobalt Blue, Gilt, Accents, Crystal Prisms, 20th Century, 10 x 5 In. 225.00
Cranberry Glass, Gold, Enamel Flowers, Cut Crystal Prisms, 14 1/2 x 7 1/2 In. 390.00
Emerald Green, Gilt Scrolls, Enamel Flowers, Scalloped Rim, 10 Pendants, 14 In., Pair . .   430.00
Green Glass, Trumpet Shape, Gilt Enameling, Continental, 1800s, 13 5/8 In. 175.00
Milk Glass, Emerald Green Cased, Floral Panels, Prisms, 14 1/2 In., Pair 1760.00
Pink, Scrolling Flowers, Hanging Cut Crystal Prisms, 20th Century, 14 1/2 x 7 In., Pair . .   530.00
Ruby, Enameled Flowers, Pendants, Scalloped Rim, Bohemia, 14 1/2 In., Pair . . . . . . *Illus*   1325.00
White Opaque, Enameled Flowers & Strawberries, 8 Pendants, 11 In., Pair 127.00

MAASTRICHT, Holland, was the city where Petrus Regout established the De Sphinx pottery in 1836. The firm was noted for its transfer-printed earthenware. Many factories in Maastricht are still making ceramics.

Bowl, Multicolored, Spatterware, Holland, c.1890, 14 1/2 In. 308.00
Bowl, Vegetable, Willow, c.1929, 8 5/8 x 2 In. 25.00
Plate, Dinner, Willow, c.1935, 8 3/4 x 1 In. 25.00
Plate, Willow, Petrus Regout, Holland, c.1930, 9 In. 65.00
Plate, Willow, Petrus Regout, Marked, 9 In. 25.00

MACINTYRE, see Moorcroft category.

MAIZE glass was made by W.L. Libbey & Son Company of Toledo, Ohio, after 1889. The glass resembled an ear of corn. The leaves were usually green, but some pieces were made with blue or red leaves. The kernels of corn were light yellow, white, or light green.

Celery Vase, Ivory, Green Leaves, 6 1/4 In. 45.00
Tumbler, Ivory, Yellow & Gold Leaves, 4 In. 80.00

The value of lustres with hanging prisms is not changed if a few of the prisms have been replaced.

Lustres, Ruby, Enameled Flowers, Pendants, Scalloped Rim, Bohemian, 14 1/2 In., Pair

MAJOLICA is a general term for any pottery glazed with an opaque tin enamel that conceals the color of the clay body. It has been made since the fourteenth century. Today's collector is most likely to find Victorian majolica. The heavy, colorful ware is rarely marked. Some famous makers include Wedgwood; Minton; Griffen, Smith and Hill (marked *Etruscan*); and Chesapeake Pottery (marked *Avalon* or *Clifton*). Majolica made by Wedgwood is listed in the Wedgwood category.

Asparagus Stand, Rectangular Tray, Arched Dish, Minton, c.1868, 10 In.	1000.00
Basket, Basket Weave, Flower Handle, Yellow, 9 3/4 x 7 1/4 In.	300.00
Basket, Blackberry Ribbon & Bow, 8 x 7 1/2 In.	280.00
Basket, Floral, Turquoise, Pink Interior, Bamboo Handle, 10 1/2 In.	280.00
Basket, Flowers, Scalloped Rim, Continental, 14 x 9 In.	630.00
Basket, Greek Eye Border, Lavender, Bamboo Style Handle, 7 3/4 x 10 3/4 x 6 3/4 In.	770.00
Basket, Pond Lily, Holdcroft, 10 1/4 In.	310.00
Basket, Shell & Seaweed, Rope Handle, 8 3/4 In.	715.00
Bell, Monk With Stein, Figural, Continental, 10 1/2 In.	65.00
Bottle, Cat, In Fancy Suit, Playing Mandolin, Figural, Continental, 12 1/2 In.	2090.00
Bowl, 6 Applied Figural Handles, Italy, 1900s, 10 In.	40.00
Bowl, Basket Weave, Twig Footed, Holdcroft, 9 In.	120.00
Bowl, Blackberry, Dragonfly, Butterfly, Brown, Yellow Rim, Footed, 3 1/4 x 10 In.	180.00
Bowl, Fan & Flower Decoration, Pedestal, 1800s, 5 1/2 x 9 1/2 In.	127.00
Bowl, Figural, Shell On Coral, Seaweed, Cobalt Blue, George Jones, 7 1/2 x 11 In.	1540.00
Bowl, Leaf Design, Green & White Ground, 5 1/2 In., 6 Piece	400.00
Bowl, Shell & Seaweed, Etruscan, 8 1/4 In.	280.00
Bowl, Strawberries, Blue Interior, Yellow Ground, Footed, 5 1/2 x 9 1/2 In.	180.00
Bowl, Swan Ends, Oval, Handles, 13 1/2 x 7 In.	495.00
Box, Cover, Asparagus Shape, 8 1/2 In.	300.00
Bread Tray, Eat Thy Bread With Thankfulness, 13 1/2 x 11 1/4 In.	145.00
Bread Tray, Shell & Seaweed, Impressed, Etruscan, c.1875, 13 1/2 In.	690.00
Butter, Cover, Cow & Wheat, Turquoise, George Jones, 7 1/2 x 4 In.	2310.00
Butter, Water Lily, Insert, Samuel Lear	175.00
Butter Chip, Ivy, Yellow Center	65.00
Butter Chip, Pond Lily, Green, Etruscan, Griffen, Smith & Hill	90.00
Butter Chip, Seaweed & Shell	215.00
Butter Tub, Cover, Relief Harvest Items, Figural	28.00
Butter Tub, Walnuts	35.00
Cake Stand, Green Leaves, White Ground, George Jones, c.1875, 9 In.	489.00
Candelabrum, Blue Ceramic Body, Brass Details, Ribbed, 40 In., Pair	290.00
Candlestick, Happy Hooligan, At Lamp Post, Figural, 6 1/2 In.	55.00
Card Tray, Vine Border, Leaves, Flowers, Oval, Griffen, Smith & Hill, 2 x 8 x 7 In.	210.00
Centerpiece, Green Leaves, Pink Ground, Rustic Base, Etruscan, c.1875, 9 1/2 In.	200.00
Chamber Jar, Albino, Haynes Pottery, 10 1/2 In.	40.00
Charger, Roman Military Leader, Trophies, Cobalt Blue Ground, Italy, 15 1/2 In., Pair	635.00
Cheese Keeper, Albino Basket Weave, Napkin & Apple Blossom, George Jones, 5 1/2 In.	450.00
Cheese Keeper, Begonia Leaf, Basket Weave, 6 1/2 x 10 In.	495.00
Cheese Keeper, Blackberry & Cow, Turquoise, 11 1/2 In.	785.00
Cheese Keeper, Fern, Pond Lily Handle, France, 11 1/2 In.	880.00
Cheese Keeper, Rustic, Flowers, 6 In.	360.00
Compote, 3 Dolphins & Shell, Holdcroft, 14 In.	670.00
Compote, Chestnut Leaf On Napkin, George Jones, 9 1/4 In.	450.00
Compote, Maple Leaf, Green, Brown, Yellow Basket Weave Ground, 2 1/2 x 9 1/2 In.	230.00
Compote, Shell, 11 x 14 In.	695.00
Creamer, Bird, Iris, Etruscan, 3 3/4 In.	165.00
Creamer, Conch Shell, Round Base, Pink Interior, 4 x 6 In.	430.00
Creamer, Hawthorne, Etruscan, 4 1/2 In.	99.00
Creamer, Leaf & Fern, 3 In.	120.00
Creamer, Red Daisy, Turquoise, 3 In.	80.00
Creamer, Shell & Seaweed, Griffen, Smith & Hill, 3 1/2 In.	170.00 to 300.00
Creamer, Swan Shape, Neck Forms Handle, Brown & Green Glaze, 4 x 6 12 In.	145.00
Cross, Mottled Green & Brown, Applied Magnolias, Pink, Green, 23 1/2 In.	280.00
Cup & Saucer, Basketry, Yellow, Green, Brown Leaves	35.00
Cup & Saucer, Bunny, Signed, Higgins & Seiter, c.1900, 3 1/2 x 8 1/2 In.	420.00
Cup & Saucer, Flowers, Blue Ground, Pink Interior, George Jones	1495.00

Decanter, Parrot, Figural, 12 3/4 In.	90.00
Desk Stand, Wooden Trough, Fronted By Well, Figural, Early 20th Century, 6 In.	120.00
Dish, Condiment, Cover, Oyster Shape, Barnacle Handle, 4 x 5 1/4 In.	230.00
Dish, Cover, Fence, Flowers, 11 x 11 In.	95.00
Dish, Game, Mottled, Liner, England, 8 3/4 In.	385.00
Dish, Game, Quail On Cover, Leaves, Ferns, Rabbits, Cobalt Blue, George Jones, 11 In.	4675.00
Dish, Leaf Shape, Blue, Brown, Yellow, Green, Griffen, Smith & Hill, 6 1/2 x 8 1/2 In.	145.00
Dog, Whippet, Seated, Multicolored, Cobalt Blue Collar, Italy, 13 1/2 In., Pair	865.00
Dolphin, Upraised Head & Tail, Mottled Glaze, c.1900, 33 x 36 In.	3290.00
Egg Basket, Picket Fence, Floral & Berry, 6 1/2 In.	112.00
Egg Stand, Basket Shape, Handle, Yellow Crisscross Pattern, 6 1/2 x 9 x 6 1/2 In.	259.00
Eggcup Set, Pineapple, 6-Cup Holder, 6 x 9 In.	990.00
Figurine, Blackamoor, Boy, With Large Hat, Lying Down Eating Watermelon, 6 In.	90.00
Figurine, Man, With Backpack, 21 In.	165.00
Figurine, Musicians, Man Holding Bagpipe, Woman Holding Guitar, 12 In., Pair	275.00
Figurine, Woman, Picking Fruit From Tree, Impressed Number On Base, 26 In.	140.00
Figurine, Woman, Seated On Rock, Feeding Swan, Art Nouveau, 9 1/4 x 11 In.	220.00
Garden Seat, Blackamoor, Holdcroft	6050.00
Garden Seat, Cobalt Blue Top, Round, Applied Vine, Flowers, 21 x 15 In.	770.00
Garden Seat, Ears Of Corn, Wheat, Lavender Ribbons, Bows, John Adams, 19 In.	3850.00
Humidor, Fish, Purple Smoking Jacket, Figural, 6 1/2 In.	770.00
Humidor, Indian Chief, 9 In.	66.00
Humidor, Indian Chief, c.1900, 6 In.	505.00
Humidor, Indian, Headdress Lid, Figural, Multicolored, 6 In.	115.00
Humidor, Man With Yellow Cap, Figural, 4 3/4 In.	45.00
Humidor, Old Friends, Blackamoor, Seated On Pillow, 7 1/2 In.	140.00
Humidor, Penguin, Figural, 7 In.	165.00
Humidor, Singing Dog, Blue Smoking Jacket, Guitar, Figural, 8 1/2 In.	715.00
Humidor, Sultan, Figural, Continental, 7 1/2 In.	110.00
Jar, Bear, Beehive, Leaves, Ferns, High Relief, 8 1/2 In.	140.00
Jardiniere, Bird's Nest, Stylized Tree Trunk, Early 20th Century, 8 5/8 In.	120.00
Jardiniere, Blackberry Twig Footed, Turquoise Ground, George Jones, 7 In.	1760.00
Jardiniere, Chestnut Leaf & Flowers, Twig Feet, George Jones, 9 In.	2240.00
Jardiniere, Cobalt Blue, Woman's Face On Each Side, Oval, Marked GB, 17 x 11 In.	310.00
Jardiniere, Egg Shape, Loop Handles, Stylized Flowers, Early 1900s, 16 In.	150.00
Jardiniere, King Fisher, Oval, Cobalt Blue Accents, France, 14 x 7 1/2 In.	330.00
Jardiniere, Multicolored, Dragon Handle, Cobalt Blue Ground, Oval, c.1885, 9 x 19 3/4 In.	200.00
Jardiniere, Pedestal, Applied Dragons, Green, Scalloped Rim, 36 x 13 1/2 In.	980.00
Jardiniere, Pedestal, Brown, Green, Pink, Blue, 37 In.	430.00
Jardiniere, Pedestal, Green, Lion's Heads, Gold Trim, Haynes Pottery, 35 In.	165.00
Jardiniere, Pedestal, Stylized Lotus Blossoms, Molded, Impressed, 30 x 11 In.	440.00
Jug, Pig, In Chef's Outfit, Onnaing, France, 10 1/2 In.	515.00
Jug, Shell & Seaweed, Albino, Etruscan, Griffen, Smith & Hill, 4 In.	58.00
Matchbox, Cover, Oak Leaf, Green, Yellow, Brown Ground, George Jones, c.1870, 4 In.	430.00
Mixing Bowl, Brown Ground, Pink Flowers, 4 1/2 x 8 1/2 In.	90.00
Mug, Handle, Flying Bird, Pond Lily, Pink Interior, Gold Rim, 4 1/4 In.	200.00
Mug, Sunflower & Butterfly, Cobalt Blue	120.00
Mug, Water Lily, Etruscan, Griffen, Smith & Hill	160.00
Mug, Woman, Art Nouveau, Flowers, 3 1/2 In.	72.00
Mug, Yellow Flower Band, Green Leaves, Green Handle, Griffen, Smith & Hill, 3 1/2 In.	200.00
Napkin Ring, Lily-Of-The-Valley, Green, White, Blue, George Jones, 1874, 6 In.	920.00
Oyster Plate, 4 Tiers, Shell-Shaped Wells, Seaweed, Minton, 10 In. ....*Illus*	6160.00
Oyster Plate, 5 Wells, Fish, Seaweed, Gold Trim, George Jones, 9 In.	305.00
Oyster Plate, 6 Wells, Black Ground, Pink Wells, Turquoise Center, 9 In.	140.00
Oyster Plate, 6 Wells, Flowers, Turquoise Wells, Holdcroft, 9 1/2 In.	1210.00
Oyster Plate, 6 Wells, Turquoise, White Center Shell, George Jones, 11 In. ......*Illus*	2128.00
Pitcher, Basket Weave, Flowers, Pink Top, 6 1/2 In.	310.00
Pitcher, Bear, Seated, Figural, 5 1/2 In.	140.00
Pitcher, Bird & Fan, 3-Sided, 6 1/2 In.	198.00
Pitcher, Bird & Fan, 3-Sided, 7 1/2 In.	70.00
Pitcher, Birds Feeding Young, In Nest, 7 1/4 In.	198.00
Pitcher, Blackberry, Treebark, 8 1/4 In.	99.00
Pitcher, Calla Lily, Cobalt Blue, Serpent Handle, 9 In.	280.00

Pitcher, Chickens, Sheaf Of Wheat, Figural, 10 1/2 In.	495.00
Pitcher, Cobalt Blue, Wild Rose, Butterfly Spout, Etruscan, 5 3/4 In.	220.00
Pitcher, Deer In Meadow, Cobalt Blue, 6 1/2 In.	175.00
Pitcher, Figural, Stock In Marsh, Cobalt Blue Base, Top, George Jones, 6 3/4 In.	2475.00
Pitcher, Fish, Cobalt Blue, Fish Handle, 7 In.	310.00
Pitcher, Flowers, Leaf, 9 In.	210.00
Pitcher, Game, Hound Handle, Pink Ground, Holdcroft, 9 1/2 In.	600.00
Pitcher, Girl With Dog, Can't You Talk, Cobalt Blue Ground, 7 1/2 In.	225.00
Pitcher, Green Ferns, White Ground, Pink Interior, Griffen, Smith & Hill, 8 1/4 In.	315.00
Pitcher, Leaves & Berries, Applied, Turquoise, France, 8 In.	330.00
Pitcher, Maple Leaf, 6 1/2 In.	35.00
Pitcher, Molded Fan Design, Flowers, Butterflies, England, 8 1/2 In.	1330.00
Pitcher, Multicolor, Lyre, Round Panel Side, Pink Interior, 6 3/4 In.	200.00
Pitcher, Owl & Fan, Tricornered, 7 1/2 In.	205.00
Pitcher, Owl, Figural, 7 In.	165.00
Pitcher, Owl, Figural, 9 3/4 In.	330.00
Pitcher, Owl, Gray, Green, Flower & Stump Handle, 6 1/2 In.	175.00
Pitcher, Parrot, Figural, 7 1/4 In.	80.00
Pitcher, Picket Fence, Water Lily, Cattail, George Jones, 5 1/2 In.	1045.00
Pitcher, Pig, Pig Spout, Figural, France, 9 In.	220.00
Pitcher, Pond Lily, Holdcroft, 7 1/2 In.	330.00
Pitcher, Ribbon, Bow & Leaf, Fielding, 4 In.	155.00
Pitcher, Robin, Mottled, 7 3/4 In.	105.00
Pitcher, Rustic, Tree Bark, Flowers, 7 3/4 In.	115.00
Pitcher, Shell & Seaweed, Etruscan, Griffen, Smith & Hill, 9 1/2 In.	255.00
Pitcher, Shell, Seaweed, Etruscan, 6 1/2 In.	330.00
Pitcher, Strawberry, Avalon, 5 In.	20.00
Pitcher, Sunflower, Cobalt Blue, Dragon Handle, 10 1/2 In.	185.00
Pitcher, Syrup, Coral & Seaweed, Pewter Top	385.00
Pitcher, Syrup, Etruscan, Sunflower, Cobalt Blue	330.00
Pitcher, Syrup, Pineapple, Pewter Top, 6 In.	250.00
Pitcher, Tree & Blackberries, 7 1/4 In.	70.00
Pitcher, U.S. Grant, Wreath, Mottled Green, Brown Ground, Pink Interior, 10 1/4 In. *Illus*	920.00
Pitcher, Water Lily, George Jones, 13 In.	4950.00
Pitcher, Water Lily, Lavender Top, Handle, Samuel Lear, 8 In.	470.00
Pitcher, Wild Rose, 5 In.	99.00
Pitcher, Wild Rose, Butterfly Spout, Cobalt Blue Rim, 7 1/2 In.	250.00
Pitcher, Wild Rose, Cobalt Blue, Butterfly Spout, 9 In.	365.00
Pitcher, Wild Rose, Tree Bark, 8 In.	179.00
Pitcher Set, Shell & Seaweed, Graduated, Etruscan, 3 1/4, 3 1/2 & 4 In., 3 Piece	110.00
Planter, Girl & Boy, Seated On Log, 8 x 9 x 6 In.	140.00
Planter, Putti, Wheat, High Relief, Palissy Style, France, 5 In.	220.00
Planter, Window Box, Flowers, Eichwald, 12 3/4 x 4 1/4 In.	120.00
Plaque, Boy, Wearing Drape, Blue Ground, White Border, Della Robbia Style, 13 In.	345.00
Plaque, Lobster, Palissy Style, Round, Seashell Border, 20th Century, 13 In.	353.00
Plate, Basket Weave, Flowers, Rustic, 12 In.	175.00

Majolica, Oyster Plate, 4 Tiers, Shell-Shaped Wells, Seaweed, Minton, 10 In.

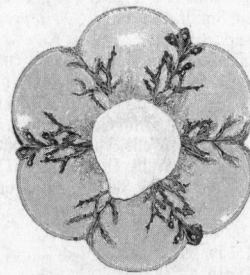

Majolica, Oyster Plate, 6 Wells, Turquoise, White Center Shell, George Jones, 11 In.

Majolica, Pitcher, U.S. Grant, Wreath, Mottled Green, Brown Ground, Pink Interior, 10 1/4 In.

Majolica, Spoon Warmer, Cracked Egg,
Turquoise, Brown, Westhead & Moore, 8 x 5 In.

Majolica, Tray, Butterflies, Wheat, Cobalt Blue,
Bamboo Border, George Jones, 13 In.

Plate, Begonia Leaf, 11 1/2 In. 130.00
Plate, Bike Rider, 7 1/2 In. 285.00
Plate, Cauliflower, Etruscan, 9 In. 165.00
Plate, Classical, Angels In Center, Etruscan, Griffen, Smith & Hill, 9 In. 66.00
Plate, Cobalt Blue & Strawberry, Brownfield, 8 3/4 In. 550.00
Plate, Dog, Green, Brown Rim, Swag Border, Etruscan, Griffen, Smith & Hill, 9 In. 175.00
Plate, Duck Motif, France, 8 1/2 In. 105.00
Plate, Fish & Cattail, Yellow Ground, Holdcroft, 8 3/4 In. 330.00
Plate, Green Central Medallion, Woman At Table, Openwork Lattice Border, 9 1/2 In. ... 99.00
Plate, Leaf, Green, Yellow, Brown, Acorns, Branch Handle, 9 x 12 In. 110.00
Plate, Man Holding Pitcher & Mug, Leaning On Keg, Pink Center, Scalloped Rim, 11 In. 95.00
Plate, Morning Glory On Napkin, Cobalt Blue Ground, 9 1/2 In. 130.00
Plate, Pineapple, 9 In. 250.00
Plate, Pineapple, George Jones, 8 3/4 In. 330.00
Plate, Shell, Red, Continental, 7 3/4 In. 140.00
Plate, Strawberry & Apple, White Ground, Etruscan, 9 In. 110.00
Plate, Strawberry, Turquoise Ground, George Jones, 8 1/4 In. 195.00
Plate, Water Lily, Turquoise Border, Mottled Center, George Jones, 7 3/4 In. 450.00
Plate, White Flowers, Yellow Centers, Pale Green Field, 6 Piece, 7 1/4 In. 305.00
Platter, Asparagus, Lift Out Asparagus Insert, France, 13 1/2 In. 475.00
Platter, Dog, Dog House, White Ground, Handles, 11 In. 115.00
Platter, Fish & Cattail, Holdcroft, 26 In. 2750.00
Platter, Fish, Multicolored, Reed Handles, Footed, Oval, Holdcroft, c.1870, 26 1/2 In. ... 3405.00
Platter, Geranium & Basket Weave, Eat Thy Bread With Thankfulness, 12 3/4 In. 365.00
Platter, Geranium, Pink Ground, Etruscan 250.00
Platter, Strawberry Ribbon & Bowl, Basket Weave Ground, 13 3/4 In. 250.00
Salt, Figural, Parakeet, Perched On Post, 2 Bowls, Frog, George Jones, 6 1/2 In. 4400.00
Sardine Box, Boat Shape, Turquoise, George Jones, 10 In. 560.00
Sauce, Flowers & Bow, Fan Shape, 6 3/4 In. 80.00
Sauce, Scalloped Edge, Etruscan 195.00
Server, Asparagus, Salins, France, 14 In. 80.00
Server, Open, 2 Handles, White, Yellow Flower Center, Corner Leaves, 11 x 8 1/2 In. 300.00
Server, Turquoise, Lily, Attached Lily Cream & Sugar, Twig Handle, George Jones 1760.00
Spoon Warmer, Cracked Egg, Turquoise, Brown, Westhead & Moore, 8 x 5 In. .... Illus 2520.00
Spoon Warmer, Frog, Open Mouth, On Lily Pad, Edward Steel, 1882, 9 In. 460.00
Spooner, Water Lily, Lear, 5 In. 120.00
Stein, Art Nouveau Woman & Grapes, Relief, Blue & Green Glaze, 1/2 Liter 220.00
Stein, Art Nouveau Woman With Flowers, Inlaid Lid, 1/2 Liter 390.00
Sugar & Creamer, Blue Ground, Basketry Band, Pink, White Flowers, 5 1/2 & 4 1/2 In. ... 1035.00
Tea Set, Cauliflower, Etruscan, 3 Piece 495.00
Tea Set, Cobalt Blue, Wild Rose, Trellis, 3 Piece 120.00
Tea Set, Crane & Water Lily, Yellow, Teapot, 7 1/2 In., 3 Piece 280.00
Teapot, Bamboo, Yellow, Brown Ground, Leaves, Griffen, Smith & Hill, 6 In. 175.00
Teapot, Fish Swallowing Fish, Figural, 11 In. 560.00
Teapot, Rooster, George Jones, 11 In. 7700.00
Teapot, Sharkskin & Floral Bow, 8 3/4 In. 280.00
Teapot, Shell & Seaweed, Etruscan, Griffen, Smith & Hill, c.1875, 9 1/2 In. 430.00
Teapot, Sugar, Corn Pattern, Cover, 6 In. 605.00

Teapot, Turquoise, Apple Blossom, George Jones 880.00
Tray, Begonia Leaf, Twig Handles, 10 1/2 In., Pair 220.00
Tray, Butterflies, Wheat, Cobalt Blue, Bamboo Border, George Jones, 13 In. .... *Illus* 3360.00
Tray, Dresser, Butterfly, Iris, Oval, George Jones, 11 In. 3300.00
Tray, Figural, Fish, Jumping On Wave, 3 3/4 x 5 1/2 In. 99.00
Tray, Figural, Squirrel, With Chestnut Leaves, Cobalt Blue, 9 1/2 In. 275.00
Tray, Figural, Turkey, Continental, 3 In. 110.00
Tray, Fish, Figural, Morley & Co., 12 1/2 In. 210.00
Tray, Leaf & Flowers, Twig Handle, 10 1/2 In. 220.00
Tray, Palissy, Fish, Bed Of Leaves, Water Center, Sealife Border, 13 3/4 In. 3025.00
Tray, Trefoil, Blue, Green, Branch Handle, George Jones, c.1875, 12 1/2 In. 865.00
Tureen, Crab Cover, Palissy Style, Crab, Shell Handles, Footed, Portugal 55.00
Umbrella Stand, Flowers, Leaves, Small, Molded, 20 In. 250.00
Umbrella Stand, Green & Brown Glaze, 21 1/2 In. 140.00
Vase, Bird, Figural, Green Stump, Blue Interior, Gold Finish, 4 3/4 In. 105.00
Vase, Black Boy Holding Basket, Tulip Shape Vase Behind, 11 1/2 In. 230.00
Vase, Bud, Bamboo, Triple Hold, 5 3/4 In. 220.00
Vase, Classically Draped Child, Seated On Rocks, Figural, Painted, 14 1/2 In., Pair 1150.00
Vase, Cornucopia, Figural, 4 3/4 In. 55.00
Vase, Ducks, Flowers, Multicolored, Germany, c.1885, 21 1/2 In. 635.00
Vase, Fish, Jumping, Open Mouth, Late 19th Century, 10 In. 145.00
Vase, Flowers, Eichwald, 13 1/2 In. 66.00
Vase, Girl With Kitten, Figural, 6 In. 30.00
Vase, Gypsy Water Boy, Multicolored, 2 Handles, Continental, c.1900, 22 1/2 In. 1955.00
Vase, Iris Decoration, Art Nouveau, Multicolored, Continental, c.1900, 16 In. 690.00
Vase, Leaf Decorated, Blue Ground, Fern, Leaf, Pink Interior, Gold Rim, 9 1/4 In. 2530.00
Vase, Peacock, Open Plumage, Vase Behind Tail, Multicolored, 14 1/2 In. 620.00
Water Cooler, Redbud Branches, Tree Stump, Ferns, Flowers, 68 x 17 x 11 In. 230.00

MALACHITE is a green stone with unusual layers or rings of darker green shades. It is often polished and used for decorative objects. Most malachite comes from Siberia or Australia.

Box, Napoleon III, Silvered Bronze, 9 1/4 In. 1300.00
Urn, Empire Style, Gilt, Bronze Mounted, 14 1/2 In., Pair 2000.00
Urn, Squat, Acanthus Leaf Pedestal, Reeded Handles, Square Base, 10 x 3 1/2 In., Pair ... 748.00

MAPS of all types have been collected for centuries. The earliest known printed maps were made in 1478. The first printed street map showed London in 1559. The first road maps for use by drivers of automobiles were made in 1901. Collectors buy maps that were pages of old books, as well as the multifolded road maps popular in this century.

Alabama, Counties, Cities, Road, Railway, Mitchell, 1846, 11 x 14 In. 1465.00
Alaska, Gold & Coal Fields, Color, Lithograph, Emmons, 1898, 29 x 24 In. 110.00
Alaska, Gold Rush, Trails, Steamer Routes, Lithograph, 1898, 28 1/2 x 23 1/2 In. 235.00
America, California As An Island, Copper Engraving, Philip Culver, 1697, 8 1/2 x 10 In. . 900.00
Amplissimae Regionis Mississippi, J.B. Homann, Nuremberg, c.1710, 19 1/2 x 23 In. 1620.00
Arizona, Indian & Military Reservations, Fort Apache, Land Office, 1896, 17 x 20 In. ... 190.00
Arizona, Territory, General Land Office, 1892, 28 1/2 x 34 In. 670.00
Australia, Colonies, Detailed Coast, 1839, 16 x 13 In. 150.00
California, Mexican-American War, Battle Of Los Angeles, Emory, 1847, 8 1/4 x 5 3/4 In. 310.00
California, Mining District, Britton & Rey, 1896, 34 x 38 In. 390.00
California, San Francisco, Streets, Buildings, 1853, 18 x 25 In. 235.00
Canada, St. Lawrence River, Exploration, Trade Route, Bellin, 1757, 12 x 8 In. 235.00
Carolina, North & South, Johnson & Browning, c.1865, 17 1/2 x 24 1/2 In. 81.00
Carte De La Floride Occidentale Et Louisiane, Les Isles De Bahama, c.1777, 20 x 47 In. 1495.00
Celestial, Constellations, Engraved H.G. Evans, New York, 1856, 17 x 14 1/2 In. 115.00
Dakotas, Railroads, Indian, Military Reservations, General Land Office, 1882, 24 x 29 In. 100.00
District Of Columbia, Streets, Building Vignette Insets, Colton, 1855, 16 x 13 In. 135.00
England & Wales, Counties, Adrian's Wall, Color Wash, VonEuler, 1755, 13 x 15 In. 110.00
Florida, 35 Counties, Roads, Railroads, Forts, Keys Inset, Colton, 1855, 15 x 12 In. 190.00
Globe, Art Nouveau, Metal Stand, Weber Costello, 12 x 21 x 8 In. 280.00
Globe, Celestial, Base Compass, Smith & Son, London, 18 x 24 x 43 In. 9775.00
Globe, Celestial, Paper On Wood, Wood Base, Delamarche, 1900s, 6 In. 2970.00

Globe, Celestial, Paper On Wood, Wood Base, Delamarche, Mid 1800s, 12 x 4 1/2 In. . . . 3025.00
Globe, Celestial, Zodiac, Calendar Scales, Turned Legs, Brass, Loring, 1841, 18 1/2 In. . . 3165.00
Globe, Paper Lithograph, Andrews, Nickel Plated, Iron Stand, Paw Feet, c.1890, 20 In. . . . 350.00
Globe, Paper Lithograph, Embossed, Mahogany Base, Repogle, 12 x 36 x 17 1/2 In. 25.00
Globe, Paper On Wood, Wood Base, Holbrook, Conn., 1840s, 11 x 6 In. 1455.00
Globe, Stand, Cast Spelter Base, Paw Feet, Animal Heads, Reeded Column, 1900s, 45 In. 489.00
Globe, Terrestrial, Brass Meridian, Zodiac, Georgian Style, Mahogany Stand, 41 In. 1610.00
Globe, Terrestrial, E. Wormley, Mahogany Stand, Brass Ring, 21 x 34 In. 1150.00
Globe, Terrestrial, J.W. Schermerhorn, New York, c.1875, 7 1/2 x 5 In. 489.00
Globe, Terrestrial, Joslin, c.1890, 16 In. 7280.00
Globe, Terrestrial, Lithograph, Mahogany Stand, Delmarche, Paris, 14 1/2 In. 920.00
Globe, Terrestrial, Metal Ring, 3 Leg Stand, Iron Stretcher, Schedler, 1900s, 18 x 17 In. . . 1430.00
Globe, Terrestrial, Meteorological, Color, Johnston, Tripod, Edinburgh, 1925, 24 In. 294.00
Globe, Terrestrial, Nickel Stand, Johnston, Edinburgh, 19th Century, 24 In. 205.00
Globe, Terrestrial, Paper On Wood, Wood Base, Shelf, Hammond, 1932, 11 x 9 x 7 In. . . . 170.00
Globe, Terrestrial, Peerless, Airplane Base, Weber Costello, 1930s, 12 x 15 1/2 In. 288.00
Globe, Terrestrial, Peerless, Color, Cardboard, Weber Costello, 1909, 8 In. 90.00
Globe, Terrestrial, Red Berries, Gold Leaf, Joslin, Iron Stand, Mid 1800s, 6 In. 1680.00
Globe, Terrestrial, Tabletop, Mahogany Stand, Rand McNally, 25 1/2 x 12 In. 1035.00
Globe, Terrestrial, Turned Wood Base, Joslin, 6 x 11 1/2 x 5 1/2 In. 870.00
Globe, Terrestrial, Turned Wooden Base, Joslin, 11 1/2 x 5 1/2 In. 850.00
Globe, Terrestrial, Zodiac Ring, Joslin, Boston, c.1890, 12 x 18 In. 6465.00
Globe, Terrestrial, Zodiac, Calendar Scales, Brass, Loring, Joslin, Boston, 17 1/2 In. 1840.00
Greece, Aegean Sea, Moire Pattern, Calligraphy, Mercator, c.1589, 18 1/2 x 14 1/4 In. . . 728.00
Gulf Coast To Red River, Union, Confederate Armies, Topographical, c.1865, 18 x 29 In. . 316.00
Holy Land, Hierusalem, Hendrik Van Schoel, c.1650, 16 1/2 x 11 1/2 In. 450.00
Jerusalem, Holy Land, Religious Icons, Temple Of Solomon, Mortier, 17 x 14 In. 390.00
Louisiana, Mississippi Valley Explorations, C.Weigel, c.1734, 16 1/2 x 12 1/2 In. 1456.00
Louisiana, Pocket Size, Pressed Cloth Boards, Gilt Lettering, Colton, c.1864, 13 x 16 In. . 575.00
Maine, Sea Coast, Pen & Ink, Frame, Luther S. Phillips, 1940, 18 1/2 x 15 1/4 In. 400.00
Maryland & Delaware, Railroads, Table Of Distances, Population Data, 1850, 14 x 11 In. . 100.00
Massachusetts & Rhode Island, Towns, Roads, Canals, Railroads, 1855, 15 1/2 x 12 In. . 50.00
New England, Boston & Harbor Insets, T. Jeffreys, 1775, 24 x 18 In., 4 Piece 3920.00
New Orleans, Plan De La Nouvelle Orleans, Streets, Compass Rose, 1750, 11 x 7 In. 310.00
New York City, Streets, Marked Proposed Central Park, Colton, 1856, 26 x 16 In. 255.00
Newfoundland, Labrador, Wool On Burlap, Grenfell, 42 x 31 1/2 In. 1435.00
North America, Alaska, Great Lakes, Baffin, Hudson Bays, Forster, 1791, 26 x 19 In. . . . 725.00
North America, Alaska, Windward Islands, Railroad System, c.1884, 17 x 13 In. 190.00
North America, European Possessions, Moll, c.1730, 10 x 7 In. 475.00
North America, Mondo Nuovo, Porcacchi, c.1686, 5 1/2 x 4 In. 560.00
North America, Multicolored, Engraved, c.1755, 24 1/2 x 18 3/4 In. 500.00
North America, National Boundaries, Indian Nations, Migeon, c.1855, 15 x 11 In. 125.00
North America, Relief, Papier-Mache, Central School Supply, Frame, 1898, 48 x 34 In. . . 110.00
North Pole, Arctic Wildlife Scenes In Corners, P. Bertius, c.1916, 56 x 45 In. 670.00
North Pole, Lands, Seas, Mountain Ranges, Tropic Of Capricorn, Cole, 1757, 5 x 8 In. . . 110.00
North Pole, Septentrionalium Terrarum, Mercator, c.1619, 15 1/2 x 14 1/2 In. 2465.00
Nova Belgica Et Anglia Nova, Willem Blaeu, Frame, c.1650, 15 1/4 x 20 In. 3520.00
Nova Virginiae, Henricus Hondius, Amsterdam, Frame, c.1633, 15 1/4 x 19 1/2 In. 1520.00
Oklahoma, Cherokee Nation, Territory Limits, 1884, 32 x 28 In., 2 Piece 280.00
Oklahoma, Indian Territory, U.S. Bureau Of Indian Affairs, 1889, 31 3/4 x 26 1/4 In. 560.00
Russia, Asia, Laurie & Whittle, 1794, 10 x 19 In. 310.00
Russia, Towns, Villages, Rivers, Forests, N. Visscher, c.1700, 27 1/2 x 20 In. 390.00
Texas, Adjoining Territories, Trails, Forts, Routes, J.E. Weyss, c.1860, 40 x 26 In. 245.00
United States, Civil War, Pro-Slavery & Union Divisions, 1861, 36 1/2 x 26 In. 200.00
United States, Eastern, Topographical, Conder, 1794, 18 x 12 In. 260.00
United States, General Land Office, 1866, 54 1/2 x 28 In. 420.00
United States, Pacific Coast, San Francisco To San Diego, 1852, 23 x 22 In. 225.00
United States, Southeastern, Copper Engraved, Bonne, c.1783, 13 x 8 1/2 In. 235.00
United States, Southwestern, Notations, Johnson & Browning, c.1861, 24 x 17 In. 900.00
United States, Traveler's Guide, Hardbound, Folding, Phelps, 1847, 20 x 24 In. 1100.00
United States, Western, Green River To Bear River, Engraved, Hayden, 1877, 35 x 26 In. 280.00
United States, Western, Indian Tribes, Forts, Missions, T. Kelly, c.1825, 9 x 7 In. 145.00
United States, Western, Mississippi To Pacific Ocean, Putnam, Colton, 1849, 18 x 11 In. . 890.00

Vermont, Battlefields, Positions Of Opposing Forces, 1780, 13 1/2 x 11 In. 160.00
Virginia, Indian Villages, Compass Rose, Engraved, 1819, 16 x 12 In. 475.00
Virginia, Maryland, Carolina, Scenic Cartouche, Hand Colored, 1714, 19 1/2 x 23 In. 715.00
Virginia, New Jersey, Manhattan, Carolinas, Hand Colored, Johan Smith, 14 x 17 1/2 In. .. 4370.00
Western Hemisphere, Americas, Gastaldi, 1565, 12 x 11 In. 1345.00
Western Hemisphere, Merian, c.1646, 14 x 11 In. 1345.00
World, Double Hemisphere, Australia, New Zealand, Stridbeck, c.1720, 5 x 6 In. 168.00
World, Double Hemisphere, Continents, Celestial Spheres, Visscher, c.1657, 19 x 12 In. ... 2570.00
World, Double Hemisphere, Oceans, Rivers, Great Lakes, Sanson, 1652, 18 3/4 x 12 In. ... 1000.00
World, Hemispheres, Orbis Terrae Compendiosa, Mercator, Frame, c.1595, 11 x 21 In. 3795.00
World, Orbis Terrarum, N. Visscher, c.1657, 19 x 12 1/2 In. 2015.00
Zanesville, Ohio, Manuscript, North Arrow Compass Star, 1819, 20 x 32 1/2 In. 1150.00

MARBLE collectors pay highest prices for glass and sulphide marbles. The game of marbles has been popular since the days of the ancient Romans. American children were able to buy marbles by the mid-eighteenth century. Dutch glazed clay marbles were least expensive. Glazed pottery marbles, attributed to the Bennington potteries in Vermont, were of a better quality. Marbles made of pink marble were also available by the 1830s. Glass marbles seem to have been made later. By 1880, Samuel C. Dyke of South Akron, Ohio, was making clay marbles and The National Onyx Marble Company was making marbles of onyx. The Navarre Glass Marble Company of Navarre, Ohio, and M. B. Mishler of Ravenna, Ohio, made the glass marbles. Ohio remained the center of the marble industry, and the Akron-made Akro Agate brand became nationally known. Other pieces made by Akro Agate are listed in this book in the Akro Agate category. Sulphides are glass marbles with frosted white figures in the center.

Agate, Light Blue With Red & Brown Stripes, Christensen, 9/16 In. 240.00
Agate, Yellow, Black, Blue, Christensen, 5/8 In. 85.00
Cat's Eyes, Akro Agate, Original Plastic Bag, 1955 .... 25.00
Cork, Blue, Yellow, Oxblood, Akro Agate, 13/16 In. 13.00
Cork, Popeye, Yellow, Red, White, Akro Agate, 9/16 In. 50.00
Helmet, Green, Akro Agate, 5/8 In. 6.00
Helmet, Green, Red, White, Vitro Agate Co., 7/8 In. 15.00
Latticinio Net, Yellow Center, Red & Blue Swirls, Germany, 1 5/16 In. 110.00
Lemonade, Oxblood, Akro Agate, 5/8 In. 85.00
Patch, Oxblood & Green, Akro Agate, 5/8 In. 8.00
Sunset, Blue & White, Mica Flecks, Peltier, 5/8 In. 10.00
Swirl, Bumblebee, Yellow, Black, Aventurine, Peltier, 5/8 In. 35.00
Swirl, Christmas Tree, White, Green, Red, Peltier, 5/8 In. 50.00
Swirl, Divided Core, 4 Ribbons, Pink, Yellow, Green, White, Blue, Germany, 13/16 In. 14.00
Swirl, Divided Core, 4 Ribbons, Red, Yellow, Pink, Blue, Black, Germany, 1 3/8 In. 110.00
Swirl, Superboy, Red & Blue, Peltier, 21/32 In. 115.00
Swirl, Turkey, White, Red, Opaque Yellow, Opaque Salmon, Christensen, 9/16 In. 200.00

MARBLE CARVINGS, such as large or small figurines, groups of people or animals, and architectural decorations, have been a special art form since the time of the ancient Greeks. Reproductions, especially of large Victorian groups, are being made of a mixture using marble dust. These are very difficult to detect and collectors should be careful. Other carvings are listed under Alabaster.

Basin, Ram Heads, Scrolled Feet, Ormolu Mounted, Pink, 10 x 25 x 22 In. ....:.... 4400.00
Box, Seated Poodle On Lid, 5 3/4 x 5 1/4 In. 75.00
Bust, Adonis, Classical Style, 20 In. 5080.00
Bust, Child, Marked, M. Hader, 13 1/4 In. 385.00
Bust, George Washington, Marbleized Column, 68 In. 9775.00
Bust, Girl, Classical Dress, Head Turned To Shoulder, Marked, Houdon, 23 In. 3520.00
Bust, Greek Slave, Nude Woman, J.A. Jackson, c.1850, 43 1/2 In. 5580.00
Bust, Julius Caesar, Youthful, 22 In. 700.00
Bust, Mare & Colt, c.1953, 14 1/2 x 7 x 18 1/2 In. 110.00
Bust, Mary Magdalene, Looking Heavenward, Cascading Hair, c.1852, 20 In. 7170.00
Bust, Napoleon, White, 17 1/4 In. 400.00

Bust, Proserpine, 2 Faces, Regency Style, 13 1/2 x 7 1/4 x 10 3/4 In. 290.00
Bust, Woman, Curly Hair, Socle Shape Base, 17 1/2 In. 1430.00
Bust, Woman, Turban, Pedestal, White, Gray, Italy, c.1900, 69 In. 3450.00
Bust, Young Girl, Twisted Braid, Laurel Wreath, Snake Around Neck, 19 1/2 In. 1760.00
Column, Brass Acorn Knob, Variegated, 42 1/2 In., 3 Piece 2310.00
Column, Louis XVI Style, Fluted, England, 40 x 10 In. 345.00
Crucifix, Sulphide, 2 In. 175.00
Garniture, Black, Green Veining, Bronze Mounts, 12 In., Pair 310.00
Jar, Horned Heads, Flower Swags, Grapevine, Green, Ormolu Mounted, 12 In., Pair 3520.00
Jardiniere, Classical Style, Cupids, Flower Garlands, 39 1/2 x 31 1/2 x 10 In. 2629.00
Obelisk, Mottled Beige, Alabaster, Continental, Early 20th Century, 22 1/2 In., Pair 750.00
Obelisk, Variegated, Slate, Continental, Early 20th Century, 13 1/4 In., Pair 520.00
Pedestal, Black, Variegated, 20th Century, 42 1/2 In. 345.00
Pedestal, Column, Ormolu Mounted, Square Platform, Octagonal Base, 42 x 12 In. 1760.00
Statue, Aphrodite, Italian, 50 In. 9200.00
Statue, Apollo, Standing, Nude, Carrara, 25 In. 489.00
Statue, Boy, Resting On Archway, Holding Ball & String, 6 In. 225.00
Statue, Bust, Madame Recamier, France, c.1813, 25 In. 1150.00
Statue, Classical Maiden, Late 18th Century, 75 In. 13800.00
Statue, Classical Woman, Green Marble Ground, Fernando Vichi, Italy, 36 x 43 In., Pair . 9775.00
Statue, Cupid & Psyche, Classical Style, 19 x 19 In. 4780.00
Statue, Girl, Hat, Crossed Arms, Grapes, C Lipini Firenze, 1884, 19 x 10 In., 2 Piece 500.00
Statue, Head Of A Soldier, Classical Style, 18 In. 1675.00
Statue, Left Hand Holding Rod, 17th Century, 7 x 5 In. 138.00
Statue, Shepherdess & Lamb, Middle Eastern, F. Vichi, 36 In. 7170.00
Statue, Slave Girl, Nude 19th Century, 29 In. 5775.00
Statue, Wolf, Seated, Verde Antico, Continental, c.1900, 6 3/4 x 5 3/4 x 3 In. 230.00
Statue, Woman, Child, Egyptian, Winged Decorations, 11 1/2 x 6 1/2 In. 415.00
Statue, Wrestlers, 2 Male Nudes, Carrara, 14 1/2 x 17 3/4 In. 1380.00
Urn, Cover, Louis XVI Style, Ormolu Mounted, 1800s, 16 1/2 In. 1955.00
Vase, Gilt Brass Mounts, 2 Handles, Pomegranate Finials, 13 3/4 In., Pair 805.00
Vase, Louis XVI Style, Gilt Brass Mounted, France, 32 x 27 In., Pair 1840.00
Woman, Fate, Veiled, Carrying Bowl, Italy, c.1885, 16 In. 230.00
Woman, Nude, Leaning Back, Holding Drape, Art Deco, 45 In. 1035.00

MARBLEHEAD Pottery was founded in 1905 by Dr. J. Hall as a rehabilitative program for the patients of a Marblehead, Massachusetts, sanitarium. Two years later it was separated from the sanitarium and it continued operations until 1936. Many of the pieces were decorated with marine motifs.

Bookends, Ship, Blue, Green, White Ground, Embossed, Marked, 5 1/2 In. 1035.00
Bowl, Blue Matte Glaze, Squat, Closed Mouth, 3 1/8 x 5 1/2 In. 330.00
Bowl, Blue, Rounded Shoulder, Tapering To Base, Impressed, 4 1/4 In. 265.00
Bowl, Caramel Matte Glaze, Oatmeal Interior, Squat, Closed Mouth, 3 In. 385.00
Bowl, Flaring, Pink Matte Glaze, 8 1/2 x 4 In. 290.00
Bowl, Low, Aqua Blue & Hunter Green Drip Glaze, Black Spatter, 1 3/4 x 6 In. 330.00
Bowl, Pink Matte Glaze, Impressed, 6 In. 175.00
Bowl, Wisteria Matte Glaze, Marked, 8 1/2 In. 200.00
Mug, Incised Black Stripe, On Green Matte Ground, Marked, 3 1/2 x 4 In. 980.00
Sugar & Creamer, Blue Matte Glaze, Early 1900s, 3 3/8 In. 205.00
Tile, Basket Of Flowers, Pink Ground, Ship Mark, Square, 4 1/2 In. 345.00
Tile, Galleon, 2 Colors, Early 1900s, 6 5/8 In. 530.00
Tile, Landscape, Green Matte Trees, Indigo Clouds, Stamped, 4 1/4 In. 1095.00
Tile, Sailboat, Blue Gray Matte, Arts & Crafts Frame, Stamped, 6 1/4 In. 4025.00
Trivet, Sea Plant, Dark Brown Matte Glaze, Speckled Matte Ocher Ground, Round, 5 In. . 690.00
Vase, Blue Matte Glaze, Aqua Interior, Relief Flowers, Berries, Squat, 3 x 5 In. 1870.00
Vase, Blue Matte Glaze, Brown Inside, Baluster Shape, Flared Mouth, 6 In. 605.00
Vase, Blue Matte Glaze, Bulbous, Marked, 4 x 5 1/4 In. 545.00
Vase, Blue Matte Glaze, Graduated Circles, Sage Green Glaze, Tapered, Art Deco, 5 In. . . 550.00
Vase, Broad Cylindrical Form, Dark Blue Matte Glaze, 4 In. 489.00
Vase, Broad Form, Brown Matte Glaze, 4 In. 430.00
Vase, Broad Form, Dark Blue Matte Glaze, Impressed Mark, 5 In. 489.00
Vase, Brown Matte Glaze, Tapered, Wide Mouth, Rolled Rim, 4 In. 530.00

Vase, Caramel Matte Glaze, Brown Speckles, Spherical Upper, Tapered Lower, 4 In. 525.00
Vase, Curdled Blue Gray Matte Glaze, Cupped Rim, Bulbous, Marked, 3 3/4 In. 865.00
Vase, Cylindrical, Blue Matte Glaze, 9 In. 690.00
Vase, Cylindrical, Gray Matte Glaze, 8 1/2 In. 575.00
Vase, Elephant Gray Glaze, Spherical Upper Body, Tapered Lower, 3 1/2 In. 330.00
Vase, Gray, Speckled, Blue Heart Shape Petals, Long Stem, Cylindrical, 8 3/4 In. 6050.00
Vase, Green Curlicues, Black Outline, Indigo Ground, Squat, Marked, 3 1/2 In. 980.00
Vase, Indigo Matte Glaze, Oval, Marked, 7 In. 690.00
Vase, Indigo Matte Glaze, Tear Form, Marked, 6 In. 980.00
Vase, Inverted Rim, Cylindrical, 3 Flowers, 3 Colors, Early 1900s, 8 3/4 In. 2940.00
Vase, Lavender Gray Matte Glaze, Purple Interior, Ovoid, Swollen Top Half, 8 1/2 In. ... 715.00
Vase, Low Form, Lavender Matte Glaze, 3 In. 430.00
Vase, Mottled Gray & Purple Matte Glaze, Cylindrical, 4 In. 385.00
Vase, Mottled Gray & Purple Matte Glaze, Tapered, Flared Lip, 8 1/2 In. 560.00
Vase, Mottled Tan & Brown Matte Glaze, Tapered, Flared Lip, 8 In. 765.00
Vase, Persian Blue Crackled Glaze, Fan Form, Marked, 6 In. 230.00
Vase, Speckled Blue Gray Matte Glaze, Oval, Marked, 5 3 1/4 In. 290.00
Vase, Speckled Green Matte Ground, Incised, Stylized Brown Design, 3 3/4 In. 4600.00
Vase, Speckled Pink Matte Glaze, Tapered, Marked, 6 1/4 In. 635.00
Vase, Stylized Blossoms, Brown, Speckled Matte Green Glaze, Incised, 3 1/2 In. 3220.00
Vase, Stylized Leaves, Brown, Incised, Speckled Matte Ground, 6 1/2 In. 6900.00
Vase, Stylized Trees, Blue, Speckled Matte Ground, Flared, Marked, 4 1/2 x 5 In. 980.00
Vase, Stylized Trees, Brown, Green Speckled Matte Ground, Tear Form, Tutt, 6 x 5 In. ... 3220.00
Vase, Tapered Oval, Green Matte Glaze, 1900s, 7 1/8 In. 765.00
Vase, Tapered, Blue Matte Glaze, 7 In. 489.00
Vase, Tapered, Gray Matte Glaze, 4 1/2 In. 520.00
Vase, Tapered, Yellow Matte Glaze, 6 1/2 In. 575.00
Vase, Trees, Stylized, Yellow Ground, Tapered, Impressed Mark, 5 1/2 In. 5580.00
Vase, Yellow Matte Glaze, Early 1900s, 5 1/4 In. 590.00
Vase, Yellow, Greenish, Blue Matte Glaze, Early 1900s, 5 1/8 In. 940.00
Wall Pocket, Lovebirds, Faceted, Speckled Green, Red, On Indigo Ground, 5 In. 2185.00

MARTIN BROTHERS of Middlesex, England, made Martinware, a salt-glazed stoneware, between 1873 and 1915. Many figural jugs and vases were made by the three brothers. Of special interest are the fanciful birds, usually made with removable heads.

Jar, Bird, 1899, 9 In. 15745.00
Jar, Bird, Head Cocked, Eyes Slightly Open 26880.00
Jug, Face, 2 Sides, Brown & Black Mottled Glaze, Incised, 1892, 8 1/4 In. 2300.00
Jug, Grotesque, Zoomorphic Spout, Gaping Mouth 5510.00
Match Holder, Hanging, Woman's Head, Bonnet, Red Clay, Stamped, 5 1/2 In. 920.00
Pitcher, Yellow Quatrefoils, Brown Leaves, Incised, 9 3/4 In. 546.00
Urn, Flowers, Yellow, Blue, Brown & Ivory Ground, Carved, Signed, 8 3/4 x 4 In. 800.00
Vase, 4 Buttresses, Incised Indigo Lines, White Matte Ground, Gourd, Tapered, 11 In. ... 1380.00
Vase, Birds, Blackberries, Butterfly, Salt Glaze, No. 10-1886, 1886, 8 3/4 In. 1380.00
Vase, Figural, Grotesque, Overlapping Fans, Stoneware, Bulbous, Flat, 8 x 4 In. 4313.00

MARY GREGORY is the name used for a type of glass that is easily identified. White figures were painted on clear or colored glass as the decoration. The figures chosen were usually children at play. The first glass known as Mary Gregory was made about 1870. Similar glass is made even today. The traditional story has been that the glass was made at the Sandwich Glass works in Boston by a woman named Mary Gregory. Recent research suggests that it is possible that none was made at Sandwich. In general, all-white figures were used in the United States, tinted faces were probably used in Bohemia, France, Italy, Germany, Switzerland, and England. Children standing, not playing, were pictured after the 1950s.

Bottle, Barber, 2 Girls, Playing Tennis, 8 1/3 In., Pair 625.00
Box, Hinged Cover, Amber, Girl & Birds, Round, 2 1/4 In. 70.00
Vase, Amethyst, Girl In Field Of Flowers, 6 1/2 In., Pair 350.00
Vase, Boy, Holding Flower, Bronze 3-Footed Base, Winged Griffins, 11 1/2 In. 1350.00
Vase, Cranberry, Girl & Hoop, Pedestal Base, 5 1/2 In. 210.00

Vase, Green, Boy, Holding Rifle, 11 1/2 In. 150.00
Wine, Cranberry, Girl Carrying Basket, 5 3/4 In. 200.00

MASON'S IRONSTONE was made by the English pottery of Charles J. Mason after 1813. Mason, of Lane Delph, was given a patent for this improved earthenware. He usually called it "Mason's Patent Ironstone China." It resisted chipping and breaking so it became popular for dinnerwares and other table service dishes. Vases and other decorative pieces were also made. The ironstone was decorated with orange, blue, gold, and other colors, often in Japanese inspired designs. The firm had financial difficulties but the molds and the name Mason were used by many owners through the years, including Francis Morley, Taylor Ashworth, George L. Ashworth, and John Shaw. Mason's joined the Wedgwood group in 1973 and the name is still found on dinnerwares.

Bowl, Vegetable, Cover, Blue, Orange, Brown, Yellow, Gilt, c.1840, 6 x 11 x 9 In. 252.00
Bowl & Pitcher, Imari Colors, Serpent Handle, c.1875, 14 1/4 x 4 1/2 x 13 In. 730.00
Dessert Service, Imari, Patent, Mid 19th Century, 13 Piece 2990.00
Jar, Potpourri, Cover, Mazarine Blue Field, Pheasants, Gilt, 2 Handles, c.1820 .... 3125.00
Pitcher, Chinoiserie Gaudy Decoration, 19th Century, 5 1/2 In. 175.00
Pitcher, Chinoiserie, 6 1/2 In., Pair 460.00
Pitcher, Ironstone, Brown, White, 6 In. 35.00
Pitcher, Ironstone, Oriental Decoration, Imari Colors, c.1880, 11 3/8 In. 290.00
Soup, Dish, 10 In., Pair 285.00
Tureen, Cover, Brown Transferware, Ladle, Underplate, 9 x 13 In. 476.00
Tureen, Sauce, Cover, Ladle, Underplate, Patent, England, 1800s, 8 In. 400.00
Tureen, Sauce, Underplate, Gaudy Ironstone, Landscape, c.1830, 8 In. 345.00

MASONIC, see Fraternal category.

MASSIER, a French art pottery, was made by brothers Jerome, Delphin, and Clement Massier in Vallauris and Golfe-Juan, France, in the late nineteenth and early twentieth centuries. It has an iridescent metallic luster glaze that resembles the Weller Sicardo pottery glaze. Most pieces are marked *J. Massier.*

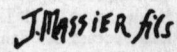

Vase, Fleur-De-Lis, Green, Purple Luster Ground, Signed, 4 x 3 In. 290.00
Vase, Flower Sprays, Metallic Glaze, Jerome, 3 1/2 In. 290.00
Vase, Lotus Blossoms, Dragonfly, Metallic Glaze, Delphin, 9 5/8 In. 865.00
Vase, Luster Glaze, Daisies, Clement Massier, Marked CM Golfe-Juan, 4 1/2 In. 259.00
Vase, Organic Form, Raised Design, 6 In. 375.00
Vase, Platinum, Pink Iridescent Glaze, Leaf Design, Clement, 7 In. 748.00

MATCH HOLDERS were made to hold the large wooden matches that were used in the nineteenth and twentieth centuries for a variety of purposes. The kitchen stove and the fireplace or furnace had to be lit regularly. One type of match holder was made to hang on the wall, another was designed to be kept on a tabletop. Of special interest today are match holders that have advertisements as part of the design.

American Manure Spreader, Tin Lithograph, 4 3/4 In. .... *Illus* 300.00
Barker's South American Fever & Ague Cure, 3 x 4 3/8 In. 190.00
Barta Photo Studio, Tin Lithograph, New Prague, Minn., 4 7/8 x 3 3/8 In. 283.00
Black Boy Kisses Pig, Tree Stump Holds Matches, 1880s, 3 3/4 In. 220.00
Black Forest, Carved, Dog On Crutch, Top Hat, Holds Matches, Cigars, 12 1/2 x 7 1/2 In. 600.00
Boy, In Grape-Covered Arch, Holding Basket, Bisque, Wall Mount, 7 3/4 In. 17.00
Bullock, Ward & Co., Tin Lithograph, Chicago, 4 3/4 In. .... *Illus* 295.00
Buster Brown Bread, 6 3/4 x 2 1/8 x 3/4 In. 2150.00
Ceresota Flour, Boy, Bread, Tin Lithograph, Die Cut, 5 3/8 x 2 1/2 In. 330.00
Ceresota Flour, Child Cutting Bread, Tin Lithograph, c.1910, 5 3/8 In. 145.00
Ceresota Flour, Embossed, Figural, Die Cut, Child Slicing Bread, 5 1/2 x 2 3/8 In. 305.00
DeLaval, Separator Shape, Tin Lithograph, c.1900, 6 1/4 In. .... 135.00 to 250.00
DeLaval, Separator, 1, 000,000 In Use 120.00
Dockash Stove Factory, Scranton Pa., Tin Lithograph, 4 7/8 In. 25.00
Dockash Stove Factory, Wood, Tin, c.1920s, 3 3/8 x 4 3/4 In. 69.00
Dr. Shoop's Health Coffee, Tin Lithograph, 3 1/2 x 5 x 1 In. .... 248.00 to 385.00

Match Holder, American
Manure Spreader, Tin Lithograph,
4 3/4 In.

Match Holder, Bullock,
Ward & Co., Tin Lithograph,
Chicago, 4 3/4 In.

Match Holder, Garland Stoves
& Ranges, Detroit, Chicago,
4 3/4 In.

Eagle White Lead Co., Celluloid Over Metal, Box, 2 3/4 x 1 1/2 x 3/8 In. 495.00
Ellwood Steel Fences, Tin Lithograph, 4 7/8 x 3 3/8 In. 140.00
Figural, Blackhead, Porkpie Hat, Chalkware, Hand Painted, 5 In. 45.00
Garland Stoves & Ranges, Detroit, Chicago, 4 3/4 In. . . . . *Illus* 245.00
Goddess Of Liberty, Glass, 19th Century, 4 1/2 In. 85.00
Green's August Flower, Cardboard, Die Cut, 7 1/2 x 4 1/2 In. 910.00
Home Insurance Company, New York, Sterling Silver, Firemen 575.00
J.C. Stevens, Old Judson Whiskey, Tin Lithograph, 3 1/2 x 5 In. 176.00
J.E. Patzlsperger, Popular Shoe Man, Tin Lithograph, 4 7/8 x 3 3/8 In. 285.00
Lax-Ets, Dr. Shoop's Laxative, Tin Lithograph, 4 7/8 x 3 3/8 In. 195.00
Monkey, Figural, Cobalt Blue Cape, Majolica, 5 1/2 In. 135.00
Moxie, Nerve Food, Tin Lithograph, Die Cut, 7 1/8 x 2 5/8 In. 660.00
New Process Gas Range, Saves Time & Gas, Tin Lithograph, 3 1/2 x 2 1/4 In. . . . .245.00 to 495.00
Pig, Matches In Head, Scratch My Back, Porcelain, Germany, 4 In. 140.00
Richardson Butane Gas, Columbus, Ms. & Tuscaloosa, Al., Wall, 5 x 3 In. 18.00
Rooster, On Leaf, Majolica, Continental 250.00
Rowe, Matches, 1 Cent, Cigarettes, 15 Cents 935.00
San Felice Cigars, Metal, Oval Celluloid Image, 1/4 x 1 5/8 x 2 3/8 In. 425.00
Sharples Separator, Daughter, Mother, Cows, Tin Lithograph, 6 3/4 x 2 1/8 In. . . .250.00 to 470.00
Shenango China, L. Barth & Son, New York, Sample, 1920s, 2 3/4 x 4 In. 115.00
Skeleton Holding Cards, E. Bohne & Sohne, 4 1/4 In. 230.00
Skull, Porcelain, E. Bohne & Sohne, 2 1/2 In. 130.00
Topsy Hosiery, Woman On Beach, 4 7/8 x 3 3/8 x 1 1/4 In. 580.00
Wm. T. Burns, Woburn, Mass., Tin, Painted, Stenciled, Early 1900s, 6 In. 20.00
Wrigley's Juicy Fruit, Made Famous, Tin Lithograph, 5 x 3 3/8 In. 440.00

MATCH SAFES were designed to be carried in the pocket. Early matches
were made with phosphorus and could ignite unexpectedly. The
matches were safely stored in the tightly closed container. Match safes
were made in sterling silver, plated silver, or other metals. The English
call these *vesta boxes.*

British Imperial Relief Fund, Celluloid, New England, Boston, Mass., c.1918 . . . . 185.00
Calendar, Cast Iron 425.00
Cement, Face, Incised Signature, E. Howard Cementer, 1906, 6 In. 345.00
Columbian Expo, Silvered, Administration Building & Art Place Relief 135.00
Gold, Chevron Decoration, Hunt & Roskell, England, 1 3/4 In. 105.00
Horse & Rider, Embossed Metal, 1/2 x 2 7/8 x 1 1/2 In. 80.00
Man, Barrel, Riding High Wheel, Silver Plate, 19th Century, Signed, James Tufts, 6 In. . . 700.00
Man Carrying A Barrel On Back, Silver Plate, James Tufts, American, 6 In. 625.00
Nickel Plated, W.J. Loth Stove Co., Waynesboro, Va. 176.00
Pan American Expo, Women As Continents In Relief, 1901 . . . . 150.00
Silver, Horse Drawn Wagon Shape, Cherub, Continental, 7/8 In. 105.00
Standard Oil Company, Celluloid Covered, 3/8 x 2 3/4 x 1 1/2 In. 495.00
US Auto Injector, American Injector Co., Detroit 165.00

MCCOY pottery was made in Roseville, Ohio. Nelson McCoy and J.W. McCoy established the Nelson McCoy Sanitary and Stoneware Company in Roseville, Ohio, in 1910. The firm made art pottery after 1926. In 1933 it became the Nelson McCoy Pottery Company. Pieces marked *McCoy* were made by the Nelson McCoy Pottery Company. Cookie jars were made from about 1940 until December 1990, when the McCoy factory closed. Since 1991 pottery with the McCoy mark has been made by firms unrelated to the original company. Because there was a company named Brush-McCoy, there is great confusion between Brush and Nelson McCoy pieces. See Brush category for more information.

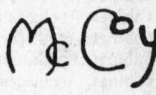

Cachepot, Bulbous, Laurel Leaf Band, Aqua Gloss Glaze, c.1925, 10 1/2 x 7 1/2 In.	145.00
Cachepot, Flower Band, Diamond Pattern, 20th Century, 7 1/2 x 8 1/2 In.	58.00
Cookie Jar, Keebler Tree House, Elf At Door, Box, 9 In.	65.00
Cookie Jar, Rocking Horse, Cream, Brown	185.00
Cookie Jar, Turkey, 11 1/2 In.	600.00
Jardniere, Pedestal, Flowers, Yellow, Orange, Brown Glaze, 29 1/2 In.	145.00
Planter, Fish, No. 7	810.00
Vase, 4 Buttresses, Mirror Black, Raspberry & Purple Glossy Glaze, 14 In.	345.00
Vase, Aqua Matte Glaze, 12 In.	115.00
Vase, Aqua Matte Glaze, Split Handles, 9 In.	45.00
Vase, Arrow Leaf, Aqua Matte Glaze, 7 1/2 In.	65.00
Vase, Art Deco, Aqua Matte Glaze, Long Handles, 9 In.	55.00
Vase, Art Deco, Pink Matte Glaze, Long Handles, 9 In.	55.00
Vase, Egg Shape, Leaf & Berry Clusters, Rose Matte Glaze, c.1925, 8 1/2 In.	80.00
Vase, Green Matte Glaze, Oval, Leaf & Berries Clusters, Early 1900s, 8 1/2 In., Pair	115.00
Vase, Loy-Nel-Art, Hand Painted, Unmarked, c.1905, 11 In.	250.00
Vase, Pink Matte Glaze, 2 Handles, 9 In.	35.00
Vase, Pink Matte Glaze, 8 1/4 In.	45.00
Vase, Swan, Aqua Matte Glaze, 9 In.	50.00
Vase, Swan, Pink Matte Glaze, 9 In.	50.00
Vase, Swan, White Matte Glaze, 9 In.	50.00
Vase, White Glossy Glaze, 8 In.	35.00
Vase, White Matte Glaze, 9 In.	50.00
Vase, Yellow Roses, On Brown Ground, Gourd Shape, Handles, 6 1/2 x 5 In.	80.00
Wall Pocket, Dog, Boxer, 8 In.	115.00

MCKEE is a name associated with various glass enterprises in the United States since 1836, including J. & F. McKee (1850), Bryce, McKee & Co. (1850 to 1854), McKee and Brothers (1865), and National Glass Co. (1899). In 1903, the McKee Glass Company was formed in Jeannette, Pennsylvania. It became McKee Division of the Thatcher Glass Co. in 1951 and was bought out by the Jeannette Corporation in 1961. Pressed glass, kitchenwares, and tablewares were produced. Jeannette Corporation closed in the early 1980s. Additional pieces may be included in the Custard Glass category.

Jade, Canister, Cover, Sugar, 4 1/4 x 5 In.	295.00
Jade, Canister, Cover, Tea, 5 In.	265.00
Jade, Towel Bar, 17 In.	55.00
Jade, Tumbler, Bath, 4 1/2 In.	160.00

MECHANICAL BANKS are listed in the Bank category.

MEDICAL office furniture, operating tools, microscopes, thermometers, and other paraphernalia used by doctors are included in this category. Veterinary collectibles are also included here. Medicine bottles are listed in the Bottle category. There are related collectibles listed under Dental.

Apothecary Sifter, Brass, 10 Cup Screens, Wengers, Etruria, 18 1/2 In.	135.00
Bleeder, Brass, Pistol Grip Shape, Spring Activated, 4 In.	85.00
Box, Glass Probes, Ultraviolet Light, Model Violetta, Chicago Electric, 1920s, 9 x 12 In.	115.00
Bust, Phrenology, Male, Half Is Delineated, Numbered, Late 1800s, 11 In.	1150.00
Cabinet, Apothecary, 8 Drawers, Oxblood Paint, 25 x 28 In.	525.00
Cabinet, Apothecary, 12 Drawers, Pine, Red Flame Graining, 36 1/2 x 9 x 12 1/2 In.	1610.00
Cabinet, Apothecary, 17 Drawers, Softwood, Painted, 16 3/4 x 33 x 11 1/2 In.	4070.00

Cabinet, Apothecary, 18 Dovetailed Drawers, Cherry, Early 1800s, 33 x 71 x 15 In. 3520.00
Cabinet, Apothecary, 18 Drawers, Pine, Porcelain Knobs, 45 x 36 In. 155.00
Cabinet, Apothecary, 25 Drawers, Painted, Peg Drawer Pulls, 36 x 45 x 14 In. 2530.00
Cabinet, Apothecary, 36 Drawers, Pine, 25 In. 325.00
Cabinet, Apothecary, 36 Drawers, Softwood, Oak Drawers, 42 x 49 In. 1400.00
Cabinet, Apothecary, 37 Drawers, Herbal, Brass Ring Pulls, Chinese, 27 x 46 1/2 In. 495.00
Cabinet, Apothecary, 60 Drawers, Scrubbed Surface, Early 1800s, 42 1/2 x 70 In. 5750.00
Capsule Filler, Eastman, 3 Extra Insert Rings, c.1900, 5 In. 1155.00
Capsule Maker, Pharmacist's, J.M. Grovsner & Co., Funnels, Labels, Instructions 138.00
Case, Venereal, 14 Instruments, Nickel Plated, USN, 1912 Patent, 4 x 8 1/2 In. 125.00
Chest, Apothecary, Drawer, Mahogany, 22 Bottles, 24 1/2 x 19 1/4 x 11 3/4 In. 460.00
Chest, Apothecary, Elm, Lacquer, Shanxi, Chinese, c.1850, 66 x 39 x 18 1/2 In. 415.00
Chest, Apothecary, George III Style, Mahogany, Traveling, c.1850, 10 1/2 x 12 1/4 In. ... 259.00
Chest, Apothecary, George III, Drawer, 2 Doors, Mahogany, c.1810, 13 3/4 x 11 1/2 In. .. 750.00
Chest, White Paint, Beveled Mirror Doors, Chrome Knobs, 28 x 21 x 7 In. 420.00
Chest, Wood, Eye Cups, Scalpel, Oil Lamp, Bottles, c.1860, 9 x 15 x 9 1/4 In. 1840.00
Cupboard, Apothecary, Corner, 5 Shelves, 96 In. 825.00
Eyecup, Bottle, Clear, 4 1/4 In. 420.00
Eyecup, Dark Brown, Faceted, Pedestal, Round Foot, 3 In. 235.00
Eyecup, Embossed Eyes, Clear, Pedestal, Pat 1-19-37, 2 In. 100.00
Eyecup, Grimes Improved Eyebath, Rubber, Red, 1 1/4 In. 835.00
Eyecup, Porcelain, Blue & White, Flower Transfer, Gold Rim, Base, Pedestal, 2 In. 285.00
Eyecup, Porcelain, Blue & White, Flower Transfer, Pedestal, 2 In. 420.00
Eyecup, Turquoise Blue, Nipped Corners, Pedestal, Ground Pontil, 3 In. 385.00
Fleam, 3 Blades, Brass & Horn Housing, Butler 60.00
Fleam, 4 Blades, Steel, Horn Handle, Brass Grip, Watkins, c.1800, 3 3/4 In. 345.00
Forceps, Birthing, Bakelite Handle, Dr. George Elliot, 1895 .... 45.00
Forceps, Black Wood Handles, Early 1800s, 13 In. 70.00
Herb Crusher, Polished Surface, Wooden, 7 1/2 In. 525.00
Lancet, 3 Blades, Borwick Cast Steel, Brass, 3 In. 56.00
Mold, Pill, 3 Sections, Brass 260.00
Mortar & Pestle, Hardstone, 2 Pestles, Wood Handle, 7 x 13 In. 635.00
Ophthalmologist's Diagnostic Instrument, F.A. Hardy & Co., 1899 Patent 800.00
Ophthalmoscope, Battery Operated, 5 Light Settings, Bausch & Lomb, Fitted Case 40.00
Pill Maker, Brass Molds, Cast Iron Base, T. Mills Bros., 12 In. 95.00
Saw, Amputation, Crosshatched, Ebony Handle, Ferguson, London 160.00
Saw, Bone, Curved Blade, Revolutionary War, c.1775, 8-In. Blade 345.00
Saw, Surgeon's, Ciencken, Stainless Frame, Brass, Ebony 55.00
Saw, Surgeon's, Disston 110.00
Sign, First-Aid, Thirsty, Nature Calling For Help, Red, Black, Tin, Embossed, 27 x 10 In. . 145.00
Surgical Kit, Scalpels, Instruments, Wood, Dovetailed, Buxton Latham, c.1850, 7 x 3 In. . 1150.00
Table, Pill Rolling, Pharmacist's, Brass, Mahogany Pill Forming Plate 130.00

MEERSCHAUM is a soft white, gray, or cream-colored mineral named magnesium silicate. The name comes from the German word for seafoam, because it was sometimes found floating in the Black Sea and people thought it was petrified seafoam. Pipes and other pieces of carved meerschaum listed here date from the nineteenth century to the present.

Pipe, Alligator, Leather Case, 6 1/2 In. 288.00
Pipe, Bearded Man, Hat, Amber Stem, Case, German, c.1885, 3 1/2 x 7 3/8 In. 403.00
Pipe, Horse, Running, Case 77.00
Pipe, Woman's Head, Gold Mount, Ludwig Hartmann, Vienna, c.1885, 3 In. 201.00
Pipe, Woman, Case, c.1880 .... 358.00
Pipe, Woman, Nude, Reclining, Servant, Leather Case, 6 1/2 x 3 1/4 In. 431.00

MEISSEN is a town in Germany where porcelain has been made since 1710. Any china made in the town can be called Meissen, although the famous Meissen factory made the finest porcelains of the area. The crossed swords mark of the great Meissen factory has been copied by many other firms in Germany and other parts of the world. Pieces of Meissen dinnerware in the Onion pattern are listed in their own category in this book.

Basket, Reticulated, Everted Sides, Flower Heads, Crabstock Handles, 9 3/4 In. 380.00

Bell, Mounted, Porcelain Base, Twist Action 475.00
Bowl, 4 Lobes, Flower Swags, Crossed Swords, 5 1/2 In. 80.00
Bowl, Bird & Bugs Front, Swirl & Basket Interior, 9 In. 226.00
Bowl, Center Flowers, Embossed Gilt Floral Border, 12 In. 339.00
Bowl, Cobalt Blue, Embossed Gilt Leaf Trim, 12 In. 310.00
Bowl, Embossed Swirls, Basket Work, Painted Flower, Insects, 9 1/2 In. 136.00
Bowl, Flowers, Embossed Basket Pattern, Oval, Footed, 6 3/4 In., Pair 396.00
Bowl, Flowers, Leaves, 19th Century, 10 In. 218.00
Bowl, Pate-Sur-Pate, Cupid, Woman, 5 Colors, Gilt Accents, Wood Frame, 10 In. 8475.00
Bowl, Serving, Oblong, Shaped Rim, Clipped Corners, Gilt Rim, Early 1900s, 8 5/8 In. ... 150.00
Box, Cover, Horse & Rider Medallion, Cobalt Blue Ground, Signed, 3 1/2 In. 80.00
Box, Flowers, Round, 20th Century, 4 3/4 In. 115.00
Bust, Girl, Flowered Kerchief, Applied Leaf Corsage, Gilt Enamel, c.1900, 6 In. 380.00
Bust, Girl, Flowers In Hair, Early 19th Century, 6 In. 575.00
Candelabrum, 3-Light, 2 Sections, Salmon Trim, 9 1/4 In. 90.00
Candlestick, Infants, Resting On Base, Applied Flowers, Crossed Swords, 12 1/2 In., Pair 1725.00
Candlestick, Woman, Grapes, Flowers, Crossed Swords, Star, Early 19th Century, 8 In. .. 259.00
Cane Handle, Woman, Hands In Muff, Crossed Swords, 3 3/4 In. 863.00
Centerpiece, Figural, Pierced, Floral Encrusted Body, c.1880, 18 1/2 In. 1955.00
Chocolate Cup, Saucer, Garden Scene, Gilt, 4 In. 970.00
Chocolate Pot, Flowers, 18th Century, 7 1/2 In. 520.00
Chocolate Pot, Ship Scene, 19th Century, 6 In. 250.00
Clock, Allegorical Figures On Rocky Outcrop, White Enamel Dial, Crossed Swords, 18 In. 8050.00
Coffee Set, Hunt Scenes, Pink Panels, Gilt Borders, Melon Shape, 6-In. Pot, 3 Piece 1495.00
Coffee Set, Multicolored Flowers, Pear Shape Coffeepot, 1800s, 8 1/4 In., 3 Piece 315.00
Coffeepot, Flowers, Gilt Trim, Rose Finial, 20th Century, 10 In. 196.00
Coffeepot, Ivy, Birds Head Handle, 20th Century, 11 1/2 In. 175.00
Compote, Figural, Young Children, Flowers, Footed, 20 In. 4780.00
Cooler, Cover, Fruit, Flower Sprigs, Crossed Swords, 7 1/2 x 9 In. 1150.00
Creamer, Lid, Blue Flowers, Flower Finial, Gilt, 5 1/2 In. 280.00
Creamer, Pink Flower, Gilt, Embossed Leaf Handle, Spout, 5 In. 310.00
Cup & Saucer, Figural, Flowers, Yellow Ground, Augustus Rex, Early 1800s 69.00
Cup & Saucer, Flower Sprays, Scattered Sprigs, Gilt, Angular Scroll Handle 320.00
Cup & Saucer, Flowers, Buildings, Gilt, Woven Serpent Handle, Footed Cup, 3 1/8 In. ... 489.00
Cup & Saucer, Garden Scene, Man, Woman, Green, 19th Century, 2 1/2 In. 160.00
Cup & Saucer, Man On Horse, Cobalt Blue Marbleized, Late 18th Century 489.00
Cup & Saucer, Portrait, Maria Theresia, 19th Century, 3 1/2 In. 350.00
Decanter, Snowball, Encrusted Flowers, Fruit, Birds, 11 1/4 In. 1245.00
Desk Set, 2 Inkwells, Cover, Rocker Blotter, Tray, Couples, Landscape, Blue, Incised 1495.00
Dish, Landscape, Bagpiper, Woman, Augustus Rex, 1700s, 6 1/4 In. 175.00
Dish, Sweetmeat, Figural, Lady & Gentleman, Flower Encrusted Dish, 12 1/2 In., Pair ... 1095.00
Figurine, Allegory Of Love, Incised 114, Stamped 52, 7 In. 1020.00
Figurine, Bacchus, Infant, Holding Flowers, Crossed Swords, 5 In. 288.00
Figurine, Bearded Man, 8 In. 550.00
Figurine, Bird, On Tree Stump, Yellow & Black, Crossed Swords, 9 3/4 In., Pair 1670.00
Figurine, Bird, Pecking Ball, Black Head, Green Body, Blue Tail Feather, 2 1/2 In. 315.00
Figurine, Bird, Sitting On Stump, 19th Century, 4 1/2 In. 259.00
Figurine, Bird, Yellow, Brown, White, On Tree Branches, 19th Century, 5 In. 375.00
Figurine, Bird, Yellow, Late 19th Century, 4 In. 315.00
Figurine, Boy & Girl Dancing, Fancy Costumes, 19th Century, 5 1/2 x 3 1/2 In. 1006.00
Figurine, Boy, Carrying Baskets Of Grapes, Signed, 5 1/2 In. 110.00
Figurine, Boy, Carrying Grapes, Early 19th Century, 4 In. 489.00
Figurine, Boy, Girl, Birdcage, Mask With Animal, Marked 120, 1800s, 4 1/2 In. .... *Illus* 1610.00
Figurine, Boy, Harvesting, Late 19th Century, 5 1/2 In. 290.00
Figurine, Boy, Holding Floral Wreath, 5 In. 125.00
Figurine, Boy, Mixing Cocoa, Marked 42, 19th Century, 4 x 4 1/2 In. 719.00
Figurine, Boy, On Ice Skates, Fur-Lined Robe, 5 In. 575.00
Figurine, Boy, Playing Flute, Marked, Early 19th Century, 4 In. 430.00
Figurine, Boy, Presenting Wreath, 19th Century, 5 In. 405.00
Figurine, Boy, Riding Toy Pull Horse, c.1905, 6 1/2 In. 1100.00
Figurine, Boy, Skating, Crossed Swords, 5 In. 345.00
Figurine, Boy, Sowing Seeds, Early 19th Century, 4 In. 140.00
Figurine, Bread Seller, Man, Large Basket Of Bread On Back, 1900s, 7 1/2 In. 588.00

Meissen, Figurine, Boy,
Girl, Bird Cage, Mask
With Animal, Marked
120, 1800s, 4 1/2 In.

Meissen, Teapot, Flowers, Birds, Gold Handle,
Early 19th Century, 4 In.

Figurine, Brown Bird, Crested, Eyeing Beetle On Branch, Crossed Swords, 12 In. 259.00
Figurine, Buddha, Nodding, Wagging Tongue, Elaborate Costume, Marked, c.1890, 12 In. 11200.00
Figurine, Cat & Dog, Watching Bird In Bath, 18th Century, 4 In. 1725.00
Figurine, Cherub, Bow & Arrow, Coup Sur Coup, 19th Century, 5 In. 1200.00
Figurine, Cherub, Boy, Le Decouvre Tout, Marked, Late 18th Century, 5 1/2 x 2 1/2 In. ... 1200.00
Figurine, Cherub, Girl, Flowers, Heart In Hand, Un Me Suffit, 19th Century, 5 x 2 1/2 In. 1200.00
Figurine, Cherub, Trimming Cloth, Blue Crossed Swords, 65 In. 860.00
Figurine, Cherub, Winged, 7 In. 1320.00
Figurine, Cherub, Winged, Wearing Quiver, Lying On Back, Faux Marble Socle, 6 In. ... 590.00
Figurine, Cherub, With Heart, 2nd Mark, Late 19th Century, 6 In. 1265.00
Figurine, Child, Bowl, Toy Pony, c.1905, 6 1/2 In. 935.00
Figurine, Child, Puppy, c.1905, 6 1/4 In. 1430.00
Figurine, Child, Seated On Cushion, c.1905, 4 1/2 In. 1980.00
Figurine, Children Playing, Signed, 4 In. 175.00
Figurine, Chocolate Lady, c.1900, 7 1/4 In. 885.00
Figurine, Couple, Child, Crossed Swords, 9 In. 1095.00
Figurine, Courting Couple, Blue Crossed Swords, 7 In. 1495.00
Figurine, Dog, Seated, Blue Crossed Swords, 9 x 12 In. 2130.00
Figurine, Fisherman, 19th Century, 4 x 3 In. 489.00
Figurine, Flower Seller, 18th Century Dress, Holding Basket, 20th Century, 6 In. 705.00
Figurine, Girl, Holding Doll, 1900s, 6 3/4 In. 500.00
Figurine, Girl, Holding Doll, Crossed Swords, 5 1/2 In. 1060.00
Figurine, Girl, Holding Flowers, Basket, 5 1/2 In. 460.00
Figurine, Girl, Holding Toy Lamb, Early 19th Century, 6 In. 920.00
Figurine, Girl, Playing Violin, Early 19th Century, 6 In. 748.00
Figurine, Girl, With Doll, Carriage, c.1905, 5 In. 1320.00
Figurine, Hen Turkey, 19th Century, 2 1/2 In. 259.00
Figurine, Lady, Fancy Dress, Hat, Early 19th Century, 6 In. 489.00
Figurine, Lady, Holding Flower Garland, 19th Century, 6 1/2 In. 575.00
Figurine, Lady, Holding Large Bowl, c.1880, 4 1/2 x 5 In. 245.00
Figurine, Lady, Wearing Mask, Fancy Gown, Early 19th Century, 6 In. 1265.00
Figurine, Magpie, Perched On Tree Trunk, Leaves, c.1934, 19 1/4 In. 750.00
Figurine, Man, Playing Bagpipes, Dog, Sheep, 19th Century, 10 1/2 In. 575.00
Figurine, Man, Singing, Sheet Music, 1700s Clothing, 5 1/4 In. 1045.00
Figurine, Man, Walking Staff, Signed, 5 1/2 In. 95.00
Figurine, Man, Woman, Rape Of Daphne, Marked, 19th Century, 9 In. 575.00
Figurine, Man, Writing, Sitting On Stump, Desk, 1700s Clothing, 5 1/2 In. 1430.00
Figurine, Melpomene, 10 1/2 In. 715.00
Figurine, Monkey Violinist, Green Coat, Straw Hat, Gilt, Early 1900s, 5 1/4 In. 705.00
Figurine, Owl, Brown, Orange, White, 19th Century, 2 In. 575.00
Figurine, Parrot, On Tree Trunk, Crossed Swords, 11 1/2 In. 405.00
Figurine, Potter, Seated At Wheel, Colorful Costume, Gilt Scroll Base, 7 3/4 In. 1955.00
Figurine, Putto, Je Les Enflamme, Crossed Swords, Incised, 5 1/4 In. 920.00
Figurine, Putto, Making A Cup Of Coffee, Crossed Swords, Incised, 4 In. 920.00
Figurine, Putto, Seminude Figure Puts Fish In Basket, Gilt Trim, c.1900, 3 3/4 In. 645.00
Figurine, Turkey, 19th Century, 2 1/2 In. 315.00
Figurine, Winged Cherub, 8 In., Pair 2270.00
Figurine, Woman, Fancy Dress, Hat, Signed, 5 3/4 In. 200.00
Figurine, Woman, Reading Letter, 8 In. 715.00

Figurine, Woman, Seated, Fan, Hat & Mask, Canceled Crossed Swords, 8 1/2 In.	2645.00
Figurine, Zeus, 15 1/4 In.	1980.00
Foot Tub, Oval, 2 Handles, Rose Pompadour Ground, Flowers, 8 x 22 1/2 x 15 In.	200.00
Group, 2 Children, Mask, 4 3/4 In.	770.00
Group, 3 Drunken Cherubs, Riding On Each Other, 19th Century, 5 1/2 x 4 1/2 In.	865.00
Group, 3 Figures, Bird In Cage, 8 In.	935.00
Group, 3 Putti, Gathered Around Easel, Gilt Base, Marked, 7 1/4 In.	1400.00 to 3000.00
Group, Bacchanalian Scene, 11 In.	1760.00
Group, Boy, Girl, Bird, In Cage, Marked 120, 19th Century, 5 1/2 x 4 1/2 In.	1495.00
Group, Boy, Holding Skull, Animal In Mouth, Girl, Holding Birdcage, 6 x 4 1/2 In.	1610.00
Group, Couple Seated, Playing Musical Instruments, PUG, Gilt Trim, 5 1/2 In.	1955.00
Group, Couple, Crossed Swords, 19th Century, 7 In.	405.00
Group, Europa The Bull, 3 Women, 7 1/2 x 4 In.	1840.00
Group, Fishing Scene, 12 In.	1760.00
Group, Juno & Jupiter, Holding Infant, Eagle, c.1870, 18 x 12 x 9 In.	3080.00
Group, Man, Lady, Playing Music In Garden, 6 x 5 In.	575.00
Group, Man, Woman, Draping Flower Garland Over Urn, Doves, Crossed Swords, 8 In.	1610.00
Group, Mythological, Triumph Of Amphitrite, Putti, Sea Nymphs, 19 x 23 In.	5290.00
Group, Perseus Presenting Head Of Medusa To Polydectes, 19th Century, 11 3/4 In.	6900.00
Group, Swan & Cygnets, Inscribed 177, Stamped 85, 5 1/4 In.	1245.00
Group, Venus & Cupid, Inscribed G72, 8 In.	1695.00
Oyster Plate, 6 Wells, Cobalt Blue, Gold, White, 9 In.	1210.00
Plaque, Swans, In Water, Birds Flying, Raised, 21 x 16 In.	2070.00
Plate, Artillery Regiment Commemorative, Laurel Wreath, Crown, 1889-1914, 9 In.	85.00
Plate, Boy, Cobalt, Jeweled, Marked, Piccolo, Nach H. Richtee, 9 In.	5465.00
Plate, Cherub, Gilt Embossed Border, 11 In.	620.00
Plate, Dessert Set, Cobalt Blue & Gold Rim, Floral Scenes, 8 In., 6 Piece	670.00
Plate, Dessert Set, Cobalt Blue & Gold Rim, Flower & Cherub Scenes, 8 In., 4 Piece	785.00
Plate, Flowers, Blue Ground, Blue Underglaze, 1850-1924, 11 In.	310.00
Plate, Flowers, Raised Gilt, Decoration Around Rim, 19th Century, 11 3/4 In.	250.00
Plate, Fruit, Painted, Fruit Sprig, Grapes, Plums, Leaf Garland Border, 8 3/4 In., Pair	705.00
Plate, Lilies Of The Valley, Scalloped, Lattice Mold, Late 19th Century, Marked, 9 In.	100.00
Plate, Modlin Honor, 2 Prussian Soldiers Survey Russian Palace, 10 In.	90.00
Plate, Panel Of Exotic Birds, Turquoise Ground, Lattice Pierced Rim, 9 1/2 In., Pair	435.00
Plate, Show, Gilt Relief Flowers, Blue Ground, c.1900, 11 In.	250.00
Platter, Figures In Water, Gilt, Handles	7500.00
Platter, Flowers, Cobalt Blue Border, Square, 16 In.	495.00
Platter, Flowers, Gold Trim, 17 x 12 In.	600.00
Platter, Mythological, Oval, Rocky Landscape, Late 18th Century, 12 1/2 In.	978.00
Platter, Purple, Black Flowers, Blue Feather Leaves, White Ground, Oval, 14 1/4 x 19 In.	275.00
Potpourri Keeper, Pierced, Urn Form, Playing Cherubs Hold Mask, 1800s, 5 1/2 In.	1380.00
Saltcellar, Double, Figural, Boy, Tricorn Hat, Double Basket, c.1900, 5 In.	646.00
Sauceboat, Flowers, Scrolled Handle, Crossed Swords, 8 In.	46.00
Stein, Crest, Porcelain, Pewter Lid, Crossed Swords, 1710-1910, 1/2 Liter	288.00
Stein, People On Horseback, Fountain, Strawberry Finial, Porcelain, 3/4 Liter, 7 In.	5750.00
Sweetmeat, Figural, Woman & Man Holding Basket, Rocaille Base, 5 In., Pair	1380.00
Sweetmeat Stand, 4 Tiers, Flowers, C Scrolls, Puce Ground, 13 1/2 In., Pair	575.00

Meissen, Teapot, Panel Scenes, Flowers,
Late 19th Century, 6 In.

Meissen, Teapot, Yellow, Flowers,
Early 19th Century, 4 1/4 In.

Tea Caddy, Yellow Ground, Shaped Panel Vignettes, Mulberry Transfer Scenes, 5 In. 75.00
Teapot, Flowers, Birds, Gold Handle, Early 19th Century, 4 In. .... *Illus* 138.00
Teapot, Flowers, Orange, Blue, Purple, Bugs, Butterflies, Twisted Handle, 19th Century .. 320.00
Teapot, Flowers, Yellow, Early 19th Century, 4 1/4 In. .... *Illus* 115.00
Teapot, Fruits, Flowers, 19th Century, 5 1/2 In. 210.00
Teapot, Ivy, 20th Century, 5 In. 105.00
Teapot, Ivy, Birds Head Spout, 20th Century, 6 1/2 In. 115.00
Teapot, Panel Scenes, Flowers, Late 19th Century, 6 In. .... *Illus* 175.00
Tray, Center Flowers, Gold Trim, Open Handles, Square, 16 In. 540.00
Tray, Flowers, Hausmalerie, Crossed Swords, 18 In. 175.00
Tray, Scrolled Acanthus, Gilt Trim, Crossed Swords, 19th Century, 13 In. 185.00
Tureen, Cover, Leaf Handles, Swirling Flower Finial, Oval, 9 1/2 x 13 3/4 In. 489.00
Urn, Classical Goddess, Angular Handles, Pate-Sur-Pate, c.1900, 12 1/2 In. 940.00
Urn, Pate-Sur-Pate, Cover, Wreath Finial, Snake Handles, Cherub, 11 In. 5650.00
Vase, Cartouche, Cobalt Blue Ground, Flared, Cylindrical, 15 3/4 In., Pair 5225.00
Vase, Cobalt Blue, Gilt Trim, 20th Century, 5 1/2 In. 140.00
Vase, Rose, 20th Century, 5 1/2 In. 105.00
Vase, Schneeballen, Vines, Yellow Bird, Thistle Shape, Crossed Swords, 9 1/2 In., Pair ... 3220.00
Vase, Snake Handles, Flower Cartouche, Germany, Early 1900s, 15 1/4 In. 1175.00
Vase, Trumpet Form, Flowers, Cobalt Blue Ground, 1800s, 6 3/4 In., Pair 489.00

MERCURY GLASS, or silvered glass, was first made in the 1850s. It lost
favor for a while but became popular again about 1910. It looks like a
piece of silver.

Gazing Ball, Pedestal, Snap Pontil, c.1850, 15 x 22 In. 1495.00
Sphere, Pedestal, Snap Pontil, Baluster Form, 1880, 15 x 22 In. 1495.00
Wig Stand, Blown, Round Base, Tapered Stem, Ball Top, Pontil, 9 1/2 In. 495.00
Witch's Ball, Pink, Mercury, 19th Century, 10 In. 35.00

MERRIMAC POTTERY Company was founded by Thomas Nickerson in
Newburyport, Massachusetts, in 1902. The company made art pottery,
garden pottery, and reproductions of Roman pottery. The pottery
burned to the ground in 1908.

Humidor, Frothy Semimatte Mottled Green Glaze, 3 Handles, Merrimac, 6 x 5 In. 920.00
Urn, Feathered Green Matte Glaze, Stamped, 6 3/4 x 6 In. 800.00
Vase, Bulbous, Textured Green Matte Glaze, Marked, Label, 10 x 8 1/2 In. 1150.00
Vase, Green Glaze, Brown Speckles, Tapered, Flared Mouth, 11 1/2 In. 2310.00
Vase, Green Glaze, Caramel Interior, Luster, Spherical, 3 1/2 x 4 In. 825.00
Vase, Green Matte Glaze, Thick, Flared Rim, Squat, Handles, Stamped, 4 1/2 In. 2070.00
Vase, Leathery Green Matte Glaze, Handles, Squat, Stamped, 4 1/4 x 4 In. 259.00
Vase, White Matte, Feathered Green, Squared Ridge, Angular Handles, 6 1/2 In. 470.00

METLOX POTTERIES was founded in 1927 in Manhattan Beach,
California. Dinnerware was made beginning in 1931. Evan K. Shaw
purchased the company in 1946 and expanded the number of patterns.
Poppytrail (1946-1989) and Vernonware (1958-1980) were divisions
of Metlox under E.K. Shaw's direction. The factory closed in 1989.

Antique Grape, Bowl, Vegetable, Round, 8 1/2 In. 44.00
Antique Grape, Gravy Boat, Underplate Attached, 1 Pt. 34.00
Antique Grape, Platter, Oval, 9 5/8 In. 50.00
Blue Dahlia, Bowl, Vegetable, Round, 9 In. 35.00
Brown-Eyed Susan, Teapot, Cover, 9 x 7 In. 95.00
California Freeform, Bowl, 8 1/4 In. 43.00
California Ivy, Bowl, Vegetable, Oval, Divided, 11 In. .... 44.00 to 55.00
California Ivy, Gravy Boat, Underplate Attached, 12 Oz. 43.00
California Ivy, Plate, Buffet Server, 13 1/4 In. 45.00
California Ivy, Platter, Oval, Or Gravy Liner, 9 In. 45.00
California Ivy, Sugar & Creamer 45.00
California Ivy, Teapot, Cover, 36 Oz., 6 Cup 89.00
California Provincial, Bowl, Vegetable, Basket Weave, 2 Tab Handles, 7 In. 50.00
California Provincial, Platter, Oval, 13 1/2 In. 49.00
California Strawberry, Bowl, Salad, 11 In. 35.00
California Strawberry, Platter, Oval, 13 In. 48.00

Colonial Heritage, Gravy Boat, 2 Spouts, Stick Handle	35.00
Cookie Jar, Cub Scout, 9 In.	400.00
Cookie Jar, Lion, 12 In.	149.00
Cookie Jar, Lucy Goosey, 14 1/4 In.	135.00
Cookie Jar, Mammy With Mixing Bowl, Blue Polka Dot, 12 1/2 In.	248.00
Cookie Jar, Mammy With Mixing Bowl, Yellow Polka Dot, 12 1/2 In.	203.00 to 550.00
Cookie Jar, Roller Skating Bear, 13 In.	149.00
Cookie Jar, Slenderella Pig, 13 In.	199.00
Cookie Jar, Squirrel On Pinecone, 12 In.	160.00
Cookie Jar, Teddy Bear In Blue Sweater, 12 In.	55.00
Cookie Jar, Topsy, Painted Ceramic, 9 3/4 In.	170.00
Della Robbia, Bowl, Vegetable, Divided, 12 x 9 In.	50.00
Fruit Basket, Bowl, Vegetable, Round, Vernonware, 8 1/4 In.	44.00
Gigi, Bowl, Vegetable, Round, Vernonware, 8 1/4 In.	44.00
Happy Time, Bowl, Vegetable, Divided, 8 In.	50.00
Happy Time, Gravy, 2 Spouts, Stick Handle, 6 In.	35.00
Heavenly Days, Tidbit, 3 Tiers, Vernonware	59.00
Homestead Provincial, Cigarette Box, 5 3/8 x 3 3/4 In.	199.00
Navajo, Teapot, Rattan Handle, 7 Cup	130.00
Organdie, Pitcher, 3 Qt., 11 1/4 In.	60.00
Provincial Blue, Tureen, Soup, Rooster Cover, Ladle, 1 Qt.	450.00
Provincial Fruit, Bowl, Vegetable, Divided, Green Stick Handle, 12 In.	50.00
Provincial Fruit, Canister Set, Covers, 1 Qt., 1 1/2 Qt., 2 Qt., 3 Qt., 4 Piece	166.00
Provincial Fruit, Sugar & Creamer	54.00
Red Rooster, Bowl, Salad, 11 1/8 In.	95.00
Red Rooster, Bowl, Vegetable, Basket Weave, 2 Tab Handles, 8 In.	50.00
Red Rooster, Bowl, Vegetable, Cover, Round, 12 In.	100.00
Red Rooster, Bowl, Vegetable, Divided, Red, 12 In.	59.00
Red Rooster, Bowl, Vegetable, Red, Round, 8 1/2 In.	65.00
Red Rooster, Bread Server, 9 In.	100.00
Red Rooster, Butter, Cover	50.00 to 65.00
Red Rooster, Carafe, Cover, Warmer, Wooden Handle, 7 Cup	140.00
Red Rooster, Gravy Boat, Handle, 2 Spouts, 1 Pt.	50.00
Red Rooster, Jam Jar, 5 In.	65.00
Red Rooster, Pitcher, Water, 2 1/4 In.	120.00
Red Rooster, Platter, Oval, 13 1/2 In.	50.00
Red Rooster, Sugar & Creamer	68.00
Red Rooster, Teapot, 7 Cup	50.00
Rose-A-Day, Tidbit, Handle, 10 In.	60.00
San Fernando, Teapot, Vernonware, 6 Cup	90.00
Sculptured Daisy, Platter, 11 In.	59.00
Sculptured Daisy, Platter, Oval, 14 1/4 In.	85.00
Sculptured Grape, Casserole, Cover, 1 Qt.	68.00
Sherwood, Bowl, Vegetable, Divided, 9 1/2 In.	50.00
Tickled Pink, Bowl, Vegetable, Divided, Vernonware, 9 1/2 In.	35.00
Tickled Pink, Celery Dish, Vernonware, 9 1/2 In.	35.00
Tickled Pink, Chop Plate, Vernonware, 13 In.	45.00
Tickled Pink, Gravy Boat, Vernonware, 1 Pt.	35.00
Tickled Pink, Pitcher, Vernonware, 8 In.	45.00
True Blue, Bowl, Vegetable, Round, Vernonware, 8 1/4 In.	35.00 to 45.00
True Blue, Casserole, Vernonware, Cover, Oval, Fluted, Scalloped Edge, 1 1/4 Qt.	80.00

METTLACH, Germany, is a city where the Villeroy and Boch factories worked. Steins from the firm are marked with the word *Mettlach* or the castle mark. They date from about 1842. Pieces marked *Mettlach* are still being made. *PUG* means painted under glaze. The steins can be dated from the marks on the bottom, which include a date-number code. Other pieces may be listed in the Villeroy & Boch category.

Ashtray, No. 2847, Art Nouveau, Etched, 5 In.	375.00
Ashtray, No. 2963, Art Nouveau, Girl's Portrait, Etched, 6 In.	230.00
Beaker, No. 2327, 1/4 Liter, Student Society, Hand Painted	255.00
Beaker, No. 2327-1032, 1/4 Liter, Dwarfs, PUG	80.00
Beaker, No. 2327-1136, 1/4 Liter, Black Forest Couple, PUG	140.00

Beaker, No. 2327-1200, 1/4 Liter, 12 Cities Of Germany, PUG 115.00
Beaker, No. 2327-1290K, 1/4 Liter, Republique Francaise, PUG 275.00
Beaker, No. 2327-1302, 1/4 Liter, American Eagle, U.S. Flag, Statue Of Liberty, PUG ... 240.00
Beaker, No. 2368, 1/4 Liter, Student Society, Alsatia Seis Panier 240.00
Beaker, No. 2368-1032, 1/4 Liter, Gnomes Drinking, PUG 100.00
Beaker, No. 2368-1095, Man Smoking, PUG, 1/4 Liter 80.00
Beer Tap, No. 2672, Knight In Castle, Etched, H. Schlitt, 18 1/2 In. 750.00
Butter, Cover, No. 3104, Etched Art Nouveau Design, 3 1/4 x 5 In. 230.00
Cake Plate, No. 2873, Cameo, 6 1/2 x 11 1/2 In. 460.00
Charger, Woman At Lake With Swans, Art Nouveau, R. Thevenin, 15 1/2 In. 2350.00
Clock, No. 2414, Brass Floral Metal Work, Etched, Art Nouveau, 23 In. 2415.00
Cup & Saucer, No. 353, Gray, Blue, White, Platinum, 2 1/4-In. Cup 80.00
Jar, No. 3101-405, Bavaria, Enameled, Cover, 3 1/4 In. 200.00
Pitcher, No. 1380, Repeating Design, Glazed Relief, 7 3/4 In. 135.00
Pitcher, No. 2433, Art Nouveau Flowers, Etched, 8 3/4 In. 690.00
Pitcher, No. 2486, Swans In Stream, Trees, 7 3/4 In. 980.00
Pitcher, No. 3322, Etched, Art Nouveau Design, Green & White, 4 1/4 In. 270.00
Pitcher, No. 6080, Green, 7 1/2 In. 65.00
Pitcher, Underplate, No. 2947, Blue & Gold, Art Nouveau, 6-In. Pitcher .... *Illus*   195.00
Planter, No. 2910, Art Nouveau, Etched, 4 3/4 x 12 In. 690.00
Plaque, Aesthetic Movement, Stoneware, Allegorical, C.Warth, Germany, c.1890, Pair ... 1060.00
Plaque, No. 1044-159, Kaub On Rhine, PUG, 12 In. 155.00
Plaque, No. 1044-991, Gnomes Picking Grapes, PUG, 7 1/2 In. 430.00
Plaque, No. 1044-1067, Man Sitting On Hillside, Barn, Water Wheel, PUG, 17 1/2 In. 280.00
Plaque, No. 1044-9041, Weggis, PUG, 12 In. 320.00
Plaque, No. 1178, Portrait Of Woman, Leaves, 16 1/2 In. 230.00
Plaque, No. 1365, Castle, Etched, 17 In. 575.00
Plaque, No. 1473, Woman Picking Flowers, Etched, C. Warth, 17 In. 1610.00
Plaque, No. 1489, Woman Picking Grapes, Etched, C. Warth, 17 In. 2530.00
Plaque, No. 2188, Haus Habsburg, Man On Horseback, Etched, 17 1/2 In. 569.00
Plaque, No. 2322, Knight Kissing Woman, Etched, 14 1/2 In. 605.00
Plaque, No. 2533, Godesburg Castle, Etched, 17 1/2 In. 750.00
Plaque, No. 2626, Drinking Cavalier, Etched, 7 1/2 In. .... *Illus*   105.00
Plaque, No. 2795, 2 Cavaliers, Serving Wench, Cameo, c.1910, 17 1/2 In. 560.00
Plaque, No. 5182, Man, With Large Hat, Delft, F. Hals, 14 In. 220.00
Plaque, No. 7066, Woman Looking Into Mirror, Phanolith, 6 In. 185.00
Pokal, No. 2171, Music Decoration, Etched, 7 3/4 In. 425.00
Punch Bowl, No. 375, 10 Liter, Dog & Cow Heads, Farm Scene, Flared Rim 425.00
Punch Bowl, No. 1888, 6 Liter, Prussian Eagle, Relief, Inlaid Lid 865.00
Punch Bowl, No. 2087, 8 Liter, Figures Dancing, Relief 470.00
Punch Bowl, No. 2226-1062, Tavern Scenes, Dwarf Lid, PUG, 1 3/4 Liter 470.00
Punch Bowl, No. 2234, 6 Liter, Birds Eating Grapes From Vines, Dwarf Finial 410.00
Punch Bowl, No. 2339-1028, 7 1/2 Liter, Dwarfs, PUG, Lid, H. Schlitt 170.00
Punch Bowl, No. 2843, 8 3/4 Liter, Dancing & Music, Etched, H. Schlitt 2130.00
Punch Bowl, No. 3334, 6 2/3 Liter, Cover, Underplate, 2 Scenes, People Drinking 575.00
Stein, No. 171, 1/2 Liter, 5 People & Dog, Inlaid Lid ....145.00 to 175.00

Mettlach, Pitcher, Underplate, No. 2947,
Blue & Gold, Art Nouveau, 6-In. Pitcher

Mettlach, Plaque, No. 2626, Drinking Cavalier,
Etched, 7 1/2 In.

Stein, No. 202, 1 Liter, Choir, Inlaid Lid 240.00
Stein, No. 285, 1/2 Liter, Fraternal, PUG, Pewter Lid 240.00
Stein, No. 328, 1/2 Liter, Man With Keg & Steins, Inlaid Lid 175.00
Stein, No. 485, 1 Liter, Musician, Inlaid Lid 365.00
Stein, No. 485, 1 Liter, Musician, Pewter Lid 195.00
Stein, No. 809, 1 Liter, Bacchus, Inlaid Lid 290.00
Stein, No. 812, 1 Liter, Hunters, Inlaid Lid . . . . .110.00 to 285.00
Stein, No. 1028, 1/2 Liter, Man, Woman With Harvest, Inlaid Lid 150.00
Stein, No. 1059, 1/2 Liter, Geometric Design, Inlaid Lid 100.00
Stein, No. 1095, 1/2 Liter, Geometric Design, Inlaid Lid 430.00
Stein, No. 1132, 1/2 Liter, Crocodile & Violinist At Pyramids, Inlaid Lid 220.00
Stein, No. 1161, 7 Liter, 2 Ladies, Verse, Etched, Inlaid Lid 3910.00
Stein, No. 1162, 1/2 Liter, Dancing Scenes, Etched, Inlaid Lid . . . . .150.00 to 240.00
Stein, No. 1163, 1/2 Liter, Musicians, Inlaid Lid 485.00
Stein, No. 1164, 1/2 Liter, Musician & Girl, Inlaid Lid 240.00
Stein, No. 1265, 1/4 Liter, Crests, Inlaid Lid 175.00
Stein, No. 1394, 1/2 Liter, German Card, Inlaid Lid . . . . .405.00 to 485.00
Stein, No. 1396, 1/2 Liter, Nymph Drinking, Etched, Inlaid Lid 500.00
Stein, No. 1403, 1/2 Liter, Cavalier Bowling, Etched, Inlaid Lid . . . . .185.00 to 365.00
Stein, No. 1471, 1/2 Liter, Musicians, Inlaid Lid, C. Warth 485.00
Stein, No. 1508, 1/2 Liter, Tavern Scene, Etched, Inlaid Lid 290.00
Stein, No. 1526, 1/2 Liter, Bavaria, Pro Fide, Hand Painted, Pewter Lid 290.00
Stein, No. 1526, 1/2 Liter, Bend In Saar River, PUG, Pewter Lid 255.00
Stein, No. 1526, 1/2 Liter, F. Schaller Hotel Du Nord, PUG, Pewter Lid 80.00
Stein, No. 1526, 1 Liter, Man Looking Into Beer Stein, Pewter Lid With Lyre 170.00
Stein, No. 1526-979, 1 Liter, Dwarfs Bowling, PUG, Pewter Lid 100.00
Stein, No. 1526-1076, 1/2 Liter, Hunter, PUG, Pewter Lid 285.00
Stein, No. 1527, 1/2 Liter, Cavaliers Drinking, Inlaid Lid 725.00
Stein, No. 1533, 1 Liter, Man Drinking, Etched, Tapestry, Pewter Lid 265.00
Stein, No. 1536, 1 Liter, Man With Pipe, Tapestry, Pewter Lid 190.00
Stein, No. 1577, 4 1/2 Liter, 12 People At Dinner, Pewter Lid 1425.00
Stein, No. 1643, 1/2 Liter, Student Drinking Beer, Tapestry, Etched, Pewter Lid 265.00
Stein, No. 1646, 1 Liter, Man Drinking, Etched, Tapestry, Pewter Lid 360.00
Stein, No. 1647, 1/2 Liter, Man, Holding Up Stein, Tapestry, Pewter Lid 150.00
Stein, No. 1654, 1/4 Liter, Geometric Design, Mosaic, Hinged Lid 127.00
Stein, No. 1655, 1/2 Liter, Dancing, Etched, Inlaid Lid 605.00
Stein, No. 1675, 1/2 Liter, Heidelberg, Etched, Inlaid Lid .489.00 to 575.00
Stein, No. 1690, 4 1/2 Liter, Man & Woman Riding Horses, Etched, Inlaid Lid 1466.00
Stein, No. 1725, 1/4 Liter, Man & Woman, Inlaid Lid, C. Warth 270.00
Stein, No. 1733, 1/2 Liter, 3 Scenes, Jockeys & Horses, Inlaid Lid 845.00
Stein, No. 1734, 1 1/2 Liter, Lovers, Etched, Inlaid Lid, C. Warth 835.00
Stein, No. 1740, 1/4 Liter, Leaves & Scroll, Relief, Hinged Lid 80.00
Stein, No. 1745, 1/4 Liter, Leaves & Scroll, Relief, Hinged Lid 125.00
Stein, No. 1756, 1 Liter, Student Drinking, Relief & Tapestry, Inlaid Lid 230.00
Stein, No. 1759, 1 Liter, Man Smoking Pipe, Relief & Tapestry, Inlaid Lid . . . . . . .325.00 to 775.00
Stein, No. 1786, 1/2 Liter, St. Florian Extinguishing Fire, Etched, Pewter Lid . . . . .570.00 to 695.00
Stein, No. 1786, 1 Liter, St. Florian Extinguishing Fire, Pewter Lid 690.00
Stein, No. 1794, 1/2 Liter, Bismarck, Etched, Inlaid Lid 405.00
Stein, No. 1795, 1/2 Liter, Freiburg, Inlaid Lid 2110.00
Stein, No. 1796, 1/2 Liter, Drunken Cavalier, Etched, Inlaid Lid, C. Warth 370.00
Stein, No. 1797, 1/2 Liter, 4 Cards, Inlaid Coin Lid 430.00
Stein, No. 1818, 6 1/4 Liter, Men Drinking At Barrel, Etched, Pewter Lid 1466.00
Stein, No. 1819, 1/2 Liter, Masonic, Etched, Inlaid Lid, C.Warth 575.00
Stein, No. 1856, 1/2 Liter, Postman, Etched, Glazed, Inlaid Lid 1840.00
Stein, No. 1861, 1/2 Liter, Kaiser Wilhelm II, Pewter Lid, PUG 230.00
Stein, No. 1863, 1/2 Liter, Stuttgart, Etched, Inlaid Lid .230.00 to 460.00
Stein, No. 1893, 1 Liter, Repeating Design, Mosaic, Pewter Lid 580.00
Stein, No. 1909-673, 1/2 Liter, Dwarfs, PUG, Pewter Lid 345.00
Stein, No. 1909-702, 1/2 Liter, Parade, PUG, Pewter Lid . . . . .190.00 to 305.00
Stein, No. 1909-715, 1/2 Liter, Hildabrand, Perkeo, Rodenstein, Falstaff, PUG, Pewter Lid 210.00
Stein, No. 1909-726, 1/2 Liter, Beer Steins To Be Filled, PUG, Pewter Lid, H. Schlitt 435.00
Stein, No. 1909-727, 1/2 Liter, Dwarfs Bowling, PUG, H. Schlitt, Pewter Lid 360.00
Stein, No. 1909-942, 1/2 Liter, Night Watchman Meets Rooster, PUG, Pewter Lid 195.00

Stein, No. 1909-983, 1/2 Liter, Falstaff, PUG, Pewter Lid 190.00
Stein, No. 1909-1010, 1/2 Liter, Dwarfs, PUG, Pewter Lid 270.00
Stein, No. 1909-1074, 1/2 Liter, Man Seated At Table, PUG, Pewter Lid, H. Schlitt 266.00
Stein, No. 1909-1102, 1/2 Liter, Festive Drinking Scene, PUG, Pewter Lid 335.00
Stein, No. 1909-1366, 1/2 Liter, Students Walking Dogs, PUG, Pewter Lid, Helmet 696.00
Stein, No. 1914, 1/2 Liter, 4F Athletic Scene, Etched, Inlaid Lid 350.00
Stein, No. 1932, 1/2 Liter, Cavaliers Toasting, Etched, Inlaid Lid, C. Warth 299.00
Stein, No. 1940, 3 Liter, Brewmeister, Etched, Inlaid Lid, C. Warth 1159.00
Stein, No. 1968, 1/4 Liter, Lovers, Etched, Inlaid Lid ....365.00 to 665.00
Stein, No. 1972, 1/4 Liter, 4 Seasons, Etched, Inlaid Lid ....196.00 to 335.00
Stein, No. 1995, 1/2 Liter, Musician Drinking, Etched, Inlaid Lid 240.00
Stein, No. 1998, 1/2 Liter, Trumpeter Of Sackingen, Etched, Inlaid Lid 520.00
Stein, No. 2001B, 1/2 Liter, Medicine, Glazed, Inlaid Lid .... *Illus* 322.00
Stein, No. 2001D, 1/2 Liter, Mathematics, Glazed, Inlaid Lid 720.00
Stein, No. 2001E, 1/2 Liter, Natural Science, Glazed, Inlaid Lid 1380.00
Stein, No. 2001F, 1/2 Liter, Architecture, Glazed, Inlaid Lid 835.00
Stein, No. 2001G, 1/2 Liter, Engineering, Glazed, Inlaid Lid 920.00
Stein, No. 2002, 1/2 Liter, Munchen Skyline, Etched, Inlaid Lid ....235.00 to 360.00
Stein, No. 2003, 1/2 Liter, Knights, 3 Scenes, Etched, Inlaid Lid 496.00
Stein, No. 2009, 1/2 Liter, Man & Woman Kissing, Inlaid Lid 725.00
Stein, No. 2024, 1/2 Liter, Berlin Skyline, Etched, Glazed, Inlaid Lid ....520.00 to 575.00
Stein, No. 2025, 1/3 Liter, Children & Cherubs, Etched, Inlaid Lid 230.00
Stein, No. 2027, 1/2 Liter, Gambrinus, Etched, Inlaid Lid 605.00
Stein, No. 2027, 1 Liter, Gambrinus, Etched, Inlaid Lid 520.00
Stein, No. 2028, 1/2 Liter, Men In Tavern, Inlaid Lid ....   *Illus* 288.00
Stein, No. 2029, 1/2 Liter, Military Scene, Etched, Inlaid Lid 230.00
Stein, No. 2030, 1/2 Liter, Military Scene, Etched, Inlaid Lid 845.00
Stein, No. 2034, 1/2 Liter, Repeating Design, Mosaic, Inlaid Lid 690.00
Stein, No. 2036, 1/2 Liter, Owl, Inlaid Lid 600.00
Stein, No. 2038, 3 3/4 Liter, Rodenstein, Relief, Etched, Inlaid Lid 3985.00
Stein, No. 2049, 1/2 Liter, Chess, Etched, Inlaid Lid 1650.00
Stein, No. 2050, 1/2 Liter, Man & Woman, Verse, Etched, Inlaid Lid 1150.00
Stein, No. 2052, 1/4 Liter, Munich Child, Etched, Inlaid Lid 485.00
Stein, No. 2053, 3 1/2 Liter, 4F Design, Etched, Inlaid Lid 3865.00
Stein, No. 2054, 1/2 Liter, Man Drinking, Etched, Inlaid Lid 605.00
Stein, No. 2057, 1/3 Liter, Festive Dancing Scene, Etched, Inlaid Lid 210.00
Stein, No. 2057, 1/2 Liter, Festive Scene, Inlaid Lid 360.00
Stein, No. 2065, 2 1/4 Liter, Cavalier & Barmaid, Inlaid Lid, H. Schlitt 690.00
Stein, No. 2074, 1/2 Liter, Bird In Cage, Etched, Inlaid Lid 2705.00
Stein, No. 2086, 1/2 Liter, Festive Scene, Relief, Inlaid Lid 105.00
Stein, No. 2089, 1/2 Liter, Man Eating At Table, Angel, Etched, Inlaid Lid, H. Schlitt 785.00
Stein, No. 2090, 1/3 Liter, Man Smoking At Table, Etched, Inlaid Lid, H. Schlitt 280.00
Stein, No. 2090, 1/2 Liter, Man Smoking At Table, Etched, Inlaid Lid, H. Schlitt 485.00
Stein, No. 2091, 1/2 Liter, St. Florian Extinguishing Fire, Etched, Inlaid Lid, H. Schlitt .. 660.00
Stein, No. 2092, 1/2 Liter, Dwarf Adjusting Clock, Etched, Inlaid Lid, H. Schlitt ..280.00 to 720.00
Stein, No. 2093, 1/2 Liter, Cards, Etched, Inlaid Lid 660.00
Stein, No. 2094, 1/2 Liter, Female Musicians, Etched, Inlaid Lid 415.00
Stein, No. 2097, 1/2 Liter, Music, Etched, Inlaid Lid 485.00
Stein, No. 2098, 4 1/4 Liter, Flowers, Mosaic, Inlaid Lid 300.00
Stein, No. 2103, 1 1/2 Liter, Drunken Man On Barrel, Etched, Inlaid Lid 1380.00
Stein, No. 2121, 1/4 Liter, Toddlers, Etched, Inlaid Lid 185.00
Stein, No. 2123, 1/3 Liter, Knight Drinking, Etched, Inlaid Lid 449.00
Stein, No. 2123, 1/2 Liter, Knight Drinking, Etched, Inlaid Lid, H. Schlitt 1449.00
Stein, No. 2133, 1/2 Liter, Dwarf In Tree, Etched, Inlaid Lid, H. Schlitt 1325.00
Stein, No. 2134, 1/2 Liter, Dwarf Sitting In Nest, Inlaid Lid, H. Schlitt 2660.00
Stein, No. 2136, 1/2 Liter, Adolphus Busch, Etched, PUG, Inlaid Lid 3105.00
Stein, No. 2176-1055, 2 Liter, Drunken Cavaliers, PUG, Pewter Lid ....545.00 to 635.00
Stein, No. 2177-960, 1/4 Liter, Jester, PUG, Pewter Lid, H. Schlitt 230.00
Stein, No. 2178-956, 2 1/2 Liter, Dwarfs Pull Barrel To Party, PUG, Pewter Lid, H. Schlitt 420.00
Stein, No. 2180-955, 3 1/3 Liter, Drinking Scenes, PUG, Pewter Lid, H. Schlitt 575.00
Stein, No. 2190, 1/2 Liter, Bicycle Race, Etched, Inlaid Lid 965.00
Stein, No. 2191, 1/2 Liter, Etruscan, Etched, H. Schlitt, Inlaid Lid 530.00
Stein, No. 2193, 3 Liter, Etruscan Scene, Etched, Pewter Lid, H. Schlitt 605.00

Mettlach, Stein, No. 2001B, 1/2 Liter, Medicine, Glazed, Inlaid Lid

Mettlach, Stein, No. 2028, 1/2 Liter, Men In Tavern, Inlaid Lid

Mettlach, Stein, No. 2880, 1/2 Liter, Men Eating At Table, Inlaid Lid

Stein, No. 2204, 1 Liter, Prussian Eagle, Relief, Inlaid Lid ....775.00 to 1180.00
Stein, No. 2205, 5 Liter, Diana & Hunters, Etched, Inlaid Lid 1810.00
Stein, No. 2206, 3 Liter, Tavern Scene, Etched, Inlaid Lid 1210.00
Stein, No. 2210, 3 1/4 Liter, Bowling Scene, Relief, Inlaid Lid 230.00
Stein, No. 2220, 3 1/4 Liter, Peacock, Flowers, Relief, Inlaid Lid 259.00
Stein, No. 2230, 1/2 Liter, Man & Barmaid, Etched, Inlaid Lid ....375.00 to 578.00
Stein, No. 2235, 1/2 Liter, Barmaid Holding Up Steins, Etched, Inlaid Lid 400.00
Stein, No. 2238, 1/2 Liter, 7th Regiment Armory, Etched, Inlaid Lid 920.00
Stein, No. 2255, 1 Liter, Etruscan Wedding Scene, Etched, Inlaid Lid 370.00
Stein, No. 2262-1014, 4 1/4 Liter, Munich Maid, PUG, Pewter Lid, H. Schlitt 978.00
Stein, No. 2262-1054, 4 1/4 Liter, Gambrinus, PUG, Pewter Lid, H. Schlitt 1550.00
Stein, No. 2271-1107, 1/2 Liter, Seven Swabians, Campfire, PUG, Pewter Lid, H. Schlitt . 460.00
Stein, No. 2277, 1/3 Liter, Heidelberg, Etched, Inlaid Lid 265.00
Stein, No. 2277, 1/3 Liter, Nurnberg, Etched, Inlaid Lid 265.00
Stein, No. 2277, 1/3 Liter, Wartburg, Etched, Inlaid Lid 360.00
Stein, No. 2282, 1/2 Liter, Father Scolding Boy For Drinking Beer, Etched, Inlaid Lid ... 175.00
Stein, No. 2285, 1/2 Liter, Lovers, Etched, Inlaid Lid 535.00
Stein, No. 2286, 3 Liter, Tavern Scene, Etched, Inlaid Lid 820.00
Stein, No. 2348-1022, 3 1/4 Liter, Musicians, PUG, Pewter Lid 259.00
Stein, No. 2363, 1/2 Liter, Black Whale Of Ascalon, Relief, Inlaid Lid 320.00
Stein, No. 2382, 1/2 Liter, Thirsty Rider, Etched, Inlaid Lid, H. Schlitt ....375.00 to 535.00
Stein, No. 2382, 1 Liter, Thirsty Rider, Inlaid Lid, H. Schlitt ....690.00 to 765.00
Stein, No. 2401, 1/2 Liter, Tannhauser In The Venusberg, Etched, Inlaid Lid 470.00
Stein, No. 2401, 1 Liter, Tannhauser In The Venusberg, Etched, Inlaid Lid 1380.00
Stein, No. 2402, 1/2 Liter, Siegfried, Etched, Inlaid Lid 710.00
Stein, No. 2441, 1/2 Liter, Men Playing Dice, Etched, Inlaid Lid 489.00
Stein, No. 2481, 1 1/4 Liter, Hildegund Aiding Wounded, Etched, Inlaid Lid 1690.00
Stein, No. 2482, 1 1/4 Liter, Shooting Festival, Inlaid Lid, F. Quidenus 665.00
Stein, No. 2501, 1/2 Liter, Drinking Scene, Etched, Inlaid Lid, F. Quidenus 605.00
Stein, No. 2520, 1/2 Liter, Student Drinking, Etched, Inlaid Lid, H. Schlitt 560.00
Stein, No. 2526, 1/2 Liter, Hunting Scene, Relief, Pewter Lid, Creussen 550.00
Stein, No. 2530, 1 Liter, Boar Hunting Scene, Inlaid Lid ....635.00 to 845.00
Stein, No. 2531, 1/2 Liter, Monk With Jug, Etched, Inlaid Lid, F. Quidenus 575.00
Stein, No. 2532, 1/2 Liter, Drunken Scene, Etched, Inlaid Lid, F. Quidenus 390.00
Stein, No. 2580, 1 Liter, Castle Scene, Etched, Inlaid Lid 489.00
Stein, No. 2581, 1/2 Liter, Choir, Etched, Inlaid Lid 345.00
Stein, No. 2582, 1 Liter, Jester Performing On Table, Inlaid Lid, F. Quidenus .....430.00 to 635.00
Stein, No. 2582, 1/2 Liter, Jester Performing On Table, Etched, Inlaid Lid, F. Quidenus .. 569.00
Stein, No. 2608, 1/3 Liter, Drinking, Courting & Music, Cameo, Inlaid Lid 210.00
Stein, No. 2639, 1/2 Liter, Blacksmith & Cavalier, Etched, Inlaid Lid 475.00
Stein, No. 2640, 1/2 Liter, Drinking Scene, Etched, Inlaid Lid ....525.00 to 575.00
Stein, No. 2652, 1/4 Liter, Man Kneeling, Cameo, Inlaid Lid 350.00
Stein, No. 2693, 1/2 Liter, Tavern Scene, Etched, Inlaid Lid 645.00
Stein, No. 2716, 1 Liter, Waitress, Etched, Inlaid Lid, F. Quidenus 965.00
Stein, No. 2718, 1/2 Liter, David & Goliath, Etched, Glazed, Inlaid Lid 1930.00
Stein, No. 2754, 1/2 Liter, 3 Panels With Couples, Etched, Cameo, Inlaid Lid 545.00
Stein, No. 2765, 1/2 Liter, Knight Riding White Horse, Etched, Inlaid Lid 2590.00
Stein, No. 2767, 1/2 Liter, Munich Child, Etched, Inlaid Lid, H. Schlitt 569.00
Stein, No. 2776, 1/2 Liter, Man In Wine Cellar, Etched, Inlaid Lid ....445.00 to 845.00
Stein, No. 2785-6130, 2 1/4 Liter, Man Playing Bagpipe, Rookwood, Pewter Lid 605.00

Stein, No. 2789-6134, 1/2 Liter, Man Smoking Pipe, Rookwood, Pewter Lid 240.00
Stein, No. 2796, 3 Liter, Heidelberg, Etched, Inlaid Lid 575.00
Stein, No. 2797, 4 Liter, Richard Wagner, Etched, Inlaid Lid 1150.00
Stein, No. 2800, 1/2 Liter, Art Nouveau, Hops, Etched, Inlaid Lid 530.00
Stein, No. 2801, 2 1/8 Liter, Art Nouveau, Etched, Inlaid Lid 1150.00
Stein, No. 2807, 1/2 Liter, Men & Women Drinking, Etched, Inlaid Lid 725.00
Stein, No. 2813, 1/2 Liter, St. Hubert, Etched, Inlaid Lid 485.00
Stein, No. 2833A, 1/2 Liter, Man Under Tree, Etched, Inlaid Lid 485.00
Stein, No. 2833D, 1/2 Liter, Man & Woman, Etched, Inlaid Lid 485.00
Stein, No. 2833E, 1/2 Liter, Soldiers, Etched, Inlaid Lid 534.00
Stein, No. 2833F, 1/2 Liter, Student Drinking, Etched, Inlaid Lid 483.00
Stein, No. 2836, 1/2 Liter, 3 Scenes Of People, Etched, Cameo, Inlaid Lid 375.00
Stein, No. 2871, 1 Liter, Cornell University, Etched, Inlaid Id 345.00
Stein, No. 2878, 1/2 Liter, 2 Bavarian Women, Tapestry, Etched, Pewter Lid 345.00
Stein, No. 2880, 1/2 Liter, Men Eating At Table, Inlaid Lid . . . . *Illus* 310.00
Stein, No. 2887, 1/2 Liter, Knights At Table, Etched, Inlaid Lid 460.00
Stein, No. 2888, 1 Liter, 3 Men Walking On Path, Etched, Inlaid Lid 845.00
Stein, No. 2894, 1/2 Liter, Heidelberg, Etched, Inlaid Lid 920.00
Stein, No. 2900, 1/2 Liter, Quilmes, Argentina, Etched, Inlaid Lid 400.00
Stein, No. 2921, 2 4/5 Liter, Campfire, Etched, Inlaid Lid 518.00
Stein, No. 2931, 1/2 Liter, Man & Barmaid, Relief, Inlaid Lid 210.00
Stein, No. 2936, 1/2 Liter, Elk's Club, Art Nouveau, Etched, Inlaid Lid 465.00
Stein, No. 2967, 1 Liter, Farmer Holding Pigs, Tapestry, Pewter Lid 230.00
Stein, No. 3078-419, 1/2 Liter, Owl & Wreath, Bavaria, Inlaid Lid 296.00
Stein, No. 3078-437, 1/2 Liter, Man & Woman, Bavaria, Inlaid Lid, F. Quidenus 310.00
Stein, No. 3080-409, 1/2 Liter, Repeating Design, Verse, Bavaria, Inlaid Lid 320.00
Stein, No. 3080-538, 1 Liter, Heidelberg Castle, Bavaria, Inlaid Lid 460.00
Stein, No. 3084, 3 Liter, Postman Tapestry, Pewter Lid 1090.00
Stein, No. 3085, 1/2 Liter, Postman, Etched, Tapestry, Relief Pewter 175.00
Stein, No. 3089, 1/2 Liter, Diogenes, Etched, Inlaid Lid, H. Schlitt 690.00
Stein, No. 3091, 1/2 Liter, Knight Drinking From Stein, Etched, Inlaid Lid 405.00
Stein, No. 3099, 3 Liter, Diogenes, Etched, Inlaid Lid, H. Schlitt 2300.00
Stein, No. 3142, 1/2 Liter, Bavarian Scene, Etched, Inlaid Lid 805.00
Stein, No. 3177, 2 1/4 Liter, Hunting Scenes, Cameo, Inlaid Lid 1825.00
Stein, No. 3219, 1/2 Liter, Men Drinking, Etched, Inlaid Lid 635.00
Stein, No. 3342-546, 1/4 Liter, Card Suits, Bavarian, Inlaid Lid 1725.00
Stein, No. 5006, 1/2 Liter, Man Drinking, Faience, Pewter Lid 285.00
Stein, No. 5016, 1 1/3 Liter, Angels, Faience, Pewter Lid 805.00
Stein, No. 5022, 1 Liter, Rural Scene, Faience, Pewter Lid 1330.00
Stein, No. 5023, 1 Liter, Prussian Eagle, Faience, Pewter Lid 1955.00
Stein, No. 5024, 1 Liter, Flowers, Faience, Pewter Lid 1449.00
Stein, No. 5188, 1 Liter, Man Drinking, Pewter Lid, Delft 1930.00
Stein, No. 5188, 1/2 Liter, Man Drinking, Pewter Lid, Delft 299.00
Vase, No. 1336, Floral, Tan, Brown, Red & White, Mosaic, 10 1/2 In. 195.00
Vase, No. 1504, Geometric Design, Tan, Pink, Green & Blue, Mosaic, 5 In. 195.00
Vase, No. 1629, Etched & Glazed, 4 1/4 In. 140.00
Vase, No. 1661, Flowers, Brown & Green, Relief, 5 In. 339.00
Vase, No. 1808, Geometric Design, Brown & Tan, Mosaic, 6 In. 470.00
Vase, No. 1857, Angel Praying, Glazed, Relief, 8 1/2 In. 489.00
Vase, No. 2172, 3 Ladies, Etched, Etruscan, Griffen, Smith & Hill, 8 In. 345.00
Vase, No. 2209, Lohengrin, Figural Woman Handles, Etched, 17 1/2 In. 3335.00
Vase, No. 2568, Eagles Flying Through Wilderness, Etched, Chevroton, 14 In. 920.00
Vase, No. 2613-6105, People Outside Building, Rookwood, 9 3/4 In. 460.00
Vase, No. 3014-453, Woman Herding Cattle To River, PUG, 13 1/2 In. 196.00
Vase, No. 3014-1250, Children With Animals, PUG, 11 1/4 In. 375.00
Vase, No. 3357, Art Nouveau Flowers, Etched, 12 In. 720.00

MILK GLASS was named for its milky white color. It was first made in
England during the 1700s. The height of its popularity in the United
States was from 1870 to 1880. It is now correct to refer to some colored glass as blue milk glass, black milk glass, etc. Reproductions of
milk glass are being made and sold in many stores. Related pieces may
be listed in the Cosmos and Westmoreland categories.

Candlestick, Lace & Dewdrop, Kemple, 4 1/8 In. . . . . *Illus* 8.50

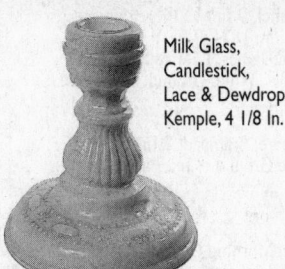

Milk Glass,
Candlestick,
Lace & Dewdrop,
Kemple, 4 1/8 In.

Milk Glass, Dish, Cover, Cabbage Head,
Blue, Vallerysthal, France, 6 In.

Dish, Cover, Cabbage Head, Blue, Vallerysthal, France, 6 In. . . . . *Illus*	85.00
Dish, Wheeling Ship Cover, 3 3/4 x 6 3/8 In.	22.00
Jar, Owl, Spread Wing Eagle Lid, Insert, 6 1/4 In.	50.00
Syrup, Alba, Enameled Flowers, Britannia Cover, 7 In.	50.00
Syrup, Peace & Plenty, Britannia Cover, 5 3/4 In.	145.00
Syrup, Swan & Cattails, Britannia Cover, 5 3/4 In.	145.00

MINTON china has been made in the Staffordshire region of England
from 1793 to the present. The firm became part of the Royal Doulton
Tableware Group in 1968, but the wares continued to be marked
Minton. The word *England* was added in 1891. Minton majolica is
listed in this book in the Majolica category.

Asparagus Server, Attached Undertray, 10 In.	670.00
Basket, Yellow Basket Weave, Oak Leaves, Twisted Handle, 11 1/2 In.	1000.00
Box, Cover, Turquoise, Pink Ribbon & Bow, 7 1/2 x 5 1/2 In.	500.00
Cachepot, Undertray, Turquoise, Cattail, c.1867, 8 In.	880.00
Centerpiece, 2 Putti, Kneeling, Lovebirds, 11 In.	3250.00
Centerpiece, Merman, Supporting Shell, Shape No. 852, 14 x 12 In.	1175.00
Charger, Winged Classical Male, England, c.1872, 11 3/4 In.	500.00
Creamer, Cobalt Blue, Flowers, Snail On Handle, Snail Feet, 5 In.	2750.00
Ewer, Cellini, Griffin Handle, Relief Putti, c.1873, 13 1/2 In.	1210.00
Figurine, Dorothea, Seated On Rock, John Bell Design, Parian, England, c.1868, 11 In. . .	440.00
Figurine, Miranda, Parian, Woman Seat On Rocky Base, Waves At Feet, 15 1/4 In.	560.00
Figurine, Vintage Figures, Carrying Tub, Rope Handles, Cobalt Blue Base, 11 x 11 In. . . .	1375.00
Flask, Pilgrim, Butterflies, Oriental Border, Sky Blue Ground, Stamped, 6 x 5 1/2 In. . . .	2990.00
Fountain, Dolphin, Pedestal, 1865, 18 In.	2800.00
Group, Mother & First Born, A. Carrier-Belleuse, Parian, England, c.1872, 12 1/4 In. . . .	1765.00
Inhaler, Beetles, Butterflies, c.1870	5700.00
Jardiniere, Bamboo, Ribbon & Bow, Undertray, 10 x 11 In.	1230.00
Jardiniere, Foxglove, Morning Glory, Fern & Leaf, 21 1/2 x 14 1/2 In.	5600.00
Jardiniere, Passion Flower, Lion's Heads Handles, Cobalt Blue, 13 1/2 x 18 In.	3300.00
Jug, Christmas, Cobalt Blue, Holly & Berries, 6 1/2 In.	800.00
Jug, Tower, Pewter & Majolica Lid, Jester Finial, Relief Medieval Figures, 13 In.	1155.00
Oyster Plate, 4 Wells, Basket Weave Ground, Aqua Wells, Rectangular, 9 x 7 1/2 In.	4180.00
Oyster Plate, 5 Wells, Cobalt Blue Wells, Green Fish Dividers	6050.00
Oyster Plate, 6 Wells, Malachite, 9 In.	1320.00
Oyster Plate, 6 Wells, Seafoam Green, Emerald Green Center, 9 In.	440.00
Oyster Plate, 7 Wells, White, Yellow, Brown, Gold Trim, 9 1/4 In.	330.00
Pedestal, Cobalt Blue, Pink Ribbon, Drapes With Fruit & Nuts, 11 In.	275.00
Pedestal, Oriental Motif, Turquoise, Open Cut Sides, 31 x 14 1/2 In.	3850.00
Pitcher, Pate-Sur-Pate Butterfly, Round Medallions, Late 19th Century, 7 1/2 In.	600.00
Plate, Butterfly, Ironstone, Multicolored, 9 1/2 In.	605.00
Plate, Cherubs, Pate-Sur-Pate Cartouche, Pierced Border, Turquoise, Gilt, Jewels, 10 In. .	600.00
Plate, Cobalt Blue, Gilt Borders, Tiffany & Co., 10 1/2 In., 12 Piece	1870.00
Plate, Dessert, Printed, Enamel Border, Leaf Swags, Blue Diapered Bands, 9 In.	25.00
Plate, Dog Portrait, Cerulean Blue Rim, Gilt Leaf Tip Edge, c.1872, 9 5/8 In.	650.00
Plate, Gold Flowers & Leaves, Bone China, England, 1900s, 10 3/4 In., 12 Piece	1530.00
Plate, India Tree Pattern, Blue Underglaze, Iron Red, 10 1/8 In.	470.00
Plate, Ivory Ground, Multiple Gold Borders, 10 1/4 In., 12 Piece	360.00

Plate, Oriental Style Transfer, Flowers, Hand Painted, Label, 9 In., 12 Piece 315.00
Plate, Peony, Prunus, Sky Blue Ground, Oriental Medallion, 1874, 9 In. 690.00
Plate, Portrait, Girl, Artistic Dress, C.H. Spiers, Howell & James, Late 1800s, 9 1/2 In. .. 440.00
Plate, Yellow Daisies, Butterfly, Pink Border, Gold Accents, White Ground, 1870, 9 In. ... 135.00
Sardine Box, Attached Undertray, Cobalt, c.1884 .... 1980.00
Tile, Bird On Branch, With Cherries, 8 In. 165.00
Tile, Medieval Organ Player, Embossed, Blue Glaze, Square, Stamped, 8 In. 145.00
Tile, Musicians, Cellist, Lyrist, Turquoise On Cobalt Blue Ground, 8 In., Pair 400.00
Tile, Violin Player, Amber, Frame, c.1880, 8 In. 315.00
Tray, Bird On Oak Leaf, Shape No. 1331, 8 In. 730.00
Tureen, Seafood, Shell & Mussel, Cover, 8 1/2 In. 990.00
Vase, Moon, Flowers, Moon Flask Form, Yellow Ground, Morning Glories, c.1910, 6 In. . 175.00
Vase, Pate-Sur-Pate, Classical Images, Cupid, Woman, Shoot Arrows, 8 3/4 In., Pair 12430.00
Vase, Pillow Shape, Embossed Chick, Cobalt Blue Ground, Signed, 5 1/2 x 5 In. 475.00
Vase, Turquoise, Figural, Peacock, Standing On Brown Base, 9 3/4 x 9 1/4 In. 220.00
Wine Cooler, Oval, Cobalt Blue Ground, Figurine Panel, Leaf Handles, 17 1/2 x 7 3/4 In. 3300.00

MIRRORS are listed in the Furniture category under Mirror.

MOCHA pottery is an English-made product that was sold in America during the early 1800s. It is a heavy pottery with pale coffee-and-cream coloring. Designs of blue, brown, green, orange, black, or white were added to the pottery and given fanciful names, such as *Tree, Snail Trail,* or *Moss.* Mocha designs are sometimes found in pearlware. A few pieces of mocha ware were made in France, the United States, and other countries.

Beaker, Geometrics, Blue Bands, Black Ground, 2 7/8 In. 520.00
Bowl, Bands, Black & Blue, White Slip Wavy Lines, Pearlware, c.1830, 6 1/2 In. 1115.00
Bowl, Bands, Blue, Marbleized Brown, Rust, Tan, White, Footed, c.1800, 3 1/8 x 4 1/2 In. 470.00
Bowl, Bands, Brown, Blue & White Heart Shape Leaves, 7 In. 375.00
Bowl, Bands, Green, Brown, Black, Cream, 7 1/4 x 4 3/8 In. 575.00
Bowl, Cover, Earthworm, Brown, White, Blue, Bands, Brown, Mustard Ground, 8 x 12 In. 5875.00
Bowl, Cover, Seaweed, Blue, Brown Stripes, White Band, Yellowware, 7 1/2 x 6 3/4 In. .. 520.00
Bowl, Earthworm, Black, Blue, White Brown, Black Rim, White Wavy Line, 6 x 3 1/4 In. 2090.00
Bowl, Earthworm, Blue Band, White, Rust, Brown, Black Strips, Tooled, Green Rim, 10 In. 3850.00
Bowl, Earthworm, Brown, White, 6 1/2 In. 850.00
Bowl, Earthworm, Pearlware, Brown, Ocher Band, White Zigzag, 4 7/8 In. 2235.00
Bowl, Earthworm, Yellow Band, Brown, Blue & White, 5 x 2 1/2 In. 460.00
Bowl, Marbleized, Brown, White, Black, Cafe Au Lait, Green Rim, 5 x 2 1/4 In. 1540.00
Bowl, Pearlware, Black & Blue Slip Bands, 1830, 6 1/2 In. 1116.00
Bowl, Pearlware, Blue Bands, Marbleized Brown, Rust, Tan, 3 1/8 In. 470.00
Bowl, Seaweed, Black, Stripes, Green & Brown Band, 6 1/4 x 3 In. 635.00
Bowl, Seaweed, Blue, Brown Stripes, White Band, Yellowware, East Liverpool, 4 x 10 In. 575.00
Bowl, Seaweed, Blue, White Slip Band, Yellowware, 6 3/4 In. 475.00
Bowl, Seaweed, Brown, Gold & Dark Brown Stripes, Band, 5 5/8 x 3 In. 495.00
Bowl, Seaweed, Butterscotch Ground, Incised Green Band, 6 1/2 In. 545.00
Bowl, Seaweed, Cobalt Blue, Olive, Brown, Taupe, White Slip, Early 19th Century, 7 In. . 1116.00
Bowl, Seaweed, White Slip Center, Brown Pinstripes, Yellowware, 12 1/2 In. 422.00
Canister, Cover, Seaweed, Conical, Cafe Au Lait, Brown Stripes, 4 1/2 In. 2090.00
Canister, Tea, Bands, Green Reeded, Brown, Ocher, Gray, Slip, Creamware, 4 3/4 In. ... 2468.00
Canister, Tea, Marbleized, Creamware, Brown Ocher, White & Gray, 1780, 5 In. 2465.00
Canister Set, Earthworm, Brown Band, Yellowware, 6 1/4 x 5 1/2 In. 495.00
Castor, Brown, Blue, White, 4 1/4 x 4 In. 920.00
Coffeepot, Tree, Baluster Form, Footed, Pearlware, Brown Bands, 10 In. 1060.00
Creamer, Bands, Balls, Light Brown, Green, Black Stripes, Leaf Handle, 4 In. 2970.00
Creamer, Geometrics, Fleur-De-Lis, Blue, Butterscotch Banding, 5 In. 230.00
Creamer, Marbleized Light Blue & Brown, Tapered, Gilt Rim, 3 1/4 In. 489.00
Crock, Butter, Earthworm, Handles, Yellowware, 6 1/2 x 7 3/4 In. 360.00
Cup & Saucer, Creamware, Blue With Black Checkered Rouletting, c.1785, 3 In. 590.00
Jar, Cover, Bands, Blue & Creamy White, Cylindrical, 1820, 5 3/8 In. 700.00
Jar, Cover, Seaweed, Blue, Thin Bands, Blue & White, c.1820, 5 3/8 x 6 In. 700.00
Jug, Bands, Blue, Black, Beaded Herringbone, Twigs, Slip Dots, Ocher, c.1820, 8 In. 7056.00
Jug, Bands, Blue, Taupe & Black, Pearlware, 1840, 7 In. 1295.00

Jug, Bands, Rust, Brown, Black, Engine Turned, Green Bands, Barrel, c.1790, 5 In. 1645.00
Jug, Barrel Form, Pearlware, Green Reeded Rim, Orange Field, 1810, 6 In. 3400.00
Jug, Barrel Form, Pearlware, Ocher, Blue & Black Rouletting Bands, 1820, 7 In. 7050.00
Jug, Barrel Form, Pearlware, Rust & Brown Bands, Ocher Field, 1810, 7 3/4 In. 1645.00
Jug, Cat's-Eye, Black, Bands, Blue, Black, Taupe, Slip Circles, Shipshape, c.1840, 7 In. ... 1293.00
Jug, Earthworm, Blue Bands, Blue Ground, 6 3/4 In. 920.00
Jug, Marbleized, Tan, Brown, White, Gold, Leaf Handle, 4 7/8 In. 2420.00
Jug, Seaweed, Black, Bands, Rust, Brown, Ocher Ground, Barrel Shape, c.1810, 7 3/4 In. . 3819.00
Jug, Seaweed, Black, Green Reeded Rim, Orange Ground, Barrel Shape, c.1810, 6 1/4 In. . 3400.00
Jug, Seaweed, Dark Brown, Bands, Brown Ground, Baluster, c.1820, 3 5/8 In. 355.00
Jug, Seaweed, Tan Ground, Butterscotch, Incised Green, Leaves, 7 In. 980.00
Jug, Trees, Brown & Green Reeded Band, c.1820, 3 5/8 In. 999.00
Mixing Bowl, Seaweed, Blue, White Band, Yellowware, 12 1/2 In. 506.00
Mixing Bowl, Seaweed, Dark Navy, Blue & White Bands, Yellowware, 12 x 5 3/4 In. 330.00
Mug, Agateware, Black & White Checkered Bands, 3 1/2 In. 805.00
Mug, Band, Blue, Brown Slip, Taupe Ground, c.1820, 1/2 Pt., 3 1/2 In. 705.00
Mug, Bands In Brown & Blue, Reeded, Wavy Rim, Black, 1820, Qt. 1525.00
Mug, Bands, Blue & Black, Yellow Edging, Incised Green Band, 5 5/8 In. 375.00
Mug, Bands, Brown & Rust, Oval, 2 3/4 In. 345.00
Mug, Bands, Olive, Brown, Slip-Filled, Engine-Turned, Foliate Terminal, c.1790, 3 3/4 In. . 440.00
Mug, Bands, Sage Green, Blue Stripes, Applied Handle, Molded Leaves, Child's, 2 5/8 In. . 250.00
Mug, Bands, Straight-Sided, Applied Loop Handle, 6 1/8 In. 155.00
Mug, Cat's-Eye, Blue, Black, Blue Bands, Pearlware, Early 1800s, 3 1/2 In. 470.00
Mug, Earthworm, Double Zigzag, Bands, Straight-Sided, Loop Handle, 5 In. 715.00
Mug, Earthworm, Loop, Bands, Straight-Sided, Applied Handle, 3 7/8 In. 690.00
Mug, Handles, Bands, Sea Worm Decoration, 19th Century, 4 1/2 In. 115.00
Mug, Marbleized, Black, White, Rust, Brown Ground, Green Reeded Band, c.1820, 6 In. . 1528.00
Mug, Pearlware, Brown & Blue With Green Bands, Black Marbleized, 1820, 6 In. 1530.00
Mug, Seaweed, Bands, Orange, Green, Blue Stripes, Leaf Handle, 5 3/4 In. 3025.00
Mug, Seaweed, Bands, Straight-Sided, Applied Loop Handle, 4 In. 145.00
Mug, Seaweed, Black Stripes, Brown Band, 3 1/2 In. 770.00
Mug, Seaweed, Black, Bands, Olive Green, White, Rust Ground, c.1820, Qt., 6 In. 2115.00
Mug, Seaweed, Brown, Blue & Black Bands, Sand Blasted, c.1900, Pt., 5 1/8 In. 355.00
Mug, Seaweed, Slate Blue Ground, Bands, 5 3/8 In. 400.00
Mug, Taupe & Blue Bands, Flowers Handle, Pearlware, 1820, 3 1/2 In. 705.00
Mug, Tree, Black, 3 Brown, 2 Blue Slip Bands, Ocher Ground, 5 7/8 In. 2705.00
Mug, Tree, Blue, Taupe Band, Pearlware, 1810, 1/2 Pt. 175.00
Mug, Tree, Reeded Blue Band, Gray Band, Pearlware, 1810, 4 3/4 In. 440.00
Mug, Trees, Bands, Black, Blue, Taupe, White, Imperial Pt., E.M. & Co., c.1900, 4 3/4 In. . 147.00
Mug, Trees, Black Mocha, Bands, White Ground, Marked, c.1810, 2 3/4 x 4 3/8 In. 500.00
Mug, Trees, Black, Bands, White Field, Extruded Handle, Mark, 1810, 3 In. 175.00
Mug, Trees, Brown Mocha, Blue Reeded Band, Gray, c.1810, Pt., 4 3/4 In. 440.00
Mug, Trees, Brown, Green Reeds, Thin Brown Lines, c.1800, Qt., 5 5/8 In. 2705.00
Mug, Trees, Whiteware, Bands, Black, White Field, 1810, 2 1/2 In. 175.00
Mustard Pot, Cat's-Eye, Bands, Bulbous, Applied Loop Handle, 3 In. 935.00
Mustard Pot, Cover, Seaweed, Black Stripes, Brown, Orange Band, Leaf Handles, 4 In. ... 1540.00
Mustard Pot, Seaweed, Brown Ground, White Handle, 3 1/2 In. 345.00
Mustard Pot, Seaweed, Dark Blown, Ocher Field, Pearlware, Barrel Form 590.00
Pepper Pot, Bands, Black & White Tooled, Blue Speckles, Light Blue Ground, 4 1/2 In. . 175.00
Pepper Pot, Bands, Black Vine Rouletting, Mustard, Creamware, 4 In. 410.00
Pepper Pot, Bands, Black, Vine, Roulette, Ocher Ground, c.1810, 2 1/2 In. 175.00
Pepper Pot, Bands, Blue & Black Ribs, Button Knop, Pearlware, 1840, 5 In. 825.00
Pepper Pot, Bands, Blue & Brown White Ground, 4 3/4 In. 259.00
Pepper Pot, Bands, Burnt Umber Stripes, Black Feather Design, 4 In. 2750.00
Pepper Pot, Cat's-Eye, Brown, Blue, Stripes, Tan, Dark Brown, 4 1/2 In. 2750.00
Pepper Pot, Checkered Center, Black, Band, Green, Light Brown Stripes, 4 In. 1320.00
Pepper Pot, Dome Top, Earthworm, Zigzag, Finial, Band Design, 4 7/8 In. 2310.00
Pepper Pot, Earthworm, White, Tan, Black, Blue, Band, Stripes, White, Black, 4 1/2 In. . 3850.00
Pepper Pot, Seaweed, Black, Band, Green, Black Stripes, 4 1/2 In. 935.00
Pepper Pot, Seaweed, Blue & White Bands, Yellowware, 5 In. 1400.00
Pepper Pot, Stripes, Light Blue, Black, Flat Top, 4 In. 800.00
Pitcher, 3 Bands, Yellowware, Stamped, Green & Co., Ltd., 4 7/8 In. 255.00
Pitcher, Bands, Barrel Shape, 6 1/2 In. 165.00

Pitcher, Bands, Blue & Gray, Black Stripes, Leaf Design In Center Band, 7 1/4 In. 230.00
Pitcher, Bands, Blue, Black, Brown, Oval, Ear Handle, 9 In. 1100.00
Pitcher, Bands, Bulbous, Applied Loop Handle, 6 3/4 In. 28.00
Pitcher, Bands, Medium Blue, Alternating White & Green, Flared Foot, 5 3/4 In. 115.00
Pitcher, Bands, Wide, Blue, Thin White Stripes, Flared Foot, 7 1/2 In. 145.00
Pitcher, Brown, Green, Yellowware, 8 1/2 In. 1705.00
Pitcher, Cat's-Eye, Black, 3 Gray Bands, Stripes, Tooled Green Lines At Neck, 6 3/4 In. . . 400.00
Pitcher, Cat's-Eye, Blue Neck, Earthworm On Base, Black, White, Ocher, 6 In. 400.00
Pitcher, Cat's-Eye, White & Black, Black Stripe, Green Band, Ocher, Handle, 6 1/2 In. . . . 1035.00
Pitcher, Earthworm, Balls, Tan Bands, Blue Stripes, Leaf Handle, 7 1/8 In. 4125.00
Pitcher, Earthworm, Black Stripes, Wide Band, Applied Leaf Ends, 6 In. 1035.00
Pitcher, Earthworm, Cat's-Eye, Blue, Black Stripes, Gray Band, Handle, 6 In. 460.00
Pitcher, Earthworm, Dot, Blue, Brown, White Background, 5 3/4 In. 225.00
Pitcher, Earthworm, Green, Blue Bands, Black Stripes, Leaf Handles, 7 1/4 In. 520.00
Pitcher, Earthworm, Loop, Cat's-Eye, Bands, Bulbous, Loop Handle, 6 In. 275.00
Pitcher, Earthworm, Zigzag, Bulbous, Loop Handle, 3 3/4 In. 95.00
Pitcher, Geometrics, Entwined Handle, Blue, Brown, 5 In. 575.00
Pitcher, Gray & Black Stripes, Tooled Lines, Feathered Lines, Applied Handle, 6 3/4 In. . . 430.00
Pitcher, Marbleized, Brown, Tan, White, Green Rim, Feathering, 5 5/8 In. 3190.00
Pitcher, Marbleized, Gray & White Body, 4 3/4 In. 248.00
Pitcher, Marbleized, Tobacco Leaf Center Band, Incised Circles, Green Bands, 6 In. 39.00
Pitcher, Seaweed, Blue, Brown & White Slip Bands, Flared Base, Yellowware, 4 3/4 In. . . 500.00
Pitcher, Seaweed, Blue, Yellowware, 3 1/2 In. 578.00
Pitcher, Seaweed, Bulbous, Applied Loop Handle, 7 1/4 In. 220.00
Pitcher, Seaweed, Green Bands, Brown Stripes, Leaf Handle, 7 In. 1045.00
Pitcher, Seaweed, Green, White, Brown Bands, Yellowware, 5 In. 440.00
Pitcher, Seaweed, Green, Yellowware, 5 1/2 In. 385.00
Porringer, Bands, Orange & Black, White, Rust Fans, Creamware, 1810, 3 In. 4110.00
Salt, Master, Cat's-Eye, Blue, White, Black, Orange Ground, Stripes, 3 1/8 x 2 In. 2090.00
Salt, Master, Seaweed, Blue, White Slip Band, Flared Pedestal Base, Yellowware, 2 In. . . 395.00
Salt, Seaweed, White Ground, Blue Banding, Footed, Yellowware, 2 1/4 In. 375.00
Saucer, Seaweed, Black, Ocher Slip Ground, c.1800, 3 1/2 In. 95.00
Serving Bowl, Pearlware, Applied Lobed Handle, Brown Band, Mustard, 8 In. 5875.00
Sugar, Bands, Brown & White, 4 1/4 x 4 In. 145.00
Sugar, Cover, Seaweed, Blue, Repeating, White Slip, Yellowware, 4 In. 500.00
Tankard, Marbleized, Brown, Caramel & Cream, 4 1/2 In., Pair 4485.00
Teapot, Cover, Seaweed, Black, Orange Ground, Bands, Blue, c.1800, 4 In. 4995.00
Tumbler, Marbleized, Gold, White, Brown, Black, Green Trim, Feathering, 2 1/2 In. 3520.00
Waste Bowl, Earthworm, Blue, Tan, Blue Stripes, Orange Band, 7 x 3 1/2 In. 220.00
Waste Bowl, Earthworm, White, Brown, Blue, Brown Stripes, Band, 6 1/2 x 3 3/8 In. 110.00
Waste Bowl, Earthworm, White, Brown, Tan, Gray, 4 3/4 x 2 3/4 In. 305.00
Waste Bowl, Speckled, Band Design, 7 1/4 In. 138.00

MONT JOYE, see Mt. Joye category.

MOORCROFT pottery was first made in Burslem, England, in 1913.
William Moorcroft had managed the art pottery department for James
Macintyre & Company of England from 1898 to 1913. The Moorcroft
pottery continues today, although William Moorcroft died in 1945. The
earlier wares are similar to the modern ones, but color and marking
will help indicate the age.

Biscuit Barrel, Japanese Style, Fall Leaves, Silver Plate Mount, Macintyre, 7 In. 200.00
Bowl, Pomegranates, 3-Footed, 7 In. 275.00
Box, Small Blue Flowers, Cover, 2 Handles, 3 3/8 In. 430.00
Jar, Cover, Multicolored Flowers, 5 3/8 x 5 3/4 In. 315.00
Lamp, Leaves & Berries, Cylindrical, Flaring Base, 24 3/4 In. 560.00
Pitcher, Pomegranate, Cobalt Blue Ground, 5 7/8 In. 690.00
Pitcher, Poppies, Stamped, 8 In. 422.00
Plate, Hibiscus, Red On Cobalt Blue, Stamped, Paper Label, 10 1/4 In. 290.00
Plate, Pomegranate, 8 In. 650.00
Trivet, Floral Cartouche, Macintyre, 7/8 x 5 1/4 In. 489.00
Vase, Anemone, Blue Ground, Bottle Shape, 6 1/4 In. 175.00
Vase, Anemone, Blue Ground, Squat, Stamped, 4 1/4 In. 200.00
Vase, Anemone, Pink, Purple, Cream, Urn Shape, 1928-1949, 5 5/8 In., Pair 590.00

Vase, Anemone, Squat, Stamped Signature, Potter To The Queen, 3 x 4 In. 230.00
Vase, Anemones, Cobalt Blue & Green Ground, Bulbous, Flared Rim, Marked, 10 In. ... 770.00
Vase, Blue Glaze, Trees, Hilly Landscape, 1900s, 8 3/8 In. 1180.00
Vase, Cornflower, Powder Blue, 3 7/8 In. 920.00
Vase, Falling Leaves, Bottle Shape, Label, 4 1/2 x 2 1/4 In. 105.00
Vase, Flambe Glaze, Viking Ship, Waves, Bernard Moore, England, 7 1/2 In. 1325.00
Vase, Florian Ware, Peacock Feather, 6 7/8 In. 1610.00
Vase, Florian Ware, Poppies, 6 In. 1150.00
Vase, Florian Ware, Poppies, Blue, W.M. Des., Macintyre, 2 3/4 In. 1725.00
Vase, Florian Ware, Poppies, Green, Yellow, Dore Base, 4-Footed, 4 5/8 In. 1725.00
Vase, Grape & Leaf, Flambe Glaze, 1947, 8 3/8 In. 1495.00
Vase, Hibiscus, Green Ground, Tapered, Impressed Mark, 10 In. 865.00
Vase, Macintyre Floral Cartouche, Poppy Decoration, 3 7/8 In. 1265.00
Vase, Macintyre Floral Spray, Gold Foot & Rim, 9 7/8 In. 1095.00
Vase, Macintyre Floral Spray, Red Slip, 3 In. 1610.00
Vase, Moonlit Blue, 3 1/4 In. 1955.00
Vase, Orchid, Green Ground, 6 1/8 In. 460.00
Vase, Orchids, Baluster Shape, 7 In. 330.00
Vase, Pomegranate, Cobalt Blue Ground, 6 3/8 In. 430.00
Vase, Pomegranate, Cobalt Blue Ground, 9 1/8 In. 690.00
Vase, Pomegranate, Deep Cobalt Blue Ground, Bulbous, Impressed Mark, 6 1/2 In. 920.00
Vase, Pomegranates, Baluster Shape, 6 In. 305.00
Vase, Seed Form, Red Leaves, Blue Ground, Early 1900s, 7 1/2 In. 520.00
Vase, Tapered Form, Pomegranate Design, Signed, 10 1/2 In. 635.00
Vase, Wisteria, Flambe Glaze, 4 In. 1095.00

MORIAGE is a special type of raised decoration used on some Japanese pottery. Sometimes pieces of clay were shaped by hand and applied to the item; sometimes the clay was squeezed from a tube in the way we apply cake frosting. One type of moriage is called *Dragonware* and is listed under that name.

Basket, Posy, Rosettes, Nippon, 1891-1921, 5 1/2 In. 127.00
Bowl, Nut, Chestnuts, Handle, Noritake, Green M Wreath, 10 In. 35.00
Ewer, Flowers, Scrolled Design, Nippon, 1891-1919, 9 1/2 In. 316.00
Humidor, Smoking Pipes, Cigar, Nippon, Blue Maple Leaf, 6 1/2 In. 719.00
Plaque, Mountains, Raised Flowers, Nippon, Maple Leaf, 9 1/2 In. 605.00
Vase, Cherry Blossoms, Handles, Nippon, 1891-1921, 9 In. 835.00
Vase, Flowers, Multicolored, Gilt Trim, Handles, Miyaro Japan Mark, 19th Century, 12 In. 200.00
Vase, Man, On Camel, Palm Trees, Handles, Blue M Wreath, 7 1/2 In. 690.00
Vase, Poppies, Beading, Scrolls, Green, Purple, Beige, On Red Ground, Nippon, 9 1/2 In. . 460.00
Vase, Purple Flowers, Blue Ground, Melon Shape, Footed, Mark, Nippon, c.1900, 6 In. ... 288.00

MOSAIC TILE COMPANY of Zanesville, Ohio, was started by Karl Langerbeck and Herman Mueller in 1894. Many types of plain and ornamental tiles were made until 1959. The company closed in 1967. The company also made some ashtrays, bookends, and related giftwares. Most pieces are marked with the entwined *MTC* monogram.

Tile, Flowers, Burgundy, Beige, Celadon Matte Glaze, Unglazed Outline, 9 In. 375.00
Tile, Nursery Rhymes, Cuerda Seca, Frame, Stamped, 4 1/2 In., 3 Piece 805.00
Tile, Sailboat, Brown & Beige, Blue Ground, Stamped, 3 In., 6 Piece 865.00

MOSER glass is made by Ludwig Moser und Sohne, a Bohemian (Czech) glasshouse founded in 1857. Art Nouveau-type glassware and iridescent glassware were made. The most famous Moser glass is decorated with heavy enameling in gold and bright colors. The firm, Moser Glassworks, is still working in Karlsbad, West Czech Republic. Few pieces of Moser glass are marked.

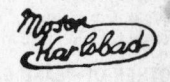

Berry Set, Cobalt Blue, Cut To Clear, Gold Enameled, 6 Piece 560.00
Bowl, Diamond Shape, Blue, Pink, Ruffled Edge, 10 x 3 1/2 In. 230.00
Box, Hinged Cover, Amethyst, Enameled Jewels, Round, 3 1/2 In. 300.00
Box, Hinged Cover, Casket, Enameled Flowers, Jewels, Amber Salamander, 3 1/2 In. 400.00
Box, Hinged Cover, Cranberry, Gold Enameled, Round, 2 1/2 In. 125.00
Box, Hinged Cover, Yellow Opaque, Enameled Flowers, Jewels, 3 In. 50.00

Ivory, opals, and pearls need to "breathe." Do not store wrapped in plastic; keep in a cloth bag.

Moser, Bride's Bowl, Enameled,
Applied Bees, Tricornered,
Gilt-Metal Holder, 10 In.

Box, Hinged Cover, Yellow Opaque, Enameled, Round, 3 1/2 x 5 1/2 In. 50.00
Bride's Bowl, Enameled, Applied Bees, Tricornered, Gilt-Metal Holder, 10 In. . . . . . *Illus* 1200.00
Chalice, Cobalt Blue, Oak Leaves, Acorns, Prunts, Gold Tracery, Signed, 7 1/2 In. 990.00
Finger Bowl, Underplate, Amber, Gold Enameled Flowers, Jewel, 3 x 6 In., Pair 355.00
Goblet, Cranberry Cut To Clear, Gold Enameled, 5 1/4 In., 9 Piece 1935.00
Goblet, Cranberry, Applied Acorns, Enameled Branches, Applied Gold Prunts, 7 1/2 In. . . . 920.00
Goblet, Cranberry, Gold Enameled, Clear Stem, Pedestal Foot, 6 1/4 In. 115.00
Goblet, Gold Encrusted, Enameled Design, Fluted, Signed, 7 3/8 In. 195.00
Goblet, Gold Encrusted, Prunts, Wash Bowl, 8 1/4 In. 345.00
Vase, Amber, Crackle, Enameled Flowers, Butterfly, 4 3/4 In. 230.00
Vase, Amethyst, Cut Facets, Gold Engraved Sovereign Frieze, 9 5/8 In. 290.00
Vase, Band Of Amazon Warriors, Ribbed, Pedestal Foot, Marked, 8 In. 290.00
Vase, Blue Rim, Band Of Cut Flower & Leaves, 10 In. 315.00
Vase, Clear Cut To Green, Enameled, Sailboats, Gold Flower Vines, c.1900, 14 In. 265.00
Vase, Cranberry, Butterflies & Berries, Enameled, Pedestal Foot, 10 In., Pair 350.00
Vase, Cranberry, Gold Enameled Morning Glory, 8 1/2 In. 345.00
Vase, Cranes, Leaves, Enameled, Bulbous, Ring Handles, c.1900, 10 In. 335.00
Vase, Cut, Enameled, Cobalt Blue, Zipper Design, Flowers, Leaves, 6 In. 260.00
Vase, Green, Jeweled Bees, Flowers, White, Pink, Gold Stem, Footed, 9 1/2 In. 335.00
Vase, Intaglio Cut Flowers, Gold Enameled Decoration, 2 1/2 In. 315.00
Vase, Jack-In-The-Pulpit, Cranberry Opalescent To Clear, Flowers, Ruffled, 16 In., Pair . . 865.00
Vase, Prism Cut, Light Amethyst, 1930, 12 In. 115.00
Vase, Roman Warriors, Engraved Frieze Band, Amber, Faceted, Signed, c.1920, 10 In. . . . 420.00
Wine, Chartreuse, Lobed, Gold Scrolling, Trumpet Foot, Signed, 6 3/4 In. 150.00
Wine, Cranberry Cut To Clear, Flowers, 8 1/8 In., 12 Piece 880.00

MOSS ROSE china was made by many firms from 1808 to 1900. It has a typical moss rose pictured as the design. The plant is not as popular now as it was in Victorian gardens, so the fuzz-covered bud is unfamiliar to most collectors. The dishes were usually decorated with pink and green flowers.

Cup & Saucer, Demitasse, Japan 10.00
Cup & Saucer, Scalloped Rim, Gold Trim 18.00
Dish, Cover, Tab Handles, 3 x 4 3/4 In. 12.00
Lighter, Japan, 3 1/4 In. 25.00
Pitcher, H.P. Co., 8 In. 145.00
Salt & Pepper 4.00
Shaving Mug, 3 1/4 In. 50.00
Sugar, Cover, Luster, Japan 10.00
Teapot, Gold Trim, Mid 1800s, 9 1/4 In. 295.00

MOTHER-OF-PEARL GLASS, or pearl satin glass, was first made in the 1850s in England and in Massachusetts. It was a special type of mold-blown satin glass with air bubbles in the glass, giving it a pearlized color. It has been reproduced. Mother-of-pearl shell objects are listed under Pearl.

Basket, Pink, Draped, 4 Camphor Feet, Thorn Handle, c.1890, 10 In. 1065.00
Biscuit Jar, Silver Cover, Opaque White, Moire Pattern, Gold Enameled, 7 In. 865.00

Bowl, Rainbow, Swirled, Pinched Edges, 2 1/4 x 4 1/2 In.	880.00
Bride's Basket, Rainbow, Enameled Scroll, White, Ruffled Edge, c.1900, 11 In.	500.00
Calling Card Case, Silver Mounted, Tortoiseshell, England, c.1885, 4 1/4 In.	430.00
Ewer, Pink, Diamond-Quilted, Thorn Handle, c.1900, 9 1/2 In.	530.00
Ewer, Rainbow, Herringbone, Oval, Tapered, Cylindrical Neck, Handle, 8 1/4 In.	715.00
Ewer, Rainbow, Herringbone, Oval, Tapered, Ruffled Edge, Rolled Rim, Handle, 8 1/2 In.	825.00
Ewer, Rainbow, Herringbone, Oval, Tapered, Tricornered Rim, Handle, 6 1/2 In. .880.00 to	1050.00
Ewer, Rainbow, Herringbone, Spherical, Knopped Neck, Handle, 10 1/4 In.	825.00
Rose Bowl, Diamond-Quilted, Rainbow, c.1890, 4 In.	450.00
Tumbler, Yellow Shaded To White, Diamond-Quilted, Enameled Flowers, 3 3/4 In.	173.00
Vase, Diamond-Quilted, Flowering Branch, Pink Ruffled Edge, c.1890, 5 1/4 In.	310.00
Vase, Diamond-Quilted, Pink, Green Highlights, 10 1/2 In., Pair	500.00
Vase, Diamond-Quilted, Yellow, 6 3/4 In.	50.00
Vase, Jack-In-The-Pulpit, Rainbow, Pinwheel, Camphor Leaf Feet, 4 In.	195.00
Vase, Light Blue, Ribbed, Ruffled Edge, 15 1/2 In.	115.00
Vase, Moire, Yellow, 9 In., Pair	300.00
Vase, Rainbow, Diamond-Quilted, Ruffled Edge, 8 In.	290.00
Vase, Rainbow, Oval, Swirled, Gold Enameled, Ribbed, Tapered, 8 1/2 In.	385.00
Vase, Rainbow, Pinched Body, Long Pulled Neck, 13 In.	460.00
Vase, Stick, Diamond-Quilted, Pink, Coralene Design, 7 1/4 In.	225.00

MOTORCYCLES and motorcycle accessories of all types are being collected today. Examples can be found that date back to the early years of the twentieth century. Toy motorcycles are listed in the Toy category.

Brochure, Indian Scout, Folded, 1929, 6 x 9 In.	220.00
Can, Harley-Davidson Two Cycle Motor Oil, Sealed, Contents, 1951, 4 In.	200.00
Catalog, Harley-Davidson, 1926, 16 Pages	130.00
Catalog, Honda, Woman & Red Motorcycle On Cover, 1966	21.00
Clock, Indian Motorcycles Sales, Lightup, Neon, 1920s, 26 In.	3840.00
Fan, Hand, Harley, Man On Motocycle, Woman In Sedan, Cardboard, 9 x 7 In.	60.00
Harley-Davidson, Knucklehead, Fire Red, c.1938	29325.00
Jacket, Biker, Horsehide, 1930s, Small	500.00
Jacket, Racing, Olive Green, Leather, Snap Collar, 1970s, Size 40	225.00
Magazine, Clincher, B.F. Goodrich Co., February 1910, 16 Pages	25.00
Matchless, 497cc, G8CS, 1960	14090.00
Moto Guzzi, 500cc Gambalunga, Ex Enrico Lorenzeti, 1948	50600.00
Moto Guzzi Dondolino, c.1949	39675.00
Pocketwatch, Indian Motorcycles Authorized Dealer, 2 In.	225.00
Postcard, Indian Motorcycle, Rider, Real Photo Postcard	196.00
Sign, BSA, Man On Motorcycle, Enameled Tin, 10 x 7 In.	155.00
Sign, Fun Runners Cycle Club, Oklahoma City, Enameled Tin, 18 1/2 x 11 In.	75.00
Sign, Mobil Oil, Specifications Chart, Cardboard, 1928, 38 1/2 x 19 1/5 In.	900.00

MOUNT WASHINGTON, see Mt. Washington category.

MOVIE memorabilia of all types is collected. Animation Art, Games, Sheet Music, Toys, and some celebrity items are listed in their own sections. Listed here are costumes and paper collectibles. A lobby card is 11 by 14 inches. A set of lobby cards includes seven scene cards and one title card. A one sheet, the standard movie poster, is 27 by 41 inches. A three sheet is 81 by 40 inches. A half sheet is 22 by 28 inches. A window card, made of cardboard, is 14 by 22 inches. An insert is 14 by 36 inches. A herald is a promotional item handed out to patrons. Press books, which contain many ad slicks, are sent to film exhibitors to aid in advertising the film. Press books and/or press kits (with photos) are sent to the media to promote a movie.

Autograph, Photograph, Jean Harlow, J. Doolittle, Frame, 1930s, 12 1/4 x 10 1/4 In.	1725.00
Autograph, Photograph, Maureen O'Sullivan, 8 x 10 In.	46.00
Autograph, Photograph, Vincent Price, Black & White, Glossy, 8 x 10 In.	35.00
Banner, Man On The Moon, Graphic On Canvas, Stan Lee, MTV, 30 x 24 In.	880.00
Herald, Clockwork Orange, Quatrefold Color, 8 Pages, 1972, 15 x 11 In.	14.00
Herald, Deliverance, Sepia, 1972, 11 x 14 In., 4 Pages	6.50

Lobby Card, America, D.W. Griffith, Set, 1924 .... 485.00
Lobby Card, Are Husbands Necessary, Ray Milland, 1942 .... 13.00
Lobby Card, Fair Warning, George O'Brien, 1931 .... 32.00
Lobby Card, Touch Of Evil, Orson Welles, Title Card, 1958 .... 360.00
Photograph, Greta Garbo, Susan Lennox, Clarence Sinclair Bull, 1931, 12 1/2 x 9 5/8 In. 500.00
Photograph, Helen Hayes, Simulated Signature, 3 1/2 x 5 1/2 In. 31.00
Photograph, Lana Turner, Studio Portrait, 1947, 8 x 10 In. 12.00
Photograph, Lust For Life, Kirk Douglas, Color, 1956, 8 x 10 In. 8.00
Photograph, Man Without A Face, Still, Silent Film, 1927, 8 x 10 In. 45.00
Photograph, Nazimova, Harold Dean Carsey, Hollywood, 13 1/2 x 10 3/8 In. 225.00
Poster, Australian Daybill, The Westerner, Gary Cooper, Linen Back, 1940, 30 x 13 In. .. 195.00
Poster, Born To Kill, Claire Trevor, Lawrence Tierney, RKO, 1946, Half Sheet .. 800.00
Poster, Casablanca, Humphrey Bogart, Ingrid Bergman, Paul Henreid, 1942, 1 Sheet 14920.00
Poster, Dillinger, Public Enemy No. 1, Midland Film Co., 1934, 1 Sheet 4945.00
Poster, Jungle Book, Walt Disney, 1967, 1 Sheet 725.00
Poster, Kiss Of Death, Victor Mature, Brian Donlevy, Coleen Gray, 1947, Half Sheet. ... 725.00
Poster, La Dama De Las Camelias, Greta Garbo, Spanish, Camille, 1936, 1 Sheet. 1500.00
Poster, Lights Of Old Santa Fe, Roy Rogers, Republic Pictures, 1944, 1 Sheet 25.00
Poster, Matri-Phony, 3 Stooges, 1942, 1 Sheet 575.00
Poster, Medicine Hat Stallion, Jack Benny, 1930, 1 Sheet 525.00
Poster, Memphis Bell, WW II Documentary, 1944, Insert 950.00
Poster, Prince & The Show Girl, Marilyn Monroe, Laurence Olivier, 1957, 1 Sheet 1200.00
Poster, Safe At Home, Mickey Mantle, Roger Maris, 1962, 3 Sheet 5032.00
Poster, The Country Girl, Bing Crosby, Grace Kelly, William Holden, 1954, 1/2 Sheet ... 20.00
Poster, Tycoon, John Wayne, Laraine Day, RKO, 1947, 1/2 Sheet 325.00
Poster, Wild One, Marlon Brando, 1953, 1/2 Sheet 341.00
Press Book, Petulia, Julie Christie, Richard Chamberlain, Uncut, 1968, 23 Pages 14.00
Press Kit, Old Man & The Sea, Spencer Tracy, 1958 .... 25.00
Press Kit, Revenge Of The Pink Panther, Peter Sellers, 1978 .... 20.00
Sheet Music, Coney Island, Put Your Arms Around Me Honey, Betty Grable, 1943 ...... 18.00
Snow Globe, Marilyn Monroe, Diamonds Are A Girl's Best Friend, No. 68/7500 .... 8.00
Wall Mural, Jayne Mansfield, Heavy Envelope, Foldout, 1950s, 21 1/2 x 62 In. 50.00
Window Card, Boston Strangler, Tony Curtis, 1968, 14 x 22 In. 24.00

MT. JOYE is an enameled cameo glass made in the late nineteenth and twentieth centuries by Saint-Hilaire Touvier de Varraux and Co. of Pantin, France. This same company made De Vez glass. Pieces were usually decorated with enameling. Most pieces are not marked.

Bowl, Bearded Iris, Gold Leaves, Frosted, Textured, Signed, 3 1/2 In. 413.00
Plate, Coupe, Purple Flowers, Green Textured Body, Gold Border, Signed, c.1920, 6 In. ... 475.00
Rose Bowl, Cyclamen, Leaves, Enameled, Crimped Rim, 4 1/4 In. 540.00
Vase, Chrysanthemums, Gold, Etched, Green Frosted, Bulbous, Stamped, 12 In. 345.00
Vase, Chrysanthemums, Yellow Enameled Sunflowers, Etched, Gilded, 16 In. 546.00
Vase, Cranberry Over Pale Green, Gold Highlights, Cylindrical, 6 7/8 In. 385.00
Vase, Flowers, Yellow, Gold, Green, Brown Chipped Ice Ground, Signed, 7 1/2 In. 660.00

MT. WASHINGTON Glass Works started in 1837 in South Boston, Massachusetts. In 1870 the company moved to New Bedford, Massachusetts. Many types of art glass were made there until 1894, when the company merged with Pairpoint Manufacturing Co. Amberina, Burmese, Crown Milano, Cut Glass, Peachblow, and Royal Flemish are each listed in their own category.

Biscuit Jar, Melon Ribbed, Gold Flowers, Silver Plated Cover, Crab, 6 1/2 In. 460.00
Bottle, Dresser, Green & Gold Leaf, 9 3/4 In. 35.00
Bowl, Russian Cutting, Oval, Ruffled Edge, 12 In. 500.00
Cake Plate, Cover, Lava, Colored Inclusions, c.1870, 8 x 14 In. 8400.00
Ewer, Purple & Pink Flowers, Opal, Rope Handle, Ruffled Spout, 13 In. 3290.00
Flower Frog, Opal Glass, c.1890, 5 In. 345.00
Jug, Syrup, Burmese 3360.00
Mustard Pot, Cover, Pansies, Colonial Ware, 3 1/4 In. 690.00
Mustard Pot, Opal Ground, Melon Ribbed, Green Loops, Daisies, 2 3/4 In. 770.00
Rose Bowl, Beige To Cream, Flowers, Leaves, Rolled Pinched Rim, 3 1/2 In. 345.00

Rose Bowl, Cream To Rose, Enameled Violets, No. 618, c.1890, 4 1/2 In.	225.00
Salt, Flowers, Opal, 1800s, 2 1/4 In., Pair	70.00
Salt, Melon Ribbed, Flowers, Enameled, Opal, 3 3/4 In., Pair	130.00
Salt & Pepper, Ribbed Pillar Shape, Flowers, Opal, 4 In.	210.00
Salt & Pepper, Swirled Body, Lavender Flowers, Gold Trim, 2 1/4 In.	175.00
Saltshaker, Fig Shape, Flowers, Leaves, Opal, 2 1/2 In.	230.00
Saltshaker, Opal Ground, Chick & Egg Shape, 2 1/2 In.	360.00
Sugar & Creamer, Cover, Embossed, Pansies, Gilt, Opal Ground, Molded, Marked	330.00
Sugar Shaker, Daisies, Blue & White, Opal, 3 3/4 x 3 1/2 In.	1450.00
Sugar Shaker, Fig Shape, Pale Green, Enameled Daisies, 4 In.	2200.00
Sugar Shaker, Fig Shape, Yellow, Enameled Flowers, 3 3/4 In.	1100.00
Sugar Shaker, Flowers, Blue, Opal, Oval, 4 1/2 In.	200.00
Sugar Shaker, Flowers, Yellow, Enameled, Leaves, Vines, Opal To Pink, Oval, 4 1/4 In.	260.00
Sugar Shaker, Melon Ribbed, Flowers, Opal, Silver Plate Lid, 4 x 2 3/4 In.	200.00
Sugar Shaker, Melon Ribbed, Raised Daisy Clusters, Opal, Embossed Lid, c.1890, 4 In.	530.00
Toothpick, Flowers, Enameled, Beaded Rim, Paneled, Opal, 2 1/4 In.	.300.00 to 400.00
Tumbler, Fish, In Net, Satin Opal, 3 3/4 In.	2990.00
Tumbler, Lemonade, Opal Satin, Applied Handle, 5 In.	200.00
Vase, Colonial Ware, Peach Flowers, Gold Enameled, Thorn Handles, Signed	2070.00
Vase, Mother-Of-Pearl, Blue To White, Diamond-Quilted, Satin, Crimped Rim, 9 In.	260.00
Vase, Rose Clusters, Opal, Pulled Handles, Signed, 9 1/2 In.	1000.00
Vase, Stick, Fall Leaves, Opal, 10 In.	1455.00
Vase, Stick, White & Pink Enameled Flowers, Green Leaves, Vines, Opal, 12 In.	865.00

MUD FIGURES are small Chinese pottery figures made in the twentieth century. The figures usually represent workers, scholars, farmers, or merchants. Other pieces are trees, houses, and similar parts of the landscape. The figures have unglazed faces and hands but glazed clothing. They were originally made for fish tanks or planters. Mud figures were of little interest and brought low prices until the 1980s. When the prices rose, reproductions appeared.

Man, Balancing Baskets On Shoulders, 1920s, 7 1/2 In.	180.00
Man, Fishing, Bamboo Pole, 5 In.	30.00
Man, Robe, Fan, Broad-Rimmed Hat, c.1910, 4 1/4 In.	50.00
Man, Robe, Fan, Broad-Rimmed Hat, Next To Urn, 6 1/2 In.	100.00
Woman, Balancing Baskets On Shoulders, 6 1/2 In.	70.00

MULBERRY ware was made in the Staffordshire district of England from about 1850 to 1860. The dishes were decorated with a reddish brown transfer design, now called *mulberry*. Many of the patterns are similar to those used for flow blue and other Staffordshire transfer wares.

Chop Plate, Oriental Scene, 19th Century, 12 1/2 In.	105.00
Plate, Corean Pattern, Podmore Walker & Co., c.1850, 9 1/2 In.	69.00
Plate, Flag & Liberty Cup, c.1840, 8 1/4 In.	290.00

MULLER FRERES, French for Muller Brothers, made cameo and other glass from about 1895 to 1933. Their factory was first located in Luneville, then in nearby Croismare, France. Pieces were usually marked with the company name.

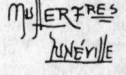

Lamp, Chandelier, Pendant, 4 Glass Shades, Scrolled Iron Frame, 22 3/4 x 24 In.	575.00
Lamp, Chandelier, Pendant, 5 Frosted Glass Shades, Iron Frame, 33 x 29 1/2 In.	865.00
Vase, African Native, Elephant, Moss Green, Signed, 5 1/2 x 7 1/4 In.	460.00
Vase, Amethyst Lady Slipper, Opalescent Ground, Cameo, Signed, 5 1/4 In.	1300.00
Vase, Autumn Leaves, Carved Insects, Brown, Green, Yellow, Signed, 6 1/4 In.	2300.00
Vase, Birds On Branches, Bulbous, 13 In.	5650.00
Vase, Cameo, Butterflies, 14 1/2 In.	7280.00
Vase, Cameo, Scenic, Bottle Shape, Birch Trees, Lake, Orange Sky, 8 3/4 In.	2875.00
Vase, Internally Decorated, Mottled Maroon & Pink Border, White Bottom, 4 In.	315.00
Vase, Peonies, Green Cut To Clear, Bulbous, Cameo, Muller Croisnare, 13 1/2 In.	1210.00
Vase, Poppies, Teal, Crimson, Leaves, Mottled Yellow, Frosted, Oval, Cameo, Signed, 6 In.	1320.00
Vase, Red, Orange & Yellow Roses, Peach Ground, Cameo, 11 In.	3105.00
Vase, Satin Glass, Mottled White Ground, Blue, Pink, Amber, Signed, 6 1/4 In.	144.00

MUNCIE Clay Products Company was established by Charles Benham in Muncie, Indiana, in 1922. The company made pottery for the florist and giftshop trade. The company closed by 1939. Pieces are marked with the name *Muncie* or just with a system of numbers and letters, like *1A*.

MuNcIE

Lamp, Nude, 5 Panels, Brown & Green Glaze, Bronze Base, Nude Finial, Marked, 28 In. .	405.00
Vase, Mottled Orange & Brown Glaze, Shouldered Form, Flared Rim, 7 1/4 In.	60.00
Vase, Ruba Rhombic, Brown Drip Glaze Over Orange, 6 In.	550.00

MURANO, see Glass-Venetian category.

MUSIC boxes and musical instruments are listed here. Phonograph records, jukeboxes, phonographs, and sheet music are listed in other categories in this book.

Accordion, Borsini, Bell, Case, Straps, Bellows, Italy	90.00
Accordion, Hohner, Diatonic, 10 Buttons, c.1950	115.00
Accordion, Hohner, Tango, Octagonal Case	35.00
Accordion, Hohner, Wood, Embossed Design, c.1900, 11 In.	200.00
Accordion, Le Mar, Straps, Case, Italy	80.00
Accordion, Tanzbar, Automatic, 28 Notes, 2 Rolls, Germany, c.1920	880.00
Banjo, 5 Strings, A.C. Fairbanks, Co., Pearl Inlay, c.1898	4255.00
Banjo, 5 Strings, Model Electric, A.C. Fairbanks, Boston, c.1910, 10 7/8 In.	1998.00
Banjo, Tenor, Gibson, Mastertone Style TB-5, Case, c.1926, 10 3/4 In.	880.00
Bow, Viola, E.M. Penzel, Silver Mounted, Round Stick	355.00
Bow, Violin, Arnold Suard, French Silver Mounted, Ebony Frog	1645.00
Bow, Violin, Eugene Sartory, French Silver Mounted, Ebony Frog	9100.00
Bow, Violin, Joseph Alfred Lamy, French Silver Mounted, Ebony Frog	7050.00
Bow, Violin, Louis Bazin, Nickel Mounted, Round Stick	825.00
Bow, Violin, Silver Mounted, Octagonal Stick, Ebony Frog	1295.00
Bow, Violin, Silver Mounted, Round Stick, Unstamped	265.00
Bow, Violoncello, Alfred Lamy, French Silver Mounted, Ebony Frog	4995.00
Box, 3 Airs, Wood Inlaid Case, Cylinder Box, Swiss, 3 In.	425.00
Box, 3 Dancing Dolls, Maple, 2 Songs, France, c.1885, 6-In. Box, 3-In. Dolls	1650.00
Box, Adler, Model 210, Mandolin, Case, 11-In. Disc, 17 x 12 1/2 In.	900.00
Box, Ariston, Wood Frame, Lithograph Top, 35 Discs, France, 16 x 16 In.	1980.00
Box, Baker Troll, Indicator, Tremolo, Mandolin, Burl Inlaid, 8 Tunes, 17 1/4-In. Cylinder .	3600.00
Box, Barbie, Susy Goose, White Plastic, Gold Trim, Candelabra, Bench	85.00
Box, Britannia, Fancy Galley, Clock, 9-In. Discs, 12 Discs, 1890, 16 x 27 In.	2530.00
Box, Criterion, Model 100, Table Model, 14 1/2 x 11 1/2 x 10 In.	520.00
Box, Cylinder, 6 Airs, Tambour, 3 Timbers, Castagnettes, Inlaid Case, Swiss, 22 In.	3280.00
Box, Cylinder, Drum, 6 Bells, Inlaid Cover, Swiss, 9 1/4-In. Cylinder	900.00
Box, Cylinder, Geneva, 12 Tunes, 16 1/2 In.	650.00
Box, Dancer, Rotates, Lithograph, Pierced Tin, Crank, 8 1/2 In.	525.00
Box, Harmonie, Cylinder, Tune Sheet, Inlaid Cover, 8 Tunes, 16 1/4-In. Split Comb	2850.00
Box, LeCoultre, Cylinder, Walnut, Inlaid, Key Wind, Tune Sheet, 6 Tunes, c.1862	550.00
Box, Lipstick, Cigarette Holder, Push Button, Doors, 17 In.	305.00
Box, Mira, Combination, Disc, Dampers, Mahogany, Patent 1805	1800.00
Box, Mira, Mahogany Case, Chromolithograph, Swiss Alps, Tin Discs, 8 x 13 1/2 x 1 In. .	1800.00
Box, Musette, Walnut Box, Top Hand Crank, Paper Rolls, Hinged Lid, 12 x 13 x 12 In. . . .	275.00
Box, Nicole Freres, Cylinder, Inlaid Case, Tune Sheet, 16 Tunes	1700.00
Box, Nicole Freres, Oratorio, Tune Card, Veneer & Crossband Front, Lid, 1860s, 22 In. . .	2470.00
Box, Orchestral, Drum, Bells, Mandolin Inlaid, Case, 16 In. Cylinder, 13 3/4 x 29 1/2 In. .	3000.00
Box, Organ Grinder, Wood, Lithograph, Windup, Germany, c.1890, 9 In.	360.00
Box, Organette, Euphonika Musikwerke, 18 Keys, Wood Case, Brass, Lithograph, c.1910 .	185.00
Box, Polyphon, 41R, Front Lever Wind, Cover Print, Single Comb, 8 1/4 In., 8 Discs	1000.00
Box, Polyphon, Excelsior, Disc, 77 Teeth, Walnut Case, c.1900, 15 1/2 In. Disc	1550.00
Box, Quality Swiss, Mandolin, Case Mounts, Handles, 17 1/4-In. Piccolo Cylinder, c.1800	1900.00
Box, Regina, Mahogany Case, Disc, Single Comb, Tabletop, 9 1/2 x 14 3/4 x 13 1/2 In. . .	2590.00
Box, Regina, Mahogany Case, Double Comb, 15-In. Disc, 21 In.	4070.00
Box, Regina, Mahogany Case, Record Stand, 15 1/2 In. Discs, 33 Discs	4675.00
Box, Regina, Reginaphone, Mahogany Case, 12 Disks, c.1910, 17 x 16 x 10 In.	2645.00
Box, Rosewood, Walnut, Urn & Flower Inlay, 12 Tunes, Bell, Drum, 27 x 15 x 13 In.	2970.00
Box, Roullet & Decamps, Teacher, Holding Book, Desk, Student, Paris, 1890, 19 In.	8225.00
Box, Singing Bird, 800 Silver Case, Bag Pipe Player, Instruments, Swiss, c.1900, 4 x 2 In.	2350.00

Box, Singing Bird, Bluebird, Birdcage, Brass, Rotating Center Clock, Austria, 5 1/2 In. ... 590.00
Box, Singing Bird, Cage, c.1950, 11 In. 230.00
Box, Singing Bird, Imitation Lapis, Gold Plate, Reuge Music, Swiss, c.1975, 4 1/2 x 2 In. 895.00
Box, Stella, Mahogany Case, Carved Acorn & Leaf Front, 12 17-In. Discs 2875.00
Box, Stella, Mahogany Case, Double Comb, Upright, 20 25 In. Discs, 86 In. 12100.00
Box, Stella, Model 126, Mahogany Case, 1897 Patent, 14 In. Disc 2900.00
Box, Sublime Harmony, 8 Airs, Tune Indicator, Inlaid Lid, 11-In. Cylinder, 23 In. 1295.00
Box, Swiss Organ, Tune Sheet, 8 Tunes, 13 In. Cylinder 1600.00
Box, Symphonion, Imperial, Single Comb, Southern California Music Co., Los Angeles .. 1175.00
Box, Symphonion, Model 6, Ebony Case, Double Offset Combs, Disc 1000.00
Box, Symphonion, Oak Stand, Black Lacquered, Double Comb, Discs 3190.00
Box, Symphonion, Walnut Case, Inlaid, Double Disc, Upright, 17 1/2 In. Disc 14850.00
Box, Tune Sheet, Inlaid Cover, Swiss, 8 Tunes, 6 In. Cylinder 500.00
Bugle, Wm. H. Horstmann Co., Brass, Phila, Deport Spec, 9 1/8 x 3 3/4 In. 280.00
Case, Violin, Elijah Hall, Traveling Musician, Buck's County, Penn., 29 x 8 1/2 x 3 1/2 In. 990.00
Cornet, Boston Musical Instruments, Silver Plate Tubing, Keys, Case 355.00
Cornet, Higham, Royal Crest Emblem, Shepherd Crook Style, Leather Case, England ... 145.00
Cornet, King, Gold Plated, Case, c.1941 .... 100.00
Cornet, Lefevre, Shepherd's Crook, Bag, Accessories, France 105.00
Drum, M. W. Stevens, Painted, Pittsfield, Mass., c.1845, 8 1/2 x 11 1/2 In. 235.00
Drum, Multicolored Wood, Tibet, c.1830, 20 1/2 x 18 In. 590.00
Drum, Shield & Flag, Painted, Spread Wing Eagle, 6 3/4 x 16 3/8 In. 110.00
Drum, Snare, Braided Cotton Head Tightening Cords, Italy, 14 x 10 In. 250.00
Drum, Snare, Mahogany, Iron Rod Brackets, Bentwood Body, Hide Surface, 8 x 17 1/2 In. 140.00
Dulcimer, Fred Martin, Redwood, Walnut, Female Head Tuner, N.C., c.1981, 42 In. 165.00
Dulcimer, Scott Hastings, Cherry, Numbered, Vermont, 1969 .... 60.00
Euphonium, C.G. Conin, Double Bell, Gold Plate Over Brass, c.1926 .... 3450.00
Flute, 8 Key, Grendilla Wood, Ivory, Silver, 6 Open Holes 200.00
Flute, Hannover, Ivory Mouth Piece, Ebony Body, Silver Keys, 15 x 5 In. 160.00
Flute, Ivory Mouth Piece, Ebony Body, Silver Keys, Oval Case, 15 x 5 In. 160.00
Flute, Jerome Thibouville Lamy, Blackwood, Nickel Keys, Fittings, Paris 2235.00
Guitar, Alvarez, Model D.Y. 55, Mahogany, Hard Shell Case, K. Yairi 225.00
Guitar, C.F. Martin, Model 000-18, Mahogany, Rosewood, Case, 1941, 19 1/4 x 15 1/8 In. 4935.00
Guitar, Electric, Silvertone, Semi Hollow, Tortoiseshell Style Pick Guard, c.1960 .... 90.00
Guitar, Gibson, Model ES225T, Birch, Case, 1959 .... 999.00
Guitar, Gibson, Model L-5, Maple, Spruce, Pearl Inlay, Ebony, Arch Top, 1947 .... 3878.00
Guitar, Gibson, Model L-5, Maple, Spruce, Pearl Inlay, Ebony, Arch Top, 1966 .... 3055.00
Guitar, Goya, Mahogany, Spruce, Tortoiseshell Style Pick Guard, Spain, c.1967 .... 58.00
Harmonica, Hohner, No. 365, Marine Band, Polished Silvertone, Box, 6 1/4 In. 29.00
Harp, Concert, Greece, 19th Century 3150.00
Harp, Erard Freres, No. 755, Gilt, 3 Pedals, Paris, 1800s, 65 In. 1955.00
Harp, Rocco Bruno, Maple, Carved, Parcel Gilt, New York, 42 In. .... *Illus* 1035.00
Harp, Rocco Bruno, Parcel Gilt, Maple, Figured, Gilt, Gesso Molding, 63 3/4 In. 800.00
Horn, Tin, 6 Soldered Sections, Bell Shape End, 59 In. 375.00
Hurdy-Gurdy, Carved Human Head, 19th Century, France 500.00
Machine, Morse Electrophone, Turntable, 8-Track, Cassette Deck, Radio Tuner, Lights ... 375.00
Mandolin, C.F. Martin, Rounded Back, Leather Case, c.1912 .... 430.00
Mandolin, Gibson, Style F4, Maple, Spruce, Cedar, Ebony, Pearl, Case, 1915, 13 1/2 In. ... 3878.00
Mandolin, Lyon & Healy, Style A, Walnut, Spruce, Mahogany, Case, 1926, 12 7/8 In. 2705.00
Melodeon, Rococo Revival, Rosewood, Gold Top, Mid 19th Century, 33 x 49 x 26 In. ... 863.00
Organ, Pump, Packard, Walnut Eastlake Case, 11 Stops, Stool, 50 x 48 In. 225.00
Organ, Roller, A.G. MacDonell & Co., Musette Paper, 3 Rolls 350.00
Organ, Roller, Crank Paper Roll, Stenciled Walnut Case, 27 x 12 In. 275.00
Organ, Roller, Gem, 1 Cob, Sears, Roebuck & Co. 300.00
Organ, Roller, Walnut Eastlake Case, 1 Roll 375.00
Organ, Wurlitzer, Style 105, Band, Artizan Movement 6500.00
Piano, Baby Grand, Cunningham, Walnut, Phila., 56 x 60 In. 575.00
Piano, Baby Grand, Franklin, Walnut, 39 1/2 x 57 1/4 x 61 1/2 In. 590.00
Piano, Baby Grand, George Steck & Co., Duo Art, Walnut Case, Bench, 100 Rolls, 62 In. 1725.00
Piano, Baby Grand, Pleyel, Rosewood, Paris, c.1910, 66 In. 5310.00
Piano, Baby Grand, Sohmer & Co., Mahogany, Fluted Column Legs, 40 x 58 x 71 In. ... 1400.00
Piano, Baby Grand, Steinway & Sons, Louis XV Style, Walnut Stained, c.1903, 72 In. ... 8050.00
Piano, Concert Grand, Wm. Knabe & Co., Rosewood, Bench, c.1865, 103 In. 3450.00

Piano, Player, Bush & Gerts, Circassian Walnut, Bench, Electrified 470.00
Piano, Seeburg, Coin-Operated, Mahogany Case, 54 x 37 In. 3300.00
Piano, Spinet, Torben Christensen, Rosewood, Stool, Hindsberg, 36 x 50 1/2 x 19 1/2 In. . . 1410.00
Pianoforte, Sheraton, Mahogany & Rosewood Veneer, 32 1/2 x 68 In. 4025.00
Saxophone, Alto, Martin, Elkhart, Nickel Horn, Case, American, 1926 . . . . 175.00
Saxophone, Alto, Selmer, Engraved Horn, Case, Paris, 1937 . . . . 1645.00
Saxophone, C.G. Conn, Elkhart, Brass Plate Horn In C, Case, American, 1906 . . . . 410.00
Saxophone, Selmer, Tenor, B-Flat, Case, France, 1957 . . . . 5750.00
Speaker, Stephens Trusonic, Eames, Quadraflex, c.1956, 21 x 16 x 29 In. 2940.00
Trombone, 2-Piece Construction, Form Fitted Leather Case, Continental, 38 In. 130.00
Trumpet, B-Flat, Amati, Pocket, Brass, 2 Lead Pipes, Mouthpiece, Case, Czechoslovakia . 150.00
Trumpet, B-Flat, Boston Wonder, Silver Plate, Case, Germany 105.00
Trumpet, King Tone, Tuning Adjuster, 2 Mouthpieces, Case 105.00
Viola, Igino & Luciano Sderci, 2-Piece Back, Italy, 1965, 16 1/2 In. 4465.00
Violin, Carlo Begonzi, 1-Piece Back, Cremona, Italy, c.1840, 13 15/16 In. 1295.00
Violin, Gasparo Da Salo, 2-Piece Back, Ribbon Carving, Tiger Inlay, Case, 2 Bows, 13 In. 175.00
Violin, Hopf, Tiger, Maple, 2 Bows, Case 56.00
Violin, Iofredus Cappa Fecit, 2-Piece Back, Plain, Case, Bow, 1682, 14 In. 5170.00
Violin, Jerome Thibouville-Lamy, Carlo Micelli, Case, 2 Bows, Paris, c.1922 . . . . 375.00
Violin, Leo Aschauer, Label, 1930, 24 In. 3050.00
Violin, Leonidas Nadegini, 1-Piece Back, Medium Curl, France, 1914, 14 1/8 In. 4700.00
Violin, Xavier Wagner, 2-Piece Back, Germany, 1812, 13 15/16 In. 3525.00
Violoncello, Joseph Bassot Luthier, 2-Piece Back, Paris, 1800, 29 5/8 In. 4585.00
Violoncello, Longman & Broderip, M-762, England, c.1780, 29 5/16 In. 8815.00
Zither, US Guitar Zither Co., Jersey City, Mezenhauers, St. Louis, 1904, 19 x 13 In. 275.00

MUSTACHE CUPS were popular from 1850 to 1900 when the large,
flowing mustache was in style. A ledge of china or silver held the hair
out of the liquid in the cup. This kept the mustache tidy and also kept
the mustache wax from melting. Left-handed mustache cups are rare
but are being reproduced.

Yellow Flower, White Lily, Pink Interior, Saucer, Majolica, 6 1/4 x 2 3/4 In. 201.00

NAILSEA glass was made in the Bristol district in England from 1788
to 1873. It was made by many different factories, not just the Nailsea
Glass House. Many pieces were made with loopings of either white or
colored glass as decoration.

Flask, Powder Horn, Opalescent Loopings, Clear Applied Rings, 10 1/2 In. 230.00
Paperweight, Bottle, Green, Flowerpot, Petunia-Type Flower, 3 3/8 In. 180.00
Paperweight, Bottle, Green, High Dome, 6 Upright Flowers, Flowing From Pot 400.00
Paperweight, Bottle, Green, High Dome, Scattered, Elongated Bubbles, 5 In. 300.00
Vase, Opal Loopings On Red, Ruffled, Rolled Edge, 6 In. 115.00
Witch's Ball, Red, Clambroth & White, Pulled Looping, 3 3/4 In. 345.00

NAKARA is a trade name for a white glassware made about 1900 by the
C. F. Monroe Company of Meriden, Connecticut. It was decorated in
pastel colors. The glass was very similar to another glass made by the
company called *Wave Crest*. The company closed in 1916. Boxes for
use on a dressing table are the most commonly found Nakara pieces.
The mark is not found on every piece.

NAKARA

Ashtray, Painted Flowers, Metal Rim, Holders, Marked, 1 1/2 x 3 3/4 In. 125.00
Box, Cover, Beaded Daisies, Pink Ground, 6 Sides, Satin Lining, Marked, 3 1/2 x 5 In. . . . 300.00
Box, Cover, Cherub Playing Lyre Transfer, Painted Flowers, Pink, Marked, 4 1/2 In. 400.00
Box, Cover, Pink Rose, Blue Ground, Metal Bottom, 3 3/4 x 3 In. 1440.00
Box, Hinged Cover, Iris, Blown Out, Light Orange, Signed, 2 1/2 x 3 1/2 In. 1000.00
Box, Hinged Cover, Pink Flowers, Beveled Interior Mirror, 2 3/4 x 4 1/2 In. 250.00
Box, Hinged Cover, Pink Flowers, Green Ground, Bishop's Hat Mold, Marked, 3 x 4 In. . . 275.00
Box, Hinged Cover, Pink Flowers, Sea Foam Mold, Satin Lining, Marked, 5 3/4 x 8 In. . . 2100.00
Box, Hinged Cover, Queen Louisa Transfer, Beaded, Bishop's Hat Mold, Marked, 4 x 4 In. 500.00
Box, Hinged Cover, Tea Party Transfer, Bishop's Hat Mold, Lining, Marked, 3 x 4 In. . . . 700.00
Box, Hinged Cover, Young Woman Transfer, Blue & Pink Ground, Marked, 2 1/2 x 4 1/2 In. 150.00
Dish, Painted Violets, Pink, Yellow Ground, Metal Rim, Marked, 2 1/2 x 5 In. 175.00
Dresser Box, Hinged Cover, Pink, Yellow, Blue Flowers, Marked, 4 x 7 1/2 In. 1400.00

Music, Harp, Rocco
Bruno, Maple, Carved,
Parcel Gilt, New York,
42 In.

Napkin Ring, Figural, Eagles, Silver Plate,
Meriden, 1 3/4 In.

Dresser Box, Hinged Cover, Queen Louise Transfer, Pink Ground, 4 x 6 In. 450.00
Fernery, Blue Flowers, Gilt Metal Rim, Embossed Cupid Feet, Marked, 6 x 8 In. 550.00
Humidor, Cigars, Hinged Cover, Enameled Beading, Blue Flowers, 6 In. 450.00
Humidor, Old Sport, English Bulldog, Rust Transfer Ground, Silver Cover, 7 In. . .530.00 to 800.00
Humidor, Tobacco, Hinged Cover, Pink Flowers, Shaded Blue, Marked, 5 1/2 In. 850.00
Jewelry Box, Hinged Cover, Pink Flowers, Green, Pink Ground, Marked, 2 1/2 x 3 3/4 In. . . 275.00
Jewelry Box, Hinged Cover, Pink Flowers, Satin Lining, Marked, 2 1/2 x 4 1/2 In. 350.00
Pin Dish, Blue, Pink, Gilt Metal Rim & Handles, Original Lining, Marked, 2 x 4 In. 125.00
Tray, Blue, Pink Poppy, Enameled Beading, Gold Handles & Rim, 2 x 6 In. 275.00
Tray, Green, Pink Flowers, Scalloped Gold Handles, 2 1/2 x 6 1/2 In. 300.00
Vase, Shaded Yellow To Pink, Green Trim, Lavender Flowers, Handles, Footed, 10 In. . . . 550.00

NANKING is a type of blue-and-white porcelain made in Canton, China, since the late eighteenth century. It is very similar to Canton, which is listed under its own name in this book. Both Nanking and Canton are part of a larger group now called *Chinese export* porcelain. Nanking has a spear-and-post border and may have gold decoration.

Bowl, Cover, Vegetable, Rectangular, Landscape, Fruit Finial, Blue, White, c.1800, 9 In. . . 748.00
Bowl, Vegetable, c.1840, 9 1/2 In. 259.00
Plate, Figural Landscape, Blue, White, 1800s, 8 In. 29.00
Platter, Blue Peony, Fence, Trees, 14 In. 385.00
Platter, Hexagonal, Clobbered Gold Trim, Blue & White, Initials, c.1800, 15 3/4 In. 705.00
Platter, Hexagonal, Fitzhugh Butterfly Border, Blue & White, c.1800, 15 3/4 In. 999.00
Platter, Well & Tree, 19th Century, 16 In. 588.00
Teapot, Lighthouse Form, Relief Berry Finial, c.1790, 10 In. 1610.00
Tureen, Sauce, Cover, Oval, Landscape, 19th Century, 8 In. 460.00

NAPKIN RINGS were in fashion from 1869 to about 1900. They were made of silver, porcelain, wood, and other materials. They are still being made today. The most popular rings with collectors are the silver plated figural examples. Small, realistic figures were made to hold the ring. Good and poor reproductions of the more expensive rings are now being made and collectors must be very careful.

Bud Vase, Cased Glass, Pink, Silver Plate, Roger Smith 1100.00
Bud Vase, Flowers, Pods, Leaves, Webster, Victorian 550.00
Cactus Pattern, Oval Shape, Sterling Silver, Georg Jensen, 2 In., Pair 325.00
Figural, 2 Engraved Fans, Silver Plate, Bridgeport, Victorian 275.00
Figural, Bashful Putto Silver Plate, J.W. Tufts, Boston, Late 1800s, 3 1/2 In. 518.00
Figural, Boy, Kate Greenway, Lying On Rectangular Base, Openwork, Tufts 995.00
Figural, Cat & Dog, Angry, Meriden, Victorian 775.00
Figural, Cherub, Holding Bud Vase, Reed & Barton 950.00
Figural, Cherub, Holding Reins To Stag, Silver Plate, Victorian 1500.00
Figural, Cherub, Looking Into Mirror, Bud Vase, Silver Plate, Rockford, Victorian 850.00
Figural, Cherub, On High Wheel, Roses, Footed, Silver Plate, Signed, Adelphi, 1890 . . . . 504.00
Figural, Cherub, Silver Plate, Pairpoint, Victorian 650.00
Figural, Chicken & Rake, Silver Plate, Webster, Victorian 650.00
Figural, Conquistador, Silver Plate, Toronto, Victorian 1500.00
Figural, Cow, Standing By Wheat Sheaf, Silver Plate, Meriden, Victorian 850.00

Figural, Crossed Rifle Leg, Silver Plate, 1850-1860, 2 1/4 x 3 1/2 In. 500.00
Figural, Dachshund, Carrying Ring On Back, Silver Plate, Victorian 1100.00
Figural, Deer, Horns, On Carpet, Toronto, Victorian 850.00
Figural, Dog, Mastiff, Silver Plate, Reed & Barton, Victorian 1700.00
Figural, Eagle, Ready To Soar, Silver Plate, Meriden, Victorian 850.00
Figural, Eagles, Silver Plate, Meriden, 1 3/4 In. ....*Illus* 250.00
Figural, Fan, Silver Plate, Marked, Pairpont, 3 1/4 x 2 In. 125.00
Figural, Flower, Closed Bud, Open Leaves, Hollow Ware, Silver Plate 225.00
Figural, Girl, Kate Greenaway, Sitting On Branches, Silver Plate, Victorian 1250.00
Figural, Girl, Rifle, Silver Plate, Simpson, Hall & Miller, American, Late 1800s, 3 In. ... 605.00
Figural, Grapes & Leaves, Silver Plate, Victorian 375.00
Figural, Lyre, Silver Plate, Victorian 395.00
Figural, Miner, Holding Pick, Death Valley, Calif., Silver Plate 475.00
Figural, Owl, On Leaf, Silver Plate, Victorian 395.00
Figural, Pan, Prancing On Earthen Mound, Silver Plate, Pairpoint, Victorian 950.00
Figural, Peacock, Silver Plate, Schade, Victorian 650.00
Figural, Perching Hawk, Silver Plate, Meriden Britannia, Conn., Late 1800s, 4 In. 430.00
Figural, Squirrel, Ring On Back, Silver Plate, Victorian 650.00
Figural, Squirrel, Silver Plate, Reed & Barton, Victorian 550.00
Figural, Squirrel, Silver Plate, Southington, Victorian 375.00
Figural, Tennis Racquets & Balls, Silver Plate, Meriden, Victorian 550.00
Figural, Turtle, Wheeled Book, Victorian 995.00
Figural, Water Lily, Pad, Hollow Ware, Silver Plate, Meriden, c.1880 .... 170.00
Sterling Silver, Amethyst, D-Shape, Hammered, Applied Thistle, Scotland, c.1900 ...... 60.00

NASH glass was made in Corona, New York, from about 1928 to 1931.
A. Douglas Nash bought the Corona glassworks from Louis C. Tiffany
in 1928 and founded the A. Douglas Nash Corporation with support
from his father, Arthur J. Nash. Arthur had worked at the Webb factory
in England and for the Tiffany Glassworks in Corona.

NASH

Bowl, Centerpiece, Deep Green, Red Chintz, Signed, c.1920, 4 x 13 In. 670.00
Bowl, Green, Red Chintz, Signed, c.1920, 4 x 13 In. 670.00
Bowl, Iridescent Gold, Signed, 7 3/4 In. 525.00
Candlestick, Aquamarine Stem, Red To Green Top, Chintz, Signed, c.1920, 4 3/4 In., Pair 840.00
Candlestick, Gold Iridescent, Flared Cup, Double Bulb Stem, Early 1900s, 3 3/4 In., Pair . 530.00
Compote, Blue & Green Ribbons, Translucent Body, Signed, c.1920, 13 In. 785.00
Compote, Iridescent Gold, Ribbed, Oval, Signed, c.1920, 4 1/2 x 6 In. 335.00
Compote, Iridescent Gold, Ribbed, Signed, c.1920, 4 1/2 x 4 In. 560.00
Goblet, Mottled Blue Bands, Green Pulled Stripes, Tapered To Knop, 6 1/2 In. 115.00
Lamp, Iridescent Gold Shade, Textured, Bronze Dore Base, Signed, c.1920, 11 3/4 In. 3080.00
Lamp, Iridescent Gold, Diamond-Quilted Shade, Bronze Dore Base, Signed, 16 x 8 In. 3240.00
Sauce, Mottled Orange Bands, Feathered Gold, Scalloped, Footed, 4 1/4 x 2 1/4 In. 60.00
Vase, Chintz, Pastel Green To Yellow, c.1920, 8 In. 745.00
Vase, Chintz, Red, Turquoise Chintz Stripes, Egg Shape, Flared Rim, c.1930, 8 In. 890.00
Vase, Iridescent Blue & Green, Translucent Foot, Oval, Signed, c.1920, 6 x 4 1/4 In. 950.00

NAUTICAL antiques are listed in this category. Any of the many objects
that were made or used by the seafaring trade, including ship parts,
models, and tools, are included. Other pieces may be found listed
under Scrimshaw.

Ax, Boarding, British Military Broad Arrow 175.00
Azimuth Circle, Brass, Dovetailed Wood Case, Extra Lenses 60.00
Azimuth Circle, ES Ritchie & Sons, Sperry Gyroscope, Brass, Case 46.00
Bell, Ship's, Bronze, 10 1/2 x 15 In. 460.00
Bell, Ship's, Bronze, Original Yoke, 26 In. 880.00
Bell, Ship's, Heywood L. Edwards, 1944, 16 In. 865.00
Bell, Ship's, Seaward, Engraved, Acorn Finial, 9 x 11 In. 865.00
Binnacle, Brass, Gimbal Liquid Compass, Kerosene Lamp, Tabletop, 9 x 9 1/2 In. 360.00
Binnacle, Brass, Sidelight, Oil Burner, Gimbaled Sestrel Compass, Case, 9 1/2 In. 255.00
Binnacle, C. Plath, Hamburg, Brass, Gimbaled Compass, 10 1/2 In. 230.00
Binnacle, Dent & Co., London, 13 1/2 x 9 In. 2875.00
Binnacle, Schooner W.W. Ker, Riggs & Bro., Phil., Wood Base, c.1890, 38 1/2 In. 4140.00
Binnacle, Ship's, K.&W.O. White Compass, Teakwood Stand, Brass, Iron Balls, 49 In. 1495.00

Binnacle, Ship's, Whyte Thomson & Co., John Hand Compass, Wood, Brass 4313.00
Binnacle, Wood, Brass Hood, Fittings, Oil, Lionel Compass, K. White Inclinometer 2760.00
Binnacle, Wood, Brass Hood, Iron Compensation, Gimbal Compass, 53 In. 1006.00
Block & Tackle, Whalebone, Brass Rivet, Double Back, 2 1/2 x 1 1/4 x 2 In., Pair 1120.00
Box, Traveling, Sailor Made, Rosewood, 3-Masted Ship, Woman's, 5 x 12 x 9 1/2 In. 1150.00
Cane, Rennoldson, London, Captain's, Brass, Leather, Ivory Knob, Telescope, Sword 2015.00
Cannon, Water, Fire Boat, Brass, 84 In. 345.00
Chart Case, England, Pine, 10 Drawers, Brass Hardware, 1800s, 38 x 50 x 30 1/2 In. 690.00
Chest, Blue Paint, Becket, Braided Canvas Wrapped Rope, Turk's Head Ends, 9 x 6 In. ... 375.00
Chest, Pine, Gray Paint, Lift Top, Interior Till, American, 17 x 46 x 19 In. 315.00
Chest, Pine, Molded Front Edge, Candle Box, Drawer, Hinges, 15 x 39 x 16 In. 275.00
Chest, Sea Captain's, Oak, 6 Gilt Decorated Bottles, 2 Tumblers, Funnel, 11 1/2 In. 805.00
Chest, Seaman's, Camphor, Teakwood, Vine & Tulip Inlay, 1800s, 19 x 37 x 17 In. 805.00
Chest, Seaman's, Dovetail Construction, Rope Handles, Black, Gold, 19 x 44 x 19 1/2 In. . 345.00
Chest, Seaman's, Recessed Panels, Painted Canvas Top, Macrame Fringe 9200.00
Chest, Seaman's, Walnut, Dovetailed, Iron Handles, Mariner's Compass Inlay, 24 In. ... 326.00
Chest, Storage, Iron Corners, Dovetailed, Anchor Closure, Early 1800s, 19 x 33 x 18 In. . 230.00
Chronometer, Charles Shepherd, Royal Navy, 48-Hour, Mahogany, c.1900, 6 In. 3080.00
Chronometer, Widenham, No. 1668, Brassbound Case, c.1830, 6 1/4 x 6 3/4 In. 3450.00
Chronometer Deck Watch, Waltham Watch Co., 8 Day, Yacht, Felt Lined Case 1095.00
Clock, Lilley & Reynolds, London, Brass Case, Hinged Bezel, c.1955, 6 In. 95.00
Clock, Ship's Bell, Chelsea Clock Co., Brass Case, Silvered Dial, c.1962, 6 In. 565.00
Clock, Ship's Bell, Chelsea, Walnut, Ship's Wheel, Anchor Shape, 6-In. Dial 396.00
Clock, Ship's Bell, Seth Thomas, 7 Jeweled, Wood Plaque Mounted, Key, 5 1/2 In. 546.00
Clock, Ship's Bell, Seth Thomas, Brass Case, c.1970, 4-In. Dial 113.00
Clock, Ship's, Boston Clock Co., 3 1/2 x 5 x 4 In. 160.00
Clock, Ship's, Chelsea, Bigelow, Kennard & Co., Brass Case, 10 1/4 In. 920.00
Clock, Ship's, Chelsea, Black Plastic, Military Time, U.S. Government, 10 1/2 In. 170.00
Clock, Ship's, Chelsea, Crosley Steam Gage & Valve Co., c.1908, 10-In. Dial 1695.00
Clock, Ship's, Chelsea, Phenolic Case, Silvered Dial, c.1942, 5 1/2 In. 198.00
Clock, Ship's, Chelsea, Polished Brass Case, Screw Bezel, c.1900, 4-In. Dial 226.00
Clock, Ship's, Chelsea, U.S. Marine Corps, Brass Case, c.1945, 5 1/2-In. Dial 463.00
Clock, Ship's, Mercer, Brass, Beveled Glass, 8 In. 175.00
Clock, Ship's, Seth Thomas, Bell, Brass, Wood Backing 430.00
Clock, Ship's, Seth Thomas, Bell, Chrome, Wood Backing, Roman Numerals 660.00
Clock, Ship's, Seth Thomas, U.S. Maritime Commission, 7 In. 403.00
Clock, Ship's, Wheel Shape, Brass Case, London, c.1965, 6-In. Dial. 140.00
Commode, Ship's, Enamel, Oval, Wood Enclosure, Brass, Wheels, 17 x 18 In. 431.00
Compass, A. Cairns, Liverpool, Tell-Tale, Bracket, 6 1/2 In. 835.00
Compass, Boxed Star No. 19534, Dry Card, Boston, 7 3/4 x 7 1/2 x 5 1/2 In. 127.00
Compass, Brass, Mahogany Case, 6 x 6 x 4 1/2 In. 160.00
Compass, Dirigo, Wooden Case, 3 In. 80.00
Compass, John Bliss & Co., N.Y., Brass, Gyroscopic, Early 1900s, 13 In. 235.00
Compass, Kelvin Bottomley & Baird, Box, 9 In. 115.00
Compass, Marine Compass Co., Pembroke, Mahogany Box, Gimbal Mount, 6 x 8 In. 150.00
Compass, Perkins Marine, Great Lakes Schooner Adrian, Brass, Glass, 12 x 9 3/4 In. 185.00
Compass, Wilcox & Crittenden, Dovetail Box, Sliding Cover, 5 x 5 x 3 1/4 In. 115.00
Compass, Yacht, Coubro & Scrutton Ltd., Brass Frame, Box, 6 x 8 x 8 In. 224.00
Course Corrector, Bain & Ainsley, Ship's, Wooden Case, 8 In. 175.00
Deck Bucket, Iron, Reliance, Captain Charles Barr, 1903, 17 1/2 x 16 1/2 In. 375.00
Desk, Captain's, Brassbound, Mahogany, Felt Writing, Surface, Brass Candle Holders ... 865.00
Desk, Captain's, Camphor Wood, Brassbound, Key, 2 Inkwells, c.1850, 19 x 11 x 7 In. ... 720.00
Desk, Captain's, Davenport, 4 Drawers, Lift-Up Top, 32 x 21 In. 1725.00
Diorama, 3-Masted, Gunboat, Village, Windmill, Lighthouse, Train, 11 1/2 x 3 In. 425.00
Diorama, Boston Harbor Pilot Boat, Hesper, Case, R. Boyd, 14 x 16 In. 489.00
Diorama, Freightliner, Smoke Stacks, Metal, Village, Church, 12 x 3 In. 175.00
Diorama, Ship In Bottle, Rigged Sailing Ship, U.S. Flag, 11 1/2 In. 315.00
Diorama, Steamship, 3 Boats, Village, Lighthouses, Windmill, 11 3/4 x 3 In. 500.00
Figurehead, Naval Officer, Mustache, Carved, Scrolled Front Leaf, 37 In. 920.00
Fire Cannon, Fire Boat's, Brass, 53 In. 316.00
Flare Gun, Cogswell & Harrison, London, Brass, Wood, Fitted Case, 12 Cartridges 316.00
Flare Pistol, U.S. Navy, International Flare, Ohio, Bronze Frame, 1944 .... 200.00
Float, Aqua, Rope Netting, 18 In., Pair 230.00

Fog Horn, Gloucester Type, 1901 Patent, 8 x 15 1/2 In. 200.00
Gauge, Gillis & Geo, Nickel, Ashcroft, New York, 9 1/2 In. 85.00
Globe, Cary & Co., Navigational, Mahogany Case, 1920s, 8 1/2 x 8 In. 1150.00
Gong, U.S. Navy, Henschel Corp., Amesbury, Mass., Brass, Mechanical, 8 x 10 In. 60.00
Half-Model, Hull, Builder's, 6 Lifts, c.1875, 27 1/2 In. 1150.00
Half-Model, Hull, Sloop DEE-DEE, Green, White, Backboard, Plaque, 12 x 30 1/2 In. . . .   374.00
Half-Model, King Lear, Packet Ship, Decorative Backboard, Ship Details, 17 x 61 In. 1955.00
Half-Model, Launch, Keel, Rudder, Laminated, Backboard Mounted, 20 1/2 In. 920.00
Half-Model, Nantucket Lightship No. 112, Folk Art Style, 28 x 48 In. 1725.00
Half-Model, Swallow, Clipper Ship, Copper Hull, Robert E. Jackson, 1855, 21 x 60 In. . . .   575.00
Harpoon, 2-Piece Handle, Brass Ferrule, Knob Latch, 7 Ft. 28.00
Harpoon, Hand Forged, Heavy Handle, Large Ferrule, 30 In. 95.00
Harpoon, Temple Form Head, Hand Forged Iron, Opened Seam Socket, c.1835, 33 In. . . .   495.00
Harpoon, Toggle, Iron, Used With Darting Gun, 42 In. 545.00
Harpoon, Toggle, New Bedford Blacksmith, 1950s, 29 1/2 In. 230.00
Harpoon, Toggle, Pole Mounted, 1800s, 96 In. 1380.00
Helmet, Deep Sea Diving, Toa Diving Apparatus Co., Yokahoma Model, Copper, 16 In. . . .   2130.00
Helmet, Diver's, Rounded Copper Bell, Brass Portholes & Fittings, 16 x 14 In. 115.00
Helmet, Diving, Miller Dunn, Miami, Diving Hook Style 2, Navy, Brass, Copper, 24 In. .   4025.00
Knife, Whaling, Wolfgang Bellach, Whale's Tooth Handle, Olympic Cruiser, 10 1/2 In. . . .   405.00
Lamp, Dressel Arlington, N.J., Mohawk, State Canal, 360 Degree Ribbed Lens, 24 In. . . .   115.00
Lamp, Ship's, USS Olympia, Copper, Brass, Pierced Panel, May 1, 1898, 29 1/2 In. 1870.00
Lantern, C. Murray, Glasgow, Masthead, Copper, Brass, Oil Burner, Fresnel Lens, 22 In. .   635.00
Lantern, National Marine Lamp Co., NY, Brass, Red & Green Lens, 9 In. 115.00
Lantern, NUC, Copper, Glass, 14 In. 120.00
Lantern, Oil, Brass, Glass Port & Starboard, Red & Blue Ribbed Lenses, 10 In., Pair 489.00
Lantern, Ship's, 360 Degree Ribbed Glass Lens, Hinged Top, Copper Plates, 20 1/2 In. . .   115.00
Lantern, Ship's, Anchor, Best & Lloyd, Brass, Copper, Ribbed Lens, Electrified, 18 In. . .   230.00
Lantern, Ship's, Brass, Kerosene, Clear Lens, 11 In. 150.00
Lantern, Ship's, Brass, Swing Handle, Caged Clear Globe, 7-Cone Top, 15 In. 330.00
Lantern, Ship's, Bronze, 360 Degrees, Russell & Stoll Co., N.Y., 19 x 7 In. 129.00
Lantern, Ship's, Bulk Head, 3 Glass Sides, Door, Key Flame Adjustment, Gray, 16 In. . . .   145.00
Lantern, Ship's, Liberty, Early 20th Century, 17 1/2 x 16 x 13 In.   230.00
Lantern, Ship's, NUC, Brass, Copper, Handle, Japan, 21 In. 200.00
Lantern, Ship's, Plume & Atwood, U.S.A., Gimbal, Brass, Pair 1440.00
Light, Beacon, Trinity House, Copper, Brass, Fresnel Glass Lens, Hinged Top, 35 x 15 In.   3335.00
Light, Running, Sea Horse GB 87003, Cast Bronze, 2 Clear Lenses, Electric, 9 x 17 In. . .   250.00
Light, Ship's, Anchor, C. Murray, Glasgow, Copper, Brass, Ribbed Glass Lens, 21 In. 719.00
Line Reel, Net Makers, Whalebone, Wood, 19th Century, 11 3/4 x 6 x 3 1/4 In. 1456.00
Line Reel, Whale Bone & Wood, 11 3/4 x 6 x 3 1/4 In. 1145.00
Liquor Set, Sea Captain's, Greene & Gladding, 1700s, 11 x 16 x 15 1/2 In. 1668.00
Log Book, Waverly Whaling Ship, Master Ephraim W. Kempton, 1849-1851 . . . .   3450.00
Log Book, Whaling, Ship Camilla, Benjamin Franklin Jones, 1867-1871 . . . .   2875.00
Mirror, Ship's Helm, Beveled Glass, Mahogany, 21 1/4 In. 100.00
Model, 1893 America's Cup Yacht, Vigilant, W. Hitchcock, Case, 30 1/2 x 31 x 10 In. 2875.00
Model, America's Cup Yacht, Puritan, Stitched Sails, Mahogany Base, 49 x 55 In. 1610.00
Model, American Clipper Ship, Sovereign Of The Seas, Full Sails, 36 x 50 In. 690.00
Model, Aphrodite, Yacht, Steam, Glass Case, 62 x 61 x 18 In. 3105.00
Model, Barque Daisy, Fully Rigged, Deadeyes, Pulleys, Long Boats, 53 x 39 In. 3165.00
Model, Basilisk, British Revenue Cutter, Robert Innis, South Dennis, Mass., 30 x 32 In. . .   1840.00
Model, Boat, Passenger, White, Turquoise, Black, Red, Saga, Micki, 1920s, 24 x 5 x 7 In.   168.00
Model, Brig, Armed, Ivory, Bone, Lion Figurehead, Anchors, Ebonized Base, 11 x 10 In. .   2185.00
Model, Brig, Case, 23 x 30 x 15 In. 518.00
Model, British Clipper Ship, Cutty Sark, Fully Fitted, Rigged, c.1900, 30 x 44 In. 1380.00
Model, British Cup Challenger, Valkyrie III, Case, 31 1/2 x 32 x 9 In. 1610.00
Model, Chesapeake Bay Flattie, Planked Deck, Sails, Case, 25 x 35 In. 748.00
Model, Clipper Ship, Cutty Sark, Wooden, Case, Table, 60 x 60 x 24 In. 2990.00
Model, Clipper, 3-Masted, Shadow Box, 8 1/2 x 5 In. 374.00
Model, Elco Steam Yacht, Caprice, Mahogany Cabins, Glass Case, 23 x 37 In. 1380.00
Model, Freighter, Charles Donnelly, American Flag, Case, 17 x 12 x 2 In. 58.00
Model, Gertrude Thiebolt, Case, 30 x 27 x 9 1/2 In. 403.00
Model, Gloucester Schooner, Case, Richard Boyd, 14 1/2 x 17 1/2 In. 259.00
Model, Lighthouse, Rock Shape Base, France, Late 19th Century, 13 1/2 x 4 1/2 In. 168.00

Model, Luxury Liner, Wood, Custom Stand, Black & Red Hull, 17 x 31 In. 405.00
Model, Maine Lobster Boat, Fully Rigging, Traps, Buoys, 10 x 21 x 7 1/2 In. 195.00
Model, Merchantman, 3-Masted, Full Sail, Clay Sea, Shadow Box, 12 x 24 x 7 In. 748.00
Model, North Sea Trawler, Case, 31 x 43 x 12 In. 748.00
Model, Privateer, Rattlesnake, Full Sail Suit, Case, Plymouth, Mass., 25 x 31 In. 920.00
Model, Sailboat, Wooden, Tan & Green Paint, Mary, C., M.Y.C., 1924, 44 1/2 In. 400.00
Model, Schooner, 2-Masted, BS Wright, Towing Launch, Shadow Box, 32 x 19 x 4 In. . . . 1265.00
Model, Schooner, 2-Masted, Corsair, J.P. Morgan's Yacht, Black & Red, Case, 22 x 48 In. 3220.00
Model, Schooner, 2-Masted, Diorama, R. Boyd, 18 1/2 x 19 1/2 In. 546.00
Model, Schooner, 2-Masted, Emma Berry, 49 In. 575.00
Model, Schooner, 2-Masted, Painted, Lead Anchors, Wood Base, 24 x 30 x 5 1/2 In. 275.00
Model, Schooner, 2-Masted, Rigging, Black Hull, Wood Platform, 8 x 11 In. 60.00
Model, Schooner, 2-Masted, Wood, Wire, Brass, Fabric, Wood Base, 36 In. 165.00
Model, Schooner, 3-Masted, Atlantic, Brass Case, 1905, 23 1/2 x 30 x 5 In. 1840.00
Model, Schooner, 3-Masted, Canvas Sails, Plastered Hull, Accessories, 52 x 50 x 8 In. . . . 880.00
Model, Schooner, 3-Masted, Cased, 39 x 27 x 15 In. 575.00
Model, Schooner, 3-Masted, Rigged Sail Suit, 27 x 33 In. 175.00
Model, Schooner, 3-Masted, Rigged, Canvas Sail, Wood Base, 1800, 52 x 50 x 7 1/2 In. . . 896.00
Model, Schooner, 3-Masted, Rocordo Isauro, Diorama, Waterline, 24 x 18 1/2 x 7 1/2 In. . 2070.00
Model, Schooner, 3-Masted, White & Black, Fully Rigged, Plank Deck, Wood, 25 x 34 In. 230.00
Model, Schooner, 4-Masted, City Of Savannah, Fully Rigged, 67 In. 2200.00
Model, Schooner, 4-Masted, Edith, Providence, Cloth Sails, Pulleys, 68 x 48 In. 1208.00
Model, Seagoing Tug, Plank On Frame Construction, Wood, Case, 26 x 39 x 14 In. 920.00
Model, Shamrock V, Full Sail Suit, Park Avenue Boom, Case, 1930s, 37 x 32 In. 1495.00
Model, Ship, Adolph, Sea, Buoy Marker, Case, 36 x 25 x 13 1/2 In. 690.00
Model, Ship, Coastal Fishing Cutter, Glass Case, England, 1860 . . . . 100.00
Model, Ship, Constitution, Carved, Poplar Case, Plexiglass Panels, 33 x 13 x 31 In. 660.00
Model, Ship, Sail, Steam, Ocean, Light House, Pilot Boat, Case, 26 x 18 x 12 In. 980.00
Model, Ship, Wood, Smoke Stack, British Flag, Cotton Waves, Pine Case, 18 x 7 x 10 In. . 250.00
Model, Steam Tugboat, Hercules, Glass Case, 17 x 26 x 6 In. 1610.00
Model, Submarine, USS Drum No. 228, Glass Case, 10 x 25 1/2 x 6 3/4 In. 865.00
Model, Tugboat, Steam, 2-Funnel, Carved Sea, Shadowbox, 15 x 18 3/4 In. 430.00
Model, Tugboat, Taurus, Mounted, Wood Base, 9 In. 145.00
Model, USS Constitution, Fully Rigged, Glass Figurehead, Glass Case, 41 x 29 In. 1035.00
Model, Whaleboat, American, Harpoons, Lances, Oars, Case, 10 1/2 x 28 x 9 1/2 In. 1075.00
Model, Whaling Ship, Fully Outfitted With Gear, Cased, 24 1/2 x 30 x 12 In. 1208.00
Model, Whaling Ship, Fully Rigged, Pulleys, Long Boats, Case, 35 x 29 In. 2300.00
Model, Yacht, Edward H., Diorama, Case, R. Boyd, 18 x 18 In. 575.00
Model, Yacht, Lighted, Mahogany, Nickeled Brass, Lucite, c.1950, 36 x 13 In. 645.00
Needle Set, Sailor's, Ropework, Case, 10 Steel Sail Needles, 19th Century, 9 1/2 In. 265.00
Net Floats, Glass, Green, Aqua, Pair 160.00
Oar, Wooden, Painted, Red, Green, 90 In., Pair 60.00
Octant, Spencer Browning & Co., Ebony, Ivory, Brass Fittings, 13 In. 489.00
Outboard Motor, Ted Williams, 7 1/2 Horsepower 22.00
Paddle, Canoe, American, Canadian Flags, 21 1/2 In., Pair 240.00
Parallel Rule, Navigator's, Dovetailed Wood Case, 18 In. 219.00
Pond Boat, Full Sails, Steel Ballast, Brass Fittings, Complete Rigging, 61 x 45 In. 2070.00
Pond Boat, Sail, Green, White Hull, Brown, Mustard Deck, Wood, 29 1/2 x 30 1/2 In. . . . 145.00
Pond Boat, Sail, Pine, White & Red Hull, Striped Sails, Wood Stand, 35 x 36 In. 345.00
Pond Boat, Sail, Red, Black Paint, Mast, Rigging, Leaded Keel, 52 In. 1035.00
Pond Boat, Sloop Rigged, Mainsail, 2 Jibs, Early 1900s, 31 x 21 In. 185.00
Porthole, Brass, Hinged Doors, 2 Dogs, 13 In., Pair 575.00
Porthole Cover, Mirror, Marked Coapind, Genova, Brass, Early 20th Century, 15 In. 175.00
Quadrant, Abraham, Liverpool, H. Duren, New York, Ebony, Ivory, Brass, c.1825, 13 In. 1006.00
Quadrant, Ebony, Ivory, Brass Fittings, 12 In. 635.00
Quadrant, Ebony, Ivory, Brass, 3 Sun Filters, c.1850, 12 In. 518.00
Quadrant, Edmund M. Blunt, N.Y, Brass, Ivory, Ebony, Green Case, 13 1/2 x 11 1/2 In. . . 920.00
Quadrant, Jones Gray & Keenan, Liverpool, Ebony, Ivory, Brass, Jones, c.1810, 12 In. . . 748.00
Quadrant, R. Miller Leith, Ebony, Ivory, Brass, Case, c.1825, 12 In. 748.00
Rudder, Wood, White & Red Paint, Tiller, 56 x 56 In. 259.00
Running Light, Ship's, Galvanized, White, Blue Green Lens, 17 In. 92.00
Sailor's Valentine, Octagonal, Heart, Multicolored Shells, 13 1/2 In. 1673.00
Sailor's Valentine, Shells, Double Sided, Heart & Rose, Home Sweet Home, 9 In. 3737.00

Sailor's Valentine, Shellwork, 8 Sided, New Curiosity Shop, St. Barbados, 17 In. 2415.00
Sailor's Valentine, Shellwork, I'm Yours Be Mine, B.A. Woodman, Frame, 10 1/2 In. 2875.00
Sailor's Valentine, Shellwork, Sailor, Mermaid, B.A. Woodman, Frame, 10 1/2 In. 2990.00
Sailor's Valentine, Shellwork, Ship, Kingston, Sign, C.J. Guise, B.A. Woodman, 10 In. ... 4600.00
Sextant, Brass, 3 Rings, Silver Scales, Dovetailed Case, 3 Eyepieces 375.00
Sextant, C. Hutchinson, John Bliss, Solid Brass, Silver Scales 635.00
Sextant, E & G.W. Blunt, New York, Silver Scales, Keystone Case, 4 Eyepieces 1725.00
Sextant, Ebony & Brass, Ivory Inlay, 3 Lens, Swing Arm, 18 1/4 In. 575.00
Sextant, Graduated Scale, Engraved Degrees, Brass, Silver Inlay, c.1870 .... 500.00
Sextant, H. Hughes & Son, Iron, Brass, Mahogany Box, 20th Century, 1920 Certificate .. 420.00
Sextant, Henry Barrow & Co., England, Brass, 1880s, 8 x 8 5/8 In. 745.00
Sextant, Henry Hughes & Son, Case, London, Oil Bottle, 10 1/2 x 11 x 5 3/4 In. 520.00
Sextant, J.D. Potter Poultry, London, Silver Scales, Case Lattice Frame, c.1870 .... 690.00
Sextant, Sestrel, 3 Ring, Dovetailed Case 315.00
Sextant, Simex MK III, Black Finish, Mahogany Box, 6 1/2 x 11 3/4 x 11 3/4 In. 365.00
Sextant, Standley, Brass, 3 x 1 1/2 In. 80.00
Sextant, Weehms, Hughes & Plath, Hand Held, Case, 1957, 6 1/2 x 12 1/2 x 12 1/2 In. .. 300.00
Sextant, Weehms, Hughes & Plath, Metal, Box, 1957 Certificate, 6 1/2 x 12 x 12 In. 335.00
Ship In Bottle, 3-Masted, 3-Sided Pinch Bottle, 8 x 4 In. 300.00
Ship In Bottle, 3-Masted, Annie, Village, 20 Buildings, 10 3/4 In. 145.00
Ship In Bottle, 3-Masted, Gun Boat, Light Green Bottle, Applied Lip, 9 3/4 x 3 3/4 In. ... 400.00
Ship In Bottle, 3-Masted, Lighthouse, 15 Buildings, 6-In. Ship, 12-In. Bottle 85.00
Ship In Bottle, 3-Masted, Upright Bottle, Green, Plaster Wave, 6 1/2 x 5 1/2 x 3 In. 225.00
Ship Model, see Nautical, Model
Ship's Wheel, Cast Brass, Glass Topped Portal, 27 In. 303.00
Ship's Wheel, Circular, Metal Band, Turned Spokes & Handles, Early 1900s, 44 In. 431.00
Ship's Wheel, Mahogany, Brass Hub, Early 1900s, 40 In. 690.00
Ship's Wheel, Seaward, Wood, Brass Hub, Bands, Pin Cap, 36 In. 1325.00
Ship's Wheel, Walnut, 8-Turned Spokes, Handles, 45 In. 275.00
Ship's Wheel, Wilcox Crittenden, Galvanized, Wood Drum, Spokes, Brass Caps, 20 In. ... 81.00
Ship's Wheel, Wood, Brass Hub, Band, 24 In. 175.00
Ship's Wheel, Wood, Brass Hub, Sailor Knot At King Pin, 42 In. 1380.00
Ship's Wheel, Wood, Iron Hub, Nickel & Brass Band, 48 In. 633.00
Ship's Wheel, Wood, Iron Mounted, Double Frame, Spindle Turned Spokes, 44 In. 165.00
Ship's Wheel, Wood, Iron, 8 Spokes, Iron Hub, Banding, 43 In. 489.00
Shoes, Diving, Canvas, Leather, Bronze Toes 316.00
Sign, Telegraph, Burkee Marine, Staten Island, Bronze, 2-Sided, 49 In. 1840.00
Signaling Cannon, 6-Sided, Flared Base, 1-In. Bore Barrel, c.1700 Century, 4 In. 415.00
Spear, Eel, Iron, 15 In. 60.00
Spotlight, Perkins Marine Lamp & Hardware, Miami, Fla., Brass, Perko, 9 1/2 x 30 In. ... 145.00
Stadimeter, Shick Corp., Original Eye Piece, Box, Early 1940s, 13 x 6 x 6 In. 430.00
Stadimeter, US Maritime Commission, Model Zero, Ajax, 1942, 4 1/2 x 11 1/4 x 5 In. 75.00
Steering Station, U.S.N.R.T.C., Salem, Mass, Brass, Wood Base, 1948, 56 In. 1670.00
Sternboard, Yacht, Wooden, Carrie May, Black Letters, White Ground, 35 In. 460.00
Table, Drop Leaf, Mahogany, 2 Lift-Top Center Compartments, 39 x 33 In. 345.00
Telegraph, Ship's, Bendix Brooklyn, CB 1318A, Brass Engine, 44 In. 1440.00
Telegraph, Ship's, Brass Signaling Device, Wood Base, Handles, 34 1/2 In. 465.00
Telegraph, Ship's, Durkee, Staten Island, Brass, Double Face, 11-In. Dials, 45 In. 3165.00
Telescope, 4 Draw, Glass, Brass, Leather, Marked, 13 x 2 3/8 In. 150.00
Telescope, Bardou A Paris, Single Draw, Brass, Leather Cover, 2 Lens Covers, 38 In. 345.00
Telescope, Captain's, Brass, Wood, 1860s, 34 1/2 In. 460.00
Telescope, Captain's, Single Draw, Solid Brass, Tapered, 60 In. 1150.00
Telescope, Petrali & Plasket, Cardiff, Bargue Assonta, Capt. Sejano, Solid Brass, 34 In. .. 460.00
Telescope, Spencer Browning & Rust, London, Single Draw, Wood Barrel, 35 In. 115.00
Telescope, U.S. Navy, Quartermaster, Oak Case, 16 Power, 1942 .... 290.00
Vanity Case, Sailor Made, Inlaid Marquetry, Hearts, US Shields, 6 x 7 1/4 x 11 1/4 In. ... 690.00
Yacht's Bridge Station, Brass Binnacle, Wheel, 2 Brass Telegraphs, c.1900, 50 In. 2415.00

NETSUKES are small ivory, wood, metal, or porcelain pieces used as toggles on the end of the cord that held a Japanese money pouch or inro. The earliest date from the sixteenth century. Many are miniature, carved works of art. This category also includes the ojime, the slide or string fastener that was used on the inro cord.

Amber, Man Seated On Treasure Sack 290.00

Bone, Karako With Hobby Horse, 19th Century 375.00
Bronze, Gourd, 19th Century 115.00
Copper, Compass, Sundial, Square, 19th Century 431.00
Ebony, 2 Monkeys Acting Like Sumo Wrestlers, Early 1800s 219.00
Ebony, Cottage Under Pine Trees, Signed Masayoshi, 19th Century.......... 259.00
Inro, 3 Stack, Star & Cube, Chrysanthemums, Leaves, 1 3/4 x 2 3/4 In., 2 Piece 275.00
Inro, 4 Compartments, Cherry Bark Surface, Gold Lacquer Flowers, Swallow, c.1890 .... 380.00
Inro, Black & Gold Lacquer, 4 Stack, Cranes & Marsh Grasses, 19th Century 2070.00
Inro, Black & Gold Lacquer, 4 Stack, Stag & Doe, 19th Century 1785.00
Inro, Cinnabar Mermaid, Carved Lacquer Peonies, 2 Compartments, 1800s 825.00
Inro, Ebony, 3 Stack, Man On Horseback, Boy On Dragon, Tortoise, 2 1/2 x 3 1/2 In. 880.00
Inro, Gold Lacquer, 4 Stack, Boatmen On River, Fortress, 19th Century 1380.00
Inro, Gold Lacquer, 4 Stack, Shoki, Oni, 19th Century 2760.00
Inro, Gold Lacquer, 5 Stack, Sage In Pine Tree Landscape, 19th Century 1035.00
Inro, Gold Lacquer, 6 Stack, Shishi On Mountainside, 19th Century 575.00
Inro, Ivory, 4 Compartments, Carved Lacquer, Boy, Flowers, Ivory Ojime, 1800s 176.00
Inro, Ivory, Swastika, Bar, Chrysanthemum, Shojo Enjoying Sake, 1 1/2 x 2 3/8 In. 1210.00
Inro, Lacquer, 4 Stack, Cockerel Hen In Bamboo Grove, 1 1/2 x 2 1/2 In............ 2460.00
Inro, Lacquer, 4 Stack, Daikoku Sitting In Bamboo Grove, 2 3/8 x 3 1/4 In. 825.00
Inro, Lacquer, 4 Stack, River, Bridge On Islet, Landscape, Dog On Leaf, 2 1/2 x 2 3/4 In. ... 660.00
Inro, Lacquer, 5 Stack, Carp Swimming Up Waterfall, 1 1/2 x 3 1/2 In. 605.00
Inro, Lacquer, Conifers, Gate, Fence, Tree Branch, 1 1/2 x 3 In. 495.00
Inro, Manju, Gold Lacquer, Maki-E, Grasses, Cinnabar Ojime, 1800s 529.00
Inro, Red & Brown Lacquer, 3 Stack, Flowers, 19th Century 489.00
Inro, Red Lacquer, Figures, Landscape, 19th Century 145.00
Inro, Wood, 1 Compartment, Jurojin, Carved Bone Puffer Fish Ojime, 1800s 176.00
Inro, Wood, 5 Stack, Man Holding Gourd, Pine Tree, 19th Century 750.00
Ivory, 2 Dancers, Costume, Foo Dog Mask, Black Ink Detail, Signed, 2 1/8 In. 145.00
Ivory, 2 Monkeys, Mountain, 1800s, 1 1/2 In. 295.00
Ivory, Basket Seller, 19th Century 978.00
Ivory, Boy, Costume, Foo Dog Mask, Hinged Lower Jaw, Stands On Drum, Seisho, 2 In. . 575.00
Ivory, Clam Shell, Carved Travelers In Woods, Rickshaw, 2 In. 115.00
Ivory, Family Of Four With Horse, Signed Minkoku, 19th Century 489.00
Ivory, Foo Dog, Guarding Ball, Inlaid Eyes 430.00
Ivory, Foo Dog, Inset Yellow Eyes, Standing On Signed Ball, 1 5/8 In. 259.00
Ivory, Foo Dog, Seated On Cushions, Black Ink Detail, Signed, 1 1/2 In., Pair .. 210.00
Ivory, Foo Dog, Smaller Dog On Its Back, 1 3/4 In............................. 200.00
Ivory, Foo Dog, With Movable Ball In Mouth, Guarding Pearl, 18th Century 550.00
Ivory, Foo Dogs, Pair, Large Himetoshi, 1700s, 2 In. 1530.00
Ivory, Frog Climbing Well Bucket, Signed, 19th Century 259.00
Ivory, Giant Crab Attacking Ship & Crew, 1800s, 2 In. 765.00
Ivory, Grazing Horse, Oval Platform, 18th Century 460.00
Ivory, Man, On Tortoise 176.00
Ivory, Man, Rocking Head, Watermelon Section, 1800s 470.00
Ivory, Man, Seated On Stump, Left Leg Over Rock, Sack Over Shoulder, 1 1/2 In. 210.00
Ivory, Man, Seated On Treasure Sack, 18th Century 605.00
Ivory, Man, Seated, Crossed Legs, Leaning On Stick, Fruit Basket, 1 1/4 In. 195.00
Ivory, Man, Seated, Holding Fan, 20th Century 375.00
Ivory, Man, Wearing Demonic Mask, Holding Axe, Basket On Hip, Marked, 1 x 1 3/4 In. . 150.00
Ivory, Manju, Chrysanthemum, Carved Leaves, Flower Petals, 18th Century 315.00
Ivory, Manju, Woman Playing With Fukurokuju, Signed Mitsuharu, 19th Century 605.00
Ivory, Monkey On Go Board, Signed Masakazu, 19th Century 375.00
Ivory, Mouse Gnawing Wood Sandal, 1700s, 2 3/4 In. 825.00
Ivory, Nesting Eaglet, Pine Branch, Signed Toyomasa, 1800s 575.00
Ivory, Pavilion In Mountain Landscape, Calligraphy, Ichiyusai 375.00
Ivory, Rat, Inlaid Eyes, On Pouch, Coral Ojime, Stained Ivory Bamboo 4715.00
Ivory, Samurai, Child Wearing Armor, 10th Century 315.00
Ivory, Seiobo, Female Divinity, 1700s, 5 1/2 In............................... 235.00
Ivory, Tangerine, Partially Peeled, 19th Century 127.00
Ivory, Water Buffalo, Head Turned Back, 19th Century 1090.00
Ivory, Woman, Seated, 19th Century 400.00
Ivory Handle, Lacquer Interior, Coconut Cup, Quail, Pheasant, Landscape, 19th Century . 127.00
Ojime, Bone, Chestnut, Early 20th Century 240.00

Ojime, Brass, Bamboo, Copper, Leaves, 19th Century 255.00
Ojime, Brass, Engraved, Peacock, 19th Century 357.00
Ojime, Bronze, Seed Shape, Baskets Of Flowers, 1800s 75.00
Ojime, Cloisonne, Flowers, Late 19th Century 69.00
Ojime, Copper, Crane, 19th Century 230.00
Ojime, Copper, Gilt Spider, Late 19th Century 360.00
Ojime, Coral, Endless Knot, c.1900 .... 175.00
Ojime, Gold, Ball Shape, Peacock, Flower, Meiji Period 1035.00
Ojime, Gold, Ball Shape, Pierced Leaf, Early 1900s 605.00
Ojime, Gold, Bird, Flower, 19th Century 1265.00
Ojime, Gold, Bird, Moonlight, 19th Century 805.00
Ojime, Gold, Flower, Butterfly, 19th Century 978.00
Ojime, Gold, Grasshopper, Flower, 19th Century 1610.00
Ojime, Gold, Pierced, Flower Garden, Signed, 19th Century 605.00
Ojime, Gold, Seed Shape, Pierced Flowers, 19th Century 690.00
Ojime, Iron, Doughnut, Gold, Silver Inlay, 19th Century 69.00
Ojime, Ivory, 2 Comic Masks, Late 19th Century 185.00
Ojime, Ivory, 6 Masks, c.1900 .... 242.00
Ojime, Ivory, Ball, Shell Carving, 19th Century 127.00
Ojime, Ivory, Lacquer, Carp, Fishing Village Scene, 20th Century 160.00
Ojime, Ivory, Mask, 19th Century 316.00
Ojime, Metal, Ball Form, Crane, Mt. Fuji Landscape, Coral Sun, 19th Century 400.00
Ojime, Metal, Silver, Chrysanthemum, Cylinder, 19th Century 170.00
Ojime, Metal, Silver, Crane, Moon, 19th Century 115.00
Ojime, Peach Pit, Seed Shape, Dragon Carving, 1800s 58.00
Ojime, Peach Pit, Songbirds, Flowering Trees, Late 19th Century 370.00
Ojime, Silver Metal, Flowers, 19th Century 375.00
Ojime, Silver, Copper, Cylinder, Silhouette Figure, Late 19th Century 400.00
Ojime, Silver, Drum, Flowers, 19th Century 345.00
Ojime, Silver, Gold, Flowers, 19th Century 1265.00
Ojime, Silver, Hexagonal, 19th Century 127.00
Ojime, Silver, Lion Dancer With Fan, 19th Century 750.00
Ojime, Staghorn, Censer, Loop Handles, 19th Century 150.00
Ojime, Staghorn, Garden Lantern, 19th Century 130.00
Porcelain, Lion Censer, 19th Century 259.00
Porcelain, Man With Pursed Lips, 19th Century 115.00
Porcelain, Monkey Wearing Vest, Hugging Peach, 19th Century 127.00
Porcelain, Shunga, Blue & White, Seated Okame, 19th Century 345.00
Stag Antler, Baying Kirin, 18th Century 4600.00
Staghorn, Bamboo Shoot, c.1800 .... 115.00
Staghorn, Entertainer With Monkey On Back, Early 19th Century 405.00
Staghorn, Samurai Seated, Laughing, Early 19th Century 276.00
Staghorn, Water Buffalo, Inlaid Eyes, 19th Century 635.00
Wood, 2 Puppies, 1800s 259.00
Wood, Ashtray, Flower Blossom, Stem, 19th Century 230.00
Wood, Child With Ivory Hands & Feet Holding Ivory Mask, Late 19th Century 520.00
Wood, Dragon, Tiger Fighting, Horn, Amber Inlaid Eyes, Ivory Fangs, c.1800 .... 4830.00
Wood, Foo Dog, Resting On Rockery Base, 1700s 345.00
Wood, Foo Dog, Resting, 19th Century 3450.00
Wood, Grazing Horse, Saddle Blanket, Early 19th Century 690.00
Wood, Man Making Mill Wheels, 19th Century 145.00
Wood, Mask, Man With Unpleasant Expression, Signed, Deme Joman, 18th Century 145.00
Wood, Metal, Pistol, Gold, Silver Inlay, Movable Hammer, Trigger, 19th Century 2070.00
Wood, Monkey, Inlaid Eyes, 19th Century 4255.00
Wood, Nio, Signed Seiichi, 1800s, 4 In. 175.00
Wood, Oni Holding Circular Drum, 18th Century 175.00
Wood, Rats On Treasure Sack, c.1800 .... 289.00
Wood, Sennin In Mugwort Cape, 1700s 150.00
Wood, Shunga, Pearl Diver, Amorous Octopus, Inlaid Eyes, 19th Century 259.00

Don't keep a house key in an obvious spot in the garage.

NEW MARTINSVILLE Glass Manufacturing Company was established in 1901 in New Martinsville, West Virginia. It was bought and renamed the Viking Glass Company in 1944. In 1987 Kenneth Dalzell, former president of Fostoria Glass Company, purchased the factory and renamed it Dalzell-Viking. Production ceased in 1998.

Addie, Creamer, Amber	14.00
Addie, Cup & Saucer, Green	12.00
Addie, Cup, Amber	9.00
Addie, Cup, Amethyst	14.00
Addie, Plate, Amber, 8 1/4 In.	9.00
Addie, Plate, Amethyst, 8 1/4 In.	12.00
Addie, Plate, Green, 6 1/8 In.	8.00
Addie, Plate, Green, 8 1/4 In.	8.00
Addie, Sandwich Server, Amethyst, Handles, 10 3/4 In.	40.00
Addie, Sandwich Server, Green, Handles, 10 3/4 In.	20.00
Addie, Saucer, Amethyst	6.00
Addie, Sherbet, Amber, 2 In.	12.00
Addie, Sugar, Amber	14.00
Carnation, Berry Bowl, Ruby Stain, Gold Trim, 4 x 8 In.	65.00
Carnation, Water Set, Ruby Stain, Gold Trim, 5 Piece	155.00
Evergreen, Cup & Saucer	30.00
Figurine, Baby Bear & Cart	130.00
Figurine, Seal, Ball On Nose, 7 1/4 In.	55.00 to 75.00
Figurine, Starfish, 7 5/8 x 7 1/8 In., Pair	230.00
Figurine, Woodsman, 7 1/4 x 4 In.	115.00
Florentine, Dish, Mayonnaise, Underplate, 2 1/2 x 5 1/2 In.	30.00
Florentine, Sugar, Footed	18.00
Frontier, Goblet, Ruby Stain, 6 1/8 In.	175.00
Janice, Basket, Black, 9 1/2 x 12 x 7 In.	190.00
Janice, Basket, Black, Clear Handle, 9 1/2 x 12 In.	190.00
Janice, Bowl, Blue, 4 x 12 1/4 In.	90.00
Janice, Bowl, Centerpiece, 3-Footed, 3 3/4 x 11 In.	45.00
Janice, Bowl, Swan Handle, 10 x 10 In.	80.00
Janice, Candle Vase, Ruby, 5 3/8 x 5 In., Pair	400.00
Janice, Candlestick, 6 In., Pair	35.00
Janice, Relish, 2 Sections, Round, Scalloped Rim, Handles, 6 In.	15.00
Janice, Sugar & Creamer, Tray, Light Blue	60.00
Moondrops, Ashtray, Ruby, 1 x 4 In.	30.00
Moondrops, Ashtray, Ruby, Round, 1 x 4 1/16 In.	30.00
Moondrops, Butter, Cover, 6 In.	250.00
Moondrops, Candlestick, 3-Light, 5 1/2 x 7 In.	50.00
Moondrops, Candlestick, Amethyst, 2 x 2 1/2 x 4 3/4 In., Pair	45.00
Moondrops, Candlestick, Pink, 3-Legged, 5 1/8 x 4 1/2 In., Pair	125.00 to 185.00
Moondrops, Candy Dish, Cobalt Blue, Metal Cover, 5 x 8 In.	150.00
Moondrops, Creamer, Ruby, 3 In.	18.00
Moondrops, Cup, Emerald Green	9.00
Moondrops, Cup, Ruby	16.00
Moondrops, Decanter Set, Ruby, 5 Piece	240.00
Moondrops, Decanter, Emerald Green, Beehive Stopper, 10 1/2 In.	150.00
Moondrops, Dish, Mayonnaise, Cobalt Blue, 3-Footed, 2 7/8 x 5 1/2 In.	90.00
Moondrops, Plate, Dinner, Emerald Green, 9 1/2 In.	15.00
Moondrops, Plate, Dinner, Ruby, 9 1/2 In.	25.00
Moondrops, Salt & Pepper, Green, 3 1/2 In.	45.00
Moondrops, Saucer, Emerald Green	6.00
Moondrops, Saucer, Ruby	6.00
Moondrops, Sherbet, Ruby	18.00
Moondrops, Soup, Dish, Ruby, 6 3/4 In.	80.00
Moondrops, Sugar, Handles, Ruby	18.00
Moondrops, Tumbler, Whiskey, Amber, 2 Oz., 2 3/4 In.	10.00
Moondrops, Tumbler, Whiskey, Ruby, Footed, Handle, 2 Oz., 2 3/4 In.	20.00
Moondrops, Tumbler, Whiskey, Ruby, Handle, 2 Oz., 2 3/4 In.	20.00
Newport, Plate, Evergreen, 8 1/2 In.	14.00
No. 606, Decanter, Ruby, Tilted, Faceted Stopper, Handle, 9 In.	145.00

No. 728, Guest Set, Pink Satin, Pitcher, Cover, Tumbler, Tray	230.00
Prelude, Candy Dish, Cover, 5 5/16 x 6 3/4 In.	90.00
Prelude, Vase, Crimped Edge, 10 In.	75.00
Radiance, Bowl, Flared, 3 Dolphin Feet, 3 1/4 In.	30.00
Radiance, Bowl, Ruby, Scalloped Edge, Brass Pedestal, Marble Base, 5 x 12 In.	250.00
Radiance, Bowl, Scalloped Edge, 12 In.	25.00
Radiance, Butter, Cover, Cutting, 4 x 6 In.	100.00
Radiance, Cheese & Cracker Set, Wild Rose Etch	55.00
Radiance, Condiment Set, Blue, Creamer, Sugar, Salt & Pepper, Tray	185.00
Radiance, Creamer	17.00
Radiance, Cup & Saucer	10.00
Radiance, Plate, 8 1/2 In.	6.00
Radiance, Punch Set, 15 Piece	180.00
Radiance, Sugar	14.00
Radiance, Sugar & Creamer, Tray	95.00
Radiance, Sugar & Creamer, Tray, Blue	100.00
Radiance, Tidbit, Ruby, Handle, 5 x 8 1/4 In.	40.00
Radiance, Vase, Meadow Wreath Etch, 9 3/4 In.	165.00
Radiance, Vase, Meadow Wreath Etch, Blue, 9 3/4 x 6 In.	170.00
Radiance, Vase, Ruby, 10 1/8 x 5 1/2 In.	170.00
Teardrop, Bowl, 3-Footed, 4 x 11 In.	45.00
Teardrop, Candlestick, 2-Light, 5 In.	40.00
Teardrop, Candlestick, 2-Light, 5 In., Pair	65.00
Teardrop, Candlestick, 2-Light, Light Blue, 5 In.	65.00
Viking, Compote, Amber, 5 1/2 In.	18.00

NEWCOMB Pottery was founded by Ellsworth and William Woodward at Sophie Newcomb College, New Orleans, Louisiana, in 1895. The work continued through the 1940s. Pieces of this art pottery are marked with the printed letters *NC* and often have the incised initials of the artist as well. Most pieces have a matte glaze and incised decoration.

Bowl, Flowers, Sadie Irvine, No. 260, 1915, 5 1/2 In.	1380.00
Bowl, Oak Trees, c.1910, 3 1/2 x 4 1/2 In.	1120.00
Bowl, Pink Trillium, Purple Ground, Sadie Irvine, 1919, 2 1/4 x 7 1/2 In.	1093.00
Bowl, Shallow, White Flowers, Blue Ground, Green Leaves, Henrietta Bailey, 8 In.	1610.00
Bowl, White Blossom Band, Flat Shoulder, A.F. Simpson, 1917, 2 x 6 1/2 In.	1380.00
Bowl, White Flowers, Teal Leaves, Blue Ground, A.F. Simpson, 2 x 7 3/4 In.	1320.00
Candlestick, Pink & Green Flowers, Pink & Purple Ground, Irvine, 7 1/2 In.	2115.00
Charger, Chapel, Trees, Newcomb College N.O. Border, c.1900, 10 3/4 In.	18400.00
Jardiniere, Celadon Glaze, 2 Ring Handles, 8 In.	935.00
Match Holder, Poplar Trees, Blue, Green, 1907, 2 x 3 In.	3450.00
Mug, Band Of Scarabs, Blue Green Ground, Desiree Roman, 1902, 4 1/2 In.	2185.00
Pitcher, You Must Still Be Bright & Quiet, Blue Green, Sadie Irvine, 1907, 3 3/4 In.	2415.00
Plaque, Spanish Moss, Over Cottage, Full Moon, Stamped, Frame, 1922, 10 x 6 In.	18400.00
Plate, Band Of Fish, Blue, On Indigo & Blue Ground, M. Baker, 1906, 9 1/2 In.	5175.00
Plate, White & Yellow Cherry Blossom Band, Indigo, Blue Green, c.1904, 8 1/4 In.	1610.00
Tile, Blue Blossoms, Green Stems, Blue Green Ground, E.A. Horner, 1911, 5 In.	2760.00
Trivet, No. TP48, Willow Tree, Green On Blue Matte, Sadie Irvine, 6 In.	1725.00

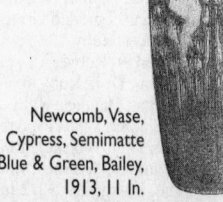

Newcomb, Vase, Cypress, Semimatte Blue & Green, Bailey, 1913, 11 In.

Trivet, White Blossoms, Green Stems, Light Blue Ground, Simpson, 1917, 6 In. 1725.00
Vase, Baluster Shape, Moss Green, Elizabeth Rogers, c.1900, 10 x 9 In. 3450.00
Vase, Band Of Bell Flowers, Blue, Squat, Alix Bettison, c.1911, 4 1/4 In. 2990.00
Vase, Blossoms, Blue Green Ground, C. Richardson, 1906, 7 1/2 x 3 1/2 In. 9200.00
Vase, Blossoms, Leaves, Blue Ground, Henrietta Bailey, 1923, 8 1/4 In. 3450.00
Vase, Blossoms, White, Yellow, Blue Ground, Bulbous, Bailey, 1932, 6 In. 1265.00
Vase, Blue Tulips, Leaves, Light Green Ground, Mary Butler, 1903, 9 1/2 In. 28750.00
Vase, Bud, Blue Green Leaves, Light Blue Ground, Marked, Urquart, 1905, 6 In. 1495.00
Vase, Bud, Spanish Moss, Oak Tree, Full Moon, Sadie Irvine, 1920, 5 x 2 1/2 In. 2990.00
Vase, Bud, White Crocuses, Corseted, A.F. Simpson, 1921, 6 1/4 x 2 3/4 In. 2300.00
Vase, Crocuses, Green, Leaves, Indigo Ground, A.F. Simpson, 1912, 8 1/4 x 3 3/4 In. 5463.00
Vase, Cylindrical, Branches, Matte Glaze, Julia Michel Hoerner, c.1913, 7 1/4 In. 5175.00
Vase, Cypress Trees, Shape No. 262, Henrietta Bailey, 1915, 6 In. 2588.00
Vase, Cypress, Semimatte Blue & Green, Bailey, 1913, 11 In. . . . . *Illus* 9200.00
Vase, Daisies, Light Blue, Yellow, Squat, A.F. Simpson, 4 1/4 x 7 1/2 In. 1093.00
Vase, Dogwood Blossoms, Pink, Yellow, Green Leaves, Bulbous, Sadie Irvine, 1922, 5 In. 2760.00
Vase, Dogwoods, Blue Ground, Cylindrical, Sadie Irvine, 1920, 10 In. 5463.00
Vase, Espanol, No. 29, Sadie Irvine, 1913, 4 5/8 In. 1495.00
Vase, Espanol, Pink, Purple Ground, A.F. Simpson, 1928, 7 x 4 In. 5750.00
Vase, Espanol, Purple, Pink Ground, Bulbous, Sadie Irvine, 1927, 5 x 2 3/4 In. 2530.00
Vase, Flowers, Leaves, Blue Ground, No. 236, Henrietta Bailey, 1922, 6 5/8 In. 2300.00
Vase, Grape Leaves, Clusters, Buff, Blue Green Ground, M. Ross, c.1902, 8 1/4 In. 10925.00
Vase, Green To Blue Matte Glaze, 4 Handles, Bottle Shape, 6 1/2 x 5 In. 1380.00
Vase, Irises, Anna Frances Simpson, Joseph Myer, 1912, 9 3/4 In. 5750.00
Vase, Irises, Blue, Yellow, Green, Blue Ground, Sadie Irvine, 1919, 6 1/2 In. 5175.00
Vase, Irises, Blue, Yellow, Green, Blue Matte Ground, Sadie Irvine, 1925, 10 1/2 In. 5175.00
Vase, Irises, Green, Glossy Indigo Ground, Sara Bloom Levy, c.1905, 10 1/2 x 4 In. 5175.00
Vase, Jonquils, Anna Frances Simpson, J.B. Hunt, No. 77, 1928, 6 7/8 In. 4715.00
Vase, Jonquils, Blue, Yellow, Green Leaves, Indigo Ground, Littlejohn, 6 3/4 x 8 1/2 In. . . 5750.00
Vase, Jonquils, Blue, Yellow, Green, A.F. Simpson, 1915, 7 x 4 In. 2415.00
Vase, Lavender Fruit Wreath, Leaves, Squat, Sadie Irvine, 1916, 3 1/4 x 5 1/2 In. 2300.00
Vase, Magnolia Blossoms, Blue, Yellow, Green Ground, Sadie Irvine, 1914, 5 In. 1725.00
Vase, Moon & Moss, Henrietta Bailey, c.1920, 4 x 5 1/2 In. 3220.00
Vase, Moon & Moss, Oval Body, Blue & Green Underglaze, 1932, 6 In. 3680.00
Vase, Moon & Moss, Shape No. 133, A.F. Simpson, 1919, 8 1/4 x 3 3/4 In. 6325.00
Vase, Moonlit Landscape, Moss Laden Trees, No. KU72, Sadie Irvine, 7 In. 5750.00
Vase, Morning Glory Wreath, Pink, Henrietta Bailey, 1926, 6 x 3 1/2 In. 2645.00
Vase, Oak Trees, Spanish Moss, Moon, Bulbous, Sadie Irvine, 1930, 6 In. 2185.00
Vase, Palm Trees, Purple, Pink Ground, Bulbous, A.F. Simpson, 1929, 5 In. 5750.00
Vase, Pine Boughs, Pink, Green, Indigo Ground, Bailey, 1930, 8 1/4 x 6 3/4 In. 8625.00
Vase, Pine Trees, Blue, Full Moon, Blue Ground, Irvine, 1931, 6 1/2 In. 1495.00
Vase, Pink Irises, Blue Ground, Bulbous, A.F. Simpson, 1923, 8 x 5 In. 3738.00
Vase, Purple Cherries, Branches, Leaves, Indigo Ground, Bailey, 1928, 7 In. 2885.00
Vase, Ribbed, Green Microcrystalline Glaze, Indigo Ground, c.1930, 5 x 3 3/4 In. 2070.00
Vase, Roses, White, Blue Ground, Bulbous, Henrietta Bailey, 1926, 4 3/4 In. 2070.00
Vase, Shoulder Flower Band, No. 3, 3 1/2 In. 865.00
Vase, Spanish Moss, Oak Tree, Landscape, Picket Fence, Irvine, 1919, 8 x 4 In. 6900.00
Vase, Spanish Moss, Oak Tree, Moon, Aurelia Arbo, c.1930, 5 x 4 In. 3450.00
Vase, Spanish Moss, Oak Tree, Moon, Bulbous, Sadie Irvine, 1932, 6 x 6 In. 5750.00
Vase, Spanish Moss, Oak Tree, Moon, Closed-In Rim, A. Arbo, c.1931, 6 x 4 In. 3450.00
Vase, Spanish Moss, Oak Tree, Moon, Sadie Irvine, 1908, 7 x 4 In. 4313.00
Vase, Spanish Moss, Oak Trees, Bulbous, A.F. Simpson, 1928, 5 1/4 x 3 In. 4313.00
Vase, Spanish Moss, Oak Trees, Pale Blue Ground, Oval, Irvine, 1918, 7 1/4 In. 3738.00
Vase, Spanish Moss, Oak Trees, Vermillion Sky, Irvine, 1930, 6 x 3 In. 4025.00
Vase, Tall Leaves, Flowers, 2 Handles, Mary Sheerer, c.1891, 9 In. 16100.00
Vase, Tobacco Leaves, Blue Green, White Blossoms, Sadie Irvine, 1925, 4 3/4 In. 2990.00
Vase, Trillium, White, Yellow, Blue Ground, De Hoa LeBlanc, 1906, 8 1/2 In. 10925.00
Vase, Trumpet Blossom Band, Pink, Blue Ground, A.F. Simpson, 1926, 5 1/4 In. 748.00
Vase, Tulips, Light Blue, Leaves, Blue, Ivory Ground, A. Roman, c.1900, 11 x 5 In. 14900.00
Vase, Wreath Of Pink Roses, Blue Ground, Bulbous, Sadie Irvine, 1927, 8 1/4 In. 5175.00
Vase, Yellow Freesias, Ivory, Trumpet Form, De Hoa LeBlanc, 1904, 10 x 4 In. 5750.00

NILOAK Pottery (Kaolin spelled backward) was made at the Hyten Brothers Pottery in Benton, Arkansas, between 1909 and 1947. Although the factory did make cast and molded wares, collectors are most interested in the marbleized art pottery line made of colored swirls of clay. It was called *Mission Ware*. By 1931 the company made cast-ware, and many of these pieces were marked with the name *Hywood*.

Urn, Marbleized, Blue, Beige, Terra-Cotta, Gray, Stamped, 23 1/2 x 12 In.	8050.00
Urn, Marbleized, Blue, Ivory, Tan, Umber, 9 In.	110.00
Vase, Marbleized Blue Green, Terra-Cotta, Brown, Beige, Stamped, 16 x 7 1/2 In.	920.00
Vase, Marbleized Red, Beige, Brown, Blue, Baluster, Stamped, 9 1/2 In.	690.00
Vase, Marbleized, Blue, Beige, Ivory, Brown, Bulbous, Stamped, 14 x 7 In.	1095.00
Vase, Marbleized, Blue, Brown, Rust & Ivory Swirls, Bulbous, 7 In.	265.00
Vase, Marbleized, Brown, Blue Gray, Ivory, Terra-Cotta Clays, Stamped, 7 1/2 In.	400.00
Vase, Marbleized, Bulbous, Brown, Blue, Tan, Swirl, 6 1/2 In.	460.00
Vase, Marbleized, Corseted, Stamped, 9 1/4 x 4 1/2 In.	175.00

NIPPON porcelain was made in Japan from 1891 to 1921. *Nippon* is the Japanese word for *Japan*. A few firms continued to use the word *Nippon* on ceramics after 1921 as a part of the company name more than as an identification of the country of origin. More pieces marked Nippon will be found in the Dragonware, Moriage, and Noritake categories.

Basket, Stylized Flowers, Cobalt Blue, Handle, Coralene, c.1909, 5 In.	175.00
Bowl, Stylized Gilt Flowers, Blue M Wreath, 1891-1919, 10 1/4 In.	115.00
Dresser Set, Gilt & Enamel, Multicolored Riverscape, Tray, Box, Hair Receiver, 11 1/4 In.	460.00
Ferner, Flowers, Butterflies, Green M Wreath, 1891-1919, 6 1/4 In.	90.00
Humidor, Stylized Flowers, Mythical Bird Mark, 1891-1919, 5 1/2 In.	160.00
Humidor, White Owl On Branch, Blue Maple Leaf Mark, 6 In. *Illus*	3565.00
Jar, Cover, Violets, Blue Maple Leaf Mark, 1891-1919, 9 In.	85.00
Jug, Wine, Elk In Wreath, Raised Scrolls, Flowers, Green M Wreath, 8 In.	1064.00
Jug, Wine, Windmill Scene, Woven Cover, Blue Maple Leaf Mark, 10 In.	175.00
Mug, Stylized Japanese Garden Scene, Green M Wreath, 1891-1919, 4 3/4 In.	70.00
Pitcher, Milk, Stylized Flowers, Green M Wreath, 1891-1919, 8 1/2 In.	105.00
Plate, Orchids, Jewels, Gold Encrusted Border, Signed, 9 1/2 In.	130.00
Powder Box, Flowers, Gilt Scroll, 3-Footed, Green M Wreath, 1891-1919, 6 In.	90.00
Rose Bowl, Stylized Flowers, Coralene, Footed, c.1900, 5 1/2 In.	575.00
Serving Dish, Hand Painted, Buff Ground, Black Stars, Multicolored Flowers, Japan, 1905	40.00
Toothpick, Palms & Lakes, 3 Handles	35.00
Urn, Lake Scene, Shield, Scrolling Flowers, Gilt Trim, Handle, Green M Wreath, 14 In.	865.00
Urn, Landscape, Gilt Chrysanthemums, Cobalt Blue, Ground, Marked, 14 1/2 In.	2300.00
Vase, 3 Eagles, Sitting On Rocks, Hand Painted, Signed, Green Mark, 10 x 6 1/4 In.	3220.00
Vase, Center Female Portrait, Red & Gold Beaded Design, Marked, 14 1/2 In.	2115.00
Vase, Chrysanthemums, Coralene, Ivory Ground, Scissor Handles, 11 In. *Illus*	1610.00
Vase, Cylindrical, Gold Enamel, White Flowers, Leaves, 10 1/2 In.	115.00
Vase, Egyptian Sailboat Scene, Handles, Green M Wreath, 5 1/4 In.	605.00
Vase, Flowers, Gilt, Cobalt Blue, Shoulder, Base, c.1909, 7 In.	978.00
Vase, Flowers, Leaves, Scrolling, Coralene, Handles, c.1909, 11 3/4 In.	1035.00

Nippon, Vase, Chrysanthemums, Coralene, Ivory Ground, Scissor Handles, 11 In.

Nippon, Humidor, White Owl On Branch, Moriage, Blue Maple Leaf Mark, 6 In.

Nippon, Vase, Pink Roses, Enameled Neck, Green M Wreath, 9 In.

Vase, Flowers, Multicolored, Handles, c.1900, 16 In. 175.00
Vase, Flowers, Multicolored, Raised Enamel Scrolling, 7 In. 200.00
Vase, Flowers, Umbrella Shape, Green, Blue, Handles, c.1909, 9 In. 1006.00
Vase, Harbor Scene, Footed, Gilt, Embossed, Handles, Green M Wreath, 10 In. 1121.00
Vase, Harbor Scene, Handles, Green M Wreath, 6 In. 547.00
Vase, Iris Blossoms, Leaves, Handles, c.1900, 11 3/4 In. 345.00
Vase, Lake Scene, Mountains, Trees, Gold, Handles, 13 In. 403.00
Vase, Landscape, Multicolored, Gilt, Coralene, 1909, 8 1/2 In. 575.00
Vase, Man In Boat, 25 1/2 In. 4313.00
Vase, Orchids, Pink, Purple, Green Ground, Gilt Curlicues, Marked, 18 1/4 In. 1955.00
Vase, Panoramic Snow Scene, 2 Gilt Handles, 10 In., Pair 201.00
Vase, Pink Roses, Enameled Neck, Green M Wreath, 9 In. .... *Illus* 230.00
Vase, Poppies, Under Raised Gilt Shoulder, Handles, Green M Wreath, 8 1/2 In. 460.00
Vase, Rose Blossoms, Coralene, Handles, c.1909, 6 3/4 In. 375.00
Vase, Roses, Gilt Bamboo, Handles, Royal Nippon Mark, c.1900, 11 3/4 In. 460.00
Vase, Roses, Petit Point Enamel Ground, 1891-1919, 8 1/2 In. 138.00
Vase, Stylized Flowers, Gilt Scrolls, Coralene, Handles, c.1909, 6 3/4 In. 546.00
Vase, Stylized Flowers, Glazed, Overshot Finish, Coralene, Handles, Kinjo, c.1910, 10 In. 605.00
Vase, Stylized Flowers, Leaves, Coralene, Handles, c.1909, 6 In. 949.00
Vase, Stylized Flowers, Molded, Buttressed Base, Coralene, Handles, 10 In. 1200.00
Vase, Stylized Flowers, Pastel, Shaded Ground, c.1909, 7 In. 949.00
Vase, Stylized Flowers, Pastel, Shaded Ground, Coralene, Handles, c.1909, 7 In. 690.00
Vase, Stylized Flowers, Shaded Ground, Yellow, Purple, Gilt, Handles, 6 1/4 In. 635.00
Vase, Stylized Iris, Coralene, c.1909, 5 3/4 In. 518.00
Vase, Stylized Water Lilies, c.1909, 5 In. 259.00
Vase, Water Lilies, Leaves, Coralene, Handles, c.1909, 7 3/4 In. 431.00
Vase, Yellow Roses, Leaves, Blue Ground, 2 Handles, Blue Maple Leaf, 7 x 5 In. 104.00

NODDERS, also called nodding figures or pagods, are figures with heads and hands that are attached to wires. Any slight movement causes the parts to move up and down. They were made in many countries during the eighteenth, nineteenth, and twentieth centuries. A few Art Deco designs are also known. Copies are being made. A more recent type of nodder is made of papier-mache or plastic. These often represent sports figures or comic characters. Sports nodders are listed in the Sports category.

Andy Gump, Bisque, Molded & Painted Features, 4 In. 70.00
Chick, Wearing Dress, Duck Under Arm, Composition, 7 1/4 In. 115.00
Donkey, Celluloid, 5 In. 20.00
Oriental Boy, Blue & White, Gold Dot Trim, Bisque, 3 3/4 x 2 1/2 In. 85.00
Oriental Man & Woman, Moving Head, Hands, Tongue, 7 In., Pair 400.00
Salt & Pepper shakers are listed in the Salt & Pepper category.
Tennis Player, Round Head, Bisque, Germany, 3 1/2 In. 44.00
Winnie Winkle, Germany 195.00

NORITAKE porcelain was made in Japan after 1904 by Nippon Toki Kaisha. The best-known Noritake pieces are marked with the M in a wreath for the Morimura Brothers, a New York City distributing company. This mark was used until the early 1950s. There may be some helpful price information in the Nippon category, since prices are comparable. Noritake Azalea is listed in the Azalea category in this book.

Ashtray, Playing Card Design, Round, 5 1/4 In. 55.00
Basket, Hand Painted Forget-Me-Nots, Luster, Gold Trim, 4 5/8 In. 230.00
Bowl, Vegetable, Oval, Arroyo, 10 x 7 In. 25.00
Bowl, Yellow, Blown-Out Acorns, Handles, Oval, 8 3/8 In. 170.00
Cup & Saucer, Arroyo 8.00
Napkin Ring, Man In Top Hat, Yellow, Gold Trim, Art Deco, 2 1/4 In. 130.00
Plate, Arroyo, 10 5/8 In. 10.00
Plate, Bread & Butter, Arroyo, 6 1/4 In. 5.00
Plate, Salad, Arroyo, 8 1/4 In. 7.00
Platter, Oval, Arroyo, 13 1/2 In. 30.00
Soup, Dish, Goldcroft, White, Gold Bands, 8 In., 6 Piece 70.00
Vase, Cottage Scene, Embossed, Hand Painted, Flared Rim, 6 3/4 In. 110.00

Vase, Egg Shape, Garden Design, Hand Painted, N. Hiwashi, 1900s, 12 In. 690.00
Vase, Hand Painted Trees, Figural Parrot At Side, 1929, 5 In. 230.00

NORSE Pottery Company started in Edgerton, Wisconsin, in 1903. In
1904 the company moved to Rockford, Illinois. The company made a
black pottery, which resembled early bronze relics of the Scandinavian
countries. The firm went out of business in 1913.

Vase, Impressed Snake, Bronze Gargoyle Handles, Feet, Squat, Stamped, 4 x 7 1/2 In. . . .   545.00

NORTH DAKOTA SCHOOL OF MINES was established in 1892 at the
University of North Dakota. A ceramic course was included and pieces
were made from the clays found in the region. Students at the university made pieces from 1909 to 1949. Although very early pieces were
marked *U.N.D.*, most pieces were stamped with the full name of the
university.

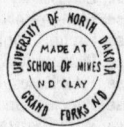

Bowl, Blossoms, Pink, Red, Purple, Celadon, Swenson, 1951, 9 In.	175.00
Bowl, Buffalo, Light Brown, Julia Mattson, UND, 5 In.	2070.00
Bowl, Fruits, Multicolored, Beige Ground, Tobiason, Signed, 9 In.	230.00
Bowl, Fruits, Multicolored, Signed, McCosh, 1 1/2 x 9 1/4 In.	200.00
Bowl, Pasque Flowers, M. Cable, UND, No. 154, 3 3/8 x 5 3/4 In.	805.00
Bowl, Radiating Pattern, Green On Oxblood Ground, Marked, 9 In.	285.00
Bowl, Russian Olive, Blue Gray, Ivory, Clark, 1942, 7 1/2 In.	430.00
Box, Cover, Scottie Finial, Carved Teepees, Turquoise Glaze, Trickey, 4 In.	460.00
Figurine, Boy, Sitting, Ivory Matte Glaze, Mountains, 7 x 9 In.	145.00
Figurine, Rabbit, Green, Brown Flowers, Brown Ground, 4 3/4 In.	635.00
Jar, Cover, Carved Birds, Branches, Yellow Glaze, Stamped, 9 1/2 x 6 In.	805.00
Jar, Temple, Carved Flowers, Cover, MJH, UND, 1947, 8 1/4 In.	1955.00
Jardiniere, Birds, Butterflies, Signed, Allen, 1955, 6 1/2 x 8 In.	260.00
Mask, Mr. Freckles, Multicolored, Buff Clay, Incised, 7 1/2 x 5 In.	1035.00
Planter, Blossoms, Full-Leaves, Brown, R. Schnell, 1945, 5 In.	805.00
Plaque, Cherry Blossom Branches, Excised, Indigo, Buff Clay, Stephens, 5 In.	145.00
Plaque, Deer, Leaves, Excised, Blue Gray, Buff Clay, 5 1/4 x 4 In.	315.00
Plate, Carved Birds, Grapevines, Multicolored, Yellow Ground, 1951, 7 3/4 In.	345.00
Plate, Flowers, Multicolored, Unglazed, Stamped, 1949, 9 1/2 In.	430.00
Plate, Flowers, Multicolored, White Ground, Marked, 1955, 8 1/4 In.	375.00
Plate, Stylized Blue Blossoms, White Ground, Stamped, 6 1/2 In.	690.00
Sugar & Creamer, Yellow, Blue Blossoms, On Lavender, Schnell, 1955	345.00
Trivet, Carved Flowers, Indigo, Yellow, On Purple Ground, Round, 6 In.	460.00
Trivet, Carved Star, Indigo, Green Chevron Ground, Round, 5 In.	290.00
Trivet, Flower, 5-Petal, Ivory, Green, On Black, Round, 5 3/4 In.	375.00
Trivet, Snowflake, Carved, Gunmetal & Green Glaze, Stamped, 5 In.	230.00
Vase, Bentonite, Indian Designs, Julia Mattson, UND, 1945, 5 In.	1035.00
Vase, Bentonite, Indian Patterns, Julia Mattson, UND, 3 5/8 In.	635.00
Vase, Birds, Black, Yellow, Terra-Cotta, Armstrong, 4 1/4 In.	1035.00
Vase, Birds, Leaves, Terra-Cotta Ground, Bentonite, Marked, 3 In.	460.00
Vase, Black Birds, Suns, Bentonite, Red Ground, Marked, 3 1/2 x 4 1/2 In.	518.00
Vase, Blue & Orange Blossoms, Pink Ground, Tapered, Huckfield, 5 In.	635.00
Vase, Blue Flower, Green Leaves, Helen Nelson, UND, c.1952, 8 In.	460.00
Vase, Brown Daffodils, Dark Brown Ground, F. Cunningham, 1950, 9 In.	1380.00
Vase, Flowers, Carved, Speckled Pink Glaze, Flared, Stamped, 1952, 6 x 7 In.	405.00
Vase, Geometric Band, White, Black Shoulder, Red To Blue Ground, 4 1/2 In.	1095.00
Vase, Green Matte Glaze, Embossed Stylized Haystacks, 4 x 5 In.	1650.00
Vase, Indigo Arabesques, Red Ground, Squat, P. McLaine, 1949, 2 3/4 In.	690.00
Vase, Pasque Flower, Blue, Shaded Ground, Flared, Huckfield, 3 3/4 In.	518.00
Vase, Persian Blue Crackled Glaze, Bulbous, Marked, 6 1/2 In.	230.00
Vase, Pink Blossoms, Leaves, Carved, Green To Pink Ground, 4 1/2 In.	635.00
Vase, Prairie Rose, Carved, Oxblood Semimatte Glaze, Cable, 8 1/2 In.	1093.00
Vase, Prairie Rose, Red Blossoms, Indigo, Red Ground, 2 1/2 x 6 In.	633.00
Vase, Rose To Blue Matte Glaze, Bulbous, Stamped, 3 1/2 In.	345.00
Vase, Sheaves Of Wheat, Carved, Sgraffito, Beige On Blue Ground, 2 1/4 In.	546.00
Vase, Stylized Blue Flowers, Carved, Indigo Ground, Tapered, Huckfield, 5 x 3 In.	920.00
Vase, Stylized Wheat Bales, Ivory To Caramel Speckled Glaze, Squat, 4 In.	460.00
Vase, Terra-Cotta Speckled Semimatte Glaze, Flared, Stamped, 6 In.	546.00
Vase, Tulip, Doris E. Brown, UND, 1934, 7 3/8 In.	2875.00

Vase, Tulips, Delft Type, Gray, Ivory Ground, 1953, 2 x 3 1/2 In.	316.00
Vase, Wheat Sheaves, Blue Ground, Carved, Sgraffito, Cooley, 9 x 5 In.	2875.00
Vase, Wild Rose, Green Blossom Band, Yellow, Green Ground, 4 1/2 x 6 In.	633.00

NORTHWOOD Glass Company was founded by Harry Northwood, a glassmaker who worked for Hobbs, Brockunier and Company, La Belle Glass Company, and Buckeye Glass Company before founding his own firm. He opened one factory in Indiana, Pennsylvania, in 1896, and another in Wheeling, West Virginia, in 1902. Northwood closed when Mr. Northwood died in 1923. Many types of glass were made, including carnival, custard, goofus, and pressed. The underlined N mark was used on some pieces.

Cherry & Cable, Berry Set, Rose-Stained Fruit, Gold Trim, 7 Piece ....120.00 to 155.00
Inverted Fan & Feather, Berry Set, Pink Slag, 9 1/2-In. Master, 7 Piece	2200.00
Leaf Umbrella, Pitcher, Topaz Over Opal, Clear Applied Handle, 8 3/4 In.	495.00
Leaf Umbrella, Tumbler, Rose Du Barry, 3 3/4 In.	155.00
No. 636, Candy Jar, Celeste Blue, Gold Trim	85.00
No. 636, Candy Jar, Jade Blue	85.00
No. 719, Candlestick, Celeste Blue, Pair	75.00
No. 719, Candlestick, Iridescent Amethyst, Pair	105.00
Posies & Pods, Berry Set, Emerald Green, Gold Trim, 10 Piece	155.00
Posies & Pods, Tumbler, Maiden's Blush Stain, Gold Trim, 4 In.	100.00
Wild Strawberry, Bowl, Basketweave, Exterior, Marked, 9 In.	230.00

NU-ART see Imperial category.

NUTCRACKERS of many types have been used through the centuries. At first the nutcracker was probably strong teeth or a hammer. But by the nineteenth century, many elaborate and ingenious types were made. Levers, screws, and hammer adaptations were the most popular. Because nutcrackers are still useful, they are still being made, some in the old styles.

Alligator, Cast Iron, Move At Jaw, 13 In., 2 Piece	330.00
Arcade, No. 9569, Insert, Box, 10 In.	165.00
Arcade, No. 9574, Deco Styled, Black, Red, Box, 10 In.	121.00
Arcade, No. 9576, Table Mount, Box	55.00
Dog, Painted, Cast Iron, 12 1/2 In.	113.00
Dog, Squirrel, Between Dog's Front Legs, Cast Iron, 6 x 12 In.	220.00
Elephant, Art Deco, Cast Iron, Twine Tail, 9 1/2 x 4 3/4 In.	275.00
Veggie Man, Pumpkin Head, Melon Body, Parsnip Arms, Carrot Nose, 13 In.	3740.00
Vindex, Cast Iron, Box, 4 1/2 In.	28.00

NYMPHENBURG, see Royal Nymphenburg.

OCCUPIED JAPAN was printed on pottery, porcelain, toys, and other goods made during the American occupation of Japan after World War II, from 1945 to 1952. Collectors now search for these pieces. The items were made for export.

Ashtray, Nude Woman On Top, Flower Border, Porcelain, 3 1/2 x 6 In.	30.00
Condiment Server, Sections, Covers, Figural Beehive, Bees, Handle, Pottery, 4 In.	50.00
Condiment Set, Figural Beehive, Bees, Pottery, 5 Piece	50.00
Creamer, Gold Dragon, Porcelain, 3 1/2 In.	35.00
Figurine, Boy Pulling Swan, Bisque, 7 In.	40.00
Figurine, Hawaiian Dancer With Ukulele, Porcelain, 4 1/4 In., Pair	25.00
Figurine, Man, Woman, Rabbits, Bisque, 7 In.	35.00
Figurine, Mermaid, Blue Tail, Bisque, Mid 20th Century, 3 1/2 In.	46.00
Lighter, Grand Piano, Silvered Metal, 3 3/4 In.	25.00
Lighter, Lucky Car, Silvered Metal, 3 In.	50.00
Range Set, Tomato Ware, Pottery, 4 Piece	125.00
Salt & Pepper, Duck, Hugger, 3 3/4 In.	65.00
Salt & Pepper, Indian Boy & Girl In Canoe, 3 1/4 In.	30.00
Salt & Pepper, Windmill, Blue & White, Pottery, 2 In.	25.00
Sugar & Creamer, Tomato Ware, Pottery	25.00
Tea Set, Peach Luster, Flowers, Child's, 3 Piece ....*Illus*	22.00

Occupied Japan,
Tea Set, Peach Luster,
Flowers, Child's,
3 Piece

Toy, Tap Dancer, Hollywood & Vine Sign, Windup, Tin, Celluloid, 8 1/2 In. 80.00
Vase, George & Martha Washington, Porcelain, 3 3/4 In., Pair 30.00

OFFICE TECHNOLOGY includes office equipment and related products, such as adding machines, calculators, and check-writing machines. Typewriters are in their own category in this book.

Adding Machine, Adix, Germany, c.1903 . . . . 660.00
Adding Machine, Pallweber & Bordt, Adix, 9-Digit, Germany, c.1900, 6 In. 499.00
Calculator, Fuller, Mahogany Handle, 1922, 17 In. 175.00
Calculator, Thatcher's, Functions Like Slide Rule, 1900s, 24 In. 1650.00
Calculator, Thatcher's, Scales, Mahogany Base, Keuffel & Esser, 21 1/2 In. 646.00
Labeler, Monarch, Cast Metal, 9 In. 39.00
Letter Case, Stenciled, Wood, 3 Letter Trays, Sample Labels, Reese's, 19 In. 330.00
Ticker Tape, Western Union, Self-Winding, Glass Dome, T.A. Edison, 1920s, 13 In. 2585.00

OHR pottery was made in Biloxi, Mississippi, from 1883 to 1906 by George E. Ohr, a true eccentric. The pottery was made of very thin clay that was twisted, folded, and dented into odd, graceful shapes. Some pieces were lifelike models of hats, animal heads, or even a potato. Others were decorated with folded clay *snakes*. Reproductions and reworked pieces are appearing on the market. These have been reglazed, or snakes and other embellishments have been added.

Bank, Squat, Bulbous, Bisque, Buff, Fold-Over Rim, Stamped, 4 x 4 In. 3375.00
Bowl, Brown High Glaze, Crimped Mouth, Inverted Body, 3 x 4 3/4 In. 825.00
Bowl, Round Form, Pinched, Brown Blistered Glaze, Green & Gunmetal Inside, 1 3/4 In. . . 1800.00
Bowl, Spherical, Green & Tan Glaze, Brown Tiger Stripe, High Glaze, 2 1/2 x 3 1/2 In. . . 1320.00
Bowl, Tobacco Glaze, Dimpled, Circular, Speckled Interior, 4 In. 2990.00
Candlestick, Flared, Bulbous Midsection, Pinched Handle, Mauve, 2 1/2 In. 2290.00
Card Holder, Square, Etched Texturing, Leaves, Green Over Yellow Glaze, 3 1/2 x 4 In. . . 3600.00
Chamber Pot, Brown Speckled, Yellow Glaze, Contents, Stilt, Stamp, 2 1/2 x 3 3/4 In. . . 1840.00
Creamer, Khaki High Glaze, Brown Speckles, Bulbous, Short Neck, Loop Handle, 3 In. . . 715.00
Inkwell, Donkey, Gunmetal Semimatte Glaze, Stamped, 2 3/4 x 5 1/4 In. 1495.00
Inkwell, House, 2 Story, Chimney, Sloping Roof, Coggled Edge, 7 x 4 x 3 1/4 In. 2350.00
Jar, Cover, Barrel Form, Mottled Deep Green Glaze, Dimpled Arrow Band, Stamped, 5 In. 3265.00
Jug, Bisque, Short Neck, Looped Handle, 4 In. 715.00
Jug, Bulbous, Mottled Green Glaze, Mottled Brown, Elongated Rim, Stamped, 5 1/4 In. . . 2475.00
Jug, Puzzle, Brown Semigloss Glaze, Stepped Handle, Stamped, 6 1/2 x 5 In. 9200.00
Mug, Cylindrical, Ribs, Squat, Oval Base, Brown Glaze, Brown & Green Handle, 5 3/8 In. 2140.00
Mug, Double Gourd, Gunmetal Brown, Speckled Caramel Interior, Pinched Top, 5 1/4 In. . . 2025.00
Mug, Flared Rim, Ear Shape Handle, Gunmetal Glaze, Signed, 5 x 4 1/2 In. 2300.00
Mug, Flared, Chartreuse, Dark Green Streaks, Orange Interior, Raised Ridge, 4 3/4 In. . . . 1650.00
Mug, Incised Here's To Your Good Health & Your Family, Dated 3-18-96, 5 5/8 In. 3375.00
Mug, Mottled Rose, Green, Blue Glaze, Ear Shape Handle, Stamped, 1896, 4 1/2 In. 4315.00
Mug, Puzzle, Mottled Brown Glaze, Green Interior Bottom, Rabbit Mask Handle, 3 1/2 In. 1406.00
Pitcher, Bisque, Marbleized Clay, Pinched Handle, Folded Rim, Signed, 5 x 6 1/2 In. 4025.00
Pitcher, Black Volcanic Glaze, Cutout Handle, Rim Folded, Pinched Spout, 4 x 5 1/4 In. . . 4900.00
Pitcher, Bulbous, Flared, Folded Rim, Applied Handle, Gunmetal Splotches, 3 3/4 In. 2925.00
Pitcher, Bulbous, Pinched, Raspberry, Green Sponging, Green To Caramel Interior, 7 In. . 33750.00
Pitcher, Dimpled, Flared, Pinched, Applied Vine Handle, Speckled Cinnamon Glaze, 4 In. 5135.00
Pitcher, Iridescent Glaze, Flared Spout Rim, Applied Handle, Stamped, 3 3/4 In. 1405.00

Pitcher, Milk, Brown & Light Green Semimatte Glaze, Cinched Waist, 3 x 4 1/2 In. 1840.00
Pitcher, Owl, Bulbous, Indents, Pinched Spout, Green Glaze, Brown Glaze Top, 4 In. 6750.00
Pitcher, Pinched, Cutout Handle, Dimpled Spout, Olive, Red, Indigo Flashes, 2 3/4 In. . . . 3450.00
Pitcher, Waisted Hourglass Shape, Gunmetal Glaze 4140.00
Pot, Bulbous, Fold-Over, Crimped Rim, Cobalt Blue Glaze, Blue To Ocher Interior, 5 In. . 6750.00
Shelf, Corner, Honeycomb, Gunmetal, Speckled Olive Green Glaze, 5 1/2 x 5 3/4 In. 865.00
Teapot, Brown, Green, Gunmetal Marbled Glaze, Ear Handle, Snake Spout, 5 x 9 1/2 In. . . 6325.00
Teapot, Cover, Mottled Green Glaze, Gooseneck, Applied Handle, Stamped, 6 In. 6300.00
Teapot, In-Body Twist, Amber, Gunmetal, Green Sponge, Crinkled Handle, 3 x 8 In. 9775.00
Vase, Bisque, Red, Brown Clay, Folded Rim, Bulbous, Signed, 3 3/4 x 4 In. 1380.00
Vase, Bud, Bulbous, Flared Rim, Mottled Green, Gunmetal Glaze, Stamped, 4 x 2 3/4 In. . 2300.00
Vase, Bud, Bulbous, Side-Thrown Neck, Tulip Top, Pink, Cobalt Blue Splotches, 5 1/2 In. 15188.00
Vase, Bud, Corseted, Gunmetal Glaze, Stamped, 5 x 2 1/4 In. 1380.00
Vase, Bulbous, Bisque, Buff, Handles, Stamped, 4 1/4 x 3 1/2 In. 1125.00
Vase, Bulbous, Body Twist On Shoulder, Indigo Glaze, Amber Interior, Stamped, 4 7/8 In. 5735.00
Vase, Bulbous, Body Twist, Flared, Apricot, Brown, Green Splotches, Speckling, 6 In. . . . 3650.00
Vase, Bulbous, Cupped Rim, Indigo, Green, Red, Amber Mottled Glaze, Stamped, 4 3/4 In. 8050.00
Vase, Bulbous, Dimpled, In-Body Twist, Green Over Green Speckled Pink Glaze, 4 In. . . . 11500.00
Vase, Bulbous, Flared Neck, In-Body Twist, Sponged Rose Glaze, Stamped, 6 1/4 In. . . . 12650.00
Vase, Bulbous, Folded & Pinched Rim, Mirrored Olive Green Glaze, 3 1/4 x 3 In. 3740.00
Vase, Bulbous, Green, Indigo Glaze, Sponged On Marbleized Clay, 4 x 5 In. 1095.00
Vase, Bulbous, Indigo, Green Speckled Glaze, Folded Rim, Stamped, 3 3/4 x 4 1/2 In. . . . 7480.00
Vase, Bulbous, Pinched Rim, 7-Point Flower, Green, Red Flambe Glaze, Stamped, 6 In. . . 4900.00
Vase, Bulbous, Pink, Green, Blue Mottled Glaze, Carved Band, Lobed Rim, 5 x 4 1/2 In. . 9775.00
Vase, Bulbous, Ruffled, Dimpled, Flared Rim, Mottled Gunmetal, Green, Amber, 4 In. . . . 4900.00
Vase, Bulbous, Tapered, Neck Ring, Blue Speckling, Green Swirls, Yellow, 5 1/4 In. 2140.00
Vase, Bulbous, Trumpet Neck, Green, Gunmetal Speckling, Brown, Interior, 8 1/2 In. 5965.00
Vase, Bulbous, Twisted At Neck, Red, Turquoise, Amber Sponge, Dripped Glaze, 3 3/4 In. 11500.00
Vase, Burnt Orange, Gunmetal Luster, Cupped, Folded Rim, Sponged, 2 1/2 x 5 1/2 In. . . 3740.00
Vase, Chartreuse, Gunmetal Brown, Flambe Glaze, White Clay, Bulbous Top, 3 3/4 In. . . . 1840.00
Vase, Cobalt Blue Glaze, Bulbous, Pinched Flowers Rim, Stamped, 3 3/4 x 3 1/4 In. 4600.00
Vase, Coffeepot, Mirrored Green Mottled Glaze, Snake Spout, Stamped, 6 x 6 1/4 In. . . . 10925.00
Vase, Cornucopia, Terra-Cotta, Unglazed, Circular Foot, c.1900, 4 In. 1095.00
Vase, Cupped Rim, Gunmetal Brown Glaze, Signed, 4 1/4 x 4 1/4 In. 1610.00
Vase, Flared, Closed-In Rim, Gunmetal, Brown Speckled, Light Green Glaze, 2 3/4 x 4 In. 2070.00
Vase, Floppy Hat Form, Gunmetal Brown Glaze, Stamped, 3 x 5 1/2 In. 3680.00
Vase, Green Speckled Amber Glaze, In-Body Twist Under Collar Neck, 6 3/4 x 4 1/4 In. . 6325.00
Vase, Gunmetal Glaze, Ringed, Gloss Russet Interior, c.1885, 3 1/2 In. 1035.00
Vase, In-Body Twist, Cobalt Blue To Pink Glossy Glaze, Stamped, 5 x 3 1/2 In. 7475.00
Vase, In-Body Twist, Flared Rim, Speckled Glossy Brown Glaze, Stamped, 4 x 3 1/4 In. . . 5750.00
Vase, In-Body Twist, Gunmetal, Star Shape Folded Rim, Squat, Marked, 3 1/4 In. 2530.00
Vase, Mottled Umber, Mahogany, Green Glaze, Speckled Brown Ground, 7 1/2 x 4 In. . . . 4600.00
Vase, Oval, Body Twist, Gunmetal, Brown, Trumpet Neck, Medial Rib, Green Interior, 6 In. 4613.00
Vase, Oval, Green, Gunmetal, Speckled Rust Glaze, In-Body Twist, Torn Rim, 5 x 4 1/2 In. 16415.00
Vase, Oval, Mahogany Ground, Sponged On Gunmetal Spots, Stamped, 3 1/2 In. 2185.00
Vase, Pear Form, Body Twist, Green, Apricot, Green Splotches, Brown Speckles, 6 1/4 In. 9640.00
Vase, Pinched Shoulder, Purple, Green, Black Speckled, Pink Matte Glaze, 3 x 4 1/2 In. . . 4900.00
Vase, Pinched Side, Bisque, Beige Clay, Signed, 3 x 6 1/2 In. 2300.00
Vase, Pinched Side, Bisque, Marbleized Clay, Signed, 4 1/4 x 6 1/2 In. 3335.00
Vase, Pinched Waist, Indigo, Green, Rose Sponged Glaze, 4 1/2 x 2 1/4 In. 3220.00
Vase, Red Bisqüe Clay, Round Neck, Protruding Shoulder, Stamped, 3 1/2 x 3 3/4 In. 1265.00
Vase, Round, Green & Brown Matte Flambe Glaze, Stamped, 3 1/2 In. 1380.00
Vase, Speckled Green Blue Flambe Glaze, Ruffled Band, Notched Rim, Etched, 5 x 6 In. . 4600.00
Vase, Speckled Pumpkin Color, Metallic Inclusions, Irregular Rim, 2 5/8 In. 2990.00
Vase, Squat, 4-Lobed, Speckled Dark Green Glaze, Ridged Base, 4 x 3 In. 5175.00
Vase, Squat, Folded Rim, Mahogany & Gunmetal, Speckled Green Glaze, 2 1/2 x 4 3/4 In. 3335.00
Vase, Squat, Gunmetal Speckled, Blue Gray Matte, Green Glaze, 3 x 4 1/4 In. 1610.00
Vase, Squat, Tapered Neck, Green, Gunmetal, Pink Mottled Glaze, Signed, 4 x 3 3/4 In. . 4600.00

OLD PARIS, see Paris category.

OLD SLEEPY EYE, see Sleepy Eye category.

OLYMPIC, see Souvenir category.

ONION PATTERN, originally named *bulb pattern*, is a white ware decorated with cobalt blue or pink. Although it is commonly associated with Meissen, other companies made the pattern in the late nineteenth and the twentieth centuries. A rare type is called *red bud* because there are added red accents on the blue-and-white dishes.

Bowl, Blue, Dome Cover, Twig Finial, Scalloped Rim, Meissen, 5 x 9 In.	200.00
Cake Plate, Blue, Lady, On Top Plate, 3 Tiers, Gilt, Crossed Swords, Meissen, 22 In.	980.00
Compote, Blue, Reticulated Border, Meissen, 8 x 9 1/4 In., Pair	385.00
Condiment Set, Blue, Round, Meissen, 16 In., 16 Piece	360.00
Kitchen Set, Canisters, Lids, Spice Jars, Oil & Vinegar, Meissen, 12 Piece	935.00
Stein, Blue, Porcelain, Lid, Meissen, 1 Liter	255.00
Stein, Porcelain Lid, Berry Finial, Crossed Swords, Meissen, 1/3 Liter, 6 In.	415.00
Urn, Blue, Baluster Form, Dome Lid, Meissen, 1900s, 15 1/4 In., Pair	590.00
Vase, Blue, Meissen, 9 3/4 In., Pair	360.00

OPALESCENT GLASS is translucent glass that has the tones of the opal gemstone. It originated in England in the 1870s and is often found in pressed glassware made in Victorian times. Opalescent glass was first made in America in 1897 at the Northwood glassworks in Indiana, Pennsylvania. Some dealers use the terms *opaline* and *opalescent* for any of these translucent wares. More opalescent pieces may be listed in Hobnail, Northwood, Pressed Glass, Spanish Lace, and other glass categories.

Alaska, Spooner, Vaseline, 3 3/8 In.	80.00
Diadem, Bowl, Vaseline, 3 1/4 In.	90.00
Herringbone, Vase, Satin, Swirled Ribs, Box Pleated Edge, 5 1/2 In.	2420.00
Klondyke, Pitcher, Blue, 8 1/8 In.	230.00
Klondyke, Rose Bowl, Vaseline, 3-Footed, 4 1/2 In.	95.00
Lattice, Tumbler, Satin, Blue, 3 1/2 In.	20.00
Opaline Brocade, Rose Bowl, Cranberry, Crimped Rim, 4 x 4 1/4 In.	140.00
Paneled Holly, Tumbler, Clear, Gold Trim, 4 1/4 In.	50.00
Poinsettia, Tumbler, Blue Opalescent, 4 In.	35.00
Reverse Swirl, Cruel, Blue, Stopper, 5 In.	130.00
Swag With Brackets, Butter, Cover, Blue	285.00
Swag With Brackets, Tumbler, Vaseline, 4 In.	45.00
Toothpicks are listed in the Toothpick category.	
Windows, Cruet, Cranberry, Stopper, 5 In.	1000.00

OPALINE, or opal glass, was made in white, green, and other colors. The glass had a matte surface and a lack of transparency. It was often gilded or painted. It was a popular mid-nineteenth-century European glassware.

Box, Cover, Enameled Leaves, Brass Hinge, Lion Mask Feet, 3 1/4 x 4 In.	150.00
Coffer, Scent Bottle, White, Napoleon III, Oval, Gilt Brass Mount, 4 3/4 In.	690.00
Encrier, Bell Shape, Gold Vines, Garland, France, c.1900, 4 x 3 In.	200.00

ORPHAN ANNIE first appeared in the comics in 1924. The redheaded girl, her dog Sandy, and her friends have been on the radio and are still on the comic pages. A Broadway musical show and a movie in the 1980s made Annie popular again and many toys, dishes, and other memorabilia are being made.

Book, A Willing Helper, c.1932	5.50
Book, Orphan Annie Circus, Die Cut Figures, American Advertising, 1935	650.00
Mug, Shake-Up, Green, Red Top, Decal	95.00
Mug, Shake-Up, Ovaltine, Game, Box, 1938	200.00
Mug, Shake-Up, Ovaltine, Plastic, Beetleware, No Lid, 1931, 3 3/4 In.	50.00
Toy, Annie Skipping Rope, Sandy Walks, Tin, Windup, Marx, 5-In. Annie	715.00
Toy, Sandy Rolls Ball, Tin Lithograph, Clockwork, Marx, Doghouse Box, 7 1/2 In.	385.00
Toy, Sandy, Magic Tail, Rubber Ears, Marx, Box	450.00
Toy, Sandy, Push Tail, Moves, Rubber Ears, Ball, Tin, Marx, Box, 8 In.	275.00
Toy, Sandy, Tin Lithograph, Clockwork, Harold Gray, Doghouse Box, USA, 5 In.	360.00
Toy, Skips Rope, Windup, Marx	350.00
Toy, Stove, 2 Doors, 3 Burners, 4 Panels Of Annie, Serving Sandy, 9 3/4 x 8 1/2 In.	80.00
Watch, Sundial, Compass, Premium, 1938	65.00

ORREFORS Glassworks, located in the Swedish province of Smaaland, was established in 1898. The company is still making glass for use on the table or as decorations. There is renewed interest in the glass made in the modern styles of the 1940s and 1950s. In 1990, the company merged with Kosta Boda. Most vases and decorative pieces are signed with the etched name *Orrefors*.

Orrefors

Bowl, Dancing Women, Intaglio, 6 Panels, P. Gabe, 1927, 9 1/2 x 8 x 3 In.	490.00
Vase, 3 Doves, Engraved, V. Lindstrom, c.1960, 6 3/4 In.	75.00
Vase, Aquatic, Rushed Fish, Plants, Green, Black, Grassl, No. 2265D, 4 3/8 In.	260.00
Vase, Ariel, No. 468F, Edvin Ohrstrom, Sweden, 1957, 4 1/2 x 6 In.	1465.00
Vase, Balinese Dancers, Intaglio, Flattened Block Shape, 11 In.	415.00
Vase, Exotic Dancer, Egg Shape, Engraved, Vicke Lindstrand, 1930s, 9 x 6 In.	345.00
Vase, Fish Graal, Amethyst Fish, Seaweed, No. 1228 L, Edward Hald, 5 In.	520.00
Vase, Fish Graal, Green Fish & Seaweed, Crystal, Oval, Signed, 5 1/2 In.	460.00 to 600.00
Vase, Fish Graal, Plants, Teal, Black Outline, No. 2511R, Edward Hald, 5 1/4 In.	490.00
Vase, Hexagonal, Women, Clear Over Amber, Ariel Glass, Olle Alberius, c.1965, 7 In.	999.00
Vase, Intaglio Carving, Nude Woman, S. Gate, 1911, 5 In.	635.00
Vase, Long Thin Neck, No. 605-60, Nils Landberg, c.1957, 11 In.	1060.00
Vase, Nude Woman, 2 Birds, Elongated, 10 3/4 x 6 In.	240.00 to 400.00

OTT & BREWER Company operated the Etruria Pottery at Trenton, New Jersey, from 1863 to 1893. They started making belleek in 1882. The firm used a variety of marks that incorporated the initials *O & B*.

Pitcher, Pink & Gold Blossom, Panel, Gold Water Lily Handle, Belleek, 9 1/4 In.	980.00
Vase, Tea Roses, Gilded Leaves, Dolphin Handles, Red Crown Stamp, 18 In.	865.00

OVERBECK pottery was made by four sisters named Overbeck at a pottery in Cambridge City, Indiana. They started in 1911. They made all types of vases, each one-of-a-kind. Small, hand-modeled figurines are the most popular pieces with today's collectors. The factory continued until 1955, when the last of the four sisters died.

Bowl, Groups Of Children, Glazed Blue Interior, 6 In.	11000.00
Bowl, Stylized Flowers, Mottled Caramel Matte Glaze, M. Frances, Incised, 2 x 6 In.	2185.00
Figurine, Cello Player, Pink Leaf Hat, Marked, 3 1/2 In.	405.00
Figurine, Fashionable Woman Seated On Sofa, 3 1/2 In.	995.00
Figurine, George & Martha Washington, 3 In.	1995.00
Figurine, Victorian Lady, White, Blue, Pink Patterned Hoop Dress, Stamped, 4 1/4 In.	375.00
Tea Set, Mauve Semimatte Glaze, Teapot, 6 Cups & Saucers, Incised OBK, 7 3/4 In.	920.00
Tile, 2 Girls, Blue Gray Outfit, Stylized Landscape, Red, White, Blue, Round, 8 In.	1440.00
Tile, Stylized Birds, Green, Yellow, Pink, Red Wings, Celtic Knots, Incised, 6 In.	8050.00
Trivet, 4 Pink Flowers, Blue Center, Green Leaves, Black Matte, Ground, Incised, 5 In.	2300.00
Vase, 3 Panels, Flower, Taupe & Green, Incised, 4 1/2 x 3 1/4 In.	2760.00

OWENS Pottery was made in Zanesville, Ohio, from 1891 to 1928. The first art pottery was made after 1896. Utopian Ware, Cyrano, Navarre, Feroza, and Henri Deux were made. Pieces were usually marked with a form of the name *Owens*. About 1907, the firm began to make tile and discontinued the art pottery wares.

Jardiniere, Utopian, Tulips, Brown Ground, Pedestal, 24 1/4 In.	805.00
Mug, Cherries, Leaves, Chocolate Brown & Caramel High Glaze, 5 1/4 In., 4 Piece	248.00
Mug, Lotus, Blackberry Vine, Charles Chilcote, 5 In.	104.00
Mug, Utopian, Berries & Leaves, Stamped, 5 x 4 1/4 In.	144.00
Tile, Geese, White, Purple, Green Ground, Raised Outline, Stamped, Frame, 6 x 6 In.	1150.00
Tile, Landscape, Raised Outline, Multicolored Matte, Frame, 14 1/2 x 30 In., 3 Piece	3738.00
Tile, Snowy Landscape, Evergreens, Stamped, 11 3/4 In., 2 Piece	6325.00
Vase, 2 Fish, Blue, Gray, White, Signed, Ferrell, 12 1/2 In.	920.00
Vase, 2 Maidens, Flowing Hair, Chocolate Ground, Squat, Handles, 9 1/2 x 7 1/2 In.	460.00
Vase, Cat Portrait, Green Matte Glaze, Bottle Shape, 16 1/2 In.	3080.00
Vase, Dragonflies, Green Matte Glaze, Squat, Impressed, 4 1/4 x 5 In.	920.00
Vase, Embossed Lines, Green Matte, Glaze, Bulbous, Shaped Tab Handles, 7 3/4 In.	385.00
Vase, Feroza, Poppies, Sheer Brown To Gunmetal Glaze, Impressed, 9 3/4 x 4 1/2 In.	1150.00
Vase, Flowers, Berries, Black High Glaze, 14 In.	1265.00
Vase, Flowers, Yellow, Orange, Brown Glaze, 12 In.	115.00

Vase, Green Matte Glaze, 4 Square Cutouts On Neck, Incised Key Pattern, 7 1/2 x 7 In. . . . 920.00
Vase, Leaves, Chocolate Brown & Caramel High Glaze, Bottle Shape, 10 1/2 In. 360.00
Vase, Lotus, 3 Swimming Fish, Charles Chilcote, No. 1258, 7 5/8 In. 2185.00
Vase, Orange Wild Rose, Oval, Stamped, 10 x 3 1/2 In. 115.00
Vase, Pansies, Bronze Crystalline Beading, Twisted Shape, 5 In. 440.00
Vase, Peonies, Under Stylized Yellow Design, Haubrich, Stamped, 11 1/2 x 4 1/2 In. 290.00
Vase, Utopian, Chrysanthemums, Bisque Ground, Impressed, 13 x 6 1/2 In. 259.00
Vase, Utopian, Dog, Brown Glaze, Flattened, Footed, Mae Timberlake, 12 x 12 In. 1880.00
Vase, Utopian, Gooseberries & Leaves, Corseted, Stamped, 10 3/4 x 4 In. 259.00
Vase, Utopian, Orange Poppies, Bulbous, Marked, 10 1/4 x 5 In. 290.00
Vase, Utopian, Wild Roses, Bottle Shape, Tod Steel, Stamped, 14 1/4 x 4 1/4 In. 315.00

OYSTER PLATES were popular from the 1880s. Each course at dinner
was served in a special dish. The oyster plate had indentations shaped
like oysters. Usually six oysters were held on a plate. There is no
greater value to a plate with more oysters, although that myth continues to haunt antiques dealers. There are other plates for shellfish,
including cockle plates and whelk plates. The appropriately shaped
indentations are part of the design of these dishes.

4 Wells, Handle, J.W. Boteler, 10 1/2 x 10 1/4 In. 4950.00
5 Wells, Ocean, Seaweed Ground, Scallop Shell Wells, 9 1/4 In. 1980.00
5 Wells, Violet Flowers, Porcelain, 8 1/2 In. 165.00
5 Wells, White, Gold Trim, Crescent Shape, Porcelain, 9 In., Pair 250.00
6 Wells, Alternating Pink & Turquoise Wells, Pink Center, Fielding, 10 In. 715.00
6 Wells, Beehive, Owls, Square, Austria, 8 1/2 In. 385.00
6 Wells, Brown Ground, Pink & Mottled Green Wells, Cobalt Blue Center, 10 In. 275.00
6 Wells, Gray, Green, Luneville, 8 3/4 In. 330.00
6 Wells, Green Gray Mottled, Shell Feet, 9 1/2 In. 55.00
6 Wells, Kissing Fish, Orange, Aqua, 10 In. 385.00
6 Wells, Lavender & White Alternating Wells, Fielding, 9 1/4 In. 385.00
6 Wells, Pink Ground, Light Blue Wells, Crescent Shape, Porcelain, 9 In. 165.00
6 Wells, Pink Ground, Mussels In Each Well, Square, Porcelain, 7 1/2 In. 110.00
6 Wells, Pink, Green, St. Clement, 9 In. 330.00
6 Wells, Seaweed, Orange, Green, Shorter & Son, 13 In. 360.00
6 Wells, Yellow, Brown, Mottled Center, Victoria Pottery Co., 10 In. 880.00
7 Wells, Flowers, Gold Trim, Porcelain, France, 7 1/2 In. 85.00
7 Wells, Sunflower, Lavender Border, Samuel Lear, 10 In. 1650.00
9 Wells, Silver Plate, Reed & Barton, 12 1/2 In. 193.00
12 Wells, Basket Weave, Longchamp, 13 1/4 In. 55.00
12 Wells, Center Handle, 6-Sided, France, 12 1/2 In. 440.00
Eagle, Russian Imperial, Rose, Ivory, Turquoise, Gold, 9 x 7 In. 825.00
Set, Singles, Chesapeake Bay Oven Oyster, Original Box, 6 Piece 165.00

PADEN CITY Glass Manufacturing Company was established in 1916
at Paden City, West Virginia. The company made more than seventy
different colors of glass. The firm closed in 1951. Paden City Pottery
is not listed here.

Ardith, Candy Dish, Cover 90.00
Ardith, Sandwich Server, Center Handle, Yellow, 4 1/2 x 10 In. 75.00
Black Forest, Plate, Dinner, 10 3/8 In. 230.00
Bunny, Cotton Holder, Pink, Frosted, 5 x 4 1/2 In. 170.00
Chaucer, Cheese & Cracker Dish, 4 x 11 3/4 In. 200.00
Crow's Foot, Bowl, Ruby, Oval, 10 3/4 x 7 In. 55.00
Crow's Foot, Cake Plate, Ruby, Orchid Etch, 11 In. 225.00
Crow's Foot, Candlestick, Black, Mushroom, 2 1/2 x 4 1/2 In., Pair 80.00
Crow's Foot, Candlestick, Cobalt Blue, Mushroom, 2 1/2 x 4 1/2 In., Pair 90.00
Crow's Foot, Candy Dish, Cobalt Blue, 3 3/4 x 7 In. 115.00
Crow's Foot, Vase, Ruby, 9 3/4 x 6 5/8 In. 150.00
Cupid, Candy Dish, Cover, Ruby, 3 3/4 x 7 In. 190.00
Esoteric, Creamer, Sugar Cube Underplate, Cheriglo, Loop Handles, 2 Piece 125.00
Esoteric, Plate, Sugar Cube, Green 55.00
Figurine, Chinese Pheasant, 13 3/4 In. 65.00
Figurine, Pheasant, Blue, 6 1/2 x 12 In. 125.00

Frost Etch, Candlestick, 2-Light, Gadroon, Pair 110.00
Frost Etch, Vase, Hummer, 8 In. 195.00
Gadroon, Sandwich Server, Etched Crocus, Center Handle, 5 1/4 x 11 In. 75.00
Gazebo, Bowl, 4 1/4 x 12 In. 50.00
Gazebo, Console, Gadroon, Rolled Rim, 3 1/2 x 13 In. 55.00
Glades, Ice Tub, Ruby, Fluted 60.00
Gothic Garden, Bowl, 4-Footed, 11 5/8 x 5 1/2 In. 85.00
Gothic Garden, Cheese & Cracker Dish, Pink 135.00
Gothic Garden, Dish, Mayonnaise, Topaz, Rolled Rim, 5 3/4 x 3 5/8 In. 90.00
Largo, Candlestick, Cobalt Blue, 4 3/4 In., Pair 300.00
Largo, Ice Bucket, Black, Wicker Handle, 6 3/4 x 7 In. 290.00
Military Hat, Candy Dish, 5 x 2 1/2 In. 50.00
No. 115, Candlestick, Amber, 6-Sided Base, 7 In., Pair 70.00
Orchid, Candlestick, Gadroon, Square Base, Rounded Corners, 5 x 4 1/2 In. 245.00
Oriental Garden, Ice Tub 95.00
Party Line, Dish, Mayonnaise, Underplate, Green, Ladle, Etched Gold Trim 125.00
Peacock & Rose, Cake Plate, Pink, 10 1/4 In. 130.00
Peacock & Wild Rose, Candlestick, Pink, 1 5/8 x 5 In. 85.00
Peacock & Wild Rose, Vase, Pink, 10 1/8 x 6 1/4 In. 290.00
Spire, Cheese & Cracker Dish, Gold Etch 65.00

PAINTINGS listed in this book are not works by major artists but rather decorative paintings on ivory, board, or glass that would be of interest to the average collector. Watercolors on paper are listed under Picture. To learn the value of an oil painting by a listed artist you must contact an expert in that area.

Casein On Board, Mercado, William Henry, c.1952, 16 x 20 In. 545.00
Oil On Artist Board, Boat Wreck, Rocky Coast, H.R. Bollinger, Frame, 27 x 31 In. 115.00
Oil On Artist Board, Landscape, Bridge Over Creek, E. Roberts, Frame, 4 3/8 x 6 In. ... 250.00
Oil On Artist Board, Moonlit, Crashing Waves, Ruins, J.A. Hekking, Frame, 14 x 18 In. . 1265.00
Oil On Artist Board, Still Life, Vegetable, Roelecke, 1890, 12 x 18 In. 1580.00
Oil On Artist's Pallet, Winter Scene, Church, Building, Landscape, Frame, 14 1/2 x 23 In. 300.00
Oil On Board, Abstraction, Hugo Lutz, Carved Wood Frame, 1961, 36 x 30 In. 345.00
Oil On Board, American 2-Masted Schooner, Willis, Frame, 1800s, 15 x 21 In. 690.00
Oil On Board, Coastal Scene, Sailing Ship, Frame, 19th Century, 11 x 15 1/4 In. 490.00
Oil On Board, Fishing Port, William Clarkson Stanfield, England, 1836, 15 3/4 x 12 In. .. 780.00
Oil On Board, Gambrel Roof House, W. Webber, Frame, c.1890, 9 x 14 In. 865.00
Oil On Board, Louisiana Bayou, Alexander J. Drysdale, c.1920, 6 x 20 In. 1265.00
Oil On Board, Mallard In Flight, Lake, John W. Taylor, Frame, 11 1/2 x 15 1/2 In. 450.00
Oil On Board, New England Landscape, Adelia Belle Beard, Frame, 8 x 13 In. 1955.00
Oil On Board, Portrait Of Young Woman, James A. Grant, Frame, 1900s, 36 x 28 In. 1840.00
Oil On Board, Rough Fishing, V.M. Stearns, 9 3/4 x 13 1/4 In. 230.00
Oil On Board, San Juan Merchant, M. Shir, Frame, 1958, 16 x 24 In. 145.00
Oil On Board, Still Life, Flowers, William L. Carrigan, Frame, 1900s, 10 x 12 In. 385.00
Oil On Board, Still Life, Fruit, Oliver Clare, Frame, 8 1/2 x 11 1/2 In. 1020.00
Oil On Board, View Of Gloucester, Sarah Kramer Glass, Frame, 10 x 8 In. 520.00
Oil On Board, Wooded River's Edge, Antoine Chintreuil, 1800s, 6 1/8 x 8 1/2 In. 1725.00
Oil On Board, Yellow House, Niles Spencer, Frame, 9 x 12 In. 1095.00
Oil On Canvas, 3-Masted Schooner On Heavy Seas, S.W. Frazer, Frame, 16 x 26 In. 776.00
Oil On Canvas, 3-Masted Ship At Sea, George Howell Gay, Frame, c.1900, 25 x 30 In. ... 400.00
Oil On Canvas, American Indian, Mountains, M.L. Sharmo, 1900s, 12 x 12 In. 115.00
Oil On Canvas, Banjo Player, V.B. Wells, Frame, c.1930, 20 x 24 In. 1380.00
Oil On Canvas, Brook, Charles Henry Harmon, Frame, c.1887, 16 x 20 In. 1440.00
Oil On Canvas, California Landscape, Paul Turner Sargent, Frame, c.1937, 20 x 24 In. ... 1150.00
Oil On Canvas, Children At Lake, Adam Emory Albright, Frame, c.1912, 24 x 30 In. 5750.00
Oil On Canvas, Chinese Export, German 3-Masted Ship Europa, 18 x 23 1/2 In. 4370.00
Oil On Canvas, Clipper Ship On High Seas, Oliver Albrutson, Frame, 24 x 30 In. 175.00
Oil On Canvas, Clipper Ship, Charles B. Kenny, Gilt Frame, 1878, 20 x 27 In. 1645.00
Oil On Canvas, Coastal Scene, Ida Pond Sylvester, Frame, c.1920, 16 x 20 In. 635.00
Oil On Canvas, Coming Day, Sunrise Landscape, Maurice Hague, Frame, 40 x 29 3/4 In. . 880.00
Oil On Canvas, Country Landscape, John Califano, 25 x 30 In. 690.00
Oil On Canvas, Early Autumn Landscape, M.V. Breitmayer, c.1930, 16 x 20 In. 690.00
Oil On Canvas, Express Train, Albert Pels, 1900s, 20 x 25 In. 3910.00

Oil On Canvas, Fleurs De Simione, Pierre Ramel, France, 1900s, 36 1/4 x 28 3/4 In. 420.00
Oil On Canvas, Folk Art, Landscape, Small Town, Pinwheel Frame, c.1897, 27 x 21 In. . . 8250.00
Oil On Canvas, Forest Pond At Dawn, J. Flier, Dutch School, Frame, c.1910, 13 x 18 In. . 460.00
Oil On Canvas, Forest Scene With Fence & Stream, A.M. Gorter, Frame, 25 x 17 In. 1150.00
Oil On Canvas, Forest Scene With Lake, Walter McDonald, Frame, 1900s, 24 x 36 In. . . . 550.00
Oil On Canvas, French Fishing Boats, Grifon, Frame, 23 1/2 x 36 1/2 In. 150.00
Oil On Canvas, French Harbor, Anne Gregory Ritter, c.1896, 11 x 13 1/2 In. 980.00
Oil On Canvas, Girl In Blue Dress, Corner Block Frame, c.1830, 30 x 38 In. 1760.00
Oil On Canvas, Governor Robie Ship, J. Arnold, Frame, 24 x 36 In. 430.00
Oil On Canvas, Hilltop Barn, Dudley Henry Morris Jr., 30 x 36 In. 2880.00
Oil On Canvas, Italian Landscape, Mountains, Lake, Gilt Gesso Frame, 15 x 25 In. 1700.00
Oil On Canvas, Landscape With Bridge, J.L. Fund, Frame, 1800s, 16 1/2 x 21 In. 1035.00
Oil On Canvas, Landscape, Western Pennsylvania, Frame, c.1850, 41 x 26 3/4 In. 1210.00
Oil On Canvas, Latin Quarter, Paris, Colette Pope Heldner, Frame, c.1930, 24 x 30 In. . . . 1150.00
Oil On Canvas, Mexican Mother & Child, Frank Perri, c.1940, 30 x 24 In. 690.00
Oil On Canvas, Midwestern Landscape, Jess Hobby, Frame, c.1920, 28 x 33 In. 1955.00
Oil On Canvas, Nude Woman, Borat-Lebraux, 38 x 45 In. 3165.00
Oil On Canvas, Ocean Liner Europa, Alex Kircher, Frame, 28 x 36 In. 575.00
Oil On Canvas, Pastoral Landscape, E. Percy Moran, c.1900, 10 x 12 In. 1725.00
Oil On Canvas, Pastoral Landscape, William B. Baird, c.1880, 22 x 32 In. 2300.00
Oil On Canvas, Pequot Ship, T. Bailey, Frame, 22 x 33 In. 520.00
Oil On Canvas, Pleased To Meet You, George Augustus Holmes, British, 24 x 36 In. 1920.00
Oil On Canvas, Poppy Red, Abstract, Emery Bopp, Frame, 1900s, 30 x 24 In. 440.00
Oil On Canvas, Rolling Landscape, James Edward McBurney, c.1925, 10 x 14 In. 315.00
Oil On Canvas, Spring Landscape, Claude Curry Bohm, Frame, 24 x 30 In. 4315.00
Oil On Canvas, Still Life, Cherries, M.A. Davis, Frame, 1800s, 6 x 9 In. 290.00
Oil On Canvas, Still Life, Dahlias In Vase, Stanley Grant Middleton, Frame, 24 x 20 In. . . . 550.00
Oil On Canvas, Still Life, Flowers, Ann Hoke, c.1928, 20 x 16 In. 490.00
Oil On Canvas, Still Life, Flowers, L. Royce, 20th Century, 15 x 20 In. 230.00
Oil On Canvas, Still Life, Fruit, Nuts, Basket, Gilt Gesso Frame, 14 x 20 In. 1075.00
Oil On Canvas, Still Life, Grapes, Peaches, Berries, A.J. Thornton, Frame, Late 1800s . . . 260.00
Oil On Canvas, Still Life, Orange, Plums, M.A. Davis, Frame, 1800s, 5 x 9 In. 200.00
Oil On Canvas, Still Life, Oranges & Pineapple, R.E. Hutchinson, 1908, 22 x 16 In. 80.00
Oil On Canvas, Still Life, Peaches & Bowl, Elmer V. Potter, Frame, 1889, 14 x 20 In. 1130.00
Oil On Canvas, Still Life, Ruby Glass With Orange, Lemons, Redelius, 1966, 18 x 32 In. . . 1580.00
Oil On Canvas, Stream In Early Autumn, Matthew A. Daly, c.1924, 24 x 30 In. 1495.00
Oil On Canvas, Summer Night, Charles Bridgeman Vickery, c.1960, 24 x 36 In. 1725.00
Oil On Canvas, Time For Bed, British School, 1800s, 33 x 29 1/2 In. 1795.00
Oil On Canvas, White Carnations & Baby Breath, E.B. Lintott, Frame, 30 x 25 In. 660.00
Oil On Canvas, Winter Troika, Rassokhym, Russia, 1900s, 14 x 17 In. 1195.00
Oil On Canvas, Young Child, Maritime Setting, Adams, 1887, 21 x 17 In. 805.00
Oil On Canvas, Young Man, Cigar, Period Frame, Early 19th Century, 30 x 36 In. 825.00
Oil On Clamshell, Schooner, High Seas, Attribution A.N.G. Jacobsen, 7 1/2 x 5 In. 6900.00
Oil On Ivory, Brothers, Black Period Frame, Oval Glass, c.1840, 3 x 2 In. 1210.00
Oil On Ivory, Child, Holding Rattle, Oval, Frame, c.1830, 2 15/16 x 1 7/8 In. 880.00
Oil On Linen, Lake, Boats, House, Hills, Mid 1800s, 10 x 15 1/2 In. 625.00
Oil On Masonite, Farm Scene, Jack Reichard, 1800s, 24 1/2 x 17 1/2 In. 1700.00
Oil On Masonite, Still Life, Flower Vase, R. H. Redelius, Frame, 30 x 24 In. 1469.00
Oil On Masonite, Still Life, Flowers In Chinese Bowl, Redelius, Frame, 25 x 17 In. 1580.00
Oil On Panel, Fountain Bleau, Agnes Middleton Raeburn, c.1910, 14 1/2 x 18 1/2 In. 980.00
Oil On Panel, Landscape, North African Figures, Mariano Nieto Bertuchi, 18 x 22 In. . . . 980.00
Oil On Panel, Monk As Artist, Morosi, Italian, c.1900, 16 1/8 x 11 1/2 In. 1315.00
Oil On Panel, Ship At Sea, Robert E. Johnston, Giltwood Frame, 15 1/2 x 20 In. 1380.00
Oil On Panel, Ships In A Harbor, Charles Gosselin, c.1874, 7 x 13 5/8 In. 375.00
Oil On Panel, Street Vendors, Agne Francois, Flemish, 1800s, 11 3/8 x 9 1/4 In. 1675.00
Oil On Panel, Temple Of Minerva, Gilt Frame, 10 x 15 In. 1800.00
Oil On Tin, Woman, Sitting In Red Painted Chair, c.1820, 6 1/2 x 8 In. 2640.00
On Ivory, European Tavern Scene, Scrimshaw Frame, 1800s, 5 7/8 x 5 1/4 In. 1035.00
On Ivory, Gentleman, William Clark, England, Frame, Early 1800s, 2 3/8 x 4 5/8 In. 470.00
On Ivory, Ladies On Exotic Terrace, H. Forster, Continental, Frame, c.1910, 7 x 4 3/4 In. . . 3525.00
On Ivory, Man, Brown Hair, Blue Eyes, Black Coat, Lois R. Killam, Frame, 2 x 1 1/2 In. . . 180.00
On Ivory, Royalty, Alexander, Cast Brass Frame, 2 In. 2260.00
On Ivory, Woman, Elaborate Lace Collar, Pink Ribbon, 1700s, 3 x 3 1/2 In. 175.00

On Ivory, Woman, Flowers In Hair, Brass Frame, 3 In. 285.00
Reverse On Glass, George & Martha Washington, c.1820, 17 1/2 x 22 In., Pair 920.00
Reverse On Glass, Woman, Black Dress, Full Length, Frame, 1800s, 8 x 9 1/2 In. 660.00
Scroll On Paper, Nanga School, Lotus, Kano Josen, 1700s, 40 x 13 1/2 In. 375.00
Scroll On Paper, Spotted Deer, Signed, Seal Marked, Japan, c.1890, 47 x 19 1/2 In. 605.00
Scroll On Silk, Bird, Red Maple Trees, Japan, Early 1900s, 12 1/2 x 15 In. 115.00
Scroll On Silk, Monkey, Monkey Netsuke, Inro, Y. Soken, Box, Late 1800s, 43 x 16 In. ... 1840.00
Scroll On Silk, Otsue Style, Man, Tree Branches, Calligraphy, 1800s, 49 1/2 x 10 1/2 In. . 415.00
Scroll On Silk, Rural Landscape, Cottages, Waterfall, Mountains, c.1900, 44 x 16 1/2 In. . 115.00

PAIRPOINT Manufacturing Company started in 1880 in New Bedford, Massachusetts. It soon joined with the glassworks nearby and made glass, silver-plated pieces, and lamps. Reverse-painted glass shades and molded shades known as *puffies* were part of the production until the 1930s. The company reorganized and changed its name several times but is still working today. Items listed here are glass or glass and metal. Silver-plated pieces are listed under Silver Plate.

Basket, Flowers, Silver Plate, Footed, 13 x 10 1/2 In. 175.00
Biscuit Jar, Silver Plated Lid, Cover, Handle, Floral & Leaf Design, Signed, 6 In. 440.00
Bottle, Dresser, Engraved Flower, Faceted Stopper, 7 3/4 In. 35.00
Bowl, Daisies & Butterflies, Sterling Silver Rim, 10 1/2 In. 250.00
Bride's Basket, Burmese Bowls, Flowers, Silver Plate Holder, 20 In. .... *Illus* 8000.00
Bride's Basket, Enameled Flowers, Pink Satin, Holder, Bird Handles, c.1900, 13 In. 616.00
Bride's Basket, Opal, Enameled Flowers, Ruffled Edge, Reticulated Holder, 9 In. 260.00
Candlestick, Engraved Flowers, Swirled Cranberry & Opal Teardrop Stem, 10 In. 385.00
Carafe, Adonis Cutting, 7 x 6 1/4 In. 155.00
Cherry Jar, 2 Cut Octagon, Hobstar Cover, 6 1/2 In. 300.00
Lamp, Berkeley Shade, Flowers, Urn Base, 27 In. .... *Illus* 1840.00
Lamp, Directoire Shade, Cone Shape, Flowers, Brass Base, Prongs, 16 x 25 1/2 In. 2015.00
Lamp, Directoire, Art Deco Design, Blue, Red, Orange, Yellow, 3 Candlesticks, 16 In. 1840.00
Lamp, Exeter Shade, Reverse Painted, Tropical, Birds, Flowers, Brass, Signed, 22 In. 8700.00
Lamp, Exeter, Reverse Painted, Signed 8970.00
Lamp, Oil, Copper, Pewter, 14 1/2 In. 130.00
Lamp, Puffy, Hummingbird, Ribbed, Frosted Shade, Flowers, Leaves, 21 x 14 In. 5230.00
Lamp, Puffy, Lilacs, Leaves, Butterflies, Tree Trunk Base, Signed, 25 x 14 In. 77625.00
Lamp, Puffy, Pansies, Signed Base, 8 1/2 x 14 In. 1610.00
Lamp, Puffy, Red & Yellow Roses, Blue & Green Leaves, Bronze Base, 16 x 10 In. 3010.00
Lamp, Puffy, Rose Clusters, Leaves, Bee, Twisted Bronze Base, Signed, 17 In. 9200.00
Lamp, Puffy, Sunflowers, 8 3/4 x 16 In. 1150.00
Lamp, Reverse Painted, Parrots, On Perch, Yellow Shaded To Orange, 15 x 7 In. 900.00
Lamp, Venice Shade, Ribs, Roses, Signed, 21 In. .... *Illus* 4485.00
Lamp Base, Disk Float, 4 Applied Floral Feet, 2 Sockets, Brass Finish, 15 In. 230.00
Paperweight, White Rose, Green Leaves, Faceted, C.O.S., 2 7/8 In. 100.00
Paperweight, Yellow Rose, Leaves, Cobalt Blue Ground, Faceted, 2 3/4 In. 80.00

Pairpoint, Bride's Basket, Burmese Bowls, Flowers, Silver Plate Holder, 20 In.

Pairpoint, Lamp, Berkeley Shade, Flowers, Urn Base, 27 In.

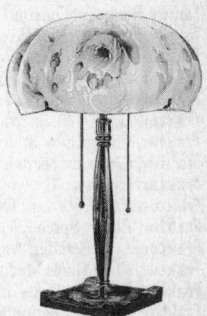

Pairpoint, Lamp, Venice Shade, Ribs, Roses, Signed, 21 In.

Plate, Fern Cutting, Diamond Border, Amethyst, 10 In. 50.00
Sandwich Server, Fork Handles, Merello Cutting, 6 1/2 x 10 In. 125.00
Shade, Reverse Painted, Landscape, Blue Clover Designs, Flared, 17 In. 2070.00
Tray, Apples On Branch, Cutting, Round, 10 1/2 In. 400.00
Tray, Colonialware, Gold Enameled, Flowers, Leaves, Opal, Folded Edges, 5 1/2 In. 30.00
Urn, Rosaria, Bubble Ball Connector, Rolled Rim, M Handles, 10 In. 230.00
Vase, Basket Shape, Fruit Cutting, 8 In. 290.00
Vase, Light Green, Vintage Engraving, c.1900, 11 In. 175.00
Vase, Paperweight, Yellow Flower, Green Leaves, Flared, 10 1/2 x 8 In. 115.00

PALMER COX, BROWNIES, see Brownies category.

PAPER collectibles, including almanacs, catalogs, children's books, some greeting cards, stock certificates, and other paper ephemera, are listed here. Paper calendars are listed separately in the Calendar category. Paper items may be found in many other sections, such as Christmas and Movie.

Almanac, Swamp Root, 1906, 6 x 9 In., 32 Pages 88.00
Birth Certificate & Baptismal, John Hoffman, Berks Co., Pa., Frame, 1786, 12 x 17 In. . . 2200.00
Book, Big Little Book, Paint, 1933, 3 3/4 x 8 1/2 In., 336 Pages 730.00
Broadside, Adam & Eve, Illuminated, Painted, Reading, Pa., 1822, 15 1/2 x 11 1/2 In. . . . 1018.00
Broadside, July 4th Excursion, To Fort Popham, Steamship, Frame, 14 x 10 1/2 In. 105.00
Brochure, Smith & Wesson Handcuffs, 1957, 8 1/2 x 11 In., 4 Pages 40.00
Catalog, Abercrombie & Fitch, 1913, Red Gods Call, 6 3/4 x 9 3/4 In., 540 Pages 605.00
Catalog, Arcade Manufacturing Company, No. 25 . . . . 495.00
Catalog, Chicago Mail Order Co., 1938, 7 3/4 x 10 1/4 In., 76 Pages 25.00
Catalog, Evinrude Motors, 1918, Color Cover, Original Order Blank, 24 Pages 360.00
Catalog, F.A.O. Schwarz, Christmas 1927 . . . . 135.00
Catalog, Henry Fields Pet, Fish & Bird Supplies, 1936, 7 1/2 x 10 1/2 In., 31 Pages 15.00
Catalog, Inter-State Nurseries, 1937, 7 1/2 x 10 3/4 In., 66 Pages 28.00
Catalog, Inter-State Nurseries, Spring 1948, 7 1/2 x 10 1/4 In., 83 Pages 25.00
Catalog, Marbles Outing Equipment, 1937-38, Moose, 4 1/8 x 7 In., 32 Pages 85.00
Catalog, Marlin Repeating Rifles, Carbines, Hunters, Campfire, c.1903, 128 Pages 125.00
Catalog, Old Town Canoes & Boats, 1930, Multicolored Cover, 6 x 8 In., 37 Pages 85.00
Catalog, Parker Guns, 1926, 9 x 6 In, 32 Pages 120.00
Catalog, Pflueger Fishing Tackle, No. 148, 1928, Color Cover & Illustrations, 128 Pages . 110.00
Catalog, Van Schaack, 1872, 4 3/4 x 7 1/4 In., 160 Pages 605.00
Catalog, Van Schaack, Stevenson & Co., 4 3/4 x 7 3/8 In., 575 Pages 1980.00
Certificate, Lincoln Monument, Contribution, 50 Cents, Frame, c.1869, 8 1/4 x 5 1/4 In. . . 80.00
Coloring Book, Prince Valiant, Hal Foster, Saalfield KFS, Box, 1954, 11 x 14 In. 65.00
Comic Book, Detective Comics, No. 27, May, 1939 . . . . 79825.00
Cut Paper, Scherenschnitte, Tree, Urn, Eagles, Frame, Pa., 6 x 6 3/4 In. 125.00
Family Record, Norton, Hearts, Cupid, Hour Glass, c.1836, 16 1/2 x 11 In. 745.00
Family Record, Pollard-Brown, Watercolor, Pillars, Vining, Flowers, 19 1/2 x 17 In. 175.00
Family Record, Valentine Doane, Lydia Nickerson, Frame, 1829-1900, 24 x 20 In. 80.00
Family Register, Daniel Howard & Patience Whitney, Calligraphy, Frame, Early 1800s . . 770.00
Family Register, Gideon Evans, Jerusha Mann, Smithfield, R.I., c.1816, 12 5/8 x 7 5/8 In. . . 715.00
Family Register, Hair Wreath, Silk Ribbons, Margaret A. Majors, c.1850, 18 x 16 In. 230.00
Fraktur, 2 Deer, Green, Brown, Exuberant Antlers, Full Gallop, c.1840, 5 x 7 In. 385.00
Fraktur, Adam Heister, Hand Drawn, Frame, 1856, 9 x 6 3/4 In. 2200.00
Fraktur, Angel, Wide Eyed, Hairy Legged, Lancaster Co., Pa., c.1825, 13 x 17 In. 1870.00
Fraktur, Bird, Branch, Watercolor, Red, Green Polka Dot, Gold Frame, c.1830, 6 x 7 In. . . 470.00
Fraktur, Calligraphy Style, Bird, Cipher Book, Brown, Red, Gold Frame, 5 1/4 x 5 3/4 In. . 175.00
Fraktur, Christian Mertel, Center Medallion, Heart Vine, c.1798, 11 1/2 x 13 1/2 In. 3940.00
Fraktur, Drawing, Brown, Black, Stylized Tulip, Flowers, Bird, Frame, c.1800, 15 x 15 In. . 880.00
Fraktur, Eagle, Reward Of Merit, Whimsical, Wood Frame, c.1885, 4 3/4 x 4 1/8 In. 300.00
Fraktur, Eagle, Spread Wing, U.S. Shield, Radiant Suns, c.1830, 8 1/4 x 7 In. 470.00
Fraktur, Elias Schafer, Angels, Birds, Frame, Berks County, Pa., 16 x 12 1/2 In. 90.00
Fraktur, Eliza Hare, Medallion, Cross, Birds, Watercolor, Frame, 11 x 9 In. 2530.00
Fraktur, Flowers, Birds, Leaping Stags, Samuel Boumann, Ephrata, c.1814, 16 x 13 In. . . 365.00
Fraktur, Johann Valentin Schuller, Griesinger & Renn Families, c.1812, 16 x 12 In. 1320.00
Fraktur, Land Grant, Farm House, Horse, Rider, Bucks County, c.1859, 19 x 17 In. 1925.00
Fraktur, Maria Sockin, Watercolor On Paper, Union County, Pa., c.1823, 15 x 11 In. 990.00
Fraktur, Marriage On Reverse, Black Frame, c.1834, 7 x 12 In. 195.00

Paper must "breathe." Don't keep it in a sealed package. It will eventually become moldy. Don't store paper collectibles in photograph albums with black pages. The acidic paper will cause damage.

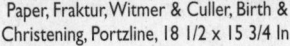
Paper, Fraktur, Witmer & Culler, Birth & Christening, Portzline, 18 1/2 x 15 3/4 In.

Fraktur, Otto Style, Heart Medallion, Flowers, Geometric, Frame, c.1788, 15 x 12 In. . . . 4220.00
Fraktur, Parrot, Stylized Tulip, Conrad Gilbert, Frame, 8 1/2 x 11 1/4 In. 470.00
Fraktur, Present, Bird, Stencil Style, Cherries, Apples, Mary Ann Lantz, c.1864, 7 x 6 In. . 578.00
Fraktur, Reward Of Merit, Man-In-Sun, Squiggle Line Border, c.1800, 8 x 7 1/2 In. 1100.00
Fraktur, Thewald & Deibert Families, Martin Brechall, Pa., Frame, c.1804, 12 x 10 In. . . 1210.00
Fraktur, Witmer & Culler, Birth & Christening, Portzline, 18 1/2 x 15 3/4 In. . . . . . . *Illus* 17600.00
Indenture, English, Hand Written, Vellum Border, Frame, 1736, 27 x 33 In. 140.00
Land Grant, 300 Acres, Burke County, North Carolina, Samuel Austin, c.1799, 9 x 5 In. . 250.00
Land Grant, Fayette County, Ind., James Monroe, Vellum, 1823, 10 x 16 In. 490.00
Land Grant, Little Miami River, Jefferson & Madison Signatures, Presidential Seal, 1807 3105.00
Magazine, American Collector, Wallace Nutting Cover, April 1975 . . . . 5.50
Magazine, American Collector, Wallace Nutting Cover, November 1977 . . . . 5.50
Magazine, American Home, Wallace Nutting Cover, May 1959 . . . . 5.50
Magazine, Fine Woodworking, Wallace Nutting Cover, 1983 . . . . 5.50
Magazine, Life, Goebbels & Goring Cover, Feb. 3, 1941 . . . . 56.00
Magazine, McCall's, Betty Ford On Cover, March 1979, Autographed 18.00
Magazine, Newsweek, Roosevelt & Willkie Cover, November 4, 1940, 68 Pages 8.00
Magazine, Saturday Evening Post, December 6, 1943 . . . . 15.00
Magazine, Time, A. Szyk, Cover Of Admiral Yamamoto, December 2, 1941 . . . . 35.00
Magazine, True, Feb. 1961, 25th Anniversary Issue, Original Wrapper 10.00
Menu, Crossroads Inn Menu, Highway 50, Kansas City, Mo. 15.00
Menu, Filene's Salad Bowl, Boston, Mass., 1946, 9 x 6 In. 25.00
Menu, Grand Canyon Lodge, Utah Park Systems, Union Pacific, 1929, 4 3/8 x 5 5/8 In. . . 25.00
Menu, Plaza Hotel, USAAF Bombers, San Antonio, New Year's, 1942 . . . . 25.00
Menu, Ringling Brothers & Barnum & Bailey, 1920 . . . . 30.00
Merit Reward, Watercolor, Jonas Tolman, Figure, White Gown, c.1810, 7 3/8 x 6 5/8 In. . 880.00
Motto, Friendship Love & Truth, Walnut Frame, Gold Liner 175.00
Motto, Home Sweet Home, Gilt Gesso Frame 115.00
Motto, Home Sweet Home, Walnut Frame, Gold Liner 130.00
Motto, Peace Be Unto This House, Gilt Gesso Frame 175.00
Motto, Vertical, After Clouds, Sunshine, Walnut Frame 165.00
Motto, We Mourn Out Loss, Tintype, Little Boy, Grain Frame 195.00
Program, Buffalo Bill's Wild West Show, 1893, 9 1/4 x 7 1/4 In., 64 Pages 865.00
Program, Ringling Bros. & Barnum & Bailey Circus, Gunther Gebel-Williams, 1974 . . . . 40.00
Push-Out Book, Tom Corbett, Unpunched, 1952, 14 x 10 In. 75.00
Stock Certificate, Nevada Territory Mining Stock, 1863 . . . . 700.00
Stock Certificate, Puget Sound Homestead Association, Gen. George Crook, 1870 . . . . . . 1320.00
Tourist Guide, Yosemite, Ansel Adams Photo, 1936 . . . . 35.00
Wallpaper, Peacocks & Lilies, Multicolored, Walter Crane, Frame, 20 1/2 x 41 In. 4315.00

PAPER DOLLS were probably inspired by the pantins, or jumping jacks, made in eighteenth-century Europe. By the 1880s, sheets of printed paper dolls and clothes were being made. The first paper doll books were made in the 1920s. Collectors prefer uncut sheets or books or boxed sets of paper dolls. Prices are about half as much if the pages have been cut.

American Lady & Her Children, Box, 6 1/2 x 9 In. 1175.00

Ballet Dancer, Tissue Costume, Gold Leaf, Fairy Wings, Taglioni Type, c.1830, 14 In.	999.00
Barbie, World Of Barbie Play Fun Box, 4 Dolls, Crayons, Wax, Whitman, Box, 1972	55.00
Barbie & Ken, Stand-Up Dolls, Plastic Stands, Punch-Out Clothes, Whitman, 1963	175.00
Brave Boy, 7 x 10 In.	3525.00
Brenda Starr, Boots, Spiral Bound Portfolio, 16 x 18 In., 4 Cut, 97 Uncut	705.00
Brenda Starr, Comic Strip, 19 Uncut	440.00
Brother & Sister, Germany, Box, Mid 19th Century, 6 1/2 x 8 1/2 In.	940.00
Chinese Dolls, 3 Dolls, Box, 5 x 7 In.	2585.00
Dancing Doll For Girls, Movable Eyes, Box, 8 x 9 x 2 In.	3878.00
Fanny Elsler, Box, c.1830, 8 x 10 In.	2468.00
Girl Queen, W. Hagelberg, London, New York	440.00
Gone With The Wind, Book, Merrill, c.1940, Uncut	325.00
Grandpapa's Rocking Chair, Envelope, Late 19th Century	380.00
Gulliver's Travels, Book, Saalfield, Paramount Pictures, 1939, Uncut	165.00
Hood's Sarsaparilla, 5 Dolls, 10 Outfits	170.00
Jenny Lind, 8 Outfits, Box, Mid 19th Century, 4 x 6 1/2 In.	940.00
Little Princess, Unsere Kaiserin, Box, c.1900	2115.00
Ma Poupee Cherie, France, Box, c.1918	645.00
Merry Mabel, Tucks, Box	705.00
Model Doll, January, February, 1866, 2 Uncut Sheets	380.00
Munsingwear, Miss Molly Munsing, Early 20th Century, 4 Uncut Sheets	225.00
Taglioni, Box, c.1830, 4 x 6 1/2 In.	2940.00
Young Riders, Tuck, Artistic Toy Novelty	380.00

PAPERWEIGHTS must have first appeared along with paper in ancient Egypt. Today's collectors search for every type, from the very expensive French weights of the nineteenth century to the modern artist weights or advertising pieces. The glass tops of the paperweights sometimes have been nicked or scratched, and this type of damage can be removed by polishing. Some serious collectors think this type of repair is an alteration and will not buy a repolished weight; others think it is an acceptable technique of restoration that does not change the value. Baccarat paperweights are listed separately under Baccarat.

Advertising, Arcade, Factory Picture, Brass, 1885-1927, 3 x 5 In.	275.00
Advertising, Arco Motor Oil Club, Cast Metal, 5 In.	110.00
Advertising, Crawford Hand-Made Shoes, 3 x 3 In.	39.00
Advertising, Firemen's Insurance Co., Brass, Velvet & Leather Case, Newark, N.J.	25.00
Advertising, James Clark Distilling Co., Cumberland, Md., 4 x 2 1/2 In.	66.00
Advertising, James Shewan & Sons Inc., Anchor, Brass, Engraved, 5 x 3 1/2 In.	295.00
Advertising, Jos. Schlitz Brewing Co., Factory Scene, c.1890-1905, 3 In.	300.00
Advertising, Maine Steamship Co., New York & Portland Me., 4 x 2 1/2 In.	105.00
Advertising, Merriam & Co. Segars, Bull Dog, Figural, Metal, 4 x 2 x 3 In.	140.00
Advertising, N.Z. Graves & Co., Varnish, Japan & Color Makers, Philadelphia, 3 In.	30.00
Advertising, Reeves Wood Burning Furnace, Cast Metal, Dover, Ohio	5.50
Advertising, Southern Fruit Julep, 5-Year Calendar, Glass, c.1927, 1 3/8 x 4 x 3 In.	360.00
Advertising, Stuart Bros., Blank Book Manufacture's, Philadelphia, 4 x 2 1/2 In.	45.00
Advertising, Tremble & Welcher Coal Company, Glass, N.J., 1 x 4 x 2 1/2 In.	195.00
Advertising, Victor Spring Beds, Noiseless, Will Never Sag, Glass, 4 x 2 1/2 x 1 In.	80.00
Apple, New England Glass Co., Rose To Off-White, Round Base, 2 5/8 x 3 5/8 In.	1045.00
Ayotte, Bird, American Redstart, Tiger Lilies, Opaque White Ground, Signed, 1986	980.00
Bacchus, Millefiori, Pastel Canes, Cogwheels, Blue, White, c.1850, 3 1/4 In.	6900.00
Bohemian, Complex Millefiori, Canes, Pink, Blue, Green, Red, Yellow, 2 5/8	800.00
Boston & Sandwich, Poinsettia, Petals, 3 Leaves, c.1880, 2 1/8 x 3 1/8 In.	560.00
Bottle, Green, Large Flower Centered, 7 Layers Of Bubbles, England, 4 3/4 In.	300.00
Broadmoor, Scarab, Ivory Semimatte Glaze, Stamped, 4 In.	105.00
Caithness, Faceted, Cane Rings, Pink Flowers, Leaves, Fuchsia, Scotland, 3 In.	145.00
Clematis Blossom, Veined Petals, Leaves, Stem, Star Cut Base, 2 1/8 x 3 In.	940.00
Clichy, 3 Flower, Pink, Red Blue, Stems Ties With Ribbon, c.1850, 3 1/4 In.	6325.00
Clichy, Interlacing Garlands, Millefiori Canes, Red Ground, c.1850, 3 In.	1380.00
Clichy, Interlacing Garlands, Pink & Green Canes, Moss Ground, c.1850, 2 1/2 In.	3910.00
Clichy, Millefiori, Large Center Cane, 6 Millefiori Circlets, Rose, 3 In.	1550.00
Clichy, Millefiori, Pastry Mold Canes, c.1850, 1 3/4 In.	489.00
Clichy, Mushroom, Concentric Canes, Double Overlay, c.1850, 2 3/4 In.	7480.00

Clichy, Pansy, Purple, Yellow, Bud, Green Stem, Leaves, c.1850, 3 In. 1265.00
Clichy, Rose, Open Concentric Millefiori, 2 1/8 In. 460.00
Clichy, Sodden Snow, Pink Rods, Canes, Latticinio, Ground, White, c.1850, 2 3/4 In. 4600.00
Clichy, Swirl, Green, White, Blue & White Center Cane, c.1850, 3 1/8 In. 3450.00
Clichy, Swirl, Purple, Pink, White, Pastry Mold Center, c.1850, 3 In. 2990.00
Clichy, Swirl, Turquoise, White, Pink Center Cane, c.1850, 2 1/2 In. 750.00
Clichy, Trefoil Garland, Rose, 3 1/16 In. . . . . *Illus* 2750.00
Cristal D'Albert, Douglas MacArthur, White, Green Ground, Box, 3 In. 176.00
Crown, Monkey, 8 Millefiori Clusters, Bohemia, 2 5/8 In. 3625.00
Czechoslovakian, 3 Lowers, 2 Pink, 1 Purple, Long Green Stems, 3 5/8 In. 250.00
Czechoslovakian, 5 Multicolored Flowers, Green, Blue, Red, Pink Ground, 4 In. 250.00
Czechoslovakian, High-Domed, Cobalt Blue Flower, Red, Black Ribbons, 2 7/8 In. 180.00
Dogwood Blossom, Leaves, Cobalt Blue Ground, 3 In. 1035.00
Figural, Black Boy's Head, Open Mouth, Bronze, c.1900, 3 In. 90.00
Floral Garland, Blue, Green, Red, White, Cinquefoil Design, 2 1/8 x 3 In. 645.00
Franklin Mint, Sulfide, Jean Jacques Rousseau, Burgundy, Signed, 1974, 2 3/4 In. 29.00
Franklin Mint, Sulphide, Thomas Jefferson, Cobalt Ground, Signed, 1974, 2 3/4 In. 35.00
G. Jones, Orient & Flume, Dogwood, Flowers, Branches, c.1975, 2 3/4 In. 175.00
Gillinder & Sons, Millefiori, Concentric, Red, White, Green, Blue, c.1861-1871, 3 In. . . . 2300.00
Grubb, 1 Blue Flower, Blue Bud, 2 Orange Flowers, Leaves, 3 In. 200.00
Grubb, Green Grape Clusters, Signed, 1991, 3 1/8 In. 690.00
Grubb, Purple, White Orchid, 2 Yellow Buds, Green Leaves, 1986, 3 In. 275.00
Kaziun, Morning Glory, Pink, On White Trellis, Cobalt Ground, Signed, 2 15/16 In. 978.00
Kaziun, Pedestal, Flower, Leaves, Cobalt Blue Aventurine Ground, 2 1/8 In. 400.00
Kaziun, Pedestal, Flower, Leaves, Green Aventurine Ground, 2 In. 290.00
Kaziun, Red, White & Yellow Flowers, Leaves, Gold Bee, 2 1/4 In. 575.00
Kaziun III, Red Poinsettia, Green Leaves, 2 1/8 In. 230.00
Kaziun Jr., Pedestal, Amethyst & White Spider Lily, Yellow Ground, 2 In. 290.00
Kaziun Jr., Pedestal, Amethyst & Yellow Spider Lily, Blue Ground, 2 In. 460.00
Kaziun Jr., Pedestal, Orange & Yellow Spider Lily, Blue Ground, 2 In. 518.00
Lundberg, 2-Petaled Flowers, Leaves, Opalescent Butterfly, Lundberg, 2 In. 230.00
Lundberg Studios, Jonquil, Pink & White Flowers, Leaves, 1990, 3 In. 460.00
Lundberg Studios, Salazar, Lamp Worked Rose, LS 90, 1991, 3 In. 200.00
Marble, Rectangular, Plum Branch, Leather Case, c.1900, 7 1/4 x 4 7/8 In. 235.00
Millefiori, Faceted, Red, White, Blue Canes, Concentric Circle, 1 5/8 x 3 In. 295.00
Millefiori, Pink & White Muslin Ground, Bohemia, 2 1/8 In. 865.00
Millville, Motto, Clasped Hands, Word Friendship, Blue Letters, 3 1/2 In. 500.00
Millville, Umbrella, Pedestal, Red, Pink, Blue & Yellow Speckled, 3 3/8 In. 550.00
Mt. Washington, Flowers, Millefiori, Turquoise Berries, c.1870-1890, 3 1/3 In. 6900.00
Mt. Washington, Red Berries, White Blossoms, Teal Leaves, Stems, c.1870-1890, 4 In. . . . 5520.00
New England Glass Co., Buttercup, White, Yellow, Bud, Jasper, Pink, 2 3/4 In. 2070.00
New England Glass Co., Cog Canes, Hollow, Clusters, Blue Carpet, 2 3/4 In. 4600.00
New England Glass Co., Concentric Millefiori, Blue, White, Pink, Green, 2 1/2 In. 690.00
New England Glass Co., Millefiori, Horse & Riders, 2 3/4 In. 345.00
New England Glass Co., Millefiori, Spoke, Canes, Sloppy Latticinio, 2 3/54 In. 403.00
New England Glass Co., Nosegay, Millefiori, 4 Green Leaves, 2 1/2 In. 1150.00

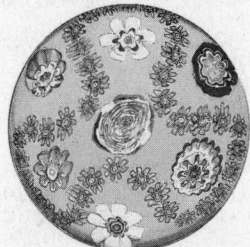

Paperweight, Clichy, Trefoil
Garland, Rose,
3 1/16 In.

Paperweight, St. Louis, Apple,
Cherries, Pears, Latticinio Basket
Ground, 3 3/16 In.

Paperweight, Wm. J. Daly To Jennie
A. Daly, Frit, American,
3 1/4 In.

New England Glass Co., Pink Pompon, Bud, Swirling White Latticinio Ground 3450.00
New England Glass Co., Poinsettia, Purple, Swirling, White Latticinio Ground, 3 In. 1380.00
New England Glass Co., Posy, Triple Garland, White Latticinio Ground, 2 1/2 In. 1840.00
Olympics, 1936, Berlin, Relay Runner, Rings, Bronze, 3 3/4 In. 240.00
Olympics, 1952, Helsinki, Medal Form, Gold Plated Bronze, 2 1/4 In. 127.00
Olympics, 1976, Winter, Innsbruck, Crystal, Swarovsky, 4 In. 115.00
Perthshire, Blue Gentian, Encircled By Millefiori Garland, 1981, 2 3/4 In. 110.00
Perthshire, Dragonfly, Bouquet, Latticinio-Winged, Hovering, Flowers, 1974, 3 In. 400.00
Perthshire, Faceted, Double Cut Overlay, Millefiori, Pond, 1974, 2 7/8 In. 345.00
Perthshire, Flower, Green Leaves, Latticinio Ground, 2 3/4 In. 185.00
Perthshire, Pink Flower, Red & White Double Overlay, White Latticinio Ground 400.00
Roman Coliseum, Marble, Black, Micro Mosaic, 1800s, 4 1/2 In. 230.00
Rosenfeld, Blue & White Flowers, Pink Rose, 1987, 3 In. 201.00
Rosenfeld, Dragonfly, Blue Flower, Red Footed Base, Signed, 2 1/2 In. 250.00
St. Louis, Apple, Cherries, Pears, Latticinio Basket Ground, 3 3/16 In. .... *Illus* 1320.00
St. Louis, Crown, Gold Aventurine, Blue, White, Latticinio Twists, c.1850, 2 3/4 In. 5645.00
St. Louis, Dahlia, Pink, Yellow Cane Center, Star-Cut Base, c.1850, 2 1/2 In. 1380.00
St. Louis, Dahlia, Yellow, Orange, Brown Stripes, Star-Cut Base, c.1850, 2 1/2 In. 4025.00
St. Louis, End Of Day, Scrambled, Silhouette Canes, c.1850, 2 3/4 In. 1840.00
St. Louis, Fruit Bouquet, 3 Pears, 4 Cherries, Latticinio Basket, 3 In. 575.00
St. Louis, Fuchsia, Buds, Twisted Orange Stem, Latticinio Ground, c.1850, 2 3/4 In. ... 3220.00
St. Louis, Marbrie, Blue, Green, White, Signed, SL, 1971 .... 575.00
St. Louis, Marbrie, Red, White, Green, Center, Blue, c.1850, 3 In. 6900.00
St. Louis, Mixed Fruit, Latticinio Ground, c.1850, 2 2/3 In. 800.00
St. Louis, Nosegay, Millefiori Canes, 5 Green Leaves, 2 3/8 In. 290.00
St. Louis, Pattern Millefiori, Green, Pin, Blue, White, 2 3/8 In. 290.00
St. Louis, Pink Double Clematis, Green Aventurine Ground, c.1850, 3 In. 4600.00
St. Louis, Pompon, White, Bud, Swirling Salmon Latticinio Ground, c.1850, 3 In. 4830.00
St. Louis, Posy, Garland, Red Flower, Translucent Red Ground, c.1850, 2 3/4 In. 4830.00
Stankard, Bouquet, 2 Roses, Yellow Foxglove, Signed, 1978 .... 1035.00
Stankard, Encased Flamework Botanical, Flowers, Berries, 3 7/8 In. 1530.00
Stankard, Encased Lampwork Orchid, 1982, 3 In. 1410.00
Stankard, Rose, 2 Pink Flowers, Leaves, 1924, 3 1/8 In. 1265.00
Sulphide, 3-D, Turkey, Spattered Ground, Bohemia, 3 1/4 x 3 In. 115.00
Sulphide, Empress Marie-Louise, Clear Ground, c.1850, 2 1/2 In. 345.00
Sulphide, Florida Singing Tower, Glass, Color Photograph, 3 1/4 In. 33.00
Sulphide, Louis Kossuth, Inscribed, Ex-Governor Of Hungaria, 2 5/8 In. 250.00
Taylors, Anchor, Dreadnought, Nickel Plate, Metal, 4 x 7 In. 95.00
The Hope Of Our Country, Wendell L. Willkie, Glass Dome, 3 1/2 In. 86.00
To Mother, Home Sweet Home, Wavy, Multicolored, Frit, American, 3 1/4 In. 150.00
Venetian, Scrambled, Twists, White Latticinio, 3 Piece Gold Veins, 2 7/8 In. 350.00
What Chicken?, Black Boy Hides Chicken Behind Back, 1890s, 4 In. 130.00
Whitefriars, Concentric, Millefiori, Red, White & Blue Canes, 2 3/4 In. 1300.00
Whitefriars, Faceted, Blue, White, Pink Millefiori, Marked, 1970, 3 1/4 In. 290.00
Whitefriars, Faceted, Sunfish Center, Marked, 1975, 3 1/8 In. 290.00
Whittemore, Lilies Of The Valley, Translucent Red Ground, c.1970, 2 1/4 In. 520.00
Whittemore, Pedestal, Blue Crimped Rose, Clear Foot, 3 In. 230.00
Wm. J. Daly To Jennie A. Daly, Frit, American, 3 1/4 In. .... *Illus* 415.00

PAPIER-MACHE is made from paper mixed with glue, chalk, and other
ingredients, then molded and baked. It becomes very hard and can be
painted. Boxes, trays, and furniture were made of papier-mache. Some
of the nineteenth-century pieces were decorated with mother-of-pearl.
Papier-mache is still being used to make small toys, figures, candy
containers, boxes, and other giftwares. Furniture made of papier-
mache is listed in the Furniture category.

Box, Desk, Black Lacquer, Polychrome, Parcel Gilt, c.1865, 5 x 8 3/4 In. 800.00
Case, Painted, 2 Women, White, Purple, Accordion Sides, 4 3/8 x 2 1/4 In. 220.00
Cigar Case, Entrance Into Port Of Boston, Fort Independence 1000.00
Spillholder, Napoleon III, Parcel Gilt, Scarlet Lacquer, 3 1/4 In., Pair 175.00
Stand, Tripod, Tip Top, Black Lacquer, Mother-Of-Pearl Inlay, 19 1/2 In. ...... *Illus* 860.00
Tray, Black Lacquer, Gold Flowers, 1850-1900, 25 In. .... *Illus* 800.00
Tray, Black Lacquer, Mother-Of-Pearl, Polychrome, c.1865, 20 x 30 x 23 In. 800.00

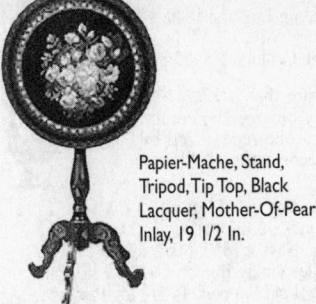

Papier-Mache, Stand,
Tripod, Tip Top, Black
Lacquer, Mother-Of-Pearl
Inlay, 19 1/2 In.

Papier-Mache, Tray, Black Lacquer,
Gold Flowers, 1850-1900, 25 In.

Tray, Black Lacquer, Parcel Gilt, Vine Border, England, c.1865, 21 x 31 1/2 In.	1090.00
Tray, Black Lacquer, Stencil, Flowers, Leaves, Butterflies, 23 x 31 In.	715.00
Tray, Chinoiserie Decor, Oval, Gilt Bronze Handles, Victorian, c.1870, 25 1/2 In.	920.00
Tray, Flower Spray, Gilt Border, Oval, Victorian, c.1865, 21 x 30 x 24 In.	375.00
Tray, Serving, Chippendale Shape, Molded Edges, Flowers, 1 1/2 x 29 1/4 x 22 In.	300.00
Tray, Stand, Black Lacquer, Gilt, Victorian, c.1850, 20 1/2 x 26 1/2 x 20 In.	1060.00

PARASOL, see Umbrella category.

PARIAN is a fine-grained, hard-paste porcelain named for the marble it
resembles. It was first made in England in 1846 and gained in favor in
the United States about 1860. Figures, tea sets, vases, and other items
were made of Parian at many English and American factories.

Bust, Classical Woman, Ivy Wreath In Hair, Round Plinth, 19th Century, 9 x 3 In.	200.00
Bust, Cower, Round Plinth, J & TB, 19th Century, 7 3/4 x 3 In.	80.00
Bust, Harriet, Duchess Of Sutherland, Lace Head Cover, Cameo, 7 5/8 x 2 3/4 In.	200.00
Bust, Napoleon Bonaparte As First Consul, France, 17 1/4 In.	400.00
Bust, Shakespeare, Round Plinth, B & C, 19th Century, 7 3/4 x 2 3/4 In.	90.00
Bust, Socrates, Round Plinth, B & C, 19th Century, 8 1/2 x 2 7/8 In.	99.00
Bust, Woman, Cloth Head Cover, Round Plinth, 9 x 3 1/4 In.	155.00
Bust, Woman, Round Plinth, 19th Century, 8 x 2 3/4 In.	66.00
Bust, Woman, Wreath In Hair, 19th Century, J. Durham, 13 x 4 1/2 In.	470.00
Bust, Woman, Wreath Of Morning Glories In Hair, Round Plinth, 19th Century, 7 x 3 In.	45.00
Bust, Youth, Grape Wreath In Hair, Round Plinth, 8 1/2 x 2 3/4 In.	330.00
Bust, Youth, Round Plinth, J & TB, 19th Century, 7 3/4 x 2 3/4 In.	120.00
Figurine, Classical Nude Woman, Holding Short Staff, 19th Century, 10 x 4 1/4 x 6 In.	120.00
Figurine, Classical Nude Woman, Seated, Holding Shell, 12 x 3 1/2 x 4 1/2 In.	255.00
Figurine, Classical Woman, Draped Gown, Arm Over Head, 1800s, 15 1/4 x 5 3/8 In.	360.00
Figurine, Classical Woman, Gown, Draped Cloak, Holding Dagger, 13 1/2 x 5 In.	130.00
Figurine, Classical Woman, Holding Flowers, Basket At Feet, 19th Century, 17 x 6 In.	330.00
Figurine, Classical Woman, Long Gown, Draped Cloak, 14 x 4 & 14 x 4 1/4 In., Pair	130.00
Figurine, Homer, Partially Draped Male & Youths, Oval Base, c.1870, 13 1/2 In.	999.00
Figurine, Man On Rock, Caduceus On Ground, 19th Century, 18 x 6 1/2 x 12 In.	880.00
Figurine, Milton, Leaning On Pedestal, Stack Of Books, England, c.1870, 14 In.	560.00
Figurine, Nude Male Athlete, Stretching, 22 1/2 x 15 1/2 In.	345.00
Figurine, Nude Woman, Arm Raised, Holding Gown, 19th Century, 14 x 4 x 4 1/4 In.	360.00
Figurine, Nude Woman, Draped, Reclining On Rock, Shells, 19th Century, 6 x 4 x 9 In.	210.00
Figurine, Nude Woman, Playing Musical Instrument, 11 1/2 x 5 x 7 1/2 In.	120.00
Figurine, Nude Woman, Rising From Cattails, Urn, 19th Century, 14 1/4 x 4 1/2 In.	880.00
Figurine, Woman, Draped Gown, Holding Ewer, 19th Century, 24 x 8 In.	275.00
Group, 2 Men Laughing, 1 Seated, 1 Reclining, 19th Century, 9 x 7 x 11 In.	210.00
Group, Classical Man & Woman, Walk Arm In Arm, England, c.1870, 18 3/4 In.	765.00
Group, Homer, Partially Draped Men & Youths, England, c.1860, 13 1/2 In.	1175.00
Group, Wrestlers, 2 Nude, Muscular Men, 15 1/4 x 17 In.	1150.00
Hand, Male, Gesturing, White, England, 10 In.	200.00
Pitcher, Cabinet, Porcelain, Morning Glories, c.1851, 7 In.	175.00
Pitcher, Cream, Imp Face, Embossed Grapes & Vines, 19th Century, 4 1/2 x 2 3/8 In.	77.00
Plate Set, Strawberries, Grapes, Leaves, Blossoms, Medium Blue, 8 1/4 In., 6 Piece	35.00

Stein, Germania Scene, Relief, Inlaid Lid, Man Holding Target, c.1840, 1/2 Liter 360.00
Teapot, Cover, Ribbed, Blue Greek Key, 19th Century, 5 1/2 x 2 5/8 In. 55.00
Wall Shelf, Woman's Face Bracket, Cornucopia, 19th Century, 5 x 4 3/8 x 4 3/4 In. 77.00

PARIS, Vieux Paris, or Old Paris, is porcelain ware that is known to
have been made in Paris in the eighteenth or early nineteenth century.
These porcelains have no identifying mark but can be recognized by
the whiteness of the porcelain and the lines and decorations. Gold dec-
oration is often used.

Basket, Reticulated, Footed, Navette Form, Blue Banding, c.1815, 8 x 13 x 6 3/4 In. 690.00
Basket, White & Gold, Round, Footed, 19th Century, 8 x 9 In. 375.00
Bottle, Leaf Stopper, 12-Sided Body, Flower Sprays, Nast, c.1850, 5 1/2 x 5 In. 690.00
Bowl, Vegetable, Cover, Round, Scrolled Leaf Handle, Vining Border, 7 1/2 x 9 In., Pair .   400.00
Candlestick, Man & Woman, 18th Century Costume, Leaf Support, 14 1/2 In., Pair 230.00
Candy Jar, Cover, Footed, Mask Head Side Handles, 2 Floral Wreaths, Souvenir, 8 In. . . .   145.00
Centerpiece, Reticulated, Cobalt Blue, White, Flared Lip, c.1865, 16 x 14 1/2 In. 1955.00
Compote, Gilt Decoration, Reticulated Bowl, Wavy Rim, Stem, Scroll Feet, c.1840, 10 In.   405.00
Cream Pot, Cover, Strawberry, Grapes, Rococo, Footed, c.1885, 4 1/4 In., 6 Piece 290.00
Garniture Set, White, Gold, Reticulated, Basket, c.1865, 9 1/2 x 8 1/4 In., 3 Piece 1150.00
Jardiniere, Pate-Sur-Pate Style Exotic Birds, Teal Cartouche, Puce Ground, 11 In. 300.00
Pastille Burner, Seated Knight, Seated Lady, 16th Century Dress, 10 x 7 x 6 In., Pair 575.00
Pastry Stand, Gilt, Multicolored, Jacob Petit, c.1835, 11 x 9 In. 3910.00
Pitcher, Flower Bouquets, Hand Painted, Gilt Highlights, 10 x 8 x 5 1/2 In. 250.00
Plate, Dessert, Pink Border, Adventures Of Eros Scenes, c.1815, 8 5/8 In., 6 Piece 1495.00
Platter, Parcel Gilt, Gilt Bands, Multicolored Flowers, Clipped Corners, c.1875, 11 3/8 In.   105.00
Pot De Creme, Peach Band, Flowers, Sprigs, Acorn Finials, Gilt, Mid 1800s, 8 Piece 630.00
Pot De Creme, Stand, Service For 12 . . . .   3220.00
Scent Bottle, Polychrome Decoration, Stopper 60.00
Scent Bottle, Square, Blue Cartouches, White Field, 4 1/2 x 4 1/4 x 4 1/4 In., Pair 635.00
Sweetmeat Basket, Tulip Shape, Rococo Base, Jacob Petit, c.1835, 3 1/4 In. 805.00
Tazza, Porcelain, White, Turquoise, Gold, Landscape Scenes, 1850s, Pair 575.00
Toiletry Set, 19 In. 1600.00
Urn, Cover, Blue, Fluted Body, Ormolu Pinecone Finials, c.1900, 15 In., Pair 1955.00
Urn, Hand Painted, Figures, Rustic Setting, Grotesque Head Mounts, 7 3/4 In., Pair 358.00
Urn, Landscape, Rustic Buildings, River Scenes, c.1860, 11 3/8 In., Pair 920.00
Urn, Pedestal Base, Hand Painted Flowers, Raspberry & Gilt Borders, 12 3/4 In. 825.00
Urn, Renaissance Style Figures, Bleu Celeste Ground, 23 In. 3470.00
Vase, Barnyard Scenes, Flowers, Blue Ground, 2 Handles, Lamp Mounted, 19 In., Pair . . .   800.00
Vase, Birds, Butterflies, 14 In., Pair 2390.00
Vase, Black & Gilt Leaf Swags, Turquoise Ground, 15 3/4 In., Pair 598.00
Vase, Cornucopia, Flower Garlands, Jacob Petit, c.1835, 4 1/2 x 3 x 2 1/4 In., Pair 1380.00
Vase, Egg Shape, Angel Handles, Classical Design, Flowers, c.1815, 15 1/4 x 6 1/2 x 8 In.   2990.00
Vase, Egg Shape, Tooled Gold Neck, Handles, Early 1800s, 13 1/2 x 7 x 4 In., Pair 520.00
Vase, Garniture, 2 Winged Nike Handles, Portrait Reserves, Gilt, c.1815, 18 In., Pair 3450.00
Vase, Garniture, Flared, Sylvan Landscape, Hound, Turkey, Fox, c.1865, 12 1/2 In., Pair . .   1610.00
Vase, Garniture, Pyriform, Noblewoman Portrait, Marble Base, Green Ground, 8 In., Pair .   1495.00
Vase, Landscape Medallions, Painted, Gilt, 11 In., Pair 285.00
Vase, Noble Woman, Gold, Urn Shape, Marble Base, 1800-1825, 8 In., Pair . . . . *Illus*   1495.00
Vase, Painted, Gold Trim, Flared Octagonal Rim, 4-Footed Base, Gargoyles, 5 1/2 x 3 In. .   140.00

Paris, Vase, Noble
Woman, Gold, Urn
Shape, Marble Base,
1800-1825, 8 In., Pair

Pearlware, Jug, Boxing
Scene, Flowers, Transfer,
Aynsley, 1824-1825, 9 In.

Vase, Portrait, Cerulean Ground, Gilt Framed Oval, Egyptian Girl, c.1880, 13 In. 175.00
Vase, Posy, Open Rose, Jacob Petit, c.1865, 5 1/4 In., Pair 1380.00

PATE-DE-VERRE is an ancient technique in which glass is made by blending and refining powdered glass of different colors into molds. The process was revived by French glassmakers, especially Galle, around the end of the nineteenth century.

Figure, Grasshopper, Berries, Leaves, Beige, 1 1/2 x 2 3/4 In. 259.00
Paperweight, 2 Butterflies On Cube, Amber, Brown Edges, Signed, 2 x 2 In. 3000.00
Sculpture, Grasshopper, Atop Berries & Flower, Beige, 1 1/2 x 2 3/4 In. 255.00
Sculpture, Woman, Seated, Yellow, Aqua Base, Impressed, Despret, 5 1/2 In. 2415.00
Tile, Scarab Beetle, On Flower, Blue, Green, Painted Yellow, 2 1/4 x 2 1/4 In. 520.00

PATE-SUR-PATE means paste on paste. The design was made by painting layers of slip on the ceramic piece until a relief decoration was formed. The method was developed at the Sevres factory in France about 1850. It became even more famous at the English Minton factory about 1870. It has since been used by many potters to make both pottery and porcelain wares.

Basin, Dragons, Flowers, Blue Ground, Chinese, 1800s, 19 In. 820.00
Brushpot, White On Blue, Cylinder Form, Bird & Flower Design, c.1800, 5 1/2 In. 690.00
Garden Seat, Hexagonal Shape, Birds, Flowers, Blue Ground, 19 1/2 In., Pair 2115.00
Plaque, Cherub Scene, Embossed, Cobalt Blue Ground, Round, 4 1/2 In. 100.00
Plaque, Nymph, Satyr, Signed, France, 1904, 13 x 5 1/2 In. 359.00
Plaque, Woman, Putti, Frame, Rectangular, France, 1800s, 5 3/4 x 7 1/2 In. 530.00
Plate, Center Flowers, Gilt Accents, 4 Colors, 8 1/2 In. 340.00
Vase, Scenes Of Children, Dogs, Flask Shape, England, 6 1/2 In. 2090.00
Vase, White Slip Ducks, Water Plants, Celadon Ground, Vietnam, 1800s, 18 1/2 In. 120.00
Vase, Woman & Cherub, Medallion, Green, 8 In. 50.00

PATENT MODELS were required as part of a patent application for a United States patent until 1880. In 1926 the stored patent models were sold as a group by the U.S. patent office and individual models are now appearing in the marketplace.

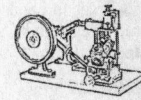

Grain Separator, Patent No. 208146, A.J. Humphrey 4485.00
Lamp, Oil, Vulcanizing, B.W. Franklin, 1863, 4 1/2 In. 633.00
Locomotive & Coal Car, Green, Ben Rhydding, W. Lynch Leeds, 5-In. Gauge 7475.00
Ox Yoke, Mahogany, Brass, Gear Ratchet System, Wooden, 9 x 4 In. 500.00
Steam Road Wagon, Wood, O.C. Harris, c.1879 . . . . 3565.00
Stove, Paperwork, String Tag, R. S. Payne, c.1837, 5 3/4 In. 225.00
Washing Machine, Tiger Maple, Armory Davidson, June 11, 1839 . . . . 4600.00
Washing Machine, Wringer, Cloth Roller, Crank, c.1881, 12 x 12 x 2 In. 275.00
Windmill, No. 207409, G.A. Roland, September 20th, 1881 . . . . 4485.00

PAUL REVERE POTTERY was made at several locations in and around Boston, Massachusetts, between 1906 and 1942. The pottery was operated as a settlement house program for teenage girls. Many pieces were signed *S.E.G.* for Saturday Evening Girls. The artists concentrated on children's dishes and tiles. Decorations were outlined in black and filled with color.

Bowl, Cereal, Cuerda Seca, Ivory Flower Band, Blue Ground, 5 1/2 In. 550.00
Bowl, Geese, Tree Trunks, Green Brown, White, Unglazed Outline, 5 x 11 1/2 In. 575.00
Bowl, Goose, Flying, Trees, Buttercup Yellow Ground, 5 In. 1210.00
Bowl, Green Trees, Landscape, Blue, Unglazed Outline, Squat, 2 3/4 x 6 1/4 In. 1610.00
Bowl, Incised Swan, Mary, Her Bowl, Matte & High Glaze, 5 3/4 In. 880.00
Bowl, Landscape, Trees, Blue Skyline, Cobalt Blue & Teal Bands, 5 In. 715.00
Bowl, Midnight Ride, Pumpkin Brown, Tan Glaze, L. Shapiro, 7 In. 415.00
Bowl, Squirrel, Lavender Gray Ground, Sylvia Louise, 4 3/4 In. 385.00
Bowl, Teal Glaze, Flared & Flattened Rim, E. Geneco, 7 1/2 In. 250.00
Bowl, Tree & Landscape Border, 1913, 10 In. 1725.00
Bowl, Yellow Jonquils, Green Grass, Blue Sky, Unglazed Outline, 8 1/4 In. 1150.00
Bowl, Yellow, White Rim, Marked, 1922, 8 1/2 In. 145.00
Candlestick, Mustard Semimatte Glaze, Marked, 3 x 7 1/2 In., Pair 200.00

Creamer, Duck, Chicory Blue Band, Black Bands, 1915, 3 1/2 In. 715.00
Cup & Saucer, Landscape, Trees, Sun, Blue Sky, Teal Ground, 2 x 5 1/2 In. 415.00
Mug, Rabbit, Chartreuse Ground, Frannie Levine, 1934, 4 3/4 In. 550.00
Pitcher, Green Leaf Band, Blue, White Ground, Marked, 3 1/2 In. 405.00
Pitcher, Milk, Goose, Landscape, Yellow, David, His Jug, Stamped, 4 1/4 In. 805.00
Pitcher, Racing Rabbit, Chartreuse Ground, 4 1/2 In. 825.00
Pitcher, Tree Band, Unglazed Outline, Blue, Beige Ground, Marked 460.00
Plate, 12 Geese, Suzanne, Her Plate, 7 1/2 In. 920.00
Plate, 3 Geese, 5 Sets, Olive Caramel Glaze, Black Band, 7 1/2 In. 415.00
Plate, 4 Chicks, Rose, Blue & Green Border, Phyllis Adrienne, Early 1900s, 6 1/4 In. 940.00
Plate, Brown & Green Trees, Mountains, Yellow & Ivory Ground, 6 1/4 In. 490.00
Plate, Brown Trees, Yellow & Ivory Ground, 6 1/4 In. ....550.00 to 635.00
Plate, Chickens & Chicks, Ivory & Blue Ground, 6 1/2 In. 865.00
Plate, Duck, Green Hillside, Buttercup Yellow, Black Bands, 6 1/4 In. 525.00
Plate, Landscape, Painted, Blue Matte Glaze, 6 In. 635.00
Plate, Rabbit On Green Hillside, Blue Clouds & Band, 1939, 7 1/2 In. 770.00
Plate, Rabbits, Blue & Ivory Ground, 6 1/2 In. 575.00
Plate, Swans, Etched, Alternating Flowers, Yellow Bands, 1913, 6 1/4 In. 1045.00
Plate, Yellow Chicks, Ivory Ground, 6 1/4 In. 690.00
Tile, Paul Revere On Horseback, c.1926, 4 1/2 In. 575.00
Tile, Tree & Landscape, 5 1/2 In. 910.00
Trivet, Geometric, Arts & Crafts Design, Green, Blue, 5 1/4 In. 575.00
Trivet, Landscape, Mustard Matte Glaze, 5 1/2 In. 1035.00
Trivet, Medallion, Stylized Tree, Cafe-Au-Lait, Ink Stamp, Paper Label, 5 1/2 In. 490.00
Tumbler, White Lotus Blossom Band, Blue & White Ground, 4 In. 315.00
Vase, Amber, Green, Blue, Mottled Semimatte Glaze, Baluster, 1920, 5 3/4 In. 290.00
Vase, Blue, Green Drip, 10 In. 985.00
Vase, Lotus Blossoms, Blue, Closed In Rim, 1913, 5 1/4 x 7 In. 1150.00
Vase, Steel Blue Glaze, Tapered, Rolled Over Mouth, 9 3/4 In. 275.00
Vase, Trees In Landscape, Mustard Matte Ground, Swollen, 4 1/2 In. 1530.00
Vase, Trees, Landscape, Unglazed Outline, Closed In Rim, 1922, 5 3/4 x 4 1/2 In. 2185.00
Vase, Wind Blown Tulips, Flaring, 4 1/2 In. 1265.00

PEACHBLOW glass was made by several factories beginning in the
1880s. New England peachblow is a one-layer glass shading from red
to white. Mt. Washington peachblow shades from pink to bluish-white.
Hobbs, Brockunier and Company of Wheeling, West Virginia, made
coral glass that they marketed as Peach Blow. It shades from yellow to
peach and is lined with white glass. Reproductions of all types of
peachblow have been made. Related pieces may be listed under
Gunderson and Webb Peachblow.

Bowl, Folded, Ruffled Edge, 4 x 5 1/2 In. 145.00
Bowl, Rigaree Collar, Scalloped Rim, Mt. Washington, 3 3/4 x 4 1/4 In. 2750.00
Bowl, Ruffled Edge, 3 x 9 1/4 In. 300.00
Bowl, Tricornered, Pink Shaded To Blue, Pontil, Mt.Washington, 2 x 3 In. 690.00
Bowl, Wild Rose, Crimped Edge, Satin, New England, 3 1/2 In. 175.00
Cruet, Bulbous, Applied Reeded Handle, Hobbs, Brockunier, 5 1/2 In. 920.00
Figurine, Pear, New England Glass Company, 5 In. 80.00
Finger Bowl, Glossy, Hobbs, Brockunier, c.1890, 4 1/2 x 2 3/4 In. 308.00
Finger Bowl, Ruffled Edge, 2 1/2 x 5 1/2 In. 145.00
Pitcher, Applied Clear Branch Handle, White Interior, 7 In. 150.00
Pitcher, Bulbous, Amber Handle, Hobbs, Brockunier, 7 1/2 In. 1438.00
Pitcher, Hobbs, Brockunier, 5 3/8 In. 1065.00
Pitcher, Squared Rim, Amber Handle, Hobbs, Brockunier, 4 5/8 In. 690.00
Pitcher, Wheeling Drape, Pink, White, Reeded Handle, Hobbs, Brockunier, 7 3/8 In. 288.00
Salt & Pepper, Bulbous, Hobbs, Brockunier, 4 In. 230.00
Spooner, Crimped Edge, 4 1/2 In. 540.00
Sugar & Creamer, Amber Handle, Silver-Plated Cover, Stand, Hobbs, Brockunier 3165.00
Tumbler, Enameled Flowers, Gold Rim, Mt.Washington, 3 3/4 In. 2300.00
Tumbler, Hobbs, Brockunier, 3 5/8 In. 260.00
Tumbler, Satin Opal, Mt.Washington, 3 3/4 In. 1300.00
Vase, Double Gourd, Flowers, Mt. Washington, 8 In. 6050.00
Vase, Double Gourd, Hobbs, Brockunier, 7 1/2 In. 2875.00

Vase, Gourd, 10 In.	180.00
Vase, Jack-In-The-Pulpit, Crimped Edge, Glossy, New England, 6 3/4 In.	863.00
Vase, Jack-In-The-Pulpit, Ruffled Edge, Mt. Washington, 7 In.	2420.00
Vase, Lily, Petaled Rim, Shaded Pink To Blue, Mt. Washington, 9 3/4 In.	2475.00
Vase, Lily, Shaded Fuchsia To Opal, Ruffled Top, Tapered, Disc, New England, 12 In.	633.00
Vase, Lily, Wild Rose, Disc Foot, New England, 5 1/2 In.	430.00
Vase, Lily, Wild Rose, Ruffled Edge, New England, 9 In.	750.00
Vase, Morgan, Amber Dragon Base, Hobbs, Brockunier	4000.00 to 4600.00
Vase, Ruffled Tricornered Rim, 3 1/4 In.	750.00
Vase, Square Mouth, Hobbs, Brockunier, 3 3/4 In.	800.00
Vase, Stick, Glossy, Hobbs, Brockunier, 11 In.	1300.00
Vase, Stick, Glossy, Hobbs, Brockunier, 10 In.	690.00
Vase, Stick, Hobbs, Brocknuier, 9 In.	1380.00
Water Set, Quatrefoil Top, Hobbs, Brockunier, 7 Piece	4750.00

PEANUTS is the title of a comic strip created by cartoonist Charles M. Schulz (1922-2000). The strip, drawn by Schulz from 1950 to 2000, features a group of children, including Charlie Brown and his sister Sally, Lucy Van Pelt and her brother Linus, Peppermint Patty, and Pig Pen, and an imaginative and independent beagle named Snoopy. The Peanuts gang has also been featured in books, television shows, and a Broadway musical.

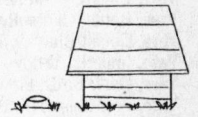

Bank, Snoopy On Doghouse, Whitman Candies, 6 1/4 In.	12.00
Snoopy, Astronaut, United Features, Box, 1969, 9 1/2 In.	390.00
Snoopy, Flying Ace, Jointed Arms & Legs, Rubber Head, Rotating Ears, 1966, 7 In.	75.00
Snoopy, Rubber Head, Jointed Arms & Legs, Rotating Ears, Plastic Bag, 1966, 7 In.	47.00
Tote Bag, Snoopy Hugging Woodstock, Love, Canvas, 2 Sides, c.1965, 12 x 13 In.	33.00
Toy Box, Snoopy On Doghouse, Fiber Board, Tension Latches, 1965, 16 In.	36.00

PEARL items listed here are made of the natural mother-of-pearl from shells. Such natural pearl has been used to decorate furniture and small utilitarian objects for centuries. The glassware known as mother-of-pearl is listed by that name. Opera glasses made with natural pearl shell are listed under Opera Glasses.

Cigarette Case, Lighter, Flowers, Birds, Seated Black Poodles, Evans	45.00
Frame, Photograph, Pieced, Edwardian Style, 8 1/4 x 6 1/4 In.	200.00
Knife, Fruit, Gold Blade, F.G. Gavet, c.1800, 8 In., 12 Piece	2070.00

PEARLWARE is an earthenware made by Josiah Wedgwood in 1779. It was copied by other potters in England. Pearlware is only slightly different in color from creamware and for many years collectors have confused the terms. Wedgwood pieces are listed in the Wedgwood category in this book. Most pearlware with mocha designs is listed under Mocha.

Pearl

Bowl, Carnation, Red, Green, Blue, Black, 12 1/2 In.	450.00
Bowl, Flower Vines, Swags On Interior Rim, 4 1/4 In.	865.00
Bowl, Paneled, Flowers, 19th Century, 2 3/4 x 6 In.	110.00
Bust, George III, c.1790, 12 1/2 In.	6400.00
Figurine, Child, England, c.1900, 8 In.	295.00
Figurine, Diana, Yellow, Green, Orange, Brown, c.1790, 11 3/4 In.	978.00
Jug, Boxing Scene, Flowers, Transfer, Aynsley, 1824-1825, 9 In. *Illus*	2875.00
Jug, Pink Luster, Green, Embossed Leaves, Ribbed Panels, 5 3/8 x 3 1/4 x 3 3/4 In.	220.00
Pitcher, Flowers, Gold, Blue, Multicolored, Bulbous, 8 In.	440.00
Pitcher, Odd Fellows, Silver Luster, God Is Our Guide, Hand Painted Transfers, 7 In.	405.00
Plate, Eagle, Spread Wings, Multicolored, 7 In.	506.00
Plate, Flower, Brown, Green, Sprig & Leaf Border, 9 1/4 In.	70.00
Plate, Flowers, Embossed Leaves, 19th Century, 8 In.	45.00
Platter, Lakeside Chinese Pavilions, Blue, Stand, c.1865, 19 x 21 In.	405.00
Platter, London Zoo, Zoological Garden, P.W. & Co., 14 3/4 x 17 3/4 In.	865.00
Platter, Oriental Village, Waterway, Boats, Geometric Border, Butterflies, 16 x 21 In.	489.00
Platter, Zoological Garden, Blue & White, c.1845, 17 3/4 In.	860.00
Sauceboat, Blue Feather, 19th Century, 4 x 3 1/2 x 7 1/4 In.	80.00
Shaker, Blue Snowflake, Bulbous Body, Flared Base, Band On Shoulder, Rim	250.00

Sugar, Cover, Blue On White, Leaves, Vine, 19th Century, 4 1/2 x 4 5/8 In. 210.00
Sugar, Reeding, Basket Weave, 4 Medallions, Blue Rope Twist Trim, 5 x 5 3/4 In. 60.00
Teapot, Stars, Leaves, Swags, Molded, Swan Finial, 7 1/4 In. 259.00

PEKING GLASS is a Chinese cameo glass first made popular in the eighteenth century. The Chinese have continued to make this layered glass
in the old manner, and many new pieces are now available that could
confuse the average buyer.

Bowl, Brick Red, Handles, 19th Century, 6 1/2 In. 60.00
Bowl, Chrysanthemums, Lotus, Mustard Yellow, 1736-1795, 6 1/2 In. 1115.00
Bowl, Leaves, Imperial Yellow, Square, Late 1800s, 4 1/2 In. 290.00
Bowl, Ruby Cut To White, Longevity Symbols, Late 1800s, 6 1/2 In., Pair 765.00
Bowl, Yellow, Flowers, Leaves, Imperial, Late 19th Century, 6 1/2 In. 540.00
Jar, Cover, Rose Snowflakes, Green Overlay, Panels, Globe Shape, 8 In., Pair 2300.00
Jar, Dresser, Green Cut To White Beehive, Tapered, Squat, Early 1900s, 3 1/2 In., Pair . . . 69.00
Vase, Blue & White, Birds & Flowers, 9 1/2 In. 259.00
Vase, Bottle, Garnet Red, 1736-1795, 7 In. 175.00
Vase, Cobalt Blue, Cylindrical, 19th Century, 4 1/4 In. 235.00
Vase, Imperial Yellow, Ku Shape, Silver Inlay, 19th Century, 9 1/2 In., Pair 1725.00
Vase, Oval, Birds, Flowering Trees, 19th Century, 5 1/2 In., Pair 470.00
Vase, Pear Shape, Birds & Flowering Trees, c.1800, 7 1/2 In. 999.00
Vase, Red & White, Egrets Among Lily Pads, Lotus Flowers, 8 In. 210.00
Vase, Red Over Yellow, Flowering Vines, Flared, Wood Stand, 4 1/2 In. 1725.00
Vase, Translucent Lavender, Square, Petals, c.1910, 7 3/4 In., Pair 1840.00
Vase, White, Carved Cobalt Blue, 20th Century, 7 1/4 In., Pair 3000.00

PELOTON glass is a European glass with small threads of colored glass
rolled onto the surface of clear or colored glass. It is sometimes called
spaghetti, or shredded coconut, glass. Most pieces found today were
made in the nineteenth century.

Butter, Cover, Chipped Ice, Pink, Yellow, Blue Opalescent Threads, Knob, 6 1/2 x 9 In. . . . 470.00
Rose Bowl, Aqua, Ribbed, Red, Yellow, White, Blue Threads, Crimped Rim, 2 1/2 x 3 In. . . 417.00
Vase, White, Pink, Blue, Green, Yellow Threads, Ribbed, 4 1/2 In. 230.00

PENS replaced hand-cut quills as writing instruments in 1780 when the
first steel pen point was made in England. But it was 100 years before
the commercial pen was a common item. The fountain pen was
invented in the 1830s but was not made in quantity until the 1880s. All
types of old pens are collected. Float pens that feature small objects
floating in a liquid as part of the handle are popular with collectors.

PEN, 18K Gold, Tennis Racket Shaped Clip, Tiffany, Pouch 206.00
Ballpoint, T-Shaped Clip, Sterling Silver, Tiffany & Co. 125.00
Dip, Oliver Hotel, Cobalt Blue Glass, Sterling Silver Inlay, 3 3/4 In. 55.00
Dip, Telescopic, Engraved Chevrons, Gold Filled, Victorian 150.00
Float, Angel & Clown Fish, Aquarium 3.25
Float, Ballerina, Moves Across Stage, Edgar Degas 4.00
Float, Boy & Girl, Snuggle In Park 3.75
Float, Car, Drive In Movie, T-Rex Chases Girl Across Screen 4.00
Float, Dragon, Over Castle 3.25
Float, Lobster, Moves Across Ocean Floor 3.25
Float, Meat, 5 Different Cuts 4.00
Float, Merry Christmas, In Different Languages, Elf Pulls Sleigh 3.75
Float, Paris 1886, People Afloat In Sunday In The Park 4.00
Float, Riverboat, On Ohio River, Cincinnati Cityscape 3.25
Float, Skier, Downhill, Dodges Evergreen Trees 4.00
Float, Statue Of Liberty, Uncle Sam, American Flag 4.00
Float, Suicide Blond, Blond Hair Dye Changes Brunette To Blond 4.00
Float, Toothpaste, Toothbrush, Yellow Teeth Turn White 4.00
Fountain, Carter's Inx, Coralite Green, Gold-Filled Trim, 14K Gold Nib, 1930 . . . . 255.00
Fountain, Pelikan, Marbleized Green Barrel, Black Cap, 14K Gold Nib, No. 100 . . . . 190.00
Fountain, Sheaffer, No. 1000, Yellow & Brown Stripe, 14K Gold Nib 70.00
Fountain, Wahl-Eversharp, Doric, Marbleized Green, 12-Sided, 1930s 330.00
Fountain, Wahl-Eversharp, Marbleized Cobalt Blue, 14K Gold Nib 300.00

Fountain, Waterman, Ideal, Filigree, Sterling Silver, 1920s 250.00
Ink, Wood, Canvas Covered, Travel Case, Roll-Up Type, Inscription, Dec. 6, 1862, 10 In. 300.00
Mother-Of-Pearl, Gold Velvet Case, Gold Tip, 8 In. 39.00
PEN & PENCIL, 14K Gold, Inscription, Box, Eversharp Skyline, c.1940, 5 1/4 In. 145.00
  Ertl Employee, 10 Years Of Service, 12K Gold, Cross, Case 75.00
  Gastown, Goldtone Metal, Revolutionary, Case 5.00
  Sheaffer, Balance, Black & Gray Pearlescent Barrel, Case, 1930-1940 .... 150.00
  Yellow Plastic, Amber Caps, Case, 1950s 5.00

PENCILS were invented, so it is said, in 1565. The eraser was not added
to the pencil until 1858. The automatic pencil was invented in 1863.
Collectors today want advertising pencils or automatic pencils of
unusual design. Boxes and sharpeners for pencils are also collected.
Advertising pencils are listed in the Advertising category. Pencil boxes
are listed in the Box category.

PENCIL, Fairchild, Mechanical, Telescoping, 14K Gold, 4 In. 33.00
  Mechanical, Chet Nichols Auto Service, Black Barrel, Redipoint, 4 3/4 In. 5.00
  Mechanical, Frigidaire, General Motors, Twice As Sure, 2 Good Names 12.00
  Mechanical, Gilt Brass, On Neck Chain, 1930-1935, 3 1/4 In. 85.00
  Mechanical, Liberty National Life Insurance, Ivory Barrel, Dor-O-Lite 12.00
  Mechanical, Philco High Fidelity Television, Black & White 15.00
  Mechanical, Phillips 66, Bovina, Texas, White Barrel, Red Trim, 4 3/4 In. 28.00
  Mechanical, Walther League, Marbleized Black & Cream, 3 5/8 In. 30.00
  Mechanical, Zippo, Black, Gold Trim 10.00
  Reddy Kilowatt, Kansas Power & Light, Magic Holetite 13.00
  Victors L'Aperitf Club, Soho, Embossed, Blue, Wood, Triangular Shaft, 1950s 7.00
PENCIL SHARPENER, 1917 Car, Burnished Copper Color, 1970s, 2 7/8 In. 10.00
  Automatic Pencil Sharpening Co., Wooden Base, Iron Wheel, 5 1/2 In. 173.00
  Black Man Head, Large Mouth, Cast Metal, Germany, 1900s, 1 1/2 In. 60.00
  Liberty Bell, Bell Swings, Burnished Copper Color, 2 7/8 In. 10.00
  Specialty Mfg. Co., Decatur, Ill., Cast Iron, 4 In. 115.00
  Steam Locomotive, Wheels Turn, Burnished Copper Color, 3 1/4 In. 10.00
  Tiger, Green Plastic, Japan, 1 1/4 In. 5.00
  Typewriter, Plastic Keys, Burnished Copper Color, 1980s, 1 7/8 In. 8.00

PENNSBURY Pottery worked in Morrisville, Pennsylvania, from 1950   *Pennsbury*
to 1971. Full sets of dinnerware as well as many decorative items were   *Pottery*
made. Pieces are marked with the name of the factory.

  Amish, Pitcher, Milk, Man & Woman, Talking By Fence, 6 1/2 In. 175.00
  Barbershop Quartet, Bowl, Oval 70.00
  Pie Plate, 1930-1950 .... 100.00
  Plaque, Baltimore & Ohio R.R., 1837, Lafayette, 5 3/4 x 8 In. 50.00
  Plaque, Baltimore & Ohio R.R., Veterans, 1955, 5 3/4 x 7 3/4 In. 65.00
  Yellow Rooster, Chamberstick, 5 1/8 In. 40.00
  Yellow Rooster, Creamer, 4 1/2 In. 45.00
  Yellow Rooster, Pitcher, Milk, 7 1/2 In. 150.00
  Yellow Rooster, Tip Tray, 6 x 8 In. 50.00

PEPSI-COLA, the drink and the name, was invented in 1898 but was not
trademarked until 1903. The logo was changed from an elaborate
script to the modern block letters in 1963. Several different logos have
been used. Until 1951, the words *Pepsi* and *Cola* were separated by 2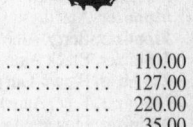
dashes. These bottles are called *double dash.* In 1951 the modern logo
with a single hyphen was introduced. All types of advertising memorabilia are collected, and reproductions are being made.

  Bottle, Escambia Bottling Co., Clear, Crown Top 110.00
  Bottle, Escambia Bottling Co., Ice Blue, 8 1/4 In. 127.00
  Bottle, Hutchinson, Clear, Escambia Bottling Co., Pensacola, Fla., 6 5/8 In. 220.00
  Can, Syrup, Red, White, Blue, No Lid, 17 x 14 In. 35.00
  Carrier, Wooden, 6-Bottle, 1940 .... 125.00
  Carrier, Wooden, 6-Bottle, c.1930 .... 198.00
  Chalkboard, Today's Specials, Tin, Embossed, Painted, 19 x 27 In. 60.00
  Coin-Operated Machine, Vending, Jacobs, Blue, Round Top 1760.00

Cooler, Double Dash, Tome, Embossed, c.1940 .... 990.00
Cooler, Gull Wing, Restored, Heintz Manufacturing, 44 In. 550.00
Cooler, Ice Cold, Sold Here, 5 Cents, Metal Stand, 36 In. 715.00
Dispenser, Syrup, Avon Faience Pottery Co., Tiltonsville, Oh, c.1904, 18 In. 27000.00
Door Push, Have A Pepsi, Yellow, Red, White, Blue, Porcelain 165.00
Door Push, Worth Twice Its Price, Yellow, Tin, c.1930, 3 1/2 x 13 1/2 In. 825.00
Drum, Bulk Syrup, Tin, Red, White, 17 In. 65.00
Figure, Crossing Guard, Sheet Metal, Lithograph, Pepsi Cap Cast Iron Base, 64 In. 300.00 to 465.00
Panel, Light-Up, Vending Machine, Polar Bear, Holding Glass, 1951, 24 x 20 In. 550.00
Record Set, Cardboard Jacket, 1960s, 6 Records 100.00
Sign, 5 Cents, Bottle Shape, Die Cut, Tin Lithograph, 1930s, 29 1/2 x 8 1/8 In. 745.00
Sign, Be Sociable, Cardboard, c.1960, 11 x 28 In. 135.00
Sign, Bigger & Better Reputation, 5 Cents, Paper, Frame, c.1920-1930, 12 x 30 In. 65.00
Sign, Bottle Cap, Enamel Painted, 1964, 60 x 42 In. 415.00
Sign, Bottle Cap, Round, 42 In. 209.00
Sign, Bottle Cap, Tin, Die Cut, Red, White, Blue, 13 1/4 x 13 7/8 In. 385.00
Sign, Bottle, 5 Cents, A Sparkling Beverage, Tin, Die Cut, c.1940, 5 x 45 In. 575.00
Sign, Drink Pepsi-Cola, Tin, Yellow, Red, White, Blue, Bottle Cap, 21 x 26 1/2 In. 240.00
Sign, Light-Up, Cup, Celluloid, Metal Frame, 20 1/2 In. 305.00
Sign, Man Carries Surfboard & 2 6-Packs, Beach, Cardboard, 24 1/2 x 36 In. 39.00
Sign, More Bounce To The Ounce, Tin, 17 1/2 x 47 In. 275.00
Sign, Pepsi Pete Cop, 5 Cent, Cardboard, 17 In. 110.00
Sign, Say Pepsi Please, Metal, 1966, 67 x 36 In. 385.00
Sign, Think Young, Say Pepsi Please, Cardboard Lithograph, Frame, 1960s, 29 In. 20.00
String Holder, Join The Swing, Bigger & Better, 5 Cent, Tin Lithograph 415.00
Thermometer, Double Dot Version, Tin, Lithograph, 27 In. 25.00
Thermometer, Say Pepsi Please, Tin, 9 In. 175.00
Toy, Truck, Bottle Cases, Nylint, 1961 .... 295.00
Toy, Truck, Delivery, Plastic, Marx, c.1950, 7 1/8 In. 150.00
Toy, Truck, Friction, Japan, 1950s, 9 In. 175.00
Tray, Pepsi Bottle Cap, Round, 2 x 13 1/8 In. 130.00
Tumbler, Aquaman, 5 1/8 In., 6 Piece 110.00
Vending Machine, Blue, Round Top, 60 In. 1760.00

PERFUME BOTTLES are made of cut glass, pressed glass, art glass, silver, metal, enamel, and even plastic or porcelain. Although the small bottle to hold perfume was first made before the time of ancient Egypt, it is the nineteenth- and twentieth-century examples that interest today's collector. DeVilbiss Company has made atomizers of all types since 1888 but no longer makes the perfume bottle tops so popular with collectors. These were made from 1920 to 1968. The glass bottle may be by any of many manufacturers even if the atomizer is marked *DeVilbiss*. The word *factice*, which often appears in ads, refers to store display bottles. Glass or porcelain examples may be found under the appropriate name such as Lalique, Czechoslovakia, Glass-Bohemian, etc.

Ahmed Soliman, Lilac, Crystal, Panels, 8-Sided, Stopper, Dabber, c.1930, 4 In. 925.00
Amber Glass, Iridescent Highlights, Stopper, Quezal, 5 In. 575.00
Amethyst, Blown, Bulbous, Tooled Flared Mouth, Pontil, 5 1/8 In. 1008.00
Amethyst, Long Neck, Tooled Lip, 12-Sided, 6 1/2 In. 175.00
Art Deco, Lavender, Diamond Shaped Stopper, 5 1/2 x 2 1/2 x 1 1/4 In. 125.00
Art Deco, Pink, Cut Glass, Clear Stopper, 5 1/2 x 3 x 2 1/2 In. 125.00
Arys, Lilas, Rectangular, Ribs, Stopper, Gaillard, 2 3/4 In. 550.00
Arys, Un Jardin La Nuit, Clear Glass, 8-Point Star Shape, Box, 1928, 3 In. 1000.00
Atomizer, Amethyst, On White, Flowers, Leaves, Stems, Cameo, Galle, 3 3/4 In. 400.00
Atomizer, Berry, Amethyst Over Blue, Cameo, Cameo, Galle, 5 1/2 In. 460.00
Atomizer, Black Amethyst, Steuben, 6 3/4 In. 220.00
Atomizer, Blown-Out Opalescent Swirl Leaf Pattern, Brass Hardware, 4 In. 60.00
Atomizer, Blue, Aurene, Intaglio Cut Flowers, Leaves, Metal Hardware, 9 3/4 In. 1035.00
Atomizer, Flowers, Leaves, Amethyst, On Burnt Orange, Cameo, Galle, 8 In. 600.00
Atomizer, Mulberry, Frosted, Straight Neck, Bulbous Base, Cameo, Richard, 9 In. 550.00
Atomizer, Opal Glass, Ball Shape, Pink, Blue Flowers, Wave Crest, 4 In. 300.00
Atomizer, Opalescent, Cut Glass, Classical Pattern, Blue Base, Fry, 7 1/2 In. 545.00
Atomizer, Ruby Flashed, White Cased, Enamel Painted, 7 In. 120.00

Atomizer, Steel, Rectangular, Round Base, On Stand, c.1930, 4 1/4 In. 1684.00
Atomizer, Stopper, Venetian Glass, 20th Century, 8 In., Pair 140.00
Babani, Pao-Pe, Crystal, Oval, Flowers, Birds, Gilding, Stopper, c.1922, 3 1/2 In. 2020.00
Baccarat, Carafe Shaped, Enameled, Stopper, c.1920, 8 In. 1685.00
Benoit, Lune De Miel, Black Glass, Crescent Stopper, Depinoix, 1926, 4 1/2 In. 5051.00
Bergdorf Goodman, No. 101, Black, Panels, 2 Sections, Depinoix, 1925, 4 1/4 In. 589.00
Blue, Champhored, Embossed Flowers, Tooled Mouth, 4-Sided, 6 1/2 In. 202.00
Blue Aurene, Flame Finial, Signed, Steuben, 10 In. 630.00
Bourjois, Ashes Of Roses, Clear Glass, Rectangular, Plastic Cap, Box, c.1950, 2 In. 168.00
Bourjois, Beau Belle, Clear Glass, Ball Shape, Screw Cap, Brosse, 1949, 2 In. 675.00
Bourjois, Evening In Paris, Cobalt Blue, Stopper, Brosse, c.1927, 2 1/2 In. 673.00
Bourjois, Glamour, Opaque, Oval, Brass Screw Cap, Brosse, Box, 1953, 4 In. 675.00
Bourjois, Kobako, Clear Glass, Disk Shape, Screw Gap, Tassel, Brosse, 1936, 2 In. 465.00
Bourjois, Lilas, Clear Glass, Rectangular, Stopper, Brosse, Box, c.1925, 3 3/4 In. 716.00
Bristol Yellow Glass, Baluster, Pointed Stopper, Stevens & Williams, 8 In. 520.00
Bull's-Eye & Waffle Block, Cut Stopper, Signed Libbey, 5 1/2 In. 75.00
Burner, Christian Dior, Silver, Metal, Louis XVI Style, Engraved, c.1948, 7 In. 340.00
Cameo Glass, Flowers, Leaves, Branches, Blue Glass, Silver Top, England, 4 In. 2015.00
Cameo Glass, Laydown, Flowers, Silver Top, Howell & James Case, 3 3/4 In. 1955.00
Cameo Glass, Laydown, Leaves, Flowers, Silver Cover, 6 In. 2160.00
Cameo Glass, Palms, Butterfly, Silver Cover, 8 In. 1380.00
Cameo Glass, Silver Top, Glass Stopper, Mappin & Webb Case, 9 3/4 In. 4370.00
Caron, L'Infini, Crystal, Round, Flower Stopper, Baccarat, 1925, 3 In. 630.00
Caron, Narcisse Noir, Lentil Shape, Stopper, Narcissus Shape, Box, 1912, 2 In. 673.00
Cherigan, Chance, Black Glass, Horseshoe Shape, Jollivet, Box, 1929, 3 In. 2105.00
Chloe, Frosted Flower-Shape Stopper, 11 In. 175.00
Christian Dior, Diorissimo, Amphora Shape, Stopper, Baccarat, 1956, 8 1/4 In. 5470.00
Christian Dior, Diorissimo, Amphora Shape, Stopper, Baccarat, Box, 1957, 5 In. 590.00
Christian Dior, Diorissimo, Clear, Frosted, Stopper, Baccarat, Box, 1956, 3 In. 295.00
Cintra, Stopper, Steuben Glass, Corning, New York, Late 1920s 2125.00
Citron, White Fronds, Butterfly, Teardrop, Cameo, Sterling Silver Cap, Webb, 4 In. 715.00
City Of Paris, Ah Paris, Frosted, Molded, Stopper, Baccarat, 1924, 6 3/4 In. 2525.00
Clear Glass, Rosaria Stripes, Flower Stopper, Pairpoint, 6 3/4 In. 180.00
Colgate, Egypt, Amphora Shape, Ribs, Stylized Flowers, Stopper, 1923, 5 3/4 In. 335.00
Cologne, 12-Sided, Lavender Blue, Boston & Sandwich Glassworks, 11 1/4 In. 225.00
Cologne, 12-Sided, Sapphire Blue, Tooled, Pontil, Boston & Sandwich, 6 1/4 In. 269.00
Cologne, Citron, Mother-Of-Pearl, Sterling Cap, Stevens & Williams, 8 1/2 In. 1650.00
Cologne, Delieuvin, Eau De Cologne, Clear, Brigantine On Sea, c.1935, 5 In. 340.00
Cologne, Enameled Zinnias, Signed, Moser, 3 1/2 In. 115.00
Cologne, Engraved Flowers, Clover, Paneled Neck, Faceted Stopper, 5 1/2 In. 145.00
Cologne, Green Jade, No. 6236, Steuben, 6 1/4 In. 1130.00
Cologne, Green, Tooled, Flutes, Cylindrical, Boston & Sandwich, 10 1/8 In. 3360.00
Cologne, Guerlain, Cologne Du Coq, Stopper, Pochet & Du Courval, 1894, 7 In. 1100.00
Cologne, Nevada Cutting, Ball Shape, Faceted Stopper, Blackmer, 3 1/2 x 5 In. 325.00
Cologne, Pinched Waist, Amethyst, Tooled Mouth, Boston & Sandwich, 4 1/4 In. 475.00
Cologne, Pinched Waist, Amethyst, Tooled Mouth, Panels, 4 1/8 In. 200.00
Cologne, Purple, Tooled Flared Mouth, Square, Herringbone Corners, 7 5/8 In. 785.00
Cologne, Ruby Cut To Clear, Hexagonal, Oval Panels, Squat, Molded Stopper, 5 In. 120.00
Corday, Femme Du Jour, Black, Stopper, Baccarat, 1926, 3 3/4 In. 1685.00
Corday, Toujours Toi, Clear Glass, Stylized Flowers, Gaillard, c.1923, 2 In. 170.00
Coty, Emeraude, Frosted Glass, 3 Panels, Stylized Flowers, c.1928, 4 1/4 In. 2275.00
Coty, Jacinthe, Inkwell Shape, Flowers, Stopper, Cristal Coty, 1914, 3 1/2 In. 4209.00
Coty, L'Aimant, 4 Panels, Square, Leaf Stopper, Baccarat, 1927, 4 In. 1095.00
Crown Perfumery Company, London, Crown Stopper, Green, Embossed, 3 1/4 In. 45.00
Crusellas, Un Amore En Venecia, Clear, Stopper, Flowers, Box, 1925, 3 1/2 In. 420.00
Cut Glass, Alternating Tusk Cut Hearts, Hobstar Hearts, Silver Flip Top Stopper 1200.00
D'Orsay, Les Fleurs, Rectangular, Stopper, Baccarat, Box, c.1923, 2 1/4 In. 4210.00
D'Orsay, Toujours Fidele, Square Pillow, Stopper, Baccarat, 1912, 2 1/2 In. 2525.00
D'Orsay, Trophee, 8 Sides, Rectangular, Brass, Screw Cap, Baccarat, 1935, 1 1/2 In. 210.00
D'Orsay, Voulez-Vous, Card, Clear Glass, Brass Screw Cap, c.1955, 1 1/2 In. 70.00
Dalon, Charme Caressant, Blue Green Opaque Glass, Stopper, Jollivet, 1924, 4 In. 3115.00
Delettrez, Crystal, Car Radiator Shape, Stopper, Baccarat, Stamped, 1927, 3 In. 5050.00
Delyna, Sensation, Black Glass, Spherical, Gilded Claws, Stopper, c.1927, 2 In. 925.00

DeVilbiss, Atomizer, Blue Aurene, Atomic Cloud Shape, Steuben, 10 In. 4440.00
DeVilbiss, Blue Aurene, Atomizer, Signed, 6 3/4 In. 460.00
Doeuillet-Doucet, Mareva, Clear Glass, Rectangular, Stopper, Box, 1929, 2 1/2 In. 340.00
Dorothy Gray, Savoir Faire, Bulbous, Oval, Enameled, Eye Mask, 1947, 2 In. 785.00
Dubarry, A Bunch Of Violets, Clear, Frosted Glass, Flowers, Stopper, c.1919, 3 In. 5895.00
Dubarry, Clear, Frosted, Drapery, 6-Point Star, Stopper, Depinoix, 1920, 5 3/4 In. 2945.00
E. Fuchs, Jasmin, Frosted Glass, Lens Shape, Stopper, Leune, Box, 1925, 1 3/4 In. 589.00
Elizabeth Arden, Blue Grass, Cobalt Blue, Enamel, Lady Bug, Box, c.1955, 1 1/4 In. 220.00
Emerald Green, Melon Ribbed, Flame Stopper, No. 1455, Steuben, 3 3/4 In. 345.00
F. Millot, Crepe De Chine, Brass, Spherical, Green Stones, Pouch, c.1935, 1 1/4 In. 340.00
F. Wolff & Sohn, Jasmin, Clear, Star Shape, Stopper, Viard, 1920, 1 3/4 In. 1179.00
Flask, Nicholas Lutz Style, Blue, Pink, Goldstone, Latticinio Twists, 4 x 1 5/8 In. 80.00
Fontanis, Fleurs De Bagdad, Clear, Stopper, Daubber, Baccarat, 1921, 1 3/4 In. 1685.00
Fragonard, Chale Indien, Egg Shape, Eggcup, Amber, White, c.1929, 1 1/4 In. 630.00
Gabilla, Chin-Li, Clear, Opaque Red Glass, Stopper, Depinoix, 1924, 2 1/2 In. 926.00
Gal, Imperial Toledo, Black Glass, Button Shape, Stopper, Ribas, 1920, 3 1/2 In. 1515.00
Gold Aurene, Bulbous, Squat, Fluted Stopper, Steuben, 4 1/2 In., Pair 4780.00
Green Over Clear, Leaves & Vines, Cameo, Silver Cover, Signed, Daum, 6 1/2 In. 600.00
Grenoville, Byzance, Black Glass, Asymmetrical, Stopper, 1934, 2 1/8 In. 5050.00
Grenoville, Chaine D'Or, Horseshoe Shape, Baccarat, Box, 1923, 3 1/2 In. 9260.00
Gueldy, Gueldiana, Black, Panels, 8-Sided, Flowers, Saumont, c.1928, 4 1/4 In. 1685.00
Gueldy, Nazir, Clear, Frosted Glass, Drapery, Flower, Stopper, c.1922, 4 In. 2020.00
Gueldy, Stellamare, Frosted Glass, Bulbous, Seascape, Viard, 1920, 3 3/4 In. 4630.00
Guerlain, Champs Elysees, Crystal, Turtle Shape Stopper, Baccarat, 1914, 6 In. 5050.00
Guerlain, Cobalt Blue, Glass, Stopper, Pochet & Du Courval, Box, 1962, 6 1/4 In. 4630.00
Guerlain, Fleur Qui Meurt, Round Shoulder, Flat Band, Stopper, 1940, 4 In. 1350.00
Guerlain, Geranium D'Espagne, Sections, Square Stopper, Box, 1938, 4 In. 1350.00
Guerlain, Guerlarose, Ribs, 8-Sided, Stopper, Baccarat, Box, 1927, 2 3/4 In. 1685.00
Guerlain, Le Mouchoir De Monsieur, Faces, Pochet & Du Courval, 1904, 4 1/2 In. 5051.00
Guerlain, Mitsouko, Opaline, Bronze Ring, Stopper, Baccarat, 1951, 6 In. 8000.00
Guerlain, Quand Vient L'Ete, Stopper, Baccarat, Stamped, Box, 1910, 3 1/2 In. 2360.00
Guerlain, Shalimar, Clear Glass, Cylindrical, Molded Ribs, 1966, 3 1/4 In. 1575.00
Hattie Carnegie, Black Glass, Flowers, Pyramid Stopper, Depinoix, 1925, 3 In. 675.00
Houbigant, La Rose France, Man With Rose, Baccarat, Box, 1908, 4 In. 675.00
Iridescent Gold Quezal Glass, Ribbed, Amber Stopper, Melba Mfg. Co., 7 3/4 In. 990.00
Isabey, Le Gardenia, Frosted, 5-Sided, Flowers, Stopper, Viard, 1925, 3 1/2 In. 1685.00
Isabey, Le Mimosa, Clear, Frosted Glass, Cone Shape, Panels, Stopper, 1925, 6 In. 550.00
J. Grossmith, White Fire, Translucent, Stopper, Cone Shape, 1928, 1 1/2 In. 255.00
Jacques Heim, J'Aime, Clear, Cylindrical, Gilded, Stopper, c.1945, 2 1/2 In. 420.00
Jade Green, Alabaster Pointed Stopper, Steuben, 4 1/2 In. 520.00
Jane Regny, Panels, Steering Wheel, Stopper, Baccarat, 1927, 3 1/4 In. 2860.00
Jaspy, Le Petit Chose, Clear, Pear Shape, Stopper, Man's Head, Hat, 1922, 4 In. 5895.00
Jean Patou, Le Sien, Panels, 8-Sided Base, Stopper, Baccarat, 1924, 6 In. 2950.00
Kanebo, Ambre, Opaque Glass, Half Moon Shape, Gilded Peaks, 1 1/4 In. 1852.00
L.T. Piver, Astris, 8-Sided, 6-Pointed Star, Baccarat, 1927, 4 In. 8420.00
L.T. Piver, Astris, Crystal, Gilt Brass, Molded, Stopper, Baccarat, 1912, 4 1/2 In. 2695.00
L.T. Piver, Violette, Sweet Pea Bud, Embossed, Stopper, Box, 1905, 5 1/4 In. 1010.00
Lancel, Le Parfum De Lancel, Clear, Rectangular, Molded Sides, c.1935, 3 In. 465.00
Lancome, Bocages, Clear, Rectangular, Stopper, 1940, 3 In. 340.00
Lancome, Conquete, Brown Frosted, 5-Sided, Stopper, Box, 1939, 7 In. 1265.00
Lancome, Envol, Clear Glass, Square, Molded Cartouche, Delhomme, 1952, 2 In. 550.00
Lancome, Envol, Clear, Rectangular, Screw Cap, Delhomme, Box, 1957, 3 1/2 In. 420.00
Lancome, Tresor, Clear Glass, Teardrop, Screw Cap, Delhomme, Box, 1952, 3 In. 340.00
Leaves, Blossoms, Branches, Lay Down, Silver Cover, Cameo, 3 1/2 In. 1080.00
Lerys, Chypre, Black Glass, Diamond Shape, 4 Panels, Beveled, 1927, 3 In. 255.00
Letheric, Miracle, Clear, Frosted, Ionic Column, Stopper, Brosse, 1924, 3 In. 675.00
Letheric, Shanghai, Clear, Frosted, Ginger Jar Shape, Handles, Brosse, 1934, 2 In. 675.00
Loulette, Mimosa, Opaque Blue, Faces, Stopper, Nancy, 1925, 7 In. 505.00
Lubin, Au Soleil, Frosted, Lighthouse, Lizard, Stopper, Depinoix, 1912, 5 3/4 In. 4209.00
Lubin, Monbrosia, Clear Glass, 8-Sided, Stopper, 1925, 3 1/2 In. 1180.00
Lucien Lelong, Jabot, Clear Glass, Drapery, Screw Cap, Box, 1939, 1 3/4 In. 379.00
Luzy, Frais Jardin, Pear Shape, Stopper, Leaves, Flowers, 1925, 3 1/2 In. 1684.00
Marcel Rochas, Femme, Opaque White Glass, Disk Shape, Cap, 1944, 2 In. 1180.00

Marcel Rochas, Moustache, Clear Glass, Rectangular, Screw Cap, 1948, 1 In.	236.00
Marques De Elorza, Argentina, Cobalt Blue, Bulbous, Sections, 1928, 3 3/4 In.	4210.00
Molinard, Amber, Bulbous, Panels, Stopper, Baccarat, 1921, 3 1/2 In.	1685.00
Molinard, Habanita, Molded Faces, Baccarat, Box, c.1934, 2 In.	380.00
Molinard, Tabatchin, Black, Cube, 4 Faces, Stopper, Baccarat, 1934, 3 1/4 In.	1850.00
Monarda, Ecrivez-Moi, Clear Tube, Pen Shape, Ivory Case, c.1939, 5 1/2 In.	235.00
Mother-Of-Pearl, Satin, Round, Flowers Resembling Moire, 1887, 5 In.	750.00
Muhlens, L'Offrande, Crystal, Oval, Ribs, Embossed, Stopper, Box, c.1920, 5 In.	1095.00
Mury, Le Narcisse Blue, 8-Sided, Narcissus, Stopper, Brosse, 1923, 2 3/4 In.	631.00
Myrurgia, A Moi, Frosted Glass, Stylized Flowers, Stopper, Viard, 1921, 4 3/4 In.	420.00
Myrurgia, Embrujo De Sevilla, Clear, Frosted Glass, Stopper, Viard, Box, 3 In.	1350.00
Myrurgia, Origanum, Frosted, Round, Stopper, Viard, Depinoix, 1921, 4 1/4 In.	465.00
Nice-Flore, Divine Chanson, Flowers, Stopper, Viard, Depinoix, c.1923, 4 In.	2105.00
Nice-Flore, Tout L'Azur, Clear, Frosted, Petals, 3 Cartouches, Depinoix, 5 1/4 In.	2360.00
Nicerose, Chypre, Panels, Arch Windows Shape, Flowers, c.1923, 4 1/4 In.	4200.00
Nissery, Le Cyclamen, Rectangular, Flowers, Embossed, Box, 1922, 3 1/2 In.	675.00
Paperweight, Deep Rose, Green Leaves, 5 1/2 In.	200.00
Paquin, Espoir, Black Glass, Circular, Drapery, Screw Cap, 1945, 2 In.	210.00
Paquin, Espoir, Clear Glass, Tube, Card, c.1945, 1 1/2 In.	170.00
Peggy Hoyt, Perfume Of Aristocrats, Woman's Head, Baccarat, 1917, 4 In.	1685.00
Poison, Christian Dior, Bracelet Shape, Black Paint, Green Sports, 14 In.	110.00
Prince Matchabelli, Abano, Clear, Cylindrical Cap, Sea Horse, c.1936, 3 In.	170.00
Prince Matchabelli, Duchess Of York, Amber, Translucent, 5-Sided, 1924, 3 In.	715.00
Prince Matchabelli, Violettes De La Reine, Amber, Stopper, 1924, 2 In.	1850.00
Prince Matchabelli, Wind Song, Clear, Crown Shape, Stopper, 1928, 8 1/4 In.	1515.00
Raquel, Orange Blossom, Clear Glass, Spheric, Stopper, Cone Shape, 1925, 2 In.	295.00
Richard Hudnut, Chypre, Cone Shape, Flowers, Viard, Box, 1926, 2 3/4 In.	1768.00
Rimmel, Mon Yvonnette, Frosted, Panels, Stopper, Viard, 1923, 3 1/2 In.	7576.00
Robj, Black Lady, Porcelain, Painted, Turban Lifts Off, Paris France, 10 1/2 In.	425.00
Roger & Gallet, Bridalis, Clear, 5 Sides, Stopper, Baccarat, 1911, 3 1/2 In.	715.00
Roger & Gallet, Fleurs D'Amour, Frosted, Rectangular, Stopper, c.1929, 3 In.	505.00
Roger & Gallet, Triomphe De France, Steel, Sunburst, Stopper, 1919, 2 3/4 In.	4040.00
Rosaline Glass, Alabaster Foot, Pointed Stopper, Steuben, 8 In.	805.00
Rosine, Chez Poiret, Clear Glass, Stopper, Lepape, 1912, 2 1/4 In.	5895.00
Rosine, Coeur En Folie, Red Glass, Heart Shape, Stopper, 1925, 1 1/2 In.	4209.00
Schiaparelli, Shocking, Body Radiance, Salvidore Dali Label, 1943, 4 3/4 In.	505.00
Schiaparelli, Si, Clear Glass, Chianti Shape, Stopper, 1957, 4 3/4 In.	758.00
Schiaparelli, Sleeping, Clear, Amber, Flame Shape, Stopper, 1938, 2 1/2 In.	1350.00
Shaded Enamel, Gilt Bronze, Champleve, Screw-Off Top, 3 In.	495.00
Silver Mounted, Chased, Embossed Silver Overlay, c.1900, 5 1/2 In., Pair	2470.00
Simonetta, Incanto, Black Glass, Lantern Shape, Stopper, c.1950, 2 In.	340.00
Verre De Soie Shoulder, Light Blue Jade Dabber, Steuben, 10 1/4 In.	980.00
Vigny, Guili-Guili, Crystal, Panels, Mahogany Foot, De Brunhoff, 1926, 6 1/4 In.	5895.00
Volnay, Firefly, Cobalt Blue Glass, 8-Sided, Stopper, Box, c.1925, 1 1/2 In.	1179.00
Volnay, Lilas De Lorraine, Pear Shape, Stopper, Normandeuse, c.1925, 6 1/2 In.	1095.00
Volnay, Perlinette, Pearlized, Stopper, Black Lacquer, Jollivet, c.1929, 2 1/4 In.	550.00
Woodworth, Karess, Frosted, Cylindrical, Geometric, Stopper, Nancy, 1920, 6 In.	2946.00
Worth, Projets, Frosted Glass, Oval Shape, Sailing Ship, Stopper, 1935, 1 3/4 In.	800.00
Ybry, Devinez, Opaque, Cube Shape, Dabber, Baccarat, 1925, 1 1/3 In.	2020.00

PETERS & REED Pottery Company of Zanesville, Ohio, was founded by John D. Peters and Adam Reed in 1897. Chromal, Landsun, Montene, Pereco, and Persian are some of the art lines that were made. The company, which became Zane Pottery in 1920 and Gonder Pottery in 1941, closed in 1957. Peters & Reed pottery was unmarked.

Bowl, Dragonfly, Brown, 5 In.	60.00
Bowl, Embossed Band Of Flowers & Leaves, 2 1/2 x 6 1/2 In.	105.00
Jardiniere, Brown, Green, Clay, Brown High Glaze Interior, 6 In.	115.00
Planter, Greek Figures, Brown, Signed, Ferrell, 5 1/4 x 12 1/2 In.	300.00
Planter, Moss Aztec, Embossed Roses, Incised, Ferrell, 5 3/4 x 7 1/4 In.	60.00
Umbrella Stand, Speckled Brown Matte Glaze, Indigo, Yellow Streaks, 15 3/4 In.	230.00
Vase, Chromal, Oval, 9 1/4 x 4 In.	800.00
Vase, Landsun, Bulbous, 6 1/2 x 4 1/2 In.	145.00

Vase, Landsun, Squat, 4 x 4 1/4 In. 90.00
Vase, Landsun, Squat, 6 3/4 x 5 In. 115.00
Vase, Oak Leaf Columns, Cylindrical, Mottled Green Glaze, 9 x 4 1/4 In. 250.00
Vase, Shadow Ware, Indigo, Ocher & Brown Dripping, Baluster, 6 3/4 x 4 In. 145.00
Vase, Shadow Ware, Indigo, Ocher, Seafoam Drip Glaze, Stamped, 13 x 7 1/2 In. ...290.00 to 400.00
Vase, Shadow Ware, Mottled Chocolate, Brown Drip, 10 1/4 In. 345.00
Vase, Shadow Ware, Mustard Matte, Dark Blue Drip, Tan, 8 1/2 In. 430.00
Vase, Shadow Ware, White, Green, Black Drip Glaze, On Yellow Ground, 6 In., Pair 145.00
Vase, Striated Black, Green, Ivory, On Russet Ground, 8 x 5 1/2 In. 60.00

PETRUS REGOUT, see Maastricht category.

PEWABIC POTTERY was founded by Mary Chase Perry Stratton in 1903 in Detroit, Michigan. The company made many types of art pottery, including pieces with matte green glaze and an iridescent crystalline glaze. The company continued working until the death of Mary Stratton in 1961. It was reactivated by Michigan State University in 1968.

Tile, Winged Animal, Iridescent Glaze, Brown Clay, 7 1/2 In. 489.00
Vase, Applied Blossoms, Swirl Stems, Green Matte Glaze, Marked, 6 1/4 x 4 1/2 In. 4315.00
Vase, Blue & Green Iridescent Glaze, Swollen Shape, Paper Labels, 9 1/2 In. 635.00
Vase, Blue Luster Glaze, Squat, Stamped, 4 1/4 x 4 In. 375.00
Vase, Blue, Green, Indigo Luster Glaze, Bulbous, Stamped, 5 1/2 x 4 1/4 In. 635.00
Vase, Celadon, Indigo, Purple Luster Glaze, Sloped Shoulder, 8 1/2 x 5 1/2 In. 1035.00
Vase, Cobalt Blue, Gray, Purple Volcanic Luster Glaze, Bulbous, 9 x 5 3/4 In. 1725.00
Vase, Cobalt Blue, Over Gold Luster Glaze, Baluster, Stamped, 4 x 3 In. 635.00
Vase, Multitone Blue, Iridescent Glaze, Bulbous, 10 In. 1095.00
Vase, Multitone Green Metallic Glaze, Waisted Shape, 4 1/2 In. 430.00
Vase, Orange Volcanic Glaze, Bulbous, Stamped, 3 x 3 In. 175.00
Vase, Pink, Luminescent Glaze, Bulbous, Elongated Neck, 8 1/2 In. 978.00
Vase, Silver Over Blue Metallic Glaze, Cabinet, 2 3/4 In. 316.00
Vase, Volcanic Luster Glaze, Purple, Black, Blue, Squat, Stamped, 3 x 4 1/2 In. 489.00

PEWTER is a metal alloy of tin and lead. Some of the pewter made after 1840 has a slightly different composition and is called *Britannia metal*. This later type of pewter was worked by machine; the earlier pieces were made by hand. In the 1920s pewter came back into fashion and pieces were often marked *Genuine Pewter*. Eighteenth-, nineteenth-, and twentieth-century examples are listed here.

Basin, Ashbil Griswold, 11 In. 715.00
Basin, Boardman, 11 1/2 In. 259.00
Basin, Flared Rim, 18th Century, 7 5/8 In. 295.00
Basin, Samuel Danforth Eagle Mark, 8 In. 499.00
Basin, Samuel Danforth, Faint Touchmark, c.1800, 6 3/4 In. 200.00
Basin, Samuel Danforth, Touchmark, 19th Century, 8 In. 115.00
Beaker, Calder, Handle, 2 7/8 In. 335.00
Beaker, Tapered, Ring At Base, 1800s, 3 In., Pair 60.00
Beaker, Wiggins, Footed, 1/2 Pt., 3 7/8 In. 40.00
Bowl, Flowers, Osiris, England, 10 In. 29.00
Bowl, Kayserzinn, Scalloped, Embossed, 3 Lobster Interior, Leaves, 3 x 9 In. 115.00
Bowl, Navette Form, Acanthus Scrolls, Continental, c.1895, 11 1/2 x 25 In. 1265.00
Bowl, Rimmed, Hebrew Letters, Continental, Late 18th Century, 8 3/4 x 14 In. 200.00
Bowl, Tooled Rim, Hammered Bouge, London, 17 3/4 In. 110.00
Box, Arts & Crafts, Hammered, Inset Turquoise To Lid, England, 4 1/2 In. 145.00
Box, Hammered, Raised Leaves, Applied Turquoise On Cover, Tudric, 4 1/2 x 2 1/2 In. ... 1175.00
Box, Orivit, Swirling Art Nouveau Design, 9 x 6 x 3 In. 345.00
Candelstick, Queen Anne, Oval Base, 4 1/2 x 4 In., Pair 345.00
Candelstick, Round Dome Base, Polished, Touchmark, c.1860, 6 1/2 In., Pair 805.00
Candelstick, Round, Step Base, Brass Push-Up, 7 1/2 In., Pair 525.00
Candlestick, Baluster Stems, Flared Drip Pan, Flagg & Homan, Cincinnati, 10 In., Pair .. 430.00
Candlestick, Flagg & Homan, Cincinnati, Ohio, 1842-1854, 9 1/2 In., Pair 345.00
Candlestick, Flower Form Base, Continental, c.1900, 8 In., Pair 80.00
Candlestick, Homan, Baluster Stem, Asa Flagg, Henry Homan, 1850-1880, 10 x 4 3/4 In. 230.00
Candlestick, Pricket, Paw Feet, Triangular Base, Continental, 12 1/2 In., Pair 489.00
Candlestick, Roswell Gleason, Flared, Knopped, Detachable Nozzle, Mass., 7 In., Pair ... 865.00

Castor, Roswell Gleason, Touchmark, 1800s, 8 1/4 In. 69.00
Castor Set, Bottles, Rufus Dunham, 12 1/2 In., 5 Piece 69.00
Chalice, Flower & Crown, Stepped, Round Base, Baluster Stem, Flared Rim, 7 7/8 In. . . . 470.00
Chalice, Timothy Brigden, Albany, N.Y., c.1816-1819, 8 3/4 In. 4840.00
Chalice, Turned Base, Tooled Stem Rings, Raised Rim Band, Engraved, c.1753, 8 In. 345.00
Chamber Pot, Circular, Handle, Dish Shape Cover, Early 1800s, 10 1/2 In. 160.00
Charger, Blakslee Barne, 13 1/8 x 1 1/2 In. 550.00
Charger, Coat Of Arms, Richard Austin, Boston, Engraved Initials, 13 1/2 In. 660.00
Charger, Colonial, Wide Rim, Beaded Edge, 13 3/4 x 1 In. 105.00
Charger, Danforth, Rampant Lion, Arched Columns, 13 1/4 x 1 1/2 In. 550.00
Charger, Engraved Coat Of Arms, 18th Century, Continental, 16 3/4 In. 295.00
Charger, Fasson & Son, Hammered Bouge, Raised Rim, Touchmark, 15 In. 460.00
Charger, Fein-Zinn, Germany, 14 In. 55.00
Charger, G. Smith, London, 18 In., c.1681 . . . . 685.00
Charger, George III, Initials, Stamped, 18th Century, 18 1/4 In., 3 Piece 520.00
Charger, John Kent, Mid 18th Century, 20 1/4 In. 550.00
Charger, Marked P I A On Rim, England, 18th Century, 16 1/4 In. 280.00
Charger, Reutlinger, Raised, Tooled Line, Around Rim, 13 7/8 In. 360.00
Charger, Robert Bush & Co., c.1780-1790, 15 1/2 In. 58.00
Charger, Semper Eadem, Boston, Late 18th Century, 15 In. 880.00
Charger, Townsend & Compton, Hammered Bouge, Tooled Rim, 15 In. 460.00
Charger, William Banckes, Multiple-Reed, Hallmarks, England, c.1690, 16 3/4 In. 595.00
Chocolate Pot, Cylindrical, Wood Handle, FWR 1850 . . . . 115.00
Cistern, Wall, 2 Parts, Mounted On Wall Shelf, Mask Decoration, c.1828, 30 In. 230.00
Coffee Mill, Red, Black Paint, 19th Century, 16 In. 865.00
Coffee Urn, Roswell Gleason, Paneled Form, Brass Spigot, Finial, Touchmark, 14 In. . . . . • 200.00
Coffeepot, Boardman & Hart, Tooled Lines, Touchmark, New York, c.1853, 11 3/4 In. . . . 748.00
Coffeepot, Dome Lid, Turned Wings, Wafer Finial, Black Handle, 12 In. 305.00
Coffeepot, George Richardson, 10 1/2 In. 200.00
Coffeepot, George Richardson, Touchmark, 1800s, 8 In. 175.00
Coffeepot, Homan & Co., Bulbous, Scrolled Handle, Applied Flower Finial, 8 1/2 In. 145.00
Coffeepot, Lighthouse, HB Ward Britannia, c.1840s, 11 1/2 In. 495.00
Coffeepot, Lighthouse, James H. Putnam Touchmark, Mid 1800s, 9 In. 345.00
Coffeepot, Lighthouse, Sheldon & Feltman, Raised Rings, Scrolled Ear Handle, 12 1/4 In. 259.00
Coffeepot, Luther Boardman, Touchmark, 19th Century, 7 1/2 In. 175.00
Coffeepot, Roswell Gleason, Octagonal, Touchmark, 1800s, 10 1/4 In. 175.00
Coffeepot, Roswell Gleason, Touchmark, 1800s, 7 1/4 In. 316.00
Coffeepot, Rufus Dunham, Straight Touchmark, 19th Century, 12 In. 375.00
Coffeepot, Tapered Cylinder, Engraved, Signed, Chinese, 1800s, 10 In. 35.00
Compote, Tudric, Hammered, Enameled Design, Arts & Crafts, 5 In. 690.00
Creamer, Hiram Yale & Co., 3 1/4 x 2 5/8 In. 265.00
Cruet, Bottles, Blown Cobalt Blue, Georgian, 3 Piece 525.00
Cup, 2 S-Scroll Handles, P. Edgar & Son, Bristol, England, 4 3/4 In., Pair 1095.00
Cup, Commemorative, Franz Joseph, Wilhelm II, Kreigsbecher 1914-1916, 6 In. 196.00
Dish, Ale Mug, England, 18th Century, 14 1/2-In. Dish 695.00
Dish, Deep, Gershom Jones, Touchmarks, 11 5/8 In. 550.00
Dish, Deep, Thomas Boardman II, 13 1/4 In. 900.00
Dish, Deep, Thomas D. Broadman, Touchmarks, 13 In. 410.00
Figure, Deity Standing On Ornate Throne, Painted Details, Chinese, 1800s, 18 In., Pair . . 590.00
Figure, Philip Kraezkowski, Buffalo Hunt, c.1971, 7 1/4 In. 60.00
Flagon, Boardman & Co., 3-Wafer Finial, N.Y., 8 1/2 In. 1100.00
Flagon, Communion, Trask, Touchmark, 19th Century, 10 5/8 In. 495.00
Flagon, Dome Lid, Flared Base, Signed, Box, 12 In. 880.00
Flagon, Dome Lid, Flared Foot, Raised Rings, Tapered Body, Scroll Handle, Finial, 12 In. 805.00
Flagon, Dome Lid, Tapered Cylindrical Shape, Disc Final, c.1850, 9 1/4 In. 3819.00
Flagon, Engraved, J.G.A., Continental, 1815, 5 1/4 In. 90.00
Flask, Round, Flattened, L & R Merry, Dublin, Ireland, 19th Century 250.00
Hour Lamp, Ribbed Glass Font, Scroll Handle, France, Early 1700s, 15 1/2 In. 200.00
Jug, Lid, Wayne & Son, 8 x 12 In. 935.00
Knife & Fork Combination, Slide Together, Bone, Pearl Handles, 18th Century 350.00
Ladle, Fiddleback, John Yates, 12 In. 110.00
Lamp, Bull's-Eye Lens, Weighted Base, Brass Whole Oil Burner, 8 1/2 In. 805.00
Lamp, Lard Oil, Saucer Base, Marked Patent 965.00

Lamp, Whale Oil, Capen & Molineux, Acorn Shaped Font, Touchmark, 1800s, 7 In. 230.00
Lamp, Whale Oil, Fuller & Smith, Double Bull's-Eye, Conn., c.1850, 10 In. 750.00
Lamp, Whale Oil, James Putnam, Double Burner, c.1830, 5 3/4 In. 400.00
Lamp, Whale Oil, Morey & Ober, Brass Collar, Burner, Scroll Handle, Boston, 3 3/4 In. . . .   145.00
Lamp, Whale Oil, Rufus Dunham, Touchmark, 1800s, 7 1/4 In. 345.00
Lamp, Whale Oil, Yale & Curtis, Gimbal, Acorn Form, New York City, 5 1/8 In. 288.00
Matchbox Holder, Ruskin Hammered Enamel Insert, Arts & Crafts, c.1905, 5 x 3 x 2 In. . .   250.00
Measure, Baluster, Brass Rim, ER522, London Country, White Swan, 1/2 Gill 700.00
Measure, Brass Trim, 6 1/4 x 4 1/2 In. 55.00
Measure, Bulbous, England, Gal. 1480.00
Measure, C. Bentley, Spout, VR, Sussex, Woodstock St., London, Qt. 200.00
Measure, Heart Terminal To Handle, Oval Disk, Crown, GR IV, Britannia, c.1825, Qt. . . .   195.00
Measure, Imperial Capacity, Embryo Shell Piece, Scotland, c.1830, 1/2 Pt., 4 1/2 In. 255.00
Measure Set, 6 Graduated Sizes, Bellied, 1 3/4 To 6 1/4 In., 6 Piece 315.00
Measure Set, Cylindrical, England, 1 3/4 To 7 In., 7 Piece 400.00
Measure Set, Graduated, England, Gill, 1 7/8 To 6 In., 6 Piece 335.00
Measure Set, Yates & Birch, Graduated, England, 1/4 Gill To Qt., 1 3/4 To 6 In., 7 Piece .   863.00
Mermaid, Holding Crystal Sphere, Amethyst Base, 3 1/2 In. 104.00
Mold, Candle, 18 Tubes, Cherry Frame, 7 In. 415.00
Mold, Candle, 18 Tubes, Walnut Frame 3190.00
Mold, Candle, 32 Tubes, Arch Cutouts, Square Cut Nails, 21 x 7 1/2 x 15 In. 1375.00
Mold, Ice Cream, Fireman Holding Trumpet 105.00
Mold, Ice Cream, Swan, 8 x 9 In. 730.00
Mug, Footed, Ball-Terminal Handle, Marked Crown X-Th, 1/2 Pt. 70.00
Mug, Tapered, Side Spout, C-Scroll Handle, G. Richardson, Rhode Island, 4 1/2 In. 575.00
Mug, Tulip Shape, Ingram & Hunt, Qt. 400.00
Pitcher, Bulbous Form, Scroll Handle, Pierced Spout Filter, 7 In. 110.00
Pitcher, R. Dunham, Bulbous, Early 19th Century, 6 3/4 In. 265.00
Pitcher, Spout, Wicker Wrapped Handle, Arts & Crafts Design, 9 In. 315.00
Pitcher, Syrup, Hinged Lid, Scroll, Thumblift, Mushroom Finial, Scrolled Handle, 6 In. . . .   310.00
Pitcher, Water, Bulbous Shape, Homan, Cincinnati, 9 1/2 x 6 1/2 In. 115.00
Pitcher, Water, Wallace, Silver Plated, Flat Bottom, Squat, Bean Pot Shape, 7 x 8 5/8 In. . .   265.00
Plate, Blakslee Barns, Touchmark, Philadelphia, 1800s, 7 3/4 In. 290.00
Plate, Compton, London, 9 In. 70.00
Plate, Crown & Tudor Rose Touchmark, Early 19th Century, 8 7/8 In. 105.00
Plate, Deep, Townsend & Compton, 12 In. 220.00
Plate, Edgar Curtis & Co., Bristol, 1793-1801, 8 In. 100.00
Plate, Elias Beyer, Maker's Mark, Bach, Germany, 8 1/2 In. 80.00
Plate, Engraved, Scrolling On Outer Edge, Sun Design, Cross, I.H.S., 1784, 12 In. 220.00
Plate, Erlangen, 3 Touchmarks, c.1827, 9 In. 60.00
Plate, George Lightner, Double Touchmark, Baltimore, 1800s, 7 7/8 In. 360.00
Plate, Jacob Danforth, Touchmark, 19th Century, 7 3/4 In. 150.00
Plate, Lovebirds, London, c.1750-1800, 11 In. 935.00
Plate, Marriage, Elisabeth Kaiserin, Wriggle Work Rim, Tulips, Penn., 1777-1801, 9 In. . . .   715.00
Plate, Octagonal, Joseph Spackman, 8 3/8 In., Pair 660.00
Plate, Oval, England, 18th Century, 22 In. 495.00
Plate, Penland, N.C., 8 In., 5 Piece 220.00
Plate, Plain Rim, Deep Well, 7 3/4 In. 28.00
Plate, Richard & Henry Joseph, Engraved, Barnards Inn-1813, London, c.1825 . . . .   250.00
Plate, Richard Austin, Polished, Touchmark, c.1817, 8 3/8 In. 575.00
Plate, Robert Bush & Co., 8 3/8 In. 100.00
Plate, Stamped E A, London, c.1774, 8 3/8 In. 170.00
Plate, T. Danfort, Touchmarks, Phila., Early 18th Century, 7 3/4 In. 330.00
Plate, Thomas Badger, Faint Touchmark, Boston, c.1800, 7 7/8 In. 175.00
Plate, Townsend & Compton, England, 7 1/2 In. . . . . .30.00 to 45.00
Plate, Townsend & Reynolds, Wavy Edge, London, c.1770, 6 Piece 1350.00
Plate, Townsend, Wide Rim, Stamped, 8 3/8 In. 55.00
Plate, Wedding, Pfeifer, Flowering Tulip, Inscribed, Maker's Name, c.1843, 8 3/4 In. 220.00
Plate, Wide Rim, Marked PB London, Early 19th Century, 8 In., 5 Piece 365.00
Plate, Wide Rim, Round, Marked, Late 18th Century, 8 3/4 In. 55.00
Plate, Wide Rim, Thistle Mark, Late 18th Century, 8 3/4 In. 60.00
Plate, William Calder, Touchmark, 1800s, 10 1/4 In. 115.00
Porringer, Bulbous Bowl, Narrow Rim Collar, Conn., 1810-1830, 1 5/8 x 4 3/8 In. 410.00

Pewter, Warming Dish, Cover, Thomas Compton,
London, Late 18th Century

Never polish Arts and Crafts copper or pewter. Even if the green patina on a piece of Heinz Art is damaged, it is better than a cleaned piece. Original finish is important.

Porringer, Cat Crown, Scrolled, Beaded, T.D. & S.B., Hartford, Ct., 2 x 7 1/4 In.	165.00
Porringer, Crown Handle, 7 1/2 In.	130.00
Porringer, Crown Handle, SG, 4 1/4 In.	250.00
Porringer, Crown Handle, TD & SB, 5 3/8 In.	600.00
Porringer, G. Jones, Flower Handle, 5 1/2 In.	805.00
Porringer, Geometric Pierced Triangular Handle, Initials, Linen Mark, 5 3/8 In.	1190.00
Porringer, Reticulated Handles, Round, 2 3/4 x 5 1/2 In.	195.00
Pot, Bachelors, Dixon & Son, Marked 82	120.00
Stamp Box, Sliding Top, Paw Feet, Bird Touchmark, 3 x 3 1/4 x 2 1/2 In.	315.00
Sugar, Egg Shape, Swirl & Flower, Cover, Continental, 1800s, 5 In.	35.00
Syrup, Spire Lid, Double C-Handle, Shell Thumbpiece, c.1840, 5 3/4 x 3 1/2 In.	195.00
Tablespoon, W. Haddsworth, Brite-Cut Design, 8 In.	8.00
Tankard, Applied Rim, Stamped, 5 7/8 x 4 7/8 In.	55.00
Tankard, Brass Rim, Engraved, Imperial Measure, Qt., 5 3/4 x 4 3/4 In.	56.00
Tankard, Dome Lid, Chair Thumbpiece, Carpenter & Hamberger, London, 8 In.	1250.00
Tankard, J.E. Kettern, Lemon Finial, Inscribed, c.1787, 10 In.	88.00
Tankard, Morgan & Gaskell, 1/2 Pt.	200.00
Tankard, Ribbed Body Bands, Acanthus Design, 19th Century, Germany, 6 In.	105.00
Tankard, Spout, Carpent & Hamburg, Pt.	350.00
Tankard, Tapered Sides, Stamped VRBH, Qt., 6 x 4 1/2 In.	56.00
Tankard, Tulip Shape, Dome Lid, Open Thumbpiece, Scrolled Handle, 7 1/2 In.	1065.00 to 1265.00
Tankard, Wide Applied Base Rim, Stamped WP, 5 7/8 x 4 7/8 In.	56.00
Tea Service, Tudric, Wicker Handles, Applied Lid Wood, Marked Archibald Knox, 17 In.	4025.00
Tea Set, Liberty & Co., Hammered, Patina, 6-In. Teapot, 4 Piece	200.00
Teapot, Boardman & Co., Black Handle, Wafer Finial, Touchmark, 7 In.	430.00
Teapot, D. Curtiss, Spherical, C-Scroll Handle, Dome Lid, Albany, 6 1/2 In.	489.00
Teapot, E. Smith, Flower & Grape Engraved Band, Touchmark, c.1813, 7 1/2 In.	1035.00
Teapot, I.C. Lewis, Cast Handle, Acanthus Leaf Ends, 8 1/4 In.	175.00
Teapot, J. Danforth, Ear Handle, Wafer Finial, Dome Lid, 8 In.	440.00
Teapot, Lighthouse, Calder, Marked	250.00
Teapot, Lighthouse, Putnam, Marked	305.00
Teapot, Lighthouse, Truncated, Roswell Gleason	300.00
Teapot, Luther Boardman, Dome Lid, Curved Spout, Scrolled Handle, c.1835, 7 3/4 In.	265.00
Teapot, Octagonal, Dixon & Son	120.00
Teapot, Pear Shape, Israel Trask, 7 1/2 In.	3080.00
Teapot, Pear Shape, Wood Wafer Finial, Continental Touchmarks, 7 In.	165.00
Teapot, R. Gleason, Black Painted Scroll Handle, Touchmark, 9 In.	345.00
Teapot, R. Gleason, Polished, Black Handle, Wafer Finial, Touchmark, c.1871, 8 3/4 In.	460.00
Teapot, Sellew & Co., Cincinnati, 5, Ear Handle, Tooled Rings, Dome Lid, 7 1/2 In.	415.00
Teapot, Sellew & Co., Cincinnati, Hinged Lid, Black Painted Handle, 7 1/2 In.	160.00
Teapot, Smith & Co., Black Paint, Marked	115.00
Teapot, William Calder, Scrolled Handle, Dome Lid, Curved Spout, c.1835, 8 3/4 In.	410.00
Teapot, Wm. McQuilkin, Philadelphia, Stamped, 1845-1853	60.00
Tobacco Container, Tulip Decoration, Stylized Pot, Diamond & Block Pattern, 2 3/4 In.	990.00
Tray, J. Von Schwarz, Tile Bottom, Cuenca, Deer, Mountain Landscape, 12 x 20 In.	1610.00
Tray, Karl Kipp, 20th Century, 9 1/2 In.	85.00
Tray, Karl Kipp, Octagonal, Hammered, 6 1/2 In.	230.00
Tray, Nude Woman, Arms Spread, Butterfly Wings, Art Nouveau, Signed, H.P., 7 1/2 In.	460.00

Tureen, Bulbous Shape, Ball & Claw Feet, Monogram, England, 18th Century 3695.00
Vase, 2 Handles, Arts & Crafts Design, Liberty, 8 In. 489.00
Vase, Raised & Incised Flowers, Santesson, Sweden, 4 In. 175.00
Vase, Tudric, 3 Buttress Shape, Stylized Design, Arts & Crafts, 9 1/2 In. 1380.00
Vase, Tudric, Hammered, Arts & Crafts Design, Liberty & Co., 8 In. 920.00
Vase, Tudric, Handles, Stylized Flower Shape, 10 In. 1035.00
Warming Dish, Cover, Thomas Compton, London, Late 18th Century .... *Illus* 690.00
Warming Dish Set, Meat Covers, Nesting, Engraved, Victorian, 9 1/2 In. 290.00
Water Tank, From Lavabo, Continental, 1821, 11 In. 69.00

PHOENIX BIRD, or Flying Phoenix, is the name given to a blue-and-
white kitchenware popular between 1900 and World War II. A variant
is known as Flying Turkey. Most of this dinnerware was made in Japan
for sale in the dime stores in America. It is still being made.

Mustard, Cover, Ladle, 2 1/2 In. 65.00
Salt & Pepper, Hexagonal Foot, 3 In. 32.00
Soup, Dish, Made In Japan, 7 1/2 In. 24.00
Sugar, Cover, Handles, Made In Japan, 5 1/2 In. 20.00
Sugar & Creamer, Nippon 10.00

PHOENIX GLASS Company was founded in 1880 in Pennsylvania. The
firm made commercial products, such as lampshades, bottles, and
glassware. Collectors today are interested in the "Sculptured Artware"
made by the company from the 1930s until the mid-1950s. Some
pieces of Phoenix glass are very similar to those made by the Consolidated Lamp and Glass Company. Phoenix made Reuben Blue, lavender, and yellow pieces. These colors were not used by Consolidated. In
1970 Phoenix became a division of Anchor Hocking, then was sold to
the Newell Group in 1987. The company is still working.

Compote, Iris, Amethyst Wash, 11 In. 200.00
Vase, Cosmos, Blue On White, 7 1/2 In. 190.00
Vase, Dancing Nudes, Brown On Ivory, 11 1/4 In. 650.00
Vase, Ferns, Coral On White, 7 In. 65.00
Vase, Freesia, Blue On Ivory, 8 1/2 In. 135.00
Vase, Geese, White, Blue Ground, Oval, Paper Label, 9 1/2 In. 317.00
Vase, Jewel, Brown On White, 4 3/4 In. 195.00
Vase, Katydid, Amethyst Wash, 8 1/4 In. 200.00
Vase, Wild Roses, Blue On White, 11 In. 175.00

PHONOGRAPHS, invented by Thomas Edison in 1877, have been made
by many firms. This category also includes other items associated
with the phonograph. Jukeboxes and Records are listed in their own
categories.

Berliner, Gram-O-Phone, Disc, Black Tin Horn, Wood Tone Arm 1750.00
Carola, Metal Case, Horn Type Reproducer, Floor Model, Child's 450.00
Columbia, Cylinder, Lyre Reproducer, Nickel Witch's Hat Horn 525.00
Columbia, Cylinder, Peerless, Lyric Reproducer, Aluminum Horn 725.00
Columbia, Disc, Columbia Reproducer, Red Morning Glory Horn, Gold Band 700.00
Columbia, Graphophone AB, Brass Horn, Plays 5-In. Cylinders, Key Wind 950.00
Columbia, Graphophone AG, Grand, Cylinder, Brass Horn, Stand 1750.00
Columbia, Graphophone B, Eagle, Cylinder, Key, Reproducer, Flared Horn, c.1894 ..... 350.00
Columbia, Graphophone BN, Disc, Red Morning Glory Horn 875.00
Columbia, Graphophone Q, Cylinder, Key Wind, Gold Band Horn, c.1898 .... 275.00 to 325.00
Columbia, Sterling, Disc, 9-Petal Nickel Horn, c.1906 .... 2000.00
Decca, Suitcase, Portable 120.00
Edison, Amberola SM, Cylinder, Mahogany Case, Floor Model 2750.00
Edison, Amberola V, Cylinder, Mahogany Case, c.1912 .... 375.00 to 400.00
Edison, Amberola VIII, Cylinder, Oak Case, c.1913 .... 325.00 to 425.00
Edison, Amberola X, Cylinder, Oak Case, Table Model 375.00
Edison, Cylinders, 2 & 4 Minute, Boxes, 18 Piece 464.00
Edison, Fireside A, Combination Type, H Reproducer, Fireside Horn 650.00
Edison, Fireside A, Combination, C Reproducer, Cygnet Horn 800.00
Edison, Fireside A, Cylinder, K Reproducer, Cygnet Horn, 2 & 4 Minute .... 700.00 to 900.00

Edison, Fireside B, Cylinder, Black Cygnet Horn 950.00
Edison, Fireside B, Diamond B Reproducer, Oak Case, Cygnet Horn, c.1913 . . . . .353.00 to 950.00
Edison, Gem, C Reproducer, Black Horn 750.00
Edison, Gem, Maroon, K Reproducer, Fireside Horn, Shroud, Cover 1200.00
Edison, Home, Cylinder, C Reproducer, Cygnet Horn, Wood Grained 750.00
Edison, Home, Cylinder, C Reproducer, Mahogany Case, Repeater, Shaver, Brass Horn . .   2700.00
Edison, Home, Cylinder, C Reproducer, Morning Glory Horn, Black 475.00
Edison, Home, Cylinder, H Reproducer, Brass Bell Horn, c.1900 . . . . .400.00 to 525.00
Edison, Home, Cylinder, K Reproducer, Cygnet Horn 950.00
Edison, Standard D, Cylinder, H Reproducer, Morning Glory Horn, c.1908 . . . .   600.00
Edison, Standard D, Cylinder, R Reproducer, Cygnet Horn, 2 & 4 Minute, c.1908 . . . .   900.00
Edison, Standard E, Cylinder, Blue Morning Glory Horn, Chrysanthemum 600.00
Edison, Standard, Cylinder, C Reproducer, 2 & 4 Minute, Brass Bell Horn, c.1910 . . . . . .   375.00
Edison, Standard, Cylinder, Latch Suitcase, Brass Bell Horn, c.1897 . . . .   475.00
Edison, Triumph D, Cylinder, 10-Panel Horn 1150.00
Edison, Triumph E, Cylinder, Combination, Oak Cygnet Horn, c.1910 . . . .   2500.00
Edison, Triumph, Oak Case, Cygnet Horn & Crane, Herzog Cabinet 1998.00
Graphophone, Coin-Operated, Oak Case, Curved Glass, Marquee, c.1898, 15 x 13 In. . . .   3300.00
Kalamazoo Duplex, Disc, 2 Brass Bell Horns, Kalamazoo, Michigan 4800.00
Little Wonder, Cast Iron Base, Black Reflector Horn, 7-In. Turntable 529.00
Melodier, Gramophone, Disc Suitcase Model, Portable 50.00
Parlophon, Carl Lindstrom, Oak Case, Berlin, 45 x 45 x 34 In., c.1925 . . . .   255.00
Peter Pan, Folding, Leather Cover, Wood Case, Horn 239.00
Peter Pan, Hand Crank, Flared Horn, Portable, 19th Century 1495.00
Silvertone, Disc, Floor Model, Windup, Mahogany Case, Hand Crank 525.00
Thorens, Spring Motor, Oak Case, Tin Horn, c.1920 . . . .   534.00
Victor, Monarch MS, Exhibition Reproducer, Brass Bell Horn, c.1901 . . . .   2600.00
Victor, Monarch, Improved, Double Spring Motor, Brass Bell Horn, 10-In. Turntable 880.00
Victor, Victrola IX, Mahogany Case, 12-In. Turntable . . . . .197.00 to 250.00
Victor, Victrola IX, Oak Case, 12-In. Turntable 375.00
Victor, Victrola VV4-7, Disc, Walnut Case, Floor 250.00
Victor, Victrola X, No. 2 Soundbox, Mahogany Cabinet, 42 In. 355.00
Victor, Victrola XI, Quartered Oak, Early 1900s, 44 x 21 x 24 In. 590.00
Victor, Victrola XVI, Oak Case, Floor Model, 49 1/2 x 23 In. 310.00
Victor II, Exhibition Reproducer, Oak Case, Brass Bell Horn, 10-In. Turntable . .1000.00 to 1100.00
Victor III, Exhibition Reproducer, Mahogany Case, Floral Horn, 10-In. Turntable 1000.00
Victor III, Exhibition Reproducer, Oak Case, Brass Bell Horn, 10-In. Turntable 1500.00
Victor M, Exhibition Reproducer, Oak Horn, Case . . . . .1800.00 to 2000.00
Victor V, Exhibition Reproducer, Brass, Bell Horn, 28 x 18 1/2 In. 1800.00
Zonophone, Concert Grand, Disc, Oak Case, Brass Horn, c.1901-1904 . . . .   1700.00
Zonophone, Concert, Disc, Oak Case, Brass Horn 1500.00
Zonophone, Concert, Disc, Oak Case, Morning Glory Horn 800.00

PHONOGRAPH NEEDLE CASES of tin are collected today by music and
phonograph enthusiasts and advertising addicts. The tins are very
small, about 2 inches across, and often have attractive graphic designs
lithographed on the top and sides.

Beestone, Contents, 2 x 1 1/4 In. 49.00
His Master's Voice, Gramophone, Nipper Dog, England, 2 x 1 1/2 In. 49.00
Leading Always, 1/2 x 1 5/8 x 1 1/4 In. 36.00
Light, Gramophone, 1/2 x 1 7/8 x 1 3/8 In. 36.00
Lux, Gramophone, Contents, Germany, 2 x 1 1/4 In. 49.00
Lux Original, 3/8 x 1 7/8 x 1 3/8 In. 25.00
Marschall, 1 5/8 x 1 1/2 In. . . . . .36.00 to 45.00
Marschall, Gramophone, Contents, 2 x 1 1/4 In. 49.00
Montgomery Ward, Contents, Slide Top 35.00
Mount Everest, Contents, Germany, 1 3/4 x 1 1/4 In. 49.00
Parrot, Gramophone, Contents, 1 3/4 x 1 1/4 In. 49.00
Pegasus Nadeln, 1 7/8 x 1 3/8 In. 38.00
Pegasus Original, 1 7/8 x 1 1/4 In. 48.00
Regal Loud Tone, 1 3/4 x 1 3/8 In. 36.00
Rojar, 1 7/8 x 1 3/8 In. 40.00
Salon-Tanz Nadeln, Gramophone Needle, Man Dancing, Germany, 1925, 2 In. 75.00

Solo, Contents, England, 1 3/4 x 1 1/4 In. 49.00
Songster, Blue, 1 7/8 x 1 1/4 In. 38.00

PHOTOGRAPHY items are listed here. The first photograph was a view
from a window in France taken in 1826. The commercially successful photograph started with the daguerreotype introduced in 1839.
Today all sorts of photographs and photographic equipment are collected. Albums were popular in Victorian times. Cartes de visite, popular after 1854, were mounted on 2 1/2-by-4-inch cardboard. Cabinet
cards were introduced in 1866. These were mounted on 4 1/4 x 6 1/2-
inch cards. Stereo views are listed under Stereo Card. The cases for
daguerreotypes are listed in the Gutta-Percha category. Stereoscopes
are listed in their own section.

Album, Gilt Brass Mounted, Parcel Gilt, Faux Morocco, 2 1/2 x 6 3/4 x 5 1/2 In. 145.00
Album, Howard Hughes, 88 Custom Prints, 1938, 24 x 19 In. 2875.00
Album, Leporello, Japan, Varnished Wood Cover, Ivory Carving 50 Photos 200.00
Albumen, 10 Indian Chiefs, Wounded Knee, Deadwood, S.D., 1891, 11 x 14 In. 3750.00
Albumen, Arba Read Steam Fire Engine, Troy, N.Y., Oval, G. Rockwood, 3 3/4 x 5 In. ... 175.00
Albumen, Civil War Soldier, Union Infantry Officer, Oval, Frame, 9 1/4 x 11 1/4 In. 405.00
Albumen, Cypress Drive, Monterey, William H. Jackson, 1880s, 16 3/4 x 21 In. 3220.00
Albumen, Dignitaries At Execution Scene, F. Aubert, Mexico, 6 5/8 x 9 1/8 In. 1200.00
Albumen, Hydraulic Gold Mining, Ivory Mount, W.H. Jackson, 7 x 8 3/4 In. 1380.00
Albumen, Lincoln At Antietam, Ostendorf, c.1865, 9 x 7 In. 9750.00
Albumen, Nervous System Of An Animal, 1882, 9 1/2 x 4 1/2 In. 460.00
Albumen, Niagara Falls, Mounted, George Baker, c.1886, 20 3/4 x 16 In. 315.00
Albumen, Oglala Sioux, Wild West Show, Horses, 5 x 8 1/4 In. 250.00
Albumen, Photographic Views Of Sherman's Campaign, George Barnard, 3 Views 920.00
Albumen, Rain In The Face & Wife, D.F. Barry, West Superior, Wisconsin 2000.00
Albumen, Rock-Tombs & Pyramid, Francis Frith, 1857, 6 x 9 In. 690.00
Albumen, Union Private, Kepi, Coat, Musket, Cartridge Box, Triple Mat, 5 x 7 In. 100.00
Albumen, Ute Man, Seated, Studio, c.1904, 7 x 5 In. 105.00
Ambrotype, Civil War, Ohio Infantryman, Fully Equipped, 1/6 Plate 1150.00
Ambrotype, Civilian, Large Cannon, Leather Case, 1/6 Plate 500.00
Ambrotype, Cobbler, Apron, Bench, Tools, Full Leather Case, 1/6 Plate 375.00
Ambrotype, Fireman, Boat, Fortress, Harbor, Lowell, Mass., 1/6 Plate 400.00
Ambrotype, Gentleman In Shiny Leather Cap, 1/9 Plate, 3 x 2 1/2 In. 35.00
Ambrotype, Girl, In Highland Dress, Gilt, Colored Highlights, Case, 1/2 Plate 940.00
Ambrotype, Henry Wilson, Grant's Vice President, c.1872, 1/6 Plate 980.00
Ambrotype, Horse & Carriage, House, Bare Tree, Separated Case, 1/4 Plate 225.00
Ambrotype, Lt. James J. Maddox, 34th Indiana, Washington Monument Case 405.00
Ambrotype, N.Y. Zouave, 146th N.Y. Infantry, Composition Case, 1/6 Plate 2070.00
Ambrotype, Ruby, 2nd VA Infantry Confederates, Piedmont Shirts, 1/6 Plate 1380.00
Ambrotype, Seated Solider, Uniform, Holding 3-Band Musket, 2 3/4 x 3 1/4 In. 550.00
Ambrotype, Southern Cheyenne Chief War Bonnet, c.1863, 3 1/4 x 2 5/8 In. 5875.00
Ambrotype, Union Corporal, Ruby Red, Leatherette Case, Glass, Brass, 1/9 Plate 290.00
Ambrotype, Union Soldier, Wearing Kepi, 2 3/4 x 3 1/4 In. 39.00
Ambrotype, Young Boy, Tinted Flag, Pressed Paper Case, Early 1860s 345.00
Balance Scale, Eastman Kodak, Measures Darkroom Chemicals, Nickel Finish 120.00
Cabinet Card, Annie Oakley, Portrait, Medals, Chicago 1955.00
Cabinet Card, Black Confederate Veteran, Holding Hat, 1903, 5 x 4 In. 790.00
Cabinet Card, Boy With His Brother, A Dog, H.E. Cutler, Morrisville, Vt. 90.00
Cabinet Card, Buffalo Soldier, Bugler, Troop A, 10th Calvary, Fort Keogh, M.T. 1265.00
Cabinet Card, Civil War, 8 Union Generals, 1864, 8 1/2 x 6 1/2 In. 95.00
Cabinet Card, Col. W.F. Cody, Silver Gelatin Print, Beaded Coat, Hat, Brooklyn 460.00
Cabinet Card, Dakota Indian Baseball Player, White's Institute, Sam Moore, Ind. 980.00
Cabinet Card, Eagle Star Sioux Chief, Holding Rifle, 1901, 8 1/2 x 5 In. 588.00
Cabinet Card, General Custer, Upper Body, Albumen, Civilian Dress 1380.00
Cabinet Card, George Osbornes, Pawnee Indian, J.H. Taylor, 1889 .... 150.00
Cabinet Card, Geronimo On One Knee, Apache, Mat, Frame, 7 x 4 1/2 In. 2300.00
Cabinet Card, Geronimo, Seated On Log, Fort Sill, O.T., Addison, 1897 .... 2760.00
Cabinet Card, Girl, Sled, Studio Snow, Rockwood, 17 Union Square 55.00
Cabinet Card, Jennie Wade, Murphy & Co., Gettysburg 115.00
Cabinet Card, Jesse James' Corpse, Graham, Lord Studio, c.1882, 6 1/2 x 4 1/4 In. 4315.00

Cabinet Card, Kiowa Maiden, Silver Gelatin, Irwin & Mankins, c.1890	520.00
Cabinet Card, Lakota Chiefs Spotted Tail & Iron Wing, c.1880, 6 x 4 In.	588.00
Cabinet Card, Lame Bear, Cheyenne Leader, Mat, Frame, 6 3/8 x 4 1/8 In.	575.00
Cabinet Card, Lilly Langtry, As Lady Teazle, Albumen, Vander Weyde Light	175.00
Cabinet Card, Man Reclining, Hat, Crossed Feet, W.M. Bostwell, East Jordan, Mich.	225.00
Cabinet Card, May Lillie, Western Outfit, Shooting Medals, Shotgun	705.00
Cabinet Card, Mountain Man, Rifle, Partridge, Boston, c.1870, 6 1/4 x 4 In.	520.00
Cabinet Card, Muggins Taylor, Found Custer Massacre, Silver Gelatin, c.1900	2530.00
Cabinet Card, Musicians, 2 Seated Men, Banjo, Guitar, Kopke, Brooklyn, 1800s	50.00
Cabinet Card, Quanah Parker, Silver Gelatin, Irwin & Mankins, c.1890	1725.00
Cabinet Card, S.F.B. Morse, Wearing Medals, Bogardus	115.00
Cabinet Card, Sandow, Profile, Flexing, Warwick Brooke	400.00
Cabinet Card, Sandow, Upper Body Pose, London Stereoscopic	480.00
Cabinet Card, Sitting Bull, Buffalo Bill, Holding Winchester, Albumen, Montreal	1530.00
Cabinet Card, Sitting Bull, Plains Style Pipe, c.1882, Bailey, Dix & Mead	690.00
Cabinet Card, Steps, Nez Perce Indian, Bailey Dix & Mead, 1882	350.00
Camera, Accessories, Rollei, Mag 150, Cartridges, Spools, Flashphoto Box	465.00
Camera, AGFA, Isolette, Folding, Leather Case, c.1955	50.00
Camera, AGFA, Viking, Folding, Box	69.00
Camera, Alta, Red, Polish, 1962	400.00
Camera, Auto Nikkor Telephoto-Zoom, 2 Caps, Case	240.00
Camera, Beau Brownie, Rose Color, Art Deco Style, Box, Carrying Case, 1930s	270.00
Camera, Eastman Kodak, No. 7A, Century Studio	1538.00
Camera, Field, Civil War Era, Oak Box, Plate Holder, Gutta Percha, Tripod, c.1858	2475.00
Camera, Heidoscop 6 x 13, 4th Model, 1931	529.00
Camera, Hologon Ultrawide, Filter, Lens Cap	3700.00
Camera, ICA A.G. Stereo-Ideal 651, 1920	463.00
Camera, Ikoflex III 853/16, 1939	320.00
Camera, Kodak AG, Retina Stereo Attachment	290.00
Camera, Kodak, Jiffy Six-20, Box	35.00
Camera, Kodak, No. 3A, Folding, Brownie, Leatherette, c.1900, 2 1/2 x 5 x 10 In.	40.00
Camera, Kodak, Retina III C, Germany	130.00
Camera, Leica IIIf, Red Dial, 1953	595.00
Camera, Lens, Zeiss Topogon, Aerial Photography, 1940	502.00
Camera, Linhof Technika, Studio Type, 5 x 7 In.	950.00
Camera, Movie Outfit, Movette, Camera, Cassette, Case, c.1917	925.00
Camera, Movie, Bell & Howell 200, 16 mm, 1957	130.00
Camera, Movie, Bell & Howell, Eymo 71/Q, 35 mm, 3 Lenses, c.1938	795.00
Camera, Movie, Cine-Kodak Special, 16 mm, c.1948	580.00
Camera, Movie, Cinoscope, 35 mm, Genova Movement, Hand Crank, c.1923	465.00
Camera, Movie, Xenon Lens, 16 mm, Arnold & Richter, Arri, c.1926	2510.00
Camera, Nikon S2, Chrome Version, Chrome Dials, Lever Advange, Japan, 1955	992.00
Camera, Obscura, Tin, 1910	212.00
Camera, Olympus OM2 SP, Zuiko 1.8/50 Lens, Pentax Stereo Adaptor, 1984	330.00
Camera, Petal, Subminiature, Round, Wooden Box, Instructions, 1948	225.00
Camera, Polizei-Exa, Mugshot Camera, East German Police	660.00
Camera, Robot II, 24 x 24 mm, 1939	200.00
Camera, Rollei TLR, Light Meter Diffusers, 25 Piece	300.00
Camera, Rolleiflex 2.8 D, Metal Lens Cap, 1955	370.00
Camera, Rolleiflex 4x4-Set, Gray, Maker's Case, Lens Cap, Box, Leaflets, 1957	360.00
Camera, Rolleiflex T, 2nd Black Model, Light Meter, Feet Scale, 1961	370.00
Camera, Rolleiflex T, 3rd Model, Penta Prism Finder, 1966	345.00
Camera, Rolleiflex T, Gray Version, Maker's Leather Case, Filters, 1958	345.00
Camera, Summicron 2/90, Black, Extendable Lens Hood, 2 Caps	660.00
Camera, Tropical, Teak, Gold Plated Brass, Brown Bellows, Germany, 1925	400.00
Camera, TV Studio, Monitor, Oscillograph, Tripod, c.1955	3235.00
Camera, Vest Pocket Watch, Expo, View Finder, Box, Instructions	500.00
Camera, Yashica YE, Lens Cap, Maker's Case, 1959	440.00
Camera, Zorki IV, 35 mm, Metal, Leatherette, Time Shutter Release, Case, Russia	80.00
Carte De Visite, Alfred H. Colquitt, Confederate Brigadier General, Anthony	300.00
Carte De Visite, Armsmear, Samuel Colt's Mansion, 2 Scenes	520.00
Carte De Visite, Black Servant & Elizabeth Blair, Henry Ulke, 1867	450.00
Carte De Visite, Brig. General John Hunt Morgan	86.00

Carte De Visite, Buffalo Bill, Standing, With Percussion Rifle 1150.00
Carte De Visite, Civil War Amputation, 3 Views 805.00
Carte De Visite, Civil War, 64th U.S. Colored Infantry, Troops, Artillery 1035.00
Carte De Visite, Comm. Cushing, Naval Officer Who Sank The CSS Albemarle 550.00
Carte De Visite, Dr. Charles H. Roemer, Thief, Medical Corp. Uniform, 1875 .... 259.00
Carte De Visite, Esticks, Pinheads As Circus Exhibits, Eisenmann, 1883 .... 395.00
Carte De Visite, Fire Company, 6 Members, North Adams, Mass., Tinted 1528.00
Carte De Visite, Frederick Douglass, Brady 1200.00
Carte De Visite, Frederick Douglass, Warren, Boston 900.00
Carte De Visite, General P.G.T. Beauregard 230.00
Carte De Visite, Indian Romance, Wylie B. Brown, Tama City, Iowa 450.00
Carte De Visite, John Reno, 1st U.S. Train Robber, 1868 .... 2070.00
Carte De Visite, Joseph Hooker, Union Major General, Anthony, N.Y. 110.00
Carte De Visite, Joseph Selby, Confederate Lieutenant 185.00
Carte De Visite, Lincoln's Tomb Interior, 2 Coffins, F.W. Ingmire, Springfield 1300.00
Carte De Visite, Lincoln's Tomb, Open Door, Guards, F.W. Ingmire, Springfield 360.00
Carte De Visite, Lyman Beecher, Harriet Beecher Stowe, Henry Ward Beecher 200.00
Carte De Visite, Pauline Cushman, Union Spy, Composite, 10 Views, c.1866 .... 265.00
Carte De Visite, Robert Anderson, Union Brigadier General 35.00
Carte De Visite, Sojourner Truth, I Sell The Shadow To Support The Substance 1150.00
Carte De Visite, William N.R. Beall, Confederate Brigadier General, Anthony, N.Y. 635.00
Chromolithograph, Paddle Wheel Boat, City Of Bangor, Frame, 32 In. 1000.00
Chromolithograph, Palisades Of The Hudson, Frame, 1900, 8 x 24 In. 405.00
Daguerreotype, 2 Men, 1 With Large Pin On Tie 30.00
Daguerreotype, Boy Holding Puppy By Head, Plaid Dress, 1/6 Plate 1265.00
Daguerreotype, Boy In Chair, 1/6 Plate 40.00
Daguerreotype, Boy In Hat, With Porcelain Dog, 1/6 Plate 105.00
Daguerreotype, Boy, Holding Puppy Around Head, 1/6 Plate 1265.00
Daguerreotype, Broadside, Splendid Daguerreotype Miniatures By E.S. Hayden 95.00
Daguerreotype, Building, Knight, Spencer & Co., Plymouth, Oh., c.1852, 1/6 Plate 865.00
Daguerreotype, Carpenter, Holding Tenon Saw, Leather Case, 1/6 Plate 880.00
Daguerreotype, Child, Sleeping On Deacons Bench, 1/4 Plate 325.00
Daguerreotype, Church, New England, Picket Fence, J.A. Becker, 1/4 Plate 2875.00
Daguerreotype, Daguerreotypist, Camera, 1/4 Plate 2015.00
Daguerreotype, Daniel Spencer, Revolutionary War Vet, 1759-1854, 1/4 Plate 1265.00
Daguerreotype, Daniel Webster, Leather Case, Flower Embossed, 1/6 Plate 1955.00
Daguerreotype, Fireman, Resealed Leather Case, 1/6 Plate 4250.00
Daguerreotype, Fireman, Trumpet, Parade Hat, Union Case, c.1850, 1/6 Plate 8500.00
Daguerreotype, French Military, 1853, 1/4 Plate 460.00
Daguerreotype, Husband Sitting, Wife Standing, Half Case, J.P. Ball, 1/4 Plate 920.00
Daguerreotype, L-Shaped House, 2 Men, Dog, Nashville, 1/4 Plate 1500.00
Daguerreotype, Lydia Wood Buckman, Oval, Frame, 1/4 Plate 325.00
Daguerreotype, Man & Microscope, Man & Son, 1/4 Plate 1265.00
Daguerreotype, Man In Suit, Waist Up, Mahogany Frame, Brady, 1846, 1/4 Plate 1095.00
Daguerreotype, Man In Top Hat, 1/6 Plate 80.00
Daguerreotype, Man, Holding A Square, Leather Case, 1/6 Plate 880.00
Daguerreotype, Man, P.C. Headley's Mary Queen Of Scots Book, 1856, 1/6 Plate 300.00
Daguerreotype, Martha Elsie Finley, About 16, 1/9 Plate 60.00
Daguerreotype, Militia Officer, Plumed Shako, Resealed Leather Case, 1/6 Plate 1350.00
Daguerreotype, Mother, Daughter, Doll, 1/4 Plate 250.00
Daguerreotype, Naval Officer, Gold Tinted Buttons, 1/6 Plate 180.00
Daguerreotype, Parleys Creek, Salt Lake City, Utah, 4 x 5 In. 175.00
Daguerreotype, Post Mortem, Mardem Family, 1/4 Plate 330.00
Daguerreotype, Silversmith, Seated At Table, Embossed Leather Case, 1/6 Plate 4900.00
Daguerreotype, Virginia Gentleman, Cane, Top Hat, Powers, Richmond, Va., 1/2 Case ... 750.00
Daguerreotype, Well To Do Couple, James Presley Ball, 1/2 Case, 1/4 Plate 920.00
Daguerreotype, William H. Prescott, Case, Early 1800s, 1/6 Plate, 4 x 3 In. 415.00
Daguerreotype, Woman, Holding Book, 1/6 Plate 20.00
Daguerreotype, Woman, In Bonnet, Blue Tinted Ribbons, Mat, Case, 1/6 Plate 445.00
Daguerreotype, Woman, In Shawl, Southworth & Hawes, Leather Case, 1/6 Plate 748.00
Daguerreotype, Woman, Lace Bonnet, Southworth & Hawes, Case, 1/6 Plate 865.00
Daguerreotype, Woman, Pearl Necklace, Southworth & Hawes, Case, 1/6 Plate 805.00
Daguerreotype, Wool Merchant, Horse Drawn Wagon, 1/6 Plate 3250.00

Daguerreotype Case, Angel, Cornucopia, B1-84, 1/6 Plate 150.00
Daguerreotype Case, Bird's Nest, Raising The Brood, 1/6 Plate 135.00
Daguerreotype Case, Catching Butterflies, 1/9 Plate 150.00
Daguerreotype Case, Fan Of Cornucopias, 1/6 Plate 125.00
Daguerreotype Case, Oval, 1/6 Plate 150.00
Enamel On Copper, 4 Children, Faulkner, London, Victorian, 3 1/2 x 4 1/4 In. 175.00
Folder, 50 Heliotypes, World Exhibition, Art Nouveau, Paris, 1900 .... 240.00
Gelatin Silver Print, Slaughter House, W.F. Puffer, Chicago, 7 3/8 x 9 3/8 In. 250.00
Locomotion, Elephants, Eadweard Muybridge, 19 x 24 In. 300.00
Locomotion, Woman Moving, Eadweard Muybridge, 13 1/2 x 19 In. 600.00
Locomotion, Woman, Bathtub, Eadweard Muybridge, 19 x 24 In. 420.00
Magic Lantern, 1860-1870, 2 Piece 240.00
Magic Lantern, Box, Germany, 8 1/2 x 7 1/2 In. 80.00
Magic Lantern, Brass, Tin, Child Shaped Support, 6 Slides, Case, Germany, 11 In. 300.00
Magic Lantern, Climax, Ernst Plank, Round Disc, Wood Box, c.1898, 8 1/2 In. 330.00
Magic Lantern, Germany, c.1860 .... 400.00
Magic Lantern, Phagmatrope, For 5-In. Slides, c.1870, 18 In. 245.00
Magic Lantern, Slides, Astronomical Scenes, Wood Frames, c.1890, 4 Piece 240.00
Magic Lantern, Slides, Hand-Painted, 4 x 6 1/2 In., 6 Piece 320.00
Magic Lantern, Slides, Jack & The Beanstalk, Wood Frame, c.1860, 8 Piece 130.00
Photograph, 2 Boys In A Factory, Lewis W. Hine, c.1909, 4 3/4 x 7 In. 550.00
Photograph, American Horse, Sioux, A. Gardner, Mat, Frame, 7 1/2 x 5 1/2 In. 1380.00
Photograph, Ansel Adams, Barn & Fence, Cape Cod, Late 1930s, 20 x 26 In. 4945.00
Photograph, Bear Legs, Osage Warrior, Sepia Tone, Carl Moon, 16 x 13 1/2 In. 1380.00
Photograph, Boyhood's Outlook, H.S. Wyer, Nantucket, Mass., 19 x 15 In. 105.00
Photograph, Brooklyn Bridge At Dusk, Jessie Tarbox Beals, 16 3/4 x 8 7/8 In. 2695.00
Photograph, Buffalo Soldiers, Officers, Fort Assiniboine, c.1896, 3 Views 2990.00
Photograph, Cavalry Band, Indian Wars, Fort Smith, Ark., c.1910, 2 Views 160.00
Photograph, Chief & His Staff, Edward S. Curtis, 1905, 12 1/2 x 17 1/4 In. 3680.00
Photograph, Child Running, Harold Edgerton, 1939, 1980s Print, 12 x 18 1/2 In. 980.00
Photograph, Coal Miners, At Portal, Mules, 4 1/2 x 7 In. 150.00
Photograph, Craters On Moon, NASA Lunar Orbiter Project, 1967, 32 1/2 x 20 In. 300.00
Photograph, Crow Foot, Sitting Bull's Son, DF Barry, Mounted, 1890s, 6 x 10 In. 650.00
Photograph, Dead Dalton Gang In Coffeyville, Daltons, Powers, Broadwell 1150.00
Photograph, El Capitan, Carleton E. Watkins, Late 1800s, 21 x 15 In. 460.00
Photograph, Eleanora Duse, Mat, Mounted, Arnold Genthe, 8 3/4 x 6 3/4 In. 350.00
Photograph, Engine Company, 1870, Charleston, S.C., George Barnard, 11 x 15 In. 635.00
Photograph, First Ladies, Truman, Roosevelt, Wilson, Signed, 16 x 12 In. 1430.00
Photograph, Georgia O'Keeffe, Dan Budnik, 1970s, 7 1/4 x 10 3/4 In. 1610.00
Photograph, Gross Anatomy Class, 6 Robed Students & Patient, 1903, 11 x 14 In. 175.00
Photograph, Hudson River, Fred Zinnemann, 1931, 10 1/4 x 13 In. 1840.00
Photograph, Indian & Child, J.G. Noble, Banff, c.1919, Frame, 19 1/2 x 15 1/2 In. 920.00
Photograph, Indian Chief, Pittsburgh Plate Glass Co., Frame, c.1899, 11 x 8 In. 575.00
Photograph, Kill Bear Sioux, Signed, F.A. Rinehart, Omaha, Frame, 17 x 13 In. 460.00
Photograph, Kutzown Fire Co., No. 1, Washington D.C., 1931, 10 x 27 In. 69.00
Photograph, Lone Wolf Dancing The War Dance, c.1890, 5 x 7 In. 400.00
Photograph, Magnolia Blossom, I. Cunningham, 1925, Reprint, 10 x 12 1/2 In. 1095.00
Photograph, Parry Sisters, Buffalo Bill's Trick Riders, Floyd, c.1912, 8 x 10 In. 1610.00
Photograph, Rain In The Face, Sioux Chief, Mat, Frame, 10 1/2 x 8 1/2 In. 1955.00
Photograph, Rough Riders, T. Roosevelt Col. 1st USV Cavalry, Frame, 16 x 20 In. 12501.00
Photograph, Sailor In Minsk, Duane Michals, 1958, 4 3/4 x 7 In. 1095.00
Photograph, Schedule, Transcontinental Railway, A.J. Russell, Citadel Rock 3105.00
Photograph, Shaker Eldress Bertha Lindsay, Inscribed, Canterbury, 9 1/2 x 7 1/2 In. 60.00
Photograph, Sitting Bull's Tepee & Family, West Superior, Wisc., 1891, 8 x 10 In. 950.00
Photograph, Some Of The Boys Who Saved Us, Civil War, Case, c.1866 .... 545.00
Photograph, Thomas Inch, Sepia Silver Print, Signed, 6 x 4 1/8 In. 150.00
Photograph, Typical Trio, Cowboys, Hand Colored, Huffman, c.1903, 8 x 9 1/2 In. 489.00
Photograph, Young, Resettled Farmer, Arkansas, Arthur Rothstein, 9 5/8 x 12 1/2 In. 350.00
Photograph, Zouave, Shaking Hands With Man In Highland Kilt, 7 3/4 x 6 In. 1125.00
Photographer's Posing Stand, Cast Iron Immobilizer, Head Clamp, Tripod 2250.00
Photogravure, Eagle Catcher, Edward S. Curtis, 1908, 7 1/2 x 5 1/2 In. 315.00
Stereo Card, Civil War, Building Bridge, Taylor & Huntington, 4 x 7 In. 138.00
Stereo Card, McKinley, Salute River Parade, Underwood, 1901, 7 x 3 1/2 In. 75.00

Stereo Card, McKinley, Speaking At Alamo, Underwood, 1901, 7 x 3 1/2 In.	75.00
Tintype, 11th New York Cavalry Sergeant, 1/4 Plate	1265.00
Tintype, African American Woman, White Child, Formal Dress, 1/2 Case, 2 3/8 x 3 In. . .	174.00
Tintype, Banjo Player, Studio Portrait, c.1890, 4 x 6 In.	575.00
Tintype, Brick Making, 8 Workmen, Windmill, Mat, 11 x 14 In., Full Plate	460.00
Tintype, Cavalryman, Union, On Horse, Leather Case, 1/4 Plate	1090.00
Tintype, Civil War Soldier, Flowers, Leaves, Case, Foil Surround, 2 x 1 3/8 In.	440.00
Tintype, Civil War, 4 Indiana Cavalry Officers, Tent, 1/2 Plate	2875.00
Tintype, Civil War, 4 Indiana Cavalrymen, Studio, Black Union Case, 1/4 Plate	1265.00
Tintype, Civil War, Caleb Glick, 114th OVI, Union Veteran Reserve Corps, 1/6 Plate	345.00
Tintype, Civil War, Soldier, Standing With Woman, Gold Painted Trim, 1/6 Plate	95.00
Tintype, Civil War, Zachariah Strickmaker, 80th OVI, Composition Case, 1/9 Plate	520.00
Tintype, Crimean War Officer, Hand Tinted, Leather Case, 1850s, 1/6 Plate	430.00
Tintype, Fireman & Wife, Bib Shirt, Hose 2, Parade Belt, Dress Cap	40.00
Tintype, Fireman, Holding Violin, North Adams, Mass., Tinted, 4 x 6 In.	259.00
Tintype, Man & Dog In Backyard, Clothes On Line, 1/2 Plate	200.00
Tintype, Scottish Child, Plaid Dress, Sash, Oval Window, Frame, 1/2 Plate	115.00
Tintype, Son Bid Off To War, Partial Composition Case, 1/6 Plate	160.00
Tintype, Union Cavalry Soldier, Saber, Sharps Carbine Rifle, 2 5/8 In.	900.00
Tintype, Union Infantry Soldier, Thermoplastic Case, 1/6 Plate	275.00
Tintype, Union Infantryman, Overcoat, Hardee Hat, Case, 1/6 Plate	430.00
Tintype, Union Soldier, At Attention, With Musket	478.00
Tintype, Union Soldier, M1860 Sword, Holstered Pistol, Case, 1/6 Plate	460.00
Tintype, Union Soldier, Standing Next To Chair, 1/4 Plate	259.00
Tintype, Young Girl, Toys, Homespun Dress, 1/2 Plate	230.00
Viewer, Carte De Visite, Concave Mirror, Square, 5 1/2 In.	200.00

PIANO BABY is a collector's term. About 1880, the well-decorated
home had a shawl on the piano. Bisque figures of babies were designed
to help hold the shawl in place. They range in size from 6 to 18 inches.
Most of the figures were made in Germany. Reproductions are being
made. Other piano babies may be listed under manufacturers' names.

Baby Lying On Back, Dutch Cap, Gebruder Heubach, c.1910, 6 In.	415.00
Baby On Back, Playful, Blond, No. 3820, Gebruder Heubach, c.1912, 10 In.	1870.00
Bisque, Baby On Back, Arms & 1 Leg Lifted, Bonnet, No. 7536, 7 1/4 In.	105.00
Bisque, Lying On Back, Blue Intaglio Eyes, Gebruder Heubach, 9 In.	250.00
Girl Holding Cup, Yellow Dress, Blue Bows, Bisque, 14 In.	175.00
Lying On Back, Uplifted Head, Waving Arms, Legs, Gebruder Heubach, c.1910, 12 In. . .	2090.00
On Chamber Pot, Scowling, Bisque, No. 9908, Heubach, c.1912, 9 In.	2200.00
Sitting, Bisque, Uplifted Arms, White Smock, Gebruder Heubach, c.1912, 11 In.	770.00
Sitting, Drawn Up Legs, Clasped Hands, Gebruder Heubach, c.1912, 11 In.	8360.00
Sitting, Inclined Forward, Blond, Gebruder Heubach, c.1912, 6 In.	600.00

PICKARD China Company was started in 1893 by Wilder Pickard.
Hand-painted designs were used on china purchased from other
sources. In the 1930s, the company began to make its own china wares
in Chicago, Illinois. The company now makes many types of porcelains, including a successful line of limited edition collector plates.

Bowl, Garden Scene, Signed, 7 In.	290.00
Plate, Tropical Scene, Marked, 8 1/2 In.	375.00
Vase, Garden Scene, 6 In.	315.00
Vase, Lake & Forest Scene, Gilt Handles, Signed, F. Vobor, c.1910, 10 1/4 x 5 In.	420.00
Vase, Tropical Scene, Handles, Marked	230.00

PICTURE FRAMES are listed in this book in the Furniture category under Frame.

PICTURES, silhouettes, and other small decorative objects framed to
hang on the wall are listed here. Sandpaper pictures are black and
white charcoal drawings done on a special sanded paper. Some other
types of pictures are listed in the Print and Painting categories.

Cutwork, Paper, Lace, Stipple Effect To Clothes, Frame, c.1824, 4 x 5 1/2 In.	115.00
Diorama, Under Glass, 2 Men At Giltwood Table, Wood Base, France, Late 1800s, 16 In.	999.00
Drawing, Ink On Paper, Waldo's Cat, Waldo Midgley, Frame, 11 1/2 x 8 1/4 In.	294.00
Drawing, Leaping Stag, Shadow Box Frame, Spencerian, 26 1/2 x 32 1/2 In.	330.00

Picture, Pyrography,
Burned & Painted
Wood, Still Life,
14 x 10 In.

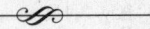

Pictures look best if hung on a
light-colored wall. Check wires and
screw eyes before hanging an old
picture. Don't forget to dust the
backs and tops of framed pictures
several times a year.

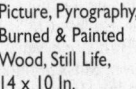

Drawing, Potted Flowers, Conrad Gilbert, Frame, Pennsylvania German, 5 x 3 In. 1320.00
Eglomise Panel, Ladies In A Garden Pavilion, Chinese, 20th Century, 29 x 21 In. 635.00
Engraving, Completion Of Pacific Railroad, Train, People Cheering, c.1869, 21 x 14 In. ... 95.00
Engraving, History Of British Birds, Rev. Francis Orpen Morris, 9 3/4 x 12 In., 8 Piece .. 60.00
Engraving On Paper, Hauling In The Nets, Sears Gallagher, New Frame, 6 x 8 3/4 In. 575.00
Etching, Covered Bridge, Wooded Landscape, E.T. Hurley, Mat, Frame, 9 x 7 In. 460.00
Etching, Hoffman, Gustave Adolph, To My Friend, John Crossley, c.1930, 11 x 14 In. 39.00
Etching, Old St. Philip's, Charleston, Alfred Heber Hutty, 9 x 12 In. 1725.00
Floral Arrangement, Fancywork, Feathers, Hair, Wool, Shadowbox Frame, 29 1/2 x 24 In. 345.00
Lithograph, Clipper Ship, Sweepstakes, Hand Colored, Gouache Highlights, 25 x 32 In... 475.00
Lithograph, Lily, Tulip, P.J. Redoute, c.1954, 20 x 13 In., Pair 805.00
Lithograph, Lincoln, Hand Colored, 10 Small Vignette Border, Frame, c.1865, 30 x 40 In. 5750.00
Merit, Sunday School, Linen, Sabbath School Hymn, Black Frame, 12 1/2 x 12 1/2 In. 275.00
Mural, Seed Art, Black & White Cows, Barn, Grazing In Field, 1936-1949 .... 4800.00
Needlework, Berlin Work, Anti-Slavery, Animals, Flowers, Frame, c.1863, 22 x 22 In. ... 1250.00
Needlework, Berlin Work, Biblical Landscape, Judges 11, Frame, c.1860, 39 x 34 In. 517.00
Needlework, Biblical Scene, Jacob Asking For Rachel's Hand, Silk, Frame, 19 x 16 In. ... 70.00
Needlework, Building, Flowers, Emeline Brown, Eglomise Mat, Frame, 18 x 23 In. 390.00
Needlework, Cloud Collar, Bird, Flower, Landscape, Silk, Frame, Late 1800s, 27 In. 230.00
Needlework, Crane, Silk, Japanese School, Gilt Frame, 44 1/2 x 22 In. 60.00
Needlework, Embroidered, Memorial, George Washington, c.1801, 13 1/2 x 11 1/2 In. ... 5225.00
Needlework, Embroidered, Silk, Phoenix, Paulownia Tree, Flowers, c.1910, 24 x 20 In. ... 230.00
Needlework, Embroidered, Women, Butterflies, Wool, Silk, On Cotton, 13 x 13 1/2 In. ... 220.00
Needlework, Flower Vase, Butterfly, Chenille Silk & Metallic Thread, 17 3/8 x 14 1/2 In.. 259.00
Needlework, Flower Vase, Polychrome On Black Silk, Frame, c.1840, 17 1/4 x 20 1/2 In. 90.00
Needlework, Gentleman & Lady On River Bank, Chenille, Watercolor, 18 x 21 1/2 In. ... 2760.00
Needlework, House, Chimneys, Windows, Flower Vase, Frame, 20 x 23 1/2 In. 440.00
Needlework, Joseph Sold Into Slavery, Frame, Continental, Victorian, 27 x 18 1/2 In. 575.00
Needlework, Landscape, Beaded Borders, Frame, Late 1800s, 10 3/8 x 10 In. 235.00
Needlework, Maidens, Fruit Trees, Flowers, Buildings, c.1900, 25 x 22 In. 150.00
Needlework, Man, Flute, Shepherdess, Silk, Frame, America, c.1810, 14 1/2 x 13 1/4 In.. 5290.00
Needlework, Man, Woman, At Well, Worked I, Elizabeth Warren, Silk, 1796, 13 x 16 In. . 440.00
Needlework, Mourning Picture, Chenille, Watercolor, Woman, Dog, Frame, 8 1/2 x 7 In. . 375.00
Needlework, Soldier Informing Family Of Bad News, Russia, 12 x 9 1/4 In. 2630.00
Needlework, Tiger, Frame, Japanese School, Early 20th Century, 10 3/4 x 19 1/4 In. 60.00
Needlework, USS Maine, Morrow Castle, Burlwood Frame, 10 x 16 In. 400.00
Needlework, Village Scene, Silk, Watercolor, Frame, 14 1/2 x 14 1/2 In. 330.00
Needlework, Watercolor, Finding Moses, Silk, Oval Reserve, 16 3/4 x 14 In. 4500.00
Needlework, Wax, Abe Lincoln, Silhouette, Bird's-Eye Maple Frame, c.1865, 8 x 9 1/4 In. 448.00
Needlework, Woman, Stream, Dog, Tree, Watercolor, c.1835, 11 5/8 x 9 1/2 In. 700.00
Needlework, Women Gathering Flowers, Yellow Grain Painted Frame, 15 1/2 x 18 In. ... 1870.00
Needlework, Wool, Flowers, Wirework Stems, Wood Base, Glass Dome Cover, 17 In. ... 175.00
Needlework, Wool, Red & White Flowers, Pot, Shadow Box Frame, c.1870, 18 x 20 In. .. 1850.00
Pastel, Hanging Game Still Life, William Henry Chandler, c.1900, 11 x 24 In. 140.00
Pastel, Landscape, Lake, Shoreline Boat, Mountains, William Henry Chandler, 14 x 28 In. 120.00
Pastel, Landscape, Man Fishing From Boat In Lake, c.1900, 4 x 24 In. 55.00

Pastel, Landscape, William Henry Chandler, c.1900, 16 x 20 In. 90.00
Pen, Ink, Watercolor On Paper, Elevation, Engine No. 174, P&K Railroad, 24 x 37 In. . . . 2629.00
Pencil, Watercolor, Gouache, Paper, Farmscape, Mat, Frame, G. Norvelle, 7 1/2 x 10 In. . . 750.00
Pencil, Young Woman, Reclining, Hands Over Head, J.W. Carroll, 1939, 13 x 9 In. 345.00
Pith Painting, Multiple Oars, Sailing Galley, Frame, Chinese, 1800s, 6 x 10 In. 345.00
Pith Painting, Sampan Boat, Floating Ducks, Chinese, 1800s, 8 x 11 In. 200.00
Portrait On Ivory, George & Martha Washington, Brass Frame, 3 1/2 x 2 1/2 In., Pair . . . 345.00
Portrait On Ivory, Young Man, Blue Coat, Pink Waistcoat, Frame, 3 1/4 x 2 1/2 In. 525.00
Pyrography, Burned & Painted Wood, Still Life, 14 x 10 In. . . . . *Illus* 85.00
Reverse Print On Glass, Africa, America, Anti-Slavery, Frame, 1807, 10 1/2 x 14 In. 6900.00
Scherenschnitte, Watercolor, Ink, Pinprick, Adam & Eve, Pa., c.1830, 13 x 17 In., Pair . . 6050.00
Silhouette, Boy With Whip, Master Reginald Bird, Frame, October 20, 1837, 11 x 9 In. . . 1840.00
Silhouette, Boy, Charles Cressor, Age 8, Lacy Collar, Hollow Cut, c.1830, 5 x 6 3/8 In. . . 275.00
Silhouette, Boy, Gold Detail, White Painted Collar, Bird's Eye Veneer Frame, 8 x 7 In. . . 173.00
Silhouette, Colonial Man, Daniel Gowing, Wilmington, Mass., Frame, 1774, 7 x 5 3/4 In. . 345.00
Silhouette, Daniell Family, 9 Children, Cutout, Gold Ink Highlights, 25 x 6 In. 385.00
Silhouette, Family, Husband, Wife, 2 Daughters, Hollow Cut, Frame, 8 1/2 x 10 1/2 In. . . 715.00
Silhouette, Full Length, Geo. Frederick Muntz, Edouart, Frame, 1838, 16 x 14 In. 220.00
Silhouette, Full Length, Hon. Oliver Hatcher, Frame, Aug. Edouart, 1841, 15 1/2 x 12 In. 990.00
Silhouette, Full Length, Man, Lithograph Balcony, Signed, Edouart, Frame, 12 x 8 1/2 In. 1650.00
Silhouette, Full Length, Rebecca Stansbury, Frame, Aug. Edouart, 1841, 14 x 11 In. 770.00
Silhouette, Gentleman, Black Paper, Gold & Black Ink Highlights, c.1840, 3 x 4 3/8 In. . . 70.00
Silhouette, Gentleman, Embossed, Peales Museum, Black Painted Frame, 5 x 4 In. 165.00
Silhouette, Gentleman, Gold Ink Detail, William Barker, Frame, 1833, 4 3/4 x 4 1/8 In. . . 290.00
Silhouette, Gentleman, Signed, W. Dudman, Frame, 1802 . . . . 330.00
Silhouette, Girl, Hair Comb, Hollow Cut, Lace Collar, Frame, c.1835, 6 1/2 x 5 1/2 In. . . 120.00
Silhouette, Husband & Wife, Hollow Cut, Curly Maple Veneer Frame, 6 x 5 In., Pair 430.00
Silhouette, Ink, Portrait, Coiffured Woman, Lace Bodice, Gilt Frame, c.1790, 5 1/2 x 5 In. 60.00
Silhouette, Lady, Hollow Cut, Embossed, Museum, Peale, Gilt Frame, 5 1/2 x 4 1/8 In. . . 220.00
Silhouette, Man, Hollow Cut, Embossed, Museum, Peale, Mahogany Frame, 6 5/8 x 6 In. . 440.00
Silhouette, Man, Hollow Cut, Impressed Designs, Pressed Brass Frame, c.1830, 5 x 5 In. . 220.00
Silhouette, Man, Hollow Cut, Ink Detail Lapels, Cravat, Hair, c.1830, 2 3/4 x 3 1/2 In. . . 330.00
Silhouette, Portrait, Man, Hollow Cut, Frame, 5 In. 175.00
Silhouette, Portrait, Woman, Blue Dress, Holding Book, c.1832, 3 1/2 x 2 1/2 In. 4700.00
Silhouette, Sisters, Cutout, Black Paper, Gold Highlights, Frame, c.1840, 7 x 5 In., Pair . . 300.00
Silhouette, Woman, Full Length, Well Dressed, Hair In Bun, Brass Frame, 8 1/2 x 6 In. . . 403.00
Silhouette, Woman, Holding Book, Hollow Cut, Gray Wash, c.1830, 4 3/8 x 5 1/8 In. . . . 440.00
Silhouette, Woman, Hollow Cut, Anna Maria Siegfried, Frame, c.1830, 5 3/4 x 8 In. 250.00
Silhouette, Woman, Hollow Cut, Upswept Hair, Hand Drawn Collar, Frame, 4 x 4 1/2 In. . 255.00
Silhouette, Woman, Lithographed Body, Hollow Cut, Frame, c.1835, 4 1/2 x 5 3/4 In. . . . 360.00
Silhouette, Woman, Ringlets, Comb, Brooch, Frame, 7 x 6 In. 375.00
Silhouette, Woman, Ringlets, Gilt Liner, Bird's-Eye Maple Frame, 7 1/4 x 6 1/8 In. 430.00
Silhouette, Woman, Standing, Marked Phelps, Frame, 1800, 4 x 2 3/4 In. 115.00
Theorem, 2 Birds, On Fruit Bowl, Bill Rank, Sponge Decorated Frame, 16 x 18 In. 715.00
Theorem, Basket Of Fruit, On Paper, Gilt Frame, 8 5/8 x 10 1/2 In. 690.00
Theorem, Bird, On Branch, Yellow, Pink Tail, Blue Wings, Frame, c.1850, 9 3/8 x 7 3/8 In. 550.00
Theorem, Bouquet Of Flowers, On Velvet, Gilt & Black Painted Frame, 19 x 19 1/2 In. . . . 460.00
Theorem, Delft Plate, Holland Scenery, Fruit, Leaves, Painted Frame, 19 3/4 x 24 1/2 In. . 385.00
Theorem, Eagle, Spread Wing, Banner, Liberty, Equality, Justice, Frame, 21 1/2 x 23 In. . 605.00
Theorem, Flower Basket, White Ground, On Paper, Gilt Frame, 20 x 24 1/2 In. 345.00
Theorem, Fruit Basket, Bird, D. Ellinger, Grain Decorated Frame, 17 3/8 x 20 3/4 In. 2200.00
Theorem, Fruit Basket, Bird, Ellie Gawron, Gesso Frame, On Flannel, 1800s, 20 x 27 In. . 115.00
Theorem, Watercolor, Basket Of Fruit, Stenciled, Cut, Frame, 1800s, 10 x 18 In. 990.00
Theorem, Watercolor, Flowers, Stenciled, Frame, 19th Century, 9 x 7 In. 415.00
Theorem, Woven Flower Basket, Gold Leaf Frame, 15 1/2 x 19 1/2 In. 1900.00
Theorem, Young Girl, On Rocking Horse, Sponge Decorated Frame, 16 x 18 In. 660.00
Watercolor, 2 Sisters, 1 Standing, 1 Seated, Frame, 11 3/4 x 9 In. 1210.00
Watercolor, American Mountain Man, Jacob, 20th Century, 27 x 13 3/4 In. 460.00
Watercolor, Arts & Crafts Interior, J.W. Johnson, Frame, 1910, 10 1/2 x 17 In. 405.00
Watercolor, Birds On Branch, Yellow, Orange, Green, Brown Ink, Frame, 9 1/2 x 13 In. . . 2185.00
Watercolor, Blue Jay, In Small Tree, Frame, 19th Century, 5 1/2 x 7 3/4 In. 770.00
Watercolor, Botanical Studies, Frame, 13 1/4 x 8 1/2 In., 4 Piece 1060.00
Watercolor, Canyon Pass, Andrew Putnam Hill, c.1915, 36 x 26 In. 920.00

Watercolor, Coastal Seascape, William C. Bauer, Frame, c.1900, 10 1/2 x 29 1/4 In. 980.00
Watercolor, Country Home, J.B. Reid, 6 x 12 1/2 In. 489.00
Watercolor, English Gentleman, Top Coat, Stove Pipe Hat, John Balt Esq., 8 1/2 x 11 In. .   620.00
Watercolor, Family Portrait, Bird's Eye Maple Frame, c.1850, 17 x 14 In. 385.00
Watercolor, Flag & Eagle, Mat, Frame, 18 x 22 In. 1050.00
Watercolor, General Wool, On Horseback, Flag, Civil War, Frame, 7 1/2 x 9 1/2 In. 565.00
Watercolor, Golden Gate Clipper Ship, F. Lundstrom, Mat, Frame, 1933, 15 x 21 In. . . .   690.00
Watercolor, Gouache, Paper, Buildings, Birch Trees, Gulbrandt Sether, Frame, 14 x 7 In. .   865.00
Watercolor, Indians On A Hillside, W.S. Burrows, c.1900, 13 x 10 1/2 In. 345.00
Watercolor, Ink On Paper, Mourning, Noah Norton, Oct. 24 1814, Age 39, 15 x 17 In. . . .   1910.00
Watercolor, Ink, Wash, Serasati, Ceiling Of A Box At La Scala Theater, Milan, 20 x 19 In.   390.00
Watercolor, Louisiana Scene, Alexander J. Drysdale, c.1910, 10 x 30 In. 1840.00
Watercolor, Man, Full Length, Lewis Miller, Painted Frame, 3 1/8 x 3 3/4 In. 550.00
Watercolor, Man, Seated, Cigar, Black Suit, Period Brown & Gold Frame, 8 3/4 x 7 In. . .   440.00
Watercolor, Man, Seated, Naively Executed, Frame, c.1864, 4 1/4 x 6 In. 415.00
Watercolor, Mariner's Compass, Red & Green, Frame, 4 1/4 x 4 1/4 In. 920.00
Watercolor, Mountain Range, E.T. Compton, c.1910, 8 x 10 In.   1380.00
Watercolor, Off The Maine Coast, Henry Webster Rice, Frame, 13 1/4 x 19 In. 230.00
Watercolor, On Paper, Salome, Dorothy Foster Brown, c.1901, 14 x 10 1/2 In. 470.00
Watercolor, Redwing Blackbird, Bruno Ertz, c.1943, 9 x 13 In.   550.00
Watercolor, Shore Side Scene, S.R. Chafee, Frame, 1800s, 9 1/2 x 13 1/2 In. 60.00
Watercolor, Well-To-Do Man, Gilt Frame, c.1840, 5 1/4 x 6 3/4 In. 440.00
Watercolor, Woman, New York State, Frame, c.1840, 4 1/2 x 4 1/4 In. 1210.00
Watercolor, Woman, Standing, Full Length, Elisabeth Tyson, c.1842, 13 x 17 In. 550.00
Watercolor, Woman, Table, Pink Dress, Emily Prinsel, 1840, 9 1/4 x 6 3/4 In. 750.00
Watercolor, Woman, Torso, White Dress, Puffy Sleeves, Frame, c.1835, 8 3/4 x 10 In. . . .   250.00
Watercolor, Wood Duck On Branch, Mat, Frame, 12 1/4 x 9 1/4 In. 140.00

PIERCE, see Howard Pierce category.

PIGEON FORGE Pottery was started in Pigeon Forge, Tennessee, in 1946. Red clay found near the pottery was used to make the pieces. Molded or thrown pottery with matte glaze and slip decoration was made. The pottery closed in 2000.

   Candleholder, Blue Snowflake, Crystalline Glaze, 2 1/2 In. 138.00

PILKINGTON Tile and Pottery Company was established in 1892 in England. The company made small pottery wares, like buttons and hatpins, but soon started decorating vases purchased from other potteries. By 1903, the company had discovered an opalescent glaze that became popular on the Lancastrian pottery line. The manufacture of pottery ended in 1937. Pilkington's Tiles Ltd. has worked from 1938 to the present.

   Plate, Royal Lancastrian, Flowers, Gladys Rogers, 1930s, 8 1/8 In. 230.00
   Vase, Bottle, Royal Lancastrian, Blue Green High Glaze, 1912, 7 1/2 In. 115.00
   Vase, Embossed Leaves, Green Matte Glaze, Round Shoulder, Inverted Neck, 7 x 7 In. . . .   500.00
   Vase, Luster, Orange, Green Streaks, Red Crystalline Glaze, Fluted Panel Body, 9 In. . . .   175.00
   Vase, Royal Lancastrian, Crystalline Glaze, 1907, 4 1/4 In. 800.00
   Vase, Royal Lancastrian, Luster, Lavender Flowers, Richard Joyce, 5 7/8 In. 1035.00
   Vase, Royal Lancastrian, Undersea Decoration, Richard Joyce, c.1910, 8 5/8 In. 3795.00

PINCUSHION DOLLS are not really dolls and often were not even pincushions. Some collectors use the term *half-doll*. The top half of each doll was made of porcelain. The edge of the half-doll was made with several small holes for thread, and the doll was stitched to a fabric body with a voluminous skirt. The finished figure was used to cover a hot pot of tea, powder box, pincushion, whisk broom, or lamp. They were made in sizes from less than an inch to over 9 inches high. Most date from the early 1900s to the 1950s. Collectors often find just the porcelain doll without the fabric skirt.

   Chocolate Lady, Opening & Returning Arms, Goebel, 3 3/4 In.   2475.00
   Flapper, 1 Open & Returning Arm, 1 Close Arm, 4 1/2 In. 49.00
   Flapper, Open & Returning Arms, Legs, 3 1/4 In. 220.00
   Nude, Arms Extended, Dressel & Kister, 6 1/4 In. 3575.00

Nude, Flowers In Hair, 1 Open & Returning Arm, 2 1/2 In. 72.00
Nude, Flowers In Hair, Arms Extended, Dressel & Kister, 5 1/4 In. 4950.00
Nude, Holding Shell, Full Figure, Open & Returning Arms, 2 1/2 In. 220.00
Peddler Type, Black Bonnet, Red Shawl, Apron, Umbrella, Red, Green, 6 3/4 In. 590.00
Woman, 1 Open & Returning & 1 Close Arm, Fur, Beads, Roses, 4 In. 385.00
Woman, Arms Extended, Fan, Fancy Hat, 6 1/4 In. 1210.00
Woman, Bodice, Hat, 1 Open & Returning & 1 Close Arm, 3 1/4 In. 60.00
Woman, Dutch, Blue, White, Hat, Dress, Marked, Schneider, Germany, 4 1/2 In. 70.00
Woman, Elaborate Blouse, Hat, Bohne & Sohne, 6 1/2 In. 5500.00
Woman, Extended Arms Hold Rose, Ruffled Blouse, Dresden China, 4 3/4 In. 3575.00
Woman, Holding Fan, Blue Hair Bow, China, Germany, 3 1/2 In. 39.00
Woman, Holding Letter, Pink Hairbow, China, Germany, 3 1/2 In. 50.00
Woman, Lavinia, Fruit Tray, Fancy Hair Piece, Bisque, 5 1/2 In. 4950.00
Woman, Shawl, Hairbow, 1 Open & Returning & 1 Close Arm, 7 3/4 In. 440.00
Woman, Spanish, Black Hair, Blue Hairbow, China, Germany, 3 In. 39.00
Woman, With Mandolin, China, Germany, 2 3/4 In. 55.00

PINK SLAG pieces are listed in this book in the Slag Glass category.

PIPES have been popular since tobacco was introduced to Europe by
Sir Walter Raleigh. Carved wooden, porcelain, ivory, and glass pipes
may be listed here. Meerschaum pipes are listed under Meerschaum.

Meerschaum, Black Woman In Turban, Gown, Case, PCF Best Made, 3 3/4 x 8 1/4 In. 660.00
Meerschaum, Carved, 2 Running Horses, Amber, Fabric Case, 7 In. 220.00
Meerschaum, Carved, Cats With Long Dress & Apron, Jacket & Bowtie, Case, 13 In. ... 196.00
Meerschaum, Carved, Figural, Nude Woman, Faux Amber Stem, Leathered Case, 4 In. .. 235.00
Meerschaum, Carved, Hunter On Horseback, Running Hounds, 7 x 3 1/4 In. 413.00
Meerschaum, Heraldic, Angel, Putti, Flower Garland, Crown, Fitted Case, 11 In. 4025.00
Meerschaum, Skull, Mounted On Coiled Snake, Marked NPW, Fabric Case, 6 1/4 In. 358.00
Meerschaum, Victorian Woman By Tree Trunk, With Walking Stick, 3 1/4 x 6 x 2 In. 330.00
Opium, Ceramic, White Crackle Glaze, Blue Designs, Copper Trim, Stem, Hook, 7 3/4 In. 115.00
Porcelain, Heidelberg Scene, Hand Painted, 1852, 4 3/4 x 12 In. 193.00
Porcelain, Reservist, Foot Artillery, Wood Shaft, Stag Fittings, Hose, 1913, 63 In. 403.00
Porcelain, Reservist, Infantry Regiment 84, 10th Co., Cherry, Prussia, 1886, 48 In. 288.00
Rosewood, Silver Mounts, Coral & Turquoise, Tibet, 1900s, 15 In. 264.00
Wood, Tyrolean, 2-Piece, Carved, Dog Chasing Horse, 13 1/2 x 3 3/4 In. 56.00

PISGAH FOREST pottery was made in North Carolina beginning in
1926. The pottery was started by Walter B. Stephen, who had been
making pottery in that location since 1914. The pottery continued in
operation after his death in 1961. The most famous kinds of Pisgah
Forest ware are the cameo type with designs made of raised glaze and
the turquoise crackle glaze wares.

Mug, Cameo, Guitar Player, Blue Ground, Raised Mark, 1950, 3 1/2 In. 115.00
Pitcher, Mottled Green Glossy Glaze, Raised Mark, 9 1/2 x 4 3/4 In. 144.00
Tea Set, Cameo Ware, Dancers, Musicians, Wedgwood Blue Ground, 1950, 4 Piece 1095.00
Teapot, Covered Wagon Scene, Teal Blue, Over White, Stephen, 5 1/2 In. 635.00
Vase, Celadon Crystalline Glaze, Baluster, Stamped Cameo Stephen, 5 In. 200.00
Vase, Covered Wagon, Green Matte Collar, Mottled Turquoise, 1939, 7 In. 865.00
Vase, Crystalline Glaze, White, Ivory Crystals, White, Stephen, c.1940, 9 1/2 In. 575.00
Vase, Ivory & Blue Crystals, Celadon Ground, Baluster, Marked, 1946, 9 x 5 In. 865.00
Vase, Ox-Drawn Wagons, Pate-Sur-Pate, Cameo, Gray, Stephen, Stamped, 5 1/2 In. 430.00
Vase, Wagon Scene, Wedgwood Blue Matte Ground, Bulbous, 11 In. 1528.00

PLANTERS PEANUTS memorabilia is collected. Planters Nut and
Chocolate Company was started in Wilkes-Barre, Pennsylvania, in
1906. The Mr. Peanut figure was adopted as a trademark in 1916. National advertising for Planters Peanuts started in 1918. The company
was acquired by Standard Brands, Inc., in 1961. Standard Brands
merged with Nabisco in 1981. Some of the Mr. Peanut jars and other
memorabilia have been reproduced and, of course, new items are being
made.

Bottle Opener, Mr. Peanut 35.00
Container, Peanut Shape, Papier-Mache, c.1930, 12 x 6 x 5 In. 44.00

Fan, Mr. Peanut, Driving Peanut Car, 1940s, 5 1/4 x 8 In. 255.00
Flashlight, Mr. Peanut, Flippo Flashlight, Tipping Hat, Bantamlite 898.00
Jar, 6-Sided, Yellow Letters & Mr. Peanut Figures, c.1936, 10 In. 80.00
Jar, Cover, 8-Sided, Embossed, 5 Cent, Peanut Finial, c.1926, 12 In. 240.00
Jar, Cover, Barrel Shape, Embossed, Mr. Peanut, Peanut Finial, c.1935, 12 In. ....305.00 to 440.00
Jar, Cover, Counter, Embossed, Mr. Peanut Corners, Peanut Finial, c.1932, 12 In. ...158.00 to 165.00
Jar, Cover, Pressed Glass, 12 In. 35.00
Jar, Cover, Salted Peanuts, Decal, Peanut Finial, 12 In. 145.00
Jar, Cover, Square, Embossed Letters, Peanut Finial, c.1934, 10 In. 60.00
Jar, Embossed, Oval, Squat, 8 In. 190.00
Jar, Embossed, Paper Label, 12 1/2 In. 169.00
Pail, High Grade Peanut Butter, Bail Handle, Lithograph, 25 Lb., c.1920, 10 In. 210.00
Peanut Butter Maker, Mr. Peanut Shape, Plastic, c.1976, 12 In. 35.00
Salt & Pepper, Plastic, 1950s, 4 In. 20.00
Tin, Egyptian Designs, c.1919, 6 1/4 x 2 In. 1155.00
Tin, Mixed Salted Nuts, Key Wind, 4 1/4 x 4 In. 105.00
Tin, Pennant, Salted Peanuts, Lid, 10 Lb., 9 1/2 In. 65.00
Tin, Redskin Spanish Peanuts, Suffolk, Va., 4 1/4 x 4 In. 68.00
Tin, Salted Almonds, 2 3/4 x 2 5/8 In. 60.00
Tin, Salted Cashew Nuts, Key Wind, 3 x 3 3/8 In. 75.00
Tin, Spanish Peanuts, Lithograph, Vacuum Pack, 1949, 3 1/8 x 3 3/8 In. 85.00

PLASTIC objects of all types are being collected. Some pieces are listed
in other categories; gutta-percha cases are listed in photography, celluloid in its own category.

Ashtray, Square, Tangerine Orange, Futura 10.00
Bowl, Salad, Turquoise Blue, Wing Handles, Boontonware, 9 3/4 In. 16.00
Bowl, Vegetable, 2 Sections, Goldenrod, Melamine, Kenro, 9 In. 10.00
Bowl, Vegetable, Charcoal Gray, Color-Flyte Royale, Branchell, 10 1/2 In. 10.00
Bowl, Vegetable, Light Blue, Melamine, No. 119, Texasware, 10 x 7 1/2 In. 23.00
Bread Box, Pink, Printed Black Antique Stove, Lustro Ware, 1950s, 13 In. 43.00
Bread Box, Red & White, Burroughs, 1950s, 3/4 In. 70.00
Canister, Light Blue & Cream Bakelite, Wing Handles, Art Deco, 5 1/4 In. 80.00
Creamer, Yellow, Royalon 10.00
Desk Organizer, 5 Connected Cylinders, Graduated, Light Blue, 1970s, 5 3/4 In. 15.00
Dinner Set, Avocado, Daisies Transfer, Artisan Deluxe, Allied Chemical, Box, 45 Piece .. 35.00
Dinner Set, Lavender, Violets Transfer, Melamine, Royalon, 36 Piece 50.00
Dinner Set, Pink, Melamine, Boonton, 56 Piece 70.00
Dinner Set, Pink, Rose Transfer, Melamine, Brookpark Modern, 56 Piece 200.00
Figurine, Palm Trees, Elephant, Butterscotch Bakelite, 7 1/4 In. 300.00
Flatware Set, Black & Cream Bakelite Handles, Fitted Box, 1930s, 22 Piece 340.00
Flatware Set, Red & Yellow Bakelite Handles, 1933, 24 Piece 225.00
Gravy Boat, Charcoal, Melamine, Colorflyte, Branchell 10.00
Gravy Boat, Mist Gray, Color-Flyte Royale, Branchell, 7 In. 28.00
Laundry Sprinkler, Blue & White, Lucky Wish Product, 6 3/8 In. 13.00
Luncheon Set, Chartreuse, Melamine, Brookpark Arrowhead, 44 Piece 185.00
Mixing Bowl, Speckled Blue, Rust, Black, Melamine, No. 125, Texasware, 11 1/2 In. 50.00
Mixing Bowl, Speckled, Brown, Texas Ware, 10 In. 20.00
Napkin Holder, Teapot Shape, Red, Rogers, 4 1/2 x 6 In. 15.00
Napkin Ring, Chick, Green Bakelite, Orange Beak, 2 1/2 In. 45.00
Napkin Ring, Duck, Red Bakelite, Green Eye, 2 1/2 In. 60.00
Napkin Ring, Scottie Dog, Orange Bakelite, Green Eye, 2 3/4 In. 40.00
Pitcher, Hinged Cover, Disk, Pink, Turquoise, 1950s, 7 In. 20.00
Planter, Girl In Sunbonnet, Lattice Frame, Yellow & Red, 9 In. 18.00
Plate, Fruit In Basket, Texas Ware, Melmac, 10 In. 9.00
Platter, Blue Onion Transfer, Melamine, Texasware, 14 x 10 In. 75.00
Poker Chip Set, Red, Black, Yellow, Tan Centers, Bakelite, 100 Piece 250.00
Salad Set, Tan & Green, Bowl, Cover, Servers, Melamine, Raffiaware, 4 Piece 20.00
Salt & Pepper, Apple & Pear, Red & Yellow Bakelite 130.00
Salt & Pepper, Semicircular, Green & Tan Bakelite, Stand, Art Deco, 1 3/4 In. 75.00
Salt & Pepper, Turquoise Blue, Oval, Boontonware Belle 10.00
Snack Set, Tan, Turquoise, Mugs, Plates, Melamine, Raffiaware, 12 Piece 35.00
Soup, Dish, Chinese Red, Florence, Prolon 8.00

Tidbit, 3 Tiers, Forest Green, Melamine, Silver Metal Handle, Brookpark Modern 45.00
Tranquil Ware, Tray, Rectangular, Yellow, Byrd's Plastics, 14 x 9 In. 12.00
Tumbler, Juice, Yellow, Printed Red Bird, Beep For Breakfast, 3 In. 20.00
Tumbler Set, The Maidens, Partially Clothed Women In Comic Poses, 5 3/4 In., 6 Piece . 88.00
Wastebasket, Cover, Pink, Gold Embossed, 1950s, 16 In. 10.00

PLATED AMBERINA was patented June 15, 1886, by Joseph Locke and
made by the New England Glass Company. It is similar in color to
amberina, but is characterized by a cream colored or chartreuse lining
(never white) and small ridges or ribs on the outside.

Bowl, Fuchsia Top, Amber Bottom, Ribs, White Interior, 7 1/2 In. 7190.00
Cruet, Tricornered Rim, Amber Handle, Faceted Stopper, 6 1/4 In. 3800.00
Cruet, Tumbler, Fuchsia To Amber, Vertical Ribs, New England Glass Co., 3 3/4 In. 1898.00
Mug, Lemonade, Handle, 4 7/8 In. 3400.00
Punch Cup, Ribbed, White Interior, Applied Handle, 2 1/2 In. 3450.00
Sugar 20125.00
Sugar Shaker, Ribbed, c.1890, 6 In. 7280.00
Syrup 8338.00
Tumbler 3910.00

PLIQUE-A-JOUR is an enameling process. The enamel is laid between
thin raised metal lines and heated. The finished piece has transparent
enamel held between the thin metal wires. It is different from cloisonne because it is translucent.

Bowl, Chubby Googly-Eyed Fish, Plants, Flower Border, 3 x 5 1/4 In. 210.00
Spoon, Silver, Beaded Edge, Demitasse, 3 3/4 In. 150.00
Vase, Flowers, Birds, Green Ground, Silver Mounts, Japan, Early 1900s, 9 1/2 In. 12925.00

POLITICAL memorabilia of all types, from buttons to banners, is col-
lected. Items related to presidential candidates are the most popular,
but collectors also search for material related to state and local offices.
Memorabilia related to social causes, minor political parties, and
protest movements are also included here. Many reproductions have
been made. A jugate is a button with photographs of both the presidential and vice presidential candidates. In this list a button is round,
usually with a straight pin or metal tab to secure it to a shirt. A pin is
brass, often figural, sometimes attached to a ribbon.

Ashtray, Glass, GOP National Convention, Elephant, San Diego, 1972, 4 1/2 x 1 In. 20.00
Ashtray, Jimmy Carter, Plains, Georgia, Conrad Crafters, 7 1/2 In. 20.00
Ashtray, We Like Ike, 1952, 5 1/4 In. 48.00
Ax, Carrie Nation's, Nickel Plated Iron, 10 In. 150.00
Badge, Bull Moose, Mechanical, Moose Has Turned Loose, Ribbon, Celluloid, 1 1/4 In. ... 620.00
Badge, Police, John F. Kennedy Inauguration, Gold Colored, 1961, 2 1/4 In. 800.00
Bandanna, Benjamin Harrison, Protection To Home Industries, 1888, 23 x 24 In. 1380.00
Bandanna, Garfield, Arthur, Red Ground, 1880, 20 1/2 x 19 1/2 In. 275.00
Bandanna, Hancock, English, White Ground, Flags In Corner, 1880, 16 1/2 x 18 1/2 In. ... 315.00
Bandanna, Harrison, Morton, U.S. Flag, Blue Star Band, 20 x 19 In. 210.00
Bandanna, Harrison, Reid, Cloth, Blue Ground, 1892, 20 1/2 x 19 1/2 In. 56.00
Bandanna, McKinley, Hobart, Waving Flag, Silk, 1896 .... 200.00
Bandanna, Roosevelt, Fairbanks, Right Men In Right Place, 1904, 16 x 17 1/4 In. 750.00
Bank, Teddy Roosevelt Bust, Cast Iron, Gold, A.C. Williams, c.1919, 5 In. 110.00
Banner, Franklin Roosevelt, America Demands, Wood, 5 x 6 1/2 In. 110.00
Banner, Kennedy, Johnson, Men For The 60's, Blue Felt, White Letters, 1960, 21 In. 345.00
Banner, Pierce, King, Grand National, 1852, 10 x 14 In. 495.00
Banner, T. Roosevelt, Admirals, Cruise Around World, Needlework, Frame, 24 x 46 In. ... 2500.00
Banner, Taylor, Fillmore, Grand National, 1848, 7 3/4 x 10 In. 495.00
Bell, Coolidge, Ring For Coolidge, Brass 50.00
Bell, Harding, Portrait, Brass 45.00
Bell, Ring For Willkie & McNary, Brass 35.00
Belt, Hannibal Hamlin, Lady's, Portrait, Brass Surround, Zinc, Silk Belt, 32 In. 920.00
Belt, Nixon, Brass, Round Plastic Letters, 38 In. 40.00
Bookends, Teddy Roosevelt As Rough Rider, Bronze Coated, Paul Herzel, 6 In. 250.00
Booklet, Bill Knowland For Governor, 12 Pages 9.00
Booklet, Henry Ford For U.S. Senator, 1918, 16 Pages 1390.00

Bookmark, Teddy Roosevelt, Heart, Silver, Black, 2 In. 55.00
Booster Tag, Dewey, Warren, Women's Republican Club, Cardboard, String, 3 x 4 1/2 In.   20.00
Box, Collar, Chester Arthur, Wood, Gutta-Percha Portrait Panel, 4 1/2 x 3 1/4 In. 125.00
Bracelet, F.D. Roosevelt, Letters, Enamel Flags 110.00
Bracelet, Stevenson, Win With Steve, Donkey, Chain 49.00
Brooch, George Washington, Picture, Color, Brass Frame, Rectangular, c.1830 . . . .   970.00
Bumper Sticker, Stevenson, Kefauver, Red, White, Blue 15.00
Bust, FDR, Bronze Finish, Heavy Metal, Signature Across Bottom, 5 1/4 In. 35.00
Bust, George Washington, Wax, 8-Sided Wood Frame, c.1797, 2 1/4 In. 960.00
Button, Adlai Stevenson, Photograph, Black, White, Orange, Celluloid, 6 In. 405.00
Button, Aircraft Workers For Eisenhower, Red, White, Blue, 1 1/4 In. 800.00
Button, Al Smith, Celluloid, Attached To Felt Derby Hat, 1 1/4 x 3 In. 75.00
Button, Al Smith, Derby Hat, Metal, Sepia Photograph, 1 3/4 In.   366.00
Button, All The Way With Adlai, Flasher, Black, White, 2 1/2 In.   20.00
Button, Anti-Goldwater, Hot Water, Bread & Water, Underwater, 1964, 6 In. 20.00
Button, Anti-Goldwater, What Me Worry, Mushroom Cloud, Celluloid, 2 1/8 In. 300.00
Button, Beat Dick, Blue On White, 1960, 7/8 In. 39.00
Button, Bedtime For Ronzo, Reagan As Monkey, Celluloid, 1984, 1 3/4 In. 30.00
Button, Black Hand Peace Sign, Blue, Black, White, 1969, 2 1/2 In. 70.00
Button, Bryan, Enemies Of Special Privilege, 4 Presidents, Celluloid, 1 3/4 In. 1585.00
Button, Bryan, Kern, 1 1/4 In. 145.00
Button, Bryan, Stevenson, Cornucopia, 16 To 1, 1900, 1 3/4 In. 1745.00
Button, Bury Goldwater, Black, Gold, Celluloid, 7/8 In. 20.00
Button, By George, Buy Utah, George W.H. Bush Caricature, Multicolor, Celluloid, 3 In.   99.00
Button, Carter, Mondale, People's Choice, Red, White, Blue, Celluloid, 1976, 3 In. 267.00
Button, Carter, Mondale, Photographs, Eagle, Bristow, 1980, 1 1/2 In. 55.00
Button, Citizens For Kennedy, Welcome Aboard, Celluloid, 1960, 3 1/2 In. 1489.00
Button, Coloradans For Goldwater, Black, White, Gold, Celluloid, 1964, 1 7/8 In. 230.00
Button, Dewey Is Dew In '48, 7/8 In. 50.00
Button, Dewey, Bricker, Jugate, Black, White, Celluloid, 1944, 1 In. 170.00
Button, Dewey, Bricker, Jugate, Photographs On White, 1944, 1 In. 138.00
Button, Dewey, Bricker, Jugate, Red, White, Blue, 1944, 1 1/4 In. 240.00
Button, District Of Columbia, Eisenhower, Nixon Club, Red, White, Blue, 7/8 In. 25.00
Button, Don't Change Front In Face Of Enemy, Nixon, Celluloid, 1960, 2 1/4 In. 240.00
Button, Dr. Martin Luther King Jr., Celluloid, c.1960, 9 In. 130.00
Button, Eisenhower In 1956, Blue, White, Celluloid, Oval, 7 3/4 In. 235.00
Button, Eisenhower, Nixon, Red, White, Blue, 9 Stars, Elephant, 3 1/2 In. 915.00
Button, Elect Kennedy President, Blue, White, Celluloid, 1960, 2 1/4 In. 410.00
Button, Elect Nixon, White House Not For Sale, Red, Blue, Celluloid, 1960, 3 1/2 In. . . .   450.00
Button, FDR, For A New Deal, Blue, Black, White, Celluloid, Picture, 3 1/2 In. 390.00
Button, FDR, God Bless America, Picture, Blue, White, Celluloid, 1940, 1 1/4 In. 440.00
Button, FDR, Our Veldt Rose, Roseveld, Red, Green, White, Black, Celluloid, 7/8 In. . . .   705.00
Button, FDR, Sweeping The Depression Out, 1 1/4 In. 150.00
Button, Ferrotype, Abraham Lincoln, Brass Frame, 1860, 7/8 In.   780.00
Button, For President, Wendell L. Willkie, Black, White, Celluloid, 9 In. 260.00
Button, For The Love Of Ike Vote Republican, Red, White, Blue, 9 In. 30.00
Button, Ford, Elephant Boxer, Green, Black, 1 3/4 In. 215.00
Button, Ford, Fighting Elephant, Green, Red, Black, 2 1/4 In. 89.00
Button, Franklin Delano Roosevelt, For President, 9 In. 300.00
Button, Franklin Roosevelt, Will Protect Our Flag, Multicolored, Celluloid, 1933, 7/8 In. .   545.00
Button, General Charles DeGaulle, Brown, Black, White, Celluloid, 7/8 In. 150.00
Button, General Nelson Miles, For President, Sepia, Celluloid, 1 1/4 In. 650.00
Button, George Wallace, Curtis Lemay, Red, White, Blue, Black, Celluloid, 1968, 9 In. . .   115.00
Button, Going Up With Lyndon, Red, White, Blue, Celluloid, 1964, 2 1/2 In. 1029.00
Button, Goldwater For President, Red, White, Blue, Black, 7 In. 40.00
Button, Goldwater In '64, Photograph, Gold Background, 9 In. 18.00
Button, Goldwater, Band Wagon Is Rolling Along, Hop On, 3 1/2 In. 369.00
Button, Harding For President, Black, Cream, Celluloid, 1920, 1 1/4 In. 685.00
Button, Harding, America First, Black, White, Celluloid, 3/4 In. 260.00
Button, Harrison & Reform, Log Cabin, Brass, Shank 45.00
Button, Harry S. Truman, Dangling Metal Donkey, 1 1/2 In. 90.00
Button, Harry Truman, For President, Center Photograph, Red, White, Blue Edge, 1 In. . .   60.00
Button, Harry Truman, Vote, For President, Celluloid, 9 In. 1830.00

Button, Henry Wallace, I'm A Vet For Wallace, Celluloid, Red, White, 1948, 1 1/4 In. 275.00
Button, Henry Wallace, Shadow Of FDR, Clue, White, Celluloid, 1948, 2 1/8 In. 100.00
Button, Herbert Hoover, 1 In. 70.00
Button, Hoo But Hoover, 7/8 In. 1690.00
Button, Hoover, 100% American, Red, White, Blue, 7/8 In. 18.00
Button, Hoover, Curtis, Jugate, Celluloid, 1928, 1 1/4 In. 1930.00
Button, Hughes, For President, Undiluted Americanism, Red, Black, Celluloid, 6 In. 860.00
Button, I Am For Alabama Cope, Carter, Mondale, Green, Black, Celluloid, 1 3/4 In. 550.00
Button, I'm For Pat & Dick, Red, White, Blue, White Ribbon, 1960, 1 1/4 In. 30.00
Button, I'm Just Wild About Harry, Blue, Cream, Celluloid, 3 1/2 In. 670.00
Button, If I Were 21 I'd Vote For Barry, Red, White, Blue, Celluloid, 1 1/4 In. 20.00
Button, Ike, Dick, Peace, Prosperity, Progress, Green On White, 1 1/4 In. 59.00
Button, Jackie Kennedy, America's First Lady, Picture, Celluloid, 3 1/2 In. 125.00
Button, James M. Cox, Red, White, Blue, Gold, Celluloid, 1920, 1 3/4 In. 7700.00
Button, Jerry Ford For Congress, Red, White, Blue, 1 3/4 In. 320.00
Button, Judge Parker, Uncle Sam, Multicolored, Celluloid, 1 1/4 In. 400.00
Button, Keep Coolidge, Blue, Black, White, Keystone, Celluloid, 5/8 In. 20.00
Button, Kennedy, All The Way With JFK, Picture, Celluloid, 1960, 1 1/4 In. 400.00
Button, Kennedy, Flasher, Plastic, 2 1/2 In. 80.00
Button, Kennedy, Johnson, Inaugural, Red, White, Blue, Black, Gold, 1961, 6 In. 70.00
Button, Khrushchev, I Hate Everybody, Celluloid, 4 In. 50.00
Button, L.B.J., Please Stay, Green, White, Celluloid, 1 1/4 In. 15.00
Button, Landon, Knox, Sunflower, Elephant, Brown, Yellow, White, Celluloid, 7/8 In. 1189.00
Button, Landon, Sunflower, Brown, Yellow, White, Celluloid, 1936, 1 3/4 In. 1997.00
Button, MacArthur For President, Celluloid, Japan, 2 3/4 In. 1230.00
Button, McGovern, Benefit Concert, Streisand, King, Taylor, Celluloid, 1972, 3 1/2 In. .. 376.00
Button, McGovern, Liberated Ladies Like McGovern & Shriver, 1 1/4 In. 80.00
Button, McKinley, Eclipse Will Be Total, Nov. 6 1900, 1 1/4 In. 2689.00
Button, McKinley, In Memoriam, Picture, Black, White, Celluloid, 1 1/4 In. 12.00
Button, McKinley, Roosevelt, Rough Rider, Celluloid, 1900, 1 3/4 In. 1390.00
Button, Nebraska For Bryan, Hand Waving Flag, Red, Cream, Blue, 7/8 In. 60.00
Button, Nebraskans For Kennedy, Red, White, Blue, Celluloid, 1960, 1 In. 310.00
Button, Nixon, Agnew, Elephant, Stars, Red, White, Celluloid, 1 3/4 In. 145.00
Button, Nixon, Lodge, Experience Counts, Jugate, 9 In. 30.00
Button, Nixon, Lodge, Red, White, Blue, Celluloid, 2 1/4 In. 100.00
Button, Nixon, Peace With Honor, Peace Sign, Black, White, Celluloid, 1968, 3 In. 110.00
Button, Parker, Davis, Jugate, National Editorial Conference, 1904, 1 3/4 In. 3974.00
Button, Parker, Davis, Shure Mike, Rooster, Multicolored, Celluloid, 1904, 1 1/4 In. 550.00
Button, Reagan Country, Vermont, Blue, White, Celluloid, 1 3/4 In. 105.00
Button, Reagan, Bush, America's New Dawn, Orange, Yellow, Black, Celluloid, 2 1/2 In. 55.00
Button, Reagan, Bush, Commitment 80, Celluloid, 2 1/4 In. 39.00
Button, Reagan, Cowboy Outfit, Gun, I Shot J.R., Black, White, Celluloid, 4 In. 250.00
Button, Reagan, I'm For Reagan For President, Yellow, Black, Celluloid, 1968, 1 1/4 In. .. 10.00
Button, Republicans For Kennedy, Blue, White, 1 1/4 In. 110.00
Button, Richard M. Nixon, For Vice President, 1952, 7/8 In. 105.00
Button, Richard Nixon, Man Of Steel, 3 1/2 In. 330.00
Button, Robert F. Kennedy, For U.S. Senator, Red, White, Blue, Celluloid, 1964, 3 1/2 In. 395.00
Button, Robert Kennedy, Return To Greatness, Celluloid, 1968, 3 1/2 In. 3155.00
Button, Ronald Reagan, Wears Cowboy Hat, Blue, White, Celluloid, 1981, 6 In. 55.00
Button, Roosevelt, Cox, Red, White, Blue, Lithograph, 5/8 In. 38.00
Button, Roosevelt, Labor's Friend, Red, White, Blue, Celluloid, 1 1/4 In. 75.00
Button, Roosevelt, Stars, Stripes, Red, White, Blue, Celluloid, 6 In. 118.00
Button, Shoeworkers For Kennedy, Celluloid, Red, White, 1960, 3 1/2 In. 665.00
Button, Smith For President, Red, White, Blue Trim, Photograph Center, 7/8 In. 30.00
Button, Stevenson, Sparkman, Vote Straight Democratic, Celluloid, 1952, 3 1/2 In. 1360.00
Button, T. Roosevelt, B.T. Washington, Equality, Celluloid, 1901, 1 3/4 In. 8650.00
Button, Taft, Black, White, Celluloid, 7/8 In. 11.00
Button, Taft, Hello Bill, 1 1/4 In. 175.00
Button, Taft, Inauguration, Washington D.C., March 4th, 1908, 1 3/4 In. 275.00
Button, Taft, Sherman, Jugate, Lady Liberty, Multicolored, Celluloid, 1 1/4 In. ...425.00 to 450.00
Button, Teddy Roosevelt, A Square Deal, Picture, Blue, Black, White, Celluloid, 7/8 In. ... 150.00
Button, Teddy Roosevelt, National Unity, Prosperity, Celluloid, 1904, 1 1/4 In. 2200.00
Button, Texas Democrats For Ike, Red, White, Blue, Celluloid, 1 1/4 In. 910.00

Button, Theodore Roosevelt, For Vice-President, Rough Rider, Celluloid, 1900, 1 1/4 In. . 2410.00
Button, Theodore Roosevelt, Rough Rider, Picture, Multicolored, Celluloid, 1 1/4 In. 215.00
Button, Truman & Civil Rights, Blue, White, Celluloid, 1948, 1 1/4 In. 975.00
Button, Truman For Senator, Blue, Black, White, 7/8 In. 410.00
Button, Truman, 8 Ball, Black, White, Lithograph, 5/8 In. 30.00
Button, Truman, 8 Ball, Black, White, Lithograph, 7/8 In. 35.00
Button, Truman, Barkley, Red, White, Blue, Lithograph, 7/8 In. 30.00
Button, Truman, Donaldson, Show Me State, Missouri, Celluloid, Ribbon, 1948, 2 In. . . . 8800.00
Button, Truman, Red, White, Blue, Celluloid, 3 1/2 In. 160.00
Button, Truman, Vote, For President, Red, White, Blue, Black, Celluloid, 1948, 3 1/2 In. . 3390.00
Button, Truman, Welcome, 42nd Ward, Celluloid, 3 1/2 In. 1158.00
Button, Uncle Sam, Home Improvement, Celluloid, Metal, So. Shaftsbury, Vt., 1 1/4 In. . . 38.00
Button, Votes For Women 1915, Sun Coming Up Over On Horizon, Celluloid, 7/8 In. . . . 242.00
Button, Votes For Women June 5, Black, Gold, 7/8 In. 396.00
Button, Votes For Women Patriotism, Multicolored, 12 Stars, Celluloid, 3/4 In. 300.00
Button, Votes For Women, 4 Stars, Gold, Cream, Celluloid, 7/8 In. 290.00
Button, Votes For Women, 12 Stars, Blue, Yellow, Black, White, Celluloid, 7/8 In. 290.00
Button, W.J. Bryan, Arthur Sewall, Victory, Jugate, Celluloid, 1896, 1 1/2 In. 660.00
Button, W.J. Bryan, John Kern, Celluloid, 1908, 1 1/4 In. 2010.00
Button, Wallace For President, Red, White, Blue, Oval, 2 3/4 In. 30.00
Button, Wallace, Illinois Volunteers, Celluloid, 1968, 2 1/4 In. 700.00
Button, Watergate Gang, Black, White, Celluloid, 2 1/4 In. 45.00
Button, William Gibbs Maddox, 1924, 4 In. 460.00
Button, William H. Taft, For President, 1 1/4 In. 45.00
Button, William Jennings Bryan, Ear Of Corn, Oval, Celluloid, 1896, 1 1/2 x 2 1/2 In. . . . 2025.00
Button, William Randolph Hearst For Governor, Celluloid, 1906, 1 3/4 In. 75.00
Button, Willkie For President, Red, White, Blue, 1940, 2 3/4 In. 373.00
Button, Willkie, America's Hope, Black, White, Celluloid, 1 1/4 In. 15.00
Button, Willkie, Every Buddy For Willkie, Picture, Celluloid, 7/8 In. 230.00
Button, Willkie, McNary, Jugate, Red, White, Blue, Lithograph, 1940, 7/8 In. 159.00
Button, Willkie, My Shoulder To The Wheel, Black, White, Lithograph, 1 1/4 In. 155.00
Button, Willkie-Ite, Capitol Building, Red, White, Blue, Celluloid, 7/8 In. 200.00
Button, Wilson, Marshall, Jugate, Celluloid, American Art Works, 1 1/4 In. 6600.00
Button, Women For Ferraro, Blue, White, Celluloid, 1984, 3 1/2 In. 200.00
Button, Woodrow Wilson, For President, Left Facing Photograph, 1912, 1 1/4 In. 70.00
Button, Young Citizens For Johnson, LBJ Center Star, Celluloid, 2 1/8 In. 390.00
Button & Ribbon, Garner For President, Celluloid, 1932, 2 1/4-In. Button 870.00
Campaign Ticket, U.S. Grant, H. Wilson, Republican Party, Lady Liberty, 7 3/4 x 5 In. . . . 85.00
Campaign Torch, 5-Point Star, Tin, Swings, Red, White & Blue Paint, Handle 1540.00
Campaign Torch, Flashing Flambeau, 2 Spouts, Handle, Signed George H. Tay & Co. . . . 1155.00
Campaign Torch, Pinecone, Tin, Handle, Campaign For James Blaine, 1884 . . . . 2970.00
Campaign Torch, Tin & Parchment, Rutherford B. Hayes, 16 In. 1540.00
Candle Lantern, Lunch Pail Form, McKinley & Roosevelt, 4 Years More, Tin, 9 In. 1430.00
Candy Container, Uncle Sam's Hat, Milk Glass, McKinley & Roosevelt, 1900, 2 1/2 In. . . 110.00
Cane, Buckeye, Harrison Tyler & Corwin, Eagle Head, Hardwood, Tippecanoe, 37 In. . . . 2300.00
Cane, Jimmy Carter, For President, Metal, Peanut Shaped Handle, 1976 . . . . 225.00
Cane, Rosewood Handle, Figural, Alton Parker, Stooped Over, Rosewood Shaft, 33 In. . . . 335.00
Cane, Teddy Roosevelt, Sepia Celluloid In Handle, 34 In. 280.00
Cane, William McKinley Portrait, Hollow Tin, 1896, 33 In. 1265.00
Canteen, Militia, Black Paint, Gold A, Early 19th Century, 4 1/2 In. 230.00
Cap, Beanie, Vote For Scranton For Governor, Felt, Blue, Gold, White 25.00
Card, Vote For Al Smith Campaign, 4 x 2 1/2 In. 15.00
Change Purse, Harding, Leather, Pewter, 1920s, 3 1/4 In. 55.00
Charm, 2-Part, McKinley, Flag, Protection Bar, Red, White, Blue 20.00
Cigar Box, Dependable, Grant, 8 1/2 x 5 1/4 In. 55.00
Cigarette Case, America Needs Stevenson, Satin Finish Brass, Blue, White Design 265.00
Cigarette Lighter, Goldwater, Portrait, Elephant, Go Conservative, Go AU H2O 50.00
Clock, Electric, Roosevelt Standing, Wheel For New Deal, 13 1/4 In. 130.00
Clothing Brush, J.Q. Adams, Contrasting Bristles Spell Name, Wood, 10 1/2 In. 2750.00
Clothing Brush, Jackson, Wood, Name & Date In Bristles, 1817, 11 1/2 In. 1250.00
Coaster, Donkey & Elephant Knock Heads, 1956, 3 1/2 In. 4.00
Coaster, Goldwater, 1964, 3 1/2 In. 9.00
Coloring Book, Jimmy Carter, Vol. 1, 1976 . . . . 17.00

Compact, Dewey For President, Celluloid, Blue, White, Gold Case, 2 3/4 In. 99.00
Compact, I Like Ike, Telephone Dial, Mirror, Enamel, 3 1/2 In. 315.00
Cup, Waxed Cardboard, Vote For Woman Suffrage, No. 6th, 3 In. 375.00
Dart Board, Anti-Nixon, Watergate, Square 11 1/4 In. 22.00
Decal, Harding, Coolidge, Red, White, Blue, Black, Yellow, Frame, 1920, 8 x 10 In. 350.00
Door Hanger, President Nixon Needs Your Vote Today, 1972, 4 x 5 1/2 In. 3.50
Door Hanger, Vote McGovern Democrat, Primary, June 6, 1972 .... 4.50
Dress, Eugene McCarthy, Peace, Zipper, 1968, 36 In. 37.00
Fan, Anti-Suffrage, Vote No Woman Suffrage, Massachusetts, November 2, 1915, 8 In. ... 303.00
Fan, Franklin D. Roosevelt 7.00
Fan, Goldwater Fan Club, Elephant Riding Donkey, 1964, 6 x 7 In. 50.00
Fan, Votes For Women, Ohio, 2-Sided, 1914, 6 3/4 x 8 1/2 In. 280.00
Fan, Woodrow Wilson, Presidents Pictures, Black, White, 1916, 9 In. 40.00
Ferrotype, Horace Greeley, Gratz Brown, Inscribed Brass Frame, Reform, 1872 .... 7290.00
Ferrotype, Lincoln, Hamlin, 1 Portrait Each Side, Velvet Frame, c.1860, 1 In. 1610.00
Field Glasses, Leather Wraps, Painted Black Finish, 19th Century 28.75
Figurine, Dog, Votes For Women, Glazed Pottery, Brown, White, 3 1/4 In. 3000.00
Figurine, Elephant, 2 1/4-In. Sepia, Taft, Celluloid, Bronzed Iron, 7 In. 550.00
Figurine, Elephant, Bobbing Head, Nixon Sash, Plaster, 6 In. 95.00
Flag, Campaign, H. Clay, Sepia Portrait, Blue, White Stripes, 26 Stars, 1844, 28 x 24 In. . 1725.00
Flag, Election, William Howard Taft, 46 Stars, Printed Cloth, 1-Sided, 34 x 23 In. 315.00
Flag, Roosevelt Battle Flag, Red, White, 1912, 22 x 23 In. 61.00
Flag, Roosevelt One Side, Fairbanks On Other, Paper, Pin, c.1908, 2 x 1 1/2 In. 69.00
Flag, Stevenson, Sparkman, Donkey, Stick, 1952, 6 x 4 In. 55.00
Flag, We Want Ike Again, Plastic, Red, White, Blue 40.00
Flasher, Eisenhower, Down With Democrats, Thumb Points Down 55.00
Flyer, In The Tradition Of John F. Kennedy, Vote Straight Demo, 5 1/2 x 8 1/2 In. 10.00
Flyer, McCarthy For President, 4 Pages 8.00
Flyer, Nobody Knows How Dry They Are, Hoover, Curtis 25.00
Flyer, Three Mile Island, Mondale & Ferraro 5.00
Flyer, Wallace For Gov. Kick-Off Rally, Black, Pink, 9/29/66, 6 x 9 In. 28.00
Folder, Dole For President, Reagan, Fold-Out, Pictures, 8 Pages 5.00
Folder, Henry Ford Tells Why He's For Hoover, 8 Pages 18.00
Folder, Jesse Jackson For President, 1984, 8 Pages 4.50
Folder, McCarthy For President, 8 Ages, New York Primary, June, 18, 1968 .... 8.00
Folder, President Hoover's Des Moines Address, October, 1932, 23 Pages 10.00
Folder, Senator McGovern On Israel, 6 Pages 5.00
Frisbee, Reagan For President, Plastic, Red, White, Blue, 9 1/4 In. 20.00
Game, President, Cutout, White House, Roosevelt, Parker, 1904, 10 1/2 x 17 In. 300.00
Game, Presidential Problem, Smith, Robinson, Hoover, Curtis, Playing Pieces, 10 x 12 In. 300.00
Garter, Campaign, Stevenson, Sparkman, Donkey, Red & White Polka Dots, 1952 ...... 75.00
Garter Belt, Ike, Dick, Cloth, Plastic, 1952 .... 40.00
Glass Slide, Ex-President Grover Cleveland At Desk 40.00
Glass Slide, Ex-President Roosevelt Riding In Carriage 45.00
Glass Slide, Franklin D. Roosevelt 45.00
Glass Slide, President Harding Driving Spike On Alaskan Railroad 40.00
Glass Slide, President Roosevelt & Peace Envoys Of Mikado & Czar 40.00
Glass Slide, President Taft Giving Speech 40.00
Glass Slide, Woodrow Wilson With War Cabinet 35.00
Golf Ball, Jerry Ford, Souvenir Gift, Signature, Presidential Seal 12.00
Golf Tees, Eisenhower, We're Fore Ike, Red, White, Blue 20.00
Greeting Card, Don't Let Your Freedom Get Flabby, Vote For LBJ & Voting Booth 10.00
Handkerchief, Presidential, Constitution James G. Blaine, John A. Logan, 24 x 23 In. 120.00
Hanger, Door, Elephant, Goldwater, Miller, Hugh Scott, 10 1/4 In. 12.00
Hanger, Wall, FDR Button, Cardboard, Black, Gray, Brown, White, 9 x 9 3/4 In. 45.00
Hanger, Wall, God Bless America, WWII, Cloth, Shield Shape, 9 x 11 In. 25.00
Hanger, Wall, War Worker WWII, Cloth, 7 1/2 x 11 1/2 In. 30.00
Hat, Adlai Stevenson, Paper, Red, White, Blue, 11 In. 25.00
Hat, I Like Ike, Paper, Red, White, Blue, 11 In. 20.00
Hat, Ike, Skull Type, 5 1/2 In. 45.00
Hat, LBJ, USA, Cloth, Red, White, Blue, Yellow, Black, White, 12 In. 20.00
Hat, Painter's, I Love Reagan, Red, Black, White 20.00
Hat Sash, LBJ For The USA, Red, White, Blue, 2 1/2 x 22 In. 20.00

Hatchet, All Nations Welcomed But Carrie, Carrie Nation Bust, Cast Iron, 11 3/4 In. 460.00
Invitation, Truman Victory Reception, February 25, 1949, Statler Hotel, 5 x 7 In. 90.00
Jug, Eisenhower, Multicolored, Presidential Seal On Handle, Barrington, England 45.00
Jug, FDR, 1932, 1936, 1940, Gold Luster, Eagle, Red, White, Blue Trim 85.00
Key, Bryan, Key To White House, Brass, 1908 . . . . 30.00
Key Chain, Flasher, Ike, Elephant, Blue, White, 1 1/8 In. 55.00
Key Chain, JFK, Ask Not Quote On Reverse 10.00
Key Chain, Jimmy & Rosalyn Carter 10.00
Label, Bryan, Sewall, Silver Standard Whiskey, 16 To 1, 2 1/2 x 3 1/2 In. 350.00
Letter Opener, Teddy Roosevelt, In Uniform, Sword, Horse, Sterling Silver, 6 In. 185.00
License Plate Attachment, Al Smith For President, Tin Lithograph, Round, 8 In. 135.00
License Plate Attachment, Al Smith, Blue, Tan, 1928, 13 3/4 In. 130.00
License Plate Attachment, Al Smith, Metal, Raised Letters, White, Green 40.00
License Plate Attachment, America Needs Roosevelt, Red, White, Blue, 10 In. 230.00
License Plate Attachment, America Needs Roosevelt, Red, White, Blue, 9 1/2 In. 105.00
License Plate Attachment, Donkey Passing Gas, LBJ Has Spoken, Red, Black, White . . . 35.00
License Plate Attachment, Eisenhower, Nixon, Inaugural, 4080, Ex. 1-31-57, 12 1/4 In. . 65.00
License Plate Attachment, Elect Landon, Knox, Red Reflector, White Letters, 10 1/2 In. . 120.00
License Plate Attachment, Forward With Roosevelt, No Retreat, 11 3/4 In. 500.00
License Plate Attachment, Goldwater For President, Gold, Black 45.00
License Plate Attachment, Inauguration 1961, District Of Columbia, 7955, 12 In. 35.00
License Plate Attachment, Land Of Lincoln, Republican National Convention, 1960 . . . . 150.00
License Plate Attachment, Landon For President, 2 Sunflowers, 1936, 6 1/2 In. 165.00
License Plate Attachment, Landon For President, Man Of The People, Portrait, 6 1/4 In. . 120.00
License Plate Attachment, Landon, Knox, Brown, Yellow, White, 1936, 11 3/4 In. 248.00
License Plate Attachment, Landon, Spirit Of 76 In 36, Save America, 11 3/4 In. 425.00
License Plate Attachment, LBJ For The USA, Red, White, Blue, Plastic 25.00
License Plate Attachment, Man Of Today, Roosevelt, Trust Of Tomorrow, 12 In. 895.00
License Plate Attachment, McGovern, Shriver, Plastic, Red, White & Blue 20.00
License Plate Attachment, Nixon In 72, Elephant, 3 Stars, Red, White, Blue, 1972 . . . . . 20.00
License Plate Attachment, Nixon, Reelect The President, Plastic, Red, White, Blue 20.00
License Plate Attachment, Roosevelt, Motor Club, Hammered Brass, 1932, 5 In. 205.00
License Plate Attachment, Vote Republican, 1968 . . . . 16.00
License Plate Attachment, Vote Truman In '48, Green Duck, Chicago, 1948, 4 3/4 In. . . . 590.00
License Plate Attachment, Wallace Kicks LBJ Faced Donkey, Ass Kickin' Time In '68 . . 65.00
License Plate Attachment, Willkie, Reflector, Blue, Orange, Silver, 13 1/2 In. 40.00
License Plate Attachment, Win With Dewey & Warren, Red, White, Blue, 1948, 10 In. . . 270.00
License Plate Attachment, Win With Roosevelt, Blue, White, 2 1/2 x 10 1/4 In. 145.00
License Plate Attachment, Win With Truman & Barkley, Red, White, Blue, 1948, 10 In. . 495.00
License Plate Attachment, Win With Willkie & McNary, Red, White, Blue, 1940, 10 In. . 190.00
Match Cover, Reagan For Governor, Red, White, Blue, 1966 . . . . 12.00
Match Cover, Reagan For Governor, Tax Payer's Choice, Let's Get Out Of Debt 11.00
Match Cover, Vote For McCarthy, Presidential Hopeful, 1968 . . . . 11.00
Match Safe, McKinley, Stamped Brass Bust, Hinged Lid, Striker, 2 3/4 In. 160.00
Match Safe, Wilson, White House, Capitol, Celluloid, Tinted 375.00
Matchbook, Eisenhower, We Like Ike, New York, Red, White, Blue 14.00
Matchbook, LBJ/HHH Inauguration, Presidential Seal, 3 In. 10.00
Matchbook, Truman, Barkley, Inaugural Dinner, Gold, Black, White 60.00
Menu, LA Silver Republicans Club, W.J. Bryan Guest, 1897, 5 x 6 In. 85.00
Mirror, FDR, Retain The New Deal, Vermillion County, Black, Tan, Cloth, 3 1/8 In. 30.00
Mirror, Zack Taylor, Pewter Rim, Hand Colored Lithograph, 1848 . . . . 7865.00
Mug, Bobby Kennedy For President, 1960s, 4 In. 40.00
Mug, FDR, This Can Be Done, It Will Be Done, Blue, Wedgwood 400.00
Mug, Jimmy Carter, Grinning Peanut Shape, Glazed Ceramic, 1976, 5 x 6 In. 20.00
Napkin, Give JFK A Republican Congress For His Own Good 4.00
Necktie, FDR On Donkey, Beer Mug, Relief, Repeal, Roosevelt 175.00
Necktie, Hoover For President, Press On, Red 135.00
Necktie, Truman, Photograph, Burgundy, Macy's Tag 135.00
Notebook, Relief George Washington Portrait, Silk Lining, Ivory Covers 1350.00
Pamphlet, Californians, American Needs Nixon Now, Fold-Out, 1968, 8 Pages 7.00
Pamphlet, Lyndon Johnson For United States Senator, 3 1/4 x 4 3/4 In., 20 Pages 168.00
Pamphlet, Muskie For President, Fold-Out, 6 Pages 8.00
Parade Torch, Brass Plated, 19th Century, 8 1/2 In. 35.00

Parade Torch, Nickel Plated, 6 In. 28.00
Parade Torch, William H. Harrison, Inaugural, Eagle, Embossed Brass, c.1841, 10 In. 2420.00
Pencil, Willkie, Mechanical, Red, Pearl, Blue, Black, Silver 30.00
Pennant, Franklin D. Roosevelt, Yellow, Blue, Felt, 11 In. 30.00
Pennant, Gen. Douglas MacArthur, Welcome Home, Our Hero, Brown, White, 28 In. 60.00
Pennant, Independence, Mo., Home Of President Truman, Orange, 26 In. 95.00
Pennant, Nixon, Agnew, Vote Republican, Red, Black, White, Felt, 1968, 20 In. 30.00
Pennant, William Howard Taft, Felt, Pride Of Ohio, Photo, Eagle, 1908, 21 In. ...120.00 to 139.00
Picture, General John Geary, Candidate For Governor, 1866, 4 3/4 x 7 1/4 In. 50.00
Pin, Ax, Carry Nation, Mother Of Pearl, Brass, 1 7/8 In. 49.00
Pin, Bar, McKinley, Brass, Celluloid, June, 1900 .... 45.00
Pin, Bowtie, Willkie, Enamel, Red, White, Blue 100.00
Pin, Brass Shell, Wilson 46.00
Pin, Bull Moose, Teddy Roosevelt, Brass 45.00
Pin, Cleveland, Script, Bronze 50.00
Pin, Derby, Al Smith, Brass, 7/8 In. 30.00
Pin, Donkey Head, Red Enamel Roosevelt Bar 10.00
Pin, Donkey, Al Smith, Brown Derby Hat, Enameled 30.00
Pin, Donkey, Derby, Al Smith, Enamel, 7/8 In. 75.00
Pin, Donkey, Stevenson, Plastic, Red, White, On Card 19.00
Pin, Eagle, Harrison, Enamel, Brass, Bar, 1888 .... 49.00
Pin, Elephant, Blue, Enameled, Our Lives Begin At 40 With Willkie 75.00
Pin, Elephant, Figural, Dewey, Red, White, Blue, Brown, Wood 36.00
Pin, Elephant, Ike, Wood 15.00
Pin, Elephant, McKinley, Picture, Mechanical, Brass, Black, White, 1 1/8 In. 81.00
Pin, Eyeglasses, Goldwater, Gold, Black 20.00
Pin, FDR, Wallace, Hand Shaped Hanger 182.00
Pin, Gold Bug, McKinley, Black, White 146.00
Pin, Goldwater, Strawberry, Gold Nugget, Water Drop, 1964 .... 90.00
Pin, Hand, Fingers Crossed, MacArthur 45.00
Pin, Harrison Reform, Log Cabin, Sulfide, Rose, Brass Frame, 1840 Election, 1 1/8 In. ... 1290.00
Pin, Harrison, Script, Gold 30.00
Pin, Hoover Volunteer, Red, White, Blue, Gold, Rectangular 30.00
Pin, Key, Willkie Will Win, Brass, 3 1/2 In. 175.00
Pin, Nixon, Pull 2nd Lever, Committeeman, Lake County, 1960, 4 In. 382.00
Pin, Nose Thumber, Mechanical, Blaine, Brass 155.00
Pin, Nose Thumber, Mechanical, Garfield, Brass 328.00
Pin, Owl, Hoover, Who, Who, Hoover, Black, Gold, Enamel ....36.00 to 49.00
Pin, Silver Bug, Bryan, Mechanical, Photograph On 1 Wing, 16/1 On Other 225.00
Pin, Silver Bug, Bryan, Sewell Jugate, Photographs On Wings, Mechanical 225.00
Pin, Silvered Shell, Harrison, Morton 29.00
Pin, Taft & Sherman, Portraits, Stars & Strips, Red, White, Blue, 1912, 7/8 In. 550.00
Pin, Teddy Roosevelt, For President, 1904, Rough Rider, San Juan, 1 1/4 In. 290.00
Pin, Woodrow Wilson, Red, White, Blue, Black Gold, Picture, 7/8 In. 172.00
Pin, Woodrow Wilson, Signature, Gold Color, 2 1/2 In. 55.00
Pitcher, Presidents, Up To Johnson, Pottery, Japan, 1965, 6 1/2 In. ....*Illus* 32.00
Pitcher, William Henry Harrison, Columbian Star, J. Ridgeway, England, 10 3/4 In. 2713.00
Plate, All In Favor Say Ike, Newspaper Headlines, August, 1956, 10 In. 25.00
Plate, FDR, Churchill, Scalloped, Brown, White, Gray, 9 In. 95.00
Plate, FDR, Portrait, Sepia, Green Leaves, Gold Border, 10 1/2 In. 25.00
Plate, Franklin Delano Roosevelt, 1882-1945, 1940s, 10 In. 30.00
Plate, Garfield, Stars, Clear, Glass, Etched, 6 In. 36.00
Plate, JFK & Family, 1962, 10 In. 19.75
Plate, Jimmy Carter, 39th President, Black, White, 10 In. 10.00
Plate, McKinley, Milk Glass, 5 1/2 In. 60.00
Plate, Roosevelt Bears, Digging Ditch At Panama, Porcelain, Scalloped Rim, 5 3/4 In. 115.00
Plate, Temperance, Man & Woman, Banner Of Sobriety, Ceramic, 5 1/2 In. 110.00
Plate, Willkie Preparedness, Peace, Prosperity, Milk Glass 22.00
Plate, Wilson With Compliments, Brown, White, Gold Trim, 5 1/4 In. 55.00
Playing Cards, Votes For Women, Interlocking Vs, Yellow, Black, White, Box 1089.00
Pocket Knife, Born Leaders, Washington, Lincoln & Reagan Portraits, Steel Handle, Box . 35.00
Pocket Knife, George Wallace, American Party, 1968 .... 23.00
Postcard, Birthplace Of Wendell Willkie, Elwood, In. 6.00

Postcard, Bryan, Kern 15.00
Postcard, Coolidge, Henry Ford, Edison 25.00
Postcard, Coolidge, Shaking Hands, Wife At Side, Sepia 6.00
Postcard, Fighters For MacArthur 13.00
Postcard, Harding, Warren, Florence, Embossed, Imprint Vall's Studios 20.00
Postcard, Hellow Bill, We Love Billy Possum, No More Teddy Bear, Possum, Verse 40.00
Postcard, Hubert Humphrey, Accomplishments, Signed 15.00
Postcard, Ike's Cafe, Ike, Nixon, Dewey, Satirical Dishes, Special Menu For Nov. 4, 1952 10.00
Postcard, Iowa State Capitol, Gov. George Wilson, 1940 .... 6.00
Postcard, Italian Earthquake Relief, Roosevelt & Taft 15.00
Postcard, Lurleen Wallace, 48th Governor Of Alabama 4.00
Postcard, McKinley, Hobart, Bryan, Sewell On Revolving Wheel, 1896 .... 14.00
Postcard, McKinley, Wife On Front Porch Of W.B. Plunkel, c.1900 .... 15.00
Postcard, Only Possums That Escaped, Taft Marching With Gun, Dog, 1909 .... 20.00
Postcard, Pres. Roosevelt Signs Lend-Lease Bill, March 11, 1941 .... 15.00
Postcard, President Reagan & Queen Elizabeth On Horses, Windsor Castle, 1982 .... 4.00
Postcard, President Roosevelt Speaking At Dedication Of Great Smoky Mountains 9.00
Postcard, President Roosevelt, A Smile For Children 6.00
Postcard, Star Of West, Billy Goat Eating Our Motto Banner 30.00
Postcard, Support Roosevelt & Johnson, Red, White, Blue, 1941 .... 402.00
Postcard, Teddy Roosevelt, African Trip, Brown Tone, 1910 .... 7.00
Postcard, Teddy Roosevelt, Bull Moose, Poem, Blue, Brown, 1912 .... 179.00
Postcard, Teddy Roosevelt, Inspecting Panama Canal 8.00
Postcard, Teddy Roosevelt, Japanese & Russian Peace Delegates 14.00
Postcard, Teddy Roosevelt, Me & Teddy, 1907 .... 6.00
Postcard, Teddy Roosevelt, President, Leading Rough Riders, 12/4/1901 .... 12.00
Postcard, Teddy Roosevelt, Shakes Hand Of Cuban President Palma, 1902 .... 100.00
Postcard, Teddy Roosevelt, Shooting Geese, Cartoon 7.00
Postcard, Teddy Roosevelt, Square Deal For Every Man 12.00
Postcard, Teddy Roosevelt, This Is My Candidate, Who's Yours?, Black, White 139.00
Postcard, Teddy Roosevelt, White House Wedding 15.00
Postcard, Teddy Roosevelt, White House, Flasher, Puzzle Postcard, 1906 .... 25.00
Postcard, Teddy's Bear, Teddy Pointing Gun At Fur-Covered Bear 20.00
Postcard, The Man Who Made Lincoln Famous 14.00
Postcard, William Howard Taft, Billy Possum 6.00
Postcard, Willkie, Portrait Over High School, 1940 Campaign 25.00
Postcard, You Believe In Women's Suffrage Don't You, Girl, Rolling Pin, Boy 35.00
Postcard, Zachary Taylor 25.00
Poster, America Roosevelt, Renneker Co., Chicago 40.00
Poster, Americans For Goldwater, Cardboard, 14 x 22 In. 136.00
Poster, Anti-Andrew Jackson, John Woods Story, Coffin, 1828, 8 1/2 x 4 1/2 In. 1080.00
Poster, Anti-Tojo, Douglas Aircraft, 9 1/4 x 12 1/2 In. 125.00
Poster, Bill Miller, Headquarters Sir Francis Drake Hotel, 8 1/2 x 11 In. 12.00
Poster, Carter, Pour Le President, J'Aime Jimmy, Baton Rouge, 1976, 13 x 22 In. 35.00
Poster, Dewey For President, 11 x 13 1/2 In. 20.00
Poster, Dewey Ohio Coattail, This Is The Year, 19 x 26 1/2 In. 66.00
Poster, El Pueblo Con Jimmy Carter 10.00
Poster, Eugene McCarthy For President, A Political Alternative, 1968, 21 x 28 In. 60.00
Poster, Get Kissinger Out Now, U.S. Labor Party, 16 3/4 x 22 In. 35.00
Poster, Hancock The Bird To Bet On, Frame, 1880, 15 x 19 In. 588.00
Poster, Harding, Coolidge, Sepia, Celluloid, 1920, 11 x 16 1/2 In. 140.00
Poster, James Cox, Black & White, 1920, 14 x 11 In. 45.00
Poster, John F. Kennedy, Blue, White, Shrine Auditorium, Los Angeles, 1960, 8 x 11 In. .. 175.00
Poster, Keep Pennsylvania Liberal, 7 1/2 x 10 1/2 In. 30.00
Poster, Kennedy For President, Healy For Congress, Vote Democratic, 13 x 21 In. 135.00
Poster, Kennedy, Johnson, Leadership For The 60s, 13 x 18 In. 75.00
Poster, Larouche For President, U.S. Labor Party, 1976, 17 x 11 1/4 In. 25.00
Poster, LBJ, Cardboard, Pull Top Lever, 14 1/4 x 21 In. 32.00
Poster, Lyndon B. Johnson, For U.S. Senate, Roosevelt & Unity, 11 x 14 In. 890.00
Poster, Lyndon Johnson For United States Senator, 13 1/2 x 22 In. 805.00
Poster, McGovern Campaign, Streisand, King, Taylor, 1972, 24 1/2 x 37 1/2 In. 1200.00
Poster, McKinley, Cleveland Strobridge, Look On This, Frame, 1896, 31 x 40 In. 14920.00
Poster, McKinley, Roosevelt, Prosperity, Lady Liberty, 1900, 28 x 40 In. 7225.00

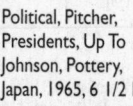

Political, Pitcher, Presidents, Up To Johnson, Pottery, Japan, 1965, 6 1/2 In.

Porcelain, Teapot, Salt Glaze, Cherub & Leaves, Hinged Lid, c.1800, 5 1/2 In.

Poster, Nixon, Lodge, Everyone Counts, Blue, Black, White, 1960, 13 3/4 x 22 In.	80.00
Poster, People Want Willkie, 6 1/2 x 16 1/2 In.	55.00
Poster, Robert F. Kennedy, Red, White, Blue, Black, 1968, 12 1/4 x 18 1/2 In.	30.00
Poster, Taft, Our Next President, Color, Board Backing, 13 x 19 In.	45.00
Poster, Teddy Roosevelt's Guiding Spirit, Frame, 1901, 19 1/2 x 26 1/2 In.	5430.00
Poster, U.S. Labor Party, 1976, 17 x 11 1/4 In.	20.00
Poster, Union Hand Made Cigars, Louisville Ky., Cardboard, 11 x 14 In.	18.00
Poster, W.J. Bryan, Octopus, Liberty, Justice, Humanity, 1900, 19 1/2 x 29 1/2 In.	5970.00
Poster, Welcome Jack, Black, White, Cardboard, 14 x 22 In.	25.00
Program, Inaugural, FDR & Garner, Official, 1933, 8 1/2 x 11 In.	25.00
Program, Inaugural, FDR, Wallace, January, 1941, 64 Pages	40.00
Program, John F. Kennedy Inauguration, Envelope, 1961, 64 Pages	100.00
Record Album, JFK & The Negro, Civil Rights Statements From His Speeches	30.00
Reverse Painting On Glass, Martin Van Buren, Portrait, Multicolored, Frame, 9 x 11 In.	865.00
Ribbon, B. Harrison, Red, White, Blue, Black, Gold, 1888, 6 In.	190.00
Ribbon, Cleveland, Black, White, Sepia, 1884, 6 In.	90.00
Ribbon, Cleveland, Gray, Indiana, Blue, Tan, 1888, 5 In.	355.00
Ribbon, Cleveland, Stevenson, Celluloid	210.00
Ribbon, Daniel Webster, Blue Silk, Albumen Oval Portrait, Welcome, 2 1/2 x 8 1/2 In.	520.00
Ribbon, Edwin Stuart For Governor, 9 1/2 In.	30.00
Ribbon, Eisenhower Inauguration, Transportation, Blue, Gold, 1953, 4 1/2 In.	25.00
Ribbon, Ford, Dole, Kansas, Mid-America Fair, 2-In. Sunflower Button, 1976, 7 In.	10.00
Ribbon, G. Washington Centennial, Woven, Multicolored, Sullivan, Fischer, c.1876	375.00
Ribbon, Garfield As Canal Boy, Garfield, Arthur 1880 Campaign, 6 3/4 In.	100.00
Ribbon, Garfield For President, Protective Tariff, Light Blue Ribbon, 6 3/4 In.	100.00
Ribbon, Harrison, Red, White, Blue, Black, Yellow, 1892, 6 In.	130.00
Ribbon, Harrison, Reid, Our Choice, President, Vice President, Woven, 5 3/4 In.	360.00
Ribbon, Hayes, Wheeler, Boys In Blue, Woven, 5 In.	140.00
Ribbon, Henry Clay, Frelinghuysen, Protection To American Industry, 8 1/2 In.	415.00
Ribbon, Henry Clay, Pride Of America, People's Choice, Silk, 2 3/4 x 9 1/4 In.	160.00
Ribbon, James Blaine, Minneapolis, Blue Ribbons, 2-In. Sepia Portrait, 1892, 8 3/4 In.	90.00
Ribbon, John A. Logan Club, Silk, Pinback Top, Tassel, c.1884, 3 x 8 In.	160.00
Ribbon, Lincoln, Union Forever, Andrew Johnson, Grant, Sherman, 1864, 7 1/4 In.	1190.00
Ribbon, McClellan, Pendleton, Purple Silk, Portrait, 1864	3650.00
Ribbon, McKinley, Hobart, Red, White, Blue, 1896, 7 In.	40.00
Ribbon, McKinley, Our Next President, Ohio, Gilt Letters, Copper Colored Silk, 6 1/2 In.	25.00
Ribbon, McKinley, Wheelman, Buffalo, Canton, Blue, Oct. 3, 1896, 5 1/4 In.	50.00
Ribbon, Millard Fillmore, Portrait, Facsimile Signature, Silk, 4 x 8 1/2 In.	1840.00
Ribbon, Mourning, Garfield, Knights Of Pythias, 6 In.	25.00
Ribbon, Mourning, JFK, Black, White, 5 1/2 In.	12.00
Ribbon, Mourning, John Quincy Adams, Silk, c.1848, 7 x 2 1/2 In.	520.00
Ribbon, Mourning, P.S. Lincoln, Black, Silver Letters, c.1865, 8 1/2 x 2 In.	690.00
Ribbon, Mourning, U.S. Grant, 8 In.	25.00
Ribbon, Mourning, U.S. Grant, Silk, Sullivan Fischer USG-M12, 1885, 6 1/4 x 2 In.	159.00
Ribbon, Mourning, William M. McKinley, In Memoriam, 5 3/4 In.	24.00
Ribbon, President Harry S. Truman, Special Guest, Davenport, Iowa, 1952, 8 1/4 In.	45.00
Ribbon, Reagan, Ford, K.C. GOP National Convention, Button At Top, 1976, 8 1/2 In.	10.00
Ribbon, Republican National Committee, Blue, Gold, Chicago, 1880	250.00
Ribbon, Republican National Convention, Vote Bush, Button, Detroit, 1980, 7 1/2 In.	10.00

Ribbon, Taft, Celluloid, Republican National League Convention, Cincinnati, 1908 ..... 150.00
Ribbon, Tammany Hall Cleveland Inauguration, Eagle Pinback, Frame, 2 1/2 x 11 In. 196.00
Ribbon, Teddy Roosevelt, Delegate, Red, White, Blue 130.00
Ribbon, U.S. Grant, Black & White, August 8, 1885 .... 20.00
Ribbon, U.S. Grant, Schuyler Colfax, Blue, 1868 .... 2200.00
Ribbon, Victory, Anti-Combine, Things Are Different Now, 7 In. 25.00
Ribbon, W.H. Harrison Memorial, Fire Engine, Biography On Reverse, 1841, 8 1/2 In. 75.00
Ribbon, W.H. Taft, Republican Party, Multicolored, 1908, 10 In. 175.00
Ribbon, William Henry Harrison, New England Convention, Silk, 1840, 6 1/2 x 3 In. 300.00
Ring, Hoover, Silver, Red, White, Blue, 1928 .... 30.00
Ring, Smith, Silver, Red, White, Blue, 1928 .... 30.00
Shaving Mug, Governor John J. Marlin Kansas, American Eagle, White, 1880, 4 In. 510.00
Sheet Music, Admiral Dewey's Grand Triumphal March, 1898 .... 25.00
Sheet Music, Cleveland's Inauguration Grand March, 1885 .... 35.00
Sheet Music, Click With Dick, Campaign Song, 1960 .... 10.00
Sheet Music, Hoover, It's An Elephant's Job, Keep Him On The Job, 1932, 9 x 12 In. ... 25.00
Sheet Music, John F. Kennedy, 1964 .... 25.00
Sheet Music, Let's Put Barry In White House, Goldwater, Miller Team, 1964 .... 10.00
Sheet Music, Lincoln Quick Step, Rail Splitting, Flatboat Scenes, Frame, 1860 .... 1250.00
Sheet Music, Lincoln's Log Cabin March, 1915 .... 25.00
Sheet Music, Our President Of 1933, FDR, 9 1/2 x 12 In. 60.00
Sheet Music, Our Teddy, Roosevelt In Rough Rider Uniform, J.W. Johnston, 10 x 13 In. . 75.00
Sheet Music, President Johnson, Grand Union March, Frame 275.00
Sheet Music, President's March, Grant, 1869 .... 40.00
Sheet Music, Spirit Of Eugene Debs, F. Zeidler, 4 Page, 8 1/2 x 11 In. 109.00
Sheet Music, That's What's The Matter, Lincoln, Davis, Slavery, 10 1/2 x 14 In. 200.00
Sheet Music, We Shall Overcome, LBJ 18.00
Sheet Music, You're The Man For Us, Harding, Coolidge 30.00
Shovel, Teddy Roosevelt, Tin Lithograph Head, Black, Blue Portrait, 5 1/2 In. 275.00
Shovel, Wilson, Tin Lithograph Head, Black, White Portrait, 5 1/2 In. 225.00
Sign, Donkey & Elephant, RCA Victor Television, Cardboard, 13 1/2 x 19 1/2 In. 50.00
Sign, Ford, Dole, Neighborhood Headquarters, Red, White, Blue, 21 x 17 In. 18.00
Sign, No Parking, Reagan's 1981 Inaugural, Cardboard, 12 x 18 In. 20.00
Silk, George Washington Centennial, Philadelphia Exhibition, 1876, 10 x 6 In. 1080.00
Song Book, Garfield, Arthur, 1880, 5 1/2 x 8 3/4 In. 60.00
Song Book, Harding, Coolidge, America First, Republican, 6 x 8 3/4 In. 30.00
Song Book, Roosevelt, Johnson, Progressive Battle Hymns, 1912, 5 1/2 x 8 In. 28.00
Sponge, John F. Kennedy For President, 2 3/4 x 4 1/2 In. 28.00
Stein, Teddy Roosevelt, On Elephant, Attacked By Lion, Germany, 13 In. 2650.00
Sticker, Coolidge, Dawes, Red, White, Blue, Black, 1924, 11 In. 165.00
Sticker, Humphrey, Muskie, Official Democratic Volunteer, Cloth, 2 x 3 1/2 In. 5.00
Sticker, Window, Dewey, Warren, All 48 In 48, 3 3/4 In. 17.00
Sticker, Window, I Like Ike, 4 In. 8.00
Sticker, Window, Ike Likes Us, Blue, White, 7 In. 9.00
Sticker, Window, Truman, Blue, Brown 25.00
Sticker, Window, Willkie, Wings For America 18.00
Stickpin, Abraham Lincoln, Ferrotype, Cloth Covered Metal, 1864, 3/4 In. 1208.00
Stickpin, Cleveland, Broom 75.00
Stickpin, Cleveland, C&T, Brass 30.00
Stickpin, Cleveland, Enamel 60.00
Stickpin, Cleveland, Gold, Enameled 25.00
Stickpin, Ferrotype, Abraham Lincoln, 1864, 5/8 In. 570.00
Stickpin, Harrison, Broom Shape 90.00
Stickpin, McKinley, Hobart, Red, Blue, Pennant Shape, Metal 30.00
Stickpin, Taft, Billy Possum Carrying TR's Big Stick 60.00
Stickpin, Taft, Ivory Portrait 118.00
Stickpin, Teddy Roosevelt, Bull Moose, Gold, 1912 .... 40.00
Straight Razor, Benjamin Harrison, Portrait, Banner, Horn Handle, 9 1/2 In. 345.00
Stud, Cleveland, Cloth, Red, Silver, 1884-1888 .... 20.00
Stud, Coffin, Anti-McKinley, Friend Of Trusts & British Gold, Mechanical, 1 In. 1315.00
Stud, Cox, Roosevelt, Man On Donkey Carrying Flag, Figural, 1920, 7/8 In. 550.00
Stud, Landon, Covered Wagon, Copper, 1 1/4 In. 65.00
Stud, Landon, Liberty Bell, Red, White, Blue, Gold, Enamel 55.00

Stud, Willkie, Dig In, Shovel, Gold, Red, White, Blue, 1 3/8 In. 110.00
Sugar & Creamer, Franklin D. Roosevelt, Brown, White, Gold Trim, 2 1/2 In. 85.00
Tab Button, Dewey, Democrats For Dewey 18.00
Tab Button, FDR, Roosevelt Now More Than Ever 25.00
Tab Button, Kennedy, Johnson, Donkey Shape, Lithograph 10.00
Tab Button, Landon, Knox, Lodge, Saltonstall, Lithograph 10.00
Tab Button, MacArthur, Red, White, Blue 20.00
Tab Button, Sinclair, Downey, Epic, Think, 1934, 7/8 In. 155.00
Tab Button, Truman, All 48 In 48, Young Democrats, 7/8 In. 99.00
Tag, Roosevelt, Johnson, Progressive Bull Moose, Celluloid 540.00
Teacup, Zachary Taylor, Snake Form Handle, Paris Porcelain, 3 3/4 x 2 3/4 In. 3750.00
Textile, George Washington, Benjamin Harrison, 1889, 22 1/2 x 22 1/2 In. 920.00
Textile, Herbert Hoover, Red, White, Blue, Brown, 1928, 14 1/2 x 18 1/2 In. 55.00
Thimble, Nixon, Governor, California, Blue, Yellow, Plastic, 1962 .... 126.00
Ticket, Delegate, Alternate, 8th Session, July, 1940 .... 25.00
Ticket, Dewey Warren Rally, Madison Square Garden, Oct. 30, 1948, Yellow, Black 30.00
Ticket, G.O.P. National Convention, Chicago, 1868, 2 1/4 x 3 1/4 In. 250.00
Ticket, Impeachment, Senate, Purple, 1868, 5 In. 445.00
Ticket, Inaugural Ball, Stubs, Gray Background 15.00
Ticket, Inaugural, FDR, Wallace, 1941, 2 1/2 x 4 3/4 In. 24.00
Ticket, Inauguration Ceremonies, Reagan, Bush, Jan., 1985, House Wing 10.00
Ticket, McKinley Inaugural Supper, Engraved, Bailey, Banks & Biddle, 1897 ....150.00 to 175.00
Ticket, Teddy Roosevelt Inauguration, President's Reviewing Stand, 1905 .... 315.00
Ticket, Truman, Barkley, Inaugural Gala, Multicolored, 1949 .... 85.00
Tie, Harry Truman, Blue, White, 1948 .... 198.00
Toby Jug, Ike In Uniform, 5-Star Hat Insignia, Sylvan, 7 1/4 In. 375.00
Token, Lincoln, Hamlin, Picture, Uniface, Brass, Ferrotype 2060.00
Top, Reagan Is Tops For 1980, Blue, White, Celluloid, Wood Stick, 1 3/4 In. 220.00
Towel, Crying, Dewey's, Lodge's, Red, White, Marshal Field, Chicago, 17 x 32 In. 100.00
Trade Card, Hancock, Garfield Campaign Cards, Flag Style, 2 3/4 x 4 1/2 In. 45.00
Trade Card, Harrison, Cleveland, Horsford's Phosphate, 1888, 7 x 4 In. 25.00
Tray, Grover Cleveland, Thomas Hendricks, Glass, Etched, 12 x 8 1/2 In. 60.00
Tray, McKinley, Roosevelt, Portraits, Oval, 16 In. 1065.00
Trivet, Emancipation Proclamation, Lincoln, Freed Slaves, Silvered Brass, 4 1/2 In. 1000.00
Trivet, President & Mrs. John F. Kennedy, White House Portrait, Tile, Metal, 5 x 8 In. ... 30.00
Tumbler, Harrison, Morton, Heavy Glass, 3 1/2 In. 250.00
Washcloth, Wash Away LBJ, Vote Republican, Cabarrus County 25.00
Watch Fob, Bryan, For President, 1908 .... 40.00
Watch Fob, Bryan, President, New Winona Assembly, Sepia, Celluloid, 1 1/2 In. 430.00
Watch Fob, Cox, Silver, 1920 .... 66.00
Watch Fob, Elephant, Roosevelt, Fairbanks, Copper 150.00
Watch Fob, Harding, Gold, 1920 .... 70.00
Watch Fob, Roosevelt, Fairbanks, Brass, 1904, 1 1/2 In. 19.00
Watch Fob, T. Roosevelt, To Washington D.C., Leather Strap, 1904 .... 30.00
Watch Fob, Taft, For President, 1908 .... 40.00
Watch Fob, Taft, Leather Strap, 1908 .... 55.00
Watch Fob, Taft, Multicolored, Celluloid 80.00
Watch Fob, Taft, White House, Brass, Leather, 1908 .... 75.00
Watch Fob, Teddy Roosevelt, Brass, 1904 ....25.00 to 39.00
Window Sticker, I'll Keep Eisenhower, 4 x 5 In. 18.00
Window Sticker, Re-Elect Roosevelt, For Freedom, 4 Freedoms, Round, 3 1/2 In. 14.00
Window Sticker, We Want Ike Again, Pennant Shape, 7 1/2 In. 24.00
Window Sticker, Willkie, We'll Win With, 3 Marching Elephants, 1940 .... 15.00

POMONA glass is a clear glass with a soft amber border decorated with pale blue or rose-colored flowers and leaves. The colors are very, very pale. The background of the glass is covered with a network of fine lines. It was made from 1885 to 1888 by the New England Glass Company. First grind was made from April 1885 to June 1886. It was made by cutting a wax surface on the glass, then dipping it in acid. Second grind was a less expensive method of acid etching that was developed later.

Bowl, Cornflower, Ruffled Edge, 2nd Grind, 2 1/2 x 5 1/4 In. 55.00

Bowl, Cornflower, Ruffled Edge, Petaled Base, 1st Grind, 3 1/2 x 8 In. 550.00
Bowl, Gold Enameled, Ruffled Edge, 1st Grind, 2 1/2 x 5 In. 55.00
Bowl, Ruffled Edge, First Grind, 1800s, 5 1/4 In. 35.00
Celery Vase, Tightly Rufled Edge, Applied Foot, Amber Stain, 6 1/2 In. 196.00
Cracker Jar, Cover, Cornflowers, 2nd Grind 952.00
Pitcher, Enameled Vines, Diamond Thumbprint, Crystal Rope Rigaree, 2nd Grind, 7 In. ... 259.00
Pitcher, Inverted Thumbprint, Trefoil, Amber Neck, Applied Handle, 2nd Grind, 7 1/4 In. 77.00
Tumbler, Blue Cornflowers, 1st Grind, 3 3/4 In. 115.00

PONTYPOOL, see Tole category.

POOLE POTTERY was started by Jesse Carter in 1873 in Poole, England. The company specialized in architectural ceramics. In 1908 the company was incorporated as Carter and Company. In 1920 it became Carter & Co. The name Poole Pottery Ltd. was taken in 1963. The company is still in business.

Blue Bird Set, Wall Mount, Graduated, No. 807/1-3, John Adams, 1930s 116.00
Bowl, No. 221, Red Body, JV Pattern, Truda Carter, Phyllis Way, 1930s 70.00
Vase, Aegean, Geometric Decoration, Yellow Ground, 1970s, 16 In. 110.00
Vase, Alfred Read, Pattern 595/PLT, 1960s, 5 In. 89.00

POPEYE was introduced to the Thimble Theatre comic strip in 1929. The character became a favorite of readers. In 1932, an animated cartoon featuring Popeye was made by Paramount Studios. The cartoon series continued and became even more popular when it was shown on television starting in the 1950s. The full-length movie with Robin Williams as Popeye was made in 1980.

Bank, Dime, Register, Tin Lithograph 30.00
Christmas Lights, Shades, Popeye, Swee'pea, General Electric, 1929, Set Of 8 .... 315.00
Christmas Tree Set, 8 Shades, Marked K.F.S., 1929 .... 315.00
Container, Popcorn, Tin, King Features, Purity Mills, 1949, 12 1/2 Oz., 4 3/4 x 3 x 2 In. . 250.00
Display, Cardboard, Lithograph On Wood, Stand Up, 55 In. 110.00
Figure, Popeye, Holding Pipe, Celluloid, 4 1/2 In. 85.00
Figure, Popeye, Jointed Wood, Hand Painted, Chein, King Features, 1932, 8 In. 495.00
Figure, Popeye, Standing, Cutout, Holds Tray, Wood, 38 In. 66.00
Game, Dexterity, Bar-Zim Toys, Tin, Glass, 1929, 3 1/2 x 5 In. 100.00
Game, Pipe Toss, Box, 10 In. 52.00
Game, Ring Toss, Rosebud Art Co., Box, 1933, 16 x 10 1/2 In. 300.00
Lantern, Popeye, Tin, Linemar, Box, 7 1/2 In. 950.00
Lunch Box, Popeye & Brutus, Arm Wrestling, Tin Lithograph, Thermos, Aladdin 55.00
Napkin Ring, Green, Bakelite, c.1930 .... 100.00
Pail, At Beach, Yellow Ground, Tin, Flat Red Tin Handle, T. Cohn, USA, 8 In. 690.00
Pencil Sharpener, Popeye, With Pipe, Tin Lithograph, Irwin, K.F.S. Mark, 2 3/4 In. 250.00
Pin, Popeye's Jeep, 1930s, 1 1/4 In. 345.00
Salt & Pepper, Popeye & Olive Oyl, 1960s-1970s, 6 1/4 In. 95.00
Soap, Popeye, Painted, Box, 6 In. 130.00
Tin, Popeye Pop Corn, Purity Mill's Lithograph, Pry Lid, 4 3/4 x 3 1/4 x 2 1/8 In. 176.00
Toy, Airplane, Eccentric, Tin Lithograph, Windup, Marx, Box, c.1930, 7 In. 1320.00
Toy, Bluto, Dippy Dumper, Crazy Action, Trailer Dumps, Tin, Windup, Marx, Box, 9 In. . 550.00
Toy, Boxer, Overhead, Tin Lithograph, Windup, Chein, American, c.1935, 10 In. 1650.00
Toy, Bubble Blowing, Tin Lithograph, Battery Operated, Linemar, Box, 11 3/4 In. 1430.00
Toy, Bubble Pipe Set, 2 Wooden Pipes, Tin Dish, King Features Syndicate, Box, 1936 .... 50.00
Toy, Handcar, Popeye, Olive Oyl, Tin Lithograph, Steel, Rubber, Box, Marx, 11 x 11 In. .. 1210.00
Toy, Olive Oyl, Ballerina, Friction, Linemar, Box, 5 1/2 In. 600.00
Toy, Popeye & Olive Oyl, On Roof, Dancing, Playing Accordion, Marx, c.1935, 9 1/2 In. .. 810.00
Toy, Popeye & Olive Oyl, Play Catch, Tin, Windup, Linemar, Japan, c.1950s, 19 In. 770.00
Toy, Popeye & Olive Oyl, Pull, On Metal Coils, Tin Lithograph, Linemar, c.1950s, 7 In. .. 715.00
Toy, Popeye Cyclist, Peddles, Tin Windup, Linemar, Box, 7 In. .... 1650.00 to 3520.00
Toy, Popeye Express, Pushing Wheelbarrow, Tin Lithograph, Marx, c.1930, 9 In. 715.00
Toy, Popeye Express, Tin Lithograph, Windup, Box, Marx, c.1935, 9 In. 1760.00
Toy, Popeye Express, Tin, Windup, Parrot On Cart, Marx, 1930s 845.00
Toy, Popeye On Barrel, Walks, Tin, Windup, Chein, 1932, 7 1/2 In. .... 440.00 to 625.00
Toy, Popeye Pilot, In Airplane, Windup, Marx, 1940 .... 675.00
Toy, Popeye, Acrobat, Tin Lithograph, Windup, Linemar, Late 1950s, 7 1/2 In. 1430.00

Toy, Popeye, Basketball Player, Tin Lithograph, Windup, Linemar, c.1950s, 9 In. .825.00 to 1100.00
Toy, Popeye, Boxer, Windup, Tin Lithograph, Celluloid, Punching Bag, Chein, 7 1/2 In. . . . 825.00
Toy, Popeye, Champ, Boxing Ring, Tin Lithograph, Celluloid, Marx, Box, 1935, 6 1/2 In. . . 3410.00
Toy, Popeye, Champ, Boxing Ring, Tin Lithograph, Clockwork, Marx, 7 1/2 In. 1540.00
Toy, Popeye, Champ, Tin Lithograph, Celluloid Figures, Louis Marx, Box, 7 1/4 In. 5225.00
Toy, Popeye, Champ, Tin Lithograph, Key, Marx, Box, 1930s, 7 In. 3960.00
Toy, Popeye, Dances On Roof, Tin Lithograph, Marx, American, 1930s, 9 In. 495.00
Toy, Popeye, Dances On Roof, Windup, Marx 650.00
Toy, Popeye, Dippy Dumper, Crazy Action, Trailer Dumps, Tin, Windup, Marx, 9 In. 850.00
Toy, Popeye, Drummer, Push Plunger, Tin, KFS, c.1930, 7 In. 2420.00
Toy, Popeye, Head Moves, Celluloid, Windup, King Features, 1929, 8 1/2 In. . . . .950.00 to 1250.00
Toy, Popeye, Heavy Hitter, Windup, Tin Lithograph, Chein, 12 In. 715.00
Toy, Popeye, Olive Oyl, In Chair, Arms Twirl, Chair Spins, Tin, Windup, Linemar, 9 In. . . 1100.00
Toy, Popeye, Olive Oyl, Juggling, Tin Lithograph, Linemar, Box, Japan, c.1960, 9 1/2 In. . . 2530.00
Toy, Popeye, Olive Oyl, Plays Accordion, Rooftop, Embossed, Tin Litho, Marx, 10 In. . . . 1155.00
Toy, Popeye, On Motorcycle, Cart, Cast Iron, Hubley, American, c.1930, 5 1/2 In. 880.00
Toy, Popeye, On Patrol Motorcycle, Cast Iron, Hubley, 8 1/4 In. 1980.00
Toy, Popeye, Parrot Cages, Tin Lithograph, Clockwork, Chein, Box, 8 1/2 In. . . . . .275.00 to 330.00
Toy, Popeye, Parrot Cages, Windup, Marx, Box, 1930s 650.00
Toy, Popeye, Pilot, Tin Lithograph, Clockwork, Louis Marx, 7 In. 770.00
Toy, Popeye, Pilot, Tin, Windup, Marx, Box, 1940s, 7 In. 1870.00
Toy, Popeye, Punching Bag, Tin Lithograph, Celluloid Bag, Clockwork, Chein, 7 In. 470.00
Toy, Popeye, Roller Skater, Bends Over, Tin, Windup, Linemar, Box, 7 In. 1155.00
Toy, Popeye, Rowboat, Tin Lithograph, Wind Up, Hoge, 1935, 15 In. 3960.00
Toy, Popeye, Rubber, 1935, 6 3/4 In. 175.00
Toy, Popeye, Smoking, Pipe Lights, Lifts To Mouth, Battery Operated, Linemar, Box 3850.00
Toy, Popeye, Smoking, Tin Lithograph, Battery Operated, Linemar, Box, 9 1/2 In. 4125.00
Toy, Popeye, Sparkling, Tin Lithograph, Chein, Box, c.1940, 5 1/2 In. 275.00
Toy, Popeye, Tank, Rubber Wheels, Tin Lithograph, Windup, Linemar, c.1950, 4 In. 385.00
Toy, Popeye, Walking, Tin Lithograph, Windup, Chein, c.1930, 6 In. 385.00
Toy, Popeye, Walking, Tin Lithograph, Windup, Marx, Box, c.1930, 8 In. . . . . . . .770.00 to 1130.00
Toy, Skating Waiter, Embossed, Tin Lithograph, Clockwork, Linemar, 6 In. 495.00
Toy, Spinach Cycle, Rubber Wheels, Cast Iron, Hubley, 5 1/2 In. 470.00
Toy, Truck, Popeye Transit Co., Friction, Linemar, 12 In. 650.00
Toy, Wimpy, Vibrates, Celluloid, Windup, Occupied Japan, 6 1/2 In. 470.00

PORCELAIN factories that are well known are listed in this book under
the factory name. This category and the two following list pieces made
by the less well-known factories. Porcelain-Contemporary lists pieces
made by artists working after 1975. Porcelain-Midcentury includes
pieces made from the 1940s to the 1980s.

Basin, Blue & White, Chinese, 19th Century, 11 In. 290.00
Basin, Blue & White, Dragon, Clouds, Vines, Phoenix, Flowers, Ming Mark, 15 1/2 In. . . . 460.00
Basket, Encrusted Flowers, Hungary, 17 In. 299.00
Basket, Flowers, Gilt Decoration, Twist Handle, 10 In. 790.00
Bowl, 5-Claw Dragon, Cover, Blue, White, Ming Mark, 1800s, 6 1/4 In. 58.00
Bowl, Bell Shape, Figural Cartouches, Keyfret Ground, Multicolored, 1800s, 6 1/2 In. . . . 58.00
Bowl, Blue Glaze, Yongzheng Mark, Chinese, Late 19th Century, 5 1/4 In., Pair 1060.00
Bowl, Blue, White, Flowering Branches, Bird, Children, Oriental, 10 1/2 x 4 1/2 In. 165.00
Bowl, Bulb, Blue & White, Butterfly Shape, Scrolling Flowers, Chinese, 10 In. 80.00
Bowl, Kylin & Phoenix Underglaze Decoration, Flower Panels, Chinese, 1800s, 7 In. 90.00
Bowl, Leaf Form, Gilt & Enamel Women, Flowers, Kakiemon Ware, Japan, 1800s, 6 In. . . 44.00
Bowl, Morning Glory, 3 Silver Ball Feet, Hand Painted, Silver Trim, 4 x 2 In. 36.00
Bowl, Parcel Gilt, Reticulated, Navette Shape, Ruffled Rim, Late 1800s, 11 3/8 In. 325.00
Bowl, Punch, Cabbage Leaf Pattern, Chinese, Early 20th Century, 15 3/4 In. 1005.00
Bowl Set, Octagonal, Enameled Flowers, Kakeimon, Late 1800s, 6 1/4 In., 5 Piece 1380.00
Box, Artist's Palette Shape, Man & Woman On Lid, France, 3 x 2 x 1 1/8 In. 180.00
Box, Butterfly, Flower, White On Blue, Rectangular, Early 1800s, 7 1/2 In. 145.00
Brush Holder, Cylinder Form, Crab, Marsh Grass, Late 1800s, 4 In. 29.00
Brush Holder, Mid 19th Century, 9 3/4 In. 290.00
Cachepot, Blue & White, Ming Style, Flowers, Chinese, 1800s, 4 3/4 x 6 1/2 In. 69.00
Cassollette, Pair, Bronze Mounted, Turquoise Ground, Ram's-Head Handles, 9 In., Pair . . 355.00
Censer, Egg Shape, 3 Stump Feet, White Glaze, 1800s, 10 In. 69.00

Charger, Bird, Flower, Blue & White, 1800s, 15 1/2 In.	127.00
Charger, Hawthorn Pattern, Blue & White, Japan, 14 1/2 In.	90.00
Charger, Octagonal, Flower Center, Bird & Flower Reserves, Hizan, 1800s, 12 In.	460.00
Chop Plate, Nicholas II Imperial, Crowned Monogram, Gilt Scrolled Rim, 10 7/8 In.	440.00
Compote, Blue Anchor, Shell Shape Bowl, Round Base, 9 3/4 x 3 5/8 In.	110.00
Compote, Bolton Abbey Ruins, Gilt Rims, John Aynsley & Sons, c.1900, 8 5/8 In.	150.00
Compote, Flower Encrusted, Figural, Germany, c.1900, 12 In.	865.00
Compote, Hand Painted, Gilt, Figural Relief, Germany, c.1900, 14 x 19 1/2 In.	785.00
Compote, Meissen Style, Baluster Stem, 3 Tiers, Trefoil Shell Shape, 24 1/2 x 16 In.	865.00
Cup, 2 Handles, Cover, Flowers, Insects, Multicolored, England, c.1815, 4 1/2 x 3 In.	290.00
Cup & Bowl, Colonial Gentlemen & Indian, Brown On White, c.1800, 4 & 6 In.	210.00
Cup & Saucer, Rococo Style, Jacob Petit, Mid 19th Century, 2 1/2 x 5 3/4 In., 2 Pair	690.00
Cup Plate, Antislavery, Kneeling Slave In Chains, 4 1/2 In.	750.00
Dish, 3-D Uncle Sam & Spaniard Fight Over Cuba, Pull On Cigar, Green Leaf, 8 In.	600.00
Dish, Fluted Oval, Ho Birds, Kakiemon, 1800s, 7 1/2 In., Pair	200.00
Dish, Nabeshima Style, Mount Fuji Landscape, Japan, 1800s, 7 In.	145.00
Dispenser, Liquor, Gilt Metal, Barrel, Cherubs, Dolphins, Continental, 11 x 9 1/2 In.	460.00
Dresser Box, Lid, Applied Flowers, Gilt, Cameo, Painted Interior, 3 1/4 x 7 x 6 In.	110.00
Ewer, Relief Cherub Decoration, Germany, Early 1900s, 12 1/2 In.	130.00
Ewer, Wine, Multicolored, Peacock, Rockery, c.1900, 10 1/4 In.	145.00
Figurine, 2 Cherubs, Holding Hands, On Gilt Ball, Scheidig, Germany, 8 x 6 1/4 In.	60.00
Figurine, Ballerina Seated On Ballroom Chair, Crinoline, Germany, c.1900, 8 In.	29.00
Figurine, Cockatoo, Oval Pedestal, Germany, c.1900, 16 In.	460.00
Figurine, Deity, Ho Ho Erh Hsien, Turquoise Robes, Chinese, c.1900, 16 In.	410.00
Figurine, Dog, German Shepherd, Dresden, 7 1/2 x 7 1/2 In., Pair	115.00
Figurine, Dog, Seated, Long Ears, Gray, S.S. Allach, 5 1/2 In.	665.00
Figurine, Gentleman With Lute, Nymphenberg, 18th Century, 4 1/2 x 4 In.	325.00
Figurine, Kannon, Standing, Yellow Robes, Japan, 1800s	355.00
Figurine, Lan Tsai Ho, Flower Basket, Chinese, Early 1900s, 16 In.	175.00
Figurine, Maidens Holding Urns, Multicolored, 19th Century, 16 1/2 In., Pair	575.00
Figurine, Man, Woman, Period Dress, Ludwigsburg, Germany, 1758-1793, 12 x 9 In.	170.00
Figurine, Monkeys On Rockery Holding Peaches, Multicolored, Chinese, 8 1/2 In.	635.00
Figurine, Monkeys On Rockery, Flowers, Multicolored, Chinese, 16 In.	345.00
Figurine, Poodle, Lying Down, Russia, 2 1/2 x 3 x 5 In., Pair	20.00
Figurine, Quan Yin, Blanc-De-Chine, Chinese, c.1850, 18 1/2 In.	325.00
Figurine, Quan Yin, Standing On Lotus, Blanc De Chine, Late 1800s, 11 In.	46.00
Figurine, Rabbit, Seated, White, Detailed Fur, Meiji Period, 6 1/2 In.	430.00
Ginger Jar, Birds, Flowers, Famille Noir, Chinese, 1800s, 14 x 13 In.	940.00
Ginger Jar, Phoenix, Peonies, Pink Ground, Chinese, Late 1800s, 9 In.	235.00
Ginger Jar, Sung, Egg Shape, Turned Wood Cover, 1800s, 8 1/2 In.	115.00
Ginger Jar, Turquoise, Hand Painted, Bluebells, 5 In.	15.00
Group, Bird, 2 Quail, Rockery Base, Japan, Early 1900s, 8 In.	345.00
Group, Dancers, 18th Century Style, Encrusted With Flowers, 7 1/2 In.	20.00
Incense Burner, 4-Footed, Foo Dog Finial, Japan, Late 19th Century, 6 In.	124.00
Jar, Cover, Blue, White, Cylinder Shape, Landscape Design, 1800s, 9 x 6 1/2 In.	80.00
Jar, Cover, Hand Painted Reserves, Cobalt Blue Ground, Lovers, 14 In., Pair	3190.00
Jar, Food, Kuang Hsu, Blue & White, Cover, Foo Dog Finial, 2 Handles, 9 x 8 In.	105.00
Jar, Temple, Cover, Oval, Coral, Gilt Glaze, Landscape, Chinese, 25 In., Pair	2070.00
Jardiniere, Blue & White, Squat Egg Shape, Shishi, Vines, Meiji Period, 9 x 10 In.	69.00
Joss Stick Holder, Coral Glazed, Kylin Shape, 5 In., Pair	315.00
Lavabo, Dolphin Shape, Embraced By Cherubs, White, Italy, 25 x 12 1/2 In., Pair	375.00
Luncheon Set, Blue, White, Plates, Serving Dish, Qianlong, c.1780, 9 & 15 In., 5 Piece	375.00
Mug, Cover, One's Happiness Is Assured If Faithful, Gold Leaf, France, 6 x 4 1/2 In.	150.00
Mug, Puzzle, Woodland Rabbits, Nude Lithograph, Transfer, 7 In.	115.00
Niddy Noddy Group, Oriental Potentate & Daughter, Jacob Petit, c.1865, 12 1/2 In.	2760.00
Pitcher, Walker Shape, Gadrooned Border, Gilt Rim, Flower Urn, Tucker, c.1830	6000.00
Plaque, Arian, Neoclassical Relief, Classical Figures Caging Cherubs, 17 x 12 In.	206.00
Plaque, Bouquet Of Flowers, Oval, Painted, Continental, 12 x 9 1/2 In., Pair	2090.00
Plaque, Das Lied, Classical Beauty, Wood Frame, Germany, c.1900, 7 x 4 In.	1175.00
Plaque, Female Nude, In The Surf, Signed Eilers, Continental, 12 x 10 In.	715.00
Plaque, Marie Louise, Sleeping Roi Du Rome, Furlaud, France, Early 1900s, 15 7/8 In.	650.00
Plaque, Peasant Girl, Gothic Style Bronze Frame, Continental, 5 x 4 In.	478.00
Plaque, Princess Louisa, Continental, 6 x 4 1/8 In.	720.00

Plaque, Ruth, Ullman, Gilt Wood Frame, Vienna, c.1865, 11 x 6 1/2 In. 2070.00
Plaque, Still Life, Fruit, Flowers, Painted, Enamel, Oval, M. Torre, c.1833, 5 3/8 In., Pair   590.00
Plaque, Virgin Mary & Christ Child, Frame, 4 x 6 1/4 In. 770.00
Plaque Set, Biscuit, White, Round, Denmark, 11 1/2 x 11 1/2 In., 4 Piece 460.00
Plate, Blue & White, Phoenix Birds, Karakusa Design, c.1860, 7 1/2 In., 8 Piece 635.00
Plate, Cobalt Blue, Gilt Border, Gilt Center Medallion, Bohemia, c.1930, 10 7/8 In. 259.00
Plate, Colonial Gentlemen, Indian, W. Penn's Treaty Banner, c.1800, 7 1/2 In. 360.00
Plate, Enamel, White, Parrot Perched On Branch, Turquoise Ground, Gilt, 9 In. 118.00
Plate, Fishing On Lake, Man, Boat, Walker China, Bedford, Ohio, c.1955, 7 1/4 In. 24.00
Plate, Gilt Accents, Scroll, Shells, Enamel, Monogram, Early 20th Century, 8 1/2 In. 175.00
Plate, Girl, Flowers, Gilt Border, Enamel Leaves, Berries, Rosen, Germany, 9 1/2 In. 2034.00
Plate, Hirado, Hibiscus Design, Scrolled Border, Late 1800s, 7 1/4 In. 138.00
Plate, Portrait, Elegant Lady, Blue Border, Fruit, Flowers, Gilt Border, 9 1/4 In. 410.00
Plate, Rothschild Bird, Basketry Edge, Crossed Swords, Late 1800s, 9 1/2 In. 160.00
Plate, Turquoise Border, Leaf, Greek Key, Medallions, 1900s, 8 3/4 In.12 Piece 440.00
Plate, Woman, Flower Wreath In Hair, Cobalt Blue, Gilt Border, Royal Vienna, 9 1/2 In. . .   960.00
Platter, Birds, Fruit, Flowers, Woodland Border, Oval, 21 1/2 In.   2260.00
Platter, Blue & White, Chinese, c.1790, 20 1/2 In. 1035.00
Platter, Floral Bouquets, Gilt Edge, Enamel Decorated, Round, Late 1800s, 17 In. 380.00
Spill Vase, Woman In Tyrolean Dress, Germany, c.1900, 9 In. 90.00
Sweetmeat Basket, Handles, Woven, Flowers, Grapevines, Jacob Petit, c.1865, 8 1/4 In. .   920.00
Sweetmeat Set, Blue & Turquoise, Chinese, 19th Century, 7 3/4 In., 9 Piece 180.00
Table Screen, Riverside Landscape, Wood Frame, 3 Panels, Late 1800s, 14 x 16 In. 230.00
Teapot, Blue & White, Bulbous, Shaped Handle, Cover, Roman Ruins, England, 5 In. 345.00
Teapot, Multicolored, Egg Shape, Figural Design, c.1890, 5 In. 29.00
Teapot, Salt Glaze, Cherub & Leaves, Hinged Lid, c.1800, 5 1/2 In. . . . . *Illus*   310.00
Teapot, Stylized Banner, Yatsushio Ware, 3 3/4 x 5 x 3 In. 250.00
Tile, 3 Storks, Leaves, Blue & White, Square, Frame, Japan, 6 In. 60.00
Tondo, Spanish Cavalier Drinking At Inn Courtyard, Germany, Late 1800s, 20 1/2 In. 980.00
Toothbrush Holder, Boy & Fire Hydrant, Japan, 1950s, 4 1/4 In. 100.00
Toothbrush Holder, Dog, Westie, Hand Painted, Marked, Goldcastle, Japan, 1950s, 6 In. . .   155.00
Tray, Footed, Twig Form Handles, Scrolling Shell & Leaf Rim, France, 23 x 14 In. 750.00
Tureen, Boar's Head Shape, Italy, Early 1900s, 11 x 10 x 17 In.   400.00
Tureen, Cover, Gilt, Cobalt Blue, Wrapped Handles, Incised Loop, 10 x 14 x 9 In. 360.00
Tureen, Dome Lid, Carl Thieme Saxonian, Late 1800s, 14 1/2 x 14 x 11 In. 1150.00
Tureen, Duck Form, Sponged Enamel, Blue, Green, Russia, c.1900, 8 In. 118.00
Tureen, Twig Handles, Flower, Leaf, Bird, Round, 1800s, 12 x 11 In. 259.00
Urn, Crackle Glaze, Foo Dog, Flowers, Birds, Lid, Chinese, c.1470, 13 In., Pair 430.00
Urn, Figures, Blue Ground, Lion's Head & Ring Mounts, Chinese, 22 1/4 In., Pair 1430.00
Urn, Italian Landscapes, Cityscapes, Pink Ground, England, 24 In., Pair 7170.00
Urn, Paneled, Baluster Shape, Flower Heads, Vine, Early 1900s, 9 1/2 In., Pair 380.00
Urn, Squat, Blue Crystalline, Squared Handles, Stamped Pierrefonds, France, 7 1/2 In. . . .   259.00
Urn, Vienna Style, Cover, Neoclassical Figures, Cobalt Blue, 29 In. 660.00
Vase, Amphora Type, Poppy, Daisy, No. 5664/2560, Ernst Wahliss, 7 1/8 In., Pair 430.00
Vase, Angenehme Begleitung, I Mag Di Leiden, Vasiform, Vienna, c.1900, 11 3/4 In. 765.00
Vase, Baluster, Animal Head Handles, White Glaze, 1800s, 9 1/2 In. 69.00
Vase, Baluster, Blue & White, 19th Century, 13 In. 355.00
Vase, Baluster, Flowers, Multicolored Fruit, Birds, Jacob Petit, c.1865, 12 1/2 In., Pair . . .   2990.00
Vase, Baluster, Robin's-Egg Blue, c.1900, 10 In. 58.00
Vase, Blanc-De-Chine, Egg Shape, Applied Lion's Mask, Ivory Glaze, 10 1/4 In. 175.00
Vase, Blue & White, Bottle Shape, Chinese, 16 In. 520.00
Vase, Blue Birds, Signed, B.E. Talmage, Austria, 1884-1909, 10 In. 750.00
Vase, Bottle Shape, Oxblood, Chinese, 13 1/4 In. 1380.00
Vase, Bottle, Birch Bark, Cloisonne Birds & Flowers, Japan, Late 1800s, 12 In. 95.00
Vase, Bottle, Double Gourd, Ribbed, Turquoise Glaze, Early 1800s, 4 In. 115.00
Vase, Chinese Deco, Silver Overlay, Dragon, Flowers, Black, Green, 10 x 7 In. 2690.00
Vase, Clair De Lune, Double Gourd, Garlic Mouth, c.1800, 7 3/4 In. 980.00
Vase, Classical Revival, Egg Shape, Classical Figures, Vienna, c.1900, 13 7/8 In. 1295.00
Vase, Cobalt Blue Decoration, Pheasant In Tree, Pond, Handles, Oriental, 16 1/2 In. 138.00
Vase, Cobalt Blue, Mountains, Pagodas, Figures, Applied Handles, Oriental, 23 In. 165.00
Vase, Cornucopia, Birds, Butterflies, Fruit, Flowers, France, c.1835, 9 x 8 1/2 In., Pair . . .   1495.00
Vase, Crackle Glaze, Ormolu Mounts, Leaf & Berry, Chinese, 8 x 5 In. 1210.00
Vase, Double Gourd, Fruit, Flower, Blue, White, 1900s, 11 3/4 In. 920.00

Vase, Dragon, Cloud, Late 1800s, 17 In. 690.00
Vase, Egg Shape, Figural Landscape Cartouches, Blue, White, Late 1800s, 3 In. 90.00
Vase, Elephant Handles, Inset Panels, Blue & White, Chinese, c.1850, 10 1/2 In. 452.00
Vase, Enameled Birds, Flowers, Fukugawa, Japan, Early 1900s, 11 1/4 In. 470.00
Vase, Flying Cranes, Blue Ground, Marked, Legrand, 10 In. 86.00
Vase, French, Painted Scene With Fountain, Figures, Garden, 18 In. 275.00
Vase, Gilded Blossoms, 2 Handles, Greenwood, Ne Plus Ultra, Purple Stamp, 10 In. 1725.00
Vase, Glazed, Flared Mouth, Dots, Upsala Ekeby, Sweden, c.1955, 5 1/2 x 16 1/2 In. 936.00
Vase, Glazed, Gold & Silver Spiral Lines, Upsala Ekeby, Sweden, c.1955, 14 1/2 In. 468.00
Vase, High Relief Dragon On Shoulder, Turquoise Blue, 1800s, 5 1/4 In. 127.00
Vase, Inverted Pear Shape, Camellia, Fukugawa, Early 1900s, 10 1/2 In., Pair 185.00
Vase, Ku Form Beaker, Archaic Designs, Blanc De Chine, Chinese, 1700s, 17 1/4 In. 5875.00
Vase, Landscape Painted Medallions, Gilt Design, 11 In. 250.00
Vase, Oriental, Cobalt On White Decoration, Outdoor Scene, Oriental, Handles, 23 In. ... 135.00
Vase, Oriental, Sand De Boeuf, Mottled Red & Brown Glaze, 21 1/2 In. 248.00
Vase, Portrait, Egg Shape, Woman, Rose, Wagner, Germany, Late 1800s, 10 1/4 In. 2115.00
Vase, Portrait, Marguerite, Egg Shape, Wagner, Germany, Late 1800s, 10 1/8 In. 2235.00
Vase, Portrait, Parcel Gilt, Egg Shape, Woman Calling Out, Austria, c.1910, 15 3/4 In. ... 3290.00
Vase, Portrait, Ruth, Slender Egg Shape, Graf, Austria, c.1900, 18 3/4 In. 2585.00
Vase, Portrait, Sommer, Egg Shape, Slender Neck, Muller, Vienna, c.1900, 10 1/4 In. 1295.00
Vase, Portrait, Spinne, Seminude Woman, Wagner, Vienna, c.1900, 12 In. 1295.00
Vase, Potpourri, Baluster, 2 Handles, Cover, Footed, Jacob Petit, c.1865, 14 1/2 In. 1150.00
Vase, Powder Blue Ground, Gilt, Chinese, 1800s, 10 1/2 In. 88.00
Vase, Putto Sitting By Pond, Bird, Flowers, Stamped 9202, Austria, 9 1/2 In. 259.00
Vase, Romeo & Juliet, Hand Painted, 2 Handles, Austria, 18 In. 550.00
Vase, Scholar's Item, Calligraphy, Gilt On Blue, Hexagonal Shape, Early 1800s, 17 In. ... 400.00
Vase, Shell Shape, Dresden Style, 3 Putti, Roses, Sitzendorf, c.1890, 12 x 16 3/4 In. 575.00
Vase, Silver Enameled, Narrow Neck, Short Gilt Handles, Dionysian Putti, Bust, 10 In. ... 500.00
Vase, Silver Overlay Dragon, Flowers, Chinese, 10 x 7 In. 2400.00
Vase, Silver Overlay, Mt. Fuji, Flowers, Blue, Green, 4 x 3 In. 365.00
Vase, Studio, Seed Form, Vine Design, Tozan, Early 1900s, 7 1/4 In. 115.00
Vase, Tanzendes Madchen, Egg Shape, Dome Cover, Wagner, c.1910, 12 1/4 In. 1645.00
Vase, Teardrop Shape, Apple Green, 1800s, 4 In. 115.00
Vase, Trumpet Mouth, Birds, Flowers, Animal Shape Handles, Japan, 1800, 23 3/4 In. ... 200.00
Vase, Undulating Leaf Shape, Woman, Art Nouveau, Germany, c.1900, 18 1/2 In. 978.00
Vase, White, Gilt Figures, In Costume, Hand Painted Faces, Japan, 11 1/2 In. 990.00
Water Dropper, Figural, 3-Legged Frog, Spotted, Underglaze, Blue, Red, Korea, 3 In. ... 489.00
Water Dropper, Reclining Lion, Korean, Yi Dynasty, 3 1/4 In. 69.00
Water Dropper, Suiteki, Puppy, Brown & Celadon Green, Japan, 1800s 69.00

PORCELAIN-CONTEMPORARY lists pieces made by artists working after 1975.
Plate Set, Dinner, White, Fornasetti, Eve, Transfer, 10 In., 12 Piece 3040.00
Plate Set, Roman Scenes, Gilt, White, Fornasetti, Italy, 10 In., 12 Piece 646.00
Smoke Dispeller, Figural, Woman, Perfume In Wine Glass, 8 1/2 In. 98.00
Vase, Bulbous, Brown, Aqua, Cobalt Rings, Maija Grotell, 9 x 9 In. 4315.00
Vase, White, Black & Yellow Stripes, Ettore Sottsass, 16 x 8 In. 489.00

PORCELAIN-MIDCENTURY includes pieces made from the 1940s to the 1980s.
Figurine, Horse, White, N.Y.C. Mayor Wagner, CC & Crown, 1964, 13 In. 115.00
Figurine, Nude Woman Holding Violin, Gerold Porzellan, 9 x 9 1/4 In. 250.00
Toothbrush Holder, Puppy, Spotted, Japan, 1950s, 6 In. 175.00
Vase, Rounded, Red, Black, No. R.2941, Raymor, Italy, c.1950s, 7 In. 55.00

POSTCARDS were first legally permitted in Austria on October 1, 1869.
The United States passed postal regulations allowing the card in 1872.
Most of the picture postcards collected today date after 1910. The
amount of postage can help to date a card. The rates are: 1872 (1 cent),
1917 (2 cents), 1919 (1 cent), 1925 (2 cents), 1928 (1 cent), 1952 (2
cents), 1959 (3 cents), 1963 (4 cents), 1968 (5 cents), 1973 (8 cents),
1975 (7 cents), 1976 (9 cents), 1978 (10 cents), 1981 (12 cents), 1981
(13 cents), 1985 (14 cents), 1988 (15 cents), 1991 (19 cents), 1995 (20
cents).

  2 Caddies, Pinehurst, North Carolina, Real Photo Postcard, 1910 .... 345.00
  American Bus Lines, Linen, Curteich Publishing, c.1940 .... 15.00

Austin Cartridge Co. Works, Factory Picture, 5 1/2 x 3 1/2 In. 88.00
Baby's Own Soap, Best For Baby, Best For You, Embossed, Canada 20.00
Betsy Ross Making First American Flag, No. 159, Raphael Tuck & Sons, Early 1900s ... 16.00
Cambridge Glass Factory, c.1909 .... 15.00
Coney Island, New Century Postcard Co., New York, 1907 .... 15.00
Cypress Point Golf Course, California, 16th Hole, 1950s, 3 1/2 x 5 1/2 In. 8.00
Fall Winter Millinery, Howard Barnes, Harrisburg, Huntington, Vermont, 1910 .... 28.00
Free Miniature Edsel For Test Driving Real One, 5 x 8 In. 35.00
Gold Red Cross Shoes, Woman On Phone, Postmarked 1947 .... 30.00
Hall Furniture & Upholstery, The Library, September Calendar, Vermont, 1913 ...... 30.00
Hayes Hosiery, A.C. Webber, Albert Line Of 100 Hose, c.1898, 3 x 5 1/2 In. 10.00
Ink Pot, Jessie Tarbox Beals 920.00
Josephine Baker, Leopard, Real Photo Postcard 138.00
Lulu Parr, Bucking Horse Rider, Real Photo Postcard, 1908 .... 316.00
Malvern's World's High Class Shooting Star, 6 1/4 x 3 5/16 In. 84.00
Odd Fellows, Fraternal Building, Kearney, Missouri, 1930s 7.00
Patriotic, 4th Of July, Hats Off, Along The Line, No. 109, Raphael Tuck & Sons, 1907 .. 20.00
Patriotic, Fireworks, Cannon, Women Carrying American Flag 18.00
Patriotic, Young Boy Shooting Off Fireworks, Embossed, Early 1900s 18.00
R.F.D. Carrier, Horse, Ringgold, Pa., Salem C. Moyer, 1907 .... 173.00
Radio City, Hollywood, NBC & CBS Studios, Postmark 1951 .... 15.00
Roosevelt Bears, At Country School 5.00
Roosevelt Bears, At Tailor's 7.00
Roosevelt Bears, In Department Store 7.00
Roosevelt Bears, On Iceberg 7.00
Roosevelt Bears, Take Auto Ride 12.00
SS Carpathia, Rescuing Titanic Survivors 144.00
SS Titanic, Real Photo Postcard 259.00
SS Titanic, Ship, Captain 196.00
United Art Publishing, Glossy View Portrait, Lover's Lane, Mayvill, Wisc., 1908 ...... 15.00

POSTERS have informed the public about news and entertainment events since ancient times. Nineteenth-century advertising or theatrical posters and twentieth-century movie and war posters are of special interest today. The price is determined by the artist, the condition, and the rarity. Other posters may be listed under Movie, Political, and World War I and II.

American Airlines, Cubistic Tourist, E.M. Kauffer, 1948, 30 x 40 In. 1000.00
Aspen Winter Jazz, Roy Lichtenstein, 1967, 40 x 26 In. 2070.00
Bally Herrenschuhe, Suited Man On Large Shoebox, Barberis, 1938, 50 1/4 x 35 3/4 In. . 750.00
Buck & Bubbles Laff Jamboree, Red, White, Blue, 41 x 27 In. 220.00
Bunco In Arizona, American Show Print Co., Milwaukee, Wis., 1902, 42 x 28 In. 1925.00
Cap Ferrat, French Riviera Hotel, C. Couronneau, 40 x 28 1/4 In. 1265.00
Carry On, Buy Liberty Bonds To Your Utmost, Edwin Bashfield, 1918, 41 x 79 In. 1035.00
Census, It's Your America, Uncle Sam, 1940, 26 x 36 In. 45.00
Clyde-Beatty-Cole Circus, Clown, 1950s, 14 x 21 In. 60.00
Cycles Wolff American, Woman, With Flowers, Riding Bike, On Linen, 58 x 41 1/2 In. .. 785.00
Dan Sullivan, Tipperary Wonder, Lifts Carriage, Hiller & Trevelen, c.1900, 30 x 20 In. ... 690.00
Dog, White, Riding Bicycle, Cyrk, c.1970, 40 1/2 x 29 In. 195.00
Firemen's Centennial, Pottstown Phillies, 1871-1971, 28 x 22 In. 35.00
Fly To Rio By Clipper, Pan American World Airways, Flamenco Dancer, 42 x 28 In. 1725.00
Fly TWA, Rome, Stylized Vatican Guard, David Klein, c.1960, 25 x 40 In. 225.00
Fly TWA Jets, Los Angeles, Sun, Mission, Doves, David Klein, c.1959, 25 x 40 In. 425.00
Grande Quinzaine De Paris A Port Aviation, A. Sorel, 1909, 31 x 46 1/2 In. 6900.00
Herman Miller Picnic, Silk Screen, Stephen Frykholm, Frame, 1983, 24 x 40 In. 460.00
Hillman Herbert Cooper Ltd. A Coventry, 23 Bould. Paris, Bicyclists, c.1888 .... 2350.00
Ithaca Guns, Extinct Passenger Pigeon, Louis Agassiz Fuertes, 1910, 27 x 16 1/2 In. 1540.00
Jesse James, Missouri Outlaw, Cowboy, Lithograph, Frame, 25 x 35 In. 176.00
Last Stand, Frank Presberry Co., Smith & Wesson, Matte, Frame, 1902, 14 3/4 x 14 In. ... 495.00
Liqueur Seve De Fine Champagne, George Meuniet, Frame, France, 1910, 50 x 35 In. ... 499.00
Little Shop Of Horrors, Mounted On Cardboard, Broadway, 72 x 42 In. 275.00
Loose Talk Can Cost Lives, Keep It Under Your Stetson, 2 Men In Life Raft, 39 x 29 In. . 980.00

Lorenzaccio, Sarah Bernhardt, Dragon, Alphonse Mucha, 1897, 40 1/4 x 14 3/4 In. 6210.00
Marilyn Monroe, Andy Warhol, Signed, 26 1/4 x 19 1/4 In. 1528.00
Mein Kampf, Adolf Hitler, 19 1/4 x 13 In. 175.00
Mistinguett, Jeanne Marie Bourgeois Stage Name, Folies Bergere, c.1913, 63 x 47 In. ... 6100.00
Nostradamus Jr., Astrologo, Ilusionista Mas Joven Del Mundo, 43 1/2 x 29 1/4 In. 575.00
Olympics, 1936, Berlin, Athlete, Lithograph, Hungarian Words, 24 x 39 In. 1700.00
Olympics, 1948, St. Moritz, City View, Logo, Color Lithograph, 25 x 40 In. 2300.00
Olympics, 1964, Tokyo, World Map, Game Venues, Multicolored, Kremling, 47 x 34 In. .. 161.00
Olympics, 1968, Mexico, Woman Leading Flags Parade, Torch, Rings, 23 x 19 1/2 In. ... 635.00
Olympics, 1972, Munich, Diver Reaching Water, Lithograph, D. Hockney, 25 x 40 In. ... 138.00
Olympics, 1976, Innsbruck, Austria, Skier Color Photo, Logo, 35 1/2 x 25 In. 200.00
Olympics, 1984, Sarajevo, Yugoslavia, Bobsled, Color Offset, 26 1/2 x 38 1/2 In. 161.00
Show With Music, His Highness The Bey, Man, Lady, Frame, 28 x 35 In. 248.00
Summer Day In Holland, Lithograph, Hendrik Cassiers, Oak Frame, c.1900, 15 x 17 In. . 374.00
Sun Valley Idaho, Gretchen Fraser, Green Olympic Bib, 38 x 25 1/2 In. 4370.00
Sun Valley Idaho, Gretchen Fraser, Skiers, Mountains, Shepler, 1948, 25 x 39 In. 1350.00
Swiss Air To Europe, Airplane, Mountain, Fisherman, Fritz Buhler, c.1955, 25 x 40 In. ... 375.00
Thurston, World's Famous Magician, Baltimore, Cardboard, 1920s, 14 x 22 In. 500.00
Uncle Tom's Cabin, Eliza's Escape From The Tavern, Lithograph, 42 x 28 In. 209.00
Will Rogers Memorial Fund, Woman, Flag, H.C. Christy, 1935, 17 x 26 In. 475.00
Yale Bulldog, Life's Sun Is Set, Love Old Yale, Abigail Kellog Hazard, 1909, 18 x 12 In. . 863.00
Years Of Dust, Man Seated On Porch, Mounted, Ben Shahn, 1936, 38 x 25 In. 10000.00

POTLIDS are just that, lids for pots. Transfer-printed potlids had their heyday from the 1840s to the early 1900s. The English Staffordshire potteries made ceramic containers with decorative lids for bear's grease, shrimp or meat paste, cold cream, and toothpaste. Printed advertising and pictures of historical events, portraits of famous people, or scenic views were designed in black and white or color. Reproductions have been made.

7 Ages Of Man, No. 230, F & R Pratt, Late 1850s, 4 In. 90.00
Allied Generals, No. 168, Pratt, Signed, J. Austin, c.1854, 4 3/4 In. 150.00
Bear, Lion, Cock, F & R Pratt, 3 1/4 In. 67.00
Bears At School, Wood Frame, F & R Pratt, 4 3/4 In. 67.00
Cherry Toothpaste, F. Newberry & Sons, London, Sailboat, 2 3/4 In. 70.00
Cherry Toothpaste, Ironstone, Jar, Transfer, 3 1/4 In. 39.00
Cherry Toothpaste, Lorimer & Co., Manufacturing, 2 3/4 In. 60.00
Cherry Toothpaste, May Roberts, Girl, Arms Folded, Leaning On Wall, 2 3/4 In. 250.00
Coral Toothpaste, Parker Chemist, Uttoxetter, 3 In. 69.00
Dogs, F & R Pratt, 4 In. 85.00
Dr. Dosteel's Cherry Toothpaste, Black Transfer, Pink Ground, Queen Victoria, 3 1/2 In. . 1837.00
Durbin's Cherry Toothpaste, Most Pleasant To Use, 3 In. 40.00
Eleanore Cross, London, 4 In. 90.00
Flowers, Piessen & Lubin, New Bond St., London, No. 131, 3 1/2 In. 125.00
Flute Player, Woman, Men, Bates, Brown, Westhead & Moore, 4 In. 85.00
Forest Scene, Ironstone, Transfer, 4 1/4 In. 8.00
Genuine Russian Bears Grease, 2 Bears, 3 In. 140.00
Genuine Russian Bears Grease, For Beautifying & Nourishing The Hair, 2 3/4 In. 175.00
Hide & Seek, No. 255, F & R Pratt, c.1860, 4 In. 90.00
Hindoo Toothpaste, M. Magor, Pharmaceutical, 3 1/2 In. 218.00
Imperial Coraline Toothpaste, Roberts & Co. Chemists, Gold Border, 3 3/4 x 2 1/4 In. .. 58.00
Inmans Stores Ltd., Hygienic, Carbolized Toothpaste, Edinburgh, Base, 3 1/2 In. 100.00
James Atkinson's Bears Cream, 24 Old Bond Street, London, 2 1/2 In. 58.00
Late Duke Of Wellington, No. 161, F & R Pratt, 4 In. 125.00
Magors Central Cold Cream Drug Stores, Birmingham, 2 1/2 In. 50.00
Man, Playing Checkers, Woman Holding Baby, Wood Frame, No. 256, J. Mayer, 4 1/2 In. 90.00
Man, Talking To Children, Woman Holding Baby, No. 214, F & R Pratt, c.1859, 3 In. 150.00
Mc Isaac & Co., Chemists, Edgbaston, Cold Cream, 2 3/4 In. 40.00
Meeting Of Garibaldi & Victor Emmanuel, No. 211, F & R Pratt, 4 In. 90.00
Otto De Rose Cold Cream, Magor Limited, Birmingham Chemists, Base, 2 3/4 In. 28.00
Peace, Trefoil Form, No. 213, Wouverman, 5 1/2 x 3 1/4 In. 58.00
Prince Albert, No. 153, F & R Pratt, 4 In. 69.00

Rifle Contest Wimbledon, 1865, Blue Marbled Rim, No. 224, 4 3/4 In. 435.00
Shurzine Antiseptic Toothpaste, Neve & Co., 12 Wellington Place, Hastings, 2 1/2 In. . . 50.00
Soap Toothpaste, John Bell & Croyden Ltd., 50 Wigmore St., 3 1/2 x 2 1/4 In. 135.00
St. Paul's Cherry Toothpaste, TM. Of St. Paul's, 2 3/4 In. 125.00
T. & W. & W. Southhall, 17 Bull Street, Birmingham, Cold Cream, 3 In. 25.00
T.F. Bristow & Cos., Cherry Toothpaste, 2-Tone, Blob Top, 3 1/4 x 2 In. 40.00
Uncle Toby, Ironstone, Transfer, Jar, 4 1/4 In. 22.00
Village Wedding, Wood Frame, No. 240, F & R Pratt, 4 In. 75.00
War, Trefoil Form, No. 212, Wouverman, 5 1/2 x 3 1/4 In. 58.00
Windsor Chapel, St. George's Chapel, No. 177, 2 3/4 In. 184.00
Wolf & Lamb, Men Fighting, People Watching, No. 361, F & R Pratt, Late 1850s, 4 In. . . 40.00
Woman Being Served On Bench, No. 98, Mayer Factory, 3 In. 35.00

POTTERY and porcelain are different. Pottery is opaque; you can't see
through it. Porcelain is translucent. If you hold a porcelain dish in front
of a strong light, you will see the light through the dish. Porcelain is
colder to the touch. Pottery is softer and easier to break and will stain
more easily because it is porous. Porcelain is thinner, lighter, and more
durable. Majolica, faience, and stoneware are all pottery. Additional
pieces of pottery are listed in this book in the categories Pottery-Art,
Pottery-Contemporary, Pottery-Midcentury, and under the factory
name. For information about pottery makers and marks, see *Kovels'
Dictionary of Marks—Pottery & Porcelain: 1650–1850* and *Kovels'
New Dictionary of Marks—Pottery & Porcelain: 1850 to the Present.*

Ashtray, Restaurant, Indian Logo, Shenango China, New Castle, Pa., c.1915, 3 3/4 In. . . . 52.00
Ashtray, Restaurant, Shenango China, New Castle, Pa., 1952, 4 In. 42.00
Basin, Lakeside Landscape, Seto, c.1900, 12 1/2 In. 105.00
Biscuit Jar, Egg Shape, Flowers, Kelp, Luster, England, c.1850, 6 In. 323.00
Bowl, Figural, Mermaid, Shell, Eichwald, Germany, 25 x 20 In. 440.00
Bowl, Footed, Sgraffito, Animals, Birds, Mottled, Henry Varnum Poor, 1928, 6 x 12 In. . 1840.00
Bowl, Iridescent, Niell Osine Ware, Austria, 3 3/4 In. 175.00
Cuspidor, Scroddle Ware, Diamond Pattern, 4 1/2 x 6 1/4 In. 805.00
Ewer, Bulbous, Flambe Glaze, Lenci, 1937, 17 x 11 In. 633.00
Ewer, Putti Handles, Leaves & Flowers, High Relief, Brownfield, England, 16 1/2 In. 385.00
Fertility Pillow, Reclining Child, Turquoise Green Glaze, c.1900, 11 In. 29.00
Figurine, Bulldog, White Brown Glaze Spots, Cobalt Blue Details, Ohio, 7 1/2 In. 175.00
Figurine, Foo Dog, Kingfisher Glazed, Wood Stand, Late 1700s, 11 In. 1725.00
Figurine, Man Seated In Chair, Mandolin & Stein, Continental, 16 In. 110.00
Figurine, Poodle, Seated, Brown & White Spotted Glaze, Nicodemus, Ohio 80.00
Figurine, Putti Holding Flower & Fruit Basket, Wiener Keramik, 11 1/2 In. 1610.00
Flowerpot, Earthenware, Copper Glaze, Gray, White, Green Detail, 4 1/8 x 4 3/4 In. 1485.00
Flowerpot, Geneva, Brown Glaze, Bluff Ground, Stripes, Squiggles, Attached Dish, 6 In. . 115.00
Fujimi, Chawan, Blue Drip Glaze, Metal Rim, Japan, 1800s, 4 1/8 In. 150.00
Humidor, Dog, Popping Out Of Barrel, Impressed, J.M., 7 1/2 x 5 In. 415.00
Humidor, Frog, Shaped Lid, Earthenware, W.T. Harris, Virginia, 9 3/4 x 6 1/2 In. 330.00
Jar, Seed Shape, Grass Type Decoration, Brown Glaze, 1800s, 20 In. 90.00
Jug, Albany Slip, Brown, Wooden Stopper, Handle, 9 In. 28.00
Jug, Galena, Orange Brown Glaze, 4 Yellow Daubs, 2 Running Stripes, Footed, 9 In. 1870.00
Jug, Harvest, Mustard Glaze, Leaf, Berry, Ring Handle, 10 In. 115.00
Jug, New Saloon, G.O. Peuse, Square, Cream, Brown, Fall Creek, Wis., c.1900, 4 3/8 In. . 220.00
Jug, Ships, Squat, Handle, Floral & Thorn Branch, Sterling Monogrammed Stopper, 7 In. . 200.00
Mustard Pot, Mocha, Ocher, Brown Design Over Ivory Glaze, 2 3/4 x 3 In. 390.00
Pitcher, Brown Glaze, Anchor & Chain, Applied Handle, 10 1/2 x 7 1/4 x 6 1/2 In. 80.00
Pitcher, Figural, Pig, With Ham, Frie Onnaing, 8 In. 250.00
Pitcher, Grape Trellis, Brown, Monmouth Raised Star, 9 In. 28.00
Pitcher, Octagonal, Flint Enamel, 1849-1858, 9 3/4 In. 235.00
Pitcher, Queen's Rose, Ribbed Body, 4 1/4 In. 360.00
Pitcher, Tavern, Windmill, Hunt Scene, Stag, Fulham, 7 1/2 In. 75.00
Pitcher, Tree Trunk Shape, Branch Handle, Applied Grapevines, Scroddle, 13 1/2 In. 220.00
Plaque, Medieval Figure, Mounted On Horse, Holding Bird, Black Frame, 9 x 6 1/2 In. . . 140.00
Plaque, Relief, Mischievous Monkeys, Ernst Wahliss, Austria, 21 In. 195.00
Pot, Candlestick Lid, Mottled Brown Glaze, Incised Designs, Laura Anderson, 12 In. 375.00
Tea Set, Oval, Paneled, Relief Decoration, Cupids, Grapes, Castleford, 3 Piece 920.00

Teapot, Cover, Relief Decoration, Classical, Blue Outlines, Castleford, 6 x 10 In. 200.00
Top Hat, Bird On Nest Top, Xmas 1902, Mr. Royle, Scroddle Ware 105.00
Trivet, Stenciled, Air-Brushed Design, Germany, 11 In. . . . . *Illus*   32.00
Vase, 3 Panels, Black Tree, Landscape, Art Nouveau, Signed, A. Cusick, 9 x 5 1/2 In. 2500.00
Vase, Blue-Gray Crystalline Glaze, Wrought Iron Floral Frame, Guerin, France, 19 In. . . .   1150.00
Vase, Bottle, Brown & Blue Stripes, Seto, Early 1900s, 13 1/4 In. 75.00
Vase, Brown Cameo Leaves, Stems, Seedpods, Frosted Ground, Moda, 4 1/4 In. 180.00
Vase, Bulbous, Cream Ground, Blue Crisscross, Kralik, 6 1/4 In.   58.00
Vase, Cream Color, Shoulder Cover, Drip Brown & Blue, Japan, c.1910, 12 In. 470.00
Vase, Cylinder, Flower Design, Gray Body, Shino, 1900s, 13 In.   40.00
Vase, Metallic Blue, Deichmann, New Brunswick, 7 In. 360.00
Vase, Purple, Blue Iridescent, Rose & Cream Threading, Signed, Kralik, Austrian, 7 In. . .   115.00
Vase, Tapered, Bulbous Top, Stylized Fish, Mottled, High Glaze, Guerin, France, 10 In. . .   403.00

POTTERY-ART Art pottery was first made in America in Cincinnati, Ohio, during the 1870s. The pieces were hand thrown and hand decorated. The art pottery tradition continued until the 1930s when studio potters began making the more artistic wares. American, English, and Continental art pottery by less well-known makers is listed here. Most makers listed in *Kovels' American Art Pottery,* such as Arequipa, Ohr, Rookwood, Roseville, and Weller, are listed in their own categories in this book. More recent pottery is listed under the name of the maker or in the Pottery category.

Bowl, Arabesque, Brown, Green, Markham, No. 5031, 2 7/8 x 5 1/4 In. 575.00
Box, Oval, Applied Brown Bug, Blue, Purple & Gray Glaze, Denbac, France, 4 1/4 In. . . .   85.00
Charger, Brown, Cream, Mottled Glaze, Blue Flowers, Brown Leaves, 15 In. 115.00
Charger, Ribbed Edge, Turquoise Matte Glaze, 12 1/2 In. 85.00
Charger, Squeezebag, Black, Gold, Crackled Vellum Ivory Ground, C. Rhead, 12 3/4 In. . .   403.00
Compote, Flared, Brown & Blue Crystalline Glaze, Marked, Guerin, 11 x 6 In. 259.00
Ewer, Organic Shape, Brown Crystalline Glaze, Signed, Denbac, France, 8 In. 85.00
Ewer, Sterling Silver Overlay, Flowers, Monogram, Mark, 5 3/4 In. 1120.00
Pitcher, Flowers, Blue, Magenta, Leaves, Metallic Brown Glaze, C. Rhead, 8 1/2 In. 250.00
Pitcher, Orange Flowers, Brown Mottled Rim, Gray Squeezebag, C. Rhead, 8 In. 175.00
Plaque, Flowers, Orange, Yellow, Swirls, Brown Squeezebag, C. Rhead, 14 In. 200.00
Plaque, Manchurian Dragon, Asian Abstracts, Squeezebag, Ribbed, C. Rhead, 12 In. 350.00
Tea Set, Teapot, 2 Pitchers, Sugar, Purple, Blue & Red Floral, Byrdcliffe, 4 Piece 690.00
Vase, 2 Applied Salamanders, Yellow Vellum Glaze, Poillon, Stamped CLP, 5 In. 345.00
Vase, Acanthus Leaves, Feathered, Green, Bulbous, Shawsheen, 1911, 9 In. 3450.00
Vase, Brown, Gray Drip, Signed, Greber, 3 1/2 In. 115.00
Vase, Bud, Squat Base, Tall Neck, Green & Amber Glaze, Chicago Crucible, 8 In. 315.00
Vase, Bulbous, Woman Carrying Bowl, Landscape, Squeezebag, Avon 2415.00
Vase, Celadon Glaze, Mottled, Red Ground, Baluster, Stamped Grand Feu, 8 3/4 In. 1265.00
Vase, Cyclamen, Impressed BACS, 2 7/8 In. 518.00
Vase, Cylindrical, Purple, Gray Matte Glaze, Rhead, 8 1/2 In. 865.00
Vase, Double Gourd, Hammered, Gunmetal Matte Glaze, Continental, 12 1/2 In. 115.00
Vase, Dragons, Green Glaze, Squeezebag, Ribbed, C. Rhead, 7 In. 60.00
Vase, Embossed Leaves, Turquoise Glaze, Pear Shape, Stamped Norweta, 8 1/4 In. 690.00
Vase, Embossed Owl On Branch, Moon, Blue, Yellow, Green, Flambe Glaze, 20 In. 575.00
Vase, Flowers, Cloisonne Enamel Shoulder, Metallic Glaze, Montieres, 4 In. 489.00

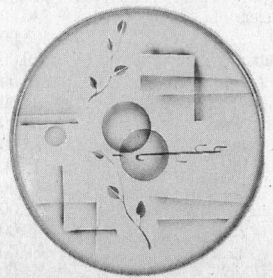

Pottery, Trivet, Stenciled, Air-Brushed Design, Germany, 11 In.

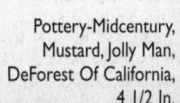

Pottery-Midcentury, Mustard, Jolly Man, DeForest Of California, 4 1/2 In.

Vase, Frogskin Glaze, Bulbous, Tapered, North State, 7 1/2 In. 635.00
Vase, Frogskin Matte Glaze, Baluster, Stamped Ouachita, 7 In. 1840.00
Vase, Gourd Form, Iridescent Glaze, Enamel Grapes, Montieres, 13 1/2 In. 980.00
Vase, Green Glaze, Charcoaling, Oatmeal Interior, Wally Volkmar, 5 1/2 In. 470.00
Vase, Kingfisher, Yellow To Rose Ground, C. Dresser, C. Ault, c.1890, 8 1/2 In. 520.00
Vase, Multisided, Long Neck, Green, Blue Crystalline Drop Glaze, Denbac, 8 In. 145.00
Vase, Oatmeal Indigo Glaze, Stamped O.L. Bachelder, Candler N.C., 4 x 4 1/2 In. 865.00
Vase, Organic Shape, Blue & Green Crystalline Handles, Signed, Denbac, 4 In., Pair 145.00
Vase, Palm Fern, Loop Handles, Cincinnati Pottery Club, Alice Belle Holabird, 8 In. 460.00
Vase, Pillow, Blue Clematis, Amber Ground, Stamped I.V.W., Jersey City, 10 In. 865.00
Vase, Robin's-Egg Blue High Glaze, Streaks, Globular, Bottle Neck, Robineau, 4 In. 1430.00
Vase, Stylized Woman & Bird, Tan & Pink Glaze, Flared Bottom, Pillin, 6 1/2 In. 355.00
Vase, Tapered Shape, Carved Leaves, Green, Tan Ground, 6 In. 430.00
Vase, Tapered, 3 Applied Snails, Blue, Green, Pink Drip Matte Glaze, Greber, 9 1/2 In. ... 520.00
Vase, Waisted Shape, Red Glaze, Turquoise Highlights, Dahpayrat, 4 In. 575.00
Vase, Woman, Carrying Bowl, Landscape, Bulbous, Avon, 14 x 7 1/2 In. 2415.00

POTTERY-CONTEMPORARY lists pieces made by artists working after 1975.
Bottle, Flattened Sides, Stopper, Gambone, 8 In. 288.00
Bowl, Glazed, Beatrice Wood, Signed Beato, c.1960, 6 3/4 x 4 1/2 In. 940.00
Bowl, Low Form, Cream, High Glaze & Matte Interior, Gambone, 23 In. 805.00
Bowl, Persian Style Paint, Lion, Wreath, Signed, Bernard Moore, 8 In. 374.00
Bowl, Raku Stoneware, Luster, Beatrice Wood, 1960s, 11 1/2 x 4 3/4 In. 4680.00
Bowl, Sgraffito, Man, Woman, Child, Scheier, 1 1/2 x 11 In. 431.00
Charger, Squeezebag, Crosshatched, Blue Ground, Stoneware, Maija Grotell, 2 1/2 x 13 In. 1095.00
Charger, Wax Resist, Figure Embraces Small Ones, Scheier, 15 3/4 In. 2070.00
Figurine, Buffalo, Glazed, Guido Gambone, Italy, 1950s, 7 x 3 x 5 In. 761.00
Figurine, Horned Animal, Glazed, Guido Gambone, Italy, 1950s, 11 x 8 In. 878.00
Ice Bucket, Cobalt Blue Glaze, Indented, Stoneware, Peter Voulkos, 1973, 4 3/4 x 7 In. .. 2990.00
Sculpture, Rooster, Ivory, Brown, Blue, Slab Built, Gambone, 12 1/2 In. 259.00
Vase, Bulbous, Small Opening, Speckled Glaze, Stoneware, Peter Voulkos, 11 x 8 3/4 In. .. 3105.00
Vase, Chalice Shape, Black & White Stripes, Ettore Sottsass, 19 x 8 In. 1610.00
Vase, Cylindrical, Opalescent Glaze, Stoneware, Maija Grotell, USA, 1940s, 4 x 6 1/4 In. . 3160.00
Vase, Cylindrical, Tapered Neck, Oatmeal Glaze, Peter Voulkous, 8 In. 2875.00
Vase, Cylindrical, White Squares, Black Matte, Stoneware, Sottsass, 1967, 18 x 6 In. 1035.00
Vase, Feelie, Bulbous, Lime Green, Celadon Vellum, Cabat, 5 1/4 x 4 In. 750.00
Vase, Flattened Sides, Tapering Neck, Gambone, 9 In. 230.00
Vase, Flattened Taper, Multicolored Lines At Waist, Gambone, 18 1/2 In. 489.00
Vase, Pinched Base, Ivory, Pastel Rectangles, Gambone, Italy, 22 x 14 In. 2645.00
Vase, Raku Stoneware, Gold Luster, Beatrice Wood, 1960s, 5 x 6 In. 4095.00
Vase, Round, Geometric Shapes, Gunmetal, Carstens, Germany, 10 x 9 In. 690.00

POTTERY-MIDCENTURY includes pieces made from the 1940s to the 1980s.
Bottle, Pillow, Unglazed, White Matte, Italy, Gambone, 17 3/4 x 8 In. 980.00
Bowl, 3 Folded Sides, Chartreuse Dead Matte Glaze, Natzler, 2 x 7 1/4 In. 520.00
Bowl, Cobalt Blue, Tan, Ivory, Matte & High Luster, Flambe Inside, Scheier, 5 In. 495.00
Bowl, Fish Within Fish, Blue Matte Glaze, Brown Accents, Scheier, 4 x 5 In. 880.00
Bowl, Glazed, Laura Anderson, c.1970, 3 x 5 3/4 In. 325.00
Bowl, Glazed, Natzler, c.1955, 4 3/4 In. 295.00
Bowl, Green To Yellow Semigloss, Paul Cox, New Orleans, 2 In. 127.00
Bowl, Ivory, Charcoal, Mottled Glaze, Natzler, 3/4 x 1 1/2 In. 978.00
Bowl, Mocha Brown Glaze, Cobalt & Brown Flecks, Flared, Scheier, 9 In. 330.00
Bowl, Mushroom Brown Glaze, Natzler, 2 1/2 x 8 In. 4406.00
Bowl, Painted Bird Design, Gray, Yellow & Green Flowers, Cazaux, 6 1/2 In. 320.00
Bowl, Women, Birds, Tree, Rooster, Multicolored, Pillin, 4 1/2 x 9 In. 1610.00
Condiment Set, Bird, Japan, c.1940s 195.00
Condiment Set, Bonzo, Dogs, Salt & Pepper, Mustard Jar, Luster, 3 Piece 150.00
Condiment Set, Hippo, 2 Blooming Cacti Shakers, Japan, 1940s, 5 In. 85.00
Dish, Oval, 2 Women, Landscape, Harris Strong, 1 1/4 x 11 x 6 1/2 In. 115.00
Figurine, Bunny, Gray & White, Kreiss, 3 1/2 In. 17.00
Figurine, Horse, Bay Foal, Kreiss, 1950s, 6 In. 32.00
Figurine, Old Gray Mare, Kreiss, 1950-1960, 5 1/4 In. 40.00
Figurine, Poodle, Seated, Turquoise, Nicodemus, Ohio 80.00
Figurine, Psycho Ceramic, Blue Man With White Hair, Kreiss, 5 1/2 In. 65.00

Figurine, Psycho Ceramic, Pink Man With White Ears, Kreiss, 5 1/8 In. 65.00
Figurine, Queen Of Spades, King Of Clubs, Kreiss, 6 1/2 In., Pair 60.00
Mustard, Jolly Man, DeForest Of California, 4 1/2 In. . . . . *Illus* 38.00
Planter, Ceramic, Hourglass, Architectural, Lagardo Tackett, 1960s, 11 x 21 In. 900.00
Plate, 2 Dancers, High Glaze, Polia Pillin, 6 In. 690.00
Tea Service, Glazed, William & Polia Pillin, USA, 1940s, 8 Piece 1053.00
Tile, Tableau, Cypress Trees, Frame, Harris Strong, 30 x 18 In. `.` 460.00
Tray, Slab Built, Antelopes, People, Bows, Arrows, Paul Bogatay, 1962, 11 x 20 In. 2645.00
Vase, Bands Of Cerulean Blue Drip Glaze, Brown Pools, Cabat, 3 1/2 In. 250.00
Vase, Birds, Leaf Branches, Flowers, Matte Glaze, L. Hjorth, Denmark, 12 In. 350.00
Vase, Blue Crystalline, Ocher, Bronze Streak Glaze, 6 Sides, Pierrefonds, 10 In. 500.00
Vase, Bottle Shape, Stoneware, Bernard Leach, c.1960, 6 3/4 In. 880.00
Vase, Cucumber Green Curdled Glaze, Wide Mouth, WJW, 5 3/4 x 5 In. 470.00
Vase, Earthenware, Crystalline Glaze, O&G Natzler, USA, 1961, 6 1/4 In. 15210.00
Vase, Flat Shoulder, Mottled Blue, Green, Gold, Pillin, 7 1/2 x 6 1/4 In. 750.00
Vase, Flower Holder, Brown Over Green Matte, Spherical, WJW, 3 x 5 In. 470.00
Vase, Glazed, Stoneware, Antonio Prieto, USA, c.1950, 6 x 10 In. 1755.00
Vase, Green, Brown, Flambe Glaze, Natzler E, 1 1/8 x 1 3/4 In. 1095.00
Vase, Green, Gray, Blue Drip Glaze, Blue Body, Bordeaux Ceramique, 3 3/4 In. 230.00
Vase, Lavender Mint Glaze, Globular, Cabat, 2 3/4 x 2 1/2 In. 220.00
Vase, Matte Brown & Black Stripes, Raymor, 1960s, 16 1/2 In. 430.00
Vase, Melon, Chartreuse, Yellow Streaks, Cabat, 4 3/4 x 4 In. 990.00
Vase, Onion, Lime Green Glaze, Brown & Tan Pools, Speckles, Cabat, 3 In. 195.00
Vase, Oxblood, Catalina Pottery, 4 7/8 In. 140.00
Vase, Red Crystals, Lime Green Drip, William & Polia Pillin, 11 1/2 In. 863.00
Vase, Ribbed, Dark Blue Green Glaze, California Faience, 5 1/2 In. 460.00
Vase, Ribbed, Multitone Brown Matte Glaze, California Faience, 5 1/2 In. 865.00
Vase, Square Form, Conical Base, Face, Stoneware, Clyde Burt, 1960s, 14 1/2 x 17 1/2 In. . 935.00
Vase, Stoneware, Lid, Glazed, Clyde Burt, USA, c.1960, 5 1/2 x 22 In. 2340.00
Vase, Teardrop, Green, Black Speckles, Gourd-Shaped Mouth, Cabat, 3 In. 165.00
Vase, Teardrop, Yellow Glaze, Tan Streaks, Green Drip Base, Cabat, 4 x 3 In. 330.00
Vase, Turquoise High Glaze, Marked, California Faience, 4 1/2 In. 115.00
Vase, Vase, Volcanic, Orange Over Blue, William & Polia Pillin, 7 1/4 In. 1265.00
Vase, Wide Mouth, White Glaze, Green Specks, Natzler, 6 1/2 x 7 1/4 In. 5750.00
Vase, Woman's Head, Black, White, Semimatte Ground, Stoneware, Picasso, 11 x 8 In. . . . 4025.00
Vase, Yellow, Brown, Charcoal, Mottled Glaze, Natzler, 1 1/8 x 7/8 In. 920.00

POWDER FLASKS AND POWDER HORNS were made to hold the gunpowder used in antique firearms. The early examples were made of
horn or wood; later ones were of copper or brass.

POWDER FLASK, Brass, Crossed Pistol Shape, Spread-Wing Eagle, Shield, Dog, 5 1/2 In. . . 310.00
Brass, Embossed Scene, Seated Dog, A.M. Flask & Cap Co., 8 In. 169.00
Brass, Indian Hunting Buffalo, 4 Side Rings, 9 1/2 x 4 1/4 In. 290.00
Brass, Ribbed, 8 x 3 1/4 In. 39.00
Brass, Scroll, Leather Strap, P. Powell & Sons, Cincinnati, 7 1/4 x 3 1/2 In. 290.00
Brass, Shell Design, Handmade Braided Strap 115.00
Copper, Engraved Leaves, Cylindrical Spout, Inscribed J.E. Scheid, 1767 . . . . 295.00
Copper, Leaf Decoration, 1800s, 8 In. 35.00
Cow Horn, Flattened, Wheel Lock Rifle, Wood Base, European, c.1600, 8 In. 575.00
Cow Horn, Flattened, Wheel Lock, Wood Base & Plug, Leather Harness, c.1700 . . . . 775.00
Eagle, E. Pluribus Unum 660.00
POWDER HORN, Birch, Horse, Man, Hexagonal Spout, Wood Stopper, Gary Birch, 13 1/2 In. 575.00
Birch, Lady & Goose, Cherry Stopper, Brass Plug, Leather Strap, Gary Birch, 8 In. 865.00
Brass & Wood Mounted, 1800s, 14 In. 145.00
Brass Base, Adjustable Spout, Spring Cut Off, Patent Top, Early 1800s 95.00
Carved, Engraved, Soft Wood Plug, Ediah Winchell, 1775, 10 2 1/2 In. 690.00
Carved, Fish Shape, Eyes, Open Mouth, 18th Century 350.00
Cherry End Plug, Brown Gold, New England Style, c.1830, 13 In. 450.00
Cherry Turned Butt Cap, Rope Twist Carving, Wood Stopper, 9 In. 255.00
Cow Horn, Black Spout, New Plugs, H.F. Clark, c.1819, 17 In. 230.00
Cow Horn, Naval, Ivory, Bone, Wood, War Ships, Flag, 19th Century, 25 In. 4185.00
Cow Horn, Nickel Plated Mounts, S. Oblinger, Troy, Ohio, 9 1/2 In. 175.00
Engraved, 2 Sailing Ships, Eagle, Shield Medallion, 13 Stars, Fish, c.1811, 14 In. 2875.00

Engraved, British Arms, Ship, Cottage Scene, 19th Century, 12 1/2 In. 956.00
Engraved, Captain, Ships, Farm House, F.E. Call, Maine, Mid 1800s, 9 x 2 In. 575.00
Engraved, Coat Of Arms, Animals, Cannons, Fort, c.1774, 13 1/2 In. 1035.00
Engraved, United We Stand, Revolutionary War, c.1779, 14 In. 13145.00
Engraved Text, Nicholas Green, American, 1865, 8 3/4 In. 489.00
Fish, Mermaid, Sea Bird, Cord Flange, Nippled End, P. Kerwin, c.1770, 12 In. 575.00
Master, Curved, Brass Decoration, c.1882, 19 In. 405.00
Master, Hearts, Animals, Samuel E. Watts, Jonesboro, Maine, c.1837, 18 1/2 In. 920.00
Sea Unicorn & Horse, Ship, Nathaniel Munden, England, 1829, 16 In. 1150.00
Ship, Buildings, Flowers, Scalloped, Geometric, Border, Inscription, 1767, 13 In. 1530.00
Silver Overlay Decoration, Scotland, 3 In. 140.00
Violin Key Stopper, 3 Neck Rings, Half Moon Base Decoration, 16 1/4 In. 60.00
Wood & Leather Mounts, North Carolina, Early 19th Century, 6 In. 90.00

PRATT ware means two different things. It was an early Staffordshire pottery, cream-colored with colored decorations, made by Felix Pratt during the late eighteenth century. There was also Pratt ware made with transfer designs during the mid-nineteenth century in Fenton, England. Reproductions of the transfer-printed Pratt are being made.

PRATT FENTON

Cradle, Cover, Yellow, Brown, 18th Century, 2 1/4 x 1 3/4 x 4 In. 385.00
Figurine, Boy, Leaning On Barrel, 4 3/4 In. 110.00
Figurine, Boy, Red Coat, Mustard Yellow Breeches, Holding Bird Nest, 6 3/4 In. 345.00
Figurine, Lion, Lying, Brown & Blue Sponge Decoration, c.1810, 4 1/2 In. 635.00
Jar, Multicolored Lid, 4 Dogs Upsetting Fish Kettle, 1800s, 4 In. 85.00
Jug, Transfer Printed, Washerwomen, Horsemen, Egg Shape, England, c.1850, 5 In. 90.00
Pitcher, 2 Scenes, Man Smoking Pipe, Man Drinking, 6 In. 290.00
Pitcher, Mephistopheles, 3 Faces, Multicolored, Shaped Handle, c.1825, 5 In. .... *Illus* 115.00
Pitcher, Mephistopheles, Single Face, Multicolored Overglaze, Pearlware Body, 5 1/2 In. .. 155.00
Vase, 2-Sided, Trooper, Lady, Farm Animals, Mottled Green Ground, 6 1/2 In. 60.00

PRESSED GLASS was first made in the United States in the 1820s after the invention of glass pressing machines. Hundreds of patterns of pressed glass were made in complete table settings. Although the Boston and Sandwich Works was the most famous of the pressed glass factories, there were about sixteen other factories making pressed glass from 1830 to 1850, and still more from 1850 to 1900, when pressed glass reached its greatest popularity. It is now being widely reproduced. The pattern names used in this listing are based on the information in the book *Pressed Glass in America* by John and Elizabeth Welker. There may be pieces of pressed glass listed in this book in other categories, such as Lamp, Ruby, Sandwich, and Souvenir.

Acanthus pattern is listed here as Ribbed Palm.
Amazon, Cordial, Ruby Stain, 3 1/8 In. 55.00
Amberette, Bowl, Oval, 9 In. 85.00
Aquarium, Pitcher, Water, 9 1/4 In. 285.00
Argus, Goblet, 5-Row Variant, 6 In. 66.00
Art Novo, Tumbler, Ruby Stain, 4 In. 28.00
Ashburton, Celery Vase, 9 In. 50.00
Austrian, Cordial, Vaseline, 3 In. 100.00

Pratt, Pitcher,
Mephistopheles, 3 Faces,
Multicolored, Shaped
Handle, c.1825, 5 In.

**Pressed glass banana
stands are being used
today to hold rolled hand
towels in a bathroom.**

Pressed Glass,
Bellflower

Pressed Glass,
Button Arches

Pressed Glass,
Deer & Dog

Baby Face, Spooner, Frosted, Scalloped Rim, 6 1/2 In.	120.00
Baby Thumbprint pattern is listed here as Dakota.	
Bakewell Block, Celery Vase, 6-Sided Stem, Circular Foot, 9 1/4 In.	440.00
Banded Portland, Cruet, Maiden's Blush Stain, Stopper, 7 1/4 In.	605.00
Banded Portland, Goblet, Maiden's Blush Stain, 5 3/4 In.	90.00
Banded Portland, Wine, Maiden's Blush, 4 1/8 In.	80.00
Beaded Grape, Sugar, Cover, Fiery Opalescent, Footed, 5 3/4 In.	175.00
Beaded Grape, Sugar, Cover, Footed, 5 3/4 In.	275.00
Beaded Oval & Scroll, Creamer, 4 1/2 In.	22.50
Bearded Head pattern is listed here as Viking.	
Bellflower, Butter, Cover, Beaded Rim, Flint, 5 x 6 1/2 In.	100.00
Bellflower, Celery Vase, Scalloped Rim, Flint, 8 In.	175.00
Bellflower, Champagne, Left Facing Vine, 5 1/4 In.	65.00
Bellflower, Compote, Cover, Wafer-Attached Base, 8 3/4 In.	805.00
Bellflower, Compote, Left Facing Vine, Scalloped Rim, 8 1/2 In.	660.00
Bellflower, Decanter, Cut Ovals Around Neck, Stopper, Pontil, 11 3/4 In.	315.00
Bellflower, Jug, Molasses, Applied Handle, Marked Pewter Cover, 8 In.	1610.00
Bellflower, Pitcher, Milk, Left Facing Vine, 7 1/4 In.	990.00
Bellflower, Pitcher, Milk, Tooled Rim, Applied Handle, Pontil, Flint, 7 1/2 In.	805.00
Bellflower, Pitcher, Tooled Flared Rim, Applied Handle, Pontil, 9 In.	520.00
Bellflower, Plate, Ground Rim, Flint, 6 1/2 In.	115.00
Bellflower, Spooner, Left Facing Vine, 5 5/8 In.	310.00
Bellflower, Sugar & Creamer, Frosted	132.00
Bellflower, Sugar, Cover, 8-Sided, Scalloped Rim, 8 1/4 In.	2860.00
Bellflower, Tumbler, Lemonade, Left Facing Vine, Handle, 2 7/8 In.	2420.00
Bellflower Double Vine, Creamer, Right Facing Vines, Rayed Foot, 7 In.	100.00
Bellflower Double Vine, Decanter, Right Facing Vines, Tapered Sides, 8 In.	770.00
Bellflower Double Vine, Eggcup, Cover, Fine Rib, Cut Decoration, Shield, 5 1/2 In.	3450.00
Bellflower Double Vine, Pitcher, Milk, Right & Left Facing Vines, 7 In.	3410.00
Bellflower Double Vine, Pitcher, Right & Left Facing Vines, 8 7/8 In.	230.00
Bellflower Double Vine, Pitcher, Right & Left Facing Vines, Straight Sides, 8 In.	605.00
Bellflower Double Vine, Tumbler, Right Facing Vine, Rayed Foot, 4 7/8 In.	440.00
Bigler, Goblet, Flared, 6 1/4 In.	20.00
Blaze & Mirror, Goblet, 6 In.	40.00
Bleeding Heart, Creamer, 6 In.	100.00
Bleeding Heart, Goblet, 6 1/4 In.	90.00
Bleeding Heart, Goblet, Barrel Shape, 6 1/4 In.	55.00
Bleeding Heart, Tumbler, 3 3/4 In.	90.00 to 100.00
Bleeding Heart, Wine, 4 In.	90.00
Block & Fan, Wine, Ruby Stain, 4 1/4 In.	30.00
Brilliant, Goblet, 6 1/4 In.	55.00
Brooklyn, Flute, Compote, Scalloped Rim, 5 1/4 In.	360.00
Bryce pattern is listed here as Ribbon Candy.	
Buckle, Pitcher, Milk, Strap Handle, 19th Century, 5 3/4 In.	115.00
Bull's-Eye, Spooner, Flared Rim, 5 1/4 In.	130.00
Bull's-Eye, Tumbler, 3 5/8 In.	110.00
Bull's-Eye & Bar, Eggcup, Cover, Starch Blue, Flint, 5 1/2 In.	405.00

Bull's-Eye & Bar, Eggcup, Jade Green, Flint, 3 1/2 In. 315.00

Bull's-Eye & Broken Columns, Goblet, 6 1/4 In. 65.00

Bull's-Eye & Buttons, Tumbler, Gold Trim, 3 3/4 In. 55.00

Bull's-Eye & Fleur-De-Lis, Celery Vase, 10 1/2 In. 415.00

Bull's-Eye & Fleur-De-Lis, Compote, 3 3/4 x 8 1/4 In. 175.00

Bull's-Eye & Fleur-De-Lis, Compote, 5 1/4 x 8 1/4 In. 255.00

Bull's-Eye & Fleur-De-Lis, Decanter, Pewter & Marble Stopper, 10 1/2 In. 345.00

Bull's-Eye & Fleur-De-Lis, Decanter, Pewter & Marble Stopper, 13 In. 300.00

Bull's-Eye & Fleur-De-Lis, Goblet, Flint, 6 1/4 In., Pair 260.00

Bull's-Eye & Fleur-De-Lis, Sugar, Cover, 6-Sided Finial 110.00

Bull's-Eye & Fleur-De-Lis, Sugar, Cover, 9 In. 175.00

Bull's-Eye & Prism, Goblet, 5 3/4 In. 20.00

Bull's-Eye With Diamond Point, Eggcup, Flint, Polished Pontil, 3 3/4 In. 70.00

Bull's-Eye With Diamond Point, Goblet, Flint, 7 In., Pair 290.00

Bull's-Eye With Diamond Point, Spooner, Cobalt Blue Stain, 5 1/2 In. 145.00

Bull's-Eye With Diamond Point, Tumbler, Flint, Polished Pontil, 3 1/2 In. 185.00

Bull's-Eye With Diamond Point, Wine, 4 3/4 In. 210.00

Bull's-Eye With Diamond Point, Wine, Flint, 4 1/4 In. 230.00

Bungalo, Goblet, Engraved Flowers & Leaves, Ruby Stain, 6 In. 285.00

Butterfly, Celery Vase, Frosted Bands, Handles, 8 1/4 In. 50.00

Button Arches, Pitcher, Tankard, Ruby Stain, Frosted Band, 11 1/2 In. 130.00

Button Arches, Sugar, Cover, 6 1/2 In. 70.00

Cable, Goblet, 5 1/2 In. 145.00

Cable With Ring, Sugar, Cover, 7 1/4 In. 110.00

California pattern is listed here as Beaded Grape.

Canadian, Compote, Cover, 11 1/4 In. 130.00

Candlewick as a pressed glass pattern is properly named *Banded Raindrop*. There is also a pattern called *Candlewick*, which has been made by Imperial Glass Corporation since 1936. It is listed in this book in the Imperial Glass category.

Candy Ribbon pattern is listed here as Ribbon Candy.

Charleston, Tumbler, Water, Fiery Opalescent, 3 5/8 In. 385.00

Church Windows pattern is listed here as Columbia.

Classic, Pitcher, Log Feet, 10 In. 220.00

Coin Spot pattern is listed in this book in its own category.

Colonial, Champagne, 5 1/4 In. 55.00

Colonial, Goblet, Knop Stem, 6 1/4 In. 45.00

Colorado, Creamer, Ruby Stain, Beaded Rim, 3 3/4 In. 65.00

Columbia, Tray, Vaseline, 9 1/2 x 12 3/4 In. 230.00

Columbian Coin, Pitcher, Gold Coins, 9 5/8 In. 300.00

Columbian Coin, Wine, Gold Coins, 4 In. 110.00

Comet, Goblet, Flint, Polished Pontil, 6 1/4 In. 115.00

Comet, Tumbler, Whiskey, Applied Handle, Flint, Polished Pontil, 3 In. 630.00

Comet, Tumbler, Whiskey, Flint, Polished Pontil, 3 In. 225.00

Compact pattern is listed here as Snail.

Cord & Tassel, Bowl, Cover, Oval, Footed, 6 In. 100.00

Cornucopia, Vase, Ruby Stain, 5 3/4 In. 175.00

Corona, Goblet, Ruby Stain, Engraved Flowers, 6 In. 45.00

Cosmos pattern is listed in this book as its own category.

Crystal Wedding, Goblet, Amber Stain, 5 3/4 In. 100.00

Currant, Compote, 9 x 10 3/4 In. 50.00

Cut Strawberry Diamond & Fan, Compote, Serrated Rim, 7 1/4 x 10 1/4 In. 360.00

Daisy & Button With Crossbar, Celery Vase, Vaseline, 7 In. 120.00

Dakota, Candy Jar, Cylindrical, 26 In., Pair 880.00

Dakota, Goblet, Ruby Stain, 6 1/2 In. 40.00

Dakota, Pitcher, Milk, Engraved Fern & Berry, 8 1/2 In. 165.00

Dakota, Wine, Flared, Ruby Stain, 3 3/4 In. 30.00

Deer & Dog, Bowl, Cover, Oval, Footed, 8 1/2 In. 1045.00

Deer & Dog, Champagne, 5 3/8 In. 190.00

Deer & Dog, Compote, Cover, 13 In. 440.00

Deer & Dog, Goblet, 6 1/2 In. 80.00

Deer & Pine Tree, Goblet, 6 1/2 In. 90.00

Delaware, Puff Box, Cover, Rose Stain, Gold Trim, 3 1/4 In. 300.00

Diamond Band With Panels, Goblet, Ruby Stain, 5 1/2 In. 55.00

Pressed Glass,
Diamond Thumbprint

Pressed Glass, Empress

Pressed Glass, Loop & Block

Diamond In Ovals, Goblet, 6 In. 65.00
Diamond Point, Compote, Cobalt Blue, Clear Stem & Foot, 9 1/2 In. 770.00
Diamond Point, Cordial, Fancy Knop Stem, 3 1/4 In. 130.00
Diamond Point, Jelly Jar, 5 1/4 In. 80.00
Diamond Point, Jug, 8-Panel Base, 6 3/8 In. 415.00
Diamond Point, Pitcher, Milk, 6-Sided Scalloped Foot, 8 1/8 In. 255.00
Diamond Point With Loops, Cordial, Knopped Stem, 3 1/4 In. 130.00
Diamond Point With Panels, Goblet, 6 1/4 In. 190.00
Diamond Thumbprint, Compote, Scalloped Rim, 6 1/4 In. 230.00
Diamond Thumbprint, Goblet, Flint, 6 3/4 In. 865.00
Diamond Thumbprint, Tumbler, 3 3/8 In. 165.00
Dodo, Goblet, 6 In. 55.00
Double Loop pattern is listed here as Ribbon Candy.
Double Vine pattern is listed here as Bellflower Double Vine.
Double Wedding Ring pattern is listed here as Wedding Ring.
Early Thumbprint, Cake Stand, 3 x 7 5/8 In. 285.00
Early Thumbprint, Compote, Double Step Base, Scalloped Rim, 10 3/4 In. 1485.00
Early Thumbprint, Mug, Barrel Shape, 4 1/4 In. 990.00
Early Thumbprint, Nappy, Cover, Scalloped Base, 6-Sided Finial, 5 In. 605.00
Elk Medallion, Goblet, 6 1/4 In. 100.00
Empress, Syrup, Green, Gold Trim, 7 1/4 In. 255.00
English Hobnail Cross pattern is listed here as Amberette.
Etched Dakota pattern is listed here as Dakota.
Excelsior, Creamer, 4 1/2 In. 550.00
Fine Rib, Champagne, 5 1/8 In. 120.00
Fine Rib, Goblet, 6 1/8 In. 55.00
Flat Diamond & Panel, Goblet, 6 1/8 In. 130.00
Flower Medallion, Goblet, 6 In. 110.00
Flying Robin pattern is listed here as Hummingbird.
Flying Stork, Goblet, 6 In. 40.00
Framed Block, Wine, 4 1/2 In. 15.00
Frog & Spider, Goblet, 6 In. 230.00
Frosted patterns may also be listed under name of main pattern.
Frosted Leaf, Wine, 3 3/4 In. 130.00
Frosted Roman Key pattern is listed here as Roman Key, Frosted.
Gargoyle, Goblet, 6 1/4 In. 415.00
Giant Baby Thumbprint, Goblet, 6 3/8 In. 55.00
Giant Prism, Goblet, 6 3/8 In. 50.00
Giant Prism With Thumbprint Band, Goblet, 6 1/4 In. 90.00
Giant Sawtooth, Goblet, Gilt Rim, 6 3/8 In. 190.00
Gothic, Celery Vase, Flared, 9 1/2 In. 385.00
Gothic, Goblet, Flint, 6 In., Pair 85.00
Gothic, Wine, 3 3/4 In. 65.00
Grape, see the related patterns Beaded Grape and Magnet & Grape.
Hairpin, Dish, Lacy, Scalloped & Pointed Rim, 1 1/8 x 6 1/8 In. 130.00
Hairpin With Rayed Base, Champagne, 5 In. 100.00
Hairpin With Thumbprint, Goblet, 6 In. 45.00

Hamilton, Champagne, 4 3/4 In.	165.00
Hamilton With Frosted Leaf, Wine, 3 3/4 In.	55.00
Hand, Cake Plate, Translucent Amethyst, Ribbed Stem, Ribbed Dome Foot, 11 In.	175.00
Hand, Compote, Blue, 9 In.	130.00
Hand, Compote, Vaseline, 8 3/4 In.	220.00
Heart With Thumbprint, Cake Stand, 9 x 5 1/4 In.	385.00
Heart With Thumbprint, Creamer, 4 1/2 In.	165.00
Heart With Thumbprint, Ice Bucket, Scalloped & Pointed Rim, 4 Points, 5 x 6 In.	155.00
Hinoto pattern is listed here as Diamond Point with Panels.	
Hobnail pattern is in this book as its own category.	
Hobstar & Feather, Punch Set, Flared Bowl, 13 Piece	360.00
Honeycomb, Celery Vase, Blue, 8 3/4 In.	120.00
Horizontal Threads, Sugar & Creamer, Cover, Ruby Stain, Child's	175.00
Horizontal Threads, Wine, Ruby Stain, 4 In.	80.00
Horn Of Plenty, Goblet, 6 1/4 In.	80.00
Horn Of Plenty, Goblet, Pair	185.00
Horn Of Plenty, Pitcher, Water, Applied Handle, Polished Pontil, 8 1/2 In.	1610.00
Horn Of Plenty, Plate, Canary, Flint, 6 1/4 In.	320.00
Huber, Tumbler, Whiskey, Handle, 3 In.	35.00
Hummingbird, Goblet, Blue, 6 In.	110.00
Icicle With Chain Band, Goblet, 6 3/8 In.	80.00
Iconoclast, Goblet, 6 1/4 In.	80.00
Inverted Fern, Goblet, Flint, 6 1/2 In., Pair	70.00
Inverted Fern, Pitcher, Water, Engraved Monogram, Applied Solid Handle, 8 3/4 In.	690.00
Inverted Fern, Wine, Flint, 4 In.	130.00
Jumbo, Compote, Cover, Elephant Finial, Circular Stepped Foot, 12 In.	9625.00
Jumbo, Compote, Cover, Frosted Elephant Finial, 12 3/4 In.	1980.00
King's Crown, Celery Vase, Ruby Stain, 6 1/2 In.	165.00
King's Crown, Spooner, Ruby Stain, Engraved Leaves, 4 1/4 In.	65.00
Krom, Goblet, High Domed Foot, 5 3/4 In.	80.00
Laminated Petals, Goblet, 6 In.	45.00
Lattice & Oval Panels pattern is listed here as Flat Diamond & Panel.	
Lee, Goblet, 6 3/4 In.	190.00
Lee, Tumbler, Flint, 3 1/4 In.	85.00
Lincoln Drape, Dish, Sweetmeat, Rayed Base, 7 1/2 In.	175.00
Lincoln Drape, Goblet, 6 In.	140.00
Lincoln Drape, Lamp, Oil, 8 3/4 In.	175.00
Little Red Riding Hood, Punch Set, Footed Bowl, 6 Cups, Child's	250.00
Loop, Pitcher, Applied Handle, 11 In.	115.00
Loop & Block, Pitcher, Ruby Stain, 9 1/4 In.	300.00
Loop & Block, Tumbler, Ruby Stain, 3 3/4 In.	30.00
Madison, Celery Vase, 6-Sided Bowl, Circular Foot, 8 5/8 In.	45.00
Magnet & Grape With Frosted Leaf, Goblet, 3 7/8 In.	110.00
Magnet & Grape With Frosted Leaf & American Shield, Goblet, 6 1/2 In.	285.00
Maine, Tumbler, Blue Green & Blood Red Amethyst Stain, 4 In.	110.00
Mardi Gras, Cracker Jar, Cover, 8 1/4 In.	55.00
Mardi Gras, Pitcher, Barrel Shape, Applied Handle, 7 3/4 In.	110.00

Pressed Glass,
Millard

Pressed Glass,
Nail

Pressed Glass,
New England Pineapple

Pressed Glass,
Paneled Forget-Me-Not

Pressed Glass,
Philadelphia

Pressed Glass,
Snail

Michigan, Celery Vase, Maiden's Blush Stain, Gold Trim, 5 3/4 In.	230.00
Michigan, Cruet, Maiden's Blush Stain, Gold Trim, Facetted Stopper, 6 1/4 In.	440.00
Michigan, Salt & Pepper, Maiden's Blush Stain, Gold Trim, Britannia Cover, 4 In.	285.00
Michigan, Tumbler, Ruby Stain, 3 3/4 In.	130.00
Michigan, Water Set, Maiden's Blush Stain, Gold Trim, 7 1/2-In. Pitcher, 7 Piece	360.00
Millard, Goblet, Amber Stain, 6 1/4 In.	90.00
Millard, Goblet, Ruby Stain, 6 1/4 In.	100.00
Minerva, Compote, Scalloped Shaped Rim, 9 In.	17.00
Mitered Bars, Cordial, Ruby Stain, 3 In.	40.00
Mitered Diamond Points pattern is listed here as Mitered Bars.	
Moorish Arch, Spooner, 6-Sided Rim, 4 3/4 In.	35.00
Morning Glory, Goblet, Flint, 6 In.	1265.00
Nail, Celery Vase, Ruby Stain, 6 1/2 In.	200.00
Nail, Goblet, Ruby Stain, 6 1/2 In.	90.00
New England Pineapple, Champagne, 5 1/8 In.	190.00
New England Pineapple, Decanter, Applied Thick Bar Lip, 8 1/2 In.	290.00
New England Pineapple, Goblet, 6 1/8 In.	65.00
New England Pineapple, Sugar, 7 1/4 In.	130.00
New England Pineapple, Tumbler, Whiskey, Flint, Polished Pontil, 3 In.	375.00
O'Hara Diamond, Claret, Ruby Stain, 4 3/4 In.	110.00
Oregon, see the related pattern Skilton.	
Owl pattern is listed here as Bull's-Eye with Diamond Point.	
Owl In Horseshoe, Goblet, 6 1/8 In.	90.00
Palm Leaf Fan, Goblet, Ruby Stain, 5 3/4 In.	145.00
Paneled Finetooth, Goblet, 6 1/4 In.	35.00
Paneled Forget-Me-Not, Goblet, Vaseline, 5 7/8 In.	230.00
Paneled Ovals, Champagne, 4 3/4 In.	90.00
Pendleton, Champagne, 5 In.	50.00
Philadelphia, Goblet, 6 1/4 In.	1155.00
Pigs In Corn, Goblet, Left-Leaning Husk, 6 In.	300.00
Pillar, Goblet, 6 1/4 In.	80.00
Pleat & Panel, Wine, 4 1/4 In.	120.00
Pleating, Goblet, Ruby Stain, 6 In.	110.00
Pleating, Pitcher, Ruby Stain, 9 7/8 In.	65.00
Plume, Tumbler, Ruby Stain, Engraved Band, 3 7/8 In.	130.00
Pointed Buckle, Goblet, 5 3/4 In.	65.00
Portland With Diamond Point Band pattern is listed here as Banded Portland.	
Prism & Bull's-Eye Column, Wine, 4 1/2 In.	50.00
Prism & Lobular Loops, Goblet, 6 1/4 In.	80.00
Prism With Arched Top, Goblet, 6 1/4 In.	50.00
Radiant Daisy, Creamer, Ruby Stain, 5 1/4 In.	45.00
Rhode Island, Goblet, 5 3/4 In.	470.00
Ribbed Palm, Creamer, 6 In.	130.00
Ribbed Palm, Pitcher, Applied Handle, 8 3/4 In.	360.00
Ribbed Palm, Tumbler, 3 1/2 In.	80.00
Ribbon Candy, Cake Plate, Emerald Green, 3 3/8 x 6 5/8 In.	100.00
Ribbon Candy, Cordial, 3 1/4 In.	90.00

Ribbon Candy, Wine, 3 3/4 In. 80.00
Roanoke, Goblet, Ruby Stain, 5 3/4 In. 50.00
Roman Key, Goblet, Frosted, 5 3/4 In. 50.00
Roman Key, Tumbler, Footed, Frosted, 5 In. 20.00
Royal Crystal, Goblet, Ruby Stain, 6 1/8 In. 155.00
Royal Crystal, Tumbler, Ruby Stain, 3 7/8 In. 20.00
Ruby Thumbprint, see the related pattern King's Crown.
Sandwich Loop, see the related pattern Hairpin.
Sandwich Star, Goblet, Polished Pontil, Flint, 6 1/2 In. 865.00
Sawtooth Band pattern is listed here as Amazon.
Scarab, Goblet, Plain Foot, 6 1/4 In. 110.00
Scarab, Goblet, Rayed Foot, 6 1/4 In. 100.00
Sheaf & Block, Pitcher, Milk, Ruby Stain, 7 1/2 In. 65.00
Short Ovals & Honeycomb, Champagne, 5 In. 45.00
Shoshone pattern is listed here as Victor.
Skilton, Compote, Ruby Stain, 4 1/2 x 6 3/4 In. 120.00
Snail, Banana Stand, 7 1/4 In. 165.00
Snail, Cracker Jar, Cover, 9 In. 240.00
Snail, Goblet, 6 1/2 In. 100.00
Spanish Coin pattern is listed here as Columbian Coin.
Squirrel, Goblet, 6 In. ....715.00 to 880.00
Star & Buckle, Spooner, 4 3/4 In. 30.00
Star In A Square, Berry Set, Ruby Stain, Gold Trim, 7 Piece 410.00
Stedman, Creamer, 7 1/4 In. 90.00
Stippled Forget-Me-Not, Plate, Cat Center, Closed Handles, 9 In. 220.00
Stippled Paneled Flower pattern is listed here as Maine.
Swan, Goblet, 5 7/8 In. 175.00
Swimming Swan, Goblet, 6 1/4 In. 880.00
Teardrop & Tassel, Goblet, 5 3/4 In. 120.00
Tennessee, Goblet, 6 In. 165.00
Tennessee, Pitcher, Milk, 7 1/2 In. 145.00
Texas, Cake Stand, 6 x 10 3/4 In. 200.00
Texas, Cake Stand, Maiden's Blush Stain, 5 3/4 x 9 In. 470.00
Texas, Goblet, 6 In. 90.00
Texas, Wine, Maiden's Blush Stain, 4 In. 130.00
Three Face, Compote, Cover, 8 1/2 In. 275.00
Three Graces, see the related pattern Three Face.
Three Sisters pattern is listed here as Three Face.
Thrush & Apple Blossom, Goblet, 6 In. ....65.00 to 120.00
Thumbprint & Draped Prism, Goblet, 6 1/4 In. 210.00
Tong, Celery Vase, 7 3/4 In. 40.00
Tong, Sugar & Creamer, Cover 155.00
Torpedo, Compote, Domed Cover, 13 1/2 In. 165.00
Trilby, Goblet, 5 3/4 In. 190.00
Tulip With Sawtooth, Decanter, Stopper, 14 1/4 In. 550.00
Tulip With Sawtooth, Goblet, 6 1/2 In. 90.00
Tulip With Sawtooth, Pitcher, Scalloped Foot, 9 In. 605.00
U.S. Coin, Pitcher, Water, Frosted Dollar, 9 1/2 In. 1375.00

Pressed Glass,
Squirrel

Pressed Glass,
Teardrop & Tassel

Pressed Glass, Wading Heron

U.S. Rib, Goblet, Ruby Stain, 6 1/8 In. 358.00
Valentine pattern is listed here as Trilby.
Victor, Goblet, Ruby Stain, 6 1/8 In. 155.00
Viking, Bowl, Cover, Oval, 4-Footed, 6 1/4 In. 40.00
Viking, Pitcher, Water, 3-Footed, 8 3/4 In. 110.00
Virginia, Cake Stand, Scalloped Rim, 6 x 9 In. 190.00
Virginia, Cracker Jar, Cover, 11 3/4 In. 175.00
Virginia, Pitcher, Applied Handle, 7 3/4 In. 220.00
Virginia, Pitcher, Straight Sides, 8 1/4 In. 100.00
Wading Heron, Pitcher, Emerald Green, 9 1/4 In. 180.00
Waffle, Goblet, 6 1/4 In. 100.00
Waffle & Thumbprint, Champagne, 5 1/2 In. 100.00
Waffle & Thumbprint, Goblet, 6 1/4 In. 100.00
Waffle & Thumbprint, Tumbler, Applied Handle, Flint, Polished Pontil, 3 In. 100.00
Washington, Celery Vase, 8 1/2 In. 80.00
Washington, Champagne, 4 7/8 In. 190.00
Washington, Goblet, 5 7/8 In. 110.00
Washington, Goblet, Oval Panels, Engraved Flowers & Fruit, 5 1/2 In. 550.00
Wedding Ring, Goblet, 6 In. 100.00
Wedding Ring, Wine, 4 1/4 In. 50.00
Wellington, Salt & Pepper, Ruby Stain, 2 1/2 In. 300.00
Westward Ho, Goblet, 6 1/2 In. 145.00
Wildflower, Salt & Pepper, Blue, 3 1/4 In. 50.00
Worcester, Tumbler, Applied Handle, Flint, 4 In. 1035.00
Wyoming, Wine, 4 In. 90.00
Zipper Slash, Wine, Amber Stain, 4 In. 50.00
Zipper Slash, Wine, Ruby Stain, 4 In. 20.00

PRINT, in this listing, means any of many printed images produced on
paper by one of the more common methods, such as lithography. The
prints listed here are of interest primarily to the antiques collector, not
the fine arts collector. Many of these prints were originally part of
books. Other prints will be found in the Advertising, Currier & Ives,
Movie, and Poster categories.

Aldin, Cecil, Animal Tea Party, Rabbits, Cat, Pig In Tuxedo, Oak Frame, 12 1/2 x 7 In. . . .   225.00
Aldin, Cecil, Drawn Blank, Hunters In Village, Arts & Crafts Oak Frame, 19 x 11 In. 550.00
Andersonville Prison, Southeast View, Bird's-Eye View, Chromolithograph, 24 x 27 In. . .   140.00

Audubon bird prints were originally issued as part of books printed
from 1826 to 1854. They were issued in two sizes, 26 1/2 inches by 39
1/2 inches and 11 inches by 7 inches. The quadrupeds were issued in
28-by-22-inch prints. Later editions of the Audubon books were done
in many sizes, and reprints of the books in the original size were also   J.W.Audubon
made. The bird pictures have been so popular they have been copied in
myriad sizes by both old and new printing methods. This list includes
originals and later copies because Audubon prints of all ages are sold
in antiques shops.

Audubon, Brown's Lark, Havell Edition, Lithograph, Frame, c.1828, 28 1/2 x 34 1/2 In. . .   590.00
Audubon, Little Auk, Birds Of America, Robert Havell, c.1836 . . . .   1795.00
Audubon, Rose-Breasted Grosbeak, Birds Of America, Robert Havell, c.1831 . . . .   5020.00
Audubon, Savannah Finch, Birds Of America, Robert Havell, c.1836 . . . .   2150.00
Bicknell, J.C., Carrabaggett Meadow, c.1910, 16 1/2 x 24 1/2 In. 65.00
Bicknell, J.C., Island Road, c.1915, 12 x 20 In. 90.00
Cacciola, Pedro, Blossomed Hills, 8 x 10 In. 115.00
Cacciola, Pedro, Bridge Of Flowers, Close Frame, 10 x 13 In. 130.00
Cacciola, Pedro, Covered Bridge, Close Frame, 8 x 10 In. 35.00
Cacciola, Pedro, Flowery Path, 11 x 14 In. 220.00
Cacciola, Pedro, Italian Scene, Hillside, Seaside Town, 8 x 10 In. 50.00
Cacciola, Pedro, Rainbow Over Garden, 11 x 14 In. 145.00
Cacciola, Pedro, Summer Joys, c.1945, 8 x 10 In. 360.00
Cacciola, Pedro, Tunnel Of Joy, 11 x 14 In. 90.00
Carlock, Royal, Lincoln Memorial, Close Frame, 8 x 10 In. 45.00
Chandler, William Henry, Dead Game, Still Life, 14 x 28 In. 160.00

Chandler, William Henry, Evening Campfire, 18 x 40 In. 500.00
Chandler, William Henry, Evening Campfire, 11 x 26 In. 300.00
Chandler, William Henry, Lake & Mountain, Pastel, 16 x 20 In. 160.00
Chandler, William Henry, Lake, Pastel, 14 x 24 In. 400.00
Chandler, William Henry, Lake, Pastel, 20 x 30 In. 725.00
Chandler, William Henry, Landscape, 18 x 40 In. 300.00
Chandler, William Henry, Landscape, Pastel, 12 x 14 In. 130.00
Chandler, William Henry, Sailboat, 16 x 26 In. 500.00
Chandler, William Henry, Seascape, Pastel, c.1900, 14 x 24 In. 220.00
Chandler, William Henry, Winter, Pastel, 13 x 22 In. 190.00
Chant, Elizabeth, Plowman Homeward Plods His Weary Way, Frame, 27 x 17 In. 290.00
Davidson, David, Dragon, c.1910, 5 x 7 In. 90.00
Davidson, David, Golden Sunset, c.1915, 10 x 12 In. 66.00
Davidson, David, Pasture Pool, c.1928, 10 x 16 In. 66.00
Davidson, David, Pres. Coolidge's Home, Plymouth, Vt., 10 x 12 In. 248.00
Fisher, Harrison, Pretty Girl, Close Frame, 9 x 12 In. 20.00
Fox, R. Atkinson, Fountain Of Love, 10 x 15 In. 35.00
Fox, R. Atkinson, Garden Of Romance, 10 x 8 In. 39.00
Fox, R. Atkinson, Magic Pool, 10 x 16 In. 50.00
Fox, R. Atkinson, Russet Gems, 9 x 12 In. 39.00
Fox, R. Atkinson, Sunset Dreams, 18 x 30 In. 80.00
Frost, A.B., Shooting Ducks From A Battery 330.00
Glorious Defeat Of Invincible Spanish Armada, Barnard's, 1783, 15 x 9 1/2 In. 140.00
Grant, Gordon, Whaling Vessel, 3-D Sails, U.S. Flag, Shadow Box, 1934, 13 x 19 In. ... 650.00
Grimball, Meta, Pies That Mother Used To Make, 14 x 18 In. 1800.00
Gutmann, Bessie Pease, Anxious Mother, 1910, 12 x 16 In. 358.00
Gutmann, Bessie Pease, Brown Study, 1910, 14 x 18 In. 1100.00
Gutmann, Bessie Pease, Dreamland's Border, 1921, 14 x 17 In. .... .99.00 to 143.00
Gutmann, Bessie Pease, Just A Little Bit Independent, 1946, 18 x 14 In. 240.00
Gutmann, Bessie Pease, Little Bo Peep, 1933, 12 x 10 In. 80.00
Gutmann, Bessie Pease, Little Boy Blue, 1933, 12 x 10 In. 110.00
Gutmann, Bessie Pease, Sonny Boy, c.1929, 18 x 14 In. 80.00
Gutmann, Bessie Pease, Thank You, God, 1951, 20 x 14 In. .... .90.00 to 120.00
Gutmann, Bessie Pease, To Love & Cherish, 1911, 18 x 13 In. 220.00
Harris, Florida Wilds, c.1915, 10 x 14 In. 80.00
Harris, Oldest House, St. Augustine, Fla., 4 x 7 In. 35.00
Haskell & Allen, Ross Castle, Colored, 19th Century 25.00
Higgins, Charles R., Apple Blossom Road, 8 x 14 In. 60.00
Higgins, Charles R., Highway & Byway, 7 x 12 In. 100.00
Higgins, Charles R., Moonlight Sail, 6 x 13 In. 145.00

Icart prints were made by Louis Icart, who worked in Paris from 1907 as an employee of a postcard company. He then started printing magazines and fashion brochures. About 1910 he created a series of etchings of fashionably dressed women and he continued to make similar etchings until he died in 1950. He is well known as a printmaker, painter, and illustrator. Original etchings are much more expensive than the later photographic copies.

Icart, Cinderella, At Fireplace, Holding Cat & Dog, Oval, Frame, 18 1/2 x 14 1/2 In. 1250.00
Icart, Japanese Garden, Frame, 1925, 22 X25 In. 2290.00
Icart, Red Riding Hood, Frame, 1927, 21 x 14 In. 2200.00
Icart, Sleeping Beauty In The Woods, Oval, Frame, 18 1/2 x 14 1/2 In. 1250.00
Icart, Speed II, Racing Greyhounds, 1937, 15 x 24 3/4 In. 5800.00
Icart, Symphony In White, Woman, White Afghan Hounds, Frame, 1932, 20 x 15 1/2 In. .. 3800.00

Jacoulet prints were designed by Paul Jacoulet (1902-1960), a Frenchman who spent most of his life in Japan. He was a master of Japanese woodblock print technique. Subjects included life in Japan, the South Seas, Korea, and China. His prints were sold by subscription and issued in series. Each series had a distinctive seal, such as a sparrow or butterfly. Most Jacoulet prints are approximately 15 x 10 inches.

Jacoulet, After The Banquet, 1951 .... 460.00
Jacoulet, Basket Weaver, 1948 .... 980.00

Jacoulet, Birds Of Paradise, 1937 .... 750.00
Jacoulet, Black Lotus, 1959 .... 1725.00
Jacoulet, Bowl Of Milk, 1958 .... 1095.00
Jacoulet, Bride, 1948 .... 575.00
Jacoulet, Butterflies Of The Tropics, 1939 .... 3450.00
Jacoulet, Cactus, 1941 .... 1955.00
Jacoulet, Chamorro Woman Of Guam, 1934, 16 x 10 1/2 In. 750.00
Jacoulet, Chinese Gamblers, 1941 .... 690.00
Jacoulet, Chinese Mask Seller, 1940 .... 460.00
Jacoulet, Chinese Writer, 1953 .... 1265.00
Jacoulet, Daughter Of The Chief, 1953 .... 1840.00
Jacoulet, Evening Flowers, 1941 .... 2185.00
Jacoulet, First Love, 1937 .... 2070.00
Jacoulet, Fisherman Of Sawara, 1936 .... 520.00
Jacoulet, Happy Man, 1955 .... 575.00
Jacoulet, Korean Baby In Ceremonial Costume, 1934 .... 750.00
Jacoulet, Love Letter, 1955 .... 1325.00
Jacoulet, Lovers Of Tarang, 1935 .... 805.00
Jacoulet, Mango Seller, 1939 .... 1840.00
Jacoulet, Master Potter, 1940 .... 1265.00
Jacoulet, Midnight Prayer, 1959 .... 1265.00
Jacoulet, Old Carp Seller, 1934 .... 575.00
Jacoulet, Red Lacquer Mirror, 1938 .... 1610.00
Jacoulet, Return From The Jungle, 1948 .... 1265.00
Jacoulet, Salt Merchant, 1936 .... 920.00
Jacoulet, Snowy Night, 1939 .... 575.00
Jacoulet, Squatting Man, Chinese, 1947 .... 890.00
Jacoulet, Tattooed Woman Of Falalap, 1935 .... 6325.00
Jacoulet, Watermelons, 1939 .... 1035.00
Jacoulet, Winter Flowers, 1955 .... 865.00
Jacoulet, Young Girl Of Fiji, 1935 .... 805.00
Jacoulet, Young Girl Of Jaluit, 1939 .... 1150.00

Japanese woodblock prints are listed as follows: Print, Japanese, name
of artist, title or description, type, and size. Dealers use the following
terms: Tate-e is a vertical composition. Yoko-e is a horizontal composition. The words Aiban (13 by 9 inches), Chuban (10 by 7 1/2 inches),
Hosoban (13 by 6 inches), Oban (15 by 10 inches), and Koban (7 by 4
inches) denote approximate size. Modern versions of some of these
prints have been made. Other woodblock prints that are not Japanese
are listed under Print, Woodblock.

Japanese, Beisaku, Sino-Japanese War Of 1894-1895, c.1895, Oban 445.00
Japanese, Chikanobu, Processional Scene, Elephant, Fete De Janno, Triptych ... 230.00
Japanese, Choki, Eishosai, Cherry Blossom Viewing At Toeizan, Oban, Yoko-e ... 2390.00
Japanese, Choki, Eishosai, Confession Of Takao, Woman, Tobacco Set, Oban Tate-e ... 5020.00
Japanese, Eisen, 47 Ronin On Snow Covered Bridge, Chuban, Triptych 520.00
Japanese, Eisen, Keisai, Karasu River At Kuragano Station, Oban, Yoko-e 3585.00
Japanese, Eisen, Keisai, Shinkiso, Melancholy Type, Modern Beauty Series, Oban, Tate-e ... 4540.00
Japanese, Eisen, Keisai, Sumida River, Roman Letter Border, Oban, Yoko-e 6575.00
Japanese, Eishi, 3 Ladies Relax Beside Stream, Oban, Tate-e 259.00
Japanese, Eisui, Geisha Holding Bound Book, Matted, Frame, Early 1900s, 21 x 17 In. ... 58.00
Japanese, Eizan, Kikugawa, Returning Boats, Yabase, Furyu Omi Series, Oban, Tate-e ... 2630.00
Japanese, Goyo, Hashiguchi, Rain At Yabakei, 1918, 16 1/8 x 20 1/4 In. 2270.00
Japanese, Goyo, Hashiguchi, Woman Holding A Towel, 1920, 18 1/8 x 12 In. 4780.00
Japanese, Hasui, Kawase, Lake Kawaguchi, 1933, Hosoban 345.00
Japanese, Hasui, Kawase, Snow Scene, Figure Holding Umbrella, Temple, Oban, Tate-e . 1440.00
Japanese, Hasui, Kawase, Temple At Zentsuji In Sanuki, Oban, Tate-e 430.00
Japanese, Hiroshige, A Bridge In Snow, Winter Scene, Mat, Frame, c.1935, 12 x 15 In. .. 260.00
Japanese, Hiroshige, Ando, Snowfall At Kambara, Mat, Frame, 12 x 15 In. 385.00
Japanese, Hiroshige, Departure From The Inn, Mat, Frame, 17 x 21 In. 230.00
Japanese, Hiroshige, Descending Geese To Katata, Oban, Tate-e 1440.00
Japanese, Hiroshige, Evening Bell At Mii Temple, Oban, Tate-e 980.00
Japanese, Hiroshige, Satta Pass, Travelers Looking From A Mountain Cliff, 17 x 21 In. .. 230.00

Japanese, Hiroshige, Shimada, Workers In Rice Paddy, Mat, Frame, 12 x 15 In. 290.00
Japanese, Hiroshige, Snow Scene, Women Under Umbrella, Canal, Frame, Oban, Tate-e . 375.00
Japanese, Hiroshige, Traveling At Night Through Hakone Mountains, Oban, Tate-e 375.00
Japanese, Hiroshige, Utagawa, Listening To Insects, Mount Dokan, Oban, Yoko-e 7770.00
Japanese, Hiroshige, Utagawa, Pocket Watch, Egoyomi Surimono, 1823, Kakuban 5975.00
Japanese, Hiroshige, View Of Edo, Figures Outside Restaurant, Oban, Yoko-e 230.00
Japanese, Hiroshige II, Utagawa, Foreign Building, Yokohama, Triptych, Oban, Tate-e .. 5975.00
Japanese, Hiroshige II, Utagawa, Panorama, Yokohama, Triptych, Oban, Tate-e 2870.00
Japanese, Hokkei, Totoya, Tokimasa Praying On Balcony, Benten Shrine, Kakuban 2390.00
Japanese, Hokusai, Fuji From Mishima Pass, Kai Province, Oban, Yoko-e 3680.00
Japanese, Hokusai, Katsushika, Ferryboat At Onmayagashi, Matted, Frame, 12 x 15 In. .. 190.00
Japanese, Hokusai, Katsushika, Urashima Entering Dragon Palace, Oban Yoko-e 4780.00
Japanese, Hokusai, Katsushika, Wild Pinks, Shells For Genroku Poems Series, Kakuban . 2390.00
Japanese, Kasamatsu, Shiro, Cherry Trees On Temple Ground, Frame, Oban, Tate-e 405.00
Japanese, Kasamatsu, Shiro, Farmer Returning Home, Frame, Oban, Tate-e 200.00
Japanese, Koitsu, Tsuchiya, Mount Fuji, Lake, Chuban 90.00
Japanese, Koitsu, Tsuchiya, Night Fishing & Ferry, Oban, Yoko-e 460.00
Japanese, Koitsu, Tsuchiya, Temple Lanterns & Gateway At Night, Oban, Tate-e 290.00
Japanese, Koitsu, Tsuchiya, Temple, Rain, Figures, Frame, Oban, Tate-e 145.00
Japanese, Koson, Goose Landing In Marsh, Frame, Hosoban 140.00
Japanese, Koson, Ohara, 2 White Geese, Grasses, Black Ground, Oban, Tate-e 405.00
Japanese, Koson, Ohara, Miyashima Shrine, Deer, Sunset, Chuban 375.00
Japanese, Koson, Ohara, Raven, Flowering Branches, Full Moon, Chuban 230.00
Japanese, Kunisada, Night Battle Scene, Silhouette Background, Frame, Oban, Triptych .. 230.00
Japanese, Kunisada, Sumo Wrestler, Red Apron, Calligraphy, Oban, Tate-e 115.00
Japanese, Kunisada, Utagawa, Actor Ichikawa Danzo, Head Portrait, Oban, Tate-e 5020.00
Japanese, Kunisada, Utagawa, Genji Admiring Morning Glories, Triptych, Oban, Tate-e .. 2390.00
Japanese, Kunisada, Women, Garden, Stone Lantern, Cherry Trees, Triptych 150.00
Japanese, Kuniyoshi, Man At Shrine, Drawn Blade, Oban, Tate-e 160.00
Japanese, Kuniyoshi, Ronin Warrior Cutting Through Shoji Screen, Oban, Tate-e 175.00
Japanese, Kuniyoshi, Yoshitsune Marching To Attack Castle, Triptych, Oban 890.00
Japanese, Sadahide, Hashimoto, American Merchant Visiting Yokohama, Oban, Tate-e .. 3346.00
Japanese, Sadahide, Hashimoto, Daimon Bridge, Yokohama, Triptych, Oban, Tate-e 2390.00
Japanese, Sadahide, Hashimoto, Tigers, Dragon, Yokohama, Triptych, Oban, Tate-e 6575.00
Japanese, Sadanobu, Hunters On Horses Chasing Wolf, Triptych 90.00
Japanese, Saito Kiyoshi, Persimmons In Aizu, 1996, 23 3/4 x 15 3/4 In. 2870.00
Japanese, Shigenobu, Yanagawa, Poem, No. 2, Collected Flowers Series, Kakuban 1555.00
Japanese, Shinsui, Ito, Nails, Modern Beauties, Second Series, 1936, 17 1/2 x 11 1/4 In. . 2630.00
Japanese, Shinsui, Ito, Snowy Night, 12 Beauties Series, 1923, 17 1/2 x 11 1/4 In. 7170.00
Japanese, Shinsui, Ito, Woman Penciling Eyebrows, Oban, Yoke-e 7670.00
Japanese, Shoson, Ohara, Shorebirds In A Marsh, Frame, Oban, Tate-e 115.00
Japanese, Shoson, Parrot On Pomegranate, Chuban 175.00
Japanese, Shun'ei, Katsukawa, Actor Ichikawa Yaozo, Waterfall, Hosoban 1793.00
Japanese, Shunko, Katsukawa, Actors Ichikawa Danjuro, Nakamura Nakazo, Oban, Tate-e 3100.00
Japanese, Shunsho, Katsukawa, Act 2 Of Chushingura, Woman, Man, Chuban, Tate-e ... 2630.00
Japanese, Shunsho, Katsukawa, Actor Nakamura Nazako I As Pilgrim, Hosoban 4780.00
Japanese, Shunsho, Women In Garden, Oban, Tate-e 259.00
Japanese, Sozan, Ito, Morning Glories In A Field, Chuban 115.00
Japanese, Takahashi Hiroaki, Famous Place At Nikko, Yomei Gate, 15 1/2 x 10 1/4 In. 2629.00
Japanese, Toshikata, Mizuno, Scenes Of Women In The Bathhouse, 13 x 9 In., Pair 230.00
Japanese, Toyokuni, Man Jumping Near River, Mat, Frame, c.1820, 21 x 17 In. 315.00
Japanese, Toyokuni I, Woman & Child, Winter Kimono, Oban, Tate-e 315.00
Japanese, Toyokuni III, 2 Women, Man, Riverboats, Frame, Triptych, Oban 605.00
Japanese, Toyokuni III, Actors, Hydrangea, Oban, Tate-e 115.00
Japanese, Toyokuni III, Armored Warrior, Sword, Blue Ground, Frame, Oban, Tate-e 115.00
Japanese, Toyokuni III, Kitchen, Samurai, 2 Servants, Triptych, Oban 145.00
Japanese, Toyokuni III, Woman In Rainstorm, Frame, Oban, Tate-e 69.00
Japanese, Toyokuni, Utagawa, Play Scene, Ghost, Sleeping Woman, Oban, Tate-e 2850.00
Japanese, Utamaro, 2 Women, Flowering Bonsai Tree, Frame, Oban, Tate-e 660.00
Japanese, Utamaro, 2 Women, Peonies, 1 Sewing, Frame, Oban, Tate-e 400.00
Japanese, Utamaro, Kitagawa, Woman Threads Needle, Landscape Series, Oban, Tate-e . 4780.00
Japanese, Yoshida, Hiroshi, Benten Shrine In Negumigaseki, 1939, Oban 710.00
Japanese, Yoshida, Hiroshi, Fishes Of Honolulu, 1925, Oban, Yoko-e 1150.00

Japanese, Yoshida, Hiroshi, Grand Canyon, U.S. Series, 1925, Oban	1535.00
Japanese, Yoshida, Hiroshi, Misty Day In Nikko, 1937, Oban	472.00
Japanese, Yoshida, Hiroshi, Osaka Castle, 1935, Oban	590.00
Japanese, Yoshida, Toshi, Chimney Forest, 1951, Oban, Yoko-e	230.00
Japanese, Yoshida, Toshi, Eagle Owl, Oban, Tate-e	160.00
Japanese, Yoshida, Toshi, Sacred Mountains In Tibet, 1987, Dai Oban, Yoko-e	403.00
Japanese, Yoshiiku, Utagawa, Large Elephant, Yokohama, 1861, Oban, Tate-e	4185.00
Japanese, Yoshikazu, Utagawa, American Man, Woman, Clock, Yokohama, Oban, Tate-e .	2850.00
Japanese, Yoshikazu, Utagawa, Steam Locomotive, Yokohama, Triptych, Oban, Tate-e . . .	2850.00
Japanese, Yoshitora, Utagawa, England, Igirisu, Yokohama, Oban, Tate-e	5020.00
Japanese, Yoshitora, Utagawa, France, Yokohama, Triptych, Oban, Tate-e	2850.00
Japanese, Yoshitoshi, Full Moon, Tatami Mats, Pine Branch Shadows, 1885, Oban, Tate-e	375.00
Japanese, Yoshitoshi, Moon Above Sea At Daimotsu Bay, 1886, Oban, Tate-e	1550.00
Keep, George C., Portland Head Light, 4 x 5 In.	55.00
Kellog, Shakers, Mode Of Worship, Hand Colored Lithograph, 12 1/2 x 16 1/2 In.	1495.00
Lamson, Moonlight, 9 x 14 In.	65.00
Leand, David, Baby's Welcome, 14 x 17 In.	50.00
Lithograph, Common American Deer, J.T. Bowen, Philadelphia, 21 1/2 x 27 1/2 In.	1495.00
Lithograph, Diana The Huntress, Alberto Vargas, 29 x 21 1/4 In.	345.00
Lithograph, Geometric Landscape, Alexander Caldwell, 6 1/4 x 11 1/4 In.	230.00
Lithograph, My Wonderful Son, My Pride For All Years, Morris & Bendien, Art Deco . . .	45.00
Maynard, King Solomon Building Temple Of Jerusalem, c.1790, 15 x 9 1/2 In.	173.00
Northend, Mary Harrod, An Early Garden, c.1910, 14 x 16 In.	55.00
Northend, Mary Harrod, Cohassett Garden, c.1910, 14 x 16 In.	28.00

Nutting prints are now popular with collectors. Wallace Nutting is known for his pictures, furniture, and books. Nutting *prints* are actually hand-colored photographs issued from 1900 to 1941. There are over 10,000 different titles. Wallace Nutting furniture is listed in the Furniture category.

Nutting, A Call In State, 12 x 17 In.	90.00
Nutting, Absorbing Tale, 13 x 16 In.	275.00
Nutting, Afternoon In Nantucket, 14 x 17 In.	130.00
Nutting, Almost Ready, 8 x 10 In.	65.00
Nutting, Along The Garden, 12 x 16 In.	110.00
Nutting, Androscoggin Elms, 13 x 16 In.	255.00
Nutting, Anxious To Please, 2 Girls, In Parlor, With Hats & Boxes, 10 x 12 In.	110.00
Nutting, As It Was In 1700, 8 x 12 In.	165.00
Nutting, At The Well, Sorrento, 7 1/2 x 13 1/2 In.	130.00
Nutting, Barnet Curve, 11 x 14 In.	85.00
Nutting, Below The Arches, 13 x 16 In.	88.00
Nutting, Between The Spruces, 12 x 16 In.	99.00
Nutting, Birch Mountain, 10 x 19 In.	187.00
Nutting, Blossoms At The Bend, 14 x 16 In.	120.00
Nutting, Breakfast Hour, 11 x 17 In.	248.00
Nutting, Bridesmaids' Procession, 9 x 15 In.	70.00
Nutting, California Hill Tops, 12 x 14 In.	220.00
Nutting, Call Of The Country, 8 x 10 In.	20.00
Nutting, Caroline's Garden, 10 x 12 In.	145.00
Nutting, Chestnut By The Bars, 11 x 14 In.	220.00
Nutting, Cliff Clingers, Lake Mohonk, N.Y., 10 x 18 In.	110.00
Nutting, Coming Out Of Rosa, 10 x 12 In. . . . . .99.00 to 110.00
Nutting, Coming Out Of Rosa, Girl, On Porch, Holding Mother's Hand, 13 x 16 In.	170.00
Nutting, Decked As A Bride, 11 x 14 In.	88.00
Nutting, Delaware Water Gap, 12 x 16 In.	900.00
Nutting, Dell Blossoms, 9 x 11 In.	65.00
Nutting, Down From Mt. Washington, 10 x 12 In.	90.00
Nutting, Draped In Blossoms, 14 x 17 In.	165.00
Nutting, Durham, 7 x 9 In.	65.00
Nutting, Elaborate Dinner, 15 x 18 In.	145.00
Nutting, Elm Drapery, 12 x 20 In.	65.00
Nutting, Evangeline Lane, 9 x 11 In.	145.00
Nutting, Eventful Journey, 13 x 16 In.	715.00

Nutting, Fireside Contentment, 14 x 17 In. 90.00
Nutting, Flume Falls, 12 x 15 In. 100.00
Nutting, Forest Side Blossoms, 13 x 16 In. 105.00
Nutting, Fryeburg Waters, 13 x 16 In. 200.00
Nutting, Gettysburg Crossing, 13 x 15 In. 300.00
Nutting, Goose Chase Pattern, 10 x 16 In. 50.00
Nutting, Gorgeous May, 10 x 12 In. 55.00
Nutting, Grace Before Meat, 10 x 12 In. 165.00
Nutting, Green Mountain Range, 11 x 17 In. 65.00
Nutting, Hawthorn Dell, 10 x 12 In. 65.00
Nutting, Heifers By The Stream, 8 1/2 x 14 In. 330.00
Nutting, Hesitancy, 13 x 16 In. 440.00
Nutting, His Move, Uncle Sam, Granny, Play Checkers, Signed, 13 x 16 In. 600.00
Nutting, His Rose, 6 x 12 In. 90.00
Nutting, Hollyhock Cottage, 14 x 17 In. ....80.00 to 120.00
Nutting, Honeymoon Cottage, 14 x 20 In. 55.00
Nutting, Honeymoon Drive, Frame, 13 x 10 In. 125.00
Nutting, Into The Birch Wood, 13 x 16 In. ....50.00 to 78.00
Nutting, Iris & Portulaca, 9 x 11 In. 39.00
Nutting, Jersey Blossoms, 11 x 14 In. 130.00
Nutting, June Beautiful, 10 x 12 In. 65.00
Nutting, Larkspur, c.1915, 17 x 21 In. 175.00
Nutting, Life Of The Golden Age, 15 x 22 In. 300.00
Nutting, Lights Of Venice, 9 x 13 In. 120.00
Nutting, Little Rose Of Ireland, 12 x 16 In. 2090.00
Nutting, Maine Coast Sky, 14 x 17 In. 77.00
Nutting, Many Happy Returns, 11 x 14 In. 50.00
Nutting, Maple Sugar Cupboard, 14 x 20 In. 121.00
Nutting, May Drive, 11 x 14 In. 100.00
Nutting, Memory Of Childhood, 10 x 12 In. 66.00
Nutting, Moat Mountain, 10 x 12 In. 132.00
Nutting, Natural Bridge, 6 x 8 In. 28.00
Nutting, Nova Scotia Idyll, 9 x 11 In. 176.00
Nutting, October Byway, 12 x 15 In. 155.00
Nutting, Old Back Door, 10 x 14 In. 66.00
Nutting, Old Time Gallant, 13 x 15 In. 176.00
Nutting, On Dress Parade, 12 x 20 In. 66.00
Nutting, On The Avon, 3 Ducks Swim In Lake, Houses, Cathedral Spire, 14 x 17 In. 370.00
Nutting, Orchard Heights, 11 x 14 In. 80.00
Nutting, Paradise Portal, 13 x 16 In. 440.00
Nutting, Pasture At Muckross, 10 x 16 In. 275.00
Nutting, Pasture Pool, 16 x 20 In. 155.00
Nutting, Path Of Roses, 13 x 16 In. 660.00
Nutting, Patriarch In Bloom, c.1915, 13 x 16 In. 110.00
Nutting, Pine Landing, 12 x 20 In. 99.00
Nutting, Pioneer Cottage, 12 x 15 In. 198.00
Nutting, Poplar Lane, Green, Grassy, Country Road, Birch & Poplar Trees, 9 x 18 In. 200.00
Nutting, Prudence Drawing Tea, 14 x 17 In. 110.00
Nutting, Purity & Grace, 16 x 20 In. 110.00
Nutting, Rangeley Shore, 13 x 16 In. 90.00
Nutting, Red Berries, 8 x 10 In. 132.00
Nutting, Red Berries, Close Frames, 3 x 4 In. 165.00
Nutting, Rest After Sewing, 12 x 15 In. 138.00
Nutting, River Meadow, 14 x 17 In. 176.00
Nutting, Robed In White, 6 x 7 In. 45.00
Nutting, Ross-On-Wye, 7 x 9 In. 55.00
Nutting, Russet & Gold, 16 x 20 In. 100.00
Nutting, Sea Ledges, 12 x 15 In. 110.00
Nutting, Shell Top Cupboard, 11 x 17 In. 85.00
Nutting, Sheltered, Country Road, Tall Trees, White Wooden Fences, 13 x 15 In. 200.00
Nutting, Silhouette, Bird, 4 x 4 In. 35.00
Nutting, Silhouette, Birdcage, 4 x 4 In. 55.00

Nutting, Silhouette, Lamb, 4 x 4 In. 35.00
Nutting, Slack Water, 7 x 9 In. 22.00
Nutting, Snow At The Bend, 14 x 17 In. 35.00
Nutting, Softness Of Spring, 17 x 21 In. 145.00
Nutting, Spinning, 13 x 16 In. 77.00
Nutting, Spring In The Dell, 13 x 15 In. 116.00
Nutting, Springfield Blossoms, 12 x 15 In. 130.00
Nutting, Stately Tea Pouring, 16 x 20 In. 66.00
Nutting, Stitch In Time, 14 x 17 In. 99.00
Nutting, Sturdy Beauty, 11 x 17 In. 110.00
Nutting, Summer Grotto, 18 x 22 In. 130.00
Nutting, Summer On The Avon, 15 x 22 In. 150.00
Nutting, Summer Wind, 16 x 20 In. 132.00
Nutting, Sunshine & Music, 13 x 17 In. 28.00
Nutting, Sweet Williams, 11 x 13 In. 825.00
Nutting, Swimming Pool, Stream, Rocky Banks, 20 x 30 In. 200.00
Nutting, There's Rosemary, Girl, Greets Friend On Porch, 13 x 16 In. 450.00
Nutting, Tranquility Farm, 13 x 16 In. 385.00
Nutting, Untrodden Shore, 13 x 16 In. 75.00
Nutting, Up The Half Stair, 11 x 17 In. 120.00
Nutting, Venice Afar, 13 x 15 In. 1320.00
Nutting, Warm Spring Day, 6 x 9 In. 39.00
Nutting, Warm Spring Day, Sheep, 14 x 17 In. 145.00
Nutting, Washington Cherry Blossoms, 8 x 10 In. 55.00
Nutting, Watersmeet, 14 x 17 In. 130.00
Nutting, Westfield Water, 10 x 16 In. 66.00
Nutting, Westfield Water, 18 x 22 In. 120.00
Nutting, Windsor Roadside, 9 x 11 In. 248.00
Nutting, World Beautiful, 10 x 12 In. 110.00
Nutting, Zinnias, 13 x 16 In. 1540.00
O'Klein, Boris, Naughty Dogs, 11 x 22 In. 50.00
Ohio Art, Cupid Asleep, Lithographed Tin Frame, Oval, 7 x 5 1/2 In. .... *Illus* 28.00

Parrish prints are wanted by collectors. Maxfield Frederick Parrish
was an illustrator who lived from 1870 to 1966. He is best known as a
designer of magazine covers, posters, calendars, and advertisements.

Parrish, Christmas Morn, c.1950, 6 x 8 In. 28.00
Parrish, Garden Of Allah, 16 x 30 In. 200.00
Parrish, King Of Black Isles, c.1907, 13 x 16 In. 100.00
Parrish, Lazy Land, c.1912, 3 3/4 x 12 In. 75.00
Parrish, Love's Pilgrimage, 3 3/4 x 12 In. 120.00
Parrish, Lute Players, 12 x 18 In. 130.00
Parrish, Lute Players, c.1924, 18 x 30 In. 385.00
Parrish, Morning, 12 x 15 In. .... 155.00 to 250.00
Parrish, Old King Cole, c.1906, 11 x 30 In. 770.00
Parrish, Peaceful Valley, c.1936, 5 1/2 x 7 1/2 In. 90.00
Parrish, Perfect Day, 12 x 15 In. 200.00
Parrish, Perfect Day, 18 x 22 In. 120.00
Parrish, Perfect Day, June Skies, 4 x 6 In. 160.00
Parrish, Royal Gorge Of The Colorado, 16 x 20 In. 200.00
Parrish, Sea Nymphs, 11 x 14 In. 180.00
Parrish, Stars, 10 x 14 In. 225.00
Parrish, Stars, Nude On Rock, Label, 6 x 10 In. 310.00
Parrish, Theater At Villa Gori, Italian Villas, Trees, Garden, c.1910, 6 x 9 In. 70.00
Parrish, Twilight, 18 x 22 In. 210.00
Parrish, Twilight, Christmas Card, 1950s, 6 x 7 In. 50.00
Parrish, Wild Geese, 12 x 15 In. 165.00
Pressier, Gene, A Fair Equestrienne, 10 x 21 In. 100.00
Redoute, Botanical, Andromeda, Daphne, Hand Tinted, Frame, 20 x 17 In., Pair 355.00
Robinson, Katherine, Miami Beach, c.1915, 10 x 12 In. 22.00
Rockwell, Doctor & Boy, Black & White, 19 x 25 In. 2094.00
Rockwell, Expected & Unexpected, Signed, Numbered, 15 x 16 In. 518.00

Rockwell, Gilding The Eagle, Old Man Painting Eagle, Signed, 21 x 26 In. 2132.00
Rockwell, Teacher's Pet, Signed, Numbered, 22 x 18 In. 978.00
Rockwell, Visit To The Doctor's Office, Signed, Numbered, 22 x 19 1/2 In. 920.00
Sawyer, Ammonoosuc At Twin Mountain, 11 x 14 In. 138.00
Sawyer, Bridge Of Flowers, 8 x 10 In. 99.00
Sawyer, Charles, Echo Lake, c.1915, 7 x 9 In. 39.00
Sawyer, Eventide, Lake Winnipesaukee, 7 x 9 In. 61.00
Sawyer, New England Road In May, 13 x 20 In. 83.00
Sawyer, Old Man Of The Mountains, 8 x 10 In. 132.00
Strand, Paul, Delta Upsilon Colgate, c.1920, 11 x 13 In. 50.00
Thompson, Fred, Autumn Twilight, c.1915, 13 x 16 In. 39.00
Thompson, Fred, Fireside Dreams, c.1915, 13 x 15 In. 88.00
Thompson, Fred, Sailing Schooner, Homeward Bound, 5 x 7 In. 94.00
Thompson, Fred, The Arbor, 6 x 12 In. 275.00
Thompson, Fred, Tired Of Spinning, 7 x 9 In. 50.00
Waugh, Ida, Infant, c.1900, 10 x 13 In. 11.00
Waugh, Ida, Young Boy, c.1900, 10 x 12 In. 22.00

Woodblock prints that are not in the Japanese tradition are listed here.
Most were made in England and the United States during the Arts and
Crafts period. Japanese woodblock prints are listed under Print,
Japanese.

Woodblock, Augis, Marcel, Moulin En Touraine, Frame, Titled & Signed, 8 1/4 x 6 In. ... 259.00
Woodblock, Bailey, Henrietta, Moss-Covered Oak Tree, Mat, Frame, 10 x 7 In. 2940.00
Woodblock, Bates, Pierce, 2 Bass, Lily Pads, 3 Colors, Signed, 10 x 13 In. 33.00
Woodblock, Bates, Pierce, 3 Trout, 3 Colors, Signed, 10 x 13 In. 45.00
Woodblock, Baumann, Gustave, Eagle Ceremony At Tesuque Pueblo, c.1932, 8 1/4 In. ... 1035.00
Woodblock, Bixler, David, Church, Painted, Lancaster Co., Frame, c.1864, 3 3/4 x 3 In. .. 4950.00
Woodblock, Bixler, David, Dove, Painted, Lancaster Co., Frame, c.1864, 3 3/4 x 3 In. ... 4675.00
Woodblock, Chase, Waldo, Dockside, Fishing Boat, Mat, Frame, Signed, 1931, 6 x 11 In. . 520.00
Woodblock, Chase, Waldo, Nomad, Fishing Boat, Silhouette, Mat, Frame, 1932, 12 x 7 In. 1265.00
Woodblock, Courtyard With Figures, c.1920, 5 1/4 x 5 1/4 In. 290.00
Woodblock, Gearhart, Frances, Monterey Cypresses, Mat, Frame, Signed, 9 x 6 3/4 In. ... 4600.00
Woodblock, Gearhart, Frances, Quiet, Mountain Scene, Mat, Frame, Signed, 9 x 5 1/2 In. 4900.00
Woodblock, Gearhart, Frances, Snowy Mountain Landscape, Mat, Frame, 6 x 4 1/2 In. ... 2185.00
Woodblock, Hall, Norma Basset, Game Creek Bridge, Landscape, Frame, 14 1/2 x 12 In. . 430.00
Woodblock, Howey, R.L., Coastal Scene, Arts & Crafts Oak Frame, 6 1/2 x 5 1/2 In. 375.00
Woodblock, Hyde, Helen, Butterflies, Child, Frame, Signed, 1908, 7 x 2 1/2 In. 230.00
Woodblock, Hyde, Helen, Children Pushing Cart, Mat, 5 x 4 1/2 In. 260.00
Woodblock, Hyde, Helen, Three Friends Of Winter, 1913, 5 x 8 In. 430.00
Woodblock, Hyde, Helen, Woman, Child, Iris Field, 1910, 7 x 15 In. 920.00
Woodblock, Lum, Bertha, Bridge, Signed, 1913, 5 x 9 3/4 In. 645.00
Woodblock, Lum, Bertha, Chinese Children At Play, Signed, 4 1/2 x 7 In. 290.00
Woodblock, Lum, Bertha, Dragon Well, Signed, 8 1/2 x 11 3/4 In. 545.00
Woodblock, Lum, Bertha, Processing, Signed, 1916, 13 1/2 x 19 1/4 In. 470.00
Woodblock, Lum, Bertha, Spinning Goddess, Signed, 1916, 13 1/2 x 19 1/4 In. 940.00
Woodblock, Patterson, Margaret, Foxglove, Pink, Blue, Green Vase, Frame, 10 x 7 In. ... 2875.00
Woodblock, Patterson, Margaret, Morning Glories, Purple, Green Vase, Frame, 10 x 7 In. .. 2875.00

Print, Ohio Art, Cupid
Asleep, Lithographed
Tin Frame, Oval,
7 x 5 1/2 In.

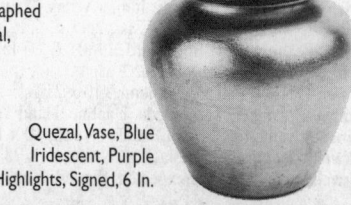

Quezal, Vase, Blue
Iridescent, Purple
Highlights, Signed, 6 In.

Woodblock, Rice, William, Glacial Lake-Sierras, Signed, Mat, Frame, 6 x 8 In.	590.00
Woodblock, Richert, Charles, Covered Bridge In Autumn, Mat, Frame, 5 x 7 In.	750.00
Woodblock, Richert, Charles, Maine Fishing Village, Birch Trees, Mat, Frame, 5 x 7 In. ...	635.00
Woodblock, Richert, Charles, Sea Gulls, Mat, Frame, Signed, 4 x 4 3/4 In.	490.00
Woodblock, Richert, Charles, Up For Repairs, Boat, Anchor, Mat, Frame, 4 3.4 x 6 3/4 In.	520.00
Woodblock, Rothby, Carl, Figures, Fall Trees, Gold, Brown, Signed, Frame, 5 x 7 In.	259.00
Woodblock, Smith, Edward C., Benjamin's Arrival Phila., Frame, 1940s, 14 x 17 In.	55.00
Woodblock, Taylor, Ora Nelson, Calla Lilies, Black Ground, Mounted, 6 1/2 x 8 1/2 In. ..	259.00
Wright, Frank Lloyd, Dana House, Wasmuth, Mat, Arts & Crafts Oak Frame, 14 x 24 In. .	980.00
Wright, Frank Lloyd, McArthur House, Wasmuth, 18 x 13 1/2 In.	430.00
Yard Long, Indian Maiden, Frame, 9 x 32 In.	285.00
Yard Long, Lady, Yellow Dress, Black Stole, Frame, 8 x 35 In.	110.00
Yard Long, Victorian Lady, Lavender Dress, Frame, 11 x 38 In.	165.00
Yard Long, Victorian Lady, White Dress, Hat, Red Ground, Frame, 8 x 35 In.	300.00
Yellin, Samuel, Washington Cathedral, Memorial Gates, Frame, 16 x 10 In.	1150.00

PURINTON POTTERY COMPANY was incorporated in Wellsville, Ohio, in 1936. The company moved to Shippenville, Pennsylvania, in 1941 and made a variety of hand-painted ceramic wares. By the 1950s Purinton was making dinnerware, souvenirs, cookie jars, and florist wares. The pottery closed in 1959.

Purinton Pottery

Apple, Jug, 4 1/2	35.00
Apple, Sugar & Creamer, Cover	30.00
Apple, Teapot, 6 Cup, 6 1/2 x 7 1/4 In.	90.00
Apple, Teapot, Round Body, 2 Cup, 4 In.	30.00
Fruit, Cookie Jar, 9 1/2 x 6 In.	100.00
Fruit, Oil & Vinegar, Square, 9 1/2 In.	80.00
Fruit, Tidbit, 2 Tiers, 14 In.	20.00
Intaglio, Baker, Ivory, Brown Slip, 7 In.	18.00
Intaglio, Bean Pot, Cover	35.00
Intaglio, Bowl, 8 In.	5.00
Intaglio, Bowl, Dessert, 4 In.	6.00
Intaglio, Cookie Jar, Brown, Square, 9 1/2 x 6 In.	75.00
Intaglio, Jug, 5 Pt., 8 In.	75.00
Intaglio, Mug, Flower & Leaf, 8 Oz., 4 In.	30.00
Intaglio, Plate, 8 1/2 In.	10.00
Intaglio, Plate, Dinner, 9 3/4 In.	13.00
Intaglio, Plate, Salad, 6 3/4 In.	7.00
Intaglio, Platter, Ivory, Brown Slip	18.00
Intaglio, Saucer, 5 1/4 In.	4.00
Mountain Rose, Teapot, 2 Cup, No Cover, 4 In.	10.00
Normandy Plaid, Casserole, Cover	39.00
Normandy Plaid, Cup & Saucer	15.00
Normandy Plaid, Jug, 2 Qt., 7 1/2 x 10 1/2 In.	88.00
Normandy Plaid, Plate, Dinner, 9 3/4 In.	9.00
Normandy Plaid, Sugar, Cover	18.00
Normandy Plaid, Teapot, Cover	50.00
Pennsylvania Dutch, Plate, Sandwich	35.00
Red Ivy, Jug, Honey, 6 1/4 In. ....20.00 to 45.00
Seaform, Plate, Dinner, 9 3/4 In.	25.00
Shooting Star, Jug, Honey, 6 1/4 In.	35.00
Shooting Star, Vase, 5 3/4 In.	45.00
Tulip & Vine, Jug, 2 Qt., 5 1/2 In.	35.00

PURSES have been recognizable since the eighteenth century, when leather and needlework purses were preferred. Beaded purses became popular in the nineteenth century, went out of style, but are again in use. Mesh purses date from the 1880s and are still being made. How to carry a handkerchief and lipstick is a problem today for every woman, including the Queen of England.

18K Gold, Flap, Diamond Scalloped Edge, Initials, Van Cleef & Arpels	5290.00
18K Gold, Sapphire, Diamond, Openwork Frame, Flower Vines	1645.00
Alligator Skin, Ebony & Rhinestone Clasp, Marked Created By Original Hand Bag Co. ...	345.00

Basket, Wood, White, Poodle, Plexiglas Lid, Rhinestones, Jerri's Of Miami, 3 1/4 x 11 In.   225.00
Beaded, Black Beaded Poodle, Back Zipper, France, 12 3/4 x 12 1/4 In. 1100.00
Beaded, Flower Petit Point Center, Gold Plate Hinge, Clasp, Chain, Lining, 6 x 5 1/2 In. .   80.00
Beaded, Flower Petit Point, Gold Plated Hinge Clasp, Chain, Lining, 6 x 5 1/2 In. 90.00
Beaded, Flowers, Geometric Design, Fringe, Suede Lining, Gilt Frame, 8 In. 69.00
Beaded, Multicolored Flowers, Beaded Handle, Silk Lining, Tiffany, c.1950s 175.00
Beaded, Multicolored, Enameled Silver Frame, Chain, Pastel, Fringe, 9 x 6 In. 70.00
Beaded, Pearl, Deco Style, Silver, Finger Loop Handles, Zipper, Lining, 5 3/4 x 7 In. 90.00
Beadwork, Art Deco, Egyptian Revival, Bakelite, Winged Scarab 355.00
Beadwork, Black, White, Green, Orange, Drawstring 195.00
Beadwork, Geometric & Floral Pattern, Dankbarheit, 4 1/2 x 3 1/4 In. 60.00
Beadwork, Petit Point, Chain, Silk Lining, Gold Plated Clasp, France, 6 x 7 In. 55.00
Briefcase, Alligator, De Vecchi, Hamilton Hodge, Italy, 13 x 17 1/2 In. 885.00
Coin, Mesh, Edwardian, Flowers, 14K Gold 355.00
Coin, Mesh, Ruby, Diamonds, 18K Gold, Edwardian 705.00
Dance, Silver, Poodle, 2 Compacts, Ivorine Dance Card, Money Clip, No. 800 & 739 . . . .   800.00
Deco, Silver, Simulated Pearl, Silk Lining, Zipper Top, Belgium, 5 3/4 x 7 In. 80.00
Decoupage, Octagonal, Wood, Poodle Design, Kay Murphy, 1973, 6 x 9 1/2 In. 325.00
Fabric, Green Floss, Satin Stitch, Geometric Flowers, Arts & Crafts, c.1910, 8 x 7 In. 230.00
Leather, Constance, Front Flap, Goldtone Fittings, Adjustable Strap, 2 Pockets, Hermes . .   499.00
Leather, Shell, Overlay Tortoise Design, Divided Compartments, Czechoslovokia, 7 In. . .   175.00
Leather, Tou Dou, Adjustable Leather Strap, Hermes, Box 175.00
Leather, Woman's High Button Shoe Shape, Late 1800s, 5 1/4 In. 35.00
Lipstick Case, Brass, Lancome, Cocktail Shaker Shape, Cupid, Bird, c.1940, 2 In. 210.00
Lipstick Case, Compact, Silver, Enameled, Red, Black Geometric, c.1925, 2 1/2 x 2 In. . .   1685.00
Lipstick Case, Silver, Column Shape, Boucheron, c.1939, 2 1/2 In. 1350.00
Lizard, Hexagonal, Blue, 2 Pockets, Goldtone Fittings, Lana Marks 765.00
Mesh, 14K Gold, 3 Colors, Leaf, Flower Frame, c.1910 . . . .   1530.00
Mesh, 14K Gold, Beaded Tassels, Engraved Openwork Frame, 4 x 2 1/2 In. 495.00
Mesh, 14K Gold, Diamond, Sapphire, Bezel Set, Engraved Frame, Carter, Gough & Co. . . .   940.00
Mesh, Colored, Gold Washed Frame, Whiting & Davis, 5 x 4 In. 195.00
Mesh, Edwardian, Sapphire Cabochon, Pierced, Engraved Frame, Link Chain, 14K Gold .   1765.00
Mesh, Silver, Arabesque Wrist Style, Beaded, 7 x 5 1/4 In. 195.00
Mesh, Steel, Gilt Frame, Tassel, Fleur-De-Lis Style, Brass & Silver Color Beads, 10 In. . .   66.00
Mesh, Sterling, 2-Part Hinged Clasp, Repousse Flowers, Leaves, Gorham, 6 1/2 x 4 1/2 In.   185.00
Mesh, Sterling, Flower Engraved Top, 5 1/4 x 7 1/2 In. .50.00 to 56.00
Mesh, Sterling, Hinged Clasp, Repouse Flowers, No. B570M, Gorham, 6 1/2 x 4 1/2 In. . .   165.00
Mesh, Sterling, Jeweled Frame, Cabochons, Bead Tassels, c.1909, 5 x 5 5/8 In. 125.00
Micro-Beaded, Castle On River, Silver Gilt Frame, Flowers, Swans, Silk Lining 290.00
Micro-Beaded, Lilacs, Leaves, Beaded Fringe, Gilt Frame, 10 1/2 In. 210.00
Nantucket, Basket, Ivory & Leather Trim, Whale, Barlow 230.00
Nantucket, Basket, Ivory Trim, Bird 115.00
Needlework, Wool Bargello, Linen, Green, Made By Harriet Jones, Penn., 5 1/2 x 10 In. . .   60.00
Patent Leather, Black, Seated Poodle, Soure Bag, New York, 11 1/2 In. 10.00
Pave Set, Stones, Tasseled Cord, Comb, Mirror, Round, Judith Leiber 529.00
Plastic, Poodle, Black, Eiffel Tower, Black Cloth, Wood Bottom, 10 1/2 In. 120.00
Plastic & Seashell, White, Poodle, Flip Top Lid, Wood Base, 9 1/2 x 10 In. 20.00
Shadowbox Frame, Blue, Gilt, Silver Beads, Gilt Chain, Art Deco, c.1920, 20 1/2 x 12 In.   355.00
Silk, Fabric, Leather, Conte De Fees, Black, Applique Landscape, Louis Vuitton 355.00
Velvet, Embossed Bird, Goldtone Fittings, Leather Interior & Handle, Mirror, Bottles 265.00
Wood, Carved, Poodle Head, Timmy Woods, Beverly Hills, 6 3/4 x 7 In. 50.00
Wool, Black, Beaded Poodle, Plastic Handle, 11 1/2 In. 20.00

QUEZAL glass was made from 1901 to 1924 by Martin Bach, Sr., in Queens, New York. Other glassware by other firms, such as Loetz, Steuben, and Tiffany, resembles this gold-colored iridescent glass. Martin Bach died in 1921. His son-in-law, Conrad Vahlsing, Jr., went to work at the Lustre Art Company about 1920 and his son, Martin Bach, Jr., worked at the Durand Art Glass division of the Vineland Flint Glass Works after 1924.

Quezal

Bottle, Scent, Gold, 4 Vertical Ribs, 6-Sided Stopper, 7 1/2 In.   750.00
Bowl, Gold Iridescent, Classical Shape, Low Pedestal, c.1905, 9 1/2 In. 115.00

Bowl, Opal Iridescent, Green, Amethyst Flowers, Gold Iridescent Interior, Signed, 12 In. . 745.00
Bowl, Silver Blue Iridescent, Pulled Feather, Brown Iridescent, 6 In. 2300.00
Candlestick, Blue Iridescent, Tapered, Knop Stem, Pulled Flat Rim, Signed, 10 In., Pair . . 1100.00
Compote, Apricot, Gold Iridescent Interior, Signed, 4 1/2 In. 880.00
Compote, Blue Opalescent, Signed, 6 x 4 1/2 In. 800.00
Compote, Gold Iridescent, Bulbous, Ruffled Rim, Signed, 5 x 6 In. 1000.00
Compote, Gold Iridescent, Raised Rim, Round, Flared Pedestal, Signed, 2 1/4 In. 315.00
Compote, Iridescent, Amber, Green Swirl Under, Shallow Dish Top, c.1900, 5 3/8 In. 885.00
Compote, Pulled Feathers, 7 In. 2530.00
Compote, Sweet Pea, Opal, Green Pulled Feathers, Ruffled Stretched Rim, Signed, 6 In. . 3575.00
Decanter, Gold Iridescent, Engraved Maud, 9 In. 360.00
Lamp, Hanging, Green & Gold, Pulled Feathers, 3 Chains, Early 1900s, 23 x 6 3/8 In. . . . 4115.00
Lamp, Lily, 8-Arm, Bronze, Iridescent Shades, Signed, 20 1/2 In. 4760.00
Plate, Gold Iridescent, Amber, Stretched Rim, Signed, 6 1/4 In. 330.00
Salt, Blue Iridescent, Gold, Ribbed, Ruffled Edge, Signed, 2 x 2 1/2 In. 385.00
Salt, Gold Iridescent, Ribbed, Signed, 1 x 2 3/4 In. 250.00
Salt, Gold Iridescent, Ribbed, Signed, 2 1/2 In. 165.00
Shade, Blue & Green Pulled Feathers, Ivory Ground, Signed, 6 In. 630.00
Shade, Candle, Gold Pulled Feathers, Ivory Ground, Signed, 3 1/2 In., 5 Piece 1840.00
Shade, Flower Form, Gold Latticework, Ivory Ground, Squat, Signed, 3 3/4 In. 345.00
Shade, Flower Form, Pulled Feather, Gold, Green, Frosted Ground, Signed, 5 In. 175.00
Shade, Gold & Green Pulled Feathers, Ivory Ground, Flared, Signed, 5 1/4 In. 345.00
Shade, Gold & Green Pulled Feathers, Ivory Ground, Signed, 4 3/4 In. 230.00
Shade, Gold Iridescent Ribbons, Opalescent Body, Ribbed, Signed, 5 In. 530.00
Shade, Green & Gold Pulled Leaves, Cream Ground, Threading, 5 In., 6 Piece 1765.00
Shade, Trumpet, Gold, Embossed Diamond Pattern, Signed, 5 1/2 In. 230.00
Shade, Tulip Form, Ribbed, Gold, Green, Pulled Feathers, Opalescent, Signed, 5 1/2 In. . . 575.00
Shade, Tulip Form, Threading, Pulled Feathers, Signed, 5 1/4 In., 4 Piece 920.00
Sherbet, Gold Iridescent, Signed, 4 In. 495.00
Vase, Automobile, Lily, Iridescent Gold, Rolled Rim, Signed, 10 1/2 In. 580.00
Vase, Blue Iridescent, Pulled Coils, Opalescent, Cylindrical, Signed, 6 1/2 In. 1200.00
Vase, Blue Iridescent, Purple Highlights, Signed, 6 In. . . . . *Illus* 635.00
Vase, Blue, Amber, Green Coils, Opalescent, Tapered, Flared Rim, Signed, 5 1/2 In. 1650.00
Vase, Calla Lily Form, Gold Iridescent, Blue Tipped Rim, Signed, 8 1/2 In. 1100.00
Vase, Flower Form, Gold Iridescent, Green Feathers, Flared, Ruffled Edge, 5 3/4 In. 3110.00
Vase, Flower Form, Green Pulled Feathers, Gold Tipped, Opal, Ruffled Edge, 5 In. 4020.00
Vase, Flower Form, Opal, Pulled Iridescent Feathers, Gold Striated, Signed, 6 1/2 In. 2700.00
Vase, Flower Form, Threaded, Gold Iridescent, Wide Mouth, Early 1900s, 8 1/4 In. 1060.00
Vase, Gold Iridescent, Baluster, Flared Neck, Footed, Signed, 9 In. 385.00
Vase, Gold Iridescent, Bulbous, Round Neck, Signed, 8 1/2 In. 1320.00
Vase, Gold Iridescent, Pinched Body, Flared Rim, Signed, 2 3/4 In. 345.00
Vase, Gold Iridescent, Pulled Vine & Leaves, 4 7/8 In. 2235.00
Vase, Gold Iridescent, Ruffled Edge, 3 In. 375.00
Vase, Gold Iridescent, Silver Overlay Flowers, Signed, c.1920, 7 In. 1800.00
Vase, Gold Iridescent, White Pulled Stripes, Ruffled Edge, Footed, c.1915, 6 1/4 In. 1910.00
Vase, Gold Zipper, Green Pulled Feather, Cream Ground, Signed, 6 In. 1725.00
Vase, Green & Gold, Hooked Swirl, 6 In. 920.00
Vase, Green & White, Pulled Feather, Gold Trim, 6 In. 1380.00
Vase, Green Iridescent, Applied Ribbed Lily Pads, 14 1/4 In. 4715.00
Vase, Jack-In-The-Pulpit, Amber Iridescent, Pink & Green Rings, c.1920, 13 In. 8800.00
Vase, Jack-In-The-Pulpit, Gold Iridescent, Green & Magenta Highlights, 1915, 14 In. 7770.00
Vase, Jack-In-The-Pulpit, Gold Iridescent, Green Pulled Feathers, 13 1/4 In. 5975.00
Vase, Jack-In-The-Pulpit, Gold Iridescent, Purple Highlights, Signed, 8 1/2 In. 2645.00
Vase, King Tut, Cover, Green, Blue, Golden Pink Iridescent Ground, Baluster, 13 In. 2300.00
Vase, King Tut, Gold Iridescent Swirls, Cream Ground, Signed, 8 1/2 In. 2070.00
Vase, King Tut, Gold Iridescent, Green & Blue Swirl, 10 In. 1550.00
Vase, Lily, Gold Iridescent, Ruffled Folds, Signed, 4 1/2 In. 385.00
Vase, Opalescent Yellow, Green Iridescent Ribs, Striated Feathers, Petals, c.1902, 9 1/2 In. 2820.00
Vase, Silvery Blue Iridescent, Gold Neck, Silver Overlay, 5 In. 980.00
Vase, Trumpet, Gold Iridescent, Blue Rim, Raised Disc Foot, Signed, 8 x 3 In. 600.00
Vase, Trumpet, Gold Iridescent, Opal, Pulled Petals & Hooks, Pillow, Signed, 4 1/4 In. . . . 3300.00
Vase, Trumpet, Opalescent, Iridescent, Petals, Green Pulled Feathers, Oval, Signed, 8 In. . 6160.00

QUILTS have been made since the seventeenth century. Early textiles were very precious, and every scrap was saved to be reused. A quilt is a combination of fabrics joined to a filler and a backing by small stitched designs known as quilting. An appliqued quilt has pieces stitched to the top of a large piece of background fabric. A patchwork, or pieced, quilt is made of many small pieces stitched together. Embroidery can be added to either type.

Amish, Block Pattern, Blue, Purple, Brown, Maroon, Frame, Child's, 30 x 33 In.	520.00
Amish, Capital T, Blue On Red Blocks, Brown Bars, Feather Stitch Border, 72 x 86 In.	770.00
Amish, Center Diamonds, Machine Stitched, Child's, 24 x 40 In.	1116.00
Amish, Irish Chain, Elsie Hostetler, Buchanan Co., Iowa, 1929, 70 x 80 In.	495.00
Amish, Patchwork, Double 9-Patch, Pink, Blue, Red Border, Flower Quilting, 82 x 82 In.	345.00
Amish, Patchwork, Green Diamond, Burgundy, Blue, Purple, Feather Quilting, 80 x 80 In.	920.00
Amish, Patchwork, Red Diamond, Pink, Green, Blue Border, Feather Quilting, 82 x 82 In.	980.00
Amish, Patchwork, Red, Dark Blue, Green, Sawtooth Border, Polished Cotton, 82 x 84 In.	2875.00
Amish, Patchwork, Wedding Ring, Blue, Green, Black, Brown, White, 84 x 88 In.	275.00
Amish, Rainbow Stripes, Diagonal Border, 20th Century, 78 x 83 In.	468.00
Amish, Trip Around The World, Multicolored, Black Binding, 82 x 84 In.	935.00
Amish, Tumbling Blocks, Multicolored, Daybed, 26 x 68 In.	220.00
Appliqued, 4 Blocks, Flowers, Diamond & Meandering Vine Borders, 83 x 81 In.	210.00
Appliqued, 12 Flower Baskets, Tan, Red, On White, Double Sawtooth Border, 72 x 90 In.	525.00
Appliqued, 12 Flower Medallions, Yellow, Gold, Red, On Green Circles, 83 x 70 In.	345.00
Appliqued, 12 Medallions, Radiating Tulips, Multiple Borders, 91 1/2 x 75 In.	410.00
Appliqued, 16 Stars, White & Red Diamonds, Sawtooth Border, 93 x 89 1/2 In.	660.00
Appliqued, Black, Red & Green Felt Tulips, Wool Serge, Flannel Backing, 65 x 67 In.	575.00
Appliqued, Central Star, Eagles In Corners, Pink, Yellow, Peach, Green, 81 x 87 In.	660.00
Appliqued, Eagles, Blue, Yellow, Red, White Cotton Ground, Blue Binding, 75 x 78 In.	190.00
Appliqued, Floral, Eagle Below Tulip, Vine, Floral Border, 1900s, 95 x 80 In. *Illus*	2090.00
Appliqued, Flower, Opening Buds, Vine Border, 84 x 88 In.	230.00
Appliqued, Flowers, Vine, Center Eagle, Spread Wing, 81 1/2 x 96 In.	440.00
Appliqued, Flowers, White Ground, Red, Green, White Sawtooth Border, 70 x 96 1/2 In.	495.00
Appliqued, Friendship, Cornucopia Basket, Strawberries, Grapes, 1849, 96 x 96 In.	525.00
Appliqued, Golden Yellow On White, Feather Quilting, Late 19th Century, 78 x 86 In.	225.00
Appliqued, Holly & Flower Medallions, Diamond & Oak Leaves, 81 x 81 In.	550.00
Appliqued, Leaf & Bud Medallions, Birth, 1832, Death, 1857, Paper Label, 78 x 78 In.	2300.00
Appliqued, Oak Leaf, Red, Green, Calico, 73 x 86 In.	145.00
Appliqued, Peony Or Carolina Lily Variation, 25 Blocks, c.1850, 102 x 101 In. *Illus*	715.00
Appliqued, Poinsettia, Flowers, Green Leaves, White Ground, c.1900, 79 x 77 In.	990.00
Appliqued, Pomegranate, Red, Gold, Beige Vines, Feather Medallions, 69 1/2 x 69 1/2 In.	440.00
Appliqued, Princess Feather Variation, White Ground, c.1865, 74 x 8 1/2 In.	400.00
Appliqued, Princess Feather, Flower Vine Serpentine Border, 1860, 96 x 96 In.	1540.00
Appliqued, Princess Feather, Pinwheels, Red, Gold, Green Border, 75 x 72 1/2 In.	330.00
Appliqued, Religious, Cross, Purple, Yellow Squares, Psalms Depictions, c.1930, 97 x 75	1430.00
Appliqued, Spread Eagle Center, Tulips, Vines, Red Petal Flowers, c.1930, 82 x 100 In.	1455.00

Quilt, Appliqued, Floral, Eagle Below Tulip,
Vine, Floral Border, 1900s, 95 x 80 In.

Quilt, Appliqued, Peony Or Carolina Lily
Variation, 25 Blocks, c.1850, 102 x 101 In.

Quilt, Crazy, Fans, Flowers, Embroidered,
   Silk, 1884 In Corner, 72 x 62 In.

> Samplers stitched with silk are usually
> more valuable than those stitched
> with wool. Alphabets and pictures
> are more popular with buyers than
> religious messages.

Appliqued, Star, Red, White, 86 x 76 In.	230.00
Appliqued, Trapunto, Carolina Lily, Red & Green Calico, c.1846, 84 x 88 In.	2990.00
Appliqued, Tulip, Red, Green, Flower Baskets, Crossed Tulips, 76 x 81 In.	110.00
Appliqued, Tulip, Red, Yellow, Blue Leaves, White, Flower Bud Border, 84 x 84 In.	560.00
Appliqued Top, 9 Potted Flowers, Red, Yellow, Green, White Ground, 80 x 81 In.	170.00
Appliqued Top, 30 White Blocks, Red, Green Tulips, Red & White Borders, 77 x 91 In.	145.00
Appliqued Top, Flower Baskets, Red, Green, On White, 89 x 91 In.	230.00
Bride's, White, 74 x 76 In.	280.00
Crazy, 8-Point Stars, Godey Design, 84 x 90 In.	140.00
Crazy, Dresden Plate, Double Border, 74 x 74 In.	1015.00
Crazy, Embroidered Flowers, Wool, Linen, M.W., 1918, 69 x 88 1/2 In.	345.00
Crazy, Embroidered, Multicolored, Maroon, Red, Yellow, Silk & Velvet, 1885, 64 x 64 In.	1290.00
Crazy, Fans, Flowers, Embroidered, Silk, 1884 In Corner, 72 x 62 In. .... *Illus*	5500.00
Crazy, Flowers, Black, Rust, Yellow, Gray, White, Wool & Linen, Dated 1918, 69 x 85 In.	345.00
Crazy, Heart In Hand, Flowers, Hand, Easter Cross, Heart, Fan, Wool, 72 x 73 In.	980.00
Crazy, Log Cabin, Pineapple, Silk, Victorian, 50 x 60 In.	3500.00
Crazy, Patchwork, Needlework, Irregular Block Pattern, Victorian, 59 x 71 In.	405.00
Crazy, Wagon Wheel Center, Crocheted Border, 1884, 66 x 66 In.	1210.00
Embroidered, Childhood, Dreams Of The Forest, White, Cotton, c.1887, 70 x 70 In.	275.00
Embroidered, Summer Spread, 42 Blocks, Verses, Sawtooth Border, 57 x 66 In.	450.00
Friendship, Autographs, Green, Pink Pattern, Orange Squares, c.1880, 86 x 83 In.	605.00
Friendship, Multiple Starburst, Vermont, c.1850, 88 x 80 In.	600.00
Lone Star, Solid Color Star Border, 79 x 81 In.	480.00
Mennonite, Patchwork, Brown Squares, Diamond, Flower Print Back, 82 x 82 In.	330.00
Mennonite, Patchwork, Drunkard's Path, Red Calico, Blue Calico Ground, 39 x 38 In.	200.00
Mennonite, Patchwork, Joseph's Coat, Feather Border, Calico Backing, 81 x 81 In.	2128.00
Mennonite, Sampler, Earth Tones, 80 x 66 In.	280.00
Patchwork, 4-Patch, Green Borders, Binding, Cotton, Muslin, 1800s, Crib, 36 x 37 In.	530.00
Patchwork, 8-Point Stars, Calico Cotton, Corner Fan Blocks, c.1860, 79 x 79 In.	260.00
Patchwork, 9-Patch, Pink & Yellow Ground, Medallion Print Border, 84 x 86 In.	365.00
Patchwork, 30 Blue & White Geometric Blocks, Print Sashing, 1800s, 88 x 70 In.	385.00
Patchwork, 49 Blocks, Star, Green Sawtooth Border, New Hampshire, 79 1/2 x 78 In.	300.00
Patchwork, Album Variation, Red, Brown, Borders, 1800s, 84 x 75 1/2 In.	193.00
Patchwork, Album Variation, Sawtooth Diamonds, Sashing, Late 1800s, 100 x 93 In.	385.00
Patchwork, Album, Orange & White, Feather Medallion, Stepped Border, 67 x 78 In.	400.00
Patchwork, Around The World, Pumpkin, Purple, Maroon, Blue, 1890s, Crib	1455.00
Patchwork, Autograph, Spicer Family, Mystic, Conn., c.1847, 102 x 98 In.	400.00
Patchwork, Bar, Red, Green Flower Print, Gray Printed Backing, 82 x 90 1/4 In.	300.00
Patchwork, Basket, Red Patches, 78 x 90 In.	380.00
Patchwork, Basket, Yellow Calico Triangles, White Diamonds, Flowers, 78 x 78 In.	518.00
Patchwork, Bear Paw Variation, Red & White, Tulip Quilting, Binding, 68 x 92 In.	230.00
Patchwork, Bowtie Variation, Calico, Prints, Blue, Brown, Coral Border, 100 x 100 In.	660.00
Patchwork, Bowtie Variation, Multicolored, Walnut Dyed Backing, Chintz, 78 x 93 In.	633.00
Patchwork, Bowties & Squares, Flowers, Calico, Cotton, c.1865, 83 x 78 In.	400.00
Patchwork, Carpenter Square, Printed Fabrics, 94 x 94 In.	110.00
Patchwork, Chimney Sweep, Calico, Cotton, c.1880, 78 x 86 In.	127.00
Patchwork, Diamond & Bar, Burgundy, Blue & White Print, Salmon Backing, 68 x 82 In.	110.00

Patchwork, Diamond Blocks, Floral, Red, White, Basket Border, Chintz, 86 x 88 In. 1800.00
Patchwork, Diamond-In-Square, Calico, Cotton, 19th Century, 85 x 87 In. 380.00
Patchwork, Diamonds, Pink & Blue Calico, Alternating Gray Squares, 68 x 80 In. 145.00
Patchwork, Double Irish Chain, Pink & White, 79 x 79 In. 165.00
Patchwork, Double Sawtooth, Center Initials AMG, Lancaster Co., 83 x 89 In. 370.00
Patchwork, Double Wedding Ring, Saskatchewan, c.1900, 82 x 84 In. 325.00
Patchwork, Drunkard's Path, Purple On White, c.1950, 68 x 76 In. 140.00
Patchwork, Exotic Birds, Flower, 4 Panels, Red, Blue, Green, Chintz, Cotton, 84 x 92 In. 1530.00
Patchwork, Feathered Star, 8-Point, Red, White, Blue, Red Sashing, 79 x 64 In. 190.00
Patchwork, Flower & Leaf Rings, Brown, Rose, Green, White Ground, 69 x 85 In. 145.00
Patchwork, Flower Basket, Green Ground, Colored Flowers, c.1930, 76 x 86 In. 695.00
Patchwork, Flower Baskets, Princess Feather, White Ground, Chintz, 78 x 91 In. 440.00
Patchwork, Flower Baskets, Printed Chintz, Mary B. Raymond, 1841, 86 1/2 x 90 In. ... 750.00
Patchwork, Geometric, 4 Heart Corners, Red, Green, Early 20th Century, 78 x 90 In. 495.00
Patchwork, Goose Track, 25 Blocks, Blue, Calico, Cotton, 77x 77 In. 580.00
Patchwork, Grandmother's Flower Garden, Scalloped Edges, 68 x 88 In. 175.00
Patchwork, Harvest Sun, 8-Point Star, Cotton, 19th Century, 103 x 103 In. 2585.00
Patchwork, Hills Of Vermont, Red Calico, White, Crib, 42 x 57 In. 520.00
Patchwork, Irish Puzzle Variation, Goldenrod, White, 90 x 90 In. 750.00
Patchwork, Lemon Star, Orange Calico, 78 x 78 In. 345.00
Patchwork, Log Cabin Variation, Brown, Amber, 85 x 85 In. 3080.00
Patchwork, Log Cabin Variation, Purple, Peach Calico, Homespun Backing, 69 x 78 In. ... 230.00
Patchwork, Log Cabin, Green, Blue, Purple, Red, Pink, Purple Binding, 74 x 84 In. 165.00
Patchwork, Log Cabin, Stepped Blocks, Plaid Back, Wool & Cotton, 62 x 78 In. 170.00
Patchwork, Mariner's Compass, Calico, New England, 76 x 78 In. 690.00
Patchwork, Ocean Wave, Red, Blue, Green, 76 x 79 In. 125.00
Patchwork, Octagons, 8-Point Stars, White Field, Feather Quilting, 101 1/2 x 94 In. 300.00
Patchwork, Odd Fellows Patch, Brown, Red Chintz, Ribbon Award, 1932, 90 x 90 In. ... 290.00
Patchwork, Odd Fellows Patch, Princess Feather Stitch, 76 x 90 In. 495.00
Patchwork, Ohio Irish Chain, Red, Green, White Ground, Cotton, 66 x 77 In. 200.00
Patchwork, One-Patch, Calico, Cotton, Mid 19th Century, 74 x 80 In. 160.00
Patchwork, Pine Tree, Leaves, Multicolored, Princess Feather Medallions, 66 x 76 In. ... 385.00
Patchwork, Pineapple, Pink, Yellow Calico, Blue Backing, 69 x 80 In. 330.00
Patchwork, Pinwheel Variation, Yellow, Red, Pennsylvania, 68 x 68 In. 290.00
Patchwork, Pinwheel, Brown, White, 83 x 86 In. 175.00
Patchwork, Pinwheel, Red, Yellow, White, Late 19th Century, 74 x 84 In. 230.00
Patchwork, Postage Stamp, Concentric Diamonds, Sawtooth Border, 78 x 98 In. 1045.00
Patchwork, Princess Feather, Blue, White, 1930, 86 x 86 In. 1100.00
Patchwork, Red & Blue Star Medallions, Scrolled Feather, Triangle Border, 84 x 85 In. ... 1380.00
Patchwork, Red Chains, White Ground, Double Red Borders, Wheel Quilting, 66 x 84 In. 460.00
Patchwork, Red Leaf Medallions, White, Princess Feather Medallions, 68 x 82 In. 260.00
Patchwork, Rocky Road To Kansas, Red, Calicos, Scalloped Edge, c.1880, 79 x 67 In. ... 650.00
Patchwork, Sawtooth Bars, Red & Green Alternating Rows, Double Border, 78 x 78 In. ... 1800.00
Patchwork, Schoolhouse, Maria Haynes, March 18, 1907, 70 x 72 In. 440.00
Patchwork, Shell & Wreath, Turquoise, Yellow, Tan & White Border, 84 x 84 In. 140.00
Patchwork, Shoo-Fly, Red, Brown Calicos, White, Pennsylvania, 74 x 84 In. 290.00
Patchwork, Star, 36 Green Calico Stars, Red Blocks, Alternating Borders, 75 x 76 In. 410.00
Patchwork, Star, Green & Yellow Calico, Homespun Backing, 1870s, 79 x 94 In. 400.00
Patchwork, Star, Yellow Ground, Purple, Yellow Borders, c.1934, 77 x 82 In. 220.00
Patchwork, Stars, White & Indigo, 68 x 85 In. 750.00
Patchwork, Stepped Squares, Blue Sashing, Brown Floral Backing, 64 x 79 In. 315.00
Patchwork, Stylized Tulips, Navy Blue, White Print, 75 x 74 In. 690.00
Patchwork, Sunflower, White Field, Pineapples, Cornucopias, Print Border, 92 x 80 In. .. 605.00
Patchwork, Sunshine & Shadow, Red, White, 78 x 91 In. 230.00
Patchwork, Texas Star, 20th Century, 76 x 76 In. 485.00
Patchwork, Tobacco Flag, Flags, Butterflies, Indian Design Patches, 70 x 90 In. 160.00
Patchwork, Tobacco Flag, Large American Flag Center, Flags, Butterflies, 69 x 76 In. ... 250.00
Patchwork, Top, Goose In The Pond, Green, Red Calico, White, 78 x 80 In. 115.00
Patchwork, Top, Irish Chain, Postage Stamp, Blue, White, Polka Dots, 88 x 90 In. 175.00
Patchwork, Touching Star, Blue, Calico & Chintz Border, Sarah Hinson, 76 x 80 In. 825.00
Patchwork, Trapunto, Flower Baskets, Calico, Sawtooth Borders, 84 x 86 In. 630.00
Patchwork, Triangles, Red, Brown, Blue, Green, White, Calico, Chintz, 82 x 94 In. 660.00
Patchwork, Trip Around The World, Multicolored, Sawtooth Border, 85 x 80 In. 495.00

Patchwork, Triple Irish Chain, Brown, Green, White, Wave Border, 81 x 85 In. 230.00
Patchwork, Triple Irish Chain, Feather Medallions, Stars, Scallops, 78 x 79 In. 690.00
Patchwork, Whirligigs, Red, Beige, Scalloped Borders, 78 x 85 In. 460.00
Patchwork, Wild Geese, Red & White, Double Border, Tulip & Fan Quilting, 68 x 84 In. .   690.00
Patchwork, Windmill, Yellow, Green, Red, Green Calico, White Blocks, 66 x 84 In. 400.00
Patchwork & Appliqued, 9 Red & Yellow Stars, White Ground, Flowers, 76 x 77 In. 315.00
Patchwork & Appliqued, 20 Blocks, Bear Paw, Pumpkin, Brown, 63 x 77 In. 415.00
Patchwork & Appliqued, 42 8-Point Stars, Cotton, 19th Century, 96 x 104 In. 1000.00
Patchwork & Appliqued, Horse Racing, 18 Diamonds, Triangles, 66 x 90 In. 2300.00
Patchwork & Appliqued, Little Red School House, Cotton, 19th Century, 74 x 77 In. 410.00
Patchwork & Appliqued, Princess Feather, 16 Blocks, Crossed Feathers, 94 x 98 In. 3335.00
Patchwork & Appliqued, Tulip, Red, Green, Sawtooth Border, Cotton, 1800s, 84 x 86 In.   2115.00
Stencil Pattern, Bird In Flight, Tulips, Tin, White Paint, Late 19th Century, 12 x 13 In. .   910.00
Stencil Pattern, Bird, Salmon Paint, Sawtooth Border, Mid 19th Century, 11 1/2 x 7 In. . .   770.00
Trapunto, Calico Star Medallions, Diamond Band Borders, Blue, White, 76 x 90 In. 2475.00
Trapunto, White, 19th Century, 111 x 103 In. 290.00
Trapunto, White, Flower Vase, Grapevine Borders, Eagles, Arrows, c.1810, 78 x 86 In. . .   1785.00

QUIMPER pottery has a long history. Tin-glazed, hand-painted pottery
has been made in Quimper, France, since the late seventeenth century.
The earliest firm, founded in 1685 by Jean Baptiste Bousquet, was
known as HB Quimper. Another firm, founded in 1772 by Francois
Eloury, was known as Porquier. The third firm, founded by Guillaume
Dumaine in 1778, was known as HR or Henriot Quimper. All three
firms made similar pottery decorated with designs of Breton peasants
and sea and flower motifs. The Eloury (Porquier) and Dumaine
(Henriot) firms merged in 1913. Bousquet (HB) merged with the oth-
ers in 1968. The group was sold to a United States family in 1984. The
American holding company is Quimper Faience Inc., located in
Stonington, Connecticut. The French firm has been called Societe
Nouvelle des Faienceries de Quimper HB Henriot since March 1984.

HR
Quimper

Bank, Pig, Maroon Flowers, Green Leaves, Tan & Brown, Marked, 4 x 8 x 3 In. 295.00
Bookends, Figural, Seated Man, Green Striped Pants, Blue Coat, 8 x 7 In. 460.00
Bowl, Peasant Woman, 10 1/2 In. 250.00
Dish, Peasant Man, Holding Staff, Fir Trees, Heart Shape, Keraluc, 5 x 5 1/4 In. 30.00
Ewer, Man & Walking Stick, Marked Henriot Quimper, France, 10 1/4 In. 165.00
Figurine, 2 Dancers, Plougastel Costumes, Multicolored Faience, c.1930, 14 In. 1675.00
Jar, Cylindrical, Short Handles, Enamel Man & Woman, Cover, c.1800, 6 3/4 In. 380.00
Oyster Plate, 7 Wells, Flower, Spongeware, Henriot, 9 In. 195.00
Pitcher, Figural, Henriot Quimper, 7 In. 150.00
Platter, Men Lawn Bowling, c.1900, 16 x 12 1/2 In. 2300.00
Platter, Wedding Party, Top Crest, Henriot Quimper, c.1950, 21 x 11 In. 1250.00
Vase, Profile Of Gentleman, Signed, 7 1/2 In. 259.00
Wall Pocket, Figural, Man, Woman, Serrated Edges, Fleur-De-Lis, 11 x 3 x 2 In., Pair . . .   335.00

RADFORD pottery was made by Alfred Radford in Broadway, Virginia,
Tiffin and Zanesville, Ohio, and Clarksburg, West Virginia, from 1891
until 1912. Jasperware, Ruko, Thera, Radura, and Velvety Art Ware
were made. The jasperware resembles the famous Wedgwood ware of
the same name. Another pottery named Radford worked in England
and is not included here.

RADURA.

Vase, Pink, Blue Gooseberries, Leaves, Green Matte Ground, Cylindrical, 10 3/4 In. 489.00
Vase, Tree, Landscape, Brown Matte Painted, Mottled Ocher Ground, Marked, 5 In. 200.00

RADIO broadcast receiving sets were first sold in New York City in
1910. They were used to pick up the experimental broadcasts of the
day. The first commercial radios were made by Westinghouse Company for listeners of the experimental shows on KDKA Pittsburgh in
1920. Collectors today are interested in all early radios, especially
those made of Bakelite plastic or decorated with blue mirrors. Figural
advertising radios and transistor radios are also collected.

Addison, Model 5E, Catalin, Tube, Marbelized Brown & Butterscotch, c.1940 . . . .   700.00
Addison, Model 5F, Catalin, Tube, Gold, Maroon, c.1940 . . . .   1150.00

Admiral, Model 5X1, AM, White 10.00
Air King, Model A600, Duchess, Catalin, Green & Yellow, c.1947 . . . . 1810.00
Bulova, Clock, Model 140 Series, Pink 20.00
Channel Master, Model 6510, Transistor, AM, Plastic, c.1960, 5 3/4 x 12 3/4 x 5 In. 10.00
Channel Master, Model 6520, Transistor, AM, Plastic, 2-Tone, c.1960 . . . . 20.00
Crosley, Model 515, AM/SW, Tube, Wood Box Case, Upright Table, 1934 . . . . 90.00
DeForest-Crosley, Metal Case, Atwater Kent Top Speaker, Canada 110.00
Emerson, Model 587, Series B, AM, White, Plastic, 1949 . . . . 20.00
Fleetwood, Model 5072, Clock, Aqua, White 15.00
Loewe EB 100, Receiver, Single Circuit, c.1931 . . . . 562.00
Marconi, Model 422, Clock, Red, Plastic, 5 Tubes, 1 Band, c.1955 . . . . 30.00
Philco, Model 20, Cathedral, Wood, Cloth Grill, c.1930 . . . . 180.00
Philco, Model 40-90, Bakelite, Gold Speaker Grill Cloth, c.1940, 6 x 8 x 12 In. 75.00
Philco, Model 610, Chassis, Wood Case, 5 Tubes, 2 Bands, c.1936 . . . . 60.00
RCA, Victor, Model 5T7, John Vassos Design, Wood, 5 Tubes, 2 Bands, c.1936 . . . . 165.00
RCA, Victor, Model Nipper 1XA, AM, Pink 15.00
RCA, Victor, Model X624, AM, White 10.00
Shelburn, Model 55C, Clock, Maroon 80.00
Sparton, Bakelite, Chrome, Cloisonne, 5 In. 9245.00
Tesla, Model 516030, Microphone, Ball Shape, Wire Mesh, Velvet & Satin Lined Box, 3 In. 51.00
Zenith, Model 1005, Wood Cabinet, Console, Push Button, 1939 . . . . 700.00
Zenith, Radio Nurse, Bakelite, Isamu Noguchi, c.1942, 7 1/2 In. 2470.00

RAILROAD enthusiasts collect any train memorabilia. Everything is wanted, from oilcans to whole train cars. The Chessie system has a store that sells many reproductions of their old dinnerware and uniforms.

Badge, CRI&P Railway Police, Star Shape, Chicago, Rock Island 225.00
Bell, Brass, Cast Iron Yoke, Brass Acorn Finial, 27 In. 690.00
Bell, Cast Brass, Cast Iron Yoke, Acorn Finial, 24 In. 1045.00
Butter Chip, U.P. Railroad Streamliner, China 29.00
Cap, Cotton, Blue & White Stripes, 4 Metal Grommets, Lee Brand, 1940-1950, Size 6 7/8 30.00
Grenade, Fire, C&NWRY, Contents, Wood Plaque, 18 In. 316.00
Headlight, Kerosene Fueled, Star Manufacturing Co., Civil War Period, 11 x 25 In. 850.00
Jug, C&NWRY, Stoneware, Brown Over White 65.00
Lamp, Brass, Wall Mounted, Openwork Shades, Clear Glass Globes, 10 1/2 In., Pair 250.00
Lantern, Copper Frame, Glass Panels, Wire Hasp, Electric, France, 12 x 9 x 21 In. 165.00
Lantern, CRRR, Tin, Clear Globe, Etched 330.00
Lantern, Dressel, 4-Lens, Red, Blue Green Lenses, Electrified, Late 1800s, 16 1/2 In. . . . 104.00
Lantern, Dressel, Arlington, N.J., Cast Iron Base, Blue Lens, 17 In. 120.00
Lantern, NYCS, Switchman's, Kerosene, Adlake, 9 1/2 In. 85.00
Map, Northern Alabama Railway & Other Companies, Jasper Area, Paper, 1917 . . . . 60.00
Notary Stamp, Iron, Woodstock Railroad, 19th Century 35.00
Photograph, Atlantic & Great Western Railway, Albumen, c.1865, 7 3/8 x 9 1/4 In. 1000.00
Photograph, Atlantic & Great Western Railway, Albumen, J.F. Ryder, 7 3/8 x 9 1/4 In. 500.00
Plate, Missouri Pacific Lines, Flower Border, 10 1/2 In. 220.00
Sign, Boston & Maine RR Tickets, Reverse Painted Glass, Black, Gold, 5 1/2 x 35 In. . . . 425.00
Sign, Chicago & Alton Railroad, Paper, Cardboard, Frame, c.1910, 15 x 39 In. . . . .635.00 to 775.00
Sign, Grand Trunk Pacific Railway, Photograph, Frame, c.1900, 29 x 35 In. . . . . . .650.00 to 750.00
Sign, Rock Island System, Reverse Painted, Mother-Of-Pearl, c.1905, 26 1/2 x 90 In. 9775.00
Sign, Stop, Look, Listen, Cast Iron, Oval, 19 In. 305.00
Sink, Adams & Westlake, Metal, 20 In. 70.00
Stepstool, Pullman, Blue Paint, 1940s 295.00
Whistle, Steam, Nathan, c.1900, 32 In. 935.00

RAZORS were used in ancient Egypt and subsequently wherever shaving was in fashion. The metal razor used in America until about 1870 was made in Sheffield, England. After 1870, machine-made hollow-ground razors were made in Germany or America. Plastic or bone handles were popular. The razor was often sold in a set of seven, one for each day of the week. The set was often kept by the barber who shaved the well-to-do man each day in the shop.

Etched, On To Cuba, 1st Vol. Cav. Rgt., Joseph Allen, Sheffield, Spanish-American War . 1000.00

Frederick Reynolds, Straight Edge, Black Celluloid Handle, Art Nouveau, England 40.00
Garland Cutlery Co., Straight Edge, Celluloid Handle, Nude Woman, Germany, 6 1/4 In. . 95.00
Hopkins, Straight Edge, Bone Handle 45.00
Joseph Allen, Straight Edge, Black Bakelite Handle, Sheffield, England 35.00
Keen Kutter, Safety, Red Bakelite Handle, Paper Label, Box, 4 In. 60.00
Keen Kutter, Straight, Model 1150, Bakelite Handle, Box, 1940s, 3-In. Blade 29.00
Otto Deutsch, Safety, Black Handle, Box, Germany 23.00
Robert Klaas, Straight Edge, Ivory Celluloid Handle, Box, Prussia 35.00

REAMERS, or juice squeezers, have been known since 1767, although
most of those collected today date from the twentieth century. Figural
reamers are among the most prized.

Ceramic, Yellow With Orange Crown, Bill & Feet, Green Tail & Wings, Deco, 1984, 3 In.   60.00
Clown, Orange Trimmed Collar, Japan, 2 1/2 In. 85.00
Custard Glass, Saucer Type, Loop Handle, McKee, 5 1/2 In. 35.00
Glass, Cheriglo, Flowers, 4-Cup Pitcher Base, 2 Piece, 8 1/4 x 7 1/2 In. 170.00
Glass, Green, Ribbed, Loop Handle, Anchor Hocking, 6 In. 25.00
Glass, Opalescent White, Embossed Sunkist, Marked Pat. No. 18764, U.S.A, McKee, 6 In.   150.00
Glass, Opaque Pink, Embossed Sunkist, Pat. No. 18764, Made In U.S.A, McKee, 6 In. 225.00
Glass & Metal, Hinged Black Metal, Clear Glass Insert, Marked Williams, 4 3/4 In. 75.00

RECORDS have changed size and shape through the years. The cylin-
der-shaped phonograph record for use with the early Edison models
was made about 1889. Disc records were first made by 1894, the dou-
ble-sided disc by 1904. High-fidelity records were first issued in 1944,
the first vinyl disc in 1946, the first stereo record in 1958. The 78 RPM
became the standard in 1926 but was discontinued in 1957. In 1932,
the first 33 1/3 RPM was made but was not sold commercially until
1948. In 1949, the 45 RPM was introduced. Compact discs became
available in the U.S. in 1982 and many companies began phasing out
the production of phonograph records.

Anita Bryant, Mine Eyes Have Seen The Glory, LP, 33 1/3 RPM, 1960s 25.00
Bob Marley & Wailers, Catch A Fire, Autographed, 33 1/3 RPM, 1973-1974 .... 4415.00
Castells, Teardrops, Warner Brothers, No. 5421, 45 RPM, 1964 .... 60.00
Del Shannon, Hey Little Girl, Big Top Records, 45 RPM, c.1961 .... 20.00
Dinah Shore, Fascination, RCA Victor, No. 47-6980, 45 RPM 5.00
Lesley Gore, All About Love, Mercury Records, No. S.R. 61066, 33 1/3 RPM, LP 20.00
Let's Dance The Square Dance, Decca, No. K-72, K-73, 33 1/3 RPM, 10 In., 2 Records .. 10.00
Monkees, More Of The Monkees, Colgems Records, No. COS-102, 33 1/3 RPM, 1967 .. 30.00
Paul Anka, Put Your Head On My Shoulder, ABC-Paramount, No. 45-10040, 45 RPM ... 4.00
Perry Como, More, RCA Victor, No. 6554, 45 RPM 20.00
Raggedy Ann's Sunny Songs, Gruelle, Luther, RCA Victor, 78 RPM, c.1930, 3 Records .. 200.00
Rosemary Clooney, Winter Wonderland, 1954 .... 35.00
Snow White, Storybook Cover, Peter Pan Records, 45 RPM 10.00
Sounds In Space, Stereo Demonstration, Victor, No. SP-33-13, LP, 1958 .... 6.00
Ventures, No Trespassing, Picture Sleeve, Dolton, No. 28, 45 RPM, 1960 .... 32.00

RED WING Pottery of Red Wing, Minnesota, was a firm started in
1878. The company first made utilitarian pottery, including stoneware
jugs and canning jars. In the 1920s art pottery was made. Many dinner
sets and vases were made before the company closed in 1967. Rumrill
pottery made by the Red Wing Pottery for George Rumrill is listed in
its own category. For more information, see *Kovels' Depression Glass
& Dinnerware Price List*.

Advertising, Jug, Garibaldi Co., Wines & Liquors, Chicago, Tan & Brown Glaze 450.00
Art Pottery, Vase, Brown & Green Crystalline Drip, Handles, Marked, 10 In. 115.00
Art Pottery, Vase, Lady & Deer, Relief, Turquoise, White Crackle Glaze, 1942, 8 In. 65.00
Art Pottery, Vase, Mottled Amber, Green Crystalline Glaze, Bulbous, Stamped, 7 1/4 In. .. 403.00
Art Pottery, Vase, Raised Rim, Egg Shape, Lions & Leaves, Sage, Blue Glaze, 8 In. 120.00
Blossom Time, Relish, Sections, Rectangular, 11 In. 32.00
Bob White, Bowl, Vegetable, 12 1/2 In. 55.00
Bob White, Butter, Cover 60.00
Bob White, Pitcher, Ice Lip, 15 In. 350.00

Bob White, Salt & Pepper, Figural 22.00
Bob White, Tray, Chip & Dip, 5 Sections, 12 1/2 In. 75.00
Brittany, Plate, Dinner, 10 In. 18.00
Capistrano, Platter, Freeform, 13 In. 35.00
Cookie Jar, Chef, Blue Glaze, 11 1/2 In. 65.00
Cooler, Iced Tea, 2 Gal. 2000.00
Country Garden, Plate, Salad, 8 In. 22.00
Damask, Tidbit, Metal Center Handle, 7 In. 13.00
Jug, Beehive, Blue Shield, Colfax Mineral Water Co., 5 Gal., 17 In. 835.00
Lute Song, Bowl, Fruit, 5 In. 18.00
Lute Song, Plate, Dinner, 10 In. 30.00
Magnolia, Plate, Bread & Butter, 6 In. 8.00
Normandy, Cup & Saucer 21.00
Oomph Village Green, Teapot, Brown & Green Glaze, 6 In. 125.00
Pepe, Cup & Saucer 25.00
Pepe, Plate, Bread & Butter, 6 In. 17.00
Pepe, Plate, Dinner, 10 In. 30.00
Pepe, Sugar & Creamer 50.00
Random Harvest, Bowl, Vegetable, 8 In. 32.00
Reamer, Ceramic, 6 3/4 In. 125.00
Stoneware, Chicken Feeder, Ko-Rec Feeder, 10 1/2 x 9 1/2 In. 58.00
Stoneware, Jug, Shoulder, 18 x 11 1/2 In. 69.00
Tampico, Plate, Dinner, 10 1/2 In. 25.00
Tweed Tex, Creamer, Black 20.00
Water Cooler, Bar Lid, 5 Gal. 580.00

REDWARE is a hard, red stoneware that originated in the late 1600s and
continues to be made. The term is also used to describe any common
clay pottery that is reddish in color.

Bank, Face, Black Man, White Eyes, Mouth Coin Slot, Late 19th Century, 3 1/2 x 3 In. ... 770.00
Bank, Manganese Splotches, Beehive Shape, Incised Museum, 4 1/4 In. 705.00
Bank, Mottled Glaze, Dome, Finial, Coggled Rim, Incised Rosette, 5 1/4 In. 1265.00
Bank, Scroddleware, 3 Birds, On Branch, Bulbous Bank, Jack Moon Risher, 9 In. ... 440.00
Bird Whistle, On Pedestal, Yellow, Brown Mottled Glaze, 9 1/4 In. 110.00
Bird Whistle, Scroddleware, Bird, Berry In Mouth, Ocher Slip, c.1898, 5 x 6 1/2 In. ... 2145.00
Birdhouse, Mottled, Glazed, Hanging Knob, 6 3/4 In. 330.00
Birdhouse, Wheel Turned, Dome Top, Incised Line Decoration, Painted Blue, 8 1/2 In. ... 250.00
Bowl, Brown & Tan Mottled Glaze, Molded Foot, 3 x 5 1/2 In. 770.00
Bowl, Brown Glaze, Black Dot Interior Design, Canted, Raised Rim, 8 1/8 x 2 3/4 In. ... 85.00
Bowl, Center Band, Manganese Splotches, 9 1/2 In. 310.00
Bowl, Flaring, Yellow, Brown Flame Glazes, Beatrice Wood, 3 x 10 In. 750.00
Bowl, Incised Lines At Rim, Brown Brush Strokes, Footed, 5 1/2 x 2 1/4 In. 415.00
Bowl, Manganese Design On Interior Rim, 11 x 3 1/2 In. 140.00
Bowl, Manganese Glazed Interior, 10 1/4 In. 730.00
Bowl, Milk, Sloped Sides, Mustard Splotch Glaze, 19th Century, 3 3/4 x 15 5/8 In. ... 295.00
Bowl, Orange Glaze, Yellow Slip Crisscross, Signed, W. Smith, Womelsdorf, 7 1/2 In. ... 330.00
Bowl, Scalloped Rim, Twig & Scroll, 13 In. 125.00
Bowl, Splayed Edge, Yellow, Green, Brown Slip, 4 1/2 In. 1320.00
Bowl, Yellow Slip Splash, Orange, Brown Glaze, 8 In. 220.00
Charger, Coggled Rim, 3-Line Bird Claw Design, Crossed Lines, 13 1/4 In. 1760.00
Charger, Coggled Rim, 6 Daubs Yellow Slip Decoration, 12 In. 660.00
Charger, Coggled Rim, Yellow Slip Bird, 13 1/2 In. 2420.00
Charger, Coggled Rim, Yellow Slip Decoration, Wavy Latticework, 13 1/4 In. 4290.00
Charger, Dimpled Rim, Singer Pottery, Signed, Dated, c.1886, 11 1/2 In. 4510.00
Compote, Sgraffito Leaf Decoration, Yellow Glaze, 6 1/4 x 7 1/2 In. 50.00
Creamer, Bulbous, Pinched Spout, Applied Handle, 2 1/2 In. 275.00
Creamer, White Drip Splotches, Applied Strap Handle, Maker's Mark, 4 x 4 In. ... 275.00
Crock, Dome Cover, 2 Incised Bands, Wide Mouth, Lug Handles, Early 1800s, 11 In. ... 353.00
Crock, Glazed, Loop Handle, 4 3/4 In. 85.00
Crock, Interior Glaze, Incised Ring, Handles, Signed, J. Feeg, 8 1/4 In. 1020.00
Crock, Orange Showing Through Green Glaze, 4 1/4 In. 115.00
Crock, Storage, 3, Double Handle, Signed, C.G., Lancaster, Penn., 1870s, 13 1/4 In. ... 275.00
Crock, Storage, Green & Orange Glaze, Molded Rim, 4 1/2 In. 165.00

Crock, Storage, Incised Squiggle & Line, Molded Lip, Mottled Glaze, 5 3/4 In.	580.00
Cup, Apple Butter, Incised Lines On Shoulder, Handle, Brown Daubs, 5 1/2 In.	460.00
Cup, Manganese Splotches, Handles, 2 1/4 In.	200.00
Dish, Loaf, Coggled Rim, Bird Claw Design, Wavy Lines, Yellow Slip, 13 3/4 x 9 In.	1890.00
Dish, Loaf, Coggled Rim, Dark Brown Glaze, 7 1/2 x 10 1/2 In.	2090.00
Dish, Loaf, Coggled Rim, Yellow Slip, 3 Rows, Script L's, 11 1/4 x 15 1/2 x 1 3/4 In.	3630.00
Dish, Loaf, Coggled Rim, Yellow Slip, Lafayette, 9 x 14 In.	3300.00
Dish, Loaf, Slip Decorated, Center Band, Crow's-Foot Border, Dashes, Lines, 14 x 9 In.	1675.00
Dish, Manganese Splotch, 6 1/4 In.	146.00
Dish, Orange Glaze, c.1680, 9 In.	250.00
Dish, Pumpkin Glaze, Brown Daubs, 6 1/4 x 1 1/2 In.	430.00
Doorstop, Upside Down Top, Red, White, Stripes, Gold, 6 1/2 x 6 In.	360.00
Figurine, Dog, Seated, With Basket, Signed, L. & B. Breininger, Aug. 1977, 9 In.	440.00
Figurine, Dog, Spaniel, Glazed, Black Paint Over Glaze, 10 1/2 In.	175.00
Figurine, Dog, Spaniel, Seated, Manganese Glaze, S. Bell, Virginia, 3 5/8 x 1 1/4 x 4 In.	440.00
Flask, Figural, Fish, Molded, Glazed, Embossed Scales, Mid 19th Century, 8 1/2 In.	250.00
Flask, Sgraffito Tree, Apple, Bell Flower & Potted Plant, 6 1/2 In.	2860.00
Flask, Squat, Green Glaze, 5 1/4 In.	130.00
Flowerpot, Saucer Base, Mottled Glaze, Signed, W. Smith, Womelsdorf, 5 1/4 x 6 In.	1155.00
Flowerpot, Serrated Rim, Lead, Manganese, Copper Glaze, Green, Brown, 5 x 6 1/4 In.	415.00
Flowerpot, Undertray, Pie Crimped Edge, Manganese Splotches, 5 3/4 In.	115.00
Flowerpot, Undertray, Yellow, Brown, Green Glaze, Manganese Splotching, 5 1/4 In.	75.00
Foot Warmer, Orange, Green Glaze, Wheel Thrown, Molded Spout, 5 x 9 3/4 In.	385.00
Inkwell, Applied Orange Alkaline Glaze, c.1820, 1 3/4 x 3 1/4 In.	90.00
Jar, Apple Butter, Brownish Green Alkaline Glaze, c.1830, Qt., 6 In.	275.00
Jar, Canning, Brown Daubs, Orange, Green Glaze, 8 In.	1485.00
Jar, Canning, Cover, Burnt Orange Peppered Applied Glaze, c.1840, Gal., 8 In.	165.00
Jar, Canning, Magnesium Decoration, 8 1/2 In.	195.00
Jar, Cover, Black Sponge Design, Raised Foot, 8 1/2 In.	770.00
Jar, Cover, Mottled Red & Orange, Green Glaze, Brown Daubs, Brown Dots, 9 In.	2185.00
Jar, Cover, Squat, Glazed, Lobbed Handles, 7 In.	220.00
Jar, Mottled Brown, Incised Line, Applied Ribbed Strap Handle, 4 1/2 x 5 1/2 In.	495.00
Jar, Mottled Brown, Tapered, Incised Ring, Applied Strap Handle, 5 1/4 x 6 In.	440.00
Jar, Oval, Multiglaze, Applied Rosette, 2 Handles, Early 19th Century, 7 3/4 x 8 In.	635.00
Jar, Storage, 2-Tone, Glazed, 5 1/2 In.	190.00
Jar, Storage, Bulbous, Flared, Manganese Splotches, Applied Handles, 8 1/2 In.	199.00
Jar, Storage, Bulbous, Incised Ring, Manganese Glaze, 9 In.	275.00
Jar, Storage, Bulbous, Molded Lip, Orange, Green Glaze, 5 In.	45.00
Jar, Storage, Bulbous, Signed, J. Feeg, 7 1/4 In.	495.00
Jar, Storage, Interior Glaze, Signed, Willoughby Smith, Womelsdorf, 5 3/4 In.	275.00
Jar, Storage, Relief Latticework At Shoulder & Base, 6 3/4 In.	105.00
Jar, Storage, Running Green Glaze, 2 Raised Bands, Sharp Shoulder, Scribed 6, 8 In.	575.00
Jug, 3 Incised Rings, Green Highlights, Strap Type Handle, Small Lip Base, Maine, 6 In.	575.00
Jug, Black Sponge Decoration, Running Glaze, Raised Bead, Flared Spout, 9 1/4 In.	330.00
Jug, Dark Brown Daubs, Oval, Applied Strap Handle, 7 In.	550.00
Jug, Face, Grotesque, Brown Ash Glaze, Mottled Green & Blue, Shard Teeth, 9 1/4 In.	81.00
Jug, Face, Grotesque, Devil, Brown Ash, Running Blue Glaze, Shard Teeth, 9 1/4 In.	98.00
Jug, Harvest, Mottled Glaze, Oval, Applied Ribbed Handle, 6 In.	1045.00
Jug, High Shoulder, Incised Lines, Ribbed Strap Handle, Early 19th Century, 8 In.	590.00
Jug, Lead, Manganese Glazed Tan, Brown, Applied Handle, 4 x 3 In.	550.00
Jug, Oval, Green Glaze, Double Lip, Orange Yellow Spots, Applied Rib Handle, 7 In.	550.00
Jug, Oval, Incised Lines, 8 1/2 In.	100.00
Jug, Oval, Mottled, Glazed Decoration, Applied Handle, 10 In.	495.00
Jug, Oval, Raised Foot, Applied Strap Handle, 11 3/4 In.	330.00
Jug, Pear Shape, Incised Shoulder Bands, Green Glaze, c.1830, 9 In.	9988.00
Loving Cup, Embossed Cherub Design, Glazed, Double Loop Handles, 5 1/4 In.	385.00
Measure, Pouring, Incised Bands, Green Seaweed, Handle, V. Rudolph, 4 1/2 In.	2600.00
Measuring Cup, Magnesium Decoration	160.00
Mold, Candle, 12-Tube, Cutout Feet, Softwood, Signed, Smedley & Co., 13 1/2 x 19 In,	1045.00
Mug, Brick Red Alkaline Glaze, c.1860, 10 In.	99.00
Mug, Bulbous, Tin Glaze, Applied Handle, 4 x 3 1/4 In.	140.00
Mug, Flared, Mottled Glaze, Applied Loop Handle, 4 1/4 In.	95.00
Mug, Incised Line, Brown Manganese Glaze, Applied Handle, 2 3/4 In.	146.00

Mug, Incised Lines, Running Yellow Glaze, Applied Handle, 4 1/4 In. 715.00
Mug, Tapered, Hand Thrown, Tin Glaze, Early 18th Century, 5 3/4 x 4 1/4 In. 50.00
Pepper Pot, Manganese Band, Orange Glaze, 5 In. 1045.00
Pie Plate, 3 Yellow Slip Stripes, 4 1/4 In. 415.00
Pie Plate, Coggled Rim, 3 Sets Of Wavy Lines, Yellow Slip, 8 In. 1430.00
Pie Plate, Coggled Rim, 3 Wavy Lines, Yellow Slip, 4 In. 1980.00
Pie Plate, Coggled Rim, 3-Line W Design, Yellow Slip, 7 3/4 In. 770.00
Pie Plate, Coggled Rim, 3-Line Yellow Slip, 4 In. 1430.00
Pie Plate, Coggled Rim, 3-Line Yellow Slip, 6 3/4 In. 220.00
Pie Plate, Coggled Rim, Brick Red Color, Yellow Slip Scrolling, 11 1/4 In. 2300.00
Pie Plate, Coggled Rim, Central Double S, Green & Dark Brown, 6 3/4 In. 2090.00
Pie Plate, Coggled Rim, Crossed Snowshoe, Dots, Yellow Slip, 8 1/2 In. 5650.00
Pie Plate, Coggled Rim, Dots, Wavy Line, Yellow Slip, 10 In. 470.00
Pie Plate, Coggled Rim, Green & Dark Brown Lines, 8 In. 4125.00
Pie Plate, Coggled Rim, Grid Design, Wavy Lines, Yellow Slip, 9 In. 1650.00
Pie Plate, Coggled Rim, James, Yellow Slip, 10 1/4 In. 3300.00
Pie Plate, Coggled Rim, Mary's Dish, Yellow Slip, 9 1/4 In. 1540.00
Pie Plate, Coggled Rim, Pinwheel, Dark Green, 8 1/4 In. 935.00
Pie Plate, Coggled Rim, Seaweed, Yellow Slip, 10 1/2 In. 1760.00
Pie Plate, Coggled Rim, Stylized 4-Leaf Clover, Yellow Slip, 9 1/4 In. 1650.00
Pie Plate, Coggled Rim, Tulip, Green, Brown Slip, Dryville, Berks County, 8 In. 7975.00
Pie Plate, Coggled Rim, Wavy Lines, Dots, Yellow Slip, 10 1/2 In. 835.00
Pie Plate, Coggled Rim, Wavy Lines, Feather Design, Yellow Slip, 8 1/2 In. 1430.00
Pie Plate, Coggled Rim, Yellow Slip Bird, 10 In. 489.00
Pie Plate, Coggled Rim, Yellow Slip Decoration, 10 1/2 In. 55.00
Pie Plate, Coggled Rim, Yellow Slip Decoration, 12 1/4 In. 1650.00
Pie Plate, Coggled Rim, Yellow Slip, Agness, 10 1/4 In. 1760.00
Pie Plate, Yellow & Brown Slip, Wavy, Cross Lines, W. Smith, Womelsdorf, 7 In. 2310.00
Pitcher, Band Of Molded Hearts, Oval, Mottled Orange & Green Glaze, 7 1/4 In. 175.00
Pitcher, Bulbous, Leaf Panel, Green & Manganese Glaze, Mexico, 9 In. 30.00
Pitcher, Bulbous, Mottled Glaze, Applied Handle, 12 1/4 In. 965.00
Pitcher, Cover, Brown Sponge Lines, Galleried Rim, Tooled, Incised Lines, 6 1/4 x 7 In. . 635.00
Pitcher, Graduated Splotches, On Shoulder, Rim, Ribbed Handle, 6 In. 1130.00
Pitcher, Green & Brown Running Glaze, Over Yellow, Ribbed Handle, 6 In. 360.00
Pitcher, Green, Orange, Yellow Dots, Green Sponge Band, 11 In. 140.00
Pitcher, Incised Bands, Mottled Green Glaze, Reeded Strap Handle, c.1830, 5 3/4 In. . . . 7638.00
Pitcher, Incised Lines, Green Stripes, Mottled Orange & Green Glaze, 3 1/2 In. 85.00
Pitcher, Lead Manganese, Slip Wash, Green, Brown, Copper Glaze, 5 1/2 x 3 3/8 In. 825.00
Pitcher, Milk, 8-Sided Base, White Splotches, Signed, Henry Swopes Pottery, 8 3/4 In. . . . 1210.00
Pitcher, Milk, Manganese Design, Applied Handle, 6 In. 280.00
Pitcher, Round, Tapered Neck, Shaped Spout, Dark Brown Glaze, Maine Glazed, 5 In. . . 60.00
Pitcher, Speckled Black Glaze, Brown Splotches, 6 1/4 In. 660.00
Pitcher, Tapered, Brown Flower, Yellow, Green Slip Leaves, Orange Glaze, 7 1/4 In. 1980.00
Pitcher, Wood Cover, Yellow Slip Daubs, Loop Handle, 6 1/4 In. 1045.00
Planter, Coggled Rim, Sgraffito Flower, Mottled Green, Brown, Orange, 9 3/4 x 10 In. . 4180.00
Plate, 3 Yellow Slip Round Decorations, Orange Glaze, 6 3/4 In. 330.00
Plate, Brown Dot, Yellow Slip, Double Quill, Orange Ground, 5 In. 1045.00
Plate, Brown Glaze, Zoar, 8 In. 80.00
Plate, Coggled Rim, 3-Line Yellow Slip, 4 In. 330.00
Plate, Coggled Rim, 5 Lines, Triple Quill Yellow Slip, Orange Glaze Ground, 12 1/4 In. . 1430.00
Plate, Coggled Rim, Center Squiggle, Leaves Around Edge, 9 In. 255.00
Plate, Coggled Rim, Triple Quill, Yellow Slip, Orange, Brown Glaze, 11 In. 350.00
Plate, Coggled Rim, X In Circle, Wavy Lines, Red Glaze, 9 1/4 In. 935.00
Plate, Coggled Rim, Yellow & Green Crisscross, Squiggles, Orange Glaze, 7 1/2 In. 3630.00
Plate, Coggled Rim, Yellow Slip Dot & Ring, Orange Glaze Ground, 9 In. 1430.00
Plate, Deep Dish, Coggled Rim, Slip Decorated, Splotches Around Upper Rim, 11 1/2 In. . 675.00
Plate, Sixth Week In Lent, Louis Scranton, Norwalk, Conn., 11 In. 1210.00
Plate, Slip Trailed Spider Web, Stamped, W. Smith, Womelsdorf, 8 In. 565.00
Plate, Stylized Tulip, Green & Brown Slip, 11 1/4 In. 770.00
Plate, Yellow Zigzag Design, 8 In. 550.00
Pot, Barrel Shape, Brown, Uneven Lead Glaze, Initials M.C.M., 5 3/4 x 4 3/4 In. 275.00
Quill Holder, Lamb, Scroddle Brown, Yellow Glaze, Scroll Work, 2 1/4 x 2 1/4 In. 140.00
Stove Rest, Sponge Daubed, Lancaster, Pa., Mid 19th Century, 3 7/8 x 4 1/4 In. 220.00

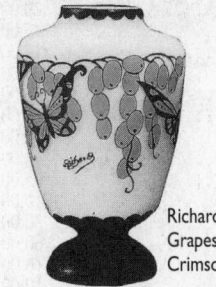
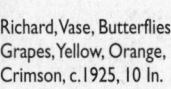

Richard, Vase, Butterflies,
Grapes, Yellow, Orange,
Crimson, c.1925, 10 In.

Don't store ceramic dishes or figurines for long periods of time in old newspaper wrappings. The ink can make indelible stains on china.

Sugar, Cover, Brown Sponge, Orange Glaze Ground, Applied Handles, 3 1/2 x 5 In.	220.00
Sugar, Flared Rim, Applied Handles, 4 1/2 In.	39.00
Tankard, Slip Decoration, Crosshatching, Trees, Applied Double Handle, 5 1/2 In.	275.00
Trencher, Plate, Mary Schooner, Slip Design, Gold Tulip, Polka Dots, 6 x 5 In.	525.00
Tumbler, Glazed, Lipped, Incised Band Decoration, 2 3/4 x 3 3/4 In.	140.00
Vase, Bulbous, Red, Tan Slip Wash, Green Glaze, 7 1/2 x 6 1/4 In.	660.00
Vase, Grand Tour Style, Greek Black Figure, Amphora Shape, Loop Handles, 22 In.	440.00

REGOUT, see Maastricht category.

RICHARD was the mark used on acid-etched cameo glass vases, bowls, night-lights, and lamps made by the Austrian company Loetz after 1918. The pieces were very similar to the French cameo glasswares made by Daum, Galle, and others.

Lamp, Mountain Village, Cylindrical, Brown Over Orange, c.1920, 16 In.	900.00
Vase, Black Cameo Flowers & Butterfly, Orange Ground, Black Foot, 4 In.	150.00
Vase, Butterflies, Grapes, Yellow, Orange, Crimson, c.1925, 10 In. *Illus*	1610.00
Vase, Castle, Mountains, Water, Trees, Tapered, Cobalt, Orange, Signed, 15 3/4 In.	605.00
Vase, Flower, Orange, Dark Brown Ground, 5 1/4 In.	680.00

RIDGWAY pottery has been made in the Staffordshire district in England since 1808 by a series of companies with the name Ridgway. The transfer-design dinner sets are the most widely known product. They are still being made. Other pieces of Ridgway are listed under Flow Blue.

Coffeepot, Windsor Pattern, Brown Transfer, Hand Colored Flowers, 8 5/8 In.	75.00
Compote, View From Ruggloes House, Black Transfer, 6 1/4 x 11 In.	660.00
Creamer, Relief Molded & Hand Painted Flowers, Gold Trim, c.1820, 4 1/2 In.	115.00
Cup & Saucer, Jolly Jinks Pattern, Child's	33.00
Cup & Saucer, Truro Pattern, Floral Border	45.00
Pitcher, Classical Design, Blue, White, 6 x 3 3/4 In.	60.00
Plate, Helical Pattern, Blue & Green Tendril & Flowers, c.1830, 6 1/2 In.	85.00
Plate, New York City Hall, 9 3/4 In.	100.00
Plate, Philadelphia Library, Blue, White, 8 In.	374.00
Platter, Beauties Of America, Almshouse, New York, 16 3/4 In.	1325.00
Platter, Lynton Pattern, Lavender & Yellow Flowers, Oval, 14 In.	75.00
Sugar & Creamer, Old English Bouquet Pattern	35.00
Syrup, Indus Pattern, Asian Birds & Plants, Hand Colored, Pewter Cover, 4 1/2 In.	425.00
Teapot, Blue Wave Pattern, Maroon Trim, 1950s, 5 In.	85.00

RIFLES that are firearms are not listed in this book. BB guns and air rifles are listed in the Toy category.

RIVIERA dinnerware was made by the Homer Laughlin Co. of Newell, West Virginia, from 1938 to 1950. The pattern was similar in coloring and in mood to Fiesta and Harlequin. The Riviera plates and cup handles were square. For more information, see *Kovels' Depression Glass & Dinnerware Price List*.

COLONIAL

Ivory, Bowl, Fruit, 5 1/4 In.	11.00
Ivory, Cup	13.00

Ivory, Platter, 11 In.	20.00
Ivory, Sauceboat, Attached Underplate	145.00
Ivory, Sugar	12.00
Light Green, Plate, 9 In.	4.00
Light Green, Platter, 11 In.	25.00
Light Green, Saltshaker	12.00
Mauve Blue, Casserole, Cover	140.00
Mauve Blue, Platter, 11 1/2 In.	8.00
Mauve Blue, Tumbler, 4 1/4 In.	65.00
Mauve Blue, Tumbler, Handle, 4 3/8 In.	110.00
Red, Bowl, Vegetable, 8 1/4 In.	30.00
Red, Butter	60.00
Red, Platter, Closed Handles, 11 1/4 In.	16.00
Red, Sugar	12.00
Yellow, Baker, Oval, 9 1/4 In.	25.00
Yellow, Eggcup, Double	20.00
Yellow, Gravy Boat	25.00
Yellow, Plate, Salad, 7 In.	14.00
Yellow, Teapot	185.00

ROCKINGHAM, in the United States, is a pottery with a brown glaze that resembles tortoiseshell. It was made from 1840 to 1900 by many American potteries. Mottled brown Rockingham wares were first made in England at the Rockingham factory. Other types of ceramics were also made by the English firm. Related pieces may be listed in the Bennington category.

Bottle, Toby, Glazed, 1849-1858, 10 3/4 In.	440.00
Bowl, Tapered, Brown Glaze, 3 3/4 x 11 1/4 In.	58.00
Creamer, Cow, Bennington Type, Brown Mottled Glaze, 5 1/2 x 7 In.	290.00
Creamer, Cow, Horns, Oval Base, Lid, 5 1/4 x 7 In.	155.00
Figurine, Dog, Poodle, Clipped, Bird In Mouth, Pedestal Base, England, 4 In.	70.00
Figurine, Dog, Poodle, Seated, Leaf Molded Base, Staffordshire, c.1850, 3 1/2 In., Pair	60.00
Figurine, Dog, Seated, Free-Standing Front Legs, Scrolls, Shell Base, 7 1/2 x 10 In.	220.00
Figurine, Dog, Seated, Long Tail, Inverted Scallop Base, Acanthus Leaves, 10 3/4 In.	550.00
Figurine, Dog, Seated, Yellowware Body, East Liverpool, Oh., c.1850, 7 1/2 x 10 In.	375.00
Figurine, Lion, Lying Down, Yellowware, East Liverpool, 9 1/2 x 5 3/4 x 6 3/4 In.	635.00
Frame, Mirror, Oval, Glazed, 9 3/4 x 8 5/8 In.	235.00
Group, 2 Poodles Flank Clock, Poodle On Top, 8 1/2 x 7 In.	350.00
Inkwell, Dog, 6 In.	635.00
Inkwell, Man, Wearing Turban, Upturned Shoes, Reclining On Sofa, 6 1/2 In.	290.00
Jug, Puzzle, Figural, Man, Open Book, On Stylized Horse, Brown Glaze, 9 1/2 In.	80.00
Mixing Bowl Set, Graduated, Mottled Brown, 7 1/8 To 13 1/8 In., 4 Piece	1725.00
Pitcher, Embossed Hunter With Dog, Brown Glaze, 9 In.	80.00
Pitcher, Hound Handle, Glazed, 1849-1858, 10 3/4 In.	380.00
Pitcher, Mottled Brown Glaze, 3 3/4 x 6 1/4 In.	69.00
Pitcher, Paneled Baluster Form, C-Scroll Handle, Bearded Mask, 8 1/2 In.	1150.00
Plate, Landscape, Green & Gold Scrollwork Borders, c.1850, 8 3/4 In., Pair	230.00
Shaving Mug, Toby, Twig Handle, Split, 4 1/4 In.	230.00
Tea Service, Gilt Shell & Scroll, Cobalt, Yellow Ground, c.1840, 39 Piece	410.00
Toby Jug, Portly Man, Tricorn Hat, Scroll Handle, Lid, England, c.1850, 10 In.	175.00

ROGERS, see John Rogers category.

ROOKWOOD pottery was made in Cincinnati, Ohio, from 1880 to 1960. All of this art pottery is marked, most with the famous flame mark. The R is reversed and placed back to back with the letter P. Flames surround the letters. After 1900, a Roman numeral was added to the mark to indicate the year. The name and some of the molds were purchased in 1984. A few new pieces were made, but these were glazed in colors not used by the original company.

Ashtray, General Electric, Light-Bulb Shape, Pomegranate Glaze, 1949, 7 1/8 In.	160.00
Ashtray, Hull Dobbs, Ford, Wine Madder Glaze, 1954, 6 1/8 x 5 1/2 In.	259.00
Ashtray, Maroon High Glaze, Scalloped Edge, 1935, 4 1/4 In.	46.00
Bookends, Collies, Brown Matte Glaze, 1929, 6 In.	980.00

Bookends, Double Owl, Blue Crystalline Glaze, 1927, 6 3/4 In. 1150.00
Bookends, Dutch Boy & Girl, Blue Matte Glaze, Pink, Green, 1914, 6 x 4 1/4 In. 345.00
Bookends, Egyptian Woman, Cream, William McDonald, 1930, 5 1/2 In. 1035.00
Bookends, Elephant, Brown, 1920, 4 1/2 In. 750.00
Bookends, Elephant, Trunk Up, Green Matte Glaze, 1929, 7 1/4 In. 1150.00
Bookends, Goddess, Indigo Matte Glaze, 1918, 8 In. 290.00
Bookends, Horse Head, Ivory Matte Glaze, William McDonald, 1934, 5 7/8 In. 520.00
Bookends, Kingfisher, Blue & Green, William McDonald, 1929, 5 1/2 In. 345.00
Bookends, Owl, 1946, 5 3/4 In. 375.00
Bookends, Panther, Dark Brown, William McDonald, 1957, 6 In. 690.00
Bookends, Panther, Ivory Matte Glaze, W. McDonald, 1951, 5 3/4 In. 546.00
Bookends, Peacock, Light Blue Matte Glaze, 1926, 4 1/2 In. 460.00
Bookends, Peacock, Yellow Matte Glaze, 1924, 4 7/8 In. 489.00
Bookends, Rook, Black, Green Ground, 1921, 7 In. 1840.00
Bookends, Rook, Celadon High Glaze, McDonald, 1948, 5 In. 400.00
Bookends, Rook, Green Black Speckle, Tan Ground, 5 1/2 In. 230.00
Bookends, Rook, Ivory Matte Glaze, 1943, 5 In. 430.00
Bookends, Scarlett With Fan, Turquoise Matte Glaze, 1932, 6 1/2 In. 290.00
Bookends, Ship, Blue, William McDonald, 1927, 5 1/2 In. 430.00
Bookends, Tree, Yellow Green, Brown Glaze, 1928, 5 3/4 x 6 In. 865.00
Bookends, Woman Reading, Green, 1921, 7 In. 800.00
Bowl, Blue Crystalline Matte, Tan Interior, Octagonal, 1924, 9 5/8 In. 140.00
Bowl, Cover, Flowers, Mocha Tan Standard Glaze, W. Purcell, 4 x 6 1/2 In. 250.00
Bowl, Flowers, Mottled Blue Green Glaze, 1921, 2 1/4 x 5 3/4 In. 230.00
Bowl, Flowers, Porcelain Glaze, Lorinda Epply, 1926, 3 3/8 In. 430.00
Bowl, Geometric Pattern, Porcelain Glaze, Footed, 1930, 10 1/2 In. 805.00
Bowl, Green Glaze, Pink Interior, Fluted, Ear Handles, 1928, 5 x 8 7/8 In. 140.00
Bowl, Ivory Matte Glaze, Celadon High Glaze, 1937, 3 5/8 x 7 3/4 In. 160.00
Bowl, Lion's Head, Yellow, Brown, Tan, Glaze, Matthew Daly, 1885, 12 1/4 In. 2750.00
Bowl, Pink Matte Glaze, 1929, 1 3/4 x 4 1/4 In. 58.00
Bowl, Red & Green Matte Glaze, 1913, 7 In. 410.00
Bowl, Red Matte Glaze, Olive, c.1910, 6 x 10 3/4 In. 330.00
Bowl, Round, Squat, Rolled Rim, Matte Glaze, c.1916, 8 x 3 1/2 In. 230.00
Bowl, Slate Blue, 6 3/4 In. 375.00
Box, Cover, Blue Crystalline Glaze, 1942, 1 3/4 x 4 In. 460.00
Box, Cover, Carved, Dark Gray Matte Glaze, 9 In. 1380.00
Box, Cover, Poppies, Red, Blue, Pink, Green, Hexagonal, 1928, 4 1/2 In. 690.00
Box, Figure On Cover, Stylized Landscape, Cylindrical, 1901, 6 In. 489.00
Bust, Woman, Amber & Brown Crystalline Matte Glaze, 1912, 8 1/4 x 7 1/2 In. 690.00
Candleholder, Dark Pink Matte Glaze, Mottled Green, 1920, 3 3/4 In. 115.00
Candleholder, Jonquils, Green Glaze, c.1950, 3 3/4 In., Pair 90.00
Candleholder, Lotus Blossom, Polychrome Matte Glaze, 1946, 3 5/8 In., Pair 400.00
Candleholder, Pink Crystalline Matte Glaze, 1921, 1 1/2 In., Pair 175.00
Candlestick, Leaf & Berry, Fluted, Constance Baker, 1894, 7 3/4 In. 750.00
Candlestick, Lotus, Green Matte Glaze, 1934, 3 1/8 In., Pair 150.00
Candlestick, Primrose, Yellow, Green, Indigo Matte Ground, 1923, 4 In., Pair 315.00
Chalice, Leaves, Berries, Dentil Work, K. Van Horne, 1917, 4 1/4 In. 690.00
Cocktail Shaker, Cover, Raspberry Porcelain Glaze, Stopper, 1932, 11 3/8 In. 520.00
Coffee Set, Blue Ship, White Ground, 1924, 5 5/8 In., 3 Piece 210.00
Compote, Tan Matte Glaze, 3-Elephant Support, 1929, 11 In. 750.00
Creamer, Tea Roses, Sadie Markland, 1892, 2 1/2 In. 575.00
Dish, Walnut-Shell Shape, Realistic Accents, Incised Flowers Inside, 6 In. 195.00
Ewer, 5-Petal Flowers, Yellow, Crimped Mouth, Sara Toohey, 1888, 6 1/4 In. 550.00
Ewer, Bellflowers, Orange, Yellow, Standard Glaze, Matt Daly, 1892, 12 3/4 In. 1035.00
Ewer, Dandelion, Slender Neck, Edith Felton, 1898, 5 1/8 In. 430.00
Ewer, Dogwood Blossoms, Mahogany Red, Standard Glaze, Ruffled Edge, 11 In. 1000.00
Ewer, Holly Berries, Sallie Coyne, 5 In. 450.00
Ewer, Jonquil, 3-Color Rim, Standard Glaze, Ed Diers, 1899, 6 3/4 In. 430.00
Ewer, Pansy, Standard Glaze, William Klemm, 1901, 5 1/2 In. 460.00
Ewer, Pine Bough, Matt Daly, 1896, 12 1/4 In. 3450.00
Ewer, Virginia Creeper, Slender Neck, Howard Altman, 1902, 6 1/4 In. 430.00
Figurine, Bird, Gray Brown Glaze, 4 1/4 x 5 x 2 3/8 In. 2310.00
Figurine, Cardinal, Jane Sacksteder, 1946, 7 1/8 In. 635.00

Figurine, Heron, Violet Gray, 1948, 8 3/4 In. 316.00
Figurine, Leopard, Wine Madder Glaze, 1951, 3 7/8 In. 375.00
Figurine, Pheasant, Polychrome, Glossy, 1949, 8 7/8 x 13 5/8 In., Pair 635.00
Figurine, Rooster, Multicolored, McDonald, 1943, 5 1/2 In. 635.00
Figurine, St. Francis, Wine Madder Glaze, C. Zanetta, 1947, 11 1/8 In. 230.00
Flask, Birds Flying, Reeds, Flowers, Cameo, 5 In. 575.00
Flower Frog, 2 Women Kneeling, Blue High Glaze, 1921, 6 x 7 In. 290.00
Flower Frog, Ivory Matte Glaze, 1920, 6 3/4 In. 185.00
Flower Frog, Turtle, Green Matte Glaze, 1914, 3 x 3 1/2 In. 500.00
Flower Frog, Yellow High Glaze, 1921, 6 3/4 In. 210.00
Ginger Jar, Flowers, Wax Matte Glaze, E. Barrett, 1924, 7 1/2 In. 865.00
Ginger Jar, Hydrangea, Butterflies, Hazy Black Ground, H. Wilcox, 1920, 6 In. 770.00
Incense Jar, Sage Green Crystalline Matte Glaze, 1923, 2 3/8 In. 259.00
Inkwell, Blue Flowers, Yellow Leaves, Frog Finial, 1894, 4 In. 635.00
Inkwell, Green Blue Matte Glaze, 3 Square Feet, Lift-Out Insert, 1917, 2 1/4 In. 70.00
Jam Pot, Blue Ship, White Ground, Lid Notch, 4 1/8 In. 160.00
Jar, Cover, Beehive, Celadon Green High Glaze, 1945, 5 1/4 In. 195.00
Jar, Cover, Glossy Green, Acorn Handle, Hexagonal, 1925, 4 In. 205.00
Jar, Cover, Turtle, Blossoms, Standard Glaze, A.R. Valentien, 1885, 9 1/2 x 6 In. 545.00
Jar, Cover, Yellow Roses, Standard Glaze, 3 3/4 x 4 3/4 In. 200.00
Jar, Potpourri, Reversible Cover, Smear Glaze, Matt Daly, 1887, 7 1/2 In. 1495.00
Jar, Potpourri, Reversible Cover, Turquoise Matte Glaze, c.1932, 4 In. 185.00
Jardiniere, Roses, White, Blue To Pink Ground, Vellum, Rothenbusch, 1912, 6 x 6 In. . . . 805.00
Jug, Cheyenne Brave, Standard Glaze, Sadie Markland, 1898, 8 In. 4830.00
Jug, Perfume, Meadow Flowers, Harriet Wenderoth, 1883, 4 1/2 In. 405.00
Jug, Perfume, Sparrow, Oriental Grasses, Albert Valentien, 1884, 4 7/8 In. 315.00
Jug, Stopper, Dogwood, Blossoms, Mottled Indigo Ground, 1885, 14 x 16 1/2 In. 805.00
Lamp, Bleeding Heart, Tan, High Glaze, Metal Foot, Gold Patina, c.1940, 23 In. 460.00
Lamp, Flowers, Leaves, Purple, Deep Rose Ground, Wax Matte, E. Lincoln, 9 1/2 In. 1540.00
Lamp Base, Purple Flowers, Green Leaves, Matte Glaze, 9 1/2 In. 1800.00
Match Holder, Wild Clover, C. Steinle, 2 In. 290.00
Mug, Embossed Leaves, Face, Feet, Olive Green High Glaze, 1962, 7 In. 115.00
Mug, Indian, 3 Handles, Sadie Markland, 1898, 4 5/8 In. 5175.00
Mug, Tendrils, Mottled Sea Green Glaze, Cylindrical, 5 1/2 In. 325.00
Mug, Yellow Blossoms, Green Leaves, Iris Glaze, A. Bookprinter, 1904, 4 1/2 In. 635.00
Paperweight, Boss Bull, Cincinnati's Butcher's Supply Company, 1949, 3 3/8 In. 115.00
Paperweight, Canary, Buff High Glaze, 1947, 4 In. 290.00
Paperweight, Carousel Horse, Celadon High Glaze, W. Rehm, 1946, 8 1/4 In. 490.00
Paperweight, Cat, Chartreuse, Louise Abel, 1946, 6 3/4 In. 805.00
Paperweight, Cat, Jewel Porcelain, Glossy Ocher Glaze, Abel, 1946, 6 1/2 x 5 In. 460.00
Paperweight, Duck, Mottled Gray, High Glaze, Starkville, 1963, 2 1/4 In. 150.00
Paperweight, Duck, Yellow Matte Glaze, 1930, 2 1/8 In. 290.00
Paperweight, Elephant, Turquoise, High Glaze, c.1945, 3 7/8 In. 460.00
Paperweight, Gazelle, Ivory Matte Glaze, 1935, 4 3/8 In. 400.00
Paperweight, Goat, Bisque, Louise Abel, 1951, 6 3/8 In. 210.00
Paperweight, Monkey, Green High Glaze, 1930, 3 7/8 In. 489.00
Paperweight, Peach Cluster, Ivory Porcelain Glaze, 1933, 5 1/2 In. 290.00
Paperweight, Penguin, Mottled Gray, Tan Matte Glaze, 1930, 5 1/4 In. 575.00
Paperweight, Rook, Blue Matte Glaze, 1934, 4 1/2 In. 660.00
Paperweight, Rook, Mottled Brown Matte Glaze, 1924, 4 1/2 In. 430.00
Paperweight, Rooster, Polychrome, High Glaze, W. McDonald, 1943, 5 In. 865.00
Pencil Holder, Rooks, Green Matte Crystalline Glaze, 1931, 4 3/4 In. 290.00
Pencil Holder, Rooks, Pink Matte Crystalline Glaze, 5-Sided, 1928, 4 3/4 In. 259.00
Pin Tray, Embossed Moth, Triangular, 1927, 5 1/2 In. 115.00
Pitcher, Berries, Iris Glaze, Kataro Shirayamadani, c.1888, 9 In. 1800.00
Pitcher, Flowers, Incised, Reddish Brown Glaze, c.1882, 9 5/8 In. 325.00
Pitcher, Grapevines, Blue Matte Glaze, Louise Abel, 1925, 6 3/4 In. 1150.00
Pitcher, Leaves, Green & Ocher, Bulbous, Crimped Mouth, A. Sprague, 9 1/4 In. 660.00
Pitcher, Maple Leaves, Standard Glaze, 3-Sided, Triple-Rolled Spout, Olga Reed, 4 In. . . 330.00
Pitcher, Spiders In Web, Bamboo Plants, Organic Shape, M.L. Nichols, 1883, 8 In. 1610.00
Pitcher, Tendrils, Green Matte Glaze, 3 Spouts, 5 1/2 In. 590.00
Plaque, Beach, Trees, Ocean, Vellum Glaze, Sara Sax, 1918, 8 3/8 x 10 3/4 In. 10060.00
Plaque, Birches, Lake, Vellum Glaze, E.T. Hurley, 1948, 8 3/4 x 11 3/4 In. 15525.00

Plaque, Creek, Spanish Moss, Oval, Vellum, Carl Schmidt, 1913, 13 1/2 x 11 1/8 In. 2350.00
Plaque, Evening Reflections, Frame, Shirayamadani, 1912, 14 1/4 x 9 In. 20700.00
Plaque, Harbor Scene, Vellum Glaze, Frame, Carl Schmidt, 1941, 8 x 5 In. 4025.00
Plaque, Hurley's Hidden Mountain Pool, Vellum, Gilt Frame, 1946, 10 x 12 In. 20700.00
Plaque, Landscape, Gray, Blue, Gold, Iris Glaze, Frame, 1896, 10 x 8 In. 6900.00
Plaque, Landscape, Green Vellum Glaze, Frame, E.T. Hurley, 1914, 10 1/2 x 8 In. 9775.00
Plaque, Landscape, River, Tree, Hillside, Frame, Sara Sax, 1907, 8 1/2 x 10 1/2 In. 9200.00
Plaque, Landscape, Stream, Cattails, Frame, E.F. McDermott, 1912, 9 1/2 x 5 In. 4600.00
Plaque, Madonna & Child, Ivory High Glaze, Round, Clotilda Zanetta, 1958, 5 In. 220.00
Plaque, Portrait Of Man, Iris Glaze, Frame, Grace Young, 1903, 6 In. 1955.00
Plaque, Portrait Of Woman, Iris Glaze, Frame, Grace Young, 1903, 6 In. 4025.00
Plaque, Snow, Trees, Twilight, Vellum, Frame, Fred Rothenbusch, 1912, 9 1/2 x 7 3/8 In. 8625.00
Plaque, Spring Landscape, House, Road, Frame, Fred Rothenbusch, 1927, 6 x 8 In. 6325.00
Plaque, Stream, Palm Trees, Vellum Glaze, Elizabeth McDermott, 7 1/4 x 9 1/4 In. 3565.00
Plaque, Tree-Lined Road, Vellum Glaze, Frame, Fred Rothenbusch, 1925, 9 x 12 In. 6900.00
Plaque, Trees Reflected In Lake, Vellum, Frame, Ed Diers, 1919, 8 3/4 x 10 3/4 In. 9200.00
Plaque, Trees, Shoreline, Vellum Glaze, Charles J. McLaughlin, 1915, 7 x 9 In. 13800.00
Plaque, Windmill, Boats, Frame, Fred Rothenbusch, 1935, 10 x 12 In. 16415.00
Plaque, Winter Landscape, Frame, E.F. McDermott, 1919, 6 x 8 In. 6325.00
Plaque, Winter Landscape, River, Frame, Fred Rothenbusch, 1912, 7 1/2 x 6 In. 4315.00
Plate, Carp, Seaweed, Cream, Porcelain Glaze, Arthur Conant, 1922, 10 1/8 In. 2875.00
Sugar & Creamer, Buttercups, No. 43, Jeanette Swing, 1899, 2 x 3 In. 690.00
Sugar & Creamer, Glossy Blue Porcelain Glaze, Marked, 1916, 4 In. 175.00
Tile, Donkey, Wax Matte Faience Glaze, Frame, c.1945, 6 In. 920.00
Tile, Fish, Tan, Green Ground, Arts & Crafts Oak Frame, 1921, 5 1/2 In. 635.00
Tile, Flowers, Green, Brown, 6 In. 230.00
Tile, Grape Clusters, Blue, Red & Green Leaves, Green Matte Ground, 6 x 11 1/2 In. 200.00
Tile, Grapes, Vines, Leaves, 1919, 5 5/8 In. 355.00
Tile, Grapevine, Azure Blue Ground, White Border, Hexagonal, 1925, 5 1/2 In. 275.00
Tile, Landscape, Bridge, Woman & Dog At Shoreline, Frame, 5 3/4 In. 470.00
Tile, Leaves, Geometric Pattern, Green, Blue Matte Ground, Arts & Crafts Frame, 9 In. . . . 999.00
Tile, Leaves, Green Glaze, Ivory Ground Faience, Arts & Crafts Frame, 6 In. 1035.00
Tile, Owl, Leaves, Oak Arts & Crafts Frame, 6 x 6 In. 1410.00
Tile, Parrot, Green, Yellow, Frame, 6 In. 750.00
Tile, Pinecones, Faience, Blue, Green Matte Glaze, Arts & Crafts Frame, 6 x 6 In. 1380.00
Tile, Rook, Oriental Trellis, Indigo, 1927, 5 3/4 In. 800.00
Tile, Swan, Blue Gray, Ivory Matte Glaze, Green Crystalline Ground, Frame, 6 In. 690.00
Tile, Trees, Mountains, Blue, Green, Brown Matte Glaze, Frame, 12 In. 3105.00
Tile, White Geese, Trees, Grass, Blue Sky, Water, Oak Frame, 1925, 5 3/4 In. 999.00
Tray, Lily Pad, Pink Matte Glaze, 1907, 7 In. 115.00
Tray, Oakleaf, Acorns, Blue Matte Glaze, 1910, 7 5/8 In. 259.00
Trivet, Flowers, Woman, Watering Can, Matte Glaze, 1940, 5 1/4 In. 635.00
Trivet, Pelican, Gold Mottled Green High Glaze, 1949, 5 5/8 In. 200.00
Trivet, Seagulls, Embossed, Green Waves, Blue Green Sky, Round, 1925, 6 1/4 In. 290.00
Trivet, White Geese, Embossed, Green Grass, Blue Pond, Sky, Frame, 1924, 6 In. 370.00
Urn, Blue Glaze Dripping Over Unglazed Ground, 2 Handles, 26 1/2 In. 1840.00
Urn, Cranes, 2 Handles, Elizabeth Barrett, 1935, 7 7/8 In. 2530.00
Urn, Greek Key, 2 Handles, Wilhelmine Rehm, 1935, 7 3/4 In. 805.00
Vase, 3 Carved Panels, Maroon, Green Matte Glaze, 1915, 5 In. 315.00
Vase, 3 Flower Clusters, Vellum, Lorinda Epply, 1933, 5 5/8 In. 805.00
Vase, Apple Blossoms Border, Rose Ground, 1922, 6 1/2 x 3 In. 750.00
Vase, Apple Blossoms, Iris Glaze, Elizabeth Lincoln, 1906, 6 5/8 In. 1840.00
Vase, Apple Blossoms, Vellum Glaze, Fred Rothenbusch, 1930, 7 7/8 In. 2070.00
Vase, Arrowroot Blossoms, Leaves, Blue To Green, Carl Schmidt, 1914, 11 x 6 In. 2415.00
Vase, Autumn Leaves, Flared Rim, Sallie Toohey, Early 1900s, 9 1/8 In. 825.00
Vase, Bearded Man, After Rembrandt, Pillow, Edith Felten, 1900, 5 1/2 In. 1035.00
Vase, Berries, Lace, Embossed, Caramel Honey Matte Glaze, Art Deco, 7 1/4 In. 305.00
Vase, Berries, Orange, Green Leaves, Glaze, K. Shirayamadani, 1889, 13 1/4 In. 1610.00
Vase, Berry Branches, Leaves, Red Matte, Purple Ground, O.G. Reed, 6 3/4 In. 1035.00
Vase, Birds, Branches, Matte Glaze, Baluster Form, 7 3/8 In. 345.00
Vase, Black Outside, Wine Inside, Hexagonal, 1919, 4 3/4 In. 195.00
Vase, Black-Eyed Susans, Standard Glaze, Cylindrical, Sallie Coyne, 1902, 7 1/2 In. 660.00
Vase, Blossom Branches, Pink, Tan, Blue, Green, Jewel, A. Conant, 1928, 5 x 3 3/4 In. . . . 2300.00

Vase, Blossoms, Pink, White, Yellow, Iris Glaze, Oval, E. Lincoln, 1909, 6 1/4 In. . . *Illus*   2070.00
Vase, Blue Crystalline Matte Glaze, Embossed Rim, 1920, 3 In. 230.00
Vase, Blue Gray & Black Drip, Mottled Rose, 1932, 3 1/8 In. 489.00
Vase, Blue Mottled Glaze, 1922, 7 In. 95.00
Vase, Boy, Frogs, Bats, Spider, Moon, Matte Glaze, Nichols, 1883, 26 In. 3450.00
Vase, Brown, Blue, Purple Drip, 1932, 3 3/4 In. 290.00
Vase, Buff High Glaze, 1944, 5 In. 140.00
Vase, Burnt Orange Glossy Glaze, Elliptical, 1961, 10 In. 315.00
Vase, Butterflies, Cardinal, Ivory, Blue Glossy Glaze, 1933, 4 5/8 In. 316.00
Vase, Butterfly, Turquoise Matte Crystalline Glaze, 1938, 4 7/8 In. 290.00
Vase, Cactus, Flowers, Yellow, Green, Vellum Glaze, F. Rothenbusch, 1912, 10 In. 2230.00
Vase, Chartreuse Matte Glaze, 2 Handles, 1929, 6 1/2 In. 230.00
Vase, Cherries, Blue, High Glaze, Jens Jensen, 1946, 7 1/4 In. 805.00
Vase, Cherry Blossoms, Blue, Purple & Green Ground, Shirayamadani, 9 In. 4700.00
Vase, Cherry Blossoms, Pink, Teal Leaves, Mauve Ground, Vellum, 1917, 7 1/4 In. 660.00
Vase, Cherry Blossoms, Vellum Glaze, E.T. Hurley, 1923, 4 1/2 In. 690.00
Vase, Chrysanthemums, Burgundy, Sea Green Ground, Wax Matte, 12 In. 2420.00
Vase, Chrysanthemums, White, Blue Gray Matte, Laura Fry, 1885, 7 1/4 In. 1380.00
Vase, Chrysanthemums, Yellow, Brown, Tan, Swollen Neck, E. Noonan, 1904, 8 In. 470.00
Vase, Clematis Vine, Turquoise, Margaret McDonald, 1928, 8 1/2 In. 980.00
Vase, Clover Blossoms, Brown & Yellow, Standard Glaze, Baluster, 7 1/4 In. 140.00
Vase, Columbines, 2 Handles, J.W. Pullman, 1929, 8 7/8 In. 1095.00
Vase, Columbines, Leafy Stalks, Vellum Glaze, Ed Diers, 1931, 7 7/8 In. 3450.00
Vase, Coppertone, Red, Orange, 5 1/4 x 5 In. 405.00
Vase, Coromandel, Narrow Neck, 1932, 3 7/8 In. 520.00
Vase, Cosmos Blossoms, Iris Glaze, Sara Sax, 1900, 9 3/4 In. 2300.00
Vase, Cranes, Yellow Ground, Iris Glaze, Sara Sax, 1899, 4 7/8 In. 1725.00
Vase, Crocus, Brown, Green Leaves, Yellow Ground, Shirayamadani, 1934, 5 1/2 In. *Illus*   1610.00
Vase, Crocuses, Blue, Vellum Glaze, Black Outline, Ed Diers, 1930, 5 3/8 In. 2760.00
Vase, Crystalline Matte Glaze, C.S. Todd, 1917, 16 1/4 In. 3680.00
Vase, Daffodils, Silver Overlay, Laura Lindeman, 1900, 6 1/2 In. 865.00
Vase, Daffodils, Vellum Glaze, E.T. Hurley, 1928, 7 3/4 In. 2300.00
Vase, Daisies, Buds, Yellow, Standard Glaze, Bulbous, Edith Felton, 1903, 7 In. 1760.00
Vase, Daisies, High Glaze, Kataro Shirayamadani, 1929, 4 1/8 In. 1725.00
Vase, Daisies, Standard Glaze, Tapered, Edith Noonan, 1905, 7 In. 770.00
Vase, Daisies, Turquoise Matte Glaze, 1937, 5 1/4 In. 210.00
Vase, Daisies, White, Iris Glaze, Kataro Shirayamadani, 1908, 12 3/4 In. 15525.00
Vase, Dandelions, Standard Glaze, Bulbous, Irene Bishop, 1903, 7 1/2 In. 175.00
Vase, Dogwood Branches, Pink & White, Kataro Shirayamadani, 1934, 4 3/4 In. 2645.00
Vase, Emerald Green Crystalline Matte Glaze, 1940, 6 1/8 In. 175.00
Vase, Ferns, Light Blue Matte Glaze, 1946, 4 5/8 In. 195.00
Vase, Fish Leaping, Blue Crystalline Matte Glaze, 1920, 7 5/8 In. 345.00
Vase, Fish, Green Ground, Iris Glaze, E.T. Hurley, 1903, 8 1/4 In. 4485.00
Vase, Fish, High Glaze, Margaret McDonald, 1944, 4 5/8 In. 1035.00
Vase, Fish, Iris Glaze, Sallie Coyne, 1911, 8 3/4 In. 1808.00
Vase, Fish, Kelp, Shirayamadani, 1929, 11 1/8 In. 1095.00
Vase, Fish, Porcelain, Jens Jensen, 1946, 7 In. 3680.00
Vase, Fish, Sea Green Glaze, Bulbous, Edward Hurley, 1903, 5 7/8 In. 2115.00

Rookwood, Vase,
Blossoms, Pink,
White, Yellow,
Iris Glaze, Oval,
E. Lincoln, 1909,
6 1/4 In.

Rookwood, Vase,
Crocus, Brown,
Green Leaves, Yellow
Ground, Shirayamadani,
1934, 5 1/2 In.

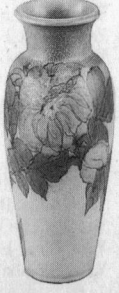

Rookwood, Vase,
Roses, Red, Blue
To Pink Ground,
Baluster,
E. Lincoln, 1929,
13 1/2 x 5 In.

Vase, Fish, Seaweed, Iris Glaze, Olga Reed, 1897, 9 1/2 In. 5175.00
Vase, Flower Band, Bottled Green Matte Glaze, C. Todd, 13 1/2 In. 2468.00
Vase, Flower Band, Egg Shape, Tapered Rim, 1932, 4 5/8 In. 205.00
Vase, Flower Band, Iris Glaze, Katherine Van Horne, 1911, 6 1/4 In. 575.00
Vase, Flower Band, Red, Blue, Green Mottled Matte Glaze, 1914, 8 1/2 In. 863.00
Vase, Flower Band, White, Magenta, Dark Blue Ground, Vellum, McDonald, 9 In. 990.00
Vase, Flower Bands, Porcelain, E.T. Hurley, 1933, 6 1/2 In. 2070.00
Vase, Flowers & Maple Leaves, Olive & Brown Ground, 5 3/4 In. 220.00
Vase, Flowers, Art Deco, Wilhelmine Rehm, 1930, 6 3/4 In. 1840.00
Vase, Flowers, Berries, Brown Crystalline Matte, Ribbed, 1931, 6 3/4 In. 230.00
Vase, Flowers, Blue Ground, Shouldered, Louise Abel, 1920, 14 In. 1998.00
Vase, Flowers, Blue Matte Glaze, Egg Shape, c.1928, 5 1/2 In. 230.00
Vase, Flowers, Blue Matte Ground, Shouldered, E. Lincoln, 19 In. 3525.00
Vase, Flowers, Blue, Flared, M.H. McDonald, 1930, 6 1/2 In. 690.00
Vase, Flowers, Blue, Green, Iris Glaze, William Hentschel, 1920, 5 1/2 In. 690.00
Vase, Flowers, Blue, Moresque, Porcelain, W. Hentschel, 1921, 9 5/8 In. 1840.00
Vase, Flowers, Blue, Round, J.W. Pullman, 1930, 6 In. 550.00
Vase, Flowers, Cream Color, J. Jensen, 1933, 8 In. 690.00
Vase, Flowers, Cylindrical, Carl Schmidt, 1911, 9 In. 1410.00
Vase, Flowers, Embossed, Mottled Blue Matte Glaze, Narrow Neck, 1920, 9 3/4 In. 345.00
Vase, Flowers, Embossed, Red & Green Matte Glaze, Tapered, Bulbous Neck, 7 In. 590.00
Vase, Flowers, Gorham Silver Overlay, Constance Baker, c.1892, 4 3/4 In. 2875.00
Vase, Flowers, Leaves, Vellum Glaze, 1936, 8 x 5 In. 840.00
Vase, Flowers, Low, Fred Rothenbusch, 1926, 4 7/8 In. 2185.00
Vase, Flowers, Matte Glaze, Janet Harris, 1931, 5 In. 978.00
Vase, Flowers, Matte Glaze, Slender Neck, Elizabeth Barrett, 1944, 9 5/8 In. 430.00
Vase, Flowers, Matte Glaze, William Hentschel, 1912, 7 1/4 In. 750.00
Vase, Flowers, Orange, High Glaze, Baluster Shape, 1898, 8 In. 460.00
Vase, Flowers, Pink, Green, Iris Glaze, Ed Diers, 1902, 5 In. 575.00
Vase, Flowers, Purple, Green Matte Glaze, William Hentschel, 1913, 8 7/8 In. 4715.00
Vase, Flowers, Red, Blue, Sara Sax, 1920, 6 1/4 In. 3565.00
Vase, Flowers, Ribbed Lower Body, Sadie Markland, 1894, 7 7/8 In. 1610.00
Vase, Flowers, Standard Glaze, Albert Valentien, 1886, 10 In. 575.00
Vase, Flowers, Standard Glaze, Flattened, Footed, Sallie Coyne, 1892, 4 In. 400.00
Vase, Flowers, Sterling Silver Overlay, Josephine Zettel, 1893, 6 3/8 In. 2300.00
Vase, Flowers, Tan Matte Glaze, Bulbous, Long Tapered Neck, E. Barrett, 17 In. 1645.00
Vase, Flowers, Vellum Glaze, Elizabeth Lincoln, 1923, 6 In. 2300.00
Vase, Flowers, Vellum Glaze, Low, E. Lincoln, 1908, 6 1/2 In. 520.00
Vase, Flowers, Vellum Glaze, Sara Sax, 1922, 8 5/8 In. 3220.00
Vase, Flowers, Vines, Matte Glaze, Margaret McDonald, 1935, 6 7/8 In. 920.00
Vase, Flowers, W. Hentschel, 1904, 9 3/8 In. 1955.00
Vase, Flowers, White, Pale Blue Ground, Matte, M.H. McDonald, 1936, 5 3/4 In. 825.00
Vase, Flowers, White, Thorny Stems, Dark To Light Gray Ground, Iris Glaze, 5 1/2 In. . . . 1100.00
Vase, Flowers, Yellow Stippled Glaze, Vellum, Katherine Jones, 1919, 4 1/8 In. 650.00
Vase, Flowers, Yellow, High Glaze, Loretta Holtkamp, 1952, 3 3/4 In. 230.00
Vase, Freesia Sprays, Iris Glaze, Bulbous, 3 In. 440.00
Vase, Fruit, Flowers, Trellis, Matte Glaze, Janet Harris, 1930, 8 3/8 In. 920.00
Vase, Fruit, Red, Green Ground, E. Diers, 1904, 4 1/2 In. 546.00
Vase, Fruit, Yellow, High Glaze, Lois Furukawa, 1946, 5 3/4 In. 400.00
Vase, Fuchsia, High Glaze, Harriet Wilcox, 1931, 5 1/2 In. 1610.00
Vase, Gazelles Leaping, Wine Madder Glaze, 1944, 4 1/2 In. 115.00
Vase, Geometric Flowers, Incised, Brown, Green Drip Matte, 1925, 9 In. 515.00
Vase, Geometric Pattern, Burnt Orange Matte Glaze, 1925, 6 1/4 In. 259.00
Vase, Geometric Pattern, Carved, Pink, Green Matte, 1914, 5 1/2 In. 545.00
Vase, Geometric Pattern, Glossy Yellow, 1934, 5 1/2 In. 185.00
Vase, Geometric Pattern, Green, Rose Matte, Angular Shoulder, 1912, 5 In. 545.00
Vase, Geometric Pattern, Incised, Porcelain Glaze, Earl Menzel, 1935, 7 1/8 In. 1725.00
Vase, Geometric Pattern, Pink, Green Matte, Tapered, Shouldered, 1914, 8 1/2 In. 690.00
Vase, Geraniums, Red, Porcelain, William Hentschel, 1925, 15 3/4 In. 2875.00
Vase, Gingko Leaves, Fruit, Purple & Green Matte Glaze, Squat, 1913, 2 1/4 In. 805.00
Vase, Glossy Turquoise Crystalline, Flared Rim, 1933, 4 3/4 In. 230.00
Vase, Goldenrod, Iris Glaze, Fechheimer, 1903, 11 In. 8700.00
Vase, Grapes, Jens Jensen, 1945, 6 1/4 In. 865.00

Vase, Grapes, Leaves, Green, Purple, Maroon Ground, Tapered, E. Lincoln, 10 1/2 In. 1880.00
Vase, Gray Drip Over Brown, 1932, 4 1/8 In. 230.00
Vase, Gray, Light Blue, Oxblood Glaze, Tapered, 1923, 8 In. 635.00
Vase, Grecian Figure, Bubbles, Charcoal Drips, Ivory Ground, 1930, 8 x 7 1/2 In. 3220.00
Vase, Greek Key, Green & Red Matte Glaze, 2 Square Handles, 6 1/4 In. 880.00
Vase, Green Blue Glaze, 1923, 7 In. 100.00
Vase, Green Matte Glaze, Cylindrical, 1915, 7 1/2 In. 405.00
Vase, Green To Pink, 1926, 6 1/8 In. 140.00
Vase, Green, Burgundy, Matte Glaze, Charles Todd, 1912, 8 In. 750.00
Vase, Harbor Scene, Blue, Aqua, Pink, Indigo Blue, Vellum, Ed Diers, 1908, 8 3/4 In. 2970.00
Vase, Hawthorn Branches, Iris Glaze, Lenore Asbury, 1910, 8 In. 1380.00
Vase, Holly & Berries, c.1900, 2 1/2 x 1 3/4 In. 220.00
Vase, Hollyhocks, Iris Glaze, Ed Diers, 1903, 17 In. 20700.00
Vase, Horse, Embossed, Blue Glaze, Signed, 4 3/4 In. 250.00
Vase, Horses, Mustard Yellow High Glaze, 1941, 4 3/8 In. 140.00
Vase, House, Mountains, Lake, Arthur Conant, 1920, 5 3/8 In. 2990.00
Vase, Hyacinth Color Matte Glaze, 1929, 4 In. 175.00
Vase, Iris Glaze, Tapering Cylindrical, Irene Bishop, 1905, 6 1/4 In. 1295.00
Vase, Iris, Purple, White, Iris Glaze, Carl Schmidt, 1902, 10 5/8 In. 16100.00
Vase, Irises, Black, Mistletoe, Cobalt Top, Matt Daly, 1900, 13 1/8 In. 18400.00
Vase, Irises, Black, Pink, White Ground, 7 In. 575.00
Vase, Irises, Iris Glaze, Elizabeth Lincoln, 1910, 5 7/8 In. 980.00
Vase, Japanese Scene, Pines, Birds, Ships, Arthur Conant, 1919, 5 1/4 In. 5175.00
Vase, Jonquil, High Glaze, 1894, 4 1/2 In. 405.00
Vase, Jonquil, Leaves, Embossed, Chartreuse Ground, High Glaze, Stegner, 3 1/2 In. 305.00
Vase, Koi Fish, Ivory Porcelain Glaze, Bulbous, MHM, 1944, 4 1/2 In. 518.00
Vase, Lake, Trees, Black & Sage Green, High Glaze, Sallie Coyne, 1917, 9 1/2 In. 1870.00
Vase, Lake, Trees, Vellum Glaze, Sallie Coyne, 1912, 8 In. 2300.00
Vase, Leaf, Green, Blue Matte, Bulbous, Footed, 1927, 8 1/2 In. 865.00
Vase, Leafy Wreath, Ruby Flowers, Elizabeth Lincoln, 1910, 7 In. 635.00
Vase, Leaves, Berries, Gorham Overlay, Olga Geneva Reed, 1893, 9 1/4 In. 4600.00
Vase, Leaves, Berries, Matte Glaze, Flared Rim, E. Lincoln, 1922, 10 1/2 In. 1380.00
Vase, Leaves, Berries, Standard Glaze, Caroline Bonsall, 1901, 4 1/2 In. 518.00
Vase, Leaves, Berries, Standard Glaze, Clara Lindeman, 1906, 5 In. 430.00
Vase, Leaves, Berries, Standard Glaze, Howard Altman, 1901, 4 1/2 In. 520.00
Vase, Leaves, Berries, Wax Matte Glaze, M.H. McDonald, 1930, 5 1/2 In. 575.00
Vase, Leaves, Blue Berries, High Glaze, Jens Jensen, 1945, 6 1/8 In. 1035.00
Vase, Leaves, Blue, Brown Crystalline Matte Glaze, 1935, 5 1/2 In. 210.00
Vase, Leaves, Carved, Brown & Ivory Matte Glaze, Wide Mouth, 4 1/2 In. 295.00
Vase, Leaves, Carved, Gunmetal Blue Matte Glaze, 1919, 12 In. 940.00
Vase, Leaves, Incised, Earl Menzel, 1937, 7 1/4 In. 259.00
Vase, Leaves, Indigo Butterfat Glaze, 1916, 24 1/2 x 11 In. 2185.00
Vase, Leaves, Rose, Green Matte Glaze, Flared, c.1929, 7 1/2 x 8 In. . . . . : 145.00
Vase, Leaves, Seeds, Flowers, Shaded Ground, Shirayamadani, 1894, 10 x 13 In. 465.00
Vase, Leaves, Standard Glaze, 2 Handles, Laura Lindeman, 1902, 4 In. 546.00
Vase, Leaves, Standard Glaze, Howard Altman, 1902, 5 1/2 In. 518.00
Vase, Leaves, Yellow, Ocher, Caramel Yellow Glaze, 7 In. 660.00
Vase, Lilies, Standard Glaze, J. Wareham, 1902, 14 In. 2710.00
Vase, Lily Blossoms, Sea Green Glaze, Sallie Toohey, 1900, 8 1/2 In. 8625.00
Vase, Magnolia, Jens Jensen, 1944, 6 1/2 In. 1035.00
Vase, Maidens, Scantily Clad, Crystalline Glaze, 2 Handles, 9 3/8 In. 430.00
Vase, Maple Leaves, Eliza Lawrence, 5 In. 565.00
Vase, Matte Green Glaze, Narrow Neck, 12 1/2 In. 940.00
Vase, Mice, Blue Ground, Porcelain, Jens Jensen, 6 1/8 In. 2645.00
Vase, Mistletoe, Low, Howard Altman, 1901, 2 5/8 In. 430.00
Vase, Morning Glories, Blue, E.T. Hurley, 1944, 7 1/2 In. 3795.00
Vase, Morning Glories, Matte Glaze, Sallie Coyne, 1925, 6 1/8 In. 1035.00
Vase, Morning Glories, Purple Matte, 1925, 11 In. 1400.00
Vase, Mosaic, Green, Cobalt, Mauve, Yellow, Sallie Coyne, 1930, 6 1/4 In. 770.00
Vase, Mottled Blue Green Matte Glaze, 1917, 5 1/2 In. 175.00
Vase, Mottled Green, Dark Pink Matte Glaze, 1910, 7 7/8 In. 575.00
Vase, Mottled Green, Rose Matte Glaze, Footed, 1916, 3 In. 220.00
Vase, Mottled Mauve Glaze, Shouldered, 1907, 4 1/2 In. 489.00

Vase, Mottled Red, Green Crystalline Drip, 1932, 4 1/4 In. 545.00
Vase, Mums, Yellow, Wasp, Terra-Cotta Ground, A.R. Valentien, 1885, 10 In. 1380.00
Vase, Mushrooms, Black To Green Ground, 1911, 10 In. 10350.00
Vase, Nasturtiums, Bulbous, Flared Rim, Anna M. Valentien, 1899, 10 1/8 In. 825.00
Vase, Nasturtiums, Matte Glaze, Sallie Coyne, 1903, 6 5/8 In. 690.00
Vase, Oak Leaves, Ferns, Brown Crystalline Glaze, 1930, 5 1/8 In. 196.00
Vase, Olive Green Over Orange Glaze, Egg Shape, Cylindrical Neck, 1932, 6 1/2 In. 460.00
Vase, Orchid Cactus Flower, Kataro Shirayamadani, 1899, 19 3/4 In. 17250.00
Vase, Panels, Inset, Pink & Mottled Green Matte Glaze, 1924, 6 1/4 In. 150.00
Vase, Pansies, Loretta Holtkamp, 1945, 4 5/8 In. 290.00
Vase, Pansies, Purple, Lavender, Iris Glaze, Bulbous, Constance Baker, 1902, 6 In. 1495.00
Vase, Path, Trees, Lake, Vellum Glaze, Rothenbusch, 1926, 11 5/8 In. 8050.00
Vase, Peach Branches, Shaded, Standard Glaze, Bulbous, M. Daly, 1890, 10 In. 2300.00
Vase, Peacock Feathers, Arts & Crafts, Charles Todd, 1913, 8 3/8 In. 920.00
Vase, Peacock Feathers, Blue To Mauve Matte Ground, Lincoln, 1920, 12 x 5 In. 1955.00
Vase, Peacock Feathers, Green Matte Glaze, Tapered, 7 1/2 In. 355.00
Vase, Peacock Feathers, Green Over Rose Matte, Buttressed Handles, 6 In. 195.00
Vase, Peacock Feathers, Pink Matte Glaze, 8 7/8 In. 290.00
Vase, Persian Rose, Cylindrical, 1915, 6 1/4 In. 470.00
Vase, Pinecone, Needles, Yellow Matte Glaze, Cylindrical, 1919, 6 1/2 In. 265.00
Vase, Pink Blossoms Raised On Green Stems, Egg Shape, 1907, 8 In. 1410.00
Vase, Pink Matte Glaze, 1949, 6 1/8 In. 58.00
Vase, Pink Matte Glaze, 2 Handles, 1928, 5 1/4 In. 127.00
Vase, Pink Matte Glaze, Baluster, 1927, 11 3/4 In. 230.00
Vase, Pink Matte Glaze, Embossed Neck, 1922, 6 3/4 In. 160.00
Vase, Pink Matte Glaze, Squared Handles, 1927, 6 1/4 In. 140.00
Vase, Poppies, Amber, Standard Glaze, 1893, 8 In. 1095.00
Vase, Poppies, Carved, Yellow, Blue, Plum Butterfat Ground, Todd, 1914, 14 In. 2070.00
Vase, Poppies, Orange, Glaze, Swirled, Ruffled Rim, Matt Daly, 1892, 8 1/2 In. 1955.00
Vase, Poppies, Pink, Pink Mottled Ground, Wax Matte, E. Lincoln, 1927, 9 In. 1540.00
Vase, Poppies, Wheat Stalks, Kataro Shirayamadani, 1934, 6 5/8 In. 1380.00
Vase, Purple Matte Glaze, Angular Handles, c.1914, 7 In. 430.00
Vase, Rain Lily, Purple Ground, Iris Glaze, Olga Geneva Reed, 1902, 9 3/8 In. 3680.00
Vase, Red Flowers, Blue Leaves, Elizabeth Barrett, 1944, 4 1/2 In. 405.00
Vase, Red Matte Glaze, Arts & Crafts, 1903, 10 3/8 In. 1095.00
Vase, Red Matte Glaze, Egg Shape, Early 1900s, 3 5/8 In. 765.00
Vase, Red Matte Glaze, Organic Shape, c.1909, 9 In. 980.00
Vase, Richard Wagner Portrait, 3 Handles, S. Markland, 1896, 8 In. 1840.00
Vase, Rooks, Blue, Green, Blue Matte, Cylindrical, Elizabeth Noonan, 1908, 7 1/2 In. 1840.00
Vase, Rooks, Embossed, Tan, Blue, Crystalline Glaze, 1924, 6 5/8 In. 489.00
Vase, Roosters, Matte, C.S. Todd, 1911, 5 7/8 In. 7475.00
Vase, Roses, Red, Blue To Pink Ground, Baluster, E. Lincoln, 1929, 13 1/2 x 5 In. . . *Illus*   1035.00
Vase, Roses, Standard Glaze, Silver Overlay, 1902, 6 3/4 In. 1840.00
Vase, Roses, Tulips, Indigo, Orange, Green Ground, Lincoln, 1925, 15 x 9 In. 1725.00
Vase, Roses, Vellum Glaze, Sara Sax, 11 In. 3850.00
Vase, Roses, Yellow, Standard Glaze, Bottle Shape, E. Lincoln, 9 In. 550.00
Vase, Sailboats, White, Blue Water, Clouds, Iris Glaze, S. Lawrence, 1903, 11 3/4 In. 4025.00
Vase, Scalloped Band, Brown Drip Rim, Elizabeth Barrett, 1945, 8 In. 575.00
Vase, Sculpted, Green, Blue Matte Glaze, Low, 1913, 7 In. 920.00
Vase, Seaweed, Applied Carved Crab, Brown Glaze, 1885, 5 In.   1495.00
Vase, Snowdrops, White, Sea Green, Sallie Coyne, 1901, 3 1/4 x 2 1/2 In. 1955.00
Vase, Spider Mums, Blue, Vellum Glaze, E.T. Hurley, 1927, 5 7/8 In. 2415.00
Vase, Stork Silhouettes, High Glaze, E.T. Hurley, 1943, 7 1/8 In.   2760.00
Vase, Sunflowers, Yellow, Blue & Ivory Ground, Vellum, Ed Diers, 1921, 5 In. 1100.00
Vase, Sunny Yellow Matte Glaze, 1931, 5 3/8 In. 140.00
Vase, Sunny Yellow Porcelain Glaze, 1921, 11 3/4 In. 259.00
Vase, Swans Flying, Blue & White Ground, Vellum, Bulbous, E. Lincoln, 1911, 6 In. 2415.00
Vase, Swirls, Incised, Indigo Blue Matte Glaze, Art Deco, 1926, 6 In. 358.00
Vase, Tea Roses, Vellum, Shirayamadani, 1933, 7 5/8 In. 1840.00
Vase, Thistle, Blue, Iris Glaze, Albert Valentien, 1903, 11 3/8 In. 10925.00
Vase, Thistle, Embossed, Brown, Lavender, Matthew Andrew Daly, 1901, 13 In. 5175.00
Vase, Tree, Embossed, Green, Yellow Matte Glaze, Arts & Crafts, 1915, 7 In. 520.00
Vase, Tree-Lined Lake, Vellum Glaze, Sallie Coyne, 1922, 7 In. 2070.00

Vase, Trees, Lake, Vellum Glaze, Lenore Asbury, 1917, 9 5/8 In. 4025.00
Vase, Trees, River, Mountains, Vellum, S. Coyne, 1924, 10 3/4 In. 3740.00
Vase, Tropical Landscape, Vellum Glaze, Kataro Shirayamadani, 1911, 10 3/4 In. 2990.00
Vase, Tulips, Green Leaves, Iris Glaze, Olga Reed, 1903, 10 In. 705.00
Vase, Tulips, Green To Apricot Ground, Iris Glaze, Fechheimer, 1903, 10 x 5 In. 1610.00
Vase, Tulips, Iris Glaze, Sara Sax, 1903, 7 3/4 In. 6900.00
Vase, Tulips, Magenta, Mottled Blue Ground, Wax Matte, 1925, 7 In. 1110.00
Vase, Tulips, Peach, Ivory To Peach To Black Ground, Iris Glaze, Fechheimer, 7 In. 1650.00
Vase, Tulips, Yellow, Iris Glaze, Lenore Asbury, 1904, 8 3/4 In. 2875.00
Vase, Turquoise Crystalline Matte Glaze, 2 Handles, 1923, 4 5/8 In. 230.00
Vase, Turquoise Crystalline Matte Glaze, Arts & Crafts, 1931, 7 1/2 In. 719.00
Vase, Turquoise Mottled Matte Glaze, 1922, 4 In. 115.00
Vase, Turquoise Over Mauve, 1932, 4 1/8 In. 259.00
Vase, Turquoise, Yellow, Wide Mouth, 1932, 4 3/4 In. 175.00
Vase, Twilight Scene, Banded, Lenore Asbury, 1913, 7 1/4 In. 920.00
Vase, Venice Harbor, Boats, Porcelain, Carl Schmidt, 1922, 9 1/2 In. 16100.00
Vase, Village, Trees, Vellum Glaze, Ed Diers, 1922, 17 3/8 In. 6325.00
Vase, Vines, Flowers, Blue Brick Wall, Carved, Ocher Ground, C.S. Todd, 1921, 12 In. . . . 2760.00
Vase, Violets, Crystalline Matte Glaze, 1937, 3 3/4 In. 92.00
Vase, Violets, High Glaze, 1946, 3 3/8 In. 259.00
Vase, Violets, Iris Glaze, Ed Diers, 1903, 7 In. 1240.00
Vase, Violets, Pink Ground, Blue Butterfat, Squat, Shirayamadani, 4 1/2 x 3 In., Pair 1840.00
Vase, Water Lilies, Kataro Shirayamadani, 11 In. 3500.00
Vase, Wild Roses, Iris Glaze, Gorham Silver Overlay, Ed Diers, 1904, 9 1/8 In. 16675.00
Vase, Wild Roses, Kataro Shirayamadani, 1945, 6 1/8 In. 1495.00
Vase, Wild Roses, Thorny Branch, Glaze, Egg Shape, E. Lincoln, 1895, 4 1/2 In. 360.00
Vase, Wild Roses, Vellum Glaze, Ed Diers, 1914, 6 3/8 In. 690.00
Vase, Wisteria, Branch, Purple, Iris Glaze, Irene Bishop, 1905, 8 1/4 In. 2300.00
Vase, Yellow To Green, Iris Glaze, Egg Shape, Sara Sax, c.1901, 8 In. 2800.00
Vase, Yellow, Brown Matte Glaze, Arts & Crafts, 1914, 8 1/2 In. 865.00
Wall Pocket, Calla Lily, Yellow Matte Glaze, 1922, 15 1/2 In. 865.00
Wall Pocket, Leaves & Branches, Green Matte Glaze, 1923, 7 1/2 In. 525.00

RORSTRAND was established near Stockholm, Sweden, in 1726. By the
nineteenth century they were making English-style earthenware, bone
china, porcelain, ironstone china, and majolica. The company is still
working. The three crown mark has been used since 1884.

Oyster Plate, 6 Wells, Scallop Shells, 11 In. 3025.00
Tea Set, Teapot, Sugar & Creamer, Marked, c.1890 . . . . 230.00
Vase, Blue Crystalline Glaze, Bulbous, Tapered Neck, Flaring Foot, 4 1/2 In. 345.00
Vase, Blue Glaze, Bottle Shape, Carl Stalhane, 5 In. 295.00
Vase, Blue, Violet Glossy Glaze, 4 Buttressed Handles, 9 3/4 In. 425.00
Vase, Brown & Gray Glaze, Ribbed, Cylindrical, Swollen, Gunnar Nylund, 9 In. 205.00
Vase, Mottled Blue & Brown Matte Glaze, Shouldered, Elongated Flared Neck, 11 In. . . . 380.00
Vase, Mottled Gray Glaze, Bottle Shape, Carl Stalhane, 8 In. 205.00
Vase, Mottled Green & Brown Matte Glaze, Bulbous, Ribbed, Carl Stalhane, 8 In. 380.00
Vase, Violet Glossy Glaze, 4 Looped Buttressed Handles, 9 3/4 In. 425.00

ROSALINE, see Steuben category.

ROSE BOWLS were popular during the 1880s. Rose petals were kept in
the open bowl to add fragrance to a room, a popular idea in a time of
limited personal hygiene. The glass bowls were made with crimped
tops, which kept the petals inside. Many types of Victorian art glass
were made into rose bowls.

Blue Satin Glass, Tooled Camphor Feet, White Berries, Stippled Branches, 4 1/2 In. 69.00
Crackle Glass, Orange Red, Folded & Crimped Top, 5 x 4 1/2 In. 75.00
Crackle Glass, Overshot, Rubina, 4 1/2 x 4 1/2 In. 150.00
Glass, Silver Overlay, Falling Leaves, 4 Ribbed Feet, 4 1/2 x 3 1/2 In. 29.00
Overshot, Tree Branch Feet, Victorian, 1890s, 4 1/2 x 4 1/2 In. 295.00
Pink Cased, White Interior, Pulled Petal Feet, 3 1/4 x 3 In. 105.00
Porcelain, Relief Cherubs, Holding Globe, Scalloped Rim, 4 Ribbed Feet, 5 1/2 In. 155.00
Satin Glass, Diamond Quilted, Turquoise, White Cased Interior, 1930s, 6 x 5 1/2 In. 160.00
Spatterware, Clear Cased, White Interior, Clear Crimped Rim, Reeded Thorn Feet, 6 In. . 295.00

Spatterware, Multicolored, White Interior, Scalloped Seashells, Stevens & Williams, 4 In.   150.00
Strawberry Diamond & Fan, 32-Point Star Base, 4 x 5 1/2 In. 250.00

ROSE CANTON china is similar to Rose Mandarin and Rose Medallion,
except no people or birds are pictured in the decoration. It was made
in China during the nineteenth and twentieth centuries in greens, pinks,
and other colors.

Bowl, Oval, Scalloped Rim, c.1840, 10 1/2 In. 310.00
Bowl, Stand, c.1840, 10 1/2 In. 365.00
Box, Cover, Rectangular, c.1840, 1 3/4 x 4 x 2 3/4 In. 260.00
Punch Bowl, Flared Mouth, Wood Stand, c.1840, 6 1/2 x 16 In. 2300.00

ROSE MANDARIN china is similar to Rose Canton and Rose Medallion.
If the panels in the design picture only people and not birds, it is called
Rose Mandarin.

Bough Pot, Cover, Cracked Ice Ground, 1800s, 7 In. 2070.00
Bowl, Cover, 2 Entwined Form Handles, 1800s, 5 3/4 In. 489.00
Bowl, Figures, Butterfly, Flower Border, Early 1800s, 9 1/2 In. 920.00
Bowl, Vegetable, Cover, Early 1800s, 9 1/2 In., Pair 2070.00
Box, Cover, Cylindrical, 19th Century, 4 3/4 In. 259.00
Box, Cylindrical, Early 1800s, 4 1/2 In. 400.00
Brushpot, Raised Figures, c.1840, 4 1/2 x 2 1/2 In. 259.00
Charger, Shaped Cartouches, Early 1800s, 15 In. 920.00
Coffeepot, c.1820, 9 In. 920.00
Cup & Saucer, Early 1800s 90.00
Cup & Saucer, Figures, 19th Century, Pair 160.00
Cup & Saucer, Figures, Butterfly & Flower Border, c.1820 . . . .   95.00
Dish, Cover, Oval, Figures, c.1800, 13 1/4 In. 3565.00
Dish, Entree, Cover, Square, c.1840, 9 1/2 In. 1380.00
Garden Seat, Hexagonal, Flowers, Early 1800s, 18 1/2 In. 1610.00
Moon Flask, Cover, Flowers, Scene, Early 1800s, 22 1/2 In., Pair 5175.00
Mug Set, Court Life Scenes, 4 Piece 1725.00
Plate, Center Design, Butterflies, Bats, Early 1800s, 10 In. 250.00
Platter, Early 1800s, 18 3/4 In. 3100.00
Platter, Houseboat, Dragons, Early 1800s, 16 In. 5980.00
Platter, Oval, c.1840, 11 In. 1035.00
Punch Bowl, 8 3/4 x 18 1/2 In. 1495.00
Soap Dish, Lid, Drainer, c.1850, 1 1/2 x 5 1/2 x 4 1/2 In. 420.00
Teapot, Entwined Handle, 1800s, 6 In. 374.00
Teapot, Globular Shape, Landscape, Early 1800s, 5 1/2 In. 489.00
Tureen, Twined Handles, c.1810, 7 1/2 In. 863.00
Vase, Arrow Style Necks, Court Scenes, c.1820, 17 In., Pair 5750.00
Vase, Baluster Form, Gilt Stylized Dragon Handles, 1800s, 7 1/2 In. 259.00
Vase, Bottle, Chinese, 1800s, 15 In. 765.00
Vase, Bottle, Rose Medallion Borders, Chinese, 1800s, 16 In.   940.00
Vase, Cylindrical, Mid 19th Century, 9 1/2 In. 315.00
Vase, Famille Rose Enamels, Dragons, Foo Dogs, Chinese, 1800s, 25 In. 2470.00
Vase, Hexagonal, Gilt Dragon Handles, 1800s, 12 In. 940.00
Vase, Hexagonal, Gold Salamanders, c.1825, 24 In., Pair 4370.00
Vase, Hexagonal, Late 1700s, 19 1/2 In., Pair 2990.00
Vase, Hu Form, Mandarin Scenes, Early 1800s, 13 In. 1200.00
Vase, Mandarin Scenes, Flower Gilt Borders, Jui-i Scepter Handles, c.1850, 18 In. 1115.00
Wall Pocket, c.1795, 9 In., Pair 2070.00
Washbowl, Figural, Turned Out Rim, c.1810, 14 1/2 In. 1783.00

ROSE MEDALLION china was made in China during the nineteenth and
twentieth centuries. It is a distinctive design with four or more panels
of decoration around a central medallion that includes a bird or a
peony. The panels show birds and people. The background is a design
of tree peonies and leaves. Pieces are colored in greens, pinks, and
other colors. It is similar to Rose Canton and Rose Mandarin.

Berry Bowl, Oriental Scene, Women, Ruffled Edge, Monogram, 1840s, 9 In. 765.00
Bottle, Water, 19th Century, 13 1/4 In. 825.00

Bowl, 20th Century, 10 In. 460.00
Bowl, c.1840, 6 In. 230.00
Bowl, c.1840, 12 In. 3450.00
Bowl, c.1840, 16 In. 1725.00
Bowl, Circular, Scalloped Rim, c.1840, 9 In. 315.00
Bowl, Cover, Side Handle, Bird & Flower, Late 1800s, 10 In. 489.00
Bowl, Cut Corner, Square, c.1840, 9 1/2 In. 865.00
Bowl, Flower Form, WAR Monogram, Early 1800s, 10 In. 575.00
Bowl, Fruit, Liner, 9 1/2 x 11 & 10 x 9 x 4 In. 1800.00
Bowl, Rim Foot, Scenes, 1800s, 6 In. 259.00
Bowl, Vegetable, Cover, Oval, Bird, Butterfly, Flower, c.1840, 11 1/2 In. 430.00
Bowl, Vegetable, Cover, Oval, Pinecone Finial, c.1840, 11 1/2 In., Pair 750.00
Bowl, Vegetable, Cover, Pinecone Finial, Monogram, c.1810, 9 1/2 In., Pair 1495.00
Bowl, Vegetable, Cover, Rectangular, 1800s, 8 In. 295.00
Box, Cover, c.1830, 4 In. 290.00
Box, Cover, Cylindrical, Figures, Bird, Flower, c.1850, 3 1/2 In. 315.00
Box, Cover, Cylindrical, Scenes, 1800s, 4 3/4 x 4 In. 460.00
Box, Cylindrical, c.1850, 4 1/2 x 4 In. 400.00
Brushpot, Cylindrical, c.1840, 4 1/4 In. 219.00
Brushpot, Cylindrical, c.1840, 5 x 5 In. 345.00
Brushpot, Cylindrical, Reserves Of Domestic Scenes, Flowers, 1800s, 6 In. 430.00
Butter, Cover, Insert, 6 In. 169.00
Butter, Dome Cover, c.1850, 7 1/2 In. 315.00
Cachepot, Hexagonal, Undertray, Birds, Figures, c.1840, 11 In. 1725.00
Cachepot, Miniature, 19th Century, 2 1/4 In., Pair 259.00
Candlestick, Scene, Flowers, c.1850, 8 In., Pair 1035.00
Candlestick, Trumpet Form, Early 1800s, 6 In., Pair 690.00
Cann, Cup, Cylindrical, Gilt Twist Handle, c.1840, 5 In. 489.00
Charger, 19th Century, 14 In. 575.00
Charger, 19th Century, 18 In. 345.00
Charger, Alternating Figures, Flower & Birds, c.1850, 16 In. 885.00
Charger, Enamel, 1800s, 13 1/2 In. 700.00
Chestnut Basket, Underplate, Famille Rose, 3 x 8 1/2 x 1/2 In. 980.00
Compote, Early 1800s, 10 In. 635.00
Compote, Oval, Footed, Birds, c.1870, 11 3/4 x 15 1/4 In. 1035.00
Creamer, Bulbous, 1800s, 3 1/2 In. 230.00
Creamer, Scalloped Rim, Paneled Sides, Late 19th Century, 4 3/4 In. 500.00
Cup, Armorial, Round Body, Loop Handle, c.1770, 2 1/2 In. 520.00
Cup & Saucer, 1800s 69.00
Dish, Cover, Oval, Gilt Fruit Finial, 1800s, 5 In. 375.00
Dish, Cover, Rectangular, Oriental Scenes, 9 1/2 In. 425.00
Dish, Egg Shape, Ring Foot, c.1840, 12 1/4 In. 430.00
Dish, Footed, Figures, Birds, Flowers, c.1840, 12 1/4 In. 430.00
Dish, Hot Water, c.1830, 10 1/2 In. 405.00
Dish, Leaf Form, Bird & Flower, Early 1800s, 7 1/2 In. 315.00
Dish, Leaf Form, WAR Monogram, Early 1800s, 7 1/4 In. 175.00
Dish, Leaf Shape, Early 1800s, 7 3/4 In. 315.00
Dish, Leaf Shape, Mandarin Scenes, Orange Peel Glaze, 8 In. 98.00
Dish, Lobed Oval, Butterflies, Gilt Ground, Flowers, Late 1800s, 10 1/2 In., Pair 430.00
Dish, Oval, Alternating Flowers & Scenes, c.1840, 12 1/2 In. 405.00
Dish, Rectangular, Scenes, People, Birds, Flowers, c.1810, 7 1/2 x 8 3/4 In., Pair 920.00
Dish, Scalloped Rim, 19th Century, 2 1/4 x 10 1/4 In. 470.00
Dish, Sweetmeat, Leaf Shape, c.1840, 7 1/4 In., Pair 460.00
Flask, Moon, Gilt Bat-Shape Handles, 1800s, 16 In., Pair 2820.00
Fruit Basket, Undertray, Bird & Flower, Open Latticework, Early 1800s, 10 In. 1610.00
Garden Seat, Barrel Form, c.1840, 18 In. 3450.00
Garden Seat, Drum Form, Landscape, Bird & Flowers, c.1810, 18 1/2 In. 4370.00
Garden Seat, Hexagonal, Figures, Gilt Flowers, 1800s, 18 1/2 In., Pair 8510.00
Gravy Boat, Double Spout, Late 1800s, 8 In. 235.00
Jar, Cover, Miniature, c.1840, 2 1/2 In. 200.00
Jar, Cover, Square, Birds & Flower, Chinese Women, 1800s, 7 1/2 In., Pair 2070.00
Lamp, Vase, Applied Gold, Carved Wood Base, 29 1/4 In., Pair 300.00
Mug, Entwined Handle, c.1840, 5 In. 375.00

Mug, Entwined Handle, Early 1800s, 4 1/4 In. 430.00
Pitcher, Cream, c.1850, 5 1/4 In. 175.00
Pitcher, Early 1800s, 3 1/2 In. 185.00
Plate, Early 1800s, 9 1/2 In., Pair 160.00
Plate, Gilt Border, Birds, Butterflies, Fruit, Flowers, 1800s, 10 In., Pair 646.00
Plate, Pierced Rim, 8 1/2 In. 85.00
Plate, Roundel, Flower Scrolls, Lavender, Late 1800s, 8 1/2 In. 150.00
Plate, Scenes, Birds, Flowers, Early 1800s, 7 3/4 In., Pair 259.00
Platter, Deep, Reticulated Liner, Early 1800s, 16 3/4 In. 2645.00
Platter, Drain Plate, People, Court Scene, Birds, Flowers, 18 x 15 In. 920.00
Platter, Oval, Bird & Flower, 1800s, 18 1/2 In. 1208.00
Platter, Oval, Historical Event Scene, Late 1800s, 14 In. 825.00
Platter, Oval, People, Separated By Birds, Flowers, 14 1/4 In. 365.00
Punch Bowl, 19th Century, 5 1/4 x 13 1/4 In. .... 765.00 ·
Punch Bowl, 19th Century, 6 3/8 x 15 1/2 In. ....1765.00 to 2000.00
Punch Bowl, Birds, Flowers, Figures, c.1840, 13 1/2 In. 290.00
Punch Bowl, Court Life Scenes, Famille Rose, 20th Century, 8 1/4 x 18 1/4 In. 2530.00
Punch Bowl, Flowers, Birds, Insects, 6 x 14 1/2 In. 1200.00
Punch Bowl, Mandarin Panels, Early 1800s, 16 In. 3450.00
Punch Bowl, Paneled, Polychrome, People, Flowers, Birds, c.1865, 10 3/4 In. 865.00
Punch Bowl, People, Butterfly, Flower Border, Early 1800s, 15 1/2 In. 3565.00
Sauceboat, Entwined Handle, 1800s, 3 x 7 In. 250.00
Sauceboat, Entwined Handle, Early 1800s, 7 1/8 In. 400.00
Sauceboat, Leaf Form, Early 1800s, 7 3/4 In. 175.00
Sauceboat, Undertray, Oval, Side Handles, Birds, Flowers, 1800s, 8 In. 546.00
Serving Dish, Circular, Birds, Flowers, Early 1800s, 14 1/2 In. 635.00
Serving Dish, Figures, Birds, Flowers, Early 1800s, 10 1/2 In. 430.00
Serving Dish, Footed, Monogram, Oval, Early 1800s, 15 1/4 In. ....520.00 to 800.00
Serving Dish, Jui-i Scepter, Monogram, Early 1800s, 10 1/2 In. 316.00
Serving Dish, Oval, Early 1800s, 10 3/4 In. 400.00
Serving Dish, Pierced Lattice Border, Oval, c.1810, 9 1/2 In. 375.00
Serving Dish, Rectangular, Panels, c.1830, 9 In. 240.00
Sugar & Creamer, 1800s, 4 3/4 In. 259.00
Sugar & Creamer, Saucer, 19th Century 145.00
Tea Service, Flower, Birds, Butterflies, Early 1800s, 8 1/4 x 9 In., 16 Piece 1035.00
Teapot, Cover, Straight Sides, Ribbon Handle, Footed, c.1800, 5 x 5 1/2 In. 690.00
Teapot, Cover, Urn Shape, Birds, Flowers, c.1860, 10 1/2 x 11 In. 920.00
Teapot, Dome Cover, 1800s, 8 x 11 In. 690.00
Teapot, Dome Cover, Early 1800s, 10 In. 805.00
Teapot, Drum Form, Wicker Handle, 1800s, 5 In. 115.00
Teapot, High Dome Cover, Baluster Form, Gilt Ball Finial, c.1840, 10 In. 460.00
Teapot, Mandarin Scenes, 2 Handleless Cups, Wicker Case, 9 x 5 In. Case 170.00
Teapot, Twig Handles, c.1820, 8 1/2 x 5 In. 1495.00
Thimble Case, Barrel Form, 19th Century, 1 1/2 In. 315.00
Tureen, Cover, Entwined Handles, Flower Form Finial, c.1850, 8 In. 660.00
Tureen, Cover, Oval, Entwined Handles, Early 1800s, 15 1/2 In. 2070.00
Tureen, Cover, Oval, Lotus Blossom Knop, Gilt, 19th Century, 7 3/8 x 8 3/4 In. 765.00
Tureen, Dome Cover, Oval, Entwined Handles, Flower Finial, c.1840, 13 1/2 In. 1265.00 to 2300.00
Tureen, Sauce, Undertray, Cover, Early 1800s, 8 1/4 In. 1265.00
Tureen, Sauce, Undertray, Monogram, c.1810, 8 1/2 In., Pair 2185.00
Tureen, Soup, Ogee Form, Dragon & Pearl Handle, Late 1800s, 11 In. 600.00
Urinal, Cover, Chinese Figures, Handle 1345.00
Urn, Scalloped Rim, Egg Shape, Figures, Birds, c.1840, 24 1/2 In., Pair 4370.00
Vase, Baluster Form, Folded Rim, 1800s, 17 1/2 In. 1150.00
Vase, Baluster Shape, Domestic Life Scenes, Applied Dragon, Late 1800s, 9 In. 200.00
Vase, Baluster Shape, Dragons, Foo Dog Handles, 1800s, 17 1/2 In., Pair 2185.00
Vase, Bottle Shape, Club Form, Relief Dragon, Early 1800s, 11 1/2 In. 545.00
Vase, Cover, Bottle Shape, Celadon Ground, 1800s, 14 In. 705.00
Vase, Cover, Bottle, Panels, Early 1800s, 18 In. 1265.00
Vase, Cover, Egg Shape, Nature, Court Life Cartouches, c.1800, 26 1/2 In., Pair 5750.00
Vase, Cylindrical, Flowers, Butterflies, 1800s, 8 1/4 x 3 3/4 In. 460.00
Vase, Cylindrical, Molded Decoration, 1800s, 4 In. 145.00
Vase, Dome Cover, Teardrop Shape, Medallions, Flowers, c.1810, 16 In. 1150.00

Vase, Flat Baluster, Figures In Courtyard, Vine, Berry, 12 In., Pair 920.00
Vase, Gilt Applique, 19th Century, 17 3/4 In., Pair 1495.00
Vase, Lion Handles, Relief Dragons At Neck, Early 1800s, 24 1/2 In. 1610.00
Vase, Mounted As Lamp, Rosewood Base, 19th Century, 7 1/2 In., Pair 200.00
Vase, Rouleau Form, Lion's Head Handle, Early 1800s, 24 In., Pair 3450.00
Warming Platter, 1800s, 16 In. 865.00
Washbowl, c.1840, 15 3/4 In. 920.00
Washbowl, Spangle, Butterfly & Flower Border, c.1810, 16 1/2 In. 970.00

ROSE O'NEILL, see Kewpie category.

ROSE TAPESTRY porcelain was made by the Royal Bayreuth factory of Tettau, Germany, during the late nineteenth century. The surface of the porcelain was pressed against a coarse fabric while it was still damp, and the impressions remained on the finished porcelain. It looks and feels like a textured cloth. Very skillful reproductions are being made that even include a variation of the Royal Bayreuth mark, so be careful when buying.

Biscuit Jar, Applied Handles, Gilt, 5 1/2 x 6 3/8 In. 805.00
Bowl, Gilt Brass Mounted, Handles, Louis XVI, 13 1/2 x 18 In. 980.00
Box, Cover, 3 Corners, 2 x 3 1/2 In. 60.00
Cake Plate, Blue Mark, 10 In. 260.00
Chocolate Set, 4 Cups & Saucers, Chocolate Pot, 9 Piece 3950.00
Creamer, Pinched Spout, Flared Base, Pink, Yellow, White, Gold Trim, 3 1/4 In. 425.00
Dresser Box, Cover, Round, 2 1/8 x 3 3/8 In. 185.00
Hair Receiver, Cover, Oval, Marked, 4 1/4 x 6 x 5 1/2 In. 200.00
Hatpin Holder, 15 Hole, 4 3/4 In. 150.00
Relish, Handles, Green Mark, 8 1/4 In. 85.00
Sugar & Creamer 335.00
Tray, Dresser, Roses, Pink, Cream, 7 3/8 x 10 In. 425.00
Tray, Green, Marked, 11 1/2 x 8 1/4 In. 200.00

ROSENTHAL porcelain was made at the factory established in Selb, Bavaria, in 1880. The factory is still making fine-quality tablewares and figurines. A series of Christmas plates was made from 1910. Other limited edition plates have been made since 1971.

Bowl, Birdcage, Raymond Loewy, Royal Continental China Porcelain, 5 1/2 x 7 In. 47.00
Charger, Water Lily, Blue Ground, 13 In. 23.00
Coffee Service, Studio Line, Flash Frisco, Dorothy Hafner, 9-In. Pot, 3 Piece 288.00
Dinner Service, Regina Pattern, 114 Piece 575.00
Figurine, Nude Boy, Holding Flower Bundles, Gray Hair, Gilt Flowers, 6 1/2 In. 144.00
Figurine, Nude Woman, Green Flowing Cloth, 7 3/4 In. 100.00
Figurine, Poodle, Dancing, Playful, Open Mouth, Black, 8 1/2 In. 130.00
Figurine, Poodle, Lying Down, White, 4 1/4 x 7 In. 100.00
Figurine, Poodle, Seated, Pet Clip, Curious, White, 5 3/4 x 5 1/2 In. 90.00
Figurine, Poodle, Seated, White, 6 In. 100.00
Figurine, Poodle, Standing On Hind Legs, Playful, 8 1/2 In. 160.00
Figurine, Poodle, Standing, Gray, 6 x 6 In. 110.00
Figurine, Poodle, Standing, Playful, White, 7 1/4 x 10 In. .... 100.00 to 140.00
Figurine, Woman, Blue Skirt, Yellow Cloth On Head, 8 In. 400.00
Vase, Glazed, Beate Kuhn, Germany, c.1952, 6 x 8 x 6 In. 350.00
Vase, Organic Form, White Porcelain, Ribbed, Martin Freyer, 3 1/2 In. 58.00
Vase, Organic Form, White Porcelain, Ribbed, Martin Freyer, 4 1/2 In. 29.00

ROSEVILLE Pottery Company was organized in Roseville, Ohio, in 1890. Another plant was opened in Zanesville, Ohio, in 1898. Many types of pottery were made until 1954. Early wares include Sgraffito, Olympic, and Rozane. Later lines were often made with molded decorations, especially flowers and fruit. Most pieces are marked *Roseville*. Many reproductions made in China have been offered for sale the past few years.

Apple Blossom, Bookends, Green, 5 In. 200.00
Apple Blossom, Pedestal, Pink, Marked, 16 1/2 In. 230.00
Apple Blossom, Vase, Blue, 12 In. 288.00
Apple Blossom, Vase, Blue, White, Cylindrical, Footed, 1948, 9 In. 200.00

Apple Blossom, Vase, Green, Handles, 7 In., Pair 230.00
Apple Blossom, Wall Pocket, Blue, 8 In., Pair 489.00
Apple Blossom, Wall Pocket, Green, Marked, 8 In., Pair 288.00
Artcraft, Jardiniere, Pedestal, Orange, 28 3/4 In. 3220.00
Autumn, Jardiniere, 8 1/2 x 11 1/2 In. 635.00
Aztec, Vase, Blue, Stylized Flowers, Squeezebag, Tapered, 11 x 3 In. 690.00
Aztec, Vase, Orange, Stylized Flowers, 9 1/4 x 3 1/2 In. 288.00
Azurean, Vase, Blue, Trees, Bulbous, Signed, 14 x 7 1/2 In. 575.00
Baneda, Jardiniere, Green, 8 x 11 1/4 In. 1610.00
Baneda, Jardiniere, Green, Handles, 4 1/4 x 5 1/2 In. 489.00
Baneda, Vase, Green, 1933, 6 In. 500.00
Baneda, Vase, Green, 9 In. 1238.00
Baneda, Vase, Green, Bulbous, Handles, Foil Label, 6 1/4 x 3 1/2 In. 460.00
Baneda, Vase, Green, Square Handles, 4 In. 330.00
Baneda, Vase, Pink, 9 In. 575.00
Baneda, Vase, Pink, Bulbous, Handles, 10 1/4 x 8 In. ....1100.00 to 1265.00
Baneda, Vase, Pink, Bulbous, Handles, 5 1/4 x 4 1/2 In. 575.00
Baneda, Vase, Pink, Flared, Footed, Handles, 7 1/2 x 4 1/4 In. ....750.00 to 805.00
Baneda, Vase, Pink, Panel, Blue, Green Leaves, Globular, Handles, 6 1/2 In. 525.00
Baneda, Vase, Pink, Purple Glazed Foot, Arched Handles, 9 1/8 In. 715.00
Baneda, Wall Pocket, Green, 8 In. 4200.00
Bittersweet, Bowl, Green, Marked, 12 In. 145.00
Blackberry, Jardiniere, Pedestal, Relief Berries & Leaves, 28 x 12 1/2 In. 3080.00
Blackberry, Vase, Bulbous, Flared, Handles, 5 1/4 x 4 3/4 In. 415.00
Blackberry, Vase, Handles, 8 In. 690.00
Blackberry, Vase, Handles, 12 In. 1840.00
Blackberry, Vase, Squat, Handles, 4 1/4 x 6 In. 489.00
Blackberry, Wall Pocket, Foil Label, 8 1/4 x 6 3/4 In. 2415.00
Blackberry, Wall Pocket, Pierced Windows, 8 In. 1650.00
Bleeding Heart, Wall Pocket, Pink, 8 In., Pair 460.00
Burmese, Bookends, Green, 7 In. 144.00
Bushberry, Bookends, Gray, Marked, 5 In. 230.00
Bushberry, Jardiniere, Green, Red Berries, Handles, 1948, 7 In. 165.00
Bushberry, Tea Set, Brown, Marked, 6-In. Teapot, 3 Piece 400.00
Bushberry, Vase, Blue, Marked, 18 In. 630.00
Bushberry, Vase, Green, 12 In. 400.00
Bushberry, Wall Pocket, Brown, 8 In., Pair 400.00
Cameo, Jardiniere, Ivory, 12 Maidens Dancing, Footed, 10 x 10 1/2 In. 220.00
Carnelian I, Vase, Green, 12 In. 288.00
Carnelian I, Vase, Yellow, Bulbous, Handles, Marked, 8 1/4 x 5 In. 230.00
Carnelian I, Wall Pocket, Blue Green, Handles, 7 1/2 In. ....175.00 to 230.00
Carnelian II, Lamp Base, Red, Mottled, Ocher, Purple Glaze, Round, 8 1/4 In. 748.00
Carnelian II, Urn, Cover, Green, Blue, Lavender Mottled Glaze, 15 x 9 In. 546.00
Carnelian II, Urn, Purple, Green, Rose & Ocher Glaze, Handles, 15 x 10 In. 1150.00
Carnelian II, Urn, Yellow, Blue, Green, Buff, Stovepipe Neck, Handles, 10 In. 374.00
Carnelian II, Vase, Blue, Gray, Lavender Glaze, Bulbous, Handles, 9 x 8 1/4 In. 300.00
Carnelian II, Vase, Mauve, Green, Ocher, Purple Glaze, Bulbous, Handles, 8 1/4 In. 575.00
Carnelian II, Vase, Ocher, Mauve, Brown, Gourd, Marked, 7 1/4 x 5 1/4 In. 345.00
Carnelian II, Vase, Ocher, Mauve, Green Glaze, Squat, Handles, 6 1/4 x 9 3/4 In. 300.00
Carnelian III, Vase, Pink, Seafoam, Ocher, Lavender Glaze, Buttresses, 16 1/2 In. 6038.00
Cherry Blossom, Bowl, Urn, Brown, Recessed Neck, Looped Handles, 4 1/2 In. 440.00
Cherry Blossom, Bowl, White, Gray, c.1932, 3 3/4 x 11 In. 105.00
Cherry Blossom, Planter, Pink, Green, Handles, 4 x 5 1/4 In. 316.00
Cherry Blossom, Vase, Brown, 7 1/8 In. 430.00
Cherry Blossom, Vase, Brown, Bulbous, 7 x 5 In. 430.00
Cherry Blossom, Vase, Brown, Handles, 12 1/2 x 6 3/4 In. 805.00
Cherry Blossom, Vase, Cerulean Blue, Panels, Looped Handles, 4 In. 358.00
Cherry Blossom, Vase, Pink, Green, Urn Shape, c.1930s, 7 1/4 In. 322.00
Chloron, Pitcher, Green, Swirled Design, Ring Handle, 7 1/2 x 4 1/2 In. 375.00
Clemana, Urn, Brown, 7 In. 316.00
Clemana, Vase, Green, Bulbous, Impressed, 9 In. 288.00
Clematis, Basket, Rust, Brown, Gold, c.1944, 10 1/2 In. 105.00
Clematis, Wall Pocket, Brown, Raised Mark, 8 In. 115.00

Clematis, Wall Pocket, Green, Raised Mark, 8 In. 230.00
Columbine, Ewer, Brown, 7 In. 144.00
Columbine, Flower Frog, Tan, 6 In. 175.00
Columbine, Vase, Brown, Bulbous, Footed, Handles, Marked, 10 In. 318.00
Columbine, Vase, Brown, Buttressed Base, Marked, 12 In. 430.00
Columbine, Vase, Ocher To Green, Bulbous, Handles, 6 1/4 x 9 In. 220.00
Columbine, Vase, Pink, 16 1/2 In. ....*Illus* 690.00
Columbine, Wall Pocket, Blue, 8 In. 635.00
Columbine, Wall Pocket, Brown, 8 In. 259.00
Corinthian, Jardiniere, Pedestal 825.00
Cosmos, Basket, Blue, Foil Label, 12 In. 578.00
Cosmos, Jardiniere, Blue, 5 3/4 In. 210.00
Cosmos, Jardiniere, Green, 3 1/2 In. 140.00
Cosmos, Vase, Blue, 6 1/4 In. 195.00
Cosmos, Vase, Blue, Oval, Flared Rim, Handles, Marked, 9 In. 460.00
Cosmos, Vase, Brown, Bulbous, Handles, Marked, 7 In. 290.00
Cremona, Vase, Pink, Blue Blossoms, 4 Sides, 10 1/4 x 3 3/4 In. 230.00
Cremona, Vase, Stylized Leaves & Berries, Yellow, Banded Branch, 10 1/4 x 5 3/4 In. 315.00
Dahlrose, Bowl, 3 5/8 x 10 In. 210.00
Dahlrose, Bowl, 4 In. 230.00
Dahlrose, Candlestick, 3 1/2 In., Pair 219.00
Dahlrose, Jardiniere, 6 In. 259.00
Dahlrose, Jardiniere, 8 In. 405.00
Dahlrose, Planter, Hanging, Ocher, Teal Green & Brown Mouth, 5 1/2 x 8 1/4 In. .. 195.00
Dahlrose, Vase, Brown, Handles, 10 In. 460.00
Dahlrose, Vase, Bud, Double, 6 In. 185.00
Dahlrose, Vase, Bud, Triple, Brown, 6 In. ....230.00 to 290.00
Dahlrose, Vase, Bulbous, 10 x 9 1/4 In. 1610.00
Dahlrose, Vase, Ocher, Blue, Panel, Relief Flowers, Square Handles, 8 x 7 In. 248.00
Dahlrose, Vase, Oval, Flared, Handles, 10 x 7 In. 460.00
Dahlrose, Vase, Pink, Green, Squat, Handles, 6 1/4 x 7 1/4 In. 145.00
Dahlrose, Wall Pocket, 2 Flowers, Pink, Green, 10 x 6 3/4 In. 316.00
Dahlrose, Wall Pocket, 8 In. 316.00
Della Robbia, Vase, 12 Fish, Mustard, Brown, 10 5/8 In. 4140.00
Della Robbia, Vase, Cavalier, Trees, Pink Tulips, Incised, G.B., 18 1/2 x 5 In. 8050.00
Della Robbia, Vase, Grape Panels, Brown, Green, Bottle Shape, 10 x 4 1/4 In. 2415.00
Della Robbia, Vase, Stylized Mums, Carved, Yellow, Green, Wafer Mark, 8 1/2 In. 4600.00
Dogwood I, Jardiniere, Pedestal, 28 In. 1495.00
Donatello, Candlestick, 8 In., Pair 115.00
Donatello, Jardiniere, 10 x 13 In. 385.00
Donatello, Jardiniere, Pedestal, 22 1/2 x 10 In. 260.00
Donatello, Vase, Bulbous, Flared Rim, 11 3/4 x 6 1/2 In. 260.00
Donatello, Vase, Flared, Footed, 11 3/4 x 6 1/2 In. 175.00
Donatello, Vase, Trial Glaze, Ribs, Cylindrical, 11 3/4 x 5 3/4 In. 145.00
Donatello, Wall Pocket, Impressed Mark, 11 x 5 1/4 In. 259.00
Donatello, Wall Pocket, Marked, 10 x 4 1/2 In. 200.00
Earlam, Vase, Blue Green, Flared, Buttressed Base, 9 1/4 x 5 1/2 In. 430.00
Earlam, Vase, Green, Blue Streak Glaze, Ocher Interior, Bulbous, Handles, 7 1/4 In. 605.00
Earlam, Vase, Green, Blue, Pink, 4 Sides, 9 x 6 In. 865.00
Egypto, Pitcher, Green, Scalloped Mouth, Vine Handle, 6 1/2 x 7 In. 550.00
Egypto, Urn, Green, Handles, 12 x 5 In. 546.00
Egypto, Vase, Dark Green Matte Glaze, Oil Lamp Shape, 9 1/2 x 9 In. 1495.00
Falline, Vase, Blue, Egg Shape, Looped Handles, 7 1/4 x 5 1/2 In. 880.00
Falline, Vase, Blue, Trumpet Shape, 2 Handles, 8 1/2 x 6 1/2 In. 1760.00
Falline, Vase, Brown, Bulbous, Handles, 8 x 8 In. 690.00
Falline, Vase, Brown, Handles, 7 In. ....315.00 to 575.00
Falline, Vase, Brown, Low Handles, 12 1/2 In. 2815.00
Falline, Vase, Brown, Pea Pods, Trumpet Shape, Handles, 8 1/2 In. 550.00
Ferella, Candlestick, Rose, Handles, 4 In. 520.00
Ferella, Vase, Brown, Handles, 8 1/2 x 7 In. 635.00
Ferella, Vase, Brown, Ocher, Torpedo Shape, Pierced, Long Curved Handles, 9 1/4 In. 770.00
Ferella, Vase, Brown, Oval, Flared, Buttressed Handles, 10 1/4 x 6 1/4 In. 920.00
Ferella, Vase, Red, Relief Flowers, Genie Bottle, Pierced, Angular Handles, 4 1/2 x 6 In. .. 470.00

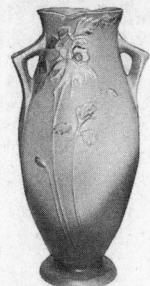

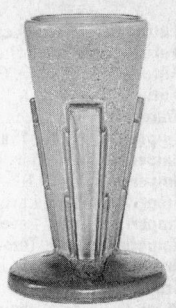

Roseville, Columbine, Vase, Pink, 16 1/2 In.

Roseville, Fuchsia, Vase, Green, Handle, 6 In.

Roseville, Futura, Vase, Brown, Green, Cone, 3 Buttresses, 8 In.

Ferella, Vase, Rose, 5 In.	690.00
Ferella, Wall Pocket, Red, Green, 6 3/4 x 6 1/2 In.	1725.00
Florentine, Basket, Hanging, Brown, 6 1/2 x 10 1/2 In.	145.00
Foxglove, Vase, Green, 16 In.	460.00
Foxglove, Vase, Pink, Handles, Marked, 16 In.	635.00
Foxglove, Wall Pocket, Green, Marked, 8 In.	520.00
Foxglove, Wall Pocket, Green, Pink, White, Marked, 8 In.	320.00
Freesia, Basket, Hanging, Yellow Brown, 5 In.	115.00
Freesia, Bowl, Blue, White, c.1945, 3 1/2 x 14 In.	115.00
Freesia, Jardiniere, Green, Handles, Marked, 8 In., Pair	635.00
Freesia, Tea Set, Green, Marked, 8-In. Teapot, 3 Piece	520.00
Freesia, Vase, Green, Handles, Raised Mark, 8 In.	175.00
Freesia, Wall Pocket, Brown, Handles, Marked, 8 In.	200.00
Freesia, Wall Pocket, Brown, Marked, 8 In.	145.00 to 200.00
Freesia, Wall Pocket, Green, 8 In., Pair	316.00
Fuchsia, Basket, Hanging, Green, 5 x 7 In.	316.00
Fuchsia, Bowl, Green, Marked, 8 In.	230.00
Fuchsia, Jardiniere, Blue, 3 1/2 In.	219.00
Fuchsia, Jardiniere, Brown, Impressed, 3 In.	200.00
Fuchsia, Jardiniere, Pedestal, Blue, 30 In.	2300.00
Fuchsia, Vase, Blue, 8 In.	345.00
Fuchsia, Vase, Brown, Looped Handles, Footed, 12 1/4 In.	440.00
Fuchsia, Vase, Green, Handle, 6 In. *Illus*	184.00
Fuchsia, Vase, Green, Handles, 7 1/2 In., Pair	430.00
Fuchsia, Vase, Green, Sheared Rim, 7 In.	290.00
Fuchsia, Wall Pocket, Blue, 8 In.	750.00
Fudji, Vase, Art Nouveau, 10 5/8 In.	2185.00
Fudji, Vase, Geometric, 1906, 10 In.	1450.00
Fujiyama, Vase, Bisque, Orange Peonies, 11 x 4 In.	750.00 to 810.00
Futura, Jardiniere, Gray, Pink & Blue Leaves, 10 x 15 In.	175.00
Futura, Jardiniere, Orange, Polychrome Leaves, Handles, 10 x 14 1/4 In.	175.00
Futura, Jardiniere, Tan, Green Borders, Handles, 9 1/2 In.	748.00
Futura, Planter, Yellow, Blue, Green, Embossed Branches, Leaves, 4-Sided, 5 x 7 In.	546.00
Futura, Vase, Beer Mug, Handles, Paper Label, 6 1/4 x 3 1/2 In.	575.00
Futura, Vase, Blue, Green Leaves, 7 In.	1150.00
Futura, Vase, Blue, Rectangular, 5 1/2 In.	545.00
Futura, Vase, Blue, Yellow, Green, Footed, 4 In.	750.00
Futura, Vase, Brown, Green, Cone, 3 Buttresses, 8 In. *Illus*	805.00
Futura, Vase, Brown, Orange, Arches, Faceted, Stepped Base, Handles, 14 x 5 3/4 In.	4600.00
Futura, Vase, Green Matte Glaze, Square Column, c.1928, 8 1/2 In.	1035.00
Futura, Vase, Ocher, Art Deco Panel At Shoulder, Square Handles, 6 1/4 In.	440.00
Futura, Vase, Orange, Green, Pink, Cone, Stepped, 10 1/2 x 4 3/4 In.	489.00
Futura, Vase, Pine Cones, Blue, Green, Yellow Drip, Buttresses, Bulbous, Flared, 10 In.	920.00
Futura, Vase, Pink, Green, Handles, 8 1/2 In.	633.00
Futura, Vase, Red Vee, 7 In.	460.00
Futura, Vase, Space Capsule, Ivory To Brown, Flowers, Raised Bands, Flared Neck, 8 In.	470.00

Futura, Vase, Table Leg, Orange, Green, Flared, Buttresses, Stepped, Geometric, 12 In. . . . 2185.00
Futura, Vase, Tank, Orange To Blue Mottled Glaze, 9 1/2 x 9 In. 9775.00
Futura, Vase, Yellow, Green, Blue Glaze, Triangular, 4 x 5 In. 345.00
Futura, Wall Pocket, Tan, Cream, Green, Handles, 8 In. . . . . *Illus* 374.00
Gardenia, Vase, Green, Handles, 16 In. 489.00
Imperial I, Planter, Round, 8 1/2 x 9 1/2 In. 345.00
Imperial I, Vase, Handles, 9 1/2 x 8 In. 405.00
Imperial II, Bowl, Blue, Frothy Yellow Glaze, Flared, 5 x 12 1/2 In. 575.00
Imperial II, Vase, Lavender Over Turquoise, 5 In. 345.00
Imperial II, Vase, Lavender, Yellow Mottled Glaze, Tear Shape, Ribs, 6 1/2 x 5 3/4 In. . . . 330.00
Imperial II, Vase, Turquoise, Lavender, 4 1/2 In. 430.00
Iris, Basket, Hanging, Brown, 5 x 8 1/2 In. 316.00
Iris, Vase, Blue, White, Green Leaves, Impressed, 15 1/2 In. 520.00
Ivory II, Basket, Velmoss, Impressed, 9 In. 200.00
Jonquil, Basket, Handle, 8 1/2 In. 460.00
Jonquil, Bowl, 4-Sided, 3 3/4 x 9 1/4 In. 405.00
Jonquil, Bowl, Flower Frog, 4-Sided, Handles, 3 1/2 x 9 1/2 In. 316.00
Jonquil, Bowl, Handles, Paper Label, 3 x 8 1/4 In. 316.00
Jonquil, Console, Handles, 3 1/2 x 12 In. 375.00
Jonquil, Jardiniere, Brown, Green, 8 x 11 In. . . . . .290.00 to 375.00
Jonquil, Jardiniere, Handles, 6 1/4 x 8 1/2 In. 345.00
Jonquil, Jardiniere, Pedestal, 28 1/2 x 14 In. 2070.00
Jonquil, Vase, Brown, Green, Handles, 6 1/4 x 5 1/2 In. 230.00
Jonquil, Vase, Bulbous, Handles, 10 1/4 x 9 1/2 In. 575.00
Jonquil, Vase, Round, Handles, 6 x 7 In. 345.00
Jonquil, Vase, Round, Handles, Paper Label, 4 1/4 x 5 1/4 In. 175.00
Jonquil, Vase, Urn, Green To Ocher Glaze, Globular, Angular Handles, 5 3/4 In. 220.00
Jonquil, Wall Pocket, Green, 8 1/4 x 6 1/2 In. 978.00
Landscape, Jardiniere, Brown, Birds Flying On Rim, 13 1/2 x 16 1/4 In. 1380.00
Laurel, Vase, Green, Bulbous, Handles, Foil Label, 7 1/2 x 5 In. 405.00
Laurel, Vase, Green, Flared, 6 3/4 x 4 In. . . . . .175.00 to 405.00
Laurel, Vase, Russet, 9 1/4 x 6 1/4 In. 405.00
Laurel, Vase, Yellow, Handles, Foil Label, 8 1/2 x 6 In. 430.00
Luffa, Candlestick, Green, Foil Label, 5 In., Pair 460.00
Luffa, Jardiniere, Green, Handles, 71/2 x 9 1/2 In. 489.00
Luffa, Vase, Brown, 9 In. 375.00
Luffa, Vase, Brown, Oval, 8 1/4 x 6 3/4 In. 345.00
Luffa, Vase, Green, Handles, 6 In. . . . . .230.00 to 290.00
Luffa, Vase, Green, Oval, 7 1/2 x 4 1/2 In. 345.00
Luffa, Wall Pocket, Green, 8 1/2 In. 865.00
Magnolia, Basket, Green, Pink Flowers, Raised Mark, 8 In. 200.00
Magnolia, Vase, Brown, Cornucopia, Raised Mark, 12 In. 175.00
Mock Orange, Basket, Green, Impressed Mark, 10 In. 345.00
Mock Orange, Basket, Pink, Impressed Mark, 8 In. 150.00
Monticello, Vase, Brown, Feathered Glaze, Bulbous, Handles, 7 1/2 x 6 1/4 In. 805.00
Monticello, Vase, Brown, Squat, Handles, 4 1/4 x 5 In. 575.00
Monticello, Vase, Green, Ocher, Looped Handles, 9 1/4 x 8 In. 935.00
Monticello, Vase, Ocher, Blue Spatter, Incised, Bulbous, Looped Handles, 5 1/2 In. 415.00
Monticello, Vase, Tan, Handles, 5 In. 145.00
Morning Glory, Vase, Green Matte, Chalice Shape, Angular Handles, 7 1/2 In. 275.00
Morning Glory, Vase, Green, Flared, 8 1/2 In. 865.00
Morning Glory, Vase, White, 5 In. 405.00
Morning Glory, Wall Pocket, White, Double, 9 In. 695.00
Moss, Basket, Hanging, Blue, 5 x 7 1/2 In. 375.00
Moss, Urn, Blue, 8 In. 290.00
Moss, Urn, Blue, Handles, 8 In. 375.00
Moss, Urn, Pink, 9 In. 259.00
Moss, Vase, Fan, Ocher To Aqua, Scalloped Mouth, 7 1/4 x 6 1/2 In. 275.00
Moss, Vase, Pink, Handles, 8 In. 375.00
Moss, Wall Pocket, Pink, 10 1/4 x 5 1/4 In. 290.00
Moss, Wall Pocket, Pink, 8 3/4 In. 316.00
Mostique, Jardinere, Yellow, Brown, Blue, Green, RV, 13 x 10 1/2 In. 748.00
Mostique, Jardiniere & Pedestal, Gray, 13 In. 1150.00

Mostique, Vase, Flared, 12 In. 403.00
Mostique, Vase, Orange, Flowers, Blue, Pink, Green, 6 x 4 1/4 In. 375.00
Mostique, Vase, Orange, Stylized Flowers, Banded, Green, White, Cylindrical, 8 x 4 In. .. 144.00
Mostique, Vase, Orange, Stylized Flowers, Green, White, Handles, Impressed, 3 In. 201.00
Mostique, Vase, Pink Flowers, Cylindrical, 10 x 5 In. 460.00
Normandy, Jardiniere, 8 In. 345.00
Orion, Vase, Red, Squat, Stepped Body, 7 1/4 x 8 In. 520.00
Pauleo, Vase, Gray, Shaded Lavender Luster, Vines, Baluster, 13 1/2 In. 1870.00
Peony, Bookends, Green, Raised Marks, 6 In. 145.00
Peony, Ewer, Green, 15 In. 430.00
Peony, Vase, Gold, Green, c.1942, 12 1/2 In. 200.00
Peony, Vase, Green, Flared, Handles, Raised Mark, 15 In. 375.00
Peony, Wall Pocket, Yellow, 8 In. 290.00
Pine Cone, Basket, Brown, Branch Handle, 11 In. 633.00
Pine Cone, Basket, Hanging, Blue, Branch Handles, 5 1/4 x 8 1/4 In. 275.00
Pine Cone, Bookends, Brown, 5 In. 430.00
Pine Cone, Cigarette Holder, Blue, 3 x 4 1/4 In. 345.00
Pine Cone, Ewer, Blue, 10 In. 690.00
Pine Cone, Jardiniere, Brown, 8 In. 345.00
Pine Cone, Jardiniere, Brown, Handles, Marked, 10 In. 290.00
Pine Cone, Mug, Blue, Marked, 4 In. 290.00
Pine Cone, Pitcher, Blue, 9 1/2 x 8 3/4 In. ....805.00 to 865.00
Pine Cone, Planter, Blue, Rectangular, Branch Handle, 12 In. 520.00
Pine Cone, Umbrella Stand, Blue, 20 In. 2795.00
Pine Cone, Vase, Blue, Branch Handles, Bulbous, Marked, 10 In. 1380.00
Pine Cone, Vase, Blue, Branch Handles, Bulbous, Marked, 12 In. 1955.00
Pine Cone, Vase, Blue, Cylindrical, 5 In. 288.00
Pine Cone, Vase, Blue, Flared Handle, 10 1/2 In. 518.00
Pine Cone, Vase, Blue, Handles, 7 1/4 x 6 In. ....*Illus* 460.00
Pine Cone, Vase, Brown, Branch Handles, 18 In. 2400.00
Pine Cone, Vase, Brown, Bulbous, Handles, 10 In. 805.00
Pine Cone, Vase, Brown, Bulbous, Marked, 4 In. 405.00
Pine Cone, Vase, Bud, Brown, Triple, 8 1/4 In. 315.00
Pine Cone, Vase, Cornucopia, Blue, Branch Handle, 8 1/2 x 8 1/2 In. 275.00
Pine Cone, Vase, Green, Flared, Basket Handle, Marked, 10 In. 315.00
Pine Cone, Vase, Pillow, Brown, 8 1/4 x 9 1/2 In. 315.00
Pine Cone, Vase, Pillow, Brown, Footed, Handles, Marked, 7 In. ....315.00 to 400.00
Pine Cone, Vase, Pillow, Green, 8 In. 460.00
Pine Cone, Vase, Trophy, Blue, Branch Handles, 7 x 6 1/2 In. 415.00
Pine Cone, Wall Pocket, Blue, Double, Branch Handle, 9 In. 1320.00
Poppy, Flower Frog, Pink, 3 1/2 In. 219.00
Poppy, Vase, Gray, Flared, Handles, Raised Mark, 15 In. 430.00
Poppy, Wall Pocket, Green, Bullet Shape, Triple, Impressed, 8 1/2 x 6 1/2 In. .....460.00 to 690.00
Primrose, Vase, Pillow, Pink, 8 In. 219.00
Rosecraft Hexagon, Vase, Blue Glossy, Marked, 5 1/2 x 3 3/4 In. 230.00

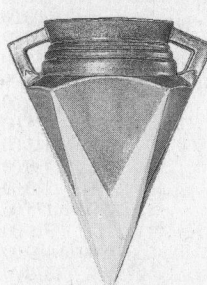

Roseville, Futura, Wall
Pocket, Tan, Cream, Green,
Handles, 8 In.

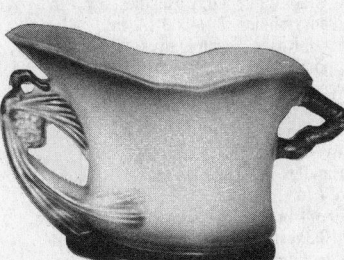

Roseville, Pine Cone,
Vase, Blue, Handles,
7 1/4 x 6 In.

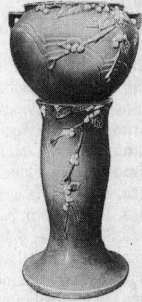

Roseville, Snowberry,
Jardiniere, Pedestal, Green,
25 In.

Rosecraft Hexagon, Vase, Brown, Flared, Marked, 7 1/2 x 5 In. 259.00
Rosecraft Hexagon, Vase, Green, Footed, 7 1/2 x 5 1/4 In. 259.00
Rosecraft Panel, Vase, Brown, Flowers, 6 In., Pair 200.00
Rosecraft Panel, Vase, Brown, Nude Figure, 7 1/4 x 5 In. 460.00
Rosecraft Vintage, Bowl, Brown, 2 x 6 In. 105.00
Rosecraft Vintage, Vase, Chocolate, 8 In. 518.00
Rosecraft Vintage, Wall Pocket, Brown, 9 1/4 In. 345.00
Rozane, Ewer, Brown, Berries & Leaves, Stamped, 10 3/4 x 5 In. 170.00
Rozane, Jug, Brown, Berries & Leaves, Stamped, 4 1/2 x 5 In. 200.00
Rozane, Jug, Orange, Pansies, Ruffled Rim, 4 1/2 x 5 In. 375.00
Rozane, Vase, Gooseberry Leaves, Squat, Stamped, 4 1/4 x 3 3/4 In. 145.00
Rozane, Vase, Orange Flowers, Tear Shape, Handles, Stamped, 6 x 5 1/2 In. 90.00
Rozane, Vase, Orange Honeysuckle, 8 x 4 1/4 In. 405.00
Russco, Urn, Green, Beige, 8 1/2 x 6 1/2 In. 375.00
Russco, Vase, Brown & Tan Crystalline Glaze, Handles, RV, 7 1/2 In. 259.00
Russco, Vase, Caramel, Vertical Incised Bands, 8-Sided Mouth, Handles, 15 In. 440.00
Russco, Vase, Green To Crystalline Glaze, Round, 6 1/2 x 7 1/2 In. 430.00
Russco, Vase, Pillow, Green, Yellow Interior, Round, 7 1/2 In. 345.00
Silhouette, Ewer, Pink, Stylized Flower, Marked, 10 In. 230.00
Snowberry, Bowl, Pink, Raised Mark, 6 In. 58.00
Snowberry, Jardiniere, Pedestal, Green, 25 In. .... *Illus* 920.00
Snowberry, Tea Set, Green, Marked, 7 3/4-In. Teapot, 3 Piece 345.00
Snowberry, Vase, Blue, 18 In. 1150.00
Snowberry, Vase, Green, 15 In. 375.00
Snowberry, Vase, Pink, Branch Handles, 15 In. 345.00
Sunflower, Bowl, Looped Handles, 4 1/4 x 7 1/2 In. 935.00
Sunflower, Vase, 7 1/4 x 8 1/4 In. 489.00
Sunflower, Vase, Broad Form, 5 In. 489.00
Sunflower, Vase, Broad, Shouldered, 7 In. 865.00
Sunflower, Vase, Bulbous, Flat Shoulder, 5 x 6 1/4 In. 1265.00
Sunflower, Vase, Cylindrical, Angular Handles, 6 1/4 x 5 In. 770.00
Sunflower, Vase, Handles, 4 1/4 In. 635.00
Sunflower, Vase, Looped Handles, 8 1/4 x 6 In. 1100.00
Sunflower, Wall Pocket, 7 1/4 x 6 In. 1610.00
Sweet Cosmos, Vase, Green, 4 In. 140.00
Thorn Apple, Bookends, Brown, 5 1/2 In. 230.00
Topeo, Bowl, Blue Matte Glaze, 10 In. 200.00
Topeo, Vase, Blue, Mauve, Green Deco Beading, Buttresses, Flared, 6 1/2 In. 330.00
Tourist, Pedestal, 21 1/2 x 11 In. 2530.00
Tourist, Vase, Flared, 12 x 7 In. 2070.00
Tourmaline, Candlestick, Blue, 4 In., Pair 150.00
Tourmaline, Urn, Blue, Beige, Ocher Matte Crystalline Glaze, 8 1/4 x 6 1/4 In. 200.00
Tourmaline, Vase, Blue, Buttressed Base, Flared, Foil Label, 9 1/2 x 5 1/4 In. 345.00
Tourmaline, Vase, Blue, Green Streaks, Embossed Squares At Neck, 4 3/4 x 6 1/2 In. 195.00
Tourmaline, Vase, Blue, Oval, 7 1/2 x 4 In. 259.00
Tourmaline, Vase, Bulbous, Handles, 6 x 6 In. 230.00
Tourmaline, Vase, Pillow, Blue, White, Gray, Handles, 6 x 7 In. 200.00
Tuscany, Vase, Pink, 4-Sided, Handles, 7 1/4 x 3 1/2 In. 259.00
Velmoss, Jardiniere, Pedestal, Roses, Green Leaves, 29 1/2 In. 1035.00
Velmoss, Vase, Blue, Cylindrical, Footed, Handles, Foil Label, 7 x 5 1/2 In. 290.00
Velmoss, Vase, Green Over Brown, 5 3/4 In. 575.00
Velmoss, Vase, Green, Cylindrical, 8 1/4 x 2 1/2 In. 575.00
Velmoss, Vase, Green, Gourd, 6 x 5 1/2 In. 345.00
Velmoss, Vase, Ocher, Olive Green, 5 In. 430.00
Vista, Basket, Hanging, Handles, 4 1/2 x 7 1/2 In. 200.00
Vista, Bowl, Fern, 3 1/2 x 7 In. ....145.00 to 175.00
Vista, Jardiniere, 8 1/4 x 9 3/4 In. 316.00
Vista, Jardiniere, 9 1/2 x 10 3/4 In. ....405.00 to 489.00
Vista, Umbrella Stand, Blue, Green Matte Glaze, 20 In. 2070.00
Vista, Vase, Bulbous, Handles, 10 x 5 1/2 In. ....345.00 to 575.00
Vista, Vase, Bulbous, Handles, 10 x 7 1/2 In. ....978.00 to 1380.00
Vista, Vase, Handles, 12 x 6 1/4 In. ....635.00 to 920.00
Vista, Vase, Handles, 18 x 8 In. 1380.00

 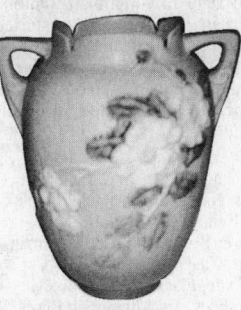 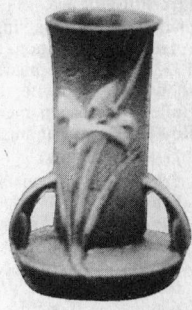

Roseville, Water Lily, Jardiniere, Blue Glaze, Handles, Signed, 10 x 16 In.

Roseville, White Rose, Vase, Pink, Green, Bulbous, Handles, 12 In.

Roseville, Zephyr Lily, Vase, Green, Handles, 10 In.

Water Lily, Jardiniere, Blue Glaze, Handles, Signed, 10 x 16 In. .... *Illus*	230.00
White Rose, Vase, Blue, Embossed, Handles, c.1940, 6 In.	80.00
White Rose, Vase, Brown, Bulbous, Handles, Marked, 12 In.	315.00
White Rose, Vase, Pink, Green, Bulbous, Handles, 12 In. .... *Illus*	315.00
Wincraft, Tea Set, Yellow, Marked, 7-In. Teapot, 3 Piece	288.00
Wincraft, Teapot, Green, Brown, 10 In.	60.00
Wisteria, Vase, Blue, 4 In.	374.00
Wisteria, Vase, Blue, Squat, Handles, 4 1/4 x 6 1/4 In.	489.00
Wisteria, Vase, Brown, Gourd, Handles, 8 1/2 x 4 1/2 In.	978.00
Wisteria, Vase, Brown, Handles, 12 1/2 x 7 1/2 In.	1150.00
Wisteria, Vase, Brown, Lavender, Flattened Sphere, Looped Handles, 5 x 6 In.	605.00
Wisteria, Vase, Brown, Squat, Handles, 4 1/2 x 6 1/4 In.	375.00
Wisteria, Wall Pocket, Blue, 8 1/4 x 7 In.	1495.00
Wisteria, Wall Pocket, Brown, Green, Purple, 8 1/2 x 7 1/4 In.	1150.00
Zephyr Lily, Bookends, Blue, 5 In.	175.00
Zephyr Lily, Console, Blue, Handles, Raised Mark, 14 In.	145.00
Zephyr Lily, Cookie Jar, Green, Raised Mark, 8 In.	430.00
Zephyr Lily, Jardiniere, Pedestal, Brown & Green Glaze, Relief, 25 x 11 1/4 In. ... .460.00 to 825.00
Zephyr Lily, Planter, Underplate, Blue, 6 In.	85.00
Zephyr Lily, Vase, Brown & Green Glaze, 19 x 10 In.	495.00
Zephyr Lily, Vase, Green, Cornucopia, 6 In.	60.00
Zephyr Lily, Vase, Green, Flattened Form, 6 x 7 In.	60.00
Zephyr Lily, Vase, Green, Handles, 10 In. .... *Illus*	145.00
Zephyr Lily, Wall Pocket, Brown, Raised Mark, 8 In.	210.00

ROWLAND & MARSELLUS Company is part of a mark that appears on historical Staffordshire dating from the late-nineteenth and early-twentieth centuries. Rowland & Marsellus is the mark used by an American importing company in New York City. The company worked from 1893 to about 1937. Some of the pieces may have been made by the British Anchor Pottery Co. of Longton, England, for export to a New York firm. Many American views were made. Of special interest to collectors are the plates with rolled edges, usually blue and white.

Plate, Asbury Park, New Jersey, Casino, Arcade, Blue Transfer, 10 In.	175.00
Plate, Bangor, Maine, Ships, Blue Transfer, 10 In.	100.00
Plate, Bridgeport, Conn., Buildings & Monuments, Blue Transfer, 10 In.	145.00
Plate, New York City, Hudson River Scenes, Blue Transfer, 10 In.	115.00
Plate, New York City, Statue Of Liberty, Blue Transfer, c.1900, 10 In.	195.00
Plate, Niagara Falls, Blue Transfer, 10 In.	50.00
Plate, Priscilla & John Alden, Blue Transfer, 10 In.	65.00
Plate, Shakespeare, Stratford-On-Avon, Blue Transfer, Rolled Edge, 10 In.	140.00
Plate, The Elm At Cambridge, Mass., Blue Transfer, 10 In.	65.00
Plate, Theodore Roosevelt, Blue Transfer, Rolled Edge, 10 In.	195.00
Plate, Valley Forge, Blue Transfer, 10 In.	25.00

ROY ROGERS was born in 1911 in Cincinnati, Ohio. In the 1930s, he made a living as a singer; in 1935, his group started work at a Los Angeles radio station. He appeared in his first movie in 1937. From 1952 to 1957, he made 101 television shows. The other stars in the show were his wife, Dale Evans, his horse, Trigger, and his dog, Bullet. Roy Rogers memorabilia is collected, including items from the Roy Rogers restaurants.

Archery Set, Box	195.00
Briefs, Boy's, Original Package	125.00
Cap Gun, Roy, On Trigger, Nickel Finish, Metal Grips, c.1950s, 8 1/4 In.	210.00
Cap Gun Set, 2 Holsters, Belt, Guns, Schmidt, 10 In.	633.00 to 900.00
Coloring Book, Roy, Dale & Bullet On Front, Whitman, 1958	35.00
Cowboy Outfit, Shirt, Vest, Chaps, Box	150.00
Dish Set, Dinner, Roy & Dale, Plastic Dishes, Box	200.00
Game, Ring Toss & Horseshoes, Tin Lithograph Bases, Rope Rings, Ohio Art, 1950s	85.00
Gun, BB, Roy Rogers & Trigger, Daisy	320.00
Gun, Flash-Draw Set, Die Cast 6-Shooters, Jeweled Grips, Schmidt, 1950s	1350.00
Gun & Holster, 2 Metal Guns, Double Holster, Gold Tone, Classy Products	375.00
Lunch Box, Saddlebag, Vinyl, Tan, Thermos, 1960, 9 1/4 x 7 x 4 In.	150.00
Modeling Clay, Unopened Box	230.00
Mug, Figural, Roy Smiling, Quaker Oats, 1950, 4 In.	56.00
Paint By Number Set, Unused, 1954	175.00
Play Set, Rodeo Ranch, Marx, Box, 1952, 22 In.	287.00
Saddle, Tooled Images, Roy Rogers, Trigger, Factory Made, 1950s	950.00
Toy, Cowboy Band Set, Plastic Musical Instruments, Box, 30 x 18 In.	325.00
Toy, Dale Evans, Buttermilk, Accessories, No. 802, Heartland Creation	150.00
Toy, Roy, Trigger, Accessories, No. 806, Heartland Creation, Box, 8 1/2 x 9 In.	125.00

ROYAL BAYREUTH is the name of a factory that was founded in Tettau, Bavaria, in 1794. It has continued to modern times. The marks have changed through the years. A stylized crest, the name *Royal Bayreuth*, and the word *Bavaria* appear in slightly different forms from 1870 to about 1919. Later dishes may include the words *U.S. Zone*, the year of the issue, or the word *Germany* instead of *Bavaria*. Related pieces may be found listed in the Rose Tapestry, Sand Babies, Snow Babies, and Sunbonnet Babies categories.

Bowl, Reticulated Vine, Molded Rim, c.1900, 10 1/2 In.	315.00
Box, Cover, Devil & Cards, 3 x 4 1/4 x 3 1/4 In.	635.00
Box, Stamp, Cover, Devil & Cards, 2 3/4 x 3 3/4 x 2 1/2 In., Pair	920.00
Box, Stamp, Cover, Peace Bringing Plenty, Brown, 3 In.	90.00
Candleholder, Devil & Cards, 2 3/4 x 6 In.	575.00
Candleholder, Devil & Cards, Climbing Devil, 4 x 4 1/2 x 4 In.	635.00
Candleholder, Dutch Girl Scene, Blue Mark, Early 20th Century, 4 1/4 In.	69.00
Creamer, Alligator	350.00
Creamer, Devil & Cards, 3 x 5 x 4 In.	219.00
Creamer, Souvenir, Catalina Island, Blue Mark, 5 1/4 In.	69.00
Cup Set, Dice, Devil & Cards, Each Different, 1 3/4 x 2 In., 3 Piece	230.00
Dish, Clock, Devil, Tan Ground, Black Roman Numerals, 4 1/2 In.	1610.00
Humidor, Cover, Devil & Cards, 7 1/4 In.	920.00
Match Holder, Devil & Cards, Wall, 4 x 5 In., Pair	460.00
Nappy, Devil & Cards, 6 3/4 In.	403.00
Pin Holder, Devil, Folded Wings, Extended Arms, 3 1/4 x 4 1/2 x 2 1/2 In., Pair	635.00
Pitcher, Black Poodle, 4 1/2 In.	80.00
Pitcher, Cattle, Standing In Pasture, Gilt Handle, 9 In.	336.00
Pitcher, Devil & Cards, 3 3/4 x 3 3/4 x 2 1/2 In., Pair	575.00
Pitcher, Devil & Cards, Green Mark, 7 1/4 In. *Illus*	520.00
Pitcher, Devil & Cards, Late 1800s, 7 1/4 In.	1035.00
Pitcher, Devil, Without Cards, 9 x 7 1/2 In.	3220.00
Pitcher, Pheasant Scene, Blue Mark, 4 3/4 In.	260.00
Pitcher, Poodle, Gray & White, 4 1/2 In.	80.00
Pitcher, Santa Claus, With Sack, 4 1/4 In.	1595.00
Plate, Child's, Children On Beach, Blue Mark, 7 1/2 In.	175.00
Salt, Master, Devil & Cards, Handle, 2 3/4 x 3 1/2 x 2 3/4 In., Pair	460.00

Always roll a rag rug for storage with the right side on the outside. This puts less stress on the backing.

Royal Bayreuth,
Pitcher, Devil &
Cards, Green
Mark, 7 1/4 In.

Salt & Pepper, Devil & Cards, 3 In., Pair	545.00
Salt & Pepper, Grape, 1950s, 3 1/2 In.	150.00
Sugar & Creamer, Tomato, Green Leaves, Handles, 3 5/8 x 3 3/4 In.	55.00
Toothpick, Devil & Cards, 2 1/2 In.	375.00
Tray, Devil & Cards, 7 1/4 x 10 In.	865.00
Vase, 4 Handles, Metallic Glaze, 4 1/4 In.	290.00
Vase, Pair Of Musketeers, Blue Mark, 5 1/2 In.	90.00

ROYAL BONN is the nineteenth- and twentieth-century trade name for the Bonn China Manufactory. It was established in 1755 in Bonn, Germany. A general line of porcelain was made. Many marks were used, most including the name *Bonn*, the initials *FM*, and a crown.

Clock, Ansonia, Mini, Actor, Violets, c.1905, 7 In.	245.00
Clock, Ansonia, Shelf, La Drome, 8-Day, Time & Strike, c.1901, 12 In.	730.00
Clock, Ansonia, Shelf, La Vendee, 8-Day, Time & Strike, c.1904, 14 1/2 In.	896.00
Pedestal, Flowers, Gilt, 36 In., Pair	1750.00
Urn, Cover, Painted, Flowers, Gilt Trim, Handles, c.1900, 24 In.	250.00
Urn, Cover, Portrait, Gilt Accents, 19th Century, 24 x 7 1/2 x 8 1/2 In., Pair	560.00
Vase, Art Nouveau, Flared Rim, Franz Anton Mehlem, Early 1900s, 12 3/8 In.	295.00
Vase, Egg Shape, Rose Bouquet, River Landscape, Late 1800s, 9 1/2 In., Pair	145.00
Vase, Portrait, Spherical, Impressionist Background, Flowers, 5 In.	375.00
Vase, Scenic Panels, Blue, White, Marked, c.1870, 8 In., Pair	175.00
Vase, Thistle, Gold Tracery, Gilt Handles, Marked, 10 3/4 In.	175.00

ROYAL COPENHAGEN porcelain and pottery have been made in Denmark since 1775. The Christmas plate series started in 1908. The figurines with pale blue and gray glazes have remained popular in this century and are still being made. Many other old and new style porcelains are made today.

Bowl, Bronze, Mottled Green Patina, Fluted, Denmark, 1950, 7 x 4 In.	1755.00
Bowl, Flora Danica, Scalloped, Gilt Rim, 9 1/4 In.	690.00
Figurine, Boy On Goat, 1905-1928, 7 1/2 In.	285.00
Figurine, Dutch Boy & Cow, Green Ink Stamp, 6 1/2 x 7 In.	175.00
Figurine, Dutch Milkmaid, Feeding Cow, Green Ink Stamp, 6 1/4 x 6 3/4 In.	175.00
Figurine, Dutch Peasant, 2 Goats, Green Ink Stamp, 9 1/2 x 7 3/4 In.	200.00
Figurine, Elephant, Trumpeting, Glazed Stoneware, Knud Kyhn	130.00
Figurine, Poodle, Gray, Standing, No. 4757, T.N., 4 1/2 In.	25.00
Figurine, White Heron, Standing, Tall Grass, Green Ink Stamp, 11 1/2 In.	345.00
Figurine, Woman Chasing Geese, 9 In.	125.00
Group, Nude Couple Kissing On Rocks, Waves, c.1900, 18 1/2 In.	546.00 to 748.00
Lamp, Scent, Sea Gull, Porcelain, French Metal Mounts, Early 1900s, 8 3/4 In.	90.00
Mirror, Flowers, Urn, Pediment, Rectangular, Arched, 30 1/2 In.	1210.00
Plate, Christmas, 1909, Danish Landscape, St. Ussing	360.00
Plate, Christmas, 1911, Danish Landscape, Oluf Jensen	220.00
Plate, Christmas, 1912, Elderly Couple By Christmas Tree	200.00 to 315.00
Plate, Christmas, 1914, Sparrows In Tree	150.00 to 270.00
Plate, Christmas, 1915, Danish Landscape, A. Krog	245.00
Plate, Christmas, 1917, Tower Of Our Savior's Church	150.00
Plate, Christmas, 1920, Mary With Child	125.00 to 150.00

Plate, Christmas, 1922, 3 Singing Angels 120.00
Plate, Christmas, 1924, Christmas Star Over The Sea 180.00
Plate, Christmas, 1925, Street Scene ....110.00 to 165.00
Plate, Christmas, 1935, Fishing Boat Off Kronborg Castle ....200.00 to 360.00
Plate, Christmas, 1937, Christmas Scene In Main Street, Copenhagen 450.00
Plate, Christmas, 1938, Round Church In Osterlars 550.00
Plate, Christmas, 1939, Expeditionary Ship In The Pack-Ice 725.00
Plate, Christmas, 1941, Danish Village Church 580.00
Plate, Christmas, 1942, Bell-Tower Of Old Church In Jutland 830.00
Plate, Christmas, 1943, Flight Of The Holy Family To Egypt 1090.00
Plate, Christmas, 1945, Peaceful Motif ....500.00 to 900.00
Plate, Christmas, 1951, Christmas Angel ....350.00 to 630.00
Plate, Christmas, 1962, Little Mermaid At Wintertime ....200.00 to 340.00
Platter, Flora Danica, Oval, Gilt Ruffled Rim, Denmark, 1900s, 18 5/8 In. 2235.00
Punch Bowl, Bicentennial, Battles, George Washington, c.1976, 13 1/4 In. 705.00
Snuff Bottle, Daisies, Porcelain, Silver Lid, 5 3/8 In. 2530.00
Teapot, Blue Flowers, White Ground, 20th Century, 6 In. 160.00
Teapot, Blue Flowers, White Ground, Baluster, 20th Century, 8 1/2 In. 230.00
Tureen, Cover, Flora Danica, Shallow, Oval, Denmark, 1900s, 15 5/8 In. 1530.00
Vase, Abstract, Cast Stoneware, Solfatara Glaze, Axel Salto, 10 x 7 1/2 In. 6435.00
Vase, Black, Brown, Knop Stem, Cast Stoneware, Axel Salto, 3 3/4 x 3 In. 1404.00
Vase, Gourd, Brown & Green Crystalline Matte Glaze, Marked, 1920, 6 In. 86.00
Vase, Ribbed, White Glaze, No. 4882, c.1950, 7 1/4 In. 120.00
Vase, Sung Glaze, Knop Stem, Cast Stoneware, Axel Salto, 5 1/4 x 7 3/4 In. 5265.00
Vase, Sung Glaze, Knop Stem, Cast Stoneware, Axel Salto, 7 1/2 x 9 1/2 In. 7020.00
Vase, Tapered Cylinder, Moths, Blossoms, Denmark, 1894-1922, 17 1/4 In. 295.00
Vase, Tapered, Painted Lady's Slipper, 8 In. 460.00

ROYAL COPLEY china was made by the Spaulding China Company of
Sebring, Ohio, from 1939 to 1960. The figural planters and the small
figurines, especially those with Art Deco designs, are of great collector interest.

Figurine, Dog, 8 1/2 In. 40.00
Figurine, Mallard, 5 5/8 x 7 3/4 In. 10.00
Figurine, Mallard, Windsor, 5 1/4 In. 20.00
Figurine, Parrot, Multicolored, 8 In. 45.00
Figurine, Parrot, Perched On Stump, 1940s, 8 In. 40.00
Figurine, Wren, 3 1/2 In. 30.00
Planter, Bamboo, 7 1/2 x 3 1/4 In. 15.00
Planter, Bear In Log, Black, Cream & Brown, 3 x 5 In. 15.00
Planter, Bird, 4 In. 17.00
Planter, Black & White, 4 In. 32.00
Planter, Boy, Thinking, Resting Elbow On Barrel, 6 In. 18.00
Planter, Boy, With Bucket, 6 1/4 In. 25.00
Planter, Bunny, Hiding Behind Large Leaf, 5 In. 15.00
Planter, Cocker Spaniel, Original Sticker, 8 In. 89.00
Planter, Deer & Fawn, 9 1/2 In. 10.00
Planter, Dog, At Mailbox, 8 In. ....25.00 to 35.00
Planter, Duck, Brown, Blue Feathers, American Bisque, 9 1/4 In. 26.00
Planter, Duckling, 5 5/8 x 7 1/2 In. 28.00
Planter, Flowers, Cream, Late 1940s, 4 x 4 In. 28.00
Planter, Flowers, Yellow, Sculpted, Green Leaves, 6 x 3 In. 10.00
Planter, Horse, Yellow Mane, 8 In. 40.00
Planter, Kitten, Yellow, Green Eyes, Pink Paw, Yellow Ball, 5 In. 20.00
Planter, Lamb, No. 293 .... 27.00
Planter, Oriental Man, Leaning, Pink, Blue & Gray, 7 x 6 1/2 In. 22.00
Planter, Peter Rabbit, 6 1/4 In. 25.00
Planter, Springer Spaniel, Basket, 5 1/2 x 5 In. 28.00
Planter, Teddy Bear, 6 3/4 In. 25.00
Planter, Vintage, Dark Brown, Ribbed, 3 1/4 x 3 1/2 In. 15.00
Vase, Bird, Black & Yellow, Gold Trim, 5 In. 6.00
Vase, Doe Nuzzling Fawn, Earth Tones, 9 x 5 1/2 In. 18.00
Vase, Flowers, Green, Yellow, Marked, 8 In. 35.00

Vase, Flowers, Yellow, Light Pink & Green, 7 3/4 In. 30.00
Vase, Head, Old Man, Wearing Hat, 8 In. 23.00
Vase, Head, Oriental, 7 1/2 In. 30.00
Vase, Leaf Design, Green, 6 1/2 In. 15.00
Vase, Leaf Design, Pink, Tan, Handles, 1940s, 5 x 5 1/2 In. 40.00
Vase, Pillow, Gray, Pink, Black, 5 1/2 In. 18.00
Vase, Pillow, Leaf Design, Brown & Green, Lime Green Ground, Art Deco, 5 1/2 In. 28.00
Vase, Pink, White, Metal Wire Flower Frog Inside, 6 3/4 In. 30.00
Wall Pocket, Angel, Blue Gown, Blond Hair, 6 1/4 In., Pair 50.00

ROYAL CROWN DERBY

ROYAL CROWN DERBY Company, Ltd., was established in England in
1890. There is a complex family tree that includes the Derby, Crown
Derby, and Royal Crown Derby porcelains. The Royal Crown Derby
mark includes the name and a crown. The words *Made in England*
were used after 1921. The company is now a part of Royal Doulton
Tableware Ltd.

Candlestick, Imari, Inverted Dolphin Base, c.1970, 10 1/2 In., Pair ....1035.00 to 1095.00
Cup & Saucer, Imari, No. 2224, Early 20th Century, 2 1/2 In. 140.00
Dish, Imari, Oval, Pierced Leaf & Acorn Handles, 11 5/8 x 8 1/4 In. 489.00
Figurine, Couples, Putting On Shoes, 11 x 6 In., Pair 615.00
Jar, Cover, Pink Ground, Gilt, Leaves, Flowers, Fruit, 9 3/4 x 6 In. 115.00
Plate, Haddon Hall, Landscape, Castle, Sheep, W.E.J. Dean, c.1900, 10 1/4 In. 489.00
Vase, Aesthetic Movement, Melon Shape, Flower Bouquet, c.1890, 9 In. 315.00
Vase, Chinoiserie, Enameled, Narrow Mouth, Multicolored, c.1886, 5 1/4 In. 265.00
Vase, Chrysanthemums, Green, Gilt, Yellow, Amphora Shape, Handles, 8 In. 262.00
Vase, Scalloped Rim, Egg Shaped, Loop Handles, Gilt, c.1901, 7 3/8 In. 316.00

ROYAL DOULTON

ROYAL DOULTON is the name used on Doulton and Company pottery
made from 1902 to the present. Doulton and Company of England was
founded in 1853. Pieces made before 1902 are listed in this book under
Doulton. Royal Doulton collectors search for the out-of-production
figurines, character jugs, vases, and series wares. Some vases and animal figurines were made with a special red glaze called flambe. Sung
and Chang glazed pieces are rare. The multicolored glaze is very thick
and looks as if it were dropped on the clay.

Animal, American Great Dane, HN 2602, 1941-1960 .... 575.00
Animal, Bullfinch, HN 2551, 1940-1946 .... 383.00
Animal, Dragon, Flambe, HN 3552 .... 825.00
Animal, Drake, Standing, HN 2635, 1952-1974 ....775.00 to 2000.00
Animal, Elephant, Young, Flambe, HN 3548, 1990-1996 .... 575.00
Animal, English Foxhound, HN 1025, 1931-1955 ....2298.00 to 2352.00
Animal, Fighter Elephant, HN 2640, 1952-1992 .... 475.00
Animal, Fox, Seated, HN 1130, 1937-1947 ....385.00 to 700.00
Animal, Fox, Seated, HN 2634, 1952-1992 ....862.00 to 1077.00
Animal, French Poodle, Lying On Cushion, DA 115, 1990-1995 ....35.00 to 50.00
Animal, Gannet, HN 195, 1920-1946 ....850.00 to 1600.00
Animal, Langur Monkey, HN 2657, 1960-1969 ....400.00 to 1149.00
Animal, Leaping Salmon, Flambe, No. 666, 1940-1950 ....460.00 to 900.00
Animal, Nyala Antelope, HN 2664, 1960-1969 ....400.00 to 1000.00
Animal, Pekinese, HN 1011, 1931-1955 ....420.00 to 800.00
Animal, Pig, Snorting, HN 968A, 1928-1936 ....1100.00 to 1500.00
Animal, Pointer, HN 2624, 1952-1985 ....300.00 to 400.00
Animal, Polar Bear, Seated, HN 121, 1912-1936 .... 1532.00
Animal, Pride Of The Shires & Foal, HN 2528, 1939-1960 ....270.00 to 500.00
Animal, Red Admiral Butterfly, HN 2607, 1941-1946 .... 1666.00
Animal, Red Setter, Collar, HN 976, 1930-1946 ....960.00 to 1200.00
Animal, Robin, HN 144, 1917-1946 .... 383.00
Animal, Scottish Terrier, HN 1015, 1931-1960 .... 383.00
Animal, Scottish Terrier, HN 1038, 1931-1946 ....3065.00 to 3200.00
Animal, Tern, Female, HN 1194, 1937-1946 .... 804.00
Animal, Thrush Chicks, HN 2552, 1941-1946 .... 536.00
Animal, West Highland Terrier, HN 1048, 1931 .... 920.00
Candlestick, Monk In Winery, 9 In. 115.00

Royal Doulton character jugs depict the head and shoulders of the subject. They are made in four sizes: large, 5 1/4 to 7 inches; small, 3 1/4 to 4 inches; miniature, 2 1/4 to 2 1/2 inches; and tiny, 1 1/4 inches. Toby jugs portray a seated, full figure.

Character Jug, Alfred Hitchcock, D 6987, 1997, Large 805.00
Character Jug, Beefeater, D 6233, 1947-1953, Small 60.00
Character Jug, Cardinal, D 6129, 1940-1960, Miniature 45.00
Character Jug, Churchill, Noke, D 6170, 1940-1941, Large 4800.00
Character Jug, Gondolier, D 6595, 1964-1969, Miniature 380.00
Character Jug, John Lennon, D 6725, 1984-1991, Mid 860.00
Character Jug, Lord Nelson, D 6336, Large 288.00
Character Jug, Mephistopheles, D 5757, 1937-1948, Large 1205.00
Character Jug, Mephistopheles, D 5758, 1937-1948, Small ....725.00 to 1530.00
Character Jug, Mr. Pickwick, D 6254, 1947-1960, Miniature 56.00
Character Jug, Old Charley, D 6144, Miniature 603.00
Character Jug, Pearly Boy, 1947, Large 6895.00
Character Jug, Pearly Boy, 1947, Small 2110.00
Character Jug, Pharaoh, D 7028, 1996, Large 536.00
Character Jug, Ronald Reagan, D 6718, 1984, Large 920.00
Character Jug, White Haired Clown, D 6322, 1951-1955, Large 958.00
Figurine, Abdullah, HN 2104, 1953-1962 .... 290.00
Figurine, Adrienne, HN 2304 ....62.00 to 75.00
Figurine, Alison, HN 2336 .... 75.00
Figurine, Angela, HN 1204, 1926-1940 .... 558.00
Figurine, Annette, HN 1471, 1931-1938 .... 385.00
Figurine, Annette, HN 1550, 1933-1949 .... 536.00
Figurine, Auctioneer, HN 2988, 1986 .... 150.00
Figurine, Automne, HN 3068, 1986 .... 345.00
Figurine, Autumn Breezes, HN 1911, 1939-1976 .... 205.00
Figurine, Autumn Breezes, HN 1913, 1913-1971 .... 113.00
Figurine, Autumn Breezes, HN 1934, 1940-1997 .... 120.00
Figurine, Bachelor, HN 2319, 1964-1975 .... 170.00
Figurine, Balloon Seller, HN 583, 1923-1949 ....520.00 to 690.00
Figurine, Beggar, HN 2175, 1956-1962 ....259.00 to 290.00
Figurine, Bernice, HN 2071, 1951-1953 .... 498.00
Figurine, Biddy, HN 1445, 1931-1937 .... 804.00
Figurine, Bon Appetit, HN 2444, 1972-1975 ....960.00 to 980.00
Figurine, Boy Evacuee, HN 3202, 1989 .... 860.00
Figurine, Bride, HN 2166, 1956-1976 ....110.00 to 220.00
Figurine, Bridget, HN 2070, 1951-1973 .... 150.00
Figurine, Broken Lance, HN 2041, 1949-1975 .... 1819.00
Figurine, Bunnykins, Astro Rocket Man, DB 20, 1983-1988 ......100.00 to 200.00
Figurine, Bunnykins, Collector Bunnykins, DB 54, 1987 .... 563.00
Figurine, Bunnykins, Cooling Off, DB 3, 1972-1987 ....100.00 to 200.00
Figurine, Bunnykins, Downhill Bunnykins, DB 31, 1985-1988 ....125.00 to 300.00
Figurine, Bunnykins, Freddie Bunnykin, 3 3/4 In. 4980.00
Figurine, Bunnykins, Mr. Bunnybeat, Strumming, DB 16, 1982-1988 ....200.00 to 250.00
Figurine, Buttercup, HN 2309, 1964-1997 .... 75.00
Figurine, Calumet, HN 2068, 1950-1953 ....345.00 to 580.00
Figurine, Camilla, HN 1711, 1935-1949 ....800.00 to 1000.00
Figurine, Celeste, HN 2237, 1959-1971 ....150.00 to 200.00
Figurine, Cellist, HN 2226, 1960-1967 ....260.00 to 400.00
Figurine, Charge Of The Light Brigade, HN 4486, 2002 .... 3639.00
Figurine, Charlie Chaplin, HN 2771, 1989 .... 3800.00
Figurine, Charlotte, HN 2421, 1972-1986 ....85.00 to 100.00
Figurine, Chelsea Pensioner, HN 689, 1924-1938 .... 1149.00
Figurine, China Repairer, HN 2943, 1982 .... 125.00
Figurine, Christmas Morn, HN 1992, 1947-1996 ....85.00 to 150.00
Figurine, Clarissa, HN 1525, 1932-1938 .... 766.00
Figurine, Clarissa, HN 2345, 1968-1981 ....65.00 to 100.00
Figurine, Cleopatra, HN 2868, 1979 ....558.00 to 920.00
Figurine, Clockmaker, HN 2279, 1961-1975 ....140.00 to 200.00

Figurine, Clown, HN 2890, 1979-1988 .... 150.00
Figurine, Coachman, HN 2282, 1963-1971 ....275.00 to 300.00
Figurine, Coralie, HN 2307, 1964-1988 .... 62.00
Figurine, Cradle Song, HN 2246, 1959-1962 ....230.00 to 400.00
Figurine, Craftsman, HN 2284, 1961-1965 ....300.00 to 500.00
Figurine, Cup Of Tea, HN 2322, 1964-1983 ....105.00 to 200.00
Figurine, Curly Knob, HN 1627, 1934-1949 ....640.00 to 1200.00
Figurine, Curly Locks, HN 2049, 1949-1953 ....275.00 to 400.00
Figurine, Daffy Down Dilly, HN 1712, 1935-1975 .... *Illus* 250.00
Figurine, Dainty May, HN 1656, 1934-1949 ....300.00 to 600.00
Figurine, Damaris, HN 2079, 1951-1952 ....500.00 to 1000.00
Figurine, Dancing Eyes & Sunny Hair, HN 1543, 1933-1949 .... 460.00
Figurine, Daydreams, HN 1731, 1935-1996 ....85.00 to 150.00
Figurine, Delphine, HN 2136, 1954-1967 .... 219.00
Figurine, Do You Wonder Where Fairies Are, HN 1544, 1933-1949 .... 748.00
Figurine, Dorcas, HN 1490, 1932-1938 ....615.00 to 1000.00
Figurine, Drummer Boy, HN 2679, 1976-1981 ....150.00 to 300.00
Figurine, Duchess Of York, HN 3086, 1986 .... 306.00
Figurine, Eagle On Rock, HN 139, 1917-1936 .... 1375.00
Figurine, Easter Day, HN 2039, 1949-1969 ....220.00 to 450.00
Figurine, Eleanor Of Provence, HN 2009, 1948-1953 .... 431.00
Figurine, Eleanore, HN 1754, 1936-1949 ....560.00 to 1000.00
Figurine, Elegance, HN 2264, 1961-1985 ....65.00 to 130.00
Figurine, Ellen, HN 3816, 1997 ....40.00 to 90.00
Figurine, Emily, HN 3806, 1996-1997 ....50.00 to 120.00
Figurine, Emir, HN 1604, 1933-1949 .... 804.00
Figurine, Empress Dowager, HN 2391, 1983 ....460.00 to 1000.00
Figurine, Enchantment, HN 2178, 1957-1982 ....50.00 to 100.00
Figurine, Ermine Coat, HN 1981, 1945-1967 ....150.00 to 200.00
Figurine, Eve, HN 2466, 1984 ....230.00 to 460.00
Figurine, Fair Lady, HN 2193, 1963-1996 ....85.00 to 120.00
Figurine, Fair Lady, HN 2832, 1977-1996 ....75.00 to 150.00
Figurine, Falstaff, HN 1606, 1933-1949 ....1340.00 to 1960.00
Figurine, Falstaff, HN 2054, 1950-1992 .... 62.00
Figurine, Family Album, HN 2321, 1966-1973 ....200.00 to 300.00
Figurine, Farmer's Wife, HN 2069, 1951-1955 ....360.00 to 720.00
Figurine, Fat Boy, HN 1893, 1938-1952 ....345.00 to 575.00
Figurine, Fat Boy, HN 555, 1923-1939 ....345.00 to 1000.00
Figurine, Fiddler, HN 2171, 1956-1962 ....520.00 to 600.00
Figurine, First Steps, HN 2242, 1959-1965 ....290.00 to 400.00
Figurine, Flora, HN 2349, 1966-1973 ....200.00 to 300.00
Figurine, Flower Seller's Children, HN 1342, 1929-1993 .... 695.00
Figurine, For You, HN 3754, 1996 ....100.00 to 200.00
Figurine, French Peasant, HN 2075, 1951-1955 ....230.00 to 400.00
Figurine, French Poodle, Standing, NH 2631, 1952-1985 ....50.00 to 100.00
Figurine, Gaffer, HN 2053, 1950-1959 ....240.00 to 400.00
Figurine, Geisha, HN 1223, 1927-1938 ....730.00 to 1200.00
Figurine, Genevieve, HN 1962, 1941-1975 ....200.00 to 300.00
Figurine, Gentlewoman, HN 1632, 1934-1949 ....540.00 to 1100.00
Figurine, George Washington At Prayer, HN 2861, 1977 .... 1053.00
Figurine, Gollywog, HN 1979, 1945-1959 ....460.00 to 900.00
Figurine, Good Day Sir, HN 2896, 1986-1989 .... 107.00
Figurine, Grandma, HN 2052, 1950-1959 ....245.00 to 400.00
Figurine, Granny's Heritage, HN 1873, 1938-1949 ....860.00 to 1100.00
Figurine, Granny's Heritage, HN 2031, 1949-1969 .... *Illus* 360.00
Figurine, Grizel, HN 1629, 1934-1938 .... 1436.00
Figurine, Harmony, HN 2824, 1978-1984 ....75.00 to 160.00
Figurine, He Loves Me, HN 2046, 1949-1962 ....275.00 to 500.00
Figurine, Helen Of Troy, HN 2387, 1981 ....575.00 to 1200.00
Figurine, Henrietta Maria, HN 2005, 1948-1953 ....345.00 to 550.00
Figurine, Henry Irving As Cardinal Wosley, HN 344, 1919-1949 ....960.00 to 1500.00
Figurine, Henry Lytton As Jack Point, HN 610, 1924-1949 ....425.00 to 900.00
Figurine, Her Majesty Queen Elizabeth II, HN 2878, 1983 .... 498.00

Royal Doulton, Figurine,
Daffy Down Dilly, HN 1712,
1935-1975

Royal Doulton, Figurine,
Granny's Heritage, HN
2031, 1949-1969

Royal Doulton, Figurine,
Pajamas, HN 1942,
1940-1949

Figurine, Hiver, HN 3069, 1988 ....345.00 to 820.00
Figurine, HRH Princess Of Wales, HN 2887, 1982 ....860.00 to 1400.00
Figurine, Jack, HN 2060, 1950-1971 ....90.00 to 150.00
Figurine, Jane, HN 3711, 1997 ....75.00 to 120.00
Figurine, Janet, HN 1916, 1939-1949 ....230.00 to 300.00
Figurine, Janice, HN 2022, 1949-1955 .... 460.00
Figurine, Janine, HN 2461, 1971-1995 ....85.00 to 150.00
Figurine, Jolly Sailor, HN 2172, 1956-1965 ....460.00 to 900.00
Figurine, Jovial Monk, HN 2144, 1954-1976 ....140.00 to 260.00
Figurine, Judith, HN 2278, 1986 ....85.00 to 170.00
Figurine, Julia, HN 2705, 1975-1990 ....60.00 to 102.00
Figurine, King Charles, HN 2084, 1952-1992 ....650.00 to 1400.00
Figurine, Kirsty, HN 2381, 1971-1996 ....90.00 to 180.00
Figurine, Lady Anne Neville, HN 2006, 1948-1953 ....460.00 to 800.00
Figurine, Lady Of The Fan, HN 52, 1916-1936 ....1535.00 to 3200.00
Figurine, Lady Pamela, HN 2718, 1974-1981 ....115.00 to 175.00
Figurine, Last Waltz, HN 2315, 1967-1993 ....65.00 to 170.00
Figurine, Lavender Woman, HN 569, 1924-1936 ....1375.00 to 2600.00
Figurine, Lilac Time, HN 2137, 1954-1969 ....200.00 to 300.00
Figurine, Lobster Man, HN 2317, 1964-1994 .... 207.00
Figurine, Long John Silver, HN 2204, 1957-1965 ....250.00 to 500.00
Figurine, Lucrezia Borgia, HN 2342, 1985 ....558.00 to 1000.00
Figurine, Lucy Lockett, HN 524, 1921-1949 ....420.00 to 800.00
Figurine, Lynne, HN 2329, 1971-1996 ....60.00 to 120.00
Figurine, Madonna Of The Square, HN 2034, 1949-1951 .... 1245.00
Figurine, Margaret Of Anjou, HN 2012, 1948-1953 ....460.00 to 750.00
Figurine, Marriage Of Art & Industry, HN 2261, 1958 .... 5171.00
Figurine, Mary Jane, HN 1990, 1947-1952 ....460.00 to 500.00
Figurine, Mask Seller, HN 2103, 1953-1995 ....160.00 to 350.00
Figurine, Masquerade, Male, HN 636, 1924-1936 ....1250.00 to 3100.00
Figurine, Master Sweep, HN 2205, 1957-1962 ....400.00 to 800.00
Figurine, Matilda, HN 2011, 1948-1953 ....345.00 to 650.00
Figurine, Mayor, HN 2280, 1963-1971 ....195.00 to 300.00
Figurine, Miss Muffet, HN 1937, 1940-1952 .... 306.00
Figurine, Modena, HN 1846, 1938-1949 ....765.00 to 1600.00
Figurine, Molly Malone, HN 1455, 1931-1937 ....670.00 to 2000.00
Figurine, Monica, HN 1458, 1931-1949 .... 383.00
Figurine, Mr. Micawber, HN 557, 1923-1939 .... 460.00
Figurine, Mr. Pickwick, HN 556, 1923-1939 .... 383.00
Figurine, Mrs. Fitzherbert, HN 2007, 1948-1953 ....430.00 to 600.00
Figurine, My Teddy, HN 2177, 1962-1967 ....375.00 to 500.00
Figurine, Nell Gwynne, HN 1882, 1938-1949 ....460.00 to 1500.00
Figurine, New Bonnet, HN 1957, 1940-1949 ....575.00 to 1500.00
Figurine, Newsboy, HN 2244, 1956-1965 ....600.00 to 1530.00

Figurine, Newsvendor, HN 2891, 1986 ....140.00 to 180.00
Figurine, Nicola, HN 2804, 1981-1987 ....80.00 to 120.00
Figurine, Odds & Ends, HN 1844, 1938-1949 .... 2185.00
Figurine, Old King Cole, HN 2217, 1963-1967 ....335.00 to 500.00
Figurine, Old King, HN 2134, 1954-1992 .... 326.00
Figurine, Old Lavender Seller, HN 1492, 1932-1949 .... 920.00
Figurine, Old Mother Hubbard, HN 2314, 1964-1975 ....185.00 to 200.00
Figurine, One That Got Away, HN 2153, 1955-1959 ....255.00 to 300.00
Figurine, Organ Grinder, HN 2173, 1956-1965 ....640.00 to 900.00
Figurine, Owd Willum, HN 2042, 1949-1973 ....150.00 to 200.00
Figurine, Painting, HN 3012, 1987 .... 2298.00
Figurine, Pajamas, HN 1942, 1940-1949 ....*Illus*   690.00
Figurine, Palio, HN 2428, 1971-1975 ....3000.00 to 5000.00
Figurine, Pecksniff, HN 553, 1923-1939 .... 766.00
Figurine, Penelope, HN 1901, 1939-1975 ....230.00 to 400.00
Figurine, Phillipine Dancer, HN 2439, 1978 ....310.00 to 450.00
Figurine, Phillippa Of Hainault, HN 2008, 1948-1953 .... 375.00
Figurine, Pied Piper, HN 1215, 1926-1938 .... 2100.00
Figurine, Pied Piper, HN 2102, 1953-1976 ....160.00 to 200.00
Figurine, Pierrette, HN 643, 1924-1938 ....1300.00 to 1700.00
Figurine, Piglet, HN 2648, 1959-1967 ....325.00 to 1340.00
Figurine, Pinkie, HN 1553, 1933-1938 .... 558.00
Figurine, Piper, HN 2907, 1980-1992 .... 575.00
Figurine, Poacher, HN 2043, 1949-1959 ....*Illus*   350.00
Figurine, Premiere, HN 2343, 1969-1979 ....75.00 to 275.00
Figurine, Pride & Joy, HN 2945, 1984 .... 127.00
Figurine, Primroses, HN 1617, 1934-1949 .... 670.00
Figurine, Prince Of Wales, HN 1217, 1926-1938 ....540.00 to 1000.00
Figurine, Princess Badoura, HN 3921, 1996-1999 .... 7500.00
Figurine, Printemps, HN 3066, 1987 .... 345.00
Figurine, Priscilla, HN 1501, 1932-1938 ....610.00 to 1100.00
Figurine, Prized Possessions, HN 2942, 1982 ....185.00 to 300.00
Figurine, Professor, HN 2281, 1965-1981 .... 127.00
Figurine, Punch & Judy Man, HN 2765, 1981-1990 ....160.00 to 240.00
Figurine, Queen Of Sheba, HN 2328, 1982 ....765.00 to 1000.00
Figurine, R.C.M.P., HN 2547, 1973 .... 862.00
Figurine, Regal Lady, HN 2709, 1975-1983 ....80.00 to 120.00
Figurine, Rhoda, HN 1574, 1933-1940 ....250.00 to 500.00
Figurine, Romany Sue, HN 1758, 1936-1949 .... 1245.00
Figurine, Rosamund, HN 1497, 1932-1938 ....1050.00 to 1800.00
Figurine, Roseanna, HN 1926, 1940-1959 ....259.00 to 400.00
Figurine, Rosebud, HN 1983, 1945-1952 .... 575.00
Figurine, Ruby, HN 1724, 1935-1949 ....600.00 to 1245.00
Figurine, Sairey Gamp, HN 1896, 1938-1952 ....259.00 to 500.00
Figurine, Schoolmarm, HN 2223, 1958-1981 ....160.00 to 220.00

Royal Doulton, Figurine,
Poacher, HN 2043, 1949-1959

Royal Doulton, Figurine, Sleepy
Head, HN 2114, 1953-1955

Royal Doulton, Figurine, Sweet
Lavender, HN 1373, 1930-1949

Figurine, Scotch Girl, HN 1269, 1928-1938 . . . . .1530.00 to 2500.00
Figurine, Sea Sprite, HN 2191, 1958-1962 . . . . .200.00 to 375.00
Figurine, Silks & Ribbons, HN 2017, 1949-2001 . . . . 115.00
Figurine, Sir Winston Churchill, HN 3057, 1985 . . . . .127.00 to 300.00
Figurine, Skater, HN 2117, 1953-1971 . . . . .200.00 to 400.00
Figurine, Sleepy Head, HN 2114, 1953-1955 . . . . *Illus* 1840.00
Figurine, Snake Charmer, HN 1317, 1929-1938 . . . . 615.00
Figurine, Sophie, HN 3790, 1996-1997 . . . . .50.00 to 100.00
Figurine, Southern Belle, HN 2229, 1958-1997 . . . . 197.00
Figurine, Spring Flowers, HN 1807, 1937-1959 . . . . .230.00 to 350.00
Figurine, Spring Walk, HN 3120, 1990-1992 . . . . .70.00 to 120.00
Figurine, St. George, HN 2051, 1950-1985 . . . . 536.00
Figurine, Sunday Best, HN 2206, 1979-1984 . . . . .95.00 to 200.00
Figurine, Sweet & Twenty, HN 1298, 1928-1969 . . . . 259.00
Figurine, Sweet & Twenty, HN 1589, 1933-1949 . . . . 306.00
Figurine, Sweet Dreams, HN 2380, 1971-1990 . . . . .90.00 to 180.00
Figurine, Sweet Lavender, HN 1373, 1930-1949 . . . . *Illus* 834.00
Figurine, Sweet Maid, HN 1504, 1932-1936 . . . . .498.00 to 1100.00
Figurine, Taking Things Easy, HN 2677, 1975-1987 . . . . .275.00 to 862.00
Figurine, Teresa, HN 1682, 1935-1949 . . . . .862.00 to 1100.00
Figurine, To Bed, HN 1805, 1937-1959 . . . . 306.00
Figurine, Top O' The Hill, HN 1834, 1937 . . . . .115.00 to 300.00
Figurine, Top O' The Hill, HN 1849, 1938-1975 . . . . .115.00 to 200.00
Figurine, Town Crier, HN 2119, 1953-1976 . . . . .150.00 to 200.00
Figurine, Toymaker, HN 2250, 1959-1973 . . . . .287.00 to 420.00
Figurine, Tracy, HN 2736, 1983-1994 . . . . .73.00 to 120.00
Figurine, Victorian Lady, HN 728, 1925-1952 . . . . .287.00 to 410.00
Figurine, Wandering Minstrel, HN 1224, 1927-1936 . . . . 3064.00
Figurine, Wee Willy Winkie, HN 2050, 1949-1953 . . . . 383.00
Figurine, Wizard, HN 2877, 1979 . . . . .175.00 to 360.00
Figurine, Young Miss Nightengale, HN 2010, 1948-1953 . . . . .430.00 to 600.00
Flask, Stopper, William Grant, 1987, Large 155.00
Jar, Tobacco, Lid, Monk, Kingsware 1149.00
Jug, Proverb, Twixt The Cup & The Lip, Buff Ground, Flower, Brown, Handle, 7 In. 160.00
Jug, Series Ware, Humanized Card Playing Figures 287.00
Jug, Shakespeare, Play Characters, Limited, 1931, 10 1/2 In. 765.00
Jug, Treasure Island, Limited Edition, 1934, 7 1/2 In. 1915.00
Model Set, Hare, HN 2593, 1941-1968, HN 2594, 1941-1985, K 37, 1940-1947 . . . . 536.00
Planter, Scalloped Rim, Gilt, Tapestry Style Band, Enameled, 8 x 10 1/2 In. 55.00
Plaque, Children, Woodland Scene, Blue Underglaze, Oval, Frame, 9 1/2 In., Pair 978.00
Plaque, Messenger's Coming Job, George Tinworth, Terra-Cotta 1245.00
Plate, Golfing Scene, St. Andrews Fife, D 5654 . . . . 245.00
Plate, Hunting Man, 10 1/2 In. 60.00
Plate, Monks Listening To Sermon, 9 3/4 In. 35.00
Plate, Service, Leaf Latticework, Flowers, Medallions, 10 1/2 In., 14 Piece 1610.00
Plate, Shakespeare, Hamlet, 9 1/4 In. 40.00
Plate, Snowman Skiing, Associated Wares, 1990-1992 . . . . 385.00
Pub Jug, Stonachie Distillery, Perthshire, Scotland, Sandy MacDonald Scotch 389.00
Punch Bowl, Venetian Canal Scene, Footed, Early 20th Century, 16 3/8 In. 295.00
Teapot, Spider Mums, Lid, 4 3/4 In. 127.00
Toby Jug, Fat Boy, D 6264, Small 65.00
Toby Jug, Mr. Pickwick, D 6261, Small 138.00
Toby Jug, Toby Phipots, No. 1114, Small 58.00
Tray, Titanian, Hunting Dog, Mounted Boar's Head, Ivy Leaves, 11 In. 345.00
Trivet, Promise Little & Do Much, c.1900, 6 1/2 In. 145.00
Vase, And When They Were Come To The Place, Calvary, George Tinworth 2680.00
Vase, Blue Roses, No. 1113, Square, 3 1/8 In. 69.00
Vase, Burgundy Crystalline Glaze, Marked, 4 x 2 3/4 In. 200.00
Vase, Cafe-Au-Lait Crystalline Glaze, Gourd, 6 3/4 x 6 In. 949.00
Vase, Chang, Geometric Design, 1925-1939, 9 In. 2875.00
Vase, Edward VII Coronation, Egg Shape, King, Queen Alexandra, c.1902, 11 In. 500.00
Vase, Flambe, Blue, Body Twists At Rim, Squat, 2 x 6 In. 460.00
Vase, Flambe, Cottage By River, Tear Shape, 7 In. 375.00

Vase, Flambe, Fruit, Blue, No. 8580, 10 In. 345.00
Vase, Flambe, Leaves, Berries, Crystalline Matte, No. 7943, 7 3/4 In. 345.00
Vase, Flambe, Stylized Flowers, Purple Glaze, 7 3/4 In. 290.00
Vase, Flambe, Stylized Leaves & Vines, Blue Ground, 9 5/8 In., Pair 175.00
Vase, Flambe, Sung Baluster, Stamped, Signed Noke, 10 x 4 1/2 In. 259.00
Vase, Pink, Daffodil Pattern, Gold Highlights, Signed Kelsall, 5 x 2 1/4 In. 250.00
Vase, Spider Mums, White Slip, 7 1/4 In., Pair 259.00
Vase, Stoneware, 3 Flower Clusters, c.1934, 9 In. 115.00
Vase, Stylized Flowers, Mottled Gray Green Ground, 11 1/8 In. 259.00
Vase, Swirls In Squares, Mottled Gray Blue, 5 7/8 In. 230.00
Vase, Titanian, Young Long-Eared Owl, Moon, Harry Allen, 5 7/8 In. 1035.00
Vase, Village, Landscape, Trees, Drill Hole, A. Eaton, Paper Label, Signed, 18 x 7 In. 920.00

ROYAL DUX is the more common name for the Duxer Porzellanmanu-
faktur, which was founded by E. Eichler in Dux, Bohemia, in 1860. By
the turn of the century, the firm specialized in porcelain statuary and
busts of Art Nouveau–style maidens, large porcelain figures, and
ornate vases with three-dimensional figures climbing on the sides. The
firm is still in business.

Bowl, 3 Dancing Women, Greek Muses, Raised Flowers, Gilt, 19 1/2 In. 385.00
Bowl, Group, Shepherd Family, Sheep, Oval, Early 20th Century, 20 In. 440.00
Bowl, Inverted Shells, Nymph, Shell, Seaweed, Czechoslovakia, c.1910, 16 1/2 In. 646.00
Bowl, Iris Blossom, Cattail, Nymph, Cherub, Egg Shape, c.1910, 14 In. 825.00
Figurine, Dancer, 22 In. 1540.00
Figurine, Girl, In Pantaloons, Blue To White Dress, Tan Bonnet, 8 1/4 x 4 1/2 In. 325.00
Figurine, Gypsy Shepherdess, Staff, Tambourine, Early 1900s, 19 1/2 In. 558.00
Figurine, Maiden, On Horse, White, Stamped, Pink Triangle, 14 x 12 In. 115.00
Figurine, Man, Woman Water Bearers, Draped Gowns, Classically Styled, 24 In., Pair ... 468.00
Figurine, Nude L'Seuse, Butterfly On Knee, Pink Triangle Mark, c.1900, 8 In. 545.00
Figurine, Woman Bather, Seated On Rocky Outcrop, Early 1900s, 18 1/2 In. 999.00
Figurine, Woman, Semi-Nude, Bathing, Signed, 21 In. 3335.00
Figurine, Youth, Riding Horse, 16 In. 478.00
Group, Hunting Dogs, Standing, Seated, Early 20th Century, 11 1/2 x 16 x 6 1/2 In. 316.00
Vase, Flower Stems, Masks, Egg Shape, Early 1900s, 10 5/8 In., Pair 410.00
Vase, Fruit, Applied, Relief, Ivory Ground, Early 1900s, 19 In., Pair 1380.00
Vase, Maiden, Oak Leaves, Acorn, Gilt, Iris, No. 1558, c.1910, 22 In. 750.00
Vase, Nymph, Filling Urn, Iris Stems, Early 1900s, 17 1/2 In. 825.00
Vase, Spill, Nymph, On Shell, Rocaille Branch Base, Early 1900s, 11 1/4 In. 825.00

ROYAL FLEMISH glass was made during the late 1880s in New Bedford,
Massachusetts, by the Mt. Washington Glass Works. It is a colored
satin glass decorated with dark colors and raised gold designs. The
glass was patented in 1894. It was supposed to resemble stained glass
windows.

Biscuit Jar, Coin Medallions, Rampant Lion, Sun, Tapered, Oval, Panels, 8 x 5 In. 1093.00
Biscuit Jar, Multicolored Foliage, Frosted Panels, Metal Lid, c.1890, 7 In. 1344.00
Cologne, Flowers, Butterflies, Enameled Gold Wings, Stopper, 5 1/2 x 4 1/2 In. 6038.00
Ewer, Cupid, Dragon, Gold Scrolling Medallion, Handle, Signed, c.1890, 11 In. 2800.00
Jug, Raised Gold Panels, Coat Of Arms, Lions, Floral Neck Band, c.1890, 12 In. 4480.00
Lamp, Banquet, Thistle Design, Filigreed Brass Foot, 1884 Patent, 24 1/2 In. 1840.00
Lamp, Renaissance Decoration 11200.00
Vase, Enameled Flowers, Bulbous, Cup Shape Neck, Handles, 9 1/2 In. 4100.00
Vase, Enameled Flowers, Translucent, Frosted, Gilt, Handles, Signed, 5 3/4 In. 2090.00
Vase, Flowers, Medallions, Black Scrolls, Gray, Russet, Gilt, Flared, c.1890, 12 In. 3685.00
Vase, Geometric Background, Winged Griffin, Dragon, 10 In. 4140.00
Vase, Mythological Bird, Tan, Brown, Raised Gold, Scrolls, c.1890, 14 1/2 In. 5600.00
Vase, Peacock, Frosted, Gold, Enamel, 12 1/2 In. 4830.00
Vase, Peacock, Gold, Beads, Leaves, Scrolls, Panels, Marked, 13 In. 7475.00
Vase, Satin, Bittersweet, Beige Panels, Gilt, Dragons, Wood Stand, 7 1/2 In. 2185.00
Vase, Stick, Flowers, Raised Medallions, Griffins, Scrolled Neck, c.1890, 12 In. 4480.00

ROYAL HAEGER, see Haeger category.

ROYAL IVY, see Northwood, Royal Ivy

ROYAL NYMPHENBURG is the modern name for the Nymphenburg porcelain factory, which was established at Neudeck-ob-der-Au, Germany, in 1753 and moved to Nymphenburg in 1761. The company is still in existence. Marks include a checkered shield topped by a crown, a crowned *CT* with the year, and a contemporary shield mark on reproductions of eighteenth-century porcelain.

Coffee & Tea Set, Solitaire, Neoclassical, Oval Landscapes, c.1885, 5 Piece	375.00
Dessert Service, Enamel, Flowers, Compote, Plates, c.1890, 7 Piece	380.00
Figurine, Lady Warrior, Shield, 14 In.	3740.00
Figurine, Lady, Fancy Gown, Holding Fan, Early 19th Century, 6 In.	230.00
Figurine, Man, Scratching Head, Marked, Bustelli, Early 1900s, 8 In.	1265.00
Group, Marte Serie De Los Dioses Antiguos, 15 In.	3530.00
Group, Mother, Nursing Baby, 3 Children, 19th Century, 7 x 5 In.	660.00

ROYAL OAK pieces are listed in the Pressed Glass category by that pattern name.

ROYAL RUDOLSTADT, see Rudolstadt category.

ROYAL VIENNA, see Beehive category.

ROYAL WORCESTER is a name used by collectors. Worcester porcelains were made in Worcester, England, from about 1751. The firm went through many different periods and name changes. It became the Worcester Royal Porcelain Company, Ltd., in 1862. Today collectors call the porcelains made after 1862 *Royal Worcester*. In 1976, the firm merged with W. T. Copeland to become Royal Worcester Spode. Some early products of the factory are listed under Worcester.

Basket, Flower & Butterfly, Embossed, Twisted Gilt Handle, Exterior, 6 In.	285.00
Candelabrum, 2-Light, Flower Bands, Dolphin, Herm Handles, Vase, 7 3/4 In.	825.00
Candlestick, Columnar, Fluted, Scrolled Sconce, England, c.1888, 8 In., Pair	560.00
Chamberstick, Stylized Lotus Blossom, Frog On Gilt Leaf, 4 5/8 In.	150.00
Compote, Rose Pink Border, Flowers, Footed, c.1860, 2 3/8 x 9 3/8 In., Pair	115.00
Compote, Shell, Pink Interior, Impressed Mark, Late 1800s, 6 1/2 In. .... *Illus*	190.00
Compote, Triple, Shell, Dolphin Footed, 7 x 10 In.	2750.00
Cup & Saucer, Flowers, Divided Panels, Marked	145.00
Demitasse Set, Imperial Chinese Yellow, 18 Piece	345.00
Dish Set, Assorted Game Birds, Scalloped Edges, 9 In., 22 Piece	2875.00
Ewer, Flowers, Plum, Blue, Gilt, No. 1116, Bailey, Banks & Biddle, c.1887, 8 In.	207.00
Ewer, Flowers, Plum, Green, Blue, Gilt, No. 1026, c.1890, 6 In.	218.00
Ewer, Gilt Feather, Pink & Gold Metallic, Patina Neck, Handles, 14 In.	785.00
Ewer, Ivory, Basket Weave, Flower Scrolls, Dragon Handle, Gilt, 12 3/4 In.	250.00
Ewer, Plum, Green, Blue, Gold Floral, No. 1026, c.1890, 6 In. .... *Illus*	218.00
Figurine, Bacchante, Tambourine, No. 1441, England, c.1892, 9 3/4 In.	380.00
Figurine, Betty, Marigold, No. 2930, 4 In.	125.00
Figurine, Blackbird, Yellow Head, Signed, Dorothy Doughty, 1950, 11 1/2 In.	2185.00
Figurine, Boer War Soldier, Black Watch, No. 2109, c.1903, 7 1/2 In.	999.00

Royal Worcester, Compote, Shell, Pink Interior, Impressed Mark, Late 1800s, 6 1/2 In.

Royal Worcester, Ewer, Plum, Green, Blue, Gold Floral, No. 1026, c.1890, 6 In.

Royal Worcester, Teapot, Double Body, Fern, Peach, Brown, Gilt, c.1877, 4 7/8 In.

Figurine, China, Boy, Eating From Bowl, No. 3073, 2 1/4 x 1 x 1 3/4 In. 25.00
Figurine, Farmer, Scythe, Porcelain Shot, England, No. 1292, 1890s, 8 1/2 In. 470.00
Figurine, Female Water Carrier, Gilt Rim, Ivory, England, c.1895, 9 1/2 In. 411.00
Figurine, Friday's Child, No. 3261, 6 1/2 In. 135.00
Figurine, Girl, Tambourine, Gilt, No. 1032, Hadley Model, c.1887, 8 1/4 In. 265.00
Figurine, Girl, With Flowers, England, No. 3075, 5 1/2 In. 225.00
Figurine, Goosey Goosey Gander, No. 3304, 5 1/2 In. 225.00
Figurine, Lark Sparrow, Red Gila, Twinpod, Doughty, c.1966, 6 In. . . . . .460.00 to 1725.00
Figurine, Mikado Characters, Hadley, c.1890, 16 In., Pair 12000.00
Figurine, Moorhen Chick, Water Lily, Doughty, c.1964, 4 1/2 x 12 1/2 In. 1150.00
Figurine, Ovenbird, Crested Iris, Doughty, No. 3533, c.1960, 10 1/2 In. 4140.00
Figurine, Ovenbird, Lady's Slipper, No. 3532, Doughty, c.1960, 11 In. 2760.00
Figurine, Parroquet, Dorothy Doughty, c.1965, 6 1/2 x 18 In. . . . . .430.00 to 546.00
Figurine, Romanian Woman, Shovel, No. 1606, England, c.1892, 13 1/4 In. 880.00
Figurine, September, Snowy, Boy, With Cat, Marked, No. 3457, 4 3/4 In. 175.00
Figurine, Wild Rose Bird, Whitethroat, Curraca, Doughty, 1964, 10 In. 1093.00
Figurine, Wren, Burnet Rose, Dorothy Doughty, c.1964, 6 1/2 In. 1725.00
Flask, Moon, Japanese Style, Angular Scroll Handles, Bronze Tones, 10 In. 2990.00
Group, Figures, With Water Jug, Hadley, 7 In. 390.00
Jug, Bottle Shape, Dragon Handle, Enamel, Yellow, England, c.1880, 10 3/4 In. 560.00
Jug, Cream, Embossed Basket Weave, c.1900, 3 In. 60.00
Jug, Double Walled, Reticulated Body, Gilt, Enameled, c.1879, 5 1/4 In. 2235.00
Jug, Flowers, Gilt Branch Handle, 5 In. 69.00
Knife Handle, Crabstock Handles, Case, 8 3/4 In., 12 Piece 175.00
Lamp, Oil, Gilt Trim, Enamel Decorated, England, Late 1800s, 13 1/4 In. 650.00
Pitcher, Claret, Flowers, Gilt Highlights, Late 1800s, 9 In. 144.00
Pitcher, Fish, Pike, Figural, 12 In. 2352.00
Pitcher, Flowers, Bamboo Form Handle, Ivoryware, 8 In. 115.00
Pitcher, Flowers, Gilt, 7 1/2 In. 105.00
Pitcher, Flowers, Vine Form Handle, Ivoryware, 6 3/4 In. 130.00
Plate, Cobalt Blue, Cream, Gilt, 1929, 10 1/2 In. 865.00
Plate Set, Flower Urns, Classical Style, Pink Rim, c.1929, 10 1/2 In., 12 Piece 1295.00
Plate Set, Pink Cartouches, Scrollwork, Scalloped Edge, Gilt, 10 1/4 In., 12 Piece 1610.00
Platter, Well & Tree, Diamond Bands, c.1950, 24 1/4 x 16 3/4 In. 145.00
Soup Set, Blue Allover Transfer, Flower Heads, Chinoiserie, 16 1/2 In. 705.00
Sugar & Creamer, Flowers, Blue, Gilt, Purple Crown Mark, c.1900, 2 1/2 In. 80.00
Teapot, Blue, Gilt, Woman's Head Spout, Bailey, Banks & Biddle, 1887, 7 1/2 In. 173.00
Teapot, Double Body, Fern, Peach, Brown, Gilt, c.1877, 4 7/8 In. . . . . *Illus* 288.00
Teapot, Flower Branch, Pink, Gilt, Ivory, Woman's Head Spout, c.1888, 7 3/4 In. 489.00
Teapot, Flowers, Brown, Plum, Green, Blue, Double Spout, c.1883, 6 In. 520.00
Teapot, Oriental Design, Raised Gilt, Ivory, No. 1339, c.1895, 6 1/2 In. 430.00
Teapot, Raised Gilt Flowers, Leaves, Ivory, c.1884, 7 1/4 In. 290.00
Teapot, Robin's-Egg Blue, Gilt, c.1887, 5 1/2 In. 265.00
Toothpick, Picket Fence, Flowers, Ivy, 2 3/4 In. 140.00
Tureen, Cover, Platter, Game Series, Brown Flowers, Scalloped Edge, 7 x 14 In. 365.00
Vase, Aesthetic Movement, Baluster Shape, Loop Handles, 15 3/8 In. 940.00
Vase, Bottle Shape, Leaves, Flowers, Ivory, No. 1192, c.1891, 14 1/2 In. 765.00
Vase, Club Shape, Molded Dragon Wrapped Around Neck, 16 In. 880.00
Vase, Egg Shape, Reticulated Neck, Gilt Handles, Multicolored, 1889, 17 In. 440.00
Vase, Enamel Flowers, Ivory, No. 1331, c.1891, 10 1/2 In. 825.00
Vase, Japanese Design, Dragon Mask Handles, Bronze Tones, 11 In., Pair 5060.00
Vase, Landscape, Crown Ware Luster, England, c.1926, 10 1/4 In. 500.00
Vase, Leaves, Butterflies, Ivory, Enamels, Persian, No. 784, c.1880, 13 1/2 In. 440.00
Vase, Samurai, Stylized Pilgrim Flask Form, 13 1/4 In. 2475.00
Vase, Shell, Raised On Pedestal, 16 In. 1870.00
Vase, Urn Shape, Geometric Design, Gilt, 3 Snake Handles, c.1890, 7 In. 258.00
Wall Pocket, Orchid Shape, Enameled Petals, c.1883, 8 1/4 In., Pair 440.00

ROYCROFT products were made by the Roycrofter community of East
Aurora, New York, in the late nineteenth and early twentieth centuries.
The community was founded by Elbert Hubbard, famous philosopher,
writer, and artist. The workshops owned by the community made furniture, metalware, leatherwork, embroidery, and jewelry. A printshop

produced many signs, books, and the magazines that promoted the sayings of Elbert Hubbard. Furniture by the Roycroft community is listed in the Furniture category.

Ashtray, Round, Copper, Hammered, 5 In. 60.00
Bookends, Copper, Hammered, Dogwood Blossoms, Medallion, Repousse, 5 x 6 In. . . . 400.00
Bookends, Copper, Hammered, Open Form, Tooled Flowers, Impressed Mark, 8 1/2 In. . . 145.00
Bookends, Copper, Hammered, Oval, Roped Panel, Orb & Cross Mark, 5 x 3 3/4 In. . . . 490.00
Bookends, Copper, Hammered, Poppy, Riveted, Orb & Cross Mark, 5 1/4 x 5 In. 430.00
Bookends, Copper, Hammered, Tooled Owl Design, Curled Corners, 6 1/2 x 4 In. 200.00
Bookends, Copper, Side Medallion, Little Journey Book Set, 8 x 6 In. 230.00
Box, Cover, Hinged, 1 x 3 1/2 x 3 1/2 In. 400.00
Box, Mahogany, Hammered Clasp, Corners, Side Handles, Signed Orb, 26 x 12 x 9 In. . . . 600.00
Candelabrum, Copper, Hammered, 6-Light, Twisted Base, Original Patina, 14 x 13 In. . . 1150.00
Candlestick, Copper, Cylinder, Round Drip Pan, Double Square Shaft, 7 1/2 In., Pair . . . 1210.00
Candlestick, Copper, Hammered, 2 Stems, Riveted, Faceted, Patina, 7 3/4 In., Pair 805.00
Candlestick, Copper, Hammered, Open Shaft, Square Base, 7 1/2 In., Pair 590.00
Card Tray, Stylized Squares, Dark Patina, Dard Hunter, Orb & Cross Mark, 5 3/4 In. . . . 690.00
Compote, Copper, Acid Etched, Dark Bronze Patina, Marked, 4 1/2 x 11 1/4 In. 145.00
Desk Pad Ends, 16 x 2 1/2 In. 230.00
Desk Set, Copper, Hammered, Glass Inkwell, 14 x 4 In. 480.00
Door Latch, Hand Forged, Rattail Ends, Colonial Style, Thumb Latch, 11 In., Pair 635.00
Dresser Set, Copper, Hammered, Quatrefoils, Ball Feet, Brass, Cover, 2 Piece, 2 3/4 In. . . 3105.00
Frame, Copper, Hammered, Embossed Quatrefoils, 4 Corners, Patina, 5 3/4 x 8 1/4 In. . . . 805.00
Inkwell, Brass Wash, 2 x 3 x 3 In. 290.00
Lamp, Copper, Hammered, Dome Shade, Mica Paneled Skirt, 10 x 14 In., Pair 9200.00
Letter Rack, 4 1/2 x 4 x 2 1/2 In. 375.00
Pen Tray, Brass Wash, 2 x 7 x 2 In. 170.00
Telephone, Copper, Hammered, Bakelite, Original Wiring, Patina, Marked, 12 In. 8050.00
Tray, Copper, Hammered, Oval, Flowers, Embossed, Handles, Marked, 9 1/2 x 23 In. 374.00
Vase, Brass, Hammered, Blown Glass, Stamped Cross & Orb, 5 7/8 In. 705.00
Vase, Bud, Copper, Hammered, 4 Buttresses, Applied Nickel Silver Squares, 8 x 4 In. 2415.00
Vase, Bud, Copper, Hammered, Cylindrical, Buttressed Handles, Riveted, 7 3/4 In. 4315.00
Vase, Copper Hammered, Original Patina, Orb & Cross Mark, 5 1/4 x 5 In. 690.00
Vase, Copper, Acid Etched, Original Patina, Orb & Cross Mark, 5 In. 259.00
Vase, Copper, Hammered, Brass Washed, American Beauty, Orb & Cross Mark, 19 In. . . . 2415.00
Vase, Copper, Hammered, Cylindrical, Applied Silver Trim, 6 1/2 In. 1295.00
Vase, Copper, Hammered, Cylindrical, Silver Overlay, 6 In. 2645.00
Vase, Copper, Hammered, Old Patina, Squat, Impressed, 4 1/2 x 6 3/4 In. 750.00
Vase, Copper, Hammered, Shouldered Shape, 4 3/4 In. 489.00

ROZANE, see Roseville category.

ROZENBURG worked at The Hague, Holland, from 1890 to 1914. The most important pieces were earthenware made in the early twentieth century with pale-colored Art Nouveau designs.

Plaque, Bucolic Scene, Trees, Cottage, Hand Painted, Frame, Marked, 11 x 16 In. 1725.00
Plaque, Landscape, Children On Haywagon, Horses, Frame, 1912, 10 x 13 In. 2070.00
Tile, Sheep, In Barn, Mauve, Sepia Tones, Panel, Frame, Signed, 7 x 15 In. 1095.00
Tile Panel, Dutch Landscape, Woman Tending Sheep, Frame, 32 x 26 In., 12 Piece 3125.00
Vase, Dandelion, Leaves, Brown Ground, Oval, Looped & Arched Handles, 8 3/4 In. 920.00
Vase, Hyacinth, Purple, Stylized Stems, Brown Ground, Bulbous, Art Nouveau, 9 In. 1095.00
Vase, Jonquils, Yellow, Leaves, Brown To Blue Ground, Baluster, Footed, 8 3/4 In. 1095.00
Vase, Peacock, Stylized Flowers, Cobalt Blue, Green, Gold, Baluster, 10 1/2 In. 690.00
Vase, Stylized Bell Flowers, Magenta, Blue Ground, Recessed Trumpet Neck, 9 3/4 In. . . 1265.00
Vase, Stylized Tulips, Tan, Blue Ground, Bulbous, Tapered, Footed, 14 1/2 x 8 In. 1380.00

RRP or RRP, Roseville, is the mark used by the firm of Robinson-Ransbottom. It is not a mark of the more famous Roseville Pottery. The Ransbottom brothers started a pottery in 1900 in Ironspot, Ohio. In 1920, they merged with the Robinson Clay Product Company of Akron, Ohio, to become Robinson-Ransbottom. The factory is still working.

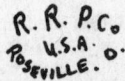

Canister Set, Covers, Spongeware, Blue & Tan, 2 Qt., Qt., Pt., 3 Piece 40.00

Casserole, Cover, Brown, Ivory Drip, Square, 9 x 9 x 4 In. 10.00
Cookie Jar, Hey Diddle-Diddle, Cow Finial, 9 3/4 In. 130.00
Cookie Jar, Jocko The Monkey, 1950s, 11 3/4 In. 55.00
Crock, Cover, Painted, Mexican Boy Sleeping, Cactus, Red, Green, Ear Handles, 9 In. ... 29.00
Pitcher, Spongeware, Ivory & Blue, 2 Qt., 8 1/4 In. 11.00
Vase, Oil Jar, Burgundy Glaze, 2 Grape Leaf Handles, Rolled Rim, 14 In. 51.00
Vase, Relief Flowers, Yellow, Blue, Orange, Shouldered, Dorothy Archer, 6 In. 65.00
Water Cooler, Stoneware, Ivory, Blue Bands, Spigot, Blue Crown Mark, 4 Gal., 15 In. ... 60.00

RS GERMANY is part of the wording in marks used by the Tillowitz, Germany, factory of Reinhold Schlegelmilch from 1914 until about 1945. The porcelain was sold decorated and undecorated. The Schlegelmilch families made porcelains marked in many ways. See also ES Germany, RS Poland, and RS Prussia.

Berry Set, Red Flowers, Gold Trim, Marked, 6 Piece 195.00
Box, Cover, White Roses, Art Deco Mold, Blue RSG Mark, 4 In. 35.00
Cake Plate, Roses, Cosmos, Scalloped Edge, Open Handles, Mold 205, 10 3/4 In. 40.00
Cake Plate, Scalloped Edge, Open Handles, Green RSG Mark, 10 3/4 In. 40.00
Card Receiver, Lily Mold Form, Hand Painted, Blue, Marked, 20th Century, 5 1/2 In. 35.00
Card Receiver, Roses, Red, Yellow, Green Mark, 20th Century, 7 In. 35.00
Celery Dish, Flowers, Multicolored, Gold Trim, Handles, Steeple Mark, 12 1/4 In. 80.00
Hatpin Holder, Painted Rose, Green Ground, Marked, 4 1/2 In. 50.00
Nappy, Vine Roses, Parrot In Cutout Handle, Heart Shape, Marked, 6 1/2 x 6 1/2 In. 40.00
Sugar Shaker, Daffodils, White, Yellow, Gold RSG Steeple Mark, 4 In. 69.00
Sugar Shaker, Flowers, Gold Steeple Mark, 20th Century, 4 In. 70.00

RS POLAND (German) is a mark used by the Reinhold Schlegelmilch factory at Tillowitz from about 1946 to 1956. After 1956, the factory made porcelain marked PT Poland. This is one of many of the RS marks used. See also ES Germany, RS Germany, RS Prussia, RS Silesia, RS Suhl, and RS Tillowitz.

Sugar & Creamer, White Roses, Fitted, Silver Plated Caddy, Red RSP Mark, 8 In. 58.00
Sugar & Creamer, White Roses, Silver Plated Caddy, Red Mark, 20th Century, 8 In. 60.00

RS PRUSSIA appears in several marks used on porcelain before 1917. Reinhold Schlegelmilch started his porcelain works in Suhl, Germany, in 1869. See also ES Germany, RS Germany, RS Poland, RS Silesia, RS Suhl, and RS Tillowitz.

Berry Set, Red Roses, Blue & Chartreuse, Green Wreath Mark, 7 Piece 335.00
Biscuit Jar, Flowers, 5 In. 150.00
Biscuit Jar, Iris, Autumn Figural Decor, Late 19th Century, 7 In. 1035.00
Biscuit Jar, Pond, Water Lilies, Side Handles, 6 In. 180.00
Bowl, Flower Bouquet, Red RSP Mark, 10 1/2 In. 80.00
Bowl, Flowers, Cranberry, Red Mark, Mold 25 Iris, Late 19th Century, 9 1/4 In. 175.00
Bowl, Flowers, Multicolored, Late 19th Century, RSP Mark, 10 In. 489.00
Bowl, Flowers, Multicolored, Mold 86, Late 19th Century, 10 In. 345.00
Bowl, Flowers, Reflection From Water's Edge, Oval Inset Rim Panels, 11 In. 160.00
Bowl, Iris, Foldover, Solid Gold 2 In. Border, 11 In. 2300.00
Bowl, Iris, Summer Central Design, Red Mark, 9 1/2 x 10 In. 1065.00
Bowl, Oak Leaf Mold, Madame Recamier Portrait, Gold Leaves, 10 1/2 In. 5000.00
Bowl, Pink Roses, Satin, Red Mark, Late 19th Century, 10 In. 260.00
Bowl, Red Flowers, Olive Green Accents, Red Mark, 10 In. 489.00
Bowl, Red Poppies, Blue Ground, Red Mark, Late 19th Century, 10 In. 175.00
Bowl, Roses, Cranberry Ground, Late 19th Century, 9 1/4 In. 173.00
Bowl, Roses, Red & Yellow, Fleur-De-Lis, Late 19th Century, Red RSP Mark, 10 In. 90.00
Bowl, Wild Roses, Yellow Ground, Red Mark, Late 19th Century, 10 In. 489.00
Cake Plate, Pink Roses, Gilt, 11 In. 460.00
Cake Plate, Water Lilies, Open Handles, 10 1/2 In. 175.00
Cake Plate, Winter Season, Iris Mold, 10 1/2 In. 5500.00
Celery Dish, Bluebird, Openwork Handles, 14 In. 115.00
Celery Dish, Flower, Spade Form Panels, Flared Rim, Openwork Handles, 13 3/4 In. 50.00
Celery Dish, Hanging Basket Decoration, Red Mark, Late 19th Century, 12 x 2 In. 250.00
Celery Tray, Red Mark, Melon Eaters Scene, Portrait Medallions, Gold Trim 1800.00

Chocolate Pot, Red Roses, Marked, Green Wreath, 9 1/2 In. 500.00
Chocolate Pot, Summer Season, Carnation Mold, Satin 5500.00
Egg Box, Cover, Rose Band, Red Mark, Late 19th Century 4 3/4 In. 115.00
Pin Tray, Dice Throwers, Gilt Trim, Pierced Handles, c.1910, 8 x 6 x 1 In. 450.00
Pin Tray, Hidden Figure Of Woman, Embossed, 4 1/2 x 3 In. 336.00
Pitcher, 4 Fruits, Yellow, Brown, Green, Gilt, c.1900, 9 3/4 In. 375.00
Plate, Lion, Male, Female, 8 1/2 In. 1975.00
Plate, Melon Eaters, Keyhole Medallion, 8 1/2 In. 900.00
Plate, Red, Yellow Flowers, Gilt Trim, Red Mark, 10 In. 575.00
Shaving Mug, Flowers, Fleur-De-Lis, Red Mark, Mold 609, Late 19th Century, 3 1/2 In. ... 115.00
Sugar & Creamer, Flower Spray, Blue Arched Panels, Late 19th Century, 5 In. 100.00
Tankard, Pink Roses, Green Ground, Gilt, c.1900, 11 1/2 In. 476.00
Tankard, Point & Clover, Dice Throwers, Melon Eaters, Gold Highlights, 15 In. 7000.00
Tankard, Stippled Floral, Summer Season, Mill Scene, 13 In. 3500.00
Tea Set, Flowers, Mold 664, Late 19th Century, 8 In., 3 Piece 200.00
Toothpick, Fall Season, Iris Mold, Satin 8500.00
Tray, Dresser, Red Roses, On Mold, Red RSP Mark, Late 19th Century, 11 3/4 In. 69.00
Vase, Couples Dancing, Garden Veranda, Green Mark, 12 In. 785.00
Vase, Gazelle, 2 Handles, 5 In. 2500.00
Vase, Poppies, Snowball, Red Mark, Late 19th Century, 6 In. 265.00

RUBINA is a glassware that shades from red to clear. It was first made
by George Duncan and Sons of Pittsburgh, Pennsylvania, about 1885.
This coloring was used on many types of glassware. The pressed glass
patterns of Royal Ivy and Royal Oak are listed under Pressed Glass.

Cruet, Bulbous Base, Slender Neck, Applied Clear Handle, Ball Stopper, 10 In. 375.00
Toothpick 125.00
Toothpick, Royal Oak 175.00
Tumbler, Engraved Cranes, 3 5/6 In., Pair 150.00
Vase, Jack-In-The-Pulpit, Bulbous Base, 7 In. 185.00

RUBINA VERDE is a Victorian glassware that was shaded from red to
green. It was first made by Hobbs, Brockunier and Company of
Wheeling, West Virginia, about 1890.

Celery Vase, Dew Drop, Hobbs Brockunier, 6 1/2 In. 180.00
Pitcher, Optic Panels, Applied Handle, 6 3/4 In. 275.00
Rose Bowl, Swirled Ribs, 3 Rigaree Handles, 3 Petal Feet, 5 In. 225.00
Vase, Lily Shape, Ruffled Rim, Silver Plated Holder, 8 3/4 In. 125.00

RUBY GLASS is the dark red color of the precious gemstone known as
a *ruby*. It was a popular Victorian color that never went completely out
of style. The glass was shaped by many different processes to make
many different types of ruby glass. There was a revival of interest in
the 1940s when modern-shaped ruby table glassware became fashionable. Sometimes the red color is added to clear glass by a process
called flashing or staining. Flashed glass is clear glass dipped in a colored glass, then pressed or cut. Stained glass has color painted on a
clear glass. Then it is refired so the stain fuses with the glass. Pieces of
glass colored in this way are indicated by the word *stained* in the
description. Related items may be found in other categories, such as
Cranberry Glass, Pressed Glass, and Souvenir.

Bowl, Gorham Sterling Pedestal Base, 6 In. 40.00
Sherry, Clear Stem & Base, 6 Piece 55.00
Vase, Beaded Flowers, Gold Trim, 9 1/4 In. 30.00
Vase, Cut To Clear, Beaded Rim, Fluted Shoulder, Fans, Vesicas, 6 1/4 In. 460.00
Vase, Gold Enameled Portrait Medallion, Girl & Dog, c.1860, 15 1/2 x 6 In. 400.00

RUDOLSTADT was a faience factory in the Thuringia region of
Germany from 1720 to about 1791. In 1854, Ernst Bohne began working in the area. From about 1887 to 1918, the New York and Rudolstadt Pottery made decorated porcelain marked with the RW and
crown familiar to collectors. This porcelain was imported by Lewis
Straus and Sons of New York, which later became Nathan Straus and

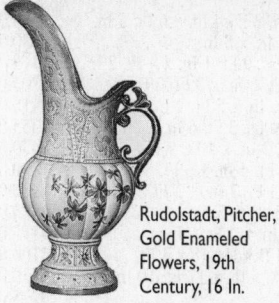

Rudolstadt, Pitcher,
Gold Enameled
Flowers, 19th
Century, 16 In.

It can be hard to thread a needle, especially with the old pure cotton thread that should be used for repairing old fabric. Put hairspray on the end of the thread to stiffen it.

Sons. The word *Royal* was included in their import mark. Collectors often call it *Royal Rudolstadt*. Most pieces found today were made in the late nineteenth or early twentieth century. Additional pieces may be listed in the Kewpie category.

Bowl, Figural, Chariot, Winged Lion, Cherub, C-Scroll Base, c.1910, 11 1/2 In.	353.00
Ewer, Flower, c.1900, 14 1/2 In.	58.00
Pitcher, Gold Enameled Flowers, 19th Century, 16 In. *Illus*	92.00
Urn, Flowers, 2 Handles, Gilt, Stamped, Germany, 1875-1910, 15 1/2 In.	84.00
Vase, Flowers, Handles, Marked, Crown RW, c.1900, 8 In.	92.00
Vase, Indian, Figural, Green, Gold, Black & White Headdress, 6 3/4 x 3 1/4 In.	165.00
Vase, Nymph, Magenta, Globular, L'Amour Desarme, Handles, 10 1/2 In.	935.00

RUGS have been used in the American home since the seventeenth century. The oriental rug of that time was often used on a table, not on the floor. Rag rugs, hooked rugs, and braided rugs were made by housewives from scraps of material.

Afghan, 3 Urns & Flowers, Olive Green, Multicolored, 3 Ft. 9 In. x 6 Ft.	495.00
Afghan, Lions, Peacocks, Maroon Field, Multicolored, 4 Ft. x 6 Ft. 10 In.	385.00
Afghan, Serapi, Central Medallion, Red Field, 20th Century, 7 Ft. 5 In. x 9 Ft. 9 In.	825.00
Afghan, Tribal Design, Lions, Peacocks, Maroon Field, Geometric Border, 4 x 6 Ft. 10 In.	390.00
Afshar, Diamond Medallions, Blue Field, Zigzag Stripes, 1800s, 4 Ft. 2 In. x 3 Ft. 10 In.	295.00
Afshar, Geometric, Flower, Meandering Border, Early 1900s, 4 Ft. 6 In. x 3 Ft. 5 In.	295.00
Agra, Gold Ground, Joined Flower Medallions, Rosette, Vine Border, 15 x 12 Ft.	3450.00
Agra, Red Ground, Palmette, Vine Field, Vine Border, c.1950, 15 Ft. 2 In. x 11 Ft. 11 In.	5290.00
Ardebil, Stylized Birds, Animals, Red, Blue, On Beige Ground, 4 Ft. 4 In. x 9 Ft. 9 In.	315.00
Azerbaijan Soumak, Burgundy, Black, Blue, Orange, 6 Ft. 9 In. x 12 Ft.	405.00
Azerbaijan Soumak, Burgundy, Green, Blue, Black, Gold, 6 Ft. 9 In. x 12 Ft. 7 In.	748.00
Azerbaijan Soumak, Plum Ground, Blue & Red Borders, 6 Ft. 10 In. x 11 Ft.	460.00
Bagface, Baluchi, Medallion, Star-In-Octagon, Blue Field, Plant Border, 2 Ft. 7 In. x 2 Ft.	205.00
Bagface, Baluchi, Medallion, Star-In-Octagon, Plum, Late 1800s, 2 Ft. 10 In. x 2 Ft. 4 In.	470.00
Bagface, Caucasian, Floral Lattice, Blue Field, Meandering Border, 2 Ft. 2 In. x 1 Ft. 9 In.	765.00
Bagface, Kurd, Serrated Hexagon, Gold Field, Blue Border, 3 Ft. 8 In. x 2 Ft. 2 In.	355.00
Bagface, Qashqai, Hooked Diamond Medallion, Meandering Border, 2 Ft. 2 In. x 2 Ft.	705.00
Bagface, Shahsevan Soumak, Medallions, 3 Ft. 5 In. x 1 Ft. 4 In.	880.00
Bagface, Shahsevan, Soumak, Blue Field, Pinwheel Border, 2 Ft. 7 In. x 2 Ft. 4 In.	470.00
Bagface, Shahsevan, Soumak, Flower Heads, Pinwheels, Cruciform Border, 22 x 17 In.	705.00
Bagface, Turkoman, Allover Guls, Red Field, 2 Ft. 5 In. x 3 Ft. 4 In.	145.00
Bakhtiari, Blue Ground, Rosette Field, Guard Border, 11 Ft. 6 In. x 5 Ft. 11 In.	520.00
Bakhtiari, Floral Panel, Flower Border, 7 Ft. 2 In. x 10 Ft. 3 In.	825.00
Bakhtiari, Floral Panels, Border, Red, Blue, Ivory, Mid 1900s, 7 Ft. 2 In. x 10 Ft. 3 In.	840.00
Bakhtiari, Flower Medallions, Vines, Navy, Red, Gold, Ivory, 7 Ft. 1 In. x 4 Ft. 5 In.	764.00
Bakhtiari, Flowers, Cypress Tree, Rosette, Vine Border, 18 Ft. 8 In. x 14 Ft.	2070.00
Bakhtiari, Shield Medallion Inset, Blue Field, Turtle Border, 17 Ft. 4 In. x 12 Ft. 6 In.	4115.00
Bakhtiari, Wildlife, People, Trees, South Persia, c.1925, 15 Ft. 7 In. x 11 Ft. 9 In.	8365.00
Baluchi, Afghanistan, Center Medallion, Geometric, 3 Ft. 10 In. x 6 Ft. 6 In.	300.00
Baluchi, Afghanistan, Double Urn, Flowers, Geometric Border, 3 Ft. 4 In. x 6 Ft. 5 In.	325.00
Baluchi, Afghanistan, Green Ground, Triple Urn, Flowers, 3 Ft. 9 In. x 6 Ft.	505.00
Baluchi, Afghanistan, Red, Ivory, Brown Ground, Navy, 4 Ft. 6 In. x 2 Ft. 9 In.	470.00

Baluchi, Blue Field, Brown, Green, Red, Urns, Flowers, Border, 3 Ft. 4 In. x 6 Ft. 5 In. ... 365.00
Baluchi, Diamond Lattice, Vines, Double Cross Border, 8 Ft. 8 In. x 5 In. 380.00
Baluchi, Red Geometric Center, Black Ground, Multiple Borders, 9 Ft. 1 In. x 4 Ft. 2 In. . 175.00
Baluchi, Serrated Medallions, Blue Field, Diamond Border, 6 Ft. 6 In. x 3 Ft. 2 In. 705.00
Baluchi, Stepped, Geometric, Green, Ivory, Red Ground, 3 Ft. 6 In. x 5 Ft. 9 In. 115.00
Baluchi, Tree Of Life, Blue, Red, Rust, Camel Ground, Late 1800s, 3 Ft. 6 In. x 2 Ft. 6 In. 355.00
Baluchi, Tree Of Life, Blue, Red, Rust, Diamond, Border, 4 Ft. 2 In. x 2 Ft. 9 In. 470.00
Baluchi, Tree Of Life, Brown, Gold, Red Field, Afghanistan, 3 Ft. 5 In. x 6 Ft. 3 In. 390.00
Baluchi, Tree Of Life, Tan Field, Triangle Border, Late 1800s, 3 Ft. 7 In. x 2 Ft. 9 In. 380.00
Bergama, Octagonal Medallion, Red Field, Border, 5 Ft. 2 In. x 4 Ft. 5 In. 3820.00
Beshir, Herati, Blue & Brown Field, Palmette Border, 10 Ft. 2 In. x 4 Ft. 6 In. 4115.00
Bidjar, Allover Herati, Salmon, Green, Blue, Plum, Blue Floral Border, 18 x 4 Ft.........'. 2100.00
Bidjar, Blue Ground, Spandrels, Burgundy Border, Runner, 1 Ft. 3 In. x 17 Ft. 10 In. ... 1430.00
Bidjar, Blue Medallion, Red Field, Red, Blue, Ivory, 14 x 25 Ft. 9775.00
Bidjar, Central Medallion, Herati, North Persia, 11 Ft. 11 In. x 8 Ft. 8 In. 4780.00
Bidjar, Floral Medallion, Spandrels, Latticework, Mid 1900s, 4 Ft. x 2 Ft. 7 In. 560.00
Bidjar, Herati, Blue, Rose, Gold, Ivory, Brown, Terra-Cotta Field, 5 Ft. 6 In. x 3 Ft. 8 In. . 1295.00
Bidjar, Madder Field, Herati Medallions, Palmette Border, c.1885, 17 Ft. 8 In. x 6 Ft. 5 In. 3885.00
Bidjar, Palmettes, Terra-Cotta Field, Meandering Flower Border, 5 Ft. 5 In. x 3 Ft. 8 In. ... 1880.00
Braided, Concentric Circles, Black Border, Frame, 39 In. 56.00
Braided, Hooked, Center Square, 8-Pointed Star, Early 20th Century, 28 x 28 In. 385.00
Braided, Table Mat, Oval, Blue, Gray, Tan, White, Cotton, c.1900, 16 1/2 x 9 1/2 In. 275.00
Braided, Table Mat, Oval, Gold, Lavender, White, Blue, Red, Silk, c.1900, 11 x 7 1/2 In. . 525.00
Braided, Table Mat, Oval, White, Tan, Red, Gold, Cotton, c.1900, 9 1/4 x 8 1/4 In....... 330.00
Braided, Table Mat, Round, Green, Tan, Yellow, Rust, Tan, Cotton, 14 3/8 In. 275.00
Caucasian, Blue Field, 3 Polygons, Double Headed Animal, 5 Ft. 5 In. x 3 Ft. 3 In. 316.00
Caucasian, Blue Ground, Rosettes, Leaf Field, 12 Medallions, Brown Border, 13 x 3 Ft. ... 920.00
Caucasian, Central Medallion, Geometric, Multiple Borders, 6 Ft. 8 In. x 4 Ft. 4 In. 2530.00
Caucasian, Karabagh, Central Panel, Diagonal Flowers, Geometric, 4 Ft. 3 In. x 9 Ft. 6 In. 715.00
Caucasian, Rectangular Panels, Flowers, Geometric, 3 Ft. 8 In. x 4 Ft. 10 In. 825.00
Caucasian, Shirvan, Central Panel, Stepped Diamonds, Geometric, 3 Ft. 1 In. x 5 Ft. 6 In. 495.00
Caucasian, South, Prayer, Blue Field, Medallion, Octagons, 5 Ft. x 2 Ft. 11 In. 920.00
Caucasian Kilim, Hexagonal Medallions, Hooked Diamonds, 9 Ft. x 5 Ft. 9 In. 880.00
Chinese, Art Deco, Flowers, Birds, Buildings, Multicolor, 8 Ft. 2 In. x 10 Ft. 10 In. 2645.00
Chinese, Art Deco, Flowers, Green, Blue, Red, Purple Field, c.1920, 6 Ft. 9 In. x 4 Ft. ... 399.00
Chinese, Art Deco, Purple & Gray Field, Vases, Lanterns, Plum Border, 7 Ft. 10 In. x 5 Ft. 395.00
Chinese, Art Deco, Trees, Birds, Blue, Gold, Ivory, Peach, 5 Ft. 4 In. x 2 Ft. 6 In. 865.00
Chinese, Bird Medallion, Flower Sprays, Blue Ground, 6 Ft. 8 In. x 3 Ft. 11 In. 200.00
Chinese, Brown Ground, Birds, Flowers, Symbols, Blue Border, 10 Ft. 6 In. x 13 Ft. 6 In. 1320.00
Chinese, Flowers, Spandrels, Blue Field, Borders, 20th Century, 11 Ft. 6 In. x 10 Ft...... 1880.00
Chinese, Green, Gray Leaves, Ivory Spandrels, Blue Border, 9 Ft. 9 In. x 13 Ft. 6 In. 635.00
Chinese, Medallion Center, Flower Vase, Blue Field, 9 Ft. 6 In. x 7 Ft. 10 In. 460.00
Chinese, Meditation Mats, 4, Floral Medallion, Vine Spandrels, 7 Ft. 4 In. x 2 Ft. 2 In. ... 765.00
Chinese, Red Ground, Blue Border, Flowers, Runner, 2 Ft. 9 In. x 11 Ft. 7 In. 580.00
Chinese, Spring Green Border, Dark Red Ground, Multicolored Flowers, 9 x 12 Ft. 660.00
Drugget, Flowers, Brown, Orange, Yellow, Beige Ground, 56 x 50 In. 175.00
Drugget, Geometric, Black, Yellow, Orange, Green, Beige Ground, 77 x 51 In. 230.00
Ersari, Columns, Octagonal Tauk Nuska Guls, Red Field, Vine Border, 11 Ft. 3 In. x 7 Ft. 1410.00
Feraghan, Blue Ground, Geometric Field, Vine Border, c.1935, 6 Ft. 8 In. x 4 Ft. 2 In. 230.00
Feraghan, Rows Of Mother & Child Boteh, Red, Blue, Brown, Ivory, 24 x 12 Ft. 5900.00
Feraghan Sarouk, Diamond Medallion, Red Field, Vine Border, 11 Ft. 9 In. x 8 Ft. 5 In. ... 7638.00
Feraghan Sarouk, Flowers On Rose Field, 4 Ft. 9 In. x 3 Ft. 1 In. 230.00
Feraghan Sarouk, Medallion Center, Rose Ground, 4 Ft. 8 In. x 3 Ft. 3 In. 290.00
French Savonnerie Style, Chain Stitch, Blue, Pink, Yellow, India, 14 Ft. 5 In. x 12 Ft. 569.00
Gendje, Diagonal Stripes, Boteh, Blue, Red, Ivory, Wineglass Border, 10 Ft. 6 In. x 3 Ft. . 2705.00
Grenfell, Eskimo, Flying Ducks, Label, 52 x 40 In. 2500.00
Grenfell, Eskimo, Flying Geese, New Moon, Pine Trees, Lake, 1900s, 24 x 36 In........ 1300.00
Grenfell, Eskimo, Marine Scene, 2-Masted Schooner, On Stretcher, 26 x 39 In. 3450.00
Grenfell, Eskimo, Sampler, Ship, Fish, House, People, Birds, Sled, Dog, 25 1/2 x 20 In. .. 3165.00
Grenfell, Mat, Hooked, Puffin, Rayon, Silk, Burlap Back, Frame, 11 7/8 x 17 3/4 In. 765.00
Grenfell, Mat, Hooked, Seal Hunt, Silk, Rayon, Burlap, Early 1900s, 17 x 11 1/2 In. 765.00
Hamadan, Blue Field, 3 Polygons, Stepped Border, Blue, Red, 4 Ft. 2 In. x 2 Ft. 8 In. 115.00

Hamadan, Branches, Leaves, Red Field, Navy Floral Border, 4 Ft. 9 In. x 2 Ft. 6 1/2 In. . . . 260.00
Hamadan, Camel Spandrels, Blue Ground, Red Border, 3 Ft. 8 In. x 5 Ft. 1 In. 145.00
Hamadan, Central Medallion, Allover Geometric, Red, Blue, 3 Ft. 5 In. x 5 Ft. 5 In. 250.00
Hamadan, Central Medallion, Tan Field, Allover Design, 1930s, 4 Ft. 4 In. x 6 Ft. 9 In. . . . 390.00
Hamadan, Floral Medallion, Repeating Background, Red Field, 7 Ft. 9 In. x 9 Ft. 11 In. . . 385.00
Hamadan, Flowers, Blue Field, Central Panel, Geometric Borders, 3 Ft. 4 In. x 6 Ft. 4 In. 330.00
Hamadan, Flowers, Red, Black, Blue, Tan, c.1930, Runner, 2 Ft. 6 In. x 8 Ft. 550.00
Hamadan, Hexagonal Medallion, Tan, Vine Border, Late 1800s, 8 Ft. 6 In. x 3 Ft. 6 In. . . 558.00
Hamadan, Indigo Ground, Geometric, Ivory Border, 4 Ft. 11 In. x 8 Ft. 259.00
Hamadan, Ivory Central Medallion, Red Field, Mid 1900s, 4 Ft. 10 In. x 6 Ft. 5 In. 165.00
Hamadan, Lobed Diamond Medallion, Red Field, Rosette Border, 4 Ft. 10 In. x 3 Ft. 6 In. 295.00
Hamadan, Multicolored Herati, Indigo Field, Vine Border, 15 Ft. 10 In. x 3 Ft. 2 In. 385.00
Hamadan, Red, Blue Field, Borders, Runner, c.1930, 3 Ft. 2 In. x 6 Ft.1 In. 330.00
Hamadan, Repeating Floral Designs, Red Field, 2 Ft. 10 In. x 11 Ft. 470.00
Hamadan, Rows Of Stars, Multicolored, 20th Century, 3 Ft. 11 In. x 7 Ft. 4 In. 195.00
Hamadan, Serrated Diamond, Central Medallion, Blue Field, Salmon, 4 Ft. 9 In. x 6 Ft. . . 440.00
Hamadan, Serrated Geometric Panel, Blue Center, Borders, 3 Ft. 1 In. x 4 Ft. 6 In. 360.00
Hamadan, Star Rows, Multicolored, Red, Blue, Early 1900s, 3 Ft. 11 In. x 7 Ft. 4 In. 195.00
Haradja, Medallions, Blue, Orange, Ivory, Red, Turquoise, Runner, 2 Ft. 3 In. x 8 Ft. 2 In. 390.00
Heriz, Blue Central Medallion, Red Field, Ivory Corners, 8 Ft. 1 In. x 10 Ft. 9 In. 1120.00
Heriz, Brown, Rosette Field, 11 Medallions, Vine Border, 15 Ft. 7 In. x 2 Ft. 10 In. 1265.00
Heriz, Central Medallion, Rose, Red, Blue, Ivory Field, 5 Ft. 9 In. x 9 Ft. 6 In. 715.00
Heriz, Flower Head, Serrated Leaf Columns, Early 20th Century, 11 Ft. 10 In. x 9 Ft. 2 In. 2115.00
Heriz, Flowers, Red Field, Flower Border, Mid 1900s, 12 Ft. x 8 Ft. 10 In. 2115.00
Heriz, Geometric, Red, Blue, Ivory, Runner, 3 Ft. 4 In. x 10 Ft. 11 In. 690.00
Heriz, Medallion, Palmettes, Blue, Rose, Ivory, 4 Ft. 5 In. x 8 Ft. 8 In. 2350.00
Heriz, Multicolored Geometric Medallion, Persia, c.1935, 15 Ft. 3 In. x 10 Ft. 11 In. 2390.00
Heriz, Multicolored Geometric Medallions, Persia, c.1925, 20 Ft. 3 In. x 2 Ft. 8 In. 2030.00
Heriz, Red Field, Blue, Goldenrod, Persia, 1930s, 7 Ft. 4 In. x 10 Ft. 5 In. 1008.00
Heriz, Red Ground, Herati Field, Star Medallion, Leaf Border, 10 Ft. 7 In. x 7 Ft. 4 In. . . . 1725.00
Heriz, Red Ground, Herati Field, Star Medallion, Spandrels, Rosettes, 21 Ft. 2 In. x 12 Ft. 10925.00
Heriz, Red Ground, Herati Field, Vine Guard Border, c.1915, 11 Ft. 5 In. x 8 Ft. 2 In. 1955.00
Heriz, Red Ground, Herati, Star Medallion, Leaf Guard Border, 12 Ft. 9 In. x 9 Ft. 4 In. . . 978.00
Heriz, Rosettes, Palmettes, Vines, Serrated Leaf Border, 11 Ft. 8 In. x 8 Ft. 2 In. 5290.00
Heriz, Salmon Ground, Ivory Spandrels, Blue Border, 6 x 6 Ft. 110.00
Heriz, Square Medallion, Palmettes, Red Field, Turtle Border, 9 Ft. 10 In. x 6 Ft. 8 In. . . . 2350.00
Hooked, 2 Red-Winged Blackbirds, Striped Border, 22 x 38 In. 575.00
Hooked, 5 Rabbits Eating Carrot, 30 x 36 In. 605.00
Hooked, Acorn, Blue, Gray, Green, Brown, 43 x 25 In. 155.00
Hooked, Basket Of Fruit, 30 x 34 1/2 In. 2400.00
Hooked, Baskets, Off-White, Red & Yellow Flowers, Blue Ground, 27 3/4 x 49 In. 460.00
Hooked, Birds & Flowers, 32 x 58 In. 145.00
Hooked, Black & White Cat, Flowers, Sawtooth Border, Mounted, 28 x 38 1/2 In. 805.00
Hooked, Black & White Dog, Flowers, 33 x 22 In. 210.00
Hooked, Black Rooster, Blue Legs, Flowers, Orange Ground, Mounted, 25 x 38 In. 990.00
Hooked, Butterfly, White, Blue, Black, Brown, Red Trim, Brown Ground, 16 x 26 1/4 In. . . . 145.00
Hooked, Cats & Kittens, 26 x 52 In. 255.00
Hooked, Center Cartouche, Burgundy, Floral Border, 74 x 89 In. 468.00
Hooked, Center Floral Panel, 72 x 92 In. 1495.00
Hooked, Center Panel, Reclining Dalmatian, Floral Border, 31 x 50 In. 415.00
Hooked, Central Medallion, Spaniel Dog, Checked Rug, Frost Pattern, 27 1/2 x 42 In. . . . 920.00
Hooked, Checkerboard Center, Corners, 34 x 24 In. 80.00
Hooked, Concentric Diamonds, Triangles, Black, Gold, Green, Felt Bound, 25 x 77 In. 127.00
Hooked, Cornucopia, Flowers, Bluebird, Green Ground, Blue Border, 42 1/2 x 65 In. 115.00
Hooked, Cornucopia, Solid & Mottled Threads, Cotton, Wool, 19th Century, 61 x 39 In. . . 1076.00
Hooked, Country Winter Scene, Horse, Sleigh, Barn, Mounted On Board, 28 x 35 1/2 In. . . 330.00
Hooked, Diamond Center, Black Border, 4-Leaf Clovers, Multicolored, 40 x 50 In. 220.00
Hooked, Dog, Egyptian, 31 x 42 In. 1250.00
Hooked, Dog, Lying Down, Canted Corners, Oval Leaf Border, 24 x 18 In. 360.00
Hooked, Dog, Terrier, Multicolored, 38 x 19 In. 70.00
Hooked, Fish Scale Pattern, Burgundy, Green, Gray, Diamond Medallions, 76 x 38 In. 1035.00
Hooked, Flower Medallion, Ivory Field, Black Ground, c.1951, 41 x 78 In. 138.00

Hooked, Flowers, Brown, Red, 35 x 60 In. 90.00
Hooked, Flowers, Green Ground, Oak Leaf & Double Braid Border, 43 x 27 In. 345.00
Hooked, Flowers, Multicolored, 55 x 34 In. 105.00
Hooked, Flowers, Red, Beige, Brown, 43 x 63 In. 58.00
Hooked, Flowers, Red, Green, Beige, Brown, 28 x 58 In. 175.00
Hooked, Flowers, Roses, Green, Ivory, Red, 20 Oval Panels, Signed, 27 x 47 In. 340.00
Hooked, Freehand Design, Flowers, Green, Red, 20 Oval Panels, MS 1949, 27 x 47 In. . . 350.00
Hooked, Freehand, Diamond Center, Black Border, 4-Leaf Clovers, 40 x 50 In. 225.00
Hooked, Fruit & Leaf, Gray Field, Red, White, Green Border, 49 x 78 In. 105.00
Hooked, Geometric Center, Rolling Log Border, 28 1/2 x 43 1/4 In. 55.00
Hooked, Geometric Design, Red, Beige, Brown, 21 x 37 In. 35.00
Hooked, Geometric Rosebud, Wool, Burlap Backing, 19th Century, 31 x 53 In. 646.00
Hooked, Half Moon, Flower Urn, Blue Ground, Frame, 41 In. 180.00
Hooked, Horse & Man, Red, Charcoal, Black, c.1880, 40 1/2 x 27 3/4 In. 6875.00
Hooked, Horse, Black, White Eye, Red Mouth, Brown Saddle, Gray Field, 29 x 20 In. . . . 825.00
Hooked, Horseshoe, 2 Horses, c.1910, 29 1/2 x 64 In. 1550.00
Hooked, Indian Portrait, Abstract Landscape, Black Border, c.1930, 41 x 38 In. 590.00
Hooked, Ivory, Gray Scrolls, Flowers, Green, Salmon, Gold, Sardinia, 117 x 112 In. 550.00
Hooked, Lamb, Yellow, Prancing, Red Eyes, Nose, 15 Stars, 39 x 22 In. 660.00
Hooked, Leaf Corners, Rose Medallion Center, 46 x 29 In. 115.00
Hooked, Leaf Pattern, Orange, Green, Brown, 72 x 108 In. 3000.00
Hooked, Leaves, Fall Colors, Tan Ground, Brown Border, 68 1/2 x 75 In. 165.00
Hooked, Leaves, Flowers, Pink, Yellow, Brown, Red, Green Ground, Borders, 29 x 45 In. 95.00
Hooked, Lion, Smiling, Yellow, Brown, White, Green Ground, Sawtooth, 23 x 38 In. 220.00
Hooked, Log Cabin, Multicolored, Wool, Burlap Backing, 75 x 64 In. 248.00
Hooked, Mallard Ducks, Mountains, Lake Scene, Multicolored, 52 x 25 In. 160.00
Hooked, Maple Sugar Making, Wool, 20th Century, 29 x 44 In. 940.00
Hooked, Mayflower Ship, 52 x 30 In. 127.00
Hooked, Multicolored Stripes, Black Border, Runner, 24 x 79 In. 230.00
Hooked, Multicolored Stripes, Leaf & Vine Borders, Runner, 121 3/4 x 15 1/2 In. 385.00
Hooked, New England Farm Scene, On Stretcher, 31 x 46 In. 345.00
Hooked, Oval Center Medallion, Flowers, Scrolls, 46 x 69 In. 55.00
Hooked, Owl, Full Moon, Gray Ground, Tree, Leaves, 19 1/2 x 34 1/2 In. 360.00
Hooked, Peacock, Purple, Green, Blue, Gray, Brown & Orange Border, 16 x 27 1/2 In. . . . 300.50
Hooked, Red House, 24 x 40 In. 58.00
Hooked, Rose Bouquets, Wool, 19th Century, 37 1/2 x 59 1/2 In. 588.00
Hooked, Samuel & Mary, Black & White, 1922, 26 x 43 In. 2400.00
Hooked, Scenic, East Machias, Maine, Catherine Walker, Wool, Cotton, 35 x 65 In. 5375.00
Hooked, Scenic, New Bedford, Mass., Alice Beaty, Wool, Cotton, 1810, 37 x 62 In. 5375.00
Hooked, Single Fish, 26 x 43 In. 2530.00
Hooked, Snake, Brown, Gold Border, 28 x 47 In. 545.00
Hooked, Stylized Tulip, Abstract Ground, On Stretcher, American, 39 x 22 In. 115.00
Hooked, Tree, 3 Horses, 2 Foals, On Stretcher, 19 3/4 x 34 1/2 In. 825.00
Hooked, Tulips, Purple Stars, 2 Dogs, Multicolored Border, Early 1900s, 51 x 32 1/2 In. . 660.00
Hooked, White Calla Lilies, Gray Leaves, Flowerpot, Black Ground, 22 x 39 In. 130.00
Isfahan, Cinnabar, Medallion, Spandrels, Flowers, Blue Border, 10 Ft. 4 In. x 15 Ft. 3 In. . 2415.00
Isfahan, Flower Vines, Plum Palmette, East Persia, c.1925, 16 Ft. x 12 Ft. 8 In. 4780.00
Isfahan, Flowers, Off-White Field, Floral Border, 6 Ft. 8 In. x 10 Ft. 6 In. 690.00
Isfahan, Garden, Beige Ground, Flower Urns, Birds, Trees, c.1935, 6 Ft. 4 In. x 4 Ft. 2 In. 2760.00
Isfahan, Ivory Field, Center Medallion, Flower Border, c.1930, 9 Ft. 9 In. x 13 Ft. 2 In. . . 2856.00
Isfahan, Medallion, Palmettes, Vines, Leaves, Ivory Field, 6 Ft. 10 In. x 4 Ft. 8 In. 470.00
Jaipur, English Garden, 4 Ft. x 16 Ft. 8 In. 1610.00
Joshaqan, Navy Diamond Center, Pomegranate Ground, Spandrels, 6 Ft. 6 In. x 4 Ft. 6 In. 259.00
Jozan, Lobed Medallion, Blue Field, Rosette & Vine Border, 5 Ft. 2 In. x 3 Ft. 5 In. 558.00
Karabagh, Blue Ground, Flowers, Diagonal Border, c.1915, 14 Ft. 10 In. x 2 Ft. 9 In. 920.00
Karabagh, Cloud Band, Blue & Green Medallions, Ivory Border, 4 Ft. 3 In. x 8 Ft. 7 In. . . 2645.00
Karabagh, Concentric Medallions, Red Field, c.1915, 8 Ft. x 4 Ft. 9 In. 1645.00
Karabagh, Dark Salmon Ground, Blue Spandrels, Ivory Border, 3 Ft. 10 In. x 7 Ft. 10 In. . 520.00
Karabagh, South Caucasus, Bessarabian Flower, Runner, 1883, 18 Ft. 7 In. x 6 Ft. 9 In. . . 2875.00
Karabagh, Square Medallion, Hooked Diamond, Stepped Border, 6 Ft. 2 In. x 4 Ft. 2 In. . 529.00
Karagashli, 3 Stepped Diamond Medallions, Flower Heads, 6 Ft. 6 In. x 3 Ft. 8 In. 1175.00
Karaja, 5 Medallions, Blue Field, Iran, Runner, c.1950, 2 Ft. 3 In. x 8 Ft. 2 In. 350.00
Karaja, Geometric Flower Heads, Red Field, Ivory Border, c.1940, 9 Ft. 2 In. x 2 Ft. 415.00

Karaja, Ivory & Green Medallions, Red Border, 2 Ft. 10 In. x 11 Ft.	230.00
Karaja, Medallion Rows, Red Field, Ivory, Blue, Iran, c.1950, 2 Ft. 2 In. x 10 Ft. 10 In.	700.00
Karaja, Medallions, Red Field, Ivory, Blue, Mid 19th Century, 2 Ft. 2 In. x 10 Ft. 10 In.	785.00
Karastan, Laver Kerman, Red, Blue, Turquoise, Tan, 8 Ft. 8 In. x 12 Ft.	895.00
Karastan Heriz, Central Medallion, Ivory Field, Flower Border, 5 Ft. 9 In. x 9 Ft. 6 In.	730.00
Kashan, Beige Ground, Palmette, Vine Field, Lobed Medallion, 7 Ft. 1 In. x 5 Ft. 2 In.	315.00
Kashan, Center Medallion, Blue Border, Late 1900s, 8 Ft. 8 In. x 10 Ft. 7 In.	1000.00
Kashan, Ivory Field, Leaf, Brown, Blue, White, 3 Ft. x 5 Ft. 2 In.	110.00
Kashan, Lobed Medallion, Palmettes, Rosettes, Red Field, Blue Border, 7 Ft. x 4 Ft. 10 In.	880.00
Kashan, Medallion, Serrated Leaves, Blue, Yellow, Red Field, 4 Ft. 11 In. x 3 Ft. 4 In.	790.00
Kashan, Red Field, Blue Flower Medallion, Off-White, Red, Green, 8 x 10 Ft.	460.00
Kashan, Red Ground, Flower Field, Palmette, Vine Border, 13 Ft. 10 In. x 9 Ft. 11 In.	1840.00
Kashmir, Beige Ground, Flowers, Animal Field, Medallion, Rust, 11 Ft. 1 In. x 7 Ft. 2 In.	575.00
Kashmir, Medallions, Brown Field, Animals, Geometric Border, 2 Ft. 11 In. x 4 Ft. 11 In.	195.00
Kashmir, Prayer, Woven, Flowers, Multiple Borders, Silk, Late 1900s, 2 Ft. 1 In. x 3 Ft.	335.00
Kashmir, Urn, Tree, Multiple Borders, Silk, 2 Ft. 6 In. x 4 Ft. 2 In.	770.00
Kasvin, Red Ground, Palmette, Vine Field, Lobed Medallion, 12 Ft. 2 In. x 8 Ft. 11 In.	690.00
Kayseri, Flowers, Green, Blue, Brown, Ivory Field, Red Ground, Turkey, 9 Ft. 6 In. x 7 Ft.	569.00
Kazak, 3 Medallions, Tan, Navy, Light Blue, Red Ground, 6 Ft. 1 In. x 9 Ft.	900.00
Kazak, 8 Square Panels, Plant Motifs, Ivory Border, Late 19th Century, 10 Ft. 4 In. x 3 Ft.	1115.00
Kazak, 8-Sided Medallion, Blue Green Ground, Late 1800s, 6 Ft. 4 In. x 3 Ft. 6 In.	590.00
Kazak, Central Medallion, Red Field, Birds, Multicolored, 5 Ft. 10 In. x 8 Ft. 2 In.	990.00
Kazak, Cloud Band, Medallions, Red Field, Ivory Border, 5 Ft. 2 In. x 8 Ft. 2 In.	5175.00
Kazak, Geometric, Flowers, Chestnut Ground, Runner, 3 Ft. 10 In. x 11 Ft. 8 In.	405.00
Kazak, Geometric, Ivory Border, Blue Ground, 1919, 4 Ft. 3 In. x 7 Ft. 2 In.	230.00
Kazak, Lozenge Medallion, Blue, Red, Green, Ivory Star Border, 5 Ft. 8 In. x 4 Ft. 4 In.	1835.00
Kazak, Medallions, 8 Cloud Bands, Red Field, 7 Ft. 4 In. x 4 Ft. 7 In.	1765.00
Kazak, Octagonal Medallions, Rust Field, Multiple Border, Early 1900s, 4 Ft. 4 In. x 5 Ft.	785.00
Kazak, Prayer, Latchhooked Diamond, Rosettes, Geometric, c.1913, 5 Ft. 5 In. x 3 Ft.	1610.00
Kazak, Prayer, Mihrab Cartouche Inset, Medallion, Red Field, 4 Ft. 9 In. x 3 Ft. 8 In.	1115.00
Kazak, Red Ground, Animal Field, Medallions, Border, 7 Ft. 6 In. x 4 Ft. 1 In.	1955.00
Kazak, Rust Ground, 3 Stepped Medallions, Leaf Guard Border, 6 Ft. 9 In. x 5 Ft.	920.00
Kazak, Star In Cruciform Medallions, 5 Narrow Borders, Early 20th Century, 9 x 6 Ft.	1880.00
Kazak, Turkoman Style Medallions, Red Field, 7 Ft. 2 In. x 4 Ft. 9 In.	2585.00
Kerman, Beige Ground, Flowers, Diamond Medallion, c.1950, 16 Ft. 3 In. x 11 Ft. 10 In.	805.00
Kerman, Blue Ground, Floral Spray Field, Vine Border, c.1950, 10 x 8 Ft.	1380.00
Kerman, Diamond Medallion, Ivory Field, Flower Border, 4 Ft. 10 In. x 2 Ft.	380.00
Kerman, Floral Medallion, Blue Field, Palmette Border, 11 Ft. 8 In. x 8 Ft. 10 In.	2090.00
Kerman, Floral Medallions, Blue, Red, Green, Black, 2 Ft. x 3 Ft. 2 In.	115.00
Kerman, Flower, Ivory Field, Palmette Border, Southeast Persia, c.1935, 7 Ft. x 4 Ft. 2 In.	329.00
Kerman, Flowers, Palmettes, Leaves, Ivory Field, 20 Ft. 4 In. x 10 Ft. 8 In.	5290.00
Kerman, Garden, Tree, Ivory Field, 4 Ft. 3 In. x 6 Ft. 11 In.	1540.00
Kerman, Ivory, Pale Blue Central Medallion, Red Field, c.1950, 3 Ft. 2 In. x 7 Ft. 1 In.	220.00
Kerman, Red Ground, Palmette, Trellis Vine Field, Medallion, 11 Ft. 5 In. x 8 Ft.	460.00
Kerman, Sky Blue Pendant Medallion, Ivory, Floral Vine Border, 11 Ft. 6 In. x 8 Ft. 8 In.	1980.00
Khamseh, Hexagonal Medallions, Red Field, Multiple Borders, 6 Ft. 2 In. x 4 Ft.	1765.00
Kilim, 2 Panels, Burgundy, Blue, Ivory, Turkey, Early 20th Century, 4 Ft. 3 In. x 9 Ft. 8 In.	225.00
Kilim, Geometric, Red, Pink, Orange, Yellow, Blue, Brown, 4 Ft. 8 In. x 11 Ft. 6 In.	175.00
Kilim, Moroccan, Stepped Hexagonal Medallions, Black Field, 8 Ft. 6 In. x 4 Ft. 4 In.	235.00
Kilim, Woven, Burgundy, Blue, Ivory, Early 1900s, 4 Ft. 3 In. x 9 Ft. 8 In.	200.00
Kuba, 3 Lesghi Stars, Blue Field, Ivory Crab Border, Late 1800s, 5 Ft. 3 In. x 3 Ft. 5 In.	1175.00
Kuba, Prayer, Lamp, Columns, Blue Field, Black Border, 5 Ft. 6 In. x 3 Ft. 8 In.	1410.00
Kuba, Red Field, Blue Bird & Palmette Border, 6 Ft. 4 In. x 4 Ft. 6 In.	2940.00
Kuba, Stepped Medallions, Flowers, Birds, c.1935, 5 Ft. 11 In. x 4 Ft. 5 In.	1610.00
Kurdish, Boteh, Brown Field, Animals, Flowers, 3 Ft. 8 In. x 10 Ft. 11 In.	1045.00
Kurdish, Geometric Medallions, Blue Field, Floral Border, 4 Ft. 6 In. x 10 Ft. 6 In.	290.00
Kurdish, Hexagonal Medallions, Ashik Guls, Blue Field, 7 Ft. x 4 Ft. 5 In.	470.00
Kurdish, Repeating Boteh, Blue Field, Ivory, Salmon Borders, 4 Ft. 6 In. x 7 Ft. 8 In.	195.00
Kurdish, Tan, Red Ground, Blue Border, Runner, 3 Ft. 4 In. x 9 Ft. 3 In.	440.00
Latin America, Hand Woven, Red, Black, Flowers, Wool, 5 Ft. 10 In. x 4 Ft. 3 In.	75.00
Laver Kerman, Floral Vines, Blue, Red, Eggplant, Blue Field, 7 Ft. x 4 Ft. 5 In.	1225.00
Laver Kerman, Gold Ground, Palmette, Vine Field, Medallion, 20 Ft. 1 In. x 13 Ft. 1 In.	11500.00
Lesghi Stars, Ashik Guls, Blue, Ivory, Gold, Olive, Red Field, 5 Ft. x 3 Ft. 6 In.	1530.00

Lillihan, Blue Spandrels, Burgundy Ground, Blue Border, 8 Ft. 11 In. x 11 Ft. 8 In. 835.00
Lillihan, Blue, Ivory & Yellow Flowers, Red Field, Palmette, Guard Borders, 10 x 8 Ft. . . . 1310.00
Lillihan, Crimson Ground, Symmetric Flowers, Indigo Border, 3 Ft. 6 In. x 10 Ft. 2 In. . . .   230.00
Lillihan, Flowers, Vines, Blue Palmette Border, 12 Ft. x 8 Ft. 7 In.   550.00
Lillihan, Mottled Plum Ground, Blue & Red Borders, 2 Ft. 4 In. x 4 Ft. 110.00
Luristan, Lobed Medallion, Salmon, Green, Claret Floral Ground, 12 Ft. x 10 Ft. 3 In. . . .   610.00
Machine Woven, Stanley Tigerman, Arrow, Wool, Edward Fields, 1971, 5 x 9 Ft. 1870.00
Machine Woven, Stanley Tigerman, Arrow, Wool, Edward Fields, 4 Ft. x 4 Ft. 9 1/2 In. . . 1405.00
Mahal, Diamond Medallion, Flowers, West Persia, c.1950, 12 Ft. x 8 Ft. 10 In. 590.00
Mahal, Floral Lattice, Serrated Leaves, Ivory, Green, Salmon, Palmette Border, 12 x 9 Ft. .   960.00
Mahal, Flowers, Madder Field, Indigo Rosette, Vine Border, 12 Ft. 2 In. x 9 Ft. 2 In. 1320.00
Mahal, Multicolored, Flower Vinery, Vine Border, Persia, c.1935, 12 Ft. 8 In. x 9 Ft. 6 In. 1075.00
Mahal, Persian, Flower Medallions, Golden Brown Field, 8 Ft. 2 In. x 10 Ft. 3 In. 5750.00
Malayer, Red, Blue, Ivory, 8 Ft. 7 In. x 11 Ft. 10 In. 2070.00
Malayer, Rows Of Flower Heads, Blue, Red, Blue Field, c.1920, 22 Ft. 10 In. x 3 Ft. 1575.00
Meshed, Ivory Ground, Gold, Dark Blue Border, 10 x 14 In. 920.00
Meshed, Multicolored Vines, Blue Field, Plum Palmette Border, 17 Ft. 8 In. x 12 Ft. 4675.00
Meshed, Red, Blue, Ivory, 20th Century, 12 Ft. 8 In. x 9 Ft. 11 In. 460.00
Nain, Medallion, Spandrels, Palmettes, Vine, Blue Field, Tan Border, 10 Ft. x 5 Ft. 10 In. . 1645.00
Needlepoint, Roses, Lilac Stems, Black Ground, Pink, Lavender, Mid 1900s, 5 x 7 Ft. 355.00
Needlepoint, Tiles, Saffron Field, England, c.1900, 5 Ft. 4 In. x 4 Ft. 3 In. 990.00
Needlework, Flowers, Ribbons, Gray Field, Striped Border, 6 Ft. 3 In. x 5 Ft. 9 In. 220.00
Needlework, Lattice, Flowers, Blue Field, Rosette Border, 19th Century, 7 Ft. x 5 Ft. 6 In.   590.00
Pakistani, Hexagonal Medallions, Ivory Field, Blue, Red, Border, 4 Ft. 2 In. x 3 Ft. 3 In. . .   120.00
Penny, Animals, Hearts, 20 Embroidered Center Medallions, Black Petals, 24 x 27 In. 2750.00
Penny, Pink Moose, Embroidered, Flowers, Vines, Mounted, c.1897, 36 x 24 In. 2860.00
Persian, Northwest, Central Medallion, Flowers, c.1950, 4 Ft. 3 In. x 6 Ft. 7 In. 650.00
Persian, Northwest, Herati, Medallion, Red Field, Vine Border, 11 Ft. 9 In. x 5 Ft. 6 In. . . .   655.00
Qashqai, 3 Diamond Medallions, Red Field, Black, Green, Ivory, 3 Ft. 10 In. x 5 Ft. 11 In.   420.00
Qashqai, Central Medallion, Red Field, Iran, c.1850, 5 Ft. 9 In. x 8 Ft. 6 In. 600.00
Qashqai, Stepped Diamond Medallions, Octagons, Rosette Border, 12 Ft. x 6 Ft. 3 In. 3055.00
Qum, Flowering Vines, Blue, Red, Ivory Field, Red Border, 12 Ft. 6 In. x 8 Ft. 10 In. 2115.00
Qum, Tree Of Life, Blue Ground, Spandrels, Salmon Border, 4 Ft. 4 In. x 6 Ft. 8 In. 1155.00
Romanian, Floral Medallion, Vines, Gray Field, Shrub Border, 21 Ft. 9 In. x 8 Ft. 3 In. . . 1320.00
Rya, Figure 8 Design, Yellow, Orange, Red, Brown, 11 x 8 Ft. 520.00
Rya, Radiating Square, Purple, Orange, Yellow, Beige, Wool, 12 Ft. 2 In. x 9 Ft. 4 1/2 In. . .   145.00
Samarkand, Rust Field, 3 Medallions, Birds, Vines, 8 Ft. 7 In. x 5 Ft. 6 In. 220.00
Sarouk, Allover Flowers, Blue, Rose, Wine Field, Ivory Border, 15 Ft. 10 In x 10 Ft. 2 In.   265.00
Sarouk, Blue Ground, Flower Sprays, Vine Guard Border, c.1935, 6 Ft. 6 In. x 4 Ft. 1 In. . .   865.00
Sarouk, Blue Ground, Millefleur Field, Flower Border, 6 Ft. 5 In. x 4 Ft. 1 In. 1495.00
Sarouk, Bouquets, Leaves, Blue, Green, Red Field, Navy Palmette, 12 Ft. x 9 Ft. 2 In. 2270.00
Sarouk, Camel Ground, Burgundy Borders, 9 Ft. 10 In. x 16 Ft. 2990.00
Sarouk, Cruciform Medallion, Rose Field, Turtle Border, 4 Ft. 10 In. x 3 Ft. 5 In. 1295.00
Sarouk, Flower Sprays, Blue, Ivory, Red Field, Palmette Border, 6 Ft. 9 In. x 4 Ft. 2 In. . . . 1410.00
Sarouk, Flower Sprays, Crimson Field, Gray Vine Border, 13 Ft. 10 In. x 10 Ft. 7 In. 3300.00
Sarouk, Flower Sprays, Ivory, Blue, Salmon, Palmette Border, 5 Ft. 2 In. x 2 Ft. 7 In. 240.00
Sarouk, Flower Sprays, Meandering Vine Border, c.1925, Runner, 16 Ft. 3 In. x 2 Ft. 9 In. 2390.00
Sarouk, Flower Vases, Red Field, Blue Flower Meandering Border, 6 Ft. 6 In. x 4 Ft. 765.00
Sarouk, Flowers, Medallions, Red Ground, Flower Border, 3 Ft. 4 In x 4 Ft. 8 In. 300.00
Sarouk, Flowers, Vase, Salmon Field, 6 Ft. 3 In. x 9 Ft. 4 In. 635.00
Sarouk, Hexagonal Medallion, Flower Heads, Blue Field, Vine Border, 2 Ft. 6 In. x 2 Ft. .   295.00
Sarouk, Medallion, Spandrels, Vine Border, North Persia, c.1915, 7 Ft. 4 In. x 4 Ft. 6 In. .   359.00
Sarouk, Midnight Blue Ground, Plum Border, 4 Ft. 6 In. x 6 Ft. 6 In. 750.00
Sarouk, Oval Medallion, Flowers, Red Field, Floral Border, Mid 1900s, 5 Ft. x 3 Ft. 4 In.   940.00
Sarouk, Red Ground, Flower Spray Field, Vine Border, c.1935, 5 Ft. x 3 Ft. 4 In. 635.00
Sarouk, Red Spandrels, Midnight Blue Border, 8 Ft. 9 In. x 12 Ft. 750.00
Sarouk, Repeating Flowers, Red Field, Ivory, Blue, Olive, 5 Ft. 10 In. x 8 Ft. 7 In. 2640.00
Sarouk, Rosette, Flower Sprays, Red Field, Flower Border, 6 Ft. 10 In. x 4 Ft. 3 In. 1000.00
Savonnerie, Madder Field, Multicolored Palmettes, Spain, 16 Ft. 4 In. x 13 Ft. 3 In. 1195.00
Senneh, Beige Ground, Flowers, Vine Guard Border, c.1935, 6 Ft. 6 In. x 4 Ft. 3 In. 520.00
Senneh, Botehs, Red Ground, Flower Vine Border, c.1935, 10 Ft. 5 In. x 7 Ft. 1 In. 3450.00
Senneh, Hexagonal Medallion, Arrowhead Pendants, Turtle Border, 6 Ft. 4 In. x 4 Ft. 2 In.   700.00

Senneh, Medallion, Allover Herati, Blue Field, Meandering Border, 6 Ft. x 4 Ft. 3 In.	2350.00
Shiraz, Center Medallion, Blue, Red Field, Border, Early 20th Century, 3 Ft. 8 In. x 5 Ft. .	365.00
Shiraz, Dark Red Ground, Blue Spandrels, Ivory Border, 5 Ft. 6 In. x 8 Ft. 10 In.	805.00
Shiraz, Geometric, Brown, Orange, Red, Black Ground, 9 Ft. x 4 Ft. 8 In.	175.00
Shiraz, Midnight Blue Ground, Border, Dark Blue, Ivory, 5 Ft. 2 In. x 6 Ft. 7 In.	405.00
Shiraz, Orange, Royal, Ivory Geometric Center, Red Ground, 9 Ft. 11 In. x 5 Ft. 5 In.	230.00
Shiraz, Red, Brown, Ivory, 20th Century, 9 Ft. x 6 Ft. 4 In.	230.00
Shirvan, Columns, Diamond Medallions, Blue Field, Vine Border, 14 Ft. x 6 Ft. 8 In.	9400.00
Shirvan, Dark Blue Ground, Multicolored Border, Medallions, c.1910, 4 Ft. 3 In. x 7 Ft. . .	1495.00
Shirvan, Geometric, Ivory Field, 4 Ft. 9 In. x 3 Ft. 8 In.	303.00
Shirvan, Lesghi Stars, Boteh, Animals, Blue Border, 5 Ft. 5 In. x 8 Ft. 10 In.	2940.00
Shirvan, Octagon-In-Square, Diagonal Stripes, Brown Border, 6 Ft. 3 In. x 3 Ft. 3 In.	1763.00
Sivas, Central Medallion, Buff Field, Rose Palmette Vine Border, 11 Ft. 11 In. x 8 Ft. 9 In.	550.00
Sivas, Flower Medallion, Spandrels, Leaf Border, Anatolia, c.1915, 6 Ft. 2 In. x 4 Ft.	715.00
Soumak, Columns, Flower Heads, Red Field, Serrated Leaf Border, 11 Ft. x 5 Ft. 8 In.	4700.00
Soumak, Embroidered Borders, Octagonal Medallion, Zigzag Border, 2 Ft. 10 In. x 3 Ft. .	605.00
Soumak, Serrated Diamonds, Blue & White Bands, Turkey, 2 Ft. 8 In. x 9 Ft. 8 In.	250.00
Soumak, Tile Design Inset, Hook Motifs, Ashik Gul Border, 4 x 4 Ft.	2940.00
Sultanabad, Blue Ground, Flowers, Gold Border, 12 Ft. 3 In. x 15 Ft.	5405.00
Sultanabad, Cartouche, Flower, Eggplant, Ivory, Gray, 6 Ft. 6 In. x 4 Ft. 1 In.	290.00
Sultanabad, Ivory Ground, Blue, Red, Pakistan, 1900s, 10 Ft. x 15 Ft. 6 In.	2250.00
Suzani, 4 Columns, Palmettes, Ivory Field, Border, 19th Century, 7 Ft. 5 In. x 5 Ft. 4 In. .	880.00
Suzani, Blossoming Plants, Ivory Field, Border, 19th Century, 5 Ft. 2 In. x 3 Ft. 2 In.	558.00
Tabriz, Allover Vase Design, Palmettes, Vine Border, 11 Ft. 6 In. x 8 Ft. 6 In.	7640.00
Tabriz, Blue Ground, Equestrian Hunting Scene, Silk, 6 Ft. 7 In. x 4 Ft. 7 In.	2185.00
Tabriz, Center Medallion, Flower Border, Persia, 10 Ft. 1 In. x 13 Ft. 10 In.	1250.00
Tabriz, Central Tree Of Life, Flowers, Brown Field, Ivory Border, 8 Ft. 11 In. x 12 Ft. . . .	1345.00
Tabriz, Flowers, Tan, Rust, Salmon, Persia, c.1910, 7 Ft. 2 In. x 11 Ft. 7 In.	2990.00
Tabriz, Ivory Floral Field, Blue Spandrels, Red Ground, 9 Ft. 3 In. x 7 Ft.	1005.00
Tabriz, Pictorial, Tree Of Life, Flowers, Animals, Figures, 8 Ft. 11 In x 12 Ft.	1320.00
Tabriz, Prayer, Blossoming Plant, Blue Border, Silk, Late 1800s, 6 Ft. 3 In. x 4 Ft. 4 In. . .	2235.00
Tabriz, Red Ground, 16-Point Medallion, Spandrels, Blue Border, 8 Ft. 7 In. x 12 Ft.	1840.00
Tabriz, Red Ground, Palmette, Vine Field, Medallion, c.1950, 9 Ft. 1 In. x 5 Ft. 7 In.	1380.00
Tabriz, Rosette, Hexagonal Pole Medallions, Tan Field, Vine Border, 4 x 3 Ft.	385.00
Tabriz, Scalloped Medallion, Floral Cartouche Border, 15 Ft. 4 In. x 10 Ft. 8 In.	3820.00
Tabriz, Vines, Flowers, Ivory Field, c.1950, 10 Ft. 2 In. x 14 Ft.	1650.00
Tekke, Asmalyks, Embroidery, Flower Heads, Leaves, Early 19th Century, 4 x 2 Ft.	1410.00
Tekke, Guls, Red Ground, Serrated Leaf Border, c.1935, 11 Ft. 7 In. x 7 Ft. 1 In.	750.00
Tekke, Rows Of Guls, Rust, Red, Blues, Chevron Guard Border, 6 Ft. 8 In. x 4 Ft. 3 In. . .	875.00
Turkish, Central Medallion, Ivory, Multicolored Panels, 3 Ft. 7 In. x 6 Ft. 8 In.	605.00
Turkish, Medallions, Floral Scrolls, Rosette & Vine Border, 13 Ft. 6 In. x 17 Ft. 4 In.	3450.00
Turkish, Pictorial, Hunting Scene, Ivory, Blue, Arabesque Border, Silk, 3 Ft. x 1 Ft. 10 In.	350.00
Turkoman, Gul Rows, Red Field, Multicolored Borders, 9 Ft. 6 In. x 12 Ft. 6 In.	3360.00
Ushak, Blue Ground, Floral Trellising, Vine Field, 13 Ft. 9 In. x 9 Ft. 1 In.	5175.00
Ushak, Green Ground, Medallion, Rosettes, Vine Border, 15 Ft. 10 In. x 10 Ft. 2 In.	4600.00
Ushak, Orange Field, Medallion, Ivory Palmette, Vine Border, 14 Ft. 9 In. x 11 Ft. 1 In. . .	1100.00
Yomud, Red Field, Border, Late 1800s, 4 Ft. x 3 Ft. 3 In.	325.00
Yomud, Staggered Dyrnak Guls, Plum Field, Ivory Border, 10 Ft. 3 In. x 5 Ft. 10 In.	705.00

RUSKIN is a British art pottery of the twentieth century. The Ruskin
Pottery was started by William Howson Taylor, and his name was used
as the mark until about 1899. The factory, at West Smethwick, Birmingham, England, stopped making new pieces in 1933 but continued
to glaze and sell the remaining wares until 1935. The art pottery is
noted for its exceptional glazes.

Candlestick, Green High Glaze, 1906, 6 1/4 In.	115.00
Vase, Blue & Green Flambe Glaze, Flared Neck, Stamped, 5 1/2 In.	489.00
Vase, Celadon, Amber & Indigo Flambe Crystalline Glaze, Bulbous, Stamped, 4 1/2 In. . .	374.00
Vase, Green Grapevines, Mottled Luster, Yellow Ground, Bulbous, Stamped, 7 In.	90.00
Vase, Lavender Luster Glaze, Baluster, Stamped, 7 1/2 In.	345.00
Vase, Orange Luster Glaze, Stamped, 1925, 10 x 4 In.	520.00
Vase, Pink Luster & Purple Flambe Glaze, Marked, 5 3/4 In.	400.00

RUSSEL WRIGHT designed dinnerwares in modern shapes for many companies. Iroquois China Company, Harker China Company, Steubenville Pottery, and Justin Tharaud and Sons made dishes marked *Russel Wright*. The Steubenville wares, first made in 1938, are the most common today. Wright was a designer of domestic and industrial wares, including furniture, aluminum, radios, interiors, and glassware. Dinnerwares and other pieces by Wright are listed here. For more information, see *Kovels' Depression Glass & Dinnerware Price List*.

Russel
Wright
MFG. BY
STEUBENVILLE

Aluminum, Pitcher, Wood Handle, 7 3/4 In.	125.00
Aluminum, Punch Set, Saturn, Wood Knob Handles, 10 Piece	1100.00
Aluminum, Spaghetti Set, Pot, Cover, Cheese Shaker, Reed Handles, 3 Piece	2100.00
Aluminum, Spaghetti Set, Rattan Trim & Handle, 4 Piece ... *Illus*	1725.00
American Modern, Bowl, Salad, Granite Gray	.75.00 to 95.00
American Modern, Bowl, Vegetable, Oval, Coral, 10 In.	14.00
American Modern, Chop Plate, White	50.00
American Modern, Creamer, Granite Gray	5.00
American Modern, Cup & Saucer, Black Chutney	28.00
American Modern, Cup & Saucer, Chartreuse	10.00 to 14.00
American Modern, Cup & Saucer, Granite Gray	28.00
American Modern, Cup, Black Chutney	13.00 to 15.00
American Modern, Cup, Cedar Green	8.00 to 19.00
American Modern, Cup, Coral	6.00 to 17.00
American Modern, Cup, Granite Gray	6.00 to 13.00
American Modern, Cup, Seafoam	14.00 to 19.00
American Modern, Dish, Pickle, Coral, 10 1/2 In.	18.00
American Modern, Flatware Set, Stainless Steel, 1951, 56 Piece	1645.00
American Modern, Plate, Bread & Butter, Granite Gray, 6 In.	5.00 to 7.50
American Modern, Plate, Dinner, Cedar Green, 10 In.	20.00
American Modern, Plate, Dinner, Chartreuse, 10 In.	15.00
American Modern, Plate, Dinner, Coral, 10 In.	8.00
American Modern, Plate, Dinner, Glacier Blue, 10 In.	30.00
American Modern, Plate, Dinner, Granite Gray, 10 In.	8.00 to 15.00
American Modern, Plate, Salad, Chartreuse, 8 In.	16.00
American Modern, Platter, Bean Brown, 13 1/4 In.	15.00
American Modern, Platter, Coral, 13 1/4 In.	30.00
American Modern, Salt & Pepper, Black Chutney	40.00
American Modern, Salt & Pepper, Chartreuse	28.00
American Modern, Salt & Pepper, Coral	25.00
American Modern, Sauceboat, Coral	75.00
American Modern, Sauceboat, Granite Gray	.20.00 to 25.00
American Modern, Stack Server, Chartreuse	300.00
American Modern, Sugar, Black Chutney	27.00
American Modern, Sugar, Coral	20.00
American Modern, Sugar, Granite Gray	22.00
American Modern, Sugar, Seafoam	30.00
American Modern, Tea Set, Child's, Plastic, Ideal, 20 Piece	125.00 to 175.00
American Modern, Teapot, Coral	.95.00 to 125.00
American Modern, Teapot, Seafoam	142.00
American Modern, Teapot, White	45.00
Antarctica, Ice Bucket, Aluminum, Tongs, Chase, 7 1/2 In.	175.00
Art Pottery, Vase, Pillow, Glazed Stoneware, Bauer, 1946, 9 1/2 x 4 In.	702.00
Art Pottery, Vase, Pillow, Speckled Apricot Glaze, Bauer, 9 x 10 In.	489.00
Bowl, Rectangular, Figured White, Glaze, Bauer, 17 x 9 1/2 In.	575.00

Russel Wright, Aluminum,
Spaghetti Set, Rattan Trim &
Handle, 4 Piece

Candlestick, Speckled Apricot Glaze, Tapered, Bauer, 11 In., Pair 1495.00
Chrome, Corn Set, Pitcher, Salt & Pepper, Blue Glass Tray, Chase, 4 Piece 300.00
Chrome, Ice Bucket, Antarctic, Tongs, Chase, 7 1/2 In. 175.00
Chrome, Pitcher, Beer, Chase 38.00
Chrome, Zoo Animal Series, Bookends, c.1928, 8 1/4 x 4 1/4 In. 18800.00
Glass, Imperial Pinch, Sherbet, Pink, 3 7/8 In. 20.00
Glass, Snow Glass, Plate, Salad 85.00
Home Decorators, Plate, White, Bow Knot, Melamine, 6 In., 4 Piece 5.00
Iroquois Casual, Berry Bowl, Avocado Yellow, 5 1/2 In. . . . . .13.00 to 15.00
Iroquois Casual, Berry Bowl, Charcoal, 5 1/2 In. 20.00
Iroquois Casual, Berry Bowl, Lemon Yellow, 5 1/2 In. 18.00
Iroquois Casual, Berry Bowl, Nutmeg Brown, 5 1/2 In. . . . . .10.00 to 15.00
Iroquois Casual, Berry Bowl, Ripe Apricot, 5 1/2 In. 15.00
Iroquois Casual, Berry Bowl, Sugar White, 5 1/2 In. 16.00
Iroquois Casual, Bowl, Cereal, Charcoal, 5 In. 28.00
Iroquois Casual, Bowl, Cereal, Gay Wings, 5 In. 20.00
Iroquois Casual, Bowl, Cereal, Ice Blue, 5 In. 7.00
Iroquois Casual, Bowl, Cereal, Lemon Yellow, 5 In. 15.00
Iroquois Casual, Bowl, Cereal, Ripe Apricot, 5 In. 13.00
Iroquois Casual, Bowl, Cereal, Shepherd's Purse, 5 In. 20.00
Iroquois Casual, Bowl, Cereal, White Violets, 5 In. 25.00
Iroquois Casual, Bowl, Divided, Sugar White, 10 In. 58.00
Iroquois Casual, Bowl, Fruit, Pink Sherbet, 5 1/2 In. 12.00
Iroquois Casual, Bowl, Vegetable, Avocado Yellow, 8 In. 35.00
Iroquois Casual, Bowl, Vegetable, Divided, Avocado Yellow, 10 In. . . . . .18.00 to 40.00
Iroquois Casual, Bowl, Vegetable, Divided, Lettuce Green, 10 In. 50.00
Iroquois Casual, Bowl, Vegetable, Divided, Oyster, 10 In. 70.00
Iroquois Casual, Bowl, Vegetable, Divided, Ripe Apricot, 10 In. 40.00
Iroquois Casual, Bowl, Vegetable, Lemon Yellow, 8 In. 35.00
Iroquois Casual, Bowl, Vegetable, Pink Sherbet, 8 In. 32.00
Iroquois Casual, Butter, Cover, Charcoal 275.00
Iroquois Casual, Butter, Cover, Lettuce Green 225.00
Iroquois Casual, Butter, Cover, Parsley 195.00
Iroquois Casual, Butter, Cover, Pink Sherbet . . . . .110.00 to 125.00
Iroquois Casual, Butter, Cover, Ripe Apricot 745.00
Iroquois Casual, Butter, No Cover, Ice Blue 45.00
Iroquois Casual, Carafe, Charcoal, 10 In. 550.00
Iroquois Casual, Carafe, Sugar White 295.00
Iroquois Casual, Casserole, Cover, Avocado Yellow, 2 Qt. . . . . .43.00 to 60.00
Iroquois Casual, Casserole, Cover, Divided, Ice Blue, 10 In. 49.00
Iroquois Casual, Casserole, Cover, Ripe Apricot, 8 In. 125.00
Iroquois Casual, Casserole, No Cover, Avocado Yellow, 2 Qt., 8 In. 32.00
Iroquois Casual, Casserole, No Cover, Ripe Apricot, 2 Qt., 8 In. 38.00
Iroquois Casual, Casserole, No Cover, Sugar White, 2 Qt., 8 In. 58.00
Iroquois Casual, Chop Plate, Pink Sherbet 60.00
Iroquois Casual, Coffeepot, Cover, Nutmeg Brown 135.00
Iroquois Casual, Coffeepot, Cover, Oyster 150.00
Iroquois Casual, Creamer, Cantaloupe 220.00
Iroquois Casual, Creamer, Ice Blue 32.00
Iroquois Casual, Creamer, Lettuce Green 40.00
Iroquois Casual, Creamer, Ripe Apricot 32.00
Iroquois Casual, Creamer, Stacking, Avocado Yellow 13.00
Iroquois Casual, Creamer, Stacking, Charcoal 30.00
Iroquois Casual, Creamer, Stacking, Ice Blue 14.00
Iroquois Casual, Creamer, Stacking, Sugar White 27.00
Iroquois Casual, Creamer, Sugar White 15.00
Iroquois Casual, Cup & Saucer, Aqua 125.00
Iroquois Casual, Cup & Saucer, Avocado Yellow . . . . .15.00 to 30.00
Iroquois Casual, Cup & Saucer, Cantaloupe 50.00
Iroquois Casual, Cup & Saucer, Ice Blue 32.00
Iroquois Casual, Cup & Saucer, Nutmeg Brown 15.00
Iroquois Casual, Cup & Saucer, Oyster 20.00
Iroquois Casual, Cup & Saucer, Sugar White 12.00

Iroquois Casual, Cup, Cantaloupe . . . . .20.00 to 35.00
Iroquois Casual, Cup, Gay Wings 18.00
Iroquois Casual, Cup, Lemon Yellow 15.00
Iroquois Casual, Cup, Lettuce Green . . . . .16.00 to 17.00
Iroquois Casual, Cup, Nutmeg Brown 11.00
Iroquois Casual, Cup, Oyster 12.00
Iroquois Casual, Cup, Ripe Apricot . . . . .10.00 to 13.00
Iroquois Casual, Cup, Sugar White 17.00
Iroquois Casual, Cup, White Violets 25.00
Iroquois Casual, Dish, Gumbo, Ripe Apricot 55.00
Iroquois Casual, Dish, Ripe Apricot 42.00
Iroquois Casual, Mug, Avocado Yellow 125.00
Iroquois Casual, Mug, Pink Sherbet 80.00
Iroquois Casual, Mug, Redesigned, Lemon Yellow 90.00
Iroquois Casual, Mug, Ripe Apricot 125.00
Iroquois Casual, Pitcher, Water, Nutmeg Brown 95.00
Iroquois Casual, Plate, Bread & Butter, Avocado Yellow, 6 1/2 In. . . . . .5.00 to 6.50
Iroquois Casual, Plate, Bread & Butter, Charcoal, 6 1/2 In. 10.00
Iroquois Casual, Plate, Bread & Butter, Gay Wings, 6 1/2 In. 7.50
Iroquois Casual, Plate, Bread & Butter, Nutmeg Brown, 6 1/2 In. 5.00
Iroquois Casual, Plate, Bread & Butter, Oyster, 6 1/2 In. 10.00
Iroquois Casual, Plate, Bread & Butter, Ripe Apricot, 6 1/2 In. . . . . .5.50 to 6.00
Iroquois Casual, Plate, Dinner, Avocado Yellow, 10 In. 15.00
Iroquois Casual, Plate, Dinner, Ice Blue, 10 In. 20.00
Iroquois Casual, Plate, Dinner, Lemon Yellow, 10 In. 15.00
Iroquois Casual, Plate, Dinner, Pink Sherbet, 10 In. 13.00
Iroquois Casual, Plate, Dinner, Sugar White, 10 In. . . . . .18.00 to 25.00
Iroquois Casual, Plate, Luncheon, Avocado Yellow, 9 1/2 In. . . . . .10.00 to 15.00
Iroquois Casual, Plate, Luncheon, Charcoal, 9 1/2 In. 26.00
Iroquois Casual, Plate, Luncheon, Oyster, 9 1/2 In. 20.00
Iroquois Casual, Plate, Luncheon, Ripe Apricot, 9 1/2 In. 19.00
Iroquois Casual, Plate, Salad, Cantaloupe, 7 1/2 In. 25.00
Iroquois Casual, Plate, Salad, Ice Blue, 7 1/2 In. 18.00
Iroquois Casual, Plate, Salad, Lemon Yellow, 7 1/2 In. . . . . .15.00 to 18.00
Iroquois Casual, Plate, Salad, Nutmeg Brown, 7 1/2 In. 20.00
Iroquois Casual, Plate, Salad, Ripe Apricot, 7 1/2 In. 20.00
Iroquois Casual, Platter, Oval, Avocado Yellow, 9 3/4 x 12 1/2 In. 10.00
Iroquois Casual, Platter, Oval, Gay Wings, 12 3/4 In. 35.00
Iroquois Casual, Platter, Oval, Nutmeg Brown, 12 3/4 In. . . . . .30.00 to 42.00
Iroquois Casual, Platter, Oval, Pink Sherbet, 14 1/2 In. 45.00
Iroquois Casual, Salt & Pepper, Stacking, Avocado Yellow, Cork Stoppers 35.00
Iroquois Casual, Salt & Pepper, Stacking, Charcoal 68.00
Iroquois Casual, Salt & Pepper, Stacking, Lemon Yellow 60.00
Iroquois Casual, Salt & Pepper, Stacking, Oyster 75.00
Iroquois Casual, Salt & Pepper, Stacking, Pink Sherbet 30.00
Iroquois Casual, Salt & Pepper, Stacking, Ripe Apricot 25.00
Iroquois Casual, Saucer, Avocado Yellow 4.00
Iroquois Casual, Saucer, Gay Wings 7.50
Iroquois Casual, Saucer, Ice Blue 4.00
Iroquois Casual, Saucer, Lemon Yellow 5.50
Iroquois Casual, Saucer, Lettuce Green 5.00
Iroquois Casual, Saucer, Nutmeg Brown 4.00
Iroquois Casual, Skillet, Cover, White, 10 1/4 In. 325.00
Iroquois Casual, Soup, Dish, Lettuce 55.00
Iroquois Casual, Sugar & Creamer, Oyster 75.00
Iroquois Casual, Sugar & Creamer, Stacking, Avocado Yellow 25.00
Iroquois Casual, Sugar & Creamer, Stacking, Ripe Apricot 30.00
Iroquois Casual, Sugar, Cover, Gay Wings 50.00
Iroquois Casual, Sugar, Lemon Yellow 50.00
Iroquois Casual, Sugar, Sugar White 55.00
Iroquois Casual, Teapot, Cover, Lemon Yellow 245.00
Iroquois Casual, Teapot, Cover, White 200.00
Iroquois Casual, Teapot, Nutmeg Brown 200.00

Iroquois Casual, Teapot, Sugar White 385.00
Ivy, Teapot, Sterling 159.00
Meladur, Plate, Green, 6 In. 11.00
Plastic, Residential, Bowl, Vegetable, Divided, Gray, Melmac, 11 x 9 In. 19.00
Plastic, Residential, Creamer, Turquoise, Melmac 15.00
Plastic, Residential, Cup, Salmon, Melmac 5.00
Plastic, Residential, Cup, Sea Mist, Melmac 5.00
Plastic, Residential, Dinner Set, Lemon Ice & Gray, Melmac, 25 Piece 78.00
Plastic, Residential, Plate, Bread & Butter, Sea Mist, Melmac, 6 In. 5.00
Plastic, Residential, Plate, Turquoise, Melmac, 6 In. 5.00
Plastic, Residential, Platter, Turquoise, Melmac, 14 3/4 x 12 3/4 In. 11.00
Queen Anne's Lace, Cup & Saucer, Knowles 10.00
Silver, Sugar & Creamer, Stacking, Charcoal Gray, Oneida, 5 In. 10.00
Tea & Coffee Set, Porcelain, Overlay Flowers, Steubenville, 4 Piece 353.00
White Clover, Ashtray, Golden Spice, Harker 20.00
White Clover, Bowl, Cereal, Coral Sand, Harker 25.00
White Clover, Creamer, Charcoal, Harker 50.00
White Clover, Plate, Dinner, Coral Sand, Harker, 10 In. 15.00
White Clover, Salt & Pepper, Large, Charcoal, Harker 10.00

SABINO glass was made in the 1920s and 1930s in Paris, France. Founded by Marius-Ernest Sabino (1878–1961), the firm was noted for Art Deco lamps, vases, figurines, and animals in clear, colored, and opalescent glass. Production stopped during World War II but resumed in the 1960s with the manufacture of nude figurines and small opalescent glass animals. The new pieces are a slightly different color and can be recognized.

Sabino France

Figurine, 2 Love Birds, White Opalescent, Marked, Sabino, France, 3 1/4 In. 92.00
Figurine, Crowing Rooster, Elaborate Tail, Opalescent, 6 3/4 In. 207.00

SALT AND PEPPER SHAKERS in matched sets were first used in the nineteenth century. Collectors are primarily interested in figural examples made after World War I. *Huggers* are pairs of shakers that appear to embrace each other. Many salt and pepper shakers are listed in other categories and can be located through the index at the back of this book.

4-Eyed Man & Toothless Woman, Barrel, Bisque, Novex, 3 1/2 x 3 In. 85.00
Acorn, Opaque Pink, Gold Enamel Trim, 3 In. 120.00
American Indian, Burgundy & Yellow Headbands, Japan, 3 In. 60.00
Aunt Jemima & Uncle Mose, F&F, Dayton, 1940s-1950s, 3 1/2 In. 75.00
Barbar The Elephant, Stacking, Japan, c.1950s, 4 7/8 In. 69.00
Baseball Catcher & Batter, Copalis Beach, Wash., 1950s, 3 1/2 In. 85.00
Baseball Catcher & Batter, Japan, 1940s-1950s, 4 In. 85.00
Baseball Catcher & Fielder, Children, Japan, 3 7/8 In. 90.00
Baseball Pitcher & Batter, Mice, 3 1/4 In. 59.00
Bear, Nodder, Flowers On Base, Japan, 1940s, 3 3/4 In. 115.00
Bear, Nodder, Rose Decorated Base, Japan, 1940s 90.00
Bears, Polka Dot, Rocking, Japan, 4 In. 65.00
Black Baby & Bottle, 1950s, 3 x 4 In. 95.00
Black Boy & Watermelon, 1950s, 2 1/2 In. 95.00
Black Boy & Watermelon, 3 1/2 In. 65.00
Black Boy On Elephant, Japan, 1950s, 5 In. 110.00
Black Boy On Gator, Ceramic, Hand Painted, Prewar Japan, 4 In. 70.00
Black Chef & Mammy, c.1943, 5 In. 275.00
Black Chef & Mammy, Just Call Me Old Salty, Just Call Me Peppy, 1952, 5 In. 110.00
Black Chef & Mammy, Lafayette, Tenn. 125.00
Black Chef & Mammy, Plastic, New Orleans, La., Box, 1950s-1960s, 2 1/2 x 3 In. 80.00
Black Chef & Mammy, Yellow Clothes, Stove Size, 8 In. 185.00
Black Chef & Mammy, Yellow Trim, Brayton Laguna, 5 1/2 In. .... .68.00 to 85.00
Black Children Eating Watermelon, Chalkware, 3 In. 80.00
Black Girl & Watermelon, Leaf Skirt, Japan, 3 1/4 In. 125.00
Black Golliwog, Playing Bagpipes, Saxophone, Silver Crane Co., England, 3 3/4 In. 225.00
Black Native & Hippo, Playing Banjo, Japan, 1940s-1950s 155.00
Black Native Boy & Girl, Japan, 1940s, 4 3/4 In. 75.00

Buzz & Woody, Treasure Craft, Box, 7 In.	135.00
Casper The Friendly Ghost, Star Jars, 5 In.	59.00
Cat, Mother & Baby, Black, Nodder, Japan, 4 In.	425.00
Cat, Nodder, Japan, 1940s, 3 1/2 In.	95.00
Cat & Mouse, Arthur Wood, England, 7 & 5 In.	65.00
Chili Pepper, Red, Green Leaves, 4 Legs, Royal Bavaria, 3 In.	148.00
Conoco, Gas Pump, R.R. Sublette's Service Station, Mo., Plastic, Box, 2 3/4 In.	95.00
Dairy Queen Girl, Japan, 4 In.	195.00
Daisy, Red, Blue Banner, Majolica, 4 1/2 In.	130.00
Deer, Nodder, 2 x 3 In.	60.00
Deer, Nodder, Flowers On Base, Japan, 1940s, 3 1/2 In.	90.00
Dinosaur, Twisted Neck Iguanadon, Japan, c.1950s, 4 1/2 In.	95.00
Donkey, Japan, 1940s-1950s	145.00
Dopey, Japan, 4 In.	65.00
Double-Eye Man & Woman, Nodder, Japan, 1940s	110.00 to 125.00
Duck, Hugger, Yellow, Van Tellingen, 3 3/4 In.	63.00
Duck, Nodder, Flowers On Base, Japan, c.1940, 3 1/2 In.	85.00 to 90.00
Dumbo, 1 Blue Trim, 1 Red Trim, 3 1/4 In.	65.00
Dutch Boy & Girl, Kissing, Nodder, Japan, 1940s-1950s	225.00
Fawn, Nodder, Japan, 1940s-1950s	98.00
Fish, Nodder, Caribou, Maine, Japan, 2 x 2 3/4 In.	75.00 to 80.00
Flamingo, Nodder, Japan, 1940s-1950s	100.00
Flowers, Purple, Gold Tops, Hand Painted, Pensee, Bavaria, c.1885, 2 3/4 x 2 In.	75.00
Foghorn Leghorn & Henry, Treasure Craft, Box, 5 1/2 In.	60.00
Fred Flintstone & Barney Rubble, Certified International, Box, 3 1/2 & 5 1/2 In.	59.00
Garfield & Arlene, Enesco, Korea, 1978, 3 1/4 In.	125.00
Giraffe, Hugger, Artmark, Japan, 1950s, 4 3/4 In.	65.00
Glass, Deep Blue, Brass Cap, Christmas, 2 1/2 x 1 1/2 In.	121.00
Glass, Prism Cut Body, Silver & Mother-Of-Pearl Tops, 2 1/2 In.	40.00
Goldilocks, Regal China, c.1940s, 4 1/2 In.	125.00
Green's, Milk & Ice Cream, Plastic, White, Green Logo, 4 In.	20.00
Hen & Rooster, Japan, c.1940	165.00
Hen & Rooster, Nodder, Japan, 1940s-1950s	100.00 to 125.00
Humpty Dumpty, 1940s, 5 1/2 In.	89.00
Humpty Dumpty, Regal China, 4 1/4 x 3 In.	190.00
Indian, Nodder, Japan, 1940s	100.00
Kangaroo, Nodder, Japan, 1940s	145.00
KFC Colonel Sanders, Plastic, Starling, Canada, 4 3/8 In.	65.00
Lamb, Range Set, 5 3/4 In.	75.00
Lawnmower, USA, 1950s	120.00
Luzianne Mammy, Green Skirt, 5 In.	165.00
Maid, Holding Tray With 2 Eggs, Lusterware, c.1930, 5 1/4 In., 3 Piece	125.00
Mammy, Nude, Nodder, Japan, 1940s, 3 1/2 In.	295.00
Mammy & Pappy, Black, Thames, 8 1/8 In.	115.00
Mammy & Pappy Yokum, Dogpatch USA, Sadiron Shape, 1968	59.00
Man In Doghouse, Woman With Rolling Pin, Vallona Starr, 3 1/2 In.	95.00
Martian In Spaceship, Vallona Starr, 2 1/2 x 4 In.	125.00
Mary Had A Little Lamb, Van Tellingen	80.00
Matador & Bull, Nodder, 1940s-1950s	195.00 to 245.00
Mickey McGuire, Toonerville Trolley, Ceramic, 3 In.	20.00
Military Bears, World War II, Aviator & Sailor, California Pottery, 1940s, 4 3/8 In.	65.00
Milk Bottle, Jones Dairy, Glass, Metal Top, 1930s, 3 1/2 In.	75.00
Milk Bottle, Warminster Farm, Hatboro, Pa., Glass, Metal Lid, 1930s, 3 3/8 In.	65.00
Miss Muffet & Spider, Poinsettia Studio, 1950s, 2 1/2 & 3 1/2 In.	85.00
Monk, McWilliams Moselle Wine, Japan, 3 1/2 In.	95.00
Monkey, Nodder, Japan, c.1940	175.00
Monkey, Nodder, Swinger, Japan, 1950s	65.00
Naughty Lady, Nodder, Japan, 1940s-1950s	125.00 to 135.00
Nude Lady In Barrel, Nodder, Anco, Japan, 1950s, 6 In.	110.00
Nugget Sam, Nugget Casino, Sparks, Nevada, Japan, 1950s, 4 In.	75.00
Old Mother Hubbard & Dog, Gold Trim, Poinsettia Studio, 3 1/2 In.	85.00
Oriental Couple, Nodder, Moriage, Dragonware, 3 1/2 In.	200.00

Oswald & Homer, Japan, Napco, 1958, 4 In. 135.00
Peek-A-Boo, Red Dots, Van Tellingen, 4 In. 225.00
Peerless Beer Men, LaCrosse Breweries, Hartland Plastic, 5 In. 95.00
Pheasant, Nodder, Japan, c.1950 ....80.00 to 85.00
Pig, Bride & Groom, Nodder, Japan, 1940s-1950s ....325.00 to 345.00
Pinnochio & Dutch Girl, Japan, 4 3/4 In. 175.00
Pixie Baseball Players, Batter & Catcher, Japan, 3 1/2 In. 75.00
Pixies Riding Rocket Ship, Gold Trim, 1950s, 2 3/4 x 3 1/2 In. 59.00
Pure Oil Company, Gas Pump, Mower County, Minn., Plastic, 2 3/4 In. 135.00
Refrigerator, GE, Milk Glass, 1940s, 3 1/4 In. 59.00
Rocket Ship & Moon, Enesco, Japan, 1950s, 4 1/4 In. 59.00
Rotary Bits, Anthracite Bit Co., Oil Centennial, Plastic, 1959, 3 In. 125.00
Sailboat, Nodder, Japan, 1940s 95.00
Salty & Peppy, Yellow Pearlware, Ceramic, 7 & 7 1/2 In. 147.00
Shmoo Couple, 1940s, 3 1/2 In. 225.00
Silly Symphony Pig, Japan, 1930s, 4 In. 59.00
Singing Nude In Bathtub, 1950s, 2 1/2 x 3 1/4 In. 59.00
Skull, Nodder, Japan, 1940s-1950s, 3 1/2 In. ....85.00 to 88.00
Skull, Nodder, Lusterware, Japan, 1940s-1950s 90.00
Stillbrook Bourbon, 4 1/2 In. 75.00
Sylvester The Cat, Japan, 1970s, 4 In. 175.00
Sympathetic Ear, Art Anson, Allentown, Pa., 1965, 4 In. 75.00
Toaster, Pop-Up, Box, 1970s, 4 1/2 x 3 In. 65.00
Uncle Sam, Bust, Painted, Ceramic, 1920, 2 1/2 x 1 1/2 In. 35.00
Whiskey, Gluckenheimer, Front Labels 75.00
Wolf, Wearing Clothes, Germany, 3 1/2 In. 75.00
Woodsy Owl, 1960s-1970s, Japan, 4 1/4 In. 125.00
Yosemite Sam, Warner Brothers, c.1960, 4 In. 95.00

SALT GLAZE has a grayish white surface with a texture like an orange peel. It is a method of decoration that has been used since the eighteenth century. Salt-glazed pieces are still being made.

Bowl, Underplate, Impressed Flowers, Reticulated, 8 1/2 x 2 1/2 In. 315.00
Churn, Egg Shape, Double Lunate Handles, Cobalt Blue Flower, 6 Gal., 11 3/4 x 20 In. . . 520.00
Cream Riser, J.D. Craven 300.00
Crock, Cobalt Blue Chicken, Hand Decorated, 2 Gal. 825.00
Crock, Macomb Pottery, 2 Gal. 110.00
Dish, Basketry Design, 1700s, 6 In., Pair 240.00
Jar, Storage, John Craven, North Carolina, 1840s-1850s 2090.00
Jug, Beehive, Pour Spout, 13 In. 80.00
Teapot, White, Morning Glories, Leaves, Vines, 19th Century, 5 1/2 x 3 1/4 In. 220.00

SAMPLERS were made in America from the early 1700s. The best examples were made from 1790 to 1840. Long, narrow samplers are usually older than square ones. Early samplers just had stitching or alphabets. The later examples had numerals, borders, and pictorial decorations. Those with mottoes are mid-Victorian. A revival of interest in the 1930s produced simpler samplers, usually with mottoes.

ABCDE

Adam & Eve, Elizabeth Pratt, July 30th 1835, Silk On Linen, 14 1/2 x 13 In. 1060.00
Adam & Eve, Flower Border, Susana Vale, Age 11, 1809, Gilt Frame, 15 x 13 In. ... 1345.00
Alphabet, Bird, Peafowl, Trees, Flowers, Catharine Wardlaw, Aged 15, 1828, 19 3/4 In. . . 690.00
Alphabet, Birds, Baskets, Mary M. Clapp, Aged 9, 1804, Frame, 13 1/4 x 12 In. 826.00
Alphabet, Birds, Vine Border, Emma Eliza Hancock, 1862, Wool, Cotton, 24 x 16 In. 660.00
Alphabet, Blue, Burgundy, Brown, Cynthia Tithelm, 1840, Gilt Frame, 18 1/2 x 20 In. ... 520.00
Alphabet, Church, Floral Border, Elizabeth Scowcroft, 1845, Linen, Frame, 17 x 16 In. .. 920.00
Alphabet, Embroidered, Pricilla Hillman, c.1873, Linen, Vine Frame, 20 x 20 In. 405.00
Alphabet, Flowers, Hearts, Sunbursts, Hannah Schell, 1818, Frame, 7 3/8 x 9 3/4 In. 253.00
Alphabet, Flowers, Inscription, GT Weston EH, c.1808, 17 x 17 In. 4140.00
Alphabet, Flowers, Mary Ann Phillips, Aged 11 Years, Mahogany Frame, 13 x 12 In. 605.00
Alphabet, Flowers, Trees, Biblical Subjects, Frame, England, c.1850, 12 x 16 In. 415.00
Alphabet, Flowers, Trees, Margaret Nancy Doughty, 1833, 12 1/2 x 21 1/2 In. 1375.00
Alphabet, Francesca, Flowers, Geometric Design, Wool On Linen, 13 1/2 x 21 In. 185.00

Alphabet, Fruit Baskets, Flowers, Deer, Pine Trees, Strawberry Vine, c.1799, 14 x 14 In. .. 1095.00
Alphabet, Girl, Dog On Leash, Bird, Monkey, Flowers & Vines, O.B., 1850, 13 x 14 In. .. 440.00
Alphabet, House, Trees, Potted Flowers, Gilt & Rosewood Frame, England, 17 x 14 In. .. 525.00
Alphabet, J. Hall Deer, c.1826, Linen Ground, Eyelet Stitch, Wool, Frame, 9 x 9 In. 275.00
Alphabet, Jean Morrison, 1840s, Frame, 13 x 18 In. 310.00
Alphabet, Leaf Border, Christiana G. Robb, 1845, Maple Frame, 21 x 20 In. 715.00
Alphabet, Mary Jastram, May 27, 1818, Bird's-Eye Maple Frame, 10 x 8 1/4 In. 805.00
Alphabet, Names, Flower Urns, Helen M. Miller, 1850, Gilt Frame, 19 x 17 1/2 In. 990.00
Alphabet, Numbers, Animals, Flowers, Figures, Greek Key Border, Pastel, 17 x 14 3/8 In. 80.00
Alphabet, Numbers, Flowers, People, 1863, Frame, 18 x 19 In. 165.00
Alphabet, Numbers, Maria Neiens Kayl, 1908, France, Frame, 12 1/2 x 14 1/2 In. 90.00
Alphabet, Numbers, Trees, Basket, Mary Watson, Aged 16 Years, Frame, 16 x 15 In. 3738.00
Alphabet, Numbers, Trees, Eliza Richardson, 1829, 16 1/2 x 16 1/2 In. 7280.00
Alphabet, Poem To Sister, Vermont, Philinda Lamb, 1820, Frame, 14 1/2 x 17 In. 3740.00
Alphabet, Red House, Trees, Birds, Verse, 1857, Frame, 10 x 14 In. 800.00
Alphabet, Strawberry Border, Flowers, Sarah Talbot, Aged 10, 1787, 10 3/4 x 8 1/2 In. .. 470.00
Alphabet, Susan Carheh, Frame, 15 7/8 x 13 1/4 In. 525.00
Alphabet, Verse, Abigail Reynolds, April 27th 1772, Frame, 7 x 8 1/2 In. 310.00
Alphabet, Verse, Birdcage, Flower, Dogs, Ann Nichols, Aged 9, 1817, 12 x 12 In. 330.00
Alphabet, Verse, Emma J. Warner, Aged 12 Years, 1842, Linen, 16 1/2 x 17 1/4 In. 1880.00
Alphabet, Verse, Sarah Jane Harris, South Boston, Aged 9, 1822, 21 1/4 x 16 In. 3565.00
Alphabet, Verses, Animals, Birds, Vining Strawberry Border, 1786, 17 x 13 In. 1265.00
Alphabets, 2 Verses, Animals, Charlot Shepardson, 1833, Silk Thread, Frame, 14 x 24 In. 170.00
Alphabets, Embroidered Lines, Ann Maxwell, Harrisburgh, c.1807, Frame, 16 3/4 x 8 In. . 935.00
Alphabets, Number String, Poem, Elizabeth Blower, 1857, Frame, 21 1/2 x 24 1/2 In. ... 690.00
Alphabets, Numbers, Strawberry Border, 1813, Silk, Linen, Frame, 18 1/2 x 19 1/2 In. ... 635.00
Alphabets, Numbers, Verse, Helen Moffat, Aged 8 Years, 1812, Frame, 20 x 12 In. 605.00
Alphabets, Various Styles, Margaret Simmons, Age 12, 19th Century, 11 1/2 x 13 3/8 In. .. 520.00
Alphabets, Verse, People, Animals, Plants, 1869, Linen, Frame, 13 x 11 In. 1045.00
Alphabets, Verses, Sarah Ashlers, Aged 11 Yrs, Norfolk, Ct., Silk On Linen, 17 In. 2530.00
Animals, Mary Heasley, 1852, Frame, 12 x 13 1/2 In. 120.00
Birds, Flowers, Hannah Flagg, Age 13, 1798, Frame, 13 3/4 x 9 In. 300.00
Birds, Flowers, Sarah Elizabeth Allen, Little Neck, 1835, 17 1/2 x 16 1/2 In. 4025.00
Cross-Stitch, German, Yesaias V. Schultz, 1854, Perforated Paper, Frame, 9 3/4 x 8 In. .. 55.00
Family Register, Borders, Cape Cod, 1843, Silk On Linen, Frame, 18 x 20 In. 1380.00
Flower Basket, Vining, Wreath, Mary Jacob, Aged 6 Yrs. 9 Mos., 1822, 13 x 18 In. 1035.00
Flower Border, Birds, Animals, Strawberries, Deborah A. Brown, 1841, 16 1/2 x 8 In. 2860.00
Flower Vase, Border Stitch Patterns, Margaret Ann Orr, 1835, Silk, Wool, 17 x 22 1/2 In. . 220.00
Flowers, Animals, Train, Elephant, Figures, Frame, 23 x 23 In. 200.00
Flowers, Prayer, Ann Maria Wood, Aged 7 Years, Alexandria, 1850, Frame, 16 x 16 In. .. 3185.00
House, God Bless Our Home, Perforated Paper, Walnut Frame, Victorian, 19 x 23 In. 395.00
Letters, Flowers, Rachel McCutcheon, Bird's-Eye Maple Frame, 19 1/2 x 24 1/2 In. 40.00
Letters, Numbers, Flower Border, Mary Montgomery, 1832, Frame, 16 3/4 x 16 1/2 In. .. 340.00
Letters, Numbers, House, Esther Woodman, Delaware Valley, 1833, Frame, 13 x 17 In. .. 2815.00
Letters, Numbers, Verse, Rebecca Bowers, Delaware Valley, 1824, Frame, 16 1/4 x 16 In. 1800.00
Lord's Prayer, Punched Paper, Wood Frame, 1880s, 19 x 15 In. 595.00
Map, England & Wales, Susanna Murphy, Ireland, 1796, Silk, 20 1/2 x 18 1/2 In. 990.00
Map, England, Part Of Scotland, Margaret Brown, 1787, Frame, 29 x 26 In. 1265.00
Motto, Cross-Stitch, Colonial Couple, Home, Notched Frame, 12 In. .... *Illus* 65.00
Petit Point, Dogs, Birds, Flowers, House, Ellen Street, Aged 12 Years, Frame, 15 x 15 In. 575.00
Rose Of Sharon, Strawberry Border, Birds, Trees, Angels, Ann Broadbent, 19 x 16 In. ... 1320.00
Scenic, 2-Story House, Willow Tree, Eliza Bare, York County, Frame, 15 x 20 1/2 In. 1540.00
Tulip & Bird Trees, Sarah Alice Salmon, Aged 13 Years, 1863, 16 1/4 x 15 1/2 In. 2420.00
Verse, 8 Lines, Silk Cross, Outline Stitches, Linen Ground, 17 x 16 In. 770.00
Verse, Alphabet, Schoolhouse, Inscription, Elisabeth Ingram Aged 14, 1848, 16 x 16 In. .. 920.00
Verse, Angels, House, Garden, Greens, Blues, Ann Reeve, 1842, England, 13 x 16 In. ... 1049.00
Verse, Biblical, Mary Rosewall, Aged 9 Years, October 1829, Linen, Silk, 13 x 19 In. 345.00
Verse, Flowers, Scrollwork, Sarah Ann Green, March 1858, Stretcher, 14 x 17 In. 345.00
Verse, Fruit Basket, Leaves, Building, Perched Birds, Flowers, Vine Border, 24 x 22 In. .. 2310.00
Verse, House, Fence, Tree, Susanna Stanley, 1823, Silk, Linen, 15 3/4 x 22 In. 2235.00
Verse, House, Willow Trees, Vining Rose Border, 1837, Maple Frame, 19 x 20 1/2 In. 1150.00
Verse, On Mortality, Figures, Gate, Birds, Sarah Kingston, 1818, Frame, 16 x 19 In. 805.00

SAMSON and Company, a French firm specializing in the reproduction of collectible wares of many countries and periods, was founded in Paris in the early nineteenth century. Chelsea, Meissen, Famille Verte, and Chinese Export porcelain are some of the wares that have been reproduced by the company. The firm uses a variety of marks on the reproductions. It is still in operation.

Basket, Heraldic Crest Design, Pierced Sides, Leaf Border, Late 1800s, 10 1/4 In.	115.00
Bowl, Duck & Marsh Grass Cartouche, Spearhead Design Border, c.1900, 14 In.	460.00
Figurine, Famille Verte, Lantern Shape Shade, Chinese Export Style, 10 1/2 In., Pair	1840.00
Group, Courting Couple, Man Kneeling At Feet Of Woman, 11 5/8 In.	150.00
Jar, Cover, Famille Verte, Louis XV Style Ormolu Mounted, 19 In.	2530.00
Plate, Heraldic Crest Design, Pierced Border, Late 1800s, 9 1/2 In.	80.00
Stand, Biscuit Bowl, 4 Neoclassical Women, 16 3/4 x 16 3/8 In., Pair	9200.00
Vase, Armorial, Chinese Export Style, Mask Handles, Mounted As Lamp, 22 In., Pair	1265.00
Vase, Meissen Schneeballen Style, Relief Flower Heads, Bird Cover, Stand, 26 In.	10925.00

SANDWICH GLASS is any of the myriad types of glass made by the Boston and Sandwich Glass Works in Sandwich, Massachusetts, between 1825 and 1888. It is often very difficult to be sure whether a piece was really made at the Sandwich factory because so many types were made there and similar pieces were made at other glass factories. Additional pieces may be listed under Pressed Glass and in related categories.

Bowl, Gaines, Fiery Opalescent, Scalloped Rim, Footed, 4 5/8 In.	285.00
Bowl, Horn Of Plenty, Scalloped Rim, Footed, 4 3/8 In.	145.00
Cake Stand, Horn Of Plenty, 6-Lobed Stem, Patterned Foot, 5 x 9 In.	1650.00
Candlestick, 6-Sided Base, 7 1/2 In.	110.00
Candlestick, Acanthus Leaf, Clambroth, Starch Blue Petal Socket, 11 In.	660.00
Candlestick, Canary, 6-Sided Base, 7 3/4 In.	220.00
Candlestick, Clambroth, 6-Sided Base, 7 In., Pair	440.00
Candlestick, Clambroth, Petal Sockets & Base, 7 In., Pair	220.00
Candlestick, Column, Canary, Petal Socket, 9 3/8 In.	155.00
Candlestick, Crucifix, 11 3/4 In., Pair	60.00
Candlestick, Dolphin, Canary, Petal Socket, Double Step, 9 3/8 In.	385.00
Candlestick, Dolphin, Canary, Petal Socket, Single Step, 10 In.	187.00
Candlestick, Dolphin, Starch Blue, 6-Sided Base, 7 In.	770.00
Candlestick, Hexagonal, Clambroth, Starch Blue Socket, 8 1/4 In., Pair	415.00
Candlestick, Lacy, Socket, Stepped Base, Extended Corners, 7 In.	130.00
Candlestick, Loop, Canary	240.00
Candlestick, Petal & Loop, Canary, 6 3/4 In., Pair	195.00
Candlestick, Petal Socket, Faceted Standard, Round Base, Canary, 7 1/4 In.	45.00
Castor, Salt, Ruby, Engraved Grapes, 2 1/2 In., Pair	70.00
Celery Vase, Ashburton, Canary, Scalloped Rim, 10 3/4 In.	2070.00
Celery Vase, Horn Of Plenty, 8 1/2 In., Pair	375.00
Celery Vase, Horn Of Plenty, Scalloped Rim, 8 1/4 In.	145.00
Celery Vase, Waffle & Thumbprint, Flared Rim, 9 1/8 In.	200.00
Celery Vase, Waffle, 9 1/2 In.	65.00
Cigar Holder, Cut, Double Overlay, Rose To White To Clear, 5 3/4 In.	265.00
Cologne, Amethyst, Corseted, 4 7/8 In.	195.00
Cologne, Amethyst, Paneled, Commercial, 4 3/4 x 1 1/4 In.	550.00
Cologne, Ring & Star, Canary, Stopper, 5 1/4 In., Pair	800.00
Compote, Horn Of Plenty, Oval, Scalloped Rim, 6-Lobed Stem, 6 1/2 In.	1650.00
Compote, Loop, 5 1/2 In.	160.00
Compote, New England Pineapple, Hollow Paneled Stem, 8 1/2 In.	265.00
Compote, Open Airtrap Stem, 8 1/2 In.	185.00
Compote, Shallow, Rolled Edge, Square Base, 4 3/4 x 6 1/2 In., Pair	1325.00
Compote, Waffle & Thumbprint, Flared Rim, 9 In.	190.00
Cordial, Horn Of Plenty, 8 Piece	750.00
Creamer, Waffle, Applied Handle, 6 3/8 In.	120.00
Cruet, Cobalt Blue, 3-Piece Mold, Ringed Base, 6 In.	165.00
Curtain Tieback, Pressed Petals & Fins, Fiery, Opalescent, 6 In., Pair	330.00
Decanter, Arch & Fern With Snake, Rayed Base, Bulbous Stopper, 10 1/2 In.	210.00
Decanter, Ashburton, Amethyst, Pewter Pouring Stopper, Bar Lip, 10 1/2 In.	1840.00

Sampler, Motto,
Cross-Stitch, Colonial
Couple, Home,
Notched Frame, 12 In.

Sarreguemines, Mustard,
Tinted Transfer, Fair
Scene, Obernais
Faienceires, 4 In.

Decanter, Canary, Ribbed, 3-Piece Mold, Flat Stopper, 8 x 2 3/4 In.	165.00
Decanter, Cordial, Ribbed Ivy, 5 7/8 In.	65.00
Decanter, Diamond & Sunburst Band, Plain Neck, 3-Piece Mold, Stopper, 9 1/4 In.	175.00
Decanter, Neck Rings, Diamond Band, Ribbed Neck, 3-Piece Mold, 9 1/4 In.	130.00
Decanter, Scroll & Reed, 3-Piece Mold, Stopper, c.1830, 11 1/2 In.	175.00
Dish, Arch & Fern, 8-Sided, Oblong, Stippled Ground, 1 1/2 x 6 x 8 In.	55.00
Dish, Canary, Lily, Scroll & Diamond, Lacy, Oval, Beaded Rim, 1 x 1 x 2 In.	1760.00
Dish, Paneled Rose & Thistle, 8-Sided, Scalloped Rim, 1 1/4 x 5 1/4 In.	55.00
Dish, Pineapple & Gothic Arch, Rectangular, Scallop & Point Rim, 7 x 10 In.	100.00
Dish, Sweetmeat, Cover, Peacock Eye, Grape, Scallop & Point Rim, 5 x 6 3/8 In.	525.00
Eggcup, Cover, Flat Diamond & Panel, Jade Green, 6 1/2 In.	4900.00
Eggcup, Diamond Point, Clambroth, 3 5/8 x 2 5/8 In.	55.00
Epergne, Ruffled Edge Bowl, Engraved, Central Trumpet, 21 In.	520.00
Goblet, 3-Piece Mold-Blown Bowl, Clear, Plain Rim, Bladed Stem, 5 1/2 In.	690.00
Goblet, Bellflower, Cut, 6 Clusters, 6 1/4 In.	2750.00
Goblet, Fine Rib, Bellflower Border, 5 1/2 In.	3410.00
Goblet, Harp, 6 3/8 In.	3300.00
Goblet, Horn Of Plenty, 6 In.	80.00
Hat, Cobalt Blue, Hairpin, Blown, Rolled Lip, Pontil, 2 3/4 In.	2090.00
Jar, Bear, Amethyst, 3 3/4 In.	175.00
Jar, Wolf Head Cover, Bear Body, Alabaster, Embossed x Basin Philada, 5 3/4 In.	1150.00
Lamp, Emerald Green, Milk White Base, Frosted Shade, 18 1/2 In.	800.00
Lamp, Fluid, Double Cut, Cobalt Blue To Opal To Clear, Jade Green Base, 15 In.	374.00
Lamp, Fluid, Horn Of Plenty, 10 1/4 In.	165.00
Lamp, Fluid, Red Overlay, 1850s, Pair	3950.00
Lamp, Fluid, Ring & Oval, 8 In.	1595.00
Lamp, Fluid, White, Blue, Double Stepped Marble Base, 13 In., Pair	1955.00
Lamp, Fluid, White, Cranberry, Marble Base, 12 1/2 In.	1495.00
Lamp, Oil, Amethyst Cut To Clear, Inverted Pear, Brass, Marble Base, 16 1/2 In.	1035.00
Lamp, Oil, Clear Font, Opal Base, 10 In.	165.00
Lamp, Oil, Onion Font, Electric Blue, Clambroth, Blue Chimney, 15 In.	1035.00
Lamp, Oil, Peg Punty, Cranberry Cut To Clear, Gilt Bronze, c.1850, 11 x 7 In., Pair	1840.00
Lamp, Oil, Waffle & Thumbprint, Finger, 4 In.	210.00
Lamp, Whale Oil, 7 Panels, Elongated Loops, Applied Handle, 3 1/2 In.	75.00
Mustard, Sunburst, 3-Piece Mold, Pontil, Clear	140.00
Nappy, Nectarine, 3 Blooms, Scalloped Rim, Footed, 4 x 6 In.	120.00
Nappy, Princes Feather Medallion, Center Diamond, Scalloped Rim, 1 7/8 x 10 In.	90.00
Newel Post, Ribbed Melon, Clambroth, Brass Fitting, 9 1/2 x 4 1/2 In.	440.00
Pan, Blown, Diamond Base, Folded Rim, 3-Piece Mold, Flint, Pontil, 1 1/8 x 5 In.	120.00
Paperweight, Nesting Hen, Cobalt Blue, 3 In.	110.00
Pitcher, Applied Crystal Twist Handle, Ice Lip, 11 1/2 In.	450.00
Pitcher, Cranberry, Straight Sides, Crystal Reeded Handle, 6 5/8 In.	115.00
Pitcher, Horn Of Plenty, Scalloped Foot, 8 3/4 In.	880.00
Plate, Diamond Check & Fan, Fan-Scalloped & Rosette Rim, 9 In.	415.00
Plate, Shell & Princess Feather Medallion, 12-Sided, Scalloped Rim, 1 x 7 In.	120.00
Salt, Beaded Scroll & Basket Of Flowers, 2 x 1 7/8 x 3 3/8 In.	265.00
Salt, Beaded Scroll & Scrolled Leaf, 1 3/4 x 2 x 2 3/4 In.	55.00
Salt, Cobalt Blue, Round, Pedestal, 1 3/4 x 2 7/8 In.	550.00

Salt, Cornucopia & Shield, Paw Feet, Oval, 2 x 2 7/16 x 3 3/8 In. 210.00
Salt, Cover, Casket, Scrolled Feet & Sides, Flower Basket, Pine Cone Finial, 3 In. 1320.00
Salt, Cover, Ribbed Ivy, Raised Rays, Tulip Finial, 4 1/2 In. 110.00
Salt, Eagle, Weeping Willow, Stars, 4 Knopped Feet, 2 x 3 x 2 1/4 In. 180.00
Salt, Horn Of Plenty, Oval, Clear, 3 1/4 In., Pair 140.00
Salt, Sapphire Blue, Heart & Club, Scrolls, Flowers, 1 3/4 x 3 1/4 x 2 In. 2760.00
Salt, Shell, Amber, 1 11/16 x 2 x 3 In. 935.00
Salt, Strawberry Diamond, 2 x 1 7/8 x 3 3/8 In. 240.00
Spill Holder, Amethyst, Inverted Diamond & Thumbprint, 5 In. 975.00
Spooner, Cable, Starch Blue, Scalloped Rim, 5 3/4 In. 2145.00
Spooner, New England Pineapple, 5 In. 45.00
Spooner, Snowflake, 5 1/4 In. 40.00
Sugar, Cover, 8-Sided, Gothic Arch, Canary, Round Foot, 5 1/2 x 5 In. 770.00
Syrup, Bellflower, Fiery Opalescent, Left-Facing, Single Vine, 5 3/4 In. 4070.00
Tumbler, Engraved Vintage Grape, Ruby, Octagonal, Footed, 4 7/8 x 3 1/4 In. 45.00
Tumbler, Whiskey, Horn Of Plenty, Handle, 3 In. 470.00
Tumbler, Whiskey, Horn Of Plenty, Pair 130.00
Tumbler, Whiskey, Ribbed Ivy, Handle, 2 3/4 In. 200.00
Tumbler, Whiskey, Teal, 3 1/4 In. 145.00
Tumbler, Whiskey, Waffle & Thumbprint, 3 1/8 In. 155.00
Vase, Hobnail, Clambroth, Plain Rim, Oval, Blown-Molded, 5 1/2 x 2 1/2 In. 50.00
Vase, Hyacinth, Blown, Teal, Rough Pontil, 6 3/4 x 2 3/4 In. 120.00
Vase, Pressed, Twisted Loop, Amethyst, Gauffered Rim, Hexagonal, 9 1/2 x 5 In. 1760.00
Vase, Three-Printie Block, Amethyst, Ruffled Rim, Knop Stem, 9 1/4 In., Pair 1265.00
Vase, Tulip, 10 In. 375.00
Wine, Horn Of Plenty, 12 Piece 1265.00
Witch's Ball, Rose, White, Blue 275.00

SARREGUEMINES is the name of a French town that is used as part of a china mark. Utzschneider and Company, a porcelain factory, made ceramics in Sarreguemines, Lorraine, France, from about 1775. Transfer-printed wares and majolica were made in the nineteenth century. The nineteenth-century pieces, most often found today, usually have colorful transfer-printed decorations showing peasants in local costumes.

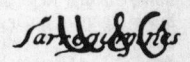

Bank, Figural, Man, With Hat, Cigar, 3 1/2 In. 130.00
Candlestick, Poodle, Top Hat In Mouth, Tail Finger Grip, 6 In., Pair 250.00
Dish, Cover, Basket, Grapes, Green, Red, Purple, Majolica, 6 x 4 In. 200.00
Figurine, Sea Gull, 10 In. 505.00
Humidor, English Gentleman, Top Hat, 7 In. 250.00
Humidor, Face, Chinese Man, 5 1/2 In. 280.00
Jar, Cover, Bear, Figural, 4 1/2 In. 385.00
Jardiniere, Flowers, Swags, Hanging, Impressed, c.1880, 12 3/4 In. 345.00
Jug, Face, French Sailor, 6 In. 90.00
Jug, Face, French Sailor, 8 3/4 In. 45.00
Jug, Face, Jolly Fellow, 8 3/4 In. 95.00
Jug, Face, Judge, 6 1/2 In. 145.00
Jug, Face, Man, Green Hat, Pink Bow, 5 1/2 In. 90.00
Jug, Face, Priest, 5 3/4 In. 90.00
Jug, Face, Puck, 7 In. 110.00
Jug, Face, Scotsman, 8 3/4 In. 45.00
Jug, Face, Sleepy Look, 8 1/2 In. 250.00
Mustard, Tinted Transfer, Fair Scene, Obernais Faienceires, 4 In. .... *Illus* 120.00
Pitcher, Cat, Figural, 8 1/4 In. 200.00
Pitcher, Corn, 7 In. 80.00
Pitcher, Jovial Man, Green Hat, Impressed, c.1890, 8 In. 185.00
Pitcher, Judy, Figural, 12 In. 495.00
Pitcher, Pig, Figural, 9 1/2 In. 280.00
Plate, Dessert, Wise Sayings, Flower Border, 1800s, 7 1/2 In., 8 Piece 170.00
Platter, 3 Dogs Fighting Wolf, Majolica, 24 x 16 In. 1980.00
Platter, Fruit, Round, 11 1/2 In. 110.00
Stein, Repeating Design, Sculpted, Gold Trim, Pottery, Pewter Lid, 1 Liter 345.00
Urn, Campana Shape, Portrait Roundels, Arabesque Trim, Majolica, 23 In., Pair 805.00

Vase, Elephant Handles, Cobalt Blue, 12 1/2 In. 195.00
Vase, Green Crystalline Glaze, Mounted In Classical Ormolu, Stamped, 11 1/2 In. 200.00
Wall Pocket, Figural, Bee, 14 1/2 x 10 In. 112.00

SATIN GLASS is a late-nineteenth-century art glass. It has a dull finish
that is caused by hydrofluoric acid vapor treatment. Satin glass was
made in many colors and sometimes has applied decorations. Satin
glass is also listed by factory name, such as Webb, or in the Mother-of-
Pearl category in this book.

Biscuit Box, Silver Plated Lid & Handle, Enameled, Copper Luster, 6 3/4 x 5 In. 165.00
Bowl, Pink, Ribbed Foot, 8 1/2 In. 30.00
Decanter, Pink, Diamond-Quilted, White Lining, Stopper, 8 1/4 In., Pair 230.00
Pitcher, Opaque Green, Amethyst & Gold Stained Rim, New England, c.1880, 3 3/4 In. . . 395.00
Rose Bowl, Green & Pink Looping, Scalloped, Berry Pontil, Camphor Foot, 5 In. 200.00
Sugar, Opaque Green, Amethyst & Gold Stained Rim, New England, c.1890, 5 1/4 In. . . . 730.00
Vase, Blue, White Lining, Spotted, Ruffled Edge, 11 In. 115.00
Vase, Dark Blue Shaded To Light Blue, Diamond-Quilted, 10 In. 60.00
Vase, Lavender, Diamond-Quilted, 12 1/2 In. 520.00
Vase, Orange Shaded To Opalescent, Diamond-Quilted, Silver Holder, 7 1/2 In. 600.00

SATSUMA is a Japanese pottery with a distinctive creamy beige crackled glaze. Most of the pieces were decorated with blue, red, green,
orange, or gold. Almost all Satsuma found today was made after 1860,
especially during the Meiji Period, 1868–1912. During World War I,
Americans could not buy undecorated European porcelains. Women
who liked to make hand painted porcelains at home began to decorate
plain Satsuma. These pieces are known today as *American Satsuma*.

Bowl, Butterflies, Flowers, Clothing, Kinkozan, Footed, 4 3/4 x 1 3/4 In. 6380.00
Bowl, Center, Asian Scene, Pink Lotus, Black Border, Footed, Handles, 6 1/2 x 14 1/2 In. . . 225.00
Bowl, Circular Reserves, Fish, Sea, Figures, Footed, 4 3/4 x 2 In. 770.00
Bowl, Figures Crossing Bridge, Mount Fuji, Early 1900s, 10 In. 69.00
Bowl, Pheasant, People, Interior Design, Men Doing Tasks, Pheasants, 2 1/2 x 6 In. 480.00
Bowl, White Ground, Molded Decoration, Painted, 6 3/4 x 1 1/2 In., Pair 259.00
Box, Cover, Cobalt Ground, Gilt, Marked Kinkozan, 4 1/4 x 2 In. 1540.00
Box, Cover, Cobalt, Gilt Ground, Cherry Blossoms, 2 Panels, Kinkozan, 2 x 4 1/4 In. 2750.00
Box, Cover, Round, Warriors, 6 In. 69.00
Box, Drum Shape, Children, Japan, 1 1/2 In. 440.00
Box, Round, Woman In Garden, Seikozan, c.1880, 1 1/4 x 2 In. 315.00
Buddha, Hands In Lap, On Lotus Shape Bowl, 6-Sided Base, Blue, Red, Gold, 12 In. 1495.00
Censer, Cylindrical, Figural Design, Dome Cover, Signed, 3 3/4 In. 690.00
Censer, Tripod, Cream Glaze, Kaizan, 4 5/8 In. 259.00
Cup & Saucer, Tree Decoration, Yabu Meizan, 1800s, 6 Sets 315.00
Cup & Saucer, Wisteria, Ho Bird, Flowers, Butterflies, Shimazu Crest, 19th Century, Pair . 635.00
Dish, 2 Overlapping Squares, Woman Watching Fireworks, 1800s, 6 In. 1295.00
Dish, Chrysanthemum Design, Gold & Enamel, Oval, Early 1800s, 5 3/4 In., 4 Piece 375.00
Dish, Square, Gods, Landscape, 3 1/4 In. 1325.00
Group, Shishi & Young, Aubergine & Black Glaze, 7 1/2 In. 405.00
Incense Burner, Cylindrical, Figural, 3 1/4 In. 115.00
Incense Burner, Rectangular, Flowers, Gyozan, c.1900, 5 1/2 x 4 1/4 x 3 1/2 In. 200.00
Jar, Cover, Amphora Shape, Gold Leaf Finial, 12 Panels, Geometric 2800.00
Jar, Cover, Egg Shape, Warrior's Accoutrements, Gosu Blue Sea, c.1860, 5 In. 1095.00
Jar, Cover, Fans, 4 Lugs Resembling Metalwork, 9 1/2 In. 765.00
Jar, Cover, Flowers, Pierced Neck, Signed, Early 20th Century, 11 In. 90.00
Jar, Cover, Money Bag Shape, Rakans, Chinese Scholars, 1800s, 22 In. 295.00
Jar, Cover, People, Gold Trim, c.1900, 10 x 8 In. 50.00
Jar, Globular, Landscape, Lacquer Technique, 2 1/2 In. 380.00
Jar, Hexagonal, Figural, Brocade Ground, Late 1800s, 5 1/2 In. 230.00
Koro, Bulbous, Flowers, Pierced Flower Cover, 4 In. 2830.00
Koro, Cover, Footed, Chrysanthemum, Crackle Glaze, 2 3/4 x 2 In. 715.00
Koro, Cover, Latticed Panels, Dome Shape, Battle Scenes, Landscape, Yokusan, 5 In. 5060.00
Pitcher, Tsuba, 1800s, 4 1/2 In. 58.00
Plate, Cherry Blossoms, Panels, Pigeons, Quails, Landscape, Kinkozan, 1 1/4 x 3 3/8 In. . . 2310.00

Don't soak old ceramic pieces in water for a long time. Old repairs may be loosened.

Satsuma, Powder Box, Cover,
Beetles & Scrolls, Beading,
Gold Details, American, 5 In.

Plate, Maple Tree, Seizan, 7 1/4 In.	40.00
Powder Box, Cover, Beetles & Scrolls, Beading, Gold Details, American, 5 In. ..... *Illus*	195.00
Saucer, Late 19th Century, 5 In., Pair	395.00
Spill, Cylindrical, 3 Footed, Raised Enamel, Quail, Cherry Blossom, 1 1/4 x 3 3/8 In., Pair	1650.00
Tea Set, Teapot, Cups, Creamer, Red, Blue, Green Border, Crackle Glaze, 4 Piece	275.00
Teapot, Scholars In Garden, Chrysanthemum Lid Finial, 1800s, 6 In.	355.00
Temple Jar, Egg Shape, Figural Panels, Dome Cover, 15 1/4 In., Pair	1210.00
Vase, Applied Dragon, Gold, Man Battles Dragon, 9 In.	460.00
Vase, Baluster Shape, Figural, 10 In.	200.00
Vase, Baluster Shape, Figural, 5 1/4 In.	300.00
Vase, Baluster Shape, Flowers, Raised Enamel, Gilt, Early 20th Century, Signed	105.00
Vase, Baluster Shape, Ribbon Handles, Lohan, Late 1800s, 7 1/4 In.	125.00
Vase, Baluster Shape, Square, Figural, 9 3/4 In.	345.00
Vase, Cherry Blossoms Festival, Gilt, Figures, Stand, Kozan, 5 1/4 In, Pair	6100.00
Vase, Cherry Blossoms, Beige & Gray Honeycomb Field, Gilt Borders, 18 In.	300.00
Vase, Cone Shape, Cobalt Ground, Reserve Panels, Landscape, Sozan, 5 3/4 x 7 In.	8250.00
Vase, Cup Shape, Trumpet Mouth, Tradesmen, Yabu Meizan, 3 In.	5290.00
Vase, Cylindrical, Lake, Shrine, Landscape, Kinkozan, 9 1/2 In.	1670.00
Vase, Egg Shape, Flowering Branches, Cobalt Blue Ground, 2 3/4 In.	2480.00
Vase, Egg Shape, Long Neck, Figures In Roundels, Flowers, Clouds, 3 1/2 In.	590.00
Vase, Egg Shape, Samurai Under Flowering Tree, 20th Century, 14 1/2 In.	710.00
Vase, Figural, Cobalt Blue & Gilt Ground, 6-Sided, 5 1/4 In.	300.00
Vase, Figural, Cobalt Blue, Gilt Ground, Taizan, 3 1/2 In., Pair	345.00
Vase, Figural, Dragon, 12 In.	489.00
Vase, Figures, Signed, Dai Nihon Teikoku, 6 In.	460.00
Vase, Globular Shape, Flowers, 1800s, 5 In.	880.00
Vase, Globular Shape, Hundred Arhats, 11 x 11 In.	2705.00
Vase, Hexagonal, Hundred Wisemen, Early 1900s, 10 In.	355.00
Vase, High Relief, Monkey Frieze, Hardwood Stand, 13 1/2 In.	6900.00
Vase, Inverted Pear Shape, Tassel Handles, Relief Figural, 25 In.	345.00
Vase, Jurojin, Nikko Shrine, Early 1900s, 6 1/4 In.	380.00
Vase, Lobated Shape, Tripod Foot, Hundred Wisemen, 7 x 6 In.	529.00
Vase, Male Royal Figures, Gilt, Enamel, 12 x 7 In.	310.00
Vase, Modified Seed Shape, Warriors, 18 1/4 In.	405.00
Vase, Oval Shape, Roosters, Mille Fleur Border, 3 3/4 In.	1060.00
Vase, Pilgrim Flask Shape, Chrysanthemums, Yellow Ground, 9 1/2 In.	80.00
Vase, Roundels, Children & Sages, Flower Borders, 1800s, 6 In.	410.00
Vase, Samurai On Horseback, Dragon, 10 In., Pair	1890.00
Vase, Seed Shape, Figural, Brocade Ground, 9 3/4 In.	170.00
Vase, Seed Shape, Thousand Flower Design, 1900s, 6 In.	69.00
Vase, Seed Shape, Warrior, c.1870, 11 1/2 In., Pair	375.00
Vase, Seed Shape, Women, Cherry Blossoms, Shunzan, 6 In., Pair	345.00
Vase, Shrine, Musicians, Owl, Landscape, Yabu Meizan, 3 In.	2470.00
Vase, Square, Figural, 4 In.	160.00
Vase, Waisted Form, Lohan, Tripod Base, 4 1/2 In.	175.00
Vase, Warriors & Geisha, 4 Panels, 4 1/2 x 4 In., Pair	100.00

SATURDAY EVENING GIRLS, see Paul Revere Pottery category.

SCALES have been made to weigh everything from babies to gold. Collectors search for all types. Most popular are small gold dust scales and special grocery scales.

Balance, Beam, Brass, Iron Ball, Double Hook, W.B. Preston, Patent Feb. 22, 1870, 17 In. ... 100.00
Balance, Brass, Marble, Baluster Form, Early 19th Century, 40 x 34 In. 440.00
Balance, Brass, Weights, Late 19th Century, 60 x 43 x 16 In. 1000.00
Balance, Countertop, Dry Goods, Cast Iron, Chrome, F. Stimpson Co., 23 x 27 x 18 In. ... 112.00
Balance, Dodge Mfg., Yonkers, N.Y., Marble Top, Brass Pan, Micrometer, 14 x 17 In. 175.00
Balance, Fitted Box, Drawer, 17 Weights, c.1900, 13 1/4 x 14 1/8 x 6 In. 1095.00
Balance, Gold, Brass Pans, Iron Beam, Oak Box 90.00
Balance, Jewelry, Mahogany Case, Becker & Sons New York, 19th Century, 15 x 19 In. ... 230.00
Balance, Wrought Iron, Copper Pans, 18th Century, 21 x 18 In. 195.00
Candy, National, c.1900, 2 Lb., 10 In. 660.00
Candy, National, Nickel Base, c.1900, 2 Lb., 10 In. 715.00
Candy, Toledo, Green, Brass Trim, 3 Lb. 440.00
Candy, Toledo, Honest Weight, 14 1/2 In. 155.00
Candy, Wrigley, Spearmint Gum, Brass, 8 1/2 In. 285.00
Counter, Chicago Scale Co., Brass Arm, Pan Stenciled A.I. Root Medina, Oh., 12 In. 35.00
Handheld, Richard Brock, 2 Copper Pans, 5 Brass Weights, Wood Case, London, c.1710 . 1495.00
Hanging, Brass, Steel, Germany 70.00
Micrometer, Dodge Scale Co., Brass, Cast Iron, Marble, 1903 Patent, 15 In. 275.00
Platform, Richmond Scale Co., Red, White, Marble, 16 x 19 x 22 1/2 In. 85.00
Postage, 4 Weights, England, c.1850, 8 1/2 In. 230.00
Postage, Day & Millward, Brass, Brass Weights, Birmingham, c.1900, 8 x 19 x 15 In. ... 920.00
Postage, Eagle & Shield, 7 1/2 In. 65.00
Postage, Howes Patent, Brandon Mfg. Co., Brandon, Vermont, 10 In. 90.00
Produce, Detroit Automatic, To 5 Lb., Detachable Weighing Pan, c.1916, 30 1/2 In. 80.00
Shopkeeper, Angldile, Glass Tray, c.1910, 20 In. 605.00
Shopkeeper, Angldile, Mirror, Open Face, Restored, 21 In. 1006.00
Shopkeeper, Toledo, No Spring, Honest Weight, Milk Glass, Light-Up, 10 Lb., 32 In. 120.00
Shopkeeper, Victorian Style, Cast Iron, 12 Lb., 11 In. 2750.00
Stimpson, Marble Top, Blue Paint, 30 In. 145.00
Weighing, Angldile, Glass Tray, c.1910, 20 In. 605.00
Weighing, Caille Company, Washington, Coin-Operated, Nickel Plated, Mirror, 69 In. 1870.00
Weighing, Coin-Operated, Character Readings, Your Future, Porcelain, Metal, 51 In. 120.00
Weighing, Coin-Operated, Porcelain, Fortunes, Polished Metal, 66 In. 330.00
Weighing, Mills Tru-Weight, Coin-Operated, Porcelain, Purple, Lavender, 46 In. 440.00
Weighing, Rhodes-Hocherim, Lollipop, Weigh Yourself Today?, Blue Enamel, 69 In. 480.00
Weighing, Royal Crown Cola, Coin-Operated, Bottle Shape, Cast Iron Base, 45 In. 1045.00
Weighing, Watling, Coin-Operated, Porcelain, Fortunes, Mirrored Marquee, 64 In. 300.00

SCHAFER & VATER, makers of small ceramic items, are best known for their amusing figurals. The factory was located in Volkstedt-Rudolstadt, Germany, from 1890 to 1962. Some pieces are marked with the crown and R mark, but many are unmarked.

Cigarette Holder, Street Urchin, Wide Mouth, Multicolored, 3 1/4 In. 80.00
Flask, Grinning Black Dandy, Umbrella, Boutonniere, Germany, 8 In. 185.00
Hatpin Holder, Man With Hangover, How Bad I Feel, Multicolored, 4 3/4 In. 80.00
Humidor, Man's Head, Smoking, Pink & Green Glaze, 4 In. 265.00
Match Holder, Boy Thumbs Nose, Big Ears, Clown Outfit, 1880s, 6 In. 120.00
Match Holder, Fallen Woman, Legs In Air, Multicolored, 4 In. 60.00
Pitcher, Chinese Man Holding Goose, Multicolored, 3 3/4 In. ....140.00 to 150.00
Pitcher, Chinese Woman Holding Crane, Multicolored, 3 3/4 In. 85.00
Pitcher, Girl & Milk Pitcher, Blue & White, 4 1/2 In. 60.00
Pitcher, Goat Dressed In Tails & Checkered Pants, Multicolored, 5 3/4 In. 265.00
Pitcher, Little Red Riding Hood, Blue & White, 5 In. 160.00
Pitcher, Mother Goose, Multicolored, 4 In. 160.00
Pitcher, Person, Upturned Umbrella, Multicolored, 5 In. 115.00
Pitcher, Screaming Man, Green Robe, Monkey, Multicolored, 5 3/4 In. 140.00
Pitcher, Screaming Man, Monkey On Back, Multicolored, 3 3/4 In. 170.00
Pitcher, Watering Can, White Roses, Green Ground, Multicolored, 4 In. 60.00
Pitcher, Winged Devil, Multicolored, 3 1/4 In. 115.00

Schafer & Vater, Tea Set, Figural,
Woman's Head, Bisque, Green Stain,
5 3/4-In. Teapot, 3 Piece

Pitcher, Winged Devil, Multicolored, 5 In.		345.00
Pitcher, Wolf As Grandmother, Blue & White, 5 In.		105.00
Pitcher, Woman In Clown Hat, Cape, Fan, Flowers, Multicolored, 4 3/4 In.		200.00
Tea Set, Figural, Woman's Head, Bisque, Green Stain, 5 3/4-In. Teapot, 3 Piece	*Illus*	650.00
Toothpick, Screaming Black Head, Germany, 4 1/2 In.		180.00

SCHNEIDER Glassworks was founded in 1913 at Epinay-sur-Seine, France, by Charles and Ernest Schneider. Art glass was made between 1913 and 1930. The company still produces clear crystal glass. See also the Le Verre Français category.

Schneider

Bowl, Applied Cherries, Bronze Base, c.1950, 8 3/8 x 9 1/2 In.	1175.00
Compote, Amethyst Stem, Mottled Rim, Art Deco, 7 1/2 x 6 1/2 In.	960.00
Goblet, Lavender, Orange, Signed, 7 1/2 In.	500.00
Vase, Amethyst, Applied Yellow Swirls, Handles, Hourglass Shape, Signed, 8 1/4 In.	690.00
Vase, Marbleized, Red, Squat, 9 x 11 In.	315.00
Vase, Orange, Applied Black Rings, Knopped Stem, Spread Foot, 10 In., Pair	1320.00
Vase, Orange, Red, Mottled, Flared Mouth, Footed, 17 1/2 In.	1035.00
Vase, Stick, Bijoux, Tangerine, Red, Ebony Cabochons, Signed, 4 In.	690.00
Vase, Trumpet, Blossoms, Fruit Pods, Purple, Brown, Cream, Orange, Cameo, 10 1/8 In.	690.00
Vase, White, Blue Stripes & Base, Orange Overlay, 10 1/4 In.	4315.00
Vase, Yellow & Lavender Swirl, 3 Applied Ribs, Orange, Signed, 3 1/2 In.	300.00

SCIENTIFIC INSTRUMENTS of all kinds are included in this category. Other categories such as Barometer, Binoculars, Dental, Nautical, Medical, and Thermometer may also price scientific apparatus.

Compass, Gimbal Mounted, Brass, Enamel, Mahogany Box, 5 x 7 x 7 In.	168.00
Compass, Iron Points, 28 In.	200.00
Compass, Kelvin Hughes, Great Britain, Prismatic, Wood Case, 3 7/8 In.	145.00
Compass, Lensatic, U.S. Army, Pouch	60.00
Compass, Magnetic, U.S. Army, Pouch, Folding Design, c.1964	85.00
Compass, Star Pathfinder, Gimbal Mounted, Mahogany Box, 4 1/2 x 5 x 5 In.	190.00
Compass, Surveyor's, James Gale, Salem, 4 Vane, Mahogany, Signed, 14 In.	881.00
Compass, Surveyor's, Scratch-Built, Brass, Wood, Early 19th Century, 3 In.	120.00
Drafting Set, Ivory Handles, Rosewood Box, Velvet Interior, Shelf, 2 x 7 x 4 In.	55.00
Electrostatic & Physical Set, Wimshurts Machine, Ebony Base	560.00
Gyroscope, Sperry, Brooklyn, N.Y., Cast Metal, 6 In.	294.00
Hydrometer, Ronsberg & Son, Manchester, Sikes, Case, 1915, 10 In.	120.00
Hydrometer, T.O. Blake, London, Sikes, Mahogany Case, 2 x 8 x 4 In.	145.00
Magnifying Glass, Gold, Enamel, Round, Late 19th Century, 3 1/8 In.	440.00
Medical, Flemming Battery, Electrical, Mahogany Case, 8 x 9 x 8 In.	110.00
Microscope, Brass, Mahogany Case, 1 Lens, 4 Slides, 8 1/2 In.	230.00
Microscope, E.F. Mahony Co., Boston, Mass., Case	110.00
Microscope, F. Waldstein, Monocular, Brass, Accessories, Case, 19th Century	1400.00
Microscope, Leitz, Revolving 3-Power Turret, 4 Eye Pieces, Case, 13 3/4 In.	518.00
Protractor, Calibrated Instruments, New York, Case, 6 1/4 x 14 1/2 In.	115.00
Protractor, Kern & Co., Aarau Suisse, Nickel Brass, 5 1/8 x 14 1/8 In.	35.00
Protractor, Keuffel & Esser, German Silver, Leather Case, 3 1/4 x 8 1/4 In.	115.00
Semi Circumferentor, S. Brown, Boston, Brass, 1700s, 10 3/4 x 6 In.	1955.00
Share Talon Draw Drum, German Stock Exchange, c.1900, 11 x 9 x 13 In.	730.00
Telegraph Key, J. H. Bunnell & Co., Oak Base Mount, Brass Plaque	340.00
Telescope, 2 Draw, Brass, Wooden Barrel, Civil War Era, 35 In.	290.00

Telescope, 2 Draw, Cherry Tripod, Brass Finial, 1840s, 52 x 3 1/2 In. 2750.00
Telescope, A. Lietz Co., Single Draw, Brass, Officer Of Deck, Germany, 23 1/2 In. 175.00
Telescope, American, Brass, Wood Tripod, Rack & Pinion, 3-1/4 In. Lens 2530.00
Telescope, Bardou & Son, Brass Tripod, Oak, Cast Iron, 39 1/2 x 61 x 49 In. 1960.00
Telescope, Bardou & Son, Paris, Brass, Extension Tube, 61 x 49 In. 1925.00
Telescope, Bardou & Son, Paris, Brass, Tripod, Wood Case 1323.00
Telescope, Brass, 11 3/8 x 2 1/2 In. 165.00
Telescope, Brass, Sliding Lens Cover, 19th Century, 14 To 34 In. 200.00
Telescope, C. Barker, London, Walnut Tripod Base, 52 In. Closed 2990.00
Telescope, Dolland, London, Mahogany Barrel, 4 Sections, 33 In. Open 460.00
Telescope, England, Wood, Brass, 19th Century, 35 In. 165.00
Telescope, England, Woven Barrel Cover, 19th Century, 35 1/2 In. 550.00
Telescope, Keuffel & Esser, N.Y., Single Draw, Brass, Leather, 21 1/2 In. 145.00
Telescope, Ross, London, Single Draw, No. 55548, Nickel, Brass, 23 1/2 In. 69.00
Telescope, Sewill Liverpool, Single Draw, Brass, Marked, 37 1/4 In. 575.00
Telescope, Single Draw, Brass, Wooden Barrel, c.1840, 38 In. 155.00
Telescope, Spencer Browning, Single Draw, Brass, Cord Wrapped, 41 In. 230.00
Telescope, Stanley, London, 3 Draw, 16 In. 225.00
Telescope, Tabletop, Brass, Box, 2 1/2 x 15 x 7 1/2 In. 60.00
Telescope, Union Cavalry, Mahogany Barrel, Leather Case, 1860s, 9 3/4 In. 620.00
Testing Glasses, Optical, Wood Case, Cloth Covered, 75 Lenses 210.00
Transit, W. & L.E. Gurly, Engraved Dial, Brass Case, 16 x 8 x 4 1/2 In. 1380.00
Tripod, Brass, T.B. Winter & Son, Newcastle, 42 x 17 In. 460.00
Weather Station, Chelsea, Brass Case, Walnut Plaque, 4 1/4 x 7 1/4 In. 250.00

SCRIMSHAW is bone or ivory or whale's teeth carved by sailors and others for entertainment during the sailing-ship days. Some scrimshaw was carved as early as 1800. There are modern scrimshanders making pieces today on bone, ivory, or plastic. Other pieces may be found in the Ivory and Nautical categories.

Basket, Sewing, Whalebone, Flowers, Leaves, 6 Side Pieces, 2 1/2 x 3/4 In. 290.00
Basket, Sewing, Whalebone, Wood, 7-Sided, Hearts, 7 1/2 x 4 3/4 In. 3565.00
Bobbin, Whalebone, Table Mount, Screw Knobs, American, 1800s, 4 1/2 In. 230.00
Bodkin, Whale's Tooth, Fist Holding Snake, Black Eyes, 4 In. 635.00
Bodkin, Whale's Tooth, Turned Ring Design, 3 1/4 In. 69.00
Bottle, Weaver At Loom, Inside Bottle, Stopper, Prisoner-Of-War, 1800s, 9 In. 8365.00
Box, Busy Port, Ships, Monogram, Round, 4 x 3 1/4 In. 345.00
Box, Ditty, Panbone, Latticework, Fruit Basket, Oval, Late 1800s, 2 x 3 1/2 x 7 In. 1435.00
Box, Sailing Ship, Stars, Continental, 2 In. 209.00
Box, Whalebone, Mahogany, Swing Handle, Early 20th Century, 10 x 8 x 6 In. 2030.00
Busk, Bone, Patriotic, Opposing Eagle Heads, Crossed Flags, 6 3/4 In. 450.00
Busk, Ship, Tree, Umbrella, Star, Crosses, Polychrome, 1800s, 11 x 1 1/4 In. 805.00
Busk, Whalebone, Baleen, Plant, Hearts, Verse, England, 1800s, 12 1/2 x 1 1/2 In. 259.00
Busk, Whalebone, Bird, Flower, 1800s, 12 1/2 In. 520.00
Busk, Whalebone, Intertwined Hearts, Arrows, Bush, Tree, 12 1/2 x 1 1/2 In. 750.00
Busk, Whalebone, Multicolored Scenes, Ship, Palm Trees, Swan, 12 1/2 x 1 1/4 In. 635.00
Busk, Whalebone, Potted Tree, Colonial House, Star In Circle, 12 3/4 x 1 3/4 In. 520.00
Button Polisher, Bone, King James II, Union Jack, John McKinley, c.1840, 7 1/2 In. 1000.00
Cane, Whalebone, Clenched Fist, Collar, Whale's Tooth Handle, 35 In. 865.00
Cane, Whalebone, Fist Clenching Snake, Whale's Tooth Handle, 34 In. 2530.00
Cane, Whalebone, Narwhal Tusk Handle, L-Shape Handle, 35 In. 1495.00
Cane, Whalebone, Turned Whale's Tooth Handle, Silver Spacer, 34 In. 750.00
Cane, Whalebone, Whale's Tooth, Knob Handle, 1850 Coin, Sweden, 33 In. 980.00
Cane, Whalebone, Woman's Leg Shaped Whale's Tooth Handle, 34 In. 635.00
Club, Whalebone, Turned, Flared Base, Leather Strap, 11 1/2 In. 1725.00
Cribbage Board, Walrus Tusk, Hunting Scenes, Carved Walrus Figures, Inuit, 21 In. 1815.00
Desk Set, Whalebone, Ship's Wheel, Anchor, Pen Holder, c.1960, 4 3/4 x 3 3/4 In. 145.00
Etui, Silver Mounted, Chocolate Tortoiseshell, Edwardian, c.1900, 4 In. 1495.00
Fid, Whalebone, 8 1/2 In. 315.00
Fid, Whalebone, Rope Working, 10 1/2 In. 430.00
Figurine, Man, Broom, Whalebone, Ivory, Japan, 1800s, 7 1/4 In. 230.00
Figurine, Nude Woman, Walrus Tusk, Wood Base, 9 3/4 In. 495.00
Figurine, Whale, Walrus Bone, Alaska, 14 In. 80.00

Fish Hook, Wood Body, Whalebone Point, Baleen Loop, Whale Carving, 8 1/2 In. 865.00
Frame, Walrus Tusk, Inscription 1100.00
Game, Whalebone, Ball In Cup, 1800s, 5 1/2 In. 240.00
Group, Man, 2 Children, Whalebone, Ivory, Japan, 1800s, 9 In. 430.00
Group, Man, Child, Whalebone, Ivory, Japan, 1800s, 6 1/2 In. 230.00
Hairpin, Walrus Ivory, 6 1/2 In. 259.00
Hat Rack, Whalebone, 3 x 17 1/2 In. 750.00
Kerchief Slide, Whalebone, Shield Shape, 2 Stars, US, c.1860s, 1 1/4 x 1 1/4 In. 290.00
Knife, Bowie Type, 8 1/2 In. 105.00
Knife, Whalebone, 10 1/2 In. 150.00
Knitting Needles, Whalebone Shaft, Whale's Tooth Clenched Fist Terminal, 14 1/2 In. 1095.00
Knitting Needles, Whalebone, Whale Ivory, Cutout Star Ends 635.00
Letter Opener, Whalebone, 10 1/2 In. 58.00
Letter Opener, Whalebone, Cutout Hearts, Red Pigment, 5 1/2 In. 60.00
Mallet, Whalebone, Panbone Handle, Ivory Head, Waffle Decoration, 1800s, 8 1/2 In. ... 345.00
Mastodon Tusk, Seal, Ice Flow, Harold Sewall, 14 1/2 x 2 In. 140.00
Ostrich Egg, On Stand, Whaling Scene, Scrollwork Band, Animal Masks, 9 In. 645.00
Ostrich Egg, Ship Under Full Sail, Wood Base, 20th Century, 7 3/8 In. 115.00
Pie Crimper, Bird On Branch, Vining Plant In Vase, c.1875, 6 In. 1725.00
Pie Crimper, Walrus Ivory, 2-Tine Fork, Leaves, Cutout Wheel, 6 7/8 In. 805.00
Pie Crimper, Whale Ivory, Ebony Spacer, Diamond Shape Inlay, 8 In. 1380.00
Pie Crimper, Whale's Tooth, 3-Tine Fork, Metal Wheel Pin, 7 7/8 In. 2130.00
Pie Crimper, Whale's Tooth, 4 Diamond Tortoise Inlay, 3-Tine Fork, 6 1/4 In. 1210.00
Pie Crimper, Whale's Tooth, Seahorse, 5-Point Star Cutting Wheel, 4 3/4 In. 1150.00
Pie Crimper, Whalebone Ivory, 4 1/4 In. 1150.00
Pie Crimper, Whalebone, Fork End, 1800s 255.00
Pie Crimper, Whalebone, Leaf, Flower, Multicolored, New Bedford, Mass., 1800s, 6 In. . 1670.00
Purse, Whalebone, Rosewood, Whaling Scenes, D. Waring, 1880, 3 3/4 x 6 x 7 In. 660.00
Rattle, Whistle, Whalebone, Turned, 2 Metal Bells, Child's, 3 In. 430.00
Scribe, Whalebone, Initial DPW, 18th Century, 8 In. 3300.00
Seal, Whalebone, Engraved Lines, Brass Seal End, 1800s, 3 In. 290.00
Seal Club, Sperm Whale Penis Bone, 23 1/4 In. 230.00
Seam Rubber, Whalebone, 1800s, 5 1/4 In. ....518.00 to 575.00
Sewing Kit, Egg Shape, Whale Ivory, 1800s, 2 1/2 x 1 1/2 In. 460.00
Thread Container, Friction Fit Cover, Thread Hole, Monogram, 1 5/8 x 1 1/4 In. 110.00
Top, Whalebone Handle, Whale Ivory Pull, Wooden Spinner, 7 x 3 1/4 In. 775.00
Trinket Box, Scenes On 4 Sides, Ship, Star, Flowers On Top, 3 7/8 x 2 x 2 In. 4600.00
Vase, Whale's Tooth, Blossom, Buds, Leaves, Wood Base, 7 x 3 1/2 x 9 In. 6040.00
Walrus Tusk, American Eagle, Whaling Scenes, Sailor, Brown Ink, 21 In. 345.00
Walrus Tusk, Artic Scene, Polar Bears, Whale Ships, Walrus, 23 In. 1495.00
Walrus Tusk, Clipper Ship, Whaling Tools, Early 20th Century, 25 1/2 In. 1150.00
Walrus Tusk, Napoleon On Horseback, Woman's Bust, 13 In. 520.00
Walrus Tusk, Woman, Child Playing, Hoop, Stick, 14 In. 950.00
Walrus Tusk Tip, Seal Killer, American Flags, Man's Portrait, Girl, J. Wennom, 8 In. 144.00
Whale's Tooth, 2 Ships Under Sail, Sperm Whale, 6 In. 230.00
Whale's Tooth, 3-Masted Ship 1 Side, Eagle, Shield & Flags Other, c.1825, 6 1/2 In. .. 4900.00
Whale's Tooth, 3-Masted Ship 1 Side, Sperm Whale Other, c.1850, 5 1/2 In. 3450.00
Whale's Tooth, 3-Masted Ship, Female Nude, 1900s, 3 3/4 In. 145.00
Whale's Tooth, 3-Masted Ship, New Bedford, Mass., Mounted, F.D.R., 9 In. 2415.00
Whale's Tooth, 3-Masted Ship, Ribbon Banner, Natchess, c.1868, 5 3/4 In. 405.00
Whale's Tooth, Amorous Couple, Engraved, Multicolored, 1800s, 7 1/2 In., Pair 3100.00
Whale's Tooth, Bell Rock Lighthouse, Seascape, 19th Century, 7 3/4 In. 5380.00
Whale's Tooth, C.W. Morgan, Ship, Fisherman, Signed LL, 6 In. 145.00
Whale's Tooth, Capt. Rodney French, New Bedford, Mass., 1861-1862, 5 In. 865.00
Whale's Tooth, Clipper Ship, 19th Century, 7 1/4 In. 2630.00
Whale's Tooth, Cutting Sections Of Whale, Taken From My First Whale, 1849, 8 In. 1265.00
Whale's Tooth, Eagle, Banner, Shield, Arrows, 21 Stars, Ship, New York Seal, 5 1/2 In. .. 2185.00
Whale's Tooth, Eagle, Flags, Where Liberty Dwells There Is My Home, 4 3/4 In. 2150.00
Whale's Tooth, Elm Tree, American Flag, Eagle, House, Multicolored, 6 In. 920.00
Whale's Tooth, Home Sweet Home, Woman, Church, Ship, 5 3/4 x 2 3/4 In. 489.00
Whale's Tooth, Kelly The Pirate, 5 3/4 In. 2070.00
Whale's Tooth, Landscape, 7 In. 7770.00
Whale's Tooth, Man, Feathered Hat, High Boots, Gloves, Crowned Woman, 5 In. 1035.00

Whale's Tooth, Masted Schooner, Full Sail, Early 19th Century, 5 In. 1093.00
Whale's Tooth, Masted Ship, K. Powers, 4 1/2 In. 480.00
Whale's Tooth, Mermaid Riding Whale, 19th Century, 5 1/4 In. 645.00
Whale's Tooth, Ships, American Flags, 6 In., Pair 11500.00
Whale's Tooth, Shunga, Carved, Open Clamshell, Oriental Woman, Teak Stand, 5 In. 460.00
Whale's Tooth, Sperm Whale, Harpooner, 6 In. 490.00
Whale's Tooth, Spread Wing Eagle, Flag, Ship, 19th Century, 5 In. 7170.00
Whale's Tooth, Whale Stoving Boat, Volcano, Mother, Children, 6 3/4 In. 920.00
Whale's Tooth, Whale, 2 Women, Triptych, 1864, 6 3/4 In. 1035.00
Whale's Tooth, Whaling Scene, 10 Whales, 4 Boats, Ship, Eagle, 6 1/2 x 2 3/4 In. 1725.00
Whale's Tooth, Whaling Scene, 19th Century, 7 In. 8965.00
Whale's Tooth, Whaling Scene, American Eagle, Flags, 1900s, 8 In. 920.00
Whale's Tooth, Whaling Scene, Fortuna, Eagle, Flag, Indian Ocean, 1845, 7 In. 1035.00
Whale's Tooth, Whaling Scene, Ship, 2 Long Boats, 2 Whales, 6 1/2 In. 2185.00
Whale's Tooth, Woman & Branch, Clothing, Young Girl & Rolling Hoop, 5 1/2 In. 690.00
Whale's Tooth, Woman On One Side, Girl On Other, 1800s, 3 3/4 In. 145.00
Whale's Tooth, Woman Sitting At Table, Curtain, c.1850, 6 In. 920.00
Whale's Tooth, Woman, 2 Girls, Rolling Hoop, Jumping Rope, Ship, 7 In. 1555.00
Whale's Tooth, Woman, Carriages, Sailing Ship, Engraved, Multicolored, 1800s, 7 In. ... 5020.00
Whale's Tooth, Woman, Carrying Fruit Basket, Multicolored, 19th Century, 5 In. 1195.00
Whale's Tooth, Woman, Victorian Dress, 1850-1870, 7 3/4 In. 2450.00
Whale's Tooth, Young Woman, Brick Garden Wall, Flower Basket, 4 1/4 In. 1150.00
Whale's Tooth, Young Woman, Victorian Dress, Bouquet, 6 In. 175.00
Yardstick, Whalebone, Length Marks, Initials, 36 In. 460.00

SEG, see Paul Revere Pottery category.

SEVRES porcelain has been made in Sevres, France, since 1769. Many copies of the famous ware have been made. The name originally referred to the works of the Royal Porcelain factory. The name now includes any of the wares made in the town of Sevres, France. The entwined lines with a center letter used as the mark is one of the most forged marks in antiques. Be very careful to identify Sevres by quality, not just by mark.

Bowl, Bronze Mount, Painted, Courting Couple Scene, Loop Handles, 17 5/8 In. 2350.00
Bowl, Louis XVI Style, Flowers, Gilt Bronze Mount, Late 1800s, 8 x 16 x 9 In. 690.00
Bowl, Lovers By River, Flowers, Gilt Scrolls, Blue Ground, Oval, Gilt Handles, 16 In. ... 1265.00
Box, 3 Children, Oval, Brass Frame, Hand Painted, R. Petit, Signed, 10 x 15 In. 3080.00
Bust, Madame De Pompadour, Parian, France, c.1907, 30 1/2 In. 1765.00
Centerpiece, Gilt Bronze, Cherubs, Musical, Late 1800s, 14 x 8 In. 3565.00
Clock, Figural, Girl, Nest Of Birds, Parian Ware, Bronze Base, 10 In. 345.00
Compote, Flowers, Pink Inside, Gilt Banding, 1800s, 6 1/4 x 10 1/2 In. 140.00
Cup & Saucer, Breakfast, King Louis Philippe, Hunting Service, 1845, 3 1/2 x 7 3/8 In. .. 460.00
Cup & Saucer, First Empire, Cabinet, Antique Cameo Decor, Plum, Gilded, c.1800, 8 In. . 1955.00
Cup & Saucer, Jeweled Turquoise, Portrait Of Henri IV, Butterflies, Flowers, Gilt Trim .. 1610.00
Cup & Saucer, Yellow, Floral, Gold Trim, c.1744, 3 1/2 In. .... *Illus* 175.00
Figure, Boar Fighting Hound, Bisque, 10 x 17 In. 2390.00
Figure, Nude Woman Among Cattails, c.1909, 14 In. 518.00
Garniture Set, Chateau De Longpre, Lovers, Green Ground, Gilt, 18 In., 3 Piece ... *Illus* 3450.00

Sevres, Cup & Saucer, Yellow, Floral, Gold Trim,
c.1744, 3 1/2 In.

Sevres, Garniture Set, Chateau De Longpre,
Lovers, Green Ground, Gilt, 18 In., 3 Piece

A two-finger Shaker box really
has three. Two are on the
bottom, one is on the lid.

Sevres, Teapot, Portrait,
Chateau Des Tuileries,
Cobalt Blue, Gilt,
c.1837, 5 1/4 In.

Garniture Set, Clock, Ormolu Mounts, 1800s, 14 & 19 1/2 In., 3 Piece	3795.00
Garniture Set, Porcelain, Ormolu Mounted, Couples, c.1900, 11 & 20 In., 3 Piece	3525.00
Group, Woman & Child, Inscribed, 6 1/4 In.	980.00
Jar, Ormolu Mounts, Women Playing Lyre, Garlands, Musical Motifs, 25 In.	880.00
Plate, Cabinet, Courting Couple, Bleu Celeste Border, c.1900, 9 1/2 In.	175.00
Plate, Multicolored Flowers, Gilt, Paneled Border, Footed Stand, Handle, 8 1/2 In., Pair	2185.00
Plate, Portrait, Woman In Ruff, Marq. De Verneuil, Jeweled, Late 1800s, 9 5/8 In.	1295.00
Plate, Portrait, Woman, Rose Corsage, Mm. De Parabere, Jeweled, Late 1800s, 9 7/8 In.	1116.00
Plate, Wide Cobalt Blue Band, Gilt Floral Sprays, c.1945, 9 3/4 In., 7 Piece	175.00
Sauceboat, Undertray, Gilt, Biscuit, Swan Boat Shape, Oval Dish, 4 x 4 x 6 In., Pair	290.00
Tazza, Louis XVI Style, Gilt Metal Mounted, Late 1800s, 4 x 12 1/2 x 8 In.	200.00
Teapot, Portrait, Chateau Des Tuileries, Cobalt Blue, Gilt, c.1837, 5 1/4 In. .... *Illus*	518.00
Tray, Medallion, Louis XIV, Blue Ground, Square, 12 In.	165.00
Urn, Cover, Classical Scenes, Ormolu Mounted, Late 1800s, 12 In., Pair	2820.00
Urn, Cover, Ormolu Base, Cream, Woman, Cupid, Acorn Finial, A. Collot, 21 1/2 In.	1570.00
Urn, Cover, Ormolu Mounted, Napoleonic, Late 19th Century, 22 1/2 In.	1090.00
Urn, Cover, Ormolu Mounted, Yellow, Enameled, Courting Scene, 25 In., Pair	4995.00
Urn, Maiden, Cherubs, Acanthus Leaf Handles, Pink & Green, Signed, E. Carelle, 23 In.	800.00
Vase, Blue Flambe Crystalline Glaze, Faceted, Flared Floral Rim, Stamped, 6 3/4 In.	175.00
Vase, Cover, Putti In Landscape, Raised Lattice, Amphora Shape, Bronze Base, 7 In.	460.00
Vase, Egg Shape Body, Trumpet Neck & Foot, Gilt Flower Sprigs, Early 1900s, 23 5/8 In.	880.00
Vase, Gilt Flowers, Cobalt Blue Ground, Marked, 7 1/4 In.	230.00
Vase, Louis XVI Style, Gilt Bronze, Blue Body, Late 19th Century, 19 1/2 x 13 x 8 In.	1840.00
Vase, Painted, Courting Couple, Flowers, Pink Ground, Gilt Surrounds, 18 3/4 In.	175.00
Vase, Stick, Orange Flowers, Long Stem, Blue, Cameo, Signed, c.1900, 12 1/2 In.	365.00

SEWER TILE figures were made by workers at the sewer tile and pipe
factories in the Ohio area during the late nineteenth and early twentieth centuries. Figurines, small vases, and cemetery vases were favored.
Often the finished vase was a piece of the original pipe with added
decorations and markings. All types of sewer tile work are now considered folk art by collectors.

Birdhouse, Wire Hanger, Wood Base, 7 1/4 In.	385.00
Doorstop, Lion, Reclining, Hollow Eyes, Ribbed Base, 9 1/2 In.	85.00
Figure, Cat, Seated, Molded, Long Tail, White Clay Eyes, Shiny Glaze, 7 3/4 In.	230.00
Figure, Deer, Reclining, Brown Glaze, 12 1/4 x 11 1/2 In.	1495.00
Figure, Dog, Seated, Free-Standing Front Legs, Hollow Body, Red Brown Glaze, 10 In.	288.00
Figure, Dog, Seated, Hand Tooled Eyes, Punched Holes, Tan Matte Glaze, 9 3/4 In.	230.00
Figure, Dog, Seated, Molded, Hand Tooled Eyelashes, Ohio, 10 In.	81.00
Figure, Dog, Seated, Upturned Head, Watchful Eyes, Curly Coat, Brown Glaze, 10 In.	450.00
Figure, Lion, Roaring, Reclining, Oval Base, Brown Glaze, 14 1/2 x 8 In.	374.00
Figure, Sheep & Lamb, Reclining, On Solid Brick, Goggle Eyes, 8 3/4 x 4 x 7 In.	865.00
Humidor, Seaman, Figural, 13 In.	169.00
Mug, Knife Point Slits, 2 Stars, Oak Leaf, Crosshatched Rim, 4 1/8 In.	259.00
Pedestal, Lion Heads, Raised, Molded Leaves, Brown Glaze, Triangular Base, 28 In.	330.00
Planter, Tree Stump, Applied Letters, 6 In., Pair	316.00
Planter, Tree Trunk, 4 Branches Around Large Center Hole, 27 1/2 In.	340.00
Umbrella Stand, Tree Stump, Snake Wrapped Around Trunk, Brown Glaze, 9 x 21 In.	489.00

SEWING equipment of all types is collected, from sewing birds that held the cloth to tape measures, needle books, and old wooden spools. Sewing machines are included here. Needlework pictures are listed in the Picture category.

Basket, Poodle, Brown Felt, Fitted Interior, Sewing Implements, Round, 11 In.	15.00
Basket, Woven Wicker, Brown Felt Poodle On Lid, Oval, 7 1/2 x 13 x 9 In.	10.00
Bird, Clamp, Brass, Silver Plate Finish, Pincushion Mount, 5 x 4 In., Pair	205.00
Bird, Table Clamp, Brass, 2 Pincushions, 1858 Patent, 5 In.	115.00
Box, Burl, Drawers, Screw Clamp, c.1820, 6 In.	825.00
Box, Chip Carved, Gilt Highlights, Banded, 9 In.	2200.00
Box, Dovetailed, Thread Spools Mounts, 19th Century, 8 1/2 x 9 x 6 3/4 In.	195.00
Box, Faux Bamboo, Chinoiserie Birds, Leaves, Quilted Inside, c.1880, 18 3/4 x 4 3/4 In.	1035.00
Box, Federal, Mahogany Inlay, Dome Top, 2 Inlaid Doors, Lion Pulls, 14 x 14 x 8 In.	5380.00
Box, Hinged Lid, Decoupage, Flower Border, Liner, Footed, Early 1800s, 5 3/8 x 11 In.	999.00
Box, Maple, Pincushion	400.00
Box, Painted, Yellow, Green & Black Leaves, Wood Handle, c.1820, 5 1/2 x 4 x 3 In.	385.00
Box, Roses, Compartments, New England, c.1815	8500.00
Box, Salmon Ground, Red, White, Yellow, Black, Applied Decal, 6 1/2 x 7 x 11 In.	11550.00
Box, Thread, Aunt Lydia's Carpet & Button Thread, 9 1/4 x 3 1/4 x 2 In.	39.00
Box, Thread, Green Paint, Steel Handle, 3 Open Compartments, Drawer, 17 1/2 In.	235.00
Box, Victorian, Faux Bamboo, Lacquered, 34 In.	359.00
Box, Work, Tunbridge, Marquetry Border, Blond Tortoiseshell, Mid 19th Century, 4 x 12 In.	2185.00
Cabinet, Spool, see also Advertising category.	
Cabinet, Spool, Walnut, 6 Drawers, Ruby Glass Inserts, c.1890, 24 x 19 In.	935.00
Caddy, Bird, Wood, Painted, Mottled Green, Platform Base, c.1905, 11 In. .... *Illus*	219.00
Caddy, Tabletop, Wood, Painted, 3 Tiers, Scalloped Feet, 15 x 15 1/2 x 16 In.	1870.00
Chest, Lift Top, 2 Drawers, Dovetailed, c.1870s, 12 In.	400.00
Darner, Curly Maple, 5 1/2 In.	288.00
Hem Gauge, Sterling Silver, Flower Top, Whiting	39.00
Kit, King Coal Trailways, Pack Up All Your Cares & Go, Needles, Buttons, 3 1/2 In.	5.00
Kit, Lydia Pinkham's Vegetable Compound, Metal Tube, Bobbin, Thread, 2 1/4 In.	20.00
Lacemaker's Lamp, Blown Glass, Baluster, Globular Font, Round Foot, Early 1800s, 8 In.	200.00
Lacemaker's Lamp, Brass, Candle, Spring-Loaded, 12 1/2 x 4 1/2 In.	345.00
Lacemaker's Lamp, Clear Glass, Bulbous Shaft, Round Footed Base, 6 In.	200.00
Lacemaker's Lamp, Cut Glass Font, Concentric Ovals, Pressed Glass Foot, 10 In.	400.00
Machine, Jones, England, c.1885	340.00
Machine, Nelson, American Sewing Machine Co., London, c.1900	167.00
Machine, Princess Of Wales, c.1880	703.00
Machine, Secor Fairy, Round Frame & Clamp, Wood Box, c.1885	2468.00
Machine, Spenser, Double Gearing, Boston, Early 20th Century, 10 In.	206.00
Machine, Wilcox & Gibbs, Portable, Wooden Base & Case, c.1885, 13 In.	144.00
Needle Book, A & P, 6 Needle Packets, Threader, Western Germany, 5 3/4 x 4 In.	11.00
Needle Book, Dirigible .... *Illus*	11.50
Needle Book, Food Fair, America's Showplace Food Values, 6 Needle Packets, Threader	8.00
Needle Book, Grand Union, 6 Needle Packets, Threader	8.00
Needle Book, Kenmore, Fine Needle Work, Needle Packet, Sears, Japan	7.00
Needle Book, Liberty National Life Insurance Co., Birmingham, Alabama, Needle Packet	5.00
Needle Book, National Life & Accident Insurance Co., Shield Shape, 2 1/2 x 2 1/2 In.	5.00

Sewing, Caddy, Bird, Wood, Painted, Mottled Green, Platform Base, c.1905, 11 In.

Sewing, Needle Book, Dirigible

Needle Book, Rexall, Make A Point Of Saving At Our Store, Threader, 3 Needle Packets .   15.00
Needle Book, Woolworth, Woolco/Woolworth Building, 6 Needle Packets, Dosco 14.00
Needle Case, Boye, Tin Lithograph, Revolving, 16 In. 120.00
Needle Case, Figural, Woman, Silver, 2-Piece Design 210.00
Needle Case, Silk, Embroidered Tulips, Silver Clasp, Silk Interior, England, c.1750 .....   595.00
Needle Threader, Prudential Has Strength Of Gibraltar, Rock Sketch, Tin 9.00
Notion, Bird, Holds Shears, Thimble, Thread, Pins, Painted, Folk Art, 1910, 11 x 11 In. ..   210.00
Pin Holder, Prudential Insurance, Cardboard, Foam, Mother, Child, Oval, 2 1/2 In. 9.00
Pincushion, Birds & Hearts, 2 Tiers, Leather, Velvet, 19th Century, 6 1/2 x 9 In. 670.00
Pincushion, Black Boy Gambling, Bisque, Hand Painted, Padded Cloth Behind, 3 1/4 In. . .   70.00
Pincushion, Chair Shape, Dark Wood, Victorian, 6 1/2 x 3 x 3 In. 250.00
Pincushion, Clamp On, Basket Shape, Crazy Quilt Top, Wood Base, Brass Clamp, 4 In. ...   169.00
Pincushion, Heart Shape, Embossed Brass Flower Trim, Victorian, 7 1/2 In. 45.00
Pincushion, Leg Shape, Lace Stocking Cover, Red Garter At Top, 12 In. 60.00
Pincushion, N.E. Velvet, Theorum 145.00
Pincushion, Pillow Shape, Victorian, 8 In. 11.00
Pincushion, Rattle, Rooster, 4 3/4 In. 28.00
Pincushion, Strawberry Shape, Victorian, Beaded, Cloth, 3 In. 44.00
Pincushion, Teakettle, Fruitwood Inlay, Bone Finial, Swing Handle, 2 In. 145.00
Pincushion, Tomato Shape, Attached Strawberry, 2 1/2 x 2 1/2 In. 11.00
Pincushion, Walnut, Screw Clamp, Painted, York Co., Pa., 1800s, 4 x 6 In. 935.00
Pincushion Dolls are listed in their own category.
Pincushion Stand, Painted, Carved Ball Feet, c.1880, 4 3/4 x 3 1/4 x 3 In. 5225.00
Pocket, Crewelwork, Purple Silk, 6 Sections, Shadowbox, c.1812, 7 1/2 x 28 In. 3850.00
Pocket, Sampler Stitchery, Pink Silk, 4 Sections, Shadowbox, c.1841, 22 1/2 x 5 1/2 In. ..   6600.00
Rule, Fitometer Tailor's, Boxwood, 3 Adjustable Arms, W.T. Raynor Patent 160.00
Shears, Tailor's, Wilkinson & Son, German Silver 370.00
Spool Cabinets are in the Advertising category under Cabinet, Spool.
Spool Caddy, Mahogany, Banded Inlay, Turned Pedestal, Velvet Pincushion, 7 1/2 In. 127.00
Spool Rack, Drawer, Scrimshaw Elements, c.1850, 8 3/4 x 6 1/4 x 11 In. 2185.00
Tape Measure, Alligator, Scared Black Man's Head In Mouth, Prewar Japan, 6 In. 165.00
Tape Measure, Black Boy Bust With Top Hat, Cast Metal, Germany, 2 1/4 In. 190.00
Tape Measure, Black Boy Head With Cigarette, Celluloid, 1 1/2 In. 150.00
Tape Measure, Black Girl Head, Red Bandana, White Dress, Celluloid, 1 3/4 In. 130.00
Tape Measure, Black Girl With Apple, Red Bandana, White Dress, Celluloid, 2 In. 135.00
Tape Measure, General Electric Refrigerators, Blue, Black, White, Green, 1 1/4 In. 70.00
Tape Measure, H. Borenstein & Sons, Taneytown, Maryland, Cloth, Cardboard Tag, 60 In.   11.00
Tape Measure, H.D. Lee Company, Cloth, Cardboard End, 60 In. 35.00
Tape Measure, Newton Manufacturing, Newton, Iowa, Our 60th Year, 1 1/2 In. 15.00
Tape Measure, Red Kap Uniforms, 60 In. 9.00
Tape Measure, Rye Straw Hat, Paulson Bros., 75 Years On Wood Str., 2 3/4 In. 140.00
Tape Measure, Singing Tower, Florida, Metal, Celluloid, Cloth, Germany, 1930s, 1 1/2 In.   48.00
Tape Measure, Stouffer, Reduce & Keep Fit, Easy Stouffer Home Plan Way, Paper 8.00
Thimble, Aluminum, Navy Enamel Ground, Absolom's Moss Bank Tea, 15/16 x 3/4 In. ...   18.00
Thread Dispenser, 6 Spools, Girl Picking Flowers, Side Openings, 4 3/4 In. 79.00
Yarn Winder, Spoked Wheel, Box Mounted, Tripod Base, 19th Century, 46 In. 80.00

SHAKER items are characterized by simplicity, functionalism, and orderliness. There were many Shaker communities in America from the eighteenth century to the present day. The religious order made furniture, small wooden pieces, and packaged medicines, herbs, and jellies to sell to *outsiders*. Other useful objects were made for use by members of the community. Shaker furniture is listed in this book in the Furniture category.

Abacus, Pine Frame, Cherry Handle, Tin Reinforced Sides, 18 1/4 x 16 1/4 In. 920.00
Apple Peeler, Cherry, Pine, Bench Style, Handled Wheels, c.1850, 12 x 26 In. 635.00
Basket, Apple, Black Ash, Hickory Hoop Handle, Wrapped Rim, N.H., 14 1/2 x 15 3/4 In.   575.00
Basket, Berry, Pierced Wood Panels, Round, Tapered, Tin Rim, 4 5/8 x 6 In. 200.00
Basket, Black Ash, Carved Handles, Double Wrapped Rim, c.1860, 14 1/2 x 22 1/2 In. ..   690.00
Basket, Black Ash, Carved Hoop Handle, Inverted Bottom, c.1850, 13 1/2 x 13 1/2 In. ..   520.00
Basket, Cat Head, Stationary Handle, Double Wrap Rim, New Lebanon, 8 x 6 3/4 In. 7820.00
Basket, Cheese, Black Ash Splint, Hexagonal Base, Round Top, 10 x 21 1/2 In. 460.00
Basket, Drying, Splint, Oblong, Loop Side Handles, Peg Feet, 14 1/2 x 19 1/4 x 26 1/2 In.   200.00

Basket, Fancywork, Black Ash Splint, Tub Form, New Lebanon, c.1860, 7 3/4 x 6 1/4 In.		6900.00
Basket, Fixed Handle, Sliding Lid, New England, 8 In.		90.00
Basket, Gathering, Black Ash Splint, Hickory Hoop Handle, T. Manchester, 15 x 12 In. . . .		1725.00
Basket, Sewing, 3-Finger, Swivel Handle, Copper Tacks, Silk Lining, 6 x 9 x 3 In.		250.00
Basket, Splint, Round, Carved Wood Handles, Domed Base, 15 1/2 x 19 1/2 In.		120.00
Basket, Woven Splint, Round, Single Lashed Wide Rim, 8 1/4 x 25 5/8 In.		705.00
Basket, Woven Splint, Upright Handle, Square Base, Round Rim, Brown Stain, 6 x 5 In. .		590.00
Biscuit Cutter, Chrome Yellow, Domed, Cylindrical, Turned Handle, Canterbury, 4 1/2 In.		230.00
Blanket, Wool, Blue Windowpane Checks, White Ground, 3 Border Stripes, 72 x 82 In. . . .		650.00
Bonnet, Poplarware, Rye Straw, Alternating Light & Dark, Labeled 8, 7 3/4 In.		400.00
Bonnet, Tight Weave, Pleated End, Cloth Rim, Paper Label, Size 6, 9 1/4 In.		105.00
Bonnet, Woven, Pink Pleated Trim, Ribbons, Miniature, 2 x 2 1/4 In.		375.00
Bonnet, Woven, Poplarware, Silk Cowl, Stand, Eldress Bertha Lindsey, Canterbury, 7 In. .		2300.00
Booklet, Declaration, Reasons For Refusing To Aid The Cause Of War, c.1815, 20 Pages .		600.00
Booklet, What Shall I Do To Be A Shaker?, East Canterbury, N.H., c.1885		125.00
Bowl, Black Walnut, Sloping Sides, Carved Handholds, Enfield, Conn., 15 5/8 x 28 In. . . .		440.00
Bowl, Wood, Round, Blue Paint, Shallow, 14 1/2 x 4 In.		499.00
Box, 1/2 Round, Poplarware, Silk Lining, Ribbons, Trademark, Alfred, Me., 3 1/2 In.		320.00
Box, 2-Finger, Lid, Oval, Rosehead Nails, Tacks, 12 In.		290.00
Box, 2-Finger, Lid, Round, Staved, Banded, Teal Blue Paint, 6 x 14 1/2 In.		460.00
Box, 2-Finger, Oval, Blue, Rosehead Nails, 7 x 8 1/2 In.		290.00
Box, 2-Finger, Oval, Cord Sewn, 13 1/4 In.		345.00
•	**Box,** 2-Finger, Oval, Red Paint, 12 3/8 In.		575.00
Box, 2-Finger, Oval, Rosehead Nails, 11 1/2 x 9 In.		489.00
Box, 3-Finger, Lid, Oval, Black Paint, 4 1/2 In.		230.00
Box, 3-Finger, Lid, Oval, Maple, Pine, Cherry, Copper Tacks, 1 3/4 x 4 1/2 In.		3450.00
Box, 3-Finger, Lid, Oval, Maple, Pine, Red, Copper Tacks, MH, 2 3/4 x 5 3/4 In.		1440.00
Box, 3-Finger, Lid, Oval, Natural Finish, 12 x 8 1/4 In.		230.00
Box, 3-Finger, Lid, Pine, Maple, Copper Tacks, 3 3/8 x 8 1/2 In.		345.00
Box, 3-Finger, Lid, Oval, Pine, Maple, Red Paint, Copper Tacks, 1 5/8 x 4 1/2 In.		5750.00
Box, 3-Finger, Lid, Oval, Red Finish, 11 1/4 x 7 1/2 In.		460.00
Box, 3-Finger, Oval, Pine, Yellow Paint, Copper Tacks, 6 x 8 3/4 x 3 1/2 In.		805.00
Box, 4-Finger, Lid, Left-Facing, Oval, Pine Top, Maple, Copper Tacks, 1893, 3 x 6 In. . . .		700.00
Box, 4-Finger, Lid, Oval, Maple, Pine, Natural Finish, E.W., 5 x 13 1/4 In.		1725.00
Box, 4-Finger, Lid, Oval, Pine, Maple, Blue, Copper Tacks, Iron Point, 4 x 10 3/8 In.		2300.00
Box, 5-Finger, Lid, Oval, Brick Red Paint, 13 3/8 In.		3450.00
Box, 5-Finger, Lid, Oval, Ivory Paint, 10 1/2 In.		4140.00
Box, 5-Finger, Lid, Oval, Pine, Maple, Cherry Red Finish, 5 1/2 x 13 1/4 In.		9200.00
Box, Bonnet, Pine, White Ash, Green, New Lebanon, N.Y., c.1845, 12 1/2 x 22 3/4 In. . . .		1265.00
Box, Chamfered Sliding Lid, Red Paint, Compartments, Front Pull, 8 x 11 x 9 1/2 In.		259.00
Box, Chip, Poplar, Hickory Handle, Dovetailed, c.1840		2530.00
Box, Cover, Round, Red Paint, Vertical Seams, Iron Tacks, Turned Knop, 10 x 14 In.		700.00
Box, Document, Tin, Hinged Lid, Turned Handle, 8 x 16 1/2 In.		29.00
Box, Dough, Lift Lid, Pine, Gray, Sabbathday Lake, Me., 13 1/4 x 27 1/4 x 12 In.		805.00
Box, Dough, Red, Tapering Rectangle, Interior Partition, 13 1/4 x 26 1/2 x 15 In.		290.00
Box, Dried Green Sweet Corn, North Family Shakers, Conn., 6 1/4 x 3 1/8 In.		300.00
Box, Hinged Lid, Pine, Dovetailed, Drawer, Canterbury, N.H., 13 x 12 1/2 x 18 1/2 In. . . .		1840.00
Box, Hinged Lid, Rectangle, Dovetailed, Cherry, Enfield, Conn., 6 x 10 1/2 x 7 1/2 In. . . .		560.00
Box, Hinged Lid, Rectangle, Dovetailed, Tiger Maple, Inlaid Diamond, 1878, 14 x 7 In. . . .		705.00
Box, Lid, Oval, Beech, Copper Tacks, Presentation, c.1812		310.00
Box, Lid, Oval, Raised Pierced Handles, Staved Construction, 16 x 22 1/2 x 28 In.		1725.00
Box, Rectangle, Pine, Green Paint, 19th Century, 4 5/8 x 8 3/8 x 5 3/8 In.		325.00
Box, Sewing, 3-Finger, Round, Red, 14 Double Thread Hole Rows, 8 3/4 In.		2070.00
Box, Sewing, 4-Finger, Lid, Oval, Pine, Maple, Swing Handle, 10 x 11 5/8 In.		575.00
Box, Sewing, Cut Corner, Woven Cover, Silk Interior, Contents, Alfred, Me., 6 x 8 1/2 In.		1006.00
Box, Sewing, Maple, Pine, Handle, Copper Tacks, Satin Interior, Contents, 5 1/2 In.		575.00
Box, Sewing, Oval, Swing Handle, Blue Lining, Contents, Sabbathday Lake, 8 1/2 x 6 In.		805.00
Box, Sewing, Presentation, Maple, Cherry, Pine, Contents, Sarah Collins		1955.00
Box, Sewing, Walnut, Gallery Top, 6 Spool Holders, Lower Drawer, 1823, 7 x 6 In.		205.00
Box, Storage, Left-Facing Finger Construction, Green Paint, 6 1/4 In.		290.00
Box, Storage, Lid, Dark Blue, 6 1/2 x 18 1/2 In.		345.00
Box, Work, Hinged Lid, Pine, Red Paint, Yellow Interior, 5 1/2 x 10 x 5 1/2 In.		1380.00
Box Set, 4-Finger, Lid, Oval, Canterbury, N.H., c.1850, 8 3/4, 10 1/4 & 11 1/4 In., 3 Piece		2875.00

Box Set, Nesting, Lid, Oval, Finger Jointed, 3 x 7 x 5 To 2 x 4 x 2 1/2 In., 3 Piece 130.00
Brush, Bent Bristled End, Removable, Turned Wooden Handle 625.00
Brush, Knopped Handle, Cylindrical Tapering Bristles, Velvet Collar, 8 1/4 In. 115.00
Bucket, Lid, Flaring, Swing Handle, Blue, R.A. Cool, Dolgeville, N.Y., 12 x 11 3/4 In. 520.00
Bucket, Pine Staves, Painted, 2 Iron Hoops, Hanger Tab, Enfield, N.H., 9 x 12 In. 440.00
Bucket, Pine Staves, Yellow Paint, 3-Hoop, Tab Hanger, North Family, 11 x 12 In. 235.00
Bucket, Pine, Blue Paint, Wire Bail Handle, Birch Handle, c.1885, 13 x 9 1/2 In. 1725.00
Butter Scale, Maple, Cherry, 23 3/4 In. 800.00
Candle Box, Slide Lid, 3 Finger Slots, Pin, Dovetailed, 6 1/2 x 8 x 16 In. 520.00
Cape, Sister's, Iridescent Silk, Linen, High Collar, Wood Hanger, 17 In. 1035.00
Carrier, 2-Finger, Maple, Pine, Fixed Handle, G. Roberts, c.1930, 7 1/2 x 11 x 14 1/2 In. . 690.00
Carrier, 3-Finger, Oval, Hickory Handle, Copper Tacks, c.1850, 7 1/2 x 9 1/8 In. 2990.00
Carrier, 3-Finger, Oval, Natural Finish, Stationary Handle, 11 In. 690.00
Carrier, 4-Finger, Oval, Cherry, Swing Handle, Silk Lining, 5 1/4 x 7 1/4 In. 460.00
Carrier, Berry Basket, Pine, Hickory Swing Handle, c.1850, 18 1/2 x 8 1/2 In. 1610.00
Carrier, Brother's, Pine, Hickory Hoop Handle, Slots, Dovetailed, 4 x 9 x 18 1/2 In. 575.00
Carrier, Food, Lid, Blue Painted, Swing Handle, Metal Liner, Contents, 9 1/2 x 12 In. 750.00
Carrier, Maple, Satin Lining, Copper Tacks, Stamp, Sabbathday Lake, 11 x 8 x 8 In. 1955.00
Carrier, Pine, Yellow Stain, Dovetailed, Hickory Hoop Handle, c.1840, 11 x 14 x 13 In. .. 800.00
Carrier, Round, Black Ash, Hickory Swing Handle, Nailed, 10 1/2 x 12 1/4 In. 405.00
Carrier, Sewing, 3-Finger, Lid, Satin Lining, Natural Finish, Accessories, 9 3/8 x 6 3/4 In. . 405.00
Carrier, Sewing, 3-Finger, Pine, Maple, Hoop Handle, Contents, 6 1/4 x 6 3/4 x 9 In. 1035.00
Carrier, Sewing, 4-Finger, Lid, Oval, Swing Handle, Fabric Lining, 13 1/2 x 9 1/2 In. 575.00
Carrier, Sewing, Swing Handle, Satin Lining, Contents, Sabbathday Lake, Me., 7 3/4 In. . 460.00
Cheese Container, Lid, Interlaced Fingers, Insert, Albert Howard, 15 1/4 In. 575.00
Churn, Pine Staves, Blue Paint, Pine Dasher, Maple Handle, Alfred, Me., 46 In. 355.00
Cloak, Dorothy, Crimson Wool Broadcloth, Hood, Shawl Collar, Canterbury, N.H. .520.00 to 590.00
Cloak, Sister's, Beige Wool, Silk Ribbon & Hood Lining, E. Canterbury, N.H., 57 In. 1035.00
Cloak, Sister's, Red Wool, Silk Ribbon & Hood Lining, Sabbathday Lake, Me., 60 In. 1150.00
Cloak, Wool, Navy Blue, Silk Lining, Satin Sashes, Bonnet, Sabbathday Lake, Me. 590.00
Coat Hanger, Double, 2 Horizontal Bars, Rounded Ends, Red, 11 1/2 x 14 In. 635.00
Cobbler's Hammer, 6 3/4 In. 145.00
Comb, Shampoo, Wood, Cylindrical, Sawtooth Edge, 2 In. 35.00
Cream Skimmer, Wood, Carved, Sabbathday Lake, Me., 19th Century, 6 1/4 In. 265.00
Dipper, Maple, Pine, Turned Handle, Copper Nails, DM, New Lebanon, c.1855, 6 x 9 In. . 2990.00
Dipper, Tiger Maple, Carved, Turned, 2 1/4 x 4 3/4 x 3 1/4 In. 1150.00
Doll's Bonnet, Woven Palm Leaf, Green Silk Bow, 4 3/4 In. 115.00
Doll's Cloak, Dorothy, Hood, Cape, Camel Wool, Ribbon Tie, Mount Lebanon, N.Y. 85.00
Drying Board, Flannel, Red Paint, 2 Pivoting Arms, Breadboard Ends, 44 x 22 1/2 In. ... 575.00
Drying Rack, Folding, Wall, 2 Horizontal Struts, Mount Lebanon, 29 1/4 x 34 1/4 In. 460.00
Drying Rack, Revolving, Folding, Pine, V-Form Legs, Watervliet, N.Y., 58 x 42 x 25 In. .. 520.00
Duster, Red Wool, Turned Maple Handle, Incised Lines, 13 1/2 In. 120.00
Dustpan, Tin, Flowers, Turned Wooden Handle, 16 1/2 In. 750.00
Embroidery Hoop, Maple, Adjustable Shaft, Screw-On Table Clamp, 14 1/2 In. 705.00
Foot Warmer, Cherry, Walnut, Tin Ember Carrier, Slide Front, Bail Handle, 5 3/4 x 9 In. . 690.00
Funnel Mold, Tin, Cherry, 8 Parts, Leather Strap, Brass Tacks, Enfield, N.H., 8 x 3 1/2 In. 635.00
Grinder, Herb, Cast Iron, Boat-Shaped, Turned Maple Handles, Incised Lines, 7 x 15 In. . 470.00
Handkerchief, White Linen, Rolled Edges, Cross-Stitched TD, 19 1/2 In. 175.00
Hanger, Curved, Chamfered Edges, Enfield, N.H., 18 1/4 In. 80.00
Hanger, Double, Pine, 2 Graduated Bars, Peg Hole, 11 x 14 In. 460.00
Hanger, Red, Incised Initials, 16 1/2 In. 430.00
Label, Apple Jelly, North Family, Society Of Shakers, Mt. Lebanon, N.Y., 2 1/2 x 1 In. ... 40.00
Label, Can, Pulverized Summer Savory, Bogle & Lyles, 7 1/2 x 2 1/8 In. 120.00
Label, Canning Fruit, Fresh Apples, Wrap-Around, D.C. Brainard & Co. 1750.00
Label, Crabapple Jelly, Society Of Shakers, Mt. Lebanon, N.Y., 2 1/2 x 1 In. 40.00
Label, Parlor Broom, Thomas Estes, New Lebanon, N.Y., 1 1/2 x 3 In. 65.00
Ladder, Blue Paint, 15 Rungs, Chamfered Pegs, Old Chatham, N.Y., 20 Ft. 400.00
Measure, Maple, Pine, Yellow Wash, Copper Nail, Canterbury, N.H., c.1850, 3 x 4 1/2 In. 1840.00
Measuring Stick, Tailor's Counter, Handwritten Ink Numerals, 36 In. 575.00
Mirror, Shaving, Swivels, Wooden Trestle Stand, T. Fisher, 1869, 10 x 9 x 5 In. 1175.00
Mitten Block, Red, Inscription, Pierced For Hanging, 13 1/4 In. 230.00
Neckerchief, Silk, Iridescent Purple, 2 Triangular Pieces, Frame, 31 x 30 In. 1035.00
Neckerchief, Silk, Saffron Yellow, Tie-Dye Dot Design, Frame, 33 x 38 In. 1380.00

Pail, Applesauce, Pine, Turned Lid, Inset Knob, Canted Sides, Steel Bands, 9 x 8 In. 690.00
Pail, Tapered, Wood Swing Handle, Painted Metal Bands, 6 x 7 In. 275.00
Pegboard, Dark Red Paint, 12 Pegs, 97 In. 460.00
Pegboard, Red Paint, 3 Pegs, 28 In. 115.00
Pegboard, Red Paint, 3 Pegs, 31 In. 90.00
Pegboard, Red Paint, 4 Pegs, 38 In. 345.00
Pegboard, Wall Mounted, Old Brown Stain, 54 In. 55.00
Picnic Basket, 2 Hinged Lids, Woven, Oblong, Stationary Handle, 10 1/2 x 14 3/4 In.. .... 60.00
Picnic Basket, Attached Lid, 2 Swing Handles, Concentric Square Designs, 10 3/4 In. ... 115.00
Pincushion, Adjustable, Butternut Turnings, Screws, Tabletop, 9 In. 405.00
Pincushion, Oval, Clamp, Maple, Yellow, Thumbscrew, Wool, Hancock, c.1870, 6 1/4 In.. . 750.00
Pincushion, Tomato, Maple Spool Stand, Green Fabric, 6 1/2 In. 290.00
Pincushion, Turned Maple Shaft, Round Cherry Base, 6 Metal Spool Holders, 6 In. 190.00
Rolling Pin, Birch, Canterbury, N.H., 34 1/2 In. 920.00
Rug, Hooked, Multicolored Diamonds Radiating, 8-Point Star, Wool, Round, 79 In. 5875.00
Rug, Rag, Geometrics, Blue, Gray, Natural, 25 x 50 In. 230.00
Rug, Rag, Woven, Stripes, Green, Red, Natural, Runner, 41 x 71 In. 230.00
Rug Beater, Wood, Salmon Paint, Signed, Shaker 0, 40 In. 325.00
Scarf, Sister's, Linen, Checkered, 4 Stripes, 22 x 21 In. 230.00
Scarf, Sister's, Linen, Windowpane Pattern, 2 Stripe Border, 23 1/2 x 24 1/2 In. 575.00
School Box, Slate Board, c.1877, 7 1/4 x 10 1/4 In. 345.00
Scoop, Apple Butter, Wood, Yellow Paint, Pierced Handle, 6 5/8 x 11 5/8 In. 206.00
Scoop, Cherry, Carved, Boat Shape, Pierced Half Moon Handle, Enfield, Conn., 4 x 10 In. 825.00
Scoop, Chrome Yellow, Curved, Chamfered Handle, 9 In. 1150.00
Seed Bag, Beet Early Blood Turnip, D.M. From The Shakers Gardens, 8 3/4 x 5 1/2 In. .. 85.00
Seed Bag, Shaker Seeds, Blue Imperial Peas, West Pittsfield, Mass., 4 1/2 x 5 1/2 In. 150.00
Seed Bag, Shakers' Yellow Onion, N.F., New Lebanon, N.Y., 7 3/4 x 5 In. 150.00
Sewing Kit, Leather Shoe, Silk Ribbon, Thimble, Scissors, Pincushion, Canterbury, 5 In. . 750.00
Shawl, Gray Wool, Striped Border, Fringed Edge, Child's, 42 x 42 In. 290.00
Shawl, Wool, Sister Mercy Howard, Fringe, Natural Border, Watervliet, N.Y., 64 x 62 In. . 400.00
Shovel, Maple, Grain Painted, Red, Open Handle, 36 In. 529.00
Sieve, Bean, Woven Ash, Oak Rim, Copper Tacks, New Lebanon, N.Y., c.1845, 19 In. 230.00
Sign, Shaker Tamar Laxative, West Gloucester, Me., 11 x 9 In. 1210.00
Spinning Wheel, Flax, Maple, c.1840, 19 x 39 In. 325.00
Spinning Wheel, Maple, Birch, Oak, Wool, FW, Watervliet, N.Y., c.1830, 48 x 54 In. 805.00
Spinning Wheel, Red Paint, Tripod Raked Legs, 60 x 48 In. 460.00
Spool, Maple, Hourglass Shape, Salmon Paint, 3 1/8 x 2 In. 235.00
Spool Holder, Birch, Pegged, Mortised, Canterbury, N.H., c.1840, 18 1/2 x 13 x 12 In. ... 460.00
Spool Holder, Pincushion, Maple, 5 Brass Pins, Sabbathday Lake, Me. 690.00
Spool Holder, Walnut, 5 Brass Pins, Walnut, S. Maria L., Enfield, Conn., c.1850, 10 In. .. 920.00
Swift, Tabletop, Maple, Thumbscrew, Hancock, Mass., c.1880, 25 In. 230.00
Swift, Tabletop, Screw Device In Base, Beehive Form Turning, 31 In. 345.00
Tailoring Rule, Cherry, Hand Stamped Numerals, Canterbury, N.H., 60 In. 1150.00
Tool Box, Yellow Paint, 30 Woodworking Tools, Leather Straps, 24 x 17 x 24 In. ...,..... 1150.00
Towel Rack, Folding, 2 Bars, Trestle Ends, Shoe Feet, 36 x 25 1/2 In. 345.00
Tray, Rectangle, Cherry, Applied Molding, Mt. Lebanon, N.Y., c.1840, 16 x 22 In. 700.00
Tray, Rectangle, Pine, Raised Sides, 2 Pierced Oval Handles, 4 3/8 x 14 5/8 x 21 In. 200.00
Winnower, Diamond Form, Collapsible, Meredith, N.H., 35 x 12 In. 345.00
Writing Board, Red, Breadboard Ends, 20 1/2 x 14 1/4 In. 230.00
Yarn Winder, 2 Cherry Spools, Iron Spokes, Adjustable Arm, 21 1/4 x 14 1/2 x 6 1/2 In. . 800.00
Yarn Winder, Birch, Oak, Flame Birch, Clock Wheel, Canterbury, N.H., c.1830, 42 In. ... 635.00
Yarn Winder, Cherry, Squirrel Cage Style, Thumbscrew, 42 x 13 3/4 In. 920.00
Yarn Winder, Folding, X-Form, Pullout Extensions, Tabletop, 16 In. 290.00

SHAVING MUGS were popular from 1860 to 1900. Many types were
made, including occupational mugs featuring pictures of men's jobs.
There were scuttle mugs, silver-plated mugs, glass-lined mugs, and
others.

2 Ducks, Grass & Water Background, China, Hand Painted, 3 5/8 x 3 5/8 In. 110.00
Automobile, D.R. Sollenberger, Bavaria, Signed Phil Eisemann 1925.00
Bicycle, Ed. Yowse, T & V, France 935.00
Duck Hunting, Hunter In Boat Shooting Duck, 3 1/2 x 3 1/2 In. 300.00
Fisherman, Fishing Rod, Fish, Gun, Lake, Boat, V/D Austria, 3 5/8 x 3 5/8 In. 145.00

Fraternal, P.O.S. Of A., Patriotic Order Sons Of American, Signed Ph. Eisemann 27.00
Fraternal, Shriner's Emblem, Egyptian Head Inside Horn, A.F.W., 3 3/8 In. 100.00
Horses, In Cartouche, Transfer, Hand Painted, 3 7/8 In. . . . . *Illus*   35.00
Hunter, 2 Dogs On Point, J.M. Garwood, 1890-1925, 3 3/4 In. 335.00
Hunter, Dog In Boat, Hunting Ducks, Frank Kithcart, 3 3/4 In. 260.00
Majolica, Wheat, Flowers, Ribbon & Bow, 3 1/2 In. 145.00
Man, Riding Horse, Over Bridge To Cottage, H.D. Carter, 4 1/8 In. 78.00
Man & Woman On Road, Cottage & Windmill, J.A. Cleveland, 3 5/8 In. 100.00
Occupational, 2 Hats & Boot, C.A. Buckholtz, 1890-1925, 4 1/8 In. 160.00
Occupational, Anvil & Hammer, Gold Wreath, Pink Roses, E.H. Wetzel, 4 In. 110.00
Occupational, Artist, Paint Pallet, John P. Wachler, 1890-1925, 3 5/8 In. 225.00
Occupational, Automobile Mechanic, M.H. Griest, Signed F.B. 3300.00
Occupational, Barber, Shop, John Schmidt, 1890-1910, 3 5/8 In. 1790.00
Occupational, Bartender, Fernand Emenes, T & V 140.00
Occupational, Beekeeper, Beehive Skep, Wm. T. Bennett, Germany 1540.00
Occupational, Blacksmith, Shoeing Horse, G.B. Crosley, 3 7/8 In.   505.00
Occupational, Blacksmith, Shoeing Horse, S.D. Canfield 275.00
Occupational, Butcher Tools, A.A. Brooks, 3 5/8 In. 179.00
Occupational, Caboose, Leslie A Gadd, 3 7/8 In. 615.00
Occupational, Carpenter, Saw 350.00
Occupational, Chicken, 12 Baby Chicks, Roy M. Wentling, 3 5/8 In. 1000.00
Occupational, Coal Delivery Wagon, D. Donte, T & V Limoges, France 440.00
Occupational, Conductor, Trolley Car, B.W. Bickley, G.B.S. Co., Felda China, Germany .   1210.00
Occupational, Cowboy, Roping Steer, Ed Sefried, 4 In. 1064.00
Occupational, Engineer, Railroad Engine, H.M. Richards, 3 3/4 In. 280.00
Occupational, Engineer, Stationary Engine, R.O. Healy, 3 7/8 In.   390.00
Occupational, Express Wagon, Horse Drawn, Hand Painted, 4 3 3/4 In. 440.00
Occupational, Farmer, Plowing Field, 2-Horse Team, CA Smith Barber Supplies 600.00
Occupational, Fire Engine, Horse Drawn Pumper, Rainbow No. 1, Frederick Baer 1500.00
Occupational, Fire Engine, Steam, Pulled By 2 Horses, Samuel S. Shive, 3 5/8 In. 950.00
Occupational, Hand, Holding Pen, Felda China, Germany, SS, 1930, 1890-1925 . . . .   160.00
Occupational, Hand, Operating Telegraph Key, T.G. McMohan, 1890-1925, 3 1/2 In. 670.00
Occupational, Horse Track, F. Bridgwater, 1890-1925 . . . .   670.00
Occupational, Horse Track, W.G. & Co., Limoges, France, 1890-1925, 3 7/8 In. 335.00
Occupational, Ice Dealer, Palmer's, T&V, France, 3 1/2 x 3 1/2 In. 910.00
Occupational, Lawyer, Alfonso Manfredi, Anchor Pottery, 1925 . . . .   3080.00
Occupational, Livery Stable, J.G. Glick, 1890-1925, 4 In. 450.00
Occupational, Livery Stable, P.A. Mathews, 1890-1925, 3 5/8 In.   530.00
Occupational, Man, Driving Horse Drawn Wagon & Bricks, Chas Kobler, 4 In. 615.00
Occupational, Man, Driving Horse Drawn Wagon, George Hunkely, 3 5/8 In. 950.00
Occupational, Man, Driving Touring Car, George Stiefuater, 3 5/8 In. 1230.00
Occupational, Man, Driving Touring Car, Vincent H. Tallorico, 1890-1925, 3 7/8 In. 560.00
Occupational, Man, Driving Touring Car, W.M. Smith, 3 5/8 In. 1000.00
Occupational, Man, Horse Drawn Bus, James McCarthy, 1890-1925, 3 3/8 In. 2800.00
Occupational, Man, Waiting On Woman, General Store, Harry Maltby, 3 3/4 In. 785.00
Occupational, Milkman, Horse Drawn Delivery Wagon, Wm. C. Hughes, 3 3/4 In. 195.00
Occupational, Miner, Holding Pickax, J.G. Hutchinson, 1890-1925, 3 5/8 In. 1790.00
Occupational, Mortar & Pestle, J.H. Garret, 1890-1925, 3 1/2 In.   200.00

Shaving Mug, Horses,
In Cartouche, Transfer,
Hand Painted, 3 7/8 In.

Shawnee, Cookie Jar,
Winnie, Pink & Blue
Flowers, Clover Bud,
Gold Trim

Occupational, Oil Derrick, H.W. Odell, 3 1/2 In. 200.00
Occupational, Painters Pallet, Chas F. Spathelf, 1890-1925, 3 5/8 In. 160.00
Occupational, Rabbit Hunting, Rabbits, Hunter, Snow, 3 1/2 x 3 5/8 In. 130.00
Occupational, Railroad Parlor Car, James Ryan, 1890-1925, 3 7/8 In. 215.00
Occupational, Restaurant, Patrons, Waiters, Bartender, G. Wilkes, 3 3/4 In. 2350.00
Occupational, Shoe Salesman, Aug. 5, 1905, Chas. Dillingham, 3 3/4 In. 785.00
Occupational, Soda Fountain, Clerk, Woman, Germany, 3 3/4 x 3 5/8 In. 2750.00
Occupational, Steam Tractor, Men Working, John White, 3 7/8 In. 2800.00
Occupational, Tailor, J.B. Coats, Elpco China 385.00
Occupational, Textiles Merchant, W.O. Chichester, A Kern B.S. Co., St. Louis 605.00
Occupational, Tinsmith, W. Macaulay, T & V Limoges, France 410.00
Occupational, Trolley On Tracks, Horse Drawn, Conductor On Rear Deck 500.00
Occupational, Tugboat, J. Green, 1890-1925 . . . . 900.00
Occupational, Undertaker, Horse Drawn Hearse, 1890-1925, 3 7/8 In. 215.00
Occupational, Wagon, Flour Sacks, Barrels 475.00
Occupational, Woman In Military Type Jacket, Standing, Ervin M. Davis, 3 5/8 In. 1065.00
Occupational, Woodworker, Cabinetmaker, J.E. Weidman, D & Co. 660.00
Patriotic, Eagle With Spread Wings On Rock, Wm. Schaefer, 3 3/4 In. 135.00
Pierrot, Silver Moon, Stringed Instrument, Limoges, 1/2 x 3 3/4 In. 130.00
Winter Scene, Horse Drawn Sleigh, Hand Colored Transfer, 3 1/2 x 3 5/8 In. 120.00

SHAWNEE POTTERY was started in Zanesville, Ohio, in 1937. The company made vases, novelty ware, flowerpots, planters, lamps, and cookie jars. Three dinnerware lines were made: Corn, Lobster Ware, and Valencia (a solid color line). White Corn pattern utility pieces were made in 1945. Corn King was made from 1946 to 1954; Corn Queen, with darker green leaves and lighter colored corn, from 1954 to 1961. Shawnee produced pottery for George Rumrill during the late 1930s. The company closed in 1961.

Bowl, Corn King, 5 In. 26.00
Cookie Jar, Winnie, Pink & Blue Flowers, Clover Bud, Gold Trim . . . . *Illus* 1200.00
Creamer, Corn King, 6 In. 15.00
Creamer, Puss 'n Boots, 4 3/4 In. 31.00
Cup & Saucer, Corn King . . . . .19.00 to 23.00
Cup & Saucer, Corn Queen 21.00
Pitcher, Corn King, No. 70 . . . . 52.00
Planter, Blow Fish, Pink, 3 1/2 In. 37.00
Planter, Dog On 3-Button Shoe, White, 4 1/2 x 8 In. 6.00
Planter, Dutch Boy & Girl At Wishing Well, 5 1/2 x 8 In. 10.00
Planter, Parrot, Brown, Cream, 4 x 3 1/2 In. 4.00
Planter, Smiling Pig, Pink Trim, 3 x 4 1/2 In. 12.00
Platter, Corn King, 8 1/2 x 6 1/2 In. 21.00
Platter, Corn King, 11 3/4 x 8 1/4 In. 20.00
Salt & Pepper, Corn King, 5 In. 17.00
Salt & Pepper, Fruit, 3 5/8 In. 6.00
Salt & Pepper, Jack & Jill, Gold Trim, 5 1/4 In. 250.00
Salt & Pepper, Puss 'n Boots, 3 1/2 In. 36.00
Salt & Pepper, Puss 'n Boots, Gold Trim, 3 1/2 In. 79.00
Salt & Pepper, Smiley & Winnie Pig, 3 In. 40.00
Salt & Pepper, Smiley Pig, 5 In. 90.00
Salt & Pepper, Tappan, Souvenir Of Atkinson, Nebr., 3 1/4 In. 85.00
Sugar & Creamer, Corn Queen 23.00
Teapot, Granny Ann, Head & Shoulders Cover 19.00
Teapot, Rose, Green Leaves, 6 1/2 In. 11.00
Teapot, Yellow Snowflake, 5 In. 26.00

SHEARWATER pottery is a family business started by Mr. and Mrs. G. W. Anderson, Sr., and their three sons. The local Ocean Springs, Mississippi, clays were used to make the wares in the 1930s. The company is still in business.

Beaker, Thunderstorm, Clouds, Rain, White Ground Underglaze, 4 1/2 In., Pair 3165.00
Bowl, Birds, Waves, Flared, White Ground, Blue Interior, 2 3/4 x 8 In. 3450.00
Plate, Blackbird, Joined Legs, Clouds, Waves, White Ground Underglaze, 6 In. 1840.00

Plate, Pelican, Black, Blue, White, Wave Border, 10 1/8 In. 4900.00
Vase, Baluster, Turquoise Glaze, c.1930, 11 1/4 In. 175.00
Vase, Sea, Earth, Sky, Molded, Metallic Brown Glaze, 11 3/4 In. 9200.00

SHEET MUSIC from the past centuries is now collected. The favorites
are examples with covers featuring artistic or historic pictures. Early
sheet music covers were lithographed, but by the 1900s photographic
reproductions were used. The early music was larger than more recent
sheets, and you must watch out for examples that were trimmed to fit
in a twentieth-century piano bench.

Ac-Cent-Tchu-Ate The Positive, Mercer & Arlen, E.H. Morris, N.Y., 1944, 4 Pages 7.00
Alabama Slide, Dancing Couple, Large Format, 1915 .... 30.00
Amazons, Billie Burke, Large Format, 1913 .... 38.00
Anchors Aweigh, C.A. Zimmerman, Robbins Music, N.Y., 1942, 2 Pages 7.00
Au Revoir, But Not Good-Bye, Brown & Von Tilzer, Broadway Music, 1917, 2 Pages 7.00
Back O'Town Blues, Steamboat, 1923 .... 25.00
Barney Google Fox Trot, Barney Rides Spark Plug, Rose & Conrad, J.H. Remick 35.00
Carolina Fox Trot, Couple In Fox Hats, Fox, Large Format, 1914 .... 33.00
Come Take A Dip In The Deep With Me, Annette Kellerman, Large Format, 1909 ...... 30.00
Daddy Boy, Art Cover, 1923 .... 40.00
Death Comes At Dawn, San Francisco Earthquake, Jennie H. Bragdon 40.00
Djer Kiss Waltz, Girl In Rose Garden, Swing, Parrish, c.1925, 13 3/4 x 10 1/2 In. 300.00
Don't Fence Me In, C. Porter, Hollywood Canteen, Harms, N.Y., 1944, 2 Pages 6.00
Fiddle Sticks, Cherubs Playing Violins, Large Format, 1910 .... 55.00
Fire Drill, March 2 Step, Harry J. Lincoln, Frame, 14 x 11 In. 15.00
Have Yourself A Merry Little Christmas, Judy Garland, 1944 .... 50.00
He's So Good To Me, Woman Pinching Man's Cheeks, Large Format, 1913 .... 120.00
Hesitating Blues, Louis Armstrong, 1942 .... 30.00
High Stepper, Woman On Horse, Large Format, 1917 .... 79.00
Hitchy-Koo, Raymond Hitchcock Caricature, Large Format, c.1918 .... 35.00
I Dreamt I Dwelt In Harlem, Glenn Miller, 1941 .... 28.00
I'm All Out Of Breath, Notes On Staff, 1937 .... 36.00
If You Don't Want My Peaches, You Better Stop Shaking The Tree, Large Format, 1914 . 118.00
Indian Chief Tecumseh, Large Format, 1906 .... 45.00
John Dillinger, Forrest Herbert, Poland, Indiana, 13 Verses, 1934 .... 75.00
Keep Away From The Fellow Who Owns An Automobile, Large Format, 1912 .... 35.00
Liberty Loan March, People By Statue Of Liberty, Large Format, 1918 .... 28.00
Mid Flame & Smoke, Burning Of Brooklyn Theatre, 1876 .... 50.00
NC-4 March, Commander A.C. Read, USN, F.E. Bigelow, 1919 .... 40.00
Neptune Polka, Neptune Engine Co. No. 6, Detroit, 1858 .... 85.00
Over There, Cohan & Feist, James Cagney, Yankee Doodle Dandy, 1942, 3 Pages 8.00
Paper Doll, J. Black, Frank Sinatra Cover, E.B. Marks Music, N.Y., 1942, 2 Pages 8.00
Race Horse Rag, Jockeys, Horses, Large Format, 1911 .... 60.00
Return Of The Victor, Dewey 90.00
Sing Birdie Sing, Colored Lithograph, S. Brainard & Co., Cleveland, Frame .... *Illus* 85.00
Sleepy Hollow Rag, Trees, Large Format, 1918 .... 55.00
Tango Tea, People Dancing, Large Format, 1913 .... 33.00
Tie A Yellow Ribbon Round Ole Oak Tree, I. Levine, R. Brown, 1972, 4 Pages 7.00
Wasn't It Yesterday, Trees, Nora Bayes, Irving Fisher, Large Format, 1917 .... 55.00
Whirl Of The World, Ragtime Of Arabian Nights, Large Format, 1914 .... 35.00

SHEFFIELD items are listed in the Silver Plate and Silver-English categories.

SHELLEY first appeared on English ceramics about 1912. The Foley
China Works started in England in 1860. Joseph Ball Shelley joined
the company in 1862 and became a partner in 1872. Percy Shelley
joined the firm in 1881. The company went through a series of name
changes, and in 1910 the then Foley China Company became Shelley
China. In 1929 it became Shelley Potteries. The company was
acquired in 1966 by Allied English Potteries, then merged with the
Doulton group in 1971. The name *Shelley* was put into use again in
1980. A trio is the name for a cup, saucer, and cake plate set.

Bowl, Moire Antique, Open Handles, Scalloped Gold Rim, 9 3/4 In. 163.00
Cake Plate, Maytime, Chintz, Center Metal Handle, 8 1/4 In. 110.00

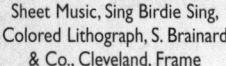

Sheet Music, Sing Birdie Sing,
Colored Lithograph, S. Brainard
& Co., Cleveland, Frame

Shirley Temple, Doll,
Ideal, Composition,
Hazel Sleep Eyes, 6
Teeth, Curly Top, 17 In.

Shirley Temple, Doll,
Ideal, Vinyl, Hazel
Sleep Eyes, 6 Teeth,
1957, 36 In.

Cake Plate, Queen Anne Cottage, Square, Rounded Corners, Tab Handles, 9 1/2 In.	110.00
Cake Plate, Red Poppy, No. 11326, Tab Handles, 8 x 9 1/2 In.	75.00
Cup & Saucer, Harebell	140.00
Cup & Saucer, Primrose, Dainty	195.00
Cup & Saucer, Queen Anne Cottage	98.00
Cup & Saucer, Rock Garden, Footed Oleander, c.1940	260.00
Cup & Saucer, Summer Glory, Footed Oleander	225.00
Cup & Saucer, Sunrise & Tall Trees, Queen Anne	195.00
Cup & Saucer, Thistle, No. 13820	135.00
Cup & Saucer, Violets, No. 13821	90.00
Eggcup, Rosebud, 2 1/2 In.	85.00
Float Bowl, Yellow, Green, Roses On Black Trellis Border, 10 x 2 1/2 In.	96.00
Jam, Cover, Metal, Holder, Bridal Rose	175.00
Juicer, Base, Harmony, Streaky Pink & Green Glaze, 2 Piece	350.00
Muffineer, Lily Of The Valley, Dainty, Dome Cover, 4 x 7 In.	245.00
Platter, Blue Rock, Queen Anne, 17 1/2 x 14 1/2 In.	185.00
Soup, Cream, Underplate, Georgian, Gold Trim	75.00
Sugar & Creamer, Begonia	130.00
Sugar & Creamer, Underplate, Blue, Dainty, Individual	249.00
Tea Set, Dainty Flower Handle, Yellow, White, 21 Piece	2100.00
Tea Set, Green Block, Vogue, Cream, Green, Brown, Black, Art Deco, 21 Piece	4750.00
Tea Set, Woodlands, 8 Piece	1000.00
Teapot, Pastoral, Windsor, Platinum Trim, 1950s	280.00
Trio, Art Nouveau, New York	125.00
Trio, Balloon Tree, Art Deco	220.00
Trio, Blue Fern, Lily, c.1896	130.00
Trio, Blue Iris, Queen Anne, Cup & Saucer & Plate	200.00
Trio, Campanula, Dainty	205.00
Trio, Forget-Me-Nots, Pansies, Roses, Dainty	220.00
Trio, Garland Of Flowers, Queen Anne	225.00
Trio, Melody, Chintz	250.00
Trio, Queen Anne Sheep & Cottage	275.00
Trio, Yellow, Dainty	134.00
Tureen, Cover, Blue Iris, Queen Anne, Square, Handles	285.00
Vase, Damsons, Squat, 3 1/2 x 4 In.	125.00

SHIRLEY TEMPLE, the famous movie star, was born in 1928. She made her first movie in 1932. Thousands of items picturing Shirley have been and still are being made. Shirley Temple dolls were first made in 1934 by Ideal Toy Company. Millions of Shirley Temple cobalt blue glass dishes were made by Hazel Atlas Glass Company and U.S. Glass Company from 1934 to 1942. They were given away as premiums for Wheaties and Bisquick. A bowl, mug, and pitcher were made as a breakfast set. Some pieces were decorated with the picture of a very young Shirley, others used a picture of Shirley in her 1936 *Captain*

January costume. Although collectors refer to a cobalt creamer, it is actually the 4 1/2-inch-high milk pitcher from the breakfast set. Many of these items are being reproduced today.

Badge, Sunday Referee Shirley Temple League, Stud Back, Roden, London, c.1930	82.00
Bracelet, Charm, Silver, Enamel, 4 Charms, c.1930, 6 In.	359.00
Doll, Composition Head, Hazel Sleep Eyes, Mohair, 6 Teeth, 17 In.	825.00
Doll, Composition Head, Shoulder, Sleep Eyes, Teeth, Mohair, Baby, 22 In.	1760.00
Doll, Ideal, Composition Head, Flirty Sleep Eyes, 6 Teeth, Cowboy Outfit, c.1939, 27 In. .	1980.00
Doll, Ideal, Composition Head, Sleep Eyes, 6 Teeth, Mohair Wig, Jointed, Child, 20 In. ..	715.00
Doll, Ideal, Composition Head, Sleep Eyes, Teeth, Tongue, Mohair, Box, 27 In.	990.00
Doll, Ideal, Composition Socket Head, Sleep Eyes, Wig, 5-Piece Body, 13 In.	1050.00
Doll, Ideal, Composition, Hazel Sleep Eyes, 6 Teeth, Curly Top, 17 In. .... *Illus*	825.00
Doll, Ideal, Composition, Hazel Sleep Eyes, 6 Teeth, Mohair Wig, Box, 18 In.	1210.00
Doll, Ideal, Composition, Hazel Sleep Eyes, 6 Upper Teeth, Scottie Dress, 13 In.	935.00
Doll, Ideal, Vinyl, Brown Flirty Eyes, Smiling, Blond Hair, 1957, 17 In.	100.00
Doll, Ideal, Vinyl, Hazel Sleep Eyes, 6 Teeth, 1957, 36 In. .... *Illus*	990.00
Doll, Ideal, Vinyl, Hazel Sleep Eyes, 6 Upper Teeth, 5-Piece Body, 1957, 12 In.	215.00
Doll, Ideal, Vinyl, Plastic, Clothes, Box, 36 In.	1840.00
Doll, Ideal, Vinyl, Sleep Eyes, 6 Teeth, Synthetic Hair, Jointed, 1957, 19 In.	413.00
Doll, Montgomery Ward, Vinyl, Sleep Eyes, Rooted Curls, 1972, 15 In.	140.00
Doll, Vinyl, Sleep Eyes, Rooted Hair, Jointed, Metal Trunk, Clothes, 1957, 12 In. . .385.00 to 660.00
Paper Doll, Her Movie Wardrobe, No. 1773, Saalfield, 1938, 10 7/8 x 12 5/8 In.	199.00
Tea Set, Pink, Plastic, Teapot, Sugar, Creamer, Cups, Metal Plates, Saucers	550.00

SHRINER, see Fraternal category.

SILVER DEPOSIT glass was first made during the late nineteenth century. Solid sterling silver is applied to the glass by a chemical method so that a cutout design of silver metal appears against a clear or colored glass. It is sometimes called silver overlay.

Bowl, Centerpiece, Clear Glass, Flowers, Leaves, Scrolls, 4-Footed, 10 3/4 In.	45.00
Candlestick, Clear Glass, 3 Ruffled Tiers, Flowers & Scrolls, 5 1/2 In., Pair	110.00
Compote, Yellow Glass, Art Nouveau Swags, Cobalt Blue Foot, 8 1/2 In.	50.00
Decanter, Black Amethyst Glass, Leaves, Scrolls, Art Deco, 8 3/4 In.	45.00
Decanter, Cobalt Blue Glass, Floral Overlay, Stopper, 8 1/2 In.	50.00
Decanter, Stopper, Clear Glass, Rococo Design, c.1900, 11 In.	385.00
Perfume Bottle, Green Glass, Leaves, Vines, 1847 & 1907 In Overlay, 2 1/2 In.	76.00
Relish, Cut Glass, Urns Of Flowers & Vines, 3 Sections, 12 1/2 x 10 In.	39.00
Vanity Bottle, Stopper, Clear Glass, Art Nouveau Flowers, 5 1/4 In.	320.00
Vase, Bud, Aqua Glass, Poppies & Leaves, Bulbous Base, 8 In.	30.00
Vase, Clear Glass, Thumbprint Pattern, Flared, Overlaid Collar & Foot, 11 1/4 In.	35.00
Vase, Cobalt Blue Glass, Grapes & Leaves, 7 3/4 In.	35.00
Vase, Floral & Leaf Overlay, Iridescent Glass, Oct. 20th, 1904, 6 1/4 In.	1210.00
Vase, Green Glass, Art Deco Flowers, Bulbous Shoulder, Flared Base, 8 In.	330.00

SILVER FLATWARE includes many of the current and out-of-production silver and silver-plated flatware patterns made in the past eighty years. Other silver is listed under Silver-American, Silver-English, etc. Most silver flatware sets that are missing a few pieces can be completed through the help of one of the many silver matching services that advertise in many of the national publications.

SILVER FLATWARE PLATED, Adoration, Pickle Fork, Rogers, 1930	14.00
Ambassador, Gravy Ladle, International	16.00
Artistry, Sugar Shell, Oneida Community, 1965	9.00
Avon, Meat Fork, Rogers Brothers International, 1901	15.00
Beacon, Pie Server, Oneida, 1931	15.00
Bird Of Paradise, Dinner Fork, Community Plate, 1923	8.00
Brookwood, Soup Spoon, Rogers, 1950	10.00
Caprice, Butter Knife, Oneida Nobility, 1937	12.00
Cedric, Jelly Spoon, Community, 1933	10.00
Chatauqua, Sugar Spoon, Oneida Service Plate, 1916	10.00
Columbia, Cake Fork, Rogers Brothers	25.00
Croydon, Serving Fork, William A. Rogers, 1932	18.00
Danish Queen, Serving Spoon, Harmony House, 1944	4.50
El California, Serving Spoon, Rogers, 1961	5.00

Enchantment, Serving Fork, Oneida Tudor, 1929	20.00
Fantasty, Slotted Spoon, Oneida, 1941	25.00
Fantasy, Dinner Fork, Oneida Tudor, 1941	13.00
Fantasy, Dinner Spoon, Oneida Tudor, 1941	15.00
Fantasy, Sugar Spoon, Oneida Tudor, 1941	13.00
First Love, Child's Spoon, Rogers	29.00
Flowertime, Gravy Ladle, Rogers, 1963	15.00
Grenoble, Jelly Knife, Oneida, 1938	10.00
Irving, Soup Ladle, W.R. Keystone, 1916	23.00
Ivy, Punch Ladle, 1867	100.00
June, Serving Fork, Oneida Tudor, 1932	12.00
Knickerbockers, Cheese Spoon, Wallace, 1934	6.50
La Touraine, Olive Fork, International, 1920	13.00
Lady Fair, Meat Fork, Rogers International, 1957	6.00
Lady Fair, Sugar Spoon, Rogers International, 1957	3.50
Lady Hamilton, Meat Fork, Oneida Community, 1932	10.00
Madelon, Teaspoon, Oneida Tudor, 1935	8.00
Manhattan, Soup Spoon, Cream, International, 1951	5.00
Maytime, Dinner Fork, Harmony House, 1944	3.00
Maytime, Dinner Knife, Harmony House, 1944	3.50
Maytime, Teaspoon, Harmony House, 1944	3.00
Monarch, Nut Spoon, Slotted, National	5.00
Old Colony, Soup Ladle, Rogers Brothers International, 1911	18.00
Orleans, Meat Fork, International, 1964	7.50
Princess Royal, Butter Knife, National, 1930	8.00
Princess Royal, Gravy Ladle, National, 1930	16.00
Princess Royal, Meat Fork, National, 1930	12.00
Princess Royal, Pie Server, National, 1930	16.00
Royal Manor, Bonbon Spoon, International, 1956	10.00
Sharon, Dinner Spoon, Wallace, 1926	4.00
Sharon, Serving Spoon, Wallace, 1926	4.50
Shelburne, Salad Fork, Gorham, 1914	9.00
Signature, Cold Meat Fork, Old Company, 1950	10.00
Silver Flowers, Sugar Shovel, Oneida, 1960	5.00
Silver Tulip, Pie Server, International, 1956	12.00
Skyline, Butter Knife, Oneida Tudor, 1930	9.00
South Seas, Child's Fork, Community, 1955	15.00
Southern Manor, Seving Spoon, Pierced, Rogers	15.00
Springtime, Cheese Server, Rogers, 1930	12.00
Springtime, Serving Spoon, Rogers, 1957	15.00
Starlight, Serving Fork, Internation, 1939	29.00
Treasure, Butter Knife, Rogers, 1940	3.50
Treasure, Dinner Spoon, Rogers, 1940	5.00
Victoria, Cream Ladle, William Rogers & Son, 1895	25.00
Woodland Rose, Salad Fork, International, 1955	
SILVER FLATWARE STERLING, Acanthus, Serving Fork, Spoon, Georg Jensen, c.1945, 9 In.	470.00
Acorn, Salad Servers, Stainless Bowls, Georg Jensen, 7 5/8 In.	295.00
Acorn, Service For 12, Georg Jensen, 1933-1944, 144 Piece	8225.00
Acorn, Spoon Set, Demitasse, Johan Rohde Design, Georg Jensen, 1915, 12 Piece	805.00
Acorn, Steak Knife, Georg Jensen, c.1915, 8 In.	80.00
Acorn, Sugar Tongs, Pointed Nips, Georg Jensen, 3 5/8 In.	206.00
Acorn, Tomato Server, Johan Rohde Design, Georg Jensen, 1915, 9 In.	230.00
Bead, Gravy Ladle, Durgin, c.1893, 7 In., Pair	230.00
Cactus, Carving Set, Georg Jensen, 2 Piece	505.00
Chantilly, Punch Ladle, Gilt, Monogram, Gorham	230.00
Chrysanthemum, Ice Cream Fork, Durgin	79.00
Chrysanthemum, Serving Fork, Durgin	259.00
Chrysanthemum, Serving Spoon, Durgin, 9 1/2 In.	450.00
Colonial, Ladle, Monogram, Gorham, 12 1/2 In.	110.00
Courtship, Knives, Forks, Spoons, International, 67 Piece	460.00
Cupid, Stuffing Spoon, Dominick & Haff, 13 3/8 In.	395.00
Du Barry, Salad Fork, Durgin	85.00
Du Barry, Serving Spoon, Durgin, 9 5/8 In.	294.00

Duke Of York, Bouillon Spoon Set, Monogram, Whiting, 5 In., 10 Piece 175.00
Egyptian, Mustard Ladle, F. Whiting 159.00
Fiorito, Serving Spoon, Gourd Shaped Bowl, G.W. Shiebler & Co., 9 In. 176.00
Florentine, Baby Food Pusher, Gorham 179.00
Fontainebleau, Dinner Fork, Gorham 89.00
Francis I, Punch Ladle, Reed & Barton, c.1907, 12 x 3 5/8 In. 545.00
Francis I, Tablespoon, Reed & Barton, c.1907, 8 1/2 In., Pair 230.00
Francis I, Tomato Server, Reed & Barton, c.1907, 9 In. 230.00
George III, Lettuce Fork, Gold Wash Tines, F. Whiting, 9 3/8 In. 139.00
George III, Salt Spoon, Gold Wash Bowl, Master, F. Whiting 69.00
George III, Spoon Set, Demitasse, F. Whiting, 6 Piece 125.00
Gio Ponti Diamond, Dinner Service, Forks, Knives, Spoons, Reed & Barton, 48 Piece ... 4113.00
Grand Baroque, Salad Set, Wallace, 2 Piece 345.00
Hepplewhite Engraved, Ladle, Reed & Barton, c.1907, 13 In. 260.00
Hyperion, Oyster Fork, Gorham, Monogram, 12 Piece 320.00
Imperial Chrysanthemum, Bouillon Spoon, Gorham 39.00
Imperial Chrysanthemum, Salad Fork, Gorham 79.00
Imperial Queen, Grapefruit Spoon, F. Whiting 60.00
Imperial Queen, Gumbo Spoon, F. Whiting 75.00
Ionic, Spoon Set, Preserves, Gorham, c.1867, 6 In., 6 Piece 69.00
Iris, Salad Serving Fork, Durgin 450.00
Iris, Tablespoon, Durgin 175.00
King George, Soup Ladle, Gorham, 11 In. 355.00
Kings III, Tablespoon, Gorham 65.00
Lady Mary, Punch Ladle, Monogram, Towle 115.00
Lily, Berry Spoon, Whiting 550.00
Lily Of The Valley, Teaspoon Set, Whiting, c.1885, 6 In., 6 Piece 69.00
Louis XV, Ladle, Whiting, c.1891, 10 1/2 In. 288.00
Louis XV, Tablespoon, Whiting Division, Gorham, 6 Piece 105.00
Love Disarmed, Servers, Fork, Spoon, Reed & Barton, 1900s, 10 1/2 In., 2 Piece 646.00
Mary Chilton, Tablespoon, Towle 55.00
Mayan, Butter Spreader, Georg Jensen .... • 140.00
Mazarin, Seafood Fork Set, Dominick & Haff, 5 3/8 In., 6 Piece 235.00
Miss Alvin, Butter Knife, Master, Alvin, 9 In. 12.00
Morning Glory, Jelly Server, Gorham 550.00
New Art, Berry Spoon, Durgin 950.00
Newcastle, Tablespoon, Gorham, Pair 35.00
No. 10, Berry Spoon, Dominick & Haff 225.00
No. 10, Cold Meat Fork, Dominick & Haff 225.00
No. 10, Sugar Sifter, Gold Wash, Dominick & Haff 159.00
Old French, Serving Fork, Gorham, c.1905, 10 In. 115.00
Old King, Soup Ladle, Monogram, Gorham, c.1890 .... 288.00
Old Lace, Butter Knife, Towle 39.00
Old Lace, Gravy Ladle, Towle 49.00
Orleans, Strawberry Fork Set, F. Whiting, 5 In., 6 Piece 225.00
Poppy, Soup Ladle, Monogram, Gorham, c.1890 .... 288.00
Putnam, Ice Tongs, Wallace 160.00
Radiant, Dinner Fork, F. Whiting 75.00
Radiant, Sardine Tongs, F. Whiting 340.00
Raphael, Berry Spoon, Alvin 975.00
Renaissance, Butter Knife, Dominick & Haff 140.00
Renaissance, Preserve Spoon, Tiffany 395.00
Renaissance, Punch Ladle, Gold Washed Bowl, Dominick & Haff, 12 In. 440.00
Renaissance, Soup Spoon, Oval, Dominick & Haff 79.00
Repousse, Berry Spoon, Embossed Bowl, S. Kirk & Son, 9 In. 150.00
Repousse, Berry Spoon, Samuel Kirk, Baltimore, c.1828, 3 x 9 In. 316.00
Repousse, Ladle, 4 Initial Monogram, Stieff, 14 In. 440.00
Rose, Engraved, Sugar Tongs, F. Whiting, 4 1/2 In. 79.00
Spartan, Tomato Server, Manchester, c.1898 .... 195.00
Strasbourg, Punch Ladle, Gorham, 12 1/2 In. 353.00
Versailles, Punch Ladle, Gorham, 12 3/4 In. 575.00
Versailles, Serving Spoon & Meat Fork, Gorham, c.1888, 9 In. 690.00
Virginia Lee, Tomato Server, Towle 85.00

SILVER PLATE is not solid silver. It is a ware made of a metal, such as nickel or copper, that is covered with a thin coating of silver. The letters *EPNS* are often found on American and English silver-plated wares. Sheffield is a term with two meanings. Sometimes it refers to sterling silver made in the town of Sheffield, England. In this section, Sheffield refers to a type of silver plate, usually English.

Basket, Aesthetic Movement, Cartouche Shape, Japanese Style, 10 x 13 x 9 In.	127.00
Basket, Fruit, Swing Handle, 22 Pieces Of Stone Fruit, Rogers & Smith, Conn., 12 In. . . .	805.00
Basket, Hinged Handle, Round Bowl, Flowers, England, c.1832, 10 1/2 x 24 In.	315.00
Basket, Looped Handle, Beaded, Open Flute Edge, Bright Cut Design, 12 In.	118.00
Basket, Reticulated, Neoclassical Style, Navette Shape, Sheffield, 4 x 16 x 8 In.	290.00
Berry Bowl, Gilt, Round, Petal Molded Lip, Fruit, Leaf Molded, 1900s, 10 In.	295.00
Berry Spoon, Repousse Bowl, Grapevines, Victorian, c.1880, 9 In., Pair	175.00
Biscuit Box, Cut Glass, Hinged Lid, Cylinder Shape, Silver Frame, 9 x 7 1/4 In.	316.00
Biscuit Box, Folding Shell, Leaf, Bellflower Support, 10 1/2 x 8 x 5 3/4 In.	400.00
Biscuit Box, Oval, Lion's-Head Ring Handles, Footed, Bone Finial, 6 1/2 x 7 x 6 In.	110.00
Biscuit Box, Tree Branch, Walker & Hall, Sheffield, Victorian, c.1880, 10 x 8 1/4 In.	315.00
Bowl, Frog, Crab, Lizard, Bat, Lobster, Turtle, Meriden, American, 7 In.	29.00
Bowl, Vegetable, Cover, Acanthus Handles, Hot Water Stand, c.1800, 15 In., Pair	1380.00
Bowl, Vegetable, Cover, Heating Stand, Burner, 16 1/2 In.	175.00
Bowl, Vegetable, Scalloped Lid, Center Handle, Rogers, American, 14 x 11 x 7 In.	259.00
Box, Repousse Design, Lift Top, 2 Lovers On Cover, Late 1800s, 6 In.	45.00
Box, Sardine, Key Fret Design, Fish Form Finial, Ridgefield & Rice, 5 1/4 In.	69.00
Butter, Regency, Old Sheffield, c.1820, 6 1/2 x 4 x 8 1/4 In., Pair	2300.00
Candelabrum is listed in its own category.	
Candlesticks are listed in their own category.	
Caviar Set, Scalloped Edge, Trefoil Stand, Cut Crystal Bowl, England, 10 1/2 x 10 In. . . .	1495.00
Centerpiece, Palm Tree, Henry Wilkinson, Sheffield, Victorian, c.1870, 9 x 7 In.	345.00
Chocolate Pot, Louis XV Style, Pear Shape, c.1940, 10 1/2 x 5 1/2 In.	259.00
Cocktail Shaker, Skyscraper Form, Cover, Bernard Rices Sons, N.Y., c.1930, 11 In.	2270.00
Coffee Urn, William Rogers, Early 20th Century	150.00
Coffeepot, Egg Shape, Banding, Wooden Handle, Charles Balaine, Paris, c.1835, 10 In. . .	230.00
Coffeepot, Pear Shape, Dome Lid, Pineapple Finial, Wood Handle, Sheffield, Eng., 12 In.	560.00
Coffeepot, Tankard Form, Children, Dolphins, Inscription, 1871, 9 1/2 In.	690.00
Compote, Cast Dolphin Stems, 8-Sided Base, 1909, 6 1/2 x 5 In., Pair	200.00
Cruet Stand, Victorian, c.1890, 16 In.	35.00
Crumber, Engraved Flowers, H. Wilkinson & Co., Sheffield, England, c.1880, 13 In.	115.00
Dessert Set, Mother-Of-Pearl, Monogram, Case, James Dixon, 1887	805.00
Dish, Cover, Gadroon, Leaf & Shell Border, Handles, 4 Paw Feet, Sheffield, England, 15 In.	300.00
Dish, Cover, Oval, Molded Rim, Finial Handle, Sheffield, England, c.1800, 17 In.	210.00
Dish, Cover, Stand, Fluted, Dart Border, Handles, 4 Paw Feet, Sheffield, England, 15 In. .	280.00
Dish, Entree, Lid, Reeded Borders, Monogram, Gorham, 5 1/4 x 11 In.	55.00
Dish, Entree, Sloped Rectangle, Lion Mask Handles, Sheffield, c.1810, 9 1/2 x 12 In.	375.00
Dish Holder, Entwined Apple Branches, Christofle, 14 In.	956.00
Dresser Box, Continental Drinking Scenes, Castles, 2 1/4 x 5 1/2 x 4 1/4 In.	110.00
Epergne, 2 Tiers, Christofle, Beaded Knops, 2 Graduated Gold Wash Tiers, 15 5/8 In. . . .	265.00
Epergne, 3 Scrolling Arms, Elkington, Mason, Birmingham, England, c.1854, 22 x 17 In.	2070.00
Epergne, 4 Arms, Rocaille Scrolls, Mold-Cut Bowls, 19th Century, 12 3/8 In.	1765.00
Epergne, Baluster Shape, S-Scroll Arms, 5 Glass Dishes, Sheffield, c.1840, 16 x 25 In. . . .	1610.00
Epergne, Detachable Bowl, Tulip Form Vase, 3 Scrolling Arms, Baskets, 11 3/4 In.	290.00
Epergne, Flowers, Leaves, J. Dixon & Sons, Sheffield, England, c.1910, 16 x 12 x 16 In. .	1035.00
Epergne, Trumpet Shape, 4 Detachable Candle Branches, Victorian, 18 x 24 In.	1325.00
Ewer, Walker & Hall, Sheffield, 20th Century, 11 In., Pair	1298.00
Fish Knife, Mother-Of-Pearl Handles, Fitted Box, Late 1800s, 7 1/2 In., 10 Piece	46.00
Fish Service, Shamrocks, Ivory, Case, Levesley, Sheffield, c.1896, 24 Piece	690.00
Flask, Remember The Maine, Relief Scene, Battleship On Water, 5 In.	250.00
Fruit & Nut Set, 2 Nutcrackers, Grape Scissors, Fitted Case, 7 1/2 x 7 1/4 In.	86.00
Grape Scissors, Walker & Hall	80.00
Hot Water Dispenser, Thompson-Brown & Sons, Sheffield, England, c.1866, 16 x 8 In. .	950.00
Hot Water Urn, 2 Handles, Egg Shape, Flower Repousse, Victorian, 20 In.	260.00
Hot Water Urn, Beehive, Scrolled Legs & Feet, Sheffield, c.1800, 19 In. . . . . *Illus*	920.00
Hot Water Urn, Masonic Moon, Ball Feet, Egyptian Head, 19th Century, 13 x 9 x 10 In. .	440.00
Humidor, 2 Compartments, Jockey & Horse Finial, Derby, 9 3/4 x 7 1/2 In.	300.00

Humidor, 2 Hunting Dog Finials, Meriden, Signed, American, 8 3/4 x 4 1/2 In. 230.00
Humidor, 4 Compartments, Putti, Match Well Finial, Meriden, American, 12 x 9 In. 230.00
Humidor, Flowers, Demons, Rectangular, Rogers Bros., 6 1/2 x 4 1/2 In. 175.00
Humidor, Hunting Dog & Game Finials, Rectangular, Meriden, American, 7 x 7 In. 230.00
Humidor, Rectangular, 2 Pug Dog Finials, Glass Eyes, Rockford, American, 6 x 7 In. 230.00
Jewelry Box, Dragonfly, Plants, Satin, Pairpoint, c.1880s, 12 x 6 x 5 1/2 In. 920.00
Knife Rest, Diagonally Fluted, W. Huhon & Sons, Sheffield, Eng., c.1872, 3 3/4 In., Pair . 230.00
Ladle, Oval Bowl, Fiddle Shape Handle, Late 19th Century, 13 1/2 In. 46.00
Meat Fork, Trident Form Blade, Chevrons, Victorian, c.1890, 1 1/2 x 9 In. 145.00
Mirror, Toilet, Art Nouveau, Germany, c.1900, 14 1/2 In. 530.00
Mug, Child's, Inscribed Anna, Aug. 22, 1869, 3 1/4 x 2 3/4 In. 11.00
Napkin Rings are listed in their own category.
Pastry Trowel, Pointed Spade, Ferns, C-Scrolls, Ivorine, c.1900, 3 1/4 x 11 1/2 In. 46.00
Perfume Tantalus, Locking Frame, Rope Twist Trim, Stoppers, Mid 1800s, 5 1/4 In. 325.00
Pitcher, Gallia, Art Nouveau, France, c.1900, 8 3/4 In. 499.00
Pitcher, Grape & Vine, Scroll Handle, Forbes, 13 In. 39.00
Pitcher, Water, Tilting, Stand, Aesthetic, Derby Silver Co., c.1880, 21 3/4 In. 230.00
Platter, Leafy Scroll & Shell Rim, Oval, J. Watson, Sheffield, England, c.1830, 15 In., Pair 370.00
Platter, Motto, Coat Of Arms, Scalloped, Smith, Sisems & Co., c.1850, 23 x 18 In. 230.00
Platter, Tree & Well, Oval, Shells, Leaves, Ellis Barker, Early 1900s, 17 x 21 1/2 In. 145.00
Platter Set, Old Sheffield, George III, c.1800, 14 x 10 & 11 x 10 In., 5 Piece 460.00
Punch Set, Vintage, Applied Grapes, Grape Handles, Pedestal, 12 Cups, Webster 385.00
Salad Servers, Ivory Ends, 19th Century 150.00
Salt & Pepper, Silver On Copper, Friction Fit Lids, Lion's-Head Paws, 4 x 2 In. 70.00
Serving Dish, 2 Sections, Shell Corners, Gadroon Edge, England, 17 1/4 In. 69.00
Spirit Dispenser, Barrel, 4-Wheel Carriage, Mappin & Webb, England, c.1863, 12 x 8 In. 1750.00
Spoon, Souvenir, see Souvenir category.
Spoon Rest, Nautilus Shell Shape, Hinged, Mappin & Webb, England, 5 1/2 x 6 In., Pair . 290.00
Spoon Warmer, Nautilus Form, Hinged, Turtle's Back, 6 3/4 x 6 1/2 x 4 In. 605.00
Sugar, Wire Type, Oval Pedestal Foot, Cobalt Blue Glass Liner, 5 1/2 x 6 In. 145.00
Sugar Nips, Scissor Action, Serpent Handles, Talon Terminals, Victorian, 6 1/2 In. 29.00
Sugar Scuttle, Shell Form, Hinged Lid, England, c.1930, 4 3/4 x 5 1/4 In. 200.00
Tankard, Glass Bottom, Banded Rim Decoration, Sheffield, England, 7 1/2 In. 375.00
Tea & Coffee Set, American Neo-Grec, Medallion, c.1865, 5 Piece 460.00
Tea & Coffee Set, Grape Cluster Finials, Barbour, Taunton, American, c.1895, 5 Piece . . . 546.00
Tea Box, Reeded Borders, Oval, 4 Teaspoons, 4 3/4 x 3 3/4 x 2 1/2 In. 90.00
Tea Caddy, Barbour, c.1920, 4 1/2 x 3 x 3 1/2 In. 35.00
Tea Set, Chippendale Style, Wood Handles, 7 1/2 x 14 In., 4 Piece 140.00
Tea Set, Scroll, Flower, Leaf, Gadroon Border, Poole Silver Co., American, 4 Piece 50.00
Tea Urn, Hepplewhite Style, Ram's Head, Square Base, Sheffield, England, 1800s, 15 In. . 750.00
Tea Urn, Neo-Grec, Oval, 2 Handles, Beaded Borders, c.1865, 15 3/4 In. 175.00
Tea Urn, Plated Lid, Tin Sleeve, Sheffield, 19th Century, 15 In. 635.00
Teapot, Engraved Flowers, Modified Oval Shape, Ball Feet, Sheffield, England, 12 In. . . . 115.00
Toast Rack, Figural, Crossed Rifles, 7 Pair, Laurel Wreath Holder, 4 Ball Feet 765.00
Tray, Chased Flowers & Scroll, Monogram, Sheffield, England, 29 1/2 x 20 In. 450.00
Tray, Double Handles, Shell & Scroll Work Border, 2 1/2 x 24 x 15 1/2 In. 50.00
Tray, Engraved, Reticulated Inner Border, Sheffield, England, 25 x 19 3/8 In. 225.00
Tray, Footed, Pierced Rim, Handles, Flowers, Sheffield, England, 20 x 14 1/2 In. 375.00
Tray, Galleried, 2 Handles, I. Freeman & Son, England, 1900s, 26 1/4 x 17 In. 460.00
Tray, Octagonal, Openwork Leaf Gallery, H. Hobson, Sheffield, England, 15 x 10 In. 525.00
Tray, Oval, Curved Border, 8 Arabesques, Victorian, c.1895, 19 1/2 x 30 1/2 In. 300.00
Tray, Oval, Flower, Scroll Rim, Rococo Scroll Band, Towle, 2 1/2 x 20 x 30 In., Pair 200.00
Tray, Oval, Pierced Gallery, Feet, England, c.1950, 3 x 16 1/4 x 24 1/4 In. 316.00
Tray, Oval, Pierced Rim, Grapevine Edge, C-Scrolls, Electroplate, c.1895, 2 x 16 x 26 In. . 259.00
Tray, Oval, Reticulated Rim, Sorley, Glasgow, c.1850, 25 3/4 x 19 1/2 In. 575.00
Tray, Rectangular, Canted Corners, Scrolled Handles, Bun Feet, 4 x 25 x 13 In. 495.00
Tray, Rectangular, Gadroon Rim, Scroll Handles, Sheffield, England, 33 1/2 In. 875.00
Tray, Rounded Rectangle, Flowers, Ellis-Barker, England, c.1925, 2 x 18 1/2 x 30 In. 1150.00
Tray, Rounded Rectangle, Gadroon Border, Shells, England, 1900s, 17 x 28 In. 200.00
Tray, Scalloped, Shell Rim, Flowers, Monogram, 2 Handles, 27 1/2 x 18 3/4 In. 145.00
Tray, Scroll & Floral, Reticulated Border, Shells, Bead, Gadroon Border, 25 x 19 In. 200.00
Tray, Tea, 2 Handles, Chased Rococo Surface, Feet, England, c.1900, 28 5/8 x 20 3/8 In. . 920.00
Tray, Tea, Egg Shape, Presentation Inscription, Bird Crest, Early 1900s, 28 1/2 In. 355.00

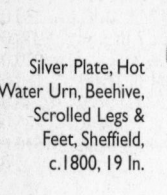

Silver Plate, Hot Water Urn, Beehive, Scrolled Legs & Feet, Sheffield, c.1800, 19 In.

Silver-American, Basket, Kensington Pattern, International Silver Co., 14 3/4 In.

Tray, Tea, Oval, Egg & Dart Decoration, Handles, James Dixon, 33 x 22 In. 175.00
Tray, Tea, Scroll & Flowers, Flared Rim, Ellis-Barker, Early 1900s, 30 5/8 x 19 In. 400.00
Tray, Turtleback Form, C-Scroll Border, Flowers, Gorham, c.1900, 19 3/4 x 27 In. 748.00
Trophy, Bowl, Jockey Figure, Galloping Mount, 20th Century, 15 In. 59.00
Trophy, Cycling, Holly, Berry Frieze, Circular Cartouche, Handles, 11 x 14 x 10 In. 195.00
Tureen, Cover, Neoclassical, Mappin Brothers, England, c.1900, 10 1/2 x 18 1/8 In. 460.00
Tureen, Cover, Regency Style, Oval, Handles, Beaded Borders, 9 3/4 x 13 1/2 x 9 1/4 In. . . 330.00
Tureen, Lid, Repousse Flowers, Engraved Initials, B.C., Meriden, 12 1/2 x 8 1/2 In. 220.00
Tureen, Oval, Lobed, Waisted, Acanthus Rim, Cover, Sheffield, c.1840, 11 x 10 x 16 In. . . 1265.00
Tureen, Revolving, Cover, 4 Lion Mask Feet, Elkington, England, 1882, 7 x 12 In. 630.00
Tureen, Sauce, Old Sheffield, George III, c.1800, 6 1/2 x 4 1/4 x 9 1/2 In. 105.00
Tureen, Sauce, Victorian, James Dixon & Sons, c.1865, 6 1/2 x 4 3/4 x 8 In. 546.00
Urn, Cover, Crested, Chased Scrolls, Leaves, Ring Handles, 15 x 8 1/2 In., Pair 1495.00
Urn, Neoclassical, Cover, Beaded Loop Handles, Artichoke Finial, Sheffield, 14 1/2 In. . . . 410.00
Vase, Cobalt Blue Glass Liner, Mythological & Garland Design, 12 x 4 1/2 In. 865.00
Vase, Seated Poodle, Ruffled Glass Vase Insert, James W. Tufts, Boston, 8 1/2 In. 110.00
Vase, Trumpet Form, Cobalt Liners, Cast Flower Swags, England, 16 1/2 In., Pair 2185.00
Vase Holder, Cutout Design, WMF, Germany, 4 In. 115.00
Waiter, Round, Circular, Elkington, Mason & Co., England, c.1860, 2 x 18 1/2 In. 980.00
Wine Coaster, Applied Grapevine Design, England, 7 In., Pair 315.00
Wine Coaster, Pierced Geometric Sides, England, 5 1/2 In., Pair 160.00
Wine Coaster, Pierced Grapevine Rim, Turned Wooden Base, Sheffield, England, 7 In., Pair 280.00
Wine Coaster, Quatrefoil Pierced, London, George III, 1776, 4 5/8 In., Pair 2940.00
Wine Coaster, Repousse, Swag Design, 4 1/2 In., Pair 195.00
Wine Coaster, Reticulated Sides, Elkington, Birmingham, c.1917, 5 7/8 In., Pair 860.00
Wine Coaster, Round, Flared Rim, Grapevine, Wood Base, c.1890, 3 1/4 x 8 1/4 In. 345.00
Wine Coaster, Wood Base, Squat Bulbous Shape, 2 x 5 1/2 In., Pair 200.00
Wine Coaster Wagon, Leaf Decoration, Double, England, 18 In. 520.00
Wine Cooler, Octagonal, Handled, Liner, Grape Clusters, Austria, c.1900, 9 3/4 In. 865.00
Wine Trolley, Cannon Form, England, 8 3/4 x 6 1/2 x 11 1/2 In. 1265.00

SILVER, SHEFFIELD, see Silver Plate; Silver-English categories.

SILVER-AMERICAN. American silver is listed here. Coin and sterling silver are included. Most of the sterling silver listed in this book is subdivided by country. There are also other pieces of silver and silver plate listed under special categories, such as Candelabrum, Napkin Ring, Silver Flatware, Silver Plate, Silver-Sterling, and Tiffany Silver. For information about makers and marks, see *Kovels' American Silver Marks: 1650 to the Present.*

SILVER-AMERICAN, Tea & Coffee Set, Gorham, c.1885, 5 Piece 1380.00
 Basket, Candy, Pierced Rim, Handle, Wayne Silver Co., 9 In. 70.00
 Basket, Fenestrated Decoration, Monogram, Gorham, 9 In. 115.00
 Basket, Fenestrated, Cobalt Blue, Glass Liner 69.00
 Basket, Gorham, 15 1/2 In. 1910.00
 Basket, Kensington Pattern, International Silver Co., 14 3/4 In. . . . . *Illus* 575.00
 Basket, Octagonal, Pierced Lattice Bands, Flower Baskets, Redlich, c.1910, 10 3/8 In. . . . 355.00
 Basket, Whiting Manufacturing Company, c.1900, 11 1/2 x 8 x 12 3/4 In. 1265.00

Beaker, Federal Coin, Flared Rim, Monogram, Thomas Fletcher, c.1815, 3 1/2 In. 558.00
Bell, Dinner, 2 Applied Rib Bands, Stem Handle, Box, c.1900, 3 1/2 In. 520.00
Bell, Rococo Repousse Decoration, Engraved K, 2 3/4 x 2 1/8 In. 25.00
Berry Spoon, Repousse, Embossed Strawberry Bowl, Jenkins & Jenkins, 10 In. 370.00
Berry Spoon, Repousse, Gilt Bowl, Jacobi & Jenkins, c.1900, 10 1/8 In. 430.00
Biscuit Basket, Melon Shape, Ebony Handle, Silver Joinery, 9 1/2 x 7 1/2 In. 1600.00
Bonbon, Basket Shape, Handle, Graff, Washbourne & Dunne, c.1915, 5 In., Pair 575.00
Bonbon, Peacock Shape, Gorham, Durgin, 9 1/2 In., Pair 920.00
Bonbon Spoon, Openwork Stem, Acanthus, G.W. Shiebler, c.1900, 5 5/8 In. 176.00
Bonbon Spoon, Reeded, Rose Wrapped Handle, Female Mask, Gorham, c.1900, 9 1/4 In. 529.00
Bosun's Whistle, Nussbaum & Hunold 200.00
Bowl, Aesthetic Movement, Oval, Monogram, Late 1800s, 17 1/4 In. 999.00
Bowl, Art Deco, Rounded Reeded, Stylized Scroll Feet, Reed & Barton, c.1931 .... 250.00
Bowl, Arts & Crafts, McAuliffe & Hadley, Early 20th Century, 13 In. 999.00
Bowl, Arts & Crafts, Round, Applied Rim, 4-Footed, Lebolt & Company, 2 x 7 In. 275.00
Bowl, Center, Oval, 2 Handles, Coin, W. Gale & Son, 1856, 5 x 15 x 10 In. 2185.00
Bowl, Center, Repousse, Floral Border, Monogram, 10 1/2 In. 175.00
Bowl, Conjoined Script Monogram, Providence, R.I., c.1902, 17 In. 805.00
Bowl, Cover, Robert E. Lee Family Crest, Jacobi & Jenkins 8625.00
Bowl, Diapered Panels, Flowers, Pedestal Base, 1800s, 5 x 5 1/2 x 5 1/2 In. 385.00
Bowl, Embossed Fruit, Scalloped & Lobed Rim, Reed & Barton, 11 1/2 In. 310.00
Bowl, Figures, Scenic Landscape, Circular Footed Base, 2 3/4 x 4 1/2 In. 545.00
Bowl, Flared Rim, Strawberry Border, Art Nouveau, Mauser, c.1900, 8 1/2 In. 315.00
Bowl, Flared, Fluted Sides, Scalloped Edges, Gyllenberg, 1 3/4 x 10 7/8 In. 825.00
Bowl, Flat Bottom, Broad Border, Panel, Magnussen, 1 5/8 x 11 5/8 In. 2750.00
Bowl, Flat Bottom, Lobed Trefoil, Undulating Rim, Gorham, 1 3/4 x 10 1/4 In. 575.00
Bowl, Flat Bottom, Lobed Trefoil, Undulating Rim, J.O. Randahl, 1 3/4 x 10 1/4 In. 575.00
Bowl, Floral Repousse, Monogram, Kirk & Son, Early 1900s, 9 x 10 1/2 In. 345.00
Bowl, Flower Form, 2 Overlapping Poppy Blossoms, Wallace, 1900s, 10 In. 235.00
Bowl, Footed, Flared Rim, Alphonse La Paglia, Meriden, 5 3/4 x 10 In. 1955.00
Bowl, Footed, Navette Form, Tuttle, Boston, c.1930, 5 x 4 1/2 x 8 In., Pair 690.00
Bowl, Francis I Pattern, Reed & Barton, c.1950, 1 1/2 x 8 In. 575.00
Bowl, Fruit, Arts & Crafts, Egg Shape, Leaf Handles, Quaker Silver Co., c.1935, 13 In. ... 380.00
Bowl, Fruit, Egg Shape, Scalloped Rim, Graff, Washbourne & Dunn, 1900s, 12 In. 176.00
Bowl, Fruit, Frontenac, Overlapping Vertical Panels, Gorham, 1900s, 10 1/2 In. 206.00
Bowl, Fruit, Gorham, Early 20th Century, 11 1/2 In. 560.00
Bowl, Fruit, Rectangular, Flared Rim, C-Scroll Cartouches, Gorham, c.1891, 8 1/4 In. 355.00
Bowl, Fruit, Stepped Trumpet Foot, Beaded, Geradus Boyce, c.1825, 9 1/2 In. 3345.00
Bowl, Fruit, Wallace, 10 1/4 In. 90.00
Bowl, Hammered, Tooled Flowers, Footed, Arthur J. Stone, 9 1/2 In. 3250.00
Bowl, Ice, Footed, Iceberg Shape, Polar Bears, c.1870, 7 1/2 x 9 1/4 In. 2760.00
Bowl, Laurel & Ribbon Band, Footed, Bailey & Co., c.1865, 4 x 5 1/2 In. 375.00
Bowl, Lobed Circular, Scrolls, Leaves, Monogram, F.W. Smith, Mass., c.1910, 12 In. 315.00
Bowl, Low, Repousse, Vermeil Interior, Howard & Co., 1885, 9 In. 848.00
Bowl, Mixed Metal, 3-Footed, Applied Copper, Gorham Mfg. Co., c.1883, 8 1/2 In. 5975.00
Bowl, Monteith, Sterling, Repousse, Removable Notched Collar, c.1881, 9 x 10 In. 2530.00
Bowl, Oblong, Flowers, Repousse, 8 3/4 In. 170.00
Bowl, Oval, Scrolled Edge Border, Graff, Washbourne & Dunn, 3 x 11 x 9 1/4 In. 180.00
Bowl, Panel & Rope Border, International, 10 In. 60.00
Bowl, Raised Ring Foot, Applied Bands, Mulholland Bros., 3 3/8 x 9 1/8 In. 615.00
Bowl, Repousse, Flower & Scroll Border, Shreve, Crump & Low, 11 3/8 x 2 1/2 In. 290.00
Bowl, Repousse, Fruit, Flowers, Pedestal, Justis & Armiger, 8 x 10 1/2 In. 2485.00
Bowl, Revere Style, No. 4010, A.G. Schulz, Baltimore, 5 1/4 x 10 In. 250.00
Bowl, Ring Foot, Chased, Punch Work, Arthur J. Stone, 2 1/8 x 5 1/8 In. 1675.00
Bowl, S. Kirk & Son, 9 1/2 In. 96.00
Bowl, Scalloped & Grape Repousse, Gorham, Late 1800s, 8 1/2 x 4 In. 252.00
Bowl, Scalloped Shape, Marked, Marshall Field, 8 1/2 In. 490.00
Bowl, Scroll & Shell Border, Footed, Monogram, 9 1/4 x 3 3/4 In. 175.00
Bowl, Silver Mounted, Ceramic, Shreve & Co., c.1910, 5 In. 956.00
Bowl, Underliner, Wedgwood Pattern, Footed, International, 3 1/2 x 6 In. 150.00
Bowl, Underplate, Footed, Greek Key, Leaf Band, Grapes, A. Coles, 3 & 6 1/8 In. 355.00
Bowl, Vegetable, Cover, Handles, Gadroon Border, Jacobi & Jenkins, 11 In., Pair 690.00
Bowl, Wedgwood Pattern, 2 Scroll Handles, Footed, Monogram, International, 7 x 12 In. .. 360.00

Box, Cartouche Body, Hinged Lid, Gorham, c.1925, 1 1/2 x 5 1/4 x 3 In. 288.00
Bread Basket, Boat Shape, Pierced & Engraved Border, Gorham, Early 1900s, 15 1/4 In. .. 880.00
Bread Fork, Chased & Entwined Wirework, S. Kirk & Son, 7 x 3 1/4 In. 145.00
Bread Tray, Art Nouveau, Round Navette Shape, Unger Brothers, 12 1/2 x 7 1/2 In. 405.00
Bread Tray, Oval, Frank W. Smith, c.1953 .... 120.00
Butter, Classical, Flower Molded Finial, Saucer Shape Cover, 5 1/2 In. 705.00
Butter, Cover, Liner, Knife, Openwork Handles, Wood & Hughes, c.1860 .... 3585.00
Butter, Repousse, Cover, Flower Finial, A.E. Warner, 5 1/2 In. 1130.00
Butter Knife, Medallion, Classical Helmeted Man, Coin, 7 1/4 In., Pair 295.00
Cake Plate, Reticulated, Durgin, Early 20th Century, 8 1/2 & 9 1/2 In., Pair 150.00
Cake Plate, Reticulated, Octagonal, Fruit Baskets, Redlich & Co., Early 1900s, 10 1/4 In. 235.00
Cake Platter, Tara Pattern, Weighted, Reed & Barton, 10 1/2 x 5 1/4 In. 220.00
Cake Stand, Arts & Crafts, Hammered, Monogram, Shreve & Co., 11 1/2 In. 259.00
Cake Stand, Footed, Chased, Repousse Border, Lebolt & Co., 1 1/8 x 10 1/2 In. 750.00
Cake Stand, Repousse, Footed, Andrew Ellicott Warner, c.1870, 6 x 9 In. 1265.00
Cake Stand, Repousse, Footed, Fruit, Flowers, Leaf Border, c.1870, 6 x 9 In. 1150.00
Cake Tray, Tree Branch Loop Handles, Rim, Repousse Border, S. Kirk & Son, 14 In. ... 1580.00
Candelabrum is listed in its own category.
Candlesticks are listed in their own category.
Cann, Cup, Engraved Monogram, Charles Louis Boehme, c.1812, 4 1/2 In. 5750.00
Card Case, Engraved Japanese Style Fans, Stylized Leaves, Wood & Hughes, 4 In. 290.00
Card Tray, International Silver Co., 6 In. 355.00
Carving Set, Bone Handle, Duhme & Co., Cincinnati, 4 Piece 35.00
Castor, Baluster, Banding, Zachariah Brigden, Boston, c.1760, 5 1/2 In. .... *Illus* 3740.00
Castor, Bell Shape Finial, High Dome, Early 19th Century, 5 1/2 In. 825.00
Christening Cup, Bulbous Form, Gorham, Rhode Island, c.1902, 2 5/8 In. 6615.00
Cigarette Case, 3 Fold, Gold Monogram, R. Blackington, c.1930, 3 x 3 1/2 In. 175.00
Cigarette Case, Repousse, Maiden Of The Sea, Art Nouveau, Unger Bros., 3 In. ......→ 90.00
Cocktail Shaker, Gorham, 9 In. 219.00
Coffee Set, Bailey & Kitchen, Philadelphia, c.1850, 11 In., 3 Piece 1695.00
Coffee Set, Burgundy, Oval, Leaf Cartouches, Handles, Reed & Barton, 1900s, 10 In. 1645.00
Coffee Set, Chased Lilies & Leaves, Gorham, 1904, 3 Piece 7768.00
Coffee Set, Francis I, Reed & Barton, c.1925, 11 1/2 In., 3 Piece 1955.00
Coffee Set, Oval, Demitasse, 3 Piece 288.00
Coffee Set, Rose Pattern, Stieff, 10 1/4-In. Pot, 4 Piece 2640.00
Coffeepot, Alabama, c.1855, 9 x 10 x 6 In. 2760.00
Coffeepot, Cover, Flower Heads, Serpentine Spout, Fluted Stem, Towle, 1900s, 11 In. 440.00
Coffeepot, Engraved Flowers, Urn Finial, Handles, Watson, 9 1/2 In. 250.00
Coffeepot, Ivory Insulator, Old Newbury Crafters, 7 3/4 x 7 1/4 In. 825.00
Coffeepot, Neoclassic Design, Slip Top, W. Ball, Baltimore, c.1795, 11 In. 2486.00
Coffeepot, Repousse, Grapevine, Branch Handle, Footed, Gale & Son, 1852, 12 In. 845.00
Coffeepot, Rococo Revival, Bulbous, Coin, Osmon Reed, Phila., c.1840, 10 3/4 In. 1076.00
Compote, Chased, Howard & Co., 4 x 8 In. 345.00
Compote, Frank Smith, Early 20th Century, 7 3/4 x 10 3/4 In. 2700.00
Compote, Marie Antoinette, No. 20033, Footed, Gorham 145.00
Compote, Pedestal, Turned In Rim, Shreve & Co., 4 1/2 x 6 1/4 In. 495.00
Compote, Repousse Pattern, Samuel Kirk & Sons, c.1905, 6 x 7 1/2 In., Pair 865.00
Compote, Trumpet Shape, Bead & Shell Border, Howard & Co., c.1904, 3 In., Pair 956.00
Cordial, Red, Green Enameled Dot, 2 3/4 x 2 3/8 In., Pair 425.00
Cream Jug, Federal, Engraved Overlapping Leaves, Coin, c.1800, 5 3/4 In. 265.00
Cream Jug, Federal, Wide Spout, Leopard Head Handle, Paw Feet, c.1805, 6 In. 705.00
Cream Jug, Gadroon Border, Beaded Rim, William Hollingshead, c.1775, 5 In. 3585.00
Cream Jug, Helmet Shape, Leaftip Lip, Scrolled Handle, Coin, c.1820, 6 In. 235.00
Cream Jug, Pyriform, 3 Hoof Feet, Double Scroll Handle, c.1765, 3 1/2 In. 3825.00
Creamer, Barrel Shape, Hammered, Hollow Handle, Dominick & Haff, 4 x 4 1/2 In. 425.00
Creamer, Bulbous Body, Square Handle, Engraved Wreath, Monogram, 5 In. 290.00
Creamer, Federal, Baluster Shape, Looped Handle, Coin, c.1795, 4 1/2 In. 206.00
Creamer, Federal, Helmet Shape, Pedestal Base, Monogram, Garlands, 5 7/8 In. 345.00
Creamer, First Baltimore Standard, c.1850, 9 x 6 In. 1095.00
Creamer, Flowers, Repousse, 4 Ball & Claw Feet, S. Kirk & Son, 3 3/4 x 2 3/4 In. 160.00
Creamer, Gadroon Rim, Embossed Leaf Band, Paw Feet, London, 1822, 6 1/4 In. 396.00
Creamer, Presentation, W. Faris, 18th Century 2530.00
Cruet, Cut Glass, Leaf Molded, Looped Handle, William Gale & Son, 12 1/2 In. 1175.00

Crumber, Aesthetic Movement, Dominick & Haff, Late 1800s, 13 In. 410.00
Crumber, Repousse, Engraved Blade, S. Kirk & Son, 13 In. 535.00
Cup, Bulbous Base, Engraved, Adolph Himmel, New Orleans, c.1861, 4 In. 1380.00
Cup, Engraved Birds & Leaves, Rope Trim & Handle, Gorham 288.00
Cup, Footed, Scroll Handle, Molded Rim, Engraved, Coin, Gorham, c.1855, 4 In. 230.00
Cup, Julep, Beaded, Impressed, McDannold, Winchester, Ky., 3 7/8 In. 1210.00
Demitasse Pot, Lighthouse Form, Acid Etched, Whiting Manufacturing, c.1865, 7 1/2 In.   1410.00
Demitasse Set, Baluster Shape, Cartouches, Dominick & Haff, 4 Piece 4405.00
Demitasse Set, Elongated Egg Shape, Durgin, Early 1900s, 8 1/2 In., 3 Piece 295.00
Demitasse Set, Plymouth, Helmet Shape, 1907, Gorham, 10 3/4 In. 265.00
Demitasse Set, Reed & Barton, c.1930, 4 Piece 1175.00
Demitasse Set, Wedgwood Pattern, International, 10 In.-Pot, 3 Piece 720.00
Desk Pad Corners, Dolphin Shape, Whiting, c.1890, 3 3/8 x 3 3/8 In. 375.00
Dessert Server, Pierced Handle, Twig, Leaves, Berries, Pansy Bowl, Wallace, 1900 . . . . .   460.00
Dessert Set, Iris Design Border, Whiting, 1905, 9 3/8 In., 12 Plates 2185.00
Dish, Entree, Cover, Oval, Molded Ribs, 11 3/8 In. 1175.00
Dish, Fluted, Kensington, Ruffled, Scalloped Edge, Arthur J. Stone, 1 x 7 1/2 In. 775.00
Dish, Oval, Fluted, Flat Bottom, Stylized Blossom, J.O. Randahl, 1 1/4 x 7 1/2 In. 495.00
Dish, Oval, Fluted, Kensington, Ruffled, Scalloped Edge, Arthur J. Stone, 3/4 x 6 1/8 In. .   325.00
Dish, Oval, Footed, Galleried, Gorham, 1896, 6 1/2 In., Pair 266.00
Dish, Ring Foot, Fluted, Scalloped Border, Chased, Arthur J. Stone, 7/8 x 7 1/4 In. 1350.00
Dish, Ring Foot, Turned Up Sides, Medallion, Grape Leaves, Arthur Stone, 3/4 x 3 5/8 In.   485.00
Dish, Ring Foot, Upturned Edge, Chased, Punch Work, M.C. Knight, 3/4 x 10 In. 975.00
Dish, Shell Shape, Ball Form Supports, Wallace, 6 In. 98.00
Dish, Shell Shape, Footed, Gorham, 9 x 9 In. 100.00
Dish, Shell Shape, Monogram P, Gorham, 9 In. 200.00
Dresser Box, Rectangular, Cover, Dominick & Haff, c.1890, 5 1/2 In. 300.00
Dresser Set, Repousse, Lilies, Women's Faces, Art Nouveau, Wm B. Kerr, 10 Piece 840.00
Dresser Set, Roger Williams Silver Company, Monogram, 4 Piece 165.00
Dressing Spoon, Federal, Monogram, Thomas Bentley, Boston, c.1800, 13 1/4 In. 1725.00
Ewer, Baluster, Vines, Engraved, Coin, Ball, Tompkins & Black, c.1865, 13 5/8 In. 1116.00
Ewer, Leaf Banding, Engraved, c.1845, 15 1/4 In. 1095.00
Ewer, Repousse, Architectural Vignettes, Flowers, S. Kirk & Son, c.1890, 11 In. 978.00
Ewer, Rococo Revival, Shouldered, Coin, Bigelow Brothers, c.1860, 6 1/2 In. 478.00
Figurine, Equestrian, Jockey Completing Jump, R. Donaldson, 7 3/4 x 9 In. 1840.00
Fish Platter, J.E. Caldwell, 22 1/2 In. 777.00
Fish Set, Engraved Blade, Entwined Dolphin, Filled Handles, Albert Cole, 12 In. 678.00
Fish Slice, Farrington & Hunnewell, 1840-1850, 11 In. 575.00
Fish Slice, Flat Handle, H.A. Griswold, Whitehall, N.Y., c.1850 . . . .   5290.00
Fish Slice, Pierced, Engraved, Heloise Boudo, Charleston, c.1835, 12 In. 3910.00
Fork, Asparagus, Scroll, Flowers, Marked 259.00
Fork Set, Fiddle & Thread, Engraved Stag Crest, c.1870, 7 1/2 In., 9 Piece 750.00
Fruit Bowl, Unger Bros., 10 In. 206.00
Goblet, Lord Saybrook, International, 6 5/8 In., 4 Piece 305.00
Goblet, Swags, Ribbons, Holly, Berries, Dominick & Haff, 7 In., 6 Piece 2310.00
Grape Scissors, Griffin Handles, 6 3/4 In. . . . . *Illus*   125.00
Gravy Boat, Shell Shape Body, Gadroon Rim, Howard & Co., c.1892, 6 In. 265.00
Gravy Boat, Undertray, Champlain, Hand Chased, Ellmore, 9 In.   430.00
Gravy Ladle, Engraved, Monogram, Coin 196.00
Hair Receiver, Undertray, Monogram 345.00

Silver-American,
Castor, Baluster,
Banding, Zachariah
Brigden, Boston,
c.1760, 5 1/2 In.

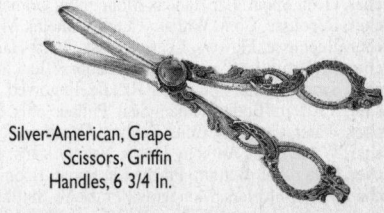

Silver-American, Grape
Scissors, Griffin
Handles, 6 3/4 In.

Ice Cream Set, Hammered, Marked, Server, Spoons, Monogram, 13 Piece 460.00
Inkwell, Undertray, Lid, Repousse, Glass, Flowers, Leaf Border, c.1893, 5 In. 375.00
Jug, Dome Lid, Pear Shape, 8-Sided, Stepped Base, Scroll Handle, Coin, 9 1/2 x 9 x 5 In. 330.00
Jug, Flat Lid, Nautical, Presentation, Barrel Shape, Lewis E. Jenks, Early 1900s, 9 1/2 In. . 7050.00
Jug, Milk, Baluster Shape, Chased, Embossed, Angular Handle, c.1850, 9 In. 470.00
Jug, Milk, Footed, Chased, Embossed, Leaves, Repousse, S. Kirk & Son, 8 1/4 In. 380.00
Jug, Milk, Hexagonal, Ivory Disks, Repousse, Samuel Kirk, c.1845, 7 1/4 In. 558.00
Jug, Milk, Squat, Flat Bottom, Looping Handle, Arthur J. Stone, 4/1 4 x 5 3/4 In. 950.00
Jug, Water, Egg Shape, Etched Flowers, Mask Spout, Kirk, c.1840, 8 1/2 In. 2070.00
Julep Cup, Agricultural Premium, John Kitts, Louisville, c.1857, 4 In. 2070.00
Julep Cup, Barrel Form, Monogram, Asa Blanchard, Kentucky, c.1820, 3 1/4 In. 2990.00
Julep Cup, Commemorative, Kentucky Derby, Canonero II, Darby House, 1971 .... 460.00
Julep Cup, Martha Harp, Banding, E. & D. Kinsey, 3 x 3 1/2 In. 520.00
Julep Cup, Tapered, Manchester Silver Co., 1900s, 4 x 3 In., 12 Piece 1955.00
Kettle, Stand, Baluster Shape, Scroll Spout, Arthur J. Stone, c.1910, 13 In. 1910.00
Kettle, Stand, Crabstock Spout, Coin, Jones, Ball & Poor, c.1854, 15 1/2 In. 1530.00
Kettle, Stand, Fluted, Melon Shape, Burner, Arthur J. Stone, 13 1/4 x 9 In. 3900.00
Kettle, Stand, Oval, Repousse, Cartouches, Scrolled Legs, Coin, 13 x 10 x 6 In. 1650.00
Knife Set, Fish, Second Baltimore Standard, Repousse Pattern, c.1828, 7 1/2 In. 401.00
Ladle, Back Tipped Handle, Oval Bowl, Coin, Mid 19th Century, 13 In. 150.00
Ladle, Back Tipped Handle, Oval, Monogrammed, Jones, Boston, 1839, 11 5/8 In. 176.00
Ladle, Coin, Richard Vincent, Baltimore, c.1810, 14 1/2 In. 920.00
Ladle, Fiddle Thread, Jones, Low & Ball, Boston, c.1840 .... 200.00
Ladle, Fleur-De-Lis Stem, Shell Bowl, Coin, Albert Coles & Co., c.1870, 11 In. 173.00
Ladle, Imperial Queen, Whiting, 1893, 10 1/2 In. 315.00
Ladle, Oval Bowl, Fiddle Handle, Coin, Boston, 11 1/8 In. 88.00
Lemon Squeezer, Rounded Triangular Form, Engraved Scroll, Gorham, 1910 .... 630.00
Loving Cup, Cast Loop Handles, Urn Shape, Tiered Spreading Foot, c.1806, 6 In. 880.00
Loving Cup, Engraved Flowers, Landscape, Inscription, Gorham, 1904, 12 3/4 In. 1380.00
Loving Cup, Oval, 3 Ear Handles, Baluster, Trumpet Foot, Hammered, Gorham, 12 In. ... 700.00
Match Cover, Rectangular, Bezel Set Bloodstone Cabochon, 2 1/4 x 1 1/2 In. 145.00
Mirror, Hand-Held, Hammered, Monogram, Stamped Lebolt Sterling 400, 10 x 6 In. 290.00
Muffineer, Cylindrical, Pierced Lid, Leaf Chased Body, Early 1900s, 6 1/4 In. 180.00
Mug, Baluster Shape, Looped Handle, Repousse, C-Scrolls, Coin, 4 1/2 In. 235.00
Mug, Engraved, Coin, Jones, Ball & Co., Boston, Child's, 3 1/2 In. 230.00
Mug, Flowers, Guilloche, Monogram, Gorham, c.1920, 4 x 4 3/4 x 3 In. 358.00
Mug, Leaftip Molded, Scrolled Handle, Baluster Body, 18th Century, 5 In. 880.00
Mug, Tapered Cylinder Shape, Coin, Gorham, Mid 1800s, 3 3/4 In. 375.00
Mustard Pot, Cover, Applied Border, Engraved Initials, c.1845, 3 In. 259.00
Mustard Pot, First Baltimore Standard, 4 x 2 1/2 In. 175.00
Mustard Pot, Silver Cover, Applied Border, Initials, Wood & Hughes, N.Y., c.1845, 3 In. . 315.00
Nut Dish, Cromwell, Gorham, c.1900, 1 x 2 1/2 x 4 In., 8 Piece 80.00
Nut Dish, Flower Form, Paneled Sides, Joel F. Hewes, Pa., c.1925, 3 3/4 In. 420.00
Nut Dish, No. A9645, Oval, Cornucopia, Flowers, Vines, Gorham, 3 3/4 In., 18 Piece ... 880.00
Pie Server, Arts & Crafts, Trefoil Handle, Shreve Co., 9 3/4 In. 705.00
Pin Tray, Repousse Flower Border, No. 101, Stieff, 8 In. 339.00
Pitcher, Baluster Form, Engraved Wreath, Monogram, c.1815, 6 1/2 In., Pair 3450.00
Pitcher, Black, Starr & Frost, 20th Century, 8 3/4 In. 175.00
Pitcher, Embossed Scrolls, Wm. Durgin, 12 In. 1290.00
Pitcher, Fairfax, Paneled Helmet Shape, Short Spout, Gorham, c.1941, 8 3/4 In. 940.00
Pitcher, Hammered, Lobed Design, Kalo, Chicago, 11 In. 4900.00
Pitcher, Helmet Shape, Acanthus Thumb Piece, Rogers, 9 1/4 x 5 1/2 In. 415.00
Pitcher, Oval, Spout, Ear Handle, Monogram, Gorham, 1919, 8 3/8 In. 470.00
Pitcher, Repousse, Coin, William Henry Calhoun, Mid 1800s 10500.00
Pitcher, Repousse, Flowers, Leaves, Mask, Twist Handle, S. Kirk & Son, 9 In. 4635.00
Pitcher, Robert E. Lee Family Crest, Jacobi & Jenkins 6613.00
Pitcher, Trophy, Oval, Spout, Ear Handle, Engraved, Watson, 1920-1930, 7 1/4 In. 206.00
Pitcher, Vasiform Body, William Seal, Philadelphia, c.1810, 8 In. 3738.00
Pitcher, Water, Classical, Coin, Baldwin Gardiner, N.Y., c.1830, 13 1/2 In. 5460.00
Pitcher, Water, Coin, Anthony Rasch, New Orleans, c.1849, 10 5/8 In. 3450.00
Pitcher, Water, Flat Bottom, Pinched In Spout, Looping Handle, 9 x 8 1/4 In. 2200.00
Pitcher, Water, Flowers, Monogram, Frank W. Smith, Early 1900s, 10 In. 805.00
Pitcher, Water, Garret Eoff, New York City, 1805-1845 .... 1785.00

Pitcher, Water, Georgian Style, Towle, 9 3/4 In. 259.00
Pitcher, Water, Gorham, J.E. Caldwell Retailer, 9 In. 325.00
Pitcher, Water, Gorham, William Gale & Son, c.1850, 13 In. 885.00
Pitcher, Water, Gourd Shape, Buildings, Flowers, New York, Mid 1900s, 12 In. 2235.00
Pitcher, Water, Hammered, Marked, Marshall Field, c.1915, 7 1/2 In. 690.00
Pitcher, Water, Helmet Shape, Ellmore Silver Company, 9 x 9 x 6 1/2 In. 275.00
Pitcher, Water, Helmet Shape, Gorham, c.1955, 8 1/2 x 9 x 5 3/4 In. 275.00
Pitcher, Water, Hexagonal, Acanthus Ear Handle, Gorham, 1895, 8 In. 355.00
Pitcher, Water, Neoclassical Urn, c.1860, 13 x 9 x 6 1/2 In. 865.00
Pitcher, Water, Octagonal, Monogram, 8 1/4 In. 489.00
Pitcher, Water, Oval Shape, Ivy Leaves, Gorham, c.1874, 10 x 5 1/2 x 7 1/2 In. 2300.00
Pitcher, Water, Repousse, Dominick & Haff, 1889 . . . . 1725.00
Pitcher, Water, Repousse, Flowers, Cartouches, Ellmore Silver Co., c.1950, 11 In. 690.00
Pitcher, Water, Repousse, Insects, Birds, Scalloped Edge, c.1890, 7 1/2 In. 2300.00
Pitcher, Water, Short Spout, Curved Handle, Globular Body, Gorham, c.1884, 7 In. 440.00
Pitcher, Water, Waisted Oval Shape, Leaf Topped Handle, Early 1900s, 8 In. 440.00
Pitcher, Water, Waisted Pear Shape, Short Spout, Gadroon Rim, Poole, Early 1900s, 9 In. 265.00
Pitcher, Water, Wedgwood Pattern, International, 10 1/2 In. 540.00
Plate, Bread & Butter, Plain, Molded Rim, Dominick & Haff, 6 5/8 In., 12 Piece 290.00
Platter, Central Tree, Shaped Rim, Shreve & Co., Early 20th Century, 24 In. 825.00
Platter, Meat, Shaped Reeded Edge, Applied Monogram, Gorham, 21 1/8 In. 380.00
Platter, Oval, Applied Rim, Gorham, 1908, 18 7/8 & 14 3/4 In., Pair 765.00
Platter, Oval, Howard & Co., New York, 17 7/8 In. 1005.00
Platter, Robert E. Lee Family Crest, Jacobi & Jenkins 3450.00
Platter, Rococo, Shells, Scrolls, Acanthus, Diapering, 1900s, 13 3/8 In. 825.00
Porringer, Engraved LIM, Samuel Casey, Rhode Island, 7 1/2 In. 5465.00
Porringer, Flared Rim, Curved Sides, Pierced Handle, 7 1/2 In. 1840.00
Porringer, Monogram Handle, Paul Revere 6210.00
Porringer, Pierced Keyhole Handle, Samuel Burt, c.1750, 8 In. 2629.00
Punch Bowl, Dome Foot, Embossed Flowers, Horse-Head Handles, c.1860, 13 In. 5975.00
Punch Bowl, Revere Reproduction, Fisher Silversmiths, c.1950, 7 x 14 1/4 In. 575.00
Punch Bowl, Robert E. Lee Family Crest, Jacobi & Jenkins 10925.00
Salad Fork, Large, Dominick & Haff, 8 7/8 In. 265.00
Salad Servers, Ebonized Handles, Monogram, A. Adler, c.1950, 13 1/2 In., 2 Piece 920.00
Salad Servers, Ebony Handles, Allan Adler, 13 In. 690.00
Salad Servers, Hammered, Kalo Shop, c.1925, 10 3/4 In., 2 Piece 375.00
Salad Servers, Hand Hammered, Arts & Crafts, A. Stowell & Co., 2 Piece 276.00
Salt, Flowers, Repousse, Tripod Supports, Pair 210.00
Salt, Master, F. Whiting, Pair 130.00
Salt, Open, Durgin, Early 20th Century, 3 1/4 In., Pair 295.00
Salt, Open, Gyllenberg, 1 1/8 x 2 1/2 In., Pair 160.00
Salt, Porringer Shape, Keyhole Pierced Handle, K. Pratt, 1 1/8 x 3 1/2 In. 335.00
Salt, Repousse Flower Band, Round, Compressed, 4 Scroll Feet, 2 1/2 In., Pair 175.00
Salt, Shell Shape, Gorham, Cartier, Boxed, 3 3/8 In., 4 Piece 176.00
Salt & Pepper, Gio Ponti Diamond, Reed & Barton, 1958, 2 In. 1175.00
Salt & Pepper, Gorham, 5 5/8 In. 115.00
Salt & Pepper, Round Bottom, Squat, 4 Ball Feet, A. Adler, 2 3/4 In. 325.00
Salt & Pepper, Stein Shape, Beaded Bands, Dome Top, Wallace, 1900-1920 . . . . 65.00
Salt & Spoon, Flat Bottom, Fluted, K.F. Leinonen, 3/4 x 1 3/4 & 2 3/8 In. 150.00
Salt & Spoon, Round, Hammered, Gaylord, 3/8 x 2 & 2 1/4 In. 85.00
Salt Cellar, Basket Shape, Inverted Rim, Whiting, c.1900, 3/4 In., 8 Piece 316.00
Salt Shaker, Flat Oval, Repousse, G.W. Shiebler, c.1920, 2 3/8 x 2 1/4 In., Pair 175.00
Salt Spoon, Shell Bowl, Coffin Terminals, Coin, William Simes, c.1810, Pair 160.00
Salt Spoon, Shell Bowl, Fiddle Handles, Coin, Robert Gray, c.1820, 4 Piece 245.00
Salver, Beaded Rim, Engraved Leaf Border, Coin, Jones, Ball & Poor, 12 In. 705.00
Salver, Round, Inner C-Scroll Rim, Flower Lappets, Reed & Barton, c.1947, 14 1/8 In. 235.00
Salver, Round, Molded Guilloche Rim, Coin, Lincoln & Foss, c.1850, 4 3/8 In. 120.00
Sauceboat, 3 Hoof Feet, Scroll Joins, Thomas Hammersley, c.1760, 7 In. 9560.00
Sauceboat, Double C-Scroll Handle, Monogram, Gorham, 5 7/8 x 9 In. 316.00
Sauceboat, Ladle, Leaf & Berry Base, Handle, Redlich & Co., N.Y., c.1940, 4 In. 895.00
Sauceboat, Undertray, Husk Rim, Acanthus Band, International Silver, 1900s, 8 3/4 In. . . . 176.00
Serving Dish, Aesthetic Movement, Stylized Palm Front, Gorham, 14 In. 1765.00
Serving Spoon, Arthur J. Stone, 20th Century, 9 3/4 In. 410.00

Serving Spoon, Coffin Style Handles, 19th Century 80.00
Serving Spoon, Franklin Porter, c.1925, 10 3/8 In. 440.00
Serving Spoon, Medallion, Coin, Wood & Hughes, N.Y., c.1865, 9 1/2 In. 230.00
Smoking Set, Ferd, Fuchs & Bros., N.Y., Late 1800s, 10 1/4 In., 5 Piece 520.00
Soup Ladle, Canfield Bros. & Co., Baltimore, 1850 . . . . 159.00
Soup Ladle, Coffin Shape Handle, Monogram, Boston, 1810 . . . . 200.00
Soup Ladle, Fiddlehead, Downturned Handle, Coin, c.1840, 14 In. 200.00
Soup Ladle, Fiddlehead, Upcurved Handle, Coin, 13 In. 290.00
Soup Spoon, New York Federal, Monogram, Garret Schank, c.1780, 6 . . . . 1495.00
Soup Spoon, Wavy Terminal, Ridged Rattail Bowl, Edward Webb, Boston, 1718 . . . . 4140.00
Spoon, Shell Shape Bowl, Coin, Bailey & Co., c.1849, 11 In. 145.00
Spoon Set, Dessert, Fiddle Pattern, Andrew Ellicott Warner, c.1827, 7 Piece 460.00
String Holder, Cover, Pierced, Ball Shape, F. Fuchs, 3 x 3 1/2 In. 440.00
Stuffing Spoon, Olive, Grotesque Mask, Coin, Mid 19th Century, 13 5/8 In. 325.00
Sugar, Andrew Ellicott Warner, Baltimore, c.1850, 10 x 5 1/2 In. 1265.00
Sugar, Cover, Acorn Finial, Round, Scrolled Handles, Coin, 1800s, 10 x 9 1/4 x 6 In. 385.00
Sugar, Cover, Coin, Meadows & Co., c.1860, 5 1/2 In. 345.00
Sugar, Cover, Repousse, Chased, Embossed, Leaves, Handles, Paw Feet, 5 1/4 In. 355.00
Sugar, Cover, Tapered, Coin, Gale, Wood & Hughes, c.1840, 10 3/4 x 8 1/2 x 5 3/4 In. . . . 715.00
Sugar & Creamer, Cover, Federal, Leaf Molded Handles, Coin, c.1810 . . . . 765.00
Sugar & Creamer, Cover, Flowers, Repousse, 3 1/2 In. 405.00
Sugar & Creamer, Flat Bottom, Strap Handles, Marshall Field, 2 1/2 In. 350.00
Sugar & Creamer, Hemisphere & Vase Shapes, Towle, c.1910, 4 3/4 In. 259.00
Sugar & Creamer, Medallion, Neo-Grec, J.R. Wendt, c.1865, 6 1/2 x 6 3/4 In. 1093.00
Sugar & Creamer, Pedestal Base, Monogram, Joshua Dorsey, c.1800, 7 1/4 In. 2415.00
Sugar & Creamer, Scrolled Handles, Flowers, Gold Wash Interior, Gorham, 3 In. 275.00
Sugar Tongs, Scissor Form, Flower Head, IT, John Tanner, c.1750, 4 1/4 In. 2070.00
Sugar Urn, Dome Lid, Angular Handles, Coin, Urn Finial, c.1800, 9 1/2 In. 470.00
Sugar Urn, Monogram, George Drewry, Philadelphia, 1763, 10 1/2 In. 2875.00
Sugar Urn, Repousse, Architectural Vignettes, Leaf Band, Samuel Kirk, 7 3/4 In. 980.00
Tablespoon, Trifid Pattern, Elongated Bowl, Samuel Vernon, c.1720, 8 1/2 In. 5019.00
Tankard, Baluster Shape, Cast Handle, Coin, Early 1800s, 6 1/4 In. 2235.00
Tazza, Durgin, Gorham, 20th Century, 3 1/2 x 8 In., Pair 705.00
Tazza, Flowers & Leaf Border, Baluster Stem, Paw Feet, Gorham, 7 x 9 In., Pair 1495.00
Tazza, Pedestal Base, Flared Rim, Art Nouveau, Gorham, c.1900, 4 x 9 1/4 In. 230.00
Tazza, Pierced Border, Carved Bell Flowers, Graff, Washbourne & Dunn, 4 x 11 In. 660.00
Tea & Coffee Set, Angular Handles, Monogram, Durgin, Early 1900s, 7 In., 6 Piece 2000.00
Tea & Coffee Set, Art Deco Leaf Tip Band, Concord Silversmiths, 1900s, 5 Piece 825.00
Tea & Coffee Set, Art Deco, Durgin, 6 Piece 1650.00
Tea & Coffee Set, Bailey, Banks & Biddle, Gorham, c.1900, 5 Piece 738.00
Tea & Coffee Set, Classical Revival, Egg Shape, Monogram, Durgin, Early 1900s, 5 Piece 1765.00
Tea & Coffee Set, Dominick & Haff, 18 1/2-In. Tray, 5 Piece 2640.00
Tea & Coffee Set, Egg Shape, Classical Revival, Graff, Washbourne, Dunn, 1900s, 5 Piece 1000.00
Tea & Coffee Set, Embossed Flowers, Georgian Style, Alvin, 6 Piece 1095.00
Tea & Coffee Set, Flowers, Wood Handle, Curry & Preston, c.1835, 5 Piece 2868.00
Tea & Coffee Set, Gorham, 16 1/2-In. Kettle, 6 Piece 6050.00
Tea & Coffee Set, Hampton Court, Reed & Barton, 6 Piece 1555.00
Tea & Coffee Set, Inverted Pear Shape, Gorham, c.1941, 5 Piece 1725.00
Tea & Coffee Set, Kent, Monogram, M. Fred Hirsch, 1920-1945, 5 Piece 1150.00
Tea & Coffee Set, Laurel & Berry Border, Dominick & Haff, N.Y., c.1918, 8 Piece 8365.00
Tea & Coffee Set, Parcel Gilt, William B. Durgin 8625.00
Tea & Coffee Set, Pointed Antique, Initials, Reed & Barton, c.1950, 5 Piece 920.00
Tea & Coffee Set, Queen Anne, Baltimore, 1900s, 6 Piece 1300.00
Tea & Coffee Set, Roger Williams, 5 Piece 1116.00
Tea & Coffee Set, Towle, Early 20th Century, 4 Piece 470.00
Tea & Coffee Set, Waisted, Paneled, Wood Handles, Gorham, 1910, 5 Piece 1060.00
Tea & Coffee Set, Whiting Manufacturing Co., c.1916, 7 Piece 5875.00
Tea & Coffee Set, Wild Rose Center Band, Gorham, c.1881, 7 Piece 12925.00
Tea Caddy, Dome Cover, Friction Fit, Vase Shape, Watson Co., 4 1/4 In. 495.00
Tea Set, Arthur Stone, 1890-1910, 5 Piece 6075.00
Tea Set, Baluster Shape, Thistle Finial, William Thomson, c.1815, 5 Piece 1435.00
Tea Set, Dolphin Finials, Coin, Chaudron & Rasch, Phila., c.1815, 3 Piece 6440.00
Tea Set, Embossed Shells, Flowers, Urn Shape Finials, Watson Co., 3 Piece 430.00

Tea Set, Federal, Egg Shape, Coin, Hugh Wishart, N.Y., c.1785, 7 1/2 In., 3 Piece 2115.00
Tea Set, Flower Head Finials, Coin, Bailey & Kitchen, 7 1/4 In. 1116.00
Tea Set, J&I Cox, New York, 1921, 11 In., 4 Piece 2360.00
Tea Set, Kettle On Stand, Teapot, Sugar, Waste Bowl, Creamer, Cover, Tongs, 7 Piece ... 1380.00
Tea Set, Melon Shape, Shreve, Crump & Low, 1900s, 11 3/4 In., 4 Piece 1528.00
Tea Set, Paul Revere Pattern, Tuttle, 3 Piece 147.00
Tea Set, Plymouth Pattern, Angled Handles, Monogram, Gorham, 1917-1928, 4 Piece ... 499.00
Tea Set, Plymouth Pattern, Gorham, 10 1/2 In., 4 Piece 1000.00
Tea Set, Repousse Flowers, Shiebler, 4 1/2 In., 3 Piece 748.00
Tea Set, Round, Flared Sides, Ivory Insulators, K.F. Leinonen, 5 1/4 x 9 1/2 In. 1750.00
Tea Set, Royal Danish, International, 4 Piece 660.00
Tea Set, Shreve, Crump & Low, Early 20th Century, 6 Piece 1645.00
Tea Set, Tete-A-Tete, Aesthetic Movement, Dominick & Haff, c.1879, 3 1/2 In. 2585.00
Tea Strainer, F. Whiting 179.00
Tea Strainer, Ivory Handle, First Baltimore Standard, c.1870, 6 3/4 In. 175.00
Tea Tray, Egg Shape, Rim Roses, Monogram, Woodside, c.1915, 28 1/2 In. 2820.00
Tea Tray, Oval, Flower Basket, Acanthus Handles, Dominick & Haff, 1900s, 30 In. 3055.00
Tea Tray, Rectangular, Rounded Corners, Black, Starr & Gorham, c.1950, 25 1/2 In. 1058.00
Teapot, Dome Lid, Pear Shape, Gooseneck Spout, Gorham, 1906, 9 x 5 In. 375.00
Teapot, First Baltimore Standard, c.1850, 11 1/2 x 10 In. 2300.00
Teapot, Hinged Cover, Round, Handle, Pedestal Base, Coin, 1839, 7 x 8 3/4 5 In. 415.00
Teapot, Repousse, Birds, Flowers, Leaves, Monogram, S. Kirk & Sons, 7 3/4 In. 1035.00
Teapot, Slender, Gooseneck Spout, Scrolled Handle, Urn Finial, Gorham, 9 1/2 In. 75.00
Teapot, Urn Shape, Scroll Handle, Repousse, Coin, John Cook, N.Y., c.1808, 9 1/4 In. ... 288.00
Thimble Holder, Unger Brothers, 1 1/4 x 1 In. 159.00
Tomato Server, Baker-Manchester Co., R.I., c.1930, 2 3/4 x 7 1/4 In. 80.00
Tongs, Stylized Leaves, 11 1/2 In. 405.00
Tray, 2 Handles, Coin, Gregg, Hayden & Co., Charleston, c.1849, 10 1/2 x 17 1/2 In. 5750.00
Tray, 2 Handles, Inscription, Flower Border, S. Kirk & Son, Late 1800s, 32 3/4 In. 14340.00
Tray, Embossed Grapes, Mauser Manuf. Co., 13 x 7 1/2 In. 110.00
Tray, Fairfax, Rolled Border, Openwork Handles, Gorham, 25 1/2 x 16 1/4 In. 2420.00
Tray, Flowers, Leaves, Monogram, Art Nouveau, Dominick & Haff, 1902, 14 In. 1380.00
Tray, Footed, Black, Starr & Frost, 13 In. 500.00
Tray, Footed, Relief Leaf Rim, Gorham, 10 3/4 In. 320.00
Tray, Gadroon, Mathews & Prior, Round, 18 In. 1035.00
Tray, Handles, Round, Footed, Towle, 12 In. 200.00
Tray, Octagonal, Landscape, Church, Pagoda, Scrolling Leaves, Shield, 12 1/8 In. 3220.00
Tray, Rectangular, Rounded Corners, Allan Adler, 1900s, 17 1/8 x 24 1/2 In. 1880.00
Tray, Round, Ring Foot, Chased, Punch, Flowers, M.C. Knight, 1907, 3/4 x 10 In. 1450.00
Tray, Sandwich, International, 10 3/4 In. 69.00
Tray, Serving, Wedgwood, Renaissance Border, International, 13 1/4 x 10 In. 330.00
Tray Set, Graduated, Oval, Gorham, c.1902, 27 1/2, 18 & 14 1/2 In., 3 Piece 2875.00
Trinket Box, Cover, Cylindrical, Dominick & Haff, 1892, 3 In. 398.00
Trophy, Anti Prohibition, Griffin Handles, Footed Urn, Inscription, 1933, 9 In. 520.00
Trophy, Bowl, New York Racing Association, Flared Rim, Low Foot, c.1975, 8 In. 175.00
Trophy, Horse Racing, 2 Handles, Gorham, 8 1/2 In. 320.00
Trophy, Platter, Meat, New York Racing Association, Gorham, c.1977, 21 1/8 In. 470.00
Trophy, Platter, New York Racing Association, Coat Of Arms, c.1976, 14 In. 355.00
Tureen, Classical Revival, Gorham, Early 20th Century, 12 In. 1880.00
Tureen, Soup, Waisted Egg Shape, Reeds, Scrolled Handles, Gorham, 1907, 15 3/4 In. ... 1295.00
Tureen, Undertray, Repousse, Dominick & Haff, c.1886, 8 1/2 x 11 1/2 In. 3819.00
Vase, Bud, Trumpet Shape, Ruffled Rim, Hammered, 8 1/2 In. 385.00
Vase, Tapered, Octagonally Scalloped Flared Lip, Flowers, c.1920, 14 x 4 In. 200.00
Vase, Trumpet Shape, Footed Pedestal, Beaded Rims, Webster Co., 10 1/4 In. 259.00
Vase, Trumpet Shape, Reticulated, Scalloped, Copper Liner, Mauser, c.1910, 13 In. 411.00
Vase, Trumpet Shape, Ruffled Rim, Hammered, 12 In. 475.00
Waste Bowl, Classical, Coin, Eoff & Shepherd, c.1850, 5 1/2 x 7 In. 575.00
Watch Holder, Repousse Pattern, Heart Shape Body, Round Foot, Kirk 115.00
Wine Set, Monogram, Gorham, 4 1/2 In., 12 Piece 315.00
Youth Set, Knife, Fork, Spoon, Embossed U.S. Seal, Pro Patria, Dominick & Haff 288.00
SILVER-AUSTRIAN, Basket, Sweetmeat, Handle, Lapis, K. Moser, c.1905, 6 1/2 x 4 1/8 In. .. 8365.00
Ewer, FW, 1802, 10 1/2 In. 405.00
Jug, Hot Milk, Maker's Mark SH, c.1900, 5 1/2 In. 325.00

Ladle, Maker's Mark ID, Vienna, 1818 .... 295.00
Pill Box, Tongs, Rose, Josef Hoffmann, Wiener Werkstatte, c.1910, 1 1/4 x 1 1/4 x 1/2 In. 2870.00
Salt, Amber Glass Liner, 3 Legs, Round Base, Josef Hoffmann, c.1902, 2 3/8 x 3 In. 7768.00
Salt, Silver Ring Base, Stepped Glass Liner, Josef Hoffmann, WW, c.1903, 2 3/8 In. 9560.00
Tray, Pierced Latticework, Laurel Garland Rim, Scroll Handles, 4 Bun Feet, Vienna, 28 In. 1575.00
SILVER-BELGIAN, Creamer, Second Standard, Wooden Handle, Swirl, Gold Wash Inside, 4 In. 145.00
SILVER-CANADIAN, Coffeepot, Flat Cover, Pear Shape, Flared Rim, Cartouches, 6 1/4 In. 470.00
Decanter, Haig's, Glass Bottle, c.1920, 9 x 5 In. 290.00
Pitcher, Water, Shell Shape, Seated Figure, Mermaid, Birks, 16 1/2 In. 1610.00
Ring Box, Bell Shape, Monogram, Birks, 1 1/2 In. 175.00
Soup Ladle, Fiddle Handle, G. Savage, Montreal, c.1830 .... 480.00
Tea & Coffee Set, Melon-Fluted, Wooden Scroll Handle & Finial, H. Birks, 4 Piece 700.00
SILVER-CHINESE, Bowl, Centerpiece, Cobalt Liner, Monogram, c.1865, 7 x 11 In. 4000.00
Butter, Cover, Dragon's Head, Early 1900s, 5 1/8 In. 410.00
Chalice, Cover, Court Scenes, Foo Dog Finial, Chicheong, c.1900, 20 In. 4500.00
Compote, Bamboo, Dragon, Dolphin Pedestal, HC, 1800s, 6 1/2 x 7 1/2 In. 978.00
Goblet, Tapered, Flared Rim, Stepped Foot Ring, 19th Century, 5 1/4 In. 1210.00
Tazza, Crenellated Top, Tree Panels, Dragon Stem, Late 1800s, 7 1/2 In. 1645.00
Tea Set, Dragon Decoration, Sing Fat, Early 1900s, 7 Piece 4000.00
Tea Set, Octagonal, Landscape, Dragon Handles, Ing Woe, c.1846, 5 Piece 2070.00
Urn, Enameled, 6 Ivory Panels, Mother-Of-Pearl, 7 1/2 In. 1840.00
SILVER-CONTINENTAL, Beaker, Tapered Cylindrical Shape, Round Foot, 3 3/4 In. 410.00
Bowl, Centerpiece, Downswept Rim, Peasants Cartouches, 1900s, 20 In. 235.00
Bowl, Fruit, Round, 4 Openwork Handles, Coin, 16 In. 880.00
Bowl, Repousse, Chased Fruit, 9 x 11 1/4 In. 896.00
Bowl, Reticulated, Oval, Flutes, Husk Swags, Urns, Wreaths, 23 Oz., 14 In. 325.00
Box, Cherub Figures, 2 1/2 In. 160.00
Box, Dolphin Feet, Swing Handle, Engraved Leaves, 1800s, 5 3/4 In. 130.00
Box, Egg Shape, 3 Leaf-Like Feet, Bird Finial, Hinged Cover, 1800s, 5 1/4 In. 230.00
Chalice, Silvered Metal Mounted, Coconut, Flared Lip, Shell Body, 6 In. 235.00
Coffee Set, Maker's Mark JD, 20th Century, 6 In., 3 Piece 355.00
Coffeepot, GG, 1800s, 8 1/2 In. 425.00
Creamer, Cow, Tail Handle, Head Spout, Fly On Lid, 3 7/8 In. 765.00
Cup, Cover, Presentation, 17 In. 1016.00
Dish, Entree, Cover, Pear Shape, Gadroon Rims, Shell Handles, 9 In. 265.00
Epergne, Fruit, Eagle Handles, Winged Cherub Panels, 12 x 11 1/2 In. 690.00
Frame, Rectangular, Serpentine Sides, Frogs, Swan Racing, 9 1/2 x 7 1/2 In. 200.00
Ladle, Coconut, Turned Handle, Silver Mount, 16 In. 345.00
Lobster, Articulated, 9 In. 460.00
Muffineer, Pierced Fruit Shape Cover, Baluster Body, Leaftips, 1700s, 7 In. 265.00
Mug, Baluster Shape, Serpentine Handle, Rococo Cartouche, 5 1/4 In. 175.00
Platter, Oval, Molded Rim, Marked FB, 24 3/4 In. 370.00
Salt, Master, Oval, JR Hallmark, 4 Legs, 2 1/4 x 3 In., Pair 80.00
Serving Dish, Oval, Beaded Edge, Bird Chasing Moth, Late 1800s, 13 1/2 In. 120.00
Sugar Basket, Rectangular, Concave, Flower Band, U Handle, 9 x 5 3/4 x 8 In. 750.00
Tankard, Cover, Pear Shape Body, Stippled, Stepped Foot, 1800s, 9 1/2 In. 660.00
Tankard, Hinged Cover, Repousse Scene, Cylindrical, 7 In. 345.00
Tea Strainer, Cherub Openwork Handle, Star Design Bowl, c.1890, 6 1/2 In. 170.00
Tray, Oblong, Gadroon Rim, Heraldic Crest Engraving, c.1800, 18 1/4 In. 380.00
Water Jug, Baluster Shape, Repousse, Fish Shape Handle, 14 In. 2070.00
Wine Cup, Timbale Shape, Flared Rim, Gilt, 2 3/4 x 2 1/2 In. 58.00
SILVER-DANISH, Bottle Opener, Acanthus, Georg Jensen 92.00
Bottle Opener, Ribbed Handle, Georg Jensen, 6 1/2 In. 160.00
Bowl, Beaded Design, Plain Bowl, Cutout Gallery Rim, Georg Jensen, 8 x 5 1/2 In. 430.00
Bowl, Footed, Berry & Leaf Pedestal, Georg Jensen, 4 1/2 In. 978.00
Bowl, Molded Rim, Handles, Footed, Horse Trial Presentation, Cohr, 10 3/4 x 3 In. 280.00
Bowl, Oval, Flared Rim, Hammered, No. 575E, Georg Jensen, c.1950, 8 In. 940.00
Cigarette Box, Dome Lid, Repousse, Stylized Shells, Coral, Georg Jensen, 5 3/4 In. 1955.00
Cigarette Case, No. 226, Stepped Edge, Georg Jensen, 1945-1951, 3 7/8 In. 175.00
Cocktail Shaker, Rectangular, Ripple Edge, c.1942, 11 In. 720.00
Coffeepot, Blossom Pattern, Egg Shape, Georg Jensen, 1926-1932, 8 1/2 In. 3290.00
Compact, Fish On Lid, Georg Jensen, 3 In. 145.00
Compote, Flared Rim, Openwork Flower Stem, Georg Jensen, 5 x 8 In. 2470.00

Compote, Flared, Footed, Peter Hertz, 9 In. 115.00
Compote, Hammered, Fruiting Grapevine, Fluted Stem, Georg Jensen, 7 1/2 In. 2705.00
Compote, No. 242, Figural Stem, Johan Rohde, Georg Jensen, 7 1/4 In. 1650.00
Cup & Saucer, Demitasse, No. 373 A, Georg Jensen, 2 In., 8 Piece 750.00
Demitasse Set, Blossom Pattern, Ivory Handles, Georg Jensen, 6 1/4 In. 3408.00
Demitasse Set, Hammered Texture, Wood Handles, Georg Jensen, 1900s, 3 Piece 1295.00
Dish, Flanged, Horse Trophy Inscription, Georg Jensen, 1936, 7 In. 326.00
Dresser Set, Brushes, Box, Mirror, File, Harald Nielsen, Georg Jensen, 5 Piece 2200.00
Ewer, Georg Jensen, 17 In. 10925.00
Magnifying Glass, No. 73, Georg Jensen, 6 1/2 x 3 In. . . . . .200.00 to 224.00
Pitcher, No. 432c, Johan Rohde, Georg Jensen, 11 1/4 In. 5500.00
Plate, Service, Round, Beaded Border, 11 In., 12 Piece 1575.00
Salad Servers, Openwork, Elongated Leaftip, Seed Pods, Georg Jensen, 7 1/2 In. 1116.00
Salad Set, Spoon & Fork, Pointed Tip, Monogram, Georg Jensen, 8 1/2 In. 330.00
Salt & Pepper, Acorn, Cobalt Glass, Johan Rohde, Georg Jensen, 6 Piece 230.00
Salt & Pepper, Cactus, Gundorph Albertus Design, Georg Jensen, 1930, 2 In. 290.00
Salt Cellar Set, No. 243 C, Georg Jensen, 3 1/4 In., 12 Piece 690.00
Salver, Horse Trophy, 13 In. 70.00
Sandwich Server, Scrolled Handles, Beaded, Fan Decoration, Georg Jensen, 8 In. 410.00
Tankard, Cover, Molded Body, Leaves, Medallion, Ear Handle, 1748, 29 Oz., 7 3/4 In. . . 1765.00
Teapot, Egg Shape, Lobed Foot, Cover, Leaves, Georg Jensen, 7 1/2 In. 288.00
SILVER-DUTCH, Beaker, Tapered Cylindrical, Embossed, c.1695, 3 1/4 In. 1998.00
Box, Cover, Hinged, Binding Of Isaac, 19th Century, 4 In. 1645.00
Coffee Jug, Hinged Lid, Cherub Finial, Leaf Body, Wood Handle, A.H.T., c.1875, 10 In. . . 620.00
Compote, Oval, Footed, c.1727, 2 x 5 1/2 x 3 1/2 In. 460.00
Salt & Pepper, Boy, Girl, Early 1900s, 3 In. 145.00
Spoon, Ragout, Double Ringed Shank, Shell At End, F.R. Precht, Amsterdam, 16 In. 745.00
Stuffing Spoon, Oval Bowl, Upturned Rib Handle, Jen Bosch, 1786, 12 In. 80.00
Tobacco Box, Oval, Chased Figural Decoration, 1 x 6 x 3 In. 105.00
SILVER-EGYPTIAN, Bowl, Boat Shape, Chased Flowers, Alexandria, c.1925, 10 x 22 In. 1610.00

SILVER-ENGLISH. English sterling silver is marked with a series of four or five small hallmarks. The standing lion mark is the most commonly seen sterling quality mark. The other marks indicate the city of origin, the maker, and the year of manufacture. These dates can be verified in many good books on silver.

SILVER-ENGLISH, Asparagus Tongs, Fiddle Handle, William Eaton, George IV, 1824 . . . . . . 750.00
Baby Rattle, Bells, Whistle, Coral End, 5 1/2 In. 460.00
Basket, Handle, Shell, Leaf Border, Vermeil Bowl, S. Davenport, George IV, 1823, 4 In. . . 370.00
Basket, Pierced Sides, Twisted Handle, Blue Glass Liner, Simkiss, George III, 4 In. 980.00
Basket, Pierced, Clover, Star, Scroll, Swing Handle, London, 4 1/2 x 13 x 11 In. 2130.00
Basket, Sweetmeat, Cutout, Swing Handle, George III, c.1775, 6 In. 375.00
Basting Spoon, Feather Edge, London, George III, c.1770, 12 3/4 In. 395.00
Basting Spoon, Fiddle Handle, William Eaton, William IV, 1830 . . . . 300.00
Basting Spoon, Hanoverian Pattern, Crest, Henry Brind 635.00
Beaker, Curved Flutes, Scroll Cartouche, Punched Acorn Border, J. Smith II, 7 In. 748.00
Beaker, Double, Barrel Shape, Marked, George III, 1787, 6 1/2 In. 1150.00
Berry Spoon, Engraved, London, George II, c.1745, 8 1/4 In. 120.00
Berry Spoon, Gold Washed Bowl, Fitted Case, Thomas Wallis, c.1798, Pair 195.00
Bowl, 1 Handle, Roman Style, Chester, 1913 . . . . 145.00
Bowl, Baluster Shape, Repousse Flower, Leaf, 1904, 5 x 6 In. 200.00
Bowl, Centerpiece, Marked, George V, 8 1/2 x 11 1/2 In. 520.00
Bowl, Elongated Loop Handle, Abalone Cabochon, C.R. Ashbee, 1905, 7 In. 3680.00
Bowl, Footed, Flower Repousse, Charles Stuart Harris, London, 1898, 8 1/2 x 14 In. 2530.00
Bowl, Pierced Sides, Chased Panels Of Flowers, Guild Of Handicraft, 1903, 6 In. 2530.00
Bowl, Pierced Sides, Engraved Leaves, Serpent Crest, c.1856, 8 1/2 In. 690.00
Bowl, Swirl Shape Base, Pedestal, London, 1786, 10 3/4 x 6 1/4 In. 1035.00
Bowl, Vegetable, Cover, Presentation Inscription, Sheffield, c.1857, 12 In. 575.00
Box, Ring, Repousse Decoration, Birmingham, c.1905, 3 1/4 In. 375.00
Box, Wave Pattern Top, Hinged Lid, S & Co., Goldsmiths Co., Newcastle, 3 1/2 In. 215.00
Brandy Saucepan, Pear Shape, Thomas Chawner, George III, 1785, 3 1/2 In. 705.00
Brandy Warmer, Stand, Eames & Barnard, c.1812 . . . . 1150.00
Bread Basket, Oval, Sheffield, c.1780, 11 1/2 x 13 3/4 In. 980.00

Bun Warmer, Ribbed Cover, Legs, 19th Century, 13 1/2 In. 230.00
Caddy Spoon, George III, c.1798, 3 x 1 5/8 In. 259.00
Caddy Spoon, Scallop Shape Bowl, Bright Cut Handle, 1795, 2 3/4 In. 230.00
Cake Basket, Garlands, Crest, John Deacon, c.1774, 10 x 13 1/2 In. 3220.00
Cake Basket, Oval, Panels, Wheat, Cable, Flowers, 1768, 10 x 13 x 11 1/2 In. 615.00
Candelabrum is listed in its own category.
Candle Snuffer, Stylized Rose, Scroll Handle, Barnard, London, 1840, 6 1/2 In., Pair 345.00
Candlesticks are listed in their own category.
Cann, Cup, Tapered Cylinder, Monogram, Etched Leaf, Bateman, George III, 1781, 6 In. . 3450.00
Card Tray, Shell Engraved Border, Thomas Hannam & Richard Mills, 1775 .... 375.00
Castor, Baluster, Pierced & Engraved Dome Top, T. Burridge, 1731, 6 3/4 In. 575.00
Castor, Baluster, Pierced Lid, Spreading Foot, George II, 1744, 6 3/8 In., Pair 590.00
Castor, Sugar, EC, London, Victorian, 1888, 10 In. 500.00
Chalice, Fenestrated, Boy Riding Dolphin, Domed Base, 1800s, 5 1/2 In., Pair 575.00
Chatelaine, 3 Graduated Egg Shape Segments, Putti, 6 Chains, 1888, 9 1/4 In. 499.00
Chocolate Pot, Stand, Fruitwood Handle, Reeded Rim, George III, c.1791, 10 In. 2350.00
Cigarette Case, Filigree, Birmingham, Square, c.1906, 3 1/2 In. 168.00
Cigarette Case, Thumb Latch, Interior Straps, George V, 1919, 6 x 3 1/2 In. 69.00
Coaster, Decanter, Gadroon Rim, W. Sharp, George III, 1817, 6 In. 345.00
Coffeepot, Beaded, Foliate Spout, Baluster, Wood Handle, Thomas Wallis, c.1823, 11 In. . 1763.00
Coffeepot, Dome Lid, Baluster, Gadroon Rim, Inscription, George II, 1759, 12 In. 2700.00
Coffeepot, Dome Lid, Baluster, Samuel Wood, George III, 1767, 10 1/4 In. 1880.00
Coffeepot, Dome Lid, Wood Handle, London, George III, 1765, 9 1/2 In. 235.00
Coffeepot, Tiered Lid, Serpentine Fruitwood Handle, George II, c.1748, 10 In. 2585.00
Condiment Set, Pierced Gallery, Richard Meach, George III, 10 In., 6 Piece 2185.00
Creamer, Egg Shape, Reeded Bands, Hannah Northcote, George III, 1809, 3 7/8 In. 175.00
Creamer, Helmet Shape, Loop Handle, Engraved, George III, 1805, 4 1/2 x 4 x 3 In. 550.00
Creamer, Squat, Chased Flowers, Leaves, J. Henry, C. Lias, 1826, 3 In. 315.00
Cruet Set, Rocaille Frame, 4 Anthemion Feet, 2 Jars, Wilkinson & Co., 10 In. 865.00
Cup, Presentation, Bulbous, Guest & Cradock, George III, c.1807, 7 1/2 In. 920.00
Decanter Label, Rectangular Shape, Rum, George III, c.1800, 3/4 x 2 In. 85.00
Decanter Label, Ribbon Scroll Form, Benedictine, George III, c.1810, 1 x 2 7/8 In. 69.00
Dish, Cover, Goose Head Crest, Sheffield, Mid 19th Century, 10 1/2 x 19 3/4 In. 635.00
Dish, Entree, Cover, Gadroon Rims, Handle, George V, 11 In. 999.00
Dish, Entree, Cover, Pierced Strainer, 2-Handled Stand, Sheffield, 15 In., Pair 1425.00
Dish, Shell Shape, 3-Footed, H. Bailey, London Hallmark, c.1750, 1 x 4 1/2 In., Pair 920.00
Egg Cruet, Circular, 6 Removable Eggcups, W. Bateman, c.1820, 8 1/2 In. 1435.00
Ewer, Cut Crystal, Cover, Egg Shape, WC, London, c.1895, 9 3/4 In. 290.00
Ewer, Presentation, Victorian, Oval Body, Short Spout, c.1854, 13 In. 1410.00
Ewer, Shaped Spout, Loop Handle, Pear Shape, Leaves, London, 1904, 9 1/4 In. 600.00
Figurine, Chinese Man, Charles Stuart Harris, London, 1874, 3 3/4 In. 175.00
Figurine, Fighting Cock, With Spurs, Thomas Of Bond St., 1904, 3 1/2 In. 350.00
Fish Server, Cutwork Decoration, Holly & Berry, George III, c.1817, 12 In. 1375.00
Fish Server, Lily Pattern, Pierced & Engraved Tines & Blade, Victorian, Pair 460.00
Fish Set, Mother-Of-Pearl Handles, Oak Case, Harrison, Sheffield, c.1910, 24 Piece 520.00
Fish Slice, Double Blade, Fiddle, Pierced, 1817, 11 3/8 In. 1050.00
Fish Slice, King's Pattern, Stag Head Crest, Eley & Fearn, George IV, 1821, 12 1/2 In. 460.00
Fish Slice, Marked, Hester Bateman, London, 1784 .... 200.00
Frame, Castor, Flower Form, Scrolled, Shell Feet & Handle, Cartouche, 10 5/8 In. 325.00
Frame, Green Enamel, Flowers, Leaves, Liberty & Co., 1902, 7 1/2 x 6 In. 1725.00
Goblet, Thistle Shape Bowl, Grapevines, Joseph Angell, c.1825, 6 x 3 1/4 In. 1840.00
Gravy Boat, Oblong, Melon Shape, Coat Of Arms, J. Pollock, c.1751, 5 In. 575.00
Inkstand, 2 Cobalt Glass Pots, Candleholder Box Lid, T.B., George IV, 1821, 7 In. 1495.00
Inkstand, Boat Shape, Beaded Edge, John Schofield, 1784, 7 3/4 In. 880.00
Jug, Cut Glass, Pear Shape, Crosshatch Cut, Edward Hutton, c.1882, 10 1/2 In. 1210.00
Jug, Hot Water, Lid, Cylindrical, 4 Reeded Bands, George III, 1786, 7 1/2 In. 705.00
Jug, Hot Water, Lobed, Baluster, Acorn Finial, 3 Feet, J. Mortimer & J.S. Hunt, 9 In. 920.00
Kettle, Stand, Base, Handle, Burner, Marked, 12 In. 575.00
Kettle, Stand, Pear Shape, Strapwork Cartouches, R. Hennell, London, 1871, 17 In. 2235.00
Knife & Fork Set, Pistol Handle, Cased, Edward VII, c.1902, 12 Piece 635.00
Ladle, Bellflower & Fern, Repousse, Stamped, Dewey & Jordan, Victorian, 12 1/2 In. ... 150.00
Ladle, Crest Engraved Handle, T B, c.1811, 13 In. 237.00
Ladle, Embossed Bowl, Rosewood Handle, 13 In. 115.00

Ladle, Fiddle, Thread & Shell, Edwardian, c.1902, 8 x 2 1/2 In., Pair 115.00
Ladle, Oval Bowl, George III, London, c.1763, 13 In. 295.00
Ladle, Oval Bowl, London, 1842, 13 3/8 In. 150.00
Ladle, Sterling, Fiddle Thread Shell, Monogram, Fearn, Eley & Chawner, 12 1/2 In. 285.00
Marrow Scoop, Double, P. & W. Bateman, London, c.1805, 9 In. 290.00
Marrow Scoop, Family Crest, Hand & Sword, George II, 1749, 8 1/2 In. 300.00
Marrow Scoop, George Smith & William Fearn, c.1792 .... 195.00
Marrow Scoop, Green Ivory Handle, P. & W. Bateman, 1811, 6 1/4 In. 575.00
Match Safe, Repousse Golfing Scene, Birmingham, Early 1900s, 1 1/2 In. 520.00
Meat Skewer, Ring Handle, Crozier, William Barrett, George III, c.1809, 11 1/2 In. 200.00
Muffineer, Pierced Pear Shape Lid, Flame Finial, c.1891, 7 In. 200.00
Muffineer, Waisted Baluster Shape, Fluted Base, Edward VII, c.1904, 8 1/4 In. 235.00
Mug, Baluster Shape, Scroll Handle, Leaftip, Monogram, George II, c.1746, 5 In. 880.00
Mug, Baluster Shape, Serpentine Handle, Reeded Foot, George III, 1797, 5 1/4 In. 940.00
Mug, Cylindrical, Leaf Shape Handle, C.H. Rawlings, William IV, 1835, 3 1/4 In. 375.00
Mug, Cylindrical, Leaf Shape Handle, William IV, 1833, 3 In. 375.00
Mug, Cylindrical, Repousse Wave & Flower, Sheffield, 1897 .... 185.00
Mug, Footed, C-Handle, GS & DF, c.1897, 2 3/4 In. 175.00
Mug, Hexagonal Baluster Shape, Joseph & John Angel, Victorian, 4 1/2 In. 259.00
Mug, Repousse, Engraved Shells, Laurel Foot, C. & G. Fox, 1852, 4 In. 345.00
Mustard Pot, Dome Lid, Oval, Dash & Dot Band, Hinged, Edwardian, 2 x 3 In. 230.00
Mustard Pot, Hinged Lid, Gibson & Longman, c.1866, 2 1/2 x 2 x 3 3/4 In., Pair 430.00
Mustard Pot, Spoon, Wire Loop Handle, Ball Finial, Guild Of Handicraft, 4 In. 2760.00
Napkin Rings are listed in their own category.
Page Turner, Rococo, Tortoiseshell Blade, George III, c.1817, 14 1/2 In. 380.00
Page Turner, Tortoiseshell Blade, Pistol Grip Handle, Engraved, Repousse, c.1882, 11 In. . 220.00
Pap Boat, Monogram, London, George I, 1726, 4 3/8 In. 235.00
Peg Tankard, Low Stepped Lid, Volute Thumbpiece, Charles II, c.1683, 6 3/4 In. 7640.00
Plate Set, Molded, Gadroon Rim, Coat Of Arms, George III, 9 1/2 In., 6 Piece 255.00
Platter, Gadroon Rim, Engraved, Sebastian & James Crespell, George III, 18 In. 1530.00
Punch Ladle, Back Tipt Handle, Engraved, George III, c.1810, 12 1/4 In. 265.00
Punch Ladle, Engraved H, George Angell, Victorian, c.1852, 13 1/2 In. 170.00
Punch Ladle, Handle, Shell Shape Bowl, London, George III, 13 In. 295.00
Punch Ladle, Monogram, WRS Hallmark, London, c.1846, 7 In. 175.00
Punch Ladle, Scallop Bowl, Chasing On Bottom, P., A. & W. Bateman, 1802 .... 290.00
Rose Bowl, Lobed, Fluted, Scroll & Shell Rim, Footed, Guild Of Handicraft, 10 In. 805.00
Salt, Georgian, Scalloped Rim, Round Body, Flowers, 3 Heads, London, 1760, Pair 345.00
Salt, London, 1917, 5 Oz., 2 1/2 In., Pair 265.00
Salt, Octagonal, Waisted, Oval Bowl, R. Pilkington, George II, 1728, 3 In., Pair 1955.00
Salt, Square, Concave Corners, Round Bowl, J.E. Terry, George III, 1788, 3 In., Pair 520.00
Salt & Pepper, Cylindrical, Reeding, Flame Finials, c.1894, 2 1/4 In., Pair 59.00
Salt Cellar, Cauldron Shape, 3 Supports, Bateman, Georgian, 1 3/8 x 2 3/8 In., Pair 345.00
Salver, 3 Pad Feet, Acanthus Engraved, Ebenezer Coker, George III, 1765, 6 3/4 In. 470.00
Salver, 4 Ball & Claw Feet, Monogram, Gadroon Rim, George V, 1928, 18 1/2 In. 1175.00
Salver, Acanthus & Scrolling Rocaille Rim, Coat Of Arms, George II, 1748, 15 In. 3290.00
Salver, Armorial, Shell Rim, Richard Rug, London, 1770, 7 5/8 In. .... *Illus* 1120.00
Salver, C-Scroll Cartouches, Monogram, Inscription, E.& J. Barnard, 1857, 12 7/8 In. ... 529.00
Salver, Daniel Holy & Co., 1825, 6 3/4 In. 339.00
Salver, Engraved, Armorial, C-Scroll Cartouche, George III, c.1770, 7 5/8 In. 1120.00
Salver, Engraved, C-Scroll, Rocaille, Leaves, Molded Rim, George II, c.1755, 7 5/8 In. .. 499.00
Salver, Footed, Peter & Ann Bateman, 1791, 7 1/4 In. 4950.00
Salver, Heraldic Shield, Swag Border, Timothy Renou, George III, 1795, 6 7/8 In. 440.00
Salver, Oval, Engraved, Hester Bateman, London, George III, 1790, 6 1/2 In. 920.00
Salver, Oval, Engraved, Tied Swags, Leaves, Scrolled Feet, 17 Oz., 10 3/8 In. 295.00
Salver, Raised Pad Feet, Marked, George V, 10 In. 400.00
Salver, Shaped Rim, Acanthus, Shells, Engraved Roundels, c.1885, 12 In. 590.00
Salver, Shell Molded, Gadroon Rim, 3 Hoof Feet, George II, 1761, 7 3/8 In. 705.00
Salver, Shell, Scroll Border, Scroll Supports, George III, c.1800, 16 1/8 In. 4900.00
Salver, William & Robert Peaston, George II, c.1758, 7 In. 560.00
Sauce Ladle, Fiddle Thread, George Smith III, W. Fearn, c.1790, 7 In., Pair 200.00
Sauce Ladle, King Pattern, William Chawner, London, 1832, 7 In. 235.00
Sauce Ladle, Old English Pattern, Hester Bateman, George III, c.1785, 7 In. 470.00
Sauceboat, 3-Footed, Scroll Open Handle, c.1889, 3 1/2 x 6 3/4 In. 60.00

Sauceboat, Crimped Edge, Hoof Feet, Shells, Acanthus Leaf Handle, 4 7/8 x 7 In. 575.00
Sauceboat, Scrolled Handle, 3 Legs, Hoofed Feet, E.B., Georgian, c.1769, 6 In. 545.00
Seal, Art Nouveau Bust, Woman In Corset, Flowers In Flowing Hair, 1901, 3 3/4 In. 385.00
Sealing Wax Stand, Shell Shape, Engraved Leaves, Oil Lamp, C. Edington, 9 In. 750.00
Serving Spoon, Aesthetic Movement, Peacock, Acanthus, c.1877, 8 3/4 In., Pair 295.00
Serving Spoon, Hester Bateman, c.1782, Pair 260.00
Serving Spoon, Monogram, William Eaton Mark, George IV, 1824, 12 1/2 In. 250.00
Shaker, Dome Pierced Cap, Pedestal Base, Cylinder Shape, London, 1811, 3 1/2 In. 115.00
Soup Ladle, William Hutton & Sons, London, c.1907 .... 230.00
Spoon, Demitasse, Enameled, Gold Wash Bowl, Edward VIII, 4 In., 12 Piece 175.00
Straining Spoon, Fiddle Shape, William IV, c.1831, 12 x 2 1/4 In. 345.00
Stuffing Spoon, Engraved Crest, Hester Bateman, c.1783 .... 575.00
Stuffing Spoon, Monogram H, London, Dated 1806, 12 In. 230.00
Sugar, Cover, Egg Shape, Ribbed Waist, Gadroon Rim, Heming, 1926, 5 1/2 In. 175.00
Sugar, Neoclassical, Vermeil Interior, 4 Ribbed Panels, c.1801, 7 1/2 In. 339.00
Sugar, Rose, C-Shape Handles, Flower Vine, J.E. Terry, c.1825, 5 1/2 x 8 In. 200.00
Sugar, Urn, Neoclassical, Bright Cut Decoration, Glass Liner, Georgian, 5 1/2 In. ... 805.00
Sugar, Waisted Oval Shape, Angular Reeded Handles, George III, c.1807, 9 In. 410.00
Sugar Basket, Handle, Beaded Edge, Engraved Flowers, Sheffield, 4 3/4 x 4 In. 110.00
Sugar Basket, Navette Shape, Swing Handle, London, George III, 1791, 4 3/4 In. 499.00
Sugar Shaker, Pierced Top, Faceted Baluster Shape, S.L. Ltd., 7 1/2 In., 1932 ...... 330.00
Sugar Tongs, Old English Pattern, George III, c.1803, 5 3/4 In. 35.00
Tablespoon, Bright Cut, John Lamb, London, 1784 .... 357.00
Tablespoon, Fiddle & Thread, George Smith, George III, 16 Piece 1380.00
Tablespoon, Fiddle Thread Design, Eley & Fearn, London, 1807, Pair 60.00
Tablespoon, Hanoverian, Rococo Shell, R. Burton, London, Georgian, c.1762, 8 In. 145.00
Tankard, Tapered Cylinder, Engraved Armorials, T. Cooke II & R. Gurney, 5 In. 2300.00
Tankard, Tapered Cylinder, Scroll Handle, W. Shaw & W. Priest, George III, 8 In. 3220.00
Tea & Coffee Set, Bun Feet, Wood Handles, J.G. Ltd., Birmingham, 4 Piece 656.00
Tea & Coffee Set, Richard Hennell, Aesthetic Period, c.1860, 4 Piece 3500.00
Tea & Coffee Set, Scrolled Leaves, Fluted Melon Shape, Scrolled Feet, J. Figg, 4 Piece .. 2990.00
Tea Caddy, Enamel, Oval, Applied Roundels, Liberty & Co., 3 3/8 x 3 3/8 x 2 1/2 In. 845.00
Tea Caddy Spoon, Leaf Shape, George III, 3 3/8 In. 695.00
Tea Set, Aesthetic Style Repousse, Bone Handle, William Fox, c.1876, 4 Piece 1675.00
Tea Set, Lobed Egg Shape, Atkins & Somersall, 1824, 3 Piece 1295.00
Tea Set, Melon Fluted, Barnard, 5 3/4-In. Pot, 3 Piece 920.00
Tea Set, Melon Shape, Chased, Embossed, William IV, c.1835, 4 Piece 3055.00
Tea Set, Oval, Creamer, Sugar, George V, 4 1/2 In. 265.00
Tea Set, Oval, Gold Wash Interior, Acanthus, T.B., London, 1822, 3 Piece 605.00
Tea Set, Sugar, Creamer, Fruitwood Handle, Edward VII, 18 Oz., 5 1/4 In., 3 Piece 235.00
Tea Urn, 3 Parts, Flowers, Alexander Johnston, George III, 20 1/4 In. 3165.00
Teapot, Bright Cut Decoration, Hinged Lid, George III, c.1787, 6 1/2 In. 520.00
Teapot, Cover, London, George III, c.1798, 6 3/4 In. 590.00
Teapot, Ivory Finial, Scrolling Vines, George III, c.1800, 11 In. 765.00
Teapot, Ivory Mushroom Shape Finial, Scrolled Spout, George III, 8 In. 764.00
Teapot, Oval, Wood Handle, Hester Bateman, London, c.1781, 5 1/2 x 9 1/2 In. 2875.00
Teapot, Pear Shape, Urn Finial, Wood Handle, George III, 11 1/2 x 9 x 5 In. 1430.00
Teapot, Repousse, Spout, Handle, Flowers, Cartouche, George III, 10 In. 440.00
Teapot, Swirl Fluted, Inverted Pear, Paul Storr, George III, 1814, 6 7/8 In. 1610.00
Teapot, Trivet, Bright Cut Decoration, Ivory Handle, Finial, George III, c.1786 .... 1610.00
Teapot, Turned Wood Finial, Cover, Flattened Ball Shape, George V, c.1921, 4 In. 355.00
Teapot, Waisted Egg Shape, Reeded Rim, 1900s, 6 3/4 In. 120.00
Teapot, Waisted Oval Shape, Reeded Girdle, Ear Handle, George IV, c.1824, 6 In. 646.00
Tete-A-Tete, Reeding, Angular Fruitwood Handles, George V, c.1912, 5 In., 3 Piece 235.00
Thimble Case, Egg Shape, Embossed, Birds, C-Scrolls, c.1893, 2 In. 325.00
Thread Pull, Stork With Baby In Stomach, 1700s, 4 3/4 In. 175.00
Toast Rack, James Dixon & Sons, Sheffield, c.1896, 4 x 3 1/4 In. 375.00
Toast Rack, Rectangular, Ball Feet, Handle, 1812, 9 Oz., 6 x 7 x 4 1/2 In. 770.00
Toast Rack, WE, London, c.1873, 7 1/2 In. 375.00
Toddy Ladle, Shaped Bowl, Chased Garlands, Horn Handle, George III, 16 3/4 In. 185.00
Tongs, Ember, Accordion Shape, Pierced & Chased Flowers & Leaves, 21 In. 1265.00
Tray, Center Crest, Handles, Sheffield, c.1820, 30 In. 430.00
Tray, Oval, Cartouche, Engraved Crest, London, c.1909, 18 1/2 & 16 In., Pair 1430.00

Silver-English, Salver,
Armorial, Shell Rim,
Richard Rug, London,
1770, 7 5/8 In.

Silver-Irish, Salver, Footed,
Armorial Engraving, Dublin,
1706-1708, 5 5/8 In.

Trophy, Coffeepot, Dome Lid, New York Racing Assn., George III, c.1777, 13 In.	2468.00
Trophy, Cup, Egg Shape, 3 Rifles, Wreath, Victorian, c.1862, 7 3/4 In.	635.00
Trophy, Cup, Silver Gilt, 2 Handles, Cover, London, William IV, 1832, 16 In.	5900.00
Trophy, Victorian, Urn Shape, Scroll, Flowers Repousse, 1863, 9 x 7 x 4 In.	330.00
Trowel, Ivory Handle, Scroll Border, c.1875, 11 In.	175.00
Tureen, Sauce, Dome Lid, Boat Shape, Loop Handles, George III, 1787, 10 1/4 In.	1175.00
Urn, Beehive, Sheffield Plate, George III, c.1800, 19 x 9 In.	920.00
Urn, Cover, Gilt, Flowers, Grapevine, Inscription, London, William IV, 1831, 14 In.	2185.00
Urn, Pinecone Finial, Lion Masks, Ring Handles, George III, c.1792, 17 1/2 In.	3290.00
Urn, Presentation, Applied Figures Chasing Horses, Edward VII, 11 x 14 x 13 In.	7700.00
Vase, 2 Handles, Berry, Garland, Leaves, JB & Son, Sheffield, c.1898, 5 1/2 In.	250.00
Vase, Trumpet, Reticulated, Comyns & Sons, Edward VII, 1903, 7 3/4 In., Pair	410.00
Vase, Trumpet, Weighted Foot, William Comyns, London, Edward VII, 1902, 15 In.	705.00
Vinaigrette & Perfume, Hunting Horn, Sampson Mordan & Co., 1873, 3 In.	2200.00
Waiter, Piecrust Rim, 3 Scroll Supports, London, George III, c.1816, 8 In.	865.00
Waiter, Piecrust Rim, 3 Scroll Supports, Victorian, c.1873, 8 1/4 In.	345.00
Wine Coaster, Gadroon Exterior, Leaf Decoration, Weighted, 7 In., Pair	489.00
Wine Cooler, Fluted Body, Beaded Rims, Sheffield, c.1800, Pair	2640.00
Wine Cooler, Urn Shape, Double Flower Handles, Gadrooning, Sheffield, 9 1/2 In.	440.00
Wine Funnel, 2 Part, R. Emes & R. Barnard, George III, 1812, 5 In.	805.00
Wine Funnel, Bell Shape, Strainer, George III, 1810, 4 Oz., 5 3/4 x 3 1/4 In.	990.00
Wine Funnel, Bucket Shape, Smith & Hayter, George III, c.1802, 5 3/4 x 2 3/4 In.	865.00
Wine Funnel, Detachable Strainer, John Deacon, George III, 1794, 6 1/4 In.	470.00
Wine Funnel, Reeded Rim, Curving Spout, George III, c.1807, 6 3/4 In.	750.00
SILVER-FRENCH, Beaker, Flared, Tapering, Circular, Pedestal Feet, 1800s, 4 x 3 1/2 In., Pair	865.00
Beaker, Paneled Cylinder, Pendant Acanthus, Round Foot, c.1800, 4 In.	355.00
Bottle Holder, Hinged, Scrolled Handles, Tapered Collar, Cartier, 9 x 4 x 1 In., Pair	1100.00
Box, Treen Lined, Art Deco, Christofle, 5 1/2 In.	330.00
Carving Set, Louis XV Pattern, Steel Blade, Monogram, c.1890, 12 1/2 In., 2 Piece	85.00
Chalice & Paten, Engraved, Enamel Plaques Of Holy Family, 8 In.	345.00
Cigar Case, First Standard, Oblong, Flowers, Mountain Lake, c.1850, 5 3/8 x 3 In.	345.00
Coffeepot, Second Standard, Pear Shape, Side Handle, 1800s, 9 1/2 In.	3680.00
Coffeepot, Urn Shape, Leaf Tip Rim & Waist Bands, Paris, Early 1800s, 12 3/4 In.	1530.00
Cream Pot, First Standard, Swirled Body, Ring Foot, Side Handle, GB, 5 In.	575.00
Cup & Saucer, Mid To Late 19th Century, 3 3/4 In.	235.00
Dresser Set, Gadroon Borders, Mirror, 2 Hair & 2 Clothes Brushes	290.00
Ewer, Heavy Leaf Repousse, Minerva Hallmark, 1873, 6 x 5 In.	420.00
Ice Bucket, Double Hinge Handles, Ice Tong Hanger, Cartier, 14 x 7 x 5 1/2 In.	550.00
Jewelry Box, Cover, Hinged, Eagle & Leaf Swag, 7 1/2 In.	999.00
Muffineer, Repousse, Flower, Cherub, Dolphin Finial, 1800s, 7 1/2 In.	259.00
Mug, Barrel Shape, Scroll Handle, 1800s, 1 1/2 In.	145.00
Mustard Pot, Cover, Oblong, Berry Finial, 18th Century, 5 Oz., 3 1/2 In.	190.00
Salad Servers, Bone, Fork & Knife, Fiddle Shape Handles, Late 1800s, 10 1/2 In.	150.00
Sugar Sifter, Standard, c.1835, 8 3/4 In.	105.00
Tea & Coffee Set, First Standard, Ivory Handles, RD, 4 Piece	1840.00
Tumbler, Machine Turning, M Monogram, 1800s, 3 In.	127.00
Tureen, Louis XV, Tetard Freres, 9 1/2 In.	1650.00
Vase, Baroque Style, Strasbourg, c.1763, 9 1/4 In.	1840.00
Water Jug, Dome Lid, Fluted, Spout, Fruitwood Handles, 3-Footed, 20 Oz., 9 In.	3290.00

Wine Coaster, Egg Shape, Scroll, Leaf Rim, Late 1800s, 11 1/4 In. 325.00
Writing Set, Cased, Ivory Blade Letter Opener, Leaf Bandwork, 3 Piece 265.00
SILVER-GERMAN, Bowl, Centerpiece, Glass, Leaf, Berry Sprigs, 19th Century, 19 1/2 In. ... 1998.00
Bowl, Centerpiece, Ribbed Panels, Basket Weave, 1884, 6 1/2 x 13 1/4 x 7 1/2 In. 385.00
Bowl, Cover, Etched Flowers, Scrolling Leaves, Putto Finial, Roses On Base, 8 3/4 In. 245.00
Bowl, Mounted, Etched Glass, Putto Driving Reindeer-Drawn Sled, c.1900, 13 In. 2185.00
Bowl, Repousse, Engraved Fruit, Leaves, Round, Lobed, Pedestal Foot, 8 1/2 In. 260.00
Bowl, Reticulated, Cherubs, Dolphins, Flowers, c.1890, 9 1/2 In. 140.00
Candy Dish, Dragon Shape Handles, 3 1/2 x 4 3/4 In. 160.00
Card Holder, Fan Shape, Figural Relief, Late 1800s, 3 1/2 In. 69.00
Castor, Cover, Emu, Cabochon Stone Eyes, Oval, Incised Feather, 4 Oz., 5 3/8 In. 175.00
Cigarette Box, Geometric Designs, Art Deco, c.1835, 1 1/2 x 3 1/4 x 4 1/4 In. 150.00
Claret Jug, Etched Glass, Flowers, Scrolls, Flattened Baluster, 11 3/4 In. 940.00
Compact, Hinged Lid, Enameled Scene, Shaped Edge, 3 1/4 In. 470.00
Cup, 3 Handles, Repousse Landscape, Shell Shape Feet, 1800s, 3 1/4 In. 230.00
Dessert Spoon, Classical Figures, Gold Wash Bowl, 13 Piece 200.00
Dish, Cover, Engraved, Cherub Finial, Acanthus Feet, 9 1/2 In. 565.00
Salt, Triple, Cherub Handle, Scallop Shell Bowls, Dolphin Feet, 1800s, 4 In. 315.00
Sauceboat, Fluted, Gilt Interior, Scroll Handle, Oval Stand, Pair 525.00
Sauceboat, Helmet Shape, Scrolled Handle, Beaded Borders, Lions, Eagles, 9 x 6 x 9 In. . 303.00
Sauceboat, Reeded Border, Handles, Acanthus Leaf Mounts, 5 x 10 x 7 In., Pair 520.00
Tea & Coffee Set, Balustrade Bodies, Chased, Embossed, 6 Piece 4110.00
Tea Set, Gourd Shape, Flower Designs, P. Bruckman & Son, c.1925, 3 Piece 260.00
Teapot, Hinged Lid, Twist Design Body, Schickmann, U.S. Zone, 8 1/2 In. 150.00
Tray, Repousse Scene, Frolicking Cherubs, 13 1/2 In. 418.00
Vase, Reticulated Silver, Etched Glass, Leaf Band, Stamped Scenes, 14 5/8 In. 705.00
SILVER-INDIAN, Coffeepot, Baluster Shape, Serpentine Spout, Handle, Early 1900s, 7 3/4 In. 235.00
SILVER-IRISH, Coffeepot, Swag & Leaf, Acorn Finial, Joseph Jackson, 1779 .... 2645.00
Cup, 2 Scroll Handles, Grape & Leaf, John Locker, Dublin, c.1770, 6 1/2 x 10 In. 920.00
Dish Ring, Pierced Concave Side, People, Animals, Victorian, c.1899, 3 3/4 x 7 3/4 In. ... 805.00
Dish Ring, Reticulated, Engraved, Flared, C Scrolls, Flower Heads, 6 3/4 In. 4400.00
Salver, Footed, Armorial Engraving, Dublin, 1706-1708, 5 5/8 In. .... *Illus* 1640.00
Stuffing Spoon, Regimental, William Fitzgerald, George III, c.1810, 10 In. 3820.00
SILVER-ITALIAN, Bowl, Centerpiece, Coquille Shape, Buccellati, Milan, 1900s, 3 x 14 x 16 In. 3220.00
Cigarette Box, Rectangular, 2 Gold Washed Vertical Bands, 1900s, 7 In. 175.00
Dish, Shell, Spiral Shell Footed, Gianmaria Buccellati, 20th Century, 6 In. 865.00
Dish, Sunflower Shape, Gianmaria Buccellati, 20th Century, 7 1/4 In. 865.00
Ewer, Fluted Sides, Scroll Handle, Pedestal Foot, 8 1/2 In. 920.00
Grape Scissors, Figural Design, Late 1800s, 5 1/2 In. 69.00
Hip Flask, Cylindrical Lid, Curved Rectangle, Rounded Corners, 1900s, 5 3/8 In. 120.00
Platter, Oval, Pierced Ovolo Gallery, Buccellati, Milan, 1900s, 16 1/2 x 20 In. 3910.00
Salad Servers, Fiddle Shape Handle, A. Cesa, Allesandria, c.1925, 10 1/2 In. 115.00
Tea Set, Georgian Style, Squat, Waisted, Egg Shape, Buccellati, 1900s, 4 Piece 2000.00
SILVER-JAPANESE, Bowl, Chrysanthemum Shape, 1900s, 7 1/4 In. 489.00
Bowl, Repousse Flower Decoration, 6 1/2 In. 561.00
Censer, Carved & Pierced Chrysanthemums, 1869-1911, 5 In. 1295.00
Cigar Box, Leaf Design, Rosewood Lining, Engraved, Early 1900s, 8 1/4 In. 690.00
Picture Frame, Dragon & Pearl Design, 1900s, 12 1/2 x 10 1/2 In. 345.00
Tea & Coffee Set, Sterling Cased, Imperial Hotel Tokyo, Mid-1900s, 7 Piece 1265.00
Tea & Coffee Set, Tray, Flower Capped Legs, Scroll Handle, 4 Piece 1840.00
Vase, Pear Shape, Crane, Wave, Handles, Nakagawa Yoshizane, c.1910, 10 1/2 In. 920.00
SILVER-MEXICAN, Ashtray, Inverted Cone, 3 Cigarette Holders, W. Spratling, 2 1/4 In., Pair . 650.00
Bowl, Ear Handles, Beads, Spratling, 6 In. 1115.00
Bowl, Kovsh Shape, Cast Shield Handle, Shell Finial, 15 In. 1115.00
Bowl, Lobed, Oval, Chased, Embossed Leaf Rim Border, Ear Handles, 9 In. 470.00
Bowl, Tapered Oval, Chased Rim, Leaf & Flower Swags, Handles, 14 Oz., 9 1/8 In. 235.00
Box, Hinged Lid, Book Shape, Clasp Closure, 20th Century, 7 1/2 In. 410.00
Coffee Set, Sanborn, c.1950, 16 x 9 1/2 In., 4 Piece 2625.00
Coffeepot, Hinged Lid, Wood Side Handle, Angled Spout, 6 In. 575.00
Dish, Entree, Cover, Oval, Scroll Handles, Rim, 20th Century, 14 5/8 In. 235.00
Julep Cup, Cylindrical, Tapered, 1900s, 4 3/4 x 2 3/4 In., 8 Piece 230.00
Nut Dish, Embossed Leaf Shape, 3 Feet, c.1940, 3 x 3 1/2 In., 5 Piece 50.00
Pitcher, Bulbous, Art Deco, Ribbed Handle, 8 3/4 In. 290.00

Pitcher, Elongated Sphere, Threaded Bands, c.1950, 8 In. 635.00
Pitcher, Modern Shape, Round Angular Spout, Flattened Foot, Spratling, 5 1/2 In. 590.00
Pitcher, Water, Elongated Sphere, C-Scroll Handle, Sanborn, 1950 . . . . 630.00
Pitcher & Stirrer, Martini, Rolled Rim, 9 3/4 x 6 1/2 In. 375.00
Plate, Repousse, Flower Rim, Star Of David, 20th Century, 11 1/4 In. 190.00
Platter, Oval, 12 1/2 In. 80.00
Platter, Oval, Molded & Reeded Rim, 20th Century, Ortega, 21 1/2 In. 295.00
Punch Bowl, Ladle, 14 x 9 In. 520.00
Punch Set, Sterling, Leafy S-Scroll Rims, Spreading Foot, 14 Piece 2235.00
Salad Servers, Danish Modern Style, Blossom Handles, c.1950, 10 In. 290.00
Salt & Spoon, Chasing, Applied Beads, W. Spratling, 1 1/8 & 2 3/8 In., Pair 495.00
Salt & Spoon, Rosewood Handle, Spratling, c.1942, 1 x 1 1/2 In., 12 Piece 690.00
Serving Bowl, Molded Sides, Reeded Rim, 20th Century, 10 1/2 In. 175.00
Shot Cup Set, Chased Band Of Flowers, c.1950, 1 3/4 x 1 1/4 In., 12 Piece 90.00
Spoon Set, Demitasse, Bamboo Shape Handles, c.1950, 5 Piece 345.00
Tray, Chippendale Style, Scalloped Edge, Hand Hammered, 16 3/4 In. 1100.00
Tray, Oval, Applied Beaded, Flowered Handles, Rolled Lip, 18 x 12 1/4 In. 475.00
Tray, Oval, Molded Edge, Cutout Handles, 4-Footed, Maciel, 1900s, 21 In. 500.00
Tray, Oval, Scrolled, Scalloped Borders, Openwork, Luella, c.1960, 30 x 19 1/4 In. 1045.00
Tray, Rectangular, Molded Rim, 2 Handles, Sanborn, 1930s, 20 1/4 In. 440.00
SILVER-MIDDLE EASTERN, Coffee Set, Demitasse, Dimpled, Chased, Early 1900s, 5 Piece . . 765.00
Tray, Raised Rim, Molded Panels, Engraved Leaves, 15 3/4 In. 470.00
SILVER-ORIENTAL, Tea Set, Repousse Dragons, Bamboo Handles, 5-In. Teapot, 3 Piece 345.00
SILVER-PERUVIAN, Bowl, Fruit, Oval, Pinched Center, Stylized Berries, 1900s, 11 1/8 In. . . . 175.00
Bowl, Fruit, Oval, Pinched Center, Stylized Berries, 1900s, 11 In. 175.00
Charger, Hand Tooled, Ancient Style Design, 14 In. 115.00
Ice Bucket, Raised Figural Decoration, 5 1/2 In. 69.00
SILVER-PORTUGUESE, Pitcher, Water, Oval, Scroll Handle, Shells, Leaves, 8 3/4 In. 315.00
Tea & Coffee Set, Classical Revival Style, Ribbon Swag, 4 Piece 1645.00
SILVER-ROMANIAN, Box, Geometric Pattern, Engraved, Rectangular, 1900s, 4 3/4 In. 115.00

SILVER-RUSSIAN. Russian silver is marked with the Cyrillic, or Russian, alphabet. The numbers 84, 88, or 91 indicate the silver content. Russian silver may be higher or lower than sterling standard. Other marks indicate maker, assayer, or city of manufacture. Many pieces of silver made in Russia are decorated with enamel. Faberge pieces are listed in their own category.

SILVER-RUSSIAN, Basket, Sweetmeat, Oval, Lobed, Leaves, Swing Handle, Footed, 7 3/4 In.   370.00
Cigarette Case, Crumpled Hide Look, Rectangular, Blue Cabochon, 4 In. 825.00
Cream Jug, Cover, Flower Finial, Wide Spout, Baluster Body, c.1784, 6 In. 175.00
Cup, Tulip Shape, Stippled & Cut Flowers, Vines, 1855, 2 3/4 In. 290.00
Ewer, Egg Shape Body, Slender Neck, Serpentine, Moscow, 1867, 9 3/4 In. 350.00
Ewer, Engraved Flower Band, Black Enamel Accent, 8 1/2 In. 395.00
Glass Beaker, Mounted, Handle, Early 1800s 4183.00
Glass Holder, Enameled, Klingert, 3 1/4 In. 255.00
Kovsh, Enamel Flowers, MC Maker's Mark, Maria Semenova, c.1912, 2 x 3 1/2 In. 1035.00
Kovsh, Enameled, Gilt, Flat Handle, Scrolling Floral Vines, 4 1/4 In. 2235.00
Ladle, EK, St. George 84, 1894, 11 3/4 x 3 1/2 In. 259.00
Salt Cellar, Hinged Lid, Gilt, Throne Shape, Leaf Scrolls, Basket Weave, c.1874, 3 In. . . . 295.00
Spoon, Engraved Buildings, Vermeil Bowls, 4 1/4 In., 6 Piece 425.00
Sugar & Creamer, Bone Handle, Finial, Hallmark, 3 3/4 In. 200.00
Tea Set, Teapot, Sugar, Creamer, Cake Basket, Late 1800s, 4 Piece 5975.00
Teapot, Bullet, Eagles, Leaf Swags, Serpentine Spout, Rocaille Base, c.1767, 4 3/4 In. 1880.00
Tray, Rectangular, Rim Of Patera In Navettes, Rosehead Band, Moscow, 1836, 15 In. 295.00
Tub, Caviar, 1860, 4 In. 1000.00
SILVER-SCOTTISH, Flatware, Child's, Old Mother Hubbard, 2 Piece 69.00
Punch Ladle, Monogram, JO Hallmark, Edinburgh, 1797, 14 In. 230.00
Soup Ladle, Fiddle Handle, WF & Co., Edinburgh, George IV, 1829 . . . . 390.00
Stuffing Spoon, Rattail Bowl, Monogram, Edinburgh, Edward VII, 1908, 11 3/4 In. 235.00
Sugar, Angular Handles, Engraved, Lappet Band, George III, c.1802, 7 3/4 In. 560.00
Sugar Tongs, Sterling, Chased, Allover Flowers, George III, c.1839, 6 In. 150.00
SILVER-SOUTH AMERICAN, Bowl, Footed, Lobed Body, Chasing, Flower Band, 7 x 2 1/2 In. . 80.00
Bowl, Rose Water, 19 In. 620.00

Cocktail Shaker, Hand Tooled Decoration, Mayan Masks, 12 x 4 1/2 In. 575.00
SILVER-SPANISH, Box, Figural Finial, Eagles, Leaves, Shells, Eagle Feet, 1800s, 12 x 9 In. . . .   1840.00
   Figurine, Birds, Parcel Gilt, 20th Century, 20 1/4 In., 2 Piece 1610.00
   Goblet, First Standard, M. Espunes Company, c.1935, 9 1/2 x 5 In. 545.00

SILVER-STERLING. Sterling silver is made with 925 parts silver out of 1,000 parts of metal. The word *sterling* is a quality guarantee used in the United States after about 1860. The word was used much earlier in England and Ireland. Pieces listed here are not identified by country. Other pieces of sterling quality silver are listed under Silver-American, Silver-English, etc.

SILVER-STERLING, Basket, Reticulated, Early 20th Century, 13 In.   765.00
   Bowl, Bulbous Body, Repousse Flowers, Scrolling, c.1895, 2 x 4 1/2 In. 115.00
   Bowl, Centerpiece, Flared Enameled Edge, Old Derby Crafters, 12 1/2 In. 1035.00
   Bowl, Hemispherical Pattern, c.1915, 6 1/2 x 6 1/2 In. 865.00
   Bowl, Medallion, Loop Handles, Classical Profiles, Ford & Tupper, c.1874, 10 In. 2235.00
   Bowl, Presentation, Jensen Style, Openwork Stem, Curved Wirework, 9 1/8 In. 355.00
   Bowl Set, Soup, 2 Handles, Porcelain Liner, 5 In., 6 Piece 380.00
   Box, Regency, c.1814, 2 x 3 1/4 x 4 1/4 In. 200.00
Candelabrum is listed in its own category.
Candlesticks are listed in their own category.
   Castor, Rococo Style, Pear Shape, Ram Feet, Flower Chased, 4 3/4 In., Pair 130.00
   Chalice, Mounted, Cabochon, Cartouches, Embossed, Trumpet Foot, 1900s, 8 In. 120.00
   Cocktail Fork, Rococo Pattern, c.1888, 5 1/4 In., 6 Piece 35.00
   Cocktail Shaker, Acid Etched, Early 20th Century, 8 In. 880.00
   Coffee Set, Mid 20th Century, 3 Piece 265.00
   Compote, Flared Rim, Engraved, Tulips, Leaves, Trumpet Foot, 1900s, 8 In. 325.00
   Compote, Hammered, Ruffled, Trumpet Foot, Flowers, 1900s, 9 In. 355.00
   Compote, Octagonal, Gadroon Edge, Monogram, Grogan & Co., 3 1/2 x 9 In. 160.00
   Cordial Cup, Crown Silver, Inverted Bell Shape, Gilt Interior, 3 In., 12 Piece 175.00
   Corncob Holder, Corncob & Husk, 2 3/4 In., 12 Piece 160.00
   Creamer, Geometric, Flowers, Vermeil Interior, Moscow, 1891, 4 1/2 In. 905.00
   Cup, Jade, 2 Nude Maiden Shaped Handles, Cartier, 1950s, 3 3/8 In. 1725.00
   Demitasse Set, Coffeepot, Creamer, Sugar, Pear Shape, Ogee Rims, 1900s, 8 In. 175.00
   Dish, Sweetmeat, Boat Shape, Scrolls, Flower Head, 4-Footed, 1902, 7 1/4 In. 470.00
   Flask, Diapered Pattern, Cut Glass Body, c.1900, 5 1/2 x 3 x 1 1/2 In. 175.00
   Frame, Victorian Style, Shield Shaped, Garland, Doves, Easel, 12 In. 235.00
   Goblet, Pinched Waist, Repousse Grapevine, Knopped Stem, 6 5/8 In., Pair 805.00
   Grape Scissors, Cast Flower Design, 6 In. 255.00
   Grape Scissors, Scroll Handle, Fine Finger Loops, 5 3/8 x 2 In. 56.00
Napkin Rings are listed in their own category.
   Pitcher, Repousse, Helmet Shape, Circular Pedestal, Scrolled Handle, 1800s 1430.00
   Pitcher, Water, Bulbous Baluster Shape, Serpentine Handle, 1900s, 8 3/4 In. 380.00
   Pitcher, Water, Oval, Vertical Ribs, Scrolled Handle, Feet, 1906, 9 3/8 In. 1175.00
   Platter, Georgian Style, Gadroon Edge, Early 20th Century, 20 In. 558.00
   Platter, Oval, Footed, Well & Tree, National Silver Deposit Ware, 17 1/2 In. 518.00
   Punch Bowl, Flared Rim, Monogram, Engraved, Early 20th Century, 9 x 15 In. 1060.00
   Riding Crop, Horsehair, Leather, Woven Handle, Horse's Leg Cap, c.1900, 22 1/4 In. 90.00
   Salt & Pepper, Open Salts, Hand Chased, 20th Century, 4 Piece 355.00
   Salver, Georgian Style, Molded, Gadroon Rim, Footed, 1900s, 11 3/4 In. 265.00
   Sauceboat, Arts & Crafts, Hammered, Ladle, Applied Scroll Feet, 3 x 4 3/4 In. 605.00
Spoon, Souvenir, see Souvenir category.
   Sugar, Cover, Shaped Body, Domed Base, Lid, Repousse, c.1743, 5 1/2 In. 1495.00
   Sugar & Creamer, Basket, Repousse, Chased, Embossed, Leaf Base, 3 3/8 In. 235.00
   Tazza Set, Reticulated, Early 20th Century, 3 1/4 In., 4 Piece 1880.00
   Tea & Coffee Set, Hand Chased, Early 20th Century, 7 Piece 4113.00
   Tea Set, Gadroon Lip, Oval Shape, c.1913, 10-In. Teapot, 3 Piece 440.00
   Tea Set, Oval Shape, Wooden Handle, Hot Milk Jug, Open Sugar, Creamer 920.00
   Tray, Gadroon & Shell Border, Scroll & Fruit Handles, Inscribed, To Roy Whittier 1250.00
   Trophy, Cylindrical, Flared Rim, Scrolled Handles, Pedestal, 14 1/4 x 11 x 6 In. 1100.00
   Trophy, Goblet Shape, Scalloped Top, Teardrop Panels, 1860, 64 Oz., 12 x 8 In. 1760.00
   Tureen, Cover, Repousse Flowers, Ring Handle, 19th Century, 11 x 15 x 9 In. 865.00
   Tureen, Soup, Cover, S-Handles, Finial, Crichton & Co., Ltd., Early 1900s, 12 In. 4140.00

Tureen, Soup, Cover, Tied Bowknots, C-Scroll Handles, Flower Finial, 12 x 10 3/4 In. 4140.00
Vase, Bust, Man, Hammered, Flared Sides, 20th Century, 10 1/4 In. 1410.00
Vase, Paneled, Trumpet Shaped, Flared Rims, 20th Century, 14 7/8 In. 325.00
Vase, Trumpet, Classical Revival, Ribbon Tied Swags, 12 3/4 In. 764.00
SILVER-SWEDISH, Bowl, Flower Form, Beaded Rim, Hammered, Early 1900s, 9 3/4 In. 81.00
   Box, Gaming Counter, Made From Coins, Gustavus III Rex On Lid 250.00
   Pill Box, Engraved Flowers, 1842, 1 3/4 In. 127.00
SILVER-TIBETAN, Cup, Cover, 2 1/4 In. 236.00
   Teapot, c.1830, 8 In. 472.00
SILVER-TURKISH, Cup, Hand Hammered, Scroll Handle, Bird Finial, 1800s, 5 In. 173.00
   Pen Case, Scholar's, Lidded Inkwell, Seal Marks, 19th Century, 9 In. 1998.00

SINCLAIRE cut glass was made by H.P. Sinclaire and Company of Corning, New York, between 1905 and 1929. He cut glass made at other factories until 1920. Pieces were made of crystal as well as amber, blue, green, or ruby glass. Only a small percentage of Sinclaire glass is marked with the S in a wreath.

   Bowl, Base, Eggnog, Alpha Cutting, Signed, 9 3/4 x 10 3/4 In. 400.00
   Bowl, Diamond & Silver Thread Style, 8-Sided, Flared, 12 In. 1150.00
   Cruet, Hobstar, Fan & Long Thumbprint, Squat, Signed, 5 1/2 In. 110.00
   Vase, Hobstar Chain, Fern Panels, Cylindrical, Flared Rim, 10 In. 375.00

SKIING, see Sports category.

SLAG GLASS resembles a marble cake. It can be streaked with different colors. There were many types made from about 1880. Caramel slag is the incorrect name for Chocolate glass. Pink slag was an American Victorian product made by Harry Barstow and Thomas E.A. Dugan at Indiana, Pennsylvania. Purple and blue slag were made in American and English factories. Red slag is a very late Victorian and twentieth-century glass. Other colors are known but are of less importance to the collector. New versions of chocolate glass and colored slag glass are being made.

   Blue, Basket, Sowerby, 1877 .... 135.00
   Green, Butter, Cover, Marquis & Marchioness Landed At Halifax, Davidson 300.00
   Purple, Candlestick, Sowerby, 8 In., Pair 75.00
   Purple, Dish, Cow, Cover, Davidson, 8 In. ....225.00 to 300.00
   Purple, Dish, Frog On Basket, Cover 60.00
   Purple, Dish, Horse On Basket, Cover 60.00
   Purple, Dish, Imperial Rooster On Basket, Cover 150.00
   Purple, Dish, Owl On Basket, Cover 45.00
   Purple, Dish, Rabbit On Basket, Cover 650.00
   Purple, Punch Set, Imperial Glass Co., 13 1/2 x 5 In., 13 Piece 2500.00
   Teal, Compote, Marquis & Marchioness Landed At Halifax, Davidson 130.00

SLEEPY EYE collectors look for anything bearing the image of the nineteenth-century Indian chief with the drooping eyelid. The Sleepy Eye Milling Co., Sleepy Eye, Minnesota, used his portrait in advertising from 1883 to 1921. It offered many premiums, including stoneware and pottery steins, crocks, bowls, mugs, and pitchers, all decorated with the famous profile of the Indian. The popular pottery was made by Western Stoneware, Weir Pottery Company, and other companies long after the flour mill went out of business in 1921. Reproductions of the pitchers are being made today. The original pitchers came in only five sizes: 4 inches, 5 1/4 inches, 6 1/2 inches, 8 inches, and 9 inches. The Sleepy Eye image was also used by companies unrelated to the flour mill.

   Cookbook, Loaf Of Bread 45.00
   Creamer, No. 1, Blue & White 115.00
   Jug, Water, Blue & White, Pioneer Woman, Log Cabin, Lid, Spigot 450.00
   Mug, Blue & White, Marked, 4 1/2 In. ....120.00 to 185.00
   Mug, Brown, 1952, 4 In. 80.00
   Paperweight 260.00
   Pin, Fat Face 350.00
   Pitcher, No. 1, Blue & Gray 75.00

Pitcher, No. 2, Blue & White, Blue Rim	900.00
Pitcher, No. 2, Green & Yellow	4500.00
Pitcher, No. 3, Blue & White, 6 1/2 In.	210.00
Pitcher, No. 4, Blue & White, Marked, 8 In.	165.00
Pitcher, No. 4, Green & White, Green Rim, 8 In.	1450.00
Pitcher, No. 5, Blue & White, Blue Rim, 9 In.	260.00
Pitcher, Standing Indian, Flemish	850.00
Print, Sleepy Eye Mills, Sleepy Eye Cream, Indian, Minn., Frame, 30 x 24 In.	68.00
Sign, Indian, Old Sleepy Eye Joe, Tin, Frame, 25 x 33 In.	690.00
Spoon, Rose Design	85.00
Stein, Brown & White	1300.00
Sugar, Blue & White, Marked	420.00
Vase, Cattail, Cobalt Blue	600.00

SLOT MACHINES are included in the Coin-Operated Machine category.

SMITH BROTHERS glass was made after 1878. Alfred and Harry Smith had worked for the Mt. Washington Glass Company in New Bedford, Massachusetts, for seven years before going into their own shop. They made many pieces with enamel decoration.

Smith Bros. Co.

Biscuit Jar, 2 Gold Medallions, Beaded Flowers, Opal, Melon Ribbed, 7 In.	345.00
Biscuit Jar, Daisies, Ribbed, Opal, Signed, 6 1/2 x 7 In.	460.00
Biscuit Jar, Flowers, Melon Ribbed, Gold, Yellow, Silver Plate Handle, 5 1/2 In.	259.00
Biscuit Jar, Flying Crane, Stalks, Bamboo, Shaded Blue To Opal, Melon Ribbed	460.00
Biscuit Jar, Girl, Gold Flowers, Opal, Melon Ribbed, 6 1/4 x 6 1/2 In.	520.00
Creamer, Gold Renaissance Medallion, Sunflowers, Silver Mount, 3 1/2 In.	224.00
Jar, Sweetmeat, Portrait Of Girl, Gold Daisies, Opal, Oval Body, 3 1/2 x 4 In.	525.00
Sugar & Creamer, Pansies, Blue, Cream Ground, Silver Plate Hardware, 3 1/4 In.	230.00
Vase, Blue Wisteria Flowers, Leafy Stems, Opal, Signed, c.1870, 9 In.	670.00
Vase, Enameled Asters, Pinched Cream Ground, Gold Rim, 4 1/2 In.	375.00
Vase, Flowers, Cream Ground, Perched Birds, 3-Footed, Silver Plate, Stand, 11 In.	420.00
Vase, Golden Irises, Opal, Waisted Neck, Beaded Rim, Signed, 4 In.	195.00
Vase, Hummingbird, Flowers, Cream Ground, Signed, 8 In.	145.00

SNOW BABIES, made from bisque and spattered with glitter sand, were first manufactured in 1864 by Hertwig and Company of Thuringia. Other German and Japanese companies copied the Hertwig designs. Originally, Snow Babies were made of candy and used as Christmas decorations. There are also Snow Babies tablewares made by Royal Bayreuth. Copies of the small Snow Babies figurines are being made today and can easily confuse the collector.

Figurine, Baby Crawling, Bear Costume, Germany, c.1920, 4 In.	660.00
Figurine, Boy On Sled, No. 6104, Gebruder Heubach, Germany, c.1915, 9 In.	1980.00
Figurine, Girl In Fur Trimmed Jacket, Seated, Gebruder Heubach, c.1910, 6 In.	2090.00
Figurine, Girl Pushing Sled, No. 6409, Gebruder Heubach, Germany, c.1915, 7 In.	2640.00
Figurine, Girls On Sled, No. 6101, Gebruder Heubach, Germany, c.1910, 7 In.	3300.00
Figurine, Standing, Sitting, Late 19th Century, 3 In., Pair	144.00
Figurine, Trio Sledding, Germany, c.1915, 5 In.	1760.00
Plate, Sledding With Dog, Ruffled, Royal Bayreuth, 5 1/4 In.	150.00

SNUFF BOTTLES are listed in the Bottle category.

SNUFFBOXES held snuff. Taking snuff was popular long before cigarettes became available. The gentleman or lady would take a small pinch of the ground tobacco or snuff in the fingers, then sniff it and sneeze. Snuffboxes were made of many materials, including gold, silver, enameled metal, and wood. Most snuffboxes date from the late eighteenth or early nineteenth centuries.

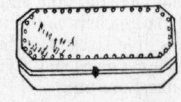

Enamel, Boar's Head, Boar Hunt Scene On Lid, England, 19th Century, 3 In.	499.00
Enamel, Boar's Head, Gilt Brass, Multicolored Lid, Boar Hunt, 3 In.	3680.00
Enamel, Flowers, Geometric Design, Signed, Limoges, France	115.00
English Oak, Carved, Mermaid, Tudor Roses, Late 17th Century	450.00
Fruitwood, Ship, Penwork, Hinged Deck Lids, England, 4 In., Pair	440.00
Gilt Metal, Oval, Engine Turned Ground, Louis XVI Style, 3 1/4 In.	175.00
Horn, Tight Curl, Horn Cap, 3 In.	169.00

Horn Mounted, Blond Tortoiseshell, Oblong, Dutch, Mid 1800s, 7/8 x 3 x 2 In. 144.00
Lacquer, Andrew Jackson, 3 1/2 In. 3980.00
Papier-Mache, Portrait, Man, Curly Hair, Gold Hoop Earring, Grain, 1 x 3 In. 403.00
Silver, Fish, Reticulated, Inset Paste Eyes, South America, 6 3/4 In. 575.00
Silver, Hinged Lid, Male Monarch Roundel, Continental, c.1800, 2 3/4 In. 90.00
Silver, Inscribed, D Foster, From His Wife Mary, Marked, 1863, 1/2 x 3 In. 125.00
Silver, Line Engraved, Thomas Shaw, George III, 1797, 2 5/8 In. 380.00
Silver, Oval, Starburst Ground, Vertical Linework, Continental, c.1800, 2 1/4 In. 355.00
Silver, Ribbon & Bow Designs, Hinged Lid, Chester, Emgland, c.1910, 5/8 x 3 3/8 In. . . . 259.00
Silver, Round Lid, Flowering Tree, Monograms, Scrolls, Naples, Italy, c.1700, 7 3/8 In. . . . 175.00
Sterling Silver, Enameled Roundel, Cavalier Bust, Chased Leaf Scroll, 2 In. 206.00
Sterling Silver, Hinged Cover, A.T., Birmingham, Victorian, c.1855, 3 1/4 x 2 3/8 In. 259.00
Tortoiseshell, Continental Silver Mounts, Domed, Late 1800s, 1 x 3 1/16 In. 489.00
Wood, Book, Chip Carved, Sliding Lid, Wales, 6 In. 350.00

SOAPSTONE is a mineral that was used for foot warmers or griddles
because of its heat-retaining properties. Soapstone was carved into figurines and bowls in many countries in the nineteenth and twentieth
centuries. Most of the soapstone seen today is from China or Japan. It
is still being carved in the old styles.

Figurine, Goddess Kuan Yin Holding Scepter, Gold Lacquer Inlay, Chinese, 1800s, 17 In. 295.00
Figurine, Meijin, Cloud Pattern Robe, Holding Peach, Flower Basket, c.1810, 8 3/4 In. . . . 145.00
Finger Moistener, Googly-Eyed Carp, Rosewood Stand, Chinese, 1800s, 2 x 5 3/4 In. . . . 690.00
Mortar & Pestle, Turned Mortar, Pedestal Base, 4 x 4 1/2 In. 145.00
Panel, Carved, Trees, Water Birds, Bamboo, Stilted Buildings, Teak Frame, 20 x 13 In. . . 460.00
Vases, 2 Vases Joined By Carved Leaves, Birds, Japan, 8 1/2 In. 345.00
Vases, 3 Vases Joined By Carved Leaves, Birds, Japan, 10 1/2 In. 345.00

SOFT PASTE is a name for a type of pottery. Although it looks very
much like porcelain, it is a chemically different material. Most of the
soft-paste wares were made in the early nineteenth century. Other
pieces may be listed under Gaudy Dutch or Leeds.

Cup & Saucer, Chinoiserie Figural Landscape, Early 1800s 75.00
Cup & Saucer, Handleless, King's Rose, Broken Border Design, Pair 105.00
Cup Plate, Queen's Rose, Strawberry Decorated, 3 7/8 In. 265.00
Mug, Blue Oriental Design, Woman In Fenced Garden, The Long Liza, 8 In. 546.00
Mug, Brown Checkered Band, Yellow, Green, Orange, Leaf Molded Handle, 4 3/4 In. 127.00
Mug, Figures In Formal Garden, England, c.1800, 3 1/2 In. 105.00
Pitcher, 2 Black Transfer Scenes, Black Banded Rim, Applied Handle, 6 In. 330.00
Pitcher, Black Transfer, Applied Handle, Pour Spout, 8 In. 385.00
Plate, Queen's Rose, Broken Floral Border, 8 1/4 In. 165.00
Plate, Toddy, Queen's Rose, Hand Painted, 5 1/4 In. 115.00
Platter, 2 Figures, Near Ruins, Palm Trees, Medium & Dark Blue, 14 x 18 1/2 In. 431.00
Teapot, Ball Form, Dome Cover, Multicolored Chinoiserie Design, 1700s, 5 3/4 In. 345.00
Teapot, Silver Luster, Floral Bands, Red Leaves, Urn Shape, 10 1/4 In. 58.00
Teapot, Strawberry, Flared Rim, Red, Green Strawberries, On Lid, Shoulder, 5 In. 300.00
Teapot, Strawberry, Swirl Rib Bands, Red, Yellow, Light Green Enamel, 6 1/4 In. 330.00
Vase, Bottle, Blue & White, Squat, 1662-1722, 5 3/8 In. 956.00
Wash Bowl, Cobalt Blue Leaves, Swags, Vining, Gaudy, 13 1/2 In. 285.00

SOUVENIRS of a trip—what could be more fun? Our ancestors enjoyed
the same thing, and souvenirs were made for almost every location.
Most of the souvenir pottery and porcelain pieces of the nineteenth
century were made in England or Germany, even if the picture showed
a North American scene. In the twentieth century, the souvenir china
business seems to have gone to the manufacturers in Japan, Taiwan,
Hong Kong, England, and America. Another popular souvenir item is
the souvenir spoon, made of sterling or silver plate. These are usually
made in the country pictured on the spoon. Related pieces may be
found in the Coronation and World's Fair categories.

Ashtray, Diplomats Resorts & Country Clubs, Hollywood By Sea, Royal China, 5 3/8 In. . . 15.00
Ashtray, Doral Hotels, Miami Beach, Harkerware, East Liverpool, Ohio, 5 1/2 In. 15.00
Ashtray, Green, Black, Graniteware, 1934 . . . . 35.00

Ashtray, Hawaii, Metal, Surfer, Surfboard, Beach, Japan, 1960s, 5 1/2 x 4 In. 16.00
Ashtray, Holiday Inn, Dixie Highway, Coral Gables, 6 In. 16.00
Ashtray, Las Vegas Casino Style, Working Roulette Wheel, Copper Toned Metal, 1978 . . . 28.00
Ashtray, Miami Beach Racket Club, Ca D' Antibes, Royal China, 1950s-1960s, 5 1/2 In. . . 30.00
Ashtray, Olympics, 1924, Paris, 3-D Boxer, Bronzed White Metal, 3 x 6 In. 127.00
Ashtray, Olympics, 1956, Winter, Squaw Valley, Logo, Blue, White, Red, Glass, 3 1/2 In. . . 190.00
Ashtray, Olympics, 1972, Munich, Rings, Slogan, White, Blue, Ceramic, 5 1/2 In. 80.00
Ashtray, Pony Swim, Chincoteague, Va., Horse Head Shape, Japan, 5 1/2 x 4 In. 26.00
Ashtray, Wright Co., Atlanta, Georgia, Syracuse China, 1938, 5 1/4 In. 25.00
Badge, Olympics, 1920, Antwerp, Italian Team, Crown, Bronze, Gold Plated, 1 1/2 In. . . . 1670.00
Badge, Olympics, 1932, Lake Placid, Participant's, Gold Plated, Blue Bar, Inscribed, 2 In. 2760.00
Badge, Olympics, 1948, St. Moritz, Radio, Yellow Enamel, Rings, 1 1/4 In. 1870.00
Badge, Olympics, 1968, Mexico City, BBC-TV, Silver, Black, Gold Plated Logo, 1 In. . . . 145.00
Bank, Olympics, 1936, Berlin, Bell Shape, Event Names, Silvered Metal, 3 In. 210.00
Bathtub, Glass, Craig, Iowa, 4 Molded Legs, Hand Painted, 5 1/4 x 2 In. 28.00
Booklet, Chicago Festival, Aluminum Cover, Linen Pages, Dewey, 1899, 3 3/4 In. 125.00
Bowl, Hotel Clavendon, J.D. Moskowitz Co., Daytona, Shenango China, 7 x 5 1/2 In. 12.00
Bowl, Niagara Falls, Canada, Open Latticework, c.1900, 7 1/2 x 2 1/4 In. 75.00
Brochure, Olympics, 1932, Lake Placid, General Rules For Games Committee, 32 Pages . 175.00
Cigarette Holder, Olympics, 1924, Paris, Boxing Scene, Ivory, Brown Design, 7 1/2 In. . . 200.00
Creamer, Mt. Tom, Summit House, Holyoke, Mass., Porcelain, Austrian Made, 2 1/4 In. . 35.00
Dish, Lakeside Pavilion, 6-Petal Shape, Grapevines, Iron, Komai Inlay, 1800s, 5 In. 546.00
Eagle, Camp Lejeune, N.C., Cast Iron, Wooden Base, 1930s, 15 x 23 1/2 x 10 In. 300.00
Figurine, Olympics, 1960, Rome, Diver, Yellow, Blue Water, Logo, Murano Glass, 13 In. . 460.00
Figurine, Olympics, 1972, Munich, Torch Bearer, Ceramic, 7 3/4 In. 115.00
Medal, Participation, Olympics, 1908, London, Winged Fame, Globe, White Metal, 2 In. . 345.00
Medal, Participation, Olympics, 1928, St. Moritz, Silvered, Enameled, 1 1/4 In. 805.00
Medal, Participation, Olympics, 1968, Grenoble, Bronze, Silver Plated, 2 In. 1380.00
Medal, Torch Relay, Olympics, 1984, Los Angeles, Torch, Runner, Bronze, 3 In. 185.00
Mug, Concord, New Hampshire, Ruby Glass, Arched Ovals, c.1900, 3 1/4 In. 23.00
Patch, Olympics, 1972, Sapporo, Japan, U.S. Committee Official, Felt, 4 In. 160.00
Pennant, Jacksonville, Florida, Beach Scene, Canvas, Felt, 1940s, 27 In. 25.00
Pennant, Miami Beach Bathing Beauty, c.1940, 27 In. 26.00
Pennant, Philadelphia Centennial Exhibition, Eagle, Flag, 38 Stars, 1776, Linen 225.00
Pill Box, New Orleans Superdome, Glass, Goldtone Metal Overlay, c.1960, 1 1/2 In. 15.00
Pin, Olympics, 1956, Cortina D'Ampezzo, Italy, Austria Team, 1 1/4 In. 145.00
Pin, Olympics, 1956, Melbourne, Rhodesia Team, Gold Plated, Enameled, 1 In. 210.00
Pin, Olympics, 1980, Moscow, East German TV, Gilt, Red & Blue Enamel, 1 1/2 In. 158.00
Pitcher, Bosque County, Texas, Centennial, 1854-1954, Yellow, San Marino, Pt. 38.00
Placemat, Blue, Pacific Far East Lines, 11 x 17 In. 4.00
Plaque, Olympics, 1972, Munich, Germany, Rings, Turquoise, For Car, 2 x 6 1/2 In. 115.00
Plate, Capitol Building, Washington, DC, Gold Border, Taylor, Smith & Taylor, 6 1/2 In. . 6.00
Plate, Luray Caverns, Gold Trim Rim, 1950s, 9 In. 28.00
Plate, Minnesota, Gopher State, Gold Trim, Homer Laughlin, 1955, 1 1/4 x 10 In. 15.00
Plate, Olympics, 1928, Amsterdam, Shield, Laurel, White Ground, Gouda, 10 1/2 In. 299.00
Plate, Olympics, 1972, Olympiade Munchen, Cityscape, Made In Copenhagen 28.00
Plate, St. Augustine, Florida, Blue Transfer, Staffordshire Ware, 7 In. 35.00
Postcard, Olympics, 1906, Athens, Stadium, Officials, Event, Cancelled Stamp 12.00
Postcard, Olympics, 1936, Berlin, Torch, Hurdler, Cancelled Stamp 75.00
Postcard, Olympics, 1936, Berlin, Torch, Rings, Brandenburg Gate, Cancelled Stamp . . . 115.00
Poster, Olympics, 1968, Grenoble, Chamrousse, Alpine Skiing, 24 1/2 x 38 In. 290.00
Program, Olympics, 1908, London, July 18, Includes Rules, 7 x 5 In., 40 Pages 460.00
Program, Olympics, 1932, Lake Placid, February 9th, 5 x 7 In., 14 Pages 140.00
Ring, Olympics, 1976, Montreal, Logo, 18K Gold 155.00
Salt & Pepper, Coney Island, N.Y., Plastic, Screw Tops, 1950s, 2 1/2 In., Pair 29.00
Scarf, 9th Olympiad Amsterdam, 1928, Athlete, Dutch Flag, Coat Of Arms, 33 x 35 In. . . . 1150.00
Spoon, Sterling Silver, Bicycle Stump, Everett, Wash., 5 1/4 In. 235.00
Spoon, Sterling Silver, Washington, D.C., Man, Riding Bicycle, 4 1/4 In. 179.00
Spoon, Uncle Sam On Handle, Sterling Silver, Engraved Bowl, 1889, 6 In. 190.00
Spoon Set, Moscow, RMS Aquitania, RMS Homeric, RMS Lusitania, Russia, 8 Piece . . . 375.00
Stein, Chicago, City Landmarks, Pewter, Hinged Pewter Lid, 1/3 Liter, 6 In. 78.00
Stein, Detroit, City Buildings, Metal, Gold Wash, Hinged Lid, 1/3 Liter, 5 In. 65.00
Stein, Olympics, 1972, Munich, Crock, Color Lithograph, Paulaner Munchen, 5 In. 58.00

Tablecloth, California, Red, Blue, Green, Yellow, State Map, 1940s, 48 x 48 In.	75.00
Teapot, Florida Flamingo, Pink Lusterware, Japan, 1940s-1950s, 7 3/4 In.	35.00
Ticket, Olympics, 1932, Lake Placid, Bleacher, Orange & Cream, Celluloid, 3 x 2 In.	140.00
Ticket, Olympics, 1964, Tokyo, Closing Ceremony, Oct. 24, Multicolored, 7 x 3 In.	145.00
Ticket, Olympics, 1980, Lake Placid, Opening Ceremony, Feb. 13, 2 1/2 x 6 In.	58.00
Tile, Olympics, 1952, Oslo, Norway, Rings, Sports, Blue, White, Pottery, 6 In., Pair	320.00
Tip Tray, Cunard Lines, Aquitania Ocean Liner, Tin Lithograph, 4 5/8 x 6 5/8 In.	385.00
Torch, Olympics, 1936, Berlin, Eagle, Bronzed Metal, Marble Base, 7 In.	690.00
Torch, Olympics, 1972, Munich, Germany, Stainless Steel, 28 In.	1815.00
Toy, Bus, Tandem, Great Lakes Exposition, 1936, Cleveland, Cast Iron, Arcade, 11 In.	415.00
Tray, San Francisco, United States Shape, Metal, Japan, 1940s-1950s, 4 x 2 1/2 In.	15.00
Tumbler, Flamingo Hotel Casino, Libbey, c.1955, 4 1/2 x 2 1/4 In.	25.00
Vase, Olympics, 1956, Stockholm, Equestrian, Engraved Logo, Clear Glass, 3 1/2 In.	316.00

SPANGLE GLASS is multicolored glass made from odds and ends of colored glass rods. It includes metallic flakes of mica covered with gold, silver, nickel, or copper. Spangle glass is usually cased with a thin layer of clear glass over the multicolored layer. Similar glass is listed in the Vasa Murrhina category.

Basket, Cased Blue, Silver Mica, Clear Twist Handle, 7 In.	80.00
Pitcher, Red, White, 8 1/2 In.	70.00
Vase, End-Of-Day, Gold, 12 1/2 In.	110.00

SPATTER GLASS is a multicolored glass made from many small pieces of different colored glass. It is sometimes called *End-of-Day* glass. It is still being made.

Pitcher, Rainbow, Square Mouth, Reeded Handle, Hobbs Brockunier, 8 1/2 In.	280.00
Pitcher, Translucent Rose, Opaque Specks, Ruffled Edge, Bulbous, 9 In.	175.00
Vase, Multicolored, Gold Enameled Neck & Rim, Austrian, 4 3/4 In.	90.00

SPATTERWARE is the creamware or soft paste dinnerware decorated with colored spatter designs. The earliest pieces were made in the late eighteenth century, but most of the spatterware found today was made from about 1800 to 1850, or it is a form of kitchen crockery with added spatter designs, made in the late nineteenth and twentieth centuries. The early spatterware was made in the Staffordshire district of England for sale in America. The later kitchen type is an American product.

Bowl, Berry Wreath, Purple, 4 1/2 In.	575.00
Bowl, Flower Center, Brown	69.00
Bowl, Flowers, Brown, 6 In.	30.00
Bowl, Rainbow, Red, Green, Striped, 3 1/4 In.	920.00
Bowl, Rose, Blue, Paneled, 4 1/4 In.	259.00
Bowl, Vegetable, Virginia Pattern, Stick, Rectangular, 9 In.	70.00
Charger, 2 Fuchsia Blossoms, Purple Stick Spatter Starflower, 16 1/2 In.	400.00
Coffeepot, Brown, Blue Flower, Paneled, 9 In.	440.00
Coffeepot, Geometric, Red, Blue, 9 1/2 In.	525.00
Creamer, Blue Spatter On Top, Molded Handle, Paneled, 5 1/2 In.	85.00
Creamer, Bud, Red, Blue, 4 3/8 In.	316.00
Creamer, Dove, On Branch, Blue, Yellow, Green Leaves, 4 1/4 In.	660.00
Creamer, Festoon, Red, Blue, Green, Paneled, 5 1/2 In.	1870.00
Creamer, Peafowl, Blue, Yellow, Red, Rainbow, Red, Green, Blue, Thumbprint, 3 1/2 In.	7475.00
Creamer, Peafowl, Purple, Green, Red, 3 5/8 In. .... *Illus*	1150.00
Creamer, Peafowl, Red, Green, Blue, Spatter Branch, Green, Leaf Handle, 4 In.	525.00
Creamer, Pinwheel, Blue, 3 3/4 In.	345.00
Creamer, Rainbow, Black, Brown, Striped, 4 3/8 In.	2760.00
Creamer, Rainbow, Blue, Green, Stripes	865.00
Creamer, Rainbow, Green, Red, Blue, 3 1/2 In.	2185.00
Creamer, Rainbow, Red & Blue, Applied Handle, 4 In.	259.00
Creamer, Rainbow, Red, Purple, Stripes, 3 1/8 In.	1095.00
Creamer, Rose, 2-Sided, Rainbow, Black, Brown, 4 3/4 In. .... 375.00 to 575.00	
Creamer, Star, Red, 2-Sided, Blue, 4 1/2 In.	375.00
Creamer, Tulip, Red, Blue, Leaves, Green, 3 1/2 In.	330.00
Cup, Cow, Green	3450.00

Cup, Cow, Green, Handleless 3450.00
Cup, Guinea Hen, Red, Handleless 825.00
Cup, Peafowl, Red, Handleless, 4 In. 120.00
Cup, Thistle, Rainbow, Red, Yellow, Handleless 415.00
Cup, Thistle, Red, Green, Blue, Handleless, 2 Piece 86.00
Cup & Saucer, 2 Buds, Red, Leaves, Yellow, Blue, Red Border 6900.00
Cup & Saucer, 2 Men On Raft, Red Border 21850.00
Cup & Saucer, Berry Wreath, Purple 805.00
Cup & Saucer, Bull's-Eye, Rainbow, Purple & Blue, Handleless 550.00
Cup & Saucer, Bull's-Eye, Rainbow, Red, Purple 1955.00
Cup & Saucer, Bull's-Eye, Red & Blue, Handleless 4140.00
Cup & Saucer, Bull's-Eye, Red, Yellow, Handleless 880.00
Cup & Saucer, Carnation, Red, Green Leaves, Blue Background 200.00
Cup & Saucer, Castle, Red, Handleless 605.00
Cup & Saucer, Cherry, Red 3680.00
Cup & Saucer, Cluster Of Buds, Red & Blue, Handleless ....345.00 to 750.00
Cup & Saucer, Dangling Tulip, Yellow, Leaves, Red Buds, Blue Border, Handleless 1650.00
Cup & Saucer, Dove, Blue & Mustard, Handleless 1430.00
Cup & Saucer, Drape & Circle, Blue 375.00
Cup & Saucer, Drape, Green, Red & Yellow Christmas Balls, Miniature 7475.00
Cup & Saucer, Drape, Rainbow, Red, Green, Yellow, Blue, Handleless 20700.00
Cup & Saucer, Drape, Red, Blue, Green Dots 1035.00
Cup & Saucer, Eagle & Shield, Blue Transfer, Purple, Paneled, Handleless 105.00
Cup & Saucer, Festoon, Yellow, Red, Green, Handleless 3300.00
Cup & Saucer, Fort, Blue, Handleless Cup, Miniature 110.00
Cup & Saucer, Fort, Red 1265.00
Cup & Saucer, Grape Clusters, Blue Sponge 1265.00
Cup & Saucer, Green, Yellow, Red Bird, Child's 4620.00
Cup & Saucer, Half Moon, Rainbow, Red, Green, Blue 2070.00
Cup & Saucer, Holly Berry, Purple, Handleless 250.00
Cup & Saucer, Morning Glory, Blue 1725.00
Cup & Saucer, Parrot, Blue, Green, Red, Handleless 715.00
Cup & Saucer, Peafowl, Blue, Red, Yellow, Blue Border, Handleless 330.00
Cup & Saucer, Peafowl, Blue, Yellow, Green, Red ....403.00 to 460.00
Cup & Saucer, Peafowl, Blue, Yellow, Red, Brown Border 1380.00
Cup & Saucer, Peafowl, Blue, Yellow, Red, Olive Green Border 1725.00
Cup & Saucer, Peafowl, Blue, Yellow, Red, Rainbow, Blue, Purple 865.00
Cup & Saucer, Peafowl, Brown, Green, Blue, Red Border, Handleless 385.00
Cup & Saucer, Peafowl, Green, Blue, Yellow, Red, Handleless 605.00
Cup & Saucer, Peafowl, On Bar, Yellow, Blue, Green, Red Border 805.00
Cup & Saucer, Peafowl, Open Body, Red, Wavy Lines, Blue, Green, Yellow, Handleless .. 920.00
Cup & Saucer, Peafowl, Red Sponge, Yellow, Blue, Green, Handleless 1155.00
Cup & Saucer, Peafowl, Red, Green Thumbprint Spatter, Handleless 920.00
Cup & Saucer, Pinwheel, Rainbow, Yellow, Red, Green, Black, Handleless, Child's 3575.00
Cup & Saucer, Rainbow, Black & Green, Thistle, Red, Handleless 23000.00
Cup & Saucer, Rainbow, Blue Squares, Red Dots 1095.00
Cup & Saucer, Rainbow, Blue, Red, Bull's-Eye Center, Handleless 200.00
Cup & Saucer, Rainbow, Drape, Red, Blue, Green, Yellow, Miniature 16100.00
Cup & Saucer, Rainbow, Teal, Red 863.00
Cup & Saucer, Rooster, Blue, Yellow, Red 3480.00
Cup & Saucer, Rooster, Yellow, Blue, Red, Blue Border 1725.00
Cup & Saucer, Rose, Rainbow, Red, Green 345.00
Cup & Saucer, Rosebud, Red, 11 Blueberries, Blue 4600.00
Cup & Saucer, School House, Red School, Yellow, Green, Brown, Handleless 1265.00
Cup & Saucer, School House, Red, Blue, Creepy Crawlers, Handleless 5220.00
Cup & Saucer, School House, Red, Green Lawn, Blue Border 2300.00
Cup & Saucer, Shed, Blue, Yellow, Red 1840.00
Cup & Saucer, Star, Bull's-Eye, Rainbow, Purple, Blue 3220.00
Cup & Saucer, Swirl, Rainbow, Red, Green, Blue 3160.00
Cup & Saucer, Swirl, Rainbow, Yellow, Red, Green 24150.00
Cup & Saucer, Thistle, Blue, Red Border 980.00
Cup & Saucer, Thistle, Rainbow, Red & Yellow, Handleless 1870.00
Cup & Saucer, Thistle, Red 750.00

Spatterware, Creamer, Peafowl, Purple, Green, Red, 3 5/8 In.

Spatterware, Pitcher, Rainbow, 5 Colors, 9 In.

Spatterware, Plate, Rose, Red Flower, Green Leaves, Blue, Paneled Rim, 9 3/4 In.

Cup & Saucer, Thistle, Red, Rainbow, Yellow & Blue, Handleless 16100.00
Cup & Saucer, Thistle, Yellow, Red, Green Leaves, Handleless 1045.00
Cup & Saucer, Tulip, Rainbow, Red, Green 546.00
Cup & Saucer, Tulip, Red 865.00
Cup & Saucer, Umbrella Flower, Blue, Purple, Green, Blue Border 575.00
Cup & Saucer, Windmill, Blue, Red, Yellow, Red Border 8625.00
Cup & Saucer, Yellow Dove, Green Branch, Purple Border, Blue, Handleless 2750.00
Cup Plate, Bull's-Eye, Rainbow, Green, Red, Striped Border, 4 1/8 In. 385.00
Cup Plate, Cockscomb, Yellow, Red, Green, Paneled Rim, 4 1/8 In. 1650.00
Cup Plate, Fort, Blue, Yellow, Red, Brown, Green, 12-Sided, 4 1/4 In. 470.00
Cup Plate, Peafowl, Green, Red, Gold, Light Blue, 3 7/8 In. 415.00
Cup Plate, Peafowl, Red, Green, Blue, Branch, Green, Feather Molded Edge, 4 In. 468.00
Cup Plate, Rose, Blue, Red, Green, 4 1/8 In. 415.00
Cup Plate, Rose, Yellow, Red, Green, 4 1/8 In. 1320.00
Dinnerware Set, Brown, Red, Child's, c.1850, 23 Piece 300.00
Jug, Cream, Tulip, Red, Green Flowers, Black Stem, Purple Border, 4 1/4 In. 550.00
Jug, Milk, Peafowl, Red, Yellow, Green Bird, Light Blue, Hexagonal 275.00
Mug, Brown, Blue, Bands, Orange, Ribbed, 2 3/4 In. 690.00
Mug, Rainbow, 5 Colors 12650.00
Mug, Rainbow, Black, Yellow, 5 In. 5175.00
Pitcher, Blue, Bulbous, Loop Handle, 9 1/4 In. 330.00
Pitcher, Cluster Of Buds, Blue, Red Buds, Green Leaves, 9 3/4 In. 525.00
Pitcher, Cream, Rainbow, Purple, Teal, Paneled, 5 1/2 In. 275.00
Pitcher, Fort, Blue, Scrolled Handle, 10 3/4 In. 290.00
Pitcher, Fort, Green, Black, Red, Gray, Paneled, 8 1/2 In. 520.00
Pitcher, Lily Of The Valley, Purple, Paneled, 5 5/8 In. 2300.00
Pitcher, Milk, Dahlia, Red, Blue, 8 1/4 In. 3680.00
Pitcher, Milk, Rainbow, Red, Blue, 7 1/4 In. 3910.00
Pitcher, Peacock At Fountain, Blue, 6 1/4 In. 85.00
Pitcher, Peafowl, Blue, Green, Red, 6 3/4 In. 880.00
Pitcher, Primrose, Red, Purple & Yellow, Paneled, 9 3/4 In. 2530.00
Pitcher, Rainbow, Blue, Green, Orange, Red, Ribbed, Hound Form Handle, 6 7/8 In. 5750.00
Pitcher, Rainbow, Red, Blue, Vertical Stripes, Hexagonal, Molded Fan, 6 1/2 In. 495.00
Pitcher, Rainbow, Red, Green, Paneled, 6 3/4 In. 920.00
Pitcher, Rainbow, Red, Green, Yellow, Blue, Black, Paneled, 9 In. ..... *Illus* 8050.00
Pitcher, Red & Blue Rainbow, Bulbous Shape, 3 1/2 In. 110.00
Pitcher, Tulips, Blue Spatter, 8 Panels, Angled Handle, Early 19th Century, 8 1/8 In. 825.00
Plate, 3 Acorns, Yellow, Purple, Paneled, 9 1/8 In. 1840.00
Plate, 6-Point Star, Red, Green, Blue, Sunburst Border, Red, 9 1/2 In. 360.00
Plate, Bowl, Vegetable, Peafowl, Blue, Yellow, Green, Red Border, Octagonal, 10 1/2 In. .. 865.00
Plate, Bull's-Eye, Rainbow, Olive Green & Red, 8 1/8 In. 4370.00
Plate, Bull's-Eye, Rainbow, Purple, Black, 7 3/8 In. 2590.00
Plate, Bull's-Eye, Rainbow, Red & Blue, 8 1/4 In. 3910.00
Plate, Christmas Balls, Red, Yellow, Drape, Green 12650.00
Plate, Creamware, Green & Blue Rainbow, 5 Sprays Of Brown, Blue, Green, 7 1/2 In. 305.00
Plate, Crisscross, Rainbow, Red, Blue, 8 1/2 In. 1035.00
Plate, Dahlia, Rainbow, Red, Blue, Green Sprigs, 8 1/4 In. 1650.00

Plate, Eagle & Shield, Blue, Paneled, 7 In. 220.00
Plate, Festoon, Rainbow, Yellow, Green, Red, 8 1/4 In. 9775.00
Plate, Fingerprint, Dark Blue, Red, Yellow, Blue Dot, Paneled, 8 1/2 In. ... 935.00
Plate, Flower, Purple Transfer, Copper Luster Border, Paneled, 9 3/4 In. 165.00
Plate, Green, Red & Yellow Christmas Balls, 9 1/2 In. 8625.00
Plate, Peafowl, Blue, Green, Red, 8 1/4 In. 385.00
Plate, Peafowl, Blue, Yellow, Green, Red Border, 9 1/4 In. 690.00
Plate, Peafowl, Blue, Yellow, Red, Ribbed, 8 3/8 In. 920.00
Plate, Peafowl, Brown, Ocher, Red Bird, Purple Border, 8 1/4 In. 120.00
Plate, Peafowl, Green, Mustard, Red, Blue Spatter, Paneled Rim, 8 7/8 In. ... 440.00
Plate, Peafowl, Purple, Blue, Yellow, Red, 8 1/4 In. 880.00
Plate, Peafowl, Red, Orange, Green, Blue Border, 9 5/8 In. 489.00
Plate, Pineapple, Blue, Red, Black Highlights, Green Leaves, 8 In. 20900.00
Plate, Pomegranate, Red, Blue, Black, Green, 7 1/4 In. 195.00
Plate, Primrose, Purple, Green, Red Border, Paneled, 8 1/4 In. 140.00
Plate, Rainbow, Blue, Red, 8 1/4 In. 7475.00
Plate, Rainbow, Drape, Red, Green, Yellow, Blue, 8 1/4 In. 17250.00
Plate, Rainbow, Rayed Design, Red, Green, 9 1/2 In. 3050.00
Plate, Rainbow, Red, Green, Alternating, 8 1/8 In. 805.00
Plate, Rose, Red Flower, Green Leaves, Blue, Paneled Rim, 9 3/4 In. .... *Illus* 230.00
Plate, Rose, Red, Green, Spatter Border, 9 1/4 In. 140.00
Plate, School House, Red, Brown & Green Tree, 8 1/2 In. 330.00
Plate, School House, Red, Brown, Green, Blue Border, 8 1/4 In. 3680.00
Plate, School House, Red, Green & Brown Lawn, Tree, 9 3/8 In. 6325.00
Plate, School House, Red, Yellow, Brown, Green, Paneled, 9 1/2 In. 5225.00
Plate, Soup, Peafowl, Blue, Yellow, Red, 10 1/2 In. 220.00
Plate, Star, Rainbow, Blue, Red, Arrow Border, 9 1/2 In. 550.00
Plate, Star, Rainbow, Red, Blue, Green, Half Moons, 9 1/8 In. 23000.00
Plate, Star, Red, Blue, Green, Red Spatter, 8 3/8 In. 430.00
Plate, Sunburst, Blue, Paneled, 9 1/2 In. 330.00
Plate, Swag, Rainbow, Green, Red, 9 5/8 In. 8050.00
Plate, Swirl, Rainbow, Green, Brown, Yellow, Red, 8 1/4 In. 20700.00
Plate, Thistle, Rainbow, Red, Black, Ribbed, 6 1/8 In. 5460.00
Plate, Thistle, Red Flower, Green Leaves, Paneled, 9 1/4 In. 440.00
Plate, Thistle, Red, Green, Yellow Border, Feather Edge, 9 1/2 In. 4290.00
Plate, Toddy, Peafowl, Blue, Red, Green, Border, Red, 3 3/8 In. 145.00
Plate, Toddy, School House, Red, Blue, Green Tree, Grass, Red Border, 3 3/8 In. 169.00
Plate, Tree, Blue, 9 In. 495.00
Plate, Tulip, Blue, Leaves, Green, Brown, Blue Border, 8 In. 165.00
Plate, Tulip, Red & Blue Flower, Green Leaves, Paneled, 8 1/4 In. 2310.00
Plate, Tulip, Red, Green, Yellow Panel Border, 8 In. 2420.00
Plate, Tulip, Yellow, Purple, Border, Red, Paneled, 9 1/8 In. 200.00
Plate, Virginia, Stick, 8 1/2 In., 4 Piece 220.00
Platter, Peafowl, Blue, Green, Red, Red Allover Spatter, 15 3/4 In. .... *Illus* 3300.00
Platter, Peafowl, Blue, Yellow, Green, Red, Octagonal, Ribbed, 9 1/4 In. 2760.00
Platter, Rainbow, Blue, Green, Octagonal, 15 1/2 In. 1495.00
Platter, Rainbow, Blue, Purple, Mottled, Octagonal, 10 1/8 In. 1150.00
Platter, Rainbow, Purple, Black, Octagonal, 18 In. 14950.00

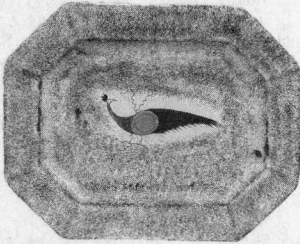

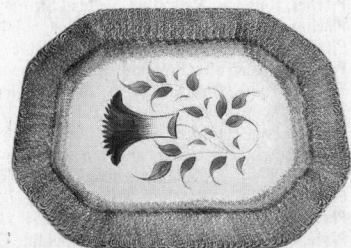

Spatterware, Platter, Peafowl, Blue, Green, Red, Red Allover Spatter, 15 3/4 In.

Spatterware, Platter, Thistle, Red, Green Leaves, Ribbed Rim, Blue, 16 In.

Platter, Rainbow, Red, Green, Blue, Crisscross, 15 1/2 In. 21850.00
Platter, Strawberry, Blue, 3 Red Strawberries, Green Leaves, 8 x 10 In. 1100.00
Platter, Sunburst, Blue, Scalloped, 13 3/4 x 17 3/4 In. 195.00
Platter, Thistle, Red, Green Leaves, Ribbed Rim, Blue, 16 In. .... *Illus* 5290.00
Salt, Rainbow, Purple, Blue, 2 1/8 In. 690.00
Sauce Dish, Peafowl, Red, 5 In. 305.00
Saucer, Festoon, Yellow, Red, Green 855.00
Saucer, Flower, Red, Yellow, Green, Blue Border 440.00
Saucer, Rooster Stick, 3 Colors, Purple Border, Crows Foot Line In Base, 5 5/8 In. 440.00
Saucer, Town House, Hipped Roof, Rainbow, Red & Purple Border 6325.00
Sugar, Cornflower, Blue, Rainbow, Drape, Red, Yellow, 4 1/2 In. 8625.00
Sugar, Cover, Blue Spatter Rims, Red & Green Open Tulips, 4 3/4 In. 230.00
Sugar, Cover, Green, Blue, Pearlware, Trees, Buildings, England, c.1810, 5 3/8 In. 3525.00
Sugar, Cover, Molded, Flowers, Blue, Squat, 4 1/2 x 4 In. 99.00
Sugar, Cover, Parrot, Red, Green, 2-Sided, Red Border, 6 In. 259.00
Sugar, Cover, Rainbow, Black, Brown, 5 In. 3450.00
Sugar, Cover, Rose, Red, Green, Blue, 9 1/4 In. 275.00
Sugar, Cover, Semicircles & Loops, Teal, Orange, Paneled, 5 1/4 In. 575.00
Sugar, Cover, Thistle, Rainbow, Red, Green, 2-Sided, Fluted, Open Handles, 3 3/4 In. ... 3080.00
Sugar, Cover, Thistle, Yellow, Red Flower, Green Leaves 2200.00
Sugar, Octagonal, Red, White, Blue 35.00
Sugar, Rose, Yellow, 4 3/4 In. 635.00
Teapot, Acorn, Blue, 2-Sided, Brown Acorns, Teal Caps, 5 1/4 In. 825.00
Teapot, Cover, 4-Petal Flower, Blue, Red 750.00
Teapot, Cover, Blue, White, Paneled Side, Scrolled Handle, 9 3/4 In. 385.00
Teapot, Dove, Blue, Blue & Yellow, 5 1/2 In. 525.00
Teapot, Eagle & Shield, Purple, Paneled, Child's, 6 In. 495.00
Teapot, Fort, Blue, Yellow, Red, Black, Green Trees, Child's, 9 1/2 In. 360.00
Teapot, Peafowl, Red, Blue, Yellow, Green, 2-Sided, 6 3/4 In. 550.00
Teapot, Rooster, Yellow, Blue, Red, Blue Border, 2-Sided, 6 In. 2760.00
Tureen, Peafowl, Blue, Hexagonal Shape, Footed, Rosette Finial, 10 x 7 In. 5465.00
Waste Bowl, Morning Glory, Red, Blue Flower, Green Leaves, Fluted, Footed, 3 1/2 In. .. 1925.00
Waste Bowl, Red & Green, Flared Edge, 3 x 5 1/2 In. 250.00

SPELTER is a synonym for a zinc alloy. Figurines, candlesticks, and other pieces were made of spelter and given a bronze or painted finish. The metal has been used since about the 1860s to make statues, tablewares, and lamps that resemble bronze. Spelter is soft and breaks easily. To test for spelter, scratch the base of the piece. Bronze is solid; spelter will show a silvery scratch.

Cigar Cutter, Eagle Head, Embossed Flowers Around Neck, Germany, 5 In. 95.00
Figurine, Roman Woman, Semireclining, Marble Base, France, c.1875, 14 x 17 1/2 In. ... 635.00
Lamp, 2 Putti Holding Urn On Pedestal Base, Bronze Finish, 14 1/2 In. 85.00
Lamp, Electric, Maiden, Flower Wreath, Czech End-Of-Day Ball Shade, 22 In. 50.00
Vase, Patinated Bronze, Relief Couple, Ancient Altar, Fitted As Lamp, c.1890, 24 1/2 In. .. 745.00

SPINNING WHEELS in the corner have been symbols of earlier times for the past 100 years. Although spinning wheels date back to medieval days, the ones found today are rarely more than 200 years old. Because the style of the spinning wheel changed very little, it is often impossible to place an exact date on a wheel.

Bentwood, Turned Spindle Spokes, Chip Carved Plank Base, Tripod Feet, 60 In. 35.00
Bold Turnings, Painted, Red, Brown, Yellow, 60 In. 605.00
Flax, Pine, Maple, Turned, 18th Century, 37 x 30 x 23 In. 125.00
Flax, Treadle Operated, Mixed Hardwoods, Turned Spindle Spokes, 34 1/2 In. 55.00
Flax, Upright, Hardwood, 3 Turned Legs, Turned Spokes, Single Flyer, 34 In. 375.00
Mixed Wood, Turnings 56.00
Pine, Maple, Oak, Turned Uprights, Pegged, Splayed Legs, 36 1/2 x 18 x 16 In. 75.00
Standard Form, Mark JH, 60 x 66 In. 90.00
Walnut, Turned, Carved Sections, Decorations, 19th Century, 42 1/2 x 46 In. 69.00
Wool Walking Type, Oak, Hickory, Maple, Wrought Iron, 58 1/2 x 68 x 46 In. 440.00
Wool Walking Type, Oak, Hickory, Maple, Wrought Iron, 60 x 62 x 46 In. 150.00
Yarn Winder, Oak, Maple 70.00

Never put your name on your mailbox. Put the street number in reflecting numerals more than 3 inches high, in clear view. Make it easy for the police & fire departments to find your house.

Spode, Pitcher, Chicago Fire, Indians, Firemen, Relief, White On Blue Ground, 8 1/2 In.

SPODE pottery, porcelain, and bone china were made by the Stoke-on-Trent factory of England founded by Josiah Spode about 1770. The firm became Copeland and Garrett from 1833 to 1847, then W.T. Copeland or W.T. Copeland and Sons until 1976. It then became Royal Worcester Spode Ltd. The word *Spode* appears on many pieces made by the factories. Most collectors include all the wares under the more familiar name of Spode. Porcelains may be listed in this book by the name that appears on the piece. Related pieces may be listed under Copeland, Copeland Spode, and Royal Worcester.

Dish, Flowers, Early 1800s, 5 1/2 In.	12.00
Dish, Soft Paste, Imari, 1800s, 8 1/4 In.	405.00
Pitcher, Chicago Fire, Indians, Firemen, Relief, White On Blue Ground, 8 1/2 In. . . . . *Illus*	489.00
Plate, Scalloped Rim, Birds, Branches, Beige Ground, c.1840, 9 1/8 In., Pair	145.00
Platter, Octagonal, Painted, Oriental Scene, Pink Flowers, 9 x 12 1/2 In.	138.00
Platter, Octagonal, Painted, Pink, Red Roses, Armorial, Rampant Lions, 9 x 12 1/2 In. . . .	82.00
Platter, Tower, Ironstone Red Transfer, Gadroon Border, 1 3/4 x 23 x 18 1/4 In.	400.00
Scent Jar, Chinese Figures, c.1825	748.00
Serving Dish, Imari, Shell Shape, Red, Blue, Green, Gold, 9 1/2 x 8 1/4 x 2 1/2 In.	325.00
Teapot, Egyptian Revival, Redware, c.1815	2185.00
Vase, Spill, Flower Encrusted, Flaring Cylinder, Gilt Rim Enamel, Early 1900s, 6 1/4 In. .	235.00

SPONGEWARE is very similar to spatterware in appearance. The designs were applied to the ceramics by daubing the color on with a sponge or cloth. Many collectors do not differentiate between sponge-ware and spatterware and use the names interchangeably. Modern pottery is being made to resemble the old spongeware, but careful examination will show it is new.

Bowl, Blue, White, Relief Column, 5 x 10 1/2 In.	66.00
Bowl, Vegetable, Blue, White, Scalloped Edge, 9 1/4 x 2 In.	99.00
Chamber Set, Blue, Cream, 10-In. Pitcher, 6 Piece	546.00
Charger, Rabbitware, Tennis, Virginia Rose Flowers, Florets, 12 1/2 In. . . . . *Illus*	1650.00
Crock, Butter, Blue, White, Navy	165.00
Cup & Saucer, Red, Royal Standard, Military Scene, Black Transfer, Handleless	195.00
Cup & Saucer, Red, Stag Pattern, Handleless	770.00
Mixing Bowl, Blue, 10 In.	165.00
Mixing Bowl, Blue, Heart Panels, 13 In. . . . . 145.00 to	170.00
Mixing Bowl, Blue, Ribbed, 11 1/2 In.	125.00
Mixing Bowl, Blue, White, 10 1/4 In.	140.00
Mixing Bowl, Blue, White, Heart Panels, Wide Band On Top Rim, 12 In.	255.00
Mug, Blue, Applied Handle, 4 1/2 In.	259.00
Mug, Teal, 5 1/4 In.	635.00
Pitcher, Batter, Blue, Short Spout, Applied Handle, 7 1/2 In.	405.00
Pitcher, Blue, 6 3/4 In.	365.00
Pitcher, Blue, Blue Rim, Applied Handle, 8 1/2 In.	230.00
Pitcher, Blue, Bulbous, Sparrow Beak Spout, 7 3/4 In.	395.00
Pitcher, Blue, White, 7 1/2 In.	145.00
Pitcher, Blue, White, 8 3/4 In. . . . . 132.00 to	225.00

Spongeware, Charger,
Rabbitware, Tennis, Virginia Rose
Flowers, Florets, 12 1/2 In.

Spongeware, Plate,
Rabbitware, Golf, Rosettes,
Virginia Rose, 9 1/4 In.

Spongeware, Plate, Rabbitware,
Reading, Walking, Eating, Virginia
Rose, 9 1/4 In.

Pitcher, Blue, White, 9 In.	210.00
Pitcher, Blue, White, Accent Band, 9 In.	175.00
Pitcher, Blue, White, Accent Bands, 8 3/4 In.	415.00
Pitcher, Blue, White, Girl & Dog, 9 In.	330.00
Pitcher, Rabbitware, 3 Rabbits, Frog, In Field, Virginia Rose, Sponge Florets, 8 1/2 In.	3740.00
Pitcher, Yellow, Diamonds, Brown & Blue Design, Cylindrical, 9 1/2 In.	350.00
Plate, Rabbitware, Baseball, Rosettes, Virginia Rose, 9 1/4 In.	1320.00
Plate, Rabbitware, Croquet, Rosettes, Virginia Rose, 9 1/4 In.	1100.00
Plate, Rabbitware, Driving A Car, Virginia Rose, 9 1/4 In.	2420.00
Plate, Rabbitware, Golf, Rosettes, Virginia Rose, 9 1/4 In. .... *Illus*	4290.00
Plate, Rabbitware, Reading, Walking, Eating, Virginia Rose, 9 1/4 In. .... *Illus*	660.00
Plate, Rabbitware, Tennis, Rosettes, Virginia Rose, 9 1/4 In.	1650.00
Plate, Tulip, Red, Green, Sponge Border, Red, Blue, Cotton & Barlow, 9 3/4 In.	220.00
Platter, Blue, White, Rectangular, Curved Sides, 10 x 13 3/4 In. ....220.00 to 250.00	
Sugar, Tulip, Blue, Paneled, 7 3/4 In.	440.00
Umbrella Stand, Blue, White, 3 Striped Accent Bands, 20 1/2 In.	770.00
Urn, Cover, Blue, White, Applied Loop Handles, Blue Accent Bands, 13 In.	965.00

SPORTS equipment, sporting goods, brochures, and related items are listed here. Items are listed by sport. Other categories of interest are Bicycle, Card, Fishing, Sword, Toy, and Trap. Kentucky Derby glasses are listed in the Decorated Tumblers category.

Auto Racing, Pennant, Indianapolis 500, Red Border, Green, Car, Driver, 1914	250.00
Baseball, Ball, Autographed, Joe DiMaggio, Official Gene Budig, American League	110.00
Baseball, Ball, Autographed, Mickey Mantle, No. 7	430.00
Baseball, Ball, Autographed, Minneapolis Millers, 19 Players, Manager, 1958	460.00
Baseball, Ball, Autographed, New York Yankees, 13 Players, 1960	345.00
Baseball, Ball, Autographed, Ted Williams	200.00
Baseball, Ball, Early Figure 8, Leather, 1860s	2840.00
Baseball, Bat, Ash, Louisvillle Slugger, Tobacco Brown Finish, 33 x 2 1/4 In.	25.00
Baseball, Bat, Autographed, Harmon Killebrew, Adirondack, 34 In.	375.00
Baseball, Bat, Autographed, Johnny Bench, Game Used, Louisville Slugger, 34 1/4 In.	805.00
Baseball, Bat, Autographed, Pete Rose, Game Used, Louisville Slugger, 34 1/4 In.	805.00
Baseball, Bat, Autographed, Roger Cedeno, Game Used, Louisville Slugger, 34 1/4 In.	115.00
Baseball, Bat, Eddie Murray, Game Used, Louisville Slugger M275, 35 1/4 In.	519.00
Baseball, Bat, Frank Thomas, Game Used, Black, Worth, 33 3/4 In.	200.00
Baseball, Bat, Kirby Puckett, Game Used, Louisville Slugger P339, 34 3/4 In.	345.00
Baseball, Bat, Louisville Slugger, Ash, Tobacco Brown Finish, 33 x 2 1/4 In.	28.00
Baseball, Bat, Mike Piazza, Game Used, Rawlings, 34 1/2 In.	865.00
Baseball, Bat, Reach, Mushroom Handle, Stamped Barrel, Pat. Aug. 1, 05, 34 In.	489.00
Baseball, Booklet, Babe Ruth, Crack Shot, Remington, 1938, 4 1/2 x 7 1/2 In., 24 Pg.	300.00
Baseball, Bust, Hank Aaron, Bronze, Resin, Genesis Productions Inc., 1974, 7 In.	25.00
Baseball, Button, Burleigh Grimes, Cubs, Multicolored, Lithograph, 7/8 In.	17.00
Baseball, Button, Butch Schmidt, First Base, Celluloid, 1913-1915, 1 1/4 In.	500.00
Baseball, Button, Don Drysdale, Celluloid, Robin's-Egg Blue Ground, 3 1/2 In.	100.00
Baseball, Button, Jimmie Foxx, Yours For Life, Red, White, Black, 1 1/4 In.	125.00
Baseball, Button, Ralph Kiner, Pittsburgh Pirates, Black, White, Celluloid, 1 3/4 In.	100.00

Baseball, Button, Washington Senators, Pitcher, Capital Building, c.1960, 3 1/3 In. 199.00
Baseball, Button, Welcome Yogi Day, Yankee Stadium, Lithograph, 1964, 1 1/2 In. 125.00
Baseball, Button, Willie Mays, Black & White, Celluloid, 1 3/4 In. 110.00
Baseball, Button, Winegarner, Pitcher, Mrs. Sherlock's 40.00
Baseball, Button, Yellow Kid, I'm Goin' To Pitch Fer De New Yorks, No. 8, 1 1/4 In. 82.00
Baseball, Cereal Box, Dizzy Dean For Post Grape-Nuts, 1936, 5 3/4 x 4 1/2 x 1 3/4 In. ... 605.00
Baseball, Clock, Babe Ruth, 2 Balls, Rotary, Bronze, Wood Base, Abbotwares, c.1948 ... 2195.00
Baseball, Figure, Babe Ruth, Hartland Plastics, 7 3/4 In. 115.00
Baseball, Figure, Cream To White, Hartland Plastics, 19 Piece 3939.00
Baseball, Figure, Dairy Queen, White Plastic, 1955, 18 Piece 1090.00
Baseball, Figure, Lou Gehrig, Hartland Plastics, 7 1/2 In. 105.00
Baseball, Figure, Mickey Mantle, Hartland Plastics, 8 1/2 In. 175.00
Baseball, Figure, Stan Musial, Hartland Plastics, 9 In. 115.00
Baseball, Figure, Yogi Berra, Hartland Plastics, 7 In. 160.00
Baseball, Glove, Autographed, Luke Appling, First Baseman's, Spalding 865.00
Baseball, Glove, D & M, c.1920 .... 185.00
Baseball, Glove, Davega, c.1920 .... 115.00
Baseball, Glove, Earl Averill 115.00
Baseball, Glove, Mickey Mantle Children's Model, Rawlings, Box, Tag, 1953 .... 5180.00
Baseball, Glove, Nippy Jones, 3-Finger Claw 69.00
Baseball, Jersey, A. Ditmar, Kansas City Athletics, Game Worn, Rawlings, 1960s 980.00
Baseball, Jersey, Autographed, Earl Battey, Charlotte Hornets, Game Worn, 1962 ..... 290.00
Baseball, Jersey, Autographed, Earl Battey, Minnesota Twins, No. 10, Game Worn, 1963 . 1095.00
Baseball, Jersey, Autographed, Pete Rose, Cincinnati Reds, No. 14, Game Worn, 1977 ... 2530.00
Baseball, Jersey, Moose Skowren, New York Yankees, No. 14, Game Worn, 1961 ...... 3220.00
Baseball, Leather, Team, Players Photographs, Red Sox, World Champs, 1915, 32 x 39 In. 3850.00
Baseball, Nodder, Baltimore Orioles, Mascot Bird, 1960-1961, 6 3/4 In. 110.00
Baseball, Pennant, N.Y. Yankees, AL Champions, Felt, Blue, Late 1940s, 27 In. 730.00
Baseball, Pennant, New York Yankees, 1960, American League Champions, Roster 150.00
Baseball, Pennant, St. Louis Cardinals, 1965, Color Team Photograph 69.00
Baseball, Photograph, 1911 N.Y. Giants, Includes Mathewson, 10 1/2 x 13 1/2 In. 1500.00
Baseball, Photograph, 1952 N.Y. Yankees, Facsimile Signatures, 12 x 19 In. 820.00
Baseball, Photograph, Autographed, Babe Ruth, Boston Braves, 1935, 2 3/4 x 3 3/4 In. .. 2350.00
Baseball, Photograph, Autographed, Billy Martin, Frame, 8 x 10 In. 80.00
Baseball, Photograph, Autographed, Mickey Mantle, Frame, 8 x 10 In. 140.00
Baseball, Photograph, Autographed, Roger Maris, Frame, 8 x 10 In. 400.00
Baseball, Photograph, Cabinet, Cap Anson, Formal Dress, Scott, Chicago 1000.00
Baseball, Photograph, DiMaggio, Mantle, Autographed, Black & White, Frame, 9 x 7 In. . 150.00
Baseball, Photograph, Jackie Robinson, Ben Chapman, Apology, 1947, 8 1/2 x 6 5/8 In. .. 500.00
Baseball, Photograph, Joe DiMaggio, Black & White, Autographed, 11 x 9 In. 99.00
Baseball, Photograph, Red Sox, 1916 World Series, Silver Print, Gray Mount, 5 x 7 In. ... 2250.00
Baseball, Pillow, Detroit Tigers, Tiger With Pennant, c.1907, 20 x 20 In. 670.00
Baseball, Postcard, Buck Weaver, Chicago, American League 430.00
Baseball, Postcard, Honus Wagner, Views Of Carnegie, Pa. 345.00
Baseball, Postcard, Jackie Robinson On WNBC, 1950s, 6 x 7 1/2 In. 50.00
Baseball, Postcard, Nick Altrock, Pitcher, Chicago White Sox, 1907 .... 259.00
Baseball, Postcard, Ted Williams, Autographed, 5 1/2 x 3 1/2 In. 1900.00
Baseball, Postcard, Tinkers, Evers, Chance, Chicago, National League, 1906 .... 175.00
Baseball, Poster, Batter, Catcher, Cheap Excursion To Rochester, 1887, 28 x 12 In. 5830.00
Baseball, Poster, Mickey Mantle, Swinging Bat, Autographed, 19 3/4 x 16 In. 259.00
Baseball, Press Pin, 1920 World Series, Brooklyn Dodgers, Goldtone & Red, 3/4 In. 1090.00
Baseball, Program, 1914 World Series, Boston Braves vs. Philadelphia A's, 16 Pages 2580.00
Baseball, Program, 1948, World Series 120.00
Baseball, Record Album, Babe Ruth's Home Run Story, Pathe, Actuelle, 78 RPM, 1930 .. 700.00
Baseball, Scorekeeper, Babe Ruth, Multicolored, 2-Sided, Celluloid, 1 1/4 In. 120.00
Baseball, Seat, Fenway Park, Green Paint, 1912-1934, Pair 5500.00
Baseball, Sign, Babe Ruth For Puffed Wheat & Rice, Cardboard, 1934, 29 1/2 x 20 In. 3890.00
Baseball, Sign, Fort Wayne Daisies, Front Office, Girls Pro League, 1940s, 13 x 24 In. 1320.00
Baseball, Tapestry, Babe Ruth Swinging Bat, Full Stands, Cranberry Border, 18 In. 600.00
Baseball, Ticket, 1911 World Series, Game 2, Phila. A's vs. N.Y. Giants, Shibe Park 1475.00
Baseball, Ticket, 1926 World Series, Game 4, Autographed By Babe Ruth & Lou Gehrig . 3335.00
Baseball, Ticket, Babe Ruth Tribute Game, Yankee Stadium, vs. Cleveland, 3/15/48 ..... 9185.00
Baseball, Ticket, N.Y. Mets, Inaugural Opening Day, Polo Grounds, April 13, 1962 ..... 1905.00

Basketball, Ball, Autographed, Harlem Globe Trotters, 4 Signatures 69.00
Basketball, Photograph, Autographed, Michael Jordan, 8 x 10 In. 100.00
Billiards, Ball, Autographed, William Mosconi, No. 14 .... 58.00
Billiards, Balls, Ivorylene, Solid Inlaid Numbers, Interior Stamped January 1929, Box ... 95.00
Boxing, Button, Johnson & Jeffries Reno Fight, Obak Cigarettes, 1910, 7/8 In. 140.00
Boxing, Figure, John L. Sullivan, Fighting Pose, Bronze, Hanging Loop, 10 In. 500.00
Boxing, Glove, 10 Champions' Autographs, Ali, Lewis, Tyson, Foreman, Ringside, 25 In. .. 675.00
Boxing, Kerchief, Jeffries & Johnson, Championship, Reno, Nevada, 1910, 16 In. 1000.00
Boxing, Photograph, Autographed, Ali & Frazier In Ring, 20 x 16 In. 115.00
Boxing, Photograph, Autographed, Jack Dempsey, Inscription, Black & White, 8 x 10 In. .. 98.00
Boxing, Photograph, Autographed, Rocky Marciano, 1950s, 10 x 8 In. 1430.00
Boxing, Poster, Ali vs. Frazier, Madison Square Garden, Yellow, 1974, 22 x 28 In. 1560.00
Boxing, Poster, Ali vs. Mildenberger, Frankfurt, Germany, Blue, 1966, 23 x 33 In. 820.00
Boxing, Poster, Louis, Tunney, Dempsey, Uniforms, Chicago Sun, 1942, 14 x 30 In. 175.00
Boxing, Program, Ali vs. Frazier, Heavyweight Championship, Thrilla In Manila, 1975 ... 1200.00
Boxing, Snuffbox, Molineaux vs. Cribb, Tin, Red Ground, c.1811, 3 x 2 In. 600.00
Football, Ball, Autographed, 1957 Cleveland Browns, With Rookie Jim Brown 1570.00
Football, Ball, Winchester American, Rugby, No. 912 .... 4305.00
Football, Cuff Links & Tie Bar, Helmets, Insignia, Green, Yellow, Goldtone, 1960s 255.00
Football, Figure, Joe Namath, Helmet, Strap, Jersey, Pants, Mego, 1970s, 12 In. 140.00
Football, Figure, Joe Namath, Leather Jacket, Shirt, Pants, Mego, 1970s, 12 In. 145.00
Football, Football, Autographed, Chicago Bears, 13 Autographs, 1963 .... 219.00
Football, Program, 1916 Rose Bowl, Washington State vs. Brown, Football Shape 10928.00
Football, Program, U. Of Minnesota At U. Of Michigan, 1910, 32 Pages 1625.00
Football, Program, U. Of Penn. At U. Of Michigan, 1911 Homecoming, 32 Pages 830.00
Football, Stock Certificate, Green Bay Packers, 5 Shares, Green, 1923, 6 x 10 In. 3780.00
Golf, Club Cover Set, Three Stooges, Dolls, Talking, Battery Operated, 3 Piece 80.00
Golf, Marker, Crow, Iron, 55 In. 210.00
Golf, Photograph, Autographed, Bobby Jones, 10 x 8 In. 5700.00
Hockey, Skates, Canadian Kiwanis Pee Wee Tournament, Miniature, 3 In. 45.00
Horse Racing, Poster, 4 Mounted Jockeys, Calvert Litho Co., Detroit, 38 1/2 x 26 3/8 In. .. 295.00
Horse Racing, Silk Hat, Willie Shoemaker, Purple, Embroidered Name 125.00
Hunting, Box, Cartridge, Western New Chief, Buff, Green, 16 Gauge, Shot Shell Lid 40.00
Hunting, Box, Clinton Cartridge Co., Pointer, 12 Gauge, Smokeless Powder, 2 Piece 395.00
Hunting, Box, Peters Target Shells, Paper Shot, 12 Gauge 335.00
Hunting, Box, Peters, Victor, Rustless, Smokeless Shotgun Shells, 12 Gauge 66.00
Hunting, Box, Winchester, Brass Shot Shells, 20 Gauge, Contents 305.00
Hunting, Box, Winchester, Leader 16 Gauge, Loaded Shotshells, Smokeless, Contents ... 996.00
Hunting, Brochure, Peters Big Game Cartridges, Grizzly Bear, 6 1/4 x 3 3/8 In. 220.00
Hunting, Brochure, Remington, Rider Revolver, Self-Cocking, Frame, Bifold, 1860s 275.00
Hunting, Button, Daisy Air Rifles, Shoot Safe Buddy, White, Blue, Red, Pinback, 7/8 In. . 17.00
Hunting, Button, Ducks Unlimited, Celluloid, 1949, 1 1/4 In. 78.00
Hunting, Button, Infallible Shotgun Smokeless, Multicolored, Celluloid, 1 1/4 In. 60.00
Hunting, Button, Peters Cartridge Co., Duck Theme, Multicolored, Celluloid, 7/8 In. 60.00
Hunting, Button, Peters Cartridge Co., Red, White, Blue, Stars & Stripes, 7/8 In. 85.00
Hunting, Button, Peters Cartridge Co., Steel Where Steel Belongs, Celluloid, 7/8 In. 45.00
Hunting, Button, Peters Shells, Hunter, Duck, Multicolored, Celluloid, 7/8 In. 105.00
Hunting, Button, Peters Superior Cartridges, Gold, Black, White, Red, Celluloid, 7/8 In. .. 39.00
Hunting, Button, Shoot Blue Rocks, Celluloid, 7/8 In. 380.00
Hunting, Button, Shoot Winchester Shotgun Shells, Red, Black, White, Celluloid, 7/8 In. .. 30.00
Hunting, Button, Sportsmans League, 2 Men, In Canoe, Fishing, Celluloid, 1 1/4 In. 99.00
Hunting, Button, Sportsmans League, Bradshaw Fancy, Celluloid, 1 1/4 In. 80.00
Hunting, Button, Sportsmans League, Johnson, Wet Fly For Trout, Celluloid, 1 1/2 In. ... 88.00
Hunting, Button, Winchester Leader, Champion Shot, W.R. Crosby, Celluloid, 1 1/4 In. .. 165.00
Hunting, Button, Winchester, Always Shoot Winchester Cartridges, Pinback, 3/4 In. 22.00
Hunting, Button, Winchester, C.G. Spencer 310.00
Hunting, Case Insert, Winchester, Shotgun, Puppies, Cardboard, Frame, 12 x 8 1/2 In. ... 825.00
Hunting, Catalog, Funsten Trapping Supplies, 1920s 117.00
Hunting, Catalog, Parker Gun, 1923 .... 127.00
Hunting, Catalog, Price List, Winchester, 1916 .... 55.00
Hunting, Catalog, Winchester Fishing Tackle, 1924, Color, 5 1/2 x 8 1/2 In., 32 Pages ... 110.00
Hunting, Counter Felt, Winchester, Cartridges, Shotgun Shells, 11 x 13 In. 650.00
Hunting, Counter Pad, Colt, A Tradition Of Safety, Blue & White, Rubber 60.00

Hunting, Counter Pad, UMC Shot Shells Are Steel Lined, Frame 400.00
Hunting, Counter Pad, Winchester, Cartridges, Loaded Shells, Rifles & Shotguns, Frame .. 325.00
Hunting, Counter Pad, Winchester, More Than A Gun, Red & White, Rubber 110.00
Hunting, Display, DuPont, Select Your Loads Here, Cardboard, Easel Back, 16 x 21 In. ... 580.00
Hunting, Display, Hornady Bullets, 119 Samples, Simulated Wood Grain 33.00
Hunting, Display, Winchester, 22 Rifles, Shotguns, Cardboard, c.1950, 18 x 12 In. 635.00
Hunting, Dummy Set, Sample, Winchester, Shot Shells, Cartridges, Box 150.00
Hunting, Hang Tag, Daisy Air Rifle, No. 12, Single Shot, $1.00, 3 5/8 x 2 1/4 In. 85.00
Hunting, Letter Opener, Peters Cartridge Co., Brass, Silver, 7 3/4 In. 325.00
Hunting, License, Button, Celluloid, Mustard, Non-Resident, Minn., 1927, 1 3/4 In. 116.00
Hunting, Loading Tool, Winchester, Cal. 32-20, Primer Extractor 200.00
Hunting, Poster, 2 Cowboys, Winchester, P.R. Goodwin, Frame, c.1906, 15 x 29 3/4 In. .. 2295.00
Hunting, Poster, DuPont, Smokeless Shotgun Powders, Trap Shoot, 17 1/2 x 20 3/4 In. ... 3545.00
Hunting, Poster, Peters Loaded Shells, Steel Where Steel Belongs, Birds, 30 1/4 x 20 In. . 990.00
Hunting, Poster, Remington UMC, 4 Gun Models, 4 Prey Animals, 24 3/4 x 13 In. 550.00
Hunting, Poster, Remington UMC, Black Powder, Bear, Cardboard, Easel, 12 x 12 In. 580.00
Hunting, Poster, We Sell Peters Shells, 3 Flying Ducks, Multicolored, c.1915, 9 x 12 In. ... 1155.00
Hunting, Poster, Western Ammunition, Moose, 1921, 30 x 16 3/4 In. 1359.00
Hunting, Poster, Winchester, 20 Gauge Shotguns, 2 Dogs, 1906, 15 7/8 x 29 1/4 In. 2700.00
Hunting, Price List, Robin Hood Ammunition Co., List No. A10, c.1911, 10 1/2 x 5 1/2 In. 289.00
Hunting, Razor, Winchester, As Good As The Gun, c.1920, 1 1/2 x 4 x 1/2 In. 125.00
Hunting, Sign, Colt Patent Firearms, Hartford, Ct., Cowboy, Horse, Frame, 28 x 38 In. ... 935.00
Hunting, Sign, Dead Shot Gunpowder, Duck, Paper, Frame, c.1910, 25 x 31 In. .1200.00 to 1800.00
Hunting, Sign, Peters Shells & Cartridges, Die Cut, 13 x 10 1/4 In. 600.00
Hunting, Sign, Remington UMC Ammunition, Dog, Bird, Ammo, Frame, 36 x 45 In. 525.00
Hunting, Sign, U.S. Ammunition Co., Man, Pulling Horse, Bear, Cardboard, 16 x 12 In. ... 440.00
Hunting, Sign, Western Lubaloy Cartridges, Cardboard, Easel Back, 12 x 20 1/2 In. 495.00
Hunting, Sign, Winchester Repeating Shotguns, Pointer & Setter, 16 1/2 x 30 1/2 In. ... 1430.00
Hunting, Sign, Winchester, Cowboy On Horse, Tin, 2-Sided, Round, 38 In. 500.00
Hunting, Sign, Winchester, Leader, Paper Shot Shells, Grouse, Die Cut, 12 1/4 x 7 3/8 In. 2130.00
Hunting, Tin, Daisy Pellets, Bullseye Brand, Brown, Yellow 35.00
Hunting, Tin, Gold Dust Smokeless Shotgun Powder, Paper Label, 1/2 Lb. 176.00
Hunting, Tin, Kentucky Rifle Gunpowder, Hazard Powder Co., Man, Dog, 1 Lb. 135.00
Hunting, Tin, Mathewson Gunpowder, Tin, Paper Label, 1 Lb., 3 1/2 x 7 x 1 In. 88.00
Hunting, Tin, Orange Ducking Powder, Laflin & Rand, Paper Label, 4 x 5 1/2 x 1 1/2 In. .. 180.00
Hunting, Tin, Orange Rifle Powder, Laflin & Rand Co., Paper Label, 4 x 6 x 1 1/2 In. 178.00
Hunting, Tin, Schultze Gunpowder, Fist, Lightning Bolts, Paper Label, 4 x 5 x 1 1/2 In. ... 325.00
Hunting, Tin, Selby B.B. Split Shot, Gold, Brown, White, Partial Contents, 1 1/2 In. 85.00
Hunting, Tin, Superior Rifle Gunpowder, Paper Label, 2 1/2 x 3 1/2 In. 225.00
Hunting, Tin, Union Gunpowder, Mills At Santa Cruz, Paper Label, Lead Cap, 1 Lb. 225.00
Hunting, Token, Robin Hood Ammunition, Game Laws Token, Maine, c.1914, 1 1/2 In. ... 270.00
Hunting, Trap Shooting Scorecard, Smokeless, Jack Panning, DuPont, 4 1/2 x 3 In. 110.00
Hunting, Trap Thrower, Hand, Allison & Faulkner 55.00
Ice Skating, Skates, No. 38 1/2 In., Steel, Box, John Wilson, Marsden Bros. 18.00
Ice Skating, Skates, Winchester, Saranac, No. 5221, Size 8 1/2, Box 360.00
Ice Skating, Skates, Wood, Red Painted, Steel Blades, Brass Ball Finials, 11 1/4 In. 316.00
Polo, Mallet, Bamboo Shaft, England, Late 19th Century 95.00
Pool, Scoring Counter, Oak, Wall Mounted, Sliding Index Points, 22 x 39 In. 230.00
Riding, Spurs, Gold Plated, Leaves, Flowers, Peal Of Duke St., London, Gentleman's 2243.00
Snowshoes, Bear Paw, Henry Ross Ltd., 12 x 29 In. 60.00
Snowshoes, Maine Style, Leather Bindings, Snocraft Inc., Norway, Maine, 12 x 42 In. ... 85.00
Snowshoes, Maine Style, Leather Bindings, Tubbs Co., Norway, Maine, 12 x 52 In. 60.00
Snowshoes, Wood Frame, Red Paint, 34 In. 99.00
Soccer, Ball, England vs. Spain, Wembley, 1955 .... 285.00

STAFFORDSHIRE, England, has been a district making pottery and porcelain since the 1700s. Hundreds of kilns are still working in the area. Thousands of types of pottery and porcelain have been made in the many factories that worked and still work in the area. Some of the most famous factories have been listed separately, such as Adams, Davenport, Ridgway, Rowland & Marsellus, Royal Doulton, Royal Worcester, Spode, Wedgwood, and others. Some Staffordshire pieces are listed under categories like Fairing, Flow Blue, Mulberry, Shaving Mug, etc.

Bank, Cat, Multicolored, Enameled, Tasseled Pillow, 4 x 4 x 4 1/2 In. 265.00

Bowl, Lafayette At Washington's Tomb, Blue Transfer, Beaded, Enoch Wood, 2 5/8 x 12 In.   2350.00
Bowl, Landing Of Fathers At Plymouth, Blue & White, Enoch Wood, 10 1/4 In. 315.00
Bowl, Vegetable, Cover, Castle, Sailboat, Fisherman, Square, Blue, 12 1/2 x 6 1/4 In. 460.00
Bowl, Vegetable, Hudson River View, Enoch Wood & Sons, 9 3/4 In. 1725.00
Bowl, Vegetable, Letter Of Introduction, James & Ralph Clews, 2 1/8 x 8 3/8 In. 355.00
Bowl, Washington, Franklin, Apotheosis, Early 1800s, 5 x 10 1/2 In. 3565.00
Bust, George Washington, Blue Jacket, Floral Vest, Cravat, Early 19th Century, 8 In. 470.00
Bust, Napoleon, Multicolored Enamel, Cobalt Blue Coat, Marbleized Base, 9 5/8 In. 165.00
Cheese Plate, Cow's Head Cover, c.1865, 8 1/2 x 10 1/4 x 7 1/2 In. 575.00
Coffeepot, Cover, Black, Glazed, Pear Shape, S-Scroll Handle, c.1775, 9 In. 645.00
Coffeepot, Lafayette At Franklin's Tomb, Enoch Wood & Sons, 11 In. 1955.00
Compote, Multicolored, Cream Ground, Marked, 9 In. 58.00
Creamer, Blue Transfer, Cottage, Castle Scene, 4 1/2 In. 165.00
Creamer, Cow & Milkmaid, c.1800 . . . .   1800.00
Creamer, Toby, 3 3/4 In. 45.00
Cup, Chancellor Livingston Ship, Blue, Handleless 330.00
Cup, Girl With Toy Hoops, Brown, White, Child's, 2 1/2 x 3 In. . . . . .70.00 to 75.00
Cup & Saucer, American Eagle & Urn, James & Ralph Clews 405.00
Cup & Saucer, Countryside Scene, People Fishing, Handleless 60.00
Cup & Saucer, Gray, Straight-Sided, Dog Chasing Rabbit 130.00
Cup & Saucer, Lafayette At Franklin's Tomb, Enoch Wood & Sons, 10 1/8 In. 1035.00
Cup & Saucer, MacDonnough's Victory, Blue, Handleless 410.00
Cup & Saucer, W. Penn Treaty, c.1850 . . . .   510.00
Cup & Saucer, Wadsworth Tower, Enoch Wood & Sons, 3 3/4 & 5 3/4 In. 345.00
Cup Plate, Arms Of South Carolina, Blue, T. Mayer, 4 1/4 In. 1155.00
Cup Plate, Arms Of The United States, Flower Border, Scalloped, Blue, 3 3/4 In. 2860.00
Cup Plate, Blue Transfer, Building Decoration, 3 3/4 In. 690.00
Cup Plate, Boston Harbor, Eagle, On Ocean Wave, Shield, Blue, Rogers, 4 In. 1210.00
Cup Plate, Boston State House, Acorn & Leaf Border, Scalloped, Blue, R.S.W, 4 1/4 In. .   990.00
Cup Plate, Boston State House, Flower Border, Scalloped, Enoch Wood, 4 3/4 In. 770.00
Cup Plate, Boston State House, Scalloped, Beaded, Enoch Wood & Sons, 3 3/4 In. 1100.00
Cup Plate, Bridge, Arched, Stone, Blue, Enoch Wood & Sons, Impressed, 3 5/8 In. 220.00
Cup Plate, Cadmus, Trefoil Border, Blue, Enoch Wood & Sons, 3 5/8 In. 330.00
Cup Plate, Castle Garden Battery, N.Y., Scalloped, Enoch Wood & Sons, 4 5/8 In. 1375.00
Cup Plate, Castle Garden Battery, Shell Border, Enoch Wood & Sons, 3 3/4 In. 385.00
Cup Plate, Customs House, Philadelphia, Flower Border, Blue, 3 1/2 In. 2090.00
Cup Plate, Holiday Street Theatre, Baltimore, Fruit & Flower Border, Blue, 3 1/2 In. 880.00
Cup Plate, Landing Of Gen. Lafayette, Scalloped Edge, Blue, J. & R. Clews, 3 1/2 In. . . .   520.00
Cup Plate, Landing Of The Pilgrims, Scalloped, Blue, Enoch Wood & Sons, 3 5/8 In. . . .   770.00
Cup Plate, Octagon Church, Boston, Oak & Leaf Border, Scalloped, Stevensons, 4 In. . . .   1980.00
Cup Plate, Peace & Plenty, Flower Border, Scalloped Rim, Blue, 3 7/8 In. 1650.00
Cup Plate, Pittsfield Elm, Floral Border, Vignettes, Scalloped, Blue, 4 5/8 In. 495.00
Cup Plate, Quebec, Ship Near Shore, Flower Border, Blue, 3 7/8 In. 550.00
Cup Plate, Scudder's American Museum, Acorn & Leaf Border, Scalloped, 4 1/4 In. 1430.00
Cup Plate, Welcome Lafayette The Nations Guest, Leaf Border, Beaded, 4 3/4 In. 1980.00
Cup Plate, Woodlands, Near Philadelphia, Scalloped Rim, Blue, Stubbs, 3 1/8 In. 330.00
Dish, Hen On Nest Cover, Multicolored Paint, Late 1800s, 9 x 7 x 8 1/2 In. 575.00
Dish, Hen On Nest Cover, Multicolored, Green, Basket, 9 x 7 1/2 x 9 1/2 In. 330.00
Dish, Letter Of Introduction, Blue Transfer, Oblong, J. & R. Clews, 2 1/4 x 9 1/2 In. 705.00
Dish, Rabbit On The Wall, Blue Transfer, Rectangular, J. & R. Clews, 1 1/2 x 5 5/8 In. . . .   529.00
Figurine, Autumn, Woman, Sickle, Sheaf Of Wheat, 1790, 9 In. 520.00
Figurine, Ben Backstay, Legs Crossed, Arm Supporting Moneybag, 8 In. 85.00
Figurine, Ben Franklin, Purple Pants, Seated, c.1825, 8 3/4 In. 520.00
Figurine, Bird, Cockatoo, J.T. Jones, 13 1/2 x 7 x 4 3/4 In., Pair 935.00
Figurine, Blind Harpist, Seated, Harp, Spaniel Standing, 14 x 3 x 7 1/4 In. 605.00
Figurine, Boy, Hand Resting On Urn, 13 3/4 x 3 1/2 x 5 In. 120.00
Figurine, Cat, Calico, Seated, On Oval Scroll Base, Early 19th Century, 3 5/8 In. 999.00
Figurine, Cat, Gray, Green Glass Eyes, Enameling, Early 1900s, 12 1/4 In., Pair 325.00
Figurine, Child On Dog, Hand Painted, 5 1/2 In. 140.00
Figurine, Cobbler & Wife, Holding Shoe, Pouring From Jug, 13 x 6 x 6 In., Pair 180.00
Figurine, Cobbler, Holding Shoe, Dog Under Chair, 12 x 5 1/2 x 6 1/4 In. 66.00
Figurine, Cow, With Young, 5 In. 150.00
Figurine, Cradle, Baby, Yellow Basket Weave, Pink Rockers, 4 1/2 x 3 1/2 In. 275.00

Figurine, Dick Turpin, Man, Pistol, Horse, 10 1/4 In. 165.00
Figurine, Dog, Black & White, Chain, Lock Collar, 9 In. 200.00
Figurine, Dog, Poodle, 19th Century, 8 In., Pair 315.00
Figurine, Dog, Seated, White, Luster Enameled Collar, Encrusted Coat, 6 In. 150.00
Figurine, Dog, Spaniel, Black & White, 8 1/2 In., Pair 468.00
Figurine, Dog, Spaniel, Black & White, Gilt Decoration, 10 1/2 In., Pair 316.00
Figurine, Dog, Spaniel, Craquelure, 19th Century, 12 In., Pair 546.00
Figurine, Dog, Spaniel, Gold Lock, Marked Old Staffordshire, 4 1/2 In., Pair 55.00
Figurine, Dog, Spaniel, Orange, White, 7 1/2 In. 660.00
Figurine, Dog, Spaniel, Red & White, 4 In. 70.00
Figurine, Dog, Spaniel, Seated, Black & White, Gilt Collar & Chain, 9 3/4 In. 145.00
Figurine, Dog, Spaniel, Seated, Copper Luster Chains, 12 1/2 In., Pair 300.00
Figurine, Dog, Spaniel, Seated, White, Gold Accents, Painted Face, 10 1/2 In., Pair 60.00
Figurine, Dog, Spaniel, White, Seated, Orange, Black, Yellow, Gold Detail, 12 1/4 In., Pr. 445.00
Figurine, Dog, Whippet, Rabbit In Mouth, 19th Century, 11 x 9 x 3 In., Pair 1350.00
Figurine, Dog, Whippet, Rabbit In Mouth, England, 5 3/4 x 1 3/4 x 5 1/4 In. 145.00
Figurine, Dog, Whippet, Red, Curled Up On Grass, 4 1/2 In. 300.00
Figurine, Elephant, Coleslaw Grass, Chimney Piece, 6 3/4 In. 260.00
Figurine, Equestrian Riding Astride, Stag Over Saddle, 14 3/4 x 3 3/4 x 8 3/4 In. 165.00
Figurine, Falstaff, Stout Man, Walking Stick, 7 In. 85.00
Figurine, Garibaldi, Mounted On A Horse, Painted, 11 x 7 1/4 x 2 1/2 In. 56.00
Figurine, Girl, Flower Basket, Seated On Rock, 7 1/4 In. 55.00
Figurine, Girl, Riding Goat, Oval Base, Gilt Lined, c.1875, 5 In. 140.00
Figurine, Girl, Sitting On Dog, 4 x 1 1/2 x 2 1/4 In. 55.00
Figurine, Girl, Standing, Rabbits, 6 3/4 x 1 3/4 x 3 1/4 In. 525.00
Figurine, Girl, With Deer, 7 In., Pair 285.00
Figurine, Grandmother, Reading To Child, c.1850, 6 In. 185.00
Figurine, John Wesley, 6 In. 145.00
Figurine, John Wesley, Green & Red Speckled Self Socle, 19th Century, 10 1/2 In. 265.00
Figurine, Lady, With Bird, Cream Dress, Blue Jacket, Yellow Bird, 8 1/8 x 2 1/2 In. 225.00
Figurine, Lamb, 2 1/4 In., Pair 55.00
Figurine, Leopard, Reclining, Mother & Cubs, c.1835, Pair 12000.00
Figurine, Lion, Reclining, 9 1/2 x 13 x 5 3/4 In., Pair 300.00
Figurine, Lion, Reclining, Splotches, Blue, Brown, Scalloped Edge Base, 3 7/8 x 6 In. 645.00
Figurine, Man & Poodle, Plumed Hat, Accordion, Flower Urn, 11 In. 350.00
Figurine, Man, Gun & Dead Stag Hanging, 17 1/4 x 3 1/4 x 7 1/2 In. 65.00
Figurine, Man, Holding Gun, Dog At Side, 14 x 3 1/2 x 6 In. 175.00
Figurine, Man, Holding Spear, Seated Dog, 18 x 5 x 7 1/4 In. 120.00
Figurine, Man, On Bicycle, 1860-1870, 3 1/4 In. 50.00
Figurine, Man, Riding Horse, Dog Races At Side, 4 1/4 x 1 1/4 x 2 3/4 In. 360.00
Figurine, Man, Standing, Hand On Cannon, Hat In Hand, Flag, 11 1/2 x 3 1/4 x 5 In. 200.00
Figurine, Maria, 7 3/4 In. 265.00
Figurine, Paperboy, Holding Daily News, 12 1/2 x 4 3/4 x 5 In. 275.00
Figurine, Peace, Woman, Classically Draped, Dove On Hand, 10 In. 280.00
Figurine, Peahen, White, Red Eye, Coleslaw Grass, Green Base, 12 5/8 In. 400.00
Figurine, Pomona, Roman Goddess Of Fruit Trees, c.1790, 8 In. 575.00
Figurine, Princess Of Wales, Early 19th Century, 6 In. 105.00
Figurine, Rebecca, Standing By Well, Holding Ewer, 9 In. 140.00
Figurine, Robin Hood, 2 Men, Feathers In Hats, Dog, 15 In. 385.00
Figurine, Rooster, White, Red Comb, Wattles, Gilt, 11 1/2 In. 1035.00
Figurine, Sailor, Standing Cross Legged, Leaning On Cannon, 7 1/2 x 1 1/2 x 3 In. 470.00
Figurine, Scotsman, Gun, Rabbit Hanging From Strap, 15 x 3 3/4 x 6 In. 385.00
Figurine, Scotsman, Holding Dog & Bird, 9 x 2 1/4 x 2 3/4 In. 360.00
Figurine, Scotsman, Holding Sword & Lion Foot, 17 x 4 1/2 x 8 In. 130.00
Figurine, Scotsman, Riding, Stag Over Saddle, 14 3/4 x 3 3/4 x 8 3/4 In. 360.00
Figurine, Scottish Highlander, Astride Horse, Gilt Highlights, 14 1/2 In., Pair 190.00
Figurine, Scottish Huntswoman, On Bay Horse, 10 In. 165.00
Figurine, Scottish Man, Holding Bagpipes, 14 1/4 x 4 1/2 x 6 In. 230.00
Figurine, Shepherdess, Holding Lamb, Blue Skirt, Jacket, Yellow Trim, 10 1/4 In. 1175.00
Figurine, Tailor Of Bath & His Wife, England, 1820-1825, 5 1/4 In., Pair 405.00
Figurine, Uncle Tom & Eva, 19th Century, 4 x 5 1/2 In. 140.00
Figurine, Uncle Tom & Eva, c.1852, 8 1/2 In. 520.00
Figurine, Woman, Arm Around Lamb, Instrument At Side, 11 3/4 x 3 x 5 1/2 In. 330.00

Figurine, Woman, Holding Dog & Bird, 16 3/4 x 5 1/4 In.	198.00
Figurine, Woman, Riding Side Saddle, Holding Tambourine, 10 1/2 x 3 x 7 In.	220.00
Figurine, Woman, Standing At Attention, Holding Flag, 12 1/2 x 3 x 3 1/2 In.	155.00
Figurine, Woman, Standing Beside Gravestone, 7 1/4 x 2 x 3 In.	165.00
Figurine, Woman, Standing In Front Of Donkey, Holding Bowl, 8 x 3 1/2 x 8 In.	145.00
Figurine, Woman, Wearing 3-Tiered Dress, Plumed Hat, Muff, 3 3/4 x 1 1/2 x 2 In.	110.00
Figurine, Zebra, Leg Raised, 7 1/2 x 3 1/4 x 6 1/4 In.	605.00
Fruit Basket, Reticulated, Double Handle, Quadrupeds Pattern, 3 1/2 x 12 x 8 In.	1725.00
Gravy Boat, Catskill Mountains, Hudson River, Enoch Wood & Sons, 7 1/2 In.	430.00
Gravy Boat, Old English Abbey, c.1942	40.00
Group, 2 Poodles, Standing, Hiding In Barrel, Cobalt Blue Base, 5 x 5 1/8 In.	430.00
Group, Boy Sitting On Clock, Holding Horn, Girl Standing, 7 x 1 3/4 x 3 In.	145.00
Group, Boy, Standing In Front Of Cow, 8 1/4 x 4 x 7 1/2 In.	440.00
Group, Dabney & Joan, Man & Woman Side By Side, 11 1/4 x 3 x 5 3/4 In.	230.00
Group, Fisherman & Wife, Holding Child, 9 x 3 x 5 In.	80.00
Group, Fishermen, Repairing Nets, Draped Jacket Over Arm, 9 1/4 x 2 1/2 x 5 In.	99.00
Group, Fisherwomen, Wearing Aprons, Scarves, Basket, 9 1/4 x 3 x 6 1/2 In.	155.00
Group, Lady Macbeth, Hamlet, Clock In Center, 8 1/2 In.	120.00
Group, Lion & Lamb, Standing, 3 1/2 x 1 1/4 x 2 1/2 In.	55.00
Group, Man & Woman, Arms Around Each Other, 3 3/4 x 1 1/4 x 1 3/4 In.	80.00
Group, Man & Woman, Head On Shoulder, Arm Around Shoulder, 8 x 3 x 3 1/2 In.	135.00
Group, Man & Woman, Seated, Holding Basket Of Fish, 10 1/4 x 3 x 5 1/2 In.	550.00
Group, Man, Dog Attacking Man, Dead Birds, 13 1/4 x 2 3/4 x 7 1/2 In.	385.00
Group, Man, Leaning Toward Woman, 8 x 2 1/4 x 3 3/4 In.	165.00
Group, Men, Woman, Flag, Seated On Bridge, 13 1/2 x 3 1/4 x 7 1/2 In.	240.00
Group, Napoleon & Duke Of Wellington, Clock, 9 x 2 1/4 x 5 In.	110.00
Group, Promenaders, Man & Woman, With Bocage, c.1820, 6 1/2 In.	173.00
Group, Samson & Lion, 12 In.	315.00
Group, Scottish Couple, Man & Bagpipe, Woman & Basket, 9 In.	250.00
Group, Uncle Tom & Eva, c.1875, 8 x 3 3/4 In.	530.00
Group, Uncle Tom & Eva, Sitting On Stump, 7 1/2 In.	260.00
Group, Woman & Man, Playing Lute & Violin, 10 1/2 x 2 3/4 x 6 In.	77.00
Group, Woman Leaning On Donkey, Carrying Sand Bag, 7 3/4 In.	105.00
Group, Woman, Holding Tambourine, Man Holding Instrument, 9 1/2 x 3 x 6 In.	220.00
Group, Woman, Mandolin, Man, Flute, Walton School, c.1815, 8 3/4 In.	575.00
Incense Burner, Cottage	140.00
Jug, Boston State House, City Hall, New York, Dark Blue, 19th Century, 4 3/4 x 3 In.	385.00
Mug, Field Sports, Child's, 3 1/2 In.	145.00
Mug, Frog & Newt, Flowers, Gilt Initials & Border, 5 In.	210.00
Mug, Frog, Bacchus' Head, Pedestal Base, 5 In.	280.00
Mug, Frog, Rose Sprigs, Brown Glazed Ground, 2 Handles, 4 In.	115.00
Mug, Frog, Spaniel & Pheasant Before & After Hunt, 2 Handles, 5 1/2 In.	210.00
Mug, Mr. Pickwick, Brown Transfer, Child's, 3 In.	110.00
Mug, Scenic, Boy Balancing Sword On Nose, Child's, c.1840, 2 1/2 In.	175.00
Mustard Pot, Man Holding Drinking Vessel, 5 1/2 x 2 1/4 In.	99.00
Mustard Pot, Man Holding Mug, 5 1/4 x 2 1/2 In.	176.00
Pendulum, Black Basalt, Round, Classical Cartouches, England, Early 1800s, 6 In.	295.00
Pitcher, Admiral Nelson, Captain Hardy, Ships Flanking Bust, 6 1/2 In.	259.00
Pitcher, Dog, Spaniel, Begging, Wearing Tricornered Hat, Gilt Collar, 9 In.	375.00
Pitcher, Famous Naval Heroes, Washington, Independence, Truxtun, 6 1/4 In.	1495.00
Pitcher, Lafayette At Franklin's Tomb, Dark Blue Transfer, Wood, 8 1/2 In.	630.00
Pitcher, Lafayette At Franklin's Tomb, Dark Blue, 6 In.	880.00
Pitcher, Landing Of General Lafayette, Castle Garden, J. & R. Clews, 6 1/2 In.	2530.00
Pitcher, Military Figures, Flags, General Hill, Lord Wellington, 5 In.	230.00
Pitcher, Persia, Light Blue Transfer, Marked, c.1850, 10 1/2 In.	140.00
Pitcher, River Scene, 4-Arch Bridge, Blue & White Transfer, J. & R. Clews, 4 3/4 In.	382.00
Pitcher, Toby, Black Coat, Blue Striped Stockings, Seated On Stump, 8 3/4 In.	230.00
Plate, 3 Colors, 20th Century, 10 In.	150.00
Plate, Abbey On Cliff, River, 2 Figures, Dark Blue, 19th Century, 9 1/8 In.	99.00
Plate, America & Independence, 2-Story Building, Curved Drive, Clews, 8 In., Pair	460.00
Plate, America & Independence, Blue Transfer, 6 3/4 In.	400.00
Plate, America & Independence, Blue Transfer, 10 3/4 In.	400.00
Plate, America & Independence, Fishermen With Net, J. & R. Clews, 10 5/8 In.	460.00

Plate, Antislavery, Justice Pardoning Slave, Scalloped Rim, 19th Century, 9 1/2 In. 470.00
Plate, Baker's Falls, Hudson River, Brown Transfer, 8 3/4 In. 145.00
Plate, Baltimore & Ohio Railroad, On Incline, Enoch Wood & Sons, 9 1/8 In. 865.00
Plate, Baltimore & Ohio Railroad, On Level, Enoch Wood & Sons, 10 1/4 In. ...., 1095.00
Plate, Bamborough Castle, Northumberland, Blue, White, 1800s, 10 In. 105.00
Plate, Boston State House, Enoch Wood & Sons, 10 In. 518.00
Plate, Boston State House, Floral Border, Light Blue Transfer, Rogers, 10 In. 230.00
Plate, Boston State House, John Rogers & Son, 8 1/2 In. 1095.00
Plate, Broadlands, Scenery, Flower Border, Blue Transfer, R. Hall, 3 7/8 In. 110.00
Plate, Cabbage Rose, Scalloped Edge, 6 1/4 In. 80.00
Plate, Cadmus, Shell Border, Enoch Wood, 10 In. 585.00
Plate, Cascade De Gresy, Pres. Chambery, Dark Blue, E. Wood & Sons, 7 1/2 In. 105.00
Plate, Castle Garden Battery, Shell Border, Blue Transfer, 3 3/4 In. 330.00
Plate, Chief Justice Marshall, Shell Border, Enoch Wood, 8 3/8 In. 705.00
Plate, City Hotel, New York, Ralph Stevenson & Williams, 8 1/2 In., Pair 690.00
Plate, City Of Albany, State Of New York, Blue, E. Wood & Son, 10 In. 415.00
Plate, Commodore MacDonnough's Victory, Blue & White Transfer, 10 1/8 In. 440.00
Plate, Commodore MacDonnough's Victory, Dark Blue, Wood & Sons, 6 1/2 In. 316.00
Plate, Commodore MacDonnough's Victory, Shell Border, Blue, 8 1/4 In. 518.00
Plate, Dam & Waterworks Philadelphia, Blue, 10 In. 495.00
Plate, Dessert, Green Majolica, Grape Leaf, Thomas Tell, c.1855, 9 1/4 In., 6 Piece 430.00
Plate, Dinner, Quadrupeds, Blue, White, Lion Stalking, R. Hall, c.1830, 10 In. 495.00
Plate, Dr. Franklin's Maxims, Child's, 7 1/4 In. 130.00
Plate, Embossed Flower Panels, Eagles, 19th Century, 5 1/2 In. 33.00
Plate, Entrance Of Erie Canal Into Hudson, Albany, Enoch Wood & Sons, 10 1/4 In. 1035.00
Plate, European Landscape, Blue, White, 10 In. 105.00
Plate, Fairmount Near Philadelphia, Dark Blue, Stubbs, 10 1/4 In. 360.00
Plate, Fisherman Drying Nets, Classic Ruins, Scalloped Edge, 9 7/8 In. 55.00
Plate, Fishermen, River, Bridge, Flower, Leaf Border, Blue & White, 1800s, 9 3/4 In. 58.00
Plate, Grecian Gardens, Green, Pink, Jackson, 10 1/2 In. 145.00
Plate, Gunton Hall, Norfolk, 7 5/8 In. 85.00
Plate, Hampton, Gold Rim, Alfred Meakin, 10 In. 29.00
Plate, Harvard College, Acorn Border, Ralph Stevenson & Williams, 10 1/4 In. 410.00
Plate, Highlands, Hudson River, Dark Blue, Wood & Sons, 6 1/2 In. 635.00
Plate, Hoboken In New Jersey, Eagle Border, Blue Transfer, 8 In. 259.00
Plate, Hoboken In New Jersey, Stubbs, 7 3/4 In., Pair 375.00
Plate, House, Man, Woman, Child Walking Near Lake, Blue, 19th Century, 10 In. 275.00
Plate, Junction Of Sacandaga & Hudson Rivers, Scallop, J. & R. Clews, 6 3/4 In. 145.00
Plate, Kent East Indiaman, Shell Border, Blue Transfer, 9 1/4 In. 315.00
Plate, La Grange, Residence Of Marquis Lafayette, Blue, Enoch Wood, 10 1/4 In. 290.00
Plate, Landing Of Gen. Lafayette, Dark Blue, Flower Border, Impressed, 10 1/8 In. 400.00
Plate, Landing Of Lafayette, At Castle Garden, August 1824, Blue & White, 10 In. 410.00
Plate, Landing Of The Fathers At Plymouth, Blue, Enoch Wood, 10 1/8 In. ......115.00 to 310.00
Plate, Mahomedan Mosque & Tomb, John Hall & Sons, c.1825, 9 3/4 In., 6 Piece 2115.00
Plate, Nahant Hotel Near Boston, Joseph Stubbs, 8 1/2 In. 635.00
Plate, Near Fishkill, Hudson River, Picturesque Views, Scalloped Rim, 10 1/2 In. 175.00
Plate, Oriental Pagoda & Fountain, Dark Blue, 10 In. 165.00
Plate, Oriental Scenery Fakeer's Rock, Fruit & Flower Border, Blue Transfer, 4 1/4 In. ... 140.00
Plate, Park Theatre, New York, Ralph Stevenson & Williams, 10 In. 175.00
Plate, Playing At Draughts, Blue Transfer, J. & R. Clews, 1817-1834, 10 1/4 In. 244.00
Plate, Race Bridge, Philadelphia, Red Transfer, Scalloped Edges, 9 1/8 In., Pair 230.00
Plate, Soup, Octagon Church, Boston, Floral Rim, 1814-1830, 10 In. 385.00
Plate, St. Paul's Church, N.Y., Dark Blue, 6 1/4 In. 880.00
Plate, Table Rock, Niagara, Shell Border, Enoch Wood, 10 1/8 In. 590.00
Plate, Tim & Bobbin, Child's, 7 In. 165.00
Plate, Tomb At Jeswuntnagur, Blue, White, I. Hall, 7 1/2 In. 45.00
Plate, Transylvania University, Lexington, Enoch Wood & Sons, 9 1/8 In. 145.00
Plate, Union Line, Dark Blue, Enoch Wood & Sons, 10 1/4 In. 525.00
Plate, View Of Trenton Falls, 3 People On Rock, 7 5/8 In., Pair 403.00
Plate, Villa In The Regent's Park, London, Blue Transfer, 8 7/8 In. 145.00
Plate, Villa In The Regent's Park, St. Paul's School, Blue Transfer, 2 Piece 259.00
Plate, Winter View Of Pittsfield, Mass., Blue Transfer, 8 3/4 In. 315.00
Plate, Woman, In Ruins, Embossed Flower Border, c.1830, 8 In. 60.00

Staffordshire, Platter, Blue Transfer, Stevenson,
Cobridge, 1816-1830, 19 In.

**If garage windows are painted,
burglars won't be able to tell if
cars are home or not. Use
translucent paint to get light in
the closed garage, if it has an
entrance to your house.**

Platter, Arms Of The States, New York, Thomas Mayer, 10 In.	1035.00
Platter, Birds With Fruit, Dark Blue, 14 1/2 In.	910.00
Platter, Birds With Fruit, Dark Blue, 18 1/2 In.	1100.00
Platter, Blue Transfer, Stevenson, Cobridge, 1816-1830, 19 In. *Illus*	575.00
Platter, Boston & Bunker's Hill, Blue & White Transfer, Thomas Godwin, 13 3/8 In.	499.00
Platter, Boston State House, John Rodgers, 16 3/4 In.	2185.00
Platter, Castle Garden Battery, New York, Enoch Wood & Sons, 18 3/4 In.	2760.00
Platter, Castle Ruins, Deer, Couples, Blue & White Transfer, 20 x 16 In.	495.00
Platter, Dublin Scene, Dark Blue, Wood & Sons, 14 3/4 In.	1760.00
Platter, Fruit, Blue, White, England, 13 In.	520.00
Platter, Italian Scenery, Genoa, Blue Transfer, Wood & Sons, 12 3/4 In.	290.00
Platter, Lake George, State Of New York, Enoch Wood & Sons, 16 3/8 In.	1840.00
Platter, Landing Of General Lafayette, Castle Garden, James & Ralph Clews, 17 In.	2645.00
Platter, Louisville, Columbus, Neff Wanton, 14 3/8 In.	2645.00
Platter, Musketeer, Oriental Series, Oblong, Beaded Edge, John Rogers, 17 In.	530.00
Platter, Niagara Falls, Pink, Thomas Cole, England, c.1831, 20 x 16 In.	1800.00
Platter, Pashkov House, Moscow, Medium Dark Blue, 1830s, 20 In.	2250.00
Platter, Peace & Plenty, Dark Blue, James & Ralph Clews, 17 In.	1840.00
Platter, Peruvian Horse Hunt, Medium Blue Transfer, Spatter Border, 10 x 13 In.	200.00
Platter, Texian Campaigne, Brown, White, 15 1/4 In.	1495.00
Platter, Vase Of Flowers, Blue, 17 x 13 3/4 In.	315.00
Platter, View Of Dublin, Dark Blue, 14 1/4 In.	1760.00
Platter, Vue Du Temple De La Philosophie Ermonville, Impressed Wood, 16 1/2 In.	405.00
Platter, Well & Tree, Christianburg Danish Settlement, Gold Coast Africa, Blue, 18 In.	2420.00
Quill Holder, 2 Poodles, Flower Shape Holder, 5 1/2 x 4 1/2 In.	100.00
Saltshaker, Man Holding Mug, Tricornered Hat, 5 1/2 x 2 1/4 In.	55.00
Sauceboat, Quadrupeds, Dark Blue, J. Hall	410.00
Saucer, Landing Of Lafayette At Castle Garden, Blue Glaze, 1824, 7 3/4 In.	375.00
Shaker, Pepper, Multicolored, Oval, Iron Red, 5 1/2 x 1 1/2 x 1 3/4 In.	110.00
Soup, Dish, America & Independence, Building, Fishermen, J. & R. Clews, 10 1/4 In.	405.00
Soup, Dish, Exchange, Baltimore, Henshall, Williamson & Co., 9 1/2 In.	750.00
Soup, Dish, Marshal Troy, Dark Blue, E. Wood & Sons, 8 1/4 In.	470.00
Soup, Dish, Table Rock, Niagara, Enoch Wood & Sons, 10 1/8 In.	575.00
Soup, Dish, View Of Trenton Falls, Dark Blue, Wood & Sons, 7 1/4 In.	308.00
Spill Holder, Dog, Poodles, Flower Shape Vase, 5 1/2 x 4 1/2 In.	125.00
Spill Holder, Dog, Reclining, At Base Of Tree, Oblong Base, 6 In.	79.00
Spill Holder, Flock Of Sheep, 3 Rams, 2 Ewes, 5 In.	300.00
Spill Holder, Little Red Riding Hood, Wold, Tree, 7 1/2 In.	105.00
Spill Holder, Milkman, Pail, Front Of Cow, 8 3/4 x 2 3/4 x 7 In. 360.00 to	470.00
Spill Holder, Sheep, Glaze, 7 1/2 In.	230.00
Stirrup Cup, Fox, Black Collar, 1800s, 5 x 2 1/2 In.	635.00
Stirrup Cup, Hound, Tan, Black, Yellow Eyes, 4 3/4 x 2 1/4 x 2 3/4 In.	415.00
Sugar & Creamer, Cover, Young Girls With Book, Dark Blue	525.00
Sugar & Milk Pitcher, Cover, Flowers, Stippled Ground, 5 1/2 & 4 1/8 In.	690.00
Tea Set, Black, Glazed, Gilt, Fruit, Leaves, Vines, Crabstock Handle, 3 Piece	940.00
Tea Set, Salopian, Flowers, Birds, Blue, Gold, Yellow, Green, Brown, 6 Piece	690.00
Teapot, Castle, Black Transfer, 19th Century, 7 1/2 x 11 1/2 In.	175.00

Teapot, Cover, Black, Glazed, Crabstock Handle, Spout, Bird Finial, Gilt, c.1780, 5 In. ...	325.00
Teapot, Cover, Black, Glazed, Globular, Crabstock Handle, c.1770, 4 3/4 In.	325.00
Teapot, Cover, Black, Glazed, Globular, Crabstock Handle, Paw Feet, c.1775, 5 1/4 In. ...	325.00
Teapot, Cover, Black, Glazed, Molded, Oval, Classical Figures, Early 1800s, 6 1/2 In. ...	355.00
Teapot, Cover, Black, Glazed, Tree Stump Shape, Branch Handle, Spout, 4 3/4 In.	500.00
Teapot, Cover, Blue & White, Flower, Bird, 1800s, 6 x 10 In.	460.00
Teapot, Cover, Flowers, Blue, Red, Green, Reverse Drape, 7 In.	220.00
Teapot, Denton Park, Yorkshire, Dark Blue	470.00
Teapot, Running Stag, Dark Blue	385.00
Teapot, Wadsworth Tower, Enoch Wood & Sons, 6 3/4 In.	690.00
Toby Jugs are listed in their own category.	
Tureen, Boston State House	1210.00
Tureen, Cover, Bird & Fruit, Dark Blue	330.00
Tureen, Cover, Fruit, Blue & White	690.00
Tureen, Cover, Upper Ferry Bridge Over River Schuylkill, Joseph Stubbs, 8 3/4 In.	1725.00
Tureen, Sauce, Underplate, Brown & White, Chinoiserie Decor, 1800s, 8 1/2 In.	259.00
Tureen, Underplate, Coastal Scenes, Shell Borders, Blue, 8 In.	385.00
Tureen, Underplate, Trinity Hall Cambridge, Christ Church Oxford, 9, 6 1/2 In.	460.00
Tureen, Vegetable, Cover, Etruscan, Blue, White, Enoch Wood & Sons, c.1830, 12 In. ...	395.00
Vase, Chimney, 2 Black & White Hunting Dogs, Tree Base, 7 1/2 In.	175.00
Vase, Chimney, 2 Children By Fireplace, Holding Bird, 10 1/4 In.	148.00
Vase, Chimney, Scottish Woman, Carrying Pheasants, 8 3/4 In.	85.00
Vase, In The Open, Fox Hunt Scene, Green, Tan, Brown, Maroon, Cecil Aldin, 12 In.	275.00
Vase, The First, Hunting Scene, Green, Tan, Brown, Maroon, Cecil Aldin, 11 3/4 In.	400.00
Watch Holder, Man & Woman, Holding Bird, 10 1/2 x 2 1/2 x 6 3/4 In.	155.00

STANGL Pottery traces its history back to the Fulper Pottery of New Jersey. In 1910, Johann Martin Stangl started working at Fulper. He left to work at Haeger Pottery from 1915 to 1920. Stangl returned to Fulper Pottery in 1920, became president in 1926, and changed the company name to Stangl Pottery in 1929. Stangl acquired the firm in 1930. The pottery is known for dinnerware and a line of bird figurines. Martin Stangl died in 1972, and the pottery was sold to Frank Wheaton, Jr., of Wheaton Industries. Production continued until 1978, when Pfaltzgraff Pottery purchased the right to the Stangl trademark, and the remaining inventory was liquidated. A single bird figurine is identified by a number. Figurines made up of two birds are identified by a number followed by the letter "D" indicating "Double."

Amber Glo, Plate, Dinner, 10 In.	5.00
Antique Gold, Bowl, Footed, 10 In.	55.00
Antique Gold, Candy Dish, Divided, Handle, 7 x 6 1/2 In.	35.00
Apple Delight, Teapot, 5 1/4 In.	28.00
Bird, Blue Bird, No. 3276S, 5 In.	85.00
Bird, Cerulean Warbler, No. 3456, 4 1/4 In.	110.00
Bird, Chickadees, Triple, No. 3581	289.00
Bird, Cockatoo, No. 3405S, 6 In.	95.00
Bird, Cockatoo, No. 3405S, Antique Ivory Crackled, 6 In.	95.00
Bird, Gazing Duck, No. 3250D, 3 3/4 In.	80.00
Bird, Oriole, No. 3402S, 3 1/4 In.	110.00
Bird, Painted Bunting, No. 3452, 5 In.	125.00
Bird, Redstarts, Double, No. 3490D, 9 In.	200.00
Bird, Yellow Warbler, No. 3447, 5 In.	110.00
Bittersweet, Bowl, Vegetable, Oval, Divided	14.00
Bittersweet, Tidbit, 10 In.	45.00
Blueberry, Bowl, Salad, 10 In.	50.00
Blueberry, Chop Plate, 14 1/2 In.	35.00
Christmas Tree, Plate, Jeweled, 8 In.	70.00
Cosmos, Vase, Sunflower Shape, Turquoise Satin Glaze, Gold Trim, 7 1/2 x 8 x 4 In.	35.00
Country Garden, Bowl, Fruit, 5 1/2 In.	15.00
Country Garden, Bowl, Vegetable, 8 In.	25.00
Country Garden, Plate, Dinner, 10 In.	35.00
Country Garden, Salt & Pepper, 3 In.	25.00
Dahlia, Tidbit, 2 Tiers, 10 In.	25.00

Fruit, Creamer, Grapes, Peach 20.00
Fruit, Mug, Grape, 2 Cup 6.00
Fruit, Plate, Bread & Butter, 6 In. 15.00
Fruit & Flowers, Cake Plate, Footed 60.00
Fruits & Flowers, Bowl, Salad, 12 In. 25.00
Garland, Butter, Cover 45.00
Garland, Cup & Saucer 15.00
Golden Blossom, Cup & Saucer 7.00
Golden Blossom, Plate, Dinner, 10 In. 12.00
Golden Blossom, Plate, Salad, 8 In. 7.00
Golden Harvest, Plate, Dinner, 10 In. 10.00
Hen & Rooster, Salt & Pepper, 3 1/2 x 5 In. 145.00
Kiddieware, Cup, ABC 55.00
Kiddieware, Kitten Kapers, Dish, 3 Sections 170.00
Magnolia, Bowl, Cereal, 6 In. 25.00
Magnolia, Chop Plate, 12 1/2 In. 30.00
Magnolia, Chop Plate, 14 In. 40.00
Magnolia, Cup & Saucer 28.00
Magnolia, Plate, 10 In. 10.00
Magnolia, Sugar, No Cover 12.00
Maize-Ware, Butter, Cover, Corn, Harvest Yellow, 1/4 Lb. 25.00
Orchard Song, Bowl, Salad, 12 In. 28.00
Orchard Song, Cake Plate, 6 In. 10.00
Orchard Song, Cup & Saucer ....11.00 to 14.00
Orchard Song, Eggcup, 3 1/4 In. 11.00
Orchard Song, Gravy Boat, Underplate 25.00
Orchard Song, Plate, Dinner, 10 In. 11.00
Orchard Song, Plate, Salad, 8 In. ....8.00 to 10.00
Paisley, Chop Plate, 12 1/2 In. 25.00
Paisley, Relish, 11 In. 14.00
Prelude, Plate, 8 In. 7.00
Provincial, Cup & Saucer 15.00
Rooster, Saltshaker, 4 1/2 x 3 1/2 In. 45.00
Sculptured Fruit, Cup 12.00
Sculptured Fruit, Saucer 4.00
Sculptured Fruit, Soup, Dish, 7 3/4 In. 12.00
Terra Rose, Vase, Brown Glaze, Fluted, 7 1/2 x 4 In. 80.00
Thistle, Cup & Saucer 14.00
Thistle, Plate, Bread & Butter, 6 In. 5.00
Thistle, Plate, Dinner, 10 In. 20.00
Thistle, Plate, Luncheon, 9 1/2 In. 22.00
Town & Country, Bowl, Salad, Blue, Ribbed, Rolled Rim, 12 In. 39.00
Town & Country, Plate, Dinner, Blue, 10 5/8 In. 40.00
Town & Country, Platter, Oval, Blue, 14 3/8 x 10 1/8 In. 145.00
Vase, Bud, Black Gold, 5 3/4 In. 65.00
Vase, Bud, Gold Tweed, 6 In. 15.00
Vase, Granada Gold, Genie Shape, 8 1/2 In. 18.00
White Dogwood, Plate, Bread & Butter, 6 In. 6.00

STAR TREK AND STAR WARS collectibles are included here. The original *Star Trek* television series ran from 1966 through 1969. The series
spawned an animated series, three sequels, and a prequel, which is still
in production. The first Star Trek movie was released in 1979 and nine
others followed, the most recent in 2002. The movie *Star Wars* opened
in 1977. Sequels were released in 1980 and 1983, prequels in 1999 and
2002. Other science fiction and fantasy collectibles can be found under
Batman, Buck Rogers, Captain Marvel, Flash Gordon, Movie,
Superman, and Toy.

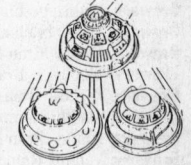

STAR TREK, Card & Sticker Set, Topps, 88 Cards, 22 Stickers, Box, 1976 .... 160.00
Figure, Cheron, Mego, 1974 .... 45.00
Figure, Romulan, Mego, 1974 .... 155.00
Figure, Spock, Mego, On Card, 1974 .... 45.00
Gun, Tracer, 20 Jet Disks, Plastic, Blister Card, Grand Toys Ltd., Canada, 1966, 6 1/2 In. .. 40.00

Lunch Box, Enterprise, Metal, Dome, Aladdin, 1968 .... 2130.00
Lunch Box, Metal, Plastic Thermos, 1979 .... 50.00
Playset, USS Enterprise, Mego, Box, 1974 .... 110.00
Shirt, Uniform, Blue, Polyester, Rubies Costumes, Paramount, Registered, Size XL 30.00
Water Gun, Phaser, Azark-Hamway International, Hong Kong, 1975, 5 3/4 In. 50.00
Water Gun, USS Enterprise, Azark-Hamway International, Hong Kong, 1976 .... 80.00
STAR WARS, Cookie Jar, R2-D2, Box, Roman Ceramics, 1977, 13 In. 120.00
Figure, Amamanan, Staff, Coin, Kenner, 1985, 5 In. 50.00
Figure, Barada, Staff, Coin, Kenner, 1985 .... 26.00
Figure, Darth Vader, 12-Back Card, Kenner, c.1978 .... 480.00
Figure, EV-9D9, Torture Droid, Coin, Kenner, 1985 .... 42.00
Figure, Imperial Dignitary, Coin, Kenner, 1985 .... 20.00
Figure, Lando Calrissian, General Pilot, Coin, Kenner, 1985 .... 30.00
Figure, Luke Skywalker, 12-Back Card, Kenner, c.1978 .... 680.00
Figure, Luke Skywalker, Stormtrooper Outfit, Helmet, Weapon, Kenner, 1985 .... 85.00
Figure, Lumat Ewok Warrior, Bow, Coin, Partial Card, Kenner, 1985 .... 20.00
Figure, Princess Leia, 12-Back Card, Kenner, c.1978 .... 720.00
Figure, R2-D2, 12-Back Card, Kenner, 1977 .... 190.00
Figure, R2-D2, Pop-Up Light Saber, Power Of The Force, Kenner, 1985 .... 175.00
Figure, Romba Ewok, Spear, Coin, Partial Card, Kenner, 1985 .... 25.00
Figure, Yak Face, Staff, Kenner, 1985 .... 110.00
Saltshaker, R2-D2, Sigma, c.1983, 4 1/4 In. 125.00
Tankard, Darth Vader, California Originals, 1977, 52 Oz., 7 1/4 In. 195.00
Tankard, Darth Vader, Ceramic, Painted, 7 1/4 In. ....25.00 to 60.00
Tankard, Obi-Wan Kenobi, Painted, 5 1/2 x 6 x 6 3/4 In. ....25.00 to 60.00
Toy, Ewok Village Action Playset, Kenner, Box, 1983, 12 In. 125.00
Toy, Millennium Falcon Spaceship, Return Of The Jedi, 21 x 18 In. 175.00

STEINS have been used by beer and ale drinkers for over 500 years. They have been made of ivory, porcelain, stoneware, faience, silver, pewter, wood, or glass in sizes up to nine gallons. Although some were made by Mettlach, Meissen, Capo-di-Monte, and other famous factories, most were made by less important German potteries. The words *Geschutz* or *Musterschutz* on a stein are the German words for *patented* or *registered design*, not company names. Steins are still being made in the old styles. Lithophane steins may be found in the Lithophane category.

2 Men, Furniture, Multicolored, Pewter Lid, Faience, Austria, c.1763, 1 Liter, 11 In. 920.00
Anchor, Flowers, Merchant Seamen, Multicolored, Pewter Ring & Lid, Faience, 1/2 Liter . 1450.00
Anheuser-Busch, Budweiser, Holiday, Clydesdales, 50th Anniversary, 1983 .... 65.00
Bicycle, Pottery, Man & Woman Riding Standard Bicycle, Relief, 1/2 Liter 360.00
Brewery, Bavaria Keller, Stoneware, Pewter Lid, 1 Liter 425.00
Brewery, Brauerei Kroneburg, Dortmund, Transfer, Enameled, Pottery, Pewter Lid, 1 Liter 230.00
Brewery, Eberl Brau Gegrundet 1593 Munchen, Etched, Pottery, Pewter Lid, 1/2 Liter ... 485.00
Brewery, Franzikaner Leist Brau Munchen, Stoneware, Enameled, Pewter Lid, 1 Liter ... 169.00
Brewery, Gerner Brau Munchen, Glass, Pressed, Pewter Lid, 1/2 Liter 240.00
Brewery, HB, With Crown, Transfer, Enameled, Stoneware, Pewter Lid, 4 In. 115.00
Brewery, Konigsbacher Brauerei Coblinez 1931, Stoneware, Pewter Lid, 1/2 Liter 145.00
Brewery, Konigsbacher Urbock, Relief, Stoneware, Pewter Lid, 1 Liter 219.00
Brewery, Lady On Horse, Braeu Rosl, Stoneware, Pewter Lid, 4-Horse Thumblift, 1 Liter 345.00
Brewery, Lothringerbrau, Devant-Les-Ponts, Pottery, Pewter Lid, Relief, 1/2 Liter 260.00
Brewery, Lowenbraukeller Munchen, Hand Engraved, Pewter Lid, 1 Liter 145.00
Brewery, Mahr's Brau Bamberg, Farm Scene, Etched, Stoneware, 1 Liter 175.00
Brewery, Mathaser, Brau Munchen, Schutz-Marke, Pewter Lid, Relief, 1 Liter 725.00
Brewery, Pschorr-Brau, Transfer, Enameled, Stoneware, Pewter Lid, 1/2 Liter 105.00
Brewery, Stadtbrauerei Einbeck, Stoneware, Pewter Lid, Relief, 1/2 Liter 99.00
Brewery, Unions Brau Munchen, Pottery, Transfer, Enameled, Pewter Lid, 1 Liter 135.00
Brewery, Vereins Brauerei Zu Greiz, Stoneware, Pewter Lid, Relief, 1/2 Liter 160.00
Character, 4 Men Under Umbrella, Porcelain, Pewter Lid, Schierholz, 1/2 Liter 430.00
Character, Alligator, Porcelain, Inlaid Lid, E. Bohne & Sohne, 1/2 Liter 747.00
Character, Alligator, Porcelain, Lid, Schierholz, 1/2 Liter 740.00
Character, Bear, Pottery, Lid, 1/2 Liter 635.00
Character, Birch Tree, Pottery, Pewter Lid, 1 Liter 365.00

Character, Bismarck, Porcelain, Lid, Schierholz, 1/2 Liter 290.00
Character, Bowling Pin, Pottery, Inlaid Lid, 1/2 Liter 250.00
Character, Bustle Lady, Stoneware, Pewter Lid, Hauber & Reuther, 1/2 Liter 980.00
Character, Card Game, Pottery, Pewter Lid, Relief, 1/2 Liter 150.00
Character, Cat Holding Fish, Pottery Lid, Eckhardt & Engler, 1/2 Liter 300.00
Character, Cat Holding Kitten, JWR, Inlaid Lid, 1/2 Liter 210.00
Character, Cat With Hangover, Porcelain, Inlaid Lid, Schierholz, 1/2 Liter 415.00
Character, Cat, Pottery, Inlaid Lid, 1/2 Liter 315.00
Character, Cavalier, Set On Lid, Stoneware, 3 Liter, 15 In. 280.00
Character, Clown, Pottery, Inlaid Lid, Diesinger, 1/2 Liter 1440.00
Character, Composers, Tan, Black, Pottery, Relief, Inlaid Lid, 1/2 Liter 135.00
Character, Devil, Porcelain, Inlaid Lid, E. Bohne & Sohne, 1/2 Liter 635.00
Character, Dog, Dressed As Hunter, Pottery, Inlaid Lid, JWR, 1/2 Liter 285.00
Character, Drinking Scene, Tan, Green, Pottery, Relief, KB, 2 Liter 145.00
Character, Drinking Scenes, Tan, Green, Black, Pottery, Relief, Pewter Lid, 1 1/2 Liter .. 80.00
Character, Elephant, Porcelain, Inlaid Lid, Schierholz, 1/2 Liter 920.00
Character, Fat Man, Blue, Stoneware, 1/2 Liter .... *Illus* 127.00
Character, Fish, Pottery, Inlaid Lid, Reinhold Merkelbach, 1/2 Liter 390.00
Character, Fox, Porcelain, Porcelain Lid, Schierholz, 1/2 Liter 2900.00
Character, Fox, Stoneware, Inlaid Lid, 1/2 Liter 275.00
Character, Frog, Porcelain, Lid, Schierholz, 1/2 Liter 710.00
Character, General Tilley, Pottery, Relief, Pewter Lid, 1/2 Liter 115.00
Character, Goose Man, Porcelain, E. Bohne & Sohne, 1/8 Liter, 6 In. 1200.00
Character, Happy Radish, Porcelain, Inlaid Lid, Schierholz, 1/2 Liter 375.00
Character, Happy Radish, Porcelain, Inlaid Lid, Schierholz, 1/8 Liter 460.00
Character, Indian, Porcelain, Inlaid Lid, E. Bohne & Sohne, 1/3 Liter 660.00
Character, Knight, Majolica, Pewter Lid Forms Helmet, 1/2 Liter 355.00
Character, Lantern, Glass, Metal Lid, 1 Liter 185.00
Character, Man & Woman Dancing, Stoneware, Munchen, Pewter Lid, T. Neu, 1/2 Liter . 135.00
Character, Man & Woman, Art Nouveau Pewter Lid, F. Ringer, Enameled, 1/2 Liter ... 316.00
Character, Man & Woman, Cherubs On Sides, Pottery, Enameled, Pewter Lid, 1/2 Liter .. 115.00
Character, Man At Table With Beer, Relief, Pewter Lid, Sarreguemines, 1 Liter 345.00
Character, Man Holding Mug, Drinking, Stoneware, Relief, White's, New York, 2 Liter .. 420.00
Character, Man's Face, Pottery, Pewter Lid, 1 Liter 280.00
Character, Man, Green Jacket, Stoneware, Enameled, Pewter Lid, Franz Ringer, 1/2 Liter 420.00
Character, Man, Woman Playing Instrument, Pottery, Relief, Metal Lid, 1 Liter 240.00
Character, Man, Woman, Martin Pauson, Munchen, Pewter Lid, Enameled, 1 Liter 240.00
Character, Men On Horseback, Pottery, Relief, Glazed, Pewter Lid, 1 1/2 Liter 255.00
Character, Monk, Pottery, Pewter Lid, Goebel, Stylized Bee, 1/2 Liter 230.00
Character, Monk, Stoneware, Purple Salt Glaze, Inlaid Lid, 1/2 Liter 370.00
Character, Moses, 10 Commandments, Porcelain, Inlaid Lid, Nymphenburg, 2 Liter 1495.00
Character, Mother-In-Law, Pottery, Inlaid Lid, Reinhold Merkelbach, 1/2 Liter 485.00
Character, Munchen, Zugspitz, Stoneware, Inlaid Lid, Martin Pauson, 1/2 Liter 415.00
Character, Munich Child, Barrel Lid, Fish Handle, Porcelain, Schierholz, 1/2 Liter 633.00
Character, Munich Child, Barrel Lid, Radish Handle, Porcelain, Schierholz, 1/2 Liter 590.00
Character, Munich Child, Pottery, Inlaid Lid, 1/4 Liter, 7 1/4 In. 360.00
Character, Munich Child, Pottery, Inlaid Lid, 1 Liter 489.00
Character, Munich Child, Pottery, Marked Lichtinger Munchen, Inlaid Lid, 1 Liter 497.00
Character, Nun, Stoneware, Purple Salt Glaze, Inlaid Lid, 1/2 Liter 255.00
Character, Nurnberg Tower, City Scenes, Pottery, Pewter Lid, Flag Finial, 1/2 Liter 400.00
Character, Nurnberg Tower, Pottery, 1/8 Liter, 5 1/2 In. 175.00
Character, Nurnberger Trichter, Porcelain, Inlaid Lid, Schierholz, 1/4 Liter 690.00
Character, Nurnberger Trichter-Funnel, Porcelain, Schierholz, Inlaid Lid, 1/2 Liter 550.00
Character, People Drinking, Music Box Base, Transfer, Enameled, Pewter Lid, 1 Liter 100.00
Character, People Sitting On Porch, Transfer, Pewter Lid, Eckhardt & Engler, 1/2 Liter .. 50.00
Character, Perkeo, Porcelain, Inlaid Lid, E. Bohne & Sohne, 1/2 Liter 1495.00
Character, Pig In Moneybag, Porcelain, Pewter Lid, 1/2 Liter 276.00
Character, Portrait Of Man, Transfer, Pottery, Enameled, Musical, Pewter Lid, 2 1/2 Liter 210.00
Character, Rabbit, Porcelain, Porcelain Lid, Schierholz, 1/2 Liter 1850.00
Character, Rhinoceros, Porcelain, Lid, Schierholz, 1/2 Liter 635.00
Character, Sad Radish, Porcelain, Inlaid Lid, Schierholz, 2 Liter 660.00
Character, Singing Pig, Porcelain, Inlaid Lid, Schierholz, 1/3 Liter .... .375.00 to 460.00
Character, Skull, Inlaid Lid, 1/2 Liter 500.00

Character, Skull, On Book, Porcelain, Inlaid Lid, E. Bohne & Sohne, 1/3 Liter 489.00
Character, Skull, On Large Book, Porcelain, Inlaid Lid, E. Bohne & Sohne, 1/2 Liter 1329.00
Character, Smoking Pig, Porcelain, Inlaid Lid, Schierholz, 1/2 Liter 360.00
Character, Student Fox, Porcelain, Inlaid Lid, 1/2 Liter 375.00
Character, Student, Inlaid Lid, c.1950, 1/2 Liter 145.00
Character, Tower, Man, Woman, Pottery, Relief, 1/2 Liter 145.00
Character, Tower, Relief, Knights Drinking, Pottery, 1/2 Liter 215.00
Character, Uncle Sam, Porcelain, Lid, Schierholz, 1/2 Liter 1255.00
Character, White Owl, Porcelain, Inlaid Lid, E. Bohne & Sohne, 1/2 Liter 2070.00
Character, Woman Holding Baby, Pottery, 1/2 Liter 365.00
Character, Woman, Wearing Large Dress, Mephistopheles Handle, Pewter, 1/2 Liter 1475.00
Cut Glass, Red & Yellow Stain, Spa Scenes From Carlsbad, 1/2 Liter 345.00
Eagle, Multicolored, Pewter Lid, Faience, Berlin, c.1780, 1/2 Liter, 8 1/4 In. 690.00
Earthenware, Tin Glaze, Hand Painted, Pewter Lid, c.1750, 9 1/4 x 4 1/2 In. 520.00
Faience, Pewter Lid, Baluster Shape, Flattened Dome, Oval Thumbpiece, 10 1/2 In. 560.00
Faux Ivory, Bacchic Revelers, Gilt, Electrotype, Elkington, Late 1800s, 11 1/2 In. 2000.00
Fleur-De-Lis, Faience Lid, Faience, France, c.1900, 1 1/2 Liter, 11 3/4 In. 520.00
Flowers, Hand Painted, Pewter Lid, Faience, Fish Mark, c.1900, 4 1/2 In. 275.00
Flowers, Hand Painted, Pottery, Pewter Lid, Faience, c.1900, 1/8 Liter, 6 In. 265.00
Flowers, High Fired, Multicolored, Pewter Lid, Faience, Schrezheim, c.1790, 1 Liter, 9 In. 575.00
Flowers, Multicolored, Pewter Base Ring & Lid, Faience, Bayreuth, 1798, 1 Liter, 9 1/2 In. 1750.00
Glass, Adam & Eve, 3 Other Couples, Inlaid Lid, Lovers, 1/2 Liter 169.00
Glass, Amber, Pewter Overlay, Faces, Pewter Lid, 18 In. 725.00
Glass, Blown, Amber, Pewter Overlay & Lid, Brewer Holding Tankard, 1 Liter 399.00
Glass, Blown, Amber, Pewter Overlay Of Child, Pewter Lid, 1/2 Liter 175.00
Glass, Blown, Amber, Prunts, Ruffle, Pewter Lid, Crossed Swords, 1/2 Liter 230.00
Glass, Blue, Thumbprint, Mary Gregory, Boy, White Opaline Inlaid Lid, 1/3 Liter 195.00
Glass, Chicago White Metal Company, Porcelain Inlaid Lid, 1/2 Liter 170.00
Glass, Clear, Enameled, Man Playing Bagpipe, Pewter Lid, 1/2 Liter 230.00
Glass, Clear, Enameled, Students Greeting New Arrival, Fluted, Pewter Lid, 1/2 Liter 278.00
Glass, Clear, Enameled, Verse, Beer, Food, Chest, Art Nouveau Pewter Lid, 1/2 Liter 225.00
Glass, Clear, Engraved Deer, Fluted, Glass Inlaid Lid, Closed Hinge, c.1860, 5 In. 200.00
Glass, Cobalt Blue, Hand Painted Flowers, Zum Andenken, Pewter Lid, 1865, 1 Liter 375.00
Ivory, Battle Scene, 2 Dogs On Handle, Dog Head Thumblift, c.1880, 11 1/2 In. 3680.00
Ivory, Children, Carved, Brass, Cast Head On Handle, 5 In. 748.00
Ivory, Hunting Scene, Ibex Handle, Brass Base, Lid Mounts, c.1880, 8 In. 1150.00
Jockey, Pottery, Jumping Over Fence, Pewter Lid, Gerz, 1/3 Liter, 4 3/4 In. 75.00
Man Playing Violin, Pewter Lid, Faience, Thuringen, c.1790, 1 Liter, 9 In. 660.00
Merkelbach & Wick, Blue Knamein Leafy Vine, Pottery, Pewter Lid, 1/2 Liter ..... *Illus* 69.00
Mettlach steins are listed in the Mettlach category.
Military, Naval, Pottery, Ship's Flag, S.S. Kaiserin Auguste Victoria, Pewter Lid, 1/2 Liter 180.00
Military, Prussian Patriotic, Eiserne Zeit, Gray, Armored Knight, Metal Lid, 1915, 1/2 Liter 175.00
Military, Soldiers On Horseback, Lithophane, Porcelain, Pewter Lid, 1/2 Liter 145.00

Stein, Character, Fat Man,
Blue, Stoneware,
1/2 Liter

Stein, Merkelbach & Wick, Blue
Knamein Leafy Vine, Pottery,
Pewter Lid, 1/2 Liter

Stein, Rosenthal, Incised Floral
Decoration, Pottery, Pewter
Lid, 1/2 Liter

Milk Glass, 3 Chicks Hatching, Transfer, Enameled, Milk Glass Inlaid Lid, 4 3/4 In. 255.00
Milk Glass, Enameled Flowers, Pewter Base Ring & Lid, c.1800, 1 Liter 1090.00
Milk Glass, Flowers, Enameled Flowers, Ribbed, Pewter Lid & Base Ring, 1820, 5 In. ... 185.00
Occupational, Baker, Baking Scene, Pretzel, Crest, Porcelain, Pewter Lid, 1/2 Liter 300.00
Occupational, Barber, Transfer, Enameled, Porcelain, Pewter Lid, 1/2 Liter 750.00
Occupational, Beer Brewer, 2 Scenes, Pewter Lid Of Trumpeter Of Sackingen, 1/2 Liter . 230.00
Occupational, Blacksmith, Lithophane Bottom, Pewter Top, Germany, 1/2 Liter, 9 1/4 In. . 160.00
Occupational, Bookbinder, Transfer, Enameled, Pewter Lid, 1/2 Liter 245.00
Occupational, Brick Manufacturer, Stoneware, Pewter Lid, 1/2 Liter 230.00
Occupational, Butcher, Animals, Pottery, Relief, Pewter Lid, 1/2 Liter 275.00
Occupational, Butcher, Transfer, Enameled, Porcelain, Pewter Lid, 1/2 Liter 275.00
Occupational, Carpenter, Multicolored, Pewter Base Lid, Faience, c.1780, 1 Liter, 9 In. .. 1090.00
Occupational, Clock Maker, Porcelain, Pewter Lid, 1/2 Liter 920.00
Occupational, Farming, Landwirtschaft, Porcelain, Pewter Lid, 1/2 Liter 90.00
Occupational, Farming, Transfer, Enameled, Porcelain, Pewter Lid, 1/2 Liter 489.00
Occupational, Flaschner, Plumber, Lions, Shield, Porcelain, Pewter Lid, 1/2 Liter 290.00
Occupational, Gardner, Transfer, Enameled, Porcelain, Pewter Lid, 1/2 Liter 460.00
Occupational, Landmann, Farming, 2 Scenes, Porcelain, Pewter Lid, 1/2 Liter 150.00
Occupational, Metal Worker, 1 Large Scene, Pewter Lid, 1/2 Liter 375.00
Occupational, Pharmacists, Stoneware, Transfer, Enameled, Pewter Lid, 1/2 Liter 100.00
Occupational, Post Coach Driver, Wilhelm Konig, Pewter Lid, 1/2 Liter 485.00
Occupational, Shoemaker, Transfer, Enameled, Porcelain, Pewter Lid, 1/2 Liter 375.00
Occupational, Stoneware, Combed Body, Pewter Lid, Lion Thumblift, c.1850, 1 Liter ... 105.00
Occupied Berlin, Tan Crockery, Berlin Map, 4 Occupied Zones, West Germany, 1/2 Liter . 75.00
Patriotic, Iron Cross, Prussian Crown, Flags, Glazed Gray, Metal Lid, 1914, 1/2 Liter ... 380.00
Pewter, German Verse, Dancing Couple, Scrolled Leaves, Engraved, RJ 1782, 9 1/2 In. .. 340.00
Porcelain, Flowers, Transfer, Enameled, Lithophane, Pewter Lid, 1/2 Liter 80.00
Porcelain, Hunters Farewell, Transfer, Enameled, Lithophane, Pewter Lid, 1/2 Liter 130.00
Porcelain, Royal Vienna Type, Ladies Dressing Venus With Jewels, Inlaid Lid, 1/2 Liter .. 3380.00
Pottery, 19 Composers, Relief, Inlaid Lid, Book With Music, Lyre Thumblift, 1/2 Liter .. 185.00
Pottery, Bicycle Scene, Marked, Crown Devon, England, 1/2 Liter 80.00
Pottery, Bicycle, Relief, Pewter Lid, 1/2 Liter 365.00
Pottery, Gasthaus, Relief, Pewter Lid, 1/2 Liter 110.00
Pottery, Interior House Scene, Relief, Thewalt, Pewter Lid, 1/2 Liter 100.00
Pottery, Lohengrin Scene, Relief, Pewter Lid, 1/2 Liter 65.00
Pottery, Sarreguemines, Art Nouveau Leaves, Inlaid Lid, Snail, Max V. Heider, 1/2 Liter . 690.00
Pottery, Wine Cellar Scene, Relief, Pewter Lid, 1 Liter 110.00
Prussian Eagle, Pewter Lid, Faience, Berlin, c.1750, 1 Liter, 10 In. 2185.00
Regimental, 2-Sided, Roster, Grolsh Hess, Lion Thumblift, Porcelain, 1/2 Liter, 11 In. ... 280.00
Regimental, 2-Sided, Roster, Pioneer, Anchor Thumblift, Stoneware, Prism Lid, 1/2 Liter . 725.00
Regimental, 2-Sided, Roster, Porcelain, Griffin Thumblift, 1/2 Liter 570.00
Regimental, 2-Sided, Roster, Pottery, Eagle Thumblift, Holes Around Edge, 15 In., 1 Liter 185.00
Regimental, 2-Sided, Roster, Rgt. 14, Hannov. Ulanen, Eagle Thumblift, 1/2 Liter, 14 In. . 865.00
Regimental, 2-Sided, Roster, S.M. Torpedo Boot V 185, Pottery, Eagle Thumblift, 1 Liter 1150.00
Regimental, 2-Sided, Roster, Tambour Bernauer, Griffin, Porcelain, 1/2 Liter, 10 In. 299.00
Regimental, 2-Sided, Soldiers Standing At Attention, Eagle Thumblift, 1/2 Liter 1845.00
Regimental, 4-Sided, Rgt. 22, Westfal Feld Artillerie, Pottery, 1/2 Liter, 13 1/2 In. 690.00
Regimental, 4-Sided, Roster, Field Artillery Rgt. 60, Pottery, Eagle Thumblift, 1/2 Liter .. 680.00
Regimental, 4-Sided, Roster, Jakob Weber, Lion Thumblift, Pottery, 1/2 Liter, 12 1/4 In. . 265.00
Regimental, 4-Sided, Roster, Porcelain, Eagle Thumblift, Stanhope, 1/2 Liter 775.00
Regimental, 4-Sided, Roster, Porcelain, Lion Thumblift, 1/2 Liter, 11 3/4 In. 475.00
Regimental, 4-Sided, Roster, Porcelain, Lion Thumblift, 1/2 Liter, 12 1/4 In. 460.00
Regimental, 4-Sided, Roster, Porcelain, Screw Lid, Blue Glass Jewel, 1/2 Liter, 12 1/2 In. 605.00
Regimental, 4-Sided, Roster, Prism Bottom, Soldiers Drinking, Porcelain, 1/2 Liter 755.00
Regimental, Roster, Relief Germania, Music Box Base, Eagle Thumblift, 1/2 Liter 430.00
Regimental, Roster, Rgt. 1, Ulan Pfrommer, Porcelain, Child Thumblift, 1/2 Liter, 9 In. .. 230.00
Regimental, Third Reich, Adolph Hitler, Porcelain, Transfer, Pewter Lid, 1924, 1/2 Liter . 690.00
Regimental, Third Reich, Infantry Scene, Porcelain, Pewter Lid, Regensburg, 1/2 Liter ... 345.00
Regimental, Third Reich, Machine Gun Scene, Porcelain, Pewter Lid, Relief, 1/2 Liter ... 320.00
Regimental, Third Reich, Motorcycle, Side Car, Porcelain, Pewter Lid, Helmet, 1/2 Liter . 360.00
Regimental, Third Reich, Soldiers With Flag, Porcelain, Pewter Lid, 1/2 Liter 725.00
Rosenthal, Incised Floral Decoration, Pottery, Pewter Lid, 1/2 Liter .... Illus 82.00
Stoneware, 12 Apostles Around Body, Relief, Pewter Lid, Base Ring, Creussen, 6 1/2 In. . 2990.00

Stoneware, Animal Wrapped Around Body, Sarraguemines, 16 In. 449.00
Stoneware, Bicycle, High Wheel Bicycle, Pewter Lid, Dumler & Breiden, 1/2 Liter 365.00
Stoneware, Birds & Flowers, Westerwald, Engraved, Pewter Lid, c.1800, 1 Liter 725.00
Stoneware, Cobalt Blue, Salt Glaze, Engraved, Pewter Lid, c.1850, 1 1/2 Liter 98.00
Stoneware, Couple, On Bicycles, All Heil, Relief, Pineapple Finial, Pewter Lid, 2 Liter .. 235.00
Stoneware, Figural Monkey Handle, Glazed, Sarraguemines, 1 Liter 275.00
Stoneware, Flowers, Birds, Engraved, Pewter Lid, Westerwald, c.1800, 1/2 Liter, 8 1/2 In. 845.00
Stoneware, Gasthaus, Etched, Pewter Lid, Matthias Girmscheid, 1/2 Liter 240.00
Stoneware, Hunter Departing, Relief, Plated Pewter Lid, 1/2 Liter 86.00
Stoneware, Knibis Design, Pewter Base Ring, Top Ring & Lid, Westerwald, 1/2 Liter ... 2175.00
Stoneware, Munich Skyline, Child, Relief Pewter Lid, 1 Liter 345.00
Stoneware, Oktoberfest 1810-1910, Transfer, Enameled, Pewter Ring, F. Ringer, 1/2 Liter 360.00
Stoneware, Outdoor Drinking Scene, Etched, Girmscheid, 1 Liter 160.00
Stoneware, Repeating Art Nouveau Design, Pewter Lid, Albin Muller, 1/2 Liter 545.00
Stoneware, Repeating Design, Engraved, Westerwald, c.1800, 8 In. 285.00
Student Society, Amiatia Ambricensis, Glass, Pewter Lid, Engraved Zirkel, 1/2 Liter 230.00
Student Society, Cheruscia Sei's Panier, Glass, Inlaid Lid, Hannover, 1914, 1/2 Liter 459.00
Student Society, Glass, Fluted, Eimbrias Sei's Panier, Pewter Lid, 1/2 Liter 275.00
Student Society, Palatia Sei's Panier, Glass, Pewter Lid, 1888, 1/4 Liter 575.00
Student Society, Porcelain, Hans Schiedler, Transfer, Enameled, Pewter Lid, 1/2 Liter ... 170.00
Student Society, Porcelain, Pewter Lid, Armor, Crossed Swords, 1/2 Liter 165.00
Student Society, Ruperfia Sei's Panier, Glass Blown, Pewter Lid, 1/2 Liter 300.00
Student Society, Saxo-Thuringia Sei's Panier, Glass, Fluted, Pewter Lid, 2 Liter, 15 In. ... 1380.00
Student Society, Starkenburgia Sei's Panier, Porcelain, Pewter Lid, 1/2 Liter 198.00
Student Society, Stoneware, Guilelmia Sei's Panier, Pewter Lid, Dated 1907/08, 1 Liter .. 290.00
Student Society, Suevia Sei's Panier, Hand Painted, Pewter Lid, c.1896, 1/2 Liter 718.00
Student Society, Textilia Sei's Panier, Pottery, Pewter Lid, 1938, 1/2 Liter 130.00
Student Society, Vandalia Sei's Panier, Hand Painted Relief, Pewter Lid, 1/2 Liter 345.00
Student Society, Vinets Sei's Panier, Hand Painted, Pewter Lid, c.1898, 1/3 Liter 299.00
Student Society, Wattia Sei's Panier, Hand Painted, Pewter Lid, 1896, 1/2 Liter 290.00
Villeroy & Boch, Stoneware, Dancing Figures, King Of Hops, Pewter Lid, 1/2 Liter 90.00
Villeroy & Boch, Stoneware, Verse, Woman Holding Goblet, Pewter Lid, 3 Liter 169.00
Woman, Basket Of Fruit, By Building, Pewter Lid, Faience, Austria, 18th Century, 1 Liter 1330.00
Woman, Picking Grapes, Pewter Lid, Faience, Austrian, c.1780, 10 In. 660.00

STEREO CARDS that were made for stereoscope viewers became popular after 1840. Two almost identical pictures were mounted on a stiff cardboard backing so that, when viewed through a stereoscope, a three-dimensional picture could be seen. Value is determined by maker and by subject. These cards were made in quantity through the 1930s.

Air Transportation, Keystone Library, Boxed Set, 25 Cards 690.00
Algiers Dry Dock, S.T. Blessing 85.00
Among Petrified Wood, Badlands, Man, Horse, Rifle, J. Jay Haynes 95.00
Aviation, Biplanes, 1904 Wright Flyer, Keystone, 8 Views 430.00
Blondin On Tightrope, Niagara, Glass View, J. McPherson, 1859 .... 440.00
Bound For Klondyke Gold Fields, Chilcoot Pass, Alaska, 1898, 3 1/2 x 7 In. 105.00
C For Chinoises, Alphabet Des Costumes, Tinted, Pierced, Blue Mount 165.00
California Street Cable R.R., Watkins' New Series 200.00
Cat On Fern Case, Tan Mount, G.H. Nickerson, Provincetown, Mass. 75.00
Chain Bridge From Moulton's Castle, Copeland, N.H. 85.00
Chicago, Court House, Yellow Mount, John Carbutt 45.00
China, Red Cloth Slipcase, Gilt Lettering, 100 Views 1060.00
Community Helpers, Keystone Library, Boxed Set, 25 Cards 290.00
Crosby's Opera House, John Carbutt 60.00
Dead At Gettysburg, 1863 .... 240.00
Denmark, Red Cloth Slipcase, Gilt Lettering, 100 Views 1060.00
Dressmakers, Women, Sewing Machine, Boy, Tan Mount 150.00
Genessee Falls, Mill, Buildings, Bridge, Langenheim, 1856 .... 710.00
Golden Gate, Watkins' Pacific Coast Views, 1867 .... 100.00
Golden Gate From Alcatraz, Muybridge, San Francisco, Helios Flying Studio 160.00
Goliath At Wadsworth, Big Bend Of Truckee River, Yellow Mount 2650.00
India, Red Cloth Slipcase, Gilt Lettering, 100 Views 520.00
Interior Of Starr Arms Factory, Stacy 170.00

Japan, Red Cloth Slipcase, Gilt Lettering, 100 Views	750.00
Miners & Packers Climbing Golden Stair Trail, Alaska, 1900, 3 1/2 x 7 In.	175.00
Netherlands, Red Cloth Slipcase, Gilt Lettering, 100 Views	575.00
Nob Hill From Telegraph Hill, Orange, Lavender Mount, J.J. Reilly	75.00
Public Helpers, Keystone Library, Boxed Set, 25 Cards	375.00
Railroad Wharves At Sacramento City, Yellow Mount, A.A. Hart	600.00
Russian Hill From Telegraph Hill, No. 359, Thomas Houseworth's San Francisco	160.00
Saint Charles Hotel, Statue, Trams, No. 302, S.T. Blessing	65.00
San Juan Or Bust, No. 240, Gray Mount, Thurlow & Weitfle	330.00
Set, First Aid, Schonstein, Raumbild Editor, 2 1/4 x 5 In., 59 Piece	345.00
Sherman House, Railway, Telegraph Office, No. 52, John Carbutt	75.00
View On The Monitor Dictator, C.W. Woodward Imprint	259.00

STEREOSCOPES were used for viewing stereo cards. The hand viewer was invented by Oliver Wendell Holmes, although more complicated table models were used before his was produced in 1859. Do not confuse the stereoscope with the stereopticon, a magic lantern that used glass slides.

Chase's Folding, 65 Cards, Patent 1878	431.00
Mahogany, Ratchet Mechanism, 4-In. Magnifying Mechanism, 9 Views	385.00
Mascher's Improved, Leather Cased Daguerreotype, 5 In.	1017.00
Negretti & Zambra, Stereo-Graphoscope, Rosewood Case, Bone, 14 x 8 1/2 In.	380.00
Stereo-Graphoscope, Wood Eye Pieces, Hinged & Pierced Bracket, 1870s	460.00
Table, For Paper Stereographs, Wood, Ivens & Co., Holland	500.00
Tabletop, Rosewood, Holds 38 Views, 9 1/2 x 18 1/2 x 9 1/2 In.	920.00
Walnut, 2 Lens Sets, Cards, Late 1800s, 23 x 16 x 10 In.	1395.00
Wood, Pine Cutlery Tray, 49 Cards, 20th Century, 12 x 7 In.	224.00

STERLING SILVER, see Silver-Sterling category.

STEUBEN glass was made at the Steuben Glass Works of Corning, New York. The factory, founded by Frederick Carder and T.G. Hawkes, Sr., was purchased by the Corning Glass Company. They continued to make glass called *Steuben*. Many types of art glass were made at Steuben. The firm is still making exceptional quality glass but it is clear, modern-style glass. Additional pieces may be found in the Aurene, Cluthra, and perfume bottle categories.

Ashtray, David Hills, 1950, 7 1/8 In.	115.00
Ashtray, David Hills, 1952, 5 1/2 In., Pair	115.00
Basket, Selenium Ruby, Silver Lattice, Vine & Flower Overlay, 14 1/2 In.	3565.00
Bottle, Scent, Bristol Yellow Pedestal, Grapevine, Candy Cane Stopper, 12 1/2 In.	2040.00
Bowl, 3 Lobes, 7 3/4 In.	105.00
Bowl, Acid-Cut, Nedra, Mirror Black Over Alabaster	3135.00
Bowl, Calcite, Gold Aurene Interior, 2 1/4 x 10 In.	230.00
Bowl, Calcite, Gold Aurene Interior, 5 1/2 In.	200.00
Bowl, Calcite, Gold Aurene Interior, 9 3/4 x 2 1/2 In.	460.00
Bowl, Calcite, Gold Aurene Interior, Broad, Rolled Rim, 10 1/2 In.	300.00
Bowl, Calcite, Gold Aurene Interior, Flared Pedestal Foot, 3 3/4 x 9 3/4 In.	520.00
Bowl, Calcite, Gold Aurene Interior, Flared Rim, 3 x 10 In.	430.00
Bowl, Calcite, Gold Aurene Interior, Footed, c.1920, 3 x 8 In.	250.00
Bowl, Centerpiece, Grotesque, Dark Blue Jade	6040.00
Bowl, Centerpiece, Low, 4 Curved Legs, 5 x 10 In.	750.00
Bowl, Centerpiece, Pomona Green, Topaz Handles, 15 3/4 x 8 1/4 x 4 1/2 In.	400.00
Bowl, Crystal, Asymmetrical, Leaf Handle, 1 7/8 x 5 1/4 In.	115.00
Bowl, Crystal, Scroll Handle, 3 3/4 x 5 3/4 In. ....290.00 to	315.00
Bowl, Crystal, Scroll Handles, 2 x 9 1/2 In.	315.00
Bowl, Footed, John Dreves, 1942, 11 In.	345.00
Bowl, Green Jade, Square, 8 x 3 3/4 In.	230.00
Bowl, Grotesque, Amethyst Shaded To Clear, Signed, 6 1/4 x 11 1/2 In.	360.00
Bowl, Grotesque, Amethyst, c.1934, 4 3/4 x 8 1/4 In.	385.00
Bowl, Grotesque, Green Shaded To Crystal, 4 Pillars, 6 3/4 x 12 In.	460.00
Bowl, Holly, Paul Schulze, 1963, 6 3/4 x 5 In.	290.00
Bowl, Ivory, Footed, Flared Rim, 10 x 3 3/4 In.	175.00

Bowl, Ivrene, 2 1/4 x 5 3/8 In. 175.00
Bowl, Raised White Flowers, Pulled Green Leaves & Vines, Flared, Ruffled Edge, 7 In. .. 590.00
Bowl, Scroll Handle, 2 3/4 x 8 3/4 In. 345.00
Bowl, Spiral, Donald Pollard, c.1954, 7 In. 375.00
Bowl, Topaz, Swirl, Flared Rim, 7 In. 230.00
Box, Cover, Pink Jade, Signed, 6 1/4 In. 400.00
Candlestick, Aquamarine, Applied Ring Handle, 4 In. 430.00
Candlestick, Rope Twist, George Thompson, 1939, 8 In. 115.00
Candlestick, Rosaline, Alabaster, Twist Stem, 10 In., Pair 1550.00
Candlestick, Ruby, Cerise, 8 In. 260.00
Candlestick, Topaz Baluster Stem, Ribbed Amethyst Foot, c.1920, 15 In. 1344.00
Champagne, Flowered Panels, c.1950, 4 1/4 In., 10 Piece 175.00
Compote, Calcite, Gold Aurene Interior, Signed, c.1910, 3 1/2 x 8 In. 390.00
Compote, Swirled, Clear Stem, Pomona Green Rim, 7 x 8 In. 290.00
Cordial, Oriental Poppy Bowl, Opalescent Foot & Stem, 5 3/4 x 3 1/4 In. 635.00
Decanter, Crystal, Pointed Spout, Curved Handle, 10 In. 345.00
Figurine, Artic Fisherman, Signed, 1900s, 6 x 6 1/2 In. 2575.00
Figurine, Deer, Rosaline, 10 In. 50.00
Figurine, Elephant, Raised Trunk, James Houston, 1964, 7 In. 400.00
Figurine, Gazelle, 6 3/4 In. 230.00
Figurine, Horse Head, Signed, 1900s, 4 1/4 In. 140.00
Figurine, Koala Bear 700.00
Figurine, Open Crown, Signed, 1900s, 4 In. 170.00
Figurine, Owl, Frosted Eyes, Donald Pollard, 1955, 5 1/4 In. 250.00
Figurine, Piece Of Cheese, Gilt Brass Mouse, Box, 4 In. 2700.00
Goblet, Celeste Blue Bowl & Foot, Clear Stem, 6 In. 180.00
Lamp, Sculptured Leaf, Yellow Quartz, c.1910, 24 x 5 In. 1345.00
Letter Opener, Camelot, Sterling Silver, Sword In Glass Stone, 9 In. 1910.00
Paperweight, Central Teardrop Bubble, White Latticinio Spiral, 3 1/2 In. 280.00
Paperweight, Mistletoe, Pearl Mounted Cut Glass, Patinated Bronze, Case, 5 3/4 In. 2070.00
Paperweight, Pear, Ivory, 3 1/2 In. 430.00
Paperweight, Purple Flower, Central Bubble, Green Ground, 1920-1930, 3 1/2 In. 345.00
Pitcher, Green Jade, Swirled Ribs, Alabaster Handle, Silver Overlay, Dancing Girls, 9 In. 525.00
Pitcher, Green, Jade, Swirled Rib, Alabaster Handle, Silver Overlay, 9 3/8 In. 525.00
Plaque, Thomas Edison, Frosted & Clear, 1929, 8 1/2 x 6 In. 690.00
Plate, Applied Glass Knot Handle, c.1950, 10 In. 85.00
Sculpture, Beehive, Gold Bees, Base, Mid 20th Century, 3 1/2 x 5 1/4 In. 3740.00
Sculpture, Thistlerock, Rock Formation, Thistle, Leather Case, c.1970, 7 1/2 In. 1455.00
Shade, Calcite, Gold Threading, Gold & Green Pulled Tendril, Tulip Form, 5 In., Pair ... 690.00
Sherbet, Amethyst Bowl & Foot, Ribbed, Clear Stems, 4 1/2 In., 4 Piece 115.00
Sherbet, Oriental Poppy Bowl, Ribbed, Green Foot & Stem, 4 3/4 In. 575.00
Sherbet, Rosaline Bowl, Alabaster Stem, 3 1/4 x 4 1/4 In. 180.00
Vase, 5 Lobes, Carder & Manoikowski, 6 In. 175.00
Vase, Acid Cut, Bird, Flowering Branches, Green Jade Over Alabaster, 9 3/8 In. 1150.00
Vase, Acid Cut, Birds, 1924, 12 In. 8400.00
Vase, Acid Cut, Dragons, Clouds, 9 In. 2130.00
Vase, Acid Cut, Floral Pattern, Green Jade Over Alabaster, 9 In. 115.00
Vase, Acid Cut, Flowers & Birds, Green Jade, Bulbous, Rolled Rim, Footed, 9 In. 1315.00
Vase, Acid Cut, Flowers & Leaves, Rose Quartz, Geometric Lip, 13 In. 2875.00
Vase, Acid Cut, Flowers, Rosaline Over Alabaster, 7 In. 1150.00
Vase, Acid Cut, Plum Jade, 8 x 10 In. 1150.00
Vase, Acid Cut, Stamford, Gazelles, Black Over Alabaster, 8 3/4 In. 5260.00
Vase, Acid Cut, Stamford, Gazelles, Ivory, Signed, 10 1/2 In. 3740.00
Vase, Alabaster, Green, Ribbed, Flared, 5 3/4 In. 520.00
Vase, Amber Swirl, Blue Ruffled Edge, 11 In., Pair 230.00
Vase, Amber, Engraved Leaves & Vines Band, Stylized Clover On Waist, 8 1/4 In. 115.00
Vase, Amethyst, Flared Top, Slight Vertical Ribbing, 9 1/2 In. 230.00
Vase, Bouquet, George Thompson, 1949, 5 In. 175.00
Vase, Cintra, Acid Cut, Stylized Flowers & Trellis, 12 In. 4025.00
Vase, Cornucopia, Rosaline, Alabaster Foot, Signed, 8 In. 300.00
Vase, Cornucopia, Ruffled Edge, Square Base, 6 1/2 In. 60.00
Vase, Dragon, Acid Cut, Black Over Amber, Baluster, 14 In. 1540.00
Vase, Fan, Pale Amethyst, 11 x 9 In. 230.00

Vase, Fan, Topaz, Pomona Green Applied Foot, 8 1/2 In.	85.00
Vase, French Blue, 6-Sided Top, Swirled Ribs, 8 In.	175.00
Vase, Green Jade, Alabaster Handles	1625.00
Vase, Green Jade, Shouldered, Swirled Ribs, 6 1/4 In.	230.00
Vase, Green Jade, Swirled Ribs, Flared Top, 5 1/2 In.	175.00
Vase, Grotesque, Flemish Blue Shaded To Crystal, 9 1/4 In.	750.00
Vase, Grotesque, Green Shaded To Clear, Clear Foot, 11 3/4 In.	230.00
Vase, Grotesque, Green Shaded To Crystal, 9 1/8 In., Pair	750.00
Vase, Grotesque, Ivory, 4 Flared Ribbed Corners, Pinched Sides, 9 1/4 x 5 3/8 In.	260.00
Vase, Inverted Thumbprint, Applied White Threading, Flared Rim, 6 1/4 In.	85.00
Vase, Irregular Cut Facets, Blown Opening, P. Schulze, 6 1/2 x 4 1/4 In.	645.00
Vase, Ivrene, Optic Ribs, Flared, Ruffled Top, c.1934, 3 3/4 x 6 In.	145.00
Vase, Lily, Celeste Blue, Optic Ribbed, 4 In., Pair	415.00
Vase, Millefiori, Iridescent Gold, Leafy Vines, Flowers, 4 3/4 In.	3335.00
Vase, Opaque White, Applied Gold Leaf & Vine, 6 1/2 In.	575.00
Vase, Pomona Green, Swirled, Flaring Top, 7 In.	85.00
Vase, Rosaline, Signed, 8 In.	145.00
Vase, Stick, Rosaline, Alabaster Foot, 8 1/4 In.	240.00
Vase, Tree Trunk, 6 In.	145.00
Vase, Tree Trunk, Amber, 6 In.	230.00
Vase, Trumpet, Ivrene, Etched, Calla Lilies, 12 1/4 In.	1150.00
Vase, Tyrian, Heart & Vine, Purple, Blue, Signed, 7 1/4 x 4 1/4 In.	8910.00
Wine, Trumpet Shape, Sidney Waugh, 7 1/4 In., 10 Piece	520.00

STEVENGRAPHS are woven pictures made like fancy ribbons. They were manufactured by Thomas Stevens of Coventry, England, and became popular in 1862. Most are marked *Woven in silk by Thomas Stevens* or were mounted on a cardboard that tells the story of the Stevengraph. Other similar ribbon pictures have been made in England and Germany.

Bookmark, Late General Stonewall Jackson, Tassel, 8 1/2 In.	600.00
Picture, For Life Or Death, Heroism On Land, Horse Drawn Steam Pumper, Frame	275.00
Picture, Houses Of Parliament, Woven, Gilt Edge Mat, 3 x 7 In.	125.00
Picture, Kenilworth Castle, Woven, Gilt Edge Mat, 3 x 7 In.	125.00
Picture, Windsor Castle, Woven, Gilt Edge Mat, 3 x 7 In.	125.00

STEVENS & WILLIAMS of Stourbridge, England, made many types of glass, including layered, etched, cameo, and art glass, between the 1830s and 1930s. Some pieces are signed *S & W.* Many pieces are decorated with flowers, leaves, and other designs based on nature.

Biscuit Jar, Silver Cover, Cameo, Opal, Pink, Signed, 5 In.	1150.00
Bowl, Aqua, Amber Pears, Green Leaves, Spherical, Ribbed, Footed, 7 3/4 In.	1430.00
Bowl, Ivory Over Pink, Scissor Cut Rim, Rectangular, 6 1/4 x 8 1/2 In.	127.00
Bowl, Lemon Yellow To White, Applied Pink Flowers, Oval, c.1890, 7 1/4 In.	345.00
Bowl, Opalescent, Applied Cherries, Plums, Amethyst Rim, Bronze Holder	1310.00
Decanter, Amberina Cut To Clear, Trees, Butterflies, c.1890, 11 1/2 In.	1065.00
Decanter, Green Cut To Clear Flowers & Leaves, Handle, 10 In.	2530.00
Jar, Oval, Pastel Green, Alabaster Pedestal, Cupped Rim, c.1890, 8 In.	165.00
Pitcher, Peachblow, Applied Yellow, White, Flowers, Amber, 15 In.	2588.00
Plate, Jewel, Light Blue, Zipper, Ruffled Edge, Ground Pontil, 7 In.	85.00
Rose Bowl, Blue, Brown, Chartreuse, Fluted, Squared Rim, 5 1/2 In.	2185.00
Rose Bowl, Diamond-Quilted, Mother-Of-Pearl, Green Shaded To Yellow, 3 In.	920.00
Vase, Amber, White, Applied Flower, Base, Pull-Up, 5 In.	345.00
Vase, Amethyst Cut To Clear, Intaglio Fruit Pods, Vines, 6 3/4 In.	575.00
Vase, Bud, Pink Pastel, Stylized Ferns, Grass, Cylindrical Neck, 5 In.	300.00
Vase, Butterscotch Shaded To Satin, Tapered, Oval, Lobed Neck, 12 In.	1155.00
Vase, Cranberry, White, Gold Mica Swirls, Rigaree, Footed, 13 In., Pair	500.00
Vase, Fruit Clusters, Crimson Martele Ground, Cameo, J. Millward, 6 1/2 In.	2520.00
Vase, Mother-Of-Pearl, Red, Yellow, Peacock Eye, Flared, Handles, 6 3/4 In.	550.00
Vase, Mother-Of-Pearl, Zipper Swirls, Flowers, Gold Leaves, Footed, 7 x 6 In.	715.00
Vase, Orange & Yellow Pulls, Opal Body, 3 Branch Feet, c.1880, 12 In.	560.00
Vase, Rainbow, Diamond-Quilted, Brass Northwind Feet, Handles, 14 1/4 In.	660.00
Vase, Red Shaded To Pearl, Peacock Eye Pattern, Fluted Rim, 7 In.	345.00

Vase, Swirl, Amber Shaded To Pink, Blue Interior, Ruffled Edge, 4 1/2 In. 863.00
Vase, Yellow Satin, Swirls, c.1890, 9 In. 730.00

STIEGEL TYPE glass is listed here. It is almost impossible to be sure a
piece was actually made by Stiegel, so the knowing collector refers to
this glass as *Stiegel type*. Henry William Stiegel, a colorful immigrant
to the colonies, started his first factory in Pennsylvania in 1763. He
remained in business until 1774. Glassware was made in a style popular in Europe at that time and was similar to the glass of many other
makers. It was made of clear or colored glass and was decorated with
enamel colors, mold blown designs, or etching.

Bottle, Multicolored Enameled Flowers, 5 In. 50.00
Cup, Oval Panel, Remember Me, Leaf Sprays, 4 1/4 In. .... : 60.00
Mug, Oval Panel, Remember Me, Leaf Sprays, 3 3/8 In. 50.00

STONE includes those articles made of stones not listed elsewhere in
this book. Micro mosaics (small decorative design, made by setting
pieces of stone in a pattern), urns, vases, and other pieces made of
natural stones are listed here. Alabaster, Jade, Malachite, Marble, and
Soapstone are in their own categories. Stoneware is pottery and is
listed in the Stoneware category.

Bowl, Agate, Chinese, Qing Dynasty, 19th Century, 5 3/4 In. 384.00
Dice, Painted, Black Ground, White Recessed Dots, 19th Century, 4 x 4 x 4 In. 470.00
Figure, Dove, Shaped Platform, 4 1/2 x 7 3/4 In. 10.00
Figure, Eagle, Carved, Wood Base, 22 In. 1210.00
Figure, Foo Dog, Limestone, Rectangular Base, Relief Decoration, 16 1/2 x 10 x 27 In. ... 220.00
Figure, Indian Maiden, Long Braids, Papoose, Sandstone, 52 In. 3850.00
Figure, Jizo, Seated, Lotus Posture, Calligraphy Carved Plinth, 23 In. 635.00
Figure, Lion, Seated, Rectangular Base, 15 x 9 x 22 In. 175.00
Figure, Monk, Cross-Legged, Dark Gray, Block Base, Chinese, 24 In. 415.00
Figure, Monk, Cross-Legged, Holding Pipe, Cloth Draped Pedestal, Gray, Oriental, 23 In. 385.00
Figure, Monk, Seated, Gray, Brown Patina, 23 In. 470.00
Figure, Putti, Holding Grapes, Representing Spring, 54 In. 375.00
Fruit Set, Pear, Peach, Apple, Lemon, Oranges, Tangerine, 2 1/2 In., 13 Piece 400.00
Group, Rock Crystal, 3 Figures Holding Fruit & Teapot, c.1900, 7 x 6 1/2 In. 290.00
Incense Holder, Carved, Pinwheel Design, Leaves On Top, Sawtooth Border, 5 x 6 In. ... 605.00
Panel, Agate, Tree, 2 Birds, High Relief, Chinese, 1800s, 6 1/4 x 5 In. 264.00
Panel, Black Stone, Inlay, Pink Roses, Green Leaves, Pietra Dura, 4 3/4 x 6 3/4 In. 330.00
Panel, Putti Pressing Grapes, Terra-Cotta Tint, Napoleon III, 32 x 55 In. 1265.00
Pipe & Match Holder, Carved, Civil War Soldier, Leaning On Tree Stump, 4 3/4 x 7 In. .. 1155.00
Plaque, Bird, Butterfly Inlaid Marble, Pietra Dura, 3 1/4 x 4 3/4 In. 339.00
Plaque, Flower Inlaid Marble, Pietra Dura, 6 x 4 In., Pair 625.00
Scholar's Rock, Limestone, Mounted, Hardwood Stand, Chinese, 20th Century, 12 In. ... 460.00
Sculpture, Agate, Nude Female, Silver Patinated Base, Art Deco, 11 1/2 In. 4950.00
Sculpture, Alabaster, Woman, Flowing Gown, Alabaster, Art Nouveau, 24 x 9 x 7 1/2 In. .. 150.00
Snuff Mull, Agate, Horn, Rhyton Form, Silver Mounted, Scotland, c.1815, 5 In. 635.00
Totem Pole, Sandstone, Deer Head, Grotesques, Metal Post, Popeye Reed, 94 In. 575.00
Urn, Nephrite, Ivory, Tan, Brown, 4 Rings, Oriental, 7 1/4 In. 190.00
Vase, Cover, Agate, Figures, High Relief, Gray Blue, Chinese, 1900s, 9 1/2 In. 705.00
Vase, Rock Crystal, Tiger Lily, Gothic Panels, Trumpet, 15 3/4 In. 1000.00

STONEWARE is a coarse, glazed, and fired potter's ceramic that is used
to make crocks, jugs, bowls, etc. It is often decorated with cobalt blue
decorations. In the nineteenth and early twentieth centuries, potters
often decorated crocks with blue numbers indicating the size of the
container. A "2" meant 2 gallons. Stoneware is still being made.

Bank, Alarm Clock, Bristol Glaze, Roman Numerals, c.1880, 4 x 2 In. 550.00
Bank, Cat, Uplifted Leg, Scratching, Applied Brown Rockingham Glaze, 6 In. 45.00
Bank, Frog, Seated, Green Alkaline Glaze, 4 In. 89.00
Barrel, Rum, England, 12 In. 145.00
Basket, Emerald Lead Glaze, Tapered Handle, c.1950, 10 1/2 In. 78.00
Basket, Green Lead Glaze, Cord Style Handle, Fluted Edge, c.1940, 4 3/4 In. 65.00
Basket, Multicolored, Swirlware, Fluted Rim, 1930s, 13 1/4 x 8 1/2 In. 360.00
Batter Jug, Tin Lid, Tin Spout Cover, Leaf Designs, Cowden & Wilcox 2970.00

Batter Pail, Bail Handle, Cobalt Blue Tree Stump Design, 1860, 6 Qt. 660.00
Batter Pail, Flowers, c.1870, Gal., 9 In. 415.00
Batter Pail, Plume, Flower, Cowden & Wilcox, c.1870, Gal., 8 In. 2530.00
Bean Pot, Cover, Blue & White, Sponged Design, Pinched Spout Strap Handle, 5 In. 115.00
Beater Jar, Blue, Gray, Wilson's Variety Store, Clarion, Iowa, 5 In. 210.00
Biscuit Jar, Cottage, Thatched Roof, Rattan Handle, 9 1/4 x 4 x 6 In. 125.00
Bottle, 5-Point Star, Impressed, 10 In. 145.00
Bottle, Beer, J. Hindles Pop 145.00
Bottle, Ginger Beer, Salt Glaze, Clinton, 10 In. 50.00
Bottle, Impressed, J. Francis, 9 1/4 In. 66.00
Bottle, Impressed, John Howell, Con Top, 10 In. 80.00
Bottle, Ink, Henry Stephens Ink Co., 5 1/2 In. 10.00
Bottle, Pig, Cobalt Blue, Cork In Tail 160.00
Bottle, Soda, Root Beer, Hathaway Stoneware 95.00
Bottle, Whiskey, Grube's Pure Rye Whiskey, Sherwood Bros., Pa., 11 1/4 In. 115.00
Bowl, Brown, Tan Lead Glaze, c.1969, 2 x 6 In. 39.00
Bowl, Chinese Blue Glaze, Red, Turquoise Speckles, Rice, c.1930, 1 7/8 x 4 1/4 In. 550.00
Bowl, Harding Black, Iron Slip Flambe Glazed, Footed, c.1956, 4 3/4 x 7 1/2 In. 345.00
Bowl, Lid, Olive, Albany Slip Glaze, Monogram, c.1937, 3 x 2 1/2 In. 195.00
Bowl, Milk, Cobalt Blue Clover, Applied Handles, Raised Rim, 12 1/8 x 4 3/4 In. 580.00
Bowl, Multicolored, Glaze, Footed, Black Speckles, c.1970, 2 1/2 x 5 In. 90.00
Bowl, Olive Green, Gray Matte Ground, Toshiko Takaezu, 4 x 7 In. 460.00
Bowl, Raised Ostriches, Cobalt Blue Interior, 9 In. 70.00
Bowl, Rooster, Cinnamon, Glaze, Protruding Eyes, Comb, Tail, c.1950, 10 x 9 In. 1265.00
Bowl, Speckled Green Glaze, Mahogany, Brown, White, Woodman, 6 x 14 3/4 In. 1035.00
Bowl, Tobacco Spit Lead Glaze, Busbee's Jugtown Shape, c.1940, 3 1/4 x 9 3/4 In. 165.00
Bust, Head, Black, Bronze, Black Lead Glaze, c.1950, 8 1/2 In. 385.00
Bust, Head, Rust, Multicolored, Incised Hair, Eyelashes, Goatee, 11 3/4 In. 165.00
Bust, Indian Chief, Orange, Yellow, Clear Lead Glaze, War Paint, 1981, 6 1/2 x 8 In. 330.00
Butter Tub, Blue & White, Embossed Fruit, 6 3/4 In. 60.00
Butter Tub, Brown Glaze, Raised Letters, 19th Century, 4 3/4 In. 35.00
Butter Tub, Flowers, Dimpled Body, Sunflower, Bail Handle, Blue, White, 7 3/4 x 6 In. . . . 135.00
Cachepot, Alkaline Glaze, Cartouche Flowers, Chinese, 25 x 28 In. . . . . .175.00 to 200.00
Candleholder, Blue Lead Glaze, Looped Handle, Candle Socket Rim, c.1982, 3 1/4 In. 35.00
Candlestick, Frogskin, Albany Slip Glaze, 1960s-1970s, 11 1/2 In., Pair 305.00
Canister, Cover, Bail Handle, Flower, Relief Diamond, 4 x 6 1/2 In. 578.00
Chamber Pot, Green, Gray, Glaze, Handle, Swirl, Early 1980s, 2 7/8 In. 195.00
Charger, Flower, Orange Lead Glaze, Signed, Seagrove, c.1978, 1 x 12 In. 550.00
Chicken Waterer, Brown Over White, Incised Maple Leaf, Western Stoneware Co., Gal. . 300.00
Chicken Waterer, Slip Glazed, Oval, Knob Finial, Albany, 8 3/4 In. 165.00
Churn, Bird, Cobalt Blue, On Branch, Gray, Impressed, H.A. White & Son, 9 1/4 In. 4675.00
Churn, Black Brown, Albany Slip, 2 Handles, c.1920, 13 7/8 In. 99.00
Churn, Brown, Albany Slip, Handle, c.1945, 13 3/4 In. 90.00
Churn, Brown, No. 4, 4 Gal. 160.00
Churn, Cobalt Blue Bird, White's, Utica, 5 Gal., 18 In. 1540.00
Churn, Cobalt Blue Design, Ear Handles, N.A. White & Son, c.1885, 5 Gal. 1695.00
Churn, Cobalt Blue Design, Stripes, Flowers, James Hamilton & Co., 17 1/4 In. 375.00
Churn, Cobalt Blue Detail, Oval, Applied Handles, Flared Lip, Signed, 18 In. 210.00
Churn, Cobalt Blue Flowers Under Glaze, Heart Over Glaze, Circle Stamp, 10 3/4 In. 940.00
Churn, Cobalt Blue Flowers, Leaves, Ballard & Brothers, 3 Gal., 15 1/4 In. 1265.00
Churn, Cobalt Blue Stenciled Label, Hamilton & Jones, Greensboro, Penn., 14 1/2 In. . . . 403.00
Churn, Cobalt Blue Tulips, Meandering Vines, 17 1/2 In., 5 Gal. 720.00
Churn, Cobalt Feather, Applied Double Handles, Flared Rim, 18 1/2 In. 495.00
Churn, Cobalt Tulip, 6, Raised Rim, Applied Handles, Oval, 19 1/2 In. 230.00
Churn, Dotted Bird On Fern Leaf, N. Clark, Jr., c.1850, 4 Gal., 16 In. 330.00
Churn, Dotted Triple Flower, c.1870, 3 Gal., 15 In. 250.00
Churn, Eagle, Shield, Leaves, Stenciled, Cobalt Blue Lines, Signed, A. Conrad, 15 1/4 In. . 345.00
Churn, Flower Wreath, White's, Utica, c.1866, 4 Gal., 17 In. 825.00
Churn, Flower, Wm. Peck Druggist & Grover, c.1865, 4 Gal., 6 1/2 In. 2200.00
Churn, Lion & Palm, John Burger, Jr., 8 Gal., 22 In. 27500.00
Churn, Loop Handle, Brown, Tan, W.D. Suggs, c.1900, 5 Gal., 17 In. 360.00
Churn, Palatine, Stenciled, Cobalt Blue, Rearing Horse, Leaves, Applied Handles, 19 In. . 460.00
Churn, Salt Glaze, 2 Handles, Incised Lines, c.1920, 18 In. 825.00

Churn, Spray Of Flowers, White's, Utica, 4 Gal. 660.00
Churn, Star Face, T. Harrington Lyons, c.1850, 4 Gal., 17 In. 6875.00
Churn, Stencil, A.P. Donaghho, Parkersburg, W. Virginia, 8 In. 200.00
Churn, Swirls, Dots, Double 4, A.O. Whittemore, c.1870, 4 Gal., 16 In. 495.00
Churn, W.S. Co., White Hall, Ill., Miniature 1400.00
Container, Poison, For External Use, St. Bartholomew's Hospital, Shield Form, 3 3/4 In. . 251.00
Cream Pot, Drooping Flower, Evan R. Jones, c.1870, Gal., 8 In. 250.00
Cream Pot, Oval, E.S. Fox, c.1832, 2 Gal., 11 In. 690.00
Cream Pot, Snowflake, Applied Strap Handle, F.H. Cowden, c.1890, Gal., 6 In. 300.00
Cream Pot, Trophy Filled With Flowers, Incised, N. Clark & Co., c.1850, 2 Gal., 12 In. ... 1070.00
Cream Riser, Olive, Alkaline Glaze, c.1900, 6 3/8 x 9 In. 300.00
Creamer, Pewter Cover, Bearded Man Profile, Bristol Glaze, 4 3/4 In. 140.00
Crock, 2 Tulips, Swirled Center, Swirl & Dot, Handles, M. Woodruff & Co., 13 1/2 In. ... 790.00
Crock, 4-Leaf Flowers, Leaf Spray, Evan Jones, Blue, Pittston, Pa., 2 Gal. 140.00
Crock, Albany Slip, White Stencil, Clinton Pottery Co., Clinton, Mo., 8 Gal. 160.00
Crock, Ayres Bros., Impressed, Blue, Dotted Leaf, c.1870, 1 1/2 Gal., 8 1/4 In. 190.00
Crock, Bird On Twig, Oval, J.A. & C. W. Underwood, c.1865, 2 Gal., 10 1/4 In. 495.00
Crock, Bird Perched On Fence, West Troy, c.1871, 3 Gal., 10 1/2 In. 2970.00
Crock, Bird, Spotted, Flowered Branch, W. Roberts, 2 Gal. 690.00
Crock, Blue Bands, Dodson & Brauns Fine Pickles, St. Louis, Swing Handle, 6 Gal. 220.00
Crock, Blue Bird, Harmon & Dearden, Springfield, Mass., 3 Gal. 440.00
Crock, Blue Bird, On Branch, J.S. Taft & Co., Keene, N.H., 4 Gal. 525.00
Crock, Blue Decoration, Flower, Handle Accents, 10 1/2 In. 450.00
Crock, Blue Decoration, Squiggle Band, 12 Gal., 21 3/4 In. 1069.00
Crock, Blue Floral Slip, Gray, Bulbous, Handle, Late 18th Century, 2 Gal., 10 x 8 In. 140.00
Crock, Blue Flower, Double, c.1870, Gal., 7 In. 250.00
Crock, Blue Highlights, Handles, Name, Goodwin & Webster, Oval, 2 Gal. 250.00
Crock, Blue Swag & Flowers, 2 In Circle, 7 3/4 In. 200.00
Crock, Blue Swans, Stamped, Gardner, Me., 6 Gal. 105.00
Crock, Bristol Glaze, Horseshoe Ink Stamp, Macomb Pottery Co., 2 Gal. 30.00
Crock, Bristol Glaze, Stag Ink Mark, Buckeye Pottery Co., Macomb, Ill., 5 Gal. 95.00
Crock, Butter, Cobalt Blue Stenciled Label, Hamilton & Jones, Pa., 6 3/8 In. 295.00
Crock, Cable Slip, Quilled Design, Wilcox & Cowden, Harrisburg, Pa., 20 In. 575.00
Crock, Cake, 3 Flowers, Trailing Vines, D.P. Shenfelder, Reading, Pa., 3 Gal., 8 1/4 In. ... 770.00
Crock, Cake, Flowers & Swags, Incised, c.1850, Gal., 9 In. 470.00
Crock, Cake, Squat Bird, Bullard & Scott, c.1870, 2 Gal., 7 3/4 In. 635.00
Crock, Chicken Pecking Corn, c.1870, 6 Gal., 13 In. 690.00
Crock, Chicken Pecking Corn, c.1880, 3 Gal., 10 In. 745.00
Crock, Chicken Pecking Feed, New York Stoneware Co., 4 Gal. 1540.00
Crock, Cobalt Blue Bird Slip Decoration, Ear Handles, 3 Gal. 275.00
Crock, Cobalt Blue Bird, Fort Edward, New York, 6 Gal. 1915.00
Crock, Cobalt Blue Decoration, Clark & Fox, 1831, 9 3/8 x 13 1/2 In. 880.00
Crock, Cobalt Blue Decoration, Fern Leaves, Rochester, N.Y., Applied Handles, 11 1/2 In. 460.00
Crock, Cobalt Blue Design, 3 Tornado-Like Designs, 2 Handles, 14 In. 520.00
Crock, Cobalt Blue Design, E.B. Hissong, Pennsylvania, 1860s, 3 Gal. 1800.00
Crock, Cobalt Blue Eagle Stencil, Salt Glaze, Wheel Thrown, 6 Gal., 9 1/2 x 14 In. 1765.00
Crock, Cobalt Blue Feather, Drooping Flower, 8 7/8 In. 250.00
Crock, Cobalt Blue Flower, J. Shumway & Co., Webster, Mass., Gal. 120.00
Crock, Cobalt Blue Flower, Jardiniere Style, I. Seymour, 2 Gal. 160.00
Crock, Cobalt Blue Flower, Jardiniere Style, Wm. E. Warner, West Troy, Gal. 205.00
Crock, Cobalt Blue Flower, Salt Glaze, Egg Shape, Double Lunate Handles, 10 x 10 In. .. 130.00
Crock, Cobalt Blue Flowers, Applied Handles, Cowden & Wilcox, 2 Gal. 500.00
Crock, Cobalt Blue Flowers, Ear Handles, F.B. Norton, Mass., c.1870, Gal. 200.00
Crock, Cobalt Blue Incised Flowers, Applied Double Handles, 2-Sided, 12 In. 605.00
Crock, Cobalt Blue Leaf Design, Impressed 2, 10 1/4 In. 200.00
Crock, Cobalt Blue Leaves, Drooping Flower, Blue Handles, Oval, Gal. 165.00
Crock, Cobalt Blue Pecking Chicken, Applied Handles, No. 3, 10 x 10 1/2 In. 690.00
Crock, Cobalt Blue Signature, Hormell & Smyth, 15 In. 865.00
Crock, Cobalt Blue Single Flower & Leaf, Ear Handles, 5 Gal., 16 1/2 In. 440.00
Crock, Cobalt Blue Slip Decoration, Ear Handles, 4 1/4 In. 660.00
Crock, Cobalt Blue Stripe, Stenciled 1 1/2, Raised Rim, Slight Egg Shape, 9 1/4 In. 440.00
Crock, Cobalt Blue Tulip, Flared Rim, 8 3/4 In. 200.00
Crock, Cobalt Blue Tulip, Large 3, Brush Marks, Handles, 13 1/2 In. 230.00

Crock, Cobalt Blue Tulip, Oval, Applied Handles, Harrington & Burger, Rochester, 11 In.   550.00
Crock, Cobalt Blue Tulip, Oval, Raised Rim, Handles, 12 3/4 In. 430.00
Crock, Cobalt Blue Vines, 3 Large Flowers, Applied Handles, 21 In. 690.00
Crock, Cover, Cobalt Blue Highlights On Handles, Front Brush Mark, Oval, 2 Gal. 160.00
Crock, Cover, Demuth's Snuff, Cobalt Blue Slip, F.H. Cowden, 9 1/4 In. 660.00
Crock, Cream, Flower, Cowden & Wilcox, Harrisburg, Pa., 1 1/2 Gal. 145.00
Crock, Dotted & Ribbed Orchid Leaf, White & Wood, c.1885, 9 In. 275.00
Crock, Dotted & Ribbed Standing Bird On Vine, W. Roberts, c.1860, 4 Gal., 11 1/2 In. 1075.00
Crock, Dotted Cone Shaped Flower, C.W. Braun, Buffalo, N.Y., c.1870, 4 Gal., 11 In. 165.00
Crock, Dotted Pheasant, On Branch, J. Burger Jr., 5 Gal. 1925.00
Crock, Dotted Triple Flower, C. Hart, Sherbourne, c.1870, 4 Gal., 11 In. 305.00
Crock, Drooping Orchid, N.A. White & Son, Gal. 330.00
Crock, Drooping Orchid, N.A. White & Son, Utica, N.Y., c.1870, 3 Gal., 10 In. 200.00
Crock, E.S. & B. Newbrighton, Pa., 6 Gal. 110.00
Crock, Eagle, With Banner, Wm. E. Warner, 2 Gal. 5280.00
Crock, Fishing Lure, Incised, Dark Slip, 4 Gal. 1540.00
Crock, Flower & Buds, T. Harrington Lyons, c.1850, 3 Gal., 9 3/4 In. 248.00
Crock, Flower Cornucopia, Blue Decoration, 8 In. 140.00
Crock, Flower Tree, Althens Pottery, c.1893, 4 Gal., 11 In. 385.00
Crock, Flying Bird Chasing Butterfly, c.1880, 3 Gal., 10 1/2 In. 495.00
Crock, Freehand Vines & Tulips, 10 At Base, 2 Handles, Raised Rim, 20 In. 750.00
Crock, Fruit, Incised Leaf Mark, Western Stoneware Co., Monmouth, Ill., 6 Gal. 145.00
Crock, Heron Standing In Pond, Leaves, N.A. White & Son, Utica, N.Y., c.1870, 2 Gal. ... 7700.00
Crock, J.S. Brophy, Liquor Dealer, Blue Script, c.1880, Gal., 11 In. 250.00
Crock, Large Stamp Flower, Synan Bros., Somerset, N.J., 4 Gal. 120.00
Crock, Leaves, Brown Slip, Cobalt Blue Trim, 6 Gal. 440.00
Crock, Leaves, Scrolls, Handle, Signed Hamilton & Jones, Greensboro, Pa., 14 In. 290.00
Crock, Oval, Cobalt Blue Tulips, Leaf Band, 2, Double Handles, Remney, 12 3/4 In. 175.00
Crock, Oval, Open Handles, C. Crolius, c.1800, 13 In. 990.00
Crock, Partridge, A.O. Whittemore, Havana, c.1870, 6 Gal., 12 1/2 In. 1210.00
Crock, Poison, Swift's Arsenate Of Lead, Merrimac Chemical, Boston, 1/2 Gal. 60.00
Crock, Ribbed Geometric, Light Blue, J.M. Pruden, c.1870, 3 Gal., 10 1/2 In. 99.00
Crock, Ribbed Leaf & Flower, Edmands & Co., c.1870, 2 Gal., 9 1/2 In. 210.00
Crock, Salt Glaze, 2 Lunate Handles, Higgens & Co., Cleveland, 3 Gal., 9 1/2 x 13 In. 575.00
Crock, Salt Glaze, Stenciled Eagle, Cobalt Blue, Eagle Pottery, Macomb, Ill., 6 Gal. 130.00
Crock, Singing Bird, G.W. Fulper & Bros., c.1880, 2 Gal., 9 In. 770.00
Crock, Spray Of Flowers, A.E. Wheeler & Co., Broad Street, Boston, Mass., 3 Gal. 300.00
Crock, Spray Of Flowers, F.B. Norton & Co., Worc., Mass., Gal. 140.00
Crock, Spray Of Flowers, F.B. Norton & Co., Worc., Mass., 2 Gal. 140.00
Crock, Spray Of Flowers, White's, Utica, 2 Gal. 275.00
Crock, Storage, Cobalt Blue Tobacco Leaf, Slip, Cowden & Wilcox, 3 Gal., 12 In. 580.00
Crock, Stylized Flower Stems, Dashes, Swags, Lug Handles, 19th Century, 13 1/4 In. 1175.00
Crock, Stylized Flower, J. Fisher, Lyons, N.Y., 2 Gal. 100.00
Crock, Stylized Leaf, c.1870, 4 Gal., 11 1/2 In. 145.00
Crock, Sunflower Style Design, B.C. Milburn, Alexandria, Virginia, 2 Gal. 3520.00
Crock, Tulip Decoration, Gray Cobalt Blue, Cowden & Wilcox, 10 1/4 x 8 3/4 In. 460.00
Crock, Tulip Decoration, Oval, Straight Top, Applied Handles, 11 3/4 In. 165.00
Crock, Tulip, Blue, 1 1/2 Gal. 110.00
Crock, Tulip, Spotted, Havana, 3 Pot Stones, Jardiniere Style, Brewer & Halm, 6 Gal. ... 360.00
Crock, Whitehead & Co., Wholesale Liquor Dealer, Blue Script, c.1885, Gal., 11 In. 330.00
Cuspidor, Butterfly, Blue & White, 6 In. 70.00
Figurine, Cat, Seated, Cobalt Blue Circles, Blue Accents, 8 x 8 In. 690.00
Figurine, Chicken, Green, Blue Lead Glaze, Incised Wings, Tail, Feathers, 7 1/4 x 8 In. .. 300.00
Figurine, Dog, Seated, Mottled Albany Slip Glaze, Jordan, New York, 9 1/2 In. 750.00
Figurine, Dog, Spaniel, Seated, Curly Coat, Brown Glaze, 8 x 10 1/2 x 10 1/2 In. 345.00
Figurine, Indian, Headdress, Canoe, Paddle, Burleigh Ware, 4 x 8 1/2 x 2 1/3 In. 135.00
Figurine, Rooster, Hand Built, Roger Capron, France, 1960, 5 x 10 x 15 In. 880.00
Figurine, Spaniel Seated, Applied Albany Glaze, c.1897, 7 In. 660.00
Flagon, Blue & White, Pewter Top, Music Mechanism, Germany, 13 1/2 In. 69.00
Flask, Brown Alkaline Glaze, Railroad Map, Anna Pottery Pig, 7 1/2 x 3 1/2 In. 6325.00
Flask, Cobalt Blue Leaves, Around Shoulder, 8 In. 495.00
Flask, Eagle Shape, Salt Glaze, Press Molded, 10 1/2 x 8 In., Pair 5750.00
Flask, Fern Flowers, Repeated, Oval, c.1830, Pt., 8 In. 1650.00

Flask, Salt Glaze, Oval, Blue Flower, 6 In. 935.00
Ginger Jar, Cobalt Blue Leaf Decoration, 3 3/4 In. 45.00
Grave Marker, Salt Glaze, Bulbous, Incised, Signed, P.S.T., Late 19th Century, 14 1/2 In. .. 2750.00
Grave Marker, Salt Glaze, Drain Hole, 1898, 12 In. 3190.00
Jar, 2 Handles, Goodwin & Webster, 2 Gal. 850.00
Jar, A.P. Donaghho, Parkersburg, W. Va. 99.00
Jar, Albany Slip, W. Emmett, 2 Gal. 60.00
Jar, Blue Lettering, Jas. Hamilton & Co., Greensboro, 10 In. 125.00
Jar, Blue Tulip, 4, Double Handles, Burger Bro's & Co., Rochester, N.Y., 15 1/2 In. 315.00
Jar, Boggs, Salt Glaze, Flared Rim, Applied Lug Handles, N.C., c.1875, 14 1/2 In. 99.00
Jar, Boston Incised On Front, Oval, Gal. 415.00
Jar, Brown Glaze, Geometric Band, 10 3/4 In. 30.00
Jar, Brown Glaze, Signed, Wm. Moyer, Harrisburg, 7 1/2 In. 85.00
Jar, Canning, Barking Dog, Stenciled, Pallatine Pottery Co., c.1875, Gal., 9 In. 660.00
Jar, Canning, Blue Stripe Decoration, Tin Lid, 6 1/2 In. 465.00
Jar, Canning, Brown Alkaline Glaze, c.1860, Qt., 5 1/2 In. 55.00
Jar, Canning, Cobalt Blue Cross & Stars, Blue Swags, J.P. Parker, West Virginia 1705.00
Jar, Canning, Cobalt Blue Stencil Label, Pear, Palatine Pottery Co., 10 3/4 In. 550.00
Jar, Canning, Cobalt Blue Stencil, J. Hamilton & Co., Greensboro, Pa., 9 1/4 In. 546.00
Jar, Canning, Cover, Dark Brown Alkaline Glaze, c.1860, Qt., 5 3/4 In. 55.00
Jar, Canning, Cover, Double Flower, Leaves, J. Mantell Penn Yan, c.1860, 2 Gal., 11 In. ... 1485.00
Jar, Canning, Cover, Double Flower, Thompson & Tyler, c.1858, 3 Gal., 13 In. 605.00
Jar, Canning, Cover, Double Flower, Tornado At Base, Cortland, c.1860, 2 Gal., 10 1/2 In. 360.00
Jar, Canning, Cover, Flower, Penn Yan, c.1860, Gal., 9 In. 360.00
Jar, Canning, Cover, Olive Green Alkaline Glaze, c.1860, Qt., 5 3/4 In. 35.00
Jar, Canning, Cylindrical, Cobalt Blue, Donagho Fredericktown, Eagle, 9 1/2 In. 935.00
Jar, Canning, Double Flower, Cylinder Shape, c.1850, 10 1/2 In. 110.00
Jar, Canning, Flower, Lyons, c.1860, 2 Gal., 12 In. 275.00
Jar, Canning, Salt Glaze, c.1850, 7 3/4 In. 2860.00
Jar, Canning, Stone Mason Fruit Jar Union Stoneware, c.1899, Gal., 10 1/2 In. 385.00
Jar, Canning, Triple Flower & Grapes, c.1860, 1/2 Gal., 9 In. 415.00
Jar, Chinese, Salt Glaze, Knitted Lines, Loop Handles, Collared Rim, c.1989, 9 x 9 1/2 In. 165.00
Jar, Cobalt Blue Flower Band, 8 1/2 In. 425.00
Jar, Cobalt Blue Flower, Tree On Reverse, Handles, S. Bell, 10 1/4 In. 1200.00
Jar, Cobalt Blue Flowers, Edmunds & Co., 3 Gal. 195.00
Jar, Cobalt Blue Highlights, Goodale & Stedman, Oval, 2 Gal. 305.00
Jar, Cobalt Blue Highlights, Oval, Gal. 205.00
Jar, Cobalt Blue Tulip, Lyons, Gal. 220.00
Jar, Cobalt Blue, 4 Bands, Western Pa., 8 In. 365.00
Jar, Cobalt Blue, Fern On Shoulder, 8 1/2 In. 115.00
Jar, Double Heart, Impressed 22, c.1870, 11 3/4 In. 745.00
Jar, Face, Chocolate, Slip Glaze, 2 Handles, Glass Melts, Mid 1900s, 12 3/4 In. 275.00
Jar, Golden Rust, Alkaline Glaze, Oval, 2 Handles, c.1850, 15 1/4 In. 1870.00
Jar, Gray Brown, Crushed Glass Glaze, 2 Handles, Incised, c.1920, 18 x 43 In. 220.00
Jar, Hamilton & Jones, Stenciled Signature, Foliage, 9 3/4 In. 330.00
Jar, Khaki, Olive, Rust, Alkaline Glaze, 2 Handles, 19th Century, 10 1/4 In. 385.00
Jar, Long-Tailed Singing Bird On Stump, Riedinger & Caire, c.1870, 4 Gal., 14 1/2 In. ... 2310.00
Jar, Multicolored, Olive, Brown, 2 Handles, Late 19th Century, 16 3/4 In. 440.00
Jar, Olive Khaki, Alkaline Glaze, Signed DAH, c.1850, 14 1/2 x 35 In. 1650.00
Jar, Olive, Alkaline Glaze, 2 Groove Top Handles, c.1860, 14 x 49 In. 3300.00
Jar, Olive, Alkaline Glaze, 2 Handles, c.1920, 14 1/4 In. 65.00
Jar, Olive, Alkaline Glaze, 2 Handles, Double Dip, c.1830, 15 1/4 In. 715.00
Jar, Olive, Alkaline Glaze, 2 Handles, Swag, Loops, Collared Rim, 1840s, 13 In. 2750.00
Jar, Olive, Alkaline Glaze, Lid Ledge, c.1850, 8 In. 330.00
Jar, Olive, Collar, Rim, Handles, 1870, 13 In. 275.00
Jar, Palm Tree, Chelsea, Pot Stone, Handles, Oval, Loammi & Kendall, 4 Gal. 385.00
Jar, Plume, C. Hart & Son, Sherburne, c.1860, 2 Gal, 10 1/2 In. 385.00
Jar, Plume, Cylinder, W.H. Lehew & Co., c.1880, Gal., 9 1/2 In. 110.00
Jar, Poison, Off-White Glaze, Black Transfer, 5 1/2 In. 17.00
Jar, Runpoint & McCormick Dry Goods, c.1870, 4 Gal., 14 1/2 In. 990.00
Jar, Salt Glaze Over Iron, Groove Top Lug Handles, Bell Shape, 1900s, 13 1/2 In. 935.00
Jar, Salt Glaze, Applied Oval Handles, Decorated Shoulders, 20 1/2 In. 110.00
Jar, Salt Glaze, Cobalt Blue Design, Jas. Hamilton, Greensboro, Pa., 1860-1880, Gal. 200.00

Jar, Soda, Olive, Alkaline Glaze, Bell Shape, Lid Ledge, 19th Century, 9 1/8 In. 195.00
Jar, Swirl Handles, Runny Green Glaze, North Carolina, 13 1/2 In. 250.00
Jar, Yellow Glaze, Stamped, John Bell, 7 1/2 In. 480.00
Jardinere, Pedestal, Knot, Fluted Column, Speckled Gray Matte Glaze, 32 x 14 In. 2490.00
Jardiniere, Double Flower, Long Stem, c.1850, Gal., 10 In. 935.00
Jardiniere, Flowering Vine, Applied Ear, Oval, c.1830, 3 Gal., 13 1/2 In. 415.00
Jardiniere, Flowering Vine, c.1850, Gal., 9 1/2 In. 190.00
Jardiniere, Swag, Repeated, c.1830, 1/2 Gal., 8 In. 130.00
Jug, 2 Flowers, H. Selby & Co., Oval, Hudson, N.Y. 415.00
Jug, 2 Flowers, Hand Painted, Oval, Charlestown, Gal. 99.00
Jug, 2 Polka Dot Flower Blooms, 2, Inscribed A. Clark Jr., Athens, N.Y., 14 In. 345.00
Jug, 2, Oval, Blue Accent, Tan, Dry Glaze, c.1850, 13 1/2 In. 330.00
Jug, 3 Blue Flowers, 8 1/4 In. 565.00
Jug, 3-Leaf Branch, Blue Design, Cowden & Wilcox, Penn., 2 Gal., 13 1/2 In. 790.00
Jug, A. Budlong & Co., Providence, R.I., 19th Century, Gal. 45.00
Jug, A.F. Parr & Co., Liquor Dealers, Stamped, c.1880, Gal., 11 In. 35.00
Jug, Albany Slip, Sgraffito, Timothy McCarty, Bird, Gin Bottle, Handles, Gal., 11 In. 935.00
Jug, Backwards Looking Bird On Branch, White's, Utica, c.1865, 2 Gal., 13 In. 745.00
Jug, Beehive, Fort Dodge Stoneware Co., 4 Gal., 15 1/2 In. 460.00
Jug, Bird On Branch, Cobalt Blue Leaf Slip, 11 x 7 In. 660.00
Jug, Bird On Branch, Egg Shape, Handle, Jacob Caire & Co., Poughkeepsie, N.Y., 4 Gal. . . 9900.00
Jug, Bird On Branch, Fort Edward Pottery Co., c.1860, Gal., 11 1/2 In. 1020.00
Jug, Bird On Plume, Cobalt Blue, c.1870, 13 1/2 In. 330.00
Jug, Bird On Twig, Dark Navy Blue, W. Roberts, c.1860, Gal., 10 In. 1020.00
Jug, Bird, Blue, Incised, Oval, N.Y. State, Gal. 1650.00
Jug, Black, Caramel, Rust, Yellow, Alkaline Glaze, 2 Handles, 1870-1880s, 19 x 40 In. 660.00
Jug, Blue 3-Branch Flower, T.H. Willson & Co., Harrisburg, Pa., 2 Gal., 14 In. 1400.00
Jug, Blue Antler, Cortland, c.1860, 1/2 Gal., 9 In. 250.00
Jug, Blue Bird, Haxston Ottman, Fort Edwards, N.Y., 2 Gal. 360.00
Jug, Blue Bird, On Branch, West Roy Pottery, 2 Gal. 470.00
Jug, Blue Bird, Ottman Bros. & Co., 2 Gal. 275.00
Jug, Blue Butterfly, Impressed, Blue Accents, c.1845, Gal., 10 In. 250.00
Jug, Blue Flower, J. Burger Jr., Rochester, N.Y., 3 Gal. 195.00
Jug, Blue Flower, Leaf, Samuel Irvine, 2 Gal., 14 1/2 In. 730.00
Jug, Blue Flower, Serpentine Stem, Oval, Raised Ring, Strap Handle, 12 In. 145.00
Jug, Blue Spray Of Cherries, Brushstroke Leaves, Cowden & Wilcox, 3 Gal., 14 In. 1500.00
Jug, Blue Stencil, Cream, Casper Co., Mail Order Whiskey House, 1890-1910, Gal. 145.00
Jug, Blue Tornado, E.H. Farrar, c.1851, Gal., 11 1/2 In. 305.00
Jug, Blue Tulip, Impressed, 3, York, Pa., 35 1/4 In. 545.00
Jug, Blue Tulips, 3, Strap Handle, Impressed, Somerset Pottery Works, 16 In. 145.00
Jug, Blue Tulips, Harrisburg, Pa., 12 In. 340.00
Jug, Blue, Bulbous, Multi-Branch Flowers, 3 Gal. 225.00
Jug, Blue, Bulbous, Swag, 15 In. 190.00
Jug, Bluebird, Spray Of Flowers, West Troy, 6 Gal. 660.00
Jug, Brown & White, Chas. Moul, York, Pa., Stencil, Bail Handle, 4 In. 280.00
Jug, Brown & White, Dongan Club, Gold Lettering, 4 In. 45.00
Jug, Brown & White, Edwin Moul, York, Pa., Stencil, 8 1/2 In. .... 250.00 to 340.00
Jug, Brown & White, H.W. Bard, Denver, Pa., 10 1/2 In. 125.00
Jug, Brown Albany Glaze, Handle, c.1860, 4 In. 35.00
Jug, Brown Alkaline Glaze, Handle, Oval, c.1840, Qt., 8 In. 130.00
Jug, Bull's-Eye Over Tornado, Dry Glaze, Tan, c.1865, 2 Gal., 13 In. 275.00
Jug, Caramel, Salt Glaze, Iron Wash, Handle, 1812-1827, 15 In. 250.00
Jug, Charlestown, Allover Brown Slip, Mass., 1/2 Gal. 55.00
Jug, Chas. A Grove, Centre Square, Lancaster, Pa., Gal., 9 1/2 In. 1430.00
Jug, Chocolate, Slip Glaze, Handle, Incised Fish, Signed, c.1903, 20 1/2 In. 5060.00
Jug, Cinnamon, Alkaline Glaze, Handle, Double Collared Rim, c.1830, 11 1/2 In. 1650.00
Jug, Cobalt Blue Bird On Branch, A. White & Co., Binghamton 2, Handle, 14 1/2 In. 805.00
Jug, Cobalt Blue Bird On Leafy Branch, Impressed, Haxton, Ottman & Co., 12 In. 525.00
Jug, Cobalt Blue Bird, Applied Handle, 3 Gal., 16 1/2 x 9 1/2 In. 225.00
Jug, Cobalt Blue Bird, Serpentine Branch, Fanned Tail Feathers, White's, Utica, 13 1/2 In. . 400.00
Jug, Cobalt Blue Brush Stains, No. 1 Inside, Gal. 165.00
Jug, Cobalt Blue Decoration, Nichols & Boynton, Vermont, c.1856, 18 In., 4 Gal. 940.00
Jug, Cobalt Blue Design, Lodde & Borguieyer Fine Pure Old Whiskey, 16 In. 230.00

Jug, Cobalt Blue Dotted Double Flower, c.1870, Gal., 10 In. 165.00
Jug, Cobalt Blue Feather, Oval, Applied Strap Handle, 13 In. 345.00
Jug, Cobalt Blue Flower, Strap Handle, Impressed, T. Harrington, Lyons, 18 In. 205.00
Jug, Cobalt Blue Flowers, 12 In. 345.00
Jug, Cobalt Blue Flowers, Applied Strap Handle, Wells, Crafts & Wells, 15 In. 170.00
Jug, Cobalt Blue Flowers, Gray Tan Glaze, E.A. Buck & Co., Boston, 11 3/4 In. 280.00
Jug, Cobalt Blue Flowers, Somerset Potters Works, 2 Gal. 116.00
Jug, Cobalt Blue Hand Painted Name, Handles, John F. Weiler, 19th Century, Gal. 150.00
Jug, Cobalt Blue Highlight On Handle, Oval, Gal. 105.00
Jug, Cobalt Blue Leaves, Bulbous, Gibson & Co., Reading, Pa., 3 Gal., 15 1/2 In. 1045.00
Jug, Cobalt Blue Stencil, Rounded Top, Spout, Strap Handle, Hamilton & Jones, 12 In. 80.00
Jug, Cobalt Blue Tulip, Oval, Applied Strap Handle, 13 1/2 In. 259.00
Jug, Cobalt Blue Tulip, Strap Handle, 11 In. 175.00
Jug, Cobalt Blue, 3 Flower Bulbs, Round, 11 In. 310.00
Jug, Dark Blue Leaf, Scrolled Stem, 4, Signed, A.K. Ballard, Burlington, Vt., 18 In. 175.00
Jug, Devil, Bulging Eyes, Mustache, China Teeth, Horns, 11 1/2 In. 1100.00
Jug, Dirt Band, L.W. Porter, Boston, 2 Gal. 1540.00
Jug, Double Flower, Ribbed, Swirls, Lines, c.1870, 2 Gal., 14 In. 300.00
Jug, Drooping Flower, Beehive Shape, A.O. Whittemore, c.1870, 2 Gal., 12 In. 250.00
Jug, E.S.B., Jefferson, York Co., Pa., Stencil, 14 In. 956.00
Jug, Eagle Carrying Banner, W.J. Seymour, c.1855, 3 Gal., 15 1/2 In. 1700.00
Jug, Egg Shape, 2 Handles, Flowers, Scroll, Hamilton & Jones, Greensboro, Pa., 5 Gal. .. 990.00
Jug, Egg Shape, J. Bennage, Ohio, 1837, 8 x 11 1/2 In. 230.00
Jug, Face, Alkaline Glaze, Olive Glaze, Broken China Teeth, 11 In. 660.00
Jug, Face, Black, Albany Slip, Cigar, China Teeth, Incised Eyelashes, Eyebrows, 5 1/2 In. 1265.00
Jug, Face, Buggy, Alkaline Glaze, Teeth, Eyes, Raised Cheeks, Chin, 5 1/2 x 9 1/4 In. 360.00
Jug, Face, Burlon Craig, Swirled Gray & White Face, 5 Teeth, C-Shape Handle, 12 In. 400.00
Jug, Face, Eyebrows, Eyelashes, Mustache, Pierced Eyes, Teeth, Royal Blue, 5 1/2 In. ... 120.00
Jug, Face, Olive Alkaline Glaze, Blue Highlights, China Teeth, Bulging Eyes, 10 1/2 In. .. 990.00
Jug, Face, Olive, Unglazed Teeth, Eyes, Blue Glazed Pupils, Slit Lid, Handle, 9 1/2 In. .. 1980.00
Jug, Face, Unglazed, Indented Cheek, Chin, Eyelids, Curled Tongue, Handle, 11 3/4 In. .. 4950.00
Jug, Figural, Head Of Bacchus, Crown Of Grapes, Leaves, Brown Glaze, Salt Glaze, 9 In. 440.00
Jug, Flower, Dark Blue, C. Boynton & Co., c.1825, Gal., 10 1/2 In. 440.00
Jug, Flower, J.F. Brayton, Utica, c.1830, Gal., 11 1/2 In. 45.00
Jug, Flower, N. Clark, Jr, c.1850, Gal., 12 In. 250.00
Jug, Flower, Oval, Scribed Lines, c.1820, 3 Gal., 15 1/2 In. 605.00
Jug, Flower, Spotted, Drooping, Edmunds & Co., Gal. 220.00
Jug, Flower, Spotted, Drooping, Script Initials, J.P.R., Edmunds, Gal. 470.00
Jug, Frogskin, Albany Slip Glaze, Oval, Handle, Grooved Top, Thumb Press, 1930s, 6 In. . 80.00
Jug, Fulton Whiskey, Capacity Exceeds 3 Gallons, Blue Stencil, 1890-1910, 3 Gal. 130.00
Jug, Gabriel Gerstley Liquor Dealer, Cylinder Shape, c.1850, Gal., 11 In. 360.00
Jug, Heckt's Hotel, Brown & White, Havre De Grace, Md., Bail Handle, 3 3/4 In. 280.00
Jug, Hennessey Brandy, Paper Label, J.H. Waters & Co., Boston, 1/2 Gal. 50.00
Jug, Hyman Browarsky Wholesale Liquor Dealer, c.1870, 3 Gal., 16 In. 385.00
Jug, John Mattews Fine Syrups & Extracts, Impressed, c.1880, Gal., 11 In. 132.00
Jug, Kishere Pottery, Mortlake Surrey, Salt Glaze, Grapes, Vines, 2-Tone, 7 1/4 In. 58.00
Jug, Leaf, Ball Shaped, Tan, c.1830, 15 In. 855.00
Jug, Long-Tailed Bird, Glaze Drip Spots, White's, Utica, c.1865, 3 Gal., 15 1/2 In. 525.00
Jug, Long-Tailed Bird, White's, Utica, c.1865, Gal., 11 In. 440.00
Jug, Louis Zapp & Co, Louisville, Ky., Brown Glaze, 1870-1890, 1/2 Gal., 9 3/4 In. 190.00
Jug, Monkey, Double Chamber, Olive, Alkaline, Crushed Glass Glaze, c.1920, 10 In. 1155.00
Jug, Olive Khaki, Alkaline Glaze, Handle, 1880s, 11 3/4 In. 525.00
Jug, Olive, Alkaline Glaze, Handle, Signed, 1875-1890, 13 1/2 In. 120.00
Jug, Olive, Alkaline Glaze, Handle, Signed, c.1860, 14 3/4 In. 1045.00
Jug, Olive, Alkaline, 2 Handles, Glass Melts, Late 19th Century, 16 3/4 In. 660.00
Jug, Olive, Alkaline, Double Handle, Bulbous, Signed TR, c.1880, 13 1/2 x 36 In. 4950.00
Jug, Olive, Glaze Dip, Handle, Flare To Square Shape, 1870-1880, 14 1/4 In. 330.00
Jug, Orange Lead Glaze, Oval, Groove Top Handle, Thumb Press, 1960s, 5 5/8 In. 66.00
Jug, Oval, Impressed Charlestown Mark, 19th Century, 12 In. 345.00
Jug, Oval, Impressed, Blue Band, c.1820, 3 Gal., 14 In. 825.00
Jug, Oval, Medford, Brown Finish, 19th Century, 11 In. 259.00
Jug, Parrot, Blue Squiggle, Flack & Van Arsdale, c.1870, 2 Gal., 14 In. 635.00
Jug, Persimmon, Crushed Glass Glaze, c.1920, 16 1/4 In. 550.00

Jug, Pine Tree, N.A. White & Son, Utica, N.Y., c.1870, Gal., 11 In. 250.00
Jug, Pine Tree, Tall Bird, N.A. White & Son, c.1870, Gal., 11 In. 770.00
Jug, Plume, c.1860, Gal., 11 In. 190.00
Jug, Pouring, Olive, Alkaline Glaze, 5, Signed H.H.H., Early 1900s, 18 In. 4400.00
Jug, Ribbed Flower, Cortland, c.1860, Gal., 11 1/2 In. 190.00
Jug, Salt Glaze, Applied Strap Handles, Incised Wavy Line, 18 3/4 In. 140.00
Jug, Salt Glaze, Cobalt Blue Flower, Stamped 2, Ohio, 2 Gal., 8 1/2 x 13 1/2 In. 260.00
Jug, Salt Glaze, Handle, Bulbous Rim, 19th Century, 6 3/4 In. 770.00
Jug, Salt Glaze, Handle, Coggle Lines, 1830s-1840s, 13 1/4 In. 2530.00
Jug, Salt Glaze, Handle, Oval, Bulbous, Signed, N. Fox, c.1840, 13 1/2 In. 2090.00
Jug, Salt Glaze, Handle, Signed Fox & Allred 2, c.1860, 13 1/4 In. 7150.00
Jug, Salt Glaze, Handle, Signed, T.W. Craven, c.1850, 12 3/4 In. 935.00
Jug, Slip-Cup Flowers, Cowden & Wilcox, 3 Gal. 11000.00
Jug, Spray Of Flowers, A.K. Ballard, Burlington, Vt., 2 Gal. 215.00
Jug, Spray Of Flowers, F.T. Wright & Son, 2 Gal. 195.00
Jug, Spray Of Flowers, J.S. Taft, Keene, N.H., 3 Gal. 330.00
Jug, Squat Bird, White's, Utica, c.1865, Gal., 10 In. 635.00
Jug, Storage, Olive, Alkaline Glaze, Oval, Handles, Signed TB 4, c.1850, 14 1/2 x 39 In. . 935.00
Jug, Storage, Olive, Alkaline Glaze, Signed JFS, c.1850, 14 3/8 x 34 In. 3080.00
Jug, Strainer, Wide Mouth, c.1870, 14 1/2 In. 798.00
Jug, Struven & Wacker Grocers & Ship Chandlers, Squat, c.1850, Gal., 8 1/2 In. 250.00
Jug, Stylized Flower, Haxstun Ottman & Co., c.1870, 2 Gal., 14 In. 155.00
Jug, Stylized Flower, W.A. Waters 133 Endicott Street, Boston, 3 Gal. 160.00
Jug, Stylized Leaf, Brady & Ryan, Ellenville, N.Y., c.1885, 3 Gal., 15 1/2 In. 220.00
Jug, Stylized Tornados, Bee Stingers, N. Clark, Jr., c.1850, 2 Gal., 14 1/2 In. 470.00
Jug, Stylized Tulip, Cobalt Blue, Sloped Shoulder, Applied Handle, Cortland, 10 1/2 In. . . 295.00
Jug, Sunflower, Incised, Cobalt Blue Highlights, I. Seymour & Co., Oval, 3 Gal. 715.00
Jug, Swirl, Applied Rattlesnake, Concentric Bands, Blue, Beige, White, 11 1/2 In. 220.00
Jug, Syrup, Blue & White, Sponge Decoration, Molded Leaf Design, 6 1/2 In. 575.00
Jug, Syrup, Blue & White, Sponge Decoration, Molded Leaf Design, 8 1/8 In. 920.00
Jug, Syrup, Blue & White, Sponge Decoration, Molded Rosette, 5 3/8 In. 575.00
Jug, Syrup, Parrot On Plume, Fort Edward Pottery, Co., c.1860, 2 Gal., 14 In. 1320.00
Jug, Tan & Brown Glaze, Compliments Of H. Endres 250.00
Jug, Triple Flower, Beehive Shape, Lehman & Riedinger, c.1855, 4 Gal., 15 1/2 In. 330.00
Jug, Welcome To Home, Honest Abe, Oatmeal, Brown Top, 1885-1900, 3 1/4 In. 385.00
Jug, White Glaze, Edwin T. Moul, York, Pa., Stencil, 6 1/2 In. 310.00
Jug, Wide Awake, Bank, White Glaze, C-Shape Handle, 3 x 4 1/2 In. 405.00
Jug, Wine, Glaze, Handle, Stopper, 8 1/2 In. 130.00
Jug, Wolff Distillery, Brown Shoulders, Oatmeal Body, 1880-1900, 1/2 Gal. 110.00
Jug, Wreath, Script 3, John Burger, Rochester, N.Y., 3 Gal. 275.00
Jug, Yellow Glaze, Blue Sponge, 1870-1890, 10 3/4 In. 160.00
Jug, Yellow Stencil, Albany Slip, Cannelton Stoneware Co., Indiana, 4 Gal. 470.00
Milk Pan, Cobalt Blue Flowers, Applied Handle, 11 1/2 In. 730.00
Milk Pan, Cobalt Blue, 3-Leaf Design, Pouring Lip, 1850, Gal, 4 In. 275.00
Milk Pan, Flower, Cowden & Wilcox, c.1870, Gal., 5 1/2 x 11 In. 415.00
Mixing Bowl, Blue Band, 10 In. 59.00
Mug, Boy & Girl, Handle, Salt Glaze, 4 3/4 In. 55.00
Mug, Cobalt Blue Tulip, Bushed, Applied Strap Handle, 4 1/2 In. 1210.00
Mug, Scrolls, Applied Loop Handle, Incised, Bettie Wheeler, 4 1/2 In. 250.00
Pitcher, Abe Lincoln Bust, Log Cabin, Blue, White, 7 1/2 In. 370.00
Pitcher, Ale, Salt Glaze, Barrel Shape, Cut Log Relief, Applied Handle, 6 x 9 1/2 In. 90.00
Pitcher, Auburn, Brown Leon Slip Glaze, Applied Handle, Semi-Flat Top, c.1900, 7 In. . . . 45.00
Pitcher, Bartmannkrug, Brown, Bottle Shape, Loop Handle, Incised Face, 1600s, 8 3/4 In. . 470.00
Pitcher, Batter, Gray Glazed, Blue Slip, Applied Handle, 1 1/2 Gal., 12 1/2 x 7 1/4 In. . . . 670.00
Pitcher, Bird On Stump, Satterlee & Mory, c.1860, Gal., 11 In. 825.00
Pitcher, Blue & White, Cows In Rope-Framed Medallion, 8 In. 175.00
Pitcher, Blue & White, Relief Scene, Dutch Boy & Girl Kissing, Windmill, 6 3/4 In. 70.00
Pitcher, Blue Bird, 1 1/2 Gal. 630.00
Pitcher, Blue Panels, Embossed, Flemish, Stamped, Robinson Clay Product Co., 8 1/2 In. . 260.00
Pitcher, Blue Ribbed Plume, Gal., c.1870, Gal., 10 1/2 In. 275.00
Pitcher, Blue Slip, Molded Pour Spout, Applied Handle, Gray Glazed, 12 1/2 x 7 1/4 In. . . 660.00
Pitcher, Blue Stylized, Dotted Flowers, 2 Gal. 385.00
Pitcher, Blue, Cream, Bands, 8 1/2 In. 99.00

Pitcher, Brown Slip Glaze, Incised Scrolling, Handle, 20th Century, 10 1/2 In. 99.00
Pitcher, Brown, Crushed Glass Glaze, Looping Swag, Collar, Rolled Rim, 1900s, 11 In. . . . 110.00
Pitcher, Caramel, Slip Glaze, Ribbed Collar, Handle, Signed, 1920-1930, 6 In. 55.00
Pitcher, Clear Lead Glaze, Crimson Double Dip, Handle, Thumb Press, c.1940, 6 1/2 In. . 90.00
Pitcher, Cobalt Blue Decoration, Oval, Flared Top, Incised Rings, 10 3/4 In. 290.00
Pitcher, Cobalt Blue Flower, Incised Rings, Wavy Lines, 11 1/2 In. 145.00
Pitcher, Cobalt Blue Flowers, Applied Strap Handle, 2 Gal., 13 1/2 In. 1045.00
Pitcher, Cobalt Blue Leaves & Blossoms, 10 1/4 In. 750.00
Pitcher, Cobalt Blue Triple Flower & Leaf, Applied Strap Handle, 2 Gal., 13 3/4 In. 2310.00
Pitcher, Cobalt Blue, Clear Crushed Glass Glaze, Handle, Square End, c.1930, 5 1/4 In. . . 165.00
Pitcher, Cobalt Blue, Geometric, Gal., c.1870, 11 In. 275.00
Pitcher, Cobalt Blue, Salt Glaze, Stylized Leaves, Bulbous Body, c.1850, 13 In. 750.00
Pitcher, Cream, Westward Ho Scene, Blue Matte Field, Aqua Glaze, 1953, 3 3/4 In. 440.00
Pitcher, Crushed Glass Glaze, Bell Shape, Handle, 2 7/8 In. 130.00
Pitcher, Doe & Fawn, Tree, Blue & White Salt Glaze, 8 1/4 In. 220.00
Pitcher, Dotted Sunflower, F. Stetzenmeyer & G. Goetzman, c.1857, 1 1/2 Gal., 11 In. . . . 1265.00
Pitcher, Emerald, Black, White, Seagrove Shape, Groove Top Handles, 1940, 8 In., Pair . 80.00
Pitcher, Frogskin Albany Slip Glaze, Lines, Groove Top, Thumb Press, 1960s, 6 7/8 In. . . 66.00
Pitcher, Gray, Orange, Chocolate, Salt Glaze, Signed, J.M. Hays, 19th Century, 12 In. . . . 1650.00
Pitcher, Grazing Cows, Oval Frame, Blue & White Salt Glaze, 8 In. 110.00
Pitcher, Green & Cream, Cows In Rope-Framed Medallion, 8 In. 115.00
Pitcher, Leaping Stag, Wreath Frame, Blue & White Salt Glaze, 8 In. 165.00
Pitcher, Love Birds, Oval Frame, Blue & White Salt Glaze, 8 In. 90.00
Pitcher, Milk, Blue & White, Sponge & Flower Decoration, 9 In. 250.00
Pitcher, Ohio Hound Handle, Vance Faience Co., c.1900, 8 3/4 x 12 3/4 In. 750.00
Pitcher, Olive Rust, Alkaline Glaze, c.1850, 10 3/4 In. 130.00
Pitcher, Olive, Alkaline Glaze, c.1930, 11 In. 90.00
Pitcher, Orange, Clear Lead Glaze, House Paint, Flowers, Handle, Cast Ware, 4 1/2 In. . . . 55.00
Pitcher, Oval, Cobalt Blue, Hormell & Smyth, Flared Rim, Applied Strap Handle, 13 In. . 1840.00
Pitcher, Remy, Blue, Tulips, Sprays Around Neck, 11 In. 500.00
Pitcher, Rose Trellis, Blue & White, 8 In. 120.00
Pitcher, Salt Glaze, 2, Roll Rim, Handle, Signed, P & C, 19th Century, 14 In. 250.00
Pitcher, Salt Glaze, Sculpted Spout, Handle, Signed, 1935-1940, 9 1/2 In. 440.00
Pitcher, Stencil, Freehand Design, Signed, Williams & Reppert, Greensboro, 13 In. 1100.00
Pitcher, Tall Tulip, Blue Swags, Impressed 2, c.1850, 13 1/2 In. 385.00
Pitcher, Tan Lead Glaze, Gold Rim, Handle, Footed, 1940-1942, 6 1/2 In. 90.00
Pitcher, Treebark Form, Incised, Miss Maria Murphy, 1881, 8 1/2 In. 440.00
Pitcher, Turquoise, Flambe Lead Glaze, Speckles, Groove Top Handle, c.1940, 3 1/2 In. . 55.00
Pitcher, Turquoise, Wine Crackle Glaze, Handle, 7 3/4 In. 90.00
Pitcher, Windmill & Tree, Blue & White Salt Glaze, 7 In. 35.00
Pitcher, Yellow, Clear Red Lead Glaze, Groove Top Handle, 1922-1923, 6 1/4 In. 165.00
Platter, Orange, Clear Lead Glaze, Groove Top Lug Handles, c.1930, 2 x 15 3/4 x 12 In. . 193.00
Pot, Blue Lead Glaze, Signed, Smithfield Pottery, c.1930, 2 2/4 In. 165.00
Pot, Preserve, Cobalt Blue, Salt Glaze, Signed, A.P. Donaghho, Parkersburg, W.Va., 10 In. 80.00
Pot, Stone Ointment For Eczema, Abscesses, Boils, Running Sores, White, 3 1/2 In. 235.00
Pot, Stone Salve, For Rheumatism Gout, Neuralgia, Sciatica, White, 3 1/2 In. 267.00
Pot, Storage, Rust, Black, Red Lead Glaze, Incised Line, Sloping Shoulder, c.1800, 6 In. . 110.00
Pot, Storage, Rust, Brown, Clear Red Lead Glaze, Square Rim, Incised Lines, 7 1/2 In. . . . 360.00
Salt Box, Blue, Indian Good Luck, Blue & White Salt Glaze, 6 x 6 In. 110.00
Sugar, Footed, Flower, Relief Accented Knob, c.1840, 5 In. 6600.00
Sugar Jar, Incised Woman, Zigzags, Dots, Circles, Albany Slip, 1889, Gal., 9 In. 2310.00
Sugar Jar, Sgraffito, Woman, Floral Hairpiece, Albany Slip, 1889, Gal., 9 In. 2310.00
Teapot, Lid, Caramel, Red Lead Glaze, Biblical Scene, Fire Proof, 1885-1887, 7 In. 880.00
Teapot, Lid, Mirror Black Lead Glaze, Groove Top, c.1930, 6 1/2 In. 145.00
Teapot, Oval, Straight Spout, Olive Alkaline Glaze, Catawba Valley, N.C., 6 In. 440.00
Tureen, Jugendstil, Glazed, Westerwald Region, Germany, c.1915, 5 1/2 x 9 x 12 In. 265.00
Urn, Clear Red Lead Glaze, 2, Groove Top Handles, c.1920, 7 1/2 In. 525.00
Vase, Baluster, Runny Glaze, Blue, Cream, Silver Collar, Chinese, 1795, 16 In. 3960.00
Vase, Black, Chocolate, Albany Slip Glaze, c.1920, 3 3/8 In. 385.00
Vase, Blue Lead Glaze, 4-Way Scallop Top, Signed, Glenn Art, 1948-1968, 5 1/2 In. 55.00
Vase, Bottle Shape, Volcanic Glaze, Harding Black, 1957, 14 1/2 x 4 In. 1380.00
Vase, Brown, Light Green Speckled Glaze, Dimples, Karen Karnes, 6 1/2 x 9 1/4 In. 575.00
Vase, Buff Matte Glaze, No. 578, Richard Devore, 1960s, 9 1/2 x 6 1/2 x 10 In. 11700.00

Vase, Bulbous, Abstract Patterns, Daniel Rhodes, 6 1/4 x 5 1/2 In. 259.00
Vase, Bulbous, Chocolate Brown Alkaline Glaze, c.1900, 6 1/2 In. 45.00
Vase, Bulbous, Mottled Matte Glaze, Erich & Ingrid Triller, Tobo, 5 1/2 x 3 1/2 In. 290.00
Vase, Bulbous, Red High Glaze, W&P Pillin, USA, 1950s, 10 x 12 1/2 In. 1055.00
Vase, Chinese Blue Glaze, Turquoise Speckles, Signed, c.1930, 5 1/2 In. 1210.00
Vase, Chinese Blue, Chinese White Mottled Glaze, Dragon Head, c.1960, 7 1/2 In. 470.00
Vase, Clear Red Lead Glaze, Manganese Drippings, c.1920, 6 7/8 In. 440.00
Vase, Cover, Sculpted, Tooling, Ivory Matte, Umber Glaze, Karen Karnes, 14 x 13 In. . . .   1035.00
Vase, Egg, Chinese Blue, Chocolate Albany Slip Glaze, Multicolored, 1930, 3 3/4 In. 360.00
Vase, Gray Cinnamon, Crushed Glass Glaze, 1920s-1930s, 9 5/8 In. 250.00
Vase, Hand Thrown, Oxide Glaze, Ruth Duckworth, USA, 1960s, 8 x 8 In. 1755.00
Vase, Jade, Aqua Lead Glaze, 3 Loop Handles, Double Dipped, Footed, c.1930, 5 5/8 In. .   99.00
Vase, Lead Glaze, Aqua Turquoise, c.1950, 8 In. 120.00
Vase, Multicolored, 2 Handles, Incised Lines, c.1940, 15 3/4 In. 195.00
Vase, Multicolored, Lead Glaze, Signed, Brown Pottery, 1930s, 8 1/4 In. 165.00
Vase, Red, Turquoise, Chinese Blue Glaze, Chocolate Albany Slip Glaze, 1930s, 5 In. 880.00
Vase, Renaissance Revival, Scrolled Loop Handles, Figural Scene, Leaf Band, 12 1/2 In. .   200.00
Vase, Salt Glaze, Cobalt Blue, Incised Scrolling, Rolled Rim, c.1920, 6 x 8 1/4 In. 525.00
Vase, Salt Glaze, Footed, Applied Handles, Umber, Cobalt Blue, Green Glaze, 12 x 18 In.   3740.00
Vase, Trophy, Clear Lead Glaze, Multicolored, 2 Handles, c.1960, 13 1/2 In. 360.00
Vase, Yellow, Clear Red Lead Glaze, Cobalt Blue, Fluted Top, Mid 1920, 5 3/4 In. 275.00
Vase, Yellow, Clear Red Lead Glaze, Cobalt Blue, Handles, Angular, 4 3/4 x 6 1/2 In. 250.00
Vase, Yellow, Orange Slip, 4 Handles, Tapering Handles, Double Dip, c.1920, 6 In. 990.00
Wagon Jug, Squat, Strap Handle, Salt Glaze, Ohio, 9 x 8 In., Gal. 230.00
Wall Pocket, Face, Brown, Cream Swirlware, Glaze, China Teeth, Pierced Hole, 7 1/4 In.   65.00
Water Cooler, 3 Pegged Legs, 19th Century, 8 x 5 x 9 In. 195.00
Water Cooler, Bee Sting, Cobalt Blue, Salt Glaze, Lunate Handles, 12 x 19 In. 590.00
Water Cooler, Bird, Blue Incised Lines, New York Stoneware Co., c.1870, 4 Gal. 1150.00
Water Cooler, Blue Bands, Crimped Spigot Hole, No Lid Or Spigot, 10 Gal. 205.00
Water Cooler, Cobalt Blue American Eagle & Flag, Incised, Iron Based Slip, 20 1/2 In. . . 29700.00
Water Cooler, Cover, Blue Leaf, Barrel Shape, N.Y. Stoneware Co., 4 Gal., 15 1/2 In. . . .   300.00
Water Cooler, Incised Birch Leaves, Union Stoneware, Red Wing, Minn., 8 Gal. 1800.00
Water Cooler, Inverted Tulip, Cobalt Blue, Lunate Handles, Dashed Circle, 9 x 11 In. . . .   290.00
Water Cooler, Leaf, Charlestown, c.1850, 5 Gal., 15 In. 495.00
Water Cooler, Niagara Falls, Cobalt Blue Flowers, 3 Colors, White's, Utica, 2 Gal. 1100.00
Water Cooler, Polar Bears, Embossed, White's, Utica, Spigot, No Lid, 2 Gal. 440.00
Water Cooler, Stenciled Eagle, Eagle Pottery, Macomb, Ill., 6 Gal. 600.00

STORE fixtures, cases, cutters, and other items that have no advertising
as part of the decoration are listed here. Most items found in an old
store are listed in the Advertising category in this book.

Bag Holder, Tin, Lithograph, Snow King 1320.00
Bag Holder, Wood, Stenciled, 1884 . . . .   2090.00
Bag Rack & String Holder, Wire, 37 In. 200.00
Bin, 3 Compartments, Slant Top, Lift Top, Porcelain Knobs, Green Paint, 73 In. 220.00
Bin, Feed, Softwood, 2 Slant Lid Compartments Over 3 Doors, Red Paint 480.00
Bin, Feed, Softwood, Dovetailed, Shoe Feet, Robin's Egg Blue Paint, 39 x 33 In. 2363.00
Bin, Grain, Lift Top, 3 Compartments, 2 Doors, Red Paint, 68 x 37 In. 198.00
Bin, Grain, Lift Top, Iron Latch, 3 Sections, New England, 26 1/2 x 73 x 19 In. 200.00
Bin, Seed, Oak Case, Slant Lid, Peaked Glass Panels, 22 x 17 1/2 x 15 In. 500.00
Bin, Seed, Oak, Walker Handles, 120 In. 1540.00
Bin, Tea, No. 35, Red Paint, Late 19th Century 2900.00
Bin, Tea, Painted Chinese Women Scene, Tin, Lift Top, Victorian, 20 x 15 x 16 In. 85.00
Cabinet, Nut & Bolt, Revolving, 72 Drawers, Stenciling 3850.00
Cabinet, Nut & Bolt, Revolving, 80 Drawers, 18-Drawer Base 2200.00
Cabinet, Oak, Pine, Multi-Divided Interior, Screen Door, 39 In.   195.00
Cabinet, Oak, Stick & Ball, Curved Glass Corners, Mirrored Back, 27 x 32 In. 578.00
Cabinet, Ribbon, Tip-Out Doors, Slide-Out Ends, 28 x 37 In. 1650.00
Cabinet, Seed, Glass Front Drawers, Item Names On Drawer Fronts, Sherer, 142 In. 5390.00
Cabinet, Spice, Decorative Paint, Countertop, 32 In. 935.00
Cabinet, Spool, Cherry, Revolving, Glazed Drawers, 3 Mirrors, Late 1800s, 38 x 18 In. . . .   1095.00
Cabinet, Spool, Mahogany, Molded Top, 3 Long Over 2 Short Drawers, 23 1/4 x 14 In. . . .   135.00
Cabinet, Spool, Oak, 4 Drawers, Brass Knobs, Concentric Circles, 21 1/2 x 16 1/2 In. 160.00

Cabinet, Spool, Oak, 7 Drawers, Glass Front, 16 In. 495.00
Candy Display Case, Glass, Wood Frame, Cast Iron Pedestal, Revolving, c.1900, 70 In. ... 5720.00
Case, Display, Collar, Glass, Oak Frame, Illinois Show Case Co., Chicago, 15 x 25 In. 715.00
Case, Display, Copper, Brass Ends, Bowed Glass Front, 29 x 12 x 18 In. 200.00
Case, Display, Curved Glass, 60 In. 1000.00
Case, Display, Curved Glass, Oak Trim, German Silver Corner Caps, Countertop, 36 In. ... 850.00
Case, Display, Garter, Oak, Stepped Down, Drawer, Stencil, 20 x 10 x 8 In. 310.00
Case, Display, Oak, Curved Glass, J. Riswig, Chicago, 10 In. 440.00
Case, Display, Oak, Curved Glass, Tower Style, Mirrored, Victorian, 21 x 17 In. 880.00
Case, Display, Oak, Slant Front, Columbus Showcase Co., Countertop, 60 In. 250.00
Case, Display, Oak, Slant Front, Shelf, 3 Doors, Countertop, 69 In. 275.00
Case, Display, Oak, Sun Mfg. Co., Columbus, Ohio, Countertop, 56 In. 230.00
Case, Display, Pine, Roof Like Top, Knob Finial, 52 x 24 In. 240.00
Case, Display, Rosewood Grain Top, 2 Shelves, Plexiglass Doors, 25 x 22 x 12 In. 320.00
Case, Display, Seeds, 6 Compartments, Pine, Green Paint, 142 In. 275.00
Case, Display, Showcase, Oak, Glass, 12 In. 2860.00
Case, Display, Slant Front, Metal Casing, 2 Sliding Doors, Countertop, 33 In. 200.00
Case, Display, Slant Front, Mirrored Back, Tabletop, 10 x 18 In. 440.00
Cheese Cutter, Cast Iron, Wood, Safe, Countertop, 20 In. 175.00
Cheese Cutter, Enterprise, Countertop, 26 In. 300.00
Cheese Cutter, Standard Computing Co., 20 In. 115.00
Cigar Cutter, Standing Poodle, Copper Patina, Musterschutz D.R.G., 5 1/4 x 6 1/2 In. ... 325.00
Coffee Bin, Slanted Lift Top, Pine, Blue Paint, 21 x 33 In. 198.00
Coffee Bin, Wood, Red Paint, 17 1/2 x 24 In. 175.00
Coffee Grinders are listed in their own category.
Counter, Wood, Mahogany Stain, Marble Kick Plate, Raised Panel Ends, 36 x 72 In. 495.00
Dispenser, Gum, Chrome, Revolving, 5-Sided, 14 In. 130.00
Dispenser, Ice Cream Cone, Metal Lid & Lifter, 15 In. 415.00
Dispenser, Julep, Crock Base, Spigot, Gallon Jug, 1900-1910, 18 In. 88.00
Dispenser, Label, Drugstore, Oak, Labels, 23 In. 605.00
Dispenser, Orange Julep, Pump, c.1918 .... 770.00
Dispenser, Tea, Toleware, Oolung Tea, 16 x 10 1/2 x 14 In. 195.00
Display, Female Head, Shoulders, Profile, Painted Gray, 1920s, 37 x 14 1/2 In. 112.00
Display, Hand, Painted Metal, Glass Stone On Bracelet, 19 1/2 In. ....*Illus* 990.00
Display, Pig, Animated, Dressed, Plush, Holding Hammer, Round Wood Base, 40 1/2 In. .. 225.00
Display, Scissors, Brass, 25 1/4 In. 825.00
Display, Tree, Wire, Countertop, 26 In. 99.00
Display, Window, Little Red Riding Hood & Wolf Grandma, 53 In. 345.00
Egg Carrier, Cabinet Style, 2 Shelves, Egg Holes, Slatted, Front Door, Wooden, 11 1/2 In. 45.00
Holder, Ice Cream Cone, Glass, Chrome, Metal Insert, Chain, 14 x 6 1/2 In. 525.00
Hot Nuts Machine, Tin, R.J. Masbach, N.Y., 38 In. 440.00
Jar, Display, Globe, Apothecary, Deco, Aluminum Tripod Base, Showglobe Stopper, 23 In. 360.00
Jar, Display, Globe, Apothecary, Showglobe Stopper, Metal Stand, 9 x 4 In. 90.00
Jar, Display, Globe, Apothecary, Stacking, Showglobe Stopper, 13 In. 95.00
Jar, Display, Globe, Apothecary, Wheel Cut, Pineapple Etched, Showglobe Stopper, 30 In. 3300.00
Mannequin, Iron Feet, Child, c.1900, 41 In. 385.00
Mannequin, Victorian Dress, 66 In. 360.00
Menu Board, Chrome, Glass, Enjoy Our Fountain Specials, 15 x 26 In. 580.00
Paper Holder, Cast Iron, Nickel Plated, 19 In. 77.00
Peanut Warmer, Uncle Sam, Burner, c.1890, 22 In. 825.00
Pill Tile, Ceramic, 0-30 Graduated Transfer, 9 3/4 x 8 In. 175.00
Popcorn & Peanut Roaster Machine, Cretors, Clown, Toy, 1918, Floor Model 3500.00
Post Office Unit, Desk, Cash Box, Slots, Alarm, Oak, Post Masters Supply Co., 101 In. ... 1650.00
Rack, Buggy Whip, Cast Iron, Painted, Locking Tops, 40 In. 360.00
Rack, Display, Biscuit, Metal, 10 Compartments, Apple Green, 54 In. 295.00
Rack, Display, Broom, 2 Brooms, Bittersweet Color, 61 In. 175.00
Rack, Paper Sack Dispensing, Wood, Stenciled Decoration, Iron Ball String Dispenser ... 2090.00
Rack, Postcard, Revolving, Cast Iron Base, Tin Racks, 25 1/2 In. 215.00
Sack Rack, Metal, c.1900, 30 In. 210.00
Seed Counter, Oak, 9 Compartments, 34 x 46 In. 1100.00
Seed Counter, Oak, 9 Drawers, 48 x 35 In. 1650.00
Shelf, Apothecary, Walnut, Pine, Black, Red Sponging, Cutouts, 39 x 10 1/2 x 37 In. 1725.00
Shelf, Corner, 5 Shelves, Wood, 64 In. 300.00

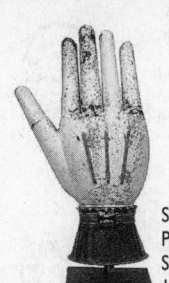

Store, Display, Hand,
Painted Metal, Glass
Stone On Bracelet,
19 1/2 In.

Stove, Parlor, Wild Rose
No. 9, Cast Iron, Pierced,
Jewett & Root,
Buffalo, N.Y., 38 In.

Sign, American Indian On Each Side, Wood, Shaped Top, 61 1/2 x 31 In.	5750.00
Sign, Cigars, Cigar Shape, Wood, c.1910, 58 In.	2090.00
Sign, Fire Escape, Green Ground, Glass, Reverse Painted, Frame, 11 x 18 In.	127.00
Sign, Rooster, White, Black, Tin, 2-Sided, 36 In.	2300.00
Sign, Top Hat, Tin, Steel Band, Brass Buckle, Black Paint, 29 x 27 x 13 In.	1295.00
Sign, Waiting Room, Red, White, Porcelain, 2-Sided, 18 1/2 x 24 In.	190.00
Sign, Women's Room, Woman, Powdering Face, Blue, Porcelain, 12 x 13 In.	99.00
Strawholder, Glass, Flared Base, Metal Insert, Brass Lid, 12 x 4 3/8 In.	360.00
Stringholder, Arcade, 4 x 5 In.	55.00
Sugar Chopper, Iron Blade, Wood Base, Shield Shape, 14 In.	39.00
Sugar Cutters, Steel, Engraved, 10 In.	130.00
Tobacco Cutter, Beaver, Star, Playing Card Symbols, Tabletop, 9 x 18 x 9 In.	1035.00
Tobacco Cutter, Horse, Tin, Applied Metal Saddle, Handle, 14 x 6 x 1 1/2 In.	2970.00

STOVES have been used in America for heating since the eighteenth century and for cooking since the nineteenth century. Most types of wood, coal, gas, kerosene, and even some electric stoves are collected.

Cast Iron, 2-Piece, Tapered Top, Ribbed Borders, Cabriole Legs, 24 x 37 1/2 x 15 In.	605.00
Cast Iron, Raised Detail, Eagles, Cornucopia, Urns Of Flowers, 28 x 19 x 21 In.	300.00
Franklin, 1876	1500.00
Heating, Ice Skater's, Oil, Brass & Wood, Patented, O.W. Taft, 1865, 9 1/2 In.	110.00
Parlor, Cast Iron, Sliding Doors, Top Lid, Peruvian Model, 27 1/2 x 23 x 20 In.	290.00
Parlor, Gas Fired, Majolica Ceramic Panels, Germany, 1911-1920, 52 In.	1300.00
Parlor, Gothic, Cast Iron, Brass Urn Finial, Rosettes, Diamond, Cabriole Legs, 40 In.	920.00
Parlor, Wild Rose No. 9, Cast Iron, Pierced, Jewett & Root, Buffalo, N.Y., 38 In. . . . *Illus*	230.00
Potbelly, Sears Roebuck & Co., No. 11957, Cast Iron, Restored, 27 In.	44.00
Quick Meal, Enamel, Gray, 38 x 55 In.	55.00
Shaker, Box, Cast Iron, Arched Legs, Penny Feet, Shallow Oval Apron, 34 In.	1725.00
Shaker, Cast Iron, 2 Piece, Union Village, Ohio, c.1850, 19 x 13 x 31 1/2 In.	165.00
Shaker, Cast Iron, Flue Pipe, Tool Holder, Tools, Hancock, 73 x 33 1/2 In.	2590.00
Shaker, Cast Iron, Oak Knob, Lipped Front Edge, Penny Feet, 20 1/2 x 33 1/2 x 10 1/2 In.	1725.00
Shaker, Cast Iron, Super Heater, Tool Holder, Mt. Lebanon, 27 x 33 1/2 x 14 1/4 In.	2590.00

STRETCH GLASS is named for the strange stretch marks in the glass. It was made by many glass companies in the United States from about 1900 to the 1920s. It is iridescent. Most American stretch glass is molded; most European pieces are blown and may have a pontil mark.

Bowl, Blue Iridescent, Northwood, 8 x 3 In.	55.00
Bowl, Canary, 9 1/2 x 3 1/4 In.	75.00
Candlestick, Blue Iridescent, Northwood, c.1920, 8 1/2 In.	60.00
Candlestick, Blue Iridescent, Northwood, No. 719, 6 3/4 In.	60.00
Compote, Blue, Black Trim, 8 Panels, 4 1/2 x 4 In.	40.00
Compote, Topaz Iridescent, 3 7/8 x 7 1/4 In.	80.00
Plate, Florentine Green, Footed, 9 1/2 In.	50.00
Plate, Rosita Amber, Raised Ring, c.1920, 10 In.	70.00
Rose Bowl, Blue Iridescent, Footed, Northwood, 7 x 5 In.	100.00
Sherbet, Topaz Iridescent, Footed, 6 3/4 In.	60.00
Vase, Red, Imperial, 10 1/2 x 3 3/4 In.	230.00

SUMIDA is a Japanese pottery that was made from about 1870 to 1941. Pieces are usually everyday objects—vases, jardinieres, bowls, teapots, and decorative tiles. Most pieces have a very heavy orange-red, blue, brown, black, green, purple, or off-white glaze, with raised three-dimensional figures as decorations. The unglazed part is painted red, green, black, or orange. Sumida was sometimes mistakenly called *Korean Pottery* or *Poo Ware* in the past.

Lamp, Modified Cylinder Shape, Relief Figural, Early 1900s, 13 In.	184.00
Vase, Baluster Shape, Child, Wine Jug, Signed, Early 1900s, 4 3/4 In.	104.00
Vase, Seed Shape, Man, Snail, Signed, Early 1900s, 4 3/4 In.	92.00

SUNDERLAND luster is a name given to a special type of pink luster made by Leeds, Newcastle, and other English firms during the nineteenth century. The luster glaze is metallic and glossy and appears to have bubbles in it. Other pieces of luster are listed in the Luster category.

Creamer, Pink Luster, Grapes, Flowers, Blue Neck Band, White Body, 4 3/4 In.	69.00
Dinner Set, Pink Luster, Woman, Children, Lamb, Multicolored Transfer, 17 Piece	125.00
Flowerpot, Undertray, Pink Luster, Flowers, Shell Handles, Pearlware, 1800s, 4 5/8 In.	294.00
Frog Mug, Compass, Figures Of The Empire, 3 3/4 In.	402.00
Jug, Pink Luster, 3 Vignettes, 4-Line Verse, 7 1/2 In. *Illus*	431.00
Mug, Hardy Sailor Transfer, Luster, Pink, Monogram, 5 1/4 In.	431.00
Pitcher, Hunting, Snipe Shooting, Luster, Nautilus Shape, Pearlware Body, 7 1/4 In.	316.00
Pitcher, Luster, Hound Handle, Pearlware Body, Running Hounds, 1840, 7 3/4 In.	230.00
Pitcher, Pink Luster, 3 Oval Medallions, Sailing Ship, Below Spout, Transfer, 7 In.	550.00
Pitcher, Pink Luster, Iron Bridge & Jacks, Safe Return, 9 1/2 In.	990.00
Pitcher, Pink Luster, Transfer, The Sailor's Return, Cast Iron Bridge, 9 1/2 In.	690.00

SUPERMAN was created by two seventeen-year-olds in 1938. The first issue of *Action* comics had the strip. Superman remains popular and became the hero of a radio show in 1940, cartoons in the 1940s, a television series, and several major movies.

Bank, Dime Register, Lithograph, Yellow, Red, Blue, c.1945	665.00
Coloring Set, National Comics Publ. Transogram, Box, 1954, 12 x 13 In., 24 Pages	275.00
Comic Book, Action Comics, No. 142, 1950	2345.00
Lunch Box, Robot, Action Pictures, Metal, Universal, 1954	798.00
Mold, For Bubble Bath Bottle, Bronze, Avon, 1970, 4 1/2 In.	345.00
Playsuit, 3-Piece Cotton, Red & Blue Silk Shirt, Emblem, Funtime Inc., 1950	165.00
Record Player, Portable, 1978, 12 x 9 1/2 In.	170.00
Tank, Linemar	575.00

SUSIE COOPER began as a designer in 1925 working for the English firm A.E. Gray & Company. In 1932 she formed Susie Cooper Pottery, Ltd. In 1950 it became Susie Cooper China, Ltd., and the company made china and earthenware. In 1966 it was acquired by Josiah Wedgwood & Sons, Ltd. The name Susie Cooper appears with the company names on many pieces of ceramics.

Bowl, Vegetable, Cover, Green Trim, Handles, Pink & Gray Feather Finial	60.00

You can use an empty vase as a bookend if you weight it. Put a resealable plastic bag in the vase. Fill the bag with sand, then seal it. The vase should be about half full.

Sunderland, Jug, Pink Luster, 3 Vignettes, 4-Line Verse, 7 1/2 In.

Creamer, Underplate, Blue Stars, White Ground, Blue Interior, Gold Trim 47.00
Cup, Saucer, Plate Set, Green Crescent, Tan Interior, 3 Piece 55.00
Cup & Saucer, Blue Stars, White Ground, Blue Interior, Gold Trim 28.00
Cup & Saucer, Gardenia 33.00
Cup & Saucer, Patricia Rose, Pink 114.00
Cup & Saucer, Plate, Glen Mist, 3 Piece 16.00
Dish, Dresden Spray, Green, Clover Shape, 3 Sections, Center Handle, 8 1/2 In. ... 119.00
Dish, Oval, Pink, Blue & Purple Flowers, Scalloped Edge, 8 In. 31.00
Eggcup, Dresden Spray, Pink, Yellow & Purple Flowers, Green Leaves 36.00
Lamp, Art Deco, Half Circle, Geometric, Parchment Shade, Laced, 15 x 13 In. 1150.00
Mustard Pot, Cover, Assyrian Motif, Gold Trim, 3 In. 47.00
Platter, Oval, Pear In Pompadour, 11 1/5 In. 55.00
Platter, Oval, Pink Camion, Blue Border, 12 In. 22.00
Soup, Cream, Underplate, Pear In Pompadour 27.00
Sugar & Creamer, Glen Mist, Footed 11.00
Tea Set, Patricia Rose, 23 Piece 1450.00
Teapot, Glen Mist 30.00
Tureen, Underplate, Dresden Spray, Green, Side Handle On Dome Cover, 7 1/2 In. 110.00
Vase, Green Matte Glaze, Stylized Leaves, c.1932, 7 In. 646.00

SWANKYSWIGS are small drinking glasses. In 1933, the Kraft Food
Company began to market cheese spreads in these decorated, reusable
glass tumblers. They were discontinued from 1941 to 1946, then made
again from 1947 to 1958. Then plain glasses were used for most of the
cheese, although a few special decorated Swankyswigs have been
made since that time. A complete list of prices can be found in *Kovels'
Depression Glass & Dinnerware Price List.*

Band No. 2, Red & Black, 3 3/8 In. 7.00
Bustlin' Betsy, Blue, 3 3/4 In. ....7.00 to 10.00
Bustlin' Betsy, Brown, 3 3/4 In. 7.00
Bustlin' Betsy, Green, 3 3/4 In. ....6.00 to 7.00
Bustlin' Betsy, Orange, 3 3/4 In. 7.00
Bustlin' Betsy, Yellow, 3 3/4 In. 10.00
Churn & Cradle, Orange, 3 3/4 In. 10.00
Clock & Coal Scuttle, Brown, 3 3/4 In. 7.00
Daisy, Red, White, Green, 3 3/4 In. 7.00
Dog & Rooster, Orange, 3 3/4 In. 6.00
Forget-Me-Not, Light Blue, 3 1/2 In. 7.00
Kiddie Kup, Bear & Pig, Blue, 3 3/4 In. 7.00
Kiddie Kup, Bird & Elephant, Red, 3 3/4 In. 7.00
Kiddie Kup, Cat & Rabbit, Green, 3 3/4 In. 7.00
Kiddie Kup, Dog & Rooster, Orange, 3 3/4 In. 7.00
Kiddie Kup, Duck & Horse, Black, 3 3/4 In. 7.00
Kiddie Kup, Squirrel & Deer, Brown, 3 3/4 In. 7.00
Posy Cornflower No. 1, Green, Light Blue, 3 1/2 In. 7.00
Posy Cornflower No. 1, Light Blue, 3 1/4 In. 8.00
Posy Cornflower No. 2, Red, 3 1/2 In. 7.00
Posy Jonquil, Green & Yellow, 3 1/2 In. 7.00
Posy Tulip, Green & Red, Leaves, 3 1/2 In. 7.00
Spinning Wheel & Bellows, Red, 3 3/4 In. 7.00
Tulip No. 1, Blue, 3 1/2 In. 6.00
Tulip No. 1, Green, 3 1/2 In. 7.00
Tulip No. 1, Red, 3 1/2 In. 7.00
Tulip No. 3, Yellow, 3 7/8 In. ....3.50 to 4.00

SWORDS of all types that are of interest to collectors are listed here. The
military dress sword with elaborate handle is probably the most wanted.
Be sure to display swords in a safe way, out of reach of children.

Andrea Ferrara Mark, Basket Hilt, Grotesque Figures, Wood Grip, 43 3/4 In. 1530.00
Antebellum Militia, Bone Grip, Curved, Etched, Iron Scabbard & Mounts, 29-In. Blade .. 920.00
Artillery, France, Curved Blade, Inscription, Brass Handle, Scabbard, 1842, 39 In. 330.00
Artillery, N.P. Ames, Springfield, Model 1832, Leather Body Scabbard, Short 748.00
Artillery Officer's, Horstmann, Phil., Bone Handle, Brass Scabbard, 29 1/2-In. Blade 2415.00

Artillery Officer's, Poland, Marine, Spear Point, Celluloid Handle, Scabbard, 1939, 14 In.   950.00
Bavarian Officer's, Dress, Etched, Composition Grip, Steel Scabbard, 32-In. Blade 210.00
Bayonet, Ames, Mass., Dahlgren, Plymouth Rifle, Leather Scabbard, 12-In. Blade 1495.00
Bayonet, Eickhorn, Dress, Checkered Grip, Black Scabbard, 12 1/2 In. 60.00
Bayonet, Fire, Police, C. Gustav Spitzer, Eagle Head Pommel, Steel Scabbard, 9 3/4 In. ...   90.00
Bayonet, For Model 95 Musket, Metal, Wood, Winchester, 15 7/8 In. 290.00
Bayonet, Japan, Arisaka Model 30, Wood Grip, Steel Scabbard, 19 7/8 In. 55.00
Bayonet, Panzer NCO, Skull On Grip, Puma, Solingen, World War II, 14-In. Blade 285.00
Bayonet, Sawtooth, Sheath, Simon & Co., World War I, Germany, 18 1/2-In. Blade 375.00
Bayonet, Solingen, Dress, Black Painted Scabbard, 13 1/2 In. 69.00
Bayonet, Zouave Rifle, Single Fuller Yatahghan Blade, Scabbard, 20-In. Blade ...230.00 to 375.00
Belgian Infantry Officer's, M.1860, Double Edged, c.1850, 32 3/4 In. 595.00
Brass Guard, Ames Mfg., Chicopee, Mass., Riveted Sheath, 1861, 26 In. 1100.00
Cavalry, Brass Hand Guard, Model 1860, Scabbard, c.1864, 35-In. Blade 750.00
Cavalry, Model 1860, Scabbard, c.1863, 34-In. Blade 635.00
Ceremonial, Hense & Ames Co., Kalamazoo, Gilt, Jewels, Engraved, Early 1900s, 36 In. .   145.00
Curved Blade, Philippines, Tapered, Ebony Handle, Mahogany Scabbard, 25 3/4 In. ...   345.00
Cutlass, U.S. Navy, Model 1917, Clip Point Blade, Leather Scabbard, 24 3/4-In. Blade ...   460.00
Cutlass, U.S.N., Naval, Model 1917, Iron Guard, Wood Grip, Scabbard, 24 3/4-In. Blade .   690.00
Diplomatic, England, Gold Plated Hilt, Leather Scabbard, Plaque Mounted, 29-In. Blade .   575.00
Dragoon Saber, N.P. Ames, Model 1833, Leather Wrapped Grip, Scabbard, c.1839 ......   978.00
Dress, William IV, Gilt Hilt, Twisted Wire Wrapped Grip, c.1830, 31 1/4-In. Blade 875.00
Executioner's, Chinese, Welded Blade, Cord Wrapped Hand Grip, Boxer Rebellion, 55 In. 1450.00
Executioner's, Tapered Cylindrical Pommel, Leather Wrapped Grip, Rounded End, 53 In.   499.00
Field Officer's, Model 1850, Etched Blade, Steel Scabbard, France, 37 1/2 In. 920.00
Foot Officer's, France, Brass Basket Handle, Scabbard, 1840s, 39 1/2 In. 230.00
Foot Officer's, Model 1850, Red Patina On Brass, 1860s 345.00
Foot Officer's, Presentation, Model 1850, Curved, Scabbard, 1859, 31-In. Blade 2645.00
Foot Officer's, Presentation, Model 1850, Scabbard, 33 1/2-In. Blade 2113.00
Foot Officer's, Solingen, Model 1850, Sharkskin Grip, Ames Scabbard 863.00
France, Steel Blade, Gilt Bronze Handle, Morocco Sheath, Late 1800s, 24 1/2 In. 2938.00
General's, Ames, US M.1832, Etched Blade, Metal Scabbard, 31-In. Blade 3450.00
General's, Royal Romanian Air Force, Leather Scabbard, Carl Eickhorn, 27 1/2-In. Blade .   978.00
Hanger, France, Infantry, Brass Grip, Braided Pommel, c.1700, 26 3/4-In. Blade 780.00
Hannover Royal Uhlan Regiment, Engraved, Steel Scabbard, 32 1/2-In. Blade 421.00
Hunting, England, Silver Mounted, Single Edge, Leather Scabbard, 1700s, 29 1/2 In. 2875.00
Hunting, Saw Back Edge, Curved Blade, Brass Hilt, Stag Grip, c.1740, 19 1/2 In. 480.00
Imperial Artillery Officer's, Kaiser Wilhem Profile, Motto, Scabbard, 34-In. Blade 403.00
Imperial Officer's, Germany, Iron Hilt, Wire Wrapped Grip, c.1880, 31 3/4-In. Blade 445.00
Infantry, Artillery Officer's, U.S., Ivory Grip, Leather Scabbard, c.1805, 28 1/4-In. Blade 1100.00
Infantry Officer's, Prussian, Brass Hilt, Imperial Eagle, M.1889, 28 3/4-In. Blade 415.00
Infantry Officer's, Sardinia, Gilt Brass Hilt, Horn Grip, c.1850, 32 1/4-In. Curved Blade .   595.00
Ivory & Bone Case, Japan, Samurai Carving, 1868-1911, 21 1/2 In. 500.00
Katana, Japan, Shinogi-Zukuri Blade, Bronze Tsuba, Steel Saya, 27-In. Blade 1725.00
Katana, Japan, Shinogi-Zukuri Blade, Iron Tsuba, Wood Saya, 27-In. Blade 644.00
Kris, Java, Wood Hilt & Scabbard, Demon Faces, 3-Wave Blade, 1700s, 12-In. Blade 195.00
Kyugunto, Japan, Shinogi-Zukuri Blade, Nickel Plated Steel Saya, Nakago, 22-In. Blade .   863.00
Mameluke, India, Straight, Gold & Blue Blade, Bone Grip, Brass Scabbard, 30 1/4 In. ... 2760.00
Military, France, Hollow Triangular Blade, Steel Hilt, Small, c.1775, 28 1/2-In. Blade 1175.00
Militia, Eagle Head, Etched Brass, Bone Grip, Blue & Gold Blade, c.1830 .... 1840.00
Militia Officer's, American Eagle Pommel, Ivory Grip, Brass Scabbard, c.1830, 35 1/2 In.   805.00
Musician's, Ames, Model 1840, Straight, Brass Throat, Leather Scabbard, 1864, 28 In. ...   575.00
Musician's, Collins & Co., Hartford, Model 1840, Scabbard, c.1862, 28-In. Blade 460.00
Naval Officer's, Non-Regulation, Etched Blade, Leather Scabbard, 1800s 201.00
Naval Officer's, Shannon, Miller & Crane, Model 1852, Sharkskin Grip, Scabbard 288.00
Non-Commissioned Officer's, France, Etched Blade, M.1780/1800, 32 1/2-In. Blade 1075.00
Officer's, England, Model 1796, Double Shell Guard, Gold Overlay, 31 1/2-In. Blade 875.00
Officer's, Etchings On Blade, Sharkskin & Wire Grip, Scabbard, Civil War Era, 38 In. ...   690.00
Officer's, General & Staff, Ames, Etching, Brass Hilt, 1832, 35 In. 575.00
Officer's, Staff & Field, Ames, Mass., Model 1850, Sharkskin Grip, Scabbard, 30 1/4 In. . 1265.00
Officer's, Staff & Field, Ames, Mass., Model 1850, Sharkskin Grip, Scabbard, 32 In. 1495.00
Officer's, Staff & Field, Ames, Mass., Model 1860, Sharkskin Grip, Brass Scabbard 3450.00

Officer's, Staff & Field, Ames, Mass., Model 1860, Sharkskin Grip, Steel Scabbard 633.00
Officer's, Staff & Field, Rochester, N.Y., Model 1860, Sharkskin Grip, Scabbard 345.00
Officer's Dress, Germany, Screaming Eagle, Wyserber, Kirschbaum, 31 3/4-In. Blade 220.00
Patriotic, Ames, Etched Eagle, Bow, Quiver, Bone Grip, Brass Scabbard, 30 3/4-In. Blade   1725.00
Presentation, Officer's, Etched Blade, Engraved Scabbard, Civil War, 41 In. 1093.00
Rapier, Continental, Cup Hilt, Lobed Grip, Crosshatched Pommel, Wavy Blade, 58 1/2 In.   705.00
Regimental, Hannover Hussar, Engraved, Steel Scabbard, Eickhorn, 30 1/2-In. Blade 607.00
Saber, Ames, Mass., Enlisted Artillery, Model 1840, Leather Grip, Scabbard, c.1848 . . . . .   1610.00
Saber, Ames, Mass., Enlisted Cavalry, Model 1840, Leather & Wire Grip, Scabbard 1495.00
Saber, Artilleria Nacional Toledo, Spain, Bronze Handle, Leather Sheath, 27 1/2-In. Blade   115.00
Saber, Cavalry, C. Hammond, Wood Handle, c.1860, 35-In. Blade 1035.00
Saber, Cavalry, France, Curved Blade, Scabbard, 1822, 45 In. 390.00
Saber, Cavalry, Roby, Model 1860, Stamped Signature, 3 Branch Hilt, Scabbard, 42 In. . .   374.00
Saber, Cavalry, Tiffany & Co., Model 1840, Leather & Wire Wrap, Steel Scabbard, 43 In.   805.00
Saber, Cavalry, U.S. Light, Model 1860, Stamped Blade, 34 1/2 In. 977.00
Saber, Cavalry, U.S., Palmetto, Model 1840, Scabbard, Civil War Era 2990.00
Saber, Dog/Lion Pommel, Silver Hilt, Silver Wire Wrap, Ebony Grip, 33 1/4 In. 7763.00
Saber, Enlisted Cavalry, Mansfield & Lamb, R.I., Model 1860, Scabbard, c.1864 . . . .   978.00
Saber, French Officer's, Brass Hilt, Copper Wire Wrapped Grip, c.1780, 20 3/4-In. Blade .   1025.00
Saber, Saxon Artillery Officer's, W K & Co., c.1870, 32-In. Curved Blade 265.00
Saber, Springfield, Dragoon, Engraved Signature, Leather Handle, Scabbard, 1837, 39 In.   575.00
Saber, Stamped Walsheid Solingen, Brass Hilt, Leather & Wire, Scabbard, 1840, 43 In. . .   661.00
Samurai, Curved Blade, Alloy Handle, Iron Scabbard, Belt, Japan, World War II, 27 In. . .   460.00
Samurai, Single Nakago-Ana, WWII Mounts, Scabbard, 36 3/4 In. 575.00
Samurai, Wakizashi, Hira-Zukuri Blade, Ivory & Wood Scabbard, 24 In. 348.00
Shin-Gunto, Japanese Army NCO, Scabbard, World War II, 27 1/2-In. Blade 853.00
Tanto, Japan, Choji Grain, Praying Mantis Menuki, Iron Kozuka, 12 1/2-In. Blade 1645.00
Tsuba, Japan, Hand Guard, Gold Inlay, Iron, 1800s 325.00
Tsuba, Japan, Inlaid, Shin No Maru-Gata, Landscape, Iron, Signed, c.1800, 2 7/8 In. 81.00
Tsuba, Japan, Kiku Form, Openwork Iron, 1600s, 3 1/4 In. 546.00
Tsuba, Japan, Kiku Form, Pierced Petal Iron, 1700s, 2 3/4 In. 345.00
Tsuba, Japan, Shin No Maru-Gata, Undulating Rim, Mokume Design, 1700s, 3 1/4 In. . . .   259.00
Umbrella, Victorian Ivory Handle, 4-Sided Blade, 32 In. 1495.00
Vatican Dress, Pope's Crown, Brass Hilt, Mother Of Pearl Grip, c.1830, 30 3/4 In. 2450.00
Wehrmacht Officer's, Composite Grip, Scabbard, Alcoso, 38 1/4 In. 374.00
Whalebone Handle, Brass Fittings, Leather Scabbard 230.00

SYRACUSE is a trademark used by the Onondaga Pottery of Syracuse, New York. The company was established in 1871. It is still working. The name became the Syracuse China Company in 1966. It is known for fine dinnerware and restaurant china.

SYRACUSE
China

Art Moderne, Platter, Oval, 1931, 13 1/2 x 9 1/2 In. 43.00
Briarcliff, Bowl, Vegetable, Oval, Federal Shape, Pastel Flowers, Gold Trim, 10 3/4 In. . .   38.00
Briarcliff, Creamer, Federal Shape, Pastel Flowers, Gold Trim 22.00
Briarcliff, Platter, Federal Shape, Pastel Flowers, Gold Trim, 13 3/4 In. 32.00
California Poppy, Cup & Saucer, Virginia Shape 22.00
California Poppy, Sugar, Cover, Virginia Shape 25.00
Concord Rose, Plate, Blue, 8 In. 6.00
Coralbel, Cup & Saucer, Virginia Shape, Green Flowers, Platinum Trim 33.00
Coralbel, Plate, Dinner, Virginia Shape, Green Flowers, Platinum Trim, 9 3/4 In. 18.00
Coralbel, Soup, Dish, Virginia Shape, Green Flowers, Platinum Trim 18.00
Governor Clinton, Platter, Oval, Virginia Shape, Gold Trim, 14 In. 65.00
Lilac Rose, Berry Bowl, Gold Trim, 4 5/8 In. 16.00
Lilac Rose, Creamer, Gold Trim 30.00
Lilac Rose, Gravy Boat, Underplate, Gold Trim 45.00
Lilac Rose, Plate, Salad, Gold Trim, 8 In. 17.00
Lilac Rose, Soup, Cream, Underplate, Gold Trim 35.00
Madame Butterfly, Casserole, Cover, Virginia Shape, Gold Trim 125.00
Madame Butterfly, Creamer, Virginia Shape 35.00
Madame Butterfly, Cup & Saucer, Virginia Shape, Gold Trim 20.00
Madame Butterfly, Platter, Oval, Virginia Shape, 16 In. 100.00
Madame Butterfly, Sugar, Cover, Virginia Shape 35.00

Portland, Sauceboat, Attached Underplate, Federal Shape, Roses, Gold Trim 35.00
Raleigh, Bowl, Vegetable, Oval, Federal Shape, Gold Trim, 10 1/4 In. 35.00
Raleigh, Gravy Boat, Attached Underplate, Federal Shape, 9 In. 44.00
Royal Rochester, Casserole, Cover, Platinum Trim, Metal Stand, 1930s, 9 x 6 In. 55.00
Sherwood, Creamer, Virginia Shape, Blue Laurel Wreath Border, Gold Trim 56.00
Sherwood, Plate, Virginia Shape, Blue Laurel Wreath Border, Gold Trim, 10 1/4 In. 43.00
Sherwood, Soup, Cream, Virginia Shape, Blue Laurel Wreath Border, Gold Trim 43.00
Springtime, Bowl, Vegetable, Oval, Federal Shape, Pastel Flowers, 10 1/2 In. 40.00
Springtime, Creamer, Federal Shape, Pastel Flowers ..′....................... 20.00
Springtime, Plate, Dinner, Federal Shape, Pastel Flowers, 9 In. 12.00
Springtime, Platter, Federal Shape, Pastel Flowers, 14 In. 40.00
Suzanne, Bowl, Vegetable, Cover, Federal Shape, Yellow, Blue, Pink Flowers, Gold Trim . 200.00
Suzanne, Creamer, Federal Shape, Yellow, Blue, Pink Flowers, Gold Trim 56.00
Suzanne, Platter, Federal Shape, Yellow, Blue, Pink Flowers, Gold Trim, 14 In. 117.00
Suzanne, Sugar, Cover, Federal Shape, Yellow, Blue, Pink Flowers, Gold Trim 75.00
Thistle, Plate, Dinner, c.1950, 9 In. 24.00
Victoria, Bowl, Vegetable, Oval, Gold Trim, 10 1/4 In. 70.00
Victoria, Creamer 62.00
Victoria, Cup & Saucer 45.00
Victoria, Gravy Boat, Attached Underplate, Gold Trim, 9 In. 125.00
Victoria, Plate, Dinner, Fluted Rim, Gold Trim, 10 In. ....35.00 to 43.00
Woodbine, Bowl, Cereal, Brown & Aqua Leaves, 6 5/8 In. 17.00
Woodbine, Bowl, Vegetable, Divided, Brown & Aqua Leaves 35.00
Woodbine, Bowl, Vegetable, Round, Brown & Aqua Leaves, 9 1/2 In. 33.00
Woodbine, Cup & Saucer, Brown & Aqua Leaves 6.00
Woodbine, Gravy Boat, Attached Underplate, Brown & Aqua Leaves 40.00
Woodbine, Plate, Dinner, Brown & Aqua Leaves, 10 1/4 In. 15.00
Woodbine, Platter, Oval, Brown & Aqua Leaves, 11 1/2 In. 26.00

TAPESTRY, PORCELAIN, see Rose Tapestry category.

TEA CADDY is the name for a small box made to hold tea leaves. In the
eighteenth century, tea was very expensive and it was stored under
lock and key. The first tea caddies were made with locks. By the nineteenth century, tea was more plentiful and the tea caddy was larger.
Often there were two sections, one for green tea, one for black tea.

Apple Wood, Apple Shape, Hinged Cover, England, 4 1/2 In. 3280.00
Black Lacquer, Gilt, Pewter Liner, Chinese, c.1850, 4 x 8 3/4 x 6 1/2 In. 550.00
Black Lacquer, Gilt, Pewter Liner, Chinese, c.1850, 5 1/2 x 10 x 7 In. 1150.00
Black Lacquer, Metal Liner, Chinese, 19th Century, 8 1/4 x 13 3/8 x 10 In. 823.00
Black Lacquer, Mother-Of-Pearl Inlay, Pewter, Chinese, 24 3/4 x 20 1/2 In. 400.00
Burl, 2 Compartments, Dome Lid, Paktong Linings, c.1885, 6 3/4 x 11 x 7 In. 1095.00
Burl, Inlaid, Cut Corner, Hinged Top, Inset Mirror, 4 3/4 x 7 3/4 x 4 1/2 In. 520.00
Burl, Shagreen Accents, Turned Wood, Apple Shape, Brass Finial, 5 1/2 In. 1528.00
Circassian Walnut, Rectangular, Hinged Lid, Cut Glass Bowl Inside, 6 In. 610.00
Fruitwood, Apple Shape, England, c.1800, 4 1/2 In. 2645.00
Fruitwood, Inlaid, 2 Compartments, Parquetry, Flowers, 1800s, 5 x 7 In. 750.00
Fruitwood, Iron Escutcheon, Georgian, Apple Shape, Late 1700s, 5 In. 3525.00
Fruitwood, Melon Shape, England, Early 1800s, 5 In. 4485.00
Fruitwood, Painted Leaf Shape Base, Pineapple Shape, England, c.1800, 6 In. 14950.00
Fruitwood, Pear Shape, England, c.1800, 6 1/4 In. 6095.00
German Silver, 8-Sided, Schleissner Sons, c.1885, 4 1/2 x 2 1/2 x 3 5/8 In. 145.00
Harewood, Crossband Satinwood, Hinged Lid, Brass Pull, George II, 5 3/4 x 12 x 6 In. .. 520.00
Harewood, Penwork, Basket Of Flowers, Ribbon, Oval, England, 5 In. 1398.00
Ivory, Tortoiseshell Inlay, Hinged Lid, Compartments, George III, c.1800, 4 x 7 x 4 In. 1265.00
Lacquer, Black, Scrolls, Medallions, Chinoiserie, Hexagonal, 5 x 6 In. 275.00
Lacquer, Gilt, Figures, In Courtyard, Dragons, Flowers, 8-Sided, Chinese, 5 3/4 x 12 In. . 990.00
Mahogany, 2 Compartments, String Inlay, England, Late 1700s, 6 1/2 In. 605.00
Mahogany, Band Inlay, Figured Veneer, Pine, Paw Feet, Basket Pull, 11 x 6 x 7 In. 175.00
Mahogany, Banded, Inlaid, Solitaire, Georgian, c.1815, 4 1/2 x 4 3/4 x 3 3/4 In. 375.00
Mahogany, Bombe, 3 Steel Liners, Brass Handle, Escutcheon, England, c.1750, 10 In. ... 750.00
Mahogany, Bombe, String Inlay, Brass Ball Feet, c.1800, 10 In. 920.00
Mahogany, Brass Ball Feet, Fruit Basket Handle, c.1800, 11 x 6 1/2 In. 460.00

Mahogany, Chippendale, 3 Compartments, Hidden Drawer, 1700s, 6 1/2 x 9 1/4 In. 1380.00
Mahogany, Chippendale, Bombe Form, Stepped Cover, Brass Handle, 6 1/4 x 10 In. 1150.00
Mahogany, Georgian Style, Brass Handle, Escutcheon, 3 Wells, 8 3/8 In. 355.00
Mahogany, Inlaid Elm Medallions, Ivory Escutcheon, Rectangular, England, 5 In. 656.00
Mahogany, Inlaid Medallion, 2 Compartments, Bone Knobs, 10 x 4 1/2 In. 169.00
Mahogany, Inlaid, Hinged Lid, Star Design, Georgian, 6 x 5 1/2 x 5 1/2 In. 290.00
Mahogany, Inlaid, Sarcophagus, Ball Feet, Georgian, 19th Century, 4 1/2 In. 295.00
Mahogany, Inlaid, Walnut, Hinged Lid, Silvered Handle, Hepplewhite, 11 3/4 In. 999.00
Mahogany, Polished Bone Grips, 2 Compartments, c.1815, 5 x 8 1/2 In. 200.00
Mahogany, Satinwood Chevron Bands, 8-Sided, Inlaid Shell Panel On Lid, 5 In. 960.00
Mahogany, String Inlay, Compartments, England, Late 1700s, 6 1/2 In. 1265.00
Mahogany Veneer, Brass Escutcheons & Feet, Acorns, Fruit Basket, 11 x 5 1/2 x 6 In. ... 345.00
Mahogany Veneer, Diamond Form Ivory Escutcheon, Early 1800s, 4 1/4 x 7 In. 290.00
Maple, Shell & Flower Inlay, Oval, England, Early 1800s, 4 3/4 In. 690.00
Mother-Of-Pearl, Abalone, Bowfront, 2 Compartments, England, 4 x 5 3/4 x 3 3/8 In. .. 920.00
Orange Peel Glaze, Hand Painted, Roses, Gilt Highlights, Chinese, 4 7/8 In. 140.00
Oriental Lacquer, Landscape, Pewter Containers, c.1850, 7 3/4 x 5 1/2 x 4 1/2 In. 230.00
Papier-Mache, Parcel Gilt Rouge De Fer Lacquered, Nested, c.1900, 5 x 4 In., Pair 29.00
Porcelain, Blue & White, 8-Sided, Leaves, French Silver Mounts, 1800s, 5 In. 345.00
Porcelain, Flower, Butterfly, Chinese Export, 1700s, 5 1/2 In. 489.00
Porcelain, Pear Shape, Openweave Base, No Cover, Chinese Export, 1700s, 3 1/2 In. 150.00
Rolled Paper, Gilt, Stylized Flowers, Under Glass, Octagonal, Hinged Lid, 5 1/2 In. 2620.00
Rosewood, Amboyna, Burl, Double, Casket Shape, Regency, c.1880, 5 1/2 x 4 1/2 In. ... `345.00
Rosewood, Brass Feet, 9 x 14 x 6 In. 500.00
Rosewood, Sarcophagus Shape, Ivorine Escutcheon, Georgian, 12 In. 500.00
Rosewood, William IV, c.1835, 6 1/4 x 11 1/2 x 6 In. 355.00
Satinwood, Inlaid, 8-Sided, Shell Inlay, 2 Compartments, Georgian, 7 1/2 x 4 3/4 In. 575.00
Satinwood, Oval Inlays, 8-Sided, Georgian, 4 3/4 x 5 In. 690.00
Satinwood & Rosewood, String Inlay, Mother-Of-Pearl Escutcheon, 16 x 12 x 6 In. 430.00
Shell Inlay, Open Interior, England, 7 1/2 In. 790.00
Silver, 6-Sided, Tapered Egg Shape, Roger Williams, Early 1900s, 4 3/4 In. 118.00
Silver, Dome Cover, Oval, Portugal, 5 3/4 In. 499.00
Silver, Eagle Finial, Flowers, Acanthus, Cupid, Continental, 1800s, 5 x 4 1/2 In. 520.00
Silver, Fish Shape, 2 Compartments, Vietnam Hallmark, 5 1/2 x 2 1/2 In. 168.00
Silver, Frolicking Peasants, Continental, 1800s, 3 3/4 In. 499.00
Silver, Hinged, Oval, Ivory Finial, George III, 1793, 5 1/2 x 4 1/2 x 3 In. 715.00
Sterling Silver, Mixed Metal, Aesthetic Revival, Dominick & Haff, 1879, 5 1/4 In. 4400.00
Sterling Silver, Scroll, Flowers, Lion, Branch, Dome Cap, England, 4 3/4 x 3 1/4 In. 1150.00
Sterling Silver, Tapering Oval Shape, Ring Handles, Hunt & Roskel, 5 x 5 In. 980.00
Tole, Flowers, Leaves, Sarcophagus Style, Brass Ring Handles, Paw Feet, 6 1/2 In. 2185.00
Tole, Leaves, Vermicelli Ground, Oval, Ring Handle On Cover, England, 5 In. 2620.00
Tortoiseshell, 2 Compartments, Oblong, Russet, Edwardian, c.1900, 6 1/2 x 7 In. 1955.00
Tortoiseshell, 2 Compartments, Russet, Edwardian, c.1900, 6 3/4 x 6 5/8 x 3 3/4 In. 2530.00
Tortoiseshell, 8-Sided, Hinged Lid, Interior Lid, Turned Ivory Handle, 4 In. 1835.00
Tortoiseshell, Blond, 8-Sided, 2 Compartments, Georgian, c.1865, 6 x 6 5/8 In. 4830.00
Tortoiseshell, Casket Shape, Brass Ring, Handles, Paw Feet, 7 1/2 x 12 In. 3505.00
Tortoiseshell, Domed Hinged Lid, Ball Finial, Ball Feet, Georgian, 6 1/2 In. 2115.00
Tortoiseshell, Inlaid Ivory, Silver Mounting, George III, c.1790, 5 3/4 x 7 In. 4140.00
Tortoiseshell, Mother-Of-Pearl, Dome Cover, c.1820, 7 1/2 x 5 1/4 In. 1610.00
Tortoiseshell, Oblong, Bone Grips, 2 Compartments, England, c.1865, 7 1/2 x 5 In. 3220.00
Tortoiseshell, Rectangular, Bun Form, 2 Compartments, Early 1800s, 4 1/2 x 6 3/4 In. ... 1265.00
Tortoiseshell, Sarcophagus Shape, Starburst Panel, Georgian, 1800s, 6 1/2 In. 2700.00
Tortoiseshell, Sarcophagus, Waisted, Bun Feet, Turned Ivory Handles, 4 3/4 In. 1748.00
Tortoiseshell, Silver Mounted, 2 Compartments, English Silver, 5 x 6 1/2 x 3 1/2 In. 2760.00
Tortoiseshell Veneer, Inlaid Mother-Of-Pearl Leaves, Insects, Bowed Front, 4 3/4 In. 875.00
Tortoiseshell Veneer, Serpentine Front, Molded Base, England, 4 1/2 In. 1575.00
Walnut Inlay, Hinged Top, Oval Reserve, Brass Ball Feet, Federal, c.1810, 7 x 11 x 6 In. . 1435.00
Yew, Inlaid, Georgian Style, Diamond Shape, Hinged Top, Georgian, 9 1/4 x 4 7/8 In. 750.00

TEA LEAF IRONSTONE dishes are named for their decorations. There
was a superstition that it was lucky if a whole tea leaf unfolded at the
bottom of your cup. This idea was translated into the pattern of dishes
known as *tea leaf*. By 1850, at least twelve English factories were

making this pattern, and by the 1870s, it was a popular pattern in many countries. The tea leaf was always a luster glaze on early wares, although now some pieces are made with a brown tea leaf. There are many variations of tea leaf designs, such as Teaberry, Pepper Leaf, and Gold Leaf. The designs were used on many different white ironstone shapes, such as Bamboo, Lily of the Valley, Empress, and Cumbow.

Bacon Rasher, Meakin	35.00
Baker, Wilkinson	35.00
Bowl, Vegetable, Cover, Chelsea, Meakin	100.00
Bowl, Vegetable, Cover, Square Ridge, Hearts, Mellor Taylor	90.00
Bowl, Vegetable, Gothic, Octagonal, Luster Band, Unmarked	100.00
Bowl, Vegetable, Simple Square, Cover, Wedgwood	70.00
Brush Box, New York Shape, Luster Band, Clementson	425.00
Brush Vase, Chelsea, Gold Design, Powell & Bishop	200.00
Brush Vase, Chelsea, Meakin	325.00
Brush Vase, Meakin	80.00
Brush Vase, Scallop, Meakin	70.00
Butter, Cover, Fishhook, Meakin	50.00
Butter, Dome Cover, Simple Pear, Meakin	525.00
Cake Plate, Bamboo, Meakin	45.00
Cake Plate, Brocade, Meakin	155.00
Cake Plate, Daisy, Shaw	325.00
Cake Plate, Gold Leaf, SB & S	10.00
Cake Plate, Quartered Rose, Plumes & Pinstripes Trim, Furnival	300.00
Cake Plate, Washington, Rose Design, Powell & Bishop	275.00
Chamber Pot, Lid, New York Shape, Luster Band, Clementson	300.00
Child's Set, Balanced Vine, Luster Band, Unmarked	750.00
Chop Plate, Kitchen Kraft, Gold Leaf, Homer Laughlin	70.00
Coffeepot, Empress, Adams	270.00
Coffeepot, Lid, Bamboo, Meakin	50.00 to 100.00
Coffeepot, Paneled Grape, Furnival	275.00
Compote, Donut, Square, Red Cliff	85.00
Compote, Footed, Red Cliff	60.00
Compote, Gold Leaf, Iona Shape, Powell & Bishop	110.00
Creamer, Bamboo, Meakin, 5 In.	80.00
Creamer, Basket Weave, Shaw	325.00
Creamer, Cable, Shaw	130.00
Creamer, Cumbow	20.00
Creamer, Gold Leaf, Iona Shape, Powell & Bishop	85.00
Creamer, Gothic III, Pinwheel Design, Unmarked	250.00
Creamer, Gothic, Luster, Red Cliff	30.00
Creamer, Paneled Grape, Furnival	450.00
Creamer, Paneled Grape, Unmarked	275.00
Creamer, Square Ridge, Red Cliff, 5 In.	60.00
Cup, Luster Band, Walley Gothic, Child's	50.00
Cup & Saucer, Basket Weave, Shaw	180.00
Cup & Saucer, Cable, Shaw	30.00
Cup & Saucer, Lily Of The Valley, Shaw	330.00
Cup & Saucer, Meakin	60.00
Cup & Saucer, Quartered Rose, Pinstripes & Plumes Trim, Furnival	200.00
Cup & Saucer, Red Cliff	20.00
Cup & Saucer, Ring Of Hearts, Pinwheel, Unmarked	70.00
Cup & Saucer, Shaw	25.00
Cuspidor, Shaw	500.00
Donut Stand, Square Ridged, Mellor Taylor	500.00
Eggcup, Empress, Adams	170.00
Ewer, Davenport	210.00
Ewer, Maidenhair Fern, Wilkinson, 9 1/2 In.	950.00
Gravy Boat, Attached Undertray, Empress, Adam	120.00
Gravy Boat, Chinese, Shaw	140.00
Gravy Boat, Daisy, Shaw	35.00
Gravy Boat, Empress, Adams	160.00
Gravy Boat, Lily Of The Valley, Shaw	220.00

Gravy Boat, Meakin 50.00
Gravy Boat, Square Ridge, Wedgwood 25.00
Ladle, Sauce, Maidenhair Fern, Wilkinson 175.00
Mug, Lily Of The Valley, Shaw 155.00
Mug, Sayers 80.00
Pancake Plate, Empress, Adam ....195.00 to 250.00
Pitcher, Bamboo, Meakin, 7 In. 170.00
Pitcher, Bamboo, Meakin, 8 1/2 In. 250.00
Pitcher, Basket Weave, Shaw, 7 1/2 In. 275.00
Pitcher, Gothic III, Full Paneled, Teaberry Design, Unmarked 300.00
Pitcher, Gothic, Pinwheel Design, 7 In. 150.00
Pitcher, Grape Octagon, Luster Band, 8 3/4 In. 110.00
Pitcher, Milk, Gothic II, Luster Band, Red Cliff 25.00
Pitcher, Milk, Meakin 110.00
Pitcher, New York, Luster Trim, Clementson, 9 In. 300.00
Pitcher, Rondeau, Davenport, 9 1/2 In. 300.00
Pitcher, Teaberry, Clementson, 9 1/2 In. 200.00
Plate, Lily Of The Valley, Shaw, 8 In. 75.00
Plate, Pomegranate, Walley, 8 1/4 In. 60.00
Plate, Thistle & Berry, Walley Gothic 100.00
Platter, Embossed, Mayer, 13 1/4 x 9 1/4 In. 20.00
Platter, Red Cliff 15.00
Relish, Gentle Square, T. Furnival 165.00
Sauce Tray, Red Cliff 35.00
Shaving Mug, Gentle Square, T. Furnival 1600.00
Soup, Dish, Shaw, 9 1/2 In. 90.00
Sugar, Cover, Fishhook, Meakin 55.00
Sugar, Cover, Portland, Morning Glory, Elsmore & Forster 80.00
Sugar, Cover, Square Ridge, Red Cliff 40.00
Sugar, Elegance, Teaberry Design, Clementson 275.00
Sugar, Fishhook, Meakin 40.00
Sugar, Luster Trim, Elsmore & Forster Ceres 70.00
Sugar, Paneled Grape, Furnival 175.00
Sugar, Prairie, Coral Design, Clementson 325.00
Sugar & Creamer, Cumbow, Child's 90.00
Teapot, Gothic III, Full Paneled, Luster Band, Livesley & Powell, 9 In. 130.00
Teapot, Portland, Morning Glory, Elsmore & Forster 200.00
Teapot, Portland, Reverse Teaberry, Elsmore & Forster 375.00
Tureen, Sauce, Bamboo, Meakin 70.00
Tureen, Sauce, Red Cliff, 4 Piece ....75.00 to 170.00
Tureen, Soup, Cable, T. Furnival, 4 Piece 325.00
Waste Bowl, East End, Child's 350.00
Waste Bowl, Lily Of The Valley, Shaw 220.00

TECO is the mark used on the art pottery line made by the American
Terra Cotta and Ceramic Company of Terra Cotta and Chicago,
Illinois. The company was an offshoot of the firm founded by William
D. Gates in 1881. The Teco line was first made in 1885 but was not
sold commercially until 1902. It continued in production until 1922.
Over 500 designs were made in a variety of colors, shapes, and glazes.
The company closed in 1930.

Bookends, Figural, Girl Reading, Tan Matte Glaze, 5 1/2 x 4 1/2 In., Pair 635.00
Bowl, Low Form, Green Matte Glaze, Marked, 6 1/2 In. 315.00
Bowl, No. 136, Wreath, Berries, Green Matte Glaze, Charcoaling, Embossed, 2 x 9 In. 1840.00
Creamer, Green Matte Glaze, Incised, 3 3/4 x 4 1/2 In. 325.00
Dish, Frog Figurine, Embossed 08, Blue Green Mottled Glossy Glaze, Stamped, 4 1/4 In. .. 430.00
Jardiniere, Garden, Architectural, Blue Glaze, W.B. Mundie, Impressed Mark, 28 x 19 In. 2645.00
Tile, Clovers At Corners, Square, Arts & Crafts, Green Matte Glaze, W. Gates, 6 In. 380.00
Vase, 3-Sided, Green Matte Glaze, Impressed Marks, 8 In. 1095.00
Vase, 4 Buttresses, Green Matte Glaze, William Gates, 10 1/2 In. 3450.00
Vase, 4 Buttresses, Panels, Handles, Green Matte Glaze, Charcoaling, 13 1/2 x 7 1/4 In. .. 13800.00
Vase, 4 Handles, Green Matte Glaze, 11 1/2 In. 460.00
Vase, Baluster, Green Matte Glaze, Stamped, 7 3/4 x 3 In. 635.00

Vase, Bud, Squat, Narrow Neck, Green Matte Glaze, Stamped, 4 3/4 x 4 In. 750.00
Vase, Bulbous, 2 Buttressed Handles, Green Matte Glaze, Marked, 5 1/2 In. 1035.00
Vase, Bulbous, Green Matte Glaze, Marked, 4 1/2 In. 805.00
Vase, Bulbous, Small Opening, Green Matte Glaze, Marked, 4 In. 748.00
Vase, Bulbous, Triangular Rim, Mottled Green Matte Glaze, 4 1/2 In. 345.00
Vase, Classic, 2 Handles, Brown Matte Glaze, Fritz Albert, 9 In. 980.00
Vase, Classic, No. 283, 2 Handles, Green Matte Glaze, Fritz Albert, 9 In. 1035.00
Vase, Cylindrical, 4 Buttresses, Green Matte Glaze, 6 1/4 In. 865.00
Vase, Flared Mouth, Recessed Panels, Antique Verde Green Glaze, Charcoaling, 3 x 3 In. . .   385.00
Vase, Flared Neck, 3 Lobes, Legged Base, Pierced, Green Matte Glaze, 9 x 7 In. 1610.00
Vase, Green Matte, Crystalline, 4 1/4 In. 375.00
Vase, Handles, Green Matte Glaze, Impressed Mark, 4 In. 315.00
Vase, Lobed Form, Green Matte Glaze, Fritz Albert, 10 In. 3450.00
Vase, Long Neck, Flattened Bottom, Green Matte Glaze, 6 In. 590.00
Vase, Low Form, Green Matte Glaze, 6 1/2 In. 430.00
Vase, No. 258, Panels, 4-Sided, Handles, Green Matte Glaze, Charcoaling, 13 1/2 In. 13800.00
Vase, No. 287, 4 Buttressed Handles, Gourd, Green Matte Glaze, Veined, 6 1/2 x 5 1/2 In. .   3450.00
Vase, No. 365, Bulbous, 4-Sided Neck, Dimpled Base, Speckled Green Matte Glaze, 4 In.   635.00
Vase, No. 402, Bulbous, Flared Rim, Speckled Green Matte Glaze, 7 x 4 1/4 In. 545.00
Vase, Oval, Cobalt Blue Matte Glaze, Stamped, 8 1/4 In. 1150.00
Vase, Ribbed, Green Matte Glaze, Impressed Marks, 4 1/2 In. 460.00
Vase, Round, Green Matte Glaze, Stamped, 3 In. 690.00
Vase, Squat, Brown Glaze, Stamped, 4 In. 690.00
Vase, Squat, Ribbed Stovepipe Neck, Green Matte Glaze, Stamped, 4 3/4 x 4 In. 690.00
Vase, Tapered, 4 Opposing Lobes, Green Matte Glaze, Fritz Albert, 8 1/2 In. 2415.00
Vase, Tapered, Feathered Green Matte Glaze, Ridged, Stamped, 4 3/4 In. 690.00
Vase, Tapered, Flaring Lip, 2 Closed Buttresses, Green Matte Glaze, W.D. Gates, 8 In. . . .   1495.00
Vase, Waisted Form, Ruffled Rim, Green Matte Glaze, 5 In. 460.00
Wall Pocket, Embossed Leaves, Green Matte Glaze, Charcoaling, Stamped, 17 x 6 1/2 In.   2300.00

TEDDY BEARS were named for a president of the United States. The
first teddy bear was a cuddly toy said to be inspired by a hunting trip
made by Teddy Roosevelt in 1902. Morris and Rose Michtom started
selling their stuffed bears as *teddy bears* and the name stayed. The
Michtoms founded the Ideal Novelty and Toy Company. The German
version of the teddy bear was made about the same time by the Steiff
Company. There are many types of teddy bears and all are collected.
The old ones are being reproduced. Other bears are listed in the Toy
section.

Bing, Mohair, Brown, Amber Eyes, Collar, Cast Iron Wheels, 14 In. 990.00
Growler, Mohair, Orange-Ginger, Jointed, Brown Glass Eyes, c.1930, 20 In. 295.00
Herman, Germany, 1930s 225.00
Ideal, Smokey The Bear, Plush, Celluloid Hat, Belt, Badge, Tag, 15 In. 115.00
Merry Thought, Mohair, Jointed, Velveteen Paw Pads, England, 12 In. 55.00
Mohair, Beige, Jointed, Glass Eyes, Embroidered Nose, c.1916, 22 In. 120.00
Mohair, Beige, Jointed, Glass Eyes, Hump, Germany, 15 In. 215.00
Mohair, Black, Arms, Legs Move, Gray Glass Eyes, Long Nose, 16 In. 525.00
Mohair, Blond, Jointed, Shoebutton Eyes, Embroidered Nose, Mouth, Hump, 12 In. 470.00
Mohair, Brown, Jointed, Button Eyes, Yarn Nose, 14 In. 90.00
Mohair, Brown, Jointed, Glass Eyes, 25 In. 98.00
Mohair, Excelsior Stuffing, Swivel Head, Jointed, Shoebutton Eyes, Hump, 14 In. 880.00
Mohair, Frosted, Glass Eyes, Straw Stuffed, Felt Pads, Germany, c.1930, 19 1/2 In. 75.00
Mohair, Gold, Brown Glass Eyes, Embroidered Nose, Mouth, c.1930, 13 In. 90.00
Mohair, Gold, Swivel Head, Excelsior Stuffing, Glass Eyes, Felt Pads, 16 In. 880.00
Mohair, Janus, 2-Face, Schuco, c.1950, 3 1/2 In. 385.00
Mohair, Jointed, Glass Button Eyes, Red Suit, Black Coat, 16 In. 200.00
Mohair, Jointed, White, Glass Eyes, Embroidered Nose, Mouth, c.1920, 25 In. 295.00
Mohair, Light Brown, Jointed, Button Eyes, Stubby Ears, Felt Pads, 22 In. 145.00
Mohair, Light Brown, Jointed, Glass Eyes, Stitched Nose, Felt Paws, 27 1/2 In. 115.00
Mohair, Light Gold, Curly, Felt Paws, Shoebutton Eyes, Germany, c.1920, 22 In. 1320.00
Mohair, White, Jointed, Button Eyes, Humpback, Cloth Paws, 16 In. 300.00
Musical, Mohair, Light Gold, Brown Glass Eyes, England, c.1920, 22 In. 605.00
Plush, Light Brown, Jointed, Shoebutton Eyes, Hump In Back, 11 1/2 In. 2200.00

Plush, Porter's Outfit, 15 In. 460.00
Scooter, Mohair, Jointed, Glass Eyes, Excelsior Stuffing, Swivel Head, 12 In. 605.00
Steiff, Berryman, 90th Anniversary, 11 In. 95.00
Steiff, Blond, Excelsior Stuffing, Swivel Head, Shoebutton Eyes, Hump, Felt Pads, 13 In. 990.00
Steiff, Dog, On Wheels, Plush Over Straw, Cast Iron, Glass Eyes, Ear Button, 10 In. 715.00
Steiff, Growler, Mohair, Blond, Shoebutton Eyes, Embroidered Mouth, Claws, 16 In. 4115.00
Steiff, Growler, Mohair, Blond, Shoebutton Eyes, Stitched Nose, c.1910, 16 In. 4400.00
Steiff, Light Brown, Jointed, Button In Ear, 5 In. 495.00
Steiff, Light Brown, Jointed, Shoebutton Eyes, Button In Ear, Hump, 11 1/2 In. 2200.00
Steiff, Mohair, Blond, Curly, Glass Eyes, Tag, Button, c.1950, 24 In. 2530.00
Steiff, Mohair, Blond, Jointed, Glass Eyes, Ear Button, Humpback, 10 In. 660.00
Steiff, Mohair, Blond, Jointed, Shoebutton Eyes, c.1905, 9 In. 590.00
Steiff, Mohair, Brown, Swivel Head, Amber Eyes, Embroidered, Muslin Paws, 13 In. 1320.00
Steiff, Mohair, Cinnamon, Swivel Head, Bead Eyes, Embroidered, Hump Back, 21 In. ... 6875.00
Steiff, Mohair, Golden, Passport Bear, 13 In. 85.00
Steiff, Mohair, Golden, Swivel Head, Snout Nose, Amber Eyes, Muslin Paws, 13 In. 935.00
Steiff, Mohair, Jointed, Button Eyes, c.1905, 7 In. 825.00
Steiff, Mohair, Light Gold, Shoebutton Eyes, Felt Pads, Ear Button, c.1910, 20 In. 6463.00
Steiff, Mohair, String Tag, Shoebutton Eyes, 3 3/4 In. 146.00
Steiff, Mohair, Swivel Head, Jointed, Glass Eyes, Floss Nose, Mouth, 13 In. 165.00
Steiff, Mohair, White, Creamy, Swivel Head, Jointed, Black Bead Eyes, Felt Paws, 16 In. . 3630.00
Steiff, Mohair, White, Glass Eyes, Embroidered Nose, Mouth, Claws, c.1910, 20 In. 7050.00
Steiff, Polar Bear, Ear Button, 20 In. 3955.00
Steiff, Reginald Oliver Smythe, Ghurka Backpack, Sack, 15 In. 137.00
Steiff, Sandey, Mohair, Purple, 12 In. 115.00
Steiff, White, Red Bandanna, 12 In. 3910.00

TELEPHONES are wanted by collectors if the phones are old enough or unusual enough. The first telephone may have been made in Havana, Cuba, in 1849, but it was not patented. The first publicly demonstrated phone was used in Frankfurt, Germany, in 1860. The phone made by Alexander Graham Bell was shown at the Centennial Exhibition in Philadelphia in 1876, but it was not until 1877 that the first private phones were installed. Collectors today want all types of old phones, phone parts, and advertising. Even recent figural phones are popular.

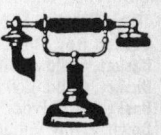

7-Up, Spot Character, 8 3/4 x 5 x 11 1/2 In. 100.00
Booth, Mahogany, Light-Up Marquee, Pay Phone, 84 In. 1430.00
Call Box, Western Union, Telegraph & Cable, 6 In. 120.00
Candlestick, Polished Brass, Bakelite Mouth & Ear Pieces, American, 12 In. 190.00
Den, Oak, Wall, 26 In. 300.00
Fire Engine, Ahrens Fox, Ladders, Telemania, 13 In. 80.00
Harley-Davidson, Heritage Softail, Instructions, Warranty Card, Box, 1993 .... 69.00
ITT, Plastic Case, Chrome Ear, Mouthpiece 45.00
Kellogg, Wall, Crank, Oak Case, 25 In. 250.00
Kellogg, Wall, Oak Case, 18 In. 190.00
Kellogg, Wall, Oak, 24 In. 275.00
Kellogg, Wall, Oak, Brass Bell, Mouthpiece Arm, 24 In. 210.00
Key, Bell Telephone, Cast Metal, 1884, 10 In. 165.00
Little Sprout, Pillsbury, Touch Tone, 1984 .... 100.00
Northern Electric, Wall, Crank, 24 In. 220.00
Sign, Bell, Underground Cable, Do Not Disturb, Bell System, Porcelain 65.00
Sign, Michigan Bell Tel. Co., Business Office, 2-Sided, Wood Stand, 16 x 34 In. 275.00
Sign, N.Y. Telephone Company, AT&T, Enamel, Blue, White, Round, 8 In. 50.00
Sign, Postal Telegraph, Telephone Your Telegrams, Flange, Porcelain, 10 1/2 In. 155.00
Sign, Public Telephone, Bell System, Flanged, Porcelain, 11 x 12 In. 305.00
Sign, Public Telephone, Sheet Metal, Flange, 13 In. 120.00
Stromberg Carlson, Wall, Oak Case, 32 In. 357.00
Stromberg Carlson, Wall, Oak, 1918, 19 In. 115.00
Wall, Oak, Adjustable Shelf, 25 1/2 In. 160.00
Western Electric, Bell System, Rotary, Blue, 1957, 8 1/2 In. ....*Illus* 80.00
Western Electric, Model 202, c.1920 .... 140.00
Western Electric, Model 302, Henry Dreyfus, 1937 .... 129.00
Western Electric, Wall, Rotary Dial, Rectangular Housing, 8 1/2 In. 60.00

Teplitz, Bust,
Woman, Ornately
Dressed, Flowers,
c.1900, 17 1/2 In.

Telephone, Western Electric, Bell System,
Rotary, Blue, 1957, 8 1/2 In.

TELEVISION sets are twentieth-century collectibles. Although the first television transmission took place in England in 1925, collectors find few sets that pre-date 1946. The first sets had only five channels, but by 1949 the additional UHF channels were included. The first color television set became available in 1951.

Philco, Futuristic Predicta, Swivel Screen, UHF, Receiver, Tabletop, 1959, 28 x 15 In. ... 4765.00
Philco, Predicta, Swivel Screen, Wireless Remote Control, c.1959 .... 1500.00

TEPLITZ refers to art pottery manufactured by a number of companies in the Teplitz-Turn area of Bohemia during the late nineteenth and early twentieth centuries. Two of these companies were the Alexandra Works and The Amphora Porcelain Works, run by Reissner, Stellmacher, and Kessel. Ernst Wahliss, connected with the RS & K wares, started his own factory after 1900.

Basket, Boy, Dog, Amphora, 8 x 10 In. 490.00
Basket, Child & Birds, Green, Low, Amphora, 7 x 6 In. 85.00
Basket, Child, Low, Amphora, 5 1/2 In. 60.00
Basket, Girl, Ivory, Low, Amphora, 7 x 8 In. 60.00
Bowl, 3 Gray Vultures, Water Lilies, Enamel, Indigo Ink Stamp, Amphora, 10 1/2 In. 375.00
Bowl, Boy, Looking At Side Of Barrel, White, Gold, Amphora, 7 In. 175.00
Bust, Woman, Ornately Dressed, Flowers, c.1900, 17 1/2 In. .... *Illus* 863.00
Compote, Leaves, Stylized, Amphora, 7 In. 400.00
Figurine, Bull, Multitone Green, Brown, Gray Matte Glaze, Amphora, 13 x 11 In. 200.00
Figurine, Elephant, Multitone Gray Matte, Green Base, Amphora, 7 1/2 In. 200.00
Figurine, Woman Draped In Baskets, Rugs, Amphora, 15 In. 1100.00
Figurine, Woman, Carrying Basket, Water Jug, Amphora, 16 1/2 In. 345.00
Jardiniere, Rooster, Chicken, Mottled Tan Ground, Amphora, 7 In. 200.00
Jardiniere, Woman, Flowing Dress, Flowers, Ram's Head, Impressed, Amphora, 19 In. . 1955.00
Planter, Tulips, Pink, Green Ground, Raised Outline, Amphora, 4 1/4 In. 200.00
Sculpture, Woman, Carrying Basket, Vase, Amphora, 12 1/2 In. 115.00
Vase, 4 Buttresses, Center Bowl, Amphora, 12 In. 175.00
Vase, Abstract Design, Mottled Blue Glaze, 2 Spouts, Handle, Amphora, 7 1/2 In. 85.00
Vase, Abstract Geometric Design, Bulbous, 3 Openings, Amphora, 8 In. 115.00
Vase, Bear In Blackberry Patch, Figural, Riesser & Kessel, Amphora, 23 In. 4600.00
Vase, Birds, Trees, Riessner, Stellmacher & Kessel, Amphora, 11 1/8 In. 489.00
Vase, Blue & White Poppies, Gold, Riessner, Stellmacher & Kessel, Amphora, 5 7/8 In. . 220.00
Vase, Butterflies, Brown Ground, 4 Buttress Bottom, 2 Top Handles, Amphora, 8 In. 145.00
Vase, Carved Mutlicolored Decoration, Bottle Shape, 2 Green Handles, Amphora, 13 In. . 290.00
Vase, Conical, 7 Women, Gilt Lilies, Art Nouveau, Amphora, Austria, c.1920, 6 1/2 In. .. 1116.00
Vase, Cyclamen, Swirl Stem Handles, Hammered Luster Ground, Amphora, 8 x 7 In. 2185.00
Vase, Doves, Pomegranate Branch, Enamel, Bulbous, Amphora, Marked, 13 1/4 In. 290.00
Vase, Egyptian Figures, Scarab, Flowers, Multicolored, Amphora, 13 1/2 In. 290.00
Vase, Flowers, Multicolored, Amphora, 12 1/2 In., Pair 145.00
Vase, Flowers, Stylized, Inset Jewels, Dragon Handles, Ivory Ground, Amphora, 6 x 11 In. 175.00
Vase, Flowers, Stylized, Multicolored, Bulbous, Brown, Tan Ground, Amphora, 14 In. ... 230.00
Vase, Flowers, Stylized, Multicolored, Bulbous, Mottled Brown Ground, Amphora, 7 In. . 85.00
Vase, Flowers, Stylized, Multicolored, Swollen, Amphora, 10 1/2 In. 115.00
Vase, Flying Ducks, Green Ground, Riessner, Stellmacher & Kessel, Amphora, 7 1/8 In. .. 460.00

Vase, Forest Silhouette, Raised Orchids, Wasps, Cobalt Blue Ground, Squat, 7 In. 300.00
Vase, Fruit, Flowers, Embossed, Green Matte Glaze, Gourd, Handles, Amphora, 6 3/4 In. . . 115.00
Vase, Herons, Marbleized Ground, 2 Handles At Shoulder, Amphora, Austria, 14 In. 316.00
Vase, Jewel Pattern, Blue & White, Ivory, Gold, Green, Amphora, 9 1/2 In. 85.00
Vase, Kingfisher, Water Lilies, Enamel, Hammered Ground, Amphora, Marked, 11 1/2 In. . 175.00
Vase, Leaves, Bulbous, 2 Gold Handles, Textured Background, Amphora, 15 1/2 In. 805.00
Vase, Leaves, Cylindrical, Multitone Green, Brown, Gold Highlights, Amphora, 6 1/2 In. . 290.00
Vase, Leaves, Gilt Tendrils, Art Nouveau, Amphora, Austria, Early 1900s, 16 In. 500.00
Vase, Leaves, Handles, Red, Gold, Iridescent Ground, Amphora, 6 1/2 In. 175.00
Vase, Lilies, Cobalt Blue Ground, Scrolling Gold Ribbon, Amphora, Marked, 14 1/2 In. . . 520.00
Vase, Lion's Mask, Leaf Swags, Amphora, Early 20th Century, 5 1/2 In. 295.00
Vase, Multicolored Jewels, Faux Verdigris & Bronze Ground, Round, Amphora, 3 1/4 In. . 115.00
Vase, Parrot, Flowers, Leaves, Stylized, Blue Ground, Swollen, Amphora, 16 1/2 In. 290.00
Vase, Polar Bear, Seagulls, Arctic Landscape, Cylindrical, Amphora, 13 In. 575.00
Vase, Poppies, Blue, Green Centers, Shouldered, 2 Handles, Amphora, 12 In. 545.00
Vase, Roses, Mottled, Textured Multicolored Ground, 4 Handles, Amphora, 7 In. 85.00
Vase, Trees, Stylized, Pheasant, Gourd Shape, Amphora, Early 1900s, 16 1/4 In. 529.00
Vase, Tropical Bird, Multicolored, 2 Handles, Amphora, 5 1/2 In. 115.00
Vase, Tropical Birds, Multicolored, Bulbous, 2 Handles, Textured Ground, Amphora, 11 In. 230.00
Vase, Tulip, Red, Gold Highlights, Handles, Amphora, 15 In. 200.00
Vase, Vertical Flowers, Ivory Ground, Slender, Bulbous Top, Amphora, 12 In. 290.00
Vase, Vulture, Olive Branches, Enameled, Multicolored, Incised, Bulbous, 19 x 12 1/2 In. . 1150.00
Vase, Woman's Head, Flowers, Leaves, Spout, Amphora, 12 In. 430.00
Vase, Woman, Sheep, Brown, Green, Gray Matte, Rectangular, Amphora, 12 x 8 In. 405.00
Vase, Young Woman, Hair Garlands, Stellmacher, Halmar, 9 1/2 In. 3335.00

TERRA-COTTA is a special type of pottery. It ranges from pale orange to
dark reddish-brown in color. The color comes from the clay, which is
fired but not always glazed in the finished piece.

Blocks, Gothic Style, Embossed, Leaves, Berries, 7 1/2 In., Pair 316.00
Bowl, Architectural, Unglazed, 1950s, 12 x 4 In. 635.00
Bowl, Architectural, Unglazed, Footed, 1950s, 10 1/2 x 4 3/4 In. 635.00
Bust, Man, Gray Marble Pedestal, France, Late 19th Century, 23 1/2 In. 4600.00
Bust, Marie Antoinette, Sepia Color, Marble Base, France, c.1890, 25 1/2 In. 1175.00
Cachepot, Bacchanal Masque Handles, 9 x 8 In., Pair 460.00
Cigar Holder, Boy, With Bagpipe, Base, 7 1/2 In. 77.00
Cigar Holder, Girl, With Grapes, Base, 5 In. 30.00
Figurine, Dog, Boxer, Reclining, Front Paw Tucked Under, Brown, White, 17 1/2 In. 790.00
Figurine, Lion's Head, White Glaze, Mouth Ring, 22 x 18 In. 880.00
Figurine, Monkey, Seated, Glass Eyes, White Glaze, France, Mid 20th Century, 15 In. . . . 440.00
Figurine, Satyr, Fromard, 13 In. 1435.00
Figurine, Worker On Horseback, Keebler Kunst, Germany, c.1930, 16 x 16 In. 1840.00
Gourd, Multicolored, 4 1/2 x 6 In., Pair 345.00
Jar, Oil, French Provincial, Amphora Shape, Handles, Ocher Glaze, c.1885, 22 1/2 In. . . . 230.00
Jardiniere, Pedestal, Raised Putti, Triangular, Lion Head Masks, Mid 1900s, 43 In. 310.00
Match Box, Embossed, Woodland Scenes, Dog Finial, 3 1/2 In. 60.00
Pipe Stand, Men Pulling Fox From Hole, Head On Reverse, 4 1/2 x 7 1/2 x 6 In. 55.00
Pitcher, Monkeys, Acting Like Humans, Relief, Mid 1800s, 9 In. 405.00
Plaque, Putti & Dog, Buff Color Clay, Matte Glaze, 9 1/2 x 15 In. 520.00
Plaque, Putti & Goat, Embossed, 9 1/2 x 15 1/4 In. 550.00
Plaque, Worship Of Virgin & Child, Architectural Frame, Cream Glaze, 16 x 11 In. 635.00
Roof Tile, Rooster Mount, Applied Glazed Shards, 19 x 15 1/2 x 12 1/2 In., Pair 550.00
Tile, Embossed, Leaf Wreath, 4 x 5 1/2 In. 405.00
Tobacco Jar, Franz Josef, Porcelain Lid, 10 In. 275.00
Tobacco Jar, Hunter With Large Target, 12 In. 1240.00
Wall Pocket, Masks, Richard The Lion-Hearted, Eleanor Of Aquitaine, 12 1/2 In., Pair . . . 145.00

TEXTILES listed here include many types of printed fabrics and table
and household linens. Some other textiles will be found under Clothing, Coverlet, Quilt, Rug, etc.

Altar Cloth, Embroided, Silk, Velvet, Continental, 1800s, 79 In. 805.00
Badge, Rank, Embroidered, Silk, Metallic Thread, Fly Catcher, 19th Century, 18 x 19 In. . 230.00
Bag, Collars, Cuffs, Linen, Arts & Crafts, Belding Brothers Co., 1908-1913, 12 x 15 In. . . 115.00

Banner, British Legion, Wool, 2-Sided, World War II Era, 34 1/2 x 46 In.	69.00
Banner, Eagle, 13 Stars, Sunburst, Shield, Blue, White, Red Stripes, c.1900, 34 x 108 In. .	375.00
Banner, Italo-American Bakers Union, Silk, New York, c.1913, 62 x 36 In.	3600.00
Banquet Cloth, Linen, Openwork, Crochet Lace, Birds, Rosettes, 132 x 76 In.	200.00
Bed Cover, Lace, Square Central Insert, Borders, 91 x 86 In.	100.00
Bed Cover, Toile, Red, Cream, 19th Century, France, 72 x 80 In.	115.00
Bedspread, Cotton, Crewel Embroidered, Geometric, Martha Burton, 1810, 84 x 82 In. . .	3410.00
Bedspread, Glasgow School, Floss, Linen, Ram's Head Style, c.1920, 63 x 96 In.	1150.00
Bedspread, Popcorn, Sunburst, Trees, Flowers, Zigzag Border, England, 93 x 104 In.	259.00
Bedspread, White-On-White, Candlewick, Flower Basket, Swags, c.1829, 97 x 102 In. . . .	1610.00
Bell Pull, Needlepoint, Wool, Felt, Brass, Embossed, Cased Glass Handle, 71 1/2 In.	230.00
Blanket, Wool, Linen, White, Red Madder Stripes, Rolled Hems, 2 Panel, 92 x 64 1/2 In. .	110.00
Bolt, Flag, 38 Stars, 6 Complete Flags, 6 Extra Stripes, Linen, 91 1/2 x 23 In.	1116.00
Book Cover, Almanac, Flame Stitch, New England, Late 18th Century	495.00
Bookmark, Silk, Green, Olive, E.J. Neale & Co., Mount Lebanon, N.Y., 8 x 3 In.	225.00
Curtain, Crewelwork, Oriental Style, Flannel Interlining, 103 x 52 In., Pair	1870.00
Curtain, Pink Flowers, Maroon Wool, Satin Stitch, Arts & Crafts, c.1910, 25 x 56 In.	260.00
Cushion, Appliqued, Forward To Victory, RCAF Emblem ·	50.00
Doily, Declaration Of Independence, Off-White Color, Machine Made, c.1876, 21 In.	315.00
Family Register, Murdoch Family, By Adeline S. Trowbidge, Age 10, c.1834, 15 x 12 In. . .	405.00
Flag, 34 Stars, 5 Rows Of 6, 1 Offset Row Of 4, Hemp Rope Hoist	2070.00
Flag, 34 Stars, 5-Point Star With 5 Smaller Stars Attached At Points, 63 x 96 In.	6325.00
Flag, American, 1776 & 1876 Star Pattern, Centennial Parade, 1876, 44 1/2 x 28 In.	4900.00
Flag, American, 20 Stars, Hand Sewn, Silk Canton, Linen Stars, Wool Stripes, 34 x 58 In. .	9200.00
Flag, American, 30 Stars, Virginia, Muslin, E.C. Williams, 17 x 25 In.	8050.00
Flag, American, 33 Stars, Wool Bunting, Cotton Stars, c.1859, 54 x 42 In.	1320.00
Flag, American, 34 Stars, Printed Cotton, Medallion Pattern, 9 1/2 x 14 1/2 In.	1840.00
Flag, American, 36 Stars, Wool, Machine Sewn, 3 Grommets, 95 x 69 In.	1035.00
Flag, American, 45 Stars, N.B. Mead, c.1900, 89 x 138 In.	200.00
Flag, American, 45 Stars, Wool, Machine Sewn, 136 x 73 In.	195.00
Flag, Civil War, Garrison, Union, 35 Stars, 90 x 144 In.	3165.00
Flag, Colonel Otter, Cotton, Portrait, Union Jack, Canada, c.1900, 19 1/4 x 27 1/4 In. . . .	219.00
Flag, Confederate First National, 7 Stars, Bannerman's Island, 29 x 19 1/2 In.	6325.00
Flag, Confederate First National, 11 Stars, Wool, 2 Red & 1 White Stripe, 45 1/2 x 25 In. .	9000.00
Flag, Confederate First National, 11 Stars, Wool, Wide Red Bottom Stripe, 35 x 26 In. . . .	9775.00
Flag, Confederate First National, 11 Stars, Wool, Wide Red Bottom Stripe, 37 x 27 In. . . .	7475.00
Flag, Pennsylvania State Seal, Hand Painted, Blue Silk, Civil War Era, 61 x 65 In.	6900.00
Flag, Queen Victoria Jubilee, Cotton, Sepia Portrait, Union Jack, 28 x 34 1/2 In.	375.00
Flag, Standard Of England, Wool, Cotton, 2 Sides, Hemp Pole Rope, 66 x 100 In.	115.00
Flag, U.S. Centennial, Concentric Circle Stars, Printed Fabric, c.1876, 34 x 57 In.	720.00
Flag, Viet Cong Souvenir, Cotton, 1968, 7 3/4 x 9 3/4 In.	69.00
Furniture Spread, Linen, Cotton Back, Flower Baskets, Grapevines, c.1850, 29 x 51 In. .	145.00
Handkerchief, Effect Of Principle, Behold The Man, Glazed Cotton, c.1806, 12 x 12 In. . . .	920.00
Handkerchief, Printed Hearts, 1901 Calendar, Frame, 10 x 10 In. . . . . *Illus*	80.00
Homespun, Blue & White Checked, Woven, Full Seam, 80 x 66 In.	220.00
Homespun, Blue & White Plaid, 40 x 70 In.	415.00
Homespun, Blue & White, Woven, White Homespun Linen Back, 70 x 58 In.	255.00
Homespun, White & Brown Plaid, Linen Back, 70 x 40 In.	880.00
Kerchief, Battleship Maine	65.00
Linen, Homespun, Blue & White Checked, 39 x 74 In.	220.00
Linen, Homespun, Blue & White Checked, 67 x 38 In.	110.00
Linen, Homespun, Blue & White Checked, 72 x 40 In.	275.00
Linen, Homespun, Brown, Natural Checked, Initials, Full Length Seam, 70 x 62 In.	3080.00
Linen, Homespun, Brown, White, Blue Checked, 42 x 39 In.	385.00
Linen, Homespun, White & Blue Plaid, Full Length Seam, 74 x 44 In.	138.00
Linen, Homespun, White & Dark Blue Checked, 42 x 72 In.	220.00
Mandarin Square, Egret, Flowers, Scrolls, Male, Civil 6th Rank, c.1900, 8 1/2 In.	130.00
Mandarin Square, K'o-Ssu, Goose, Gold Ground, Male, Civil 4th Rank, c.1810, 11 In. . . .	345.00
Mandarin Square, Lion, Buddhist Symbols, Female, Military 2nd Rank, c.1890, 11 1/2 In. .	430.00
Mandarin Square, Paradise Flycatcher, Male, Civil 9th Rank, Frame, c.1810, 11 1/2 In. . .	259.00
Mandarin Square, Quail, Couchwork, Female, Civil 8th Rank, Frame, c.1900, 8 3/4 In. . . .	145.00
Mandarin Square, Spotted Leopard, Gold Couchwork, Satin Stitch, Frame, 1800s, 12 In. .	1065.00
Mat, Flower Design, Brown Stenciling, Floss, Linen, Arts & Crafts, c.1910, 24 In.	175.00

Mat, Flower Design, Floss, Linen, Arts & Crafts, Belding Brothers, c.1913, 23 In. 374.00
Mat, Flowers, Oatmeal Linen, Herringbone Stitches, Arts & Crafts, c.1910, 36 In. 230.00
Mat, French Knots, Trellis Stitches, Arts & Crafts, H.E. Verran, Royal Society, 1910, 26 In. 545.00
Mat, Oval, Floss, Linen, Arts & Crafts, H.E. Verran, Royal Society, 23 x 34 In. 375.00
Mat, Round, French Knots, Flowers, Linen, Arts & Crafts, c.1910, 26 In. 85.00
Mattress Cover, Linen, Blue & White Checked, Full Seam, String Ties, 86 x 58 In. 358.00
Mattress Ticking, Homespun, Blue, Red, White Plaid, 60 x 76 In. 175.00
Naval Jack, 40 Stars, Double Appliqued Stars, Blue Canton, Wool, 52 x 35 In. 2415.00
Needlepoint, Renaissance Style, Maidens, Trees, Flowers, Brown Ground, 25 x 22 In. ... 170.00
Needlework, Family Record, Walton & Appleby, Maine, 1825, 18 1/2 x 19 1/2 In. 1150.00
Needlework, Picture, Wool, Felt & Paper, Couple, Tree, House, Frame, 20 In. 940.00
Needlework, Silk, Memorial, Woman In Mourning, Church, Cemetery, 1870, 17 x 15 In. . 2235.00
Panel, Brocade, Hundred Children Playing Design, Chinese, 1800s, 80 x 56 In. 295.00
Panel, Brocade, Moroccan Silk, Metal Thread, Red Field, 67 x 19 In. 705.00
Panel, Crewelwork, Metallic, Tree Of Life, Flowering Vine Frame, 71 x 41 1/2 In. 1880.00
Panel, Ecclesiastical, Appliqued, Saint, Scroll Leaf, Velvet Ground, 71 1/2 x 7 1/2 In. ... 1100.00
Panel, Embroidered, Bird & Butterfly, Leaves, Silk, Early 19th Century, 9 1/2 x 7 1/2 In. . 230.00
Panel, Embroidered, Phoenixes, Sun, Moon, Island Of Immortals, 1700s, 31 1/2 In. 1763.00
Panel, Embroidered, Silk, Dragon Boat Festival, Emperor, Frame, 38 x 53 1/2 In. 3335.00
Panel, Embroidered, Silk, Gold Thread, Figures, Armorial Crest, Continental, 19 x 23 In. . 480.00
Panel, Embroidered, Silk, Iris, Peony, Morning Glory, Japan, Late 1800s, 69 x 65 In. 295.00
Panel, Embroidered, Silk, Samurai, Gray Ground, Japan, c.1890, 22 1/2 x 53 1/2 In. 175.00
Panel, Embroidered, Silk, Woven, Satin Stitch Flowers, Fruit, Frame, 12 1/2 x 11 In. 375.00
Panel, Embroidery, Silk, Flowers, Continental, Gilt Wood Frame, c.1830, 11 1/2 In. 175.00
Panel, Needlepoint, Mrs. Wimpfheimer, Flowers, Taupe Ground 95.00
Panel, Silk Brocade, Dragons, Clouds, Chinese Zodiac, Chinese, 1600s, 70 x 38 1/4 In. .. 690.00
Panel, Silk, Ikat, Lattice, Stepped Diamond, Red, Gold, Ivory, 1800s, 76 x 53 In. 235.00
Panel, Tapestry Weave, Luo Han, Rocky Throne, Books, Incense, c.1800, 38 x 20 In. 765.00
Panel, Tapestry, Aubusson Style, Palm Fronds, Hanging Flower Basket, 102 x 39 In. 1175.00
Panel, Tapestry, Aubusson Style, Rose Garlands, Paneled Frame, Early 1900s, 87 x 45 In. 880.00
Panel, Tapestry, K'o-Ssu Of Insects, Fruit, Flowers, Gold Dragon, Chinese, 1800s, 73 In. . 825.00
Panel, Tapestry, Petit Point, 4 Men, Guns, Boat, Lakeside Cottage, Frame, 23 x 26 In. ... 85.00
Pillow, 2 Floss Flowers, Linen, Arts & Crafts, Richardson Silk, c.1912, 20 x 14 In. 750.00
Pillow, Aubusson Type, Silk, Woven, Roses, Tulips, Iris, White Ground, 23 x 23 In. 360.00
Pillow, Dragonfly, Arts & Crafts, Hemmingway & Sons, c.1910, 20 x 15 In. 635.00
Pillow, Egyptian Designs, Arts & Crafts, H.E. Verran, Royal Society, c.1911, 24 x 20 In. ... 575.00
Pillow, Egyptian Flower Design, Oatmeal Linen, Arts & Crafts, c.1916, 20 x 16 In. 550.00
Pillow, Embroidered, Flowers, Ribbon, Oatmeal Linen, Tassels, Arts & Crafts, 16 x 23 In. 550.00
Pillow, Embroidered, Moth, Green Bands, Oatmeal Linen, Arts & Crafts, 20 x 14 In. 499.00
Pillow, Embroidered, Roses, Thorny Vines, Oatmeal Linen, Arts & Crafts, 24 x 14 In. 265.00
Pillow, Flower Design, Floss, Oatmeal Linen, Arts & Crafts, c.1910, 20 x 16 In. 518.00
Pillow, Flowers, Checkerboard, Linen, Arts & Crafts, H.E. Verran, c.1918, 20 x 17 In. 230.00
Pillow, Flowers, Floss, Arts & Crafts, Richardson Silk, No. 5002, c.1914, 19 x 15 In. 375.00
Pillow, Flowers, Floss, Linen, Buttonhole Stitches, Arts & Crafts, c.1908, 23 x 16 In. 489.00
Pillow, Flowers, Leaves, Linen, Arts & Crafts, H.E. Verran, No. 381, c.1924, 23 x 17 In. ... 405.00
Pillow, Flowers, Multicolor Floss, Oatmeal Linen, Arts & Crafts, c.1910, 20 x 14 In. 635.00
Pillow, Flowers, Oatmeal Linen, Arts & Crafts, H.E. Verran, c.1911, 19 x 15 In. 635.00
Pillow, Japanese Chasing Comma Design, Linen, Arts & Crafts, c.1910, 22 x 16 In. 750.00
Pillow, Linen, Floss, Arts & Crafts, H.E. Verran, Royal Society, c.1911, 20 x 15 In. 460.00
Pillow, Paisley Design, Floss, Oatmeal Linen, Arts & Crafts, c.1910, 20 x 15 In. 430.00
Pillow, Tapestry, Aubusson Type, Goats, Flowers, Swag, Silk Backing, 18 x 18 In. 99.00
Pillow, Tapestry, Birds, South American Jungle, Tassels, 15 x 25 In. 110.00
Pillow Sham, Linen, Blue & White Plaid, Homespun, 47 x 18 In. 60.00
Pillowcase, Chinese Boy, Characters, R. Behrendt, San Francisco, c.1902, 20 In. 100.00
Pot Holder, Needlework, Multicolored Diamonds, New England, 18th Century 295.00
Purse, Linen, Embroidered, Red Yarn Fringe, Frame, c.1832, 10 1/2 x 12 In. 635.00
Runner, Celesta, Needleweave, H.E. Verran, Royal Society, c.1920, 22 x 50 In. 316.00
Runner, Flower Design, Gold Floss, White Linen, Arts & Crafts, c.1910, 14 x 44 In. 230.00
Runner, Flowers, Floss, Linen, Arts & Crafts, H.E. Verran Co., c.1920, 16 x 48 In. 575.00
Runner, Flowers, Multicolored Floss, Felt, Satin, Arts & Crafts, 1900-1920, 11 x 49 In. ... 430.00
Runner, Flowers, White Linen, Fringe Border, Arts & Crafts, 1908-1913, 46 x 16 In. 115.00
Runner, Linen, Blue Hand Block Design, Tan Ground, Arts & Crafts, c.1910, 20 x 56 In. . 430.00
Runner, Linen, Embroidered Flowers, Blue, Green, Brown, 19 x 66 In. 460.00

Runner, Linen, Embroidered Red Flowers, Yellow, Green, 20 x 46 In. 520.00
Runner, Lotus, Multicolored Floss, Linen, Tassels, Arts & Crafts, c.1905, 19 x 52 In. 690.00
Runner, Yellow, Gold Designs, Arts & Crafts, c.1910, 17 1/2 x 46 In. 405.00
Saddlebag, Persian, Stuffed As A Pillow, 22 In. 130.00
Sculpture, Bird, Beaded, Cloth, Victorian, 6 1/2 In. 95.00
Shirt Bag, Flowers, Floss, Linen, Ribbon, Arts & Crafts, H.E. Verran, c.1912, 26 x 14 In. . 290.00
Silk, Embroidered, Flowers, Feather Medallions, Fringe, Persian, Victorian, 40 x 44 In. . . . 275.00
Sleeve Band, Embroidered, Birds, Cloud Ground, Silk Thread, 31 x 10 1/2 In., Pair 635.00
Sleeve Panel, Embroidered, Chinese, 19th Century, 34 1/2 x 15 In. 865.00
Table Mat, Acorn, Linen, Fringe, Arts & Crafts, H.E. Verran, Round, c.1910, 26 In. 490.00
Table Mat, Celtic Design, Floss, Linen, Arts & Crafts, Home Pattern, c.1913, 21 In. 490.00
Table Mat, Dragonfly, Multicolored Floss, Linen, Arts & Crafts, Round, 1908-1913, 25 In. 460.00
Tablecloth, Flower Design, Green, Yellow, Floss, Cotton, c.1915, 52 x 64 In. 460.00
Tablecloth, Flowers, Floss, Linen, Cross Outline Stitches, c.1920, 38 x 38 In. 460.00
Tablecloth, Jacquard Weave, Flowers, Leaves, Hearts, Arts & Crafts, c.1910, 62 x 116 In. 460.00
Tablecloth, Lace, Ecru, 3 Floral Medallions, Openwork Field, Scrolled Border, 97 x 64 In. 200.00
Tablecloth, Normandy Lace, Medallion Center, 36 x 108 In. 5465.00
Tablecloth, Poppy, Floss, Linen, Lace, Satin, Arts & Crafts, c.1915, 35 x 32 In. 145.00
Tapestry, 18th Century Scene, Figures In A Room, Continental, 53 x 32 In. 144.00
Tapestry, Allegorical, Elder & Attendants, Aubusson, c.1700, 9 Ft. 8 In. x 12 Ft. 6 In. . . . 8050.00
Tapestry, Angel Communicating With Woman, Flemish, 17th Century, 63 x 99 In. 4840.00
Tapestry, Annunciation, Angel, Doves, Multicolored, Continental, 1700s, 15 x 21 In. 470.00
Tapestry, Aubusson, Draperie Rouge, Temple, River, Wool, Silk, 1800s, 10 x 17 Ft. 9400.00
Tapestry, Battle Scene, Flemish Design, 74 x 105 In. 405.00
Tapestry, Biblical, King, Queen, Attendants, Flemish, c.1700, 10 Ft. 3 In. x 14 Ft. 8 In. . . 6325.00
Tapestry, Figures In Romantic Landscape, Continental, 20th Century, 40 x 30 In. 45.00
Tapestry, Last Supper, Needlepoint, Petit Point, 17 1/2 x 33 1/8 In. 115.00
Tapestry, Needlepoint, Hunting Scene, France, c.1950, 94 x 70 In. 1435.00
Tapestry, Needlework, 4 Ladies, 3 Men, Robes, Dresses, Gothic Doorways, 57 x 51 In. . . . 715.00
Tapestry, Needlework, Aubusson Type, Palm Trees, Storks, Monkeys, 101 x 137 In. 440.00
Tapestry, Needlework, Fleur-De-Lis, Rust, Red, Off-White, 47 x 69 1/2 In. 145.00
Tapestry, Needlework, Flowers, Black, Off-White Ground, 47 x 71 1/2 In. 230.00
Tapestry, Pictorial, Courting Couple On Rope Swing, 72 x 86 In. 2010.00
Tapestry, Wool On Cotton, Wooded Landscape, Birds, 20th Century, 74 x 101 In. 3960.00
Tapestry Fragment, Wool, Green Leaves, Cream Flowers, Continental, 38 x 10 In. 259.00
Towel, Show, Homespun, Pink, Blue Cross-Stitch, Sarahann Renninger, 1850, 15 x 56 In. . 115.00
Wall Hanging, Composition, Yellow & Orange, Evelyn Ackerman, c.1969, 33 x 48 In. 470.00
Wall Hanging, Embroidered, Silk, Incense Burner, Phoenix, Japan, c.1830, 68 x 44 In. . . . 7190.00
Wall Hanging, Geometric, Aurelia Munoz, Barcelona, 1963, 63 x 47 1/2 In. 355.00
Wall Hanging, Silk, Children, Fruit, Flowering Branches, Chinese, 30 x 68 In. 110.00
Wallet, Folded, Silk, Embroidered, France, c.1750 . . . . 395.00
Weaving, Alexander Calder, Jute, Guatemala, c.1874, 82 x 57 In. 3105.00
Work Bag, Drawstring, Flowers, Floss, Linen, H.E. Verran, c.1911, 9 x 12 In. 259.00

THERMOMETER is a name that comes from the Greek word for heat.
The thermometer was invented in 1731 to measure the temperature of
either water or air. All kinds of thermometers are collected, but those
with advertising messages are the most popular.

4 Pinkham Medicines, For Better Health, Blue, Cardboard, 4 3/4 x 6 3/4 In. 190.00
7-Up, Orange, Yellow, Round, 12 In. 99.00
American Brakeblok, Dog, Yellow, Metal, 20 x 6 In. 259.00
American Manufacturing Co., Metal, Glass Cover, 9 In. 155.00
Baltimore Tank & Tower Co., Celluloid, 6 1/4 x 2 In. 95.00
Barq's, Drink Barq's, It's Good, Tin Lithograph, 26 In. 220.00
Baugh's Fertilizers, Painted Wood, 12 In. 95.00
Bear, Wooden, Glass Eyes, Swiss, c.1900, 9 1/4 x 4 1/2 In. 360.00
Bear, Wooden, Glass Eyes, Swiss, c.1910, 6 3/4 In. 240.00
Bronze, Victorian Style, C.S. Wilder, c.1890, 54 In. 110.00
Bronze Figure, Cast Iron Base, C.S. Wilder, Peterboro, N.H., c.1890, 10 1/2 In. 420.00
Calumet, Call For Calumet, Wood, 27 x 7 1/4 In. 1210.00
Chaney Tru-Temp, Metal, Beige Ground, Black Letters, Made In USA, 7 x 3/4 In. 27.00
Cloverdale Soft Drink, Stay Lively Longer, Round, 12 In. 300.00
Country Fair Bourbon, Tin Lithograph, Paperboard Back, Round, 9 In. 35.00

Crystal Laundry, Wood, Cumberland, Md., 21 In. 99.00
Desk, Cast Brass, Scales, Barley Twist Supports, 3 Dolphin Feet, France, c.1880 .... 380.00
Diet Rite Cola, Sugar Free, Blue, Glass Cover, Round, 12 In. 140.00
Dr. A.C. Daniels, Quimby Druggist, White, Black, Wood, 21 x 5 In. 385.00
Ex-Lax, Chocolate Laxative, Sheet Steel, 36 In. 250.00
Ex-Lax, Safe Chocolate Laxative, Keep Regular, Porcelain, 36 In. 330.00
Franklin Fire Insurance, Philadelphia, Round, 9 1/4 In. 46.00
Hills Bros. Coffee, Robed Man, Porcelain Enamel, 20 3/4 x 8 3/4 In. 300.00
Hires Root Beer, Bottle Shape, Tin Lithograph, 28 In. 120.00
Icy Hot, Puts Pain To Sleep, Metal, 38 In. 60.00
Kentucky Club Pipe Tobacco, Painted Metal, 38 1/2 x 8 In. 220.00
Kentucky Fuel Co., As Good As Gold, Union Central Bldg., 21 1/2 x 5 In. 60.00
Mail Pouch, Chew Mail Pouch, Red, White, Blue, Sheet Steel Lithograph, 38 In. 95.00
Mail Pouch, Treat Yourself To The Best, Black Ground, Yellow, Porcelain, 34 In. 130.00
Man, Mounting High Wheel Bicycle, Spelter, Cast Iron, 1800s, 7 1/2 x 7 In. 950.00
Mason's Root Beer, 14 1/4 x 4 1/2 In. 140.00
Moxie, Drink Moxie, Frank Archer, Tin, Die Cut, Wood Crate, 38 x 12 In. 1900.00
Nesbitt's Orange Soda, Plein De Soleil, French Writing, Canada, 17 x 5 In. 165.00
Prestone Antifreeze, You're Safe & You Know It, Porcelain, 36 In. 145.00
Ramon's Brownie Pills, Wood, Dorfmass Bros., Corona, N.Y., 21 In. 220.00
Red Goose, Finest & Best, Porcelain, Friedman & Shelby, 27 In. 470.00
Red Seal Battery, Porcelain, 27 In. 165.00
Royal Crown Cola, Embossed, Tin Lithograph, 13 In. 220.00
Royal Crown Cola, Sheet Metal, Painted, 25 In. 120.00
Schmidt's Bread, Blue Ribbon, Round, Pam Clock Co., 1958, 12 In. 415.00
Squirt, Banner, Bottle, 5 3/4 x 13 5/8 In. 145.00
SunCrest, Bottle Shape, Die Cut, Tin, 17 In. 330.00
USS American Fence & Posts, Porcelain, 19 In. 220.00
Westinghouse, Betty Furness, 3 Thermometers, Skewer, Set, Manual, Box, 4 Piece 30.00
Wethrometer, Female Mechanic, 1930-1940, 2 1/2 x 6 In. 625.00
Wool Soap, Metal Case, Glass Front, Dial, Round, c.1895, 6 In. 660.00

TIFFANY is a name that appears on items made by Louis Comfort
Tiffany, the American glass designer who worked from about 1879 to
1933. His work included iridescent glass, Art Nouveau styles of
design, and original contemporary styles. He was also noted for
stained glass windows, unusual lamps, bronze work, pottery, and sil-
ver. Other types of Tiffany are listed under Tiffany Glass, Tiffany Gold, *Louis C. Tiffany*
Tiffany Pottery, or Tiffany Silver. The famous Tiffany lamps are listed
in this section. Tiffany jewelry is listed in the jewelry and wristwatch
categories. Some Tiffany Studio desk sets have matchingclocks. They
are listed here. Clocks made by Tiffany & Co. are listed in the Clock
category. Reproductions of some types of Tiffany are being made.

Ashtray, 3 Rests, Footed, Bronze, Gold Dore, Insert, 3 1/2 x 3 1/4 In. 400.00
Ashtray, Fluted Bronze Base, 3 Arms, No. 1658, 9 x 25 In. 1265.00
Ashtray, Match Safe, Venetian, Bronze, Gold Dore, 5 x 3 1/2 x 3 In. 550.00
Ashtray, Match Safe, Zodiac, Octagonal, Bronze, Dark Patina, 4 1/2 x 4 1/2 x 4 In. 250.00
Ashtray, Pedestal Foot, Matchbox, Cigar Holder, Sailing Ship, Bronze, 6 1/4 x 5 In. 460.00

Textile, Handkerchief,
Printed Hearts, 1901
Calendar, Frame,
10 x 10 In.

Tiffany Glass, Vase, Amber
Iridescent, Ribbed Baluster,
Favrile, 3 In.

Ashtray, Venetian, Bronze, Gold Dore, 5 x 3 1/2 x 3 1/2 In. 550.00
Ashtray Set, Nested, Ribbed, Bronze, Signed, 3 To 4 1/2 In., 3 Piece 225.00
Ashtray Set, Nesting, Swirl Edge, Bronze, Gold Dore, 3 1/2 To 5 1/4 In., 4 Piece 375.00
Bill File, Bookmark, Octagonal, Bronze, Gold Dore, 3 3/4 x 6 1/2 In. 650.00
Bill File, Byzantine, Beaded, Bronze, Gold Dore, 3 3/4 x 8 In. 1500.00
Bill File, Paperweight, Pine Needle, Green Slag Glass, Bronze, 3 1/2 x 7 1/2 In. 750.00
Bill File, Zodiac, Bronze, Signed, 7 1/2 x 3 1/2 In. 518.00
Blotter, American Indian, Knob Handle, Bronze, Signed, 5 3/4 x 3 In. 250.00
Blotter, Louis XVI, Bronze, Signed, 5 1/4 x 2 3/4 In. 450.00
Blotter, Pine Needle, Green Slag Glass, Bronze, Dark Patina, Signed, 5 1/4 x 2 3/4 In. ... 550.00
Blotter, Venetian, Bronze, 5 1/4 x 2 3/4 In. 250.00
Blotter Ends, Adam, Bronze, Gold Dore, Signed, 12 x 2 In., Pair 250.00
Blotter Ends, American Indian, Bronze, Signed, 12 x 2 In., Pair 250.00
Blotter Ends, Chinese, Bronze, Signed, 19 x 2 1/2 In., Pair 350.00
Blotter Ends, Heraldic, Red Enamel, Bronze, Signed, 19 3/4 x 2 1/4 In., Pair 350.00
Blotter Ends, Louis XVI, Bronze, Signed, 12 1/4 x 1 1/4 In., Pair 350.00
Blotter Ends, Pine Needle, Bronze, Dark Patina, 12 x 2 In., Pair 450.00
Blotter Ends, Spanish Bronze, Gold Dore, 19 x 2 In., Pair 750.00
Blotter Ends, Zodiac, Bronze, Gold Dore, Signed, 3 1/2 x 3 1/2 In., 4 Piece 450.00
Bonbon, Scallop Edge, Pedestal Base, Bronze, Gold Dore, 4 1/2 x 1 1/2 x 3 3/4 In. 150.00
Bookends, Abalone, Blue Green Enamel, Bronze, Gold Dore, Signed, 5 1/2 In. .1800.00 to 2000.00
Bookends, Abalone, Enamel, Multicolor Jewels, Bronze, Gold Dore 1500.00
Bookends, Bookmark, Enamel, Bronze, Gold Dore 1500.00
Bookends, Bronze, Egyptian Hieroglyphic Symbols, Spread Wings, 5 3/4 x 5 1/4 In. 2500.00
Bookends, Buddha, Bronze, Gold Dore, Signed, 6 In. 750.00
Bookends, Grapevine, Amber Slag Glass, Bronze, Gold Dore, 5 1/2 In. 1500.00
Bookends, Lakeside Press Chicago, Indian Chief, Cabin, Bronze, 6 1/4 In. 2115.00
Bookends, Landscape Scene, Cast Bronze, Relief, Rounded Top, Signed, 5 x 4 1/2 In. ... 2200.00
Bookends, Peacock, Portal, Birds, Urns, Bronze, Gold Dore, Signed, 4 1/2 x 6 In. 1200.00
Bookends, Venetian, Bronze, Gold Dore, Signed, 5 x 6 In. 1500.00
Bookends, Zodiac, Camel Back Rim, Enameled, Gold Dore, Impressed, 6 x 5 In. 1325.00 to 1785.00
Bookrack, Pine Needle, Amber Slag Glass, Bronze, Gold Dore, 6 x 5 3/4 x 23 In. 2500.00
Bowl, Glass, Blue & Purple Iridescent, Ribbed, Favrile, 6 In. 780.00
Bowl, Glass, Etched, Stylized Leaf Pattern, Islamic Style, Flared Rim, c.1947, 9 In. 1434.00
Bowl, Glass, Slight Scallop Top, Ribs, Gold Iridescent, Favrile, 6 x 2 1/2 In. 400.00
Bowl, Relief Flowers With Lattice, Etched, Bronze, Gold Dore, 8 3/4 In. 138.00
Box, Bookmark, Bronze, Gold Dore, 6 1/4 x 5 3/4 x 2 1/2 In. 1200.00
Box, Card, Hinged Cover, Grapevine, Sections, Amber Slag Glass, Bronze, 3 x 2 x 4 In. .. 1200.00
Box, Hinged Cover, Abalone, Bronze, Gold Dore, Signed, 5 1/4 x 3 1/2 x 1 In. 850.00
Box, Hinged Cover, American Indian, Signed, 5 1/2 x 3 In. 500.00
Box, Hinged Cover, Grapevine, Amber Slag Glass, Bronze, Signed, 6 1/2 x 4 x 3 In. 1500.00
Box, Hinged Cover, Grapevine, Beaded, Green Slag Glass, Bronze, 4 x 3 x 1 1/2 In. 850.00
Box, Hinged Cover, Grapevine, Green Slag Glass, Bronze, Gold Dore, 4 x 3 x 1 1/2 In. ... 850.00
Box, Hinged Cover, Heraldic, Green Enamel, Silvered Edges, Bronze, 4 3/4 x 3 1/2 In. ... 750.00
Box, Hinged Cover, Zodiac, Bronze, Green Patina, Signed, 1 3/4 x 6 3/4 x 3 In. 460.00
Box, Pine Needle, Beaded, Green Slag Glass, Bronze, 4 1/4 x 3 In. 850.00
Box, Stamp, Abalone, Bronze, Gold Dore, 2 1/4 x 4 x 1 1/2 In. 600.00
Box, Stamp, Grapevine, Sectioned, Amber Slag Glass, Bronze, Gold Dore, 4 1/2 x 2 1/2 In. 550.00
Box, Stamp, Hinged Cover, Graduate, 3 Sections, Bronze, Gold Dore, Signed, 4 x 2 In. .. 400.00
Box, Stamp, Hinged Cover, Venetian, Bronze, Gold Dore, 4 x 2 x 2 In. 650.00
Box, Stamp, Hinged Cover, Zodiac, 3 Sections, Bronze, Gold Dore, 3 3/4 x 2 1/4 In. 550.00
Box, Stamp, Pine Needle, Green Slag Glass, Bronze, Footed, 4 x 2 1/2 x 1 1/2 In. 600.00
Box, Stamp, Zodiac Pattern, 3 Compartment Tray, 3 3/4 x 2 1/4 x 1 In. 550.00
Bridge Pad, Egyptian Design, Enamel, Bronze, Gold Dore, Signed, 4 x 6 1/4 In. 550.00
Calendar, Venetian, Bronze, Gold Dore, Easel, Signed, 6 1/2 x 6 In. 1200.00
Calendar, Zodiac, Bronze, Gold Dore, 1 5/8 x 4 3/8 x 3 1/2 In. 500.00
Calendar, Zodiac, Gold Dore, Cardboard Insert, 8 1/8 x 7 1/2 In. 800.00
Candlestick, 3-Legged Stand, Bronze, c.1905, 8 In. 430.00
Candlestick, 6 Leaf Arms, Stick Body, Bronze, Gold Dore, Signed, 10 In., Pair 2500.00
Candlestick, 6-Sided Column, Brass, Arts & Crafts, 21 3/4 In., Pair 1380.00
Candlestick, Blown Green Glass Cup, Bobeche, Bronze, 3-Footed, Signed, 8 In. 2000.00
Candlestick, Bulbous Candle Cup, 4 Ribbed Legs, Bronze, Gold Dore, 11 1/4 In., Pair ... 2235.00
Candlestick, Tripod, Ribbed, Bobeche, Commemorative, Bronze, Signed, 8 In. 750.00

Candlestick-Light, Organic Design, Bronze, Snuffer, No. 1232, 9 In. 3100.00
Card Tray, Enamel, Intaglio Leaves & Vines, Ivory Iridescent, Handle, Favrile, 6 In. 2500.00
Chamberstick, 2 Arms, Round Base, Bronze, Green Glass, 7 x 6 1/4 In. 4000.00
Chamberstick, Enamel, Bronze, Gold Dore, 3 1/2 x 4 In., Pair 1500.00
Chest, Bronze, Gold Dore, Handle, Signed, 4 x 2 1/2 x 3 In. 950.00
Chest, Hinged Cover, Bronze, Gold Dore Textured Finish, 5 3/4 x 3 1/2 x 2 3/4 In. 650.00
Cigar Box, Zodiac, Bronze, Wood Liner, 6 1/2 x 6 x 2 1/2 In. 1200.00
Cigarette Box, Grapevine, Green Slag Glass, Bronze, Patina, Signed, 2 x 4 1/2 x 3 1/4 In. 690.00
Cigarette Box, Zodiac, Bronze, Gold Dore, Wood Liner, Signed, 4 3/8 x 3 1/4 In. 403.00
Clock, Desk, Bookmark, Cathedral Shape, Key, Bronze, Signed, 5 3/4 x 4 1/4 In. 3335.00
Clock, Desk, Partner's, 2 Dials, Bronze Case, Onyx Base, Swiss Works, c.1930 . . . . 339.00
Clock, Desk, Zodiac, Cathedral Shape, Bronze, Gold Dore, Brass Dials, 5 1/4 x 4 1/4 In. . 2070.00
Compote, Abalone, Silvered Bronze, 3 1/4 x 6 3/4 In. 550.00
Compote, Bronze, Gold Dore, Blue Enameled Flowers & Lines Around Rim, 10 In. 1500.00
Compote, Bronze, Gold Dore, Favrile, Signed, c.1900, 6 1/4 In. 392.00
Compote, Gold Iridescent, Ruffled Edge, Pedestal, Favrile, 6 1/4 x 2 1/4 x 3 1/4 In. 800.00
Compote, Stylized Flowers, Embedded Malachite-Like Stones, Greek Key Border, 7 In. . . . 415.00
Compote, Sunburst, Bronze, Gold Dore, 3 1/2 x 6 In. 550.00
Daily Memoranda, Zodiac, Bronze, Gold Dore, 6 x 4 x 2 In. 850.00
Desk Set, Abalone, Bronze, 12 Piece 6900.00
Desk Set, Grape Leaves, Mother-Of-Pearl Inlay, Bronze, Gold Dore, 9 Piece 1725.00
Desk Set, Grapevine, Slag Glass, Bronze, 8 Piece 3850.00
Desk Set, Ninth Century, Bronze, Gold Dore, 8 Piece 1840.00
Desk Set, Pine Needle Design, 4 Piece 1725.00
Desk Set, Zodiac, Bronze, 5 Piece 1035.00
Desk Set, Zodiac, Bronze, 9 Piece 1265.00
Dish, Enamel, Bronze, Gold Dore, Signed, 8 x 1 In. 1500.00
Dish, Red, Blue & Green Enamel, Brozne, Signed, 1 x 8 In. 1500.00
Figurine, Puppy, Seated, Patinated Bronze, Stamped, 9 1/2 In. 325.00
Finger Bowl, Underplate, Gold Iridescent, Ribbed, Scalloped Rim, 6 1/4 x 4 1/2 In. 660.00
Flower Arranger, Bronze, Gold Dore Finish, Glass Tubes, Center Handle, 8 x 4 In. 2500.00
Frame, Abalone, Bronze, 7 1/2 x 10 1/4 In. 3000.00
Frame, Adam, Bronze, Gold Dore, Easel, Signed, 9 x 12 In. 2500.00
Frame, Chinese, Bronze, Dark Patina Finish, Easel, Signed, 8 3/4 x 7 1/4 In. 950.00
Frame, Grapevine, Amber Slag Glass, Bronze, Gold Dore, Easel, 8 x 10 In. . . . .2000.00 to 3500.00
Frame, Grapevine, Amber Slag Glass, Bronze, Gold Dore, Easel, 12 x 14 In. 3500.00
Frame, Grapevine, Green Slag Glass, Bronze, 7 1/4 x 6 In. 2200.00
Frame, Grapevine, Slag Glass, Bronze, Folding, Signed, 10 In. 2090.00
Frame, Heraldic, Enamel, Bronze, Easel, 9 x 12 In. 2500.00
Frame, Louis XVI, Bronze, Gold Dore, Signed, 6 x 5 1/2 In. 950.00
Frame, Pine Needle, Green Slag Glass, Bronze, Easel, 8 1/2 x 7 In. 2200.00
Frame, Pine Needle, Green Slag Glass, Bronze, Easel, Signed, 7 x 6 In. 1500.00
Frame, Pinecone, Amber Slag Glass, Brass, No. 947, 9 In. 865.00
Frame, Venetian, Bronze, Gold Dore, 9 x 12 . . . . 2500.00
Frame, Zodiac, Bronze, Brown Patina, Signed, 7 x 8 In. 1200.00
Frame, Zodiac, Bronze, Gold Dore, Easel, Signed, 14 x 12 In. 2760.00
Humidor, Cover, Bronze, Leaf, Vine, Gold Iridescent, Glass Insert, 9 1/2 x 5 1/2 In. 2500.00
Humidor, Cover, Pine Needle, Bronze, 6 1/2 x 5 In. 2500.00
Inkwell, Abalone, Bronze, Gold Dore, Octagonal, Glass Insert, 3 1/2 In. 750.00
Inkwell, Bookmark, Bronze, Gold Dore, Octagonal, Glass Insert, Signed, 4 1/2 In. 750.00
Inkwell, Cover, Modeled, Bronze, Gold Dore, Cone Shape, 5 x 3 1/2 x 3 1/4 In. 750.00
Inkwell, Graduate, Bronze, Gold Dore, Glass Insert, Square, Signed, 4 x 4 x 2 In. 450.00
Inkwell, Grapevine, Beaded, Green Slag Glass, Bronze, 4 Ball Feet, 4 x 3 In. 850.00
Inkwell, Grapevine, Green Slag Glass, Bronze, Patina, 4 x 6 1/2 In. 1100.00
Inkwell, Hinged Cover, Adam, Bronze, Gold Dore, Oval, 4 x 3 x 2 1/2 In. 550.00
Inkwell, Hinged Cover, American Indian, Bronze, Signed, 5 1/2 In. 750.00
Inkwell, Hinged Cover, Chinese, Bronze, Octagonal, Signed, 4 1/2 In. 1200.00
Inkwell, Hinged Cover, Geometric, Bronze, Enamel, Signed, 3 3/4 x 2 1/2 In. 1500.00
Inkwell, Hinged Cover, Heraldic, Bronze, Signed, 3 x 3 1/2 In. 950.00
Inkwell, Hinged Cover, Louis XVI, Bronze, Signed, 3 x 4 In. 1200.00
Inkwell, Hinged Cover, Modeled, Bronze, Gold Dore, Signed, 3 1/2 x 3 x 2 1/2 In. 550.00
Inkwell, Hinged Cover, Pine Needle, Green Slag Glass, Bronze, 4 In. 850.00
Inkwell, Hinged Cover, Zodiac, Bronze, Gold Dore, Octagonal, Glass Insert, 2 x 4 In. . . . 550.00

Inkwell, Hinged Cover, Zodiac, Hexagonal, Bronze, Gold Dore, Signed, 3 3/4 x 6 3/4 In. . 400.00
Inkwell, Hinged Cover, Zodiac, Octagonal, Bronze, Silvered Finish, 2 x 4 In. 550.00
Inkwell, Pine Needle, Green Slag Glass, Bronze, 7 In. 2000.00
Inkwell, Pine Needle, Slag Glass, Bronze, Dark Patina, Ball Feet, 3 1/2 x 3 In. . . . .550.00 to 850.00
Inkwell, Spanish, Bronze, Gold Dore, 4 1/2 x 6 In. 2200.00
Inkwell, Venetian, 2 Wells, Bronze, Gold Dore, 5 x 3 x 2 In. 1500.00
Jam Jar, Gold Iridescent, Blue, Sterling Silver, Mechanical Bale, Cover, Signed, 6 x 3 In. . 1840.00
Jewelry Box, Abalone, Bronze, Gold Dore, 6 1/2 x 4 1/2 x 2 1/2 In. 2000.00
Jewelry Box, Bronze, Enamel, Antique Gold Finish, Scrolling, 8 x 3 3/4 x 3 In. 3900.00
Jewelry Box, Grapevine, Amber Slag Glass, Bronze, Gold Dore, 6 1/2x 4 x 3 In. 1500.00
Jewelry Box, Hinged Cover, Abalone, Bronze, 6 1/2 x 4 1/2 x 2 1/2 In. 1500.00
Jewelry Box, Hinged Cover, Enamel, Arches, Squares, Ball Feet, Bronze, 8 x 3 3/4 x 3 In. 3900.00
Lamp, 3-Light, Lily, Draped Stems, Bronze, Gold Dore, 8 3/4 In. 1765.00
Lamp, Amber Glass, Screen Shade, 3 Parts, Bronze, Urn Shape Base, 16 1/2 In. 3500.00
Lamp, Amber, Hooked Feather Shade, Opalescent Gold, Bronze Base, c.1900, 26 In. 2130.00
Lamp, Damascene, Gold, Bronze, Gold Dore, 9 3/4 x 15 3/4 In. 8815.00
Lamp, Damascene, Opal Ground, Gold Iridescent Swirl, Bronze Base, Favrile, 13 In. 5000.00
Lamp, Geometric Shade, Amber, Bronze, Dark Red Patina, Fluted Shaft, 23 x 18 In. 18400.00
Lamp, Geometric Shade, Flowers, Green, Bronze Patina, Oil Font Base, 22 x 16 In. 10925.00
Lamp, Glass Shade, Bronze, Patina, Raised Leaf, Diagonal Arm, Signed, 15 In. 6000.00
Lamp, Gold Iridescent Glass Shade, Curved Arm, Bronze, 19 x 4 1/2 x 5 In. 4000.00
Lamp, Grapevine, Green Slag Glass Shade, Bronze Base, 6 1/2 x 18 In. 4500.00
Lamp, Green Pulled Feather Shade, Bronze Base, Fluted, No. 424, 17 1/2 In. 8050.00
Lamp, Green Slag Glass Shade, Hampshire Pottery Base, Green Matte Glaze, 17 x 12 In. . 5750.00
Lamp, Hanging, Globe, Gold Iridescent, Pulled Feathers, Bronze Holder, Favrile, 13 In. . . 3500.00
Lamp, Hanging, Gold Iridescent Shade, Feather Line & Swirl, Bronze, Favrile, 6 x 13 In. . 3500.00
Lamp, Hanging, Turtleback Tiles, Leaded Pomegranate, Bronze, 27 x 16 In. 9990.00
Lamp, Harp, Metal Shade, Brass, Signed, 10 x 55 In. 5175.00
Lamp, Hydrangea, Leaded, Stained, Bronze Base, No. 376, Signed, 71 x 25 In. 11200.00
Lamp, Linenfold Shade, Bronze Base, No. 580 Base, 14 In. 14850.00
Lamp, Lotus, Leaded, Stained, Bronze Base, Marked, 31 x 27 In. 15680.00
Lamp, Oil, Zodiac, Handle, Bronze, Impressed, 2 1/2 x 3 In. 2990.00
Lamp, Peacock Blue, Twisted Ribbed Body, Favrile, Signed, 14 In. 6000.00
Lamp, Poinsettia, Leaded, Domed Shade, Green, Red, Bronze Base, Signed, 26 x 18 In. . . 47000.00
Lamp, Red & Blue Pulled Feather Shade, Gold Spots, Gold Iridescent Base, 18 1/8 In. . . . 1725.00
Lamp, Student, Bronze, Dark Patina, Signed, 19 In. 4000.00
Lamp, Zodiac, Bell Shade, Gold Iridescent Feather, Bronze Base, 6 x 18 In. 4500.00
Lamp, Zodiac, Gold Iridescent Shade, Purple, Bronze, Signed, 13 1/2 In. 6900.00
Lamp, Zodiac, Green Slag Glass, Geometric, Leaded, Bronze Base, 16 1/2 x 11 In. 8050.00
Lamp, Zodiac, Harp, Green Feather Shade, Cream, Orange, Bronze, Gold Dore, 13 In. . . . 3840.00
Lamp, Zodiac, Harp, Turtleback Tile, Blue, Green, Gold Iridescent, Bronze Base, 15 In. . . 9775.00
Lamp, Zodiac, Hexagonal, Bronze, Gold Dore, Adjustable, 13 1/2 In. 5500.00
Letter Opener, Abalone, Bronze, Gold Dore, Signed, 10 In. 450.00
Letter Opener, Adam, Bronze, Gold Dore, Curved Handle, Signed, 9 In. 350.00
Letter Opener, Bookmark Pattern, Bronze, Gold Dore, Signed, 10 1/2 In. 350.00
Letter Opener, Chinese Bronze, Gold Dore, Signed, 11 In. 250.00
Letter Opener, Grapevine, Amber Slag Glass, Bronze, Gold Dore, 9 1/4 In. 550.00
Letter Opener, Pine Needle, Green Slag Glass, Beaded, Bronze, Dark Patina, Signed, 9 In. 550.00
Letter Opener, Scissors, Chinese, Bronze, Leather Case, Signed, 10 3/4 In., 3 Piece 2300.00
Letter Rack, Abalone, 2 Sections, Bronze, Gold Dore, Signed, 9 1/4 In. 1200.00
Letter Rack, Abalone, Bronze, Gold Dore Finish, 4 1/2 x 6 1/4 x 2 1/2 In. 1500.00
Letter Rack, Adam, 2 Sections, Bronze, Gold Dore, 9 x 2 x 6 In. 700.00
Letter Rack, American Indian, 2 Sections, Bronze, Gold Dore, 11 x 5 3/4 In. 950.00
Letter Rack, American Indian, Bronze, 4 1/2 x 6 1/4 x 2 3/4 In. 900.00
Letter Rack, Byzantine, Jeweled, Bronze, Gold Dore 2500.00
Letter Rack, Chinese, 3 Sections, Bronze, Dark Patina, Signed, 8 x 12 In. 1500.00
Letter Rack, Graduate, 2 Sections, Bronze, Gold Dore, Signed, 9 1/2 x 2 3/4 In. 750.00
Letter Rack, Grapevine, 2 Sections, Green Slag Glass, Bronze, 10 x 6 1/2 In. 1500.00
Letter Rack, Grapevine, 2 Sections, Green Slag Glass, Bronze, 6 1/4 x 4 1/2 x 2 3/4 In. . . 1200.00
Letter Rack, Grapevine, 3 Sections, Bronze, Brown Patina, 9 x 12 1/2 In. 999.00
Letter Rack, Modeled, 3 Sections, Bronze, Gold Dore, 12 x 3 1/2 x 8 1/2 In. 1200.00
Letter Rack, Ninth Century, Bronze, Gold Dore, Signed, 4 1/2 x 6 In. 1200.00
Letter Rack, Pine Needle, 2 Compartments, Green Slag Glass, Bronze, 10 x 6 In. 1500.00

Letter Rack, Spanish, Bronze, Gold Dore, 10 x 8 x 3 In. 1800.00
Letter Rack, Zodiac, 3 Sections, Bronze, Green Patina, Signed, 12 x 8 1/4 x 3 1/2 In. 1955.00
Letter Rack, Zodiac, Bronze, 6 x 9 1/2 x 2 1/2 In. 575.00
Magnifying Glass, Adam, Beaded, Bronze, Gold Dore, 4 x 8 1/4 In. 1500.00
Magnifying Glass, Bookmark, Bronze, Gold Dore, Signed, 4 x 8 3/4 In. 1500.00
Magnifying Glass, Graduate, Bronze, Gold Dore, Signed, 4 x 8 3/4 In. 1500.00
Magnifying Glass, Venetian, Bronze, Gold Dore, Signed, 4 x 9 In. 1500.00
Magnifying Glass, Zodiac, Bronze, Gold Dore, Signed, 4 x 8 3/4 In. . . . . .900.00 to 1500.00
Match Holder, Bookmark, Gold Dore, Impressed, 4 1/2 x 3 3/4 In. 345.00
Match Holder, Nautical, Bronze, Gold Dore, 6 1/2 x 5 1/4 x 4 1/2 In. 1200.00
Mirror, Grapevine, Amber Slag Glass, Bronze, Gold Dore, Curved Handle, 1 3/4 In. 1800.00
Notepad Holder, Bookmark, Bronze, Wood Back, Signed, 4 1/4 x 8 1/2 In. 550.00
Notepad Holder, Pine Needle, Slag Glass, Bronze, Dark Patina, Signed, 7 1/2 x 5 In. 650.00
Notepad Holder, Spanish, Bronze, Gold Dore, 4 1/2 x 7 1/2 In. 1500.00
Orchid Arranger, Bronze, Scrolls, 6 Openings, Signed, 22 In. 3500.00
Paper Clip, American Indian, Bronze, Signed, 2 3/4 x 4 In. 450.00
Paper Clip, Bookmark, Bronze, Gold Dore, Signed, 2 1/4 x 3 1/4 In. 450.00
Paper Clip, Byzantine, Beaded, Jewels, Bronze, Gold Dore, 2 1/4 x 3 1/4 In. 650.00
Paper Clip, Chinese, Bronze, Signed, 2 3/4 x 4 In. 600.00
Paper Clip, Pine Needle, Green Slag Glass, Bronze, 2 1/2 x 3 3/4 In. 650.00
Paper Clip, Zodiac, Bronze, Gold Dore, 2 1/2 x 3 3/4 In. . . . . .450.00 to 600.00
Paperweight, Bulldog, Bronze, Signed, 2 1/4 In. 335.00
Paperweight, Dog, Pointer, Bronze, 3 1/4 x 2 x 2 1/2 In. 850.00
Paperweight, Owl, Bronze, Dark Patina, Signed, 3 x 1 1/4 In. 850.00
Paperweight, Sphinx, Bronze, Dark Patina, Signed, 1 1/4 x 1 x 2 1/4 In. 850.00
Paperweight, Zodiac, Bronze, Red Brown Patina, Green Highlights, 3 1/2 x 2 1/8 In. 520.00
Pen, Pine Needle, Bronze Handle, 6 In. 540.00
Pen Brush, Abalone, Bronze, Gold Dore, 2 1/4 x 2 In. 650.00
Pen Brush, Pine Needle, Bronze, Urn Shape, 2 x 2 x 2 1/4 In. 500.00
Pen Holder, American Indian, 2 Openings, Bronze, 7 x 4 1/2 x 1 In. 2500.00
Pen Holder, Heraldic, Red Enamel, Bronze, Signed, 7 x 4 1/2 In.   750.00
Pen Holder, Zodiac, 2 Bakelite Holders, Bronze, Gold Dore, Signed, 7 x 4 1/2 In. 1680.00
Pen Tray, Abalone, 3 Sections, Ball Feet, Bronze, 8 1/2 x 2 1/2 In. 300.00
Pen Tray, Adam, 3 Sections, Bronze, Signed, 9 1/4 x 2 3/4 In. 250.00
Pen Tray, Chinese, Bronze, Signed, 9 1/2 x 3 In. 350.00
Pen Tray, Graduate, 3 Sections, Ball Feet, Bronze, Gold Dore, Signed, 8 1/2 x 2 1/2 In. . .   225.00
Pen Tray, Grapevine, Green Slag Glass, 4 Bronze Feet, 9 1/2 x 2 3/4 In. 550.00
Pen Tray, Louis XVI, Oval, 2 Ribbed Handles, Bronze, Signed, 8 1/4 x 3 1/4 In. 450.00
Pen Tray, Pine Needle, 3 Sections, Ball Feet, Green Slag Glass, Signed, 9 1/2 x 2 3/4 In. .   550.00
Pen Tray, Spanish, Bronze, Gold Dore, 9 3/4 x 3 3/4 In. 650.00
Pen Tray, Venetian, Bronze, Gold Dore, 10 x 3 In. 805.00
Plant Stand, Medallion, Winged Horse, Figure, Tripod, Paw Feet, Bronze, 31 x 18 In. 1430.00
Planter, Abalone, Bronze, Gold Dore, Copper Liner, 2 1/2 x 8 1/2 In. 999.00
Platter, Enameled Florets, Pink, Blue, Geometric Band, Bronze, 10 In. 750.00
Postage Scale, Grapevine, Green Slag Glass, Bronze, 1 1/2 x 3 x 3 In. 1500.00
Postage Scale, Pine Needle, Green Slag Glass, Bronze, Signed, 1 1/2 x 3 x 3 In. 1500.00
Postage Scale, Zodiac, Bronze, Dark Patina, 3 x 3 1/4 In. . . . . .920.00 to 1500.00
Punch Cup, Handle, Blue, Purple Highlights, Gold Iridescent, Favrile, 2 1/2 x 3 1/4 In. . .   750.00
Tazza, Heart Shape Enamel, Gold Iridescent Glass, Bronze, 7 x 6 1/2 In. 3500.00
Thermometer, Byzantine, Gold Dore, Easel, 8 x 3 3/4 In. 2000.00
Thermometer, Grapevine, Green Slag Glass, Bronze, Easel, 8 x 3 3/4 In. . . . . . .1800.00 to 2000.00
Thermometer, Venetian, Bronze, Easel, Signed, 8 x 4 In. 2000.00
Thermometer, Zodiac, Bronze, Easel, Signed, 8 x 4 In. . . . . .1140.00 to 2000.00
Tray, Braided Rim, Swirl, Bronze, Gold Dore, Impressed, 11 x 9 In. 431.00
Tray, Enamel, Fleur-De-Lis Corners, Bronze, 5 x 2 5/8 In. 489.00
Tray, Geometric Border, Bronze, Gold Dore, 12 In. 300.00
Tray, Green Enameled Highlights, Bronze, Gold Dore, Signed, 10 In. 672.00
Vase, Baluster, Bronze, Mottled Patina, 16 In. 1955.00
Vase, Curved Wreath, Berries & Leaves, Fluted Edge, Bronze, 3 1/2 x 4 1/2 In. 1500.00
Vase, Green Iridescent, Gold Pulled Feathers, Bronze Holder, Signed, 14 1/4 In., Pair 2415.00
Vase, Molded Flowers, Stems, Bronze, 1910-1914, 6 3/4 In. 2250.00
Vase, Trumpet, Amber Iridescent, Bronze, Gold Dore Base, 1918-1928, 14 1/4 In. 2124.00
Vase, Trumpet, Blue Enameled Foot, Bronze, Signed, c.1900, 13 3/4 In. 1120.00

Vase, Trumpet, Gold Iridescent, Brass Holder, 3 Dragon Supports, Favrile, 18 In. 1100.00
TIFFANY GLASS, Bonbon, Gold Iridescent, Green, Flared, Footed, Favrile, 5 x 2 3/4 x 1 1/2 In.   650.00
Bottle, Scent, Applied Ribs, Silver Cap, Favrile, 4 In. 3970.00
Bottle, Scent, Blue Iridescent, Pulled Heart & Vine, Stopper, 5 1/2 In. 6040.00
Bowl, Blue Iridescent, Flared Rim, Footed, Favrile, 11 1/2 In. 1380.00
Bowl, Blue Iridescent, Ribbed, Flared Rim, Favrile, 10 1/4 x 3 1/2 In. 1210.00
Bowl, Blue Iridescent, Scalloped Rim, Favrile, 6 In. 775.00
Bowl, Blue Pastel, Opalescent Pulled Feathers, Favrile, Signed, c.1920, 4 x 12 In. 2015.00
Bowl, Blue, Ribbed, Scalloped Rim, Favrile, Signed, c.1900, 2 3/4 x 6 In. 1065.00
Bowl, Centerpiece, Blue, Intaglio Cut, Cone Shape Well, Favile, 7 1/2 x 4 In. 2500.00
Bowl, Flower Shape, Footed, Gold, Pink Band, Ruffled Edge, Favrile, 7 x 6 In. 1670.00
Bowl, Gold Favrile, Blue, Green, Amber Highlights, 7 1/2 In. 575.00
Bowl, Gold Iridescent Ribs, Clear Body, 3 1/2 x 2 1/4 In. 173.00
Bowl, Gold Iridescent, Flared, Red-Violet Rim, Favrile, Signed, 3 1/4 x 4 1/2 In. 950.00
Bowl, Gold Iridescent, Green Pods, Vines, Oval, Flared, Favrile, 3 1/4 x 4 1/2 In. 495.00
Bowl, Gold Iridescent, Irregularly Ruffled Rim, Signed, Favrile, 4 1/2 In. 355.00
Bowl, Gold Iridescent, Ribbed, Scalloped Rim, No. 6940, Favrile, 8 In. 720.00
Bowl, Gold Iridescent, Scalloped Rim, Favrile, Signed, c.1910, 2 1/4 x 9 In. 504.00
Bowl, Gold Iridescent, Scalloped Rim, Favrile, Signed, c.1910, 3 1/2 x 10 In. 1460.00
Bowl, Gold Iridescent, Swirled Ribs, Scalloped Edge, Favrile, Signed, 3 1/4 x 8 In. 880.00
Bowl, Gold Iridescent, Vertical Ribs, Scalloped Edge, Favrile, Signed, 8 1/4 In. 480.00
Bowl, Gold Iridescent, Vertical Ribs, Scalloped Rim, Signed, 5 In. 200.00
Bowl, Green Iridescent To Opalescent, Flared Rim, Favrile, 2 x 5 In. 330.00
Bowl, Green Opalescent, Pulled Feather, Signed, 2 3/4 x 8 1/4 In. 920.00
Bowl, Iridescent Gold, Blue, Purple Highlights, Scalloped Rim, Signed, 9 In. 540.00
Bowl, Ivory, Melon Ribbed, Molded Fruit, Signed, 5 x 9 In. 21000.00
Bowl, Pastel Blue, Opalescent, Stretch Rim, Favrile, 7 x 3 In. 1840.00
Bowl, Pastel, Green Iridescent, Diamond-Quilted Opalescent, Amber, Favrile, 8 In. 600.00
Bowl, Pastel, Opalescent Optic, Leaves, Electric Blue Rim, 6 1/4 x 2 In. 950.00
Bowl, Yellow Iridescent, Opalescent, Diamond-Quilted, Favrile, Signed, 9 1/2 In. 1670.00
Bowl, Yellow Pastel, Footed, No. 1561, Favrile, 6 In. 518.00
Bowl, Yellow, Lattice Design, Ruffled Edge, Signed, 8 1/4 In. 715.00
Box, Gold Iridescent Base, Enameled Bronze Cover, 5 In. 2875.00
Candle Lamp, Gold Iridescent, Favrile, Signed, c.1900, 15 In. 1345.00
Candle Lamp, Gold Iridescent, Twisted Stem, Favrile, 6 3/4 In. 770.00
Candle Lamp, Green Iridescent Base, Cream, Green Shade, c.1900, 13 1/2 In. 1900.00
Candle Lamp, King Tut, Green, Gold Iridescent, Ruffled Edge, 6 1/2 In. 1035.00
Candle Lamp, Shade, Gold Iridescent, Pulled Feather Stem, 13 1/2 In. 1840.00
Candlestick, Gold Amber Iridescent, Cupped, Ruffled Rim, Spiral Ribs, 9 In., Pair 880.00
Candlestick, Gold Iridescent, Banded Ring, Ribbed Base, 7 In., Pair 1000.00
Candlestick, Gold Iridescent, Twisted Spiral, Favrile, Signed, 7 In. 715.00
Candlestick, Gold Iridescent, Twisted Stem, Cupped Bobeche, 5 x 4 In., Pair 1265.00
Candlestick, Iridescent Blue, Gold, Spiral Stem, Cord Opening In Base, 5 1/8 In. 460.00
Candlestick, Pastel, Opalescent, Tapered, Favrile, c.1925, 9 1/2 In., Pair 2600.00
Candlestick, Reeded, Tapered Stem, Leaf Bobeche, Favrile, 14 1/2 In. 1000.00
Candlestick, Yellow, White Opalescent, Twisted Stem, Paper Label, 12 In., Pair 2700.00
Card Tray, Intaglio Cut Leaves, Vines, Enamel, Green Border, Favrile, 6 x 2 In. 2500.00
Chalice, Green Pulled Feather, Gold Iridescent, Trumpet, Signed, c.1900 . . . . 560.00
Compote, Amber, Diamond-Quilted, Pink Iridescent Rim, c.1920, 2 1/2 x 9 In. 1900.00
Compote, Amethyst, Clear Stem, Frosted Foot, c.1900, 5 1/4 x 6 1/2 In. 1000.00
Compote, Blue Iridescent, Favrile, Signed, 5 1/2 x 10 In. 3500.00
Compote, Blue Iridescent, Gold Border, Favrile, c.1900, 9 x 3 In. 840.00
Compote, Blue, Silver Iridescent, Ribbed, Double Inverted Rim, Favrile, 6 In. 2185.00
Compote, Clear, Opalescent Rays, Aqua Petaled Rim, Trumpet, Favrile, 4 1/2 x 6 In. 880.00
Compote, Gold Iridescent, Amber Green, Ribbed, Stretch Rim, Favrile, 5 In. 715.00
Compote, Gold Iridescent, Bulbous Ruffled Rim, Disk Foot, c.1910, 5 x 4 1/2 In. 785.00
Compote, Gold Iridescent, Diamond-Quilted, Favrile, 6 In. 750.00
Compote, Gold Iridescent, Favrile, c.1910, 2 x 7 3/4 In. 560.00
Compote, Gold Iridescent, Purple, Incised Leaves & Vines, Favrile, 4 In. 1175.00
Compote, Gold Iridescent, Ribbed, Ruffled Edge, Green Intaglio Leaves, 2 1/4 In. 1495.00
Compote, Gold Iridescent, Ribbed, Scalloped Rim, Pedestal Base, Favrile, 3 3/4 In. 750.00
Compote, Gold Iridescent, Ruffled Edge, Favrile, c.1920, 4 x 5 1/2 In. 840.00
Compote, Gold Iridescent, Scalloped Rim, 3 x 6 In. . . . . .635.00 to 800.00

Compote, Gold Iridescent, Scalloped Rim, Knop Stem, Raised Disc Foot, 3 x 6 In. 690.00
Compote, Gold Iridescent, Shallow Rim, Swollen Stem, Favrile, 9 3/4 In. 940.00
Compote, Gold Iridescent, Swollen Stem, Favrile, c.1900, 5 1/2 x 3 1/2 In. 475.00
Compote, Gold Iridescent, Violet Highlights, Ruffled Edge, Footed, 6 1/4 In. 800.00
Compote, Grape Leaf & Vine, Gold Iridescent, Favrile, Signed, 2 3/4 x 6 3/4 In. 770.00
Compote, Green Iridescent, Opalescent, Scalloped Rim, Signed, 5 x 6 1/2 In. 2300.00
Compote, Green Pastel, Opalescent Rays, Pedestal, Favrile, 2 1/4 x 4 3/4 In. 440.00
Compote, Green, Intaglio Butterfly, Favrile, c.1920, 2 1/4 x 5 1/4 In. 950.00
Compote, Iridescent Gold, Scalloped Top, Vertical Ribs, Applied Foot, 6 x 6 In. 1095.00
Compote, Low, Footed, Ruffled Rim, Iridescent Gold, Favrile, c.1900, 6 In. 448.00
Compote, Pastel, Radiating Bands, Irregular Top, Favrile, 5 1/4 x 2 In. 850.00
Compote, Pink Iridescent, Diamond Optic, Footed, Favrile, Signed, 3 x 8 In. 1500.00
Compote, Pink, Opalescent Rayed Body, Ruffled Edge, Favrile, 4 1/4 In. 800.00
Compote, Stars, Opalescent, Turquoise Pulled Feathers, Oval, Favrile, 7 x 5 In. 1800.00
Compote, Yellow Stretched Rim, Opalescent Foot, Favrile, c.1920, 5 1/2 x 7 In. 950.00
Cordial, Gold Iridescent, Pulled Design, Yellow Stem, Cut Diamond, 3 1/2 In. 460.00
Cordial Set, Iridescent & Opalescent Green Bowls, Favrile, 4 3/4 In., 6 Piece 2070.00
Cup & Saucer, Opal, Gold Iridescent Interior, Green Iridescent Rim, Signed 840.00
Dish, Gold Iridescent, Blue Tipped Ruffled Edge, Signed, 2 1/2 In. 190.00
Finger Bowl, Gold Iridescent, 10 Twisted Prunts, Favrile, 2 1/2 x 5 In. . . . . .480.00 to 615.00
Finger Bowl, Underplate, Gold Iridescent, Intaglio Grapes & Leaves, Favrile 600.00
Finger Bowl, Underplate, Gold Iridescent, Intaglio, Draped Chain, 2 1/2 x 6 In. 635.00
Finger Bowl, Underplate, Gold, Green & Magenta Iridescent, Favrile, 4 3/8 In. 717.00
Finger Bowl, Underplate, Paperweight, Amber, Green Lily Pad, Vine, Flared, 2 x 4 In. 690.00
Finger Bowl, Underplate, Waterlily Shape, Gold Iridescent, Favrile, 6 x 3 In. 520.00
Goblet, Gold Iridescent, Pink, Purple & Blue Highlights, 3 3/4 In., 4 Piece 2350.00
Goblet, Green Opalescent, Reeded, Pastel Stem, Rayed Base, Favrile, 7 1/2 In. 360.00
Goblet, Green Pastel, Favrile, Signed, c.1910, 4 1/4 In. 400.00
Goblet, Seafoam Green Bowl, Opalescent Rim, Ribbed Stem, Favrile, 7 1/4 In. 800.00
Goblet, Tulip Shape, Shaded Pearl To Aqua To Yellow, Clear Stem, Favrile, 7 1/2 In. 495.00
Inkwell, Acid-Cut Flowers, Silver Collar & Cap, 5 x 4 3/4 In. 1265.00
Jar, Cover, Blue Iridescent, Bulbous Body, Long Neck, Stepped Foot, 9 1/2 In. 1200.00
Jar, Cover, Gold Iridescent, Cut Sunburst Knob, Favrile, 4 x 7 1/2 In. 1800.00
Loving Cup, Gold Iridescent, Green Pulled Leaf & Vine, 3 Applied Handles, 7 In. 2590.00
Loving Cup, Gold, 3 Applied Handles, Green Leaf & Vines, Favrile, 7 1/4 In. 2590.00
Nappy, Gold Iridescent, Applied Finger Holder, Favrile, c.1910, 5 1/2 x 4 In. 560.00
Nut Dish, Ruffled Top, Steel Blue Top Rim, Gold Iridescent, Favrile, 2 x 2 In. 400.00
Paperweight, Scarab, Blue Iridescent, 5 x 2 1/2 x 1 1/2 In. 750.00
Paperweight, Scarab, Blue, Favrile, 5 3/8 x 2 3/4 In. 825.00
Parfait, Aqua, Opal Vertical Bands, Favrile, 6 1/4 In. 580.00
Parfait, Green, Aqua Stripes, Opal Ring, Ruffled Edge, Favrile, Signed, 9 In. 980.00
Perfume Bottle, Gold, Iridescent, Veining, Ribbed, Stopper, Favrile, 5 1/2 x 3 In. 730.00
Pitcher, Blue Iridescent, Straight Sides, Favrile, c.1900, 8 1/4 In. 840.00
Pitcher, Gold Iridescent, Green Leaves, Vines, Straight Sides, Favrile, 6 1/2 In. 3795.00
Plate, Gold Iridescent, Ribbed, Scalloped Edge, Favrile, 7 1/4 In. 260.00
Plate, Pastel, Gold Iridescent, White Opalescent, No. 558T, Favrile, 8 In. 290.00
Punch Cup, Gold Iridescent, Applied Lily Pads, Favrile, 2 1/8 x 3 1/8 In. 385.00
Punch Cup, Gold Iridescent, Blue Highlights, Applied Tendrils, Signed, 2 In. 1000.00
Punch Cup, Gold Iridescent, Purple, Green Pulled Geometric Design, 2 1/2 In. . . . .765.00 to 800.00
Punch Cup, Tel El Amarna, Gold Iridescent, Swollen, Scroll Handle, Favrile, 3 In. 1175.00
Salt, Gold Iridescent, 4-Footed, Flared Rim, Signed, 2 1/4 In. . . . . .180.00 to 300.00
Salt, Gold Iridescent, Applied Pods, Trailing Vines, Favrile, 1 1/4 x 2 1/4 In. 550.00
Salt, Gold Iridescent, Flat Bottom, Ruffled Edge, Favrile, Signed, 2 1/2 x 1 In. 200.00
Salt, Gold Iridescent, Ruffled Edge, Favrile, Signed, 2 1/2 x 1 In. 200.00
Salt, Gold Iridescent, Ruffled Rim, Polished Pontil, Favrile, 2 3/8 In. 300.00
Salt, Gold Iridescent, Tapered, Flared Rim, Signed, 1 1/2 x 2 1/4 In. 195.00
Salt, Green, Gold Iridescent, Ruffled Edge, Signed, c.1900, 2 3/4 x 1 In. 335.00
Salt, Pink Pastel, Ruffled Edge, Favrile, c.1920, 2 3/4 In. 1345.00
Scarab Seal, Triangular, Glass Beaded Edge, Gold Iridescent, Favrile, 1 3/4 In. 750.00
Shade, Amber To Orange Iridescent, Diamond-Quilted, Ruffled Edge, c.1900 . . . . 1065.00
Shade, Geometric, Leaded, Vines, Leaves, Green To Yellow Slag Glass, 14 In. 6600.00
Shade, Gold, Ruffled Edge, Favrile, c.1910, 7 x 2 1/2 In. 670.00
Shade, Lily, Glass, Ribbed, Green Pulled Feathers, Ruffled Rim, Favrile, 4 3/8 In. 1380.00

Shade, Linenfold, Green, Signed, 8 In. 3450.00
Shade, Nasturtium, Leaded, Domed, 22 In. 48400.00
Shade, Red Swirl Opal, Favrile, 5 1/8 In. 865.00
Sherbet, Gold Iridescent, Facet-Cut Stem, 4 In. 345.00
Spice Dish, Gold Iridescent, Favrile, Inscribed, 3 In. 259.00
Tazza, Stretched Rim, Pink Over Opalescent, N.Y., 5 7/8 x 6 1/2 In. 1175.00
Tazza, White Opalescent, Leaf Design, Ruffled Rim, Favrile, 5 1/2 x 4 1/8 In. 800.00
Tile, Turtleback, Blue Iridescent, Favrile, 7 3/4 x 5 1/2 In. 420.00
Tumbler, Gold Iridescent, Pinched, Threaded, Favrile, Signed, 4 In. 300.00
Tumbler, Whiskey, Gold Iridescent, Twisted, Signed, 1 3/4 In. 300.00
Vase, Amber Iridescent, Ribbed Baluster, Favrile, 3 In. . . . . *Illus*   690.00
Vase, Amber, Gold Iridescent Pulled Feathers, 3 1/2 In. 1265.00
Vase, Blue Iridescent, Bulbous, Pinched Shoulders, Favrile, 5 In. 1910.00
Vase, Blue Iridescent, Pulled Feathers, Reverse Trumpet, Favrile, 10 1/4 In. 3450.00
Vase, Blue Iridescent, Pulled Heart & Vine, Button Pontil, Favrile, 7 In. 2875.00
Vase, Blue Iridescent, Pulled Lappets, Oval, Cylindrical Neck, Favrile, 7 5/8 In. 4675.00
Vase, Blue Iridescent, Twisted, Pinched Sides, Water-Dropper Neck, 7 3/4 In. 4185.00
Vase, Blue Iridescent, Vertical Ribbing, Enameled Bronze Base, 17 1/4 In. 2015.00
Vase, Blue Translucent Iridescent, Green Lappets, Opal Rolled Rim, Oval, 2 3/4 In. 1705.00
Vase, Blue, Cylindrical, Flared Rim & Base, Favrile, 15 In., Pair 3820.00
Vase, Blue, Ribs, Dimples, Bulbous, Scalloped Rim, Favrile, Signed, 4 In. 2000.00
Vase, Bud, Blue Iridescent, Metal Base, Enameled, c.1900, 12 In. 840.00
Vase, Bud, Blue Iridescent, Stick, Flared Rim, Bronze Holder, Signed, 12 In. 1265.00
Vase, Deep Red, Frosted, Cut Broad Leaves, Relief, Baluster, Cameo, 9 1/4 In. 7130.00
Vase, Double Gourd, Blue Exterior, White Interior, Favrile, 12 In. 1955.00
Vase, Double Gourd, Butterscotch, Gold Iridescent, Favrile, Signed, 6 1/2 In. 2185.00
Vase, Double Gourd, Gold Iridescent, Long Neck, Signed, 11 3/4 In. 2590.00
Vase, Flower Form, 5-Fold Flare Out Top, Gold Iridescent, Red-Violet, 5 1/2 In. 1800.00
Vase, Flower Form, Amber, Waisted, Scalloped Rim, Favrile, c.1907, 3 3/4 In. 1060.00
Vase, Flower Form, Blue Iridescent, Ribbed, Applied Foot, Favrile, 11 3/4 In. 2070.00
Vase, Flower Form, Blue Iridescent, Waisted Onion, Ruffled Edge, Ribbed, 10 1/2 In. 4400.00
Vase, Flower Form, Gold Iridescent, 5-Crimp Rim, Pedestal, Signed, 5 1/2 In. 1800.00
Vase, Flower Form, Gold Iridescent, Blue Pulled Feather Leaves, 10 1/4 In. 2587.00
Vase, Flower Form, Gold Iridescent, Bulbous, 4-Footed, Flared Rim, 2 1/2 In. 580.00
Vase, Flower Form, Gold Iridescent, Magenta, Ruffled Edge, Knop Stem, 14 In. 5175.00
Vase, Flower Form, Gold Iridescent, Ribbed, Favrile, c.1910, 11 1/4 In. 335.00
Vase, Flower Form, Gold Iridescent, Violet Highlights, Ribbed, 4 x 5 1/2 In. 1800.00
Vase, Flower Form, Gold Iridescent, White Pulled Feathers, Ruffled Edge, 5 In. 2760.00
Vase, Flower Form, Gold, Orange Iridescent, Green Pulled Feather, 14 In. 2990.00
Vase, Flower Form, Pale Amber Iridescent, Feathered Trails, Engraved, c.1899 . . . . 4140.00
Vase, Flower Form, Pink Opalescent, Clear Foot, Favrile, Signed, c.1920, 8 3/4 In. 1232.00
Vase, Flower Form, White, Green Iridescent Pulled Feathers, Signed, 16 In. 6325.00
Vase, Gold Iridescent, 2 Pulled-Out Handles, Flared Lip, Signed, 6 In. 780.00
Vase, Gold Iridescent, 4 Pigtail Prunts, Favrile, 3 1/4 In. 750.00
Vase, Gold Iridescent, Blue, Amethyst, 8 Applied, Pulled Prunts, Signed, 4 In. 540.00
Vase, Gold Iridescent, Bulbous, Raised Zipper Design, Favrile, 4 x 6 In. 1800.00
Vase, Gold Iridescent, Bulbous, Ruffled Stretch Edge, Footed, Favrile, 2 1/2 In. 385.00
Vase, Gold Iridescent, Flared Ruffled Edge, 4-Footed, 2 3/4 In. 315.00
Vase, Gold Iridescent, Green Hearts & Vines, Ruffled Edge, Favrile, 11 In. 1980.00
Vase, Gold Iridescent, Green Pulled Hearts & Vines, Favrile, 2 1/2 x 3 In. 2200.00
Vase, Gold Iridescent, Hooked Design, Square Mouth, Bulbous, Favrile, 9 1/4 In. 460.00
Vase, Gold Iridescent, Pinched Sides, Pulled Prunts, Egg Shape, c.1900, 7 1/2 In. 1000.00
Vase, Gold Iridescent, Platinum Highlights, Gourd Shape, 4 In. 635.00
Vase, Gold Iridescent, Platinum, Purple, Blue Highlights, 4 1/2 In. 805.00
Vase, Gold Iridescent, Raised Zipper, Raised Collar, Bulbous, Favrile, 4 x 6 In. 1800.00
Vase, Gold Iridescent, Red Violet, Pinched, Tricornered, Favrile, Signed, 2 1/4 In. 650.00
Vase, Gold Iridescent, Ribbed Shape, Urn, Pedestal Foot, Favrile, Signed, 8 1/4 In. 1870.00
Vase, Gold Iridescent, Ribbed Sides, Favrile, 3 1/2 In. 420.00
Vase, Gold Iridescent, Ribbed, 2 Applied Threads, Favrile, 11 In. 1380.00
Vase, Gold Iridescent, Ribbed, 5 Pulled & Folded Petals, Button Pontil, 4 1/4 In. . . . . · 920.00
Vase, Gold Iridescent, Squat, Pedestal Base, Raised Collar, 2 1/2 x 4 x 2 In. 400.00
Vase, Gold Iridescent, Translucent Green Shoulder, Oval, Tapered, Signed, 7 In. 1430.00
Vase, Gold Iridescent, Twisted Pigtail Prunts, Flared, Favrile, Signed, 2 In. 1000.00

Vase, Gold, Applied Lily Pads, Ruffled Edge, Favrile, c.1910, 8 In. 225.00
Vase, Gold, Green Highlights, 3 Handles, Hourglass, Favrile, 4 1/2 In. 1265.00
Vase, Gold, Narrow Neck, Bulbous Body, Favrile, 3 1/2 In. 325.00
Vase, Green Leaves, Blue Iridescent Outline, Favrile, Signed, 4 In. 3970.00
Vase, Green Pulled Decoration, Gold Iridescent, Favrile, Cone Shape, 14 1/4 In. 2475.00
Vase, Green, Blue, Gold Iridescent, Bulbous, Shouldered, 4 1/2 x 6 1/4 In. 2860.00
Vase, Green, Gold Pulled Waves, On Shoulder, Pulled Chains, 5 1/2 In. 2240.00
Vase, Iridescent Gold To Blue, Pulled Feather, Bulbous, 8 1/2 In. 5750.00
Vase, Ivory, Pulled Feather, Gold Iridescent, Swollen Shoulder, 6 3/4 In. 1725.00
Vase, Leaves, Green, Blue, Favrile, 1 3/4 x 2 1/2 In. 1900.00
Vase, Lily, Amethyst Opalescent, Ruffled Rim, 7 In. 220.00
Vase, Mirror Blue Iridescent, Favrile, 2 3/4 In. 290.00
Vase, Paperweight, Brown, Green Leaves, White & Brown Flowers, 2 3/4 In. 4600.00
Vase, Paperweight, Flowers, Yellow Opalescent, Stylized Leaves, 4 1/2 In. 2200.00
Vase, Paperweight, Green, Leaves, Vines, Blossoms, Favrile, 7 x 4 In. 4000.00
Vase, Paperweight, Internal Luster, Delphiniums, Green Lily Pad, Vine, 4 3/4 In. 5750.00
Vase, Peacock Blue, Applied Ribs, Pinched Top, Favrile, 5 x 3 1/2 x 1 1/4 In. 1800.00
Vase, Pink Iridescent, Bulbous, Gold, Narrow Neck, Favrile, c.1912, 6 3/4 In. 805.00
Vase, Pink To Fiery Opalescent, Flared Petals, Bands, Pedestal, Favrile, 5 1/2 In. 880.00
Vase, Pulled Double Hook, Yellow, Green, Pink, Orange, Iridescent, 3 1/2 In. 2415.00
Vase, Purple Blue Iridescent, Oval, Elongated Neck, Favrile, 13 1/4 In. 5225.00
Vase, Raised Swirling White On Yellow Ground, Bulbous, 3 1/2 In. 1840.00
Vase, Red Iridescent, Bulbous, Tapered, Extended Neck, Flared, 6 In. 4675.00
Vase, Red Iridescent, Double Gourd, Favrile, c.1915, 6 In. 3465.00
Vase, Red Iridescent, Yellow Interior, Oval, Lobed Shoulder, Favrile, 6 In. 3575.00
Vase, Red, Flared, Tapered, Internal Luster, Signed, c.1906, 10 In. 4890.00
Vase, Silver & Green Pulled Feathers, Baluster Shape, Favrile, 7 1/2 In. 3575.00
Vase, Swirling Green, Rose, White Lines, No. 406, Favrile, 7 1/2 In. 3220.00
Vase, Swirls, Light Blue, Orange, Amber, Yellow, Green, Agate, Oval, 4 1/2 In. 3850.00
Vase, Tel El Amarna, Brown, Iridescent Gold Collar, Herringbone Band, 5 In. 4315.00
Vase, Tel El Amarna, Gold Iridescent, Bulbous Body, Tall Neck, 5 In. 6615.00
Vase, Trumpet, Gold Iridescent, Footed, Favrile, c.1900, 7 In. 785.00
Vase, Trumpet, Gold Iridescent, Ribbed Lower Body, Knop Stem, 7 7/8 In. 805.00
Vase, Yellow Iridescent, 4 Green Leaves, Copper Base, Signed, 13 In. 2530.00
Vase, Yellow Iridescent, Swirling Lines, Stretched Rim, Favrile, 6 1/2 In. 1100.00
Vase, Yellow Swirl, Green, Silver, Blue & Purple Iridescent, Ribbed, 3 In. 1150.00
Wine, Gold Iridescent, Amber & Purple Highlights, 5 1/2 In. 1035.00
Wine, Gold Iridescent, Amber Highlights, Etched Leaves, 5 1/2 In. 489.00
Wine, Gold Iridescent, Amber, Rose Highlights, 6 In. 800.00
Wine, Gold Iridescent, Applied Pods & Vines, Favrile, 3 1/2 x 3 1/4 In. 750.00
Wine, Gold, Yellow Iridescent, Etched Highlights, Favrile, 6 In. 345.00
Wine, Green Shaded To Opalescent, Yellow Applied Stem & Base, 6 In. 400.00
Wine, Pink, Opalescent Ribs, Clear Stem, Disc Foot, 5 3/4 In. 375.00
TIFFANY GOLD, Coffee Set, Gadroon Border, Floral Chased, 18K Gold, c.1897, 3 Piece 13145.00
Dresser Set, Reed Border, 18K Gold, c.1930, 6 Piece 3585.00
Flask, Hip, 18K Gold, 4-Leaf Clover, Edwardian, c.1910 .... 3175.00
TIFFANY POTTERY, Vase, Green Glaze, Blossoms & Vines, Raised Border, 13 1/4 x 7 In. 2000.00
Vase, Green Glaze, Carved Leaves, Bulbous, 4 1/2 x 2 In. 950.00
Vase, Green Leaf, Yellow, Brown Ground, Ruffled Edges, 3 1/4 x 4 1/4 In. 3600.00
Vase, Molded Trees, Leaves, Cream, Green, Black, Handles, c.1910, 6 3/4 In. 8525.00
Vase, White, Carved Tulip Design, Bisque, Signed, LCT, 7 In. 1725.00
TIFFANY SILVER, Basket, Candy, Reticulated, Swing Handle, 4 1/2 x 2 1/2 In. 145.00
Basket, Egg Shape, Pierced Rim, Quatrefoil Band, Upright Handle, 1907-1938, 9 In. 350.00
Basket, Egg Shape, Reticulated, Flared Sides, Rocaille Scroll, 1902-1907, 10 In. 825.00
Basket, Raised Reticulated Rim, Beaded Edge, Oval, Monogram, 2 1/2 x 12 In. 325.00
Berry Spoon, Strawberry Handle, Reeded, Leaf, Monogram, 9 5/8 In. 380.00
Berry Spoon, Strawberry, Monogram, c.1905, 9 5/8 In. ....260.00 to 300.00
Bonbon, Beaded Edge, Handle Monogram, c.1900, 3 x 4 x 1 1/2 In., 12 Piece 750.00
Bowl, Art Deco, Tapered, Engraved, Scrolled, Sterling, 1930, 9 1/2 x 9 1/2 In. 495.00
Bowl, Centerpiece, 4 Candle Sockets, Scrolled Legs, Impressed, 4 x 8 3/4 In. 865.00
Bowl, Chased Flower Garlands, Geometric Band, Circular Base, 5 1/4 In. 440.00
Bowl, Clover Border, Gothic Monogram, 2 1/2 x 9 In. 495.00
Bowl, Floral, Sterling, Gilt Brass Frog, c.1938, 12 In. 1530.00

Bowl, Footed, Monogram, Sterling, Inscribed 1973, 3 1/2 In. 160.00
Bowl, Modernist, Boat Shape, Monogram, Flared Foot, 1947-1956, 16 1/4 In. 940.00
Bowl, Oval, Pieced Edge, Monogram, 1 3/4 x 10 1/2 x 6 3/4 In. 180.00
Bowl, Repousse, Chased Flowers, Parcel Gilt, Removable Pedestal, c.1891, 6 In. 5020.00
Bowl, Scalloped Rim, Beaded Border, Monogram, 2 x 10 In. 300.00
Bowl, Scalloped, Pierced Flower, Rolled Rim, Early 20th Century, 2 3/4 x 10 In. 460.00
Bowl, Serving, Sections, Egg Shape, Stepped Rim, Monogram, 1907-1938, 13 In. 700.00
Bowl, Spiral Gadrooning, Shell & Scroll Rim, Sterling, 8 1/2 x 3 1/2 In. 2185.00
Bowl, Trefoil Shape, 3 Ball Feet, Sterling, 7 In. 165.00
Bowl, Trophy, Best Irish Setter, Morris & Essex Dog Show, 1936, 4 1/2 x 8 In. 750.00
Bowl, Vegetable, Shaped Rim, Monogram, 1907-1938, 9 3/8 In. 410.00
Bread Tray, Reticulated, Oval, Pierced Rim, 1902-1907, 11 1/8 In. 530.00
Butter Spreader, Chrysanthemum, Sterling, 6 Piece 630.00
Cake Basket, Oval, Pedestal, Scalloped Border, Embossed, Swing Handle, 11 In. 2868.00
Cake Plate, Round, Incised Border, Swags, 1947, 10 5/8 In. 355.00
Cake Stand, Square, Canted Corners, Impressed, 10 1/4 In. 800.00
Cigarette Box, Sterling, c.1907, 6 1/2 In. 500.00
Cocktail Tray, Pierced Gallery Rim, Black Lacquer Wood Base, c.1938, 13 3/4 In. 410.00
Coffee Set, Flowers, Leaves, 7-In. Pot, 3 Piece 1575.00
Coffee Set, Neoclassical Style, Sterling, c.1907, 3 Piece 1725.00
Coffee Set, Putti, Cherubs, Garlands Over Flower Baskets, Repousse, 3 Piece 2970.00
Coffeepot, Chrysanthemum, 8 In. 3025.00
Coffeepot, Hammered Dandelions, Tapered Cylinder, Hinged Lid, c.1891, 7 In. 19120.00
Cold Meat Fork, Ailanthus, Sterling 495.00
Compote, Blackberry, 10 In., Pair 2750.00
Compote, Openwork Border, Spades, Teardrops, Dots, Bars, 3 x 7 1/2 In. 275.00
Compote, Scrolling Vine Rim, Beaded Trumpet Foot, Oval, c.1891, 7 1/2 In. 380.00
Compote, Upswept Rim, Baluster Pedestal, Early 20th Century, 4 1/2 x 9 In. 375.00
Creamer, 3-Footed, Scroll Handle, Wavy Top, Gold Wash, c.1900, 4 3/4 In. 180.00
Crumber, Palm Pattern, Monogram, 1871-1891, 13 1/4 In. 325.00
Cup, Urn Shape, Molded Round Foot, Leaf Scroll Handles, c.1956, Pair 3345.00
Demitasse Set, Persian Style Coffeepot, Monogram, 1907-1938, 4 Piece 1530.00
Dish, Arts & Crafts Style, Budding Leaf Handles, Melon Shape, 1907-1938, 10 In. 235.00
Dish, Entree, Cover, Rectangular, Repousse Flowers, 4 1/2 x 8 1/2 In., Pair 6900.00
Dish, Heart Shaped Ivy Leaf, Handle, Arts & Crafts Style, 1956-1965, 6 In. 380.00
Dresser Set, Enamel, Mint Green, Glass, Marked, 5 Piece 1265.00
Dresser Tray, Reticulated Rim, Husks, Quatrefoil Flowers, Oval, c.1938, 8 1/2 In. 235.00
Fish Slice, Wave Edge, Monogram, 1884, 12 In. 345.00
Fork, Serving, Wave Edge, Monogram, 1884, 9 1/2 In. 400.00
Frame, Sterling, c.1947, 14 x 11 In. 1530.00
Grape Shears, Stylized Grapevine Handles, 1938-1947, 6 5/8 In. 206.00
Gravy Ladle, English King, Sterling 398.00
Gravy Spoon, Chrysanthemum, Back Button, 12 1/4 In. 1155.00
Jug, Cover, Hinged, Squat, Ebony Handle, Undertray, Sterling, 5 x 4 7/8 In. 695.00
Kettle, Stand, Hot Water, Inverted Pear Shape, Sterling, c.1865, 13 In. 1410.00
Ladle, Chrysanthemum, Sterling, Vermeil Bowl, 12 In. 1580.00
Ladle, English King Pattern, Shell Form, 7 1/2 In. 190.00
Ladle, Gramercy Sterling, c.1921, 7 In. 90.00
Ladle, Palm Pattern, Engraved Eagle & Corona Crest, New York, 7 In. 345.00
Ladle, Persian, Oval, Spiral Reeded Bowl, Sterling, 1891, 11 In. 940.00
Mug, Openwork Base, Sterling, Vermeil Interior, Baby's, 1870s, 4 In. 480.00
Mug, Presentation, Cherubs Picking Grapes, Handle, 3 7/8 x 3 x 5 In. 1400.00
Mug, Presentation, Engraved Inscription, 3 Handles, 7 In. 1650.00
Mustard Spoon, Colonial, Sterling 115.00
Nut Dish, Heart Shape, Leaf Handles, 3 Ball Feet, 3 1/4 In., 4 Piece 250.00
Pan, Flambe, Dome Cover, Initials, 1900s, 5 1/2 x 9 x 14 3/4 In. 345.00
Pitcher, Baluster Shape, Scroll Handle, Angled Spout, Marked, c.1953, 11 3/4 In. 4780.00
Pitcher, Lilies, Cattail Handle, Sterling, Young & Ellis, 10 1/2 x 8 x 6 In. 5600.00
Pitcher, Repousse, Flowering Vines, Baluster Shape, c.1854, 11 1/2 In. 2820.00
Place Card Holder, Pineapple Shape, Round Base, 5 1/4 In. 1050.00
Plate, Renaissance Style, Footed, Octagonal, Panels, Sterling, 1900s, 1 1/4 x 7 1/2 In. . . . 440.00
Porringer, Single Pierced Handle, Engraved Rim, Husk Band, c.1938, 7 1/4 In. 410.00
Punch Bowl, Oval, Applied Band, Low Foot, Monogram, Sterling, 14 1/8 In. 1998.00

Relish, Melon Shape, Stylized Leaf Cluster Handles, Ball Feet, Sterling, 10 In.	206.00
Salad Servers, Poppy Pattern, Sterling, Late 19th Century, 10 5/8 In.	1115.00
Salt, Chased Flowers, 3 Cabriole Legs, c.1875, 1 1/2 x 2 1/3 In.	230.00
Salver, Round, Plain Applied Rim, Sterling, 1947-1956, 13 In.	499.00
Salver, Strapwork Griffin Band, Beaded Rim, 4-Footed, 1854-1870, 12 In.	1175.00
Sauceboat, Silver Soldered, Monogram, 2 Pt., 10 1/2 In.	450.00
Serving Dish, Sterling, Gold Chased, Square, 9 1/2 In.	1765.00
Serving Fork, Olympian, Sterling	175.00
Serving Spoon, Grapevine, Sterling, c.1870, 8 1/2 x 2 In.	105.00
Serving Spoon, Olympian, Gilt Bowl, Sterling	1265.00
Soup Ladle, Saratoga, Sterling	950.00
Spoon, Demitasse, Wave Edge, Monogram, 4 3/4 In., 12 Piece	215.00
Spoon, Strawberry, Parcel Gilt, 20th Century, 9 1/2 In.	561.00
Sugar, Cover, Egg Shape, Angular Handles, Monogram, 1907-1938, 7 1/2 In.	325.00
Sugar & Creamer, Acanthus Leaf, Classical Head, Gold Chased Interior, c.1873	978.00
Sugar & Creamer, Molded Egg Shape, Reeded Waistbands, Early 1900s, 3 3/4 In.	440.00
Sugar Basket, Cobalt Blue Glass Liner, Swivel Handle, Monogram, 5 1/2 In.	175.00
Sugar Spoon, Audubon, Sterling	200.00
Tablespoon, Chrysanthemum, Monogram, c.1880, 4 Piece	489.00
Tazza, Egg Shape Plate, Scalloped Rim, 1907-1938, 4 1/2 x 11 3/4 In., Pair	2940.00
Tazza, Floral Repousse Border, Reticulated Edge, Marked, 3 1/2 x 7 In., Pair	1000.00
Tazza, Floral Repousse, Footed, 5 1/2 x 9 In.	935.00
Tea & Coffee Set, Kettle-On-Stand, Baluster Finial, c.1918, 7 Piece	5975.00
Tea & Coffee Set, Repousse, Vine, Acanthus Handles, Gold Chased, 5 Piece	3525.00
Tea Set, Neoclassical, Egg Shape Bodies, c.1860, 9 1/2 In., 3 Piece	2760.00
Tea Strainer, Laurel Garland Rim, Monogram, 1907, 2 1/2 x 5 In.	270.00
Teapot, Dome Lid, Egg Shape, Gooseneck Spout, Ivory Handle, c.1940, 8 In.	750.00
Tomato Server, Windham, Sterling	295.00
Toothpick Holder, Basket Form, Rope, Tassel, Marked, Sterling, 7 3/4 In.	605.00
Tray, Asparagus, Oblong, Beaded Edge, Footed, Sterling, 1902, 12 3/4 In.	2350.00
Tray, Engraved Heron On Branch Over Lily Pad, Indented Corners, 10 3/4 In.	2270.00
Tray, Oval, Beaded Border, Monogram, 14 x 10 In.	330.00
Tray, Oval, Gadroon, Shell Borders, Sterling, 20 x 15 In.	1100.00
Tray, Pierced Gallery Border, Open Rocaille Feet, Edward Moore, c.1870, 20 In.	6573.00
Tray, Presentation, Genesee Valley Cup, New York, 1907-1938, 13 In.	400.00
Tray, Scroll & Relief Border, Monogram, Footed, 10 5/8 In.	315.00
Tray, Threaded Edge, Oval, Monogram, 11 3/4 x 6 1/2 In.	250.00
Tumbler Set, Nesting, Stamped, 4 Piece	375.00
Tureen, Domed Cover, Flower & Shell Finial, Bent Twig Handles, 8 x 10 3/4 In.	400.00
Vase, Fluted Hammered Body, Flared Rim, Pedestal Foot, Monogram, 9 In.	3585.00
Vase, Tapered, Flared, Enameled Grapevine, Sterling, 7 1/2 x 2 1/2 In.	2900.00
Vase, Trumpet, Fluted, Flared, Hammered, 1907-1938, 9 1/8 In.	2000.00
Vase, Trumpet, Single Band, Monogram, Gold Wash, 1907-1938, 7 In., Pair	440.00

TIFFIN Glass Company of Tiffin, Ohio, was a subsidiary of the United
States Glass Co. of Pittsburgh, Pennsylvania, in 1892. The U.S. Glass
Co. went bankrupt in 1963, and the Tiffin plant employees purchased
the building and the inventory. They continued running it from 1963 to
1966, when it was sold to Continental Can Company. In 1969, it was
sold to Interpace, and in 1980, it was closed. The black satin glass,
made from 1923 to 1926, and the stemware of the last twenty years are
the best-known products.

Amberina, Compote, Frosted, 1920s, 5 1/8 x 7 In.	75.00
Amberina, Sugar & Creamer, Handles, 1920s, 3 3/8 In.	75.00
Amberina, Vase, Flower Arranger, 1920s	100.00
Apollo-Diana, Plate, Gold Trim, 6 1/4 In.	8.00
Apollo-Diana, Sherbet, Gold Rim, 4 3/4 In.	25.00
Byzantine, Cocktail, 5 1/2 x 3 In.	35.00
Byzantine, Goblet, 8 1/2 x 3 1/2 In.	25.00
Byzantine, Sherbet, 5 1/2 x 4 In.	30.00
Cadena, Goblet, Amber, Clear Stem & Base, 7 1/2 In.	50.00
Canterbury, Nappy, Chartreuse, Handle, 6 1/4 In.	20.00
Cherokee Rose, Champagne, 5 1/2 Oz., 4 1/4 In.	20.00

Cherokee Rose, Vase, Bud, 6 In. .... 25.00 to 45.00
Dolores, Compote, Beaded Stem, 6 1/2 x 6 1/4 In. 40.00
Drape & Pointed Knob, Candlestick, 2-Light, 6 x 7 In. 30.00
Draped Nude, Cordial, Frosted 180.00
Elinor, Grapefruit, Green 75.00
Empress Modern, Basket, Blue Pulled Wings, 17 In. 150.00
Empress Modern, Basket, Blue To Pink Pulled Wings, 15 In. 150.00
Figurine, Pheasant, Paperweight Base, 6 1/8 x 12 3/4 In. 100.00
Flanders, Champagne, 6 3/16 x 4 In. 18.00
Flanders, Nut Dish, Pink, Footed, 1 7/8 In. 115.00
Flanders, Pitcher, 9 1/2 In. 260.00
Flanders, Tumbler, Iced Tea, Pink, Footed, 12 Oz., 5 3/4 In. 100.00
Flanders, Tumbler, Seltzer, Pink, Footed, 5 Oz., 3 7/8 In. 70.00
Fontaine, Wine, 2 1/2 Oz., 4 7/8 In. 80.00
Franciscan Ondine, Champagne 60.00
Franciscan Ondine, Goblet 100.00
Franciscan Ondine, Tumbler, Iced Tea 100.00
Franciscan Ondine, Wine 100.00
Fuchsia, Candlestick, 2-Light 70.00
Fuchsia, Champagne, 5 1/2 Oz., 5 3/8 In. 30.00
Fuchsia, Cocktail, 3 Oz., 4 1/4 In. 25.00
Fuchsia, Plate, Salad, 8 In. 20.00
Fuchsia, Relish, 3 Sections, 9 1/4 In. 25.00
Fuchsia, Vase, Bud, 8 In. 40.00
June Night, Dish, Sundae, 5 1/2 Oz., 4 1/2 In. 18.00
June Night, Sherbet, 5 1/2 Oz., 6 In. 20.00
King's Crown, Cake Plate, Amber 30.00
King's Crown, Candleholder, Amber, 3 In., Pair 25.00
King's Crown, Compote, 5 1/2 x 5 In. 20.00
King's Crown, Compote, Amber 30.00
King's Crown, Compote, Platinum Rim 25.00
King's Crown, Compote, Ruby Flashed, 5 1/4 In. 15.00
King's Crown, Goblet, Cranberry Flashed, 5 1/2 In. 18.00
King's Crown, Goblet, Gold Stain, 9 Oz. 13.00
King's Crown, Goblet, Ruby Stain, Gold Trim, 9 Oz. 8.00
King's Crown, Platter, Amber, Round, 13 In. 22.00
King's Crown, Sugar & Creamer, Green 15.00
King's Crown, Wine, 4 Oz. 13.00
Mandarin, Creamer, Red, 3 1/8 x 6 In. 25.00
Mandarin, Sugar, Handles, Red, 3 1/8 x 7 1/2 In. 25.00
Modern, Bowl, Handles, 4 x 11 1/2 In. 135.00
Modern, Vase, Copen Blue, Cylindrical, 12 x 4 In. 140.00
Old Gold, Creamer, Amber, 3 1/8 x 6 In. 25.00
Poppy, Vase, Black Amethyst, Satin, 1920s, 6 1/2 x 5 In. 35.00
Poppy, Vase, Satin, Oval, 8 3/4 x 8 1/4 In. 95.00
Poppy, Vase, Sky Blue, Round, 5 In. 95.00
Rambler Rose, Cordial, Gold Trim, 2 Oz. 45.00
Rambler Rose, Dish, Mayonnaise, Ladle, Footed, Gold Trim, 3 1/4 x 6 1/4 In. 95.00
Rambler Rose, Relish, 6 Sections, 6 1/2 In. 40.00
Rose Marie, Champagne, 6 Oz., 5 7/8 In. 15.00
Rose Marie, Cocktail, 3 Oz., 4 3/4 In. 18.00
Rose Marie, Goblet, Low Foot, 10 Oz. 18.00
Swedish Optic, Vase, Copen Blue, Footed, 9 1/4 x 5 1/4 In. 85.00
Thistle, Cordial, 4 3/4 In. 70.00
Thistle, Sherbet, 3 5/8 In. 10.00
Twilight, Basket, 3 x 5 In. 140.00
Twilight, Bowl, Crimped, 4 1/4 x 9 1/2 In. 90.00
Twilight, Bowl, Square, 4 Scrolled Feet, 4 x 10 In. 290.00
Twilight, Vase, 4 3/4 x 5 3/4 In. 70.00
Twilight, Vase, 7 x 5 1/2 In. 240.00
Twilight, Vase, Contour, 7 7/8 x 8 1/2 In. 130.00
Twilight, Vase, Orchid Pink, Scroll Feet, 9 In. 695.00
Wisteria, Vase, 4 Scroll Feet, 7 5/8 x 4 3/16 In. 145.00

TILES have been used in most countries of the world as a sturdy building material for floors, roofs, fireplace surrounds, and surface toppings. Many of the American tiles are listed in this book under the factory name.

Birds Of Tintern Alley, Ivory, Blue Ground, Diagonal, Moravian, 5 1/2 In.	115.00
Boy, Fishing, Dog, Silhouette, Mustard Ground, Green Foreground, Franklin Pottery, 9 In.	980.00
Castles, Mountains, Brown, Ivory, Matte Glaze, Stamped, California Art Tile, 6 In.	145.00
City Of God, Ivory, Blue Glossy Glaze, Moravian, 5 1/2 In.	520.00
Daffodils, Yellow, Blue Ground, Raised Outline, Franklin, Arts & Crafts Frame, 9 In.	345.00
Figures, Moravian Mercer, 6 x 6 In., 4 Piece	29.00
Fish, Coral, Embossed, Sheer Celadon Glaze, Raised S.O.F. Votm E.T.M., 6 In.	345.00
Flowers, Bowl, Black Ground, Raised Outline, Stamped, Square, Claycraft, 7 3/4 In.	690.00
Flowers, Pink, Green Stems, Stylized, Arts & Crafts, 6 In.	316.00
Fox, Grapevines, Carved, Molded, Semimatte Glaze, Faience, Terra-Cotta Co., 14 In.	920.00
Fruit, Multicolored, Blue Ground, Round, California Faience, 5 1/2 In.	295.00
Gentleman & Lady, Elegantly Dressed, Art Pottery, 3 Tile Panels, 6 x 18 In., Pair	259.00
Girl, Geese, Village In Distance, Amber, Blue Green Glaze, Moravian, 6 In.	115.00
Girl, Geese, Village In Distance, Ivory, Blue Ground, Red Clay, Moravian, 6 In.	175.00
Greek Goddesses, Around Flower Urn, Green Glaze, Stoneware, 10 1/4 x 8 1/4 In.	35.00
Indian Brave, On Horse, Looking Over Canyon, Multicolored, Taylor, 12 x 18 In., 6 Piece	2185.00
Knights Dueling, On Horseback, Village, Matte, California Art Tile, 5 3/4 x 19 1/2 In.	1380.00
Landscape, Trees, Hills, Green, Brown, Square, Arts & Crafts Oak Frame, 6 In.	3055.00
Lantern Lighter, Holding Lamps, Black Silhouette, Mustard, Franklin Pottery, 9 In.	690.00
Lion, Profile, White Matte Glaze, Celadon Matte Ground, American, Frame, 4 x 9 In.	865.00
Lisbon Harbor, Ships, Castle, Blue, Gold, Signed, L.R. R.S., 22 x 33 In., 2 Piece	250.00
Maiden, Long Hair, Red, Poppies, Yellow, Green Ground, Outline, 10 x 3 3/4 In., Pair	2070.00
Marble Veneer, Green, Red, Acanthus Scrolls, Black, Ivory Border, 12 x 12 x 1 1/2 In.	95.00
Mission Courtyard, Fountain, Trees, Matte Glaze, Claycraft, Frame, 8 1/2 x 16 1/2 In.	1840.00
Moose, Geese, Purple Silhouette, Yellow Crystalline, Franklin Pottery, 13 1/2 x 9 In.	2530.00
Muses, Dancing, Art Pottery, Frame, 6 x 18 In., Pair	865.00
Organic Design, Stylized, Green, Yellow, Arts & Crafts, 6 In.	145.00
Panel, Fall Landscape, Trees, Water, Squeezebag Decoration, 18 x 24 In., 12 Piece	5175.00
Parthenia, Greek Goddess, Olive Green Glossy Glaze, Isaac Broome, Frame, 13 x 10 In.	1150.00
Peacock, Stylized, Matte Glaze, Hotel Dacea, Romania, 1901, 11 1/2 x 19 1/2 In.	173.00
Peacock Pair, Floral Border, Blue Engobe, Stamped Batchelder, 5 3/4 In.	230.00
Pine Tree, River, Village, Brown Engobe, California Art Tile, Frame, 15 1/2 x 3 3/4 In.	920.00
Rooster, Blue Green Semimatte Ground, Porcelain, Robineau, Carved AR 584, 6 1/2 In.	6325.00
Roses, Yellow, Green Leaves, Stylized, Arts & Crafts, 6 In.	375.00
Round, Colorful Fruit, Blue Ground, California Faience, 5 1/2 In.	403.00
Round, Colorful Fruit, Green Matte Ground, California Faience, 5 1/2 In.	1380.00
Sailboat, Blue Green Waves, Blue Sky, White Clouds, Raised Outline, Flint, 6 In., Pair	750.00
Sailing Ship, Matte, Multicolored Glaze, Stamped, Franklin Pottery, 9 In.	575.00
She Loves Me, She Loves Me Not, Frame, Arts & Crafts, Signed, M. Wintermote, 10 In.	520.00
Tree, Village, Blue Engobe, Batchelder Style, Square, 6 In.	115.00
Windmill, Birds, Embossed, Red Glossy Glaze, Square, England, 6 In.	60.00
Zodiac, Cancer Crab, Embossed, Terra-Cotta, Mustard Matte Glaze, Mueller, 7 1/2 In.	430.00

TINWARE containers for household use have been made in America since the seventeenth century. The first tin utensils were brought from Europe, but by 1798, tin plate was imported and local tinsmiths made the wares. Painted tin is called *tole* and is listed separately. Some tin kitchen items may be found listed under Kitchen. The lithographed tin containers used to hold food and tobacco are listed in the Advertising category under Tin.

Apple Container, Chromolithograph, Wood Finial, Shenandoah Valley, 4 1/2 In.	275.00
Bathtub, White Paint, Child's, 17 x 29 x 24 In.	375.00
Bed Warmer, Pierced, Wood Handle, 21 In.	28.00
Candleholder, Painted, Glass Front, Peaked Roof, Handle, 3 3/4 x 2 1/4 x 5 1/2 In.	385.00
Canteen, Union, Blue Wool, Cork Stopper, Linen Strap, Pewter Spout, c.1858, 9 In.	173.00
Coffeepot, Applied Handle, Straight Spout, Ram Horn Finial, 14 In.	169.00
Coffeepot, Flared Base, Applied Strap Handle, Pennsylvania, 9 1/2 In.	220.00
Coffeepot, Formed Handled, Spout, Raised Decorative Bands, Finial, Penn., 10 1/2 In.	525.00
Coffeepot, Raised Neck Rings, 9 1/4 In.	115.00

Cream Can, Cover, Applied Handles, Blue Paint, Early 1800s, 1 Qt., 11 x 5 1/4 In. 125.00
Figure, Man, Dancing, Silhouette, Cutout, Articulated Joints, Painted, 11 1/4 In. 230.00
Foot Warmer, Heart Decoration, Iron Carry Handle, Wooden, 11 x 7 In. 225.00
Foot Warmer, Pierced, Turned Maple Frame, 6 x 9 x 8 In. 69.00
Foot Warmer, Punched, Wooden Frame, Bail Handle, 8 3/4 In. 105.00
Humidor, Brass Lid & Trim, Leather Base, Rumidor, New York, 4 1/2 x 5 1/4 In. 38.00
Mold, Candle, 8 Tube, Arched Base 120.00
Mold, Candle, 8 Tube, Footed, Handle, 12 In. 578.00
Mold, Candle, 8 Tube, Rolled Edge Top, Base, Applied C-Scroll Handle, 10 3/4 In. 30.00
Mold, Candle, 8 Tube, Round, 2 Handles 440.00
Mold, Candle, 12 Tube, 10 In. 58.00
Mold, Candle, 12 Tube, 19th Century, 11 In. 80.00
Mold, Candle, 12 Tube, Loop Handle, 11 x 8 1/4 In. 60.00
Mold, Candle, 12 Tube, Rectangular Base, Loop Carry Handle, 9 3/4 In. 115.00
Mold, Candle, 12 Tube, Rolled Edge Base, Applied Handle, Wire Reinforced Top, 11 In. . 35.00
Mold, Candle, 12 Tube, Round, Crimped Base & Top 340.00
Mold, Candle, 24 Tube, Cut Nail Construction, Dovetail Shelf, 18 x 22 1/2 x 7 In. 525.00
Mold, Candle, 36 Tube, Wood Frame 2310.00
Mold, Candle, 36 Tube, Wood Frame, Painted Red, Bootjack Ends, 13 x 11 x 12 In. 765.00
Sconce, Candle, Floral Tole Decoration, Wire Reinforced Sides, Hanging Loop, 10 1/2 In. 198.00
Squirrel Cage, Cream Paint, Peaked Roof, Glass, Exercise Wheel, 20 x 11 x 17 In. 375.00
Squirrel Cage, Exercise Wheel, Wood, House Shape, Green Paint, 16 x 12 x 30 In. 385.00
Stencil, Name, Jacob Baumgardner, 6 1/4 x 19 1/4 In. 80.00
Top Hat, Galvanized, Old Gray Surface, 8 1/2 x 11 1/8 In. 230.00
Torch, Oil, 8 Long Side Spouts, Cover, Handle, Handmade, 11 In. 495.00
Tub, Grain Painted, 24 In. 176.00

TOBACCO CUTTERS may be listed in either the Advertising or Store categories.

TOBACCO JAR collectors search for those made in odd shapes and colors. Because tobacco needs special conditions of humidity and air, it has been stored in special containers since the eighteenth century.

Arab Man, 2-Tone Blue, Baghdad, 19th Century 230.00
Baby On Top Hat, Humidor, Bernhard Block, 7 1/2 In. 310.00
Bearded Man, Humidor, 6 In. 75.00
Bison Hoof, Cover, Silver Lidded Rim, Acorn Finial, 8 1/2 x 5 x 7 In. 690.00
Black Man Holding White Baby, Terra-Cotta, Marked, 9 1/2 In. 4115.00
Black Man In Barrel, Terra-Cotta, Czechoslovakia, Marked, 7 1/4 In. 605.00
Boy, Sitting On Dog, Terra-Cotta, Marked, 10 x 12 1/2 In. 1150.00
Boy, Sitting On Nut, Terra-Cotta, Marked, 9 In. 350.00
Cat, Brown & White, Green Glass Eyes, Terra-Cotta, Marked, 10 1/4 In. 920.00
Chinaman, Composition, Glass Eyes, Real Hair, Fly On Head, Humidor, c.1890, 7 In. ... 330.00
Composite, Bearded Man, Nightcap, Barrel, Pipe, Humidor, Germany, 6 In. 50.00
Cover, Alpine Man, Porcelain, Schierholz, 8 1/2 In. 290.00
Dog, Begging, Terra-Cotta, Marked, 6 In. 365.00
Dog & Cat, Terra-Cotta, 7 In. 520.00
Driver, Terra-Cotta, 5 1/2 In. 690.00
Duke Of Wellington, Heavy Pottery, Humidor, 7 1/2 In. 169.00
Elephants, Tigers, Birds, Rabbit, Deer, Carved, Skirt, Ivory, India, 7 1/2 x 4 3/4 x 4 In. .. 800.00
Fox Hunt & Dogs Scenes, White On Sage Green, Wedgwood, 4 1/2 x 4 1/4 In. 78.00
Girl, In Bonnet, Tobacco Bag, Humidor, 4 1/2 In. 115.00
Girl, In Hat, Seated, Terra-Cotta, 6 1/2 In. 255.00
Globe, Yellow, Tin Lid, Sample 195.00
Gypsy Woman, Terra-Cotta, Marked, 9 In. 635.00
Hunter, Terra-Cotta, Marked, Czechoslovakia, 11 3/4 In. 750.00
Indian Head, Figural, Bisque, 5 x 3 3/4 In. 145.00
Man, Baseball Cap, Smoking Cigar, Humidor, 5 In. 50.00
Man, Fly On Nose, Painted, Continental, 6 In. 138.00
Man, On Barrel, Mug, Monkey, 2 Open Barrels, Humidor, Austria, 10 In. 205.00
Man, Sitting On Tree Stump, Dog, Terra-Cotta, 10 1/4 In. 690.00
Man, Sitting On Tree Stump, Terra-Cotta, 11 1/2 In. 605.00
Man, With Large Hat, Terra-Cotta, Marked, 11 1/2 In. 949.00
Monk, Humidor, 9 1/4 In. 85.00
Monk, Humidor, Bernard Bloch, 10 In. 340.00

Monk, Standing Next To Barrel, Terra-Cotta, 7 In. 605.00
Ottoman Woman, Humidor, 6 In. 140.00
Painted, Flowers, Gold Lettering, Cover, Pipe Finial, Ironstone, 6 x 5 x 3 In. 90.00
Skull, Humidor, Carlsbad Austria Victoria, 4 3/4 In. 200.00
Woman, With Flowers, Art Nouveau, Porcelain, Austria, 8 1/4 In. 170.00

TOBY JUG is the name of a very special form of pitcher. It is shaped like
the full figure of a man or woman. A pitcher that shows just the top half
of a person is not correctly called a toby. More examples of toby jugs
can be found under Royal Doulton and other factory names.

Lady Snuff Taker, Holding Snuffbox, Staffordshire, 10 x 4 3/4 In. 300.00
Man, Brown Coat, Yellow Tricorner Hat, Breeches, Blue Stockings, 9 1/2 In. 460.00
Man, Holding Jug & Cup, Staffordshire, 5 1/4 x 4 1/4 x 5 In. 110.00
Man, Holding Jug & Pipe, Staffordshire, 9 1/4 x 4 1/4 x 4 1/2 In. 190.00
Man, On Barrel, Home Brewed Ale, Adams Rose, Staffordshire, 11 3/8 In. 345.00
Man, With Snuff, Blue Jacket, Green Pants, Staffordshire, 8 In. 290.00
Mr. Pickwick, Seated On Tree, Glass In Hand, Monocle, Staffordshire, 8 1/2 x 4 x 5 In. ... 495.00
Pearlware, Pratt Type, Underglaze, Brown, Orange, Yellow, Black, c.1800, 9 3/4 In. 705.00
Peary, Artic Coat, Hat, 5 In. 90.00
Roger Giles, Squatting Man In Semiformal Attire, Staffordshire, 10 1/2 x 5 In. 230.00
Snuff Taker, Staffordshire, Mid 19th Century, 9 1/2 In. 105.00
Squire, Holding Mug & Pipe, Staffordshire, 11 x 6 x 6 In. 360.00

TOLE is painted tin. It is sometimes called *japanned ware*, *pontypool*,
or *toleware*. Most nineteenth-century tole is painted with an orange-
red or black background and multicolored decorations. Many recent
versions of toleware are made and sold. Related items may be listed in
the Tinware category.

Bookends, Cutout Silhouettes, Fruit Baskets, Hand Painted 220.00
Bowl, Sugar, Cover, Red, Flower Band, Leaves, Swags, 3 1/2 In. 395.00
Box, Copper Luster, Fruit, Leaves, Feather, Swag, Ring Top, 3 1/2 x 6 1/2 x 3 In. 1035.00
Box, Document, Flowers, Red, Green, Yellow, White, Ring Handle, 5 1/2 x 9 x 4 1/2 In. ... 798.00
Box, Turnip Decoration, Hand Painted, Round, Peter Hunt, 6 1/2 In. 69.00
Bread Tray, Flowers, Flared, Scalloped Rim, 11 1/4 In. 60.00
Cachepot, French Provincial, Embossed, Ocher Ground, Branches, 13 x 18 1/2 In., Pair .. 259.00
Canister, Slant Lid, Fruit & Flowers, Red-Orange Ground, 5 1/2 In. 110.00
Coffeepot, Dome Lid, Hinged, 2-Sided, Gooseneck, C-Scroll Handle, Flowers, 10 1/2 In. . 4675.00
Coffeepot, Dome Lid, Medallions, Fillips, Tapered Cylinder, Applied Handle, 7 3/4 In. 1550.00
Coffeepot, Lid, Gooseneck, Black Ground, Sunburst Red, Yellow Leaf, 11 In. .....*Illus* 1430.00
Coffeepot, Lid, Gooseneck, Red Ground, Yellow Designs, Flowers, Leaves, 11 In. ..*Illus* 1925.00
Dipper, Black Ground, Red, Mustard Decoration, Tapered Handle, 3 1/2 x 8 In. 480.00
Planter, Cylindrical Shape, Oriental Manner Paint, Cabriole Legs, 19 1/2 x 16 1/2 In. 315.00
Plaque, Washington, Stamped, Gilt, Commemoration, Initialed LW, 3 7/8 x 5 3/4 In. 115.00
Salver, Painted, Swing Handled, Molded Edge, Hoho Bird, Leaves, Gilt Metal, 9 5/8 In. .. 150.00
Spice Box, Fruit & Flowers, 6 Canisters, Button Finial, Multicolored, 3 x 9 1/4 x 6 1/4 In. . 415.00
Storage Bin, Red Paint, Italy, Late 1800s, 19 1/2 In. 856.00
Sugar, Cover, Fruit, Leaves, Red, Yellow, Green, Japanned Ground, Scroll Handle, 4 In. ... 1150.00

Tole, Coffeepot, Lid, Gooseneck,
Black Ground, Sunburst Red,
Yellow Leaf, 11 In.

Tole, Coffeepot, Lid, Gooseneck,
Red Ground, Yellow Designs,
Flowers, Leaves, 11 In.

Tole, Tray, Eagle, Cornucopias,
Stenciled, Metal, Cutout Handles,
1800s, 22 x 16 In.

Sugar, Cover, Red & Yellow Berries, Leaves, Gray Band, Japanned Ground, Handle, 4 In. 860.00
Sugar, Cover, Red Ground, Fruit & Flowers, 3 1/2 In. 220.00
Tea Chest, Rotating Cylinder, Oriental Figures, Tea Name Inscriptions, 14 1/2 x 14 In. 175.00
Teapot, Brown Japanned Ground, Red, Green Flowers, 10 1/2 In. 115.00
Teapot, Hinged Lid, Side Spout, Strap Type Handle, 6 1/2 In. 50.00
Teapot, Rose Decoration, Oval, Hinged Lid, Angled Spout, Strap Handle, 6 x 9 1/2 In. 1840.00
Tin, Cinnamon Spice, Black Ground, Palm Trees & Exotic Birds, 1880s, 10 x 9 x 8 In. 345.00
Tinder Box, Circular, Candleholder, Looped Finger Hole, 3 1/2 x 4 1/2 In. 316.00
Tray, Apple Decoration, 4 Lobes, 12 1/2 x 2 1/2 In. 300.00
Tray, Apple, Rectangular, Slope Ends, Japanned, Yellow Stripe, Berries, Leaves, 8 x 12 In. 495.00
Tray, Apple, Yellow Stripes, White Border, Red Berries, Green Leaves, 7 3/4 x 13 x 3 In. . 1495.00
Tray, Bird, Flower Border, Fruit Basket, Peaches, Stenciled, Rectangular, 18 x 24 In. 190.00
Tray, Central Medallion, Basket Of Fruit, Demilune, Flowers, 27 In. 360.00
Tray, Chippendale, Bird, Floral Spray, Mother-Of-Pearl Accents, Flared Rim, 24 In. 125.00
Tray, Eagle, Cornucopias, Stenciled, Metal, Cutout Handles, 1800s, 22 x 16 In. ...... *Illus* 743.00
Tray, Flowers, Gilt Scroll Borders, Rectangular, Early 1800s, 26 x 20 In. 115.00
Tray, Landscape, Woman Tending Goats, Cows, Border Leaves, c.1825, 16 x 21 3/4 In. .. 403.00
Tray, Octagonal, Red, Gold Stenciled Decoration, Mass., c.1975, 26 1/4 In. 127.00
Tray, Oval, Sienna Ground, Transfer Decorated, Military Portraits, France, c.1850, 24 In. . 345.00
Tray, Pheasant, Leaves, Pagoda, Floral, Bird Corners, Black & Gold Stencil, 22 In. 70.00
Tray, Red, Yellow, Blue, Green, Peter Hunt, 1949, 18 In. ....300.00 to 400.00

TOM MIX was born in 1880 and died in 1940. He was the hero of over
100 silent movies from 1910 to 1929, and 25 sound films from 1929
to 1935. There was a Ralston Tom Mix radio show from 1933 to 1950,
but the original Tom Mix was not in the show. Tom Mix comics were
published from 1942 to 1953.

Branding Iron, 28 In. 949.00
Film Viewer, 5 Films, Original Mailer, R.C.A. Victor 195.00
Hobbyhorse, Tony, Wood, Lithograph Paper, 4 Wheels, 1930s 825.00
Horse, Rocking, Tony, Wood, 1950s ....325.00 to 600.00
Ring, Magnet, Ralston Cereal, 1947 .... 79.00
Ring, Marlin Gun, Eagle, Shield, Brass, c.1937 .... 325.00

TOOLS of all sorts are listed here, but most are related to industry. Other
tools may be found listed under Iron, Kitchen, Tinware, and Wooden.

Adze, Shipwright's, Sorby, No. 1 .... 60.00
Angle Divider, Stanley, No. 30, Pamphlet, Box, 7 3/8 In. 138.00
Auger, Pod, Tee Handle, 18th Century 165.00
Auger Bit Set, Russell Jennings, Chestnut Box, 13 Piece 138.00
Ax, Camp, Marbles, No. 10, 14-In. Handle 175.00
Ax, Goosewing, Mark, 11 1/2 In. 28.00
Ax, Goosewing, Pine Tree, 3 Stars, 9-In. Head, 15-In. Edge 165.00
Ax, Marbles, No. 2, Safety Guard, Embossed Rabbit & Dog, Gladstone, Mich. 210.00
Ax, Mortising, Stamped 175.00
Ax, Shingling, Winchester, U.S.A. 50.00
Ax, Side, Cooper's, Wheat Ears, Stamped Rubin, 19th Century, 14 In. 69.00
Ax, Turf, Horton & Arnold, Pear Shape, 1950 .... 275.00
Barrel Pump, Enterprise, 8 In. 35.00
Bellows, Blacksmith, Forge, Elm, Leather, Iron, Perigord, France, Early 1800s, 31 x 62 In. 660.00
Bench & Chest, Doelger's, Oak, Maple, Drawers, Trays, Tills, Vise, Patented, July 28, 1896 1870.00
Bevel, Brass, Rosewood, Engraved, c.1761, 7 In. 740.00
Bevel, James Howarth, Ebony, Brass Frame, Sheffield 80.00
Boot Form, Cobbler's, Maple, American, 1800s, 13 3/4 In. 35.00
Box, Farrier's, Software, Drawer In Base, Cutout Handle In Center Divider, 21 1/2 In. 200.00
Box, Harness Maker's, Pine, Walnut, Dovetailed Drawer, Sections, Tools Inside, 23 x 10 In. 1438.00
Brace, Carpenter's, Sheffield Plated, England 125.00
Brace, Chairmaker's, Dowelling Bit, Beech, Rosewood, 1800s 246.00
Brace, Iron Rings, 7 Pods, Barnboard Frame, 18th Century 305.00
Brace, James Howarth, Ebony, Sheffield Brass Plated 1140.00
Brace, Mathieson, Beech 145.00
Brace, Mathieson, Cocobolo Head, Beech Brace, 13 Bits, Brass 350.00
Brace, Ultimatum, Colquhoun & Cadman, Ebony, Lever 415.00

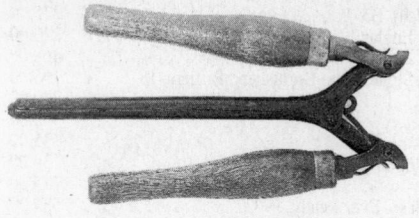

Torquay, Plate,
One Today Is
Worth Two
Tomorrow,
6 1/4 In.

Tool, Curling Iron, Folding, Wood Handles, 8 3/4 In.

Brace, Ultimatum, William Marples, Beech, Ebony, Ivory	330.00
Brace, Ultimatum, William Marples, Brass Frame	555.00
Broadax, Evansville, 7 In.	110.00
Buck Saw, Walnut Frame, Forged Iron Wing Nut, 15 1/2 In.	85.00
Cabinet, Hardware, Nut & Bolt, 72 Drawers, 6-Sided, Spins, 33 In.	1100.00
Caliper, Lady's Leg, Iron, 1807, 6 In.	285.00
Caliper, Log, Brass Ferrules	715.00
Caliper Rule, F.M. Greenleaf, Loggers, Brass, Wood, 10 Scale, Mass., 48 In.	748.00
Caliper Rule, Loggers, Pooler, Brass, Wood, 10-Spoke Wheel, Spike Ends, 56 In.	1785.00
Caliper Rule, Rabone, 4-Fold, Ivory, German Silver, 12 In.	499.00
Caliper Rule, Stanley, No. 38, Ivory, German Silver	195.00
Caliper Rule, Stanley, No. 83 1/2, Boxwood, 4-Fold, Arch Joint, 24 In.	110.00
Can, Kerosene, Embossed Glass, Tin, Wood Bail Handle, 13 In.	230.00
Capper & Cork Press, Gem, Mounted On Wood Board, 13 In.	22.00
Carving Set, Chisels, Box, 19 Piece	195.00
Chamfer Spoke Shave, Stanley, No. 65, 10 In.	70.00
Chest, Carpenter's, Sliding Tray, Locking Hasp, 16 x 37 x 17 In.	350.00
Chest, Cover, Chestnut, Mahogany, Dovetailed Case, 2 Drawers, 23 1/2 x 15 1/2 x 10 In.	275.00
Chest, Shipwright's, P.A. Travers, New York City, 25 1/4 x 39 In.	5600.00
Chisel, Cabinetmaker's, Marples, Bevel Edged, Boxwood Handle, 2 In.	86.00
Chisel, Hand Forged, 1848, 3 x 11 1/2 In.	275.00
Chisel, Ibbotson, Lock Mortise, 1/2 In.	45.00
Chisel, Paring, Sorby, Bevel Edged, Boxwood Handle, 1 1/4 In.	80.00
Coin Sorter, Hoey Improved, Oak Case, Handles, Rochester Novelty Works, 15 x 18 In.	920.00
Combination, Edward Helb, Level, Compass, Inclinometer, Plumb, Bubbles, Sighting	248.00
Combination, Inclinometer, Chaplin-Stephens, No. 036, Pitch Gauge	70.00
Combination, Moore & Wright, Engineer's, Square	89.00
Combination, Moore & Wright, Square, Center Finder, Protractor, Case	139.00
Combination, Stanley, No. 1, Odd Jobs, 10 Functions	305.00
Combination, Stephens, No. 36, Boxwood, Brass Bound, Level, Rule, c.1870, 12 In.	127.00
Combination Rule, Stanley, No. 036, Inclinometer, Pitch Gauge, 1929-1942	358.00
Cord Winder, Geared Wheel, Rotating Hook, Brass Frame, Tabletop Clamps	330.00
Cork Driver, Brevetto, 2 Handles, 12 In.	110.00
Cork Press, Brass, 7 1/2 In.	230.00
Cork Press, Sleeping Dog, Cast Iron, 10 In.	385.00
Cork Press, Yankee, Mounted On Board, 13 In.	22.00
Cork Press & Cutter, Prize, 12 In.	110.00
Corn Sheller, Gray & Bros., Cast Iron, 2-Sided Hinge, 1870	275.00
Cranberry Scoop, 19th Century, 19 In.	290.00
Cranberry Scoop, A.D. Makepeace, Wood Tines, Tin Bottom, Mesh, Mass., 17 x 22 In.	374.00
Cranberry Scoop, Chandler Mfg. Co., Canvas Liner, Whiting Patent, 1906, 15 3/4 In.	605.00
Cranberry Scoop, Wood Tines, 22 In.	345.00
Curling Iron, Folding, Wood Handles, 8 3/4 In. ....*Illus*	25.00
Curling Iron, Wooden Handles, Metal Spring Action Shaft, 8 In.	11.00
Dividers, Bronze, Steel Tip, Circular Design, 1700s, 5 In.	356.00
Drafting Set, McAllister, Signed Brass Compass, Sharkskin Covered, Philada., 6 In.	330.00
Drawknife, Gentlemen's, W. Kent, 10 In.	54.00
Drawknife, Hand Wrought, Wing Nut, Wood Handle	195.00
Drill, Beam, Wood Frame	70.00

Drill, Bow, Ivory Spool, Rosewood Handle, 1/4-In. Bit 275.00
Drill, Hand, Glasgow Gyro, Pull Chain, Caddy, England 220.00
Dynamometer, Fairbanks & Co., Walnut Case, Brass Face, Japanned 468.00
Engraver's Set, Wesley Wilcox, Graveurs, Pad, Stone, Wax, Burnishers, Rifflers, 1872 ... 165.00
Fid, Ebony, Knot Work Sheath, 8 In. 200.00
Fire Extinguisher, Automatic, Glass, Red Comet 95.00
Fire Extinguisher, Shur-Stop 35.00
Flashlight, Penlight, Winchester, Marbleized, No. 6613, c.1938, 5 3/16 x 11 1/6 In. 130.00
Flashlight, Reliable, Deluxe 1775.00
Flashlight, Shield Contact, Deluxe, Vulcanite Case, Ever Ready, 1902 .... 589.00
Flashlight, Shield Contact, Standard, Paper Case, Ever Ready, 1902 .... 560.00
Flax Hackle, Oak, Incised Hearts & Rosettes, Wrought Iron Toothed Comb, 23 In. 173.00
Flax Hackle, Wood, Tin Cover, Punched Decoration, Hearts, Tulips, 1800, 12 1/4 In. 11.00
Flax Spindle, Wood, 2 Maple Blades, Green Painted Base, 32 In. 155.00
Gauge, Butt & Mortise, H.G. Fulton, Stamped, July 17, 88, 1888 Patent 50.00
Gauge, Marking & Mortise, Joseph Marples, Rosewood, Brass 50.00
Gauge, Marking & Mortise, Marden's Type, Mahogany, Brass 85.00
Gauge, Marking, Bennet D. Burley, Brass Face & Fittings 50.00
Gauge, Mortise, Osborne, Rosewood, Brass Stem 80.00
Gauge, Murrays, Dovetail, Brass, Expanding, Instructions 70.00
Gauge, Panel, Stanley, No. 85 1/2, Rosewood, Brass, 20 1/2 In. 83.00
Gauge, Pressure, American LaFrance 52.00
Gauge, Splitting, Wood, Brass Tip, Wedged Cutters, 16 In. 72.00
Gauge, Steam, Lonergan, Brass, Auxiliary Steam Heat System, Phila., 5 1/2 In. 17.00
Glue Furnace, Double Boiler, Copper 116.00
Gold Detector, Chromed Metal, Spring, Glass Tube, Nickeled Brass Dial, 20 In. 633.00
Grape Crusher, Hopper, Wood, Cast Iron, Peters Seed, Cincinnati, 25 x 11 1/4 x 11 3/4 In. 173.00
Hammer, Cramping, Strap 55.00
Hammer, Double Claw 116.00
Hammer, Floor Laying, Cheney, 28 Oz. 99.00
Hammer, Strapped, Holtzapffel, 12 In. 225.00
Hatchet, Winchester, Wood Shaft, 14 In. 115.00
Hay Fork, Iron, Wooden Pulley, Salesman's Sample, 9 3/4 x 11 1/4 In. 85.00
Hay Fork, Wood Tines, Patent Dates 1856-1867 .... 170.00
Inclinometer, Brass, Wood Plaque, 8 3/4 x 11 3/4 In. 138.00
Inclinometer, Davis Level & Tool Co., Mahogany, 12 In. 358.00
Inclinometer, L.L. Davis, No. 14, Mahogany, 30 In. 1045.00
Inclinometer, Level, L.L. Davis, Mahogany, 30 In. 2420.00
Inclinometer, Mathieson, No. 96C, Rosewood, Brass, Scotland, 12 x 1 x 2 1/2 In. 2049.00
Inclinometer, Wood, Bronze, 10 x 12 In. 90.00
Insect Sprayer, Lyon Manufacturing, Tin Lithograph, New York, 3 1/2 In. 145.00
Iron, Heating, Electric, Carpentry, Turned Up Front Edge, 1891, 5 In. 635.00
Jack, Simplex, No. 141, Yellow Cab Co., 12 In. 35.00
Key, Joshua Blake, Wine Cellar, Engraved Silver Tag, Winthrop, Boston, c.1820, 7 7/8 In. 410.00
Kit, Combination, Timmins, Figured Rosewood Handles, Carrying Case 570.00
Level, Bubble, Stanley Rule & Level Co., Wood, Brass, US, LSS, 1896 Patent, 24 In. 430.00
Level, O. Hanks, Cast Iron, Sighting Porthole, Vial Holder, Patented 1847, 21 5/8 In. 330.00
Level, Rabone, Rosewood, Brass, 10 In. 55.00
Level, Sighting, Mahogany, 12 In. 70.00
Level, Skeleton, L.L. Davis, Springfield, Mass., 18 In. 4950.00
Level, Spirit, Boissel, Engineer's, Brass, Mahogany Case, Paris, 1800s 285.00
Level, Spirit, Mathieson, Cylindrical, Rosewood, Brass, 12 In. 178.00
Level, Stanley, No. 324, EAIA Medallion, Box, 1947-1957 .... 330.00
Level, Surveyor's, Bostrom No. 5, Wood Case, Tripod 350.00
Lock, Winchester, Key, 6 Lever 110.00
Mill, Wheat Fanning, Hand Cranked, Red Wash, 1897, 47 x 54 x 36 In. 695.00
Mold, Bullet, Iron, 38 Caliber, Wood Handles, Stamped 38 W C F, 9 In. 20.00
Mold, Minnie Ball, 3 3/4 In. 10.00
Mold, Spoon, Bronze, 2 Parts, 8 1/2 In. 145.00
Mold, Spoon, Bronze, 2 Parts, 9 1/4 In. 200.00
Mower, Sickle, Salesman's Sample, Horse Drawn 1760.00
Padlock, C.C.K. Ltd., Brass, Iron, Key, 12 Lever, Bandgladesh, c.1910, 6 x 2 x 10 3/4 In. 75.00
Parallel Rule & Protractor, J. Dod, Brass, Mendham, 12 In. 615.00

Pipe Tongs, Iron, 18th Century 1540.00
Plane, Bayley Core, Japanned 195.00
Plane, Bench, Bed Rock, Stanley, No. 604 1/2, Type 2, Japanned 248.00
Plane, Bench, Bed Rock, Stanley, No. 605 1/2, Type 3, Japanned 165.00
Plane, Bench, Bed Rock, Stanley, No. 605, Type 3, Japanned 110.00
Plane, Bench, Bed Rock, Stanley, No. 606 . . . . 55.00
Plane, Bench, Bed Rock, Stanley, No. 607, Japanned 165.00
Plane, Bench, Fulton, No. 3708BB, No. 2, Japanned 140.00
Plane, Bench, Gage Jack, Stanley, No. G5, 14 x 2 In. 85.00
Plane, Bench, Smooth, Stanley, No. 4, Box, 9 x 2 In. 85.00
Plane, Bench, Smooth, Stanley, No. 4C, Label, Box, 9 x 2 In. 55.00
Plane, Bevelling, James Howarth, Brass Frame, Walnut Handle, Interchangeable Blades . . 115.00
Plane, Block, Stanley, No. 9, Cabinet Maker's 4180.00
Plane, Bookcase, Mahogany Wedge, Fully Boxed, Parry 125.00
Plane, Butcher Block, Stanley, No. 64, Original Toothing Blade, 1915-1923, 12 1/2 x 2 In. 4180.00
Plane, Chamfer, Adjustable, Beeche, Preston 150.00
Plane, Circular, Stanley No. 20, Japanned 140.00
Plane, Circular, Stanley, No. 113, Patented 1877 . . . . 105.00
Plane, Combination, Lewin Universal, Blades, Instructions, Japanned 85.00
Plane, Combination, Sargent, No. 1080PB, Cardboard Box 285.00
Plane, Combination, Stanley, No. 45, Box, Canada 145.00
Plane, Crown Molding, Marked W. Martin, 1773-1801, 4 In. 2200.00
Plane, Dado, Stanley, No. 39 1/4, Japanned 138.00
Plane, Dado, Stanley, No. 39 3/8, Japanned 110.00
Plane, Dado, Stanley, No. 39 5/8, Japanned 220.00
Plane, Dado, Stanley, No. 39 7/8, Japanned 110.00
Plane, Fall & Cunningham, Wood, Brass, Fence 55.00
Plane, Howkins, Model C, Instructions, 24 Cutters, Box 1300.00
Plane, Jack, Siegley, No. 5, Adjustable Blade, Textured Handle 215.00
Plane, Molding, Mathieson, No. 100, Twin Iron, 2 1/4 In. 145.00
Plane, Molding, Stanley, No. 45, Rosewood Handles, 18 Blades, Box, 6 x 12 x 5 3/4 In. . . 300.00
Plane, Norris, Model A5, Dovetailed, Rosewood Infill 1426.00
Plane, Panel Raiser, Adjustable Fence, Top Wedge, Flat Chamfers, Wooden 165.00
Plane, Panel, Mathieson, Dovetailed, Rosewood Infill, 13 1/2 In. 855.00
Plane, Plow, Andruss, Wedge Arm, Beech, Brass Tips & Stop 85.00
Plane, Plow, C. Warren, Screw Arm, Rosewood 385.00
Plane, Plow, Casey, Kitchell & Co., Ebony, Auburn, N.Y. 5500.00
Plane, Plow, Coach Maker's, Adjustable, Brass, Beechwood 1870.00
Plane, Plow, Rosewood, 4 Ivory Tips, Handle, Screw Arm 470.00
Plane, Plow, S. Perrin, Coach Maker's, Router Style, Brass Wear 605.00
Plane, Rabbet, Spiers Ayr, Steel Shouldered Rebate, Ebony Wedge, 6 In. 144.00
Plane, Rabbet, Stanley, No. 10, Carriage Maker's, Japanned, c.1884 . . . . 250.00
Plane, Rounding, Mortised, Tenoned Frame, Adjustable Mechanism 110.00
Plane, Sandusky's Morris, Handle, Mushroom-Shaped Knob, Patented 1870 . . . . 1320.00
Plane, Sash Filletster, Cotman, Ivory Rules 220.00
Plane, Scraper, Stanley, No. 212, Japanned, 1911-1935, 5 1/2 x 1 3/8 In. 990.00
Plane, Smoothing, Norris, No. 2, Dovetailed Steel, Rosewood Infill 320.00
Plane, Spelk, 2 Pull Handles, 1822 . . . . 110.00
Plane, Stanley, No. 41, Type II, Miller's Patent, 10 1/2 In. 2640.00
Plane, Stanley, No. 97, Cabinet Maker's, Japanned, 10 x 2 1/4 In. 220.00
Plane, Try, Felix Emanuel Bortoz 220.00
Plane, Wood, Lakeside, Wood Body, Black Finish Metal Fitting, Adjustable, 5 x 10 In. . . . 29.00
Plane, Wood, Sheffield Blade, 14 In. 45.00
Pliers, Wick, Internal Springs, Crescent Form Blades, Hinged Back Lock, 1700s, 9 1/4 In. 275.00
Plow, Leatherworker's, Blanchard, Brass, Steel, Rosewood, 6 In. 116.00
Plumb Bob, Bronze, Steel Tip, 1800s, 4 1/2 In. 130.00
Powder Dispenser, Ideal Manufacturing, No. 5, Tabletop, 1892 Patent 58.00
Pump Oiler, Handlan, Brass Can 70.00
Rake, Cranberry, A D Makepeace Co., Wood, Metal, 2 Handles, 19th Century, 8 x 18 In. . . 125.00
Rake, Grass, Wood, Twig Detail, Primitive, 64 In. 55.00
Rake, Wood, Metal Bracket, Primitive, 66 In. 28.00
Router, Pistol Grip, Boxwood, Steel Fence 385.00
Rule, Board Stick, H. Chapin, 8-Sided Scales, Brass Tipped, Capped 165.00

Rule, Boxwood, Hay's, 4-Fold, Steel Tips, Scales, c.1900, 3 Ft. 165.00
Rule, Boxwood, J.A. Rabone & Sons, Ironmonger's, 3-Fold, Brass Caliper 70.00
Rule, Brass, Rolling, Dovetail Case, Stanley Great Turnstile Holborn, London, 15 1/4 In. . 127.00
Rule, Gunter, Box, Wood, 24 In. 90.00
Rule, Parallel, Capt. Fields Improved, Box, Wood, Brass Hinges, 18 In. 46.00
Rule, Pattern, Lufkin Rule Co., Chart, Box 55.00
Rule, Preston, No. 5111, Eesesee Rule 36.00
Rule, Stanley, No. 40, German Silver, Ivory, Sliding Caliper, Folding 259.00
Rule, Stanley, No. 86, Ivory, German Silver, 4-Fold, 24 In. 415.00
Rule, Stanley, No. 94, Carriage Maker's, Folding, Boxwood 195.00
Rule Set, Draftsman's, Troughton & Simms, Steel, 2 Rules, Set Square, Velvet Lined Box 145.00
Safe, Floor, Victorian, Black Paint, Wheels, Victor Safe & Lock Co., 27 x 16 x 17 In. 730.00
Saw, 2-Handed, 1808 .... 195.00
Saw, Atkins, No. 53, c.1950 .... 70.00
Saw, Back, Fenn, Wood, 8 In. 80.00
Saw, Bow, Ebony, Scrimshaw Whalebone, Iron Blade, Locking Wedge, 17 x 7 In. 635.00
Saw, Bow, Ivory, Ebony Handles, 1800s, 10 1/2 In. 378.00
Saw, Dovetailing, Iron, Wood, Bird Form, Punch Decoration, 1886, 11 In. 275.00
Saw, Hand, T. Tillotson & Co., Brass Plate, Steam-Powered Clipper Ship, Sheffield 495.00
Saw, Iron, Ivory & Ebony Handle, 1700s, 20 In. 535.00
Saw, Scroll, Cast Iron, Treadle Powered, Leather Belt, Oak Arms, New Rogers, 36 x 26 In. 175.00
Saw, Tenon, Disston, Brass Back, 14 In. 98.00
Saw, Tenon, Mathieson, Brass Back, 14 In. 89.00
Scissors, Wilkinson, Brass Handle 250.00
Scraper, Stanley, No. 283, Rosewood Handles, 1929-1942, 9 1/2 x 2 7/8 In. 419.00
Screwbox & Tap, Fenn, Beech, 3/4 In. 60.00
Screwbox & Tap, Holtzapffel, Boxwood, 1/2 In. 146.00
Screwdriver, Beech Handle, Late 1700s, 17 In. 169.00
Screwdriver, Boxwood Handle, 24 In. 75.00
Screwdriver, Fruitwood Handle, 1700s, 22 In. 215.00
Screwdriver, Walnut Handle, c.1800, 30 In. 55.00
Shave, Handrail, Gleave, Oldham St., Manchester 178.00
Shipwright's Set, Caulking Mallet, Irons 138.00
Slater's Set, Ripper, Hammer, Stake, 3 Piece 70.00
Slick, Clapboard, Iron Handle 70.00
Slide Rule, Publican's, Farmars, Boxwood, 1 3/4 In. 270.00
Spokeshave, L. Bailey, Cutter, New Britain, Conn. 120.00
Spokeshave, Preston, Round, Nickel Plated 89.00
Square, Brass, Decorated Ends, Inch Calibrations, 1700s, 9 In. 89.00
Square, J.K. Sommes, Wood, 8 Measuring Sides, Sheffield, Mass., 1876 Patent, 36 In. 105.00
Square, Mathieson, Ebony, Brass Bound, Glasgow, 6 In. 190.00
Sundial, Pocket, Wooden, Folding, Embossed, Inked Interior, 3 1/2 x 2 1/8 x 1/4 In. 55.00
Tap Box, Wooden Bolts, Turn Heads & Tips, 2 In. 165.00
Timber Scribe, Marples, Rosewood Handle 60.00
Tobacco Shredder, Hand Crank, Iron, c.1900, 13 x 8 In. 145.00
Trammel, Incised Crosshatch Design, Scrolling Terminals, 2 Parts, Iron, 30 In. 460.00
Transit, L.E. Gurley, Mahogany Case, Brass Plum Bob, Walnut Tripod, Troy, N.Y., 1900s 345.00
Trowel, Stonemason's, Rosewood, Brass, Bouvais, Bordeaux 180.00
Vise, Harness Maker's, Leather 125.00
Vise, Pattern Maker's, Emmert's, Rotates 305.00
Vise, Pattern Maker's, Wooden, Turn Crank, 22 x 12 In. 60.00
Wagon Jack, Forged Iron, Wood Shaft, c.1838 .... 96.00
Wagon Jack, Forged Iron, Wood Shaft, c.1847 .... 113.00
Wagon Jack, Hand Forged Crank, Wood Frame, 1818 .... 248.00
Wagon Jack, Iron, Wood Shaft, c.1844 .... 113.00
Water Motor, Chicago, Patent 1872, 15 1/2 In. 385.00
Wheelbarrow, Red, Yellow Stencil, 74 In. 360.00
Wheelbarrow, S.A. Smith, Oak, Finger-Jointed, Iron Rim Wheel, Vt., 30 1/2 In. 60.00
Wheelbarrow, Wooden, Painted Red, Yellow Decoration, 25 1/2 x 70 In. 230.00
Wrench, Coachbuilder's, Adjustable, Petch's Pattern, 17 1/2 In. 196.00
Wrench, Colbrooks, Adjustable, No. 1, 4 In. 36.00
Wrench, Spanner, American LaFrance Foamite Corp., 11 1/2 In. 69.00
Wrench Brace, Lowentraut, Metal Crank Handle, Screwdriver Tip, Patented 1894 .... 75.00

Wrench Brace, Lowentraut, Rosewood Handle, Newark, N.J., Patented May 21, 1901 ... 125.00
Yarn Winder, Clock Work, 39 x 22 In. 69.00
Yoke, Ox, Double, Wood, Red Paint, 50 In. 80.00

TOOTHPICK HOLDERS are sometimes called *toothpicks* by collectors. The variously shaped containers used to hold small wooden toothpicks are made of glass, china, or metal. Most of the toothpick holders are Victorian. Additional items may be found in other categories, such as Bisque, Silver Plate, Slag Glass, etc.

Advertising, Ruby Stain, Dissinger's New Store, 1906, 2 1/2 In. 39.00
Amberette, 2 1/4 In. 88.00
Basket, Oval, Amber, Opal 35.00
Beaded Grape, Green, Gold Trim 55.00
Beatty Honeycomb, White Opalescent 35.00
Beatty Rib, Opalescent 22.00
Bethlehem Star 15.00
Bohemian, Cranberry, Gold Trim 200.00
Bohemian, Green, Gold Trim, 2 5/8 In. 145.00
Box-In-Box, Green 85.00
Buckingham 40.00
Bulging Loops, Yellow 325.00
Butterfly, Milk Glass, 2 3/4 In. 6.00
Carnival Glass, Souvenir Of Millersburg Glass Co., Founded 1909, Marigold 45.00
Columbian Coin, Frosted 170.00
Cradle, Amber 60.00
Daisy & Button, Amber, Blue 35.00
Daisy & Button, Amberina 225.00
Daisy Kettle, Amber, Handle, 2 In. 25.00
Delaware, Rose, Gold Trim, 2 1/2 In. 44.00
Diamond & Long Sunburst, Green, Gold Trim, 2 1/4 In. 11.00
Diamond Spearhead 125.00
Diamond Spearhead, Vaseline Opalescent, 2 1/4 In. ....50.00 to 75.00
Dog, With Top Hat, 3 1/2 x 3 1/2 In. 39.00
Double Dahlia With Petal 60.00
Double Eye Hobnail 30.00
Empress, Green, Gold Trim, 2 3/4 In. 165.00
Eureka, Ruby Stain 85.00
Fancy Loop, Green 225.00
Feather, Green 375.00
Figural Soldier & Sailor On Either Side Of Cup, Embossed, Preparedness 330.00
Footed Palm Leaf, Milk Glass 20.00
Forget-Me-Not, Blue 40.00
Gable, Handles, 2 1/4 In. 42.00
Galloway 20.00
Georgia Gem, Custard 45.00
Harvard 40.00
Heart Band, Ruby Stain 35.00
Hickman 40.00
Hobnail 40.00
Hobnail, Blue Opalescent 65.00
Hobnail, White Opalescent 42.00
Idyll, Blue Opalescent, 2 1/2 In. 145.00
Inverted Fan & Feather, Ivory 350.00
Inverted Fan & Feather, Pink Slag 875.00
Iris With Meander 145.00
Iris With Meander, Amethyst, Gold Trim, 2 1/2 In. 20.00
Iris With Meander, Blue Opalescent, 2 1/2 In. 39.00
Iris With Meander, Vaseline Opalescent, 2 1/2 In. 90.00
Iris With Meander, White Opalescent, 2 1/2 In. 17.00
Jefferson Colonial, Apple Green, Gold Trim, 2 1/2 In. 17.00
Jefferson Optic, Enameled Flowers 35.00
Jefferson Optic, Ruby Stain 65.00
Kittens, Marigold Carnival 175.00

Majolica, English Monkey, Figural, Cobalt Blue Cape, Before Darwin, 5 1/4 In. 187.00
Majolica, Flower Shape, White Crocus, Leaf Base, 3 3/4 In. 90.00
Manhattan, Gold Spots 18.00
Michigan, Maiden's Blush, Gold Trim, 2 1/2 In. 145.00
Milk Glass, 3 Swan Handles, Westmoreland, 2 3/8 In. 30.00
Mother-Of-Pearl, Raindrop, Pink 465.00
Nursery Tales 30.00
Oaken Bucket, Opal, Metal Insert 35.00
One-Hundred-One, White 85.00
Opaline, Pink 25.00
Oregon 90.00
Owl, Spread Wings, Blue Mist, Westmoreland, 3 In. 24.00
Owl, Spread Wings, Milk Glass, Westmoreland, 3 x 2 1/4 In. 20.00
Peachblow, Aurora Company Silver Plated Holder 1250.00
Peek-A-Boo, Gold Trim 40.00
Peerless, Gold Trim, Heisey 45.00
Pillar 125.00
Pineapple & Fan, Green, Gold Trim 200.00
Plain Panel, Green, Scalloped Edge 25.00
Pomona 250.00
Porcelain, Cabbage Roses, Germany ....22.00 to 25.00
Porcelain, Flowers, Art Deco, Germany 25.00
Porcelain, Flowers, Lay-Down Shape 30.00
Porcelain, Flowers, Swags, Hand Painted, Handles, Bavaria 28.00
Porcelain, Hand Painted, Roses, 3 Handles, RS Prussia 90.00
Porcelain, Molded Rose, Pink Luster & Gold 20.00
Porcelain, Yellow Flowers, Gold Trim, Germany 25.00
Portland, Banded 85.00
Portland, Maiden's Blush Stain, Banded, 2 3/8 In. 39.00
Portland, Maiden's Blush, Banded 45.00
Prize, Ruby Stain 95.00
Punty Band, Ruby, Beaded Rim 50.00
Quartered Block 32.00
Ribbed Kettle, Purple Slag 40.00
Ribbed Pillar, Pink Spatter 55.00
Ribbed Spiral, Blue Opalescent 55.00
Ribbed Spiral, White Opalescent, 2 3/8 In. 18.00
Ring & Beads, Amethyst, Gold Trim 25.00
Ring & Beads, Apple Green 25.00
Ring & Beads, Custard, Gold Trim 30.00
Ring Band, Custard 130.00
Rising Sun, Amethyst Stain 49.00
Rising Sun, Gold Trim 25.00
Royal Ivy, Frosted 75.00
Royal Ivy, Rubina, Northwood 165.00
Sawtooth Honeycomb 45.00
Scroll With Cane Band 30.00
Scroll With Cane Band, Amber Stain 110.00
Scrolled Shell, Milk Glass, Gold Trim 20.00
Seaweed, Blue Milk Glass, 2 1/4 In. 22.00
Seaweed, White Opalescent 55.00
Shamrock, Green 60.00
Shoshone 28.00
Simple Scroll, Milk Glass 36.00
Souvenir, Bead Swag, Opal, W.W. Smith, Lisbon, Mo. 95.00
Souvenir, Bead Swag, Ruby Stain, Mrs. D.J. Garrett, 1907 .... 50.00
Souvenir, Custard Glass, Flag Staff Park, Mauchchunk, Pa., Flowers 39.00
Souvenir, Jefferson Optic, Amethyst, 1909 .... 45.00
Sunbeam, Cobalt Blue, Gold Trim 75.00
Swirl, Cranberry Opalescent, Satin 350.00
Texas Star, Clear, Frosted Base 100.00
Thumbnail 45.00
Thumbprint 45.00

Truncated Cube, Ruby Stain	30.00
Venetian Diamond, Amberina	425.00
Wellington, Ruby Stain, 2 1/4 In.	303.00
Windows, White Opalescent	100.00
Winged Scroll, Custard	150.00
Witch's Kettle, Clam Broth, Flowers	15.00
Witch's Kettle, Green, Gold Trim, Handle	15.00
Zipper Slash, Frosted, Amber-Stained Vines	90.00

TORQUAY is the name given to ceramics by several potteries working near Torquay, England, from 1870 until 1962. Until about 1900, the potteries used local red clay to make classical-style art pottery vases and figurines. Then they turned to making souvenir wares. Items were dipped in colored slip and decorated with painted slip and sgraffito designs. They often had mottoes or proverbs, and scenes of cottages, ships, birds, or flowers. The *Scandy* design was a symmetrical arrangement of brushstrokes and spots done in colored slips. Potteries included Watcombe Pottery (1870–1962); Torquay Terra-Cotta Company (1875–1905); Aller Vale (1881–1924); Torquay Pottery (1908–1940); and Longpark (1883–1957).

TORQUAY

Bowl, Ash, Motto Ware, Mind The Carpet, Round, St. Ives, Cornwall, 3 1/2 In.	49.00
Jug, Cream, Motto Ware, Fresh From The Farm, Royal Watcombe, 3 3/4 In.	59.00
Pitcher, Motto Ware, Fresh From The Farm, Farm House, Trees, 2 1/4 In.	49.00
Plate, One Today Is Worth Two Tomorrow, 6 1/4 In. .... *Illus*	45.00

TORTOISESHELL is the shell of the tortoise. It has been used as inlay and to make small decorative objects since the seventeenth century. Some species of tortoise are now on the endangered species list, and old and new objects made from these shells cannot be sold legally.

Bottle, Scent, Brown, Amber, Silver Collar, Amber Blown Stopper, 4 1/4 In.	127.00
Box, Perfume, Rectangular, Serpentine Front, Fitted Interior, 2 Bottles, 4 In.	1049.00
Card Case, Chinese, 1800s, 3 1/2 x 2 1/2 In.	150.00
Comb, Diamond, Blond, Rose Gold Flower Garland, Edwardian	700.00
Etui, Belt, Bronze Mount, Blond, Anglo-Indian, Late 19th Century, 10 3/4 In.	173.00
Pitcher, Applied Amber Handle, Ground Pontil, 5 x 7 In.	90.00
Workbox, Georgian, Blond, Mid 1800s, 8 Compartments, 3 x 7 1/2 x 5 1/2 In.	2070.00

TOY collectors have special clubs, magazines, and shows. Toys are designed to entice children, and today they have attracted new interest among adults who are still children at heart. All types of toys are collected. Tin toys, iron toys, battery operated toys, and many others are collected by specialists. Dolls, Games, Teddy Bears, and Bicycles are listed in their own categories. Other toys may be found under company or celebrity names.

Accordion Player, Minstrel, Sitting On Stump, Bisque, Painted, 1880s, 3 3/4 In.	140.00
Acrobat, Aerial, Windup, Tin Lithograph, Marx Big 3, Box, 12 In.	195.00
Acrobat, Windup, Celluloid, Japan, 15 In.	100.00
Acrobats, Bisque, Molded Clothes, Ball, Germany, Box, c.1880	410.00
Action Figure, Aquaman, Uniform, Equipment, Captain Action, Ideal, Box, 1966 . .205.00 to 230.00	
Action Figure, Evil-Lyn, Masters Of The Universe, On Card, Mattel, 1983	45.00
Action Figure, Incredible Hulk, Flyaway Action, Mego, Box, 1970s, 12 In.	160.00
Action Figure, Mary Marvel, Plastic, R.W. Kerr, Box, 1946	575.00
Action Figure, Oddjob, Throws Hat, Karate Chop, James Bond 007, Gilbert, Box, 1965	885.00
Action Figure, Spiderman, Mego, Box, 1978, 12 1/2 In.	120.00
Aeroswing, Windup, Tin Lithograph, Chein, Box, 10 In.	770.00
Airplane, 2 Airplanes Circle Globe, Tin Lithograph, Spring Powered, West Germany	55.00
Airplane, 2 Engines, Silver, Red, Wyandotte, 7 In.	55.00
Airplane, Air Devil, No. 56, Windup, Blue, Red, Yellow, Tin Lithograph, Pat. 1926, 8 In.	700.00
Airplane, Air France, F-ALBA, Joustra, 21 x 24 In.	1000.00
Airplane, American Airlines, Flagship, Tin, 27 1/2-In. Wingspan	220.00
Airplane, Army, Windup, Tin Lithograph, Marx, 18-In. Wingspan	220.00
Airplane, Avion X115, Windup, Tin Lithograph, Joustra Toys, France, Box, 1950s, 16 In.	345.00
Airplane, Biplane, German Fighter, Tippco, 11 In.	2450.00

Airplane, Biplane, Tin Lithograph, Friction, Japan, 15-In. Wingspan 145.00
Airplane, Boeing B-50 Superfortress, Double Machine Guns, Tin, Yonezawa, 15 In. 1075.00
Airplane, Bomber, Exploding Tank, Metal, Sears Exclusive, Japan, 24 In. 215.00
Airplane, Bomber, Olive, Wyandotte, 7 In. 120.00
Airplane, China Clipper, Tin, Wyandotte, 1930, 10 In. .... 305.00 to 525.00
Airplane, Circling, Control Tower, Battery Operated, Tin Litho., Cragstan, Japan, Box, 9 In. 138.00
Airplane, Coast Defense, Circling, Windup, Tin, Marx, Box, 9 In. 908.00
Airplane, Dagwood's Solo, Tin Lithograph, Marx, Box, c.1935, 9 In. .... 715.00 to 1430.00
Airplane, F-14A, Tin, Battery Operated, Japan, 12 In. .... 28.00 to 55.00
Airplane, Fighter, Jet, Battery Operated, KO, Box, 9 In. 145.00
Airplane, Fighter, Tin Lithograph, Plastic, Battery Operated, Grumman, Japan, Box, 16 In. 90.00
Airplane, Folding Wings, Green, Yellow, Hubley, 6 In. 40.00
Airplane, Go-Round, Tin Lithograph, Box, 1940s 675.00
Airplane, Gull Clipper, Spinning Prop, Tin, Windup, Yonezawa, Box, 10 In. 550.00
Airplane, Heinkel, Fighter, Nazi, Box, 1930s 450.00
Airplane, Jet, Pressed Tin, U.S.A.F., Japan, 4 In. 35.00
Airplane, Jet, Starfire, Tin, Friction, Sparks, Japan, Box, c.1950, 8 1/2 In. 140.00
Airplane, Jet, Y-53, Tin Lithograph, Madson, Japan, 12 In. 160.00
Airplane, Lockheed Sirrus, Pull Type, Steelcraft, 21 1/2-In. Wingspan 1320.00
Airplane, Military, Green, Stars & Stripes, Tin Lithograph, Windup, Marx, c.1945, 13 In. . 224.00
Airplane, Moncoupe, Pressed Steel, Wyandotte, 10-In. Wingspan 60.00
Airplane, Monoplane, 3 Engines, Cast Iron, Kilgore TAT 4785.00
Airplane, Mystery, Bump & Go, Pilot Steers, Tin, Battery Operated, Japan, Box, 10 In. .. 330.00
Airplane, Northwest, 4 Engines, Metal Props, Tin, Asahitoy, Box, 19 In. 1210.00
Airplane, P-31 Lightning, Hubley, 10 In. 130.00
Airplane, Pan American, 4 Props, Wheels, Tin, Friction, Yonezawa, Box, c.1950, 9 1/2 In. 310.00
Airplane, Pressed Steel, 1 Engine, Red Wings, Gray Body, 20-In. Wingspan 275.00
Airplane, Propellers, Pressed Steel, Marx, 15 7/8-In. Wingspan 96.00
Airplane, Quick Draw McGraw, Hanna-Barbera, Linemar, Box, 1961, 9 In. 1540.00
Airplane, Shieble, Pressed Steel, 3 Engines, 1930s, 27-In. Wingspan 660.00
Airplane, Skyhawk, Control Tower, 2 Airplanes, Tin Lithograph, Windup, 9 In. 120.00
Airplane, Strato-Jet, Tin Lithograph, Battery Operated, TN Japan, Box, 1950s, 12 x 14 In. 195.00
Airplane, TC-1029, 4 Bombs, Tipp, 14 1/2 In. 2200.00
Airplane, Tiger, X-15, Moves, Props Spin, Tin, Friction, Usagiya, Box, 7 1/2 In. 155.00
Airplane, Tin, Red, Marx, 10 In. 99.00
Airplane, Tin, Red, Silver, Wyandotte, 7 In. 55.00
Airplane, TWA, Windup, Tin Lithograph, Japan, 11 1/2-In. Wingspan 110.00
Airplane, U.S. Army, Tin, Windup, Marx, 18-In. Wingspan 195.00
Airplane, U.S. Mail, NX131, 3 Engines, Steelcraft, 26 1/2-In. Wingspan 1045.00
Airplane, United Airlines, Boeing 747, Battery Operated, Tin, TN, Box, 14 In. 130.00
Airplane, Viscount Capitol Airlines, Tin, Remote Control, Linemar, Box, c.1950, 11 In. .. 635.00
Airplane, Windup, Tin Lithograph, Chein, 11-In. Wingspan, Box 1320.00
Airplane Hangar, Windup, Tin, Marx 350.00
Airport Set, Hanger, Tin, 2 Mack U.S. Mail Trucks, Searchlight Tower, Tootsietoy 725.00 to 775.00
Airport Set, Metal, Windup, Germany, Box, 1950s 295.00
Alabama Coon Jigger, Tin Lithograph, Clockwork, Lehmann, Box, 10 In. 660.00
Alabama Coon Jigger, Tombo, Tin, Mechanical, Strauss, c.1910, 10 In. .... 440.00 to 675.00
Alligator, Alley, Cloth Over Tin, Rubber Back Spikes, Marx, Box, 17 1/2 In. .... 200.00 to 385.00
Alligator, Amazing, Tin Lithograph, Battery Operated, Japan, 13 In. 110.00
Alligator, Green, Yellow, Painted, Wood, Glass Eyes, Schoenhut, 12 1/2 In. ...... 275.00 to 525.00
Alligator, Squeeze Tail & Jaw, Handle, Tin Lithograph, Embossed, 7 In. 45.00
Ambulance, 4 Figures, Windup, No. 914, Tippco, Germany, 1937, 9 In. 995.00
Ambulance, Buick, Tin, Friction, Japan, 14 1/2 In. 295.00
Ambulance, Ford, White, Friction, Box, 1959, 10 In. 115.00
Ambulance, Horse Drawn, Figures, Elastolin, 8 1/2 In. 210.00
Ambulance, Horse Drawn, Tin Lithograph, Nonpariel, 12 In. 220.00
Ambulance, LCC, No. 14, Matchbox, Lesney, Box, 1962 .... 80.00
Ambulance, Military, Die Cast Metal, No. 30HM, Daimler, Dinky Toys, England 89.00
Andy, Walker, Tin Lithograph, Windup, Marx, Box, c.1930, 12 In. 1018.00
Animals, Skip Rope, Windup, T.P.S., Japan, Box 175.00
Ape, King Of The Jungle, Tin Lithograph, Plastic Head, Windup, TN, Box 6160.00
Arthur A Go Go, Beating Drum, Battery Operated, 9 In. 250.00
Astronaut, Astro Boy, Swimming, Vinyl Head & Arms, Atom, Tokyo, Japan, Box, 8 In. .. 850.00

Astronaut, Astro Man, Tin Lithograph, Plastic, Windup, TN 3300.00
Astronaut, Boy, Tin Lithograph, Battery Operated, Daiya, Japan, Box, c.1950s, 14 In. 880.00
Astronaut, Rotate-O-Matic, Tin Litho., Battery Operated, Horikawa, Japan, Box, 11 1/2 In. 165.00
Baby, Crawling, Plastic, Box, Irwin, 5 1/2 In. 70.00
Badge, G-Man, Celluloid, Pep Comics Premium, 1944 .... 145.00
Baking Kit, Betty Crocker, 20 Utensils, 11 Mixes, Baking Book, Mirro, Box, 1953 ...... 135.00
Ballerina, Tin Lithograph, Gyro Motor, Marx, 5 1/2 In. 99.00
Ballerina, Twirls On Rod, Tin Lithograph, Marx, Box, c.1940, 6 In. 225.00
Balloon Seller, Clockwork, Tin Lithograph, Distler, 6 1/2 In. 470.00
Barber Shop, Animal, Bear Gives Rabbit A Shave, Tin, T.P.S., Box, 5 In. 495.00
Barbie Compact, Mirror, 2 Pieces, Brass Hinge 230.00
Barn, Wood, Lithograph, Animals, Germany, 12 In. 130.00
Barnacle Bill, Tin, Windup, Chein, 6 1/2 In. 475.00
Barney Google, 4-Wheeled Platform, Tin, Pull Toy, 1920s 975.00
Bartender, Charley Weaver, Battery Operated, Rosko, Japan, Box 20.00
Baseball Catcher, Celluloid, Windup, Occupied Japan, Box, 5 1/4 In. 55.00
Bat, Eric The Bat, Plush, Steiff, Button, Tag, Large 975.00
Bathtub, Doll's, Cream, Gold Stripe, Handles, 18 x 14 1/2 x 8 In. 95.00
Bears are also listed in the Teddy Bears category.
Bear, Accordion, Battery Operated, Bruno, Box, 10 In. 350.00
Bear, Baby, Sitting In Chair, Eats Ice Cream, Eyes Light Up, Modern Toys, Japan, Box .. 415.00
Bear, Barber, Mixed Material, Battery Operated, TN, Box, 10 In. ....650.00 to 935.00
Bear, Barney, Drummer Boy, Walks, Plays Drum, Remote Control, Alps, Box, 11 In. 220.00
Bear, Busy Housekeeper, Pushes Vacuum, Tin, Plush, Battery Operated, Alps, Box, 8 In. . 390.00
Bear, Camera, Tin Lithograph, Battery Operated, 6 In. 20.00
Bear, Cashier, Phone Rings, Tin, Plush, Battery Operated, Masudaya, Box, 8 In. 330.00
Bear, Clever, Windup, Japan, Box, 5 In. 39.00
Bear, Coffeetime, Battery Operated, TN, Box, 10 In. 385.00
Bear, Crawls, Mohair, Shoebutton Eyes, Tin Legs, Wheels, Pull Toy, 9 In. 470.00
Bear, Dentist, Mixed Material, Battery Operated, TN, Box, 10 In. 935.00
Bear, Drinking, Battery Operated, 10 In. ....35.00 to 55.00
Bear, Father, Battery Operated, Modern Toys, Box, 10 In. 170.00
Bear, Golfer, Shoots Hole-In-One, Tin, Windup, Box 105.00
Bear, Grandma, Knitting, Battery Operated, Modern Toys, c.1950, 9 3/4 In. ...... 60.00 to 100.00
Bear, Grandpa, Battery Operated, Alps, Box, 9 In. 220.00
Bear, Grandpa, Rocking In Chair, Pipe Lit, Battery Operated, Alps, Japan, Box 105.00
Bear, Growls, Mohair, Papier-Mache, Glass Eyes, Wheels, 10 1/2 In. 415.00
Bear, Hungry, Mama Feeds Baby Bottle, Squeals, Battery Operated, Japan, Box, 9 1/2 In. 195.00
Bear, In Rocking Chair, Telephone Ringing, Talking, Battery Operated, MT Mark, 10 In. . 110.00
Bear, Jointed, Wood, Leather Ears, Rope Tail, Schoenhut, 7 1/4 In. 250.00
Bear, Marching, Battery Operated, Alps, Box, 10 In. 50.00
Bear, Maxwell Coffee Loving, Battery Operated, Rosko, Box, 10 In. 385.00
Bear, Mechanical, Ives, Box, c.1890, 8 In. 525.00
Bear, Muzzle, Rattle, Fur Covering, Clockwork, Germany, 13 In. 275.00
Bear, On Scooter, Tin Lithograph, Friction, 6 In. 980.00
Bear, On Wheels, Plush, Straw Stuffed, Glass Eyes, Muzzle, Pull Chain, 12 In. 470.00
Bear, Papa, Walks, Lifts Pipe, Smokes, Plush, Tin, Remote Control, Marusan, Box, 9 In. . 99.00
Bear, Playing Ball, Nods, Umbrella Spins, Duck, Tin, Battery Operated, Japan, Box, 11 In. 880.00
Bear, Polar, Ball, Tin Lithograph, Windup, Japan, 6 In. 50.00
Bear, Polar, Fishing, Eyes Light Up, Catches Fish, Battery Operated, Cragstan, Japan 175.00
Bear, Shoeshine, Battery Operated, Alps, 1950s, 10 In. ....90.00 to 120.00
Bear, Shooting Cine, Lifts Camera, Plush, Tin, Battery Operated, Linemar, Box, 11 In. 550.00
Bear, Sleeping, Bed, Battery Operated, Linemar, Box, 9 In. 395.00
Bear, Telephone, Tin, Plush, Battery Operated, Masudaya, Box, 9 In. 230.00
Bear, Telephone, Writes On Paper, Tin, Plush, Battery Operated, Linemar, Box, 7 1/2 In. . 330.00
Bear, Walking, Windup, Modern Toys, Japan, Box, 3 1/2 In. 28.00
Bear, Wee Little Baby, Flips Pages, Tin, Plush, Battery Operated, Alps, Box, 10 In. 355.00
Bear, Xylophone, Eyes Light, Plush, Tin, Battery Operated, Swallow, Box, 10 In. 300.00
Beaver, Nagy, Mohair, Tag, Ear Button, Steiff, c.1950, 4 In. 70.00
Bed, Doll's, Arched Headboard & Footboard, Cornucopia & Leaf Stencil, 20 In. 140.00
Bed, Doll's, Empire, Oak, 13 1/2 x 17 1/4 In. 259.00
Bed, Doll's, Iron, Blue & White Paint, 18 x 14 1/2 x 24 In. 110.00
Bed, Doll's, Pierced Headboard & Footboard, Red, Cast Iron, Victorian Style, 15 In. 138.00

Bed, Doll's, Spindle Posts, Canopy, Shaped Head, Footboards, Wood, 19th Century, 17 In.   1540.00
Bed, Doll's, Walnut, Scalloped & Shaped Headboard & Footboard, Victorian, 21 x 14 In. .   60.00
Beetle, Crawls, 6 Legs, Tin Lithograph, Windup, Lehmann, Box, 4 x 3 In. . . . . . . .200.00 to 325.00
Beetle, Magic, Battery Operated, Linemar, Box, 7 In. 55.00
Bell Ringer, Black Wooden Figure, Tin Base, Articulated Axle, Spoke Wheels, 6 In. 715.00
Bell Ringer, Landing Of Columbus, Ship, 4 Oarsmen, Cast Iron, c.1892, 7 1/2 In. 450.00
Bicycles that are large enough to ride are listed in their own category.
Big Joe Chef, Windup, Tin Lithograph, Japan, Box, 6 1/2 In. 130.00
Bigo-Bello, Schuco, 10 In. 39.00
Bird, Blue Birds Spin Around Post, Tin, Lever, Reeves Mfg. Co., Box, c.1925, 10 In. 250.00
Bird, Dancing, Pine, Hand Crank, Handmade, Signed H.L. Wallace, 12 In. 99.00
Bird, Pheasant, Tin Lithograph, Windup, Germany, 10 1/2 In. 220.00
Bird, Singing, Windup, Tin, Kohler, 9 In. 255.00
Black Dude, Jointed Body, Molded Head, Felt Jacket, Schoenhut, 8 1/4 In. 550.00
Black Man Carrying Bananas, Tin Lithograph, Distler, Germany, 7 1/2 In. 990.00
Blender, Dollee, Battery Operated, Box, 7 1/2 In. 39.00
Blocks, Alphabet, Birds, Wood, Paper Lithograph, McLoughlin, c.1890, 15 x 10 In. 2530.00
Blocks, Animals, Sound Effects, Cardboard, Paper Lithograph, Pull String, Box, 17 x 12 In.   300.00
Blocks, Building, Dovetailed Wooden Box, Label, Germany, 1930s, 12 x 10 x 2 In. 125.00
Blocks, Nesting, ABC, Circus, Animals, Wood, Paper Lithograph, Germany, 8 x 8 x 7 In. .   935.00
Blocks, Plastic, Blue, Red, Black, Verner Panton, Kurt Naef, Swiss, c.1975 . . . .   575.00
Blocks, Railroad, Alphabet, Box 1200.00
Blushing Willie, Battery Operated, Box, 10 In. 69.00
Bo Jangle, Dances, Wood, Tin Base, Clown Toy Co., Brooklyn, Box, 8 In. 120.00
Boar, Mohair, Brown, Tan, Studio, Steiff, Ear Button, 23 In. 385.00
Boat, Aircraft Carrier, Plastic, Battery Operated, Ventura, 22 In. 99.00
Boat, Aircraft Carrier, Tin Lithograph, Friction, Japan, 14 1/2 In. 120.00
Boat, Apollo, Tin Lithograph, Plastic, Battery Operated, Japan, 12 In. 40.00
Boat, Barbie, Irwin, Light Green, Plastic, Orange Seats, 1964 . . . .   95.00
Boat, Battleship, 4 Guns, 3 Sailors, Wood, Paper Lithograph, Reed, 31 In. 745.00
Boat, Battleship, Metal, Windup, Wolverine, U.S.A., 1950s, 14 1/2 In. 145.00
Boat, Battleship, Potemkin, Tin, Windup, Tucher & Walther, Box, 21 In. 220.00
Boat, Cabin Cruiser, Chris Craft, Red & Blue Stripes On White, Wood, Metal, 48 In. 205.00
Boat, Canoe, Li'l Abner & Lonesome Polecat, Ideal, Box, c.1951, 12 In. 935.00
Boat, Champion Racer, Driver, Tin, Friction, Haji, Box, 10 In. 220.00
Boat, Fleet Set, Naval Ships, Die Cast, Tootsietoy, Box, 6-In. Ships, 12 Piece 440.00
Boat, Gunboat, 2 Lifeboats, Wheels, Stained, Tin, Germany, 9 1/2 In. 195.00
Boat, Gunboat, Imperator, Tin, Windup, Tucher & Walther, Box, 24 In. 165.00
Boat, Man, Rowing, Wood, Tin, Cloth, Key, Clockwork, Ives, Feb. 1869, 12 In. 4115.00
Boat, Motor, Wood Hull, Pressed Steel Cabin, Windup, Key, Orkin, 29 In. 2530.00
Boat, Navy Set, Die Cast, Tootsietoy, Box, 6-In. Ships, 6 Piece 385.00
Boat, Ocean Liner, Painted Tin, Clockwork, Marklin, 18 In. 5720.00
Boat, Ocean Liner, SS America, Tin Lithograph, Pressed Steel Hull, Wyandotte, 12 In. . . .   130.00
Boat, Ocean Liner, SS United States, Tin, Battery Operated, Linemar, Box, 14 In. 1045.00
Boat, Ocean Liner, Tin Lithograph Deck, Windup, Germany, 8 In.   155.00
Boat, Ocean Liner, Tin Lithograph, Windup, Wolverine, Box, 15 In. 165.00
Boat, Ocean Liner, Tin, Germany, 16 In. 3520.00
Boat, Queen Of The Sea, Bump & Go, Horn, Battery Operated, Masudaya, Box, 22 In. . . .   330.00
Boat, Riverboat, Great Swanee, Tin, Spinning Paddlewheels, TN, 10 1/2 In. 385.00
Boat, Riverboat, KronPrinz, Paddlewheel, Painted, Germany, 17 In. 3160.00
Boat, Riverboat, Sailor, 3 Wheels, 2 Flags, Tin Lithograph, Germany, 1800s, 4 1/2 x 2 In.   300.00
Boat, Riverboat, Side-Wheeler, Packet Morning Mail, Handmade, Wood, c.1883, 74 In. . . .   935.00
Boat, Riverboat, Tin Lithograph, Battery Operated, Modern Toys, Japan, Box, 14 In. 77.00
Boat, Rowboat, Lady & Sailor, Rocking Action, Tin Lithograph, Meier, 3 In. 770.00
Boat, Rowboat, Man, Cap, Boots, Tin Lithograph, Rubber Band Powered, 9 In. 176.00
Boat, Sail, Endeavor, Wood, Star Yacht, England, 19 In. 35.00
Boat, Sail, Peggy Jane, Tin Lithograph, Hercules, Chein, 36 In. 130.00
Boat, Sail, Wood, Siefert, Germany, Box, 13 In. 110.00
Boat, Sail, Wood, Steel, Star Productions, England, Box, 24 In. 55.00
Boat, Sailor Figures, Metal Gears, Hinged Top Section, c.1840, 48 In. 2950.00
Boat, Shore Patrol, Tin, Battery Operated, Yonezawa, Box, 8 1/2 In. 99.00
Boat, Speedboat, Gas Powered, Wood, c.1950, 30 In. 1155.00
Boat, Speedboat, Go Racing, Tin, Windup, Japan, 8 In. 395.00

Boat, Speedboat, Liberty Flash, Driver, Propeller Spins, Tin, Wood, 16 In. 220.00
Boat, Speedboat, Mercury, Crank, Tin, No. 25, Japan, Box, 1950s, 6 In. 175.00
Boat, Speedboat, Miss America, Wood, Windup, Liberty, 18 In. 360.00
Boat, Speedboat, Spark Action, Masudaya, Box, Early 1950s, 6 1/2 In. 275.00
Boat, Speedboat, Tin, Plastic, Windup, Hornby, Box, 13 In. 145.00
Boat, Speedboat, Woman Driver, Flywheel, Tin Lithograph, Meier, 4 3/4 In. 275.00
Boat, Steamboat, Torpedo, Bing, 39 In. 4620.00
Boat, Tugboat, Annie, Tin Lithograph, Battery Operated, Japan, Box, 13 In. 99.00
Boat, Tugboat, Noises, Puffs Smoke, Battery Operated, Cragstan, Box, 14 In. 225.00
Boat, Wood, Battery Operated, Box, 11 In. 190.00
Boob McNut, Tin Lithograph, Windup, Strauss, 8 1/2 In. 535.00
Box, Peep, Rural Scenes, Engravings, Colored, Skylight, Case, Germany, 19th Century, 8 In. 765.00
Box, Uncle Sam Mechanical Band, Stenciled, Shepard Hardware, Box Only 1100.00
Boxers, Knockout Champs, In Ring, Tin Lithograph, Celluloid, Windup, Marx. 185.00
Boxers, Knockout, Tin, Mechanical, In Ring, Bob Up & Down, Strauss, 1921, 4 x 5 In. .. 365.00
Boxers, Slugger Champions, Louis-Schmelling Fight, Metal, Windup, 1950s 450.00
Boy, Black, Dangles Legs Riding On Cart, Windup, Martin, France, 1910 .... 950.00
Boy, In Highchair, Converts To Table, Embossed, Tin Lithograph, Distler, 4 In. 220.00
Boy, On Horse, Windup, Celluloid, 4 1/2 In. 80.00
Boy, On Scooter, Kicks Leg, Bisque Head, Wood, Composition, Clockwork, 13 In. 1210.00
Boy, On Sled, Plastic, Metal, Windup, Kenkosha Toys, Occupied Japan, Box, 4 1/2 In. ... 110.00
Boy, On Sled, Steel, Painted, Friction, Clark, 12 In. 310.00
Boy, On Sled, Tin, Friction, Red, Yellow, Green Paint, 9 x 6 In. 580.00
Boy, On Turtle, Tin, Painted, Embossed, Windup, 5 1/2 In. 250.00
Boy, Pulling Girl In Cart, Tin Lithograph, Germany, 7 1/4 In. 525.00
Boy, Whistling, Windup, Plastic, Irwin, Box, 9 1/2 In. 120.00
Brewster The Rooster, Battery Operated, Marx, Box, 10 In. 80.00
Bridge, Greyhound Bus On George Washington Bridge, Tin, Box, 1937, 25 In. 995.00
Bridge, Trestle, Steel, Electric Spotlight, Marx, Box, 24 In. 55.00
Bridge, Windup, Tin Lithograph, 24 In. 415.00
Bucking Bronco, Tin Lithograph, Embossed, Painted, Lehmann, Box, 7 1/2 In. 880.00
Buffalo, Jointed Wood, Leather Horns, Rope Tail, Painted Eyes, Schoenhut, 8 In. 250.00
Bugs Bunny, Baseball Player, Plastic Mask Face, Cloth Body, Carrot, 18 In. 11.00
Building Set, Wooden, Ge. Gesch., Germany, Box, Prewar, 12 x 8 1/2 In. 135.00
Bull, Bubbling, Battery Operated, Linemar, Box, 7 In. 155.00
Bulldozer, Moves, Lights, Horn, Tin, Battery Operated, Linemar, Box, 12 1/2 In. 440.00
Bus, Autobus, Penny Toy, Lehmann, 8 In. 990.00
Bus, Autobus, Spoke Wheels, Tin Lithograph, Windup, No. 590, Lehmann, c.1910, 8 In. . 990.00
Bus, Carnival, Tin, Friction, Japan, Box, 1950s, 9 In. 545.00
Bus, Cast Iron, Nickel Wheels, Freidag, 9 In. 440.00
Bus, City, Red, Green Trim, Rubber Tires, Kenton, 6 1/2 In. ....750.00 to 850.00
Bus, Coast To Coast, Keystone, Blue, Pressed Steel, Box, 31 In. 24200.00
Bus, Double-Decker, Blue, Arcade, 1929, 8 In. 650.00
Bus, Double-Decker, Cast Iron, Nickel Wheels, Freidag, 9 In. 440.00
Bus, Double-Decker, Green, Red Stripe, Kenton, 10 In. ....850.00 to 1500.00
Bus, Double-Decker, Green, Rubber Tires, Cast Iron, Arcade, 8 In. 360.00
Bus, Double-Decker, Interstate, Tin Lithograph, Mechanical, Strauss, c.1920s, 10 In. 605.00
Bus, Double-Decker, Tin Lithograph, Penny Toy, Fischer, Germany, c.1910, 4 In. ..,.... 440.00
Bus, Double-Decker, Tin Lithograph, Windup, Wells, England, Box, 4 1/2 In. 120.00
Bus, Double-Decker, Yellow, Cast Iron, White Rubber Tires, 13 1/2 In. 2090.00
Bus, GM Coach, Bump & Go, Lights, Tin, Battery Operated, Yonezawa, 16 In. 330.00
Bus, Greyhound Lines, Driver, Lady, Black Man, Tin, Friction, Marusan, Box, 12 1/2 In. . 825.00
Bus, Greyhound Lines, Tin Lithograph, Chein, 9 In. 180.00
Bus, Greyhound Scenic Cruiser, Tin, Friction, Japan, Box, 1960s, 14 1/2 In. 145.00
Bus, Greyhound, Tin, Hadson, Box, c.1956, 7 1/4 In. 220.00
Bus, Imperial Bus Lines, Tin Lithograph, Nonpareil, 9 1/2 In. 275.00
Bus, Inter-City, Pressed Steel, Electric Lights, Steelcraft, 24 In. 660.00
Bus, Interstate, Tin Lithograph, Strauss, 10 In. 605.00
Bus, Interstate, Windup, Tin Lithograph, Strauss, 11 In. 330.00
Bus, Junior, Tin Lithograph, Chein, 9 In. 385.00
Bus, Night Coach, Cast Iron, Kenton, 6 1/2 In. 470.00
Bus, Night Coach, Pick-Wick, Cast Iron, Kenton, 11 In. 5720.00
Bus, School, Children, Honks, Moves, Tin, Friction, Kanto, Box, 9 In. 99.00

Bus, School, Driver, Yellow, Friction, Toymaster, Box, c.1960, 9 In. 135.00
Bus, Shore Line Cannon Ball Express, Tin Lithograph, Upton, 9 1/2 In. 120.00
Bus, Sightseeing, Tin Lithograph, Battery Operated, Yonezawa, Japan, Box, 1950s, 9 In. ... 285.00
Bus, Trailways, Mystery Action, Silver, Red, Battery Operated, c.1960, 12 In. 225.00
Bus, Traveling Library, Tin, Japan, 6 In. 145.00
Busy Delivery, Black Pinocchio Figure, Tin Lithograph, Windup, Marx, 9 In. 600.00
Busy Lizzie, Windup, Tin Lithograph, Germany, 6 1/2 In. ....470.00 to 550.00
Butter & Egg Man, With Duck, Tin Lithograph, Windup, Marx, c.1930, 7 1/2 In. 495.00
Calypso Joe, Drummer, Native Rocks, Plays Drum, Tin, Windup, Japan, Box, 6 In. 325.00
Calypso Joe, Drummer, Walks, Tin, Cloth, Remote Control, Linemar, Box, 11 In. 495.00
Camel, Bactrian, Glass Eyes, Schoenhut, 7 In. 800.00
Camel, Steiff, 1950s, 11 In. 105.00
Cannon, Big Bang, No. 6F, Instructions, Box, 9 In. 99.00
Cannon, Civil War, Wood Carriage, Metal Rim Wheels, 12 Lb., 27 x 13 x 11 In. 290.00
Cannon, Wood, Blue, Red Stripes, Schoenhut, 23 In. 220.00
Cap Bomb, Admiral Dewey's Head 215.00
Cap Bomb, Admiral Dewey, Nickel Plated, Embossed Ring, 1900, 1 3/4 In. ....66.00 to 88.00
Cap Bomb, Cannibal Head, 1900, 2 3/4 In. 880.00
Cap Bomb, Congo Fire Bug, Cast Iron, Directions, Box, 3 In. 825.00
Cap Bomb, Devil's Head, 1 1/2 In. 440.00
Cap Bomb, Hobo, Nickel Plated, Ideal, 1896, 2 1/8 In. 195.00
Cap Bomb, McKinley, Nickel Plated, 1900, 2 1/4 In. 715.00
Cap Bomb, Pickaninny, 2-Piece Casting, Ives, 1890, 2 1/2 In. 360.00
Cap Gun, 6-Shooter, Revolving Cylinder, Single Action, Cast Iron, Kilgore, 6 7/8 In. 55.00
Cap Gun, 9-Petal Flower, Cast Iron, Logan Best, c.1878 .... 125.00
Cap Gun, Alligator, Animated, Cast Molded, 1887, 3 1/4 In. 1760.00
Cap Gun, Buster, Single Shot, Double Action, Cast Iron, Nickel Plated, 1900, 5 In. 330.00
Cap Gun, Butting Match, 2 Men Butt Heads, Cast Iron, Japanned, Ives, 1885, 5 In. 1045.00
Cap Gun, Cat, Animated, Paw Strikes Cap, Cast Iron, Japanned, 1882, 4 3/4 In. 5775.00
Cap Gun, Chinese Must Go, Animated, Man Kicks Man, Iron, Ives, 1892, 3 7/8 In. 880.00
Cap Gun, Duck, Animated, Beak Snaps Cap, Iron, Japanned Finish, Ives, 1884, 3 3/4 In. . 2200.00
Cap Gun, Dude, Black Paint, Single Shot & Action, Cast Iron, Stevens, 1887, 3 5/8 In. 140.00
Cap Gun, Go Bang, Single Action & Shot, Open Handle, Cast Iron, 1878, 3 3/8 In. 65.00
Cap Gun, Leo, Single Shot & Action, Cast Iron, 1890, 3 1/2 In. 250.00
Cap Gun, Man On Alligator, Animated, Iron, Japanned Finish, Ives, 1883, 5 1/8 In. 3850.00
Cap Gun, Monkey & Coconut, Animated, Cast Iron, J. & E. Stevens, 1890, 4 1/4 In. 1100.00
Cap Gun, Parole, Single Shot & Action, Cast Iron, Japanned Barrel, Ives, 1880, 3 5/8 In. .. 195.00
Cap Gun, Police Action, .38 Special, 12-Shot, Die Cast, Pistol Team Badge, Coibel, Box .. 40.00
Cap Gun, Polo, Single Shot & Action, Embossed, Cast Iron, Ives, 1878, 6 In. 90.00
Cap Gun, Rex, Single Shot & Action, Cast Iron, Nickel Plated, Kenton, 1923, 3 1/2 In. 65.00
Cap Gun, Volunteer, Single Shot & Action, Iron, Japanned Finish, Stevens, c.1873, 5 In. ... 55.00
Cap Gun, Zip, Cast Iron, Nickel Plated, Stevens, c.1890, 4 7/8 In. 140.00
Cap Machine Gun, Pump Action, McDowell, Box, 1920s, 13 1/2 In. 140.00
Captain, Drinks, Lamp Lights, Belly Expands, Battery Operated, S & E, Box, 12 In. 130.00
Car, Airflow, Cast Iron, Nickel Plated Grille, White Rubber Tires, Hubley, 4 In. 605.00
Car, Airflow, Cast Iron, Nickel Plated Grille, White Rubber Tires, Hubley, 6 In. ...170.00 to 275.00
Car, Airflow, Clockwork, Kingsbury, 14 In. 495.00
Car, Airflow, Coupe, Iron, Nickel Plated Grille, White Rubber Tires, Hubley, 4 1/2 In. .·.. 330.00
Car, Airflow, Coupe, Pressed Steel, Friction Motor, Wyandotte, 1930s, 5 1/2 In. 99.00
Car, Andy Gump, Cast Iron, Arcade, c.1930, 7 In. ....770.00 to 2300.00
Car, Archie's Jalopy, Windup, Tin Lithograph Of Archie Gang, Marx, 1960s 290.00
Car, Armored, Die Cast Metal, No. 80A, Dinky Toys, France, 3 1/2 In. 75.00
Car, Army, Driver, 22nd BN, Mettoy, England, 1940s, 11 In. 495.00
Car, Artie Clown, Windup, Tin Lithograph, Unique Art, 7 In. 250.00
Car, Aston Martin, James Bond, Tin, Battery Operated, Instructions, Box, 11 In. . ..385.00 to 715.00
Car, Aston Martin, Stunt, Turnover, Tin Lithograph, Windup, Japan, Box, 1960s, 7 In. ... 145.00
Car, Atom Robot, Driver, Tin, Rubber Tires, Friction, Yonezawa, Box, 16 In. 5445.00
Car, Austin Healey, No. 103, Dinky Toys, 1957, 3 1/2 In. 75.00
Car, Barbie, Orange, Turquoise Interior, Chrome Trim, Irwin 100.00
Car, Beetle, Tin Lithograph, Battery Operated, Bandai, Japan, 11 In. 55.00
Car, Blondie's Jalopy, Tin Lithograph, Windup, Marx, American, c.1930s, 15 In. 1375.00
Car, BMW, Tin, Windup, 3 Speeds, Distler, West Germany, Box, 9 1/2 In. 450.00
Car, Buick, 1939 Model, Prototype, Sample Tag, Marx, 26 In. 3960.00

Car, Buick, 1947 Model, Moves, Tin, Windup, Gama, U.S. Zone Germany, Box, 6 1/2 In. . 170.00
Car, Buick, 1951 Model, Convertible, Japan, 11 In. 775.00
Car, Buick, 1959 Model, Remote Control, Tin Lithograph, Cragstan, Japan, 11 1/2 In. 115.00
Car, Buick, 1966 Model, Bump & Go, Lights Flash, Tin, Battery Operated, A-1, 11 1/2 In. 250.00
Car, Buick, Bump & Go, Windup, KO, Japan, 1950s, 6 1/2 In. 225.00
Car, Buick, Century, Black, Gold, Silver Chrome, Japan, 1950s, 14 In. 1575.00
Car, Buick, Police, Friction, Japan, 1959, 11 In. 295.00
Car, Buick, Riviera, Removable Roof, Doors Open, Tin, Friction, Haji, Box, 11 In. 275.00
Car, Buick, Station Wagon, Tin, Friction, Japan, Box, 1960s, 6 1/2 In. 195.00
Car, Buick, Take Apart, Battery Operated Headlights, 1950s, 7 In. 450.00
Car, Bumper, Driver, Tin Lithograph, Rubber Bumper, Clockwork, Lindstrom, 9 In. 275.00
Car, Cabrio Super, Tin, Friction, Box, CKO 1000.00
Car, Cadillac, 1933 Model, Tin Lithograph, Friction, Bandai, 8 1/2 In. 50.00
Car, Cadillac, 1954 Model, Battery Operated, Japan, 9 In. 195.00
Car, Cadillac, 1954 Model, Tin, Friction, Marusan, Box, 12 1/2 In. 1465.00
Car, Cadillac, 1959 Model Auto Series, Convertible, Tin, Friction, Bandai, Box, 11 1/2 In. 465.00
Car, Cadillac, 1960 Model, 2 Door, Hard Top, Black, Marusan, 11 In. 375.00
Car, Cadillac, 1962 Model, Tin, Friction, Yonezawa, Box, 14 In. 660.00
Car, Cadillac, 1963 Model, Convertible, Tin, Battery Operated, Bandai, Box, 17 In. 635.00
Car, Cadillac, 1964 Model, Tin, Friction, Japan, Box, 22 In. 2860.00
Car, Cadillac, Convertible, Key Ignition, Tin, Battery Operated, Bandai, Box, 17 In. 1020.00
Car, Cadillac, Eldorado Broughman, 1967 Model, Marusan, Box, 15 In. 280.00
Car, Cadillac, Electricmobile, Convertible, Maroon, Japan, Box, 13 1/2 In. 1260.00
Car, Cadillac, Fleetwood Eldorado, Tin, Friction, Japan, Box, 10 1/2 In. 380.00
Car, Cadillac, Musical, Convertible, Driver, Tin, Battery Operated, Japan, Box, 9 In. 415.00
Car, Cadillac, Romance Car, Friction, Man Waving Hat, Woman Waving Arm, Japan, 1950 245.00
Car, Cadillac, Stunt, Battery Operated, No. 27, TM, Japan, Box, 11 In. 145.00
Car, Camaro, 1967 Model, Big Spots, Tin, Friction, Japan, 13 1/2 In. 375.00
Car, Chevrolet, 1928 Model, Coupe, Cast Iron, Arcade, 8 In. . . . . .495.00 to 715.00
Car, Chevrolet, 1960 Model, 2 Door, Hard Top, 2-Tone Blue, Alps, 9 In. 235.00
Car, Chevrolet, 1961 Model, Tin, Friction, ATC, Japan, 12 In. 440.00
Car, Chevrolet, Corvair, Fire Chief, Lonestar, Red, Die Cast, 1960, 4 In. 75.00
Car, Chevrolet, Corvair, Red, Tin, Friction, Bandai, Box, 8 1/4 In. 280.00
Car, Chevrolet, Coupe, Cast Iron Wheels, Rear Mounted Spare, Arcade, 8 1/2 In. 1155.00
Car, Chevrolet, Friction, Blue & Cream, Japan, 1960, 11 1/2 In. 375.00
Car, Chevrolet, Impala, Sports Sedan, Tin, Friction, Bandai, Box, 11 In. 248.00
Car, Chevrolet, Siren Service, Battery Operated, Japan, 1964, 14 1/2 In. 295.00
Car, Chevrolet, Station Wagon, Model Auto Series, Tin, Friction, Bandai, Box, 6 In. 150.00
Car, Chevrolet, Superior Sedan, Cast Iron, Arcade, c.1925, 3 3/4 x 3 x 6 3/4 In. 300.00
Car, Chevrolet, Tin, Friction, Japan, 1959 . . . . 295.00
Car, Chinese Man, Parasol, Tin Lithograph, Embossed, Distler, 3 In. 360.00
Car, Chrysler, 1950s Model, Tin, Friction, Japan, 1959, 8 1/2 In. 95.00
Car, Chrysler, Battery Operated, Premium, 1959 . . . . 1600.00
Car, Chrysler, Driver, Rubber Tires, Tin, Friction, Yonezawa, Box, 10 In. 290.00
Car, Circus, Tin Lithograph, Friction, Japan, A.T.C., 8 In. 495.00
Car, Circus, Tin, Windup, Japan, 1950s, 5 1/2 In. 145.00
Car, Citroen, 2CV, Clacking Noise, Tin, Friction, Daiya, Box, 8 1/4 In. . . . . .330.00 to 475.00
Car, Citroen, DS 19, Yellow, White, Tin, Battery Operated, Box, 12 In. 198.00
Car, Citroen, Metal, Friction, France, 1950s, 8 1/2 In. 295.00
Car, Citroen, Tin Lithograph, Electric Lights, Doors Open, Windup, 19 1/2 In. . .1265.00 to 1320.00
Car, Coo Coo Crazy, Tin Lithograph, Windup, Shellacked Wheels, Marx, 8 In. . . . .210.00 to 248.00
Car, Corvette Stingray, Bump & Go, Tin, Battery Operated, Ichida, Box, 12 In. 250.00
Car, Corvette Y Body, 1960 Model, 10 In. 850.00
Car, Coupe, Airflow, Tin Lithograph, Paya, Spain, 4 3/4 In. 50.00
Car, Coupe, Cast Iron, Crimson, Black, Kenton, 8 In. 880.00
Car, Coupe, Red, Black, White Rubber Tires, Electric, Headlight Bulbs, Wyandotte, 8 In. . 195.00
Car, Coupe, Reversible, Pressed Steel, Windup, Marx, 15 In. . . . . .259.00 to 350.00
Car, Coupe, Rumble Seat, Pressed Steel, Painted, Rubber Tires, Wyandotte, 8 In. 100.00
Car, Coupe, Tin Lithograph, Electric Lights, Marx, 15 In. 385.00
Car, Coupe, Tin Wheels, Tin Trunk Lid, Cast Iron, Green, Arcade, 6 In. 250.00
Car, Coupe, Tin, Windup, Folding Luggage Rack, Battery Lights, Girard, 1934, 14 In. . . . 200.00
Car, Coupe, Windup, Tin Lithograph, Marx, 12 In. 495.00
Car, Dagwood The Driver, Tin Lithograph, Windup, Marx, c.1930s, 15 In. . . . . . . .660.00 to 995.00

Car, Dodge, 1957 Model, Streamline Electric Sedan, Tin, Battery Operated, Box, 9 1/2 In.   140.00
Car, Dodge, 1957 Model, Tin, Friction, Japan, Box, 9 In. 798.00
Car, Dragster, Front Motor, Piston, Japan, 1950s, 9 In. 295.00
Car, Dream, Tin Lithograph, Friction, Japan, Box, 1950s, 16 In. 4950.00
Car, Drive Ur Self, Pull String To Direct Car, Tin, Windup, Marx, Box, 13 In. 2200.00
Car, Driver, Tiller Steering, Black, Red, Yellow, Cast Iron, 5 In. 259.00
Car, Ferrari, Friction, Bandai, Super America, Box, 11 In. . . . . .575.00 to 715.00
Car, Ferrari, Gear Shift, Moves, Lights, Tin, Battery Operated, Bandai, Box, 11 1/4 In. 250.00
Car, Ferrari, Silver, Red Interior, Battery Operated, Bandai, Japan, Box, 1960s, 11 In. 385.00
Car, Fiat, 600, Sunroof Sedan, Tin, Friction, Bandai, Box, 7 In. . . . . .275.00 to 415.00
Car, Fire Bird, Battery Operated, Japan, Box, 1950s, 10 1/2 In. . . . . .495.00 to 595.00
Car, Fire Chief, Red, Pressed Steel, Girard, 14 In. 220.00
Car, Fire Chief, Tin Lithograph, Battery Operated, Box, 11 In. 45.00
Car, Fire Chief, Tin Lithograph, Rubber Tires, Clockwork, Marx, Box, 11 In. 300.00
Car, Fire Department, Tin, Friction, 1950s, 8 1/2 In. 110.00
Car, Flivver, Coupe, Spoke Wheels, Buddy L, 1930, 11 In. . . . . .745.00 to 1430.00
Car, Flivver, Model T, Driver, Windup, Tin, Black, Bing, Germany, 6 In. 315.00
Car, Flivver, Roadster, Pressed Steel, Aluminum Wheels, Buddy L, 1920s, 11 1/2 In. 2200.00
Car, Ford, 1939 Model, Coupe, Classic Cast, 10 1/2 In. 935.00
Car, Ford, 1950 Model, Convertible, Red, Tootsietoy, 5 1/4 In. 125.00
Car, Ford, 1955 Model, 2 Door, Asahi, 9 In. 425.00
Car, Ford, 1965 Model, 2-Tone Blue, 10 In. 115.00
Car, Ford, America's Exposition, San Diego, Hard Rubber, 1935, 5 In. 415.00
Car, Ford, Convertible, Blue, Tin, Friction, Masaduya, Box, 7 In.   215.00
Car, Ford, Corsair, Green, Boattail, No. 46, Matchbox, Lesney, Box, 1965 . . . .   160.00
Car, Ford, Cougar, Metal, Battery Operated, Japan, 10 In. 145.00
Car, Ford, Dog Driver, Tin, Friction, Japan, 1962, 10 1/2 In. 245.00
Car, Ford, Fairlane 500, Sunliner, Tin, Bandai, Box, 1950s, 12 In. 880.00
Car, Ford, Fat Boy, Red, Silver, Yonezawa, Japan, c.1950, 15 In.   345.00
Car, Ford, Flower Delivery Wagon, 1955 Model, Tin Litho., Friction, Bandai, Box, 12 In. .   1100.00
Car, Ford, Galaxie 500, Station Wagon, Wood Grain, Friction, Yonezawa, 1965, 10 In. . . .   285.00
Car, Ford, Model A, Carrier, Arcade, 26 1/2 In., 5 Piece 4000.00
Car, Ford, Model A, Cast Iron, Iron Spoke Wheels, Arcade, 5 In.   220.00
Car, Ford, Model A, Sedan, Blue, Cast Iron, Arcade, 7 In. 440.00
Car, Ford, Model T, Center Door, Driver, Black, Arcade, 6 1/2 In.   650.00
Car, Ford, Model T, Coupe, Pressed Steel, Aluminum Wheels, Buddy L, 1920s, 11 In. . . .   1320.00
Car, Ford, Model T, Roadster, Pressed Steel, Aluminum Wheels, Buddy L, 1920s, 11 In. . .   770.00
Car, Ford, Model T, Roadster, Windup, Tin, Black, Bing, Germany, 6 1/2 In. . . . . .200.00 to 490.00
Car, Ford, Model T, Sedan, Center Door, Arcade, 6 1/2 In. 650.00
Car, Ford, Model T, Sedan, Center Door, Pressed Steel, Cowdry, 11 In. 825.00
Car, Ford, Model T, Sedan, Windup, Tin, Orobr, Germany, 6 In. 145.00
Car, Ford, Model T, Touring, Pressed Steel, Cowdry, Box, 11 In.   1155.00
Car, Ford, Model T, Touring, Windup, Tin, Orobr, Germany, 8 In.   358.00
Car, Ford, Mustang, Flower Power Stock Racing, No. 348, Corgi, England, Box, 1967 . . .   70.00
Car, Ford, Mustang, Tin, Bandai, Japan, 1960s, 11 1/2 In. 77.00
Car, Ford, Ranchero, 1957 Model, Bandai, Friction, Box, 12 In. 895.00
Car, Ford, Sedan, Tin, Windup, Black, Bing, 6 In. 225.00
Car, Ford, Skyliner, Bump & Go, Roof Slides, Tin, Battery Operated, Japan, Box, 9 In. . . .   165.00
Car, Ford, Skyliner, Roof Slides Into Trunk, Tin, Friction, Japan, Box, 7 1/2 In. 275.00
Car, Ford, Standard Coffee, 1955 Model, Tin Lithograph, Friction, Bandai, Japan, 12 In. . .   3520.00
Car, Ford, Taurus, Tin, Friction, Bandai, Japan, Box, 1960s, 8 1/2 In. 120.00
Car, Ford, Thunderbird, Convertible, Tin, Roof & Windows Move, Sears, Japan, 15 1/2 In.   495.00
Car, Ford, Thunderbird, Friction, Free Gift, Box, 1957, 1 7/8 x 3 x 7 1/4 In. 295.00
Car, Ford, Thunderbird, Retractable Hardtop, Lever, Tin Steering Wheel, 9 1/2 In. 250.00
Car, Ford, Thunderbird, Tin, Battery Operated, 1955, 11 In. 595.00
Car, Futuristic, No. 3, Friction, Japan, 1962, 11 In. 395.00
Car, Futuristic, Tin, Linemar, Japan, 8 1/4 In. 275.00
Car, Futuristic, Woman Driver, Sparks, Tin, Friction, Linemar, Box, 1955, 12 In. 1345.00
Car, G-Man Pursuit, Plate Metal, Windup, Marx, c.1930s, 14 In.   1155.00
Car, G-Man Pursuit, Tin, Rubber Tires, Sparking Machine Gun, Marx, 15 In. 1570.00
Car, Graham Paige, No. 3, Tin Lithograph, Windup, Japan, Box, Prewar, 6 In. 330.00
Car, Green Hornet Black Beauty, 1966, 2 3/4 In. 145.00
Car, Happy Chick, Rooster, Tin, Friction, Yonezawa, Box, 5 1/2 In. 170.00

Car, Happy Chick, Tin Lithograph, Friction, Yonezawa, Box, 5 1/2 In. 145.00
Car, Hercules, Roadster, Tin, Chein, 18 In. 550.00
Car, Hot Rod, Battery Operated, Tin Lithograph, Japan, Box, 7 In. 385.00
Car, Hot Rod, Dreamboat, Driver, Bump & Go, Tin, Battery Operated, Japan, Box, 7 In. . . 250.00
Car, Hot Rod, Friction, Tin Lithograph, Japan, Box, 1950s, 7 1/2 In. 295.00
Car, Humphrey Mobile, Tin, Windup, Wyandotte, Box, 8 In. 340.00
Car, Indian Crash, 3 Wheeler, Cast Iron, Champion, 7 In. 385.00
Car, International Agent, Tin, Friction, Marx, Japan, Box, 1966, 4 In. 105.00
Car, Isetta, Red, White, Tin, Friction, Bandai, Box, 6 1/2 In. 385.00
Car, Jaguar, Coupe, 1960s Model, Bandai, 9 1/2 In. 365.00
Car, Jaguar, Driver's Arm Moves, Tin, Friction, Japan, 1950s, 7 1/2 In. 195.00
Car, Jaguar, Metallic Blue, Friction, TN, c.1960, 11 In. 325.00
Car, Jaguar, XK120, Tin Lithograph, Friction, Alps, Box, 7 In. . . . . .70.00 to 160.00
Car, Jaguar, XK150, Tin Lithograph, Battery Operated, Cable Steering, Japan, 8 In. 39.00
Car, Jalopy, Limping Lizzie, Driver, Windup, Marx, Original Box, 1930s 650.00
Car, James Bond, 007, Battery Operated, Windscreen, Ejector Seat, Gilbert, 1965, 12 In. . 265.00
Car, James Bond, 007, Bump & Go, Tin, Battery Operated, Japan, Box, 14 1/2 In. 798.00
Car, James Bond, 007, Chevrolet Impala, 5 Actions, Joy Toy Co., Box, 1963, 15 In. 650.00
Car, Jolly Joe, Man Driving Jeep, Gun On Hood, Clockwork, Marx 170.00
Car, Karmann Ghia, Tin, Friction, Bandai, Japan, Box, 7 1/2 In. 275.00
Car, Kingsbury Airflow, Pressed Steel, Clockwork, Rubber Wheels, 14 In. 255.00
Car, LaSalle, Sedan, Pressed Steel, Marx, 11 In. 250.00
Car, Leaping Lena, Black, Graffiti, I Do Not Choose To Run, Tin, Mechanical, 7 In. 140.00
Car, Leaping Lena, Black, New York To Frisco, Tin, Mechanical, Strauss, 8 In. 365.00
Car, Leaping Lena, Rolls Forward, Hops, Windup, Tin Lithograph, Strauss, 1930, 8 1/2 In. 230.00
Car, Limousine, Driver, Orange, Black, Luggage Rack, Windup, G & K, c.1910, 7 In. 650.00
Car, Limousine, Driver, Pressed Steel, Flywheel Motor, Dayton, 1920s, 12 In. 470.00
Car, Limousine, Driver, Red, Black, Tin, Windup, Fischer, Germany, 8 In. 270.00
Car, Limousine, Driver, Tin Lithograph, Penny Toy, Germany, 5 1/2 In. 300.00
Car, Limousine, Driver, Tin Lithograph, Windup, Bing, 5 1/2 In. 180.00
Car, Limousine, Driver, Tin, Electric Lights, Clockwork, Gunthermann, 18 In. . .1540.00 to 2200.00
Car, Limousine, Driver, Tin, Passengers Lithograph, Chein, 8 In. 130.00
Car, Limousine, Driver, Windshield, Lanterns, Windup, Carette, France, 1908, 8 3/4 In. . . 1800.00
Car, Limousine, Driver, Windup, Rear Opening Doors, Tin Litho., Orobr, Germany, 6 In. . 660.00
Car, Limousine, Family, Girl, Doll, Tin Lithograph, Windup, Chein, 1930s, 6 In. 300.00
Car, Limousine, Mechanical, Tin Lithograph, Moko, Germany, 9 1/2 In. 495.00
Car, Lincoln, Airport Limousine, Tin, Friction, Japan, Box, 1960s, 9 In. 195.00
Car, Lincoln, Concept, Friction, Tin, Japan, 1950s, 7 1/2 In. 395.00
Car, Lincoln, Fire Chief, Siren, Bump & Go, Tin, Battery Operated, Bandai, Box, 11 In. . . 165.00
Car, Lincoln, Touring, Blue, Spoke Wheels, A.C. Williams, 7 In. 550.00
Car, Man From U.N.C.L.E., Thrush Buster, Die Cast, Corgi, Box, 4 1/4 In. 495.00
Car, Mercedes-Benz, 220S, Automatic Jack, Lug Wrench, Tire, Tin, SSS, Box, 12 In. 330.00
Car, Mercedes-Benz, 250SE, Bump & Go, Horn, Tin, Battery Operated, Ichiko, Box, 13 In. 220.00
Car, Mercedes-Benz, 250SL, Driver, Lights, Tin, Battery Operated, Bandai, Box, 10 In. . . 165.00
Car, Mercedes-Benz, Fire Chief, Mystery, Bump & Go, Tin, Battery, Sanshi, Box, 9 In. . . . 495.00
Car, Mercedes-Benz, Metal, Lights, Battery Operated, Japan, 1950s, 7 1/2 In. 95.00
Car, Mercedes-Benz, Super Racer, Driver, Plastic, Tin, Friction, Linemar, Box, 10 In. 275.00
Car, Mercury, 1954 Model, Metal, Battery Operated, Japan, 10 In. 295.00
Car, Mercury, Station Wagon, Tin, 3 Colors, Plastic Windshields, Bandai, Box, 8 In. 275.00
Car, MG, 1018, Fold-Down Window, Tin, Friction, Japan, Box, 6 1/2 In. 275.00
Car, MG, Red, Battery Operated, KO, c.1950, 8 In. 265.00
Car, MGA, Sports, Red, Tin, Friction, Japan, Box, 9 1/2 In. 495.00
Car, MGB GT, No. 327, Corgi, England, Box, 1967 . . . . 79.00
Car, Military, Police, Green, White, Friction, Taiyo, Japan, Box, c.1960, 10 In. 145.00
Car, Milton Berle, Tin Lithograph, Windup, Marx, Box, c.1950, 6 In. 525.00
Car, Monkee Mobile, Pontiac GTO, Tin, Plastic Figures, Raybert ASC, Japan, 1967, 12 In. 495.00
Car, Moon, Bump & Go, Moon Spins, Lights, Tin, Battery Operated, Linemar, Box, 13 In. 1540.00
Car, Mr. Magoo, Rises In Seat, Tin, Battery Operated, Hubley, Box, 1961, 9 In. 330.00
Car, Nash, Touring, Open, Tin Lithograph, Friction, Fabric Top, 1930s Model, Japan, 11 In. 25.00
Car, Naughty Boy, Father & Son, Windup, Lehmann 575.00
Car, Nutty Mad, Driver, Moves, Kicks Back, Tin, Battery Operated, Marx, Japan, 9 1/2 In. 170.00
Car, Oho, Driver, Tin Lithograph, Mechanical, Lehmann, Germany, c.1910, 4 In. 525.00
Car, Old Jalopy, Tin Lithograph, Friction, Linemar, Japan, 6 In. 66.00

Car, Old Jalopy, Tin Lithograph, Windup, Marx, Box, c.1930s, 7 In. 385.00
Car, Oldsmobile, 1958 Model, Convertible, Red, White Interior, Tin, Friction, Japan, 13 In.   570.00
Car, Oldsmobile, Sedan, Battery Operated, Tin Lithograph, Radicon, 1950s, 14 In. 635.00
Car, Plymouth, 1957 Model, Japan, 11 1/2 In. 625.00
Car, Plymouth, 1959 Model, Tin, Friction, 8 1/4 In. 245.00
Car, Plymouth, 1960s Model, Station Wagon, Tin, Friction, Japan, 10 In. 175.00
Car, Plymouth, Fury, 1961 Model, Tin, Friction, Japan, Box, 14 In. 300.00
Car, Plymouth, Tin, Friction, Japan, Box, 1957, 8 1/2 In. 195.00
Car, Police, Battery Operated, Metal, Japan, 1962, 10 In. 175.00
Car, Police, Battery Operated, Tin Lithograph, Japan, Box, 8 In. 175.00
Car, Police, Battery Operated, Tin, Linemar, Japan, Box, 7 In. .... 90.00 to 120.00
Car, Police, Chevrolet, Gang Buster, Light, Gun, Tin, Friction, Ichiko, Box, 1950, 11 In. ... 195.00
Car, Police, Coupe, Tin Lithograph, Friction, Siren, Green, Marx, 8 In. 330.00
Car, Police, Electric Remote Control, Linemar, Box 85.00
Car, Police, Highway Patrol, Broderick Crawford, Guns, Tin, Friction, Japan, Box, 5 1/2 In.   255.00
Car, Police, Mystery, Tin, Battery Operated, Japan, Box, 1960s, 10 In. 285.00
Car, Police, Oldsmobile, Black, White, Friction, Box, 1959, 10 In. 115.00
Car, Police, Siren, Friction, Tin Lithograph, Lupor, Box, c.1950, 11 In. 245.00
Car, Police, Siren, Plate Metal, Windup, Marx, c.1930, 14 In. 495.00
Car, Police, Talking, Battery Operated, Cragstan, Japan, Box, 1960s, 14 In. 285.00
Car, Police, Tin Lithograph, Plastic, Siren, Battery Operated, Japan, Box, 13 In. 39.00
Car, Police, Tin, Friction, SSS Toys, Japan, Box, 1950s, 5 1/4 In. 95.00
Car, Pontiac, 1953 Model, Tin, Friction, Japan, 14 1/2 In. 660.00
Car, Pontiac, Baby, Tin, Windup, TM, Occupied Japan, Box, 3 3/8 In. 125.00
Car, Pontiac, Convertible, Cast Iron, Kilgore, 10 1/4 In. 1550.00
Car, Pontiac, Convertible, Yellow, No. 39, Matchbox, Lesney, Box, 1962 .... 65.00
Car, Porsche, 7500, Electromatic, Tin, Battery Operated, Distler, West Germany, 10 In. ... 415.00
Car, Prop Rod, Plastic, Gas Power, Aluminum Belly Pan, Thimble Drome, Box, 13 In. ... 155.00
Car, Puzzle, Metal, Occupied Japan, Box, 6 In. 75.00
Car, Race Track Set, Johnny Lightning Indy 500, Topper, 1970s, 24 x 24-In. Box 65.00
Car, Race Track Set, Streamline Speedway, Tin Lithograph, Windup Cars, Marx, Box 165.00
Car, Racing, 2 Seats, George Fisher, Penny Toy 1760.00
Car, Racing, Atom Jet, Land Speed, Tin, Friction, Japan, 1950s, 28 In. 3850.00
Car, Racing, Battery Operated, Tin, Japan, Box, 8 In. 250.00
Car, Racing, Benz, Battery Operated, Marusan, Japan, Box, 10 In. 395.00
Car, Racing, Bluebird, Land Speed, Tin Lithograph, Gunthermann, Germany, 20 In. 1265.00
Car, Racing, Boat Tail, Pressed Steel, Electric Headlights, Wyandotte, 9 In. 250.00
Car, Racing, Buffalo Silver Bullet, Spring Motor, 26 In. 489.00
Car, Racing, Cast Iron, Original Paint, Hubley, 8 In. 175.00
Car, Racing, Citroen, Driver, Rubber Tires, Steel, Windup, France, Box, 17 In. 825.00
Car, Racing, Don Edmunds, White, Aluminum, 20 1/2 In. 9900.00
Car, Racing, Driver, Battery Operated, Tin Lithograph, Yonezawa, Japan, 1950s, 6 1/4 In. .. 185.00
Car, Racing, Driver, Leather Helmet, Blue, Cast Iron, 6 1/2 In. 200.00
Car, Racing, Driver, Red, Remote Control, Electric, Domo, Box, c.1952, 16 1/2 In. 6050.00
Car, Racing, Driver, Tin Lithograph, Windup, Matarazzo, Argentina, Box, 9 1/2 In. 305.00
Car, Racing, Driver, Tin Lithograph, Windup, No. 7, Marx, 5 In. 80.00
Car, Racing, Electric, Racing Course, Domo, Box, c.1952, 16 1/2 In. 6050.00
Car, Racing, Electro, No. 21, Tin Lithograph, Battery Operated, Japan, Box, 1950s, 10 In.   4400.00
Car, Racing, Fiction, Siren, Tin Lithograph, Metal Wheels, 1940s, 5 In. 95.00
Car, Racing, Flying Goose, No. 3, Tin Lithograph, Windup, Japan, 13 1/2 In. 660.00
Car, Racing, Golden Jet, No. 18, Japan, Box, 1950s, 12 In. 295.00
Car, Racing, Indianapolis 500, Rod Lifts Car, Tin, Battery Operated, Sears, Box, 15 1/2 In.   525.00
Car, Racing, Indy Champion, No. 1, Tin, Friction, Y-Japan, 1950s, 9 1/2 In. 395.00
Car, Racing, Indy Racer, No. 4, Friction, MAR Japan, 1950s, 7 In. 195.00
Car, Racing, JC Agajanian, No. 98, Tin Lithograph, Friction, Japan, Box, 19 In. 7370.00
Car, Racing, Jetspeed, Driver, 2 Speeds, Lights, Tin, Battery Operated, Marx, Box, 17 In. .. 550.00
Car, Racing, King Jet, Bubble Canopy, Sparking Engine, Japan, 12 In. 2200.00
Car, Racing, King, Driver, Yellow, Black, Tin, Windup, Marx, Box, 1930s, 9 In. 8645.00
Car, Racing, Lupor, Tin Lithograph, Windup, Box, 11 1/2 In. 190.00
Car, Racing, Mercedes-Benz, 2 Figures, Friction, Tin Lithograph, Japan, 6 1/2 In. 140.00
Car, Racing, Metal, Rack & Pinion Steering, Flags, Windup, Kingsbury, 3 1/2 x 19 In. ... 375.00
Car, Racing, Midget, No. 4, Tin, Friction, Japan, 7 In. 635.00
Car, Racing, Midget, No. 63, Tin Lithograph, Friction, Japan, 7 In. .... 360.00 to 935.00

Car, Racing, Nickel Plated Driver, Rubber Tires, Cast Iron, Hubley, 8 1/2 In. 275.00
Car, Racing, Nickel Plated Driver, White Rubber Tires, Cast Iron, Hubley, 6 In. 180.00
Car, Racing, No. 1, Painted, Hubley, 8 In. 175.00
Car, Racing, No. 5, Hood Opens, Cast Iron, Hubley, 9 In. 605.00
Car, Racing, No. 13, Tin, Windup, Ingap, Italy, 7 1/2 In. 935.00
Car, Racing, No. 52, Metal, Friction, 1950s, 11 1/2 In. 275.00
Car, Racing, Open Wheel, Red Paint, Cast Iron, Hubley, 5 In. 115.00
Car, Racing, Pressed Steel, Electric Headlights, Wyandotte, 1940s, 8 1/2 In. 275.00
Car, Racing, Propeller Driven, Friction, Chrome Exhaust Pipes, Japan, 1960s, 9 1/2 In. 245.00
Car, Racing, Road Wizard, Tin, Windup, Driver Raises Arm & Turns, TBC, 7 1/2 In. 155.00
Car, Racing, Rocket Racer, Wyandotte, 1935 . . . .   395.00
Car, Racing, Silver Bullet, Driver, Passenger, Tin, Windup, Buffalo Toy, 26 In. 715.00
Car, Racing, Speed Racer, Driver, Clicking Noise, Windup, Tin, Marx, Box, 6 1/4 In. 205.00
Car, Racing, Speedway Racer, No. 20, Tin Lithograph, Elenee, Japan, Box, 10 1/2 In. 200.00
Car, Racing, Super Racer, No. 42, Red Flame, Tin Lithograph, Friction, 1950s, 19 In. 3080.00
Car, Racing, Thunderbolt, Driver, Tin, Friction, Japan, Box, 11 In. 385.00
Car, Racing, Windup, Electric Spotlight, Tin Lithograph, Tipp, Germany, 14 1/2 In. 908.00
Car, Racing, Windup, Pressed Steel, Tin Lithograph, Marx, 12 In. 360.00
Car, Racing, Windup, Tin Lithograph, Burnett Ubuilda, England, 11 In. 170.00
Car, Racing, Windup, Tin Lithograph, France, 10 In. 275.00
Car, Racing, Windup, Tin Lithograph, Germany, 1950s, 10 In., Pair 95.00
Car, Racing, Windup, Tin Lithograph, Lupor, Box, 12 In. 190.00
Car, Racing, Windup, Tin Lithograph, Mettoy, Great Britain, 15 1/2 In. 470.00
Car, Racing, Windup, Tin Lithograph, Silver Flash, 19 In. 440.00
Car, Racing, Windup, Tin, H.J., Germany, 1950s, 5 In. 120.00
Car, Racing, Y53, Tin, Friction, Japan, 1950s, 12 1/2 In. . . . . .195.00 to 375.00
Car, Railroad Dredge, Pressed Steel, Buddy L, 1920s, 30 In. 1320.00
Car, Renault, Windup, Tin, Bavaria, 6 In. 385.00
Car, Rheo, Coupe, Driver, Nickel Plated Wheels, Cast Iron, Arcade, 9 In. 2640.00
Car, Roadster, Red, Schieble, 1920s, 18 In. 625.00
Car, Rocket Express, Tin Lithograph, Windup, Technofix, Germany, 15 In. 110.00
Car, Rocket Jupiter, Tin Lithograph, Friction, Japan, Box, 9 In.   105.00
Car, Rocket Racer, Moves, Click Noise, Tin, Friction, Masudaya, Box, 7 In. 360.00
Car, Rolls-Royce, No. 152, Dinky Toys, Box 375.00
Car, Rolls-Royce, Silver Cloud, Tin, Bandai, Box, 12 In. . . . . .104.00 to 385.00
Car, Royal Coupe, Driver, Windup, Spare Tire On Trunk, Tin, Marx, Box, c.1930, 9 In. . . .   1430.00
Car, Sedan, Driver, Windup, Gunthermann, 1930s, 9 1/2 In. 550.00
Car, Sedan, Nickel Plated Grille, Rear Bumper, White Rubber Tires, Hubley, 7 1/2 In. . . .   190.00
Car, Sedan, Windup, C. Rossignol, France, 8 In. 485.00
Car, Space Patrol, Astronaut Driver, Bump & Go, Battery, Tin, Bandai, Box, 12 In. 715.00
Car, Space Patrol, Bump & Go, Noise, Lights, Tin, Battery Operated, Japan, Box, 8 In. . . .   260.00
Car, Space, Tin Lithograph, Friction, Yellow Dome, Tin Driver, 1950s, 9 In. 95.00
Car, Sports, Cunningham, Tin, Asahitoy, Box, 7 1/2 In. 171.00
Car, State Police, Blue, White, Friction, Japan, Box, c.1960, 10 In. 195.00
Car, Station Wagon, Tin, Friction, Lithographed Luggage, Japan, Box 325.00
Car, Streamline, Windup, Tin Lithograph, Marx, 13 In. 210.00
Car, Studebaker, Friction, Tin, Japan, 1950s, 8 1/2 In. 195.00
Car, Studebaker, Power Station, Distler, Electromatic, Box 375.00
Car, Take-A-Part, 3 Different Bodies, Cast Iron, Hubley, 4 In. 165.00
Car, Telephone Service, Friction, Japan, Box, 1950s, 8 In. 145.00
Car, Tin Lithograph, Windup, Japan, 7 1/2 In. 580.00
Car, Tin, Composition Figures, Remote Control, Steering, Arnold, Germany, 10 In. 110.00
Car, Tin, Windup, No. 700, Germany, 1903 Patent 200.00
Car, Touring, Cast Iron, Iron Spoke Wheels, 12 In. 580.00
Car, Touring, Driver, Open, Windup, Germany, 11 In. 750.00
Car, Touring, Driver, Woman Passenger, Tin Lithograph, Embossed, Meier, 3 1/2 In. 470.00
Car, Touring, Windup, Tin Lithograph, Strauss, 10 In. 920.00
Car, Toy Town Delivery, Pressed Steel, Lithograph, Doors Open, Wyandotte, 1940s, 21 In.   330.00
Car, Toyota, Celica, Yellow, Japan, Box, c.1971, 14 1/2 In. 345.00
Car, Trikauto, Crazy, Circus, Driver, Tin, Windup, Strauss, Box, 7 1/2 In. 550.00
Car, Tut-Tut, Driver Blows Horn, Lehmann, Box 1840.00
Car, Uncle Wiggily, Crazy, Rabbit Driver, Tin, Windup, CK, Prewar, 7 1/2 In. 1705.00
Car, Uncle Wiggily, Tin Lithograph, Windup, Marx, c.1935, 7 In. . . . . .605.00 to 1265.00

Toy, Carriage, Doll's,
Red, Spokes, Stenciling,
Lace Fringe, Wood Frame,
27 x 39 In.

Toy, Carriage, Doll's,
Wicker, Rolled Edge,
F.A. Whitney Carriage
Co., 37 x 37 In.

Car, Volkswagen, Bump & Go, Convertible, Tin, Plastic, Battery, TN, Box, 13 In. 1045.00
Car, Volkswagen, Bump & Go, Sedan, Driver, Lights, Tin, Battery, Bandai, Box, 10 In. . . 250.00
Car, Volkswagen, Space Patrol, Astronaut Driver, Battery, Lights, Tin, Japan, 13 In. 1650.00
Car, What's It, Tin, Mechanical, Erratic, Strauss, 1925, 10 In. 1456.00
Car, Whoopee, Driver, Crazy Action, Tin, Windup, Marx, Box, 7 1/2 In. 440.00
Car, Whoopee, Flivver, Model T, Driver, Dog, Suitcase, Spins, Windup, Tin, Marx, 7 In. . 180.00
Car, Woman Driving In Open Air, 3 Wheels, Tin Lithograph, DRGM, Germany, 4 1/2 In. . 700.00
Car, Woody, Convertible, Pressed Steel, Lithograph, Wyandotte, 12 1/2 In. 250.00
Car, Woody, Station Wagon, Tin Lithograph, Friction, Marx, 7 1/2 In. . . . . .100.00 to 150.00
Car, Woody, Station Wagon, Toy Town, Lithograph Man & Girl, Tin, Wyandotte, 21 In. . . 335.00
Car, World Circus, Clown Decorations, Japan, 1950s, 7 In. 125.00
Car, Zigzag, Tin Lithograph, Windup, Lehmann, Germany, c.1910, 6 In. 1210.00
Car & Boat Trailer, Pontiac, Tin, Friction, Japan, 1950s, 11 1/2 In. 145.00
Car & Boat Trailer, Station Wagon, Tin Litho., Friction, Haji, Japan, Box, 1950s, 11 In. . . 155.00
Caroplane, XY-302, Plane Converts To Car, Friction, MSK, Japan, 1950s 290.00
Carousel, Indian, Motorcycles, 1940s, 45 In. 3520.00
Carousel, Swans & Airplanes, Windup, Wyandotte, 6 In. 350.00
Carriage, Doll's, Battery Operated, Baby, Mother, Rosko, Box, 8 In. 115.00
Carriage, Doll's, Canopy, Garton, 25 In. 55.00
Carriage, Doll's, Lithograph Paper On Wood, Tin Wire Wheels, c.1900, 9 In. 220.00
Carriage, Doll's, Red, Spokes, Stenciling, Lace Fringe, Wood Frame, 27 x 39 In. . . . *Illus* 345.00
Carriage, Doll's, Tin, Painted, Wood Push Handle, Marklin, 9 In. 1980.00
Carriage, Doll's, Wicker, Opera Window Top, 26 In. . . . . .35.00 to 45.00
Carriage, Doll's, Wicker, Rolled Edge, F.A. Whitney Carriage Co., 37 x 37 In. . . . . . *Illus* 175.00
Carriage, Doll's, Wicker, Wire, Spoke Wheels, Wood Handle, 30 In. 85.00
Carriage, Doll's, Wicker, Wood Seat, Handle, Metal Spokes, 17 In. 79.00
Carriage, Doll's, Wood, Black, Gold Stencil, Spoke Wheels, Velvet Cover, 26 In. 55.00
Carriage, Horse Drawn, Painted Wood, Lutz Type, Germany, 21 In. 210.00
Carriage, Horse Team, Cast Iron, Aluminum, Stanley Toys, 11 1/2 In. 50.00
Carriage, Horse, Wood, Platform, Metal Wheels, F.A.O. Schwarz, 14 x 12 In. 275.00
Cart, Chinese Man, Tin Lithograph, Black Image On Cart, Germany, G & K, 6 In. 489.00
Cart, Delivery, Horse Drawn, High Grade Goods Department Store, Tin Litho., 10 In. . . . 115.00
Cart, Delivery, Man Peddling, Tin, Vebe, France, 1930s, 6 In. 145.00
Cart, Horse Drawn, Carved Coach, Wood, Wheel Platform, F.A.O. Schwarz, 26 In. 275.00
Cart, Horse Drawn, Woman Driver, c.1890, 10 1/4 In. 995.00
Cart, Ice Cream, Vendor, Celluloid, Tin, Windup, Occupied Japan 250.00
Cart, Ice Cream, Vendor, Plastic, Helados, Commando, Spain, Box, 5 x 6 In. 95.00
Cart, Ice Cream, Vendor, Tin Lithograph, Windup, Japan, Box, c.1960, 4 1/2 x 5 In. 195.00
Cart, Ice Cream, Vendor, Tin, Rico, Spain, 1926, 5 x 5 In. 695.00
Cart, Ice Cream, Vendor, Umbrella, Pewter, 6 x 4 In. 65.00
Cart, Ostrich, Monkey, Windup, Tin Lithograph, Japan, 9 In. 259.00
Cart, Vendor, Jolly Popcorn, Bear Pushes, Tin, Plastic, Battery Operated, TN, Japan, Box . 185.00
Cart, Zulu, Driver, Ostrich, Tin Litho., Embossed, Clockwork, Lehmann, 7 In. . . . .495.00 to 525.00
Case, Barbie & Francie, Hat Box, Light Blue Vinyl, White Handle, Mirror, 1965 . . . . 80.00
Case, Barbie & Francie, Light Blue Vinyl, White Handle, Mirror . . . . .85.00 to 165.00
Case, Barbie & Midge, Travel Pals, Hat Box, Black Vinyl, 1963 . . . . 85.00
Case, Barbie Goes Travelin', Car, Plane, Pink, Black Handle, Vinyl, 1965 . . . . 180.00
Case, Barbie, Ballet, Black Vinyl, Ballerinas, 1966 . . . . 65.00

Case, Barbie, Carry-All, 3 Barbies, Black Vinyl, Red Vinyl Interior ....25.00 to 160.00
Case, Barbie, International Mod, Pink Vinyl, Hat Box, 1971 .... 75.00
Case, Barbie, Perk Up, Red Vinyl, Zipper, 1962 .... 80.00
Case, Skipper & Skooter, Beach Scene, Blue Vinyl, Black Handle 55.00
Case, Skipper, Doll, Purse-Pal, Blue Vinyl, 2 Compartments 130.00
Cash Register, Black, Silver Trim, 1 Cent To 10 Dollars, American Flyer, 9 x 10 In. 35.00
Cat, Blinkey, Meows, Begs, Battery Operated, Remote Control, Alps, Japan, Box 80.00
Cat, Felix & Mice, Tin, Red Wheels, Pull Toy, Nifty, Germany, c.1920s, 7 1/2 In. 580.00
Cat, Felix, Black, White, Painted, Wood, Schoenhut, 7 3/4 In. 165.00
Cat, Felix, Dancer, Tin Lithograph, Crank, Distler, 3 3/4 In. 2750.00
Cat, Felix, Jointed, Leather-Eared, Schoenhut, 4 In...........................95.00 to 115.00
Cat, Felix, Squeeze Toy, Germany, 1920s 385.00
Cat, Felix, Standing Figure, Tin Lithograph, Windup, Germany, c.1925, 6 In. 385.00
Cat, Felix, Wood Jointed, Rubber Head, Black, Red, Yellow, KFS, 9 1/2 In. 275.00
Cat, Felix, Wood, Jointed, Decal On Chest, Pat Sullivan, 1924, 8 In. ....350.00 to 386.00
Cat, Hungry, Eyes Light Up, Battery Operated, Linemar, Japan, Box, 9 In. ....210.00 to 525.00
Cat, Knitting, Tin, Felt, Windup, Japan 11.00
Cat, Playful, Tin Lithograph, Windup, Alps, Japan, Box, 5 In. 17.00
Cat, Puss In Boots, Fabric, Molded Composition Boots, Plastic Eyes, Grissly, 23 In. 20.00
Cat, Puss In Boots, Felt, Sword, Italy, 18 In. 220.00
Cat, Squeak, Stripes, Googly Glass Eyes, Flannel, 6 In. 150.00
Cat, Sylvester, Posable, Cloth, 15 In. 149.00
Cat, Tabby, Tag, Steiff, c.1950, 4 In. 60.00
Cat, Velvet, Painted Markings, Shoebutton Eyes, Jointed, 3 1/2 In. 185.00
Cat, Walking, Battery Operated, Box, 7 In. 88.00
Cat, Walking, Fur, White, Glass Eyes, Open Mouth, Clockwork, Descamps, 12 In. 385.00
Cat & Fiddle, Papier-Mache, Pip-Squeak, 4 1/2 In. 83.00
Caterpillar, Green, Battery Operated, Box, 17 In. 470.00
Caterpillar, Green, Tin, Windup, Box, 10 In. 33.00
Caterpiller, Yellow, Cast Iron, Arcade, 8 In................................. 990.00
Chair, Doll's, Ebony Frame, Silk, Brass Studs, c.1875, 9 In., Pair 935.00
Chair, Doll's, Maple, Spindles, Faux Bamboo, Cane Seat, c.1875, 12 In. 360.00
Chair, Doll's, Metal, Gilded, Arched, Splayed Legs, Upholstered, France, c.1860, 12 In. .. 1980.00
Chair, Doll's, Wood Frame, Legs, Brocade, Tufted, Fringe, c.1860, 8 In. 1100.00
Charleston Trio, Minstrel Show, Tin Lithograph, Marx, c.1930, 9 1/2 In............. 578.00
Charlie Weaver, Bartender, Tin, Plastic, Battery Operated, TN, Box, 1962, 12 In. 90.00
Chef, Roller Skating, Tin Lithograph, Windup, T.P.S., 6 In. 315.00
Cherry The Cook, Windup, Celluloid, Box, 4 1/2 In. ....80.00 to 135.00
Chest, Doll's, Empire, Hand Carved, 3 Drawers, Porcelain Knobs, c.1840, 12 In. 880.00
Chimpanzee, Wandering, Windup, Japan, Box, 5 In. 125.00
Chinese Boy, Roly Poly, Papier-Mache, 4 In. 250.00
Chinese Man, Nu-Nu, Pulling Tea Cart, Lehmann, 1924 .... 750.00
Chipmunk, Chipper, Windup, Tin, Plastic, J. Chein & Co., Box 105.00
Chipmunk, Chippy, Battery Operated, Remote Control, Alps, Japan, Box 28.00
Circus, Battery Operated, Tomiyama-Japan, Box 550.00
Circus, Flying, Battery Operated, Box, 14 In. 470.00
Circus, Flying, Elephant, Plane, Clown, Tin, Windup, Unique Art, Box, 13 In. 2285.00
Circus, Monkeys Move, Tin, Windup, American, 6 In. 330.00
Circus, Ring-A-Ling, Ringmaster, Animals, Tin Lithograph, Windup, Marx, c.1930, 7 In. .. 700.00
Circus Acrobat, Strongman, 2-Part Head, Felt Costume, Schoenhut 825.00
Circus Drum, Tin Lithograph, Box, 8 1/2 In. 130.00
Circus Girl, Standing On Horse, Painted Wood, Schoenhut, 9 In. 165.00
Circus Hand Car, Hokey Pokey, Clowns, Metal, Windup, Wyandotte, 1950s, 6 In. .245.00 to 275.00
Circus Lion, Battery Operated, Box, 10 In.................................. 430.00
Circus Parade, Tin Lithograph, Pull Toy, Courtland, 12 In. 120.00
Circus Parade, Tin, Friction, Japan, 1960s, 7 1/2 In. 175.00
Circus Ringmaster, Jointed Wood, Painted Face, Schoenhut, 8 In. 165.00
Circus Set, 2 Clowns, Ringmaster, Trapeze, Girl, Schoenhut, 13 Piece 430.00
Circus Set, The Big Top, Lithograph, Contents, Woodette, 1940s 75.00
Circus Set, Transport, Corgi, Box 425.00
Circus Tent, Humpty Dumpty, Flags, Ring, Trapeze, Schoenhut, Box 660.00
Circus Trapeze, Man, Flips, Spins, Tin, Windup, Wyandotte, Box, 9 In. ....160.00 to 255.00
Clancy The Cop, Face Moves, Waddles, Tin Lithograph, Clockwork, Marx, 10 1/2 In. 935.00

Clown, Balances Whirligig On Nose, Windup, Gely, Germany, 1920s, 10 In. 280.00
Clown, Bimbo, Drumming, Battery Operated, Cragstan, Box, 11 In. 220.00
Clown, Bisque Head, Blinking, Hinged Jaw, Muslin Body, Jointed, 12 In. 1430.00
Clown, Blinky, Plays Xylophone, Tin, Cloth, Battery Operated, Amico, Box, 11 In. 325.00
Clown, Bozo, Parasol, Tin Lithograph, Windup, Joustra Toys, France, Box, 1940s, 5 In. . . 135.00
Clown, Chair & Pedestal, Leather Ears, Schoenhut, 8 In. 250.00
Clown, Composition, Tin Lithograph, Windup, Japan, 11 In. 110.00
Clown, Dodgem Car, Windup, England, Box, 1940s, 3 1/2 x 4 1/2 In. 95.00
Clown, Donkey, Windup, Celluloid, Japan, 5 In. 90.00
Clown, Funny Charlie, Battery Operated, Alps, Box, 10 In. 425.00
Clown, Guitarist, Head Bobs, Lithograph, Windup, Distler, Germany, 8 1/2 In. 550.00
Clown, Happy & Sad, Magic Face, Plays Accordion, Battery, Yonezawa, Box, 10 In. 165.00
Clown, Happy Fiddler, Sways, Plays Fiddle, Battery Operated, Alps, Box, 10 In. 355.00
Clown, Happy, Puppet Show, Sways, Battery Operated, Yonezawa, Box, 10 In. . . . .220.00 to 449.00
Clown, Hobo, Whistle, Monkey, Plays Cymbal, Battery Operated, Japan, 13 1/2 In. 130.00
Clown, Hobo, Windup, Tin, Japan, 6 1/2 In. 66.00
Clown, In Barrel, Rolls, Tin Lithograph, Embossed, Weighted, 2 3/4 In. . . . . .360.00 to 495.00
Clown, Ioto, Beloved, Windup, Celluloid, Box, 13 In. 90.00
Clown, Jalopy Cycle, Bump & Go, Tin, Friction, Japan, Box, 9 In. 965.00
Clown, Jenny The Balking Mule, Strauss, Windup . . . . .595.00 to 935.00
Clown, Juggler, 4 Balls, Tin, Windup, Schuco, U.S. Zone Germany, Box, 5 In. 220.00
Clown, Lester The Jester, Twirls Cane, Celluloid, Tin, Cloth, Windup, Alps, Box, 9 In. . . . 275.00
Clown, Lifting Weight, Windup, Bends Forward & Back, Tin, Germany, 1920s, 7 1/2 In. . 785.00
Clown, Magician, Lifts Hat, Rabbit, Tin, Cloth, Windup, Japan, Box, 7 In. 330.00
Clown, Magician, Puffs Smoke, Tips Hat, Tin, Remote Control, Marusan, Box, 12 In. 215.00
Clown, On Donkey, Bucks, Moves Ears, Composition, Spring Mounted, Pull Toy, 8 In. . . . 660.00
Clown, On Motorcycle, Tin Lithograph, Windup, Japan, Prewar, 6 In. 180.00
Clown, On Motorcycle, Upsy Down, Tin, Alps, 6 1/2 In. 715.00
Clown, On Pig, Celluloid, Tin Lithograph, Made In Japan, 3 In. 120.00
Clown, On Roller Skates, Windup, Tin Lithograph, Japan, Box, 7 In. . . . . .315.00 to 475.00
Clown, On Rope, Hand Over Hand, Mechanical, Cragston, Box, 9 In. 495.00
Clown, On Unicycle, Tin Lithograph, Windup, Japan, 6 In. 160.00
Clown, Painted Wood, Hat, Cloth Costume, Schoenhut, 9 In. 35.00
Clown, Performing Parrots, On Wheel, Tin, Windup, Late 19th Century, 9 In. 3470.00
Clown, Peter, Cloth Covered, Celluloid Hands, Head, Feet, Windup, Japan, 1930s, 7 In. . . . 185.00
Clown, Pinky, Juggler, Battery Operated, Tin, Cloth, Plastic, Japan, Box, 1950s, 19 In. . . . 289.00
Clown, Pinky, Juggler, Lighted Balls, Alps, Box, 8 In. 195.00
Clown, Roly Poly, Orange Costume, Papier-Mache, 5 1/2 In. 250.00
Clown, Roly Poly, Papier-Mache, Musical, 8 In. 75.00
Clown, Roly Poly, Yellow, Green, Red, Papier-Mache, 2 1/2 In. 39.00
Clown, Stretch Body, Neck, Tin Lithograph, Windup, Germany, 1950s, 6 In. 145.00
Clown, Tambourine, Tin Lithograph, Cloth Costume, Windup, Japan, 1960s, 7 1/2 In. 75.00
Clown, Unique Artie, Crazy Car, Tin, Windup, Unique Art, Box, 7 In. 455.00
Clown, Violinist, Tin, Cloth, Clockwork, Schuco, Box, 4 1/2 In. 265.00
Clown, Windup, Alps, Japan, Box, 6 In. 35.00
Clown, Windup, Tin, Schuco, 4 1/2 In. 25.00
Clown, With Poodle, Circles, Tin, Windup, Germany, 3 1/2 In. 250.00
Clown, Zilotone, Plays Xylophone, Windup, Wolverine, c.1930 . . . . 450.00
Clown & Lion, Battery Operated, Mixed Material, Modern Toys, Box, 13 In. . . . . .360.00 to 575.00
Clowns, Sitting, Throwing Ball, Tin Lithograph, Embossed, Lever, Penny Toy, Meier, 4 In. 770.00
Clowns, Windup, Tin Lithograph, Germany, Lehmann, Box, 9 In. 865.00
Coney Island Rocket Ride, Tin, Battery Operated, Alps, Box, 14 In. 990.00
Coney Island Scooter, Windup, Tin, Rubber Head, 1950s, Japan, 5 1/2 In. 155.00
Construction Set, Dump & Cement Trucks, Bulldozer, Plastic, Friction, Japan, Box, 7 In. 90.00
Construction Set, Road Building, Die Cast, No. 75, Hubley, Box, 1950s, 11 x 18 In. 715.00
Construction Set, Truck, Trailer, Steam Shovel, Pressed Steel, Wyandotte, 1950s, 23 In. . 155.00
Contractor Set, Pressed Steel, Plastic, No. M-965, Structo, Box, 1960s 85.00
Cow, Moos, Glass Eyes, Horns, Hide Covered, Wood, Papier-Mache, Platform, 15 1/2 In. . 1430.00
Cowboy, Juggler, Windup, 4 Balls, Vibrates, Schuco, Box, 4 3/4 In. . . . . .1025.00 to 1350.00
Cowboy, On Horse, Plastic, Windup, Box, 4 3/4 In. 30.00
Cowboy, On Horse, Twirling Lariat, Moving Gun, Windup, Marx, 6 x 8 1/2 In. 138.00
Cowboy, On Rocking Horse, Windup, Tin Lithograph, Cragstan, Box, 7 In. 250.00
Cowboy Set, 5 Cowboys On Horses, Britains, London, Box, 1930s, 5 Piece 125.00

Cradle, Doll's, Painted, Carved, America, 19th Century, 7 1/2 x 7 3/8 x 11 In. 235.00
Cradle, Doll's, Papier-Mache, Flowers, Scrolls, Blue, Black, England, c.1860, 10 x 14 In. . 650.00
Cradle, Doll's, Pine, Red Paint, 13 x 11 In. 80.00
Cradle, Doll's, Tin, Painted, Green, Hood, Tin-Covered Rockers, 17 x 12 1/4 In. 200.00
Crane, Dockyard, Logs, Pallet, Lifts, Tin, Windup, Linemar, Box, 9 In. 120.00
Crane, Railroad Wrecking, Pressed Steel, Buddy L, 1920s, 30 In. 2530.00
Crane, Tin, Windup, Germany, 18 In. 165.00
Crawling Black Baby, Celluloid, Fabric, 5 1/2 In. 80.00
Cricket Cage, Bone, Tree Stump Form, Carved, 2 Crickets, Japan, c.1890, 2 1/2 In. 242.00
Cyclist, High Wheel, Crescent Weights, A.C. Gilbert Toy Co., 5 x 9 1/2 In. 448.00
Cyclist, Monkey, Windup, Tin Lithograph, Paperboard, Marx, 6 In. 155.00
Cyclist, Skippy, Tricky, Tin Lithograph, Windup, Cragstan, Japan, Box, 1950s, 6 In. 215.00
Dancer, Black Man, Windup, 8 1/2 In. 210.00
Dancer, Pango Pango, African, Tin, Windup, Vibrates, 6 In. 200.00
Dancer, Tin, Windup, Box, 5 1/2 In. 35.00
Dancing Dan, Articulated Black Dancer, Mystery Mike, Mechanical, 13 1/2 In. 213.00
Dancing Dan, Battery Operated, Box, 16 In. 175.00
Dancing Sambo, Paper, Framed, 12 x 21 In. 55.00
Dancing Senorita, Windup, Plastic, Irwin, Box, 10 In. 65.00
Dapper Dan Coon Jigger, Tin Lithograph, Marx, Box, 10 In. 715.00
Dennis The Menace, Battery Operated, Box, 8 In. 315.00
Derrick, Pressed Steel, Buddy L, 24 In. 1815.00
Derrick, Pressed Steel, Triang, 1930s, 36 In. 525.00
Dinnerware Set, American Modern, Russel Wright, Ideal, 22 Piece 80.00
Dino Dinosaur, Windup, Linemar, Japan, 1961, 9 In. 295.00
Dino On Tricycle, Celluloid, Tin, Windup, Marx, Box, 4 1/4 In. 850.00
Dinosaur, Steiff, 1950s, 10 In. 415.00
Dirigible, Silver, Los Angeles, Tootsietoy, 5 In. 175.00
Doctor Moon, Oversized Glasses, Moves, Head Turns, Tin, Windup, Daiya, Box, 7 1/2 In. 990.00
Dog, Astro, Battery Operated, Box, 11 In. 175.00
Dog, Basset Hound, Plush, Mohair, Ear Button, Steiff, 8 In. 55.00
Dog, Bee Dog, Key Wind, Alps, Occupied Japan, Box, 5 In. 135.00
Dog, Boxer, Tag, Ear Button, Steiff, c.1950, 6 1/2 In. 65.00
Dog, Brown Mohair, Glass Eyes, Stitched Snout, Steiff, 8 1/2 In. 140.00
Dog, Bulldog, Growls When Chain Is Pulled, Pull Toy, c.1890, 14 In. 2235.00
Dog, Bulldog, Mohair, Straw Stuffed, Ear Button, Steiff, 15 1/2 In. 565.00
Dog, Bulldog, Painted Wood, Tin Lithograph Base, Pull, Hustler, 8 In. 30.00
Dog, Bulldog, Straw Stuffed, Shoebutton Eyes, Jointed Legs, Steiff, 15 In. 358.00
Dog, Bulldog, Walks, Head Turns, Wheels, Hide Cover, Clockwork, Descamps, 12 In. . . . 415.00
Dog, Clever Puppy, Tin Lithograph, Windup, TN, Box, 6 In. 28.00
Dog, Collie, Battery Operated, Box, 7 In. 70.00
Dog, Collie, Mohair, Tag, Steiff, c.1950, 5 In. 83.00
Dog, Dachshund, Steiff, 1950s, 14 In. 52.00
Dog, Fido, Battery Operated, Cragstan, Box, 9 In. 120.00
Dog, Happy Doggy, Windup, Japan, Rosko, 6 In. 50.00
Dog, Holding Basket, Tin, Black, Green Platform, Brown & Fallows, 1870s, 6 1/2 In. 375.00
Dog, In House, Musical, Ohio Art, Box, 8 In. 175.00
Dog, Lazy Bones, Sleepy, Plush, 4 Actions, Tin, Windup, Japan, Box, c.1950, 5 1/2 In. . . . 155.00
Dog, Mohair, Glass Eyes, Jointed, c.1910, 3 In. 115.00
Dog, On Wheels, Plush, Glass Eyes, Straw Stuffed, Collar, Ear Button, Steiff, 10 In. 715.00
Dog, Outer Space, Opens Mouth, Eyes Roll, Ears Flap, Tin, Friction, Japan, Box, 6 In. . . . 385.00
Dog, Pateena Poodle, Ballerina Leotards, Dress, Extra Clothes, Hasbro, 9 1/4 In. 100.00
Dog, Pip-Squeak, Barking, Cream, Tan, Hinged Jaw, Squeeze Base, 6 In. 935.00
Dog, Plush, Rubber Wheels, Push, Ireland, 21 In. 69.00
Dog, Poodle, Black Lamb's Wool, Plush, Articulated Arms, Steiff, 33 In. 570.00
Dog, Poodle, Erect, Velvet, Yarn, Madame Alexander, 13 In. 50.00
Dog, Poodle, Glass Eyes, Cloth Mane, Open Mouth, Schoenhut . . . . 95.00 to 195.00
Dog, Poodle, Gray, Cloth, Movable Legs, Glass Eyes, Wooden, Schoenhut, 4 1/2 x 7 In. . . 160.00
Dog, Poodle, Gray, Pull Ring For Bark, Wheels, Steiff, 22 1/2 x 23 In. 70.00
Dog, Poodle, Green, Pink Bow, Yarn, Felt Heart On Nose, Madame Alexander, 13 1/2 In. . 50.00
Dog, Poodle, Painted Eyes, Nose, Mouth, String Tail, Schoenhut, 6 x 7 In. 90.00
Dog, Poodle, White, Painted Eyes, Schoenhut, 7 3/4 In. 115.00
Dog, Puppy, Barky, Battery Operated, Alps, Box, 9 In. 80.00

Dog, Puppy, Friendly, Battery Operated, Box, 8 In. 35.00
Dog, Puppy, Peppy, Battery Operated, Box, 7 In. 40.00
Dog, Puppy, Skipping, Windup, Tin Lithograph, Box, 5 1/2 In. 130.00
Dog, Radio Rex, Celluloid, Battery Operated, John Hugo Mfg., Box, 1922 .... 115.00
Dog, Scottie, Ball, Windup, Tin, Schuco, 5 In. 16.00
Dog, Scottie, Guid-A-Dog, Tin, Windup, Pull Toy, Marx, Box, 12 In. 245.00
Dog, Scottie, Windup, Tin Lithograph, Marx, 11 In. 145.00
Dog, Snappy Puppy, Battery Operated, Alps, 9 In. 45.00
Dog, Stuffed, Leather Leash, Tin, Rubber Wheels, Pull, 18 In. 95.00
Dog, Terrier, Barking, Battery Operated, Marx, Japan, Box, 8 In. 99.00
Dog, Tin Lithograph, Windup, Marx, Japan, 6 In. 5.00
Dog, Trickey Tom, Tin Lithograph, Windup, Japan, Marx, 6 In. 55.00
Dog, Wood Legs, Hide, Glass Eyes, Leather Muzzle, Brass Collar, French, c.1900, 6 In. ... 470.00
Dolls are listed in their own category.
Dollhouse, 2 Story, 4 Rooms, Dutch Colonial, Red Roof, Electrified, 20 x 18 x 10 In. 700.00
Dollhouse, 2 Story, Bubble-Glass Windows, c.1875, 49 x 23 x 19 In. 3500.00
Dollhouse, 2 Story, Paper Interior, Paper Roof, Christian Hacker, 21 x 11 x 27 In. 150.00
Dollhouse, 2 Story, Paper Lithograph, Tower, Gottschalk, Germany, 1890, 16 x 19 1/2 In. .. 8800.00
Dollhouse, 2 Story, Porches, Wood, Blue Roof, Furniture, Gottschalk, c.1900, 24 x 14 In. .. 1790.00
Dollhouse, 2 Story, Victorian, Gambrel Roof, Wallpaper, Hinge Doors, Shingles, c.1900 .. 2800.00
Dollhouse, 2 Story, Wood, Lithograph, Glass Windows, Chimneys, 15 x 9 x 6 In. 990.00
Dollhouse, 2 Story, Wood, Mansard Roof, Furniture, Germany, c.1890, 24 x 22 In. 7840.00
Dollhouse, 3 Story, Gothic Revival, Turret, Shingles, Windows, 1890s, 46 x 32 x 20 In. .. 3585.00
Dollhouse, 3 Story, Normandy, Mansard Roof, Dormers, Green Paint, Early 1900s, 35 In.. 1410.00
Dollhouse, 3 Story, Porch, Scalloped Molding, Glass Windows, 44 x 26 x 31 1/2 In. 1015.00
Dollhouse, 3 Story, Shaker Style, Wood, 9 Rooms, Shaker Furniture, 34 x 36 x 24 In. 7050.00
Dollhouse, 3 Story, Swiss Chalet, Balconies, Gottschalk Style, Germany, 1910, 23 x 25 In. 2800.00
Dollhouse, 4 Rooms, Porch, Red Roof, Cardboard, Wood Frame, Schoenhut, 23 x 24 In. . 305.00
Dollhouse, 4 Story, Jubilee Villa, Brick Interior, P. Lewis Builder, c.1887, 52 x 29 x 9 In. . 900.00
Dollhouse, Mobile Home, Pressed Steel, Plastic Furniture, Ny-Lint, Box, 1960s, 29 In. 365.00
Dollhouse Furniture, Bathroom Set, Tub, Pedestal Sink, Stool, Toilet, Green, 1930s, 3 In. 310.00
Dollhouse Furniture, Bathroom Set, Tub, Pedestal Sink, Toilet, Original Green, Arcade .. 575.00
Dollhouse Furniture, Bed, Four Poster, c.1830 .... 3800.00
Dollhouse Furniture, Bedroom Set, Bed, Dresser, Armoire, Mirror, 2 Chairs, Table 235.00
Dollhouse Furniture, Birdcage, Ormolu, Moroccan, Parrot, Germany, c.1880, 3 3/4 In. .. 1530.00
Dollhouse Furniture, Birdcage, Ormolu, Square, Parrot, Swing, Germany, c.1880, 2 In. .. 440.00
Dollhouse Furniture, Carriage, Metal, Gilt, Parasol, Baby, Jointed, 4 1/2 x 5 1/2 In. 590.00
Dollhouse Furniture, Chess Set, Ivory, Red, White, Tripod Base, Filigree, 2 1/2 In. 380.00
Dollhouse Furniture, Cradle, Metal, Hood, Scroll Feet, Gilt, Germany, c.1880, 4 x 7 In. .. 355.00
Dollhouse Furniture, Desk, Silver, Baroque, Urns, Inkwell, Drawer, 4 x 3/4 x 5 1/2 In. .. 380.00
Dollhouse Furniture, Dresser, Oak, Swivel Mirror, Curved Top Drawer, 6 3/4 x 9 3/4 In. . 105.00
Dollhouse Furniture, Hutch, Step Back, Drawer, Door, Paper Interior, c.1847, 10 x 5 In. . 120.00
Dollhouse Furniture, Parlor Set, Settee, 4 Chairs, Upholstered, 1865, 9 In. 935.00
Dollhouse Furniture, Parlor Set, Sofa, 2 Armchairs, 2 Side Chairs, Desk, Biedermeier ... 646.00
Dollhouse Furniture, Parlor Set, Sofa, Chairs, Rocker, Bamboo, Fabric, 1900, 5 In. 2100.00
Dollhouse Furniture, Parlor Set, Stained Wood, Upholstered, Biedermeier, 8 Piece 235.00
Dollhouse Furniture, Settee, Pedestal Table, Sidechair, Armchair, Upholstery, 1860, 11 In. 3080.00
Dollhouse Furniture, Table, Checkerboard Top, Lithograph Paper, Wood, Bliss, 6 In. 250.00
Dollhouse Furniture, Table, Rosewood, Marquetry, Tilt Top, Round, c.1840, 4 x 3 1/2 In. . 380.00
Dolly Dressmaker, Girl At Sewing Machine, Battery Operated, TN, Japan 110.00
Dolphin, Tail Moves, Floats, Windup, French, 1890s, 15 In. 550.00
Donkey, Walking, Battery Operated, Linemar, Box, 9 In. 145.00
Donkey, Winking, Windup, Japan, Box, 5 1/2 x 4 3/4 In. 50.00
Dragon, Snappy Bubble Blowing, Plush, Battery Operated, Japan, Box, 37 In. ..2700.00 to 3520.00
Dragonfly, Tin Lithograph, Plastic, Windup, Cragstan, Japan, Box, 8 1/2 In. 65.00
Drink Mixer, Go-Go Girl, Battery Operated, Pointer Prods, Japan, Box, c.1969, 21 1/4 In. . 35.00
Drum, Children, Revolutionary War Costumes, Tin Lithograph, Embossed, 12 In. 330.00
Drum, Soldiers, American, German, English, French, Flags, Stenciled, Wood, 8 In. 470.00
Drum Major, Windup, Tin Lithograph, Chein, 8 1/2 In. 130.00
Drum Major, Windup, Tin Lithograph, Wolverine, 14 In. ....198.00 to 275.00
Drummer, Head, Hands & Eyes Move, Stained Wood, Ivory Lever, Kobe, 4 1/2 In. 155.00 to 500.00
Drummer, Russian, Windup, Marx, Japan, 6 1/2 In. ....22.00 to 52.00
Drummer, Uniform, Metal, Windup, Marx, England, 10 In. 75.00

Drummer Boy, George, Plays Drum, Tin, Windup, Marx, Box, 9 In. . . . . .190.00 to 220.00
Drummer Boy, Tin, Windup, Chein, c.1930, 9 In. . . . . .250.00 to 275.00
Drunkard, Lifts Bottle, Raises Cup To Mouth, Cloth Dress, Tin, Wire, Martin, 8 In. 250.00
Duck, 3 Ducklings In Wicker Basket, Wheels, Tin, Windup, Lehmann, c.1920, 7 1/2 In. . . 390.00
Duck, Amphibious Taxi, Monkey, 2 Squirrels, Tin, Windup, Japan, Box, 6 1/2 In. 490.00
Duck, Battery Operated, Linemar, Box, 8 In. 39.00
Duck, Mama Duck & Ducklings, Tin Lithograph, Windup, T.P.S., Japan 45.00
Duck, On Tricycle, Quacking, Windup, Tin Lithograph, 6 In. 69.00
Duck, Plastic, Friction, Wyandotte, Box, 4 1/2 In. 11.00
Duck, Quaggi, Mohair, Wing Button, Steiff, c.1950, 5 In. 116.00
Duck, Strutting, Windup, Alps, Box, 7 In. 35.00
Duck, Tin Lithograph, Wyandotte, 1950s, 9 In. 75.00
Duck, Walking, Windup, Tin Lithograph, Japan, Box, 8 In. 145.00
Dune Buggy, Driver, Surfboard, Tin, Plastic, Battery Operated, T.P.S., Japan, Box, 10 In. . . 99.00
Elephant, Composition, Nodding Head, Pull Toy, 8 In. 75.00
Elephant, Felt, Composition, Glass Eyes, Carved Tusk, Wheels, Pull Toy, 12 In. 175.00
Elephant, Glass Eyes, Schoenhut, 9 In. 115.00
Elephant, Holding Umbrella, Ball, HRD Japan, Box, 7 In. 195.00
Elephant, Jumbo, Bubble Blowing, Battery Operated, Box, 8 In. 160.00
Elephant, Jumbo, On Tricycle, Windup, Tin, Germany, 4 In. 115.00
Elephant, Jumbo, Windup, Alps, Japan, Box, 6 In. 29.00
Elephant, On Ball, Boy Riding, Tin Lithograph, Windup, Japan, Box, 7 In. 190.00
Elephant, On Tricycle, Tin, Windup, Germany, 9 In. 63.00
Elephant, Rajah, King Of The Jungle, Windup, Alps, Japan, Box 28.00
Elephant, Reading, Trunk Turns Pages, Tin Book, Windup, Alps, Japan, Box, 6 1/2 In. 75.00
Elephant, Red Blanket, Bells, Neck, Ear Button, Steiff, 7 1/2 In. 80.00
Elephant, Walks, Free Flying Ball, Remote Control, Modern Toys, Japan, Box 50.00
Elephant, Windy, Holding Umbrella, Juggling, Battery Operated, TN, Japan, Box 127.00
Elves, Drums, Wood, Spring Heads, Pull Toy, Japan, 6 In. 28.00
Erector Set, A.C. Gilbert, Booklet, Box, 1938 . . . . 60.00
Erector Set, Automatic Radar Scope, No. 10042, Gilbert, Box, 1959, 16 1/4 x 8 1/4 In. . . 90.00
Erector Set, Mark 30, Motor, Plastic Carrying Case, Gilbert, 1971, 12 x 7 1/2 In. 40.00
Erector Set, No. 7 1/2, Electric Motor, Manual, 10 x 18 In. 65.00
Erector Set, No. 7 1/2, Trumodel, Built Truck, Wood Box 220.00
Erector Set, Rocket Launcher, Motor, Instructions, 1959 . . . . 85.00
Fashion Shop, Barbie, Cardboard, Box 220.00
Ferdinand The Bull, Bounces, Flower, Bee, Tin, Windup, WDE, Marx, Box, 1938, 6 In. . . 435.00
Ferris Wheel, Chein, Box, 1941 . . . . 695.00
Ferris Wheel, Giant Ride, Ohio Art 200.00
Ferris Wheel, Hercules, 4 Cars, Windup, Tin Lithograph, Chein, Box, c.1945, 16 In. 335.00
Ferris Wheel, Windup, Tin Lithograph, Bell, Chein, c.1950, 16 3/4 In. 230.00
Ferris Wheel, Windup, Tin Lithograph, Chein, Box, 16 In. 440.00
Film Projector, Magic Lantern, Tin, On Wood, Shutter, Sprocket Drive, 12 In. 85.00
Finnegan The Porter, Tin, Windup, Unique Art 345.00
Fire Pumper, 2 Horses, Driver, Hubley, 1910, 11 1/2 In. 325.00
Fire Pumper, 2 Horses, Steam, Pratt & Letchworth, 1880s, 18 In. 1200.00
Fire Pumper, 3 Horses, Driver, Cast Iron, Wilkins, 12 1/2 In. 375.00
Fire Pumper, 6 Firemen, Cast Iron, Rubber Tires, Arcade, 1930s, 13 In. 775.00
Fire Pumper, Blue Paint, Yellow Wheels, Gold Accents, Hubley, 9 1/4 In. 115.00
Fire Pumper, Cast Iron, Nickel Plated Boiler, Hubley, 13 1/2 In. 1980.00
Fire Pumper, Driver, Cast Iron, Iron Wheels, Kenton, 12 1/2 In. 1595.00
Fire Pumper, Headlights, Bumper, Tires, Buddy L, 24 In. 6820.00
Fire Pumper, Horse Drawn, Cast Iron, Hubley, 18 In. 1295.00
Fire Pumper, Horse Drawn, Cast Iron, Wilkins, 19 In. 525.00
Fire Pumper, Kenton, 11 1/2 In. 1250.00
Fire Pumper, Pressed Steel, Buddy L, 1940s, 12 1/2 In. 99.00
Fire Pumper, Pressed Steel, Friction Motor, Dayton, 1920s, 8 1/2 In. 230.00
Fire Pumper, Tonka, 1961 . . . . 225.00
Fire Pumper, Tonka, Box, 1960 . . . . 350.00
Fire Truck, 3 Firemen, Ladder, Cast Iron, Arcade, 16 In. 550.00
Fire Truck, 5 Firemen, Crank Operated Ladder, Tin Lithograph, Distler, 4 In. 350.00
Fire Truck, Aerial Ladder, Pressed Steel, Red, Smith-Miller, 1950s, 14 1/2 In. 825.00,
Fire Truck, Aerial Ladder, Tonka, 1959 . . . . 295.00

Fire Truck, Boiler, Hose Reel, Pressed Steel, Double Friction, Dayton, 14 1/2 In. 310.00
Fire Truck, Chemical, Pressed Steel, 2 Ladders, Bell, Toledo Bulldog, Mack, 28 In. 3520.00
Fire Truck, GMC, Pressed Steel, Buddy L, 1950s, 26 In. 99.00
Fire Truck, Hook & Ladder, Buddy L, 1923, 26 In. 2600.00
Fire Truck, Hook & Ladder, Hydraulic, Pressed Steel, Structo, 1950s, 32 In. 110.00
Fire Truck, Hook & Ladder, Pressed Steel, Buddy L, 1940s, 20 In. 770.00
Fire Truck, L.A.F.D., Die Cast, Doors Open, Smith-Miller, Box, 1950s, 24 In. 1100.00
Fire Truck, Ladder Goes Up & Down, Friction, Japan, 1950s, 8 In. 145.00
Fire Truck, Ladder, Aerial, Pressed Steel, Aluminum Wheels, Buddy L, 1920s, 40 In. 1400.00
Fire Truck, Ladder, Aerial, Pressed Steel, Kingsbury, 1920s, 36 In. 1650.00
Fire Truck, Ladder, Driver, Rider, Red Paint, Cast Iron, Hubley, 16 In. 370.00
Fire Truck, Ladder, Metal, Running Board, Removable Hood, Lights, Structo, 7 x 22 In. .. 200.00
Fire Truck, Ladder, Pressed Steel, Aluminum Ladders, Doepke, 1940s, 34 In. 198.00
Fire Truck, Ladder, Pressed Steel, Friction, Dayton, 1920s, 18 In. 489.00
Fire Truck, Ladder, Pressed Steel, Girard, U.S.A., 1920s, 11 In. 195.00
Fire Truck, Ladder, Pressed Steel, Turner, 1930s, 25 In. 4950.00
Fire Truck, Ladder, Pressed Steel, Yellow Ladders, Rubber Tires, 5 x 14 x 5 In. 275.00
Fire Truck, Ladder, Red, Gold, Flywheel Drive, Schieble, 1909, 20 In. 525.00
Fire Truck, Metal, Aluminum Wheels, Rack & Pinion Steering, 8 x 24 x 7 1/2 In. 325.00
Fire Truck, Metal, Red Paint, Extending Nozzle, Bell, Windup, Rubber Tires, 24 In. 220.00
Fire Truck, NYCFD, Lights, Plastic, Windup, Marx, Box, c.1950, 13 In. 200.00
Fire Truck, Pressed Steel, Structo, Box, 1960s, 30 In. ....:.................... 149.00
Fire Truck, Pressed Steel, Tin Lithograph, Wyandotte, 1940s, 12 In. ....145.00 to 360.00
Fire Truck, Pressed Steel, Tin Lithograph, Wyandotte, 1940s, 18 In. 120.00
Fire Truck, Pressed Steel, Tin Lithograph, Wyandotte, 1950s, 20 In. 110.00
Fire Truck, Rolled Sheet Metal, Red, Bench Seat, Friction, Kingsbury, 5 x 14 x 4 3/4 In. . 2600.00
Fire Truck, Searchlight, Friction, Japan, 1950s, 7 1/2 In. 175.00
Fire Truck, Tanker, Tonka, 1959 .... 295.00
Fire Truck, Tin Lithograph, Bandai, Box, 6 1/2 In. 99.00
Fire Truck, Tin Lithograph, Pressed Steel, Wyandotte, 1950s, 24 In. 275.00
Fire Truck, Tin Lithograph, Wyandotte, 1950s, 10 In. 99.00
Fire Truck, Tin, Friction, Japan, Box, 7 1/2 In. 60.00
Fire Truck, Tom & Jerry, Metal, Battery Operated, Japan, 1950s, 16 In. 195.00
Fire Truck, Wood, Red, Yellow, Buddy L, 1943, 20 In. ....275.00 to 295.00
Fire Wagon, 2 Horses, 2 Wood Ladders, 2 Firemen, Gong Bell, Hubley, 1915, 27 1/2 In. . 1295.00
Fire Wagon, 2 Horses, 7 Firemen, Embossed Fire Patrol, Kenton Hardware Co., 1920s ... 450.00
Fire Wagon, 2 Horses, Driver, Rider, Hose Reel, Cast Iron, 10 1/2 In. 85.00
Fire Wagon, Hook & Ladder, 2 Horses, 2 Firemen, Bell, Hubley, 1915, 27 1/2 In. 1195.00
Fire Wagon, Hook & Ladder, 2 Horses, 2 Firemen, Carpenter, c.1880, 28 In. 1995.00
Fire Wagon, Hook & Ladder, 2 Horses, Driver, Carpenter, 1888, 28 In. 2495.00
Fire Wagon, Hook & Ladder, 2 Horses, Firemen, Yellow Frame, Ives, 1880s, 26 In. 1995.00
Fire Wagon, Hook & Ladder, 3 Horses, 3 Ladders, Gong Bell, Dent, 1905, 27 1/2 In. 1295.00
Fire Wagon, Hook & Ladder, Metal Wheels, Buddy L, 1920s 2420.00
Fire Wagon, Patrol, 2 Horses, 4 Firemen, Hubley, 1910, 5 1/2 & 13 1/2 In. 995.00
Fire Wagon, Patrol, 3 Horses, 5 Firemen, Dent, 1905, 21 In. 1195.00
Fire Wagon, Patrol, Converts To Sleigh, Red, Paris Manufacturing, c.1900, 56 In. 3410.00
Fire Wagon, Pumper, Cast Iron, Hubley, 18 In. 190.00
Fireman, Climbing, Windup, Tin Lithograph, Plastic, Marx, Box, 12 In. 250.00
Fisherman, Tin, Windup, Spins Fish, No Fishing Sign, Japan, 1950s 80.00
Flashlight, Ringling Bros. & Barnum & Bailey, Tiger Head, 9 1/2 In. 5.00
Flintstones, Bedrock Band, Battery Operated, Alps, Box, 9 In. ....325.00 to 430.00
Flintstones, Fred, On Tricycle, Windup, Tin Lithograph, Celluloid, Marx, 4 In. 175.00
Flintstones, Pals On Dino, Barney, Mechanical, Box, 8 In. ....235.00 to 470.00
Flintstones, Rubble's Wreck, Marx, 1962 .... 135.00
Flintstones, Turnover Tank, Tin, Windup, Linemar, 1960s, 4 In. 495.00
Flintstones, Wilma, In Car, Tin Lithograph, Rubber Head, Friction, Marx, 4 In. 110.00
Flintstones, Wilma, Tricycle, Tin Lithograph, Celluloid, Windup, Marx, Japan, 1962, 4 In. 155.00
Flying Man, Swings In Space Car, Mouth Opens, Closes, Tin, Windup, Japan, Box, 6 In. . 495.00
Flying Saucer, Battery Operated, Japan, Box, 1950s 395.00
Flying Saucer, Mercury X-1, Bump & Go, Lights, Tin, Battery, Yonezawa, Box, 8 In. 275.00
Flying Saucer, Pilot, Bump & Go, Lights, Siren, Tin, Battery Operated, KO, Box, 8 In. 240.00
Flying Saucer, Z-101, Spark Action, Masudaya, Box, 7 In. 440.00
Football Player, Kicker, Pull Leg Back, Kicks Rubber Ball, Cast Iron, c.1930, 8 1/2 In. .. 520.00

Football Player, Sandy Andy Fullback, Tin, Celluloid Ball, Wolverine, Box, c.1920s, 8 In.	2640.00
Frankenstein, Battery Operated, Paper Body, Rubber, Rosko, Japan, Box, 14 In.	400.00
Frankenstein, Walks, Purple Face, Hands, Blue Body, Windup, Marx, c.1960, 5 1/2 In. . . .	325.00
Fred Astaire, Dances By Street Sign, Windup, Celluloid, Cloth	275.00
Funny Face, Harold Lloyd, Sways, Swings Cane, Tin, Windup, Marx, Box, 10 1/2 In.	550.00
Furnace, Cast Aluminum, Thatcher Co., N.Y., Patent June 6 86, Salesman's Sample	220.00
Furnace, No. 250A, Cast Iron, Pressed Steel, Carrying Case, Dutch, Salesman's Sample . .	303.00
G.I. Joe, Blond Hair & Beard, Orange Jumpsuit, Gun In Shoulder Rig, 1970s	105.00
G.I. Joe, Brown Hair & Beard, Camouflage Uniform, 1970s	75.00
G.I. Joe, Desert Patrol Attack, Jeep, Gun, Box, 1967	505.00
G.I. Joe, Jumping Jeep, Metal, Unique Art, 1950s, 7 In.	245.00
G.I. Joe, K-9 Pups, Metal, Windup, Unique Art, Box, 9 In.	275.00
G.I. Joe, Marine, Hard Head, Rifle, 1964	65.00
G.I. Joe, Marine, Paperwork, Dog Tag, Stickers, Hasbro, 1964	4355.00
G.I. Joe, Ring, Black Stone, Box	400.00
G.I. Joe, Sailor, Web Belt, Gun In Holster, Binoculars, 1964	80.00
G.I. Joe, Space Capsule, Figure, Box, 1966	395.00
Gambler, Roulette, Battery Operated, Box, 9 In.	220.00
Games are listed in their own category.
Garage, Honeymoon, Coupe, Tin Lithograph, Marx	85.00
Garage, Wood, Green Roof, White Door, 13 x 18 In.	50.00
Gas Pump, Cast Iron, Arcade, 3 In.	80.00
Gas Pump, Red, Cast Iron, Arcade, 6 In.	470.00
Gas Station, 2 Pumps, Brightlite, Tin Lithograph, Marx	385.00
Gas Station, Brightlite, Lights, Tin, Battery Operated, Marx, Box, 9 1/2 In.	440.00
Gas Station, Paper Lithograph On Wood, Gibbs, 12 1/2 In.	300.00
Gas Station, Pumps, Car Lift, Marx, 1925	495.00
Gas Station, Roadside Rest, Tin Lithograph, Watering Can, Oil Cart, Car, Marx . . .415.00 to 495.00
Gas Station, Tin Lithograph, Battery Operated, Marx, 9 In.	105.00
Gino Neapolitan, Balloon Blower, Battery Operated, Japan, Box	130.00
Giraffe, Bounces From Hands To Chin, Tin, Windup, Linemar, Box, 9 In.	305.00
Giraffe, Glass Eyes, Schoenhut, 11 In. . . . . .470.00 to 700.00
Giraffe, Orange, Yellow, Painted, Wood, Schoenhut, 10 In.	195.00
Girl, Black, Checkered Dress, Windup, Tin, Cloth, Fisher-Price, 6 In.	575.00
Girl, On Swing, Painted Tin, Wood, Gibbs, Canton, Ohio	145.00
Gnomes Sawing, Tin Lithograph, Lever, Embossed, Meier, 4 In.	275.00
Goat, Mountain, Mohair, Glass Eyes, Straw Stuffed, 9 In.	75.00
Goat, Nodding Head, Fur, Collar, Glass Eyes, Wood, Iron Wheels, Pull, 10 1/2 x 11 In. . .	395.00
Goat, Tin Body, Cast Steel Wheels, c.1880, 7 x 6 1/2 In.	345.00
Goat Cart, Wood, Green, Red Paint, 1800s, 35 In.	316.00
Godzilla, Battery Operated, Box, 10 In.	935.00
Godzilla, Tin, Vinyl Fins, Smoke From Mouth, Walks, Bullmark, Box, 13 In.	1330.00
Golfer, Bob Hope, Radio Control, Amazon Industries Ltd., Box	50.00
Golfer, Windup, Tin Lithograph, Strauss, Box, 12 In.	385.00
Good Time Charlie, Cigar Lights, Lifts Bottle, Battery Operated, Illfielder, Box, 13 In.	165.00
Goose, Bobbing Head, Wheeled Base, Tin Lithograph, Embossed, Distler, 4 In.	99.00
Goose, Flapping Wings, Windup, Japan, Box	11.00
Gorilla, Celluloid, Rabbit Fur, Windup, Japan, 5 1/2 In.	125.00
Gorilla, Cloth, Celluloid Hands & Face, Windup, Japan, 5 In.	16.00
Gorilla, Roaring, Battery Operated, Box, 9 In.	127.00
Gorilla, Shooting, Battery Operated, Modern Toys, Box, 10 In.	489.00
Gorilla, Windup, Marx, Box, 7 1/2 In.	360.00
Grasshopper, Cast Iron, Original Paint, Pull, Hubley, 9 1/4 In.	650.00
Guitar, Barbie, Ge-Tar, Black Plastic, Ponytail Barbie, Blond, Crank Handle, 1963	110.00
Gun, Air Pistol, Benjamin, Single Shot, Tin Pellets, Paper Targets, Flyer, Box	80.00
Gun, Anti-Aircraft, Tin Lithograph, Steel, Wood Bullets, Marx, 10 In.	495.00
Gun, Atomic Space Patrol, Flashlight, Super Beam Signal, Plastic, Marx, c.1950, 7 3/4 In. . .	250.00
Gun, BB, Daisy Red Rider, No. 1938B, Wood Stock, Box	60.00
Gun, BB, Mini, Gatling, Bolt Upgrade, CO2 Powered, Electric, Paul Piper	2800.00
Gun, Bell Ringer, Multishot, Dual Action, Iron, Brass Bell, May 22, 1877 Patent, 4 7/8 In.	990.00
Gun, Cosmic Ray, Plastic, Spark Action, Ranger Steel, Box, 1950s, 8 In.	165.00
Gun, Flashy Flickers, Magic Picture, 116 Frames, Battery Operated, Marx, Box	14.00
Gun, Flashy-Ray, Rat-A-Tat Noise, Lights, Tin, Battery Operated, Japan, Box, 18 In.	220.00

Gun, Machine, X-5, Legs, Tin Lithograph, Tada, Japan, Box, 1960s, 7 x 11 In. 26.00
Gun, Pop Gun, Cork, Double BBL, Daisy 175.00
Gun, Rifle, Camouflage, Smokes, Noise, Scope, Instructions, Box, 5 x 31 x 1 1/2 In. 120.00
Gun, Rifle, Tom Corbett Space Cadet, Colorful Metal 250.00
Gun, Rocket Dart Pistol, Darts, Target, Steel, Daisy, 7 In. 330.00
Gun, Space Gun, Tom Corbett, Tin, Clicker, Marx, 1950s, 10 In.   255.00
Gun, Space Spun, Space Scout, Box, Instructions, 1950s 85.00
Gun, Spiderman, Signal, Plastic, Battery Operated, Marvel Comics, Blister Card, 3 1/2 In.   20.00
Gun, Spitfire, Hip, Clip, Cap Cartridge Loading, Nichols, Box, 1950s, 9 In. 48.00
Gun, Wizard Liquid Pistol, Nickel Plated, Parker Stearns Co., Box 165.00
Gypsy, Fortune Teller, Battery Operated, Box, 10 In. 1265.00
Ham & Sam, Dancing Man, Piano Player, Tin, Windup, Linemar, Japan, 1950s, 4 1/2 In.   525.00
Ham & Sam, Minstrels, Play Piano, Banjo, Windup, Tin, Strauss, 1921, 6 1/2 In. . .650.00 to 868.00
Handcar, Jerry, Tom & Jerry, Tin, Vinyl Head, Battery Operated, Masudaya, Box, 9 In. . .   385.00
Handcar, Moon Mullins & Kayo, Tin, Windup, Marx, Box, 6 In. . . . . .385.00 to 715.00
Handcar, Tom, Tom & Jerry, Tin, Vinyl Head, Battery Operated, Masudaya, Box, 9 In. . .   195.00
Hansom Cab, Driver, Passenger, Cast Iron, Kenton, 16 In. . . . . .185.00 to 550.00
Hansom Cab, Driver, Pratt & Letchworth, 1892, 3 In. 1650.00
Hansom Cab, Tin, Hand Enameled, Heavy Cast Metal Wheels, Marklin, 21 In. 3740.00
Happy Hooligan, Police Patrol, 3 People, 2 Horses, Cart, Cast Iron, Kenton, 17 In. 2420.00
Happy Hooligan, Roly Poly, Schoenhut, 1910, 5 In. 245.00
Happy Hooligan, Walker, Windup, Chein, 1930s 485.00
Happy Jigger Tap Dancer, Tin, Celluloid, Alps, Japan, Box, 8 In.   440.00
Haunted House, 8 Functions, Tin, Battery Operated, Marx, 11 In. . . . . .489.00 to 745.00
Helicopter, Circus, Windup, Tin, Japan, 1950s, 6 In. 145.00
Helicopter, Flies Around Satellite On Base, Brussels World's Fair, Windup, 1958 . . . .   95.00
Helicopter, Sikorsky, U.S. Air Force, Lithograph, Pilot, Copilot, Tin, Marusan, Box, 12 In.   250.00
Helicopter, Space Bus, Tin, Battery Operated, Bandai, Box, 14 In. 495.00
Helicopter, Vertol 107, Stop & Go, Lights, Battery, Alps, Japan, Box, c.1950, 14 In. 190.00
Helmet, Steve Canyon, Jet, Ideal, Box, 1959 . . . .   230.00
Henry, Riding White Elephant, Celluloid, Windup, Japan, 1940s, 8 In. 880.00
Henry & Brother, Windup, Celluloid, Japan, Prewar 1100.00
Henry & Henrietta, Windup, Celluloid, Tin Lithograph Suitcase, 7 In. 2750.00
Hey Hey Chicken Snatcher, Wide Mouth, Dog, Windup, Tin, Marx, 8 1/2 In. 1090.00
Hi-Way Henry, Windup, Fischer, 1927 . . . .   2250.00
Hillclimber, Woman Chasing Duck, Friction, Tin, D.L. Clark Co., c.1915, 10 1/2 x 7 In. . .   550.00
Hobo, Painted Facial Features, Felt Jacket, Schoenhut, 7 3/4 In.   195.00
Hobo, Rubber Neck, Windup, Celluloid, Box, 8 In. 250.00
Hockey Player, Big League, Tin, Windup, T.P.S., Box, 1950s, 6 1/2 In. 345.00
Hooligan's Hack, Tin, Mechanical, 2-Wheeled Cart, Driver, Horses, Strauss, 1925, 8 In. . .   730.00
Horse, Composition, Tin Wheels, Pull Toy, 7 1/2 In. 62.00
Horse, Jockey, Rocking Base, Tin Lithograph, Embossed, Meier, 3 1/2 In. . . . . .1100.00 to 1400.00
Horse, Jockey, Tin Lithograph, Penny Toy, Germany, 19th Century, 3 3/4 x 3 1/2 In. 700.00
Horse, Leaping, Mohair, Glass Eyes, Composition, Saddle, Steiff, 27 x 38 In. 6900.00
Horse, Mohair, Brown, Saddle, Red Wooden Base, Tin Wheels, Pull Toy, 29 x 27 In. 215.00
Horse, Mohair, Glass Eyes, Steel Frame, Wood Wheels, Ear Button, Steiff, 23 x 22 In. . . .   480.00
Horse, Papier-Mache, Wood Legs, Fur Tail, Tin Wheels, Germany, 5 1/4 In. 160.00
Horse, Push & Pull, Ear Button, Steiff, 19 x 19 In. 1650.00
Horse, Rocking, Black, Silver Canvas Saddle, Felt Blanket, Hair Mane, Tail, 38 x 28 In. .   340.00
Horse, Rocking, Cowhide, Wood Base, Blue Leather Straps, 31 1/2 x 43 x 15 In. 2990.00
Horse, Rocking, Platform, Dapple, Horsetail Mane, Tail, Saddle, Foot Rings, 54 x 44 In. .   1915.00
Horse, Rocking, Shoofly, Red, Black, Yellow Trim, Wood, Iron Legs, c.1880, 34 In. 415.00
Horse, Rocking, Smoke Decoration, Saddle, Cast Iron Brackets, 44 x 16 x 35 1/2 In. 1760.00
Horse, Rocking, Square Mortise Construction, American, 38 x 25 In. 1265.00
Horse, Rocking, Wood, Dappled White, Felt Saddle, Burlap Mane, Tail, Red Base, 33 In. .   200.00
Horse, Rocking, Wood, Handmade, Painted, 44 In. 190.00
Horse, Rocking, Wood, Step-In Seat, Red, White, 34 In. 59.00
Horse, Rocking, Wood, White, Red Canvas Saddle, Green Felt Blanket, 48 x 36 In. 450.00
Horse, Rocking, Wool Body, Wooden Mouth & Feet, 1880s, 30 In. 360.00
Horse, Sparkplug, Barney Google, Painted, Wood, Jointed, Cloth, Schoenhut, 9 In. 250.00 to 275.00
Horse, Swinging, Whitney Reed Co., Mass., c.1905 . . . .   4800.00
Horse, Walking, Battery Operated, Tin Lithograph, Linemar, Japan, Box, 7 In. 190.00
Horse, Woman Rider, Wheels, Cast Iron, Pull Toy, 1950s, 6 3/4 In. 235.00

Horse, Wood, Wheels, Pull Toy, Germany, 13 x 12 1/2 In. 125.00
Horse & Rider, Galloping, Battery Operated, Cragstan, Box, 12 In. 230.00
Horse & Sulky, Black Horse, Red Wheels, Cast Iron, 4 3/4 x 8 x 4 In. 125.00
Horse & Wagon, 2 Horses, Pratt & Letchworth, 1893, 17 1/2 In. 3395.00
Horse & Wagon, 2 Horses, Sand & Gravel, Driver, Kenton, 1930s, 15 In. 725.00
Horse & Wagon, American Cuzner Trotter, Tan, Tin, Red Wagon, Clockwork, 1872, 10 In. 6600.00
Horse & Wagon, Driver, Cast Iron, Kenton, 5 In. 85.00
Horse & Wagon, Driver, Fine Bread, Crate Of Bread, Painted, Wood, Schoenhut, 23 In. . . . 4400.00
Horse & Wagon, Log, Kenton, 1911, 14 In. 1295.00
Horse & Wagon, Milk, Toylands Farm Products, Windup, Tin, Marx, 10 In. 149.00
Horse & Wagon, National Biscuit Co., Uneeda Bakery 470.00
Horse & Wagon, Wood, Metal Tires, S.A. Smith Mfg. Co., Brattleboro, 26 In. 275.00
Housekeeper, Battery Operated, Cragstan, Box, 10 In. 220.00
Hovercraft, Brave, Tin, Battery Operated, Remote Control, Japan, Box, 8 In. 250.00
Hula Girl, Composition, Japan, Box, 7 In. 60.00
Humphrey Mobile, Joe Palooka, Windup, Wyandotte, Original Box . . . . .525.00 to 750.00
Ice Skater, Couple, Celluloid, Windup, Occupied Japan 39.00
Indian, Baby, Roly Poly, Papier-Mache, 4 In. 250.00
Indian, Galloping, Tin, Full Headdress, Moves As Horse Moves, 6 In. . . . . .175.00 to 195.00
Indian, Nutty Mad, Windup, Tin Lithograph, Marx, Japan, Box, 7 In. 115.00
Indian, Wild West, Windup, 1970s 15.00
Indiana Jones, Gun, Accessories, Kenner, Box, 1970s, 12 In. 285.00
Jack-In-The-Box, Krusty Clown 34.00
Jackie, Hornpipe Dancer, Moves, Sailor Dances, Tin, Windup, Strauss, Box, 9 In. 1760.00
Jazzbo Jim, Dancer On Roof, Tin Lithograph, Unique Art, Box, 1921, 7 x 5 In. . .715.00 to 1000.00
Jazzbo Jim, Song & Dance Man, White Version, Windup, Linemar, 6 In. 1350.00
Jeep, Anti-Aircraft, Soldiers, Guns Rotate, Tin, Friction, SSS, Box, 11 1/2 In. 169.00
Jeep, Circus, Clown Driver, Elephant Spins Globe, Tin, Friction, Exelo, Box, 6 In. 440.00
Jeep, Construction, Tin, Friction, Marusan, Japan, Box, 8 In. 120.00
Jeep, Danny's Fast Food, Red, Friction, Japan, 1960s, 9 In. 195.00
Jeep, Flying, Moves, Rotor Spins, 3 Drivers, Tin, Friction, Japan, Box, 8 In. 400.00
Jeep, Jouncing, G.I. Joe, Tin Lithograph, Clockwork, Unique Art, Box, 7 In. 319.00
Jeep, Jumper, Tin, Windup, Marx 195.00
Jeep, Jumpin', Soldiers, Tin Lithograph, Clockwork, Marx, 5 1/4 In. . . . . .195.00 to 250.00
Jeep, Navy, Searchlight Trailer, Pressed Steel, Marx, 1940s, 13 In. 140.00
Jeep, Police, Driver, Tin, Battery Operated, Japan, TN, Box, 10 In. 127.00
Jeep, Smokey The Bear, Tin Lithograph, Battery Operated, Japan, Box, 1950s, 10 1/2 In. . 975.00
Jeep, Tipping, Battery Operated, Linemar, Box, 8 In. 185.00
Jeep, Willys, Headlights, Hood Opens, Pressed Steel, Marx, 11 In. 70.00
Jigger, Dancing, Tin Lithograph, Crank, Distler, 3 1/2 In. 220.00
Joe Penner, Duck, Tin Lithograph, Windup, Marx, Box, c.1930, 8 In. . . . . .470.00 to 850.00
Jolly Black Joe, Celluloid, CK, Flapless Box, Tokyo, 7 3/4 In. 798.00
Jolly Drummer, Battery Operated, Alps, Box, 9 In. 198.00
Jolly Peanut Vendor, Bear, Walks, Pushes Cart, Tin, Battery Operated, Japan, Box, 9 In. . . . 330.00
Judo Man, Walks, Arms Move, White Cloth Outfit, Tin, Windup, Japan, Box, 9 1/2 In. 635.00
Juggler, Famous, Spins Rings On Sticks, Plastic, Cloth, Clockwork, Box, 10 1/2 In. 200.00
Jungle Trio, Battery Operated, Linemar, Box, 8 In. 300.00
Kaleidoscope, Telescopic, Brass Tip, Wooden Stand, 6 In. 150.00
Kaleidoscope, Wood, Marquetry, Hexagonal, 10 1/8 x 3 1/2 In. . . . . .150.00 to 170.00
Kangaroo & Baby, Mohair, Glass Eyes, Swivel Neck, Arms, Steiff, 21 In. 440.00
Katzenjammer Mama, Tea Cozy, Red Blouse, Green Skirt, Felt, Ear Button, Steiff, 16 In. 440.00
Kennedy Airport, Voice Control, Remco, 1960s, 19 x 14 In. 260.00
Keystone Kop, Roly Poly, Papier-Mache, 4 In. 250.00
Kitchen, Barbie, Refrigerator, Stove, Dishes, Steel, Wood Grain 80.00
Kitten, With Ball, Celluloid, Tin, Windup, Occupied Japan, Box, 5 In. 55.00
Knitting Grandma, Battery Operated, TN, Box, 9 In. 130.00
Lady Bug Train, 4 Lady Bugs, Tin, Windup, T.P.S., Japan, 12 1/2 In. 28.00
Lady Marvel, Windup, Celluloid, Japan, Prewar, 7 In. 160.00
Lamb, Baas When Head Is Pulled, Cast Wheels, Wooden Platform, 14 In. 1045.00
Lamb, Mohair, Glass Eyes, Embroidered Nose, Mouth, Bell, Steiff, c.1920, 7 x 9 In. 590.00
Land & Air Set, Die Cast, Tootsietoy, Box, 8 Piece 360.00
Landrover, Green, Tin, Friction, Japan, Box, 7 1/2 In. 385.00
Lantern, Battery Operated, Linemar, Box, 7 In. 60.00

Launching Station, ICBM, Moves Down Ramp, Tin, Crank, Horikawa, Box, 19 In. 275.00
Leopard, Mechanical, Windup, Marx, Japan, Box, 11 In. 95.00
Li'l Abner Dogpatch Band, Tin Lithograph, Unique Art, Box, c.1950 .... 990.00
Li'l Abner Dogpatch Band, Tin Lithograph, Unique Art, c.1950 ....385.00 to 550.00
Light Bulb, Magic, Battery Operated, Box, 5 In. 30.00
Lighthouse, Circling Train, Balls Spin, Bell, Tin, Battery Operated, Alps, Box, 7 In. 908.00
Lion, Bubble Blowing, Tin, Battery Operated, Modern Toys, Japan, Box 95.00
Lion, Mohair, Glass Eyes, Straw Stuffed, Ear Button, Steiff, 11 In. 115.00
Lion, Painted, Wood, Schoenhut, 7 1/2 In. 165.00
Lion, Roars, Sits, Springs Forward, Stuffed, Plush, Clockwork, Descamps, 16 In. 470.00
Loader, High Lift, Pressed Steel, Wyandotte, 1950s, 15 In. 27.00
Lop-Ear Looie, Fisher-Price, c.1934 .... 285.00
Louis Armstrong, Playing Trumpet, Rubber, Tin, Plastic, Windup, Japan, 10 In. 170.00
Lucky Crane, Lever, Picks Up Prizes, Tin, Battery Operated, Maruyoshi, Box, 9 x 5 In. .. 550.00
Maggie & Jiggs, Red Shirt, Black Pants, Blouse, Skirt, Painted, Wood, Schoenhut, 9 In. .. 440.00
Maggie & Jiggs, Tin, Windup, Wheels Move Back & Forth, 5 1/2 In. 265.00
Magic Set, Mysto Magic, Tricks, Illusions, Gilbert, 1938 .... 250.00
Magician, Happy Go Lucky, Windup, Tin Lithograph, TN, Japan, Box 315.00
Magician, Mr. Fox & Disappearing Rabbit, Tin, Battery Operated, Japan, 1950s, 9 1/2 In. . 340.00
Magician, Wolf, Lifts Hat To Reveal Rabbit, Windup, Japan, 6 1/4 In. 55.00
Mammy, Sweeping, Windup, Lindstrom, Box ....425.00 to 750.00
Mammy, Walker, Wood & Fabric, 4 1/4 In. 40.00
Man, With Pig, Pip-Squeak, Man Moves, Pig Bucks, Wood, Papier-Mache, Cloth, 8 In. .. 275.00
Man, With Suitcase, Blue Coat, Tin, Paya, Spain, Box, 7 In. 50.00
Man From Mars, Windup, Plastic, Irwin, Box, 11 In. 300.00
Man From U.N.C.L.E., Counter Spy, Trench Coat, Decoder, Cigarette Lighter, Marx, 1966 350.00
Man From U.N.C.L.E., Illya Kuryakin, Badge, Secret Agent Card, Gun, Handgrip, 12 In. .. 250.00
Man From U.N.C.L.E., Napoleon Solo, Briefcase, Weapons, Handgun, 12 In. 155.00
Man From U.N.C.L.E., Shooting Gallery, Tin, Plastic, Marx, Box, 1966, 11 In. 275.00
Mandarin, Sedan Chair, 2 Coolies, Windup, Lehmann, Germany, 1905 .... 2500.00
Manure Spreader, Cast Iron, McCormick Deering 700.00
Marionette Theater, 50 Lithograph Backdrops, 20 1/2 x 27 x 17 In. 315.00
Marionette Theater, Windup, Celluloid Clowns, Box, 10 In. 605.00
Marionette Theater, Windup, Celluloid Figures, Box, 11 In. 1095.00
Marionette Theater, Windup, Celluloid Figures, Box, 13 In. 715.00
Marionette Theater, Windup, Celluloid Figures, Japan, Prewar, Box 895.00
Mary & Lamb, Celluloid, Tin, On Wheels, Occupied Japan 475.00
Mary & Lamb, Glass Eyes, Bell, School Desk, Schoenhut, 7 1/2 In. 1430.00
Mason & Parker Runabout, Wood & Metal, Cast Iron Driver, Pull Toy, 9 In. .....385.00 to 475.00
Matador & Bull, Platform, Wheels, Tin Lithograph, Einfalt, c.1920, 8 In. 505.00
McGregor, Cigar Smoker, Battery Operated, Rosko, Box, 12 In. 115.00
Merry-Go-Round, Plastic, Airplanes, Tin Lithograph, Wolverine, Box, 12 In. 440.00
Merry-Go-Round, Spring Motor, Tin Lithograph, Wolverine, 13 In. 250.00
Merry-Go-Round, Tea Cup, Tin, Plastic, Windup, Japan, 8 In. 90.00
Merry-Go-Round, Windup, Tin Lithograph, Chein, Box, 10 In. ....495.00 to 965.00
Merrymakers Band, Mice Play Instruments, Windup, Tin, Marx, c.1930, 10 In. ...460.00 to 770.00
Mexicali Pete, Battery Operated, Alps, Box, 10 In. 175.00
Mighty Kong, Battery Operated, Marx, Box, 11 In. 525.00
Missile Erector, Missile, Launching Platform, No. 666, Dinky Toys, England, Box 330.00
Mister Machine, Ideal, 1960 .... 500.00
Mixer, Battery Operated, Box, 10 In. 110.00
Model Kit, Addams Family Haunted House, Plastic, Aurora Plastic Corp., Box, 1964-1965 730.00
Model Kit, Boat, Laughing Whale, Plank On Frame, Unopened, Box, 1982 .... 50.00
Model Kit, Boat, Thunderbolt, Fleet Line, Mahogany, K&O, Box, 1950s, 12 In. 130.00
Model Kit, Car, Chevrolet, Coupe, 1932 Model, Die Cast, Plastic, Hubley, Box, 10 In. ... 22.00
Model Kit, Car, MG, Assembled, Aluminum, Doepke, Box, 16 In. 305.00
Model Kit, Car, Raceabout, Mercer, 1/8th Scale 8250.00
Model Kit, Gigantic Tarantula, 1975 .... 25.00
Model Kit, Moon Bus, 2001 A Space Odyssey, Aurora, 1969, 15 x 10 1/2 In. 165.00
Model Kit, SJ Duesenberg, Metal, Die Cast, Plastic, Hubley, Box, 13 In. 28.00
Model Kit, Sport Roadster, Balsa Wood, Models Of Merit, California, 1940s, 8 In. 35.00
Model Kit, Stagecoach, Wells Fargo Overland, Lindberg Toys, Box, c.1979 .... 200.00
Monkey, Acrobat, Tin Lithograph, Windup, Marx, 12 In. 120.00

Monkey, Artist, Windup, TN, Japan, Box, 6 1/2 In. 230.00
Monkey, Balloon Blowing, Battery Operated, Alps, Box, 12 In. 130.00
Monkey, Banjo Player, Windup, Japan, 4 1/2 In. 50.00
Monkey, Big John, Chimpee Chief, Battery Operated, Alps, Japan, Box 22.00
Monkey, Bombo, Acrobat, Windup, Unique Art, Box 250.00
Monkey, Bongo Playing, Eyes Light Up, Battery Operated, Alps, Japan 60.00
Monkey, Brown, Red Hat, Outfit, Painted, Wood, Schoenhut, 8 1/2 In. 330.00
Monkey, Bubble Blowing, Eyes Light, Ring In Coconut, Battery, Alps, Box, 11 In. 85.00
Monkey, Climbing, Fez, Tin, Lehmann, Box, 8 In. 220.00
Monkey, Climbs Palm Tree, Tin Lithograph, Paper, Steel Balls, Emporium, 17 1/2 In. 70.00
Monkey, Climbs String When Pulled, Tin Lithograph, Lehmann, Box, 8 In. 110.00
Monkey, Cymbal Playing, Battery Operated, Box, 12 In. 45.00
Monkey, Dark Brown, Red Outfit, Wood, Schoenhut, 8 1/2 In. 330.00
Monkey, Dino, Hat On-Walks, Hat Off-Stops, Plastic, Battery Operated, Box, 9 3/4 In. ... 45.00
Monkey, Drinking, Eyes Light, Battery Operated, Inserts, Rock Valley, Alps, Box 200.00
Monkey, Drummer, Tin, Cloth, Clockwork, Schuco, Box, 4 1/2 In. 310.00
Monkey, Jocko, Musical, Mohair, Plush, Red Patch, Ear Button, Steiff, c.1950 .... 525.00
Monkey, Jocko, Tips Hat, Plays Cymbals, Remote Control, Alps, Box, 10 In. 149.00
Monkey, Jolly Bambino, In Highchair, Eats, Battery Operated, Japan, Box 140.00
Monkey, Jumbo, Climbing, Marx, 10 In. 105.00
Monkey, On Tricycle, Cast Iron, Bell, Stevens & Co., c.1890, 8 In. 1120.00
Monkey, On Tricycle, Rides Bike, Tin, Plastic, Windup, Occupied Japan, Box 220.00
Monkey, Plush, Felt Features, Glass Eyes, Schuco, 14 In. 45.00
Monkey, Plush, Glass Eyes, Jointed, Steiff, 12 In. 99.00
Monkey, Pushes Wagon, With Cane, Tin, Windup, U.S. Zone Germany, Box, 4 In. 120.00
Monkey, Riding Horse, Monkey Jumps, Wheels, Painted, Windup, Germany 650.00
Monkey, Rock & Roll Taps Foot, Plays Guitar, Battery Operated, Alps, Box, 12 In. 280.00
Monkey, Rock & Roll, Microphone, Tin, Fur, Battery Operated, 12 In. .....75.00 to 195.00
Monkey, Rooster, Tin Lithograph, Embossed, Lever, 4 In. 275.00
Monkey, Short Snort, Windup, Marx, Box, 12 In. 110.00
Monkey, Skipping, Battery Operated, TN, Box, 10 In. 65.00
Monkey, Suzette, Eating, Battery Operated, Linemar, Box, 9 In. 345.00
Monkey, Thirsty, Windup, Tin, TN, Japan, 6 In. 69.00
Monkey, Trumpet Playing, Battery Operated, Cragstan, Box, 10 In. 160.00
Monkey, Tumbling, Battery Operated, Box, 9 In. 45.00
Monkey, Weight Lifter, Champion, Battery Operated, Box, 10 In. 115.00
Monkey, Windup, Steel, Tin Lithograph, Cragstan, Box, 5 In. 230.00
Monkey, Windup, Tin, Cloth, Schuco, 4 1/2 In. 58.00
Monkey, Zippo, Climbing, Tin Lithograph, Marx, 10 In. 50.00
Monkey & Bell, Cast Iron, Animated, 6 1/2 In. 525.00
Monkey & Rooster, Tin Lithograph, Embossed, Lever, Meier, 4 In. 275.00
Monkey Cycle, Monkey Peddles Bike, Tin, Windup, Bandai, Box, 5 In. 260.00
Monster, Creature From Black Lagoon, Arms Move, Plastic, 1960s, 13 In. 190.00
Moon Explorer, Tin, Crank Action, Clear Plastic Helmet, KO, Box, 7 1/2 In. 745.00
Moon Mullins, On Handcar, Kayo, Tin, Windup, Marx, Box, c.1930, 6 In. 550.00
Mother, Rocking Baby, Composition, Windup, Germany, Box, 8 1/2 In. 99.00
Mother Bear, Rocks, Knits, Lights, Plush, Tin, Battery Operated, MT Mark, Box, 10 In. . 205.00
Mother Duck, Baby, Battery Operated, Box, TN, 7 In. ....22.00 to 99.00
Mother Goose, Bobbing Neck, Tin Lithograph, Clockwork, Marx, 6 1/2 In. 470.00
Motorcycle, Army, Rider, Sparking, Tin Lithograph, Windup, Japan, 5 1/2 In. 205.00
Motorcycle, Arnold Mac, Dismounts, Clockwork, Tin Litho, U.S. Zone Germany, 7 In. .. 520.00
Motorcycle, Cable Rider, Tin Lithograph, Windup, Modern Toys, Japan, Box, 1950s, 5 In. 195.00
Motorcycle, Cart, Arctic Ice Cream, Driver, White, Hubley, 9 In. 695.00
Motorcycle, Cart, Delivery, Tin Lithograph, Clockwork, JML, 14 In. 935.00
Motorcycle, Cast Iron, Blue, Champion, 8 In. ....190.00 to 275.00
Motorcycle, Cast Iron, Green, Champion, 8 In. 330.00
Motorcycle, Cast Iron, Hubley, 9 In. 385.00
Motorcycle, Condor, Tin, Friction, IY, Japan, 12 In. 1155.00
Motorcycle, Delivery, Rubber Tires, Tin, Windup, Ny-Lint, 7 In. 195.00
Motorcycle, Driver, Sidecar, Rider, Red, Silver, Metal Spokes, Cast Iron, Hubley, 5 x 8 In. 1000.00
Motorcycle, Expert Cyclist, Dismounts, Tin, Battery Operated, Masudaya, Box, 12 In. ... 1165.00
Motorcycle, Friction, IY Metal Toys, Box, c.1940, 12 In. 8800.00
Motorcycle, Harley-Davidson, Moves, Sparks, Tin, Friction, Japan, Box, 9 In. 675.00

Motorcycle, Harley-Davidson, Parcel Post, Driver, Cast Iron, Hubley, 10 In. 1980.00
Motorcycle, Harley-Davidson, Sidecar, 2 Policemen, Cast Iron, Hubley, 9 1/2 In. 1320.00
Motorcycle, Harley-Davidson, Tin Lithograph, Friction, Japan, 15 In. 1540.00
Motorcycle, Harley-Davidson, Tin Lithograph, Friction, TN, Japan, 9 In. 275.00
Motorcycle, Highway Patrol, Driver Dismounts, Tin, Battery, Masudaya, Box, 12 In. 800.00
Motorcycle, Mac, Driver, Dismounts, Clockwork, Tin Litho., U.S. Zone Germany, 7 In. . . . 725.00
Motorcycle, Moto Flash Cycle, Tin, Windup, Technofix, France, 7 1/2 In. 330.00
Motorcycle, No. 49, Tin, Windup, Australia, 7 1/2 In. 245.00
Motorcycle, Policeman, 3 Wheels, Tin, Battery Operated, Japan, 1950s, 10 In. 475.00
Motorcycle, Policeman, Blue, White Rubber Tires, Hubley, 1920s, 4 In. 125.00
Motorcycle, Policeman, Cast Iron, Green, White Rubber Tires, Champion, 7 1/2 In. 385.00
Motorcycle, Policeman, Cast Iron, Red, Rubber Tires, U.S.A., 6 1/2 In. 120.00
Motorcycle, Policeman, Rookie, Falls Over, Tin, Windup, Marx, Box, c.1930, 9 In. 580.00
Motorcycle, Policeman, Sidecar, Cast Iron, Rubber Tires, 4 In. 145.00
Motorcycle, Policeman, Sidecar, Windup, Marx, 8 1/2 In. 325.00
Motorcycle, Policeman, State Trooper, Sparks, Tin, Friction, 10 In. 570.00
Motorcycle, Policeman, Tin Lithograph, Clockwork, 7 1/2 In. 385.00
Motorcycle, Policeman, Tin Lithograph, Windup, Siren, Marx, 8 In. 195.00
Motorcycle, Policeman, Tin, Battery Operated, Bandai, Box, c.1950, 12 In. 1250.00
Motorcycle, Policeman, Windup, Tin Lithograph, Box, 6 In. 330.00
Motorcycle, Racing, Driver, Windup, Tin Lithograph, 1940s, 7 In. 315.00
Motorcycle, Racing, Rider, Friction, Japan, 1960s, 8 In. 155.00
Motorcycle, Red, Driver, Clockwork, Tin Lithograph, Mettoy, 7 1/2 In. 385.00
Motorcycle, Rider, Battery Operated, Tin Lithograph, Modern Toys, Japan, Box, 12 In. . . 935.00
Motorcycle, Rider, Tin Lithograph, Windup, 8 1/2 In. 180.00
Motorcycle, Rider, Tin Lithograph, Windup, No. 2, Technofix, U.S. Zone Germany, 7 In. . 220.00
Motorcycle, Rider, Tin Lithograph, Windup, No. 15, Technofix, 7 In. 70.00
Motorcycle, Sidecar, 2 Policemen, Hubley, 8 1/2 In. 875.00
Motorcycle, Sidecar, Balloon Tires, Tin, Original Key, Russia, 8 3/4 In. 225.00
Motorcycle, Sidecar, Cast Iron, Champion, 6 In. 415.00
Motorcycle, Sidecar, Cast Iron, Hubley, 9 In. 660.00
Motorcycle, Sidecar, Driver, Passenger, Meier, Penny Toy 1760.00
Motorcycle, Sidecar, Passenger, Windup, Japan, 1930s, 4 In. 335.00
Motorcycle, Sidecar, Sparking Gun, Tin Lithograph, Windup, CKO, Germany, 4 In. 250.00
Motorcycle, Sidecar, Tin Lithograph, Windup, Marx, 8 1/2 In. 220.00
Motorcycle, Sidecar, Tin, Friction, M.E., Japan, 1950s, 5 1/2 In. 175.00
Motorcycle, Sidecar, Tin, Windup, Tucher & Walther, Box . . . . .22.00 to 39.00
Motorcycle, Tin, Friction, Blue, 7 In. 30.00
Motorcycle, Triumph, Sidecar, 3 People, Tin Lithograph, Embossed, Meier, 4 1/4 In. 1760.00
Motorcycle, U.S. Air Mail, Driver, Cast Iron, Indian, Hubley, 1929, 9 1/4 In. 1700.00
Motorcycle, Windup, Tin Lithograph, Marx, 8 1/2 In. 145.00
Motorcycle, Windup, Tin Lithograph, Schuco, 5 In. 330.00
Motorcycle, Windup, Tin Lithograph, Siren, Marx, 8 1/2 In. 275.00
Motorcycle, Windup, Tin Lithograph, TCO-59, Technofix, Germany, 7 In. 330.00
Mouse, Girl, Felt, Ratina, Italy, 15 In. 330.00
Mouse, Mother Lifts Baby Mouse, Tin, Flannel, Windup, Schuco, Germany, 1935, 4 In. . . 170.00
Mower, Reel, Arcade, 22 In. 120.00
Mower, Reel, Arcade, 26 In. 198.00
Moxiemobile, Moxie Soda, White Horse, Jockey On Top, Die Cut, 6 1/2 In. 2860.00
Mr. & Mrs. Potato Head, Family, General Mills Premium, Box, 1952 . . . . 325.00
Mr. Baseball, Battery Operated, Box, 8 In. 825.00
Mr. Caterpillar, Windup, Tin Lithograph, Japan, Box, 12 In. 85.00
Mr. Dan, Tin Lithograph, Windup, TN, Japan, Box, 6 In. 39.00
Mr. Mercury, Battery Operated, Gold Tin, Marx, 1960s, 13 In. 435.00
Mule, Dancing, Hand Crank, Folk Art, Hessler Wallace, 14 In. 130.00
Mule & Wagon, Hubley, 1910, 10 1/4 In. 450.00
Munsters, Herman Munster, Windup, Japan, 1960s, 5 1/2 In. 225.00
Music Hall, Battery Operated, Linemar, Box, 6 In. 495.00
Musicians, Cymbal Player, Drummer, Bisque Head, Wood Base, Pull Toy, 10 1/2 In. 1540.00
Mysto Magic Set, Tricks, Sleight Of Hand, Illusions, Gilbert, 1938 . . . . 250.00
Noah's Ark, 12 Animals, Converse, c.1915, 19 In. 220.00
Old Timer, Tin Lithograph, TN, Japan, Box, 9 1/2 In. 99.00
One-Man Band, Xylophone, Drum, Bell, Harmonica, Triangle, Tin, Box, c.1940, 11 In. . . . 110.00

Orange Vendor, Woman, Pushing Cart, Cloth Dress, Over Wire, Tin, Martin, 7 In. 660.00
Organ, Church, Windup, Tin Lithograph, Chein, Box, 10 In. 175.00
Organ, Tin, Pipes, Birds, Harps, Winding Handle, Germany, 6 3/4 x 4 1/2 In. 85.00
Organ Grinder, Monkey, Tin Lithograph, Mechanical, Distler, Germany, c.1923, 6 1/2 In. . 1100.00
Oscar The Seal, Tin Lithograph, Windup, Japan, Box, 4 In. 45.00
Ostrich, Painted Eyes, Schoenhut, 10 In. 275.00
Ostrich, Pulling Cart, Tin Lithograph, No. 170, Lehmann, Germany, c.1910, 6 In. 825.00
Ostrich, With Monkey In Cart, Windup, Japan, Box, 9 In. 259.00
Owl, Wittie, Mohair, Tag, Steiff, c.1950, 3 In. 45.00
Ox Cart, Red, Silver, Orange, Spoke Wheels, 2 Piece, Cast Iron, 2 1/2 x 7 1/4 x 3 1/2 In. . 50.00
Pail, 3 Little Pigs Leaving Home, Red Handle, Tin, J. Chein, USA, 3 1/2 In. 140.00
Pail, 3 Wise Men Of Gotham, Black Silhouettes On Red, Tin, Wire Bail Handle, 4 In. 165.00
Pail, 4 Children, Goat Cart At Beach, Flower & Leaf Border, Gilded Bail Handle, Tin, 5 In. 300.00
Pail, Atlantic City, Stars & Stripes, Red, White, Blue, Wire Bail Handle, Tin, 5 1/2 In. ... 630.00
Pail, Baby & Baby Farm Animals, Tin, Flat Tin Bail Handle, T. Cohn, USA, 4 1/4 In. 110.00
Pail, Boy & Donkey, 3 Children In Rowboat, Gilt Borders & Bail Handle, Tin, 3 In. 165.00
Pail, Children & Toy Boat, Children Gathering Seashells, Gilded Bail Handle, Tin, 5 In. .. 220.00
Pail, Children Building Sand Castles, Flower, Leaf Border, Gilded Bail Handle, Tin, 7 In. . 690.00
Pail, Clown Faces, Tin, Red Flat Tin Handle, Ohio Art, 7 3/4 In. 55.00
Pail, Girl Riding Goat, Boy Riding Horse, Tin, Wire Bail Handle, Wood Grip, 5 3/4 In. .. 415.00
Pail, Jungle Animals, Gilt Flowered Scroll Border, Tin, T. Bros., 6 1/2 In. 440.00
Pail, Nursery Rhymes, Square, Yellow Flat Tin Handle, J. Chein, USA, 5 3/4 In. 110.00
Pail, Playing Pirates, Yellow Interior, Flat Red Handle, Kirchhof, USA, 5 In. 85.00
Pail, Punch & Judy, Tin, Wire Bail Handle, USA, 4 In. 360.00
Pail, Scenes At Beach, Red Border, Tin, Flat Tin Bail Handle, Ohio Art, 6 In. 605.00
Pail, Ships At Harbor & Calm Seas, Red Ground, Tin, Wire Bail Handle, 3 In. 275.00
Pail, Simple Simon, Black Silhouette On Red Ground, Tin, Wire Bail Handle, 4 In. 300.00
Pail, Treasure Island, Red Flat Tin Bail Handle, U.S. Metal Toy Mfg. Co., 7 1/2 In. 55.00
Panda, Battery Operated, Alps, Box, 11 In. 275.00
Pango Pango African Dancer, Tin Lithograph, Mechanical, Japan, 6 In. 150.00
Parrot, Peggy, Battery Operated, Rosko, Box, 11 In. 145.00
Parrot, Pip-Squeak, Pink, Orange & Maroon Feathers, Blue Comb, Green Base, 7 3/4 In. . 220.00
Peacock, Chirps, Clockwork, Tin Lithograph, EBO, 10 1/2 In. 220.00
Peahen, Pip-Squeak, White Body, Blue Feathers, Wire Legs, 8 In. 1760.00
Pedal Car, Airplane, Army Scout, Wood, Steel, Gendron, 1920s, 41 In. 1610.00
Pedal Car, Chrysler, Airflow, Hood Ornament, Windshield, Horn, Steelcraft, 46 In. 1265.00
Pedal Car, Chrysler, Bumper, Windshield, Headlight, Steelcraft, 1941, 37 In. 1430.00
Pedal Car, Comet, Maroon, Horn, Murray, c.1950, 38 In. 660.00
Pedal Car, Essex, Electric Headlights, Steelcraft, 1930s, 34 In. 2420.00
Pedal Car, Ford, Wood, Steel, Adjustable Seat, 42 In. 2530.00
Pedal Car, Pacesetter, Yellow & Blue, Hubcap, Steering Wheel & Windshield, AMF 40.00
Pedal Car, Packard Style, Accessories, American National, 1920s, 45 In. 4025.00
Pedal Car, Packard, Leather Seats, Gendron, 1931 .... 8800.00
Pedal Car, Pressed Steel, Yellow, Gravel Dump, Jet Flow Drive, Murray, 1948, 45 In. 310.00
Pedal Car, Red & Yellow Paint, c.1930 .... 630.00
Pedal Car, Red, Pressed Steel, Spoke Wheels, Headlights, American National, 46 In. 1375.00
Pedal Car, Tin, Wood, Wire Wheels, Red & Yellow Paint, c.1910 .... 660.00
Pedal Car, Torpedo, Beehive Wheels, Trim, Murray, 1940s, 39 In. 635.00
Pedal Car, Tractor, McCormick Farmall, Eska, Box 770.00
Pedal Cart, Horse Drawn, Articulated, 48 In. 1980.00
Penguin, Skier, On Leash, Windup, Remote Control, Japan, Box 28.00
Periscope, Battery Operated, Cragstan, Box, 9 In. 95.00
Peter Rabbit, Drumming, Yellow, Alps, Iwaya, Japan, Box, 13 In. 250.00
Peter Rabbit Chick-Mobile, Tin, Windup, Ringing Bell, Lionel, 1930s 975.00
Pianist, Jolly, Battery Operated, Box, 8 1/2 In. ....220.00 to 300.00
Piano, Candleholders, Wood, Cast Iron Legs, Schoenhut, 16 x 13 In. 275.00
Piano, Grand, Red, Storybook Decal, Schoenhut, c.1940, 10 In. 35.00
Piano, Jaymar, Pat. Date 1953, 18 In. 42.00
Piano, Play Away, Songbook, Tin, Marx, Box, 9 x 10 In. 110.00
Piano, Schoenhut, 21 In. 35.00
Piano, Upright, Bliss, c.1900, 12 In. 120.00
Piano, Upright, Schoenhut, 13 1/8 x 9 1/4 x 7 In. 46.00
Pig, Glass Eyes, Painted Wood, 1-Part Head & Neck, Schoenhut, 6 3/4 In. 385.00

Piggy Cook, Pig Cooks Egg, Battery Operated, Y, Japan, 10 3/4 In. 45.00
Pink Panther, 1-Man Band, Battery Operated, Illco, Box 105.00
Pistol Pete, Battery Operated, Marusan, Box, 10 In. 360.00
Play Set, Rin Tin Tin, Fort Apache, Series 1000, No. 3658, Marx, Box, 1956, 22 In. 510.00
Play Set, Strawberry Shortcake, 3 Figures, American Greetings, 1980, 10 In. 119.00
Play Set, Voyage To Bottom Of Sea, Sub, Crawler, Missiles, Divers, Chest, Remco, 1960 . 945.00
Playboy, Man Drinks, Spins, Battery Operated, Cragstan, Japan 70.00
Playground, Mechanical, Tin Lithograph, Lee, Box, 15 In. 137.00
Playground, Tin, Windup, T.P.S., Japan, 1950s, 9 1/2 In. 245.00
Pleasant Kappa, Funny River Monster, Laughs, Tin, Battery Operated, Japan, Box, 11 In. 880.00
Policeman, Casey The Cop, Walks, Windup, Unique Art, 1930s, 9 In. 575.00
Policeman, Traffic, Tin Lithograph, Plastic, Battery Operated, TN, Box, 14 In. 360.00
Policeman, Traffic, Tin, Germany, Prewar, 5 1/2 In. 325.00
Pony & Cart, Brown Pony, Red Wheels, Victorian, c.1880 . . . . 450.00
Pool Player, Shoots Balls On Table, Tin Lithograph, Embossed, Lever, Kellermann, 4 In. . 120.00
Pool Players, Tin, Mechanical, Men Standing At Pool Table, Kico, Germany, 14 In. 420.00
Poor Pete, Black, Celluloid, Fabric, Windup, Japan, Original Box 385.00
Poor Pete, Black, Tin Lithograph, Windup, Germany, 6 In. 450.00
Popcorn Machine, Junior, Wilson Bros., Memphis, Tenn., Unopened Box, 20 In. 110.00
Popcorn Vendor, Battery Operated, Tin Lithograph, Japan, Box, 8 In. 250.00
Porky Pig, Umbrella, Marx, 8 In. 550.00
Porter, Busy, Battery Operated, Modern Toys, Box, 8 In. 130.00
Porter, Red Cap, Tin, Windup, Walks Along Holding Suitcases, Marx, 8 In. . . . . . .650.00 to 715.00
Powerful Katrinka, Tin, Windup, Jimmy In Wheelbarrow, Germany, 1923, 7 In. .1430.00 to 1760.00
Printing Press, Baltimore No. 9, Cast Iron, Painted, Raised Letters, 8 In. 110.00
Punching Bag, Bozo Bop Bag, Sand Filled Base, Rocket USA, Box, 46 In. 20.00
Puppet Stage, Paper Accessories, Lithograph, Pollock, 20 x 19 In. 80.00
Queen Elizabeth, Coronation Coach Set, Glass Enclosure, Britains, c.1950, 25 x 5 1/4 In. 200.00
Rabbit, Busy Bunny, Holds Camera, Iwaya, Alps, Japan, Box, 6 In. 95.00
Rabbit, Busy Bunny, Holds Ice Cream Cone, Iwaya, Alps, Japan, Box, 6 In. 95.00
Rabbit, Drumming, Windup, Alps, Iwaya, Japan, Box, 1950s, 7 In. 95.00
Rabbit, Easter Delivery, Motorcycle, Sidecar, Wyandotte, 9 1/2 In. . . . . .140.00 to 165.00
Rabbit, Easter, Pulls Chick, Duckling, Celluloid, Tin, Windup, Daihachi, Japan, 7 In. 195.00
Rabbit, Musical, Windup, Tin Lithograph, Celluloid, 8 In. 99.00
Rabbit, Musical, Xylophone, Windup, Pink, Fuji Press, Japan, Box, 10 In. 165.00
Rabbit, Picnic Bunny, Battery Operated, Alps, Japan, Box, 10 In. 50.00
Rabbit, Wheelbarrow, Tin Lithograph, Chein, 6 In. 20.00
Rabbit, With Camera, Windup, Tin, Alps, Japan, Box, 8 In. 120.00
Radar Station, Lights Flash, Antenna Spins, Tin, Battery Operated, Masudaya, Box, 7 In. 370.00
Rattle, Policeman, Celluloid, Japan, Prewar, 4 1/2 In. 45.00
Red Cross Field Station, Penny Toy, Meier, 4 In. 470.00
Refrigerator, Doll's, Metal, Marx, Box, 14 In. 127.00
Reg'lar Fellers Paint Set, American Toy Works, Box, c.1930, 10 x 15 In. 70.00
Rickshaw, Masuyama, Clockwork, Lehmann, 1920s 1985.00
Rider, On Horse, Composition, Wood, Red Rockers, Clockwork, Germany, 25 x 18 In. . . . 415.00
Rip Van Winkle, Ol' Sleepy Head, Sits Up, Yawns, Battery, Yonezawa, Box, 9 In. 250.00
Road Roller, Model, Steam Powered, Solid Fuel Burning, Instructions, Germany, 12 In. . . 350.00
Robot, Astronaut, Battery Operated, Tin Lithograph, Cragstan, Japan, 13 In. 489.00
Robot, Astronaut, Walks, Click Noise, Red, Tin, Crank, Yonezawa, Box, 10 In. 3080.00
Robot, Astronaut, Walks, Fires Gun, Tin, Battery Operated, Cragstan, Daiya, Box, 11 In. . 1430.00
Robot, Astronaut, Walks, Lifts Rifle, Fires, Red, Tin, Battery Operated, Daiya, Box, 14 In. 2255.00
Robot, Atomic, Walks, Steps Over, Head Turns, Tin, Windup, Yonezawa, 6 1/2 In. 385.00
Robot, Atomic, Walks, Steps Over, Tin, Windup, Japan, Box, 5 In. 1020.00
Robot, Baby Swinging, Tin Lithograph, Clockwork, Japan, Box, 7 In. 250.00
Robot, Blazer, Tin Lithograph, Windup, Red, Japan, Box, 9 1/4 In. 300.00
Robot, Blink A Gear, Walks, Lights, Tin, Battery Operated, Taiyo, Box, 14 1/2 In. 990.00
Robot, Brazer, Tin Lithograph, Rubber Head, Clockwork, Bullmark, Japan, Box, 8 1/2 In. 275.00
Robot, Bulldozer, Marvelous Mike, Moves, Tin, Battery Operated, Saunders, Box, 13 In. . 385.00
Robot, Chief Smoky, Bump & Go, Arms Swing, Tin, Battery Operated, Japan, Box, 12 In. 960.00
Robot, Chief, White, Tin Lithograph, Plastic Chest Panel, Yoshida, Japan, 1950s, 12 In. . . 990.00
Robot, Clown, Moves, Mouth Opens, Plastic, Battery Operated, Waco, Box, 14 In. 220.00
Robot, Conehead, Walks, Eyes Spark, Tin, Windup, Yonezawa, 8 3/4 In. 2860.00
Robot, D Fighter, Tin Lithograph, Spiked Head, Clockwork, ST, Japan, 9 1/2 In. 195.00

Robot, Diamond Planet, Walks, Sparks, Tin, Windup, Yonezawa, Box, 10 1/2 In. 33000.00
Robot, Diaparon, Tin Lithograph, Clockwork, Bullmark, Japan, Box, 8 1/4 In. 250.00
Robot, Dino-Robot, Tin Lithograph, Helmet, Monster Head, Horikawa, Japan, Box, 11 In. 1320.00
Robot, Elephant, Rocks, Ears Flap, Sparks, Tin, Windup, Japan, Box, 5 In. 1320.00
Robot, Etsuko, Kamen, Tin Lithograph, Clockwork, Bullmark, Japan, Box, 9 In. . .440.00 to 550.00
Robot, Gears Spin, Light On Head, Tin, Battery Operated, Horikawa, Box, 9 In. 495.00
Robot, Getter Dragon, Walks, Arms Move, Tin, Windup, Popy, Box, 9 In. 195.00
Robot, Gurendaiza, Walks, Tin, Windup, Popy, Box, 9 In. 195.00
Robot, High Wheel, Walks, Gears Spin, Sparks, Tin, Windup, Japan, Box, 10 In. 440.00
Robot, Hysterical Harry, Laughing, Battery Operated, Plastic, Japan, 1960s, 13 In. 355.00
Robot, Jupiter, Red Plastic, Tin Face Guard, Windup, Japan, Box, 7 In. 165.00
Robot, Lost In Space, Battery Operated, Hong Kong, Box, 1977, 10 1/2 In. . . . . . .165.00 to 250.00
Robot, Machine Man, Red, Tin Lithograph, Battery Operated, Modern Toys, 14 In. 14300.00
Robot, Martin The Martian, Bump & Go, Light-Up, Battery, Yonezawa, Box, 15 In. 495.00
Robot, Mekanda, Walks, Arms Move, Tin, Windup, Bullmark, Box, 8 1/2 In. 275.00
Robot, Mighty, Tin Lithograph, Battery Operated, Yoshiya, Japan, 12 In. 1100.00
Robot, Mighty, Windup, Tin Lithograph, Box, Japan, 6 In. 140.00
Robot, Mirror Man, Tin Litho., Clockwork, Rubber Mask, Bullmark, Japan, Box, 9 In. . . . 400.00
Robot, Moon Scout, Hi-Bouncer, Walks, Balls Shoot, Tin, Battery, Marx, Box, 12 In. 2750.00
Robot, Moon, Tin, Sparking Action, Rubber Ears & Hands, Yonezawa, Box, 11 In. 3520.00
Robot, Moon, Walks, Sparks, Tin, Plastic, Windup, Yonezawa, Box, 7 1/2 In. 440.00
Robot, Mr. Mercury, Walks, Arms Move, Tin, Remote Control, Marx, Box, 13 1/2 In. . . . 440.00
Robot, Mr. Robot, Bump & Go, Antenna Spins, Tin, Battery Operated, Japan, Box, 11 In. 1430.00
Robot, Mr. Robot, Tin, Battery Operated, Yonezawa, Box, 11 1/2 In. 1650.00
Robot, Planet, Tin Body, Plastic Helmet, Windup, Yoshiya, Japan, Box, 9 In. 140.00
Robot, Planet, Walks, Sparks, Black Body, Red Hands & Feet, Windup, KO, Box, 9 In. . . 340.00
Robot, Radar, Walks, Lights, Flashes, Tin, Remote Control, Japan, Box, 10 In. . .1320.00 to 1760.00
Robot, Ranger, Walks, Arms Swing, Voice Noise, Lights, Plastic, Daiya, Box, 10 In. 2035.00
Robot, Remote Control, Battery Operated, Linemar, Box, 7 1/2 In. 965.00
Robot, Robby, Battery Operated, Box, 1950s, 13 1/2 In. 2000.00
Robot, Smoking Lantern, Walks, Swings Lantern, Tin, Remote Control, Linemar, 8 In. . . . 2200.00
Robot, Smoking, Walks, Red Eyes, Tin, Battery Operated, Linemar, Box, 12 In. 2200.00
Robot, Space Explorer, Battery Operated, Yonezawa, Japan, Box, 7 1/2 In. 1760.00
Robot, Space Explorer, Box Becomes Robot, Tin, Battery Operated, Yonezawa, Box, 12 In. 1100.00
Robot, Space Patrol, In Car, Tin Lithograph, Friction, Cragston, Japan, Box, 8 In. 2310.00
Robot, Space Scout, Walks, Lights, Plastic, Tin, Battery, Horikawa, Box, 9 1/2 In. 155.00
Robot, Space Scout, White, Tin, Siren Sound, Yonezawa, Japan, 9 5/8 In. 2860.00
Robot, Sparks, Walks, Mechanical, Japan, Box, 6 1/2 In. 525.00
Robot, Sparky, Tin, Windup, Japan, Box, 7 1/2 In. . . . . .495.00 to 520.00
Robot, ST1, Walks, Tin, Windup, West Germany, Box, 7 1/2 In. 550.00
Robot, Super Hero, Tin Lithograph, Clockwork, Bullmark, Japan, Box, 8 3/4 In. 770.00
Robot, Super Moon Explorer, Plastic, Hong Kong, Box, 11 1/2 In. 90.00
Robot, Swinging Baby, Swings On Girders, Flag, Tin, Windup, Yone, Box, 6 In. 495.00
Robot, Thunder, Walks, Antenna Spins, Gun, Tin, Battery Operated, Asakusa, Box, 12 In. 5850.00
Robot, Tin Man, Wizard Of Oz, Walks, Plastic, Battery, Remco, Box, 1969, 22 In. 440.00
Robot, Tin, Battery Operated, Claw Hands, Easel Back, Yonezawa, Box, 6 In. 1580.00
Robot, Topalino, Radar, Battery Operated, Tin Lithograph, Plastic, TN, Box, 12 In. 11000.00
Robot, Ultra Man Leo, Tin Litho., Clockwork, Rubber Head, Bullmark, Japan, 9 In. 495.00
Robot, Urutora Man, Tin Litho., Clockwork, Rubber Head, Bullmark, Japan, Box, 9 In. . . 600.00
Robot, Winky, Walks, Sparks, Eyes, Moves, Tin, Windup, Yonezawa, Box, 9 1/2 In. 3080.00
Robot, X-70, Tulip Head, Camera Inside Head, Nomura, Japan, 12 1/2 In. 715.00
Robot, Zabitan, Tin Lithograph, Clockwork, Plastic Head, Bullmark, Japan, Box, 9 In. . . . 275.00
Robot, Zoomer, Walks, Eyes Light, Blue, Red, Tin, Battery Operated, Japan, 8 In. 965.00
Rocker, Doll's, Elephant Shape, Lithograph, Wood, Converse, c.1900, 13 In. 300.00
Rocket, Saturn X-5, Tin Lithograph, Plastic, Alps, Japan, Box, 1960s, 11 1/2 In. 195.00
Rocket, Solar X, Tin Lithograph, Battery Operated, TN, Japan, Box 90.00
Rocket, Sonicon, Moves, Whistles, Lights Flash, Tin, Remote Control, Japan, Box, 14 In. 825.00
Rocket, Space, Tin Lithograph, Friction, Holdrakete, 16 In. 55.00
Rocket, Tiger, Cape, Tin, Friction, MT Mark, Box, 12 1/2 In. 465.00
Rocket Ride, Twirly Whirly, Spins, Lights, Tin, Battery Operated, Alps, Box, 13 In. 495.00
Rocket Ride, Twirly Whirly, Tin Lithograph, Cragstan, Box, 10 1/2 In. 250.00
Rocket Ship, Tin Lithograph, Monorail, Linemar, Japan, 1950, 10 In. 235.00
Rocky, Waves Stick & Stone Ax, Tin, Battery Operated, Japan, Box, 4 1/2 In. 195.00

Rodeo Joe, Cowboy, On Tractor, Tin, Windup, England, Box, 7 In. 300.00
Roll-Around, Tin Wheel, Figure Inside, Tin, Occupied Japan, Box, 6 In. 395.00
Roller Chimes, Cylinder, Orchestra Scenes, Tin Lithograph, Marx, c.1940, 9 1/2 In. 56.00
Roller Coaster, Windup, Tin Lithograph, Chein, 19 In. . . . . .200.00 to 450.00
Rollo Chair, Atlantic City, Black Porter, Tin Lithograph, Mechanical, Germany, 8 In. 1650.00
Rooster, Cock Fighting, On Wheels, Tin, Windup, Box, 6 In. 130.00
Rooster, Mohair, Steiff, c.1950, 3 In. 50.00
Rooster, Pip-Squeak, Multicolored, Blue Feathers, Red Comb, Wire Legs, 5 1/4 In. 165.00
Royal Couple, Prince, Princess, Dance, Plastic, Windup, Irwin, Box, 5 1/2 In. . . . . · 95.00
Sailor, Tin, Windup, Lehmann, c.1900, 7 1/2 In. . . . . .310.00 to 750.00
Sailor, Woman, In Rowboat, Rocking Action, Tin Lithograph, Meier, 3 In. 770.00
Sammy, The Strolling Skeleton, Windup, Japan, Original Box, 1950s, 5 1/2 In. 410.00
Sammy Wong, The Tea Totaler, Pours Teapot, Lifts Cup, Japan, Box, 10 In. 330.00
Sand, Captain Sandy, Pirates, Cylinder, No.63C, Wolverine Supply, Box, 13 1/2 In. 220.00
Sand, Handcar, Pulley, Tin Lithograph, Silver Base, Red, Blue Liner, Yellow, USA, 11 In. 55.00
Sand, Mill, Hod Carrier, No. 69, Tin Litho., Boy Catching Sand, Automatic, Chein, 10 In. 140.00
Sand, Mill, One Excelsior, Cast Iron Chute, Man, Tin Bucket, Wooden Box, 13 In. 468.00
Sand, Mill, Tin Lithograph, Children At Beach, Revolving, J. Chein, USA, 6 In. 300.00
Sand, Sandmaster, Children At Beach, Tin, Midwest Industries, Cleveland, 10 1/2 In. 28.00
Sand, Water Pump, Tin Lithograph Elephant, Children, Ohio Art, 10 In. 99.00
Sand, Windmill, Dutch, Pour Sand, Blades Turn, Tin, McDowell, Box, c.1930, 12 In. 230.00
Sandwich Man, Windup, Tin Lithograph, TN, Japan, Box, 7 In. . . . . .65.00 to 130.00
Sandy Andy, No. 1, Tin Lithograph, Green, Orange, Pittsburgh, USA, 1909-1917, 18 In. . . 110.00
Sandy Andy, Seesaw, No. 61, Black Rabbit Silhouettes, Wolverine, Box, 9 In. 140.00
Satellite, In Orbit, Tin Lithograph, Battery Operated, Cragstan, Japan, Box, 1950s, 10 In. . 285.00
Satellite, Tracking Station, Mobile, Battery Operated, Tin Lithograph, Japan, Box, 9 In. . 1045.00
Scooter, Ice Cream, Vendor Hits Bell, Tin, Windup, Courtland, Box, c.1930, 6 1/2 In. 385.00
Scooter, Ice Cream, Windup, Courtland, U.S.A., Box, 1948, 6 In. 495.00
Scooter, Shooting Star, 39 In. 65.00
Seal, Brown, Steiff, c.1950, 5 In. 39.00
Seal, Glass Eyes, Leather Flippers, Schoenhut 990.00
Seesaw, Elephant & Zebra, Metal, Windup, Japan, 1950, 7 1/4 x 6 1/2 In. 595.00
Sewing Kit, Little Travelers, Doll, Patterns, Sewing Utensils, Transogram Co., Box 30.00
Sewing Kit, Moderne Sewing For Little Girls, Cardboard Dolls, American Toy Works, Box 60.00
Sewing Machine, Bing, Iron Case, Gold Stencil, Original Box, 8 In. 169.00
Sewing Machine, Gold Flower Stencil, Tin, 5 3/4 In. 96.00
Sewing Machine, Midget, Cast Iron, Decals, 7 1/2 In. 305.00
Sewing Machine, Singer, Cast Iron, Box, c.1914 . . . . 248.00
Sewing Machine, Singer, Crank, Iron, Nickel Plated, Just Like Mom's, Box, 6 1/2 In. 155.00
Sewing Machine, Singer, Sew Handy, Box, c.1940 . . . . 105.00
Sewing Machine, Tin Lithograph, Embossed, Crank Operates Needle, Meier, 3 In. 99.00
Sharpshooter, Celluloid, Windup, Original Key, Gun Noise, Head Turns, Japan 215.00
Shoeshine Joe, Eyes Light Up, Battery Operated, TN, Japan, Box, 9 In. . . . . .70.00 to 160.00
Shooting Gallery, Rubber Ball, 9 Targets, Paper Lithograph On Wood, Schoenhut, 16 In. . 248.00
Shovel, Pressed Steel, Ny-Lint, Michigan, 31 1/2 In. 45.00
Sign, Do Not Park Here, Freidag Base, 12 x 12 1/2 In. 690.00
Sign, Go, Cast Iron, May 1925, 5 In. 415.00
Sign, Stop, Go, Tin Lithograph, Chein, 11 In. 440.00
Sign, Stop-N-Go, Arcade, 3 3/4 In. 250.00
Sign, U.S. Highway 41, Round Base, Arcade, 5 In. 495.00
Ski Jumper, Does Flip, Flags, Painted, Wood, Metal, Schoenhut, Box, 26 In. 250.00
Ski Slope, Tin Lithograph, Wolverine, 26 In. 115.00
Skier, Windup, Chein, 5 x 7 1/2 In. 165.00
Sky Ranger, Tin Lithograph, Unique Art, 24 In. . . . . .220.00 to 275.00
Sled, Bentwood, Stenciled Seat, Red, Paris Mfg., Maine, 33 1/2 x 11 1/4 In. 345.00
Sled, Bird's-Eye Maple, Mahogany, Painted, Indians, Pilgrims, Gov. Robie, 45 x 19 In. . . 19120.00
Sled, Flexible Flyer, Wood, Steel, 4 Man, 102 In. 550.00
Sled, Ironbound Runners, Red Paint, 42 x 11 In. 155.00
Sled, Oak, Iron, Flowers, Robert J., America, Late 1800s, 7 x 12 x 42 5/8 In. 880.00
Sled, Painted, Eagle, Shield, Arrows, Child Sledding, Bay State Banner, 1800s, 45 In. 2300.00
Sled, Red & Black, Gold Pinstripes, Initials B.C.B., 19th Century, 15 x 43 x 8 In. 650.00
Sled, Red Paint, Steel Runners, Oval Medallion, 1900, 36 In. . . . . .145.00 to 176.00
Sled, Running Horse, Red Glides, American, c.1880 . . . . 2850.00

Sled, Steel Runners, Green, Yellow Pinstripes, Bird, Vine, Leaves, 23 x 7 1/4 In. 340.00
Sled, Wagon Seat, Pony Hitch, Bradley Junior, 36 In. 525.00
Sled, Wood, Iron, Painted Flowers, Mustard Paint, 36 In. 250.00
Sled, Wood, Iron, Painted Flowers, Red Paint, 15 In. 990.00
Sled, Wood, Iron, Painted Scene, Green Paint, Wabash, 36 In. 615.00
Sled, Wood, Metal Braces & Runners, Stenciled Scene, Lake & Trees, 1910, 39 In. 615.00
Sled, Wood, Metal, 19th Century, 63 In. 230.00
Sled, Wood, Red Paint, Stenciled Gold Flowers, 30 x 12 x 7 1/2 In. 425.00
Sled, Wood, Steel Runners, Green Paint, 34 In. 120.00
Sled, Wood, Steel Streamlined Nose, Bo-Bo Link Decal, 1940s, 50 In. 80.00
Sled, Yellow Seat, Red Sides, Flowers, Original Paint, Iron Runners, 35 In. 478.00
Sleigh, Horse Drawn, Lutz, 27 In. 5720.00
Sleigh, Iron, Upholstered Seat, Handle, Wooden Runners, Victorian, 38 x 56 x 16 In. 300.00
Sleigh, Wood, Stenciling, Velvet, Pennsylvania, 41 In. 360.00
Snowmobile, Battery Operated, TM, Japan, Box, 1950s, 8 In. 495.00
Soccer Players, Kicking Ball, Tin Lithograph, Embossed, Lever, Penny Toy, Meier, 4 In. . 1100.00
Soldier, Alymer, Artillery Elephant Drag, Box, 18 In. 115.00
Soldier, Alymer, Boer War Cow Gun, Box, 16 In. 150.00
Soldier, Nazi, Mechanical, Tin, 1930s, 5 1/4 In. 195.00
Soldier Set, 100 Soldiers On Parade, Die Cut, McLoughlin Bros., Box, 1900, 21 x 12 In. . 365.00
Soldier Set, Composition, Painted Wood, Various Nationalities, Horses, c.1909, 129 Piece 470.00
Soldier Set, Paper Lithograph, Box, 10 To 20 In. 120.00
Soldier Set, Soldiers Of Fortune, Tin Lithograph, Marx, Box, 1930s 675.00
Soldier Set, Soldiers On Parade, No. 3, McLoughlin, Box, 25 Piece 225.00
Space Capsule, Tin Lithograph, Plastic, Battery Operated, Japan, 10 In. 330.00
Space Capsule, Tin Lithograph, Plastic, Battery Operated, Japan, Box, 9 In. 110.00
Space Dog, Rocks Back & Forth, Windup, Japan, Box, 7 1/2 In. 650.00
Space Shuttle, Columbia, Bump & Go, Lights, Tin, Battery Operated, Spain, Box, 14 In. . 220.00
Space Sled, Land Of Giants, Battery Operated, 4 Disks, Remco, 1968, 10 1/2 In. 475.00
Space Station, Tin Lithograph, Battery Operated, Japan, 9 In. 230.00
Space Tank, Tin Lithograph, Friction, Japan, 6 In. 90.00
Space Tank, Tin Lithograph, Plastic, Battery Operated, Japan, 8 In. 198.00
Spaceman, Sparks In Chest, Tin Lithograph, Windup, Nomura Toys, Japan, Box, 5 1/2 In. 195.00
Spaceman, Tin Lithograph, Mechanical, Yoshia, Japan, Box, 6 In. 330.00
Spaceship, Apollo, Docking, Battery Operated, Tin Lithograph, Masudaya, Box, 18 In. . . . 440.00
Spaceship, Apollo, Spacewalker, Bump & Go, Tin, Lights, TM, Japan, Box, 1960s, 11 In. 300.00
Spaceship, Apollo, Tin Lithograph, Plastic, Battery Operated, Japan, Box, 9 In. 39.00
Spaceship, Battery Operated, Tin Lithograph, Modern Toys, Japan, Box, 8 In. 80.00
Spaceship, Friendship 7, Tin Lithograph, Friction, Japan, 13 In. 220.00
Spaceship, Gemini, Astronaut, Tin, Battery Operated, Masudaya, Box, 9 1/2 In. 165.00
Spaceship, Patrol, Bump & Go, Noise, Tin, Battery Operated, Yonezawa, Box, 8 In. 385.00
Spaceship, Patrol, Tin Lithograph, Battery Operated, Modern Toys, Box, 11 1/2 In. 210.00
Spaceship, Ranger, Battery Operated, Tin Lithograph, Plastic, Box, 8 In. 90.00
Spaceship, Red Man From Space, Tin Lithograph, Friction, Japan, 6 In. 95.00
Spaceship, Tin Lithograph, Battery Operated, Japan, 8 1/2 In. 195.00
Spaceship, Tom Corbett, Sparking, Windup, Marx Rockhill, Box, 12 In. 1430.00
Spaceship, X-8, Bump & Go, Lights, Tin, Battery Operated, Tada, Box, 9 In. 200.00
Sparkler, Archie, Celluloid, Eyes Spark, Pull String, Ronson, 1923 . . . . 175.00
Speed Boy Delivery, Tin Lithograph, Mechanical, Marx, 10 In. . . . . .360.00 to 480.00
Speedway, U.S.A. 500 Miles, Pittsburgh, Pa., Metal Box, 1950s, 24 In. 95.00
Spinning Wheel, Red, Remco, Box, c.1983 . . . . 17.00
Squirmy Hermy, Tin Lithograph, Box, 12 In. 77.00
Squirrel Skipper, Tin, Windup, Japan, Box, 8 In. 50.00
Squirt Gun, Atomic, Plastic, Reliable Toys, Toronto, Box, Early 1950s, 8 In. 175.00
Squirt Gun, Dragnet, Black Plastic, 714 L.A. Shield On Grip, 1950s, 6 In. 40.00
Squirt Gun, Eagle Spaceship, Space 1999, Azark-Hamway, Hong Kong, 1975 . . . . 60.00
Squirt Gun, Green Hornet, Knuckle, Late 1960s 50.00
Squirt Gun, Spiderman, Durham Plastics, Hong Kong, 1975 . . . . 40.00
Squirt Gun, Stun, Space 1999, Azark-Hamway International, Hong Kong, 1975 . . . . 45.00
Squirt Gun, Tiny, Plastic, Reliable Toys, Toronto, 1950, 4 1/2 In. 35.00
Stagecoach, Overland, Battery Operated, Cragston, Box, 15 In. 99.00
Steam Engine, Alcohol Fueled, Vertical, Weeden 110.00
Steam Shovel, Cast Iron, Red, Nickel Plated, Rubber Tread, 3 1/4 In. 115.00

Steam Shovel, Pressed Steel, Buddy L, 1920s, 22 In. 209.00
Steam Shovel, Pressed Steel, Buddy L, 1940s, 20 In. 35.00
Steam Shovel, Pressed Steel, Structo, 12 In. 85.00
Steam Shovel, Pressed Steel, Structo, Box, 1950s, 18 In. 130.00
Steam Shovel, Pressed Steel, Turner, 1930s, 15 In. 55.00
Steamroller, Ride 'Em, Red, Gray, Keystone, 1930s, 20 In. 395.00
Steamroller, U.S. Army, Green, Driver, Rollers, Nickel Plated, Cast Iron, Hubley, 8 In. . . 400.00
Steamroller, Windup, Tin, Lindstrom, Box, 11 1/2 In. 210.00
Stereopticon, Walnut, 2 Sides, 15 Glass Views, Becker, 17 x 10 1/2 x 9 In. 1265.00
Stork, With Baby, Flies Around Chimney, Tin, Plastic, Windup, West Germany, 13 In. . . . 210.00
Stove, Eagle, Cast Aluminum, Accessories, 14 In. 115.00
Stove, Empire, Electric, Cord, Instructions 130.00
Stove, Royal, Cast Iron, Copper Flash, Kenton, 11 In. 50.00
Street Car, Tin, Momoya, Japan, Box, 1955, 10 In. 550.00
Street Cleaner, Metal, Japan, 1950s 95.00
Stroller, Doll's, Art Deco, Plastic Wicker, Fenders, 32 In. 110.00
Stroller, Doll's, Victorian, Painted, Stenciling, Fringed Canopy 350.00
Stroller, Doll's, Victorian, Wicker, Wire Spoke Wheels, Wooden Handle, 32 In. 56.00
Strutting Sam, Black Man, Dances, Tin, Battery Operated, Japan, Box, 11 In. 470.00
Submarine, Diving, Windup, Key, Cork, Wolverine, Box, 1940s, 13 In. . . . . .185.00 to 300.00
Submarine, Tin, Windup, Japan, Box, 9 1/2 In. 300.00
Surrey, Fringed, 2 Horses, Woman Rider, Man Driver, Kenton, 1940s, 13 In. . . . . .525.00 to 675.00
Surrey, Horse Drawn, Cast Iron, 7 1/2 In. 90.00
Surrey, Horse Drawn, Driver, Passenger, Cast Metal, Stanley, Box, 14 3/4 In. 190.00
Susi, Black Baby, Riding Turtle, Windup, Tin, Celluloid, Lehmann, Box, c.1950 . . . . 225.00
Suzy, Bouncing Ball, Tin, Vinyl, Windup, T.P.S., Japan, Box, 5 1/4 In. 160.00
Swing, Dog & Bear, Tin, Windup, Japan, 1950s 225.00
Switchboard Operator, Plugs In Lines, Lights, Battery, Linemar, 1950s, 8 In. . . .825.00 to 1450.00
Switchboard Operator, Tin, Vinyl Head, Linemar, Box, 1950s, 8 In. 1595.00
Table, Doll's, Pedestal, Fruitwood Inlay, Tilt Top, Beveled Edge, Tea Service, 5 In. 1980.00
Table, Doll's, Pedestal, Twisted Metal, Gilt, Wooden Top, Brass Studs, c.1860, 9 In. 2090.00
Table, Doll's, Walnut, Ebony, 2 Drawers, Drop Leaves, Leather, Brass, c.1880, 7 In. 1650.00
Tank, Anti-Tank Set, Exploding Tanks, Soldiers, Marx, Box, c.1939, 16 x 22 In. 640.00
Tank, Army Tank Corps 12, Sparking, Climbing, Fighting, Marx, Box, c.1935, 9 1/2 In. . . 635.00
Tank, Army, No. 12, Moves, On Rubber Treads, Sparks, Tin, Windup, Marx, 1930s, 10 In. 130.00
Tank, Aurora Expedition, Driver, Pulls Vehicle, Tin, Battery, Yonezawa, Box, 14 In. 1045.00
Tank, Casper Ghost, Tin, Harvey Features, Linemar, Box, 4 In. . . . . .231.00 to 440.00
Tank, Friction, Tin, White Rubber Tread, Gama, Germany, Box, 7 1/2 In. 90.00
Tank, Looping Space, Moves, Lights, Flips, Tin, Battery Operated, Daiya, 8 In. 275.00
Tank, Metal, Windup, U.S. Zone Germany, Box, 5 1/2 In. 95.00
Tank, Rollover, Sparks, White Treads, Windup, Gama, 3 In. 95.00
Tank, Sandy & Yankee, Metal, Wyandotte, 1930s, 14 1/2 In. 175.00
Tank, Torpedo, Cannon, Spinner Missiles, 3 Defenders, Remco, 1964, 12 x 6 1/2 In. 675.00
Tank, Wonder Sparking, Windup, Japan, Prewar, Box, 3 In. 125.00
Tank, X-75, Target, Tin, Battery Operated, Japan, Box, 1950s, 10 In. 190.00
Tap Dancer, Black, White Face On Box, Alps, Occupied Japan, 8 1/2 In. 395.00
Tap Dancer, Tap Rhythm On Pedal Mechanism, Mechanical, Box, 7 In. 90.00
Tarzan, Swimming, Arms Move, Celluloid, Tin, c.1930 . . . . 980.00
Taxi, Amos 'n' Andy, Embossed, Tin Lithograph, Clockwork, Marx, 8 In. . . . . .650.00 to 895.00
Taxi, Driver, Windup, Tin Lithograph, Strauss, 9 In. 575.00
Taxi, Driver, Women, Windup, Tin, Fischer, Germany, 12 In. 2640.00
Taxi, Mercedes-Benz, Bump & Go, Lights, Tin, Battery Operated, Bandai, Box, 10 1/4 In. 225.00
Taxi, Rollover, Windup, Tin Lithograph, Marx, Box, 6 In. 120.00
Taxi, Tin, Friction, Japan, Box, 6 In. 55.00
Taxi, Tricky, Tin Lithograph, Windup, Marx, Box, 4 1/2 In. 175.00
Taxi, Yell-O-Taxi, Driver, Windup, Strauss, 8 In. 650.00
Taxi, Yellow Cab, Cast Iron, Friedag, 8 In. 440.00
Taxi, Yellow Cab, Cast Iron, Kenton, 6 1/2 In. 305.00
Taxi, Yellow Cab, No. 3, Arcade, c.1927, 5 1/2 In. 1000.00
Taxi, Yellow Cab, Tin Lithograph, Gunthermann, Germany, 9 In. 1320.00
Taxi, Yellow Cab, Tin Lithograph, Windup, Marx, 6 In. 70.00
Taxi, Yellow Cab, Tin Lithograph, Windup, Mohawk, 7 In. 60.00
Tea Set, Cherry Blossom, Depression Glass, 14 Piece 99.00

Tea Set, Children At Play, 4 Scenes, Porcelain, Germany, c.1890, 5-In. Teapot, 11 Piece .. 530.00
Tea Set, Flower & Gold Design, Porcelain, Box, 17 Piece 115.00
Tea Set, Mulberry Transfer, Ironstone, Storybook, England 80.00
Tea Set, Raised Flowers, Leaves, Gilt, Porcelain, Germany, 5-In. Teapot, 9 Piece 200.00
Tea Set, Red Riding Hood, Tin Litho., Story Characters, Ohio Art, Box, 1930, 5 Piece ... 410.00
Teddy, Artist, Tin, Cloth, Battery Operated, Electro Toy, Box 250.00
Teddy Bears are also listed in the Teddy Bear category.
Teddy Roosevelt, Safari Outfit, Helmet, Rifle, Schoenhut, 9 In................. 3080.00
Telephone, Calling Dr. Kildare, Plastic, Rienzi, 1950s 55.00
Threshing Machine, McCormick Deering, Arcade, 9 In. 550.00
Tiger, On Trike, Tin Lithograph, Plastic, Windup, Box, 4 In. 60.00
Tiger, Walker, Battery Operated, Marx, Box, 12 In. 330.00
Tiger, Walker, Holds Flower, Tin, Plush, Windup, Marx, Rock Valley, Japan, Box, 8 In. .. 225.00
Tiger, Windup, Marx, Rock Valley, Japan, Box, 11 In............................ 95.00
Toboggan, Wood, Red Paint, Black Trim, 72 In................................. 110.00
Toonerville Trolley, Driver Shifts Gear, Tin, Windup, Fontaine Fox, 1922, 7 In. . . .440.00 to 850.00
Toonerville Trolley, Tin Lithograph, Windup, H. Fischer, Germany, c.1925, 5 In. 990.00
Top, Humming, Multicolored, Vent Hole, Painted, 19th Century, 6 In. 440.00
Top, Whistling, Red, White, Blue, Yellow, 12 In. 105.00
Top, Whistling, Wood, Painted, 7 In. 300.00
Topo Gigio, On Motorcycle, Tin, Vinyl, Friction, Argentina, Box, c.1960, 8 In. 275.00
Tractor, Caterpillar, Plastic, Black Letters, Peoria, Ill. 105.00
Tractor, Climbs Ramp, Trailer, Tin, Battery, On Platform, Japan, Box, 9 In. ....85.00 to 145.00
Tractor, Die Cast, No. 1601, Hubley, Box 50.00
Tractor, Driver, Tin Lithograph, Windup, Box, 8 1/4 In. 110.00
Tractor, Farmall M, Cast Iron, Arcade, 7 In. 470.00
Tractor, Ford, Battery Operated, Japan, 1950s, 12 In. 175.00
Tractor, Fordson, Green, Red, Arcade, 5 1/2 In. 385.00
Tractor, Handy Hank, Mystery, Battery Operated, Box, 11 In. 90.00
Tractor, Marvelous Mike Robot, Bump & Go, Tin, Battery, Saunders, Box, 13 In. 300.00
Tractor, Robot Driver, Fan Belt Turns, Tin, Battery Operated, Japan, Box, 9 1/2 In. 470.00
Tractor & Spreader, Cast Iron, Red, Green, Leather Tires, Allis Chalmers, Lever, 12 In. . . 98.00
Trailer, 1 Axle, No. 23B, Verkehrs, 26 x 15 In. 150.00
Trailer, 2 Axles, No. DS30, Hohm, 39 1/2 x 14 In. 300.00
Trailer, Car & House, Tin, Friction, Japan, 16 In. 415.00
Train, Arnold, Cat, Pushes & Pulls, Station, Tin, Windup, U.S. Zone Germany, Box, 15 In. 500.00
Train, Buddy L, Locomotive & Tender, Pressed Steel, Outdoor, 1920s, 40 In. ....1045.00 to 2530.00
Train, Carlisle & Finch, Locomotive & Tender, 45 Steam, Standard Gauge 13310.00
Train, Cragstan, Locomotive, Tooting, Chugging, Battery Operated, Box, 24 In. 100.00
Train, Daiya, Passenger, Tin Lithograph, Rubber Tires, Noise, Friction, Box, 21 In....... 85.00
Train, Engine & Car, Tin, Spoke Wheels, Germany, c.1910, 11 In.................... 605.00
Train, Ernst Plank, Locomotive, Steam, Brass, Germany, 6 1/2 In.................... 660.00
Train, Lionel, Engine, Western Pacific, 1970s 115.00
Train, Locomotive, Firebird, Tin, Battery Operated, Japan, Box, 8 In. 55.00
Train, Locomotive, Horse Special, Battery Operated, Japan, Box 39.00
Train, Locomotive, Tin Lithograph, Friction, Japan, 6 In......................... 28.00
Train, Marx, Choo-Choo, Musical, Tin Lithograph, Windup, Japan 28.00
Train, Marx, Honeymoon Express, Tin Lithograph, Windup, 9 In................60.00 to 99.00
Train, Marx, Locomotive, Battery Operated, Box, 6 In. 90.00
Train, Marx, Toy Town Locomotive, Plastic, Box, 9 1/2 In. 11.00
Train, Silver Mountain Express, Battery Operated, Japan, Box 35.00
Train, Streamline, Tin Lithograph, Friction, Japan, 20 In......................... 115.00
Train, TN, Tin Lithograph, Battery Operated, Box, 5 In. 46.00
Train, Western Special Locomotive, Tin Lithograph, Battery Operated, Japan, Box, 14 In. . 22.00
Train Accessory, American Flyer, Log Loader, Pressed Steel, Plastic, No. 571, Box 275.00
Train Accessory, Baggage Cart, Driver, Tin, Eastern Europe, 7 In. 75.00
Train Accessory, Billboard, Building Top, Reddy Kilowatt, Plastic Box 33.00
Train Accessory, Fuchs, Baggage Cart, Driver, Tin, U.S. Zone Germany, 1948, 6 In. 59.00
Train Accessory, Ives, Bell Signal, Red Cast Iron Base, Tin Pole, Brass Sign, 10 1/4 In. .. 195.00
Train Accessory, Ives, Station, Tin Lithograph, 12 3/4 In. 99.00
Train Accessory, Marklin, Foot Bridge, Painted, Germany, 3 Piece 220.00
Train Accessory, Marx, Water Tower, Plastic, Box, 8 In. 33.00
Train Accessory, Rossignol, Baggage Cart, Luggage, Tin, France, c.1930s 125.00

Train Accessory, Station, Water Tower, Light Poles, Signal Light 135.00
Train Car, Buddy L, Ballast, Pressed Steel, Outdoor, Side Doors, 1920s, 22 In. . . .770.00 to 1320.00
Train Car, Buddy L, Bottom Dump, Pressed Steel, Outdoor, 1920s, 22 In. . . . . . . .990.00 to 1045.00
Train Car, Buddy L, Boxcar, Pressed Steel, Outdoor, 1920s, 22 In. 1155.00
Train Car, Buddy L, Coal, Pressed Steel, Outdoor, 1920s, 22 In. . . . . .300.00 to 1000.00
Train Car, Buddy L, Ore, Pressed Steel, Outdoor, Side Dump, 1920s, 12 In. 2420.00
Train Car, Buddy L, Steam Shovel, Railroad, Pressed Steel, 1920s, 28 In. 1430.00
Train Car, Buddy L, Stock Car, Pressed Steel, 1920s, 20 In. 2200.00
Train Car, Buddy L, Tank, Pressed Steel, Outdoor, 1920s, 19 In. . . . . .1150.00 to 1430.00
Train Car, Lehmann, Engine Cab, Berlin Pedal, Tin Litho., Windup, No. 345, c.1895, 5 In. 935.00
Train Car, Lionel, Boxcar, Rio Grande, 1970s 35.00
Train Car, Lionel, Hopper, No. 516, Standard Gauge, 11 1/2 In. 165.00
Train Car, Strauss, Engine, All Aboard Limited, Tin, Mechanical, 17 In. 645.00
Train Set, American Flyer, Engine No.290, Tender, 3 Cars, Transformer, Bridge, O Gauge 219.00
Train Set, American Flyer, Silver Streak, Engine, Baggage, Passenger & Vista Dome Cars   56.00
Train Set, Cragstan, Locomotive, Frontier, Tin Litho., Battery Operated, Japan, Box, 13 In. 50.00
Train Set, Fisher, Tin Lithograph, Clockwork, Germany, Box 415.00
Train Set, Hafner, Locomotive, Windup, Tin Lithograph, Box, 14 x 17 In. 130.00
Train Set, Ives, Engine No. 3252, 3 Cars, No. 70, 72, 73, O Gauge 69.00
Train Set, Ives, Engine No. 3253, Passenger Car, 2 Baggage Cars, Transformer 39.00
Train Set, Ives, Locomotive, Pullman Parlor Car, Pullman Observation Car, O Gauge 225.00
Train Set, Karl Bub, Locomotive, Tender, 2 Coaches, Tin Lithograph, Clockwork, Box . . . 330.00
Train Set, Lionel, Engine No. 1688, Tender, 4 Cars, Depot, Gates, Lights, Transformers . . 255.00
Train Set, Lionel, Locomotive, Pullman Passenger Car, Observation Car, O Gauge 170.00
Train Set, Lionel, No. 252, 8 In., 7 Piece 345.00
Train Set, Lionel, No. 262, 5 In., 5 Piece 195.00
Train Set, Lionel, No. 2149B, Diesel No. 622 Freight, 1949 . . . . 495.00
Train Set, Lionel, No. 2163WS, Berkshire Freight, 1950 . . . . 495.00
Train Set, Lionel, No. 2190W, Santa Fe Passenger, 1952 . . . . 795.00
Train Set, Lionel, No. 2270, Jersey Central Passenger, 1956 . . . . 995.00
Train Set, Lionel, No. 2296W, Canadian No. 2373 Passenger, 1957 . . . . 2995.00
Train Set, Lionel, No. 2501W, Minn. St. Louis, Box, 1958 . . . . 1495.00
Train Set, Lionel, No. 2517W, Rio Grande No. 2379, 1958 . . . . 1095.00
Train Set, Marx, Engine No. 666, Tender, 6 Cars, Transformer, Accessories, Box, c.1950 . 310.00
Train Set, Marx, MarLine, Locomotive, 7 Cars, Electric, Plastic, 1 1/4 Gauge 75.00
Train Set, Overland Express, Tin Lithograph, Battery Operated, Japan, Box, 1960s, 17 In. 33.00
Tree, Kookie Spookie, Battery Operated, Marx, 15 In. 770.00
Tree, Whistling Spooky, Eyes, Tin, Battery Operated, Marx, Box, 15 In. . . . . . . .1760.00 to 1930.00
Tricycle, Boy Rider, Metal, Windup, Unique Art, U.S.A., 1950s . . . . *Illus* 295.00
Tricycle, Fireman Steps On Clutch, Tin, Battery Operated, Japan, Box, 10 In. 660.00
Tricycle, Police, Blows Whistle, Figure 8 Pattern, Tin, Battery, Japan, Box, 10 In. 330.00
Tricycle, Police, Tin Lithograph, Battery Operated, TN, Japan, Box, 10 In. 415.00
Tricycle, Tricky Trike, Mechanical, Japan, Box 70.00
Tricycle, Wood, Upholstered Seat, Metal Rim Wheels, 1800s, 37 1/2 x 58 In. 980.00
Trinity Chimes, Paper On Wood, 8 Chimes, Schoenhut, 17 In. 155.00
Trolley, Battery Operated, Modern Toys, 10 In. 45.00
Trolley, Broadway, Tin Lithograph, Masudaya, Japan, c.1950s, 11 In. 50.00
Trolley, Kingsbury 782, Pressed Steel Bell, Windup, 1920s, 9 1/2 In. 395.00

Toy, Tricycle, Boy Rider,
Metal, Windup,
Unique Art,
U.S.A., 1950s

Use a blow dryer to heat and soften tape on boxes that once held toys. If you see some of the colored parts of the box coming up when you pull the tape, stop removing the tape.

Trolley, L.C.C., Embossed, Tin Lithograph, London, Penny Toy, 3 In. 495.00
Trolley, Passengers, Tin Lithograph, Embossed, Meier, 3 1/4 In. 110.00
Trolley, Tin, Windup, SG Germany, 1920s, 12 In. 575.00
Truck, 245, Driver, Tin Lithograph, Embossed, Georg Fischer, 3 1/2 In. 190.00
Truck, 7-Up, Friction, Japan, T.P.S., 1950s, 9 In. 175.00
Truck, ABC Television, Tin Lithograph, Rotating Camera, 1950s, Japan, 9 In. 375.00
Truck, Aerial, Tonka, 1969 .... 295.00
Truck, Airport Mail, Tin Lithograph, Structo 880.00
Truck, Airway, GMC, Pressed Steel, Buddy L, 1950s, 15 In. 250.00
Truck, American Express, Green, Red Wheels, Pressed Steel, Keystone, 1930, 26 In. 525.00
Truck, American Oil Co., Painted, Cast Iron, Spoke Wheels, Dent, 15 In. 1100.00
Truck, Anti-Aircraft, GMC, Pressed Steel, Searchlight Trailer, Buddy L, 1950s, 24 In. ... 415.00
Truck, Arctic Ice, Blue, Red, Cast Iron, Kenton, 8 In. 770.00
Truck, Army Combat Carrier, Tin, Friction, Japan, Box, 1960s, 19 In. 60.00
Truck, Army Supply Corps, No. 42, Pressed Steel, Wyandotte, 1940s, 18 In. .....130.00 to 165.00
Truck, Army Supply, Pressed Steel, Buddy L, 1950s, 14 1/2 In. 55.00
Truck, Army, GMC, Pressed Steel, Buddy L, 1950s, 14 1/2 In. 330.00
Truck, Army, Metal, Die Cast, No. 151B, Dinky Toys, England 65.00
Truck, Army, Pressed Steel, Buddy L, 1940s, 17 1/2 In. 90.00
Truck, Army, Pressed Steel, Keystone, 22 In. 400.00
Truck, Army, Pressed Steel, Tin Lithograph, Marx, 1950s, 14 In. 88.00
Truck, Army, Searchlight, 3 Soldiers, Windup, Wells Of London, Box, 1940s, 9 In. 485.00
Truck, Army, Tin Lithograph, Marx, 1950s, 13 In. 80.00
Truck, Army, Transport, Pressed Steel, Box, 18 1/2 In. 85.00
Truck, Baggage, Pressed Steel, Barrel Skid, No. 401, Buddy L, Box, c.1948 .... 440.00
Truck, Bank Of America, Smith-Miller, 15 In. 210.00
Truck, Bell Telephone, Cast Iron, Nickel Plated Wheels, Rubber Tires, Hubley, 8 1/2 In. ... 345.00
Truck, Bell Telephone, Cast Iron, Tools, White Rubber Tires, Hubley, 11 In. 385.00
Truck, Bell Telephone, Cast Iron, White Rubber Tires, Hubley, 5 In. ....175.00 to 275.00
Truck, Black Diamond Coal Co., Tin Lithograph, Plastic, Windup, 10 1/2 In. 130.00
Truck, Borden's Milk, Cream, Die Cast, Divco, 4 In. 120.00
Truck, Borden's Milk, Iron, Nickel Grille, White Rubber Tires, Hubley, 7 In. ....990.00 to 1100.00
Truck, Borden's, Kingsbury 395.00
Truck, Camper, Raggedy Ann & Andy, Blue & Orange, Buddy L, 1967, 12 In. 65.00
Truck, Camper, Rubber Tires, Tin, Friction, Japan, Box, 8 In. 115.00
Truck, Camper, Tin Lithograph, Friction, Cragstan, Japan, Box, 8 In. 145.00
Truck, Canada Dry, Metal, Buddy L, 1960s, 9 1/2 In. 55.00
Truck, Car Carrier, 3 Austins, Red, Green, Yellow, Arcade, 14 1/2 In. 1500.00
Truck, Car Carrier, 4 Cars, Arcade, 11 In. ....305.00 to 385.00
Truck, Car Carrier, 4 Cars, Hubley, 10 In. 385.00
Truck, Car Carrier, 4 Cars, Pressed Steel, Lincoln, Canada, 24 In. 395.00
Truck, Car Carrier, Diamond T, Tootsietoy, 1949 .... 500.00
Truck, Car Carrier, Pressed Steel, No. 350, Wyandotte, 22 In. 150.00
Truck, Cargo Carrier, Pressed Steel, Tonka, 1950s, 23 In. 405.00
Truck, Cargo Lines, Motor Transport Fleet, Pressed Steel, Wyandotte, 1950s, 26 In. 155.00
Truck, Cargo, No. 702, Steel, Red, Blue, Structo, 21 In. 80.00
Truck, Cast Iron, Stake Back, Rubber Tires, Arcade, 11 1/2 In. 605.00
Truck, Cattle, Buckeye, Pressed Steel, Box, 1950s, 23 In. 155.00
Truck, Cattle, Green Valley Ranch, Tin Litho., Pressed Steel, Wyandotte, 1950s, 17 In. 150.00
Truck, Cattle, Shady Glen Ranch, Tin Lithograph, Pressed Steel, Wyandotte, 1950s, 17 In. .. 140.00
Truck, Cement Mixer, Battery Operated, Japan, 1950s, 10 1/2 In. 105.00
Truck, Cement Mixer, Ford, Bulldog, Pressed Steel, Gears, Japan, 12 In. 95.00
Truck, Cement Mixer, Green, Orange, Rubber Wheels, Metal, Structo, 9 x 21 x 8 In. 175.00
Truck, Cement Mixer, Orange, Kenton Jaeger, 8 In. 415.00
Truck, Cement Mixer, Pressed Steel, Plastic, Drum Turns, Buddy L, 1960s, 15 In. 220.00
Truck, Cement Mixer, Red, Kenton Jaeger, 8 In. 910.00
Truck, Cement Mixer, Red, Metallic Blue, Friction, SSS, c.1960, 14 In. 135.00
Truck, Cement Mixer, Super Constructor, Tin, Friction, SSS, Japan, Box, 20 In. 4620.00
Truck, Chevrolet, Pickup, Metal, Friction, Argentina, Box, 1960s, 11 1/2 In. 195.00
Truck, Circus Parade, Battery Operated, TM, Japan, Box, 1950s, 13 In. 495.00
Truck, Circus, Battery Operated, Tin, Plastic, Japan, 10 1/2 In. 80.00
Truck, Circus, Menagerie, Tin, Friction, Japan, 10 In. 120.00
Truck, Coal, Cast Iron, Green, Driver, Wheels, Shovel, Nickel Plated, Dent, 6 1/2 In. 259.00

Truck, Coal, Front Scoop, Fuel & Supply Co., Pressed Steel, Wyandotte, 13 In. 146.00
Truck, Coal, Tin Lithograph, Pressed Steel, Wyandotte, 1950s, 11 In. 70.00
Truck, Communications, Morse Code Units, Tin, Battery Operated, MT Mark, Box, 12 In. 275.00
Truck, Communications, Pressed Steel, Structo, 1960s, 21 In. 250.00
Truck, Confectionary Store, Strauss, Boston, 9 In. 1500.00
Truck, Construction, Tin Lithograph, Pressed Steel, Side Dump, Wyandotte, 1950s, 17 In. 330.00
Truck, Construction, Tin Lithograph, Pressed Steel, Side Dump, Wyandotte, 1950s, 20 In. 195.00
Truck, Contractor, Model T, Pressed Steel, Aluminum Wheels, Buddy L, 1920s, 12 In. . . . 1760.00
Truck, Crane, Yellow, Blue, Metal, Mechanical, Ny-Lint, 8 1/2 x 27 x 6 In. 25.00
Truck, Curtiss Candies, Baby Ruth, Butterfinger, Buddy L, 39 In. 1650.00
Truck, Custom, Red Back, Yellow Van Body, Wyandotte, 17 In. 210.00
Truck, Dairy, Marcrest Dairy, Bottles, Pressed Steel, Marx, Box, 14 In. 660.00
Truck, Dairy, Sheffield Farms, Macy Label, Buddy L, 25 In. 2530.00
Truck, Delivery, Boston Store, Tin, Windup, Diamond T, Germany, 1922, 8 x 4 1/4 In. . . . 1075.00
Truck, Delivery, Carlysle Drygoods, Pressed Steel, Friction, Dayton, 1920s, 12 In. 580.00
Truck, Delivery, Cast Iron, Nickel Plated Grille, White Rubber Tires, Arcade, 9 1/2 In. . . . 2415.00
Truck, Delivery, Deluxe, Red, Yellow, Boxes, Tin, Marx, Box, 11 In. 550.00
Truck, Delivery, Green, Black, Metalcraft, St. Louis, 1935, 11 In. 350.00
Truck, Delivery, Groceries, Windup, Tin Lithograph, 1918, 6 In. 385.00
Truck, Delivery, Inter City, Tin Lithograph, Marx, 1940s, 18 In. 120.00
Truck, Delivery, Jet, Pressed Steel, Tonka, 1962-1963, 13 3/4 In. 200.00
Truck, Delivery, Model T, Pressed Steel, Aluminum Wheels, Buddy L, 1920s, 14 In. 7150.00
Truck, Delivery, Model T, Richfield, Pressed Steel, Cowdry, 11 1/2 In. 1430.00
Truck, Delivery, Pressed Steel, Flywheel Motor, Dayton, 1920s, 11 In. 200.00
Truck, Delivery, Pressed Steel, Marx, 1950s, 13 1/2 In. 130.00
Truck, Delivery, Studebaker, Super, Tin, Friction, I.Y., Japan, Box, 16 In. 3960.00
Truck, Delivery, Tin Lithograph, Germany, Penny Toy, 4 1/2 In. 120.00
Truck, Dippy Dumper, Tin Lithograph, Celluloid Driver, Windup, Marx, c.1930s, 10 In. . . 690.00
Truck, Dodge, Tin, Marusan, Japan, Lithograph Box, 19 In. 4620.00
Truck, Dray, Motor Driven, Pressed Steel, Cast Iron Driver, Wilkins, Kingsbury, 10 In. . . . 470.00
Truck, Dray, Tin Lithograph, Windup, Germany, 5 In. 95.00
Truck, Dump & Scoop, Pressed Steel, Buddy L, 1950s, 18 In. . . . . .80.00 to 90.00
Truck, Dump & Scoop, Pressed Steel, Roberts, Box, 1960s, 18 In. 210.00
Truck, Dump, Anthony, Cast Iron, Arcade, 8 1/4 In. 975.00
Truck, Dump, Battery Operated, Wyandotte, 1930s, 10 3/4 In. 425.00
Truck, Dump, Big Mike, Pressed Steel, 2 Hydraulic Pumps, V-Plow, Tonka, 1950s, 20 In. 580.00
Truck, Dump, Buddy L, 1961 . . . . 295.00
Truck, Dump, Cast Iron, Green, Arcade, 1931, 10 1/2 In. 1020.00
Truck, Dump, Cast Iron, Hubley, 7 In. 300.00
Truck, Dump, Cast Iron, Nickel Plated Grille, Rubber Tires, Arcade International, 9 3/4 In. 1320.00
Truck, Dump, Chevrolet, Tin, Friction, Japan, Box, 15 In. 155.00
Truck, Dump, Crank, Pressed Steel, Buddy L, 1920s 825.00
Truck, Dump, Deluxe Rider, Pressed Steel, Shovel, No. 802, Buddy L, Box, c.1948 . . . . . 825.00
Truck, Dump, Diamond T, Green, Structo, Box, 1940s, 21 In. 525.00
Truck, Dump, Die Cast Cab, Black Decal, Smith-Miller, Box, 1940s, 12 In. . . . . . .495.00 to 580.00
Truck, Dump, Front Loading Scoop, Tin Lithograph, Wyandotte, 1950s, 15 In. 240.00
Truck, Dump, Glendale Coal Co., High Lift, Tin, Marx, 12 In. 485.00
Truck, Dump, GMC, Tin, Friction, Yonezawa, Box, c.1950, 14 In. 195.00
Truck, Dump, Green Body, Yellow Bed, Cast Iron, Arcade, 11 In. 169.00
Truck, Dump, Green, Buddy L, Box, 1963 . . . . 350.00
Truck, Dump, Harvester, Red Paint, Cast Iron, Arcade International, 10 1/2 In. 565.00
Truck, Dump, Heavy Duty, Dumping Action, Steel, Tin, Marx, Box, 20 In. 180.00
Truck, Dump, Hi-Lift, Glendale Coal Company, Tin, Marx, Box, 12 In. 535.00
Truck, Dump, Hydraulic, Pressed Steel, Aluminum Wheels, Buddy L, 1920s, 24 In. 2200.00
Truck, Dump, Hydraulic, Pressed Steel, Wyandotte, 1950s, 21 In. 60.00
Truck, Dump, Keystone, Ride-On, Pressed Steel, Painted, Wooden Handle, 24 In. 660.00
Truck, Dump, Little Jim, Steelcraft, 1935, 24 In. 475.00
Truck, Dump, Mack, Driver, Green, Arcade, 8 1/2 In. 1750.00
Truck, Dump, Model A, Cast Iron, Blue, Red, Arcade, 7 In. 330.00
Truck, Dump, Model T, Pressed Steel, Aluminum Spoke Wheels, Buddy L, 1920s, 11 In. . 385.00
Truck, Dump, Open Cab, Pressed Steel, Buddy L, c.1930, 26 In. 550.00
Truck, Dump, Powerhouse Hydraulic, Engine Noise, Pressed Steel, Marx, Box, 21 In. 195.00
Truck, Dump, Pressed Aluminum, Smith-Miller, 11 1/2 In. 230.00

Truck, Dump, Pressed Steel, Buddy L, 1940s, 17 In. 110.00
Truck, Dump, Pressed Steel, Marx, 1940s, 20 In. 90.00
Truck, Dump, Pressed Steel, Marx, Box, 1950s, 18 In. 358.00
Truck, Dump, Pressed Steel, Side Dump, Wyandotte, 1950s, 19 In. 130.00
Truck, Dump, Pressed Steel, Structo, 1960s, 12 In. 35.00
Truck, Dump, Pressed Steel, Tin Lithograph, Marx, Box, 1950s, 18 In. 165.00
Truck, Dump, Pressed Steel, Tin Lithograph, Wyandotte, 1950s, 10 In. 145.00
Truck, Dump, Pressed Steel, Tin Lithograph, Wyandotte, 1950s, 17 In. 95.00
Truck, Dump, Pressed Steel, Wyandotte, 1930s, 15 In. .... 275.00 to 325.00
Truck, Dump, Pressed Steel, Wyandotte, 1940s, 12 In. ....110.00 to 145.00
Truck, Dump, Pressed Steel, Wyandotte, 1960s, 22 In. 90.00
Truck, Dump, Red, Blue, Wyandotte, 22 In. 80.00
Truck, Dump, Red, Green, Tonka, 1955, 13 In. 85.00
Truck, Dump, Red, Silver, Hubley, 4 1/2 In. 225.00
Truck, Dump, Remote Control, Die Cast Cab Over, Smith-Miller, 1940s, 12 In. 525.00
Truck, Dump, Rope Lift, Pressed Steel, Aluminum Disk Wheels, Buddy L, 1920s, 24 In. . 1210.00
Truck, Dump, Sand & Gravel, Pressed Steel, Buddy L, 1940s, 13 1/2 In. 80.00
Truck, Dump, Sand & Gravel, Pressed Steel, Cast Aluminum Cab, Slik Toy, 13 In. 140.00
Truck, Dump, Sand & Gravel, Tin, Black, White, Marx, 12 In. 658.00
Truck, Dump, Sand & Stone, Pressed Steel, Buddy L, 1950s, 14 1/2 In. 220.00
Truck, Dump, Side Dump, Pressed Steel, Marx, 1940s, 10 1/2 In. 130.00
Truck, Dump, Side Dump, Pressed Steel, Tin Lithograph, Wyandotte, 1950s, 17 In. 100.00 to 275.00
Truck, Dump, Side, Pressed Steel, Lift Lever, Wyandotte, Box, 17 In. 440.00
Truck, Dump, Sit & Ride, Pressed Steel, Painted, Buddy L, 25 In. 1045.00
Truck, Dump, State H-Way Dept., Plows, Hydraulic, Pressed Steel, Tonka, 13 In. 226.00
Truck, Dump, Super Constructor, SSS International, Japan, Box, 23 In. 2640.00
Truck, Dump, Tin Lithograph, Pressed Steel, Wyandotte, 1950s, 11 In. 130.00
Truck, Dump, Tin Lithograph, Pressed Steel, Wyandotte, 1950s, 13 In. 155.00
Truck, Dump, Tin Lithograph, Pressed Steel, Wyandotte, 1950s, 17 In. 90.00
Truck, Dump, Wyandotte, 1930s, 6 In. 400.00
Truck, Dump, Yellow, Hydraulic, Rubber Wheels, Removable Hood, Structo, 7 x 21 In. .. 175.00
Truck, Dump, Yellow, Wyandotte, 1930s, 6 In. 150.00
Truck, Eagle Crane, Tin, Marusan, Hayashi, Japan, 16 In. 275.00
Truck, Emergency, Air Corps, Japan, 9 In. 195.00
Truck, Esso Service, 2 Express Baggage Carts, Arnold, Box 1500.00
Truck, Express Line, Black, Green, Red, Steel, Buddy L 580.00
Truck, Express, Pressed Steel, Tin Lithograph, Wyandotte, 1950s, 17 In. 175.00
Truck, Farm, Lazy Days Farm, Tin Lithograph, Wyandotte, 1950s, 17 In. 130.00
Truck, Farm, Tin Lithograph, TN, Japan, Box, 9 1/2 In. 210.00
Truck, Farm, Trailer, Tonka, 1961 .... 195.00
Truck, Fast Freight, Tin Lithograph, Friction, Modern Toys, Japan, Box, 8 1/2 In. 155.00
Truck, Ferris Wheel, Tin, Friction, TN, Japan, 8 In. 300.00
Truck, Flatbed, Black, Red, Oak Bed, Keystone, 1930s, 24 In. 495.00
Truck, Flatbed, Painted Green, Cast Iron, 4 1/2 In. 75.00
Truck, Ford, Pickup, Model T, Cast Iron, Arcade, 8 1/2 In. 715.00
Truck, Ford, Pickup, Model T, Pressed Steel, Cowdry, 12 In. 1320.00
Truck, Ford, Pickup, Model T, Roadster, Pressed Steel, Buddy L, 1920s, 12 In. ...770.00 to 1320.00
Truck, Ford, Stake, Red, Pressed Steel, Japan, 9 In. 35.00
Truck, Freight, Die Cast Cab, Pressed Steel & Wood Trailer, Wyandotte, 1950s, 23 In. 240.00
Truck, Freight, GMC, Pressed Steel, Buddy L, 1950s, 22 In. 198.00
Truck, Freight, Pressed Steel, Structo, Box, 1960s, 24 In. 190.00
Truck, Freighter, Trans-Continental, Die Cast, Wood, Smith-Miller, 1940s, 24 In. 495.00
Truck, Garbage, Dept. Of Sanitation, Tin, Friction, Yamaichi, Box, 9 In. 205.00
Truck, Garbage, Pressed Steel, Marx, 13 In. 226.00
Truck, Garbage, Pressed Steel, Structo, 1960s, 19 In. 105.00
Truck, GMC Service, Pressed Steel, Buddy L, 1950s, 15 In. 385.00
Truck, GMC, Missile, Pressed Steel, Buddy L, Box, 1950s, 15 In. 440.00
Truck, GMC, Stake, Bump & Go, Lights Flash, Tin, Friction, Yonezawa, Box, 10 In. 330.00
Truck, Grader, Pressed Steel, Doepke Adams, 1940s, 25 In. 99.00
Truck, Grader, Pressed Steel, Wyandotte, 1950s, 18 In. 22.00
Truck, Grain Hauler, Pressed Steel, Tonka, 1940s, 22 In. 120.00
Truck, Grain Hauler, Pressed Steel, Tonka, 1950s, 23 In. 220.00
Truck, Green, Hubley, 10 In. 330.00

Truck, Grocery, Fancy Groceries, Tin Lithograph, Chein, 6 In. 250.00
Truck, Grocery, Motor Market Delivery, Boxes, Tin, Plastic, Marx, Box, 15 In. 495.00
Truck, Grocery, Toy Town, Pressed Steel, Metalcraft, Box, c.1930, 11 In. 2145.00
Truck, Heavy Duty Express, Pressed Steel, Plastic Cab, Marx, Box, 1950s, 19 In. 250.00
Truck, Heavy Machinery Service, Pressed Steel, Buddy L, 1950s, 20 In. 120.00
Truck, Heinz Pickle, Electric Lights, Rubber Tires, Spare Tire, Metalcraft, 12 In. 855.00
Truck, Heinz Rice Flakes, Metalcraft, 11 1/2 In. 150.00
Truck, Hercules, Ratchet Lift, Tin, Chein, Box, 19 1/2 In. 825.00
Truck, Highway Freight, Tin Lithograph, Pressed Steel, Wyandotte, 1950s, 17 In. 130.00
Truck, Horse Trailer, Pressed Steel, Ny-Lint, Box, 1960s, 23 In. 220.00
Truck, Horse Van, Vista Dome, Pressed Steel, No. 417, Structo, Box 170.00
Truck, Huckster, Pressed Steel, Aluminum Spoke Wheels, Buddy L, 1920s, 14 In. 2200.00
Truck, Ice Cream, Friction, Bell, Rear Hatch Door, Canopy, Japan, 1950s, 8 In. 135.00
Truck, Ice Cream, Mister Buddy, White, Buddy L, 1963 . . . .   250.00
Truck, Ice Cream, Pop Up, Tin, Plastic, Battery Operated, Bandai, Japan, 1950s, 10 In. . . .   95.00
Truck, Ice, Bulldog Mac, Cast Iron, Nickel Plated Iron Wheels, Driver, Arcade, 11 In. . . .   1430.00
Truck, Ice, Cast Iron, Blue, Arcade, 11 In. 745.00
Truck, Ice, Driver, Ice, Tongs, Arcade, 11 In. 3500.00
Truck, Ice, International, Pure Ice, Pressed Steel, Buddy L, 1930s, 22 In. 825.00
Truck, Ice, Model T, Pressed Steel, Cowdry, 15 1/2 In. 1540.00
Truck, Ice, Pressed Steel, Buddy L, c.1930, 26 In. 1375.00
Truck, Jalopy, Driver, Passenger, Tin, Windup, MAR, 1950s, 7 In. 195.00
Truck, Jewel Tea & Housewares, Pressed Steel, 1940s, 9 1/2 In.   360.00
Truck, Kroehler Furniture, Pressed Steel, Structo, Box, 1960s, 23 In. 330.00
Truck, Laura Secord Candies, Rubber, Canada, 1950s, 11 In. 145.00
Truck, Livestock, Cast Iron, Nickel Plated Iron Wheels, Kilgore, 7 In. 580.00
Truck, Log Trailer, Pressed Steel, Windup, Logs, Chain, Marx, Box, c.1948, 13 1/2 In. . . .   495.00
Truck, Log, Tandem, Mack, Die Cast, Pup Trailer, Smith-Miller, 1940s, 32 In. 605.00
Truck, Lumber, Steel, Rubber Tires, 5 Pieces Of Lumber, Wyandotte, Box, 11 In. 250.00
Truck, Machinery, Pressed Steel, Buddy L, 1950s, 23 In. 250.00
Truck, Mack, Hercules Dairy Products, Yellow, Blue, Tin, Chein, 19 1/2 In. 1430.00
Truck, Mack, Hoist, Arcade, 1932, 11 In. 2530.00
Truck, Mack, Panama Steam Shovel, Hubley, 12 In. 1980.00
Truck, Marine Supply, Buddy L, 1959 . . . .   395.00
Truck, Mazda, Detailed Interior, Rubber Tires, Tin, Windup, Marx, Box, 7 In. 1430.00
Truck, Merry-Go-Round, Bell Noise, Tin, Friction, Japan, Box, 8 1/2 In. 575.00
Truck, Merry-Go-Round, Pressed Steel, Wooden Carousel, Buddy L, 1960s, 13 In. 330.00
Truck, Merry-Go-Round, Tin, Friction, Japan, 8 In. 120.00
Truck, Mobile Artillery, Tin Lithograph, Pressed Steel Flatbed, Wyandotte, 1950s, 13 In. .   80.00
Truck, Motor Fleet Hauling Service, Arrow Lines, Dump Trailer, Steel, Wyandotte, 17 In.   135.00
Truck, Motor Freight, Tin Lithograph Cab, Pressed Steel Trailer, Wyandotte, 1950s, 17 In.   145.00
Truck, Moving Van, All American, Cast Aluminum, Pressed Steel, 24 In. 385.00
Truck, Moving Van, Allied Van Lines, Pressed Steel, Tonka, 24 In. 145.00
Truck, Moving Van, Allied Van Lines, Tonka, 1950s 600.00
Truck, Moving Van, Bekins, Die Cast Cab, Steel Trailer, Smith-Miller, 1950s, 26 In. 1705.00
Truck, Moving Van, Canadian Lincoln, Pressed Steel, 1950s, 24 In. 395.00
Truck, Moving Van, Friction, Tin, Ichiko, Japan, 1960s, 19 In. 175.00
Truck, Moving Van, Hi-Way Express, Doors Open, Tin, Steel, Marx, Box, 27 In. 275.00
Truck, Moving Van, Long Distance Moving, Buddy L, 1940s 525.00
Truck, Moving Van, North American Van Lines, Tin Lithograph, Windup, Marx, 15 In. . . .   130.00
Truck, Moving Van, North American, Tin, Steel, Windup, Marx, Box, 14 In. 635.00
Truck, Moving Van, Plastic, Tin Lithograph Trailer, Wyandotte, 1950s, 15 In. 200.00
Truck, Moving Van, Pressed Steel, Aluminum Disc Wheels, Buddy L, 1920s, 21 In. 1100.00
Truck, Moving Van, Pressed Steel, Tin Lithograph, Wyandotte, 14 In. 190.00
Truck, NBC Television, Cameras, Friction, Japan, 6 In. 165.00
Truck, Overland Transport Express, Battery Operated, Modern Toys, Box, 17 In. 155.00
Truck, Panel, Black, Silver, Gold, Red, Friction, Metal, Kingsbury, 5 x 14 x 5 In. 7500.00
Truck, Panel, Cast Iron, Nickel Plated Wheels, Driver, Arcade, 8 1/2 In. 3080.00
Truck, Panel, Cast Iron, White Rubber Tires, Rear Door Opens, Arcade, 9 In. 2420.00
Truck, Panel, Yellow Cab Delivery, Stukenberg & Borchers, Rubber Tires, Arcade, 8 In. . .   12100.00
Truck, Payloader, Pressed Steel, Brochure, Ny-Lint, 1960s, 17 In. 165.00
Truck, Payloader, Pressed Steel, Ny-Lint, 1950s, 17 In. 120.00

Truck, Payloader, Pressed Steel, Ny-Lint, 1960s, 17 In. 75.00
Truck, Phillips 66, Model T Fuel, Cast Iron, Arcade, 9 In. 330.00
Truck, Pickup, 2-Tone Green, Metal, Japan, 1950s, 7 In. 175.00
Truck, Pickup, Cast Metal, White Rubber Tires, Tootsietoy, 1930s, 5 3/4 In. 29.00
Truck, Pickup, No. 302, Tonka, Box, 1963 . . . . 295.00
Truck, Pickup, Pressed Steel, Black, Silver Tires, Red Rims, Label, Buddy L, 12 In. 750.00
Truck, Pickway Pastures Livestock, Stake, Steel, Rubber Tires, Wyandotte, Box, 12 In. . . 385.00
Truck, Pie, Mack, Die Cast, Aluminum Trailer, Smith-Miller, 28 In. 715.00
Truck, Pile Driver, Pressed Steel, Buddy L, 1920s, 27 In. 1210.00
Truck, Popcorn Vendor, Battery Operated, TN, Box, 9 In. 330.00
Truck, Power Shovel, Ride 'Em, Orange & Green, Keystone 450.00
Truck, Power Shovel, Tin, Friction, 10 Wheel, Asakusa, Japan, 16 In. 225.00
Truck, Pressed Steel, Buddy L, 1930s, 23 In. 295.00
Truck, Railway Express, Cast Iron, White Rubber Tires, Hubley, 5 In. 300.00
Truck, Railway Express, Pressed Steel, Tin Lithograph, Wyandotte, 1940s, 12 In. 130.00
Truck, Ranger, Trailer Fleet, Tin, Windup, Ranger Steel, Box, 6 In. 250.00
Truck, RCA Television Service, Ladders, Plastic, Marx, Box, 8 1/2 In. 195.00
Truck, Red Baby, Buddy L, 1920s 3500.00
Truck, Rescue, Pressed Steel, Tonka, 1960s, 13 In. 120.00
Truck, Road Roller, Driver, Tin, Battery Operated, Yonezawa, Box, 9 In. 140.00
Truck, Road Roller, Huber, Orange, Cast Iron, Hubley, 8 In. 495.00
Truck, Roadster, Pressed Steel, Aluminum Spoke Wheels, Buddy L, 1920s, 12 In. 1155.00
Truck, Saddledump, No. 960, Buddy L, Box, c.1940 . . . . 660.00
Truck, Sand Conveyor, Tin, Graphics, T.P.S., Japan, 24 In. 275.00
Truck, Satellite Launching, Tin Lithograph, Friction, Japan, 12 In. 219.00
Truck, Satellite Launching, Tin, Battery Operated, Yonezawa, Box, 12 In. 745.00
Truck, Scoop-A-Dump, Pressed Steel, Marx, 12 In. 90.00
Truck, Semi-Trailer, Open Van, Tin Lithograph, Windup, Cortland, 12 1/2 In. 85.00
Truck, Semi-Trailer, Toy R Us, White, Ertl, 1979, 22 In. 45.00
Truck, Service, Hard Plastic, Battery Operated, Andy Gard, U.S.A., Box 95.00
Truck, Shell, Pressed Steel, Buddy L, 1940s, 13 In. 130.00
Truck, Shell, Pressed Steel, Electric Headlights, Rubber Tires, 7 Barrels, Metalcraft, 12 In. 550.00
Truck, Shell, Pressed Steel, England Triang, 1950s, 14 In. 325.00
Truck, Shovel, General, Red & Green, Hubley, 10 1/2 In. 650.00
Truck, Shovel, Mack, Green, Red, Hubley, 10 1/2 In. 550.00
Truck, Shovel, Red, Green, Hubley, 10 1/2 In. 650.00
Truck, Sit & Ride, Stone & Gravel, Pressed Steel, No. 5732, Buddy L, Box, c.1957 . . . . . 468.00
Truck, Sportsman, Pressed Steel, Plastic Boats, Tonka, 1960s, 13 In. 120.00
Truck, Stake, 5 Ton, Cast Iron, Hubley, 17 In. 1705.00
Truck, Stake, Cast Iron, Champion, 7 1/2 In. 195.00
Truck, Stake, Cast Iron, Nickel Wheels, A.C. Williams, 7 In. 195.00
Truck, Stake, International, Green, Arcade, 12 In. 3000.00
Truck, Stake, Mack, Hercules, Balloon Tires, Yellow, Black, Tin, Chein, 19 In. 1100.00
Truck, Stake, Pressed Steel, Ny-Lint, 1960s, 14 In. 155.00
Truck, Stake, Pressed Steel, Painted, Rubber Tires, Wyandotte, 12 In. 149.00
Truck, Stake, Pressed Steel, Tin Lithograph, Wyandotte, 1950s, 16 In. 95.00
Truck, Stake, Pressed Steel, Tonka, 1961, 14 In. 60.00
Truck, Stake, Red, Green, Wyandotte, 1938, 16 In. 225.00
Truck, Steel Carrier, Pressed Steel, Dunwell, 1950s, 23 In. 220.00
Truck, Sunshine Biscuit, Black Fenders, Yellow Body, White Tires, Red Wheels, 15 In. . . 225.00
Truck, T.V. Service, Rentaset, Blue Windows, No. 62, Matchbox, Lesney, Box, 1962 . . . . 127.00
Truck, Tanker, Aviation Gas, Cast Iron, Kilgore, 12 In. 3630.00
Truck, Tanker, B-A, Pressed Steel, Minnitoys 800.00
Truck, Tanker, Gasoline, Black Fenders, Orange Body, Yellow Wheels, Wyandotte, 18 In. 250.00
Truck, Tanker, Gasoline, Cast Iron, Green, Kenton, 8 In. 550.00
Truck, Tanker, Gasoline, Champion Gas & Motor Oil, Cast Iron, Red, Champion, 8 In. . . . 330.00
Truck, Tanker, Gasoline, Holiday, Tin, Japan, Box, 12 In. 115.00
Truck, Tanker, Gasoline, Mobile, Tin Lithograph, Japan, 11 In. 45.00
Truck, Tanker, Gasoline, Texaco, Painted Pressed Steel, Buddy L, 23 1/2 In. 50.00
Truck, Tanker, Gasoline, Tin Lithograph, Windup, Green, Red, Marx, 9 In. 470.00
Truck, Tanker, Jet Fuel, Texaco, Metal, Box, 1965 . . . . 250.00
Truck, Tanker, Metal Wheels, Buddy L, Box, 1920s 3080.00

Truck, Tanker, Oil, Electric Headlights, Cap, Pull Rod, Buddy L, c.1934 . . . . 2530.00
Truck, Tanker, Oil, Shell, Cast Metal, Black Rubber Tires, Tootsietoy, 1940s, 6 In. 45.00
Truck, Tanker, Oil, Standard Oil, Driver, Red, Green, Tin, Windup, Strauss, c.1930, 10 In. 450.00
Truck, Tanker, Painted, Decals, Sturditoy, 1920, 33 In. 8250.00
Truck, Telephone Service, Lincoln Toys, 11 In. 330.00
Truck, Telephone Service, Painted, Lincoln Toys, 11 In. 330.00
Truck, Television, Tin Lithograph, Battery Operated, Linemar, Box, 12 In. 1540.00
Truck, Tow, AA, 24-Hour Service, Tonka, 1963 . . . . 350.00
Truck, Tow, Austin, Red, Arcade, 4 1/2 In. 375.00
Truck, Tow, Auto Service, Plastic Cab, Tin Litho. Body, Wyandotte, 1950s, 15 In. .190.00 to 210.00
Truck, Tow, Chain, Hook, Tin, Friction, Japan, Box, 8 In. 165.00
Truck, Tow, Cities Service Towing, Green, White, Metal, 18 In. 165.00
Truck, Tow, Dodge, Cities Service, Fix All, Green, Yellow, Box, 1959, 9 In. 195.00
Truck, Tow, Emergency, Pressed Steel, Buddy L, 1940s, 13 In. 55.00
Truck, Tow, Emergency, Pressed Steel, Buddy L, 1950s, 17 In. 130.00
Truck, Tow, Fix It, Jack, Buddy L, Box, 1955 . . . . 295.00
Truck, Tow, Mack, Red, Champion, 4 1/2 In. 175.00
Truck, Tow, Model A, Weaver, Cast Iron, Rubber Over Tires, Arcade, 8 In. . . . . . . .385.00 to 550.00
Truck, Tow, Model T, Pressed Steel, Cowdry, 16 In. 1430.00
Truck, Tow, Moto Fix, Tin Lithograph, Pressed Steel, Wyandotte, 1950s, 15 In. 230.00
Truck, Tow, Packard, Pressed Steel, Rubber Tires, Keystone, 1920s, 27 In. 545.00
Truck, Tow, Pressed Steel, Buddy L, 1930s, 15 In. 110.00
Truck, Tow, Pressed Steel, Lincoln, Canada, 1950s, 14 In. 245.00
Truck, Tow, Pressed Steel, Rubber Tires, Sturditoy, 1920s, 31 In. 1495.00
Truck, Tow, Red, Cast Iron, Champion, 8 In. 195.00
Truck, Tow, Red, White, Marx, c.1940, 12 1/2 In. 165.00
Truck, Tow, Running Boards, Rubber Tires, Metal, Friction, Kingsbury, 9 x 13 x 5 In. . . . 4600.00
Truck, Tow, Service, Rider, Horn, Pressed Steel, No. 5840, Buddy L, Box, c.1957 . . . . . . 605.00
Truck, Tow, Service, Tin Lithograph, Pressed Steel, Wyandotte, 1950s, 13 1/2 In. 330.00
Truck, Tow, Steel, Rubber Tires, Wyandotte, Box, 9 In. 440.00
Truck, Tow, Tin Lithograph, Pressed Steel, Wyandotte, 1950s, 9 1/2 In. 265.00
Truck, Tow, Tin Lithograph, Wyandotte, 1950s, 14 In. .255.00 to 440.00
Truck, Tow, Weaver Boom, Cast Iron, Arcade, 8 1/2 In. 935.00
Truck, Tow, Weaver Boom, Cast Iron, Arcade, Box, 11 1/2 In. 3850.00
Truck, Tractor Trailer, Shop-Rite, Tin, Steel, Marx, Box, 25 In. 305.00
Truck, Trailer & Hauler, Acme Van, Doors Open, Tin, Steel, Marx, Box, c.1950, 25 In. . . . 510.00
Truck, Trailer, Army, Pressed Steel, Marx, 1950s, 36 In. 65.00
Truck, Trailer, Rubber Tires, Plastic, Marx, 9 1/2 In. 115.00
Truck, Trailer, Sunshine Fruit Growers, Tin Lithograph, Pressed Steel, Marx, 15 In. 50.00
Truck, Trailer, U-Haul, Pressed Steel, Ny-Lint, 1960s, 21 In. 80.00
Truck, Trailer, U.S. Army, Marx, 1940s, 30 In. 165.00
Truck, U.S. Army, With Searchlight, Tin, Steel, Canvas Roof, Marx, Box, c.1950, 19 In. . . 635.00
Truck, U.S. Mail, 18-Gauge Steel Grid Cargo Area, Keystone 1210.00
Truck, U.S. Mail, Pressed Steel, Removable Roof, Buddy L, c.1950 . . . . 385.00
Truck, U.S. Mobile Guided Missile Squadron, Tin Lithograph, Marx, 18 In. 145.00
Truck, Utility Service, Tin Lithograph, Marx, 1950s, 19 1/2 In. 190.00
Truck, Volkswagen, Talking Camping Car, Tin, Battery Operated, Yonezawa, Box, 9 In. . . 195.00
Truck, Water Tower, Pressed Steel, Headlights, Bumpers, Tires, Sturditoy, 1920s, 33 In. . . 8250.00
Truck, Water, Windup, Tin Lithograph, Strauss, 11 In. 489.00
Truck, Wrigley's Spearmint Gum, Electric Headlights, Buddy L, 1930s, 23 In. 2310.00
Truck, Wyandotte Trucking Line, Pressed Steel, Green, Red, Wyandotte, 25 In. 185.00
Truck, Zoo, Traveling, Animals, Buddy L, Box, 1963 . . . . 350.00
Trunk, Doll's, Around The World, Paper Lithograph, Hinged, Latch, Bliss, 7 In. 255.00
Trunk, Doll's, Doll Clothes, Dolls, Clown, 32 In. 115.00
Trunk, Doll's, Dome Top, Clothes, Accessories, 19th Century, 18 In. 207.00
Tug Of War, Children, Spring Bounce, Wheels, Einfalt, c.1920, 8 1/2 In. 1510.00
Turkey, Tucky, Mohair, Tag, Steiff, c.1950, 4 In. 160.00
Turkey, Walks, Tin Lithograph, Windup, U.S. Zone Germany 105.00
Turtle, Crawling, Celluloid, Windup, Alps, Occupied Japan, Box, 5 1/2 In. 140.00
Turtle, Mack, Battery Operated, Rosko, Box, 9 In. 275.00
Turtle, Yellow, Green, Red, Lithograph, Windup, 1950s, 5 In. 85.00
Typewriter, Types Capital & Small Letters, Red Metal, Berwin, 1930s, 12 x 12 x 8 In. . . . 110.00
Typist, Miss Friday, Battery Operated, Typewriter, Desk, Phone, Japan, Box, 8 In. 300.00

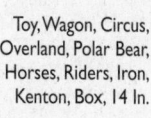

Toy, Wagon, Circus,
Overland, Polar Bear,
Horses, Riders, Iron,
Kenton, Box, 14 In.

Uncle Sam, Walks, With Flag, Plastic, Windup, Japan, Box 11.00
Vacuum Cleaner, Battery Operated, Box, 13 1/2 In. . . . . .28.00 to 39.00
Velocipede, Driver Bends Forward & Back, Windup, Tin Lithograph, Marx, c.1925, 5 In. .   590.00
Ventriloquist Dummy, Black Man, Checked Pants, Papier-Mache, c.1900, 38 In. 990.00
View-Master, Barbie's Around-The-World Trip, Unit & 3 Reels, Talking 75.00
Wagon, Band, Bandsmen, Reeds Band Chariot, Wood, Paper Lithograph, 25 In. 8470.00
Wagon, Band, Wood, Built-In Phonograph, Charles Belknap 2000.00
Wagon, Blue Bird Coaster, Green, Red Paint, Mustard Letters, Cast Iron Wheels 1025.00
Wagon, Buddy Coaster, Wood, Red, Rubber Tires, Indian Head, Paris Mfg. Co., c.1900 . . .   1600.00
Wagon, Champion Express, Red, White Tires, 4 In. 80.00
Wagon, Circus Band, Overland, Cast Iron, 16 In. 440.00
Wagon, Circus, Humpty Dumpty, 7 People, 4 Horses, Wood, Schoenhut, 20 x 42 In. 26400.00
Wagon, Circus, Overland, 6 Musicians, Driver, 2 Riders, Horses, Cast Iron, Kenton 750.00
Wagon, Circus, Overland, Polar Bear, Horses, Riders, Iron, Kenton, Box, 14 In. . . . . . *Illus*   520.00
Wagon, Circus, Tent, Bimbo & Barany, Wood, Paper Label, Rubber Tires, c.1950s, 23 In. . .   95.00
Wagon, Dray, Hand Enameled Tin & Heavy Cast Metal Wheels, Marklin, 23 In. 3740.00
Wagon, Elevating, Wood, Cast Aluminum, 34 In. 325.00
Wagon, Express, Buckboard, Wood, Steel, Removable Seat, Wooden Spokes, 20 x 35 In. . .   980.00
Wagon, Farm, Ford, White Ground, Blue Trim, 40 In. 1210.00
Wagon, Farm, Horse Drawn, Tin Lithograph, Windup, Marx, 10 In. . . . . .145.00 to 175.00
Wagon, Farm, Wood, Iron Wheels, Bittersweet Paint, 34 In. 140.00
Wagon, Fine Bread, Painted, Decals, Schoenhut, 23 In. 4400.00
Wagon, Hay, Wood, Brown Stripes, 27 In. 175.00
Wagon, Ladder, Cast Iron, Arcade, 16 In. 290.00
Wagon, Milk, Borden, Driver, Bottle Case, Tin Lithograph, Wood, Rich Toy 230.00
Wagon, Milk, Cast Iron, Kenton, 13 In. 110.00
Wagon, Milk, Horse Drawn, Tin Lithograph, 13 In. 190.00
Wagon, Milk, Plastic, Wyandotte, Box, 1950s, 8 In. 35.00
Wagon, Police Patrol, Yellow, 4 Blue Policemen, 3 Horses, Hubley, 1915, 15 In. 995.00
Wagon, Pressed Steel, Wyandotte, 1940s, 5 1/2 In. 95.00
Wagon, Pressed Steel, Wyandotte, 1940s, 12 In. 70.00
Wagon, Radio Flyer, Radio Line, Red, Decals, 4 3/4 In. 150.00
Wagon, Red Cross, Penny Toy, Meier 300.00
Wagon, Sand & Gravel, Cast Iron, Arcade, 15 1/2 In. 155.00
Wagon, Studebaker Junior, Green Paint, Gilt Trim, 42 x 24 In. 2310.00
Wagon, U.S. Mail, Tin Lithograph, 11 In. 70.00
Wagon, Wood, Iron Rim, Wooden Wheels, 42 In. 600.00
Warm Air Generator, Cast Aluminum, Kelsey, Syracuse, N.Y., Salesman's Sample 220.00
Washboard, Doll's, Arcade Crystal, 11 In. 22.00
Washing Machine, 3 Little Pigs, Tin Lithograph, Chein, 8 In. 415.00
Washing Machine, Copper & Tin Plated, Hinged Cover, Drain Spigot, c.1885, 6 In. 770.00
Washing Machine, Sunny Suzy, Tin Lithograph, Wood Board, 21 x 10 1/2 In. 85.00
Washing Machine, Wood, Gray Paint, 16 x 18 In. 60.00
Washing Machine, Wringer, Busy Betty, Hoge Mfg., 10 1/2 In. 255.00
Water Heater, Cast Iron, Copper Tubing, Wire Base, No. 25, Ruud, Salesman's Sample . .   358.00
Watering Can, Dutch Children Watering Tulips, Tin, Ohio Art, 4 1/4 In. 28.00
Western Bad Man, Shoots Gun At Bottles, Tin, Battery Operated, Japan, Box, 10 In. 1020.00
Wheelbarrow, Red, Black Pinstripes, Tin Bucket, Spoke Wheel, Wood Frame, 36 In. 169.00
Wheelbarrow, Stenciled, Wood, 34 In. 275.00
Wheelbarrow, Wood, Painted, Blue, Red, Gold Designs, 32 In. 145.00
Wheelbarrow, Wood, Stamped, No. 1, Paris, Me. 220.00

Whip Ride, Playland, No. 340, Chein, Box, 1953 . . . .   1995.00
Wienermobile, Oscar Mayer, Pull, 1950s, 4 1/4 x 9 1/2 In. 295.00
Windmill, 4 Blades, Red, White, Blue, Green, Tin Lithograph, Embossed, 4 1/2 In. 550.00
Windmill, 4 Blades, Tin Lithograph, On Stand, Germany, 19th Century, 4 1/2 x 2 1/4 In. . .   100.00
Woman, Chasing Duck, Whip, Steel, Painted, Friction, Inertia Drive, Clark, 11 In. 415.00
Xylophone, Instructions, Schoenhut, 20 In. 39.00
Xylophone, Schoenhut, 12 In. 35.00
Xylophone, Schoenhut, 14 In. 44.00
Xylophone Player, Tin Lithograph, Windup, Linemar, 5 In. 138.00
Xylophone Player, Tin, Windup, Celluloid Figure, 6 In. 185.00
Zebra, Pulling Cart, Windup, Tin Lithograph, Germany, Lehmann, Box, 8 In. . . . . .375.00 to 415.00
Zeppelin, SR-47, Tin Lithograph, Windup, Strauss, Box, c.1935, 11 In. 700.00
Zilotone, Tin Lithograph, Steel, Clockwork, Wolverine, 7 1/2 In. 275.00
Zoetrope, Milton Bradley, 1867 Patent, 12 x 12 In. 248.00

TRAMP ART is a form of folk art made since the Civil War. It is usually
made from chip-carved cigar boxes. Examples range from small boxes
and picture frames to full-sized pieces of furniture.

Bank, Cathedral, Notch Carved, 2 Slotted Peaks, 6 Drawers, 26 1/4 x 14 In. . . . . *Illus*   2350.00
Box, 2-Tier Pyramid, Notched, Hinged, Early 1900s, 8 1/2 x 11 x 8 In. 210.00
Box, Applied Chip Carved Trim, Cutouts, Painted, Blue, 8 x 6 x 4 1/2 In. 200.00
Box, Chip Carved, Lift Top, Stars, Gilding, 1800s, 6 3/8 x 7 1/2 x 9 1/4 In. 225.00
Cabinet, Medicine, 4 Interior Shelves, Chip Carved, White, Blue Paint 330.00
Chest, Flowers & Diamonds, 2 Drawers, Late 1800s, 9 3/4 x 9 5/8 x 7 1/2 In. 295.00
Chest, Notched, Geometric, 5 Drawers, Late 1800s, 12 1/2 x 9 3/4 x 5 1/2 In. 176.00
Cigar Box, Stacked Diamond Designs, Hinged Lid, Handle, c.1900 . . . .   59.00
Frame, 1 Over 3 Over 1 Picture Openings, Porcelain Button Tacks, 20 x 15 In. 107.00
Frame, Carte De Visite, Porcelain Tack Buttons, Holds 13 Pictures, 27 1/2 x 20 In. 25.00
Frame, Chip Carved, Alligator Varnish Finish, 20 x 17 1/2 In. 120.00
Frame, Double, Crown-Of-Thorns Pattern, Cedar, 20 x 17 In. 1050.00
Frame, Extended Corner Blocks, Center Crest, c.1898, 31 1/2 x 28 In. 358.00
Frame, Notch Carved, Diamond, Heart, Circles, 7 Openings, 1800s, 19 x 21 1/4 In. 558.00
Frame, Notch Carved, Stepped, Gilding, 1800s, 15 1/2 x 14 1/4 In. 380.00
Frame, Puzzle Work, Crucifix Crest, 5 Openings, c.1900, 29 x 15 7/8 In. 176.00
Frame, Queen Anne Style, Pediment Top, Oak Leaves, Acorns, Glass Stars, 24 x 49 In. . . .   1150.00
Frame, Star Shape, Carved Flowers, Stars, Fretwork, 20th Century, 21 In. . . . . *Illus*   558.00
Frame, Sunburst Medallions, Scalloped Opening, Green, 1800s, 31 x 27 In. 440.00
Jewelry Box, Interior Tray, Chip Carved, Brass Mounts, Feet, 7 x 12 1/2 x 8 1/2 In. 165.00
Lamp, Eiffel Tower, Notch Carved, Early 1900s, 33 5/8 x 12 1/4 In. 1645.00
Lantern, Hanging, Notch Carved, c.1900, 11 1/2 x 5 5/8 x 5 7/8 In. 705.00
Mirror, Sawtooth Border, Arrow Corners, Applied Star & Leaf, 19 1/2 x 24 1/2 In. 338.00
Plaque, Eagle, Spread Wings, Arrow, 1800s, 9 1/4 x 16 In. 825.00
Shelf, Corner, Chip Carved, Hemispherical, 1800s, 22 x 16 x 13 3/4 In. 765.00

Tramp Art, Bank, Cathedral,
Notch Carved, 2 Slotted Peaks,
6 Drawers, 26 1/4 x 14 In.

Tramp Art, Frame, Star Shape,
Carved Flowers, Stars,
Fretwork, 20th Century, 21 In.

Tramp Art, Table, Sewing, Notch
Carved, Carved Mother, Lift
Top, Hinged, 31 x 33 In.

Sideboard, Chip Carved, 2 Drawers, 2 Doors, c.1900, 36 1/2 x 46 1/2 x 22 3/4 In. 1528.00
Table, End, Drawer, Chip Carved Geometric, Early 1900s, 22 x 15 3/4 x 14 In. 1998.00
Table, Sewing, Notch Carved, Carved Mother, Lift Top, Hinged, 31 x 33 In. .... *Illus* 2350.00
Wall Pocket, Carved, Applied Ship Carving Design, 10 3/4 x 8 1/4 In. 220.00
Wall Pocket, Peaked Arch, Diamond Shape Mirror, c.1900, 36 x 15 3/8 In. 235.00
Wall Pocket, Valentines, Mirror, Drawer, 1800s, 42 1/2 x 11 3/4 In. 2000.00
Wall Rack, Newspaper, Lattice Tilt Out Front, Late 1800s, 22 x 24 7/8 In. 148.00

TRAPS for animals may be handmade. One of the most unusual is the
mousetrap made so that when the mouse entered the trap, it was hit on
the head with a mallet. Other traps were commercially manufactured
and often are marked with the name of the manufacturer. Many traps
were designed to be as humane as possible, and they would trap the
live animal so it could be released in the woods.

Bear, Hand Forged, Single Spring, Toothed, 36-In. Chain, Open 12 x 16 In. 330.00
Bear, Steel, Newhouse, No. 5 .... 1150.00
Bear, Steel, Newhouse, No. 15 .... 1300.00
Fly, Apothecary Jar Shape, Satin Glass, Stopper 550.00
Fly, Blown Glass, Wire Bail Handle, Blue ....95.00 to 180.00
Fly, Blown Glass, Wire Bail Handle, Green 105.00
Fly, Glass, Amber, Inverted Thumbprint, 3-Footed, Stopper 525.00
Fly, Glass, Blue, Inverted Thumbprint, 3-Footed, Stopper 440.00
Fly, Glass, Cone Shape, 3-Footed, Tin Lid, Unique Fly Trap, Pat. 468.00
Fly, Glass, Swirled, Ribbed Design, Amber Base, 1890 Patent, 2 Piece 385.00
Fly, Glass, Swirled, Ribbed Design, Blue Base, 1890 Patent, 2 Piece 468.00
Flycatcher, Blown Glass, Etched, c.1850, 7 1/2 In. 9775.00
Flycatcher, Footed, Neckband, Blown Glass, Mid 19th Century, 7 1/2 x 6 3/4 In. 200.00
Mouse, Glass, Otto Kampfe Mfg. Co. 360.00
Mouse, Side Lying, Tin, Iron, Trap Door, Otto Kampfe Mfg. Co., Newark N.J. 360.00
Rat, Glass, Otto Kampfe Mfg. Co. 580.00
Rat, Molded Glass, Tin & Iron Screw Lid, Otto Kampfe Mfg. Co., Newark, N.J. 580.00
Roach, Glass, Otto Kampfe Mfg. Co. 248.00

TREEN, see Wooden category.

TRENCH ART is a form of folk art made by soldiers. Metal casings from
bullets and mortar shells were cut and decorated to form useful objects,
such as vases.

Andirons, Brass Casings, Aluminum, Cast Metal Base, World War I, 18 In. 114.00
Ashtray, Amphibious Vehicle, U.S. Army, Brass, Shell Wheels & Headlights 49.00
Ashtray, Large Caliber Shell Base, P-38 Plane On Post, Brass, 6 3/4 In. 85.00
Bracelet, Aircraft Aluminum, Camel, Palm Tree, Africa, 1944 .... 29.00
Bracelet, Shell, Brass, Iron Cross, Oak Leaves, Acorns, Prussia, c.1915 .... 58.00
Candelabra, 2-Light, Chrome Shell, 1916, 3 1/2 In. 70.00
Inkwell, Artillery Shell, Brass Casing, Engraved, World War I, 1918 .... 300.00
Inkwell, Pen Rack, Artillery Shell, Brass, Projectiles, c.1870 .... 259.00
Vase, Artillery Shell, 75 mm., Birds, Trees, Imperial Era, WWI, 1915, 11 3/4 In. 58.00
Vase, Artillery Shell, German, Brass Case, Flowers, Leaves, Reims, 9 In. 49.00
Vase, Shell Casing, Brass, Twisted, Fluted Base, Grapes, Leaves, France, WWI, 12 3/4 In. 56.00
Vase, Shell, Imperial German, Woodland Scene, Shield, 1936, 9 x 3 1/2 In. 58.00
Vase, Shells, Brass, Leaves, Scalloped Rims, Argonne, 1918 France, 12 In., Pair 158.00

TRIVETS are now used to hold hot dishes. Most trivets of the late nineteenth and early twentieth centuries were made to hold hot irons. Iron
or brass reproductions are being made of many of the old styles.

Brass, Bronze, Spade Shape, Rub While The Iron Is Hot 72.00
Brass, Cast, Hearth, Pierced Geometric, Scroll Top, Paw & Ball Feet, 4 x 11 x 5 3/4 In. .. 60.00
Brass, Openwork Top, Pad Feet, 19th Century, 3 1/2 x 10 x 5 In. 80.00
Brass, Rectangular, Pierced Top, Post Legs, 3 1/2 x 9 x 4 1/4 In. & 6 x 12 x 4 1/2 In. 58.00
Brass, Tiger, Paw Feet, 19th Century, 4 x 10 x 5 1/2 In. 375.00
Brass, Tilt Top, Tripod, Round, Pierced, Double Knop, 19th Century, 11 3/4 In. 150.00
Cast Iron, Openwork Heart, Eagle, Arrows, 3-Footed, Handle, J. English, 11 x 4 In. 440.00
Cast Iron, Twisted Loop Handle, 9 1/4 x 16 3/4 x 10 1/4 In. 1380.00
Hearts & Scrolls, Wrought Iron, Footed 220.00

Iron, Heart Shape, Blacksmith Made, 18th Century 325.00
Redware, Mammy, Exaggerated 3-Dimensional Mammy, 8 In. 75.00
Wrought Iron, Openwork Star, 3-Footed, 2 1/2 x 5 1/2 In. 195.00
Wrought Iron, Ram's Horn Handle, 4 Riveted Bars, 2 Fleur-De-Lis, 13 1/2 x 3 1/2 In. 275.00
Wrought Iron, Scrolled Legs, Wood Handle, 8 3/4 x 30 x 12 3/4 In. 290.00

TRUNKS of many types were made. The nineteenth-century sea chest was often handmade of unpainted wood. Brass-fitted camphorwood chests were brought back from the Orient. Leather-covered trunks were popular from the late eighteenth to mid-nineteenth centuries. By 1895, trunks were covered with canvas or decorated sheet metal. Embossed metal coverings were used from 1870 to 1910. By 1925, trunks were covered with vulcanized fiber or undecorated metal. Suitcases are listed here.

Bow Top, Iron Straps, c.1800, 17 1/2 x 37 x 16 1/2 In. 140.00
Camphor Wood, 6-Board, Dovetailed, Iron Handles, 16 x 30 1/2 In. 345.00
Carriage, Dome Top, Leather Straps, Inner Tray, 14 1/2 x 27 x 14 In. 140.00
Dome Top, Basswood, Birds, Wallpaper Covering, White, Green, Square Nails, 31 x 16 In. 490.00
Dome Top, Dovetailed Construction, Iron Lock, Blue Paint, 28 In. 480.00
Dome Top, Pine, Grain Painted, Ocher, New England, Early 1800s, 11 1/2 x 28 x 14 In. .. 1765.00
Dome Top, Pine, Iron Mounted, Carrying Handles, 26 x 45 x 21 1/2 In. 110.00
Dome Top, Softwood, Iron Straps, Handles, Lid, Dovetailed, 27 x 15 In. 200.00
Dome Top, Softwood, Theorem Style Flower Basket, Flowers, Birds, 24 x 12 x 13 In. ... 1520.00
Feather Painted, Bessie E. Martin, 64 x 28 In. 175.00
Hide Covered, Forged Iron Lock, Brass Tacks, Newspaper Lining, 1800s, 9 x 20 x 10 In. . 165.00
Immigrant's, Hand Wrought Hardware, Blue Paint, K.O.S. Initials, c.1862, 32 In. 80.00
Immigrant's, Pine, Dovetailed, Iron Straps, Flowers, Norway, 1860, 49 x 25 x 26 In. 415.00
Immigrant's, Pine, Wrought Hardware, Oxblood Paint, T.A. Brandt, 1888, 40 In. 150.00
Louis Vuitton, Steamer, Brass Trim, Shelf, Hanging, 2 Trays, Labeled, 28 x 20 x 22 In. .. 310.00
Louis Vuitton, Steamer, Hinged Top, 2 Trays, Red Striped Interior, 22 1/2 x 39 1/2 In. .. 500.00
Louis Vuitton, Steamer, Hinged Top, Drop In Tray, Quilted Top, 13 x 39 1/2 x 21 In. 600.00
Louis Vuitton, Wardrobe, Mustard Exterior, 4 Drawers, Hat Box 3000.00
Oak, North European, c.1775, 30 3/4 x 47 1/2 x 24 In. 770.00
Pine, Arched Top, Locking Hasp, 1800s, 13 x 23 x 12 In. 295.00
Pine, Dovetailed Case, Rope Handles, Iron Strap Hinges, c.1810, 47 x 24 x 25 In. 230.00
Pine, Metal Strapping, Brass Nails, Interior Tray, 24 x 15 In. 175.00
Softwood, Tin Banding, Punched Initials On Tin 50.00
Storage, Softwood, Green Background, Multicolored Scroll, Flowers, Strap Hinges 280.00
Suitcase, Leather, Brass Mounts, 15 x 24 x 8 In. 30.00
Wood, Beveled Lid, Wrought Iron Handle, 1852, 22 x 13 1/4 In. 259.00
Wood, Multicolored, Tibet, c.1850, 26 x 53 1/4 x 18 7/8 In. 885.00

TYPEWRITER collectors divide typewriters into two main classifications: the index machine, which has a pointer and a dial for letter selection, and the keyboard machine, most commonly seen today. The first successful typewriter was made by Sholes and Glidden in 1874.

Blickensderfer, Model 7 .... 150.00
Blickensderfer, Model 9 .... 299.00
Caligraph, Model 2 .... 385.00
Caligraph, New Century 340.00
Carlsson, Writing Apparatus, For The Blind, Sweden, c.1905 .... 529.00
Chicago, Typesleeve Machine, c.1898 .... 925.00
Corona, Model 3, Folding 110.00
Corona, Simplified Qwerty Keyboard, Carrying Case, 1917 Patent 75.00
Hammond, Model 2, Curved Keyboard, Square Keys 685.00
Imperial, Model B, c.1908 .... 345.00
Oak Base, Metal Cover 110.00
Oliver, Model 11 .... 150.00
Pittsburgh Visible, Model 10 .... 600.00
Smith Premier, Model 1 .... 340.00
Sun, Model 2 .... 340.00
Woodstock, 42 Key, World War II 58.00
Yost, Model 4 .... 470.00

TYPEWRITER RIBBON TINS are now being collected. The lithographed tin containers have been used since the 1870s. Most popular with collectors are tins with pictorial graphics.

A.P. Little, Black Boy Popping Out Of Paper, Lithograph, 1920s, 2 1/2 In.	70.00
Allied Typewriter Ribbon, Allied Cabon & Ribbon Mfg. Corp., New York	34.00
Amneco Typewriter Ribbon, Square	75.00
Carter's Midnight Typewriter Ribbon, Carter's Ink Company, Boston	16.00
Hallmark Typewriter Ribbon, Round, Cameron Manufacturing, Dallas	20.00
Keelox Brand Typewriter Ribbon	24.00
Park Avenue Typewriter Ribbon, Unopened, 2 1/2 In.	12.00
Thorobred Typewriter Ribbon, Underwood Corporation, Burlington, N.J.	25.00
Type Bar Brand Typewriter Tin, LC Smith Corona Typewriters Inc.	18.00
Vertex Roytype Typewriter Ribbon, Unopened, 2 1/2 In.	12.00
Webster Star Brand Non-Filling Typewriter Ribbons, F.S. Webster Co., Boston	18.00

UMBRELLA collectors like rain or shine. The first known umbrella was owned by King Louis XIII of France in 1637. The earliest umbrellas were sunshades, not designed to be used in the rain. The umbrella was embellished and redesigned many times. In 1852, the fluted steel rib style was developed, and it has remained the most useful style.

Parasol, Silver Handle, Rope & Leaves, 10 Purple Stones, Ball Shape Handle	115.00
Parasol, Whalebone Handle, Baleen Ribs, Brass Mounts, Cloth Cover, 1800s, 24 In.	115.00
Silk, Red, White & Blue, 1890s	275.00

UNION PORCELAIN WORKS was established at Greenpoint, New York, in 1848 by Charles Cartlidge. The company went through a series of ownership changes and finally closed in the early 1900s. The company made a fine quality white porcelain that was often decorated in clear, bright colors.

Dish Set, Nesting, Shaker, Oval, Cream Color, Flowers, 3 Piece	4485.00
Oyster Plate, 5 Wells, Shell Shape, 8 1/2 In.	385.00
Pitcher, Figural, Sea Lion Face Spout, Bear Handle, Peach, Pink, 1875, 10 In.	9075.00
Pitcher, Gambler, Chinese Man, Uncle Sam, Goat, Walrus Spout	7280.00

UNIVERSITY CITY POTTERY, of University, Missouri, worked from 1909 to 1915. Well-known artists, including Taxile Doat, Adelaide Alsop Robineau, and Frederick Hurten Rhead, worked there.

Vase, Stylized Gray Trees, Green Mottled Ground, F. Rhead, 1911, 6 1/2 In.	4600.00

UNIVERSITY OF NORTH DAKOTA, see North Dakota School of Mines category.

VAL ST. LAMBERT Cristalleries of Belgium was founded by Messieurs Kemlin and Lelievre in 1825. The company is still in operation. All types of table glassware and decorative glassware have been made. Pieces are often decorated with cut designs.

Cordial, Cranberry Cut To Clear, Berncastle, 5 In., Pair	150.00
Figurine, Cat, Sleeping, 6 In.	235.00
Figurine, Monkey, Seated, 6 In.	60.00
Paperweight, Rock Shape, Medical Emblem, Signed, 4 In.	45.00
Vase, Trees, Sailboat, Mountains, Frosted Citron Over Teal Blue, Cameo, Signed, 6 In.	935.00

VALLERYSTHAL Glassworks was founded in 1836 in Lorraine, France. In 1854, the firm became Klenglin et Cie. It made table and decorative glass, opaline, cameo, and art glass. A line of covered, pressed glass animal dishes was made in the nineteenth century. The firm is still working.

Vase, Amethyst Jonquil, Cut Gold Highlights, Green, Cameo, Cylindrical, 12 In.	1093.00
Vase, Maiden, Roman Warrior, Animals, Enamel, Gilded Panels, Acid Relief, 6 1/8 In.	2070.00

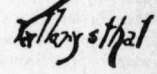

VAN BRIGGLE pottery was made by Artus Van Briggle in Colorado Springs, Colorado, after 1901. Van Briggle had been a decorator at Rookwood Pottery of Cincinnati, Ohio. He died in 1904. His wares usually had modeled relief decorations and a soft, dull glaze. The pottery is still working and still making some of the original designs.

Bookends, Bison, Turquoise Glaze, Stamped, AA, 6 x 8 1/2 In.	345.00

Bookends, Elephant, Multitone Blue Matte Glaze, 3 1/2 In. 175.00
Bookends, Squirrel, Blue, Paper Label, 27 In. 190.00
Bookends, Squirrel, Maroon, Blue Matte Glaze, 7 In. 145.00
Bowl, Dragonflies, Maroon, Blue, 9 In. 200.00
Bowl, Flower Frog, Lady Of The Lake, Turquoise, c.1926, 14 In. . . . . .375.00 to 520.00
Bowl, Ivy Leaves, Purple Glaze, c.1903, 2 x 4 5/8 In. 1035.00
Figurine, Colonial Peasants, Boy, Girl, Persian Rose Glaze, Stamped, 8 1/2 In., Pair 175.00
Figurine, Dos Cabezas, 2 Women, Flowing Gowns, Maroon, Blue Matte Glaze, 7 1/2 In. . . 2350.00
Figurine, Seated Woman Holding Large Shell In Lap, Green, 7 In. 470.00
Incense Burner, Gnome, Crouching In Crescent, Purple & Indigo Glaze, 4 1/2 In. 375.00
Lamp, Woman With Vase By Stream, Blue Glaze, 16 1/2 In. 495.00
Paperweight, Rabbit, Turquoise, 2 5/8 In. 140.00
Paperweight, Scarab, Brown Matte Glaze, Mottled, Carved, 2 1/2 In. 645.00
Pitcher, Gray Matte Glaze, Marked 1906, 4 3/4 In. 520.00
Plate, Dogwood Blossoms, Turquoise & Brown Matte Glaze, 8 1/4 In. 690.00
Plate, Grapes, Blue, Green Matte Glaze, 1907-1912, 8 1/2 In. 460.00
Plate, Leaf, Stylized, Multitone Blue Matte Glaze, 1907-1912, 6 In. 575.00
Vase, 3-Headed Indian, Green, Brown Matte Glaze, c.1928, 11 1/4 In. 745.00
Vase, Baluster Shape, Green Matte Glaze, Marked, 1905, 9 In. 920.00
Vase, Blossoms, Lavender To Chartreuse Matte Glaze, 3 3/4 In. 230.00
Vase, Bud, Squat, Chartreuse, Beige Glaze, 1902, 6 In. 2300.00
Vase, Bud, Trillium, Handles, Turquoise Matte Glaze, c.1907, 5 In. 145.00
Vase, Butterflies, Brown Green Matte Glaze, 1913, 4 1/8 In. 705.00
Vase, Butterflies, Green Glaze, c.1915, 2 3/4 In. 375.00
Vase, Butterflies, Squat, Persian Rose Glaze, 4 In. 105.00
Vase, Daffodils, Blue & Green Matte Glaze, c.1916, 9 In. 375.00
Vase, Daffodils, Pink Glaze, c.1907, 6 1/2 x 4 In. 750.00
Vase, Daisies, Tear Shape, Blue Green Glaze, 1908-1911, 4 x 2 1/4 In. 635.00
Vase, Dragonflies, Brown Matte Glaze, Mottled, c.1906, 3 1/2 In. 633.00
Vase, Flower Design, Carved, Green & Blue Matte Glaze, 4 1/2 In. 85.00
Vase, Flowers, Flared, Blue, Red Matte Glaze, c.1930, 9 1/2 In. 405.00
Vase, Flowers, Green & Blue, 9 3/4 In. 2305.00
Vase, Flowers, Leaves, Carved, Tapered, Maroon Matte Glaze, Blue, 6 In. 1530.00
Vase, Flowers, Leaves, Swirled, Green Matte Glaze, 1902, 10 1/2 In. 2530.00
Vase, Flowers, Stylized, Handles, Maroon, Blue Matte Glaze, 7 In. 489.00
Vase, Flowers, Stylized, Squat, Ocher Glaze, 1908-1911, 4 3/4 In. 750.00
Vase, Gourd Shape, Speckled Green & Blue Glaze, 1905, 5 1/4 In. 1150.00
Vase, Indian Chief, Brown Glaze, Green, c.1920, 11 In. 520.00
Vase, Leaf, Blue Glaze, 8 1/2 In. 220.00
Vase, Leaves, 2-Tone Green Glaze, 1915, 7 In. 575.00
Vase, Leaves, Berries, Light Green Matte Glaze, 1908-1911, 13 1/4 In. 920.00
Vase, Leaves, Broad, Yellow, Blue Matte Glaze, c.1915, 8 In. 805.00
Vase, Leaves, Carved, Baluster Shape, Green Matte Glaze, 6 In. 1645.00
Vase, Leaves, Green Matte Glaze, c.1915, 7 In. 865.00
Vase, Leaves, Maroon, Blue Matte Glaze, c.1920, 4 1/2 In. 230.00
Vase, Leaves, Squat, Mountain Craig Brown, 1930, 4 1/4 x 5 In. 175.00
Vase, Leaves, Squat, Mustard Matte Glaze, c.1905, 2 1/4 x 6 1/4 In. 460.00
Vase, Leaves, Stylized, Maroon, Blue Matte Glaze, c.1920, 4 1/2 In. 145.00
Vase, Leaves, Swirled, Gray Glaze, 1908-1911, 4 1/2 In. 635.00
Vase, Leaves, Tapered, Blue, Green Matte Glaze, c.1915, 5 1/2 In. 805.00
Vase, Leaves, Whiplash, Maroon, Blue Matte Glaze, 7 1/2 In. 374.00
Vase, Lorelei, Blue, Green Matte Glaze, c.1920, 10 In. 575.00
Vase, Lorelei, Turquoise & Blue Glaze, 1950s, 11 In. 145.00
Vase, Poppies, Brown Matte Glaze, Mottled, 10 1/2 In. 6463.00
Vase, Poppy Pod, Green, Blue Matte Glaze, 8 1/2 In. 200.00
Vase, Poppy Pod, Maroon, Blue Matte Glaze, 4 In. 230.00
Vase, Poppy Pod, Stem, Maroon, 3 3/4 In. 115.00
Vase, Poppy Pod, Stems, Turquoise, 3 1/2 In. 115.00
Vase, Squat, Carved Rim, Brown Glaze, 1905, 3 1/2 In. 490.00
Vase, Trillium, Pinched Waist, Chartreuse & Turquoise Glaze, c.1907, 7 1/4 In. 865.00
Vase, Vertical Leaf Design, Green, Blue Matte Glaze, c.1920, 6 In. 200.00

VASA MURRHINA is the name of a glassware made by the Vasa Murrhina Art Glass Company of Sandwich, Massachusetts, about 1884. The glassware was transparent and was embedded with small pieces of colored glass and metallic flakes. The mica flakes were coated with silver, gold, copper, or nickel. Some of the pieces were cased. The same type of glass was made in England. Collectors often confuse Vasa Murrhina glass with aventurine, spatter, or spangle glass. There is uncertainty about what actually was made by the Vasa Murrhina factory. Related pieces may be listed under Spangle Glass.

Bride's Basket, Golden Amber To Cream, Silver Mica Flecks, Petaled, 10 1/2 In. 230.00
Vase, Rainbow, Bulbous, Clear Ruffled Edge, Mica Flecks, 10 1/4 In. 635.00

VASELINE GLASS is a greenish-yellow glassware resembling petroleum jelly. Some vaseline glass is still being made in old and new styles. Pressed glass of the 1870s was often made of vaseline-colored glass. Additional pieces of vaseline glass may also be listed under Pressed Glass in this book.

Butter, Cover, Shamrock, Hummingbird & Leaf Design, 4 1/2 In. 155.00
Pitcher, Milk, Fish Shape, Open Mouth Forms Rim, 7 1/2 In. 470.00
Vase, Trumpet, Folded Rim, Ribbed Ball Knop, c.1910, 11 5/8 In. 90.00

VENETIAN GLASS, see Glass-Venetian category.

VERLYS glass was made in Rouen, France, by the Societe Holophane Francais, a company that started in 1920. It was made in Newark, Ohio, from 1935 to 1951. The glass is either blown or molded. The American glass is signed with a diamond-point-scratched name, but the French pieces are marked with a molded signature. The designs resemble those used by Lalique.

Bowl, Console, Chrysanthemum, 4 1/4 x 10 1/8 x 6 1/8 In. 250.00
Bowl, Pinecone, Frosted, Molded, 6 1/4 x 1 3/4 In. 175.00
Bowl, Poppy, 2 1/2 x 13 3/4 In. 125.00
Vase, Frosted Background, Leaves, Stems, 3 Rows Of Flowers, 6 1/2 In. 288.00

VERNON KILNS was the name used by Vernon Potteries, Ltd. The company, which started in 1931 in Vernon, California, made dinnerware and figurines until it went out of business in 1958. The molds were bought by Metlox, which continued to make some patterns. Collectors search for the brightly colored dinnerware and the pieces designed by

Rockwell Kent, Walt Disney, and Don Blanding. For more information, see *Kovels' Depression Glass & Dinnerware Price List.*

Bits Of The Old South, Plate, Cypress Swamp, Multicolored, 8 1/2 In. 33.00
Bits Of The Old South, Plate, Southern Mansion, 8 1/2 In. 3.00
Bits Of The Old South, Plate, Tapping For Sugar, Multicolored, 8 1/2 In. 35.00
Bits Of The Old South, Plate, Tobacco Field, Multicolored, 8 1/2 In. 35.00
Brown Eyed Susan, Bowl, Casserole, Cover, Chicken Pie, Stick Handle, 4 In. 45.00
Brown Eyed Susan, Butter, Cover 50.00
Brown Eyed Susan, Teapot 80.00
Casual California, Pitcher, Lime Green, 2 Qt., 11 In. 70.00
Frontier Days, Ashtray, 5 1/2 In. 50.00
Frontier Days, Casserole, Cover, Chicken Pie, Stick Handle, 4 In. 50.00
Fruitdale, Platter, 14 In. 20.00
Gingham, Coffeepot 35.00
Gingham, Flowerpot, Saucer, 3 In. 50.00
Gingham, Mixing Bowl, 7 In. 44.00
Gingham, Mixing Bowl, 8 In. 47.00
Gingham, Pitcher, 1/2 Pt., 5 In. 80.00
Gingham, Soup, Dish, Rim, 8 1/2 In. 12.00
Homespun, Bowl, Fruit, 5 1/2 In. 8.00
Homespun, Carafe, Stopper 45.00
Homespun, Chop Plate, 12 In. 30.00
Homespun, Flowerpot 55.00

Homespun, Plate, Bread & Butter, 6 1/2 In. 6.00
Linda, Chop Plate, 17 In. 150.00
Linda, Teapot 125.00
Organdie, Bowl, Vegetable, 9 In. 28.00
Organdie, Carafe, Stopper 45.00
Organdie, Cup & Saucer 11.00
Organdie, Sugar & Creamer 18.00
Raffia, Chop Plate, 13 In. 12.00
Raffia, Pitcher, Pt. 35.00
Raffia, Pitcher, Qt. 50.00
Raffia, Plate, Salad, 7 1/2 In. 5.00
Raffia, Platter, Oval, 11 In. 15.00
Raffia, Salt & Pepper 11.00
Raffia, Sauceboat 23.00
Raffia, Soup, Dish, 8 In. 8.00
Raffia, Sugar, Cover 10.00
Souvenir, Coaster, Alaska, Siberian Husky, Maroon, 4 1/4 In. 29.00
Souvenir, Plate, 48th National Convention Of Postmasters, 1952 .... 29.00
Souvenir, Plate, Alamo, San Antonio Landmarks, Maroon, 10 1/2 In. 43.00
Souvenir, Plate, Arkansas, Brown, 1943, 10 1/2 In. 35.00
Souvenir, Plate, Arkansaw Traveler, Blue, 1936, 10 1/2 In. 35.00
Souvenir, Plate, Black Hills Passion Play, Multicolored, 1953, 10 1/2 In. 35.00
Souvenir, Plate, Cedar Rapids, Iowa, Brown, 10 1/2 In. 27.00
Souvenir, Plate, Colorful San Francisco, Brown, 10 1/2 In. 20.00
Souvenir, Plate, Corpus Christi, Blue, 10 1/2 In. 20.00
Souvenir, Plate, Franciscan Monastery, Transfer, Blue Underglaze 20.00
Souvenir, Plate, Knott's Berry Farm, Gold Rush, Transfer, Blue Underglaze, 1949 ...... 25.00
Souvenir, Plate, Letchworth State Park, Brown, 10 1/2 In. 25.00
Souvenir, Plate, MacArthur, World War II Scenes, Blue, White, 1942, 11 In. 40.00
Souvenir, Plate, Missouri, Maroon, Ultra, 10 1/2 In. 29.00
Souvenir, Plate, Pennsylvania Turnpike, Howard Johnson's, 1940-1950 .... 35.00
Souvenir, Plate, Santa Fe, New Mexico, Pie Crust Rim, Maroon 35.00
Souvenir, Plate, Sonoma, Calif., Valley Of The Moon, Maroon, Ultra, 10 1/2 In. 29.00
Souvenir, Plate, Statue Of Liberty, 4 Images, Blue, 10 1/2 In. 35.00
Souvenir, Plate, Texas State, Cattle Brand Border, Maroon, 10 1/2 In. 45.00
Souvenir, Plate, Texas, Blue, Flat, 10 1/2 In. 20.00
Souvenir, Plate, Tuscumbia, Ala., Maroon, 10 1/2 In. 40.00
Souvenir, Plate, University Of Oregon, Maroon, Ultra, 10 1/2 In. 29.00
Souvenir, Plate, Wyckoff's, Stroudsburg, Pa., Maroon, 10 1/2 In. 30.00
Tam O'Shanter, Cup 10.00
Tam O'Shanter, Flowerpot, 5 In. 55.00
Tam O'Shanter, Pitcher, Qt. 60.00
Tam O'Shanter, Platter, Oval, 13 In. 25.00
Tickled Pink, Chop Plate, 13 In. 30.00
Tweed, Chop Plate, 14 In. 50.00
Tweed, Pitcher, 1/2 Pt., 5 In. 80.00

VERRE DE SOIE glass was first made by Frederick Carder at the
Steuben Glass Works from about 1905 to 1930. It is an iridescent glass
of soft white or very, very pale green. The name means *glass of silk*,
and it does resemble silk. Other factories have made verre de soie, and
some of the English examples were made of different colors. Verre de
soie is an art glass and is not related to the iridescent, pressed, white
carnival glass mistakenly called by its name. Related pieces may be
found in the Steuben category.

Bowl, Rolled Rim, Raised, Round Pedestal, Molded Supports, c.1914, 5 x 8 In. 400.00
Perfume Bottle, Stopper, Steuben, 3 1/2 In. 315.00
Rose Bowl, Iridescent, Bulbous, Ruffled Top, Steuben, 3 1/2 x 4 In. 290.00
Vase, Iridescent, Cobalt Sprays, Textured Base, Boda 4909, Vallien, Sweden, 3 In. 288.00
Vase, Ruffled Rim, 10 In. 375.00
Vase, Turquoise Ring, Prunts, Threading, Ruffled Rim, Iron Holder, Vines, 12 In. 175.00
Vase, Wheel-Cut Medallions, Garlands, 7 3/4 In. 140.00

VIENNA, see Beehive category.

VILLEROY & BOCH Pottery of Mettlach was founded in 1836. The firm made many types of wares, including the famous Mettlach steins. Collectors can be confused because although Villeroy & Boch made most of its pieces in the city of Mettlach, Germany, they also had factories in other locations. The dating code impressed on the bottom of most pieces makes it possible to determine the age of the piece. Additional items, including steins and earthenware pieces marked with the famous castle mark or the word *Mettlach,* may be found in the Mettlach category.

Ashtray, Monkey Holding Basket, Glass Eyes, 5 1/2 In.	105.00
Beaker, Man Bowling, Dresden Factory, PUG, 1/4 Liter	115.00
Beaker, Woman Playing Tennis, Dresden Factory, PUG, 1/4 Liter	430.00
Chop Plate, Gaudy, Flowers, Red, Blue, Yellow, Transfer Label, Germany, 12 In.	29.00
Dinner Service, Sienna, Platter, Serving Bowl, Salad Bowl, 63 Piece	430.00
Jardiniere, Cinderella's Pumpkin Coach, Marked, c.1880, 12 In.	2645.00
Paperweight, Dwarf Lying On Stomach, Majolica, Dresden, 3 x 6 1/2 In.	240.00
Plaque, Patriotic, Shield, Eagle, Flag, Laurel, Statue Of Liberty, 13 1/4 x 11 In.	1035.00
Plaque, Sessionist Design, Oval, 17 1/2 In.	290.00
Punch Bowl, Transferware, Flower Decoration, Medallion, 10 x 19 x 18 In.	415.00
Tile, Frieze, Carp Swimming, Lotus Blossom, Stamped Mark, 6 x 11 In., 2 Piece	490.00
Tile, Stylized Blossoms, Ivory, Amber, Red, Raised Outline, Green Leaves, 5 3/4 In.	185.00
Vase, Red Luster Glaze, Mottled, Black Streaks, Globular, Flat Mouth, 10 In.	425.00

VOLKMAR pottery was made by Charles Volkmar of New York from 1879 to about 1911. He was associated with several firms, including the Volkmar Ceramic Company, Volkmar and Cory, and Charles Volkmar and Son. Volkmar had been a painter, and his designs often look like oil paintings drawn on pottery.

Charger, Native American Brave, Large Feathers, Underglaze Painted, Stamped, 14 In.	1495.00
Charger, Native American Chief, Stilt Pulls, Underglaze Painted, Stamped, 14 In.	1035.00
Vase, Wide, Flattened, Tapered Neck, Green, Yellow, Brown High Glaze, 12 x 7 1/2 In.	430.00

WADE pottery is made by the Wade Group of Potteries started in 1810 near Burslem, England. Several potteries merged to become George Wade & Son, Ltd. early in the twentieth century, and other potteries have been added through the years. The best-known Wade pieces are the small figurines given away with Red Rose Tea and other promotional items. The Disney figures are listed in this book in the Disneyana category.

Bowl, Bramble, 7 In.	25.00
Building, Post Office, No. 12, Whimsey-On-Why, 1 1/2 x 1 1/2 x 7/8 In.	22.00
Figurine, Baa Baa Black Sheep, Nursery Rhyme	30.00
Figurine, Cat & The Fiddle, Nursery Rhyme	36.00
Figurine, Gingerbread Man, Nursery Rhyme	.40.00 to 65.00
Figurine, Mary, Lamb, Nursery Rhyme, 3 In.	45.00
Figurine, Puss In Boots, Nursery Rhyme	30.00
Jug, Cream, Fruit, White Ground, 5 In.	24.00
Napkin Ring, Chintz Thistle, 2 3/4 x 2 1/4 In.	18.00
Napkin Ring, Sweetpea, 2 3/4 x 2 1/4 In.	15.00
Plate, Child's, Quack-Quacks, Nursery Ware, 6 1/2 In.	68.00
Plate, Dinner, Meadow, Scalloped Rim, 10 3/4 In.	20.00
Stag Hotel, No. 15, Whimsey-On-Why, 1 7/8 x 2 1/2 In.	28.00

WALL POCKETS were popular in the 1930s. They were made by many American and European factories. Glass, pottery, porcelain, majolica, chalkware, and metal wall pockets can be found in many fanciful shops.

Cone Shape, Embossed Parrot, Blue & Yellow, Majolica, 6 x 3 1/2 In.	50.00
Cone Shape, Green Luster Glaze, Hand Painted Bird Of Paradise, 9 In.	50.00
Cone Shape, Painted Flowers, Tin Glaze, France, c.1920, 12 x 5 In.	250.00
Cuckoo Clock, Bird Sticking Head Out, Green Leaves, Japan, 5 x 3 In.	35.00
Cup & Saucer, Ivory Glaze, Embossed & Painted Fruit On Cup, 8 In.	35.00
Dustpan, Ivory Glaze, Embossed Orange, Painted Word California, 8 x 8 In.	25.00
Elephant, Blue Luster Glaze, Red & Green Trim, Art Deco, Japan, 7 x 4 1/4 In.	60.00

Flying Duck On Cornucopia, Purple & Brown, c.1948, 7 x 5 1/2 In. 50.00
Girl In Tulip, Pink & Green, Gold Trim, Marked, HB, 7 In. 35.00
Heart Shape, Brass, England, 18th Century, Pair 250.00
Love Birds, Atop Nest With Ribbon, Morton, 4 x 4 In. 15.00
Parrot, Wings Spread, Purple, Green, Yellow, 8 x 4 In. 40.00
Scoop Shape, Pink, 7 1/2 In. 35.00
Woman's Profile, Asian, Red & Black Trim, Art Deco, 8 1/2 x 5 3/4 In. 45.00

WALLACE NUTTING photographs are listed under Print, Nutting. His
reproduction furniture is listed under Furniture.

WALRATH was a potter who worked in New York City; Rochester, New
York; and at the Newcomb Pottery in New Orleans, Louisiana. Frederick
Walrath died in 1920. Pieces listed here are from his Rochester period.

Walrath
Pottery

Candlestick, 3-Light, Putto On Column, Green Matte Glaze, 12 In. 690.00
Vase, Arts & Crafts Design, Brown, Mottled Green Ground, Tapered, 5 In. 1765.00

WALT DISNEY, see Disneyana category.

WALTER, see A. Walter category.

WARWICK china was made in Wheeling, West Virginia, in a pottery
working from 1887 to 1951. Many pieces were made with hand
painted or decal decorations. The most familiar Warwick has a shaded
brown background. The name *Warwick* is part of the mark and sometimes the mysterious word *IOGA* is also included.

IOGA

Ashtray, White, Gold Trim, Warwick China Script, Knight's Helmet In Black, 1940s 75.00
Creamer, White, 2 Green Bands, Sumter Hospital Logo, 3 In. 22.00
Cup, Demitasse, Alcoa, 1946, 2 1/2 In. 14.00
Cup & Saucer, Tan, Red, Santone Finish 25.00
Cup & Saucer, White, Crestwood Pattern 25.00
Cup & Saucer, White, Dakota Pattern 20.00
Cup & Saucer, White, Duckwall's Logo 40.00
Cup & Saucer, White, St. Gregory's Logo 22.00
Dish, Fern, Pansy Design, Flow Blue Ground, Gold Trim, Marked, 1896, 4 3/4 In. 475.00
Ewer, Brown, Tan & Cream, Gold Rim, Pink Poppies, Knight's Helmet In Green, 1905 .. 70.00
Humidor, Cover, Brown & Tan, Elk's Head & Clock, Cigars, c.1903, 6 1/2 In. 295.00
Mug, Elk Head & BPOE Emblem 45.00
Mug, White, Green Drape, Security Benefit Assoc. Emblem, 3 1/2 In. 15.00
Mustard, Cover, White, Duckwall's Logo 28.00
Pitcher, Lemonade Shape, Pink Ground, Christy Girl, Purple Flowers, 9 In. 265.00
Pitcher, Tobio No. 2, Overall White Ground, Bird Design, 7 In. 185.00
Plate, White, 2 Green Bands, 4 H Camp, 1944, 7 1/4 In. 20.00
Plate, White, Black & Red Bands, Masonic Temple Of Austin Emblem 18.00
Plate, White, Compliments Of Dine Furniture Company 40.00
Plate, White, The Washington Duke, 10 1/4 In. 35.00
Platter, White, Gold Band, Railroad Symbol, Knight's Helmet In Green, 1938, 8 In. 125.00
Platter, White, Maroon Band, Wentworth Military Academy Crest, 1930s, 15 In. 25.00
Sugar, White, 2 Green Bands, Sumter Hospital Logo, 3 3/4 In. 25.00
Tankard Set, Turquoise & Salmon, Shriner Emblem, Knight's Helmet, 1909 .... 925.00
Teapot, Covered, Gibson Girl, Turquoise & Pink, 1910, 7 1/2 In. 425.00
Vase, Bouquet, Gypsy Girl, Red Dress & Headscarf, 1908, 10 In. 240.00
Vase, Carnation, Brown Shaded To Brown Ground, Flowers, 9 In. 200.00
Vase, Carol, Green Shaded To Green Ground, Red Roses, 8 In. 255.00
Vase, Chicago, Brown Shaded To Brown Ground, Red & Green Flowers, 8 In. 300.00
Vase, Clytie, Red Ground, Poinsettias, 6 1/2 In. 210.00
Vase, Dainty, Brown Shaded To Brown Ground, Flowers, 4 1/2 In. 145.00
Vase, Den, Brown Shaded To Brown, Pinecones, 6 1/2 In. 325.00
Vase, Duchess, Brown Shaded To Brown Ground, Flowers, 8 In. 155.00
Vase, Duchess, White Ground, Birds, 8 In. 185.00
Vase, Louise, Brown Shaded To Brown Ground, Roses, 9 1/2 In. 250.00
Vase, Penn, Brown Shaded To Brown Ground, Acorns, 9 1/2 In. 195.00
Vase, Thelma, Pink, Gibson Girl Decal, 1909, 9 1/2 In. 245.00
Vase, Victoria, White, Gold Rim, Herons, 1909, 8 1/4 In. 190.00
Vase, Violet, Brown Shaded, Tan Ground, 4 In. 110.00

WATCH pockets held the pocket watch that was important in Victorian times because it was not until World War I that the wristwatch was used. All types of watches are collected: silver, gold, or plated. Watches are arranged by company name or by style. Wristwatches are a separate category.

A. Lunser, Stopwatch, German Military Officer's, Field Case	220.00
Agassiz, Tiffany & Co., 18K Yellow Gold, 17 Jewel, Pocket, 1 3/4 x 2 1/4 In.	560.00
Aurora, Guild, Dueber Silverine Case	275.00
Buchet, Hunting Case, 18K Gold, Flower Medallions, No. 19273, Swiss, c.1860, Pocket .	205.00
C.H. Meylan, Hunting Case, Woman's, 18K Gold, Enamel, c.1899, Size 0	600.00
Cartier, 18K Gold, Open Face, Model 88537, European Watch & Clock	1410.00
Champion, State Of Vermont Seal Dial, Nickel Silver Case	440.00
Chas. A. Gaudette, Open Face, Gold Rope Twist Chain, Intaglio Fob, Pocket, 12 3/4 In. ..	440.00
Columbus, Hunting Case, Silveroid, Northstar, No. 245561, Size 18, Pocket	135.00
Dohaie & Co., Open Face, 1/4 Hour Repeater, Calendar, Swing Out, 18K Case, 1800	300.00
E. Howard, Hunting Case, White Enamel Dial, 18K Gold, Boston, c.1880	1495.00
E. Howard, Monogram, Scalloped Edge, Porcelain Dial, 14K Gold, 1886, Pocket	1765.00
E. Howard, Open Face, 14K Gold, Mahogany Box, Series 7, 1908 Model, Size 12	255.00
E. Howard, Open Face, Indian Teepee On Dial, Yellow Gold Fill Case	250.00
E. Howard, Open Face, O'Hara Dial, Crescent, Yellow Gold Fill Case	99.00
E. Howard Bros., Open Face, Model 1, Coin Silver Case	195.00
Edgemere, Open Face, Silveroid Case, No. 3031554, Size 18, Pocket	45.00
Elgin, 14K Gold, Hunting Case, Flowers, Monogram, No. 8240771, Size 6, Pocket	115.00
Elgin, 15 Jewel, Engraved Case, Flowers, Cartouche, 14K Yellow Gold, c.1904, Pocket ..	330.00
Elgin, 18K Gold, Hunting Case, Wreath, Medallion, No. 1454801, c.1884, Size 6, Pocket .	146.00
Elgin, Father Time, US Flag, Plane, Metal Case, Model 15, No. 23385627, Size 16, Pocket	225.00
Elgin, Gold, No. 6866227, Pendant	56.00
Elgin, High Wheel Bicycle, Signed, B.W. Raymond	225.00
Elgin, Hunting Case, 15 Jewel, 3-Color Gold Design, Woman's	300.00
Elgin, Hunting Case, Gold Filled Box Case, No. 2490185, Size 18, Pocket	225.00
Elgin, Hunting Case, Model 1, Engraved Stag, Yellow Gold Fill	305.00
Elgin, Hunting Case, No. 6301516, Gold Filled Chain	68.00
Elgin, Lapel, Woman's, Presentation, Lever Set, Stem Wound, 14K Scalloped Case, c.1886	250.00
Elgin, Lord, 14K, Yellow Gold Fill Case, Box, Papers	165.00
Elgin, Lord, No. 543, Open Face, Chevrolet Presentation, 14K Gold	140.00
Elgin, Open Face, 14K Gold, 17 Jewel, Inside Cover Initialed, Size 16, Pocket	145.00
Elgin, Open Face, Chevrolet Logo On Dial, Yellow Gold Fill, Shaped Case	220.00
Elgin, Open Face, Model 7, Green Enamel, Engine Turned Dial, Dueber Special	250.00
Elgin, Open Face, Multicolored Dial, Star Scepter, Yellow Gold Fill	330.00
Ernest Duval, Hunting Case, 18K Gold, 2 Key Wind Holes, Geneva	575.00
Eska, 20 Dollar Gold Coin, Manual Wind, 18K Gold, c.1960, Pocket	750.00
Georges Roulet Movement, Hunting Case, 14K Gold, Engraved Edges, Box, Size 8	500.00
Hamilton, 21 Jewel, 5 Positions, Lever Set, No. 992, 10K Gold Plate, Illinois Case	250.00
Hamilton, Masonic Dial, Pendant Set, No. 968, 10K Yellow Gold	415.00
Hamilton, Open Face, Model 1, Coil Silver	275.00
Hamilton, Open Face, No. 921, 14K Gold, Rex Fob, 5 Positions	165.00
Hamilton, Open Face, No. 926, Rear Display Crystal	305.00
Hamilton, Railroad, 14K Bicolor Gold, Elk Design, Pocket	2160.00
Hamilton, Railroad, 14K Gold Filled Case, No. 936, No. 973405, Size 18, Pocket	225.00
Hamilton, Railroad, Open Face, No. 940, No. 160253, Size 18, Pocket	250.00
Hamilton, Railway Special, Open Face, Gold Filled, Model 11, No. 992B, Pocket	340.00
Hampden, Dueber Series, 5 Positions, Yellow Gold Fill	210.00
Hampden, John Hancock Series IV, Open Face, Locomotive, Tender On Dial, Nickel	190.00
Hampden, Open Face, Railway, Yellow Gold Fill Case	120.00
Heuer, Gold, Open Face, Moon Phase, Chain, Oval Disc, Documents, Box, 1 3/4 In.	350.00
Huguenin, Pendant, Black Enamel, Key Wind, 18K Gold	290.00
Humbert, Hunting Case, Sterling, No. 30747, Size 18, Pocket	68.00
Illinois, Burlington, Pillow Style, Yellow Gold Fill, 14K Gold Case	100.00
Illinois, Hunting Case, Gold Filled, Santa Fe Special, Railroad Grade, Pocket	450.00
Illinois, Open Face, Model 1, Wadsworth Gold Filled Case, Size 12, Pocket	50.00
Ingersoll, Waterbury Bee Movement, Back Wind, Brass Plated, Tin Case, 1893	495.00
Lapel, 18K Gold, 8 Diamonds, Enameled Woman's Profile, Swiss, c.1896, 3 x 1 1/2 In. ..	1495.00
Longines, Hunting Case, 14K Gold, Black Arabic Numerals, Blue Hands, 17 Jewel, 1920 .	690.00

Longines, Manual Wind, 14K Gold, c.1925 .... 1725.00
Montauk, Hunting Case, Multicolored Dial, Yellow Gold Fill 130.00
Observature, Hunting Case, Duplex Captina's, 3 Dials, Black Enamel On Silver, Swiss .. 358.00
Omega, Lapel, De Ville, Enamel, Manual Wind, Silver, Swiss, c.1960 .... 175.00
Pendant, Ball Shape, Enameled, Green, Swiss 140.00
Pendant, Diamond, Ruby, Rose Cut, Open Face, Enamel Dial, Roman Numerals 1765.00
Pendent, Art Deco, Enamel, Diamond, Wind, 14K Gold, c.1920 .... 865.00
Rockford, Hunting Case, Argentine Silver, Jeweled, No. 7949, Size 18, Pocket 215.00
Rockford, Hunting Case, Model 8, Yellow Gold Fill 90.00
Rockford, Swing Out Case, Gold Inlay, Wood Fired Engine 100.00
Samuel Curtis, Roxbury, No. 418, Original No. 101 Case, Anchor & Eagle Hallmark 6100.00
Sandoz, Hunting Case, 15 Jewel, Key Wind, Gold Filled, Swiss, Size 16, Pocket 50.00
Seth Thomas, Hunting Case, Model 2, Yellow Gold Fill 255.00
Seth Thomas, Swing Out, Yellow Gold Fill Case 175.00
Sloan, Alarm, Brass Case, White Face, Japan Movement, 2 1/2 In. 60.00
South Bend, Studebaker, Double Roller, Star, 10K Yellow Gold Fill Case 215.00
Tiffany & Co., Hunting Case, 18K Gold, Enamel Dial, Monogram, Triple Signed 415.00
Tobias, George Washington, Rose, Patent Lever, No. 75307, Key, Liverpool 1500.00
Tobias, Open Face, Flowers, 18K Gold, No. 173080, Liverpool, England, Pocket 96.00
Tortoiseshell Case, Hinged Fusee Movement, White Enamel Dial, 2 x 2 x 1 In. 275.00
Trenton, Open Face Silveroid Case, Elk, Model 1, Size 18, Pocket 135.00
Vacheron & Constantin, Woman's, Enamel Dial, 18K Gold, Swiss Movement 880.00
Waltham, Demi-Hunting Case, Slim, 14K Gold, Swing Out Movement, 1 3/4 In., Pocket . 60.00
Waltham, Gold Plate, Hunting Case, 14K Gold Chain, Garnet 255.00
Waltham, Hunting Case, 14K Gold, Jeweled Nickel Movement, Size 6 .... 205.00
Waltham, Hunting Case, 14K Gold, Movement No. 7169222 .... 169.00
Waltham, Hunting Case, 18K Gold, Size 6, Pocket 380.00
Waltham, Hunting Case, Arabic Numerals, Engraved, Diamond Crescent, Star, Size 6 ... 205.00
Waltham, Hunting Case, Coin Silver, Model 1883, No. 5851313, Size 18, Pocket 95.00
Waltham, Hunting Case, Enamel Dial, Nickel Movement, 14K Gold, 2 In. 320.00
Waltham, Hunting Case, Giant, White Enamel Dial, Size 16 1/2, Pocket 85.00
Waltham, Hunting Case, Royal, Gilt, Enamel Dial, Yellow Gold Fill, Box 300.00
Waltham, Hunting Case, Shell Engraving, Model 88, Gold Filled, c.1893 .... 56.00
Waltham, Hunting Case, Tricolor Gold, No. 5608816, Engraved, Mary E. Baker, 1893 ... 225.00
Waltham, Hunting Case, Vest Chain, 9K Gold, Monogram Fob, c.1928, 2 x 16 1/2 In. ... 259.00
Waltham, Model 77, Wm. Ellery, 11 Jewel, Initials, c.1883 .... 195.00
Waltham, Open Face, 14K Gold, 17 Jewel, Monogram, Engraved, c.1907 .... 295.00
Waltham, Open Face, 14K Gold, 19 Jewel, Colonial Case, c.1916, Size 12, Pocket 140.00
Waltham, Open Face, 14K Gold, Presentation Engraving, Size 16, Pocket 169.00
Waltham, Open Face, Coil Silver Case 90.00
Waltham, Open Face, Ellery, Sterling, Elk Head, Model 1879, No. 2085696, Size 18 ....
Waltham, Open Face, Gold Filled, No. 13360098, Chain, Mesh Fob, Pocket 85.00
Waltham, Open Face, Non Magnetic, Peoria Movement, Swing Out, Coil Silver Case ... 95.00
Waltham, White Enamel Dial, Roman Numerals, Chain, 17 Jewel, Engraved, 14K Gold .. 1998.00
Waltham, White Enamel Dial, Roman Numerals, Chain, Pansies, 14K Gold, 27 In. 470.00
Waltham, White Enamel Dial, Roman Numerals, Rose Gold Case, 15 Jewel, Size 6 ..... 499.00
Waltham, Woman's, Gold Filigree, Heart Slide, Opal, 24 In. Chain, Pocket, 1 3/8 In. 70.00
Welch, E.N., Open Face, Mascot, Back Wind & Set, Plated Brass Case, 1891 .... 105.00 ⟍

WATCH FOBS were worn on watch chains. They were popular during
Victorian times and after. Many styles, especially advertising designs,
are still made today.

Airedale Terrier In Horseshoe, Crystal, Link Chain, 14K Gold Mount 470.00
National Sportsman's, Raised Deer, Fishing Rods, Leather Belt, 1 1/2 In. 28.00
Putti On Dolphin, 14K Gold, Carnelian, Late 1800s, 1 3/4 x 1 1/4 In. 1955.00
Savage Automatic Pistol 90.00

WATERFORD type glass resembles the famous glass made from 1783 to
1851 in the Waterford Glass Works in Ireland. It is a clear glass that
was often decorated by cutting. Modern glass is being made again in
Waterford, Ireland, and is marketed under the name *Waterford.*

Biscuit Jar, Cut Decoration, 4 3/4 x 7 In. 175.00
Candlestick, Round Base, Signed, 8 In., Pair 60.00

Clock, Shelf, 2 7/8 In. 86.00
Lamp, Vase, Diamond Point, Paneled Neck, Urn Shape, Square Plinth Base, 18 In. 144.00
Sherbet, Diamond Crosshatch Band, 3 1/2 In., 6 Piece 90.00
Vase, Diamond, Fan & Zipper, Cut Crystal, 12 In. 230.00

WATT family members bought the Globe pottery of Crooksville, Ohio, in 1922. They made pottery mixing bowls and tableware of the type made by Globe. In 1935 they changed the production and made the pieces with the freehand decorations that are popular with collectors today. Apple, Starflower, Rooster, Tulip, and Autumn Foliage are the best-known patterns. Pansy, also called Rio Rose, was the earliest pattern. Apple, the most popular pattern, can be dated from the leaves. Originally, the apples had three leaves; after 1958 two leaves were used. The plant closed in 1965. For more information, see *Kovels' Depression Glass & Dinnerware Price List.*

Apple, Baker, Cover, 2-Leaf, No. 67, 8 1/4 x 3 1/2 In. 65.00
Apple, Baker, Open, 2-Leaf, No. 67, 8 1/4 x 3 1/2 In. 45.00
Apple, Baker, Open, No. 96, 8 1/2 x 2 3/4 In. ....55.00 to 95.00
Apple, Baker, Ribbed, Adams Feed & Hatchery, Storm Lake, Iowa, No. 600, 7 3/4 In. ... 70.00
Apple, Bean Pot, No. 76, 2 1/2 Qt., 6 1/2 In. ....92.00 to 125.00
Apple, Bowl, Salad, 2-Leaf, No. 55, 11 3/4 x 5 In. 75.00
Apple, Bowl, Salad, Individual, No. 23, 5 5/8 x 1 1/2 In. 160.00
Apple, Bowl, Salad, Individual, No. 74, 5 1/2 x 2 In. 30.00
Apple, Bowl, Salad, No. 73, 9 1/2 x 4 In. 30.00
Apple, Bowl, Salad, Olson Grain Co. Wilmont, Minn, No. 73, 9 1/2 x 4 In. 85.00
Apple, Bowl, Salad, Pelican Rapids, Minn., No. 73, 9 1/2 x 4 In. 65.00
Apple, Bowl, Spaghetti, No. 24, 11 x 2 1/2 In. 165.00
Apple, Bowl, Spaghetti, No. 25, 15 x 3 1/2 In. 165.00
Apple, Bowl, Spaghetti, No. 39, 13 x 3 1/4 In. ....80.00 to 100.00
Apple, Casserole, Cover, 2-Leaf, Handle, No. 18, 5 In. 135.00
Apple, Casserole, Cover, Ribbed, No. 600, 7 3/4 x 5 1/4 In. 80.00
Apple, Casserole, Cover, Tab Handle, No. 18, 5 In. ....115.00 to 155.00
Apple, Chop Plate, No. 49, 12 In. 245.00
Apple, Creamer, 2-Leaf, No. 62, 1/2 Pt., 4 1/4 In. ....125.00 to 195.00
Apple, Creamer, Fitzs Hatchery & Produce, Ivanhoe, Minn., No. 62, 1/2 Pt., 4 1/4 In. 85.00
Apple, Creamer, Just A Little Thank You Winnebago Co-Op Creamery, No. 62, 1/2 Pt., 4 In. 95.00
Apple, Creamer, Kiel Hardware 1957 Pease, Minn., No. 62, 1/2 Pt., 4 1/4 In. 185.00
Apple, Creamer, Lake Benton Hatchery Dutch & Chuck Phone 2451, No. 62, 1/2 Pt., 4 In. 95.00
Apple, Creamer, No. 62, 1/2 Pt., 4 1/4 In. 65.00
Apple, Creamer, Onida Electric Paul-Bob-Ethel-Gladys, No. 62, 1/2 Pt., 4 1/4 In. 65.00
Apple, Creamer, Open, No. 62, 1/2 Pt., 4 1/4 In. 1300.00
Apple, Creamer, Ryan Grain & Feed Bird Island, No. 62, 1/2 Pt, 4 1/4 In. 85.00
Apple, Creamer, Schori & Kuster Lbr. Co. Elgin, Iowa, No. 62, 1/2 Pt., 4 1/4 In. 85.00
Apple, Ice Bucket, Cover, No. 59, 7 1/2 x 7 In. 165.00
Apple, Ice Bucket, No. 59, 7 1/2 In. 55.00
Apple, Mixing Bowl, 2-Leaf, No. 6, 6 In. 40.00
Apple, Mixing Bowl, A Thank You From Kinnards Dairy Estherville, Iowa, No. 7, 7 In. .. 46.00
Apple, Mixing Bowl, No. 7, 7 In. 30.00
Apple, Mixing Bowl, Wide Lip, Gilman, Minn., No. 9, 9 In. 70.00
Apple, Mug, Hourglass, No. 121, 3 x 3 3/4 In. 150.00
Apple, Nappy, Ribbed, No. 07, 7 1/4 x 3 3/4 In. 40.00
Apple, Pie Plate, Buffalo Lake, Minn., No. 33, 9 1/4 In. 60.00
Apple, Pie Plate, Compliments Of Murdock Farmers Elev., No. 33, 9 1/4 In. 80.00
Apple, Pie Plate, Elroy Co-Op Dairy, Elroy, Wisc., No. 33, 9 1/4 In. 100.00
Apple, Pie Plate, H.J. Schult Son, Sumner, Iowa, 9 In., 9 1/4 In. 140.00
Apple, Pie Plate, Haugen-Johnson Impl. Allis Chalmers Benson, Minn., No. 33, 9 1/4 In. .. 125.00
Apple, Pie Plate, Kingston Co-Op Dairy Ass'n & Feed Mill, No. 33, 9 1/4 In. 105.00
Apple, Pie Plate, No. 33, 9 1/4 In. 95.00
Apple, Pie Plate, Plaza Park State Bank Established 1910, St. Cloud, Minn., No. 33, 9 In. . 95.00
Apple, Pie Plate, Seasons Greetings Edinburg Farmers Elev. Co., No. 33, 9 1/4 In. 145.00
Apple, Pie Plate, Seasons Greetings Howard Lake, Minn., No. 33, 9 1/4 In. 70.00
Apple, Pitcher, 2-Leaf, No. 15, Pt., 5 1/4 In. 105.00
Apple, Pitcher, 2-Leaf, No. 16, 2 Pt., 6 1/2 In. 155.00

Apple, Pitcher, Baker Equip. Monticello, Minn, No. 15, Pt., 5 1/4 In. 85.00
Apple, Pitcher, Cokato Co-Op Creamery, No. 15, Pt., 5 1/4 In. 75.00
Apple, Pitcher, Dolly's Garage New Auburn, Minn., No. 15, Pt., 5 1/4 In. 85.00
Apple, Pitcher, Fred Sorenson Lory Brunberg, No. 15, Pt., 5 1/4 In. 55.00
Apple, Pitcher, Hector Elevator Co., Hector Minn., No. 15, 5 1/4 In. 69.00
Apple, Pitcher, Ice Lip, Flat Sides, No. 69, 8 In. 150.00
Apple, Pitcher, Ice Lip, No. 17, 5 Pt., 8 In. 205.00
Apple, Pitcher, Kiel Hardware, Pease, Minn. 1954, No. 15, Pt., 5 1/4 In. 125.00
Apple, Pitcher, Let Us Serve You Cockatoo Co-Op, Cokato, Minn., No. 15, Pt., 5 1/4 In. . 125.00
Apple, Pitcher, No. 15, Pt., 5 1/4 In. . . . . .55.00 to 75.00
Apple, Pitcher, No. 16, 2 Pt., 6 1/2 In. . . . . .80.00 to 110.00
Apple, Pitcher, No. 17, 5 Pt., 8 In. 190.00
Apple, Plate, Dinner, Coons Corner, Oxford, Jct., No. 29, 9 1/2 In. 600.00
Apple, Plate, Dinner, No. 29, 9 1/2 In. 500.00
Apple, Salt & Pepper, Hourglass, 2 1/4 x 4 3/4 In. 195.00
Apple, Shaker, Pepper, Barrel, No. 46, 2 1/2 x 4 In. 195.00
Apple, Sugar, Joe Miller Land O' Lakes, Janesville, Minn., No. 98 . . . . 175.00
Apple, Sugar, Kiel Hardware 1959, Pease, Minn, No. 98 . . . . 205.00
Arcs, Casserole, Cover, Brown & White Stripes, No. 8, 8 3/4 In. 35.00
Autumn Foliage, Casserole, Cover, No. 110, 8 1/2 In. 55.00
Autumn Foliage, Chop Plate, No. 31, 15 In. 65.00
Autumn Foliage, Cookie Jar, No. 503, 6 1/2 In. 155.00
Autumn Foliage, Electric Warmer, Cut Away, No. 133 . . . . 105.00
Autumn Foliage, Mug, Beer, Bulged Waist, No. 501, 2 3/4 x 4 1/2 In. 85.00
Autumn Foliage, Pitcher, No. 16, 2 Pt., 6 1/2 In. 95.00
Autumn Foliage, Shaker, Pepper, Hourglass, Raised P, No. 118, 2 1/4 x 4 3/4 In. 40.00
Brownstone, Bean Cup, Blue, No. 75, 8 Oz., 3 1/2 x 2 1/4 In. 15.00
Brownstone, Mug, Blue, Hourglass, No. 121, 3 x 3 3/4 In. 15.00
Brownstone, Nappy, Blue, Ribbed, No. 603, 5 3/4 x 2 1/2 In. 5.00
Butterfly, Pitcher, Ice Lip, No. 69, 8 In. 2000.00
Cabinart, Baking Dish, Cover, 6 1/2 In. 15.00
Cherry, Baker, Cover, No. 54, 8 1/4 x 3 1/4 In. 60.00
Cherry, Bowl, Salad, No. 55, 11 3/4 x 4 In. 90.00
Cherry, Chop Plate, No. 49, 12 In. 200.00
Cookie Jar, Policeman, Cover, White, Blue, Head Knob, 10 1/2 In. 619.00
Daisy, Bowl, Wide Lip, No. 7, 7 In. 35.00
Dogwood, Plate, Salad, 6 1/2 In. 95.00
Double Apple, Bowl, Salad, No. 73, 9 1/2 x 4 In. 90.00
Double Apple, Casserole, Cover, No. 96, 8 1/2 In. 120.00
Double Apple, Creamer, No. 62, 1/2 Pt., 4 1/4 In. 275.00
Double Apple, Nappy, Ribbed, No. 07, 7 1/4 x 3 3/4 In. 65.00
Dutch Tulip, Baker, Cover, No. 66, 7 1/4 x 3 1/2 In. 105.00
Dutch Tulip, Baker, Cover, No. 67, 8 1/4 x 3 1/2 In. 165.00
Dutch Tulip, Bowl, Salad, No. 73, 9 1/2 x 4 In. 145.00
Dutch Tulip, Canister, Coffee, Cover, No. 82, 5 In. 195.00
Dutch Tulip, Canister, Tea, Cover, No. 82, 5 In. 210.00
Dutch Tulip, Cheese Crock, Cover, No. 80, 8 1/2 x 8 In. 325.00
Dutch Tulip, Creamer, No. 62, 1/2 Pt., 4 1/4 In. 165.00
Dutch Tulip, Ice Bucket, Cover, No. 59, 7 1/2 x 7 In. 500.00
Dutch Tulip, Mixing Bowl, No. 64, 4 Pt., 7 1/2 x 4 3/4 In. 65.00
Dutch Tulip, Pitcher, No. 15, Pt., 5 1/4 In. 135.00
Dutch Tulip, Pitcher, No. 16, 2 Pt., 6 1/2 In. 185.00
Dutch Tulip, Pitcher, Refrigerator, Ice Lip, No. 69, 8 In. 425.00
Eagle, Bowl, Salad, No. 73, 9 1/2 x 4 In. 145.00
Esmond, Cookie Jar, Wood Cover, Pear, Apple, No. 34, 8 1/2 x 8 In. 50.00
Keg, Iced Tea, Cover, Base, Russet, 2 Gal. 22.50
Keg, Lacas Iced Tea, Brown, Cover 15.00
Keg, Lemonade, Cover, Yellow 35.00
Keg, Nestea Iced Tea, Aqua, No Cover 12.00
Kitch-N-Queen, Bowl, No. 6, 6 1/4 x 2 1/4 In. 15.00
Kitch-N-Queen, Mixing Bowl, Ribbed, No. 7, 7 In. 12.50
Kitch-N-Queen, Mixing Bowl, Ribbed, No. 9, 9 In. 15.00
Moonflower, Casserole, Cover, Green, No. 8, 8 3/4 x 4 1/2 In. 35.00

Moonflower, Casserole, Cover, Lug Handle, Green, No. 18, 5 In. 40.00
Morning Glory, Sugar & Creamer, No. 98, 3 1/2 x 4 1/4 In. 400.00
Orchard Ware, Greenbriar, Baker, Cover, No. 54, 8 1/4 x 3 1/4 In. 10.00
Orchard Ware, Greenbriar, Bowl, Salad, Individual, No. 52, 6 1/4 x 2 1/4 In. 5.00
Orchard Ware, Greenbriar, Tumbler, Slanted Sides, No. 56, 4 x 4 1/2 In. 15.00
Pansy, Berry Bowl, Bullseye, No. 22, 5 1/2 x 2 In. 50.00
Pansy, Bowl, Spaghetti, Cut-Leaf, No. 39, 13 x 3 1/4 In. 30.00
Pansy, Casserole, Cover, Crosshatch 175.00
Pansy, Casserole, Cover, Cut-Leaf, No. 18, 5 In. 25.00
Pansy, Chop Plate, Cut-Leaf, No. 31, 15 In. 50.00
Pansy, Chop Plate, No. 31, 15 In. 25.00
Pansy, Pie Plate, Bullseye, No. 33, 9 1/4 In. 185.00
Pansy, Pie Plate, Crosshatch, No. 33, 9 1/4 In. 150.00
Pansy, Pitcher, No. 15, Pt., 5 1/4 In. 185.00
Pansy, Plate, Luncheon, Cut-Leaf, No. 43, 8 3/4 In. 30.00
Pansy, Plate, Snack, Bullseye, No. 30, 11 1/2 In. 40.00
Pansy, Soup, Dish, Cut-Leaf, No. 44, 8 x 1 1/2 In. 15.00
Pansy, Soup, Dish, No. 44, 8 x 1 1/2 In. 45.00
Par-T-Que, Mug, Hourglass, No. 121, 3 x 3 3/4 In. 80.00
Par-T-Que, Pitcher, Ice Lip, No. 17, 5 Pt., 8 In. 70.00
Rio Rose, see Pansy
Rooster, Baker, Cover, No. 67, 8 1/4 x 3 1/2 In. . . . . .65.00 to 135.00
Rooster, Baker, No. 68, 5 1/4 x 5 In. 80.00
Rooster, Casserole, Cover, French Handle, No. 18, 5 In. 125.00
Rooster, Casserole, Cover, Handles, Round Knob, No. 18, 5 In. 135.00
Rooster, Creamer, Manannah Store, Grove City, Minn., No. 62, 4 1/4 In. 185.00
Rooster, Creamer, No. 62, 1/2 Pt., 4 1/4 In. 130.00
Rooster, Dutch Oven, Cover, No. 70, 9 1/2 x 7 1/4 In. 245.00
Rooster, Ice Bucket, No. 59, 7 1/2 x 5 3/4 In. 165.00
Rooster, Mixing Bowl, No. 63, 2 Pt., 6 1/2 x 4 1/4 In. 70.00
Rooster, Mixing Bowl, Tri-County Chickery, Cedar Mills, Minn., No. 8, 8 In. 65.00
Rooster, Pitcher, Compliments Of Rahs Produce, Waldorf, Minn., No. 15, Pt., 5 1/4 In. . . 105.00
Rooster, Pitcher, Lange's Grade A Dairy Products, No. 15, Pt., 5 1/4 In. 65.00
Rooster, Pitcher, No. 15, Pt., 5 1/4 In. 95.00
Rooster, Pitcher, No. 16, 2 Pt., 6 1/2 In. . . . . .115.00 to 125.00
Rooster, Pitcher, Refrigerator, Ice Lip, No. 69, 8 In. 300.00
Rooster, Shaker, Pepper, Barrel, No. 46, 2 1/2 x 4 In. 175.00
Silhouette, Bowl, Spaghetti, No. 39, 13 x 3 1/4 In. 20.00
Silhouette, Chop Plate, No. 31, 15 In. 45.00
Starflower, Baker, 4-Petal, Ribbed, Renville, Minn., No. 600, 7 3/4 In. 80.00
Starflower, Baker, Cover, No. 54, 8 1/4 x 3 1/4 In. . . . . .45.00 to 70.00
Starflower, Baker, Cover, No. 66, 7 1/4 x 3 1/2 In. 85.00
Starflower, Baker, Cover, No. 67, 8 1/4 x 3 1/2 In. 85.00
Starflower, Baker, No. 68, 5 1/4 x 4 In. 40.00
Starflower, Bowl, 4-Petal, No. 120, 5 x 2 In. 20.00
Starflower, Bowl, 4-Petal, Ribbed, No. 6, 6 1/4 x 2 1/4 In. 40.00
Starflower, Bowl, Inter-State Lumber Company, 9 x 4 1/2 In. 69.00
Starflower, Bowl, No. 4, 5 x 1 3/4 In. 35.00
Starflower, Bowl, No. 55, 11 3/4 x 4 In. 45.00
Starflower, Casserole, Cover, 2 Tab Handles, No. 18-N, 5 x 3 3/4 In. 60.00
Starflower, Chop Plate, No. 31, 15 In. 65.00
Starflower, Cookie Jar, No. 21, 7 x 6 In. 195.00
Starflower, Creamer, 1907-55 Farmers Co-Op Creamery, Milaca, No. 62, 1/2 Pt., 4 1/4 In. 145.00
Starflower, Mixing Bowl, No. 63, 2 Pt., 6 1/2 x 4 1/4 In. 35.00
Starflower, Mixing Bowl, Renville Co-Op Creamery, Renville, Minn., No 7, 7 In. 55.00
Starflower, Mug, 4-Petal, No. 501, 2 3/4 x 5 1/2 In. 55.00
Starflower, Nappy, 4-Petal, Ribbed, No. 06, 6 1/4 x 3 In. 50.00
Starflower, Pie Plate, 4-Petal, Renville, Minn., No. 33, 9 1/4 In. 115.00
Starflower, Pitcher, 4-Petal, Ice Lip, No. 17, 5 Pt., 8 In. 185.00
Starflower, Pitcher, 4-Petal, No. 15, Pt., 5 1/4 In. 75.00
Starflower, Pitcher, 4-Petal, No. 16, 2 Pt., 6 1/2 In. 85.00
Starflower, Pitcher, Christmas 1955 Figge-Nelson Annandale, Minn., No. 15, Pt., 5 1/4 In. 115.00
Starflower, Pitcher, Compliments Of Gibson Farm Supply, No. 15, Pt., 5 1/4 In. 75.00

Starflower, Pitcher, No. 15, Pt., 5 1/4 In. 80.00
Starflower, Pitcher, No. 16, 2 Pt., 6 1/2 In. 40.00
Starflower, Pitcher, No. 17, 5 Pt., 8 In. . . . . .70.00 to 86.00
Starflower, Salt & Pepper, Barrel, No. 45 & 46, 2 1/2 x 4 In., Pair 135.00
Starflower, Saltshaker, 4-Petal, Hourglass, Raised S, No. 117, 2 1/4 x 4 3/4 In. 50.00
Stoneware, Churn, Eagle, Wire Handles, 4 Gal. 95.00
Stoneware, Crock, Eagle, 2 Gal. 45.00
Stoneware, Jug, Eagle, 3 Gal. 30.00
Tear Drop, Bean Pot, No. 76, 2 1/2 Qt., 5 1/2 x 6 1/2 In. 50.00
Tear Drop, Bowl, Salad, Individual, No. 74, 5 1/2 x 2 In. . . . . 35.00.
Tear Drop, Bowl, Salad, No. 73, 9 1/2 x 4 In. 55.00
Tear Drop, Cheese Crock, No. 80, 8 1/2 x 8 In. 300.00
Tear Drop, Creamer, No. 62, 1/2 Pt., 4 1/4 In. 250.00
Tear Drop, Pitcher, No. 15, Pt., 5 1/4 In. 50.00
Tear Drop, Pitcher, No. 16, 2 Pt., 6 1/2 In. 125.00
Tear Drop, Saltshaker, Barrel, No. 45, 2 1/2 x 4 In. 75.00
Tulip, Baker, Cover, No. 600, 7 3/4 x 5 1/4 In. 80.00
Tulip, Bowl, Nappy, No. 602, 4 3/4 x 1 1/2 In. 165.00
Tulip, Bowl, Salad, No. 73, 9 1/2 x 4 In. 80.00
Tulip, Creamer, No. 62, 1/2 Pt., 4 1/4 In. . . . . .115.00 to 195.00
Tulip, Mixing Bowl, Deep, No. 65, 6 Pt., 9 x 5 In. 50.00
Tulip, Pitcher, Ice Lip, No. 17, 5 Pt., 8 In. 210.00
Tulip, Pitcher, No. 16, 2 Pt., 6 1/2 In. . . . . .125.00 to 140.00
Wavy, Planter, Green, No. 901, 6 1/4 x 7 In. 12.50
Wavy, Planter, White, No. 902, 7 1/4 x 7 In. 10.00

WAVE CREST glass is an opaque white glassware manufactured by the Pairpoint Manufacturing Company of New Bedford, Massachusetts, and some French factories. It was decorated by the C.F. Monroe Company of Meriden, Connecticut. The glass was painted in pastel colors and decorated with flowers. The name *Wave Crest* was used after 1898.

**WAVE CREST
WARE**

Biscuit Jar, Cream, Pink, Blue Flowers, Silver Plated Cover & Bail, 8 In. 225.00
Biscuit Jar, Egg Crate Mold, Flower Transfer, Metal Cover & Bail, 8 x 5 1/4 In. 175.00
Biscuit Jar, Egg Crate Mold, Pink Flowers, 8 In. 250.00
Biscuit Jar, Flowers, Paneled, Silver Plated Collar, Cover, Bail, 7 1/2 In. . . . . .115.00 to 175.00
Biscuit Jar, Frame Mold, Yellow Flowers, Silver Plated Cover & Bail, 8 In. 175.00
Biscuit Jar, Helmschmied Swirl, Flowers, Beading, Embossed Metal Cover, 7 3/4 In. 575.00
Biscuit Jar, Helmschmied Swirl, Flowers, Metal Hardware, 7 1/4 In. 430.00
Biscuit Jar, Pink Flowers, Concave, Scrolls, Silver Plated Collar, Cover, Bail, 7 1/2 In. . . . 200.00
Biscuit Jar, Pink Flowers, Square, Brass Cover, Bail, 9 In. 155.00
Biscuit Jar, Pink, White, Yellow Flowers, Oval, Silver Plated Cover, Bail, 7 1/2 In. 175.00
Biscuit Jar, Red, Yellow, Blue Flowers, Silver Plated Collar, Cover, Bail, 8 1/2 In. 175.00
Biscuit Jar, Rococo, Blue & Opal Body, Enameled Flowers, Putti, 5 1/2 x 7 In. 575.00
Blotter, Enameled Flowers, Brass Mounts, 2 3/4 x 5 1/4 In. 345.00
Box, Blue & White, Pink Flowers, Footed, Hinged Cover, Marked, 4 x 3 In. 250.00
Box, Blue Flowers, White Ground, Hinged Cover, 2 1/2 x 3 In. 130.00
Box, Blue, White, Pink Flowers, Baroque Shell, Hinged Cover, Marked, 3 x 4 1/4 In. 250.00
Box, Collars, Rococo, Chrysanthemums, 9 x 6 In. 835.00
Box, Cover, African Violets, Footed, Gilt Metal, Satin Lining, 4 1/2 In. 175.00
Box, Cover, Flowers, Green Ground, Footed, c.1900, 5 x 7 In. 110.00
Box, Cover, Helmschmied Swirl, Flowers, 7 In. Diameter 490.00
Box, Cream, Helmschmied Swirl, Pink & White Flowers, Hinged Cover, 3 x 4 1/2 In. 150.00
Box, Cream, Pink Flowers, Swirl Mold, Hinged Cover, 4 1/2 x 6 In. 325.00
Box, Egg Crate Mold, Flowers, Metal Hardware, 5 1/2 x 3 1/4 x 3 In. 230.00
Box, Embossed Ribbon Border, Mums, Hinged Cover, Marked, 3 1/2 x 7 1/2 In. 950.00
Box, Glove, Blue, White, Pink Flowers, Marked, 3 1/2 x 8 1/2 In. 900.00
Box, Glove, Cover, Cobalt Blue, Chrysanthemums, Blown Out, 9 3/4 x 5 1/2 In. 2590.00
Box, Glove, Rococo Lattice, Flowers, Gilt Metal Feet, Marked, 5 1/2 x 9 1/2 In. 275.00
Box, Handkerchief, Blue, Flowers, Footed, 5 1/2 x 10 In. 1680.00
Box, Helmschmied Swirl, Flowers, Metal Hardware, 6 x 4 1/2 In. 575.00
Box, Helmschmied Swirl, Flowers, Metal Hardware, 7 x 4 In. 173.00
Box, Pansies, Blown-Out, Enamel Painted, Hinged Cover, Signed, 4 1/2 In. . . . . . .770.00 to 865.00
Box, Puffy Mold, Pink Thistle, Hinged Cover, 3 1/2 x 7 In. 275.00

Box, Rococo, Enameled Daisies, Hinged Cover, 7 x 4 x 5 In. 1440.00
Box, Storks, Sunrise, Clear Frosted Ground, Lining, Hinged Cover, 3 1/2 x 5 In. 2600.00
Brush & Pin Tray, Rococo, Flowers, Gilt Metal Rim, Marked, 4 1/2 x 9 In. 1600.00
Card Holder, Flowers & Satin Lining, 2 1/2 x 4 1/8 In. 345.00
Cigar Box, Egg Crate Mold, Red Mums, Hinged Cover, 5 x 7 In. 1570.00
Dresser Box, Egg Crate Mold, Apple Blossoms, 6 x 7 In. 750.00
Dresser Box, Helmschmied Swirl, Ferns, Berries, Satin Lining, 3 1/2 x 5 1/2 In. 545.00
Dresser Box, Helmschmied Swirl, Flowers, Hinged Cover, 4 x 7 In. . . . . .260.00 to 345.00
Dresser Box, Helmschmied Swirl, Holly Leaves & Berries, Clear, Frosted, 4 x 7 In. 1150.00
Dresser Box, Helmschmied Swirl, Pink Christmas Cactus Flowers, Yellow, 5 1/2 In. 220.00
Dresser Box, Helmschmied Swirl, Roses, 4 1/2 x 6 In. 365.00
Dresser Box, Pink Blossoms, Cream, Gilt Metal Base & Feet, 6 x 7 In. 600.00
Fernery, Bishop's Hat Mold, Blue Ground, Pink Flowers, Metal Insert, 3 1/4 x 9 In. 250.00
Fernery, Blue Daisies, Metal Insert, Signed, 3 1/2 x 8 In. 250.00
Fernery, Egg Crate Mold, Pink Thistle, Blue, White, Metal Rim, 3 1/2 x 7 In. 225.00
Fernery, Egg Crate Mold, Yellow Flowers, Metal Rim, 3 1/2 x 7 In. 150.00
Fernery, Loyal, Round, Silver Plated Rim, 3 3/4 x 7 In. 100.00
Hair Receiver, Blue, Pink Flowers, Metal Top, Round, 2 1/4 x 3 1/2 In. 175.00
Humidor, Cigar, Blue & Purple Flowers, Cover, Baroque Shell, Marked, 6 In. 425.00
Humidor, Cigarette, Blue Flowers, Shell Mold Cover, Round, Hinged, Marked, 4 In. 350.00
Jardiniere, Floral Transfer, Enameled, Beaded Rim, 7 3/4 In. 315.00
Jewelry Box, Egg Crate Mold, Blue, Pink Flowers, Hinged Cover, Marked, 3 x 3 In. 275.00
Lamp Base, Woman, Fish, Corset Shape, Signed, 13 In. 3080.00
Letter Holder, Egg Crate Mold, Metal Rim, Marked, 4 x 5 1/2 In. 250.00
Letter Holder, Egg Crate Mold, White, Pink Flowers, Gilt Metal Rim, 4 x 5 1/2 In. 275.00
Letter Holder, Puffy Mold, Flowers, 4 x 5 1/2 In. 400.00
Match Holder, Pink Flowers, Blue Ground, Footed, 2 1/4 In. 200.00
Match Safe, Rococo, Flowers, Gilt Metal Wall Mount, Marked, 4 In. 1000.00
Photo Receiver, Egg Crate Mold, Enameled Flowers, Ormolu Mount, 4 x 6 In. 490.00
Photo Receiver, Pink Daisies, Rectangular, Banner Mark, 4 x 6 In. 420.00
Pin Tray, Cream, Blue Flowers, Swirl Mold, Gilt Metal Rim, Handles, 2 x 5 In. 150.00
Pin Tray, Gold Gilt Handles, Bonnet Baby, Satin Lining, Marked, 1 1/2 x 3 In. 125.00
Pin Tray, Rococo, Blue & White, Pink Flowers, Gilt Metal, Marked, 3 1/4 In. 70.00
Pin Tray, White, Pink Flowers, Oval, Gilt Metal Feet, Marked, 1 1/2 x 6 1/2 In. 400.00
Planter, Pink Flower Cluster, Leafy Stems, Opal Ground, Moorish Rim, 8 x 11 In. 365.00
Plaque, Pink Roses, Blue & Gold Scrolling, Leaf Embossed Frame, 15 x 12 In. 7280.00
Powder Jar, Hinged Cover, Flowers, Signed, 3 x 5 In. 125.00
Salt & Pepper, Cat & Spider, Creased Neck, 4 1/2 In. 250.00
Salt & Pepper, Chick, On Pedestal, Yellow, Green, Enameled Daisies, 3 In. 1100.00
Salt & Pepper, Enameled Birds, Flowers, White Opal, Silver Plated Holder 200.00
Sugar & Creamer, Helmschmied Swirl, Flowers, 4 1/2 x 6 In. 290.00
Sugar & Creamer, Helmschmied Swirl, Yellow Flowers, Silver Plated Cover, Bail, Handle 250.00
Sugar & Creamer, White, Pink Flower, Silver Plated Cover, Spout, Handles 100.00
Tobacco Jar, Opaque White, Yellow Diagonal Bands, Brass Collar, 5 1/4 In. 145.00
Tooth Powder Shaker, Rococo, Blue, Flowers, Gold Metal Cap, Marked, 3 1/2 In. 800.00
Toothbrush Holder, Silver, Scroll Mold, Blue & White, Flowers, Marked, 7 1/4 In. 900.00
Toothpick Holder, Blue, Pink Flowers, Gilt Metal Feet, Marked, 2 1/2 In. . . . . .70.00 to 100.00
Tray, Pink Flowers, Blue, White Ground, Beveled Mirror, 4 3/4 x 4 In. 225.00
Tray, Pink Roses, Gilt Metal Rim, Turkey Feet, Marked, 4 1/4 x 5 In. 250.00
Vase, Aphrodite Riding Dolphin Transfer, Pink Rose, Brass Feet, Marked, 13 1/2 In. 4200.00
Vase, Footed, Red Ground, Yellow Flowers, Handles, Marked, 12 In. 225.00
Vase, Pink Flowers, Green Fields, Gilt Metal Handles, Footed, Marked, 12 In. 1300.00
Vase, Rococo Blue Flowers, Gilt Metal, Footed, Marked, 10 1/2 In. 275.00
Vase, Rococo, Wild Rose, Metal Base, 6 1/4 In. . . . . .175.00 to 260.00
Vase, Shaded Yellow To Pink, Pink Flowers, Handles, 9 1/4 In. 250.00
Vase, Stick, Pink Mums, Opal Body, Green Tracery, 9 In. . . . . .280.00 to 400.00
Vase, Yellow, Pink Thistle, Gilt Metal Handles, Footed, Marked, 12 In. 475.00
Whisk Broom Holder, Pink Flowers, Gilt Metal Wall Mount, Marked, 10 In. 800.00

WEAPONS listed here include instruments of combat other than guns,
knives, rifles, or swords. Firearms are not listed in this book. Knives
and Swords are listed in their own categories.

    Ax, Executioner's, Wood Hilt, Brass, Beaded Copper, Curved Blade, 14 In. 775.00

Billy Club, Whalebone, Rosewood Handle, Ebony, Ivory Dividers, 14 1/2 In. 805.00
Bullet Mold, Ball, 60 Caliber, Revolutionary War, c.1775, 7 In. 190.00
Cannon, Lantanka, Swivel, Bronze, 41 In. 4025.00
Cannon, Salute, Gun Powder Tester, Bronze, England, 18th Century, 4 In. 425.00
Gauntlet, Hinged Steel, Finger Protection, Leather Mounts, Early 1900s, 14 1/2 In., Pair .   165.00
Halberd, Iron Head, Crescent Axe, Black Painted Shaft, Switzerland, c.1700, 78 In. 950.00
Shield, Oblong, Cast Iron, Chased Scene, Equestrian Battle, Castler, 1800s, 25 In. 176.00
Spear, Eel, Stamped, 16 1/4 In. 46.00
Spear, Naga Headhunter's, Palm Wood Haft, Iron Head, Rattan Wrap, Hair, c.1850, 68 In.   465.00
Truncheon, Military Or Constable's, Gilt Painted, GR III, England, c.1780 . . . . . . .600.00 to 850.00

WEATHER VANES were used in seventeenth-century Boston. The direction of the wind was an indication of coming weather, important to the
seafaring and farming communities. By the mid-nineteenth century,
commercial weather vanes were made of metal. Today's collectors
often consider weather vanes to be examples of folk art, even though
they may not have been handmade.

American Indian, Headdress, Bow & Arrow, Sheet Metal, c.1900, 12 x 17 In. 310.00
Arrow, Copper & Iron, Small Ball, Mounted On Vertical Rod, 1890s, 16 x 20 In. 1290.00
Arrow, Copper, Ball Finial, Corrugated Sheet Tail, Late 1800s, 14 x 30 In. 1175.00
Arrow, Copper, Iron, Corrugated Tail, Paint, American, 19th Century, 10 5/8 x 32 In. 881.00
Arrow, Pineapple Finial, Ball & Pedestal, 4 Flower Stems, Zinc, 43 In. 360.00
Banner, Arrow, Scroll, Copper, Zinc, American, 1800s, 16 3/8 x 38 In. 1645.00
Banner, Cutout Scroll Design, Ball Shape Finial, Late 1800s, 16 1/2 x 48 In. 4112.00
Banner, Geometric Cutouts, Flowers, Ball Finial, Late 19th Century, 24 x 32 In. 1410.00
Banner, Pierced Copper, Iron, Scrolled Foliate, Gilt, Fiske, 19th Century, 18 x 37 In. 940.00
Banner, Wavy Edge, Sheet Iron, Painted Black, c.1841, 19 1/2 x 14 1/4 In. 823.00
Banner, Zinc & Copper, Scroll, Tulips, J. Howard & Co., 7 3/4 x 33 3/4 In. 3175.00
Bannerette & Arrow, Cast Iron, Scrolled, Iron Stand, 19th Century, 79 x 50 1/2 In. 1175.00
Blacksmith Scene, Wrought Iron, Cutout, 35 In. 176.00
Codfish, Wood, Carved, Gilded, Applied Eyes, Metal Fins, 36 1/4 x 19 3/4 In. 11950.00
Copper, Mythological Bird & 1905, Continental, 52 x 33 In. 4900.00
Copper, Quill Form, 32 1/2 x 36 In. 960.00
Cow, Copper & Zinc, Molded, Rust Paint, Gilt, Iron Rod, Wood, 25 x 42 1/2 In. 14100.00
Cow, Copper, Curved Horns, Applied Ears, Bird's-Eye Maple Base, 18 x 28 In. 10450.00
Cow, Yellow Paint, Full Figure, Applied Horns, Tail, Molded Copper, 19 x 32 In. 8365.00
Cyclist, Whirligig, On Stand, 20th Century, 36 In. . . . .'.   1200.00
Dog, Holding Game Bird In Mouth, Iron, Black & White Paint, 28 x 21 In. 310.00
Eagle, Ball & Arrow, Spread Wings, Copper, 29 In. 520.00
Eagle, Copper, Full-Bodied, Spread Wings, Pierced Arrow, 20 x 26 In. 1015.00
Eagle, Copper, Gilt, Spread Wings, Standing On Ball, 19th Century, 25 1/2 x 31 In. 2000.00
Eagle, Copper, Zinc, Standing On Ball, Boston Metal Workers Co., c.1850, 16 x 20 In. . . .   7050.00
Eagle, Green, Painted, Sheet Iron, Silhouette, Riveted, 24 7/8 x 38 1/2 In. 2235.00
Eagle, Molded Copper, Zinc, Outstretched Wings, Gilding, 1800s, 11 1/2 In. 3995.00
Eagle, Perched On Ball, Arrow Directional, Copper, Gilt, 19th Century, 31 In. 6615.00
Eagle, Spread Wings, Copper & Zinc, Gilt, 2 Balls, 19th Century, 20 In. 1530.00
Eagle, Spread Wings, Perched, Copper, Gilt, Verdigris, 19th Century, 21 x 24 In. 1293.00
Eagle, Spread Wings, Perched, Gilt, Copper, American, 19th Century, 20 x 20 In. 911.00
Eagle, Wings Tucked, Galvanized Tin, Red, Gray, Blue Paint, c.1950, 27 1/2 In. 370.00
Eagle On Ball, Arrow, Copper, 74 x 36 x 36 In. 440.00
Fish, Wood, Green Paint, Applied Tin Fins, Large Tack Eyes, Mounted, 46 In. 7810.00
Fox, Leaping, Cast, Molded, Cut Eyes, Ear, Tail, A. Jewel & Co., c.1865, 15 x 42 In. 20315.00
Fox, Running, Copper, Zinc, 15 1/8 x 29 1/4 In. 4780.00
High Wheel, Copper, Brass Directional, 33 x 19 In. 115.00
Horse, Cast Iron, Dempster Mill Mfg., Beatrice, Nebraska, 16 x 17 In. 303.00
Horse, Prancing, Cast Iron, Weathered Gilt, Paint, Rochester Ironworks, 19 x 25 In. 25850.00
Horse, Prancing, Copper, Index, Molded, J. Howard Company, c.1868, 14 x 17 In. 11355.00
Horse, Prancing, Copper, Verdigris Patina Over Gold Gilt, 1800s, 25 x 22 In. 10350.00
Horse, Prancing, Index, Molded Zinc, Copper, Mass., 25 1/2 x 29 In. 8965.00
Horse, Rider, Full-Bodied, Main, 32 In. 6900.00
Horse, Rider, Molded Copper, Zinc, J.W. Fiske & Co., c.1893, 37 1/2 x 18 1/2 In. 15535.00
Horse, Running, Carved, Painted, On Stand, American, 43 In. 1265.00
Horse, Running, Cast Zinc Head, Wood Base, Directionals, Verdigris, 30 x 89 In. 1045.00

Horse, Running, Copper, Molded, Full-Bodied, 15 1/2 x 25 In. 3825.00
Horse, Running, Copper, Molded, Full-Bodied, J.W. Fiske & Co., c.1893, 17 x 25 In. 8365.00
Horse, Running, Copper, Zinc Head, Verdigris, Gilt Traces, Iron Base, 18 x 29 In. 1540.00
Horse, Running, Copper, Zinc, Ethan Allen, 19th Century, 18 1/4 x 30 3/8 In. 2233.00
Horse, Running, Copper, Zinc, Molded, Iron Directional, Late 19th Century, 18 x 21 In. ... 1998.00
Horse, Running, Copper, Zinc, Verdigris, 19th Century, 16 x 29 3/4 In. 1880.00
Horse, Running, Full-Bodied, Copper, Zinc Ears, 1800s, 17 1/2 x 22 1/4 In. 2820.00
Horse, Running, Patchen, Full-Bodied, Gilt Copper, c.1882, 20 x 32 In. 3055.00
Horse, Running, Sheet Iron, Shaft, Directionals, 60 x 39 In. 955.00
Horse, Running, Wooden, Carved, Painted, 20 x 55 In. 580.00
Horse, Running, Zinc, Arrow, 31 x 31 1/2 In. 2025.00
Horse, Sulky, Rider, Directionals, Copper, Iron, 67 x 34 In. 195.00
Horse, Trotting, 4-Legged Stand, Copper Lightning Rod, c.1900, 31 In. 230.00
Horse, Trotting, Black Hawk Style, Finders, 19th Century, 26 1/4 In. 550.00
Horse, Trotting, Black Hawk, Yellow Paint, 18 1/4 x 24 In. 5740.00
Horse, Trotting, Copper, Brass Rod, 68 1/2 x 29 1/2 In. 635.00
Horse, Trotting, Gold Patina, Verdigris, Open Mouth, Pointed Ears, 1800s, 36 In. 4315.00
Horse & Jockey, Copper Horse, Cast Jockey, Verdigris, 32 x 18 1/2 In. 2875.00
Horse & Man, Tin, Hand Cutout, 11 1/2 x 19 In. 90.00
Horse & Rider, Silhouette, Riveted, Sheet Iron, 14 x 32 1/2 In. 880.00
Horse & Rider, Tin, Sheet Metal, Yellow Paint, 17 1/2 x 30 In. 85.00
Indian, In Headdress, Tomahawk Raised, Gun, Painted, Tin, c.1950, 29 1/4 In. 169.00
Mermaid, Silhouette, Copper, Cutout, Arrow, Iron Spike Top, 21 1/2 In. 120.00
Pig, Copper, Hollow, c.1900 .... 10500.00
Ram, Copper, Molded, Full-Bodied, Rod Support, 19th Century, 28 x 35 In. 13145.00
Rooster, Copper, 21 x 18 1/2 In. 550.00
Rooster, Copper, Zinc, 13 x 12 1/4 In. 16730.00
Rooster, Directional Arrow, Metal, Folk Art, 15 x 25 In. 495.00
Rooster, Hand Wrought, Dimensional Wings, Tail Feather, Blue, 36 In. 299.00
Rooster, Molded, Copper, Corrugated Tail, 18th Century, 22 3/8 x 26 In. 5875.00
Rooster, Molded, Copper, Verdigris Patina, L.W. Cushing & Sons, 1800s, 28 x 29 In. 25850.00
Rooster, Sheet Iron, 29 In. 7500.00
Rooster, Zinc, Gilt Traces, Early 20th Century, 14 1/2 x 16 1/2 In. 1045.00
Sailboat, Rippling Flags, Sails, Molded Copper, Early 20th Century, 37 x 37 In. ., ... 7770.00
Sailboat, Sheet Copper, 38 x 37 In. 6575.00
Ship, 3-Masted, Copper, 42 x 44 In. 550.00
Ship, Wood, Zinc, Carved, Painted, 3-Masted, Copper Rigging, 19 1/4 x 25 1/2 In. 1060.00
Stag, Leaping, Sheet Iron, 15 x 16 In. 340.00
Sulky, Horse, Driver, Directional Arrows, Lightning Rod, Ball, Copper, 60 x 32 In. 1320.00
Sulky & Driver, Silhouette, Sheet Metal, Serrated Horse's Tail, 31 x 68 In. 2530.00
Swan, In Flight, Carved, Thomas Langan, New York, 60 In. 935.00
Swordfish, Wood, Painted, Finders, 20th Century, 23 In. 430.00
Whale, Copper, Handmade, Dovetailed Seams, Applied Fin & Tail, 33 In. 2300.00
Windmill Lighthouse, Whalebone, 4 Wind Vanes, Wood Base, 8 3/4 In. 175.00

WEBB glass is made by Thomas Webb & Sons of Ambelcot, England.
Many types of art and cameo glass were made by them during the
Victorian era. Production ceased by 1991, and the factory was demol-
ished in 1995. Webb Burmese and Webb Peachblow are special colored glasswares of the Victorian era. They are listed at the end of this
section. Glassware that is not Burmese or Peachblow is included here.

Webb

Bottle, Scent, Blossoms, Leaves, Cameo, Sterling Silver Cap, 6 1/4 In. 4600.00
Bottle, Scent, Duck's Head Shape, White Over Yellow, Cameo, Silver Cover, 8 3/4 In. ... 4600.00
Bottle, Scent, Ivory, Flower Medallions, Wheat Sprays, 4 1/2 In. 1035.00
Bottle, Scent, Lily Of The Valley, Butterfly, Cameo, Silver Cover, 4 In. 2015.00
Bottle, Scent, Lily Of The Valley, Cameo, Silver Cap, 5 1/4 In. 3740.00
Bottle, Scent, Morning Glory, White, Amethyst, Blue, Cameo, Silver Cover, 2 In. 3450.00
Bottle, Scent, Teardrop Shape, Flowers, Stems, Leaves, Bee, Cameo, 3 1/2 In. 1380.00
Bottle, Scent, Teardrop Shape, Water Lilies, Dragonfly, Lay Down, Cameo, Cap, 3 1/2 In. 4140.00
Bowl, Citron, Red & White Flowers, Cameo, 1 1/2 x 2 In. 185.00
Bowl, Mother-Of-Pearl, Ribbed, Blue, Pink Interior, Ruffled Edge, c.1890, 11 x 5 In. 1065.00
Bowl, Pink Satin, Enameled Flowers, Thorny Feet, Ruffled Rim, c.1890, 5 x 9 In. 225.00
Bride's Basket, Mother-Of-Pearl, Herringbone, Ruffled Edge, Metal Frame, 10 x 14 In. .. 1570.00

Webb, Vase, Red
Morning Glories,
Green Leaves,
White, Camphor,
Cameo, 1889, 7 In.

If red wine spills on the carpet, dilute it with white wine, clean the spot with cold water, then cover it with salt. Wait at least ten minutes, then vacuum.

Bride's Basket, Mother-Of-Pearl, Ribbed, Yellow, Pink, Ruffled Edged, c.1890, 11 x 5 In.	615.00
Creamer, Ribbed White Over Pink, Applied Amber Handle & Feet, 4 x 5 In.	155.00
Ewer, Green, Bronze Iridescence, Applied Handle, Pontil, 5 1/2 x 3 3/4 In.	115.00
Ewer, Mother-Of-Pearl, Apricot, Swirled, Ruffled Edge, Camphor Thorn Handles, 7 In.	220.00
Flask, Citron, White Flower, Veined Leaves, Cameo, Sterling Silver Cap, 10 In.	1705.00
Flask, Fish Shape, Citron, Opaque Scales, Ribbed, Lay Down, Sterling Cap, 12 In.	4675.00
Perfume Bottle, Swan's Head, White Over Cranberry, Lay Down, Cameo, Box, 9 In.	14950.00
Perfume Bottle, Vines, Leaves, Butterfly, Cameo, Gorham Silver Top, 10 1/2 In.	2185.00
Perfume Bottle, White Over Citron, Carved Swan, Cameo, Gilt Cap, 5 3/4 In.	5750.00
Rose Bowl, Alexandrite, Cranberry, Silver, Gold Enameled Flowers, Butterflies, 6 In., Pair	400.00
Vase, Branches Leaves, Pink, Yellow, Green, Pearl Ground, Double Gourd, Cameo, 6 In.	1610.00
Vase, Branches, Butterflies, Blue Satin, Gold Enameled, c.1890, 10 1/2 In.	420.00
Vase, Burmese, Spherical Body, Cylindrical Neck, Ruffled Edge, Handles, 6 5/8 In.	990.00
Vase, Citron, Flowers, Leaves, Red, White, Bulbous, Cameo, Signed, 5 In.	2875.00
Vase, Coralene, Red Shaded To Cream, Baluster, Rolled Ruffled Rim, 5 1/2 In.	633.00
Vase, Flowers, Leaf, Butterfly, Citron, Teardrop, Cupped Mouth, Cameo, 10 1/2 In.	1045.00
Vase, Flowers, Leaves, Elephant Head Handles, Cameo, 6 x 6 In.	2245.00
Vase, Flowers, Roses, Leaves, Tiffany & Co., Cameo, Paris Exposition, 1889, 7 1/2 In.	3280.00
Vase, Green Vine, Red Blossoms, Cameo, 7 In.	9200.00
Vase, Iridescent Amber, Purple, Blue, Moorish-Style Flowers, 10 1/2 In.	575.00
Vase, Ivory, Flowers, Leaves, Ruffled Edge, Tapered, Bulbous, Cameo, Signed, 3 3/4 In.	720.00
Vase, Mother-Of-Pearl, Coralene Flowers, Diamond-Quilted, Ruffled Rim, 6 3/4 In.	110.00
Vase, Mother-Of-Pearl, Pink Satin, Handles, c.1890, 12 In.	365.00
Vase, Opal Morning Glory, Bird, Salmon To Cream, Satin, Oval, Flat Rim, Cameo, 5 In.	145.00
Vase, Opal, Leaves, Flowers, Shaded Butterscotch To Salmon, Cameo, Marked, 4 1/4 In.	605.00
Vase, Opalescent White & Russet Swirls, Gold Garland, Oval, Rolled Rim, 7 1/2 In.	220.00
Vase, Orange, Enameled, Flowers, Rolled Ruffled Rim, Bulbous, Cased, c.1890, 9 In.	110.00
Vase, Persian Design, Yellow, White, Blue, Raisin Ground, Flared Cameo, 4 1/2 In.	4315.00
Vase, Pink Satin, Enameled Flowers & Leaves, Signed, 10 1/4 In.	360.00
Vase, Red Morning Glories, Green Leaves, White, Camphor, Cameo, 1889, 7 In. .... *Illus*	9200.00
Vase, White Flowers, Leaves, Prussian Blue, Bulbous, Ringed Neck, Cameo, Signed, 7 In.	1100.00
Vase, White Fuchsia Flowers, Raisin Ground, Rolled Rim, Oval, Cameo, 4 1/2 In.	495.00
Vase, White Passion Flowers, Leaves, Rose To Gray, Double Gourd, Cameo, 11 1/2 In.	9900.00

WEBB BURMESE is a colored Victorian glass made by Thomas Webb
& Sons of Stourbridge, England, from 1886.

Bowl, 5-Point Rolled Rim, Ruffled Edge, Satin, Signed, 2 3/4 x 3 3/4 In.	220.00
Epergne, Fairy Lamp Center, 4 Lily Vases, Berry Pontils	1320.00
Figurine, Pig, 1 1/8 In.	440.00
Rose Bowl, Ruffled Rim, 2 7/8 x 3 In.	275.00
Sugar, Egg Shape, c.1890, 4 In.	230.00
Sugar, Enameled Leaves & Grapes, 6-Sided Rim, 3 1/2 In.	430.00
Tumbler, Lemonade, Satin, Applied Handle, 4 3/4 In.	330.00
Vase, Applied Berries, Branches, Leaves, Bulbous, Flared, Signed, 3 In.	420.00
Vase, Cascading Ivy, Pinched, Bulbous, c.1890, 5 3/4 In., Pair	1000.00
Vase, Enameled Flowers, Bulbous, Rolled Rim, Saucer Foot, 4 3/4 In.	460.00
Vase, Jack-In-The-Pulpit, Tapered, 4 3/4 In., Pair	550.00

Vase, Lily, Branches, Cherries, Tricornered, Footed, 4 In. 550.00
Vase, Peacock, Flowers, Ferns, Bulbous Body, Stick Neck, Signed, 8 1/2 In. 920.00
Vase, Ribbed, 4 In. 250.00
Vase, Teardrop, 8 1/4 In. 330.00

WEBB PEACHBLOW is a colored Victorian glass made by Thomas
Webb & Sons of Stourbridge, England, from 1885.

Bride's Basket, Enameled Flowers, Leaves, Ribbed, Ruffled Edge, Holder, c.1890, 11 In. . . 1232.00
Bride's Bowl, Enameled Daisy, 12 3/4 In. 400.00
Jar, Enameled Flower Sprigs, Brass, Cover, 5 In. 260.00
Jardiniere, Gold Enameled, Clematis, Oval, Handles, Footed, c.1895, 6 1/2 In. 440.00
Paperweight, Apple, c.1890, 3 In. 250.00
Vase, Blue Jay, Pinecone Branch, Gold Enameled Leaves, Gilt, 14 In. 520.00
Vase, Cascading Flower Vines, Gold Enameled, Squat, c.1890, 5 1/2 In. 420.00
Vase, Coralene Design, Shouldered, 5 1/2 In. 575.00
Vase, Fall Scene, Butterfly, Gold Leaves, Teardrop, Signed 385.00
Vase, Gold Enameled Flowers, Butterflies, Insects, 7 1/2 In. 90.00
Vase, White Enameled Flowers, Applied Handles, 6 In. 260.00

WEDGWOOD, one of the world's most successful potteries, was
founded by Josiah Wedgwood, who was considered a cripple by his
brother and was forbidden to work at the family business. The pottery
was established in England in 1759. A large variety of wares has been
made, including the well-known jasperware, basalt, creamware, and
even a limited amount of porcelain. There are two kinds of jasperware.   WEDGWOOD
One is made from two colors of clay, the other is made from one color
of clay with a color dip to create the contrast in design. The firm is still
in business. Other Wedgwood pieces may be listed under Flow Blue,
Majolica, Tea Leaf Ironstone or in other porcelain categories.

Barber Bottle, Cover, Black Basalt, Bacchus Heads, Late 19th Century, 10 1/8 In. 999.00
Biscuit Jar, Cover, Egyptian Style, Green, Brown, Silver Plated, Mounts, c.1875, 7 In. ... 200.00
Biscuit Jar, Cover, Jasper Dip, Crimson, Classical Relief, Oak Leaves, c.1920, 8 In. 2235.00
Bough Pot, Cover, Brown, Slip, Swags, Fluting, c.1800, 9 3/4 In. 590.00
Bough Pot, Cover, Jasper Dip, Blue, Square, Late 18th Century, 6 1/8 In. 1060.00
Bough Pot, Cover, Jasperware, Blue, Arched, Recessed Panels, Late 1700s, 6 3/8 In., Pair 4406.00
Bough Pot, Cover, Pearlware, Chrysanthemum, Early 1800s, 6 In., Pair 560.00
Bough Pot, Cover, Queen's Ware, Brown Slip, Flower Band, Late 1700s, 5 1/4 In. 2115.00
Bowl, Agate, Glazed Black & White, Norman Wilson, Mid 20th Century, 4 In. 295.00
Bowl, Black Basalt, Engine Turned, Ribbed Banded Border, 1967, 10 In. 205.00
Bowl, Black Basalt, Oval, Scrolled Leaf Handles, Late 18th Century, 6 3/4 In. 1175.00
Bowl, Black Basalt, Red, White Bands, Etruscan Pattern, 12 In. 4700.00
Bowl, Black Basalt, Rosso Antico, Loop Handles, Applied Palmette Band, 9 1/4 In. 590.00
Bowl, Black Basalt, Turned Rim Band, Keith Murray, c.1940, 6 1/2 In. 999.00
Bowl, Bone China, Brown, Green, Blue Glaze, Flared Rim, Elwyn James, c.1973, 7 In. ... 1156.00
Bowl, Brown Matte, Gray Exterior, Mottled Blue Interior, Mid 20th Century, 4 In. 380.00
Bowl, Caneware, Applied Gray Green Fern Relief, Stars, Early 1800s, 7 In. 880.00
Bowl, Caneware, Smear Glaze, Applied Grapevine Border, 19th Century, 10 7/8 In. 470.00
Bowl, Copper Luster, Cane, Glazed, Flowers, Millicent Taplin, c.1928, 10 In. 325.00
Bowl, Drab Ware, Leaf Molded, c.1820, 7 In. 650.00
Bowl, Dragon Luster, Dragons, Gold Highlights, 3 5/8 x 8 7/8 In. 1150.00
Bowl, Dragon Luster, Mottled Blue, c.1920, 9 1/8 In. 645.00
Bowl, Dragon Luster, Mottled Green Exterior, Mother-Of-Pearl, c.1920, 5 1/2 In. 265.00
Bowl, Dragon Luster, Scalloped, Lobed, Mottled Blue, Mother-Of-Pearl, c.1920, 7 In. ... 1410.00
Bowl, Egret, Black Basalt, Rocky Base, Glass Eyes, c.1915, 10 3/4 In. 175.00
Bowl, Fairyland Luster, Empire, Leapfrogging Elves, Mother-Of-Pearl, c.1920, 5 In. 4405.00
Bowl, Jasperware, Blue, White Relief Bacchanalian Boys, Footed, c.1785, 8 7/8 In. 7050.00
Bowl, Jasperware, Lilac, Dancing Hours, Laurel Band, England, 1961, 8 In. 265.00
Bowl, Jasperware, Lilac, White Dancing Hours Figures, Laurel Border, c.1960, 10 In. 470.00
Bowl, Lahore, Luster, Imperial, Black Ground, Yellow Ground Interior, c.1920, 8 In. 3290.00
Bowl, Lobster & Radish, Cobalt Blue, Turquoise Interior, Footed, 10 1/2 In. 1230.00
Bowl, Ornament, Luster, Celtic, Black Matte, Yellow Ground Exterior, c.1920, 5 In. 825.00
Bowl, Pedestal, Jasperware, Classical Figures, Dark Blue, White, c.1875, 8 1/2 In. 85.00
Bowl, Potpourri, Cover, Stoneware, Smear Glaze, Loop Handles, Blue Acanthus, 9 In. ... 1115.00

Bowl, Queen's Ware, Oval, Center Bail Handle, Late 18th Century, 13 In. 705.00
Bowl, Queen's Ware, Painted, Landscapes, 3 Fluted Legs, c.1865, 4 1/8 In. 410.00
Bowl, Queen's Ware, Servers, Lobster, Transfer, Sea Scenes, Footed, c.1884, 10 In. 880.00
Bowl, Stand, Stoneware, Nautilus Shell, Oval, Early 19th Century, 8 1/2 In. 590.00
Bowl, Stone China, Blue Transfer, Square Shape, Water Lily Pattern, c.1840, 9 1/2 In. . . . 410.00
Bowl, Stoneware, Green Glaze, Black Spatter Design, Elwyn James, c.1976, 11 In. 1295.00
Bowl, Vegetable, Cover, Annular Shape, Green Matte Glaze, c.1935, 11 1/4 In. 355.00
Box, Cover, Jasper Dip, Crimson, Round, Applied Classical Relief, Flowers, c.1920, 5 In. . 1645.00
Box, Cover, Moonstone Glaze, Depicting Muse Erato, Arnold Machin, c.1945, 5 In. 235.00
Box, Dip, Cover, Jasperware, Crimson, Classical & Floral Relief, England, c.1920, 4 In. . . 1295.00
Bread Tray, Argenta Ware, Grape Pattern, Marked, 1883, 11 3/4 In. 230.00
Bust, Aristotle, Black Basalt, Waisted Socle, Late 18th Century, 7 3/4 In. 590.00
Bust, Byron, Carrara, Waisted Circular Socle, England, c.1855, 15 1/2 In. 880.00
Bust, Lord Zetland, Carrara, Waisted Socle, c.1868, 19 3/4 In. 999.00
Bust, Socrates, Black Basalt, Mounted On Waisted Socle, 18th Century, 7 3/4 In. 590.00
Butter Tub, Cover, Jasperware, Blue, Cylindrical Shape, White Borders, 3 1/4 In. 1000.00
Cabaret Set, Black Basalt, Red Enamel Trim, Mid 1800s, 7 Piece 1880.00
Cake Plate, Cover, Jasper Dip, Blue, An Offering To Peace, 11 1/4 x 7 In. 645.00
Cake Stand, Majolica, Stanley Pattern, 1870, 8 3/4 In. 230.00
Candle Vase, Cover, Variegated Agate, Leaf Handle, Swags, c.1775, 9 1/2 In. 2235.00
Candleholder, Black Basalt, Sphinx, Plinth Mount, 19th Century, 10 1/2 In, Pair 2940.00
Candleholder, Jasper Dip, Crimson, Applied Classical Relief, Leaf Border, c.1920, 3 In. . . 1998.00
Candlestick, Black Basalt, Enamel, Multicolored Flowers, Mid 1800s, 7 3/4 In., Pair 1115.00
Candlestick, Black Basalt, Triton, Cornucopia Sconce, Early 19th Century, 11 In. 3820.00
Candlestick, Drab Ware, Glazed, Columnar, Square Plinth, Gilt Trim, c.1840, 8 In., Pair . . 410.00
Candlestick, Figures, Black Basalt, Juno, Ceres, Gilt, Bronze, c.1880, 10 7/8 In., Pair 2350.00
Candlestick, Jasper Dip, Dark Blue, White Wreathed Laurel, Early 1800s, 8 In., Pair 560.00
Candlestick, Jasperware, Early 20th Century, Impressed, 7 In., Pair 175.00
Candlestick, Jasperware, White Standing Figures, Flora & Pomona, Lilac, 9 1/4 In. 3820.00
Candlestick, Queen's Ware, Acanthus Leaf Border, Fluting, Late 1700s, 11 In., Pair 380.00
Candlestick, Queen's Ware, Figural, Cornucopia Shape Sconce, c.1883, 10 In., Pair 560.00
Canister, Cover, Jasper Dip, Crimson, Classical Relief, Flowers, c.1920, 6 1/2 In. 1765.00
Cann, Cup, Saucer, Jasper Dip, Lilac, White Leaf Relief, Late 1700s, 4 5/8 In. 1295.00
Cann, Cup, Saucer, Jasperware, Blue Ground, Lilac Medallions, Late 1800s, 5 1/2 In. 440.00
Cann, Cup, Saucer, Jasperware, Tricolor, White Ground, Lilac Medallions, 5 1/4 In. 1410.00
Cann, Cup, Saucer, Rosso Antico, Applied Relief, Hieroglyphs, Early 1800s, 5 1/4 In. 705.00
Cheese Keeper, Argenta, Primrose, 9 1/2 In. 560.00
Coffee Biggin, Drab Ware, Smear Glaze, Applied Flower Band, Mid 1800s, 6 3/4 In. 590.00
Coffee Set, Black Basalt, Robert Minkin, c.1964, 3 Piece 235.00
Coffee Set, Bone China, Persian Ponies Pattern, Victor Skellern, c.1935, 3 Piece 1765.00
Coffeepot, Cover, Caneware, Basket Weave Body, Sibyl Finial, c.1800, 7 3/4 In. 115.00
Coffeepot, Cover, Caneware, Smear Glaze, Arabesque Flowers, Leaves, 8 3/4 In. 440.00
Coffeepot, Cover, Queen's Ware, Gilt, Shell Shape Trim, Flower Knop, 1700s, 9 In. 1295.00
Coffeepot, Cover, Queen's Ware, Transfer, Tea Party, Shepherd, Late 1700s, 9 1/2 In. 350.00
Compote, Argenta, Monkey Support, 10 x 9 1/2 In. 2800.00
Compote, Drab Ware, Glazed, Footed, Oval, Upturned Loop Handles, c.1830, 10 x 6 In. . 380.00
Compote, Hummingbird Luster, Mottled Blue Exterior, c.1920, 10 3/4 In. 2115.00
Compote, Jasperware, Blue, Impressed, c.1900, 12 In. 345.00
Compote, Oval, Loop Handles, Ivy Pattern Borders, Late 18th Century, 5 1/2 In., Pair . . . 1115.00
Compote, Queen's Ware, Oval, Scalloped Rim, Enamel Transfers, c.1872, 10 1/2 In. 295.00
Compote, Stand, Earthenware, Can Glazed, Scroll Handles, Early 1800s, 13 In. 325.00
Cooler, Wine, Jasperware, Applied Designs, Bear Handles, No. 3151, 10 1/2 In., Pair 1356.00
Crocus Pot, Pierced Cover, Agate Ware, Pearl Glazed Ground, Late 1800s, 6 1/2 In. 1880.00
Crocus Pot, Stand, Black Basalt, Hedgehog, England, c.1975, 9 1/2 x 11 1/4 In. 470.00
Crocus Pot, Stand, Black Basalt, Hedgehog, Oval, Pierced Body, 19th Century, 10 In. 1645.00
Cup, Stand, Jasper Dip, Black, Applied Flowers, Flower Festoons, c.1800, 4 1/2 In. 1410.00
Cup & Saucer, Caneware, Relief, Boy Playing, Turned Band, Late 1700s, 5 In. 470.00
Cup & Saucer, Cobalt Blue, Yellow Rim, Turquoise Interior 215.00
Cup & Saucer Sets, Harvard, Blue Transfer, Demitasse, 24 Piece 145.00
Custard Cup, Cover, Jasper Dip, Blue, White Lattice, Twisted Loop Handle, 2 1/2 In. 355.00
Dessert Set, Bird & Fan, Cobalt Blue, 14-In. Platter, 8 6 1/2 In. Plates, 9 Piece 3360.00
Dessert Set, Blue Rim, Sanded Look, Greek Key Trim, 24 Piece 220.00
Dip Jug, Jasperware, Yellow, Black Classical Figures, England, c.1930, 7 1/2 In. 1115.00

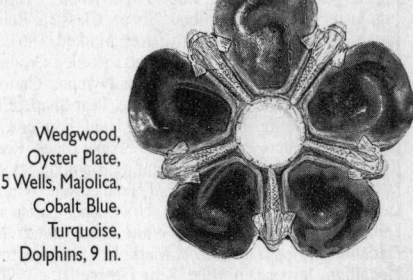

Wedgwood, Dish, Game, Cover, Flowers,
Leaves, Lovebirds Finial, Griffin Ends, 9 1/2 In.

Wedgwood,
Oyster Plate,
5 Wells, Majolica,
Cobalt Blue,
Turquoise,
Dolphins, 9 In.

Dish, Black Basalt, Leaf Shape, Iron Red Enamel, Multicolored, Mid 1800s, 10 In.	295.00
Dish, Cover, Rabbit Finial, Terra-Cotta, 11 In.	385.00
Dish, Game, Cover, Flowers, Leaves, Lovebirds Finial, Griffin Ends, 9 1/2 In. . . . . . *Illus*	896.00
Dish, Game, Cover, Majolica, Oval, Brown Ground, Bird Finial, c.1875, 11 In.	560.00
Dish, Oval, Jasperware, Blue Dip, Birds On Branches, England, c.1934, 10 3/4 In.	355.00
Dish, Queen's Ware, Brown, Blue Enamel, Sailing Scene, Alfred Powell, c.1928, 12 In.	2233.00
Dish, Queen's Ware, Oval, Scallop Rim, Soldier Looking At Sea, c.1865, 11 1/2 In.	940.00
Dresser Set, Bone China, Blue Transfer, Scrolled Leaves, Cipriani Print, c.1900, 5 Piece	205.00
Ewer, Black Basalt, Tall Scrolled Handle, Applied Leaves, Bentley, c.1775, 14 1/2 In.	2705.00
Ewer, Ivory Vellum, Porcelain, Gilt Trim, Enamel & Raised Gilt, c.1890, 11 In., Pair	880.00
Ewer, Jasper Dip, Light Blue, Goddesses, Drapery Banding, c.1890, 7 3/4 In., Pair	750.00
Ewer, Wine, Water, Black Basalt, Triton, Satyr, Holding Spout, 15 1/2 In., Pair	3290.00
Figurine, Chess, Jasperware, Modeled Warrior Bearing Sword, Late 1700s, 2 3/8 In.	295.00
Figurine, Cupid, Jasperware, Drum, Swags, Late 1700s, 7 In.	1880.00
Figurine, Fallow Deer, Cream Glaze, Skeaping, 20th Century, 7 1/4 In.	440.00
Figurine, Girl Seated By Basket Shape Vase, Queen's Ware, Pink Enamel, c.1876, 7 In.	265.00
Figurine, Hebe, Jasperware, White, Blue Jasper Drum, Festoons, Ram's Heads, 1700s, 7 In.	3290.00
Figurine, Kangaroo, Cane Colored Glaze, John Skeaping, 20th Century, 8 3/4 In.	765.00
Figurine, King Charles I, Black Basalt, Cavalier Standing By Spaniel, c.1910, 6 3/8 In.	470.00
Figurine, Monkey, Creamware, John Skeaping, 20th Century, 6 3/4 In.	355.00
Figurine, Polar Bear, White Moonstone Glaze, John Skeaping, 20th Century, 7 1/4 In.	235.00
Figurine, Raven, Black Basalt, Glass Eyes, Ernest Light, c.1915, 4 1/2 In.	235.00
Figurine, Sea Lion, Creamware, John Skeaping, 20th Century, 7 3/4 In.	440.00
Figurine, Skills Of The Nation, Potter, Wheelwright, Black Basalt, c.1980, 9 1/2 In.	560.00
Footbath, Creamware, Oval, Molded Bands, Acorn, Oak Leaf, 8 3/4 x 19 1/2 In.	1035.00
Frame, Jasper Dip, Dark Blue, Buckle, Cut Steel Mount, Cupid Unmasked, 3 1/8 In.	590.00
Fruit Basket, Stand, Queen's Ware, Oval, Openwork, Entwined Handles, 1700s, 13 In.	500.00
Garniture, Agate Ware, Scroll Handles, Leaf Swags, Terra-Cotta Plinths, c.1775, 3 Piece	4400.00
Garniture, Pearlware, Slip, Flower Festoons, Relief Border, Late 1700s, 3 Piece	1530.00
Group, Interpretation, Joseph Before Pharaoh, Carrara, Creamware, c.1860, 19 In.	3525.00
Inkpot, Caneware, Globular, Loop Handles, Late 18th Century, 2 1/8 In.	825.00
Inkstand, Green Matte Ground, Rectangular Shape, Pen Tray, Wells, Pots, c.1936, 10 In.	590.00
Inkstand, Queen's Ware, Bird's-Head Handles, Vine Borders, 19th Century, 8 In.	529.00
Inkstand Dish, Drab Ware, Glazed, Leaf Molded Tray, 3 Pots, c.1830, 9 1/4 In.	700.00
Inkstand Dish, Drab Ware, Glazed, Rectangular, Cut Corners, Blue Glaze, c.1872, 9 In.	265.00
Jardiniere, Jasper Dip, Olive Green, Relief Muse Figures, c.1920, 7 1/4 In.	410.00
Jardiniere, Jasperware, Green, Impressed, 8 1/4 In.	265.00
Jardiniere, Majolica, Tree Bark Body, Raised Branch Rim, Argenta, c.1880, 8 3/4 In.	999.00
Jug, Black Basalt, Silver Mounted, Loop Handle, Satyr Mask, Late 1700s, 7 1/2 In.	1645.00
Jug, Caneware, Classical Relief, Domestic Employment, Early 1800s, 7 In.	999.00
Jug, Caterer's, Drab Ware, Jewel & Motto Bands, Blue Underglaze, c.1870, 9 In.	150.00
Jug, Caterer's, Majolica, Raised Bands Of Jewel & Mottoes, c.1869, 8 1/2 In.	235.00
Jug, Celadon Slip, Cream Ground, Keith Murray, c.1940, 8 In.	205.00
Jug, Cover, Black Basalt, Bacchanalian Boys, Silver Mounted, Sibyl Finial, 9 1/4 In.	2115.00
Jug, Cover, Majolica, Silver Plate, Mottled Blue, c.1876, 9 In.	175.00
Jug, Cream, Caneware, Bamboo Molded Body, Late 1700s, 2 1/2 In.	1295.00
Jug, Hot Water, Ivory Glaze, Tapered Sides, Rope Twist Handle, c.1880, 8 1/4 In.	1115.00
Jug, Jasper Dip, Crimson, Applied Classical Relief, Grapevine Border, c.1920, 4 In.	999.00

Jug, Jasper Dip, Crimson, Applied White Classical Muses, Leaves, c.1920, 3 7/8 In. 825.00
Jug, Jasper Dip, Crimson, Rope Twist Handle, Classical Relief, Border, c.1920, 6 In. 1998.00
Jug, Jasper Dip, Lilac, Bulbous Shape, Classical Relief, Floral Festoons, 5 5/8 In. 645.00
Jug, Majolica, Hinged Pewter Cover, Marked, 1867, 12 In. 230.00
Jug, Majolica, Leaf & Flower Bands, Mottled Ground, c.1869, 8 3/4 In. 205.00
Jug, Majolica, Molded, Classical Sea Nymphs, Cartouche, c.1867, 8 5/8 In. 410.00
Jug, Queen's Ware, Entwined Handle, Pear Shape, Embossed, Late 1700s, 7 1/2 In. 825.00
Jug, Queen's Ware, Transfer, Rabbit Hunt, Farmer's Arms, c.1770, 10 1/2 In. 2705.00
Jug, Rosso Antico, Egyptian, Club Shape, Black, Red, White, c.1854, 8 In. 1765.00
Jug, Water, Caneware, Turned Fluting, Bamboo Style Handle, c.1800, 6 1/2 In. 470.00
Kettle, Cover, Black Basalt, Bail Handle, Red, White Enamel, c.1800, 10 1/2 In. 9695.00
Lamp, Jasperware, Blue, White, Urn Shape, Classical Figures, c.1910, 11 1/2 In. 200.00
Lamp, Oil, Jasper Dip, Black, White Laurel Bands, Mid 19th Century, 5 7/8 In. 1060.00
Medallion, Jasper Dip, Black, Maria I Of Portugal, c.1787, 4 In. 2470.00
Medallion, Jasper Dip, Blue, King George III, c.1776, 3 7/8 In. 2470.00
Medallion, Jasper Dip, Blue, Oval, Applied White Relief Seasonal Figure, 3 1/8 In. 295.00
Medallion, Jasper Dip, Dark Blue, Applied White Classical Relief, Codex, 2 1/8 In. 265.00
Medallion, Jasper Dip, Liberty, Peace, Art & Labor, White Relief, 2 1/2 In. 530.00
Medallion, Jasperware, Blue, George Washington, Oval, White Relief, c.1779, 4 In. 2470.00
Medallion, Jasperware, Blue, Governor William Franklin, c.1784, 4 1/4 In. 2470.00
Medallion, Jasperware, Blue, James Stuart, White Relief, c.1780, 3 5/8 In. 1410.00
Medallion, Jasperware, Blue, Sir Isaac Newton, White Relief, c.1779, 4 In. 1645.00
Mug, Caneware, Applied Gray Green Fern, Star Relief, Late 1700s, 3 3/8 In. 880.00
Mug, Caneware, Barrel Shape, Boys Playing Relief, Turned Band, 3 1/2 In. 1530.00
Mug, Creamware, c.1800, 6 In. 740.00
Oyster Plate, 5 Wells, Majolica, Cobalt Blue, Turquoise, Dolphins, 9 In. .... *Illus* 5600.00
Oyster Plate, 5 Wells, Majolica, Turquoise, Dolphin Dividers, 5 Piece 12320.00
Oyster Plate, 6 Wells, Argenta, Oriental Flowers, 9 1/2 In. 1045.00
Pancake Server, Cover, Jasperware, Light Green, Early 20th Century 380.00
Pedestal, Jasper Dip, Blue & Lilac Ram's Heads, Swags, c.1890, 4 5/8 In., Pair 690.00
Perfume Flask, Jasperware, Blue, White Classical Relief, Oval, England, 1800s, 4 In. 880.00
Pie Dish, Cover, Caneware, Oval, Crust Rim, Acanthus Handle, Late 1700s, 13 1/2 In. .. 1528.00
Pie Dish, Cover, Caneware, Oval, Crust Rim, c.1800, 8 1/2 In. 705.00
Pie Dish, Cover, Majolica, Grapevine Pattern, Marked, c.1870, 7 1/2 In. 405.00
Pin, Jasperware, Blue, Cut Steel Mount, Applied Classical Relief, Poor Maria, 1800s, 3 In. 590.00
Plaque, Black Basalt, Claudius, Oval, Incised Title, Late 18th Century, 6 1/4 In. 1765.00
Plaque, Black Basalt, King Tut, Rectangular, Gilt, c.1977, 8 1/2 x 15 3/8 In. 765.00
Plaque, Black Basalt, Vesputian, Oval, Incised Title, Late 18th Century, 6 1/4 In. 1295.00
Plaque, Fairyland Luster, Picnic By A River, c.1920, 4 3/4 x 10 5/8 In. 7640.00
Plaque, Jasper Dip, Green, Relief Depicting Achilles Dragging Hector, 6 x 18 1/2 In. 4995.00
Plaque, Jasper Dip, Green, Relief, Offerings, Sacrifice To Peace, 4 1/2 x 17 1/2 In. 1060.00
Plaque, Jasperware, Blue, Cupid & Psyche, Relief, Oval, 19th Century, 3 1/2 In. 295.00
Plaque, Jasperware, Blue, Depicting Adam, Relief, Anna Zinkeisen, c.1924, 7 1/4 In. 1115.00
Plaque, Jasperware, Blue, Fall Of Phaeton, Applied Relief, c.1977, 11 x 19 In. 940.00
Plaque, Jasperware, Prince Regent, Early 19th Century, Brass Frame, 3 3/4 x 3 In. 210.00
Plaque, Jasperware, Seasons, 4 Cherubs, Velvet Liner, England, 8 1/4 x 14 1/4 In. 195.00
Plate, Anti-Slavery, Kneeling Slave, Am I Not A Man & Brother, 6 1/2 In. 1375.00
Plate, Caneware, Blue Enamel, Greek Key Border, White Glaze, c.1800, 8 1/8 In., Pair .. 1645.00
Plate, Cauliflower, 9 In. 335.00
Plate, Chapoo, Ironstone, Flow Blue, 1800s, 9 In., Pair 100.00
Plate, Harvard, Blue Transfer, 1941, 10 1/4 In., 12 Piece 290.00
Plate, Ivanhoe, Flow Blue, 9 1/2 In. 125.00
Plate, Jasperware, Bicentennial, 5 Colors, Light Blue, White Portrait Bust, c.1976, 9 In. ... 440.00
Plate, Majolica, Pierced, Scalloped Basket Weave Border, c.1874, 9 In., 8 Piece 1600.00
Plate, Old Coffyn House, Nantucket, Blue & White, Etruria & Barlston, 10 In. 240.00
Plate, Queen's Ware, Commemorative, Embossed, c.1939, 9 3/8 In., Pair 295.00
Plate, Queen's Ware, Dog & The Shadow, Emile Lessore, c.1865, 9 1/4 In. 765.00
Plate, Reticulated, Hummingbird, Butterfly & Flower, Cobalt Blue, 9 In. 365.00
Plate, Rosso Antico, Black Basalt, Egyptian, Hieroglyphs, Mid 19th Century, 9 1/4 In. ... 705.00
Plate, Seafood, Blue Ground, Scallop Shell Center Section, Majolica, 7 In., 4 Piece 1095.00
Plate, Strawberry & Leaf, Yellow Ground, 9 In. ....440.00 to 450.00
Plate, Sunflower & Wicker Argenta, 8 3/4 In. 250.00
Plate, Sunflower, Dark Green, Albino, 8 1/2 In., Pair 45.00

Plate, Urn Design, Blue & Gilt Border, 10 In., 12 Piece 1810.00
Plate, Zinnias, Stipple Gray Ground, Majolica, 9 In. 360.00
Platter, Corn & Poppy, Basket, 12 3/4 In. 605.00
Platter, Creamware, Oval Shape, Border Decoration, Motto, c.1800, 17 x 13 In. 145.00
Platter, Fish, Mazarin, Red, Blue, Gold, White Ground, Oval, 20 1/2 In. 345.00
Platter, Insert, Queen's Ware, Strawberry Leaf Border, Dot & Green Trim, 18 1/2 In. 120.00
Platter, Queen's Ware, Japonica, Printed, Enameled, Oval, c.1880, 18 1/2 In. 120.00
Platter, Queen's Ware, Red Transfer, Exotic Birds, Late 1700s, 15 In. 1765.00
Platter, Transferware, Ironstone, Oval, Blue Willow, Scallop Rim, c.1900, 16 x 11 In. ... 145.00
Platter, Transferware, Willow, Ironstone, Rectangular, c.1900, 15 1/4 x 12 In. 405.00
Pot, Hot Water, Cover, Caneware, Egyptian, Brown Relief, Hieroglyphs, 8 1/2 In. 3820.00
Punch Service, Argenta, Majolica, Fruiting Grape Leaves, c.1875, 10 Piece 880.00
Rum Keg, Queen's Ware, Raised Banding, Brown Transfer, Mid 1800s, 12 7/8 In. 410.00
Rum Pot, Cover, Black Basalt, Bail Handle, Bacchanalian Boys, Late 1700s, 8 3/8 In. ... 1530.00
Salt, Figural, Conch Shell, On Coral, 3 1/4 In. 385.00
Salt Cellar, Majolica, Figural, Fish Supporting Shell Shape Bowl, 1872, 4 1/4 In. 765.00
Sardine Box, Cover, Argenta Oriental Flower, 9 In. 280.00
Sardine Box, Cover, Ocean Crate, Cobalt Blue 670.00
Sardine Box, Cover, Queen's Ware, Tray, Transfers, Flowers, Butterflies, c.1875, 8 In. ... 470.00
Serving Dish, Majolica, Tremblay, Double Twig & Ribbon Handle, c.1877, 9 In. 205.00
Shell, Stand, Nautilus, Alpine Pink, Bone China, 20th Century, 8 In. 205.00
Spoon Warmer, Majolica, Nautilus, Shell Shape Bowl, Oval Base, c.1879, 5 1/2 In. 1645.00
Strawberry Set, Majolica, Blue Ground, Heart Shape Tray, c.1871, 3 Piece 175.00
Sucrier, Cover, Jasperware, Yellow, Applied Classical Relief, 20th Century, 3 1/2 In. 410.00
Sucrier, Cover, Stand, Jasper Dip, Green, Classical Relief Children At Play, 4 3/4 In. 765.00
Sugar, Cover, Argenta, Ocean 99.00
Tankard, Black Basalt, Bringing Home The Game, Silver Mounted, 1700s, 5 In. 2235.00
Tankard, Black Basalt, Dimpled Ground, Oak Leaf Ground, Bentley, c.1778, 4 1/4 In. 1765.00
Tankard, Black Basalt, Oak Leaf Band, Stippled, Silver Mounted, Late 1700s, 5 In. 1060.00
Tankard, Black Basalt, Oak Leaves, Stippled, Silver Mounted, Late 1700s, 3 3/4 In. 1115.00
Tankard, Pearlware, Multicolored Enamel, Black Transfer, Early 19th Century, 5 In. 235.00
Tea Set, Black Basalt, Classical Medallions, Anthemion Border, 3 Piece 1763.00
Tea Set, Bone China, Oval, Fluted Body, Flowers, Late 19th Century, 3 Piece 120.00
Tea Set, Bone China, Squat, Fluted, Imari Style Enamel, c.1900, 3 Piece 175.00
Tea Set, Jasperware, Dice Ware, Tricolor, Black Ground, White Vinework, 3 Piece 7640.00
Tea Set, Queen's Ware, Commemorative, Embossed, Edward VIII Coronation, c.1937 .... 59.00
Tea Set, Stoneware, Smear Glaze, Gothic Style, Satyr Masks, c.1830, 3 Piece 999.00
Tea Tray, Jasperware, Blue, Oval, Applied White Arabesque Border, Sunflower, 14 In. ... 590.00
Tea Tray, Jasperware, Blue, Oval, White Acanthus & Leaf Border, Late 1700s, 17 1/2 In. . 2056.00
Teabowl, Saucer, Jasper Dip, Lilac, White Leaf Relief, Late 1700s, 5 1/4 In. 1295.00
Teapot, Cover, Black Basalt, Applied Rosso Antico Acanthus, Bell Flowers, 7 1/4 In. 880.00
Teapot, Cover, Caneware, Silver, Octagonal, Brown Relief Classical Figures, 5 3/8 In. ... 590.00
Teapot, Cover, Caneware, Smear Glaze, Green Leaf Relief, 19th Century, 4 In. 530.00
Teapot, Cover, Drab Ware, Blue Fern & Star Relief, England, c.1830, 5 1/8 In. 645.00
Teapot, Cover, Jasper Dip, Yellow, Applied Black Classical Relief, Leaves, 4 1/4 In. 500.00
Teapot, Cover, Queen's Ware, Globular, Leaf Spout, Entwined Handle, c.1770, 4 3/4 In. . 1175.00
Teapot, Cover, Rosso Antico, Applied White Prunus, Twig Handle, Late 1700s, 4 5/8 In. . 1410.00
Teapot, Cover, Stand, Caneware, Beehive Shape, Early 1800s, 6 1/2 In. 1295.00
Teapot, Cover, SYP, Rockingham, c.1900, 8 In. 235.00
Teapot, Ferrara, Italian Harbor Scene, Blue & White, c.1900, 5 1/2 In. 45.00
Teapot, Man, Woman, Drinking Tea In Garden, Black Transfer, Ribbon Handle, 5 In. 1575.00
Teapot, Stoneware, Salt Glazed, Scrolled Leaves & Flowers, Spaniel Finial, 7 1/2 In. 345.00
Tile, Majolica, Fruit, Vegetable High Relief, Leaves, Late 19th Century, 6 In., Pair 355.00
Toast Rack, Queen's Ware, Green Enamel Trim, 19th Century, 7 1/4 In. 265.00
Tobacco Jar, White On Green, Fox Hunting Scenes, 4 1/2 x 4 1/4 In. 70.00
Tray, Fairyland Luster, Lily, Green Fish Border, Mother-Of-Pearl, c.1920, 9 1/4 In. 880.00
Tray, Ice Cream, Argenta, Majolica, Rectangular, Scalloped Rim, c.1880, 10 1/2 In. 825.00
Tray, Leaf & Lily Of The Valley, 9 1/2 In. 335.00
Tray, Majolica, Trefoil, Mottled Blue, Brown, Yellow, Branch Shape Handle, 12 In. 295.00
Tureen, Cover, Stand, Ladle, Queen's Ware, Scrolled Handles, Leaf Knop, c.1800, 10 In. . 590.00
Tureen, Cover, Underplatter, Queen's Ware, Japan Pattern, c.1882, 12 3/4 In. 529.00
Tureen, Sauce, Cover, Stand, Stoneware, White Glaze, Shell Shape, Finial, 5 1/4 In. 410.00
Umbrella Stand, Bird & Fan, Turquoise Ground, Cobalt Blue Accents, 22 In. 4820.00

Urn, Crater, Black Basalt, Encaustic Decorated, Cover, England, c.1862, 5 1/4 In. 2115.00
Urn, Crater, Pierced Cover, Black Basalt, Enamel, Painted Sprays, Mid 1800s, 6 In. 1410.00
Urn, Jasperware, Cover, Coral, Blue, Gray Field, Musicians, Orators, Impressed, 8 In. . . . 1300.00
Urn, Jasperware, Green, White, Classical Sprigging, c.1890, 8 3/4 In., Pair 460.00
Vase, Basalt, Auro, Raised Foliage, Iron Red Enamel Band, c.1885, 11 1/2 In. 235.00
Vase, Black Basalt, Lion's Head Handles, Masks, Bentley, c.1775, 16 1/2 In. 5875.00
Vase, Black Basalt, Relief Leaves, Trumpet Shape, England, Early 1900s, 9 1/2 In., Pair . . 470.00
Vase, Black Basalt, Scrolled Handles, Goat Masks, Festoons, Bentley, 5 1/2 In. 2350.00
Vase, Black Basalt, Sphinx Head Handles, Classical, Bentley, c.1775, 13 In. 999.00
Vase, Bone China, Shell Shape, White Glaze, Coral Stem, Late 1800s, 10 In. 500.00
Vase, Caneware, Bamboo, Free-Form Base, Blue, Green, Late 1700s, 10 In. 7930.00
Vase, Caneware, Multicolored Enamel, Millicent Taplin, c.1930, 8 In. 380.00
Vase, Copper Luster, Cane Glazed, Multicolored Flowers, Millicent Taplin, c.1928, 8 In. . 500.00
Vase, Cover, Black Basalt, Fluted Neck, Sphinx Handles, Bentley, c.1775, 13 1/2 In. 2235.00
Vase, Cover, Jasper Dip, Black, White Swag Band, Bacchus Head Handles, 8 In. 560.00
Vase, Cover, Jasper Dip, Dice Ware, Tricolor, Dancing Hours Relief, 1900s, 8 3/4 In. 2000.00
Vase, Cover, Jasper Dip, Dice Ware, Tricolor, White Classical Relief, 11 1/2 In. 1410.00
Vase, Cover, Jasper Dip, Green, White Classical Relief, Leaf Borders, 1800s, 13 In. 1175.00
Vase, Cover, Jasperware, Blue, Double Handles, Arabesque Flowers, Borders, 9 In., Pair . 1295.00
Vase, Cover, Queen's Ware, Horn Handles, Masks, Emile Lessore, c.1860, 15 1/2 In. 1645.00
Vase, Cover, Queen's Ware, Trophies Within Festoons, c.1880, 10 1/8 In. 2235.00
Vase, Cover, Terra-Cotta, White, Beaded Borders, Late 18th Century, 4 In. 1645.00
Vase, Cover, Variegated Agate, Bacchus Head Handles, Bentley, c.1770, 8 3/4 In. 2820.00
Vase, Dragon Luster, Blue Iridescent, Gold, 5 In. 290.00
Vase, Earthenware, Silver Luster, Cane Ground, Flaring Rim, Louise Powell, c.1930, 8 In. 645.00
Vase, Fairyland Luster, Argus Pheasant, Birds, Flowers, c.1920, 9 In. 7050.00
Vase, Fairyland Luster, Candlemas, Black Ground Panel, c.1920, 7 1/2 In. 9400.00
Vase, Fairyland Luster, Torches, Stairs, Lead To Temple, Trees, Birds, Marked, 11 In. 5175.00
Vase, Fish Luster, Mottled Blue Exterior, Multicolored, Gilt, c.1920, 8 7/8 In. 1880.00
Vase, Jasper Dip, Blue, Classical Scene, Pedestal Base, c.1876, 20 In. 1095.00
Vase, Jasper Dip, Cylindrical, Flaring Rim, Green Basket Weave, c.1800, 5 In. 2820.00
Vase, Jasper Dip, Dark Blue, Classical Relief Figures, Portland, 1800s, 10 1/4 In. 1060.00
Vase, Jasper Dip, Portland, Black, Applied White Classical Relief, c.1900, 8 In. 440.00
Vase, Jasper Dip, Tricolor, White Leaf Border, Cylindrical Shape, c.1800, 5 In. 2820.00
Vase, Jasperware, Black, White Trim, Orange Peel Ground, Frank Brookes, c.1979, 6 In. . 1175.00
Vase, Jasperware, Blue, Classical Relief, Frank Brookes, c.1980, 5 3/4 In. 499.00
Vase, Jasperware, Blue, Fluted Rim, White Mask Relief, Octagonal Plinth, 5 1/2 In. 590.00
Vase, Jasperware, Blue, Relief Portraits, Floral Band, Frank Brookes, c.1980, 5 1/2 In. . . . 120.00
Vase, Jasperware, Blue, White, Portland, Impressed, 8 In. 880.00
Vase, Jasperware, Cobalt Blue Field, Figures Standing, Holding Mask, 8 In. 475.00
Vase, Majolica, Chinese Style, Looped Foo Dog Handles, Green, Brown, Cream, 10 In. . . 705.00
Vase, Majolica, Figural, Child Seated On Log, Oval Base, c.1868, 6 3/4 In. 264.00
Vase, Marsden Art Ware, Bottle Shape, Slip Flowers, Vines, c.1885, 12 3/4 In. 940.00
Vase, Marsden Art Ware, Slip, Blue Ground, Oranges On Branches, c.1890, 10 1/2 In. . . . 1645.00
Vase, Potpourri, Cover, Jasperware, Lilac, White Medallions, Swags, c.1961, 12 In., Pair . 2470.00
Vase, Queen's Ware, Bottle Shape, Pierced, Gilding, Harry Barnard, c.1900, 11 1/2 In. . . . 205.00
Vase, Queen's Ware, Game Birds, Flowers, Upturned Loop Handles, c.1862, 12 In., Pair . . 3525.00
Vase, Queen's Ware, Molded, Squat Bottle Shape, Processional, Military Relief, 7 In. 650.00
Vase, Queen's Ware, Pierced Trumpet Shape, Acanthus Leaves, Early 1900s, 10 1/4 In. . . 940.00
Vase, Queen's Ware, Scroll Handles, Emile Lessore, c.1864, 8 1/2 In. 825.00
Vase, Terra-Cotta, White, Meander Border, Late 18th Century, 6 In. 705.00
Vase, Wall, Jasperware, Blue, 3 Winged Putti, Late 19th Century, 6 In. 69.00
Veilleuse, Queen's Ware, Insert Bowl, Cover, Bail Handle, 18th Century, 11 1/2 In. 1115.00
Wall Plaque, Majolica, Yellow Glaze Roundel, Relief Of Medusa, c.1870, 6 In. 1058.00
Wall Pocket, Moonlight Luster, Shell Shape, Pierced Insert Grid, c.1810, 9 3/4 In. 825.00
Washbowl, Willow Ware, 19th Century, 16 In. 173.00

WELLER pottery was first made in 1872 in Fultonham, Ohio. The firm
moved to Zanesville, Ohio, in 1882. Artwares were introduced in
1893. Hundreds of lines of pottery were produced, including
Louwelsa, Eocean, Dickens Ware, and Sicardo, before the pottery
closed in 1948.

LOUWELSA
WELLER

Ansonia, Pitcher, Orange, Green, Highly Textured, 8 1/2 In. 115.00

Arcola, Lamp Base, Ruby Grapes, Brown & Green Ground, 9 5/8 In. 185.00
Ardsley, Bowl, Bulb, Green White, 5 In. 70.00
Ardsley, Flower Frog, Fish, Purple, Green, Signed, 6 In. 545.00
Art Nouveau, Vase, Panels Of Poppies & Grapes, 11 x 3 1/4 In. 290.00
Aurelian, Vase, Blossoms, Berries, Marked, 10 1/4 x 4 In. 115.00
Aurelian, Vase, Carnations, Twisted, Faceted, 7 1/2 x 6 In. 305.00
Baldin, Vase, Apples, Stems, Leaves, Squat, 7 x 5 In. . . . . *Illus* 115.00
Baldin, Vase, Blue, Apples, Leaves, Branches, Trumpet Neck, 6 3/4 x 10 In. 250.00
Barcelona, Bowl, Low, Hand Thrown, 2 1/2 x 10 1/2 In. 150.00
Barcelona, Jardiniere, Hand Thrown, 10 1/4 x 14 5/8 In. 405.00
Barcelona, Jardiniere, Hand Thrown, 9 x 10 3/4 In. 375.00
Blossom, Jardiniere, Blue, Urn Shape, 2 Looped Handles, 9 1/2 In. 80.00
Blue Drapery, Pedestal, Red Roses, Blue Ground, 22 In. 290.00
Blue Ware, Compote, 4 5/8 x 8 1/8 In. 45.00
Blue Ware, Vase, Grecian Maiden Dancing, Stamped, 8 3/4 x 4 1/2 In. 115.00
Blue Ware, Vase, Grecian Maiden, Yellow Dress, Oval, 7 1/4 x 3 3/4 In. 200.00
Bonito, Vase, Blue Blossom, Cream Ground, Green Interior, Flared, Etched, 9 1/4 x 6 In. . . 115.00
Bonito, Vase, Pink Daisies, Bulbous, Marked, 6 In. 115.00
Brighton, Vase, Wall, Kingfisher, Branches, 11 7/8 In. 575.00
Chase, Vase, Blue, White Relief, Horse & Rider Jumping Fence, 5 1/2 In. 290.00
Chase, Vase, Hunter, On Horse, Dogs, Blue, White, Marked, 10 x 7 1/4 In. 435.00
Chase, Vase, Man On Horseback, Jumping Fence, Blue Ground, Incised, 5 1/2 x 5 In. 260.00
Chengtu, Vase, Orange, Faceted, Stamped, 9 1/4 x 4 In. 290.00
Claywood, Pedestal, Roses, Marked, 18 In. 175.00
Clinton Ivory, Umbrella Stand, Leaves, Scrolls, Bisque, Cylindrical, 19 In. 210.00
Clinton Ivory, Vase, Oak Leaf Rows, Cylindrical, 9 1/4 x 4 1/2 In. 105.00
Cloudburst, Vase, Blue, 5 1/4 In. 175.00
Coppertone, Bowl, Bass, Sentry Frog On Edge, 5 x 10 In. 1035.00
Coppertone, Bowl, Frog On Lily Pad, Stamped, 2 x 15 In. 490.00
Coppertone, Bowl, Frog, On Lily Pad, Marked, 15 x 10 1/2 In. 345.00
Coppertone, Bowl, Lily & Pods, 3 x 12 In. 290.00
Coppertone, Bowl, Mottled Green, Copper Highlights, Water Lilies, Frog, 3 x 12 1/2 In. . . 575.00
Coppertone, Candlestick, Frog On Lily Pad, 3 1/4 x 5 In., Pair 520.00
Coppertone, Candlestick, Turtle, Lily Pad, 3 1/4 In., Pair 550.00
Coppertone, Candlestick, Turtles, Blossoms, Lily Pad, Marked, 3 1/4 x 5 1/4 In., Pair . . . 550.00
Coppertone, Console, Frog, Perched On Lily Pad, Green, Brown Glaze, 4 x 11 In. 605.00
Coppertone, Dish, Frog Perched On Edge, Green, Marked, 3 x 6 1/4 In. 315.00
Coppertone, Figurine, Frog, Green, 2 1/4 x 2 3/4 In. 290.00
Coppertone, Figurine, Frog, Lily Pad, Marked, 4 In. 230.00
Coppertone, Figurine, Frog, Stamped, 2 1/2 x 2 1/4 In. 290.00
Coppertone, Fountain, Frog, Stamped, 8 1/2 x 11 In. 1725.00
Coppertone, Vase, 2 Frogs Perched On Sides, Bulbous, Stamped, 8 x 8 In. 1610.00
Coppertone, Vase, Beaker Shape, Incised Z, 6 In. 230.00
Coppertone, Vase, Flared, Brown, Green Matte Glaze, 8 1/2 In. 345.00
Coppertone, Vase, Frog, Clinging To Base, Brown To Green Glaze, Flared, 9 x 3 1/2 In. . . 430.00
Coppertone, Vase, Frog, Clinging To Base, Flared, Stamped, 9 x 3 1/2 In. 575.00
Coppertone, Vase, Green & Black Glaze, Bulbous, Flared Rim, Tab Handles, 7 1/2 In. 195.00
Coppertone, Vase, Lily Pad, Trefoil, 4 Frog Heads, Flared, 11 1/4 x 5 1/2 In. 4025.00

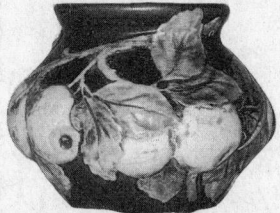

Weller, Baldin, Vase, Apples, Stems,
Leaves, Squat, 7 x 5 In.

Weller, Hudson, Vase,
Irises, On Lavender To
Pink Ground, Oval,
Signed, 6 1/4 x 3 1/4 In.

Cornish, Vase, Blue, Marked, 7 1/4 x 4 1/4 In. 175.00
Creamware, Jar, Tobacco, Cover, Embossed Pipes & Flowers, 7 1/2 x 5 1/2 In. 259.00
Dickens Ware, Humidor, Chinese Man, Signed, 6 1/4 x 4 1/4 In. 1035.00
Dickens Ware, Jug, American Indian, Blue Hawk, Painted, Incised, 6 In. . . . . .430.00 to 520.00
Dickens Ware, Mug, A Chirping Cupid's My Mating Song, Blue Ground, 5 In. 375.00
Dickens Ware, Mug, Garlands, Yellow Blossoms, Fishscale Base, Green Ground, 7 In. . . . 460.00
Dickens Ware, Mug, Incised Monk Design, Signed, 5 1/2 In. 145.00
Dickens Ware, Tankard, Indian Chief, Headdress, 12 In. 2000.00
Dickens Ware, Tobacco Jar, Turk, 7 1/2 x 6 In. 715.00
Dickens Ware, Umbrella Stand, Sailboat, Lake, Sunset, Trees, Second Line, 21 In. 4850.00
Dickens Ware, Vase, American Indian, Black Bird, 7 1/2 In. 575.00
Dickens Ware, Vase, American Indian, Incised, 6 In. 260.00
Dickens Ware, Vase, Colonial Scene, Man, Woman, Path, Second Line, 15 1/4 In. 3680.00
Dickens Ware, Vase, Etched Monk, Painted Green Flowers, Pillow, 4 3/4 x 6 In. 200.00
Dickens Ware, Vase, Man Golfer, Signed, 10 1/4 In. 2200.00
Dickens Ware, Vase, Portrait, Ghost Bull, 8 1/2 In. 1500.00
Dickens Ware, Vase, Swimming Fish, Incised, 3 Sides, Marked, 7 x 4 3/4 In. 430.00
Dickens Ware, Vase, Woman Golfer, Signed, 9 1/2 In. 2300.00
Eocean, Jardiniere, Pink Carnations, 7 x 8 1/2 In. 115.00
Eocean, Vase, Blue Berries, Leaves, Cylindrical, Stamped, 9 3/4 x 4 1/4 In. 175.00
Eocean, Vase, Bud, Forget-Me-Nots, 5 7/8 In. 140.00
Eocean, Vase, Cherries, Oval, Stamped, 9 x 4 In. 315.00
Eocean, Vase, Corset Form, Honeysuckle Blossoms, 8 3/8 In. 375.00
Eocean, Vase, Cylindrical, Hollyhocks, 6 Loop Handles, 15 3/8 In. 1610.00
Eocean, Vase, Flowers & Berries, 9 In. 140.00
Eocean, Vase, Forget-Me-Nots, Mae Timberlake, 8 1/4 In. 290.00
Eocean, Vase, Gooseberries, Leaves, Oval, Etched, 10 1/2 x 3 3/4 In. 489.00
Eocean, Vase, Grape Branches, Leaves, Marked, 11 3/4 x 6 1/2 In. 1265.00
Eocean, Vase, Gray Kitten, Elizabeth Blake, 6 1/2 In. 1725.00
Eocean, Vase, Painted Berries, Leaves, Shaded Green Ground, Tapered, 7 x 2 1/2 In. 430.00
Eocean, Vase, Painted Daisies, Tapered, Stamped, 3 1/4 x 3 In. 230.00
Eocean, Vase, Pansies, Purple, Cream, Brown, Cylindrical, Signed, 8 x 2 1/2 In. 345.00
Eocean, Vase, Pink, Yellow, 12 3/8 In. 405.00
Eocean, Vase, Red Berries, Leaves, Flat Shoulder, Cupped Rim, Etched, 7 1/4 x 5 1/4 In. . 415.00
Eocean, Vase, Toy Spaniel, Elizabeth Blake, 12 In. 1840.00
Eocean Rose, Mug, Red Cherry Decoration, 6 In. 115.00
Etched Matte, Mug, Woman, Flowing Blond Hair, Incised, 5 x 4 3/4 In. 175.00
Etched Matte, Vase, Stylized Stems, Flowers, Orange, Corseted, Marked, 11 x 4 In. 375.00
Etna, Mug, Fruit & Leaf, Signed, 6 In. 190.00
Etna, Vase, Blue Blossoms, Tapered, Stamped, 5 3/4 x 2 1/2 In. 58.00
Etna, Vase, Daffodils, Marked, 11 1/4 x 4 1/2 In. 375.00
Etna, Vase, Pink Blossoms, 2 Crossed Handles, Marked, 4 3/4 x 8 3/4 In. 175.00
Etna, Vase, Pink Flowers, Corseted, Stamped, 4 1/2 x 3 3/4 In. 230.00
Etna, Vase, Pink Roses, Shaded Gray Ground, Stamped, 10 1/4 x 4 In. 345.00
Flemish, Basket, Pink Roses, Handles, 5 x 6 1/4 In. 145.00
Flemish, Jardiniere, Lion's Heads, Sprays Of Roses, Green, Brown, 9 3/4 x 12 In. 250.00
Flemish, Jardiniere, Stylized Roses, 18 In. 175.00
Flemish, Planter, Band Of Leaves, Fruit, 10 1/2 x 12 In. 200.00
Fleron, Bowl, Green, Fluted Rim, Braided Handles, 4 x 8 7/8 In. 90.00
Fleron, Vase, Blue, Mottled Pink Interior, Marked, 8 1/4 x 5 1/4 In. 175.00
Fleron, Vase, Tan Over Yellow, 9 5/8 In. 115.00
Floretta, Vase, Bulbous, Stamped, 12 x 8 In. 144.00
Forest, Jardiniere, 8 1/2 In. 140.00
Forest, Jardiniere, Pedestal, Landscape, 27 In. 1725.00
Forest, Vase, Flared, Stamped, 8 In., Pair 345.00
Glendale, Candlestick, Chirping Bird, Nest, Blue Eggs, 2 In., Pair 345.00
Glendale, Vase, Double Bud, Blue Bird & Nest, Leaves, Berries, Tree Trunks, 7 x 7 In. . . 220.00
Greenbriar, Ewer, Double Ring Handle, 11 1/4 In. 259.00
Greora, Bowl, Brown, Green, 8-Sided, Flared, Marked, 2 1/2 x 14 1/2 In. 230.00
Greora, Vase, Flared Rim, 6 1/2 x 5 1/4 In. 145.00
Greora, Vase, Rust Shaded To Green, Marked, 8 1/2 x 5 3/4 In. 520.00
Hobart, Bowl, Flower Frog, Boy & Swan, 9 1/4 In. 374.00
Hobart, Vase, Bud, Woman, Holding Her Dress, Green Blue Glaze, Stamped, 11 x 8 In. . . 460.00

Hudson, Irises, Blue, White, Orange, Green, Gray Green Ground, 12 1/2 In. 825.00
Hudson, Vase, Berries & Leaves, On Cream Ground, Signed, Pillsbury, 8 3/4 x 4 In. 345.00
Hudson, Vase, Blooming Irises, Buds, Hester Pillsbury, 6 5/8 In. 920.00
Hudson, Vase, Blue Freesia, Baluster, Stamped, 8 1/4 x 3 1/2 In. 315.00
Hudson, Vase, Blue, Cluster Of Pink Blossoms, Flared, Stamped, 7 x 3 In. 405.00
Hudson, Vase, Blue, Pink Blossoms, Green, Pink Band, Oval, Stamped, 8 x 5 In. 290.00
Hudson, Vase, Blue, White Irises, 2 Handles, Signed, Sarah McLaughlin, 16 x 7 In. 4600.00
Hudson, Vase, Daffodils, Cylindrical, Stamped, 8 1/2 x 3 1/2 In. 290.00
Hudson, Vase, Dogwood Blossoms, Sara Timberlake, 6 3/4 In. 375.00
Hudson, Vase, Dogwood, Pink, White, Faceted, 12 x 5 1/2 In. 290.00
Hudson, Vase, Irises, On Lavender To Pink Ground, Oval, Signed, 6 1/4 x 3 1/4 In. . *Illus* 575.00
Hudson, Vase, Jonquils, Ivory, Yellow, Faceted, Stamped, 9 3/4 x 4 3/4 In. 315.00
Hudson, Vase, Lily Of The Valley, Teal To Blue Ground, Naomi Walch, 8 3/4 In. 1430.00
Hudson, Vase, Multitone Blue Matte Glaze, Bulbous, Signed, Walch, 10 In. 920.00
Hudson, Vase, Owl, In Tree, Under Full Moon, Oval, Signed, Ed Abel, 14 1/2 x 7 1/2 In. . 2990.00
Hudson, Vase, Painted Acorns, Oak Leaves, Oval, Stamped, 10 x 4 3/4 In. 315.00
Hudson, Vase, Pink & White Roses, Hester Pillsbury, 13 1/4 In. 2415.00
Hudson, Vase, Pink Poppies, Shaded Gray To Pink Ground, Bulbous, 10 1/2 x 5 1/2 In. ... 920.00
Hudson, Vase, Pink Primrose, Oval, Stamped, 9 x 4 1/2 In. 230.00
Hudson, Vase, Pink Tulips, Green Leaves, Blue, Green Ground, McLaughlin, 12 In. 1795.00
Hudson, Vase, Poppies, Pink, Blue, Ivory, Stamped, Timberlake, 12 x 6 1/2 In. 2415.00
Hudson, Vase, Purple & White Iris, Lavender Gray To Ivory Ground, 10 1/2 In. 715.00
Hudson, Vase, Rose, Hester Pillsbury, 10 5/8 In. 90.00
Hudson, Vase, Sweet Violet Bouquet, Dorothy England, 6 5/8 In. 575.00
Hudson, Vase, Twin Morning Glory Blossoms, Sarah McLaughlin, 7 7/8 In. 750.00
Hudson, Vase, Violets, Oval, Stamped, 10 x 4 In. 575.00
Hudson, Vase, White & Yellow Roses On Shoulder, Blue Ground, Corseted, 13 1/2 In. ... 1100.00
Hudson, Vase, Wild Roses, Bulbous, Stamped, 8 3/4 x 3 3/4 In. .... *Illus* 400.00
Hudson, Vase, Yellow Roses, 2 Handles, Hester Pillsbury, 9 1/4 In. 1150.00
Hunter, Vase, Duck Over Choppy Water, 3-Sided, Charles B. Upjohn, No. 353, 6 7/8 In. . 690.00
Hunter, Vase, Seagulls, Flying Over Ocean, 7 1/4 x 3 In. 630.00
Ivory, Planter, Panels Of Flowers, 5 x 6 In. 60.00
Jap Birdimal, Creamer, Dutch Landscape, Blue, Marked, 2 1/4 x 3 1/2 In. 145.00
Jap Birdimal, Hair Receiver, 4 Ships, Tan, Ivory, Black, Cobalt Blue Ground, 1 3/4 x 4 In. 520.00
Jap Birdimal, Mug, Blue Viking Ship, Ivory Ground, Handles, Stamped, 4 x 6 1/4 In. 85.00
Jap Birdimal, Pedestal, Trees, Rocky Path, 25 3/4 In. 1150.00
Jap Birdimal, Planter, Green Matte Glaze, 4 Loop Handles, 5 1/2 x 8 In. 90.00
Jap Birdimal, Planter, Stylized Trees, Geese On Rim, 4 Loop Handles, 5 1/2 x 7 1/4 In. .. 1150.00
Jap Birdimal, Vase, Man, Handles, Signed, Rhead, 5 In. 750.00
Jardiniere, Green Matte Glaze, Embossed Elephant Ear Leaves, 11 x 12 1/4 In. 635.00
Jardiniere, Leaf & Fern, Cream, Green, Wrought Iron Stand, 12 x 11 In., 34-In. Stand ... 980.00
Jardiniere, Yellow & Amber Peonies, Brown Ground, 9 1/4 x 11 1/2 In. 115.00
Kenova, Vase, Green, Applied Twisted Stems, Leaves, 8 3/4 x 5 In. 260.00
L'Art Nouveau, Vase, Pillow, Embossed, Long-Haired Woman, Profile, Stamp, 6 x 5 3/4 In. 520.00
LaSa, Bowl, Landscapes, Pink, Gold, 9 In. 230.00
LaSa, Vase, Bud, Lake, Trees, Brown, Gold, 7 1/4 In., Pair 520.00
LaSa, Vase, Palm Trees, Mountains, Building, Marked, 15 In. 920.00
LaSa, Vase, Winter Riverscape, 5 1/8 In. 315.00

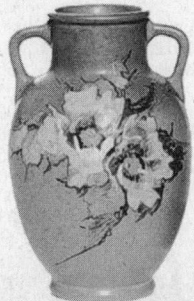

Weller, Hudson,
Vase, Wild Roses,
Bulbous, Stamped,
8 3/4 x 3 3/4 In.

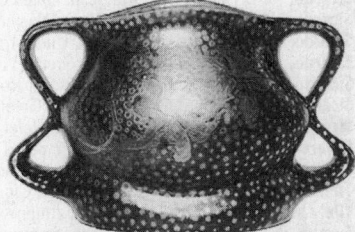

Weller, Sicardo, Vase, Iridescent Metallic Glaze,
Handles, Stylized Design, Signed, 9 In.

Louwelsa, Ewer, Nasturtium, Bulbous, Marked, 7 x 6 1/4 In. 200.00
Louwelsa, Jardiniere, Pedestal, Yellow Daffodils, 24 x 10 In. 316.00
Louwelsa, Jug, Berries & Leaves, Round, Marked, 6 1/2 x 5 1/2 In. 175.00
Louwelsa, Jug, Blackberries, Leaves, Spherical, Marked, 6 1/2 x 5 3/4 In. 259.00
Louwelsa, Jug, Egg Shape, Pansy Design, Early 1900s, 4 In. 230.00
Louwelsa, Lamp, Oil, Nasturtiums, Marked, 17 In. 690.00
Louwelsa, Mug, Arabian Man Portrait, Marked, 6 1/2 x 4 1/4 In. 345.00
Louwelsa, Mug, Portrait Of Man, With Glasses, Stamped, 6 x 5 3/4 In. 200.00
Louwelsa, Pitcher, Ear Of Corn, Stamped, 13 1/2 x 6 1/2 In. 315.00
Louwelsa, Tankard, Flowers, Leaves, Stems, Impressed, 12 1/4 In. 175.00
Louwelsa, Vase, Orange Blossoms, Around Shoulder, Squat, Stamped, 3 1/4 x 5 1/4 In. ... 175.00
Louwelsa, Vase, Pansies In Relief, Stylized Stems, Blue, High Glaze, 6 1/2 x 8 1/2 In. 935.00
Louwelsa, Vase, Pillow, Painted Orange, White Carnations, Marked, 4 In. 105.00
Louwelsa, Vase, Spider Mums, Orange, Yellow, Frank Ferrell, 14 3/8 In. 865.00
Louwelsa, Vase, Wild Roses, Brown, Tan, Squat, Marked, A.S., 3 x 5 1/2 In. 260.00
Malvern, Vase, Pillow, Bud, Leaves, Red, Green, Yellow, Marked, 8 x 6 1/2 In. 175.00
Manhattan, Vase, Flared, 9 x 5 In. 200.00
Marbleized, Vase, High Gloss Glaze, Signed, 5 1/4 In. 95.00
Marengo, Vase, Gray, 9 3/4 x 4 1/4 In. 750.00
Marvo, Vase, Brown, Bulbous, Stamped, 8 x 5 1/4 In. 145.00
Muskota, Figurine, Woman Kneeling, Stamped, 7 1/2 x 6 In. 315.00
Muskota, Flower Frog, Boy, Fishing, 7 x 5 In. 145.00
Muskota, Flower Frog, Boy, Fishing, Green & Ocher Glaze, 6 1/2 x 5 In. 110.00
Muskota, Flower Frog, Frog, On Lily Pad, 4 1/2 x 5 In. 110.00
Noval, Compote, Fruit, Black Bands, 5 5/8 In. 60.00
Orris, Hanging Basket, Red Flowers, Scalloped Rim, 3 1/2 x 6 1/2 In. 90.00
Parian, Vase, Etched Flowers, Rolled Rim, 9 1/4 In. 80.00
Rhead Faience, Vase, Squeezebag Peacock Feathers, Blue, Green Ground, 6 1/2 In. 1295.00
Roma, Bowl, Garlands, Birds, Footed, Handles, 5 1/4 x 11 In. 90.00
Roma, Planter, Flower Panels, Faceted, 6 1/2 x 7 In. 145.00
Roma, Vase, Cylindrical, 4 Panels, Flowers, Branches, 9 In. 140.00
Roma, Vase, Fan Shape, 6 1/4 In. 50.00
Rosemont, Bowl, Glasgow Roses, Glossy Black, Stamped, 9 In. Diam. 90.00
Rosemont, Vase, Bird, Black Ground, Signed, 10 In. 460.00
Sabrinian, Vase, Mauve Shell, Aqua Seaweed, Seahorse Handles, Fan Shape, 7 x 8 In. ... 440.00
Sabrinian, Vase, Shell Design, 2 Seahorse Handles, Trumpet Neck, Ocher Matte, 10 1/2 In. ... 330.00
Sicardo, Bowl, Clover, Under Red, Purple, Green Glaze, 4 Buttresses, 2 1/2 x 6 1/2 In. ... 518.00
Sicardo, Vase, Blue, Green, Gold Iridescent, Flowers, 6 In. 520.00
Sicardo, Vase, Chrysanthemums, Copper Glaze, Purple Iridescent, 5 1/4 x 3 1/4 In. 550.00
Sicardo, Vase, Daffodils, Blizzard, Swirled Body, 9 1/2 In. 980.00
Sicardo, Vase, Daisies, 10 In. 2895.00
Sicardo, Vase, Flowers, Dots, Iridescent Purple, Blue, Green, Gold, Bulbous, 3 3/4 In. ... 550.00
Sicardo, Vase, Holly & Leaves, Nacreous Purple, Gold, Green, 4-Sided, Signed, 16 In. ... 1380.00
Sicardo, Vase, Iridescent Metallic Glaze, Handles, Stylized Design, Signed, 9 In. ... *Illus* 2070.00
Sicardo, Vase, Iridescent Ruby Crackle Laze, Holly Silhouette, Green Blue, 4 3/8 In. 949.00
Sicardo, Vase, Iridescent, Flowers & Leaf, Art Nouveau, Signed, 7 1/4 In. 275.00
Sicardo, Vase, Leaves, Wavy Lines, Under Iridescent Purple, Green, Yellow, Tapered, 5 In. 750.00
Sicardo, Vase, Mistletoe, Marked, 10 x 3 In. 750.00
Sicardo, Vase, Mottled Iridescent Glaze, Magenta, Gold, Blue, Green, Butterflies, 5 1/2 In. 1200.00
Sicardo, Vase, Oak Leaves, Iridescent Green Ground, 16 In. 8900.00
Sicardo, Vase, Peacock Feathers, Vines, Nacreous Purple, Red, Gold, Green, 4-Sided, 16 In. 1380.00
Sicardo, Vase, Pillow, Spider Mums, Under Iridescent Green, Orange, Marked, 10 1/2 In. . 1840.00
Sicardo, Vase, Stylized Ferns, Blue, Green, Violet Iridescent, Tapered, Swollen Top, 6 In. . 550.00
Sicardo, Vase, Stylized Flowers, Iridescent Body, 3 7/8 In. 705.00
Sicardo, Vase, Stylized Grapes & Vines, Green & Amethyst Iridescent, 14 1/2 In. 3300.00
Sicardo, Vase, Stylized Vines, Green & Violet Iridescent, Cylindrical Neck, 9 3/4 In. 1100.00
Silvertone, Jardiniere, Hydrangea, Stamped, 11 x 10 1/2 In. 865.00
Silvertone, Vase, Rambling Roses, Bee, Hester Pillsbury, 8 1/8 In. 430.00
Tile, Castle, Lavender Roof, Bushes, Shy, Clouds, 6 x 6 In. 1600.00
Tile, Castle, White, Pink, Green, Blue, Impressed Mark, 6 In. 805.00
Turada, Bowl, Corseted, Squeezebag, Stamped, 3 1/4 x 8 In. 145.00
Turada, Vase, Oil Lamp Shape, Gold Lattice Lid, 6 x 9 1/2 In. 345.00
Turkis, Vase, Flared, Signed, 8 3/4 x 6 In. 145.00

Velva, Vase, Cover, Brown, Handles, Marked, 11 1/4 x 6 In. 375.00
Warwick, Planter, Handles, Stamped, 4 1/2 x 9 3/4 In. 60.00
Warwick, Vase, Pillow, Handles, Stamped, 10 x 7 In. 173.00
Woodcraft, Candlestick, Double, Owl, 14 In. 490.00
Woodcraft, Dish, Squirrel, Perched On Rim, Stamped, 5 x 6 1/2 In. 290.00
Woodcraft, Planter, Foxes In Den, 6 x 7 In. 315.00
Woodcraft, Vase, Branches & Pink Blossoms, 8 1/2 x 4 1/4 In. 145.00
Woodcraft, Vase, Bud, Double, Fruit Trees, 7 1/2 x 8 In. 175.00
Woodcraft, Vase, Foxes, Handle, Impressed Mark, 12 1/2 In. 520.00
Woodcraft, Vase, Tree Shape, Stamped, 10 1/2 x 4 1/4 In. 115.00
Woodcraft, Wall Pocket, Squirrel, 9 In. 520.00
Woodland, Planter, Foxes In Den, Stamped, 4 1/2 x 7 In. 259.00
Zona, Jardiniere, Pedestal, Bands Of Flowers, Columns, 32 1/2 In. 460.00
Zona, Pitcher, Cattails & Kingfisher Panels, Stamped, 8 x 8 1/2 In. 115.00

WESTMORELAND GLASS was made by the Westmoreland Glass
Company of Grapeville, Pennsylvania, from 1890 to 1984. They made
clear and colored glass of many varieties, such as milk glass, pressed
glass, and slag glass.

Beaded Bouquet, Candy Jar, Cover, Opaque Almond, Footed, 8 In. 40.00
Beaded Bouquet, Vase, Bud, Opaque Almond, Hexagonal Foot, 9 3/4 In. 35.00
Beaded Edge, Bowl, Milk Glass, Pansy, Footed, 9 In. 28.00
Beaded Edge, Cup & Saucer, Milk Glass, Daisies 65.00
Beaded Edge, Cup & Saucer, Milk Glass, Flowers, Blue, Red Centers 65.00
Beaded Edge, Cup & Saucer, Milk Glass, Flowers, Pink 65.00
Beaded Edge, Torte Plate, Milk Glass, Zodiac, Gold Star, 14 5/8 In. 125.00
Beaded Grape, Ashtray, Milk Glass, Hand Painted, Square, 1 1/4 x 4 In. 30.00
Beaded Grape, Box, Cover, Golden Sunset, 5 1/4 x 3 5/8 In. 30.00
Beaded Grape, Candy Jar, Cover, Milk Glass, Square, Footed, 4 1/2 x 5 1/4 In. 40.00
Beaded Grape, Cigarette Box, Cover, Milk Glass, 4 x 6 In. 40.00
Beaded Grape, Cigarette Box, Cover, Milk Glass, Gold Trim, 2 x 5 7/8 In. 50.00
Beaded Grape, Compote, Cover, Milk Glass, 7 In. 30.00
Beaded Grape, Compote, Cover, Milk Glass, Blue Trim, 6 1/2 In. 40.00
Beaded Grape, Compote, Cover, Square, Milk Glass, 8 x 4 In. 40.00
Beaded Grape, Compote, Cover, Square, Milk Glass, 9 x 4 1/2 In. 50.00
Beaded Grape, Compote, Square, Milk Glass, 4 3/4 x 4 1/2 In. 25.00
Beaded Grape, Tumbler, Milk Glass, 10 Oz., 6 In. 45.00
Beaded Grape, Vase, Milk Glass, Green Leaves, Gold Grapes, Footed, 5 1/2 In. 34.00
Beaded Grape, Vase, Milk Glass, Scalloped Rim, Footed, 6 In. 25.00
Block & Star, Salt & Pepper, 3 3/8 x 1 1/4 In. 30.00
Brandywine, Basket, Picnic, Cover, Blue, Basket Weave, 5 1/4 x 5 x 3 1/2 In. 70.00
Cherry, Cookie Jar, Handles, 7 1/2 x 7 1/2 In. 85.00
Cherry, Cookie Jar, Milk Glass, Footed, Handles, 11 3/4 In. 225.00
Colonial Harvest, Dish, Cover, Milk Glass, Footed, 7 In. 40.00
Della Robbia, Bowl, Oval, Pointed Rim, 4 x 12 1/2 x 8 1/2 In. 350.00
Della Robbia, Candy Dish, Milk Glass, Roses & Bows, 7 In. 90.00
Della Robbia, Candy Dish, Multicolored Stain, 4 5/8 x 6 3/8 In. 130.00
Della Robbia, Candy Dish, Multicolored Stain, 7 In. 100.00
Della Robbia, Console Set, Cranberry Stain, 3 Piece 350.00
Della Robbia, Iced Tea, Multicolored Stain, 6 x 3 3/8 In. 45.00
Della Robbia, Rose Bowl, Ruby Stain, Footed, 5 3/4 In. 80.00
Della Robbia, Sugar, Multicolored Stain, Footed, Handles, 3 1/4 In. 25.00
Dolphin, Candlestick, 4 In., Pair 30.00
Doric, Candlestick, Green, 4 1/2 In. 20.00
Doric, Candlestick, Milk Glass, 4 1/2 In. 20.00
Duck On Nest, Dish, Cover, Milk Glass, Amber Glass Eyes, 8 1/2 In. 120.00
Eagle & Flag, Bell, 5 1/8 x 2 1/2 In. 30.00
Eagle On Basket, Dish, Cover, Spread Wings, Blue, Oval, Amber Glass Eyes 150.00
English Hobnail, Bowl, 10 x 4 1/2 In. 35.00
English Hobnail, Bowl, Brandywine Blue, Footed, Handles, 5 3/4 x 8 In. 160.00
English Hobnail, Bowl, Ivy, Square Foot, 6 3/4 x 5 In. 25.00
English Hobnail, Bowl, Laurel Green, 3-Footed, 2 3/4 x 7 In. 75.00
English Hobnail, Candlestick, Laurel Green, 3 3/4 In., Pair 80.00

English Hobnail, Candlestick, Laurel Green, 9 In., Pair 190.00
English Hobnail, Candy Dish, Cover, Milk Glass, Square Foot, 9 x 2 3/4 In. 30.00
English Hobnail, Candy Dish, Cranberry Stain, Footed, 11 3/4 x 4 1/2 In. 70.00
English Hobnail, Candy Jar, Pink, Square Foot, 9 In. 180.00
English Hobnail, Celery Dish, Pink, Oval, 9 In. 45.00
English Hobnail, Compote, Golden Sunset, Footed, 7 3/4 x 5 1/2 In. 30.00
English Hobnail, Cordial, Square Foot 15.00
English Hobnail, Creamer, Pink, Footed, 5 3/4 In. 30.00
English Hobnail, Goblet, Green, Round Foot, 8 Oz., 6 In. 35.00
English Hobnail, Goblet, Ice Blue, 8 Oz., 6 In. 50.00
English Hobnail, Ivy Ball, Square Foot, 6 3/4 x 7 1/2 In. 40.00
English Hobnail, Jar, Marmalade, Spoon, Milk Glass 65.00
English Hobnail, Pitcher, Milk Glass, Applied Crystal Handle, 7 In. 40.00
English Hobnail, Punch Set, Bowl, Base, Cups, 14 Piece 445.00
English Hobnail, Saltshaker, Crystal, Square Foot 15.00
English Hobnail, Soup, Cream, Handles, 5 In. 30.00
English Hobnail, Sugar & Creamer, Hexagonal Foot 30.00
English Hobnail, Tumbler, Footed, 7 Oz. 15.00
English Hobnail, Vase, Flared, 8 1/2 In. 35.00
English Hobnail, Vase, Milk Glass, Square Foot, 4 1/2 x 6 In. 30.00
Figurine, Bulldog, Green, Rhinestone Eyes, 2 1/2 In. 45.00
Figurine, Cardinal, Dark Blue Mist 30.00
Figurine, Cardinal, Ruby 30.00
Figurine, Owl, On Tree Stump, Antique Blue, 5 1/2 In. 35.00
Figurine, Robin, Pink, 2 x 3 1/2 In. 30.00
Forget-Me-Not, Box, Cover, Square, Milk Glass, 5 x 3 3/4 In. 65.00
Grape & Cherry, Sugar, Cover, Milk Glass, 5 x 4 3/8 In. 15.00
Hen On Nest Cover, Dish, Bermuda Blue, 5 1/2 x 4 1/4 In. ....25.00 to 26.00
Hen On Nest Cover, Dish, Blue Marble, 5 1/2 x 4 1/4 In. 25.00
Hen On Nest Cover, Dish, Brown Marble, 4 1/2 x 7 In. 25.00
Hen On Nest Cover, Dish, Marigold, 5 1/2 x 4 1/4 In. 25.00
Hen On Nest Cover, Dish, Red Carnival, 5 1/2 x 4 1/2 In. 30.00
Hen On Nest Cover, Dish, Ruby Marble, 5 1/2 x 4 1/2 In. 25.00
Lattice Edge, Candlestick, Milk Glass, 4 1/2 In., Pair 30.00
Lotus, Candlestick, 3-Light, Milk Glass, 8 1/2 x 5 In. 30.00
Lotus, Compote, Green Satin Mist, Scalloped Rim, 3 1/2 x 6 In. 15.00
Maple Leaf, Sugar & Creamer, Black Milk Glass 85.00
Mary Gregory, Bell, Boy Flying Kite 35.00
Mary Gregory, Plate, Boy Fishing, Black, Forget-Me-Not Border, 8 1/2 In. 35.00
Mary Gregory, Plate, Girl With Dog, Black, Forget-Me-Not Border, 8 1/2 In. 35.00
Old Quilt, Bowl, Cover, Milk Glass, 4 3/4 x 4 In. 35.00
Old Quilt, Bowl, Milk Glass, Square, Footed, 2 3/4 x 4 3/4 In. 15.00
Old Quilt, Box, Cover, 5 x 4 In. 40.00
Old Quilt, Butter, Cover, Gold Trim, Blue Flowers, 2 3/8 x 7 1/2 In. 80.00
Old Quilt, Candy Dish, Cover, Milk Glass, Square, 7 In. 40.00
Old Quilt, Candy Dish, Cover, Milk Glass, Square, Footed, 5 x 4 7/8 In. 25.00
Old Quilt, Creamer, Milk Glass, 3 1/2 x 5 5/8 In. 20.00
Old Quilt, Dish, Mayonnaise, Spoon, Milk Glass, Footed, 3 3/4 x 4 1/2 In. 25.00
Old Quilt, Pitcher, Antique Blue, 8 x 7 3/8 In. 75.00
Old Quilt, Pitcher, Milk Glass, Pt., 7 1/4 In. 28.00
Old Quilt, Sugar, Cover, Roses & Bows, 6 1/2 In. 40.00
Old Quilt, Sugar, Milk Glass, 3 1/2 x 3 3/4 In. 18.00
Old Quilt, Tumbler, 5 Oz., 4 In. 15.00
Old Quilt, Vase, Milk Glass, 9 x 5 1/2 In. 75.00
Owl, Plate, Milk Glass, 7 1/4 x 7 3/8 In. 30.00
Paneled Grape, Basket, Blue Mist Satin, Footed, Oval, Crimped, 7 1/2 x 6 3/8 In. 75.00
Paneled Grape, Basket, Blue Mist Satin, Oval, Crimped Rim, 7 In. 95.00
Paneled Grape, Basket, Crimped Rim, Milk Glass, 7 1/2 x 6 3/8 In. 100.00
Paneled Grape, Basket, Laurel Green, 11 x 7 1/4 In. 175.00
Paneled Grape, Basket, Milk Glass, 11 x 7 1/4 In. ....150.00 to 170.00
Paneled Grape, Basket, Milk Glass, Split Handle, Oval, 4 x 6 5/8 In. 40.00
Paneled Grape, Bowl, Milk Glass, Crimped, Footed, 6 3/8 x 7 1/2 In. 30.00
Paneled Grape, Bowl, Milk Glass, Footed, 7 7/8 x 9 3/4 In. 38.00

Paneled Grape, Bowl, Milk Glass, Oval, Scalloped Rim, Footed, 4 7/8 x 11 7/8 In. 75.00
Paneled Grape, Bowl, Milk Glass, Scalloped Rim, Footed, 3 3/4 x 8 In. 28.00
Paneled Grape, Candlestick, 3-Light, 4 1/2 x 8 In., Pair 390.00
Paneled Grape, Candlestick, Milk Glass, 4 x 2 In., Pair 28.00
Paneled Grape, Candlestick, Milk Glass, 4 x 4 In. 25.00
Paneled Grape, Candy Dish, Cover, Milk Glass, 5 1/4 x 6 1/2 In. 70.00
Paneled Grape, Candy Jar, Cover, Blue Mist Satin, Daisies, 6 1/2 In. 42.00
Paneled Grape, Compote, Cover, Footed, Bermuda Blue, 7 In. 35.00
Paneled Grape, Compote, Cover, Milk Glass, 7 In. 25.00
Paneled Grape, Compote, Golden Sunset, Footed, Crimped Rim, 5 3/4 x 7 1/2 In. 32.00
Paneled Grape, Compote, Milk Glass, 6 x 8 In. 28.00
Paneled Grape, Cruet, Milk Glass, Stopper, Handle, 2 Oz., 4 3/4 In. 25.00
Paneled Grape, Cup & Saucer, Golden Sunset 30.00
Paneled Grape, Egg Plate, Salt & Pepper, 13 In. 275.00
Paneled Grape, Epergne, Milk Glass, 2 Lilies, 13 1/2 In. 345.00
Paneled Grape, Epergne, Milk Glass, Lily, 9 In. 185.00
Paneled Grape, Fruit Cocktail, Underplate, Milk Glass, 2 3/4 x 4 In. 28.00
Paneled Grape, Gravy Boat, Underplate, Milk Glass, 5 1/4 x 6 1/2 In. 70.00
Paneled Grape, Jar, Pickle, Milk Glass, 12 x 6 In. 175.00
Paneled Grape, Jardiniere, Milk Glass, 6 1/2 x 6 3/8 In. 45.00
Paneled Grape, Nappy, Handle, Milk Glass, 5 In. 28.00
Paneled Grape, Pitcher, Milk Glass, 32 Oz. 28.00
Paneled Grape, Pitcher, Milk Glass, 8 1/8 In. 40.00
Paneled Grape, Planter, Milk Glass, 9 1/8 In. 50.00
Paneled Grape, Plate, Dinner, Milk Glass, 10 1/2 In. 45.00
Paneled Grape, Punch Bowl, Base, Milk Glass, Flared Rim, 8 1/2 x 12 1/2 In. 195.00
Paneled Grape, Punch Bowl, Base, Milk Glass, Flat Sides, Scalloped Rim, 9 x 11 In. 185.00
Paneled Grape, Punch Bowl, Base, Milk Glass, Scalloped Rim, 9 1/4 x 12 In. 185.00
Paneled Grape, Salt & Pepper, Milk Glass, 4 1/2 In. 30.00
Paneled Grape, Soap Dish, Milk Glass, 6 3/4 x 5 3/16 In. 145.00
Paneled Grape, Tidbit, 2 Tiers, Handle .... .95.00 to 115.00
Paneled Grape, Tumbler, Child's, Laurel Green, 2 3/8 x 2 In. 35.00
Paneled Grape, Tumbler, Iced Tea, Milk Glass, 12 Oz. 25.00
Paneled Grape, Vase, Milk Glass, 13 1/4 In. 113.00
Paneled Grape, Vase, Milk Glass, Scalloped Rim, 4 x 4 3/4 In. 27.00
Paneled Grape, Vase, Milk Glass, Straight Sides, Footed, 9 1/4 x 4 1/2 In. 45.00
Paneled Grape, Vase, Swung, 14 1/2 x 4 1/2 In. 31.00
Paneled Grape, Window Box, Milk Glass, 4 1/16 x 9 x 5 In. 30.00
Princess Feather, Cake Plate, Golden Sunset, Footed, 4 1/4 x 10 1/4 In. 70.00
Princess Feather, Plate, Applied Handle, 7 1/4 In. 125.00
Princess Feather, Salt & Pepper, Golden Sunset 32.00
Princess Feather, Saltshaker 14.00
Ring & Petal, Cake Plate, Milk Glass, Square, 5 x 10 3/4 In. 125.00
Ring & Petal, Candlestick, Milk Glass, 3 1/2 x 5 1/4 In. 18.00
Robin On Twig Cover, Dish, Nest, Pedestal, Milk Glass, 6 In. 107.00
Rose & Lattice, Basket, Milk Glass, 8 1/4 x 6 1/2 x 7 In. 40.00
Rose & Lattice, Candy Dish, Cover, Footed, Milk Glass, 6 In. 45.00
Rose & Lattice, Vase, Milk Glass, 8 3/4 In. 40.00
Rose Trellis, Vase, 9 x 4 1/2 In. 40.00
Roses & Bows, Candlestick, Milk Glass, 4 1/2 x 3 5/16 In., Pair 125.00
Shell & Jewel, Pitcher, 8 1/2 In. 40.00
Spoke & Rim, Bowl, Milk Glass, Gold Design, 4 1/4 x 8 1/4 In. 125.00
Strawberries, Canister Set, 4 Piece 165.00
Swan & Rushes, Sugar, Cover, Handles, Milk Glass, 5 x 6 In. 25.00
Swan On Basket Cover, Dish, Cobalt Carnival 300.00
Swan On Basket Cover, Dish, Milk Glass, Lace Edge 200.00
Thousand Eye, Basket, Oval, 8 3/4 x 12 In. 295.00
Thousand Eye, Basket, Oval, 9 1/2 x 11 3/8 In. 125.00
Thousand Eye, Candlestick, 2-Light, 5 1/2 x 6 In. 45.00
Thousand Eye, Candlestick, Dome Foot, 5 x 4 1/4 In. 16.00
Thousand Eye, Coaster, 3 1/4 In. 15.00
Thousand Eye, Fairy Light, Pink, 6 1/2 x 2 3/4 In. 135.00
Thousand Eye, Torte Plate, 18 3/8 In. 45.00

Thousand Eye, Tray, Handles, 12 1/2 In. 145.00
Thousand Eye, Tumbler, Amberina Stain, 10 Oz., 4 1/4 In. 25.00

WHEATLEY Pottery was established in 1880. Thomas J. Wheatley had worked in Cincinnati, Ohio, with the founders of the art pottery movement, including M. Louise McLaughlin of the Rookwood Pottery. Wheatley Pottery was purchased by the Cambridge Tile Manufacturing Company in 1927.

Bowl, Embossed Ridged Leaves, Brown Speckled Matte Glaze, Stamped, 9 3/4 In. 1035.00
Planter, Mythological Figures, Green Matte Glaze, 9 1/2 In. 210.00
Tile, Black Rooster, Marked, 4 In. 144.00
Tile, Spanish Sailing Ship, Waves, Sky, Multicolored, Oak Frame, 8 x 12 In., 6 Piece 1045.00
Vase, 2 Handles, Green Matte Glaze, Raised Mark, 6 In. 920.00
Vase, Burgundy & Gray Streak High Glaze, Blue Flowers, Diamond Shape, 6 3/4 In. 220.00
Vase, Carved Dragonflies, Green Matte Glaze, Tapered, 14 In. 7650.00
Vase, Green Matte Glaze, Incised Wild Roses, Stems, Bulbous, Short Neck, 11 In. 715.00
Wall Pocket, Curdled Mustard Matte Glaze, Tin Lining, 10 x 9 1/2 In. 1495.00

WHEELING Pottery Company of Wheeling, West Virginia, worked from 1879 to about 1923. The firm went through a number of mergers and name changes during that time. Pottery, semiporcelain, artware, and sanitary wares were made.

Bone Dish, Flowers, Gold Trim, Crescent Shape, c.1885, 6 1/2 x 3 1/2 In. 30.00
Paperweight, Knights Templar Design, Dated 1901, 3 3/4 In. 75.00
Pitcher, White, Painted Pink Tulips, Green Stems & Leaves, c.1900, 7 In. 25.00

WHIELDON was an English potter who worked alone and with Josiah Wedgwood in eighteenth-century England. Whieldon made many pieces in natural shapes, like cauliflowers or cabbages.

Jar, Lid, Woman's Face, Threaded, Concentric Beading, England, 19th Century, 1 7/8 In. .. 590.00
Plate, 10 1/4 In. 460.00

WILLOW pattern has been made in England since 1780. The pattern has been copied by factories in many countries, including Germany, Japan, and the United States. It is still being made. Willow was named for a pattern that pictures a bridge, birds, willow trees, and a Chinese landscape. Most pieces are blue and white.

Bowl, Marked, Morijuna, 9 1/2 x 4 1/2 In. 60.00
Bowl, Marked, Ye Old Willow England, 1936, 3 1/2 x 5 1/2 In. 40.00
Casserole, Child's, 2 3/4 x 5 3/4 In. 60.00
Casserole, Child's, Made In Occupied Japan, 5 x 3 x 2 1/2 In. 50.00
Casserole, Cover, 3 1/2 Qt. 43.00
Casserole, Cover, Warming Base, 10 In. 60.00
Chop Plate, Made In England 30.00
Chop Plate, Pink, c.1920, 13 In. 50.00
Creamer, Child's, Marked, Made In Occupied Japan, 2 In. 35.00
Creamer, Cow Form 385.00
Cup, After Dinner, 2 1/4 x 2 1/2 In. 5.00
Cup & Saucer, Demitasse, Solian, Early 1900s, 12 Piece 69.00
Cup & Saucer, Kang-He, Marked, Tillson, c.1900 .... 80.00
Eggcup, Transferware 35.00
Gravy Boat, Attached Underplate, Child's, Made In Occupied Japan 50.00
Grill Plate, Signed, Grindley, England, c.1920, 10 In. 35.00
Jug, Gold Trim, 6 1/2 In. 50.00
Oil & Vinegar, c.1950, 4 Piece 145.00
Plate, Transfer, Scalloped Edges, Ironstone, Allerton's Ltd., 10 In., 6 Piece 115.00
Platter, Black Willow, 2 x 18 x 14 In. 40.00
Platter, Blue, 22 1/2 In. 39.00
Platter, Handles, Child's, 5 1/4 In. 30.00
Platter, Marked, Japan, 12 3/4 x 9 In. 38.00
Platter, Oval, Combed Back, Stand, c.1815, 19 x 18 x 14 In. 315.00
Salt & Pepper, Churchill, 3 In. 30.00
Sugar, Cover, 7 x 5 1/2 In. 28.00
Sugar & Creamer, Cover, Marked, Royal Wessex 40.00

Tea Set, Marked Ironstone, 15 Piece 95.00
Teapot, Child's, Made In Japan, 4 In. 25.00
Teapot, Gold Design, Gold Rim, Gold Ring-Shaped Finial, 4 3/4 x 6 1/2 In. 58.00
Teapot, Old Cream Ground, 8 1/2 x 6 3/4 In. 50.00
Teapot, Stamped, Saddler, England 130.00
Tray, Octagonal, Mounted As Table, X-Stretcher, 18 1/2 x 17 x 13 1/2 In. 315.00
Tumbler, 5 1/8 In. 38.00

WINDOW glass that was stained and beveled was popular for houses during the late nineteenth and early twentieth centuries. The old windows became popular with collectors in the 1970s; today, old and new examples are seen.

Leaded, Amber, Gothic Cross, 21 x 13 1/4 In. ....110.00 to 125.00
Leaded, Dragonflies, Green, Yellow Jewel Eyes, Red Tails, Filigree Wings, 25 x 25 In. 2875.00
Leaded, Prairie Style, Clear, Frosted & Green Iridescent, Arts & Crafts, 34 x 9 In., Pair .. 590.00
Leaded, Stained Glass, Birds, Branches, Leaves, Frame, Early 1900s, 49 3/4 x 20 In. 500.00
Leaded, Stained Glass, Crests, Painted, Giltwood Frame, Continental, 11 In., Pair 144.00
Leaded, Stained Glass, Hammered, Glasgow Rose, Amber, Green, Frame, 16 x 15 In. 520.00
Leaded, Stained Glass, Red Hearts, Red & Green Swags, Frame, 23 x 24 1/2 In. 115.00
Leaded, Stained Glass, Red Stylized Tulip, Green Leaves, Frame, 21 1/2 x 25 1/2 In. 460.00
Leaded, Stained Glass, Stylized Tulip, Green Leaves, Amber, Pine Frame, 13 x 20 In. 115.00
Stained Glass, Abraham Lincoln, Commemorative, Lighted Box, c.1900, 83 x 59 In. 3450.00
Stained Glass, American Eagle, Shield, Star Border, 44 1/4 x 52 In. 220.00
Stained Glass, Green Border, Jeweled Anthemion, Frame, 44 x 30 In. 360.00
Stained Glass, Green Rectangular Pattern, 51 1/2 x 27 1/2 In., Pair 60.00
Stained Glass, Painted, George Washington, Arched, American, 54 x 31 In. 1840.00
Stained Glass, Peacock, Mottled Border, Amber Inserts, Pine Frame, 53 x 37 In. 1925.00
Stained Glass, Thistle Design, c.1900, 16 1/2 x 13 1/4 In. 65.00

WOOD CARVINGS and wooden pieces are listed separately in this book. Many of the wood carvings are figurines or statues. There are also wooden pieces found in other categories, such as Kitchen.

2 Nodding Men, Whistling Device, Carved, Painted, 14 In. 555.00
Altar Figure, Polychrome, Gesso, Back Opening, Asian, 26 In. 795.00
Angel, Detailed Face With Wings, Beaded Shaped Top, 36 1/2 x 7 3/4 In. 375.00
Ashtray, Bear, Holding Tree Stump, Glass Eyes, Swiss, c.1890, 13 In. 4140.00
Bear, Glass Eyes, Swiss, c.1920, 6 1/4 x 11 1/4 In. 605.00
Bear, Looking Up, Glass Eyes, Glass Vase Inset, Swiss, c.1900, 15 In. 1691.00
Bear, Paws Together, Holding Vase, Glass Eyes, Swiss, c.1910, 7 In. 193.00
Bear, Standing, Glass Eyes, Swiss, c.1900, 10 1/2 In. 1200.00
Bear, Standing, Glass Eyes, Swiss, c.1920, 13 x 4 3/4 In. 1900.00
Bear, Standing, Holding Rifle, Glass Eyes, Swiss, c.1920, 10 In. 405.00
Bear, Standing, Next To Barren Tree, Glass Eyes, Black Forest, 79 In. 4125.00
Bear, Walking, Swiss, c.1900, 6 x 11 In. 575.00
Bear, Walking, With Cub In Basket, Glass Eyes, Swiss, c.1940, 12 In. 1660.00
Bears, Seated, Holding Bowl, Oval, Glass Eyes, Swiss, c.1890, 9 x 19 1/2 In. 3680.00
Beaver, Paw Caught In Split Tree Stump, c.1900, 10 In. 520.00
Bighorn Ram Head, 19th Century, 15 x 13 1/2 x 13 3/4 In., Pair 5975.00
Bird, Cherry, Amber, Teak Wood Stand, 9 In. 75.00
Bird, Red, Gray Body, Yellow Wings, Red & White Tail, 19th Century 880.00
Bishop, Saint, Fruitwood, Standing, Wearing Mitre, 18 1/4 In. 645.00
Bishop, Saint, Holding Book, Stepping On Demon, Continental, 30 In. 705.00
Bobwhite Quail, Miniature, Chip Carved Base, Abercrombie & Fitch 375.00
Brant, Driftwood Base, Miniature, Signed, H. Gibbs, 1967 .... 518.00
Bull, Walnut, Black Forest, Standing, Grasses, 19th Century, 14 1/2 x 21 In. 2000.00
Candle Sconce, Pine, Spread Wing Eagle, Drapery Motif, 46 In., Pair 1130.00
Cello Top, Carved Face, Decorated, Punched Stars, 7 x 2 1/2 x 3 In. 690.00
Cherub Faces, Winged, Classical, Austrian Style, 4 1/2 x 6 1/4 x 2 1/2 In. 140.00
Chinese Immortal, Customs Seal On Base, Polychrome, 12 In. 88.00
Christ, 1900s, 47 x 19 1/2 x 14 In. 575.00
Circus Figure, Blond, Tights, Middy Blouse, Polychrome, Gesso, 47 In. 8900.00
Cow, Pine, Red Paint, 5 In. 325.00
Cross, Red, Green & Gold Paint, Southwestern, 16 1/2 In. 115.00

Crow, Mounted On Log, Signed C. Schaal, c.1976, 10 In. 215.00
Deer, On Rock, Branch Base, Swiss, c.1900, 24 In. 860.00
Deer, Palmwood, Reclining, Detachable Antlers, 28 x 15 In. 150.00
Dove, Mounted On Round Tree Base, Signed Mike Waoercak 110.00
Drake, Bufflehead, Miniature, Driftwood Base, J. Lapham, Dennisport, Mass, 1957 ..... 430.00
Eagle, Bellamy Style 1760.00
Eagle, Full-Bodied, Nail Head Eyes, Wooden Plinth, 19th Century, 6 1/2 In. 235.00
Eagle, Shield, Arrows, 42 In. 25.00
Eagle, Shield, Pine, Gold Head, Red, White, Blue, Arrows, 17 x 44 In. 1210.00
Eagle, Shield, Pine, Painted, Early 20th Century, 26 1/2 In. 600.00
Eagle, Spread Wings, Crouching, Facing Right, American, 15 x 14 In. 1955.00
Eagle, Spread Wings, Giltwood, Standing On Rock, Demilune Frame, 42 x 78 In. 5288.00
Eagle, Spread Wings, On Ball, Flag Staff, Pine, Scrubbed, 13 x 11 In. 1650.00
Eagle, Spread Wings, On Rocks, Swiss, c.1890, 29 1/2 In. 7245.00
Eagle, Spread Wings, Pine, Blue Shield, 11 x 26 x 3 In. 325.00
Eagle, Spread Wings, Pine, C. Bellamy, 20th Century, 8 1/4 x 27 In. 385.00
Eagle, Spread Wings, Walnut, Gold Disc, Oak Leaves, Acorns, 24 x 12 In. 1035.00
Figure, Blackamoor, Female, Gesso, Art Nouveau, c.1890, 86 In. 4830.00
Figure, Blackamoor, Polychrome, Gilt, 31 In. 1265.00
Figure, Buddha, Brown Finish, Carved Robe, Facial Features, Chinese, 20 In. 150.00
Figure, Buddha, Polychrome Wood, 20th Century 295.00
Figure, Hardwood, Arms Raised, Abalone Eyes, Maori, 12 x 6 x 2 In. 50.00
Figure, Japanese Woodcarver, Chisel, Mallet, Ivory, Boxwood, 8 In. 4366.00
Figure, Saint, Female, Holding Book, c.1800, 20 In. 345.00
Figure, Santos, Polychrome, Spain, Mid 19th Century, 23 1/4 In. 345.00
Finial, Gilded, Treen, Late 18th Century, 18 x 6 3/4 x 3 3/4 In., Pair 390.00
Fish, Pine, Scales, Fins, Eyes, Iron Hanging Brackets, 72 In. 1610.00
Game Rack, Steer Center, Scrolled Leaves, 8 Wrought Iron Hooks, 53 In. 630.00
Girl, Holding Flower, Sattler, 1926, 10 1/2 x 6 In. 545.00
Goldeneye, Flying, Miniature, Russ Burr, Hingham, Mass., Pair 1205.00
Hand, James Prestini, c.1940, 6 In. 3819.00
Head, Boy's, Pine, Simeon Skillen, Early 19th Century, 10 1/4 x 7 x 8 In. 1880.00
Head, Liberty, Mahogany, Black Metal & Wood Stand, 19th Century, 12 3/4 In. 765.00
Head, Putto, Baroque Style, Continental, Late 1800s, 17 x 26 1/2 In. 690.00
Horse, Galloping, Painted, Ocher Over Gesso, Black Mane, 38 x 27 1/2 In. 880.00
Horse, On Platform, Painted, 19th Century, 21 x 19 x 5 1/2 In. 3850.00
Horse, Rider, Hat, Sword, Scabbard At Saddle, Dark Red, Black Finish, 16 x 15 In. 115.00
Humidor, Bear, Seated, Glass Eyes, Hinged Head, Swiss, c.1930, 10 1/4 In. 920.00
Hunter, Wearing Backpack, Smoking Pipe, Rifle, Dog, 32 1/2 In. 1210.00
Hunter, With Dog, At Tree Stump, Walnut, Swiss, c.1890, 15 In. 2990.00
Indian, Headdress, Pine, Painted, 1920s, 48 In. 650.00
Joseph, Santos, 47 x 14 x 11 1/2 In. 575.00
Man, Plowing Field, Oxen, Basswood, A. Dule, 8 1/2 x 28 1/2 x 9 1/2 In. 315.00
Man, Walnut, Long Flowing Hair, Draped Gown, 16 In. 2530.00
Mannequin Head, Base, Painted, Black, White, Natural, 14 x 7 In. 200.00
Merchant Sea Captain, Holding Sextant, c.1900, 77 In. 7475.00
Mermaid, Painted, Multicolor, 49 1/2 In. 1035.00
Mule Deer Head, Applied Antlers, Gold Leaf, Late 1800s, 32 x 34 In., Pair 2475.00
Okimono, Tortoise & Young, Yoshiharu, 19th Century, 11 1/2 In. 403.00
Owl, 20th Century, 9 3/4 In., Pair 575.00
Owl, Hinged, Contains Box, Black Forest, c.1900, 6 1/2 In. 150.00
Oxen Pair, Black Forest, J. Huggler, A Brienz, c.1900, 9 1/4 x 13 In. 940.00
Peacock, Tin Fan Tail, Blue, Green Polka Dots, Late 19th Century, 9 1/4 x 5 In. 2200.00
Penguin, Painted, Charles Hart, 1930s, 37 In. 7475.00
Photographer, Man, Camera On Tripod, Italy, 1970s, 11 In. 45.00
Plaque, American Eagle, Spread Wings, Shield, 19 Stars, Pine Board, 17 In. 575.00
Plaque, Birds, Trees, Relief, 20th Century, 21 x 16 In. 170.00
Plaque, Man Holding Head Of Beheaded Man, Gesso, Gilt, 13 1/4 x 10 In. 140.00
Print Block, For Fabric, Pakistan, 15 x 12 1/2 In. 55.00
Putti, Painted, 20th Century, 29 1/2 In., Pair 1035.00
Raven, Inset Wings, Tail, Stand, c.1895, 41 In. 5700.00
Retablo, Our Lady Of Guadalupe, Juan Diego, Gesso, Painted, Spanish Colonial, 11 In. ... 646.00

Rooster, Pennsylvania German Style, Painted, 11 1/2 x 12 1/2 In. 3520.00
Rooster, Red Comb, Early 19th Century, 6 x 11 1/2 In. 60.00
Sconce, Cherub, Gilt, 9 In. 226.00
Snow Goose, Shaped Wood Base, Signed Mike Wavercak, c.1975, 8 1/2 In. 90.00
Soldier, On Horseback, Movable Arms, Legs, 19th Century, 11 x 8 1/2 In. 3850.00
Spruce Goose, Log Mount, Signed T. Smith, c.1984, 7 1/4 In. 60.00
Squaw Duck, Wood Base, Mike Wavercak, c.1976, 13 1/2 In. 200.00
St. Francis Of Assisi, Spain, 17th Century, 10 In. ...., 2800.00
St. Peter, Multicolored, Gilt Flowered Robe, 1700s, 41 x 19 x 11 In. 4315.00
Stag, Standing, Continental, c.1900, 19 x 16 In. 230.00
Temple Goddess, Barefoot, Kwan Yin, Chinese, Ming Dynasty, 48 In. 3220.00
Tray, Leaves, Vine, Eagle Finial, 5 Sections, c.1890, 14 x 12 In. 230.00
Uncle Sam, Standing, Hands In Pocket, Stovepipe Hat, 12 1/4 In. 45.00
Vase, Dwarf, Holding Cornucopia, Glass Insert, Swiss, c.1930, 9 In. 175.00
Whale Man, Stocking Cap, Mustache, Pine, c.1950, 15 In. 85.00
Whimsy, Ball In Box, In Bottle, Prisoner Carved, T.W. Weaver, 1876, 15 3/4 In. 265.00
Woman, Dress, Apron, Movable Leather Arms, Painted, 8 In. 1760.00
Woman, Profile, Elaborate Headdress, 20th Century, 16 x 16 In. 140.00
Woman, Seated, Stylized, Lacquered, Walnut, Frank Varga, 1969, 29 1/4 In. 85.00
Woman, Standing, Signed, M. Franchi, 10 In. 440.00
Wood Skull, 3 Ivory Oni, Gyokuzan, 1868-1912, 6 1/2 In. 5060.00

WOODEN wares were used in all parts of the home. Wood was used for
many containers and tools. Small wooden pieces are called *treenware*
in England, but the term woodenware is more common in the United
States. Additional pieces may be found in the Advertising, Kitchen,
and Tool categories.

Altar Sticks, Rococo Style, Silvered Wood, 28 1/2 In., Pair 1016.00
Apple Box, Softwood, Dovetailed, Arched Sides, 10 In. 205.00
Arrow Holder, Polychrome Wood, Tibet, c.1850, 36 3/4 In. 212.00
Barrel, Oak, Brass Bands, Copper Rivets, Brass Swing Handle, 17 1/2 x 11 In. 880.00
Barrel, Oak, Brass Bound, Oval Staved Form, England, c.1850, 25 x 15 x 12 In. 632.00
Barrel, Tea, Oriental, Painted Decoration, Diamond Panels, Octagonal, 13 x 18 In. 345.00
Bottle Stopper, Bear, Doing Handstand On Pedestal, Cork, Swiss, c.1920, 4 In. 145.00
Bowl, Ash Burl, Raised Rim & Foot, 12 1/2 x 4 1/2 In. 550.00
Bowl, Blue Paint, Poplar, Ring Turnings, Scrubbed Interior, 18 x 5 In. 575.00
Bowl, Burl, 18th Century, 3 3/4 x 6 x 7 In. 250.00
Bowl, Burl, Carved Finger Ring Handle, 9 1/2 In. 635.00
Bowl, Burl, Carved, Treen, America, 19th Century, 4 5/8 x 16 3/4 In. 1295.00
Bowl, Burl, Cover, Turned Knob Finial, Austin Smith, 4 3/4 In. 460.00
Bowl, Burl, Molded Collar, 18th Century, 18 In. 2760.00
Bowl, Burl, Raised Foot, Broad Rim Band, 13 1/2 x 4 1/4 In. 1045.00
Bowl, Elm, 19th Century, 7 x 20 1/2 In. 1265.00
Bowl, Maple, Red Paint, Scrubbed Interior, Turned Foot, Raised Rim, 19 x 6 In. 880.00
Bowl, Maple, Treen, 18th Century, 6 1/4 x 16 1/4 In. 825.00
Bowl, Teak, Henning Koppel, Georg Jensen, Denmark, 1960s, 19 x 4 1/2 In. 1640.00
Bowl, Treen, Green Paint, Penn., 19th Century, 7 1/8 x 19 In. 1058.00
Bowl, Treen, James Prestini, c.1948, 10 3/4 In. 3525.00
Bowl, Treen, James Prestini, c.1948, 11 1/2 In. 2115.00
Bowl, Walnut, Burl, 18th Century, 5 1/2 x 5 x 2 1/2 In. 500.00
Bowl, Yellow Paint, Scrubbed Interior, Raised Rim, Footed, 21 1/2 x 7 3/8 In. 750.00
Brush Holder, Rosewood, Chinese, 19th Century, 5 1/2 In. 649.00
Bucket, Cover, Salmon Paint, Squiggled Lines, Lehnware, 8 1/2 x 9 1/4 In. 1265.00
Bucket, George III, Mahogany, Brass Bound, Navette Shape, c.1800, 15 x 11 x 15 In. 1725.00
Bucket, Iron Bands, Loop Handle 45.00
Bucket, Metal Bands, Bail Handle, Yellow Paint, 12 In. 55.00
Bucket, Red, Lidded, Stave, Brass Hoop, Impressed E. Murdock & Co., 5 In. 205.00
Bucket, Sap, Hand Painted, Stamped, Whitney & Adams, Miss., 7 1/2 x 10 In. 145.00
Bucket, Stave Construction, 2 Wood Bands, Cha. Wilder, So. Hingham, Mass., 10 In. 520.00
Bucket, Stave Construction, Bail Handle, Bittersweet Paint, Apple Butter Label, 7 3/4 In. .. 489.00
Bucket, Stave Construction, Finger Band, Wire Bail Handle, 6 3/4 In. 520.00
Bucket, Stave Construction, Rose & Square Head Nails, Green Paint, 17 In. 345.00

Bucket, Stave Construction, Shaker Style, Steel Bands, Bail Handle, 6 3/8 x 10 In. 85.00
Bucket, Sugar, Green Over Yellow Paint, 12 In. 99.00
Bucket, Sugar, Hand Forged Handle, Copper Trim, 7 1/2 x 7 In. 75.00
Bucket, Sugar, Stave Construction, 3 Bands, Swing Handle, Yellow Paint, 12 5/8 In. 490.00
Bucket, Sugar, Stave Construction, 3 Wooden Bands, Handle, GR Sugar, 12 1/2 In. 490.00
Bucket, Sugar, Wire & Wood Bail, White, Blue Bands, 6 In. 45.00
Canteen, Painted, Oval, Initials, Sunburst, Red, Mustard, Black, 1800s, 6 x 5 3/4 In. 1645.00
Canteen, Red Paint, Iron Handle, 11 In. 175.00
Card Case, Teakwood, China, 4 1/2 x 2 3/4 x 1/2 In. 45.00
Compote, Mahogany, Stepped Base, Urn Shaped Column, Shallow Bowl, 10 x 8 In. 345.00
Cup, Acorn Finial, 4-Ring Base, Hardwood, Treen, 12 In. 85.00
Cup, Cover, Heart Band, Snowflake, Treen, Polychrome, Elizabeth Sheely 1859, 4 In. ... 4250.00
Cup & Saucer, Salmon Ground, Strawberry, 1 1/2 x 1 1/4 In. 2090.00
Egg, Green, Yellow Striped Border, Snowflakes, February 24 A.D. 1860, 2 In. 3263.00
Firkin, Cover, Green Paint, Impressed, Our Centennial Best, 10 1/2 x 9 1/2 In. 315.00
Firkin, Cover, Medium Brown, 19th Century, 9 1/2 In. 69.00
Firkin, Open, 19th Century, 14 x 13 1/2 In. 45.00
Firkin, Pickle, Yellow, Red Bands, Stencil, Monarch No. 12, Bail Handle, 7 1/2 In. 225.00
Floral Display, Fruit, Dried Flowers, Seeds, Flow Blue Bowl, 1900s, 9 1/2 x 12 x 9 In. ... 265.00
Foot Measure, Shoe Shape Decoration, Old Patina, 18 1/2 In. 360.00
Gavel, Presentation, Rosewood, Sterling, Inscription, Pottsville YMCA, 1926, 9 In. 375.00
Glove Stretcher, Stamped, Wisconsin Textile Mfg. Co., 15 1/4 In. 330.00
Humidor, Cabinet Shape, Barham Hunt Jockey, Polychrome, 13 x 11 x 18 In. 115.00
Humidor, Cat In Shoe, Hand Carved, c.1880s, 9 x 5 In. 230.00
Humidor, Mahogany, Geometric Inlay, Star Shape Medallion, 5 x 15 x 8 In. 140.00
Humidor, Pool Table Shape, Cue & Balls On Top, Walnut, Hinged Top, 6 x 12 In. 750.00
Ice Bucket, Teak, Plastic Liner, Dansk, 19 1/4 x 9 In. 90.00
Jar, Cover, Mushroom Shape, Red Paint, Yellow Accents, Treen, 3 In. 205.00
Jar, Tobacco, Cover, Burlwood, Squat, 4 1/2 x 6 3/4 In. 605.00
Jardiniere, Burl, Lozenge Shape, Gilt Metal Mounts, Late 1800s, 6 x 13 In. 518.00
Jardiniere, Serpentine Shape, Parquetry, Late 1800s, 18 In. 2760.00
Keg, Powder, Blue Paint, 5 In. 90.00
Knife Carrier, Mahogany, Slope Sides, Center Divider, Turned Handle, 6 x 15 x 10 In. ... 196.00
Lazy Susan, Walnut, Dish Top, Rotating Molded Base, 30 In. 1855.00
Mannequin, Artist's, Featureless Head, Articulated Neck, Torso & Limbs, 22 In. 750.00
Master Salt, Turned, Salmon Ground, Strawberries, Blue, Green, Red, 1 7/8 In. 715.00
Master Salt, Turned, Tan Ground, Red, Blue Flowers, 3 In. 770.00
Mitten Dryer, Hinged Thumb, Pine, Signed G.S. Bumell, 14 1/2 In. 330.00
Mold, Walnut, Soldier, Saluting, Epaulets, Carrying Rifle, 16 1/4 x 6 3/4 x 3 1/2 In. 440.00
Ox Yoke, Curly Maple, Red Paint, Wrought Iron Hardware, 54 x 12 In. 230.00
Pail, 2 Handles, Green Paint, 11 In. 200.00
Pail, Maple, Painted, Lehnware, 12 In. 6000.00
Pitcher, Brass Spout, Handle, Graduated Barrel Hoops, c.1900, 23 x 11 In. 115.00
Pitcher, Stave Construction, Cane Wrapped, Carved Lid, Handle, 7 In. 140.00
Plaque, Oval, Ivory, Relief, Staghorn, Man & Waterwheel, 17 x 13 1/2 In. 165.00
Pricket Stand, Painted, Turned, 46 1/2 In., Pair 415.00
Propeller, Brass Trim, Hartzell, Piqua, Ohio, 84 In. 495.00
Quilt Blocks, Walnut, Yellow, Red, Green, Blue, Black, 3 Shapes, 12 x 12 In. 405.00
Receiving Card Tray, Boy Holding Tray, Pedestal, 64 In. 2000.00
Seed Tray, Red Oak, New England, 18th Century 195.00
Shoe, Lady's, Black Paint, Carved Upper, 7 3/4 In. 201.00
Tankard, Lift Lid, Decorations, Norway, 1850, 12 In. 150.00
Tazza, Carved, c.1800, 29 1/4 x 27 1/4 x 7 1/4 In. 1050.00
Tray, Butternut, House, Leaf, Religious Text, 1834, 7 3/4 x 18 1/2 In. 825.00
Tray, Marquetry, Elephants, Sun, Palm Trees, Handles, Signed, Galle, 22 3/4 x 15 In. 2520.00
Trencher, 50 x 14 In. 100.00
Trencher, Hand Hewn, Figured Birch, Ached Ends, Tapered Ear Handle, 17 x 38 In. 345.00
Trencher, Hand Planed, Blue Paint, 12 1/4 x 21 1/2 x 5 1/2 In. 440.00
Truncheon, Leather, Red Paint, Arrow Mark, Revolutionary War 295.00
Urn, Knife, Mahogany, Georgian Style, Oval, Bellflower Swags, 25 x 9 In., Pair 1840.00
Wash Tub, Blue, Green Paint, Openwork Handles, Iron Rod Supports, 17 x 25 In. 305.00
Watch Holder, Walnut, Tall Case Clock Shape, J. Curtis Watch, London, c.1810, 11 In. ... 575.00
Wine Bucket, Mahogany, Brass Bands, Handle, Liner, Dutch, 1800, 13 1/2 x 14 1/2 In. ... 690.00

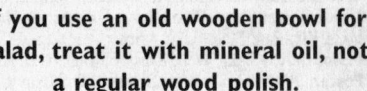

If you use an old wooden bowl for salad, treat it with mineral oil, not a regular wood polish.

Worcester, Teapot, Blue & White, Dr. Wall, Crescent Mark, 4 1/2 In.

WORCESTER porcelains were made in Worcester, England, from 1751. The firm went through many name changes and eventually, in 1862, became The Royal Worcester Porcelain Company Ltd. Collectors often refer to *Dr. Wall, Barr, Flight,* and other names that indicate time periods or artists at the factory. It became part of Royal Worcester Spode Ltd. in 1976. Related pieces may be found in the Royal Worcester category.

Bowl, Blue & White Flowers, Dr. Wall, 1700s, 3 1/2 In.	720.00
Bowl, Kakiemon Pattern, Dr. Wall, 1700s, 3 1/4 In.	230.00
Bowl, Landscape Design, Dr. Wall, 1700s, 4 In.	460.00
Bowl, Pagoda Center, 3 Bird Panels, Oval, 5 x 13 1/2 In.	1580.00
Cann, Cup, Porcelain, 3 Oval Leaf Scenes, Cobalt Blue & Gilt Band, 3 1/2 In.	160.00
Cup, Bishop Sumner Pattern, Dr. Wall, 1700s	200.00
Cup, Blue & White, Flowers, Dr. Wall, 1700s, 2 In.	60.00
Cup, Imari Pattern, Flight Barr Period, c.1820, 2 1/2 In.	109.00
Cup & Saucer, Chamberlain, Bengal Tiger Design, c.1800	460.00
Cup & Saucer, Exotic Bird, Cobalt Blue & Gilt Ground, 1700s	865.00
Dish, Scalloped Edge, Fruit, Pinecones, Flowers, Dr. Wall, 6 1/4 In.	330.00
Dish, Shell Shape, Figural Landscape, Dr. Wall, 1700s, 4 1/2 In.	11385.00
Dish, Sweetmeat, 3 Scallop Shell Shape, Seaweed, 18th Century, 9 In.	705.00
Inkwell, 4 Scallop Shell Decorations, Birds, Seascape, 5 1/4 x 3 In.	230.00
Jar, Potpourri, Cobalt Blue, Gilt, Flowers, Paw Feet, 4 1/4 In.	480.00
Jardiniere, Flowers, Dragonflies, Embossed Mold, Reticulated Rim, c.1900, 8 In.	315.00
Mug, Robert Hancock Transfer, Frederick The Great, King Of Prussia, Baluster	2000.00
Mug, Robert Hancock Transfer, Marquis Of Granbay, Fame, Cylindrical	2000.00
Plate Set, Molded Blackberry Pattern, Polychrome Flowers, c.1800, 8 In., 4 Piece	230.00
Sauceboat, Flowers, Blue & White	385.00
Sauceboat, Flowers, Tulip On Interior, Strap Flute, Blue Underglaze, 7 In.	865.00
Sauceboat, Imari Pattern, Early 1800s, 6 In.	290.00
Spoon Tray, Egg Shape, Cobalt Blue Glaze, Enameled Flowers, Gilt, 1800s, 7 7/8 In.	175.00
Spoon Tray, Hexagonal, Imari Flowers, Blue Ground, Dr. Wall, 1700s, 5 1/4 In.	260.00
Spoon Tray, Kakiemon Flower Design, Fishscale Ground, Dr. Wall, 1700s, 5 3/4 In.	460.00
Tazza & Bowl, Tree, Pagoda Center, Bird, Flower Border, Gilt Edge, 10 In.	450.00
Tea Caddy, Blue Transfer, Flowers, Butterfly, No Lid, Marked, 3 3/4 In.	290.00
Tea Caddy, Egg Shape, Kakiemon Design, Wood Cover, Dr. Wall, 1700s, 4 1/2 In.	430.00
Teapot, Blue & White, Dr. Wall, Crescent Mark, 4 1/2 In. *Illus*	750.00
Teapot, Dome Top, Soft Paste, 9 In.	1045.00
Tray, Birds, Cobalt Blue & Gilt Border, Openwork Leaf Handles, Gilt, 10 In., Pair	339.00
Tray, Fish Scale Design, Dark Blue, Polychrome Flowers, Gilt, Marked, 6 3/4 x 10 In.	230.00

WORLD WAR I and World War II souvenirs are collected today. Be careful not to store anything that includes live ammunition. Your local police will tell you how to dispose of the explosives. See also Sword and Trench Art.

WORLD WAR I, Ammunition Box, Olive, Oak, Steel Fittings, Leather Handle, U.S. Army	40.00
Belt Buckle, Telegrapher, Brass, 2 Riveted Loops, 1 3/4 x 4 In.	259.00
Binoculars, Leather Covered Tubes, Neck Strap, Brass, Feldschar 8 Fach, Carl Zeiss	210.00
Bugle, Field, Nickel Plated, Brass Mouthpiece, Leather Wrapped, France, 11 1/2 In.	115.00
Button, Welcome Home, Red, White, Blue, Gold, Black, Celluloid	25.00

Canteen, Aluminum, U.S. Army 12.00
Case, Ammunition, Leather, Strap, Holds 6 Clips Of Rifle Cartridges, 12 x 6 x 4 In. 145.00
Grenade Ball, Cast Iron, Alloy Fuse, Germany, 1915 .... 70.00
Lantern, Kerosene, Blue Globe, U.S. Army, 10 In. 109.00
Mess Kit, Pan, Plate, U.S. Army 14.00
Pistol Belt, Khaki, Web, Brass Fittings, U.S. Army 22.00
Poster, 20,000 Apprentice Seamen, U.S. Navy, Charles Stafford, c.1917, 38 x 28 In. 633.00
Poster, Be A U.S. Marine, First In Fight, J.M. Flagg, 1918, 29 x 40 In. 775.00
Poster, Blot It Out With Liberty Bonds, J. Allen St. John, 19 3/4 x 30 1/4 In. 138.00
Poster, Buy Bonds, Clear The Way, Fourth Liberty, H.C. Christy, 1918, 20 x 30 In. 375.00
Poster, Buy W.S.S. & Keep Him Out Of America, A. Treidler, c.1918, 20 x 28 In. 325.00
Poster, Buy War Savings Stamps, Our Soldiers In Siberia, Petrtyl, 1918, 23 x 33 In. 425.00
Poster, Clear The Way, Columbia & Navy Gun Crew, H.C. Christy, 1918, 20 x 30 In. 375.00
Poster, Daddy What Did You Do In The Great War, c.1916, 20 x 30 In. 1800.00
Poster, Everything For The War, Woman Worker, Linen, Russia, 1916, 28 x 38 In. 1000.00
Poster, Gee, I Wish I Were A Man, I'd Join Navy, Cardstock, Christy, 27 x 41 In. 1495.00
Poster, Get In The Game With Uncle Sam, J.C. Leyendecker, 1917, 19 x 26 In. 1900.00
Poster, Give The World The Once Over, U.S. Navy, Daugherty, c.1919, 28 x 42 In. 450.00
Poster, Go Over The Top, U.S. Marines, J.A. Coughlin, 1917, 21 x 28 In. 475.00
Poster, Help Him Win By Saving & Serving, Buy War Savings Stamps, 20 x 30 In. 161.00
Poster, There's Room For You, Enlist Today, Linen, England, c.1915, 20 x 30 In. 450.00
Poster, Third Liberty Loan, Good Bye, Dad, Paper Lithograph, L.S. Harris, 30 x 20 In. .. 450.00
Poster, Uncle Sam Is Looking For Every Fit Man, Herbert Paus, c.1916, 19 x 26 In. 700.00
Poster, War Clouds Gather, Join Navy League, Hazel Roberts, c.1917, 19 x 25 In. 500.00
Poster, YMCA, Help Us Help Our Boys, Haskell Coffin, 1918, 21 x 28 In. 500.00
Poster, You Are Wanted By U.S. Army, K.M. Bara, 1917, 27 x 41 In. 3000.00
Sheet Music, I Want To Be Loved By A Soldier, Fink, Silver, Morris, 1918, 2 Pages 8.00
Sheet Music, K-K-K-Katy, G. O'Hara, L. Feist, N.Y., 1918, 7 x 10 1/2 In., 2 Pages 6.00
Sheet Music, On The Sidewalks Of Berlin, 1918 .... 18.00
Sheet Music, The Fight Is On, 1918 .... 15.00
Sheet Music, Victory, 1918 .... 18.00
Sheet Music, We Won't Be With You Tomorrow, Today We March Away, 1917 .... 18.00
Sheet Music, When A Yankee Got His Eye Down The Barrel Of A Gun, 1918 .... 19.00
Sheet Music, You Can't Stop The Yanks, 1918 .... 45.00
Sheet Music, Your Country Needs You, Dubin, Cormack, McConnell, 1917, 2 Pages 6.00
Sign, Liberty Loan, Ring It Again, c.1917, 34 x 24 In. 110.00
WORLD WAR II, Bag, Drawstring, Khaki, Marked P-4979, U.S. Army, 14 x 16 In. 14.00
Belt, Garrison, Leather, Brown, Square Buckle, Brass, U.S. Army, Size 36 .... 28.00
Belt, Web, Khaki, Roller Buckle, Brown, U.S. Army, Size 34 .... 8.00
Binnacle, W&C Compass, Lionel Corp., Copper, Brass 405.00
Blanket, Wool, Olive Drab, U.S. Army 30.00
Blouse, Dress, U.S. Army, Medical Officer, 4 Pockets, Gabardine Wool 55.00
Boots, Riding, SS Officer, Leather, Cloth Pulls, 16 1/2 In., Size 6 1/2 .... 345.00
Briefcase, Field, Cotton Canvas, Officer, Army, Japan, 9 x 13 In. 45.00
Bugle, U.S. Army, Rexcraft Regulation 78.00
Cane, WH Reservist, Cloth Covered Shaft, Metal Tip, Bust, Tassels, 36 1/2 In. 93.00
Canteen, Army, Web Skeleton Straps, Rubber Stopper, Japan 60.00
Cap, Crusher, Officer's, Gabardine, Olive Drab, Leather Bill, Band, Straps, USAAF 85.00
Cap, Seaman's, Navy, Wool, U.S. Navy, Size 6 3/4 .... 20.00
Cap, SS General, Peaked Visor, Wool, Satin Interior, Eagle, Skull, Size 56 .... 1925.00
Chart, Navigation, Linen, England Northwest, Royal Air Force, 1942, 24 x 32 In. 40.00
Chart, Navigation, Rumania, Waterproof, 2-Sided, c.1943, 48 x 40 In. 60.00
Coat, Jeep, Macinaw, Olive Drab, U.S. Army, 1943, Size 36 .... 40.00
Field Glasses, Nazi, 6 x 30, Diensigles 77.00
Field Glasses, U.S. Signal Service Day & Night, Leather Covered Barrels, Paris 450.00
First Aid Pouch, Web, Khaki, U.S. Army 8.00
Flag, Brigadier General, White Linen Star, Red Wool Ground, 36 x 48 In. 75.00
Flashlight, TL-122-Banglehead, U.S. Army 90.00
Gas Mask, Rubberized Cloth, Canvas Carrier, Japan 52.00
Gloves, Leather Palm, Wool, U.S. Army, Ross Glove Co., Size 10 .... 50.00
Greeting Card, Good Luck To You In The Service, Tires Rotate, Driver Moves 11.00
Hatchet, Wood, D-Day, June 6, 1944, Invasion Of Normandy, Frank Feathers, 16 In. 3263.00
Headnet, Mosquito, Khaki Cloth, Olive Drab Net, U.S. Army 15.00

Helmet, Combat, Wehrmacht, Single Eagle Decal, Steel, Leather Liner & Chin Strap 370.00
Holster, Luger PO8, Black Leather, Hardshell, Magazine Pouch, Tool Pocket 110.00
Jacket, Bush, Officer's, CBI Patch, Tan Cotton, USAAF Medium 100.00
Jacket, Senior Pilot Maj., Patches, Insignia, Pilot Wings, USAAF 85.00
Life Vest, Aviators, CO2 Inflatable, Blue, U.S. Navy 60.00
Map, France, Card Stock Folder, U.S. Army, Corps Of Engineers, 1944 .... 62.00
Mess Kit, Utensils, Nazi Eagle, Steel Knife & Holder, Aluminum Fork, Spoon 80.00
Mirror, Souvenir, Roosevelt, Churchill, Stalin, 3 1/2 In. 85.00
Mittens, Trigger Finger, Wool Shell, Leather Palms, Japan 75.00
Pin, Don't Let Him Down, MacArthur, Red, White, Blue, Celluloid 20.00
Pin, Let's Pull Together, Uncle Sam, Multicolored, Lithograph, Mechanical 98.00
Pin, Uncle Sam, Kick 'Em In The Axis, Red, White, Blue, Celluloid 50.00
Playing Cards, American Red Cross, U.S. Playing Card Co., Cincinnati, 1945 .... 40.00
Poster, Buy U.S. War Stamps Bonds, Girl & Mother Pasting Stamps, 14 x 20 In. 105.00
Poster, Buy War Bonds, Let's All Fight, G.I. With Bayonet, 22 x 14 In. 58.00
Poster, Buy War Bonds, Uncle Sam Leads Battle, N.C. Wyeth, 1942, 29 x 40 In. 675.00
Poster, Churchill Octopus, Amputated Tentacles, Linen, Germany, 31 x 46 In. 900.00
Poster, Do With Less, So They'll Have Enough, Smiling G.I. & Coffee Mug, 28 x 40 In. . 86.00
Poster, Enemy Ears Are Listening, 3 Axis Figures, G. Illian, 1942, 14 x 26 In. 525.00
Poster, Fire Away, Buy Extra Bonds, Submarine, 20 x 28 In. 85.00
Poster, General Eisenhower, Back 'Em Up, Buy Extra Bonds, 20 x 28 In. 210.00
Poster, I Want You For The U.S. Army, Uncle Sam, J.M. Flagg, c.1944, 35 x 38 In. 900.00
Poster, Let's Go, U.S. Marines, Linen Mount, Thomason, 1942, 28 x 40 In. 550.00
Poster, Little Jap Is A Big Job, Japanese Soldier, Rising Sun, 1945, 29 x 40 In. 425.00
Poster, Marines Have Landed, Marines Wade Ashore, J.M. Flagg, 1941, 30 x 40 In. 500.00
Poster, Save For The Brave, War Bonds, Purple Heart, C.C. Beall, 1944, 13 x 16 In. 60.00
Poster, Someone Talked, Drowning Man, Siebel, 1942, 22 x 28 In. 350.00
Poster, To Have & To Hold, Buy War Bonds, Little Girl, 20 x 28 In. 110.00
Poster, U.S. War Bonds, Statue Of Liberty, Hebrew & English, 1943, 28 x 22 In. 1150.00
Poster, Watch Out For Fire, C.A.A. War Training, E.M. Kauffer, 1943, 31 x 44 In. 975.00
Poster, We Can, We Will, We Must, Buy Bonds, Flag, 1942, 11 1/4 x 21 1/2 In. 175.00
Poster, Wings Over America, Bald Eagle, Planes, Tom Woodburn, 1941, 25 x 38 In. 1500.00
Sextant, Bunav Mark 11, Cased, U.S. Navy, David White Co., Milwaukee, Wis. 316.00
Sheet Music, Bring New Glory To Old Glory, Gordon, Warren, Mayfair, 1942, 3 Pages .. 6.00
Sheet Music, I'm Getting Tired So I Can Sleep, I. Berlin, 1942, 2 Pages 8.00
Sheet Music, Men Of The Merchant Marine, 1942 .... 18.00
Sheet Music, Song Of The Marines, 1942 .... 25.00
Sheet Music, The Yanks Are On Their Way, 1942 .... 22.00
Sheet Music, We're The Yanks, B. Gardner, Lancaster, Pa., 1943, 2 Pages 7.00
Sleeping Bag, Wool, Olive Drab, Case, U.S. Army 45.00
Spoon, Wooden, Carved, Remember Pearl Harbor, Dec. 7, 1941, Frank Feathers, 12 In. .. 900.00
Sunglasses, Comfortable Cable, USAAF, Nickel Frames, Green Lenses, Case 144.00
Tent, Shelter, Half, Khaki, U.S. Army 35.00
Tunic, Officer's, Wool, 5-Button Front, 4 Pockets, Army, Japan, Medium 138.00
Tunic, Work, Enlisted, Cotton, 5-Button Front, 4 Pockets, Army, Japan, Medium 92.00
Visor, Crusher Style, Officer, Wool, Copper Finish Badge, Army, Medium 86.00

WORLD'S FAIR souvenirs from all of the fairs are collected. The first
fair was the Great Exhibition of 1851 in London. Some other impor-
tant exhibitions and fairs include Philadelphia, 1876 (Centennial);
Chicago, 1893 (World's Columbian); Buffalo, 1901 (Pan-American);
St. Louis, 1904 (Louisiana Purchase); San Francisco, 1915 (Panama-
Pacific); Philadelphia, 1926 (Sesquicentennial); Chicago, 1933 (Cen-
tury of Progress); Cleveland, 1936 (Great Lakes); San Francisco, 1939
(Golden Gate International); New York, 1939 (World of Tomorrow);
Seattle, 1962 (Century 21); New York, 1964; Montreal, 1967; New
Orleans, 1984; Tsukuba, Japan, 1985; Vancouver, B.C., 1986; Bris-
bane, Australia, 1988; Seville, Spain, 1992; and Genoa, Italy, 1992;
Seoul, Korea, 1993; and Lisbon, Portugal, 1998. Memorabilia of fairs
include directories, pictures, fabrics, ceramics, etc. Memorabilia from
other similar celebrations may be listed in the Souvenir category.

Ashtray, 1964, New York, Pink, Melmac, Made In USA 18.00
Badge, 1939, New York, Elsie The Cow, Borden, Brass, 2 1/4 In. 38.00

Bank, 1964, New York, Dime Register, On Card, 1964, 3 x 5 In. 75.00
Booklet, 1939, Golden Gate International Exposition, Magic In The Night, 18 Pages 20.00
Bookmark, Letter Opener, 1904, St. Louis, Cherub Top, Teardrop Body, Gilt, Brass 165.00
Cup & Saucer, 1893, Chicago Exposition, Turquoise, Coalport, Demitasse, 2 1/4 In. 185.00
Electric Candle, 1933, Chicago, Eveready, Box 480.00
Handkerchief, 1876, Centennial Exhibition, Memorial Hall Art Gallery, 20 x 23 In. 18.00
Handkerchief, 1876, Philadelphia International Exhibition, Frame, 29 1/2 x 33 In. 220.00
Leather, 1933, Chicago, Cowboy, Bucking Steer, 101 Ranch, Ray Larson, 7 x 11 1/2 In. . .   950.00
Letter Opener, 1904, St. Louis, Indian Relief, Bronze, 11 In. 375.00
Medal, 1904, St. Louis, Grand Prize, Eagle, America, Shield, Bronze, 2 1/2 In. 230.00
Paperweight, 1893, Chicago, Globe, Metal Stand, Schedler, 2 3/4 x 4 In. 615.00
Paperweight, 1893, Chicago, Pear, Peachblow, 4 1/2 In. 100.00
Pennant, 1876, Philadelphia Exhibition, Linen, 38 Stars, Eagle, 18 x 24 In. 225.00
Pennant, 1926, Philadelphia Sesquicentennial, Green Felt, Liberty Bell, Shield, 21 In. . . .   50.00
Plate, 1904, St. Louis, Cascades, 5 Views, Fair Buildings, Copper, Gilt, 7 1/4 In. 175.00
Plate, 1968, San Antonio, Hemisfair, River Court, Alamo, Fair Attractions 25.00
Playing Cards, 1904, St. Louis, Fair Scenes, Thomas Jefferson, Aluminum, Holder 1840.00
Poster, 1939, New York, Via New York Central System, Joseph Binder, 30 x 20 In. 2232.00
Quilt, 1939, New York, Trylon, Perisphere, Multicolored, Sawtooth Border, 90 x 75 In. . . 8250.00
Ribbon, 1893, Chicago, Administration Building, Red, White, Blue, Black, Silk, 5 In. 75.00
Salt & Pepper, 1933, Chicago, Plated Metal, Handle, 2 In. 75.00
Spoon, 1915, San Francisco, Expo Designs, Gold, Dirigold 29.00
Spoon, 1933, Chicago, Century Of Progress, Dirigold, Green Duck, Co. 25.00
Sugar, 1893, Chicago, Peachblow, Ribbing, Applied Handles, 2 3/4 In. 316.00
Ticket, 1904, St. Louis, Day 220, Aug. 7, Light Brown, 2 3/4 x 1 1/4 In. 130.00
Tile, 1904, St. Louis Exposition, Embossed, Knight, Hartford Faience, 4 1/2 In. 460.00
Toy, 1939, New York, Bus, Greyhound, Cast Iron, Rubber Tires, Arcade, 6 3/4 In. 220.00
Toy, 1939, New York, Bus, Greyhound, Cast Iron, Rubber Tires, Arcade, 8 1/2 In. 330.00
Toy, 1939, New York, Bus, Greyhound, Cast Iron, Rubber Tires, Arcade, 10 1/2 In. 525.00
Tray, 1933, Chicago, Buckingham Fountain, Relief, Bronze, 4 1/2 In. 29.00
Vase, 1893, Chicago, Jack-In-The-Pulpit, Amberina, Tapered Neck, Bulbous, 7 In. 345.00

WRISTWATCHES came into use during World War I. Wristwatches are
listed here by manufacturer or as advertising or character watches.
Pocket watches are listed in the Watch category.

Art Deco, Platinum, Diamond, Blue Sapphire, 14K Gold 400.00
Audemars Piguet, Silvertone Dial, 18K Gold Bezel, Lugs, Lizard Band, 8 3/4 In. 1175.00
Audemars Piguet, Woman's, Diamond, Platinum, Gold, 17 Jewel, 6 In. 1265.00
Baume & Mercier, 14K Gold, Black Dial, Box 1180.00
Baume & Mercier, Baumatic, Matte Gold Dial, Black Hands, 18K Gold Case 1265.00
Baume & Mercier, Silvertone Dial, 14K Gold, Braided Band, Box, 7 1/4 In. 590.00
Baume & Mercier, Woman's, Diamond, Flexible Band, 14K White Gold, 6 1/2 In. 355.00
Buccellati, Mother-Of-Pearl Dial, 18K Bicolor Gold, Silk Pouch, 7 In. 1880.00
Bucherer, Woman's, Ivorytone Dial, Stick Numerals, 17 Jewel, Mesh Bracelet, 18K 530.00
Bulgari, 20th Anniversary, Stainless Steel, Skeleton Band, Leather Band 590.00
Bulgari, Scuba, Luminescent Numeral Indicators, Stainless Steel 2350.00
Bulgari, Woman's, Black Dial, Quartz, Leather Band, Box, 18K Gold 1295.00
Bulova, Accutron, 14K Gold, Gold Filled Mesh Band, c.1968 . . . .   169.00
Bulova, Accutron, Stainless Steel, 10K Gold, Quartz 325.00
Bulova, Stem Hack Wind, USAF Pilot, Korean War, Expandable Band 115.00
Bulova, U.S. Army Issue, Leather Band, Wrapper, World War II 278.00
Bulova, Woman's, Gold Filled, Movement Marked, 15 Jewel, 3 Adjustments, No. 48029 .   45.00
Cartier, Baignoire, Oval Dial, Leather Band, Sapphire Winding Stem, 18K Gold 1998.00
Cartier, Panther, Black Dial, Gold Hands, Diamonds, 18K Gold Band 13800.00
Cartier, Stainless Steel, Second Hand, Date Window, 7 In. 1265.00
Cartier, Tank Francaise, Stainless Steel, Automatic Movement, Flexible Link Band 1880.00
Cartier, White Dial, Roman Numeral, Quartz, Alligator Band, Box 1880.00
Cartier, Woman's, Gray Dial, Roman Numerals, Vermeil Bezel, Lugs, Leather Band 470.00
Cartier, Woman's, Must 21, Stainless Steel, 2 Leather Bands, Quartz Movement 470.00
Cartier, Woman's, Must De Cartier, Yellow Dial, Roman Numerals, Vermeil Bezel, Box . . 1528.00
Chanel, Woman's, 18K Gold, Alligator Band, Swiss Quartz Movement 1880.00
Character, Barbie, Gold, Blue Denim, Pink, White Vinyl Band, Box, 1971 . . . .   90.00
Character, Barbie, Gold, Light Blue Band, Box, 1964 . . . .   105.00

Character, Dan Dare, Spaceman, Ingersoll, Box, England, c.1953 . . . . 715.00
Character, Underdog, Flexing Muscles, Leonardo, Japan, 1 1/4 In. Diam. 85.00
Concord, Circular Dial, Roman & Arabic Numerals, Date, Moon Phase, 14K Gold 705.00
Concord, Woman's, Rectangular Goldtone Dial, Quartz Movement, 14K Gold 355.00
Corum, Stainless Steel, Diamonds, 8 In. 1955.00
E.P. Pequignet, Woman's, Stainless Steel, Rectangular Dial, 7 Bands, Case 380.00
Elgin, Woman's, Art Deco, Platinum, Diamond, 17 Jewel, Manual Wind, c.1938 . . . . 635.00
Eterna, Woman's, Platinum, Sapphires, Diamonds, Blue Steel Hands, c.1925 . . . . 1150.00
Girard Perregaux, Emerald, Diamond, 17 Jewel, Art Deco 5580.00
Glashuette, Silvertone Dial, Louisiana Alligator Strap, 18K Gold, Wood Box 4406.00
Gubelin, Jubilee, Woman's, 18K Gold, Diamond, Manual Wind, c.1960, 6 3/4 In. 750.00
Gubelin, Woman's, 18K Gold, Gold Mesh Band, 17 Jewel, Swiss 635.00
Hamilton, Gemini II, Electric 79.00
Hamilton, Lindsay, Gold Filled, 17 Jewel, c.1952 . . . . 96.00
Hamilton, Military, OD-86093, WWII Issue 158.00
Hamilton, Roland, Gold Filled, 17 Jewel, c.1937 . . . . 79.00
Hamilton, Square White Dial, 17 Jewel, Bezel & Lugs, Silk Cord Band 441.00
Hamilton, Woman's, 14K Gold, Diamond, 17 Jewel, Silk Cord Band 380.00
Hamilton, Woman's, Art Deco, 14K Gold, Gold Filled, Diamond, c.1930, 7 In. 259.00
Hamilton, Woman's, Diamond, Platinum, Arabic Numerals, 17 Jewel, 6 1/2 In. 1528.00
International, 18K Gold, Malachite, Automatic, No. 9318, Swiss, c.1970, 8 In. 2300.00
International, Gold, Schaffhausen, Gold Case, Leather Band 920.00
Jaeger LeCoultre, Automatic, Memovox Alarm, 18K Gold, c.1959 . . . . 1380.00
Jos. Boillat, Woman's, 14K Gold, Diamond, Sapphire, Concealed Face, c.1950 . . . . 575.00
Jules Jurgensen, Woman's, Oval, Goldtone Dial, Black Roman Numerals, 14K Gold 206.00
Katherine Tess, Woman's, Magnum, Aluminum, Diamond, Blue Dial, Suede Pouch 411.00
Keith Haring, 2 Red Figures, Chasing Bunny, Red Bow Tie, Leather Bands, 1986 . . . . 65.00
Lamarne, Woman's, Silvertone Dial, 17 Jewel, Platinum, 14K White Gold Band, 7 In. . . . 1175.00
LeCoultre, Goldtone Dial, 17 Jewel, Leather Band, c.1950 . . . . 823.00
LeCoultre, Goldtone Dial, 18K Gold, Arched Lugs, Leather Band 382.00
LeCoultre, Silvertone Dial, 14K Gold, Automatic Movement, Leather Band 347.00
Movado, Woman's, Platinum, Diamond, Manual Wind, 17 Jewel, c.1960 . . . . 805.00
Moviga, Concealed Face, Wind, Diamond, 14K Gold, c.1950 . . . . 748.00
Normandie, 14K Gold, Ruby, Manual Wind, Swiss, c.1935, 6 1/2 In. 1380.00
Omega, 18K Gold, Manual Wind, Swiss, c.1960, 7 x 1 1/2 In. 690.00
Omega, De Ville, Stainless Steel, Wind, 18K Gold, 6 In. 173.00
Omega, Seamaster Professional Chronometer, Stainless Steel, Luminescent 441.00
Omega, Woman's, Platinum, 14K White Gold, Manual Wind, 17 Jewel, c.1965 . . . . 805.00
Omega, Woman's, Platinum, Diamond, Marquise Cut, 7 In. 5288.00
Patek Philippe, Calatrava, 18K Gold, Damascened Movement, Leather Band 3290.00
Patek Philippe, Silvertone Dial, 18 Jewel, 18K Gold, Leather Band 3525.00
Patek Philippe, Silvertone Dial, Back Wind Movement, 18K Gold, Leather Band 2938.00
Patek Philippe, Woman's, Calatrava, 18K Gold, Adjustable Mesh Band, 6 In. 2585.00
Patek Philippe, Woman's, Diamond, Enamel, 18K Gold, c.1895, Size 0 . . . . 9400.00
Piaget, Goldtone Dial, Brickwork Band, 18K Gold, 7 3/4 In. 1763.00
Rolex, Diamond, Automatic, 18K Gold, c.1984 . . . . 7475.00
Rolex, Oyster Perpetual, Bubbleback, Matte Black Dial, Arabic & Roman Numerals 1840.00
Rolex, Oyster Perpetual, Datejust, Gray Dial, Gold Hands, Baton Numerals 2645.00
Rolex, Oyster Perpetual, Day Date, 18K Gold, Papers, Extra Links, c.1985 . . . . 4995.00
Rolex, Oyster Perpetual, Ivorytone Dial, Triangular Numerals, Red To Black, 14K Gold . . 940.00
Rolex, Oyster Perpetual, President, Silvertone Dial, Stick Numerals, 18K Gold 5525.00
Rolex, Oyster Perpetual, Silvertone Dial, Baton Numerals, Stainless Steel, 14K Gold 1115.00
Rolex, Oyster Royal, Silvertone Dial, Stainless Steel, Leather Band, No. 6144 . . . . 1060.00
Rolex, Oyster, Stainless Steel, Automatic, 18K Gold, c.1984 . . . . 1495.00
Rolex, Oyster, White Enamel Dial, Arabic Numerals, 15 Jewel, Sterling Silver 1410.00
Rolex, Woman's, 18K Gold, Diamond, Manual Wind, Concealed Face, 1960, 6 1/2 In. 520.00
Rolex, Woman's, Matte Silver Dial, Diamonds, 14K White Gold Mesh Band, 1965 . . . . . . 3450.00
Rolex, Woman's, Oyster Perpetual, Silvertone Dial, Gold Stick Numerals, 18K Gold 2940.00
Rolex, Woman's, Perpetual Date, Champagne Dial, Gold, Stainless Steel Band, 14K Gold . 1998.00
Royal Dynasty, Bangle, Bakelite, Butterscotch, 17 Jewel, 1-In. Band 80.00
Tiffany, 14K Gold, 17 Jewel Swiss Movement, Gold Mesh Band 700.00
Tiffany, Woman's, Atlas, Goldtone Dial, Roman Numerals, Quartz, 18K Gold 590.00
Vacheron & Constantin, Woman's, Diamond, Sapphire, Gold Bracelet, 7 In. 2705.00

Vacheron & Constantin, Woman's, Platinum, Arabic Numerals, 18K Gold, c.1935 ...... 2468.00
Van Cleef & Arpels, Stainless Steel, Black Dial, Leather Band 999.00
Woman's, Art Deco, Silvertone Dial, Arabic Numerals, Grosgrain Band, c.1930 .... 410.00
Woman's, Diamond, Platinum, Ivorytone Dial, Arabic Numerals, 17 Jewel, 6 1/2 In. 440.00
Woman's, Edwardian, Platinum, Diamond, 17 Jewel, Swiss Movement, 7 In. 1765.00
Woman's, Platinum, White Dial, Arabic Numerals, 17 Jewel, Mesh Band, 5 3/4 In. 2235.00
Yurman, Ivorytone Dial, Square Gold Bezel, Gold Link Band 1765.00

YELLOWWARE is a heavy earthenware made of a yellowish clay. It
varies in color from light yellow to orange-yellow. Many nineteenth-
and twentieth-century kitchen bowls and jugs were made of yellowware. It was made in England and in the United States. Another
form of pottery that is sometimes classed as yellowware is listed in this
book in the Mocha category.

Batter Pail, Bristol Glaze, Bail Handle, c.1890, 9 1/2 In. 22.00
Beater Jar, Compliments Of Ringger Dairy, Double Brown Slip Stripes, 5 1/4 In. 90.00
Bowl, Blue Center Band, White Pinstripes, 2 x 4 1/4 In. 169.00
Bowl, Blue Slip Band, White Pinstripes, 2 x 4 1/4 In. 366.00
Bowl, Brown Bands, 15 In. 165.00
Bowl, Dark Brown Rockingham Glaze, 3 3/4 x 11 1/2 In. 45.00
Bowl, Dark Brown Rockingham Glaze, 4 3/4 x 10 In. 20.00
Bowl, Dark Brown Rockingham Glaze, 5 x 11 In. 99.00
Bowl, Rockingham Glaze, Footed, 3 1/2 In. 30.00
Bowl, Rockingham Glaze, Shaped, 8 In. 55.00
Bowl Set, Nesting, 7 1/4, 8 1/2 & 9 In., 3 Piece 95.00
Coffeepot, Cover, Rockingham Glaze, 4 1/2 In. 360.00
Colander, Relief Drape, Pierced, Footed, 3 1/2 x 8 In. 175.00
Corn Tray, 9 5/8 In. 225.00
Cream Pitcher, Rockingham Glaze, Man's Profile, Flowered Frame, 4 1/2 In. 121.00
Creamer, Brown Bands, Impressed Tooled Rim, 3 In. 90.00
Crock, Butter, White & Blue Bands, Handles, 6 x 8 In. 140.00
Crock, White Slip, Pinstripes, Stamped Butter, 4 1/2 In. 75.00
Cuspidor, Green & Brown Glaze, Signed, Lyman Fenton & Co. 165.00
Custard Cup, Brown Rockingham Glaze, 2 1/2 In., 4 Piece 66.00
Dish, Brown Rockingham Glaze, Oval, 2 x 8 In. 10.00
Figurine, Dog, Poodle, Holding Fruit Basket, Rockingham Glaze, 8 1/2 x 9 In. 1100.00
Flask, Boot Shape, Rockingham Glaze, 6 1/4 In. 120.00
Humidor, Tree Stump, Applied Vines & Snake, Bird On Nest Lid, 6 5/8 In. 60.00
Jar, Canning, Cover, Double Handle, 7 1/2 In. 45.00
Jar, Canning, Qt., 6 1/4 In. 110.00
Mixing Bowl, Brown & Blue Sponging, 11 1/4 In. 145.00
Mixing Bowl, Quadruple Banded Decoration, 19th Century, 10 1/2 In. 115.00
Mixing Bowl, Semi Sunburst, 6 1/2 x 12 1/4 In. 45.00
Mixing Bowl, White Band, 11 In. 55.00
Mold, Relief Swirl, Footed, 2 3/4 x 4 3/4 In. 75.00
Mug, 2 White Slip Bands, Brown Border, Applied Handle, Leaf Terminals, 3 5/8 In. 394.00
Mug, Applied Dark Brown Rockingham Glaze, Applied Strap Handle, 3 1/2 In. ....80.00 to 100.00
Mug, Straight-Sided, Applied Handle, Black & White Bands, 3 7/8 x 4 In. 330.00
Mug, Straight-Sided, Brown & White Bands, Applied Loop Handle, 3 7/8 x 4 In. 220.00
Mustard Pot, Cover, 3 White Slip Pinstripes, 2 1/2 In. 395.00
Nappy, Brown Rockingham Glaze, Heart Shaped Footed, 2 3/4 x 9 1/2 In. 65.00
Nappy, Brown Rockingham Glaze, Ribbed Footed, 3 x 10 1/2 In. 65.00
Pail, Clam, Black Band, Barrel Shape, 7 In. 420.00
Pepper Pot, 2 Brown Slip Bands, 4 1/4 In. 365.00
Pepper Pot, Stripes, Light Blue, 2 White Bands, 4 1/4 In. 1100.00
Pie Plate, Brown Rockingham Glaze, 9 1/2 In. 35.00
Pie Plate, Dark Brown Rockingham Glaze, 9 3/4 In. ....45.00 to 65.00
Pie Plate, Dark Brown Rockingham Glaze, 10 In. 45.00
Pie Plate, Dark Brown Rockingham Glaze, 10 3/4 In. 20.00
Pie Plate, Light Brown Rockingham Glaze, 11 1/2 In. 22.00
Pitcher, Brown & Greenish Blue, Accent Bands, 8 In. 99.00
Pitcher, Brown & White Bands, Applied Handle, 8 3/4 In. 440.00
Pitcher, Peacock & Palm Trees, Brown Rockingham Glaze, 8 1/4 In. 90.00

Pitcher, Petal & Column, Footed, Applied Brown Rockingham Glaze, 8 In. 65.00
Platter, Serving, Light Brown Rockingham Glaze, 12 1/2 x 9 1/2 In. 175.00
Salt, White Band, Pale Blue Stripes, 3 x 2 In. 430.00
Soap Dish, Brown Rockingham Glaze, 6 1/2 x 1 3/4 In. 110.00
Soap Dish, Round, 3 1/4 x 5 3/4 In. 145.00
Sugar, Cover, Ribbed, Applied Brown Rockingham Glaze, 4 1/2 In. 35.00
Umbrella Stand, Ribs, Embossed Arched Panels, Flowers, Green Glaze, 18 1/2 In. 75.00
Washboard, Manganese Splotches, Softwood Frame, Impressed R, 24 x 11 1/2 In. 356.00
Washbowl & Pitcher, Blue Slip Pinstripes, 2 7/8-In. Pitcher, 3 3/4-In. Bowl 535.00

ZANESVILLE Art Pottery was founded in 1900 by David Schmidt in Zanesville, Ohio. The firm made faience umbrella stands, jardinieres, and pedestals. The company closed in 1962. Many pieces are marked with just the words *La Moro*.

LA MORO

Jardiniere, Pedestal, Embossed Irises, Blue Green Matte Glaze, 21 1/2 In. 259.00
Jardiniere, Pedestal, Roses, Glossy Multicolored Glaze, 29 1/2 In. 175.00
Planter, Light Green Matte Glaze, Embossed Elephant Ear Leaves, 7 1/4 x 8 1/2 In. 259.00
Vase, Flowers, Embossed, Green Matte Glaze, Bottle Shape, 9 1/2 x 6 In. 259.00
Vase, Panel Of Trees, Blue, Faceted Base, Handles, 15 1/2 x 7 In. 290.00
Vase, Pink & Green Mottled Glaze, Ring Handles, Incised, 6 1/2 x 5 3/4 In. 80.00
Vase, Wild Rose, Brown, Tan, Marked, SO, 8 1/4 x 4 In. 175.00

ZSOLNAY pottery was made in Hungary after 1862 and was characterized by Persian, Art Nouveau, or Hungarian motifs. A series of new Zsolnay figurines with green-gold luster finish is available in many shops today. Early Zsolnay was not marked, but by 1878 the tower trademark was used.

Candlestick, Mottled Multicolored Lustered Glaze, Handles, Marked, 6 x 5 In., Pair 635.00
Ewer, Lusterware, c.1900, 12 x 7 In., Pair 475.00
Figurine, Bird, Eosin Glaze, Green, Judith Nador, 4 3/8 In. 125.00
Figurine, Bison, Blue Green, Eosin Glaze, Rectangular Base, 6 In. 175.00
Figurine, Dog, Stylized, Ribbed, Eosin Glaze, 1925-1970, 6 1/2 In. . : 127.00
Figurine, Frog, Eosin Glaze, Green, Judith Nador, 6 In. 290.00
Figurine, Seated Musician, Green & Gold Luster, Earthenware, Early 1900s, 9 In. 500.00
Jug, Egg Shape, Dragon Handle, Earthenware, Japonesque, c.1890, 10 1/4 In. 295.00
Pitcher, Relief Scrolls, Flower, White Buttons, Pinched Spout, Blue Mark, 6 1/4 In. 60.00
Tumbler, Metallic Glaze, Spots, White, 5 Churches, 1 3/8 In. 230.00
Vase, Blue Crystalline Glaze, Shouldered, Short Neck, Rolled Rim, 5 In. 590.00
Vase, Embossed Leaves, Metallic Glaze, 10 7/8 In. 3680.00
Vase, Figural, Girl With Flowing Skirt, Red Iridescent Metallic Glaze, 5 1/2 In. 1060.00
Vase, Stylized Leaves & Trees, Gold & Green Luster Glaze, Embossed, c.1970, 3 3/4 In. . . 115.00

INDEX

This index is computer-generated, making it as complete as possible. References in uppercase type are category listings. Those in lowercase letters refer to additional pages where pieces can be found. There is also an internal cross-referencing system used in the main part of the book, so if you look for a Kewpie doll in the Doll category, you will be told it is in its own category. There is additional information at the end of many paragraphs about where to find prices of pieces similar to yours.

KOVELS'
AMERICAN ANTIQUES
1750-1900

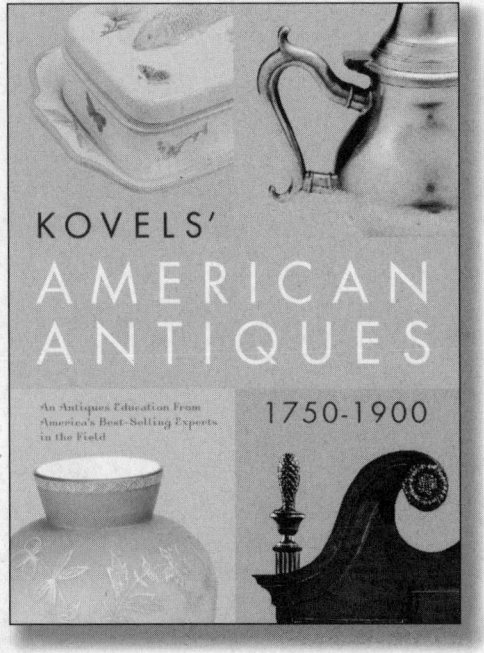

THE ULTIMATE GUIDE TO OUR
AMERICAN TREASURES!

A full-color reference complete with basic facts, fresh information, helpful historical details, and hundreds of photographs, all designed to make you a smarter, more discerning collector

- Furniture, pottery and porcelain, jewelry, silver, glass, and more

- Over 400 color photographs, plus hundreds of identifying marks

- Extensive lists of designers and manufacturers, with locations, dates, and marks

400 PAGES • PAPERBACK • $24.95 • ISBN: 0-609-80892-3